JOB HUNTER'S SOURCEBOOK

Explore your options!
Gale databases offered in
a variety of formats

DISKETTE/MAGNETIC TAPE

Many Gale databases are available on diskette or magnetic tape, allowing systemwide access to your most-used information sources through existing computer systems. Data can be delivered on a variety of mediums (DOS-formatted diskette, 9-track tape, 8mm data tape) and in industry-standard formats (comma-delimited, tagged, fixed-field)

CD-ROM

A variety of Gale titles are available on CD-ROM, offering maximum flexibility and powerful search software.

The information in this Gale publication is also available in some or all of the formats described here. Your Gale Representative will be happy to fill you in.

ONLINE

For your convenience, many Gale databases are available through popular online services, including DIALOG, NEXIS, DataStar, ORBIT, OCLC, Thomson Financial Network's I/Plus Direct, HRIN, Prodigy, Sandpoint's HOOVER, The Library Corporation's NLightN, and Telebase Systems.

A number of Gale databases are available on an annual subscription basis through GaleNet, a new online information resource that features an easy-to-use end-user interface, the powerful search capabilities of BRS/SEARCH retrieval software and ease of access through the World-Wide Web.

For information, call

GALE
1-800-877-GALE

ISSN: 1053-1874

A GALE CAREER INFORMATION GUIDE

JOB HUNTER'S SOURCEBOOK

Where to find employment leads and other job search resources

THIRD EDITION

Kathleen E. Maki, Editor

David Bianco, Contributing Editor

GALE

DETROIT · NEW YORK · TORONTO · LONDON

Kathleen E. Maki, *Editor*

David Bianco, Amy R. Hall, Jan Klisz, Theresa J. MacFarlane, Tyra Y. Phillips, Tara E. Sheets, *Contributors*
Michelle LeCompte, *Advisor*

Research Staff

Victoria B. Cariappa, *Research Manager*
Gary J. Oudersluys, *Research Specialist*

Julia C. Daniel, Tamara C. Nott, Michele P. Pica, Tracie A. Richardson,
and Cheryl L. Warnock, *Research Associates*

Production Staff

Mary Beth Trimper, *Production Director*
Shanna Heilveil, *Production Associate*

Gwendolyn S. Tucker, *Data Entry Supervisor*
Timothy Alexander, Johnny Carson, Sr., and Elizabeth Pilette, *Data Entry Associates*

Barbara Yarrow, *Graphic Services Supervisor*
C.J. Jonik, *Desktop Publisher*

Theresa Rocklin, *Manager of Systems and Programming*
Sheila R. Printup, *Programmer/Analyst*

⊗™   This book is printed on acid-free paper that meets the minimum requirements of American National Standard for Information Sciences—Permanence Paper for Printed Library Materials, ANSI Z39.48-1984.

⊛   This book is printed on recycled paper that meets Environmental Protection Agency standards.

ISBN 0-8103-9075-2
ISSN 1053-1874

Printed in the United States of America

Contents

Provides sources of help-wanted ads, placement and job referral services, employer directories and networking lists, handbooks and manuals, employment agencies and search firms, and other leads for the following careers:

Part Two: Sources of Essential Job-Hunting Information **755**

Includes reference works; newspapers, magazines, and journals; audio/visual resources; online and database services; software; and other sources about the following topics:

Highlights

This new edition of a work selected for Library Journal's annual list of best reference sources and the New York Public Library's outstanding reference sources tally serves job seekers and career changers at all levels as the essential first step in launching a job search.

One Central Source

Job Hunter's Sourcebook pulls together all of the research and the resources for a successful job hunt in one central place. Part One profiles 179 high-interest professional and vocational occupations--from accountant to aircraft mechanic and sports official to stockbroker. Each profile lists a variety of sources of job-opportunity information organized into six easy-to-use categories:

- Sources of Help-Wanted Ads
- Placement and Job Referral Services
- Employer Directories and Networking Lists
- Handbooks and Manuals
- Employment Agencies and Search Firms
- Other Sources, including internships and such innovative resources as job hotlines, computerized resume banks, and electronic bulletin boards

A Master List of Profiled Professions and Occupations identifies hundreds of alternate, popular, and related job titles and links them to the occupations profiled in *JHS*.

Essential Job-Hunting Information

In addition, *JHS* serves as a clearinghouse in organizing the wide-ranging information available to today's job seeker. From resources on resumes, to alternative ways to work, to opportunities for a diverse work force, Part Two of *JHS* features such topics as:

- Interviewing Skills
- Employment Issues for Disabled Workers
- Electronic Job Search Information
- Working at Home
- Opportunities for Gay and Lesbian Workers
- Working Part-Time, Summer Employment, and Internships

Each category includes:

- Reference Works
- Newspapers, Magazines, and Journals
- Audio/visual Resources
- Online and Database Services
- Software
- Other Sources, such as special associations, job-hunting kits, and organizers

New in This Edition

The third edition is a complete revision incorporating thousands of updates to organization and publication data. Changes and additions include:

- Fully updated contact/order information--including addresses and phone numbers
- E-Mail and Website addresses listed when available
- Fourteen new occupational profiles
- New chapters on electronic job search information--including using the Internet for job hunting, and opportunities for gay and lesbian workers
- Entries for career-related websites include a description of the site and the online address (URL)--most sites offer job banks or job postings, as well as providing other services for job hunters

Preface

"The person who gets hired is not necessarily the one who can do that job best; but, the one who knows the most about how to get hired."

--Richard Bolles
What Color Is Your Parachute?

Job hunting is often described as a campaign, a system, a strategic process. According to Joan Moore, principal of The Arbor Consulting Group, Inc. in Plymouth, Michigan, "Launching a thorough job search can be a full-time job in itself. It requires as much energy as you would put into any other major project--and it requires a creative mix of approaches to ensure its success."

Job Hunting Is Increasingly Complex

Today's competitive job market has become increasingly complex, requiring new and resourceful approaches to landing a position. The help-wanted ads are no longer the surest route to employment. In fact, most estimates indicate that only a small percentage of all jobs are found through the classified sections of local newspapers.

Though approaches vary among individual job seekers and the levels of jobs sought, a thorough job search today should involve the use of a wide variety of resources. Professional associations, library research, executive search firms, college placement offices, direct application to employers, professional journals, and networking with colleagues and friends are all approaches commonly in use. Job hotlines and resume referral services may be elements of the search as well. High-tech components might include the use of resume databases, and electronic bulletin boards that list job openings.

Over 7 Million Job Seekers

Just as the methods of job seeking have changed, so have the job hunters themselves. By choice or by chance, the U.S. Department of Labor, Bureau of Labor Statistics, Current Population Survey estimates that at any given time over 7 million Americans are seeking employment. This number includes the ranks of students pursuing their first--but probably not only--jobs. As Joyce Slayton Mitchell notes in College to Career, "Today, the average young person can look forward to six or seven different jobs, six or seven minicareers, that will make up his or her lifetime of work." Lifelong commitment to one employer is no longer the norm; professionals seeking to change companies, workers reentering the job market after a period of absence, and people exploring new career options are also represented in significant numbers in the job seeking pool. And in a time of significant corporate change, restructuring, divestiture, and downsizing, many job seekers are in the market unexpectedly. These include a growing number of white-collar workers who find themselves competing against other professionals in a shrinking market.

Help for Job Hunters

As the job market has become more competitive and complex, job seekers have increasingly looked for job search assistance. The rapid growth in the number of outplacement firms and employment agencies during the last 24 years reflects the perceived need for comprehensive help. Similarly, the library has become an increasingly important and valuable resource in the job hunt. In fact, some librarians report that their most frequently asked reference questions pertain to job seeking. In response to this need, many libraries have developed extensive collections of career and job-hunting publications, periodicals that list job openings, and directories of employers. Some libraries have developed centralized collections of career information, complemented by such offerings as resume preparation software, career planning databases, and interviewing skills videotapes.

Valuable Guide for Job Seekers

Job Hunter's Sourcebook (JHS) was designed to assist those planning job search strategies. Any job hunter--the student looking for an internship, the recent graduate, the executive hoping to relocate--will find *JHS* an important first step in the job search process because it identifies and organizes employment leads quickly and comprehensively. Best of all, JHS provides all the information a job hunter needs to turn a local public library into a customized employment agency, available free-of-charge. Library Journal and the New York Public Library concurred, and gave the first edition of this work their annual outstanding reference awards.

Introduction

Job Hunter's Sourcebook (JHS) is a comprehensive guide to sources of information on employment leads and other job search resources. It streamlines the job-seeking process by identifying and organizing the wide array of publications, organizations, audio-visual and electronic resources, and other job hunting tools.

JHS completes much of the research needed to begin a job search, with in-depth coverage of information sources for 179 specific professional and vocational occupations. Listings of resources on 26 essential topics of interest to job hunters complement the profiles on specific occupations, providing the job seeker with leads to all the information needed to design a complete job search strategy.

Job Hunter's Sourcebook can be used to:

• **Find a job.** *JHS* is designed for use by job seekers at all levels-from those seeking a first job to executives on the move to those in transition. Each individual can select from the wide range of resources presented to develop a customized job campaign.

• **Use career resources more effectively.** As library research becomes an increasingly important component in the job hunting process, librarians are providing more information and support to job seekers. *JHS* helps users go directly to the most appropriate library material by providing comprehensive lists of job hunting resources on high-interest professional and vocational occupations.

• **Build a better career resources collection.** Librarians, career counselors, outplacement firms, spouse relocation services, job referral agencies, and others who advise job seekers can use *JHS* to start or expand their collections of career and job hunting materials.

Comprehensive Coverage and Convenient Arrangement

The job search resources in *JHS* are conveniently arranged into two parts, which are followed by a master index:

•**Sources of Job-Hunting Information by Professions and Occupations** identifies information sources on employment opportunities for 179 specific types of jobs. A Master List of Profiled Professions and Occupations lists hundreds of alternate, popular, synonymous, and related job titles and links them to the jobs profiled in *JHS*, providing quick access to information sources on specific occupations or fields of interest by all their variant names. Entries contain complete contact information and are arranged by type of resource.

•**Sources of Essential Job-Hunting Information** addresses 26 employment topics, from resume writing to interviewing skills to using recruiters and employment agencies. In addition, this section provides information on such high-interest topics as electronic job search information and international and government job opportunities. The information sources listed under each topic are arranged by type of resource and include complete contact information.

•**Index to Information Sources** comprehensively lists all of the publications, organizations, electronic resources, and other sources of job hunting information contained in JHS.

Please consult the User's Guide for more information about the arrangement, content, and indexing of the information sources cited in JHS.

JHS Profiles 179 High-Interest Professions and Occupations

JHS catalogs job hunting resources for 179 professional, technical, and trade occupations, carefully selected to provide a broad cross-section of occupations of interest to today's job seekers. The majority are profiled in the Department of Labor's *Occupational Outlook Handbook* (*OOH*), a leading career resource containing detailed descriptions of some 250 professional and vocational occupations. Most of the professions cited in *OOH* are also included in *JHS*, as are representative vocational occupations selected from the those listed in *OOH*. To round out this list, additional occupations were included on the basis of Bureau of Labor Statistics data projecting them as high-growth positions.

Coverage of Employment Alternatives and Trends

In addition to focusing on such "how-to" topics as resume-writing and interviewing, the Sources of Essential Job-Hunting Information offers resources for non-traditional work options and diverse segments of the work force. Working part-time, at home, and in your own business are featured chapters, as are opportunities for minorities, older workers, women, disabled workers, and gay and lesbian job seekers. In response to growing interest, a chapter covering sources of electronic job search information has been included.

Method of Compilation

JHS contains citations compiled from direct contact with a wide range of associations and organizations, from dozens of publisher catalogs and other secondary sources, and from selected information from other Gale databases. While many resources cited in *JHS* contain career planning information, their usefulness in the job hunting process was the primary factor in their selection. Their annotations are tailored to support that function.

Acknowledgments

Special thanks go out to Michelle LeCompte, editor of the two previous editions of *JHS*. Acting as an advisor for this edition, her career expertise and subject area knowledge provided invaluable assistance in the planning and updating of the third edition.

Comments and Suggestions Are Welcome

Libraries, associations, employment agencies, executive search firms, referral services, publishers, database producers, and other organizations involved in helping job seekers find opportunities orcompanies find candidates are encouraged to submit information about their activities and products for use in future editions of *JHS*. Comments and suggestions for improving this guide are also welcome. Please contact:

Job Hunter's Sourcebook
Gale Research
835 Penobscot Bldg.
Detroit, MI 48226-4094
Telephone: (313)961-2242
Toll-free: (800)877-GALE
Facsimile: (313)961-6815

User's Guide

Job Hunter's Sourcebook (*JHS*) is divided into two parts:

•Part One: Sources of Job-Hunting Information by Professions and Occupations

•Part Two: Sources of Essential Job-Hunting Information

Access to entries is facilitated by a Master List of Profiled Professions and Occupations and an Index to Information Sources. Users should consult each section to benefit fully from the information in JHS.

Master List of Profiled Professions and Occupations

A Master List of Profiled Professions and Occupations alphabetically lists the job titles used to identify the professions and occupations appearing in Part One of *JHS*, as well as alternate, popular, synonymous, and related job titles and names, and occupational specialties contained within job titles. Citations include "See" references to the appropriate occupational profiles and their beginning page numbers.

JHS is designed to meet the needs of job seekers at all levels of experience in a wide range of fields. Managers as well as entry-level job hunters will find information sources that will facilitate their career-specific searches. In addition, information on professions and occupations related to those profiled also will be found.

▲ **All career levels.** The title assigned to each profile identifies its occupational field or subject area; these titles are not meant to indicate the level of positions for which information is provided. Information systems managers, for example, will find highly useful information in the "Computer Programmers" and "Computer Systems Analysts" profiles, while financial analysts will benefit from information in the "Financial Managers" profile. The "General Managers and Top Executives" profile, on the other hand, is broad in nature and useful to any management-level search; it does not focus upon a specific profession or occupation.

▲ **Other occupations.** Job seekers not finding their specific career fields listed in this guide will discover that related profiles yield valuable sources of information. For example, legal secretaries will find relevant information about employment agencies serving the legal profession and about prospective employers in the "Legal Assistants" and "Lawyers" profiles. An individual interested in finding a position in radio advertising sales might look to the entries in the broadcasting- and sales-related profiles to find appropriate resources. Career changers, too, can use JHS profiles to identify new professions to which their previously acquired skills would be transferable.

Part One: Sources of Job-Hunting Information by Professions and Occupations

This section features profiles of job-hunting information for 179 specific careers. Profiles are listed alphabetically by profession or occupation. Each profile contains up to six categories of information sources, as described below. Within each category, entries are arranged in alphabetical order by name or title. Entries are numbered sequentially, beginning with the first entry in the first profile. All resources listed are included in each relevant profile (and in Part Two chapters, as appropriate) providing a complete selection of information sources in each occupational profile.

Categories of Information in Profession and Occupation Profiles

★ **Sources of Help-Wanted Ads.** Includes professional journals, industry periodicals, association newsletters, placement bulletins, and online services. In most cases, periodicals that focus on a specific field are cited here; general periodical sources such as the *National Business Employment Weekly* are listed in Part Two under "Help-Wanted Ads." Publications specific to an industry will be found in all profiles related to that industry. Candidates in some occupational areas, such as word processors are usually recruited from the local marketplace and therefore are not as likely to find openings through a professional publication. Profiles for these occupations may contain fewer ad sources as job hunters are better served by local newspapers and periodicals.

•**Entries include:** the source's title and the name, address, and phone number of its publisher or producer; publication frequency; subscription rate; description of contents; toll-free or additional phone numbers; and facsimile numbers, when applicable. Source titles appear in italics.

★ **Placement and Job Referral Services.** Various services that are designed to match job seekers with opportunities are included in this category. Primarily offered by professional associations, these services range from job banks to placement services to employment clearinghouses, operating on the national and local levels.

•**Entries include:** the association's or organization's name, address, and phone number; its membership, activities, and services; toll-free or additional phone numbers; and facsimile numbers. E-mail and website addresses are provided, when available.

★ **Employer Directories and Networking Lists.** Covers directories and rankings of companies, membership rosters from professional associations, and other lists of organizations or groups that can be used to target prospective employers and identify potential contacts for networking purposes. In some cases, Who's Who titles are included where these can provide a source of contact information in a specialized field. General directories of companies such as Standard and Poor's Register of Corporations, Directors, and Executives are cited in Part Two in the "Identifying Prospective Employers" profile.

•**Entries include:** the title and name, address, and phone number of the publisher or distributor; publication date or frequency; price; description of contents; arrangement; indexes; toll-free or additional phone numbers; and facsimile numbers, when available. Directory titles appear in italics.

★ **Handbooks and Manuals.** This category notes books, pamphlets, brochures, and other published materials that provide guidance and insight to the job-hunting process in a particular occupational field.

•**Entries include:** the title and name, address, and phone number of its publisher or distributor; editor's or author's name; publication date or frequency; price; number of pages; description of contents; toll-free or additional phone numbers; and facsimile numbers, when known. Publication titles appear in italics.

★ **Employment Agencies and Search Firms.** Features firms used by companies to recruit candidates for positions and, at times, by individuals to pursue openings. Covered are:

▲**Employment agencies,** which are generally geared toward filling openings at entry- to mid-levels in the local job market. Candidates sometimes pay a fee for using their services. When possible, *JHS* lists agencies where the employer pays the fee.

▲**Executive search firms,** which are paid by the hiring organization to recruit professional and managerial candidates, usually for higher-level openings and from a regional or national market. Executive search firms are of two types: contingency, where the firm is paid only if it fills the position, and retainer, where the firm is compensated to undertake a recruiting assignment, regardless of whether or not that firm actually fills the opening. The majority of the search firms cited in *JHS* are contingency firms. Although executive search firms work for the hiring organization and contact candidates only when recruiting for a specific postion, most will accept unsolicited resumes, and some may accept phone calls.

▲**Temporary employment agencies,** which also are included in some profiles because they can be a way to identify and obtain regular employment.

For the most part, each profile lists firms that typically service that career. Firms specializing in a particular industry are included in all profiles relevant to that industry. A mix of large and small firms are covered. Major national search firms, which are quite broad in scope, are listed only under the "General Managers and Top Executives" profile. Some occupations are not served by employment agencies or search firms (fire fighter, for example); therefore, there are no entries for this category in such profiles.

•**Entries include:** the firm's name, address, and phone number; whether it's an employment agency, executive search firm, or temporary agency; descriptive information, as appropriate; toll-free and additional phone numbers; and facsimile numbers, when applicable.

★ **Other Sources.** This category comprises a variety of resources available to the job seeker in a specific field: job hotlines providing 24-hour recordings of openings; lists of internships, fellowships, and apprenticeships; bibliographies of job-hunting materials; databases; video and audio cassettes; and salary surveys to be used as a guide when discussing compensation. Professional associations of significance or those that provide job hunting assistance (but not full placement services) are also included here. Because of the trend towards entrepreneurship, this section offers information sources on being one's own boss in a given field as well. Resources on job and career alternatives are provided for certain professions (such as educators), as is information on working abroad.

•**Entries for associations and organizations include:** name, address, and phone number; the membership, activities, and services of associations; toll-free or additional phone numbers; and facsimile numbers. E-mail and website addresses are provided, when available.

•**Entries for other resources include:** title of the publication or name of the product or service; the name, address, and phone number of its publisher, distributor, or producer; editor's or author's name; publication date or frequency; price; special formats or arrangements; descriptive information; hotline, toll-free, or additional phone numbers; and facsimile numbers, when available. Publication, videocassette, and audiocassette titles appear in italics.

Part Two: Sources of Essential Job-Hunting Information

This section presents 26 profiles on topics of interest to any job hunter, such as resume writing or interviewing, as well as those of specialized interest, such as working at home (see "Contents" pages for the complete list). Profiles are arranged alphabetically by topic and contain up to six categories of information, as listed below. Within each category, citations are organized alphabetically by name or title. Entries are also numbered sequentially, continuing the number sequence from Part One. The publications, periodicals, and other sources listed are fully cited in all relevant chapters (and in Part One profiles, as appropriate), providing the reader with a complete selection of resources in a single, convenient location.

Categories of Information in Part Two's Chapters

★**Reference Works.** Includes handbooks and manuals, directories, pamphlets, and other published sources of information.

•**Entries include:** the title and name, address, and phone number of its publisher or distributor; editor's or author's name; publication date or frequency; price; number of pages; description of contents; toll-free or additional phone numbers; and facsimile numbers, when known. Publication titles appear in italics.

★**Newspapers, Magazines, and Journals.** Lists items published on a serial basis.

•**Entries include:** the title and name, address, and phone number of its publisher or distributor; frequency; price; description of contents; toll-free or additional phone numbers; and facsimile numbers, when known. Publication titles appear in italics.

★**Audio/visual Resources.** Features audiocassettes, videocassettes, and filmstrips.

•**Entries include:** the title and name, address, and phone number of its distributor or producer; date; price; special formats; descriptive information; toll-free or additional phone numbers; and facsimile numbers, when applicable. Videocassette and audiocassette titles appear in italics.

★**Online and Database Services.** Publicly available electronic databases, including websites that facilitate matching job hunters with openings are cited.

•**Entries include:** the name of the product or service; the name, address, and phone number of the distributor or producer; price; special formats or arrangements; descriptive information; toll-free or additional phone numbers; and facsimile numbers, when applicable. For websites: the online address (URL) is included along with descriptive information.

★**Software.** This category notes software programs designed to help with various aspects of job hunting, such as resume preparation.

•**Entries include:** the name of the product or service; the name, address, and phone number of the distributor or producer; price; special formats or arrangements; hardware compatibility, if relevant; descriptive information; toll-free or additional phone numbers; and facsimile numbers, when applicable.

★**Other Sources.** Varied resources such as special associations and organizations and job-hunting bibliographies, kits, and organizers are covered in this section. Citations for journal and newspaper articles are provided if a topic is relatively new.

Entries include: the title of the publication or name of the organization, product, or service; the name, address, and phone number of the organization, publisher, distributor, or producer; editor's or author's name; publication date or frequency; price; special formats or arrangements; descriptive information; toll-free or additional phone numbers; and facsimile numbers, when applicable. Publication titles appear in italics. For article citations: the article title, publication date, and journal or newspaper title, as well as a description of the article.

Index to Information Sources

JHS provides a comprehensive Index to Information Sources that lists all publications, periodicals, associations, organizations, firms, online and database services, and other resources cited in Parts One and Two. Entries are arranged alphabetically and are referenced by their entry numbers. Titles of publications, audiocassettes, and videocassettes appear in italics.

Master List Of Profiled Professions and 0ccupations

This list outlines references to covered occupations and professions by job titles, alternate names, occupation names contained within job titles, popular names, and synonymous and related names. Beginning page numbers for each occupation's profile are provided. Titles of profiles appear in boldface.

JOB HUNTER'S
SOURCEBOOK

Part One:
Sources of Job-Hunting Information by Professions and Occupations

Provides sources of help-wanted ads, placement and job referral services, employer directories and networking lists, handbooks and manuals, employment agencies and search firms, and other sources for the following careers:

Accountants and Auditors

★14★ Association for Accounting Administration (AAA)

136 S. Keowee St.
Dayton, OH 45402
Ph: (513)222-0030   Fax: (513)222-5794

Purpose: Promotes the profession of accounting administration and office management in accounting firms and corporate accounting departments. **Activities:** Sponsors activities, including consulting and placement services, seminars, salary and trends surveys, and speakers' bureau. Provides a forum for representation and exchange. Offers group purchasing opportunities.

★15★ Association of Chartered Accountants in the United States (ACAUS)

666 5th Ave., Ste. 350
New York, NY 10103
Ph: (212)713-5724

Members: Chartered accountants from England, Wales, Scotland, Ireland, Canada, Australia, New Zealand, and South Africa in commerce and public practice. **Purpose:** Represents the interests of chartered accountants; promotes career development and international mobility of professionals. **Activities:** Offers educational and research programs. Maintains speakers' bureau and placement service.

★16★ Association of Healthcare Internal Auditors (AHIA)

1200 19th St. NW, Ste. 300
Washington, DC 20036
Ph: (202)429-5134   Fax: (202)223-4579

Members: Health care internal auditors and other interested individuals. **Purpose:** Promotes cost containment and increased productivity in health care institutions through internal auditing. Serves as a forum for the exchange of experience, ideas, and information among members; provides continuing professional education courses and informs members of developments in health care internal auditing. **Activities:** Offers employment clearinghouse services.

★17★ Association of Water Transportation Accounting Officers (AWTAO)

PO Box 53, Bowling Green Sta.
New York, NY 10004
Ph: (212)264-1384

Members: Accountants, financial officers, and other management employees in the accounting and financial departments of companies engaged in marine transportation. **Purpose:** Promotes general systematization and greater uniformity in marine transportation accounting systems and government reports. **Activities:** Maintains placement service; conducts seminars.

★18★ Christian Management Association (CMA)

PO Box 4638
Diamond Bar, CA 91765
Ph: (909)861-8861   Fax: (909)860-8247
Fr: 800-727-4CMA

Members: Managers, lawyers, auditors, pastors, church administrators, and other individ-

uals who serve Christian organizations. **Purpose:** To promote the general welfare of Christian nonprofit organizations by assisting those involved in management and administration. Emphasizes areas such as: accounting and finance; media; legal and tax issues; general, church, fundraising, financial, time, and personnel management; deferred giving; women in management; executive development; marketing and communications; public relations; information development. Maintains task forces that consider emerging and potentially troubling issues. **Activities:** Offers national and regional seminars in all areas of management through its annual national conference, the Christian Management Institute. Holds bimonthly fellowship meeting for training and information reports. Provides job referral and professional referral service to assist Christian managment personnel.

★19★ International Association of Hospitality Accountants (IAHA)

PO Box 203008
Austin, TX 78720-3008
Ph: (512)346-5680   Fax: (512)346-5760

Members: Accountants and financial officers in 50 countries working in hotels, resorts, casinos, restaurants, and clubs. **Purpose:** Develops uniform system of accounts. **Activities:** Offers placment service. Conducts education, training, and certification programs; maintains hall of fame.

★20★ International Newspaper Financial Executives (INFE)

11600 Sunrise Valley Dr.
Reston, VA 22091
Ph: (703)648-1160   Fax: (703)476-5961

Members: Controllers, chief accountants, auditors, business managers, treasurers, secretaries and related newspaper executives, educators, and public accountants. **Purpose:** Conducts research projects on accounting methods and procedures for newspapers. Offers placement service; maintains speakers' bureau.

★21★ National Association of Black Accountants (NABA)

7249A Hanover Pky.
Greenbelt, MD 20770
Ph: (301)474-6222   Fax: (301)474-3114

Members: CPAs, accountants, and accounting students. **Purpose:** To unite accountants and accounting students who have similar interests and ideals, who are committed to professional and academic excellence, who possess a sense of professional and civic responsibility, and who are concerned with enhancing opportunities for minorities in the accounting profession. **Activities:** Maintains placement service. Programs include: free income tax preparation; high school and university career seminars; regional student conferences; technical seminars and lectures. Maintains speakers' bureau.

EMPLOYER DIRECTORIES AND NETWORKING LISTS

★22★ Accountants Directory

American Business Directories, Inc.
American Business Information, Inc.
5711 S. 86th Cir.
Omaha, NE 68127
Ph: (402)593-4600   Fax: (402)331-1505

Annual. $3,590, U.S. edition; $210.00, (Canad. ed.). Number of listings: 117,953 (U.S. edition); 4,272 (Canadian edition). Entries include: Name, address, phone (including area code), size of advertisement, year first in Yellow Pages, name of owner or manager, number of employees. Regional editions available: Compiled from telephone company Yellow Pages, nationwide. Arrangement: Geographical.

★23★ Accounting Firms Directory

American Business Directories, Inc.
American Business Information, Inc.
5711 S. 86th Cir.
Omaha, NE 68127
Ph: (402)593-4600   Fax: (402)331-1505

Updated continuously; printed on request. $1495.00, U.S. edition; $145.00, (Canad. ed.). Entries include: Name, address, phone (including area code), size of advertisement, year first in Yellow Pages, name of owner of manager, number of employees. Regional editions available: Eastern $945.00; Western $610.00. Compiled from telephone company Yellow Pages, nationwide. Arrangement: Geographical.

★24★ American Association of Attorney-Certified Public Accountants Directory

American Association of Attorney-Certified Public Accountants
24196 Alicia Pkwy., Ste. K
Mission Viejo, CA 92691
Ph: (714)768-0336

Annual, November/December. $175.00. Covers Approximately 1,400 individuals licensed as both attorneys and CPAs. Entries include: Name, company name, address, phone, fax, biographical data, and areas of specialization. Arrangement: Geographical.

★25★ American Society of Women Accountants—Membership Directory

American Society of Women Accountants
1755 Lynnfield Rd., Ste. 222
Memphis, TN 38119
Ph: (901)680-0470   Fax: (901)680-0505

Annual. $500.00. Covers Approximately 7,600 member accountants and educators in the accounting field. Entries include: Name, address, phone. Arrangement: Alphabetical.

★26★ American Woman's Society of Certified Public Accountants—Roster

American Woman's Society of Certified
  Public Accountants
401 N. Michigan Ave.
Chicago, IL 60611
Ph: (312)644-6610   Fax: (312)321-6869
Fr: 800-297-2721

Annual, October. Available to members only. Number of listings: 4,000. Entries include: Name, title; company name, address, phone; home address and phone; membership classification. Arrangement: Classified by type of membership, then geographical. Indexes: Alphabetical.

★27★ Asian American Certified Public Accountants—Membership Directory

Asian American Certified Public
  Accountants
PO Box 110
Pacific Ave.
San Francisco, CA 94111
Ph: (415)957-3000

Annual. Covers about 400 member accountants.

★28★ Bookkeeping Service Directory

American Business Directories, Inc.
American Business Information, Inc.
5711 S. 86th Cir.
Omaha, NE 68127
Ph: (402)593-4600   Fax: (402)331-1505

Annual. $960.00, U.S. edition; $150.00, (Canad. ed.). Entries include: Name, address, phone (including area code), size of advertisement, year first in Yellow Pages, name of owner or manager, number of employees. Regional editions available. Compiled from telephone company Yellow Pages, nationwide. Arrangement: Geographical.

★29★ Careers in Public Accounting: A Comprehensive Comparison of the Top Tier Firms

The Emerson Co.
12356 Northrup Way, No. 103
Bellevue, WA 98005
Ph: (206)869-0655

James C. Emerson. Fourth edition, 1993. $155.00. 215 pages. Profiles of the top firms from a job hunting perspective.

★30★ Directory of Canadian Chartered Accountants

Canadian Institute of Chartered
  Accountants
277 Wellington St. W.
Toronto, ON, Canada M5V 3H2
Ph: (416)204-3331   Fax: (416)977-8585

Biennial, spring of even years. $125.00. Covers over 52,000 chartered accountants, over 4,500 accounting firms, sole practitioners, professional accounting corporations, and national and provincial accounting associations. Entries include: For chartered accountants: name, address. For accounting firms, practitioners, and corporations: name, address, phone, names of partners and principals. For associations: name, address, phone, names of executive officers. Arrangement: Accountants are alphabetical; others are geographical.

★31★ Emerson's Directory of Leading Accounting Firms Worldwide

The Emerson Co.
12356 Northup Way, No. 103
Bellevue, WA 98005
Ph: (206)869-0655   Fax: (206)869-0746

Biennial, March of even years. $275.00. Covers 10,000 CPA firms worldwide. Entries include: Company name, address, phone, telex, names and titles of key personnel, number of employees, geographical area served, subsidiary and branch names and locations, description of services provided and industries served. Arrangement: Geographical. Indexes: Alphabetical.

★32★ Institute of Internal Auditors— Membership Directory

Institute of Internal Auditors
249 Maitland Ave.
Altamonte Springs, FL 32701-4201
Ph: (407)830-7600   Fax: (407)831-5171

Available to members only. Covers Approximately 50,000 member internal auditors; comptrollers, accountants, educators, computer specialists in the auditing field.

★33★ National Society of Public Accountants—Yearbook

National Society of Public Accountants
1010 N. Fairfax St.
Alexandria, VA 22314
Ph: (703)549-6400   Fax: (703)549-2984

Formerly annual; latest edition February, 1995. Free to members, government agencies and libraries; Not available to others. Covers association members and committees; also includes lists of affiliated state organizations and members of governing board. Entries include: Member listings include name, address, phone, and code indicating type of membership. Other listings include name, address, and phone. Arrangement: Geographical.

★34★ Peterson's Job Opportunities in Business 1996

Peterson's
PO Box 2123
Princeton, NJ 08543-2123
Ph: (609)243-9111   Fax: (609)243-9150
Fr: 800-338-3282

Compiled by the Peterson's staff. Annual. $19.95 (paper). 416 pages. Profiles 2,000 companies that are hiring employees in a number of nontechnical fields, including financial services, management consulting, retailers, utilities, and consumer products companies. Contains job-search strategies and career options to help match education and expertise to the job market. Indexed geographically, by industry, and by hiring needs.

★35★ Tax Return Preparation Service Directory

American Business Directories, Inc.
American Business Information, Inc.
5711 S. 86th Cir.
Omaha, NE 68127
Ph: (402)593-4600   Fax: (402)331-1505

Annual. $1,880.00, U.S. edition; $190.00, (Canad. ed.); payment with order. Number of

listings: 58,200 (U.S. edition); 3,637 (Canadian edition). Entries include: Name, address, phone (including area code), size of advertisement, year first in Yellow Pages, name of owner or manager, number of employees. Regional editions available. Compiled from telephone company Yellow Pages, nationwide. Arrangement: Geographical.

★36★ Who Audits America

Data Financial Press
PO Box 668
Menlo Park, CA 94026
Ph: (415)321-4553

Reported as semiannual, June and December; latest edition June 1994. $142.00. Covers 8,500 publicly held corporations that report to the Securities and Exchange Commission, and their accounting firms. Companies are alphabetical; accounting firms are geographical. There is a separate alphabetical section of Big Eight accounting firms, with list of their clients having more than $200 million annual sales.

HANDBOOKS AND MANUALS

★37★ Business and Finance Career Directory

Gale Research
835 Penobscot Bldg.
Detroit, MI 48226-4094
Ph: (313)961-2242   Fax: (313)961-6083
Fr: 800-877-GALE

Bradley Morgan. Second edition, 1992. $39.00. 413 pages. Features a basic and comprehensive job search section, articles by top professionals in the field, and detailed listings of hundreds of top companies who hire individuals in this field. Aimed particularly at entry-level job hunters.

★38★ Career Choices for the 90's for Students of Business

Walker and Company
435 Hudson St.
New York, NY 10014
Ph: (212)727-8300   Fax: (212)727-0984
Fr: 800-289-2553

Prepared by the Career Associates staff. 1990. $9.95. 166 pages. Discusses alternatives for students of business. Offers advice on how to break into the field and how to move up. Covers where and who the employers are, internship possibilities, and professional networking associations. Comprehensive guide to career and job search planning.

★39★ Career Choices for the 90's for Students Considering an MBA

Walker and Company
435 Hudson St.
New York, NY 10014
Ph: (212)727-8300   Fax: (212)727-0984
Fr: 800-289-2553

Prepared by the Career Associates staff. 1990. $8.95. 166 pages. Discusses career alternatives and offers advice on how to break in and move up. Covers where and who the employers are, internship possibilities, and professional networking associations. Comprehensive guide to career and job search planning.

★40★ Career Choices for the 90's for Students of Economics

Walker and Company
435 Hudson St.
New York, NY 10014
Ph: (212)727-8300   Fax: (212)727-0984
Fr: 800-289-2553

Prepared by the Career Associates staff. 1990. $8.95. 166 pages. Discusses alternatives for students of economics. Offers advice on how to break into the field and how to move up. Covers where and who the employers are, internship possibilities, and professional networking associations. Comprehensive guide to career and job search planning.

★41★ Careers in Accounting

VGM Career Horizons
4255 W. Touhy Ave.
Lincolnwood, IL 60646-1975
Ph: (847)679-5500   Fax: (847)679-2494
Fr: 800-323-4900

Gloria Gaylord and Glenda E. Ried. 1991. $17.95; $13.95 (paper). Details opportunities in public, corporate, government, and not-for-profit accounting. Topics range from choosing a specialty to finding a mentor and networking on the job.

★42★ Careers for Number Crunchers and Other Quantitative Types

VGM Career Horizons
4255 W. Touhy Ave.
Lincolnwood, IL 60646-1975
Ph: (847)679-5500   Fax: (847)679-2494
Fr: 800-323-4900

Rebecca Burnett. 1993. $14.95; $9.95 (paper). Provides information to math-oriented job hunters on how to become statisticians, field researchers, computer programmers, stock analysts, investment managers, bankers, engineers, accountants, underwriters, economists, market analysts, mathematicians, systems analysts, and more.

★43★ Encyclopedia of Careers and Vocational Guidance

J. G. Ferguson Publishing Co.
200 W. Monroe, Ste. 250
Chicago, IL 60606
Ph: (312)580-5480

William E. Hopke. Ninth edition, 1993. $129.95; $199.95 (CD-ROM). Four-volume set that profiles 900 occupations and describes job trends in 71 industries. Includes career description, educational requirements, history of the job, methods of entry, advancement, employment outlook, earnings, conditions of work, social and psychological factors, and sources of further information. Contains career and employment information for this field.

★44★ How to Market Your Accounting Services, Vol. 1: Developing Your Plan

Irwin Professional Publishing
1333 Burr Ridge Pky.
Burr Ridge, IL 60521
Ph: (708)789-4000   Fax: 800-926-9495
Fr: 800-634-3961

Stuart C. Rogers. 1994. $75.00. 400 pages.

★45★ How to Market Your Accounting Services, Vol. 2: Implementing Your Plan

Irwin Professional Publishing
1333 Burr Ridge Pky.
Burr Ridge, IL 60521
Ph: (708)789-4000   Fax: 800-926-9495
Fr: 800-634-3961

Stuart C. Rogers. 1994. $75.00. 304 pages.

★46★ Liberal Arts Jobs: What They Are and How to Get Them

Peterson's
PO Box 2123
Princeton, NJ 08543-2123
Ph: (609)243-9111   Fax: (609)243-9150
Fr: 800-338-3282

Burton Jay Nadler. Second edition, 1989. $9.95. 153 pages. Presents a list of the top 20 fields for liberal arts majors, covering more than 300 job opportunities. Discusses strategies for going after those jobs, including guidance on the language of a successful job search, informational interviews, and making networking work.

★47★ 100 Best Careers for the Year 2000

Prentice Hall General Reference
15 Columbus Cir.
New York, NY 10023
Ph: (212)373-8500   Fr: 800-223-2348

Shelly Field. 1992. $15.00 (paper). Covers 100 of the fastest growing jobs. The publication is divided into 11 general employment sections. Specific careers are covered within each section. Provides job description, responsibilities, employment opportunities, earnings, education and training, advancement opportunities, and experience and qualifications for each occupation.

★48★ Opportunities in Accounting Careers

VGM Career Horizons
4255 W. Touhy Ave.
Lincolnwood, IL 60646-1975
Ph: (847)679-5500   Fax: (847)679-2494
Fr: 800-323-4900

M. Rosenberg. 1991. $14.95; $11.95 (paper). 160 pages. Covers job opportunities in a variety of fields and specialties and how to pursue them. Illustrated.

★49★ Opportunities in Financial Careers

VGM Career Horizons
4255 W. Touhy Ave.
Lincolnwood, IL 60646-1975
Ph: (847)679-5500   Fax: (847)679-2494
Fr: 800-323-4900

Michael Sumichrast and Dean A. Christ. 1991. $14.95; $11.95 (paper). A guide to planning for and seeking opportunities in this challenging field.

★50★ Opportunities in Hotel and Motel Careers

VGM Career Horizons
4255 W. Touhy Ave.
Lincolnwood, IL 60646-1975
Ph: (847)679-5500   Fax: (847)679-2494
Fr: 800-323-4900

Shepard Henkin. 1992. $14.95; $11.95 (paper). 160 pages. A guide to planning for and seeking opportunities in this growing field. Illustrated.

★51★ Opportunities in Insurance Careers

VGM Career Horizons
4255 W. Touhy Ave.
Lincolnwood, IL 60646-1975
Ph: (847)679-5500   Fax: (847)679-2494
Fr: 800-323-4900

Robert Schrayer. 1994. $14.95; $11.95 (paper). A guide to planning for and seeking opportunities in the field. Contains bibliography and illustrations.

★52★ Opportunities in International Business Careers

VGM Career Horizons
4255 W. Touhy Ave.
Lincolnwood, IL 60646-1975
Ph: (847)679-5500   Fax: (847)679-2494
Fr: 800-323-4900

Jeffrey Arpan. 1995. $14.95; $11.95 (paper). 160 pages. Describes what types of jobs exist in international business, where they are located, what challenges and rewards they bring, and how to prepare for and obtain jobs in international business.

★53★ Opportunities in Office Occupations

VGM Career Horizons
4255 W. Touhy Ave.
Lincolnwood, IL 60646-1975
Ph: (847)679-5500   Fax: (847)679-2494
Fr: 800-323-4900

Blanche Ettinger. 1995. $14.95; $11.95 (paper). Covers a variety of office positions and discusses trends for the next decade. Describes the job market, opportunities, job duties, educational preparation, the work environment, and earnings.

★54★ Opportunities in State and Local Government Careers

VGM Career Horizons
4255 W. Touhy Ave.
Lincolnwood, IL 60646-1975
Ph: (847)679-5500   Fax: (847)679-2494
Fr: 800-323-4900

Neale Baxter. 1993. $13.95; $10.95 (paper). 160 pages. Points out the incentives and drawbacks of a government career. Describes hiring procedures and provides tips on filling out applications, taking physical and aptitude tests, handling interviews, and finding jobs. Describes the jobs in which 75% of all state and local government workers are employed. For each occupation, covers the nature of the work and the training required.

★55★ *Where the Jobs Are: The Hottest Careers for the '90s*

The Career Press, Inc.
3 Tice Rd.
PO Box 687
Franklin Lakes, NJ 07417
Ph: (201)848-0310   Fax: (201)848-1727
Fr: 800-237-3371

Joyce Hadley. Second edition, 1995. $9.99. 300 pages. Describes careers in fifteen general fields, from accounting to travel and hospitality.

EMPLOYMENT AGENCIES AND SEARCH FIRMS

★56★ **Accountants Overload Group**
10990 Wilshire Blvd.
Los Angeles, CA 90024-3913
Ph: (213)629-2800

Employment agency.

★57★ **Addington Personnel Services**
2401 Fountainview, Ste.104
Houston, TX 77057
Ph: (713)780-8810

Employment agency. Places individuals in regular or temporary positions.

★58★ **Best Personnel Services**
8901 State Line Rd.
Kansas City, MO 64114-3200
Ph: (816)361-3100

Employment agency. Fills openings on a regular or temporary basis. Office also located in Independence, MO.

★59★ **Don Richard Associates of Washington D.C.**
1717 K St. NW, Ste. 1000
Washington, DC 20006-1587
Ph: (202)463-7210   Fax: (202)331-9743

Employment agency.

★60★ **Financial Search Corp.**
2720 Des Plaines Ave., Ste. 154
Des Plaines, IL 60018
Ph: (708)297-4900   Fax: (708)297-0294

Executive search firm.

★61★ **Insurance Personnel**
65 Franklin St.
Boston, MA 02110-1303
Ph: (617)357-5380   Fax: (617)482-6581

Employment agency.

★62★ **Jim King and Associates**
1301 Gulf Life Dr., Ste. 1901
Jacksonville, FL 32207-9062
Ph: (904)398-5464

Employment agency.

★63★ **Kanon Personnel Inc.**
8 W. 40th St., 11th Fl.
New York, NY 10018-3994
Ph: (212)391-2610

Employment agency.

★64★ **New Boston Associates**
146 Bowdoin St.
Boston, MA 02108-2797
Ph: (617)720-0990   Fax: (617)723-8822

Employment agency. Located in Boston, Woburn, and Quincy, Massachusetts.

★65★ **Rocky Mountain Recruiters, Inc.**
1801 Broadway, Ste. 810
Denver, CO 80202
Ph: (303)296-2000

Executive search firm.

★66★ **Romac International, Inc.**
120 Hyde Park Pl., Ste. 200
Tampa, FL 33606
Fr: 800-341-0263

Executive search firm. More than 30 locations throughout the U.S.

★67★ **Source Finance**
5580 LBJ Fwy., Ste. 300
Dallas, TX 75240
Ph: (214)385-3002   Fax: (214)717-0075

Executive search firm. Many affiliate offices located in most major cities throughout the U.S.

OTHER SOURCES

★68★ **Accreditation Council for Accountancy and Taxation (ACAT)**
1010 N. Fairfax St.
Alexandria, VA 22314-1574
Ph: (703)549-2228   Fax: (703)549-2984

Members: Participants include accounting and tax practitioners, enrolled agents, certified public accountants, students, and others interested in attaining accreditation in accounting or taxation. **Purpose:** Strives to raise professional standards and improve the practices of accountancy and taxation; to identify persons with demonstrated knowledge of the principles and practices of accountancy and taxation, to ensure the continued professional growth of accredited individuals by setting stringent continuing education requirements, to foster increased recognition for the profession in the public, private, and educational sectors. **Activities:** Conducts semiannual accreditation examination in accountancy. Tax credentials obtained through coursework and examination. Designations are: Accredited in Accountancy/Accredited Business Accountant, Accredited Tax Advisor and Accredited Tax Preparer.

★69★ **Affiliated Conference of Practicing Accountants International (ACPA)**
30 Massachusetts Ave.
North Andover, MA 01845-3413
Ph: (508)689-9420   Fax: (508)689-9404

Members: Certified public and chartered accounting firms. **Purpose:** Encourages the interchange of professional and legislative information among members with the aim of: enhancing service and technical and professional competency; maintaining effective management administration and practice development; increasing public awareness of members' capabilities. Facilitates availability and use of specialists and industry expertise among members in areas such as manufacturing, real estate, legal and medical services, finance, wholesaling, retailing, and municipal government. Makes client referrals; compiles revenue, operating expense, and cost ratio comparisons among firms. **E-Mail:** acpa@delphi.com.

★70★ **American Institute of Certified Public Accountants (AICPA)**
1211 Avenue of the Americas
New York, NY 10036-8775
Ph: (212)596-6200   Fax: (212)596-6213
Fr: 800-862-4272

Members: Professional society of accountants certified by the states and territories. **Purpose:** Responsibilities include establishing auditing and reporting standards; influencing the development of financial accounting standards underlying the presentation of U.S. corporate financial statements; preparing and grading the national Uniform CPA Examination for the state licensing bodies. **Activities:** Conducts research and continuing education programs and surveillance of practice. Maintains over 100 committees including Accounting Standards, Accounting and Review Services, AICPA Effective Legislation Political Action, Auditing Standards, Federal Taxation, Management Consulting Services, Professional Ethics, Quality Review, Women and Family Issues, and Information Technology. Maintains speakers' bureau.

★71★ **American Society of Tax Professionals (ASTP)**
PO Box 1024
Sioux Falls, SD 57101
Ph: (605)335-1185

Members: Tax preparers, accountants, attorneys, bookkeepers, accounting services, and public accounting firms seeking to uphold high service standards in professional tax preparation. **Purpose:** Works to enhance the image of tax professionals and make tax practice more profitable; keep members abreast of tax law and service and delivery changes; promote networking among members for mutual assistance. **Activities:** Offers continuing education and training courses and public relations and marketing planning and preparation services. Supports Certified Tax Preparer Program.

★72★ Asian American Certified Public Accountants (AACPA)

580 California St., 16th Fl.
San Francisco, CA 94104

Members: Asian-American certified public accountants and other accountants aspiring to become CPAs. **Purpose:** Unites Asian-American CPAs improves professionalism; encourages the exchange of expertise and knowledge in the field. Works to gain better opportunities for Asian-Americans in the field of accounting, including an equal share of economic advantages for Asian-American CPAs. Sponsors speakers' bureau.

★73★ Association of Government Accountants (AGA)

2200 Mount Vernon Ave.
Alexandria, VA 22301-1314
Ph: (703)684-6931   Fax: (703)548-9367

Members: Professional society of financial managers employed by federal, state, county, and city governments in management and administrative positions. **Activities:** Conducts research; offers education and professional development programs.

★74★ BKR International (BKR)

40 Exchange Pl., Ste. 1100
New York, NY 10005
Ph: (212)809-5796   Fax: (212)809-5965

Members: Accounting firms in the U.S. and abroad. **Purpose:** Seeks to create an international group of competent professional firms which will provide full services in major markets of the world and enable member firms to send and receive referrals. Helps reduce operating costs of member firms by: developing consolidated purchasing arrangements for services and supplies at the lowest possible cost; developing recruiting programs, marketing materials, and advertising to reduce the collective recruiting effort of group members; expanding the group to reduce the burden on individual member firms and increase their potential scope of services. **Activities:** Compiles statistics to provide member firms with data helpful to sound management decisions. Organizes

clinical and administrative peer reviews to insure quality and provide managment with professional counsel. Develops forms, procedures, and manuals to provide guidance and accommodate the needs of partners. Conducts 12 continuing education programs per year in all areas of expertise.

★75★ Information Systems Audit and Control Association (ISACA)

3701 Algonquin Rd., Ste. 1010
Rolling Meadows, IL 60008
Ph: (708)253-1545   Fax: (708)253-1443

Purpose: Dedicated to the establishment of standards and systems of control designed to effectively organize and utilize data processing resources. Aids auditors, managers, and systems specialists in addressing problems related to controls in data processing systems. Offers Certified Information Systems Auditor Professional Designation Program. Administers the Information Systems Audit & Control Foundation, which sponsors research in the field.

★76★ Institute of Internal Auditors (IIA)

249 Maitland Ave.
Altamonte Springs, FL 32701-4201
Ph: (407)830-7600   Fax: (407)831-5171

Members: International professional organization of internal auditors, comptrollers, accountants, educators, and computer specialists in functions of internal auditing in corporations, government agencies, and institutions. **Activities:** Grants professional certification. Offers benchmarking subscription service and quality reviews.

★77★ Institute of Management Accountants (IMA)

10 Paragon Dr.
Montvale, NJ 07645
Ph: (201)573-9000   Fax: (201)573-8185
Fr: 800-638-4427

Members: Management accountants in industry, public accounting, government, and academia; other persons interested in internal and management uses of accounting. **Activities:** Conducts research on accounting

methods and procedures and the management purposes served. Established Institute of Certified Management Accountants to implement and administer examination for the Certified Management Accountant (CMA) program. Annually presents chapter medals for competition, manuscripts and for the highest scores on the CMA Examination. Offers continuing education programs comprising courses, conferences, and a self-study program in management accounting areas. Offers ethics counseling services for members by telephone. Sponsors the Stuart Cameron McLeod Society, the Continuous Improvement Center, and the Foundation for Applied Research.

★78★ National Association of Tax Practitioners (NATP)

720 Association Dr.
Appleton, WI 54914
Ph: (414)749-1040   Fax: (414)749-1062

Members: Persons engaged in the practice of preparing federal or state tax returns including tax preparers, enrolled agents, certified public accountants, licensed public accountants, public accountants, and attorneys. **Purpose:** To foster high standards in the tax preparation profession; to promote and protect the interest of tax practitioners. **Activities:** Provides and promotes continuing tax educational seminars for tax preparers. Compiles statistics; offers tax research service.

★79★ National Society of Public Accountants (NSPA)

1010 N. Fairfax St.
Alexandria, VA 22314-1574
Ph: (703)549-6400   Fax: (703)549-2984
Fr: 800-966-6679

Members: Professional society of practicing accountants and tax practitioners. **Purpose:** Represents the independent practitioner. **Activities:** Conducts correspondence courses and seminars; operates speakers' bureau. Maintains 21 committees.

Actors, Directors, and Producers

SOURCES OF HELP-WANTED ADS

★80★ American Cinematographer

ASC Holding Corp.
PO Box 2230
Los Angeles, CA 90078
Ph: (213)969-4333   Fax: (213)876-4973

Monthly. $24.00/year for individuals; $4.00 for single issue. Magazine of the American Society of Cinematographers; covering film and video production.

★81★ Art Direction

Advertising Trade Publications, Inc.
10 E. 39th St., 6th Fl.
New York, NY 10016-0199
Ph: (212)889-6500   Fax: (212)889-6504

Monthly. Magazine on advertising art and photography.

★82★ ARTJOB

Western States Arts Federation
236 Montezuma Ave.
Santa Fe, NM 87501
Ph: (505)988-1166

Biweekly. $45.00, for 24-issue subscription. Covers national full- and part-time positions and temporary paid positions in visual, performing, and literary arts, arts education, and general arts administration, competitions, internships, conferences. Entries include: Job title, salary, description of responsibilities, qualifications, application procedure and deadline, name and address of contact. Arrangement: Classified by field.

★83★ Audio

Hachette Filipacchi Magazines, Inc.
500 W. Putham Ave.
Greenwich, CT 06830
Ph: (203)622-2700   Fax: (203)622-2725

Monthly. $3.50/year for single issue. Consumer stereo equipment magazine.

★84★ AV Video

Knowledge Industry Publications, Inc.
701 Westchester Ave.
White Plains, NY 10604
Ph: (914)328-9157   Fax: (914)328-9093
Fr: 800-800-5474

Monthly. $48.00/year for individuals; $60.00/year for Canada and Mexico; $80.00/year for other countries. Magazine covering audiovisual and video production and presentation technology and techniques.

★85★ Billboard

BPI Communications
1515 Broadway, 11th Fl.
New York, NY 10036
Ph: (212)536-5167   Fax: (212)536-5351
Fr: 800-274-4100

Weekly. $229.00/year. International magazine of music and home entertainment geared toward professionals in the music and home video industries and related fields.

★86★ Broadcasting and Cable

Conners Publishing
245 W. 17th St.
New York, NY 10011
Ph: (212)463-6835   Fax: (212)463-6836

Weekly. $85.00/year for individuals; $3.00/year for single issue. News magazine covering ''The Fifth Estate'' (radio, TV, cable, and satellite), and the regulatory commissions involved.

★87★ Daily Variety

Cahners Business Newspapers
5700 Wilshire Blvd., Ste. 120
Los Angeles, CA 90036
Ph: (213)857-6600   Fax: (213)857-0494

Daily (morn.). Global entertainment newspaper (tabloid).

★88★ Electronic Media

Crain Communications, Inc.
740 N. Rush St.
Chicago, IL 60611
Ph: (312)649-5260   Fax: (312)649-5228

Weekly (Mon.). $69.00/year for individuals. Tabloid covering management, programing, syndication, technology, and trends in the television, radio, and electronic media industry.

★89★ The Hollywood Reporter

Billboard Magazine
33 Commercial St.
Gloucester, MA 01930
Ph: (508)281-3110   Fax: (508)281-0136

Daily (morn.). $149.00/year for individuals. Film, TV, and entertainment trade newspaper.

★90★ HOW

F&W Publications, Inc.
1507 Dana Ave.
Cincinnati, OH 45207
Ph: (513)531-2222   Fax: (513)531-1843

Bimonthly. $49.00/year for individuals. Instructional trade magazine.

★91★ Millimeter Magazine

Penton Publishing
611 Rte. 46 W.
Hasbrouck Heights, NJ 07604
Ph: (201)393-6060   Fax: (201)393-6297

Monthly. $45.00/year; $7.00/single issue.

★92★ Multichannel News

Capital Cities/ABC, Inc.
825 7th Ave., 6th Fl.
New York, NY 10019
Ph: (212)887-8400   Fax: (212)887-8384

Weekly (Mon.). $84.00/year for individuals. Cable and pay TV magazine.

★93★ Post

Post Pro Publishing, Inc.
25 Willowdale Ave.
Port Washington, NY 11050
Ph: (516)767-2500   Fax: (516)767-9335

Monthly. Magazine serving the field of television, film, video production and post-production.

★94★ Producer's Masterguide

Producer's Masterguide
60 E. 8th St., 31st Fl.
New York, NY 10003-6514
Ph: (212)777-4002   Fax: (212)777-4101
Fr: 800-622-6111

Annual. $125.00/year for individuals; $145.00/year for out of country. Magazine for the professional motion picture, TV commercial, cable, and videotape industries in the U.S. Canada, the U.K., the Caribbean Islands, Mexico, Europe, Israel, the Far East and South America.

★95★ Puppetry Journal

Puppeteers of America
5 Cricklewood Path
Pasadena, CA 91107
Ph: (818)797-5748

Quarterly.

★96★ Religious Broadcasting

National Religious Broadcasters
7839 Ashton Ave.
Manassas, VA 22110
Ph: (703)330-7000

Monthly. $24.00/year.

★97★ TCI (Theatre Crafts International)

Theatre Crafts
32 W. 18th St.
New York, NY 10011-4612
Ph: (212)229-2965   Fax: (212)229-2084

$40.00/year for individuals; $5.00 for single issue. The business of entertainment technology and design.

★98★ Variety

Cahners Publishing Co.
249 W. 17th St.
New York, NY 10011
Ph: (212)645-0067   Fax: (212)463-6410

Weekly (Mon.). Newspaper (tabloid) reporting on theatre, television, radio, music, records, and movies.

PLACEMENT AND JOB REFERRAL SERVICES

★99★ Actors' Fund of America (AFA)

1501 Broadway, Ste. 518
New York, NY 10036
Ph: (212)221-7300   Fax: (212)764-0238

Purpose: Human service organization of the entertainment industry. Provides emergency financial assistance to those in need; makes available social services, counseling and psychotherapy, health and education services, and nursing home care and retirement housing. **Activities:** Conducts substance abuse programs and blood drives; sponsors survival jobs program to provide employment for those between engagements.

★100★ American Conservatory Theater Foundation (ACT)

30 Grant Ave.
San Francisco, CA 94108
Ph: (415)834-3200   Fax: (415)834-3360

Purpose: Provides resources for the American Conservatory Theatre which functions as a repertory theatre and accredited acting school, offering a Master of Fine Arts degree. Holds national auditions for the MFA program in Chicago, IL, New York City, and Los Angeles, CA, usually in February. Holds student matinees, school outreach programs, and in-theatre discussions between

artist and audiences. Conducts professional actor-training programs, a summer training congress, and a young conservatory evening academy program for children aged 8-18. **Activities:** Operates speakers' bureau and placement service.

★101★ Association for Theatre in Higher Education (ATHE)

PO Box 15282
Evansville, IN 47716-0282
Ph: (812)474-0549   Fax: (812)476-4168

Members: Universities, colleges, and professional education programs; artists, scholars, teachers, and other individuals; students. **Purpose:** Promotes the exchange of information among individuals engaged in theatre study and research, performance, and crafts. Provides advocacy and support services. Encourages excellence in postsecondary theatre training, production, and scholarship. **Activities:** Operates placement service.

★102★ Black Filmmaker Foundation (BFF)

375 Greenwich, Ste. 600
New York, NY 10013
Ph: (212)941-3944   Fax: (212)941-3943

Purpose: Serves as media arts center. **Activities:** Fosters audience development by screening films by black filmmakers and by programming local and national film festivals. Operates Talent Directory (skills bank) for job referrals. Conducts educational programs.

★103★ Black Stuntmen's Association (BSA)

8949 W. 24th St.
Los Angeles, CA 90034
Ph: (213)870-9020   Fax: (310)842-7182

Members: Men and women (ages 18 to 50) who are members of the Screen Actors Guild and the American Federation of Television and Radio Artists. **Purpose:** Serves as an agency for stuntpeople in motion pictures and television. Conducts stunt performances at various local schools. Plans to operate school for black stuntpeople. **Activities:** Offers placement service.

★104★ Health Sciences Communications Association (HESCA)

1 Wedgewood Dr.
Jewett City, CT 06351
Ph: (203)376-5915   Fax: (203)376-6621

Members: Media managers, graphic artists, biomedical librarians, producers, faculty members of health science and veterinary medicine schools, health professional organizations, and industry representatives. **Purpose:** Acts as a clearinghouse for information used by professionals engaged in health science communications. Coordinates Media Festivals Program which recognizes outstanding media productions in the health sciences. **Activities:** Offers placement service.

★105★ International Theatrical Arts Society (ITAA)

3101 N. Fitzhugh, Ste. 301
Dallas, TX 75204
Ph: (214)528-6112

Purpose: Theatrical agencies working to book entertainers and international acts into all live music venues. **Activities:** Provides placement service; conducts educational seminars.

★106★ National Association of Broadcasters (NAB)

1771 N St. NW
Washington, DC 20036
Ph: (202)429-5300   Fax: (202)429-5343

Members: Representatives of radio and television stations and networks; associate members include producers of equipment and programs. **Purpose:** Seeks to ensure the viability, strength, and success of free, over-the-air broadcasters; serves as an information resource to the industry. **Activities:** Offers minority placement service and employment clearinghouse. Monitors and reports on events regarding radio and television broadcasting. Maintains Broadcasting Hall of Fame.

★107★ National Association of Dramatic and Speech Arts (NADSA)

208 Cherokee Dr.
Blacksburg, VA 24060
Ph: (703)552-6862

Purpose: Persons interested in educational, community, children's, and professional theater. Area of interest is black and ethnic theater and writers. **Activities:** Provides placement service. Sponsors competitions and educational programs.

★108★ National Council for Culture and Art (NCCA)

1600 Broadway, Ste. 611C
New York, NY 10019
Ph: (212)757-7933

Members: Artists, civic and business leaders, professional performers, and visual arts organizations. **Purpose:** To provide exposure and employment opportunities for rural Americans, disabled Americans, and other minorities including blacks, Hispanics, American Indians, and European-Americans. Sponsors arts programs and spring and fall concert series. Operates Opening Night, a cable television show. Bestows annual Monarch Award and President's Award, and sponsors annual Monarch Scholarship Program. **Activities:** Offers children's and placement services; conducts charitable program; maintains hall of fame. Plans to conduct Minority Playwrights Forum, Dance Festival U.S.A., Vocal and Instrumental Competition, Film and Video Festival, and Concerts U.S.A.

★109★ New England Theatre Conference (NETC)

Northeastern University
Department of Theatre
360 Huntington Ave.
Boston, MA 02115
Ph: (617)424-9275   Fax: (617)424-9275

Members: Individuals and theatre-producing groups in New England who are actively engaged in or have a particular interest in theatre activity either professionally or as an avocation. **Purpose:** To develop, expand, and assist theatre activity on community, educational, and professional levels in New England. **Activities:** Auditions for jobs in New England summer and equity theatres; workshops on performance, administrative, and technical aspects of production. Divisions and committees hold workshops throughout the year geared to particular theatre areas.

★110★ Non-Traditional Casting Project (NTCP)

1560 Broadway, Ste. 1600
New York, NY 10036
Ph: (212)730-4750   Fax: (212)730-4830

Purpose: Advocates the elimination of discrimination in theatre, film, and television. Works to increase the employment of artists of color, female artists, and artists with disabilities by encouraging cultural diversity throughout the artistic process and all levels of production and administration, and offering consultative services. **Activities:** Maintains the Artist Files containing pictures and resumes of 3,700 actors, directors, writers, designers, and stage managers of color as well as those with disabilities. Sponsors forums.

★111★ Southeastern Theatre Conference (SETC)

PO Box 9868
Greensboro, NC 27429-0868
Ph: (919)272-3645   Fax: (919)272-8810

Members: Individuals and theatre organizations involved in university, college, community, professional, children's, and secondary school theatres. **Purpose:** Purpose is to bring together people interested in theatre and theatre artists and craftsmen from 10 southeastern states of the U.S. in order to promote high standards and to stimulate creativity in all phases of theatrical endeavor. **Activities:** Services include: central office for business and communication; job contact service; new play project; annual auditions for summer indoor and outdoor theatres; fall auditions for professional theatres. Compiles statistics.

★112★ University Film and Video Association (UFVA)

Donald J. Zirpola
Loyola Marymount University
Communication Arts Department
Loyola Blvd. W. 80th St.
Los Angeles, CA 90045
Ph: (310)338-3033   Fax: (310)338-3030

Members: Professors and video/filmmakers concerned with the production and study of film and video in colleges and universities. **Activities:** Conducts research programs; operates placement service; presents annual grants; bestows scholarships and awards.

EMPLOYER DIRECTORIES AND NETWORKING LISTS

★113★ Academy Players Directory

Academy of Motion Picture Arts & Sciences
8949 Wilshire Blvd.
Beverly Hills, CA 90211-1972
Ph: (310)247-3058   Fax: (310)550-5034

Three times yearly: January, May, September. $20.00 per issue; $65.00 per year. Covers over 20,000 members of Actors Equity Association (AEA), American Federation of Television and Radio Artists (AFTRA), and Screen Actors Guild (SAG). All listings are paid. Entries include: Name of actor, name of agency and/or personal manager with address and phone; types of roles sought (leading man or woman, character, comedy, child, etc.); photograph, contact number.

★114★ Billboard's International Talent and Touring Directory

BPI Communications
1515 Broadway, 39th Fl.
New York, NY 10036
Ph: (212)536-5025   Fax: (212)525-5055
Fr: 800-344-7119

Annual, October. $70.00, plus $3.00 shipping. Covers tour facilities and services; venues; entertainers, managers, booking agents, and others in the entertainment industry; international coverage. Entries include: Company name, address, phone, fax, names and titles of key personnel. Arrangement: Classified by line of business; venues are then geographical. Indexes: Product/service.

★115★ Broadcasting & Cable Yearbook

R. R. Bowker Co.
Reed Reference Publishing
121 Chanlon Rd.
New Providence, NJ 07974
Ph: (908)464-6800   Fax: (908)464-3553
Fr: 800-521-8110

Annual, March. $169.95. Covers all television and radio stations in the United States, its territories, and Canada; cable MSOs and their individual systems; television and radio networks, broadcast and cable group owners, station representatives, satellite networks and services, film companies, advertising agencies, government agencies, trade associations and schools. Entries include: Company name, address, phone, fax, names of executives. Station listings include broadcast power, other operating details. Arrangement: Stations and systems are geographical, others are alphabetical. Indexes: Alphabetical.

★116★ Celebrity Directory: How to Reach over 7,000 Movie, TV Stars and Other Famous Celebrities

Axiom Information Resources
PO Box 8015
Ann Arbor, MI 48107
Ph: (313)761-4842   Fax: (313)761-3276

Biennial, even years. $39.95. Covers stars, agents, networks, studios, and other celebrities. Entries include: Name and address. Arrangement: Alphabetical.

★117★ Celebrity Service International Contact Book

Celebrity Service, Inc.
1780 Broadway, Ste. 300
New York, NY 10019
Ph: (212)245-1540   Fax: (212)397-8197

Irregular, latest edition February 1993. $45.00. Covers Stage, motion pictures, television-radio, music, dance, sports, producers, agents, managers, publicity agents, advertising agencies, recording companies, newspapers, magazines, publishers, hotels, restaurants, night clubs, airlines, etc., in New York, Washington, DC, Los Angeles, London, Paris, and Rome. Entries include: Name, address, phone, contact. Arrangement: Geographical, then by category.

★118★ Cinematographers, Production Designers, Editors and Costume Designers Guide

Lone Eagle Publishing Co.
2337 Roscomare Rd., Ste. 9
Los Angeles, CA 90077
Ph: (310)471-8066   Fax: (310)471-4969
Fr: 800-345-6257

Annual. $45.00, plus $6.00 shipping. Covers Approximately 2,500 motion picture and television cinematographers, editors, production designers, and costume designers. Entries include: Personal name; name, address, phone of agent or contact; chronological list of films or shows. Arrangement: Classified by line of business. Indexes: Film/show title, contact name, agents and managers.

★119★ Contemporary Theatre, Film, and Television

Gale Research
835 Penobscot Bldg.
Detroit, MI 48226-4094
Ph: (313)961-2242   Fax: (313)961-6083
Fr: 800-877-GALE

Annual. $125.00. Covers in 12 volumes, more than 6,500 leading and up-and-coming performers, directors, writers, producers, designers, managers, choreographers, technicians, composers, executives, and dancers in the United States and Great Britain. Each volume includes updated biographies for people listed in previous volumes and in *Who's Who in the Theatre*, which this series has superseded. Entries include: Name, agent and/or office addresses, personal and career data; stage, film, and television credits; writings, awards, other information. Arrangement: Alphabetical. Indexes: Cumulative name index also covers entries in *Who's Who in the Theatre* editions 1-17 and in *Who Was Who in the Theatre*.

★120★ CRTentertainment

Sofprotex
PO Box 271
Belmont, CA 94002

$39.00. Diskette; requires a FileMaker compatible database. Database covers: over 500 theatrical agencies and entertainment industry organizations and 1,000 movie stars, musicians, producers, directors, and writers in the U.S. Database includes: Name, home address, business address and phone.

★121★ Directors Guild of America—Directory of Members

Directors Guild of America
7920 Sunset Blvd.
Los Angeles, CA 90046
Ph: (213)289-2000   Fax: (213)289-5340

Annual, February. $22.00 plus $2.90 shipping. Covers over 9,700 motion picture and television directors and their assistants providing films and tapes for entertainment, commercial, industrial, and other non-entertainment fields; international coverage. Entries include: DGA member name; contact or representative address, phone; specialty; brief description of experience and credits. Arrangement: Alphabetical. Indexes: Geographical, women and minority members, agents.

★122★ Directory of Minority Arts Organizations

Civil Rights Division
National Endowment for the Arts
1100 Pennsylvania Ave. NW, Rm. 812
Washington, DC 20506
Ph: (202)682-5454   Fax: (202)682-5674

Irregular, latest edition February 1987. Free. Covers almost 1,000 performing groups, presenters, galleries, art and media centers, literary organizations, and community centers with significant arts programming that have leadership and constituency that is predominantly Asian-American, African-American, Hispanic, Native American, or multi-racial. Entries include: Organization name, address, phone, name and title of contact, description of activities. Arrangement: Geographical. Indexes: Organization name, activity.

★123★ Dramatics Magazine—Summer Theatre Directory Issue

International Thespian Society
3368 Central Pkwy.
Cincinnati, OH 45225
Ph: (513)559-1996

Annual, February. $3.50, postpaid. Publication includes: List of over 150 study and performance opportunities in summer schools and summer theater education programs. Entries include: Organization, school or group name, address, phone, name of contact; description of program, dates, requirements, cost, financial aid availability, etc. Arrangement: Geographical.

★124★ Dramatists Guild Quarterly—Directory Issue

Dramatists Guild, Inc.
234 W. 44th St., 11th FL.
New York, NY 10036
Ph: (212)398-9366   Fax: (212)944-0420

Annual, August. Available to members only. Publication includes: Lists of Broadway and off-Broadway producers; off off-Broadway groups; agents; regional theaters; sources of grants, fellowships, residencies; conferences and festivals; sponsors of playwriting contests; and sources of financial assistance. Arrangement: Contests are by deadline; others are classified.

★125★ Film Producers, Studios, Agents, and Casting Directors Guide

Lone Eagle Publishing Co.
2337 Roscomare Rd., Ste. 9
Los Angeles, CA 90077-1851
Ph: (310)471-8066   Fax: (310)471-4969
Fr: 800-FIL-MBKS

Annual. $50.00. Covers Approximately 4500 television and motion picture producers, 200 studios and production companies, 100 agents and casting directors, and over 14,000 film credits. Entries include: For producers: name, address, phone, films worked on; name, address, phone of contact. For studios: name, address, phone, names and titles of key personnel. For agents: agency name, address, phone, individual agents' names, job titles. For casting directors: credits. Arrangement: Classified by line of business. Indexes: Film title, producer, studio executive, agent, casting director, academy awards and nominations by year.

★126★ HOLA Directory of Hispanic Talent

Hispanic Organization of Latin Actors
250 W. 65th St.
New York, NY 10023
Ph: (212)595-8286   Fax: (212)799-6718

Biennial, January of odd years. $12.50 plus tax. Covers about 500 Hispanic performing artists from New York, New Jersey, and California; all listings are paid. Entries include: Name, photograph, profession(s), phone number(s). Persons listed are contacted through the publisher. Arrangement: Alphabetical.

★127★ Hollywood Agents Directory

M & A Communications
3000 Olympic Blvd.
Santa Monica, CA 90404
Ph: (310)315-4815   Fax: (310)315-4816
Fr: 800-815-0503

Semiannual, February and August. $40.00, plus $3.00 shipping. Covers Over 1,025 talent and literary agencies and managers, and 475 casting directors and talent executives in Los Angeles and New York. Entries include: Agency name, address, phone, fax, names and titles of key personnel, product or service. Arrangement: Alphabetical. Indexes: Company name.

★128★ Hollywood Creative Directory

M & A Communications
3000 Olympic Blvd.
Santa Monica, CA 90404
Ph: (310)315-4815   Fax: (310)315-4816
Fr: 800-815-0503

Three times per year in March, July, and November. $45.00, per issue, plus $3.00 shipping. Covers more than 1,600 motion picture and television production companies employing 5,800 development and production personnel, primarily in Hollywood, California, and New York City, with some companies in other parts of the country. Entries include: Company name, address, phone, fax, names and titles of key personnel (with produced credits where applicable). Arrangement: Alphabetical. Indexes: Personal name, companies with studio contracts.

★129★ Humor Correspondence Club—List of Members

Humor Correspondence Club
Box 023304
Brooklyn, NY 11202
Ph: (718)855-5057

Annual, January. $10.00. Covers persons interested in humor, including entertainers and performers, comedy writers, and others with an avocational interest. Entries include: Name and address. Arrangement: In sequence as admitted to membership.

★130★ International Dictionary of Films and Filmmakers

St. James Press
835 Penobscot Bldg.
Detroit, MI 48226-4094
Ph: (313)961-2242   Fax: (313)961-6083
Fr: 800-877-GALE

Description: Every five years, new edition expected September 1996. $525.00 per set; $145.00 individual volumes. Covers in an illustrated multi-volume set, approximately 500 directors and filmmakers,750 actors and actresses, and 500 writers and production artists (in volumes 2, 3, and 4 respectively). Both historical and contemporary artists are listed, chosen on the basis of international importance in film history. Entries include: Name; personal, education and career data; address, when available; filmography; bibliography of monographs and articles on and by the subject, critical essay, illustrations. Volume 1 contains entries describing approximately 750 significant films. Arrangement: Alphabetical in each volume. Indexes: Film title.

★131★ International Motion Picture Almanac

Quigley Publishing Co., Inc.
159 W. 53rd St.
New York, NY 10019
Ph: (212)247-3100   Fax: (212)489-0871

Annual, January. $88.50, plus $6.00 shipping. Covers motion picture producing companies, firms serving the industry, equipment manufacturers, casting agencies, literary agencies, advertising and publicity representatives, motion picture theater circuits, buying and booking organizations, independent theaters, international film festivals, associations, theatre equipment supply companies.

Arrangement: Classified by service or activity.

★132★ International Television and Video Almanac

Quigley Publishing Co., Inc.
159 W. 53rd St.
New York, NY 10019
Ph: (212)247-3100   Fax: (212)489-0871

Annual, January. $88.50, plus shipping. Covers Who's Who in Motion Pictures and Television and Home Video, television networks, major program producers, major group station owners, cable television companies, distributors, firms serving the television and home video industry, equipment manufacturers, casting agencies, literary agencies, advertising and publicity representatives, television stations, associations, list of feature films produced for television; statistics, industry's year in review, award winners. Entries include: Generally, company name, address, phone; manufacturer and service listings may include description of products and services and name of contact; producing, distributing, and station listings include additional detail. Arrangement: Classified by service or activity, then generally geographical.

★133★ Madison Avenue Handbook: The Image Makers Source

Peter Glenn Publications
42 W. 38th St., No. 802
New York, NY 10018
Ph: (212)869-2020   Fax: (212)869-3287
Fr: 800-223-1254

Annual, spring. $45.00. Covers advertising agencies and related services in the U.S. and Canada. Includes television, film, and music producers; photographers, agents, suppliers, sources of props and rentals, fashion houses, beauty services, locations, and film commissions. Entries include: Company name, address, phone; paid listings include description of products or services, key personnel. Arrangement: Classified by line of business.

★134★ Michael Singer's Film Directors: A Complete Guide

Lone Eagle Publishing Co.
2337 Roscomare Rd., Ste. 9
Los Angeles, CA 90077
Ph: (310)471-8066   Fax: (310)471-4969
Fr: 800-FIL-MBKS

Annual. $50.00 plus $6.00 shipping. Covers over 3,700 living and primarily active theatrical and television film directors who have made films with running times of one hour or more; over 350 deceased directors; directors of videotaped television dramas are not included. Entries include: Name, date and place of birth, address and phone (or that of agent), and chronological list of films that meet stated criteria. Arrangement: Alphabetical. Indexes: Director, agent/manager, film title, foreign director name, academy awards and nominations by year, guilds.

★135★ New England Theatre Conference—Membership Directory and Resource Book

New England Theatre Conference
c/o Department of Theatre
Northeastern University
360 Huntington Ave.
Boston, MA 02115
Ph: (617)424-9275   Fax: (617)424-9275

Annual, November. $10.00. Covers 1,810 individuals and 165 groups. Entries include: For individuals: name, address, code indicating type or level of theater activity, theater affiliation. For groups: name, address; names and addresses of delegates. Arrangement: Alphabetical.

★136★ New York Casting and Survival Guide

Peter Glenn Publications
42 W. 38th St., Ste. 802
New York, NY 10018-6210
Ph: (212)869-2020   Fr: 800-223-1254

Annual, September. $15.95. Covers about 10,000 services and facilities for actors, models, and performers in the New York area, including agents in New York and Los Angeles, theaters, producers and casting agencies, casting personnel in advertising agencies, music clubs, typing services, schools, unions, health food stores, apartment and roommate referral agencies. Entries include: Company name, address, phone, and contact. Arrangement: Classified by service.

★137★ The Official Southwest Talent Directory

Cobb-Rendish Publishing
2908 McKinney Ave.
Dallas, TX 75204
Ph: (214)754-4729   Fax: (214)855-0643

Annual, latest edition March, 1995. $25.00. Covers over 500 adult and juvenile actors, actresses, and models; motion picture and audio/videotape production facilities in the Southwest. Entries include: Name, acting or performing specialties, and agency contact; production services are presented in individual suppliers' ads. Arrangement: Talent classified by sex and age of performers; production sources classified by product or service. Indexes: Personal name, ethnic group, talent abilities.

★138★ Performing Arts Career Directory

Gale Research
835 Penobscot Bldg.
Detroit, MI 48226-4094
Ph: (313)961-2242   Fax: (313)961-6083
Fr: 800-877-GALE

First edition March 1994. $34.00; $17.95(paper). Covers over 360 organizations in the performing arts offering entry-level positions and internships, including commercial and nonprofit performing arts centers, companies, and festivals; Broadway, Off-Broadway, regional and community theater companies; music ensembles; dance companies and troupes; and theater production companies. Also lists sources of help-wanted ads, professional associations, producers of videos, databases, career guides, and professional guides and handbooks. Entries include: For employers: Name, address, phone, fax, description, names and titles of key personnel, number of employees, average number of entry-level positions available, human resources contact, description of internship opportunities including contact, type and number available, application procedures, qualifications, and duties. For others: Name or title, address, phone, description. Paperback edition is available from Visible Ink Press. Arrangement: Employers are alphabetical; others are classified by type of resource. Indexes: Name and keyword.

★139★ Regional Theater Directory

American Theatre Works, Inc.
PO Box 519
Dorset, VT 05251
Ph: (802)867-2223   Fax: (802)867-0144

Annual, May. $15.95. Covers regional theater companies with employment opportunities in acting, design, production, and management. Entries include: Company name, address, phone, name and title of contact; type of company, activities, and size of house; whether union affiliated, whether nonprofit or commercial; year established; hiring procedure and number of positions hired annually, season; description of stage; internships, description of artistic policy and audience. Arrangement: Geographical. Indexes: Company name, type of play produced.

★140★ Scriptwriters Market

Scriptwriters - Film Makers Publishing
8033 Sunset Blvd., Ste. 306
Hollywood, CA 90046
Ph: (818)505-1236   Fax: (818)505-0562

Annual, February. $39.95 plus $3.00 shipping. Covers 450 literary agents, 375 film producers, over 3,000 actors and actresses, 325 directors, and 275 television producers. Entries include: For agents: firm name, address, phone. For actors: name, address, phone. For television producers: firm name, address, phone, program title, name of executive producer or other contact. For film producers: name, address, phone, contact name and title. Arrangement: Separate alphabetical sections for agents, producers, actors.

★141★ Stage Managers Directory

Stage Managers' Association
PO Box 2234
New York, NY 10108-2020
Ph: (212)691-5633

Biennial, August. $25.00. Covers about 350 stage managers experienced in theater, ballet, opera, music, and other productions. Entries include: Name, address, phone, union affiliations, name of production or theater company, position held, contract or type of production (stock, opera, dance, etc.), related skills, etc. Arrangement: Alphabetical. Indexes: Name, type of experience (Broadway, Off-Broadway, opera, dance, etc.), foreign language skill, geographical.

★142★ Summer Theater Directory

American Theatre Works, Inc.
PO Box 519
Dorset, VT 05251
Ph: (802)867-2223   Fax: (802)867-0144

Annual, December. $15.95. Covers summer theater companies that offer employment opportunities in acting, design, production, and management; summer theater training programs. Entries include: Company name, address, phone, name and title of contact; type of company, activities and size of house; whether union affiliated, whether non-profit or commercial; year established; hiring procedure and number of positions hired annually, season; description of stage; internships; description of company's artistic goals and audience. Arrangement: Geographical. Indexes: Company name.

★143★ Television Program Producers Directory

American Business Directories, Inc.
American Business Information, Inc.
5711 S. 86th Cir.
Omaha, NE 68127
Ph: (402)593-4600   Fax: (402)331-1505

Entries include: Name, address, phone (including area code), size of advertisement, year first in Yellow Pages, name of owner or manager, number of employees. Compiled from telephone company Yellow Pages, nationwide. Arrangement: Geographical.

★144★ Theatrical Agencies Directory

American Business Directories, Inc.
American Business Information, Inc.
5711 S. 86th Cir.
Omaha, NE 68127
Ph: (402)593-4600   Fax: (402)331-1505

Updated continuously; printed on request. Please inquire. Entries include: Name, address, phone, size of advertisement, name of owner or manager, number of employees, year first in Yellow Pages. Compiled from telephone company Yellow Pages, nationwide. Arrangement: Geographical.

★145★ Who's Where in American Theatre

Feedback Theatrebooks & Prospero Press
305 Madison Ave., Ste. 1146
New York, NY 10165
Ph: (212)359-2781   Fax: (212)359-5532

Irregular, latest edition 1992. $14.95. Covers over 3,300 producers, directors, performers, designers, writers, theater artists and scholars in the U.S. Entries include: Name, title or position, name of organization with which affiliated, address, phone. Arrangement: Alphabetical. Indexes: Field of specialty, geographical.

★146★ Who's Who in the Motion Picture Industry

Packard Publishing Co.
PO Box 2187
Beverly Hills, CA 90213
Ph: (310)854-0276   Fax: (818)501-7392

Annual, February; supplement. $29.00. Covers about 1,200 cinematographers, directors, producers, writers, and studio executives in the theatrical and television motion picture

industries. Entries include: For production companies and studios: name, address, phone, names and titles of key personnel. For others: name, company or agent name, address, phone, credits. Arrangement: Classified by professional status (director, studio executive, etc.) in separate sections for theatrical and television films. Indexes: Alphabetical.

★147★ Who's Who in Television

Packard Publishing Co.
PO Box 2187
Beverly Hills, CA 90213
Ph: (310)854-0276   Fax: (818)501-7392

Latest edition February 1991. $16.95. Covers Approximately 2,000 studios, production companies, networks, writers, directors, and other professionals involved in cable and network television. Entries include: Individual or company name, address, phone, description of projects; names and titles of key personnel and name and title of contact given for companies; biographical data for individuals. Arrangement: Alphabetical. Indexes: Personal name.

HANDBOOKS AND MANUALS

★148★ Acting Professionally: Raw Facts about Careers in Acting

Mayfield Publishing Co.
1280 Villa St.
Mountain View, CA 94041
Ph: (415)960-3222   Fr: 800-433-1279

Robert Cohen. Fourth edition, 1990. $13.95. 168 pages. Includes bibliography.

★149★ Career Choices for the 90's for Students of Art

Walker and Company
435 Hudson St.
New York, NY 10014
Ph: (212)727-8300   Fax: (212)727-0984
Fr: 800-289-2553

Prepared by the Career Associates staff. 1990. $9.95. 166 pages. Discusses alternatives for students of art. Offers advice on how to break into the field and how to move up. Covers where and who the employers are, internship possibilities, and professional networking associations. Comprehensive guide to career and job search planning.

★150★ Career Information Center

Macmillan Publishing Co.
200 Old Tappan Rd.
Old Tappan, NJ 07675
Ph: (609)461-6500   Fr: 800-223-2336

Visual Education Center Staff. Fifth edition, 1992. $229.00. This 13-volume set profiles over 600 occupations. Each occupational profile describes job duties, educational requirements, how to get the job, advancement possibilities, employment outlook, working conditions, earnings and benefits, and where to write for more information.

★151★ Career Opportunities in Television, Cable and Video

Facts on File, Inc.
11 Penn Plaza, 15th Fl.
New York, NY 10001-2006
Ph: (212)967-8800   Fax: 800-678-3633
Fr: 800-322-8755

Maxine K. Reed and Robert M. Reed. Third edition, 1991. $29.95; $15.95 (paper). 272 pages.

★152★ Career Opportunities in Theater and the Performing Arts

Facts on File, Inc.
11 Penn Plaza, 15th Fl.
New York, NY 10001-2006
Ph: (212)967-8800   Fax: 800-678-3633
Fr: 800-322-8755

Shelly Field. 1992. $29.95; $15.95 (paper). 256 pages. Offers a complete range of information about job opportunities in the performing arts.

★153★ Careers for Culture Lovers and Other Artsy Types

VGM Career Horizons
4255 W. Touhy Ave.
Lincolnwood, IL 60646-1975
Ph: (847)679-5500   Fax: (847)679-2494
Fr: 800-323-4900

Marjorie Eberts and Margaret Gisler. 1994. $14.95; $9.95 (paper). Describes how to get work in a variety of fields related to art and culture. Opportunities include picture framer, curator, art restorer, symphony manager, disk jockey, music reviewer, dance teacher, choreographer, costume designer, theater manager, light designer, drama teacher, bookstore owner, interior decorator, antique store owner, and others.

★154★ Careers Inside the World of Sports and Entertainment

Rosen Publishing Group, Inc.
29 E. 21st St.
New York, NY 10010
Ph: (212)777-3017   Fax: (212)777-0277
Fr: 800-237-9932

Bruce McGlothlin. 1995. $14.95.

★155★ The Encyclopedia of Career Choices for the 1990s: Guide to Entry-Level Jobs

Perigree Books
The Berkley Publishing Group
PO Box 506
East Rutherford, NJ 07073
Ph: (201)933-9292   Fr: 800-223-0510

Career Associates Staff. 1992. $19.95. 862 pages. Describes 500 entry-level careers in a variety of industries. Presents qualifications required, working conditions, salary, internships, and professional associations.

★156★ *For the Working Artists: A Survival Guide for Performing, Visual and Media Artists Who Choose to Manage Their Own Careers*

National Network for Artist Placement
935 West Ave. 37
Los Angeles, CA 90065
Ph: (213)255-3096

Judith Luther. Second edition, 1991. $30.00. 338 pages.

★157★ *The Harvard Guide to Careers in the Mass Media*

Bob Adams, Inc.
260 Center St.
Holbrook, MA 02343
Ph: (617)767-8100   Fax: (617)767-0994
Fr: 800-872-5627

John Noble. 1989. $7.95. 202 pages. Each section of the book evaluates one media profession in depth and contains an industry profile, a career profile that describes positions available in that area, information about current salary ranges, industry-specific job-hunting tips and strategies, and a case study outlining the methods that were used in a successful job hunt.

★158★ *Jobs in Arts and Media Management: What They Are and How to Get One!*

American Council for the Arts
1 E. 53rd St.
New York, NY 10022-4201
Ph: (212)223-2787   Fr: 800-321-4510

Stephen Langley and James Abruzzo. Revised edition, 1990. $21.95. 281 pages. Includes lists of about 150 sources of information on job opportunities in the arts, including organizations offering internships, job listings, graduate programs, and short-term study; professional groups concerned with theater, music, dance, opera, museum and gallery management, film, and telecommunication management. (Does not include popular music performing or music recording.) Entries include: For internships Organization name, address, phone, description, requirements. For job referral associations and periodicals - Association or publisher name, address, fields covered, services offered, turn-around time, average number of jobs, cost of subscription or dues, comments. Arrangement: Classified by type of source.

★159★ *Liberal Arts Jobs: What They Are and How to Get Them*

Peterson's
PO Box 2123
Princeton, NJ 08543-2123
Ph: (609)243-9111   Fax: (609)243-9150
Fr: 800-338-3282

Burton Jay Nadler. Second edition, 1989. $9.95. 153 pages. Presents a list of the top 20 fields for liberal arts majors, covering more than 300 job opportunities. Discusses strategies for going after those jobs, including guidance on the language of a successful job search, informational interviews, and making networking work.

★160★ *The Los Angeles Agent Book*

Sweden Press
Box 1612
Studio City, CA 91604
Ph: (818)995-4250

K. Nolte. Fifth edition, 1994. $15.95. 301 pages. Describes the actor-agent relationship, provides guidance for selecting the right agent, and gives a list of agents in Los Angeles with background information on each.

★161★ *The Movie Business Book*

Simon and Schuster Trade
Simon and Schuster Bldg.
1230 Avenue of the Americas
New York, NY 10020
Ph: (212)698-7000   Fr: 800-223-2348

Jason E. Squire. Second edition, 1992. $14.00. Producers, distributors, and agents reveal the workings of the motion picture business.

★162★ *The New York Agent Book*

Sweden Press
Box 1612
Studio City, CA 91604
Ph: (818)995-4250

Third edition, 1992. $15.95. 250 pages.

★163★ *100 Best Careers in Entertainment*

Prentice Hall General Reference & Travel
15 Columbus Cir.
New York, NY 10023
Ph: (212)373-8500   Fr: 800-223-2348

Shelly Field. 1994. $15.00 (paper).

★164★ *Opportunities in Acting Careers*

VGM Career Horizons
4255 W. Touhy Ave.
Lincolnwood, IL 60646-1975
Ph: (847)679-5500   Fax: (847)679-2494
Fr: 800-323-4900

Dick Moore. 1993. $14.95; $11.95 (paper). 160 pages. A guide to planning for and seeking opportunities in acting.

★165★ *Opportunities in Film Careers*

VGM Career Horizons
4255 W. Touhy Ave.
Lincolnwood, IL 60646-1975
Ph: (847)679-5500   Fax: (847)679-2494
Fr: 800-323-4900

Jan Bone. 1990. $14.95; $11.95 (paper). 160 pages. Provides advice on obtaining a job in film and in corporate non-broadcast film/video production. Illustrated.

★166★ *Opportunities in Performing Arts Careers*

VGM Career Horizons
4255 W. Touhy Ave.
Lincolnwood, IL 60646-1975
Ph: (847)679-5500   Fax: (847)679-2494
Fr: 800-323-4900

Bonnie Bjorguine Bekken. 1991. $14.95; $11.95 (paper). Examines opportunities in classical and popular music; theater, television, and movie acting; classical and modern dance; performance art; and teaching and therapy careers. Assists aspiring performers

with developing a portfolio and preparing for interviews, tests, and auditions.

★167★ *Radio and Television Career Directory*

Gale Research
835 Penobscot Bldg.
Detroit, MI 48226-4094
Ph: (313)961-2242   Fax: (313)961-6083
Fr: 800-877-GALE

Bradley Morgan. Second edition, 1993. $39.00. 334 pages. Features extensive listings of contacts and entry-level job opportunities. Provides information on internships and sources of help-wanted ads.

★168★ *Television and Video: A VGM Career Planner*

VGM Career Horizons
4255 W. Touhy Ave.
Lincolnwood, IL 60646-1975
Ph: (847)679-5500   Fax: (847)679-2494
Fr: 800-323-4900

Shonan Noronha. 1989. $7.95. Describes career opportunities in broadcasting organizations. Discusses working conditions, compensation, education, professional development and job search strategies.

★169★ *Where the Jobs Are: The Hottest Careers for the '90s*

The Career Press, Inc.
3 Tice Rd.
PO Box 687
Franklin Lakes, NJ 07417
Ph: (201)848-0310   Fax: (201)848-1727
Fr: 800-237-3371

Joyce Hadley. Second edition, 1995. $9.99. 300 pages. Describes careers in fifteen general fields, from accounting to travel and hospitality.

★170★ *Your Film Acting Career*

Gorham House Publishing
2118 Wilshire Blvd., Ste. 777
Santa Monica, CA 90403
Ph: (310)826-2299

M.K. Lewis and Rosemary R. Lewis. Third edition, 1993. $15.95. 320 pages. Subtitled: "How to Break into the Movies and T.V. and Survive in Hollywood." Includes index and illustrations.

OTHER SOURCES

★171★ Academy of Television Arts and Sciences (ATAS)

5220 Lankershim Blvd.
North Hollywood, CA 91601
Ph: (818)754-2800   Fax: (818)761-2827

Members: Professionals in the television and film industry. **Purpose:** To advance the arts and sciences of television through services to the industry in education, preservation of television programs, and information and community relations; to foster creative leadership in the television industry. Sponsors Television Academy Hall of Fame. Maintains library on television credits and historical material, the Television Academy Archives, and archives at UCLA of over 35,000 television programs. Offers internships to students.

★172★ **Alliance of Resident Theatres/ New York (ART/NY)**

131 Varick St., Rm. 904
New York, NY 10013
Ph: (212)989-5257   Fax: (212)989-4880

Members: Nonprofit professional theatres in New York City and interested theatre-related associations. Promotes recognition of the nonprofit theatre community. **Purpose:** Provides members with administrative services and resources pertinent to their field. Facilitates discussion among the theatres; helps to solve real estate problems; serves as a public information source. Acts as advocate on behalf of members with government, corporate, and foundation funders to encourage greater support for New York's not-for-profit theatres. Sponsors seminars, roundtables, and individual consultations for members in areas such as financial management, board development and marketing. Organizes Passports to Off Broadway, an industry-wide marketing campaign.

★173★ **American Association of Community Theatre (AACT)**

4712 Enchanted Oaks
College Station, TX 77845
Ph: (409)774-0611   Fax: (409)776-8718

Members: Community theatre organizations; individuals involved in community theatre. **Purpose:** Promotes excellence in community theatre through networking, workshops, publications, and festivals of community theatre productions. **E-Mail:** ange loaact@aol.com

★174★ **American Film Marketing Association (AFMA)**

10850 Wilshire Blvd., 9th Fl.
Los Angeles, CA 90024-4305
Ph: (310)447-1555   Fax: (310)447-1666

Members: Independent producers and distributors of feature length theatrical films; private and governmental organizations involved in selling film rights to domestic and foreign territories. **Purpose:** Contributes to negotiations with foreign producer associations; has developed standardized theatrical and video contracts in English, French, Italian, and Spanish. Established and maintains the International Arbitration Tribunal, a system through which prominent entertainment attorneys throughout the world assist members and consenting clients in reaching equitable and binding agreements. Facilitates the formulation of policies, standardized private and governmental contracts, and the exchange of information and experience among members. Deals with predominantly English language products, but handles a limited number of foreign films. Sponsors fundraising events. Future plans include establishment of a reference library, employment referral service, insurance and travel assistance programs, and a liaison among international markets and producers organizations.

★175★ **Association of Asian/Pacific American Artists (AAPAA)**

10153 1/2 Riverside Dr., No. 199
Toluca Lake, CA 91602-2533
Ph: (213)874-0786   Fax: (213)874-4755

Members: Active members are individuals in the entertainment industry, including performers, producers, designers, directors, technicians, and writers. Supporting members include students, individuals, and organizations. **Purpose:** Encourages equal employment opportunities in all aspects of the entertainment industry in order to assure realistic images and portrayals of Asian/Pacific peoples as they exist in real life and in the mainstream of America. Sponsors business and professional seminars with industry leaders to expand members' knowledge of theatre, motion pictures, and television. Maintains speakers' bureau. Offers specialized education.

★176★ **Association of Independent Video and Filmmakers (AIVF)**

625 Broadway, 9th Fl.
New York, NY 10012
Ph: (212)473-3400   Fax: (212)677-8732

Members: Independent film- and videomakers, producers, directors, writers, and individuals involved in film and television. **Purpose:** Champions independent work as a vital expression of American culture. Attempts, through joint effort, to open pathways for financing and exhibiting independent work. Has established Foundation for Independent Video and Film, its educational arm, dedicated to increasing the public's appreciation of independent video and film. **Activities:** Offers Festival Bureau, seminars, publications, and referrals.

★177★ *Celebrity Bulletin*

Celebrity Service, Inc.
1780 Broadway, Ste. 300
New York, NY 10019
Ph: (212)757-7979   Fax: (212)397-4626

New York and Hollywood editions are daily; London, and Rome editions are biweekly. $250.00 New York edition, per month; $1,750 per year. New York edition is typical of the five editions published. It indicates arrivals of celebrities in the vicinity (including dates, purpose, etc.), their upcoming activities, and contacts for them during their visits. Separate list of daily activities for celebrities already in the area. Editions are published for New York, Hollywood, London, and Rome. Subscribers accepted only after interview.

★178★ **Directors Guild of America (DGA)**

7920 Sunset Blvd.
Hollywood, CA 90046
Ph: (310)289-2000   Fax: (310)289-2029

Purpose: Negotiates agreements for members.

★179★ **International Television Association (ITVA)**

6311 N. O'Connor Rd., Ste. 230
Irving, TX 75039
Ph: (214)869-1112   Fax: (214)869-2980

Members: Individuals engaged in video communications needs analysis, scriptwriting, producing, directing, consulting, and operations management in the videotape and nonbroadcast television fields. **Purpose:** Seeks to advance the arts and sciences of the field for professionals working outside of the broadcast area.

★180★ *National Directory of Arts Internships*

National Network for Artist Placement
935 W. Ave. 37
Los Angeles, CA 90065
Ph: (213)222-4035   Fax: (213)222-4035

Biennial, odd years. $40.00, postpaid; payment with order. Covers Approximately 2,000 internship opportunities in dance, music, theater, art, design, film, and video. Entries include: Name of sponsoring organization, address, name of contact; description of positions available, eligibility requirements, stipend or salary (if any), application procedures. Arrangement: Classified by discipline, then geographical.

★181★ *The Overnight Resume*

Ten Speed Press
PO Box 7123
Berkeley, CA 94707
Ph: (510)559-1600   Fax: (510)559-1629
Fr: 800-841-BOOK

Donald Asher. 1990. $7.95. Discusses how to write aggressive business resumes, with additional information on special styles for technical, legal, and advertising personnel, actors, speakers, and students with no experience. Covers medical curricula vitae.

★182★ *Screen Actor*

Screen Actor Guild
7065 Hollywood Blvd.
Hollywood, CA 90028
Ph: (213)856-6650   Fax: (213)856-6802

Trade magazine for professional performers.

★183★ *Theatrical Index*

Theatrical Index Ltd.
888 8th Ave., 16th Fl.
New York, NY 10019
Ph: (212)586-6343

Weekly. $10.00 per issue; $105.00 monthly updates; $200.00 bimonthly updates. Covers theatrical presentations in pre-production stage which are seeking investors; also covers producers, agents, and theaters. Entries include: For productions: production name, brief details, contact. For agents and producers: name, address, phone. For theaters: name, address, box office and backstage phone numbers.

★184★ **Women in Film (WIF)**

6464 Sunset Blvd., Ste. 530
Hollywood, CA 90028
Ph: (213)463-6040   Fax: (213)463-0963

Purpose: Supports women in the film and television industry and serves as a network for information on qualified women in the entertainment field. **Activities:** Sponsors screenings and discussions of pertinent issues. Provides speakers' bureau. Maintains Women in Film Foundation, which offers financial assistance to women for education, research, and/or completion of film projects.

Actuaries

SOURCES OF HELP-WANTED ADS

★185★ Best's Review (Life/Health Edition)

A.M. Best Co.
Ambest Rd.
Oldwick, NJ 08858
Ph: (908)439-2200   Fax: (908)439-3363

Monthly. $21.00/year for individuals; $7.50/year for single issue. Magazine covering issues and trends for the management personnel of life/health insurers, the agents, and brokers who market their products.

★186★ Business Insurance

Crain Communications, Inc.
740 N. Rush St.
Chicago, IL 60611-2590
Ph: (312)649-5311   Fax: (312)280-3189

Weekly. $80.00/year for individuals. Magazine for executives in the corporate risk, employee benefit, and finance fields.

★187★ Contingencies

American Academy of Actuaries
1100 Seventeenth St. NW, 7th Fl.
Washington, DC 20036
Ph: (202)223-8196   Fax: (202)872-1948

Bimonthly. Magazine on actuarial science and its relevance to current social issues.

★188★ National Underwriter Property and Casualty/Risk and Benefits Management

National Underwriter Co.
505 Gest St.
Cincinnati, OH 45203-1716
Ph: (513)721-2140   Fax: (513)721-0126

Weekly (Mon.). Newsweekly for agents, brokers, executives, and managers in risk and benefit insurance.

★189★ PENSION Management

Argus Business
6151 Powers Ferry Rd.
Atlanta, GA 30339
Ph: (404)955-9970   Fax: (404)256-3116

Monthly. $68.00/year for individuals. Magazine on pension investment and fund administration.

★190★ Pensions and Investments

Crain Communications, Inc.
220 E. 42nd St.
New York, NY 10017
Ph: (212)210-0259   Fax: (212)210-0499

Biweekly. $180.00/year. Magazine containing news and features on investment management, pension management, corporate finance, and cash management.

EMPLOYER DIRECTORIES AND NETWORKING LISTS

★191★ Best's Agents Guide

A. M. Best Co.
Ambest Rd.
Oldwick, NJ 08858
Ph: (908)439-2200   Fax: (908)439-3296

Annual, August. $95.00. Covers over 1,700 life and health insurance companies nationwide. Entries include: Company name, address, names of president and secretary, phone, whether a stock or mutual company, states where licensed, Best's rating, current and historical financial data. Arrangement: Alphabetical.

★192★ Best's Insurance Reports

A. M. Best Co.
Ambest Rd.
Oldwick, NJ 08858
Ph: (908)439-2200   Fax: (908)439-3296

Annual, August. $570.00, per edition; monthly publications included. Published in two editions: Life-health insurance, covering about 1,800 companies, and property-casualty insurance, covering over 2,000 companies; scope includes Canada. Each edition lists state insurance commissioners and re-lated companies and agencies (mutual funds, worker compensation funds, underwriting agencies, etc.). Entries include: For each company, company name, address, phone; history; states in which licensed; names of officers and directors; financial data; editorial comment and rating. Arrangement: Alphabetical.

★193★ Insurance Almanac

Underwriter Printing and Publishing Co.
50 E. Palisade Ave.
Englewood, NJ 07631
Ph: (201)569-8808   Fr: 800-526-4700

Annual, July. $115.00. Covers over 3,000 insurance companies that write fire, casualty, accident and health, life, and Lloyd's policies; also lists mutual and reciprocal companies. Includes national, state, and local insurance associations; state insurance officials; and about 800 agents, brokers, actuaries, and adjusters. Arrangement: Classified by insurance lines, type of activity, etc. Indexes: Company name.

★194★ Insurance Phone Book and Directory

U.S. Directory Service
Reed Reference Publishing
121 Chanlon Rd.
New Providence, NJ 07974
Ph: (908)464-6800   Fax: (908)665-6688
Fr: 800-521-8110

Annual. $89.95, plus $6.30 shipping. Covers about 4,000 life, accident and health, worker's compensation, auto, fire and casualty, marine, surety, and other insurance companies. Entries include: Company name, address, phone, fax, toll-free number, type of insurance provided. Arrangement: Alphabetical.

★195★ Moody's Bank and Finance Manual

Moody's Investors Service, Inc.
99 Church St.
New York, NY 10007
Ph: (212)553-0300   Fax: (212)553-4700
Fr: 800-342-5647

Annual, July; supplements in *Moody's Bank & Finance News Reports*. $1,475.00, per year, including supplements. Covers in four volumes, over 20,000 national, state, and private banks, savings and loans, mutual funds, unit investment trusts, and insurance and real estate companies in the United States. Entries include: Company name, headquarters and branch offices, phones, names and titles of principal executives, directors, history, Moody's rating, and extensive financial and statistical data. Arrangement: Classified by type of business. Indexes: Company name.

★196★ **Who's Who in Insurance**

Underwriter Printing and Publishing Co.
50 E. Palisade Ave.
Englewood, NJ 07631
Ph: (201)569-8808   Fr: 800-526-4700

Annual, February. $115.00. Covers over 5,000 insurance officials, brokers, agents, and buyers. Entries include: Name, title, company name, address, home address, educational background, professional club and association memberships, personal and career data. Arrangement: Alphabetical.

HANDBOOKS AND MANUALS

★197★ **Actuaries Make a Difference**

Society of Actuaries
475 N. Martingale Rd., Ste. 800
Schaumburg, IL 60173
Ph: (708)706-3500

Booklet. Free. 24 pages. Describes job opportunities, in addition to career information.

★198★ **Business and Finance Career Directory**

Gale Research
835 Penobscot Bldg.
Detroit, MI 48226-4094
Ph: (313)961-2242   Fax: (313)961-6083
Fr: 800-877-GALE

Bradley Morgan. Second edition, 1992. $39.00. 413 pages. Features a basic and comprehensive job search section, articles by top professionals in the field, and detailed listings of hundreds of top companies who hire individuals in this field. Aimed particularly at entry-level job hunters.

★199★ **Career Choices for the 90's for Students of Economics**

Walker and Company
435 Hudson St.
New York, NY 10014
Ph: (212)727-8300   Fax: (212)727-0984
Fr: 800-289-2553

Prepared by the Career Associates staff. 1990. $8.95. 166 pages. Discusses alternatives for students of economics. Offers advice on how to break into the field and how to move up. Covers where and who the employers are, internship possibilities, and professional networking associations. Comprehensive guide to career and job search planning.

★200★ **Career Choices for the 90's for Students of Mathematics**

Walker and Company
435 Hudson St.
New York, NY 10014
Ph: (212)727-8300   Fax: (212)727-0984
Fr: 800-289-2553

Prepared by the Career Associates staff. 1990. $8.95. 166 pages. Discusses alternatives for students of mathematics. Offers advice on how to break into the field and how to move up. Covers where and who the employers are, internship possibilities, and professional networking associations. Comprehensive guide to career and job search planning.

★201★ **Career Information Center**

Macmillan Publishing Co.
200 Old Tappan Rd.
Old Tappan, NJ 07675
Ph: (609)461-6500   Fr: 800-223-2336

Visual Education Center Staff. Fifth edition, 1992. $229.00. This 13-volume set profiles over 600 occupations. Each occupational profile describes job duties, educational requirements, how to get the job, advancement possibilities, employment outlook, working conditions, earnings and benefits, and where to write for more information.

★202★ **Careers for Number Crunchers and Other Quantitative Types**

VGM Career Horizons
4255 W. Touhy Ave.
Lincolnwood, IL 60646-1975
Ph: (847)679-5500   Fax: (847)679-2494
Fr: 800-323-4900

Rebecca Burnett. 1993. $14.95; $9.95 (paper). Provides information to math-oriented job hunters on how to become statisticians, field researchers, computer programmers, stock analysts, investment managers, bankers, engineers, accountants, underwriters, economists, market analysts, mathematicians, systems analysts, and more.

★203★ **The Encyclopedia of Career Choices for the 1990s: Guide to Entry-Level Jobs**

Perigree Books
The Berkley Publishing Group
PO Box 506
East Rutherford, NJ 07073
Ph: (201)933-9292   Fr: 800-223-0510

Career Associates Staff. 1992. $19.95. 862 pages. Describes 500 entry-level careers in a variety of industries. Presents qualifications required, working conditions, salary, internships, and professional associations.

★204★ **Encyclopedia of Careers and Vocational Guidance**

J. G. Ferguson Publishing Co.
200 W. Monroe, Ste. 250
Chicago, IL 60606
Ph: (312)580-5480

William E. Hopke. Ninth edition, 1993. $129.95; $199.95 (CD-ROM). Four-volume set that profiles 900 occupations and describes job trends in 71 industries. Includes career description, educational requirements, history of the job, methods of entry, advancement, employment outlook, earnings, conditions of work, social and psychological factors, and sources of further information. Contains career and employment information for this field.

★205★ **100 Best Careers for the Year 2000**

Prentice Hall General Reference
15 Columbus Cir.
New York, NY 10023
Ph: (212)373-8500   Fr: 800-223-2348

Shelly Field. 1992. $15.00 (paper). Covers 100 of the fastest growing jobs. The publication is divided into 11 general employment sections. Specific careers are covered within each section. Provides job description, responsibilities, employment opportunities, earnings, education and training, advancement opportunities, and experience and qualifications for each occupation.

★206★ **Opportunities in Insurance Careers**

VGM Career Horizons
4255 W. Touhy Ave.
Lincolnwood, IL 60646-1975
Ph: (847)679-5500   Fax: (847)679-2494
Fr: 800-323-4900

Robert Schrayer. 1994. $14.95; $11.95 (paper). A guide to planning for and seeking opportunities in the field. Contains bibliography and illustrations.

EMPLOYMENT AGENCIES AND SEARCH FIRMS

★207★ **Avery Crafts Associates, Ltd.**

116 John St., Ste. 820
New York, NY 10038
Ph: (212)285-1074   Fax: (212)732-1039

Executive search firm.

★208★ **Blake and Associates Executive Search**

PO Box 1425
Pleasantville, NJ 08232
Ph: (609)645-3330   Fax: (609)383-0320

Executive search firm.

★209★ **The Canon Group**

27936 Lost Canyon Rd.
Santa Clarita, CA 91351
Ph: (805)252-7400

Employment agency and search firm.

★210★ **E.J. Ashton and Associates, Ltd.**

3125 N. Wilke Rd.
Arlington Heights, IL 60004-1452
Ph: (708)577-7900

Employment agency. Executive search firm.

★211★ **Godfrey Personnel Inc.**

300 W. Adams, Ste. 612
Chicago, IL 60606-5194
Ph: (312)236-4455

Employment agency.

★212★ Insurance Personnel
65 Franklin St.
Boston, MA 02110-1303
Ph: (617)357-5380   Fax: (617)482-6581
Employment agency.

★213★ Insurance Personnel Service
120 Kearny St., Ste. 1480
San Francisco, CA 94108-4803
Ph: (415)391-5900
Employment agency.

★214★ International Insurance Personnel, Inc.
PO Box 28408
Atlanta, GA 30358
Ph: (404)257-9685

★215★ The Oxford Group
901 Waterfall Way
Richardson, TX 75080
Ph: (214)644-5544   Fax: (214)644-7134
Executive search firm.

★216★ Questor Consultants, Inc.
2515 N. Broad St.
Colmar, PA 18915
Ph: (215)997-9262   Fax: (215)997-9226
Executive search firm.

OTHER SOURCES

★217★ Alliance of American Insurers (ALLIANCE)
1501 Woodfield Rd., Ste. 400 W
Schaumburg, IL 60173-4980
Ph: (708)330-8500   Fax: (708)330-8602
Members: Property and casualty insurance companies.

★218★ American Academy of Actuaries
1100 17th NW, 7th Fl.
Washington, DC 20036
Ph: (202)223-8196   Fax: (202)872-1948
Members: Qualified actuaries (professionals trained in the application of mathematical probability and statistics to the design of insurance and pension programs). **Purpose:** Seeks to: facilitate relations between actuaries and government bodies; conduct public relations activities; promulgate standards of practice for the actuarial profession.

★219★ American Council of Life Insurance (ACLI)
1001 Pennsylvania Ave. NW
Washington, DC 20004-2599
Ph: (202)624-2000   Fax: (202)624-2319
Fr: 800-942-4242
Members: Legal reserve life insurance companies authorized to do business in the U.S. **Purpose:** Works to advance the interests of the life insurance industry and to provide effective government relations. **Activities:** Conducts investment and social research programs; compiles statistics. Maintains Insurance Industry's Citizen Action Network and Center for Corporate Public Involvement and Medical Research Fund.

★220★ American Society of Pension Actuaries (ASPA)
4350 N. Fairfax Dr., Ste. 820
Arlington, VA 22203
Ph: (703)516-9300   Fax: (703)516-9308
Members: Individuals involved in the consulting, administrative, and design aspects of the employee benefit business. **Purpose:** Promotes high standards in the profession; provides nine-part educational program.

★221★ Casualty Actuarial Society (CAS)
1100 N. Glebe Rd., Ste. 600
Arlington, VA 22201
Ph: (703)276-3100   Fax: (703)276-3108
Purpose: Professional society of insurance actuaries promoting actuarial and statistical science as applied to insurance problems (such as casualty, fire, and social) other than life insurance. Examinations required for membership.

★222★ Conference of Consulting Actuaries (CCA)
1110 W. Lake Cook Rd., Ste. 235
Buffalo Grove, IL 60089-1968
Ph: (708)419-9090   Fax: (708)706-3599
Members: Full-time consulting actuaries or governmental actuaries.

★223★ Insurance Information Institute (III)
110 William St.
New York, NY 10038
Ph: (212)669-9200   Fax: (212)732-1916
Members: Property and liability insurance companies. **Purpose:** Provides information and educational services to mass media, educational institutions, trade associations, businesses, government agencies, and the public. Conducts public opinion surveys. Sponsors seminars and briefings on insurance, safety, research, public policy, and economic topics.

★224★ Life Office Management Association (LOMA)
2300 Windy Ridge Pkwy., Ste. 600
Atlanta, GA 30339-8443
Ph: (404)951-1770   Fax: (404)984-0441
Members: Life and health insurance companies and financial services in the U.S. and Canada; and overseas in 45 countries; affiliate members are firms that provide professional support to member companies. **Purpose:** Provides research, information, training, and educational activities in areas of operations and systems, human resources, financial planning and employee development. Administers FLMI Insurance Education Program, which awards FLMI (Fellow, Life Management Institute) designation to those who complete the ten-examination program.

★225★ National Association of Insurance Women - International (NAIW)
1847 E. 15th
PO Box 4410
Tulsa, OK 74159
Ph: (918)744-5195   Fax: (918)743-1968
Fr: 800-766-6249
Members: Insurance industry professionals. **Purpose:** Promotes continuing education and networking for the professional advancement of its members. **Activities:** Offers education programs, meetings, services, and leadership opportunities.

★226★ Society of Actuaries (SOA)
475 N. Martingale Rd., Ste. 800
Schaumburg, IL 60173-2226
Ph: (708)706-3500   Fax: (708)706-3599
Purpose: Professional organization of individuals trained in the application of mathematical probabilities to the design of insurance, pension, and employee benefit programs. Sponsors series of examinations leading to designation of fellow or associate in the society.

Administrative Assistants

HANDBOOKS AND MANUALS

★227★ Careers in Business

VGM Career Horizons
4255 W. Touhy Ave.
Lincolnwood, IL 60646-1975
Ph: (847)679-5500   Fax: (847)679-2494
Fr: 800-323-4900

Lila B. Stair and Dorothy Domkowski. 1992. $17.95; $13.95 (paper). 196 pages. Examines careers and job opportunities in business, including management and supervision. A separate chapter sketches the entrepreneurial opportunities of consulting or owning a small business.

★228★ Careers Inside the World of Offices

Rosen Publishing Group, Inc.
29 E. 21st St.
New York, NY 10010
Ph: (212)777-3017   Fax: (212)777-0277
Fr: 800-237-9932

Carolyn Simpson. 1995. $14.95. 64 pages. Describes skills needed to work in office settings for reluctant readers.

★229★ Careers Without College: Office Careers

New Careers Center
1515 23rd St.
Box 339-CT
Boulder, CO 80306
Ph: (303)447-1087
$7.95.

★230★ Charting the Career of the Professional Secretary

Professional Secretaries International
10502 Northwest Ambassador Dr.
PO Box 20404
Kansas City, MO 64195-0404
Ph: (816)891-6600

Free. 5-page pamphlet.

★231★ The Complete Job-Finding Guide for Secretaries and Administrative Support Staff

New Careers Center
1515 23rd St.
Box 339-CT
Boulder, CO 80306
Ph: (303)447-1087

Paul Falcone. 1995. $16.95. 258 pages. Covers several secretarial and administrative staff support positions and includes tips on resume writing, interview preparation, and other aspects of the job search.

★232★ Encyclopedia of Careers and Vocational Guidance

J. G. Ferguson Publishing Co.
200 W. Monroe, Ste. 250
Chicago, IL 60606
Ph: (312)580-5480

William E. Hopke. Ninth edition, 1993. $129.95; $199.95 (CD-ROM). Four-volume set that profiles 900 occupations and describes job trends in 71 industries. Includes career description, educational requirements, history of the job, methods of entry, advancement, employment outlook, earnings, conditions of work, social and psychological factors, and sources of further information. Contains career and employment information for this field.

★233★ Executive Secretary

National Association of Executive
  Secretaries
900 S. Washington St., Ste. G-13
Falls Church, VA 22046
Ph: (703)237-8616

Free. 8 pages. Career brief.

★234★ From Secretary Track to Fast Track

AMACOM
135 W. 50th St., 15th Fl.
New York, NY 10020
Ph: (212)903-8315   Fr: 800-262-9699

Ken Lizotte and Barbara A. Litwak. 1996. $15.95. 192 pages. Subtitled: *The Get Ahead Guide for Administrative Assistants, Secretaries, Office Managers, Receptionists, and Everyone Who Wants More.*

★235★ Jobs Rated Almanac: Ranks the Best and Worst Jobs by More Than a Dozen Vital Criteria

John Wiley and Sons
605 Third Ave.
New York, NY 10158-0012
Ph: (212)850-6000   Fr: 800-225-5945

Les Krantz. Third edition, 1995. $16.95. 340 pages. Ranks 250 jobs by environment, salary, outlook, physical demands, stress, security, travel opportunities, and geographic location.

★236★ 100 Best Careers for the Year 2000

Prentice Hall General Reference
15 Columbus Cir.
New York, NY 10023
Ph: (212)373-8500   Fr: 800-223-2348

Shelly Field. 1992. $15.00 (paper). Covers 100 of the fastest growing jobs. The publication is divided into 11 general employment sections. Specific careers are covered within each section. Provides job description, responsibilities, employment opportunities, earnings, education and training, advancement opportunities, and experience and qualifications for each occupation.

★237★ Opportunities in Federal Government Careers

VGM Career Horizons
4255 W. Touhy Ave.
Lincolnwood, IL 60646-1975
Ph: (847)679-5500   Fax: (847)679-2494
Fr: 800-323-4900

Neale Baxter. 1992. $13.95; $10.95 (paper). 160 pages. Describes the spectrum of government employment, including professional, administrative, scientific, blue-collar, clerical, and technical opportunities, and how to land a job. Illustrated.

★238★ Opportunities in Office Occupations

VGM Career Horizons
4255 W. Touhy Ave.
Lincolnwood, IL 60646-1975
Ph: (847)679-5500   Fax: (847)679-2494
Fr: 800-323-4900

Blanche Ettinger. 1995. $14.95; $11.95 (paper). Covers a variety of office positions and discusses trends for the next decade. Describes the job market, opportunities, job duties, educational preparation, the work environment, and earnings.

★239★ Opportunities in Secretarial Careers

VGM Career Horizons
4255 W. Touhy Ave.
Lincolnwood, IL 60646-1975
Ph: (847)679-5500   Fax: (847)679-2494
Fr: 800-323-4900

Blanche Ettinger. 1992. $14.95; $11.95 (paper). Includes a chapter on finding a secretarial job with sample resumes and interview questions.

★240★ Opportunities in State and Local Government Careers

VGM Career Horizons
4255 W. Touhy Ave.
Lincolnwood, IL 60646-1975
Ph: (847)679-5500   Fax: (847)679-2494
Fr: 800-323-4900

Neale Baxter. 1993. $13.95; $10.95 (paper). 160 pages. Points out the incentives and drawbacks of a government career. Describes hiring procedures and provides tips on filling out applications, taking physical and aptitude tests, handling interviews, and finding jobs. Describes the jobs in which 75% of all state and local government workers are employed. For each occupation, covers the nature of the work and the training required.

★241★ Peterson's Job Opportunities in Business 1996

Peterson's
PO Box 2123
Princeton, NJ 08543-2123
Ph: (609)243-9111   Fax: (609)243-9150
Fr: 800-338-3282

Compiled by the Peterson's staff. Annual. $19.95 (paper). 416 pages. Profiles 2,000 companies that are hiring employees in a number of nontechnical fields, including financial services, management consulting, retailers, utilities, and consumer products companies. Contains job-search strategies and career options to help match education and expertise to the job market. Indexed geographically, by industry, and by hiring needs.

★242★ Secretaries: Secretaries are Moving Up

Chronicle Guidance Publications, Inc.
66 Aurora St.
PO Box 1190
Moravia, NY 13118-1190
Ph: (315)497-0330   Fax: (315)497-3359
Fr: 800-622-7284

Chronicle Guidance Staff. 1992. $2.00. Reprint of a journal article.

★243★ Secretaries and Stenographers

Chronicle Guidance Publications, Inc.
66 Aurora St.
PO Box 1190
Moravia, NY 13118-1190
Ph: (315)497-0330   Fax: (315)497-3359
Fr: 800-622-7284

Chronicle Guidance Staff. 1995. $2.00. Pro-

vides concise career information and sources of additional information.

★244★ Your Opportunities as a Secretary (Executive and Legal)

Energeia Publishing, Inc.
PO Box 985
Salem, OR 97308
Ph: (503)362-1480   Fax: (503)362-2123

Laurie Bean. 1994. $2.00.

EMPLOYMENT AGENCIES AND SEARCH FIRMS

★245★ Alper and Associates Personnel Services

353 Sacramento St., Ste. 1760
San Francisco, CA 94111
Ph: (415)397-6611   Fax: (415)397-6479

Temporary help service.

★246★ Apple One Employment Agency

18538 Hawthorne Blvd.
Torrance, CA 90504
Ph: (310)542-8534

Employment agency.

★247★ Budget Quality Staffing, Inc.

9500 S. Dadeland Blvd., Ste. 430
Miami, FL 33156
Ph: (305)670-6660   Fax: (305)670-4808

Temporary help service.

★248★ Career Center, Inc.

194 Passaic St.
PO Box 1036
Hackensack, NJ 07601
Ph: (201)342-1777

Employment agency.

★249★ Dial Personnel Associates

1033 E. Imperial Hwy., Ste. E-10
Brea, CA 92621
Ph: (714)671-1726

Employment agency.

★250★ Don Richard Associates of Washington, DC

1717 K St. NW, Ste. 1000
Washington, DC 20006
Ph: (202)463-7210   Fax: (202)331-9743

Temporary help service.

★251★ Egar Employment

23200 Chagrin Blvd., Bldg. 4
Cleveland, OH 44122
Ph: (216)464-4400   Fax: (216)464-8461

Temporary help service.

★252★ Executemps, Inc.

6000 E. Evans Ave., #3-201
Denver, CO 80222
Ph: (303)758-9353   Fax: (303)758-0032

Temporary help service.

★253★ Express Personnel Services

2360 N. Broadway
Rochester, MN 55906
Ph: (507)285-1616   Fax: (507)285-1830

Temporary help service.

★254★ Grafton Staffing Companies

600 Broadway, Ste. 250
Kansas City, MO 64105
Ph: (816)842-7700   Fax: (816)842-3054

Temporary help service.

★255★ Greer Personnel Consultants

5500 McNeeley Dr., Ste. 102
Raleigh, NC 27612
Ph: (919)571-0051   Fax: (919)571-7450

Temporary help service.

★256★ Group Agency, Inc.

1419 Avenue J
Brooklyn, NY 11230
Ph: (718)258-9202

Employment agency.

★257★ J. Morrissey & Co.

50 Columbus Blvd.
Hartford, CT 06106
Ph: (203)246-9000   Fax: (203)246-6051

Temporary help service.

★258★ The Linde Group, Inc.

515 Olive, Ste. 1500
St. Louis, MO 63101
Ph: (314)621-2950   Fax: (314)621-2891

Temporary help service.

★259★ Normann Personnel Consultants

1200 MacArthur Blvd., Ste. 13
Mahwah, NJ 07430-2331
Ph: (201)818-0200   Fax: (201)818-0004

Temporary help service. Another office is located in Paramus, NJ.

★260★ Opportunities Unlimited

53 W. Jackson, Ste. 215
Chicago, IL 60604
Ph: (312)922-8898   Fax: (312)347-1206

Employment agency.

★261★ Snelling Personnel Services

1350 Old Bayshore Hwy., Ste. 468
Burlingame, CA 94010-1813
Ph: (415)344-0374   Fax: (415)344-1066

Temporary help service.

★262★ Steverson & Co., Inc.

PO Box 219226
Houston, TX 77218-9226
Ph: (713)496-5313   Fax: (713)496-4975

Temporary help service.

★263★ The Sullivan and Cogliano Companies

230 Second Ave.
Waltham, MA 02154-1102
Ph: (617)890-7890

Regular and temporary help agency.

★264★ **Winters and Ross**
442 Main St.
Fort Lee, NJ 07024
Ph: (201)947-8400

OTHER SOURCES

★265★ *The Executive Secretary in Europe: International Administration and Secretarial Procedures*
Trans-Atlantic Publications, Inc.
311 Bainbridge
Philadelphia, PA 19147
Ph: (215)925-5038   Fax: (215)925-1912

Carol Maclay and John Harrison. 1994. $44.50.

★266★ *Executive Secretary Salary Survey*
National Association of Executive Secretaries
900 S. Washington St., Ste. G-13
Falls Church, VA 22046
Ph: (703)237-8616

Biennial. $5.00.

★267★ *Video Career Library: Administration and Management*
Chronicle Guidance Publications, Inc.
66 Aurora St.
PO Box 1190
Moravia, NY 13118-1190
Ph: (315)497-0330   Fax: (315)497-3359
Fr: 800-622-7284

Video. $79.95. 30 minutes. Full-color video shows workers performing tasks and provides information on job duties, working conditions, salaries, outlook, education, training, and other aspects of the job.

Adult and Vocational Education Teachers

SOURCES OF HELP-WANTED ADS

★268★ Adult and Continuing Education Today

LERN
1544 Hayes Dr.
Manhattan, KS 66502
Ph: (913)539-5376   Fr: 800-678-5376

Biweekly. $95.00/year. Provides news and information on adult education.

★269★ Adult Learning

American Association for Adult &
  Continuing Education
1200 19th St. NW, Ste. 300
Washington, DC 20036
Ph: (202)429-5131   Fax: (202)223-4579

Bimonthly. $27.00/year. Journal covering instructional techniques and issues relating to adult and continuing education.

★270★ Community College Journal

American Association of Community and
  Junior Colleges
1 Dupont Circle NW, Ste. 410
Washington, DC 20036-1176
Ph: (202)728-0200   Fax: (202)223-9390

Bimonthly. $22.00/year for individuals; $4.00 for single issue; $28.00/year for other countries. Educational magazine.

★271★ Community Jobs: The Employment Newspaper for the Non-Profit Sector

ACCESS: Networking in the Public
  Interest
30 Irving Pl.
New York, NY 10003
Ph: (212)475-1001   Fax: (212)475-1199

Monthly. $69.00. Covers jobs and internships available with nonprofit organizations active in issues such as the environment, foreign policy, consumer advocacy, housing, education, etc. Entries include: Position title; name, address, and phone of contact; description, responsibilities; requirements; salary. Arrangement: Geographical.

★272★ EIS English as a Second Language Lists

Education Information Services (EIS)
PO Box 660662
Newton, MA 02162-0662
Ph: (617)443-0125

$5.00-$10.00 for each list. Provides lists of names and addresses of schools seeking teachers of English As A Second Language in most countries of the world.

★273★ NABE News

National Association for Bilingual
  Education (NABE)
1220 L St. NW, Ste. 605
Washington, DC 20005-4018
Ph: (202)898-1829

Eight issues/year.

PLACEMENT AND JOB REFERRAL SERVICES

★274★ American Association of Women in Community and Junior Colleges (AAWCJC)

Amarillo College
PO Box 447
Amarillo, TX 79178-0001
Ph: (806)371-5000   Fax: (806)371-5370

Members: Women faculty members, administrators, staff members, students, and trustees of community colleges. **Purpose:** Objectives are to: develop communication and disseminate information among women in community, junior, and technical colleges; encourage educational program development; obtain grants for educational projects for community college women. Disseminates information on women's issues and programs. **Activities:** Conducts regional and state professional development workshops and forums. Maintains placement services.

★275★ International Educator's Institute (TIE)

PO Box 513
Cummaquid, MA 02637
Ph: (508)362-1414

Purpose: Facilitates the placement of teachers and administrators in American, British, and international schools. Seeks to create a network that provides for professional development opportunities and improved financial security of members. Offers advice and information on international school news, recent educational developments, job placement, and investment, consumer, and professional development opportunities. Makes available insurance and travel benefits. Operates International Schools Internship Program. Sponsors competitions. Bestows awards.

★276★ National Association for the Advancement of Black Americans in Vocational Education (NAABAVE)

PO Box 04437
Detroit, MI 48204
Ph: (313)494-1660   Fax: (313)494-1132

Members: Educational institutions, teachers, administrators, students, and government employees committed to the greater involvement of black Americans in all areas of vocational/technical education. **Purpose:** Goal is to generate national leadership and increase the impact of blacks in the field of vocational/technical education by: assuring opportunities and promoting recruitment and the retention of black Americans in all areas and levels; utilizing research discoveries as a basis for influencing key funding sources at the national, state, and local levels; providing a career information exchange system. Develops training models for marketable skills; links black talent with vocational/technical employment opportunities in the public and private sectors at the federal, state, and local levels; identifies, assesses, and evaluates critical issues that affect the extent of participation of blacks and offers recommendations for improvement. **Activities:** Conducts regional workshops. Maintains placement service for blacks and other minorities. Operates speakers' bureau; compiles statistics.

EMPLOYER DIRECTORIES AND NETWORKING LISTS

★277★ American Trade Schools Directory

Croner Publications, Inc.
34 Jericho Tpke.
Jericho, NY 11753
Ph: (516)333-9085   Fax: (516)338-4986
Fr: 800-441-4033

Base volume supplied upon subscription; monthly supplements. $95.00, plus $4.95 shipping, payment with order. Covers over 12,000 private and public trade, technical, and vocational schools. Entries include: School name, address, phone, contact person, year school founded, private or public, accrediting agencies, whether approved by state or Veterans Administration, home study courses offered. Arrangement: Geographical. Indexes: Occupation.

★278★ Chronicle Two-Year College Databook

Chronicle Guidance Publications, Inc.
PO Box 1190
Moravia, NY 13118
Ph: (315)497-0330   Fax: (315)497-3359
Fr: 800-622-7284

Annual, September. $22.46, plus $2.25 shipping. Covers over 725 associate, certificate, occupational, and transfer programs offered by more than 2,400 technical institutes, two-year colleges, and universities in the United States. Entries include: College charts section gives college name, address, phone; accreditation, enrollment, admissions, costs, financial aid; accrediting associations' names, addresses, and phone numbers. Arrangement: Part I is classified by college major; part II is geographical. Indexes: College name.

★279★ Chronicle Vocational School Manual

Chronicle Guidance Publications, Inc.
PO Box 1190
Moravia, NY 13118
Ph: (315)497-0330   Fax: (315)497-3359
Fr: 800-622-7284

Annual, September. $22.48, plus $2.25 shipping. Covers over 920 programs of study offered by more than 4,000 vocational schools. Entries include: School name, city and ZIP code, phone, programs offered, admissions requirements, costs, enrollment, financial aid programs, year established, student services. Arrangement: Geographical. Indexes: Vocation/course.

★280★ Directory of Accredited Institutions

Indiana Commission on Proprietary Education
302 W. Washington St., Rm. E201
Indianapolis, IN 46204
Ph: (317)232-1320   Fax: (317)233-4219
Fr: 800-227-5695

Irregular, latest edition April 1994. Free. Covers about 220 vocational, trade and technical, and home study schools regulated by the Indiana Commission on Proprietary Education. Entries include: School name, address, phone, name and title of contact, description of courses, accreditation. Arrangement: Alphabetical. Indexes: Subject (courses).

★281★ Directory of Public Vocational-Technical Schools and Institutes in the U.S.A.

Media Marketing Group, Inc.
Box 611
DeKalb, IL 60115
Ph: (815)895-6842

Biennial, January of even years. $65.00. Covers over 1,400 post-secondary vocational and technical education programs in public education; private trade and technical schools are not included. Also includes state agencies responsible for vocational and technical education. Entries include: For institutions: name, address, phone, contact person, relevant programs offered. For agencies: name, address. Arrangement: Geographical. Indexes: Institution name, program, subject.

★282★ National Profile of Community Colleges: Trends and Statistics

American Association of Community Colleges (AACC)
1 Dupont Cir. NW, Ste. 410
Washington, DC 20036-1136

$65.00 for nonmembers; $50.00 for members. Covers about 1,500 community, technical, and junior colleges in the United States; state directors for community colleges. Entries include: Institution name, address, phone, name of chief executive officer, year established, total credit and non-credit enrollment, number of faculty and administrators, tuition. Arrangement: Geographical.

★283★ Opportunities Abroad for Educators

Fulbright Teacher Exchange Program
600 Maryland Ave., SW, Rm. 235
Washington, DC 20024-2520
Ph: (202)382-8586   Fax: (202)426-0657
Fr: 800-726-0479

Annual, May. Free. Covers opportunities available for elementary and secondary teachers, college and university instructors and professors, and school administrators to attend seminars or to teach abroad under the Mutual Educational and Cultural Exchange Act of 1961. Entries include: Countries of placement, dates, eligibility requirements, teaching assignments. Arrangement: Geographical.

★284★ Peterson's Guide to Vocational and Technical Schools

Peterson's Guides, Inc.
202 Carnegie Ctr.
Box 2123
Princeton, NJ 08543-2123
Ph: (609)243-9111   Fax: (609)243-9150
Fr: 800-338-3282

Published 1993. $34.95. Covers approximately 7,400 accredited vocational and technical schools that offer training programs in over 240 career fields. Available in separate eastern and western U.S. regional editions. Entries include: Institution name, address, phone, name and title of contact, type of institution, year founded, accreditation, enrollment, faculty-to-student ratio, registration fee, student body profile, programs offered, student services, financial aid. Arrangement: Classified by by program type.

★285★ School Guide

School Guide Publications
210 North Ave.
New Rochelle, NY 10801
Ph: (914)632-7771   Fax: (914)632-3412
Fr: 800-433-7771

Annual, March. $10.00. Covers over 1,000 colleges, vocational schools, and nursing schools in the United States. Entries include: Institution name, address, phone, courses offered, degrees awarded. Arrangement: Classified by type of institution, then geographical. Indexes: Subject.

★286★ Schools—Business & Vocational Directory

American Business Directories, Inc.
American Business Information, Inc.
5711 S. 86th Cir.
Omaha, NE 68127
Ph: (402)593-4600   Fax: (402)331-1505

Annual. $445.00, payment with order. Entries include: Name, address, phone (including area code), size of advertisement, year first in Yellow Pages, name of owner or manager, number of employees. Compiled from telephone company Yellow Pages, nationwide. Arrangement: Geographical.

★287★ Schools Industrial, Technical, & Trade Directory

American Business Directories, Inc.
American Business Information, Inc.
5711 S. 86th Cir.
Omaha, NE 68127
Ph: (402)593-4600   Fax: (402)331-1505

Annual. $290.00, U.S. edition. Entries include: Name, address, phone (including area code), size of advertisement, year first in Yellow Pages, name of owner or manager, number of employees. Compiled from telephone company Yellow Pages, nationwide. Arrangement: Geographical.

★288★ Tech Prep Guide: Technical, Trade, & Business School Data Handbook

Wintergreen/Orchard House, Inc.
PO Box 15899
New Orleans, LA 70175-5899
Ph: (504)866-8658   Fax: (504)866-8710
Fr: 800-321-9479

Biennial, even years. $150.00, national edition, plus $9.00 shipping; $45.00, each, regional editions, $2.70 shipping. Covers over 5,170 accredited public and proprietary post-secondary schools offering programs in auto mechanics, aviation, business, electronics, and other technical, trade, or business fields. Available in a four-volume national edition or as four regional editions. Entries include: School name, address, phone, accrediting body, admissions contact, course offerings, placement services, and profile. Arrangement: Geographical. Indexes: Subject.

HANDBOOKS AND MANUALS

★289★ Career Choices for the 90's for Students of Art

Walker and Company
435 Hudson St.
New York, NY 10014
Ph: (212)727-8300   Fax: (212)727-0984
Fr: 800-289-2553

Prepared by the Career Associates staff. 1990. $9.95. 166 pages. Discusses alternatives for students of art. Offers advice on how to break into the field and how to move up. Covers where and who the employers are, internship possibilities, and professional networking associations. Comprehensive guide to career and job search planning.

★290★ Career Choices for the 90's for Students of Political Science and Government

Walker and Company
435 Hudson St.
New York, NY 10014
Ph: (212)727-8300   Fax: (212)727-0984
Fr: 800-289-2553

Prepared by the Career Associates staff. 1990. $8.95. 166 pages. Discusses alternatives for students of political science and government. Offers advice on how to break into the field and how to move up. Covers where and who the employers are, internship possibilities, and professional networking associations. Comprehensive guide to career and job search planning.

★291★ Career Information Center

Macmillan Publishing Co.
200 Old Tappan Rd.
Old Tappan, NJ 07675
Ph: (609)461-6500   Fr: 800-223-2336

Visual Education Center Staff. Fifth edition, 1992. $229.00. This 13-volume set profiles over 600 occupations. Each occupational profile describes job duties, educational requirements, how to get the job, advancement possibilities, employment outlook, working conditions, earnings and benefits, and where to write for more information.

★292★ Careers in Education

VGM Career Horizons
4255 W. Touhy Ave.
Lincolnwood, IL 60646-1975
Ph: (847)679-5500   Fax: (847)679-2494
Fr: 800-323-4900

Roy A. Edelfeldt. 1993. $17.95; $13.95 (paper). 192 pages. Explores opportunities for teachers, administrators, and specialists in elementary and secondary schools, as well as teaching, research, and administrative positions in higher education. Additional focus on adult and continuing education and industry opportunities for educators. Provides detailed background on careers in state boards and state departments of education, accrediting agencies, federal agencies, and national associations and councils.

★293★ The Encyclopedia of Career Choices for the 1990s: Guide to Entry-Level Jobs

Perigree Books
The Berkley Publishing Group
PO Box 506
East Rutherford, NJ 07073
Ph: (201)933-9292   Fr: 800-223-0510

Career Associates Staff. 1992. $19.95. 862 pages. Describes 500 entry-level careers in a variety of industries. Presents qualifications required, working conditions, salary, internships, and professional associations.

★294★ How to Get a Job in Education

Bob Adams, Inc.
260 Center St.
Holbrook, MA 02343
Ph: (617)767-8100   Fax: (617)767-0994
Fr: 800-872-5627

Joel Levin. Second edition, 1995. $12.95. 320 pages. Prepared for recent college graduates, seasoned educators, and career-changing professionals, this publication guides the job-seeker through the necessary steps to obtaining a job in education at the elementary, secondary, and university levels. Offers advice on how to prepare for state and local examinations, how to locate teaching opportunities nationwide, and how to obtain certification. Includes a nationwide salary survey. Covers public, private, summer, and overseas opportunities.

★295★ Liberal Arts Jobs: What They Are and How to Get Them

Peterson's
PO Box 2123
Princeton, NJ 08543-2123
Ph: (609)243-9111   Fax: (609)243-9150
Fr: 800-338-3282

Burton Jay Nadler. Second edition, 1989. $9.95. 153 pages. Presents a list of the top 20 fields for liberal arts majors, covering more than 300 job opportunities. Discusses strategies for going after those jobs, including guidance on the language of a successful job search, informational interviews, and making networking work.

★296★ Non-Profits and Education Job Finder

Planning/Communications
7215 Oak Ave.
River Forest, IL 60305-1935
Ph: (708)366-5200   Fr: (888)366-5200

Daniel Lauber. 1996. $32.95; $16.95 (paper). 350 pages. Covers 1600 sources. Discusses how to use sources of non-profit sector job vacancies in a number of specialties and state-by-state, including job-matching services, job hotlines, specialty periodicals with job ads, salary surveys, and directories. Covers a variety of fields from education to religion. Includes chapters on resume and cover letter preparation and interviewing.

★297★ 100 Best Careers for the Year 2000

Prentice Hall General Reference
15 Columbus Cir.
New York, NY 10023
Ph: (212)373-8500   Fr: 800-223-2348

Shelly Field. 1992. $15.00 (paper). Covers 100 of the fastest growing jobs. The publication is divided into 11 general employment sections. Specific careers are covered within each section. Provides job description, responsibilities, employment opportunities, earnings, education and training, advancement opportunities, and experience and qualifications for each occupation.

★298★ Opportunities in Marketing Careers

VGM Career Horizons
4255 W. Touhy Ave.
Lincolnwood, IL 60646-1975
Ph: (847)679-5500   Fax: (847)679-2494
Fr: 800-323-4900

Margery Steinberg. 1994. $14.95; $11.95 (paper). 160 pages. Includes guidance on identifying and pursuing job opportunities. Illustrated.

EMPLOYMENT AGENCIES AND SEARCH FIRMS

★299★ Educational Placement Service

5050 Poplar Ave., Ste. 1700
Memphis, TN 38157-1701
Ph: (901)767-1884

Employment agency. Focuses on teaching, administrative, and education-related openings.

OTHER SOURCES

★300★ American Association for Adult and Continuing Education (AAACE)

1200 19th St. NW, Ste. 300
Washington, DC 20036
Ph: (202)429-5131   Fax: (202)223-4579

Purpose: Provides leadership in advancing adult education as a lifelong learning process. Serves as a central forum for a wide variety of adult and continuing education special interest groups. Works to stimulate local, state, and regional adult continuing education efforts; encourage mutual cooperation and support; monitor proposed legislation and offer testimony to Congress.

★301★ American Association of Community Colleges (AACC)

National Center for Higher Educ.
1 Dupont Cir. NW, Ste. 410
Washington, DC 20036-1176
Ph: (202)728-0200   Fax: (202)833-2467

Members: Community colleges; individual associates interested in community college development; corporate, educational, foundation, and international associate members. **Purpose:** Office of Federal Relations monitors federal educational programming and legislation. **Activities:** Compiles statistics through data collection and policy analysis. Conducts seminars and professional training programs.

★302★ American Association of Cosmetology Schools (AACS)

901 N. Washington St., Ste. 206
Alexandria, VA 22314-1535
Ph: (703)845-1333   Fax: (703)845-1336

Members: Owners and instructors of schools of cosmetology; associate members are manufacturers and jobbers of beauty products and others interested in beauty culture and training. Sponsors competitions and seminars.

★303★ American Vocational Association (AVA)

1410 King St.
Alexandria, VA 22314
Ph: (703)683-3111   Fax: (703)683-7424
Fr: 800-892-2274

Members: Teachers, supervisors, administrators, and others interested in the development and improvement of vocational, technical, and practical arts education. Areas of interest include: secondary, postsecondary, and adult vocational education; education for special population groups; cooperative education. **Purpose:** Works with such government agencies as: Bureau of Apprenticeship in Department of Labor; Office of Vocational Rehabilitation in Department of Health and Human Services; Veterans Administration; Office of Vocational and Adult Education of the Department of Education. Maintains hall of fame; bestows awards.

★304★ A Career for the 21st Century

International Technology Education
  Association
Publications Dept.
1914 Association Dr.
Reston, VA 22091
Ph: (703)860-2100

Video. $20.00. 10 minutes. Career profile of technology teachers covers benefits and necessary preparation.

★305★ College Reading and Learning Association (CRLA)

University of North Colorado
McKee 213
Greeley, CO 80639
Ph: (303)351-2189   Fax: (303)351-2312

Members: Professionals involved in college/adult reading, learning assistance, developmental education, and tutorial services. **Purpose:** Promotes communication for the purpose of professional growth.

★306★ International Reading Association (IRA)

800 Barksdale Rd.
PO Box 8139
Newark, DE 19714-8139
Ph: (302)731-1600   Fax: (302)731-1057

Members: Teachers, reading specialists, consultants, administrators, supervisors, researchers, psychologists, librarians, and parents interested in promoting literacy. **Purpose:** Seeks to improve the quality of reading instruction and promote literacy worldwide. Disseminates information pertaining to research on reading, including information on adult literacy, early childhood and literacy development, international education, literature for children and adolescents, and teacher education and professional development. **Activities:** Maintains over 40 special interest groups and over 70 committees. **E-Mail:** 74673.3646@compuserve.com

★307★ International Technology Education Association - Council for Supervisors (ITEA-CS)

George R. Willcox
Virginia Department of Education
PO Box 2120, 21st Fl.
Richmond, VA 23216-2120
Ph: (804)225-2020   Fax: (804)371-0249

Members: Technology education supervisors from the U.S. Office of Education; local school department chairpersons; state departments of education, local school districts, territories, provinces, and foreign countries. **Purpose:** To improve instruction and supervision of programs in technology education. **Activities:** Conducts research; compiles statistics. Sponsors competitions. Maintains speakers' bureau.

★308★ National Association for Industry-Education Cooperation (NAIEC)

235 Hendricks Blvd.
Buffalo, NY 14226
Ph: (716)834-7047   Fax: (716)834-7047

Members: Representatives of business, industry, education, government, labor, and the professions. **Purpose:** Fosters industry-education collaboration in school improvement in order to form responsive academic and vocational programs which will more effectively serve the needs of both the students and employers as well as further human resources and economic development. Provides technical assistance to schools implementing business- or industry-sponsored programs. Promotes improved career and entrepreneurship education and supports school-based job placement. Provides staff development programs to improve instruction and curricula through use of corporate and volunteer services. Acts as national clearinghouse for information on industry involvement in education; serves as liaison between organizations involved in industry-education cooperation, including Chamber of Commerce of the United States-U.S. Chamber, Council of Chief State School Officers, and American Society for Training and Development.

★309★ North American Council of Automotive Teachers (NACAT)

11956 Bernardo Plaza Dr., Dept. 436
San Diego, CA 92128-9713
Ph: (619)487-8126   Fax: (619)487-3617

Members: Automotive teachers. **Purpose:** To cooperate with all members of the automotive industry, and federal and state governments to improve educational levels and educational resources for the automotive teacher. Encourages use of uniform curricula on specific types of car repair and replacement. **Activities:** Maintains speakers' bureau; conducts educational programs.

★310★ Overseas Employment Opportunities for Educators: Department of Defense Dependents Schools

Diane Publishing Co.
600 Upland Ave.
Upland, PA 19015
Ph: (610)499-7415

1993. $29.95. 52 pages.

★311★ Randax Education Guide to Colleges Seeking Students

Education Guide, Inc.
PO Box 63
Hingham, MA 02043
Ph: (617)740-2040   Fax: (617)740-0018

Annual, January. $17.95, postpaid; payment with order. Covers about 200 two-year and four-year colleges, health care schools, and vocational schools that are actively recruiting students and that advertise in the publication. Entries include: School name, address, phone, degrees and courses offered, date founded, type of control, enrollment, costs, admission requirements. Arrangement: Geographical. Indexes: Major study, state, school name.

★312★ Resumes for Education Careers

VGM Career Horizons
4255 W. Touhy Ave.
Lincolnwood, IL 60646-1975
Ph: (847)679-5500   Fax: (847)679-2494
Fr: 800-323-4900

1992. $9.95. Sample resumes cover a variety of education careers and reflect education professionals at all levels of experience.

★313★ Vocational Careers Sourcebook

Gale Research
835 Penobscot Bldg.
Detroit, MI 48226-4094
Ph: (313)961-2242   Fax: (313)961-6083
Fr: 800-877-GALE

Second edition, 1995. $79.00. 1,100 pages. Directs users to career information sources related to specific occupations, such as insurance and real estate sales, corrections and police work, mechanics, armed forces options, agriculture and forestry, production work, and the trades. Contains information on general career guides, career information and services provided by trade associations, standards and certification agencies, directories of educational programs and institutions, basic reference guides and handbooks related to the occupation, trade periodicals, and more. Indexes: Alphabetical.

Aerospace Engineers

SOURCES OF HELP-WANTED ADS

★314★ Aerospace Engineering

Society of Automotive Engineers, Inc.
400 Commonwealth Dr.
Warrendale, PA 15096
Ph: (412)776-4841   Fax: (412)776-4026

Monthly. $44.00/year; $96.00/year for other countries. Magazine for aerospace manufacturing engineers providing technical and design information.

★315★ Aerospace Products News

Gordon Publications, Inc.
301 Gibraltar Dr.
PO Box 231
Cooperstown, NY 13326
Ph: (607)547-2591   Fax: (607)547-2923

Seven times/year. $17.50/year; $2.50/issue.

★316★ Aviation Equipment Maintenance

Phillips Business Information, Inc.
1201 Seven Locks Rd.
Potomac, MD 20854
Ph: (301)340-1520   Fax: (301)340-0542

Monthly. Free to qualified subscribers. Magazine covering aviation maintenance.

★317★ Aviation Week and Space Technology

New York Construction News
1221 Avenue of the Americas, 41st Fl.
New York, NY 10020
Ph: (212)512-4773   Fax: (212)512-4770

Weekly (Mon.). Magazine focusing on aviation space engineering.

★318★ Captsule Job Listings

Publications and Communications, Inc.
12416 Hymeadow Dr.
Austin, TX 78750
Ph: (512)250-9023   Fax: (512)331-3900
Fr: 800-678-9724

Online database. Lists current job openings in the contract (temporary) technical services industry. Includes the Action Hot List, which provides information on job seekers. Includes employment opportunities in technical/professional engineering, computing, and design/drafting. Entries generally contain company name, address, and job opening.

★319★ Engineering Times

National Society of Professional Engineers
1420 King St.
Alexandria, VA 22314
Ph: (703)684-2875   Fax: (703)836-4875

Monthly. Magazine (tabloid) covering professional, legislative, and techology issues for an engineering audience.

★320★ ENR: Engineering News Record

New York Construction News
1221 Avenue of the Americas
New York, NY 10020
Ph: (212)512-4773   Fax: (212)512-4770

Weekly. $42.00/year; $2.00/issue.

★321★ High Technology Careers Magazine

HTC
4701 Patrick Henry Dr., No. 1901
Santa Clara, CA 95054
Ph: (408)970-8800   Fax: (408)980-5103

Bimonthly. Magazine (tabloid) containing employment opportunity information for the engineering and technical community.

★322★ Minority Engineer

Equal Opportunity Publications, Inc.
150 Motor Pkwy., Ste. 420
Hauppauge, NY 11788-5145
Ph: (516)273-0066   Fax: (516)273-8936

Affirmative-action recruitment magazine serving college graduating and professional minority engineers.

★323★ NASA Tech Briefs

Associated Business Publications Co., Ltd.
41 E. 42nd St.
New York, NY 10017
Ph: (212)490-3999   Fax: (212)986-7864

Monthly. Free to qualified subscribers. Publication covering technology for American industry and government in the fields of electronics, computers, physical sciences, materials, mechanics, machinery, fabrication technology, math and information sciences, and the life sciences.

★324★ NSBE Magazine

NSBE Publications
1454 Duke St.
Alexandria, VA 22314
Ph: (703)549-2207   Fax: (703)683-5312

$10.00/year for individuals; $2.00 for single issue. Journal providing information on engineering careers, self-development, and cultural issues for recent graduates with technical majors.

★325★ SWE

Society of Women Engineers
120 Wall St., 11th Fl.
New York, NY 10005-3902
Ph: (212)509-9577   Fax: (212)509-0224

Bimonthly. $30.00/year for nonmembers. Magazine for engineering students and for women and men working in the engineering and technology fields. Covers career guidance, continuing development and topical issues.

★326★ Technology Review

The Tech
PO Box 397029
Cambridge, MA 02139
Ph: (617)253-1541   Fax: (617)258-8226

$30.00/year for individuals; $3.75 for single issue; $42.00/year for other countries. Magazine reviewing new developments in technology with an emphasis on economic, political, and social implications. Not a new product publication.

★327★ TEST Engineering & Management

The Mattingley Publishing Co., Inc.
3756 Grand Ave., Ste. 205
Oakland, CA 94610
Ph: (510)839-0909   Fax: (510)839-2950

Bimonthly. $30.00/year for individuals; $40.00/year for other countries; $5.00 for single issue. Reliability/qualifications test engineering magazine.

★328★ Woman Engineer

Equal Opportunity Publications, Inc.
150 Motor Pkwy., Ste. 420
Hauppauge, NY 11788-5145
Ph: (516)273-0066   Fax: (516)273-8936

Engineer recruitment magazine.

PLACEMENT AND JOB REFERRAL SERVICES

★329★ American Indian Science and Engineering Society (AISES)

1630 30th St., Ste. 301
Boulder, CO 80301
Ph: (303)492-8658   Fax: (303)492-3400

Members: American Indian and non-Indian students and professionals in science, technology, and engineering fields; corporations representing energy, mining, aerospace, electronic, and computer fields. **Purpose:** Seeks to motivate and encourage students to pursue undergraduate and graduate studies in science, engineering, and technology. **Activities:** Sponsors science fairs in grade schools, teacher training workshops, summer math/science sessions for 8th-12th graders, professional chapters, and student chapters in colleges. Offers scholarships. Adult members serve as role models, advisers, and mentors for students. Operates placement service. **E-Mail:** aise sha@spot.colorado.edu

★330★ American Institute of Aeronautics and Astronautics (AIAA)

370 L'Enfant Promenade SW
Washington, DC 20024
Ph: (202)646-7400   Fax: (202)646-7508

Members: Scientists and engineers in the field of aeronautics and astronautics. **Purpose:** Facilitates interchange of technological information through publications and technical meetings in order to foster overall technical progress in the field and increase the professional competence of members. Operates Public Policy program to provide federal decision-makers with the technical information and policy guidance needed to make effective policy on aerospace issues. Public Policy program activities include congressional testimony, position papers, section public policy activities, and workshops. **Activities:** Offers placement assistance; compiles statistics; offers educational programs. Provides abstracting services through its Acroplus Access.

★331★ Engineering Society of Detroit (ESD)

100 Farnsworth Ave.
Detroit, MI 48202
Ph: (313)832-5400   Fax: (313)832-5920

Members: Engineers from all disciplines; scientists and technologists. **Activities:** Offers placement services. Conducts technical programs and engineering refresher courses; sponsors conferences and expositions. Maintains speakers' bureau. Although based in Detroit, MI, society membership is international.

★332★ ISA

PO Box 12277
67 Alexander Dr.
Research Triangle Park, NC 27709
Ph: (919)549-8411   Fax: (919)549-8288

Purpose: Educational organization dedicated to advancing knowledge and practice related to the theory, design, manufacture, and use of instruments and controls in science and industry. Operates training center for industry; conducts symposia; develops standards; recognizes individual achievement. **Activities:** Maintains speakers' bureau and placement service.

★333★ Korean Scientists and Engineers Association in America (KSEA)

6261 Executive Blvd.
Rockville, MD 20852
Ph: (301)984-7048   Fax: (301)984-1231

Members: Scientists and engineers holding single or advanced degrees. **Purpose:** Goals are to: promote friendship and mutuality among Korean and American scientists and engineers; contribute to Korea's scientific, technological, industrial, and economic developments; strengthen the scientific, technological, and cultural bonds between Korea and the U.S. Sponsors symposium. **Activities:** Maintains speakers' bureau, placement service, and biographical archives. Compiles statistics. Maintains 100 volume library of scientific handbooks and yearbooks in Korean.

★334★ Society of Hispanic Professional Engineers (SHPE)

5400 E. Olympic Blvd., Ste. 210
Los Angeles, CA 90022
Ph: (213)725-3970

Purpose: Engineers, student engineers, and scientists seeking to increase the number of Hispanic engineers by providing motivation and support to students. Sponsors competitions and educational programs. **Activities:** Maintains placement service and speakers' bureau; compiles statistics.

EMPLOYER DIRECTORIES AND NETWORKING LISTS

★335★ Aerospace Technology Centres

Longman Publishing Group
The Longman Bldg.
10 Bank St.
White Plains, NY 10606-1951
Ph: (914)993-5000   Fr: 800-266-8855

Second edition, 1991. $475.00. Profiles more than 700 research and technical laboratories, public as well as private, furnish administrators, scientists, engineers, consultants, and others. Arrangement: By country.

★336★ American Institute of Aeronautics and Astronautics—Roster

American Institute of Aeronautics and Astronautics
370 L'Enfant Promenade SW
Washington, DC 20024
Ph: (202)646-7400   Fax: (202)646-7508
Fr: 800-682-2422

Biennial, January of odd years. $79.95. Covers 34,000 member scientists, managers and engineers in the fields of aeronautics and astronautics; international coverage. Entries include: Name, title, affiliation, address, phone. Arrangement: Alphabetical. Indexes: Affiliation.

★337★ American Men and Women of Science

R. R. Bowker Co.
Reed Reference Publishing
121 Chanlon Rd.
New Providence, NJ 07974
Ph: (908)464-6800   Fax: (908)665-6688
Fr: 800-521-8110

Triennial, latest edition January 1995. $106.00, per volume; $850.00, set. Covers over 123,000 U.S. and Canadian scientists active in the physical, biological, mathematical, computer science, and engineering fields; includes references to previous edition for deceased scientists and nonrespondents. Entries include: Name, address, education, personal and career data, memberships, honors and awards, research interest. Arrangement: Alphabetical. Indexes: Discipline (in separate volume).

★338★ Directory of Contract Service Firms

C. E. Publications, Inc.
PO Box 97000
Kirkland, WA 98083
Ph: (206)823-2222   Fax: (206)821-0942

Annual, January. $10.00. Covers Approximately 900 contract firms actively engaged in the employment of engineering and technical personnel for temporary contract assignments throughout the world. Entries include: Company name, address, phone, name of contact. Arrangement: Alphabetical. Indexes: Geographical.

★339★ Directory of Engineering Societies and Related Organizations

American Association of Engineering Societies
1111 19th St. NW, Ste. 608
Washington, DC 20036
Ph: (202)296-2237   Fax: (202)296-1151
Fr: 800-658-8897

1992. $185.00. Lists 1,000 national, regional, Canadian, and international organizations concerned with engineering and related fields.

★340★ Directory of Engineers in Private Practice

National Society of Professional Engineers
1420 King St.
Alexandria, VA 22314
Ph: (703)684-2862   Fax: (703)836-4875

Annual. $85.00. Covers 600 consulting engineering firms and 7,200 individuals who are members of the society's Professional Engineers in Private Practice division. Entries include: For companies, name, address, phone, name of principal executive, list of services. For individuals, name, address; most listings include phone. Arrangement: Firms are geographic, then by specialty; individuals are alphabetical.

★341★ Engineering Research Centres

Stockton Press
Groves Dictionaries
345 Park Ave. S., 10th Fl.
New York, NY 10010
Ph: (212)689-9200   Fr: 800-221-2123

Fourth edition, 1995. $515.00. 768 pages. Contains over 8,000 entries describing research and technology laboratories in over 70 countries. Provides details on industrial research centers and educational establishments with research and development activity. Indexes: Subject and title of establishments.

★342★ Peterson's Job Opportunities in Engineering and Technology 1996

Peterson's
PO Box 2123
Princeton, NJ 08543-2123
Ph: (609)243-9111   Fax: (609)243-9150
Fr: 800-338-3282

Compiled by the Peterson's staff. Annual. $19.95 paperback. 432 pages. Profiles 2,000 high-tech companies looking primarily for technical personnel in such fields as biotechnology, telecommunications, software, computers and peripherals, defense, and aerospace. Contains job-search strategies and career options to help match education and expertise to the job market. Indexed geographically, by industry, and by hiring needs.

★343★ Scientific and Technical Organizations and Agencies Directory

Gale Research
835 Penobscot Bldg.
Detroit, MI 48226-4094
Ph: (313)961-2242   Fax: (313)961-6083
Fr: 800-877-GALE

Irregular; latest edition December 1993. $195.00. Covers over 25,600 national and international organizations and agencies concerned with the physical and applied sciences, engineering, and technology, including associations, computer information services, consulting firms, educational institutions, foundations, government advisory organizations, federal government agencies, general grant and assistance programs, libraries and information centers, patent sources and services, research and development centers, scholarships, fellowships, and loans, science-technology centers, standards organizations, state academies of science, and state government agencies in the fields of aeronautics and space sciences, chemistry, computer science specialties, electronics, geography, geology, machinery, mathematics, metallurgy, meteorology, mineralogy, nuclear science, petroleum and gas, physics, plastics, transportation, water resources, and other areas. Entries include: Organization name, address, phone, and name of contact; additional descriptive text for most entries. Arrangement: Classified by type of organization. Indexes: Organization name/key word.

★344★ Space Industry International

Gale Research
835 Penobscot Bldg.
Detroit, MI 48226
Ph: (313)961-2242   Fax: (313)961-6083
Fr: 800-877-GALE

Second edition, 1994. $522.00. Provides global coverage of companies, organizations, agencies, and similar bodies active in the space industry. Regional chapters cover national programs as well as the specifics on private firms, associations, and institutes. Indexes: Company and organization name, product area, and personal name.

★345★ Who's Who in Technology

Gale Research
835 Penobscot Bldg.
Detroit, MI 48226-4094
Ph: (313)961-2242   Fax: (313)961-6083
Fr: 800-877-GALE

Irregular, new edition expected June 1995. $380.00. Covers 38,000 engineers, scientists, inventors, and researchers. Entries include: Name, title, affiliation, address; personal, education, and career data; publications, patents; technical field of activity; area of expertise. Arrangement: Alphabetical. Indexes: Geographical, employer, technical discipline, expertise.

HANDBOOKS AND MANUALS

★346★ The Aerospace Careers Handbook

Simon and Schuster Trade
1230 Avenue of the Americas
New York, NY 10020
Ph: (212)698-7000   Fr: 800-223-2348

Anne Cardoza and Suzee J. Vlk. Contains index, bibliography, and illustrations.

★347★ The Best Resumes for Scientists and Engineers

John Wiley and Sons
605 3rd Ave.
New York, NY 10158
Ph: (212)850-6000   Fr: 800-225-5945

Adele Lewis. Second edition, 1993. $37.50; $14.95 (paper). Presents an extensive collection of scientific and engineering resumes, highlighting the important differences between these and resumes written for other occupations.

★348★ Careers in Engineering

VGM Career Horizons
4255 W. Touhy Ave.
Lincolnwood, IL 60646-1975
Ph: (847)679-5500   Fax: (847)679-2494
Fr: 800-323-4900

Geraldine O. Gardner. 1994. $17.95; $13.95 (paper). Covers careers in the public or private sector, in industry, the university, or the military, from applications in computer architecture design to high temperature ceramics.

★349★ Careers in High Tech

VGM Career Horizons
NTC Publishing Group
4255 W. Touhy Ave.
Lincolnwood, IL 60646-1975
Ph: (847)679-5500   Fax: (847)679-2494
Fr: 800-323-4900

Nick Basta. 1994. $17.95; $13.95 (paper). 160 pages. Examines new career opportunities in such fields as biotechnology, computers, aerospace, telecommunications, and others.

★350★ Engineering Success

Kendall Hunt Publishing
4050 Westmark Dr.
PO Box 1840
Dubuque, IA 52004-1840
Ph: (319)589-1000   Fax: 800-772-9165
Fr: 800-228-0810

Bill Osher. 1994. $27.96.

★351★ Engineering Your Job Search: A Job-Finding Resource for Engineering Professionals

Professional Publications, Inc.
1250 5th Ave.
Belmont, CA 94002
Ph: (415)593-9119   Fax: (415)592-4519
Fr: 800-426-1178

Compiled by Professional Publications editors. 1995. $12.95 (paper).

★352★ Introduction to the Engineering Profession

HarperCollins Publishers, Inc.
10 E. 53rd. St.
New York, NY 10022-5299
Ph: (212)207-7000   Fax: (212)207-7145
Fr: 800-331-3761

David M. Burghardt. 1995. $30.00 (paper).

★353★ Job Opportunities in Engineering and Technology

Peterson's Guides, Inc.
PO Box 2123
Princeton, NJ 08543-2123
Ph: (609)243-9111   Fax: (609)243-9150
Fr: 800-338-3282

1994. $18.95 (paper).

★354★ Majoring in Engineering: How to Get from Your Freshman Year to Your First Job

Farrar, Straus & Giroux, Inc.
19 Union Sq., W
New York, NY 10003
Ph: (212)741-6900   Fr: 800-788-6262

John Garcia. 1995. $20.00; $10.00 (paper).

★355★ Opportunities in Aerospace Careers

VGM Career Horizons
4255 W. Touhy Ave.
Lincolnwood, IL 60646-1975
Ph: (847)679-5500   Fax: (847)679-2494
Fr: 800-323-4900

Wallace R. Maples. 1995. $14.95; $11.95 (paper). Surveys jobs with the airlines, airports, the government, the military, in manufacturing, and in research and development.

Includes information on job opportunities with NASA in the U.S. space program.

★356★ **Opportunities in Engineering Careers**
VGM Career Horizons
4255 W. Touhy Ave.
Lincolnwood, IL 60646-1975
Ph: (847)679-5500   Fax: (847)679-2494
Fr: 800-323-4900

Nicholas Basta. 1995. $14.95; $11.95 (paper). Outlines typical job titles, salaries, career paths, and employment prospects.

★357★ **Opportunities in High Tech Careers**
VGM Career Horizons
4255 W. Touhy Ave.
Lincolnwood, IL 60646-1975
Ph: (847)679-5500   Fax: (847)679-2494
Fr: 800-323-4900

Gary D. Golter and Deborah Yanuck. 1995. $14.95; $11.95 (paper). 160 pages. Explores high technology careers. Describes job opportunities, how to make a career decision, how to prepare for high technology jobs, job hunting techniques, and future trends.

★358★ **Resumes for Engineering Careers**
VGM Career Horizons
NTC Publishing Group
4255 W. Touhy Ave.
Lincolnwood, IL 60646-1975
Ph: (847)679-5500   Fax: (847)679-2494
Fr: 800-323-4900

1994. $9.95. 160 pages. Contains sample resumes and cover letters applicable to any engineering field.

★359★ **Where the Jobs Are: The Hottest Careers for the '90s**
The Career Press, Inc.
3 Tice Rd.
PO Box 687
Franklin Lakes, NJ 07417
Ph: (201)848-0310   Fax: (201)848-1727
Fr: 800-237-3371

Joyce Hadley. Second edition, 1995. $9.99. 300 pages. Describes careers in fifteen general fields, from accounting to travel and hospitality.

EMPLOYMENT AGENCIES AND SEARCH FIRMS

★360★ **ABC Employment Service**
25 S. Bemiston, Ste. 214
Clayton, MO 63105
Ph: (314)725-3140
Employment agency.

★361★ **Amtec Engineering Corp.**
2749 Saturn St.
Brea, CA 92621
Ph: (714)993-1900   Fax: (714)993-2419
Employment agency.

★362★ **B and M Associates, Inc.**
199 Cambridge Rd.
Woburn, MA 01801-4705
Ph: (617)938-9120
Employment agency.

★363★ **Colli Associates of Tampa**
PO Box 2865
Tampa, FL 33601
Ph: (813)681-2145
Employment agency. Executive search firm.

★364★ **Engineer One, Inc.**
10124 Dutchtown Rd.
Knoxville, TN 37932-2611
Ph: (615)690-2611   Fax: (615)690-2611
Employment agency.

★365★ **Hayden and Associates, Inc.**
7825 Washington Ave. S., Ste. 120
Minneapolis, MN 55439-2431
Ph: (612)941-6300   Fax: (612)941-9602
Employment agency. Executive search firm. Fills openings in a variety of fields.

★366★ **Industrial Recruiters Associates, Inc.**
630 Oakwood Ave., Ste. 318
West Hartford, CT 06110
Ph: (203)953-3643
Employment agency.

★367★ **International Staffing Consultants**
500 Newport Center Dr., Ste. 300
Newport Beach, CA 92660-7003
Ph: (714)721-7990
Employment agency. Provides placement on regular or temporary basis. Affiliate office in London.

★368★ **The Jobs Co.**
8900 E. Sprague Ave.
Spokane, WA 99212-2927
Ph: (509)928-3151   Fax: (509)928-3168
Employment agency. Has division specializing in engineering and scientific openings. Also operates division specializing in sales openings.

★369★ **JR Professional Search**
PO Box 18356
Tucson, AZ 85731
Ph: (520)721-1855   Fax: (520)721-1855
Employment agency.

★370★ **LOR Personnel Division**
418 Wall St.
Princeton, NJ 08540
Ph: (609)921-6580
Employment agency. Executive search firm.

★371★ **Main Line Personnel Service, Inc.**
401 City Ave.
Bala Cynwyd, PA 19004-1122
Ph: (610)667-1820
Employment agency.

★372★ **Search and Recruit International**
4455 South Blvd.
Virginia Beach, VA 23452
Ph: (804)490-3151

Employment agency. Headquartered in Virginia Beach. Other offices in Bremerton, WA; Charleston, SC; Jacksonville, FL; Memphis, TN; Pensacola, FL; Sacramento, CA; San Bernardino, CA; San Diego, CA.

★373★ **Sierra Technology Corporation**
4150 Manzanita Ave., Ste. 100
Carmichael, CA 95608-1700
Ph: (916)488-4960   Fax: (916)488-7058

Employment agency. Provides placement on a temporary basis.

★374★ **Source Engineering**
5580 LBJ Fwy., Ste. 300
Dallas, TX 75240
Ph: (214)385-3002   Fax: (214)717-0075

Executive search firm. Many affiliate offices located throughout the U.S.

★375★ **T.R. Employment Agency**
409 Wilshire Blvd.
Santa Monica, CA 90401
Ph: (310)393-4107
Employment agency.

★376★ **Tri-Serv Inc.**
22 W. Padonia Rd., Ste. C53
Timonium, MD 21093
Ph: (301)561-1740
Employment agency.

OTHER SOURCES

★377★ **American Association of Engineering Societies (AAES)**
1111 19th St. NW, Ste. 608
Washington, DC 20036
Ph: (202)296-2237   Fax: (202)296-1151

Purpose: Seeks to promote leadership in public affairs for the engineering community, work in support of math and science education for young persons. Disseminates of information about the profession. Provides statistics about engineers.

★378★ **Association for International Practical Training (AIPT)**
10400 Little Patuxent Pkwy. Ste. 250
Columbia, MD 21044
Ph: (410)997-2200   Fax: (410)992-3924

Purpose: Helps coordinate training around the world in fields such as travel, the culinary arts, and hotel management. **Activities:** Conducts programs in career development and hospitality/tourism exchanges. Operates a student exchange program. Provides reciprocal practical training experience for recent graduates from the U.S., Austria, Germany, Finland, France, Hungary, Ireland, Japan, Malaysia, Netherlands, Switzerland, and the United Kingdom. Arranges training programs in the U.S. and abroad. Serves as U.S. affiliate to IAESTE (International Association for the Exchange of Students for Technical Experience) and operates a Professional Visitors Program to arrange short-term educational and training visits to the U.S. **E-Mail:** aipt@aipt.org

★379★ Engineering Salary Survey

Source Engineering
1290 Oakmead, Ste. 318
Sunnyvale, CA 94086
Ph: (408)738-8440

Annual. Discusses the structure of the engineering profession, trends, and compensation. Salaries are listed by job function, industry, and years of experience.

★380★ Graduating Engineer

Peterson's/COG Publishing Group
16030 Ventura Blvd., No. 560
Encino, CA 91436
Ph: (818)789-5293

Eight issues/year. Magazine focusing on employment, education, and career development for entry-level engineers.

★381★ National Action Council for Minorities in Engineering (NACME)

3 W. 35th St.
New York, NY 10001-2281
Ph: (212)279-2626   Fax: (212)629-5178

Purpose: Seeks to increase the number of African American, Latino, and Native American students enrolled in and graduating from engineering schools. Through the Corporate Scholars Program, offers comprehensive scholarships to engineering students that include leadership development, corporate mentors and summer internships. Works with local, regional, and national education organizations to motivate and encourage precollege students to engage in engineering careers. Conducts educational and research programs; operates project to assist engineering schools in improving the retention and graduation rates of minority students. Maintains speakers' bureau; compiles statistics.

★382★ National Society of Professional Engineers (NSPE)

1420 King St.
Alexandria, VA 22314
Ph: (703)684-2800   Fax: (703)836-4875

Members: Professional engineers and engineers-in-training in all fields registered in accordance with the laws of states or territories of the U.S. or provinces of Canada; qualified graduate engineers, student members, and registered land surveyors. **Purpose:** Is concerned with social, professional, ethical, and economic considerations of engineering as a profession; encompasses programs in public relations, employment practices, ethical considerations, education, and career guidance. Monitors legislative and regulatory actions of interest to the engineering profession. **Website:** http.//www.hspc.org

★383★ Salaries of Scientists, Engineers, and Technicians: A Summary of Salary Surveys

Commission on Professionals in Science and Technology (CPST)
1500 Massachusetts Ave. NW, Ste. 831
Washington, DC 20005
Ph: (202)223-6995

1993.

★384★ Society of Women Engineers (SWE)

120 Wall St., 11th Fl.
New York, NY 10005
Ph: (212)509-9577   Fax: (212)509-0224

Members: Educational service society of women engineers; membership is also open to men. **Purpose:** Supplies information on the achievements of women engineers and the opportunities available to them; assists women engineers in preparing for return to active work following temporary retirement. Serves as an informational center on women in engineering. **Activities:** Administers several certificate and scholarship programs. Offers tours and career guidance; conducts surveys. Compiles statistics.

Agricultural Scientists

★385★ **Agricultural Engineering**
American Society of Agricultural Engineers
2950 Niles Rd.
St. Joseph, MI 49085-9659
Ph: (616)429-0300   Fax: (616)429-3852
Bimonthly. Magazine covering technology for food and agriculture.

★386★ **BioWorld Magazine**
American Health Consultants, Inc.
PO Box 740021
Atlanta, GA 30374
Ph: (404)262-7436   Fax: (404)814-0759
Magazine covering the biotechnology industry.

★387★ **Cell**
Cell Press
50 Church St.
Cambridge, MA 02138
Ph: (617)661-7057   Fax: (617)661-7061
Biweekly. $325.00/year for individuals. Journal on molecular and cell biology.

★388★ **Environmental Opportunities**
Environmental Opportunities
PO Box 788
Walpole, NH 03608
Ph: (603)756-4553
Monthly. $47.00/year. Lists full-time openings in environmental positions as well as short-term opportunities and internships.

★389★ **Farm Journal**
Farm Journal, Inc.
230 W. Washington Sq.
Philadelphia, PA 19106
Ph: (215)829-4700   Fax: (215)829-4757
Fr: 800-523-1538
$14.00/year for individuals. Agricultural news magazine for people who own or operate farms or ranches.

★390★ **Farmland News**
104 Depot St.
PO Box 240
Archbold, OH 43502-0240
Ph: (419)445-9456   Fax: (419)445-4444
Weekly (Tues.). $21.00/year for individuals; $35.00 for two years. Agriculture and human-interest newspaper (tabloid).

★391★ **Feedstuffs**
Miller Publishing Co.
12400 Whitewater Dr., Ste. 1600
Minnetonka, MN 55343
Ph: (612)931-0211   Fax: (612)938-1832
Weekly (Mon.). Magazine serving the grain and feed industries.

★392★ **Nature: International Weekly Journal of Science**
Nature Publishing Co.
65 Bleecker St.
New York, NY 10012-2467
Ph: (212)477-9600   Fax: (212)505-1364
Weekly. Magazine covering science and technology, including the fields of biology, biochemistry, genetics, medicine, earth sciences, physics, pharmacology, and behavioral sciences.

★393★ **The Scientist**
The Scientist, Inc.
3501 Market St.
Philadelphia, PA 19104
Ph: (215)386-0100   Fax: (215)387-7542
Biweekly. $58.00/year for individuals; $82.00/year for Canada and Mexico; $79.00/year for other countries. Newspaper (tabloid) for scientists featuring news, opinions, research, and professional section.

★394★ **American Society of Agronomy (ASA)**
677 S. Segoe Rd.
Madison, WI 53711
Ph: (608)273-8080   Fax: (608)273-2021
Members: Professional society of agronomists, plant breeders, physiologists, soil scientists, chemists, educators, technicians, and others concerned with crop production and soil management, and conditions affecting them. **Activities:** Sponsors fellowship program and student essay and speech contests. Provides placement service.

★395★ **American Society for Horticultural Science (ASHS)**
113 S. West St., Ste. 400
Alexandria, VA 22314-2824
Ph: (703)836-4606   Fax: (703)836-2024
Members: Educators and government workers engaged in research, teaching, or extension work in horticultural science; firms, associations, and others interested in horticulture. **Purpose:** Promotes and encourages interest in scientific research and education in horticulture. **Activities:** Maintains hall of fame. Offers placement service. Operates 42 committees and 46 working groups. **E-Mail:** ashs@ashs.org

★396★ **Association of Applied Insect Ecologists (AAIE)**
1008 10th St., Ste. 549
Sacramento, CA 95814
Ph: (916)441-5224   Fax: (916)441-5224
Members: Professional agricultural pest management consultants, entomologists, and field personnel. **Purpose:** Promotes the implementation of integrated pest management in agricultural and urban environments. Provides a forum for the exchange of technical information on pest control. **Activities:** Offers placement service.

★397★ Federation of American Societies for Experimental Biology (FASEB)

9650 Rockville Pike
Bethesda, MD 20814-3998
Ph: (301)530-7000   Fax: (301)530-7001

Members: Federation of scientific societies with a total of 40,000 members: The American Physiological Society; American Society for Biochemistry and Molecular Biology; American Society for Pharmacology and Experimental Therapeutics; American Society for Investigative Pathology; American Institute of Nutrition; The American Association of Immunologists; The American Society for Cell Biology; Biophysical Society; American Association of Anatomist. **Activities:** Maintains placement service. Administers Welcome Visiting Professorships program.

★398★ Korean Scientists and Engineers Association in America (KSEA)

6261 Executive Blvd.
Rockville, MD 20852
Ph: (301)984-7048   Fax: (301)984-1231

Members: Scientists and engineers holding single or advanced degrees. **Purpose:** Goals are to: promote friendship and mutuality among Korean and American scientists and engineers; contribute to Korea's scientific, technological, industrial, and economic developments; strengthen the scientific, technological, and cultural bonds between Korea and the U.S. Sponsors symposium. **Activities:** Maintains speakers' bureau, placement service, and biographical archives. Compiles statistics. Maintains 100 volume library of scientific handbooks and yearbooks in Korean.

★399★ National Network of Minority Women in Science (MWIS)

Directorate for Education and Human Resources Programs
1333 H St. NW
Washington, DC 20005
Ph: (202)326-6757   Fax: (202)371-9849

Members: Asian, Black, Mexican American, Native American, and Puerto Rican women involved in science related professions; other interested persons. **Purpose:** Promotes the advancement of minority women in science fields and the improvement of the science and mathematics education and career awareness of minorities. Supports public policies and programs in science and technology that benefit minorities. **Activities:** Maintains placement servce. Compiles statistics; serves as clearinghouse for identifying minority women scientists. Offers writing and conference presentations, seminars, and workshops on minority women in science and local career conferences for students. Local chapters maintain speakers' bureaus, and children's services. **E-Mail:** ggilbert@aaas.org

★400★ National Postsecondary Agricultural Student Organization (PAS)

PO Box 15440
Alexandria, VA 22309
Ph: (703)780-4922   Fax: (703)780-4378

Members: Two-year agricultural educational institutions and students. **Activities:** Promotes leadership experiences and assists students in job placement. Sponsors Speakers for Agriculture and Employment Interview. Conducts Planning for Progress Project to recognize achievement by students.

★401★ Women in Agribusiness (WIA)

PO Box 414937
Kansas City, MO 64141-4937

Members: Women in agribusiness. **Purpose:** Provides a forum for the discussion of ideas and information related to agribusiness. **Activities:** Offers placement, networking, and peer/mentor support services.

Employer Directories and Networking Lists

★402★ Agricultural Research Centres

Stockton Press
Groves Dictionaries
345 Park Ave. S., 10th Fl.
New York, NY 10010
Ph: (212)689-9200   Fr: 800-221-2123

Twelfth edition, 1995. $595.00. 1000 pages. Covers 2,000 main organizations controlling over 7,500 departments engaged in research in agriculture, fisheries, food, forestry, horticulture, and the veterinary sciences.

★403★ Agricultural Research Institute— Membership Directory

Agricultural Research Institute
9650 Rockville Pke.
Bethesda, MD 20814
Ph: (301)530-7122   Fax: (301)530-7007

Annual. $10.00, postpaid. Covers 125 member institutions; also lists study panels and committees interested in environmental issues, pest control, agricultural meteorology, biotechnology, food irradiation, agricultural policy, research and development, food safety, technology transfer, and remote sensing. Entries include: Name, title of primary contact, address, phone. fax. Arrangement: Alphabetical.

★404★ Agricultural and Veterinary Sciences International Who's Who

Stockton Press
Groves Dictionaries
345 Park Ave. S., 10th Fl.
New York, NY 10010
Ph: (212)689-9200   Fr: 800-221-2123

Fifth edition, 1994. $595.00. 1248 pages. Provides biographical profiles of about 7,500 senior agricultural and veterinary scientists from approximately 100 countries.

★405★ American Men and Women of Science

R. R. Bowker Co.
Reed Reference Publishing
121 Chanlon Rd.
New Providence, NJ 07974
Ph: (908)464-6800   Fax: (908)665-6688
Fr: 800-521-8110

Triennial, latest edition January 1995.
$106.00, per volume; $850.00, set. Covers over 123,000 U.S. and Canadian scientists active in the physical, biological, mathematical, computer science, and engineering fields; includes references to previous edition for deceased scientists and nonrespondents. Entries include: Name, address, education, personal and career data, memberships, honors and awards, research interest. Arrangement: Alphabetical. Indexes: Discipline (in separate volume).

★406★ Directory of State Departments of Agriculture

Financial Management Division
Agricultural Marketing Service
U.S. Department of Agriculture
14 Independence Ave. SW, Rm. 3964-S. Bldg.
Washington, DC 20250
Ph: (202)720-6920

Biennial, late summer of odd years. Free. Covers state departments of agriculture and their officials. Entries include: Department name, address, phone, names and titles of key personnel, department branches. Arrangement: Geographical.

★407★ Healthy Harvest: A Global Directory of Sustainable Agriculture and Horticulture Organizations

AgAccess
603 4th St.
Davis, CA 95616
Ph: (916)756-7177   Fax: (916)756-7177

Biennial, even years. $19.95, plus $4.00 shipping. Covers more than 1,400 agriculture and horticulture training institutions, research institutes, development programs, political organizations, appropriate technology institutes, and sustainable agriculture design groups worldwide. Entries include: Organization name, address, phone, contact name, geographical area served, description of activities. Arrangement: Alphabetical. Indexes: Subject, geographical, periodicals, educational opportunities.

★408★ Life Sciences Organizations and Agencies Directory

Gale Research
835 Penobscot Bldg.
Detroit, MI 48226-4094
Ph: (313)961-2242   Fax: (313)961-6083
Fr: 800-877-GALE

$175.00. Covers about 7,500 associations, government agencies, research centers, educational institutions, libraries and information centers, museums, consultants, electronic information services, and other organizations and agencies active in agriculture, biology, ecology, forestry, marine science, nutrition, wildlife and animal sciences, and other natural and life sciences. Entries include: Organization or agency name, address, phone, name and title of contact, description. Arrangement: Classified by type of organization. Indexes: Organization/agency name and keyword.

★409★ Peterson's Job Opportunities in Engineering and Technology 1996

Peterson's
PO Box 2123
Princeton, NJ 08543-2123
Ph: (609)243-9111   Fax: (609)243-9150
Fr: 800-338-3282

Compiled by the Peterson's staff. Annual. $19.95 paperback. 432 pages. Profiles 2,000 high-tech companies looking primarily for technical personnel in such fields as biotechnology, telecommunications, software, computers and peripherals, defense, and aerospace. Contains job-search strategies and career options to help match education and expertise to the job market. Indexed geographically, by industry, and by hiring needs.

★410★ Professional Workers in State Agricultural Experiment Stations and Other Cooperating State Institutions

Cooperative State Research Service
U.S. Department of Agriculture
Ag Box 2202
Washington, DC 20250-2202

Annual, January. $15.00. Covers academic and research personnel in all agricultural, forestry, aquacultural, home economics, and animal husbandry fields at experiment stations and academic institutions with agricultural programs. Entries include: Station or institution name, address, phone; names of personnel; their degrees and titles, and, in some cases, individual phone numbers and Internet address. Arrangement: Geographical; personnel are listed by major scientific or administrative areas. Indexes: Personal name.

★411★ Scientific and Technical Organizations and Agencies Directory

Gale Research
835 Penobscot Bldg.
Detroit, MI 48226-4094
Ph: (313)961-2242   Fax: (313)961-6083
Fr: 800-877-GALE

Irregular; latest edition December 1993. $195.00. Covers over 25,600 national and international organizations and agencies concerned with the physical and applied sciences, engineering, and technology, including associations, computer information services, consulting firms, educational institutions, foundations, government advisory organizations, federal government agencies, general grant and assistance programs, libraries and information centers, patent sources and services, research and development centers, scholarships, fellowships, and loans, science-technology centers, standards organizations, state academies of science, and state government agencies in the fields of aeronautics and space sciences, chemistry, computer science specialties, electronics, geography, geology, machinery, mathematics, metallurgy, meteorology, mineralogy, nuclear science, petroleum and gas, physics, plastics, transportation, water resources, and other areas. Entries include: Organization name, address, phone, and name of contact; additional descriptive text for most entries. Arrangement: Classified by type of organization. Indexes: Organization name/key word.

★412★ Who's Who in Technology

Gale Research
835 Penobscot Bldg.
Detroit, MI 48226-4094
Ph: (313)961-2242   Fax: (313)961-6083
Fr: 800-877-GALE

Irregular, new edition expected June 1995. $380.00. Covers 38,000 engineers, scientists, inventors, and researchers. Entries include: Name, title, affiliation, address; personal, education, and career data; publications, patents; technical field of activity; area of expertise. Arrangement: Alphabetical. Indexes: Geographical, employer, technical discipline, expertise.

HANDBOOKS AND MANUALS

★413★ The Best Resumes for Scientists and Engineers

John Wiley and Sons
605 3rd Ave.
New York, NY 10158
Ph: (212)850-6000   Fr: 800-225-5945

Adele Lewis. Second edition, 1993. $37.50; $14.95 (paper). Presents an extensive collection of scientific and engineering resumes, highlighting the important differences between these and resumes written for other occupations.

★414★ Career Information Center

Macmillan Publishing Co.
200 Old Tappan Rd.
Old Tappan, NJ 07675
Ph: (609)461-6500   Fr: 800-223-2336

Visual Education Center Staff. Fifth edition, 1992. $229.00. This 13-volume set profiles over 600 occupations. Each occupational profile describes job duties, educational requirements, how to get the job, advancement possibilities, employment outlook, working conditions, earnings and benefits, and where to write for more information.

★415★ Careers in Health Care

VGM Career Horizons
4255 W. Touhy Ave.
Lincolnwood, IL 60646-1975
Ph: (847)679-5500   Fax: (847)679-2494
Fr: 800-323-4900

Barbara M. Swanson. 1995. $17.95; $13.95 (paper). Describes job duties, work settings, salaries, licensing and certification requirements, educational preparation, and future outlook. Gives ideas on how to secure a job.

★416★ Careers for Nature Lovers and Other Outdoor Types

VGM Career Horizons
4255 W. Touhy Ave.
Lincolnwood, IL 60646-1975
Ph: (847)679-5500   Fax: (847)679-2494
Fr: 800-323-4900

Louise Miller. 1992. $12.95; $9.95 (paper). Examines career opportunities in biology, agriculture, landscaping, forestry and conservation, geology, and waste management, and pollution control. Offers insight into preparing for and finding outdoor jobs in federal and state government, as well as private industry.

★417★ Careers in Science

VGM Career Horizons
4255 W. Touhy Ave.
Lincolnwood, IL 60646-1975
Ph: (847)679-5500   Fax: (847)679-2494
Fr: 800-323-4900

Thomas Easton. Third edition, 1996. 192 pages. $17.95; $13.95 (paper). Discusses careers in life science, earth science, physical and space science, social science, engineering, mathematics, and computer science. Offers job hunting advice.

★418★ Careers With the Agricultural Research Service

United States Department of Agriculture
Agricultural Research Service
6305 Ivy Ln., Rm. 117
Greenbelt, MD 20770-1435
Ph: (301)344-3964

Free. 16 pages. Describes the federal hiring process, eligibility requirements, salaries and benefits, and training opportunities with the agricultural service.

★419★ Encyclopedia of Careers and Vocational Guidance

J. G. Ferguson Publishing Co.
200 W. Monroe, Ste. 250
Chicago, IL 60606
Ph: (312)580-5480

William E. Hopke. Ninth edition, 1993. $129.95; $199.95 (CD-ROM). Four-volume set that profiles 900 occupations and describes job trends in 71 industries. Includes career description, educational requirements, history of the job, methods of entry, advancement, employment outlook, earnings, conditions of work, social and psychological factors, and sources of further information. Contains career and employment information for this field.

★420★ Exploring Careers in Agronomy, Crops, and Soils

American Society of Agronomy (ASA)
Career Development and Placement
 Service
677 S. Segoe Rd.
Madison, WI 53711
Ph: (608)273-8080

1995. Single copy free. 26 pages. Describes agronomic sciences and the various roles which agronomists, crop scientists, and soil scientists fulfill. Includes description of various job opportunities as well as salaries in the agronomic sciences. Includes a list of colleges and universities offering degrees in agronomic science.

★421★ Opportunities in Biotechnology Careers

VGM Career Horizons
4255 W. Touhy Ave.
Lincolnwood, IL 60646-1975
Ph: (847)679-5500   Fax: (847)679-2494
Fr: 800-323-4900

Sheldon Brown. 1990. $14.95; $11.95 (paper). Discusses typical jobs, their income potential, and career opportunities.

★422★ Opportunities in Environmental Careers

VGM Career Horizons
4255 W. Touhy Ave.
Lincolnwood, IL 60646-1975
Ph: (847)679-5500   Fax: (847)679-2494
Fr: 800-323-4900

Odom Fanning. 1995. $14.95; $11.95 (paper). 160 pages. Describes a broad range of opportunities in fields such as environmental health, recreation, physics, and hygiene, and provides job search advice.

★423★ Opportunities in Farming and Agriculture Careers

VGM Career Horizons
4255 W. Touhy Ave.
Lincolnwood, IL 60646-1975
Ph: (847)679-5500   Fax: (847)679-2494
Fr: 800-323-4900

William C. White and Donald N. Collins. 1995. $14.95; $11.95 (paper). 160 pages. Covers opportunities in such fields as agricultural engineering, management, experimental farming, agricultural sales, teaching, and others, and provides job-hunting advice. Illustrated.

★424★ A PhD Is Not Enough: A Guide to Survival in Science

Addison-Wesley Publishing Co., Inc.
1 Jacob Way
Reading, MA 01867
Ph: (617)944-3700   Fax: (617)942-1117
Fr: 800-447-2226

Peter J. Feibelman. 1993. $12.95 (paper).

★425★ A Scientific Career with the Agricultural Research Service

United States Department of Agriculture
Agricultural Research Service
6305 Ivy Ln., Rm. 117
Greenbelt, MD 20770-1435
Ph: (301)344-3964

Brochure. Free. 16 pages. Describes the work of the agricultural research service and jobs with the service.

★426★ Where the Jobs Are: The Hottest Careers for the '90s

The Career Press, Inc.
3 Tice Rd.
PO Box 687
Franklin Lakes, NJ 07417
Ph: (201)848-0310   Fax: (201)848-1727
Fr: 800-237-3371

Joyce Hadley. Second edition, 1995. $9.99. 300 pages. Describes careers in fifteen general fields, from accounting to travel and hospitality.

EMPLOYMENT AGENCIES AND SEARCH FIRMS

★427★ ABC Employment Service

25 S. Bemiston, Ste. 214
Clayton, MO 63105
Ph: (314)725-3140

Employment agency.

★428★ Agra Placements, Ltd.

4949 Pleasant St., Ste. 1
W. 50th Pl. III
West Des Moines, IA 50266-5494
Ph: (515)225-6562   Fax: (515)225-7733

Executive search firm. Branch offices in Peru, IN, Lincoln, IL, and Minneapolis, MN.

★429★ Agri-Associates

500 Nichols Rd.
Kansas City, MO 64112
Ph: (816)531-7980   Fax: (816)531-7982

Executive search firm.

★430★ Agri-Personnel

5120 Old Bill Cook Rd.
Atlanta, GA 30349
Ph: (404)768-5701

Executive search firm.

★431★ Hansen Agri-Placement

PO Box 1172
Grand Island, NE 68802
Ph: (308)382-7350

Employment agency. Handles placements in a variety of fields on a regular or temporary basis.

★432★ Hayden and Associates, Inc.

7825 Washington Ave. S., Ste. 120
Minneapolis, MN 55439-2431
Ph: (612)941-6300   Fax: (612)941-9602

Employment agency. Executive search firm. Fills openings in a variety of fields.

★433★ The Jobs Co.

8900 E. Sprague Ave.
Spokane, WA 99212-2927
Ph: (509)928-3151   Fax: (509)928-3168

Employment agency. Has division specializing in engineering and scientific openings. Also operates division specializing in sales openings.

★434★ Management Search, Inc.

2800 W. Country Club Dr.
Oklahoma City, OK 73116
Ph: (405)842-3173

Executive search firm.

★435★ Sierra Technology Corporation

4150 Manzanita Ave., Ste. 100
Carmichael, CA 95608-1700
Ph: (916)488-4960   Fax: (916)488-7058

Employment agency. Provides placement on a temporary basis.

OTHER SOURCES

★436★ American Institute of Biological Sciences (AIBS)

730 11th St. NW
Washington, DC 20001-4521
Ph: (202)628-1500   Fax: (202)628-1509
Fr: 800-992-AIBS

Members: Professional biological associations and laboratories whose members have an interest in the life sciences. **Purpose:** Promotes unity and effectiveness of effort among persons engaged in biological research, education, and application of biological sciences, including agriculture, environment, and medicine. Seeks to further the relationships of biological sciences to other sciences, the arts, and industries. **Activities:** Conducts symposium series; provides names of prominent biologists who are willing to serve as speakers and curriculum consultants; provides advisory committees and other services to the Department of Energy, Environmental Protection Agency, National Science Foundation, Department of Defense, and National Aeronautics and Space Administration. Maintains educational consultant panel.

★437★ Association for International Practical Training (AIPT)

10400 Little Patuxent Pky. Ste. 250
Columbia, MD 21044
Ph: (410)997-2200   Fax: (410)992-3924

Purpose: Helps coordinate training around the world in fields such as travel, the culinary arts, and hotel management. **Activities:** Conducts programs in career development and hospitality/tourism exchanges. Operates a student exchange program. Provides reciprocal practical training experience for recent graduates from the U.S., Austria, Germany, Finland, France, Hungary, Ireland, Japan, Malaysia, Netherlands, Switzerland, and the United Kingdom. Arranges training programs in the U.S. and abroad. Serves as U.S. affiliate to IAESTE (International Association for the Exchange of Students for Technical Experience) and operates a Professional Visitors Program to arrange short-term educational and training visits to the U.S. **E-Mail:** aipt@aipt.org

★438★ Council for Agricultural Science and Technology (CAST)

4420 Lincoln Way
Ames, IA 50010-3447
Ph: (515)292-2125   Fax: (515)292-4512

Members: Scientific societies, associate societies, individuals, corporations, foundations, and trade associations. **Purpose:** To disseminate information to the public, news media, and the government on the science and technology of food and agricultural matters of broad public concern. **Activities:** Sponsors educational programs.

★439★ Discover Entomology

Entomological Society of America
PO Box 177
Hyattsville, MD 20781

Video. $49.00. 15 minutes. Explores the careers and contributions of entomologists.

★440★ New Careers Directory: Internships and Professional Opportunities in Technology and Social Change

Student Pugwash USA
815 15th St. NW, Ste. 814
Washington, DC 20005
Ph: (202)393-6555   Fax: (202)393-6550
Fr: 800-WOW-A-PUG

Irregular; latest edition spring 1993. $13.00

for students; $21.00 for institutions, plus $3.00 shipping. Covers about 300 research institutes, think tanks, laboratories, government agencies, professional, science, and other non-profit organizations offering public policy, science, and technology internships and jobs. Entries include: Sponsoring organization name, description of organization, programs offered, work environment and application procedures, compensation offered. Arrangement: Alphabetical and classified by subject. Indexes: Geographical, subject.

★441★ *Resumes for Scientific and Technical Careers*
VGM Career Horizons
NTC Publishing Group
4255 W. Touhy Ave.
Lincolnwood, IL 60646-1975
Ph: (847)679-5500   Fax: (847)679-2494
Fr: 800-323-4900

1994. $9.95. 160 pages. Provides resume

advice for individuals interested in working in scientific and technical careers. Includes sample resumes and cover letters.

★442★ *Salaries of Scientists, Engineers, and Technicians: A Summary of Salary Surveys*
Commission on Professionals in Science and Technology (CPST)
1500 Massachusetts Ave. NW, Ste. 831
Washington, DC 20005
Ph: (202)223-6995

1993.

★443★ **Soil Science Society of America (SSSA)**
677 S. Segoe Rd.
Madison, WI 53711
Ph: (608)273-8080   Fax: (608)273-2021

Members: Professional soil scientists, including soil physicists, soil classifiers, land use and management specialists, chemists, mi-

crobiologists, soil fertility specialists, soil cartographers, conservationists, mineralogists, engineers, and others interested in fundamental and applied soil science.

Aircraft Mechanics and Engine Specialists

SOURCES OF HELP-WANTED ADS

★444★ Aerospace Engineering

Society of Automotive Engineers, Inc.
400 Commonwealth Dr.
Warrendale, PA 15096
Ph: (412)776-4841   Fax: (412)776-4026

Monthly. $44.00/year; $96.00/year for other countries. Magazine for aerospace manufacturing engineers providing technical and design information.

★445★ Aviation Equipment Maintenance

Phillips Business Information, Inc.
1201 Seven Locks Rd.
Potomac, MD 20854
Ph: (301)340-1520   Fax: (301)340-0542

Monthly. Free to qualified subscribers. Magazine covering aviation maintenance.

★446★ Commuter Air International

6151 Powers Ferry Rd. NW
Atlanta, GA 30339-2941
Ph: (404)955-2500   Fax: (404)955-0400

Monthly. Free to qualified subscribers; $45.00/year for institutions.

★447★ Flying

Hachette Filipacchi Magazines, Inc.
500 W. Putham Ave.
Greenwich, CT 06830
Ph: (203)622-2700   Fax: (203)622-2725

Monthly. $18.97/year; $3.50 for single issue. General aviation magazine.

★448★ General Aviation News and Flyer

General Aviation News Flyer
PO Box 39099
Tacoma, WA 98439-0099
Ph: (206)471-9888   Fax: (206)471-9911

Biweekly. General aviation newspaper (tabloid) for aircraft pilots and owners.

★449★ Rotor & Wing

Phillips Business Information, Inc.
1201 Seven Locks Rd., Ste.300
Potomac, MD 20854
Ph: (301)340-1520   Fax: (301)340-0542

Monthly. $36.00/year for individuals; $44.00/year for other countries; $4.00 for single issue. Magazine covering helicopters.

PLACEMENT AND JOB REFERRAL SERVICES

★450★ Aircraft Electronics Association (AEA)

PO Box 1963
Independence, MO 64055-0963
Ph: (816)373-6565   Fax: (816)478-3100

Members: Companies engaged in the sales, engineering, installation, and service of electronic aviation equipment and systems. **Purpose:** Purposes are to: advance the science of aircraft electronics; promote uniform and stable regulations and uniform standards of performance; establish and maintain a code of ethics; gather and disseminate technical data; advance the education of members and the public in the science of aircraft electronics. Is active in the areas of supplement type certificates, test equipment licensing, temporary FCC licensing for new installations, spare parts availability and pricing, audiovisual technician training, equipment and spare parts loan, profitable installation, and service facility operation. **Activities:** Provides employment information, equipment exchange information, stolen equipment lists, and service assistance on member installations anywhere in the U.S. and Canada. Compiles statistics.

★451★ Aviation Maintenance Foundation International (AMFI)

PO Box 2826
Redmond, WA 98073
Ph: (206)827-2295   Fax: (206)827-2320

Members: Trade association consisting of licensed aircraft mechanics, students, and schools as well as companies involved in the aviation maintenance industry. **Purpose:** To promote and improve the industry through education and research. Conducts surveys and market studies. Appoints professional aviation maintenance delegates to foreign countries. Sponsors competitions. **Activities:** Maintains placement service. Conducts seminars; maintains speakers' bureau; compiles statistics. Operates charitable program; compiles statistics.

★452★ Professional Aviation Maintenance Association (PAMA)

1200 18th St. NW, Ste. 401
Washington, DC 20036-2598
Ph: (202)296-0545   Fax: (202)296-0618

Members: General aviation airframe and powerplant (A & P) technicians and aviation industry-related companies. **Purpose:** Strives to increase the professionalism of the individual aviation technician through greater technical knowledge and better understanding of safety requirements. Establishes communication among technicians throughout the country. **Activities:** Maintains job referral assistance program. Fosters and improves methods, skills, learning, and achievement in the aviation maintenance field.

EMPLOYER DIRECTORIES AND NETWORKING LISTS

★453★ Aircraft Servicing & Maintenance Directory

American Business Directories, Inc.
American Business Information, Inc.
5711 S. 86th Cir.
Omaha, NE 68127
Ph: (402)593-4600   Fax: (402)331-1505

Annual. $345.00, U.S. edition. Entries include: Name, address, phone, size of advertisement, name of owner or manager, number of employees, year first in Yellow Pages. Compiled from telephone company Yellow Pages, nationwide. Arrangement: Geographical.

★454★ Airline Companies Directory

American Business Directories, Inc.
American Business Information, Inc.
5711 S. 86th Cir.
Omaha, NE 68127
Ph: (402)593-4600   Fax: (402)331-1505

Annual. $255.00, U.S. edition. Entries include: Name, address, phone (including area code), size of advertisement, year first in Yellow Pages, name of owner or manager, number of employees. Compiled from telephone company Yellow Pages, nationwide. Arrangement: Geographical.

★455★ AOPA's Aviation U.S.A.

Aircraft Owners and Pilots Association
421 Aviation Way
Frederick, MD 21701
Ph: (301)695-2000   Fax: (301)695-2375
Fr: 800-872-2672

Annual, January. $24.95. Covers almost 6,000 international public-use landing facilities, including airports, U.S. customs airports, heliports, seaplane bases, and approximately 1,800 private-use landing facilities; 5,000 aviation service companies. Entries include: For landing facilities: Airport type and name, city, phone, runway dimensions, types of instrument approaches, hours operated, communications frequencies, runway light system, local attractions, ground transportation, restaurants, hotels. For aviation service companies: Company name, phone, airport affiliation, operating hours, fuel type, unicom frequency. Arrangement: Geographical. Indexes: Facility name.

★456★ National Air Transportation Association—Official Membership Directory

National Air Transportation Association
4226 King St.
Alexandria, VA 22302
Ph: (703)845-9000   Fax: (703)845-8176

Annual, October. $95.00. Covers more than 1,000 regular, associate, and affiliate members; regular members include airport service organizations, air taxi operators, and commuter airlines. Entries include: Company name, address, phone, fax number, name and title of contact. Arrangement: Regular members are classified by service; associate and affiliate members are alphabetical in separate sections. Indexes: Geographical.

★457★ World Aviation Directory

Aviation Week Group
McGraw-Hill, Inc.
1200 G St. NW
Washington, DC 20005
Ph: (202)822-4600   Fax: (202)383-2388
Fr: 800-551-2015

Semiannual, March and September. $175.00. Covers aviation, aerospace, and missile manufacturers, including manufacturers of aircraft, spacecraft, piston and jet engines, and component manufacturers and major subcontractors; support services (fuel companies, repair stations, etc.); airports and heliports; airlines; government agencies and associations; airline caterers; air freight companies; international coverage. Arrangement: Classified by major activity (manufacturers, airlines, etc.). Indexes: Company and organization, personnel, product, trade name.

Handbooks and Manuals

★458★ Career Information Center

Macmillan Publishing Co.
200 Old Tappan Rd.
Old Tappan, NJ 07675
Ph: (609)461-6500   Fr: 800-223-2336

Visual Education Center Staff. Fifth edition, 1992. $229.00. This 13-volume set profiles over 600 occupations. Each occupational profile describes job duties, educational requirements, how to get the job, advancement possibilities, employment outlook, working conditions, earnings and benefits, and where to write for more information.

★459★ The Complete Aviation/ Aerospace Career Guide

TAB/McGraw Hill, Inc.
PO Box 182607
Columbus, OH 43218
Ph: (614)759-3773   Fax: (614)759-3644
Fr: 800-722-4726

Robert Calderone. 1989. $15.95. A comprehensive guide to hundreds of aviation-related jobs. Provides job description, training requirements, advancement opportunities, and employment outlook.

★460★ Encyclopedia of Careers and Vocational Guidance

J. G. Ferguson Publishing Co.
200 W. Monroe, Ste. 250
Chicago, IL 60606
Ph: (312)580-5480

William E. Hopke. Ninth edition, 1993. $129.95; $199.95 (CD-ROM). Four-volume set that profiles 900 occupations and describes job trends in 71 industries. Includes career description, educational requirements, history of the job, methods of entry, advancement, employment outlook, earnings, conditions of work, social and psychological factors, and sources of further information. Contains career and employment information for this field.

★461★ Exploring Nontraditional Jobs for Women

Rosen Publishing Group, Inc.
29 E. 21st St.
New York, NY 10010
Ph: (212)777-3017   Fax: (212)777-0277
Fr: 800-237-9932

Rose Neufeld. 1989. $14.95. Describes occupations where few women are found. Covers job duties, training routes, where to apply for jobs, tools used, salary, and advantages and disadvantages of the job.

★462★ Flying High in Travel

John Wiley and Sons
605 3rd Ave.
New York, NY 10158
Ph: (212)850-6000   Fr: 800-225-5945

Karen Rubin. Second edition, 1992. $19.95. 336 pages. A guide to careers and job hunting in the travel industry. Describes the many job opportunities available, from writing to hotel management to law. Includes information on educational preparation, training, and job hunting.

★463★ Opportunities in Aerospace Careers

VGM Career Horizons
4255 W. Touhy Ave.
Lincolnwood, IL 60646-1975
Ph: (847)679-5500   Fax: (847)679-2494
Fr: 800-323-4900

Wallace R. Maples. 1995. $14.95; $11.95 (paper). Surveys jobs with the airlines, airports, the government, the military, in manufacturing, and in research and development. Includes information on job opportunities with NASA in the U.S. space program.

★464★ Opportunities in Travel Careers

VGM Career Horizons
4255 W. Touhy Ave.
Lincolnwood, IL 60646-1975
Ph: (847)679-5500   Fax: (847)679-2494
Fr: 800-323-4900

Robert Scott Milne. 1996. $14.95; $11.95 (paper). 160 pages. Discusses what the jobs are and where to find them in airlines, shipping lines, and railroads. Discusses related opportunities in hotels, motels, resorts, travel agencies, public relation firms, and recreation departments. Illustrated.

Employment Agencies and Search Firms

★465★ Amtec Engineering Corp.

2749 Saturn St.
Brea, CA 92621
Ph: (714)993-1900   Fax: (714)993-2419

Employment agency.

Aircraft Pilots and Flight Engineers

SOURCES OF HELP-WANTED ADS

★466★ AOPA Pilot

AOPA Pilot
421 Aviation Way
Frederick, MD 21701
Ph: (301)695-2350   Fax: (301)695-2180

Monthly. $21.00/year for individuals; $2.00 for single issue. Magazine for general aviation pilots and aircraft owners who are members of the Aircraft Owners and Pilots Association. Articles are tailored to address the special informational requirements of both recreational and business pilots.

★467★ Commuter Air International

6151 Powers Ferry Rd. NW
Atlanta, GA 30339-2941
Ph: (404)955-2500   Fax: (404)955-0400

Monthly. Free to qualified subscribers; $45.00/year for institutions.

★468★ Flight Training

405 Main St.
Parkville, MO 64152
Ph: (816)741-5151   Fax: (816)741-6458

Monthly. $20.00/year; $2.95/single issue.

★469★ Flying

Hachette Filipacchi Magazines, Inc.
500 W. Putham Ave.
Greenwich, CT 06830
Ph: (203)622-2700   Fax: (203)622-2725

Monthly. $18.97/year; $3.50 for single issue. General aviation magazine.

★470★ General Aviation News and Flyer

General Aviation News Flyer
PO Box 39099
Tacoma, WA 98439-0099
Ph: (206)471-9888   Fax: (206)471-9911

Biweekly. General aviation newspaper (tabloid) for aircraft pilots and owners.

★471★ Private Pilot Magazine

Fancy Publications, Inc.
PO Box 6050
Mission Viejo, CA 92690
Ph: (714)855-8822   Fax: (714)855-3045

Monthly. $21.97/year for individuals. Magazine covering general aviation interests.

★472★ Professional Pilot

Queensmith Communications Corp.
3014 Colvin St.
Alexandria, VA 22314
Ph: (703)370-0606   Fax: (703)370-7082

Monthly. $36.00/year for individuals; $5.00 for single issue; $8 .00 for directory issue. Magazine serving pilots of corporate, charter, commuter, and major airlines.

★473★ Rotor & Wing

Phillips Business Information, Inc.
1201 Seven Locks Rd., Ste.300
Potomac, MD 20854
Ph: (301)340-1520   Fax: (301)340-0542

Monthly. $36.00/year for individuals; $44.00/year for other countries; $4.00 for single issue. Magazine covering helicopters.

PLACEMENT AND JOB REFERRAL SERVICES

★474★ International Agricultural Aviation Foundation (IAAF)

PO Box 1607
Mount Vernon, WA 98273
Ph: (360)336-9738   Fax: (360)336-2506

Members: Crop duster pilots, aerial applicators, fire bomber pilots, and agricultural aviation operators licensed by the FAA. **Purpose:** To increase public knowledge about the activities and responsibilities of crop dusters and to provide educational institutions with an understanding of the industry. **Activities:** Aids survivors of decedents of the industry. Maintains speakers' bureau, and placement service. Conducts specialized education.

★475★ National Black Coalition of Federal Aviation Employees (NBCFAE)

Washington Headquarters
PO Box 44392
Washington, DC 20026-4392
Ph: (202)267-7911   Fax: (202)267-5632

Members: Federal Aviation Administration employees. **Purpose:** To promote professionalism and equal opportunity in the workplace; locate and train qualified minorities for FAA positions; help the FAA meet its affirmative action goals; monitor black, female, and minority trainees; educate members and the public about their rights and FAA personnel and promotion qualifications; develop a voice for black, female, and minority FAA employees. **Activities:** Recruits minorities from community and schools who qualify for employment; sponsors seminars for members and for those who wish to be employed by the FAA.

★476★ Negro Airmen International (NAI)

8891 Airport Rd.
Cluster One-Box 9
Minneapolis, MN 55449
Ph: (612)786-7153

Members: Individuals holding at least a student pilot license who are active in some phase of aviation; members include both aviation professionals and others who are qualified pilots. **Purpose:** Seeks greater participation by blacks in the field of aviation through the encouragement of broader job opportunities; promotes awareness by government and industry of the needs, attitudes, and interests of blacks concerning aviation. Encourages black youth to remain in school and to enter the field of aviation. **Activities:** Maintains Summer Flight Academy for teenagers each July at Morton Field, Tuskegee, AL. Operates speakers' bureau and placement service.

★477★ Ninety-Nines, International Women Pilots

PO Box 59965
Oklahoma City, OK 73159
Ph: (405)685-7969   Fax: (405)685-7985

Members: Women pilots united to foster a better understanding of aviation. **Activities:** Operates placement service. Encourages cross-country flying; provides consulting service and gives indoctrination flights; flies missions for charitable assistance programs; endorses air races. Develops programs and courses for schools and youth organizations and teaches ground school subjects. Participates in flying competitions. Maintains resource center. Conducts lecture on personal aviation experience, and charitable event. Compiles statistics.

★478★ Organization of Black Airline Pilots (OBAP)

PO Box 5793
Englewood, NJ 07631
Ph: (201)568-8145   Fax: (201)712-9775

Members: Cockpit crew members of commercial air carriers, corporate pilots, and other interested individuals. **Purpose:** Seeks to enhance minority participation in the aerospace industry. Maintains liaison with airline presidents and minority and pilot associations. Conducts lobbying efforts, including congressional examinations into airline recruitment practices. Provides scholarships; cosponsors Summer Flight Academy for Youth at Tuskegee Institute in Alabama. **Activities:** Offers job placement service and charitable program; operates speakers' bureau; compiles statistics on airline hiring practices.

★479★ Pilots International Association (PIA)

PO Box 907
Minneapolis, MN 55440
Ph: (612)588-5175   Fax: (612)520-6760

Members: Private, commercial, airline, military, and student pilots in 49 countries; associate members are persons other than pilots who are interested in flying. **Purpose:** Promotes airplane use and cooperates with government agencies and private and public flying organizations to increase the general safety of flying. Encourages the development of convenient landing and service facilities and the use of aircraft fuel taxes for aviation development. Fosters international understanding of common aircraft problems. **Activities:** Services include: job placement; group life and health insurance. Maintains film-lending library and collection of general flying periodicals.

EMPLOYER DIRECTORIES AND NETWORKING LISTS

★480★ Airline Companies Directory

American Business Directories, Inc.
American Business Information, Inc.
5711 S. 86th Cir.
Omaha, NE 68127
Ph: (402)593-4600   Fax: (402)331-1505

Annual. $255.00, U.S. edition. Entries include: Name, address, phone (including area code), size of advertisement, year first in Yellow Pages, name of owner or manager, number of employees. Compiled from telephone company Yellow Pages, nationwide. Arrangement: Geographical.

★481★ National Air Transportation Association—Official Membership Directory

National Air Transportation Association
4226 King St.
Alexandria, VA 22302
Ph: (703)845-9000   Fax: (703)845-8176

Annual, October. $95.00. Covers more than 1,000 regular, associate, and affiliate members; regular members include airport service organizations, air taxi operators, and commuter airlines. Entries include: Company name, address, phone, fax number, name and title of contact. Arrangement: Regular members are classified by service; associate and affiliate members are alphabetical in separate sections. Indexes: Geographical.

★482★ Private Pilot—Directory of Aviation Clubs Issue

Fancy Publications, Inc.
Box 6050
Mission Viejo, CA 92690
Ph: (714)855-8822   Fax: (714)855-3045

Annual, August. $2.95. Publication includes: List of aviation clubs and pilot organizations. Entries include: Organization name, address, contact person, phone, number of members, annual fees, publications, purpose, date of annual meeting. Arrangement: Alphabetical.

★483★ World Aviation Directory

Aviation Week Group
McGraw-Hill, Inc.
1200 G St. NW
Washington, DC 20005
Ph: (202)822-4600   Fax: (202)383-2388
Fr: 800-551-2015

Semiannual, March and September. $175.00. Covers aviation, aerospace, and missile manufacturers, including manufacturers of aircraft, spacecraft, piston and jet engines, and component manufacturers and major subcontractors; support services (fuel companies, repair stations, etc.); airports and heliports; airlines; government agencies and associations; airline caterers; air freight companies; international coverage. Arrangement: Classified by major activity (manufacturers, airlines, etc.). Indexes: Company and organization, personnel, product, trade name.

HANDBOOKS AND MANUALS

★484★ The Aerospace Careers Handbook

Simon and Schuster Trade
1230 Avenue of the Americas
New York, NY 10020
Ph: (212)698-7000   Fr: 800-223-2348

Anne Cardoza and Suzee J. Vlk. Contains index, bibliography, and illustrations.

★485★ Career Information Center

Macmillan Publishing Co.
200 Old Tappan Rd.
Old Tappan, NJ 07675
Ph: (609)461-6500   Fr: 800-223-2336

Visual Education Center Staff. Fifth edition, 1992. $229.00. This 13-volume set profiles

over 600 occupations. Each occupational profile describes job duties, educational requirements, how to get the job, advancement possibilities, employment outlook, working conditions, earnings and benefits, and where to write for more information.

★486★ Encyclopedia of Careers and Vocational Guidance

J. G. Ferguson Publishing Co.
200 W. Monroe, Ste. 250
Chicago, IL 60606
Ph: (312)580-5480

William E. Hopke. Ninth edition, 1993. $129.95; $199.95 (CD-ROM). Four-volume set that profiles 900 occupations and describes job trends in 71 industries. Includes career description, educational requirements, history of the job, methods of entry, advancement, employment outlook, earnings, conditions of work, social and psychological factors, and sources of further information. Contains career and employment information for this field.

★487★ Flying High in Travel

John Wiley and Sons
605 3rd Ave.
New York, NY 10158
Ph: (212)850-6000   Fr: 800-225-5945

Karen Rubin. Second edition, 1992. $19.95. 336 pages. A guide to careers and job hunting in the travel industry. Describes the many job opportunities available, from writing to hotel management to law. Includes information on educational preparation, training, and job hunting.

★488★ 100 Best Careers for the Year 2000

Prentice Hall General Reference
15 Columbus Cir.
New York, NY 10023
Ph: (212)373-8500   Fr: 800-223-2348

Shelly Field. 1992. $15.00 (paper). Covers 100 of the fastest growing jobs. The publication is divided into 11 general employment sections. Specific careers are covered within each section. Provides job description, responsibilities, employment opportunities, earnings, education and training, advancement opportunities, and experience and qualifications for each occupation.

★489★ Opportunities in Aerospace Careers

VGM Career Horizons
4255 W. Touhy Ave.
Lincolnwood, IL 60646-1975
Ph: (847)679-5500   Fax: (847)679-2494
Fr: 800-323-4900

Wallace R. Maples. 1995. $14.95; $11.95 (paper). Surveys jobs with the airlines, airports, the government, the military, in manufacturing, and in research and development. Includes information on job opportunities with NASA in the U.S. space program.

★490★ *Opportunities in Travel Careers*

VGM Career Horizons
4255 W. Touhy Ave.
Lincolnwood, IL 60646-1975
Ph: (847)679-5500   Fax: (847)679-2494
Fr: 800-323-4900

Robert Scott Milne. 1996. $14.95; $11.95 (paper). 160 pages. Discusses what the jobs are and where to find them in airlines, shipping lines, and railroads. Discusses related opportunities in hotels, motels, resorts, travel agencies, public relation firms, and recreation departments. Illustrated.

★491★ *Opportunities in Vocational and Technical Careers*

VGM Career Horizons
4255 W. Touhy Ave.
Lincolnwood, IL 60646-1975
Ph: (847)679-5500   Fax: (847)679-2494
Fr: 800-323-4900

Adrian A. Paradis. 1992. $14.95; $11.95 (paper). 160 pages. Provides information on a variety of opportunities and advice on breaking into the field.

OTHER SOURCES

★492★ *American Almanac of Jobs and Salaries 1994-95*

Avon Books
1350 Avenue of the Americas, 2nd Fl.
New York, NY 10019
Ph: (212)261-6800   Fr: 800-238-0658

John Wright. Revised edition, 1993. $17.00. 704 pages. This is a comprehensive guide to the wages of hundreds of occupations in a wide variety of industries and organizations.

Air Traffic Controllers

SOURCES OF HELP-WANTED ADS

★493★ Federal Career Opportunities
Federal Research Service, Inc.
243 Church St. NW
PO Box 1059
Vienna, VA 22183
Ph: (703)281-0200   Fax: (703)281-7639
Fr: 800-822-5627

Biweekly. $7.95, per copy; $39.00, 6 issues; $77.00, 12 issues; $175.00, 26 issues. Covers more than 4,000 current federal job vacancies in the United States and overseas; includes permanent, part-time, and temporary positions. Entries include: Position title, location, series and grade, job requirements, special forms, announcement number, closing date, application address. Arrangement: Classified by federal agency and occupation.

★494★ Federal Jobs Digest
Federal Jobs Digest
325 Pennsylvania Ave. SE
Washington, DC 20003
Ph: (202)762-5111   Fax: (202)762-4818
Fr: 800-824-5000

Biweekly. $4.50, per issue; $29.00, for three months; $110.00, per year. Covers over 10,000 specific job openings in the federal government in each issue. Entries include: Position name, title, General Schedule (GS) grade, and Wage Grade (WG), closing date for applications, announcement number, application address, phone, and name of contact. Arrangement: By federal department or agency, then geographical.

★495★ General Aviation News and Flyer
General Aviation News Flyer
PO Box 39099
Tacoma, WA 98439-0099
Ph: (206)471-9888   Fax: (206)471-9911

Biweekly. General aviation newspaper (tabloid) for aircraft pilots and owners.

PLACEMENT AND JOB REFERRAL SERVICES

★496★ National Black Coalition of Federal Aviation Employees (NBCFAE)
Washington Headquarters
PO Box 44392
Washington, DC 20026-4392
Ph: (202)267-7911   Fax: (202)267-5632

Members: Federal Aviation Administration employees. **Purpose:** To promote professionalism and equal opportunity in the workplace; locate and train qualified minorities for FAA positions; help the FAA meet its affirmative action goals; monitor black, female, and minority trainees; educate members and the public about their rights and FAA personnel and promotion qualifications; develop a voice for black, female, and minority FAA employees. **Activities:** Recruits minorities from community and schools who qualify for employment; sponsors seminars for members and for those who wish to be employed by the FAA.

EMPLOYER DIRECTORIES AND NETWORKING LISTS

★497★ National Air Transportation Association—Official Membership Directory
National Air Transportation Association
4226 King St.
Alexandria, VA 22302
Ph: (703)845-9000   Fax: (703)845-8176

Annual, October. $95.00. Covers more than 1,000 regular, associate, and affiliate members; regular members include airport service organizations, air taxi operators, and commuter airlines. Entries include: Company name, address, phone, fax number, name and title of contact. Arrangement: Regular members are classified by service; associate and affiliate members are alphabetical in separate sections. Indexes: Geographical.

HANDBOOKS AND MANUALS

★498★ Air Traffic Control Specialist
Chronicle Guidance Publications, Inc.
66 Aurora St.
PO Box 1190
Moravia, NY 13118-1190
Ph: (315)497-0330   Fax: (315)497-3359
Fr: 800-622-7284

Chronicle Guidance Staff. 1993. $2.00. Provides concise career information and sources of additional information.

★499★ Career Information Center
Macmillan Publishing Co.
200 Old Tappan Rd.
Old Tappan, NJ 07675
Ph: (609)461-6500   Fr: 800-223-2336

Visual Education Center Staff. Fifth edition, 1992. $229.00. This 13-volume set profiles over 600 occupations. Each occupational profile describes job duties, educational requirements, how to get the job, advancement possibilities, employment outlook, working conditions, earnings and benefits, and where to write for more information.

★500★ Career Options in Air Traffic Control and Airway Facilities
Chronicle Guidance Publications, Inc.
66 Aurora St.
PO Box 1190
Moravia, NY 13118-1190
Ph: (315)497-0330   Fax: (315)497-3359
Fr: 800-622-7284

Chronicle Guidance Staff. 1994. $2.00. Article reprint from current professional or trade journal.

★501★ Encyclopedia of Careers and Vocational Guidance
J. G. Ferguson Publishing Co.
200 W. Monroe, Ste. 250
Chicago, IL 60606
Ph: (312)580-5480

William E. Hopke. Ninth edition, 1993. $129.95; $199.95 (CD-ROM). Four-volume set that profiles 900 occupations and describes job trends in 71 industries. Includes career description, educational requirements, history of the job, methods of entry, advancement, employment outlook, earnings, conditions of work, social and psychological factors, and sources of further information. Contains career and employment information for this field.

★502★ Jobs Rated Almanac: Ranks the Best and Worst Jobs by More Than a Dozen Vital Criteria

John Wiley and Sons
605 Third Ave.
New York, NY 10158-0012
Ph: (212)850-6000   Fr: 800-225-5945

Les Krantz. Third edition, 1995. $16.95. 340 pages. Ranks 250 jobs by environment, salary, outlook, physical demands, stress, security, travel opportunities, and geographic location.

★503★ Liberal Arts Jobs: What They Are and How to Get Them

Peterson's
PO Box 2123
Princeton, NJ 08543-2123
Ph: (609)243-9111   Fax: (609)243-9150
Fr: 800-338-3282

Burton Jay Nadler. Second edition, 1989. $9.95. 153 pages. Presents a list of the top 20 fields for liberal arts majors, covering more than 300 job opportunities. Discusses strategies for going after those jobs, including guidance on the language of a successful job search, informational interviews, and making networking work.

★504★ Opportunities in Aerospace Careers

VGM Career Horizons
4255 W. Touhy Ave.
Lincolnwood, IL 60646-1975
Ph: (847)679-5500   Fax: (847)679-2494
Fr: 800-323-4900

Wallace R. Maples. 1995. $14.95; $11.95 (paper). Surveys jobs with the airlines, airports, the government, the military, in manufacturing, and in research and development.

Includes information on job opportunities with NASA in the U.S. space program.

OTHER SOURCES

★505★ Air Traffic Control Association (ATCA)

2300 Clarendon Blvd., Ste. 711
Arlington, VA 22201
Ph: (703)522-5717   Fax: (703)527-7251

Members: Air traffic controllers; private, commercial, and military pilots; private and business aircraft owners and operators; aircraft and electronics engineers; airlines, aircraft manufacturers, and electronic and human engineering firms interested in the establishment and maintenance of a safe and efficient air traffic control system. **Activities:** Conducts special surveys and studies on air traffic control problems. Participates in aviation community conferences.

Animal Caretakers, Technicians, and Trainers

SOURCES OF HELP-WANTED ADS

★506★ The Chronicle of the Horse
The Chronicle of the Horse, Inc.
PO Box 46
Middleburg, VA 22117
Ph: (703)687-6341   Fax: (703)687-3937

Weekly. Magazine covering English riding and horse sports.

★507★ Dog World
Intertec Publishing Co.
29 N. Wacker Dr.
Chicago, IL 60606
Ph: (312)435-2330   Fax: (312)726-4103
Fr: 800-621-9907

Monthly. $28.00/year for individuals; $3.75 for single issue. Magazine serving breeders, exhibitors, hobbyists and professionals in kennel operations, groomers, veterinarians, animal hospitals/clinics and pet suppliers.

★508★ DVM Newsmagazine
Advanstar Communications, Inc.
7600 Old Oak Blvd.
Cleveland, OH 44130
Ph: (216)243-8100   Fax: (216)891-2733

Monthly. $38.00/year; $3.00 for single issue. Recipients are veternarians in private practices in the U.S.

★509★ Equus
Fleet Street Publishing Corp.
656 Quince Orchard Rd.
Gaithersburg, MD 20878
Ph: (301)977-3900   Fax: (301)990-9015

Monthly. $24.00/year for individuals; $3.00 for single issue. Magazine featuring health, care, and understanding of horses.

★510★ Horse Illustrated
Fancy Publications, Inc.
PO Box 6050
Mission Viejo, CA 92690
Ph: (714)855-8822   Fax: (714)855-3045

Monthly. Horse riding (English and western styles).

★511★ Horse & Rider
Cowles Magazines Inc.
1060 Calle Cordillera, Ste. 103
San Clemente, CA 92673
Ph: (714)361-1955   Fax: (714)361-0333

Monthly. $19.95/year for individuals; $2.50 for single issue. Magazine devoted to Western style riding, apparel, products, lifestyle, and general horse care.

★512★ Horsemen's Journal
American Equine Publishers, Inc.
PO Box 2106
Ocala, FL 34478-2106
Ph: (904)237-6444   Fax: (904)237-5610

Monthly. Tabloid with features and statistics for thoroughbred racehorse owners and trainers.

★513★ The Morgan Horse
American Morgan Horse Association
PO Box 960
Shelburne, VT 05482-0960
Ph: (802)985-4944   Fax: (802)985-8897

Monthly. $27.50/year for individuals. Magazine for Morgan horse enthusiasts.

★514★ Pet Age
H.H. Backer Associates, Inc.
20 E. Jackson Blvd.
Chicago, IL 60604
Ph: (312)663-4040   Fax: (312)663-5676

Monthly. Free to qualified subscribers; $25.00/year for individuals; $50.00/year for other countries; $2.50 for single issue. Trade magazine for pet supplies retailers, wholesalers, and manufacturers.

★515★ Rocky Mountain Employment Newsletter
Intermountain Publishing & Referral
311-NP 14th St.
Glenwood Springs, CO 81601
Ph: (303)945-8991   Fax: (303)945-5140

Semimonthly. $13.00/year, per month for one edition; $16.00/year, for two editions; $19.00/year, for three editions; $21.00/year, for four editions. Lists information on current job openings in Colorado, Idaho, Montana, Arizona, New Mexico, Washington, Oregon, and Wyoming. Provides job titles, descriptions, requirements, and employer name and address or telephone number. Covers all occupational fields. Specializes in summer-winter seasonal openings, and in ranch, horse, livestock and farm opportunities. Available in four editions: Colorado-Wyoming, Arizona-New Mexico, Idaho-Montana, and Washington-Oregon.

★516★ Saddle Horse Report
Saddle Horse Report
PO Box 1007
Shelbyville, TN 37160
Ph: (615)684-8123   Fax: (615)684-8196

Weekly (Mon.). $50.00/year for individuals. Newspaper containing national coverage of horse shows and sales.

★517★ The Thoroughbred of California
California Thoroughbred Breeders
  Association
201 Colorado Pl.
PO Box 750
Arcadia, CA 91066
Ph: (818)445-7800   Fax: (818)574-0852

Monthly. $42.00/year for nonmembers. Magazine about horse breeding and racing.

★518★ Trends Magazine
American Animal Hospital Association
12575 W. Bayaud Ave.
Lakewood, CO 80228
Ph: (303)986-2800

Bimonthly. $60.00/year. Covers the management of small animal veterinary practices.

★519★ Veterinary Technician
Veterinary Learning Systems
9300 W. 110th St., Ste. 145
Overland Park, KS 66210
Ph: (913)451-3475   Fax: (913)451-3929

Official journal of the North American Veterinary Technician Association. Published for veterinary technicians, nurses, and assistants.

★520★ Western Horseman
PO Box 7980
Colorado Springs, CO 80933-7980
Ph: (719)633-5524   Fax: (719)633-1392

Monthly. $18.00/year for individuals; $25.00/year for other countries; $2.50 for single issue. Magazine covering forms of horsemanship and all breeds of horses; emphasizing western stock horses and western lifestyle.

PLACEMENT AND JOB REFERRAL SERVICES

★521★ American Veterinary Medical Association (AVMA)

1931 N. Meacham Rd., Ste. 100
Schaumburg, IL 60173-4360
Ph: (708)925-8070   Fax: (708)925-1329
Fr: 800-248-2862

Members: Professional society of veterinarians. **Activities:** Conducts educational and research programs. Provides placement service. Maintains the American Society of Laboratory Animal Practitioners. Sponsors American Veterinary Medical Association Foundation (also known as AVMA Foundation) and Educational Commission for Foreign Veterinary Graduates. Compiles statistics.

★522★ National Animal Control Association (NACA)

PO Box 480851
Kansas City, MO 64148-0851
Fax: (913)768-0607   Fr: 800-828-6474

Members: Animal control agencies, humane societies, public health and safety agencies, corporations, and individuals. **Purpose:** Works to educate and train personnel in the animal care and control professions. Seeks to teach the public responsible pet ownership; operates the NACA Network to provide animal control information; evaluates animal control programs. Provides training guides for animal control officers; makes available audiovisual materials. **Activities:** Operates placement service and speakers' bureau.

★523★ National Dog Groomers Association of America (NDGAA)

Box 101
Clark, PA 16113
Ph: (412)962-2711   Fax: (412)962-1919

Members: Dog groomers and supply distributors organized to upgrade the profession. **Activities:** Conducts state and local workshops; sponsors competitions and certification testing. Makes groomer referrals.

EMPLOYER DIRECTORIES AND NETWORKING LISTS

★524★ Animal Hospitals Directory

American Business Directories, Inc.
American Business Information, Inc.
5711 S. 86th Cir.
Omaha, NE 68127
Ph: (402)593-4600   Fax: (402)331-1505

Annual. $965.00, payment with order. Entries include: Name, address, phone (including area code), size of advertisement, year first in Yellow Pages, name of owner or manager, number of employees. Compiled from telephone company Yellow Pages nationwide. Arrangement: Geographical.

★525★ Directory of Animal Care and Control Agencies

American Humane Association
63 Iverness Dr. E.
Englewood, CO 80112
Ph: (303)792-9900   Fax: (303)792-5333
Fr: 800-227-4645

Updated continuously; printed on request. $75.00, Base edition, to nonprofit organizations; $500.00, Base edition, to others. Covers over 4,500 animal protection agencies; Canadian and some other foreign agencies are available; national and individual state editions are available. Entries include: Agency name, address, phone, contact. Arrangement: Geographical.

★526★ Kennels Directory

American Business Directories, Inc.
American Business Information, Inc.
5711 S. 86th Cir.
Omaha, NE 68127
Ph: (402)593-4600   Fax: (402)331-1505

Annual. $800.00, U.S. edition. Entries include: Name, address, phone (including area code), size of advertisement, year first in Yellow Pages, name of owner or manager, number of employees. Compiled from telephone company Yellow Pages, nationwide. Arrangement: Geographical.

★527★ Pet Washing & Grooming Directory

American Business Directories, Inc.
American Business Information, Inc.
5711 S. 86th Cir.
Omaha, NE 68127
Ph: (402)593-4600   Fax: (402)331-1505

Annual. $1,295.00, U.S. edition. Entries include: Name, address, phone (including area code) size of advertisement, year first in Yellow Pages, name of owner or manager, number of employees. Compiled from telephone company Yellow Pages, nationwide. Arrangement: Geographical.

HANDBOOKS AND MANUALS

★528★ Career Information Center

Macmillan Publishing Co.
200 Old Tappan Rd.
Old Tappan, NJ 07675
Ph: (609)461-6500   Fr: 800-223-2336

Visual Education Center Staff. Fifth edition, 1992. $229.00. This 13-volume set profiles over 600 occupations. Each occupational profile describes job duties, educational requirements, how to get the job, advancement possibilities, employment outlook, working conditions, earnings and benefits, and where to write for more information.

★529★ Careers for Animal Lovers and Other Zoological Types

VGM Career Horizons
4255 W. Touhy Ave.
Lincolnwood, IL 60646-1975
Ph: (847)679-5500   Fax: (847)679-2494
Fr: 800-323-4900

Louise Miller. 1995. $14.95; $9.95 (paper). Surveys a range of opportunities working with animals in both the public and profit sectors. Includes such possibilities as groomers, trainers, zookeepers, researchers, veterinarians, pet psychologists, pet shelter operators, wildlife biologists, and animal writers, photographers, and illustrators.

★530★ Careers in Veterinary Medicine

Rosen Publishing Group, Inc.
29 E. 21st St.
New York, NY 10010
Ph: (212)777-3017   Fax: (212)777-0277
Fr: 800-237-9932

Jane Caryl Duncan. Revised edition, 1994. $13.95; $9.95 (paper). Surveys job opportunities in teaching, private practice, private industry, and zoos.

★531★ The Challenge of a Lifetime: Careers in Laboratory Animal Science

American Association for Laboratory Animal Science
70 Timber Creek Dr., Ste. 5
Cordova, TN 38018
Ph: (901)754-8620

8 pages. This booklet surveys careers in animal laboratory science. Covers entry-level positions and places of employment.

★532★ Encyclopedia of Careers and Vocational Guidance

J. G. Ferguson Publishing Co.
200 W. Monroe, Ste. 250
Chicago, IL 60606
Ph: (312)580-5480

William E. Hopke. Ninth edition, 1993. $129.95; $199.95 (CD-ROM). Four-volume set that profiles 900 occupations and describes job trends in 71 industries. Includes career description, educational requirements, history of the job, methods of entry, advancement, employment outlook, earnings, conditions of work, social and psychological factors, and sources of further information. Contains career and employment information for this field.

★533★ Opportunities in Animal and Pet Care Careers

VGM Career Horizons
4255 W. Touhy Ave.
Lincolnwood, IL 60646-1975
Ph: (847)679-5500   Fax: (847)679-2494
Fr: 800-323-4900

Mary Price Lee and Richard S. Lee. 1994. $14.95; $11.95 (paper). 160 pages. Covers the field from small animal medicine to large animal medicine, and provides job-hunting advice. Illustrated.

★534★ Opportunities in Veterinary Medicine

VGM Career Horizons
4255 W. Touhy Ave.
Lincolnwood, IL 60646-1975
Ph: (847)679-5500   Fax: (847)679-2494
Fr: 800-323-4900

Robert E. Swope. 1993. $14.95; $11.95 (paper). Covers all types of today's practice opportunities, including research, zoological careers, government agency positions at local, state, national, and world levels, and private practice. Illustrated.

★535★ Robert Half's Success Guide for Accountants

Prentice Hall General Reference
15 Columbus Cir.
New York, NY 10023
Ph: (212)373-8500   Fr: 800-922-0577

Robert Half. 1990. $9.95. 167 pages. Includes index.

★536★ Your Career in Veterinary Technology

American Veterinary Medical Association
1931 N. Mecham Rd.
Schaumburg, IL 60173
Ph: (708)605-8070

Brochure. Single copy free. 8 pages. Discusses the work, places of employment, educational preparation, and earnings of veterinary medical technologists.

EMPLOYMENT AGENCIES AND SEARCH FIRMS

★537★ Temporary Horse Care and Service

807 SW 3rd Ave.
Ocala, FL 34474-4233
Ph: (904)622-2040

Employment agency. Provides placements on regular or temporary basis.

OTHER SOURCES

★538★ American Association for Laboratory Animal Science (AALAS)

70 Timber Creek, Ste. 5
Cordova, TN 38018
Ph: (901)754-8620   Fax: (901)753-0046

Members: Persons and institutions professionally concerned with the production, use, care, and study of laboratory animals. **Purpose:** Serves as clearinghouse for collection and exchange of information on all phases of laboratory animal care and management and on the care, use, and procurement of laboratory animals used in biomedical research. **Activities:** Conducts examinations and certification through its Animal Technician Certification Program.

★539★ American Boarding Kennels Association (ABKA)

4575 Galley Rd., No. 400A
Colorado Springs, CO 80915
Ph: (719)591-1113   Fax: (719)597-0006

Members: Persons or firms that board pets; kennel suppliers; others interested in the boarding kennel industry. **Purpose:** Seeks to upgrade the industry through educational programs, seminars and conventions. **Activities:** Provides insurance plans for members and supplies pet care information to the public. Promotes code of ethics and accreditation program for recognition and training of superior kennel operators. Compiles statistics.

★540★ Career Encounters: Veterinary Medicine

Cambridge Career Products
PO Box 2153
Dept. CC15
Charleston, WV 25328-2153
Ph: (304)744-9323   Fax: (304)744-9351
Fr: 800-468-4227

Video. $99.95. 25 minutes. Professionals shown in a variety of settings discuss different aspects of their careers.

★541★ Pet Hotel and Grooming Service Business Guide

Entrepreneur, Inc.
2392 Morse Ave.
Box 19787
Irvine, CA 92713-9787
Fax: (714)851-9088   Fr: 800-421-2300

$79.50 (includes business guide and software). Provides information on how to start a pet hotel and grooming service. Includes data on equipment, profits and costs, advertising and promotion, and related topics.

Anthropologists

PLACEMENT AND JOB REFERRAL SERVICES

★542★ African Studies Association (ASA)

Emory University
Credit Union Bldg.
Atlanta, GA 30322
Ph: (404)329-6410   Fax: (404)329-6433

Members: Persons specializing in teaching, writing, or research on Africa including political scientists, historians, geographers, anthropologists, economists, librarians, linguists, and government officials; persons who are studying African subjects; institutional members are universities, libraries, government agencies, and others interested in receiving information about Africa. **Purpose:** Seeks to foster communication and to stimulate research among scholars on Africa. **Activities:** Sponsors placement service; conducts panels and discussion groups; presents exhibits and films. **E-Mail:** africa@mony.edu

★543★ American Academy of Forensic Sciences (AAFS)

410 N. 21st St., Ste. 203
PO Box 669
Colorado Springs, CO 80901-0669
Ph: (719)636-1100   Fax: (719)636-1993

Members: Professional society of criminalists, scientists, members of the bench and bar, pathologists, biologists, psychiatrists, examiners of questioned documents, toxicologists, odontologists, anthropologists, and engineers. **Purpose:** Works to: encourage the study, improve the practice, elevate the standards, and advance the cause of the forensic sciences; improve the quality of scientific techniques, tests, and criteria; plan, organize, and administer meetings, reports, and other projects for the stimulation and advancement of these and related purposes. **Activities:** Maintains Forensic Sciences Job Listing; conducts selected research for the government; offers forensic expert referral service.

★544★ American Anthropological Association (AAA)

4350 N. Fairfax Dr., Ste. 640
Arlington, VA 22203
Ph: (703)528-1902   Fax: (703)528-3546

Purpose: Professional society of anthropologists, educators, students, and others interested in the biological and cultural origin and development of humanity. Sponsors visiting lecturers, congressional fellowship, and departmental services programs. **Activities:** Maintains speakers' bureau, consultants' bureau, and placement service. Sponsors competitions. Conducts research programs and compiles statistics.

★545★ Commission on the Study of Peace (CSP)

Syracuse University
Anthropology Department
Syracuse, NY 13244-1090
Ph: (315)443-2367   Fax: (315)443-3818

Members: Anthropologists. **Purpose:** Fosters research on the social and cultural dynamics of peace and war. **Activities:** Operates placement service. Provides curricular services; compiles statistics. Sponsors seminars and professional workshops. **E-Mail:** Internet, rar@.mailbox.syr.edu

★546★ Social Sciences Services and Resources

PO Box 153
Wasco, IL 60183
Ph: (708)897-5345

Members: Consulting associates in social sciences. **Purpose:** Established to advance the teaching, consulting, and practice of the social sciences basic disciplines including sociology, anthropology, political science, geography, history, economics, and their applied disciplines: social work, community development, planning, and public administration. Serves as: a center for dissemination of current and comprehensive social research findings. Provides consultants for citizen groups, community projects, and governmental units on written request. Upon request from colleges, school boards, and citizens groups, conducts in-service workshops on teaching, consulting, and new developments in the social sciences. Provides consultant evaluation services for small

colleges throughout the U.S. **Activities:** Maintains speakers' bureau and placement information service. Conducts research programs.

EMPLOYER DIRECTORIES AND NETWORKING LISTS

★547★ American Journal of Physical Anthropology—American Association of Physical Anthropologists Membership Directory Issue

American Association of Physical Anthropologists
Department of Anthropology
State University of New York/Buffalo
380 MFAC
Buffalo, NY 14261
Ph: (716)636-2414

Annual, December. Available to members only. Publication includes: 1,500 physical anthropologists and scientists in closely related fields interested in the advancement of the science of physical anthropology through research and teaching of human variation, primate paleoanthropology, and primate evolution. Entries include: Name, affiliation, address. Arrangement: Alphabetical.

★548★ Historical Archaeology Newsletter—Society for Historical Archaeology Membership Directory Issue

Society for Historical Archaeology
Box 30446
Tucson, AZ 85751
Ph: (602)886-8006   Fax: (602)886-0182

Annual, June. Available to members only. Publication includes: List of about 2,100 member archaeologists, historians, anthropologists, and ethnohistorians, and other individuals and institutions having an interest in historical archeology or allied fields. Entries include: Name, address. Arrangement: Alphabetical.

Handbooks and Manuals

★549★ Opportunities in Social Science Careers

VGM Career Horizons
4255 W. Touhy Ave.
Lincolnwood, IL 60646-1975
Ph: (847)679-5500   Fax: (847)679-2494
Fr: 800-323-4900

Rosanne J. Marek. 1990. $14.95; $11.95 (paper). 160 pages. Profiles job opportunities in education, government, and business, along with their salary levels and outlook in the years to come. Illustrated.

★550★ A PhD Is Not Enough: A Guide to Survival in Science

Addison-Wesley Publishing Co., Inc.
1 Jacob Way
Reading, MA 01867
Ph: (617)944-3700   Fax: (617)942-1117
Fr: 800-447-2226

Peter J. Feibelman. 1993. $12.95 (paper).

Other Sources

★551★ American Association of Physical Anthropologists (AAPA)

925 Koarney St.
NCSE
El Cerrito, CA 94530-2810
Ph: (510)526-1674   Fax: (510)526-1675

Purpose: Professional society of physical anthropologists and scientists in closely related fields interested in the advancement of the science of physical anthropology through research and teaching of human variation, primate paleoanthropology, and primate evolution.

★552★ American Society of Primatologists (ASP)

Rush-Presbyterian, St. Lukes Medical Center
Department OB/GYN
1653 W. Congress Pky.
Chicago, IL 60612
Ph: (312)942-2152   Fax: (312)942-4043

Purpose: Promotes the discovery and exchange of information regarding nonhuman primates, including all aspects of their anatomy, behavior, development, ecology, evolution, genetics, nutrition, physiology, reproduction, systematics, conservation, husbandry, and use in biomedical research.

★553★ Amerind Foundation (AF)

PO Box 400
Dragoon, AZ 85609
Ph: (520)586-3666   Fax: (520)586-4679

Purpose: Conducts research in anthropology and archaeology of the greater American southwest and northern Mexico and ethnology in the Western Hemisphere. **Activities:** Offers guided tours, artist shows; volunteer opportunities, internship program, and visiting scholar program. Operates museum.

★554★ Anthropology Film Center Foundation (AFCF)

PO Box 493
Santa Fe, NM 87501
Ph: (505)983-4127

Members: General anthropologists, visual anthropologists, culture and communication specialists, applied anthropologists, musicologists, linguists, and educators. **Purpose:** Seeks to further scholarship, research, and practice in visual anthropology by using consultation and research services, seminars, publications, teaching, equipment outfitting, and specialized facilities. **Activities:** Generation and publication of research films and reports; consultation with universities and institutions; resident fellow program. Offers Ethnographic and Documentary Film Program which provides introductory basics in photography, film making and ethnology, and hands on training with story boarding, camera, sound, editing and lighting exercises.

★555★ Association of Black Anthropologists (ABA)

4350 N. Fairfax Dr., Ste. 640
Arlington, VA 22203
Ph: (703)528-1902   Fax: (703)528-3546

Members: A section of the American Anthropological Association. Anthropologists and others interested in the study of blacks and other peoples subjected to exploitation and oppression. **Purpose:** Works to: formulate conceptual and methodological frameworks to advance understanding of all forms of human diversity and commonality; advance theoretical efforts to explain the conditions that produce social inequalities based on race, ethnicity, class, or gender; develop research methods that involve the peoples studied and local scholars in all stages of investigation and dissemination of findings.

★556★ Foundation for Latin American Anthropological Research (FLAAR)

Brevard Community College
1519 Clearlake Rd.
Cocoa, FL 32922
Ph: (407)632-1111   Fax: (407)633-4565

Purpose: Works to promote a better public understanding of professional archaeology. **Activities:** Sponsors research in the fields of archaeology, pre-Columbian art and architecture, and ethnohistory. Sponsors annual two-week study trips to archaeological sites in Mexico, Guatemala, and Peru. Together with WBCC-TV Channel 68 FLAAR produces television documentaries on Maya art, pyramid architecture, and archaeology. Offers a traveling photo exhibit to museums, colleges, and associations. Provides professional consultant services to museums galleries, universities, television and film on interactive multi-media computer programs in archaeology, pyramid architecture, and ancient art.

★557★ Institute for the Study of Man (ISM)

1133 13th St. NW, No. C-2
Washington, DC 20005
Ph: (202)371-2700   Fax: (202)371-1523

Purpose: To publish books and journals in areas related to anthropology and the human sciences.

★558★ International Studies Association (ISA)

Brigham Young University
David M. Kennedy Center
216 HRCB
Provo, UT 84602
Ph: (801)378-5459   Fax: (801)378-7075

Members: Social scientists and other scholars from a wide variety of disciplines who are specialists in international affairs and cross-cultural studies; academicians; government officials; officials in international organizations; business executives; students. **Purpose:** Promotes research, improved teaching, and the orderly growth of knowledge in the field of international studies; emphasizes a multidisciplinary approach to problems. **Activities:** Holds conferences with government officials; conducts workshops and discussion groups; sponsors development of modular curriculum materials.

★559★ International Women's Anthropology Conference (IWAC)

Anthropology Department
25 Waverly Pl.
New York, NY 10003
Ph: (212)998-8550

Members: Women anthropologists and sociologists who are researching and teaching topics such as women's role in development, feminism, and the international women's movement. **Purpose:** Encourages the exchange of information on research, projects, and funding; addresses policies concerning women from an anthropological perspective. Conducts periodic educational meetings with panel discussions.

★560★ Society for Applied Anthropology (SFAA)

PO Box 24083
Oklahoma City, OK 73124
Ph: (405)843-5113   Fax: (405)843-8553

Members: Professional society of anthropologists, sociologists, psychologists, health professionals, industrial researchers, and educators. **Purpose:** Promotes scientific investigation of the principles controlling relations between human beings, and to encourage wide application of these principles to practical problems.

★561★ Wenner-Gren Foundation for Anthropological Research (WGFAR)

220 5th Ave., 16th Fl.
New York, NY 10001
Ph: (212)683-5000   Fax: (212)683-9151

Purpose: Supports research in all branches of anthropology including cultural/social, biological/physical, ethnological, archaeological, and anthropological linguistics, and in closely related disciplines concerned with human origins, development, and variation.

Archaeologists

★562★ Photogrammetric Engineering and Remote Sensing

American Society for Photogrammetry and Remote Sensing (ASPRS)
5410 Grosvenor Ln., Ste. 210
Bethesda, MD 20814-2160
Ph: (301)493-0290   Fax: (301)493-0208

Monthly. Free to members; $120.00/year for nonmembers. Provides technical information about the applications of photogrammetry, remote sensing, and geographic information systems.

PLACEMENT AND JOB REFERRAL SERVICES

★563★ American Philological Association (APA)

Department of Classics
Worcester, MA 01610-2395
Ph: (508)793-2203   Fax: (508)793-3428

Members: Teachers of Latin and Greek, classical archaeologists with literary interests, and comparative linguists. **Purpose:** For the advancement and diffusion of philological information. **Activities:** Sponsors placement service and campus advisory service to provide advice on instructional programs in classical studies.

★564★ Archaeological Institute of America (AIA)

656 Beacon St.
Boston, MA 02215
Ph: (617)353-9361   Fax: (617)353-6550

Purpose: Educational and scientific society of archaeologists and others interested in archaeological study and research. Founded five schools of archaeology. **Activities:** Maintains annual lecture program for all branch societies. Operates placement service for archeology educators. Sponsors educational

programs for middle school children. **E-Mail:** majordomo@brynmawr.edu

★565★ Society for American Archaeology (SAA)

900 2nd St. NE, No. 12
Washington, DC 20002
Ph: (202)789-8200   Fax: (202)789-0284

Members: Professionals, avocationals, students, and others interested in American archaeology. **Purpose:** Stimulates scientific research in the archaeology of the New World by: creating closer professional relations among archaeologists, and between them and others interested in American archaeology; advocating the conservation of archaeological data and furthering the control or elimination of commercialization of archaeological objects; promoting a more rational public appreciation of the aims and limitations of archaeological research. **Activities:** Maintains placement service and educational programs.

EMPLOYER DIRECTORIES AND NETWORKING LISTS

★566★ Archaeological Institute of America Bulletin

Archaeological Institute of America
656 Beacon St.
Boston, MA 02215-2010
Ph: (617)353-9361

Annual. $6.50, plus $2.50 shipping. Publication includes: List of local society officers and staff. Entries include: Name, address, phone. Arrangement: Geographical.

★567★ Guide to Prehistoric Ruins of the Southwest

Pruett Publishing Co.
2928 Pearl St.
Boulder, CO 80301
Ph: (303)449-4919   Fax: (303)443-9019
Fr: 800-247-8224

Irregular, latest edition May 1989. $12.95, plus $2.50 shipping; payment with order. Covers over 200 archeological sites in Arizona, New Mexico, Utah and Colorado. Entries

include: Site name, location, size, features and description of site, names of excavators or sponsoring organization, discoveries, whether accessible to the handicapped, active parts of site. Arrangement: Geographical.

★568★ Historical Archaeology Newsletter—Society for Historical Archaeology Membership Directory Issue

Society for Historical Archaeology
Box 30446
Tucson, AZ 85751
Ph: (602)886-8006   Fax: (602)886-0182

Annual, June. Available to members only. Publication includes: List of about 2,100 member archaeologists, historians, anthropologists, and ethnohistorians, and other individuals and institutions having an interest in historical archeology or allied fields. Entries include: Name, address. Arrangement: Alphabetical.

HANDBOOKS AND MANUALS

★569★ Careers in Archaeology

Chronicle Guidance Publications, Inc.
66 Aurora St.
PO Box 1190
Moravia, NY 13118-1190
Ph: (315)497-0330   Fax: (315)497-3359
Fr: 800-622-7284

Chronicle Guidance Staff. 1993. $2.00. Reprint of a journal article.

★570★ Opportunities for Contract Work in Archaeology and Historic Preservation

American Anthropological Association
4350 N. Fairfax Dr., Ste. 640
Arlington, VA 22203

This pamphlet describes career opportunities with federal, state, and local agencies which are required by law to identify and preserve historic properties. Gives a list of agencies employing archivists.

★571★ Opportunities in Historical Archaeology

Chronicle Guidance Publications, Inc.
66 Aurora St.
PO Box 1190
Moravia, NY 13118-1190
Ph: (315)497-0330   Fax: (315)497-3359
Fr: 800-622-7284

Chronicle Guidance Staff. 1991. $2.00. Reprint of a journal article.

★572★ Opportunities in Social Science Careers

VGM Career Horizons
4255 W. Touhy Ave.
Lincolnwood, IL 60646-1975
Ph: (847)679-5500   Fax: (847)679-2494
Fr: 800-323-4900

Rosanne J. Marek. 1990. $14.95; $11.95 (paper). 160 pages. Profiles job opportunities in education, government, and business, along with their salary levels and outlook in the years to come. Illustrated.

★573★ A PhD Is Not Enough: A Guide to Survival in Science

Addison-Wesley Publishing Co., Inc.
1 Jacob Way
Reading, MA 01867
Ph: (617)944-3700   Fax: (617)942-1117
Fr: 800-447-2226

Peter J. Feibelman. 1993. $12.95 (paper).

OTHER SOURCES

★574★ American Society for Photogrammetry and Remote Sensing (ASPRS)

5410 Grosvenor Ln., Ste. 210
Bethesda, MD 20814-2160
Ph: (301)493-0290   Fax: (301)493-0208

Members: Firms, individuals, government employees, and academicians engaged in photogrammetry, photointerpretation, remote sensing, and geographic information systems and their application to such fields as archaeology, geographic information systems, military reconnaissance, urban planning, engineering, traffic surveys, meteorological observations, medicine, geology, forestry, agriculture, construction, and topographic mapping. **Activities:** Offers voluntary certification program open to persons associated with one or more functional area of photogrammetry, remote sensing, and GIS. Surveys the profession of private firms in photogrammetry and remote sensing in the areas of products and services.

★575★ Amerind Foundation (AF)

PO Box 400
Dragoon, AZ 85609
Ph: (520)586-3666   Fax: (520)586-4679

Purpose: Conducts research in anthropology and archaeology of the greater American southwest and northern Mexico and ethnology in the Western Hemisphere. **Activities:** Offers guided tours, artist shows; volunteer opportunities, internship program, and visiting scholar program. Operates museum.

★576★ Archaeological Conservancy (AC)

5301 Central Ave. NE, Ste. 1218
Albuquerque, NM 87108
Ph: (505)266-1540

Members: People interested in preserving prehistoric and historic sites for interpretive or research purposes (most members are not professional archaeologists). **Purpose:** Seeks to acquire for permanent preservation, through donation or purchase, the ruins of past American cultures, primarily those of American Indians. Works throughout the U.S. to preserve cultural resources presently on private lands and protect them from the destruction of looters, modern agricultural practices, and urban sprawl. **Activities:** Operates with government agencies, universities, and museums to permanently preserve acquired sites.

★577★ Center for American Archeology (CAA)

PO Box 366
Kampsville, IL 62053
Ph: (618)653-4316   Fax: (618)653-4232

Members: Philanthropic organizations, foundations, corporations, professional and amateur archaeologists, students, and others interested in archaeology in the U.S. **Purpose:** Conducts archaeological research and disseminates the results. Excavates, analyzes, and conserves archaeological sites and artifacts. Through the Kampsville Archeological Center sponsors tours, lectures, and educational and outreach programs, including university, middle school and junior high, and high school field schools; offers professional training at levels of detail ranging from secondary to postgraduate. Maintains speakers' bureau. Operates Kampsville Archeological Museum.

★578★ Epigraphic Society (ES)

2443 Filmore St., Ste. 328
San Francisco, CA 94115
Ph: (619)571-1344   Fax: (619)571-1124

Members: Individuals interested in deciphering ancient inscriptions, including professional and amateur epigraphers (specialists in engraved inscriptions) and linguists. **Purpose:** Members launch expeditions to North America and overseas. Reports discoveries and decipherments and assesses their historical implications. Participates in group lecture and teaching programs with other archaeological societies and university departments of archaeology and history. Conducts specialized education and research programs. Operates museum. Maintains numerous committees.

★579★ Foundation for Latin American Anthropological Research (FLAAR)

Brevard Community College
1519 Clearlake Rd.
Cocoa, FL 32922
Ph: (407)632-1111   Fax: (407)633-4565

Purpose: Works to promote a better public understanding of professional archaeology. **Activities:** Sponsors research in the fields of archaeology, pre-Columbian art and architecture, and ethnohistory. Sponsors annual two-week study trips to archaeological sites in Mexico, Guatemala, and Peru. Together with

WBCC-TV Channel 68 FLAAR produces television documentaries on Maya art, pyramid architecture, and archaeology. Offers a traveling photo exhibit to museums, colleges, and associations. Provides professional consultant services to museums galleries, universities, television and film on interactive multi-media computer programs in archaeology, pyramid architecture, and ancient art.

★580★ Society for Historical Archaeology (SHA)

PO Box 30446
Tucson, AZ 85751
Ph: (602)886-8006   Fax: (602)886-0182

Members: Archaeologists, historians, anthropologists, and ethnohistorians; other individuals and institutions with an interest in historical archaeology or allied fields. **Purpose:** Aim is to bring together persons interested in studying specific historic sites, manuscripts, and published sources, and to develop generalizations concerning historical periods and cultural dynamics as these emerge through the techniques of archaeological excavation and analysis.

★581★ Society of Professional Archaeologists (SOPA)

Planning and Environmental Branch
North Carolina Department of Transportation
Raleigh, NC 27611
Ph: (919)733-3141   Fax: (919)733-9794

Members: Professional archaeologists satisfying basic requirements in training and experience, including private consultants, individuals working with large firms, and academic personnel. **Purpose:** Objectives are to define professionalism in archaeology; provide a measure against which to evaluate archaeological actions and research; establish certification standards; provide for grievance procedures; demonstrate to other archaeologists and the public the nature of professional archaeology. **Activities:** Monitors related legislative activities; maintains society archives. Is developing educational programs and drafting standards and guidelines for field schools.

★582★ Working Holidays

Central Bureau for Educational Visits & Exchanges
Seymour Mews House
Seymour Mews
London W1H 9PE, England
Ph: 71 4865101   Fax: 71 9355741

Annual, November. $9.99, postpaid. Covers 1,000 organizations offering short-term paid and voluntary work opportunities in Britain and over 70 countries worldwide, for periods of three days to a year or longer; jobs include archeological digs, au pair/childcare, children's projects, couriers, guides, monitors, teachers, work camps, conservation, community works, hotel work, farm work, teaching, simple construction, etc. Entries include: Organization name, address, name of contact, objectives, projects available, conditions and terms of work. Arrangement: Geographical, then by type of work. Indexes: Organization name.

Architects

SOURCES OF HELP-WANTED ADS

★583★ Architectural Record
New York Construction News
1221 Avenue of the Americas, 41st Fl.
New York, NY 10020
Ph: (212)512-4773   Fax: (212)512-4770

Magazine focusing on architecture.

★584★ Builder
Hanley-Wood, Inc.
1 Thomas Cir., Ste. 600
Washington, DC 20005
Ph: (202)452-0800   Fax: (202)785-1974

Monthly. $29.95/year for individuals. Magazine covering housing, commercial, and industrial building.

★585★ Civil Engineering-ASCE
American Society of Civil Engineers
345 E. 47th St.
New York, NY 10017-2398
Ph: (212)705-7463   Fax: (212)705-7712

Monthly. $81.00/year for individuals. Professional magazine.

★586★ Custom Home
Hanley-Wood, Inc.
1 Thomas Cir., Ste. 600
Washington, DC 20005
Ph: (202)452-0800   Fax: (202)785-1974

Bimonthly. Trade publication.

★587★ Design Cost & Data
L.M Rector Corp.
8602 N. 40th St.
Tampa, FL 33604
Ph: (813)989-9300   Fax: (813)980-3982

Quarterly. $48.00/year for individuals. Publication providing real cost data case studies of various types completed around the country. Used by design and building professionals.

★588★ Fabrics and Architecture
Industrial Fabrics Association Intl.
345 Cedar St., Ste. 800
St. Paul, MN 55101
Ph: (612)222-2508   Fax: (612)222-8215

Bimonthly. $21.00/year. Magazine specializing in interior and exterior design ideas for fabric applications in architecture.

★589★ INTERIORS
BPI Communications
1515 Broadway, 11th Fl.
New York, NY 10036
Ph: (212)536-5167   Fax: (212)536-5351
Fr: 800-274-4100

Monthly. Magazine for interior designers and architects.

★590★ Kitchen and Bath Design News
PTN Publications
2 University Plaza, Ste. 11
Hackensack, NJ 07601
Ph: (201)487-7800   Fax: (201)487-1061

Monthly.

★591★ Metal Architecture
Modern Trade Communications, Inc.
7450 N. Skokie Blvd.
Skokie, IL 60077
Ph: (708)674-2200   Fax: (708)674-3676

Monthly.

★592★ Metal Construction News
Modern Trade Communications, Inc.
7450 N. Skokie Blvd.
Skokie, IL 60077
Ph: (708)674-2200   Fax: (708)674-3676

Monthly. $35.00/year for individuals. Magazine focusing on metal building, metal roof, and sidewall news.

★593★ The Military Engineer
Society of American Military Engineers
607 Prince St.
Alexandria, VA 22314-3117
Ph: (703)549-3800   Fax: (703)684-0231

Journal on military and civil engineering.

★594★ PM Network
Project Management Institute
130 S. State Rd.
Upper Darby, PA 19082
Ph: (610)734-3330   Fax: (610)734-3266

Monthly. $90.00/year for members. Magazine covering project and program management.

★595★ Professional Builder
Cahners Publishing Co.
1350 E. Touhy Ave.
PO Box 5080
Des Plaines, IL 60018-5080
Ph: (708)635-8800   Fax: (708)635-9950

Monthly. $10.00 for single issue; $139.95/year by mail.

★596★ Progressive Architecture
600 Summer St.
PO Box 1361
Stamford, CT 06904
Ph: (203)348-7531

Monthly. $48.00/year; $7.50/issue. National magazine on architecture, interior designs, and planning.

★597★ Texas Architect
Texas Society of Architects
114 W. 7th, Ste. 1400
Austin, TX 78701
Ph: (512)478-7386   Fax: (512)478-0528

Bimonthly. Magazine for design professionals and their clients.

★598★ Tile World
Tradelink Publishing Co., Inc.
1 Kalisa Way, No. 205
Paramus, NJ 07652
Ph: (201)599-0136   Fax: (201)599-2378

Bimonthly. $38.00/year; $7.00/single issue.

PLACEMENT AND JOB REFERRAL SERVICES

★599★ Asian American Architects and Engineers
1670 Pine St.
San Francisco, CA 94109
Ph: (415)928-5910   Fax: (415)921-0182
Members: Minorities. **Purpose:** Provides contracts and job opportunities for minorities in the architectural and engineering fields. **Activities:** Serves as a network for the promotion in professional fields.

★600★ Council of Educational Facility Planners, International (CEFPI)
8687 E. Via de Ventura, Ste. 311
Scottsdale, AZ 85258-3347
Ph: (602)948-2337   Fax: (602)948-4420
Members: Individuals and firms who are responsible for planning, designing, creating, maintaining, and equipping the physical environment of education. **Purpose:** Sponsors an exchange of information, professional experiences, research results, and other investigative techniques concerning educational facility planning. **Activities:** Activities include publication and review of current and emerging practices in educational facility planning; identification and execution of needed research; development of professional training programs; strengthening of planning services on various levels of government and in institutions of higher learning; leadership in the development of higher standards for facility design and the physical environment of education. Operates speakers' bureau; sponsors placement service; compiles statistics.

★601★ Nacore International (NACORE)
440 Columbia Dr., Ste. 100
West Palm Beach, FL 33409
Ph: (407)683-8111   Fax: (407)697-4853
Members: Executives, attorneys, real estate department heads, architects, engineers, analysts, researchers, and anyone responsible for the management, administration, and operation of national and regional real estate departments of national and international corporations. **Purpose:** Provides a meeting ground for the exchange of ideas, experience, and problems among members; encourages professionalism within corporate real estate through education and communication; protects the interests of corporate realty in dealing with adversaries, public or private; maintains contact with other real estate organizations; publicizes the availability of fully qualified members to the job market. Maintains Institute for Corporate Real Estate as educational arm. **Activities:** Maintains placement service.

★602★ Professional Women in Construction (PWC)
342 Madison Ave., Rm. 451
New York, NY 10173
Ph: (212)687-0610   Fax: (212)490-1213
Members: Management-level women and men in construction and allied industries; owners, suppliers, architects, engineers, field personnel, office personnel, and bonding/surety personnel. **Purpose:** Provides a forum for exchange of ideas and promotion of political and legislative action, education, and job opportunities for women in construction and related fields; forms liaisons with other trade and professional groups; develops research programs. Strives to reform abuses and to assure justice and equity within the construction industry. Sponsors mini-workshops. **Activities:** Maintains Action Line which provides members with current information on pertinent legislation and on the association's activities and job referrals.

★603★ Society of American Registered Architects (SARA)
1245 S. Highland Ave.
Lombard, IL 60148
Ph: (708)932-4622
Members: Architects registered or licensed under the laws of states and territories of the U.S. **Activities:** Offers placement service. Sponsors seminars and professional and student design competitions.

EMPLOYER DIRECTORIES AND NETWORKING LISTS

★604★ Architects Directory
American Business Directories, Inc.
American Business Information, Inc.
5711 S. 86th Cir.
Omaha, NE 68127
Ph: (402)593-4600   Fax: (402)331-1505
Annual. $1,155.00, U.S. edition; $170.00, (Canad. ed.): Entries include: Name, address, phone, size of advertisement, year first in Yellow Pages, name of owner or manager, number of employees. Regional editions available: Eastern, $725; Western, $645.00. Compiled from telephone company Yellow Pages, nationwide. Arrangement: Geographical.

★605★ Art Marketing Sourcebook
ArtNetwork
18757 Wildflower Dr.
Penn Valley, CA 95946-9717
Ph: (916)432-7630   Fax: (916)432-1633
Biennial, spring 1995. $22.95, plus 4.00 shipping; payment must accompany order; libraries, schools may send purchase orders. Covers over 2,000 representatives, consultants, galleries, critics, architects, interior designers, corporations, museum curators. Entries include: Company name, address, phone, description of services, style represented, mediums, years in business, types of companies dealt with, geographical limitations, number of clients, requirements for viewing slides. Arrangement: Classified by type of organization.

★606★ Association of University Interior Designers—Membership List
Association of University Interior Designers
c/o Denise Beard
Ohio State University
The Office of the University Architect and Physical Planning
2009 Millikin Rd.
Columbus, OH 43210
Ph: (614)292-4458
Twice yearly, June and October. Available to members only. Covers nearly 100 in-house interior designers, landscape designers, architects, and purchasing agents associated with universities. Entries include: Name, title, affiliation, address, phone. Arrangement: Alphabetical.

★607★ Athletic Business—Professional Directory Section
Athletic Business Publications, Inc.
1846 Hoffman St.
Madison, WI 53704
Ph: (608)249-0186   Fax: (608)249-1153
Fr: 800-722-8764
Monthly. $5.00 per issue. Publication includes: List of architects, engineers, contractors, and consultants in athletic facility planning and construction; all listings are paid. Entries include: Company name, address, phone. Arrangement: Alphabetical.

★608★ Construction Employment Guide in the National and International Field
World Trade Academy Press
50 E. 42nd St., Ste. 509
New York, NY 10017
Ph: (212)697-4999
$16.50. Covers More than 200 U.S. and international construction, engineering and design companies. Also covers U.S. government construction employment opportunities, job centers and employment agencies. Entries include: Company name, address, specialties.

★609★ Directory of African American Design Firms
San Francisco Redevelopment Agency
770 Golden Gate Ave.
San Francisco, CA 94102-3120
Ph: (415)749-2423   Fax: (415)749-2526
Annual, December. Free. Covers over 100 architectural, engineering, planning, and landscape design firms. Entries include: Firm name, address, phone names and titles of key personnel, particular type of work. Arrangement: Alphabetical.

★610★ Directory of Latino Design Firms
San Francisco Redevelopment Agency
770 Golden Gate Ave.
San Francisco, CA 94102-3120
Ph: (415)749-2423
Irregular, latest edition August 1994. Free. Covers over 100 professional consulting firms in the U.S. wherein at least one principal is Latino. Entries include: Company name, address, phone, contact name. Arrangement: Alphabetical. Indexes: Business organization.

★611★ ENR Directory of Design Firms

McGraw-Hill, Inc.
1221 Ave. of the Americas
New York, NY 10020
Ph: (212)512-2534

Biennial, fall of even years; issue of *Engineering News Record*. $85.00. Covers 133 architects, architectural engineers, consultants, and other design firms; limited to advertisers. Mini-profiles on about 3,400 U.S. firms and 500 foreign firms or foreign offices of U.S. firms. Also includes lists of top 500 design firms in the United States, top 200 international design firms, top 50 United States design-construction firms, and top 50 international design-construction firms, based on total amount of billings. Entries include: For advertisers: company name, address, branch locations, subsidiaries, list of key personnel, territory served, capabilities. In ranked lists: company name, address, phone; international firms include telex. Arrangement: Alphabetical (profiles); geographical (mini-profiles).

★612★ ENR—Top 500 Design Firms Issue

McGraw-Hill, Inc.
1221 Ave. of the Americas
New York, NY 10020
Ph: (212)512-4635

Annual, April. $10.00, reprint, payment must accompany order. Publication includes: List of 500 leading architectural, engineering, and specialty design firms selected on basis of annual billings. Entries include: Company name, headquarters location, type of firm, current and prior year rank in billings, types of services, countries in which operated in preceding year. Arrangement: Ranked by billings.

★613★ ENR—Top International Design Firms Issue

McGraw-Hill, Inc.
1221 Ave. of the Americas
New York, NY 10020
Ph: (212)512-4635

Annual, July. $10.00, reprint, payment with order. Publication includes: List of 200 design firms (including United States firms) competing outside their own national borders who received largest dollar volume of foreign contracts in preceding calendar year. Entries include: Company name, headquarters location, type of firm, current and previous year rankings in total billings, types of services, countries in which operated in preceding year. Arrangement: By amount billed to international clients in previous year.

★614★ Illinois Architecture Reference Directory

Metropolitan Press Publications
Box 3680
Merchandise Mart Plaza
Chicago, IL 60654
Ph: (312)829-9650

Annual, December. $20.00, plus $3.00 shipping. Publication includes: List of architects who reside in Illinois, and a directory of architectural, engineering, preservationist, allied professional, educational, art, historical, and construction organizations throughout the United States. Entries include: For Illinois

architects: name, address, phone, whether a member of the American Institute of Architects (AIA). For organizations: name of firm or association, address, phone, director. Arrangement: Illinois architects list is alphabetical; organizations are classified by type (professional, governmental, etc.). Indexes: AIA members.

★615★ Military Engineer—Directory Issue

Society of American Military Engineers
607 Prince St.
Alexandria, VA 22314-3117
Ph: (703)549-3800   Fax: (703)548-6153
Fr: 800-336-3097

Annual, January/February. $50.00. Publication includes: List of about 2,600 member architects, engineers, engineering and information systems equipment manufacturers, suppliers, contractors, and other engineering-related firms providing products and services to the U.S. Government and private sector, firms with experience and equipment useable in event of disasters. Entries include: Firm name, address, phone, names of principals, activities, type of ownership (public, private, parent company name), number of employees, and the engineering capabilities of the firm. Arrangement: Alphabetical.

★616★ ProFile/The Directory of U.S. Architectual Design Firms

American Institute of Architects
1735 New York Ave. NW
Washington, DC 20006
Ph: (202)626-7300   Fr: 800-365-2724

Annual. $145.00, plus $8.00 shipping. Covers more than 14,500 architectural firms, one or more of whose principals is a member of the American Institute of Architects. Entries include: For firms, firm name, address, phone, fax, year established, parent organization, key staff and their primary responsibilities, branches, number of staff personnel by discipline, types of work, geographical area served, projects. Arrangement: Firms are geographical. Indexes: Firm name, key individuals, specialization by category.

★617★ Saskatchewan Design Directory

Design Council of Saskatchewan, Inc.
642 Broadway Ave., Ste. 200
Saskatoon, SK, Canada S7N 1A9
Ph: (306)242-0733   Fax: (306)664-2598

Biennial, spring of odd years. $5.00. Covers members of the Saskatchewan Association of Architects, the Association of Professional Community Planners of Saskatchewan, the Saskatchewan Graphic Arts Association, the Interior Designers of Saskatchewan, Association of Consulting Engineers of Saskatchewan, Saskatchewan Society of Illustrators and Designers, and the Saskatchewan Association of Landscape Architects, which are members of the council; about 380 persons and firms listed. Entries include: Name, address, phone, fax, professional association with which affiliated. Arrangement: Classified by professional group.

★618★ Society of American Registered Architects—National Directory

Society of American Registered Architects
1245 S. Highland Ave.
Lombard, IL 60148
Ph: (708)932-4622   Fax: (312)495-3054

Annual, January. Available only to members and advertisers. Covers 1,000 architects registered or licensed under the laws of states and territories of the United States. Entries include: Name, affiliation, address, phone, office size, specialties, and dollar volume of work. Arrangement: Alphabetical. Indexes: Cross-referenced by state registration.

HANDBOOKS AND MANUALS

★619★ Architect's Handbook of Professional Practice

American Institute of Architects Press
1735 New York Ave.
Washington, DC 20006
Ph: (202)626-7575   Fax: (703)435-6757

David Haviland. 1994. $20.00.

★620★ Architectural Practice Management

John Wiley & Sons, Inc.
605 3rd Ave.
New York, NY 10158-0012
Ph: (212)850-6000   Fr: 800-225-5945

F.Stasiowski. 1993. $225.00.

★621★ Career Information Center

Macmillan Publishing Co.
200 Old Tappan Rd.
Old Tappan, NJ 07675
Ph: (609)461-6500   Fr: 800-223-2336

Visual Education Center Staff. Fifth edition, 1992. $229.00. This 13-volume set profiles over 600 occupations. Each occupational profile describes job duties, educational requirements, how to get the job, advancement possibilities, employment outlook, working conditions, earnings and benefits, and where to write for more information.

★622★ Career Profile: Architect

American Institute of Architects
1735 New York Ave. NW
Washington, DC 20006-5292
Ph: (202)626-7300   Fr: 800-365-ARCH

Free brochure provides an overview of the professional, education and training requirements, and career opportunities.

★623★ Encyclopedia of Careers and Vocational Guidance

J. G. Ferguson Publishing Co.
200 W. Monroe, Ste. 250
Chicago, IL 60606
Ph: (312)580-5480

William E. Hopke. Ninth edition, 1993. $129.95; $199.95 (CD-ROM). Four-volume set that profiles 900 occupations and describes job trends in 71 industries. Includes career description, educational requirements, history of the job, methods of entry, advancement, employment outlook, earnings, conditions of work, social and psychological factors, and sources of further information. Contains career and employment information for this field.

★624★ How to Start and Operate Your Own Design Firm

McGraw-Hill Companies
1221 Avenue of the Americas
New York, NY 10020
Ph: (212)512-2000   Fr: 800-262-4729

Albert W. Rubeling, Jr. 1994. $33.00.

★625★ Liberal Arts Jobs: What They Are and How to Get Them

Peterson's
PO Box 2123
Princeton, NJ 08543-2123
Ph: (609)243-9111   Fax: (609)243-9150
Fr: 800-338-3282

Burton Jay Nadler. Second edition, 1989. $9.95. 153 pages. Presents a list of the top 20 fields for liberal arts majors, covering more than 300 job opportunities. Discusses strategies for going after those jobs, including guidance on the language of a successful job search, informational interviews, and making networking work.

★626★ Opportunities in Architecture Careers

VGM Career Horizons
4255 W. Touhy Ave.
Lincolnwood, IL 60646-1975
Ph: (847)679-5500   Fax: (847)679-2494
Fr: 800-323-4900

Robert J. Piper and Richard D. Rush. 1994. $14.95; $11.95 (paper). A guide to planning for and seeking opportunities in the field. Illustrated.

★627★ Opportunities in Computer-Aided Design and Computer-Aided Manufacturing

VGM Career Horizons
4255 W. Touhy Ave.
Lincolnwood, IL 60646-1975
Ph: (847)679-5500   Fax: (847)679-2494
Fr: 800-323-4900

Jan Bone. 1994. $14.95; $11.95 (paper). 160 pages. Defines cad (computer-aided design), cam (computer-aided manufacturing), and map (manufacturing automation protocol). Explains career opportunities in the cad/cam field, and education and training needed. Gives job-hunting tips.

★628★ Opportunities in Environmental Careers

VGM Career Horizons
4255 W. Touhy Ave.
Lincolnwood, IL 60646-1975
Ph: (847)679-5500   Fax: (847)679-2494
Fr: 800-323-4900

Odom Fanning. 1995. $14.95; $11.95 (paper). 160 pages. Describes a broad range of opportunities in fields such as environmental health, recreation, physics, and hygiene, and provides job search advice.

EMPLOYMENT AGENCIES AND SEARCH FIRMS

★629★ Agra Placements, Ltd.

4949 Pleasant St., Ste. 1
W. 50th Pl. III
West Des Moines, IA 50266-5494
Ph: (515)225-6562   Fax: (515)225-7733

Executive search firm. Branch offices in Peru, IN, Lincoln, IL, and Minneapolis, MN.

★630★ B W and Associates, Inc.

4415 W. Harrison St.
Hillside, IL 60162-1910
Ph: (708)449-5400

Employment agency.

★631★ Claremont-Branan, Inc.

2150 Parklake Dr., Ste. 212
Atlanta, GA 30345
Ph: (404)491-1292

Employment agency. Executive search firm.

★632★ Connelly Search

PO Box 30926
Tucson, AZ 85751-0926
Ph: (602)327-7999

Executive search firm.

★633★ Consultants and Designers Inc.

7240 Parkway Dr., Ste. 250
Hanover, MD 21076-1367
Ph: (410)712-0052

Places staff in temporary positions. West Coast office located in Santa Clara, CA.

★634★ JR Professional Search

PO Box 18356
Tucson, AZ 85731
Ph: (520)721-1855   Fax: (520)721-1855

Employment agency.

★635★ RitaSue Siegel Associates, Inc.

20 E. 46th St.
New York, NY 10017-2417
Ph: (212)682-2100

Executive search firm.

★636★ Sierra Technology Corporation

4150 Manzanita Ave., Ste. 100
Carmichael, CA 95608-1700
Ph: (916)488-4960   Fax: (916)488-7058

Employment agency. Provides placement on a temporary basis.

★637★ Specialized Search Associates

15200 Carter Rd.
Delray Beach, FL 33446
Ph: (407)499-3711   Fax: (407)499-3770

Executive search firm.

OTHER SOURCES

★638★ American Institute of Architects (AIA)

1735 New York Ave. NW
Washington, DC 20006
Ph: (202)626-7300   Fax: (202)626-7421

Members: Professional society of architects: regular members are professional, licensed architects; associate members are graduate architects, not yet licensed; emeritus members are retired architects. **Purpose:** Fosters professionalism and accountability among members through continuing education and training; promotes design excellence by influencing change in the industry. Sponsors educational programs with schools of architecture, graduate students, and elementary and secondary schools; conducts professional development programs. Advises on professional competitions; supplies construction documents. **Activities:** Established the American Architectural Foundation. Sponsors Octagon Museum; operates bookstore; stages exhibitions; compiles statistics. Provides monthly news service on design and construction.

★639★ Association for International Practical Training (AIPT)

10400 Little Patuxent Pky. Ste. 250
Columbia, MD 21044
Ph: (410)997-2200   Fax: (410)992-3924

Purpose: Helps coordinate training around the world in fields such as travel, the culinary arts, and hotel management. **Activities:** Conducts programs in career development and hospitality/tourism exchanges. Operates a student exchange program. Provides reciprocal practical training experience for recent graduates from the U.S., Austria, Germany, Finland, France, Hungary, Ireland, Japan, Malaysia, Netherlands, Switzerland, and the United Kingdom. Arranges training programs in the U.S. and abroad. Serves as U.S. affiliate to IAESTE (International Association for the Exchange of Students for Technical Experience) and operates a Professional Visitors Program to arrange short-term educational and training visits to the U.S. **E-Mail:** aipt@aipt.org

★640★ Career Encounters: Architecture

Cambridge Career Products
PO Box 2153
Dept. CC15
Charleston, WV 25328-2153
Ph: (304)744-9323   Fax: (304)744-9351
Fr: 800-468-4227

Video. $99.95. 25 minutes. Professionals shown in a variety of settings discuss different aspects of their careers.

★641★ Construction Education Foundation (MSF)

1300 N. 17th St.
Rosslyn, VA 22209
Ph: (703)812-2000   Fax: (703)812-8235

Purpose: Works to promote the merit shop for the benefit of the construction industry. (A merit shop is an open, nonunion shop that competes for business on the basis of price and quality rather than union status.) Conducts annual grants program to fund research and education projects aimed at improving the technology and environment of the construction industry and to promote the merit shop philosophy. Sponsors college programs and activities including: informational mailings to construction programs; financial aid for construction students; assistance to educators traveling to merit shop meetings; merit shop nights. Provides grants for publications and research studies to forecast trends in open shop construction, to compile information on the economic impact of wage laws, and to create an awareness of merit shop principles among students. Distributes study summaries, reports, and information about merit shop construction to

public officials, contractors, educators, and students. Sponsors Wheels of Learning to provide apprenticeship and task training in 15 trade areas. Holds annual Job Fair for construction management, engineering, architecture, and building science students.

★642★ National Council of Architectural Registration Boards (NCARB)
1735 New York Ave. NW, Ste. 700
Washington, DC 20006
Ph: (202)783-6500   Fax: (202)783-0290

Members: Federation of state boards for the registration of architects in the United States, District of Columbia, Puerto Rico, Virgin Islands, Guam, and the Northern Mariana Islands.

★643★ National Organization of Minority Architects (NOMA)
Howard University
School of Architecture and Planning
2366 6th St.
Washington, DC 20059

Purpose: Seeks to increase the number and influence of minority architects by encouraging minority youth and taking an active role in the education of new architects. **Activities:** Works in cooperation with other associations, professionals, and architectural firms to promote the professional advancement of members.

Archivists and Curators

SOURCES OF HELP-WANTED ADS

★644★ ARTJOB

Western States Arts Federation
236 Montezuma Ave.
Santa Fe, NM 87501
Ph: (505)988-1166

Biweekly. $45.00, for 24-issue subscription. Covers national full- and part-time positions and temporary paid positions in visual, performing, and literary arts, arts education, and general arts administration, competitions, internships, conferences. Entries include: Job title, salary, description of responsibilities, qualifications, application procedure and deadline, name and address of contact. Arrangement: Classified by field.

★645★ Historic Preservation News

National Trust for Historic Preservation
1785 Massachusetts Ave. NW
Washington, DC 20036
Ph: (202)673-4075

Monthly. $15.00/year for members only. Newspaper featuring historic preservation and architecture.

★646★ History News

American Association for State and Local History
530 Church St., #600
Nashville, TN 37219-2325
Ph: (615)255-2971   Fax: (615)255-2979

Bimonthly. Magazine for employees of historic sites, museums, and public history agencies. Coverage includes museum education programs and techniques for working with volunteers.

★647★ Sky & Telescope

Sky Publishing Corp.
PO Box 9111
Belmont, MA 02178-9111
Ph: (617)864-7360   Fax: (617)864-6117

Monthly. $33.00/year for individuals; $24.00/year for students; $3.95 for single issue. Magazine on astronomy and space science.

★648★ Technology and Conservation of Art, Architecture and Antiquities

The Technology Organization, Inc.
1 Emerson Pl.
Boston, MA 02114
Ph: (617)227-8581

Quarterly. Magazine on art, architecture, and archeology.

PLACEMENT AND JOB REFERRAL SERVICES

★649★ American Association of Museums (AAM)

1225 Eye St. NW, Ste. 200
Washington, DC 20005
Ph: (202)289-1818   Fax: (202)289-6578

Members: Art, history, and science museums, art associations and centers, historic houses and societies, preservation projects, planetariums, zoos, aquariums, botanical gardens, college and university museums, libraries, and special museums; trustees and professional employees of museums and others interested in the museum field. **Activities:** Has established an accrediting system for museums. Maintains placement service for museum professionals.

★650★ American Society for Information Science (ASIS)

8720 Georgia Ave., Ste. 501
Silver Spring, MD 20910-3602
Ph: (301)495-0900   Fax: (301)495-0810

Members: Information specialists, scientists, librarians, administrators, social scientists, and others interested in the use, organization, storage, retrieval, evaluation, and dissemination of recorded specialized information. **Purpose:** Seeks to improve the information transfer process through research, development, application, and education. Provides a forum for the discussion, publication, and critical analysis of work dealing with the theory, practice, research, and development of elements involved in communication of information. **Activities:** Maintains placement service. Members are engaged in a variety of activities and specialties including classification and coding systems, automatic and associative indexing, machine translation of languages, special librarianship and library systems analysis, and copyright issues. Sponsors National Auxiliary Publications Service, which provides reproduction services and a central depository for all types of information (operated for ASIS by Microfiche Publications). Sponsors numerous special interest groups. Conducts continuing education programs and professional development workshops. **E-Mail:** asis@cni.org

★651★ Natural Science for Youth Foundation (NSYF)

130 Azalea Dr.
Roswell, GA 30075
Ph: (404)594-9367   Fax: (404)594-7738

Purpose: Sponsors natural science centers, junior nature museums, native animal parks, and trailside museums. Provides information service. Conducts training courses in museum and nature center management. Maintains museum and placement service.

★652★ Print Council of America (PCA)

Dept. of Prints, Drawings, and Photographs
Yale University Art Gallery
2006 Yale Sta.
New Haven, CT 06520
Ph: (203)432-0628   Fax: (203)432-8150

Members: Museum professionals. **Purpose:** Fosters the study and appreciation of new and old prints, drawings, and photographs; stimulates discussion. **Activities:** Sponsors educational programs and research publications; offers placement services.

★653★ Special Libraries Association (SLA)

1700 18th St. NW
Washington, DC 20009-2508
Ph: (202)234-4700   Fax: (202)265-9317

Members: International association of information professionals who work in special libraries serving business, research, government, universities, newspapers, museums, and institutions that use or produce specialized information. **Purpose:** Seeks to advance the leadership role of special librarians. Offers consulting services to organizations that wish to establish or expand a library or information services. Conducts continuing education courses, public relations, and government relations programs. **Activities:** Provides employment services. Operates Information Resources Center on topics pertaining to the development and management of special libraries. Maintains Hall of Fame. **E-Mail:** SLA@CAPON.NET

EMPLOYER DIRECTORIES AND NETWORKING LISTS

★654★ American Art Directory
R. R. Bowker Co.
Reed Reference Publishing
121 Chanlon Rd.
New Providence, NJ 07974
Ph: (908)464-6800   Fax: (908)771-7704
Fr: 800-521-8110

Approximately biennial. $186.00. Covers over 7,000 museums, art libraries, and art organizations, and 1,700 art schools; also includes lists of state directors and supervisors of art education in schools, traveling exhibition booking agencies, corporations having art holdings for public viewing, newspapers that carry art notes, art scholarships and fellowships; and 190 national, regional, and state open art exhibitions. Arrangement: Geographical. Indexes: Geographical, collection/subject/name, personal name, institution name.

★655★ Art Marketing Sourcebook
ArtNetwork
18757 Wildflower Dr.
Penn Valley, CA 95946-9717
Ph: (916)432-7630   Fax: (916)432-1633

Biennial, spring 1995. $22.95, plus 4.00 shipping; payment must accompany order; libraries, schools may send purchase orders. Covers over 2,000 representatives, consultants, galleries, critics, architects, interior designers, corporations, museum curators. Entries include: Company name, address, phone, description of services, style represented, mediums, years in business, types of companies dealt with, geographical limitations, number of clients, requirements for viewing slides. Arrangement: Classified by type of organization.

★656★ Directory of Consultants
Society of American Archivists
600 S. Federal, Ste. 504
Chicago, IL 60605
Ph: (312)922-0140   Fax: (312)347-1452

Biennial, odd years. Free. Covers Approximately 48 archivists, 17 conservators and preservation administrators, and 23 manuscript appraisers in the U.S. Entries include: Name, address, phone, fax, e-mail, description of services or areas of specialty. Arrangement: Classified by line of business, then alphabetical. Indexes: Geographical.

★657★ Directory of Special Libraries and Information Centers
Gale Research
835 Penobscot Bldg.
Detroit, MI 48226-4094
Ph: (313)961-2242   Fax: (313)961-6083
Fr: 800-877-GALE

Annual. Three volumes: Volume 1, "Directory of Special Libraries and Information Centers", $475.00; Volume 2 "Geographic and Personnel Indexes", $395.00; Volume 3, "New Special Libraries", $390.00. Covers over 19,000 special libraries, information centers, documentation centers, etc., in the United States, Canada, and 80 other countries. Provides comprehensive information about the library or information center's services, facilities, holdings, availability, and staff.

★658★ International Directory of Arts
K.G. Saur
121 Chanlon Rd.
New Providence, NJ 07974
Ph: (908)464-6800   Fr: 800-521-8110

Annual. Two volumes. $225.00/set. Guide to art sources and markets in 137 countries. Contains over 130,000 names and addresses, including working artists, individual collectors, and art dealers and galleries, art museums, and more.

★659★ International Directory of Corporate Art Collections
ARTnews
48 W. 38th St., 9th Fl.
New York, NY 10018
Ph: (212)398-1690   Fax: (212)819-0394

Biennial, March of odd years. $109.95, payment must accompany order. Covers about 1,300 art collections maintained or sponsored by businesses and corporations in the United States, Canada, Europe, and Japan. Entries include: Collection name; company name, name of contact, address, phone; line of business, description of collection, size and location of collection; publications, exhibitions, loan and viewing policies, other corporate arts activities. Arrangement: Alphabetical. Indexes: Geographical, personal name, media and type of art, type of business, collection status.

★660★ List of 96 Ethnic and Religious Genealogical and Historical Societies and Archives
Summit Publications
Box 222
Munroe Falls, OH 44262

Irregular, latest edition March 1989. $4.00 postpaid.

★661★ Midwest Archives Conference— Membership Directory
Midwest Archives Conference
c/o Becky Haglund Tousey
Kraft General Foods, Inc.
6350 Kirk St.
Morton Grove, IL 60053
Ph: (708)998-2981   Fr: 800-545-2433

Annual. $4.00, postpaid. Covers more than 1,000 individual and institutional members, largely librarians, archivists, records manag-

ers, manuscripts curators, historians, and museum and historical society personnel; about 25 archival associations in the Midwest. Entries include: For institutions: name of archives, parent organization, address, phone. For individuals: name, title, business address, phone. Arrangement: Separate alphabetical sections for individuals and institutions.

★662★ Museums Directory
American Business Directories, Inc.
American Business Information, Inc.
5711 S. 86th Cir.
Omaha, NE 68127
Ph: (402)593-4600   Fax: (402)331-1505

Annual. $485.00, U.S. edition. Number of listings: 6,756 (U.S. edition); 900 (Canadian edition). Entries include: Name, address, phone (including area code), size of advertisement, year first in Yellow Pages, name of owner or manager, number of employees. Compiled from telephone company Yellow Pages, nationwide. Arrangement: Geographical.

★663★ Official Museum Directory
R. R. Bowker Co.
Reed Reference Publishing
121 Chanlon Rd.
New Providence, NJ 07974
Ph: (908)464-6800   Fax: (908)665-6688
Fr: 800-521-8110

Annual, November. $185.00. Covers Approximately 7,000 institutions of art, history, and science in the United States, including general museums, college and university museums, children's and junior museums, company museums, national park and nature center displays, and highly specialized museums. Entries include: For museums: name, address, phone, date established, personnel, governing authority, brief description of museum and type of collections, facilities, activities, publications, hours of operation, admission prices, membership fees, attendance figures. Arrangement: Museums are geographical. Indexes: Museum personnel (with name, title, affiliation, city, and state); type of museum (with name, city, and state); alphabetical; special collection.

★664★ Society of American Archivists Yellow Pages: Directory of Members
Society of American Archivists
600 S. Federal, Ste. 504
Chicago, IL 60605
Ph: (312)922-0140   Fax: (312)347-1452

Irregular, Latest edition 1994. $50.00, plus $5.00 shipping. Covers 4,600 individual and institutional members concerned with management and custody of current and historical records, and with archival administration. Entries include: Member name, company or institution where member works, address, phone, fax, computer network names and identification. Arrangement: Alphabetical. Indexes: Institution/company name, section membership, geographic listing of individual members.

★665★ State Archives and Records Management Programs Directory

National Association of Government Archives and Records Administrators (NAGARA)
48 Howard St.
Albany, NY 12207
Ph: (518)463-8644

Annual, latest edition 1995. $10.00. Covers state government records management and archival programs in the fifty states, the District of Columbia, American Samoa, Guam, Northern Mariana Islands, Puerto Rico, and the Virgin Islands; individual archivists and records managers. Entries include: For state government records management and archival programs: name, address, phone, names and titles of key personnel. For individuals: name, address. Arrangement: Separate geographical sections for state programs and individuals.

★666★ Subject Collections

R. R. Bowker Co.
Reed Reference Publishing
121 Chanlon Rd.
New Providence, NJ 07974
Ph: (908)464-6800   Fax: (908)771-7704
Fr: 800-521-8110

Irregular, latest edition March 1993. $275.00. Covers collections of books, recordings, manuscripts, and other library materials devoted to specific subjects housed in 5,900 academic, public, and special libraries and museums in the U.S. and Canada. Entries include: For each collection: Name of institution, library name, address, phone, fax, electronic mail address, number of items, topic of collection, type of materials, photocopying and interlibrary loan policies, and other information. Arrangement: Classified by subject, then geographical.

★667★ Who's Who in American Art

R. R. Bowker Co.
Reed Reference Publishing
121 Chanlon Rd.
New Providence, NJ 07974
Ph: (908)464-6800   Fax: (908)771-7704
Fr: 800-521-8110

Biennial, May of odd years. $189.00, plus $13.23 shipping. Covers about 11,800 people active in visual arts, including sculptors, painters, illustrators, printmakers, collectors, curators, writers, educators, dealers, critics, patrons, and museum executives. Also includes cumulative necrology from 1953. Entries include: Name, professional classification, address; artists' listings include dealer's name and address, preferred media, works in public collections, awards, publications, teaching positions, etc. Arrangement: Alphabetical. Indexes: Geographical, professional classification.

HANDBOOKS AND MANUALS

★668★ Career Choices for the 90's for Students of Art

Walker and Company
435 Hudson St.
New York, NY 10014
Ph: (212)727-8300   Fax: (212)727-0984
Fr: 800-289-2553

Prepared by the Career Associates staff. 1990. $9.95. 166 pages. Discusses alternatives for students of art. Offers advice on how to break into the field and how to move up. Covers where and who the employers are, internship possibilities, and professional networking associations. Comprehensive guide to career and job search planning.

★669★ Career Opportunities in Art

Facts on File, Inc.
11 Penn Plaza, 15th Fl.
New York, NY 10001-2006
Ph: (212)967-8800   Fax: 800-678-3633
Fr: 800-322-8755

Susan H. Haubenstock and David Joselit. Revised edition, 1994. $29.95; $15.95 (paper). 208 pages. This book profiles seventy-five jobs that can be found in the art field. Each profile includes a career description, career ladder, employment and advancement prospects, education, experience and skills required, salary range, and tips for entry into the field.

★670★ Career Resource Guide

Smithsonian Institution
Center for Museum Studies
2235 Arts and Industries Bldg.
Washington, DC 20560
Ph: (202)357-3101

Free. Lists sources of museum job listings, with bibliography and career tips.

★671★ Careers for Culture Lovers and Other Artsy Types

VGM Career Horizons
4255 W. Touhy Ave.
Lincolnwood, IL 60646-1975
Ph: (847)679-5500   Fax: (847)679-2494
Fr: 800-323-4900

Marjorie Eberts and Margaret Gisler. 1994. $14.95; $9.95 (paper). Describes how to get work in a variety of fields related to art and culture. Opportunities include picture framer, curator, art restorer, symphony manager, disk jockey, music reviewer, dance teacher, choreographer, costume designer, theater manager, light designer, drama teacher, bookstore owner, interior decorator, antique store owner, and others.

★672★ Careers in the Visual Arts: A Guide to Jobs, Money, Opportunities, and an Artistic Life

Watson-Guptill Publications, Inc.
BPI Communications, Inc.
1515 Broadway
New York, NY 10036
Ph: (212)536-5121   Fr: 800-451-1741

Dee Ito. 1993. $14.95. 320 pages. Gives a broad overview of each field included, with educational requirements and employment opportunities. Includes ideas on how to get started.

★673★ The Encyclopedia of Career Choices for the 1990s: Guide to Entry-Level Jobs

Perigree Books
The Berkley Publishing Group
PO Box 506
East Rutherford, NJ 07073
Ph: (201)933-9292   Fr: 800-223-0510

Career Associates Staff. 1992. $19.95. 862 pages. Describes 500 entry-level careers in a variety of industries. Presents qualifications required, working conditions, salary, internships, and professional associations.

★674★ Jobs in Arts and Media Management: What They Are and How to Get One!

American Council for the Arts
1 E. 53rd St.
New York, NY 10022-4201
Ph: (212)223-2787   Fr: 800-321-4510

Stephen Langley and James Abruzzo. Revised edition, 1990. $21.95. 281 pages. Includes lists of about 150 sources of information on job opportunities in the arts, including organizations offering internships, job listings, graduate programs, and short-term study; professional groups concerned with theater, music, dance, opera, museum and gallery management, film, and telecommunication management. (Does not include popular music performing or music recording.) Entries include: For internships Organization name, address, phone, description, requirements. For job referral associations and periodicals - Association or publisher name, address, fields covered, services offered, turn-around time, average number of jobs, cost of subscription or dues, comments. Arrangement: Classified by type of source.

★675★ Museum Careers & Training: A Professional Guide

Greenwood Publishing Group, Inc.
88 Post Rd., W., Box 5007
Westport, CT 06881
Ph: (203)226-3571   Fax: (203)222-1502
Fr: 800-225-5800

Victor J. Danilov. 1994. $85.00. Describes various museum positions and training programs available.

★676★ Museum Jobs from A-Z: What They Are, How to Prepare, and Where to Find Them

Batax Museum Publishing
2051 Wheeler Ln.
Switzerland, FL 32259

G.W. Bates. 1994. $9.95 (paper). Provides information, including descriptions and training needs, for 62 museum occupations.

★677★ Opportunities for Contract Work in Archaeology and Historic Preservation

American Anthropological Association
4350 N. Fairfax Dr., Ste. 640
Arlington, VA 22203

This pamphlet describes career opportunities with federal, state, and local agencies which are required by law to identify and preserve historic properties. Gives a list of agencies employing archivists.

★678★ Opportunities in Crafts Careers

VGM Career Horizons
4255 W. Touhy Ave.
Lincolnwood, IL 60646-1975
Ph: (847)679-5500   Fax: (847)679-2494
Fr: 800-323-4900

Marianne Munday. 1993. $14.95; $11.95 (paper). 160 pages. Provides information about careers and job opportunities in such areas as fine and applied arts, antiques and collectibles, ceramics, woodworking, sewing and needlecraft, and more. Illustrated.

EMPLOYMENT AGENCIES AND SEARCH FIRMS

★679★ Gossage Regan Associates

25 W. 43rd St., Ste. 812
New York, NY 10036
Ph: (212)869-3348

Employment agency. Concentrates in placement of library and information professionals on permanent basis nationwide.

OTHER SOURCES

★680★ AAMD Salary Survey

Association of Art Museum Directors (AAMD)
1130 Sherbrooke St. W, Ste. 530
Montreal, PQ, Canada H3G 1G1
Ph: (514)842-3832

Annual. Survey of art museum salaries from 142 museums.

★681★ American Institute for Conservation of Historic and Artistic Works (AIC)

1717 K St. NW, Ste. 301
Washington, DC 20006
Ph: (202)452-9545   Fax: (202)452-9328

Members: Professionals, scientists, administrators, and educators in the field of art conservation; interested individuals. **Purpose:** Advances the practice and promotes the importance of the preservation of cultural property. **Activities:** Coordinates the exchange of knowledge, research, and publications. Establishes and upholds professional standards.

★682★ Art Libraries Society/North America (ARLIS/NA)

4101 Lake Boone Trl., Ste. 201
Raleigh, NC 27607-7506
Ph: (919)787-5181   Fax: (919)787-4916
Fr: 800-89-ARLIS

Members: Individuals and institutions interested in art librarianship and visual resources curatorship (in public libraries, museums, galleries, art schools, universities, colleges, and publishing houses). **Purpose:** Acts as forum for exchange of materials and information on documentation of the visual arts.

★683★ Careers in Art

Cambridge Career Products
PO Box 2153
Dept. CC15
Charleston, WV 25328-2153
Ph: (304)744-9323   Fax: (304)744-9351
Fr: 800-468-4227

Video. $49.95. 21 minutes. Covers many professional options available in the world of art.

★684★ College Art Association (CAA)

275 7th Ave.
New York, NY 10001
Ph: (212)691-1051   Fax: (212)627-2381

Members: Professional organization of artists, art historians and fine art educators, museum directors, and curators. **Purpose:** Seeks to raise the standards of scholarship and of the teaching of art and art history throughout the country. **E-Mail:** cad@pipeline.com

★685★ Society of American Archivists (SAA)

600 S. Federal St., Ste. 504
Chicago, IL 60605
Ph: (312)922-0140   Fax: (312)347-1452

Purpose: Individuals and institutions concerned with the identification, preservation, and use of records of historical value. **E-Mail:** info@saa.mbs.compuserve.com

★686★ Women's Caucus for Art (WCA)

Moore College of Art
20th The Parkway
Philadelphia, PA 19103
Ph: (215)854-0922   Fax: (215)854-0915

Members: Professional women in visual art fields: artists, critics, art historians, museum and gallery professionals, arts administrators, educators and students, and collectors of art. **Purpose:** Objectives are to: increase recognition for contemporary and historical achievements of women in art; ensure equal opportunity for employment, art commissions, and research grants; encourage professionalism and shared information among women in art; stimulate and publicize research and publications on women in the visual arts. **Activities:** Conducts workshops, periodic affirmative action research, and statistical surveys. Presents annual honor awards to senior women in the visual arts.

Auto and Diesel Mechanics

SOURCES OF HELP-WANTED ADS

★687★ Automotive Body Repair News

Chilton Publications
825 7th Ave.
New York, NY 10019
Ph: (212)887-8400   Fax: (212)887-8484

Monthly. Magazine reporting automotive repair industry news.

★688★ Automotive Cooling Journal

NARSA
PO Box 97
East Greenville, PA 18041
Ph: (215)541-4500   Fax: (215)679-4977

Monthly. $30.00/year. Automotive trade magazine.

★689★ Automotive Fleet

Bobit Publishing
2512 Artesia Blvd.
Redondo Beach, CA 90278
Ph: (310)376-8788   Fax: (310)374-7878

Monthly. $35.00/year for individuals; $42.00/year for Canada; $53.00/year for other countries. Automotive magazine covering the car and light truck fleet market.

★690★ Automotive News

Crain Communications, Inc.
1400 Woodbridge Ave.
Detroit, MI 48207
Ph: (313)446-1600   Fax: (313)446-0383

Weekly. $85.00/year for individuals. Tabloid reporting on all facets of the automotive and truck industry, as well as related businesses.

★691★ Automotive Rebuilder

Babcox Publications
11 S. Forge St.
Akron, OH 44304
Ph: (216)535-7011   Fax: (216)535-0874

Monthly. Magazine covering management topics, technical information, and new product news for owners and managers of leading volume rebuilding businesses.

★692★ BodyShop Business

Babcox Publications
11 S. Forge St.
Akron, OH 44304
Ph: (216)535-7011   Fax: (216)535-0874

Monthly. Magazine providing management and technical information that can be applied to running an efficient and profitable collision repair shop.

★693★ Brake and Front End

Babcox Publications
11 S. Forge St.
Akron, OH 44304
Ph: (216)535-7011   Fax: (216)535-0874

Monthly. Free to qualified subscribers; $41.00/year for institutions; $69.00 for two years. Magazine covering automotive brake, front end, and chassis systems.

★694★ Bus Ride

Friendship Publications, Inc.
PO Box 1472
Spokane, WA 99210-1472
Ph: (509)328-9181   Fax: (509)325-0405

Magazine for managers of bus operations.

★695★ Import Automotive Parts and Accessories

Meyers Publishing
6211 Van Nuys Blvd., Ste. 200
Van Nuys, CA 91401
Ph: (818)785-3900   Fax: (818)785-4397

Monthly. $34.00/year for individuals; $50.00/year for Canada and Mexico; $85.00/year for other countries. Trade magazine for the automotive aftermarket.

★696★ Import Car & Truck

Babcox Publications
11 S. Forge St.
Akron, OH 44304
Ph: (216)535-7011   Fax: (216)535-0874

Monthly. Free to qualified subscribers; $41.00/year for individuals; $69.00 for two years. Magazine servicing the import automotive aftermarket.

★697★ Import Service

Gemini Communications
306 N. Cleveland Massillon Rd.
Akron, OH 44333
Ph: (216)666-9553   Fax: (216)666-8912

Monthly. Magazine covering the service and repair of imported cars.

★698★ Motor/Age

Chilton Publications
825 7th Ave.
New York, NY 10019
Ph: (212)887-8400   Fax: (212)887-8484

Monthly. Trade magazine for the automotive service industry.

★699★ Motor Service

Adams/Hunter Publishing Co.
25 Northwest Pt. Blvd., Ste. 800
Elk Grove Village, IL 60007
Ph: (708)427-9512   Fax: (708)427-2079

Monthly. $36.00/year for individuals. Magazine for auto repair shops.

★700★ Passenger Transport

American Public Transit Association
1201 New York Ave. NW, Ste. 400
Washington, DC 20005
Ph: (202)898-4119   Fax: (202)898-4095

Weekly (Mon.). $65.00/year for individuals; $2.00 for single issue. Magazine covering the public transit industry in the U.S. and Canada.

★701★ Popular Mechanics

The Hearst Corp.
224 W. 57th St., 2nd Fl.
New York, NY 10019
Ph: (212)649-3192   Fax: (212)586-5467

Monthly. $15.94/year; $2.50   for single issue. Magazine focusing on autos, the home, and leisure. Prints Latin American Edition.

★702★ The PT Distributor

Peter Li
1100 Superior Ave.
Cleveland, OH 44114
Ph: (216)696-7000   Fax: (216)696-7670

Bimonthly. $20.00/year for individuals; $25.00/year for Canada; $35.00/year for other countries. Magazine devoted exclusively to helping power transmission distributors add value to products for customers and suppliers.

★703★ School and Community

Missouri State Teachers Association
PO Box 458
Columbia, MO 65205-0458
Ph: (314)442-3127   Fax: (314)443-5079

Quarterly. Education magazine.

★704★ ServiceInsights

Heather Publishing Co., Inc.
PO Box 201427
Arlington, TX 76006
Ph: (817)860-2375   Fax: (817)548-0004

Monthly. $35.00/year; $85.00/year for other countries. Automotive magazine.

★705★ Specialty and Custom Dealer

Babcox Publications
11 S. Forge St.
Akron, OH 44304
Ph: (216)535-7011   Fax: (216)535-0874

Monthly. Magazine serving owners and managers of automotive specialty/performance retail and wholesale operations.

★706★ Transmission Digest

MD Publications, Inc.
3057 E. Cairo
PO Box 2210
Springfield, MO 65801-2210
Ph: (417)866-3917   Fax: (417)866-2781

Monthly. $34.00/year for individuals; $3.50 for single issue.

★707★ Transport Topics

American Trucking Association
2200 Mill Rd.
Alexandria, VA 22314
Ph: (703)838-1770   Fax: (703)548-3662

Weekly. $69.00/year for individuals; $79.00/year for other countries. Newspaper (tabloid) covering the trucking industry, for executives and managers of large and small fleets at for-hire and private carriers.

★708★ Undercar Digest

M D Publications, Inc.
PO Box 2210
Springfield, MO 65801-2210
Ph: (417)866-3917   Fax: (417)866-2781
Fr: 800-274-7890

Monthly. $34.00/year; $3.00 for single issue. Magazine for the undercar service and supply industry.

PLACEMENT AND JOB REFERRAL SERVICES

★709★ Automotive Technicians Association International (ATA)

222 Meirill St., Ste. 101
Birmingham, MI 48009
Ph: (810)644-6190   Fax: (810)642-3239

Members: Technicians working in the automotive service industry. **Purpose:** Seeks to

create an industry-wide communications program to enhance the public and professional image of the automotive technician. Represents members before federal regulatory agencies, domestic and foreign manufacturers, trade groups, and the public; offers professional recognition program for technicians who have superior diagnostic skills and a high customer satisfaction rating. **Activities:** Maintains placement services; compiles statistics.

HANDBOOKS AND MANUALS

★710★ Career Information Center

Macmillan Publishing Co.
200 Old Tappan Rd.
Old Tappan, NJ 07675
Ph: (609)461-6500   Fr: 800-223-2336

Visual Education Center Staff. Fifth edition, 1992. $229.00. This 13-volume set profiles over 600 occupations. Each occupational profile describes job duties, educational requirements, how to get the job, advancement possibilities, employment outlook, working conditions, earnings and benefits, and where to write for more information.

★711★ Careers in Trucking

Rosen Publishing Group, Inc.
29 E. 21st St.
New York, NY 10010
Ph: (212)777-3017   Fax: (212)777-0277
Fr: 800-237-9932

Donald D. Schauer. 1991. $14.95. 144 pages. Describes employment in the trucking industry including driving, operations, maintenance, sales, and administration. Covers qualifications, training, future outlook, and salaries. Offers career planning and job hunting advice.

★712★ Encyclopedia of Careers and Vocational Guidance

J. G. Ferguson Publishing Co.
200 W. Monroe, Ste. 250
Chicago, IL 60606
Ph: (312)580-5480

William E. Hopke. Ninth edition, 1993. $129.95; $199.95 (CD-ROM). Four-volume set that profiles 900 occupations and describes job trends in 71 industries. Includes career description, educational requirements, history of the job, methods of entry, advancement, employment outlook, earnings, conditions of work, social and psychological factors, and sources of further information. Contains career and employment information for this field.

★713★ Exploring Nontraditional Jobs for Women

Rosen Publishing Group, Inc.
29 E. 21st St.
New York, NY 10010
Ph: (212)777-3017   Fax: (212)777-0277
Fr: 800-237-9932

Rose Neufeld. 1989. $14.95. Describes occupations where few women are found. Covers job duties, training routes, where to

apply for jobs, tools used, salary, and advantages and disadvantages of the job.

★714★ Opportunities in Automotive Service Careers

VGM Career Horizons
4255 W. Touhy Ave.
Lincolnwood, IL 60646-1975
Ph: (847)679-5500   Fax: (847)679-2494
Fr: 800-323-4900

Robert Weber. 1995. $14.95; $11.95 (paper). Covers the whole scope of opportunities from mechanic to specialists in parts, body, hydraulic, security, electronics, and management, and discusses how to pursue employment. Illustrated.

★715★ Opportunities in Vocational and Technical Careers

VGM Career Horizons
4255 W. Touhy Ave.
Lincolnwood, IL 60646-1975
Ph: (847)679-5500   Fax: (847)679-2494
Fr: 800-323-4900

Adrian A. Paradis. 1992. $14.95; $11.95 (paper). 160 pages. Provides information on a variety of opportunities and advice on breaking into the field.

EMPLOYMENT AGENCIES AND SEARCH FIRMS

★716★ Action Plus Employer Services

1211 W. Imperial Hwy., Ste. 100
Brea, CA 92621
Ph: (714)773-1506   Fax: (714)773-9201

Employment agency.

★717★ Jobs, Training, and Services, Inc.

101 S. Moberly Ave.
Longview, TX 75602-1433
Ph: (903)757-3046

Employment agency. Another office is located in Henderson, TX.

OTHER SOURCES

★718★ Automotive Service Association (ASA)

1901 Airport Fwy., Ste. 100
PO Box 929
Bedford, TX 76095-0929
Ph: (817)283-6205   Fax: (817)685-0225
Fr: 800-272-7467

Members: Automotive service businesses including body, paint, and trim shops, engine rebuilders, radiator shops, brake and wheel alignment services, transmission shops, tune-up services, and air conditioning services; associate members are manufacturers and wholesalers of automotive parts, and the trade press. **Purpose:** Represents independent business owners and managers before private agencies and national and state legislative bodies. Promotes confidence between consumer and automotive technician, safety inspection of motor vehicles, and better highways.

★719★ Career Tracks

National Automotive Technicians Education Foundation (NATEF)
13505 Dulles Technology Dr.
Herndon, VA 22071
Ph: (703)713-0100

Video. $19.95. 12 minutes. Encourages teenagers to consider careers in the automotive industry.

★720★ Gasoline and Automotive Service Dealers Association (GASDA)

9520 Seaview Ave.
Brooklyn, NY 11236
Ph: (718)241-1111   Fax: (718)763-6589

Members: Owners/operators or dealers of service stations or automotive repair facilities; interested individuals. **Purpose:** Aim is to educate, inform, and help increase professionalism of members and of the industry.

Activities: Offers periodic technical training clinics, and other educational programs including advanced automotive technical training, prepaid group legal services plan and group health insurance, and liaison with government agencies. Informs members of political and legislative action or changes affecting their industry.

★721★ National Institute for Automotive Service Excellence (ASE)

13505 Dulles Technology Dr.
Herndon, VA 22071-3415
Ph: (703)713-3800   Fax: (703)713-0727

Members: Governed by a 40-member board of directors selected from all sectors of the automotive service industry and from education, government, and consumer groups. **Purpose:** Encourages and promotes the highest standards of automotive service in the public interest. **Activities:** Conducts continuing research to determine the best methods for training automotive technicians; encourages the development of effective training programs. Tests and certifies the compe-

tence of automobile, medium/heavy truck, collision repair, and engine machinist technicians as well as parts specialists.

★722★ Truck-Frame and Axle Repair Association (TARA)

PO Box 122
Adelphia, NJ 07710-0122
Ph: (908)577-8485   Fax: (908)577-9474

Members: Owners and operators of heavy-duty truck repair facilities and their mechanics; allied and associate members are manufacturers of heavy-duty trucks and repair equipment, engineers, trade press, and insurance firms. **Purpose:** Seeks to help members share skills and technical knowledge and keep abreast of new developments and technology to better serve customers in areas of minimum downtime, cost, and maximum efficiency. **Activities:** Conducts studies and surveys regarding safety, fuel conservation, and heavy-duty truck maintenance and repairs.

Bakers

SOURCES OF HELP-WANTED ADS

★723★ Milling & Baking News

Sosland Publishing Co.
4800 Main St., Ste. 100
Kansas City, MO 64112
Ph: (816)756-1000   Fax: (816)756-0494

Weekly (Tues.). $89.00/year for individuals. Trade magazine covering the grain-based food industries.

HANDBOOKS AND MANUALS

★724★ Bakers and Bakery Products Workers

Chronicle Guidance Publications, Inc.
66 Aurora St.
PO Box 1190
Moravia, NY 13118-1190
Ph: (315)497-0330   Fax: (315)497-3359
Fr: 800-622-7284

Chronicle Guidance Staff. 1993. $2.00. Provides concise career information and sources of additional information.

★725★ Careers for Gourmets and Others Who Relish Food

VGM Career Horizons
4255 W. Touhy Ave.
Lincolnwood, IL 60646-1975
Ph: (847)679-5500   Fax: (847)679-2494
Fr: 800-323-4900

Mary Donovan. 1993. $14.95; $9.95 (paper). 158 pages. Discusses such job prospects as foods columnist, cookbook writer, test kitchen worker, pastry chef, recipe developer, food festival organizer, restaurant manager, and food stylist.

★726★ Careers in the Restaurant Industry

Rosen Publishing Group, Inc.
29 E. 21st St.
New York, NY 10010
Ph: (212)777-3017   Fax: (212)777-0277
Fr: 800-237-9932

Richard S. Lee and Mary Price Lee. 1990. $14.95. 160 pages. Explores various jobs in the restaurant industry. Describes job duties, salaries, educational preparation, and job hunting. Contains information about fast food, catering, and small businesses.

★727★ Encyclopedia of Careers and Vocational Guidance

J. G. Ferguson Publishing Co.
200 W. Monroe, Ste. 250
Chicago, IL 60606
Ph: (312)580-5480

William E. Hopke. Ninth edition, 1993. $129.95; $199.95 (CD-ROM). Four-volume set that profiles 900 occupations and describes job trends in 71 industries. Includes career description, educational requirements, history of the job, methods of entry, advancement, employment outlook, earnings, conditions of work, social and psychological factors, and sources of further information. Contains career and employment information for this field.

★728★ Grain Science and Industry

Kansas State University
Dept. of Grain Science and Industry
201 Shellenberger Hall
Manhattan, KS 66506

Free. 3 pages. Brochure describes career opportunities in bakery science and management and related fields.

★729★ Opportunities in Culinary Careers

VGM Career Horizons
4255 W. Touhy Ave.
Lincolnwood, IL 60646-1975
Ph: (847)679-5500   Fax: (847)679-2494
Fr: 800-323-4900

Mary Deirdre Donovan. 1990. $14.95; $11.95 (paper). 160 pages. Describes the educational preparation and training of chefs and cooks and explores a variety of food service jobs in restaurants, institutions, and research and development. Lists major culinary professional associations and schools. Offers guidance on landing a first job in cooking and related fields.

★730★ Opportunities in Food Service Careers

VGM Career Horizons
4255 W. Touhy Ave.
Lincolnwood, IL 60646-1975
Ph: (847)679-5500   Fax: (847)679-2494
Fr: 800-323-4900

Carol Caprione. 1992. $14.95; $11.95 (paper). 160 pages. Discusses how to secure employment and provides information on identifying openings, resume writing, and interviewing. Lists recruiters and associations to contact for further information and leads. Illustrated.

★731★ Opportunities in Restaurant Careers

VGM Career Horizons
4255 W. Touhy Ave.
Lincolnwood, IL 60646-1975
Ph: (847)679-5500   Fax: (847)679-2494
Fr: 800-323-4900

Carol Caprione Chmelynski. 1992. $14.95; $11.95 (paper). Covers opportunities in the food service industry and details salaries, benefits, training opportunities, and professional associations. Special emphasis is put on becoming a successful restaurant manager by working up through the ranks. Illustrated.

OTHER SOURCES

★732★ Bakery Technology and Engineering

Pan-Tech International
PO Box 4548
McAllen, TX 78502
Ph: (210)383-4473   Fax: (210)702-7085

Samuel A. Matz. 1992. $129.00

★733★ Council on Hotel, Restaurant, and Institutional Education (CHRIE)

1200 17th St. NW
Washington, DC 20036-3097
Ph: (202)331-5990   Fax: (202)785-2511

Purpose: Schools and colleges offering specialized education and training in cooking, baking, tourism and hotel, restaurant, and institutional administration; individuals, executives, and students. **Activities:** Provides networking opportunities and professional development. Sponsors competitions.

★734★ *The Guide to Cooking Schools*

ShawGuides, Inc.
10 W. 66th St., Ste. 30H
New York, NY 10023
Ph: (212)799-6464

Dorlene V. Kaplan. 1995. $22.95. 337 pages. In addition to describing cooking school and travel programs, this work provides contact information for 122 approved culinary apprenticeship programs.

★735★ Independent Bakers Association (IBA)

1223 Potomac St. NW
Washington, DC 20007
Ph: (202)333-8190   Fax: (202)337-3809

Members: Bakers owning small- and medium-sized wholesale bakeries; persons in allied fields. **Purpose:** Represents independent wholesale bakers on federal legislative and regulatory issues. **Activities:** Offers annual Smith-Schaus-Smith internships.

★736★ *Professional Baking*

John Wiley and Sons
605 3rd Ave.
New York, NY 10158
Ph: (212)850-6000   Fr: 800-225-5945

Wayne Gisslen. Second edition, 1993. $29.50. 400 pages.

Biological Scientists

★749★ American Academy of Forensic Sciences (AAFS)

410 N. 21st St., Ste. 203
PO Box 669
Colorado Springs, CO 80901-0669
Ph: (719)636-1100   Fax: (719)636-1993

Members: Professional society of criminalists, scientists, members of the bench and bar, pathologists, biologists, psychiatrists, examiners of questioned documents, toxicologists, odontologists, anthropologists, and engineers. **Purpose:** Works to: encourage the study, improve the practice, elevate the standards, and advance the cause of the forensic sciences; improve the quality of scientific techniques, tests, and criteria; plan, organize, and administer meetings, reports, and other projects for the stimulation and advancement of these and related purposes. **Activities:** Maintains Forensic Sciences Job Listing; conducts selected research for the government; offers forensic expert referral service.

★750★ American Society for Biochemistry and Molecular Biology (ASBMB)

9650 Rockville Pike
Bethesda, MD 20814-3996
Ph: (301)530-7145   Fax: (301)571-1824

Members: Biochemists and molecular biologists who have conducted and published original investigations in biological chemistry and/or molecular biology. **Activities:** Operates placement service.

★751★ American Society for Cell Biology (ASCB)

9650 Rockville Pike
Bethesda, MD 20814
Ph: (301)530-7153   Fax: (301)530-7139

Members: Scientists with educational or research experience in cell biology or an allied field. **Activities:** Offers placement service.

★752★ American Society for Histocompatibility and Immunogenetics (ASHI)

PO Box 15804
Lenexa, KS 66285-5804
Ph: (913)541-0009   Fax: (913)541-0156

Members: Scientists, physicians, and technologists involved in research and clinical activities related to histocompatibility testing (a state of mutual tolerance that allows some tissues to be grafted effectively to others). **Activities:** Conducts proficiency testing and educational programs. Maintains liaison with regulatory agencies; offers placement services and laboratory accreditation. Has developed histocompatability specialist certification program.

★753★ American Society for Microbiology (ASM)

1325 Massachusetts Ave. NW
Washington, DC 20005-4171
Ph: (202)737-3600

Members: Scientific society of microbiologists. **Purpose:** Promotes the advancement of scientific knowledge in order to improve education in microbiology. Encourages the highest professional and ethical standards, and the adoption of sound legislative and regulatory policies affecting the discipline of microbiology at all levels. Communicates microbiological scientific achievements to the public. **Activities:** Maintains numerous committees and 23 divisions, and placement services; compiles statistics.

★754★ American Society of Plant Physiologists (ASPP)

15501 Monona Dr.
Rockville, MD 20855-2768
Ph: (301)251-0560   Fax: (301)279-2996

Members: Professional society of plant physiologists, plant biochemists, and other plant scientists engaged in research and teaching. **Activities:** Offers placement service for members; conducts educational programs. **Website:** http://www.aspp.org

★755★ American Water Works Association (AWWA)

6666 W. Quincy Ave.
Denver, CO 80235
Ph: (303)794-7711   Fax: (303)795-1440
Fr: 800-926-7337

Members: Water utility managers, superintendents, engineers, chemists, bacteriologists, and other individuals interested in public water supply; municipal- and investor-owned water departments; boards of health; manufacturers of waterworks equipment; government officials and consultants interested in water supply. **Purpose:** Develops standards and supports research programs in waterworks design, construction, operation, and management. **Activities:** conducts in-service training schools and prepares manuals for waterworks personnel. Maintains hall of fame. Offers placement service via member newsletter; compiles statistics. Offers training; children's services; and information center on the water utilities industry, potable water, and water reuse.

★756★ Association of Applied Insect Ecologists (AAIE)

1008 10th St., Ste. 549
Sacramento, CA 95814
Ph: (916)441-5224   Fax: (916)441-5224

Members: Professional agricultural pest management consultants, entomologists, and field personnel. **Purpose:** Promotes the implementation of integrated pest management in agricultural and urban environments. Provides a forum for the exchange of technical information on pest control. **Activities:** Offers placement service.

★757★ Biophysical Society (BPS)

Emily M. Gray
Biophysical Society Office
9650 Rockville Pike, Rm. 0512
Bethesda, MD 20814
Ph: (301)530-7114   Fax: (301)530-7133

Members: Biophysicists, physical biochemists, and physical and biological scientists interested in the application of physical laws and techniques to the analysis of biological or living phenomena. **Activities:** Maintains placement service.

★758★ Engineering Society of Detroit (ESD)

100 Farnsworth Ave.
Detroit, MI 48202
Ph: (313)832-5400   Fax: (313)832-5920

Members: Engineers from all disciplines; scientists and technologists. **Activities:** Offers placement services. Conducts technical programs and engineering refresher courses; sponsors conferences and expositions. Maintains speakers' bureau. Although based in Detroit, MI, society membership is international.

★759★ Environmental Mutagen Society (EMS)

11250 Roger Bacon Dr., Ste. 8
Reston, VA 22090-5202
Ph: (703)525-1191   Fax: (703)276-8196

Members: Bioscientists in universities, governmental agencies, and industry. **Purpose:** Promotes basic and applied studies of mutagenesis (the area of genetics dealing with mutation); disseminates information relating to environmental mutagenesis. **Activities:** Offers placement service.

★760★ Federation of American Societies for Experimental Biology (FASEB)

9650 Rockville Pike
Bethesda, MD 20814-3998
Ph: (301)530-7000   Fax: (301)530-7001

Members: Federation of scientific societies with a total of 40,000 members: The American Physiological Society; American Society for Biochemistry and Molecular Biology; American Society for Pharmacology and Experimental Therapeutics; American Society for Investigative Pathology; American Institute of Nutrition; The American Association of Immunologists; The American Society for Cell Biology; Biophysical Society; American Association of Anatomist. **Activities:** Maintains placement service. Administers Welcome Visiting Professorships program.

★761★ Forensic Sciences Foundation (FSF)

410 N. 21st St., Ste. 203
Colorado Springs, CO 80904
Ph: (719)636-1100   Fax: (719)636-1993

Purpose: Purposes are to: conduct research in the procedures and standards utilized in the practice of forensic sciences; develop and implement useful educational and training programs and methods of benefit to forensic sciences; conduct programs of public education concerning issues of importance to the forensic sciences; engage in activities which will promote, encourage, and assist the development of the forensic sciences. **Activities:** Provides referral service for forensic scientists. Compiles statistics. Operates the Forensic Sciences Foundation Press.

★762★ Korean Scientists and Engineers Association in America (KSEA)

6261 Executive Blvd.
Rockville, MD 20852
Ph: (301)984-7048   Fax: (301)984-1231

Members: Scientists and engineers holding single or advanced degrees. **Purpose:** Goals are to: promote friendship and mutuality among Korean and American scientists and engineers; contribute to Korea's scientific, technological, industrial, and economic developments; strengthen the scientific, technological, and cultural bonds between Korea and the U.S. Sponsors symposium. **Activities:** Maintains speakers' bureau, placement service, and biographical archives. Compiles statistics. Maintains 100 volume library of scientific handbooks and yearbooks in Korean.

★763★ National Network of Minority Women in Science (MWIS)

Directorate for Education and Human
  Resources Programs
1333 H St. NW
Washington, DC 20005
Ph: (202)326-6757   Fax: (202)371-9849

Members: Asian, Black, Mexican American, Native American, and Puerto Rican women involved in science related professions; other interested persons. **Purpose:** Promotes the advancement of minority women in science fields and the improvement of the science and mathematics education and career awareness of minorities. Supports public policies and programs in science and technology that benefit minorities. **Activities:** Maintains placement servce. Compiles statistics; serves as clearinghouse for identifying minority women scientists. Offers writing and conference presentations, seminars, and workshops on minority women in science and local career conferences for students. Local chapters maintain speakers' bureaus, and children's services. **E-Mail:** ggilbert@aaas.org

★764★ Society for Cryobiology (SC)

Dept of Mechanical Engineering
University of Texas
Austin, TX 78712
Ph: (512)471-7167   Fax: (512)530-7001

Purpose: Basic and applied research in the field of low temperature biology and medicine. Promotes interdisciplinary approach to freezing, freeze-drying, hypothermia, hibernation, physiological effects of low environmental temperature on animals and plants, medical applications of reduced temperatures, cryosurgery, hypothermic perfusion and cryopreservation of organs, cryoprotective agents and their pharmacological action, and pertinent methodologies. **Activities:** Operates charitable program and placement service.

★765★ Society for In Vitro Biology (SIVB)

8815 Centre Park Dr., Ste. 210
Columbia, MD 21045
Ph: (410)992-0946   Fax: (410)992-0949
Fr: 800-741-7476

Members: Professional society of individuals using mammalian, invertebrate, plant cell tissue, and organ cultures as research tools in chemistry, physics, radiation, medicine, physiology, nutrition, and cytogenetics. **Purpose:** Aims are to foster collection and dissemination of information concerning the maintenance and experimental use of tissue cells in vitro and to establish evaluation and development procedures. **Activities:** Operates placement service.

★766★ Society for Industrial Microbiology (SIM)

3929 Old Lee Hwy., No. 92A
Fairfax, VA 22030-2421
Ph: (703)941-5373   Fax: (703)941-8790

Members: Mycologists, bacteriologists, biologists, chemists, engineers, zoologists, and others interested in biological processes as applied to industrial materials and processes concerning microorganisms. **Purpose:** Serves as liaison between the specialized fields of microbiology. **Activities:** Maintains placement service; conducts surveys and scientific workshops in industrial microbiology.

EMPLOYER DIRECTORIES AND NETWORKING LISTS

★767★ American Men and Women of Science

R. R. Bowker Co.
Reed Reference Publishing
121 Chanlon Rd.
New Providence, NJ 07974
Ph: (908)464-6800   Fax: (908)665-6688
Fr: 800-521-8110

Triennial, latest edition January 1995. $106.00, per volume; $850.00, set. Covers over 123,000 U.S. and Canadian scientists active in the physical, biological, mathematical, computer science, and engineering fields; includes references to previous edition for deceased scientists and nonrespondents. Entries include: Name, address, education, personal and career data, memberships, honors and awards, research interest. Arrangement: Alphabetical. Indexes: Discipline (in separate volume).

★768★ The Biotechnology Directory

Stockton Press
Groves Dictionaries
345 Park Ave. S., 10th Fl.
New York, NY 10010
Ph: (212)689-9200   Fr: 800-221-2123

Annual. $265.00. Covers biotechnology firms.

★769★ Federation of American Societies for Experimental Biology— Directory of Members

Federation of American Societies for
  Experimental Biology (FASEB)
9650 Rockville Pke.
Bethesda, MD 20814
Ph: (301)530-7000   Fax: (301)571-1855

Annual, Fall. $50.00. Covers about 41,000 members of the American Physiological Society, American Society for Biochemistry and Molecular Biology, American Society for Pharmacology and Experimental Therapeutics, American Society for Investigative Pathology, American Institute of Nutrition, American Association of Immunologists, American Society for Cell Biology, Biophysical Society, and American Association of Anatomists. Entries include: Name, address, title, affiliation, memberships in federation societies, highest degree, year elected to membership, phone, fax and electronic mail address. Arrangement: Alphabetical. Indexes: Geographical.

★770★ Life Sciences Organizations and Agencies Directory

Gale Research
835 Penobscot Bldg.
Detroit, MI 48226-4094
Ph: (313)961-2242   Fax: (313)961-6083
Fr: 800-877-GALE

$175.00. Covers about 7,500 associations, government agencies, research centers, educational institutions, libraries and information centers, museums, consultants, electronic information services, and other organizations and agencies active in agriculture, biology, ecology, forestry, marine science, nutrition, wildlife and animal sciences, and other natural and life sciences. Entries include: Organization or agency name, address, phone, name and title of contact, description. Arrangement: Classified by type of organization. Indexes: Organization/agency name and keyword.

★771★ Peterson's Job Opportunities in Engineering and Technology 1996

Peterson's
PO Box 2123
Princeton, NJ 08543-2123
Ph: (609)243-9111   Fax: (609)243-9150
Fr: 800-338-3282

Compiled by the Peterson's staff. Annual. $19.95 paperback. 432 pages. Profiles 2,000 high-tech companies looking primarily for technical personnel in such fields as biotechnology, telecommunications, software, computers and peripherals, defense, and aerospace. Contains job-search strategies and career options to help match education and expertise to the job market. Indexed geographically, by industry, and by hiring needs.

★772★ Who's Who in Technology

Gale Research
835 Penobscot Bldg.
Detroit, MI 48226-4094
Ph: (313)961-2242   Fax: (313)961-6083
Fr: 800-877-GALE

Irregular, new edition expected June 1995. $380.00. Covers 38,000 engineers, scientists, inventors, and researchers. Entries include: Name, title, affiliation, address; personal, education, and career data; publications, patents; technical field of activity; area of expertise. Arrangement: Alphabetical. Indexes: Geographical, employer, technical discipline, expertise.

HANDBOOKS AND MANUALS

★773★ The Best Resumes for Scientists and Engineers
John Wiley and Sons
605 3rd Ave.
New York, NY 10158
Ph: (212)850-6000   Fr: 800-225-5945

Adele Lewis. Second edition, 1993. $37.50; $14.95 (paper). Presents an extensive collection of scientific and engineering resumes, highlighting the important differences between these and resumes written for other occupations.

★774★ Business and Careers in Marine Sciences
Hydrodryne Marine, Inc.
595 Arrowhead Tr.
Knoxville, TN 37919
Ph: (615)523-1198   Fax: (615)588-6922

James S. McNutt, Jr. 1993. $24.00 (paper).

★775★ Careers in Industrial Microbiology
Society for Industrial Microbiology
3929 Old Lee Hwy., Ste. 92A
Fairfax, VA 22030
1995. Brochure.

★776★ Careers for Nature Lovers and Other Outdoor Types
VGM Career Horizons
4255 W. Touhy Ave.
Lincolnwood, IL 60646-1975
Ph: (847)679-5500   Fax: (847)679-2494
Fr: 800-323-4900

Louise Miller. 1992. $12.95; $9.95 (paper). Examines career opportunities in biology, agriculture, landscaping, forestry and conservation, geology, and waste management, and pollution control. Offers insight into preparing for and finding outdoor jobs in federal and state government, as well as private industry.

★777★ Careers in Science
VGM Career Horizons
4255 W. Touhy Ave.
Lincolnwood, IL 60646-1975
Ph: (847)679-5500   Fax: (847)679-2494
Fr: 800-323-4900

Thomas Easton. Third edition, 1996. 192 pages. $17.95; $13.95 (paper). Discusses careers in life science, earth science, physical and space science, social science, engineering, mathematics, and computer science. Offers job hunting advice.

★778★ Conducting Meaningful Experiments: 40 Steps to Becoming a Scientist
Sage Publications, Inc.
2455 Teller Rd.
Thousand Oaks, CA 91320
Ph: (805)499-0871   Fax: (805)499-0871

Barker R. Bausell. 1994. $39.95; $17.95 (paper).

★779★ Encyclopedia of Careers and Vocational Guidance
J. G. Ferguson Publishing Co.
200 W. Monroe, Ste. 250
Chicago, IL 60606
Ph: (312)580-5480

William E. Hopke. Ninth edition, 1993. $129.95; $199.95 (CD-ROM). Four-volume set that profiles 900 occupations and describes job trends in 71 industries. Includes career description, educational requirements, history of the job, methods of entry, advancement, employment outlook, earnings, conditions of work, social and psychological factors, and sources of further information. Contains career and employment information for this field.

★780★ Meeting the Nation's Needs for Biomedical and Behavioral Scientists
National Academy Press
2101 Constitution Ave. NW, Lockbox 285
Washington, DC 20055
Fax: (202)334-2793   Fr: 800-624-6242

Compiled by the National Research Council, Committee on Vision Staff. 1994. $27.00 (paper).

★781★ Opportunities in Biological Sciences
VGM Career Horizons
4255 W. Touhy Ave.
Lincolnwood, IL 60646-1975
Ph: (847)679-5500   Fax: (847)679-2494
Fr: 800-323-4900

Charles A. Winter. 1993. $14.95; $11.95 (paper). Identifies employers and outlines opportunities in plant and animal biology, biological specialties, biomedical sciences, applied biology, and other areas. Illustrated.

★782★ Opportunities in Biotechnology Careers
VGM Career Horizons
4255 W. Touhy Ave.
Lincolnwood, IL 60646-1975
Ph: (847)679-5500   Fax: (847)679-2494
Fr: 800-323-4900

Sheldon Brown. 1990. $14.95; $11.95 (paper). Discusses typical jobs, their income potential, and career opportunities.

★783★ Opportunities in Environmental Careers
VGM Career Horizons
4255 W. Touhy Ave.
Lincolnwood, IL 60646-1975
Ph: (847)679-5500   Fax: (847)679-2494
Fr: 800-323-4900

Odom Fanning. 1995. $14.95; $11.95 (paper). 160 pages. Describes a broad range of opportunities in fields such as environmental health, recreation, physics, and hygiene, and provides job search advice.

★784★ Opportunities in High Tech Careers
VGM Career Horizons
4255 W. Touhy Ave.
Lincolnwood, IL 60646-1975
Ph: (847)679-5500   Fax: (847)679-2494
Fr: 800-323-4900

Gary D. Golter and Deborah Yanuck. 1995.

$14.95; $11.95 (paper). 160 pages. Explores high technology careers. Describes job opportunities, how to make a career decision, how to prepare for high technology jobs, job hunting techniques, and future trends.

★785★ A PhD Is Not Enough: A Guide to Survival in Science
Addison-Wesley Publishing Co., Inc.
1 Jacob Way
Reading, MA 01867
Ph: (617)944-3700   Fax: (617)942-1117
Fr: 800-447-2226

Peter J. Feibelman. 1993. $12.95 (paper).

★786★ Resumes for Environmental Careers
VGM Career Horizons
NTC Publishing Group
4255 W. Touhy Ave.
Lincolnwood, IL 60646-1975
Ph: (847)679-5500   Fax: (847)679-2494
Fr: 800-323-4900

1994. $9.95. 160 pages. Provides resume advice tailored to people pursuing careers focusing on the environment. Includes sample resumes and cover letters.

★787★ Science (Career Portraits)
VGM Career Horizons
NTC Publishing Group
4255 W. Touhy Ave.
Lincolnwood, IL 60646-1975
Ph: (847)679-5500   Fax: (847)679-2494
Fr: 800-323-4900

Jane Kelsey. 1996. $13.95. 96 pages. Practicing professionals describe their work in challenging science careers.

★788★ Where the Jobs Are: The Hottest Careers for the '90s
The Career Press, Inc.
3 Tice Rd.
PO Box 687
Franklin Lakes, NJ 07417
Ph: (201)848-0310   Fax: (201)848-1727
Fr: 800-237-3371

Joyce Hadley. Second edition, 1995. $9.99. 300 pages. Describes careers in fifteen general fields, from accounting to travel and hospitality.

EMPLOYMENT AGENCIES AND SEARCH FIRMS

★789★ ABC Employment Service
25 S. Bemiston, Ste. 214
Clayton, MO 63105
Ph: (314)725-3140
Employment agency.

★790★ Amtec Engineering Corp.
2749 Saturn St.
Brea, CA 92621
Ph: (714)993-1900   Fax: (714)993-2419
Employment agency.

★791★ Biomedical Search Consultants

PO Box 1070
Danbury, CT 06813
Ph: (203)744-4027   Fax: (203)748-2122

Employment agency.

★792★ Erspamer Associates

7300 France Ave. S., Ste. 402
Edina, MN 55435
Ph: (612)831-5564   Fax: (612)831-5981

Executive search firm.

★793★ Hayden and Associates, Inc.

7825 Washington Ave. S., Ste. 120
Minneapolis, MN 55439-2431
Ph: (612)941-6300   Fax: (612)941-9602

Employment agency. Executive search firm.
Fills openings in a variety of fields.

★794★ Health and Science Center

209 Hunter St.
Media, PA 19063-5726
Ph: (610)891-0714

Employment agency. Executive search firm.

★795★ Intech Summit Group, Inc.

6540 Lusk Blvd., C-228
San Diego, CA 92121
Ph: (619)452-2100

Employment agency and executive recruiter.

★796★ The Jobs Co.

8900 E. Sprague Ave.
Spokane, WA 99212-2927
Ph: (509)928-3151   Fax: (509)928-3168

Employment agency. Has division specializing in engineering and scientific openings. Also operates division specializing in sales openings.

★797★ JPM International

4665 MacArthur Ct., Ste. 100B
Newport Beach, CA 92660
Ph: (714)955-2545   Fax: (714)757-1320

Executive search firm and employment agency.

★798★ Lybrook Associates, Inc.

PO Box 572
Newport, RI 02840
Ph: (401)683-6990

Executive search firm.

★799★ The Personnel Institute

1000 Connecticut Ave. NW, Ste. 1108
Washington, DC 20036
Ph: (202)223-4911

Consulting firm.

★800★ Professional Placement Associates, Inc.

11 Rye Ridge Plaza
Rye Brook, NY 10573
Ph: (914)251-1000   Fax: (914)939-1959

Employment agency.

★801★ Sierra Technology Corporation

4150 Manzanita Ave., Ste. 100
Carmichael, CA 95608-1700
Ph: (916)488-4960   Fax: (916)488-7058

Employment agency. Provides placement on a temporary basis.

★802★ T.R. Employment Agency

409 Wilshire Blvd.
Santa Monica, CA 90401
Ph: (310)393-4107

Employment agency.

OTHER SOURCES

★803★ American Association of Anatomists (AAA)

Dr. Robert D. Yates
Tulane Med. Center
1430 Tulane Ave.
New Orleans, LA 70112
Ph: (504)584-2727   Fax: (504)584-1687

Members: Professional society of anatomists and scientists in related fields.

★804★ American Institute of Biological Sciences (AIBS)

730 11th St. NW
Washington, DC 20001-4521
Ph: (202)628-1500   Fax: (202)628-1509
Fr: 800-992-AIBS

Members: Professional biological associations and laboratories whose members have an interest in the life sciences. **Purpose:** Promotes unity and effectiveness of effort among persons engaged in biological research, education, and application of biological sciences, including agriculture, environment, and medicine. Seeks to further the relationships of biological sciences to other sciences, the arts, and industries. **Activities:** Conducts symposium series; provides names of prominent biologists who are willing to serve as speakers and curriculum consultants; provides advisory committees and other services to the Department of Energy, Environmental Protection Agency, National Science Foundation, Department of Defense, and National Aeronautics and Space Administration. Maintains educational consultant panel.

★805★ Association for International Practical Training (AIPT)

10400 Little Patuxent Pky. Ste. 250
Columbia, MD 21044
Ph: (410)997-2200   Fax: (410)992-3924

Purpose: Helps coordinate training around the world in fields such as travel, the culinary arts, and hotel management. **Activities:** Conducts programs in career development and hospitality/tourism exchanges. Operates a student exchange program. Provides reciprocal practical training experience for recent graduates from the U.S., Austria, Germany, Finland, France, Hungary, Ireland, Japan, Malaysia, Netherlands, Switzerland, and the United Kingdom. Arranges training programs in the U.S. and abroad. Serves as U.S. affiliate to IAESTE (International Association

for the Exchange of Students for Technical Experience) and operates a Professional Visitors Program to arrange short-term educational and training visits to the U.S. **E-Mail:** aipt@aipt.org

★806★ New Careers Directory: Internships and Professional Opportunities in Technology and Social Change

Student Pugwash USA
815 15th St. NW, Ste. 814
Washington, DC 20005
Ph: (202)393-6555   Fax: (202)393-6550
Fr: 800-WOW-A-PUG

Irregular; latest edition spring 1993. $13.00 for students; $21.00 for institutions, plus $3.00 shipping. Covers about 300 research institutes, think tanks, laboratories, government agencies, professional, science, and other non-profit organizations offering public policy, science, and technology internships and jobs. Entries include: Sponsoring organization name, description of organization, programs offered, work environment and application procedures, compensation offered. Arrangement: Alphabetical and classified by subject. Indexes: Geographical, subject.

★807★ Radiation Research Society (RRS)

2021 Spring Rd., Ste. 600
Oak Brook, IL 60521
Ph: (708)571-2881   Fax: (708)571-7837

Members: Professional society of biologists, physicists, chemists, and physicians contributing to knowledge of radiation and its effects. **Purpose:** Promotes original research in the natural sciences relating to radiation; facilitates integration of different disciplines in the study of radiation effects.

★808★ Resumes for Scientific and Technical Careers

VGM Career Horizons
NTC Publishing Group
4255 W. Touhy Ave.
Lincolnwood, IL 60646-1975
Ph: (847)679-5500   Fax: (847)679-2494
Fr: 800-323-4900

1994. $9.95. 160 pages. Provides resume advice for individuals interested in working in scientific and technical careers. Includes sample resumes and cover letters.

★809★ Salaries of Scientists, Engineers, and Technicians: A Summary of Salary Surveys

Commission on Professionals in Science and Technology (CPST)
1500 Massachusetts Ave. NW, Ste. 831
Washington, DC 20005
Ph: (202)223-6995

1993.

★810★ Soil Science Society of America (SSSA)

677 S. Segoe Rd.
Madison, WI 53711
Ph: (608)273-8080   Fax: (608)273-2021

Members: Professional soil scientists, including soil physicists, soil classifiers, land use and management specialists, chemists, microbiologists, soil fertility specialists, soil cartographers, conservationists, mineralogists, engineers, and others interested in fundamental and applied soil science.

★811★ **Teratology Society (TS)**
9650 Rockville Pike
Bethesda, MD 20814
Ph: (301)571-1841   Fax: (301)571-1852
Members: Individuals from academia, government, private industry, and the professions. **Purpose:** Objective is to stimulate scientific interest in, and promote the exchange of ideas and information about, problems of abnormal biological development and malformations at the fundamental or clinical level. Sponsors annual education course, and presentations. Is establishing archives of society documents and history.

Biomedical Engineers

SOURCES OF HELP-WANTED ADS

★812★ American Biotechnology Laboratory

International Scientific Communications, Inc.
30 Controls Dr.
PO Box 870
Shelton, CT 06484-0870
Ph: (203)926-9300   Fax: (203)926-9310

$128.00/year for individuals. Biotechnology magazine.

★813★ Bio/Technology

Nature Publishing Co.
345 Park Ave. S, 10th Fl.
New York, NY 10010-1707
Ph: (212)726-9200   Fax: (212)696-9006

Monthly. $59.00/year for individuals. Scientific research journal.

★814★ Cell

Cell Press
50 Church St.
Cambridge, MA 02138
Ph: (617)661-7057   Fax: (617)661-7061

Biweekly. $325.00/year for individuals. Journal on molecular and cell biology.

★815★ High Technology Careers Magazine

HTC
4701 Patrick Henry Dr., No. 1901
Santa Clara, CA 95054
Ph: (408)970-8800   Fax: (408)980-5103

Bimonthly. Magazine (tabloid) containing employment opportunity information for the engineering and technical community.

★816★ Minority Engineer

Equal Opportunity Publications, Inc.
150 Motor Pkwy., Ste. 420
Hauppauge, NY 11788-5145
Ph: (516)273-0066   Fax: (516)273-8936

Affirmative-action recruitment magazine serving college graduating and professional minority engineers.

★817★ SWE

Society of Women Engineers
120 Wall St., 11th Fl.
New York, NY 10005-3902
Ph: (212)509-9577   Fax: (212)509-0224

Bimonthly. $30.00/year for nonmembers. Magazine for engineering students and for women and men working in the engineering and technology fields. Covers career guidance, continuing development and topical issues.

★818★ Technology Review

The Tech
PO Box 397029
Cambridge, MA 02139
Ph: (617)253-1541   Fax: (617)258-8226

$30.00/year for individuals; $3.75 for single issue; $42.00/year for other countries. Magazine reviewing new developments in technology with an emphasis on economic, political, and social implications. Not a new product publication.

★819★ Woman Engineer

Equal Opportunity Publications, Inc.
150 Motor Pkwy., Ste. 420
Hauppauge, NY 11788-5145
Ph: (516)273-0066   Fax: (516)273-8936

Engineer recruitment magazine.

PLACEMENT AND JOB REFERRAL SERVICES

★820★ American Indian Science and Engineering Society (AISES)

1630 30th St., Ste. 301
Boulder, CO 80301
Ph: (303)492-8658   Fax: (303)492-3400

Members: American Indian and non-Indian students and professionals in science, technology, and engineering fields; corporations representing energy, mining, aerospace, electronic, and computer fields. **Purpose:** Seeks to motivate and encourage students to pursue undergraduate and graduate studies in science, engineering, and technology. **Activities:** Sponsors science fairs in grade schools, teacher training workshops, summer math/science sessions for 8th-12th graders, professional chapters, and student chapters in colleges. Offers scholarships. Adult members serve as role models, advisers, and mentors for students. Operates placement service. **E-Mail:** aise sha@spot.colorado.edu

★821★ Engineering Society of Detroit (ESD)

100 Farnsworth Ave.
Detroit, MI 48202
Ph: (313)832-5400   Fax: (313)832-5920

Members: Engineers from all disciplines; scientists and technologists. **Activities:** Offers placement services. Conducts technical programs and engineering refresher courses; sponsors conferences and expositions. Maintains speakers' bureau. Although based in Detroit, MI, society membership is international.

★822★ Korean Scientists and Engineers Association in America (KSEA)

6261 Executive Blvd.
Rockville, MD 20852
Ph: (301)984-7048   Fax: (301)984-1231

Members: Scientists and engineers holding single or advanced degrees. **Purpose:** Goals are to: promote friendship and mutuality among Korean and American scientists and engineers; contribute to Korea's scientific, technological, industrial, and economic developments; strengthen the scientific, technological, and cultural bonds between Korea and the U.S. Sponsors symposium. **Activities:** Maintains speakers' bureau, placement service, and biographical archives. Compiles statistics. Maintains 100 volume library of scientific handbooks and yearbooks in Korean.

★823★ Society of Hispanic Professional Engineers (SHPE)

5400 E. Olympic Blvd., Ste. 210
Los Angeles, CA 90022
Ph: (213)725-3970

Purpose: Engineers, student engineers, and scientists seeking to increase the number of Hispanic engineers by providing motivation and support to students. Sponsors competitions and educational programs. **Activities:**

Maintains placement service and speakers' bureau; compiles statistics.

★824★ **Society for Industrial Microbiology (SIM)**

3929 Old Lee Hwy., No. 92A
Fairfax, VA 22030-2421
Ph: (703)941-5373   Fax: (703)941-8790

Members: Mycologists, bacteriologists, biologists, chemists, engineers, zoologists, and others interested in biological processes as applied to industrial materials and processes concerning microorganisms. **Purpose:** Serves as liaison between the specialized fields of microbiology. **Activities:** Maintains placement service; conducts surveys and scientific workshops in industrial microbiology.

EMPLOYER DIRECTORIES AND NETWORKING LISTS

★825★ *American Men and Women of Science*

R. R. Bowker Co.
Reed Reference Publishing
121 Chanlon Rd.
New Providence, NJ 07974
Ph: (908)464-6800   Fax: (908)665-6688
Fr: 800-521-8110

Triennial, latest edition January 1995. $106.00, per volume; $850.00, set. Covers over 123,000 U.S. and Canadian scientists active in the physical, biological, mathematical, computer science, and engineering fields; includes references to previous edition for deceased scientists and nonrespondents. Entries include: Name, address, education, personal and career data, memberships, honors and awards, research interest. Arrangement: Alphabetical. Indexes: Discipline (in separate volume).

★826★ *Directory of Engineers in Private Practice*

National Society of Professional Engineers
1420 King St.
Alexandria, VA 22314
Ph: (703)684-2862   Fax: (703)836-4875

Annual. $85.00. Covers 600 consulting engineering firms and 7,200 individuals who are members of the society's Professional Engineers in Private Practice division. Entries include: For companies, name, address, phone, name of principal executive, list of services. For individuals, name, address; most listings include phone. Arrangement: Firms are geographic, then by specialty; individuals are alphabetical.

★827★ *International Cytogenetic Laboratory Directory*

Association of Cytogenetic Technologists
c/o Turid Knutsen
National Institutes of Health
Cytogenetic Oncology Section, NCI
Building 10, Rm. 12N-226
Bethesda, MD 20892
Ph: (301)496-6501   Fax: (301)541-0156

Annual, fall/winter. $50.00 for members; $60.00 for nonmembers. Covers about 520 laboratories studying heritable and acquired chromosomal disorders using cytogenetic, genetics, and cellular biology techniques. Entries include: Laboratory name, address, phone, areas of specialization, techniques, numbers and types of laboratory tests performed, and names of director and cytogenetic technologists. Arrangement: Geographical. Indexes: Director name, ACT member name.

★828★ *Medical Research Centres*

Stockton Press
Groves Dictionaries
345 Park Ave. S., 10th Fl.
New York, NY 10010
Ph: (212)689-9200   Fr: 800-221-2123

Eleventh edition, 1995. $595.00. 856 pages. Covers medical and biochemical research conducted in over 100 countries. Entries include information on industrial enterprises, research laboratories, universities, societies, and professional associations engaged in research in medicine and related subjects like dentistry, nursing, pharmacy, psychiatry, and surgery.

★829★ *Scientific and Technical Organizations and Agencies Directory*

Gale Research
835 Penobscot Bldg.
Detroit, MI 48226-4094
Ph: (313)961-2242   Fax: (313)961-6083
Fr: 800-877-GALE

Irregular; latest edition December 1993. $195.00. Covers over 25,600 national and international organizations and agencies concerned with the physical and applied sciences, engineering, and technology, including associations, computer information services, consulting firms, educational institutions, foundations, government advisory organizations, federal government agencies, general grant and assistance programs, libraries and information centers, patent sources and services, research and development centers, scholarships, fellowships, and loans, science-technology centers, standards organizations, state academies of science, and state government agencies in the fields of aeronautics and space sciences, chemistry, computer science specialties, electronics, geography, geology, machinery, mathematics, metallurgy, meteorology, mineralogy, nuclear science, petroleum and gas, physics, plastics, transportation, water resources, and other areas. Entries include: Organization name, address, phone, and name of contact; additional descriptive text for most entries. Arrangement: Classified by type of organization. Indexes: Organization name/key word.

★830★ *Who's Who in Technology*

Gale Research
835 Penobscot Bldg.
Detroit, MI 48226-4094
Ph: (313)961-2242   Fax: (313)961-6083
Fr: 800-877-GALE

Irregular, new edition expected June 1995. $380.00. Covers 38,000 engineers, scientists, inventors, and researchers. Entries include: Name, title, affiliation, address; personal, education, and career data; publications, patents; technical field of activity; area of expertise. Arrangement: Alphabetical. Indexes: Geographical, employer, technical discipline, expertise.

HANDBOOKS AND MANUALS

★831★ *The Best Resumes for Scientists and Engineers*

John Wiley and Sons
605 3rd Ave.
New York, NY 10158
Ph: (212)850-6000   Fr: 800-225-5945

Adele Lewis. Second edition, 1993. $37.50; $14.95 (paper). Presents an extensive collection of scientific and engineering resumes, highlighting the important differences between these and resumes written for other occupations.

★832★ *Biomedical Engineering*

John Wiley & Sons
605 3rd Ave.
New York, NY 10158-0012
Fr: 800-225-5945

Edward A. Profio. 1993. $89.95.

★833★ *Biomedical Engineering Careers*

Biomedical Engineering Society
PO Box 2399
Culver City, CA 90231
Ph: (310)618-9322

Free. 8-page brochure.

★834★ *The Biomedical Engineering Handbook*

CRC Press, Inc.
2000 Corporate Blvd. NW
Boca Raton, FL 33431
Ph: (407)994-0555   Fax: (407)997-0949
Fr: 800-272-7737

Joseph D. Bronzino, editor. 1995. $129.95.

★835★ *Biomedical Engineers*

Chronicle Guidance Publications, Inc.
66 Aurora St.
PO Box 1190
Moravia, NY 13118-1190
Ph: (315)497-0330   Fax: (315)497-3359
Fr: 800-622-7284

Chronicle Guidance Staff. 1994. $2.00. Provides concise career information and sources of additional information.

★836★ Biomedical Engineers: Biomedical Engineering Careers

Chronicle Guidance Publications, Inc.
66 Aurora St.
PO Box 1190
Moravia, NY 13118-1190
Ph: (315)497-0330   Fax: (315)497-3359
Fr: 800-622-7284

Chronicle Guidance Staff. 1994. $2.00. Reprint of a journal article.

★837★ Careers in Engineering

VGM Career Horizons
4255 W. Touhy Ave.
Lincolnwood, IL 60646-1975
Ph: (847)679-5500   Fax: (847)679-2494
Fr: 800-323-4900

Geraldine O. Gardner. 1994. $17.95; $13.95 (paper). Covers careers in the public or private sector, in industry, the university, or the military, from applications in computer architecture design to high temperature ceramics.

★838★ Careers in High Tech

VGM Career Horizons
NTC Publishing Group
4255 W. Touhy Ave.
Lincolnwood, IL 60646-1975
Ph: (847)679-5500   Fax: (847)679-2494
Fr: 800-323-4900

Nick Basta. 1994. $17.95; $13.95 (paper). 160 pages. Examines new career opportunities in such fields as biotechnology, computers, aerospace, telecommunications, and others.

★839★ Careers in Science

VGM Career Horizons
4255 W. Touhy Ave.
Lincolnwood, IL 60646-1975
Ph: (847)679-5500   Fax: (847)679-2494
Fr: 800-323-4900

Thomas Easton. Third edition, 1996. 192 pages. $17.95; $13.95 (paper). Discusses careers in life science, earth science, physical and space science, social science, engineering, mathematics, and computer science. Offers job hunting advice.

★840★ Careers in Science and Engineering

National Academy Press
2101 Constitution Ave. NW
Washington, DC 20418
Ph: (202)334-3313   Fr: 800-624-6242

1996. $9.95. 70 pages. Covers planning for graduate school and beyond.

★841★ Encyclopedia of Careers and Vocational Guidance

J. G. Ferguson Publishing Co.
200 W. Monroe, Ste. 250
Chicago, IL 60606
Ph: (312)580-5480

William E. Hopke. Ninth edition, 1993. $129.95; $199.95 (CD-ROM). Four-volume set that profiles 900 occupations and describes job trends in 71 industries. Includes career description, educational requirements, history of the job, methods of entry, advancement, employment outlook, earnings, conditions of work, social and psychological factors, and sources of further information. Contains career and employment information for this field.

★842★ Engineering Success

Kendall Hunt Publishing
4050 Westmark Dr.
PO Box 1840
Dubuque, IA 52004-1840
Ph: (319)589-1000   Fax: 800-772-9165
Fr: 800-228-0810

Bill Osher. 1994. $27.96.

★843★ Engineering Your Job Search: A Job-Finding Resource for Engineering Professionals

Professional Publications, Inc.
1250 5th Ave.
Belmont, CA 94002
Ph: (415)593-9119   Fax: (415)592-4519
Fr: 800-426-1178

Compiled by Professional Publications editors. 1995. $12.95 (paper).

★844★ Introduction to the Engineering Profession

HarperCollins Publishers, Inc.
10 E. 53rd. St.
New York, NY 10022-5299
Ph: (212)207-7000   Fax: (212)207-7145
Fr: 800-331-3761

David M. Burghardt. 1995. $30.00 (paper).

★845★ Job Opportunities in Engineering and Technology

Peterson's Guides, Inc.
PO Box 2123
Princeton, NJ 08543-2123
Ph: (609)243-9111   Fax: (609)243-9150
Fr: 800-338-3282

1994. $18.95 (paper).

★846★ Majoring in Engineering: How to Get from Your Freshman Year to Your First Job

Farrar, Straus & Giroux, Inc.
19 Union Sq., W
New York, NY 10003
Ph: (212)741-6900   Fr: 800-788-6262

John Garcia. 1995. $20.00; $10.00 (paper).

★847★ Meeting the Nation's Needs for Biomedical and Behavioral Scientists

National Academy Press
2101 Constitution Ave. NW, Lockbox 285
Washington, DC 20055
Fax: (202)334-2793   Fr: 800-624-6242

Compiled by the National Research Council, Committee on Vision Staff. 1994. $27.00 (paper).

★848★ Opportunities in Biological Sciences

VGM Career Horizons
4255 W. Touhy Ave.
Lincolnwood, IL 60646-1975
Ph: (847)679-5500   Fax: (847)679-2494
Fr: 800-323-4900

Charles A. Winter. 1993. $14.95; $11.95 (paper). Identifies employers and outlines opportunities in plant and animal biology, biological specialties, biomedical sciences, applied biology, and other areas. Illustrated.

★849★ Opportunities in Biotechnology Careers

VGM Career Horizons
4255 W. Touhy Ave.
Lincolnwood, IL 60646-1975
Ph: (847)679-5500   Fax: (847)679-2494
Fr: 800-323-4900

Sheldon Brown. 1990. $14.95; $11.95 (paper). Discusses typical jobs, their income potential, and career opportunities.

★850★ Opportunities in Engineering Careers

VGM Career Horizons
4255 W. Touhy Ave.
Lincolnwood, IL 60646-1975
Ph: (847)679-5500   Fax: (847)679-2494
Fr: 800-323-4900

Nicholas Basta. 1995. $14.95; $11.95 (paper). Outlines typical job titles, salaries, career paths, and employment prospects.

★851★ Opportunities in High Tech Careers

VGM Career Horizons
4255 W. Touhy Ave.
Lincolnwood, IL 60646-1975
Ph: (847)679-5500   Fax: (847)679-2494
Fr: 800-323-4900

Gary D. Golter and Deborah Yanuck. 1995. $14.95; $11.95 (paper). 160 pages. Explores high technology careers. Describes job opportunities, how to make a career decision, how to prepare for high technology jobs, job hunting techniques, and future trends.

★852★ Peterson's Hidden Job Market 1996

Peterson's
PO Box 2123
Princeton, NJ 08543-2123
Ph: (609)243-9111   Fax: (609)243-9150
Fr: 800-338-3282

Fifth edition, 1995. $17.95. Guide to 2,000 fast-growing companies that are hiring now. Focuses on high technology companies in such fields as environmental consulting, genetic engineering, home health care, telecommunications, alternative energy systems, and others.

★853★ Peterson's Job Opportunities in Engineering and Technology 1996

Peterson's
PO Box 2123
Princeton, NJ 08543-2123
Ph: (609)243-9111   Fax: (609)243-9150
Fr: 800-338-3282

Compiled by the Peterson's staff. Annual. $19.95 paperback. 432 pages. Profiles 2,000 high-tech companies looking primarily for technical personnel in such fields as biotechnology, telecommunications, software, computers and peripherals, defense, and aerospace. Contains job-search strategies and career options to help match education and expertise to the job market. Indexed geographically, by industry, and by hiring needs.

★854★ A PhD Is Not Enough: A Guide to Survival in Science

Addison-Wesley Publishing Co., Inc.
1 Jacob Way
Reading, MA 01867
Ph: (617)944-3700   Fax: (617)942-1117
Fr: 800-447-2226

Peter J. Feibelman. 1993. $12.95 (paper).

★855★ Resumes for Engineering Careers

VGM Career Horizons
NTC Publishing Group
4255 W. Touhy Ave.
Lincolnwood, IL 60646-1975
Ph: (847)679-5500   Fax: (847)679-2494
Fr: 800-323-4900

1994. $9.95. 160 pages. Contains sample resumes and cover letters applicable to any engineering field.

★856★ Science (Career Portraits)

VGM Career Horizons
NTC Publishing Group
4255 W. Touhy Ave.
Lincolnwood, IL 60646-1975
Ph: (847)679-5500   Fax: (847)679-2494
Fr: 800-323-4900

Jane Kelsey. 1996. $13.95. 96 pages. Practicing professionals describe their work in challenging science careers.

★857★ Where the Jobs Are: The Hottest Careers for the '90s

The Career Press, Inc.
3 Tice Rd.
PO Box 687
Franklin Lakes, NJ 07417
Ph: (201)848-0310   Fax: (201)848-1727
Fr: 800-237-3371

Joyce Hadley. Second edition, 1995. $9.99. 300 pages. Describes careers in fifteen general fields, from accounting to travel and hospitality.

EMPLOYMENT AGENCIES AND SEARCH FIRMS

★858★ ABC Employment Service

25 S. Bemiston, Ste. 214
Clayton, MO 63105
Ph: (314)725-3140

Employment agency.

★859★ Action Plus Employer Services

1211 W. Imperial Hwy., Ste. 100
Brea, CA 92621
Ph: (714)773-1506   Fax: (714)773-9201

Employment agency.

★860★ Amtec Engineering Corp.

2749 Saturn St.
Brea, CA 92621
Ph: (714)993-1900   Fax: (714)993-2419

Employment agency.

★861★ Arancio Associates

542 High Rock St.
Needham, MA 02192
Ph: (617)449-4436

Employment agency. Executive search firm.

★862★ Biomedical Search Consultants

PO Box 1070
Danbury, CT 06813
Ph: (203)744-4027   Fax: (203)748-2122

Employment agency.

★863★ Blake and Associates Executive Search

PO Box 1425
Pleasantville, NJ 08232
Ph: (609)645-3330   Fax: (609)383-0320

Executive search firm.

★864★ Erspamer Associates

7300 France Ave. S., Ste. 402
Edina, MN 55435
Ph: (612)831-5564   Fax: (612)831-5981

Executive search firm.

★865★ JPM International

4665 MacArthur Ct., Ste. 100B
Newport Beach, CA 92660
Ph: (714)955-2545   Fax: (714)757-1320

Executive search firm and employment agency.

★866★ Lloyd Personnel Consultants

445 Broad Hollow Rd., Ste. 120
Melville, NY 11747
Ph: (516)777-7600   Fax: (516)777-7626

Personnel agency.

★867★ O'Keefe and Associates

3420 Executive Center Dr., Ste. 114
Austin, TX 78731
Ph: (512)343-1134   Fax: (512)343-0142

Personnel agency.

★868★ The Personnel Institute

1000 Connecticut Ave. NW, Ste. 1108
Washington, DC 20036
Ph: (202)223-4911

Consulting firm.

★869★ Pomerantz Staffing Services

1375 Plainfield Ave.
Watchung, NJ 07060
Ph: (908)754-3092   Fax: (908)757-0298

Personnel agency.

★870★ Roger G. Gilmer and Associates

14581 Grand Ave. S.
Burnsville, MN 55306
Ph: (612)435-6565

Executive search firm.

★871★ The Sullivan and Cogliano Companies

230 Second Ave.
Waltham, MA 02154-1102
Ph: (617)890-7890

Regular and temporary help agency.

★872★ Temporary Tech Corp.

PO Box 12509
Research Triangle Park, NC 27709
Ph: (919)544-7515   Fax: (919)544-0162

Personnel agency.

OTHER SOURCES

★873★ American Association of Engineering Societies (AAES)

1111 19th St. NW, Ste. 608
Washington, DC 20036
Ph: (202)296-2237   Fax: (202)296-1151

Purpose: Seeks to promote leadership in public affairs for the engineering community, work in support of math and science education for young persons. Disseminates of information about the profession. Provides statistics about engineers.

★874★ Biotechnology: An Introduction

American Council on Science and Health
1995 Broadway, 2nd Fl.
New York, NY 10023-5860
Ph: (212)362-7044

$3.85. 39 pages.

★875★ Biotechnology: Careers for the 21st Century

National Association of Biology Teachers
11250 Roger Bacon Dr., No. 19
Reston, VA 22090
Ph: (703)471-1134

Video. $10.00. 14 minutes. Explores careers in the field of biotechnology for middle and high school students.

★876★ The Biotechnology Directory

Stockton Press
Groves Dictionaries
345 Park Ave. S., 10th Fl.
New York, NY 10010
Ph: (212)689-9200   Fr: 800-221-2123

Annual. $265.00. Covers biotechnology firms.

★877★ Emerging Careers Library: Biotechnology and Biogenetics

Chronicle Guidance Publications, Inc.
66 Aurora St.
PO Box 1190
Moravia, NY 13118-1190
Ph: (315)497-0330   Fax: (315)497-3359
Fr: 800-622-7284

Video. $89.95. 29 minutes. Full-color video features interviews with actual workers talking about their occupation and its challenges.

★878★ Engineering Salary Survey

Source Engineering
1290 Oakmead, Ste. 318
Sunnyvale, CA 94086
Ph: (408)738-8440

Annual. Discusses the structure of the engineering profession, trends, and compensation. Salaries are listed by job function, industry, and years of experience.

★879★ Evolution of the Clinical Engineering Profession

Quest Publishing Co.
1351 Titan Way
Brea, CA 92621
Ph: (714)738-6400   Fax: (714)525-6258
Allan F. Pacela, editor. 1991. $26.00 (paper).

★880★ Graduating Engineer

Peterson's/COG Publishing Group
16030 Ventura Blvd., No. 560
Encino, CA 91436
Ph: (818)789-5293

Eight issues/year. Magazine focusing on employment, education, and career development for entry-level engineers.

★881★ National Action Council for Minorities in Engineering (NACME)

3 W. 35th St.
New York, NY 10001-2281
Ph: (212)279-2626   Fax: (212)629-5178

Purpose: Seeks to increase the number of African American, Latino, and Native American students enrolled in and graduating from engineering schools. Through the Corporate Scholars Program, offers comprehensive scholarships to engineering students that include leadership development, corporate mentors and summer internships. Works with local, regional, and national education organizations to motivate and encourage precollege students to engage in engineering careers. Conducts educational and research programs; operates project to assist engineering schools in improving the retention and graduation rates of minority students. Maintains speakers' bureau; compiles statistics.

★882★ National Society of Professional Engineers (NSPE)

1420 King St.
Alexandria, VA 22314
Ph: (703)684-2800   Fax: (703)836-4875

Members: Professional engineers and engineers-in-training in all fields registered in accordance with the laws of states or territories of the U.S. or provinces of Canada; qualified graduate engineers, student members, and registered land surveyors. **Purpose:** Is concerned with social, professional, ethical, and economic considerations of engineering as a profession; encompasses programs in public relations, employment practices, ethical considerations, education, and career guidance. Monitors legislative and regulatory actions of interest to the engineering profession. **Website:** http://www.hspc.org

★883★ Resumes for High Tech Careers

VGM Career Horizons
4255 W. Touhy Ave.
Lincolnwood, IL 60646-1975
Ph: (847)679-5500   Fax: (847)679-2494
Fr: 800-323-4900

1992. $9.95. 160 pages. Demonstrates how to tailor a resume that catches a high tech employer's attention.

★884★ Resumes for Scientific and Technical Careers

VGM Career Horizons
NTC Publishing Group
4255 W. Touhy Ave.
Lincolnwood, IL 60646-1975
Ph: (847)679-5500   Fax: (847)679-2494
Fr: 800-323-4900

1994. $9.95. 160 pages. Provides resume advice for individuals interested in working in scientific and technical careers. Includes sample resumes and cover letters.

★885★ Salaries of Scientists, Engineers, and Technicians: A Summary of Salary Surveys

Commission on Professionals in Science and Technology (CPST)
1500 Massachusetts Ave. NW, Ste. 831
Washington, DC 20005
Ph: (202)223-6995

1993.

★886★ Society of Women Engineers (SWE)

120 Wall St., 11th Fl.
New York, NY 10005
Ph: (212)509-9577   Fax: (212)509-0224

Members: Educational service society of women engineers; membership is also open to men. **Purpose:** Supplies information on the achievements of women engineers and the opportunities available to them; assists women engineers in preparing for return to active work following temporary retirement. Serves as an informational center on women in engineering. **Activities:** Administers several certificate and scholarship programs. Offers tours and career guidance; conducts surveys. Compiles statistics.

Bricklayers and Cement Masons

SOURCES OF HELP-WANTED ADS

★887★ Builder

Hanley-Wood, Inc.
1 Thomas Cir., Ste. 600
Washington, DC 20005
Ph: (202)452-0800　　Fax: (202)785-1974

Monthly. $29.95/year for individuals. Magazine covering housing, commercial, and industrial building.

★888★ Concrete Construction Magazine

The Aberdeen Group
426 S. Westgate
Addison, IL 60101-9929
Ph: (708)543-0870　　Fax: (708)543-3112
Fr: 800-837-0870

Monthly. $18.00/year for individuals; $25.00/year for Canada and Mexico; $77.00/year for other countries. Trade magazine for contractors, subcontractors, and others involved in concrete construction.

★889★ Concrete Products

Intertec Publishing Co.
29 N. Wacker Dr.
Chicago, IL 60606
Ph: (312)435-2330　　Fax: (312)726-4103
Fr: 800-621-9907

Monthly. Magazine on concrete products and ready-mixed concrete.

★890★ Construction Digest

Construction Magazine Group, Inc.
PO Box 6132
Indianapolis, IN 46206-6132
Ph: (317)329-3100　　Fax: (317)329-3110
Fr: 800-860-3105

Semimonthly. $3.00 for single issue. Magazine for the public works and construction engineering industries.

★891★ CONSTRUCTOR

Associated General Contractors
　Information
1957 E St. NW
Washington, DC 20006-5199
Ph: (202)393-2040　　Fax: (202)628-7369

Monthly. $15.00/year for members; $4.00 for single issue.

★892★ Professional Builder

Cahners Publishing Co.
1350 E. Touhy Ave.
PO Box 5080
Des Plaines, IL 60018-5080
Ph: (708)635-8800　　Fax: (708)635-9950

Monthly. $10.00 for single issue; $139.95/year by mail.

★893★ Summer Jobs: Opportunities in the Federal Government

Office of Personnel Management
1900 E St. NW
Washington, DC 20415
Ph: (202)606-0950

Formerly annual; latest edition January 1993; suspended indefinitely. Free. Covers GS-1 through GS-4 clerical jobs and other jobs at GS-5 and above which are expected to be available in federal agencies and departments throughout the United States during the season. Most jobs are in Metropolitan Washington, D.C. Latest application date is generally April 15; many are earlier. Includes general information on applying for jobs in trades and labor occupations and summer employment for needy youth programs. Entries include: Agency name, filing deadline, titles of jobs available, brief information on qualifications needed, location, etc. Complete agency names and addresses are given in separate list. Publication is available from Federal Employment Information Center offices and agency personnel offices. Arrangement: By job level, then alphabetical by agency name.

★894★ Tradeswomen

Tradeswomen, Inc.
PO Box 2622
Berkeley, CA 94702
Ph: (510)649-6260

Bimonthly. $35.00/year. Subtitled: "A Quarterly Magazine for Women in Blue Collar Work". Reports activities of the organization and other events in the California Bay Area and of national interest to women working or wishing to work in nontraditional and blue collar jobs. Recurring features include announcements of apprenticeship opportunities and job openings, information on unions and government agencies, and U.S. Department of Labor statistics.

PLACEMENT AND JOB REFERRAL SERVICES

★895★ Associated Builders and Contractors (ABC)

1300 N. 17th St.
Rosslyn, VA 22209
Ph: (703)812-2000　　Fax: (703)812-8200

Members: Construction contractors, subcontractors, suppliers, and associates. **Purpose:** Aim is to foster and perpetuate the principles of rewarding construction workers and management on the basis of merit. **Activities:** Maintains placement service. Sponsors management education programs and craft training; also sponsors apprenticeship and skill training programs. Disseminates technological and labor relations information. Compiles statistics.

★896★ National Association of Home Builders of the U.S. (NAHB)

1201 15th St. NW
Washington, DC 20005
Ph: (202)822-0200　　Fax: (202)822-0559

Members: Single and multifamily home builders, commercial builders, and others associated with the building industry. **Purpose:** Lobbies on behalf of the housing industry and conducts public affairs activities to increase public understanding of housing and the economy. Collects and disseminates data on current developments in home building and home builders' plans through its Economics Department and nationwide Metropolitan Housing Forecast. **Activities:** Maintains NAHB Research Center, which functions as the research arm of the home building industry. Sponsors seminars and workshops on construction, mortgage credit, labor relations, cost reduction, land use, remodeling, and business management. Compiles statistics; offers charitable program, spokesman training, and placement service; maintains speakers' bureau, and hall of fame.

EMPLOYER DIRECTORIES AND NETWORKING LISTS

★897★ ABC Today—Associated Builders and Contractors Membership Directory Issue

Associated Builders and Contractors
1300 N. 17th St.
Rosslyn, VA 22209
Ph: (703)812-2000   Fax: (703)812-8200

Annual, November. $150.00, plus $7.00 shipping. Publication includes: List of approximately 17,000 member construction contractors and suppliers. Entries include: Company name, address, phone, name of principal executive, code to volume of business, business specialty. Arrangement: Classified by chapter, then by work specialty.

★898★ Constructor—Directory of Membership and Services Issue

AGC Information, Inc.
Associated General Contractors of
  America
1957 E St. NW
Washington, DC 20006
Ph: (202)393-2040   Fax: (202)347-4004

Annual, July. $135.00. Publication includes: List of more than 8,500 member firms and 9,000 national associate member firms engaged in building, highway, heavy, industrial, municipal utilities, and railroad construction, listing of state and local chapter officers. Arrangement: Geographical. Indexes: Company name.

★899★ ENR—Top 400 Construction Contractors Issue

McGraw-Hill, Inc.
1221 Ave. of the Americas
New York, NY 10020
Ph: (212)512-4635   Fax: (212)512-2820

Annual, May issue of *Engineering News Record*. $10.00, Reprint, payment with order. Publication includes: List of 400 United States contractors receiving largest dollar volumes of contracts in preceding calendar year. Separate lists of 50 largest design/construct management firms; 50 largest program and construction managers; 25 building contractors; 25 heavy contractors. Entries include: Company name, headquarters location; total value of contracts received in preceding year, value of foreign contracts, countries in which operated, construction specialities. Arrangement: By total value of contracts received.

★900★ Masonry Contractors Directory

American Business Directories, Inc.
American Business Information, Inc.
5711 S. 86th Cir.
Omaha, NE 68127
Ph: (402)593-4600   Fax: (402)331-1505

Annual. $800.00, U.S. edition. Number of listings: 11,188 (U.S. edition); 2,320 (Canadian edition). Entries include: Name, address, phone (including area code), size of advertisement, year first in Yellow Pages, name of owner or manager, number of employees. Compiled from telephone company Yellow Pages, nationwide. Arrangement: Geographical.

HANDBOOKS AND MANUALS

★901★ Bricklaying

Brick Institute of America
11490 Commerce Park Dr.
Reston, VA 22091-1525
Ph: (703)620-0010

$.50. This four-page pamphlet describes skills, benefits, and how to get started as a bricklayer.

★902★ Construction Job Directory-Worldwide

Rector Press, Ltd.
130 Rattlesnake
Leverett, MA 01054-9726
Ph: (413)548-9708   Fax: (413)367-2853
Fr: 800-247-3473

1994. $125.00 (paper).

★903★ Exploring Careers in the Construction Industry

Rosen Publishing Group
29 E. 21st St.
New York, NY 10010
Ph: (212)777-3017   Fax: (212)777-0277
Fr: 800-237-9932

Elizabeth Stewart Lytle. 1992. $14.95.

★904★ Exploring Nontraditional Jobs for Women

Rosen Publishing Group, Inc.
29 E. 21st St.
New York, NY 10010
Ph: (212)777-3017   Fax: (212)777-0277
Fr: 800-237-9932

Rose Neufeld. 1989. $14.95. Describes occupations where few women are found. Covers job duties, training routes, where to apply for jobs, tools used, salary, and advantages and disadvantages of the job.

★905★ How to Get Started As a Contractor

Summertree Books
811 Moundridge Dr.
Lawrence, KS 66049
Ph: (913)841-7643

J.L. McCabe. 1994. $8.95 (paper).

★906★ Opportunities in Building Construction Trades

VGM Career Horizons
4255 W. Touhy Ave.
Lincolnwood, IL 60646-1975
Ph: (847)679-5500   Fax: (847)679-2494
Fr: 800-323-4900

Michael Sumichrast. 1993. $14.95; $11.95 (paper). From custom builder to rehabber, the many kinds of companies that employ craftspeople and contractors are explored. Includes job descriptions, requirements, and salaries for dozens of specialties within the construction industry. Contains a complete list of Bureau of Apprenticeship and Training state and area offices. Illustrated.

★907★ The Trowel Trades: How to Build a Career that Builds Nations

International Masonry Institute
Apprenticeship and Training Program
823 15th St. NW, Ste. 1001
Washington, DC 20005
Ph: (202)783-3908

Brochure. Free. Presents information on apprenticeship opportunities.

★908★ You Can Become a Tile, Marble, Terrazzo and Dimensional Stone Installer

United Brotherhood of Carpenters and
  Joiners of America
Apprenticeship and Training Dept.
101 Constitution Ave. NW
Washington, DC 20001
Ph: (202)546-6206

Free. 6 pages. Brochure describing apprenticeship training.

★909★ Your Opportunities in the Trades

Energeia Publishing, Inc.
PO Box 985
Salem, OR 97308
Ph: (503)362-1480   Fax: (503)362-2123

Ramel Waltman. 1994. $2.00 (paper). Covers the construction and building industries.

OTHER SOURCES

★910★ Associated General Contractors of America (AGC)

1957 E St. NW
Washington, DC 20006
Ph: (202)393-2040   Fax: (202)347-4004

Members: General construction contractors; subcontractors; industry suppliers; service firms.**Purpose:** Provides market services through its divisions. Conducts special conferences and seminars designed specifically for construction firms. Compiles statistics on job accidents reported by member firms. Maintains 65 committees, including joint cooperative committees with other associations and liaison committees with federal agencies.

★911★ Associated Specialty Contractors (ASC)

3 Bethesda Metro Ctr., Ste. 1100
Bethesda, MD 20814
Ph: (301)657-3110   Fax: (301)215-4500

Members: Subcontractor associations with a total of 25,000 members representing electrical, heating, piping, mechanical, air conditioning, sheet metal, plumbing, ventilating, masonry, painting and decorating, and roofing and insulation contractors. **Purpose:** Promotes liaison with general contractors, architects, and engineers on inter-industry matters, codes, bidding, and contracting procedures. Coordinates governmental affairs, research, and educational matters.

★912★ COIN Career Guidance System

COIN Educational Products
3361 Executive Pky., Ste. 302
Toledo, OH 43606
Ph: (419)536-5353   Fr: 800-274-8515

CD-ROM product; also available on diskette. Provides career information through seven cross-referenced files covering postsecondary schools, college majors, vocational programs, military service, apprenticeship programs, financial aid, and scholarships. Apprenticeship file describes national apprenticeship training programs, including information on how to apply, contact agencies, and program content. Military file describes more than 200 military occupations and training opportunities related to civilian employment.

★913★ *Concrete Pavers, My Career*

National Concrete Masonry Association
Publications Dept.
2302 Horse Pen Rd.
Herndon, VA 22071
Ph: (703)713-1900

Video. $40.00. 6 minutes. Explains the paver industry, the demand for contractors, and career advancement possibilities.

★914★ Mason Contractors Association of America (MCAA)

1550 Spring Rd., Ste. 320
Oak Brook, IL 60521
Ph: (708)782-6767   Fax: (708)782-6786

Members: Masonry construction firms. **Purpose:** Conducts specialized education and research programs. Compiles statistics.

★915★ The Masonry Society (TMS)

3775 Iris Ave., Ste. 6
Boulder, CO 80301-9215
Ph: (303)939-9700   Fax: (303)541-2043

Members: Architects, engineers, manufacturers, mason contractors, craftsmen, students, educators, and other individuals interested in the use of masonry. **Purpose:** Seeks to unite the specialized disciplines involved in the design, manufacture, and construction of masonry structures for the exchange of technical and practical information. Provides a forum for design professionals (architects and engineers) to become involved with the masonry industry. Advocates the establishment of a national building standard for masonry. **Activities:** Sponsors educational programs and publishes technical documents on all aspects of masonry.

★916★ National Association of Women in Construction (NAWIC)

327 S. Adams St.
Fort Worth, TX 76104
Ph: (817)877-5551   Fax: (817)877-0324
Fr: 800-552-3506

Purpose: NAWIC is an international association of women employed in the construction industry which promotes that industry and supports the advancement of women within it.

★917★ Tradeswomen, Inc.

PO Box 40664 B
San Francisco, CA 94140
Ph: (415)821-7334   Fax: (415)861-8969

Members: Women who work in nontraditional, blue-collar occupations including construction, transportation, and industrial work; women who seek to enter these fields or who support the right of others to do so. **Purpose:** Serves as a network for women in the trades. Conducts social gatherings and local and regional forums on topics such as: health and safety on the job; racism and sexism in the trades; sexual harassment; working within unions. Makes available children's services; maintains speakers' bureau. Compiles statistics.

★918★ *WIT*

Northern New England Tradeswomen
26 Railroad St.
St. Johnsbury, VT 05819
Ph: (802)748-3308   Fax: (802)748-1768

Quarterly. Included in membership; $10.00/year for nonmembers. Provides a network of support, information, and skill sharing for women in trade professions.

Broadcast Technicians

SOURCES OF HELP-WANTED ADS

★919★ Audio

Hachette Filipacchi Magazines, Inc.
500 W. Putham Ave.
Greenwich, CT 06830
Ph: (203)622-2700   Fax: (203)622-2725

Monthly. $3.50/year for single issue. Consumer stereo equipment magazine.

★920★ AV Video

Knowledge Industry Publications, Inc.
701 Westchester Ave.
White Plains, NY 10604
Ph: (914)328-9157   Fax: (914)328-9093
Fr: 800-800-5474

Monthly. $48.00/year for individuals; $60.00/year for Canada and Mexico; $80.00/year for other countries. Magazine covering audiovisual and video production and presentation technology and techniques.

★921★ Broadcasting and Cable

Conners Publishing
245 W. 17th St.
New York, NY 10011
Ph: (212)463-6835   Fax: (212)463-6836

Weekly. $85.00/year for individuals; $3.00/year for single issue. News magazine covering "The Fifth Estate" (radio, TV, cable, and satellite), and the regulatory commissions involved.

★922★ CED (Communications Engineering & Design)

600 S. Cherry St., No. 400
Denver, CO 80222
Ph: (303)393-7449   Fax: (303)393-6654

Monthly. Technical journal for engineers who design, install, operate, and maintain broadband/cable TV networks.

★923★ Communications Technology

Phillips Business Information, Inc.
1900 Grant St., Ste. 720
Denver, CO 80203-4307
Ph: (303)839-1565   Fax: (303)839-1564

Monthly. Free to qualified subscribers. Magazine catering to cable TV industry's technical community; written by industry engineers, technicians, managers, and professionals.

★924★ db, The Sound Engineering Magazine

203 Commack Rd., No. 1010
Commack, NY 11725
Ph: (516)586-6530

Bimonthly. Technical magazine for recording, broadcast, and sound reinforcement audio engineers.

★925★ Electronic Media

Crain Communications, Inc.
740 N. Rush St.
Chicago, IL 60611
Ph: (312)649-5260   Fax: (312)649-5228

Weekly (Mon.). $69.00/year for individuals. Tabloid covering management, programing, syndication, technology, and trends in the television, radio, and electronic media industry.

★926★ ETV Newsletter

Charles Tepfer, Publisher
PO Box 597
Ridgefield, CT 06877
Ph: (203)454-2618   Fax: (203)454-2618

Biweekly. $195.00/year for U.S. and Canada; $220.00/year for elsewhere. Offers inside information on what's happening in Public Television (PTV), Instructional Television (ITV), and Educational Television (ETV). Monitors government telecommunications policy changes; new marketing policies, grants and funding sources; and requests for bids on equipment, services, and programs. Recurring features include meetings and conference reports, a calendar of events, job listings, book reviews, and market studies.

★927★ The Hollywood Reporter

Billboard Magazine
33 Commercial St.
Gloucester, MA 01930
Ph: (508)281-3110   Fax: (508)281-0136

Daily (morn.). $149.00/year for individuals. Film, TV, and entertainment trade newspaper.

★928★ Journal of the Audio Engineering Society

Audio Engineering Society
60 E. 42nd St., Rm. 2520
New York, NY 10165-2520
Ph: (212)661-2355   Fax: (212)682-0477

Monthly. $130.00/year for individuals; $11.00 for single issue. Journal reporting engineering developments and scientific progress in audio engineering for audio professionals, educators, executives, consumers, and students.

★929★ Millimeter Magazine

Penton Publishing
611 Rte. 46 W.
Hasbrouck Heights, NJ 07604
Ph: (201)393-6060   Fax: (201)393-6297

Monthly. $45.00/year; $7.00/single issue.

★930★ Mix

Cardinal Business Media
6400 Hollis St., Ste. 12
Emeryville, CA 94608
Ph: (510)653-3307   Fax: (510)653-5142

Monthly. $38.00/year for individuals. Magazine focusing on audio and video music production in the recording industry.

★931★ Post

Post Pro Publishing, Inc.
25 Willowdale Ave.
Port Washington, NY 11050
Ph: (516)767-2500   Fax: (516)767-9335

Monthly. Magazine serving the field of television, film, video production and post-production.

★932★ *Producer's Masterguide*

Producer's Masterguide
60 E. 8th St., 31st Fl.
New York, NY 10003-6514
Ph: (212)777-4002   Fax: (212)777-4101
Fr: 800-622-6111

Annual. $125.00/year for individuals; $145.00/year for out of country. Magazine for the professional motion picture, TV commercial, cable, and videotape industries in the U.S. Canada, the U.K., the Caribbean Islands, Mexico, Europe, Israel, the Far East and South America.

★933★ *QST: American Radio Relay League*

225 Main St.
Newington, CT 06111
Ph: (203)666-1541

Monthly.

★934★ *Religious Broadcasting*

National Religious Broadcasters
7839 Ashton Ave.
Manassas, VA 22110
Ph: (703)330-7000

Monthly. $24.00/year.

★935★ *SMPTE Journal*

Society of Motion Picture and Television Engineers
595 W. Hartsdale Ave.
White Plains, NY 10607
Ph: (914)761-1100   Fax: (914)761-3115

Monthly. $90.00/year; $100.00/year for out of country. Journal containing articles pertaining to new developments in motion-picture and television technology; standards and recommended practices; general news of the industry.

PLACEMENT AND JOB REFERRAL SERVICES

★936★ **Armed Forces Broadcasters Association (AFBA)**

PO Box 335
Sun Valley, CA 91353-0335
Ph: (213)256-3482   Fax: (213)256-3482

Members: Former and current military and commercial broadcasters. **Purpose:** Provides an opportunity for military broadcasters and supporters to meet and socialize. Assists broadcasters returning to the U.S. from overseas. **Activities:** Provides job information center.

★937★ **Association for Educational Communications and Technology (AECT)**

1025 Vermont Ave. NW, Ste. 820
Washington, DC 20005
Ph: (202)347-7834   Fax: (202)347-7839

Members: Technology and instructional materials specialists, educational technologists, audiovisual and television production personnel, and teacher educators. **Purpose:** Seeks to improve education through the systematic planning, application, and production of communications media for instruction. **Activities:** Maintains placement service.

★938★ **Broadcast Foundation of College/University Students (BROADCAST)**

89 Longview Rd.
Port Washington, NY 11050
Ph: (516)883-2897   Fax: (516)883-7460

Members: College students interested in broadcasting and professional broadcasters interested in encouraging practical broadcasting experience in colleges and universities. **Activities:** Conducts annual survey of all professional broadcasting stations for part-time and summer employment for college students. Sponsors job advisory and placement service.

★939★ **Health Sciences Communications Association (HESCA)**

1 Wedgewood Dr.
Jewett City, CT 06351
Ph: (203)376-5915   Fax: (203)376-6621

Members: Media managers, graphic artists, biomedical librarians, producers, faculty members of health science and veterinary medicine schools, health professional organizations, and industry representatives. **Purpose:** Acts as a clearinghouse for information used by professionals engaged in health science communications. Coordinates Media Festivals Program which recognizes outstanding media productions in the health sciences. **Activities:** Offers placement service.

★940★ **Media Alliance (MA)**

814 Mission St., Ste. 205
San Francisco, CA 94103

Members: Writers, photographers, editors, broadcast workers, public relations people, and others who support free press and independent journalism. **Purpose:** Seeks to change what the alliance calls the characteristic cutthroat competitive attitude among its practitioners by encouraging contact and discussion and developing structures enabling members to assist each other and to mobilize the group's resources on behalf of mutually agreed-upon projects. **Activities:** Maintains job file. Conducts continuing professional education classes. Maintains speakers' bureau.

★941★ **National Association of Broadcasters (NAB)**

1771 N St. NW
Washington, DC 20036
Ph: (202)429-5300   Fax: (202)429-5343

Members: Representatives of radio and television stations and networks; associate members include producers of equipment and programs. **Purpose:** Seeks to ensure the viability, strength, and success of free, over-the-air broadcasters; serves as an information resource to the industry. **Activities:** Offers minority placement service and employment clearinghouse. Monitors and reports on events regarding radio and television broadcasting. Maintains Broadcasting Hall of Fame.

★942★ **National Religious Broadcasters (NRB)**

7839 Ashton Ave.
Manassas, VA 22110
Ph: (703)330-7000   Fax: (703)330-7100

Members: Religious radio and television program producers; religious radio and television station owners and operators within the U.S. and Canada; foreign broadcasters interested in religious broadcasting throughout the world. **Purpose:** Seeks to support those providing programming for radio and television and those engaging in the operation of religious radio and television stations. Is dedicated to the communication of the gospel and complete access to broadcast media for religious broadcasting. Serves as a central source of information concerning Christian radio and television. Sponsors seven regional conventions, international tours, and professional training courses. **Activities:** Compiles statistics; provides placement service; maintains hall of fame.

EMPLOYER DIRECTORIES AND NETWORKING LISTS

★943★ *Bacon's Radio/TV/Cable Directory, Volume 1*

Bacon's Publishing Co.
332 S. Michigan Ave., Ste. 900
Chicago, IL 60604
Ph: (312)922-2400   Fax: (312)922-3127
Fr: 800-621-0561

Annual, November; interedition supplement. $270.00 postpaid; includes updates. Covers over 10,300 radio and television stations, including college radio and public television stations, and cable companies. Entries include: For radio and television stations: call letters, address, phone, names and titles of key personnel, programs, times broadcast, name of contact, network affiliation, frequency or channel number, target audience data. For cable companies: name, address, phone, description of activities. Arrangement: Geographical.

★944★ *Broadcasting & Cable Yearbook*

R. R. Bowker Co.
Reed Reference Publishing
121 Chanlon Rd.
New Providence, NJ 07974
Ph: (908)464-6800   Fax: (908)464-3553
Fr: 800-521-8110

Annual, March. $169.95. Covers all television and radio stations in the United States, its territories, and Canada; cable MSOs and their individual systems; television and radio networks, broadcast and cable group owners, station representatives, satellite networks and services, film companies, advertising agencies, government agencies, trade associations and schools. Entries include: Company name, address, phone, fax, names of executives. Station listings include broadcast power, other operating details. Arrangement: Stations and systems are geographical, others are alphabetical. Indexes: Alphabetical.

★945★ Burrelle's New York Media Directory

Burrelle's Information Services
75 E. Northfield Rd.
Livingston, NJ 07039
Ph: (201)992-6600   Fr: 800-876-3342

Annual. $95.00. Includes information on radio and television stations, newspapers, and other media companies. Regional editions available for some Northeastern states.

★946★ Chicago Media Directory

Chicago Convention and Tourism Bureau
McCormick Place-on-the-Lake
Chicago, IL 60616
Ph: (312)567-8500   Fax: (312)567-8533

Quarterly. $5.00. Covers executive and editorial personnel at Chicago's major daily newspapers, downtown weeklies, and wire services, as well as radio and television station personnel. Entries include: For newspapers: publication name, address, phone, names and titles of key personnel. For radio and TV Station: name, address, phone, names and titles of key personnel. Arrangement: Classified by type of medium or outlet.

★947★ CPB Public Broadcasting Directory

Corporation for Public Broadcasting
901 E St. NW
Washington, DC 20004-2037
Ph: (202)879-9600   Fax: (202)783-1019

Annual, fall. $15.00. Covers public television and radio stations, national and regional public broadcasting organizations and networks, state government agencies and commissions, and other related organizations. Entries include: For radio and television stations: station call letters, frequency or channel, address, phone, licensee name, licensee type, date on air, antenna height, area covered, names and titles of key personnel. For organizations: name, address, phone, name and title of key personnel. Arrangement: National and regional listings are alphabetical; state groups and the public radio and television stations are each geographical; other organizations and agencies are alphabetical. Indexes: Geographical, personnel, call letter, licensee type (all in separate indexes for radio and television).

★948★ Directory of Women in Sports Business

Women's Sports Guide
3306 Maynard Rd.
Shaker Heights, OH 44122
Ph: (216)751-0910

$15.00. Covers Approximately 1,500 women involved in all aspects of sports business, including broadcasting and corporate sponsorship.

★949★ Film and Video Career Directory

Gale Research
835 Penobscot Bldg.
Detroit, MI 48226-4094
Ph: (313)961-2242   Fax: (313)961-6083
Fr: 800-877-GALE

First edition March 1994. $29.95; $17.95(paper). Covers over 210 U.S. film and video production companies, postproduction facilities, and other companies providing services related to film and video that offer entry-level positions and internships; sources of help-wanted ads, professional associations, producers of videos, databases, career guides, and professional guides and handbooks. Entries include: For companies: Name, address, phone, fax, business description, names and titles of key personnel, number of employees, average number of entry-level positions available, human resources contact, description of internship opportunities including contact, type and number available, application procedures, qualifications, and duties. For others: Name or title, address, phone, description. Paperback edition is available from Visible Ink Press. Arrangement: Companies are alphabetical; others are classified by type of resource. Indexes: Name and keyword.

★950★ FM Atlas

FM Atlas Publishing and Electronics
PO Box 24
Adolph, MN 55701
Ph: (218)879-7676   Fax: (218)879-8333

Irregular, previous edition December 1993; latest edition 1995. $14.95, plus $1.05 shipping. Covers approximately 7,000 FM stations located in North America. Entries include: Call letters, location, musical format, transmitting radius in kilometers, whether stereo or monaural, FM subcarriers, etc. Arrangement: Geographical, then by frequency.

★951★ Hollywood Creative Directory

M & A Communications
3000 Olympic Blvd.
Santa Monica, CA 90404
Ph: (310)315-4815   Fax: (310)315-4816
Fr: 800-815-0503

Three times per year in March, July, and November. $45.00, per issue, plus $3.00 shipping. Covers more than 1,600 motion picture and television production companies employing 5,800 development and production personnel, primarily in Hollywood, California, and New York City, with some companies in other parts of the country. Entries include: Company name, address, phone, fax, names and titles of key personnel (with produced credits where applicable). Arrangement: Alphabetical. Indexes: Personal name, companies with studio contracts.

★952★ Hudson's State Capitals News Media Contacts Directory

Howard Penn Hudson Associates, Inc.
44 W. Market St.
PO Box 311
Rhinebeck, NY 12572
Ph: (914)876-2081   Fax: (914)876-2561

Annual. $108.00. Covers about 1,500 media outlets located in or near the state capitals; includes wire services, radio and television broadcasting stations, newspapers, magazine and newsletter publishers. Entries include: Name, address, phone, name of editorial contact. Arrangement: Alphabetical.

★953★ International Radio and Television Society Foundation–Roster Yearbook

International Radio and Television Society Foundation
420 Lexington Ave.
New York, NY 10170
Ph: (212)867-6650   Fax: (212)867-6653

Annual, April. Available to members only. Covers Approximately 1,600 professionals in the communications industry. Entries include: Name, title (where applicable), business address, phone. Arrangement: Alphabetical.

★954★ International Television and Video Almanac

Quigley Publishing Co., Inc.
159 W. 53rd St.
New York, NY 10019
Ph: (212)247-3100   Fax: (212)489-0871

Annual, January. $88.50, plus shipping. Covers Who's Who in Motion Pictures and Television and Home Video, television networks, major program producers, major group station owners, cable television companies, distributors, firms serving the television and home video industry, equipment manufacturers, casting agencies, literary agencies, advertising and publicity representatives, television stations, associations, list of feature films produced for television; statistics, industry's year in review, award winners. Entries include: Generally, company name, address, phone; manufacturer and service listings may include description of products and services and name of contact; producing, distributing, and station listings include additional detail. Arrangement: Classified by service or activity, then generally geographical.

★955★ Media Directory San Diego County

San Diego Chamber of Commerce
402 W. Broadway, Ste. 1000
San Diego, CA 92101
Ph: (619)232-0124

Annual. $5.00. Covers San Diego county newspapers, magazines, news bureaus, radio and television stations. Entries include: For publications: name of publication, address, phone. For radio and television stations: call letters, frequency, address, mailing address, phone. Arrangement: Classified by type of media.

★956★ Metro California Media

Public Relations Plus, Inc.
Box 1197
New Milford, CT 06776
Ph: (203)354-9361   Fax: (203)355-8048
Fr: 800-999-8448

Semiannual, May and November. $149.50 per year. Covers newspapers, radio and television stations, magazines, and broadcast programs in California. Entries include: Name, address, phone, names of editors and creative staff, with titles or indication of assignments. Arrangement: Geographical. Indexes: Alphabetical.

★957★ Minority Employment Report

Federal Communications Commission
1919 M St. NW
Washington, DC 20554
Ph: (202)632-7000   Fax: (202)418-0200

Annual, December. Free. Covers television and radio stations with ten or more full-time employees. Entries include: Station name (call letters or channel), city and state, class of station; total, female, and minority full-time employment in higher and lower pay occupations, and part-time employment for previous five years. Arrangement: By state and community.

★958★ Pocket Station Listing Guide

Publications Dept.
National Association of Television Program Executives
2425 Olympic Blvd., Ste. 550E
Santa Monica, CA 90404
Ph: (310)453-4440   Fax: (310)453-5258

Quarterly. $30.00. Covers 1,500 network-affiliated, independent, and public television stations in the U.S., Canada, and Latin America. Entries include: Station name, address, phone, fax, names and titles of key personnel, geographical area served, call letters, channel station numbers, owner, sales representative. Arrangement: Geographical by state/province; separate sections for the U.S., Canada, and Latin America. Indexes: Market ranking.

★959★ Radio Programming Profile

BF/Communication Services, Inc.
66 Chestnut Ln.
Woodbury, NY 11797
Ph: (516)364-2593

Three times yearly. $310.00, per vol.; no single copies sold. Covers about 3,000 AM and FM radio stations in top 200 markets, with hour-by-hour format information. Entries include: Station call letters, address, phone, names of executives, hour-by-hour format information. Arrangement: Alphabetical by market and call letters. Volume 1 has top 70 ranking markets; volume 2 has markets 71-200.

★960★ Television & Cable Factbook

Warren Publishing, Inc.
2115 Ward Ct. NW
Washington, DC 20037
Ph: (202)872-9200   Fax: (202)293-3435

Annual, January. Weekly updates available. $405.00, plus $15.00 shipping. Covers commercial and noncommercial television stations and networks, including educational, low-power and instructional TV stations, and translators; United States cable television systems; cable and television group owners; national sales representatives of television stations; equipment manufacturers and distributors; program and service suppliers; brokerage and financing companies; consulting engineers; brokers; attorneys practicing before the Federal Communications Commission; cable system sales representatives; international coverage. Arrangement: Geographical by state, province, city, county, or country. Indexes: Call letters, product/service, name, general subject.

★961★ Television Stations & Broadcasting Companies Directory

American Business Directories, Inc.
American Business Information, Inc.
5711 S. 86th Cir.
Omaha, NE 68127
Ph: (402)593-4600   Fax: (402)331-1505

Updated continuously; printed on request. Please inquire. Entries include: Name, address, phone (including area code), size of advertisement, year first in Yellow Pages, name of owner or manager, number of employees. Compiled from telephone company Yellow Pages, nationwide. Arrangement: Geographical.

★962★ The Television Yearbook

BIA Publications
14595 Avion Pkwy., Ste. 500
Chantilly, VA 22021
Ph: (703)818-2425   Fax: (703)803-3299

Annual, March. $84.00. Covers U.S. television markets and their inclusive stations, television equipment manufacturers, and related service providers and trade associations. Entries include: For stations: Call letters, address; name and phone of general manager, owner, and other key personnel; technical attributes, rep firm, network affiliation, last acquistion date and price and ratings for total day and prime time. For others: Company or organization name, address, phone, description. Arrangement: Classified by market. Indexes: Numerical by market rank; call letters.

★963★ The Top 200 National TV News, Talk and Magazine Shows

Todd Publications
PO Box 301
West Nyack, NY 10994
Fax: (914)358-6213   Fr: 800-747-1056

Annual. $35.00. Covers The 200 most popular information shows on U.S. television. Entries include: Name, address, phone of company, name and title of contact and description of format. Arrangement: By rank.

★964★ TV and Cable Source

Standard Rate & Data Service
3004 Glenview Rd.
Wilmette, IL 60091
Ph: (708)441-2243   Fax: (708)441-2400
Fr: 800-851-7737

Quarterly. $164.00 single copy; $369.00 year subscription. Covers all commercial television stations and networks; public television stations, cable networks, systems, interconnects, rep firms, and group owners. Includes separate section showing production specifications of stations and systems. Entries include: Call letters, parent company, address, phone, representative, personnel, facilities, special features, programming. Production specifications section shows call letters or system name, address, and preferred specifications for ad copy. Arrangement: Classified by by DMA ranking, then by call letters.

★965★ Who's Who in Television

Packard Publishing Co.
PO Box 2187
Beverly Hills, CA 90213
Ph: (310)854-0276   Fax: (818)501-7392

Latest edition February 1991. $16.95. Covers Approximately 2,000 studios, production companies, networks, writers, directors, and other professionals involved in cable and network television. Entries include: Individual or company name, address, phone, description of projects; names and titles of key personnel and name and title of contact given for companies; biographical data for individuals. Arrangement: Alphabetical. Indexes: Personal name.

★966★ Women in Broadcast Technology—Directory

Women in Broadcast Technology
PO Box 370772
Denver, CO 80237-0772

Annual, June. $4.00 postpaid. Covers more than 100 women technicians and operators of audio and video broadcasting equipment. Entries include: Name, address, phone, specialty, employment interests. Arrangement: Classified by specialty.

★967★ Working Press of the Nation

Reed Reference Publishing
121 Chanlon Rd.
New Providence, NJ 07974
Ph: (908)665-3561   Fax: (908)665-2894
Fr: 800-521-8110

Annual, September. $385.00, four-volume set; Covers in four separate volumes, syndicates and over 8,400 daily and weekly newspapers; 1,400 newsletters; over 14,900 radio and television stations; 10,600 magazines; 3,200 feature writers, photographers, and professional speakers; and 2,700 internal house organs. Entries include: All listings include name of publication or station, address, phone, names of executives, editors, writers, etc., as appropriate. Broadcasting and magazine volumes include data on kinds of material needed. Technical and mechanical requirements for publications are given. Arrangement: Magazines are classified by audience; newspapers and broadcasting stations are geographical.

★968★ World Radio TV Handbook

BPI Communications, Inc.
Affiliated Publications, Inc.
1515 Broadway, 39th Fl.
New York, NY 10036
Ph: (212)764-7300

Annual, January. $19.95, plus $2.50 shipping. Covers 25,000 radio and television stations worldwide; national regulatory bodies. Entries include: For stations: name, frequency, address, phone, telex, name and title of contact and key personnel, description of programming. For agencies: name, address, phone. Arrangement: Separate geographical sections for radio and television stations. Indexes: Station name and geographical.

HANDBOOKS AND MANUALS

★969★ Career Information Center

Macmillan Publishing Co.
200 Old Tappan Rd.
Old Tappan, NJ 07675
Ph: (609)461-6500   Fr: 800-223-2336

Visual Education Center Staff. Fifth edition, 1992. $229.00. This 13-volume set profiles over 600 occupations. Each occupational profile describes job duties, educational requirements, how to get the job, advancement possibilities, employment outlook, working conditions, earnings and benefits, and where to write for more information.

★970★ Career Opportunities in Television, Cable and Video

Facts on File, Inc.
11 Penn Plaza, 15th Fl.
New York, NY 10001-2006
Ph: (212)967-8800   Fax: 800-678-3633
Fr: 800-322-8755

Maxine K. Reed and Robert M. Reed. Third edition, 1991. $29.95; $15.95 (paper). 272 pages.

★971★ Careers in Communications

VGM Career Horizons
4255 W. Touhy Ave.
Lincolnwood, IL 60646-1975
Ph: (847)679-5500   Fax: (847)679-2494
Fr: 800-323-4900

Shonan Noronha. 1994. $17.95; $13.95 (paper). 176 pages. Examines the fields of journalism, photography, radio, television, film, public relations, and advertising. Gives concrete details on job locations and how to secure a job. Suggests many resources for job hunting.

★972★ Careers in Radio

National Association of Broadcasters (NAB)
1771 N. St., NW
Washington, DC 20036
Fr: 800-368-5644

Compiled by NAB Staff. 1991. $3.50.

★973★ Exploring Nontraditional Jobs for Women

Rosen Publishing Group, Inc.
29 E. 21st St.
New York, NY 10010
Ph: (212)777-3017   Fax: (212)777-0277
Fr: 800-237-9932

Rose Neufeld. 1989. $14.95. Describes occupations where few women are found. Covers job duties, training routes, where to apply for jobs, tools used, salary, and advantages and disadvantages of the job.

★974★ The Harvard Guide to Careers in the Mass Media

Bob Adams, Inc.
260 Center St.
Holbrook, MA 02343
Ph: (617)767-8100   Fax: (617)767-0994
Fr: 800-872-5627

John Noble. 1989. $7.95. 202 pages. Each section of the book evaluates one media profession in depth and contains an industry profile, a career profile that describes positions available in that area, information about current salary ranges, industry-specific job-hunting tips and strategies, and a case study outlining the methods that were used in a successful job hunt.

★975★ How to Land a Job in TV News: The Insider's Guide

Mustang Publishing
PO Box 3004
Memphis, TN 38173
Ph: (901)521-1406   Fax: (901)521-1412

Carl Filoreto. 1995. $14.95 (paper).

★976★ Opportunities in Broadcasting Careers

VGM Career Horizons
4255 W. Touhy Ave.
Lincolnwood, IL 60646-1975
Ph: (847)679-5500   Fax: (847)679-2494
Fr: 800-323-4900

Elmo I. Ellis. 1994. $14.95; $11.95 (paper). Discusses opportunities and job search techniques in broadcasting, television, and radio. Illustrated.

★977★ Opportunities in Cable Television Careers

VGM Career Horizons
4255 W. Touhy Ave.
Lincolnwood, IL 60646-1975
Ph: (847)679-5500   Fax: (847)679-2494
Fr: 800-323-4900

Jan Bone. 1993. $14.95; $11.95 (paper). 160 pages. Focuses on what the jobs are, where they are, and how to get them. Illustrated.

★978★ Opportunities in Television and Video Careers

VGM Career Horizons
4255 W. Touhy Ave.
Lincolnwood, IL 60646-1975
Ph: (847)679-5500   Fax: (847)679-2494
Fr: 800-323-4900

Shonan Noronha. 1993. $14.95; $11.95 (paper). Details the employment opportunities open in television, cable, corporate video, institutional and government media, including independent production, and discusses how to land a job. Illustrated.

★979★ Radio and Television Career Directory

Gale Research
835 Penobscot Bldg.
Detroit, MI 48226-4094
Ph: (313)961-2242   Fax: (313)961-6083
Fr: 800-877-GALE

Bradley Morgan. Second edition, 1993. $39.00. 334 pages. Features extensive listings of contacts and entry-level job opportunities. Provides information on internships and sources of help-wanted ads.

OTHER SOURCES

★980★ Corporation for Public Broadcasting (CPB)

901 E St. NW
Washington, DC 20004-2037
Ph: (202)879-9600   Fax: (202)783-1019

A private, nonprofit corporation authorized under Public Broadcasting Act of 1967. Funded by U.S. government. **Purpose:** To promote and finance the growth and development of noncommercial radio and television. Makes grants to local public television and radio stations, program producers, and regional networks; studies emerging technologies; works to provide adequate long-range financing from the U.S. government and other sources for public broadcasting.

★981★ Country Radio Broadcasters (CRB)

PO Box 120429
Nashville, TN 37212
Ph: (615)327-4487   Fax: (615)329-4492

Members: Country radio station owners, managers, and program and music directors. **Activities:** Conducts charitable and educational programs.

★982★ Guide to Volunteer and Internship Programs in Public Broadcasting

Corporation for Public Broadcasting
Publications Dept.
901 E St. NW
Washington, DC 20004-2037
Ph: (202)879-9600

1991. Free.

★983★ National Association of Black Owned Broadcasters (NABOB)

1333 New Hampshire Ave., N.W., Ste. 1000
Washington, DC 20036
Ph: (202)463-8970   Fax: (202)429-0657

Members: Black broadcast station owners; black formatted stations not currently owned or controlled by blacks; organizations having an interest in the black consumer market or black broadcast industry; individuals interested in becoming owners; and communications schools, departments, and professional groups and associations. **Purpose:** Represents the interests of existing and potential black radio and television stations. Is currently working with the Office of Federal Procurement Policy to determine which government contracting major advertisers and advertising agencies are complying with government initiatives to increase the amount of advertising dollars received by minority-owned firms. Conducts lobbying activities; provides legal representation for the protection of minority ownership policies. Participates in the reorganization of the Advisory Committee on Radio Broadcasting. Sponsors annual Communications Awards Dinner each March. Conducts workshops; compiles statistics.

★984★ National Cable Television Association (NCTA)

1724 Massachusetts Ave. NW
Washington, DC 20036
Ph: (202)775-3550   Fax: (202)775-3695

Members: Franchised cable operators, programmers, and cable networks; associate members are cable hardware suppliers and distributors; affiliate members are brokerage and law firms and financial institutions; state and regional cable television associations cooperate, but are not affiliated, with NCTA. **Purpose:** Serves as national medium for exchange of experiences and opinions through research, study, discussion, and publications. Represents the cable industry before Congress, the Federal Communications Commission, and various courts on issues of primary importance. **Activities:** Conducts research program in conjunction with National Academy of Cable Programming. Sponsors, in conjunction with Motion Picture Association of America, the Coalition Opposing Signal Theft, an organization designed to deter cable signal theft and to develop antipiracy materials. Provides promotional aids and information on legal, legis-lative, and regulatory matters. Compiles statistics.

★985★ Society of Broadcast Engineers (SBE)

8445 Keystone Crossing, Ste. 140
Indianapolis, IN 46240
Ph: (317)253-1640   Fax: (317)253-0418

Members: Broadcast engineers, students, and broadcast professionals in closely allied fields. **Purpose:** Promotes professional abilities of members and provides information exchange. **Activities:** Provides support to local chapters. Maintains certification program; represents members' interests before the Federal Communications Commission and other governmental and industrial groups.

★986★ Student Guide to Mass Media Internships

Intern Research Group
Box 52, Regent Hall
University of Colorado
Boulder, CO 80309
Ph: (303)442-8340

Annual, latest edition 1995. $35.00, payment with order; $40.00, billed. Covers about 10,000 internships offered by 2,700 newspapers, radio and television stations, cable television companies, magazines, advertising agencies, and other firms. Entries include: Organization name, address, type and number of internships offered, eligibility requirements, application deadline, salary or other stipend offered, name and title of contact; many listings also include description of intern's duties. Arrangement: Classified by type of medium, then geographical.

★987★ Women in Cable & Telecommunications (WIC)

230 W. Monroe St., Ste. 730
Chicago, IL 60606-4702
Ph: (312)634-2330   Fax: (312)634-2345
Fr: 800-628-WICT

Members: Individuals engaged in professional activity in cable and telecommunications. **Purpose:** Through leadership, education, and advocacy, works to empower women in cable and telecommunications to achieve their economic, professional, and personal goals while influencing the future of the industries they serve. **Activities:** Provides educational programs.

Carpenters

SOURCES OF HELP-WANTED ADS

★988★ Builder

Hanley-Wood, Inc.
1 Thomas Cir., Ste. 600
Washington, DC 20005
Ph: (202)452-0800   Fax: (202)785-1974

Monthly. $29.95/year for individuals. Magazine covering housing, commercial, and industrial building.

★989★ Cabinet Manufacturing & Fabricating

PTN Publications
2 University Plaza, Ste. 11
Hackensack, NJ 07601
Ph: (201)487-7800   Fax: (201)487-1061

Monthly.

★990★ Construction Digest

Construction Magazine Group, Inc.
PO Box 6132
Indianapolis, IN 46206-6132
Ph: (317)329-3100   Fax: (317)329-3110
Fr: 800-860-3105

Semimonthly. $3.00 for single issue. Magazine for the public works and construction engineering industries.

★991★ CONSTRUCTOR

Associated General Contractors
  Information
1957 E St. NW
Washington, DC 20006-5199
Ph: (202)393-2040   Fax: (202)628-7369

Monthly. $15.00/year for members; $4.00 for single issue.

★992★ Kitchen and Bath Design News

PTN Publications
2 University Plaza, Ste. 11
Hackensack, NJ 07601
Ph: (201)487-7800   Fax: (201)487-1061

Monthly.

★993★ Professional Builder

Cahners Publishing Co.
1350 E. Touhy Ave.
PO Box 5080
Des Plaines, IL 60018-5080
Ph: (708)635-8800   Fax: (708)635-9950

Monthly. $10.00 for single issue; $139.95/year by mail.

★994★ Summer Jobs: Opportunities in the Federal Government

Office of Personnel Management
1900 E St. NW
Washington, DC 20415
Ph: (202)606-0950

Formerly annual; latest edition January 1993; suspended indefinitely. Free. Covers GS-1 through GS-4 clerical jobs and other jobs at GS-5 and above which are expected to be available in federal agencies and departments throughout the United States during the season. Most jobs are in Metropolitan Washington, D.C. Latest application date is generally April 15; many are earlier. Includes general information on applying for jobs in trades and labor occupations and summer employment for needy youth programs. Entries include: Agency name, filing deadline, titles of jobs available, brief information on qualifications needed, location, etc. Complete agency names and addresses are given in separate list. Publication is available from Federal Employment Information Center offices and agency personnel offices. Arrangement: By job level, then alphabetical by agency name.

★995★ Tradeswomen

Tradeswomen, Inc.
PO Box 2622
Berkeley, CA 94702
Ph: (510)649-6260

Bimonthly. $35.00/year. Subtitled: "A Quarterly Magazine for Women in Blue Collar Work". Reports activities of the organization and other events in the California Bay Area and of national interest to women working or wishing to work in nontraditional and blue collar jobs. Recurring features include announcements of apprenticeship opportunities and job openings, information on unions and government agencies, and U.S. Department of Labor statistics.

★996★ World Fence News

World Fence & Data Center
6101 W. Courtyard Dr.
Bldg. 3 Ste.115
Austin, TX 78730
Ph: (512)349-2536   Fax: (512)349-2567
Fr: 800-231-0275

Monthly. Trade magazine featuring news, technical articles, new products, and humor for fencing and access control industries.

PLACEMENT AND JOB REFERRAL SERVICES

★997★ Associated Builders and Contractors (ABC)

1300 N. 17th St.
Rosslyn, VA 22209
Ph: (703)812-2000   Fax: (703)812-8200

Members: Construction contractors, subcontractors, suppliers, and associates. **Purpose:** Aim is to foster and perpetuate the principles of rewarding construction workers and management on the basis of merit. **Activities:** Maintains placement service. Sponsors management education programs and craft training; also sponsors apprenticeship and skill training programs. Disseminates technological and labor relations information. Compiles statistics.

★998★ National Association of Home Builders of the U.S. (NAHB)

1201 15th St. NW
Washington, DC 20005
Ph: (202)822-0200   Fax: (202)822-0559

Members: Single and multifamily home builders, commercial builders, and others associated with the building industry. **Purpose:** Lobbies on behalf of the housing industry and conducts public affairs activities to increase public understanding of housing and the economy. Collects and disseminates data on current developments in home building and home builders' plans through its Economics Department and nationwide Metropolitan Housing Forecast. **Activities:** Maintains NAHB Research Center, which functions as the research arm of the home building industry. Sponsors seminars and workshops on construction, mortgage credit, labor relations, cost reduction, land use, remodeling, and business management. Compiles statistics; offers charitable program, spokesman training, and placement service; maintains speakers' bureau, and hall of fame.

EMPLOYER DIRECTORIES AND NETWORKING LISTS

★999★ ABC Today—Associated Builders and Contractors Membership Directory Issue

Associated Builders and Contractors
1300 N. 17th St.
Rosslyn, VA 22209
Ph: (703)812-2000   Fax: (703)812-8200

Annual, November. $150.00, plus $7.00 shipping. Publication includes: List of approximately 17,000 member construction contractors and suppliers. Entries include: Company name, address, phone, name of principal executive, code to volume of business, business specialty. Arrangement: Classified by chapter, then by work specialty.

★1000★ Cabinet Makers Directory

American Business Directories, Inc.
American Business Information, Inc.
5711 S. 86th Cir.
Omaha, NE 68127
Ph: (402)593-4600   Fax: (402)331-1505

Annual. $1,270.00, U.S. edition. Number of listings: 17,771 (U.S. edition); 3,265 (Canadian edition). Entries include: Name, address, phone (including area code), size of advertisement, year first in Yellow Pages, name of owner or manager, number of employees. Compiled from telephone company Yellow Pages, nationwide. Arrangement: Geographical.

★1001★ Carpenters Directory

American Business Directories, Inc.
American Business Information, Inc.
5711 S. 86th Cir.
Omaha, NE 68127
Ph: (402)593-4600   Fax: (402)331-1505

Annual. $460.00, U.S. edition. Entries include: Name, address, phone (including area code), size of advertisement, year first in Yellow Pages, name of owner or manager, number of employees. Compiled from telephone company Yellow Pages, nationwide. Arrangement: Geographical.

★1002★ Constructor—Directory of Membership and Services Issue

AGC Information, Inc.
Associated General Contractors of America
1957 E St. NW
Washington, DC 20006
Ph: (202)393-2040   Fax: (202)347-4004

Annual, July. $135.00. Publication includes: List of more than 8,500 member firms and 9,000 national associate member firms engaged in building, highway, heavy, industrial,

municipal utilities, and railroad construction, listing of state and local chapter officers. Arrangement: Geographical. Indexes: Company name.

★1003★ ENR—Top 400 Construction Contractors Issue

McGraw-Hill, Inc.
1221 Ave. of the Americas
New York, NY 10020
Ph: (212)512-4635   Fax: (212)512-2820

Annual, May issue of Engineering News Record. $10.00, Reprint, payment with order. Publication includes: List of 400 United States contractors receiving largest dollar volumes of contracts in preceding calendar year. Separate lists of 50 largest design/construct management firms; 50 largest program and construction managers; 25 building contractors; 25 heavy contractors. Entries include: Company name, headquarters location, total value of contracts received in preceding year, value of foreign contracts, countries in which operated, construction specialities. Arrangement: By total value of contracts received.

★1004★ Woodworkers Directory

American Business Directories, Inc.
American Business Information, Inc.
5711 S. 86th Cir.
Omaha, NE 68127
Ph: (402)593-4600   Fax: (402)331-1505

Annual. $465.00, U.S. edition. Number of listings: 6,179 (U.S. edition); 1,406 (Canadian edition). Entries include: Name, address, phone (including area code), size of advertisement, year first in Yellow Pages, name of owner or manager, number of employees. Compiled from telephone company Yellow Pages, nationwide. Arrangement: Geographical.

HANDBOOKS AND MANUALS

★1005★ Exploring Careers in the Construction Industry

Rosen Publishing Group
29 E. 21st St.
New York, NY 10010
Ph: (212)777-3017   Fax: (212)777-0277
Fr: 800-237-9932

Elizabeth Stewart Lytle. 1992. $14.95.

★1006★ Exploring Nontraditional Jobs for Women

Rosen Publishing Group, Inc.
29 E. 21st St.
New York, NY 10010
Ph: (212)777-3017   Fax: (212)777-0277
Fr: 800-237-9932

Rose Neufeld. 1989. $14.95. Describes occupations where few women are found. Covers job duties, training routes, where to apply for jobs, tools used, salary, and advantages and disadvantages of the job.

★1007★ Opportunities in Building Construction Trades

VGM Career Horizons
4255 W. Touhy Ave.
Lincolnwood, IL 60646-1975
Ph: (847)679-5500   Fax: (847)679-2494
Fr: 800-323-4900

Michael Sumichrast. 1993. $14.95; $11.95 (paper). From custom builder to rehabber, the many kinds of companies that employ craftspeople and contractors are explored. Includes job descriptions, requirements, and salaries for dozens of specialties within the construction industry. Contains a complete list of Bureau of Apprenticeship and Training state and area offices. Illustrated.

★1008★ Opportunities in Carpentry Careers

VGM Career Horizons
4255 W. Touhy Ave.
Lincolnwood, IL 60646-1975
Ph: (847)679-5500   Fax: (847)679-2494
Fr: 800-323-4900

Roger Sheldon. 1993. $14.95; $11.95 (paper). 160 pages. Discusses how to get started and covers the job market. Illustrated.

★1009★ Opportunities in Crafts Careers

VGM Career Horizons
4255 W. Touhy Ave.
Lincolnwood, IL 60646-1975
Ph: (847)679-5500   Fax: (847)679-2494
Fr: 800-323-4900

Marianne Munday. 1993. $14.95; $11.95 (paper). 160 pages. Provides information about careers and job opportunities in such areas as fine and applied arts, antiques and collectibles, ceramics, woodworking, sewing and needlecraft, and more. Illustrated.

OTHER SOURCES

★1010★ Associated General Contractors of America (AGC)

1957 E St. NW
Washington, DC 20006
Ph: (202)393-2040   Fax: (202)347-4004

Members: General construction contractors; subcontractors; industry suppliers; service firms. **Purpose:** Provides market services through its divisions. Conducts special conferences and seminars designed specifically for construction firms. Compiles statistics on job accidents reported by member firms. Maintains 65 committees, including joint cooperative committees with other associations and liaison committees with federal agencies.

★1011★ Associated Specialty Contractors (ASC)

3 Bethesda Metro Ctr., Ste. 1100
Bethesda, MD 20814
Ph: (301)657-3110   Fax: (301)215-4500

Members: Subcontractor associations with a total of 25,000 members representing electrical, heating, piping, mechanical, air conditioning, sheet metal, plumbing, ventilating, masonry, painting and decorating, and roofing and insulation contractors. **Purpose:** Promotes liaison with general contractors, architects, and engineers on inter-industry matters, codes, bidding, and contracting procedures. Coordinates governmental affairs, research, and educational matters.

★1012★ COIN Career Guidance System
COIN Educational Products
3361 Executive Pky., Ste. 302
Toledo, OH 43606
Ph: (419)536-5353   Fr: 800-274-8515

CD-ROM product; also available on diskette. Provides career information through seven cross-referenced files covering postsecondary schools, college majors, vocational programs, military service, apprenticeship programs, financial aid, and scholarships. Apprenticeship file describes national apprenticeship training programs, including information on how to apply, contact agencies, and program content. Military file describes more than 200 military occupations and training opportunities related to civilian employment.

★1013★ National Association of Women in Construction (NAWIC)
327 S. Adams St.
Fort Worth, TX 76104
Ph: (817)877-5551   Fax: (817)877-0324
Fr: 800-552-3506

Purpose: NAWIC is an international association of women employed in the construction industry which promotes that industry and supports the advancement of women within it.

★1014★ Tradeswomen, Inc.
PO Box 40664 B
San Francisco, CA 94140
Ph: (415)821-7334   Fax: (415)861-8969

Members: Women who work in nontraditional, blue-collar occupations including construction, transportation, and industrial work; women who seek to enter these fields or who support the right of others to do so. **Purpose:** Serves as a network for women in the trades. Conducts social gatherings and local and regional forums on topics such as: health and safety on the job; racism and sexism in the trades; sexual harassment; working within unions. Makes available children's services; maintains speakers' bureau. Compiles statistics.

★1015★ WIT
Northern New England Tradeswomen
26 Railroad St.
St. Johnsbury, VT 05819
Ph: (802)748-3308   Fax: (802)748-1768

Quarterly. Included in membership; $10.00/year for nonmembers. Provides a network of support, information, and skill sharing for women in trade professions.

Caterers

SOURCES OF HELP-WANTED ADS

★1016★ Modern Food Service News

Grocers Publishing Co., Inc.
15 Emerald St.
Hackensack, NJ 07601
Ph: (201)488-1800

Monthly. Magazine for restaurateurs, chefs, caterers, purchasing agents in the food service industry.

★1017★ Restaurant Business

Bill Communications, Inc.
355 Park Ave. S
New York, NY 10010-1789
Ph: (212)592-6200   Fax: (212)592-6309
Fr: 800-821-6897

Trade magazine for restaurants and commercial food service.

PLACEMENT AND JOB REFERRAL SERVICES

★1018★ Inflight Food Service Association (IFSA)

304 W. Liberty St., Ste. 201
Louisville, KY 40202
Ph: (502)583-3783   Fax: (502)589-3602

Members: Airline companies and airline catering companies. **Purpose:** Seeks to resolve mutual problems and achieve a greater uniformity in standards and policies between airlines and inflight caterers. Promotes the enactment of laws, ordinances, rules, and regulations advantageous to inflight catering operations. **Activities:** Maintains placement service. Prepares studies, gathers data, and provides an open forum for resolving technical and operational problems.

★1019★ Les Amis d'Escoffier

1230 Main St.
Leicester, MA 01524
Ph: (508)892-8000

Members: An educational organization of professionals in the food and wine industries. **Activities:** Maintains museum, speakers' bureau, hall of fame, and placement service. Sponsors charitable programs.

EMPLOYER DIRECTORIES AND NETWORKING LISTS

★1020★ Caterers Directory

American Business Directories, Inc.
American Business Information, Inc.
5711 S. 86th Cir.
Omaha, NE 68127
Ph: (402)593-4600   Fax: (402)331-1505

Annual. $1,495.00, U.S. edition; $360.00, (Canadian edition); payment with order. Entries include: Company name, address, and phone (including area code), size of advertisement, year first in Yellow Pages, name of owner or manager, number of employees. Regional editions also available: Eastern, $945.00; Western, $610.00. Compiled from telephone company Yellow Pages, nationwide. Arrangement: Geographical.

★1021★ Directory of Chain Restaurant Operators

Chain Store Guide Information Services
3922 Coconut Palm Dr.
Tampa, FL 33619
Ph: (813)664-6700   Fax: 800-846-8047
Fr: 800-927-9292

Annual, June. $290.00. Covers over 4,000 3-or-more unit chain restaurant firms operating or franchising over nearly 200,000 restaurants, drive-ins, cafeterias, restaurants in hotels and motels, contract feeders, industrial caterers, and leased units in retail stores; includes hotel and motel chains operating food service units. Entries include: Company name, address, phone, fax, numbers of units company-owned and franchised, store names, whether private or public ownership, executive names, type of menus, type of

food service, sales, territory, ownership, whether alcoholic beverages are served, year established. Also available in state editions. Arrangement: Geographical. Indexes: Type of menu, type of food service; top 100 ranked by sales, standard complete file index.

★1022★ Party Planning Service Directory

American Business Directories, Inc.
American Business Information, Inc.
5711 S. 86th Cir.
Omaha, NE 68127
Ph: (402)593-4600   Fax: (402)331-1505

Annual. $460.00, U.S. edition. Entries include: Name, address, phone (including area code), size of advertisement, year first in Yellow Pages, name of owner or manager, number of employees. Compiled from telephone company Yellow Pages, nationwide. Arrangement: Geographical.

HANDBOOKS AND MANUALS

★1023★ The Best Home-Based Businesses for the 90s

G.P. Putnam's Sons
Putnam Berkley Group
200 Madison Ave.
New York, NY 10016
Ph: (212)951-8400   Fr: 800-631-8571

Paul Edwards and Sarah Edwards. Second edition, 1994. $12.95. 400 pages. Profiles 95 businesses and careers that can be conducted from one's home. Lists sources of additional information.

★1024★ Breaking into the Catering Business

Carol Publishing Group
600 Madison Ave., 11th Fl.
New York, NY 10022
Ph: (212)486-2200   Fax: (212)486-2231

Kara Levine. 1994. $8.95.

★1025★ Career Opportunities in the Food and Beverage Industry

Facts on File, Inc.
11 Penn Plaza, 15th Fl.
New York, NY 10001-2006
Ph: (212)967-8800   Fax: 800-678-3633
Fr: 800-322-8755

Barbara Sims-Bell. 1994. $29.95; $15.95 (paper). 256 pages. Provides the job seeker with information about locating and landing 80 skilled and unskilled jobs in the industry. Includes detailed job descriptions for many specific positions and lists trade associations, recruiting organizations, and major agencies. Contains index and bibliography.

★1026★ Careers for Gourmets and Others Who Relish Food

VGM Career Horizons
4255 W. Touhy Ave.
Lincolnwood, IL 60646-1975
Ph: (847)679-5500   Fax: (847)679-2494
Fr: 800-323-4900

Mary Donovan. 1993. $14.95; $9.95 (paper). 158 pages. Discusses such job prospects as foods columnist, cookbook writer, test kitchen worker, pastry chef, recipe developer, food festival organizer, restaurant manager, and food stylist.

★1027★ Careers in the Restaurant Industry

Rosen Publishing Group, Inc.
29 E. 21st St.
New York, NY 10010
Ph: (212)777-3017   Fax: (212)777-0277
Fr: 800-237-9932

Richard S. Lee and Mary Price Lee. 1990. $14.95. 160 pages. Explores various jobs in the restaurant industry. Describes job duties, salaries, educational preparation, and job hunting. Contains information about fast food, catering, and small businesses.

★1028★ Careers and Training in Hotels, Catering, and Journalism

Butterworth-Heinemann
313 Washington St.
Newton, MA 02158
Ph: (617)928-2500   Fax: (617)928-2620
Fr: 800-366-2665

Hayler. 1993. $32.95.

★1029★ Caterers

Chronicle Guidance Publications, Inc.
66 Aurora St.
PO Box 1190
Moravia, NY 13118-1190
Ph: (315)497-0330   Fax: (315)497-3359
Fr: 800-622-7284

Chronicle Guidance Staff. 1992. $2.00. Provides concise career information and sources of additional information.

★1030★ Catering Service Business Possibility Encyclopedia

Prosperity & Profits Unlimited Distribution Services
PO Box 416
Denver, CO 80201
Ph: (303)575-5676

1991. $59.95 (ringbound).

★1031★ The Complete Caterer: A Practical Guide to the Craft and Business of Catering

Doubleday & Co., Inc.
1540 Broadway
New York, NY 10036-4094
Ph: (212)354-6500   Fax: (212)492-9700
Fr: 800-223-6834

Elizabeth Lawrence. 1992. $15.00 (paper).

★1032★ Dictionary of Hotels, Tourism, and Catering Management

IBD Ltd.
24 Hudson St.
Kinderhook, NY 12106
Ph: (518)758-1959   Fax: (518)758-1959
Fr: 800-343-3531

1994. $16.95 (paper).

★1033★ Encyclopedia of Careers and Vocational Guidance

J. G. Ferguson Publishing Co.
200 W. Monroe, Ste. 250
Chicago, IL 60606
Ph: (312)580-5480

William E. Hopke. Ninth edition, 1993. $129.95; $199.95 (CD-ROM). Four-volume set that profiles 900 occupations and describes job trends in 71 industries. Includes career description, educational requirements, history of the job, methods of entry, advancement, employment outlook, earnings, conditions of work, social and psychological factors, and sources of further information. Contains career and employment information for this field.

★1034★ Food Service Supervisors

Chronicle Guidance Publications, Inc.
66 Aurora St.
PO Box 1190
Moravia, NY 13118-1190
Ph: (315)497-0330   Fax: (315)497-3359
Fr: 800-622-7284

Chronicle Guidance Staff. 1993. $2.00. Provides concise career information and sources of additional information.

★1035★ How to Open and Operate a Home-Based Catering Business

New Careers Center
1515 23rd St.
Box 339-CT
Boulder, CO 80306
Ph: (303)447-1087

Denise Vivaldo. 1993. $15.95. Written by a successful homebased caterer.

★1036★ 100 Best Careers for the Year 2000

Prentice Hall General Reference
15 Columbus Cir.
New York, NY 10023
Ph: (212)373-8500   Fr: 800-223-2348

Shelly Field. 1992. $15.00 (paper). Covers 100 of the fastest growing jobs. The publication is divided into 11 general employment sections. Specific careers are covered within each section. Provides job description, responsibilities, employment opportunities, earnings, education and training, advancement opportunities, and experience and qualifications for each occupation.

★1037★ Opportunities in Culinary Careers

VGM Career Horizons
4255 W. Touhy Ave.
Lincolnwood, IL 60646-1975
Ph: (847)679-5500   Fax: (847)679-2494
Fr: 800-323-4900

Mary Deirdre Donovan. 1990. $14.95; $11.95 (paper). 160 pages. Describes the educational preparation and training of chefs and cooks and explores a variety of food service jobs in restaurants, institutions, and research and development. Lists major culinary professional associations and schools. Offers guidance on landing a first job in cooking and related fields.

★1038★ Opportunities in Food Service Careers

VGM Career Horizons
4255 W. Touhy Ave.
Lincolnwood, IL 60646-1975
Ph: (847)679-5500   Fax: (847)679-2494
Fr: 800-323-4900

Carol Caprione. 1992. $14.95; $11.95 (paper). 160 pages. Discusses how to secure employment and provides information on identifying openings, resume writing, and interviewing. Lists recruiters and associations to contact for further information and leads. Illustrated.

★1039★ Opportunities in Restaurant Careers

VGM Career Horizons
4255 W. Touhy Ave.
Lincolnwood, IL 60646-1975
Ph: (847)679-5500   Fax: (847)679-2494
Fr: 800-323-4900

Carol Caprione Chmelynski. 1992. $14.95; $11.95 (paper). Covers opportunities in the food service industry and details salaries, benefits, training opportunities, and professional associations. Special emphasis is put on becoming a successful restaurant manager by working up through the ranks. Illustrated.

★1040★ Start and Run a Profitable Catering Business

Self-Counsel Press
1704 N. State St.
Bellingham, WA 98225
Ph: (360)676-4530   Fr: 800-663-3007

George Erdosh. 1994. $14.95. 168 pages.

★1041★ Working in Hotels and Catering

Routledge
29 W. 35th St.
New York, NY 10001-2299
Ph: (212)244-3336   Fax: 800-248-4724

Roy C. Wood. 1992. $79.95.

Other Sources

★1042★ The Complete Off-Premise Caterer

Van Nostrand Reinhold
115 Fifth Ave.
New York, NY 10003
Ph: (212)254-3232

Judy Lieberman. Second edition, 1996. $49.95. Includes recipes plus marketing, sales, and pricing strategies.

★1043★ Council on Hotel, Restaurant, and Institutional Education (CHRIE)

1200 17th St. NW
Washington, DC 20036-3097
Ph: (202)331-5990   Fax: (202)785-2511

Purpose: Schools and colleges offering specialized education and training in cooking, baking, tourism and hotel, restaurant, and institutional administration; individuals, executives, and students. **Activities:** Provides networking opportunities and professional development. Sponsors competitions.

★1044★ International Association of Culinary Professionals (IACP)

304 W. Liberty St., Ste. 201
Louisville, KY 40202
Ph: (502)581-9786   Fax: (502)589-3602

Members: Cooking school owners, food writers, chefs, caterers, culinary specialists, directors, teachers, cookbook authors, food stylists, food photographers, student/apprentices, and individuals in related industries in 20 countries. **Purpose:** Objectives are to: promote the interests of cooking schools, teachers, and culinary professionals; encourage the exchange of information and education; promote professional standards and accreditation procedures. **Activities:** Maintains IACP Foundation to award culinary scholarships and grants. Holds regional seminars.

★1045★ National Restaurant Association (NRA)

1200 17th St. NW
Washington, DC 20036
Ph: (202)331-5900   Fax: (202)331-2429

Members: Restaurants, cafeterias, clubs, contract foodservice management, drive-ins, caterers, institutional food services, and other members of the foodservice industry; also represents establishments belonging to nonaffiliated state and local restaurant associations in governmental affairs. **Purpose:** Supports foodservice education and research in several educational institutions; conducts traveling management courses and seminars for restaurant personnel. Affiliated with the Educational Foundation of the National Restaurant Association to provide training and education for operators, food and equipment manufacturers, distributors, and educators. Offers waiter/waitress training programs. Conducts the Great Menu Contest.

★1046★ Personnel Resources (PR)

PO Box 4498
4131 N. Broad St.
Philadelphia, PA 19140
Ph: (215)324-3821

Purpose: Agency for upgrading human services careers "to an economic level of decency and dignity." Provides training and fieldwork in personal, professional, social, and skill development; provides medical screening and supervised follow-up remedial health care for trainees; acquaints trainees with varied community and cultural enrichment resources; offers educational seminars for employers and field work supervisors and postgraduate counseling for employees and employers. Has worked towards changing community attitudes about working conditions, job standards, personnel practices, compliance with Social Security laws, and salary upgrading. Future goals lie in the areas of legislation, day care group homes, solutions to transportation problems, union affiliation, group insurance coverage, and a national training center to provide training experiences for those interested in beginning similar programs. Offers guidance on other vocations such as caterers, pet and plant sitters, tour guides, and vacation parents.

★1047★ Professional Caterer

Van Nostrand Reinhold
115 Fifth Ave.
New York, NY 10003
Ph: (212)254-3232

Denis Ruffel. 1990. Four volumes. $229.95/set. $59.95/vol.

★1048★ Successful Catering

Van Nostrand Reinhold Co
115 5th Ave., 4th Fl.
New York, NY 10003
Ph: (212)254-3232   Fax: (212)254-9499
Fr: 800-926-2665

Bernard Splaver. Third edition, 1991. $44.95. A guide to the catering industry that covers costs, legalitites, and the requirements of starting a business.

Chefs and Cooks

SOURCES OF HELP-WANTED ADS

★1049★ Chef

Talcott Communications Corp.
20 N. Wacker Dr., Ste. 3230
Chicago, IL 60606
Ph: (312)849-2220   Fax: (312)849-2174
Fr: 800-229-1967

$20.00/year for individuals; $2.95 for single issue. Covers the food service field for executive chefs.

★1050★ Hotel & Motel Management

Advanstar Communications, Inc.
7600 Old Oak Blvd.
Cleveland, OH 44130
Ph: (216)243-8100   Fax: (216)891-2733

Magazine (tabloid) covering the global lodging industry.

★1051★ Midwest Foodservice News

Metropolitan Publishing Services
PO Box 596
Worthington, OH 43085
Ph: (614)848-6151   Fax: (614)888-7695

Bimonthly. Restaurant trade newspaper featuring new products and suppliers and other industry news including food news, restaurant association updates, news of chefs, restaurant concepts, earnings, and openings and closings.

★1052★ Nation's Restaurant News

Lebhar-Friedman, Inc.
425 Park Ave.
New York, NY 10022
Ph: (212)756-5257   Fax: (212)756-5270

Weekly (Mon.). $34.50/year for individuals.

★1053★ Restaurant Business

Bill Communications, Inc.
355 Park Ave. S
New York, NY 10010-1789
Ph: (212)592-6200   Fax: (212)592-6309
Fr: 800-821-6897

Trade magazine for restaurants and commercial food service.

★1054★ Restaurant Hospitality

1100 Superior Ave.
Cleveland, OH 44114
Ph: (216)696-7000

Monthly. $60.00/year; $5.25/issue.

★1055★ Restaurants & Institutions

Cahners Publishing Co.
1350 E. Touhy Ave.
Des Plaines, IL 60018
Ph: (708)635-8800   Fax: (708)390-2770

Semimonthly. $99.95/year for individuals. Magazine focusing on foodservice and lodging management.

PLACEMENT AND JOB REFERRAL SERVICES

★1056★ Chefs de Cuisine Association of America (CCAA)

155 E. 55th St., Ste. 302B
New York, NY 10022
Ph: (212)832-4939   Fax: (212)832-4939

Members: Professional executive chefs; chefs who own restaurants; pastry chefs for hotels, clubs, and restaurants. **Activities:** Maintains 350 volume library and placement service for members.

★1057★ Les Amis d'Escoffier

1230 Main St.
Leicester, MA 01524
Ph: (508)892-8000

Members: An educational organization of professionals in the food and wine industries. **Activities:** Maintains museum, speakers' bureau, hall of fame, and placement service. Sponsors charitable programs.

EMPLOYER DIRECTORIES AND NETWORKING LISTS

★1058★ College/University Foodservice Who's Who

Information Central, Inc.
Box 3900
Prescott, AZ 86302
Ph: (602)778-1513   Fax: (602)445-6407

Triennial, latest edition January 1993; $255.00. Covers over 2,200 food service programs in colleges and universities. Entries include: Institution name, address, phone, enrollment, total annual food purchases, number of meals served per day; name of management company, principal food service official, services, fast food chains on campus. Arrangement: Geographical. Indexes: Alphabetical.

★1059★ Restaurant Hospitality—Hospitality 500 Issue

Penton Publishing Co.
1100 Superior Ave.
Cleveland, OH 44114
Ph: (216)696-7000   Fax: (216)696-0836

Annual, June. $25.00. Publication includes: 500 independent restaurants selected on basis of sales. Entries include: Restaurant name, city and state, total sales, cost of food sales, cost of beverage sales, cost of labor, number of employees, number of seats, average dinner check. Arrangement: Ranked by total sales. Indexes: Restaurant name.

★1060★ School Foodservice Who's Who

Information Central, Inc.
Box 3900
Prescott, AZ 86302
Ph: (602)778-1513   Fax: (602)445-6407

Triennial, latest edition January 1995. $285.00, per volume; $500.00, per two-volume set. Covers about 5,500 food service programs in public and Catholic school systems with enrollments in excess of 1,500 students. Separate listings of the biggest buyers (school districts reporting over $1.5 million in foodservice purchases), state school foodservice officials, and co-op buying groups and food management companies involved in food service. Entries include: School district name, address, phone, fax; food service budget, key food service executive, number of meals served daily, types of food and services, food management company, fast food brands. Arrangement: Geographical.

HANDBOOKS AND MANUALS

★1061★ **Becoming a Chef**
Van Nostrand Reinhold
115 5th Ave.
New York, NY 10003
Ph: (212)254-3232   Fax: (212)254-9499

A. Dornenburg. 1995. $29.95 (paper).

★1062★ **Career Opportunities in the Food and Beverage Industry**
Facts on File, Inc.
11 Penn Plaza, 15th Fl.
New York, NY 10001-2006
Ph: (212)967-8800   Fax: 800-678-3633
Fr: 800-322-8755

Barbara Sims-Bell. 1994. $29.95; $15.95 (paper). 256 pages. Provides the job seeker with information about locating and landing 80 skilled and unskilled jobs in the industry. Includes detailed job descriptions for many specific positions and lists trade associations, recruiting organizations, and major agencies. Contains index and bibliography.

★1063★ **Careers for Gourmets and Others Who Relish Food**
VGM Career Horizons
4255 W. Touhy Ave.
Lincolnwood, IL 60646-1975
Ph: (847)679-5500   Fax: (847)679-2494
Fr: 800-323-4900

Mary Donovan. 1993. $14.95; $9.95 (paper). 158 pages. Discusses such job prospects as foods columnist, cookbook writer, test kitchen worker, pastry chef, recipe developer, food festival organizer, restaurant manager, and food stylist.

★1064★ **Careers in the Restaurant Industry**
Rosen Publishing Group, Inc.
29 E. 21st St.
New York, NY 10010
Ph: (212)777-3017   Fax: (212)777-0277
Fr: 800-237-9932

Richard S. Lee and Mary Price Lee. 1990. $14.95. 160 pages. Explores various jobs in the restaurant industry. Describes job duties, salaries, educational preparation, and job hunting. Contains information about fast food, catering, and small businesses.

★1065★ **Flying High in Travel**
John Wiley and Sons
605 3rd Ave.
New York, NY 10158
Ph: (212)850-6000   Fr: 800-225-5945

Karen Rubin. Second edition, 1992. $19.95. 336 pages. A guide to careers and job hunting in the travel industry. Describes the many job opportunities available, from writing to hotel management to law. Includes information on educational preparation, training, and job hunting.

★1066★ **The Guide to Cooking Schools**
ShawGuides, Inc.
10 W. 66th St., Ste. 30H
New York, NY 10023
Ph: (212)799-6464

Dorlene V. Kaplan. 1995. $22.95. 337 pages. In addition to describing cooking school and travel programs, this work provides contact information for 122 approved culinary apprenticeship programs.

★1067★ **How to Get a Job with a Cruise Line**
Ticket to Adventure, Inc.
PO Box 41005
St. Petersburg, FL 33743
Ph: (813)544-6440   Fr: 800-929-7447

Mary Fallon Miller. Third edition, 1994. $14.95. 224 pages. Explores jobs with cruise ships, describing duties, responsibilities, benefits, and training. Lists cruise ship lines and schools offering cruise line training. Offers job hunting advice.

★1068★ **Opportunities in Culinary Careers**
VGM Career Horizons
4255 W. Touhy Ave.
Lincolnwood, IL 60646-1975
Ph: (847)679-5500   Fax: (847)679-2494
Fr: 800-323-4900

Mary Deirdre Donovan. 1990. $14.95; $11.95 (paper). 160 pages. Describes the educational preparation and training of chefs and cooks and explores a variety of food service jobs in restaurants, institutions, and research and development. Lists major culinary professional associations and schools. Offers guidance on landing a first job in cooking and related fields.

★1069★ **Opportunities in Fast Food Careers**
VGM Career Horizons
4255 W. Touhy Ave.
Lincolnwood, IL 60646-1975
Ph: (847)679-5500   Fax: (847)679-2494
Fr: 800-323-4900

Marjorie Eberts and Margaret Gisler. 1989. $14.95; $11.95 (paper). 160 pages. Details opportunities at local restaurants, restaurant chains, and in related support areas. Also contains information on acquiring and operating a franchise. Illustrated.

★1070★ **Opportunities in Food Service Careers**
VGM Career Horizons
4255 W. Touhy Ave.
Lincolnwood, IL 60646-1975
Ph: (847)679-5500   Fax: (847)679-2494
Fr: 800-323-4900

Carol Caprione. 1992. $14.95; $11.95 (paper). 160 pages. Discusses how to secure employment and provides information on identifying openings, resume writing, and interviewing. Lists recruiters and associa-tions to contact for further information and leads. Illustrated.

★1071★ **Opportunities in Hotel and Motel Careers**
VGM Career Horizons
4255 W. Touhy Ave.
Lincolnwood, IL 60646-1975
Ph: (847)679-5500   Fax: (847)679-2494
Fr: 800-323-4900

Shepard Henkin. 1992. $14.95; $11.95 (paper). 160 pages. A guide to planning for and seeking opportunities in this growing field. Illustrated.

★1072★ **Opportunities in Restaurant Careers**
VGM Career Horizons
4255 W. Touhy Ave.
Lincolnwood, IL 60646-1975
Ph: (847)679-5500   Fax: (847)679-2494
Fr: 800-323-4900

Carol Caprione Chmelynski. 1992. $14.95; $11.95 (paper). Covers opportunities in the food service industry and details salaries, benefits, training opportunities, and professional associations. Special emphasis is put on becoming a successful restaurant manager by working up through the ranks. Illustrated.

★1073★ **Opportunities in Vocational and Technical Careers**
VGM Career Horizons
4255 W. Touhy Ave.
Lincolnwood, IL 60646-1975
Ph: (847)679-5500   Fax: (847)679-2494
Fr: 800-323-4900

Adrian A. Paradis. 1992. $14.95; $11.95 (paper). 160 pages. Provides information on a variety of opportunities and advice on breaking into the field.

EMPLOYMENT AGENCIES AND SEARCH FIRMS

★1074★ **Grosse Pointe Employment**
18514 Mack Ave
Grosse Pointe Farms, MI 48236
Ph: (313)885-4576

Employment agency.

★1075★ **HRI Services Inc.**
150 Wood Rd., Ste. 303
Braintree, MA 02184
Ph: (617)848-9110

Employment agency.

★1076★ **Poston Personnel**
16 E. 79th St., Ste. G-4
New York, NY 10021
Ph: (212)535-4116   Fax: (212)988-7080

Employment agency.

OTHER SOURCES

★1077★ American Culinary Federation (ACF)

10 San Bartola Rd.
PO Box 3466
St. Augustine, FL 32085-3466
Ph: (904)824-4468   Fax: (904)825-4758

Members: State and local chapters of professional chefs. **Purpose:** Works to advance the culinary profession by sponsoring a continuing education program to keep members informed on food preparation and new equipment, apprenticeship training, and demonstrations for charitable and professional groups. **Activities:** Maintains the Educational Institute of the ACF which operates the National Apprenticeship Program for Cooks.

★1078★ Association for International Practical Training (AIPT)

10400 Little Patuxent Pky. Ste. 250
Columbia, MD 21044
Ph: (410)997-2200   Fax: (410)992-3924

Purpose: Helps coordinate training around the world in fields such as travel, the culinary arts, and hotel management. **Activities:** Conducts programs in career development and hospitality/tourism exchanges. Operates a student exchange program. Provides reciprocal practical training experience for recent graduates from the U.S., Austria, Germany, Finland, France, Hungary, Ireland, Japan, Malaysia, Netherlands, Switzerland, and the United Kingdom. Arranges training programs in the U.S. and abroad. Serves as U.S. affiliate to IAESTE (International Association for the Exchange of Students for Technical Experience) and operates a Professional Visitors Program to arrange short-term educational and training visits to the U.S. **E-Mail:** aipt@aipt.org

★1079★ Cooking Schools

Educational Travel
Marketing and Communications
Athabasca University
Athabasca, AB, Canada T0G 2R0
Ph: (403)675-6369   Fax: (403)675-6467

Biennial. $13.05. Covers schools and tours worldwide for people interested in cooking. Entries include: School name, address; description of specialties; class and tour dates and costs. Arrangement: Geographical.

★1080★ Council on Hotel, Restaurant, and Institutional Education (CHRIE)

1200 17th St. NW
Washington, DC 20036-3097
Ph: (202)331-5990   Fax: (202)785-2511

Purpose: Schools and colleges offering specialized education and training in cooking, baking, tourism and hotel, restaurant, and institutional administration; individuals, executives, and students. **Activities:** Provides networking opportunities and professional development. Sponsors competitions.

★1081★ International Association of Culinary Professionals (IACP)

304 W. Liberty St., Ste. 201
Louisville, KY 40202
Ph: (502)581-9786   Fax: (502)589-3602

Members: Cooking school owners, food writers, chefs, caterers, culinary specialists, directors, teachers, cookbook authors, food stylists, food photographers, student/apprentices, and individuals in related industries in 20 countries. **Purpose:** Objectives are to: promote the interests of cooking schools, teachers, and culinary professionals; encourage the exchange of information and education; promote professional standards and accreditation procedures. **Activities:** Maintains IACP Foundation to award culinary scholarships and grants. Holds regional seminars.

★1082★ Travel Agent

Prentice Hall
113 Sylvan Ave.
Rte. 9W
Englewood Cliffs, NJ 07632
Ph: (201)592-2000   Fr: 800-922-0579

Wilma Boyd. 1989. $14.95. 256 pages. Outlines entry-level positions in the airline, car rental, and hospitality industries as well as in travel agencies and related travel services. Explains travel agency operations, sales techniques, and the use of computers in travel services. Gives job hunting advice and sales tips.

Chemical Engineers

SOURCES OF HELP-WANTED ADS

★1083★ Analytical Chemistry
American Chemical Society
1155 16th St. NW
Washington, DC 20036
Ph: (202)872-4600   Fax: (202)872-6005
Fr: 800-227-5558

Biweekly. $33.00/year for members; $76.00/year for nonmembers. Journal covering measurement science.

★1084★ ASTM Standardization News
ASTM
1916 Race St.
Philadelphia, PA 19103
Ph: (215)299-5400   Fax: (215)299-5511

Monthly. Magazine publishing news on the testing and evaluation industry.

★1085★ Captsule Job Listings
Publications and Communications, Inc.
12416 Hymeadow Dr.
Austin, TX 78750
Ph: (512)250-9023   Fax: (512)331-3900
Fr: 800-678-9724

Online database. Lists current job openings in the contract (temporary) technical services industry. Includes the Action Hot List, which provides information on job seekers. Includes employment opportunities in technical/professional engineering, computing, and design/drafting. Entries generally contain company name, address, and job opening.

★1086★ Chemical Business
Schnell Publishing Co., Inc.
80 Broad St.
New York, NY 10004-2203
Ph: (212)248-4177   Fax: (212)248-4901

Monthly. Magazine covering important aspects of chemical industry management.

★1087★ Chemical Engineering
New York Construction News
1221 Avenue of the Americas, 41st Fl.
New York, NY 10020
Ph: (212)512-4773   Fax: (212)512-4770

Biweekly. Chemical process industries magazine.

★1088★ Chemical and Engineering News
American Chemical Society
1155 16th St. NW
Washington, DC 20036
Ph: (202)872-4600   Fax: (202)872-6005
Fr: 800-227-5558

Weekly. Free to qualified subscribers; $105.00/year for individuals. Chemical process industries trade journal.

★1089★ Chemical Engineering Progress
American Institute of Chemical Engineers
345 E. 47th St.
New York, NY 10017
Ph: (212)705-7576   Fax: (212)752-3294

Monthly. $60.00/year for individuals. Chemical process industries magazine.

★1090★ Chemical Equipment
Curpier/ Group Publishing
301 Gibraltar Dr.
PO Box 231
Cooperstown, NY 13326
Ph: (607)547-2591   Fax: (607)547-2923
Fr: 800-733-1284

Monthly. Tabloid on the chemical process industry.

★1091★ Chemical Week
Chemical Week Associates
888 7th Ave., 26th Fl.
New York, NY 10106
Ph: (212)621-4900   Fax: (212)621-4949

Weekly (Wed.). $99.00/year for individuals. Chemical process industries magazine.

★1092★ CHEMTECH
American Chemical Society
1155 16th St. NW
Washington, DC 20036
Ph: (202)872-4600   Fax: (202)872-6005
Fr: 800-227-5558

Monthly. $41.00/year for members; $75.00/year for nonmembers. Magazine for chemists and chemical engineers.

★1093★ Electrochemical Society Interface
The Electrochemical Society
10 S. Main St.
Pennington, NJ 08534
Ph: (609)737-1902   Fax: (609)737-2743

Quarterly. 40.00/year.

★1094★ Engineering Times
National Society of Professional Engineers
1420 King St.
Alexandria, VA 22314
Ph: (703)684-2875   Fax: (703)836-4875

Monthly. Magazine (tabloid) covering professional, legislative, and techology issues for an engineering audience.

★1095★ ENR: Engineering News Record
New York Construction News
1221 Avenue of the Americas
New York, NY 10020
Ph: (212)512-4773   Fax: (212)512-4770

Weekly. $42.00/year; $2.00/issue.

★1096★ Environmental Science & Technology
American Chemical Society
1155 16th St. NW
Washington, DC 20036
Ph: (202)872-4600   Fax: (202)872-4615

Monthly. $44.00/year for members; $90.00/year for nonmembers.

★1097★ High Technology Careers Magazine
HTC
4701 Patrick Henry Dr., No. 1901
Santa Clara, CA 95054
Ph: (408)970-8800   Fax: (408)980-5103

Bimonthly. Magazine (tabloid) containing employment opportunity information for the engineering and technical community.

★1098★ Minority Engineer

Equal Opportunity Publications, Inc.
150 Motor Pkwy., Ste. 420
Hauppauge, NY 11788-5145
Ph: (516)273-0066   Fax: (516)273-8936

Affirmative-action recruitment magazine serving college graduating and professional minority engineers.

★1099★ Modern Plastics

New York Construction News
1221 Avenue of the Americas, 41st Fl.
New York, NY 10020
Ph: (212)512-4773   Fax: (212)512-4770

Monthly. Magazine for the plastics industry.

★1100★ NSBE Magazine

NSBE Publications
1454 Duke St.
Alexandria, VA 22314
Ph: (703)549-2207   Fax: (703)683-5312

$10.00/year for individuals; $2.00 for single issue. Journal providing information on engineering careers, self-development, and cultural issues for recent graduates with technical majors.

★1101★ Plastics Compounding

Advanstar Communications, Inc.
859 Williamette St.
Eugene, OR 97401-6806
Ph: (503)343-1200   Fax: (503)687-5732

Bimonthly. Magazine on formulation, production, and compounding of plastics, resins, alloys, and blends.

★1102★ Plastics Design Forum

Advanstar Communications, Inc.
466 Southern Blvd.
PO Box 448
Chatham, NJ 07928
Ph: (201)514-1422   Fax: (201)514-1404

Bimonthly. Trade magazine on plastics design engineering.

★1103★ Plastics Engineering

Society of Plastics Engineers
14 Fairfield Dr.
PO Box 0403
Brookfield, CT 06804-0403
Ph: (203)775-0471   Fax: (203)775-8490

Monthly. $50.00/year for individuals; $80.00 for two years. Plastics trade magazine.

★1104★ Plastics News

Crain Communications, Inc.
1725 Merriman Rd., Ste. 300
Akron, OH 44313-5251
Ph: (216)836-9180   Fax: (216)836-2831

Weekly. Magazine (tabloid) for the plastics industry.

★1105★ Powder and Bulk Engineering

CSC Publishing, Inc.
1300 E. 66th St.
Minneapolis, MN 55423
Ph: (612)866-2242   Fax: (612)866-1939

Monthly.

★1106★ Power

New York Construction News
1221 Avenue of the Americas, 41st Fl.
New York, NY 10020
Ph: (212)512-4773   Fax: (212)512-4770

Monthly. Magazine for engineers in electric utilities, process and manufacturing plants, commercial and service establishments, and consulting, design, and construction engineering firms working in the power technology field.

★1107★ Rubber World

1867 W. Market St.
PO Box 5451
Akron, OH 44313
Ph: (216)864-2122   Fax: (216)864-5298

Monthly. Rubber manufacturing magazine.

★1108★ SWE

Society of Women Engineers
120 Wall St., 11th Fl.
New York, NY 10005-3902
Ph: (212)509-9577   Fax: (212)509-0224

Bimonthly. $30.00/year for nonmembers. Magazine for engineering students and for women and men working in the engineering and technology fields. Covers career guidance, continuing development and topical issues.

★1109★ Technology Review

The Tech
PO Box 397029
Cambridge, MA 02139
Ph: (617)253-1541   Fax: (617)258-8226

$30.00/year for individuals; $3.75 for single issue; $42.00/year for other countries. Magazine reviewing new developments in technology with an emphasis on economic, political, and social implications. Not a new product publication.

★1110★ Woman Engineer

Equal Opportunity Publications, Inc.
150 Motor Pkwy., Ste. 420
Hauppauge, NY 11788-5145
Ph: (516)273-0066   Fax: (516)273-8936

Engineer recruitment magazine.

PLACEMENT AND JOB REFERRAL SERVICES

★1111★ American Academy of Environmental Engineers (AAEE)

130 Holiday Ct., No. 100
Annapolis, MD 21401
Ph: (410)266-3311   Fax: (410)266-7653

Members: Environmentally oriented registered professional engineers certified by examination as diplomates of the academy. **Purpose:** Purposes are: to improve the standards of environmental engineering; to certify those with special knowledge of environmental engineering; to furnish lists of those certified to the public. **Activities:** Maintains speakers' bureau. Recognizes areas of specialization: Air Pollution Control; General En-

vironmental; Hazardous Waste Management; Industrial Hygiene; Radiation Protection; Solid Waste Management; Water Supply and Wastewater. Requires written and oral examinations for certification. Works with other professional organizations on environmentally oriented activities. Identifies potential employment candidates through Talent Search Service.

★1112★ American Chemical Society (ACS)

1155 16th St. NW
Washington, DC 20036
Ph: (202)872-4600   Fax: (202)872-4615
Fr: 800-227-5558

Members: Scientific and educational society of chemists and chemical engineers. **Activities:** Conducts: studies and surveys; special programs for disadvantaged persons; legislation monitoring, analysis, and reporting; courses for graduate chemists and chemical engineers; radio and television programming. Offers career guidance counseling; administers the Petroleum Research Fund and other grants and fellowship programs. Operates Employment Clearing Houses. Compiles statistics. Maintains 33 divisions. **E-Mail:** mem info@acs.org

★1113★ American Indian Science and Engineering Society (AISES)

1630 30th St., Ste. 301
Boulder, CO 80301
Ph: (303)492-8658   Fax: (303)492-3400

Members: American Indian and non-Indian students and professionals in science, technology, and engineering fields; corporations representing energy, mining, aerospace, electronic, and computer fields. **Purpose:** Seeks to motivate and encourage students to pursue undergraduate and graduate studies in science, engineering, and technology. **Activities:** Sponsors science fairs in grade schools, teacher training workshops, summer math/science sessions for 8th-12th graders, professional chapters, and student chapters in colleges. Offers scholarships. Adult members serve as role models, advisers, and mentors for students. Operates placement service. **E-Mail:** aise sha@spot.colorado.edu

★1114★ American Institute of Chemical Engineers (AICHE)

345 E. 47th St.
New York, NY 10017
Ph: (212)705-7338   Fax: (212)752-3294
Fr: 800-242-4365

Members: Professional society of chemical engineers. **Activities:** Establishes standards for chemical engineering curricula; offers employment services. Sponsors petrochemical and refining, exposition, and continuing education programs. Sponsors competitions. Offers speakers' bureau; compiles statistics. Maintains numerous committees including: Career Guidance; Chemical Engineering Education Projects; International Activities; Research.

★1115★ **American Oil Chemists' Society (AOCS)**

PO Box 3489
Champaign, IL 61826-3489
Ph: (217)359-2344   Fax: (217)351-8091

Members: Chemists, biochemists, chemical engineers, research directors, plant personnel, and others in laboratories and chemical process industries concerned with animal, marine, and vegetable oils and fats, and their extraction, refining, safety, packaging, quality control, and use in consumer and industrial products such as foods, drugs, paints, waxes, lubricants, soaps, and cosmetics. **Activities:** Sponsors short courses; certifies referee chemists; distributes cooperative check samples; sells official reagents. Maintains 100 committees. Operates job placement service for members only.

★1116★ **Engineering Society of Detroit (ESD)**

100 Farnsworth Ave.
Detroit, MI 48202
Ph: (313)832-5400   Fax: (313)832-5920

Members: Engineers from all disciplines; scientists and technologists. **Activities:** Offers placement services. Conducts technical programs and engineering refresher courses; sponsors conferences and expositions. Maintains speakers' bureau. Although based in Detroit, MI, society membership is international.

★1117★ **International Society of India Chemists and Chemical Engineers (ISICCE)**

c/o Dr. Dayal T. Meshri
Advanced Research Chemicals
1085 Ft. Gibson Rd.
Catoosa, OK 74015
Ph: (918)266-6789   Fax: (918)266-6796

Members: Chemists and chemical engineers from India. **Purpose:** Goal is to bring together Indians in the chemical profession who live in the U.S. Aids members in securing jobs in their fields. Provides consultation to industries in India and helps individuals to start their own chemical companies in the U.S. Provides a forum for the exchange of social and technical issues. Plans to organize symposia, short courses, and exchange program. Compiles statistics.

★1118★ **ISA**

PO Box 12277
67 Alexander Dr.
Research Triangle Park, NC 27709
Ph: (919)549-8411   Fax: (919)549-8288

Purpose: Educational organization dedicated to advancing knowledge and practice related to the theory, design, manufacture, and use of instruments and controls in science and industry. Operates training center for industry; conducts symposia; develops standards; recognizes individual achievement. **Activities:** Maintains speakers' bureau and placement service.

★1119★ **Korean Scientists and Engineers Association in America (KSEA)**

6261 Executive Blvd.
Rockville, MD 20852
Ph: (301)984-7048   Fax: (301)984-1231

Members: Scientists and engineers holding single or advanced degrees. **Purpose:** Goals are to: promote friendship and mutuality among Korean and American scientists and engineers; contribute to Korea's scientific, technological, industrial, and economic developments; strengthen the scientific, technological, and cultural bonds between Korea and the U.S. Sponsors symposium. **Activities:** Maintains speakers' bureau, placement service, and biographical archives. Compiles statistics. Maintains 100 volume library of scientific handbooks and yearbooks in Korean.

★1120★ **National Organization for the Professional Advancement of Black Chemists and Chemical Engineers (NOBCChE)**

525 College St. NW
Washington, DC 20059
Ph: (202)667-1699   Fax: (202)667-1705
Fr: 800-776-1419

Members: Black professionals in science and chemistry. **Purpose:** Seeks to aid black scientists and chemists in reaching their full professional potential; encourages black students to pursue scientific studies and employment; promotes participation of blacks in scientific research. Provides volunteers to teach science courses in selected elementary schools; sponsors scientific field trips for students; maintains speakers' bureau for schools; provides summer school for students of the U.S. Naval Academy. Conducts technical seminars in Africa; operates exchange program of scientific and chemical professionals with the People's Republic of China. Sponsors competitions; presents awards for significant achievements to individuals in the field. Maintains library of materials pertaining to chemistry, science, and black history; keeps archive of organization's books and records. **Activities:** Maintains placement service; compiles statistics.

★1121★ **Society of Hispanic Professional Engineers (SHPE)**

5400 E. Olympic Blvd., Ste. 210
Los Angeles, CA 90022
Ph: (213)725-3970

Purpose: Engineers, student engineers, and scientists seeking to increase the number of Hispanic engineers by providing motivation and support to students. Sponsors competitions and educational programs. **Activities:** Maintains placement service and speakers' bureau; compiles statistics.

EMPLOYER DIRECTORIES AND NETWORKING LISTS

★1122★ *American Men and Women of Science*

R. R. Bowker Co.
Reed Reference Publishing
121 Chanlon Rd.
New Providence, NJ 07974
Ph: (908)464-6800   Fax: (908)665-6688
Fr: 800-521-8110

Triennial, latest edition January 1995. $106.00, per volume; $850.00, set. Covers over 123,000 U.S. and Canadian scientists active in the physical, biological, mathematical, computer science, and engineering fields; includes references to previous edition for deceased scientists and nonrespondents. Entries include: Name, address, education, personal and career data, memberships, honors and awards, research interest. Arrangement: Alphabetical. Indexes: Discipline (in separate volume).

★1123★ *Analytical Chemistry—Lab Guide*

American Chemical Society
1155 16th St. NW
Washington, DC 20036
Ph: (202)872-4600   Fax: (202)872-6067
Fr: 800-227-5558

Annual, August. $50.00. Publication includes: List of about 2,200 manufacturers of scientific instruments, equipment, chemicals, and other supplies for scientific research and chemical laboratories; laboratory supply houses; analytical and research services. Entries include: Company name, address, phone, products and services. Arrangement: Alphabetical. Indexes: Product, chemical, service, instrument, company name.

★1124★ *Chemical Engineering Catalog*

Penton Publishing Co.
1100 Superior Ave.
Cleveland, OH 44114-2543
Ph: (216)696-7000   Fax: (216)696-0177

Annual, fall. $60.00. Publication includes: List of approximately 2,000 manufacturers of equipment for the chemical processing industries. Entries include: Company name, address, phone, district sales offices. Arrangement: Alphabetical within product categories. Indexes: Company name, product, trade name.

★1125★ *Consulting Services*

Association of Consulting Chemists and Chemical Engineers
40 W. 45th St.
New York, NY 10036
Ph: (212)983-3160   Fax: (212)983-3161

Biennial, even years. $25.00, postpaid. Covers about 150 member consultants in chemistry, chemical engineering, metallurgy, etc. Entries include: Individual name, address, certificate number, qualifications, affiliation, experience, facilities, staff. Arrangement: Classified by area of expertise. Indexes: Personal name, geographical.

★1126★ CPI Purchasing—Chemicals Yellow Pages

Cahners Publishing Co.
275 Washington St.
Newton, MA 02158
Ph: (617)964-3030   Fax: (617)558-4327

Annual, September. $85.00. Covers manufacturers and distributors of 10,000 chemicals and raw materials; manufacturers and distributors of containers and packaging; transportation services and storage facilities; environmental services companies. Entries include: Company name, address, branch and district office names and locations, phone. Arrangement: Separate alphabetical sections for suppliers, chemicals, and trade names; distributors are georgraphical.

★1127★ Directory of Chemical Producers—U.S.A.

SRI International
333 Ravenswood Ave.
Menlo Park, CA 94025
Ph: (415)859-3627   Fax: (415)859-4623

Annual, May. Covers over 1,500 United States basic chemical producers manufacturing nearly 10,000 chemicals in commercial quantities at 4,500 plant locations. Arrangement: Companies are alphabetical by parent company; products are alphabetical and by group (dyes, pesticides, etc.); manufacturing plants are geographical.

★1128★ Directory of Contract Service Firms

C. E. Publications, Inc.
PO Box 97000
Kirkland, WA 98083
Ph: (206)823-2222   Fax: (206)821-0942

Annual, January. $10.00. Covers Approximately 900 contract firms actively engaged in the employment of engineering and technical personnel for temporary contract assignments throughout the world. Entries include: Company name, address, phone, name of contact. Arrangement: Alphabetical. Indexes: Geographical.

★1129★ Directory of Engineering Societies and Related Organizations

American Association of Engineering Societies
1111 19th St. NW, Ste. 608
Washington, DC 20036
Ph: (202)296-2237   Fax: (202)296-1151
Fr: 800-658-8897

1992. $185.00. Lists 1,000 national, regional, Canadian, and international organizations concerned with engineering and related fields.

★1130★ Directory of Engineers in Private Practice

National Society of Professional Engineers
1420 King St.
Alexandria, VA 22314
Ph: (703)684-2862   Fax: (703)836-4875

Annual. $85.00. Covers 600 consulting engineering firms and 7,200 individuals who are members of the society's Professional Engineers in Private Practice division. Entries include: For companies, name, address, phone, name of principal executive, list of services. For individuals, name, address; most listings include phone. Arrangement: Firms are geographic, then by specialty; individuals are alphabetical.

★1131★ Directory of World Chemical Producers

Chemical Information Services Ltd.
PO Box 8344, University Sta.
Dallas, TX 75205
Ph: (214)340-4345   Fax: (214)349-6286

Previous edition 1992; latest edition October 1994. Covers About 7,000 chemical producers in 81 countries; does not include producers of chemical and pharmaceutical specialities or formulated mixtures. Entries include: Company name, address, phone, telex, TWX numbers, cable address. Arrangement: Geographical. Indexes: Product.

★1132★ Engineering Research Centres

Stockton Press
Groves Dictionaries
345 Park Ave. S., 10th Fl.
New York, NY 10010
Ph: (212)689-9200   Fr: 800-221-2123

Fourth edition, 1995. $515.00. 768 pages. Contains over 8,000 entries describing research and technology laboratories in over 70 countries. Provides details on industrial research centers and educational establishments with research and development activity. Indexes: Subject and title of establishments.

★1133★ Peterson's Job Opportunities in Engineering and Technology 1996

Peterson's
PO Box 2123
Princeton, NJ 08543-2123
Ph: (609)243-9111   Fax: (609)243-9150
Fr: 800-338-3282

Compiled by the Peterson's staff. Annual. $19.95 paperback. 432 pages. Profiles 2,000 high-tech companies looking primarily for technical personnel in such fields as biotechnology, telecommunications, software, computers and peripherals, defense, and aerospace. Contains job-search strategies and career options to help match education and expertise to the job market. Indexed geographically, by industry, and by hiring needs.

★1134★ Scientific and Technical Organizations and Agencies Directory

Gale Research
835 Penobscot Bldg.
Detroit, MI 48226-4094
Ph: (313)961-2242   Fax: (313)961-6083
Fr: 800-877-GALE

Irregular; latest edition December 1993. $195.00. Covers over 25,600 national and international organizations and agencies concerned with the physical and applied sciences, engineering, and technology, including associations, computer information services, consulting firms, educational institutions, foundations, government advisory organizations, federal government agencies, general grant and assistance programs, libraries and information centers, patent sources and services, research and development centers, scholarships, fellowships, and loans, science-technology centers, standards organizations, state academies of science, and state government agencies in the fields of aeronautics and space sciences, chemistry, computer science specialties, electronics, geography, geology, machinery, mathematics, metallurgy, meteorology, mineralogy, nuclear science, petroleum and gas, physics, plastics, transportation, water resources, and other areas. Entries include: Organization name, address, phone, and name of contact; additional descriptive text for most entries. Arrangement: Classified by type of organization. Indexes: Organization name/key word.

★1135★ Who's Who in Technology

Gale Research
835 Penobscot Bldg.
Detroit, MI 48226-4094
Ph: (313)961-2242   Fax: (313)961-6083
Fr: 800-877-GALE

Irregular, new edition expected June 1995. $380.00. Covers 38,000 engineers, scientists, inventors, and researchers. Entries include: Name, title, affiliation, address; personal, education, and career data; publications, patents; technical field of activity; area of expertise. Arrangement: Alphabetical. Indexes: Geographical, employer, technical discipline, expertise.

HANDBOOKS AND MANUALS

★1136★ The Best Resumes for Scientists and Engineers

John Wiley and Sons
605 3rd Ave.
New York, NY 10158
Ph: (212)850-6000   Fr: 800-225-5945

Adele Lewis. Second edition, 1993. $37.50; $14.95 (paper). Presents an extensive collection of scientific and engineering resumes, highlighting the important differences between these and resumes written for other occupations.

★1137★ Careers in Engineering

VGM Career Horizons
4255 W. Touhy Ave.
Lincolnwood, IL 60646-1975
Ph: (847)679-5500   Fax: (847)679-2494
Fr: 800-323-4900

Geraldine O. Gardner. 1994. $17.95; $13.95 (paper). Covers careers in the public or private sector, in industry, the university, or the military, from applications in computer architecture design to high temperature ceramics.

★1138★ Engineering Success

Kendall Hunt Publishing
4050 Westmark Dr.
PO Box 1840
Dubuque, IA 52004-1840
Ph: (319)589-1000   Fax: 800-772-9165
Fr: 800-228-0810

Bill Osher. 1994. $27.96.

★1139★ *Engineering Your Job Search: A Job-Finding Resource for Engineering Professionals*

Professional Publications, Inc.
1250 5th Ave.
Belmont, CA 94002
Ph: (415)593-9119   Fax: (415)592-4519
Fr: 800-426-1178

Compiled by Professional Publications editors. 1995. $12.95 (paper).

★1140★ *From Microchips to Potato Chips: Chemical Engineers Make a Difference*

American Institute of Chemical Engineers
Communications Dept.
345 E. 47th St.
New York, NY 10017-2395
Ph: (212)705-7657

Booklet. Single copy free. 8 pages. Includes employment opportunities.

★1141★ *Introduction to the Engineering Profession*

HarperCollins Publishers, Inc.
10 E. 53rd. St.
New York, NY 10022-5299
Ph: (212)207-7000   Fax: (212)207-7145
Fr: 800-331-3761

David M. Burghardt. 1995. $30.00 (paper).

★1142★ *Majoring in Engineering: How to Get from Your Freshman Year to Your First Job*

Farrar, Straus & Giroux, Inc.
19 Union Sq., W
New York, NY 10003
Ph: (212)741-6900   Fr: 800-788-6262

John Garcia. 1995. $20.00; $10.00 (paper).

★1143★ *Opportunities in Biotechnology Careers*

VGM Career Horizons
4255 W. Touhy Ave.
Lincolnwood, IL 60646-1975
Ph: (847)679-5500   Fax: (847)679-2494
Fr: 800-323-4900

Sheldon Brown. 1990. $14.95; $11.95 (paper). Discusses typical jobs, their income potential, and career opportunities.

★1144★ *Opportunities in Chemical Engineering*

NTC Publishing Group
4255 W. Touhy Ave.
Lincolnwood, IL 60646-1975
Ph: (708)679-5500   Fax: (708)679-6375
Fr: 800-323-4900

David L. Olsson. 1995. $13.95 (paper).

★1145★ *Opportunities in Engineering Careers*

VGM Career Horizons
4255 W. Touhy Ave.
Lincolnwood, IL 60646-1975
Ph: (847)679-5500   Fax: (847)679-2494
Fr: 800-323-4900

Nicholas Basta. 1995. $14.95; $11.95 (paper). Outlines typical job titles, salaries, career paths, and employment prospects.

★1146★ *Opportunities in High Tech Careers*

VGM Career Horizons
4255 W. Touhy Ave.
Lincolnwood, IL 60646-1975
Ph: (847)679-5500   Fax: (847)679-2494
Fr: 800-323-4900

Gary D. Golter and Deborah Yanuck. 1995. $14.95; $11.95 (paper). 160 pages. Explores high technology careers. Describes job opportunities, how to make a career decision, how to prepare for high technology jobs, job hunting techniques, and future trends.

★1147★ *Resumes for Engineering Careers*

VGM Career Horizons
NTC Publishing Group
4255 W. Touhy Ave.
Lincolnwood, IL 60646-1975
Ph: (847)679-5500   Fax: (847)679-2494
Fr: 800-323-4900

1994. $9.95. 160 pages. Contains sample resumes and cover letters applicable to any engineering field.

EMPLOYMENT AGENCIES AND SEARCH FIRMS

★1148★ **ABC Employment Service**
25 S. Bemiston, Ste. 214
Clayton, MO 63105
Ph: (314)725-3140

Employment agency.

★1149★ **Channel Personnel Services, Inc.**
7007 Gulf Fwy., Ste. 214
Houston, TX 77087-2540
Ph: (713)643-8001

Executive search firm.

★1150★ **Chemical Scientific Services**
141 S. Cassady Ave.
Columbus, OH 43209
Ph: (614)231-4401   Fax: (614)231-9601

Employment agency.

★1151★ **Colli Associates of Tampa**
PO Box 2865
Tampa, FL 33601
Ph: (813)681-2145

Employment agency. Executive search firm.

★1152★ **Executive Recruiters Agency**
14 Office Park Dr.
PO Box 21810
Little Rock, AR 72221-1810
Ph: (501)224-7000   Fax: (501)224-8534

Personnel service firm.

★1153★ **Hayden and Associates, Inc.**
7825 Washington Ave. S., Ste. 120
Minneapolis, MN 55439-2431
Ph: (612)941-6300   Fax: (612)941-9602

Employment agency. Executive search firm. Fills openings in a variety of fields.

★1154★ **Industrial Recruiters Associates, Inc.**
630 Oakwood Ave., Ste. 318
West Hartford, CT 06110
Ph: (203)953-3643

Employment agency.

★1155★ **The Jobs Co.**
8900 E. Sprague Ave.
Spokane, WA 99212-2927
Ph: (509)928-3151   Fax: (509)928-3168

Employment agency. Has division specializing in engineering and scientific openings. Also operates division specializing in sales openings.

★1156★ **JR Professional Search**
PO Box 18356
Tucson, AZ 85731
Ph: (520)721-1855   Fax: (520)721-1855

Employment agency.

★1157★ **LOR Personnel Division**
418 Wall St.
Princeton, NJ 08540
Ph: (609)921-6580

Employment agency. Executive search firm.

★1158★ **Main Line Personnel Service, Inc.**
401 City Ave.
Bala Cynwyd, PA 19004-1122
Ph: (610)667-1820

Employment agency.

★1159★ **Rand Personnel Agency**
1200 Truxtun, Ste. 130
Bakersfield, CA 93301
Ph: (805)325-0751   Fax: (805)325-4120

Personnel service firm.

★1160★ **Search and Recruit International**
4455 South Blvd.
Virginia Beach, VA 23452
Ph: (804)490-3151

Employment agency. Headquartered in Virginia Beach. Other offices in Bremerton, WA; Charleston, SC; Jacksonville, FL; Memphis, TN; Pensacola, FL; Sacramento, CA; San Bernardino, CA; San Diego, CA.

★1161★ **Sierra Technology Corporation**
4150 Manzanita Ave., Ste. 100
Carmichael, CA 95608-1700
Ph: (916)488-4960   Fax: (916)488-7058

Employment agency. Provides placement on a temporary basis.

★1162★ **Source Engineering**
5580 LBJ Fwy., Ste. 300
Dallas, TX 75240
Ph: (214)385-3002   Fax: (214)717-0075

Executive search firm. Many affiliate offices located throughout the U.S.

★1163★ Systems One Ltd.

1100 E. Woodfield Rd.
Schaumburg, IL 60173
Ph: (708)619-9300   Fax: (708)619-0071

Personnel service firm.

★1164★ T.R. Employment Agency

409 Wilshire Blvd.
Santa Monica, CA 90401
Ph: (310)393-4107

Employment agency.

★1165★ Tri-Serv Inc.

22 W. Padonia Rd., Ste. C53
Timonium, MD 21093
Ph: (301)561-1740

Employment agency.

OTHER SOURCES

★1166★ American Association of Engineering Societies (AAES)

1111 19th St. NW, Ste. 608
Washington, DC 20036
Ph: (202)296-2237   Fax: (202)296-1151

Purpose: Seeks to promote leadership in public affairs for the engineering community, work in support of math and science education for young persons. Disseminates of information about the profession. Provides statistics about engineers.

★1167★ American Institute of Chemists (AIC)

501 Wythe St.
Alexandria, VA 22314-1917
Ph: (703)836-2090   Fax: (703)836-2091

Members: Chemists and chemical engineers. **Purpose:** Promotes advancement of chemical professions in the U.S.; protects public welfare by establishing and enforcing high practice standards; represents professional interests of chemists and chemical engineers. **Activities:** Sponsors American Board of Clinical Chemistry; National Registry in Clinical Chemistry; National Certification Commission in Chemistry and Chemical Engineering; AIC Foundation; National Inventors Hall of Fame; Public Education Fund.

★1168★ Association for International Practical Training (AIPT)

10400 Little Patuxent Pky. Ste. 250
Columbia, MD 21044
Ph: (410)997-2200   Fax: (410)992-3924

Purpose: Helps coordinate training around the world in fields such as travel, the culinary arts, and hotel management. **Activities:** Conducts programs in career development and hospitality/tourism exchanges. Operates a student exchange program. Provides reciprocal practical training experience for recent graduates from the U.S., Austria, Germany, Finland, France, Hungary, Ireland, Japan, Malaysia, Netherlands, Switzerland, and the United Kingdom. Arranges training programs in the U.S. and abroad. Serves as U.S. affiliate to IAESTE (International Association for the Exchange of Students for Technical Experience) and operates a Professional Visitors Program to arrange short-term educational and training visits to the U.S. **E-Mail:** aipt@aipt.org

★1169★ *Engineering Salary Survey*

Source Engineering
1290 Oakmead, Ste. 318
Sunnyvale, CA 94086
Ph: (408)738-8440

Annual. Discusses the structure of the engineering profession, trends, and compensation. Salaries are listed by job function, industry, and years of experience.

★1170★ *Graduating Engineer*

Peterson's/COG Publishing Group
16030 Ventura Blvd., No. 560
Encino, CA 91436
Ph: (818)789-5293

Eight issues/year. Magazine focusing on employment, education, and career development for entry-level engineers.

★1171★ National Action Council for Minorities in Engineering (NACME)

3 W. 35th St.
New York, NY 10001-2281
Ph: (212)279-2626   Fax: (212)629-5178

Purpose: Seeks to increase the number of African American, Latino, and Native American students enrolled in and graduating from engineering schools. Through the Corporate Scholars Program, offers comprehensive scholarships to engineering students that include leadership development, corporate mentors and summer internships. Works with local, regional, and national education organizations to motivate and encourage precollege students to engage in engineering careers. Conducts educational and research programs; operates project to assist engineering schools in improving the retention and graduation rates of minority students. Maintains speakers' bureau; compiles statistics.

★1172★ National Society of Professional Engineers (NSPE)

1420 King St.
Alexandria, VA 22314
Ph: (703)684-2800   Fax: (703)836-4875

Members: Professional engineers and engineers-in-training in all fields registered in accordance with the laws of states or territories of the U.S. or provinces of Canada; qualified graduate engineers, student members, and registered land surveyors. **Purpose:** Is concerned with social, professional, ethical, and economic considerations of engineering as a profession; encompasses programs in public relations, employment practices, ethical considerations, education, and career guidance. Monitors legislative and regulatory actions of interest to the engineering profession. **Website:** http://www.hspc.org

★1173★ *Salaries of Scientists, Engineers, and Technicians: A Summary of Salary Surveys*

Commission on Professionals in Science and Technology (CPST)
1500 Massachusetts Ave. NW, Ste. 831
Washington, DC 20005
Ph: (202)223-6995

1993.

★1174★ Society of Women Engineers (SWE)

120 Wall St., 11th Fl.
New York, NY 10005
Ph: (212)509-9577   Fax: (212)509-0224

Members: Educational service society of women engineers; membership is also open to men. **Purpose:** Supplies information on the achievements of women engineers and the opportunities available to them; assists women engineers in preparing for return to active work following temporary retirement. Serves as an informational center on women in engineering. **Activities:** Administers several certificate and scholarship programs. Offers tours and career guidance; conducts surveys. Compiles statistics.

Chemists

SOURCES OF HELP-WANTED ADS

★1175★ Adhesives Age

Communication Channels, Inc.
6255 Barfield Rd.
Atlanta, GA 30328
Ph: (404)955-9970   Fax: (404)256-3116

Monthly. $45.00/year for individuals. Magazine containing news and technology for those engaged in the manufacture, application, research, and marketing of adhesives, sealants, and related products.

★1176★ American Biotechnology Laboratory

International Scientific Communications, Inc.
30 Controls Dr.
PO Box 870
Shelton, CT 06484-0870
Ph: (203)926-9300   Fax: (203)926-9310

$128.00/year for individuals. Biotechnology magazine.

★1177★ American Paint and Coatings Journal

American Paint Journal Co.
2911 Washington Ave.
St. Louis, MO 63103
Ph: (314)534-0301   Fax: (314)534-4458

Weekly (Mon.). Magazine serving paint, varnish and lacquer manufacturers.

★1178★ Analytical Chemistry

American Chemical Society
1155 16th St. NW
Washington, DC 20036
Ph: (202)872-4600   Fax: (202)872-6005
Fr: 800-227-5558

Biweekly. $33.00/year for members; $76.00/year for nonmembers. Journal covering measurement science.

★1179★ Applied Occupational & Environmental Hygiene

Applied Industrial Hygiene, Inc.
1330 Kemper Meadow Dr., Ste. 600
Cincinnati, OH 45240
Ph: (513)742-2020   Fax: (513)742-3355

Monthly. $85.00/year for individuals; $155.00/year for institutions. Magazine presenting solutions in occupational and environmental hygiene.

★1180★ ASTM Standardization News

ASTM
1916 Race St.
Philadelphia, PA 19103
Ph: (215)299-5400   Fax: (215)299-5511

Monthly. Magazine publishing news on the testing and evaluation industry.

★1181★ Bio/Technology

Nature Publishing Co.
345 Park Ave. S, 10th Fl.
New York, NY 10010-1707
Ph: (212)726-9200   Fax: (212)696-9006

Monthly. $59.00/year for individuals. Scientific research journal.

★1182★ Chemical Business

Schnell Publishing Co., Inc.
80 Broad St.
New York, NY 10004-2203
Ph: (212)248-4177   Fax: (212)248-4901

Monthly. Magazine covering important aspects of chemical industry management.

★1183★ Chemical and Engineering News

American Chemical Society
1155 16th St. NW
Washington, DC 20036
Ph: (202)872-4600   Fax: (202)872-6005
Fr: 800-227-5558

Weekly. Free to qualified subscribers; $105.00/year for individuals. Chemical process industries trade journal.

★1184★ Chemical Equipment

Curpier/ Group Publishing
301 Gibraltar Dr.
PO Box 231
Cooperstown, NY 13326
Ph: (607)547-2591   Fax: (607)547-2923
Fr: 800-733-1284

Monthly. Tabloid on the chemical process industry.

★1185★ Chemical Processing

Putman Publishing Co., Inc.
301 E. Erie St.
Chicago, IL 60611
Ph: (312)644-2020   Fax: (312)644-2437

Monthly. $35.00/year for individuals. Magazine for the chemical process industry.

★1186★ Chemical Week

Chemical Week Associates
888 7th Ave., 26th Fl.
New York, NY 10106
Ph: (212)621-4900   Fax: (212)621-4949

Weekly (Wed.). $99.00/year for individuals. Chemical process industries magazine.

★1187★ CHEMTECH

American Chemical Society
1155 16th St. NW
Washington, DC 20036
Ph: (202)872-4600   Fax: (202)872-6005
Fr: 800-227-5558

Monthly. $41.00/year for members; $75.00/year for nonmembers. Magazine for chemists and chemical engineers.

★1188★ Drug & Cosmetic Industry

Advanstar Communications, Inc.
270 Madison Ave.
New York, NY 10016-0601
Ph: (212)951-6600   Fax: (212)481-6561

Monthly. $32.00/year; $5.00 for single issue. Trade magazine for manufacturers and merchandisers of personal products and health and beauty aids.

★1189★ Electrochemical Society Interface

The Electrochemical Society
10 S. Main St.
Pennington, NJ 08534
Ph: (609)737-1902   Fax: (609)737-2743

Quarterly. 40.00/year.

★1190★ Environmental Science & Technology

American Chemical Society
1155 16th St. NW
Washington, DC 20036
Ph: (202)872-4600   Fax: (202)872-4615

Monthly. $44.00/year for members; $90.00/year for nonmembers.

★1191★ Journal of Chemical Education

Centcom Ltd.
1599 Post Rd. E
PO Box 231
Westport, CT 06881-0231
Ph: (203)256-8211   Fax: (203)256-8175

Monthly. $17.00/year for individuals. Magazine on chemical research and education.

★1192★ Journal of Chemical Information and Computer Sciences

American Chemical Society
1155 16th St. NW
Washington, DC 20036
Ph: (202)872-4600   Fax: (202)872-6005
Fr: 800-227-5558

Bimonthly. $20.00/year for members; $180.00/year for nonmembers. Research journal for chemists, computer scientists and information specialists.

★1193★ Modern Plastics

New York Construction News
1221 Avenue of the Americas, 41st Fl.
New York, NY 10020
Ph: (212)512-4773   Fax: (212)512-4770

Monthly. Magazine for the plastics industry.

★1194★ Nature: International Weekly Journal of Science

Nature Publishing Co.
65 Bleecker St.
New York, NY 10012-2467
Ph: (212)477-9600   Fax: (212)505-1364

Weekly. Magazine covering science and technology, including the fields of biology, biochemistry, genetics, medicine, earth sciences, physics, pharmacology, and behavioral sciences.

★1195★ Paper, Film & Foil Converter

Intertec Publishing Co.
29 N. Wacker Dr.
Chicago, IL 60606
Ph: (312)435-2330   Fax: (312)726-4103
Fr: 800-621-9907

Monthly. $125.00/year for individuals. Magazine focusing on flexible packaging, paperboard, and film.

★1196★ Plastics Engineering

Society of Plastics Engineers
14 Fairfield Dr.
PO Box 0403
Brookfield, CT 06804-0403
Ph: (203)775-0471   Fax: (203)775-8490

Monthly. $50.00/year for individuals; $80.00 for two years. Plastics trade magazine.

★1197★ Plastics World

PTN Publishing Co.
445 Broad Hollow Rd., Ste. 21
Melville, NY 11747
Ph: (516)845-2700   Fax: (516)845-7109

Monthly. $20.00/year for individuals. Plastics magazine.

★1198★ Powder and Bulk Engineering

CSC Publishing, Inc.
1300 E. 66th St.
Minneapolis, MN 55423
Ph: (612)866-2242   Fax: (612)866-1939

Monthly.

★1199★ Science

American Association for the Advancement of Science
1333 H St. NW
Washington, DC 20005
Ph: (202)326-6500   Fax: (202)682-0816

Weekly (Fri.). $87.00/year for individuals; $6.00 for single issue. Magazine devoted to science, scientific research, and public policy.

★1200★ The Scientist

The Scientist, Inc.
3501 Market St.
Philadelphia, PA 19104
Ph: (215)386-0100   Fax: (215)387-7542

Biweekly. $58.00/year for individuals; $82.00/year for Canada and Mexico; $79.00/year for other countries. Newspaper (tabloid) for scientists featuring news, opinions, research, and professional section.

★1201★ Soap/Cosmetics/Chemical Specialties

PTN Publishing Co.
445 Broad Hollow Rd., Ste. 21
Melville, NY 11747-3601
Ph: (516)845-2700   Fax: (516)845-2797

Monthly. Free to qualified subscribers; $60.00/year for individuals. Soap, cosmetics, and chemical specialties trade magazine.

★1202★ Spray Technology MKH

SA Industry Publications
389 Passaic Ave.
Fairfield, NJ 07004
Ph: (201)227-5151   Fax: (201)227-9219

Monthly. $30.00/year; $40.00/year for Canada and Mexico; $100.00/year for other countries. Magazine for the spray and pressure packaging industry.

★1203★ Textile Chemist and Colorist

American Association of Textile Chemists and Colorists
PO Box 12215
Research Triangle Park, NC 27709
Ph: (919)549-8141   Fax: (919)549-8933

Monthly. $40.00/year for U.S. and Canada; $55.00/year for other countries. Magazine focusing on dyeing, finishing of fibers and fabrics.

★1204★ Today's Chemist at Work

American Chemical Society
1155 16th St. NW
Washington, DC 20036
Ph: (202)872-4600   Fax: (202)872-6005
Fr: 800-227-5558

Bimonthly. Magazine containing non-technical articles for chemists. Editorial content and commentary focus on the everyday concerns of the practicing scientist.

PLACEMENT AND JOB REFERRAL SERVICES

★1205★ American Academy of Clinical Toxicology (AACT)

Pittsburgh Poison Center
3705 5th Ave.
Pittsburgh, PA 15213
Ph: (412)692-6669   Fax: (412)692-7497

Members: Physicians, veterinarians, pharmacists, research scientists, and analytical chemists. **Purpose:** Objectives are to: unite medical scientists and facilitate the exchange of information; encourage the development of therapeutic methods and technology; establish a mechanism for the certification of medical scientists in clinical toxicology. **Activities:** Conducts professional training in poison information and emergency service personnel. Maintains placement services. **E-Mail:** Internet, krenzee@chplink.chp.edu

★1206★ American Association of Cereal Chemists (AACC)

3340 Pilot Knob Rd.
St. Paul, MN 55121-2097
Ph: (612)454-7250   Fax: (612)454-0766

Members: Professional society of scientists and other individuals in the cereal processing industry (milling, baking, convenience foods, and feeds). **Purpose:** Encourages research on cereal grains, oil seeds, pulses, and related materials, and studies their processing, utilization, and products. Seeks to develop and standardize analytical methods used in cereal and seed chemistry and to disseminate scientific and technical information through workshops and publications. Offers honors for outstanding research. **Activities:** Maintains placement service and 32 technical subcommittees. Conducts short courses for continuing education and annual sanitation certification program.

★1207★ American Association of Textile Chemists and Colorists (AATCC)

PO Box 12215
Research Triangle Park, NC 27709-2215
Ph: (919)549-8141   Fax: (919)549-8933

Members: Technical and scientific society of textile chemists and colorists in textile and related industries using colorants and chemical finishes. **Purpose:** Recognized as an authority for test methods including: colorfastness to light, washing, perspiration, and pleating; damage caused by retained chlorine; crease resistance; shrinkage; durable press; water resistance; biological and dyeing properties. **Activities:** Develops standard test methods; conducts textile test method research; disseminates scientific information. Maintains 66 research committees. Resources include placement service and speakers' bureau.

★1208★ American Chemical Society (ACS)

1155 16th St. NW
Washington, DC 20036
Ph: (202)872-4600   Fax: (202)872-4615
Fr: 800-227-5558

Members: Scientific and educational society of chemists and chemical engineers. **Activities:** Conducts: studies and surveys; special programs for disadvantaged persons; legislation monitoring, analysis, and reporting; courses for graduate chemists and chemical engineers; radio and television programming. Offers career guidance counseling; administers the Petroleum Research Fund and other grants and fellowship programs. Operates Employment Clearing Houses. Compiles statistics. Maintains 33 divisions. **E-Mail:** mem info@acs.org

★1209★ American Crystallographic Association (ACA)

PO Box 96, Ellicott Sta.
Buffalo, NY 14205-0096
Ph: (716)856-9600   Fax: (716)852-4846

Members: Chemists, biochemists, physicists, mineralogists, and metallurgists interested in crystallography and in the application of X-ray, electron, and neutron diffraction. **Purpose:** Promotes the study of the arrangement of atoms in matter, its causes, its nature, and its consequences, and of the tools and methods used in such studies. **Activities:** Maintains employment clearinghouse for members and employers.

★1210★ American Microchemical Society (AMS)

FMC Corp.
PO Box 8
Princeton, NJ 08543
Ph: (609)951-3422   Fax: (609)951-3809

Purpose: Promotes interest in the practice and teaching of microchemistry. **Activities:** Participates in exhibits and symposia. Maintains placement service.

★1211★ American Oil Chemists' Society (AOCS)

PO Box 3489
Champaign, IL 61826-3489
Ph: (217)359-2344   Fax: (217)351-8091

Members: Chemists, biochemists, chemical engineers, research directors, plant personnel, and others in laboratories and chemical process industries concerned with animal, marine, and vegetable oils and fats, and their extraction, refining, safety, packaging, quality control, and use in consumer and industrial products such as foods, drugs, paints, waxes, lubricants, soaps, and cosmetics. **Activities:** Sponsors short courses; certifies referee chemists; distributes cooperative check samples; sells official reagents. Maintains 100 committees. Operates job placement service for members only.

★1212★ American Society for Neurochemistry (ASN)

200 University Blvd., No. 519
Galveston, TX 77555-0843
Ph: (409)772-2108   Fax: (409)762-9382

Members: Members are investigators in the field of neurochemistry and scientists who are qualified specialists in other disciplines and are interested in the activities of the society. **Purpose:** To advance and promote the science of neurochemistry and related neurosciences and to increase and enhance neurochemical knowledge; to facilitate the dissemination of information concerning neurochemical research; to encourage the research of individual neurochemists. Conducts roundtables; distributes research communications. **Activities:** Maintains placement service.

★1213★ American Society of Plant Physiologists (ASPP)

15501 Monona Dr.
Rockville, MD 20855-2768
Ph: (301)251-0560   Fax: (301)279-2996

Members: Professional society of plant physiologists, plant biochemists, and other plant scientists engaged in research and teaching. **Activities:** Offers placement service for members; conducts educational programs. **Website:** http://www.aspp.org

★1214★ American Water Works Association (AWWA)

6666 W. Quincy Ave.
Denver, CO 80235
Ph: (303)794-7711   Fax: (303)795-1440
Fr: 800-926-7337

Members: Water utility managers, superintendents, engineers, chemists, bacteriologists, and other individuals interested in public water supply; municipal- and investor-owned water departments; boards of health; manufacturers of waterworks equipment; government officials and consultants interested in water supply. **Purpose:** Develops standards and supports research programs in waterworks design, construction, operation, and management. **Activities:** conducts in-service training schools and prepares manuals for waterworks personnel. Maintains hall of fame. Offers placement service via member newsletter; compiles statistics. Offers training; children's services; and information

center on the water utilities industry, potable water, and water reuse.

★1215★ Engineering Society of Detroit (ESD)

100 Farnsworth Ave.
Detroit, MI 48202
Ph: (313)832-5400   Fax: (313)832-5920

Members: Engineers from all disciplines; scientists and technologists. **Activities:** Offers placement services. Conducts technical programs and engineering refresher courses; sponsors conferences and expositions. Maintains speakers' bureau. Although based in Detroit, MI, society membership is international.

★1216★ Federation of Analytical Chemistry and Spectroscopy Societies (FACSS)

201-B Broadway St.
Frederick, MD 21701
Ph: (301)846-4797   Fax: (301)694-6860

Members: Professional societies representing 9000 analytical chemists and spectroscopists. Members are: Analysis Instrumentation Division of the Instrument Society of America; Association of Analytical Chemists; Coblentz Society; Division of Analytical Chemistry of the American Chemical Society; Division of Analytical Chemistry of the Royal Society of Chemistry; Society for Applied Spectroscopy. **Purpose:** Objective is to provide a forum to address the challenges of analytical chemistry, chromatography, and spectroscopy. **Activities:** Reviews technical papers; maintains placement service.

★1217★ International Society of India Chemists and Chemical Engineers (ISICCE)

c/o Dr. Dayal T. Meshri
Advanced Research Chemicals
1085 Ft. Gibson Rd.
Catoosa, OK 74015
Ph: (918)266-6789   Fax: (918)266-6796

Members: Chemists and chemical engineers from India. **Purpose:** Goal is to bring together Indians in the chemical profession who live in the U.S. Aids members in securing jobs in their fields. Provides consultation to industries in India and helps individuals to start their own chemical companies in the U.S. Provides a forum for the exchange of social and technical issues. Plans to organize symposia, short courses, and exchange program. Compiles statistics.

★1218★ Korean Scientists and Engineers Association in America (KSEA)

6261 Executive Blvd.
Rockville, MD 20852
Ph: (301)984-7048   Fax: (301)984-1231

Members: Scientists and engineers holding single or advanced degrees. **Purpose:** Goals are to: promote friendship and mutuality among Korean and American scientists and engineers; contribute to Korea's scientific, technological, industrial, and economic developments; strengthen the scientific, technological, and cultural bonds between Korea and the U.S. Sponsors symposium. **Activities:** Maintains speakers' bureau, placement service, and biographical archives. Compiles statistics. Maintains 100 volume library of scientific handbooks and yearbooks in Korean.

★1219★ National Network of Minority Women in Science (MWIS)

Directorate for Education and Human Resources Programs
1333 H St. NW
Washington, DC 20005
Ph: (202)326-6757   Fax: (202)371-9849

Members: Asian, Black, Mexican American, Native American, and Puerto Rican women involved in science related professions; other interested persons. **Purpose:** Promotes the advancement of minority women in science fields and the improvement of the science and mathematics education and career awareness of minorities. Supports public policies and programs in science and technology that benefit minorities. **Activities:** Maintains placement servce. Compiles statistics; serves as clearinghouse for identifying minority women scientists. Offers writing and conference presentations, seminars, and workshops on minority women in science and local career conferences for students. Local chapters maintain speakers' bureaus, and children's services. **E-Mail:** ggilbert@aaas.org

★1220★ National Organization for the Professional Advancement of Black Chemists and Chemical Engineers (NOBCChE)

525 College St. NW
Washington, DC 20059
Ph: (202)667-1699   Fax: (202)667-1705
Fr: 800-776-1419

Members: Black professionals in science and chemistry. **Purpose:** Seeks to aid black scientists and chemists in reaching their full professional potential; encourages black students to pursue scientific studies and employment; promotes participation of blacks in scientific research. Provides volunteers to teach science courses in selected elementary schools; sponsors scientific field trips for students; maintains speakers' bureau for schools; provides summer school for students of the U.S. Naval Academy. Conducts technical seminars in Africa; operates exchange program of scientific and chemical professionals with the People's Republic of China. Sponsors competitions; presents awards for significant achievements to individuals in the field. Maintains library of materials pertaining to chemistry, science, and black history; keeps archive of organization's books and records. **Activities:** Maintains placement service; compiles statistics.

★1221★ Society of Cosmetic Chemists (SCC)

120 Wall St., Ste. 2400
New York, NY 10005
Ph: (212)668-1500   Fax: (212)668-1504

Members: Professional society of scientists involved in the cosmetic industry. **Purpose:** Sponsors educational institution support programs to stimulate growth of cosmetic science-related programs. **Activities:** Maintains placement service.

★1222★ Society for In Vitro Biology (SIVB)

8815 Centre Park Dr., Ste. 210
Columbia, MD 21045
Ph: (410)992-0946   Fax: (410)992-0949
Fr: 800-741-7476

Members: Professional society of individuals using mammalian, invertebrate, plant cell tissue, and organ cultures as research tools in chemistry, physics, radiation, medicine, physiology, nutrition, and cytogenetics. **Purpose:** Aims are to foster collection and dissemination of information concerning the maintenance and experimental use of tissue cells in vitro and to establish evaluation and development procedures. **Activities:** Operates placement service.

EMPLOYER DIRECTORIES AND NETWORKING LISTS

★1223★ American Board of Clinical Chemistry—Directory of Diplomates

American Board of Clinical Chemistry
c/o Thomas C. Stewart Ph.D., DABCC
Louisiana Reference Laboratories
6746 Goya Ave.
Baton Rouge, LA 70806
Ph: (504)926-9173   Fax: (504)926-2521
Fr: 800-888-4758

Annual, winter. Available to members only. Covers about 800 chemists trained in clinical and toxicological chemistry and certified by the board. Entries include: Name, office address. Arrangement: Alphabetical.

★1224★ American Institute of Chemists—Professional Directory

American Institute of Chemists
7315 Wisconsin Ave.
Bethesda, MD 20814
Ph: (301)652-2447   Fax: (301)657-3549

Annual, spring. $65.00. Covers more than 3,500 member chemists. Entries include: Individual name and title, address, phone, name of employer, position title, principal job responsibility, principal field of chemistry, highest academic degree, certification, year elected to membership, membership category, local affiliation. Arrangement: Alphabetical. Indexes: Geographical.

★1225★ American Men and Women of Science

R. R. Bowker Co.
Reed Reference Publishing
121 Chanlon Rd.
New Providence, NJ 07974
Ph: (908)464-6800   Fax: (908)665-6688
Fr: 800-521-8110

Triennial, latest edition January 1995. $106.00, per volume; $850.00, set. Covers over 123,000 U.S. and Canadian scientists active in the physical, biological, mathematical, computer science, and engineering fields; includes references to previous edition for deceased scientists and nonrespondents. Entries include: Name, address, education, personal and career data, memberships, honors and awards, research interest. Ar-

rangement: Alphabetical. Indexes: Discipline (in separate volume).

★1226★ Analytical Chemistry—Lab Guide

American Chemical Society
1155 16th St. NW
Washington, DC 20036
Ph: (202)872-4600   Fax: (202)872-6067
Fr: 800-227-5558

Annual, August. $50.00. Publication includes: List of about 2,200 manufacturers of scientific instruments, equipment, chemicals, and other supplies for scientific research and chemical laboratories; laboratory supply houses; analytical and research services. Entries include: Company name, address, phone, products and services. Arrangement: Alphabetical. Indexes: Product, chemical, service, instrument, company name.

★1227★ Chemical Engineering Catalog

Penton Publishing Co.
1100 Superior Ave.
Cleveland, OH 44114-2543
Ph: (216)696-7000   Fax: (216)696-0177

Annual, fall. $60.00. Publication includes: List of approximately 2,000 manufacturers of equipment for the chemical processing industries. Entries include: Company name, address, phone, district sales offices. Arrangement: Alphabetical within product categories. Indexes: Company name, product, trade name.

★1228★ Chemical Week—Buyers Guide Issue

Chemical Week
888 7th Ave., 26th Fl.
New York, NY 10106-2698
Ph: (212)621-4900   Fax: (212)621-4949

Annual. $99.00, Included in subscription. $125.00, sold separately. Publication includes: About 4,200 manufacturers and suppliers of chemical raw materials to the chemical process industries; 400 manufacturers of packaging materials; and suppliers of products and services to the chemical process industries, including hazardous waste/environmental services, computer services, plant design, contruction, consulting, shipping, and transportation. Arrangement: Separate alphabetical sections for chemical, packaging, and hazardous waste/environmental services. Indexes: Product (all sections); trade name (chemical and packaging sections only).

★1229★ CPI Purchasing—Chemicals Yellow Pages

Cahners Publishing Co.
275 Washington St.
Newton, MA 02158
Ph: (617)964-3030   Fax: (617)558-4327

Annual, September. $85.00. Covers manufacturers and distributors of 10,000 chemicals and raw materials; manufacturers and distributors of containers and packaging; transportation services and storage facilities; environmental services companies. Entries include: Company name, address, branch and district office names and locations, phone. Arrangement: Separate alphabetical sections for suppliers, chemicals, and trade names; distributors are georgraphical.

★1230★ **Directory of Chemical Producers—U.S.A.**

SRI International
333 Ravenswood Ave.
Menlo Park, CA 94025
Ph: (415)859-3627   Fax: (415)859-4623

Annual, May. Covers over 1,500 United States basic chemical producers manufacturing nearly 10,000 chemicals in commercial quantities at 4,500 plant locations. Arrangement: Companies are alphabetical by parent company; products are alphabetical and by group (dyes, pesticides, etc.); manufacturing plants are geographical.

★1231★ **Directory of Custom Chemical Manufacturers**

Delphi Marketing Services, Inc.
400 E. 89th St., Ste. 2J
New York, NY 10028
Ph: (212)534-4868

Annual, late spring. $295.00. Covers over 280 custom chemical manufacturers. Entries include: Company name, address, phone, name and title of contact, unit processes and reactions carried out, areas of expertise, equipment available. Arrangement: Alphabetical. Indexes: Product/service, subject, and geographical.

★1232★ **Directory of World Chemical Producers**

Chemical Information Services Ltd.
PO Box 8344, University Sta.
Dallas, TX 75205
Ph: (214)340-4345   Fax: (214)349-6286

Previous edition 1992; latest edition October 1994. Covers About 7,000 chemical producers in 81 countries; does not include producers of chemical and pharmaceutical specialities or formulated mixtures. Entries include: Company name, address, phone, telex, TWX numbers, cable address. Arrangement: Geographical. Indexes: Product.

★1233★ **Life Sciences Organizations and Agencies Directory**

Gale Research
835 Penobscot Bldg.
Detroit, MI 48226-4094
Ph: (313)961-2242   Fax: (313)961-6083
Fr: 800-877-GALE

$175.00. Covers about 7,500 associations, government agencies, research centers, educational institutions, libraries and information centers, museums, consultants, electronic information services, and other organizations and agencies active in agriculture, biology, ecology, forestry, marine science, nutrition, wildlife and animal sciences, and other natural and life sciences. Entries include: Organization or agency name, address, phone, name and title of contact, description. Arrangement: Classified by type of organization. Indexes: Organization/agency name and keyword.

★1234★ **Peterson's Job Opportunities in Engineering and Technology 1996**

Peterson's
PO Box 2123
Princeton, NJ 08543-2123
Ph: (609)243-9111   Fax: (609)243-9150
Fr: 800-338-3282

Compiled by the Peterson's staff. Annual. $19.95 paperback. 432 pages. Profiles 2,000 high-tech companies looking primarily for technical personnel in such fields as biotechnology, telecommunications, software, computers and peripherals, defense, and aerospace. Contains job-search strategies and career options to help match education and expertise to the job market. Indexed geographically, by industry, and by hiring needs.

★1235★ **Physical Science Career Directory**

Gale Research
835 Penobscot Bldg.
Detroit, MI 48226-4094
Ph: (313)961-2242   Fax: (313)961-6083
Fr: 800-877-GALE

First edition March 1994. $34.95; $17.95 (paper). Covers over 210 chemical companies, testing and research laboratories, and consulting firms in the U.S. offering entry-level positions and internships; sources of help-wanted ads, professional associations, producers of videos, databases, career guides, and professional guides and handbooks. Entries include: For companies: Name, address, phone, fax, business description, research activities, names and titles of key personnel, number of employees, average number of entry-level positions available, human resources contact, description of internship opportunities including contact, type and number available, application procedures, qualifications, and duties. For others: Name or title, address, phone, description. Paperback edition is available from Visible Ink Press. Arrangement: Companies are alphabetical; others are classified by type of resource. Indexes: Name and keyword.

★1236★ **Scientific and Technical Organizations and Agencies Directory**

Gale Research
835 Penobscot Bldg.
Detroit, MI 48226-4094
Ph: (313)961-2242   Fax: (313)961-6083
Fr: 800-877-GALE

Irregular; latest edition December 1993. $195.00. Covers over 25,600 national and international organizations and agencies concerned with the physical and applied sciences, engineering, and technology, including associations, computer information services, consulting firms, educational institutions, foundations, government advisory organizations, federal government agencies, general grant and assistance programs, libraries and information centers, patent sources and services, research and development centers, scholarships, fellowships, and loans, science-technology centers, standards organizations, state academies of science, and state government agencies in the fields of aeronautics and space sciences, chemistry, computer science specialties, electronics, geography, geology, machinery, mathematics, metallurgy, meteorology, mineralogy, nu-

clear science, petroleum and gas, physics, plastics, transportation, water resources, and other areas. Entries include: Organization name, address, phone, and name of contact; additional descriptive text for most entries. Arrangement: Classified by type of organization. Indexes: Organization name/key word.

★1237★ **U.S. National Committee for the International Union of Pure and Applied Chemistry—Directory**

U.S. National Committee for the International Union of Pure and Applied Chemistry
National Academy of Sciences
Washington, DC 20418
Ph: (202)334-2156   Fax: (202)334-2154

Annual, July. Covers 29 member chemists and chemical engineers in the United States.

★1238★ **Who's Who in Technology**

Gale Research
835 Penobscot Bldg.
Detroit, MI 48226-4094
Ph: (313)961-2242   Fax: (313)961-6083
Fr: 800-877-GALE

Irregular, new edition expected June 1995. $380.00. Covers 38,000 engineers, scientists, inventors, and researchers. Entries include: Name, title, affiliation, address; personal, education, and career data; publications, patents; technical field of activity; area of expertise. Arrangement: Alphabetical. Indexes: Geographical, employer, technical discipline, expertise.

Handbooks and Manuals

★1239★ **The Best Resumes for Scientists and Engineers**

John Wiley and Sons
605 3rd Ave.
New York, NY 10158
Ph: (212)850-6000   Fr: 800-225-5945

Adele Lewis. Second edition, 1993. $37.50; $14.95 (paper). Presents an extensive collection of scientific and engineering resumes, highlighting the important differences between these and resumes written for other occupations.

★1240★ **Career Transitions for Chemists: Making It Happen**

American Chemical Society
1155 16th St., NW
Washington, DC 20036
Ph: (202)872-4363   Fax: (202)872-6067
Fr: 800-227-5558

Dorothy Rodmann, editor. 1994. $29.95; $14.95 (paper).

★1241★ **Careers in Science**

VGM Career Horizons
4255 W. Touhy Ave.
Lincolnwood, IL 60646-1975
Ph: (847)679-5500   Fax: (847)679-2494
Fr: 800-323-4900

Thomas Easton. Third edition, 1996. 192 pages. $17.95; $13.95 (paper). Discusses careers in life science, earth science, physical and space science, social science, engineering, mathematics, and computer science. Offers job hunting advice.

★1242★ Chemistry and Your Career: Questions and Answers

American Chemical Society
Education Division
1155 16th St. NW
Washington, DC 20036
Ph: (202)872-4600

Single copy free. 16 pages. Gives an overview of chemistry careers, salaries, and employment outlook.

★1243★ Clinical Chemistry: Is the Challenge for You?

American Association for Clinical Chemistry
Education Department
2101 L St. NW, Ste. 202
Washington, DC 20037

12 pages. Single copy free. Career information brochure. Includes section on job opportunities.

★1244★ Employment Outlook

American Chemical Society (ACS)
1155 16th St., NW
Washington, DC 20036
Ph: (202)872-4600

Annual. Single copy free. Describes career opportunities for chemists, demands, salaries, and trends in education. Charts the supply and demand for chemists. Gives career planning and job hunting advice.

★1245★ Encyclopedia of Careers and Vocational Guidance

J. G. Ferguson Publishing Co.
200 W. Monroe, Ste. 250
Chicago, IL 60606
Ph: (312)580-5480

William E. Hopke. Ninth edition, 1993. $129.95; $199.95 (CD-ROM). Four-volume set that profiles 900 occupations and describes job trends in 71 industries. Includes career description, educational requirements, history of the job, methods of entry, advancement, employment outlook, earnings, conditions of work, social and psychological factors, and sources of further information. Contains career and employment information for this field.

★1246★ Liberal Arts Jobs: What They Are and How to Get Them

Peterson's
PO Box 2123
Princeton, NJ 08543-2123
Ph: (609)243-9111   Fax: (609)243-9150
Fr: 800-338-3282

Burton Jay Nadler. Second edition, 1989. $9.95. 153 pages. Presents a list of the top 20 fields for liberal arts majors, covering more than 300 job opportunities. Discusses strategies for going after those jobs, including guidance on the language of a successful job search, informational interviews, and making networking work.

★1247★ Opportunities in Biotechnology Careers

VGM Career Horizons
4255 W. Touhy Ave.
Lincolnwood, IL 60646-1975
Ph: (847)679-5500   Fax: (847)679-2494
Fr: 800-323-4900

Sheldon Brown. 1990. $14.95; $11.95 (paper). Discusses typical jobs, their income potential, and career opportunities.

★1248★ Opportunities in Environmental Careers

VGM Career Horizons
4255 W. Touhy Ave.
Lincolnwood, IL 60646-1975
Ph: (847)679-5500   Fax: (847)679-2494
Fr: 800-323-4900

Odom Fanning. 1995. $14.95; $11.95 (paper). 160 pages. Describes a broad range of opportunities in fields such as environmental health, recreation, physics, and hygiene, and provides job search advice.

★1249★ Opportunities in High Tech Careers

VGM Career Horizons
4255 W. Touhy Ave.
Lincolnwood, IL 60646-1975
Ph: (847)679-5500   Fax: (847)679-2494
Fr: 800-323-4900

Gary D. Golter and Deborah Yanuck. 1995. $14.95; $11.95 (paper). 160 pages. Explores high technology careers. Describes job opportunities, how to make a career decision, how to prepare for high technology jobs, job hunting techniques, and future trends.

★1250★ Where the Jobs Are: The Hottest Careers for the '90s

The Career Press, Inc.
3 Tice Rd.
PO Box 687
Franklin Lakes, NJ 07417
Ph: (201)848-0310   Fax: (201)848-1727
Fr: 800-237-3371

Joyce Hadley. Second edition, 1995. $9.99. 300 pages. Describes careers in fifteen general fields, from accounting to travel and hospitality.

EMPLOYMENT AGENCIES AND SEARCH FIRMS

★1251★ ABC Employment Service

25 S. Bemiston, Ste. 214
Clayton, MO 63105
Ph: (314)725-3140

Employment agency.

★1252★ Amtec Engineering Corp.

2749 Saturn St.
Brea, CA 92621
Ph: (714)993-1900   Fax: (714)993-2419

Employment agency.

★1253★ Biomedical Search Consultants

PO Box 1070
Danbury, CT 06813
Ph: (203)744-4027   Fax: (203)748-2122

Employment agency.

★1254★ Chemical Scientific Services

141 S. Cassady Ave.
Columbus, OH 43209
Ph: (614)231-4401   Fax: (614)231-9601

Employment agency.

★1255★ Erspamer Associates

7300 France Ave. S., Ste. 402
Edina, MN 55435
Ph: (612)831-5564   Fax: (612)831-5981

Executive search firm.

★1256★ Hayden and Associates, Inc.

7825 Washington Ave. S., Ste. 120
Minneapolis, MN 55439-2431
Ph: (612)941-6300   Fax: (612)941-9602

Employment agency. Executive search firm. Fills openings in a variety of fields.

★1257★ Health and Science Center

209 Hunter St.
Media, PA 19063-5726
Ph: (610)891-0714

Employment agency. Executive search firm.

★1258★ Industrial Recruiters Associates, Inc.

630 Oakwood Ave., Ste. 318
West Hartford, CT 06110
Ph: (203)953-3643

Employment agency.

★1259★ Intech Summit Group, Inc.

6540 Lusk Blvd., C-228
San Diego, CA 92121
Ph: (619)452-2100

Employment agency and executive recruiter.

★1260★ The Jobs Co.

8900 E. Sprague Ave.
Spokane, WA 99212-2927
Ph: (509)928-3151   Fax: (509)928-3168

Employment agency. Has division specializing in engineering and scientific openings. Also operates division specializing in sales openings.

★1261★ JR Professional Search

PO Box 18356
Tucson, AZ 85731
Ph: (520)721-1855   Fax: (520)721-1855

Employment agency.

★1262★ LOR Personnel Division

418 Wall St.
Princeton, NJ 08540
Ph: (609)921-6580

Employment agency. Executive search firm.

★1263★ Lybrook Associates, Inc.

PO Box 572
Newport, RI 02840
Ph: (401)683-6990

Executive search firm.

★1264★ Professional Placement Associates, Inc.

11 Rye Ridge Plaza
Rye Brook, NY 10573
Ph: (914)251-1000   Fax: (914)939-1959

Employment agency.

★1265★ Sierra Technology Corporation

4150 Manzanita Ave., Ste. 100
Carmichael, CA 95608-1700
Ph: (916)488-4960   Fax: (916)488-7058

Employment agency. Provides placement on a temporary basis.

★1266★ T.R. Employment Agency

409 Wilshire Blvd.
Santa Monica, CA 90401
Ph: (310)393-4107

Employment agency.

★1267★ Tri-Serv Inc.

22 W. Padonia Rd., Ste. C53
Timonium, MD 21093
Ph: (301)561-1740

Employment agency.

OTHER SOURCES

★1268★ ACS Salary Survey

American Chemical Society
1155 16th St. NW
Washington, DC 20036
Ph: (202)872-4600

Annual. Gives salaries for chemists and notes how they vary by degree level, years of experience, industry, and job function.

★1269★ American Institute of Chemists (AIC)

501 Wythe St.
Alexandria, VA 22314-1917
Ph: (703)836-2090   Fax: (703)836-2091

Members: Chemists and chemical engineers. **Purpose:** Promotes advancement of chemical professions in the U.S.; protects public welfare by establishing and enforcing high practice standards; represents professional interests of chemists and chemical engineers. **Activities:** Sponsors American Board of Clinical Chemistry; National Registry in Clinical Chemistry; National Certification Commission in Chemistry and Chemical Engineering; AIC Foundation; National Inventors Hall of Fame; Public Education Fund.

★1270★ Association for International Practical Training (AIPT)

10400 Little Patuxent Pky. Ste. 250
Columbia, MD 21044
Ph: (410)997-2200   Fax: (410)992-3924

Purpose: Helps coordinate training around the world in fields such as travel, the culinary arts, and hotel management. **Activities:** Conducts programs in career development and hospitality/tourism exchanges. Operates a student exchange program. Provides reciprocal practical training experience for recent graduates from the U.S., Austria, Germany, Finland, France, Hungary, Ireland, Japan, Malaysia, Netherlands, Switzerland, and the United Kingdom. Arranges training programs in the U.S. and abroad. Serves as U.S. affiliate to IAESTE (International Association for the Exchange of Students for Technical Experience) and operates a Professional Visitors Program to arrange short-term educational and training visits to the U.S. **E-Mail:** aipt@aipt.org

★1271★ Career Encounters: Chemistry

Cambridge Career Products
PO Box 2153
Dept. CC15
Charleston, WV 25328-2153
Ph: (304)744-9323   Fax: (304)744-9351
Fr: 800-468-4227

Video. $99.95. 25 minutes. Professionals shown in a variety of settings discuss different aspects of their careers.

★1272★ International Society of Chemical Ecology (ISCE)

University of South Florida
Department of Biology
Tampa, FL 33620
Ph: (813)974-3250   Fax: (813)974-3263

Members: Chemists, ecologists, biologists, and others with an interest in chemical ecology. **Purpose:** To promote understanding of the origin, function, and importance of natural chemicals that mediate interactions within and among organisms. Seeks to broaden the scope of chemical ecology and to stimulate cooperation and exchange of information among members of diverse scientific fields. **Activities:** Conducts educational programs designed to foster knowledge in the area of chemical ecology. **E-Mail:** romeo@chuma.cas.usf.edu

★1273★ New Careers Directory: Internships and Professional Opportunities in Technology and Social Change

Student Pugwash USA
815 15th St. NW, Ste. 814
Washington, DC 20005
Ph: (202)393-6555   Fax: (202)393-6550
Fr: 800-WOW-A-PUG

Irregular; latest edition spring 1993. $13.00 for students; $21.00 for institutions, plus $3.00 shipping. Covers about 300 research institutes, think tanks, laboratories, government agencies, professional, science, and other non-profit organizations offering public policy, science, and technology internships and jobs. Entries include: Sponsoring organization name, description of organization, programs offered, work environment and application procedures, compensation offered. Arrangement: Alphabetical and classified by subject. Indexes: Geographical, subject.

★1274★ Radiation Research Society (RRS)

2021 Spring Rd., Ste. 600
Oak Brook, IL 60521
Ph: (708)571-2881   Fax: (708)571-7837

Members: Professional society of biologists, physicists, chemists, and physicians contributing to knowledge of radiation and its effects. **Purpose:** Promotes original research in the natural sciences relating to radiation; facilitates integration of different disciplines in the study of radiation effects.

★1275★ Resumes for Scientific and Technical Careers

VGM Career Horizons
NTC Publishing Group
4255 W. Touhy Ave.
Lincolnwood, IL 60646-1975
Ph: (847)679-5500   Fax: (847)679-2494
Fr: 800-323-4900

1994. $9.95. 160 pages. Provides resume advice for individuals interested in working in scientific and technical careers. Includes sample resumes and cover letters.

★1276★ Salaries of Scientists, Engineers, and Technicians: A Summary of Salary Surveys

Commission on Professionals in Science and Technology (CPST)
1500 Massachusetts Ave. NW, Ste. 831
Washington, DC 20005
Ph: (202)223-6995

1993.

★1277★ Soil Science Society of America (SSSA)

677 S. Segoe Rd.
Madison, WI 53711
Ph: (608)273-8080   Fax: (608)273-2021

Members: Professional soil scientists, including soil physicists, soil classifiers, land use and management specialists, chemists, microbiologists, soil fertility specialists, soil cartographers, conservationists, mineralogists, engineers, and others interested in fundamental and applied soil science.

★1278★ Water Environment Federation (WEF)

601 Wythe St.
Alexandria, VA 22314-1994
Ph: (703)684-2400   Fax: (703)684-2492
Fr: 800-666-0206

Members: Technical societies representing chemists, biologists, ecologists, geologists, operators, educational and research personnel, industrial wastewater engineers, consultant engineers, municipal officials, equipment manufacturers, and university professors and students dedicated to the enhancement and preservation of water quality and resources. **Purpose:** Seeks to advance fundamental and practical knowledge concerning the nature, collection, treatment, and disposal of domestic and industrial wastewaters, and the design, construction, operation, and management of facilities for these purposes. Disseminates technical information; promotes good public relations and regulations that improve water quality and the status of individuals working in this field. **Activities:**

Conducts educational and research programs.

Child Care Workers and Nannies

PLACEMENT AND JOB REFERRAL SERVICES

★1279★ American Council of Nanny Schools (ACNS)
Delta Coll.
University Center, MI 48710
Ph: (517)686-9417   Fax: (517)686-8736
Members: Schools involved in training programs for nannies. **Purpose:** To promote professionalism of nannies and others in the field of child care; compile information on nanny training programs and placement agencies available; establish and maintain a national competency test for nannies; create standards for schools initiating nanny programs, and provide a means for exchanging experiences in the curriculum. **Activities:** Maintains placement service.

EMPLOYER DIRECTORIES AND NETWORKING LISTS

★1280★ Child Care Database (CCARE)
Care Connectors, Inc.
PO Box 14452
Research Triangle Park, NC 27709
Ph: (919)544-7300   Fax: (919)544-3558
Monthly. Database covers: over 100,000 licensed, registered, or certified child care establishments in 45 states. Database includes: Facility name, address, phone, county, business type, days and hours of operation, caregiver training in first aid and CPR, training frequency, professional program managers on staff, type of care available (full-day, half-day, before and after school, hourly, or part-week), maximum child care capacity, youngest and oldest ages accepted, and other pertinent data.

★1281★ Child Care Service Directory
American Business Directories, Inc.
American Business Information, Inc.
5711 S. 86th Cir.
Omaha, NE 68127
Ph: (402)593-4600   Fax: (402)331-1505
Annual. $1,650.00, U.S. edition; $280.00, (Canad. ed.); payment with order. Entries include: Name, address, phone (including area code), size of advertisement, year first in Yellow Pages, name of owner or manager, number of employees. Regional editions available: Compiled from telephone company Yellow Pages, nationwide. Arrangement: Geographical.

★1282★ Directory of Family Day Care Associations & Support Groups
Children's Foundation
725 15th St. NW, Ste. 505
Washington, DC 20005-2109
Ph: (202)347-3300   Fax: (202)347-3382
Annual, February. $15.00. Covers over 1,400 organizations and support groups for child care providers in the U.S. Entries include: Organization name, address, phone, subsidiary and branch names and locations. Arrangement: Geographical.

★1283★ Sitting Services Directory
American Business Directories, Inc.
American Business Information, Inc.
5711 S. 86th Cir.
Omaha, NE 68127
Ph: (402)593-4600   Fax: (402)331-1505
Updated continuously; printed on request. Please inquire. Entries include: Name, address, phone, size of advertisement, name of owner or manager, number of employees, year first in Yellow Pages. Compiled from telephone company Yellow Pages, nationwide. Arrangement: Geographical.

★1284★ So You Want to Open a Profitable Day Care Center: A Basic How to Do It Guide
Young Sparrow Press
PO Box 265
Worcester, PA 19490
Ph: (215)364-1945   Fr: 800-ALL-BOOK
Irregular, latest edition 1994. $19.95. Publication includes: Lists of government bureaus, business administration offices, small business information, and early childhood education resources which issue licenses necessary for the legal operation of child care centers; organizations and associations that provide assistance to child care operators; child care related publications that provide practical easy to follow instructions that will assist entrepreneurs who are considering the operation of day care centers. Includes professionals to contact, assessment of day care needs, education curriculum guidance, child safety, and business considerations. Entries include: For government bureaus: name, address. For organizations and associations: name, address, phone. For publications: title, publisher name, address, phone, price, brief description of publication. Arrangement: Separate sections for government bureaus, organizations and associations, and publications. Indexes: Subject.

HANDBOOKS AND MANUALS

★1285★ Careers in Child Care
NTC Publishing Group
4255 W. Touhy Ave
Lincolnwood, IL 60646-1975
Ph: (708)679-5500   Fax: (708)679-6375
Fr: 800-323-4900
Marjorie Eberts. 1994. $16.95; $12.95 (paper).

★1286★ Careers in Child Care
Child Care Action Campaign
330 7th Ave., 17th Fl.
New York, NY 10001
Ph: (212)239-0138
Pamphlet. 2 pages. Addresses job opportunities in day care.

★1287★ Careers for Kids at Heart and Others Who Adore Children
NTC Publishing Group
4255 W. Touhy Ave.
Lincolnwood, IL 60646-1975
Ph: (708)679-5500   Fax: (708)679-6375
Fr: 800-323-4900
Marjorie Eberts. 1994. $12.95; $9.95 (paper).

★1288★ Household Careers: Nannies, Butlers, Maids and More: The Complete Guide for Finding Household Employment or "If the Dog Likes You, You're Hired!"

Five Star Publications
4696 W. Tyson St.
Chandler, AZ 85226
Ph: (602)940-8182   Fax: (602)940-8787
Fr: 800-545-7827

Linda F. Radke. 1993. $14.95 (paper).

★1289★ 100 Best Careers for the Year 2000

Prentice Hall General Reference
15 Columbus Cir.
New York, NY 10023
Ph: (212)373-8500   Fr: 800-223-2348

Shelly Field. 1992. $15.00 (paper). Covers 100 of the fastest growing jobs. The publication is divided into 11 general employment sections. Specific careers are covered within each section. Provides job description, responsibilities, employment opportunities, earnings, education and training, advancement opportunities, and experience and qualifications for each occupation.

★1290★ Opportunities in Child Care Careers

VGM Career Horizons
4255 W. Touhy Ave.
Lincolnwood, IL 60646-1975
Ph: (847)679-5500   Fax: (847)679-2494
Fr: 800-323-4900

Renee Wittenberg. 1995. $14.95; $11.95 (paper). 160 pages. Discusses various job opportunities and how to secure a position. Illustrated.

★1291★ Profitable Child Care: How to Start and Run a Successful Business

Facts on File, Inc.
460 Park Ave., S
New York, NY 10016
Ph: (212)683-2244   Fax: (212)213-4578
Fr: 800-322-8755

Nan L. Howkins. 1993. $24.95.

★1292★ Start and Run a Profitable Home Daycare: Your Step-by-Step Business Plan

Self-Counsel Press, Inc.
1704 N. State St.
Bellingham, WA 98225
Ph: (360)676-4530   Fax: (360)676-4549
Fr: 800-663-3007

Catherine Pruissen. 1993. $14.95 (paper).

★1293★ Starting and Operating A Child Care Center: A Guide

Readers Press
1115 Jerome Rd.
PO Box 52522
Durham, NC 27713
Ph: (919)596-2530

Lillie M. Robinson. 1994. $29.95.

EMPLOYMENT AGENCIES AND SEARCH FIRMS

★1294★ Arbor Associates, Inc.

15 Court Sq., Ste. 1050
Boston, MA 02108
Ph: (617)227-8829

Handles temporary placements.

★1295★ Capitol Search

215 E. Ridgewood Ave.
Ridgewood, NJ 07450
Ph: (201)444-6666   Fax: (201)444-4121

Employment agency. Second location in Ridgewood, NJ.

★1296★ Contemporary Family Care Services Inc./Chevy Chase Babysitters

9222 Woodland Dr.
Silver Spring, MD 20910
Ph: (301)587-0135

Employment agency.

★1297★ Grosse Pointe Employment

18514 Mack Ave
Grosse Pointe Farms, MI 48236
Ph: (313)885-4576

Employment agency.

★1298★ Poston Personnel

16 E. 79th St., Ste. G-4
New York, NY 10021
Ph: (212)535-4116   Fax: (212)988-7080

Employment agency.

★1299★ Youth Employment Project, Inc.

208 City Hall
Rochester, MN 55902
Ph: (507)287-2345

Employment agency. Provides regular and temporary employment assistance.

OTHER SOURCES

★1300★ Au Pair & Nanny's Guide to Working Abroad

Vacation-Work Publications
9 Park End St.
Oxford OX1 1HJ, England
Ph: 865 241978   Fax: 865 790885

Quadrennial, latest edition March 1993. $8.95. Lists agencies specializing in obtaining employment abroad for persons interested in working as nannies or other domestic jobs in exchange for room and board; international coverage. Entries include: Organization name, address, contact name, description of jobs offered, etc. Principal content of publication is a guide to working abroad as a nanny or au pair in 20 countries in Europe and North America. Arrangement: Alphabetical.

★1301★ Child Care Action Campaign (CCAC)

330 7th Ave., 17th Fl.
New York, NY 10001
Ph: (212)239-0138   Fax: (212)268-6515

Members: Individuals and organizations interested and active in child care; corporations and financial institutions; labor organizations; editors of leading women's magazines; leaders in government and representatives of civic organizations. **Purpose:** To alert the country to the problems of and need for child care services; prepare and disseminate information responsive to inquiries resulting from publicity; analyze existing services and identify gaps; work directly with communities to stimulate the development of local task forces and long-range plans for improved and coordinated services. Brings pressing legislative action or inaction to public attention. Has worked to help make liability insurance available for child care providers. Compiles statistics. **E-Mail:** hn5746@igc.org

★1302★ Child Services Business Guide

Entrepreneur, Inc.
2392 Morse Ave.
PO Box 19787
Irvine, CA 92713-9787
Fax: (714)851-9088   Fr: 800-421-2300

$79.50 (includes business guide and software). Provides an overview of the child services industry, including Nanny Placement and Day Care Services.

★1303★ Directory of Federal Programs Helping Child Care

ERIC Document Reproduction Service
7420 Fullerton Rd., Ste. 110
Springfield, VA 22153-2852
Ph: (703)440-1400   Fax: (703)440-1408
Fr: 800-443-ERIC

Covers Federal programs that assist child care professionals. Entries include: Name, address, phone of program name and title of contact, description of program and financial information.

★1304★ International Nanny Association (INA)

125 S. 4th St.
Norfolk, NE 68701
Ph: (402)691-9628   Fax: (402)379-3606
Fr: 800-297-1477

Members: Nannies, nanny employers, educators, and nanny placement agencies. **Purpose:** Promotes in-home professional child care; serves as a clearinghouse of information on nannies; conducts advocacy on behalf of members. Makes available educational programs; compiles statistics.

★1305★ National Association for the Education of Young Children (NAEYC)

1509 16th St. NW
Washington, DC 20036
Ph: (202)232-8777   Fax: (202)328-1846
Fr: 800-424-2460

Members: Teachers and directors of preschool and primary schools, kindergartens, child care centers, cooperatives, church schools, and groups having similar programs for young children; early childhood education and child development professors, trainers, and researchers. **Activities:** Offers voluntary accreditation for early childhood schools and centers through the National Academy of Early Childhood Programs.

★1306★ **National Center for the Early Childhood Work Force (CCEP)**

733 15th St. NW, Ste. 1037
Washington, DC 20005-2112
Ph: (202)737-7700   Fax: (202)737-0370
Fr: 800-879-6784

Purpose: Purposes are: to develop innovative solutions to the child care crisis to improve salaries, working conditions, and status of child care workers; to increase public awareness about the importance of child care work and the training and skill it demands; to develop resources and create an information sharing network for child care workers nationwide. **Activities:** Gathers current information on salaries and benefits; offers consultation services.

★1307★ **Summer Jobs in Britain**

Vacation-Work Publications
9 Park End St.
Oxford OX1 1HJ, England
Ph: 865 241978   Fax: 865 790885

Annual, November. $15.95. Covers over 30,000 farm, hotel, au pair, voluntary, and other summer jobs in Scotland, Wales, England, the Channel Islands and Northern Ireland. Entries include: Employer name, address, positions offered, description of duties, length of service, wages, other amenities. Arrangement: Classified by line of work.

★1308★ **Working Holidays**

Central Bureau for Educational Visits & Exchanges
Seymour Mews House
Seymour Mews
London W1H 9PE, England
Ph: 71 4865101   Fax: 71 9355741

Annual, November. $9.99, postpaid. Covers 1,000 organizations offering short-term paid and voluntary work opportunities in Britain and over 70 countries worldwide, for periods of three days to a year or longer; jobs include archeological digs, au pair/childcare, children's projects, couriers, guides, monitors, teachers, work camps, conservation, community works, hotel work, farm work, teaching, simple construction, etc. Entries include: Organization name, address, name of contact, objectives, projects available, conditions and terms of work. Arrangement: Geographical, then by type of work. Indexes: Organization name.

Chiropractors

★1309★ **The American Chiropractor**
Busch Publishing Co.
5005 Riviera Ct.
Fort Wayne, IN 46825
Ph: (219)484-9600   Fax: (219)484-9604
Fr: 800-837-4424

Bimonthly. $56.00/year for individuals; $10.00 for single issue. Journal covering chiropractic science and research.

★1310★ **The Digest of Chiropractic Economics**
Chiropractic News Publishing Co.
29229 6 Mile Rd.
Livonia, MI 48152
Ph: (313)427-5720   Fax: (313)427-2760

Bimonthly. Independent magazine serving the chiropractic profession. Features profession/trade industry news, articles on the business and practice of the doctor of chiropractic, as well as original scientific manuscripts.

★1311★ **Today's Chiropractic**
Today's Chiropractic, Inc.
1269 Barclay Circle
Marietta, GA 30060
Ph: (404)499-9824   Fax: (404)419-0568
Fr: 800-394-5433

Bimonthly. Professional chiropractic magazine.

PLACEMENT AND JOB REFERRAL SERVICES

★1312★ **Christian Chiropractors Association (CCA)**
PO Box 9715
Fort Collins, CO 80525-0500
Ph: (303)482-1404   Fax: (303)482-1538
Fr: 800-999-1970

Members: Christian chiropractors organized to spread the gospel of Christ throughout the U.S. and abroad. **Purpose:** Works to unify Christian chiropractors around the essentials of Christianity, leaving Lesser Points of doctrine to the conscience of the individual believers. Focus is on world missions; seeks to expand the variety of mission fields. **Activities:** Aids in placement of Christian chiropractors as missionaries. Sponsors missions in Ecuador, Ethiopia, France, Kenya, Monaco, Peru, C.I.S., Philippines, the U.S., and Canada.

EMPLOYER DIRECTORIES AND NETWORKING LISTS

★1313★ **Chiropractors Directory**
American Business Directories, Inc.
American Business Information, Inc.
5711 S. 86th Cir.
Omaha, NE 68127
Ph: (402)593-4600   Fax: (402)331-1505

Annual. $1,650.00, U.S. edition; $265.00, (Canad. ed.); payment with order. Entries include: Name, address, phone (including area code), size of advertisement, year first in Yellow Pages, name of owner or manager, number of employees. Regional editions available; please inquire. Compiled from telephone company Yellow Pages nationwide. Arrangement: Geographical.

★1314★ **Women's Auxiliary of the International Chiropractors Association—Membership Roster**
Women's Auxiliary of the International Chiropractors Association
1925 Apple Ave.
Muskegon, MI 49442
Ph: (616)777-2622   Fax: (616)777-4814

Biennial. Covers about 500 women who are chiropractic assistants, chiropractors, or related to members of the ICA.

HANDBOOKS AND MANUALS

★1315★ **Careers in Medicine**
VGM Career Horizons
4255 W. Touhy Ave.
Lincolnwood, IL 60646-1975
Ph: (847)679-5500   Fax: (847)679-2494
Fr: 800-323-4900

Terence J. Sacks. Second edition, 1996. $17.95; $13.95 (paper). 192 pages. Examines the many paths open to M.D.s, D.O.s, and M.D./Ph.D.s, including clinical private or group practice, hospitals, public health organizations, the armed forces, emergency rooms, research institutions, medical schools, pharmaceutical companies and private industry, and research/advocacy groups like the World Health Organization. A special chapter on osteopathy and chiropractic explores this branch of medicine.

★1316★ **Careers in Medicine: Traditional and Alternative Opportunities**
Garrett Park Press
PO Box 190 C
Garrett Park, MD 20896-0190
Ph: (301)946-2553

Donald T. Rucker and Martin D. Keller. 1990. $15.95. 346 pages. Cites training requirements, illustrative work activities, and a summary of the advantages and disadvantages in a variety of specialized areas. Includes hundreds of career alternatives and discusses ways to break into these fields for persons trained in medicine. Features contributions from over 40 professionals in all phases of medicine and provides 200 sources of information on specialties and subspecialties.

★1317★ **100 Best Careers for the Year 2000**
Prentice Hall General Reference
15 Columbus Cir.
New York, NY 10023
Ph: (212)373-8500   Fr: 800-223-2348

Shelly Field. 1992. $15.00 (paper). Covers 100 of the fastest growing jobs. The publication is divided into 11 general employment sections. Specific careers are covered within each section. Provides job description, responsibilities, employment opportunities, earnings, education and training, advancement opportunities, and experience and qualifications for each occupation.

★1318★ Opportunities in Chiropractic Careers

VGM Career Horizons
4255 W. Touhy Ave.
Lincolnwood, IL 60646-1975
Ph: (847)679-5500   Fax: (847)679-2494
Fr: 800-323-4900

R.C. Shafer and Louis Sportelli. 1994. $14.95; $11.95 (paper). A guide to planning for and building a career in the field. Illustrated.

★1319★ Opportunities in Sports and Athletics

VGM Career Horizons
4255 W. Touhy Ave.
Lincolnwood, IL 60646-1975
Ph: (847)679-5500   Fax: (847)679-2494
Fr: 800-323-4900

William Ray Heitzmann. 1994. $14.95; $11.95 (paper). A guide to planning for and seeking opportunities in this growing field. Illustrated.

★1320★ Opportunities in Sports Medicine Careers

VGM Career Horizons
4255 W. Touhy Ave.
Lincolnwood, IL 60646-1975
Ph: (847)679-5500   Fax: (847)679-2494
Fr: 800-323-4900

William Ray Heitzmann. 1995. $14.95; $11.95 (paper). 160 pages. Discusses a variety of opportunities in this field and how to pursue them. Contains bibliography and illustrations.

★1321★ Resumes for Health and Medical Careers

4255 W. Touhy Ave.
Lincolnwood, IL 60646-1975
Ph: (708)679-5500   Fax: (708)679-6375
Fr: 800-323-4900

Compiled by VGM Career Horizons Staff 1995. $9.95 (paper).

★1322★ Therapists and Allied Health Professionals Career Directory

Gale Research
835 Penobscot Bldg.
Detroit, MI 48226-4094
Ph: (313)961-2242   Fax: (313)961-6083
Fr: 800-877-GALE

Bradley Morgan. 1993. $39.00. 326 pages. Essays on specific careers provide an insider's perspective. Also features extensive listings of contacts and entry-level job opportunities. Provides information on internships and sources of help-wanted ads.

OTHER SOURCES

★1323★ American Chiropractic Association (ACA)

1701 Clarendon Blvd.
Arlington, VA 22209
Ph: (703)276-8800   Fax: (703)243-2593
Fr: 800-986-4636

Purpose: Enhances the philosophy, science, and art of chiropractic, and the professional welfare of individuals in the field. Promotes legislation defining chiropractic health care and improves the public's awareness and utilization of chiropractic. Conducts chiropractic survey and statistical study; maintains library.

★1324★ Council on Chiropractic Education (CCE)

7975 N. Hayden Rd., No. A-210
Scottsdale, AZ 85258-3246
Ph: (602)443-8877   Fax: (602)483-7333

Members: Representatives of member colleges. **Purpose:** Advocates high standards in chiropractic education; establishes criteria of institutional excellence for educating chiropractic physicians; acts as national accrediting agency for chiropractic colleges. Conducts workshops for college teams, consultants, and chiropractic college staffs.

★1325★ Holistic Dental Association (HDA)

c/o Dr. Paul Plowman
4801 Richmond Sq.
Oklahoma City, OK 73118
Ph: (405)840-5600   Fax: (405)843-0417

Members: Dentists, chiropractors, dental hygienists, physical therapists, and medical doctors. **Purpose:** Goals are: to provide a holistic approach to better dental care for patients; to expand techniques, medications, and philosophies that pertain to extractions, anesthetics, fillings, crowns, and orthodontics. Encourages use of homeopathic medications, acupuncture, cranial osteopathy, nutritional techniques, and physical therapy in treating patients in addition to conventional treatments. **Activities:** Classifies therapies; has developed a referral questionnaire for holistic practitioners. Sponsors training and educational seminars.

★1326★ International Chiropractors Association (ICA)

1110 N. Glebe Rd., Ste. 1000
Arlington, VA 22201
Ph: (703)528-5000   Fax: (703)528-5023

Members: Professional society of chiropractors, chiropractic educators, students, and laypersons. **Activities:** Sponsors professional development programs and practice management seminars.

Civil Engineers

★1342★ *PM Network*

Project Management Institute
130 S. State Rd.
Upper Darby, PA 19082
Ph: (610)734-3330   Fax: (610)734-3266

Monthly. $90.00/year for members. Magazine covering project and program management.

★1343★ *Public Works*

Public Works Journal Corp., Inc.
200 S. Broad St.
Ridgewood, NJ 07451
Ph: (201)445-5800   Fax: (201)445-5170
Fr: 800-524-2364

Monthly. Trade magazine covering the public works industry nationwide for city, county, and state.

★1344★ *SWE*

Society of Women Engineers
120 Wall St., 11th Fl.
New York, NY 10005-3902
Ph: (212)509-9577   Fax: (212)509-0224

Bimonthly. $30.00/year for nonmembers. Magazine for engineering students and for women and men working in the engineering and technology fields. Covers career guidance, continuing development and topical issues.

★1345★ *Technology Review*

The Tech
PO Box 397029
Cambridge, MA 02139
Ph: (617)253-1541   Fax: (617)258-8226

$30.00/year for individuals; $3.75 for single issue; $42.00/year for other countries. Magazine reviewing new developments in technology with an emphasis on economic, political, and social implications. Not a new product publication.

★1346★ *Water Engineering & Management*

Scranton Gillette Communications, Inc.
380 E. Northwest Hwy.
Des Plaines, IL 60016-2282
Ph: (708)298-6622   Fax: (708)390-0408

Monthly. $25.00/year, $3.00 for single issue. Trade magazine dedicated to the advancement of the state of the art and the transfer of technology in the field of municipal, county and regional water supply and water pollution control. Serves consulting sanitary engineers and managers of water/wastewater facilities who specify/buy products and services.

★1347★ *Western City*

League of California Cities
1400 K St.
Sacramento, CA 95814
Ph: (916)444-5790   Fax: (916)658-8240

Monthly. $30.00/year for individuals; $49.00 for two years. Municipal interest magazine.

★1348★ *Woman Engineer*

Equal Opportunity Publications, Inc.
150 Motor Pkwy., Ste. 420
Hauppauge, NY 11788-5145
Ph: (516)273-0066   Fax: (516)273-8936

Engineer recruitment magazine.

PLACEMENT AND JOB REFERRAL SERVICES

★1349★ **American Academy of Environmental Engineers (AAEE)**

130 Holiday Ct., No. 100
Annapolis, MD 21401
Ph: (410)266-3311   Fax: (410)266-7653

Members: Environmentally oriented registered professional engineers certified by examination as diplomates of the academy. **Purpose:** Purposes are: to improve the standards of environmental engineering; to certify those with special knowledge of environmental engineering; to furnish lists of those certified to the public. **Activities:** Maintains speakers' bureau. Recognizes areas of specialization: Air Pollution Control; General Environmental; Hazardous Waste Management; Industrial Hygiene; Radiation Protection; Solid Waste Management; Water Supply and Wastewater. Requires written and oral examinations for certification. Works with other professional organizations on environmentally oriented activities. Identifies potential employment candidates through Talent Search Service.

★1350★ **American Association of Blacks in Energy (AABE)**

927 15th St. NW, Ste. 200
Washington, DC 20005
Ph: (202)371-9530   Fax: (202)371-9218

Members: Blacks in energy-related professions, including engineers, scientists, consultants, academicians, and entrepreneurs; government officials and public policymakers; interested students. **Purpose:** Represents blacks and other minorities in matters involving energy use and research, the formulation of energy policy, the ownership of energy resources, and the development of energy technologies. Seeks to increase the knowledge, understanding, and awareness of the minority community in energy issues by serving as an energy information source for policymakers, recommending blacks and other minorities to appropriate energy officials and executives, encouraging students to pursue professional careers in the energy industry, and advocating the participation of blacks and other minorities in energy programs and policymaking activities. Updates members on key legislation and regulations being developed by the Department of Energy, the Department of Interior, the Department of Commerce, the Small Business Administration, and other federal and state agencies. **Activities:** Offers information on current job openings.

★1351★ **American Indian Science and Engineering Society (AISES)**

1630 30th St., Ste. 301
Boulder, CO 80301
Ph: (303)492-8658   Fax: (303)492-3400

Members: American Indian and non-Indian students and professionals in science, technology, and engineering fields; corporations representing energy, mining, aerospace, electronic, and computer fields. **Purpose:** Seeks to motivate and encourage students

to pursue undergraduate and graduate studies in science, engineering, and technology. **Activities:** Sponsors science fairs in grade schools, teacher training workshops, summer math/science sessions for 8th-12th graders, professional chapters, and student chapters in colleges. Offers scholarships. Adult members serve as role models, advisers, and mentors for students. Operates placement service. **E-Mail:** aise sha@spot.colorado.edu

★1352★ **American Water Works Association (AWWA)**

6666 W. Quincy Ave.
Denver, CO 80235
Ph: (303)794-7711   Fax: (303)795-1440
Fr: 800-926-7337

Members: Water utility managers, superintendents, engineers, chemists, bacteriologists, and other individuals interested in public water supply; municipal- and investor-owned water departments; boards of health; manufacturers of waterworks equipment; government officials and consultants interested in water supply. **Purpose:** Develops standards and supports research programs in waterworks design, construction, operation, and management. **Activities:** conducts in-service training schools and prepares manuals for waterworks personnel. Maintains hall of fame. Offers placement service via member newsletter; compiles statistics. Offers training; children's services; and information center on the water utilities industry, potable water, and water reuse.

★1353★ **Asian American Architects and Engineers**

1670 Pine St.
San Francisco, CA 94109
Ph: (415)928-5910   Fax: (415)921-0182

Members: Minorities. **Purpose:** Provides contracts and job opportunities for minorities in the architectural and engineering fields. **Activities:** Serves as a network for the promotion in professional fields.

★1354★ **Engineering Society of Detroit (ESD)**

100 Farnsworth Ave.
Detroit, MI 48202
Ph: (313)832-5400   Fax: (313)832-5920

Members: Engineers from all disciplines; scientists and technologists. **Activities:** Offers placement services. Conducts technical programs and engineering refresher courses; sponsors conferences and expositions. Maintains speakers' bureau. Although based in Detroit, MI, society membership is international.

★1355★ **Korean Scientists and Engineers Association in America (KSEA)**

6261 Executive Blvd.
Rockville, MD 20852
Ph: (301)984-7048   Fax: (301)984-1231

Members: Scientists and engineers holding single or advanced degrees. **Purpose:** Goals are to: promote friendship and mutuality among Korean and American scientists and engineers; contribute to Korea's scientific, technological, industrial, and economic developments; strengthen the scientific, technological, and cultural bonds between Korea and the U.S. Sponsors symposium. **Activities:** Maintains speakers' bureau, placement service, and biographical archives. Compiles statistics. Maintains 100 volume library of scientific handbooks and yearbooks in Korean.

★1356★ Society of Hispanic Professional Engineers (SHPE)

5400 E. Olympic Blvd., Ste. 210
Los Angeles, CA 90022
Ph: (213)725-3970

Purpose: Engineers, student engineers, and scientists seeking to increase the number of Hispanic engineers by providing motivation and support to students. Sponsors competitions and educational programs. **Activities:** Maintains placement service and speakers' bureau; compiles statistics.

EMPLOYER DIRECTORIES AND NETWORKING LISTS

★1357★ American Men and Women of Science

R. R. Bowker Co.
Reed Reference Publishing
121 Chanlon Rd.
New Providence, NJ 07974
Ph: (908)464-6800   Fax: (908)665-6688
Fr: 800-521-8110

Triennial, latest edition January 1995. $106.00, per volume; $850.00, set. Covers over 123,000 U.S. and Canadian scientists active in the physical, biological, mathematical, computer science, and engineering fields; includes references to previous edition for deceased scientists and nonrespondents. Entries include: Name, address, education, personal and career data, memberships, honors and awards, research interest. Arrangement: Alphabetical. Indexes: Discipline (in separate volume).

★1358★ American Society of Civil Engineers—Official Register

American Society of Civil Engineers
345 E. 47th St.
New York, NY 10017
Ph: (212)705-7517   Fax: (212)980-4681
Fr: 800-548-ASCE

Annual, December. Free. Publication includes: Rosters of technical, professional, educational, and research committees, national officers, regional councils, sections and branches, award recipients. Indexes: Alphabetical.

★1359★ Construction Employment Guide in the National and International Field

World Trade Academy Press
50 E. 42nd St., Ste. 509
New York, NY 10017
Ph: (212)697-4999

$16.50. Covers More than 200 U.S. and international construction, engineering and design companies. Also covers U.S. govern-

ment construction employment opportunities, job centers and employment agencies. Entries include: Company name, address, specialties.

★1360★ Directory of African American Design Firms

San Francisco Redevelopment Agency
770 Golden Gate Ave.
San Francisco, CA 94102-3120
Ph: (415)749-2423   Fax: (415)749-2526

Annual, December. Free. Covers over 100 architectural, engineering, planning, and landscape design firms. Entries include: Firm name, address, phone names and titles of key personnel, particular type of work. Arrangement: Alphabetical.

★1361★ Directory of Contract Service Firms

C. E. Publications, Inc.
PO Box 97000
Kirkland, WA 98083
Ph: (206)823-2222   Fax: (206)821-0942

Annual, January. $10.00. Covers Approximately 900 contract firms actively engaged in the employment of engineering and technical personnel for temporary contract assignments throughout the world. Entries include: Company name, address, phone, name of contact. Arrangement: Alphabetical. Indexes: Geographical.

★1362★ Directory of Engineering Societies and Related Organizations

American Association of Engineering Societies
1111 19th St. NW, Ste. 608
Washington, DC 20036
Ph: (202)296-2237   Fax: (202)296-1151
Fr: 800-658-8897

1992. $185.00. Lists 1,000 national, regional, Canadian, and international organizations concerned with engineering and related fields.

★1363★ Directory of Engineers in Private Practice

National Society of Professional Engineers
1420 King St.
Alexandria, VA 22314
Ph: (703)684-2862   Fax: (703)836-4875

Annual. $85.00. Covers 600 consulting engineering firms and 7,200 individuals who are members of the society's Professional Engineers in Private Practice division. Entries include: For companies, name, address, phone, name of principal executive, list of services. For individuals, name, address; most listings include phone. Arrangement: Firms are geographic, then by specialty; individuals are alphabetical.

★1364★ Engineering Research Centres

Stockton Press
Groves Dictionaries
345 Park Ave. S., 10th Fl.
New York, NY 10010
Ph: (212)689-9200   Fr: 800-221-2123

Fourth edition, 1995. $515.00. 768 pages. Contains over 8,000 entries describing research and technology laboratories in over 70 countries. Provides details on industrial

research centers and educational establishments with research and development activity. Indexes: Subject and title of establishments.

★1365★ Engineers—Civil Directory

American Business Directories, Inc.
American Business Information, Inc.
5711 S. 86th Cir.
Omaha, NE 68127
Ph: (402)593-4600   Fax: (402)331-1505

Annual. $660.00, payment with order. Entries include: Name, address, phone (including area code), size of advertisement, year first in Yellow Pages, name of owner or manager, number of employees. Compiled from telephone company Yellow Pages, nationwide. Arrangement: Geographical.

★1366★ Engineers—Structural Directory

American Business Directories, Inc.
American Business Information, Inc.
5711 S. 86th Cir.
Omaha, NE 68127
Ph: (402)593-4600   Fax: (402)331-1505

Annual. $405.00, payment with order. Entries include: Name, address, phone (including area code), size of advertisement, year first in Yellow Pages, name of owner or manager, number of employees. Compiled from telephone company Yellow Pages, nationwide. Arrangement: Geographical.

★1367★ ENR Directory of Design Firms

McGraw-Hill, Inc.
1221 Ave. of the Americas
New York, NY 10020
Ph: (212)512-2534   Fax: (212)512-4178

Biennial, fall of even years; issue of *Engineering News Record*. $85.00. Covers 133 architects, architectural engineers, consultants, and other design firms; limited to advertisers. Mini-profiles on about 3,400 U.S. firms and 500 foreign firms or foreign offices of U.S. firms. Also includes lists of top 500 design firms in the United States, top 200 international design firms, top 50 United States design-construction firms, and top 50 international design-construction firms, based on total amount of billings. Entries include: For advertisers: company name, address, branch locations, subsidiaries, list of key personnel, territory served, capabilities. In ranked lists: company name, address, phone; international firms include telex. Arrangement: Alphabetical (profiles); geographical (mini-profiles).

★1368★ ENR—Top 500 Design Firms Issue

McGraw-Hill, Inc.
1221 Ave. of the Americas
New York, NY 10020
Ph: (212)512-4635   Fax: (212)512-2820

Annual, April. $10.00, reprint, payment must accompany order. Publication includes: List of 500 leading architectural, engineering, and specialty design firms selected on basis of annual billings. Entries include: Company name, headquarters location, type of firm, current and prior year rank in billings, types of services, countries in which operated in preceding year. Arrangement: Ranked by billings.

★1369★ ENR—Top International Design Firms Issue

McGraw-Hill, Inc.
1221 Ave. of the Americas, Rm. 4188
New York, NY 10020
Ph: (212)512-4635

Annual, July. $10.00, reprint, payment with order. Publication includes: List of 200 design firms (including United States firms) competing outside their own national borders who received largest dollar volume of foreign contracts in preceding calendar year. Entries include: Company name, headquarters location, type of firm, current and previous year rankings in total billings, types of services, countries in which operated in preceding year. Arrangement: By amount billed to international clients in previous year.

★1370★ Municipal/County Directory Library Edition

Carroll Publishing
1058 Thomas Jefferson St. NW
Washington, DC 20007
Ph: (202)333-8620   Fax: (202)337-7020
Fr: 800-336-4240

Annual, July. $137.00, plus $8.00 shipping; payment must accompany order. Covers officials of 1,400 county governments (with populations over 25,000) and 2,000 municipalities (with populations over 1,000); includes elected, appointed, and career office holders. Entries include: Name, title, agency, address, phone. Arrangement: County officials are geographical, then by agency; municipal officials are by city. Indexes: personal name (with phone), agency.

★1371★ Municipal Year Book

Newman Books Ltd.
32 Vauxhall Bridge Rd.
London SW1V 2SS, England
Ph: 71 9736400   Fax: 71 2335057

Annual, December. $140.00, postpaid. Covers local and central government agencies and officials of the United Kingdom; municipal art galleries, associations, development organizations, fairs, libraries, museums, airports, and other local authorities. Entries include: Name of authority or governing agency, address, phone, fax, names of elected councillors, officers, names and titles of key personnel, contacts, population, and pay. Arrangement: Geographical. Indexes: Subject, place names.

★1372★ Peterson's Job Opportunities in Engineering and Technology 1996

Peterson's
PO Box 2123
Princeton, NJ 08543-2123
Ph: (609)243-9111   Fax: (609)243-9150
Fr: 800-338-3282

Compiled by the Peterson's staff. Annual. $19.95 paperback. 432 pages. Profiles 2,000 high-tech companies looking primarily for technical personnel in such fields as biotechnology, telecommunications, software, computers and peripherals, defense, and aerospace. Contains job-search strategies and career options to help match education and expertise to the job market. Indexed geographically, by industry, and by hiring needs.

★1373★ Scientific and Technical Organizations and Agencies Directory

Gale Research
835 Penobscot Bldg.
Detroit, MI 48226-4094
Ph: (313)961-2242   Fax: (313)961-6083
Fr: 800-877-GALE

Irregular; latest edition December 1993. $195.00. Covers over 25,600 national and international organizations and agencies concerned with the physical and applied sciences, engineering, and technology, including associations, computer information services, consulting firms, educational institutions, foundations, government advisory organizations, federal government agencies, general grant and assistance programs, libraries and information centers, patent sources and services, research and development centers, scholarships, fellowships, and loans, science-technology centers, standards organizations, state academies of science, and state government agencies in the fields of aeronautics and space sciences, chemistry, computer science specialties, electronics, geography, geology, machinery, mathematics, metallurgy, meteorology, mineralogy, nuclear science, petroleum and gas, physics, plastics, transportation, water resources, and other areas. Entries include: Organization name, address, phone, and name of contact; additional descriptive text for most entries. Arrangement: Classified by type of organization. Indexes: Organization name/key word.

★1374★ Who's Who in Technology

Gale Research
835 Penobscot Bldg.
Detroit, MI 48226-4094
Ph: (313)961-2242   Fax: (313)961-6083
Fr: 800-877-GALE

Irregular, new edition expected June 1995. $380.00. Covers 38,000 engineers, scientists, inventors, and researchers. Entries include: Name, title, affiliation, address; personal, education, and career data; publications, patents; technical field of activity; area of expertise. Arrangement: Alphabetical. Indexes: Geographical, employer, technical discipline, expertise.

HANDBOOKS AND MANUALS

★1375★ The Best Resumes for Scientists and Engineers

John Wiley and Sons
605 3rd Ave.
New York, NY 10158
Ph: (212)850-6000   Fr: 800-225-5945

Adele Lewis. Second edition, 1993. $37.50; $14.95 (paper). Presents an extensive collection of scientific and engineering resumes, highlighting the important differences between these and resumes written for other occupations.

★1376★ Careers in Engineering

VGM Career Horizons
4255 W. Touhy Ave.
Lincolnwood, IL 60646-1975
Ph: (847)679-5500   Fax: (847)679-2494
Fr: 800-323-4900

Geraldine O. Gardner. 1994. $17.95; $13.95 (paper). Covers careers in the public or private sector, in industry, the university, or the military, from applications in computer architecture design to high temperature ceramics.

★1377★ Engineering Success

Kendall Hunt Publishing
4050 Westmark Dr.
PO Box 1840
Dubuque, IA 52004-1840
Ph: (319)589-1000   Fax: 800-772-9165
Fr: 800-228-0810

Bill Osher. 1994. $27.96.

★1378★ Engineering Your Job Search: A Job-Finding Resource for Engineering Professionals

Professional Publications, Inc.
1250 5th Ave.
Belmont, CA 94002
Ph: (415)593-9119   Fax: (415)592-4519
Fr: 800-426-1178

Compiled by Professional Publications editors. 1995. $12.95 (paper).

★1379★ Introduction to the Engineering Profession

HarperCollins Publishers, Inc.
10 E. 53rd. St.
New York, NY 10022-5299
Ph: (212)207-7000   Fax: (212)207-7145
Fr: 800-331-3761

David M. Burghardt. 1995. $30.00 (paper).

★1380★ Job Opportunities in Engineering and Technology

Peterson's Guides, Inc.
PO Box 2123
Princeton, NJ 08543-2123
Ph: (609)243-9111   Fax: (609)243-9150
Fr: 800-338-3282

1994. $18.95 (paper).

★1381★ Majoring in Engineering: How to Get from Your Freshman Year to Your First Job

Farrar, Straus & Giroux, Inc.
19 Union Sq., W
New York, NY 10003
Ph: (212)741-6900   Fr: 800-788-6262

John Garcia. 1995. $20.00; $10.00 (paper).

★1382★ 100 Best Careers for the Year 2000

Prentice Hall General Reference
15 Columbus Cir.
New York, NY 10023
Ph: (212)373-8500   Fr: 800-223-2348

Shelly Field. 1992. $15.00 (paper). Covers 100 of the fastest growing jobs. The publication is divided into 11 general employment sections. Specific careers are covered within each section. Provides job description, responsibilities, employment opportunities, earnings, education and training, advancement opportunities, and experience and qualifications for each occupation.

★1383★ Opportunities in Civil Engineering Careers

VGM Career Horizons
NTC Publishing Group
4255 W. Touhy Ave.
Lincolnwood, IL 60646-1975
Ph: (847)679-5500   Fax: (847)679-2494
Fr: 800-323-4900

Joseph Hagerty and Louis F. Cohn. 1996. $14.95; $11.95 (paper). 160 pages. Describes career opportunities in the different fields of civil engineering and tells how to prepare for and launch such a career.

★1384★ Opportunities in Engineering Careers

VGM Career Horizons
4255 W. Touhy Ave.
Lincolnwood, IL 60646-1975
Ph: (847)679-5500   Fax: (847)679-2494
Fr: 800-323-4900

Nicholas Basta. 1995. $14.95; $11.95 (paper). Outlines typical job titles, salaries, career paths, and employment prospects.

★1385★ Opportunities in High Tech Careers

VGM Career Horizons
4255 W. Touhy Ave.
Lincolnwood, IL 60646-1975
Ph: (847)679-5500   Fax: (847)679-2494
Fr: 800-323-4900

Gary D. Golter and Deborah Yanuck. 1995. $14.95; $11.95 (paper). 160 pages. Explores high technology careers. Describes job opportunities, how to make a career decision, how to prepare for high technology jobs, job hunting techniques, and future trends.

★1386★ Opportunities in State and Local Government Careers

VGM Career Horizons
4255 W. Touhy Ave.
Lincolnwood, IL 60646-1975
Ph: (847)679-5500   Fax: (847)679-2494
Fr: 800-323-4900

Neale Baxter. 1993. $13.95; $10.95 (paper). 160 pages. Points out the incentives and drawbacks of a government career. Describes hiring procedures and provides tips on filling out applications, taking physical and aptitude tests, handling interviews, and finding jobs. Describes the jobs in which 75% of all state and local government workers are employed. For each occupation, covers the nature of the work and the training required.

★1387★ Our Past, The Present, Your Future in Civil Engineering

American Society of Civil Engineers
345 E. 47th St.
New York, NY 10017
Fr: 800-548-ASCE

This 32-page brochure contains career information about the seven major branches of civil engineering, including environmental engineering.

★1388★ Partnering for Success

American Society of Civil Engineers
345 E. 47th St.
New York, NY 10017
Ph: (212)705-7496   Fax: (212)705-7712
Fr: 800-548-2723

Thomas R. Warne. 1994. $16.00.

★1389★ Resumes for Engineering Careers

VGM Career Horizons
NTC Publishing Group
4255 W. Touhy Ave.
Lincolnwood, IL 60646-1975
Ph: (847)679-5500   Fax: (847)679-2494
Fr: 800-323-4900

1994. $9.95. 160 pages. Contains sample resumes and cover letters applicable to any engineering field.

★1390★ Where the Jobs Are: The Hottest Careers for the '90s

The Career Press, Inc.
3 Tice Rd.
PO Box 687
Franklin Lakes, NJ 07417
Ph: (201)848-0310   Fax: (201)848-1727
Fr: 800-237-3371

Joyce Hadley. Second edition, 1995. $9.99. 300 pages. Describes careers in fifteen general fields, from accounting to travel and hospitality.

EMPLOYMENT AGENCIES AND SEARCH FIRMS

★1391★ ABC Employment Service

25 S. Bemiston, Ste. 214
Clayton, MO 63105
Ph: (314)725-3140

Employment agency.

★1392★ B W and Associates, Inc.

4415 W. Harrison St.
Hillside, IL 60162-1910
Ph: (708)449-5400

Employment agency.

★1393★ Claremont-Branan, Inc.

2150 Parklake Dr., Ste. 212
Atlanta, GA 30345
Ph: (404)491-1292

Employment agency. Executive search firm.

★1394★ Engineer One, Inc.

10124 Dutchtown Rd.
Knoxville, TN 37932-2611
Ph: (615)690-2611   Fax: (615)690-2611

Employment agency.

★1395★ Hayden and Associates, Inc.

7825 Washington Ave. S., Ste. 120
Minneapolis, MN 55439-2431
Ph: (612)941-6300   Fax: (612)941-9602

Employment agency. Executive search firm. Fills openings in a variety of fields.

★1396★ Industrial Recruiters Associates, Inc.

630 Oakwood Ave., Ste. 318
West Hartford, CT 06110
Ph: (203)953-3643

Employment agency.

★1397★ International Staffing Consultants

500 Newport Center Dr., Ste. 300
Newport Beach, CA 92660-7003
Ph: (714)721-7990

Employment agency. Provides placement on regular or temporary basis. Affiliate office in London.

★1398★ The Jobs Co.

8900 E. Sprague Ave.
Spokane, WA 99212-2927
Ph: (509)928-3151   Fax: (509)928-3168

Employment agency. Has division specializing in engineering and scientific openings. Also operates division specializing in sales openings.

★1399★ JR Professional Search

PO Box 18356
Tucson, AZ 85731
Ph: (520)721-1855   Fax: (520)721-1855

Employment agency.

★1400★ LOR Personnel Division

418 Wall St.
Princeton, NJ 08540
Ph: (609)921-6580

Employment agency. Executive search firm.

★1401★ Main Line Personnel Service, Inc.

401 City Ave.
Bala Cynwyd, PA 19004-1122
Ph: (610)667-1820

Employment agency.

★1402★ Search and Recruit International

4455 South Blvd.
Virginia Beach, VA 23452
Ph: (804)490-3151

Employment agency. Headquartered in Virginia Beach. Other offices in Bremerton, WA; Charleston, SC; Jacksonville, FL; Memphis, TN; Pensacola, FL; Sacramento, CA; San Bernardino, CA; San Diego, CA.

★1403★ Sierra Technology Corporation

4150 Manzanita Ave., Ste. 100
Carmichael, CA 95608-1700
Ph: (916)488-4960   Fax: (916)488-7058

Employment agency. Provides placement on a temporary basis.

★1404★ Source Engineering

5580 LBJ Fwy., Ste. 300
Dallas, TX 75240
Ph: (214)385-3002   Fax: (214)717-0075

Executive search firm. Many affiliate offices located throughout the U.S.

★1405★ T.R. Employment Agency

409 Wilshire Blvd.
Santa Monica, CA 90401
Ph: (310)393-4107

Employment agency.

★1406★ Tri-Serv Inc.

22 W. Padonia Rd., Ste. C53
Timonium, MD 21093
Ph: (301)561-1740

Employment agency.

OTHER SOURCES

★1407★ American Association of Engineering Societies (AAES)

1111 19th St. NW, Ste. 608
Washington, DC 20036
Ph: (202)296-2237   Fax: (202)296-1151

Purpose: Seeks to promote leadership in public affairs for the engineering community, work in support of math and science education for young persons. Disseminates of information about the profession. Provides statistics about engineers.

★1408★ American Society of Civil Engineers (ASCE)

1015 15th St. NW, Ste. 600
Washington, DC 20005
Ph: (202)789-2200   Fr: 800-548-2723

Members: Professional society of civil engineers. **Purpose:** Enhances the welfare of humanity by advancing the science and profession of engineering. Offers continuing education courses and technical specialty conferences. Develops technical codes and standard published technical and professional journals, manuals and a variety of books. Works closely with congress, the White House and federal agencies to build sound national policy on engineering issues. Supports research of new civil engineering technology and material.

★1409★ Association for International Practical Training (AIPT)

10400 Little Patuxent Pky. Ste. 250
Columbia, MD 21044
Ph: (410)997-2200   Fax: (410)992-3924

Purpose: Helps coordinate training around the world in fields such as travel, the culinary arts, and hotel management. **Activities:** Conducts programs in career development and hospitality/tourism exchanges. Operates a student exchange program. Provides recipro-

cal practical training experience for recent graduates from the U.S., Austria, Germany, Finland, France, Hungary, Ireland, Japan, Malaysia, Netherlands, Switzerland, and the United Kingdom. Arranges training programs in the U.S. and abroad. Serves as U.S. affiliate to IAESTE (International Association for the Exchange of Students for Technical Experience) and operates a Professional Visitors Program to arrange short-term educational and training visits to the U.S. **E-Mail:** aipt@aipt.org

★1410★ Career Encounters: Women in Engineering

Cambridge Career Products
PO Box 2153
Dept. CC15
Charleston, WV 25328-2153
Ph: (304)744-9323   Fax: (304)744-9351
Fr: 800-468-4227

Video. $99.95. 25 minutes. Professionals shown in a variety of settings discuss different aspects of their careers.

★1411★ Engineering Salary Survey

Source Engineering
1290 Oakmead, Ste. 318
Sunnyvale, CA 94086
Ph: (408)738-8440

Annual. Discusses the structure of the engineering profession, trends, and compensation. Salaries are listed by job function, industry, and years of experience.

★1412★ Graduating Engineer

Peterson's/COG Publishing Group
16030 Ventura Blvd., No. 560
Encino, CA 91436
Ph: (818)789-5293

Eight issues/year. Magazine focusing on employment, education, and career development for entry-level engineers.

★1413★ National Action Council for Minorities in Engineering (NACME)

3 W. 35th St.
New York, NY 10001-2281
Ph: (212)279-2626   Fax: (212)629-5178

Purpose: Seeks to increase the number of African American, Latino, and Native American students enrolled in and graduating from engineering schools. Through the Corporate Scholars Program, offers comprehensive scholarships to engineering students that include leadership development, corporate mentors and summer internships. Works with local, regional, and national education organizations to motivate and encourage precollege students to engage in engineering careers. Conducts educational and research

programs; operates project to assist engineering schools in improving the retention and graduation rates of minority students. Maintains speakers' bureau; compiles statistics.

★1414★ Salaries of Scientists, Engineers, and Technicians: A Summary of Salary Surveys

Commission on Professionals in Science and Technology (CPST)
1500 Massachusetts Ave. NW, Ste. 831
Washington, DC 20005
Ph: (202)223-6995

1993.

★1415★ Society of Women Engineers (SWE)

120 Wall St., 11th Fl.
New York, NY 10005
Ph: (212)509-9577   Fax: (212)509-0224

Members: Educational service society of women engineers; membership is also open to men. **Purpose:** Supplies information on the achievements of women engineers and the opportunities available to them; assists women engineers in preparing for return to active work following temporary retirement. Serves as an informational center on women in engineering. **Activities:** Administers several certificate and scholarship programs. Offers tours and career guidance; conducts surveys. Compiles statistics.

★1416★ Water Environment Federation (WEF)

601 Wythe St.
Alexandria, VA 22314-1994
Ph: (703)684-2400   Fax: (703)684-2492
Fr: 800-666-0206

Members: Technical societies representing chemists, biologists, ecologists, geologists, operators, educational and research personnel, industrial wastewater engineers, consultant engineers, municipal officials, equipment manufacturers, and university professors and students dedicated to the ehancement and preservation of water quality and resources. **Purpose:** Seeks to advance fundamental and practical knowledge concerning the nature, collection, treatment, and disposal of domestic and industrial wastewaters, and the design, construction, operation, and management of facilities for these purposes. Disseminates technical information; promotes good public relations and regulations that improve water quality and the status of individuals working in this field. **Activities:** Conducts educational and research programs.

Claims Examiners

SOURCES OF HELP-WANTED ADS

★1417★ Best's Review (Life/Health Edition)

A.M. Best Co.
Ambest Rd.
Oldwick, NJ 08858
Ph: (908)439-2200   Fax: (908)439-3363

Monthly. $21.00/year for individuals; $7.50/year for single issue. Magazine covering issues and trends for the management personnel of life/health insurers, the agents, and brokers who market their products.

★1418★ Business Insurance

Crain Communications, Inc.
740 N. Rush St.
Chicago, IL 60611-2590
Ph: (312)649-5311   Fax: (312)280-3189

Weekly. $80.00/year for individuals. Magazine for executives in the corporate risk, employee benefit, and finance fields.

★1419★ CLAIMS

Insurance Week Publications
1001 4th Ave., Ste. 3029
Seattle, WA 98154

Monthly. $41.00/year. Magazine for the property-casualty insurance claims industry.

★1420★ National Underwriter Property and Casualty/Risk and Benefits Management

National Underwriter Co.
505 Gest St.
Cincinnati, OH 45203-1716
Ph: (513)721-2140   Fax: (513)721-0126

Weekly (Mon.). Newsweekly for agents, brokers, executives, and managers in risk and benefit insurance.

EMPLOYER DIRECTORIES AND NETWORKING LISTS

★1421★ Best's Agents Guide

A. M. Best Co.
Ambest Rd.
Oldwick, NJ 08858
Ph: (908)439-2200   Fax: (908)439-3296

Annual, August. $95.00. Covers over 1,700 life and health insurance companies nationwide. Entries include: Company name, address, names of president and secretary, phone, whether a stock or mutual company, states where licensed, Best's rating, current and historical financial data. Arrangement: Alphabetical.

★1422★ Best's Insurance Reports

A. M. Best Co.
Ambest Rd.
Oldwick, NJ 08858
Ph: (908)439-2200   Fax: (908)439-3296

Annual, August. $570.00, per edition; monthly publications included. Published in two editions: Life-health insurance, covering about 1,800 companies, and property-casualty insurance, covering over 2,000 companies; scope includes Canada. Each edition lists state insurance commissioners and related companies and agencies (mutual funds, worker compensation funds, underwriting agencies, etc.). Entries include: For each company, company name, address, phone; history; states in which licensed; names of officers and directors; financial data; editorial comment and rating. Arrangement: Alphabetical.

★1423★ Business Insurance—Third-Party Claims Administrators Directory Issue

Crain Communications, Inc.
740 N. Rush St.
Chicago, IL 60611-2590
Ph: (312)649-5279   Fax: (312)280-3174

Annual, late January/early February. $4.00. Publication includes: List of over 300 third-party claims administration, adjusting, and auditing firms that process claims for self-insured clients, including employee benefit-

and property/casualty claims. Entries include: Company name, address, phone, fax, number of employees, number of claims processing staff, number of clients, method of compensation, prior year's revenues (when available), along with percent attributed to claims administration, adjusting and auditing for self-insured clients; claims volume by number of projects conducted; specialty or area of expertise. Arrangement: Alphabetical.

★1424★ Insurance Almanac

Underwriter Printing and Publishing Co.
50 E. Palisade Ave.
Englewood, NJ 07631
Ph: (201)569-8808   Fr: 800-526-4700

Annual, July. $115.00. Covers over 3,000 insurance companies that write fire, casualty, accident and health, life, and Lloyd's policies; also lists mutual and reciprocal companies. Includes national, state, and local insurance associations; state insurance officials; and about 800 agents, brokers, actuaries, and adjusters. Arrangement: Classified by insurance lines, type of activity, etc. Indexes: Company name.

★1425★ Insurance Phone Book and Directory

U.S. Directory Service
Reed Reference Publishing
121 Chanlon Rd.
New Providence, NJ 07974
Ph: (908)464-6800   Fax: (908)665-6688
Fr: 800-521-8110

Annual. $89.95, plus $6.30 shipping. Covers about 4,000 life, accident and health, worker's compensation, auto, fire and casualty, marine, surety, and other insurance companies. Entries include: Company name, address, phone, fax, toll-free number, type of insurance provided. Arrangement: Alphabetical.

★1426★ Moody's Bank and Finance Manual

Moody's Investors Service, Inc.
99 Church St.
New York, NY 10007
Ph: (212)553-0300   Fax: (212)553-4700
Fr: 800-342-5647

Annual, July; supplements in *Moody's Bank & Finance News Reports*. $1,475.00, per year, including supplements. Covers in four volumes, over 20,000 national, state, and private banks, savings and loans, mutual funds, unit investment trusts, and insurance and real estate companies in the United States. Entries include: Company name, headquarters and branch offices, phones, names and titles of principal executives, directors, history, Moody's rating, and extensive financial and statistical data. Arrangement: Classified by type of business. Indexes: Company name.

★1427★ **National Association of Catastrophe Adjusters–Membership Roster**
National Association of Catastrophe Adjusters
PO Box 821864
North Richland Hills, TX 76182
Ph: (817)498-3466   Fax: (817)498-0480
Annual, March. Free. Covers about 500 insurance catastrophe claims adjusters and adjusting firms; about 100 related insurance firms (associate members). Entries include: Name, address, phone, spouse's name. Arrangement: Separate geographical sections for regular and associate members. Indexes: Alphabetical; geographical.

★1428★ **Underwriters' Handbook Series**
National Underwriter Co.
505 Gest St.
Cincinnati, OH 45203-1716
Ph: (513)721-2140   Fax: (513)721-0126
Fr: 800-543-0874
Annual. $48.50, per state volume; 5th edition. Covers 142,000 insurance agents and agencies in 35 states and the District of Columbia; also names field representatives, managing general agents and general agents for both property/casualty and life/health insurance, adjusters, consultants, appraisers, audit and inspection services, and related insurance groups and associations and state departments of insurance. Published in 22 separate editions for Rocky Mountain States (Arizona, Colorado, Idaho, Montana, Nevada, New Mexico, Utah, and Wyoming); Georgia-Alabama; Missouri; Nebraska; North Dakota-South Dakota; Arkansas; Minnesota; Oklahoma; West Virginia; Maryland-Delaware-District of Columbia; Indiana; Florida-U.S. Caribbean; Pennsylvania; Iowa; Michigan; Illinois; Massachusetts; Ohio; Wisconsin; Connecticut-Rhode Island; Maine-New Hampshire-Vermont; and Kansas. Entries include: For companies Name, address, year established, divisions, key personnel (with addresses and phone numbers). Many list assets, liabilities, capital, and surplus. Arrangement: Separate alphabetical sections for insurance companies and field agents; other agents and activity are listed geographically, then by activity. Indexes: Type of insurance.

★1429★ **Who's Who in Insurance**
Underwriter Printing and Publishing Co.
50 E. Palisade Ave.
Englewood, NJ 07631
Ph: (201)569-8808   Fr: 800-526-4700
Annual, February. $115.00. Covers over 5,000 insurance officials, brokers, agents, and buyers. Entries include: Name, title,

company name, address, home address, educational background, professional club and association memberships, personal and career data. Arrangement: Alphabetical.

HANDBOOKS AND MANUALS

★1430★ **Opportunities in Insurance Careers**
VGM Career Horizons
4255 W. Touhy Ave.
Lincolnwood, IL 60646-1975
Ph: (847)679-5500   Fax: (847)679-2494
Fr: 800-323-4900
Robert Schrayer. 1994. $14.95; $11.95 (paper). A guide to planning for and seeking opportunities in the field. Contains bibliography and illustrations.

EMPLOYMENT AGENCIES AND SEARCH FIRMS

★1431★ **Avery Crafts Associates, Ltd.**
116 John St., Ste. 820
New York, NY 10038
Ph: (212)285-1074   Fax: (212)732-1039
Executive search firm.

★1432★ **Best Personnel Services**
8901 State Line Rd.
Kansas City, MO 64114-3200
Ph: (816)361-3100
Employment agency. Fills openings on a regular or temporary basis. Office also located in Independence, MO.

★1433★ **The Canon Group**
27936 Lost Canyon Rd.
Santa Clarita, CA 91351
Ph: (805)252-7400
Employment agency and search firm.

★1434★ **E.J. Ashton and Associates, Ltd.**
3125 N. Wilke Rd.
Arlington Heights, IL 60004-1452
Ph: (708)577-7900
Employment agency. Executive search firm.

★1435★ **Employment Advisors**
526 Nicollet Mall
Minneapolis, MN 55402-0521
Ph: (612)339-0521
Employment agency. Also located in Bloomington, Minnesota. Places candidates in variety of fields.

★1436★ **Godfrey Personnel Inc.**
300 W. Adams, Ste. 612
Chicago, IL 60606-5194
Ph: (312)236-4455
Employment agency.

★1437★ **Insurance Personnel**
65 Franklin St.
Boston, MA 02110-1303
Ph: (617)357-5380   Fax: (617)482-6581
Employment agency.

★1438★ **Insurance Personnel Service**
120 Kearny St., Ste. 1480
San Francisco, CA 94108-4803
Ph: (415)391-5900
Employment agency.

★1439★ **International Insurance Personnel, Inc.**
PO Box 28408
Atlanta, GA 30358
Ph: (404)257-9685

★1440★ **The Oxford Group**
901 Waterfall Way
Richardson, TX 75080
Ph: (214)644-5544   Fax: (214)644-7134
Executive search firm.

★1441★ **Questor Consultants, Inc.**
2515 N. Broad St.
Colmar, PA 18915
Ph: (215)997-9262   Fax: (215)997-9226
Executive search firm.

OTHER SOURCES

★1442★ **Alliance of American Insurers (ALLIANCE)**
1501 Woodfield Rd., Ste. 400 W
Schaumburg, IL 60173-4980
Ph: (708)330-8500   Fax: (708)330-8602
Members: Property and casualty insurance companies.

★1443★ **Insurance Information Institute (III)**
110 William St.
New York, NY 10038
Ph: (212)669-9200   Fax: (212)732-1916
Members: Property and liability insurance companies. **Purpose:** Provides information and educational services to mass media, educational institutions, trade associations, businesses, government agencies, and the public. Conducts public opinion surveys. Sponsors seminars and briefings on insurance, safety, research, public policy, and economic topics.

★1444★ **Life Office Management Association (LOMA)**
2300 Windy Ridge Pkwy., Ste. 600
Atlanta, GA 30339-8443
Ph: (404)951-1770   Fax: (404)984-0441
Members: Life and health insurance companies and financial services in the U.S. and Canada; and overseas in 45 countries; affiliate members are firms that provide professional support to member companies. **Purpose:** Provides research, information, training, and educational activities in areas of operations and systems, human resources,

financial planning and employee development. Administers FLMI Insurance Education Program, which awards FLMI (Fellow, Life Management Institute) designation to those who complete the ten-examination program.

★1445★ National Association of Claims Assistance Professionals (NACAP)

5329 S. Main St., Ste. 102
Downers Grove, IL 60515-4845
Ph: (708)963-3500   Fax: (708)963-1997

Members: Claims assistance professionals and electronic claims professionals. **Purpose:** Promotes interests of members through education and certification. Thru marketing, public relations lobbying and referral services seeks to increase public awareness of claims assistance professionals and electronic claims professionals.

★1446★ National Association of Insurance Women - International (NAIW)

1847 E. 15th
PO Box 4410
Tulsa, OK 74159
Ph: (918)744-5195   Fax: (918)743-1968
Fr: 800-766-6249

Members: Insurance industry professionals. **Purpose:** Promotes continuing education and networking for the professional advancement of its members. **Activities:** Offers education programs, meetings, services, and leadership opportunities.

★1447★ National Association of Public Insurance Adjusters (NAPIA)

300 Water St., Ste. 400
Baltimore, MD 21202
Ph: (410)539-4141   Fax: (410)659-9491

Members: Professional society of public insurance adjusters. **Activities:** Sponsors certification and professional education programs.

Clinical Laboratory Technologists and Technicians

SOURCES OF HELP-WANTED ADS

★1448★ ACTA Cytologica

Science Printers and Publishers, Inc.
PO Drawer 12425
8342 Olive Blvd.
St. Louis, MO 63132
Ph: (314)991-4440   Fax: (314)991-4654

Bimonthly. Journal publishing scientific articles offering significant contributions to the advancement of clinical cytology.

★1449★ American Clinical Laboratory

International Scientific Communications, Inc.
30 Controls Dr.
PO Box 870
Shelton, CT 06484-0870
Ph: (203)926-9300   Fax: (203)926-9310

$190.00/year for individuals. Technical magazine on clinical laboratory techniques.

★1450★ American Laboratory News

International Scientific Communications, Inc.
30 Controls Dr.
PO Box 870
Shelton, CT 06484-0870
Ph: (203)926-9300   Fax: (203)926-9310

Bimonthly.

★1451★ CAP Today

College of American Pathologists
325 Waukegan Rd.
Northfield, IL 60093-2750
Ph: (708)446-8800   Fax: (708)446-3563

Monthly. $15.00/year for individuals; $40.00/year for other countries. Magazine covering advances in pathology tests and equipment, clinical lab management and operations trends, and related regulatory and legislative changes.

★1452★ Cell

Cell Press
50 Church St.
Cambridge, MA 02138
Ph: (617)661-7057   Fax: (617)661-7061

Biweekly. $325.00/year for individuals. Journal on molecular and cell biology.

★1453★ Clinical Laboratory News

American Association for Clinical Chemistry
2101 L St. NW, Ste. 202
Washington, DC 20037
Ph: (202)857-0717   Fax: (202)887-5093
Fr: 800-892-1400

Monthly. $30.00/year, $4.00 for single issue. Scholarly magazine providing current news in the field of clinical laboratory science.

★1454★ Cytometry

John Wiley and Sons, Inc.
605 3rd Ave.
New York, NY 10158
Ph: (212)850-8800   Fax: (212)850-6021
Fr: 800-225-5945

Research magazine.

★1455★ Laboratory Medicine

American Society of Clinical Pathologists
2100 W. Harrison St.
Chicago, IL 60612
Ph: (312)738-1336   Fax: (312)738-0101

Monthly. $50.00/year for individuals; $8.00 for single issue. Professional journal covering medical technology and pathology.

★1456★ Medical Laboratory Observer

Medical Economics Publishing
5 Paragon Dr.
Montvale, NJ 07645
Ph: (201)358-7200   Fax: (201)573-0440
Fr: 800-526-4870

Monthly. Trade journal.

★1457★ Nature: International Weekly Journal of Science

Nature Publishing Co.
65 Bleecker St.
New York, NY 10012-2467
Ph: (212)477-9600   Fax: (212)505-1364

Weekly. Magazine covering science and technology, including the fields of biology, biochemistry, genetics, medicine, earth sciences, physics, pharmacology, and behavioral sciences.

PLACEMENT AND JOB REFERRAL SERVICES

★1458★ American Association for Clinical Chemistry (AACC)

2101 L St. NW, Ste. 202
Washington, DC 20037-1526
Ph: (202)857-0717   Fax: (202)887-5093
Fr: 800-892-1400

Members: Clinical laboratory scientists and others engaged in the practice of clinical chemistry in independent laboratories, hospitals, and allied institutions. Maintains Endowment Fund for Research in Clinical Chemistry. **Activities:** Maintains employment service. Sponsors: therapeutic drug monitoring and endocrinology programs; continuing education programs; quality control programs.

★1459★ American Medical Technologists (AMT)

710 Higgins Rd.
Park Ridge, IL 60068
Ph: (708)823-5169   Fax: (708)823-0458
Fr: 800-275-1268

Members: National professional registry of medical laboratory technologists, technicians, medical assistants, dental assistants, and phlebotomists. **Activities:** Maintains job information service. Sponsors AMT Institute for Education, which has developed continuing education programs.

★1460★ Clinical Ligand Assay Society (CLAS)

3139 S. Wayne Rd.
Wayne, MI 48184
Ph: (313)722-6290   Fax: (313)722-7006

Members: Clinical laboratory directors and doctors, hospital technologists, private laboratories, industry, and other individuals interested in ligand. **Purpose:** Objectives are to establish and promote high standards in the science and application of ligand assay technology by encouraging research, educating practitioners, and fostering communication and cooperation among individuals in laboratories, medicine, academia, and industry. **Activities:** Sponsors job placement service.

★1461★ Endocrine Society (ES)

4350 East West Hwy., Ste. 500
Bethesda, MD 20814-4410
Ph: (301)941-0200   Fax: (301)941-0259

Purpose: Promotes excellence in research, education, and clinical practice in endocrinology and related disciplines. **Activities:** Maintains placement service.

★1462★ International Society for Clinical Laboratory Technology (ISCLT)

818 Olive St., Ste. 918
St. Louis, MO 63101-1598
Ph: (314)241-1445   Fax: (314)241-1449

Members: Clinical laboratory supervisors, technologists and technicians; physician's office laboratory technicians. **Activities:** Conducts educational programs; maintains placement service; offers specialized education.

EMPLOYER DIRECTORIES AND NETWORKING LISTS

★1463★ AHA Guide to the Health Care Field

Health Statistics Group
American Hospital Association (AHA)
1 N. Franklin
Chicago, IL 60606
Ph: (312)422-3501   Fax: (312)280-6015

Annual, July. $195.00, payment with order. Covers hospitals, multi-health care systems, freestanding ambulatory surgery centers, psychiatric facilities, long-term care facilities, substance abuse programs, hospices, Health Maintenance Organizations (HMOs), and other health-related organizations. Entries include: For hospitals: facility name, address, phone, administrator's name, number of beds, facilities and services, number of employees, expenses, other statistics. For other organizations: name, address, phone, name and title of contact. Arrangement: Geographical. Indexes: Hospital name.

★1464★ Directory of Accredited Laboratories

American Association for Laboratory Accreditation (A2LA)
656 Quince Orchard Rd., Ste. 620
Gaithersburg, MD 20878-1409
Ph: (301)670-1377   Fax: (301)869-1495

Annual, January. $40.00. Covers nearly 577 testing laboratories and inspection agencies accredited for technical competence as measured against national and international standards in the following fields of testing: metrology, acoustics and vibration, construction materials, biology, chemistry, electricity, environmental, geotechnical, mechanical, thermal, and nondestructive. Entries include: Name of laboratory, address, phone, contact, certificate number, current period of accreditation, fields of testing, testing technologies and methodologies. Arrangement: Alphabetical. Indexes: Fields of testing.

★1465★ Directory of Hospital Personnel

Medical Economics
5 Paragon Dr.
Montvale, NJ 07645-1725
Ph: (201)358-7500   Fax: (201)573-4956
Fr: 800-222-3045

Annual, September. $325.00, plus 7.50 shipping. Covers 200,000 executives at 7,100 U.S. hospitals. Entries include: Name of hospital, address, phone, number of beds, type and JCAHO status of hospital, names and titles of key department heads and staff, medical and nursing school affiliations; number of residents, interns, and nursing students. Arrangement: Geographical. Indexes: Hospital name, personnel, hospital size.

★1466★ Hospital Blue Book

Billian Publishing Co.
2100 Powers Ferry Rd., Ste. 300
Atlanta, GA 30339
Ph: (404)955-5656   Fax: (404)952-0669

Annual, spring. $154.50, national edition, plus $20.00 shipping. Covers more than 7,100 hospitals; some listings also appear in a separate southern edition of this publication. Entries include: Name of hospital, accreditation, mailing address, phone, fax, number of beds, type of facility (nonprofit, general, state, etc.); list of administrative personnel and chiefs of medical services, with specific titles. Arrangement: Geographical.

★1467★ Hospital Market Atlas

SMG Marketing Group, Inc.
1342 N. LaSalle Dr.
Chicago, IL 60610
Ph: (312)642-3026   Fax: (312)642-9729
Fr: 800-678-3026

Biennial, odd years. $495.00, payment with order. Covers over 7,000 hospitals, hospital systems and 480 group purchasing organizations. Entries include: Hospital or organization name, address, phone, county code, management, type of hospital service, number of beds, admissions, surgical operations, and emergency room visits. Arrangement: Geographical.

★1468★ Hospitals Directory

American Business Directories, Inc.
American Business Information, Inc.
5711 S. 86th Cir.
Omaha, NE 68127
Ph: (402)593-4600   Fax: (402)331-1505

Annual. $870.00, U.S. edition. Entries include: Name, address, phone (including area code), size of advertisement, year first in Yellow Pages, name of owner or manager, number of employees. Compiled from telephone company Yellow Pages, nationwide. Arrangement: Geographical.

★1469★ International Cytogenetic Laboratory Directory

Association of Cytogenetic Technologists
c/o Turid Knutsen
National Institutes of Health
Cytogenetic Oncology Section, NCI
Building 10, Rm. 12N-226
Bethesda, MD 20892
Ph: (301)496-6501   Fax: (301)541-0156

Annual, fall/winter. $50.00 for members; $60.00 for nonmembers. Covers about 520 laboratories studying heritable and acquired chromosomal disorders using cytogenetic, genetics, and cellular biology techniques. Entries include: Laboratory name, address, phone, areas of specialization, techniques, numbers and types of laboratory tests performed, and names of director and cytogenetic technologists. Arrangement: Geographical. Indexes: Director name, ACT member name.

★1470★ Laboratories Medical Directory

American Business Directories, Inc.
American Business Information, Inc.
5711 S. 86th Cir.
Omaha, NE 68127
Ph: (402)593-4600   Fax: (402)331-1505

Annual. $590.00, U.S. edition. Entries include: Name, address, phone (including area code), size of advertisement, year first in Yellow Pages, name of owner or manager, number of employees. Compiled from telephone company Yellow Pages, nationwide. Arrangement: Geographical.

★1471★ Medical and Health Information Directory

Gale Research
835 Penobscot Bldg.
Detroit, MI 48226-4094
Ph: (313)961-2242   Fax: (313)961-6083
Fr: 800-877-GALE

Approximately biennial; latest edition 1994. $195.00, per volume; $485.00, for the three-volume set. Covers in Volume 1, almost 18,600 medical and health oriented associations, organizations, institutions, and government agencies, including health maintenance organizations (HMOs), preferred provider organizations (PPOs), insurance companies, pharmaceutical companies, research centers, and medical and allied health schools. In Volume 2, nearly 11,800 medical book publishers; medical periodicals, directories, audiovisual producers and services, medical libraries and information centers, and electronic resources. In Volume 3, nearly 26,000 clinics, treatment centers, care programs, and counseling/diagnostic services for 30 subject areas. Entries include: Institution, service, or firm name, address, phone; many include names of key personnel and, when pertinent, descriptive annotation. Arrangement: Classified by organization activity, service, etc. Indexes: Each volume has a complete alphabetical name and keyword index.

★1472★ **Medical Research Centres**

Stockton Press
Groves Dictionaries
345 Park Ave. S., 10th Fl.
New York, NY 10010
Ph: (212)689-9200   Fr: 800-221-2123

Eleventh edition, 1995. $595.00. 856 pages. Covers medical and biochemical research conducted in over 100 countries. Entries include information on industrial enterprises, research laboratories, universities, societies, and professional associations engaged in research in medicine and related subjects like dentistry, nursing, pharmacy, psychiatry, and surgery.

★1473★ **Osteopathic Membership Directory—AOHA**

American Osteopathic Healthcare
  Association
5301 Wisconsin Ave. NW, Ste. 630
Washington, DC 20015-2015
Ph: (202)686-1700   Fax: (202)686-7615

Annual, summer. $125.00, payment with order. Covers about 110 osteopathic hospitals. Includes list of individual and institutional members; also lists osteopathic colleges, and directors of medical education. Entries include: For hospitals: name of hospital, name of chief executive officer, address, phone, number of beds and other hospital data. Arrangement: Geographical. Indexes: Name, institution.

HANDBOOKS AND MANUALS

★1474★ **Careers in Health Care**

VGM Career Horizons
4255 W. Touhy Ave.
Lincolnwood, IL 60646-1975
Ph: (847)679-5500   Fax: (847)679-2494
Fr: 800-323-4900

Barbara M. Swanson. 1995. $17.95; $13.95 (paper). Describes job duties, work settings, salaries, licensing and certification requirements, educational preparation, and future outlook. Gives ideas on how to secure a job.

★1475★ **Clinical Lab Technician**

R & E Publishers, Inc.
468 Auzerais Ave., Ste. A
San Jose, CA 95126
Ph: (408)977-0691   Fax: (408)977-0693

Ronald R. Smith. 1993. $1.95 (paper).

★1476★ **100 Best Careers for the Year 2000**

Prentice Hall General Reference
15 Columbus Cir.
New York, NY 10023
Ph: (212)373-8500   Fr: 800-223-2348

Shelly Field. 1992. $15.00 (paper). Covers 100 of the fastest growing jobs. The publication is divided into 11 general employment sections. Specific careers are covered within each section. Provides job description, responsibilities, employment opportunities, earnings, education and training, advancement opportunities, and experience and qualifications for each occupation.

★1477★ **Opportunities in Health and Medical Careers**

VGM Career Horizons
4255 W. Touhy Ave.
Lincolnwood, IL 60646-1975
Ph: (847)679-5500   Fax: (847)679-2494
Fr: 800-323-4900

Donald Snook, Jr. and Leo D'Orazio. 1993. $14.95; $11.95 (paper). Covers the full range of medical and health occupations. Illustrated.

★1478★ **Opportunities in Medical Imaging Careers**

VCH Publishers, Inc.
220 E. 23rd St., Ste. 909
New York, NY 10010-4606
Ph: (212)683-8333   Fax: (212)481-0897

Clifford J. Sherry. 1993.

★1479★ **Opportunities in Medical Technology Careers**

VGM Career Horizons
4255 W. Touhy Ave.
Lincolnwood, IL 60646-1975
Ph: (847)679-5500   Fax: (847)679-2494
Fr: 800-323-4900

Karen R. Karni and Sidney Oliver. 1990. $14.95; $11.95 (paper). Details opportunities for various technical medical personnel and supplies up-to-date information on salary levels and employment outlook. Appendices list associations and unions in each field. Illustrated.

★1480★ **Opportunities in Public Health Careers**

VGM Career Horizons
4255 W. Touhy Ave.
Lincolnwood, IL 60646-1975
Ph: (847)679-5500   Fax: (847)679-2494
Fr: 800-323-4900

George E. Pickett and Terry W. Pickett. 1995. $14.95; $11.95 (paper). 160 pages. Defines the public health field and describes a variety of health, science, and business opportunities as well as educational preparation and the future of the public health field. Offers job-hunting tips. The appendixes list public health organizations, state and federal public health agencies, and graduate schools offering public health programs.

★1481★ **Opportunities in Vocational and Technical Careers**

VGM Career Horizons
4255 W. Touhy Ave.
Lincolnwood, IL 60646-1975
Ph: (847)679-5500   Fax: (847)679-2494
Fr: 800-323-4900

Adrian A. Paradis. 1992. $14.95; $11.95 (paper). 160 pages. Provides information on a variety of opportunities and advice on breaking into the field.

★1482★ **Resumes for Health and Medical Careers**

4255 W. Touhy Ave.
Lincolnwood, IL 60646-1975
Ph: (708)679-5500   Fax: (708)679-6375
Fr: 800-323-4900

Compiled by VGM Career Horizons Staff 1995. $9.95 (paper).

★1483★ **Your Opportunities in Medical Support**

Energeia Publishing, Inc.
PO Box 985
Salem, OR 97308
Ph: (503)362-1480   Fax: (503)362-2123

Margie Sherman. 1994. $2.00 (paper).

EMPLOYMENT AGENCIES AND SEARCH FIRMS

★1484★ **Action Plus Employer Services**
1211 W. Imperial Hwy., Ste. 100
Brea, CA 92621
Ph: (714)773-1506   Fax: (714)773-9201
Employment agency.

★1485★ **Midwest Medical Consultants**
8910 Purdue Rd., Ste. 200
Indianapolis, IN 46268-1155
Ph: (317)872-1053
Employment agency. Executive search firm.

★1486★ **Sue Carroll Personnel, Inc.**
16 E. 79th St.
New York, NY 10021
Ph: (212)288-8866   Fax: (212)988-7191
Employment agency and executive search firm.

OTHER SOURCES

★1487★ **Accrediting Bureau of Health Education Schools (ABHES)**
Oak Manor Office
29089 U.S. 20 W.
Elkhart, IN 46514
Ph: (219)293-0124   Fax: (219)295-8564
Purpose: Serves as a nationally recognized accrediting agency of health education institutions and schools conducting medical laboratory technician and medical assistant edu-

cation programs. Establishes criteria and standards for the administration and operation of health education institutions. Seeks to enhance the profession through the improvement of schools, courses, and the competence of graduates. Schools must apply voluntarily for accreditation; once accredited, they must report to the bureau annually and be reexamined at least every 6 years. Has accredited 15 programs for medical laboratory technicians, 124 medical assistants, and 80 institutions of allied health.

★1488★ American Society for Clinical Laboratory Science ((ASCLS))

7910 Woodmont Ave., Ste. 1301
Bethesda, MD 20814
Ph: (301)657-2768   Fax: (301)657-2909

Members: Primarily clinical laboratory personnel who have an associate or baccalaureate degree and clinical training and specialists who hold at least a master's degree in one of the major fields of clinical laboratory science such as bacteriology, mycology, or biochemistry; also includes technicians, specialists, and educators with limited certificates and students enrolled in approved programs of clinical laboratory studies and military medical technology schools. **Purpose:** Promotes and maintains high standards in clinical laboratory methods and research and advances standards of education and training of personnel. **Activities:** Conducts educational program of seminars

and workshops. Approves programs of continuing education and maintains records on participation in continuing education programs for members.

★1489★ American Society of Cytopathology (ASC)

400 W. 9th St., Ste. 201
Wilmington, DE 19801
Ph: (302)429-8802   Fax: (302)429-8807

Members: Cytologists, pathologists, and clinicians with M.D.s; nonmedical professional personnel (Ph.D.s); associate members are cytotechnologists. **Purpose:** Seeks to make the cytological method of early cancer detection universally available to potential victims. Promotes establishment of additional educational and training facilities; encourages implementaion of research programs; inspects and accredits cytology laboratories; assists in preparation of national registry examination for cytotechnologists. Reviews cytotechnology training programs for accreditation.

★1490★ *Career Encounters: Clinical Laboratory Science*

Cambridge Career Products
PO Box 2153
Dept. CC15
Charleston, WV 25328-2153
Ph: (304)744-9323   Fax: (304)744-9351
Fr: 800-468-4227

Video. $99.95. 25 minutes. Professionals

shown in a variety of settings discuss different aspects of their careers.

★1491★ Commission on Accreditation of Allied Health Education Programs (CAAHEP)

515 N. State St., Ste. 7530
Chicago, IL 60610
Ph: (312)464-4636   Fax: (312)464-5830

Purpose: Serves as an nationally recognized accrediting agency for allied health programs in 19 occupational areas.

★1492★ National Certification Agency for Medical Lab Personnel (NCA)

PO Box 15945-289
Lenexa, KS 66285
Ph: (913)654-1622   Fax: (913)657-2909

Members: Persons who direct, educate, supervise, or practice in clinical laboratory science. **Purpose:** To assure the public and employers of the competence of clinical laboratory personnel; to provide a mechanism for individuals demonstrating competency in the field to achieve career mobility. Develops and administers competency-based examinations for certification of clinical laboratory personnel; provides for periodic recertification by examination or through documentation of continuing education. Compiles statistics.

College and University Faculty

SOURCES OF HELP-WANTED ADS

★1493★ ASCUS Annual: Job Search Handbook for Educators

Association for School, College and University Staffing (ASCUS)
820 Davis St., Ste. 222
Evanston, IL 60201
Ph: (708)864-1999

Annual. Includes employment notices from public school systems. Contains articles for educators seeking employment. Also includes "Directory of State Teacher Certification Offices."

★1494★ Change

Heldref Publications
Helen Dwight Reid Educational Foundation
1319 18th St. NW
Washington, DC 20036-1802
Ph: (202)296-6267   Fax: (202)296-5149
Fr: 800-365-9753

Bimonthly. $36.00/year for individuals; $11.75 for single issue; $70.00/year for institutions; $84.00/year for institutions, other countries. Magazine dealing with contemporary issues in higher learning.

★1495★ The Chronicle of Higher Education

The Chronicle of Higher Education
1255 23rd St. NW, Ste. 700
Washington, DC 20037
Ph: (202)466-1000   Fax: (202)296-2691
Fr: 800-347-6969

Weekly. $67.50/year for individuals; $2.75 for single issue. Higher education magazine (tabloid).

★1496★ Columbia Journalism Review

Columbia Journalism Review
700 Journalism Bldg.
Columbia University
New York, NY 10027
Ph: (212)854-1881   Fax: (212)854-8580

Bimonthly. Magazine focusing on journalism.

★1497★ Current Openings in Education in U.S.A.

Education Information Service
PO Box 660662
Newton, MA 02162-0662
Ph: (617)443-0125

Seven times/year. $8.00/issue. Publication is a booklet listing about 140 institutions or school systems, each with one to a dozen or more openings for teachers, librarians, counselors, administrators, and other personnel.

★1498★ Educational Researcher

American Educational Research Association
1230 17th St. NW
Washington, DC 20036-3078
Ph: (202)223-9485   Fax: (202)775-1824

$39.00/year for individuals; $7.00 for single issue; $51.00/year for institutions; $48.00/year for out of country. Educational research journal.

★1499★ Financial Management

Financial Management Association
University of South Florida
College of Business Admin.
Tampa, FL 33620
Ph: (813)974-2084   Fax: (813)974-3318

Quarterly. $40.00/year for individuals; $10.00 for single issue. Magazine covering business, economics, finance and management.

★1500★ Foreign Faculty and Administrative Openings

Education Information Service
Box 662
Newton, MA 02162
Ph: (617)237-0887

Approximately every six weeks. $9.00. Covers approximately 150 specific openings in administration, counseling, library, teaching and other disciplines for American teachers in American schools overseas and in international schools, both of which must teach English as a primarily language. Entries include: Institution name, address.

★1501★ Journal of Chemical Education

Centcom Ltd.
1599 Post Rd. E
PO Box 231
Westport, CT 06881-0231
Ph: (203)256-8211   Fax: (203)256-8175

Monthly. $17.00/year for individuals. Magazine on chemical research and education.

★1502★ Journal of Nursing Education

6900 Grove Rd.
Thorofare, NJ 08086-9447
Ph: (609)848-1000   Fax: (609)853-5991

Bimonthly. $44.00/year.

★1503★ Modern Language Association of America—Job Information List

Modern Language Association of America
10 Astor Pl.
New York, NY 10003-6981
Ph: (212)614-6321   Fax: (212)477-9863

Quarterly, February, April, October, and December. $35.00, per year, payment with order. Covers available positions for college teachers of English and foreign languages in four-year colleges and universities; February issue includes separate section of openings in two-year institutions. Separate editions for English and American language and literature and for foreign language openings. Entries include: Department chair statement, including institution name; contact name, address, phone; definite or possible openings; related information for job seekers (change in deadline date, or job description, notice of a vacancy filled, etc.). Arrangement: First section, statements of department chairmen. Second section (in October and February only), list of departments reporting no vacancies.

★1504★ NABE News

National Association for Bilingual Education (NABE)
1220 L St. NW, Ste. 605
Washington, DC 20005-4018
Ph: (202)898-1829

Eight issues/year.

★1505★ Nurse Educator

Pharmaceutical Media, Inc.
30 E. 33rd St.
New York, NY 10016
Ph: (212)685-5010   Fax: (212)685-5010

Bimonthly. Journal for nursing educators.

★1506★ OECD Observer

Organization for Economic Cooperation
and Development
Publications & Information Center
2001 L St. NW
Washington, DC 20036-4910
Ph: (202)785-6323   Fax: (202)785-0350
Fr: 800-456-OECD

Bimonthly. $25.00/year for individuals. Magazine on economic affairs, science, and technology.

★1507★ Opening List in U.S. Colleges, Public & Private Schools

Education Information Services
PO Box 662
Newton, MA 02162-0002
Ph: (617)237-0887

Every 6 weeks. $9.00. Covers about 150 current professional openings in U.S. public schools, and private schools. Entries include: Institute name, address, names and titles of key personnel, available openings.

★1508★ The Physics Teacher

American Association of Physics Teachers
1 Physics Ellipse
College Park, MD 20740-3845
Ph: (301)209-3300   Fax: (301)209-0845

Scientific education magazine.

★1509★ The Science Teacher

National Science Teachers Association
1840 Wilson Blvd.
Arlington, VA 22201
Ph: (703)312-9232   Fax: (703)243-7177

$52.00/year for individuals. Magazine on science education.

PLACEMENT AND JOB REFERRAL SERVICES

★1510★ Academy of International Business (AIB)

University of Hawaii at Manoa - SBA
2404 Maile Way
Honolulu, HI 96822
Ph: (808)956-3665   Fax: (808)956-3261

Members: University professors, researchers, writers, managers, executives, and attorneys in the international business education field. **Purpose:** Facilitates information exchange among people in academia, business, and government and encourages research activities that advance the knowledge of international business operations and increase the available body of teaching materials. Has compiled an inventory of collegiate courses in international business, a survey of research projects, and statistics. **Activities:**

Maintains placement service. **E-Mail:** aib@gusadm.cba.hawaii.edu

★1511★ Academy of Legal Studies in Business (ALSB)

Department of Finance
120 Upham Hall
Miami University
Oxford, OH 45056
Ph: (513)529-2945   Fax: (513)529-6992
Fr: 800-831-2903

Members: Teachers of business law and legal environment in colleges and universities. **Purpose:** Promotes and encourages business law scholarship and teaching outside of the law school environment. **Activities:** Maintains placement service.

★1512★ Academy of Management (AM)

PO Box 3020
Briarcliff Manor, NY 10510-8020
Ph: (914)923-2607   Fax: (914)923-2615

Members: Professors in accredited universities and colleges who teach management; selected business executives who have made significant written contributions to the literature in the field of management and organization. **Activities:** Offers placement service.

★1513★ Academy of Marketing Science (AMS)

University of Miami
School of Bus. Admin.
PO Box 248012
Coral Gables, FL 33124
Ph: (305)284-6673   Fax: (305)284-3762

Members: Marketing academicians and practitioners; individuals interested in fostering education in marketing science. **Purpose:** To promote the advancement of knowledge and the furthering of professional standards in the field of marketing. Explores the special application areas of marketing science and its responsibilities as an economic, ethical, and social force; promotes research and the widespread dissemination of findings. Facilitates exchange of information and experience among members, and the transfer of marketing knowledge and technology to developing countries; promotes marketing science on an international level. Encourages members to utilize their marketing talents to the fullest through redirection, reassignment, and relocation. **Activities:** Offers placement service; sponsors competitions.

★1514★ American Academy of Religion (AAR)

1703 Clifton Rd. NE, Ste. G5
Atlanta, GA 30329-4019
Ph: (404)727-7920   Fax: (404)727-7959

Members: Professional society of scholars and teachers in the field of religion. **Purpose:** Encourages scholarship, research, and publications in the study of religion, and stimulates effective teaching. **Activities:** Conducts research programs; offers research grants and placement services; compiles statistics.

★1515★ American Association of Teachers of French (AATF)

57 E. Armory Ave.
Champaign, IL 61820
Ph: (217)333-2842   Fax: (217)333-5850

Members: Teachers of French in public and private elementary and secondary schools, colleges, and universities. **Activities:** Maintains Pedagogical Aids Bureau, offering French maps, postcards, and medals, at cost; conducts annual French contest in elementary and secondary schools and awards prizes to the winners; maintains a placement bureau and a high school honor society. Furnishes traveling exhibits and provides a pen pal agency for exchange of letters between French and American boys and girls.

★1516★ American Association of Teachers of Spanish and Portuguese (AATSP)

University of Northern Colorado
106 Gunter Hall
Greeley, CO 80639
Ph: (303)351-1090   Fax: (303)351-1095

Members: Teachers of Spanish and Portuguese languages and literatures and others interested in Hispanic culture. **Activities:** Operates placement bureau and maintains pen pal registry. Sponsors honor society, Sociedad Honoraria Hispanica and National Spanish Examinations for secondary school students.

★1517★ American Association of Women in Community and Junior Colleges (AAWCJC)

Amarillo College
PO Box 447
Amarillo, TX 79178-0001
Ph: (806)371-5000   Fax: (806)371-5370

Members: Women faculty members, administrators, staff members, students, and trustees of community colleges. **Purpose:** Objectives are to: develop communication and disseminate information among women in community, junior, and technical colleges; encourage educational program development; obtain grants for educational projects for community college women. Disseminates information on women's issues and programs. **Activities:** Conducts regional and state professional development workshops and forums. Maintains placement services.

★1518★ American Classical League (ACL)

Miami University
Oxford, OH 45056
Ph: (513)529-7741   Fax: (513)529-7742

Members: Teachers of classical languages in high schools and colleges. **Purpose:** To promote the teaching of Latin and other classical languages. Presents scholarship. **Activities:** Maintains placement service, teaching materials, and resource center at Miami University in Oxford, OH to sell teaching aids to Latin and Greek teachers.

★1519★ American Philosophical Association (APA)

University of Delaware
Newark, DE 19716
Ph: (302)831-1112   Fax: (302)831-8690

Members: College and university teachers of philosophy and others with an interest in philosophy. **Purpose:** Facilitates exchange of ideas in philosophy, encourages creative and scholarly activity in philosophy, and fosters the professional work of teachers of philosophy. **Activities:** Participates in international congresses of philosophy and maintains affiliations with national and international philosophical organizations. Maintains placement service; sponsors competitions. Oversees selection of Romanell, Schutz and Carus lecturers.

★1520★ American Political Science Association (APSA)

1527 New Hampshire Ave. NW
Washington, DC 20036
Ph: (202)483-2512   Fax: (202)483-2657

Members: College and university teachers of political science, public officials, research workers, and businessmen. **Purpose:** Encourages the impartial study and promotes the development of the art and science of government. Develops research projects of public interest and educational programs for political scientists and journalists; seeks to improve the knowledge of and increase citizen participation in political and governmental affairs. **Activities:** Serves as clearinghouse for teaching and research positions in colleges, universities, and research bureaus in the U.S. and abroad and for positions open to political scientists in government and private business. Offers placement service.

★1521★ Association of American Law Schools (AALS)

1201 Connecticut Ave. NW, Ste. 800
Washington, DC 20036-2605
Ph: (202)296-8851   Fax: (202)296-8869

Members: Law schools. **Purpose:** Seeks to improve the legal profession through legal education. Cooperates with state and federal government, other legal education and professional associations, and other national higher education and learned society organizations. **Activities:** Compiles statistics; sponsors teacher placement service.

★1522★ Association for Direct Instruction (ADI)

PO Box 10252
Eugene, OR 97440
Ph: (503)485-1293   Fax: (503)683-7543

Members: Public school regular and special education teachers and university instructors. **Purpose:** Encourages, promotes, and engages in research aimed at improving educational methods. Promotes dissemination of developmental information and skills that facilitate the education of adults and children. **Activities:** Maintains placement service. Administers a preschool for developmentally delayed children. Offers educational training workshops for instructors.

★1523★ Association for Education in Journalism and Mass Communication (AEJMC)

1621 College St.
University of South Carolina
Columbia, SC 29208
Ph: (803)777-2005   Fax: (803)777-4728

Members: Professional organization of college and university journalism and communication teachers. **Purpose:** Works to improve methods and standards of teaching and stimulate research. Compiles statistics on enrollments and current developments in journalism education. **Activities:** Maintains a listing of journalism and communication teaching positions available and teaching positions wanted, revised bimonthly.

★1524★ Association for Library and Information Science Education (ALISE)

4101 Lake Boone Trl., Ste. 201
Raleigh, NC 27607
Ph: (919)787-5181   Fax: (919)787-4916

Members: Graduate schools offering degree programs in library science and their faculties. **Purpose:** Seeks to: promote excellence in education for library and information science as a means of increasing the effectiveness of library and information services; provide a forum for the active interchange of ideas and information among library educators; promote research related to teaching and to library and information science; formulate and promulgate positions on matters related to library education. **Activities:** Offers employment program.

★1525★ Association of Southern Baptist Colleges and Schools (ASBCS)

901 Commerce, Ste. 600
Nashville, TN 37203
Ph: (615)244-2362   Fax: (615)242-2153

Members: Southern Baptist seminaries, senior colleges, universities, junior colleges, academies, and Bible schools. **Purpose:** Promotes Christian education through literature, faculty workshops, student recruitment, teacher placement, trustee orientation, statistical information, and other assistance to members. Emphasizes Baptist Seminary, College, and School Day throughout the Southern Baptist Convention.

★1526★ Association of University Professors of Ophthalmology (AUPO)

PO Box 420369
San Francisco, CA 94142-0369
Ph: (415)561-8548   Fax: (415)561-8575

Members: Heads of departments or divisions of ophthalmology in accredited medical schools throughout the U.S.; directors of ophthalmology residency programs in institutions not connected to medical schools. **Purpose:** Promotes medical education, research, and patient care relating to ophthalmology. **Activities:** Operates Ophthalmology Matching Program and faculty placement service, which aids ophthalmologists interested in being associated with university ophthalmology programs to locate such programs.

★1527★ College Language Association (CLA)

Clark Atlanta University
James P. Brawley Dr. at Fair St. SW
Atlanta, GA 30314
Ph: (404)880-8524   Fax: (404)880-8222

Members: eachers of English and modern foreign languages, primarily in historically black colleges and universities. **Activities:** Maintains placement service; operates speakers' bureau.

★1528★ College Media Advisers (CMA)

Memphis State University
Department of Journalism
MJ-300
Memphis, TN 38152
Ph: (901)678-2403   Fax: (901)678-4798

Members: Professional association serving advisers, directors, and chairmen of boards of college student media (newspapers, yearbooks, magazines, handbooks, directories, and radio and television stations); heads of schools and departments of journalism; and others interested in junior college, college, and university student media. **Purpose:** Serves as clearinghouse for student media; acts as consultant on student theses and dissertations on publications. Encourages high school journalism and examines its relationships to college and professional journalism. **Activities:** Maintains placement service. Conducts national survey of student media in rotation each year by type: newspapers, magazines, and yearbooks; radio and television stations.

★1529★ Convention of American Instructors of the Deaf (CAID)

PO Box 377
Bedford, TX 76095-0377
Ph: (817)354-8414

Members: Professional organization of teachers, administrators, and professionals in allied fields related to education of the deaf and hard-of-hearing. **Purpose:** Objectives are: to provide opportunities for a free interchange of views concerning methods and means of educating the deaf and hard-of-hearing; to promote such education by the publication of reports, essays, and other information; to develop more effective methods of teaching deaf and hard-of-hearing children. **Activities:** Maintains speakers' bureau; offers placement services.

★1530★ Council for Jewish Education (CJE)

730 Broadway
New York, NY 10003
Ph: (212)529-2000   Fax: (212)529-2009

Members: Teachers of Hebrew in universities; heads of Bureaus of Jewish Education and their administrative departments; faculty members of Jewish teacher training schools. **Purpose:** Seeks to: further the cause of Jewish education in America; raise professional standards and practices; promote the welfare and growth of Jewish educational workers; improve and strengthen Jewish life. **Activities:** Conducts educational programs; cosponsors a Personnel Placement Committee with Jewish Education Service of North America.

★1531★ Decision Sciences Institute (DSI)

University Plz.
Atlanta, GA 30303
Ph: (404)651-4000   Fax: (404)651-2804

Members: Businesspersons and members of business school faculties. **Activities:** Maintains placement service.

★1532★ Financial Management Association (FMA)

School of Bus.
University of South Florida
Tampa, FL 33620-5500
Ph: (813)974-2084   Fax: (813)974-3318

Members: Professors of financial management; corporate financial officers. **Purpose:** Facilitates exchange of ideas among persons involved in financial management or the study thereof. **Activities:** Conducts workshops for comparison of current research projects and development of cooperative ventures in writing and research. Sponsors honorary society for superior students at 300 colleges and universities. Offers placement services.

★1533★ International Educator's Institute (TIE)

PO Box 513
Cummaquid, MA 02637
Ph: (508)362-1414

Purpose: Facilitates the placement of teachers and administrators in American, British, and international schools. Seeks to create a network that provides for professional development opportunities and improved financial security of members. Offers advice and information on international school news, recent educational developments, job placement, and investment, consumer, and professional development opportunities. Makes available insurance and travel benefits. Operates International Schools Internship Program. Sponsors competitions. Bestows awards.

★1534★ Modern Language Association of America (MLA)

10 Astor Pl., 5th Fl.
New York, NY 10003
Ph: (212)475-9500   Fax: (212)477-9863

Members: College and university teachers of English and of modern foreign languages. **Purpose:** Seeks to advance all aspects of literary and linguistic study. Under its Foreign Language Program, researches foreign language teaching primarily at the postsecondary level of U.S. education. Under its English Program, acts as a clearinghouse for information of interest to teachers of English literature and composition. **Activities:** Conducts Job Information Service. Operates 81 divisions.

★1535★ NAFSA/Association of International Educators (NAFSA)

1875 Connecticut Ave. NW, Ste. 1000
Washington, DC 20009
Ph: (202)462-4811   Fax: (202)667-3419

Members: Individuals, organizations, and institutions dealing with international educational exchange, including foreign student advisers, overseas educational advisers, credentials and admissions officers, administrators and teachers of English as a second language, community support personnel, study-abroad administrators, and embassy cultural or educational personnel. **Purpose:** Promotes self-regulation standards and responsibilities in international educational exchange; offers professional development opportunities primarily through publications, workshops, grants, and regional and national conferences. Advocates for increased awareness and support of international education and exchange on campuses, in government, and in communities. **Activities:** Offers services including: a job registry for employers and professionals involved with international education; a consultant referral service. Sponsors joint liaison activities with a variety of other educational and government organizations to conduct a census of foreign student enrollment in the U.S.; conducts workshops about specific subjects and countries.

★1536★ National Art Education Association (NAEA)

1916 Association Dr.
Reston, VA 22091-1590
Ph: (703)860-8000   Fax: (703)860-2960

Members: Teachers of art at elementary, secondary, and college levels; colleges, libraries, museums, and other educational institutions. **Purpose:** Studies problems of teaching art; encourages research and experimentation. **Activities:** Maintains placement services. Serves as clearinghouse for information on art education programs, materials, and methods of instruction. Sponsors special institutes. Cooperates with other national organizations for the furtherance of creative art experiences for youth.

★1537★ National Association of Black Professors (NABP)

PO Box 526
Crisfield, MD 21817
Ph: (410)968-2393

Members: College professors of African descent. **Purpose:** Goals are to: provide a forum for the exchange of information among college professors; enhance education for black people and enrich the educational process in general; support and promote intellectual interests of black students. Disseminates professional improvement information. **Activities:** Sponsors annual public lecture. Compiles statistics; maintains placement service and speakers' bureau.

★1538★ National Association for Sport and Physical Education (NASPE)

1900 Association Dr.
Reston, VA 22091
Ph: (703)476-3410   Fax: (703)476-8316

Members: Men and women professionally involved with physical activity and sports. **Purpose:** Seeks to improve the total sport and physical activity experience in America. Conducts research and education programs in such areas as sport psychology, curriculum development, kinesiology, history, philosophy, sport sociology, and the biological and behavioral basis of human activity. Develops and distributes public information materials which explain the value of physical education programs. **Activities:** Maintains placement service, and media resource center for public information and professional preparation. Sponsors skills clinics and foreign coach exchange programs.

★1539★ National Association of Teachers' Agencies (NATA)

PO Box 223
Georgetown, MA 01833-0323
Ph: (508)352-8473   Fax: (508)352-8680

Purpose: Private employment agencies engaged primarily in the placement of teaching and administration personnel. Works to standardize records and promote a strong ethical sense in the placement field. Maintains speakers' bureau.

★1540★ National Council for Black Studies (NCBS)

Ohio State University
208 Mount Hall
1050 Carmack Rd.
Columbus, OH 43210
Ph: (614)292-1035   Fax: (614)292-7363

Purpose: Faculty members, students, and institutions united to promote and strengthen academic and community programs in black and/or African-American studies. Sponsors undergraduate and graduate student essay contests. **Activities:** Offers professional opportunities referral service; compiles statistics on black studies activities including information on students, faculty, research, and curricula.

★1541★ National Faculty Exchange (NFE)

4656 W. Jefferson, Ste. 140
Fort Wayne, IN 46804
Ph: (219)436-2634   Fax: (219)436-5676

Members: Accredited colleges and universities, federal agencies, and education associations. **Purpose:** Facilitates the exchange of faculty and administrative staff among colleges and universities in the United States, Australia, Canada, and Mexico. **Activities:** Maintains an exchange pool which accommodates multilateral placement.

★1542★ Organization of American Historians (OAH)

112 N. Bryan St.
Bloomington, IN 47408
Ph: (812)855-7311   Fax: (812)855-0696

Members: Professional historians, including college faculty members, secondary school teachers, graduate students, and other individuals in related fields; institutional subscribers are college, university, high school and public libraries, and historical agencies. **Purpose:** Promotes historical research and study. Sponsors 12 prize programs for historical writing; maintains speakers' bureau. **Activities:** Operates a professional job registry at annual meeting. Conducts educational programs. **E-Mail:** OAH@INDIANA.EDU

★1543★ **Speech Communication Association (SCA)**

5105 Backlick Rd., Bldg. E
Annandale, VA 22003
Ph: (703)750-0533   Fax: (703)914-9471
Members: Elementary, secondary, college, and university teachers, speech clinicians, media specialists, communication consultants, students, theater directors, and other interested persons; libraries and other institutions. **Purpose:** To promote study, criticism, research, teaching, and application of the artistic, humanistic, and scientific principles of communication, particularly speech communication. Sponsors the publication of scholarly volumes in speech. **Activities:** Maintains placement service.

★1544★ **Tennessee Association of Economics Educators**

c/o Dr. S.Z. Barr
Univ. of Tennessee at Martin
112 School of Business Bldg.
Martin, TN 38238
Ph: (901)587-7208   Fax: (901)587-7241
Members: Professors, teachers, chairholders, directors of centers, foundation officers, business executives, and government leaders. **Purpose:** To promote an accurate understanding of the American economic system through teaching, research, and communication between academe and business. Encourages dialogue with representatives of other economic systems and entrepreneurship throughout the world. **Activities:** Sponsors scholarly forums and competitions. Conducts placement service.

★1545★ **U.S.-China Education Foundation (USCEF)**

5345 Light Circle
Norcross, GA 30071
Ph: (770)729-1779   Fax: (770)448-1859
A project of the Society for the Advancement of Global Education. **Purpose:** To promote the learning of the Chinese languages (including Mandarin, Cantonese, and minority languages such as Mongolian) by Americans, and the learning of English by Chinese. **Activities:** Operates teacher placement service. Conducts short-term travel-study program to prepare Americans and Chinese for stays of four, six, or eight months or one to four years in China or the U.S., respectively. A project of S.A.G.E. the Society for the Development of Global Education.

★1546★ **University Photographers Association of America (UPAA)**

News Services
Western Michigan University
Kalamazoo, MI 49008
Ph: (616)387-4111   Fax: (616)387-4124
Members: College and university personnel engaged professionally in photography, teaching of photography, audiovisual work, or journalism for universities. **Purpose:** Seeks to advance applied photography and the profession through the exchange of thoughts and opinions among its members. **Activities:** Operates placement services. Awards fellowship for exceptional work in the advancement of photography. Provides a medium for exchange of ideas and technical information on photography, especially university photographic work.

EMPLOYER DIRECTORIES AND NETWORKING LISTS

★1547★ *Accredited Institutions of Postsecondary Education*

Oryx Press
4041 N. Central, Ste. 700
Phoenix, AZ 85012-3397
Ph: (602)265-2651   Fax: 800-279-4663
Fr: 800-279-6799
Annual, September. $39.95. Covers more than 5,500 accredited institutions and programs of postsecondary education in the United States and U.S.-chartered schools in 14 countries. Entries include: Institution name, address, phone, whether public or private, any religious affiliation, type of institution and student body, branch campuses or affiliated institutions, date of first accreditation and latest reaffirmation of accrediting body, accredited programs in professional fields, level of degrees offered, name of chief executive officer, size and composition of enrollment, type of academic calendar. Arrangement: Geographical. Indexes: Institution.

★1548★ *American Association of Colleges for Teacher Education— Directory*

American Association of Colleges for Teacher Education
1 Dupont Cir. NW, Ste. 610
Washington, DC 20036
Ph: (202)293-2450   Fax: (202)457-8095
Annual, fall. $50.00. Covers over 700 member schools, colleges, and departments of education offering programs in teacher education, including more than 6,000 academic administrators and faculty. Entries include: Institution name, address, phone, fax names and titles of key administrators and faculty. Separate section gives profile of program, including degrees offered, affiliations, and national accreditation status. Arrangement: Alphabetical. Indexes: Institution name, representative name.

★1549★ *American Association of Community Colleges—AACC Membership Directory*

American Association of Community Colleges (AACC)
1 Dupont Cir. NW, Ste. 410
Washington, DC 20036-1136
Ph: (202)728-0200   Fax: (202)223-9390
Annual, spring. $75.00 for members, payment with order; $100.00 for nonmembers, payment with order. Covers 1,125 two-year colleges, primarily in the United States, but including entries from American Samoa, British Honduras, Canada, Korea, Panama, Puerto Rico, Switzerland, and Germany. Entries include: College name, chief administrator staff, address, phone, chief executive officer, enrollment, number of campuses, year founded. Arrangement: Geographical. Indexes: College name, administrator name.

★1550★ *American Universities and Colleges*

Walter de Gruyter, Inc.
200 Saw Mill River Rd.
Hawthorne, NY 10532
Ph: (914)747-0110   Fax: (914)747-1326
Quadrennial, latest edition September 1992. $149.95, plus $4.00 shipping. Covers over 1,900 accredited four-year and graduate colleges and universities. Includes a list of statewide coordinating boards of higher education. Entries include: For schools: name, address, history, governing board, calendar, freshmen and general student body characteristics, distinctive programs, student life, whether it has a reserve officers training corps (ROTC), graduate work, degrees conferred, fees, student financial aid, departments and teaching staff, enrollment, foreign students, publications, library, finances, buildings and grounds, administration; separate descriptions of each major division within a university. For boards: name, address, name of director. Arrangement: Geographical. Indexes: Institution name, general.

★1551★ *Chronicle Four-Year College Databook*

Chronicle Guidance Publications, Inc.
PO Box 1190
Moravia, NY 13118
Ph: (315)497-0330   Fax: (315)497-3359
Fr: 800-622-7284
Annual, September. $22.49, plus $2.25 shipping. Covers more than 780 baccalaureate, master's, doctoral, and first professional programs offered by more than 2,130 colleges and universities in the United States. Entries include: College charts section gives college name, address, phone; accreditation, enrollment, admissions, costs, financial aid; accreditation associations' names, addresses, and phone numbers. Arrangement: Part I, classified by college major; part II, geographical. Indexes: College name.

★1552★ *Chronicle Two-Year College Databook*

Chronicle Guidance Publications, Inc.
PO Box 1190
Moravia, NY 13118
Ph: (315)497-0330   Fax: (315)497-3359
Fr: 800-622-7284
Annual, September. $22.46, plus $2.25 shipping. Covers over 725 associate, certificate, occupational, and transfer programs offered by more than 2,400 technical institutes, two-year colleges, and universities in the United States. Entries include: College charts section gives college name, address, phone; accreditation, enrollment, admissions, costs, financial aid; accrediting associations' names, addresses, and phone numbers. Arrangement: Part I is classified by college major; part II is geographical. Indexes: College name.

★1553★ The Directory of Schools, Colleges, and Universities Overseas

Overseas Employment Services
PO Box 460
Mount Royal, PQ, Canada H3P 3C7
Ph: (514)739-1108   Fax: (514)739-0795

Annual. $15.00, postpaid. Covers Approximately 300 educational institutions worldwide that hire teachers to teach various subjects in English.

★1554★ Education Career Directory

Gale Research
835 Penobscot Bldg.
Detroit, MI 48226-4094
Ph: (313)961-2242   Fax: (313)961-6083
Fr: 800-877-GALE

First edition March 1994. $34.00; $17.95(paper). Covers over 220 public school districts, universities, and colleges offering entry-level positions, internships, and student teaching opportunities in the U.S.; sources of help-wanted ads, professional associations, producers of videos, databases, career guides, and professional guides and handbooks. Entries include: For schools: Name, address, phone, fax, names and titles of key personnel, number of employees, average number of entry-level positions available, human resources contact, description of internship and student teaching opportunities including contact, type and number available, application procedures, qualifications, and duties. For others: Name or title, address, phone, description. Paperback edition is available from Visible Ink Press. Arrangement: Schools are alphabetical; others are classified by type of resource. Indexes: Name and keyword.

★1555★ Educators Hiring Guide for Alaska, Hawaii, Idaho, Nevada, Montana, Oregon, Utah, Washington, and Wyoming

Career Center
Boise State University
Boise, ID 83725
Ph: (208)385-1747   Fax: (208)385-3437
Fr: 800-824-7017

Annual, February. $48.00 plus 2.00 shipping. Covers about 1,300 public school districts and 1,200 private schools in Alaska, Hawaii, Idaho, Montana, Nevada, Oregon, Utah, Washington, and Wyoming; also includes colleges and universities that provide educational employment information as a service. Entries include: For districts and private schools: name, address, phone, names and titles of contacts, job application and interview information, enrollment, number of elementary, middle, and high schools, starting salary. For universities and colleges: name, address, phone, description of services and fees. Arrangement: Geographical by city within state sections. Indexes: Geographical by county within state.

★1556★ Fulbright Scholar Program Grants for Faculty and Professionals

Council for International Exchange of Scholars
3007 Tilden St. NW, Ste. 5M
Washington, DC 20008-3009
Ph: (202)686-7866   Fax: (202)362-3442

Annual, March. Free. Covers about 1,000 grants available under the Mutual Educational and Cultural Exchange Act of 1961 for postdoctoral university lecturing and advanced research by American citizens in more than 100 countries. Entries include: Periods in which grants are tenable; number of grants available for the country; language or other requirement; fields in which lectures and research are desired; stipend, housing; additional income for dependents, applications and reference forms. Arrangement: Geographical.

★1557★ Higher Education Directory

Higher Education Publications, Inc.
6400 Arlington Blvd., Ste. 648
Falls Church, VA 22042
Ph: (703)532-2300   Fax: (703)532-2305

Annual, October. $47.00. Covers over 3,600 degree granting colleges and universities accredited by approved agencies recognized by the U.S. Secretary of Education; 101 systems offices; over 550 related associations and state government agencies; recognized accrediting agencies. Entries include: For institutions: name, address, congressional district, phone, fax, year established; enrollment; type of student body; religious or other affiliation; undergraduate tuition and fees; type of academic calendar; highest degree offered; accreditations; IRS status; names, titles and job classification codes for academic and administrative officers. For associations and state agencies: name, address, phone, name of chief executive officer. Arrangement: Geographical. Indexes: Administrator name (with phone), accreditation, college or university name.

★1558★ How to Find Jobs Teaching Overseas

KSJ Publishing Co.
7600 Washington Ave.
Sebastopol, CA 95473
Ph: (707)829-9109   Fr: 800-356-9315

Latest edition 1992. $7.95. Publication includes: List of 200 schools and agencies in 65 counties providing information on teaching opportunities abroad. Principal content of publication is step-by-step guide on how to locate teaching positions outside the United States, including the author's personal experiences in locating teaching positions in England, Spain, Saudi Arabia, and Japan. Arrangement: Alphabetical.

★1559★ Jobs Clearing House

Association for Experiential Education
2885 Aurora Ave., Ste. 28
Boulder, CO 80303-2252
Ph: (303)440-8844   Fax: (303)440-9581

Monthly. $5.00 per issue; $40.00 per year. Covers organizations and firms offering jobs, apprenticeships, internships, and other positions in experiential education in schools and colleges, wilderness leadership, therapeutic adventure programming, environmental education, and experiential/outdoor education; coverage includes Canada. Entries include: Position title, organization name, address, name of contact, description of duties, requirements, pay, and benefits. Arrangement: Geographical by state.

★1560★ National Directory of College Athletics

Collegiate Directories, Inc.
PO Box 450640
Cleveland, OH 44145
Ph: (216)835-1172   Fax: (216)835-8835
Fr: 800-42-NACDA

Annual, August. $14.95. Covers women's athletic departments at 2,000 senior and junior colleges. Entries include: School name, address; enrollment, colors, stadium and/or gym capacity, team nicknames; names of president, women's athletic director and physical education director, and coaches for each sport; athletic department phone number; and association affiliations. Arrangement: Alphabetical.

★1561★ National Directory of College Athletics

Collegiate Directories, Inc.
PO Box 450640
Cleveland, OH 44145
Ph: (216)835-1172   Fax: (216)835-8835
Fr: 800-42-NACDA

Annual, August. $19.95. Covers men's athletic departments of 2,100 senior and junior colleges in the United States and Canada. Entries include: School name, address, enrollment, colors, team nicknames, stadium and/or gym capacity; names of president, men's athletic director and physical education director and coaches for each sport; athletic department phone; association affiliations. Arrangement: Alphabetical.

★1562★ National Faculty Directory

Gale Research
835 Penobscot Bldg.
Detroit, MI 48226-4094
Ph: (313)961-2242   Fax: (313)961-6083
Fr: 800-877-GALE

Annual, summer; winter supplement. $665.00, Base edition; $215.00, supplement. Covers more than 630,000 (44,000 more in supplement) teaching faculty members at over 3,840 junior colleges, colleges, and universities in the United States and those in Canada that give instruction in English. Entries include: Name, department name, institution, and address. Directory combines main edition and supplement. Arrangement: Alphabetical.

★1563★ National Profile of Community Colleges: Trends and Statistics

American Association of Community Colleges (AACC)
1 Dupont Cir. NW, Ste. 410
Washington, DC 20036-1136

$65.00 for nonmembers; $50.00 for members. Covers about 1,500 community, technical, and junior colleges in the United States; state directors for community colleges. Entries include: Institution name, address, phone, name of chief executive officer, year established, total credit and non-credit enrollment, number of faculty and administrators, tuition. Arrangement: Geographical.

★1564★ *NCA Quarterly—Roster Issues*

North Central Association of Colleges and Schools
Arizona State University
PO Box 873011
Tempe, AZ 85287-3011
Ph: (602)965-8700   Fax: (602)965-9423
Fr: 800-525-9517

Annual, school issue, summer; college issue, spring. $7.00. Publication includes: Elementary schools and secondary schools (summer issue), and colleges (spring issue) accredited by the association in a 19-state region. Entries include: School name, address, year first accredited, staffing, enrollment, name of president or principal. Arrangement: Geographical.

★1565★ *Opportunities Abroad for Educators*

Fulbright Teacher Exchange Program
600 Maryland Ave., SW, Rm. 235
Washington, DC 20024-2520
Ph: (202)382-8586   Fax: (202)426-0657
Fr: 800-726-0479

Annual, May. Free. Covers opportunities available for elementary and secondary teachers, college and university instructors and professors, and school administrators to attend seminars or to teach abroad under the Mutual Educational and Cultural Exchange Act of 1961. Entries include: Countries of placement, dates, eligibility requirements, teaching assignments. Arrangement: Geographical.

★1566★ *Patterson's Schools Classified*

Educational Directories, Inc.
PO Box 199
Mount Prospect, IL 60056-0199
Ph: (708)459-0605   Fax: (708)459-0608

Annual, April. $13.00, plus $2.00 shipping. Covers over 7,000 accredited colleges, universities, community colleges, junior colleges, career schools and teaching hospitals. Entries include: School name, address, name of administrator or admissions officer, description, professional accreditation (where applicable). Arrangement: Geographical by state, then classified by type of school.

★1567★ *School Guide*

School Guide Publications
210 North Ave.
New Rochelle, NY 10801
Ph: (914)632-7771   Fax: (914)632-3412
Fr: 800-433-7771

Annual, March. $10.00. Covers over 1,000 colleges, vocational schools, and nursing schools in the United States. Entries include: Institution name, address, phone, courses offered, degrees awarded. Arrangement: Classified by type of institution, then geographical. Indexes: Subject.

HANDBOOKS AND MANUALS

★1568★ *Career Information Center*

Macmillan Publishing Co.
200 Old Tappan Rd.
Old Tappan, NJ 07675
Ph: (609)461-6500   Fr: 800-223-2336

Visual Education Center Staff. Fifth edition, 1992. $229.00. This 13-volume set profiles over 600 occupations. Each occupational profile describes job duties, educational requirements, how to get the job, advancement possibilities, employment outlook, working conditions, earnings and benefits, and where to write for more information.

★1569★ *Career Opportunities for Writers*

Facts on File, Inc.
11 Penn Plaza, 15th Fl.
New York, NY 10001-2006
Ph: (212)967-8800   Fax: 800-678-3633
Fr: 800-322-8755

Rosemary Guiley. Third edition, 1995. $29.95; $15.95 (paper). Describes more than 100 jobs in eight major fields, offering such details as duties, salaries, perquisites, employment and advancement opportunities, organizations to join, and opportunities for women and minorities.

★1570★ *Careers in Education*

VGM Career Horizons
4255 W. Touhy Ave.
Lincolnwood, IL 60646-1975
Ph: (847)679-5500   Fax: (847)679-2494
Fr: 800-323-4900

Roy A. Edelfeldt. 1993. $17.95; $13.95 (paper). 192 pages. Explores opportunities for teachers, administrators, and specialists in elementary and secondary schools, as well as teaching, research, and administrative positions in higher education. Additional focus on adult and continuing education and industry opportunities for educators. Provides detailed background on careers in state boards and state departments of education, accrediting agencies, federal agencies, and national associations and councils.

★1571★ *Customizing Your Resume for Teaching Positions*

University Press of America
4720 Boston Way
Lanham, MD 20706
Ph: (301)459-3366   Fax: (301)459-2118
Fr: 800-462-6420

Edward G. Pultorak. 1993. $17.50 (paper).

★1572★ *Educator's Job Search: The Ultimate Guide to Finding Positions in Education*

National Education Association
1201 16th St., NW
Washington, DC 20036
Ph: (202)822-7252   Fax: (202)822-7206

Martin Kimeldorf. 1993. $15.95 (paper).

★1573★ *How to Get a Job in Education*

Bob Adams, Inc.
260 Center St.
Holbrook, MA 02343
Ph: (617)767-8100   Fax: (617)767-0994
Fr: 800-872-5627

Joel Levin. Second edition, 1995. $12.95. 320 pages. Prepared for recent college graduates, seasoned educators, and career-changing professionals, this publication guides the job-seeker through the necessary steps to obtaining a job in education at the elementary, secondary, and university levels. Offers advice on how to prepare for state and local examinations, how to locate teaching opportunities nationwide, and how to obtain certification. Includes a nationwide salary survey. Covers public, private, summer, and overseas opportunities.

★1574★ *How to Get the Teaching Position You Want: Teacher Candidate Guide*

Education Enterprises
PO Box 1836
Spring Valley, CA 91979
Ph: (619)660-7740

M. Phyllis Murton. 1993.

★1575★ *100 Best Careers for the Year 2000*

Prentice Hall General Reference
15 Columbus Cir.
New York, NY 10023
Ph: (212)373-8500   Fr: 800-223-2348

Shelly Field. 1992. $15.00 (paper). Covers 100 of the fastest growing jobs. The publication is divided into 11 general employment sections. Specific careers are covered within each section. Provides job description, responsibilities, employment opportunities, earnings, education and training, advancement opportunities, and experience and qualifications for each occupation.

★1576★ *Opportunities in Teaching Careers*

VGM Career Horizons
4255 W. Touhy Ave.
Lincolnwood, IL 60646-1975
Ph: (847)679-5500   Fax: (847)679-2494
Fr: 800-323-4900

Janet Fine. 1995. $14.95; $11.95 (paper). 160 pages. Discusses licensing and accreditation programs, sources of placement information, job-seeking correspondence, selection procedures, and paths to advancement. Also covers professional associations, non-traditional teaching opportunities, and jobs abroad.

OTHER SOURCES

★1577★ *Alternative Careers for Ph.D.'s in the Humanities: A Selected Bibliography*

Books on Demand
300 N. Zeeb Rd.
Ann Arbor, MI 48106-1346
Ph: (313)761-4700   Fr: 800-521-0600

Christine F. Donaldson and Elizabeth A. Flynn. Reprint edition (originally published by Modern Language Association). $25.00. 48 pages. Bibliography of job-hunting resources and alternative occupations for Ph.D.'s in the humanities. Includes information on foreign language careers.

★1578★ *American Almanac of Jobs and Salaries 1994-95*

Avon Books
1350 Avenue of the Americas, 2nd Fl.
New York, NY 10019
Ph: (212)261-6800   Fr: 800-238-0658

John Wright. Revised edition, 1993. $17.00. 704 pages. This is a comprehensive guide to the wages of hundreds of occupations in a wide variety of industries and organizations.

★1579★ American Association of Community Colleges (AACC)

National Center for Higher Educ.
1 Dupont Cir. NW, Ste. 410
Washington, DC 20036-1176
Ph: (202)728-0200   Fax: (202)833-2467

Members: Community colleges; individual associates interested in community college development; corporate, educational, foundation, and international associate members. **Purpose:** Office of Federal Relations monitors federal educational programming and legislation. **Activities:** Compiles statistics through data collection and policy analysis. Conducts seminars and professional training programs.

★1580★ American Association of Teachers of German (AATG)

112 Haddontowne Ct., No. 104
Cherry Hill, NJ 08034
Ph: (609)795-5553   Fax: (609)795-9398

Members: Teachers of German at all levels; individuals interested in German language and culture. **Activities:** Offers in-service teacher-training workshops.

★1581★ American Catholic Philosophical Association (ACPA)

Catholic University of America
Administration Bldg., Rm. 403
620 Michigan Ave. NE
Washington, DC 20064
Ph: (202)319-5518   Fax: (202)319-5518

Members: College and university teachers of philosophy; students engaged in research; writers and others interested in philosophical knowledge. **E-Mail:** druart@cua.edu

★1582★ Association for the Advancement of Health Education (AAHE)

1900 Association Dr.
Reston, VA 22091
Ph: (703)476-3437   Fax: (703)476-6638

Members: Professionals who have responsibility for health education in schools, colleges, communities, hospitals and clinics, and industries. **Purpose:** Advancement of health education through program activities and federal legislation; encouragement of close working relationships between all health education and health service organizations; achievement of good health and well-being for all Americans automatically, without conscious thought and endeavor. Member of the American Alliance for Health, Physical Education, Recreation and Dance.

★1583★ Association of Departments of English (ADE)

10 Astor Pl.
New York, NY 10003
Ph: (212)614-6317   Fax: (212)477-9863

Members: Administrators of college and university departments of English, humanities, rhetoric, and communications. **Purpose:** To improve the teaching of English and the administration of English departments. Conducts studies and surveys of literature and writing courses. Sponsors sessions at major English conventions and conferences nationwide.

★1584★ Association for School, College and University Staffing (ASCUS)

820 Davis St., Ste. 222
Evanston, IL 60201-4445
Ph: (708)864-1999   Fax: (708)864-8303

Purpose: Educational institutions, school systems, associates and affiliates, and emeritus members; institutions that prepare teachers and other educational personnel for employment in public and private schools, colleges, and universities; other educational organizations related to educational staffing or procurement. Promotes the concept of career planning and placement as an integral part of the educational process. Fosters adoption of high professional standards among persons and associations engaged in career planning, placement, recruitment, or the selection of staff. Encourages member institutions to extend cooperative placement services to other members. Monitors placement offices and staffing. Compiles statistics; disseminates information on research studies in the field. Operates archives at Bowling Green State University. Does not provide a personal placement service.

★1585★ *Career Encounters: Teaching*

Cambridge Career Products
PO Box 2153
Dept. CC15
Charleston, WV 25328-2153
Ph: (304)744-9323   Fax: (304)744-9351
Fr: 800-468-4227

Video. $99.95. 25 minutes. Professionals shown in a variety of settings discuss different aspects of their careers.

★1586★ Conference on College Composition and Communication (CCCC)

1111 W. Kenyon Rd.
Urbana, IL 61801
Ph: (217)328-3870   Fax: (217)328-0977

Members: Teachers of English in colleges and universities.

★1587★ Eastern Finance Association (EFA)

Department of Finance
Florida State University
Tallahassee, FL 32306-1042
Ph: (904)644-4220

Members: College and university professors and financial officers; corporations, banks, and nonprofit organizations. **Purpose:** Provides a meeting place for persons interested in any aspect of finance, including financial management, investments, and banking. **Activities:** Sponsors research competitions.

★1588★ Friends Council on Education (FCE)

1507 Cherry St.
Philadelphia, PA 19102
Ph: (215)241-7245

Members: Representatives appointed by Friends Yearly Meetings; heads of Quaker secondary and elementary schools and colleges; members-at-large. **Purpose:** Acts as a clearinghouse for information on Quaker schools and colleges. **Activities:** Holds meetings and conferences on education and provides in-service training for teachers, administrators, and trustees in Friends schools.

★1589★ *How to Prepare Your Curriculum Vitae*

VGM Career Horizons
4255 W. Touhy Ave.
Lincolnwood, IL 60646-1975
Ph: (847)679-5500   Fax: (847)679-2494
Fr: 800-323-4900

Acy L. Jackson. 1993. $14.95. Dozens of examples from academics in all disciplines and at all career levels illustrate the principles of writing an effective C.V. Worksheets guide the reader through a step-by-step process that begins with describing, in draft form, all pertinent experiences, and then helps shape, organize, and edit experiences and credentials into a professional curriculum vitae. Includes sample cover letters tailored to academic institutions.

★1590★ National Association of Blind Teachers (NABT)

1155 15th St. NW, Ste. 720
Washington, DC 20005
Ph: (202)467-5081   Fr: 800-424-8666

Members: Public school teachers, college and university professors, and teachers in residential schools for the blind. **Purpose:** To promote employment and professional goals of blind persons entering the teaching profession or those established in their respective teaching fields. Serves as a vehicle for the dissemination of information and the exchange of ideas addressing special problems of members.

★1591★ *Overseas Employment Opportunities for Educators: Department of Defense Dependents Schools*

Diane Publishing Co.
600 Upland Ave.
Upland, PA 19015
Ph: (610)499-7415

1993. $29.95. 52 pages.

★1592★ *Resumes for Education Careers*

VGM Career Horizons
4255 W. Touhy Ave.
Lincolnwood, IL 60646-1975
Ph: (847)679-5500   Fax: (847)679-2494
Fr: 800-323-4900

1992. $9.95. Sample resumes cover a variety of education careers and reflect education professionals at all levels of experience.

Computer Operators

SOURCES OF HELP-WANTED ADS

★1593★ Captsule Job Listings

Publications and Communications, Inc.
12416 Hymeadow Dr.
Austin, TX 78750
Ph: (512)250-9023   Fax: (512)331-3900
Fr: 800-678-9724

Online database. Lists current job openings in the contract (temporary) technical services industry. Includes the Action Hot List, which provides information on job seekers. Includes employment opportunities in technical/professional engineering, computing, and design/drafting. Entries generally contain company name, address, and job opening.

★1594★ Computerworld

500 Old Connecticut Path
Framingham, MA 01701-9208
Ph: (508)872-0080   Fax: (508)879-7784
Fr: 800-669-1002

Weekly. $48.00/year; $6.00/issue. Newspaper for information systems management professionals.

★1595★ Datamation

Cahners Publishing Co.
275 Washington St.
Newton, MA 02158-1630
Ph: (617)964-3030   Fax: (617)558-4470

Semimonthly. Magazine on computers and information processing.

★1596★ DEC Professional

Cardinal Business Media, Inc.
1300 Virginia Dr., Ste.400
Fort Washington, PA 19034
Ph: (215)643-8064   Fax: (215)643-3901

Monthly. Magazine covering Digital Equipment Corporation's computers and related products.

★1597★ IEEE Software

IEEE Computer Society
10662 Los Vaqueros Cir.
PO Box 3014
Los Alamitos, CA 90720-3014
Ph: (714)821-8380   Fax: (714)821-4010
Fr: 800-272-6657

Bimonthly. $25.00/year for individuals. Magazine covering the computer software industry.

★1598★ MIDRANGE Systems

Professional Press, Inc.
101 Witmer Rd.
Horsham, PA 19044
Ph: (215)957-1500   Fax: (215)957-4230

Biweekly.

★1599★ NEWS 3X/400

Duke Communications, Intl.
221 E. 29th St., Ste. 242
Loveland, CO 80538
Ph: (303)663-4700   Fax: (303)669-3016
Fr: 800-621-1544

Monthly. $119.00/year for individuals. Trade magazine for programmers and data processing managers who use IBM minicomputers (System/34, System/36, System/38, and AS/400).

EMPLOYER DIRECTORIES AND NETWORKING LISTS

★1600★ Computer Directory

Computer Directories, Inc.
13205 Cypress N. Houston Rd.
Cypress, TX 77429-3606
Ph: (713)955-9791   Fax: (713)955-9793
Fr: 800-234-4353

Annual, fall. Covers Approximately 130,000 computer installations; 19 separate volumes for Alaska/Hawaii, Connecticut/New Jersey, Dallas/Ft. Worth, Eastern Seaboard, Far Midwest, Houston, Illinois, Midatlantic, Midcentral, Mideast, Minnesota/Wisconsin, North Central, New England, New York Metro, Northwest, Ohio, Pennsylvania/West Virginia, Southeast, and Southwest Texas. Entries include: Company name, address, phone, fax, name and title of contact, hardware used, software application, operating system, programming language, computer graphics, networking system. Arrangement: Geographical. Indexes: Alphabetical, industry, hardware.

★1601★ Directory of Top Computer Executives

Applied Computer Research, Inc.
11242 N. 19th Ave.
Phoenix, AZ 85029
Ph: (602)995-5929   Fax: (602)995-0905
Fr: 800-234-2227

Semiannual, May and November. Covers in three volumes, over 41,000 U.S. and 6,900 Canadian executives with major data processing or communications responsibilities in over 14,100 U.S. sites and 3,400 Canadian sites companies with gross annual sales of over $50 million and/or EDP (Electronic Data Processing) budgets over $250,000. Entries include: Company name, address, phone, subsidiary and/or division names, major systems installed, names and titles of top EDP executives. Arrangement: Geographical within separate eastern, western, and Canadian volumes. Indexes: Industry; alphabetical by company name.

★1602★ Dun & Bradstreet Reference Book of Corporate Managements

Dun & Bradstreet Information Services
Dun & Bradstreet Corp.
3 Sylvan Way
Parsippany, NJ 07054-3896
Ph: (201)605-6000   Fax: (201)605-6911
Fr: 800-526-0651

Annual, April. $785.00, lease basis; $635.00, for public libraries, lease basis. Covers nearly 200,000 presidents, directors, vice presidents, officers, and managers in 12,000 companies of greatest economic, marketing, and investment interests; those firms whose revenues are the highest in the United States. Arrangement: Alphabetical by company name. Indexes: Personal name (with abbreviated title and company affiliation), geographical, SIC code, advanced education institution, military affiliation.

★1603★ How and Where to Get the Best Computer Jobs

Information Resource Group
50495 Corporate Dr., Ste. 112
Shelby Township, MI 48315
Ph: (810)254-8500   Fax: (810)254-8500

Annual. $69.95. per directory. Publication includes: Listing of the top dataprocessing employers in United States and Canada. Information divided among 67 editions, according to state/province. Principal content of publication is hiring/interview tips, salary surveys. Entries include: Company name, address, phone, name and title of contact. Arrangement: Geographical.

★1604★ Northwest High Tech: Fast Facts on the $7 Billion Computer Industry of Washington, Oregon, Idaho, British Columbia, and Alberta

Resolution Business Press
11101 NE 8th St., Ste. 208
Bellevue, WA 98004
Ph: (206)455-4611   Fax: (206)455-9143

Annual. $34.95. Covers over 1,800 computer-related companies in Washington, Oregon, and Idaho, and British Columbia and Alberta, Canada. Entries include: Company; name, address, phone, fax; toll-free number; names and titles of key personnel; product/service, programming languages, financial data, names and titles of key personnel, number of employees, operating systems, expansion plans (including hiring and site expansion plans), company market information, Standard Industrial Classification (SIC) code. Arrangement: Geographical, industry sector. Indexes: Company name, SIC.

HANDBOOKS AND MANUALS

★1605★ ACE the Technical Interview: How to Get Your Next Job in the Computer Industry

The McGraw-Hill Companies
1221 Avenue of the Americas
New York, NY 10020
Ph: (212)512-2000   Fr: 800-262-4729

Michael Rothstein. 1994. $19.95 (paper).

★1606★ America's 50 Fastest Growing Jobs

JIST Works, Inc.
720 N. Park Ave.
Indianapolis, IN 46202
Ph: (317)264-3720   Fr: 800-648-5478

Third edition, 1995. $14.95. 288 pages. Each job profile explains the nature of the work, skills and abilities required, employment outlook, average earnings, related occupations, education and training requirements, and employment opportunities. Also contains career planning information and job search tips.

★1607★ Career Choices for the 90's for Students of Computer Science

Walker and Company
435 Hudson St.
New York, NY 10014
Ph: (212)727-8300   Fax: (212)727-0984
Fr: 800-289-2553

Prepared by the Career Associates staff. 1990. $8.95. 166 pages. Discusses alternatives for students of computer science. Offers advice on how to break into the field and how to move up. Covers where and who the employers are, internship possibilities, and professional networking associations. Comprehensive guide to career and job search planning.

★1608★ Careers for Computer Buffs and Other Technological Types

NTC Publishing Group
4255 W. Touhy Ave.
Lincolnwood, IL 60646-1975
Ph: (708)679-5500   Fax: (708)679-6375
Fr: 800-323-4900

Marjorie Eberts. 1994. $12.95; $9.95 (paper).

★1609★ Careers in Computer Fields

Rosen Publishing Group, Inc.
29 E 21st St.
New York, NY 10010
Ph: (212)777-3017   Fax: (212)777-0277
Fr: 800-237-9932

Joseph Weintraub. 1993. $14.95; $9.95 (paper).

★1610★ Careers in Computers

VGM Career Horizons
4255 W. Touhy Ave.
Lincolnwood, IL 60646-1975
Ph: (847)679-5500   Fax: (847)679-2494
Fr: 800-323-4900

Lila B. Stair. Second edition, 1995. $17.95; $13.95 (paper). Describes trends affecting computer careers and explores a wide range of job opportunities from programming to consulting. Provides job qualifications, salary data, job market information, personal and educational requirements, career paths, and the place of the job in the organizational structure. Offers advice on education, certification, and job search.

★1611★ Computer Jobs Worldwide: Support Staff Plus Electronics Plus Telecommunications

Zinks International Career Guidance
PO Box 790
Richland, MI 49083
Ph: (313)584-7529

Richard M. Zink. 1995. $14.95 (paper).

★1612★ Covin's Mid-West Computer Job Guide

Vandamere Press
PO Box 5243
Arlington, VA 22205
Ph: (703)525-5488   Fax: (703)524-4105

Carol L. Covin. 1994. $13.95 (paper).

★1613★ The Digital Frontier Job & Opportunity Finder

Moon Lake Media
PO Box 251466
Los Angeles, CA 90025
Ph: (310)535-2453

Don B. Altman. 1995. $24.95 (paper).

★1614★ Downsized but Not Out: How to Get Your Next Computer Job

The McGraw-Hill Companies
1221 Avenue of the Americas
New York, NY 10020
Ph: (212)512-2000   Fr: 800-262-4729

Alan Simon. 1994. $30.00; $17.95 (paper).

★1615★ Exploring Careers in the Computer Field

Rosen Publishing Group, Inc.
29 E. 21st St.
New York, NY 10010
Ph: (212)777-3017   Fax: (212)777-0277
Fr: 800-237-9932

Joseph Weintraub. Revised edition, 1993. Discusses entry into the field, salaries, future trends, and offers job search advice. Surveys the newest growth areas in the computer industry including artificial intelligence, desktop publishing, and personal computers.

★1616★ Exploring High-Tech Careers

Rosen Publishing Group, Inc.
29 E. 21st St.
New York, NY 10010
Ph: (212)777-3017   Fax: (212)777-0277
Fr: 800-237-9932

Scott Southworth. Revised edition, 1993. $14.95; $9.95 (paper). 118 pages. Gives an orientation to the field of high technology and high-tech jobs. Describes educational preparation and job hunting. Includes a glossary and bibliography.

★1617★ 100 Best Careers for the Year 2000

Prentice Hall General Reference
15 Columbus Cir.
New York, NY 10023
Ph: (212)373-8500   Fr: 800-223-2348

Shelly Field. 1992. $15.00 (paper). Covers 100 of the fastest growing jobs. The publication is divided into 11 general employment sections. Specific careers are covered within each section. Provides job description, responsibilities, employment opportunities, earnings, education and training, advancement opportunities, and experience and qualifications for each occupation.

★1618★ Opportunities in Computer Science Careers

VGM Career Horizons
4255 W. Touhy Ave.
Lincolnwood, IL 60646-1975
Ph: (847)679-5500   Fax: (847)679-2494
Fr: 800-323-4900

Julie Lepick Kling. 1995. $14.95; $11.95 (paper). Discusses how to enter the field and build a career. Illustrated.

★1619★ Opportunities in Data Processing Careers

VGM Career Horizons
4255 W. Touhy Ave.
Lincolnwood, IL 60646-1975
Ph: (847)679-5500   Fax: (847)679-2494
Fr: 800-323-4900

Norman Noerper. 1989. $14.95; $11.95 (paper). 160 pages. Extensive information on education, training, and job prospecting make this a useful guide to an important career field. Illustrated.

★1620★ Opportunities in Information Systems Careers

VGM Career Horizons
4255 W. Touhy Ave.
Lincolnwood, IL 60646-1975
Ph: (847)679-5500   Fax: (847)679-2494
Fr: 800-323-4900

Douglas B. Hoyt. 1991. $14.95; $11.95 (paper). Describes prospects in information specialties such as computer operations, programming, and documentation; telecommunications; records management; micrographics; and project planning and management. Offers advice about job hunting and advancement.

★1621★ Opportunities in Office Occupations

VGM Career Horizons
4255 W. Touhy Ave.
Lincolnwood, IL 60646-1975
Ph: (847)679-5500   Fax: (847)679-2494
Fr: 800-323-4900

Blanche Ettinger. 1995. $14.95; $11.95 (paper). Covers a variety of office positions and discusses trends for the next decade. Describes the job market, opportunities, job duties, educational preparation, the work environment, and earnings.

★1622★ Opportunities in Vocational and Technical Careers

VGM Career Horizons
4255 W. Touhy Ave.
Lincolnwood, IL 60646-1975
Ph: (847)679-5500   Fax: (847)679-2494
Fr: 800-323-4900

Adrian A. Paradis. 1992. $14.95; $11.95 (paper). 160 pages. Provides information on a variety of opportunities and advice on breaking into the field.

★1623★ Your Opportunities in Computers

Energeia Publishing, Inc.
PO Box 985
Salem, OR 97308
Ph: (503)362-1480   Fax: (503)362-2123

John Tribbett. 1994. $2.00 (paper).

EMPLOYMENT AGENCIES AND SEARCH FIRMS

★1624★ B and M Associates, Inc.

199 Cambridge Rd.
Woburn, MA 01801-4705
Ph: (617)938-9120

Employment agency.

★1625★ Computer Engineering Consortium

7353 McWhorten Pl., Ste. 212
Annandale, VA 22003-5648
Ph: (703)658-0016

Employment agency.

★1626★ Computer Network Resources Inc.

7000 Central Pkwy. NE
Atlanta, GA 30328-4579
Ph: (404)391-9009

Employment agency.

★1627★ Data Careers Personnel Services, Inc.

3320 4th Ave.
San Diego, CA 92103
Ph: (619)291-9994

Employment agency. Places staff on a regular or temporary basis.

★1628★ Data Systems Search Consultants

1756 Lacassie Ave.
Walnut Creek, CA 94596-4015
Ph: (510)256-0635

Employment agency. Executive search firm.

★1629★ DP Career Associates

6405 Metcalf, Ste. 425
Shawnee Mission, KS 66202
Ph: (913)236-8288

Employment agency.

★1630★ Electronic Systems Personnel

701 Fourth Ave. S., Ste. 1800
Minneapolis, MN 55415
Ph: (612)337-3000

Employment agency.

★1631★ Hayden and Associates, Inc.

7825 Washington Ave. S., Ste. 120
Minneapolis, MN 55439-2431
Ph: (612)941-6300   Fax: (612)941-9602

Employment agency. Executive search firm. Fills openings in a variety of fields.

★1632★ Linn-Truett, Inc.

7800 I.H. 10 W, Ste. 512
San Antonio, TX 78230
Ph: (210)340-3690   Fax: (210)340-2158

Employment agency.

★1633★ LOR Personnel Division

418 Wall St.
Princeton, NJ 08540
Ph: (609)921-6580

Employment agency. Executive search firm.

★1634★ The Murphy Group

1211 W. 22nd St., Ste. 221
Oak Brook, IL 60521-2115
Ph: (708)574-2840

Employment agency. Places personnel in a variety of positions.

★1635★ Romac International, Inc.

120 Hyde Park Pl., Ste. 200
Tampa, FL 33606
Fr: 800-341-0263

Executive search firm. More than 30 locations throughout the U.S.

★1636★ Source EDP

5580 LBJ Fwy., Ste. 300
Dallas, TX 75240
Ph: (214)385-3002

Executive search firm. Many affiliate offices located in most major cities in the U.S.

★1637★ Tri-Serv Inc.

22 W. Padonia Rd., Ste. C53
Timonium, MD 21093
Ph: (301)561-1740

Employment agency.

★1638★ Worlco Computer Resources, Inc.

901 Route 38
Cherry Hill, NJ 08002-2890
Ph: (609)665-4700   Fax: (609)665-8142

Employment agency. Second location in Philadelphia, PA.

OTHER SOURCES

★1639★ Association for Computer Operations Management (AFCOM)

742 E. Chapman Ave.
Orange, CA 92666
Ph: (714)997-7966   Fax: (714)997-9743

Members: Data center and data processing operations management professionals from medium and large scale main frame, midrange and client/server data centers worldwide. **Purpose:** Dedicated to meeting the professional needs of the data center management community. **Activities:** Provides information and support through educational events, research and assistance hotlines, and surveys.

★1640★ Black Data Processing Associates (BDPA)

1250 Connecticut Ave. NW, Ste. 700
Washington, DC 20036-2603
Ph: (202)775-4301   Fax: (202)775-1344
Fr: 800-727-BDPA

Members: Persons employed in the information processing industry, including electronic data processing, electronic word processing, and data communications; others interested in information processing. **Purpose:** Seeks to accumulate and share information processing knowledge and business expertise in order to increase the career and business potential of minorities in the information processing field. **Activities:** Conducts professional seminars, workshops, tutoring services, and community introductions to data processing. Makes annual donation to the United Negro College Fund.

★1641★ *The Computer Industry Almanac*

Computer Industry Almanac
225 Allen Way
Incline Village, NV 89451
Ph: (702)831-2288

Annual. $63.00. Also available on CD-ROM, $63.00. A compendium of information on the computer industry compiled from newsletters, reports, and magazines.

★1642★ *Computer Salary Survey and Career Planning Guide*

Source EDP
120 Broadway, Ste. 1010
New York, NY 10271
Ph: (212)557-8611

Annual. Describes career paths in the computer field and trends in the computer field. Lists job titles. Charts salaries by job titles, years of experience, and industry.

★1643★ **Data Processing Management Association (DPMA)**

505 Busse Hwy.
Park Ridge, IL 60068
Ph: (708)825-8124   Fax: (708)825-1693

Members: Managerial personnel, staff, educators, and individuals interested in the management of information resources. Founder of the Certificate in Data Processing examination program, now administered by an intersociety organization. **Purpose:** Maintains Legislative Communications Network. Professional education programs include EDP-oriented business and management principles self-study courses and a series of videotaped management development seminars. Sponsors student organizations around

the country interested in data processing and encourages members to serve as counselors for the Scout computer merit badge. Conducts research projects, including a business information systems curriculum for two- and four-year colleges.

★1644★ **Special Interest Group for Computers and the Physically Handicapped (SISCAPH)**

Association for Computing Machinery
1515 Broadway, 17th Fl.
New York, NY 10036
Ph: (212)626-0613   Fax: (212)302-5826

Members: A special interest group of the Association of Computing Machinery. Physically disabled computer professionals; persons involved in the application of computers to aid the disabled; persons involved in the training or employment of physically disabled computer professionals; others interested in aiding the disabled. **Purpose:** To promote application of computer technology to aid the physically disabled; to educate the public about disabled computer professionals. **Activities:** Sponsors lectures and sessions at computer conferences on hiring and training disabled computer professionals. Compiles statistics.

Computer Programmers

★1645★ ACM Computing Surveys

Association for Computing Machinery
1515 Broadway, 17th Fl.
New York, NY 10036-9998
Ph: (212)869-7440   Fax: (212)869-0481

Quarterly. $17.00/year for individuals; $105.00/year for nonmembers;Journal presenting surveys and tutorials in computer science.

★1646★ BYTE

McGraw-Hill, Inc.
1 Phoenix Mill Ln.
Peterborough, NH 03458
Ph: (603)924-9281   Fax: (603)924-2550
Fr: 800-232-2983

Monthly. Magazine covering microcomputing for major brands of hardware and software. Includes reviews, features, and technology news for experienced and knowledgeable purchasers and users of microcomputers.

★1647★ Captsule Job Listings

Publications and Communications, Inc.
12416 Hymeadow Dr.
Austin, TX 78750
Ph: (512)250-9023   Fax: (512)331-3900
Fr: 800-678-9724

Online database. Lists current job openings in the contract (temporary) technical services industry. Includes the Action Hot List, which provides information on job seekers. Includes employment opportunities in technical/professional engineering, computing, and design/drafting. Entries generally contain company name, address, and job opening.

★1648★ Communications of the ACM

Association for Computing Machinery
1515 Broadway 17th fl.
New York, NY 10036
Ph: (212)869-7440   Fax: (212)869-0481

Monthly. $32.00/year for individuals; $124.00/year for nonmembers. Computing news magazine.

★1649★ Communications Week

CMP Publications
PO Box 1094
Skokie, IL 60076
Ph: (708)647-6834

Weekly. $143.00/year. Magazine subtitled: "The Newspaper for Enterprise Networking."

★1650★ Computer

IEEE Computer Society
1730 Massachusetts Ave. NW
Washington, DC 20036
Ph: (202)371-0101

Monthly. Covers major trends in computer science and engineering.

★1651★ Computerworld

500 Old Connecticut Path
Framingham, MA 01701-9208
Ph: (508)872-0080   Fax: (508)879-7784
Fr: 800-669-1002

Weekly. $48.00/year; $6.00/issue. Newspaper for information systems management professionals.

★1652★ Data Based Advisor

Data Based Solutions, Inc.
4010 Morena Blvd., Ste. 200
San Diego, CA 92117
Ph: (619)483-6400   Fax: (619)483-9851

Monthly. $35.00/year for individuals. Magazine covering microcomputer database management system topics; offering software reviews and programming tips and techniques.

★1653★ Database Programming and Design

Miller Freeman, Inc.
600 Harrison St.
San Francisco, CA 94107
Ph: (415)905-2200

Monthly. Computer magazine.

★1654★ Datamation

Cahners Publishing Co.
275 Washington St.
Newton, MA 02158-1630
Ph: (617)964-3030   Fax: (617)558-4470

Semimonthly. Magazine on computers and information processing.

★1655★ DBMS

Miller Freeman Publishing, Inc.
501 Galveston Dr.
Redwood City, CA 94063
Ph: (415)366-3600

Monthly. $24.00/year; $2.95/issue. Magazine for developers and users of client-server database applications.

★1656★ DEC Professional

Cardinal Business Media, Inc.
1300 Virginia Dr., Ste.400
Fort Washington, PA 19034
Ph: (215)643-8064   Fax: (215)643-3901

Monthly. Magazine covering Digital Equipment Corporation's computers and related products.

★1657★ Digital News and Review

Cahners Publishing Co.
275 Washington St.
Newton, MA 02158-1630
Ph: (617)964-3030   Fax: (617)558-4470

Semimonthly. Free to qualified subscribers.

★1658★ Enterprise Systems Journal

Cardinal Business Media, Inc.
12225 Greenville Ave., Ste. 700
Dallas, TX 75243
Ph: (214)669-9000   Fax: (214)669-9909

Monthly. Journal providing authoritative, in-depth information for all IS professionals in IBM host-based enterprises.

★1659★ Government Computer News

Conners Publishing
245 W. 17th St.
New York, NY 10011
Ph: (212)463-6835   Fax: (212)463-6836

Biweekly. $74.95/year for individuals; $8.00 for single issue. Newspaper for government technical and management executives responsible for managing and buying information technology products and services. Covers computer/communications news, trends, applications, and products impacting government operations.

★1660★ IEEE Software

IEEE Computer Society
10662 Los Vaqueros Cir.
PO Box 3014
Los Alamitos, CA 90720-3014
Ph: (714)821-8380   Fax: (714)821-4010
Fr: 800-272-6657

Bimonthly. $25.00/year for individuals. Magazine covering the computer software industry.

★1661★ InformationWEEK

CMP Publications, Inc.
600 Community Dr.
Manhasset, NY 11030
Ph: (516)562-5000   Fax: (516)562-5055

Weekly. Magazine focusing on data and information processing news and strategies.

★1662★ Job Express

FVI & Wendy Vandamme
105 N. Main St.
Boonton, NJ 07005
Ph: (201)299-1535

Biweekly. $43.50/year. Contains surveys of billing rates for contract computer services, listings of open assignments and contracts, and situations wanted.

★1663★ MIDRANGE Systems

Professional Press, Inc.
101 Witmer Rd.
Horsham, PA 19044
Ph: (215)957-1500   Fax: (215)957-4230
Biweekly.

★1664★ Network World

161 Worcester Rd.
Framingham, MA 01701-9172
Ph: (508)875-6400

Weekly (Mon.). $95.00/year for individuals. The newsweekly of enterprise network computing.

★1665★ NEWS 3X/400

Duke Communications, Intl.
221 E. 29th St., Ste. 242
Loveland, CO 80538
Ph: (303)663-4700   Fax: (303)669-3016
Fr: 800-621-1544

Monthly. $119.00/year for individuals. Trade magazine for programmers and data processing managers who use IBM minicomputers (System/34, System/36, System/38, and AS/400).

★1666★ 3X/400 Systems Management

Adams/Hunter Publishing Co.
25 Northwest Pt. Blvd., Ste. 800
Elk Grove Village, IL 60007
Ph: (708)427-9512   Fax: (708)427-2079

Monthly. $42.00/year for individuals. Management-oriented magazine for DP/MIS managers with an IBM AS/400, System/36 or RS 16000 on site.

★1667★ UNIX Review

Miller Freeman Publications, Inc.
600 Harrison St.
San Francisco, CA 94107
Ph: (415)905-2200

Monthly. Magazine for professional users of UNIX and UNIX-like systems.

PLACEMENT AND JOB REFERRAL SERVICES

★1668★ American Indian Science and Engineering Society (AISES)

1630 30th St., Ste. 301
Boulder, CO 80301
Ph: (303)492-8658   Fax: (303)492-3400

Members: American Indian and non-Indian students and professionals in science, technology, and engineering fields; corporations representing energy, mining, aerospace, electronic, and computer fields. **Purpose:** Seeks to motivate and encourage students to pursue undergraduate and graduate studies in science, engineering, and technology. **Activities:** Sponsors science fairs in grade schools, teacher training workshops, summer math/science sessions for 8th-12th graders, professional chapters, and student chapters in colleges. Offers scholarships. Adult members serve as role models, advisers, and mentors for students. Operates placement service. **E-Mail:** aisesha@spot.colorado.edu

★1669★ Association of Computer Professionals (ACP)

9 Forest Dr.
Plainview, NY 11803
Ph: (516)938-8223   Fax: (516)938-3073

Members: Authors, consultants, programmers, publishers, and teachers in the computer field who provide products or services to users or to other professionals. **Purpose:** Purpose is to advance the art and science of computer professionals through educational means. Encourages education and instruction of the public regarding what the association views as the beneficial use of computers and computer technology. **Activities:** Provides members with information on accounting, business management, creative marketing techniques, law, microcomputer advances, tax matters, technical developments, and special earning opportunities. Addresses issues of software protection, contract law, tax benefits, potential tax problems, and financial subjects such as sources of capital for new ventures and expanding businesses.

EMPLOYER DIRECTORIES AND NETWORKING LISTS

★1670★ Computer Directory

Computer Directories, Inc.
13205 Cypress N. Houston Rd.
Cypress, TX 77429-3606
Ph: (713)955-9791   Fax: (713)955-9793
Fr: 800-234-4353

Annual, fall. Covers Approximately 130,000 computer installations; 19 separate volumes for Alaska/Hawaii, Connecticut/New Jersey, Dallas/Ft. Worth, Eastern Seaboard, Far Midwest, Houston, Illinois, Midatlantic, Midcentral, Mideast, Minnesota/Wisconsin, North Central, New England, New York Metro, Northwest, Ohio, Pennsylvania/West Virginia, Southeast, and Southwest Texas. Entries include: Company name, address, phone, fax, name and title of contact, hardware used, software application, operating system, programming language, computer graphics, networking system. Arrangement: Geographical. Indexes: Alphabetical, industry, hardware.

★1671★ Computers and People— Computer Directory and Buyers' Guide Issue

Berkeley Enterprises, Inc.
368 Crescent St., No. 2
Waltham, MA 02154-3804

Annual, October. $24.50, plus $1.00 shipping. Publication includes: List of over 3,600 companies offering hardware, software, and computing or data processing services; societies and associations in computer fields. Entries include: For companies: name, address, phone, products or services; some have name of principal executive or contact person, number of employees, year established, year information was verified. For organizations: name, address, phone, name of president or secretary. Arrangement: Alphabetical. Indexes: Product or service.

★1672★ Computing and Software Design Career Directory

Gale Research
835 Penobscot Bldg.
Detroit, MI 48226-4094
Ph: (313)961-2242   Fax: (313)961-6083
Fr: 800-877-GALE

Latest edition 1993. $34.00; $17.95 (paper). Covers over 200 companies and organizations with entry-level opportunities as computer programmers, software engineers, technical writers, information center analysts, and similar positions; sources of help-wanted ads, professional associations, producers of videos, databases, career guides, and professional guides and handbooks. Entries include: For companies and organizations: name, address, phone, business description, names and titles of key personnel, number of employees, average number of entry-level positions available, human resources contact, description of internship opportunities including contact, type and number available, application procedures, qualifications, and duties. For others: name or title, address, phone, description. Paperback edition is available from Visible Ink Press. Arrangement: Companies and organizations are alphabetical; others are classified by type of resource. Indexes: Name, keyword.

★1673★ **Directory of Top Computer Executives**

Applied Computer Research, Inc.
11242 N. 19th Ave.
Phoenix, AZ 85029
Ph: (602)995-5929   Fax: (602)995-0905
Fr: 800-234-2227

Semiannual, May and November. Covers in three volumes, over 41,000 U.S. and 6,900 Canadian executives with major data processing or communications responsibilities in over 14,100 U.S. sites and 3,400 Canadian sites companies with gross annual sales of over $50 million and/or EDP (Electronic Data Processing) budgets over $250,000. Entries include: Company name, address, phone, subsidiary and/or division names, major systems installed, names and titles of top EDP executives. Arrangement: Geographical within separate eastern, western, and Canadian volumes. Indexes: Industry; alphabetical by company name.

★1674★ **Dun & Bradstreet Reference Book of Corporate Managements**

Dun & Bradstreet Information Services
Dun & Bradstreet Corp.
3 Sylvan Way
Parsippany, NJ 07054-3896
Ph: (201)605-6000   Fax: (201)605-6911
Fr: 800-526-0651

Annual, April. $785.00, lease basis; $635.00, for public libraries, lease basis. Covers nearly 200,000 presidents, directors, vice presidents, officers, and managers in 12,000 companies of greatest economic, marketing, and investment interests; those firms whose revenues are the highest in the United States. Arrangement: Alphabetical by company name. Indexes: Personal name (with abbreviated title and company affiliation), geographical, SIC code, advanced education institution, military affiliation.

★1675★ **The Hidden Job Market: A Job Seeker's Guide to America's 2,000 Little-Known, Fastest-Growing High-Tech Companies**

Peterson's Guides, Inc.
202 Carnegie Center
PO Box 2123
Princeton, NJ 08543-2123
Ph: (609)243-9111   Fax: (609)243-9150
Fr: 800-338-3282

Annual, October. $16.95. Covers Approximately 2,000 technology firms with under 1,000 employees, which have added the most employees in the survey year. Entries include: Company name, address, phone, fax, name and title of contact, number of employees, year founded, number of employees added in last year, percentage of growth, line of business. Arrangement: Geographical by state, then by area code. Indexes: Alphabetical by industry.

★1676★ **How and Where to Get the Best Computer Jobs**

Information Resource Group
50495 Corporate Dr., Ste. 112
Shelby Township, MI 48315
Ph: (810)254-8500   Fax: (810)254-8500

Annual. $69.95. per directory. Publication includes: Listing of the top dataprocessing employers in United States and Canada. Information divided among 67 editions, according to state/province. Principal content of publication is hiring/interview tips, salary surveys. Entries include: Company name, address, phone, name and title of contact. Arrangement: Geographical.

★1677★ **Northwest High Tech: Fast Facts on the $7 Billion Computer Industry of Washington, Oregon, Idaho, British Columbia, and Alberta**

Resolution Business Press
11101 NE 8th St., Ste. 208
Bellevue, WA 98004
Ph: (206)455-4611   Fax: (206)455-9143

Annual. $34.95. Covers over 1,800 computer-related companies in Washington, Oregon, and Idaho, and British Columbia and Alberta, Canada. Entries include: Company; name, address, phone, fax; toll-free number; names and titles of key personnel; product/service, programming languages, financial data, names and titles of key personnel, number of employees, operating systems, expansion plans (including hiring and site expansion plans), company market information, Standard Industrial Classification (SIC) code. Arrangement: Geographical, industry sector. Indexes: Company name, SIC.

★1678★ **Peterson's Job Opportunities in Engineering and Technology 1996**

Peterson's
PO Box 2123
Princeton, NJ 08543-2123
Ph: (609)243-9111   Fax: (609)243-9150
Fr: 800-338-3282

Compiled by the Peterson's staff. Annual. $19.95 paperback. 432 pages. Profiles 2,000 high-tech companies looking primarily for technical personnel in such fields as biotechnology, telecommunications, software, computers and peripherals, defense, and aerospace. Contains job-search strategies and career options to help match education and expertise to the job market. Indexed geographically, by industry, and by hiring needs.

HANDBOOKS AND MANUALS

★1679★ **ACE the Technical Interview: How to Get Your Next Job in the Computer Industry**

The McGraw-Hill Companies
1221 Avenue of the Americas
New York, NY 10020
Ph: (212)512-2000   Fr: 800-262-4729

Michael Rothstein. 1994. $19.95 (paper).

★1680★ **ASIS Jobline**

American Society for Information Science (ASIS)
8720 Georgia Ave., Ste. 501
Silver Spring, MD 20910
Ph: (301)495-0900

Monthly periodical provides job listings in information science.

★1681★ **Career Choices for the 90's for Students of Computer Science**

Walker and Company
435 Hudson St.
New York, NY 10014
Ph: (212)727-8300   Fax: (212)727-0984
Fr: 800-289-2553

Prepared by the Career Associates staff. 1990. $8.95. 166 pages. Discusses alternatives for students of computer science. Offers advice on how to break into the field and how to move up. Covers where and who the employers are, internship possibilities, and professional networking associations. Comprehensive guide to career and job search planning.

★1682★ **Career Choices for the 90's for Students of Mathematics**

Walker and Company
435 Hudson St.
New York, NY 10014
Ph: (212)727-8300   Fax: (212)727-0984
Fr: 800-289-2553

Prepared by the Career Associates staff. 1990. $8.95. 166 pages. Discusses alternatives for students of mathematics. Offers advice on how to break into the field and how to move up. Covers where and who the employers are, internship possibilities, and professional networking associations. Comprehensive guide to career and job search planning.

★1683★ **Career Information Center**

Macmillan Publishing Co.
200 Old Tappan Rd.
Old Tappan, NJ 07675
Ph: (609)461-6500   Fr: 800-223-2336

Visual Education Center Staff. Fifth edition, 1992. $229.00. This 13-volume set profiles over 600 occupations. Each occupational profile describes job duties, educational requirements, how to get the job, advancement possibilities, employment outlook, working conditions, earnings and benefits, and where to write for more information.

★1684★ **Careers for Computer Buffs and Other Technological Types**

NTC Publishing Group
4255 W. Touhy Ave.
Lincolnwood, IL 60646-1975
Ph: (708)679-5500   Fax: (708)679-6375
Fr: 800-323-4900

Marjorie Eberts. 1994. $12.95; $9.95 (paper).

★1685★ *Careers in Computer Fields*

Rosen Publishing Group, Inc.
29 E 21st St.
New York, NY 10010
Ph: (212)777-3017   Fax: (212)777-0277
Fr: 800-237-9932

Joseph Weintraub. 1993. $14.95; $9.95 (paper).

★1686★ *Careers in Computers*

VGM Career Horizons
4255 W. Touhy Ave.
Lincolnwood, IL 60646-1975
Ph: (847)679-5500   Fax: (847)679-2494
Fr: 800-323-4900

Lila B. Stair. Second edition, 1995. $17.95; $13.95 (paper). Describes trends affecting computer careers and explores a wide range of job opportunities from programming to consulting. Provides job qualifications, salary data, job market information, personal and educational requirements, career paths, and the place of the job in the organizational structure. Offers advice on education, certification, and job search.

★1687★ *Careers in Information Science*

American Society for Information Science (ASIS)
8720 Georgia Ave., Ste. 501
Silver Spring, MD 20910
Ph: (301)495-0900

Free brochure describes career opportunities in information science, communications, computer science, and research.

★1688★ *Careers for Number Crunchers and Other Quantitative Types*

VGM Career Horizons
4255 W. Touhy Ave.
Lincolnwood, IL 60646-1975
Ph: (847)679-5500   Fax: (847)679-2494
Fr: 800-323-4900

Rebecca Burnett. 1993. $14.95; $9.95 (paper). Provides information to math-oriented job hunters on how to become statisticians, field researchers, computer programmers, stock analysts, investment managers, bankers, engineers, accountants, underwriters, economists, market analysts, mathematicians, systems analysts, and more.

★1689★ *Careers in Science*

VGM Career Horizons
4255 W. Touhy Ave.
Lincolnwood, IL 60646-1975
Ph: (847)679-5500   Fax: (847)679-2494
Fr: 800-323-4900

Thomas Easton. Third edition, 1996. 192 pages. $17.95; $13.95 (paper). Discusses careers in life science, earth science, physical and space science, social science, engineering, mathematics, and computer science. Offers job hunting advice.

★1690★ *Computer Jobs Worldwide: Support Staff Plus Electronics Plus Telecommunications*

Zinks International Career Guidance
PO Box 790
Richland, MI 49083
Ph: (313)584-7529

Richard M. Zink. 1995. $14.95 (paper).

★1691★ *Covin's Mid-West Computer Job Guide*

Vandamere Press
PO Box 5243
Arlington, VA 22205
Ph: (703)525-5488   Fax: (703)524-4105

Carol L. Covin. 1994. $13.95 (paper).

★1692★ *The Digital Frontier Job & Opportunity Finder*

Moon Lake Media
PO Box 251466
Los Angeles, CA 90025
Ph: (310)535-2453

Don B. Altman. 1995. $24.95 (paper).

★1693★ *Downsized but Not Out: How to Get Your Next Computer Job*

The McGraw-Hill Companies
1221 Avenue of the Americas
New York, NY 10020
Ph: (212)512-2000   Fr: 800-262-4729

Alan Simon. 1994. $30.00; $17.95 (paper).

★1694★ *The Encyclopedia of Career Choices for the 1990s: Guide to Entry-Level Jobs*

Perigree Books
The Berkley Publishing Group
PO Box 506
East Rutherford, NJ 07073
Ph: (201)933-9292   Fr: 800-223-0510

Career Associates Staff. 1992. $19.95. 862 pages. Describes 500 entry-level careers in a variety of industries. Presents qualifications required, working conditions, salary, internships, and professional associations.

★1695★ *Exploring Careers in the Computer Field*

Rosen Publishing Group, Inc.
29 E. 21st St.
New York, NY 10010
Ph: (212)777-3017   Fax: (212)777-0277
Fr: 800-237-9932

Joseph Weintraub. Revised edition, 1993. Discusses entry into the field, salaries, future trends, and offers job search advice. Surveys the newest growth areas in the computer industry including artificial intelligence, desktop publishing, and personal computers.

★1696★ *Exploring High-Tech Careers*

Rosen Publishing Group, Inc.
29 E. 21st St.
New York, NY 10010
Ph: (212)777-3017   Fax: (212)777-0277
Fr: 800-237-9932

Scott Southworth. Revised edition, 1993. $14.95; $9.95 (paper). 118 pages. Gives an orientation to the field of high technology and high-tech jobs. Describes educational preparation and job hunting. Includes a glossary and bibliography.

★1697★ *100 Best Careers for the Year 2000*

Prentice Hall General Reference
15 Columbus Cir.
New York, NY 10023
Ph: (212)373-8500   Fr: 800-223-2348

Shelly Field. 1992. $15.00 (paper). Covers 100 of the fastest growing jobs. The publication is divided into 11 general employment sections. Specific careers are covered within each section. Provides job description, responsibilities, employment opportunities, earnings, education and training, advancement opportunities, and experience and qualifications for each occupation.

★1698★ *Opportunities in Computer-Aided Design and Computer-Aided Manufacturing*

VGM Career Horizons
4255 W. Touhy Ave.
Lincolnwood, IL 60646-1975
Ph: (847)679-5500   Fax: (847)679-2494
Fr: 800-323-4900

Jan Bone. 1994. $14.95; $11.95 (paper). 160 pages. Defines cad (computer-aided design), cam (computer-aided manufacturing), and map (manufacturing automation protocol). Explains career opportunities in the cad/cam field, and education and training needed. Gives job-hunting tips.

★1699★ *Opportunities in Computer Science Careers*

VGM Career Horizons
4255 W. Touhy Ave.
Lincolnwood, IL 60646-1975
Ph: (847)679-5500   Fax: (847)679-2494
Fr: 800-323-4900

Julie Lepick Kling. 1995. $14.95; $11.95 (paper). Discusses how to enter the field and build a career. Illustrated.

★1700★ *Opportunities in Data Processing Careers*

VGM Career Horizons
4255 W. Touhy Ave.
Lincolnwood, IL 60646-1975
Ph: (847)679-5500   Fax: (847)679-2494
Fr: 800-323-4900

Norman Noerper. 1989. $14.95; $11.95 (paper). 160 pages. Extensive information on education, training, and job prospecting make this a useful guide to an important career field. Illustrated.

★1701★ *Opportunities in High Tech Careers*

VGM Career Horizons
4255 W. Touhy Ave.
Lincolnwood, IL 60646-1975
Ph: (847)679-5500   Fax: (847)679-2494
Fr: 800-323-4900

Gary D. Golter and Deborah Yanuck. 1995. $14.95; $11.95 (paper). 160 pages. Explores high technology careers. Describes job opportunities, how to make a career decision, how to prepare for high technology jobs, job hunting techniques, and future trends.

★1702★ Opportunities in Information Systems Careers

VGM Career Horizons
4255 W. Touhy Ave.
Lincolnwood, IL 60646-1975
Ph: (847)679-5500   Fax: (847)679-2494
Fr: 800-323-4900

Douglas B. Hoyt. 1991. $14.95; $11.95 (paper). Describes prospects in information specialties such as computer operations, programming, and documentation; telecommunications; records management; micrographics; and project planning and management. Offers advice about job hunting and advancement.

★1703★ Opportunities in Office Occupations

VGM Career Horizons
4255 W. Touhy Ave.
Lincolnwood, IL 60646-1975
Ph: (847)679-5500   Fax: (847)679-2494
Fr: 800-323-4900

Blanche Ettinger. 1995. $14.95; $11.95 (paper). Covers a variety of office positions and discusses trends for the next decade. Describes the job market, opportunities, job duties, educational preparation, the work environment, and earnings.

★1704★ The Programmer's Survival Guide: Career Strategies for Computer Professionals

Prentice Hall
113 Sylvan Ave.
Rte. 9W
Englewood Cliffs, NJ 07632
Ph: (201)592-2000   Fr: 800-922-0579

Janet Lehrman Ruhl. 1989. $16.95. 280 pages. Contains information on career planning, job hunting, and job changing. Gives advice on the software packages needed in corporate America, how to interview, and when to change jobs.

★1705★ Your Opportunities in Computers

Energeia Publishing, Inc.
PO Box 985
Salem, OR 97308
Ph: (503)362-1480   Fax: (503)362-2123

John Tribbett. 1994. $2.00 (paper).

★1706★ Your Resume: Key to a Better Job

Prentice Hall General Reference and Travel
15 Columbus Cir.
New York, NY 10023
Ph: (212)373-8500

Leonard Corwen. Fifth edition, 1993. $11.00. Provides guidelines for resume writing; explains what employers look for in a resume, including contents and style. Includes model resumes for high-demand careers such as computer programmers, health administrators, and high-tech professionals. Notes basic job-getting information and strategies.

EMPLOYMENT AGENCIES AND SEARCH FIRMS

★1707★ B and M Associates, Inc.

199 Cambridge Rd.
Woburn, MA 01801-4705
Ph: (617)938-9120

Employment agency.

★1708★ Beard Management, Inc.

245 Fifth Ave.
New York, NY 10016
Ph: (212)545-7777   Fax: (212)545-7796

Executive search firm.

★1709★ Cavan Systems Ltd.

10 Cuttermill Rd.
Great Neck, NY 11021
Ph: (516)487-7777   Fax: (516)487-7857

Executive search firm.

★1710★ Computer Engineering Consortium

7353 McWhorten Pl., Ste. 212
Annandale, VA 22003-5648
Ph: (703)658-0016

Employment agency.

★1711★ Computer Network Resources Inc.

7000 Central Pkwy. NE
Atlanta, GA 30328-4579
Ph: (404)391-9009

Employment agency.

★1712★ The Computer Resources Group, Inc.

275 Battery St., #800
San Francisco, CA 94111
Ph: (415)398-3535

Employment agency. Places staff on regular or contract basis.

★1713★ Data Systems Search Consultants

1756 Lacassie Ave.
Walnut Creek, CA 94596-4015
Ph: (510)256-0635

Employment agency. Executive search firm.

★1714★ The Datafinders Group, Inc.

25 Spring Valley Ave.
Maywood, NJ 07607
Ph: (201)845-7700   Fax: (201)845-7365

Executive search firm.

★1715★ DP Career Associates

6405 Metcalf, Ste. 425
Shawnee Mission, KS 66202
Ph: (913)236-8288

Employment agency.

★1716★ Electronic Systems Personnel

701 Fourth Ave. S., Ste. 1800
Minneapolis, MN 55415
Ph: (612)337-3000

Employment agency.

★1717★ Hayden and Associates, Inc.

7825 Washington Ave. S., Ste. 120
Minneapolis, MN 55439-2431
Ph: (612)941-6300   Fax: (612)941-9602

Employment agency. Executive search firm. Fills openings in a variety of fields.

★1718★ Huntington Personnel Consultants, Inc.

PO Box 1077
Huntington, NY 11743-0640
Ph: (516)549-8888   Fax: (516)549-3012

Employment agency.

★1719★ JR Professional Search

PO Box 18356
Tucson, AZ 85731
Ph: (520)721-1855   Fax: (520)721-1855

Employment agency.

★1720★ Linn-Truett, Inc.

7800 I.H. 10 W, Ste. 512
San Antonio, TX 78230
Ph: (210)340-3690   Fax: (210)340-2158

Employment agency.

★1721★ LOR Personnel Division

418 Wall St.
Princeton, NJ 08540
Ph: (609)921-6580

Employment agency. Executive search firm.

★1722★ Romac International, Inc.

120 Hyde Park Pl., Ste. 200
Tampa, FL 33606
Fr: 800-341-0263

Executive search firm. More than 30 locations throughout the U.S.

★1723★ Software Services Corp.

2850 S. Industrial Hwy, Ste. 300
Ann Arbor, MI 48104-6796
Ph: (313)971-2300

Employment agency.

★1724★ Source EDP

5580 LBJ Fwy., Ste. 300
Dallas, TX 75240
Ph: (214)385-3002

Executive search firm. Many affiliate offices located in most major cities in the U.S.

★1725★ Technical Talent Locators Ltd.

8850 Stanford Blvd., Ste. 3400
Columbia, MD 21045
Ph: (410)995-6051   Fax: (410)995-6281

Executive search firm.

★1726★ Techsearch Services, Inc.

6 Hachaliah Brown Dr.
Somers, NY 10589
Ph: (914)277-2727   Fax: (212)575-2618

Executive search firm.

★1727★ Tri-Serv Inc.

22 W. Padonia Rd., Ste. C53
Timonium, MD 21093
Ph: (301)561-1740

Employment agency.

★1728★ Version 2.0 Corp.

303 Congress St.
Boston, MA 02210
Ph: (617)439-0321

Executive search firm.

★1729★ Worlco Computer Resources, Inc.

901 Route 38
Cherry Hill, NJ 08002-2890
Ph: (609)665-4700   Fax: (609)665-8142

Employment agency. Second location in Philadelphia, PA.

OTHER SOURCES

★1730★ Association for Women in Computing (AWC)

41 Sutter St., Ste. 1006
San Francisco, CA 94104
Ph: (415)905-4663

Purpose: Individuals interested in promoting the education, professional development, and advancement of women in computing. E-Mail: awc@acm.org

★1731★ Black Data Processing Associates (BDPA)

1250 Connecticut Ave. NW, Ste. 700
Washington, DC 20036-2603
Ph: (202)775-4301   Fax: (202)775-1344
Fr: 800-727-BDPA

Members: Persons employed in the information processing industry, including electronic data processing, electronic word processing, and data communications; others interested in information processing. **Purpose:** Seeks to accumulate and share information processing knowledge and business expertise in order to increase the career and business potential of minorities in the information processing field. **Activities:** Conducts professional seminars, workshops, tutoring services, and community introductions to data processing. Makes annual donation to the United Negro College Fund.

★1732★ Career Encounters: Information Science and Technology

Cambridge Career Products
PO Box 2153
Dept. CC15
Charleston, WV 25328-2153
Ph: (304)744-9323   Fax: (304)744-9351
Fr: 800-468-4227

Video. $99.95. 25 minutes. Professionals shown in a variety of settings discuss different aspects of their careers.

★1733★ The Computer Industry Almanac

Computer Industry Almanac
225 Allen Way
Incline Village, NV 89451
Ph: (702)831-2288

Annual. $63.00. Also available on CD-ROM, $63.00. A compendium of information on the computer industry compiled from newsletters, reports, and magazines.

★1734★ Computer Salary Survey and Career Planning Guide

Source EDP
120 Broadway, Ste. 1010
New York, NY 10271
Ph: (212)557-8611

Annual. Describes career paths in the computer field and trends in the computer field. Lists job titles. Charts salaries by job titles, years of experience, and industry.

★1735★ Data Processing Management Association (DPMA)

505 Busse Hwy.
Park Ridge, IL 60068
Ph: (708)825-8124   Fax: (708)825-1693

Members: Managerial personnel, staff, educators, and individuals interested in the management of information resources. Founder of the Certificate in Data Processing examination program, now administered by an intersociety organization. **Purpose:** Maintains Legislative Communications Network. Professional education programs include EDP-oriented business and management principles self-study courses and a series of videotaped management development seminars. Sponsors student organizations around the country interested in data processing and encourages members to serve as counselors for the Scout computer merit badge. Conducts research projects, including a business information systems curriculum for two- and four-year colleges.

★1736★ Day in a Career: Computer Programmer

Cambridge Career Products
PO Box 2153
Dept. CC15
Charleston, WV 25328-2153
Ph: (304)744-9323   Fax: (304)744-9351
Fr: 800-468-4227

Video. $89.00. About 20 minutes. Profile of a day in the life includes candid interviews and work situations, along with information on educational requirements, credentials, job outlook, salaries, contacts, and other aspects of the job.

★1737★ Entrepreneurial Software Engineering: A Practical Guide to Developing and Marketing Computer Software

Ipser Publishing Co.
2616 Stadium Dr., Ste. 200
Fort Worth, TX 76109-1371
Ph: (817)927-2838   Fax: (817)927-0032

Edward A. Ipser, Jr. 1993. $24.95 (paper).

★1738★ InfoWorld

PO Box 1172
Skokie, IL 60076
Ph: (708)647-7925

Weekly. $130.00/year. Magazine subtitled: "The Voice of Personal Computing in the Enterprise."

★1739★ Institute for Certification of Computing Professionals (ICCP)

2200 E. Devon Ave., Ste. 247
Des Plaines, IL 60018
Ph: (708)299-4227   Fax: (708)299-4280

Purpose: Professional societies united to promote the development of computer examinations which are of high quality, directed toward information technology professionals, and designed to encourage competence and professionalism. Individuals passing the exams automatically become members of the Association of the Institute for Certification of Computer Professionals. **Activities:** Has developed code of ethics and good practice to which those taking the exams promise to adhere. Maintains speakers' bureau; compiles statistics.

★1740★ Resumes for High Tech Careers

VGM Career Horizons
4255 W. Touhy Ave.
Lincolnwood, IL 60646-1975
Ph: (847)679-5500   Fax: (847)679-2494
Fr: 800-323-4900

1992. $9.95. 160 pages. Demonstrates how to tailor a resume that catches a high tech employer's attention.

★1741★ Special Interest Group for Computers and the Physically Handicapped (SISCAPH)

Association for Computing Machinery
1515 Broadway, 17th Fl.
New York, NY 10036
Ph: (212)626-0613   Fax: (212)302-5826

Members: A special interest group of the Association of Computing Machinery. Physically disabled computer professionals; persons involved in the application of computers to aid the disabled; persons involved in the training or employment of physically disabled computer professionals; others interested in aiding the disabled. **Purpose:** To promote application of computer technology to aid the physically disabled; to educate the public about disabled computer professionals. **Activities:** Sponsors lectures and sessions at computer conferences on hiring and training disabled computer professionals. Compiles statistics.

Computer Service Technicians

SOURCES OF HELP-WANTED ADS

★1742★ Computerworld

500 Old Connecticut Path
Framingham, MA 01701-9208
Ph: (508)872-0080   Fax: (508)879-7784
Fr: 800-669-1002

Weekly. $48.00/year; $6.00/issue. Newspaper for information systems management professionals.

★1743★ DEC Professional

Cardinal Business Media, Inc.
1300 Virginia Dr., Ste.400
Fort Washington, PA 19034
Ph: (215)643-8064   Fax: (215)643-3901

Monthly. Magazine covering Digital Equipment Corporation's computers and related products.

★1744★ Machine Design

Peter Li
1100 Superior Ave.
Cleveland, OH 44114
Ph: (216)696-7000   Fax: (216)696-7670

$100.00/year. Magazine on design engineering function.

PLACEMENT AND JOB REFERRAL SERVICES

★1745★ Electronics Technicians Association, International (ETA-I)

602 N. Jackson
Greencastle, IN 46135
Ph: (317)653-8262   Fax: (317)653-8262

Members: Skilled electronics technicians. **Activities:** Provides placement service; offers certification examinations for electronics technicians and satellite installers. Compiles wage and manpower statistics. Administers FCC Commercial License examinations.

★1746★ North American Computer Service Association (NACSA)

10221 Chesham Dr.
Orlando, FL 32817
Ph: (407)447-1500

Members: Computer service and repair companies; suppliers to the industry; computer repair schools; professional consultants. **Purpose:** Promotes orderly growth for the computer service industry and assists members with tasks such as contract negotiation, training, legislative liaising, and parts and supplies purchasing. **Activities:** Maintains placement service.

EMPLOYER DIRECTORIES AND NETWORKING LISTS

★1747★ Computer Directory

Computer Directories, Inc.
13205 Cypress N. Houston Rd.
Cypress, TX 77429-3606
Ph: (713)955-9791   Fax: (713)955-9793
Fr: 800-234-4353

Annual, fall. Covers Approximately 130,000 computer installations; 19 separate volumes for Alaska/Hawaii, Connecticut/New Jersey, Dallas/Ft. Worth, Eastern Seaboard, Far Midwest, Houston, Illinois, Midatlantic, Midcentral, Mideast, Minnesota/Wisconsin, North Central, New England, New York Metro, Northwest, Ohio, Pennsylvania/West Virginia, Southeast, and Southwest Texas. Entries include: Company name, address, phone, fax, name and title of contact, hardware used, software application, operating system, programming language, computer graphics, networking system. Arrangement: Geographical. Indexes: Alphabetical, industry, hardware.

★1748★ Directory of Top Computer Executives

Applied Computer Research, Inc.
11242 N. 19th Ave.
Phoenix, AZ 85029
Ph: (602)995-5929   Fax: (602)995-0905
Fr: 800-234-2227

Semiannual, May and November. Covers in three volumes, over 41,000 U.S. and 6,900 Canadian executives with major data processing or communications responsibilities in over 14,100 U.S. sites and 3,400 Canadian sites companies with gross annual sales of over $50 million and/or EDP (Electronic Data Processing) budgets over $250,000. Entries include: Company name, address, phone, subsidiary and/or division names, major systems installed, names and titles of top EDP executives. Arrangement: Geographical within separate eastern, western, and Canadian volumes. Indexes: Industry; alphabetical by company name.

★1749★ How and Where to Get the Best Computer Jobs

Information Resource Group
50495 Corporate Dr., Ste. 112
Shelby Township, MI 48315
Ph: (810)254-8500   Fax: (810)254-8500

Annual. $69.95. per directory. Publication includes: Listing of the top dataprocessing employers in United States and Canada. Information divided among 67 editions, according to state/province. Principal content of publication is hiring/interview tips, salary surveys. Entries include: Company name, address, phone, name and title of contact. Arrangement: Geographical.

★1750★ Who's Who Electronics Buyers' Guide

Harris Publishing Co.
2057-2 Aurora Rd.
Twinsburg, OH 44087
Ph: (216)425-9000   Fax: (216)425-4328
Fr: 800-888-5900

Annual, February. $65.00, per volume. Covers Approximately 15,000 manufacturers and nearly 8,300 distributors of electronics products in five regional volumes (Northeastern, Southeastern, Midwestern, Southwestern, and Western). Entries include: For manufacturers: name, address, phone, fax, key contact names, information on facilities or plants, products manufactured or handled, year established, estimated annual sales, local sources. For distributors: company name, address, phone, fax, product lines carried. Arrangement: Alphabetical. Indexes: Product/service (with manufacturer and distributor location, and phone); manufacturer name (with distributor); manufacturer name (with local sources); distributor name (with lines carried).

HANDBOOKS AND MANUALS

★1751★ ACE the Technical Interview: How to Get Your Next Job in the Computer Industry

The McGraw-Hill Companies
1221 Avenue of the Americas
New York, NY 10020
Ph: (212)512-2000   Fr: 800-262-4729

Michael Rothstein. 1994. $19.95 (paper).

★1752★ America's 50 Fastest Growing Jobs

JIST Works, Inc.
720 N. Park Ave.
Indianapolis, IN 46202
Ph: (317)264-3720   Fr: 800-648-5478

Third edition, 1995. $14.95. 288 pages. Each job profile explains the nature of the work, skills and abilities required, employment outlook, average earnings, related occupations, education and training requirements, and employment opportunities. Also contains career planning information and job search tips.

★1753★ Careers for Computer Buffs and Other Technological Types

NTC Publishing Group
4255 W. Touhy Ave.
Lincolnwood, IL 60646-1975
Ph: (708)679-5500   Fax: (708)679-6375
Fr: 800-323-4900

Marjorie Eberts. 1994. $12.95; $9.95 (paper).

★1754★ Careers in Computer Fields

Rosen Publishing Group, Inc.
29 E 21st St.
New York, NY 10010
Ph: (212)777-3017   Fax: (212)777-0277
Fr: 800-237-9932

Joseph Weintraub. 1993. $14.95; $9.95 (paper).

★1755★ Careers in Computers

VGM Career Horizons
4255 W. Touhy Ave.
Lincolnwood, IL 60646-1975
Ph: (847)679-5500   Fax: (847)679-2494
Fr: 800-323-4900

Lila B. Stair. Second edition, 1995. $17.95; $13.95 (paper). Describes trends affecting computer careers and explores a wide range of job opportunities from programming to consulting. Provides job qualifications, salary data, job market information, personal and educational requirements, career paths, and the place of the job in the organizational structure. Offers advice on education, certification, and job search.

★1756★ Computer Jobs Worldwide: Support Staff Plus Electronics Plus Telecommunications

Zinks International Career Guidance
PO Box 790
Richland, MI 49083
Ph: (313)584-7529

Richard M. Zink. 1995. $14.95 (paper).

★1757★ Covin's Mid-West Computer Job Guide

Vandamere Press
PO Box 5243
Arlington, VA 22205
Ph: (703)525-5488   Fax: (703)524-4105

Carol L. Covin. 1994. $13.95 (paper).

★1758★ The Digital Frontier Job & Opportunity Finder

Moon Lake Media
PO Box 251466
Los Angeles, CA 90025
Ph: (310)535-2453

Don B. Altman. 1995. $24.95 (paper).

★1759★ Downsized but Not Out: How to Get Your Next Computer Job

The McGraw-Hill Companies
1221 Avenue of the Americas
New York, NY 10020
Ph: (212)512-2000   Fr: 800-262-4729

Alan Simon. 1994. $30.00; $17.95 (paper).

★1760★ Exploring Careers as a Computer Technician

Rosen Publishing Group, Inc.
29 E. 21st St.
New York, NY 10010
Ph: (212)777-3017   Fax: (212)777-0277
Fr: 800-237-9932

Jean W. Spencer. 1989. $14.95. Covers job prospects and duties, educational preparation, equipment, tools, work environment, advancement possibilities, job satisfaction, and salaries. Lists schools, journals, and professional associations.

★1761★ 100 Best Careers for the Year 2000

Prentice Hall General Reference
15 Columbus Cir.
New York, NY 10023
Ph: (212)373-8500   Fr: 800-223-2348

Shelly Field. 1992. $15.00 (paper). Covers 100 of the fastest growing jobs. The publication is divided into 11 general employment sections. Specific careers are covered within each section. Provides job description, responsibilities, employment opportunities, earnings, education and training, advancement opportunities, and experience and qualifications for each occupation.

★1762★ Opportunities in Computer Maintenance Careers

VGM Career Horizons
4255 W. Touhy Ave.
Lincolnwood, IL 60646-1975
Ph: (847)679-5500   Fax: (847)679-2494
Fr: 800-323-4900

Elliott Kanter. 1995. $14.95; $11.95 (paper).

160 pages. Offers advice on job hunting and where the jobs are. Illustrated.

★1763★ Opportunities in Computer Science Careers

VGM Career Horizons
4255 W. Touhy Ave.
Lincolnwood, IL 60646-1975
Ph: (847)679-5500   Fax: (847)679-2494
Fr: 800-323-4900

Julie Lepick Kling. 1995. $14.95; $11.95 (paper). Discusses how to enter the field and build a career. Illustrated.

★1764★ Opportunities in Data Processing Careers

VGM Career Horizons
4255 W. Touhy Ave.
Lincolnwood, IL 60646-1975
Ph: (847)679-5500   Fax: (847)679-2494
Fr: 800-323-4900

Norman Noerper. 1989. $14.95; $11.95 (paper). 160 pages. Extensive information on education, training, and job prospecting make this a useful guide to an important career field. Illustrated.

★1765★ Opportunities in High Tech Careers

VGM Career Horizons
4255 W. Touhy Ave.
Lincolnwood, IL 60646-1975
Ph: (847)679-5500   Fax: (847)679-2494
Fr: 800-323-4900

Gary D. Golter and Deborah Yanuck. 1995. $14.95; $11.95 (paper). 160 pages. Explores high technology careers. Describes job opportunities, how to make a career decision, how to prepare for high technology jobs, job hunting techniques, and future trends.

★1766★ Opportunities in Vocational and Technical Careers

VGM Career Horizons
4255 W. Touhy Ave.
Lincolnwood, IL 60646-1975
Ph: (847)679-5500   Fax: (847)679-2494
Fr: 800-323-4900

Adrian A. Paradis. 1992. $14.95; $11.95 (paper). 160 pages. Provides information on a variety of opportunities and advice on breaking into the field.

★1767★ The Professional Electronics Technician

International Electronics Technicians Association
602 N. Jackson St.
Greencastle, IN 46135
Ph: (317)653-8262

Pamphlet. $1.00. Describes job duties, training, skills and aptitudes, salaries, employment outlook, and certification.

★1768★ Where the Jobs Are: The Hottest Careers for the '90s

The Career Press, Inc.
3 Tice Rd.
PO Box 687
Franklin Lakes, NJ 07417
Ph: (201)848-0310   Fax: (201)848-1727
Fr: 800-237-3371

Joyce Hadley. Second edition, 1995. $9.99.

300 pages. Describes careers in fifteen general fields, from accounting to travel and hospitality.

★1769★ Your Opportunities in Computers

Energeia Publishing, Inc.
PO Box 985
Salem, OR 97308
Ph: (503)362-1480   Fax: (503)362-2123

John Tribbett. 1994. $2.00 (paper).

EMPLOYMENT AGENCIES AND SEARCH FIRMS

★1770★ Computer Network Resources Inc.

7000 Central Pkwy. NE
Atlanta, GA 30328-4579
Ph: (404)391-9009

Employment agency.

★1771★ Data Careers Personnel Services, Inc.

3320 4th Ave.
San Diego, CA 92103
Ph: (619)291-9994

Employment agency. Places staff on a regular or temporary basis.

★1772★ DP Career Associates

6405 Metcalf, Ste. 425
Shawnee Mission, KS 66202
Ph: (913)236-8288

Employment agency.

★1773★ Electronic Systems Personnel

701 Fourth Ave. S., Ste. 1800
Minneapolis, MN 55415
Ph: (612)337-3000

Employment agency.

★1774★ Hayden and Associates, Inc.

7825 Washington Ave. S., Ste. 120
Minneapolis, MN 55439-2431
Ph: (612)941-6300   Fax: (612)941-9602

Employment agency. Executive search firm. Fills openings in a variety of fields.

★1775★ Linn-Truett, Inc.

7800 I.H. 10 W, Ste. 512
San Antonio, TX 78230
Ph: (210)340-3690   Fax: (210)340-2158

Employment agency.

★1776★ LOR Personnel Division

418 Wall St.
Princeton, NJ 08540
Ph: (609)921-6580

Employment agency. Executive search firm.

★1777★ The Murphy Group

1211 W. 22nd St., Ste. 221
Oak Brook, IL 60521-2115
Ph: (708)574-2840

Employment agency. Places personnel in a variety of positions.

OTHER SOURCES

★1778★ The Computer Industry Almanac

Computer Industry Almanac
225 Allen Way
Incline Village, NV 89451
Ph: (702)831-2288

Annual. $63.00. Also available on CD-ROM, $63.00. A compendium of information on the computer industry compiled from newsletters, reports, and magazines.

★1779★ Computer Repair Service Business Guide

Entrepreneur, Inc.
2392 Morse Ave.
PO Box 19787
Irvine, CA 92713-9787
Fax: (714)851-9088   Fr: 800-421-2300

$79.50 (includes business guide and software). Provides step-by-step instructions on how to start a computer repair service. Topics covered include market potential, profits and costs, equipment, location, advertising and promotion, employees, and customers.

★1780★ Data Processing Management Association (DPMA)

505 Busse Hwy.
Park Ridge, IL 60068
Ph: (708)825-8124   Fax: (708)825-1693

Members: Managerial personnel, staff, educators, and individuals interested in the management of information resources. Founder of the Certificate in Data Processing examination program, now administered by an intersociety organization. **Purpose:** Maintains Legislative Communications Network. Professional education programs include EDP-oriented business and management principles self-study courses and a series of videotaped management development seminars. Sponsors student organizations around the country interested in data processing and encourages members to serve as counselors for the Scout computer merit badge. Conducts research projects, including a business information systems curriculum for two- and four-year colleges.

★1781★ International Society of Certified Electronics Technicians (ISCET)

2708 W. Berry, Ste. 3
Fort Worth, TX 76109
Ph: (817)921-9101   Fax: (817)921-3741

Members: Technicians in 37 countries who have been certified by the society. **Purpose:** Seeks to provide a fraternal bond among certified electronics technicians, raise their

public image, and improve the effectiveness of industry education programs for technicians. Offers training programs in new electronics information. **Activities:** Maintains library of service literature for consumer electronic equipment, including manuals and schematics for out-of-date equipment. Offers all FCC licenses. Sponsors testing program for certification of electronics technicians in the fields of audio, communications, computer, consumer, industrial, medical electronics, radar, radio-television, and video.

★1782★ National Association of Retail Dealers of America (NARDA)

10 E. 22nd St.
Lombard, IL 60148
Ph: (708)953-8950   Fax: (708)953-8957

Members: Retailers of appliances, home electronics, computers, furniture, and audio components; associate members include manufacturers, utilities, distributors of appliances and consumer electronics, and financial institutions. **Purpose:** Works to create more profitable dealerships. **Activities:** Services include management consulting, sales training, advertising workshops, computer service bureau, School of Service Management, Institute of Management, surveys, credit union, bank card program, and management training.

★1783★ National Electronics Service Dealers Association (NESDA)

2708 W. Berry St., Ste. 3
Fort Worth, TX 76109
Ph: (817)921-9061   Fax: (817)921-3741
Fr: 800-797-9197

Members: Local and state electronic service associations and companies representing 4200 individuals. **Purpose:** Provides educational assistance in electronic training to public schools; supplies technical service information on business management training to electronic service dealers. **Activities:** Offers certification, apprenticeship, and training programs through International Society of Certified Electronics Technicians. Compiles statistics on electronics service business; conducts technical service and business management seminars.

★1784★ Special Interest Group for Computers and the Physically Handicapped (SISCAPH)

Association for Computing Machinery
1515 Broadway, 17th Fl.
New York, NY 10036
Ph: (212)626-0613   Fax: (212)302-5826

Members: A special interest group of the Association of Computing Machinery. Physically disabled computer professionals; persons involved in the application of computers to aid the disabled; persons involved in the training or employment of physically disabled computer professionals; others interested in aiding the disabled. **Purpose:** To promote application of computer technology to aid the physically disabled; to educate the public about disabled computer professionals. **Activities:** Sponsors lectures and sessions at computer conferences on hiring and training disabled computer professionals. Compiles statistics.

Computer Systems Analysts

SOURCES OF HELP-WANTED ADS

★1785★ ACM Computing Surveys
Association for Computing Machinery
1515 Broadway, 17th Fl.
New York, NY 10036-9998
Ph: (212)869-7440   Fax: (212)869-0481

Quarterly. $17.00/year for individuals; $105.00/year for nonmembers;Journal presenting surveys and tutorials in computer science.

★1786★ BYTE
McGraw-Hill, Inc.
1 Phoenix Mill Ln.
Peterborough, NH 03458
Ph: (603)924-9281   Fax: (603)924-2550
Fr: 800-232-2983

Monthly. Magazine covering microcomputing for major brands of hardware and software. Includes reviews, features, and technology news for experienced and knowledgeable purchasers and users of microcomputers.

★1787★ Captsule Job Listings
Publications and Communications, Inc.
12416 Hymeadow Dr.
Austin, TX 78750
Ph: (512)250-9023   Fax: (512)331-3900
Fr: 800-678-9724

Online database. Lists current job openings in the contract (temporary) technical services industry. Includes the Action Hot List, which provides information on job seekers. Includes employment opportunities in technical/professional engineering, computing, and design/drafting. Entries generally contain company name, address, and job opening.

★1788★ Communications of the ACM
Association for Computing Machinery
1515 Broadway 17th fl.
New York, NY 10036
Ph: (212)869-7440   Fax: (212)869-0481

Monthly. $32.00/year for individuals; $124.00/year for nonmembers. Computing news magazine.

★1789★ Communications Week
CMP Publications
PO Box 1094
Skokie, IL 60076
Ph: (708)647-6834

Weekly. $143.00/year. Magazine subtitled: "The Newspaper for Enterprise Networking."

★1790★ Computer
IEEE Computer Society
1730 Massachusetts Ave. NW
Washington, DC 20036
Ph: (202)371-0101

Monthly. Covers major trends in computer science and engineering.

★1791★ Computerworld
500 Old Connecticut Path
Framingham, MA 01701-9208
Ph: (508)872-0080   Fax: (508)879-7784
Fr: 800-669-1002

Weekly. $48.00/year; $6.00/issue. Newspaper for information systems management professionals.

★1792★ Data Based Advisor
Data Based Solutions, Inc.
4010 Morena Blvd., Ste. 200
San Diego, CA 92117
Ph: (619)483-6400   Fax: (619)483-9851

Monthly. $35.00/year for individuals. Magazine covering microcomputer database management system topics; offering software reviews and programming tips and techniques.

★1793★ Database Programming and Design
Miller Freeman, Inc.
600 Harrison St.
San Francisco, CA 94107
Ph: (415)905-2200

Monthly. Computer magazine.

★1794★ Datamation
Cahners Publishing Co.
275 Washington St.
Newton, MA 02158-1630
Ph: (617)964-3030   Fax: (617)558-4470

Semimonthly. Magazine on computers and information processing.

★1795★ DBMS
Miller Freeman Publishing, Inc.
501 Galveston Dr.
Redwood City, CA 94063
Ph: (415)366-3600

Monthly. $24.00/year; $2.95/issue. Magazine for developers and users of client-server database applications.

★1796★ DEC Professional
Cardinal Business Media, Inc.
1300 Virginia Dr., Ste.400
Fort Washington, PA 19034
Ph: (215)643-8064   Fax: (215)643-3901

Monthly. Magazine covering Digital Equipment Corporation's computers and related products.

★1797★ Digital News and Review
Cahners Publishing Co.
275 Washington St.
Newton, MA 02158-1630
Ph: (617)964-3030   Fax: (617)558-4470

Semimonthly. Free to qualified subscribers.

★1798★ Enterprise Systems Journal
Cardinal Business Media, Inc.
12225 Greenville Ave., Ste. 700
Dallas, TX 75243
Ph: (214)669-9000   Fax: (214)669-9909

Monthly. Journal providing authoritative, in-depth information for all IS professionals in IBM host-based enterprises.

★1799★ Government Computer News
Conners Publishing
245 W. 17th St.
New York, NY 10011
Ph: (212)463-6835   Fax: (212)463-6836

Biweekly. $74.95/year for individuals; $8.00 for single issue. Newspaper for government technical and management executives responsible for managing and buying information technology products and services. Covers computer/communications news, trends, applications, and products impacting government operations.

★1800★ IEEE Software

IEEE Computer Society
10662 Los Vaqueros Cir.
PO Box 3014
Los Alamitos, CA 90720-3014
Ph: (714)821-8380   Fax: (714)821-4010
Fr: 800-272-6657

Bimonthly. $25.00/year for individuals. Magazine covering the computer software industry.

★1801★ InformationWEEK

CMP Publications, Inc.
600 Community Dr.
Manhasset, NY 11030
Ph: (516)562-5000   Fax: (516)562-5055

Weekly. Magazine focusing on data and information processing news and strategies.

★1802★ MIDRANGE Systems

Professional Press, Inc.
101 Witmer Rd.
Horsham, PA 19044
Ph: (215)957-1500   Fax: (215)957-4230

Biweekly.

★1803★ Network World

161 Worcester Rd.
Framingham, MA 01701-9172
Ph: (508)875-6400

Weekly (Mon.). $95.00/year for individuals. The newsweekly of enterprise network computing.

★1804★ 3X/400 Systems Management

Adams/Hunter Publishing Co.
25 Northwest Pt. Blvd., Ste. 800
Elk Grove Village, IL 60007
Ph: (708)427-9512   Fax: (708)427-2079

Monthly. $42.00/year for individuals. Management-oriented magazine for DP/MIS managers with an IBM AS/400, System/36 or RS 16000 on site.

★1805★ UNIX Review

Miller Freeman Publications, Inc.
600 Harrison St.
San Francisco, CA 94107
Ph: (415)905-2200

Monthly. Magazine for professional users of UNIX and UNIX-like systems.

PLACEMENT AND JOB REFERRAL SERVICES

★1806★ American Indian Science and Engineering Society (AISES)

1630 30th St., Ste. 301
Boulder, CO 80301
Ph: (303)492-8658   Fax: (303)492-3400

Members: American Indian and non-Indian students and professionals in science, technology, and engineering fields; corporations representing energy, mining, aerospace, electronic, and computer fields. **Purpose:** Seeks to motivate and encourage students to pursue undergraduate and graduate studies in science, engineering, and technology. **Activities:** Sponsors science fairs in grade schools, teacher training workshops, summer math/science sessions for 8th-12th graders, professional chapters, and student chapters in colleges. Offers scholarships. Adult members serve as role models, advisers, and mentors for students. Operates placement service. **E-Mail:** aise sha@spot.colorado.edu

★1807★ Association of Computer Professionals (ACP)

9 Forest Dr.
Plainview, NY 11803
Ph: (516)938-8223   Fax: (516)938-3073

Members: Authors, consultants, programmers, publishers, and teachers in the computer field who provide products or services to users or to other professionals. **Purpose:** Purpose is to advance the art and science of computer professionals through educational means. Encourages education and instruction of the public regarding what the association views as the beneficial use of computers and computer technology. **Activities:** Provides members with information on accounting, business management, creative marketing techniques, law, microcomputer advances, tax matters, technical developments, and special earning opportunities. Addresses issues of software protection, contract law, tax benefits, potential tax problems, and financial subjects such as sources of capital for new ventures and expanding businesses.

EMPLOYER DIRECTORIES AND NETWORKING LISTS

★1808★ Computer Directory

Computer Directories, Inc.
13205 Cypress N. Houston Rd.
Cypress, TX 77429-3606
Ph: (713)955-9791   Fax: (713)955-9793
Fr: 800-234-4353

Annual, fall. Covers Approximately 130,000 computer installations; 19 separate volumes for Alaska/Hawaii, Connecticut/New Jersey, Dallas/Ft. Worth, Eastern Seaboard, Far Midwest, Houston, Illinois, Midatlantic, Midcentral, Mideast, Minnesota/Wisconsin, North Central, New England, New York Metro, Northwest, Ohio, Pennsylvania/West Virginia, Southeast, and Southwest Texas. Entries include: Company name, address, phone, fax, name and title of contact, hardware used, software application, operating system, programming language, computer graphics, networking system. Arrangement: Geographical. Indexes: Alphabetical, industry, hardware.

★1809★ Directory of Top Computer Executives

Applied Computer Research, Inc.
11242 N. 19th Ave.
Phoenix, AZ 85029
Ph: (602)995-5929   Fax: (602)995-0905
Fr: 800-234-2227

Semiannual, May and November. Covers in three volumes, over 41,000 U.S. and 6,900 Canadian executives with major data processing or communications responsibilities in over 14,100 U.S. sites and 3,400 Canadian sites companies with gross annual sales of over $50 million and/or EDP (Electronic Data Processing) budgets over $250,000. Entries include: Company name, address, phone, subsidiary and/or division names, major systems installed, names and titles of top EDP executives. Arrangement: Geographical within separate eastern, western, and Canadian volumes. Indexes: Industry; alphabetical by company name.

★1810★ Dun & Bradstreet Reference Book of Corporate Managements

Dun & Bradstreet Information Services
Dun & Bradstreet Corp.
3 Sylvan Way
Parsippany, NJ 07054-3896
Ph: (201)605-6000   Fax: (201)605-6911
Fr: 800-526-0651

Annual, April. $785.00, lease basis; $635.00, for public libraries, lease basis. Covers nearly 200,000 presidents, directors, vice presidents, officers, and managers in 12,000 companies of greatest economic, marketing, and investment interests; those firms whose revenues are the highest in the United States. Arrangement: Alphabetical by company name. Indexes: Personal name (with abbreviated title and company affiliation), geographical, SIC code, advanced education institution, military affiliation.

★1811★ The Hidden Job Market: A Job Seeker's Guide to America's 2,000 Little-Known, Fastest-Growing High-Tech Companies

Peterson's Guides, Inc.
202 Carnegie Center
PO Box 2123
Princeton, NJ 08543-2123
Ph: (609)243-9111   Fax: (609)243-9150
Fr: 800-338-3282

Annual, October. $16.95. Covers Approximately 2,000 technology firms with under 1,000 employees, which have added the most employees in the survey year. Entries include: Company name, address, phone, fax, name and title of contact, number of employees, year founded, number of employees added in last year, percentage of growth, line of business. Arrangement: Geographical by state, then by area code. Indexes: Alphabetical by industry.

★1812★ How and Where to Get the Best Computer Jobs

Information Resource Group
50495 Corporate Dr., Ste. 112
Shelby Township, MI 48315
Ph: (810)254-8500   Fax: (810)254-8500

Annual. $69.95. per directory. Publication includes: Listing of the top dataprocessing employers in United States and Canada. Information divided among 67 editions, according to state/province. Principal content of publication is hiring/interview tips, salary surveys. Entries include: Company name, address, phone, name and title of contact. Arrangement: Geographical.

★1813★ **Northwest High Tech: Fast Facts on the $7 Billion Computer Industry of Washington, Oregon, Idaho, British Columbia, and Alberta**

Resolution Business Press
11101 NE 8th St., Ste. 208
Bellevue, WA 98004
Ph: (206)455-4611   Fax: (206)455-9143

Annual. $34.95. Covers over 1,800 computer-related companies in Washington, Oregon, and Idaho, and British Columbia and Alberta, Canada. Entries include: Company; name, address, phone, fax; toll-free number; names and titles of key personnel; product/service, programming languages, financial data, names and titles of key personnel, number of employees, operating systems, expansion plans (including hiring and site expansion plans), company market information, Standard Industrial Classification (SIC) code. Arrangement: Geographical, industry sector. Indexes: Company name, SIC.

★1814★ **Peterson's Job Opportunities in Engineering and Technology 1996**

Peterson's
PO Box 2123
Princeton, NJ 08543-2123
Ph: (609)243-9111   Fax: (609)243-9150
Fr: 800-338-3282

Compiled by the Peterson's staff. Annual. $19.95 paperback. 432 pages. Profiles 2,000 high-tech companies looking primarily for technical personnel in such fields as biotechnology, telecommunications, software, computers and peripherals, defense, and aerospace. Contains job-search strategies and career options to help match education and expertise to the job market. Indexed geographically, by industry, and by hiring needs.

HANDBOOKS AND MANUALS

★1815★ **ACE the Technical Interview: How to Get Your Next Job in the Computer Industry**

The McGraw-Hill Companies
1221 Avenue of the Americas
New York, NY 10020
Ph: (212)512-2000   Fr: 800-262-4729

Michael Rothstein. 1994. $19.95 (paper).

★1816★ **ASIS Jobline**

American Society for Information Science
(ASIS)
8720 Georgia Ave., Ste. 501
Silver Spring, MD 20910
Ph: (301)495-0900

Monthly periodical provides job listings in information science.

★1817★ **Career Choices for the 90's for Students of Computer Science**

Walker and Company
435 Hudson St.
New York, NY 10014
Ph: (212)727-8300   Fax: (212)727-0984
Fr: 800-289-2553

Prepared by the Career Associates staff. 1990. $8.95. 166 pages. Discusses alternatives for students of computer science. Offers advice on how to break into the field and how to move up. Covers where and who the employers are, internship possibilities, and professional networking associations. Comprehensive guide to career and job search planning.

★1818★ **Career Choices for the 90's for Students of Mathematics**

Walker and Company
435 Hudson St.
New York, NY 10014
Ph: (212)727-8300   Fax: (212)727-0984
Fr: 800-289-2553

Prepared by the Career Associates staff. 1990. $8.95. 166 pages. Discusses alternatives for students of mathematics. Offers advice on how to break into the field and how to move up. Covers where and who the employers are, internship possibilities, and professional networking associations. Comprehensive guide to career and job search planning.

★1819★ **Career Information Center**

Macmillan Publishing Co.
200 Old Tappan Rd.
Old Tappan, NJ 07675
Ph: (609)461-6500   Fr: 800-223-2336

Visual Education Center Staff. Fifth edition, 1992. $229.00. This 13-volume set profiles over 600 occupations. Each occupational profile describes job duties, educational requirements, how to get the job, advancement possibilities, employment outlook, working conditions, earnings and benefits, and where to write for more information.

★1820★ **Careers for Computer Buffs and Other Technological Types**

NTC Publishing Group
4255 W. Touhy Ave.
Lincolnwood, IL 60646-1975
Ph: (708)679-5500   Fax: (708)679-6375
Fr: 800-323-4900

Marjorie Eberts. 1994. $12.95; $9.95 (paper).

★1821★ **Careers in Computer Fields**

Rosen Publishing Group, Inc.
29 E 21st St.
New York, NY 10010
Ph: (212)777-3017   Fax: (212)777-0277
Fr: 800-237-9932

Joseph Weintraub. 1993. $14.95; $9.95 (paper).

★1822★ **Careers in Computers**

VGM Career Horizons
4255 W. Touhy Ave.
Lincolnwood, IL 60646-1975
Ph: (847)679-5500   Fax: (847)679-2494
Fr: 800-323-4900

Lila B. Stair. Second edition, 1995. $17.95;

$13.95 (paper). Describes trends affecting computer careers and explores a wide range of job opportunities from programming to consulting. Provides job qualifications, salary data, job market information, personal and educational requirements, career paths, and the place of the job in the organizational structure. Offers advice on education, certification, and job search.

★1823★ **Careers in Information Science**

American Society for Information Science
(ASIS)
8720 Georgia Ave., Ste. 501
Silver Spring, MD 20910
Ph: (301)495-0900

Free brochure describes career opportunities in information science, communications, computer science, and research.

★1824★ **Careers for Number Crunchers and Other Quantitative Types**

VGM Career Horizons
4255 W. Touhy Ave.
Lincolnwood, IL 60646-1975
Ph: (847)679-5500   Fax: (847)679-2494
Fr: 800-323-4900

Rebecca Burnett. 1993. $14.95; $9.95 (paper). Provides information to math-oriented job hunters on how to become statisticians, field researchers, computer programmers, stock analysts, investment managers, bankers, engineers, accountants, underwriters, economists, market analysts, mathematicians, systems analysts, and more.

★1825★ **Computer Jobs Worldwide: Support Staff Plus Electronics Plus Telecommunications**

Zinks International Career Guidance
PO Box 790
Richland, MI 49083
Ph: (313)584-7529

Richard M. Zink. 1995. $14.95 (paper).

★1826★ **Covin's Mid-West Computer Job Guide**

Vandamere Press
PO Box 5243
Arlington, VA 22205
Ph: (703)525-5488   Fax: (703)524-4105

Carol L. Covin. 1994. $13.95 (paper).

★1827★ **The Digital Frontier Job & Opportunity Finder**

Moon Lake Media
PO Box 251466
Los Angeles, CA 90025
Ph: (310)535-2453

Don B. Altman. 1995. $24.95 (paper).

★1828★ **Downsized but Not Out: How to Get Your Next Computer Job**

The McGraw-Hill Companies
1221 Avenue of the Americas
New York, NY 10020
Ph: (212)512-2000   Fr: 800-262-4729

Alan Simon. 1994. $30.00; $17.95 (paper).

★1829★ The Encyclopedia of Career Choices for the 1990s: Guide to Entry-Level Jobs

Perigree Books
The Berkley Publishing Group
PO Box 506
East Rutherford, NJ 07073
Ph: (201)933-9292   Fr: 800-223-0510

Career Associates Staff. 1992. $19.95. 862 pages. Describes 500 entry-level careers in a variety of industries. Presents qualifications required, working conditions, salary, internships, and professional associations.

★1830★ Encyclopedia of Careers and Vocational Guidance

J. G. Ferguson Publishing Co.
200 W. Monroe, Ste. 250
Chicago, IL 60606
Ph: (312)580-5480

William E. Hopke. Ninth edition, 1993. $129.95; $199.95 (CD-ROM). Four-volume set that profiles 900 occupations and describes job trends in 71 industries. Includes career description, educational requirements, history of the job, methods of entry, advancement, employment outlook, earnings, conditions of work, social and psychological factors, and sources of further information. Contains career and employment information for this field.

★1831★ Exploring Careers in the Computer Field

Rosen Publishing Group, Inc.
29 E. 21st St.
New York, NY 10010
Ph: (212)777-3017   Fax: (212)777-0277
Fr: 800-237-9932

Joseph Weintraub. Revised edition, 1993. Discusses entry into the field, salaries, future trends, and offers job search advice. Surveys the newest growth areas in the computer industry including artificial intelligence, desktop publishing, and personal computers.

★1832★ Exploring High-Tech Careers

Rosen Publishing Group, Inc.
29 E. 21st St.
New York, NY 10010
Ph: (212)777-3017   Fax: (212)777-0277
Fr: 800-237-9932

Scott Southworth. Revised edition, 1993. $14.95; $9.95 (paper). 118 pages. Gives an orientation to the field of high technology and high-tech jobs. Describes educational preparation and job hunting. Includes a glossary and bibliography.

★1833★ 100 Best Careers for the Year 2000

Prentice Hall General Reference
15 Columbus Cir.
New York, NY 10023
Ph: (212)373-8500   Fr: 800-223-2348

Shelly Field. 1992. $15.00 (paper). Covers 100 of the fastest growing jobs. The publication is divided into 11 general employment sections. Specific careers are covered within each section. Provides job description, responsibilities, employment opportunities, earnings, education and training, advance-ment opportunities, and experience and qualifications for each occupation.

★1834★ Opportunities in Computer Science Careers

VGM Career Horizons
4255 W. Touhy Ave.
Lincolnwood, IL 60646-1975
Ph: (847)679-5500   Fax: (847)679-2494
Fr: 800-323-4900

Julie Lepick Kling. 1995. $14.95; $11.95 (paper). Discusses how to enter the field and build a career. Illustrated.

★1835★ Opportunities in Data Processing Careers

VGM Career Horizons
4255 W. Touhy Ave.
Lincolnwood, IL 60646-1975
Ph: (847)679-5500   Fax: (847)679-2494
Fr: 800-323-4900

Norman Noerper. 1989. $14.95; $11.95 (paper). 160 pages. Extensive information on education, training, and job prospecting make this a useful guide to an important career field. Illustrated.

★1836★ Opportunities in High Tech Careers

VGM Career Horizons
4255 W. Touhy Ave.
Lincolnwood, IL 60646-1975
Ph: (847)679-5500   Fax: (847)679-2494
Fr: 800-323-4900

Gary D. Golter and Deborah Yanuck. 1995. $14.95; $11.95 (paper). 160 pages. Explores high technology careers. Describes job opportunities, how to make a career decision, how to prepare for high technology jobs, job hunting techniques, and future trends.

★1837★ Opportunities in Information Systems Careers

VGM Career Horizons
4255 W. Touhy Ave.
Lincolnwood, IL 60646-1975
Ph: (847)679-5500   Fax: (847)679-2494
Fr: 800-323-4900

Douglas B. Hoyt. 1991. $14.95; $11.95 (paper). Describes prospects in information specialties such as computer operations, programming, and documentation; telecommunications; records management; micrographics; and project planning and management. Offers advice about job hunting and advancement.

★1838★ Opportunities in Office Occupations

VGM Career Horizons
4255 W. Touhy Ave.
Lincolnwood, IL 60646-1975
Ph: (847)679-5500   Fax: (847)679-2494
Fr: 800-323-4900

Blanche Ettinger. 1995. $14.95; $11.95 (paper). Covers a variety of office positions and discusses trends for the next decade. Describes the job market, opportunities, job duties, educational preparation, the work environment, and earnings.

★1839★ Where the Jobs Are: The Hottest Careers for the '90s

The Career Press, Inc.
3 Tice Rd.
PO Box 687
Franklin Lakes, NJ 07417
Ph: (201)848-0310   Fax: (201)848-1727
Fr: 800-237-3371

Joyce Hadley. Second edition, 1995. $9.99. 300 pages. Describes careers in fifteen general fields, from accounting to travel and hospitality.

★1840★ Your Opportunities in Computers

Energeia Publishing, Inc.
PO Box 985
Salem, OR 97308
Ph: (503)362-1480   Fax: (503)362-2123

John Tribbett. 1994. $2.00 (paper).

EMPLOYMENT AGENCIES AND SEARCH FIRMS

★1841★ B and M Associates, Inc.

199 Cambridge Rd.
Woburn, MA 01801-4705
Ph: (617)938-9120

Employment agency.

★1842★ Beard Management, Inc.

245 Fifth Ave.
New York, NY 10016
Ph: (212)545-7777   Fax: (212)545-7796

Executive search firm.

★1843★ Cavan Systems Ltd.

10 Cuttermill Rd.
Great Neck, NY 11021
Ph: (516)487-7777   Fax: (516)487-7857

Executive search firm.

★1844★ Computer Engineering Consortium

7353 McWhorten Pl., Ste. 212
Annandale, VA 22003-5648
Ph: (703)658-0016

Employment agency.

★1845★ Computer Network Resources Inc.

7000 Central Pkwy. NE
Atlanta, GA 30328-4579
Ph: (404)391-9009

Employment agency.

★1846★ The Computer Resources Group, Inc.

275 Battery St., #800
San Francisco, CA 94111
Ph: (415)398-3535

Employment agency. Places staff on regular or contract basis.

★1847★ Data Systems Search Consultants

1756 Lacassie Ave.
Walnut Creek, CA 94596-4015
Ph: (510)256-0635

Employment agency. Executive search firm.

★1848★ The Datafinders Group, Inc.

25 Spring Valley Ave.
Maywood, NJ 07607
Ph: (201)845-7700   Fax: (201)845-7365

Executive search firm.

★1849★ DP Career Associates

6405 Metcalf, Ste. 425
Shawnee Mission, KS 66202
Ph: (913)236-8288

Employment agency.

★1850★ Electronic Systems Personnel

701 Fourth Ave. S., Ste. 1800
Minneapolis, MN 55415
Ph: (612)337-3000

Employment agency.

★1851★ Hayden and Associates, Inc.

7825 Washington Ave. S., Ste. 120
Minneapolis, MN 55439-2431
Ph: (612)941-6300   Fax: (612)941-9602

Employment agency. Executive search firm.
Fills openings in a variety of fields.

★1852★ JR Professional Search

PO Box 18356
Tucson, AZ 85731
Ph: (520)721-1855   Fax: (520)721-1855

Employment agency.

★1853★ Linn-Truett, Inc.

7800 I.H. 10 W, Ste. 512
San Antonio, TX 78230
Ph: (210)340-3690   Fax: (210)340-2158

Employment agency.

★1854★ LOR Personnel Division

418 Wall St.
Princeton, NJ 08540
Ph: (609)921-6580

Employment agency. Executive search firm.

★1855★ Romac International, Inc.

120 Hyde Park Pl., Ste. 200
Tampa, FL 33606
Fr: 800-341-0263

Executive search firm. More than 30 locations throughout the U.S.

★1856★ Software Services Corp.

2850 S. Industrial Hwy., Ste. 300
Ann Arbor, MI 48104-6796
Ph: (313)971-2300

Employment agency.

★1857★ Source EDP

5580 LBJ Fwy., Ste. 300
Dallas, TX 75240
Ph: (214)385-3002

Executive search firm. Many affiliate offices located in most major cities in the U.S.

★1858★ Technical Talent Locators Ltd.

8850 Stanford Blvd., Ste. 3400
Columbia, MD 21045
Ph: (410)995-6051   Fax: (410)995-6281

Executive search firm.

★1859★ Techsearch Services, Inc.

6 Hachaliah Brown Dr.
Somers, NY 10589
Ph: (914)277-2727   Fax: (212)575-2618

Executive search firm.

★1860★ Tri-Serv Inc.

22 W. Padonia Rd., Ste. C53
Timonium, MD 21093
Ph: (301)561-1740

Employment agency.

★1861★ Version 2.0 Corp.

303 Congress St.
Boston, MA 02210
Ph: (617)439-0321

Executive search firm.

★1862★ Worlco Computer Resources, Inc.

901 Route 38
Cherry Hill, NJ 08002-2890
Ph: (609)665-4700   Fax: (609)665-8142

Employment agency. Second location in Philadelphia, PA.

OTHER SOURCES

★1863★ Association for Systems Management (ASM)

1433 W. Bagley Rd.
PO Box 38370
Cleveland, OH 44138-0370
Ph: (216)243-6900   Fax: (216)234-2930

Members: International professional organization of executives and specialists in management information systems serving business, commerce, education, government, and the military. **Purpose:** Expresses concern with communications, electronics, equipment, forms control, human relations, organization, procedure writing, and systems applications. **Activities:** Offers seminars, conferences, and courses in all phases of information systems and management.

★1864★ Association for Women in Computing (AWC)

41 Sutter St., Ste. 1006
San Francisco, CA 94104
Ph: (415)905-4663

Purpose: Individuals interested in promoting the education, professional development, and advancement of women in computing. **E-Mail:** awc@acm.org

★1865★ Black Data Processing Associates (BDPA)

1250 Connecticut Ave. NW, Ste. 700
Washington, DC 20036-2603
Ph: (202)775-4301   Fax: (202)775-1344
Fr: 800-727-BDPA

Members: Persons employed in the information processing industry, including electronic data processing, electronic word processing, and data communications; others interested in information processing. **Purpose:** Seeks to accumulate and share information processing knowledge and business expertise in order to increase the career and business potential of minorities in the information processing field. **Activities:** Conducts professional seminars, workshops, tutoring services, and community introductions to data processing. Makes annual donation to the United Negro College Fund.

★1866★ Career Encounters: Information Science and Technology

Cambridge Career Products
PO Box 2153
Dept. CC15
Charleston, WV 25328-2153
Ph: (304)744-9323   Fax: (304)744-9351
Fr: 800-468-4227

Video. $99.95. 25 minutes. Professionals shown in a variety of settings discuss different aspects of their careers.

★1867★ The Computer Industry Almanac

Computer Industry Almanac
225 Allen Way
Incline Village, NV 89451
Ph: (702)831-2288

Annual. $63.00. Also available on CD-ROM, $63.00. A compendium of information on the computer industry compiled from newsletters, reports, and magazines.

★1868★ Computer Salary Survey and Career Planning Guide

Source EDP
120 Broadway, Ste. 1010
New York, NY 10271
Ph: (212)557-8611

Annual. Describes career paths in the computer field and trends in the computer field. Lists job titles. Charts salaries by job titles, years of experience, and industry.

★1869★ Data Processing Management Association (DPMA)

505 Busse Hwy.
Park Ridge, IL 60068
Ph: (708)825-8124   Fax: (708)825-1693

Members: Managerial personnel, staff, educators, and individuals interested in the management of information resources. Founder of the Certificate in Data Processing examination program, now administered by an intersociety organization. **Purpose:** Maintains Legislative Communications Network. Professional education programs include EDP-oriented business and management principles self-study courses and a series of videotaped management development seminars. Sponsors student organizations around the country interested in data processing and encourages members to serve as counselors for the Scout computer merit badge. Conducts research projects, including a business information systems curriculum for two- and four-year colleges.

★1870★ *Day in a Career: Computer Analyst*

Cambridge Career Products
PO Box 2153
Dept. CC15
Charleston, WV 25328-2153
Ph: (304)744-9323   Fax: (304)744-9351
Fr: 800-468-4227

Video. 1994. $89.00. 15-22 minutes. Includes candid interviews and work situations, plus outlines of relevant career information.

★1871★ *InfoWorld*

PO Box 1172
Skokie, IL 60076
Ph: (708)647-7925

Weekly. $130.00/year. Magazine subtitled: "The Voice of Personal Computing in the Enterprise."

★1872★ Institute for Certification of Computing Professionals (ICCP)

2200 E. Devon Ave., Ste. 247
Des Plaines, IL 60018
Ph: (708)299-4227   Fax: (708)299-4280

Purpose: Professional societies united to promote the development of computer examinations which are of high quality, directed toward information technology professionals, and designed to encourage competence and professionalism. Individuals passing the exams automatically become members of the Association of the Institute for Certification of Computer Professionals. **Activities:** Has developed code of ethics and good practice to which those taking the exams promise to adhere. Maintains speakers' bureau; compiles statistics.

★1873★ *Resumes for High Tech Careers*

VGM Career Horizons
4255 W. Touhy Ave.
Lincolnwood, IL 60646-1975
Ph: (847)679-5500   Fax: (847)679-2494
Fr: 800-323-4900

1992. $9.95. 160 pages. Demonstrates how to tailor a resume that catches a high tech employer's attention.

★1874★ Special Interest Group for Computers and the Physically Handicapped (SISCAPH)

Association for Computing Machinery
1515 Broadway, 17th Fl.
New York, NY 10036
Ph: (212)626-0613   Fax: (212)302-5826

Members: A special interest group of the Association of Computing Machinery. Physically disabled computer professionals; persons involved in the application of computers to aid the disabled; persons involved in the training or employment of physically disabled computer professionals; others interested in aiding the disabled. **Purpose:** To promote application of computer technology to aid the physically disabled; to educate the public about disabled computer professionals. **Activities:** Sponsors lectures and sessions at computer conferences on hiring and training disabled computer professionals. Compiles statistics.

Construction and Building Inspectors

155

reference by governmental entities. **Activities:** Provides services for maintaining the codes up-to-date. Supplies information on quality and acceptability of building materials and systems and on new construction techniques and materials. Maintains services for all members in connection with codes and their administration; provides consulting, training and education, plan review, and other advisory services; conducts correspondence courses; prepares in-service training programs and assists local organizations in such activities. Maintains placement services.

★1890★ **National Association of Home Builders of the U.S. (NAHB)**

1201 15th St. NW
Washington, DC 20005
Ph: (202)822-0200   Fax: (202)822-0559

Members: Single and multifamily home builders, commercial builders, and others associated with the building industry. **Purpose:** Lobbies on behalf of the housing industry and conducts public affairs activities to increase public understanding of housing and the economy. Collects and disseminates data on current developments in home building and home builders' plans through its Economics Department and nationwide Metropolitan Housing Forecast. **Activities:** Maintains NAHB Research Center, which functions as the research arm of the home building industry. Sponsors seminars and workshops on construction, mortgage credit, labor relations, cost reduction, land use, remodeling, and business management. Compiles statistics; offers charitable program, spokesman training, and placement service; maintains speakers' bureau, and hall of fame.

★1891★ **Professional Women in Construction (PWC)**

342 Madison Ave., Rm. 451
New York, NY 10173
Ph: (212)687-0610   Fax: (212)490-1213

Members: Management-level women and men in construction and allied industries; owners, suppliers, architects, engineers, field personnel, office personnel, and bonding/surety personnel. **Purpose:** Provides a forum for exchange of ideas and promotion of political and legislative action, education, and job opportunities for women in construction and related fields; forms liaisons with other trade and professional groups; develops research programs. Strives to reform abuses and to assure justice and equity within the construction industry. Sponsors mini-workshops. **Activities:** Maintains Action Line which provides members with current information on pertinent legislation and on the association's activities and job referrals.

EMPLOYER DIRECTORIES AND NETWORKING LISTS

★1892★ *ABC Today—Associated Builders and Contractors Membership Directory Issue*

Associated Builders and Contractors
1300 N. 17th St.
Rosslyn, VA 22209
Ph: (703)812-2000   Fax: (703)812-8200

Annual, November. $150.00, plus $7.00 shipping. Publication includes: List of approximately 17,000 member construction contractors and suppliers. Entries include: Company name, address, phone, name of principal executive, code to volume of business, business specialty. Arrangement: Classified by chapter, then by work specialty.

★1893★ *American Society of Home Inspectors—Membership Directory*

American Society of Home Inspectors
85 W. Algonquin, Ste. 360
Arlington Heights, IL 60005
Ph: (708)290-1919   Fax: (708)290-1920
Fr: 800-743-2744

Annual. Available to members only. Covers Approximately 3,500 member professional home inspectors. Entries include: Name, address, phone, fax, date the inspector joined the American Society of Home Inspectors. Arrangement: Alphabetical; geographical by state.

★1894★ *Construction Employment Guide in the National and International Field*

World Trade Academy Press
50 E. 42nd St., Ste. 509
New York, NY 10017
Ph: (212)697-4999

$16.50. Covers More than 200 U.S. and international construction, engineering and design companies. Also covers U.S. government construction employment opportunities, job centers and employment agencies. Entries include: Company name, address, specialties.

★1895★ *Constructor—Directory of Membership and Services Issue*

AGC Information, Inc.
Associated General Contractors of
  America
1957 E St. NW
Washington, DC 20006
Ph: (202)393-2040   Fax: (202)347-4004

Annual, July. $135.00. Publication includes: List of more than 8,500 member firms and 9,000 national associate member firms engaged in building, highway, heavy, industrial, municipal utilities, and railroad construction, listing of state and local chapter officers. Arrangement: Geographical. Indexes: Company name.

★1896★ *ENR Directory of Design Firms*

McGraw-Hill, Inc.
1221 Ave. of the Americas
New York, NY 10020
Ph: (212)512-2534   Fax: (212)512-4178

Biennial, fall of even years; issue of *Engineering News Record*. $85.00. Covers 133 architects, architectural engineers, consultants, and other design firms; limited to advertisers. Mini-profiles on about 3,400 U.S. firms and 500 foreign firms or foreign offices of U.S. firms. Also includes lists of top 500 design firms in the United States, top 200 international design firms, top 50 United States design-construction firms, and top 50 international design-construction firms, based on total amount of billings. Entries include: For advertisers: company name, address, branch locations, subsidiaries, list of key personnel, territory served, capabilities. In ranked lists: company name, address, phone; international firms include telex. Arrangement: Alphabetical (profiles); geographical (mini-profiles).

★1897★ *ENR—Top 400 Construction Contractors Issue*

McGraw-Hill, Inc.
1221 Ave. of the Americas
New York, NY 10020
Ph: (212)512-4635   Fax: (212)512-2820

Annual, May issue of *Engineering News Record*. $10.00, Reprint, payment with order. Publication includes: List of 400 United States contractors receiving largest dollar volumes of contracts in preceding calendar year. Separate lists of 50 largest design/construct management firms; 50 largest program and construction managers; 25 building contractors; 25 heavy contractors. Entries include: Company name, headquarters location, total value of contracts received in preceding year, value of foreign contracts, countries in which operated, construction specialities. Arrangement: By total value of contracts received.

★1898★ *Inspection Bureaus Directory*

American Business Directories, Inc.
American Business Information, Inc.
5711 S. 86th Cir.
Omaha, NE 68127
Ph: (402)593-4600   Fax: (402)331-1505

Updated continuously; printed on request. Entries include: Name, address, phone, size of advertisement, name of owner or manager, number of employees, year first in Yellow Pages. Compiled from telephone company Yellow Pages, nationwide. Arrangement: Geographical.

★1899★ *Municipal/County Directory Library Edition*

Carroll Publishing
1058 Thomas Jefferson St. NW
Washington, DC 20007
Ph: (202)333-8620   Fax: (202)337-7020
Fr: 800-336-4240

Annual, July. $137.00, plus $8.00 shipping; payment must accompany order. Covers officials of 1,400 county governments (with populations over 25,000) and 2,000 municipalities (with populations over 1,000); includes elected, appointed, and career office holders. Entries include: Name, title, agency, address, phone. Arrangement: County officials are geographical, then by agency; municipal officials are by city. Indexes: personal name (with phone), agency.

★1900★ **Municipal Year Book**

Newman Books Ltd.
32 Vauxhall Bridge Rd.
London SW1V 2SS, England
Ph: 71 9736400   Fax: 71 2335057

Annual, December. $140.00, postpaid. Covers local and central government agencies and officials of the United Kingdom; municipal art galleries, associations, development organizations, fairs, libraries, museums, airports, and other local authorities. Entries include: Name of authority or governing agency, address, phone, fax, names of elected councillors, officers, names and titles of key personnel, contacts, population, and pay. Arrangement: Geographical. Indexes: Subject, place names.

HANDBOOKS AND MANUALS

★1901★ **Construction Job Directory-Worldwide**

Rector Press, Ltd.
130 Rattlesnake
Leverett, MA 01054-9726
Ph: (413)548-9708   Fax: (413)367-2853
Fr: 800-247-3473

1994. $125.00 (paper).

★1902★ **Encyclopedia of Careers and Vocational Guidance**

J. G. Ferguson Publishing Co.
200 W. Monroe, Ste. 250
Chicago, IL 60606
Ph: (312)580-5480

William E. Hopke. Ninth edition, 1993. $129.95; $199.95 (CD-ROM). Four-volume set that profiles 900 occupations and describes job trends in 71 industries. Includes career description, educational requirements, history of the job, methods of entry, advancement, employment outlook, earnings, conditions of work, social and psychological factors, and sources of further information. Contains career and employment information for this field.

★1903★ **Opportunities in Building Construction Trades**

VGM Career Horizons
4255 W. Touhy Ave.
Lincolnwood, IL 60646-1975
Ph: (847)679-5500   Fax: (847)679-2494
Fr: 800-323-4900

Michael Sumichrast. 1993. $14.95; $11.95 (paper). From custom builder to rehabber, the many kinds of companies that employ craftspeople and contractors are explored. Includes job descriptions, requirements, and salaries for dozens of specialties within the construction industry. Contains a complete list of Bureau of Apprenticeship and Training state and area offices. Illustrated.

★1904★ **Opportunities in State and Local Government Careers**

VGM Career Horizons
4255 W. Touhy Ave.
Lincolnwood, IL 60646-1975
Ph: (847)679-5500   Fax: (847)679-2494
Fr: 800-323-4900

Neale Baxter. 1993. $13.95; $10.95 (paper). 160 pages. Points out the incentives and drawbacks of a government career. Describes hiring procedures and provides tips on filling out applications, taking physical and aptitude tests, handling interviews, and finding jobs. Describes the jobs in which 75% of all state and local government workers are employed. For each occupation, covers the nature of the work and the training required.

EMPLOYMENT AGENCIES AND SEARCH FIRMS

★1905★ **B W and Associates, Inc.**

4415 W. Harrison St.
Hillside, IL 60162-1910
Ph: (708)449-5400

Employment agency.

★1906★ **Construction Personnel Service**

14697 E. Easter Ave., Ste. B
Englewood, CO 80112-4207
Ph: (303)766-0509

Employment agency. Provides temporary staffing services.

★1907★ **Real Estate Executive Search, Inc.**

PO Box 40
Santa Rosa, CA 95402-0040
Ph: (707)525-4591

Executive search firm.

★1908★ **Roper Personnel Services**

220 Executive Center Dr., Ste. 110
Columbia, SC 29210-8421
Ph: (803)798-8500

Employment agency. Fills openings on temporary or regular basis.

★1909★ **Specialized Search Associates**

15200 Carter Rd.
Delray Beach, FL 33446
Ph: (407)499-3711   Fax: (407)499-3770

Executive search firm.

OTHER SOURCES

★1910★ **American Society of Home Inspectors (ASHI)**

85 W. Algonquin Rd.
Arlington Heights, IL 60005
Ph: (708)290-1919   Fax: (708)290-1920

Purpose: Professional home inspectors whose goals are to: establish home inspector qualifications; set standards of practice for home inspections; adhere to a code of ethics; keep the concept of objective third party intact; inform members of the most advanced methods and techniques. **Activities:** Conducts seminars through regional chapters.

★1911★ **Associated General Contractors of America (AGC)**

1957 E St. NW
Washington, DC 20006
Ph: (202)393-2040   Fax: (202)347-4004

Members: General construction contractors; subcontractors; industry suppliers; service firms.**Purpose:** Provides market services through its divisions. Conducts special conferences and seminars designed specifically for construction firms. Compiles statistics on job accidents reported by member firms. Maintains 65 committees, including joint cooperative committees with other associations and liaison committees with federal agencies.

★1912★ **Construction Education Foundation (MSF)**

1300 N. 17th St.
Rosslyn, VA 22209
Ph: (703)812-2000   Fax: (703)812-8235

Purpose: Works to promote the merit shop for the benefit of the construction industry. (A merit shop is an open, nonunion shop that competes for business on the basis of price and quality rather than union status.) Conducts annual grants program to fund research and education projects aimed at improving the technology and environment of the construction industry and to promote the merit shop philosophy. Sponsors college programs and activities including: informational mailings to construction programs; financial aid for construction students; assistance to educators traveling to merit shop meetings; merit shop nights. Provides grants for publications and research studies to forecast trends in open shop construction, to compile information on the economic impact of wage laws, and to create an awareness of merit shop principles among students. Distributes study summaries, reports, and information about merit shop construction to public officials, contractors, educators, and students. Sponsors Wheels of Learning to provide apprenticeship and task training in 15 trade areas. Holds annual Job Fair for construction management, engineering, architecture, and building science students.

★1913★ **International Conference of Building Officials (ICBO)**

5360 Workman Mill Rd.
Whittier, CA 90601-2298
Ph: (310)699-0541   Fax: (310)692-3853
Fr: 800-336-1963

Members: Representatives of local, regional, and state governments. **Purpose:** Seeks to publish, maintain, and promote the Uniform Building Code and related documents; investigate and research principles underlying safety to life and property in the construction, use, and location of buildings and related structures; develop and promulgate uniformity in regulations pertaining to building construction; educate the building official; formulate guidelines for the administration of building inspection departments. **Activities:** Conducts training programs, courses, and certification programs for code enforcement inspectors. Maintains speakers' bureau.

★1914★ National Association of Women in Construction (NAWIC)
327 S. Adams St.
Fort Worth, TX 76104
Ph: (817)877-5551   Fax: (817)877-0324
Fr: 800-552-3506
Purpose: NAWIC is an international association of women employed in the construction industry which promotes that industry and

supports the advancement of women within it.

★1915★ Southern Building Code Congress, International (SBCCI)
900 Montclair Rd.
Birmingham, AL 35213
Ph: (205)591-1853   Fax: (205)592-7001
Members: Active members are state, county, municipal, or other government subdivisions; associate members are trade associations, architects, engineers, contractors, and related groups or persons. **Purpose:** Seeks

to develop, maintain, and promote the adoption of the Standard Building, Gas, Plumbing, Mechanical, Fire Prevention, and Housing Codes. Encourages uniformity in building regulations through the Standard Codes and their application and enforcement. **Activities:** Provides technical and educational services to members and others; participates in the development of nationally recognized consensus standards. Provides research on new materials and methods of construction; conducts seminars on code enforcement, inspection, and special topics.

Correction Officers and Parole Officers

SOURCES OF HELP-WANTED ADS

★1916★ ACJS Today

Academy of Criminal Justice Sciences
Northern Kentucky University
402 Nunn Hall
Highland Heights, KY 41099-5998
Ph: (606)572-5634   Fax: (606)572-6665
Fr: 800-757-ACJS

Four issues/year. Included in membership. Contains criminal justice information.

★1917★ American City and County

Communication Channels, Inc.
6255 Barfield Rd.
Atlanta, GA 30328
Ph: (404)955-9970   Fax: (404)256-3116

Monthly. $54.00/year for individuals. Municipal and county administration magazine.

★1918★ Law and Order

1000 Skokie Blvd.
Wilmette, IL 60091
Ph: (708)256-8555   Fax: (708)256-8574

Monthly. $20.00/year for individuals. Law enforcement trade magazine.

★1919★ The Municipality

League of Wisconsin Municipalities
122 W. Washington Ave., Ste. 301
Madison, WI 53703-2757
Ph: (608)267-2380   Fax: (608)267-0645

Monthly. Magazine for officials of Wisconsin's local municipal governments.

★1920★ National Employment Listing Service Bulletin

Criminal Justice Center
Sam Houston State University
Huntsville, TX 77341
Ph: (409)294-1692   Fax: (409)294-1653

Free. Covers job openings in police departments, sheriff's departments, courts, and other law enforcement and security agencies; correctional agencies; community agencies; and universities and schools offering educational programs in criminal justice and related disciplines. Entries include: Name of position, qualifications sought, salary, name and address of office for contact. Arrangement: Geographical within field.

★1921★ Western City

League of California Cities
1400 K St.
Sacramento, CA 95814
Ph: (916)444-5790   Fax: (916)658-8240

Monthly. $30.00/year for individuals; $49.00 for two years. Municipal interest magazine.

PLACEMENT AND JOB REFERRAL SERVICES

★1922★ American Society of Criminology (ASC)

1314 Kinnear Rd., Ste. 212
Columbus, OH 43212
Ph: (614)292-9207   Fax: (614)292-6767

Members: Professional and academic criminologists; students of criminology in accredited universities; psychiatrists, psychologists, and sociologists. **Purpose:** To develop criminology as a science and academic discipline; to aid in the construction of criminological curricula in accredited universities; to upgrade the practitioner in criminological fields (police, prisons, probation, parole, delinquency workers). Conducts research programs; sponsors three student paper competitions. **Activities:** Provides placement service at annual convention.

★1923★ CEGA Services (CC)

PO Box 81826
Lincoln, NE 68501
Ph: (402)464-0602   Fax: (402)464-5931

Purpose: A service information agency working to link people, resources, and information. Maintains a Human Services Department that refers individuals to programs providing assistance with employment, housing, counseling, and other services. Provides information in the fields of criminal justice, corrections, human services, and adult functional illiteracy.

★1924★ National Association of Juvenile Correctional Agencies (NAJCA)

55 Albin Rd.
Bow, NH 03304-3703
Ph: (603)224-9749

Members: Institutions and agencies for the study, care, training, and treatment of children in the juvenile justice systems; adjudged delinquents; executive and staff personnel of residential centers for delinquent children. **Purpose:** Disseminates ideas on the function, philosophy, and goals of the juvenile correctional field with emphasis on institutional rehabilitative programs. Promotes evaluative research; fosters progressive legislation; cooperates with other agencies and organizations having kindred interests. Encourages recruitment and retention of qualified personnel and is concerned with training, working conditions, remuneration and other related matters. **Activities:** Maintains speakers bureau and placement service.

★1925★ Nine Lives Associates (NLA)

Arcadia Manor
Rte. 2, Box 3645
Berryville, VA 22611
Ph: (703)955-1128

Members: Law enforcement, correctional, military, and security professionals who have been granted Personal Protection Specialist certification through completion of the protective services program offered by the Executive Protection Institute; conducts research. EPI programs emphasize personal survival skills and techniques for the protection of others. **Purpose:** Provides professional recognition for qualified individuals engaged in executive protection assignments. **Activities:** Maintains placement service.

EMPLOYER DIRECTORIES AND NETWORKING LISTS

★1926★ Directory of Juvenile and Adult Correctional Departments, Institutions, Agencies and Paroling Authorities

American Correctional Association
8025 Laurel Lakes Ct.
Laurel, MD 20707-5075
Ph: (301)206-5100   Fax: (301)206-5061
Fr: 800-825-2665

Annual, January. $75.00, payment with order. Covers about 4,000 juvenile and adult state and federal correctional departments, institutions, agencies, programs, paroling authorities, and military correctional facilities in the United States and Canada. Entries include: Agency name, locations, phone, name of administrative officer (and other personnel for agencies), how long in operation, average number and types of inmates, cost of care, degree of security, number of staff. Arrangement: Primarily geographical within authority (federal, states, military, Canada, etc.).

★1927★ Municipal/County Directory Library Edition

Carroll Publishing
1058 Thomas Jefferson St. NW
Washington, DC 20007
Ph: (202)333-8620   Fax: (202)337-7020
Fr: 800-336-4240

Annual, July. $137.00, plus $8.00 shipping; payment must accompany order. Covers officials of 1,400 county governments (with populations over 25,000) and 2,000 municipalities (with populations over 1,000); includes elected, appointed, and career office holders. Entries include: Name, title, agency, address, phone. Arrangement: County officials are geographical, then by agency; municipal officials are by city. Indexes: personal name (with phone), agency.

★1928★ Municipal Year Book

Newman Books Ltd.
32 Vauxhall Bridge Rd.
London SW1V 2SS, England
Ph: 71 9736400   Fax: 71 2335057

Annual, December. $140.00, postpaid. Covers local and central government agencies and officials of the United Kingdom; municipal art galleries, associations, development organizations, fairs, libraries, museums, airports, and other local authorities. Entries include: Name of authority or governing agency, address, phone, fax, names of elected councillors, officers, names and titles of key personnel, contacts, population, and pay. Arrangement: Geographical. Indexes: Subject, place names.

★1929★ National Directory of Law Enforcement Administrators and Correctional Institutions

National Police Chiefs and Sheriffs Information Bureau
PO Box 365
Stevens Point, WI 54481
Ph: (715)345-2772   Fax: (715)345-7288
Fr: 800-647-7579

Annual, August. $64.95, postpaid. Covers police departments and police chiefs in cities and towns with populations of more than 1,600; sheriffs and criminal prosecutors in all counties in the nation; state law enforcement and criminal investigation agencies; federal criminal investigation and related agencies; state and federal correctional institutions; campus law enforcement departments; airport and harbor police, Bureau of Indian Affairs officials, and Canadian law enforcement personnel. Entries include: Name, address, phone, fax, names and titles of key personnel. Arrangement: Separate geographical sections for sheriffs and prosecutors, city police chiefs, and state criminal investigation agencies; also separate sections for federal agencies and miscellaneous law enforcement and related agencies.

HANDBOOKS AND MANUALS

★1930★ America's 50 Fastest Growing Jobs

JIST Works, Inc.
720 N. Park Ave.
Indianapolis, IN 46202
Ph: (317)264-3720   Fr: 800-648-5478

Third edition, 1995. $14.95. 288 pages. Each job profile explains the nature of the work, skills and abilities required, employment outlook, average earnings, related occupations, education and training requirements, and employment opportunities. Also contains career planning information and job search tips.

★1931★ Career Planning in Criminal Justice

Anderson Publishing Co.
2035 Reading Rd.
Cincinnati, OH 45202
Ph: (513)421-4142

Robert C. DeLucia and Thomas J. Doyle. Second edition, 1993. 178 pages. Surveys a wide range of career and employment opportunities in law enforcement, the courts, corrections, forensic science, and private security. Contains career planning and job hunting advice.

★1932★ Careers in Law Enforcement and Security

Rosen Publishing Group, Inc.
29 E. 21st St.
New York, NY 10010
Ph: (212)777-3017   Fax: (212)777-0277
Fr: 800-237-9932

Paul Cohen and Shari Cohen. Revised edition, 1994. $14.95; $9.95 (paper). Describes jobs such as police, sheriff, detective, FBI, CIA, and Secret Service agents, parole and probation officers, security guards, and private investigators. Covers job duties, qualifications, education, training, income, and advancement possibilities. Offers advice about where and how to apply for jobs.

★1933★ Law Enforcement Employment Guide

Lawman Press
PO Box 1468
Mt. Shasta, CA 96067
Ph: (818)344-6146

Ron Stern. Second edition, 1990. $19.95. Directed toward law enforcement applicants, officers, and career changers. Lists requirements for the scores of law enforcement agencies, from very small departments to the largest federal agencies. Includes potential number of openings in the field.

★1934★ 100 Best Careers for the Year 2000

Prentice Hall General Reference
15 Columbus Cir.
New York, NY 10023
Ph: (212)373-8500   Fr: 800-223-2348

Shelly Field. 1992. $15.00 (paper). Covers 100 of the fastest growing jobs. The publication is divided into 11 general employment sections. Specific careers are covered within each section. Provides job description, responsibilities, employment opportunities, earnings, education and training, advancement opportunities, and experience and qualifications for each occupation.

★1935★ Opportunities in Law Enforcement and Criminal Justice

VGM Career Horizons
4255 W. Touhy Ave.
Lincolnwood, IL 60646-1975
Ph: (847)679-5500   Fax: (847)679-2494
Fr: 800-323-4900

James Stinchcomb. 1994. $14.95; $11.95 (paper). Offers information on opportunities at the city, county, state, military, and federal levels. Contains bibliography and illustrations.

★1936★ Opportunities in Vocational and Technical Careers

VGM Career Horizons
4255 W. Touhy Ave.
Lincolnwood, IL 60646-1975
Ph: (847)679-5500   Fax: (847)679-2494
Fr: 800-323-4900

Adrian A. Paradis. 1992. $14.95; $11.95 (paper). 160 pages. Provides information on a variety of opportunities and advice on breaking into the field.

OTHER SOURCES

★1937★ American Correctional Association (ACA)

4380 Forbes Blvd.
Lanham, MD 20706-4322
Ph: (301)918-1800   Fax: (301)918-1900
Fr: 800-222-5646

Members: Correctional administrators, wardens, superintendents, members of prison and parole boards, probation officers, psychologists, educators, sociologists, and other individuals; institutions and associations involved in the correctional field. **Purpose:** Promotes improved correctional standards, including selection of personnel, care, supervision, education, training, employment, treatment, and post-release adjustment of inmates. Studies causes of crime and juvenile delinquency and methods of crime control and prevention through grants and contracts. Conducts research programs.

Cosmetologists and Hairdressers

SOURCES OF HELP-WANTED ADS

★1938★ American Salon
Advanstar Communications, Inc.
270 Madison Ave.
New York, NY 10016-0601
Ph: (212)951-6600   Fax: (212)481-6561
Monthly. Magazine for beauty salon owners and managers.

★1939★ Modern Salon
Vance Publishing Corp.
400 Knightsbridge Pkwy.
Lincolnshire, IL 60069
Ph: (708)634-2600   Fax: (708)634-4379
Fr: 800-621-2845
Monthly. $20.00/year for individuals; $3.00 for single issue. Magazine focusing on hairstyling salons for men and women.

★1940★ NAILpro
Summer Communications, Inc.
7626 Densmore Ave.
Van Nuys, CA 91406
Ph: (818)782-7328   Fax: (818)782-7450
Monthly. $31.00/year; $5.00/single issue.

★1941★ Skin Inc.
Allured Publishing Corp.
362 S. Schmale Rd.
Carol Stream, IL 60188-2787
Ph: (708)653-2155   Fax: (708)653-2192
Bimonthly. $46.00/year for individuals. The business magazine for skin care professionals.

★1942★ TCI (Theatre Crafts International)
Theatre Crafts
32 W. 18th St.
New York, NY 10011-4612
Ph: (212)229-2965   Fax: (212)229-2084
$40.00/year for individuals; $5.00 for single issue. The business of entertainment technology and design.

PLACEMENT AND JOB REFERRAL SERVICES

★1943★ Aestheticians International Association (AIA)
3939 E. Hwy. 80, Ste. 408
Mesquite, TX 75150
Ph: (214)686-2540   Fax: (214)686-2340
Members: Aestheticians (persons licensed to manage or own a skin care salon) and students of certified schools; associate members are manufacturers and distributors representing the cosmetic industry. **Purpose:** Objectives are to: improve the education and upgrade the standards of aestheticians, cosmetologists, and related persons in the industry; promote public awareness of research results and information relating to the professions of aesthetics and cosmetology; educate the public and the aesthetic and cosmetology professions through seminars and lectures. **Activities:** Offers Placement Service; conducts charitable programs; research programs, and maintains speakers bureau.

★1944★ World International Nail and Beauty Association (WINBA)
1221 N. Lake View
Anaheim, CA 92807
Ph: (714)779-9883   Fax: (714)779-9971
Members: Professionals in the nail and skin care industries. **Purpose:** Objectives are to: represent the manicure and skin care industry; promote the effective use and application of manicuring and skin care products and equipment; provide a means for mutual communication and joint study; represent the industry before state boards, the Food and Drug Administration, and other regulatory agencies. **Activities:** Maintains speakers' bureau and placement service. Conducts seminars; secures discounts on supplies; offers special insurance plans and rates; conducts public relations program; sponsors research and educational programs; compiles statistics.

EMPLOYER DIRECTORIES AND NETWORKING LISTS

★1945★ Beauty Salons Directory
American Business Directories, Inc.
American Business Information, Inc.
5711 S. 86th Cir.
Omaha, NE 68127
Ph: (402)593-4600   Fax: (402)331-1505
Annual. $6,575.00, U.S. edition; $920.00, (Canadian edition); payment with order. Number of listings: 214,469 (U.S. edition); 24,799 (Canadian edition). Entries include: Salon name, address, phone (including area code), size of advertisement, year first in Yellow Pages, name of owner or manager, number of employees. Regional editions available. Compiled from telephone company Yellow Pages, nationwide. Arrangement: Geographical.

★1946★ Manicuring Salons Directory
American Business Directories, Inc.
American Business Information, Inc.
5711 S. 86th Cir.
Omaha, NE 68127
Ph: (402)593-4600   Fax: (402)331-1505
Annual. $1,155.00, payment with order. Number of listings: 35,303. Entries include: Name, address, phone (including area code), size of advertisement, year first in Yellow Pages, name of owner or manager, number of employees. Regional editions available. Compiled from telephone company Yellow Pages, nationwide. Arrangement: Geographical.

HANDBOOKS AND MANUALS

★1947★ Career After Cosmetology School: Step-by-Step Guide to a Lucrative Career and Salon Ownership

Step-by-Step Publications
PO Box 1492
Cupertino, CA 95015-1492
Ph: (408)255-6610   Fax: (408)255-6650

Jessica Brooks. 1995. $29.95; $19.95 (paper).

★1948★ Career Opportunities in Television, Cable and Video

Facts on File, Inc.
11 Penn Plaza, 15th Fl.
New York, NY 10001-2006
Ph: (212)967-8800   Fax: 800-678-3633
Fr: 800-322-8755

Maxine K. Reed and Robert M. Reed. Third edition, 1991. $29.95; $15.95 (paper). 272 pages.

★1949★ Careers in Beauty Culture

Rosen Publishing Group, Inc.
29 E. 21st St.
New York, NY 10010
Ph: (212)777-3017   Fax: (212)777-0277
Fr: 800-237-9932

Barbara L. Johnson. 1989. $14.95. Offers advice on job hunting and succeeding on the job. Discusses job opportunities for cosmetologists. Describes personal characteristics, training, licensing requirements, working conditions, advancement opportunities, employment outlook, and advantages and disadvantages of the job. Contains information on owning a salon.

★1950★ Cosmetology as a Career

National Cosmetology Association
3510 Olive St.
St. Louis, MO 63103

Pamphlet. Free. Discusses how to build a career as a cosmetologist.

★1951★ Cosmetology: Excellent Opportunities

National Cosmetology Association, Inc.
3510 Olive St.
St. Louis, MO 63103
Ph: (314)534-7980

This leaflet surveys job opportunities for cosmetologists as salon managers, owners, and teachers.

★1952★ Hair, Makeup & Styling Career Guide

Set the Pace Publishing Group
4237 Los Nietos Dr.
Los Angeles, CA 90027
Ph: (213)913-0773   Fax: (213)913-0900

Wright. 1995. $39.95 (paper).

★1953★ How to Get a Job with a Cruise Line

Ticket to Adventure, Inc.
PO Box 41005
St. Petersburg, FL 33743
Ph: (813)544-6440   Fr: 800-929-7447

Mary Fallon Miller. Third edition, 1994. $14.95. 224 pages. Explores jobs with cruise ships, describing duties, responsibilities, benefits, and training. Lists cruise ship lines and schools offering cruise line training. Offers job hunting advice.

★1954★ 100 Best Careers for the Year 2000

Prentice Hall General Reference
15 Columbus Cir.
New York, NY 10023
Ph: (212)373-8500   Fr: 800-223-2348

Shelly Field. 1992. $15.00 (paper). Covers 100 of the fastest growing jobs. The publication is divided into 11 general employment sections. Specific careers are covered within each section. Provides job description, responsibilities, employment opportunities, earnings, education and training, advancement opportunities, and experience and qualifications for each occupation.

★1955★ Opportunities in Beauty Culture Careers

VGM Career Horizons
4255 W. Touhy Ave.
Lincolnwood, IL 60646-1975
Ph: (847)679-5500   Fax: (847)679-2494
Fr: 800-323-4900

Susan Wood Gearhart. 1989. $14.95; $11.95 (paper). 160 pages. Outlines how to enter the field and build a career. Independent salon ownership in also covered. Contains bibliography and illustrations.

★1956★ Opportunities in Vocational and Technical Careers

VGM Career Horizons
4255 W. Touhy Ave.
Lincolnwood, IL 60646-1975
Ph: (847)679-5500   Fax: (847)679-2494
Fr: 800-323-4900

Adrian A. Paradis. 1992. $14.95; $11.95 (paper). 160 pages. Provides information on a variety of opportunities and advice on breaking into the field.

★1957★ Planning Your Cosmetology Career

Prentice Hall
113 Sylvan Ave., Rte. 9W
Englewood Cliffs, NJ 07632
Ph: (201)592-2000   Fax: 800-445-6991
Fr: 800-922-0579

Mary Murphy-Martin. 1993. $17.20 (paper).

OTHER SOURCES

★1958★ Association of Cosmetologists and Hairdressers (ACH)

1811 Monroe
Dearborn, MI 48124
Ph: (313)563-0360   Fax: (313)563-0360

Members: Cosmetologists and beauticians; beauty product manufacturers, wholesalers, buyers, and retailers. **Purpose:** Seeks to keep members informed of current trends in the beauty culture industry. Conducts demonstrations. Compiles statistics. Sponsors educational programs.

★1959★ Hair International/Associated Master Barbers and Beauticians of America (HI/AMBBA)

124-B E. Main St.
PO Box 273
Palmyra, PA 17078
Ph: (717)838-0795   Fax: (717)838-0796

Members: Barber styling and cosmetology school and business owners and employees; manufacturers.

★1960★ Milady's Guide to Cosmetology Licensing

Milady Publishing Co.
Delmar Publishers
3 Columbia Cir.
PO Box 12519
Albany, NY 12212-2519
Ph: 800-836-5239   Fax: (518)464-0301
Fr: 800-836-5239

Biennial, odd years. $34.50. Covers state boards for licensing cosmetologists and barbers in the United States and Canada. Entries include: Board name, address, phone, name and title of contact, names and titles of key personnel, outline of requirements to become certified, licensing fees and expiration dates. Arrangement: Geographical.

★1961★ National Beauty Culturists' League (NBCL)

25 Logan Cir. NW
Washington, DC 20005
Ph: (202)332-2695

Members: Beauticians, cosmetologists, and beauty products manufacturers. **Purpose:** Encourages standardized, scientific, and approved methods of hair, scalp, and skin treatments. **Activities:** Offers scholarships and plans to establish a research center. Sponsors: National Institute of Cosmetology, a training course in operating and designing and business techniques; National Beauty Week. Maintains hall of fame; conducts research programs; compiles statistics.

★1962★ National Cosmetology Association (NCA)

3510 Olive St.
St. Louis, MO 63103
Ph: (314)534-7980   Fax: (314)534-8618
Fr: 800-527-1683

Members: Owners of cosmetology salons; cosmetologists. **Activities:** Sponsors: advanced cosmetology courses at universities throughout the U.S.; National Cosmetology

Month; National Beauty Show. Provides special sections for estheticians, school owners, salon owners, and nail technicians. Maintains hall of fame and museum. Conducts educational and charitable programs.

Cost Estimators

SOURCES OF HELP-WANTED ADS

★1963★ **Builder**

Hanley-Wood, Inc.
1 Thomas Cir., Ste. 600
Washington, DC 20005
Ph: (202)452-0800   Fax: (202)785-1974

Monthly. $29.95/year for individuals. Magazine covering housing, commercial, and industrial building.

★1964★ **Construction Digest**

Construction Magazine Group, Inc.
PO Box 6132
Indianapolis, IN 46206-6132
Ph: (317)329-3100   Fax: (317)329-3110
Fr: 800-860-3105

Semimonthly. $3.00 for single issue. Magazine for the public works and construction engineering industries.

★1965★ **CONSTRUCTOR**

Associated General Contractors
  Information
1957 E St. NW
Washington, DC 20006-5199
Ph: (202)393-2040   Fax: (202)628-7369

Monthly. $15.00/year for members; $4.00 for single issue.

★1966★ **Cost Engineering**

AACE International
PO Box 1557
Morgantown, WV 26507-1557
Ph: (304)296-8444

Monthly. Magazine.

★1967★ **Design Cost & Data**

L.M Rector Corp.
8602 N. 40th St.
Tampa, FL 33604
Ph: (813)989-9300   Fax: (813)980-3982

Quarterly. $48.00/year for individuals. Publication providing real cost data case studies of various types completed around the country. Used by design and building professionals.

★1968★ **ENR: Engineering News Record**

New York Construction News
1221 Avenue of the Americas
New York, NY 10020
Ph: (212)512-4773   Fax: (212)512-4770

Weekly. $42.00/year; $2.00/issue.

★1969★ **Professional Builder**

Cahners Publishing Co.
1350 E. Touhy Ave.
PO Box 5080
Des Plaines, IL 60018-5080
Ph: (708)635-8800   Fax: (708)635-9950

Monthly. $10.00 for single issue; $139.95/year by mail.

PLACEMENT AND JOB REFERRAL SERVICES

★1970★ **AACE International (AACE)**

209 Prairie Ave.
Morgantown, WV 26505
Ph: (304)296-8444   Fax: (304)291-5728
Fr: 800-858-2678

Members: Professional society of cost managers, cost engineers, estimators, schedulers and planners, economic evaluators, educators, representatives of all branches of engineering, engineering students, and others. **Activities:** Conducts technical and educational programs. Offers placement service. Compiles statistics.

★1971★ **Associated Builders and Contractors (ABC)**

1300 N. 17th St.
Rosslyn, VA 22209
Ph: (703)812-2000   Fax: (703)812-8200

Members: Construction contractors, subcontractors, suppliers, and associates. **Purpose:** Aim is to foster and perpetuate the principles of rewarding construction workers and management on the basis of merit. **Activities:** Maintains placement service. Sponsors management education programs and craft training; also sponsors apprenticeship and skill training programs. Dissemi-

nates technological and labor relations information. Compiles statistics.

★1972★ **International Society of Parametric Analysts (ISPA)**

PO Box 6402
Town & Country Branch
Chesterfield, MO 63006-6402
Ph: (314)527-2955   Fax: (314)256-8358

Members: Engineers, designers, statisticians, estimators, and managers in industry, the military, and government who develop and use computerized, parametric cost-estimating models. **Activities:** Conducts educational activities aimed at promoting usage of parametric modeling techniques for purposes of cost estimating, risk analysis, and technology forecasting. Sponsors placement service.

★1973★ **National Association of Home Builders of the U.S. (NAHB)**

1201 15th St. NW
Washington, DC 20005
Ph: (202)822-0200   Fax: (202)822-0559

Members: Single and multifamily home builders, commercial builders, and others associated with the building industry. **Purpose:** Lobbies on behalf of the housing industry and conducts public affairs activities to increase public understanding of housing and the economy. Collects and disseminates data on current developments in home building and home builders' plans through its Economics Department and nationwide Metropolitan Housing Forecast. **Activities:** Maintains NAHB Research Center, which functions as the research arm of the home building industry. Sponsors seminars and workshops on construction, mortgage credit, labor relations, cost reduction, land use, remodeling, and business management. Compiles statistics; offers charitable program, spokesman training, and placement service; maintains speakers' bureau, and hall of fame.

★1974★ **Professional Women in Construction (PWC)**

342 Madison Ave., Rm. 451
New York, NY 10173
Ph: (212)687-0610   Fax: (212)490-1213

Members: Management-level women and men in construction and allied industries;

owners, suppliers, architects, engineers, field personnel, office personnel, and bonding/surety personnel. **Purpose:** Provides a forum for exchange of ideas and promotion of political and legislative action, education, and job opportunities for women in construction and related fields; forms liaisons with other trade and professional groups; develops research programs. Strives to reform abuses and to assure justice and equity within the construction industry. Sponsors mini-workshops. **Activities:** Maintains Action Line which provides members with current information on pertinent legislation and on the association's activities and job referrals.

EMPLOYER DIRECTORIES AND NETWORKING LISTS

★1975★ ABC Today—Associated Builders and Contractors Membership Directory Issue

Associated Builders and Contractors
1300 N. 17th St.
Rosslyn, VA 22209
Ph: (703)812-2000   Fax: (703)812-8200

Annual, November. $150.00, plus $7.00 shipping. Publication includes: List of approximately 17,000 member construction contractors and suppliers. Entries include: Company name, address, phone, name of principal executive, code to volume of business, business specialty. Arrangement: Classified by chapter, then by work specialty.

★1976★ Constructor—Directory of Membership and Services Issue

AGC Information, Inc.
Associated General Contractors of America
1957 E St. NW
Washington, DC 20006
Ph: (202)393-2040   Fax: (202)347-4004

Annual, July. $135.00. Publication includes: List of more than 8,500 member firms and 9,000 national associate member firms engaged in building, highway, heavy, industrial, municipal utilities, and railroad construction, listing of state and local chapter officers. Arrangement: Geographical. Indexes: Company name.

★1977★ Directory of African American Design Firms

San Francisco Redevelopment Agency
770 Golden Gate Ave.
San Francisco, CA 94102-3120
Ph: (415)749-2423   Fax: (415)749-2526

Annual, December. Free. Covers over 100 architectural, engineering, planning, and landscape design firms. Entries include: Firm name, address, phone names and titles of key personnel, particular type of work. Arrangement: Alphabetical.

★1978★ ENR Directory of Design Firms

McGraw-Hill, Inc.
1221 Ave. of the Americas
New York, NY 10020
Ph: (212)512-2534   Fax: (212)512-4178

Biennial, fall of even years; issue of *Engineering News Record.* $85.00. Covers 133 architects, architectural engineers, consultants, and other design firms; limited to advertisers. Mini-profiles on about 3,400 U.S. firms and 500 foreign firms or foreign offices of U.S. firms. Also includes lists of top 500 design firms in the United States, top 200 international design firms, top 50 United States design-construction firms, and top 50 international design-construction firms, based on total amount of billings. Entries include: For advertisers: company name, address, branch locations, subsidiaries, list of key personnel, territory served, capabilities. In ranked lists: company name, address, phone; international firms include telex. Arrangement: Alphabetical (profiles); geographical (mini-profiles).

★1979★ ENR—Top 500 Design Firms Issue

McGraw-Hill, Inc.
1221 Ave. of the Americas
New York, NY 10020
Ph: (212)512-4635   Fax: (212)512-2820

Annual, April. $10.00, reprint, payment must accompany order. Publication includes: List of 500 leading architectural, engineering, and specialty design firms selected on basis of annual billings. Entries include: Company name, headquarters location, type of firm, current and prior year rank in billings, types of services, countries in which operated in preceding year. Arrangement: Ranked by billings.

★1980★ ENR—Top 400 Construction Contractors Issue

McGraw-Hill, Inc.
1221 Ave. of the Americas
New York, NY 10020
Ph: (212)512-4635   Fax: (212)512-2820

Annual, May issue of *Engineering News Record.* $10.00, Reprint, payment with order. Publication includes: List of 400 United States contractors receiving largest dollar volumes of contracts in preceding calendar year. Separate lists of 50 largest design/construct management firms; 50 largest program and construction managers; 25 building contractors; 25 heavy contractors. Entries include: Company name, headquarters location, total value of contracts received in preceding year, value of foreign contracts, countries in which operated, construction specialities. Arrangement: By total value of contracts received.

★1981★ ENR—Top International Design Firms Issue

McGraw-Hill, Inc.
1221 Ave. of the Americas, Rm. 4188
New York, NY 10020
Ph: (212)512-4635

Annual, July. $10.00, reprint, payment with order. Publication includes: List of 200 design firms (including United States firms) competing outside their own national borders who received largest dollar volume of foreign

contracts in preceding calendar year. Entries include: Company name, headquarters location, type of firm, current and previous year rankings in total billings, types of services, countries in which operated in preceding year. Arrangement: By amount billed to international clients in previous year.

EMPLOYMENT AGENCIES AND SEARCH FIRMS

★1982★ B W and Associates, Inc.

4415 W. Harrison St.
Hillside, IL 60162-1910
Ph: (708)449-5400

Employment agency.

★1983★ Real Estate Executive Search, Inc.

PO Box 40
Santa Rosa, CA 95402-0040
Ph: (707)525-4591

Executive search firm.

★1984★ Roper Personnel Services

220 Executive Center Dr., Ste. 110
Columbia, SC 29210-8421
Ph: (803)798-8500

Employment agency. Fills openings on temporary or regular basis.

★1985★ Specialized Search Associates

15200 Carter Rd.
Delray Beach, FL 33446
Ph: (407)499-3711   Fax: (407)499-3770

Executive search firm.

OTHER SOURCES

★1986★ American Society of Professional Estimators (ASPE)

11141 Georgia Ave., Ste. 412
Wheaton, MD 20902
Ph: (301)929-8848   Fax: (301)929-0231

Members: Construction cost estimators; firms allied to the construction industry; construction educators. **Purpose:** Fosters and upholds high professional and ethical standards in construction estimating. **Activities:** Sponsors efforts to enhance the education of young people entering the estimating profession; offers continuing education to established professionals; provides certification for estimators. Encourages the use of estimators throughout the construction industry. Conducts charitable program. Library is under development.

★1987★ Associated General Contractors of America (AGC)

1957 E St. NW
Washington, DC 20006
Ph: (202)393-2040   Fax: (202)347-4004

Members: General construction contractors; subcontractors; industry suppliers; service firms.**Purpose:** Provides market services through its divisions. Conducts special conferences and seminars designed specifically for construction firms. Compiles statistics on job accidents reported by member firms. Maintains 65 committees, including joint cooperative committees with other associations and liaison committees with federal agencies.

★1988★ **Construction Education Foundation (MSF)**

1300 N. 17th St.
Rosslyn, VA 22209
Ph: (703)812-2000   Fax: (703)812-8235

Purpose: Works to promote the merit shop for the benefit of the construction industry. (A merit shop is an open, nonunion shop that competes for business on the basis of price and quality rather than union status.) Conducts annual grants program to fund research and education projects aimed at improving the technology and environment of the construction industry and to promote the merit shop philosophy. Sponsors college programs and activities including: informational mailings to construction programs; financial aid for construction students; assis-

tance to educators traveling to merit shop meetings; merit shop nights. Provides grants for publications and research studies to forecast trends in open shop construction, to compile information on the economic impact of wage laws, and to create an awareness of merit shop principles among students. Distributes study summaries, reports, and information about merit shop construction to public officials, contractors, educators, and students. Sponsors Wheels of Learning to provide apprenticeship and task training in 15 trade areas. Holds annual Job Fair for construction management, engineering, architecture, and building science students.

★1989★ **National Association of Women in Construction (NAWIC)**

327 S. Adams St.
Fort Worth, TX 76104
Ph: (817)877-5551   Fax: (817)877-0324
Fr: 800-552-3506

Purpose: NAWIC is an international association of women employed in the construction industry which promotes that industry and supports the advancement of women within it.

★1990★ **Society of Cost Estimating and Analysis (SCEA)**

101 S. Whiting St., Ste. 201
Alexandria, VA 22304
Ph: (703)751-8069   Fax: (703)461-7328

Members: Individuals in cost estimating and analysis and price analysis-oriented professions. **Purpose:** Facilitates the professional association of the cost estimating and analysis disciplines; enhances the efficiency and effectiveness of cost estimating and analysis activities in proprietary industry, nonprofit organizations, and government. **Activities:** Activities include: identification of technical and ethical standards; establishment and maintenance of standards; assistance in the identification of qualified members for industry and government. Maintains code of ethics to promote cooperation and good relations among members of the profession and to enhance the stature of the profession. Provides certification program that supports technical and ethical standards through participation in oral workshops, involvement in professional programs, completion of accredited university courses, and successful completion of certification examination.

Counselors

SOURCES OF HELP-WANTED ADS

★1991★ Addiction & Recovery's National Treatment Resource Issue

Medquest Communications, Inc.
629 Euclid Ave., Ste. 500
Cleveland, OH 44114
Ph: (216)522-9700   Fax: (216)522-9707

Annual. Covers 3000 drug and alcohol treatment programs and facilities, addiction counselors, and physicians. Entries include institution name and address, addictions treated, type of facility, size.

★1992★ Alcoholism: Clinical and Experimental Research

Williams & Wilkins
351 W. Camden St.
Baltimore, MD 21201-2436
Ph: (410)361-8004   Fax: (410)528-4312
Fr: 800-222-3790

Bimonthly. $155.00/year for individuals; $300.00/year for institutions. Publishing original clinical and research studies on alcoholism and alcohol-induced organ damage.

★1993★ American Annals of the Deaf

Conference of Educational Administrators Serving the Deaf
KDES, PAS-6
800 Florida Ave. NE
Washington, DC 20002-3625
Ph: (202)651-5340   Fax: (202)651-5708

$50.00/year for individuals; $55.00/year for Canada; $65.00/year for other countries. Magazine focusing on education of the deaf.

★1994★ ARCA News

American Rehabilitation Counseling Association (ARCA)
5999 Stevenson Ave.
Alexandria, VA 22304
Ph: (703)823-9800   Fax: (703)823-0252
Fr: 800-347-6647

Quarterly.

★1995★ ASCUS Annual: Job Search Handbook for Educators

Association for School, College and University Staffing (ASCUS)
820 Davis St., Ste. 222
Evanston, IL 60201
Ph: (708)864-1999

Annual. Includes employment notices from public school systems. Contains articles for educators seeking employment. Also includes "Directory of State Teacher Certification Offices."

★1996★ The Chronicle of Higher Education

The Chronicle of Higher Education
1255 23rd St. NW, Ste. 700
Washington, DC 20037
Ph: (202)466-1000   Fax: (202)296-2691
Fr: 800-347-6969

Weekly. $67.50/year for individuals; $2.75 for single issue. Higher education magazine (tabloid).

★1997★ Community Jobs: The Employment Newspaper for the Non-Profit Sector

ACCESS: Networking in the Public Interest
30 Irving Pl.
New York, NY 10003
Ph: (212)475-1001   Fax: (212)475-1199

Monthly. $69.00. Covers jobs and internships available with nonprofit organizations active in issues such as the environment, foreign policy, consumer advocacy, housing, education, etc. Entries include: Position title; name, address, and phone of contact; description, responsibilities; requirements; salary. Arrangement: Geographical.

★1998★ Counseling Today

American Counseling Association
5999 Stevenson Ave.
Alexandria, VA 22304-3300
Ph: (703)823-9800

Mary Morrissey, editor. Monthly. $37.00/year; $2.00/single issue. Newsletter of the American Counseling Association, a partnership of associations representing professional counselors.

★1999★ Current Openings in Education in U.S.A.

Education Information Service
PO Box 660662
Newton, MA 02162-0662
Ph: (617)443-0125

Seven times/year. $8.00/issue. Publication is a booklet listing about 140 institutions or school systems, each with one to a dozen or more openings for teachers, librarians, counselors, administrators, and other personnel.

★2000★ Family Therapy News

American Association for Marriage & Family Therapy
1100 17th St. NW, 10th Fl.
Washington, DC 20036
Ph: (202)452-0109   Fax: (202)223-2329

Bimonthly. $25.00/year for individuals; $40.00/year for institutions, Canada; $35.00/year for other countries; $4.00 for single issue. Newspaper on family therapy.

★2001★ Foreign Faculty and Administrative Openings

Education Information Service
Box 662
Newton, MA 02162
Ph: (617)237-0887

Approximately every six weeks. $9.00. Covers approximately 150 specific openings in administration, counseling, library, teaching and other disciplines for American teachers in American schools overseas and in international schools, both of which must teach English as a primarily language. Entries include: Institution name, address.

★2002★ The New Social Worker

White Hat Communications
PO Box 5390
Harrisburg, PA 17110-0390
Ph: (717)238-3787

$13.25/year. Publication offering career guidance for social work students.

★2003★ The NonProfit Times

The Davis Information Group, Inc.
190 Tamarack Cir.
Skillman, NJ 08558-9662
Ph: (609)466-4600

Monthly. $39.00/year.

★2004★ Social Service Jobs

10 Angelica Dr.
Framingham, MA 01701
Ph: (508)620-8644

Biweekly. $109.00/year.

★2005★ Spotlight: On Career Planning, Placement, and Recruitment

National Association of Colleges and Employers
62 Highland Ave.
Bethlehem, PA 18017
Ph: (610)868-1421

Biweekly (except monthly in July, August, and December). Free to members; $72.00/year for nonmembers. Price includes subsription to the Journal of Career Planning and Employment.

★2006★ TeamRehab Report

Miramar Publishing
6133 Bristol Pkwy.
Box 3640
Culver City, CA 90231-3640
Ph: (213)337-9717

Bimonthly.

PLACEMENT AND JOB REFERRAL SERVICES

★2007★ American Association of Psychiatric Technicians (AAPT)

PO Box 14014
Phoenix, AZ 85063
Ph: (602)873-1890   Fax: (602)873-4616
Fr: 800-391-7589

Members: Psychiatric technicians, behavioral health technicians, mental health workers, counselors, social workers, psychiatric nurses, psychologists, and other individuals and companies interested in mental health. **Purpose:** Promotes professionalism in mental health industry. Encourages further education of mental health workers and provides national certification of mental health workers. Works with colleges, schools, and mental health facilities to develop education and training. Awards accreditation to mental health worker training programs. **Activities:** Offers placement informations.

★2008★ American College Personnel Association (ACPA)

1 Dupont Cir. NW, Ste. 300
Washington, DC 20036-1110
Ph: (202)835-2272   Fax: (202)296-3286

Members: Individuals employed in higher education and involved in student personnel work, including administration, counseling, research, and teaching. **Purpose:** Fosters student development in higher education in areas of service, advocacy, and standards by offering professional programs for educators committed to the overall development of post-secondary students. **Activities:** Sponsors professional and educational activities in cooperation with other organizations. Offers placement service.

★2009★ Association on Higher Education and Disability (AHEAD)

PO Box 21192
Columbus, OH 43221-0192
Ph: (614)488-4972   Fax: (614)488-1174

Members: Individuals interested in promoting the equal rights and opportunities of disabled postsecondary students, staff, faculty, and graduates. **Purpose:** Provides an exchange of communication for those professionally involved with disabled students; collects, evaluates, and disseminates information; encourages and supports legislation for the benefit of disabled students. **Activities:** Conducts surveys on issues pertinent to college students with disabilities; offers resource referral system and employment exchange for positions in disability student services. Conducts research programs; compiles statistics.

★2010★ Association for Multicultural Counseling and Development (AMCD)

5999 Stevenson Ave.
Alexandria, VA 22304
Ph: (703)823-9800   Fax: (703)823-0252
Fr: 800-347-6647

Members: A division of the American Counseling Association. Professionals involved in counseling careers in educational settings, social services, and community agencies; interested individuals; students. Seeks to: develop programs aimed at improving ethnic and racial empathy and understanding; foster personal growth and improve educational opportunities for all minorities in the U.S.; defend human and civil rights; provide in-service and pre-service training for members and others in the profession. Works to enhance members' ability to serve as behavioral change agents. **Activities:** Offers placement service.

★2011★ Association for Specialists in Group Work (ASGW)

5999 Stevenson Ave.
Alexandria, VA 22304
Ph: (703)823-9800   Fax: (703)823-0252
Fr: 800-347-6647

Members: A division of the American Counseling Association . Individuals interested in group counseling holding master's or doctoral degrees, and engaged in practice, teaching, or research in group work; persons holding undergraduate degrees who are interested in group work, but not actively engaged in practice, teaching, or research; students. **Purpose:** Seeks to assist and further interests of children, youth, and adults by providing effective services through the group medium, preventing problems, providing maximum development, and remediating disabling behaviors. Sponsors programs to advance group work in schools, clinics, universities, private practice, and mental health institutions. **Activities:** Conducts placement service.

★2012★ Family Service America (FSA)

11700 W. Lake Park Dr.
Milwaukee, WI 53224
Ph: (414)359-1040   Fax: (414)359-1074
Fr: 800-221-3726

Purpose: Federation of local agencies in more than 1000 communities providing family counseling, family life education and family advocacy services, and other programs to help families with parent-child, marital, mental health, and other problems of family living. Assists member agencies in developing and providing effective family services. Works with the media, government, and corporations to promote strong family life. Compiles statistics; conducts research. Maintains extensive files of unpublished materials from member agencies. **Activities:** Offers placement services.

★2013★ International Association of Counselors and Therapists (IACT)

10915 Bonita Beach Rd., Ste. 2142
Bonita Springs, FL 33923
Ph: (941)498-9710

Members: Mental health professionals, medical professionals, social workers, clergy, philosophers, educators, hypnotherapists, counselors, and individuals interested in the helping professions. **Purpose:** Promotes enhanced professional image and prestige for hypnotherapists. Provides a forum for exchange of information and ideas among practitioners of traditional and nontraditional therapies and methodologies; fosters unity among "grassroots" practitioners and those with advanced academic credentials. Facilitates the development of new therapy programs. **Activities:** Operates referral and placement services.

★2014★ International Educator's Institute (TIE)

PO Box 513
Cummaquid, MA 02637
Ph: (508)362-1414

Purpose: Facilitates the placement of teachers and administrators in American, British, and international schools. Seeks to create a network that provides for professional development opportunities and improved financial security of members. Offers advice and information on international school news, recent educational developments, job placement, and investment, consumer, and professional development opportunities. Makes available insurance and travel benefits. Operates International Schools Internship Program. Sponsors competitions. Bestows awards.

★2015★ National Academic Advising Association (NACADA)

Kansas State Univ.
2323 Anderson Ave., Ste. 225
Manhattan, KS 66502
Ph: (913)532-5717   Fax: (913)532-7732

Members: Academic program advisers, faculty, administrators, counselors, and others concerned with the intellectual, personal, and career development of students in all types of postsecondary educational institutions. **Purpose:** Is dedicated to the support and professional growth of academic advising and academic advisers. Provides a forum for discussion, debate, and exchange of ideas regarding academic advising. Serves as advocate for standards and quality programs in academic advising. **Activities:** Operates consultants bureau to assist advising services on college campuses. Conducts professional training and holds personal and professional development workshops and conferences. Maintains placement service, speakers' bureau, and clearinghouse. **E-Mail:** naca da@ksuvm.ksu.edu

★2016★ National Career Development Association (NCDA)

5999 Stevenson Ave.
Alexandria, VA 22304
Ph: (703)823-9800   Fax: (703)823-0252
Fr: 800-347-6647

A division of the American Counseling Association . **Members:** Professionals and others interested in career development or counseling in various work environments. **Purpose:** Supports counselors, education and training personnel, and allied professionals working in schools, colleges, business/industry, community and government agencies, and in private practice. **Activities:** Provides publications, support for state and local activities, human equity programs, and continuing education and training for these professionals. Provides networking opportunities for career professionals in business, education, and government.

★2017★ National Council on Rehabilitation Education (NCRE)

Dr. Garth Eldredge
Utah State University
Department of Special Education and Rehabilitation
Logan, UT 84322-2870
Ph: (801)797-3241   Fax: (801)797-3572

Members: Academic institutions and organizations; professional educators, researchers, and students. **Purpose:** Goals are to: assist in the documentation of the effect of education in improving services to persons with disability; determine the skills and training necessary for effective rehabilitation services; develop role models, standards, and uniform licensure and certification requirements for rehabilitation personnel; interact with consumers and public and private sector policy makers. Disseminates information and provides forum for discussion. **Activities:** Sponsors specialized education and placement service. Compiles statistics. Serves as an advisory body to the National Rehabilitation Association and the Rehabilitation Services Administration; works closely with other agencies and associations in the field.

EMPLOYER DIRECTORIES AND NETWORKING LISTS

★2018★ American Association for Correctional Psychology—Directory

American Association for Correctional Psychology
c/o Robert R. Smith
Counseling Program
West Virginia Graduate College
PO Box 1003
Institute, WV 25112-1003
Ph: (304)766-1929   Fax: (304)766-1942

Continuously updated. Free to members only. Covers 400 mental health professionals engaged in correctional and rehabilitative work in prisons, reformatories, juvenile institutions, probation and parole agencies, and in other aspects of criminal justice. Entries include: Name, affiliation, address, phone. Arrangement: Alphabetical.

★2019★ American Group Psychotherapy Association—Membership Directory

American Group Psychotherapy Association
25 E. 21st St., 6th Fl.
New York, NY 10010
Ph: (212)477-2677

Annual, fall. $45.00. Covers 3,700 physicians, psychologists, clinical social workers, psychiatric nurses, and other mental health professionals interested in treatment of emotional problems by group methods. Entries include: Name, office or home address, highest degree held, office or home phone number. Arrangement: Alphabetical. Indexes: Geographical.

★2020★ American Society for Adolescent Psychiatry—Membership Directory

American Society for Adolescent Psychiatry
4330 East-West Hwy., No. 1117
Bethesda, MD 20814
Ph: (301)718-6502   Fax: (301)656-0989

Biennial, fall of even years. $15.00. Covers 1,500 members. Entries include: Name, office address and phone, fax, home address and phone (when given). Arrangement: Alphabetical. Indexes: Geographical, chapter.

★2021★ Boarding Schools Directory

The Association of Boarding Schools (TABS)
National Association of Independent Schools (NAIS)
1620 L St. NW
Washington, DC 20036
Ph: (202)973-9700   Fax: (202)973-9790
Fr: 800-541-5908

Annual, August. Free. Covers 276 boarding schools that are members of the National Association of Independent Schools. Entries include: School name, address, phone, contact name, grades for which boarding students are accepted, enrollment, brief description. Arrangement: Classified by type of school. Indexes: Geographical; program.

★2022★ Child Welfare League of America—Directory of Member Agencies

Child Welfare League of America
440 1st St. NW, Ste. 310
Washington, DC 20001
Ph: (202)638-2952   Fax: (202)638-4004

Biennial. $14.00, payment with order. Covers accredited provisional, and general members, associates and supporting advocates. Includes member agencies of the Florence Crittenton Division. Entries include: Agency name, type of membership region, address, phone number, fax number, name of executive director, list of services. Arrangement: Geographical, then alphabetical.

★2023★ Christian Association for Psychological Studies International— Membership Directory

Christian Association for Psychological Studies
PO Box 310400
New Braunfels, TX 78131-0400
Ph: (210)629-2277   Fax: (210)629-2342

Biennial, May, even years. $10.00. Covers 2,300 Christians involved in psychology, psychiatry, counseling, sociology, social work, ministry, and nursing. Entries include: Name, office address and phone number, highest degree held, area of occupational specialization, and career data. Arrangement: Geographical. Indexes: Alphabetical.

★2024★ Christian Schools International—Directory

Christian Schools International
3350 E. Paris Ave. SE
Grand Rapids, MI 49512
Ph: (616)957-1070   Fax: (616)957-5022

Annual, November. $45.00. Covers nearly 450 Reformed Christian elementary and secondary schools; related associations; societies without schools. Entries include: School name, address, phone; name, title, and address of officers; names of faculty members. Arrangement: Geographical.

★2025★ College Placement Council Directory: Who's Who in Career Planning, Placement, and Recruitment

College Placement Council (CPC)
62 Highland Ave.
Bethlehem, PA 18017
Ph: (610)868-1421   Fax: (610)868-0208
Fr: 800-544-5272

Annual, January. $47.95, plus $4.50 shipping. Covers about 2,400 college and university offices concerned with securing employment for graduates and about 2,300 companies with staff assigned to recruiting and hiring college graduates. Entries include: For colleges: college name and address; names, titles, phone, fax, and e-mail addresses of career planning and placement personnel; interview dates for undergraduates and graduates; months of graduation; whether alumni placement is also handled, student enrollment (including minority data), and dates of career/job fairs. For employers: company name; names, addresses, phone, and fax of recruitment staff; names of secondary contacts; nature of business; number of employees. Arrangement: Colleges are geographical; employers are alphabetical. Indexes: Institutional name, personal name (college personnel); geographical, personal name (in company recruitment).

★2026★ Counseling Services Directory

American Business Directories, Inc.
American Business Information, Inc.
5711 S. 86th Cir.
Omaha, NE 68127
Ph: (402)593-4600   Fax: (402)331-1505

Annual. $575.00, payment with order. Entries include: Name, address, phone (including area code), size of advertisement, year first in Yellow Pages, name of owner or manager, number of employees. Compiled from telephone company Yellow Pages, nationwide. Arrangement: Geographical.

★2027★ Directory of Counseling Services

International Association of Counseling Services
101 S. Whiting St., Ste. 211
Alexandria, VA 22304-3416
Ph: (703)823-9840   Fax: (703)823-9843

Annual, September. $50.00, payment with order. Covers about 200 accredited services in the United States and Canada concerned with psychological, educational, and vocational counseling, including those at colleges and universities, community and technical colleges, and public and private agencies. Entries include: Name, address, phone, hours of operation, director's name, service, clientele served. Arrangement: Geographical.

★2028★ Directory of Experiential Therapy and Adventure-Based Counseling Programs

Association for Experiential Education
2885 Aurora Ave., Ste. 28
Boulder, CO 80303-2252
Ph: (303)440-8844   Fax: (303)440-9581

Updated regularly. $15.00 for nonmembers; $12.50 for members. Covers 257 organizations that offer experiential/adventure-based therapy programs. Entries include: Organization name, address, phone, name of director, description of program, and coded indication of target population location, sex, and age. Arrangement: Alphabetical. Indexes: Geographical.

★2029★ Directory of Public School Systems in the U.S.

Association for School, College and University Staffing
1600 Dodge Ave., S-330
Evanston, IL 60201-3451
Ph: (708)864-1999   Fax: (708)864-8303

Annual, August. $65.00. Covers about 14,500 public school systems in the United States and their administrative personnel. Entries include: System name, address, phone, name and title of personnel administrator. Arrangement: Geographical by state.

★2030★ Directory of Refugee Mental Health Professionals and Paraprofessionals

Refugee Assistance Program–Mental Health Technical Assistance Center
University of Minnesota
Box 85
Mayo
Minneapolis, MN 55455

Covers Professionals who specialize in refugee mental health. Entries include: Name, address, phone, geographical area served and area of specialty. Arrangement: Geographical.

★2031★ Handbook of Private Schools

Porter Sargent Publishers, Inc.
11 Beacon St., Ste. 1400
Boston, MA 02108
Ph: (617)523-1670   Fax: (617)523-1021

Annual, June. $85.00, plus $2.41 shipping: Covers 1,700 elementary and secondary boarding and day schools in the United States. Entries include: School name, address, phone, fax, type of school (boarding or day), sex and age range, names and titles of administrators, grades offered, academic orientation, curriculum, new admissions yearly, tests required for admission, enrollment and faculty, graduate record, number of alumni, tuition and scholarship figures, summer session, plant evaluation and endowment, date of establishment, calendar, association membership, description of school's offerings and history. Arrangement: Geographical. Indexes: Alphabetical by school name.

★2032★ Marriage & Family Counselors Directory

American Business Directories, Inc.
American Business Information, Inc.
5711 S. 86th Cir.
Omaha, NE 68127
Ph: (402)593-4600   Fax: (402)331-1505

Annual. $1,955.00. Entries include: Name, address, phone (including area code), size of advertisement, year first in Yellow Pages, name of owner or manager, number of employees. Regional editions also available. Compiled from telephone company Yellow Pages, nationwide. Arrangement: Geographical.

★2033★ Mental Health Directory

Office of Consumer, Family & Public Information
Center for Mental Health Services
U.S. Substance Abuse & Mental Health Services Administration
5600 Fishers Ln., Rm. 15-18
Rockville, MD 20857
Ph: (301)443-2792

Irregular, latest edition 1990. $23.00. Covers hospitals, treatment centers, outpatient clinics, day/night facilities, residential treatment centers for emotionally disturbed children, residential supportive programs such as halfway houses, and mental health centers offering mental health assistance; not included are substance abuse programs, Veteran's Administration programs, nursing homes, programs for the developmentally disabled, and organizations in which fees are retained by individual members. Entries include: Name, address, phone. Arrangement: Geographical.

★2034★ Mental Health Services Directory

American Business Directories, Inc.
American Business Information, Inc.
5711 S. 86th Cir.
Omaha, NE 68127
Ph: (402)593-4600   Fax: (402)331-1505

Annual. $1,095.00, payment with order. Entries include: Name, address, phone (including area code), size of advertisement, year first in Yellow Pages, name of owner or

manager, number of employees. Compiled from telephone company Yellow Pages, nationwide. Arrangement: Geographical.

★2035★ Mental Health and Social Work Career Directory

Gale Research
835 Penobscot Bldg.
Detroit, MI 48226-4094
Ph: (313)961-2242   Fax: (313)961-6083
Fr: 800-877-GALE

Latest edition 1993. $34.00; $17.95 (paper). Covers over 300 agencies, organizations, and companies offering entry-level positions in mental health, social work, counseling, psychology, etc.; sources of help-wanted ads, professional associations, producers of videos, databases, career guides, and professional guides and handbooks. Entries include: For organizations offering positions: name, address, phone, description, names and titles of key personnel, number of employees, average number of entry-level positions available, human resources contact, description of internship opportunities including contact, type and number available, application procedures, qualifications, and duties. For others: name or title, address, phone, description. Paperback edition is available from Visible Ink Press. Arrangement: Organizations offering positions are alphabetical; others are classified by type of resource. Indexes: Name, keyword.

★2036★ National Directory of Certified Counselors

National Board for Certified Counselors
3-D Terrace Way
Greensboro, NC 27403
Ph: (919)547-0607   Fax: (919)547-0017

Irregular, latest edition spring 1994. $10.00. Covers 20,000 certified counselors, career counselors, and clinical mental health counselors. Entries include: Personal name, address, phone. Arrangement: Geographical. Indexes: Personal name.

★2037★ National Directory of Children, Youth & Families Services

Marion L. Peterson, Publisher
PO Box 1837
Longmont, CO 80502-1837
Ph: (303)776-7539   Fax: 800-845-6452
Fr: 800-343-6681

Annual, July. $78.00, plus $6.00 shipping, postpaid. Covers child, youth, and family-oriented social services, health and mental health services, and juvenile/family court and youth advocacy services in state and private agencies, major cities, and 3,100 counties; also covers runaway youth centers, child abuse projects, congressional committees, clearinghouses, and national organizations concerned with family health and welfare; buyers' guide to specialized services and products. Entries include: Agency listings include agency name, address, phone, names of principal executives and staff, description of services. Arrangement: Geographical.

★2038★ *National Directory for Employment in Education*

Association for School, College and
  University Staffing
1600 Dodge Ave., S-330
Evanston, IL 60201-3451
Ph: (708)864-1999   Fax: (708)864-8303

Annual, winter. $20.00. Covers about 550 placement offices maintained by teacher-training institutions and 450 school district personnel officers and/or superintendents responsible for hiring professional staff. Entries include: Institution name, address, phone, contact name. Arrangement: Geographical. Indexes: Personal name, subject-field of teacher training, institutions which provide vacancy bulletins and placement services to non-enrolled students.

★2039★ *National Register*

American Association of Sex Educators,
  Counselors, and Therapists
435 N. Michigan Ave., Ste. 1717
Chicago, IL 60611
Ph: (312)644-0828   Fax: (312)644-8557

Annual. $15.00, payment with order. Covers about 2,279 association members. Entries include: Name, address, phone, highest degree, certification status. Arrangement: Separate geographical sections for educators, therapists, and counselors.

★2040★ *Opportunities Abroad for Educators*

Fulbright Teacher Exchange Program
600 Maryland Ave., SW, Rm. 235
Washington, DC 20024-2520
Ph: (202)382-8586   Fax: (202)426-0657
Fr: 800-726-0479

Annual, May. Free. Covers opportunities available for elementary and secondary teachers, college and university instructors and professors, and school administrators to attend seminars or to teach abroad under the Mutual Educational and Cultural Exchange Act of 1961. Entries include: Countries of placement, dates, eligibility requirements, teaching assignments. Arrangement: Geographical.

★2041★ *Private Independent Schools*

Bunting and Lyon, Inc.
238 N. Main St.
Wallingford, CT 06492
Ph: (203)269-3333   Fax: (203)269-5697

Annual, March. $96.00. Covers 1,200 English-speaking elementary and secondary private schools and summer programs in the U.S. and abroad. Entries include: School name, address, phone, enrollment, tuition and other fees, scholarship information, administrator's name and educational background, director of admissions, regional accreditation, description of programs, curriculum, activities. Arrangement: Geographical. Indexes: School name; geographical.

★2042★ *Public Welfare Directory*

American Public Welfare Association
810 1st St. NE, Ste. 500
Washington, DC 20002-4267
Ph: (202)682-0100   Fax: (202)289-6555

Annual, August. $70.00, postpaid, payment with order; $75.00, billed. Covers federal, state, territorial, county, and major municipal human service agencies; coverage includes Canadian federal and provincial agencies. Entries include: Agency name, address, phone, names of key personnel, type of service or clientele. Arrangement: Geographical.

★2043★ *Register of Marriage & Family Therapy Providers*

American Association for Marriage and
  Family Therapy
1100 17th St. NW, 10th Fl.
Washington, DC 20036
Ph: (202)452-0109   Fax: (202)223-2329

Irregular, Latest edition 1995. $50.00. Covers 15,000 members throughout the United States and Canada. Entries include: Name, office address, phone, highest degree held. Arrangement: Same information in alphabetical and geographical lists. Indexes: Approved supervisors and fellows.

★2044★ *State Vocational Rehabilitation Agencies*

U.S. Office of Special Education and
  Rehabilitative Services
Rehabilitation Services Service
  Administration
330 C St. SW, Rm. 3042-MES
Washington, DC 20202-2551
Ph: (202)205-8358   Fax: (202)205-9772

Three times a year; April, August, and December. Free. Covers state government agencies responsible for vocational rehabilitation activities, including those for the blind. Entries include: Agency name, address, phone, name and title of director, federal Rehabilitation Services Administration region number. Arrangement: Geographical.

★2045★ *Who's Who Among Human Services Professionals*

National Register Publishing
Reed Reference Publishing
121 Chanlon Rd.
New Providence, NJ 07974-1541
Ph: (908)464-6400   Fr: 800-621-9669

Latest edition February 1992; suspended indefinitely. $129.00. Covers nearly 20,000 human service professionals, in such fields as counseling, social work, psychology, audiology, and speech pathology. Entries include: Name, address, education, work experience, professional association memberships. Arrangement: Alphabetical.

HANDBOOKS AND MANUALS

★2046★ *Career Choices for the 90's for Students of Psychology*

Walker and Company
435 Hudson St.
New York, NY 10014
Ph: (212)727-8300   Fax: (212)727-0984
Fr: 800-289-2553

Prepared by the Career Associates staff. 1990. $9.95. 166 pages. Discusses alternatives for students of psychology. Offers advice on how to break into the field and how to move up. Covers where and who the employers are, internship possibilities, and professional networking associations. Comprehensive guide to career and job search planning.

★2047★ *Career Information Center*

Macmillan Publishing Co.
200 Old Tappan Rd.
Old Tappan, NJ 07675
Ph: (609)461-6500   Fr: 800-223-2336

Visual Education Center Staff. Fifth edition, 1992. $229.00. This 13-volume set profiles over 600 occupations. Each occupational profile describes job duties, educational requirements, how to get the job, advancement possibilities, employment outlook, working conditions, earnings and benefits, and where to write for more information.

★2048★ *Careers in Education*

VGM Career Horizons
4255 W. Touhy Ave.
Lincolnwood, IL 60646-1975
Ph: (847)679-5500   Fax: (847)679-2494
Fr: 800-323-4900

Roy A. Edelfeldt. 1993. $17.95; $13.95 (paper). 192 pages. Explores opportunities for teachers, administrators, and specialists in elementary and secondary schools, as well as teaching, research, and administrative positions in higher education. Additional focus on adult and continuing education and industry opportunities for educators. Provides detailed background on careers in state boards and state departments of education, accrediting agencies, federal agencies, and national associations and councils.

★2049★ *Careers for Good Samaritans and Other Humanitarian Types*

VGM Career Horizons
4255 W. Touhy Ave.
Lincolnwood, IL 60646-1975
Ph: (847)679-5500   Fax: (847)679-2494
Fr: 800-323-4900

Marjorie Eberts and Margaret Gisler. 1991. $12.95; $9.95 (paper). Contains hundreds of ideas for turning good work into paid work. Inventories opportunities in service organizations like the Red Cross, Goodwill, and the Salvation Army; religious groups, VISTA, the Peace Corps, and UNICEF; and agencies at all levels of the government.

★2050★ *Careers in Health Care*

VGM Career Horizons
4255 W. Touhy Ave.
Lincolnwood, IL 60646-1975
Ph: (847)679-5500   Fax: (847)679-2494
Fr: 800-323-4900

Barbara M. Swanson. 1995. $17.95; $13.95 (paper). Describes job duties, work settings, salaries, licensing and certification requirements, educational preparation, and future outlook. Gives ideas on how to secure a job.

★2051★ *The Encyclopedia of Career Choices for the 1990s: Guide to Entry-Level Jobs*

Perigree Books
The Berkley Publishing Group
PO Box 506
East Rutherford, NJ 07073
Ph: (201)933-9292   Fr: 800-223-0510

Career Associates Staff. 1992. $19.95. 862 pages. Describes 500 entry-level careers in a variety of industries. Presents qualifications required, working conditions, salary, internships, and professional associations.

★2052★ *How to Get a Job in Education*

Bob Adams, Inc.
260 Center St.
Holbrook, MA 02343
Ph: (617)767-8100   Fax: (617)767-0994
Fr: 800-872-5627

Joel Levin. Second edition, 1995. $12.95. 320 pages. Prepared for recent college graduates, seasoned educators, and career-changing professionals, this publication guides the job-seeker through the necessary steps to obtaining a job in education at the elementary, secondary, and university levels. Offers advice on how to prepare for state and local examinations, how to locate teaching opportunities nationwide, and how to obtain certification. Includes a nationwide salary survey. Covers public, private, summer, and overseas opportunities.

★2053★ *Liberal Arts Jobs: What They Are and How to Get Them*

Peterson's
PO Box 2123
Princeton, NJ 08543-2123
Ph: (609)243-9111   Fax: (609)243-9150
Fr: 800-338-3282

Burton Jay Nadler. Second edition, 1989. $9.95. 153 pages. Presents a list of the top 20 fields for liberal arts majors, covering more than 300 job opportunities. Discusses strategies for going after those jobs, including guidance on the language of a successful job search, informational interviews, and making networking work.

★2054★ *Non-Profits and Education Job Finder*

Planning/Communications
7215 Oak Ave.
River Forest, IL 60305-1935
Ph: (708)366-5200   Fr: (888)366-5200

Daniel Lauber. 1996. $32.95; $16.95 (paper). 350 pages. Covers 1600 sources. Discusses how to use sources of non-profit sector job vacancies in a number of specialties and state-by-state, including job-matching ser-vices, job hotlines, specialty periodicals with job ads, salary surveys, and directories. Covers a variety of fields from education to religion. Includes chapters on resume and cover letter preparation and interviewing.

★2055★ *100 Best Careers for the Year 2000*

Prentice Hall General Reference
15 Columbus Cir.
New York, NY 10023
Ph: (212)373-8500   Fr: 800-223-2348

Shelly Field. 1992. $15.00 (paper). Covers 100 of the fastest growing jobs. The publication is divided into 11 general employment sections. Specific careers are covered within each section. Provides job description, responsibilities, employment opportunities, earnings, education and training, advancement opportunities, and experience and qualifications for each occupation.

★2056★ *Opportunities in Counseling and Development Careers*

VGM Career Horizons
4255 W. Touhy Ave.
Lincolnwood, IL 60646-1975
Ph: (847)679-5500   Fax: (847)679-2494
Fr: 800-323-4900

Neale Baxter. 1994. $14.95; $11.95 (paper). A guide to planning for and seeking opportunities in this challenging field. Illustrated.

★2057★ *Opportunities in Health and Medical Careers*

VGM Career Horizons
4255 W. Touhy Ave.
Lincolnwood, IL 60646-1975
Ph: (847)679-5500   Fax: (847)679-2494
Fr: 800-323-4900

Donald Snook, Jr. and Leo D'Orazio. 1993. $14.95; $11.95 (paper). Covers the full range of medical and health occupations. Illustrated.

EMPLOYMENT AGENCIES AND SEARCH FIRMS

★2058★ **Arbor Associates, Inc.**

15 Court Sq., Ste. 1050
Boston, MA 02108
Ph: (617)227-8829

Handles temporary placements.

★2059★ **Educational Placement Service**

5050 Poplar Ave., Ste. 1700
Memphis, TN 38157-1701
Ph: (901)767-1884

Employment agency. Focuses on teaching, administrative, and education-related openings.

OTHER SOURCES

★2060★ **American Counseling Association (ACA)**

5999 Stevenson Ave.
Alexandria, VA 22304-3300
Ph: (703)823-9800   Fax: (703)823-0252
Fr: 800-347-6647

Members: Counseling professionals in elementary and secondary schools, higher education, community agencies and organizations, rehabilitation programs, government, industry, business, private practice, career counseling, and mental health counseling. **Activities:** Conducts professional development institutes and provides liability insurance. Maintains Counseling and Human Development Foundation to fund counseling projects.

★2061★ **Association for Humanistic Education and Development (AHEAD)**

5999 Stevenson Ave.
Alexandria, VA 22304
Ph: (703)823-9800   Fax: (703)823-0252
Fr: 800-347-6647

Members: A division of the American Counseling Association. Teachers, educational administrators, community agency workers, counselors, school social workers, and psychologists; others interested in the area of human development. **Purpose:** Aims to assist individuals in improving their quality of life. Provides forum for the exchange of information about humanistically-oriented administrative and instructional practices. Supports humanistic practices and research on instructional and organizational methods for facilitating humanistic education; encourages cooperation among related professional groups.

★2062★ **Council of Rehabilitation Specialists (CRS)**

American Council of the Blind
1155 15th St. NW, Ste. 720
Washington, DC 20005
Ph: (202)467-5081   Fr: 800-424-8666

Members: Rehabilitation and social service professionals, students pursuing careers in these fields, and interested individuals. **Purpose:** Promotes the establishment of academic and professional standards; advocates adequate rehabilitation services for all blind and visually impaired persons.

★2063★ *Educational Placement Sources Abroad*

Education Information Services (EIS)
PO Box 660662
Newton, MA 02162-0662
Ph: (617)443-0125

Annual, August. Includes about 150 organizations in the United States and abroad which place English-speaking teachers and education administrators in positions abroad. Provides organization name and address. Classified by type of organization.

★2064★ *Educational Placement Sources—U.S.A.*

Education Information Service
PO Box 662
4523 Andes Dr.
Newton, MA 02162-0002
Ph: (617)237-0887

Annual, fall. $4.95. Covers about 75 organizations in the United States that find positions for teachers, educational administrators, and counselors. Entries include: Organization name, address, phone. Arrangement: Alphabetical.

★2065★ Employee Assistance Society of North America (EASNA)

2728 Phillips
Berkley, MI 48072
Ph: (810)545-3888   Fax: (810)545-5528

Members: Individuals in the field of employee assistance, including psychiatrists, psychologists, and managers. **Purpose:** Facilitates communication among members; provides resource information; serves as a network for employee assistance programs nationwide. Conducts research.

★2066★ International Association of Addictions and Offender Counseling (IAAOC)

5999 Stevenson Ave.
Alexandria, VA 22304-3300
Ph: (703)823-9800   Fax: (703)823-0252
Fr: 800-347-6647

A division of the American Counseling Association. **Members:** Professionals concerned with improving the quality of substance abuse treatment and rehabilitation programs offered to public offenders. **Purpose:** Purposes are to: provide leadership in further developing the professions of substance abuse counseling and public offender counseling; improve working conditions for substance abuse and public offender counselors; promote the delivery of effective counseling services to substance abuse and public offenders. Seeks the development of new counseling strategies and of research to support these counseling approaches.

★2067★ *NACE Salary Survey*

National Association of Colleges and
   Employers (NACE)
62 Highland Ave.
Bethlehem, PA 18017

Quarterly. Free to members. Lists offers of starting salaries made to recent graduates. Data is compiled from career planning and placement offices of colleges and universities.

★2068★ National Association of Alcoholism and Drug Abuse Counselors (NAADAC)

3717 Columbia Pike, Ste. 300
Arlington, VA 22204-4254
Ph: (703)920-4644   Fax: (703)920-4672
Fr: 800-548-0497

Members: Counselors in alcoholism and drug abuse treatment. **Purpose:** Objective is

to provide national representation for counselors as well as for their training and education. Works to gain public recognition of alcoholism as a disease. Seeks legislation establishing accreditation standards for counselors. Informs the public about chemical dependency and the availability of assistance.

★2069★ National Association of State Directors of Special Education (NASDSE)

1800 Diagonal Rd., Ste. 320
Alexandria, VA 22314
Ph: (703)519-3800   Fax: (703)519-3808

Members: Professional society of state directors; consultants, supervisors, and administrators who have statewide responsibilities for administering special education programs. **Purpose:** Provides services to state agencies to facilitate their efforts to maximize educational outcomes for individuals with disabilities.

★2070★ National Council for Accreditation of Teacher Education (NCATE)

2010 Massachusetts Ave. NW, Ste. 500
Washington, DC 20036-1023
Ph: (202)466-7496   Fax: (202)296-6620

Members: Representatives from constituent colleges and universities, state departments of education, school boards, teacher, and other professional groups. **Purpose:** Voluntary accrediting body devoted exclusively to: evaluation and accreditation of institutions for preparation of elementary and secondary school teachers; preparation of school service personnel, including school principals, supervisors, superintendents, school psychologists, instructional technologists, and other specialists for school-oriented positions.

★2071★ National Employment Counseling Association (NECA)

5999 Stevenson Ave.
Alexandria, VA 22304
Ph: (703)823-9800   Fax: (703)823-0252

A division of the American Counseling Association. **Members:** Those engaged in employment counseling, counselor education, research, administration or supervision in business and industry, colleges and universities, and federal and state governments; students. **Activities:** Offers professional leadership and development services; provides opportunities for professional growth through workshops and special projects.

★2072★ National Rehabilitation Association (NRA)

633 S. Washington St.
Alexandria, VA 22314
Ph: (703)836-0850   Fax: (703)836-0848

Members: Administrators, instructors, placement specialists, secretaries, counselors, therapists, vocational evaluators, ADA specialists and others interested in rehabilitation of persons with disabilities. **Activities:** Con-

ducts legislative activities; develops accessibility guidelines; offers specialized education.

★2073★ National Rehabilitation Counseling Association (NRCA)

8807 Sudley Rd., Ste. 102
Manassas, VA 22110-4719
Ph: (703)361-2077   Fax: (703)361-2489

Members: A division of the National Rehabilitation Association . Professional and student rehabilitation counselors. **Purpose:** Works to expand the role of counselors in the rehabilitation process and seeks to advance members' professional development. Supports legislation favoring the profession.

★2074★ Northstar Center for Career Management Professionals

PO Box 532
Washington Crossing, PA 18977
Ph: (908)238-6898   Fax: (908)238-5717

Purpose: Provides comprehensive and ongoing training, certification, and support for professional career consultants. Conducts research and surveys on employment trends and career management issues; sponsors seminars and workshops on career management and placement issues at colleges and universities. Makes available individual career advice through publications. Offers low-cost professional consulting.

★2075★ *Opportunities in Psychology Careers*

VGM Career Horizons
4255 W. Touhy Ave.
Lincolnwood, IL 60646-1975
Ph: (847)679-5500   Fax: (847)679-2494
Fr: 800-323-4900

Donald E. Super and Charles McAfee Super. 1994. $14.95; $11.95 (paper). A guide to planning for and building a career in the field. Includes bibliography and illustrations.

★2076★ *Overseas Employment Opportunities for Educators: Department of Defense Dependents Schools*

Diane Publishing Co.
600 Upland Ave.
Upland, PA 19015
Ph: (610)499-7415

1993. $29.95. 52 pages.

★2077★ *Requirements for Certification of Teachers, Counselors, Librarians, Administrators for Elementary and Secondary Schools*

University of Chicago Press
5801 Ellis Ave., 4th Fl.
Chicago, IL 60637
Ph: (312)702-7648   Fax: 800-621-8476
Fr: 800-621-2736

Annual, June. $34.00. Publication includes: List of state and local departments of education. Entries include: Office name, address, phone. Principal content of publication is summaries of each state's teaching and administrative certification requirements. Arrangement: Geographical.

Credit Analysts

SOURCES OF HELP-WANTED ADS

★2078★ **American Banker**

American Banker, Inc.
1 State St. Plaza
New York, NY 10004
Ph: (212)943-6700   Fax: (212)943-2984

Daily (morn.). Newspaper for senior executives in banking and other financial services industries. Coverage includes news on the financial service industry, news analysis, statistical data ranking financial institutions, investigative pieces, and financial industry trend stories for decision-makers.

★2079★ **Bankers Monthly**

Hanover Publishers
200 W. 57th St.
New York, NY 10019
Ph: (212)399-1084   Fax: (212)245-1973

Monthly. Magazine covering current banking topics of interest to senior bank executives.

★2080★ **Business Credit**

National Association of Credit
  Management
8815 Centre Park Dr., Ste. 200
Columbia, MD 21045
Ph: (301)740-5560   Fax: (301)740-5574

Monthly. $33.00/year for individuals; $29.00/year for libraries; $5.00/year for single issue. Magazine covering finance, business credit management, providing information for the extension, and maintenance of accounts receivable cash asset management.

★2081★ **Financial Management**

Financial Management Association
University of South Florida
College of Business Admin.
Tampa, FL 33620
Ph: (813)974-2084   Fax: (813)974-3318

Quarterly. $40.00/year for individuals; $10.00 for single issue. Magazine covering business, economics, finance and management.

★2082★ **Northwestern Financial Review**

NFR Communications
2850 Metro Dr., Ste. 524
Minneapolis, MN 55425
Ph: (612)854-2177   Fax: (612)854-2627

Weekly. $65.00/year for individuals; $4.00. for single issue. Bank and financial magazine and newsletter.

★2083★ **United States Banker**

Faulkner and Gray, Inc.
11 Penn Plaza, 17th Fl.
New York, NY 10001
Ph: (212)967-7000   Fax: (212)967-2162
Fr: 800-535-8403

Monthly. $59.00/year for individuals. Magazine serving the financial services industry.

PLACEMENT AND JOB REFERRAL SERVICES

★2084★ **Commercial Finance Association (CFA)**

225 W. 34th St.
New York, NY 10122
Ph: (212)594-3490   Fax: (212)564-6053

Members: Organizations engaged in asset-based financial services including commercial financing and factoring and lending money on a secured basis to small- and medium-sized business firms. **Purpose:** Acts as a forum for information and consideration about ideas, opportunities, and legislation concerning asset-based financial services. Seeks to improve the industry's legal and operational procedures. **Activities:** Offers job placement and reference services for members. Sponsors School for Field Examiners and other educational programs.

★2085★ **National Association of Federal Credit Unions (NAFCU)**

PO Box 3769
Washington, DC 20007
Ph: (703)522-4770   Fax: (703)524-1082
Fr: 800-336-4644

Members: Federally chartered credit unions united for financial reform legislation and regulations impacting members. **Purpose:** Provides information on the latest industry developments and proposed and final regulations issued by the National Credit Union Administration, the Federal Reserve, and other regulatory agencies. Represents members' interests before federal regulatory bodies and Congress. **Activities:** Maintains speakers' bureau and research information service; offers placement service; compiles statistics.

★2086★ **National Institute of Credit (NIC)**

Credit Research Foundation of the NACM
8815 Centre Park Dr., Ste. 200
Columbia, MD 21045
Ph: (410)740-5499   Fax: (410)740-4620

Purpose: A division of the National Association of Credit Management. Offers, through local chapter classes (independently and in cooperation with local colleges), courses in credit and financial management to students; grants certificates, and Credit Business Associate, Credit Business Fellow, and Certified Credit Executive designations to persons satisfactorily completing the required points courses and examinations. Also offers the NIC Credit Administration Certificate program, which provides new members with the basic principles of business credit and financial management. Cooperates with over 55 colleges and universities in curriculum development; serves as national accrediting body for approval of business credit course curricula. Administers the Graduate School of Credit and Financial Management, an intensive college program offering classes in TQM, treasury management, management strategy, advanced credit policy making, legal environment of credit, leading the credit department, competitive strategy, and competing in the global marketplace. **Activities:** Maintains National Registry of Credit and Financial Education. Serves as national repository for transcript records, continuing education units, and recertification units. Maintains placement service and speakers' bureau. Compiles statistics.

★2087★ Society of Certified Credit Executives (SCCE)

PO Box 419057
St. Louis, MO 63141-1757
Ph: (314)991-3030   Fax: (314)991-3029
Members: A division of the International Credit Association. Credit executives who have been certified through SCCE's professional certification programs. **Purpose:** Seeks to improve industry operations while expanding the knowledge of its members. **Activities:** Maintains placement service.

EMPLOYER DIRECTORIES AND NETWORKING LISTS

★2088★ American Bank Directory

Thomson Financial Publishing Inc.
4709 W. Golf Rd.
Skokie, IL 60076-1253
Ph: (708)676-9600   Fax: (708)933-8101
Fr: 800-321-3373

Semiannual, April and October. $249.00, single issue of national edition; $26.00, for single state edition; $11.00, each additional state in same binder. Covers over 12,000 banks and registered multi-bank holding companies nationwide; also published in editions for individual states. Entries include: Bank name, address (including county and Federal Reserve District), phone, fax, fedwire number, year established, ABA number, names of officers, condensed statement of condition, principal correspondents, branches. Arrangement: Geographical.

★2089★ American Banker—Top Commercial Banks by Assets, Deposits

American Banker-Bond Buyer
International Thomson Publishing Corp.
1 State St. Plaza
New York, NY 10004
Ph: (212)943-5288   Fax: (212)480-0165
Fr: 800-367-3989

Semiannual, March and September. $25.00. Publication includes: List of the top 300 commercial banks. Entries include: Name of bank, headquarters, amount of deposits at the previous quarter, place in rank at quarter. Arrangement: Ranked by deposits and assets. Indexes: Geographical.

★2090★ American Banker—Top Finance Companies Issue

American Banker-Bond Buyer
International Thomson Publishing Corp.
1 State St. Plaza
New York, NY 10004
Ph: (212)943-5288   Fax: (212)480-0165
Fr: 800-367-3989

Annual, December. $25.00. Publication includes: List of top finance companies with $10 million or more in capital funds. Entries include: Finance company name, headquarters, city; rankings of net receivables by type, business, consumer, and other; total capital funds for two preceding years; capital and surplus, total assets, net receivables, net income, deferred income, receivables ac-

quired, and amount of bank credit at end of the preceding year. Arrangement: Ranked by size of capital funds.

★2091★ American Banker—Top 300 Mortgage Companies Issue

American Banker-Bond Buyer
International Thomson Publishing Corp.
1 State St. Plaza
New York, NY 10004
Ph: (212)943-5288   Fax: (212)943-8815
Fr: 800-238-8422

Annual, October. $25.00. Entries include: Company name, headquarters city, rank; dollar value of mortgages serviced for current and prior year; prior year's rank and gain in rank; number of mortgages; number of investors. Arrangement: Ranked by total dollar value of mortgages.

★2092★ American Banker—Top 300 Thrifts by Deposits

American Banker-Bond Buyer
International Thomson Publishing Corp.
1 State St. Plaza
New York, NY 10004
Ph: (212)943-5288   Fax: (212)480-0165
Fr: 800-367-3989

Semiannual, May and November. $25.00. Publication includes: List of top 300 thrift institutions. Entries include: Name of institution, city, rank; total assets, deposits, and total capital. Arrangement: Ranked by deposits, assets, and risk-based capital ratios.

★2093★ American Banker—Top World Banks by Deposits and Assets

American Banker-Bond Buyer
International Thomson Publishing Corp.
1 State St. Plaza
New York, NY 10004
Ph: (212)943-5288   Fax: (212)480-0165
Fr: 800-367-3989

Annual, July. $25.00. Publication includes: List of 500 largest banks in the world by assets with total deposits and deposit rank; also, the risk-based capital position of the 100 largest banking companies in the world as measured by total assets. Entries include: Bank name, headquarters, rankings by assets and amount of deposits and assets for two previous years. Arrangement: Ranked by assets. Indexes: Geographic listing of largest banks outside United States.

★2094★ Branches of Your State: Banks, Savings and Loans, Credit Unions, & Savings Banks

Sheshunoff Information Services, Inc.
Box 13202, Capitol Sta.
Austin, TX 78711-3203
Ph: (512)472-2244   Fax: (512)476-1251
Fr: 800-456-2340

Annual, February. $345.00. Covers in separate state editions, banks, savings and loan branches, and credit unions. For those states without branch banking, individual banks, savings and loan institutions, and credit unions are listed. Entries include: Institution name, address, institution type, deposit totals, percent change over 12 months, percentage share of parent company's total deposits. Arrangement: Geographical.

★2095★ Credit Reporting Agencies Directory

American Business Directories, Inc.
American Business Information, Inc.
5711 S. 86th Cir.
Omaha, NE 68127
Ph: (402)593-4600   Fax: (402)331-1505

Annual. $230.00, payment with order. Number of listings: 2,583. Entries include: Name, address, phone (including area code), size of advertisement, year first in Yellow Pages, name of owner or manager, number of employees. Compiled from telephone company Yellow Pages, nationwide. Arrangement: Geographical.

★2096★ Credit Union Directory

National Credit Union Administration
1775 Duke St.
Alexandria, VA 22314-3428
Ph: (703)518-6540

Annual, summer. $15.00, payment must accompany order. Covers federal credit unions and state-chartered credit unions that are insured by the National Credit Union Share Insurance Fund; coverage includes United States possessions. Entries include: Credit union name, address, phone, charter number, principal operating officer, year-end total assets, number of members. Arrangement: Geographical.

★2097★ Directory of Consumer Credit Counseling Service Agencies

National Foundation for Consumer Credit
8611 2nd Ave., Ste. 100
Silver Spring, MD 20910
Ph: (301)589-5600   Fax: (301)495-5623
Fr: 800-388-CCCS

Semiannual, January and July. $2.50. Covers about 1,180 affiliated non-profit Consumer Credit Counseling Services in the United States, Puerto Rico, and Canada, which provide non-profit education, counseling, and debt management programs for financial and housing issues. Entries include: Service name, address, phone, fax, name and title of contact, subsidiary and branch names and locations, names and titles of key personnel, description. Arrangement: Geographical. Indexes: Agency name.

★2098★ Directory of the Savings & Community Bankers of America

Savings & Community Bankers of America
900 19th St. NW
Washington, DC 20006
Ph: (202)857-3100   Fax: (202)659-4816

Annual, July. $55.00 for members; $95.00 for nonmembers. Covers about 2,000 community banks and savings and loan associations; related state and regional trade organizations; other affiliated members. Entries include: For savings banks and savings and loan associations Name, address, phone, fax, names and titles of key personnel, year established, type of charter, name of insuring agency, type of ownership, whether a member of the Federal Home Loan Board system; financial data of assets and deposits. Arrangement: Classified by type of membership; community banks and savings and loan associations are then geographical. Indexes: Alphabetical.

★2099★ Dun & Bradstreet Reference Book of Corporate Managements

Dun & Bradstreet Information Services
Dun & Bradstreet Corp.
3 Sylvan Way
Parsippany, NJ 07054-3896
Ph: (201)605-6000   Fax: (201)605-6911
Fr: 800-526-0651

Annual, April. $785.00, lease basis; $635.00, for public libraries, lease basis. Covers nearly 200,000 presidents, directors, vice presidents, officers, and managers in 12,000 companies of greatest economic, marketing, and investment interests; those firms whose revenues are the highest in the United States. Arrangement: Alphabetical by company name. Indexes: Personal name (with abbreviated title and company affiliation), geographical, SIC code, advanced education institution, military affiliation.

★2100★ Employment Opportunities, USA

Washington Research Associates
1660 S. Albion, Ste. 390
Denver, CO 80222
Ph: (303)756-9038   Fax: (303)770-1945

Annual, quarterly updates. $184.00, includes quarterly updates. Publication includes: List of over 1,000 employment contacts in companies and agencies in the banking, arts, telecommunications, education, and 14 other industries and professions, including the federal government. Entries include: Company name, name of representative, address, description of products or services, hiring and recruiting practices, training programs, and year established. Principal content is industry overviews, carrer news, and employment opportunity information on 14 different job markets. Arrangement: Classified by industry. Indexes: Occupation.

★2101★ Moody's Bank and Finance Manual

Moody's Investors Service, Inc.
99 Church St.
New York, NY 10007
Ph: (212)553-0300   Fax: (212)553-4700
Fr: 800-342-5647

Annual, July; supplements in *Moody's Bank & Finance News Reports*. $1,475.00, per year, including supplements. Covers in four volumes, over 20,000 national, state, and private banks, savings and loans, mutual funds, unit investment trusts, and insurance and real estate companies in the United States. Entries include: Company name, headquarters and branch offices, phones, names and titles of principal executives, directors, history, Moody's rating, and extensive financial and statistical data. Arrangement: Classified by type of business. Indexes: Company name.

★2102★ National Bankers Association— Roster of Minority Banking Institutions

National Bankers Association
1802 T St. NW
Washington, DC 20009
Ph: (202)588-5432   Fax: (202)588-5443

Annual, October. $5.00. Covers about 140 banks owned or controlled by minority group persons or women. Entries include: Bank name, address, phone, name of one executive. Arrangement: Geographical.

★2103★ Polk Financial Institutions Directory

R. L. Polk & Co.
PO Box 305100
Nashville, TN 37230-5100
Ph: (615)889-3350   Fax: (615)885-3081
Fr: 800-827-2265

Semiannual. $303.75. Covers 15,000 banks and their branches; over 2,000 head offices, and 15,500 branches of savings and loan associations; over 5,500 credit unions with assets over $5 million; Federal Reserve System and other U.S. government and state government banking agencies; bank holding, commercial finance, and leasing companies; ocverage includes the United States, Canada, Mexico, and Central America. Arrangement: Geographical. Indexes: Alphabetical.

★2104★ Roster of Minority Financial Institutions

U.S. Department of the Treasury
401 14th St. SW, Rm. 523-C
Washington, DC 20227
Ph: (202)874-6846   Fax: (202)874-6907

Biennial. Free. Covers about 170 commercial, minority-owned and controlled financial institutions participating in the Department of the Treasury's Minority Bank Deposit Program. Entries include: Name of institution, name and title of chief officer, address, phone, fax. Arrangement: Geographical.

★2105★ Thomson Bank Directory

Thomson Financial Publishing
4709 W. Golf Rd., 6th Fl.
Skokie, IL 60076-1253
Ph: (708)676-9600   Fax: (708)933-8101
Fr: 800-321-3373

Semiannual, May and November. $369.00, for 4-volume set. Covers in four volumes, about 11,000 banks and 50,000 branches of United States banks, and 60,000 foreign banks and branches engaged in foreign banking; Federal Reserve system and other United States government and state government banking agencies; 500 largest North American and International commercial banks; paper and automated clearinghouses. Entries include: For domestic banks, bank name, address, phone, telex, cable, date established, routing number, charter type, bank holding company affiliation, memberships in Federal Reserve System and other banking organizations, principal officers by function performed, principal correspondent banks, and key financial data (deposits, etc.). For international banks, bank name, address, phone, fax, telex, cable, SWIFT address, transit or sort codes within home country, ownership, financial data, names and titles of key personnel, branch locations. For branches, bank name, address, phone, charter type, ownership, and other details comparable to domestic bank listings. Arrangement: Geographical. Indexes: Alphabetical, geographical.

★2106★ Who's Who in Finance and Industry

Marquis Who's Who
Reed Reference Publishing
121 Chanlon Rd.
New Providence, NJ 07974
Ph: (908)464-6800   Fax: (908)665-6688
Fr: 800-521-8110

Biennial, July of odd years. $249.95, plus $17.50 shipping. Covers over 24,500 individuals. Entries include: Name, home and office addresses, personal, career, and family data; civic and political activities; memberships, publications, awards. Arrangement: Alphabetical.

HANDBOOKS AND MANUALS

★2107★ Opportunities in Banking Careers

VGM Career Horizons
4255 W. Touhy Ave.
Lincolnwood, IL 60646-1975
Ph: (847)679-5500   Fax: (847)679-2494
Fr: 800-323-4900

Adrian A. Paradis. 1993. $14.95; $11.95 (paper). 160 pages. Discusses banking opportunities in a variety of settings: commercial banks, savings and loans, finance companies, and mortgage banks.

★2108★ Opportunities in Hospital Administration Careers

VGM Career Horizons
4255 W. Touhy Ave.
Lincolnwood, IL 60646-1975
Ph: (847)679-5500   Fax: (847)679-2494
Fr: 800-323-4900

I. Donald Snook. 1989. $14.95; $11.95 (paper). 160 pages. Discusses opportunities for administrators in a variety of management settings: hospital, department, clinic, group practice, HMO, mental health, and extended care facilities.

EMPLOYMENT AGENCIES AND SEARCH FIRMS

★2109★ Accountants Overload Group

10990 Wilshire Blvd.
Los Angeles, CA 90024-3913
Ph: (213)629-2800

Employment agency.

★2110★ Addington Personnel Services

2401 Fountainview, Ste.104
Houston, TX 77057
Ph: (713)780-8810

Employment agency. Places individuals in regular or temporary positions.

★2111★ Best Personnel Services

8901 State Line Rd.
Kansas City, MO 64114-3200
Ph: (816)361-3100

Employment agency. Fills openings on a regular or temporary basis. Office also located in Independence, MO.

★2112★ Employment Advisors

526 Nicollet Mall
Minneapolis, MN 55402-0521
Ph: (612)339-0521

Employment agency. Also located in Bloomington, Minnesota. Places candidates in variety of fields.

★2113★ Financial Professionals

4100 Spring Valley Rd.
Farmers Branch, TX 75244-3618
Ph: (214)991-8999

Executive search consultants.

★2114★ Jim King and Associates

1301 Gulf Life Dr., Ste. 1901
Jacksonville, FL 32207-9062
Ph: (904)398-5464

Employment agency.

★2115★ Kanon Personnel Inc.

8 W. 40th St., 11th Fl.
New York, NY 10018-3994
Ph: (212)391-2610

Employment agency.

★2116★ The Murphy Group

1211 W. 22nd St., Ste. 221
Oak Brook, IL 60521-2115
Ph: (708)574-2840

Employment agency. Places personnel in a variety of positions.

★2117★ Riethmiller and Associates

8044 Montgomery Rd.
Cincinnati, OH 45236-2919
Ph: (513)793-7373   Fax: (513)793-6834

Employment agency.

★2118★ Source Finance

5580 LBJ Fwy., Ste. 300
Dallas, TX 75240
Ph: (214)385-3002   Fax: (214)717-0075

Executive search firm. Many affiliate offices located in most major cities throughout the U.S.

OTHER SOURCES

★2119★ American Bankers Association (ABA)

1120 Connecticut Ave. NW
Washington, DC 20036
Ph: (202)663-5000   Fax: (202)663-7533

Members: Members are principally commercial banks and trust companies; combined assets of members represent approximately 90% of the U.S. banking industry; approximately 94% of members are community banks with less than $500 million in assets. **Purpose:** Seeks to enhance the role of commerical bankers as preeminent providers of financial services through communications, research, legal action, lobbying of federal legislative and regulatory bodies, and education and training programs. Serves as spokesperson for the banking industry; facilitates exchange of information among members. **Activities:** Maintains the American Institute of Banking, an industry-sponsored adult education program. Conducts educational and training programs for bank employees and officers through a wide range of banking schools and national conferences. Maintains liaison with federal bank regulators; submits draft legislation and lobbies Congress on issues affecting commercial banks; testifies before congressional committees; represents members in U.S. postal rate proceedings. Serves as secretariat of the International Monetary Conference and the Financial Institutions Committee for the American National Standards Institute. Files briefs and lawsuits in major court cases affecting the industry. Conducts teleconferences with state banking associations on such issues as regulatory compliance; works to build consensus and coordinate activities of leading bank and financial service trade groups.

★2120★ Associated Credit Bureaus (ACB)

1090 Vermont Ave. NW, No. 200
Washington, DC 20005-4905
Ph: (202)371-0910   Fax: (202)371-0134

Members: International association of credit reporting and collection service offices. **Activities:** Maintains hall of fame and biographical archives; conducts specialized educational programs. Offers computerized services and compiles statistics.

★2121★ Credit Professionals International (CPI)

50 Crestwood Exec. Center
St. Louis, MO 63126
Ph: (314)842-6280   Fax: (314)842-6310

Members: Individuals employed in credit or collection departments of business firms or professional offices. **Activities:** Conducts educational program in credit work. Sponsors Career Club composed of members who have been involved in credit work at least 25 years.

★2122★ Credit Union Executives Society (CUES)

6410 Enterprise Ln., Ste. 300
Madison, WI 53719-1143
Ph: (608)271-2664   Fax: (608)271-2303
Fr: 800-252-2664

Purpose: Serves the professional development and competency enhancement needs of credit union chief executives and their vice presidents. Supports related credit union board development and its contribution to executvie effectiveness. Encourages senior management development.

★2123★ Direct Marketing Credit Association (DMCA)

Heritage House
2451 Atrium Way
Nashville, TN 37214
Ph: (615)391-2968

Members: Company representatives of the credit and marketing and/or credit and operational fields. **Purpose:** Informs members of matters concerning credit, collections, operational areas, and state and federal legislation dealing with the mail order industry. Provides speakers from industry, federal and state government, and the postal system. Conducts forums for discussion and annual facility tours.

★2124★ International Credit Association (ICA)

243 N. Lindbergh Blvd.
St. Louis, MO 63141
Ph: (314)991-3030   Fax: (314)991-3029

Members: Credit executives and professionals. **Activities:** Conducts educational seminars and conferences; offers group insurance plans. Through its Society of Certified Credit Executives , gives specific designations to members meeting its professional certification program requirements. Sponsors National Credit Education Week. Maintains speakers' bureau.

★2125★ National Association of Credit Management (NACM)

8815 Centre Park Dr.
Columbia, MD 21045
Ph: (410)740-5560   Fax: (410)740-5574

Members: Credit and financial executives representing manufacturers, wholesalers, financial institutions, insurance companies, utilities, and other businesses interested in business credit. **Purpose:** Promotes sound credit practices and legislation. Conducts Graduate School of Credit and Financial Management at Dartmouth College, Hanover, NH.

★2126★ Robert Morris Associates - Association of Bank Loan and Credit Officers (RMA)

1 Liberty Pl.
1650 Market St., Ste. 2300
Philadelphia, PA 19103
Ph: (215)851-9100   Fax: (215)851-9206

Members: Commercial and savings banks and savings and loan institutions represented by more than 15,000 commercial loan and credit officers. **Activities:** Conducts research and professional development activities in areas of loan administration, asset management, and commercial lending and credit to increase professionalism. Named in honor of Robert Morris (1734-1806), a financier and politician. Provides Mentor training curriculum for commercial lending professionals. From more than 90,000 financial statements supplied by member institutions, annually compiles the Statement Studies containing average composite balance sheets for more than 360 different lines of business in manufacturing, wholesaling, retailing, and contracting.

Dancers and Choreographers

Sources of Help-Wanted Ads

★2127★ ARTJOB

Western States Arts Federation
236 Montezuma Ave.
Santa Fe, NM 87501
Ph: (505)988-1166

Biweekly. $45.00, for 24-issue subscription. Covers national full- and part-time positions and temporary paid positions in visual, performing, and literary arts, arts education, and general arts administration, competitions, internships, conferences. Entries include: Job title, salary, description of responsibilities, qualifications, application procedure and deadline, name and address of contact. Arrangement: Classified by field.

★2128★ Billboard

BPI Communications
1515 Broadway, 11th Fl.
New York, NY 10036
Ph: (212)536-5167   Fax: (212)536-5351
Fr: 800-274-4100

Weekly. $229.00/year. International magazine of music and home entertainment geared toward professionals in the music and home video industries and related fields.

★2129★ Daily Variety

Cahners Business Newspapers
5700 Wilshire Blvd., Ste. 120
Los Angeles, CA 90036
Ph: (213)857-6600   Fax: (213)857-0494

Daily (morn.). Global entertainment newspaper (tabloid).

★2130★ Dance Magazine

33 W. 60th St.
New York, NY 10023-7990
Ph: (212)245-9050   Fax: (212)956-6487

Monthly. $34.95/year for individuals. Performing arts magazine featuring all forms of dance with profiles, news, photos, reviews of performances, and information on books, videos, films, schools, health, and technique.

★2131★ Strategies

American Alliance for Health, Physical Education, Recreation, and Dance
1900 Association Dr.
Reston, VA 22091
Ph: (703)476-3495   Fax: (703)476-9527

$20.00/year for members; $40.00/year for individuals; $50.00/year for libraries. Journal providing practical, hands-on information to physical educators and coaches.

★2132★ Variety

Cahners Publishing Co.
249 W. 17th St.
New York, NY 10011
Ph: (212)645-0067   Fax: (212)463-6410

Weekly (Mon.). Newspaper (tabloid) reporting on theatre, television, radio, music, records, and movies.

Placement and Job Referral Services

★2133★ American Dance Guild (ADG)

31 W. 21st St., 3rd Fl.
New York, NY 10018
Ph: (212)627-3790   Fax: (212)675-9657

Members: Teachers, performers, historians, critics, writers, and students in the field of dance, including ballet, modern dance, modern jazz dance, tap dance, and ethnological dance forms. **Purpose:** Initiates programs of national significance in the field. **Activities:** Maintains speakers' bureau; operates career counseling service and Job Express Registry, a monthly job listing for people looking for work in the dance field.

★2134★ Association of Laban Movement Analysts (ALMA)

11 E. 4th St., 3rd Fl.
New York, NY 10003
Ph: (212)477-4299   Fax: (212)477-3702

Members: Anthropologists, choreographers, dancers, dance instructors, actors, movement researchers, physical therapists, dance therapists, psychotherapists, management consultants, physical educators, and sports trainers. **Purpose:** Seeks to foster communication among Laban Movement Analysts throughout the country. Informs and demonstrates to other professionals the benefits of Laban Movement Analysis in their respective fields. **Activities:** Provides job referrals and some job placement assistance.

★2135★ Choreographers Guild (CG)

256 S. Robertson
Beverly Hills, CA 90211
Ph: (310)275-2533

Purpose: Choreographers united to promote their professional status and establish criteria for their responsibilities, salaries, and credentials. **Activities:** Maintains library of records, videotapes, and Labanotations. Bestows awards; operates placement service, hall of fame, and biographical archives. Compiles statistics; conducts research.

★2136★ Choreographers Theatre (CT)

94 Chambers St.
New York, NY 10007
Ph: (212)227-9067

Purpose: Provides a wide variety of production, administrative, management, and employment services to the dance and arts community. Serves as the in-residence Dance Department of the New School for Social Research in New York City.

★2137★ Dance Notation Bureau (DNB)

31 W. 21st St., 3rd Fl.
New York, NY 10010
Ph: (212)807-7899

Purpose: Documents and preserves dance works through the use of graphic notation. Awards certification for all levels of Labanotation, Teacher of Labanotation, and Professional Notator. Conducts research into movement-related analysis techniques and programs. **Activities:** Maintains placement service; assists choreographers in copyrighting, licensing, and restaging of their dance works. Offers dance reconstruction service to members.

★2138★ Institute of American Indian Arts (IAIA)

PO Box 20007
Santa Fe, NM 87504
Ph: (505)988-6463   Fax: (505)988-6446

Purpose: Federally chartered private institution. Offers learning opportunities in the arts and crafts to Native American youth (Indian, Eskimo, or Aleut). Emphasis is placed upon Indian traditions as the basis for creative expression in fine arts including painting, sculpture, museum studies, creative writing, printmaking, photography, communications, design, and dance, as well as training in metal crafts, jewelry, ceramics, textiles, and various traditional crafts. Students are encouraged to identify with their heritage and to be aware of themselves as members of a race rich in architecture, the fine arts, music, pageantry, and the humanities. All programs are based on elements of the Native American cultural heritage that emphasize differences between Native American and non-Native American cultures. **Activities:** Provides placement service. Sponsors Indian arts-oriented junior college offering Associate of Fine Arts degrees in various fields as well as seminars, an exhibition program, and traveling exhibits. Maintains extensive library, museum, and biographical archives.

★2139★ International Theatrical Arts Society (ITAA)

3101 N. Fitzhugh, Ste. 301
Dallas, TX 75204
Ph: (214)528-6112

Purpose: Theatrical agencies working to book entertainers and international acts into all live music venues. **Activities:** Provides placement service; conducts educational seminars.

★2140★ National Council for Culture and Art (NCCA)

1600 Broadway, Ste. 611C
New York, NY 10019
Ph: (212)757-7933

Members: Artists, civic and business leaders, professional performers, and visual arts organizations. **Purpose:** To provide exposure and employment opportunities for rural Americans, disabled Americans, and other minorities including blacks, Hispanics, American Indians, and European-Americans. Sponsors arts programs and spring and fall concert series. Operates Opening Night, a cable television show. Bestows annual Monarch Award and President's Award, and sponsors annual Monarch Scholarship Program. **Activities:** Offers children's and placement services; conducts charitable program; maintains hall of fame. Plans to conduct Minority Playwrights Forum, Dance Festival U.S.A., Vocal and Instrumental Competition, Film and Video Festival, and Concerts U.S.A.

★2141★ National Dance Association (NDA)

1900 Association Dr.
Reston, VA 22091
Ph: (703)476-3436   Fax: (703)476-9527
Fr: 800-321-0789

Members: Dancers, choreographers, dance educators, therapists, and arts administrators. **Purpose:** Promotes the development of sound philosophies and policies for dance as education through conferences, convention programs, special projects, and publications. Acts as advocate for better dance education programs through liaison activities with government, foundations, and special agencies. **Activities:** Provides reports and publications on dance research, career opportunities, current information on dance education, professional preparation, and certification. Maintains oral history archives of leaders in dance. Makes consultant referrals. **E-Mail:** nda@aahpend.org.

★2142★ United States National Institute of Dance (USNID)

38 S. Arlington Ave.
PO Box 245
East Orange, NJ 07019
Ph: (201)673-9225

Members: Participants include dance teachers, students, colleges and universities, dance companies, and local and international dance teachers' organizations. **Purpose:** Seeks to: provide dance teachers with international variations and techniques for improving artistic qualities and teaching methods; establish a uniform method of teaching all forms of dance at the highest professional level; provide an international network of consultation and counseling services for dance teachers and dancers. **Activities:** Offers placement and children's services; sponsors competitions. Conducts demonstrations, lectures, and certificate correspondence courses.

★2143★ World Congress of Teachers of Dancing (WCTD)

38 S. Arlington Ave.
PO Box 245
East Orange, NJ 07019
Ph: (201)673-9225

Members: A division of the United States National Institute of Dance. Colleges, universities, professional dance schools, and teachers of dancing. **Purpose:** Seeks to maintain global standards of excellence in dance. **Activities:** Maintains placement service. Conducts educational programs and examinations; certifies teachers of dancing. Researches and disseminates information on the history and status of dance from local to international levels. Bestows honorary degrees, including Professor of Dance, Companion of Dance, and Danseur/Premier Danseuse Supreme.

EMPLOYER DIRECTORIES AND NETWORKING LISTS

★2144★ *Contemporary Theatre, Film, and Television*

Gale Research
835 Penobscot Bldg.
Detroit, MI 48226-4094
Ph: (313)961-2242   Fax: (313)961-6083
Fr: 800-877-GALE

Annual. $125.00. Covers in 12 volumes, more than 6,500 leading and up-and-coming performers, directors, writers, producers, designers, managers, choreographers, technicians, composers, executives, and dancers in the United States and Great Britain. Each volume includes updated biographies for people listed in previous volumes and in *Who's Who in the Theatre*, which this series has superseded. Entries include: Name, agent and/or office addresses, personal and career data; stage, film, and television credits; writings, awards, other information. Arrangement: Alphabetical. Indexes: Cumulative name index also covers entries in *Who's Who in the Theatre* editions 1-17 and in *Who Was Who in the Theatre*.

★2145★ *Dancing Studios/Instruction Directory*

American Business Directories, Inc.
American Business Information, Inc.
5711 S. 86th Cir.
Omaha, NE 68127
Ph: (402)593-4600   Fax: (402)331-1505

Annual. $900.00, U.S. edition. Number of listings: 12,621 (U.S. edition); 1,058 (Canadian edition). Entries include: Name, address, phone (including area code), size of advertisement, year first in Yellow Pages, name of owner or manager, number of employees. Compiled from telephone company Yellow Pages, nationwide. Arrangement: Geographical.

★2146★ *Directory of Minority Arts Organizations*

Civil Rights Division
National Endowment for the Arts
1100 Pennsylvania Ave. NW, Rm. 812
Washington, DC 20506
Ph: (202)682-5454   Fax: (202)682-5674

Irregular, latest edition February 1987. Free. Covers almost 1,000 performing groups, presenters, galleries, art and media centers, literary organizations, and community centers with significant arts programming that have leadership and constituency that is predominantly Asian-American, African-American, Hispanic, Native American, or multi-racial. Entries include: Organization name, address, phone, name and title of contact, description of activities. Arrangement: Geographical. Indexes: Organization name, activity.

★2147★ *Employment Opportunities, USA*

Washington Research Associates
1660 S. Albion, Ste. 390
Denver, CO 80222
Ph: (303)756-9038   Fax: (303)770-1945

Annual, quarterly updates. $184.00, includes quarterly updates. Publication includes: List of over 1,000 employment contacts in companies and agencies in the banking, arts, telecommunications, education, and 14 other industries and professions, including the federal government. Entries include: Company name, name of representative, address, description of products or services, hiring and recruiting practices, training programs, and year established. Principal content is industry overviews, career news, and employment opportunity information on 14 different job markets. Arrangement: Classified by industry. Indexes: Occupation.

★2148★ Musical America's International Directory of the Performing Arts

K-III Directory Corp.
424 W. 33rd St., 11th Fl.
New York, NY 10001
Ph: (212)714-3100   Fax: (212)714-3157
Fr: 800-221-5488

Annual, December. $90.00, (1992 ed.). Covers U.S., Canadian, and international orchestras, musicians, singers, performing arts series, dance and opera companies, festivals, contests, foundations and awards, publishers of music, artist managers, booking agents, music magazines, and service and professional music organizations. Entries include: Name of organization, institution, address, phone, fax, telex, key personnel; most entries include name of contact, manager, conductor, etc. For schools: Number of students and faculty. For orchestras: Number of concerts and seats. Arrangement: Geographical. Indexes: Alphabetical and by category.

★2149★ New York Casting and Survival Guide

Peter Glenn Publications
42 W. 38th St., Ste. 802
New York, NY 10018-6210
Ph: (212)869-2020   Fr: 800-223-1254

Annual, September. $15.95. Covers about 10,000 services and facilities for actors, models, and performers in the New York area, including agents in New York and Los Angeles, theaters, producers and casting agencies, casting personnel in advertising agencies, music clubs, typing services, schools, unions, health food stores, apartment and roommate referral agencies. Entries include: Company name, address, phone, and contact. Arrangement: Classified by service.

★2150★ Performing Arts Career Directory

Gale Research
835 Penobscot Bldg.
Detroit, MI 48226-4094
Ph: (313)961-2242   Fax: (313)961-6083
Fr: 800-877-GALE

First edition March 1994. $34.00; $17.95(paper). Covers over 360 organizations in the performing arts offering entry-level positions and internships, including commercial and nonprofit performing arts centers, companies, and festivals; Broadway, Off-Broadway, regional and community theater companies; music ensembles; dance companies and troupes; and theater production companies. Also lists sources of help-wanted ads, professional associations, producers of videos, databases, career guides, and professional guides and handbooks. Entries include: For employers: Name, address, phone, fax, description, names and titles of key personnel, number of employees, average number of entry-level positions available, human resources contact, description of internship opportunities including contact, type and number available, application procedures, qualifications, and duties. For others: Name or title, address, phone, description. Paperback edition is available from Visible Ink Press. Arrangement: Employers

are alphabetical; others are classified by type of resource. Indexes: Name and keyword.

★2151★ Regional Theater Directory

American Theatre Works, Inc.
PO Box 519
Dorset, VT 05251
Ph: (802)867-2223   Fax: (802)867-0144

Annual, May. $15.95. Covers regional theater companies with employment opportunities in acting, design, production, and management. Entries include: Company name, address, phone, name and title of contact; type of company, activities, and size of house; whether union affiliated, whether nonprofit or commercial; year established; hiring procedure and number of positions hired annually, season; description of stage; internships, description of artistic policy and audience. Arrangement: Geographical. Indexes: Company name, type of play produced.

★2152★ Stern's Performing Arts Directory

Dance Magazine Inc.
33 W. 60th St., 10th Fl.
New York, NY 10023
Ph: (212)245-8937   Fax: (212)956-6487
Fr: 800-458-2845

Annual, September. $65.00. Covers over 13,000 dance and classical music performing groups, managers and artists' representatives, support services presenting organizations, festivals funding sources, booking organizations, and dance schools. Entries include: Company, institution or personal name, address, phone, cable, telex, fax, names of key personnel, and brief descriptions of services offered. Arrangement: Classified by performing arts category as well as product or service.

★2153★ Summer Theater Directory

American Theatre Works, Inc.
PO Box 519
Dorset, VT 05251
Ph: (802)867-2223   Fax: (802)867-0144

Annual, December. $15.95. Covers summer theater companies that offer employment opportunities in acting, design, production, and management; summer theater training programs. Entries include: Company name, address, phone, name and title of contact; type of company, activities and size of house; whether union affiliated, whether nonprofit or commercial; year established; hiring procedure and number of positions hired annually, season; description of stage; internships; description of company's artistic goals and audience. Arrangement: Geographical. Indexes: Company name.

HANDBOOKS AND MANUALS

★2154★ Career Information Center

Macmillan Publishing Co.
200 Old Tappan Rd.
Old Tappan, NJ 07675
Ph: (609)461-6500   Fr: 800-223-2336

Visual Education Center Staff. Fifth edition, 1992. $229.00. This 13-volume set profiles

over 600 occupations. Each occupational profile describes job duties, educational requirements, how to get the job, advancement possibilities, employment outlook, working conditions, earnings and benefits, and where to write for more information.

★2155★ Career Opportunities in Theater and the Performing Arts

Facts on File, Inc.
11 Penn Plaza, 15th Fl.
New York, NY 10001-2006
Ph: (212)967-8800   Fax: 800-678-3633
Fr: 800-322-8755

Shelly Field. 1992. $29.95; $15.95 (paper). 256 pages. Offers a complete range of information about job opportunities in the performing arts.

★2156★ Careers for Culture Lovers and Other Artsy Types

VGM Career Horizons
4255 W. Touhy Ave.
Lincolnwood, IL 60646-1975
Ph: (847)679-5500   Fax: (847)679-2494
Fr: 800-323-4900

Marjorie Eberts and Margaret Gisler. 1994. $14.95; $9.95 (paper). Describes how to get work in a variety of fields related to art and culture. Opportunities include picture framer, curator, art restorer, symphony manager, disk jockey, music reviewer, dance teacher, choreographer, costume designer, theater manager, light designer, drama teacher, bookstore owner, interior decorator, antique store owner, and others.

★2157★ Dance: A Career for You

National Dance Association (NDA)
1900 Association Dr.
Reston, VA 22091-1599
Ph: (703)476-3436

Brochure. Free. 8 pages. Suggests career opportunities as a teacher, therapist, performer, recreation leader, and choreographer. Describes employment opportunities, personal qualifications, training, knowledge, and skills required for a career in dance.

★2158★ The Dancer's Complete Guide to Health Care and a Long Career

Bonus Books
160 E. Illinois St.
Chicago, IL 60611
Ph: (312)467-0580   Fr: 800-225-3775

Allan J. Ryan and Robert E. Stephens. 1989. $9.95. 224 pages. Contains advice on starting, maintaining, and extending a career in dance. Includes information on training, diet, nutrition, and preventing and treating injuries.

★2159★ Dancing . . . for a Living

Rafter Publishing
10800 Peachgrove St., Apt. 5
North Hollywood, CA 91601-4676
Ph: (818)766-6403   Fax: (818)506-7944

Don Mirault. 1994. $15.95 (paper).

★2160★ For the Working Artists: A Survival Guide for Performing, Visual and Media Artists Who Choose to Manage Their Own Careers

National Network for Artist Placement
935 West Ave. 37
Los Angeles, CA 90065
Ph: (213)255-3096

Judith Luther. Second edition, 1991. $30.00. 338 pages.

★2161★ The Harvard Guide to Careers in the Mass Media

Bob Adams, Inc.
260 Center St.
Holbrook, MA 02343
Ph: (617)767-8100   Fax: (617)767-0994
Fr: 800-872-5627

John Noble. 1989. $7.95. 202 pages. Each section of the book evaluates one media profession in depth and contains an industry profile, a career profile that describes positions available in that area, information about current salary ranges, industry-specific job-hunting tips and strategies, and a case study outlining the methods that were used in a successful job hunt.

★2162★ Jobs in Arts and Media Management: What They Are and How to Get One!

American Council for the Arts
1 E. 53rd St.
New York, NY 10022-4201
Ph: (212)223-2787   Fr: 800-321-4510

Stephen Langley and James Abruzzo. Revised edition, 1990. $21.95. 281 pages. Includes lists of about 150 sources of information on job opportunities in the arts, including organizations offering internships, job listings, graduate programs, and short-term study; professional groups concerned with theater, music, dance, opera, museum and gallery management, film, and telecommunication management. (Does not include popular music performing or music recording.) Entries include: For internships Organization name, address, phone, description, requirements. For job referral associations and periodicals - Association or publisher name, address, fields covered, services offered, turn-around time, average number of jobs, cost of subscription or dues, comments. Arrangement: Classified by type of source.

★2163★ The New York Agent Book

Sweden Press
Box 1612
Studio City, CA 91604
Ph: (818)995-4250

Third edition, 1992. $15.95. 250 pages.

★2164★ Opportunities in Performing Arts Careers

VGM Career Horizons
4255 W. Touhy Ave.
Lincolnwood, IL 60646-1975
Ph: (847)679-5500   Fax: (847)679-2494
Fr: 800-323-4900

Bonnie Bjorguine Bekken. 1991. $14.95; $11.95 (paper). Examines opportunities in classical and popular music; theater, television, and movie acting; classical and modern dance; performance art; and teaching and therapy careers. Assists aspiring performers with developing a portfolio and preparing for interviews, tests, and auditions.

OTHER SOURCES

★2165★ International Tap Association (ITA)

PO Box 356
Boulder, CO 80306
Ph: (303)443-7989   Fax: (303)449-7732

Members: Tap dancers, choreographers, teachers, scholars, students, and interested individuals. **Purpose:** Promotes the understanding, preservation, and development of tap dance as an art form. Encourages the creation of new performance venues, touring circuits, and presentation methods. **Activities:** Maintains biographical and video archives covering historical figures in tap dance. Publishes the ITA newsletter six times per year. Houses information clearing house for tap resources.

★2166★ National Directory of Arts Internships

National Network for Artist Placement
935 W. Ave. 37
Los Angeles, CA 90065
Ph: (213)222-4035   Fax: (213)222-4035

Biennial, odd years. $40.00, postpaid; payment with order. Covers Approximately 2,000 internship opportunities in dance, music, theater, art, design, film, and video. Entries include: Name of sponsoring organization, address, name of contact; description of positions available, eligibility requirements, stipend or salary (if any), application procedures. Arrangement: Classified by discipline, then geographical.

★2167★ Research in Dance: A Guide to Resources

G. K. Hall & Co., Inc.
PO Box 159
Thorndike, ME 04986
Ph: (207)948-2962   Fr: 800-343-2806

Published 1994. $50.00. Covers Approximately 100 dance collections and archives; dance publishers, book dealers, dance associations/organizations, bookstores specializing in dance literature; coverage is primarily of North America, with some international listings. Second section is bibliographic information on reference literature on dance. Entries include: For collections and archives: Name, size of repository, access policy, description of collection. For others: Name, address, phone. Arrangement: Classified by repository.

★2168★ Social Dance Instruction: Steps to Success

Human Kinetics Publishers
PO Box 5076
Champaign, IL 61825-5076
Ph: (217)351-5076   Fr: 800-747-4457

Judy P. Wright. 1995. $19.95 (paper).

Database Administrators

SOURCES OF HELP-WANTED ADS

★2169★ ACM Computing Surveys

Association for Computing Machinery
1515 Broadway, 17th Fl.
New York, NY 10036-9998
Ph: (212)869-7440   Fax: (212)869-0481

Quarterly. $17.00/year for individuals; $105.00/year for nonmembers;Journal presenting surveys and tutorials in computer science.

★2170★ ASIS Jobline

American Society for Information Science (ASIS)
8720 Georgia Ave., Ste. 501
Silver Spring, MD 20910
Ph: (301)495-0900

Monthly periodical provides job listings in information science.

★2171★ BYTE

McGraw-Hill, Inc.
1 Phoenix Mill Ln.
Peterborough, NH 03458
Ph: (603)924-9281   Fax: (603)924-2550
Fr: 800-232-2983

Monthly. Magazine covering microcomputing for major brands of hardware and software. Includes reviews, features, and technology news for experienced and knowledgeable purchasers and users of microcomputers.

★2172★ Captsule Job Listings

Publications and Communications, Inc.
12416 Hymeadow Dr.
Austin, TX 78750
Ph: (512)250-9023   Fax: (512)331-3900
Fr: 800-678-9724

Online database. Lists current job openings in the contract (temporary) technical services industry. Includes the Action Hot List, which provides information on job seekers. Includes employment opportunities in technical/professional engineering, computing, and design/drafting. Entries generally contain company name, address, and job opening.

★2173★ Communications of the ACM

Association for Computing Machinery
1515 Broadway 17th fl.
New York, NY 10036
Ph: (212)869-7440   Fax: (212)869-0481

Monthly. $32.00/year for individuals; $124.00/year for nonmembers. Computing news magazine.

★2174★ Communications Week

CMP Publications
PO Box 1094
Skokie, IL 60076
Ph: (708)647-6834

Weekly. $143.00/year. Magazine subtitled: "The Newspaper for Enterprise Networking."

★2175★ Computer

IEEE Computer Society
1730 Massachusetts Ave. NW
Washington, DC 20036
Ph: (202)371-0101

Monthly. Covers major trends in computer science and engineering.

★2176★ Computerworld

500 Old Connecticut Path
Framingham, MA 01701-9208
Ph: (508)872-0080   Fax: (508)879-7784
Fr: 800-669-1002

Weekly. $48.00/year; $6.00/issue. Newspaper for information systems management professionals.

★2177★ Database Programming and Design

Miller Freeman, Inc.
600 Harrison St.
San Francisco, CA 94107
Ph: (415)905-2200

Monthly. Computer magazine.

★2178★ Datamation

Cahners Publishing Co.
275 Washington St.
Newton, MA 02158-1630
Ph: (617)964-3030   Fax: (617)558-4470

Semimonthly. Magazine on computers and information processing.

★2179★ DBMS

Miller Freeman Publishing, Inc.
501 Galveston Dr.
Redwood City, CA 94063
Ph: (415)366-3600

Monthly. $24.00/year; $2.95/issue. Magazine for developers and users of client-server database applications.

★2180★ DEC Professional

Cardinal Business Media, Inc.
1300 Virginia Dr., Ste.400
Fort Washington, PA 19034
Ph: (215)643-8064   Fax: (215)643-3901

Monthly. Magazine covering Digital Equipment Corporation's computers and related products.

★2181★ Digital News and Review

Cahners Publishing Co.
275 Washington St.
Newton, MA 02158-1630
Ph: (617)964-3030   Fax: (617)558-4470

Semimonthly. Free to qualified subscribers.

★2182★ InformationWEEK

CMP Publications, Inc.
600 Community Dr.
Manhasset, NY 11030
Ph: (516)562-5000   Fax: (516)562-5055

Weekly. Magazine focusing on data and information processing news and strategies.

★2183★ Network World

161 Worcester Rd.
Framingham, MA 01701-9172
Ph: (508)875-6400

Weekly (Mon.). $95.00/year for individuals. The newsweekly of enterprise network computing.

★2184★ NEWS 3X/400

Duke Communications, Intl.
221 E. 29th St., Ste. 242
Loveland, CO 80538
Ph: (303)663-4700   Fax: (303)669-3016
Fr: 800-621-1544

Monthly. $119.00/year for individuals. Trade magazine for programmers and data processing managers who use IBM minicomputers (System/34, System/36, System/38, and AS/400).

★2185★ *UNIX Review*

Miller Freeman Publications, Inc.
600 Harrison St.
San Francisco, CA 94107
Ph: (415)905-2200

Monthly. Magazine for professional users of UNIX and UNIX-like systems.

EMPLOYER DIRECTORIES AND NETWORKING LISTS

★2186★ *Computer Directory*

Computer Directories, Inc.
13205 Cypress N. Houston Rd.
Cypress, TX 77429-3606
Ph: (713)955-9791   Fax: (713)955-9793
Fr: 800-234-4353

Annual, fall. Covers Approximately 130,000 computer installations; 19 separate volumes for Alaska/Hawaii, Connecticut/New Jersey, Dallas/Ft. Worth, Eastern Seaboard, Far Midwest, Houston, Illinois, Midatlantic, Midcentral, Mideast, Minnesota/Wisconsin, North Central, New England, New York Metro, Northwest, Ohio, Pennsylvania/West Virginia, Southeast, and Southwest Texas. Entries include: Company name, address, phone, fax, name and title of contact, hardware used, software application, operating system, programming language, computer graphics, networking system. Arrangement: Geographical. Indexes: Alphabetical, industry, hardware.

★2187★ *Computers and People—Computer Directory and Buyers' Guide Issue*

Berkeley Enterprises, Inc.
368 Crescent St., No. 2
Waltham, MA 02154-3804

Annual, October. $24.50, plus $1.00 shipping. Publication includes: List of over 3,600 companies offering hardware, software, and computing or data processing services; societies and associations in computer fields. Entries include: For companies: name, address, phone, products or services; some have name of principal executive or contact person, number of employees, year established, year information was verified. For organizations: name, address, phone, name of president or secretary. Arrangement: Alphabetical. Indexes: Product or service.

★2188★ *The Hidden Job Market: A Job Seeker's Guide to America's 2,000 Little-Known, Fastest-Growing High-Tech Companies*

Peterson's Guides, Inc.
202 Carnegie Center
PO Box 2123
Princeton, NJ 08543-2123
Ph: (609)243-9111   Fax: (609)243-9150
Fr: 800-338-3282

Annual, October. $16.95. Covers Approximately 2,000 technology firms with under 1,000 employees, which have added the most employees in the survey year. Entries include: Company name, address, phone, fax, name and title of contact, number of employees, year founded, number of employees added in last year, percentage of growth, line of business. Arrangement: Geographical by state, then by area code. Indexes: Alphabetical by industry.

★2189★ *How and Where to Get the Best Computer Jobs*

Information Resource Group
50495 Corporate Dr., Ste. 112
Shelby Township, MI 48315
Ph: (810)254-8500   Fax: (810)254-8500

Annual. $69.95. per directory. Publication includes: Listing of the top dataprocessing employers in United States and Canada. Information divided among 67 editions, according to state/province. Principal content of publication is hiring/interview tips, salary surveys. Entries include: Company name, address, phone, name and title of contact. Arrangement: Geographical.

★2190★ *Information Sources: The IIA Annual Directory*

Information Industry Association (IIA)
555 New Jersey Ave. NW, Ste. 800
Washington, DC 20001
Ph: (202)639-8262   Fax: (202)638-4403

Annual, November. $95.00. Covers more than 500 companies involved in the creation, distribution, and use of information products, services, and technology. Entries are prepared by companies described. Entries include: Company name, address, phone, names of executives, international partners, regional offices, trade and brand names, and description of products and services. Arrangement: Alphabetical. Indexes: Product, personal name, trade name, geographical, corporate parents, international and niche markets.

★2191★ *Northwest High Tech: Fast Facts on the $7 Billion Computer Industry of Washington, Oregon, Idaho, British Columbia, and Alberta*

Resolution Business Press
11101 NE 8th St., Ste. 208
Bellevue, WA 98004
Ph: (206)455-4611   Fax: (206)455-9143

Annual. $34.95. Covers over 1,800 computer-related companies in Washington, Oregon, and Idaho, and British Columbia and Alberta, Canada. Entries include: Company; name, address, phone, fax; toll-free number; names and titles of key personnel; product/service, programming languages, financial data, names and titles of key personnel, number of employees, operating systems, expansion plans (including hiring and site expansion plans), company market information, Standard Industrial Classification (SIC) code. Arrangement: Geographical, industry sector. Indexes: Company name, SIC.

★2192★ *Signal Magazine—AFCEA Source Book Issue*

Armed Forces Communications and Electronics Association (AFCEA)
4400 Fair Lakes Ct.
Fairfax, VA 22033-3899
Ph: (703)631-6191   Fax: (703)631-4693
Fr: 800-336-4583

Annual, January. $44.00, Included in subscription. Publication includes: List of member companies concerned with communications, design, production, maintenance and operation of communications, electronics, command and control, computers, intelligence systems and imagery. Entries include: Company name, address, phone, names and titles of key personnel, financial keys, trade and brand names, products or services, affiliations, description of organizational purpose, objectives. Arrangement: Alphabetical.

HANDBOOKS AND MANUALS

★2193★ *ACE the Technical Interview: How to Get Your Next Job in the Computer Industry*

The McGraw-Hill Companies
1221 Avenue of the Americas
New York, NY 10020
Ph: (212)512-2000   Fr: 800-262-4729

Michael Rothstein. 1994. $19.95 (paper).

★2194★ *Career Choices for the 90's for Students of Computer Science*

Walker and Company
435 Hudson St.
New York, NY 10014
Ph: (212)727-8300   Fax: (212)727-0984
Fr: 800-289-2553

Prepared by the Career Associates staff. 1990. $8.95. 166 pages. Discusses alternatives for students of computer science. Offers advice on how to break into the field and how to move up. Covers where and who the employers are, internship possibilities, and professional networking associations. Comprehensive guide to career and job search planning.

★2195★ *Career Portraits: Computers*

VGM Career Horizons
NTC Publishing Group
4255 W. Touhy Ave.
Lincolnwood, IL 60646-1975
Ph: (847)679-5500   Fax: (847)679-2494
Fr: 800-323-4900

Marjorie Eberts and Margaret Gisler. 1995. $13.95. 96 pages. Designed to capture the interest of middle school and reluctant readers.

★2196★ *Careers for Computer Buffs and Other Technological Types*

NTC Publishing Group
4255 W. Touhy Ave.
Lincolnwood, IL 60646-1975
Ph: (708)679-5500   Fax: (708)679-6375
Fr: 800-323-4900

Marjorie Eberts. 1994. $12.95; $9.95 (paper).

★2197★ Careers in Computer Fields

Rosen Publishing Group, Inc.
29 E 21st St.
New York, NY 10010
Ph: (212)777-3017   Fax: (212)777-0277
Fr: 800-237-9932

Joseph Weintraub. 1993. $14.95; $9.95 (paper).

★2198★ Careers in Computers

VGM Career Horizons
4255 W. Touhy Ave.
Lincolnwood, IL 60646-1975
Ph: (847)679-5500   Fax: (847)679-2494
Fr: 800-323-4900

Lila B. Stair. Second edition, 1995. $17.95; $13.95 (paper). Describes trends affecting computer careers and explores a wide range of job opportunities from programming to consulting. Provides job qualifications, salary data, job market information, personal and educational requirements, career paths, and the place of the job in the organizational structure. Offers advice on education, certification, and job search.

★2199★ Careers in Information Science

American Society for Information Science (ASIS)
8720 Georgia Ave., Ste. 501
Silver Spring, MD 20910
Ph: (301)495-0900

Free brochure describes career opportunities in information science, communications, computer science, and research.

★2200★ Computer Careers

Data Processing Management Association
505 Busse Hwy.
PArk Ridge, IL 60068
Ph: (708)825-8124

Free booklet.

★2201★ Computer Jobs Worldwide: Support Staff Plus Electronics Plus Telecommunications

Zinks International Career Guidance
PO Box 790
Richland, MI 49083
Ph: (313)584-7529

Richard M. Zink. 1995. $14.95 (paper).

★2202★ Computer Science and Related Fields

AMIDEAST
1100 17th St. NW
Washington, DC 20036-4601
Ph: (202)776-9600

$1.15. 4 pages. Describes career opportunities, educational programs, and additional sources of information.

★2203★ Covin's Mid-West Computer Job Guide

Vandamere Press
PO Box 5243
Arlington, VA 22205
Ph: (703)525-5488   Fax: (703)524-4105

Carol L. Covin. 1994. $13.95 (paper).

★2204★ Data Base Managers

Chronicle Guidance Publications, Inc.
66 Aurora St.
PO Box 1190
Moravia, NY 13118-1190
Ph: (315)497-0330   Fax: (315)497-3359
Fr: 800-622-7284

Chronicle Guidance Staff. 1991. $2.00. Provides concise career information and sources of additional information.

★2205★ Database Administrator

R & E Publishers
468 Auzerais Ave., Ste. A
San Jose, CA 95126
Ph: (408)977-0691

1995. $1.95. One of a series of booklets on careers that require two years or less of education and training.

★2206★ The Digital Frontier Job & Opportunity Finder

Moon Lake Media
PO Box 251466
Los Angeles, CA 90025
Ph: (310)535-2453

Don B. Altman. 1995. $24.95 (paper).

★2207★ Downsized but Not Out: How to Get Your Next Computer Job

The McGraw-Hill Companies
1221 Avenue of the Americas
New York, NY 10020
Ph: (212)512-2000   Fr: 800-262-4729

Alan Simon. 1994. $30.00; $17.95 (paper).

★2208★ Encyclopedia of Careers and Vocational Guidance

J. G. Ferguson Publishing Co.
200 W. Monroe, Ste. 250
Chicago, IL 60606
Ph: (312)580-5480

William E. Hopke. Ninth edition, 1993. $129.95; $199.95 (CD-ROM). Four-volume set that profiles 900 occupations and describes job trends in 71 industries. Includes career description, educational requirements, history of the job, methods of entry, advancement, employment outlook, earnings, conditions of work, social and psychological factors, and sources of further information. Contains career and employment information for this field.

★2209★ Exploring Careers in the Computer Field

Rosen Publishing Group, Inc.
29 E. 21st St.
New York, NY 10010
Ph: (212)777-3017   Fax: (212)777-0277
Fr: 800-237-9932

Joseph Weintraub. Revised edition, 1993. Discusses entry into the field, salaries, future trends, and offers job search advice. Surveys the newest growth areas in the computer industry including artificial intelligence, desktop publishing, and personal computers.

★2210★ Opportunities in Computer Science Careers

VGM Career Horizons
4255 W. Touhy Ave.
Lincolnwood, IL 60646-1975
Ph: (847)679-5500   Fax: (847)679-2494
Fr: 800-323-4900

Julie Lepick Kling. 1995. $14.95; $11.95 (paper). Discusses how to enter the field and build a career. Illustrated.

★2211★ Opportunities in Information Systems Careers

VGM Career Horizons
4255 W. Touhy Ave.
Lincolnwood, IL 60646-1975
Ph: (847)679-5500   Fax: (847)679-2494
Fr: 800-323-4900

Douglas B. Hoyt. 1991. $14.95; $11.95 (paper). Describes prospects in information specialties such as computer operations, programming, and documentation; telecommunications; records management; micrographics; and project planning and management. Offers advice about job hunting and advancement.

★2212★ Peterson's Job Opportunities in Engineering and Technology 1996

Peterson's
PO Box 2123
Princeton, NJ 08543-2123
Ph: (609)243-9111   Fax: (609)243-9150
Fr: 800-338-3282

Compiled by the Peterson's staff. Annual. $19.95 paperback. 432 pages. Profiles 2,000 high-tech companies looking primarily for technical personnel in such fields as biotechnology, telecommunications, software, computers and peripherals, defense, and aerospace. Contains job-search strategies and career options to help match education and expertise to the job market. Indexed geographically, by industry, and by hiring needs.

★2213★ Your Opportunities in Computers

Energeia Publishing, Inc.
PO Box 985
Salem, OR 97308
Ph: (503)362-1480   Fax: (503)362-2123

John Tribbett. 1994. $2.00 (paper).

EMPLOYMENT AGENCIES AND SEARCH FIRMS

★2214★ Audit Data Search Ltd.

535 Broadhollow Rd.
Melville, NY 11747
Ph: (516)454-6666   Fax: (516)454-1595

Executive search firm.

★2215★ Career Development Services

14 Franklin St., Ste. 1200
Rochester, NY 14604
Ph: (716)325-2275   Fax: (716)325-2133

Employment agency.

★2216★ **Cavan Systems Ltd.**
10 Cuttermill Rd.
Great Neck, NY 11021
Ph: (516)487-7777   Fax: (516)487-7857

Executive search firm.

★2217★ **Huntington Personnel Consultants, Inc.**
PO Box 1077
Huntington, NY 11743-0640
Ph: (516)549-8888   Fax: (516)549-3012

Employment agency.

★2218★ **Professional Recruiters and Temporaries**
220 E. 3900 S., #9
Salt Lake City, UT 84107
Ph: (801)268-9940

Employment agency.

★2219★ **Version 2.0 Corp.**
303 Congress St.
Boston, MA 02210
Ph: (617)439-0321

Executive search firm.

OTHER SOURCES

★2220★ **Association for Systems Management (ASM)**
1433 W. Bagley Rd.
PO Box 38370
Cleveland, OH 44138-0370
Ph: (216)243-6900   Fax: (216)234-2930

Members: International professional organization of executives and specialists in management information systems serving business, commerce, education, government, and the military. **Purpose:** Expresses concern with communications, electronics, equipment, forms control, human relations, organization, procedure writing, and systems applications. **Activities:** Offers seminars, conferences, and courses in all phases of information systems and management.

★2221★ **Business Database Finder**
The Information Advisor
300 McLeod Ave.
Missoula, MT 59801
Ph: (406)728-1171

Annual, October. $99.00. Covers Business databases and online hosts. Entries include: Name of database, description of product/ service. Arrangement: Classified by by database type. Indexes: Database name.

★2222★ **Career Encounters: Information Science and Technology**
Cambridge Career Products
PO Box 2153
Dept. CC15
Charleston, WV 25328-2153
Ph: (304)744-9323   Fax: (304)744-9351
Fr: 800-468-4227

Video. $99.95. 25 minutes. Professionals shown in a variety of settings discuss different aspects of their careers.

★2223★ **The Computer Industry Almanac**
Computer Industry Almanac
225 Allen Way
Incline Village, NV 89451
Ph: (702)831-2288

Annual. $63.00. Also available on CD-ROM, $63.00. A compendium of information on the computer industry compiled from newsletters, reports, and magazines.

★2224★ **Computer Salary Survey and Career Planning Guide**
Source EDP
120 Broadway, Ste. 1010
New York, NY 10271
Ph: (212)557-8611

Annual. Describes career paths in the computer field and trends in the computer field. Lists job titles. Charts salaries by job titles, years of experience, and industry.

★2225★ **Gale Guide to Internet Databases**
Gale Research
835 Penobscot Bldg.
Detroit, MI 48226-4094
Ph: (313)961-2242   Fax: (313)961-6083
Fr: 800-877-GALE

$95.00. Covers 2,000 authoritative databases available on the Internet focusing on government, academic, research and education. Entries include: Gopher, telnet, ftp, e-mail and URL addresses.

★2226★ **InfoWorld**
PO Box 1172
Skokie, IL 60076
Ph: (708)647-7925

Weekly. $130.00/year. Magazine subtitled: "The Voice of Personal Computing in the Enterprise."

★2227★ **Link-Up—New Lines Section**
Learned Information, Inc.
143 Old Marlton Pike
Medford, NJ 08055-8750
Ph: (609)654-6266   Fax: (609)654-4309

Bimonthly. $3.00, per issue. Publication includes: List of companies offering new online services, databases, and computer software and hardware. Entries include: Company name, address, phone, description of product, price. Arrangement: Classified by product.

★2228★ **Resumes for Computer Careers**
VGM Career Horizons
NTC Publishing Group
4255 W. Touhy Ave.
Lincolnwood, IL 60646-1975
Ph: (847)679-5500   Fax: (847)679-2494
Fr: 800-323-4900

1996. $9.95. 160 pages. Offers complete instructions on producing quality resumes and cover letters for all areas and levels of the computer industry.

Dental Assistants

SOURCES OF HELP-WANTED ADS

★2229★ Dental Hygiene

American Dental Hygienists Association
444 N. Michigan Ave., Ste. 3400
Chicago, IL 60611
Ph: (312)440-8900   Fax: (312)440-8929

Six issues/year. $40.00/year; $5.00/issue.
Professional Journal on dental hygiene.

★2230★ Hawaiian Dental Journal

1360 S. Beretania
Honolulu, HI 96814
Ph: (808)528-2376   Fr: 800-591-6832

Bimonthly.

★2231★ Journal of the California Dental Association

California Dental Association
1201 'K' St. Mall
PO Box 13749
Sacramento, CA 95853
Ph: (916)443-0505   Fax: (916)443-2943

Monthly. $24.00/year; $60.00/year for non-members; $6.00 for single issue. Professional magazine for dentists.

★2232★ Journal of Dental Research

American Association for Dental Research
1619 Duke St.
Alexandria, VA 22314
Ph: (703)548-0066

Monthly. $350.00/year for individuals; $360.00/year for other countries. Dental science journal.

PLACEMENT AND JOB REFERRAL SERVICES

★2233★ American Medical Technologists (AMT)

710 Higgins Rd.
Park Ridge, IL 60068
Ph: (708)823-5169   Fax: (708)823-0458
Fr: 800-275-1268

Members: National professional registry of medical laboratory technologists, technicians, medical assistants, dental assistants, and phlebotomists. **Activities:** Maintains job information service. Sponsors AMT Institute for Education, which has developed continuing education programs.

★2234★ American Public Health Association (APHA)

1015 15th St. NW
Washington, DC 20005
Ph: (202)789-5600   Fax: (202)789-5681

Members: Professional organization of physicians, nurses, educators, academicians, environmentalists, epidemiologists, new professionals, social workers, health administrators, optometrists, podiatrists, pharmacists, dentists, nutritionists, health planners, other community and mental health specialists, and interested consumers. **Purpose:** Seeks to protect and promote personal, mental, and environmental health. **Activities:** Services include: promulgation of standards; establishment of uniform practices and procedures; development of the etiology of communicable diseases; research in public health; exploration of medical care programs and their relationships to public health. Sponsors job placement service.

★2235★ American School Health Association (ASHA)

7263 State Rte. 43
PO Box 708
Kent, OH 44240
Ph: (216)678-1601   Fax: (216)678-4526

Members: School physicians, school nurses, dentists, nurses, nutritionists, health educators, dental hygienists, school-based professionals, and public health workers. **Purpose:** Promotes comprehensive and constructive school health programs including the teaching of health, health services, and promotion of a healthful school environment. **Activities:** Offers a professional referral service, classroom teaching aids, and professional reference materials. Conducts research programs; maintains placement service; compiles statistics. Sponsors foreign travel study tour.

EMPLOYER DIRECTORIES AND NETWORKING LISTS

★2236★ American Academy of Pediatric Dentistry—Membership Roster

American Academy of Pediatric Dentistry
211 E. Chicago Ave., Ste. 1036
Chicago, IL 60611
Ph: (312)337-2169

Annual, November. $500.00. Covers 3,700 pediatric dentists in practice, teaching, and research. Entries include: Name, address, phone. Arrangement: Alphabetical. Indexes: Geographical.

★2237★ American Dental Directory

American Dental Association
211 E. Chicago Ave.
Chicago, IL 60611
Ph: (312)440-2500   Fax: (312)440-3542
Fr: 800-947-4746

Annual, January. $154.00. Covers over 170,000 dentists. Also includes list of active and historic dental schools, dental organizations, and state dental examining boards. Entries include: Name, address, year of birth, educational data, specialty, membership status. Arrangement: Geographical. Indexes: Alphabetical.

★2238★ Dentists Directory

American Business Directories, Inc.
American Business Information, Inc.
5711 S. 86th Cir.
Omaha, NE 68127
Ph: (402)593-4600   Fax: (402)331-1505

Annual. $4,860.00, U.S. edition; $685.00, (Canad. ed). Entries include: Name, address, phone (including area code), size of advertisement, code indicating specialty, year first in Yellow Pages, name of owner or manager, number of employees. Regional editions available. Compiled from telephone company Yellow Pages, nationwide. Arrangement: Geographical.

★2239★ **International Association of Oral Pathologists–Membership List**
International Association of Oral Pathologists
c/o Dr. Peter R. Morgan
Department of Oral Medicine and Pathology
Guy's Hospital Dental School
London SE1 9RT, England
Ph: 71 9554288

Annual. Free. Covers 325 dentists who have had postgraduate instruction in oral pathology. Entries include: Personal name, address. Arrangement: Geographical.

★2240★ **International Association for Orthodontics and American Orthodontic Society—Membership Directory**
International Association for Orthodontics
1100 Lake St., No. 240
Oak Park, IL 60301
Ph: (708)445-0320   Fax: (708)445-0321

Annual, June. $45.00. Covers 4,000 general and children's dentists specializing in prevention or correction of facial and jaw irregularities. Entries include: Name, office address and phone, orthodontic techniques practiced. Arrangement: Geographical. Indexes: Personal name.

★2241★ **Washington Physicians Directory**
National Directories, Inc.
PO Box 4436
Silver Spring, MD 20914
Ph: (301)384-1506   Fax: (301)384-6854

Annual, April. $33.50, payment with order. Covers 8,400 physicians in private practice or on full-time staff at hospitals in the Washington, DC, metropolitan area. Entries include: Name, medical school and year of graduation; up to four office addresses with phone numbers for each; up to four medical specialties, Unique Physician Identification Numbers (UPIN). Arrangement: Alphabetical. Indexes: Geographical (within medical specialty); foreign language.

HANDBOOKS AND MANUALS

★2242★ **Careers in Dentistry: Is It for You**
DSH Publishing Co.
9433 Elmhurst Ct.
Brentwood, TN 37027
Ph: (615)371-1927

S. Adele Doherty. 1992. $25.00.

★2243★ **Careers in Health Care**
VGM Career Horizons
4255 W. Touhy Ave.
Lincolnwood, IL 60646-1975
Ph: (847)679-5500   Fax: (847)679-2494
Fr: 800-323-4900

Barbara M. Swanson. 1995. $17.95; $13.95 (paper). Describes job duties, work settings, salaries, licensing and certification requirements, educational preparation, and future outlook. Gives ideas on how to secure a job.

★2244★ **Dental Assisting Exam Preparation**
W.B. Saunders Co.
Curtis Ctr., Independence Sq., W.
Philadelphia, PA 19106-3399
Ph: (215)238-7800   Fax: (215)238-7883

Hazel O. Torres. 1993. $19.95 (paper).

★2245★ **100 Best Careers for the Year 2000**
Prentice Hall General Reference
15 Columbus Cir.
New York, NY 10023
Ph: (212)373-8500   Fr: 800-223-2348

Shelly Field. 1992. $15.00 (paper). Covers 100 of the fastest growing jobs. The publication is divided into 11 general employment sections. Specific careers are covered within each section. Provides job description, responsibilities, employment opportunities, earnings, education and training, advancement opportunities, and experience and qualifications for each occupation.

★2246★ **Opportunities in Dental Care Careers**
VGM Career Horizons
4255 W. Touhy Ave.
Lincolnwood, IL 60646-1975
Ph: (847)679-5500   Fax: (847)679-2494
Fr: 800-323-4900

Bonnie Bendall. 1991. $14.95; $11.95 (paper). 160 pages. A guide to planning for and seeking opportunities in the field. Contains bibliography and illustrations.

★2247★ **Opportunities in Health and Medical Careers**
VGM Career Horizons
4255 W. Touhy Ave.
Lincolnwood, IL 60646-1975
Ph: (847)679-5500   Fax: (847)679-2494
Fr: 800-323-4900

Donald Snook, Jr. and Leo D'Orazio. 1993. $14.95; $11.95 (paper). Covers the full range of medical and health occupations. Illustrated.

★2248★ **Opportunities in Paramedical Careers**
VGM Career Horizons
4255 W. Touhy Ave.
Lincolnwood, IL 60646-1975
Ph: (847)679-5500   Fax: (847)679-2494
Fr: 800-323-4900

Alex Kacen. 1994. $14.95; 11.95 (paper). 160 pages. Discusses a variety of opportunities in this field and how to pursue them. Illustrated.

★2249★ **Resumes for Health and Medical Careers**
4255 W. Touhy Ave.
Lincolnwood, IL 60646-1975
Ph: (708)679-5500   Fax: (708)679-6375
Fr: 800-323-4900

Compiled by VGM Career Horizons Staff 1995. $9.95 (paper).

★2250★ **Skills Competencies for the Dental Assistant**
Delmar Publishers
3 Columbia Cir.
Box 15015
Albany, NY 12212
Ph: (518)464-0358   Fax: (518)464-0358
Fr: 800-347-7707

Charline M. Dofka. 1994. $32.95.

★2251★ **Your Opportunities as a Dental Assistant**
Energeia Publishing, Inc.
PO Box 985
Salem, OR 97308
Ph: (503)362-1480   Fax: (503)362-2123

Margie Sherman. 1994. $2.00 (paper).

EMPLOYMENT AGENCIES AND SEARCH FIRMS

★2252★ **Action Plus Employer Services**
1211 W. Imperial Hwy., Ste. 100
Brea, CA 92621
Ph: (714)773-1506   Fax: (714)773-9201

Employment agency.

★2253★ **DDS Staffing Resources, Inc.**
863 Holcolm Bridge Rd., Ste. 230
Roswell, GA 30076
Ph: (404)998-7779   Fax: (404)552-0176

Employment agency.

★2254★ **Dent-Assist Personnel Service**
725 30th St., Ste. 206
Sacramento, CA 95816
Ph: (916)443-1113

Employment agency. Provides placement on regular or temporary basis.

★2255★ **Eden Temporary Services**
280 Madison Ave.
New York, NY 10016-0801
Ph: (212)685-4666

Employment agency. Places individuals in regular or temporary positions.

★2256★ **EHS and Associates, Inc.**
3033 Excelsior Blvd., Ste. 303
Minneapolis, MN 55416
Ph: (612)924-2366   Fax: (612)924-2367

Executive search firm and employment agency.

★2257★ Sue Carroll Personnel, Inc.
16 E. 79th St.
New York, NY 10021
Ph: (212)288-8866   Fax: (212)988-7191
Employment agency and executive search firm.

OTHER SOURCES

★2258★ American Dental Assistants Association (ADAA)
203 N. LaSalle St., Ste. 1320
Chicago, IL 60601-1225
Ph: (312)541-1550   Fax: (312)541-1496
Members: Individuals employed as dental assistants in dental offices, clinics, hospitals, or institutions; instructors of dental assistants; dental students. **Purpose:** Sponsors workshops and seminars; maintains governmental liaison. Offers group insurance; maintains scholarship trust fund. Dental Assisting National Board examines members who are candidates for title of Certified Dental Assistant.

★2259★ American Dental Association (ADA)
211 E. Chicago Ave.
Chicago, IL 60611
Ph: (312)440-2500   Fax: (312)440-7494
Members: Professional society of dentists. **Purpose:** Encourages the improvement of the health of the public and promotes the art and science of dentistry in matters of legislation and regulations. Inspects and accredits dental schools and schools for dental hygienists, assistants, and laboratory technicians. Conducts research programs at ADA Health Foundation Research Institute. Produces most of the dental health education material used in the U.S. Sponsors National Children's Dental Health Month. Compiles statistics on personnel, practice, and dental care needs and attitudes of patients with regard to dental health.

★2260★ National Association of Dental Assistants (NADA)
900 S. Washington St., No. G-13
Falls Church, VA 22046
Ph: (703)237-8616
Members: Professional dental auxiliaries. **Purpose:** Seeks to: bring added stature and purpose to the profession through continuing education; make available to dental assistants the special benefits normally limited to members of specialized professional and fraternal groups. **Activities:** Conducts seminars.

★2261★ National Dental Assistants Association (NDAA)
Robert Johns
5506 Connecticut Ave. NW, Ste. 24
Washington, DC 20015
Ph: (202)244-7555   Fax: (202)244-5992
Purpose: An auxiliary of the National Dental Association. Works to encourage education and certification among dental assistants. **Activities:** Conducts clinics and workshops to further the education of members. Bestows annual Humanitarian Award; offers scholarships.

★2262★ National Rural Health Association (NRHA)
1 W. Armour Blvd., Ste. 301
Kansas City, MO 64111
Ph: (816)756-3140   Fax: (816)756-3144
Members: Administrators, physicians, nurses, physician assistants, health planners, academicians, and others interested or involved in rural health care. **Purpose:** To create a better understanding of health care problems unique to rural areas; utilize a collective approach in finding positive solutions; articulate and represent the health care needs of rural America; supply current information to rural health care providers; serve as a liaison between rural health care programs throughout the country. Offers continuing education credits for medical, dental, nursing, and management courses.

Dental Hygienists

★2263★ **Dental Hygiene**

American Dental Hygienists Association
444 N. Michigan Ave., Ste. 3400
Chicago, IL 60611
Ph: (312)440-8900   Fax: (312)440-8929

Six issues/year. $40.00/year; $5.00/issue. Professional Journal on dental hygiene.

★2264★ **Hawaiian Dental Journal**

1360 S. Beretania
Honolulu, HI 96814
Ph: (808)528-2376   Fr: 800-591-6832

Bimonthly.

★2265★ **Journal of the California Dental Association**

California Dental Association
1201 'K' St. Mall
PO Box 13749
Sacramento, CA 95853
Ph: (916)443-0505   Fax: (916)443-2943

Monthly. $24.00/year; $60.00/year for non-members; $6.00 for single issue. Professional magazine for dentists.

★2266★ **Journal of Dental Research**

American Association for Dental Research
1619 Duke St.
Alexandria, VA 22314
Ph: (703)548-0066

Monthly. $350.00/year for individuals; $360.00/year for other countries. Dental science journal.

★2267★ **RDH**

Stevens Publishing Corp.
PO Box 2573
Waco, TX 76702-2573
Ph: (817)776-9000   Fax: (817)662-7075
Fr: 800-727-7573

Monthly. Magazine for dental hygiene professionals covering practice management, patient motivation, practice options, financial planning, personal development, preventive oral health care and treatment, home care instruction, radiology, anesthesia, nutrition, and new products.

★2268★ **American Public Health Association (APHA)**

1015 15th St. NW
Washington, DC 20005
Ph: (202)789-5600   Fax: (202)789-5681

Members: Professional organization of physicians, nurses, educators, academicians, environmentalists, epidemiologists, new professionals, social workers, health administrators, optometrists, podiatrists, pharmacists, dentists, nutritionists, health planners, other community and mental health specialists, and interested consumers. **Purpose:** Seeks to protect and promote personal, mental, and environmental health. **Activities:** Services include: promulgation of standards; establishment of uniform practices and procedures; development of the etiology of communicable diseases; research in public health; exploration of medical care programs and their relationships to public health. Sponsors job placement service.

★2269★ **American School Health Association (ASHA)**

7263 State Rte. 43
PO Box 708
Kent, OH 44240
Ph: (216)678-1601   Fax: (216)678-4526

Members: School physicians, school nurses, dentists, nurses, nutritionists, health educators, dental hygienists, school-based professionals, and public health workers. **Purpose:** Promotes comprehensive and constructive school health programs including the teaching of health, health services, and promotion of a healthful school environment. **Activities:** Offers a professional referral service, classroom teaching aids, and professional reference materials. Conducts research programs; maintains placement service; compiles statistics. Sponsors foreign travel study tour.

★2270★ **American Academy of Pediatric Dentistry—Membership Roster**

American Academy of Pediatric Dentistry
211 E. Chicago Ave., Ste. 1036
Chicago, IL 60611
Ph: (312)337-2169

Annual, November. $500.00. Covers 3,700 pediatric dentists in practice, teaching, and research. Entries include: Name, address, phone. Arrangement: Alphabetical. Indexes: Geographical.

★2271★ **American Dental Directory**

American Dental Association
211 E. Chicago Ave.
Chicago, IL 60611
Ph: (312)440-2500   Fax: (312)440-3542
Fr: 800-947-4746

Annual, January. $154.00. Covers over 170,000 dentists. Also includes list of active and historic dental schools, dental organizations, and state dental examining boards. Entries include: Name, address, year of birth, educational data, specialty, membership status. Arrangement: Geographical. Indexes: Alphabetical.

★2272★ **Dentists Directory**

American Business Directories, Inc.
American Business Information, Inc.
5711 S. 86th Cir.
Omaha, NE 68127
Ph: (402)593-4600   Fax: (402)331-1505

Annual. $4,860.00, U.S. edition; $685.00, (Canad. ed.) Entries include: Name, address, phone (including area code), size of advertisement, code indicating specialty, year first in Yellow Pages, name of owner or manager, number of employees. Regional editions available. Compiled from telephone company Yellow Pages, nationwide. Arrangement: Geographical.

★2273★ *International Association of Oral Pathologists–Membership List*

International Association of Oral
  Pathologists
c/o Dr. Peter R. Morgan
Department of Oral Medicine and
  Pathology
Guy's Hospital Dental School
London SE1 9RT, England
Ph: 71 9554288

Annual. Free. Covers 325 dentists who have had postgraduate instruction in oral pathology. Entries include: Personal name, address. Arrangement: Geographical.

★2274★ *International Association for Orthodontics and American Orthodontic Society—Membership Directory*

International Association for Orthodontics
1100 Lake St., No. 240
Oak Park, IL 60301
Ph: (708)445-0320   Fax: (708)445-0321

Annual, June. $45.00. Covers 4,000 general and children's dentists specializing in prevention or correction of facial and jaw irregularities. Entries include: Name, office address and phone, orthodontic techniques practiced. Arrangement: Geographical. Indexes: Personal name.

★2275★ *Washington Physicians Directory*

National Directories, Inc.
PO Box 4436
Silver Spring, MD 20914
Ph: (301)384-1506   Fax: (301)384-6854

Annual, April. $33.50, payment with order. Covers 8,400 physicians in private practice or on full-time staff at hospitals in the Washington, DC, metropolitan area. Entries include: Name, medical school and year of graduation; up to four office addresses with phone numbers for each; up to four medical specialties, Unique Physician Identification Numbers (UPIN). Arrangement: Alphabetical. Indexes: Geographical (within medical specialty); foreign language.

HANDBOOKS AND MANUALS

★2276★ *Career Directions for Dental Hygienists*

Career Directions Press
171 Hwy. 34
Holmdel, NJ 07733
Ph: (908)946-8457

Regina A. Dreyer. Third edition, 1992. $16.50. 224 pages. Describes the personal characteristics needed to be a dental hygienist. Explores career opportunities in public health, the federal government, long-term care facilities, education, dental centers, health maintenance organizations, industry, working abroad, and private practice. Gives job hunting advice including how to write the resume and preparing for the interview.

★2277★ *Careers in Dentistry: Is It for You*

DSH Publishing Co.
9433 Elmhurst Ct.
Brentwood, TN 37027
Ph: (615)371-1927

S. Adele Doherty. 1992. $25.00.

★2278★ *Careers in Health Care*

VGM Career Horizons
4255 W. Touhy Ave.
Lincolnwood, IL 60646-1975
Ph: (847)679-5500   Fax: (847)679-2494
Fr: 800-323-4900

Barbara M. Swanson. 1995. $17.95; $13.95 (paper). Describes job duties, work settings, salaries, licensing and certification requirements, educational preparation, and future outlook. Gives ideas on how to secure a job.

★2279★ *Dental Hygienist*

R & E Publishers, Inc.
468 Auzerais Ave., Ste. A
San Jose, CA 95126
Ph: (408)977-0691   Fax: (408)977-0693

Ronald R. Smith. 1993. $1.95 (paper).

★2280★ *100 Best Careers for the Year 2000*

Prentice Hall General Reference
15 Columbus Cir.
New York, NY 10023
Ph: (212)373-8500   Fr: 800-223-2348

Shelly Field. 1992. $15.00 (paper). Covers 100 of the fastest growing jobs. The publication is divided into 11 general employment sections. Specific careers are covered within each section. Provides job description, responsibilities, employment opportunities, earnings, education and training, advancement opportunities, and experience and qualifications for each occupation.

★2281★ *Opportunities in Dental Care Careers*

VGM Career Horizons
4255 W. Touhy Ave.
Lincolnwood, IL 60646-1975
Ph: (847)679-5500   Fax: (847)679-2494
Fr: 800-323-4900

Bonnie Bendall. 1991. $14.95; $11.95 (paper). 160 pages. A guide to planning for and seeking opportunities in the field. Contains bibliography and illustrations.

★2282★ *Opportunities in Health and Medical Careers*

VGM Career Horizons
4255 W. Touhy Ave.
Lincolnwood, IL 60646-1975
Ph: (847)679-5500   Fax: (847)679-2494
Fr: 800-323-4900

Donald Snook, Jr. and Leo D'Orazio. 1993. $14.95; $11.95 (paper). Covers the full range of medical and health occupations. Illustrated.

★2283★ *Opportunities in Medical Technology Careers*

VGM Career Horizons
4255 W. Touhy Ave.
Lincolnwood, IL 60646-1975
Ph: (847)679-5500   Fax: (847)679-2494
Fr: 800-323-4900

Karen R. Karni and Sidney Oliver. 1990. $14.95; $11.95 (paper). Details opportunities for various technical medical personnel and supplies up-to-date information on salary levels and employment outlook. Appendices list associations and unions in each field. Illustrated.

★2284★ *Opportunities in Paramedical Careers*

VGM Career Horizons
4255 W. Touhy Ave.
Lincolnwood, IL 60646-1975
Ph: (847)679-5500   Fax: (847)679-2494
Fr: 800-323-4900

Alex Kacen. 1994. $14.95; 11.95 (paper). 160 pages. Discusses a variety of opportunities in this field and how to pursue them. Illustrated.

★2285★ *Opportunities in Public Health Careers*

VGM Career Horizons
4255 W. Touhy Ave.
Lincolnwood, IL 60646-1975
Ph: (847)679-5500   Fax: (847)679-2494
Fr: 800-323-4900

George E. Pickett and Terry W. Pickett. 1995. $14.95; $11.95 (paper). 160 pages. Defines the public health field and describes a variety of health, science, and business opportunities as well as educational preparation and the future of the public health field. Offers job-hunting tips. The appendixes list public health organizations, state and federal public health agencies, and graduate schools offering public health programs.

★2286★ *Opportunities in Vocational and Technical Careers*

VGM Career Horizons
4255 W. Touhy Ave.
Lincolnwood, IL 60646-1975
Ph: (847)679-5500   Fax: (847)679-2494
Fr: 800-323-4900

Adrian A. Paradis. 1992. $14.95; $11.95 (paper). 160 pages. Provides information on a variety of opportunities and advice on breaking into the field.

★2287★ *Resumes for Health and Medical Careers*

4255 W. Touhy Ave.
Lincolnwood, IL 60646-1975
Ph: (708)679-5500   Fax: (708)679-6375
Fr: 800-323-4900

Compiled by VGM Career Horizons Staff 1995. $9.95 (paper).

★2288★ **Therapists and Allied Health Professionals Career Directory**

Gale Research
835 Penobscot Bldg.
Detroit, MI 48226-4094
Ph: (313)961-2242   Fax: (313)961-6083
Fr: 800-877-GALE

Bradley Morgan. 1993. $39.00. 326 pages. Essays on specific careers provide an insider's perspective. Also features extensive listings of contacts and entry-level job opportunities. Provides information on internships and sources of help-wanted ads.

EMPLOYMENT AGENCIES AND SEARCH FIRMS

★2289★ **Action Plus Employer Services**

1211 W. Imperial Hwy., Ste. 100
Brea, CA 92621
Ph: (714)773-1506   Fax: (714)773-9201
Employment agency.

★2290★ **DDS Staffing Resources, Inc.**

863 Holcolm Bridge Rd., Ste. 230
Roswell, GA 30076
Ph: (404)998-7779   Fax: (404)552-0176
Employment agency.

★2291★ **Dent-Assist Personnel Service**

725 30th St., Ste. 206
Sacramento, CA 95816
Ph: (916)443-1113

Employment agency. Provides placement on regular or temporary basis.

★2292★ **Eden Temporary Services**

280 Madison Ave.
New York, NY 10016-0801
Ph: (212)685-4666

Employment agency. Places individuals in regular or temporary positions.

★2293★ **EHS and Associates, Inc.**

3033 Excelsior Blvd., Ste. 303
Minneapolis, MN 55416
Ph: (612)924-2366   Fax: (612)924-2367

Executive search firm and employment agency.

★2294★ **Sue Carroll Personnel, Inc.**

16 E. 79th St.
New York, NY 10021
Ph: (212)288-8866   Fax: (212)988-7191

Employment agency and executive search firm.

OTHER SOURCES

★2295★ **American Association of Dental Examiners (AADE)**

211 E. Chicago Ave., Ste. 844
Chicago, IL 60611
Ph: (312)440-7464   Fax: (312)440-7494

Members: Present and past members of state dental examining boards and board administrators. **Purpose:** To assist member agencies with problems related to state dental board examinations and licensure, and enforcement of the state dental practice act.

★2296★ **American Dental Association (ADA)**

211 E. Chicago Ave.
Chicago, IL 60611
Ph: (312)440-2500   Fax: (312)440-7494

Members: Professional society of dentists. **Purpose:** Encourages the improvement of the health of the public and promotes the art and science of dentistry in matters of legislation and regulations. Inspects and accredits dental schools and schools for dental hygienists, assistants, and laboratory technicians. Conducts research programs at ADA Health Foundation Research Institute. Produces most of the dental health education material used in the U.S. Sponsors National Children's Dental Health Month. Compiles statistics on personnel, practice, and dental care needs and attitudes of patients with regard to dental health.

★2297★ **American Dental Hygienists' Association (ADHA)**

444 N. Michigan Ave., Ste. 3400
Chicago, IL 60611
Ph: (312)440-8929   Fax: (312)440-8929
Fr: 800-243-ADHA

Members: Professional organization of licensed dental hygienists possessing a degree or certificate in dental hygiene granted by an accredited school of dental hygiene. **Purpose:** Administers Dental Hygiene Candidate Aptitude Testing Program and makes available scholarships, research grants, and continuing education programs. Maintains accrediting service through the American Dental Association's Commission on Dental Accreditation.

★2298★ **Dental Hygiene: A Profession of Opportunities**

American Dental Hygienists Association
444 N. Michigan Ave., Ste. 3400
Chicago, IL 60611
Fr: 800-243-2342

Video. $20.00.

★2299★ **Holistic Dental Association (HDA)**

c/o Dr. Paul Plowman
4801 Richmond Sq.
Oklahoma City, OK 73118
Ph: (405)840-5600   Fax: (405)843-0417

Members: Dentists, chiropractors, dental hygienists, physical therapists, and medical doctors. **Purpose:** Goals are: to provide a holistic approach to better dental care for patients; to expand techniques, medications, and philosophies that pertain to extractions, anesthetics, fillings, crowns, and orthodontics. Encourages use of homeopathic medications, acupuncture, cranial osteopathy, nutritional techniques, and physical therapy in treating patients in addition to conventional treatments. **Activities:** Classifies therapies; has developed a referral questionnaire for holistic practitioners. Sponsors training and educational seminars.

★2300★ **National Dental Hygienists' Association (NDHA)**

28315 Kalong Cir. W.
Southfield, MI 48034-5658
Ph: (810)358-0432   Fax: (313)446-1839

Members: Minority dental hygienists. **Purpose:** To cultivate and promote the art and science of dental hygiene and to enhance the professional image of dental hygienists. Attempts to meet the needs of society through educational, political, and social activities while giving the minority dental hygienist a voice in shaping the profession. Encourages cooperation and mutual support among minority professionals. Seeks to increase opportunities for continuing education and employment in the field of dental hygiene. Works to improve individual and community dental health. **Activities:** Sponsors annual seminar, fundraising events, and scholarship programs; participates in career orientation programs; counsels and assists students applying for or enrolled in dental hygiene programs. Maintains liaison with American Dental Hygienists' Association.

★2301★ **National Rural Health Association (NRHA)**

1 W. Armour Blvd., Ste. 301
Kansas City, MO 64111
Ph: (816)756-3140   Fax: (816)756-3144

Members: Administrators, physicians, nurses, physician assistants, health planners, academicians, and others interested or involved in rural health care. **Purpose:** To create a better understanding of health care problems unique to rural areas; utilize a collective approach in finding positive solutions; articulate and represent the health care needs of rural America; supply current information to rural health care providers; serve as a liaison between rural health care programs throughout the country. Offers continuing education credits for medical, dental, nursing, and management courses.

Dental Lab Technicians

SOURCES OF HELP-WANTED ADS

★2302★ Hawaiian Dental Journal

1360 S. Beretania
Honolulu, HI 96814
Ph: (808)528-2376   Fr: 800-591-6832
Bimonthly.

★2303★ Journal of the California Dental Association

California Dental Association
1201 'K' St. Mall
PO Box 13749
Sacramento, CA 95853
Ph: (916)443-0505   Fax: (916)443-2943

Monthly. $24.00/year; $60.00/year for non-members; $6.00 for single issue. Professional magazine for dentists.

★2304★ Journal of Dental Research

American Association for Dental Research
1619 Duke St.
Alexandria, VA 22314
Ph: (703)548-0066

Monthly. $350.00/year for individuals; $360.00/year for other countries. Dental science journal.

★2305★ The Journal of Prosthetic Dentistry

Mosby Year Book
11830 Westline Industrial Dr.
St. Louis, MO 63146
Ph: (314)872-8370   Fax: 800-535-9935
Fr: 800-633-6699

Monthly. $99.00/year for individuals; $138.03/year for Canada; $129.00/year for other countries; $53.00/year for students. Journal emphasizing new techniques, evaluation of dental materials, pertinent basic science concepts, and patient psychology in restorative dentistry.

EMPLOYER DIRECTORIES AND NETWORKING LISTS

★2306★ American Dental Directory

American Dental Association
211 E. Chicago Ave.
Chicago, IL 60611
Ph: (312)440-2500   Fax: (312)440-3542
Fr: 800-947-4746

Annual, January. $154.00. Covers over 170,000 dentists. Also includes list of active and historic dental schools, dental organizations, and state dental examining boards. Entries include: Name, address, year of birth, educational data, specialty, membership status. Arrangement: Geographical. Indexes: Alphabetical.

★2307★ Dental Laboratories Directory

American Business Directories, Inc.
American Business Information, Inc.
5711 S. 86th Cir.
Omaha, NE 68127
Ph: (402)593-4600   Fax: (402)331-1505

Annual. $855.00, U.S. edition. Entries include: Name, address, phone (including area code), size of advertisement, year first in Yellow Pages, name of owner of manager, number of employees. Compiled from telephone company Yellow Pages nationwide. Arrangement: Geographical.

★2308★ Dentists Directory

American Business Directories, Inc.
American Business Information, Inc.
5711 S. 86th Cir.
Omaha, NE 68127
Ph: (402)593-4600   Fax: (402)331-1505

Annual. $4,860.00, U.S. edition; $685.00, (Canad. ed). Entries include: Name, address, phone (including area code), size of advertisement, code indicating specialty, year first in Yellow Pages, name of owner or manager, number of employees. Regional editions available. Compiled from telephone company Yellow Pages, nationwide. Arrangement: Geographical.

★2309★ Who's Who in the Dental Laboratory Industry

National Association of Dental Laboratories
555 E. Braddock Rd.
Alexandria, VA 22314-2106
Ph: (703)683-5263   Fax: (703)549-4788

Annual, September. $55.00. Covers about 3,300 dental laboratories; 12,000 certified dental technicians, manufacturers, and schools of dental technology. Entries include: Company name, address, phone, name of owner, certification status, product or service. Arrangement: Geographical. Indexes: Subject, product/service.

HANDBOOKS AND MANUALS

★2310★ Careers in Dentistry: Is It for You

DSH Publishing Co.
9433 Elmhurst Ct.
Brentwood, TN 37027
Ph: (615)371-1927

S. Adele Doherty. 1992. $25.00.

★2311★ Careers in Health Care

VGM Career Horizons
4255 W. Touhy Ave.
Lincolnwood, IL 60646-1975
Ph: (847)679-5500   Fax: (847)679-2494
Fr: 800-323-4900

Barbara M. Swanson. 1995. $17.95; $13.95 (paper). Describes job duties, work settings, salaries, licensing and certification requirements, educational preparation, and future outlook. Gives ideas on how to secure a job.

★2312★ Dental Laboratory Technology: Basic Sciences

Gordon Press Publishers
PO Box 459, Bowling Green Sta.
New York, NY 10004
Ph: (718)624-8419

1993. $299.95.

★2313★ *Hands That Think: A Word about Careers in Modern Dental Laboratory Technology*

National Association of Dental Laboratories
555 E. Braddock Rd.
Alexandria, VA 22314
Ph: (703)683-5263

This free brochure describes the work, employment opportunities, earnings, training, and qualifications for dental laboratory technicians.

★2314★ *Opportunities in Dental Care Careers*

VGM Career Horizons
4255 W. Touhy Ave.
Lincolnwood, IL 60646-1975
Ph: (847)679-5500   Fax: (847)679-2494
Fr: 800-323-4900

Bonnie Bendall. 1991. $14.95; $11.95 (paper). 160 pages. A guide to planning for and seeking opportunities in the field. Contains bibliography and illustrations.

★2315★ *Opportunities in Health and Medical Careers*

VGM Career Horizons
4255 W. Touhy Ave.
Lincolnwood, IL 60646-1975
Ph: (847)679-5500   Fax: (847)679-2494
Fr: 800-323-4900

Donald Snook, Jr. and Leo D'Orazio. 1993. $14.95; $11.95 (paper). Covers the full range of medical and health occupations. Illustrated.

★2316★ *Opportunities in Medical Technology Careers*

VGM Career Horizons
4255 W. Touhy Ave.
Lincolnwood, IL 60646-1975
Ph: (847)679-5500   Fax: (847)679-2494
Fr: 800-323-4900

Karen R. Karni and Sidney Oliver. 1990. $14.95; $11.95 (paper). Details opportunities for various technical medical personnel and supplies up-to-date information on salary levels and employment outlook. Appendices list associations and unions in each field. Illustrated.

★2317★ *Opportunities in Paramedical Careers*

VGM Career Horizons
4255 W. Touhy Ave.
Lincolnwood, IL 60646-1975
Ph: (847)679-5500   Fax: (847)679-2494
Fr: 800-323-4900

Alex Kacen. 1994. $14.95; 11.95 (paper). 160 pages. Discusses a variety of opportunities in this field and how to pursue them. Illustrated.

★2318★ *Opportunities in Vocational and Technical Careers*

VGM Career Horizons
4255 W. Touhy Ave.
Lincolnwood, IL 60646-1975
Ph: (847)679-5500   Fax: (847)679-2494
Fr: 800-323-4900

Adrian A. Paradis. 1992. $14.95; $11.95 (paper). 160 pages. Provides information on a variety of opportunities and advice on breaking into the field.

★2319★ *Resumes for Health and Medical Careers*

4255 W. Touhy Ave.
Lincolnwood, IL 60646-1975
Ph: (708)679-5500   Fax: (708)679-6375
Fr: 800-323-4900

Compiled by VGM Career Horizons Staff 1995. $9.95 (paper).

EMPLOYMENT AGENCIES AND SEARCH FIRMS

★2320★ **DDS Staffing Resources, Inc.**
863 Holcolm Bridge Rd., Ste. 230
Roswell, GA 30076
Ph: (404)998-7779   Fax: (404)552-0176
Employment agency.

★2321★ **Dent-Assist Personnel Service**
725 30th St., Ste. 206
Sacramento, CA 95816
Ph: (916)443-1113

Employment agency. Provides placement on regular or temporary basis.

★2322★ **Eden Temporary Services**
280 Madison Ave.
New York, NY 10016-0801
Ph: (212)685-4666

Employment agency. Places individuals in regular or temporary positions.

OTHER SOURCES

★2323★ **American Dental Association (ADA)**
211 E. Chicago Ave.
Chicago, IL 60611
Ph: (312)440-2500   Fax: (312)440-7494

Members: Professional society of dentists. **Purpose:** Encourages the improvement of the health of the public and promotes the art and science of dentistry in matters of legislation and regulations. Inspects and accredits dental schools and schools for dental hygienists, assistants, and laboratory technicians. Conducts research programs at ADA Health Foundation Research Institute. Produces most of the dental health education material used in the U.S. Sponsors National Children's Dental Health Month. Compiles statistics on personnel, practice, and dental care needs and attitudes of patients with regard to dental health.

★2324★ **National Association of Dental Laboratories (NADL)**
555 E. Braddock Rd.
Alexandria, VA 22314-2106
Ph: (703)683-5263   Fax: (703)549-4788
Fr: 800-950-1150

Members: Federation of state associations representing 2900 commercial dental laboratories serving the dental profession. **Purpose:** Develops criteria for ethical dental laboratories. **Activities:** Offers business and personal insurance programs, Hazardous Materials Training Program, and an infectious disease prevention training program.

Dentists

SOURCES OF HELP-WANTED ADS

★2325★ American Journal of Orthodontics and Dentofacial Orthopedics

Mosby Year Book
11830 Westline Industrial Dr.
St. Louis, MO 63146
Ph: (314)872-8370   Fax: 800-535-9935
Fr: 800-633-6699

Monthly. $100.00/year for individuals; $47.00/year for students; $250.38/year for institutions. Journal for orthodontists and dentists who include orthodontics as a portion of their practice.

★2326★ CDS Review

Chicago Dental Society
401 N. Michigan Ave., Ste. 300
Chicago, IL 60611-4205
Ph: (312)836-7300   Fax: (312)836-7337

$25.00/year for individuals; $4.00 for single issue. Dental journal.

★2327★ Dental Economics

PennWell Publishing Co.
1421 S. Sheridan
PO Box 3408
Tulsa, OK 74101
Ph: (918)835-3161   Fax: (918)831-9804
Fr: 800-633-1681

Monthly. Magazine featuring business-related articles for dentists.

★2328★ Dentistry Today

Dentistry Today
26 Park St.
Montclair, NJ 07042
Ph: (201)783-3935   Fax: (201)783-7112

$40.00/year; $50.00/year for Canada. Dental magazine (tabloid).

★2329★ Hawaiian Dental Journal

1360 S. Beretania
Honolulu, HI 96814
Ph: (808)528-2376   Fr: 800-591-6832
Bimonthly.

★2330★ Illinois Dental Journal

Illinois State Dental Society
1010 S. 2nd St.
PO Box 376
Springfield, IL 62705
Ph: (217)525-1406   Fax: (217)525-8872

Bimonthly. $20.00/year for members; $30.00/year for nonmembers; $5.00 for single issue. Dental magazine.

★2331★ JADA

JADA Publishers Inc.
211 E. Chicago Ave.
Chicago, IL 60611
Ph: (312)440-2740   Fax: (312)440-2550
Fr: 800-621-8099

Monthly. $60.00/year for individuals; $8.00 for single issue. Dental magazine.

★2332★ Journal of the California Dental Association

California Dental Association
1201 'K' St. Mall
PO Box 13749
Sacramento, CA 95853
Ph: (916)443-0505   Fax: (916)443-2943

Monthly. $24.00/year; $60.00/year for nonmembers; $6.00 for single issue. Professional magazine for dentists.

★2333★ Journal of Dental Education

American Association of Dental Schools
1625 Massachusetts Ave. NW
Washington, DC 20036
Ph: (202)667-9433   Fax: (202)667-0642

Monthly. $75.00/year; $100.00/year for Canada; $125.00/year for other countries. Peer-reviewed journal for scholarly research and reviews on dental education.

★2334★ Journal of Dental Research

American Association for Dental Research
1619 Duke St.
Alexandria, VA 22314
Ph: (703)548-0066

Monthly. $350.00/year for individuals; $360.00/year for other countries. Dental science journal.

★2335★ The Journal of Prosthetic Dentistry

Mosby Year Book
11830 Westline Industrial Dr.
St. Louis, MO 63146
Ph: (314)872-8370   Fax: 800-535-9935
Fr: 800-633-6699

Monthly. $99.00/year for individuals; $138.03/year for Canada; $129.00/year for other countries; $53.00/year for students. Journal emphasizing new techniques, evaluation of dental materials, pertinent basic science concepts, and patient psychology in restorative dentistry.

★2336★ Pennsylvania Dental Journal

Pennsylvania Dental Association
Box 3341
Harrisburg, PA 17105
Ph: (717)234-5941   Fax: (717)232-7169

Bimonthly. Professional dentistry magazine containing treatment/procedure news, ADA activities information, continuing education courses, and legislation updates.

PLACEMENT AND JOB REFERRAL SERVICES

★2337★ American Public Health Association (APHA)

1015 15th St. NW
Washington, DC 20005
Ph: (202)789-5600   Fax: (202)789-5681

Members: Professional organization of physicians, nurses, educators, academicians, environmentalists, epidemiologists, new professionals, social workers, health administrators, optometrists, podiatrists, pharmacists, dentists, nutritionists, health planners, other community and mental health specialists, and interested consumers. **Purpose:** Seeks to protect and promote personal, mental, and environmental health. **Activities:** Services include: promulgation of standards; establishment of uniform practices and procedures; development of the etiology of communicable diseases; research in public health; exploration of medical care programs and their relationships to public health. Sponsors job placement service.

★2338★ American School Health Association (ASHA)

7263 State Rte. 43
PO Box 708
Kent, OH 44240
Ph: (216)678-1601   Fax: (216)678-4526

Members: School physicians, school nurses, dentists, nurses, nutritionists, health educators, dental hygienists, school-based professionals, and public health workers. **Purpose:** Promotes comprehensive and constructive school health programs including the teaching of health, health services, and promotion of a healthful school environment. **Activities:** Offers a professional referral service, classroom teaching aids, and professional reference materials. Conducts research programs; maintains placement service; compiles statistics. Sponsors foreign travel study tour.

★2339★ Ukrainian Medical Association of North America (UMANA)

2247 W. Chicago Ave.
Chicago, IL 60622
Ph: (312)278-6262

Members: Physicians, surgeons, dentists, and persons in related professions who are of Ukrainian descent. **Purpose:** Provides assistance to members; sponsors lectures. **Activities:** Maintains placement service, museum, biographical and medical archives, and library of 1800 medical books and journals in Ukrainian.

EMPLOYER DIRECTORIES AND NETWORKING LISTS

★2340★ American Academy of Pediatric Dentistry—Membership Roster

American Academy of Pediatric Dentistry
211 E. Chicago Ave., Ste. 1036
Chicago, IL 60611
Ph: (312)337-2169

Annual, November. $500.00. Covers 3,700 pediatric dentists in practice, teaching, and research. Entries include: Name, address, phone. Arrangement: Alphabetical. Indexes: Geographical.

★2341★ American Dental Directory

American Dental Association
211 E. Chicago Ave.
Chicago, IL 60611
Ph: (312)440-2500   Fax: (312)440-3542
Fr: 800-947-4746

Annual, January. $154.00. Covers over 170,000 dentists. Also includes list of active and historic dental schools, dental organizations, and state dental examining boards. Entries include: Name, address, year of birth, educational data, specialty, membership status. Arrangement: Geographical. Indexes: Alphabetical.

★2342★ Dentists Directory

American Business Directories, Inc.
American Business Information, Inc.
5711 S. 86th Cir.
Omaha, NE 68127
Ph: (402)593-4600   Fax: (402)331-1505

Annual. $4,860.00, U.S. edition; $685.00, (Canad. ed). Entries include: Name, address, phone (including area code), size of advertisement, code indicating specialty, year first in Yellow Pages, name of owner or manager, number of employees. Regional editions available. Compiled from telephone company Yellow Pages, nationwide. Arrangement: Geographical.

★2343★ Health & Medical Industry Directory

American Business Directories, Inc.
American Business Information, Inc.
5711 S. 86th Cir.
Omaha, NE 68127
Ph: (402)593-4600   Fax: (402)331-1505

Released 1993. $79.00. CD-ROM. Lists over 1.1 million physicians and surgeons, dentists, clinics, health clubs, and other health-related businesses in the U.S. and Canada. Entries include: Name, address, phone. IBM-compatible equipment required.

★2344★ International Association of Oral Pathologists–Membership List

International Association of Oral Pathologists
c/o Dr. Peter R. Morgan
Department of Oral Medicine and Pathology
Guy's Hospital Dental School
London SE1 9RT, England
Ph: 71 9554288

Annual. Free. Covers 325 dentists who have had postgraduate instruction in oral pathology. Entries include: Personal name, address. Arrangement: Geographical.

★2345★ International Association for Orthodontics and American Orthodontic Society—Membership Directory

International Association for Orthodontics
1100 Lake St., No. 240
Oak Park, IL 60301
Ph: (708)445-0320   Fax: (708)445-0321

Annual, June. $45.00. Covers 4,000 general and children's dentists specializing in prevention or correction of facial and jaw irregularities. Entries include: Name, office address and phone, orthodontic techniques practiced. Arrangement: Geographical. Indexes: Personal name.

★2346★ Meetings Inmed

Scientific Meetings Publications
Box 81662
San Diego, CA 92138
Ph: (619)270-2910   Fax: (619)270-2910

Quarterly, February, May, August, and November. $50.00, postpaid. Covers medical, dental, and health science conferences scheduled for the forthcoming 12 months; international coverage. Entries include: Conference name, address. Arrangement: Alphabetical. Indexes: Subject, Geographical, chronological.

★2347★ Physicians and Dentists Database

FIRSTMARK, Inc.
34 Juniper Ln.
Newton Center, MA 02159-2861
Ph: (617)965-7989   Fax: (617)965-8510
Fr: 800-729-2600

Updated continuously; printed on request. Please inquire. Database covers: More than 400,000 physicians and 160,000 dentists nationwide. Entries include: Individual name, address, phone, medical specialty, whether in single or group practice.

★2348★ Washington Physicians Directory

National Directories, Inc.
PO Box 4436
Silver Spring, MD 20914
Ph: (301)384-1506   Fax: (301)384-6854

Annual, April. $33.50, payment with order. Covers 8,400 physicians in private practice or on full-time staff at hospitals in the Washington, DC, metropolitan area. Entries include: Name, medical school and year of graduation; up to four office addresses with phone numbers for each; up to four medical specialties, Unique Physician Identification Numbers (UPIN). Arrangement: Alphabetical. Indexes: Geographical (within medical specialty); foreign language.

HANDBOOKS AND MANUALS

★2349★ Business Skills for Young Dentists: A Hands-on Guide for the Young Professional

Pronet Press
PO Box 486
Naperville, IL 60566
Ph: (708)653-5588

John P. Sullivan. 1993. $29.95 (paper).

★2350★ Careers in Dentistry: Is It for You

DSH Publishing Co.
9433 Elmhurst Ct.
Brentwood, TN 37027
Ph: (615)371-1927

S. Adele Doherty. 1992. $25.00.

★2351★ The Dentists' Handbook

Andent, Inc.
1000 North Ave.
Waukegan, IL 60085
Ph: (708)223-5077

E. J. Neiburger. 1993. $37.50 (paper).

★2352★ Healthcare Career Directory–Nurses and Physicians

Gale Research
835 Penobscot Bldg.
Detroit, MI 48226-4094
Ph: (313)961-2242   Fax: (313)961-6083
Fr: 800-877-GALE

Bradley Morgan. Second edition, 1993. $39.00. 327 pages. Essays on specific careers provide an insider's perspective. Features extensive listings of contacts and entry-level job opportunities. Provides information on internships and sources of help-wanted ads.

★2353★ *100 Best Careers for the Year 2000*

Prentice Hall General Reference
15 Columbus Cir.
New York, NY 10023
Ph: (212)373-8500   Fr: 800-223-2348

Shelly Field. 1992. $15.00 (paper). Covers 100 of the fastest growing jobs. The publication is divided into 11 general employment sections. Specific careers are covered within each section. Provides job description, responsibilities, employment opportunities, earnings, education and training, advancement opportunities, and experience and qualifications for each occupation.

★2354★ *Opportunities in Dental Care Careers*

VGM Career Horizons
4255 W. Touhy Ave.
Lincolnwood, IL 60646-1975
Ph: (847)679-5500   Fax: (847)679-2494
Fr: 800-323-4900

Bonnie Bendall. 1991. $14.95; $11.95 (paper). 160 pages. A guide to planning for and seeking opportunities in the field. Contains bibliography and illustrations.

★2355★ *Opportunities in Health and Medical Careers*

VGM Career Horizons
4255 W. Touhy Ave.
Lincolnwood, IL 60646-1975
Ph: (847)679-5500   Fax: (847)679-2494
Fr: 800-323-4900

Donald Snook, Jr. and Leo D'Orazio. 1993. $14.95; $11.95 (paper). Covers the full range of medical and health occupations. Illustrated.

★2356★ *Opportunities in Public Health Careers*

VGM Career Horizons
4255 W. Touhy Ave.
Lincolnwood, IL 60646-1975
Ph: (847)679-5500   Fax: (847)679-2494
Fr: 800-323-4900

George E. Pickett and Terry W. Pickett. 1995. $14.95; $11.95 (paper). 160 pages. Defines the public health field and describes a variety of health, science, and business opportunities as well as educational preparation and the future of the public health field. Offers job-hunting tips. The appendixes list public health organizations, state and federal public health agencies, and graduate schools offering public health programs.

★2357★ *Resumes for Health and Medical Careers*

4255 W. Touhy Ave.
Lincolnwood, IL 60646-1975
Ph: (708)679-5500   Fax: (708)679-6375
Fr: 800-323-4900

Compiled by VGM Career Horizons Staff. 1995. $9.95 (paper).

EMPLOYMENT AGENCIES AND SEARCH FIRMS

★2358★ DDS Staffing Resources, Inc.

863 Holcolm Bridge Rd., Ste. 230
Roswell, GA 30076
Ph: (404)998-7779   Fax: (404)552-0176

Employment agency.

★2359★ EHS and Associates, Inc.

3033 Excelsior Blvd., Ste. 303
Minneapolis, MN 55416
Ph: (612)924-2366   Fax: (612)924-2367

Executive search firm and employment agency.

★2360★ Sue Carroll Personnel, Inc.

16 E. 79th St.
New York, NY 10021
Ph: (212)288-8866   Fax: (212)988-7191

Employment agency and executive search firm.

★2361★ Team Placement Service, Inc.

5113 Leesburg Pike
Falls Church, VA 22041-3242
Ph: (703)820-8618   Fax: (703)820-3368

Employment agency.

OTHER SOURCES

★2362★ American Association of Dental Examiners (AADE)

211 E. Chicago Ave., Ste. 844
Chicago, IL 60611
Ph: (312)440-7464   Fax: (312)440-7494

Members: Present and past members of state dental examining boards and board administrators. **Purpose:** To assist member agencies with problems related to state dental board examinations and licensure, and enforcement of the state dental practice act.

★2363★ American Association of Dental Schools (AADS)

1625 Massachusetts Ave. NW
Washington, DC 20036
Ph: (202)667-9433   Fax: (202)667-0642

Members: Individuals interested in dental education; schools of dentistry, graduate dentistry, and dental auxiliary education in the U.S., Canada, and Puerto Rico; affiliated institutions of the federal government. **Purpose:** To promote better teaching and education in dentistry and dental research and to facilitate exchange of ideas among dental educators. **Activities:** Sponsors meetings, conferences, and workshops; conducts surveys, studies, and special projects and publishes their results. Maintains 37 sections representing teaching and administrative areas of dentistry.

★2364★ American Dental Association (ADA)

211 E. Chicago Ave.
Chicago, IL 60611
Ph: (312)440-2500   Fax: (312)440-7494

Members: Professional society of dentists. **Purpose:** Encourages the improvement of the health of the public and promotes the art and science of dentistry in matters of legislation and regulations. Inspects and accredits dental schools and schools for dental hygienists, assistants, and laboratory technicians. Conducts research programs at ADA Health Foundation Research Institute. Produces most of the dental health education material used in the U.S. Sponsors National Children's Dental Health Month. Compiles statistics on personnel, practice, and dental care needs and attitudes of patients with regard to dental health.

★2365★ American Society of Dentistry for Children (ASDC)

875 N. Michigan Ave., Ste. 4040
Chicago, IL 60611-1901
Ph: (312)943-1244   Fax: (312)943-5341

Members: General practitioners and specialists interested in dentistry for children. **Activities:** Conducts specialized education and research programs.

★2366★ *Dental Care Today*

R.J. Kitson Publishing
4400 NE 29th Ave.
Lighthouse Point, FL 33064
Ph: (305)946-7905

Robert J. Kitson. 1993. $7.95 (paper).

★2367★ Holistic Dental Association (HDA)

c/o Dr. Paul Plowman
4801 Richmond Sq.
Oklahoma City, OK 73118
Ph: (405)840-5600   Fax: (405)843-0417

Members: Dentists, chiropractors, dental hygienists, physical therapists, and medical doctors. **Purpose:** Goals are: to provide a holistic approach to better dental care for patients; to expand techniques, medications, and philosophies that pertain to extractions, anesthetics, fillings, crowns, and orthodontics. Encourages use of homeopathic medications, acupuncture, cranial osteopathy, nutritional techniques, and physical therapy in treating patients in addition to conventional treatments. **Activities:** Classifies therapies; has developed a referral questionnaire for holistic practitioners. Sponsors training and educational seminars.

★2368★ International Congress of Oral Implantologists (ICOI)

248 Lorraine Ave., 3rd Fl.
Upper Montclair, NJ 07043
Ph: (201)783-6300   Fax: (201)783-1175

Purpose: Dentists and oral surgeons dedicated to the teaching of and research in oral implantology (branch of dentistry dealing with dental implants placed into or on top of the jaw bone). **Activities:** Offers fellowship and course certification programs. Compiles statistics and maintains registry of current research in the field. Sponsors classes, seminars, and workshops at universities, hospitals, and societies worldwide.

★2369★ National Rural Health Association (NRHA)

1 W. Armour Blvd., Ste. 301
Kansas City, MO 64111
Ph: (816)756-3140   Fax: (816)756-3144

Members: Administrators, physicians, nurses, physician assistants, health planners, academicians, and others interested or involved in rural health care. **Purpose:** To create a better understanding of health care problems unique to rural areas; utilize a collective approach in finding positive solutions; articulate and represent the health care needs of rural America; supply current information to rural health care providers; serve as a liaison between rural health care programs throughout the country. Offers continuing education credits for medical, dental, nursing, and management courses.

Designers

★2370★ Art Direction

Advertising Trade Publications, Inc.
10 E. 39th St., 6th Fl.
New York, NY 10016-0199
Ph: (212)889-6500　　Fax: (212)889-6504

Monthly. Magazine on advertising art and photography.

★2371★ Builder

Hanley-Wood, Inc.
1 Thomas Cir., Ste. 600
Washington, DC 20005
Ph: (202)452-0800　　Fax: (202)785-1974

Monthly. $29.95/year for individuals. Magazine covering housing, commercial, and industrial building.

★2372★ Captsule Job Listings

Publications and Communications, Inc.
12416 Hymeadow Dr.
Austin, TX 78750
Ph: (512)250-9023　　Fax: (512)331-3900
Fr: 800-678-9724

Online database. Lists current job openings in the contract (temporary) technical services industry. Includes the Action Hot List, which provides information on job seekers. Includes employment opportunities in technical/professional engineering, computing, and design/drafting. Entries generally contain company name, address, and job opening.

★2373★ Design News

Cahners Publishing Co.
275 Washington St.
Newton, MA 02158-1630
Ph: (617)964-3030　　Fax: (617)558-4470

Semimonthly. $55.00/year for individuals. Magazine covering design engineering.

★2374★ DISPLAY & DESIGN IDEAS

Shore Communications, Inc.
180 Allen Rd. NE, Bldg. N, Ste. 300
Atlanta, GA 30328
Ph: (404)252-8831　　Fax: (404)252-4436

Magazine.

★2375★ Electronics

Peter Li
1100 Superior Ave.
Cleveland, OH 44114
Ph: (216)696-7000　　Fax: (216)696-7670

Bimonthly. $98.00/year; $120.00/year for Canada; $5.00 for single issue. Magazine covering global news, trends, competition, and new technologies, with an emphasis on developments in the U.S., Europe, and the Far East. Topics include computers, communications, semiconductors, and international trade.

★2376★ ENR: Engineering News Record

New York Construction News
1221 Avenue of the Americas
New York, NY 10020
Ph: (212)512-4773　　Fax: (212)512-4770

Weekly. $42.00/year; $2.00/issue.

★2377★ Fabrics and Architecture

Industrial Fabrics Association Intl.
345 Cedar St., Ste. 800
St. Paul, MN 55101
Ph: (612)222-2508　　Fax: (612)222-8215

Bimonthly. $21.00/year. Magazine specializing in interior and exterior design ideas for fabric applications in architecture.

★2378★ HOW

F&W Publications, Inc.
1507 Dana Ave.
Cincinnati, OH 45207
Ph: (513)531-2222　　Fax: (513)531-1843

Bimonthly. $49.00/year for individuals. Instructional trade magazine.

★2379★ Hydraulics & Pneumatics

Peter Li
1100 Superior Ave.
Cleveland, OH 44114
Ph: (216)696-7000　　Fax: (216)696-7670

Monthly. $50.00/year; $65.00/year for Canada; $85.00/year for other countries. Magazine of hydraulic and pneumatic systems and engineering.

★2380★ Jobline News

Graphic Artists Guide of New York
11 W. 20th St., 8th Fl.
New York, NY 10011-3704
Ph: (212)463-7759

Weekly. $100.00/year for nonmembers. Lists jobs for freelance artists in such areas as graphic design, illustration, art education. Most jobs listed are in the New York area.

★2381★ Paperboard Packaging

Advanstar Communications, Inc.
7600 Old Oak Blvd.
Cleveland, OH 44130
Ph: (216)243-8100

Monthly. $30.00/year.

★2382★ Print

R.C. Publications, Inc.
104 5th Ave., 19th Fl.
New York, NY 10011
Ph: (212)463-0600　　Fax: (212)989-9891

Bimonthly. Covers all aspects of graphic design for visual communication.

★2383★ Producer's Masterguide

Producer's Masterguide
60 E. 8th St., 31st Fl.
New York, NY 10003-6514
Ph: (212)777-4002　　Fax: (212)777-4101
Fr: 800-622-6111

Annual. $125.00/year for individuals; $145.00/year for out of country. Magazine for the professional motion picture, TV commercial, cable, and videotape industries in the U.S. Canada, the U.K., the Caribbean Islands, Mexico, Europe, Israel, the Far East and South America.

★2384★ Professional Builder

Cahners Publishing Co.
1350 E. Touhy Ave.
PO Box 5080
Des Plaines, IL 60018-5080
Ph: (708)635-8800　　Fax: (708)635-9950

Monthly. $10.00 for single issue; $139.95/year by mail.

★2385★ TCI (Theatre Crafts International)

Theatre Crafts
32 W. 18th St.
New York, NY 10011-4612
Ph: (212)229-2965   Fax: (212)229-2084

$40.00/year for individuals; $5.00 for single issue. The business of entertainment technology and design.

★2386★ VM & SD: Visual Merchandising and Store Design

ST Publications
407 Gilbert Ave.
Cincinnati, OH 45202
Ph: (513)421-2050   Fax: (513)421-5144
Fr: 800-925-1110

Monthly. $36.00/year.

★2387★ Wire Technology International

Initial Publications, Inc.
3869 Darrow Rd., Ste. 101
Stow, OH 44224
Ph: (216)686-9544   Fax: (216)686-9563

Bimonthly. $35.00/year for individuals; $68.00/year for other countries. Magazine for manufacturers of ferrous, nonferrous, bare, and insulated wire.

PLACEMENT AND JOB REFERRAL SERVICES

★2388★ Advertising Production Club of New York (APC)

60 E. 42nd St., Ste. 721
New York, NY 10165
Ph: (212)983-6042   Fax: (212)983-6043

Members: Production and traffic department personnel from advertising agencies, corporate or retail advertising departments, and publishing companies; college level graphic arts educators. Meetings include educational programs on graphic arts procedures and plant tours. **Activities:** Maintains employment service for members.

★2389★ American Society of Furniture Designers (ASFD)

PO Box 2688
High Point, NC 27261
Ph: (910)884-4074   Fax: (910)884-1737

Members: Professional furniture designers, teachers, students, corporate suppliers of products and services; others who supply products and services related to furniture design. **Purpose:** Seeks to promote the profession of furniture design. Conducts and cooperates in educational courses and seminars for furniture designers and persons planning to enter the field. **Activities:** Maintains placement service.

★2390★ Broadcast Designers' Association International (BDA)

145 W. 45th St., Ste. 1100
New York, NY 10036-4008
Ph: (212)376-6222   Fax: (212)376-6202

Members: Designers, artists, art directors, illustrators, photographers, animators, and other professionals in the electronic media industry; educators and students; commercial and industrial companies that manufacture products related to design. **Purpose:** Objectives are to promote understanding between designers, clients, and management; to stimulate innovative ideas and techniques; to encourage and provide a resource for young talent; and to provide a forum for discussion on industry issues and concerns. **Activities:** Maintains placement service; conducts surveys and compiles statistics.

★2391★ International Association of Clothing Designers (IACD)

475 Park Ave. S, 17th Fl.
New York, NY 10016
Ph: (212)685-6602   Fax: (212)545-1709

Members: Men's and women's apparel designers. **Purpose:** Forecasts clothing styles for manufacturers and retailers. **Activities:** Sponsors placement service Compiles statistics. Conducts research programs.

★2392★ National Association of Milliners, Dressmakers and Tailors (NAMDT)

157 W. 126th St.
New York, NY 10027
Ph: (212)666-1320

Members: Designers, dressmakers, tailors, milliners, fashion commentators and coordinators, and others engaged in the fashion industry. **Purpose:** Sponsors education programs, workshops, and seminars. Maintains speakers' bureau, biographical archives, and Black Fashion Museum. Is developing library and placement service.

★2393★ Professional Services Management Association (PSMA)

4726 Park Rd., Ste. A
Charlotte, NC 28209
Ph: (704)521-8890   Fax: (704)521-8873

Members: Individuals responsible for any or all aspects of business management in a professional design firm. **Purpose:** Purpose is to improve the effectiveness of professional design firms through the growth and development of business management skills. Seeks to: provide a forum for the exchange of ideas and information and discussion and resolution of common problems and issues; establish guidelines for approaches to common management concerns; initiate and maintain professional relationships among members; improve recognition and practice of management as a science in professional design firms; advance and improve reputable service to clients; offer a variety of comprehensive educational programs and opportunities. **Activities:** Maintains speakers' bureau and placement service. Holds seminars. Conducts surveys and research programs. Compiles statistics.

★2394★ University and College Designers Association (UCDA)

209 Commerce St.
Alexandria, VA 22314
Ph: (703)548-1770   Fax: (703)548-1936

Members: Colleges, universities, junior colleges, or technical institutions that have an interest in visual communication design; individuals who are involved in the active production of such communication design or as teachers or students of these related disciplines. **Purpose:** To aid, assist, and educate members through various programs of education; improve members' skills and techniques in communication and design areas such as graphics, photography, signage, films, and other related fields of communication design; be concerned with the individual members' relationships within their own institutions as well as the larger communities in which they serve; aid and assist members in their efforts to be professionals in their respective fields through programs of education and information. **Activities:** Maintains placement service.

EMPLOYER DIRECTORIES AND NETWORKING LISTS

★2395★ Creative Black Book

Black Book Marketing Group
866 3rd Ave.
New York, NY 10022
Ph: (212)702-9700   Fax: (212)605-4808

Annual, January. $140.00, plus $7.00 shipping. Publication includes: photographers and photographic services, design firms, advertising agencies, and other firms whose products or services are used in advertising. Entries include: Company name, address, phone. Principal content of publication is 4-color samples from the leading commercial photographers. Arrangement: Classified by product/service.

★2396★ Design Firm Directory

Wefler & Associates, Inc.
PO Box 1167
Evanston, IL 60204
Ph: (708)475-1866

Annual, volume 1, April; volume 2, October. $57.00, volume 1; $47.00, volume 2; postpaid, payment with order. Covers more than 2,200 commercial and private design and consulting firms, including industrial, graphic, interior, landscape and environmental design; in two volumes: Design Firm Directory Graphic and Industrial Design Edition (volume 1), and Design Firm Directory Environmental and Interior Design Edition (volume 2). Entries include: Firm name, address, phone; year established; number of employees; locations of branches (if any); names and titles of key personnel; areas of specialization; clients. Arrangement: Geographical. Indexes: Alphabetical.

★2397★ Editor & Publisher—Directory of Syndicated Services Issue

Editor & Publisher Co., Inc.
11 W. 19th St., 10th Fl.
New York, NY 10011
Ph: (212)675-4380   Fax: (212)691-6939

Annual, July. $8.00. Publication includes: Directory of several hundred syndicates serving newspapers in the United States and abroad with news, columns, features, comic strips, editorial cartoons, etc. Entries include: Syndicate name, address, phone, names of executives. Arrangement: Alphabetical. Indexes: Personnel, feature title.

★2398★ ENR Directory of Design Firms

McGraw-Hill, Inc.
1221 Ave. of the Americas
New York, NY 10020
Ph: (212)512-2534   Fax: (212)512-4178

Biennial, fall of even years; issue of *Engineering News Record*. $85.00. Covers 133 architects, architectural engineers, consultants, and other design firms; limited to advertisers. Mini-profiles on about 3,400 U.S. firms and 500 foreign firms or foreign offices of U.S. firms. Also includes lists of top 500 design firms in the United States, top 200 international design firms, top 50 United States design-construction firms, and top 50 international design-construction firms, based on total amount of billings. Entries include: For advertisers: company name, address, branch locations, subsidiaries, list of key personnel, territory served, capabilities. In ranked lists: company name, address, phone; international firms include telex. Arrangement: Alphabetical (profiles); geographical (mini-profiles).

★2399★ ENR—Top 500 Design Firms Issue

McGraw-Hill, Inc.
1221 Ave. of the Americas
New York, NY 10020
Ph: (212)512-4635   Fax: (212)512-2820

Annual, April. $10.00, reprint, payment must accompany order. Publication includes: List of 500 leading architectural, engineering, and specialty design firms selected on basis of annual billings. Entries include: Company name, headquarters location, type of firm, current and prior year rank in billings, types of services, countries in which operated in preceding year. Arrangement: Ranked by billings.

★2400★ ENR—Top International Design Firms Issue

McGraw-Hill, Inc.
1221 Ave. of the Americas, Rm. 4188
New York, NY 10020
Ph: (212)512-4635

Annual, July. $10.00, reprint, payment with order. Publication includes: List of 200 design firms (including United States firms) competing outside their own national borders who received largest dollar volume of foreign contracts in preceding calendar year. Entries include: Company name, headquarters location, type of firm, current and previous year rankings in total billings, types of services, countries in which operated in preceding year. Arrangement: By amount billed to international clients in previous year.

★2401★ Furniture Designers and Custom Builders Directory

American Business Directories, Inc.
American Business Information, Inc.
5711 S. 86th Cir.
Omaha, NE 68127
Ph: (402)593-4600   Fax: (402)331-1505

Annual. $480.00, U.S. edition. Entries include: Name, address, phone (including area code), size of advertisement, year first in Yellow Pages, name of owner or manager, number of employees. Compiled from telephone company Yellow Pages, nationwide. Arrangement: Geographical.

HANDBOOKS AND MANUALS

★2402★ Career Choices for the 90's for Students of Art

Walker and Company
435 Hudson St.
New York, NY 10014
Ph: (212)727-8300   Fax: (212)727-0984
Fr: 800-289-2553

Prepared by the Career Associates staff. 1990. $9.95. 166 pages. Discusses alternatives for students of art. Offers advice on how to break into the field and how to move up. Covers where and who the employers are, internship possibilities, and professional networking associations. Comprehensive guide to career and job search planning.

★2403★ Career Information Center

Macmillan Publishing Co.
200 Old Tappan Rd.
Old Tappan, NJ 07675
Ph: (609)461-6500   Fr: 800-223-2336

Visual Education Center Staff. Fifth edition, 1992. $229.00. This 13-volume set profiles over 600 occupations. Each occupational profile describes job duties, educational requirements, how to get the job, advancement possibilities, employment outlook, working conditions, earnings and benefits, and where to write for more information.

★2404★ Career Opportunities in Art

Facts on File, Inc.
11 Penn Plaza, 15th Fl.
New York, NY 10001-2006
Ph: (212)967-8800   Fax: 800-678-3633
Fr: 800-322-8755

Susan H. Haubenstock and David Joselit. Revised edition, 1994. $29.95; $15.95 (paper). 208 pages. This book profiles seventy-five jobs that can be found in the art field. Each profile includes a career description, career ladder, employment and advancement prospects, education, experience and skills required, salary range, and tips for entry into the field.

★2405★ Career Opportunities in Theater and the Performing Arts

Facts on File, Inc.
11 Penn Plaza, 15th Fl.
New York, NY 10001-2006
Ph: (212)967-8800   Fax: 800-678-3633
Fr: 800-322-8755

Shelly Field. 1992. $29.95; $15.95 (paper). 256 pages. Offers a complete range of information about job opportunities in the performing arts.

★2406★ Careers in Advertising

VGM Career Horizons
4255 W. Touhy Ave.
Lincolnwood, IL 60646-1975
Ph: (847)679-5500   Fax: (847)679-2494
Fr: 800-323-4900

S. William Pattis. Second edition, 1996. $17.95; $13.95 (paper). 192 pages. Explains the role of the media in advertising, personal characteristics needed to succeed in this field, educational requirements, and related jobs. Covers copy writing, art, design, account management, media, and research. Gives job hunting tips.

★2407★ Careers for Culture Lovers and Other Artsy Types

VGM Career Horizons
4255 W. Touhy Ave.
Lincolnwood, IL 60646-1975
Ph: (847)679-5500   Fax: (847)679-2494
Fr: 800-323-4900

Marjorie Eberts and Margaret Gisler. 1994. $14.95; $9.95 (paper). Describes how to get work in a variety of fields related to art and culture. Opportunities include picture framer, curator, art restorer, symphony manager, disk jockey, music reviewer, dance teacher, choreographer, costume designer, theater manager, light designer, drama teacher, bookstore owner, interior decorator, antique store owner, and others.

★2408★ Careers in the Graphic Arts

Rosen Publishing Group, Inc.
29 E. 21st St.
New York, NY 10010
Ph: (212)777-3017   Fax: (212)777-0277
Fr: 800-237-9932

Virginia Lee Roberson. Revised edition, 1995. $14.95; $9.95 (paper). Discusses a career in graphic arts; outlines educational requirements, training, and skills needed to become an illustrator, layout artist, designer, and paste-up artist. Gives job hunting advice, describes how to write a resume, prepare a portfolio, and interview preparation. Gives a state-by-state listing of schools offering graphic arts.

★2409★ Careers in the Visual Arts: A Guide to Jobs, Money, Opportunities, and an Artistic Life

Watson-Guptill Publications, Inc.
BPI Communications, Inc.
1515 Broadway
New York, NY 10036
Ph: (212)536-5121   Fr: 800-451-1741

Dee Ito. 1993. $14.95. 320 pages. Gives a broad overview of each field included, with educational requirements and employment opportunities. Includes ideas on how to get started.

★2410★ **The Designer's Commonsense Business Book**

NTC Publishing Group
4255 W. Touhy Ave.
Lincolnwood, IL 60646-1975
Ph: (708)679-5500   Fax: (708)679-6375
Fr: 800-323-4900

Barbara Ganim. 1994. $29.95; $27.99 (paper).

★2411★ **Directory of Designers**

State Mutual Book & Periodical Service, Ltd.
521 5th Ave., 17th Fl.
New York, NY 10175
Ph: (718)261-1704   Fax: (516)537-0412

Design Council Staff. 1993. $175.00.

★2412★ **The Encyclopedia of Career Choices for the 1990s: Guide to Entry-Level Jobs**

Perigree Books
The Berkley Publishing Group
PO Box 506
East Rutherford, NJ 07073
Ph: (201)933-9292   Fr: 800-223-0510

Career Associates Staff. 1992. $19.95. 862 pages. Describes 500 entry-level careers in a variety of industries. Presents qualifications required, working conditions, salary, internships, and professional associations.

★2413★ **Graphic Design Career Guide**

Watson-Guptill Publications
1515 Broadway
New York, NY 10036
Ph: (212)764-7300

James Craig. Revised edition, 1992. $19.95. 160 pages. Includes advice on the job-hunting process. Contains index, bibliography, and illustrations.

★2414★ **Liberal Arts Jobs: What They Are and How to Get Them**

Peterson's
PO Box 2123
Princeton, NJ 08543-2123
Ph: (609)243-9111   Fax: (609)243-9150
Fr: 800-338-3282

Burton Jay Nadler. Second edition, 1989. $9.95. 153 pages. Presents a list of the top 20 fields for liberal arts majors, covering more than 300 job opportunities. Discusses strategies for going after those jobs, including guidance on the language of a successful job search, informational interviews, and making networking work.

★2415★ **1996 Artist's & Graphic Designer's Market**

Writer's Digest Books
1507 Dana Ave.
Cincinnati, OH 45207
Ph: (513)531-2690   Fax: (513)531-4082
Fr: 800-289-0963

Mary Cox, editor. 1995. $23.99.

★2416★ **100 Best Careers for the Year 2000**

Prentice Hall General Reference
15 Columbus Cir.
New York, NY 10023
Ph: (212)373-8500   Fr: 800-223-2348

Shelly Field. 1992. $15.00 (paper). Covers 100 of the fastest growing jobs. The publication is divided into 11 general employment sections. Specific careers are covered within each section. Provides job description, responsibilities, employment opportunities, earnings, education and training, advancement opportunities, and experience and qualifications for each occupation.

★2417★ **Opportunities in Commercial Art and Graphic Design Careers**

VGM Career Horizons
4255 W. Touhy Ave.
Lincolnwood, IL 60646-1975
Ph: (847)679-5500   Fax: (847)679-2494
Fr: 800-323-4900

Barbara Gordon. Second edition, 1992. $14.95; $11.95 (paper). 160 pages. Provides a survey of job opportunities in advertising and public relations, publishing, fashion, architecture, and newspapers, as well as in a variety of specialty markets. Illustrated.

★2418★ **Opportunities in Fashion Careers**

VGM Career Horizons
4255 W. Touhy Ave.
Lincolnwood, IL 60646-1975
Ph: (847)679-5500   Fax: (847)679-2494
Fr: 800-323-4900

Roslyn Dolber. 1993. $14.95; $11.95 (paper). 160 pages. Covers job opportunities in the textile industry, design and manufacturing, apparel production, and fashion merchandising, and how to pursue them. Illustrated.

★2419★ **Opportunities in Publishing Careers**

VGM Career Horizons
4255 W. Touhy Ave.
Lincolnwood, IL 60646-1975
Ph: (847)679-5500   Fax: (847)679-2494
Fr: 800-323-4900

Robert A. Carter and S. William Pattis. 1995. $11.95 paperback. $14.95 hardcover. 160 pages. Covers all positions in book and magazine publishing, including new opportunities in multimedia publishing.

★2420★ **Opportunities in Visual Arts Careers**

VGM Career Horizons
4255 W. Touhy Ave.
Lincolnwood, IL 60646-1975
Ph: (847)679-5500   Fax: (847)679-2494
Fr: 800-323-4900

Mark Salmon. 1993. $14.95; $11.95 (paper). Points the way to a career in the visual arts, examining opportunities for designers, painters, sculptors, illustrators, animators, photographers, art therapists, educators, and others. Offers a view of the pros and cons of working for an art or design company or on your own.

★2421★ **Power Freelancing: Home-Based Careers for Writers, Designers, & Consultants**

Mid-List Press
4324 12th Ave., S
Minneapolis, MN 55407-3218
Ph: (612)822-3733

George Sorenson. 1995. $14.95 (paper).

★2422★ **The Professional and Business Guide to Design Services**

State Mutual Book and Periodical Service, Limited
521 5th Ave., 17th Fl.
New York, NY 10175
Ph: (718)261-1704   Fax: (516)537-0412

Lanre. 1993. $185.00.

★2423★ **Where the Jobs Are: The Hottest Careers for the '90s**

The Career Press, Inc.
3 Tice Rd.
PO Box 687
Franklin Lakes, NJ 07417
Ph: (201)848-0310   Fax: (201)848-1727
Fr: 800-237-3371

Joyce Hadley. Second edition, 1995. $9.99. 300 pages. Describes careers in fifteen general fields, from accounting to travel and hospitality.

EMPLOYMENT AGENCIES AND SEARCH FIRMS

★2424★ **ABC Employment Service**

25 S. Bemiston, Ste. 214
Clayton, MO 63105
Ph: (314)725-3140

Employment agency.

★2425★ **B and M Associates, Inc.**

199 Cambridge Rd.
Woburn, MA 01801-4705
Ph: (617)938-9120

Employment agency.

★2426★ **Capitol Search**

215 E. Ridgewood Ave.
Ridgewood, NJ 07450
Ph: (201)444-6666   Fax: (201)444-4121

Employment agency. Second location in Ridgewood, NJ.

★2427★ **Claremont-Branan, Inc.**

2150 Parklake Dr., Ste. 212
Atlanta, GA 30345
Ph: (404)491-1292

Employment agency. Executive search firm.

★2428★ **Colli Associates of Tampa**

PO Box 2865
Tampa, FL 33601
Ph: (813)681-2145

Employment agency. Executive search firm.

★2429★ Consultants and Designers Inc.

7240 Parkway Dr., Ste. 250
Hanover, MD 21076-1367
Ph: (410)712-0052

Places staff in temporary positions. West Coast office located in Santa Clara, CA.

★2430★ Industrial Recruiters Associates, Inc.

630 Oakwood Ave., Ste. 318
West Hartford, CT 06110
Ph: (203)953-3643

Employment agency.

★2431★ The Jobs Co.

8900 E. Sprague Ave.
Spokane, WA 99212-2927
Ph: (509)928-3151   Fax: (509)928-3168

Employment agency. Has division specializing in engineering and scientific openings. Also operates division specializing in sales openings.

★2432★ JR Professional Search

PO Box 18356
Tucson, AZ 85731
Ph: (520)721-1855   Fax: (520)721-1855

Employment agency.

★2433★ Randolph Associates, Inc.

950 Massachusetts Ave., Ste. 105
Cambridge, MA 02139-3174
Ph: (617)441-8777   Fax: (617)441-8778

Employment agency. Provides regular or temporary placement of staff.

★2434★ RitaSue Siegel Associates, Inc.

20 E. 46th St.
New York, NY 10017-2417
Ph: (212)682-2100

Executive search firm.

★2435★ Search and Recruit International

4455 South Blvd.
Virginia Beach, VA 23452
Ph: (804)490-3151

Employment agency. Headquartered in Virginia Beach. Other offices in Bremerton, WA; Charleston, SC; Jacksonville, FL; Memphis, TN; Pensacola, FL; Sacramento, CA; San Bernardino, CA; San Diego, CA.

OTHER SOURCES

★2436★ Career Connections Video Series

Cambridge Career Products
PO Box 2153
Dept. CC15
Charleston, WV 25328-2153
Ph: (304)744-9323   Fax: (304)744-9351
Fr: 800-468-4227

Series of six videos. 1993. $219.95/set. $39.95/each. 15-20 minutes. Each video contains interviews with workers and on-the-job footage. Titles include Graphic Design, Welding, Electrician, Plumber, Pipefitter, and HVAC.

★2437★ Careers in Art

Cambridge Career Products
PO Box 2153
Dept. CC15
Charleston, WV 25328-2153
Ph: (304)744-9323   Fax: (304)744-9351
Fr: 800-468-4227

Video. $49.95. 21 minutes. Covers many professional options available in the world of art.

★2438★ Florists' Transworld Delivery Association (FTDA)

29200 Northwestern Hwy.
Southfield, MI 48034
Ph: (810)355-9300

Members: Retail florist shops in North America selling flowers, gifts, candy, and fruit by wire. **Purpose:** Conducts specialized advertising, education, and research programs; compiles statistics. Conducts ZIP code marketing service.

★2439★ Home Economics Careers

Cambridge Career Products
PO Box 2153
Dept. CC15
Charleston, WV 25328-2153
Ph: (304)744-9323   Fax: (304)744-9351
Fr: 800-468-4227

Video. $79.95. 30 minutes. Presents a series of interviews with men and women working in different areas of home economics, including dietetics, foods and nutrition, child development, interior design, and fashion. Covers educational, personal, and professional requirements for each occupation.

★2440★ Industrial Designers Society of America (IDSA)

1142-E Walker Rd.
Great Falls, VA 22066
Ph: (703)759-0100   Fax: (703)759-7679

Members: Professional society of industrial designers. **Purpose:** Maintains the standards of the profession in its relations with business, industry, government, and international designers; promotes the industrial design profession. **Activities:** Sponsors children's services; conducts research, educational, and charitable programs. Compiles statistics.

★2441★ Society of American Florists (SAF)

1601 Duke St.
Alexandria, VA 22314-3406
Ph: (703)836-8700   Fax: (703)836-8705
Fr: 800-336-4743

Members: Growers, wholesalers, retailers, and allied tradesmen in the floral industry. **Purpose:** Lobbies Congress on behalf of the industry; sponsors educational programs; promotes the floral industry; prepares materials for consumers and for high school and college students; provides business resources. Sponsors Floricultural Hall of Fame, American Academy of Floriculture, American Floral Marketing Council, and Professional Floral Commentators - International. Compiles statistics; sponsors competitions.

Dietitians and Nutritionists

SOURCES OF HELP-WANTED ADS

★2442★ American Journal of Clinical Nutrition

American Society of Clinical Nutrition
9650 Rockville Pke.
Bethesda, MD 20814-3998
Ph: (301)530-7038   Fax: (301)571-1892

Monthly. $45.00/year for members; $90.00/year for nonmembers; $135.00/year for institutions; $35.00/year for students; $250.00/year for students, other countries. Journal of basic and clinical studies relevant to human nutrition.

★2443★ Chef

Talcott Communications Corp.
20 N. Wacker Dr., Ste. 3230
Chicago, IL 60606
Ph: (312)849-2220   Fax: (312)849-2174
Fr: 800-229-1967

$20.00/year for individuals; $2.95 for single issue. Covers the food service field for executive chefs.

★2444★ Food Management

Peter Li
1100 Superior Ave.
Cleveland, OH 44114
Ph: (216)696-7000   Fax: (216)696-7670

Monthly. $50.00/year. Professional magazine for foodservice directors.

★2445★ Food Technology

Institute of Food Technologists
221 N. La Salle St., Ste. 300
Chicago, IL 60601
Ph: (312)782-8424   Fax: (312)782-8348

Monthly. $72.00/year for individuals. Food technology and science magazine.

★2446★ FoodService Director

Bill Communications, Inc.
355 Park Ave. S.
New York, NY 10010
Ph: (212)592-6200   Fax: (212)592-6539

Monthly. Tabloid newspaper of the noncommercial foodservice market.

★2447★ Foodservice East

The Newbury Street Group, Inc.
76 Summer St.
Boston, MA 02110
Ph: (617)695-9080   Fr: 800-852-5212

$20.00/year for individuals. Tabloid covering restaurant, hotel, school, college, and hospital food service in the Northeast.

★2448★ Journal of the American Dietetic Association

American Dietetic Association
216 W. Jackson Blvd.
Chicago, IL 60606-6695
Ph: (312)899-0040   Fax: (312)899-1757

Monthly. $100.00/year; $9.75/issue. Magazine reporting original research on nutrition, diet therapy, education, and administration.

★2449★ Journal of Nutrition Education

Decker Periodicals
1 James St. S.
PO Box 620, LCD 1
Hamilton, ON, Canada L8N 3K7
Ph: (416)522-7017   Fax: (416)522-7839
Fr: 800-568-7281

Bimonthly.

★2450★ Modern Food Service News

Grocers Publishing Co., Inc.
15 Emerald St.
Hackensack, NJ 07601
Ph: (201)488-1800

Monthly. Magazine for restaurateurs, chefs, caterers, purchasing agents in the food service industry.

★2451★ Southeast Food Service News

Southeast Publishing Co., Inc.
PO Box 47719
Atlanta, GA 30362
Ph: (404)452-1807   Fax: (404)457-3829

Monthly. $23.00/year for individuals. Magazine (tabloid) serving the food industry.

★2452★ Sunbelt Foodservice

Shelby Publishing Co., Inc.
517 Green St.
Gainesville, GA 30501
Ph: (404)534-8380   Fax: (404)535-0110

Monthly. $25.00/year for individuals. Trade newspaper (tabloid) covering the food industry geared toward restaurant operators.

★2453★ Yankee Food Service

Griffin Publishing Co., Inc.
1099 Hingham St.
Rockland, MA 02370
Ph: (617)878-5300   Fax: (617)871-4721

Monthly. $40.00/year for individuals. Newspaper (tabloid) covering business news, personnel changes, food trends, and trade events of the New England food service industry.

PLACEMENT AND JOB REFERRAL SERVICES

★2454★ American Public Health Association (APHA)

1015 15th St. NW
Washington, DC 20005
Ph: (202)789-5600   Fax: (202)789-5681

Members: Professional organization of physicians, nurses, educators, academicians, environmentalists, epidemiologists, new professionals, social workers, health administrators, optometrists, podiatrists, pharmacists, dentists, nutritionists, health planners, other community and mental health specialists, and interested consumers. **Purpose:** Seeks to protect and promote personal, mental, and environmental health. **Activities:** Services include: promulgation of standards; establishment of uniform practices and procedures; development of the etiology of communicable diseases; research in public health; exploration of medical care programs and their relationships to public health. Sponsors job placement service.

★2455★ American School Health Association (ASHA)

7263 State Rte. 43
PO Box 708
Kent, OH 44240
Ph: (216)678-1601   Fax: (216)678-4526

Members: School physicians, school nurses, dentists, nurses, nutritionists, health educators, dental hygienists, school-based professionals, and public health workers. **Purpose:** Promotes comprehensive and constructive school health programs including the teaching of health, health services, and promotion of a healthful school environment. **Activities:** Offers a professional referral service, classroom teaching aids, and professional reference materials. Conducts research programs; maintains placement service; compiles statistics. Sponsors foreign travel study tour.

★2456★ Dietary Managers Association (DMA)

1 Pierce Pl., No. 1220W
Itasca, IL 60143
Ph: (708)775-9200   Fax: (708)775-9250
Fr: 800-323-1908

Purpose: Dietary managers united to maintain a high level of competency and quality in dietary departments through continuing education. **Activities:** Provides educational programs and placement service.

EMPLOYER DIRECTORIES AND NETWORKING LISTS

★2457★ AHA Guide to the Health Care Field

Health Statistics Group
American Hospital Association (AHA)
1 N. Franklin
Chicago, IL 60606
Ph: (312)422-3501   Fax: (312)280-6015

Annual, July. $195.00, payment with order. Covers hospitals, multi-health care systems, freestanding ambulatory surgery centers, psychiatric facilities, long-term care facilities, substance abuse programs, hospices, Health Maintenance Organizations (HMOs), and other health-related organizations. Entries include: For hospitals: facility name, address, phone, administrator's name, number of beds, facilities and services, number of employees, expenses, other statistics. For other organizations: name, address, phone, name and title of contact. Arrangement: Geographical. Indexes: Hospital name.

★2458★ Directory of Hospital Personnel

Medical Economics
5 Paragon Dr.
Montvale, NJ 07645-1725
Ph: (201)358-7500   Fax: (201)573-4956
Fr: 800-222-3045

Annual, September. $325.00, plus 7.50 shipping. Covers 200,000 executives at 7,100 U.S. hospitals. Entries include: Name of hospital, address, phone, number of beds, type and JCAHO status of hospital, names and titles of key department heads and staff,

medical and nursing school affiliations; number of residents, interns, and nursing students. Arrangement: Geographical. Indexes: Hospital name, personnel, hospital size.

★2459★ Directory of Nursing Homes

HCIA Inc.
300 E. Lombard St.
Baltimore, MD 21202
Ph: (410)576-9600   Fax: (410)539-5220
Fr: 800-568-3282

Annual. $249.00. Covers over 16,000 state-licensed long-term care facilities. Entries include: Facility name, address, phone, names and titles of key personnel, licensure status, number of beds; number of nursing, dietary, and auxiliary staff members; program/services; medicaid/medicare certification status; admission and referral requirements; age and gender restrictions; languages spoken; management or chain company name. Arrangement: Geographical. Indexes: Alphabetical, geographical (county) and by chain headquarters.

★2460★ Hospital Blue Book

Billian Publishing Co.
2100 Powers Ferry Rd., Ste. 300
Atlanta, GA 30339
Ph: (404)955-5656   Fax: (404)952-0669

Annual, spring. $154.50, national edition, plus $20.00 shipping. Covers more than 7,100 hospitals; some listings also appear in a separate southern edition of this publication. Entries include: Name of hospital, accreditation, mailing address, phone, fax, number of beds, type of facility (nonprofit, general, state, etc.); list of administrative personnel and chiefs of medical services, with specific titles. Arrangement: Geographical.

★2461★ Hospital Market Atlas

SMG Marketing Group, Inc.
1342 N. LaSalle Dr.
Chicago, IL 60610
Ph: (312)642-3026   Fax: (312)642-9729
Fr: 800-678-3026

Biennial, odd years. $495.00, payment with order. Covers over 7,000 hospitals, hospital systems and 480 group purchasing organizations. Entries include: Hospital or organization name, address, phone, county code, management, type of hospital service, number of beds, admissions, surgical operations, and emergency room visits. Arrangement: Geographical.

★2462★ Hospitals Directory

American Business Directories, Inc.
American Business Information, Inc.
5711 S. 86th Cir.
Omaha, NE 68127
Ph: (402)593-4600   Fax: (402)331-1505

Annual. $870.00, U.S. edition. Entries include: Name, address, phone (including area code), size of advertisement, year first in Yellow Pages, name of owner or manager, number of employees. Compiled from telephone company Yellow Pages, nationwide. Arrangement: Geographical.

★2463★ Life Sciences Organizations and Agencies Directory

Gale Research
835 Penobscot Bldg.
Detroit, MI 48226-4094
Ph: (313)961-2242   Fax: (313)961-6083
Fr: 800-877-GALE

$175.00. Covers about 7,500 associations, government agencies, research centers, educational institutions, libraries and information centers, museums, consultants, electronic information services, and other organizations and agencies active in agriculture, biology, ecology, forestry, marine science, nutrition, wildlife and animal sciences, and other natural and life sciences. Entries include: Organization or agency name, address, phone, name and title of contact, description. Arrangement: Classified by type of organization. Indexes: Organization/agency name and keyword.

★2464★ Medical and Health Information Directory

Gale Research
835 Penobscot Bldg.
Detroit, MI 48226-4094
Ph: (313)961-2242   Fax: (313)961-6083
Fr: 800-877-GALE

Approximately biennial; latest edition 1994. $195.00, per volume; $485.00, for the three-volume set. Covers in Volume 1, almost 18,600 medical and health oriented associations, organizations, institutions, and government agencies, including health maintenance organizations (HMOs), preferred provider organizations (PPOs), insurance companies, pharmaceutical companies, research centers, and medical and allied health schools. In Volume 2, nearly 11,800 medical book publishers; medical periodicals, directories, audiovisual producers and services, medical libraries and information centers, and electronic resources. In Volume 3, nearly 26,000 clinics, treatment centers, care programs, and counseling/diagnostic services for 30 subject areas. Entries include: Institution, service, or firm name, address, phone; many include names of key personnel and, when pertinent, descriptive annotation. Arrangement: Classified by organization activity, service, etc. Indexes: Each volume has a complete alphabetical name and keyword index.

★2465★ Osteopathic Membership Directory—AOHA

American Osteopathic Healthcare Association
5301 Wisconsin Ave. NW, Ste. 630
Washington, DC 20015-2015
Ph: (202)686-1700   Fax: (202)686-7615

Annual, summer. $125.00, payment with order. Covers about 110 osteopathic hospitals. Includes list of individual and institutional members; also lists osteopathic colleges, and directors of medical education. Entries include: For hospitals: name of hospital, name of chief executive officer, address, phone, number of beds and other hospital data. Arrangement: Geographical. Indexes: Name, institution.

HANDBOOKS AND MANUALS

★2466★ *Career Inside the World of Health Care*

Rosen Publishing Group
219 E. 21st. St.
New York, NY 10010
Ph: (212)777-3017   Fax: (212)777-0277
Fr: 800-237-9932

Beth Wilkinson. 1994. $14.95.

★2467★ *Career Opportunities in the Food and Beverage Industry*

Facts on File, Inc.
11 Penn Plaza, 15th Fl.
New York, NY 10001-2006
Ph: (212)967-8800   Fax: 800-678-3633
Fr: 800-322-8755

Barbara Sims-Bell. 1994. $29.95; $15.95 (paper). 256 pages. Provides the job seeker with information about locating and landing 80 skilled and unskilled jobs in the industry. Includes detailed job descriptions for many specific positions and lists trade associations, recruiting organizations, and major agencies. Contains index and bibliography.

★2468★ *Careers in Health Care*

VGM Career Horizons
4255 W. Touhy Ave.
Lincolnwood, IL 60646-1975
Ph: (847)679-5500   Fax: (847)679-2494
Fr: 800-323-4900

Barbara M. Swanson. 1995. $17.95; $13.95 (paper). Describes job duties, work settings, salaries, licensing and certification requirements, educational preparation, and future outlook. Gives ideas on how to secure a job.

★2469★ *Careers in Health and Fitness*

Rosen Publishing Group, Inc.
29 E. 21st St.
New York, NY 10010
Ph: (212)777-3017   Fax: (212)777-0277
Fr: 800-237-9932

Jackie Heron. Revised edition, 1990. $14.95. 160 pages. Contains occupational profiles for this field, including information on job duties, skills, advantages, basic equipment used, employment possibilities, certification, and salary.

★2470★ *Careers in Medicine: Traditional and Alternative Opportunities*

Garrett Park Press
PO Box 190 C
Garrett Park, MD 20896-0190
Ph: (301)946-2553

Donald T. Rucker and Martin D. Keller. 1990. $15.95. 346 pages. Cites training requirements, illustrative work activities, and a summary of the advantages and disadvantages in a variety of specialized areas. Includes hundreds of career alternatives and discusses ways to break into these fields for persons trained in medicine. Features contributions from over 40 professionals in all phases of medicine and provides 200 sources of information on specialties and subspecialties.

★2471★ *Careers Without College: Health Care*

Peterson's Guides Inc.
PO Box 2123
Princeton, NJ 08543-0261
Ph: (609)243-9150   Fax: (609)243-9150

Susan Gordon. 1992. $7.95 (paper).

★2472★ *100 Best Careers for the Year 2000*

Prentice Hall General Reference
15 Columbus Cir.
New York, NY 10023
Ph: (212)373-8500   Fr: 800-223-2348

Shelly Field. 1992. $15.00 (paper). Covers 100 of the fastest growing jobs. The publication is divided into 11 general employment sections. Specific careers are covered within each section. Provides job description, responsibilities, employment opportunities, earnings, education and training, advancement opportunities, and experience and qualifications for each occupation.

★2473★ *Opportunities in Food Service Careers*

VGM Career Horizons
4255 W. Touhy Ave.
Lincolnwood, IL 60646-1975
Ph: (847)679-5500   Fax: (847)679-2494
Fr: 800-323-4900

Carol Caprione. 1992. $14.95; $11.95 (paper). 160 pages. Discusses how to secure employment and provides information on identifying openings, resume writing, and interviewing. Lists recruiters and associations to contact for further information and leads. Illustrated.

★2474★ *Opportunities in Health and Medical Careers*

VGM Career Horizons
4255 W. Touhy Ave.
Lincolnwood, IL 60646-1975
Ph: (847)679-5500   Fax: (847)679-2494
Fr: 800-323-4900

Donald Snook, Jr. and Leo D'Orazio. 1993. $14.95; $11.95 (paper). Covers the full range of medical and health occupations. Illustrated.

★2475★ *Opportunities in Nutrition Careers*

VGM Career Horizons
4255 W. Touhy Ave.
Lincolnwood, IL 60646-1975
Ph: (847)679-5500   Fax: (847)679-2494
Fr: 800-323-4900

Carol Coles Caldwell. 1994. $14.95; $11.95 (paper). 160 pages. Focuses on job opportunities in therapeutic nutrition, health maintenance nutrition, hospital and medical diet nutrition, research and biochemical manufacturing, and others. Illustrated.

★2476★ *Opportunities in Public Health Careers*

VGM Career Horizons
4255 W. Touhy Ave.
Lincolnwood, IL 60646-1975
Ph: (847)679-5500   Fax: (847)679-2494
Fr: 800-323-4900

George E. Pickett and Terry W. Pickett.

1995. $14.95; $11.95 (paper). 160 pages. Defines the public health field and describes a variety of health, science, and business opportunities as well as educational preparation and the future of the public health field. Offers job-hunting tips. The appendixes list public health organizations, state and federal public health agencies, and graduate schools offering public health programs.

★2477★ *Opportunities in Sports Medicine Careers*

VGM Career Horizons
4255 W. Touhy Ave.
Lincolnwood, IL 60646-1975
Ph: (847)679-5500   Fax: (847)679-2494
Fr: 800-323-4900

William Ray Heitzmann. 1995. $14.95; $11.95 (paper). 160 pages. Discusses a variety of opportunities in this field and how to pursue them. Contains bibliography and illustrations.

★2478★ *Resumes for Health and Medical Careers*

4255 W. Touhy Ave.
Lincolnwood, IL 60646-1975
Ph: (708)679-5500   Fax: (708)679-6375
Fr: 800-323-4900

Compiled by VGM Career Horizons Staff. 1995. $9.95 (paper).

★2479★ *Therapists and Allied Health Professionals Career Directory*

Gale Research
835 Penobscot Bldg.
Detroit, MI 48226-4094
Ph: (313)961-2242   Fax: (313)961-6083
Fr: 800-877-GALE

Bradley Morgan. 1993. $39.00. 326 pages. Essays on specific careers provide an insider's perspective. Also features extensive listings of contacts and entry-level job opportunities. Provides information on internships and sources of help-wanted ads.

EMPLOYMENT AGENCIES AND SEARCH FIRMS

★2480★ *Academy Medical Personnel Services*

571 High St.
Columbus, OH 43085-4132
Ph: (614)848-6011

Employment agency. Fills openings on a regular or temporary basis.

★2481★ *Eden Temporary Services*

280 Madison Ave.
New York, NY 10016-0801
Ph: (212)685-4666

Employment agency. Places individuals in regular or temporary positions.

★2482★ Harper Associates
29870 Middlebelt
Farmington Hills, MI 48334
Ph: (810)932-1170
Employment agency.

★2483★ Health and Science Center
209 Hunter St.
Media, PA 19063-5726
Ph: (610)891-0714
Employment agency. Executive search firm.

★2484★ Professional Placement Associates, Inc.
11 Rye Ridge Plaza
Rye Brook, NY 10573
Ph: (914)251-1000   Fax: (914)939-1959
Employment agency.

★2485★ Ritt-Ritt and Associates
424 Swan Blvd.
Deerfield, IL 60015
Ph: (708)520-9999
Employment agency.

★2486★ Sue Carroll Personnel, Inc.
16 E. 79th St.
New York, NY 10021
Ph: (212)288-8866   Fax: (212)988-7191
Employment agency and executive search firm.

OTHER SOURCES

★2487★ American Association of Nutritional Consultants (AANC)
880 Canarios Court, Ste. 210
Chula Vista, CA 91910
Ph: (619)482-8533   Fax: (619)482-0938
Members: Professional nutritional consultants. **Purpose:** Seeks to: develop a certification board; create a forum for exchange of nutritional information; establish state chapters.

★2488★ American Dietetic Association (ADA)
216 W. Jackson Blvd., Ste. 800
Chicago, IL 60606
Ph: (312)899-0040   Fax: (312)899-1979
Members: Dietetic professionals, registered dietitians and dietetic technicians serving the public through promotion of optimal nutrition, health and well being. **Purpose:** Seeks to shape the food choices and impact the nutritional status of the public in hospitals, colleges, universities, schools, day care centers, research, business and industry. Sets and approves standards of education and practice. Provides career guidance.

★2489★ Dietary Manager Magazine
Dietary Managers Association
1 Pierce Pl., Ste. 1220 W
Itasca, IL 60143
Ph: (708)775-9200   Fax: (708)775-9250
Fr: 800-323-1908
Bimonthly. $24.00/year; $5.00/year for single issue.

★2490★ Home Economics Careers
Cambridge Career Products
PO Box 2153
Dept. CC15
Charleston, WV 25328-2153
Ph: (304)744-9323   Fax: (304)744-9351
Fr: 800-468-4227
Video. $79.95. 30 minutes. Presents a series of interviews with men and women working in different areas of home economics, including dietetics, foods and nutrition, child development, interior design, and fashion. Covers educational, personal, and professional requirements for each occupation.

Disc Jockeys

EMPLOYER DIRECTORIES AND NETWORKING LISTS

★2491★ ADJA Affiliate Directory
American Disc Jockey Association (ADJA)
c/o Bruce Kessler
PO Box 151
Horsham, PA 19044
Ph: (215)675-9567   Fax: (215)675-9611
Quarterly.

★2492★ Radio Stations and Broadcasting Companies Directory
American Business Directories, Inc.
American Business Information, Inc.
5711 S. 86th Cir.
Omaha, NE 68127
Ph: (402)593-4600   Fax: (402)331-1505
Annual. $765.00 U.S. edition. Entries include: Name, address, phone (including area code), size of advertisement, year first in Yellow Pages, name of owner or manager, number of employees. Franchise editions available: AM Stations, $245.00; FM Stations, $430.00. Compiled from telephone company Yellow Pages, nationwide. Arrangement: Geographical.

HANDBOOKS AND MANUALS

★2493★ Announcers and Disc Jockeys
Chronicle Guidance Publications, Inc.
66 Aurora St.
PO Box 1190
Moravia, NY 13118-1190
Ph: (315)497-0330   Fax: (315)497-3359
Fr: 800-622-7284
Chronicle Guidance Staff. 1994. $2.00. Provides concise career information and sources of additional information.

★2494★ Announcing: Broadcast Communications Today
Wadsworth Publishing Co.
10 Davis Dr.
Belmont, CA 94002
Ph: (415)595-2350   Fax: (606)525-0978
Lewis B. O'Donnell. 1992. $55.95.

★2495★ The Best Home-Based Businesses for the 90s
G.P. Putnam's Sons
Putnam Berkley Group
200 Madison Ave.
New York, NY 10016
Ph: (212)951-8400   Fr: 800-631-8571
Paul Edwards and Sarah Edwards. Second edition, 1994. $12.95. 400 pages. Profiles 95 businesses and careers that can be conducted from one's home. Lists sources of additional information.

★2496★ Breakin' in...To the Music Business
Cherry Lane Books
10 Midland Ave.
PO Box 430
Port Chester, NY 10573
Ph: (914)937-8601   Fr: 800-354-4004
Alan H. Siegel. 1993. $19.95. 276 pages. Describes the record deal; the artist-manager relationship; working with copyrights, demos, and the terminology used in the industry.

★2497★ Careers for Culture Lovers and Other Artsy Types
VGM Career Horizons
4255 W. Touhy Ave.
Lincolnwood, IL 60646-1975
Ph: (847)679-5500   Fax: (847)679-2494
Fr: 800-323-4900
Marjorie Eberts and Margaret Gisler. 1994. $14.95; $9.95 (paper). Describes how to get work in a variety of fields related to art and culture. Opportunities include picture framer, curator, art restorer, symphony manager, disk jockey, music reviewer, dance teacher, choreographer, costume designer, theater manager, light designer, drama teacher, bookstore owner, interior decorator, antique store owner, and others.

★2498★ Careers for Music Lovers and Other Tuneful Types
VGM Career Horizons
NTC Publishing Group
4255 W. Touhy Ave.
Lincolnwood, IL 60646-1975
Ph: (847)679-5500   Fax: (847)679-2494
Fr: 800-323-4900
Jeff Johnson. 1996. $14.95; $9.95 (paper). 160 pages. Describes hundreds of music industry jobs and careers.

★2499★ Encyclopedia of Careers and Vocational Guidance
J. G. Ferguson Publishing Co.
200 W. Monroe, Ste. 250
Chicago, IL 60606
Ph: (312)580-5480
William E. Hopke. Ninth edition, 1993. $129.95; $199.95 (CD-ROM). Four-volume set that profiles 900 occupations and describes job trends in 71 industries. Includes career description, educational requirements, history of the job, methods of entry, advancement, employment outlook, earnings, conditions of work, social and psychological factors, and sources of further information. Contains career and employment information for this field.

★2500★ Jobs Rated Almanac: Ranks the Best and Worst Jobs by More Than a Dozen Vital Criteria
John Wiley and Sons
605 Third Ave.
New York, NY 10158-0012
Ph: (212)850-6000   Fr: 800-225-5945
Les Krantz. Third edition, 1995. $16.95. 340 pages. Ranks 250 jobs by environment, salary, outlook, physical demands, stress, security, travel opportunities, and geographic location.

★2501★ Making it in Broadcasting: An Insider's Guide to Career Opportunities
Macmillan Publishing Co.
200 Old Tappan Rd.
Old Tappan, NJ 07675
Fax: 800-223-2336   Fr: 800-445-6991
Leonard Mogel. 1994. $15.00 (paper).

★2502★ On the Air

Writers Publishing Service Co.
PO Box 1868
Seattle, WA 98111-1868
Ph: (206)467-6735

Mark Carlson. 1991. $16.95 (paper).

★2503★ 100 Best Careers in Entertainment

Prentice Hall General Reference & Travel
15 Columbus Cir.
New York, NY 10023
Ph: (212)373-8500   Fr: 800-223-2348

Shelly Field. 1994. $15.00 (paper).

★2504★ Opportunities in Broadcasting Careers

VGM Career Horizons
4255 W. Touhy Ave.
Lincolnwood, IL 60646-1975
Ph: (847)679-5500   Fax: (847)679-2494
Fr: 800-323-4900

Elmo I. Ellis. 1994. $14.95; $11.95 (paper). Discusses opportunities and job search techniques in broadcasting, television, and radio. Illustrated.

★2505★ Opportunities in Music Careers

VGM Career Horizons
4255 W. Touhy Ave.
Lincolnwood, IL 60646-1975
Ph: (847)679-5500   Fax: (847)679-2494
Fr: 800-323-4900

Robert Gerardi. $14.95; $11.95 (paper). De-scribes the job market and where to find work. Covers careers in performing, writing, musical directing, management, and technical areas. Illustrated.

★2506★ Radio & Television Broadcasting Workers

Chronicle Guidance Publications, Inc.
66 Aurora St.
PO Box 1190
Moravia, NY 13118-1190
Ph: (315)497-0330   Fax: (315)497-3359
Fr: 800-622-7284

Chronicle Guidance Staff. 1992. $2.00. Provides concise career information and sources of additional information.

OTHER SOURCES

★2507★ ADJA News

American Disc Jockey Association (ADJA)
c/o Bruce Kessler
PO Box 151
Horsham, PA 19044
Ph: (215)675-9567   Fax: (215)675-9611

Bimonthly. $10.00/year for nonmembers. Newsletter.

★2508★ American Disc Jockey Association (ADJA)

c/o Bruce Kessler
PO Box 151
Horsham, PA 19044
Ph: (215)675-9567   Fax: (215)675-9611

Members: Mobile and night club disc jockeys. **Purpose:** Seeks to promote the disc jockey as a professional form of entertainment; improves the industry by establishing standards, procedures, and benefits. Assists and trains members; acts as a lobby and special interest group; provides forums for professional disc jockeys; conducts educational, charitable, and research programs.

★2509★ The Video Guide to Earning Money as a Mobile Disc Jockey

Outpost DJ Video Productions
PO Box 424
Commack, NY 11725
Fr: 800-225-0000

Video. $ 39.95. 75 minutes. Covers the basics of setting up a business as a mobile disc jockey.

Dispensing Opticians

★2510★ Review of Optometry

Chilton Publications
825 7th Ave.
New York, NY 10019
Ph: (212)887-8400   Fax: (212)887-8484

Monthly. $42.00/year. Journal for the optometric profession and optical industry.

EMPLOYER DIRECTORIES AND NETWORKING LISTS

★2511★ Contact Lenses—Retail Directory

American Business Directories, Inc.
American Business Information, Inc.
5711 S. 86th Cir.
Omaha, NE 68127
Ph: (402)593-4600   Fax: (402)331-1505

Annual. $1,055.00, U.S. edition. Entries include: Name, address, phone (including area code), size of advertisement, year first in Yellow Pages, name of owner or manager, number of employees. Compiled from telephone company Yellow Pages, nationwide. Arrangement: Geographical.

★2512★ Guild of Prescription Opticians of America—Guild Reference Directory

Guild of Prescription Opticians of America
Opticians Association of America
10341 Democracy Ln.
Fairfax, VA 22030
Ph: (703)691-8355   Fax: (703)691-3929

Annual, January. $60.00, postpaid, payment with order. Covers 250 member firms with a total of 350 retail locations. Entries include: Company name, address, name of manager, services. Arrangement: Geographical.

★2513★ Opticians Directory

American Business Directories, Inc.
American Business Information, Inc.
5711 S. 86th Cir.
Omaha, NE 68127
Ph: (402)593-4600   Fax: (402)331-1505

Annual. $1,110.00, U.S. edition. Entries include: Company name, address, phone (including area code), size of advertisement, year first in Yellow Pages, name of owner or manager, number of employees. Compiled from telephone company Yellow Pages, nationwide. Arrangement: Geographical.

HANDBOOKS AND MANUALS

★2514★ Careers in Health Care

VGM Career Horizons
4255 W. Touhy Ave.
Lincolnwood, IL 60646-1975
Ph: (847)679-5500   Fax: (847)679-2494
Fr: 800-323-4900

Barbara M. Swanson. 1995. $17.95; $13.95 (paper). Describes job duties, work settings, salaries, licensing and certification requirements, educational preparation, and future outlook. Gives ideas on how to secure a job.

★2515★ Dispensing Optician

R & E Publishers
468 Auzerais Ave., Ste. A
San Jose, CA 95126
Ph: (408)977-0693   Fax: (408)977-0693

Diane Parker. 1993. $1.95 (paper).

★2516★ 100 Best Careers for the Year 2000

Prentice Hall General Reference
15 Columbus Cir.
New York, NY 10023
Ph: (212)373-8500   Fr: 800-223-2348

Shelly Field. 1992. $15.00 (paper). Covers 100 of the fastest growing jobs. The publication is divided into 11 general employment sections. Specific careers are covered within each section. Provides job description, responsibilities, employment opportunities, earnings, education and training, advance-ment opportunities, and experience and qualifications for each occupation.

★2517★ Opportunities in Eye Care Careers

VGM Career Horizons
4255 W. Touhy Ave.
Lincolnwood, IL 60646-1975
Ph: (847)679-5500   Fax: (847)679-2494
Fr: 800-323-4900

Kathleen M. Ahrens. 1994. $14.95; $11.95 (paper). Explores careers in ophthalmology, optometry, and support positions. Describes the work, salary, and employment outlook and opportunities.

★2518★ Opportunities in Health and Medical Careers

VGM Career Horizons
4255 W. Touhy Ave.
Lincolnwood, IL 60646-1975
Ph: (847)679-5500   Fax: (847)679-2494
Fr: 800-323-4900

Donald Snook, Jr. and Leo D'Orazio. 1993. $14.95; $11.95 (paper). Covers the full range of medical and health occupations. Illustrated.

★2519★ Opportunities in Vocational and Technical Careers

VGM Career Horizons
4255 W. Touhy Ave.
Lincolnwood, IL 60646-1975
Ph: (847)679-5500   Fax: (847)679-2494
Fr: 800-323-4900

Adrian A. Paradis. 1992. $14.95; $11.95 (paper). 160 pages. Provides information on a variety of opportunities and advice on breaking into the field.

EMPLOYMENT AGENCIES AND SEARCH FIRMS

★2520★ Retail Recruiters/Spectrum Consultants, Inc.

111 Presidential Blvd., Ste. 211
Bala Pointe
Bala Cynwyd, PA 19004
Ph: (610)667-6565   Fax: (610)667-5323

Employment agency. Affiliate offices in many locations across the country.

OTHER SOURCES

★2521★ American Board of Opticianry (ABO)

10341 Democracy Ln.
Fairfax, VA 22030
Ph: (703)691-8356   Fax: (703)691-3929

Purpose: Provides uniform standards for dispensing opticians by administering the National Opticianry Competency Examination and by issuing the Certified Optician Certificate to those passing the exam. Also administers the Master in Ophthalmic Optics Examination and issues certificates to opticians at the advanced level passing the exam. Maintains records of persons certified for competency in eyeglass dispensing. Adopts and

enforces continuing education requirements; assists and encourages state licensing boards in the use of the National Opticiary Competency Examination for licensure purposes.

★2522★ National Academy of Opticianry (NAO)

10111 Martin Luther King, Jr. Hwy., Ste. 112
Bowie, MD 20720
Ph: (301)577-4828   Fax: (301)577-3880

Purpose: Offers review courses for national certification and state licensure examinations to members. Maintains speakers' bureau and Career Progression Program.

★2523★ National Association of Optometrists and Opticians (NAOO)

18903 S. Miles Rd.
Cleveland, OH 44128
Ph: (216)475-8925   Fax: (216)475-8862

Members: Licensed optometrists, opticians, and corporations. **Activities:** Conducts public affairs programs of mutual importance to members; serves as an organizational center for special purpose programs; acts as a clearinghouse for information affecting the retail optical industry.

★2524★ National Contact Lens Examiners (NCLE)

10341 Democracy Ln.
Fairfax, VA 22030
Ph: (703)691-1061   Fax: (703)691-3929

Members: National certifying agency promoting continued development of opticians and technicians as contact lens fitters by formulating standards and procedures for determination of entry-level competency. **Purpose:** Assists in the continuation, development, administration, and monitoring of a national Contact Lens Registry Examination (CLRE), which verifies entry-level competency of contact lens fitters. Issues certificates. Activities include: maintaining records of those certified in contact lens fitting; encouraging state occupational licensing and credentialing agencies to use the CLRE for licensure purposes; identifying contact lens dispensing education needs as a result of findings of examination programs; disseminating information to sponsors of contact lens continuing education programs.

★2525★ Opticians Association of America (OAA)

10341 Democracy Ln.
Fairfax, VA 22030
Ph: (703)691-8355   Fax: (703)691-3929

Members: Retail dispensing opticians who fill prescriptions for glasses or contact lenses written by a vision care specialist. **Purpose:** Works to advance the science of ophthalmic optics. **Activities:** Conducts research and educational programs.

Drafters

contact. Arrangement: Alphabetical. Indexes: Geographical.

★2540★ Directory of Engineers in Private Practice

National Society of Professional Engineers
1420 King St.
Alexandria, VA 22314
Ph: (703)684-2862   Fax: (703)836-4875

Annual. $85.00. Covers 600 consulting engineering firms and 7,200 individuals who are members of the society's Professional Engineers in Private Practice division. Entries include: For companies, name, address, phone, name of principal executive, list of services. For individuals, name, address; most listings include phone. Arrangement: Firms are geographic, then by specialty; individuals are alphabetical.

★2541★ Drafting Services Directory

American Business Directories, Inc.
American Business Information, Inc.
5711 S. 86th Cir.
Omaha, NE 68127
Ph: (402)593-4600   Fax: (402)331-1505

Annual. $420.00, U.S. edition. Number of listings: 4,646 (U.S. edition); 1,234 (Canadian edition). Entries include: Name, address, phone (including area code), size of advertisement, year first in Yellow Pages, name of owner or manager, number of employees. Compiled from telephone company Yellow Pages, nationwide. Arrangement: Geographical.

★2542★ ENR Directory of Design Firms

McGraw-Hill, Inc.
1221 Ave. of the Americas
New York, NY 10020
Ph: (212)512-2534   Fax: (212)512-4178

Biennial, fall of even years; issue of *Engineering News Record*. $85.00. Covers 133 architects, architectural engineers, consultants, and other design firms; limited to advertisers. Mini-profiles on about 3,400 U.S. firms and 500 foreign firms or foreign offices of U.S. firms. Also includes lists of top 500 design firms in the United States, top 200 international design firms, top 50 United States design-construction firms, and top 50 international design-construction firms, based on total amount of billings. Entries include: For advertisers: company name, address, branch locations, subsidiaries, list of key personnel, territory served, capabilities. In ranked lists: company name, address, phone; international firms include telex. Arrangement: Alphabetical (profiles); geographical (mini-profiles).

★2543★ ENR—Top 500 Design Firms Issue

McGraw-Hill, Inc.
1221 Ave. of the Americas
New York, NY 10020
Ph: (212)512-4635   Fax: (212)512-2820

Annual, April. $10.00, reprint, payment must accompany order. Publication includes: List of 500 leading architectural, engineering, and specialty design firms selected on basis of annual billings. Entries include: Company name, headquarters location, type of firm, current and prior year rank in billings, types of services, countries in which operated in

preceding year. Arrangement: Ranked by billings.

★2544★ ENR—Top International Design Firms Issue

McGraw-Hill, Inc.
1221 Ave. of the Americas, Rm. 4188
New York, NY 10020
Ph: (212)512-4635

Annual, July. $10.00, reprint, payment with order. Publication includes: List of 200 design firms (including United States firms) competing outside their own national borders who received largest dollar volume of foreign contracts in preceding calendar year. Entries include: Company name, headquarters location, type of firm, current and previous year rankings in total billings, types of services, countries in which operated in preceding year. Arrangement: By amount billed to international clients in previous year.

★2545★ Peterson's Job Opportunities in Engineering and Technology 1996

Peterson's
PO Box 2123
Princeton, NJ 08543-2123
Ph: (609)243-9111   Fax: (609)243-9150
Fr: 800-338-3282

Compiled by the Peterson's staff. Annual. $19.95 paperback. 432 pages. Profiles 2,000 high-tech companies looking primarily for technical personnel in such fields as biotechnology, telecommunications, software, computers and peripherals, defense, and aerospace. Contains job-search strategies and career options to help match education and expertise to the job market. Indexed geographically, by industry, and by hiring needs.

★2546★ ProFile/The Directory of U.S. Architectual Design Firms

American Institute of Architects
1735 New York Ave. NW
Washington, DC 20006
Ph: (202)626-7300   Fr: 800-365-2724

Annual. $145.00, plus $8.00 shipping. Covers more than 14,500 architectural firms, one or more of whose principals is a member of the American Institute of Architects. Entries include: For firms, firm name, address, phone, fax, year established, parent organization, key staff and their primary responsibilities, branches, number of staff personnel by discipline, types of work, geographical area served, projects. Arrangement: Firms are geographical. Indexes: Firm name, key individuals, specialization by category.

HANDBOOKS AND MANUALS

★2547★ Career Information Center

Macmillan Publishing Co.
200 Old Tappan Rd.
Old Tappan, NJ 07675
Ph: (609)461-6500   Fr: 800-223-2336

Visual Education Center Staff. Fifth edition, 1992. $229.00. This 13-volume set profiles over 600 occupations. Each occupational profile describes job duties, educational re-

quirements, how to get the job, advancement possibilities, employment outlook, working conditions, earnings and benefits, and where to write for more information.

★2548★ Exploring Drafting: Basic Fundamentals

Goodheart Wilcox Co.
123 W. Taft Dr.
South Holland, IL 60473-2089
Ph: (708)333-7200   Fax: (708)333-9130
Fr: 800-323-0440

John R. Walker. 1995.

★2549★ Exploring High-Tech Careers

Rosen Publishing Group, Inc.
29 E. 21st St.
New York, NY 10010
Ph: (212)777-3017   Fax: (212)777-0277
Fr: 800-237-9932

Scott Southworth. Revised edition, 1993. $14.95; $9.95 (paper). 118 pages. Gives an orientation to the field of high technology and high-tech jobs. Describes educational preparation and job hunting. Includes a glossary and bibliography.

★2550★ Liberal Arts Jobs: What They Are and How to Get Them

Peterson's
PO Box 2123
Princeton, NJ 08543-2123
Ph: (609)243-9111   Fax: (609)243-9150
Fr: 800-338-3282

Burton Jay Nadler. Second edition, 1989. $9.95. 153 pages. Presents a list of the top 20 fields for liberal arts majors, covering more than 300 job opportunities. Discusses strategies for going after those jobs, including guidance on the language of a successful job search, informational interviews, and making networking work.

★2551★ Opportunities in Computer-Aided Design and Computer-Aided Manufacturing

VGM Career Horizons
4255 W. Touhy Ave.
Lincolnwood, IL 60646-1975
Ph: (847)679-5500   Fax: (847)679-2494
Fr: 800-323-4900

Jan Bone. 1994. $14.95; $11.95 (paper). 160 pages. Defines cad (computer-aided design), cam (computer-aided manufacturing), and map (manufacturing automation protocol). Explains career opportunities in the cad/cam field, and education and training needed. Gives job-hunting tips.

★2552★ Opportunities in Drafting Careers

VGM Career Horizons
4255 W. Touhy Ave.
Lincolnwood, IL 60646-1975
Ph: (847)679-5500   Fax: (847)679-2494
Fr: 800-323-4900

Mark Rowh. 1994. $14.95; $11.95 (paper). Provides information on opportunities in mechanical, landscape, marine, and topographical drafting in civil service, architecture, electronics, and other fields. Contains index and illustrations.

★2553★ *Opportunities in High Tech Careers*

VGM Career Horizons
4255 W. Touhy Ave.
Lincolnwood, IL 60646-1975
Ph: (847)679-5500   Fax: (847)679-2494
Fr: 800-323-4900

Gary D. Golter and Deborah Yanuck. 1995. $14.95; $11.95 (paper). 160 pages. Explores high technology careers. Describes job opportunities, how to make a career decision, how to prepare for high technology jobs, job hunting techniques, and future trends.

★2554★ *Your Opportunities in Drafting*

Energeia Publishing Inc.
860 Commercial St., S.
Salem, OR 97302
Ph: (503)362-1480   Fax: (503)362-2123

Vcitor D. Tognazzini. 1994. $2.00 (paper). 8p.

EMPLOYMENT AGENCIES AND SEARCH FIRMS

★2555★ Agra Placements, Ltd.
4949 Pleasant St., Ste. 1
W. 50th Pl. III
West Des Moines, IA 50266-5494
Ph: (515)225-6562   Fax: (515)225-7733

Executive search firm. Branch offices in Peru, IN, Lincoln, IL, and Minneapolis, MN.

★2556★ B and M Associates, Inc.
199 Cambridge Rd.
Woburn, MA 01801-4705
Ph: (617)938-9120

Employment agency.

★2557★ Industrial Recruiters Associates, Inc.
630 Oakwood Ave., Ste. 318
West Hartford, CT 06110
Ph: (203)953-3643

Employment agency.

★2558★ International Staffing Consultants
500 Newport Center Dr., Ste. 300
Newport Beach, CA 92660-7003
Ph: (714)721-7990

Employment agency. Provides placement on regular or temporary basis. Affiliate office in London.

★2559★ LOR Personnel Division
418 Wall St.
Princeton, NJ 08540
Ph: (609)921-6580

Employment agency. Executive search firm.

★2560★ Main Line Personnel Service, Inc.
401 City Ave.
Bala Cynwyd, PA 19004-1122
Ph: (610)667-1820

Employment agency.

★2561★ Sierra Technology Corporation
4150 Manzanita Ave., Ste. 100
Carmichael, CA 95608-1700
Ph: (916)488-4960   Fax: (916)488-7058

Employment agency. Provides placement on a temporary basis.

★2562★ Source Engineering
5580 LBJ Fwy., Ste. 300
Dallas, TX 75240
Ph: (214)385-3002   Fax: (214)717-0075

Executive search firm. Many affiliate offices located throughout the U.S.

★2563★ Tri-Serv Inc.
22 W. Padonia Rd., Ste. C53
Timonium, MD 21093
Ph: (301)561-1740

Employment agency.

OTHER SOURCES

★2564★ American Design Drafting Association (ADDA)
PO Box 799
Rockville, MD 20848-0799
Ph: (301)460-6875   Fax: (301)460-8591

Members: Designers, drafters, drafting managers, chief drafters, supervisors, administrators, instructors, and students of design and drafting. **Purpose:** Encourages a continued program of education for self-improvement and professionalism in design and drafting and computer-aided design/drafting. Informs members of effective techniques and materials used in drawings and other graphic presentations. **Activities:** Evaluates curriculum of educational institutions through certification program; sponsors drafter certification program. **E-Mail:** addanatl@aol.com

Economists

SOURCES OF HELP-WANTED ADS

★2565★ Business Insurance
Crain Communications, Inc.
740 N. Rush St.
Chicago, IL 60611-2590
Ph: (312)649-5311   Fax: (312)280-3189
Weekly. $80.00/year for individuals. Magazine for executives in the corporate risk, employee benefit, and finance fields.

★2566★ Financial Management
Financial Management Association
University of South Florida
College of Business Admin.
Tampa, FL 33620
Ph: (813)974-2084   Fax: (813)974-3318
Quarterly. $40.00/year for individuals; $10.00 for single issue. Magazine covering business, economics, finance and management.

★2567★ OECD Observer
Organization for Economic Cooperation and Development
Publications & Information Center
2001 L St. NW
Washington, DC 20036-4910
Ph: (202)785-6323   Fax: (202)785-0350
Fr: 800-456-OECD
Bimonthly. $25.00/year for individuals. Magazine on economic affairs, science, and technology.

PLACEMENT AND JOB REFERRAL SERVICES

★2568★ African Studies Association (ASA)
Emory University
Credit Union Bldg.
Atlanta, GA 30322
Ph: (404)329-6410   Fax: (404)329-6433
Members: Persons specializing in teaching, writing, or research on Africa including political scientists, historians, geographers, an-thropologists, economists, librarians, linguists, and government officials; persons who are studying African subjects; institutional members are universities, libraries, government agencies, and others interested in receiving information about Africa. **Purpose:** Seeks to foster communication and to stimulate research among scholars on Africa. **Activities:** Sponsors placement service; conducts panels and discussion groups; presents exhibits and films. **E-Mail:** africa@mony.edu

★2569★ American Agricultural Economics Association (AAEA)
1110 Buckeye Ave.
Ames, IA 50010-8063
Ph: (515)233-3202   Fax: (515)233-3101
Members: Professional society of state, federal, and industrial agricultural economists, teachers, and extension workers. **Purpose:** Works to further knowledge of agricultural economics through scientific research, instruction, publications, meetings, and other activities. **Activities:** Offers placement service.

★2570★ Committee on the Status of Women in the Economics Profession (CSWEP)
Northwestern University
Department of Economics
Evanston, IL 60208
Ph: (708)491-4145   Fax: (708)491-7001
A standing committee of American Economic Association. Women economists in the U.S. **Purpose:** Purpose is to support and facilitate equality of opportunity for women economists. **Activities:** Disseminates information about job opportunities, research funding, and research related to the status of women in economics. Sponsors technical sessions.

★2571★ National Association of Business Economists (NABE)
1233 20th St. NW, Ste. 505
Washington, DC 20036
Ph: (202)463-6223   Fax: (202)463-6239
Purpose: Professional society of institutions, businesses, and students with an active interest in business economics and individuals who are employed by academic, private, or governmental concerns in the area of business-related economic issues. **Activities:** Maintains placement service for members; conducts several seminars per year. Maintains speakers' bureau.

★2572★ Social Sciences Services and Resources
PO Box 153
Wasco, IL 60183
Ph: (708)897-5345
Members: Consulting associates in social sciences. **Purpose:** Established to advance the teaching, consulting, and practice of the social sciences basic disciplines including sociology, anthropology, political science, geography, history, economics, and their applied disciplines: social work, community development, planning, and public administration. Serves as: a center for dissemination of current and comprehensive social research findings. Provides consultants for citizen groups, community projects, and governmental units on written request. Upon request from colleges, school boards, and citizens groups, conducts in-service workshops on teaching, consulting, and new developments in the social sciences. Provides consultant evaluation services for small colleges throughout the U.S. **Activities:** Maintains speakers' bureau and placement information service. Conducts research programs.

★2573★ Southern Economic Association (SEA)
Oklahoma State University
College of Bus. Admin.
Stillwater, OK 74078-0555
Ph: (405)744-7645   Fax: (405)744-5180
Members: Professional economists in government, business, and academic institutions. **Activities:** Provides placement service for economists.

EMPLOYER DIRECTORIES AND NETWORKING LISTS

★2574★ American Bank Directory

Thomson Financial Publishing Inc.
4709 W. Golf Rd.
Skokie, IL 60076-1253
Ph: (708)676-9600   Fax: (708)933-8101
Fr: 800-321-3373

Semiannual, April and October. $249.00, single issue of national edition; $26.00, for single state edition; $11.00, each additional state in same binder. Covers over 12,000 banks and registered multi-bank holding companies nationwide; also published in editions for individual states. Entries include: Bank name, address (including county and Federal Reserve District), phone, fax, fedwire number, year established, ABA number, names of officers, condensed statement of condition, principal correspondents, branches. Arrangement: Geographical.

★2575★ American Banker—Top Commercial Banks by Assets, Deposits

American Banker-Bond Buyer
International Thomson Publishing Corp.
1 State St. Plaza
New York, NY 10004
Ph: (212)943-5288   Fax: (212)480-0165
Fr: 800-367-3989

Semiannual, March and September. $25.00. Publication includes: List of the top 300 commercial banks. Entries include: Name of bank, headquarters, amount of deposits at the previous quarter, place in rank at quarter. Arrangement: Ranked by deposits and assets. Indexes: Geographical.

★2576★ American Banker—Top World Banks by Deposits and Assets

American Banker-Bond Buyer
International Thomson Publishing Corp.
1 State St. Plaza
New York, NY 10004
Ph: (212)943-5288   Fax: (212)480-0165
Fr: 800-367-3989

Annual, July. $25.00. Publication includes: List of 500 largest banks in the world by assets with total deposits and deposit rank; also, the risk-based capital position of the 100 largest banking companies in the world as measured by total assets. Entries include: Bank name, headquarters, rankings by assets and amount of deposits and assets for two previous years. Arrangement: Ranked by assets. Indexes: Geographic listing of largest banks outside United States.

★2577★ Association for University Business and Economic Research— Membership Directory

Association for University Business and Economic Research
c/o Indiana Business Research Center
801 W. Michigan St., BS4015
Indianapolis, IN 46223
Ph: (317)274-2204   Fax: (317)274-3312

Annual, January. $10.00. Covers member institutions in the United States and abroad with centers, bureaus, departments, etc., concerned with business and economic research. Entries include: Name of bureau, center, etc., sponsoring institution name, address, phone, names and titles of director and staff, publications and frequency. Arrangement: Geographical. Indexes: Director name, institution name.

★2578★ Business Economics— Membership Directory Issue

National Association of Business Economics
28790 Chagrin Blvd., Ste. 300
Cleveland, OH 44122
Ph: (216)464-7986   Fax: (216)464-6352

Annual, March. $17.95. Publication includes: List of about 3,600 members of the association, including students. Entries include: Name, address, phone, corporate affiliation, economic specialization, industries of research specialization, NABE activities, educational background, work experience. Arrangement: Alphabetical by member name, company, and roundtable affiliation.

★2579★ Moody's Bank and Finance Manual

Moody's Investors Service, Inc.
99 Church St.
New York, NY 10007
Ph: (212)553-0300   Fax: (212)553-4700
Fr: 800-342-5647

Annual, July; supplements in *Moody's Bank & Finance News Reports.* $1,475.00, per year, including supplements. Covers in four volumes, over 20,000 national, state, and private banks, savings and loans, mutual funds, unit investment trusts, and insurance and real estate companies in the United States. Entries include: Company name, headquarters and branch offices, phones, names and titles of principal executives, directors, history, Moody's rating, and extensive financial and statistical data. Arrangement: Classified by type of business. Indexes: Company name.

★2580★ National Association of Business Economics—Membership Directory

National Association of Business Economics
1233 20th St. NW, Ste. 505
Washington, DC 20036
Ph: (202)463-6223   Fax: (202)463-6239

Annual, March. $55.00, with membership. Covers about 3,600 members internationally. Entries include: Name, address, phone, company affiliation, educational background, prior employment history, areas of specialization and industries of research specialization, roundtable affiliation. Arrangement: Alphabetical. Indexes: Company name, association roundtable affiliation.

★2581★ National Economists Club— Membership Roster

National Economists Club
Box 19281
Washington, DC 20036
Ph: (202)532-9048   Fax: (202)534-2137

Biennial. Free to members. Covers nearly 800 professional economists and others having an interest in economic subjects. Entries include: Name, address, phone. Arrangement: Alphabetical by organization.

★2582★ Polk Financial Institutions Directory

R. L. Polk & Co.
PO Box 305100
Nashville, TN 37230-5100
Ph: (615)889-3350   Fax: (615)885-3081
Fr: 800-827-2265

Semiannual. $303.75. Covers 15,000 banks and their branches; over 2,000 head offices, and 15,500 branches of savings and loan associations; over 5,500 credit unions with assets over $5 million; Federal Reserve System and other U.S. government and state government banking agencies; bank holding, commercial finance, and leasing companies; ocverage includes the United States, Canada, Mexico, and Central America. Arrangement: Geographical. Indexes: Alphabetical.

★2583★ Roster of Women Economists

Committee on the Status of Women in the Economics Profession
c/o Joan G. Haworth
4901 Tower Ct.
Tallahassee, FL 32303
Ph: (904)562-1211   Fax: (904)562-3838

Biennial, even years. $35.00. Covers 6,000 women in economics. Entries include: Name, address, phone, title, affiliation, degrees, honors, specialty, number of articles and books published. e-mail, fax. Arrangement: Alphabetical. Indexes: Geographical, employer, fields of specialization.

★2584★ Thomson Bank Directory

Thomson Financial Publishing
4709 W. Golf Rd., 6th Fl.
Skokie, IL 60076-1253
Ph: (708)676-9600   Fax: (708)933-8101
Fr: 800-321-3373

Semiannual, May and November. $369.00, for 4-volume set. Covers in four volumes, about 11,000 banks and 50,000 branches of United States banks, and 60,000 foreign banks and branches engaged in foreign banking; Federal Reserve system and other United States government and state government banking agencies; 500 largest North American and International commercial banks; paper and automated clearinghouses. Entries include: For domestic banks, bank name, address, phone, telex, cable, date established, routing number, charter type, bank holding company affiliation, memberships in Federal Reserve System and other banking organizations, principal officers by function performed, principal correspondent banks, and key financial data (deposits, etc.). For international banks, bank name, address, phone, fax, telex, cable, SWIFT address, transit or sort codes within home country, ownership, financial data, names and titles of key personnel, branch locations. For branches, bank name, address, phone, charter type, ownership and other details comparable to domestic bank listings. Arrangement: Geographical. Indexes: Alphabetical, geographical.

★2585★ Who's Who in Finance and Industry

Marquis Who's Who
Reed Reference Publishing
121 Chanlon Rd.
New Providence, NJ 07974
Ph: (908)464-6800   Fax: (908)665-6688
Fr: 800-521-8110

Biennial, July of odd years. $249.95, plus $17.50 shipping. Covers over 24,500 individuals. Entries include: Name, home and office addresses, personal, career, and family data; civic and political activities; memberships, publications, awards. Arrangement: Alphabetical.

HANDBOOKS AND MANUALS

★2586★ Business and Finance Career Directory

Gale Research
835 Penobscot Bldg.
Detroit, MI 48226-4094
Ph: (313)961-2242   Fax: (313)961-6083
Fr: 800-877-GALE

Bradley Morgan. Second edition, 1992. $39.00. 413 pages. Features a basic and comprehensive job search section, articles by top professionals in the field, and detailed listings of hundreds of top companies who hire individuals in this field. Aimed particularly at entry-level job hunters.

★2587★ Career Choices for the 90's for Students of Business

Walker and Company
435 Hudson St.
New York, NY 10014
Ph: (212)727-8300   Fax: (212)727-0984
Fr: 800-289-2553

Prepared by the Career Associates staff. 1990. $9.95. 166 pages. Discusses alternatives for students of business. Offers advice on how to break into the field and how to move up. Covers where and who the employers are, internship possibilities, and professional networking associations. Comprehensive guide to career and job search planning.

★2588★ Career Choices for the 90's for Students of Economics

Walker and Company
435 Hudson St.
New York, NY 10014
Ph: (212)727-8300   Fax: (212)727-0984
Fr: 800-289-2553

Prepared by the Career Associates staff. 1990. $8.95. 166 pages. Discusses alternatives for students of economics. Offers advice on how to break into the field and how to move up. Covers where and who the employers are, internship possibilities, and professional networking associations. Comprehensive guide to career and job search planning.

★2589★ Career Choices for the 90's for Students of Mathematics

Walker and Company
435 Hudson St.
New York, NY 10014
Ph: (212)727-8300   Fax: (212)727-0984
Fr: 800-289-2553

Prepared by the Career Associates staff. 1990. $8.95. 166 pages. Discusses alternatives for students of mathematics. Offers advice on how to break into the field and how to move up. Covers where and who the employers are, internship possibilities, and professional networking associations. Comprehensive guide to career and job search planning.

★2590★ Career Choices for the 90's for Students of Psychology

Walker and Company
435 Hudson St.
New York, NY 10014
Ph: (212)727-8300   Fax: (212)727-0984
Fr: 800-289-2553

Prepared by the Career Associates staff. 1990. $9.95. 166 pages. Discusses alternatives for students of psychology. Offers advice on how to break into the field and how to move up. Covers where and who the employers are, internship possibilities, and professional networking associations. Comprehensive guide to career and job search planning.

★2591★ Careers in Finance

NTC Publishing Group
4255 W. Touhy Ave.
Lincolnwood, IL 60646-1975
Ph: (708)679-5500   Fax: (708)679-6375
Fr: 800-323-4900

Trudy Ring. 1994. $16.95; $12.95 (paper).

★2592★ Careers for Number Crunchers and Other Quantitative Types

VGM Career Horizons
4255 W. Touhy Ave.
Lincolnwood, IL 60646-1975
Ph: (847)679-5500   Fax: (847)679-2494
Fr: 800-323-4900

Rebecca Burnett. 1993. $14.95; $9.95 (paper). Provides information to math-oriented job hunters on how to become statisticians, field researchers, computer programmers, stock analysts, investment managers, bankers, engineers, accountants, underwriters, economists, market analysts, mathematicians, systems analysts, and more.

★2593★ The Encyclopedia of Career Choices for the 1990s: Guide to Entry-Level Jobs

Perigree Books
The Berkley Publishing Group
PO Box 506
East Rutherford, NJ 07073
Ph: (201)933-9292   Fr: 800-223-0510

Career Associates Staff. 1992. $19.95. 862 pages. Describes 500 entry-level careers in a variety of industries. Presents qualifications required, working conditions, salary, internships, and professional associations.

★2594★ Encyclopedia of Careers and Vocational Guidance

J. G. Ferguson Publishing Co.
200 W. Monroe, Ste. 250
Chicago, IL 60606
Ph: (312)580-5480

William E. Hopke. Ninth edition, 1993. $129.95; $199.95 (CD-ROM). Four-volume set that profiles 900 occupations and describes job trends in 71 industries. Includes career description, educational requirements, history of the job, methods of entry, advancement, employment outlook, earnings, conditions of work, social and psychological factors, and sources of further information. Contains career and employment information for this field.

★2595★ Liberal Arts Jobs: What They Are and How to Get Them

Peterson's
PO Box 2123
Princeton, NJ 08543-2123
Ph: (609)243-9111   Fax: (609)243-9150
Fr: 800-338-3282

Burton Jay Nadler. Second edition, 1989. $9.95. 153 pages. Presents a list of the top 20 fields for liberal arts majors, covering more than 300 job opportunities. Discusses strategies for going after those jobs, including guidance on the language of a successful job search, informational interviews, and making networking work.

★2596★ Opportunities in Social Science Careers

VGM Career Horizons
4255 W. Touhy Ave.
Lincolnwood, IL 60646-1975
Ph: (847)679-5500   Fax: (847)679-2494
Fr: 800-323-4900

Rosanne J. Marek. 1990. $14.95; $11.95 (paper). 160 pages. Profiles job opportunities in education, government, and business, along with their salary levels and outlook in the years to come. Illustrated.

EMPLOYMENT AGENCIES AND SEARCH FIRMS

★2597★ David P. Cordell Associates

82 Wall St., Ste. 1105
New York, NY 10005
Ph: (212)285-0634

Executive search firm.

★2598★ Dussick Management Associates

149 Durham Rd.
Madison, CT 06443
Ph: (203)245-9311   Fax: (203)245-9570

Executive search firm.

★2599★ **E.J. Ashton and Associates, Ltd.**

3125 N. Wilke Rd.
Arlington Heights, IL 60004-1452
Ph: (708)577-7900

Employment agency. Executive search firm.

★2600★ **Hansen Agri-Placement**

PO Box 1172
Grand Island, NE 68802
Ph: (308)382-7350

Employment agency. Handles placements in a variety of fields on a regular or temporary basis.

★2601★ **Hawkes Peers**

805 3rd Ave., 28th Fl.
New York, NY 10022
Ph: (212)593-3131   Fax: (212)593-3249

Executive search firm.

★2602★ **Hayden and Associates, Inc.**

7825 Washington Ave. S., Ste. 120
Minneapolis, MN 55439-2431
Ph: (612)941-6300   Fax: (612)941-9602

Employment agency. Executive search firm. Fills openings in a variety of fields.

★2603★ **International Staffing Consultants**

500 Newport Center Dr., Ste. 300
Newport Beach, CA 92660-7003
Ph: (714)721-7990

Employment agency. Provides placement on regular or temporary basis. Affiliate office in London.

★2604★ **Kanon Personnel Inc.**

8 W. 40th St., 11th Fl.
New York, NY 10018-3994
Ph: (212)391-2610

Employment agency.

★2605★ **The Murphy Group**

1211 W. 22nd St., Ste. 221
Oak Brook, IL 60521-2115
Ph: (708)574-2840

Employment agency. Places personnel in a variety of positions.

★2606★ **The Pathfinder Group**

295 Danbury Rd.
Wilton, CT 06897-3095
Ph: (203)834-2467

Employment agency. Executive search firm. Recruits staff in a variety of fields.

★2607★ **The Personnel Institute**

1000 Connecticut Ave. NW, Ste. 1108
Washington, DC 20036
Ph: (202)223-4911

Consulting firm.

★2608★ **Ritt-Ritt and Associates**

424 Swan Blvd.
Deerfield, IL 60015
Ph: (708)520-9999

Employment agency.

★2609★ **Sales Executives Inc.**

755 W. Big Beaver Rd., Ste. 2107
Troy, MI 48084
Ph: (810)362-1900

Employment agency. Executive search firm.

★2610★ **Sales Recruiters International, Ltd.**

660 White Plains Rd.
Tarrytown, NY 10591-5107
Ph: (914)631-0090

Employment agency.

★2611★ **Werbin Associates Executive Search, Inc.**

521 5th Ave., Ste. 1749
New York, NY 10175
Ph: (212)953-0909

Employment agency. Executive search firm.

★2612★ **The Wright Group**

5902 Windmier Ct.
Dallas, TX 75252
Ph: (214)733-7245

Executive search firm.

OTHER SOURCES

★2613★ *American Almanac of Jobs and Salaries 1994-95*

Avon Books
1350 Avenue of the Americas, 2nd Fl.
New York, NY 10019
Ph: (212)261-6800   Fr: 800-238-0658

John Wright. Revised edition, 1993. $17.00. 704 pages. This is a comprehensive guide to the wages of hundreds of occupations in a wide variety of industries and organizations.

★2614★ **American Economic Association (AEA)**

2014 Broadway, Ste. 305
Nashville, TN 37203-2418
Ph: (615)322-2595   Fax: (615)343-7590

Members: Educators, business executives, government administrators, journalists, lawyers, and others interested in economics and its application to present-day problems. **Purpose:** Encourages historical and statistical research into actual conditions of industrial life and provides a nonpartisan forum for economic discussion.

★2615★ **Economic Policy Institute (EPI)**

1600 L St., NW, Ste. 1200
Washington, DC 20036
Ph: (202)775-8810   Fax: (202)775-0819

Purpose: Conducts research and provides a forum for the exchange of information on economic policy issues. Promotes educational programs to encourage discussion of economic policy and economic issues, particularly the economics of poverty, unemployment, inflation, American industry, international competitiveness, and problems of economic adjustment as they affect the community and the individual. **Activities:** Sponsors seminars for economists and citizens.

★2616★ **Institute for Economic Analysis (IEA)**

508 Thayer Ave.
Silver Spring, MD 20910
Ph: (301)588-4569   Fax: (301)588-4569

Purpose: Seeks to develop more effective tools of economic analysis and policy to achieve and maintain stable full employment without inflation. Focuses on monetary and credit aspects of economics. **Activities:** Conducts research and educational programs. Plans to sponsor seminars to help increase public understanding of the basic requirements for sound economic policy.

★2617★ **International Studies Association (ISA)**

Brigham Young University
David M. Kennedy Center
216 HRCB
Provo, UT 84602
Ph: (801)378-5459   Fax: (801)378-7075

Members: Social scientists and other scholars from a wide variety of disciplines who are specialists in international affairs and cross-cultural studies; academicians; government officials; officials in international organizations; business executives; students. **Purpose:** Promotes research, improved teaching, and the orderly growth of knowledge in the field of international studies; emphasizes a multidisciplinary approach to problems. **Activities:** Holds conferences with government officials; conducts workshops and discussion groups; sponsors development of modular curriculum materials.

★2618★ **National Council on Economic Education (NCEE)**

1140 Avenue of the Americas
New York, NY 10036
Ph: (212)730-7007   Fax: (212)730-1793
Fr: 800-336-1192

Members: Economists, educators, and representatives from business, labor, and finance dedicated to improving economic education by improving the quality and increasing the quantity of economics being taught in all levels of schools and colleges. **Purpose:** Initiates curriculum development and research; experiments with new economics courses and ways to prepare teachers and students; provides updated teacher-pupil materials; coordinates national and local programs in economics education. Provides consulting services to educators; sponsors workshops; tests new methods in practical school situations.

Education Administrators

SOURCES OF HELP-WANTED ADS

★2619★ American School Board Journal

National School Boards Association
1680 Duke St.
Alexandria, VA 22314-3407
Ph: (703)838-6227   Fax: (703)683-7590

Monthly. Magazine serving school board members and superintendents.

★2620★ American School and University

Intertec Publishing
9800 Metcalf
Overland Park, KS 66212
Ph: (913)341-1300   Fax: (913)967-1905

Monthly. $65.00/year for individuals. Trade magazine.

★2621★ ASCUS Annual: Job Search Handbook for Educators

Association for School, College and University Staffing (ASCUS)
820 Davis St., Ste. 222
Evanston, IL 60201
Ph: (708)864-1999

Annual. Includes employment notices from public school systems. Contains articles for educators seeking employment. Also includes "Directory of State Teacher Certification Offices."

★2622★ Change

Heldref Publications
Helen Dwight Reid Educational Foundation
1319 18th St. NW
Washington, DC 20036-1802
Ph: (202)296-6267   Fax: (202)296-5149
Fr: 800-365-9753

Bimonthly. $36.00/year for individuals; $11.75 for single issue; $70.00/year for institutions; $84.00/year for institutions, other countries. Magazine dealing with contemporary issues in higher learning.

★2623★ The Chronicle of Higher Education

The Chronicle of Higher Education
1255 23rd St. NW, Ste. 700
Washington, DC 20037
Ph: (202)466-1000   Fax: (202)296-2691
Fr: 800-347-6969

Weekly. $67.50/year for individuals; $2.75 for single issue. Higher education magazine (tabloid).

★2624★ Community College Journal

American Association of Community and Junior Colleges
1 Dupont Circle NW, Ste. 410
Washington, DC 20036-1176
Ph: (202)728-0200   Fax: (202)223-9390

Bimonthly. $22.00/year for individuals; $4.00 for single issue; $28.00/year for other countries. Educational magazine.

★2625★ Community Jobs: The Employment Newspaper for the Non-Profit Sector

ACCESS: Networking in the Public Interest
30 Irving Pl.
New York, NY 10003
Ph: (212)475-1001   Fax: (212)475-1199

Monthly. $69.00. Covers jobs and internships available with nonprofit organizations active in issues such as the environment, foreign policy, consumer advocacy, housing, education, etc. Entries include: Position title; name, address, and phone of contact; description, responsibilities; requirements; salary. Arrangement: Geographical.

★2626★ Current Openings in Education in U.S.A.

Education Information Service
PO Box 660662
Newton, MA 02162-0662
Ph: (617)443-0125

Seven times/year. $8.00/issue. Publication is a booklet listing about 140 institutions or school systems, each with one to a dozen or more openings for teachers, librarians, counselors, administrators, and other personnel.

★2627★ Education Week

Editorial Projects in Education, Inc.
4301 Connecticut Ave. NW
Washington, DC 20008
Ph: (202)686-0800   Fax: (202)686-0797

Weekly. $59.94/year for individuals. Professional newspaper for elementary and secondary school educators.

★2628★ EIS Current Openings in Education Abroad

Education Information Services (EIS)
PO Box 660662
Newton, MA 02162-0662
Ph: (617)443-0125

$10.95. Monthly. List providing teaching and other professional education openings in American overseas schools and international schools.

★2629★ Electronic Learning

Scholastic, Inc.
411 Lafayette
New York, NY 10003
Ph: (212)505-4900   Fax: (212)260-8587

Magazine focusing on electronic education.

★2630★ Executive Educator

National School Boards Association
1680 Duke St.
Alexandria, VA 22314-3407
Ph: (703)838-6227   Fax: (703)683-7590

Monthly. $53.00/year for individuals; $58.00/year for Canada; $74.00/year for other countries. Magazine for school principals and central office administrators.

★2631★ Foreign Faculty and Administrative Openings

Education Information Service
Box 662
Newton, MA 02162
Ph: (617)237-0887

Approximately every six weeks. $9.00. Covers approximately 150 specific openings in administration, counseling, library, teaching and other disciplines for American teachers in American schools overseas and in international schools, both of which must teach English as a primarily language. Entries include: Institution name, address.

★2632★ NJEA Review

New Jersey Education Association
180 W. State St.
Box 1211
Trenton, NJ 08607
Ph: (609)599-4561   Fax: (609)392-6321

Educational journal for public school employees.

★2633★ Opening List of Professional Openings in American Overseas & International Schools

Education Information Services
Instant Alert
PO Box 662
Newton, MA 02162-0002
Ph: (617)237-0887

Every 6 weeks. $9.00. Covers about 150 current professional openings for teachers, administrators, counselors, librarians, and educational specialists in American overseas schools and international schools at which the teaching language is primarily English. Also covers English as a Second/Foreign Language (ESL-EFL) at all age levels. Entries include: Institute name, address, names and titles of key personnel, positions available.

★2634★ Opening List in U.S. Colleges, Public & Private Schools

Education Information Services
PO Box 662
Newton, MA 02162-0002
Ph: (617)237-0887

Every 6 weeks. $9.00. Covers about 150 current professional openings in U.S. public schools, and private schools. Entries include: Institute name, address, names and titles of key personnel, available openings.

★2635★ School Business Affairs

ASBO International
11401 N. Shore Dr.
Reston, VA 22090
Ph: (703)478-0405   Fax: (703)478-0205

Monthly. Magazine about school administration and business management.

★2636★ School and College

Peter Li
1100 Superior Ave.
Cleveland, OH 44114
Ph: (216)696-7000   Fax: (216)696-7670

Monthly. Educational business magazine covering business systems, services, and administration.

★2637★ Spotlight: On Career Planning, Placement, and Recruitment

National Association of Colleges and Employers
62 Highland Ave.
Bethlehem, PA 18017
Ph: (610)868-1421

Biweekly (except monthly in July, August, and December). Free to members; $72.00/year for nonmembers. Price includes subsription to the *Journal of Career Planning and Employment*.

PLACEMENT AND JOB REFERRAL SERVICES

★2638★ American Association of Christian Schools (AACS)

PO Box 2189
Independence, MO 64055
Ph: (816)795-7709   Fax: (816)795-7462

Activities: Maintains teacher/administrator certification program and placement service. Participates in school accreditation program. Sponsors National Academic Tournament and high school sports tournaments. Maintains American Christian Honor Society. Compiles statistics; maintains speakers' bureau and placement service.

★2639★ American Association of Women in Community and Junior Colleges (AAWCJC)

Amarillo College
PO Box 447
Amarillo, TX 79178-0001
Ph: (806)371-5000   Fax: (806)371-5370

Members: Women faculty members, administrators, staff members, students, and trustees of community colleges. **Purpose:** Objectives are to: develop communication and disseminate information among women in community, junior, and technical colleges; encourage educational program development; obtain grants for educational projects for community college women. Disseminates information on women's issues and programs. **Activities:** Conducts regional and state professional development workshops and forums. Maintains placement services.

★2640★ American College Personnel Association (ACPA)

1 Dupont Cir. NW, Ste. 300
Washington, DC 20036-1110
Ph: (202)835-2272   Fax: (202)296-3286

Members: Individuals employed in higher education and involved in student personnel work, including administration, counseling, research, and teaching. **Purpose:** Fosters student development in higher education in areas of service, advocacy, and standards by offering professional programs for educators committed to the overall development of post-secondary students. **Activities:** Sponsors professional and educational activities in cooperation with other organizations. Offers placement service.

★2641★ American Education Finance Association (AEFA)

5249 Cape Leyte Dr.
Sarasota, FL 34242
Ph: (941)349-7580   Fax: (941)349-7580

Members: State and national teacher organizations, university personnel, school administrators, state educational agency personnel, legislators and legislative staff, federal agency personnel, and interested foundations and students. **Purpose:** Facilitates communication among groups and individuals in the field of educational finance including academicians, researchers, and policymakers. Main interests include traditional school finance

concepts, public policy issues, and the review and debate of emerging issues of educational finance. **Activities:** Conducts workshop. Compiles statistics. Maintains placement service. **E-Mail:** gbabigi-anc@aol.com.

★2642★ Association of College and University Housing Officers–International (ACUHO-I)

364 W. Lane Ave., Ste. C
Columbus, OH 43201-1062
Ph: (614)292-0099   Fax: (614)292-3205

Members: Officials of educational institutions in 11 countries concerned with all aspects of student housing and food service operation. **Activities:** Offers placement service. Supports and conducts research. Organizes seminars and workshops. Offers internships. Maintains biographical archives. Compiles statistics.

★2643★ Association on Higher Education and Disability (AHEAD)

PO Box 21192
Columbus, OH 43221-0192
Ph: (614)488-4972   Fax: (614)488-1174

Members: Individuals interested in promoting the equal rights and opportunities of disabled postsecondary students, staff, faculty, and graduates. **Purpose:** Provides an exchange of communication for those professionally involved with disabled students; collects, evaluates, and disseminates information; encourages and supports legislation for the benefit of disabled students. **Activities:** Conducts surveys on issues pertinent to college students with disabilities; offers resource referral system and employment exchange for positions in disability student services. Conducts research programs; compiles statistics.

★2644★ Association of Southern Baptist Colleges and Schools (ASBCS)

901 Commerce, Ste. 600
Nashville, TN 37203
Ph: (615)244-2362   Fax: (615)242-2153

Members: Southern Baptist seminaries, senior colleges, universities, junior colleges, academies, and Bible schools. **Purpose:** Promotes Christian education through literature, faculty workshops, student recruitment, teacher placement, trustee orientation, statistical information, and other assistance to members. Emphasizes Baptist Seminary, College, and School Day throughout the Southern Baptist Convention.

★2645★ College Media Advisers (CMA)

Memphis State University
Department of Journalism
MJ-300
Memphis, TN 38152
Ph: (901)678-2403   Fax: (901)678-4798

Members: Professional association serving advisers, directors, and chairmen of boards of college student media (newspapers, yearbooks, magazines, handbooks, directories, and radio and television stations); heads of schools and departments of journalism; and others interested in junior college, college, and university student media. **Purpose:** Serves as clearinghouse for student media;

acts as consultant on student theses and dissertations on publications. Encourages high school journalism and examines its relationships to college and professional journalism. **Activities:** Maintains placement service. Conducts national survey of student media in rotation each year by type: newspapers, magazines, and yearbooks; radio and television stations.

★2646★ Convention of American Instructors of the Deaf (CAID)

PO Box 377
Bedford, TX 76095-0377
Ph: (817)354-8414

Members: Professional organization of teachers, administrators, and professionals in allied fields related to education of the deaf and hard-of-hearing. **Purpose:** Objectives are: to provide opportunities for a free interchange of views concerning methods and means of educating the deaf and hard-of-hearing; to promote such education by the publication of reports, essays, and other information; to develop more effective methods of teaching deaf and hard-of-hearing children. **Activities:** Maintains speakers' bureau; offers placement services.

★2647★ Council of Educational Facility Planners, International (CEFPI)

8687 E. Via de Ventura, Ste. 311
Scottsdale, AZ 85258-3347
Ph: (602)948-2337   Fax: (602)948-4420

Members: Individuals and firms who are responsible for planning, designing, creating, maintaining, and equipping the physical environment of education. **Purpose:** Sponsors an exchange of information, professional experiences, research results, and other investigative techniques concerning educational facility planning. **Activities:** Activities include publication and review of current and emerging practices in educational facility planning; identification and execution of needed research; development of professional training programs; strengthening of planning services on various levels of government and in institutions of higher learning; leadership in the development of higher standards for facility design and the physical environment of education. Operates speakers' bureau; sponsors placement service; compiles statistics.

★2648★ Council for Jewish Education (CJE)

730 Broadway
New York, NY 10003
Ph: (212)529-2000   Fax: (212)529-2009

Members: Teachers of Hebrew in universities; heads of Bureaus of Jewish Education and their administrative departments; faculty members of Jewish teacher training schools. **Purpose:** Seeks to: further the cause of Jewish education in America; raise professional standards and practices; promote the welfare and growth of Jewish educational workers; improve and strengthen Jewish life. **Activities:** Conducts educational programs; cosponsors a Personnel Placement Committee with Jewish Education Service of North America.

★2649★ International Educator's Institute (TIE)

PO Box 513
Cummaquid, MA 02637
Ph: (508)362-1414

Purpose: Facilitates the placement of teachers and administrators in American, British, and international schools. Seeks to create a network that provides for professional development opportunities and improved financial security of members. Offers advice and information on international school news, recent educational developments, job placement, and investment, consumer, and professional development opportunities. Makes available insurance and travel benefits. Operates International Schools Internship Program. Sponsors competitions. Bestows awards.

★2650★ Jesuit Association of Student Personnel Administrators (JASPA)

Creighton University
2500 California Plz.
Omaha, NE 68178
Ph: (402)280-2775   Fax: (402)280-3450
Fr: 800-426-7123

Members: Administrators of student personnel programs in 28 Jesuit colleges and universities in the United States. ACX Maintains placement service. Sponsors institutes and seminars for personnel in Jesuit colleges. Bestows Rev. Victor R. Yanitelli Award; compiles statistics. Cooperates with Catholic and non-Catholic educational associations in various projects. Conducts workshops. Operates organizational archives; compiles statistics.

★2651★ Jewish Educators Assembly (JEA)

106-06 Queens Blvd.
Flushing, NY 11375-4248
Ph: (718)268-9452   Fax: (718)520-4369

Members: Educational and supervisory personnel serving Jewish educational institutions. **Purpose:** Seeks to: advance the development of Jewish education in the congregation on all levels in consonance with the philosophy of the Conservative Movement; cooperate with the United Synagogue of America Commission on Jewish Education as the policy-making body of the educational enterprise; join in cooperative effort with other Jewish educational institutions and organizations; establish and maintain professional standards for Jewish educators; serve as a forum for the exchange of ideas; promote the values of Jewish education as a basis for the creative continuity of the Jewish people. **Activities:** Maintains placement service.

★2652★ NAFSA/Association of International Educators (NAFSA)

1875 Connecticut Ave. NW, Ste. 1000
Washington, DC 20009
Ph: (202)462-4811   Fax: (202)667-3419

Members: Individuals, organizations, and institutions dealing with international educational exchange, including foreign student advisers, overseas educational advisers, credentials and admissions officers, administrators and teachers of English as a second language, community support personnel, study-abroad administrators, and embassy cultural or educational personnel. **Purpose:** Promotes self-regulation standards and responsibilities in international educational exchange; offers professional development opportunities primarily through publications, workshops, grants, and regional and national conferences. Advocates for increased awareness and support of international education and exchange on campuses, in government, and in communities. **Activities:** Offers services including: a job registry for employers and professionals involved with international education; a consultant referral service. Sponsors joint liaison activities with a variety of other educational and government organizations to conduct a census of foreign student enrollment in the U.S.; conducts workshops about specific subjects and countries.

★2653★ National Academic Advising Association (NACADA)

Kansas State Univ.
2323 Anderson Ave., Ste. 225
Manhattan, KS 66502
Ph: (913)532-5717   Fax: (913)532-7732

Members: Academic program advisers, faculty, administrators, counselors, and others concerned with the intellectual, personal, and career development of students in all types of postsecondary educational institutions. **Purpose:** Is dedicated to the support and professional growth of academic advising and academic advisers. Provides a forum for discussion, debate, and exchange of ideas regarding academic advising. Serves as advocate for standards and quality programs in academic advising. **Activities:** Operates consultants bureau to assist advising services on college campuses. Conducts professional training and holds personal and professional development workshops and conferences. Maintains placement service, speakers' bureau, and clearinghouse. **E-Mail:** nacada@ksuvm.ksu.edu

★2654★ National Alliance of Black School Educators (NABSE)

2816 Georgia Ave. NW
Washington, DC 20001
Ph: (202)483-1549   Fax: (202)483-8323

Members: Black educators from all levels; others indirectly involved in the education of black youth. **Purpose:** To promote awareness, professional expertise, and commitment among black educators. Goals are to: eliminate and rectify the results of racism in education; work with state, local, and national leaders to raise the academic achievement level of all black students; increase members' involvement in legislative activities; facilitate the introduction of a curriculum that more completely embraces black America; improve the ability of black educators to promote problem resolution; create a meaningful and effective network of strength, talent, and professional support. **Activities:** Plans to establish a National Black Educators Data Bank and offer placement service.

★2655★ **National Association of Episcopal Schools (NAES)**

815 2nd Ave.
New York, NY 10017-4594
Ph: (212)922-5173   Fax: (212)286-9366
Fr: 800-334-7626

Members: Episcopal church-related boarding and day schools. **Purpose:** Promotes the educational ministry of the Episcopal Church; helps strengthen programs, teaching, and pastoral roles of Episcopal schools; develops criteria and curriculum materials. Provides worship materials and resources geared specifically to the needs of Episcopal schools. Works to aid communication between the National Episcopal Church and its schools and among member schools. **Activities:** Celebrates Episcopal School Week annually. Maintains charitable program, world partnership programs, and placement service.

★2656★ **National Association of Student Personnel Administrators (NASPA)**

1875 Connecticut Ave. NW, Ste. 418
Washington, DC 20009
Ph: (202)265-7500

Members: Representatives of degree-granting institutions of higher education which have been fully accredited. **Purpose:** Works to enrich the educational experience of all students. Serves colleges and universities by providing leadership and professional growth opportunities for the chief student affairs officer and other professionals who consider higher education and student affairs issues from an institutional perspective. Provides professional development; improves information and research; acts as an advocate for students in higher education. Promotes diversity in NASPA and the profession. **Activities:** Maintains career service and conducts the Richard F. Stevens Institute. Supports minority undergraduate fellows program.

★2657★ **National Association of Teachers' Agencies (NATA)**

PO Box 223
Georgetown, MA 01833-0323
Ph: (508)352-8473   Fax: (508)352-8680

Purpose: Private employment agencies engaged primarily in the placement of teaching and administration personnel. Works to standardize records and promote a strong ethical sense in the placement field. Maintains speakers' bureau.

★2658★ **National Association of Temple Educators (NATE)**

Richard Morin
707 Summerly Dr.
Nashville, TN 37209-4253
Ph: (615)352-6800   Fax: (615)352-7800

Members: Directors of education in Reform Jewish religious schools, principals, heads of departments, supervisors, educational consultants, students, and authors. **Purpose:** To assist in the growth and development of Jewish religious education consistent with the aims of Reform Judaism; stimulate communal interest in Jewish religious education; represent and encourage the profession of temple educator. **Activities:** Maintains placement service. Conducts surveys on personnel practices, confirmation practices, reli-

gious school organization and administration, curricular practices, and other aspects of religious education. Sponsors institutes for principals and educational directors. **E-Mail:** nateoff@aol.com

★2659★ **National Council of Administrative Women in Education (NCAWE)**

331 Churchill Rd.
Pittsburgh, PA 15235
Ph: (412)824-7950

Members: Women educators in administrative or supervisory positions in a public or private school system, college or university, foundation, agency, government or nongovernment education programs; also offers auxiliary and associate memberships. **Purpose:** Encourages women to prepare for careers in educational administration and to urge educational institutions, systems, and agencies to employ and advance women in this field. Monitors national and local legislation pertaining to women's education. Works to eliminate discrimination against women in educational administration. **Activities:** Circulates information on job openings. Maintains speakers' bureau; conducts research. Sponsors competitions.

★2660★ **National Council of Secondary School Athletic Directors (NCSSAD)**

1900 Association Dr.
Reston, VA 22091
Ph: (703)476-3410   Fax: (703)476-9527

Members: A council of the National Association for Sport and Physical Education, which is a division of the American Alliance for Health, Physical Education, Recreation and Dance. Professional athletic directors in secondary schools. **Purpose:** To improve the educational aspects of interscholastic athletics; to provide for an exchange of ideas; to establish closer working relationships with related professional groups and promote greater unity; to establish and implement standards for the professional preparation of secondary school athletic directors. **Activities:** Provides in-service training programs. Maintains placement service and speakers' bureau.

★2661★ **School Management Study Group (SMSG)**

860 18th Ave.
Salt Lake City, UT 84103
Ph: (801)532-5340

Members: School administrative bodies and college personnel. **Purpose:** Seeks to improve schools and to involve educators in critical school problems. **Activities:** Operates placement services. Offers services for continuing education of professional staff; sponsors seminars and training programs. Areas of interest include integration, policy development, conflict management, evaluation, shared governance, and others, most involving change. Maintains speakers' bureau; conducts research programs; compiles statistics.

★2662★ **Solomon Schecher Day School Association (SSDSA)**

155 5th Ave.
New York, NY 10010
Ph: (212)260-8450   Fax: (212)353-9439

Members: A division of the United Synagogue of America Commission on Jewish Education. Jewish elementary day schools and high schools with a total of over 17,000 students. Named for Solomon Schecher (1850-1915), reader of Talmud and rabbinical literature and founder of the United Synagogue of America and the Jewish Theological Seminary. **Purpose:** Provides educational consultation via telephone, mail, and personal visits to the school. Encourages maintenance of high standards for members; coordinates accreditation visits to each school. **Activities:** Cosponsors Master Program to Prepare Principals for Jewish Day Schools with the graduate school of the Jewish Theological Seminary of America, New York City; develops curriculum for day schools. Offers seminars, workshops, and consulting service. Provides educational services, materials, and statistics.

★2663★ **University Council for Educational Administration (UCEA)**

212 Rackley Bldg.
University Park, PA 16802-3200
Ph: (814)863-7916   Fax: (814)863-7918

Members: Consortium of departments of educational administration in universities. **Purpose:** Promotes and disseminates information on the improvement of pre-service and in-service training of school and higher education administrators. **Activities:** Conducts research and development in educational administration through interuniversity cooperation. Operates placement service.

EMPLOYER DIRECTORIES AND NETWORKING LISTS

★2664★ *Boarding Schools Directory*

The Association of Boarding Schools (TABS)
National Association of Independent Schools (NAIS)
1620 L St. NW
Washington, DC 20036
Ph: (202)973-9700   Fax: (202)973-9790
Fr: 800-541-5908

Annual, August. Free. Covers 276 boarding schools that are members of the National Association of Independent Schools. Entries include: School name, address, phone, contact name, grades for which boarding students are accepted, enrollment, brief description. Arrangement: Classified by type of school. Indexes: Geographical; program.

★2665★ Christian Schools International—Directory

Christian Schools International
3350 E. Paris Ave. SE
Grand Rapids, MI 49512
Ph: (616)957-1070   Fax: (616)957-5022

Annual, November. $45.00. Covers nearly 450 Reformed Christian elementary and secondary schools; related associations; societies without schools. Entries include: School name, address, phone; name, title, and address of officers; names of faculty members. Arrangement: Geographical.

★2666★ College Placement Council Directory: Who's Who in Career Planning, Placement, and Recruitment

College Placement Council (CPC)
62 Highland Ave.
Bethlehem, PA 18017
Ph: (610)868-1421   Fax: (610)868-0208
Fr: 800-544-5272

Annual, January. $47.95, plus $4.50 shipping. Covers about 2,400 college and university offices concerned with securing employment for graduates and about 2,300 companies with staff assigned to recruiting and hiring college graduates. Entries include: For colleges: college name and address; names, titles, phone, fax, and e-mail addresses of career planning and placement personnel; interview dates for undergraduates and graduates; months of graduation; whether alumni placement is also handled, student enrollment (including minority data), and dates of career/job fairs. For employers: company name; names, addresses, phone, and fax of recruitment staff; names of secondary contacts; nature of business; number of employees. Arrangement: Colleges are geographical; employers are alphabetical. Indexes: Institutional name, personal name (college personnel); geographical, personal name (in company recruitment).

★2667★ Directory of Public Elementary and Secondary Education Agencies

U.S. National Center for Education Statistics
555 New Jersey Ave. NW
Washington, DC 20208-5651
Ph: (202)219-1335   Fax: (202)219-1728
Fr: 800-424-1616

Annual. $22.00. Covers about 17,000 local education agencies in the United States, the District of Columbia, and five territories which operate their own schools or pay tuition to other local education agencies. Also lists intermediate education agencies. Entries include: Agency name, address, phone, county, description of district, grade span, membership, special education students, metropolitan status, number of high school graduates, teachers, and schools. Also available from Superintendent of Documents, U.S. Government Printing Office. Arrangement: Geographical, then by type of agency.

★2668★ Directory of Public School Systems in the U.S.

Association for School, College and University Staffing
1600 Dodge Ave., S-330
Evanston, IL 60201-3451
Ph: (708)864-1999   Fax: (708)864-8303

Annual, August. $65.00. Covers about 14,500 public school systems in the United States and their administrative personnel. Entries include: System name, address, phone, name and title of personnel administrator. Arrangement: Geographical by state.

★2669★ Directory of State Education Agencies

Council of Chief State School Officers
1 Massachusetts Ave. NW, Ste. 700
Washington, DC 20001-1431
Ph: (202)408-5505   Fax: (202)408-8072

Annual. Covers about 1,500 top officers of federal, state, and territorial education agencies responsible at that level for administration of elementary, secondary, and vocational/technical education. Entries include: Department or agency name, address, phone, names and phone numbers of superintendent or commissioner and principal staff members. Arrangement: Geographical. Indexes: Personal name.

★2670★ Employment Opportunities, USA

Washington Research Associates
1660 S. Albion, Ste. 390
Denver, CO 80222
Ph: (303)756-9038   Fax: (303)770-1945

Annual, quarterly updates. $184.00, includes quarterly updates. Publication includes: List of over 1,000 employment contacts in companies and agencies in the banking, arts, telecommunications, education, and 14 other industries and professions, including the federal government. Entries include: Company name, name of representative, address, description of products or services, hiring and recruiting practices, training programs, and year established. Principal content is industry overviews, career news, and employment opportunity information on 14 different job markets. Arrangement: Classified by industry. Indexes: Occupation.

★2671★ 50 State Educational Directories

Career Guidance Foundation
8090 Engineer Rd.
San Diego, CA 92111
Ph: (619)560-8051   Fax: (619)278-8960
Fr: 800-854-2670

Annual, latest edition June 1996. $89.00. Microfiche. Collection consists of reproductions of the state educational directories published by the departments of education of individual states. Directory contents vary, but the majority contain listings of elementary and secondary schools, colleges and universities, and state education officials. Amount of detail in each also varies. Entries include: Usually, institution name, address, and name of one executive.

★2672★ Handbook of Private Schools

Porter Sargent Publishers, Inc.
11 Beacon St., Ste. 1400
Boston, MA 02108
Ph: (617)523-1670   Fax: (617)523-1021

Annual, June. $85.00, plus $2.41 shipping. Covers 1,700 elementary and secondary boarding and day schools in the United States. Entries include: School name, address, phone, fax, type of school (boarding or day), sex and age range, names and titles of administrators, grades offered, academic orientation, curriculum, new admissions yearly, tests required for admission, enrollment and faculty, graduate record, number of alumni, tuition and scholarship figures, summer session, plant evaluation and endowment, date of establishment, calendar, association membership, description of school's offerings and history. Arrangement: Geographical. Indexes: Alphabetical by school name.

★2673★ Headmasters Association—Membership List

Headmasters Association
c/o Agnes C. Underwood
National Cathedral School
Mount St. Alban
Washington, DC 20016
Ph: (202)537-6353

Annual, February. Available to members only. Covers about 290 active, associate, and honorary members who are headmasters or principals of secondary schools. Entries include: Name, school name, address, date of membership. Arrangement: By type of membership.

★2674★ Independent School Guide for Washington DC and Surrounding Area

Independent School Guides
7315 Brookville Rd.
Chevy Chase, MD 20815
Ph: (301)986-5370   Fax: (301)718-4651

Biennial, summer of odd years. $12.95 plus $2.00 shipping. Covers over 300 independent schools (including parochial schools) in the Washington, DC area, including Maryland and Virginia. Entries include: School name, address, phone, name and title of contact, number of faculty, geographical area served, tuition, courses, admission procedures, summer programs, LD/ED programs, scholarships available. Arrangement: Alphabetical. Indexes: Geographical.

★2675★ Independent Schools Association of the Southwest—Membership List

Independent Schools Association of the Southwest
Box 52297
Tulsa, OK 74152-0297
Ph: (918)749-5927   Fax: (918)749-5937
Fr: 800-880-0527

Annual, August. Free. Covers over 60 independent elementary and secondary schools accredited by the association. Entries include: School name, address, phone, chief administrative officer, structure, and enrollment. Arrangement: Geographical. Indexes: Alphabetical.

★2676★ National Association of College Deans, Registrars and Admissions Officers—Directory

National Association of College Deans, Registrars and Admissions Officers
917 Dorsett Ave.
Albany, GA 31701
Ph: (912)435-4945

Annual, February. $5.00. Covers about 325 member deans, registrars, and admissions officers at nearly 90 predominantly Black schools. Entries include: Institution name, address, phone, names and titles of key personnel, enrollment, whether a public or private institution. Arrangement: Alphabetical.

★2677★ National Association of College and University Business Officers—Membership Directory

National Association of College and University Business Officers
1 Dupont Cir. NW, Ste. 500
Washington, DC 20036
Ph: (202)861-2500   Fax: (202)861-2583

Annual, winter. $115.00. Number of listings: 2,100. Entries include: Name of institution, address, names of primary representatives. Arrangement: Alphabetical.

★2678★ National Association of Teachers' Agencies—Membership Directory

National Association of Teachers' Agencies
104 S. Central Ave., Ste. 12
Valley Stream, NY 11580
Ph: (516)568-8871   Fax: (516)872-1944

Annual, January. Free. Covers approximately 20 private employment agencies engaged primarily in the placement of teaching and administrative personnel in education. Entries include: Name, address, phone, names of key officials. Arrangement: Alphabetical.

★2679★ National Association for Women in Education—Member Handbook

National Association for Women in Education
1325 18th St. NW, Ste. 210
Washington, DC 20036
Ph: (202)659-9330   Fax: (202)457-0946

Annual. Available to members only. Covers 2,000 American and foreign members. Entries include: Name, institution, office and home addresses, phone, education, position, committee membership. Arrangement: Geographical. Indexes: Alphabetical.

★2680★ National Directory of Alternative Schools

National Coalition of Alternative Community Schools
PO Box 15036
Santa Fe, NM 87506
Ph: (505)474-4312

Biennial, even years. $15.00. Covers over 400 alternative education programs, including home schools, and state and regional coalitions of alternative schools and colleges; also lists organizations and networks offering services and resources to those working with children; international coverage. Entries include: Name, address, phone, name of contact; some also include descriptions of programs. Arrangement: Schools are geographical.

★2681★ National Directory for Employment in Education

Association for School, College and University Staffing
1600 Dodge Ave., S-330
Evanston, IL 60201-3451
Ph: (708)864-1999   Fax: (708)864-8303

Annual, winter. $20.00. Covers about 550 placement offices maintained by teacher-training institutions and 450 school district personnel officers and/or superintendents responsible for hiring professional staff. Entries include: Institution name, address, phone, contact name. Arrangement: Geographical. Indexes: Personal name; subject-field of teacher training, institutions which provide vacancy bulletins and placement services to non-enrolled students.

★2682★ National School Public Relations Association—Directory

National School Public Relations Association
1501 Lee Hwy.
Arlington, VA 22209
Ph: (703)528-6713   Fax: (703)528-7017
Fr: 800-48-NSPRA

Annual, January. Available to members only. Covers approximately 2,800 school system public relations directors, school administrators, principals, and others who are members of the National School Public Relations Association. Entries include: Name, affiliation, address, phone. Arrangement: Geographical.

★2683★ Opportunities Abroad for Educators

Fulbright Teacher Exchange Program
600 Maryland Ave., SW, Rm. 235
Washington, DC 20024-2520
Ph: (202)382-8586   Fax: (202)426-0657
Fr: 800-726-0479

Annual, May. Free. Covers opportunities available for elementary and secondary teachers, college and university instructors and professors, and school administrators to attend seminars or to teach abroad under the Mutual Educational and Cultural Exchange Act of 1961. Entries include: Countries of placement, dates, eligibility requirements, teaching assignments. Arrangement: Geographical.

★2684★ Private Independent Schools

Bunting and Lyon, Inc.
238 N. Main St.
Wallingford, CT 06492
Ph: (203)269-3333   Fax: (203)269-5697

Annual, March. $96.00. Covers 1,200 English-speaking elementary and secondary private schools and summer programs in the U.S. and abroad. Entries include: School name, address, phone, enrollment, tuition and other fees, scholarship information, administrator's name and educational background, director of admissions, regional accreditation, description of programs, curriculum, activities. Arrangement: Geographical. Indexes: School name; geographical.

HANDBOOKS AND MANUALS

★2685★ Career Information Center

Macmillan Publishing Co.
200 Old Tappan Rd.
Old Tappan, NJ 07675
Ph: (609)461-6500   Fr: 800-223-2336

Visual Education Center Staff. Fifth edition, 1992. $229.00. This 13-volume set profiles over 600 occupations. Each occupational profile describes job duties, educational requirements, how to get the job, advancement possibilities, employment outlook, working conditions, earnings and benefits, and where to write for more information.

★2686★ Careers in Education

VGM Career Horizons
4255 W. Touhy Ave.
Lincolnwood, IL 60646-1975
Ph: (847)679-5500   Fax: (847)679-2494
Fr: 800-323-4900

Roy A. Edelfeldt. 1993. $17.95; $13.95 (paper). 192 pages. Explores opportunities for teachers, administrators, and specialists in elementary and secondary schools, as well as teaching, research, and administrative positions in higher education. Additional focus on adult and continuing education and industry opportunities for educators. Provides detailed background on careers in state boards and state departments of education, accrediting agencies, federal agencies, and national associations and councils.

★2687★ Educator's Job Search: The Ultimate Guide to Finding Positions in Education

National Education Association
1201 16th St., NW
Washington, DC 20036
Ph: (202)822-7252   Fax: (202)822-7206

Martin Kimeldorf. 1993. $15.95 (paper).

★2688★ Encyclopedia of Careers and Vocational Guidance

J. G. Ferguson Publishing Co.
200 W. Monroe, Ste. 250
Chicago, IL 60606
Ph: (312)580-5480

William E. Hopke. Ninth edition, 1993. $129.95; $199.95 (CD-ROM). Four-volume set that profiles 900 occupations and describes job trends in 71 industries. Includes career description, educational requirements, history of the job, methods of entry, advancement, employment outlook, earnings, conditions of work, social and psychological factors, and sources of further information. Contains career and employment information for this field.

★2689★ How to Get a Job in Education

Bob Adams, Inc.
260 Center St.
Holbrook, MA 02343
Ph: (617)767-8100   Fax: (617)767-0994
Fr: 800-872-5627

Joel Levin. Second edition, 1995. $12.95. 320 pages. Prepared for recent college graduates, seasoned educators, and career-changing professionals, this publication guides the job-seeker through the necessary steps to obtaining a job in education at the elementary, secondary, and university levels. Offers advice on how to prepare for state and local examinations, how to locate teaching opportunities nationwide, and how to obtain certification. Includes a nationwide salary survey. Covers public, private, summer, and overseas opportunities.

★2690★ Liberal Arts Jobs: What They Are and How to Get Them

Peterson's
PO Box 2123
Princeton, NJ 08543-2123
Ph: (609)243-9111   Fax: (609)243-9150
Fr: 800-338-3282

Burton Jay Nadler. Second edition, 1989. $9.95. 153 pages. Presents a list of the top 20 fields for liberal arts majors, covering more than 300 job opportunities. Discusses strategies for going after those jobs, including guidance on the language of a successful job search, informational interviews, and making networking work.

★2691★ Non-Profits and Education Job Finder

Planning/Communications
7215 Oak Ave.
River Forest, IL 60305-1935
Ph: (708)366-5200   Fr: (888)366-5200

Daniel Lauber. 1996. $32.95; $16.95 (paper). 350 pages. Covers 1600 sources. Discusses how to use sources of non-profit sector job vacancies in a number of specialties and state-by-state, including job-matching services, job hotlines, specialty periodicals with job ads, salary surveys, and directories. Covers a variety of fields from education to religion. Includes chapters on resume and cover letter preparation and interviewing.

★2692★ Opportunities in State and Local Government Careers

VGM Career Horizons
4255 W. Touhy Ave.
Lincolnwood, IL 60646-1975
Ph: (847)679-5500   Fax: (847)679-2494
Fr: 800-323-4900

Neale Baxter. 1993. $13.95; $10.95 (paper). 160 pages. Points out the incentives and drawbacks of a government career. Describes hiring procedures and provides tips on filling out applications, taking physical and aptitude tests, handling interviews, and finding jobs. Describes the jobs in which 75% of all state and local government workers are employed. For each occupation, covers the nature of the work and the training required.

★2693★ Straight Talk About School Administrators

Association of California School Administrators
1517 L St.
Sacramento, CA 95814
Ph: (916)444-3216   Fax: (916)444-3245

Association of California School Administrators. 1994. $5.00 (paper).

★2694★ Where the Jobs Are: The Hottest Careers for the '90s

The Career Press, Inc.
3 Tice Rd.
PO Box 687
Franklin Lakes, NJ 07417
Ph: (201)848-0310   Fax: (201)848-1727
Fr: 800-237-3371

Joyce Hadley. Second edition, 1995. $9.99. 300 pages. Describes careers in fifteen general fields, from accounting to travel and hospitality.

EMPLOYMENT AGENCIES AND SEARCH FIRMS

★2695★ Educational Placement Service

5050 Poplar Ave., Ste. 1700
Memphis, TN 38157-1701
Ph: (901)767-1884

Employment agency. Focuses on teaching, administrative, and education-related openings.

OTHER SOURCES

★2696★ ACE Fellows Program

1 Dupont Cir. NW, 8th Fl.
Washington, DC 20036-1193
Ph: (202)939-9420   Fax: (202)785-8056

Purpose: Service of the American Council on Education to strengthen leadership in American postsecondary education by identifying and preparing individuals who have shown promise for responsible positions in higher education administration. Objectives are: to encourage and prepare individuals making higher education administration their professional career; to provide opportunities for planned observation and experience in decision making; to identify and develop potential leaders. Arranges internships whereby promising professors and administrators are given the opportunity to study higher education leadership as an intern at a host institution or the home institution.

★2697★ American Almanac of Jobs and Salaries 1994-95

Avon Books
1350 Avenue of the Americas, 2nd Fl.
New York, NY 10019
Ph: (212)261-6800   Fr: 800-238-0658

John Wright. Revised edition, 1993. $17.00. 704 pages. This is a comprehensive guide to the wages of hundreds of occupations in a wide variety of industries and organizations.

★2698★ American Association of Collegiate Registrars and Admissions Officers (AACRAO)

1 Dupont Cir. NW, Ste. 330
Washington, DC 20036
Ph: (202)293-9161   Fax: (202)872-8857

Members: Degree-granting postsecondary institutions, government agencies, and higher education coordinating boards, private educational organizations, and education-oriented businesses. **Purpose:** Promotes higher education and furthers the professional development of members working in admissions, enrollment management, institutional research, records, and registration. **E-Mail:** harrisonj@aacrao.nche.edu

★2699★ American Association of School Administrators (AASA)

1801 N. Moore St.
Arlington, VA 22209
Ph: (703)528-0700   Fax: (703)841-1543

Members: Professional association of administrators and executives of school systems and educational service agencies; school district superintendents; central, building, and service unit administrators; presidents of colleges, deans, and professors of educational administration; placement officers; executive directors and administrators of education associations; heads of private schools.

★2700★ American Association of University Administrators (AAUA)

PO Box 2183
Tuscaloosa, AL 35403
Ph: (205)758-0636   Fax: (205)345-9778

Purpose: Promotes excellence in the administration of higher education and assists career administrators in continuing their professional growth. Conducts periodic professional development program.

★2701★ American Federation of School Administrators (AFSA)

1729 21st St. NW
Washington, DC 20009
Ph: (202)986-4209   Fax: (202)986-4211

Members: Principals, vice-principals, directors, supervisors, and administrators involved in pedagogical education. **Purpose:** To achieve the highest goals in education; maintain and improve standards, benefits, and conditions for personnel without regard to color, race, sex, background, or national origin; obtain job security; protect seniority and merit; cooperate with all responsible organizations in education; promote understanding, participation, and support of the public, communities, and agencies; be alert to resist attacks and campaigns that would create or entrench a spoils system; promote democratic society by supporting full educational opportunities for every child and student in the nation.

★2702★ Association of Christian Schools International (ACSI)

PO Box 35097
Colorado Springs, CO 80935-3509
Ph: (719)528-6906   Fax: (719)531-0631

Purpose: Service organization for Christian schools. Represents members in legislative efforts and First Amendment confrontations with the government. **Activities:** Sponsors student activities such as academic and speech meets, sports events, piano and choir festivals, and science fairs. Holds Christian Cheerleader Camp for high school students. Offers volume-reduced cost purchasing for school supplies and curriculum materials; recommends additional sources for purchasing. Sponsors ACSI Missionary Fund to send teams of Christian school educators throughout the world to conduct conventions, and in-service training programs. Provides speakers.

★2703★ Association of Departments of English (ADE)

10 Astor Pl.
New York, NY 10003
Ph: (212)614-6317   Fax: (212)477-9863

Members: Administrators of college and university departments of English, humanities, rhetoric, and communications. **Purpose:** To improve the teaching of English and the administration of English departments. Conducts studies and surveys of literature and writing courses. Sponsors sessions at major English conventions and conferences nationwide.

★2704★ Association for Humanistic Education and Development (AHEAD)

5999 Stevenson Ave.
Alexandria, VA 22304
Ph: (703)823-9800   Fax: (703)823-0252
Fr: 800-347-6647

Members: A division of the American Counseling Association. Teachers, educational administrators, community agency workers, counselors, school social workers, and psychologists; others interested in the area of human development. **Purpose:** Aims to assist individuals in improving their quality of life. Provides forum for the exchange of information about humanistically-oriented administrative and instructional practices. Supports humanistic practices and research on instructional and organizational methods for facilitating humanistic education; encourages cooperation among related professional groups.

★2705★ Association for the Study of Higher Education (ASHE)

Texas A&M University
Department of Educational Admin.
College Station, TX 77843-4226
Ph: (409)845-0393   Fax: (409)862-4347

Members: Professors, researchers, administrators, policy analysts, graduate students, and others concerned with the study of higher education. **Purpose:** To advance the study of higher education and facilitate and encourage discussion of priority issues for research in the study of higher education.

★2706★ Educational Placement Sources Abroad

Education Information Services (EIS)
PO Box 660662
Newton, MA 02162-0662
Ph: (617)443-0125

Annual, August. Includes about 150 organizations in the United States and abroad which place English-speaking teachers and education administrators in positions abroad. Provides organization name and address. Classified by type of organization.

★2707★ Educational Placement Sources—U.S.A.

Education Information Service
PO Box 662
4523 Andes Dr.
Newton, MA 02162-0002
Ph: (617)237-0887

Annual, fall. $4.95. Covers about 75 organizations in the United States that find positions for teachers, educational administrators, and counselors. Entries include: Organization name, address, phone. Arrangement: Alphabetical.

★2708★ Friends Council on Education (FCE)

1507 Cherry St.
Philadelphia, PA 19102
Ph: (215)241-7245

Members: Representatives appointed by Friends Yearly Meetings; heads of Quaker secondary and elementary schools and colleges; members-at-large. **Purpose:** Acts as a clearinghouse for information on Quaker schools and colleges. **Activities:** Holds meetings and conferences on education and provides in-service training for teachers, administrators, and trustees in Friends schools.

★2709★ The Landscape of Leadership Preparation: Reframing the Education of School Administrators

Corwin Press, Inc.
2455 Teller Rd.
Thousand Oaks, CA 91320-2218
Ph: (805)499-9734   Fax: (805)499-0871

Joseph Murphy. 1993. $42.95; $21.95 (paper).

★2710★ National Association of College and University Business Officers (NACUBO)

1 Dupont Cir. NW, Ste. 500
Washington, DC 20036
Ph: (202)861-2500   Fax: (202)861-2583

Members: Colleges, universities, and companies that are members of a regional association. **Purpose:** Develops and maintains national interest in improving the principles and practices of business and financial administration in higher education. **Activities:** Sponsors workshops in fields such as cash management, grant and contract maintenance, accounting, investment, student loan administration, and costing. Conducts research and information exchange programs between college and university personnel; compiles statistics.

★2711★ National Association of Elementary School Principals (NAESP)

1615 Duke St.
Alexandria, VA 22314
Ph: (703)684-3345   Fax: (703)548-6021

Members: Professional association of principals, assistant or vice principals, and aspiring principals; persons engaged in educational research and in the professional education of elementary and middle school administrators. **Purpose:** Sponsors National Distinguished Principals Program, President's Award for Educational Excellence, American Student Council Association, National Fellows Program, and Institute for Reflective Practice. **Activities:** Offers professional development workshops throughout the year.

★2712★ National Association of Independent Schools (NAIS)

1620 L St. NW
Washington, DC 20036-5605
Ph: (202)973-9700   Fax: (202)973-9790

Members: Independent elementary and secondary school members; regional associations of independent schools and related associations. **Purpose:** Provides curricular and administrative research and services. Conducts educational programs; compiles statistics.

★2713★ National Association of Secondary School Principals (NASSP)

1904 Association Dr.
Reston, VA 22091
Ph: (703)860-0200   Fax: (703)476-5432
Fr: 800-253-7746

Members: Secondary school principals and assistant principals; other persons engaged in secondary school administration and/or supervision; college professors teaching courses in secondary education. **Activities:** Sponsors National Association of Student Councils, National Honor Society, National Association of Student Activity Advisors, Partnerships International and National Junior Honor Society.

★2714★ National Association of State Directors of Special Education (NASDSE)

1800 Diagonal Rd., Ste. 320
Alexandria, VA 22314
Ph: (703)519-3800   Fax: (703)519-3808

Members: Professional society of state directors; consultants, supervisors, and administrators who have statewide responsibilities for administering special education programs. **Purpose:** Provides services to state agencies to facilitate their efforts to maximize educational outcomes for individuals with disabilities.

★2715★ National Community Education Association (NCEA)

3929 Old Lee Hwy., Ste. 91-A
Fairfax, VA 22032
Ph: (703)359-8973   Fax: (703)359-0972

Members: Community school directors, principals, superintendents, professors, teachers, students, and laypeople. **Purpose:** Promotes and establishes community schools as an integral part of the educational plan of every community. Serves as a clearinghouse for the exchange of ideas and information, and the sharing of efforts. **Activities:** Offers leadership training.

★2716★ **National Council for Accreditation of Teacher Education (NCATE)**
2010 Massachusetts Ave. NW, Ste. 500
Washington, DC 20036-1023
Ph: (202)466-7496   Fax: (202)296-6620
Members: Representatives from constituent colleges and universities, state departments of education, school boards, teacher, and other professional groups. **Purpose:** Voluntary accrediting body devoted exclusively to: evaluation and accreditation of institutions for preparation of elementary and secondary school teachers; preparation of school service personnel, including school principals, supervisors, superintendents, school psychologists, instructional technologists, and other specialists for school-oriented positions.

★2717★ *Overseas Employment Opportunities for Educators: Department of Defense Dependents Schools*
Diane Publishing Co.
600 Upland Ave.
Upland, PA 19015
Ph: (610)499-7415
1993. $29.95. 52 pages.

★2718★ *Requirements for Certification of Teachers, Counselors, Librarians, Administrators for Elementary and Secondary Schools*
University of Chicago Press
5801 Ellis Ave., 4th Fl.
Chicago, IL 60637
Ph: (312)702-7648   Fax: 800-621-8476
Fr: 800-621-2736
Annual, June. $34.00. Publication includes: List of state and local departments of education. Entries include: Office name, address, phone. Principal content of publication is

summaries of each state's teaching and administrative certification requirements. Arrangement: Geographical.

★2719★ *Resumes for Education Careers*
VGM Career Horizons
4255 W. Touhy Ave.
Lincolnwood, IL 60646-1975
Ph: (847)679-5500   Fax: (847)679-2494
Fr: 800-323-4900
1992. $9.95. Sample resumes cover a variety of education careers and reflect education professionals at all levels of experience.

EEG Technologists and Technicians

SOURCES OF HELP-WANTED ADS

★2720★ Clinical EEG

American Medical EEG Association
850 Elm Grove Rd.
Elm Grove, WI 53122
Ph: (414)797-7800   Fax: (414)782-8788

Quarterly. Medical journal focusing on electroencephalography and related neurological practices.

PLACEMENT AND JOB REFERRAL SERVICES

★2721★ American Society of Electroneurodiagnostic Technologists (ASET)

204 W. 7th St.
Carroll, IA 51401-2317
Ph: (712)792-2978   Fax: (712)792-6962

Members: Persons engaged mainly in clinical electroencephalographic technology, with some doing both clinical and research EEG and related neurodiagnostic procedures, such as Evoked Potential Responses and polysomnography. **Purpose:** Objective is the advancement of electroneurodiagnostic technology and the development and maintenance of high standards of training and practice in this field. **Activities:** Provides employment exchange service. Conducts a scientific program and structured,short courses in various aspects of EEG technology and electroneurodiagnostics. Joint projects with the American Electroencephalographic Society include the drawing up of job descriptions in EEG technology as guidelines for classification of personnel and working toward approved programs for training EEG technologists.

EMPLOYER DIRECTORIES AND NETWORKING LISTS

★2722★ AHA Guide to the Health Care Field

Health Statistics Group
American Hospital Association (AHA)
1 N. Franklin
Chicago, IL 60606
Ph: (312)422-3501   Fax: (312)280-6015

Annual, July. $195.00, payment with order. Covers hospitals, multi-health care systems, freestanding ambulatory surgery centers, psychiatric facilities, long-term care facilities, substance abuse programs, hospices, Health Maintenance Organizations (HMOs), and other health-related organizations. Entries include: For hospitals: facility name, address, phone, administrator's name, number of beds, facilities and services, number of employees, expenses, other statistics. For other organizations: name, address, phone, name and title of contact. Arrangement: Geographical. Indexes: Hospital name.

★2723★ Directory of Hospital Personnel

Medical Economics
5 Paragon Dr.
Montvale, NJ 07645-1725
Ph: (201)358-7500   Fax: (201)573-4956
Fr: 800-222-3045

Annual, September. $325.00, plus 7.50 shipping. Covers 200,000 executives at 7,100 U.S. hospitals. Entries include: Name of hospital, address, phone, number of beds, type and JCAHO status of hospital, names and titles of key department heads and staff, medical and nursing school affiliations; number of residents, interns, and nursing students. Arrangement: Geographical. Indexes: Hospital name, personnel, hospital size.

★2724★ Hospital Blue Book

Billian Publishing Co.
2100 Powers Ferry Rd., Ste. 300
Atlanta, GA 30339
Ph: (404)955-5656   Fax: (404)952-0669

Annual, spring. $154.50, national edition, plus $20.00 shipping. Covers more than 7,100 hospitals; some listings also appear in a separate southern edition of this publication. Entries include: Name of hospital, accreditation, mailing address, phone, fax, number of beds, type of facility (nonprofit, general, state, etc.); list of administrative personnel and chiefs of medical services, with specific titles. Arrangement: Geographical.

★2725★ Hospital Market Atlas

SMG Marketing Group, Inc.
1342 N. LaSalle Dr.
Chicago, IL 60610
Ph: (312)642-3026   Fax: (312)642-9729
Fr: 800-678-3026

Biennial, odd years. $495.00, payment with order. Covers over 7,000 hospitals, hospital systems and 480 group purchasing organizations. Entries include: Hospital or organization name, address, phone, county code, management, type of hospital service, number of beds, admissions, surgical operations, and emergency room visits. Arrangement: Geographical.

★2726★ Hospitals Directory

American Business Directories, Inc.
American Business Information, Inc.
5711 S. 86th Cir.
Omaha, NE 68127
Ph: (402)593-4600   Fax: (402)331-1505

Annual. $870.00, U.S. edition. Entries include: Name, address, phone (including area code), size of advertisement, year first in Yellow Pages, name of owner or manager, number of employees. Compiled from telephone company Yellow Pages, nationwide. Arrangement: Geographical.

★2727★ Medical and Health Information Directory

Gale Research
835 Penobscot Bldg.
Detroit, MI 48226-4094
Ph: (313)961-2242   Fax: (313)961-6083
Fr: 800-877-GALE

Approximately biennial; latest edition 1994. $195.00, per volume; $485.00, for the three-volume set. Covers in Volume 1, almost 18,600 medical and health oriented associations, organizations, institutions, and government agencies, including health maintenance organizations (HMOs), preferred provider organizations (PPOs), insurance companies, pharmaceutical companies, research centers, and medical and allied health schools. In Volume 2, nearly 11,800 medical book publishers; medical periodicals, directories, audiovisual producers and services, medical libraries and information centers, and electronic resources. In Volume 3, nearly 26,000 clinics, treatment centers, care programs, and counseling/diagnostic services for 30 subject areas. Entries include: Institution, service, or firm name, address, phone; many include names of key personnel and, when pertinent, descriptive annotation. Arrangement: Classified by organization activity, service, etc. Indexes: Each volume has a complete alphabetical name and keyword index.

★2728★ Osteopathic Membership Directory—AOHA

American Osteopathic Healthcare Association
5301 Wisconsin Ave. NW, Ste. 630
Washington, DC 20015-2015
Ph: (202)686-1700   Fax: (202)686-7615

Annual, summer. $125.00, payment with order. Covers about 110 osteopathic hospitals. Includes list of individual and institutional members; also lists osteopathic colleges, and directors of medical education. Entries include: For hospitals: name of hospital, name of chief executive officer, address, phone, number of beds and other hospital data. Arrangement: Geographical. Indexes: Name, institution.

HANDBOOKS AND MANUALS

★2729★ Careers in Health Care

VGM Career Horizons
4255 W. Touhy Ave.
Lincolnwood, IL 60646-1975
Ph: (847)679-5500   Fax: (847)679-2494
Fr: 800-323-4900

Barbara M. Swanson. 1995. $17.95; $13.95 (paper). Describes job duties, work settings, salaries, licensing and certification requirements, educational preparation, and future outlook. Gives ideas on how to secure a job.

★2730★ EEG Technician Curriculum: 110, 111, 112, 114, 120

Allied Health Publications
222 W. 24th St.
National City, CA 91950
Ph: (619)477-4800   Fax: (619)477-5202

K. Ballinger. 1994.

★2731★ Medical Technologists and Technicians Career Directory

Gale Research
835 Penobscot Bldg.
Detroit, MI 48226-4094
Ph: (313)961-2242   Fax: (313)961-6083
Fr: 800-877-GALE

Bradley Morgan. 1993. $39.00. 324 pages. Essays on specific careers provide an insider's perspective. Features extensive listings of contacts and entry-level job opportunities. Provides information on internships and sources of help-wanted ads.

★2732★ 100 Best Careers for the Year 2000

Prentice Hall General Reference
15 Columbus Cir.
New York, NY 10023
Ph: (212)373-8500   Fr: 800-223-2348

Shelly Field. 1992. $15.00 (paper). Covers 100 of the fastest growing jobs. The publication is divided into 11 general employment sections. Specific careers are covered within each section. Provides job description, responsibilities, employment opportunities, earnings, education and training, advancement opportunities, and experience and qualifications for each occupation.

★2733★ Opportunities in Health and Medical Careers

VGM Career Horizons
4255 W. Touhy Ave.
Lincolnwood, IL 60646-1975
Ph: (847)679-5500   Fax: (847)679-2494
Fr: 800-323-4900

Donald Snook, Jr. and Leo D'Orazio. 1993. $14.95; $11.95 (paper). Covers the full range of medical and health occupations. Illustrated.

★2734★ Opportunities in Medical Imaging Careers

VCH Publishers, Inc.
220 E. 23rd St., Ste. 909
New York, NY 10010-4606
Ph: (212)683-8333   Fax: (212)481-0897

Clifford J. Sherry. 1993.

★2735★ Opportunities in Medical Technology Careers

VGM Career Horizons
4255 W. Touhy Ave.
Lincolnwood, IL 60646-1975
Ph: (847)679-5500   Fax: (847)679-2494
Fr: 800-323-4900

Karen R. Karni and Sidney Oliver. 1990. $14.95; $11.95 (paper). Details opportunities for various technical medical personnel and supplies up-to-date information on salary levels and employment outlook. Appendices list associations and unions in each field. Illustrated.

★2736★ Opportunities in Vocational and Technical Careers

VGM Career Horizons
4255 W. Touhy Ave.
Lincolnwood, IL 60646-1975
Ph: (847)679-5500   Fax: (847)679-2494
Fr: 800-323-4900

Adrian A. Paradis. 1992. $14.95; $11.95 (paper). 160 pages. Provides information on a variety of opportunities and advice on breaking into the field.

★2737★ Resumes for Health and Medical Careers

4255 W. Touhy Ave.
Lincolnwood, IL 60646-1975
Ph: (708)679-5500   Fax: (708)679-6375
Fr: 800-323-4900

Compiled by VGM Career Horizons Staff 1995. $9.95 (paper).

EMPLOYMENT AGENCIES AND SEARCH FIRMS

★2738★ Action Plus Employer Services

1211 W. Imperial Hwy., Ste. 100
Brea, CA 92621
Ph: (714)773-1506   Fax: (714)773-9201

Employment agency.

★2739★ Blake and Associates Executive Search

PO Box 1425
Pleasantville, NJ 08232
Ph: (609)645-3330   Fax: (609)383-0320

Executive search firm.

★2740★ Midwest Medical Consultants

8910 Purdue Rd., Ste. 200
Indianapolis, IN 46268-1155
Ph: (317)872-1053

Employment agency. Executive search firm.

★2741★ Shiloh Careers International, Inc.

7105 Peach Ct., Ste. 102
PO Box 831
Brentwood, TN 37024-0831
Ph: (615)373-3090

Employment agency.

★2742★ Sue Carroll Personnel, Inc.

16 E. 79th St.
New York, NY 10021
Ph: (212)288-8866   Fax: (212)988-7191

Employment agency and executive search firm.

EKG Technicians

SOURCES OF HELP-WANTED ADS

★2743★ American Heart Journal

Mosby Year Book
11830 Westline Industrial Dr.
St. Louis, MO 63146
Ph: (314)872-8370   Fax: 800-535-9935
Fr: 800-633-6699

Monthly. $121.00/year for individuals; $51.00/year for students. Medical journal serving practicing cardiologists, university-affiliated clinicians, and physicians keeping abreast of developments in the diagnosis and management of cardiovascular disease.

★2744★ The American Journal of Cardiology

Conners Publishing
245 W. 17th St.
New York, NY 10011
Ph: (212)463-6835   Fax: (212)463-6836

Semimonthly. Journal for heart specialists.

★2745★ Heart and Lung: The Journal of Acute and Critical Care

Mosby Year Book
11830 Westline Industrial Dr.
St. Louis, MO 63146
Ph: (314)872-8370   Fax: 800-535-9935
Fr: 800-633-6699

Bimonthly. $39.00/year for individuals; $57.78 /year for Canada; $54.00/year for other countries; $21.00/year for students. Journal offering articles prepared by nurse and physician members of the critical care team, recognizing the nurse's role in the care and management of major organ-system conditions in critically ill patients.

★2746★ Journal of the American Society of Echocardiography

Mosby Year Book
11830 Westline Industrial Dr.
St. Louis, MO 63146
Ph: (314)872-8370   Fax: 800-535-9935
Fr: 800-633-6699

Bimonthly. $83.00/year for individuals; $109.14/year for Canada; $102.00/year for other countries; $40.00/year for students.

Official journal of the American Society of Echocardiography serving as a source of information on the technical basis and clinical application of echocardiography. Peer-reviewed publication featuring research, reviews, and case studies.

★2747★ Journal of Cardiopulmonary Rehabilitation

Pharmaceutical Media, Inc.
30 E. 33rd St.
New York, NY 10016
Ph: (212)685-5010   Fax: (212)685-5010

Bimonthly. Medical journal.

EMPLOYER DIRECTORIES AND NETWORKING LISTS

★2748★ AHA Guide to the Health Care Field

Health Statistics Group
American Hospital Association (AHA)
1 N. Franklin
Chicago, IL 60606
Ph: (312)422-3501   Fax: (312)280-6015

Annual, July. $195.00, payment with order. Covers hospitals, multi-health care systems, freestanding ambulatory surgery centers, psychiatric facilities, long-term care facilities, substance abuse programs, hospices, Health Maintenance Organizations (HMOs), and other health-related organizations. Entries include: For hospitals: facility name, address, phone, administrator's name, number of beds, facilities and services, number of employees, expenses, other statistics. For other organizations: name, address, phone, name and title of contact. Arrangement: Geographical. Indexes: Hospital name.

★2749★ Directory of Hospital Personnel

Medical Economics
5 Paragon Dr.
Montvale, NJ 07645-1725
Ph: (201)358-7500   Fax: (201)573-4956
Fr: 800-222-3045

Annual, September. $325.00, plus 7.50 shipping. Covers 200,000 executives at 7,100 U.S. hospitals. Entries include: Name of

hospital, address, phone, number of beds, type and JCAHO status of hospital, names and titles of key department heads and staff, medical and nursing school affiliations; number of residents, interns, and nursing students. Arrangement: Geographical. Indexes: Hospital name, personnel, hospital size.

★2750★ Hospital Blue Book

Billian Publishing Co.
2100 Powers Ferry Rd., Ste. 300
Atlanta, GA 30339
Ph: (404)955-5656   Fax: (404)952-0669

Annual, spring. $154.50, national edition, plus $20.00 shipping. Covers more than 7,100 hospitals; some listings also appear in a separate southern edition of this publication. Entries include: Name of hospital, accreditation, mailing address, phone, fax, number of beds, type of facility (nonprofit, general, state, etc.); list of administrative personnel and chiefs of medical services, with specific titles. Arrangement: Geographical.

★2751★ Hospital Market Atlas

SMG Marketing Group, Inc.
1342 N. LaSalle Dr.
Chicago, IL 60610
Ph: (312)642-3026   Fax: (312)642-9729
Fr: 800-678-3026

Biennial, odd years. $495.00, payment with order. Covers over 7,000 hospitals, hospital systems and 480 group purchasing organizations. Entries include: Hospital or organization name, address, phone, county code, management, type of hospital service, number of beds, admissions, surgical operations, and emergency room visits. Arrangement: Geographical.

★2752★ Hospitals Directory

American Business Directories, Inc.
American Business Information, Inc.
5711 S. 86th Cir.
Omaha, NE 68127
Ph: (402)593-4600   Fax: (402)331-1505

Annual. $870.00, U.S. edition. Entries include: Name, address, phone (including area code), size of advertisement, year first in Yellow Pages, name of owner or manager, number of employees. Compiled from telephone company Yellow Pages, nationwide. Arrangement: Geographical.

★2753★ **Medical and Health Information Directory**

Gale Research
835 Penobscot Bldg.
Detroit, MI 48226-4094
Ph: (313)961-2242   Fax: (313)961-6083
Fr: 800-877-GALE

Approximately biennial; latest edition 1994. $195.00, per volume; $485.00, for the three-volume set. Covers in Volume 1, almost 18,600 medical and health oriented associations, organizations, institutions, and government agencies, including health maintenance organizations (HMOs), preferred provider organizations (PPOs), insurance companies, pharmaceutical companies, research centers, and medical and allied health schools. In Volume 2, nearly 11,800 medical book publishers; medical periodicals, directories, audiovisual producers and services, medical libraries and information centers, and electronic resources. In Volume 3, nearly 26,000 clinics, treatment centers, care programs, and counseling/diagnostic services for 30 subject areas. Entries include: Institution, service, or firm name, address, phone; many include names of key personnel and, when pertinent, descriptive annotation. Arrangement: Classified by organization activity, service, etc. Indexes: Each volume has a complete alphabetical name and keyword index.

★2754★ **Osteopathic Membership Directory—AOHA**

American Osteopathic Healthcare Association
5301 Wisconsin Ave. NW, Ste. 630
Washington, DC 20015-2015
Ph: (202)686-1700   Fax: (202)686-7615

Annual, summer. $125.00, payment with order. Covers about 110 osteopathic hospitals. Includes list of individual and institutional members; also lists osteopathic colleges, and directors of medical education. Entries include: For hospitals: name of hospital, name of chief executive officer, address, phone, number of beds and other hospital data. Arrangement: Geographical. Indexes: Name, institution.

HANDBOOKS AND MANUALS

★2755★ **Careers in Health Care**

VGM Career Horizons
4255 W. Touhy Ave.
Lincolnwood, IL 60646-1975
Ph: (847)679-5500   Fax: (847)679-2494
Fr: 800-323-4900

Barbara M. Swanson. 1995. $17.95; $13.95 (paper). Describes job duties, work settings, salaries, licensing and certification requirements, educational preparation, and future outlook. Gives ideas on how to secure a job.

★2756★ **Medical Technologists and Technicians Career Directory**

Gale Research
835 Penobscot Bldg.
Detroit, MI 48226-4094
Ph: (313)961-2242   Fax: (313)961-6083
Fr: 800-877-GALE

Bradley Morgan. 1993. $39.00. 324 pages. Essays on specific careers provide an insider's perspective. Features extensive listings of contacts and entry-level job opportunities. Provides information on internships and sources of help-wanted ads.

★2757★ **100 Best Careers for the Year 2000**

Prentice Hall General Reference
15 Columbus Cir.
New York, NY 10023
Ph: (212)373-8500   Fr: 800-223-2348

Shelly Field. 1992. $15.00 (paper). Covers 100 of the fastest growing jobs. The publication is divided into 11 general employment sections. Specific careers are covered within each section. Provides job description, responsibilities, employment opportunities, earnings, education and training, advancement opportunities, and experience and qualifications for each occupation.

★2758★ **The Only EKG Book You'll Ever Need**

J. B. Lippincott
227 E. Washington Sq.
Philadelphia, PA 19106-3780
Ph: (215)238-4436   Fax: (215)238-4227
Fr: 800-777-2295

Malcolm S. Thaler. 1994. $29.95.

★2759★ **Opportunities in Health and Medical Careers**

VGM Career Horizons
4255 W. Touhy Ave.
Lincolnwood, IL 60646-1975
Ph: (847)679-5500   Fax: (847)679-2494
Fr: 800-323-4900

Donald Snook, Jr. and Leo D'Orazio. 1993. $14.95; $11.95 (paper). Covers the full range of medical and health occupations. Illustrated.

★2760★ **Opportunities in Medical Imaging Careers**

VCH Publishers, Inc.
220 E. 23rd St., Ste. 909
New York, NY 10010-4606
Ph: (212)683-8333   Fax: (212)481-0897

Clifford J. Sherry. 1993.

★2761★ **Opportunities in Medical Technology Careers**

VGM Career Horizons
4255 W. Touhy Ave.
Lincolnwood, IL 60646-1975
Ph: (847)679-5500   Fax: (847)679-2494
Fr: 800-323-4900

Karen R. Karni and Sidney Oliver. 1990. $14.95; $11.95 (paper). Details opportunities for various technical medical personnel and supplies up-to-date information on salary levels and employment outlook. Appendices list associations and unions in each field. Illustrated.

★2762★ **Opportunities in Vocational and Technical Careers**

VGM Career Horizons
4255 W. Touhy Ave.
Lincolnwood, IL 60646-1975
Ph: (847)679-5500   Fax: (847)679-2494
Fr: 800-323-4900

Adrian A. Paradis. 1992. $14.95; $11.95 (paper). 160 pages. Provides information on a variety of opportunities and advice on breaking into the field.

★2763★ **Resumes for Health and Medical Careers**

4255 W. Touhy Ave.
Lincolnwood, IL 60646-1975
Ph: (708)679-5500   Fax: (708)679-6375
Fr: 800-323-4900

Compiled by VGM Career Horizons Staff 1995. $9.95 (paper).

EMPLOYMENT AGENCIES AND SEARCH FIRMS

★2764★ **Blake and Associates Executive Search**

PO Box 1425
Pleasantville, NJ 08232
Ph: (609)645-3330   Fax: (609)383-0320

Executive search firm.

★2765★ **Midwest Medical Consultants**

8910 Purdue Rd., Ste. 200
Indianapolis, IN 46268-1155
Ph: (317)872-1053

Employment agency. Executive search firm.

★2766★ **Shiloh Careers International, Inc.**

7105 Peach Ct., Ste. 102
PO Box 831
Brentwood, TN 37024-0831
Ph: (615)373-3090

Employment agency.

★2767★ **Sue Carroll Personnel, Inc.**

16 E. 79th St.
New York, NY 10021
Ph: (212)288-8866   Fax: (212)988-7191

Employment agency and executive search firm.

OTHER SOURCES

★2768★ **American Society of Cardiovascular Professionals (ASCP)**

120 Falcon Dr.
Fredericksburg, VA 22408
Ph: (703)891-0079   Fax: (703)898-2393
Fr: 800-683-NSCT

Purpose: Dedicated to determining educational needs, developing programs to meet those needs, and providing a structure to offer the cardiovascular and pulmonary technology professional a key to the future as a valuable member of the medical team. Seeks advancement for members through communication and education. Provides coordinated programs to orient the newer professional to his field and continuing educational opportunities for technologist personnel. Has established guidelines for educational programs in the hospital and university setting. Works with educators and physicians to provide basic, advanced, and in-service programs for technologists. Sponsors registration and certification programs which provide technology professionals with further opportunity to clarify their level of expertise. Compiles statistics.

Electrical and Electronic Equipment Repairers

SOURCES OF HELP-WANTED ADS

★2769★ Appliance Service News

Gamit Enterprises, Inc.
110 W. St. Charles Rd.
PO Box 789
Lombard, IL 60148
Ph: (708)932-9550   Fax: (708)932-9552

Monthly. $13.50/year for individuals. Magazine for appliance repairmen.

★2770★ Electric Light & Power

PennWell Publishing Co.
1421 S. Sheridan
Tulsa, OK 74112
Ph: (918)835-3161   Fax: (918)831-9834
Fr: 800-331-4463

Monthly. Free to qualified subscribers; $42.00/year for institutions; $5.00 for single issue. Tabloid providing news of electric utility industry developments and activities and coverage of new products and technology.

★2771★ Electrical World

McGraw-Hill, Inc.
11 W. 19th St., 2nd Fl.
New York, NY 10011
Ph: (212)337-4062   Fax: (212)627-3811

Monthly. Trade magazine on the business of generating, transmitting, and distributing electric power.

★2772★ Electronic Servicing and Technology

CQ Communications
76 N. Broadway
Hicksville, NY 11801
Ph: (516)681-2922   Fax: (516)681-2926

Monthly. $24.00/year. Consumer electronics servicing magazine.

★2773★ Electronics

Peter Li
1100 Superior Ave.
Cleveland, OH 44114
Ph: (216)696-7000   Fax: (216)696-7670

Bimonthly. $98.00/year; $120.00/year for Canada; $5.00 for single issue. Magazine covering global news, trends, competition, and new technologies, with an emphasis on developments in the U.S., Europe, and the Far East. Topics include computers, communications, semiconductors, and international trade.

★2774★ Machine Design

Peter Li
1100 Superior Ave.
Cleveland, OH 44114
Ph: (216)696-7000   Fax: (216)696-7670

$100.00/year. Magazine on design engineering function.

★2775★ Popular Electronics

Gernsback Publications, Inc.
500-B Bicounty Blvd.
Farmingdale, NY 11735
Ph: (516)293-3000   Fax: (516)293-3115

Monthly. Electronics magazine featuring audio and video electronics, computers, construction, and how-to information.

★2776★ Professional Electronics

National Electronic Service Dealers
  Association
2708 W. Berry St.
Fort Worth, TX 76109
Ph: (817)921-9062   Fax: (817)921-3741

Bimonthly. Magazine for owners, managers, operators, and employees of retail electronics service firms.

★2777★ Security Sales

Bobit Publishing
2512 Artesia Blvd.
Redondo Beach, CA 90278
Ph: (310)376-8788   Fax: (310)374-7878

Monthly. $35.00/year for individuals; $42.00/year for Canada; $53.00/year for other countries. Magazine covering the alarm manufacturing industry.

PLACEMENT AND JOB REFERRAL SERVICES

★2778★ Electronics Technicians Association, International (ETA-I)

602 N. Jackson
Greencastle, IN 46135
Ph: (317)653-8262   Fax: (317)653-8262

Members: Skilled electronics technicians. **Activities:** Provides placement service; offers certification examinations for electronics technicians and satellite installers. Compiles wage and manpower statistics. Administers FCC Commercial License examinations.

EMPLOYER DIRECTORIES AND NETWORKING LISTS

★2779★ American Electronics Association—Directory

American Electronics Association
PO Box 54990
Santa Clara, CA 95056-0990
Ph: (408)987-4200   Fax: (408)970-8565

Annual, June. $175.00, plus $5.00 shipping; payment with order. Covers over 2,500 member electronics and high-technology companies and 500 associate member firms including financial institutions, law firms, and accounting firms. Entries include: Company name, address, phone, telex, cable address, fax, names of executives, number of employees, list of products or services, date founded, whether a public or private company, stock market where traded, ticker symbol. Arrangement: Alphabetical. Indexes: Geographical, product.

★2780★ Appliance Dealers—Major Household Directory

American Business Directories, Inc.
American Business Information, Inc.
5711 S. 86th Cir.
Omaha, NE 68127
Ph: (402)593-4600   Fax: (402)331-1505

Annual. $815.00, U.S. edition; $210.00, (Canadian ed.); payment with order. Significant discounts offered for standing orders. Number of listings: 21,501 (U.S. edition); 4,166 (Canadian edition). Entries include: Company name, address, phone (including area code), size of advertisement, year first in Yellow Pages, name of owner or manager, number of employees. Compiled from telephone company Yellow Pages, nationwide. Arrangement: Geographical.

★2781★ **Appliance Manufacturer— Directory Issue**

Business News Publishing Co.
5900 Harper Rd., Ste. 105
Solon, OH 44139
Ph: (216)349-3060   Fax: (216)349-2889

Annual, December. $25.00. Directory of 4,500 manufacturers and suppliers of equipment, material, and components to the appliance industry; trade associations. Entries include: Company name, address, phone, fax. Arrangement: Classified by product or service. Indexes: Product/service, company and association name.

★2782★ **Electric Equipment Manufacturers Directory**

American Business Directories, Inc.
American Business Information, Inc.
5711 S. 86th Cir.
Omaha, NE 68127
Ph: (402)593-4600   Fax: (402)331-1505

Annual. $185.00, payment with order. Number of listings: 2,076. Entries include: Name, address, phone (including area code). Compiled from telephone company Yellow Pages, nationwide. Arrangement: Geographical.

★2783★ **Electronic News—Looking at the Leaders**

Electronic News
488 Madison Ave.
New York, NY 10022
Ph: (212)909-5900

Formerly annual; suspended indefinitely. $2.00. Includes: List of 50 leading United States electronic firms in terms of electronic sales; similar data on about 25 leading foreign companies. Entries include: Company name, headquarters address; plant locations, activities, number of employees; officers; electronic sales, percent of sales in electronics, gross sales in all lines; other financial data. Arrangement: Alphabetical.

★2784★ **IEC Quarterly—Directory**

Independent Electrical Contractors, Inc.
507 Wythe St.
Alexandria, VA 22314
Ph: (703)549-7351   Fax: (703)549-7448

Annual. $75.00. Covers member electrical contracting firms. Entries include: Name of company, address, names of principals. Arrangement: Geographical.

★2785★ **Television/Radio Service & Repair Directory**

American Business Directories, Inc.
American Business Information, Inc.
5711 S. 86th Cir.
Omaha, NE 68127
Ph: (402)593-4600   Fax: (402)331-1505

Annual. $1,260.00, U.S. edition. Number of listings: 17,629 (U.S. edition); 501 (Canadian edition). Entries include: Name, address, phone (including area code), size of advertisement, year first in Yellow Pages, name of owner or manager, number of employees. Compiled from telephone company Yellow Pages, nationwide. Arrangement: Geographical.

★2786★ **Who's Who Electronics Buyers' Guide**

Harris Publishing Co.
2057-2 Aurora Rd.
Twinsburg, OH 44087
Ph: (216)425-9000   Fax: (216)425-4328
Fr: 800-888-5900

Annual, February. $65.00, per volume. Covers Approximately 15,000 manufacturers and nearly 8,300 distributors of electronics products in five regional volumes (Northeastern, Southeastern, Midwestern, Southwestern, and Western). Entries include: For manufacturers: name, address, phone, fax, key contact names, information on facilities or plants, products manufactured or handled, year established, estimated annual sales, local sources. For distributors: company name, address, phone, fax, product lines carried. Arrangement: Alphabetical. Indexes: Product/service (with manufacturer and distributor location, and phone); manufacturer name (with distributor); manufacturer name (with local sources); distributor name (with lines carried).

HANDBOOKS AND MANUALS

★2787★ **America's 50 Fastest Growing Jobs**

JIST Works, Inc.
720 N. Park Ave.
Indianapolis, IN 46202
Ph: (317)264-3720   Fr: 800-648-5478

Third edition, 1995. $14.95. 288 pages. Each job profile explains the nature of the work, skills and abilities required, employment outlook, average earnings, related occupations, education and training requirements, and employment opportunities. Also contains career planning information and job search tips.

★2788★ **The Complete Guide to Electronics Troubleshooting**

Delmar Publishers
3 Columbia Cir., Box 15015
Albany, NY 12212
Ph: (518)464-3500   Fax: (518)464-0358
Fr: 800-347-7707

James Perozzo. 1994. $52.95.

★2789★ **Opportunities in Electrical Trades**

VGM Career Horizons
4255 W. Touhy Ave.
Lincolnwood, IL 60646-1975
Ph: (847)679-5500   Fax: (847)679-2494
Fr: 800-323-4900

Robert Wood. 1990. $14.95; $11.95 (paper). 160 pages. Offers advice on job hunting and where the jobs are. Includes index, bibliography, and illustrations.

★2790★ **Opportunities in Electronics Careers**

VGM Career Horizons
4255 W. Touhy Ave.
Lincolnwood, IL 60646-1975
Ph: (847)679-5500   Fax: (847)679-2494
Fr: 800-323-4900

Mark Rowh. 1992. $14.95; $11.95 (paper). Discusses career opportunities in commercial and industrial electronics equipment repair, electronics home entertainment repair, electronics engineering, and engineering technology. Includes job outlook and how to get off to a good start on the job.

★2791★ **Opportunities in High Tech Careers**

VGM Career Horizons
4255 W. Touhy Ave.
Lincolnwood, IL 60646-1975
Ph: (847)679-5500   Fax: (847)679-2494
Fr: 800-323-4900

Gary D. Golter and Deborah Yanuck. 1995. $14.95; $11.95 (paper). 160 pages. Explores high technology careers. Describes job opportunities, how to make a career decision, how to prepare for high technology jobs, job hunting techniques, and future trends.

★2792★ **Opportunities in Installation and Repair Careers**

NTC Publishing Group
4255 W. Touhy Ave.
Lincolnwood, IL 60646-1975
Ph: (708)679-5500   Fax: (708)679-6375
Fr: 800-323-4900

Mark Rowh. 1995. $13.95; $10.95 (paper).

★2793★ **Opportunities in Vocational and Technical Careers**

VGM Career Horizons
4255 W. Touhy Ave.
Lincolnwood, IL 60646-1975
Ph: (847)679-5500   Fax: (847)679-2494
Fr: 800-323-4900

Adrian A. Paradis. 1992. $14.95; $11.95 (paper). 160 pages. Provides information on a variety of opportunities and advice on breaking into the field.

★2794★ **The Professional Electronics Technician**

International Electronics Technicians Association
602 N. Jackson St.
Greencastle, IN 46135
Ph: (317)653-8262

Pamphlet. $1.00. Describes job duties, training, skills and aptitudes, salaries, employment outlook, and certification.

★2795★ Troubleshooting Electrical-Electronic Systems

American Technical Publishers, Inc.
1155 W. 175th St.
Homewood, IL 60430
Ph: (708)957-1100   Fax: (708)957-1137
Fr: 800-323-3471

Glen A. Mazur. 1993. $32.96.

★2796★ Troubleshooting and Repairing Major Appliances

T A B Books
PO Box 40
Blue Ridge Summit, PA 17294-0850
Ph: (717)794-2191   Fax: (717)794-2080
Fr: 800-233-1128

Eric Kleinert. 1995. $44.95; $29.95 (paper).

EMPLOYMENT AGENCIES AND SEARCH FIRMS

★2797★ Careers Unlimited Inc.

1911 Hillandale Rd., Ste. 1210
Durham, NC 27705
Ph: (919)383-7431   Fax: (919)383-5706

Employment agency.

★2798★ Information Specialists Co.

242 Mustang Trail
Virginia Beach, VA 23452
Ph: (804)340-0022   Fax: (804)340-1505

Employment agency.

★2799★ Omni Recruiting, Inc.

275 Madison Ave.
New York, NY 10016-1101
Ph: (212)683-7800   Fax: (212)779-0342

Employment agency. Places individuals in a variety of fields.

★2800★ Opportunity Consultants, Inc.

435 Elm St., Ste. 400
Cincinnati, OH 45238-5409
Ph: (513)241-8675   Fax: (513)241-6285

Employment agency.

★2801★ S.D. Kelly and Associates, Inc.

990 Washington St.
Dedham, MA 02026-6704
Ph: (617)326-8038   Fax: (617)326-6123

Employment agency.

★2802★ Stephen Sellers Associates

805 Augusta Ave.
Elgin, IL 60120
Ph: (708)888-1568   Fax: (708)888-0028

Employment agency.

OTHER SOURCES

★2803★ COIN Career Guidance System

COIN Educational Products
3361 Executive Pky., Ste. 302
Toledo, OH 43606
Ph: (419)536-5353   Fr: 800-274-8515

CD-ROM product; also available on diskette. Provides career information through seven cross-referenced files covering postsecondary schools, college majors, vocational programs, military service, apprenticeship programs, financial aid, and scholarships. Apprenticeship file describes national apprenticeship training programs, including information on how to apply, contact agencies, and program content. Military file describes more than 200 military occupations and training opportunities related to civilian employment.

★2804★ Electronic Industries Association (EIA)

2500 Wilson Blvd.
Arlington, VA 22201
Ph: (703)907-7500   Fax: (202)457-4985

Purpose: Trade organization representing manufacturers of electronic components, parts, systems and equipment for communications, industrial, government, and consumer use.

★2805★ Electronic Troubleshooting and Repair Handbook

TAB Books
PO Box 40
Blue Ridge Summit, PA 17294-0850
Ph: (717)794-2191   Fax: (717)794-2080
Fr: 800-233-1128

Homer L. Davidson. 1995. $69.00.

★2806★ Electronics: Back to Your Future

Electronic Industries Association
Consumer Electronics Group, Dept. PS
2500 Wilson Blvd.
Arlington, VA 22201

Video. Free loan. 23 minutes. Illustrates opportunities of a career as a consumer electronics technician.

★2807★ International Society of Certified Electronics Technicians (ISCET)

2708 W. Berry, Ste. 3
Fort Worth, TX 76109
Ph: (817)921-9101   Fax: (817)921-3741

Members: Technicians in 37 countries who have been certified by the society. **Purpose:** Seeks to provide a fraternal bond among certified electronics technicians, raise their public image, and improve the effectiveness of industry education programs for technicians. Offers training programs in new electronics information. **Activities:** Maintains library of service literature for consumer electronic equipment, including manuals and schematics for out-of-date equipment. Offers all FCC licenses. Sponsors testing program for certification of electronics technicians in the fields of audio, communications, computer, consumer, industrial, medical electronics, radar, radio-television, and video.

★2808★ McGraw-Hill Electronic Troubleshooting Handbook

McGraw-Hill Companies
1221 Avenue of the Americas
New York, NY 10020
Ph: (212)512-2000   Fr: 800-262-4729

John D. Lenk. 1995. $39.50.

★2809★ National Association of Retail Dealers of America (NARDA)

10 E. 22nd St.
Lombard, IL 60148
Ph: (708)953-8950   Fax: (708)953-8957

Members: Retailers of appliances, home electronics, computers, furniture, and audio components; associate members include manufacturers, utilities, distributors of appliances and consumer electronics, and financial institutions. **Purpose:** Works to create more profitable dealerships. **Activities:** Services include management consulting, sales training, advertising workshops, computer service bureau, School of Service Management, Institute of Management, surveys, credit union, bank card program, and management training.

★2810★ National Electronics Service Dealers Association (NESDA)

2708 W. Berry St., Ste. 3
Fort Worth, TX 76109
Ph: (817)921-9061   Fax: (817)921-3741
Fr: 800-797-9197

Members: Local and state electronic service associations and companies representing 4200 individuals. **Purpose:** Provides educational assistance in electronic training to public schools; supplies technical service information on business management training to electronic service dealers. **Activities:** Offers certification, apprenticeship, and training programs through International Society of Certified Electronics Technicians. Compiles statistics on electronics service business; conducts technical service and business management seminars.

Electrical and Electronics Engineers

★2811★ Automotive Engineering

Society of Automotive Engineers
400 Commonwealth Dr.
Warrendale, PA 15096
Ph: (412)776-4841   Fax: (412)776-4026

Monthly. $72.00/year for individuals; $126.00/year for other countries. Magazine for automotive engineers providing technical and design information.

★2812★ Captsule Job Listings

Publications and Communications, Inc.
12416 Hymeadow Dr.
Austin, TX 78750
Ph: (512)250-9023   Fax: (512)331-3900
Fr: 800-678-9724

Online database. Lists current job openings in the contract (temporary) technical services industry. Includes the Action Hot List, which provides information on job seekers. Includes employment opportunities in technical/professional engineering, computing, and design/drafting. Entries generally contain company name, address, and job opening.

★2813★ Circuits Assembly

Miller Freeman, Inc.
2000 Powers Ferry Ctr., Ste. 450
Marietta, GA 30067
Ph: (404)952-1303   Fax: (404)952-6461

Monthly. $85.00/year for individuals; $135.00/year for other countries. Magazine for circuit board assemblers. Reports on new developments in technology, equipment, and materials involved in the manufacturing process.

★2814★ Communications of the ACM

Association for Computing Machinery
1515 Broadway 17th fl.
New York, NY 10036
Ph: (212)869-7440   Fax: (212)869-0481

Monthly. $32.00/year for individuals; $124.00/year for nonmembers. Computing news magazine.

★2815★ Computer

IEEE Computer Society
1730 Massachusetts Ave. NW
Washington, DC 20036
Ph: (202)371-0101

Monthly. Covers major trends in computer science and engineering.

★2816★ Computer Design

PennWell Publishing Co.
10 Tara Blvd., 5th Fl.
Nashua, NH 03062-2801
Ph: (603)891-0123   Fax: (603)891-0597

Free to qualified subscribers; $88.00/year. Printed in two editions. Magazine covers microprocessor-based systems design; news edition covers the systems time-to-market team.

★2817★ Connector Specifier

IHS Publishing Group
17730 W. Peterson Rd.
Libertyville, IL 60048
Ph: (708)362-8711   Fax: (708)362-3484

Free to qualified subscribers. Magazine on the use of connectors and interconnection products.

★2818★ Consulting-Specifying Engineer

Cahners Publishing Co.
1350 E. Touhy Ave.
Des Plaines, IL 60018
Ph: (708)635-8800   Fax: (708)390-2770

$74.95. /year for individuals. The integrated engineering magazine of the building construction industry.

★2819★ Control Engineering

Cahners Publishing Co.
1350 E. Touhy Ave.
Des Plaines, IL 60018
Ph: (708)635-8800   Fax: (708)390-2770

Free to qualified subscribers; $75.00/year for institutions. Magazine covering control and instrumentation systems.

★2820★ Defense Electronics

Argus Business
6300 S. Syracuse Way, Ste. 650
Englewood, CO 80111-9912
Ph: (303)220-0600   Fax: (303)770-0253

Monthly. $38.00/year for individuals. Electronic engineering magazine.

★2821★ ECN (Electronic Component News)

Chilton Publications
825 7th Ave.
New York, NY 10019
Ph: (212)887-8400   Fax: (212)887-8484

Monthly. Free to qualified subscribers; $60.00/year. Magazine (tabloid) for electronics design engineers and engineering management.

★2822★ EDN Products and Careers

Cahners Publishing Co.
275 Washington St.
Newton, MA 02158-1630
Ph: (617)964-3030   Fax: (617)558-4470

Biweekly. Free to qualified subscribers. Newspaper (tabloid) of technology, products, and careers for engineers and engineering managers.

★2823★ EE Evaluation Engineering

Nelson Publishing
2504 N. Tamiami Tr.
Nelson Bldg.
Nokomis, FL 34275
Ph: (813)966-9521   Fax: (813)966-2590

Monthly. $80.00/year for individuals; $105.00/year for Canada; $120.00/year for other countries; $7.50/year for single issue. Trade journal covering electronic engineering, evaluation and test.

★2824★ Electric Light & Power

PennWell Publishing Co.
1421 S. Sheridan
Tulsa, OK 74112
Ph: (918)835-3161   Fax: (918)831-9834
Fr: 800-331-4463

Monthly. Free to qualified subscribers; $42.00/year for institutions; $5.00 for single issue. Tabloid providing news of electric utility industry developments and activities and coverage of new products and technology.

★2825★ Electrical Design and Manufacturing

IHS Publishing Group
17730 W. Peterson Rd.
Libertyville, IL 60048
Ph: (708)362-8711   Fax: (708)362-3484
Bimonthly.

★2826★ Electrical World

McGraw-Hill, Inc.
11 W. 19th St., 2nd Fl.
New York, NY 10011
Ph: (212)337-4062   Fax: (212)627-3811
Monthly. Trade magazine on the business of generating, transmitting, and distributing electric power.

★2827★ Electrochemical Society Interface

The Electrochemical Society
10 S. Main St.
Pennington, NJ 08534
Ph: (609)737-1902   Fax: (609)737-2743
Quarterly. 40.00/year.

★2828★ Electronic Design

Penton Publishing
611 Rte. 46 W
Hasbrouck Heights, NJ 07604
Ph: (201)393-6060   Fax: (201)393-6297
Quarterly. Professional magazine covering current information in the field of electronic design.

★2829★ Electronic Engineering Times

CMP Publications, Inc.
600 Community Dr.
Manhasset, NY 11030
Ph: (516)562-5000   Fax: (516)562-5055
Weekly. Weekly Trade Newspaper.

★2830★ Electronic Products

Hearst Business Communications, Inc.
645 Stewart Ave.
Garden City, NY 11530
Ph: (516)227-1300   Fax: (516)227-1444
Magazine for electronic design engineers and management.

★2831★ Electronic Servicing and Technology

CQ Communications
76 N. Broadway
Hicksville, NY 11801
Ph: (516)681-2922   Fax: (516)681-2926
Monthly. $24.00/year. Consumer electronics servicing magazine.

★2832★ Electronics

Peter Li
1100 Superior Ave.
Cleveland, OH 44114
Ph: (216)696-7000   Fax: (216)696-7670
Bimonthly. $98.00/year; $120.00/year for Canada; $5.00 for single issue. Magazine covering global news, trends, competition, and new technologies, with an emphasis on developments in the U.S., Europe, and the

Far East. Topics include computers, communications, semiconductors, and international trade.

★2833★ Engineering Times

National Society of Professional Engineers
1420 King St.
Alexandria, VA 22314
Ph: (703)684-2875   Fax: (703)836-4875
Monthly. Magazine (tabloid) covering professional, legislative, and techology issues for an engineering audience.

★2834★ ENR: Engineering News Record

New York Construction News
1221 Avenue of the Americas
New York, NY 10020
Ph: (212)512-4773   Fax: (212)512-4770
Weekly. $42.00/year; $2.00/issue.

★2835★ High Technology Careers Magazine

HTC
4701 Patrick Henry Dr., No. 1901
Santa Clara, CA 95054
Ph: (408)970-8800   Fax: (408)980-5103
Bimonthly. Magazine (tabloid) containing employment opportunity information for the engineering and technical community.

★2836★ Machine Design

Peter Li
1100 Superior Ave.
Cleveland, OH 44114
Ph: (216)696-7000   Fax: (216)696-7670
$100.00/year. Magazine on design engineering function.

★2837★ Microwave Journal

Horizon House Publications, Inc.
685 Canton St.
Norwood, MA 02062
Ph: (617)769-9750   Fax: (617)762-9071
Fr: 800-966-6326
Monthly. Free to qualified subscribers; $75.00/year. Electronic engineering magazine.

★2838★ Minority Engineer

Equal Opportunity Publications, Inc.
150 Motor Pkwy., Ste. 420
Hauppauge, NY 11788-5145
Ph: (516)273-0066   Fax: (516)273-8936
Affirmative-action recruitment magazine serving college graduating and professional minority engineers.

★2839★ NSBE Magazine

NSBE Publications
1454 Duke St.
Alexandria, VA 22314
Ph: (703)549-2207   Fax: (703)683-5312
$10.00/year for individuals; $2.00 for single issue. Journal providing information on engineering careers, self-development, and cultural issues for recent graduates with technical majors.

★2840★ PCIM

Intertec International, Inc.
2472 Eastman Ave., Bldg. 33-34
Ventura, CA 93003
Ph: (805)650-7070   Fax: (805)650-7079
Monthly. Magazine on electronic engineering, power conversion, and electronic motion control.

★2841★ Photogrammetric Engineering and Remote Sensing

American Society for Photogrammetry and Remote Sensing (ASPRS)
5410 Grosvenor Ln., Ste. 210
Bethesda, MD 20814-2160
Ph: (301)493-0290   Fax: (301)493-0208
Monthly. Free to members; $120.00/year for nonmembers. Provides technical information about the applications of photogrammetry, remote sensing, and geographic information systems.

★2842★ Power

New York Construction News
1221 Avenue of the Americas, 41st Fl.
New York, NY 10020
Ph: (212)512-4773   Fax: (212)512-4770
Monthly. Magazine for engineers in electric utilities, process and manufacturing plants, commercial and service establishments, and consulting, design, and construction engineering firms working in the power technology field.

★2843★ Printed Circuit Design

Miller Freeman, Inc.
2000 Powers Ferry Ctr., Ste. 450
Marietta, GA 30067
Ph: (404)952-1303   Fax: (404)952-6461
Monthly. Free to qualified subscribers; $50.00 for institutions; $4.00/year for single issue. Magazine for designers of PCB's and related technologies.

★2844★ RF Design

Argus Business
6300 S. Syracuse Way, Ste. 650
Englewood, CO 80111-9912
Ph: (303)220-0600   Fax: (303)770-0253
Monthly. $42.00/year for individuals; $62.00/year for other countries; $102.00/year by mail. Magazine covering the R.F. engineering field.

★2845★ Semiconductor International

Cahners Publishing Co.
1350 E. Touhy Ave.
Des Plaines, IL 60018
Ph: (708)635-8800   Fax: (708)390-2770
Monthly. Magazine profiling semiconductor manufacturing issues.

★2846★ SMT

IHS Publishing Group
17730 W. Peterson Rd.
Libertyville, IL 60048
Ph: (708)362-8711   Fax: (708)362-3484
Monthly.

★2847★ Solid State Technology

PennWell Publishing Co.
10 Tara Blvd., 5th Fl.
Nashua, NH 03062-2801
Ph: (603)891-0123   Fax: (603)891-0597

Monthly. $145.00/year. Magazine containing electronic and semiconductor engineering news and information.

★2848★ SWE

Society of Women Engineers
120 Wall St., 11th Fl.
New York, NY 10005-3902
Ph: (212)509-9577   Fax: (212)509-0224

Bimonthly. $30.00/year for nonmembers. Magazine for engineering students and for women and men working in the engineering and technology fields. Covers career guidance, continuing development and topical issues.

★2849★ Technology Review

The Tech
PO Box 397029
Cambridge, MA 02139
Ph: (617)253-1541   Fax: (617)258-8226

$30.00/year for individuals; $3.75 for single issue; $42.00/year for other countries. Magazine reviewing new developments in technology with an emphasis on economic, political, and social implications. Not a new product publication.

★2850★ Test and Measurement World

Cahners Publishing Co.
275 Washington St.
Newton, MA 02158-1630
Ph: (617)964-3030   Fax: (617)558-4470

Monthly. Electronic engineering magazine specializing in test, measurement, and inspection of electronic components.

★2851★ Transmission and Distribution

Intertec Publishing Corp.
9800 Metcalf
PO Box 12901
Overland Park, KS 66212-2215
Ph: (913)341-1300   Fax: (913)967-1898
Fr: 800-441-0294

Monthly. Magazine about powerline construction, transmission, and distribution.

★2852★ Woman Engineer

Equal Opportunity Publications, Inc.
150 Motor Pkwy., Ste. 420
Hauppauge, NY 11788-5145
Ph: (516)273-0066   Fax: (516)273-8936

Engineer recruitment magazine.

PLACEMENT AND JOB REFERRAL SERVICES

★2853★ Aircraft Electronics Association (AEA)

PO Box 1963
Independence, MO 64055-0963
Ph: (816)373-6565   Fax: (816)478-3100

Members: Companies engaged in the sales, engineering, installation, and service of electronic aviation equipment and systems. **Purpose:** Purposes are to: advance the science of aircraft electronics; promote uniform and stable regulations and uniform standards of performance; establish and maintain a code of ethics; gather and disseminate technical data; advance the education of members and the public in the science of aircraft electronics. Is active in the areas of supplement type certificates, test equipment licensing, temporary FCC licensing for new installations, spare parts availability and pricing, audiovisual technician training, equipment and spare parts loan, profitable installation, and service facility operation. **Activities:** Provides employment information, equipment exchange information, stolen equipment lists, and service assistance on member installations anywhere in the U.S. and Canada. Compiles statistics.

★2854★ American Indian Science and Engineering Society (AISES)

1630 30th St., Ste. 301
Boulder, CO 80301
Ph: (303)492-8658   Fax: (303)492-3400

Members: American Indian and non-Indian students and professionals in science, technology, and engineering fields; corporations representing energy, mining, aerospace, electronic, and computer fields. **Purpose:** Seeks to motivate and encourage students to pursue undergraduate and graduate studies in science, engineering, and technology. **Activities:** Sponsors science fairs in grade schools, teacher training workshops, summer math/science sessions for 8th-12th graders, professional chapters, and student chapters in colleges. Offers scholarships. Adult members serve as role models, advisers, and mentors for students. Operates placement service. **E-Mail:** aisesha@spot.colorado.edu

★2855★ American Society of Test Engineers (ASTE)

PO Box 669
Charlton City, MA 01508
Ph: (508)765-0087   Fax: (508)765-0087

Members: Companies involved in the electronic testing industry and instrumentation are corporate members; engineers who work in test engineering related fields are regular members. **Purpose:** Seeks to foster improved communication among individuals and companies in the testing industry. **Activities:** Offers job referral service.

★2856★ Association for the Advancement of Medical Instrumentation (AAMI)

3330 Washington Blvd., Ste. 400
Arlington, VA 22201
Ph: (703)525-4890   Fax: (703)276-0793
Fr: 800-332-2264

Members: Clinical engineers, biomedical equipment technicians, physicians, hospital administrators, consultants, engineers, manufacturers of medical devices, nurses researchers and others interested in medical instrumentation. Purpose is to improve the quality of medical care through the application, development, and management of technology. **Activities:** Maintains placement service. Offers certification programs for bio-

medical equipment technicians and clinical engineers. Produces numerous standards and recommended practices on medical devices and procedures. Offers educational programs.

★2857★ Engineering Society of Detroit (ESD)

100 Farnsworth Ave.
Detroit, MI 48202
Ph: (313)832-5400   Fax: (313)832-5920

Members: Engineers from all disciplines; scientists and technologists. **Activities:** Offers placement services. Conducts technical programs and engineering refresher courses; sponsors conferences and expositions. Maintains speakers' bureau. Although based in Detroit, MI, society membership is international.

★2858★ International Society for Hybrid Microelectronics (ISHM)

1850 Centennial Park Dr., Ste. 105
Reston, VA 22091
Ph: (703)758-1060   Fax: (703)758-1066
Fr: 800-535-ISHM

Members: Electronics engineers and specialists in industry, business, and education. **Purpose:** Encourages the exchange of information across boundaries of fields of specialization; supports close interactions between the complementary technologies of ceramics, thick and thin films, semiconductor packaging, discrete semiconductor devices, and monolithic circuits. Promotes and assists in the development and expansion of microelectronics instruction in schools and departments of electrical and electronic engineering. **Activities:** Conducts seminars at international, national, regional, and chapter levels. Maintains placement service and equipment donation program for universities.

★2859★ ISA

PO Box 12277
67 Alexander Dr.
Research Triangle Park, NC 27709
Ph: (919)549-8411   Fax: (919)549-8288

Purpose: Educational organization dedicated to advancing knowledge and practice related to the theory, design, manufacture, and use of instruments and controls in science and industry. Operates training center for industry; conducts symposia; develops standards; recognizes individual achievement. **Activities:** Maintains speakers' bureau and placement service.

★2860★ Korean Scientists and Engineers Association in America (KSEA)

6261 Executive Blvd.
Rockville, MD 20852
Ph: (301)984-7048   Fax: (301)984-1231

Members: Scientists and engineers holding single or advanced degrees. **Purpose:** Goals are to: promote friendship and mutuality among Korean and American scientists and engineers; contribute to Korea's scientific, technological, industrial, and economic developments; strengthen the scientific, technological, and cultural bonds between Korea and the U.S. Sponsors symposium. **Activities:** Maintains speakers' bureau, placement service, and biographical archives. Compiles statistics. Maintains 100 volume library of scientific handbooks and yearbooks in Korean.

★2861★ Robotics International of the Society of Manufacturing Engineers (RI/SME)

1 SME Dr.
PO Box 0930
Dearborn, MI 48121-0930
Ph: (313)271-1500   Fax: (313)271-2861

Members: Engineers, managers, educators, and government officials in 50 countries working or interested in the field of robotics. **Purpose:** Promotes efficient and effective use of current and future robot technology. Serves as a clearinghouse for the industry trends and developments. Areas of interest include: aerospace; assembly systems; casting and forging; education and training; human factors and safety; human and food service; material handling; military systems; nontraditional systems; research and development; small shop applications; welding. Offers professional certification. **Activities:** Operates placement service; compiles statistics. Maintains speakers' bureau.

★2862★ Society of Hispanic Professional Engineers (SHPE)

5400 E. Olympic Blvd., Ste. 210
Los Angeles, CA 90022
Ph: (213)725-3970

Purpose: Engineers, student engineers, and scientists seeking to increase the number of Hispanic engineers by providing motivation and support to students. Sponsors competitions and educational programs. **Activities:** Maintains placement service and speakers' bureau; compiles statistics.

★2863★ SPIE–The International Society for Optical Engineering (SPIE)

PO Box 10
1000 20th St.
Bellingham, WA 98227
Ph: (206)676-3290   Fax: (206)647-1445

Purpose: Technical society dedicated to advancing engineering and scientific applications of optical, electro-optical, and photo-electronic instrumentation systems and technology. Fosters information exchange and technical communication among scientific, engineering, and user communities. Organizes educational programs; conducts annual Optics Education survey. **Activities:** Offers professional placement exchange.

EMPLOYER DIRECTORIES AND NETWORKING LISTS

★2864★ American Electronics Association—Directory

American Electronics Association
PO Box 54990
Santa Clara, CA 95056-0990
Ph: (408)987-4200   Fax: (408)970-8565

Annual, June. $175.00, plus $5.00 shipping; payment with order. Covers over 2,500

member electronics and high-technology companies and 500 associate member firms including financial institutions, law firms, and accounting firms. Entries include: Company name, address, phone, telex, cable address, fax, names of executives, number of employees, list of products or services, date founded, whether a public or private company, stock market where traded, ticker symbol. Arrangement: Alphabetical. Indexes: Geographical, product.

★2865★ American Men and Women of Science

R. R. Bowker Co.
Reed Reference Publishing
121 Chanlon Rd.
New Providence, NJ 07974
Ph: (908)464-6800   Fax: (908)665-6688
Fr: 800-521-8110

Triennial, latest edition January 1995. $106.00, per volume; $850.00, set. Covers over 123,000 U.S. and Canadian scientists active in the physical, biological, mathematical, computer science, and engineering fields; includes references to previous edition for deceased scientists and nonrespondents. Entries include: Name, address, education, personal and career data, memberships, honors and awards, research interest. Arrangement: Alphabetical. Indexes: Discipline (in separate volume).

★2866★ Design News OEM Directory

Cahners Publishing Co.
Design News
275 Washington St.
Newton, MA 02158
Ph: (617)558-4553   Fax: (617)558-4402

Annual, December. $50.00. Covers about 7,000 manufacturers and suppliers of power transmission products, fluid power products, and electrical/electronic components to the OEM (original equipment manufacturer) market. Entries include: Company name, address, phone, fax. Arrangement: Alphabetical. Indexes: Product, trade name.

★2867★ Directory of Contract Service Firms

C. E. Publications, Inc.
PO Box 97000
Kirkland, WA 98083
Ph: (206)823-2222   Fax: (206)821-0942

Annual, January. $10.00. Covers Approximately 900 contract firms actively engaged in the employment of engineering and technical personnel for temporary contract assignments throughout the world. Entries include: Company name, address, phone, name of contact. Arrangement: Alphabetical. Indexes: Geographical.

★2868★ Directory of Engineering Societies and Related Organizations

American Association of Engineering Societies
1111 19th St. NW, Ste. 608
Washington, DC 20036
Ph: (202)296-2237   Fax: (202)296-1151
Fr: 800-658-8897

1992. $185.00. Lists 1,000 national, regional, Canadian, and international organizations

concerned with engineering and related fields.

★2869★ Directory of Engineers in Private Practice

National Society of Professional Engineers
1420 King St.
Alexandria, VA 22314
Ph: (703)684-2862   Fax: (703)836-4875

Annual. $85.00. Covers 600 consulting engineering firms and 7,200 individuals who are members of the society's Professional Engineers in Private Practice division. Entries include: For companies, name, address, phone, name of principal executive, list of services. For individuals, name, address; most listings include phone. Arrangement: Firms are geographic, then by specialty; individuals are alphabetical.

★2870★ Electric Equipment Manufacturers Directory

American Business Directories, Inc.
American Business Information, Inc.
5711 S. 86th Cir.
Omaha, NE 68127
Ph: (402)593-4600   Fax: (402)331-1505

Annual. $185.00, payment with order. Number of listings: 2,076. Entries include: Name, address, phone (including area code). Compiled from telephone company Yellow Pages, nationwide. Arrangement: Geographical.

★2871★ Electronic News—Looking at the Leaders

Electronic News
488 Madison Ave.
New York, NY 10022
Ph: (212)909-5900

Formerly annual; suspended indefinitely. $2.00. Includes: List of 50 leading United States electronic firms in terms of electronic sales; similar data on about 25 leading foreign companies. Entries include: Company name, headquarters address; plant locations, activities, number of employees; officers; electronic sales, percent of sales in electronics, gross sales in all lines; other financial data. Arrangement: Alphabetical.

★2872★ Engineering Research Centres

Stockton Press
Groves Dictionaries
345 Park Ave. S., 10th Fl.
New York, NY 10010
Ph: (212)689-9200   Fr: 800-221-2123

Fourth edition, 1995. $515.00. 768 pages. Contains over 8,000 entries describing research and technology laboratories in over 70 countries. Provides details on industrial research centers and educational establishments with research and development activity. Indexes: Subject and title of establishments.

★2873★ Engineers—Electrical Directory

American Business Directories, Inc.
American Business Information, Inc.
5711 S. 86th Cir.
Omaha, NE 68127
Ph: (402)593-4600   Fax: (402)331-1505

Updated continuously; printed on request. Entries include: Name, address, phone, size of advertisement, year first in Yellow Pages, name of owner or manager, number of employees. Compiled from telephone company Yellow Pages, nationwide. Arrangement: Geographical.

★2874★ Peterson's Job Opportunities in Engineering and Technology 1996

Peterson's
PO Box 2123
Princeton, NJ 08543-2123
Ph: (609)243-9111   Fax: (609)243-9150
Fr: 800-338-3282

Compiled by the Peterson's staff. Annual. $19.95 paperback. 432 pages. Profiles 2,000 high-tech companies looking primarily for technical personnel in such fields as biotechnology, telecommunications, software, computers and peripherals, defense, and aerospace. Contains job-search strategies and career options to help match education and expertise to the job market. Indexed geographically, by industry, and by hiring needs.

★2875★ Scientific and Technical Organizations and Agencies Directory

Gale Research
835 Penobscot Bldg.
Detroit, MI 48226-4094
Ph: (313)961-2242   Fax: (313)961-6083
Fr: 800-877-GALE

Irregular; latest edition December 1993. $195.00. Covers over 25,600 national and international organizations and agencies concerned with the physical and applied sciences, engineering, and technology, including associations, computer information services, consulting firms, educational institutions, foundations, government advisory organizations, federal government agencies, general grant and assistance programs, libraries and information centers, patent sources and services, research and development centers, scholarships, fellowships, and loans, science-technology centers, standards organizations, state academies of science, and state government agencies in the fields of aeronautics and space sciences, chemistry, computer science specialties, electronics, geography, geology, machinery, mathematics, metallurgy, meteorology, mineralogy, nuclear science, petroleum and gas, physics, plastics, transportation, water resources, and other areas. Entries include: Organization name, address, phone, and name of contact; additional descriptive text for most entries. Arrangement: Classified by type of organization. Indexes: Organization name/key word.

★2876★ Who's Who Electronics Buyers' Guide

Harris Publishing Co.
2057-2 Aurora Rd.
Twinsburg, OH 44087
Ph: (216)425-9000   Fax: (216)425-4328
Fr: 800-888-5900

Annual, February. $65.00, per volume. Covers Approximately 15,000 manufacturers and nearly 8,300 distributors of electronics products in five regional volumes (Northeastern, Southeastern, Midwestern, Southwestern, and Western). Entries include: For manufacturers: name, address, phone, fax, key contact names, information on facilities or

plants, products manufactured or handled, year established, estimated annual sales, local sources. For distributors: company name, address, phone, fax, product lines carried. Arrangement: Alphabetical. Indexes: Product/service (with manufacturer and distributor location, and phone); manufacturer name (with distributor); manufacturer name (with local sources); distributor name (with lines carried).

★2877★ Who's Who in Technology

Gale Research
835 Penobscot Bldg.
Detroit, MI 48226-4094
Ph: (313)961-2242   Fax: (313)961-6083
Fr: 800-877-GALE

Irregular, new edition expected June 1995. $380.00. Covers 38,000 engineers, scientists, inventors, and researchers. Entries include: Name, title, affiliation, address; personal, education, and career data; publications, patents; technical field of activity; area of expertise. Arrangement: Alphabetical. Indexes: Geographical, employer, technical discipline, expertise.

HANDBOOKS AND MANUALS

★2878★ The Best Resumes for Scientists and Engineers

John Wiley and Sons
605 3rd Ave.
New York, NY 10158
Ph: (212)850-6000   Fr: 800-225-5945

Adele Lewis. Second edition, 1993. $37.50; $14.95 (paper). Presents an extensive collection of scientific and engineering resumes, highlighting the important differences between these and resumes written for other occupations.

★2879★ Careers in Engineering

VGM Career Horizons
4255 W. Touhy Ave.
Lincolnwood, IL 60646-1975
Ph: (847)679-5500   Fax: (847)679-2494
Fr: 800-323-4900

Geraldine O. Gardner. 1994. $17.95; $13.95 (paper). Covers careers in the public or private sector, in industry, the university, or the military, from applications in computer architecture design to high temperature ceramics.

★2880★ Engineering Success

Kendall Hunt Publishing
4050 Westmark Dr.
PO Box 1840
Dubuque, IA 52004-1840
Ph: (319)589-1000   Fax: 800-772-9165
Fr: 800-228-0810

Bill Osher. 1994. $27.96.

★2881★ Engineering Your Job Search: A Job-Finding Resource for Engineering Professionals

Professional Publications, Inc.
1250 5th Ave.
Belmont, CA 94002
Ph: (415)593-9119   Fax: (415)592-4519
Fr: 800-426-1178

Compiled by Professional Publications editors. 1995. $12.95 (paper).

★2882★ Introduction to the Engineering Profession

HarperCollins Publishers, Inc.
10 E. 53rd. St.
New York, NY 10022-5299
Ph: (212)207-7000   Fax: (212)207-7145
Fr: 800-331-3761

David M. Burghardt. 1995. $30.00 (paper).

★2883★ Job Opportunities in Engineering and Technology

Peterson's Guides, Inc.
PO Box 2123
Princeton, NJ 08543-2123
Ph: (609)243-9111   Fax: (609)243-9150
Fr: 800-338-3282

1994. $18.95 (paper).

★2884★ Majoring in Engineering: How to Get from Your Freshman Year to Your First Job

Farrar, Straus & Giroux, Inc.
19 Union Sq., W
New York, NY 10003
Ph: (212)741-6900   Fr: 800-788-6262

John Garcia. 1995. $20.00; $10.00 (paper).

★2885★ Opportunities in Electronics Careers

VGM Career Horizons
4255 W. Touhy Ave.
Lincolnwood, IL 60646-1975
Ph: (847)679-5500   Fax: (847)679-2494
Fr: 800-323-4900

Mark Rowh. 1992. $14.95; $11.95 (paper). Discusses career opportunities in commercial and industrial electronics equipment repair, electronics home entertainment repair, electronics engineering, and engineering technology. Includes job outlook and how to get off to a good start on the job.

★2886★ Opportunities in Engineering Careers

VGM Career Horizons
4255 W. Touhy Ave.
Lincolnwood, IL 60646-1975
Ph: (847)679-5500   Fax: (847)679-2494
Fr: 800-323-4900

Nicholas Basta. 1995. $14.95; $11.95 (paper). Outlines typical job titles, salaries, career paths, and employment prospects.

★2887★ Opportunities in High Tech Careers

VGM Career Horizons
4255 W. Touhy Ave.
Lincolnwood, IL 60646-1975
Ph: (847)679-5500   Fax: (847)679-2494
Fr: 800-323-4900

Gary D. Golter and Deborah Yanuck. 1995.

$14.95; $11.95 (paper). 160 pages. Explores high technology careers. Describes job opportunities, how to make a career decision, how to prepare for high technology jobs, job hunting techniques, and future trends.

★2888★ **Resumes for Engineering Careers**

VGM Career Horizons
NTC Publishing Group
4255 W. Touhy Ave.
Lincolnwood, IL 60646-1975
Ph: (847)679-5500   Fax: (847)679-2494
Fr: 800-323-4900

1994. $9.95. 160 pages. Contains sample resumes and cover letters applicable to any engineering field.

★2889★ **Where the Jobs Are: The Hottest Careers for the '90s**

The Career Press, Inc.
3 Tice Rd.
PO Box 687
Franklin Lakes, NJ 07417
Ph: (201)848-0310   Fax: (201)848-1727
Fr: 800-237-3371

Joyce Hadley. Second edition, 1995. $9.99. 300 pages. Describes careers in fifteen general fields, from accounting to travel and hospitality.

EMPLOYMENT AGENCIES AND SEARCH FIRMS

★2890★ **ABC Employment Service**

25 S. Bemiston, Ste. 214
Clayton, MO 63105
Ph: (314)725-3140

Employment agency.

★2891★ **B and M Associates, Inc.**

199 Cambridge Rd.
Woburn, MA 01801-4705
Ph: (617)938-9120

Employment agency.

★2892★ **Bell Oaks Co.**

3390 Peachtree Rd., Ste. 1124
Atlanta, GA 30326
Ph: (404)261-2170

Personnel service firm.

★2893★ **Claremont-Branan, Inc.**

2150 Parklake Dr., Ste. 212
Atlanta, GA 30345
Ph: (404)491-1292

Employment agency. Executive search firm.

★2894★ **Colli Associates of Tampa**

PO Box 2865
Tampa, FL 33601
Ph: (813)681-2145

Employment agency. Executive search firm.

★2895★ **Engineer One, Inc.**

10124 Dutchtown Rd.
Knoxville, TN 37932-2611
Ph: (615)690-2611   Fax: (615)690-2611

Employment agency.

★2896★ **Executive Recruiters Agency**

14 Office Park Dr.
PO Box 21810
Little Rock, AR 72221-1810
Ph: (501)224-7000   Fax: (501)224-8534

Personnel service firm.

★2897★ **Hayden and Associates, Inc.**

7825 Washington Ave. S., Ste. 120
Minneapolis, MN 55439-2431
Ph: (612)941-6300   Fax: (612)941-9602

Employment agency. Executive search firm. Fills openings in a variety of fields.

★2898★ **Industrial Recruiters Associates, Inc.**

630 Oakwood Ave., Ste. 318
West Hartford, CT 06110
Ph: (203)953-3643

Employment agency.

★2899★ **The Jobs Co.**

8900 E. Sprague Ave.
Spokane, WA 99212-2927
Ph: (509)928-3151   Fax: (509)928-3168

Employment agency. Has division specializing in engineering and scientific openings. Also operates division specializing in sales openings.

★2900★ **JR Professional Search**

PO Box 18356
Tucson, AZ 85731
Ph: (520)721-1855   Fax: (520)721-1855

Employment agency.

★2901★ **LOR Personnel Division**

418 Wall St.
Princeton, NJ 08540
Ph: (609)921-6580

Employment agency. Executive search firm.

★2902★ **Main Line Personnel Service, Inc.**

401 City Ave.
Bala Cynwyd, PA 19004-1122
Ph: (610)667-1820

Employment agency.

★2903★ **Rand Personnel Agency**

1200 Truxtun, Ste. 130
Bakersfield, CA 93301
Ph: (805)325-0751   Fax: (805)325-4120

Personnel service firm.

★2904★ **Search and Recruit International**

4455 South Blvd.
Virginia Beach, VA 23452
Ph: (804)490-3151

Employment agency. Headquartered in Virginia Beach. Other offices in Bremerton, WA; Charleston, SC; Jacksonville, FL; Memphis,

TN; Pensacola, FL; Sacramento, CA; San Bernardino, CA; San Diego, CA.

★2905★ **Sierra Technology Corporation**

4150 Manzanita Ave., Ste. 100
Carmichael, CA 95608-1700
Ph: (916)488-4960   Fax: (916)488-7058

Employment agency. Provides placement on a temporary basis.

★2906★ **Software Services Corp.**

2850 S. Industrial Hwy, Ste. 300
Ann Arbor, MI 48104-6796
Ph: (313)971-2300

Employment agency.

★2907★ **Source Engineering**

5580 LBJ Fwy., Ste. 300
Dallas, TX 75240
Ph: (214)385-3002   Fax: (214)717-0075

Executive search firm. Many affiliate offices located throughout the U.S.

★2908★ **Systems One Ltd.**

1100 E. Woodfield Rd.
Schaumburg, IL 60173
Ph: (708)619-9300   Fax: (708)619-0071

Personnel service firm.

★2909★ **Technical Talent Locators Ltd.**

8850 Stanford Blvd., Ste. 3400
Columbia, MD 21045
Ph: (410)995-6051   Fax: (410)995-6281

Executive search firm.

★2910★ **T.R. Employment Agency**

409 Wilshire Blvd.
Santa Monica, CA 90401
Ph: (310)393-4107

Employment agency.

★2911★ **Tri-Serv Inc.**

22 W. Padonia Rd., Ste. C53
Timonium, MD 21093
Ph: (301)561-1740

Employment agency.

OTHER SOURCES

★2912★ **American Almanac of Jobs and Salaries 1994-95**

Avon Books
1350 Avenue of the Americas, 2nd Fl.
New York, NY 10019
Ph: (212)261-6800   Fr: 800-238-0658

John Wright. Revised edition, 1993. $17.00. 704 pages. This is a comprehensive guide to the wages of hundreds of occupations in a wide variety of industries and organizations.

★2913★ **American Association of Engineering Societies (AAES)**

1111 19th St. NW, Ste. 608
Washington, DC 20036
Ph: (202)296-2237   Fax: (202)296-1151

Purpose: Seeks to promote leadership in public affairs for the engineering community, work in support of math and science education for young persons. Disseminates of information about the profession. Provides statistics about engineers.

★2914★ American Society for Photogrammetry and Remote Sensing (ASPRS)

5410 Grosvenor Ln., Ste. 210
Bethesda, MD 20814-2160
Ph: (301)493-0290   Fax: (301)493-0208

Members: Firms, individuals, government employees, and academicians engaged in photogrammetry, photointerpretation, remote sensing, and geographic information systems and their application to such fields as archaeology, geographic information systems, military reconnaissance, urban planning, engineering, traffic surveys, meteorological observations, medicine, geology, forestry, agriculture, construction, and topographic mapping. **Activities:** Offers voluntary certification program open to persons associated with one or more functional area of photogrammetry, remote sensing, and GIS. Surveys the profession of private firms in photogrammetry and remote sensing in the areas of products and services.

★2915★ Association for International Practical Training (AIPT)

10400 Little Patuxent Pky. Ste. 250
Columbia, MD 21044
Ph: (410)997-2200   Fax: (410)992-3924

Purpose: Helps coordinate training around the world in fields such as travel, the culinary arts, and hotel management. **Activities:** Conducts programs in career development and hospitality/tourism exchanges. Operates a student exchange program. Provides reciprocal practical training experience for recent graduates from the U.S., Austria, Germany, Finland, France, Hungary, Ireland, Japan, Malaysia, Netherlands, Switzerland, and the United Kingdom. Arranges training programs in the U.S. and abroad. Serves as U.S. affiliate to IAESTE (International Association for the Exchange of Students for Technical Experience) and operates a Professional Visitors Program to arrange short-term educational and training visits to the U.S. **E-Mail:** aipt@aipt.org

★2916★ Electronic Industries Association (EIA)

2500 Wilson Blvd.
Arlington, VA 22201
Ph: (703)907-7500   Fax: (202)457-4985

Purpose: Trade organization representing manufacturers of electronic components, parts, systems and equipment for communications, industrial, government, and consumer use.

★2917★ *Engineering Salary Survey*

Source Engineering
1290 Oakmead, Ste. 318
Sunnyvale, CA 94086
Ph: (408)738-8440

Annual. Discusses the structure of the engineering profession, trends, and compensation. Salaries are listed by job function, industry, and years of experience.

★2918★ *Graduating Engineer*

Peterson's/COG Publishing Group
16030 Ventura Blvd., No. 560
Encino, CA 91436
Ph: (818)789-5293

Eight issues/year. Magazine focusing on employment, education, and career development for entry-level engineers.

★2919★ Institute of Electrical and Electronics Engineers (IEEE)

345 E. 47th St.
New York, NY 10017
Ph: (212)705-7900   Fax: (212)705-4929

Members: Engineers and scientists in electrical engineering, electronics, and allied fields; membership includes 47,000 students. **Purpose:** Conducts lecture courses at the local level on topics of current engineering and scientific interest. **Activities:** Assists student groups. Supports Engineering Societies Library in New York City in conjunction with other groups.

★2920★ National Action Council for Minorities in Engineering (NACME)

3 W. 35th St.
New York, NY 10001-2281
Ph: (212)279-2626   Fax: (212)629-5178

Purpose: Seeks to increase the number of African American, Latino, and Native American students enrolled in and graduating from engineering schools. Through the Corporate Scholars Program, offers comprehensive scholarships to engineering students that include leadership development, corporate mentors and summer internships. Works

with local, regional, and national education organizations to motivate and encourage precollege students to engage in engineering careers. Conducts educational and research programs; operates project to assist engineering schools in improving the retention and graduation rates of minority students. Maintains speakers' bureau; compiles statistics.

★2921★ National Society of Professional Engineers (NSPE)

1420 King St.
Alexandria, VA 22314
Ph: (703)684-2800   Fax: (703)836-4875

Members: Professional engineers and engineers-in-training in all fields registered in accordance with the laws of states or territories of the U.S. or provinces of Canada; qualified graduate engineers, student members, and registered land surveyors. **Purpose:** Is concerned with social, professional, ethical, and economic considerations of engineering as a profession; encompasses programs in public relations, employment practices, ethical considerations, education, and career guidance. Monitors legislative and regulatory actions of interest to the engineering profession. **Website:** http://www.hspc.org

★2922★ *Salaries of Scientists, Engineers, and Technicians: A Summary of Salary Surveys*

Commission on Professionals in Science and Technology (CPST)
1500 Massachusetts Ave. NW, Ste. 831
Washington, DC 20005
Ph: (202)223-6995

1993.

★2923★ Society of Women Engineers (SWE)

120 Wall St., 11th Fl.
New York, NY 10005
Ph: (212)509-9577   Fax: (212)509-0224

Members: Educational service society of women engineers; membership is also open to men. **Purpose:** Supplies information on the achievements of women engineers and the opportunities available to them; assists women engineers in preparing for return to active work following temporary retirement. Serves as an informational center on women in engineering. **Activities:** Administers several certificate and scholarship programs. Offers tours and career guidance; conducts surveys. Compiles statistics.

Electricians

and coverage of new products and technology.

SOURCES OF HELP-WANTED ADS

★2924★ Builder

Hanley-Wood, Inc.
1 Thomas Cir., Ste. 600
Washington, DC 20005
Ph: (202)452-0800   Fax: (202)785-1974

Monthly. $29.95/year for individuals. Magazine covering housing, commercial, and industrial building.

★2925★ CEE News

Intertec Publishing Corp.
9800 Metcalf
PO Box 12901
Overland Park, KS 66212
Ph: (913)341-1300

Monthly.

★2926★ Construction Digest

Construction Magazine Group, Inc.
PO Box 6132
Indianapolis, IN 46206-6132
Ph: (317)329-3100   Fax: (317)329-3110
Fr: 800-860-3105

Semimonthly. $3.00 for single issue. Magazine for the public works and construction engineering industries.

★2927★ CONSTRUCTOR

Associated General Contractors
 Information
1957 E St. NW
Washington, DC 20006-5199
Ph: (202)393-2040   Fax: (202)628-7369

Monthly. $15.00/year for members; $4.00 for single issue.

★2928★ Electric Light & Power

PennWell Publishing Co.
1421 S. Sheridan
Tulsa, OK 74112
Ph: (918)835-3161   Fax: (918)831-9834
Fr: 800-331-4463

Monthly. Free to qualified subscribers; $42.00/year for institutions; $5.00 for single issue. Tabloid providing news of electric utility industry developments and activities

★2929★ Electrical World

McGraw-Hill, Inc.
11 W. 19th St., 2nd Fl.
New York, NY 10011
Ph: (212)337-4062   Fax: (212)627-3811

Monthly. Trade magazine on the business of generating, transmitting, and distributing electric power.

★2930★ Professional Builder

Cahners Publishing Co.
1350 E. Touhy Ave.
PO Box 5080
Des Plaines, IL 60018-5080
Ph: (708)635-8800   Fax: (708)635-9950

Monthly. $10.00 for single issue; $139.95/year by mail.

★2931★ Summer Jobs: Opportunities in the Federal Government

Office of Personnel Management
1900 E St. NW
Washington, DC 20415
Ph: (202)606-0950

Formerly annual; latest edition January 1993; suspended indefinitely. Free. Covers GS-1 through GS-4 clerical jobs and other jobs at GS-5 and above which are expected to be available in federal agencies and departments throughout the United States during the season. Most jobs are in Metropolitan Washington, D.C. Latest application date is generally April 15; many are earlier. Includes general information on applying for jobs in trades and labor occupations and summer employment for needy youth programs. Entries include: Agency name, filing deadline, titles of jobs available, brief information on qualifications needed, location, etc. Complete agency names and addresses are given in separate list. Publication is available from Federal Employment Information Center offices and agency personnel offices. Arrangement: By job level, then alphabetical by agency name.

★2932★ Tradeswomen

Tradeswomen, Inc.
PO Box 2622
Berkeley, CA 94702
Ph: (510)649-6260

Bimonthly. $35.00/year. Subtitled: "A Quarterly Magazine for Women in Blue Collar Work". Reports activities of the organization and other events in the California Bay Area and of national interest to women working or wishing to work in nontraditional and blue collar jobs. Recurring features include announcements of apprenticeship opportunities and job openings, information on unions and government agencies, and U.S. Department of Labor statistics.

PLACEMENT AND JOB REFERRAL SERVICES

★2933★ Associated Builders and Contractors (ABC)

1300 N. 17th St.
Rosslyn, VA 22209
Ph: (703)812-2000   Fax: (703)812-8200

Members: Construction contractors, subcontractors, suppliers, and associates. **Purpose:** Aim is to foster and perpetuate the principles of rewarding construction workers and management on the basis of merit. **Activities:** Maintains placement service. Sponsors management education programs and craft training; also sponsors apprenticeship and skill training programs. Disseminates technological and labor relations information. Compiles statistics.

★2934★ National Association of Home Builders of the U.S. (NAHB)

1201 15th St. NW
Washington, DC 20005
Ph: (202)822-0200   Fax: (202)822-0559

Members: Single and multifamily home builders, commercial builders, and others associated with the building industry. **Purpose:** Lobbies on behalf of the housing industry and conducts public affairs activities to increase public understanding of housing and the economy. Collects and disseminates data on current developments in home building and home builders' plans through its Economics Department and nationwide Metropolitan Housing Forecast. **Activities:** Maintains NAHB Research Center, which functions as the research arm of the home building industry. Sponsors seminars and workshops on construction, mortgage credit, labor relations, cost reduction, land use, remodeling, and business management. Compiles statistics; offers charitable program, spokesman training, and placement service; maintains speakers' bureau, and hall of fame.

EMPLOYER DIRECTORIES AND NETWORKING LISTS

★2935★ *ABC Today—Associated Builders and Contractors Membership Directory Issue*

Associated Builders and Contractors
1300 N. 17th St.
Rosslyn, VA 22209
Ph: (703)812-2000   Fax: (703)812-8200

Annual, November. $150.00, plus $7.00 shipping. Publication includes: List of approximately 17,000 member construction contractors and suppliers. Entries include: Company name, address, phone, name of principal executive, code to volume of business, business specialty. Arrangement: Classified by chapter, then by work specialty.

★2936★ *Constructor—Directory of Membership and Services Issue*

AGC Information, Inc.
Associated General Contractors of
  America
1957 E St. NW
Washington, DC 20006
Ph: (202)393-2040   Fax: (202)347-4004

Annual, July. $135.00. Publication includes: List of more than 8,500 member firms and 9,000 national associate member firms engaged in building, highway, heavy, industrial, municipal utilities, and railroad construction, listing of state and local chapter officers. Arrangement: Geographical. Indexes: Company name.

★2937★ *Electric Contractors Directory*

American Business Directories, Inc.
American Business Information, Inc.
5711 S. 86th Cir.
Omaha, NE 68127
Ph: (402)593-4600   Fax: (402)331-1505

Annual. $1,875.00, U.S. edition; $420.00, (Canadian edition); payment with order. Significant discounts offered for standing orders. Number of listings: 55,984 (U.S. edition); 9,454 (Canadian edition). Entries include: Name, address, phone (including area code), size of advertisement, year first in Yellow Pages, name of owner or manager, number of employees. Regional editions available: Compiled from telephone company Yellow Pages, nationwide. Arrangement: Geographical.

★2938★ *ENR—Top 400 Construction Contractors Issue*

McGraw-Hill, Inc.
1221 Ave. of the Americas
New York, NY 10020
Ph: (212)512-4635   Fax: (212)512-2820

Annual, May issue of *Engineering News Record*. $10.00, Reprint, payment with order. Publication includes: List of 400 United States contractors receiving largest dollar volumes of contracts in preceding calendar year. Separate lists of 50 largest design/construct management firms; 50 largest program and construction managers; 25 building contractors; 25 heavy contractors. Entries include: Company name, headquarters location, total value of contracts received in preceding year, value of foreign contracts, countries in which operated, construction specialities. Arrangement: By total value of contracts received.

★2939★ *IEC Quarterly—Directory*

Independent Electrical Contractors, Inc.
507 Wythe St.
Alexandria, VA 22314
Ph: (703)549-7351   Fax: (703)549-7448

Annual. $75.00. Covers member electrical contracting firms. Entries include: Name of company, address, names of principals. Arrangement: Geographical.

★2940★ *International Association of Electrical Inspectors—Membership Directory*

International Association of Electrical
  Inspectors
901 Waterfall Way, Ste. 602
Richardson, TX 75080
Ph: (214)235-1455   Fax: (214)235-3855
Fr: 800-786-4234

Annual, March. $10.00. Covers 24,000 state and federal government, industrial, utility, and insurance electrical inspectors, and, as associate members, electricians, manufacturers, engineers, architects, and wiremen. Entries include: Name, title, type of member, address, company affiliation. Arrangement: Geographical, then by division, chapter, or section, and type of membership, then alphabetical. Indexes: Committees; personal name.

HANDBOOKS AND MANUALS

★2941★ *Careers as an Electrician*

Rosen Publishing Group
29 E. 21st St.
New York, NY 10010
Ph: (212)777-3017   Fax: (212)777-0277
Fr: 800-237-9932

Elizabeth S. Lytle. 1993. $14.95.

★2942★ *Electrician's Exam Preparation Guide*

Craftsman Book Co.
6058 Corte del Cedro
Carlsbad, CA 92009
Ph: (619)438-7828   Fax: (619)438-0398
Fr: 800-829-8123

John E. Traister. 1993. $23.00 (paper).

★2943★ *Exploring Careers in the Construction Industry*

Rosen Publishing Group
29 E. 21st St.
New York, NY 10010
Ph: (212)777-3017   Fax: (212)777-0277
Fr: 800-237-9932

Elizabeth Stewart Lytle. 1992. $14.95.

★2944★ *Exploring Careers as an Electrician*

Rosen Publishing Group, Inc.
29 E. 21st St.
New York, NY 10010
Ph: (212)777-3017   Fax: (212)777-0277
Fr: 800-237-9932

Elizabeth Stewart Lyle. 1993. $14.95; $9.95 (paper). 150 pages. Takes the reader through each of the steps to becoming an electrician. Bibliography and index.

★2945★ *Exploring Nontraditional Jobs for Women*

Rosen Publishing Group, Inc.
29 E. 21st St.
New York, NY 10010
Ph: (212)777-3017   Fax: (212)777-0277
Fr: 800-237-9932

Rose Neufeld. 1989. $14.95. Describes occupations where few women are found. Covers job duties, training routes, where to apply for jobs, tools used, salary, and advantages and disadvantages of the job.

★2946★ *How to Start and Manage a Construction Electrician Business: Step-by-Step Guide to Business Success*

Lewis and Renn Associates
10315 Harmony Dr.
Interlochen, MI 49643
Ph: (616)275-7287

Jerre G. Lewis. 1994. $9.95 (paper).

★2947★ *The IBEW Leads to Electrifying Careers*

International Brotherhood of Electrical
  Workers
1125 15th St. NW
Washington, DC 20005
Ph: (202)833-7000

Free brochure. Covers the electrician apprenticeship program.

★2948★ *The New Handbook for Electricians*

Prentice Hall
113 Sylvan Ave., Rte. 9W
Englewood Cliffs, NJ 07632
Ph: (201)592-2000   Fax: 800-445-6991
Fr: 800-223-2336

Martin Clifford. 1993. $48.00.

★2949★ Opportunities in Building Construction Trades

VGM Career Horizons
4255 W. Touhy Ave.
Lincolnwood, IL 60646-1975
Ph: (847)679-5500   Fax: (847)679-2494
Fr: 800-323-4900

Michael Sumichrast. 1993. $14.95; $11.95 (paper). From custom builder to rehabber, the many kinds of companies that employ craftspeople and contractors are explored. Includes job descriptions, requirements, and salaries for dozens of specialties within the construction industry. Contains a complete list of Bureau of Apprenticeship and Training state and area offices. Illustrated.

★2950★ Opportunities in Electrical Trades

VGM Career Horizons
4255 W. Touhy Ave.
Lincolnwood, IL 60646-1975
Ph: (847)679-5500   Fax: (847)679-2494
Fr: 800-323-4900

Robert Wood. 1990. $14.95; $11.95 (paper). 160 pages. Offers advice on job hunting and where the jobs are. Includes index, bibliography, and illustrations.

★2951★ Questions and Answers for Electricians' Examinations

Macmillan Publishing Co.
200 Old Tappan Rd.
Old Tappan, NJ 07675
Fax: 800-445-6991   Fr: 800-223-2336

Paul Rosenberg. 1993.

OTHER SOURCES

★2952★ Associated General Contractors of America (AGC)

1957 E St. NW
Washington, DC 20006
Ph: (202)393-2040   Fax: (202)347-4004

Members: General construction contractors; subcontractors; industry suppliers; service firms.**Purpose:** Provides market services through its divisions. Conducts special conferences and seminars designed specifically for construction firms. Compiles statistics on job accidents reported by member firms. Maintains 65 committees, including joint cooperative committees with other associations and liaison committees with federal agencies.

★2953★ Associated Specialty Contractors (ASC)

3 Bethesda Metro Ctr., Ste. 1100
Bethesda, MD 20814
Ph: (301)657-3110   Fax: (301)215-4500

Members: Subcontractor associations with a total of 25,000 members representing electrical, heating, piping, mechanical, air conditioning, sheet metal, plumbing, ventilating, masonry, painting and decorating, and roofing and insulation contractors. **Purpose:** Promotes liaison with general contractors, architects, and engineers on inter-industry matters, codes, bidding, and contracting procedures. Coordinates governmental affairs, research, and educational matters.

★2954★ Career Connections Video Series

Cambridge Career Products
PO Box 2153
Dept. CC15
Charleston, WV 25328-2153
Ph: (304)744-9323   Fax: (304)744-9351
Fr: 800-468-4227

Series of six videos. 1993. $219.95/set. $39.95/each. 15-20 minutes. Each video contains interviews with workers and on-the-job footage. Titles include Graphic Design, Welding, Electrician, Plumber, Pipefitter, and HVAC.

★2955★ COIN Career Guidance System

COIN Educational Products
3361 Executive Pky., Ste. 302
Toledo, OH 43606
Ph: (419)536-5353   Fr: 800-274-8515

CD-ROM product; also available on diskette. Provides career information through seven cross-referenced files covering postsecondary schools, college majors, vocational programs, military service, apprenticeship programs, financial aid, and scholarships. Apprenticeship file describes national apprenticeship training programs, including information on how to apply, contact agencies, and program content. Military file describes more than 200 military occupations and training opportunities related to civilian employment.

★2956★ Independent Electrical Contractors (IEC)

507 Wythe St.
Alexandria, VA 22314
Ph: (703)549-7351   Fax: (703)549-7448

Members: Independent electrical contractors, small and large, primarily open shop. **Purpose:** Promotes the interests of members; works to eliminate unwise and unfair business practices, and to protect its members against unfair or unjust taxes and legislative enactments. **Activities:** Sponsors electrical apprenticeship programs; conducts

educational programs on cost control and personnel motivation. Represents independent electrical contractors to the National Electrical Code panel. Has formulated National Pattern Standards for Apprentice Training for Electricians.

★2957★ National Association of Women in Construction (NAWIC)

327 S. Adams St.
Fort Worth, TX 76104
Ph: (817)877-5551   Fax: (817)877-0324
Fr: 800-552-3506

Purpose: NAWIC is an international association of women employed in the construction industry which promotes that industry and supports the advancement of women within it.

★2958★ National Electrical Contractors Association (NECA)

3 Bethesda Metro Ctr., Ste. 1100
Bethesda, MD 20814
Ph: (301)657-3110   Fax: (301)215-4500

Members: Contractors erecting, installing, repairing, servicing, and maintaining electric wiring, equipment, and appliances. **Activities:** Provides management services and labor relations programs for electrical contractors; conducts seminars for contractor sales and training. Conducts research and educational programs; compiles statistics. Sponsors honorary society, the Academy of Electrical Contracting.

★2959★ Tradeswomen, Inc.

PO Box 40664 B
San Francisco, CA 94140
Ph: (415)821-7334   Fax: (415)861-8969

Members: Women who work in nontraditional; blue-collar occupations including construction, transportation, and industrial work; women who seek to enter these fields or who support the right of others to do so. **Purpose:** Serves as a network for women in the trades. Conducts social gatherings and local and regional forums on topics such as: health and safety on the job; racism and sexism in the trades; sexual harassment; working within unions. Makes available children's services; maintains speakers' bureau. Compiles statistics.

★2960★ WIT

Northern New England Tradeswomen
26 Railroad St.
St. Johnsbury, VT 05819
Ph: (802)748-3308   Fax: (802)748-1768

Quarterly. Included in membership; $10.00/year for nonmembers. Provides a network of support, information, and skill sharing for women in trade professions.

Emergency Medical Technicians

SOURCES OF HELP-WANTED ADS

★2961★ *American Fire Journal*

9072 E. Artesia Blvd., Ste. 7
Bellflower, CA 90706-6299
Ph: (310)866-1664   Fax: (310)867-6434

Monthly. $19.95/year for individuals; $36.00/year for institutions, other countries; $3.00 for single issue. Magazine about fire protection.

★2962★ *Emergency Medical Services*

Summer Communications, Inc.
7626 Densmore Ave.
Van Nuys, CA 91406-2042
Ph: (818)782-7328   Fax: (818)782-7450

Monthly. $18.95/year for individuals. Magazine covering emergency care, rescue and transportation.

★2963★ *The Municipality*

League of Wisconsin Municipalities
122 W. Washington Ave., Ste. 301
Madison, WI 53703-2757
Ph: (608)267-2380   Fax: (608)267-0645

Monthly. Magazine for officials of Wisconsin's local municipal governments.

★2964★ *Rescue-EMS Magazine*

Lifesaving Communications, Inc.
PO Box 100
Nassau, DE 19969-0100

Bimonthly. $15.00/year for individuals; $2.50 for single issue. Magazine (tabloid) serving the emergency medical services directors and field personnel.

PLACEMENT AND JOB REFERRAL SERVICES

★2965★ **National Association of Emergency Medical Technicians (NAEMT)**

102 W. Leake St.
Clinton, MS 39056
Ph: (601)924-7744   Fax: (601)924-7325
Fr: 800-34-NAEMT

Members: Nationally registered or state certified emergency medical technicians (EMTs) and EMT-paramedics. **Purpose:** Promotes the professional status of EMTs and national acceptance of a uniform standard of recognition for their skills; encourages constant upgrading of these skills and EMT qualifications and educational requirements; engages in scientific research related to the care and transportation of the sick and injured; supports the establishment of emergency medical services systems. **Activities:** Maintains placement services.

EMPLOYER DIRECTORIES AND NETWORKING LISTS

★2966★ *AHA Guide to the Health Care Field*

Health Statistics Group
American Hospital Association (AHA)
1 N. Franklin
Chicago, IL 60606
Ph: (312)422-3501   Fax: (312)280-6015

Annual, July. $195.00, payment with order. Covers hospitals, multi-health care systems, freestanding ambulatory surgery centers, psychiatric facilities, long-term care facilities, substance abuse programs, hospices, Health Maintenance Organizations (HMOs), and other health-related organizations. Entries include: For hospitals: facility name, address, phone, administrator's name, number of beds, facilities and services, number of employees, expenses, other statistics. For other organizations: name, address, phone, name and title of contact. Arrangement: Geographical. Indexes: Hospital name.

★2967★ *Directory of Hospital Personnel*

Medical Economics
5 Paragon Dr.
Montvale, NJ 07645-1725
Ph: (201)358-7500   Fax: (201)573-4956
Fr: 800-222-3045

Annual, September. $325.00, plus 7.50 shipping. Covers 200,000 executives at 7,100 U.S. hospitals. Entries include: Name of hospital, address, phone, number of beds, type and JCAHO status of hospital, names and titles of key department heads and staff, medical and nursing school affiliations; number of residents, interns, and nursing students. Arrangement: Geographical. Indexes: Hospital name, personnel, hospital size.

★2968★ *Hospital Blue Book*

Billian Publishing Co.
2100 Powers Ferry Rd., Ste. 300
Atlanta, GA 30339
Ph: (404)955-5656   Fax: (404)952-0669

Annual, spring. $154.50, national edition, plus $20.00 shipping. Covers more than 7,100 hospitals; some listings also appear in a separate southern edition of this publication. Entries include: Name of hospital, accreditation, mailing address, phone, fax, number of beds, type of facility (nonprofit, general, state, etc.); list of administrative personnel and chiefs of medical services, with specific titles. Arrangement: Geographical.

★2969★ *Hospital Market Atlas*

SMG Marketing Group, Inc.
1342 N. LaSalle Dr.
Chicago, IL 60610
Ph: (312)642-3026   Fax: (312)642-9729
Fr: 800-678-3026

Biennial, odd years. $495.00, payment with order. Covers over 7,000 hospitals, hospital systems and 480 group purchasing organizations. Entries include: Hospital or organization name, address, phone, county code, management, type of hospital service, number of beds, admissions, surgical operations, and emergency room visits. Arrangement: Geographical.

★2970★ Hospitals Directory

American Business Directories, Inc.
American Business Information, Inc.
5711 S. 86th Cir.
Omaha, NE 68127
Ph: (402)593-4600   Fax: (402)331-1505

Annual. $870.00, U.S. edition. Entries include: Name, address, phone (including area code), size of advertisement, year first in Yellow Pages, name of owner or manager, number of employees. Compiled from telephone company Yellow Pages, nationwide. Arrangement: Geographical.

★2971★ Medical and Health Information Directory

Gale Research
835 Penobscot Bldg.
Detroit, MI 48226-4094
Ph: (313)961-2242   Fax: (313)961-6083
Fr: 800-877-GALE

Approximately biennial; latest edition 1994. $195.00, per volume; $485.00, for the three-volume set. Covers in Volume 1, almost 18,600 medical and health oriented associations, organizations, institutions, and government agencies, including health maintenance organizations (HMOs), preferred provider organizations (PPOs), insurance companies, pharmaceutical companies, research centers, and medical and allied health schools. In Volume 2, nearly 11,800 medical book publishers; medical periodicals, directories, audiovisual producers and services, medical libraries and information centers, and electronic resources. In Volume 3, nearly 26,000 clinics, treatment centers, care programs, and counseling/diagnostic services for 30 subject areas. Entries include: Institution, service, or firm name, address, phone; many include names of key personnel and, when pertinent, descriptive annotation. Arrangement: Classified by organization activity, service, etc. Indexes: Each volume has a complete alphabetical name and keyword index.

★2972★ Municipal/County Directory Library Edition

Carroll Publishing
1058 Thomas Jefferson St. NW
Washington, DC 20007
Ph: (202)333-8620   Fax: (202)337-7020
Fr: 800-336-4240

Annual, July. $137.00, plus $8.00 shipping; payment must accompany order. Covers officials of 1,400 county governments (with populations over 25,000) and 2,000 municipalities (with populations over 1,000); includes elected, appointed, and career office holders. Entries include: Name, title, agency, address, phone. Arrangement: County officials are geographical, then by agency; municipal officials are by city. Indexes: personal name (with phone), agency.

★2973★ Municipal Year Book

Newman Books Ltd.
32 Vauxhall Bridge Rd.
London SW1V 2SS, England
Ph: 71 9736400   Fax: 71 2335057

Annual, December. $140.00, postpaid. Covers local and central government agencies and officials of the United Kingdom; municipal art galleries, associations, development

organizations, fairs, libraries, museums, airports, and other local authorities. Entries include: Name of authority or governing agency, address, phone, fax, names of elected councillors, officers, names and titles of key personnel, contacts, population, and pay. Arrangement: Geographical. Indexes: Subject, place names.

★2974★ National Directory of Fire Chiefs & Emergency Departments

SPAN Publishing
1308 Main St.
Stevens Point, WI 54481
Ph: (715)345-2772   Fax: (715)345-7288
Fr: 800-647-7579

Annual, February. $49.00. Covers Approximately 38,000 fire and emergency departments in the U.S. Entries include: Department name, address, phone, fax, telex, county, name of chief. Arrangement: Geographical.

★2975★ Osteopathic Membership Directory—AOHA

American Osteopathic Healthcare Association
5301 Wisconsin Ave. NW, Ste. 630
Washington, DC 20015-2015
Ph: (202)686-1700   Fax: (202)686-7615

Annual, summer. $125.00, payment with order. Covers about 110 osteopathic hospitals. Includes list of individual and institutional members; also lists osteopathic colleges, and directors of medical education. Entries include: For hospitals: name of hospital, name of chief executive officer, address, phone, number of beds and other hospital data. Arrangement: Geographical. Indexes: Name, institution.

★2976★ Registry of Ambulance Services

Emergency Medical Services Division
Oklahoma Department of Health
1000 NE 10th St.
Oklahoma City, OK 73117-1299
Ph: (405)271-4027   Fax: (405)271-3442

Annual, August. $38.00, postpaid. Covers Approximately 202 licensed ambulance services in Oklahoma. Entries include: Company, name, address, phone, geographical area served, names and titles of key personnel, number of employees, number of vehicles, description of service, number of primary hospitals. An abridged version containing only names and addresses is available for $13.00. Arrangement: Alphabetical.

HANDBOOKS AND MANUALS

★2977★ Careers in Health Care

VGM Career Horizons
4255 W. Touhy Ave.
Lincolnwood, IL 60646-1975
Ph: (847)679-5500   Fax: (847)679-2494
Fr: 800-323-4900

Barbara M. Swanson. 1995. $17.95; $13.95 (paper). Describes job duties, work settings, salaries, licensing and certification require-

ments, educational preparation, and future outlook. Gives ideas on how to secure a job.

★2978★ Emergency Medical Technician

R & E Publishers
468 Auzerais Ave., Ste. A
San Jose, CA 95126
Ph: (408)977-0691   Fax: (408)977-0693

Ronald R. Smith. 1993. $1.95 (paper).

★2979★ Emergency Medical Technician: Intermediate

Gordon Press Publishers
PO Box 459, Bowling Green Sta.
New York, NY 10004
Ph: (718)624-8419

1992. $355.00.

★2980★ Emergency Medical Technician: Paramedic

Gordon Press Publishers
PO Box 459, Bowling Green Sta.
New York, NY 10004
Ph: (718)624-8419

1992. $375.00.

★2981★ Emergency Medical Technician Workbook

Little, Brown & Co.
Time and Life Bldg.
1271 Avenue of the Americas
New York, NY 10020
Ph: (212)522-8700   Fax: (212)522-2067
Fr: 800-343-9204

Nancy L. Caroline. 1991. $15.95.

★2982★ 100 Best Careers for the Year 2000

Prentice Hall General Reference
15 Columbus Cir.
New York, NY 10023
Ph: (212)373-8500   Fr: 800-223-2348

Shelly Field. 1992. $15.00 (paper). Covers 100 of the fastest growing jobs. The publication is divided into 11 general employment sections. Specific careers are covered within each section. Provides job description, responsibilities, employment opportunities, earnings, education and training, advancement opportunities, and experience and qualifications for each occupation.

★2983★ Opportunities in Health and Medical Careers

VGM Career Horizons
4255 W. Touhy Ave.
Lincolnwood, IL 60646-1975
Ph: (847)679-5500   Fax: (847)679-2494
Fr: 800-323-4900

Donald Snook, Jr. and Leo D'Orazio. 1993. $14.95; $11.95 (paper). Covers the full range of medical and health occupations. Illustrated.

★2984★ Opportunities in Paramedical Careers

VGM Career Horizons
4255 W. Touhy Ave.
Lincolnwood, IL 60646-1975
Ph: (847)679-5500   Fax: (847)679-2494
Fr: 800-323-4900

Alex Kacen. 1994. $14.95; 11.95 (paper).

160 pages. Discusses a variety of opportunities in this field and how to pursue them. Illustrated.

★2985★ Opportunities in State and Local Government Careers

VGM Career Horizons
4255 W. Touhy Ave.
Lincolnwood, IL 60646-1975
Ph: (847)679-5500   Fax: (847)679-2494
Fr: 800-323-4900

Neale Baxter. 1993. $13.95; $10.95 (paper). 160 pages. Points out the incentives and drawbacks of a government career. Describes hiring procedures and provides tips on filling out applications, taking physical and aptitude tests, handling interviews, and finding jobs. Describes the jobs in which 75% of all state and local government workers are employed. For each occupation, covers the nature of the work and the training required.

★2986★ Opportunities in Vocational and Technical Careers

VGM Career Horizons
4255 W. Touhy Ave.
Lincolnwood, IL 60646-1975
Ph: (847)679-5500   Fax: (847)679-2494
Fr: 800-323-4900

Adrian A. Paradis. 1992. $14.95; $11.95 (paper). 160 pages. Provides information on a variety of opportunities and advice on breaking into the field.

★2987★ Resumes for Health and Medical Careers

4255 W. Touhy Ave.
Lincolnwood, IL 60646-1975
Ph: (708)679-5500   Fax: (708)679-6375
Fr: 800-323-4900

Compiled by VGM Career Horizons Staff 1995. $9.95 (paper).

EMPLOYMENT AGENCIES AND SEARCH FIRMS

★2988★ JPM International

4665 MacArthur Ct., Ste. 100B
Newport Beach, CA 92660
Ph: (714)955-2545   Fax: (714)757-1320

Executive search firm and employment agency.

★2989★ Sue Carroll Personnel, Inc.

16 E. 79th St.
New York, NY 10021
Ph: (212)288-8866   Fax: (212)988-7191

Employment agency and executive search firm.

OTHER SOURCES

★2990★ Commission on Accreditation of Allied Health Education Programs (CAAHEP)

515 N. State St., Ste. 7530
Chicago, IL 60610
Ph: (312)464-4636   Fax: (312)464-5830

Purpose: Serves as an nationally recognized accrediting agency for allied health programs in 19 occupational areas.

★2991★ National Registry of Emergency Medical Technicians (NREMT)

PO Box 29233
Columbus, OH 43229
Ph: (614)888-4484

Purpose: Promotes the improved delivery of emergency medical services by assisting in the development and evaluation of educational programs to train emergency medical technicians; establishing qualifications for eligibility to apply for registration; preparing and conducting examinations designed to assure the competency of emergency medical technicians and paramedics; establishing a system for biennial registration; establishing procedures for revocation of certificates of registration for cause; maintaining a directory of registered emergency medical technicians.

Employment Interviewers

SOURCES OF HELP-WANTED ADS

★2992★ EMAnet

Employment Management Association (EMA)
4101 Lake Boone Tr., Ste. 201
Raleigh, NC 27607
Ph: (919)787-6010   Fax: (919)787-4916

Online database. Contains the following: *EMA Journal*, a magazine published four times a year; and *EMA Reporter*, a newsletter published three times a year. Provides listings of job opportunities and scholarships, an EMA member directory, as well as access to databases from the American Compensation Association and the Society for Human Resource Management.

★2993★ *Personnel Journal*

ACC Communications, Inc.
245 Fischer Ave., B-2
Costa Mesa, CA 92626
Ph: (714)751-1883   Fax: (714)751-4106

Monthly. $59.00/year for individuals; $6.00 for single issue.

PLACEMENT AND JOB REFERRAL SERVICES

★2994★ Employment Management Association (EMA)

4101 Lake Boone Tr., Ste. 201
Raleigh, NC 27607
Ph: (919)787-6010   Fax: (919)787-5302

Members: Employment and personnel executives in business, education, and industry; individuals in organizations servicing the employment community. **Purpose:** Seeks to: investigate and recommend solutions to the personnel and employment problems facing American business; provide a forum for the exchange of ideas and information on these matters among members. Topics of discussion include employment, advertising, work force planning, organization development, job posting, outplacement, college recruiting, professional placement, human resources, affirmative action, management development, and job enrichment. **Activities:** Conducts advisory programs, surveys, and panels; operates member placement service. Special projects have included: participation in civic, professional, and legislative conferences and panels as a voice on employment matters. Maintains placement services; compiles statistics; sponsors charitable programs.

★2995★ Employment Support Center (ESC)

5 Thomas Cir. NW, 4th Fl.
Washington, DC 20005
Ph: (202)462-8004   Fax: (202)462-8448

Purpose: Trains individuals to lead support groups for job-seekers. **Activities:** Operates a job bank for employment assistance; helps people learn to network for job contacts; provides technical assistance to employment support self help groups.

EMPLOYER DIRECTORIES AND NETWORKING LISTS

★2996★ *The Directory of Executive Recruiters*

Consultants Bookstore
Templeton Rd.
Fitzwilliam, NH 03447
Ph: (603)585-6544   Fax: (603)585-9555
Fr: 800-531-0007

James H. Kennedy. Twenty-fifth edition, 1995. $44.95 (paper). 900 pages. Lists and describes more than 3,200 firms in North America and indexes these by function, industry, and geographic area. Names key principals of recruiting firms. Includes narrative section on executive search and how it affects job candidates. Also available: Corporate Edition, expanded for use by corporate staffs, $99.00 (hardcover).

★2997★ *Employment Agencies Directory*

American Business Directories, Inc.
American Business Information, Inc.
5711 S. 86th Cir.
Omaha, NE 68127
Ph: (402)593-4600   Fax: (402)331-1505

Annual. $1,185.00, U.S. edition. Number of listings: 16,550 (U.S. edition); 1,780 (Canadian edition). Entries include: Name, address, phone (including area code), size of advertisement, year first in Yellow Pages, name of owner or manager, number of employees. Compiled from telephone company Yellow Pages, nationwide. Arrangement: Geographical.

★2998★ *Employment Contractors-Temporary Help Directory*

American Business Directories, Inc.
American Business Information, Inc.
5711 S. 86th Cir.
Omaha, NE 68127
Ph: (402)593-4600   Fax: (402)331-1505

Annual. $1,040.00, U.S. edition. Number of listings: 14,511 (U.S. edition); 730 (Canadian edition). Entries include: Name, address, phone (including area code), size of advertisement, year first in Yellow Pages, name of owner or manager, number of employees. Compiled from telephone company Yellow Pages, nationwide. Arrangement: Geographical.

★2999★ *Employment Marketplace Resource Directory*

Employment Marketplace
PO Box 31112
St. Louis, MO 63131
Ph: (314)569-3095

Irregular, latest edition 1993. $40.00, plus $4.00 shipping; payment must accompany order. Covers over 1,500 firms and organizations supplying information, products, or services to the personnel and employment industry, including recruitment advertising agencies; trainers and training consultants; publishers of databases, newsletters, directories, periodicals, books, and computer software; associations; job fair coordinators; incentive merchandise suppliers; clipping services; speakers; insurance firms; and testing/assessment/evaluation firms. Entries include: Company name, address, phone, name and title of contact, publications (if any), description, field of activity. Arrangement: Alphabetical. Indexes: Business or service.

★3000★ *Executive Employment Guide*

AMACOM Books
American Management Association
135 W. 50th St.
New York, NY 10020
Ph: (212)903-7912   Fax: (212)903-8163

Monthly. $20.00. Covers over 150 executive search firms, personnel agencies, outplacement services, job registers, job counselors, resume writers, pre-employment investigators, and salary survey corporate guides. Entries include: Firm name, address, phone, subsidiary and branch names and locations, type of firm, kinds of positions handled, minimum salary of jobs handled, whether firm will review resumes and interview uninvited applicants, geographic placement capability. Arrangement: Alphabetical.

★3001★ *Executive Recruitment Firms*

JNN International, Inc.
6821 Sutherland Ct.
Mentor, OH 44060
Ph: (216)974-1959

Annual, September. $7.00, per volume. Covers firms providing services such as executive search, job counseling, and marketing (resume preparation, mailing, etc.); personnel agencies and job registers. Published in 18 industry-specific volumes under title, "Executive Recruitment Firms Specializing in (industry name)" and a general volume titled, "Executive Recruitment Firms Specializing in Most Industries". Entries include: Company name, contact name, address. Arrangement: Separate geographical sections for firms that do not charge fees and those that do charge.

★3002★ *Executive Search Consultants Directory*

American Business Directories, Inc.
American Business Information, Inc.
5711 S. 86th Cir.
Omaha, NE 68127
Ph: (402)593-4600   Fax: (402)331-1505

Annual. $460.00, payment with order. Entries include: Name, address, phone (including area code), size of advertisement, year first in Yellow Pages, name of owner or manager, number of employees. Compiled from telephone company Yellow Pages, nationwide. Arrangement: Geographical.

★3003★ *Executive Search Research Directory*

The Recruiting & Search Report
Box 9433
Panama City Beach, FL 32407
Ph: (904)235-3733   Fax: (904)233-9695
Fr: 800-634-4548

Biennial, with yearly updates. $88.00 postpaid. Covers over 300 freelance executive search researchers or independent executive search research firms that specialize in candidate locating, screening, and development for executive recruiters and corporate (inhouse) recruiters; publishers of directories, books, periodicals, and other resources related to recruitment research. Entries include: For researchers: name, address, phone,

rates, year established, first year listed, whether a retainer relationship with the search firm is required, description of services and specialties, hourly rates. For resource publishers: name, address, phone, evaluation of publication. Arrangement: Researchers are geographical by zip code; publishers are classified by subject. Indexes: Geographical; means of industry or functional concentration; unusual expertise; specialty.

★3004★ *Hoover's Directory of Human Resources Executives 1996*

The Reference Press, Inc.
PO Box 140375
Austin, TX 78714-0375
Fax: (512)454-9401   Fr: 800-486-8666

1996. $39.95 (paper). Lists names of key hiring executives for over 5,000 companies. Includes company profiles.

★3005★ *International Association for Personnel Women—Membership Roster*

National Human Resources Association (NHRA)
909 North Mayfair Rd.
Milwaukee, WI 53226
Fax: (414)475-5959

Annual, latest edition November, 1994. Free, included in membership; $150.00, nonmembers. Covers 1,200 members-at-large and members of affiliated chapters. Entries include: Individual name, title, company name, mailing address, office phone. Arrangement: Classified by type of membership.

★3006★ *Key European Executive Search Firms and Their U.S. Links*

Consultants Bookstore
Templeton Rd.
Fitzwilliam, NH 03447
Ph: (603)585-6544   Fax: (603)585-9555
Fr: 800-531-0007

James H. Kennedy. 1991. $39.00. 210 pages. Identifies linkages between more than 500 search offices in the United States and many European countries.

★3007★ *National Directory of Personnel Service Firms*

National Association of Personnel Services
3133 Mt. Vernon Ave.
Alexandria, VA 22305
Ph: (703)684-0180   Fax: (703)684-0071

Annual, spring. $15.95, plus $5.00 shipping. Covers over 1,100 member private (for-profit) personnel service firms and temporary service firms. Entries include: Firm name, address, phone, fax, contact, area of specialization. Arrangement: Same information given geographically by employment specialty.

HANDBOOKS AND MANUALS

★3008★ *Directory of U.S. Executive Search Firms*

Market Advantage Group
51 Meadow Ridge
Avon, CT 06001
Ph: (203)673-2124   Fax: (203)593-5028

Biennial. $45.00. Covers over 2,700 executive search firms in the U.S., half of which work on a retained basis, the other half of which work mainly on a contingency basis. Entries include: Company name, address, phone, name and title of contact, description of firm, codes indicating firm's industry and functional specialization, minimum salary level handled. Arrangement: Alphabetical. Indexes: Geographical, industry specialization, functional specialization.

★3009★ *Employment Firm Workers*

Chronicle Guidance Publications, Inc.
Aurora Street Extension
PO Box 1190
Moravia, NY 13118-1190
Ph: (315)497-0330   Fax: (315)497-3359
Fr: 800-622-7284

1992. Career brief describing the nature of the job, entry methods, working conditions, hours and earnings, education and training, licensure, certification, unions, personal qualifications, social and psychological factors, location, employment outlook, advancement, and related occupations.

★3010★ *Hiring: More Than a Gut Feeling*

Career Press, Inc.
3 Tice Rd.,
PO Box 687
Franklin Lakes, NJ 07417-1322
Ph: (201)848-0310   Fax: (201)848-1727
Fr: 800-227-3371

Richard Deems. 1995. $12.99 (paper).

★3011★ *How to Become a Skillful Interviewer*

AMACOM
135 W. 50th St., 15th Fl.
New York, NY 10020
Ph: (212)903-8315   Fax: (212)903-8168

Randi T. Sachs. 1994. $10.95.

★3012★ *Interviewer Approaches*

Ashgate Publishing Co.
Old Post Rd.
Brookfield, VT 05036
Ph: (802)276-3162

Jean Morton-Williams. 1993. $57.95.

★3013★ *Interviewing*

John Wiley & Sons, Inc.
605 3rd Ave.
New York, NY 10158-0012
Ph: (212)850-6000   Fr: 800-225-5945

Arlene S. Hirsch. 1994. $32.50; $10.95 (paper).

★3014★ *Interviewing the World's Top Interviewers*

Sure Sellers, Inc.
136 W. 22nd St.
New York, NY 10011
Ph: (212)633-2022   Fax: (212)633-2123

Jack Huper. 1993. $5.50 (paper)

★3015★ *Opportunities in Human Resources Management Careers*

VGM Career Horizons
4255 W. Touhy Ave.
Lincolnwood, IL 60646-1975
Ph: (847)679-5500   Fax: (847)679-2494
Fr: 800-323-4900

William Traynor and J. Steven McKenzie. 1994. $14.95; $11.95 (paper). 160 pages. A guide to planning for and seeking opportunities in this growing field. Contains bibliography and illustrations.

★3016★ *Successful Selection Interviewing*

Blackwell Publishers
238 Main St.
Cambridge, MA 02142
Ph: (617)547-7110   Fax: (617)547-0789

Neil Anderson. 1993. $39.95 (paper).

★3017★ *Where the Jobs Are: The Hottest Careers for the '90s*

The Career Press, Inc.
3 Tice Rd.
PO Box 687
Franklin Lakes, NJ 07417
Ph: (201)848-0310   Fax: (201)848-1727
Fr: 800-237-3371

Joyce Hadley. Second edition, 1995. $9.99. 300 pages. Describes careers in fifteen general fields, from accounting to travel and hospitality.

EMPLOYMENT AGENCIES AND SEARCH FIRMS

★3018★ **Abbott Smith Associates, Inc.**

PO Box 318
Franklin Ave.
Millbrook, NY 12545
Ph: (914)677-5300   Fax: (914)677-3315

Executive search firm. Affiliate offices in Chicago and London.

★3019★ **Addington Personnel Services**

2401 Fountainview, Ste.104
Houston, TX 77057
Ph: (713)780-8810

Employment agency. Places individuals in regular or temporary positions.

★3020★ **B and M Associates, Inc.**

199 Cambridge Rd.
Woburn, MA 01801-4705
Ph: (617)938-9120

Employment agency.

★3021★ **Dankowski and Associates, Inc.**

842 Corporate Way, Ste. 820
Cleveland, OH 44145
Ph: (216)892-2800

Executive search firm.

★3022★ **Hayden and Associates, Inc.**

7825 Washington Ave. S., Ste. 120
Minneapolis, MN 55439-2431
Ph: (612)941-6300   Fax: (612)941-9602

Employment agency. Executive search firm. Fills openings in a variety of fields.

★3023★ **Karras Personnel, Inc.**

2 Central Ave.
Madison, NJ 07940
Ph: (201)966-6800

Executive search firm.

★3024★ **The Pathfinder Group**

295 Danbury Rd.
Wilton, CT 06897-3095
Ph: (203)834-2467

Employment agency. Executive search firm. Recruits staff in a variety of fields.

★3025★ **Protocol Inc.**

300 N. Lake Ave., Ste. 208
Pasadena, CA 91101-4106
Ph: (818)449-2214   Fax: (818)577-0484

Executive search firm.

★3026★ **Willmott and Associates**

922 Waltham St., Ste. 103
Lexington, MA 02173
Ph: (617)863-5400   Fax: (617)863-8000

Executive search firm.

OTHER SOURCES

★3027★ *American Almanac of Jobs and Salaries 1994-95*

Avon Books
1350 Avenue of the Americas, 2nd Fl.
New York, NY 10019
Ph: (212)261-6800   Fr: 800-238-0658

John Wright. Revised edition, 1993. $17.00. 704 pages. This is a comprehensive guide to the wages of hundreds of occupations in a wide variety of industries and organizations.

★3028★ **Association of Outplacement Consulting Firms International (AOCFI)**

1200 19th St. NW, Ste. 300
Washington, DC 20036
Ph: (202)857-1185   Fax: (202)857-1115

Members: Firms providing displaced employees, who are sponsored by their organization, with counsel and assistance in job searching and the techniques and practices of choosing a career. **Purpose:** To develop, improve, and encourage the art and science of outplacement consulting and the professional standards of competence, objectivity, and integrity in the service of clients. Cooperates with other industrial, technical, educational, professional, and governmental bodies in areas of mutual interest and concern.

★3029★ *Employment Agency Business Guide*

Entrepreneur, Inc.
2392 Morse Ave.
Box 19787
Irvine, CA 92713-9787
Fax: (714)851-9088   Fr: 800-421-2300

$79.50 (includes business guide and software). Provides data on starting and operating an employment agency. Includes information on profits, costs, and related items.

★3030★ **International Association of Personnel in Employment Security (IAPES)**

1801 Louisville Rd.
Frankfort, KY 40601
Ph: (502)223-4459   Fax: (502)223-4127

Members: Officials and others engaged in job placement, unemployment compensation, and labor market information administration through municipal, state, provincial, and federal government employment agencies and unemployment compensation agencies. **Activities:** Conducts workshops and research. Offers professional development program of study guides and tests.

★3031★ **Labor Policy Association (LPA)**

1015 15th St. NW
Washington, DC 20005
Ph: (202)789-8670   Fax: (202)789-0064

Members: Senior human resource officers of industrial, service and commercial employers. **Purpose:** Conducts research and publishes findings on matters relating to federal employment policy and its application and effects. Maintains task force to study pending employment issues; conducts seminars.

★3032★ **National Association of Personnel Services (NAPS)**

3133 Mt. Vernon Ave.
Alexandria, VA 22305
Ph: (703)684-0180   Fax: (703)684-0071

Members: Private employment and temporary service firms. **Purpose:** Compiles statistics on professional agency growth and development; conducts certification program and educational programs. Association is distinct from former name of National Personnel Consultants.

★3033★ **National Association of Temporary and Staffing Services (NATSS)**

119 S. St. Asaph St.
Alexandria, VA 22314
Ph: (703)549-6287   Fax: (703)549-4808

Members: Companies supplying workers to other firms on a temporary basis. **Purpose:** Sponsors ten to 12 regional workshops and in-depth industry studies.

★3034★ *Temporary-Help Service Business Guide*
Entrepreneur, Inc.
2392 Morse Ave.
Box 19787
Irvine, CA 92713-9787
Fax: (714)851-9088   Fr: 800-421-2300
$79.50 (includes business guide and software). Explains how to start a temporary help agency. Covers topics such as acquiring a pool of qualified personnel and ensuring their demand in the maximum number of markets.

Engineering Technicians

SOURCES OF HELP-WANTED ADS

★3035★ Automotive Engineering

Society of Automotive Engineers
400 Commonwealth Dr.
Warrendale, PA 15096
Ph: (412)776-4841   Fax: (412)776-4026

Monthly. $72.00/year for individuals; $126.00/year for other countries. Magazine for automotive engineers providing technical and design information.

★3036★ Captsule Job Listings

Publications and Communications, Inc.
12416 Hymeadow Dr.
Austin, TX 78750
Ph: (512)250-9023   Fax: (512)331-3900
Fr: 800-678-9724

Online database. Lists current job openings in the contract (temporary) technical services industry. Includes the Action Hot List, which provides information on job seekers. Includes employment opportunities in technical/professional engineering, computing, and design/drafting. Entries generally contain company name, address, and job opening.

★3037★ Chemical and Engineering News

American Chemical Society
1155 16th St. NW
Washington, DC 20036
Ph: (202)872-4600   Fax: (202)872-6005
Fr: 800-227-5558

Weekly. Free to qualified subscribers; $105.00/year for individuals. Chemical process industries trade journal.

★3038★ Connector Specifier

IHS Publishing Group
17730 W. Peterson Rd.
Libertyville, IL 60048
Ph: (708)362-8711   Fax: (708)362-3484

Free to qualified subscribers. Magazine on the use of connectors and interconnection products.

★3039★ EE Evaluation Engineering

Nelson Publishing
2504 N. Tamiami Tr.
Nelson Bldg.
Nokomis, FL 34275
Ph: (813)966-9521   Fax: (813)966-2590

Monthly. $80.00/year for individuals; $105.00/year for Canada; $120.00/year for other countries; $7.50/year for single issue. Trade journal covering electronic engineering, evaluation and test.

★3040★ Electronic Engineering Times

CMP Publications, Inc.
600 Community Dr.
Manhasset, NY 11030
Ph: (516)562-5000   Fax: (516)562-5055

Weekly. Weekly Trade Newspaper.

★3041★ Electronic Products

Hearst Business Communications, Inc.
645 Stewart Ave.
Garden City, NY 11530
Ph: (516)227-1300   Fax: (516)227-1444

Magazine for electronic design engineers and management.

★3042★ Engineering Times

National Society of Professional Engineers
1420 King St.
Alexandria, VA 22314
Ph: (703)684-2875   Fax: (703)836-4875

Monthly. Magazine (tabloid) covering professional, legislative, and techology issues for an engineering audience.

★3043★ ENR: Engineering News Record

New York Construction News
1221 Avenue of the Americas
New York, NY 10020
Ph: (212)512-4773   Fax: (212)512-4770

Weekly. $42.00/year; $2.00/issue.

★3044★ High Technology Careers Magazine

HTC
4701 Patrick Henry Dr., No. 1901
Santa Clara, CA 95054
Ph: (408)970-8800   Fax: (408)980-5103

Bimonthly. Magazine (tabloid) containing employment opportunity information for the engineering and technical community.

★3045★ Mechanical Engineering

American Society of Mechanical Engineers
345 E. 47th St.
New York, NY 10017-2392
Ph: (212)705-7723   Fax: (212)705-7841
Fr: 800-843-2763

Monthly. Mechanical engineering.

★3046★ Microwave Journal

Horizon House Publications, Inc.
685 Canton St.
Norwood, MA 02062
Ph: (617)769-9750   Fax: (617)762-9071
Fr: 800-966-6326

Monthly. Free to qualified subscribers; $75.00/year. Electronic engineering magazine.

★3047★ Minority Engineer

Equal Opportunity Publications, Inc.
150 Motor Pkwy., Ste. 420
Hauppauge, NY 11788-5145
Ph: (516)273-0066   Fax: (516)273-8936

Affirmative-action recruitment magazine serving college graduating and professional minority engineers.

★3048★ Modern Metals

Trend Publishing
625 N. Michigan Ave.
Chicago, IL 60611-5503
Ph: (312)654-2300   Fax: (312)654-2323

Monthly. $70.00/year for individuals; $6.00 for single issue. Metals fabrication magazine.

★3049★ NSBE Magazine

NSBE Publications
1454 Duke St.
Alexandria, VA 22314
Ph: (703)549-2207   Fax: (703)683-5312

$10.00/year for individuals; $2.00 for single issue. Journal providing information on engineering careers, self-development, and cultural issues for recent graduates with technical majors.

★3050★ PCIM

Intertec International, Inc.
2472 Eastman Ave., Bldg. 33-34
Ventura, CA 93003
Ph: (805)650-7070   Fax: (805)650-7079

Monthly. Magazine on electronic engineering, power conversion, and electronic motion control.

★3051★ Power

New York Construction News
1221 Avenue of the Americas, 41st Fl.
New York, NY 10020
Ph: (212)512-4773   Fax: (212)512-4770

Monthly. Magazine for engineers in electric utilities, process and manufacturing plants, commercial and service establishments, and consulting, design, and construction engineering firms working in the power technology field.

★3052★ Printed Circuit Design

Miller Freeman, Inc.
2000 Powers Ferry Ctr., Ste. 450
Marietta, GA 30067
Ph: (404)952-1303   Fax: (404)952-6461

Monthly. Free to qualified subscribers; $50.00 for institutions; $4.00/year for single issue. Magazine for designers of PCB's and related technologies.

★3053★ SMT

IHS Publishing Group
17730 W. Peterson Rd.
Libertyville, IL 60048
Ph: (708)362-8711   Fax: (708)362-3484

Monthly.

★3054★ SWE

Society of Women Engineers
120 Wall St., 11th Fl.
New York, NY 10005-3902
Ph: (212)509-9577   Fax: (212)509-0224

Bimonthly. $30.00/year for nonmembers. Magazine for engineering students and for women and men working in the engineering and technology fields. Covers career guidance, continuing development and topical issues.

★3055★ Technology Review

The Tech
PO Box 397029
Cambridge, MA 02139
Ph: (617)253-1541   Fax: (617)258-8226

$30.00/year for individuals; $3.75 for single issue; $42.00/year for other countries. Magazine reviewing new developments in technology with an emphasis on economic, political, and social implications. Not a new product publication.

★3056★ Test and Measurement World

Cahners Publishing Co.
275 Washington St.
Newton, MA 02158-1630
Ph: (617)964-3030   Fax: (617)558-4470

Monthly. Electronic engineering magazine specializing in test, measurement, and inspection of electronic components.

★3057★ 33 MetalProducing

Peter Li
1100 Superior Ave.
Cleveland, OH 44114
Ph: (216)696-7000   Fax: (216)696-7670

Monthly. $50.00/year for individuals. Magazine covering the metal-producing industry.

★3058★ Tooling and Production

Huebcore Communications, Inc.
29100 Aurora Rd., Ste. 200
Solon, OH 44139
Ph: (216)248-1125   Fax: (216)248-0187

Monthly. Magazine concerning metalworking.

PLACEMENT AND JOB REFERRAL SERVICES

★3059★ Aircraft Electronics Association (AEA)

PO Box 1963
Independence, MO 64055-0963
Ph: (816)373-6565   Fax: (816)478-3100

Members: Companies engaged in the sales, engineering, installation, and service of electronic aviation equipment and systems. **Purpose:** Purposes are to: advance the science of aircraft electronics; promote uniform and stable regulations and uniform standards of performance; establish and maintain a code of ethics; gather and disseminate technical data; advance the education of members and the public in the science of aircraft electronics. Is active in the areas of supplement type certificates, test equipment licensing, temporary FCC licensing for new installations, spare parts availability and pricing, audiovisual technician training, equipment and spare parts loan, profitable installation, and service facility operation. **Activities:** Provides employment information, equipment exchange information, stolen equipment lists, and service assistance on member installations anywhere in the U.S. and Canada. Compiles statistics.

★3060★ American Indian Science and Engineering Society (AISES)

1630 30th St., Ste. 301
Boulder, CO 80301
Ph: (303)492-8658   Fax: (303)492-3400

Members: American Indian and non-Indian students and professionals in science, technology, and engineering fields; corporations representing energy, mining, aerospace, electronic, and computer fields. **Purpose:** Seeks to motivate and encourage students to pursue undergraduate and graduate studies in science, engineering, and technology. **Activities:** Sponsors science fairs in grade schools, teacher training workshops, summer math/science sessions for 8th-12th graders, professional chapters, and student chapters in colleges. Offers scholarships. Adult members serve as role models, advisers, and mentors for students. Operates placement service. **E-Mail:** aisesha@spot.colorado.edu

★3061★ American Society of Certified Engineering Technicians (ASCET)

PO Box 1348
Flowery Branch, GA 30542
Ph: (770)967-9173   Fax: (770)967-8049

Members: Certified and noncertified engineering technicians and technologists. **Purpose:** Works to obtain recognition of the contribution of engineering technicians and engineering technologists as an essential part of the engineering-scientific team; cooperate with engineering and scientific societies; improve the utilization of the engineering technician and technologist; assist the educational, social, economic, and ethical development of the engineering technician and technologist. **Activities:** Conducts triennial survey among members to determine employer support, pay scales, and fringe benefits. Offers referral service.

★3062★ Electronics Technicians Association, International (ETA-I)

602 N. Jackson
Greencastle, IN 46135
Ph: (317)653-8262   Fax: (317)653-8262

Members: Skilled electronics technicians. **Activities:** Provides placement service; offers certification examinations for electronics technicians and satellite installers. Compiles wage and manpower statistics. Administers FCC Commercial License examinations.

★3063★ Engineering Society of Detroit (ESD)

100 Farnsworth Ave.
Detroit, MI 48202
Ph: (313)832-5400   Fax: (313)832-5920

Members: Engineers from all disciplines; scientists and technologists. **Activities:** Offers placement services. Conducts technical programs and engineering refresher courses; sponsors conferences and expositions. Maintains speakers' bureau. Although based in Detroit, MI, society membership is international.

★3064★ ISA

PO Box 12277
67 Alexander Dr.
Research Triangle Park, NC 27709
Ph: (919)549-8411   Fax: (919)549-8288

Purpose: Educational organization dedicated to advancing knowledge and practice related to the theory, design, manufacture, and use of instruments and controls in science and industry. Operates training center for industry; conducts symposia; develops standards; recognizes individual achievement. **Activities:** Maintains speakers' bureau and placement service.

★3065★ Robotics International of the Society of Manufacturing Engineers (RI/SME)

1 SME Dr.
PO Box 0930
Dearborn, MI 48121-0930
Ph: (313)271-1500   Fax: (313)271-2861

Members: Engineers, managers, educators, and government officials in 50 countries working or interested in the field of robotics. **Purpose:** Promotes efficient and effective use of current and future robot technology. Serves as a clearinghouse for the industry trends and developments. Areas of interest include: aerospace; assembly systems; casting and forging; education and training; human factors and safety; human and food service; material handling; military systems; nontraditional systems; research and development; small shop applications; welding. Offers professional certification. **Activities:** Operates placement service; compiles statistics. Maintains speakers' bureau.

★3066★ Society of Hispanic Professional Engineers (SHPE)

5400 E. Olympic Blvd., Ste. 210
Los Angeles, CA 90022
Ph: (213)725-3970

Purpose: Engineers, student engineers, and scientists seeking to increase the number of Hispanic engineers by providing motivation and support to students. Sponsors competitions and educational programs. **Activities:** Maintains placement service and speakers' bureau; compiles statistics.

★3067★ Society for Mining, Metallurgy, and Exploration (SME)

PO Box 625002
Littleton, CO 80162-5002
Ph: (303)973-9550   Fax: (303)973-3845
Fr: 800-763-3132

Members: Member society of the American Institute of Mining, Metallurgical and Petroleum Engineers. Persons engaged in the finding, exploitation, treatment, and marketing of all classes of minerals (metal ores, industrial minerals, and solid fuels) except petroleum. **Purpose:** Promotes the arts and sciences connected with the production of useful minerals and metals. **Activities:** Provides placement service. Offers specialized education programs; compiles enrollment and graduation statistics from schools offering engineering degrees in mining, mineral, mineral processing/metallurgical, geological, geophysical, and mining technology. **E-Mail:** smeaime@aol.com

EMPLOYER DIRECTORIES AND NETWORKING LISTS

★3068★ Directory of African American Design Firms

San Francisco Redevelopment Agency
770 Golden Gate Ave.
San Francisco, CA 94102-3120
Ph: (415)749-2423   Fax: (415)749-2526

Annual, December. Free. Covers over 100 architectural, engineering, planning, and landscape design firms. Entries include: Firm name, address, phone names and titles of key personnel, particular type of work. Arrangement: Alphabetical.

★3069★ Directory of Contract Service Firms

C. E. Publications, Inc.
PO Box 97000
Kirkland, WA 98083
Ph: (206)823-2222   Fax: (206)821-0942

Annual, January. $10.00. Covers Approximately 900 contract firms actively engaged in the employment of engineering and technical personnel for temporary contract assignments throughout the world. Entries include: Company name, address, phone, name of contact. Arrangement: Alphabetical. Indexes: Geographical.

★3070★ Directory of Engineering Societies and Related Organizations

American Association of Engineering Societies
1111 19th St. NW, Ste. 608
Washington, DC 20036
Ph: (202)296-2237   Fax: (202)296-1151
Fr: 800-658-8897

1992. $185.00. Lists 1,000 national, regional, Canadian, and international organizations concerned with engineering and related fields.

★3071★ Directory of Engineers in Private Practice

National Society of Professional Engineers
1420 King St.
Alexandria, VA 22314
Ph: (703)684-2862   Fax: (703)836-4875

Annual. $85.00. Covers 600 consulting engineering firms and 7,200 individuals who are members of the society's Professional Engineers in Private Practice division. Entries include: For companies, name, address, phone, name of principal executive, list of services. For individuals, name, address; most listings include phone. Arrangement: Firms are geographic, then by specialty; individuals are alphabetical.

★3072★ Electronic News—Looking at the Leaders

Electronic News
488 Madison Ave.
New York, NY 10022
Ph: (212)909-5900

Formerly annual; suspended indefinitely. $2.00. Includes: List of 50 leading United States electronic firms in terms of electronic sales; similar data on about 25 leading foreign companies. Entries include: Company name, headquarters address; plant locations, activities, number of employees; officers; electronic sales, percent of sales in electronics, gross sales in all lines; other financial data. Arrangement: Alphabetical.

★3073★ Engineering Research Centres

Stockton Press
Groves Dictionaries
345 Park Ave. S., 10th Fl.
New York, NY 10010
Ph: (212)689-9200   Fr: 800-221-2123

Fourth edition, 1995. $515.00. 768 pages. Contains over 8,000 entries describing research and technology laboratories in over 70 countries. Provides details on industrial research centers and educational establishments with research and development activity. Indexes: Subject and title of establishments.

★3074★ Engineers—Mechanical Directory

American Business Directories, Inc.
American Business Information, Inc.
5711 S. 86th Cir.
Omaha, NE 68127
Ph: (402)593-4600   Fax: (402)331-1505

Updated continuously: Entries include: Name, address, phone, size of advertisement, year first in Yellow Pages, name of owner or manager, number of employees. Compiled from telephone company Yellow Pages, nationwide. Arrangement: Geographical.

★3075★ ENR—Top 500 Design Firms Issue

McGraw-Hill, Inc.
1221 Ave. of the Americas
New York, NY 10020
Ph: (212)512-4635   Fax: (212)512-2820

Annual, April. $10.00, reprint, payment must accompany order. Publication includes: List of 500 leading architectural, engineering, and specialty design firms selected on basis of annual billings. Entries include: Company name, headquarters location, type of firm, current and prior year rank in billings, types of services, countries in which operated in preceding year. Arrangement: Ranked by billings.

★3076★ Peterson's Job Opportunities in Engineering and Technology 1996

Peterson's
PO Box 2123
Princeton, NJ 08543-2123
Ph: (609)243-9111   Fax: (609)243-9150
Fr: 800-338-3282

Compiled by the Peterson's staff. Annual. $19.95 paperback. 432 pages. Profiles 2,000 high-tech companies looking primarily for technical personnel in such fields as biotechnology, telecommunications, software, computers and peripherals, defense, and aerospace. Contains job-search strategies and career options to help match education and expertise to the job market. Indexed geographically, by industry, and by hiring needs.

★3077★ Scientific and Technical Organizations and Agencies Directory

Gale Research
835 Penobscot Bldg.
Detroit, MI 48226-4094
Ph: (313)961-2242   Fax: (313)961-6083
Fr: 800-877-GALE

Irregular; latest edition December 1993. $195.00. Covers over 25,600 national and international organizations and agencies concerned with the physical and applied sciences, engineering, and technology, including associations, computer information services, consulting firms, educational institutions, foundations, government advisory organizations, federal government agencies, general grant and assistance programs, libraries and information centers, patent sources and services, research and development centers, scholarships, fellowships, and loans, science-technology centers, standards organizations, state academies of science, and state government agencies in the fields of aeronautics and space sciences, chemistry, computer science specialties, electronics, geography, geology, machinery, mathematics, metallurgy, meteorology, mineralogy, nuclear science, petroleum and gas, physics, plastics, transportation, water resources, and other areas. Entries include: Organization name, address, phone, and name of contact; additional descriptive text for most entries. Arrangement: Classified by type of organization. Indexes: Organization name/key word.

HANDBOOKS AND MANUALS

★3078★ Career Information Center
Macmillan Publishing Co.
200 Old Tappan Rd.
Old Tappan, NJ 07675
Ph: (609)461-6500   Fr: 800-223-2336
Visual Education Center Staff. Fifth edition, 1992. $229.00. This 13-volume set profiles over 600 occupations. Each occupational profile describes job duties, educational requirements, how to get the job, advancement possibilities, employment outlook, working conditions, earnings and benefits, and where to write for more information.

★3079★ Careers in Engineering
VGM Career Horizons
4255 W. Touhy Ave.
Lincolnwood, IL 60646-1975
Ph: (847)679-5500   Fax: (847)679-2494
Fr: 800-323-4900
Geraldine O. Gardner. 1994. $17.95; $13.95 (paper). Covers careers in the public or private sector, in industry, the university, or the military, from applications in computer architecture design to high temperature ceramics.

★3080★ Engineering Success
Kendall Hunt Publishing
4050 Westmark Dr.
PO Box 1840
Dubuque, IA 52004-1840
Ph: (319)589-1000   Fax: 800-772-9165
Fr: 800-228-0810
Bill Osher. 1994. $27.96.

★3081★ Engineering Your Job Search: A Job-Finding Resource for Engineering Professionals
Professional Publications, Inc.
1250 5th Ave.
Belmont, CA 94002
Ph: (415)593-9119   Fax: (415)592-4519
Fr: 800-426-1178
Compiled by Professional Publications editors. 1995. $12.95 (paper).

★3082★ Introduction to the Engineering Profession
HarperCollins Publishers, Inc.
10 E. 53rd. St.
New York, NY 10022-5299
Ph: (212)207-7000   Fax: (212)207-7145
Fr: 800-331-3761
David M. Burghardt. 1995. $30.00 (paper).

★3083★ Job Opportunities in Engineering and Technology
Peterson's Guides, Inc.
PO Box 2123
Princeton, NJ 08543-2123
Ph: (609)243-9111   Fax: (609)243-9150
Fr: 800-338-3282
1994. $18.95 (paper).

★3084★ Majoring in Engineering: How to Get from Your Freshman Year to Your First Job
Farrar, Straus & Giroux, Inc.
19 Union Sq., W
New York, NY 10003
Ph: (212)741-6900   Fr: 800-788-6262
John Garcia. 1995. $20.00; $10.00 (paper).

★3085★ Opportunities in Electronics Careers
VGM Career Horizons
4255 W. Touhy Ave.
Lincolnwood, IL 60646-1975
Ph: (847)679-5500   Fax: (847)679-2494
Fr: 800-323-4900
Mark Rowh. 1992. $14.95; $11.95 (paper). Discusses career opportunities in commercial and industrial electronics equipment repair, electronics home entertainment repair, electronics engineering, and engineering technology. Includes job outlook and how to get off to a good start on the job.

★3086★ Resumes for Engineering Careers
VGM Career Horizons
NTC Publishing Group
4255 W. Touhy Ave.
Lincolnwood, IL 60646-1975
Ph: (847)679-5500   Fax: (847)679-2494
Fr: 800-323-4900
1994. $9.95. 160 pages. Contains sample resumes and cover letters applicable to any engineering field.

★3087★ Where the Jobs Are: The Hottest Careers for the '90s
The Career Press, Inc.
3 Tice Rd.
PO Box 687
Franklin Lakes, NJ 07417
Ph: (201)848-0310   Fax: (201)848-1727
Fr: 800-237-3371
Joyce Hadley. Second edition, 1995. $9.99. 300 pages. Describes careers in fifteen general fields, from accounting to travel and hospitality.

EMPLOYMENT AGENCIES AND SEARCH FIRMS

★3088★ ABC Employment Service
25 S. Bemiston, Ste. 214
Clayton, MO 63105
Ph: (314)725-3140
Employment agency.

★3089★ B and M Associates, Inc.
199 Cambridge Rd.
Woburn, MA 01801-4705
Ph: (617)938-9120
Employment agency.

★3090★ Colli Associates of Tampa
PO Box 2865
Tampa, FL 33601
Ph: (813)681-2145
Employment agency. Executive search firm.

★3091★ Hayden and Associates, Inc.
7825 Washington Ave. S., Ste. 120
Minneapolis, MN 55439-2431
Ph: (612)941-6300   Fax: (612)941-9602
Employment agency. Executive search firm. Fills openings in a variety of fields.

★3092★ Industrial Recruiters Associates, Inc.
630 Oakwood Ave., Ste. 318
West Hartford, CT 06110
Ph: (203)953-3643
Employment agency.

★3093★ The Jobs Co.
8900 E. Sprague Ave.
Spokane, WA 99212-2927
Ph: (509)928-3151   Fax: (509)928-3168
Employment agency. Has division specializing in engineering and scientific openings. Also operates division specializing in sales openings.

★3094★ JR Professional Search
PO Box 18356
Tucson, AZ 85731
Ph: (520)721-1855   Fax: (520)721-1855
Employment agency.

★3095★ LOR Personnel Division
418 Wall St.
Princeton, NJ 08540
Ph: (609)921-6580
Employment agency. Executive search firm.

★3096★ Main Line Personnel Service, Inc.
401 City Ave.
Bala Cynwyd, PA 19004-1122
Ph: (610)667-1820
Employment agency.

★3097★ Search and Recruit International

4455 South Blvd.
Virginia Beach, VA 23452
Ph: (804)490-3151

Employment agency. Headquartered in Virginia Beach. Other offices in Bremerton, WA; Charleston, SC; Jacksonville, FL; Memphis, TN; Pensacola, FL; Sacramento, CA; San Bernardino, CA; San Diego, CA.

★3098★ Sierra Technology Corporation

4150 Manzanita Ave., Ste. 100
Carmichael, CA 95608-1700
Ph: (916)488-4960   Fax: (916)488-7058

Employment agency. Provides placement on a temporary basis.

★3099★ Software Services Corp.

2850 S. Industrial Hwy, Ste. 300
Ann Arbor, MI 48104-6796
Ph: (313)971-2300

Employment agency.

★3100★ Source Engineering

5580 LBJ Fwy., Ste. 300
Dallas, TX 75240
Ph: (214)385-3002   Fax: (214)717-0075

Executive search firm. Many affiliate offices located throughout the U.S.

★3101★ T.R. Employment Agency

409 Wilshire Blvd.
Santa Monica, CA 90401
Ph: (310)393-4107

Employment agency.

★3102★ Tri-Serv Inc.

22 W. Padonia Rd., Ste. C53
Timonium, MD 21093
Ph: (301)561-1740

Employment agency.

OTHER SOURCES

★3103★ American Association of Engineering Societies (AAES)

1111 19th St. NW, Ste. 608
Washington, DC 20036
Ph: (202)296-2237   Fax: (202)296-1151

Purpose: Seeks to promote leadership in public affairs for the engineering community, work in support of math and science education for young persons. Disseminates of information about the profession. Provides statistics about engineers.

★3104★ Association for International Practical Training (AIPT)

10400 Little Patuxent Pky. Ste. 250
Columbia, MD 21044
Ph: (410)997-2200   Fax: (410)992-3924

Purpose: Helps coordinate training around the world in fields such as travel, the culinary arts, and hotel management. **Activities:** Conducts programs in career development and hospitality/tourism exchanges. Operates a student exchange program. Provides reciprocal practical training experience for recent graduates from the U.S., Austria, Germany, Finland, France, Hungary, Ireland, Japan, Malaysia, Netherlands, Switzerland, and the United Kingdom. Arranges training programs in the U.S. and abroad. Serves as U.S. affiliate to IAESTE (International Association for the Exchange of Students for Technical Experience) and operates a Professional Visitors Program to arrange short-term educational and training visits to the U.S. **E-Mail:** aipt@aipt.org

★3105★ Career Encounters: Mechanical Engineering

Cambridge Career Products
PO Box 2153
Dept. CC15
Charleston, WV 25328-2153
Ph: (304)744-9323   Fax: (304)744-9351
Fr: 800-468-4227

Video. $99.95. 25 minutes. Professionals shown in a variety of settings discuss different aspects of their careers.

★3106★ International Society of Certified Electronics Technicians (ISCET)

2708 W. Berry, Ste. 3
Fort Worth, TX 76109
Ph: (817)921-9101   Fax: (817)921-3741

Members: Technicians in 37 countries who have been certified by the society. **Purpose:** Seeks to provide a fraternal bond among certified electronics technicians, raise their public image, and improve the effectiveness of industry education programs for technicians. Offers training programs in new electronics information. **Activities:** Maintains library of service literature for consumer electronic equipment, including manuals and schematics for out-of-date equipment. Offers all FCC licenses. Sponsors testing program for certification of electronics technicians in the fields of audio, communications, computer, consumer, industrial, medical electronics, radar, radio-television, and video.

★3107★ National Institute for Certification in Engineering Technologies (NICET)

1420 King St.
Alexandria, VA 22314-2794
Ph: (703)684-2835   Fr: 800-787-0034

Purpose: Grants and issues certificates to engineering technicians and technologists who voluntarily apply for certification and satisfy competency criteria through examinations and verification of work experience. Requirements for certification involve work experience in terms of job task proficiency and length of progressively more responsible experience. Levels of certification are Associate Engineering Technician, Engineering Technician, Senior Engineering Technician, Associate Engineering Technologist, and Certified Engineering Technologist.

★3108★ Salaries of Scientists, Engineers, and Technicians: A Summary of Salary Surveys

Commission on Professionals in Science and Technology (CPST)
1500 Massachusetts Ave. NW, Ste. 831
Washington, DC 20005
Ph: (202)223-6995

1993.

★3109★ Society of Women Engineers (SWE)

120 Wall St., 11th Fl.
New York, NY 10005
Ph: (212)509-9577   Fax: (212)509-0224

Members: Educational service society of women engineers; membership is also open to men. **Purpose:** Supplies information on the achievements of women engineers and the opportunities available to them; assists women engineers in preparing for return to active work following temporary retirement. Serves as an informational center on women in engineering. **Activities:** Administers several certificate and scholarship programs. Offers tours and career guidance; conducts surveys. Compiles statistics.

Environmental Engineers

SOURCES OF HELP-WANTED ADS

★3110★ Applied Occupational & Environmental Hygiene

Applied Industrial Hygiene, Inc.
1330 Kemper Meadow Dr., Ste. 600
Cincinnati, OH 45240
Ph: (513)742-2020   Fax: (513)742-3355

Monthly. $85.00/year for individuals; $155.00/year for institutions. Magazine presenting solutions in occupational and environmental hygiene.

★3111★ Earth Work

Student Conservation Association
PO Box 550, Rte. 12A, River Rd.
Charlestown, NH 03603-0550
Ph: (603)543-1700

Eleven issues/year. $29.95/year. Includes career information for those working in conservation.

★3112★ Environmental Opportunities

Environmental Opportunities
PO Box 788
Walpole, NH 03608
Ph: (603)756-4553

Monthly. $47.00/year. Lists full-time openings in environmental positions as well as short-term opportunities and internships.

★3113★ Environmental Protection

Stevens Publishing Corp.
PO Box 2573
Waco, TX 76702-2573
Ph: (817)776-9000   Fax: (817)662-7075
Fr: 800-727-7573

Monthly.

★3114★ Environmental Science & Technology

American Chemical Society
1155 16th St. NW
Washington, DC 20036
Ph: (202)872-4600   Fax: (202)872-4615

Monthly. $44.00/year for members; $90.00/year for nonmembers.

★3115★ Environmental Solutions

Advanstar Communications
800 Roosevelt Rd., Bldg. E, Ste. 300
233 N. Michigan Ave.
Glen Ellyn, IL 60137
Ph: (708)545-8150   Fax: (708)469-7497

Monthly. Free to qualified subscribers; $50.00/year for individuals. Environmental magazine for industry.

★3116★ High Technology Careers Magazine

HTC
4701 Patrick Henry Dr., No. 1901
Santa Clara, CA 95054
Ph: (408)970-8800   Fax: (408)980-5103

Bimonthly. Magazine (tabloid) containing employment opportunity information for the engineering and technical community.

★3117★ The Job Seeker

The Job Seeker
Rt. 2, Box 16, Dept. J
Warrens, WI 54666
Ph: (608)378-4290

Semimonthly. $19.50/year. Specializes "in environmental and natural resource vacancies nationwide." Lists current vacancies from federal, state, local, private, and non-profit employers.

★3118★ Minority Engineer

Equal Opportunity Publications, Inc.
150 Motor Pkwy., Ste. 420
Hauppauge, NY 11788-5145
Ph: (516)273-0066   Fax: (516)273-8936

Affirmative-action recruitment magazine serving college graduating and professional minority engineers.

★3119★ SWE

Society of Women Engineers
120 Wall St., 11th Fl.
New York, NY 10005-3902
Ph: (212)509-9577   Fax: (212)509-0224

Bimonthly. $30.00/year for nonmembers. Magazine for engineering students and for women and men working in the engineering and technology fields. Covers career guidance, continuing development and topical issues.

★3120★ Technology Review

The Tech
PO Box 397029
Cambridge, MA 02139
Ph: (617)253-1541   Fax: (617)258-8226

$30.00/year for individuals; $3.75 for single issue; $42.00/year for other countries. Magazine reviewing new developments in technology with an emphasis on economic, political, and social implications. Not a new product publication.

★3121★ Water Environment Research

Water Environment Federation
601 Wythe St.
Alexandria, VA 22314
Ph: (703)684-2400   Fax: (703)684-2492
Fr: 800-666-0206

Bimonthly. Technical journal covering municipal and industrial water pollution control, water quality, and hazardous wastes.

★3122★ Woman Engineer

Equal Opportunity Publications, Inc.
150 Motor Pkwy., Ste. 420
Hauppauge, NY 11788-5145
Ph: (516)273-0066   Fax: (516)273-8936

Engineer recruitment magazine.

PLACEMENT AND JOB REFERRAL SERVICES

★3123★ American Academy of Environmental Engineers (AAEE)

130 Holiday Ct., No. 100
Annapolis, MD 21401
Ph: (410)266-3311   Fax: (410)266-7653

Members: Environmentally oriented registered professional engineers certified by examination as diplomates of the academy. **Purpose:** Purposes are: to improve the standards of environmental engineering; to certify those with special knowledge of environmental engineering; to furnish lists of those certified to the public. **Activities:** Maintains speakers' bureau. Recognizes areas of specialization: Air Pollution Control; General Environmental; Hazardous Waste Management;

Industrial Hygiene; Radiation Protection; Solid Waste Management; Water Supply and Wastewater. Requires written and oral examinations for certification. Works with other professional organizations on environmentally oriented activities. Identifies potential employment candidates through Talent Search Service.

★3124★ American Indian Science and Engineering Society (AISES)

1630 30th St., Ste. 301
Boulder, CO 80301
Ph: (303)492-8658   Fax: (303)492-3400

Members: American Indian and non-Indian students and professionals in science, technology, and engineering fields; corporations representing energy, mining, aerospace, electronic, and computer fields. **Purpose:** Seeks to motivate and encourage students to pursue undergraduate and graduate studies in science, engineering, and technology. **Activities:** Sponsors science fairs in grade schools, teacher training workshops, summer math/science sessions for 8th-12th graders, professional chapters, and student chapters in colleges. Offers scholarships. Adult members serve as role models, advisers, and mentors for students. Operates placement service. **E-Mail:** aisesha@spot.colorado.edu

★3125★ Engineering Society of Detroit (ESD)

100 Farnsworth Ave.
Detroit, MI 48202
Ph: (313)832-5400   Fax: (313)832-5920

Members: Engineers from all disciplines; scientists and technologists. **Activities:** Offers placement services. Conducts technical programs and engineering refresher courses; sponsors conferences and expositions. Maintains speakers' bureau. Although based in Detroit, MI, society membership is international.

★3126★ Environmental Careers Organization (ECO)

286 Congress St., 3rd Fl.
Boston, MA 02210-1038
Ph: (617)426-4375   Fax: (617)423-0998

Members: Seeks to protect and enhance the environment through the development of professionals, the promotion of careers, and the inspiration of individual action. **Activities:** Offers placement series, career advisement, career publications, and research and consulting. Participants in programs are mostly upper-level undergraduate, graduate, and doctoral students, or recent graduates seeking professional experience relevant to careers in the environmental fields. Individual subject areas of placement service include biology, chemistry, community development, hazardous waste, natural resources, pollution, public/occupational health, transportation, and wildlife. Maintains high-school speaker's bureau, leadership training, mentoring, outreach to minority institutions, and the Technical Advisor Program for Toxics Use Reduction. **Website:** http://www.eco.org

★3127★ Korean Scientists and Engineers Association in America (KSEA)

6261 Executive Blvd.
Rockville, MD 20852
Ph: (301)984-7048   Fax: (301)984-1231

Members: Scientists and engineers holding single or advanced degrees. **Purpose:** Goals are to: promote friendship and mutuality among Korean and American scientists and engineers; contribute to Korea's scientific, technological, industrial, and economic developments; strengthen the scientific, technological, and cultural bonds between Korea and the U.S. Sponsors symposium. **Activities:** Maintains speakers' bureau, placement service, and biographical archives. Compiles statistics. Maintains 100 volume library of scientific handbooks and yearbooks in Korean.

★3128★ Society of Hispanic Professional Engineers (SHPE)

5400 E. Olympic Blvd., Ste. 210
Los Angeles, CA 90022
Ph: (213)725-3970

Purpose: Engineers, student engineers, and scientists seeking to increase the number of Hispanic engineers by providing motivation and support to students. Sponsors competitions and educational programs. **Activities:** Maintains placement service and speakers' bureau; compiles statistics.

EMPLOYER DIRECTORIES AND NETWORKING LISTS

★3129★ American Men and Women of Science

R. R. Bowker Co.
Reed Reference Publishing
121 Chanlon Rd.
New Providence, NJ 07974
Ph: (908)464-6800   Fax: (908)665-6688
Fr: 800-521-8110

Triennial, latest edition January 1995. $106.00, per volume; $850.00, set. Covers over 123,000 U.S. and Canadian scientists active in the physical, biological, mathematical, computer science, and engineering fields; includes references to previous edition for deceased scientists and nonrespondents. Entries include: Name, address, education, personal and career data, memberships, honors and awards, research interest. Arrangement: Alphabetical. Indexes: Discipline (in separate volume).

★3130★ Association of Conservation Engineers—Membership Directory

Association of Conservation Engineers
c/o Terry N. Boyd
Engineering Section
Alabama Department of Conservation and Natural Resources
64 N. Union St.
Montgomery, AL 36130
Ph: (205)242-3476   Fax: (205)242-0289

Annual, June. Available to members only. Covers 280 persons with administrative or engineering background in conservation. Entries include: Member name, address, phone, company or institution name. Arrangement: Alphabetical.

★3131★ Directory of Contract Service Firms

C. E. Publications, Inc.
PO Box 97000
Kirkland, WA 98083
Ph: (206)823-2222   Fax: (206)821-0942

Annual, January. $10.00. Covers Approximately 900 contract firms actively engaged in the employment of engineering and technical personnel for temporary contract assignments throughout the world. Entries include: Company name, address, phone, name of contact. Arrangement: Alphabetical. Indexes: Geographical.

★3132★ Directory of Engineers in Private Practice

National Society of Professional Engineers
1420 King St.
Alexandria, VA 22314
Ph: (703)684-2862   Fax: (703)836-4875

Annual. $85.00. Covers 600 consulting engineering firms and 7,200 individuals who are members of the society's Professional Engineers in Private Practice division. Entries include: For companies, name, address, phone, name of principal executive, list of services. For individuals, name, address; most listings include phone. Arrangement: Firms are geographic, then by specialty; individuals are alphabetical.

★3133★ Engineers—Environmental Directory

American Business Directories, Inc.
American Business Information, Inc.
5711 S. 86th Cir.
Omaha, NE 68127
Ph: (402)593-4600   Fax: (402)331-1505

Updated continuously; printed on request. $330.00. Entries include: Name, address, phone, size of advertisement, name of owner or manager, number of employees, year first in Yellow Pages. Compiled from telephone company Yellow Pages, nationwide. Arrangement: Geographical.

★3134★ Environmental Career Directory

Gale Research
835 Penobscot Bldg.
Detroit, MI 48226-4094
Ph: (313)961-2242   Fax: (313)961-6083
Fr: 800-877-GALE

Latest edition 1993. $34.00; $17.95 (paper). Covers over 250 companies and organizations offering entry-level positions in environment-related careers, including forestry management, fish and wildlife management, and air and water quality control; sources of help-wanted ads, professional associations, producers of videos, databases, career guides, and professional guides and handbooks. Entries include: For companies: name, address, phone, business description, names and titles of key personnel, number of employees, average number of entry-level positions available, human resources contact, description of internship opportunities including contact, type and number available, application procedures, qualifications, and duties. For others: name or title, address, phone, description. Paperback edition is available from Visible Ink Press. Arrangement: Companies are alphabetical; others are classified by type of resource. Indexes: Name, keyword.

★3135★ Environmental Engineering Selection Guide

American Academy of Environmental Engineers
130 Holiday Ct., Ste. 100
Annapolis, MD 21401
Ph: (410)266-3311

1995. Single copy free. 128 pages. Covers a range of contacts in environmental engineering, including university professors, certified environmental engineering specialists, and accredited university programs.

★3136★ Life Sciences Organizations and Agencies Directory

Gale Research
835 Penobscot Bldg.
Detroit, MI 48226-4094
Ph: (313)961-2242   Fax: (313)961-6083
Fr: 800-877-GALE

$175.00. Covers about 7,500 associations, government agencies, research centers, educational institutions, libraries and information centers, museums, consultants, electronic information services, and other organizations and agencies active in agriculture, biology, ecology, forestry, marine science, nutrition, wildlife and animal sciences, and other natural and life sciences. Entries include: Organization or agency name, address, phone, name and title of contact, description. Arrangement: Classified by type of organization. Indexes: Organization/agency name and keyword.

★3137★ Peterson's Job Opportunities in the Environment

Peterson's Guides, Inc.
202 Carnegie Ctr.
Box 2123
Princeton, NJ 08543-2123
Ph: (609)243-9111   Fax: (609)243-9150
Fr: 800-338-3282

Annual, August. $18.95. Covers Approximately 1,500 companies and government agencies hiring environmental professionals, including waste-management companies, state and federal agencies, advocacy groups, and environmental design firms. Entries include: Organization name, address, phone, name and title of contact, type of organization, number of employees, Standard Industrial Classification (SIC) code; description of opportunities available including disciplines, level of education required, starting locations and salaries, level of experience accepted, benefits. Arrangement: Alphabetical. Indexes: Employer by type of organization, industry classification, number of employees, starting location, special interest area; education level, company.

★3138★ Scientific and Technical Organizations and Agencies Directory

Gale Research
835 Penobscot Bldg.
Detroit, MI 48226-4094
Ph: (313)961-2242   Fax: (313)961-6083
Fr: 800-877-GALE

Irregular; latest edition December 1993. $195.00. Covers over 25,600 national and international organizations and agencies concerned with the physical and applied sciences, engineering, and technology, including associations, computer information services, consulting firms, educational institutions, foundations, government advisory organizations, federal government agencies, general grant and assistance programs, libraries and information centers, patent sources and services, research and development centers, scholarships, fellowships, and loans, science-technology centers, standards organizations, state academies of science, and state government agencies in the fields of aeronautics and space sciences, chemistry, computer science specialties, electronics, geography, geology, machinery, mathematics, metallurgy, meteorology, mineralogy, nuclear science, petroleum and gas, physics, plastics, transportation, water resources, and other areas. Entries include: Organization name, address, phone, and name of contact; additional descriptive text for most entries. Arrangement: Classified by type of organization. Indexes: Organization name/key word.

★3139★ Who's Who in Environmental Engineering

American Academy of Environmental Engineers
130 Holiday Ct., Ste. 100
Annapolis, MD 21401
Ph: (410)266-3311   Fax: (410)266-7653

Annual, April. $75.00, payment with order. Covers about 2,600 licensed professional environmental engineers that have been certified by examination in one or more of seven specialties: air pollution control, general environmental engineering, industrial hygiene, hazardous waste management, radiation protection, solid waste management, water supply and wastewater. Entries include: Name, affiliation, address, phone, area of specialization, biographical data. Arrangement: Alphabetical, geographical, area of specialization.

★3140★ Who's Who in Technology

Gale Research
835 Penobscot Bldg.
Detroit, MI 48226-4094
Ph: (313)961-2242   Fax: (313)961-6083
Fr: 800-877-GALE

Irregular, new edition expected June 1995. $380.00. Covers 38,000 engineers, scientists, inventors, and researchers. Entries include: Name, title, affiliation, address; personal, education, and career data; publications, patents; technical field of activity; area of expertise. Arrangement: Alphabetical. Indexes: Geographical, employer, technical discipline, expertise.

HANDBOOKS AND MANUALS

★3141★ The Best Resumes for Scientists and Engineers

John Wiley and Sons
605 3rd Ave.
New York, NY 10158
Ph: (212)850-6000   Fr: 800-225-5945

Adele Lewis. Second edition, 1993. $37.50; $14.95 (paper). Presents an extensive collection of scientific and engineering resumes, highlighting the important differences between these and resumes written for other occupations.

★3142★ Careers in Engineering

VGM Career Horizons
4255 W. Touhy Ave.
Lincolnwood, IL 60646-1975
Ph: (847)679-5500   Fax: (847)679-2494
Fr: 800-323-4900

Geraldine O. Gardner. 1994. $17.95; $13.95 (paper). Covers careers in the public or private sector, in industry, the university, or the military, from applications in computer architecture design to high temperature ceramics.

★3143★ Careers in the Environment

VGM Career Horizons
NTC Publishing Group
4255 W. Touhy Ave.
Lincolnwood, IL 60646-1975
Ph: (847)679-5500   Fax: (847)679-2494
Fr: 800-323-4900

Michael Fasulo and Paul Walker. 1995. $17.95; $13.95 (paper). 160 pages. Comprehensive information on the diverse career opportunities available in environmental services.

★3144★ Careers for Environmental Types and Others Who Respect the Earth

VGM Career Horizons
NTC Publishing Group
4255 W. Touhy Ave.
Lincolnwood, IL 60646-1975
Ph: (847)679-5500   Fax: (847)679-2494
Fr: 800-323-4900

Jane Kinney and Mike Fasulo. 1993. $14.95; $9.95 (paper). 160 pages. Describes environmentally friendly positions with corporations, government, and environmental organizations.

★3145★ Careers Inside the World of Environmental Science

Rosen Publishing Group, Inc.
29 E. 21st St.
New York, NY 10010
Ph: (212)777-3017   Fax: (212)777-0277
Fr: 800-237-9932

Bob Gartner. 1995. $14.95. 64 pages. Describes jobs in environmental studies and related fields for reluctant readers.

★3146★ Careers in Science

VGM Career Horizons
4255 W. Touhy Ave.
Lincolnwood, IL 60646-1975
Ph: (847)679-5500   Fax: (847)679-2494
Fr: 800-323-4900

Thomas Easton. Third edition, 1996. 192 pages. $17.95; $13.95 (paper). Discusses careers in life science, earth science, physical and space science, social science, engineering, mathematics, and computer science. Offers job hunting advice.

★3147★ Careers in Science and Engineering

National Academy Press
2101 Constitution Ave. NW
Washington, DC 20418
Ph: (202)334-3313   Fr: 800-624-6242

1996. $9.95. 70 pages. Covers planning for graduate school and beyond.

★3148★ Encyclopedia of Careers and Vocational Guidance

J. G. Ferguson Publishing Co.
200 W. Monroe, Ste. 250
Chicago, IL 60606
Ph: (312)580-5480

William E. Hopke. Ninth edition, 1993. $129.95; $199.95 (CD-ROM). Four-volume set that profiles 900 occupations and describes job trends in 71 industries. Includes career description, educational requirements, history of the job, methods of entry, advancement, employment outlook, earnings, conditions of work, social and psychological factors, and sources of further information. Contains career and employment information for this field.

★3149★ Engineering Success

Kendall Hunt Publishing
4050 Westmark Dr.
PO Box 1840
Dubuque, IA 52004-1840
Ph: (319)589-1000   Fax: 800-772-9165
Fr: 800-228-0810

Bill Osher. 1994. $27.96.

★3150★ Engineering Your Job Search: A Job-Finding Resource for Engineering Professionals

Professional Publications, Inc.
1250 5th Ave.
Belmont, CA 94002
Ph: (415)593-9119   Fax: (415)592-4519
Fr: 800-426-1178

Compiled by Professional Publications editors. 1995. $12.95 (paper).

★3151★ Environmental Engineers

Chronicle Guidance Publications, Inc.
66 Aurora St.
PO Box 1190
Moravia, NY 13118-1190
Ph: (315)497-0330   Fax: (315)497-3359
Fr: 800-622-7284

Chronicle Guidance Staff. 1993. $2.00. Provides concise career information and sources of additional information.

★3152★ Environmental Sciences

AMIDEAST
1100 17th St. NW
Washington, DC 20036-4601
Ph: (202)776-9600

$.90. 3 pages. Describes career opportunities, educational programs, and additional sources of information.

★3153★ Great Jobs for Engineering Majors

VGM Career Horizons
NTC Publishing Group
4255 W. Touhy Ave.
Lincolnwood, IL 60646-1975
Ph: (847)679-5500   Fax: (847)679-2494
Fr: 800-323-4900

Geraldine O. Garner. 1996. $11.95. 224 pages. Covers all the career options open to students majoring in engineering.

★3154★ Introduction to the Engineering Profession

HarperCollins Publishers, Inc.
10 E. 53rd. St.
New York, NY 10022-5299
Ph: (212)207-7000   Fax: (212)207-7145
Fr: 800-331-3761

David M. Burghardt. 1995. $30.00 (paper).

★3155★ Job Opportunities in Engineering and Technology

Peterson's Guides, Inc.
PO Box 2123
Princeton, NJ 08543-2123
Ph: (609)243-9111   Fax: (609)243-9150
Fr: 800-338-3282

1994. $18.95 (paper).

★3156★ Job Opportunities in the Environment 1995

Peterson's Guides, Inc.
PO Box 2123
Princeton, NJ 08543-2123
Ph: (609)243-9111   Fax: (609)243-9150
Fr: 800-225-0261

1994. $18.95 (paper).

★3157★ Jobs from Recyclables Possibility Newsletter

Prosperity & Profits Unlimited Distribution Services
PO Box 416
Denver, CO 80201
Ph: (303)575-5676

Annual. $4.50. Describes employment options for environmentalists, waste management, and businesses.

★3158★ Majoring in Engineering: How to Get from Your Freshman Year to Your First Job

Farrar, Straus & Giroux, Inc.
19 Union Sq., W
New York, NY 10003
Ph: (212)741-6900   Fr: 800-788-6262

John Garcia. 1995. $20.00; $10.00 (paper).

★3159★ Nature (Career Portraits)

VGM Career Horizons
NTC Publishing Group
4255 W. Touhy Ave.
Lincolnwood, IL 60646-1975
Ph: (847)679-5500   Fax: (847)679-2494
Fr: 800-323-4900

Marjorie Eberts. 1996. $13.95. 96 pages. Highlights a range of careers that focus on the environment, with descriptions of a typical day on the job and interactive exercises for readers.

★3160★ 100 Best Careers for the Year 2000

Prentice Hall General Reference
15 Columbus Cir.
New York, NY 10023
Ph: (212)373-8500   Fr: 800-223-2348

Shelly Field. 1992. $15.00 (paper). Covers 100 of the fastest growing jobs. The publication is divided into 11 general employment sections. Specific careers are covered within each section. Provides job description, responsibilities, employment opportunities, earnings, education and training, advancement opportunities, and experience and qualifications for each occupation.

★3161★ Opportunities in Engineering Careers

VGM Career Horizons
4255 W. Touhy Ave.
Lincolnwood, IL 60646-1975
Ph: (847)679-5500   Fax: (847)679-2494
Fr: 800-323-4900

Nicholas Basta. 1995. $14.95; $11.95 (paper). Outlines typical job titles, salaries, career paths, and employment prospects.

★3162★ Opportunities in Environmental Careers

VGM Career Horizons
4255 W. Touhy Ave.
Lincolnwood, IL 60646-1975
Ph: (847)679-5500   Fax: (847)679-2494
Fr: 800-323-4900

Odom Fanning. 1995. $14.95; $11.95 (paper). 160 pages. Describes a broad range of opportunities in fields such as environmental health, recreation, physics, and hygiene, and provides job search advice.

★3163★ Our Past, The Present, Your Future in Civil Engineering

American Society of Civil Engineers
345 E. 47th St.
New York, NY 10017
Fr: 800-548-ASCE

This 32-page brochure contains career information about the seven major branches of civil engineering, including environmental engineering.

★3164★ Peterson's Hidden Job Market 1996

Peterson's
PO Box 2123
Princeton, NJ 08543-2123
Ph: (609)243-9111   Fax: (609)243-9150
Fr: 800-338-3282

Fifth edition, 1995. $17.95. Guide to 2,000 fast-growing companies that are hiring now.

Focuses on high technology companies in such fields as environmental consulting, genetic engineering, home health care, telecommunications, alternative energy systems, and others.

★3165★ *Peterson's Job Opportunities in Engineering and Technology 1996*

Peterson's
PO Box 2123
Princeton, NJ 08543-2123
Ph: (609)243-9111   Fax: (609)243-9150
Fr: 800-338-3282

Compiled by the Peterson's staff. Annual. $19.95 paperback. 432 pages. Profiles 2,000 high-tech companies looking primarily for technical personnel in such fields as biotechnology, telecommunications, software, computers and peripherals, defense, and aerospace. Contains job-search strategies and career options to help match education and expertise to the job market. Indexed geographically, by industry, and by hiring needs.

★3166★ *Resumes for Engineering Careers*

VGM Career Horizons
NTC Publishing Group
4255 W. Touhy Ave.
Lincolnwood, IL 60646-1975
Ph: (847)679-5500   Fax: (847)679-2494
Fr: 800-323-4900

1994. $9.95. 160 pages. Contains sample resumes and cover letters applicable to any engineering field.

★3167★ *Resumes for Environmental Careers*

VGM Career Horizons
NTC Publishing Group
4255 W. Touhy Ave.
Lincolnwood, IL 60646-1975
Ph: (847)679-5500   Fax: (847)679-2494
Fr: 800-323-4900

1994. $9.95. 160 pages. Provides resume advice tailored to people pursuing careers focusing on the environment. Includes sample resumes and cover letters.

★3168★ *Where the Jobs Are: The Hottest Careers for the '90s*

The Career Press, Inc.
3 Tice Rd.
PO Box 687
Franklin Lakes, NJ 07417
Ph: (201)848-0310   Fax: (201)848-1727
Fr: 800-237-3371

Joyce Hadley. Second edition, 1995. $9.99. 300 pages. Describes careers in fifteen general fields, from accounting to travel and hospitality.

EMPLOYMENT AGENCIES AND SEARCH FIRMS

★3169★ ABC Employment Service
25 S. Bemiston, Ste. 214
Clayton, MO 63105
Ph: (314)725-3140

Employment agency.

★3170★ Amtec Engineering Corp.
2749 Saturn St.
Brea, CA 92621
Ph: (714)993-1900   Fax: (714)993-2419

Employment agency.

★3171★ Bell Oaks Co.
3390 Peachtree Rd., Ste. 1124
Atlanta, GA 30326
Ph: (404)261-2170

Personnel service firm.

★3172★ Career Center, Inc.
194 Passaic St.
PO Box 1036
Hackensack, NJ 07601
Ph: (201)342-1777

Employment agency.

★3173★ Environmental Professional Associates
3857 Birch St., Ste. 186
Newport Beach, CA 92660
Ph: (310)273-5320

Executive search firm. Focuses on environmental positions.

★3174★ Erspamer Associates
7300 France Ave. S., Ste. 402
Edina, MN 55435
Ph: (612)831-5564   Fax: (612)831-5981

Executive search firm.

★3175★ Executive Recruiters Agency
14 Office Park Dr.
PO Box 21810
Little Rock, AR 72221-1810
Ph: (501)224-7000   Fax: (501)224-8534

Personnel service firm.

★3176★ Hansen Agri-Placement
PO Box 1172
Grand Island, NE 68802
Ph: (308)382-7350

Employment agency. Handles placements in a variety of fields on a regular or temporary basis.

★3177★ JPM International
4665 MacArthur Ct., Ste. 100B
Newport Beach, CA 92660
Ph: (714)955-2545   Fax: (714)757-1320

Executive search firm and employment agency.

★3178★ JR Professional Search
PO Box 18356
Tucson, AZ 85731
Ph: (520)721-1855   Fax: (520)721-1855

Employment agency.

★3179★ Rand Personnel Agency
1200 Truxtun, Ste. 130
Bakersfield, CA 93301
Ph: (805)325-0751   Fax: (805)325-4120

Personnel service firm.

★3180★ Randolph Associates, Inc.
950 Massachusetts Ave., Ste. 105
Cambridge, MA 02139-3174
Ph: (617)441-8777   Fax: (617)441-8778

Employment agency. Provides regular or temporary placement of staff.

★3181★ Systems One Ltd.
1100 E. Woodfield Rd.
Schaumburg, IL 60173
Ph: (708)619-9300   Fax: (708)619-0071

Personnel service firm.

OTHER SOURCES

★3182★ Air and Waste Management Association (A&WMA)
1 Gateway Ctr., 3rd Fl.
Pittsburgh, PA 15222
Ph: (412)232-3444   Fax: (412)232-3450
Fr: 800-270-3444

Purpose: Environmental, educational, and technical organization. Seeks to provide a neutral forum for the exchange of technical information on a wide variety of environmental topics.

★3183★ American Association of Engineering Societies (AAES)
1111 19th St. NW, Ste. 608
Washington, DC 20036
Ph: (202)296-2237   Fax: (202)296-1151

Purpose: Seeks to promote leadership in public affairs for the engineering community, work in support of math and science education for young persons. Disseminates of information about the profession. Provides statistics about engineers.

★3184★ *Computer Salary Survey and Career Planning Guide*

Source EDP
120 Broadway, Ste. 1010
New York, NY 10271
Ph: (212)557-8611

Annual. Describes career paths in the computer field and trends in the computer field. Lists job titles. Charts salaries by job titles, years of experience, and industry.

★3185★ *Engineering Salary Survey*

Source Engineering
1290 Oakmead, Ste. 318
Sunnyvale, CA 94086
Ph: (408)738-8440

Annual. Discusses the structure of the engineering profession, trends, and compensation. Salaries are listed by job function, industry, and years of experience.

★3186★ *Future Trends in Environmental Engineering*

American Academy of Environmental Engineers
130 Holiday Ct., Ste. 100
Annapolis, MD 21401
Ph: (410)266-3311

Free. 5 pages.

★3187★ Graduating Engineer

Peterson's/COG Publishing Group
16030 Ventura Blvd., No. 560
Encino, CA 91436
Ph: (818)789-5293

Eight issues/year. Magazine focusing on employment, education, and career development for entry-level engineers.

★3188★ Journal of Environmental Engineering

American Society of Civil Engineers
345 E. 47th St.
New York, NY 10017-2398
Ph: 800-548-2723   Fax: (212)705-7300

Bimonthly. Journal on the practice and status of research in environmental engineering science, systems engineering, and sanitation.

★3189★ National Action Council for Minorities in Engineering (NACME)

3 W. 35th St.
New York, NY 10001-2281
Ph: (212)279-2626   Fax: (212)629-5178

Purpose: Seeks to increase the number of African American, Latino, and Native American students enrolled in and graduating from engineering schools. Through the Corporate Scholars Program, offers comprehensive scholarships to engineering students that include leadership development, corporate mentors and summer internships. Works with local, regional, and national education organizations to motivate and encourage precollege students to engage in engineering careers. Conducts educational and research programs; operates project to assist engineering schools in improving the retention and graduation rates of minority students.

Maintains speakers' bureau; compiles statistics.

★3190★ National Society of Professional Engineers (NSPE)

1420 King St.
Alexandria, VA 22314
Ph: (703)684-2800   Fax: (703)836-4875

Members: Professional engineers and engineers-in-training in all fields registered in accordance with the laws of states or territories of the U.S. or provinces of Canada; qualified graduate engineers, student members, and registered land surveyors. **Purpose:** Is concerned with social, professional, ethical, and economic considerations of engineering as a profession; encompasses programs in public relations, employment practices, ethical considerations, education, and career guidance. Monitors legislative and regulatory actions of interest to the engineering profession. **Website:** http://www.hspc.org

★3191★ Resumes for High Tech Careers

VGM Career Horizons
4255 W. Touhy Ave.
Lincolnwood, IL 60646-1975
Ph: (847)679-5500   Fax: (847)679-2494
Fr: 800-323-4900

1992. $9.95. 160 pages. Demonstrates how to tailor a resume that catches a high tech employer's attention.

★3192★ Resumes for Scientific and Technical Careers

VGM Career Horizons
NTC Publishing Group
4255 W. Touhy Ave.
Lincolnwood, IL 60646-1975
Ph: (847)679-5500   Fax: (847)679-2494
Fr: 800-323-4900

1994. $9.95. 160 pages. Provides resume advice for individuals interested in working in scientific and technical careers. Includes sample resumes and cover letters.

★3193★ Salaries of Scientists, Engineers, and Technicians: A Summary of Salary Surveys

Commission on Professionals in Science and Technology (CPST)
1500 Massachusetts Ave. NW, Ste. 831
Washington, DC 20005
Ph: (202)223-6995

1993.

★3194★ Society of Women Engineers (SWE)

120 Wall St., 11th Fl.
New York, NY 10005
Ph: (212)509-9577   Fax: (212)509-0224

Members: Educational service society of women engineers; membership is also open to men. **Purpose:** Supplies information on the achievements of women engineers and the opportunities available to them; assists women engineers in preparing for return to active work following temporary retirement. Serves as an informational center on women in engineering. **Activities:** Administers several certificate and scholarship programs. Offers tours and career guidance; conducts surveys. Compiles statistics.

Fashion Models

SOURCES OF HELP-WANTED ADS

★3195★ Daily Variety

Cahners Business Newspapers
5700 Wilshire Blvd., Ste. 120
Los Angeles, CA 90036
Ph: (213)857-6600   Fax: (213)857-0494

Daily (morn.). Global entertainment newspaper (tabloid).

EMPLOYER DIRECTORIES AND NETWORKING LISTS

★3196★ Creative Black Book

Black Book Marketing Group
866 3rd Ave.
New York, NY 10022
Ph: (212)702-9700   Fax: (212)605-4808

Annual, January. $140.00, plus $7.00 shipping. Publication includes: photographers and photographic services, design firms, advertising agencies, and other firms whose products or services are used in advertising. Entries include: Company name, address, phone. Principal content of publication is 4-color samples from the leading commercial photographers. Arrangement: Classified by product/service.

★3197★ Directory of Modeling/Talent Agencies and Schools International

Peter Glenn Publications
42 W. 38th St.
New York, NY 10018
Ph: (212)869-2020   Fax: (212)869-3287
Fr: 800-223-1254

Annual. $29.95. Covers over 2,800 schools and agencies; international coverage. Entries include: School or agency name, address, phone. Arrangement: Geographical.

★3198★ Directory of New York City Model Agencies

Peter Glenn Publications Ltd.
42 W. 38th St., Ste. 802
New York, NY 10018
Ph: (212)869-2020   Fax: (212)869-3287
Fr: 800-723-1254

Annual, November. $11.95. Covers Approximately 125 modeling agencies in the New York City area. Entries include: Agency name, address, phone, names and titles of key personnel, restrictions and requirements. Arrangement: Alphabetical. Indexes: Agency name.

★3199★ Modeling Agencies Directory

American Business Directories, Inc.
American Business Information, Inc.
5711 S. 86th Cir.
Omaha, NE 68127
Ph: (402)593-4600   Fax: (402)331-1505

Updated continuously; printed on request. Entries include: Name, address, phone, size of advertisement, name of owner or manager, number of employees, year first in Yellow Pages. Compiled from telephone company Yellow Pages, nationwide. Arrangement: Geographical.

★3200★ New York Casting and Survival Guide

Peter Glenn Publications
42 W. 38th St., Ste. 802
New York, NY 10018-6210
Ph: (212)869-2020   Fr: 800-223-1254

Annual, September. $15.95. Covers about 10,000 services and facilities for actors, models, and performers in the New York area, including agents in New York and Los Angeles, theaters, producers and casting agencies, casting personnel in advertising agencies, music clubs, typing services, schools, unions, health food stores, apartment and roommate referral agencies. Entries include: Company name, address, phone, and contact. Arrangement: Classified by service.

★3201★ New York Model Agency Directory

Peter Glenn Publications
42 W. 38th St.
New York, NY 10018
Ph: (212)869-2020   Fax: (212)869-3287
Fr: 800-223-1254

Annual, winter. $11.95. Covers about 80 modeling agencies in New York. Entries include: Company name, address, phone, fax, name and title of contact, type of modeling work handled, interview information, years of operation. Arrangement: Alphabetical. Indexes: Name.

★3202★ The Official Southwest Talent Directory

Cobb-Rendish Publishing
2908 McKinney Ave.
Dallas, TX 75204
Ph: (214)754-4729   Fax: (214)855-0643

Annual, latest edition March, 1995. $25.00. Covers over 500 adult and juvenile actors, actresses, and models; motion picture and audio/videotape production facilities in the Southwest. Entries include: Name, acting or performing specialties, and agency contact; production services are presented in individual suppliers' ads. Arrangement: Talent classified by sex and age of performers; production sources classified by product or service. Indexes: Personal name, ethnic group, talent abilities.

HANDBOOKS AND MANUALS

★3203★ Beginner's Guide to Model Photography: Techniques for the Photographer and Tips for the Aspiring Model

Reference Desk Books
430 Quintana Rd., Ste. 146
Morro Bay, CA 93442
Ph: (805)772-8806   Fax: (805)528-0218

Valentine DelVecchio. 1993. $29.95 (paper).

★3204★ Careers for Fashion Plates and Other Trendsetters

VGM Career Horizons
NTC Publishing Group
4255 W. Touhy Ave.
Lincolnwood, IL 60646-1975
Ph: (847)679-5500   Fax: (847)679-2494
Fr: 800-323-4900

Lucia Mauro. 1996. $14.95; $9.95 (paper). 160 pages. Describes career opportunities in fashion, entertainment, retail, and promotion, with advice from fashion professionals.

★3205★ Exposed: How to Become a Model Without Getting Scammed

Maiwald Productions
PO Box 370853
Denver, CO 80237-0853
Ph: (303)290-9609

Sue Maiwald. 1994. $4.95 (paper).

★3206★ The Harvard Guide to Careers in the Mass Media

Bob Adams, Inc.
260 Center St.
Holbrook, MA 02343
Ph: (617)767-8100   Fax: (617)767-0994
Fr: 800-872-5627

John Noble. 1989. $7.95. 202 pages. Each section of the book evaluates one media profession in depth and contains an industry profile, a career profile that describes positions available in that area, information about current salary ranges, industry-specific job-hunting tips and strategies, and a case study outlining the methods that were used in a successful job hunt.

★3207★ Modeling in the 90's: Avoid the Delusion & Pitfalls

Saratu's
774 E. Colorado Blvd.
Pasadena, CA 91101
Ph: (818)683-3758   Fax: (818)796-5181

Amie Bongay. 1995. $14.95 (paper).

★3208★ Models

Chronicle Guidance Publications, Inc.
66 Aurora St.
PO Box 1190
Moravia, NY 13118-1190
Ph: (315)497-0330   Fax: (315)497-3359
Fr: 800-622-7284

Chronicle Guidance Staff. 1991. $2.00. Provides concise career information and sources of additional information.

★3209★ Opportunities in Modeling Careers

VGM Career Horizons
4255 W. Touhy Ave.
Lincolnwood, IL 60646-1975
Ph: (847)679-5500   Fax: (847)679-2494
Fr: 800-323-4900

Susan Wood Gearhart. 1993. $14.95; $11.95 (paper). Addresses opportunities in modeling, ranging from artist's model to photographic model. Includes bibliography and illustrations.

EMPLOYMENT AGENCIES AND SEARCH FIRMS

★3210★ Barbizon School of Modeling

80 Broad St.
Red Bank, NJ 07701-1930
Ph: (908)842-6161

Employment agency. Fills needs for fashion models on temporary basis.

★3211★ Charm Unlimited Inc.

880 E. Sahara Ave.
Las Vegas, NV 89104
Ph: (702)735-2335

Employment agency.

★3212★ Fairfield Resources, Ltd.

Empire State Bldg.
350 5th Ave., Rm. 7605
New York, NY 10118
Ph: (212)268-0220   Fax: (212)268-8849

Employment agency.

Financial Managers

SOURCES OF HELP-WANTED ADS

★3213★ American Banker

American Banker, Inc.
1 State St. Plaza
New York, NY 10004
Ph: (212)943-6700   Fax: (212)943-2984

Daily (morn.). Newspaper for senior executives in banking and other financial services industries. Coverage includes news on the financial service industry, news analysis, statistical data ranking financial institutions, investigative pieces, and financial industry trend stories for decision-makers.

★3214★ Bank Systems and Technology

Miller Freeman, Inc.
1515 Broadway
New York, NY 10036
Ph: (212)626-2380   Fax: (212)944-7164
Fr: 800-950-1314

Monthly. Magazine covering banking systems, automation, and operations.

★3215★ Bankers Monthly

Hanover Publishers
200 W. 57th St.
New York, NY 10019
Ph: (212)399-1084   Fax: (212)245-1973

Monthly. Magazine covering current banking topics of interest to senior bank executives.

★3216★ Barron's National Business and Financial Weekly

Dow Jones & Co., Inc.
World Financial Center
200 Liberty
New York, NY 10281
Ph: (212)416-2700   Fax: (212)416-2829

Weekly (Mon.). $119.00/year for individuals; $2.50 for single issue. Business and finance magazine.

★3217★ Business Credit

National Association of Credit
  Management
8815 Centre Park Dr., Ste. 200
Columbia, MD 21045
Ph: (301)740-5560   Fax: (301)740-5574

Monthly. $33.00/year for individuals; $29.00/year for libraries; $5.00/year for single issue. Magazine covering finance, business credit management, providing information for the extension, and maintenance of accounts receivable cash asset management.

★3218★ Business Insurance

Crain Communications, Inc.
740 N. Rush St.
Chicago, IL 60611-2590
Ph: (312)649-5311   Fax: (312)280-3189

Weekly. $80.00/year for individuals. Magazine for executives in the corporate risk, employee benefit, and finance fields.

★3219★ CFO

CFO Publishing
253 Summer St.
Boston, MA 02210
Ph: (617)345-9700   Fax: (617)951-4090

Monthly. Business magazine for small to mid-sized companies.

★3220★ Estate Planning

Warren, Gorham and Lamont, Inc.
1 Penn Plaza
New York, NY 10119
Ph: (212)971-5000   Fax: (212)971-5113

Bimonthly. $135.00/year.

★3221★ Financial Management

Financial Management Association
University of South Florida
College of Business Admin.
Tampa, FL 33620
Ph: (813)974-2084   Fax: (813)974-3318

Quarterly. $40.00/year for individuals; $10.00 for single issue. Magazine covering business, economics, finance and management.

★3222★ Financial World

Financial World Partners
1328 Broadway, 3rd Fl.
New York, NY 10001-2116
Ph: (212)594-5030   Fax: (212)629-0021
Fr: 800-829-5916

Biweekly. Magazine focusing on finance and business.

★3223★ Journal of Accountancy

The American Institute of Certified Public
  Accountants
1211 Avenue of the Americas
New York, NY 10036
Ph: (212)596-6200   Fax: (212)596-6213

Monthly. Accounting journal.

★3224★ Journal of Financial and Quantitative Analysis

Journal of Financial and Quantitative
  Analysis
University of Washington
Graduate School of Business
  Administration
326 Lewis Hall, DJ-10
Seattle, WA 98195
Ph: (206)543-4598   Fax: (206)543-6872

Quarterly. Journal on research in finance.

★3225★ The Journal of Taxation

Warren, Gorham Lamont
1 Penn Plaza
New York, NY 10119
Ph: (212)971-5185   Fax: (212)971-5025
Fr: 800-950-1252

Monthly. $170.00/year for individuals. Journal for professional tax practitioners.

★3226★ Management Accounting

Institute of Management Accountants
10 Paragon Dr.
Montvale, NJ 07645-1760
Ph: (201)573-9000   Fax: (201)573-0639
Fr: 800-638-4427

Monthly. $130.00/year; $65.00/year for Libraries. Journal reporting on corporate finance, accounting, cash management, and budgeting.

★3227★ Mortgage Banking

Mortgage Bankers Association of America
1125 15th St. NW
Washington, DC 20005
Ph: (202)861-6500   Fax: (202)872-0186

Monthly. $40.00/year for individuals. Magazine on the real estate finance industry.

★3228★ National Mortgage News

National News, Inc.
212 W. 35th St., 13th Fl.
New York, NY 10001
Ph: (212)563-4008   Fax: (212)564-8879

$199.00/year. Newspaper for mortgage lenders and investment bankers.

★3229★ Northwestern Financial Review

NFR Communications
2850 Metro Dr., Ste. 524
Minneapolis, MN 55425
Ph: (612)854-2177   Fax: (612)854-2627

Weekly. $65.00/year for individuals; $4.00. for single issue. Bank and financial magazine and newsletter.

★3230★ PENSION Management

Argus Business
6151 Powers Ferry Rd.
Atlanta, GA 30339
Ph: (404)955-9970   Fax: (404)256-3116

Monthly. $68.00/year for individuals. Magazine on pension investment and fund administration.

★3231★ Pensions and Investments

Crain Communications, Inc.
220 E. 42nd St.
New York, NY 10017
Ph: (212)210-0259   Fax: (212)210-0499

Biweekly. $180.00/year. Magazine containing news and features on investment management, pension management, corporate finance, and cash management.

★3232★ Servicing Management

LDJ Corp.
70 Edwin Ave.
PO Box 2330
Waterbury, CT 06722
Ph: (203)755-0158   Fax: (203)755-3480
Fr: 800-325-6745

Monthly. Trade magazine.

★3233★ United States Banker

Faulkner and Gray, Inc.
11 Penn Plaza, 17th Fl.
New York, NY 10001
Ph: (212)967-7000   Fax: (212)967-2162
Fr: 800-535-8403

Monthly. $59.00/year for individuals. Magazine serving the financial services industry.

PLACEMENT AND JOB REFERRAL SERVICES

★3234★ American Society of Bank Directors (ASBD)

PO Box 2739
Alexandria, VA 22301
Ph: (202)402-1200

Members: Bank directors. **Activities:** Sponsors placement service; offers specialized education programs.

★3235★ Commercial Finance Association (CFA)

225 W. 34th St.
New York, NY 10122
Ph: (212)594-3490   Fax: (212)564-6053

Members: Organizations engaged in asset-based financial services including commercial financing and factoring and lending money on a secured basis to small- and medium-sized business firms. **Purpose:** Acts as a forum for information and consideration about ideas, opportunities, and legislation concerning asset-based financial services. Seeks to improve the industry's legal and operational procedures. **Activities:** Offers job placement and reference services for members. Sponsors School for Field Examiners and other educational programs.

★3236★ Financial Management Association (FMA)

School of Bus.
University of South Florida
Tampa, FL 33620-5500
Ph: (813)974-2084   Fax: (813)974-3318

Members: Professors of financial management; corporate financial officers. **Purpose:** Facilitates exchange of ideas among persons involved in financial management or the study thereof. **Activities:** Conducts workshops for comparison of current research projects and development of cooperative ventures in writing and research. Sponsors honorary society for superior students at 300 colleges and universities. Offers placement services.

★3237★ National Association of Corporate Treasurers (NACT)

11250 Roger Bacon Dr. Ste. 8
Reston, VA 22090
Ph: (703)318-4227   Fax: (703)435-4390

Purpose: Serves as a forum for high-level finance executives who perform all or a substantial part of the duties of corporate treasureship. Seeks to produce and facilitate the exchange of information relevant to the management of corporate treasury operations. Sponsors general sessions on such topics as Cash Management Issues for the 90s, Corporate Finance, Data Processing/Electronic Services, International Liquidity Management. **Activities:** Offers job clearinghouse services.

★3238★ National Bankers Association (NBA)

1802 T St. NW
Washington, DC 20009
Ph: (202)588-5432   Fax: (202)588-5443

Members: Minority banking institutions owned by minority individuals and institutions. **Purpose:** Serves as an advocate for the minority banking industry. Organizes banking services, government relations, marketing, scholarship, and technical assistance programs. **Activities:** Offers placement services; compiles statistics.

★3239★ Treasury Management Association (TMA)

7315 Wisconsin Ave., Ste. 1250W
Bethesda, MD 20814-3211
Ph: (301)907-2862   Fax: (301)907-2864

Purpose: Seeks to establish a national forum for the exchange of concepts and techniques related to improving the management of treasury and the careers of professionals through research, education, publications, and recognition of the treasury management profession through a certification program. **Activities:** Conducts educational programs. Offers placement service.

EMPLOYER DIRECTORIES AND NETWORKING LISTS

★3240★ American Bank Directory

Thomson Financial Publishing Inc.
4709 W. Golf Rd.
Skokie, IL 60076-1253
Ph: (708)676-9600   Fax: (708)933-8101
Fr: 800-321-3373

Semiannual, April and October. $249.00, single issue of national edition; $26.00, for single state edition; $11.00, each additional state in same binder. Covers over 12,000 banks and registered multi-bank holding companies nationwide; also published in editions for individual states. Entries include: Bank name, address (including county and Federal Reserve District), phone, fax, fedwire number, year established, ABA number, names of officers, condensed statement of condition, principal correspondents, branches. Arrangement: Geographical.

★3241★ American Banker—Top Commercial Banks by Assets, Deposits

American Banker-Bond Buyer
International Thomson Publishing Corp.
1 State St. Plaza
New York, NY 10004
Ph: (212)943-5288   Fax: (212)480-0165
Fr: 800-367-3989

Semiannual, March and September. $25.00. Publication includes: List of the top 300 commercial banks. Entries include: Name of bank, headquarters, amount of deposits at the previous quarter, place in rank at quarter. Arrangement: Ranked by deposits and assets. Indexes: Geographical.

★3242★ American Banker—Top Finance Companies Issue

American Banker-Bond Buyer
International Thomson Publishing Corp.
1 State St. Plaza
New York, NY 10004
Ph: (212)943-5288   Fax: (212)480-0165
Fr: 800-367-3989

Annual, December. $25.00. Publication includes: List of top finance companies with $10 million or more in capital funds. Entries include: Finance company name, headquarters, city; rankings of net receivables by type, business, consumer, and other; total capital funds for two preceding years; capital and surplus, total assets, net receivables, net income, deferred income, receivables acquired, and amount of bank credit at end of the preceding year. Arrangement: Ranked by size of capital funds.

★3243★ American Banker—Top 300 Mortgage Companies Issue

American Banker-Bond Buyer
International Thomson Publishing Corp.
1 State St. Plaza
New York, NY 10004
Ph: (212)943-5288   Fax: (212)943-8815
Fr: 800-238-8422

Annual, October. $25.00. Entries include: Company name, headquarters city, rank; dollar value of mortgages serviced for current and prior year; prior year's rank and gain in rank; number of mortgages; number of investors. Arrangement: Ranked by total dollar value of mortgages.

★3244★ American Banker—Top 300 Thrifts by Deposits

American Banker-Bond Buyer
International Thomson Publishing Corp.
1 State St. Plaza
New York, NY 10004
Ph: (212)943-5288   Fax: (212)480-0165
Fr: 800-367-3989

Semiannual, May and November. $25.00. Publication includes: List of top 300 thrift institutions. Entries include: Name of institution, city, rank; total assets, deposits, and total capital. Arrangement: Ranked by deposits, assets, and risk-based capital ratios.

★3245★ American Banker—Top World Banks by Deposits and Assets

American Banker-Bond Buyer
International Thomson Publishing Corp.
1 State St. Plaza
New York, NY 10004
Ph: (212)943-5288   Fax: (212)480-0165
Fr: 800-367-3989

Annual, July. $25.00. Publication includes: List of 500 largest banks in the world by assets with total deposits and deposit rank; also, the risk-based capital position of the 100 largest banking companies in the world as measured by total assets. Entries include: Bank name, headquarters, rankings by assets and amount of deposits and assets for two previous years. Arrangement: Ranked by assets. Indexes: Geographic listing of largest banks outside United States.

★3246★ America's Corporate Finance Directory

National Register Publishing
Reed Reference Publishing
121 Chanlon Rd.
New Providence, NJ 07974
Ph: (908)464-6800   Fax: (908)665-6688
Fr: 800-521-8110

Annual, September. $525.00. Covers financial personnel and outside financial services relationships of 5,000 United States corporations and their wholly-owned United States subsidiaries. Entries include: Company name, address, phone, fax, telex, stock exchange information, earnings, total assets, size of pension/profit-sharing fund portfolio, number of employees, description of business, wholly-owned U.S. subsidiaries of parent company; name and title of key executives; outside suppliers of financial services. Arrangement: Alphabetical. Indexes: Financial responsibilities, Standard Industrial Classification (SIC) code, geographical, Who's Where, private companies, company.

★3247★ Association for Investment Management and Research— Membership Directory

Association for Investment Management & Research (AIMR)
PO Box 3668
Charlottesville, VA 22903
Ph: (804)977-6600   Fax: (804)980-3685
Fr: 800-789-AIMR

Annual, November. $150.00. Covers 25,000 security and financial analysts who are practicing investment analysis. Entries include: Name, firm affiliation and address, phone, fax, specialty codes. Arrangement: Geographical by constituent local or state societies.

★3248★ Branches of Your State: Banks, Savings and Loans, Credit Unions, & Savings Banks

Sheshunoff Information Services, Inc.
Box 13202, Capitol Sta.
Austin, TX 78711-3203
Ph: (512)472-2244   Fax: (512)476-1251
Fr: 800-456-2340

Annual, February. $345.00. Covers in separate state editions, banks, savings and loan branches, and credit unions. For those states without branch banking, individual banks, savings and loan institutions, and credit unions are listed. Entries include: Institution name, address, institution type, deposit totals, percent change over 12 months, percentage share of parent company's total deposits. Arrangement: Geographical.

★3249★ Corporate Finance Sourcebook

National Register Publishing
Reed Reference Publishing
121 Chanlon Rd.
New Providence, NJ 07974
Ph: (908)464-6800   Fax: (908)665-6688
Fr: 800-521-8110

Annual, September. $450.00. Covers securities research analysts; major private lenders; merger and acquisition summaries; investment banking firms; commercial banks; United States-based foreign banks; commercial finance firms; leasing companies; foreign investment bankers in the United States; pension managers; banks that offer master trusts; cash managers; business insurance brokers; business real estate specialists; lists about 3,700 firms; 15,000 key financial experts. Arrangement: Classified by line of business. Indexes: Firm name, personnel name, geographical.

★3250★ Directory of Minority and Women-Owned Investment Bankers

San Francisco Redevelopment Agency
770 Golden Gate Ave.
San Francisco, CA 94102
Ph: (415)749-2423   Fax: (415)749-2526

Approximately biennial, even years. Covers about 18 minority-owned investment banking firms. Entries include: Company name, address, phone, owner's name and title, fax and toll free numbers if available. Arrangement: Alphabetical.

★3251★ Directory of the Savings & Community Bankers of America

Savings & Community Bankers of America
900 19th St. NW
Washington, DC 20006
Ph: (202)857-3100   Fax: (202)659-4816

Annual, July. $55.00 for members; $95.00 for nonmembers. Covers about 2,000 community banks and savings and loan associations; related state and regional trade organizations; other affiliated members. Entries include: For savings banks and savings and loan associations Name, address, phone, fax, names and titles of key personnel, year established, type of charter, name of insuring agency, type of ownership, whether a member of the Federal Home Loan Board system; financial data of assets and deposits. Arrangement: Classified by type of membership; community banks and savings and loan associations are then geographical. Indexes: Alphabetical.

★3252★ Dun & Bradstreet Reference Book of Corporate Managements

Dun & Bradstreet Information Services
Dun & Bradstreet Corp.
3 Sylvan Way
Parsippany, NJ 07054-3896
Ph: (201)605-6000   Fax: (201)605-6911
Fr: 800-526-0651

Annual, April. $785.00, lease basis; $635.00, for public libraries, lease basis. Covers nearly 200,000 presidents, directors, vice presidents, officers, and managers in 12,000 companies of greatest economic, marketing, and investment interests; those firms whose revenues are the highest in the United States. Arrangement: Alphabetical by company name. Indexes: Personal name (with abbreviated title and company affiliation), geographical, SIC code, advanced education institution, military affiliation.

★3253★ Employment Opportunities, USA

Washington Research Associates
1660 S. Albion, Ste. 390
Denver, CO 80222
Ph: (303)756-9038   Fax: (303)770-1945

Annual, quarterly updates. $184.00, includes quarterly updates. Publication includes: List of over 1,000 employment contacts in companies and agencies in the banking, arts, telecommunications, education, and 14 other industries and professions, including the federal government. Entries include: Company name, name of representative, address, description of products or services, hiring and recruiting practices, training programs, and year established. Principal content is industry overviews, carrer news, and employment opportunity information on 14 different job markets. Arrangement: Classified by industry. Indexes: Occupation.

★3254★ Moody's Bank and Finance Manual

Moody's Investors Service, Inc.
99 Church St.
New York, NY 10007
Ph: (212)553-0300   Fax: (212)553-4700
Fr: 800-342-5647

Annual, July; supplements in *Moody's Bank & Finance News Reports.* $1,475.00, per year, including supplements. Covers in four volumes, over 20,000 national, state, and private banks, savings and loans, mutual funds, unit investment trusts, and insurance and real estate companies in the United States. Entries include: Company name, headquarters and branch offices, phones, names and titles of principal executives, directors, history, Moody's rating, and extensive financial and statistical data. Arrangement: Classified by type of business. Indexes: Company name.

★3255★ National Bankers Association— Roster of Minority Banking Institutions

National Bankers Association
1802 T St. NW
Washington, DC 20009
Ph: (202)588-5432   Fax: (202)588-5443

Annual, October. $5.00. Covers about 140 banks owned or controlled by minority group persons or women. Entries include: Bank name, address, phone, name of one executive. Arrangement: Geographical.

★3256★ Peterson's Job Opportunities in Business 1996

Peterson's
PO Box 2123
Princeton, NJ 08543-2123
Ph: (609)243-9111   Fax: (609)243-9150
Fr: 800-338-3282

Compiled by the Peterson's staff. Annual. $19.95 (paper). 416 pages. Profiles 2,000 companies that are hiring employees in a number of nontechnical fields, including financial services, management consulting, retailers, utilities, and consumer products companies. Contains job-search strategies and career options to help match education and expertise to the job market. Indexed geographically, by industry, and by hiring needs.

★3257★ Polk Financial Institutions Directory

R. L. Polk & Co.
PO Box 305100
Nashville, TN 37230-5100
Ph: (615)889-3350   Fax: (615)885-3081
Fr: 800-827-2265

Semiannual. $303.75. Covers 15,000 banks and their branches; over 2,000 head offices, and 15,500 branches of savings and loan associations; over 5,500 credit unions with assets over $5 million; Federal Reserve System and other U.S. government and state government banking agencies; bank holding, commercial finance, and leasing companies; ocverage includes the United States, Canada, Mexico, and Central America. Arrangement: Geographical. Indexes: Alphabetical.

★3258★ Roster of Minority Financial Institutions

U.S. Department of the Treasury
401 14th St. SW, Rm. 523-C
Washington, DC 20227
Ph: (202)874-6846   Fax: (202)874-6907

Biennial. Free. Covers about 170 commercial, minority-owned and controlled financial institutions participating in the Department of the Treasury's Minority Bank Deposit Program. Entries include: Name of institution, name and title of chief officer, address, phone, fax. Arrangement: Geographical.

★3259★ Thomson Bank Directory

Thomson Financial Publishing
4709 W. Golf Rd., 6th Fl.
Skokie, IL 60076-1253
Ph: (708)676-9600   Fax: (708)933-8101
Fr: 800-321-3373

Semiannual, May and November. $369.00, for 4-volume set. Covers in four volumes, about 11,000 banks and 50,000 branches of United States banks, and 60,000 foreign banks and branches engaged in foreign banking; Federal Reserve system and other United States government and state government banking agencies; 500 largest North American and International commercial banks; paper and automated clearinghouses. Entries include: For domestic banks, bank name, address, phone, telex, cable, date established, routing number, charter type, bank holding company affiliation, memberships in Federal Reserve System and other banking organizations, principal officers by function performed, principal correspondent banks, and key financial data (deposits, etc.). For international banks, bank name, address, phone, fax, telex, cable, SWIFT address, transit or sort codes within home country, ownership, financial data, names and titles of key personnel, branch locations. For branches, bank name, address, phone, charter type, ownership and other details comparable to domestic bank listings. Arrangement: Geographical. Indexes: Alphabetical, geographical.

★3260★ Who's Who in Finance and Industry

Marquis Who's Who
Reed Reference Publishing
121 Chanlon Rd.
New Providence, NJ 07974
Ph: (908)464-6800   Fax: (908)665-6688
Fr: 800-521-8110

Biennial, July of odd years. $249.95, plus $17.50 shipping. Covers over 24,500 individuals. Entries include: Name, home and office addresses, personal, career, and family data; civic and political activities; memberships, publications, awards. Arrangement: Alphabetical.

★3261★ Who's Who in the Securities Industry

Economist Publishing Co.
11 E. Hubbard St., No. 3A
Chicago, IL 60611-3536
Ph: (312)467-1888   Fax: (312)467-0225
Fr: 800-THE-ECON

Annual, December. $15.00. Covers about 1,000 investment bankers. Entries include: Name, company affiliation, city, position, birth date, educational and business background, directorships, club memberships, interests and hobbies. Arrangement: Alphabetical.

HANDBOOKS AND MANUALS

★3262★ Business and Finance Career Directory

Gale Research
835 Penobscot Bldg.
Detroit, MI 48226-4094
Ph: (313)961-2242   Fax: (313)961-6083
Fr: 800-877-GALE

Bradley Morgan. Second edition, 1992. $39.00. 413 pages. Features a basic and comprehensive job search section, articles by top professionals in the field, and detailed listings of hundreds of top companies who hire individuals in this field. Aimed particularly at entry-level job hunters.

★3263★ Career Choices for the 90's for Students of Business

Walker and Company
435 Hudson St.
New York, NY 10014
Ph: (212)727-8300   Fax: (212)727-0984
Fr: 800-289-2553

Prepared by the Career Associates staff. 1990. $9.95. 166 pages. Discusses alternatives for students of business. Offers advice on how to break into the field and how to move up. Covers where and who the employers are, internship possibilities, and professional networking associations. Comprehensive guide to career and job search planning.

★3264★ Career Choices for the 90's for Students Considering an MBA

Walker and Company
435 Hudson St.
New York, NY 10014
Ph: (212)727-8300   Fax: (212)727-0984
Fr: 800-289-2553

Prepared by the Career Associates staff. 1990. $8.95. 166 pages. Discusses career alternatives and offers advice on how to break in and move up. Covers where and who the employers are, internship possibilities, and professional networking associations. Comprehensive guide to career and job search planning.

★3265★ Career Opportunities in Art

Facts on File, Inc.
11 Penn Plaza, 15th Fl.
New York, NY 10001-2006
Ph: (212)967-8800   Fax: 800-678-3633
Fr: 800-322-8755

Susan H. Haubenstock and David Joselit. Revised edition, 1994. $29.95; $15.95 (paper). 208 pages. This book profiles seventy-five jobs that can be found in the art field. Each profile includes a career description, career ladder, employment and advancement prospects, education, experience and skills required, salary range, and tips for entry into the field.

★3266★ Careers in Banking and Finance

Rosen Publishing Group, Inc.
29 E. 21st St.
New York, NY 10010
Ph: (212)777-3017   Fax: (212)777-0277
Fr: 800-237-9932

Patricia Haddock. 1990. $14.95. Offers advice on job hunting. Describes jobs at all levels in banking and finance. Contains information about the types of financial organizations where the jobs are found, educational requirements, job duties, and salaries.

★3267★ Careers for Number Crunchers and Other Quantitative Types

VGM Career Horizons
4255 W. Touhy Ave.
Lincolnwood, IL 60646-1975
Ph: (847)679-5500   Fax: (847)679-2494
Fr: 800-323-4900

Rebecca Burnett. 1993. $14.95; $9.95 (paper). Provides information to math-oriented job hunters on how to become statisticians, field researchers, computer programmers, stock analysts, investment managers, bankers, engineers, accountants, underwriters, economists, market analysts, mathematicians, systems analysts, and more.

★3268★ Encyclopedia of Careers and Vocational Guidance

J. G. Ferguson Publishing Co.
200 W. Monroe, Ste. 250
Chicago, IL 60606
Ph: (312)580-5480

William E. Hopke. Ninth edition, 1993. $129.95; $199.95 (CD-ROM). Four-volume set that profiles 900 occupations and describes job trends in 71 industries. Includes career description, educational requirements, history of the job, methods of entry, advancement, employment outlook, earnings, conditions of work, social and psychological factors, and sources of further information. Contains career and employment information for this field.

★3269★ Jobs in Arts and Media Management: What They Are and How to Get One!

American Council for the Arts
1 E. 53rd St.
New York, NY 10022-4201
Ph: (212)223-2787   Fr: 800-321-4510

Stephen Langley and James Abruzzo. Revised edition, 1990. $21.95. 281 pages. Includes lists of about 150 sources of information on job opportunities in the arts, including organizations offering internships, job listings, graduate programs, and short-term study; professional groups concerned with theater, music, dance, opera, museum and gallery management, film, and telecommunication management. (Does not include popular music performing or music recording.) Entries include: For internships Organization name, address, phone, description, requirements. For job referral associations and periodicals - Association or publisher name, address, fields covered, services offered, turn-around time, average number of jobs, cost of subscription or dues, comments. Arrangement: Classified by type of source.

★3270★ Opportunities in Banking Careers

VGM Career Horizons
4255 W. Touhy Ave.
Lincolnwood, IL 60646-1975
Ph: (847)679-5500   Fax: (847)679-2494
Fr: 800-323-4900

Adrian A. Paradis. 1993. $14.95; $11.95 (paper). 160 pages. Discusses banking opportunities in a variety of settings: commercial banks, savings and loans, finance companies, and mortgage banks.

★3271★ Opportunities in Financial Careers

VGM Career Horizons
4255 W. Touhy Ave.
Lincolnwood, IL 60646-1975
Ph: (847)679-5500   Fax: (847)679-2494
Fr: 800-323-4900

Michael Sumichrast and Dean A. Christ. 1991. $14.95; $11.95 (paper). A guide to planning for and seeking opportunities in this challenging field.

★3272★ Opportunities in Hospital Administration Careers

VGM Career Horizons
4255 W. Touhy Ave.
Lincolnwood, IL 60646-1975
Ph: (847)679-5500   Fax: (847)679-2494
Fr: 800-323-4900

I. Donald Snook. 1989. $14.95; $11.95 (paper). 160 pages. Discusses opportunities for administrators in a variety of management settings: hospital, department, clinic, group practice, HMO, mental health, and extended care facilities.

★3273★ Where the Jobs Are: The Hottest Careers for the '90s

The Career Press, Inc.
3 Tice Rd.
PO Box 687
Franklin Lakes, NJ 07417
Ph: (201)848-0310   Fax: (201)848-1727
Fr: 800-237-3371

Joyce Hadley. Second edition, 1995. $9.99. 300 pages. Describes careers in fifteen general fields, from accounting to travel and hospitality.

EMPLOYMENT AGENCIES AND SEARCH FIRMS

★3274★ Accountants Overload Group

10990 Wilshire Blvd.
Los Angeles, CA 90024-3913
Ph: (213)629-2800

Employment agency.

★3275★ Addington Personnel Services

2401 Fountainview, Ste.104
Houston, TX 77057
Ph: (713)780-8810

Employment agency. Places individuals in regular or temporary positions.

★3276★ The Ahrens Agency, Inc.

3285 Wolfson Dr.
Baldwin, NY 11510
Ph: (516)223-5627

Employment agency. Fills positions in real estate and other fields.

★3277★ Cross Employment Agency

150 Broadway, Ste. 902
New York, NY 10038-4389
Ph: (212)227-6705

Employment agency. Temporary and regular placement of personnel.

★3278★ Don Richard Associates of Washington D.C.

1717 K St. NW, Ste. 1000
Washington, DC 20006-1587
Ph: (202)463-7210   Fax: (202)331-9743

Employment agency.

★3279★ Financial Professionals

4100 Spring Valley Rd.
Farmers Branch, TX 75244-3618
Ph: (214)991-8999

Executive search consultants.

★3280★ Financial Search Corp.

2720 Des Plaines Ave., Ste. 154
Des Plaines, IL 60018
Ph: (708)297-4900   Fax: (708)297-0294

Executive search firm.

★3281★ Jim King and Associates

1301 Gulf Life Dr., Ste. 1901
Jacksonville, FL 32207-9062
Ph: (904)398-5464

Employment agency.

★3282★ J.R. Scott and Associates

222 S. Riverside Plaza, Ste. 320
Chicago, IL 60606
Ph: (312)648-4630

Executive search firm specializing in retail securities sales, investment banking, and equity and debt trading.

★3283★ Kanon Personnel Inc.

8 W. 40th St., 11th Fl.
New York, NY 10018-3994
Ph: (212)391-2610

Employment agency.

★3284★ The Murphy Group

1211 W. 22nd St., Ste. 221
Oak Brook, IL 60521-2115
Ph: (708)574-2840

Employment agency. Places personnel in a variety of positions.

★3285★ New Boston Associates

146 Bowdoin St.
Boston, MA 02108-2797
Ph: (617)720-0990   Fax: (617)723-8822

Employment agency. Located in Boston, Woburn, and Quincy, Massachusetts.

★3286★ Phillip Thomas Personnel, Inc.

545 5th Ave., Ste., 606
New York, NY 10017
Ph: (212)867-0860

Employment agency.

★3287★ Rocky Mountain Recruiters, Inc.

1801 Broadway, Ste. 810
Denver, CO 80202
Ph: (303)296-2000

Executive search firm.

★3288★ Romac International, Inc.

120 Hyde Park Pl., Ste. 200
Tampa, FL 33606
Fr: 800-341-0263

Executive search firm. More than 30 locations throughout the U.S.

★3289★ Source Finance

5580 LBJ Fwy., Ste. 300
Dallas, TX 75240
Ph: (214)385-3002   Fax: (214)717-0075

Executive search firm. Many affiliate offices located in most major cities throughout the U.S.

OTHER SOURCES

★3290★ American Bankers Association (ABA)

1120 Connecticut Ave. NW
Washington, DC 20036
Ph: (202)663-5000   Fax: (202)663-7533

Members: Members are principally commercial banks and trust companies; combined assets of members represent approximately 90% of the U.S. banking industry; approximately 94% of members are community banks with less than $500 million in assets. **Purpose:** Seeks to enhance the role of commerical bankers as preeminent providers of financial services through communications, research, legal action, lobbying of federal legislative and regulatory bodies, and education and training programs. Serves as spokesperson for the banking industry; facilitates exchange of information among members. **Activities:** Maintains the American Institute of Banking, an industry-sponsored adult education program. Conducts educational and training programs for bank employees and officers through a wide range of banking schools and national conferences. Maintains liaison with federal bank regulators; submits draft legislation and lobbies Congress on issues affecting commercial banks; testifies before congressional committees; represents members in U.S. postal rate proceedings. Serves as secretariat of the International Monetary Conference and the Financial Institutions Committee for the American National Standards Institute. Files briefs and lawsuits in major court cases affecting the industry. Conducts teleconferences with state banking associations on such issues as regulatory compliance; works to build consensus and coordinate activities of leading bank and financial service trade groups.

★3291★ American Financial Services Association (AFSA)

919 18th St. NW
Washington, DC 20006
Ph: (202)296-5544   Fax: (202)223-0321

Members: Companies whose business is primarily direct credit lending to consumers and/or the purchase of sales finance paper on consumer goods. Some members have insurance and retail subsidiaries; some are themselves subsidiaries of highly diversified parent corporations. **Purpose:** Encourages the business of financing individuals and families for necessary and useful purposes, at reasonable charges, including interest; promotes consumer understanding of basic money management principles as well as constructive uses of consumer credit. Educational services include films, textbooks, and study units for the classroom and budgeting guides for individuals and families. Compiles statistical reports; offers seminars.

★3292★ American League of Financial Institutions (ALFI)

900 19th St. NW, Ste. 400
Washington, DC 20006
Ph: (202)857-3176   Fax: (202)296-8716

Members: Federal and state chartered minority savings and loan associations in 25 states and the District of Columbia. **Purpose:** Undertakes programs to increase the income of and savings flow into the associations including a direct solicitation effort; provides counseling and technical assistance for member associations; offers consultant services to assist individual associations and groups wishing to organize new associations or acquire existing associations with development potential; collects, organizes, and distributes materials that will aid member associations. **Activities:** Conducts research to improve investment capability, resolve common management problems, and evaluate statistical data on an industry-wide basis to develop and institute training programs for management personnel. Conducts research programs.

★3293★ Bank Administration Institute (BAI)

1 N. Franklin St.
Chicago, IL 60606
Ph: (312)553-4600   Fax: (312)683-2373
Fr: 800-323-8552

Purpose: Works to provide research, technical studies, publications, professional development programs, and advisory services to bank managers seeking to improve bank performance. **Activities:** Offers educational programs through conferences and research and technical studies in retail, payment systems, human resources, operations, lending, finance, executive education, audit, security, and compliance. Maintains The BAI School.

★3294★ Financial Executives Institute (FEI)

10 Madison Ave.
PO Box 1938
Morristown, NJ 07962-1938
Ph: (201)898-4600   Fax: (201)898-4649

Members: Professional organization of corporate financial executives performing duties of chief financial officer, controller, treasurer, or vice-president-finance. **Activities:** Sponsors research activities through its affiliated Financial Executives Research Foundation. Maintains offices in Toronto, Canada, and Washington, DC.

★3295★ Financial Managers Society (FMS)

8 S. Michigan Ave., Ste. 500
Chicago, IL 60603-3307
Ph: (312)578-1300   Fax: (312)578-1308

Purpose: Technical information exchange for financial managers of financial institutions.

★3296★ Risk and Insurance Management Society (RIMS)

655 3rd Ave., 2nd Fl.
New York, NY 10017
Ph: (212)286-9292   Fax: (212)986-9716

Members: Corporate risk, insurance, and employee benefits managers. **Purpose:** Exchanges ideas in the field of risk management, sponsors educational forums, and provides a basis for recommendations from risk manager to management. Aids in maintaining and fostering a competitive market in the public interest; supplies information to assist in the efficient purchase of insurance. Conducts research programs; compiles statistics. Maintains speakers' bureau.

★3297★ Robert Morris Associates - Association of Bank Loan and Credit Officers (RMA)

1 Liberty Pl.
1650 Market St., Ste. 2300
Philadelphia, PA 19103
Ph: (215)851-9100   Fax: (215)851-9206

Members: Commercial and savings banks and savings and loan institutions represented by more than 15,000 commercial loan and credit officers. **Activities:** Conducts research and professional development activities in areas of loan administration, asset management, and commercial lending and credit to increase professionalism. Named in honor of Robert Morris (1734-1806), a financier and politician. Provides Mentor training curriculum for commercial lending professionals. From more than 90,000 financial statements supplied by member institutions, annually compiles the Statement Studies containing average composite balance sheets for more than 360 different lines of business in manufacturing, wholesaling, retailing, and contracting.

★3298★ Society of Cost Estimating and Analysis (SCEA)

101 S. Whiting St., Ste. 201
Alexandria, VA 22304
Ph: (703)751-8069   Fax: (703)461-7328

Members: Individuals in cost estimating and analysis and price analysis-oriented professions. **Purpose:** Facilitates the professional association of the cost estimating and analysis disciplines; enhances the efficiency and effectiveness of cost estimating and analysis activities in proprietary industry, nonprofit organizations, and government. **Activities:** Activities include: identification of technical and ethical standards; establishment and maintenance of standards; assistance in the identification of qualified members for industry and government. Maintains code of ethics to promote cooperation and good relations among members of the profession and to enhance the stature of the profession. Provides certification program that supports technical and ethical standards through participation in oral workshops, involvement in professional programs, completion of accredited university courses, and successful completion of certification examination.

Fire Fighters

SOURCES OF HELP-WANTED ADS

★3299★ American City and County
Communication Channels, Inc.
6255 Barfield Rd.
Atlanta, GA 30328
Ph: (404)955-9970   Fax: (404)256-3116

Monthly. $54.00/year for individuals. Municipal and county administration magazine.

★3300★ American Fire Journal
9072 E. Artesia Blvd., Ste. 7
Bellflower, CA 90706-6299
Ph: (310)866-1664   Fax: (310)867-6434

Monthly. $19.95/year for individuals; $36.00/year for institutions, other countries; $3.00 for single issue. Magazine about fire protection.

★3301★ Fire News
National Fire Protection Association
  (NFPA)
1 Batterymarch Park
PO Box 9101
Quincy, MA 02269-9101
Ph: (617)770-3000   Fax: (617)770-0700

Bimonthly. Features calendar of events and lists job openings.

★3302★ Firefighter's News
Lifesaving Communications, Inc.
PO Box 100
Nassau, DE 19969-0100

Bimonthly. $15.00/year for individuals; $2.50 for single issue. Magazine (tabloid) reporting on issues affecting professional and volunteer fire and rescue personnel.

★3303★ Firehouse Magazine
PTN Publishing Co.
445 Broad Hollow Rd., Ste. 21
Melville, NY 11747
Ph: (516)845-2700   Fax: (516)845-7109

Monthly. Magazine focusing on fire protection.

★3304★ International Fire Fighter
International Association of Fire Fighters
1750 New York Ave. NW
Washington, DC 20006
Ph: (202)737-8484   Fax: (202)737-8418

Bimonthly. Free to qualified subscribers; $18.00/year for individuals. Union tabloid.

★3305★ The Municipality
League of Wisconsin Municipalities
122 W. Washington Ave., Ste. 301
Madison, WI 53703-2757
Ph: (608)267-2380   Fax: (608)267-0645

Monthly. Magazine for officials of Wisconsin's local municipal governments.

★3306★ NFPA Journal
National Fire Protection Association
  (NFPA)
1 Batterymarch Park
PO Box 9101
Quincy, MA 02269-9101
Ph: (617)770-3000   Fax: (617)770-0700

Bimonthly. $75.00/year.

★3307★ Western City
League of California Cities
1400 K St.
Sacramento, CA 95814
Ph: (916)444-5790   Fax: (916)658-8240

Monthly. $30.00/year for individuals; $49.00 for two years. Municipal interest magazine.

EMPLOYER DIRECTORIES AND NETWORKING LISTS

★3308★ American Fire Services
American Fire Services
39 Sherbrooke Ave.
Hartford, CT 06106-3839
Ph: (203)521-7056

Reported as biennial, Jan. of odd years; latest edition Nov. 1993. $50.00. Covers Approximately 2,700 municipal fire departments; coverage includes Canada. Entries include: Department name, headquarters address, fire station locations, number of employees, population, units geographical area served, description of operations, radio frequencies, chief/administrator, phone, statistics. Arrangement: Geographical. Indexes: Department name, geographical.

★3309★ Fellowship of Christian Firefighters International–Directory
Fellowship of Christian Firefighters
  International
Box 9324
Denver, CO 80209-0324
Ph: (303)861-7472

Biennial, odd years. Available to members only. Covers about 1,000 member Christian firefighters. Entries include: Name, address, phone. Arrangement: Alphabetical. Indexes: Local chapter.

★3310★ Handbook of the American Fire Service
American Fire Services
39 Sherbrooke Ave.
Hartford, CT 06106-3839
Ph: (203)521-7056

Biennial, latest edition January 1995. $50.00. Covers Approximately 46,000 municipal, state, federal, military, industrial, and private fire protection services and fire chiefs in the United States and Canada. Entries include: Organization name, address, phone, name and title of contact, stations, units, frequencies, apparatus, personnel, payscales, manning, population, area, hours worked per week, budget, organizational structure. Arrangement: Geographical.

★3311★ Municipal/County Directory Library Edition
Carroll Publishing
1058 Thomas Jefferson St. NW
Washington, DC 20007
Ph: (202)333-8620   Fax: (202)337-7020
Fr: 800-336-4240

Annual, July. $137.00, plus $8.00 shipping; payment must accompany order. Covers officials of 1,400 county governments (with populations over 25,000) and 2,000 municipalities (with populations over 1,000); includes elected, appointed, and career office holders. Entries include: Name, title, agency, address, phone. Arrangement: County officials are geographical, then by agency; municipal officials are by city. Indexes: personal name (with phone), agency.

★3312★ **Municipal Year Book**

Newman Books Ltd.
32 Vauxhall Bridge Rd.
London SW1V 2SS, England
Ph: 71 9736400   Fax: 71 2335057

Annual, December. $140.00, postpaid. Covers local and central government agencies and officials of the United Kingdom; municipal art galleries, associations, development organizations, fairs, libraries, museums, airports, and other local authorities. Entries include: Name of authority or governing agency, address, phone, fax, names of elected councillors, officers, names and titles of key personnel, contacts, population, and pay. Arrangement: Geographical. Indexes: Subject, place names.

★3313★ **National Directory of Fire Chiefs & Emergency Departments**

SPAN Publishing
1308 Main St.
Stevens Point, WI 54481
Ph: (715)345-2772   Fax: (715)345-7288
Fr: 800-647-7579

Annual, February. $49.00. Covers Approximately 38,000 fire and emergency departments in the U.S. Entries include: Department name, address, phone, fax, telex, county, name of chief. Arrangement: Geographical.

HANDBOOKS AND MANUALS

★3314★ **The Complete Firefighter's Exam Preparation Book**

Bob Adams, Inc.
260 Center St.
Holbrook, MA 02343
Ph: (617)767-8100   Fax: (617)767-0994
Fr: 800-872-5627

Norman Hall. 1991. $9.95. 272 pages. Includes complete practice exams, answer keys, and self-scoring tables; tips for boosting scores; advice for passing the physical examination; and a glossary of terms.

★3315★ **Fire Service Administration**

National Fire Protection Association
Batterymarch Pk.
Quincy, MA 02269
Ph: (617)770-3000   Fax: (617)770-0700
Fr: 800-344-3555

Nancy K. Grant. 1994. $53.50.

★3316★ **Opportunities in Fire Protection Services**

VGM Career Horizons
4255 W. Touhy Ave.
Lincolnwood, IL 60646-1975
Ph: (847)679-5500   Fax: (847)679-2494
Fr: 800-323-4900

Ronny J. Coleman. 1994. $14.95; $11.95 (paper). 160 pages. Surveys opportunities in local, state, and federal fire departments and forestry services, as well as with fire equipment and fire insurance companies. Contains bibliography and illustrations.

★3317★ **Opportunities in Vocational and Technical Careers**

VGM Career Horizons
4255 W. Touhy Ave.
Lincolnwood, IL 60646-1975
Ph: (847)679-5500   Fax: (847)679-2494
Fr: 800-323-4900

Adrian A. Paradis. 1992. $14.95; $11.95 (paper). 160 pages. Provides information on a variety of opportunities and advice on breaking into the field.

★3318★ **Professional Qualifications for Fire Inspector, Fire Investigator, and Fire Prevention Education Officer: NFPA 1031**

National Fire Protection Association
Batterymarch Pk.
Quincy, MA 02269
Ph: (617)770-3000   Fax: (617)770-0700
Fr: 800-344-3555

Compiled by the NFPA staff. 1993. $16.75.

OTHER SOURCES

★3319★ **International Association of Fire Chiefs (IAFC)**

4025 Fair Ridge Dr.
Fairfax, VA 22033-2868
Ph: (703)273-0911   Fax: (703)273-9363

Members: Fire Dept. chief officers, emergency services administrators and emergency medical services directors/managers and supervisors, career, volunteer, municipal and private, who are interested in improving fire, resuce, and EMS coverage to the general public. **Purpose:** Provides leadership to career and volunteer chiefs, chief fire officers and managers of emergency service organizations throughout the international community through vision, information, education, services and representation to enhance their professionalism and capabilities.

Fitness Trainers

Sources of Help-Wanted Ads

★3320★ **Physical Education Digest**

111 Kingsmount Blvd.
Sudbury, ON, Canada P3E 1K8
Ph: (705)675-7055   Fax: (705)675-5539

Quarterly. $24.00/year; $6.00/single issue. Trade magazine featuring health, sports, and fitness topics.

★3321★ **TennisPro**

U.S. Professional Tennis Registry
PO Box 4739
Hilton Head Island, SC 29938
Ph: (803)686-8732   Fax: (803)686-2033

Bimonthly. Included in membership. Focuses on programs and techniques for teaching tennis. Contains profiles of tennis teaching pros, and information about new equipment. Recurring features include columns titled Sport Science, New Drills, New Products, Sports Medicine, and Sport Psychology.

Placement and Job Referral Services

★3322★ **Exer-Safety Association (ESA)**

10151 University Blvd., No. 138
Orlando, FL 32817-1981
Ph: (407)677-9501

Members: Fitness instructors, personal trainers, health spas, YMCAs, community recreation departments, and hospital wellness programs. **Purpose:** To improve the qualifications of exercise instructors; to train instructors to develop safe exercise routines that will help people avoid injury while exercising; to prepare instructors for national certification. **Activities:** Offers training in aerobics and exercise and on the physiological aspects of exercise. Conducts exercise safety and research programs. Sponsors charitable program; maintains speakers' bureau. Offers placement and children's services.

★3323★ **National Athletic Trainers Association (NATA)**

2952 Stemmons Fwy., Ste. 200
Dallas, TX 75247-6103
Ph: (214)637-6282   Fax: (214)637-2206
Fr: 800-879-6282

Members: Athletic trainers from universities, colleges, and junior colleges; professional football, baseball, basketball, and ice hockey; high schools, preparatory schools, military establishments, sports medicine clinics, and business/industrial health programs. **Activities:** Maintains hall of fame and placement service. Conducts research programs; compiles statistics.

Employer Directories and Networking Lists

★3324★ **American Fitness Association— Fitness Directory**

American Fitness Association
6285 E. Spring St., Ste. 404
Long Beach, CA 90808
Ph: (310)596-8660

Annual, summer. Available to members only. Entries include: Name, address, phone, products or services, geographical area covered, sports and fitness interests. Arrangement: Alphabetical.

★3325★ **Exer-Safety Association— Member Directory**

Exer-Safety Association
10151 University Blvd., No. 138
Orlando, FL 32817-1981
Ph: (407)677-9501

Biennial, January of odd years. $25.00, plus $2.00 shipping. Covers over 6,000 fitness instructors, health clubs and spas, YMCA's, community recreation departments, aerobics studios, universities, hospital wellness programs, and others concerned with educational aspects of exercise; international coverage. Entries include: Member name, membership status, location (city, state, country). Arrangement: Geographical. Indexes: Member name.

★3326★ **Exercise and Physical Fitness Programs Directory**

American Business Directories, Inc.
American Business Information, Inc.
5711 S. 86th Cir.
Omaha, NE 68127
Ph: (402)593-4600   Fax: (402)331-1505

Annual. $560.00, payment with order. Number of listings: 7,843. Entries include: Name, address, phone (including area code), size of advertisement, year first in Yellow Pages, name of owner or manager, number of employees. Compiled from telephone company Yellow Pages, nationwide. Arrangement: Geographical.

★3327★ **Health Clubs Directory**

American Business Directories, Inc.
American Business Information, Inc.
5711 S. 86th Cir.
Omaha, NE 68127
Ph: (402)593-4600   Fax: (402)331-1505

Updated continuously; printed on request. $875.00, U.S. edition. Entries include: Name, address, phone (including area code). Compiled from telephone company Yellow Pages, nationwide. Arrangement: Geographical.

★3328★ **Health & Fitness Program Consultants Directory**

American Business Directories, Inc.
American Business Information, Inc.
5711 S. 86th Cir.
Omaha, NE 68127
Ph: (402)593-4600   Fax: (402)331-1505

Annual. $265.00, U.S. edition. Entries include: Name, address, phone (including area code), size of advertisement, year first in Yellow Pages, name of owner or manager, number of employees. Compiled from telephone company Yellow Pages, nationwide. Arrangement: Geographical.

★3329★ **Who's Who in Sports & Fitness**

American Fitness Association
6285 E. Spring St., Ste. 404
Long Beach, CA 90808
Ph: (310)596-8660

Annual, January. Available to members only. Entries include: Name, address, phone, biographical data, products or services, geographical area covered. Arrangement: Alphabetical. Indexes: Geographical.

HANDBOOKS AND MANUALS

★3330★ The Best Home-Based Businesses for the 90s

G.P. Putnam's Sons
Putnam Berkley Group
200 Madison Ave.
New York, NY 10016
Ph: (212)951-8400   Fr: 800-631-8571

Paul Edwards and Sarah Edwards. Second edition, 1994. $12.95. 400 pages. Profiles 95 businesses and careers that can be conducted from one's home. Lists sources of additional information.

★3331★ Careers in Health and Fitness

Rosen Publishing Group, Inc.
29 E. 21st St.
New York, NY 10010
Ph: (212)777-3017   Fax: (212)777-0277
Fr: 800-237-9932

Jackie Heron. Revised edition, 1990. $14.95. 160 pages. Contains occupational profiles for this field, including information on job duties, skills, advantages, basic equipment used, employment possibilities, certification, and salary.

★3332★ Careers Without College: Fitness Careers

New Careers Center
1515 23rd St.
Box 339-CT
Boulder, CO 80306
Ph: (303)447-1087

$7.95.

★3333★ Encyclopedia of Careers and Vocational Guidance

J. G. Ferguson Publishing Co.
200 W. Monroe, Ste. 250
Chicago, IL 60606
Ph: (312)580-5480

William E. Hopke. Ninth edition, 1993. $129.95; $199.95 (CD-ROM). Four-volume set that profiles 900 occupations and describes job trends in 71 industries. Includes career description, educational requirements, history of the job, methods of entry, advancement, employment outlook, earnings, conditions of work, social and psychological factors, and sources of further information. Contains career and employment information for this field.

★3334★ 100 Best Careers for the Year 2000

Prentice Hall General Reference
15 Columbus Cir.
New York, NY 10023
Ph: (212)373-8500   Fr: 800-223-2348

Shelly Field. 1992. $15.00 (paper). Covers 100 of the fastest growing jobs. The publication is divided into 11 general employment sections. Specific careers are covered within each section. Provides job description, responsibilities, employment opportunities, earnings, education and training, advance-

ment opportunities, and experience and qualifications for each occupation.

★3335★ Opportunities in Fitness Careers

VGM Career Horizons
4255 W. Touhy Ave.
Lincolnwood, IL 60646-1975
Ph: (847)679-5500   Fax: (847)679-2494
Fr: 800-323-4900

Jean Rosenbaum. 1992. $14.95; $11.95 (paper). Surveys fitness related careers. Describes career opportunities, education and experience needed, how to get into entry-level jobs and what income to expect. Schools are listed in the appendix.

★3336★ Opportunities in Recreation and Leisure

VGM Career Horizons
4255 W. Touhy Ave.
Lincolnwood, IL 60646-1975
Ph: (847)679-5500   Fax: (847)679-2494
Fr: 800-323-4900

Clayne R. Jensen and Jay H. Naylor. 1990. $14.95; $11.95 (paper). 160 pages. Presents information on pursuing a position in a variety of fields, including senior citizen recreation, corporate employee recreation programs, and urban fitness centers. Illustrated.

★3337★ Personal Fitness Trainer

Vocational Biographies, Inc.
PO Box 31
Sauk Centre, MN 56378

$2.00. Four pages. This career case history includes suggestions for finding employment.

★3338★ Personal Trainer Manual: The Resource for Fitness Instructors

American Council on Exercise
5820 Oberlin Dr., No. 102
San Diego, CA 92121-3743
Ph: (619)535-8227   Fax: (619)535-2709
Fr: 800-825-3636

Mitchell Sudy, editor. 1992. $34.95.

OTHER SOURCES

★3339★ ACE Fitness Matters

American Council on Exercise (ACE)
5820 Oberlin Dr., Ste. 102
San Diego, CA 92121-3787
Ph: (619)535-8227   Fax: (619)535-1778
Fr: 800-825-3636

Bimonthly. $17.95/year.

★3340★ American College of Sports Medicine (ACSM)

PO Box 1440
Indianapolis, IN 46206-1440
Ph: (317)637-9200   Fax: (317)634-7817

Purpose: Promotes and integrates scientific research, education, and practical applications of sports medicine and exercise science to maintain and enhance physical performance, fitness, health, and quality of life. **Activities:** Certifies fitness leaders, fitness instructors, exercise test technologists, exercise specialists, health/fitness program direc-

tors, and U.S. military fitness personnel. Grants continuing medical education (CME) and continuing education credits (CEC). Operates more than 50 committees.

★3341★ American Council on Exercise (ACE)

5820 Oberlin Dr., Ste. 102
San Diego, CA 92121-3787
Ph: (619)535-8227   Fax: (619)535-1778
Fr: 800-825-3636

Members: Certified fitness professionals and interested others. **Purpose:** Keeps fitness professionals aware of new information in the health and fitness industry. Offers continuing education programs and research and charitable programs.

★3342★ Aspire Higher: Sports Careers for Women

Cambridge Career Products
PO Box 2153
Dept. CC15
Charleston, WV 25328-2153
Ph: (304)744-9323   Fax: (304)744-9351
Fr: 800-468-4227

Video. $29.95. 24 minutes. This motivational video includes profiles of women who have succeeded in sports careers such as marketing, corporate fitness, sports journalism, coaching, and officiating.

★3343★ IDEA: International Association of Fitness Professionals (IDEA)

6190 Cornerstone Ct. E., Ste. 204
San Diego, CA 92121
Ph: (619)535-8979   Fax: (619)535-8234
Fr: 800-999-IDEA

Purpose: Provides continuing education for fitness professionals including; fitness instructors, personal trainers, program directors, and club/studio owners. **Activities:** Offers workshops for continuing education credits.

★3344★ National Federation of Professional Trainers (NFPT)

PO Box 4579
Lafayette, IN 47903
Ph: (317)447-3296   Fax: (317)447-3648

Purpose: Seeks to provide affordable, convenient, comprehensive, and applicable information; offer organizational certification credentials for consumer recognition of competence; provide certified affiliates with on ongoing education; establish a network of support, and provide professional products and services to trainers and consumers; and facilitate and encourage the exchange of ideas, knowledge, business experiences, and financial opportunities between all fitness administrators internationally. Offers educational programs.

★3345★ NFPT Review

National Federation of Professional Trainers (NFPT)
PO Box 4579
Lafayette, IN 47903
Ph: (317)447-3296   Fax: (317)447-3648

Monthly. Newsletter.

Flight Attendants

SOURCES OF HELP-WANTED ADS

★3346★ Flying
Hachette Filipacchi Magazines, Inc.
500 W. Putnam Ave.
Greenwich, CT 06830
Ph: (203)622-2700   Fax: (203)622-2725
Monthly. $18.97/year; $3.50 for single issue. General aviation magazine.

EMPLOYER DIRECTORIES AND NETWORKING LISTS

★3347★ Airline Companies Directory
American Business Directories, Inc.
American Business Information, Inc.
5711 S. 86th Cir.
Omaha, NE 68127
Ph: (402)593-4600   Fax: (402)331-1505
Annual. $255.00, U.S. edition. Entries include: Name, address, phone (including area code), size of advertisement, year first in Yellow Pages, name of owner or manager, number of employees. Compiled from telephone company Yellow Pages, nationwide. Arrangement: Geographical.

★3348★ National Air Transportation Association—Official Membership Directory
National Air Transportation Association
4226 King St.
Alexandria, VA 22302
Ph: (703)845-9000   Fax: (703)845-8176
Annual, October. $95.00. Covers more than 1,000 regular, associate, and affiliate members; regular members include airport service organizations, air taxi operators, and commuter airlines. Entries include: Company name, address, phone, fax number, name and title of contact. Arrangement: Regular members are classified by service; associate and affiliate members are alphabetical in separate sections. Indexes: Geographical.

★3349★ World Aviation Directory
Aviation Week Group
McGraw-Hill, Inc.
1200 G St. NW
Washington, DC 20005
Ph: (202)822-4600   Fax: (202)383-2388
Fr: 800-551-2015
Semiannual, March and September. $175.00. Covers aviation, aerospace, and missile manufacturers, including manufacturers of aircraft, spacecraft, piston and jet engines, and component manufacturers and major subcontractors; support services (fuel companies, repair stations, etc.); airports and heliports; airlines; government agencies and associations; airline caterers; air freight companies; international coverage. Arrangement: Classified by major activity (manufacturers, airlines, etc.). Indexes: Company and organization, personnel, product, trade name.

HANDBOOKS AND MANUALS

★3350★ Airline Flight Attendants
Chronicle Guidance Publications, Inc.
66 Aurora St.
PO Box 1190
Moravia, NY 13118-1190
Ph: (315)497-0330   Fax: (315)497-3359
Fr: 800-622-7284
Chronicle Guidance Staff. 1994. $2.00. Provides concise career information and sources of additional information.

★3351★ America's 50 Fastest Growing Jobs
JIST Works, Inc.
720 N. Park Ave.
Indianapolis, IN 46202
Ph: (317)264-3720   Fr: 800-648-5478
Third edition, 1995. $14.95. 288 pages. Each job profile explains the nature of the work, skills and abilities required, employment outlook, average earnings, related occupations, education and training requirements, and employment opportunities. Also contains career planning information and job search tips.

★3352★ Careers as a Flight Attendant: Flight to the Future
Rosen Publishing Group, Inc.
29 E. 21st St.
New York, NY 10010
Ph: (212)777-3017   Fax: (212)777-0277
Fr: 800-237-9932
Catherine Okray Lobus. Revised edition, 1994. $14.95. Discusses the work, personal characteristics of successful flight attendants, physical and educational qualifications, the application process, and airline training programs. Lists major airlines and outlines their application processes, policies and benefits, and training programs.

★3353★ The Complete Aviation/ Aerospace Career Guide
TAB/McGraw Hill, Inc.
PO Box 182607
Columbus, OH 43218
Ph: (614)759-3773   Fax: (614)759-3644
Fr: 800-722-4726
Robert Calderone. 1989. $15.95. A comprehensive guide to hundreds of aviation-related jobs. Provides job description, training requirements, advancement opportunities, and employment outlook.

★3354★ The Flight Attendant Career Guide
TK Enterprises
PO Box 6455
Delray Beach, FL 33484-6455
Ph: (407)495-4604
Tim Kirkwood. 1993. $14.95 (paper).

★3355★ Flying High in Travel
John Wiley and Sons
605 3rd Ave.
New York, NY 10158
Ph: (212)850-6000   Fr: 800-225-5945
Karen Rubin. Second edition, 1992. $19.95. 336 pages. A guide to careers and job hunting in the travel industry. Describes the many job opportunities available, from writing to hotel management to law. Includes information on educational preparation, training, and job hunting.

★3356★ *100 Best Careers for the Year 2000*

Prentice Hall General Reference
15 Columbus Cir.
New York, NY 10023
Ph: (212)373-8500   Fr: 800-223-2348

Shelly Field. 1992. $15.00 (paper). Covers 100 of the fastest growing jobs. The publication is divided into 11 general employment sections. Specific careers are covered within each section. Provides job description, responsibilities, employment opportunities, earnings, education and training, advancement opportunities, and experience and qualifications for each occupation.

★3357★ *Opportunities in Travel Careers*

VGM Career Horizons
4255 W. Touhy Ave.
Lincolnwood, IL 60646-1975
Ph: (847)679-5500   Fax: (847)679-2494
Fr: 800-323-4900

Robert Scott Milne. 1996. $14.95; $11.95 (paper). 160 pages. Discusses what the jobs are and where to find them in airlines, shipping lines, and railroads. Discusses related opportunities in hotels, motels, resorts, travel agencies, public relation firms, and recreation departments. Illustrated.

★3358★ *Opportunities in Vocational and Technical Careers*

VGM Career Horizons
4255 W. Touhy Ave.
Lincolnwood, IL 60646-1975
Ph: (847)679-5500   Fax: (847)679-2494
Fr: 800-323-4900

Adrian A. Paradis. 1992. $14.95; $11.95 (paper). 160 pages. Provides information on a variety of opportunities and advice on breaking into the field.

★3359★ *Travel Agent*

Prentice Hall
113 Sylvan Ave.
Rte. 9W
Englewood Cliffs, NJ 07632
Ph: (201)592-2000   Fr: 800-922-0579

Wilma Boyd. 1989. $14.95. 256 pages. Outlines entry-level positions in the airline, car rental, and hospitality industries as well as in travel agencies and related travel services. Explains travel agency operations, sales techniques, and the use of computers in travel services. Gives job hunting advice and sales tips.

OTHER SOURCES

★3360★ **Independent Federation of Flight Attendants (IFFA)**

720 Olive St., Ste. 1700
St. Louis, MO 63101
Ph: (314)621-1177   Fax: (314)621-3722

Members: Flight attendants employed by Trans World Airlines. **Purpose:** Works to establish, through collective bargaining, equitable wage and salary standards, shorter hours, and improved conditions of employment; to engage in civic, community, educational, legislative, social welfare, and other activities; to advance the economic security and social welfare of workers; to achieve greater in-flight safety for employees and the public. **Activities:** Maintains speakers' bureau.

Florists

Employer Directories and Networking Lists

★3361★ California State Floral Association—Directory

California State Floral Association
1715 Capitol Ave.
Sacramento, CA 95814
Ph: (916)448-5266   Fax: (916)446-1063

Irregular, latest edition January 1994. $35.00. Covers about 500 member growers, retailers, wholesalers and related firms. Entries include: Name, office address and phone, home address and phone. Arrangement: Geographical.

★3362★ Florists-Retail Directory

American Business Directories, Inc.
American Business Information, Inc.
5711 S. 86th Cir.
Omaha, NE 68127
Ph: (402)593-4600   Fax: (402)331-1505

Annual. $1,650.00, U.S. edition; $265.00, (Canad. ed.); payment with order. Entries include: Name, address, phone (including area code), size of advertisement, year first in Yellow Pages, name of owner or manager, number of employees. Regional editions available; please inquire. Compiled from telephone company Yellow Pages, nationwide. Arrangement: Geographical.

★3363★ Florists-Wholesale Directory

American Business Directories, Inc.
American Business Information, Inc.
5711 S. 86th Cir.
Omaha, NE 68127
Ph: (402)593-4600   Fax: (402)331-1505

Annual. $325.00, U.S. edition. Entries include: Name, address, phone (including area code), size of advertisement, year first in Yellow Pages, name of owner of manager, number of employees. Compiled from telephone company Yellow Pages, nationwide. Arrangement: Geographical.

★3364★ Michigan Florist—Membership Directory

Michigan Floral Association
5815 Executive Dr., Ste. B
PO Box 24065
Lansing, MI 48909
Ph: (517)394-2900   Fax: (517)394-3011
Fr: 800-968-6000

Annual, spring. $75.00. Publication includes: List of about 1,100 member floral retailers and wholesalers, nurseries and garden centers, and individual members. Entries include: Company name, owner's name, address, phone, type of business. Arrangement: Separate geographical and alphabetical lists.

★3365★ National Florist Directory and Buyer's Guide

National Florist Directory, Inc.
3309 E. Kings Hwy.
Paragould, AR 72450
Ph: (501)236-7731   Fax: (501)239-3561
Fr: 800-643-0100

Annual, October. $90.00. Covers over 45,000 retail florist shops, wholesale florists, greenhouses, nurseries, and manufacturers and suppliers of equipment and services to floral dealers. Entries include: Company name, address, phone, wire service affiliations. Arrangement: Separate geographical sections for retailers and wholesalers. Suppliers are classified by product.

★3366★ Nurseries Directory

American Business Directories, Inc.
American Business Information, Inc.
5711 S. 86th Cir.
Omaha, NE 68127
Ph: (402)593-4600   Fax: (402)331-1505

Updated continuously; printed on request. Entries include: Name, address, phone (including area code), size of advertisement, year first in Yellow Pages, name of owner or manager, number of employees. Compiled from telephone company Yellow Pages, nationwide. Arrangement: Geographical.

★3367★ Professional Floral Commentators-International—Directory

Professional Floral Commentators-
International (PFCI)
Society of American Florists
1601 Duke St.
Alexandria, VA 22314
Ph: (703)836-8700   Fax: (703)836-8705

Annual, fall. $28.50, plus $4.00 shipping. Covers about 80 member floral commentators. Entries include: Name, address, phone, professional affiliation, education, career data, interests, design and commentating techniques. Arrangement: Alphabetical.

★3368★ Teleflora Subscribers Directory

Teleflora
12233 W. Olympic Blvd., Ste. 118
Los Angeles, CA 90064
Ph: (213)826-5253   Fax: (213)207-1597
Fr: 800-421-2815

Bimonthly. Available only to Teleflora subscribers. Covers about 20,000 florists who subscribe to Teleflora, a flower delivery wire service; military bases and installations; Teleflora Canada; foreign affiliates; and suppliers of flower arranging materials and equipment. Indexes: Foreign cities served through headquarters only.

★3369★ Wholesale Florists and Florist Suppliers of America—Membership Directory

Wholesale Florists and Florist Suppliers of America
5313 Lee Hwy.
Arlington, VA 22207
Ph: (703)241-1100   Fax: (703)237-6438

September. $100.00. Number of listings: 1,275. Entries include: Company name, address, phone, names of executives, list of products or services. Arrangement: Geographical. Indexes: Alphabetical.

★3370★ Who's Who in Floriculture

Society of American Florists
1601 Duke St.
Alexandria, VA 22314
Ph: (703)836-8700   Fax: (703)836-8705

Biennial, latest edition February 1992. Available to members only. Covers 7,000 retailers, 500 growers, 550 wholesale florists, 120 manufacturers and wholesalers of supplies and hardgoods; 120 affiliated organizations, 400 associate individuals who are members of the Society of American Florists. Entries include: Company name, address, phone, telex, fax, name of principal executive, products or services, wire service memberships. Arrangement: Information given both geographically and alphabetically.

HANDBOOKS AND MANUALS

★3371★ Careers in Floriculture
Society of American Florists
1601 Duke St.
Alexandria, VA 22314
Ph: (703)836-8700   Fr: 800-336-4743
Free. 8-page brochure.

★3372★ Careers in Floriculture
Wholesale Florists and Florist Suppliers of America
PO Box 7308
Arlington, VA 22207
Ph: (703)241-1100
Brochure. Free. Discusses different careers in floriculture, including floral design and sales and greenhouse production.

★3373★ Careers for Plant Lovers and Other Green Thumb Types
VGM Career Horizons
NTC Publishing Group
4255 W. Touhy Ave.
Lincolnwood, IL 60646-1975
Ph: (847)679-5500   Fax: (847)679-2494
Fr: 800-323-4900
Blythe Camenson. 1995. $14.95; $9.95 (paper). 160 pages. Describes careers for people who love working with plants and flowers.

★3374★ Encyclopedia of Careers and Vocational Guidance
J. G. Ferguson Publishing Co.
200 W. Monroe, Ste. 250
Chicago, IL 60606
Ph: (312)580-5480
William E. Hopke. Ninth edition, 1993. $129.95; $199.95 (CD-ROM). Four-volume set that profiles 900 occupations and describes job trends in 71 industries. Includes career description, educational requirements, history of the job, methods of entry, advancement, employment outlook, earnings, conditions of work, social and psychological factors, and sources of further information. Contains career and employment information for this field.

★3375★ Floral Designers (Florists)
Chronicle Guidance Publications, Inc.
66 Aurora St.
PO Box 1190
Moravia, NY 13118-1190
Ph: (315)497-0330   Fax: (315)497-3359
Fr: 800-622-7284
Chronicle Guidance Staff. 1993. $2.00. Provides concise career information and sources of additional information.

★3376★ Florists: Careers in Floriculture
Chronicle Guidance Publications, Inc.
66 Aurora St.
PO Box 1190
Moravia, NY 13118-1190
Ph: (315)497-0330   Fax: (315)497-3359
Fr: 800-622-7284
Chronicle Guidance Staff. 1994. $2.00. Reprint of a journal article.

★3377★ Flowers for Sale: Growing and Marketing Cut Flowers
New Careers Center
1515 23rd St.
Box 339-CT
Boulder, CO 80306
Ph: (303)447-1087
Sturdivant. 1992. $15.95. Describes how to start a flower growing and selling business and profiles numerous successful flower businesses.

★3378★ How About a Floristry Career?
Rittners School of Floral Design
345 Marlborough St.
Boston, MA 02115
Ph: (617)267-3824
Brochure. 2 pages. Discusses career opportunities in floristry.

★3379★ Jobs Rated Almanac: Ranks the Best and Worst Jobs by More Than a Dozen Vital Criteria
John Wiley and Sons
605 Third Ave.
New York, NY 10158-0012
Ph: (212)850-6000   Fr: 800-225-5945
Les Krantz. Third edition, 1995. $16.95. 340 pages. Ranks 250 jobs by environment, salary, outlook, physical demands, stress, security, travel opportunities, and geographic location.

★3380★ Looking for a Job with a Future? Floral Wholesaling: A Growing Industry for Growth-Minded People
Wholesale Florists and Florists Suppliers of America, Inc.
PO Box 7308
Arlington, VA 22207
Ph: (703)241-1100
Free. 6-page pamphlet on the field of wholesale florists.

★3381★ The Now Profession: Floral Designing
Rittners School of Floral Design
345 Marlborough St.
Boston, MA 02115
Ph: (617)267-3824
Brochure. 8 pages. Covers employment opportunities, selfemployment, and other aspects of the profession. Also available on diskette for Windows or Mac.

★3382★ Opportunities in Horticulture Careers
VGM Career Horizons
NTC Publishing Group
4255 W. Touhy Ave.
Lincolnwood, IL 60646-1975
Ph: (847)679-5500   Fax: (847)679-2494
Fr: 800-323-4900
Jan Goldberg. 1995. $14.95; $11.95 (paper). 160 pages. Describes careers in horticulture, the nursery industry, and floriculture, among others.

★3383★ Owning and Managing a Florist Service
New Careers Center
1515 23rd St.
Box 339-CT
Boulder, CO 80306
Ph: (303)447-1087
Ramsey. 1995. $15.95. Covers different business options for florists.

★3384★ The Retail Florist Business
Interstate Publishers, Inc.
PO Box 50
Danville, IL 61834-0050
Ph: (217)446-0500   Fax: (217)446-9706
Fr: 800-843-4774
Peter B. Pfahl. Fifth edition, 1994. $45.25.

OTHER SOURCES

★3385★ Floral Design Career Video
Rittners School of Floral Design
345 Marlborough St.
Boston, MA 02115
Ph: (617)267-3824
Video. Available on 10-day free loan east of the Mississippi. 45 minutes. Includes a floral demonstration and discussion about floral designing as a career.

★3386★ Florists' Transworld Delivery Association (FTDA)
29200 Northwestern Hwy.
Southfield, MI 48034
Ph: (810)355-9300
Members: Retail florist shops in North America selling flowers, gifts, candy, and fruit by wire. **Purpose:** Conducts specialized advertising, education, and research programs; compiles statistics. Conducts ZIP code marketing service.

★3387★ Society of American Florists (SAF)
1601 Duke St.
Alexandria, VA 22314-3406
Ph: (703)836-8700   Fax: (703)836-8705
Fr: 800-336-4743
Members: Growers, wholesalers, retailers, and allied tradesmen in the floral industry. **Purpose:** Lobbies Congress on behalf of the industry; sponsors educational programs; promotes the floral industry; prepares materials for consumers and for high school and college students; provides business resources. Sponsors Floricultural Hall of Fame,

American Academy of Floriculture, American Floral Marketing Council, and Professional Floral Commentators - International. Compiles statistics; sponsors competitions.

★3388★ The Upstart Guide to Owning and Managing a Florist Service

Upstart Publishing Co., Inc.
163 Central Ave., Ste. 4
Dover, NH 03820-4043
Ph: (603)749-5071   Fax: (603)742-9121
Fr: 800-235-8866

1995. $15.95 (paper).

★3389★ Vocational Visions: Florist

Cambridge Career Products
PO Box 2153
Dept. CC15
Charleston, WV 25328-2153
Ph: (304)744-9323   Fax: (304)744-9351
Fr: 800-468-4227

Video. $39.95. 15 minutes. On-location interviews answer questions about educational requirements, skills needed, opportunities, and outlook for the future.

Foresters and Conservation Scientists

SOURCES OF HELP-WANTED ADS

★3390★ Appalachian Trailway News

Appalachian Trail Conference
PO Box 807
Harpers Ferry, WV 25425
Ph: (304)535-6331   Fax: (304)535-2667

$15.00/year for individuals. Magazine on hiking, Appalachian Trail protection, and general conservation issues.

★3391★ Earth Work

Student Conservation Association
PO Box 550, Rte. 12A, River Rd.
Charlestown, NH 03603-0550
Ph: (603)543-1700

Eleven issues/year. $29.95/year. Includes career information for those working in conservation.

★3392★ Environmental Opportunities

Environmental Opportunities
PO Box 788
Walpole, NH 03608
Ph: (603)756-4553

Monthly. $47.00/year. Lists full-time openings in environmental positions as well as short-term opportunities and internships.

★3393★ The Job Seeker

The Job Seeker
Rt. 2, Box 16, Dept. J
Warrens, WI 54666
Ph: (608)378-4290

Semimonthly. $19.50/year. Specializes "in environmental and natural resource vacancies nationwide." Lists current vacancies from federal, state, local, private, and nonprofit employers.

★3394★ Journal of Forestry

Society of American Foresters
5400 Grosvenor Ln.
Bethesda, MD 20814-2198
Ph: (301)897-8720   Fax: (301)897-3690

Monthly. Journal covering measurement, protection, management, and use of forests for wildlife, recreation, water, wilderness, and graying, as well as the growing and harvesting for timber and energy.

★3395★ Nature: International Weekly Journal of Science

Nature Publishing Co.
65 Bleecker St.
New York, NY 10012-2467
Ph: (212)477-9600   Fax: (212)505-1364

Weekly. Magazine covering science and technology, including the fields of biology, biochemistry, genetics, medicine, earth sciences, physics, pharmacology, and behavioral sciences.

★3396★ Park and Grounds Management

Madisen Publishing Division
PO Box 1936
Appleton, WI 54913-1936
Ph: (414)733-2301

Bimonthly. $16.00/year for individuals. Magazine for managers of large outdoor grounds areas: college campuses, public parks and schools, resort hotels, and golf courses, covering technical material relating to turf, trees, facilities, equipment, and products.

★3397★ Photogrammetric Engineering and Remote Sensing

American Society for Photogrammetry and Remote Sensing (ASPRS)
5410 Grosvenor Ln., Ste. 210
Bethesda, MD 20814-2160
Ph: (301)493-0290   Fax: (301)493-0208

Monthly. Free to members; $120.00/year for nonmembers. Provides technical information about the applications of photogrammetry, remote sensing, and geographic information systems.

PLACEMENT AND JOB REFERRAL SERVICES

★3398★ Korean Scientists and Engineers Association in America (KSEA)

6261 Executive Blvd.
Rockville, MD 20852
Ph: (301)984-7048   Fax: (301)984-1231

Members: Scientists and engineers holding single or advanced degrees. **Purpose:** Goals are to: promote friendship and mutuality among Korean and American scientists and engineers; contribute to Korea's scientific, technological, industrial, and economic developments; strengthen the scientific, technological, and cultural bonds between Korea and the U.S. Sponsors symposium. **Activities:** Maintains speakers' bureau, placement service, and biographical archives. Compiles statistics. Maintains 100 volume library of scientific handbooks and yearbooks in Korean.

★3399★ National Network of Minority Women in Science (MWIS)

Directorate for Education and Human Resources Programs
1333 H St. NW
Washington, DC 20005
Ph: (202)326-6757   Fax: (202)371-9849

Members: Asian, Black, Mexican American, Native American, and Puerto Rican women involved in science related professions; other interested persons. **Purpose:** Promotes the advancement of minority women in science fields and the improvement of the science and mathematics education and career awareness of minorities. Supports public policies and programs in science and technology that benefit minorities. **Activities:** Maintains placement servce. Compiles statistics; serves as clearinghouse for identifying minority women scientists. Offers writing and conference presentations, seminars, and workshops on minority women in science and local career conferences for students. Local chapters maintain speakers' bureaus, and children's services. **E-Mail:** ggilbert@aaas.org

★3400★ Natural Science for Youth Foundation (NSYF)

130 Azalea Dr.
Roswell, GA 30075
Ph: (404)594-9367   Fax: (404)594-7738

Purpose: Sponsors natural science centers, junior nature museums, native animal parks, and trailside museums. Provides information service. Conducts training courses in museum and nature center management. Maintains museum and placement service.

★3401★ Society for Range Management (SRM)

1839 York St.
Denver, CO 80206
Ph: (303)355-7070   Fax: (303)355-5059

Members: Professional international society of scientists, technicians, ranchers, administrators, teachers, and students interested in the study, use, and management of rangeland resources for livestock, wildlife, watershed, and recreation. **Activities:** Sponsors placement service.

★3402★ Student Conservation Association (SCA, Inc.)

PO Box 550, Rte. 12A, River Rd.
Charlestown, NH 03603-0550
Ph: (603)543-1700   Fax: (603)543-1828

Members: Individuals, foundations, corporations, and groups who support the association's programs. **Purpose:** In cooperation with the National Park Service, the U.S. Forest Service, and other federal, state, local, and private agencies which manage public lands and natural resources, the association offers educational programs for high school and college students and other adults to assist with the stewardship of national parks, forests, and other resource areas. **Activities:** High school participants build and repair structures and trails, and carry out ecological restoration work. College students and other adults assist professionals with wildlife research, wilderness management, environmental education, archaeological surveys, and other tasks. Conducts educational and vocational programs providing job skill training, work experience, and exposure to career options in natural resource fields. Operates AmeriCorps programs for Corporation for National Service.

EMPLOYER DIRECTORIES AND NETWORKING LISTS

★3403★ Agricultural Research Centres

Stockton Press
Groves Dictionaries
345 Park Ave. S., 10th Fl.
New York, NY 10010
Ph: (212)689-9200   Fr: 800-221-2123

Twelfth edition, 1995. $595.00. 1000 pages. Covers 2,000 main organizations controlling over 7,500 departments engaged in research in agriculture, fisheries, food, forestry, horticulture, and the veterinary sciences.

★3404★ American Men and Women of Science

R. R. Bowker Co.
Reed Reference Publishing
121 Chanlon Rd.
New Providence, NJ 07974
Ph: (908)464-6800   Fax: (908)665-6688
Fr: 800-521-8110

Triennial, latest edition January 1995. $106.00, per volume; $850.00, set. Covers over 123,000 U.S. and Canadian scientists active in the physical, biological, mathematical, computer science, and engineering fields; includes references to previous edition for deceased scientists and nonrespondents. Entries include: Name, address, education, personal and career data, memberships, honors and awards, research interest. Arrangement: Alphabetical. Indexes: Discipline (in separate volume).

★3405★ Association of Consulting Foresters—Membership Specialization Directory

Association of Consulting Foresters
5400 Grosvenor Ln., Ste. 300
Bethesda, MD 20814-2198
Ph: (301)530-6795   Fax: (301)530-5128

Annual, August. $18.00, postpaid. Covers nearly 450 member forestry consulting firms and professional foresters who earn the largest part of their income from consulting. Entries include: Name, address, phone, specialties, background, career data, staff (if a consulting firm), geographic area served, capabilities, including equipment available and foreign language proficiency. Arrangement: Alphabetical. Indexes: Name, office location, language, international capability.

★3406★ Conservation Directory

National Wildlife Federation
1400 16th St. NW
Washington, DC 20036
Ph: (202)790-4402   Fax: (202)442-7332
Fr: 800-432-6564

Annual, January. $20.00, plus shipping; payment with orders from individuals. Covers about 90 federal agencies, 600 national and international organizations, over 1,000 state government agencies and citizens groups, and 117 Canadian agencies and groups concerned with conservation of natural resources and preservation of the environment; colleges and universities with environmental education programs. Entries include: Agency name, address, branch or subsidiary office name and address, names and titles of key personnel, interests, activities, publications. Arrangement: Classified by type of organization. Indexes: Personal name, subject, publication title.

★3407★ Directory of National Environmental Organizations

U.S. Environmental Directories
Box 65156
St. Paul, MN 55165
Ph: (612)331-6050

Irregular, latest edition October 1994. $59.00, postpaid; payment must accompany order. Covers over 775 organizations outside of government concerned with the environment and conservation. Entries include: Or-

ganization name, address, phone, contact name, year established, number of members, short description of activities and aims. Arrangement: Alphabetical. Indexes: Subject, geographical, federal agency (with address and phone numbers).

★3408★ International Union of Societies of Foresters—Membership Directory

International Union of Societies of Foresters (IUSF)
c/o Society of American Foresters
5400 Grosvenor Ln.
Bethesda, MD 20816
Ph: (301)897-8720   Fax: (301)897-3690

Semiannual. Free. Covers approximately 34 national forestry societies representing over 34,000 individuals.

★3409★ Life Sciences Organizations and Agencies Directory

Gale Research
835 Penobscot Bldg.
Detroit, MI 48226-4094
Ph: (313)961-2242   Fax: (313)961-6083
Fr: 800-877-GALE

$175.00. Covers about 7,500 associations, government agencies, research centers, educational institutions, libraries and information centers, museums, consultants, electronic information services, and other organizations and agencies active in agriculture, biology, ecology, forestry, marine science, nutrition, wildlife and animal sciences, and other natural and life sciences. Entries include: Organization or agency name, address, phone, name and title of contact, description. Arrangement: Classified by type of organization. Indexes: Organization/agency name and keyword.

★3410★ National Directory Conservation Land Trusts

Land Trust Alliance
1319 F St. NW, Ste. 510
Washington, DC 20004-1106
Ph: (202)638-4725   Fax: (202)638-4730

Biennial, even years. Formerly *National Directory of Local and Regional Land Conservation Organizations*. Profiles 900 nonprofit land conservation organizations at the local and regional levels.

★3411★ National Parks: Index

U.S. National Park Service
1849 C St. NW
Washington, DC 20240
Ph: (202)512-2250

Biennial, odd years. $5.00, payment with order. Covers over 368 areas administered by the National Park Service, including parks, shores, historic sites, 80 national trails, and wild and scenic rivers. Entries include: Name, location, address, acreage (federal, non-federal, and gross), federal facilities, brief description. Arrangement: Most areas are geographical; wild and scenic rivers and national trails are alphabetical. Indexes: Alphabetical by area name.

★3412★ *Peterson's Job Opportunities in Engineering and Technology 1996*

Peterson's
PO Box 2123
Princeton, NJ 08543-2123
Ph: (609)243-9111   Fax: (609)243-9150
Fr: 800-338-3282

Compiled by the Peterson's staff. Annual. $19.95 paperback. 432 pages. Profiles 2,000 high-tech companies looking primarily for technical personnel in such fields as biotechnology, telecommunications, software, computers and peripherals, defense, and aerospace. Contains job-search strategies and career options to help match education and expertise to the job market. Indexed geographically, by industry, and by hiring needs.

★3413★ *Professional Workers in State Agricultural Experiment Stations and Other Cooperating State Institutions*

Cooperative State Research Service
U.S. Department of Agriculture
Ag Box 2202
Washington, DC 20250-2202

Annual, January. $15.00. Covers academic and research personnel in all agricultural, forestry, aquacultural, home economics, and animal husbandry fields at experiment stations and academic institutions with agricultural programs. Entries include: Station or institution name, address, phone; names of personnel; their degrees and titles; and, in some cases, individual phone numbers and Internet address. Arrangement: Geographical; personnel are listed by major scientific or administrative areas. Indexes: Personal name.

★3414★ *Scientific and Technical Organizations and Agencies Directory*

Gale Research
835 Penobscot Bldg.
Detroit, MI 48226-4094
Ph: (313)961-2242   Fax: (313)961-6083
Fr: 800-877-GALE

Irregular; latest edition December 1993. $195.00. Covers over 25,600 national and international organizations and agencies concerned with the physical and applied sciences, engineering, and technology, including associations, computer information services, consulting firms, educational institutions, foundations, government advisory organizations, federal government agencies, general grant and assistance programs, libraries and information centers, patent sources and services, research and development centers, scholarships, fellowships, and loans, science-technology centers, standards organizations, state academies of science, and state government agencies in the fields of aeronautics and space sciences, chemistry, computer science specialties, electronics, geography, geology, machinery, mathematics, metallurgy, meteorology, mineralogy, nuclear science, petroleum and gas, physics, plastics, transportation, water resources, and other areas. Entries include: Organization name, address, phone, and name of contact; additional descriptive text for most entries. Arrangement: Classified by type of organization. Indexes: Organization name/key word.

★3415★ *Who's Who in Technology*

Gale Research
835 Penobscot Bldg.
Detroit, MI 48226-4094
Ph: (313)961-2242   Fax: (313)961-6083
Fr: 800-877-GALE

Irregular, new edition expected June 1995. $380.00. Covers 38,000 engineers, scientists, inventors, and researchers. Entries include: Name, title, affiliation, address; personal, education, and career data; publications, patents; technical field of activity; area of expertise. Arrangement: Alphabetical. Indexes: Geographical, employer, technical discipline, expertise.

HANDBOOKS AND MANUALS

★3416★ *The Best Resumes for Scientists and Engineers*

John Wiley and Sons
605 3rd Ave.
New York, NY 10158
Ph: (212)850-6000   Fr: 800-225-5945

Adele Lewis. Second edition, 1993. $37.50; $14.95 (paper). Presents an extensive collection of scientific and engineering resumes, highlighting the important differences between these and resumes written for other occupations.

★3417★ *Career Information Center*

Macmillan Publishing Co.
200 Old Tappan Rd.
Old Tappan, NJ 07675
Ph: (609)461-6500   Fr: 800-223-2336

Visual Education Center Staff. Fifth edition, 1992. $229.00. This 13-volume set profiles over 600 occupations. Each occupational profile describes job duties, educational requirements, how to get the job, advancement possibilities, employment outlook, working conditions, earnings and benefits, and where to write for more information.

★3418★ *Career Information Question and Answer Sheet*

Society of American Foresters (SAF)
5400 Grosvenor Ln.
Bethesda, MD 20814-2198
Ph: (301)897-8720

Annual. 2 pages. Describes the differences between foresters and forestry technicians, including job duties, educational preparation, and employment opportunities.

★3419★ *Careers in the Environment*

VGM Career Horizons
NTC Publishing Group
4255 W. Touhy Ave.
Lincolnwood, IL 60646-1975
Ph: (847)679-5500   Fax: (847)679-2494
Fr: 800-323-4900

Michael Fasulo and Paul Walker. 1995. $17.95; $13.95 (paper). 160 pages. Comprehensive information on the diverse career opportunities available in environmental services.

★3420★ *Careers for Environmental Types and Others Who Respect the Earth*

VGM Career Horizons
NTC Publishing Group
4255 W. Touhy Ave.
Lincolnwood, IL 60646-1975
Ph: (847)679-5500   Fax: (847)679-2494
Fr: 800-323-4900

Jane Kinney and Mike Fasulo. 1993. $14.95; $9.95 (paper). 160 pages. Describes environmentally friendly positions with corporations, government, and environmental organizations.

★3421★ *Careers in National Park Service*

National Park Service
U.S. Department of the Interior
Public Information Office
PO Box 37127
Washington, DC 20013-7127
Ph: (202)208-5228

Booklet. Free. 20 pages. Information about the hiring process for park service opportunities.

★3422★ *Careers for Nature Lovers and Other Outdoor Types*

VGM Career Horizons
4255 W. Touhy Ave.
Lincolnwood, IL 60646-1975
Ph: (847)679-5500   Fax: (847)679-2494
Fr: 800-323-4900

Louise Miller. 1992. $12.95; $9.95 (paper). Examines career opportunities in biology, agriculture, landscaping, forestry and conservation, geology, and waste management, and pollution control. Offers insight into preparing for and finding outdoor jobs in federal and state government, as well as private industry.

★3423★ *Encyclopedia of Careers and Vocational Guidance*

J. G. Ferguson Publishing Co.
200 W. Monroe, Ste. 250
Chicago, IL 60606
Ph: (312)580-5480

William E. Hopke. Ninth edition, 1993. $129.95; $199.95 (CD-ROM). Four-volume set that profiles 900 occupations and describes job trends in 71 industries. Includes career description, educational requirements, history of the job, methods of entry, advancement, employment outlook, earnings, conditions of work, social and psychological factors, and sources of further information. Contains career and employment information for this field.

★3424★ *Job Opportunities in the Environment 1995*

Peterson's Guides, Inc.
PO Box 2123
Princeton, NJ 08543-2123
Ph: (609)243-9111   Fax: (609)243-9150
Fr: 800-225-0261

1994. $18.95 (paper).

★3425★ Liberal Arts Jobs: What They Are and How to Get Them

Peterson's
PO Box 2123
Princeton, NJ 08543-2123
Ph: (609)243-9111   Fax: (609)243-9150
Fr: 800-338-3282

Burton Jay Nadler. Second edition, 1989. $9.95. 153 pages. Presents a list of the top 20 fields for liberal arts majors, covering more than 300 job opportunities. Discusses strategies for going after those jobs, including guidance on the language of a successful job search, informational interviews, and making networking work.

★3426★ Make a Difference: Challenge Yourself with a Forest Service Career

U.S. Department of Agriculture
Forest Service
PO Box 96090
Washington, DC 20090-6090
Ph: (202)447-3760

Brochure. Free. 20 pages. Covers careers managing timber, land, wildlife, and water. Explains how to apply and qualifications needed for entry-level employment in forestry.

★3427★ Nature (Career Portraits)

VGM Career Horizons
NTC Publishing Group
4255 W. Touhy Ave.
Lincolnwood, IL 60646-1975
Ph: (847)679-5500   Fax: (847)679-2494
Fr: 800-323-4900

Marjorie Eberts. 1996. $13.95. 96 pages. Highlights a range of careers that focus on the environment, with descriptions of a typical day on the job and interactive exercises for readers.

★3428★ Now Hiring! Outdoor Jobs: The Insider's Guide to Gaining Seasonal & Year-Round Employment in America's National Parks and Forests

Progressive Media, Inc.
4556 University Way NE., Ste. 2222
Seattle, WA 98105
Ph: (206)545-7950   Fax: (206)545-7951

Kevin Lustgarten. 1993. $17.95 (paper).

★3429★ Opportunities in Biological Sciences

VGM Career Horizons
4255 W. Touhy Ave.
Lincolnwood, IL 60646-1975
Ph: (847)679-5500   Fax: (847)679-2494
Fr: 800-323-4900

Charles A. Winter. 1993. $14.95; $11.95 (paper). Identifies employers and outlines opportunities in plant and animal biology, biological specialties, biomedical sciences, applied biology, and other areas. Illustrated.

★3430★ Opportunities in Environmental Careers

VGM Career Horizons
4255 W. Touhy Ave.
Lincolnwood, IL 60646-1975
Ph: (847)679-5500   Fax: (847)679-2494
Fr: 800-323-4900

Odom Fanning. 1995. $14.95; $11.95 (pa-per). 160 pages. Describes a broad range of opportunities in fields such as environmental health, recreation, physics, and hygiene, and provides job search advice.

★3431★ Opportunities in Farming and Agriculture Careers

VGM Career Horizons
4255 W. Touhy Ave.
Lincolnwood, IL 60646-1975
Ph: (847)679-5500   Fax: (847)679-2494
Fr: 800-323-4900

William C. White and Donald N. Collins. 1995. $14.95; $11.95 (paper). 160 pages. Covers opportunities in such fields as agricultural engineering, management, experimental farming, agricultural sales, teaching, and others, and provides job-hunting advice. Illustrated.

★3432★ Opportunities in Forestry Careers

VGM Career Horizons
4255 W. Touhy Ave.
Lincolnwood, IL 60646-1975
Ph: (847)679-5500   Fax: (847)679-2494
Fr: 800-323-4900

Christopher M. Wille. 1992. $13.95; $10.95 (paper). 160 pages. Describes the forestry opportunities available in governmental agencies, commercial enterprises, education, and private conservation association, and how to pursue openings. Illustrated.

★3433★ Opportunities in State and Local Government Careers

VGM Career Horizons
4255 W. Touhy Ave.
Lincolnwood, IL 60646-1975
Ph: (847)679-5500   Fax: (847)679-2494
Fr: 800-323-4900

Neale Baxter. 1993. $13.95; $10.95 (paper). 160 pages. Points out the incentives and drawbacks of a government career. Describes hiring procedures and provides tips on filling out applications, taking physical and aptitude tests, handling interviews, and finding jobs. Describes the jobs in which 75% of all state and local government workers are employed. For each occupation, covers the nature of the work and the training required.

★3434★ A PhD Is Not Enough: A Guide to Survival in Science

Addison-Wesley Publishing Co., Inc.
1 Jacob Way
Reading, MA 01867
Ph: (617)944-3700   Fax: (617)942-1117
Fr: 800-447-2226

Peter J. Feibelman. 1993. $12.95 (paper).

★3435★ Resumes for Environmental Careers

VGM Career Horizons
NTC Publishing Group
4255 W. Touhy Ave.
Lincolnwood, IL 60646-1975
Ph: (847)679-5500   Fax: (847)679-2494
Fr: 800-323-4900

1994. $9.95. 160 pages. Provides resume advice tailored to people pursuing careers focusing on the environment. Includes sample resumes and cover letters.

★3436★ So You Want to Be a Forester

American Forestry Assn.
PO Box 2000
Washington, DC 20013
Ph: (202)667-3300

Booklet. Free. 16 pages. Includes information on job prospects and opportunities.

★3437★ View from the Top: Forest Service Research

Forest History Society, Inc.
701 Vickers Ave.
Durham, NC 27701
Ph: (919)682-9319

Keith R. Arnold. 1994. $16.95 (paper).

★3438★ A Wildlife Conservation Career for You

The Wildlife Society, Inc.
5410 Grosvenor Lane
Bethesda, MD 20814-2197
Ph: (301)897-9770

Booklet. $.50. 12 pages. Describes career opportunities in wildlife conservation.

OTHER SOURCES

★3439★ American Forests

1516 P St. NW
PO Box 2000
Washington, DC 20005
Ph: (202)667-3300   Fax: (202)667-7751
Fr: 800-368-5748

Members: A citizens' conservation organization working to advance the intelligent management and use of forests, soil, water, wildlife, and all other natural resources. **Purpose:** Promotes public appreciation of natural resources and the part they play in the social, recreational, and economic life of the U.S.

★3440★ American Society for Photogrammetry and Remote Sensing (ASPRS)

5410 Grosvenor Ln., Ste. 210
Bethesda, MD 20814-2160
Ph: (301)493-0290   Fax: (301)493-0208

Members: Firms, individuals, government employees, and academicians engaged in photogrammetry, photointerpretation, remote sensing, and geographic information systems and their application to such fields as archaeology, geographic information systems, military reconnaissance, urban planning, engineering, traffic surveys, meteorological observations, medicine, geology, forestry, agriculture, construction, and topographic mapping. **Activities:** Offers voluntary certification program open to persons associated with one or more functional area of photogrammetry, remote sensing, and GIS. Surveys the profession of private firms in photogrammetry and remote sensing in the areas of products and services.

★3441★ **Association of Consulting Foresters of America (ACF)**

5400 Grosvenor Ln., Ste. 300
Bethesda, MD 20814-2198
Ph: (301)530-6795   Fax: (301)530-5128

Members: Professional foresters in the field of applied forestry and forest utilization who work for private landowners or industry on a contract or contingency basis. Members must be graduates of an association-approved forestry school and have five years experience in forest administration and management. **Activities:** Provides client referral service. Compiles statistics. **E-Mail:** acf@igc.apc.org

★3442★ **Association for International Practical Training (AIPT)**

10400 Little Patuxent Pky. Ste. 250
Columbia, MD 21044
Ph: (410)997-2200   Fax: (410)992-3924

Purpose: Helps coordinate training around the world in fields such as travel, the culinary arts, and hotel management. **Activities:** Conducts programs in career development and hospitality/tourism exchanges. Operates a student exchange program. Provides reciprocal practical training experience for recent graduates from the U.S., Austria, Germany, Finland, France, Hungary, Ireland, Japan, Malaysia, Netherlands, Switzerland, and the United Kingdom. Arranges training programs in the U.S. and abroad. Serves as U.S. affiliate to IAESTE (International Association for the Exchange of Students for Technical Experience) and operates a Professional Visitors Program to arrange short-term educational and training visits to the U.S. **E-Mail:** aipt@aipt.org

★3443★ *Exploring a Profession in Forest Products*

Society of Wood Science and Technology
One Gifford Pinchot Dr.
Madison, WI 53705
Ph: (608)231-9347

Video. $10.00.

★3444★ **National Association of Conservation Districts (NACD)**

509 Capitol Ct. NE
Washington, DC 20002
Ph: (202)547-6223   Fax: (202)547-6450

Members: Soil and water conservation districts organized by the citizens of watersheds, counties, or communities under provisions of state laws. **Purpose:** Directs and coordinates, through local self-government efforts, the conservation and development of soil, water, and related natural resources. Districts include over 90% of the nation's privately owned land. **Activities:** Conducts educational programs and children's services.

★3445★ *Resumes for Scientific and Technical Careers*

VGM Career Horizons
NTC Publishing Group
4255 W. Touhy Ave.
Lincolnwood, IL 60646-1975
Ph: (847)679-5500   Fax: (847)679-2494
Fr: 800-323-4900

1994. $9.95. 160 pages. Provides resume advice for individuals interested in working in scientific and technical careers. Includes sample resumes and cover letters.

★3446★ *Salaries of Scientists, Engineers, and Technicians: A Summary of Salary Surveys*

Commission on Professionals in Science and Technology (CPST)
1500 Massachusetts Ave. NW, Ste. 831
Washington, DC 20005
Ph: (202)223-6995

1993.

★3447★ *Seasonal Employment*

U.S. National Park Service
PO Box 37127
Washington, DC 20013-7127
Ph: (202)208-5074

Updated as needed. Free. Publication includes: List of 10 regional offices and branches of the National Park Service that accept applications for seasonal jobs. Entries include: Name, address, phone, geographical area served. Principal content of publication is information on seasonal jobs offered by the National Park Services, with description of duties, qualifications, and application procedures for each type of job offered. Arrangement: Geographical.

★3448★ **Society of American Foresters (SAF)**

5400 Grosvenor Ln.
Bethesda, MD 20814
Ph: (301)897-8720   Fax: (301)897-3690

Members: Professional society of foresters and scientists working in related fields. **Purpose:** Serves as accrediting agency for professional forestry education. **Activities:** Provides professional training. Supports 28 subject-oriented working groups.

★3449★ *Summer Opportunities in Marine and Environmental Science*

Summer Opportunities Guide
38 Litchfield Rd.
Londonderry, NH 03053

Herriott and Herrin. Second edition, 1994. $14.95. 60 pages. Subtitled: "A Student's Guide to Jobs, Internships and Study, Camp and Travel Programs". Prepared for both high school and college students.

★3450★ *Working Holidays*

Central Bureau for Educational Visits & Exchanges
Seymour Mews House
Seymour Mews
London W1H 9PE, England
Ph: 71 4865101   Fax: 71 9355741

Annual, November. $9.99, postpaid. Covers 1,000 organizations offering short-term paid and voluntary work opportunities in Britain and over 70 countries worldwide, for periods of three days to a year or longer; jobs include archeological digs, au pair/childcare, children's projects, couriers, guides, monitors, teachers, work camps, conservation, community works, hotel work, farm work, teaching, simple construction, etc. Entries include: Organization name, address, name of contact, objectives, projects available, conditions and terms of work. Arrangement: Geographical, then by type of work. Indexes: Organization name.

Fund Raisers

SOURCES OF HELP-WANTED ADS

★3451★ The Chronicle of Philanthropy

The Chronicle of Philanthrophy
1255 23rd St. NW, Ste. 775
Washington, DC 20037
Ph: (202)466-1200   Fax: (202)466-2078

Biweekly. Magazine covering fundraising, philanthropy, and non-profit organizations. Includes information on tax rulings, new grants, and statistics, reports on grant makers, and profiles of foundations.

★3452★ Community Jobs: The Employment Newspaper for the Non-Profit Sector

ACCESS: Networking in the Public
  Interest
30 Irving Pl.
New York, NY 10003
Ph: (212)475-1001   Fax: (212)475-1199

Monthly. $69.00. Covers jobs and internships available with nonprofit organizations active in issues such as the environment, foreign policy, consumer advocacy, housing, education, etc. Entries include: Position title; name, address, and phone of contact; description, responsibilities; requirements; salary. Arrangement: Geographical.

★3453★ DM News

Mill Hollow Publications
19 W. 21st St.
New York, NY 10010
Ph: (212)741-2095   Fax: (212)633-9367

Weekly. Tabloid newspaper for publishers, fund raisers, financial marketers, catalogers, package goods advertisers and their agencies, and other marketers who use direct mail, mail order advertising, catalogs, or other direct response media to sell their products or services.

★3454★ The NonProfit Times

The Davis Information Group, Inc.
190 Tamarack Cir.
Skillman, NJ 08558-9662
Ph: (609)466-4600

Monthly. $39.00/year.

PLACEMENT AND JOB REFERRAL SERVICES

★3455★ Association of Professional Researchers for Advancement (APRA)

414 Plaza Dr., Ste. 209
Westmont, IL 60559
Ph: (708)655-0177   Fax: (708)655-0391

Members: Individuals involved in educational, medical, cultural, and religious organizations; fundraising consultants. **Purpose:** Facilitates education and dissemination of information about prospect research; encourages professional development and cooperative relationships among members. (Prospect research is aimed at securing gifts, grants, and charitable donations for nonprofit organizations.) **Activities:** Bestows Information Prospector Award; provides placement and speaker referral services. **E-Mail:** apra@adinsys.com

★3456★ Direct Mail Fundraisers Association (DMFA)

445 W. 45th St.
New York, NY 10036
Ph: (212)489-4929   Fax: (212)489-7155

Members: Fundraisers and fundraising consultants; list brokers, printers, and others from closely allied businesses. **Purpose:** Works to: help members in their professional efforts; promote and advance the direct mail fundraising industry; encourage an exchange of ideas among members; function as a clearinghouse through which trade news may be channeled, trade guidelines established, and ethical practices delineated. **Activities:** Maintains placement service; conducts seminars and workshops.

★3457★ Society for Nonprofit Organizations (SNPO)

6314 Odana Rd., Ste. 1
Madison, WI 53719
Ph: (608)274-9777   Fax: (608)274-9978
Fr: 800-424-7367

Members: Executive directors, staff, board members, volunteers, and other professionals who serve nonprofit organizations. **Purpose:** Purpose is to provide a forum for the exchange of information, knowledge, and ideas on strengthening and increasing productivity within nonprofit organizations and among their leaders. **Activities:** Offers professional support services, training and referral.

EMPLOYER DIRECTORIES AND NETWORKING LISTS

★3458★ American Association of Fund-Raising Counsel Membership Directory

American Association of Fund-Raising
  Counsel
25 W. 43rd St., Ste. 820
New York, NY 10036
Ph: (212)354-5799   Fax: (212)768-1795

Annual, January. Free. Covers member fundraising consulting firms. Entries include: Company name, address, phone, fax, geographical area served, types of clients, description of services. Arrangement: Alphabetical.

★3459★ Charitable Organizations of the U.S.

Gale Research
835 Penobscot Bldg.
Detroit, MI 48226-4094
Ph: (313)961-2242   Fax: (313)961-6083
Fr: 800-877-GALE

Latest edition 1992. $150.00. Covers Approximately 800 organizations in the U.S. actively soliciting funds from the public to support their charitable programs and activities. Entries include: Organization name, address, phone, telex, names and titles of key personnel, number of employees, financial data, description of services, projects, charitable programs, activities, product/service provided, history/purpose, fundraising methods, funding application information, supporters. Arrangement: Alphabetical. Indexes: Personal name, geographical, alphabetical/subject.

★3460★ Complete Guide to Public Employment

Impact Publications
9104-N Manassas Dr.
Manassas Park, VA 22111-5211
Ph: (703)361-7300   Fax: (703)335-9486

Ron and Caryl Krannich. Third edition, 1995. $19.95 (paper). List of federal, state, and local government agencies and departments, trade and professional associations, contracting and consulting firms, nonprofit organizations, foundations, research organizations, political support groups, and other organizations offering public service career opportunities. Entries include: Organization name, address, phone, name and title of contact. Arrangement: Classified by type of service. Indexes: Subject.

★3461★ Finding a Job in the Nonprofit Sector

The Taft Group
Gale Research
835 Penobscot Bldg.
Detroit, MI 48226-4094
Ph: (313)961-2242   Fax: (313)961-6083
Fr: 800-877-GALE

Published 1990. $95.00. Covers nearly 5,000 educational institutions, health and human services organizations, charities, social and recreational organizations, and cultural and historical societies in the U.S. Entries include: Organization name, address, phone, estimated annual income, description of activities, name and title of contact, representative job titles, typical employment requirements, application guidelines, number of employees, benefits, internship and training opportunities. Arrangement: Alphabetical. Indexes: Geographical, subject.

★3462★ Fund Raising Counselors & Organizations Directory

American Business Directories, Inc.
American Business Information, Inc.
5711 S. 86th Cir.
Omaha, NE 68127
Ph: (402)593-4600   Fax: (402)331-1505

Updated continuously; printed on request. $275.00, Please inquire. Covers Name, address, phone (including area code), size of advertisement, year first in Yellow Pages, name of owner or manager, number of employees. Compiled from telephone company Yellow Pages, nationwide. Arrangement: Geographical.

★3463★ Who's Who in Fundraising

National Society of Fund Raising
  Executives
1101 King St., Ste. 700
Alexandria, VA 22314
Ph: (703)684-0410   Fax: (703)684-0540
Fr: 800-666-FUND

Annual, January. Available to members only. Covers about 15,000 fund raisers and development officers for private and public non profit organizations. Entries include: Name, organization name, address, phone, fax. Arrangement: Classified by chapter, then alphabetical.

HANDBOOKS AND MANUALS

★3464★ Careers for Good Samaritans and Other Humanitarian Types

VGM Career Horizons
4255 W. Touhy Ave.
Lincolnwood, IL 60646-1975
Ph: (847)679-5500   Fax: (847)679-2494
Fr: 800-323-4900

Marjorie Eberts and Margaret Gisler. 1991. $12.95; $9.95 (paper). Contains hundreds of ideas for turning good work into paid work. Inventories opportunities in service organizations like the Red Cross, Goodwill, and the Salvation Army; religious groups, VISTA, the Peace Corps, and UNICEF; and agencies at all levels of the government.

★3465★ Encyclopedia of Careers and Vocational Guidance

J. G. Ferguson Publishing Co.
200 W. Monroe, Ste. 250
Chicago, IL 60606
Ph: (312)580-5480

William E. Hopke. Ninth edition, 1993. $129.95; $199.95 (CD-ROM). Four-volume set that profiles 900 occupations and describes job trends in 71 industries. Includes career description, educational requirements, history of the job, methods of entry, advancement, employment outlook, earnings, conditions of work, social and psychological factors, and sources of further information. Contains career and employment information for this field.

★3466★ Fund-Raisers

Chronicle Guidance Publications, Inc.
66 Aurora St.
PO Box 1190
Moravia, NY 13118-1190
Ph: (315)497-0330   Fax: (315)497-3359
Fr: 800-622-7284

Chronicle Guidance Staff. 1993. $2.00. Provides concise career information and sources of additional information.

★3467★ Fund-Raising Fundamentals: A Guide to Annual Giving for Professionals and Volunteers

John Wiley and Sons
605 Third Ave.
New York, NY 10158-0012
Ph: (212)850-6000   Fr: 800-225-5945

James M. Greenfield. 1994. $49.95; $19.95 (paper).

★3468★ Fund Raising 101: How to Raise Money for Charities

John Wiley and Sons
605 Third Ave.
New York, NY 10158-0012
Ph: (212)850-6000   Fr: 800-225-5945

William L. Doyle. 1993. $34.50. 237 pages.

★3469★ Jobs & Careers with Nonprofit Organizations

Impact Publications
9104N Manassas Dr.
Manassas Park, VA 22111-5211
Ph: (703)361-7300   Fax: (703)335-9486

Ron Krannich. 1995. $15.95 (paper).

★3470★ The Makings of a Philanthropic Fundraiser: The Instructive Example of Milton Murray

Jossey-Bass Inc.
350 Sansome St.
San Francisco, CA 94101
Ph: (415)433-1767   Fr: 800-223-2336

Ronald Alan Knott. 1992. $29.95. 237 pages.

★3471★ Non-Profits and Education Job Finder

Planning/Communications
7215 Oak Ave.
River Forest, IL 60305-1935
Ph: (708)366-5200   Fr: (888)366-5200

Daniel Lauber. 1996. $32.95; $16.95 (paper). 350 pages. Covers 1600 sources. Discusses how to use sources of non-profit sector job vacancies in a number of specialties and state-by-state, including job-matching services, job hotlines, specialty periodicals with job ads, salary surveys, and directories. Covers a variety of fields from education to religion. Includes chapters on resume and cover letter preparation and interviewing.

★3472★ Opportunities in Nonprofit Organizations

VGM Career Horizons
NTC Publishing Group
4255 W. Touhy Ave.
Lincolnwood, IL 60646-1975
Ph: (847)679-5500   Fax: (847)679-2494
Fr: 800-323-4900

Adrian Paradis. 1994. $14.95; $11.95 (paper). 160 pages. Covers a range of career opportunities with nonprofit organizations.

OTHER SOURCES

★3473★ Achieving Excellence in Fund Raising: A Comprehensive Guide to Principles, Strategies, and Methods

Jossey-Bass Inc.
350 Sansome St.
San Francisco, CA 94101
Ph: (415)433-1767   Fr: 800-223-2336

Henry A. Rosso and Associates. 1991. $38.95. 345 pages.

★3474★ The Corporate Contributions Handbook

Jossey-Bass Inc.
350 Sansome St.
San Francisco, CA 94101
Ph: (415)433-1767   Fr: 800-223-2336

James P. Shannon. 1991. $42.95. 440 pages.

★3475★ Earning More Funds: Fundraising Strategies

Publishers Distribution Service
6893 Sullivan Rd.
Grawn, MI 49637
Fax: 800-950-9793   Fr: 800-345-0096

1996. 196 pages. $19.95. A practical guide with applications to many areas of fundraising.

★3476★ Fund-Raising Regulation Report

John Wiley and Sons, Inc.
605 3rd Ave.
New York, NY 10158
Ph: (212)850-6000   Fax: (212)850-6799

Bimonthly. $96.00/year. Journal publishing information the impact of new laws on fundraising and charitable giving.

★3477★ National Directory of Nonprofit Organizations

Gale Research
835 Penobscot Bldg.
Detroit, MI 48226-4094
Ph: (313)961-2242   Fax: (313)961-6083
Fr: 800-877-GALE

Annual, spring. $425.00. Covers over 260,000 nonprofit organizations; volume 1 covers organizations with annual incomes of over $100,000; volume 2 covers organizations with incomes between $25,000 and $99,999. Entries include: Organization name, address, phone, annual income, IRS filing status, employer identification number, tax deductible status, activity description. Arrangement: Alphabetical. Indexes: Area of activity, geographical.

★3478★ Principles of Professional Fundraising

Jossey-Bass Inc.
350 Sansome St.
San Francisco, CA 94101
Ph: (415)433-1767   Fr: 800-223-2336

Joseph R. Mixer. 1993. $29.95. 255 pages.

★3479★ Successful Nonprofits

Development and Technical Assistance Center, Inc.
70 Audubon St.
New Haven, CT 06510
Ph: (203)772-1345   Fax: (203)777-1614
Fr: 800-788-5598

Quarterly. $18.00/year. Offers brief items on planning, management, and fund-raising.

General Managers and Top Executives

plan information for association executives and meeting planners.

SOURCES OF HELP-WANTED ADS

★3480★ CFO

CFO Publishing
253 Summer St.
Boston, MA 02210
Ph: (617)345-9700   Fax: (617)951-4090
Monthly. Business magazine for small to mid-sized companies.

★3481★ Forbes

Forbes, Inc.
60 5th Ave.
New York, NY 10011
Ph: (212)620-2200   Fr: 800-888-9896
Biweekly. Magazine reporting on industry, business and finance management.

★3482★ Industry Week

Peter Li
1100 Superior Ave.
Cleveland, OH 44114
Ph: (216)696-7000   Fax: (216)696-7670
Semimonthly. Magazine containing articles to help industry executives sharpen their managerial skills and increase their effectiveness.

★3483★ National Business Employment Weekly

Dow Jones & Co., Inc.
PO Box 300
Princeton, NJ 08543
Ph: (609)520-4306   Fax: (609)520-4309
Fr: 800-323-NBEW
Weekly. $52.00/year. Magazine (tabloid) containing help-wanted advertising from the regional editions of the Wall Street Journal. Includes statistics and articles about employment opportunities and career advancement.

★3484★ Western Association News

Western Assoc. News
13275 FIJI WAN, 4th Fl.
Marina Del Rey, CA 90292
Ph: (310)577-3700   Fax: (310)577-3715
Monthly. $48.00/year for individuals. Magazine containing management and meeting

PLACEMENT AND JOB REFERRAL SERVICES

★3485★ American Chamber of Commerce Executives (ACCE)

4232 King St.
Alexandria, VA 22302
Ph: (703)998-0072   Fax: (703)931-5624
Fr: 800-394-2223
Members: Professional society of chamber of commerce executives and staff members.

★3486★ American Society of Association Executives (ASAE)

1575 Eye St. NW
Washington, DC 20005
Ph: (202)626-2723   Fax: (202)371-8825
Members: Professional society of paid executives of national, state, and local trade, professional, and philanthropic associations. **Purpose:** Seeks to educate association executives on effective management, including: the proper objectives, functions, and activities of associations; the basic principles of association organization; the legal aspects of association activity; policies relating to association management; efficient methods, procedures, and techniques of association management; the responsibilities and professional standards of association executives. **Activities:** Maintains central resource center. Conducts referral, resume, guidance, and consultation services; compiles statistics in the form of reports, surveys, and studies; carries out research and education. Offer executive search services and insurance programs. Provides CEO center for chief staff executives. Conducts Certified Association Executive (CAE) program. **E-Mail:** asac@asae.asaenet.org

★3487★ National Black MBA Association (NBMBAA)

180 N. Michigan Ave., Ste. 1515
Chicago, IL 60601
Ph: (312)236-2622   Fax: (312)236-4131
Members: Business professionals, lawyers, accountants, and engineers concerned with the role of blacks who hold advanced management degrees. **Purpose:** Works to create economic and intellectual wealth for the black community. Encourages blacks to pursue continuing business education; assists students preparing to enter the business world. Provides programs for minority youths, students, and professionals, and entrepreneurs including workshops, panel discussions, and Destination MBA seminar. **Activities:** Sponsors job fairs. Works with graduate schools. Operates job placement service.

★3488★ National Society of Hispanic MBAs (NSHMBA)

PO Box 2903
Chicago, IL 60690-2903
Ph: (312)472-5545
Members: Hispanic individuals with Master of Business Administration degrees; MBA candidates; interested others. **Purpose:** Promotes business education among hispanics; works to increase hispanic representation in business. **Activities:** Sponsors speaker series and educational programs; maintains job bank.

★3489★ National Women's Economic Alliance Foundation (NWEAF)

1440 New York Ave. NW, Ste. 300
Washington, DC 20005
Ph: (202)393-5257   Fax: (202)639-8685
Members: Executive-level women and men. **Purpose:** Promotes dialogue among men and women in industry, business, and government. Focuses on professional, economic, and career concerns and how to address these issues within the framework of the free enterprise system. **Activities:** Offers placement service, conducts research programs.

EMPLOYER DIRECTORIES AND NETWORKING LISTS

★3490★ Dun & Bradstreet Reference Book of Corporate Managements

Dun & Bradstreet Information Services
Dun & Bradstreet Corp.
3 Sylvan Way
Parsippany, NJ 07054-3896
Ph: (201)605-6000   Fax: (201)605-6911
Fr: 800-526-0651

Annual, April. $785.00, lease basis; $635.00, for public libraries, lease basis. Covers nearly 200,000 presidents, directors, vice presidents, officers, and managers in 12,000 companies of greatest economic, marketing, and investment interests; those firms whose revenues are the highest in the United States. Arrangement: Alphabetical by company name. Indexes: Personal name (with abbreviated title and company affiliation), geographical, SIC code, advanced education institution, military affiliation.

★3491★ Financial World—FW 500 Fastest Growing Companies

Financial World Partners
1328 Broadway, 3rd Fl.
New York, NY 10001
Ph: (212)594-5030   Fax: (212)629-0026
Fr: 800-829-5916

Annual, every January. $3.95. Publication includes: Lists of 500 United States firms showing greatest growth in net earnings for the year. Entries include: Company name, rank, net earnings for two previous years, total assets, other financial and statistical data. Arrangement: Main list arranged by net earnings, other lists arranged by return on equity and other measures and by industry.

★3492★ Financial World—FW 200 Hottest Growth Companies

Financial World Partners
1328 Broadway, 3rd Fl.
New York, NY 10001
Ph: (212)594-5030   Fax: (212)629-0026

Annual, May. $3.95. Publication includes: List of companies selected on the basis of earnings per share growth rate over a 10-year period ending with current year; minimum growth rate used is 5 percent. Entries include: Company name, current and prior year's ranking, earnings growth rate (over prior 10 years), number of years of increase over prior 10 years, revenues, dividends per share, earnings per share for current year and 10 years ago. Arrangement: Classified by sales and earnings growth rate. Indexes: Company ranked within industry.

★3493★ Forbes—Up-and-Comers 200: Best Small Companies in America Issue

Forbes, Inc.
60 5th Ave.
New York, NY 10011
Ph: (212)620-2200   Fax: (212)620-1863

Annual, November. $4.50. Publication includes: List of 200 small companies judged to be exceptionally fast-growing on the basis

of 5-year return on equity and other qualitative measurements. Entries include: Company name, address; biographical data and compensation data on chief executive officer; financial data. Arrangement: Alphabetical. Indexes: Ranking.

★3494★ Fortune Directory

Fortune Directories
Time, Inc.
Time Life Bldg.
Rockefeller Center
New York, NY 10020
Ph: (212)586-1212

Annual, August. $25.00, payment with order. Covers combined, in a fall reprint, 500 largest United States industrial corporations (published in an April issue each year) and the Service 500 (published in a June issue). The Service 500 comprises 100-company rankings of each of the largest diversified service, and commercial banking companies, and 50-company rankings each of the largest, diversified financial, savings institutions, life insurance, retailing, transportation, and utility companies. Entries include: Company name, address, headquarters city, sales, assets, net income, market value, comparative earnings per share for ten years, names and titles of key personnel, phone, and various other statistical and financial information. Arrangement: Classified by annual sales, where appropriate; otherwise by assets; chart format. Indexes: Separate alphabetical indexes for industrials and service companies.

★3495★ Inc.—The Inc. 500 Issue

Inc. Publishing Corp.
38 Commercial Wharf
Boston, MA 02110
Ph: (617)248-8000   Fax: (617)248-8090
Fr: 800-842-1343

Annual, October. $3.50 postpaid. Publication includes: List of 500 fastest-growing privately held companies based on percentage increase in sales over the five year period prior to compilation of current year's list. Entries include: Company name, headquarters city, description of business, year founded, number of employees, sales five years earlier and currently, profitability range, and growth statistics. Arrangement: Ranked by sales growth.

★3496★ Inc.—The Inc. 100 Issue

The Goldhirsh Group
38 Commercial Wharf
Boston, MA 02110
Ph: (617)248-8000   Fax: (617)248-8090
Fr: 800-842-1343

Annual, May. $3.50, postpaid. Publication includes: List of 100 fastest-growing publicly held companies in manufacturing and service industries that had revenues greater than $100,000 but less than $25 million five years prior to compilation of current year's list. Entries include: Company name, headquarters city, type of business, date incorporated, date public, number of employees, return on equity, sales, and net income five years earlier and currently, and five-year growth rate. Arrangement: Ranked by sales growth.

★3497★ MBA Employment Guide Report

Association of MBA Executives
5 Summit Pl.
Branford, CT 06405

Database covers: more than 4,000 firms that employ persons with Master of Business Administration degrees. More detailed profiles are given for 100 firms selected on the basis of their on-campus recruitment activity. Custom reports are issued upon request at $10.00 per report. Database includes: For companies covered in detail: name, headquarters location, description of business, current recruitment objectives, employment policies, benefits offered, name and address of employment representative, financial data. For others: name, location, contact person and telephone number, parent company (if any), code for primary line of business.

★3498★ Million Dollar Directory Series

Dun & Bradstreet Information Services
Dun & Bradstreet Corp.
3 Sylvan Way
Parsippany, NJ 07054-3896
Ph: (201)605-6000   Fax: (201)605-6911
Fr: 800-526-0651

Annual, March. $1,350.00, lease basis; $1,225.00, for public libraries, lease basis. Covers 160,000 businesses with either a net worth of $500,000 or more, 250 or more employees at that location, or $25,000,000 or more in sales volume; includes industrial corporations, utilities, transportation companies, bank and trust companies, stock brokers, mutual and stock insurance companies, wholesalers, retailers, and domestic subsidiaries of foreign corporations. Arrangement: Alphabetical. Indexes: Geographical (with address and SIC), product by SIC (with address).

★3499★ Peterson's Job Opportunities in Business 1996

Peterson's
PO Box 2123
Princeton, NJ 08543-2123
Ph: (609)243-9111   Fax: (609)243-9150
Fr: 800-338-3282

Compiled by the Peterson's staff. Annual. $19.95 (paper). 416 pages. Profiles 2,000 companies that are hiring employees in a number of nontechnical fields, including financial services, management consulting, retailers, utilities, and consumer products companies. Contains job-search strategies and career options to help match education and expertise to the job market. Indexed geographically, by industry, and by hiring needs.

★3500★ Standard & Poor's Register of Corporations, Directors and Executives

Standard & Poor's
25 Broadway, 14th Fl.
New York, NY 10004
Ph: (212)208-8283   Fax: (212)412-0305

Annual, January; supplements in April, July, and October. $595.00, lease basis. Covers over 55,000 public and privately held corporations in the United States, including names and titles of over 400,000 officials (Volume 1); 70,000 biographies of directors and executives (Volume 2). Entries include: For companies, Name, address, phone, names of principal executives and accountants; primary bank, primary law firm, number of employees, estimated annual sales, outside directors, Standard Industrial Classification (SIC) code, product or service provided. For directors and executives, name, home and principal business addresses, date and place of birth, fraternal organization memberships, business affiliations. Arrangement: Alphabetical. Indexes: Volume 3 indexes companies geographically, by Standard Industrial Classification (SIC) code, and by corporate family groups.

HANDBOOKS AND MANUALS

★3501★ **Better Resumes for Executives and Professionals**

Barron's Educational Series, Inc.
250 Wireless Blvd.
PO Box 8040
Hauppauge, NY 11788
Ph: (516)434-3311   Fr: 800-645-3476

Robert F. Wilson. Second edition, 1991. $11.95 (paper). Explains how to write resumes and cover letters for executives and professionals in most fields.

★3502★ **Career Choices for the 90's for Students of Business**

Walker and Company
435 Hudson St.
New York, NY 10014
Ph: (212)727-8300   Fax: (212)727-0984
Fr: 800-289-2553

Prepared by the Career Associates staff. 1990. $9.95. 166 pages. Discusses alternatives for students of business. Offers advice on how to break into the field and how to move up. Covers where and who the employers are, internship possibilities, and professional networking associations. Comprehensive guide to career and job search planning.

★3503★ **Career Choices for the 90's for Students Considering an MBA**

Walker and Company
435 Hudson St.
New York, NY 10014
Ph: (212)727-8300   Fax: (212)727-0984
Fr: 800-289-2553

Prepared by the Career Associates staff. 1990. $8.95. 166 pages. Discusses career alternatives and offers advice on how to break in and move up. Covers where and who the employers are, internship possibilities, and professional networking associations. Comprehensive guide to career and job search planning.

★3504★ **Careers in Business**

VGM Career Horizons
4255 W. Touhy Ave.
Lincolnwood, IL 60646-1975
Ph: (847)679-5500   Fax: (847)679-2494
Fr: 800-323-4900

Lila B. Stair and Dorothy Domkowski. 1992. $17.95; $13.95 (paper). 196 pages. Examines careers and job opportunities in busi-

ness, including management and supervision. A separate chapter sketches the entrepreneurial opportunities of consulting or owning a small business.

★3505★ **Encyclopedia of Careers and Vocational Guidance**

J. G. Ferguson Publishing Co.
200 W. Monroe, Ste. 250
Chicago, IL 60606
Ph: (312)580-5480

William E. Hopke. Ninth edition, 1993. $129.95; $199.95 (CD-ROM). Four-volume set that profiles 900 occupations and describes job trends in 71 industries. Includes career description, educational requirements, history of the job, methods of entry, advancement, employment outlook, earnings, conditions of work, social and psychological factors, and sources of further information. Contains career and employment information for this field.

★3506★ **Opportunities in Business Management Careers**

VGM Career Horizons
4255 W. Touhy Ave.
Lincolnwood, IL 60646-1975
Ph: (847)679-5500   Fax: (847)679-2494
Fr: 800-323-4900

Irene Place. 1991. $14.95; $11.95 (paper). 160 pages. Provides guidance on the most effective channels to management positions.

★3507★ **Rites of Passage at $100,000-Plus: The Insider's Guide to Absolutely Everything About Executive Job-Changing**

Henry Holt
John Lucht. Revised edition, 1993. $29.95. 640 pages. Aimed at top executives, this book covers a range of topics from networking and personal contacts to direct mail, resumes, references, interviewing, and negotiating. Includes large section on dealing with recruiters.

EMPLOYMENT AGENCIES AND SEARCH FIRMS

★3508★ **Boyden**

375 Park Ave., Ste. 1008
New York, NY 10152
Ph: (212)980-6480

Executive search firm. Affiliate offices across the country and abroad.

★3509★ **Dunhill Personnel Systems, Inc.**

1000 Woodbury Rd.
Woodbury, NY 11797
Ph: (516)364-8800   Fax: (516)364-8920

Executive search firm. Over 300 affiliated locations coast-to-coast.

★3510★ **Egon Zehnder International Inc.**

55 E. 59th St., 14th Fl.
New York, NY 10022
Ph: (212)838-9199   Fax: (212)750-0574

Executive search firm. A number of U.S. and foreign affiliate offices.

★3511★ **Fox-Morris**

1617 JFK Blvd., Ste. 210
Philadelphia, PA 19103
Ph: (215)561-6300   Fax: (215)561-6333

Executive search firm. Branch locations in many states throughout the U.S.

★3512★ **Heidrick and Struggles, Inc.**

125 S. Wacker Dr., Ste. 2800
Chicago, IL 60606-4590
Ph: (312)372-8811   Fax: (312)372-8641

Executive search firm. International organization with a variety of affiliate offices.

★3513★ **Korn/Ferry International**

237 Park Ave.
New York, NY 10017
Ph: (212)687-1834   Fax: (212)986-5684

Executive search firm. International organization with a variety of affiliate offices.

★3514★ **Management Recruiters International, Inc. (MRI)**

1127 Euclid Ave., Ste. 1400
Cleveland, OH 44115-1638
Ph: (216)696-1122

Executive search firm. More than 300 offices throughout the U.S.

★3515★ **Roth Young Executive Recruiters**

4620 W. 77th St., Ste. 290
Minneapolis, MN 55435
Ph: (612)831-6655

Executive search firm. Over 25 affiliated offices across the nation.

★3516★ **Russell Reynolds Associates, Inc.**

200 Park Ave.
New York, NY 10166-0002
Ph: (212)351-2000   Fax: (212)370-0896

Executive search firm. Affiliate offices across the country and abroad.

★3517★ **Sanford Rose Associates (SRA Intern)**

265 S. Main St., Ste. 100
Akron, OH 44308
Ph: (216)762-7162

Executive search firm. Over 80 franchised office locations nationwide.

★3518★ **Snelling Personnel Services**

4000 S. Tamiami Tr., Ste. 407
Sarasota, FL 34231
Ph: (813)923-3611   Fax: (813)925-2360

Employment agency. Over 50 offices across the country.

★3519★ **SpencerStuart**

277 Park Ave., 29th Fl.
New York, NY 10172
Ph: (212)336-0200

Executive search firm. A number of U.S. and foreign affiliate offices.

★3520★ **Ward Howell International Inc.**

99 Park Ave., 20th Fl.
New York, NY 10016-1699
Ph: (212)697-3730

Executive search firm. International organization with a variety of affiliate locations.

OTHER SOURCES

★3521★ *American Almanac of Jobs and Salaries 1994-95*

Avon Books
1350 Avenue of the Americas, 2nd Fl.
New York, NY 10019
Ph: (212)261-6800   Fr: 800-238-0658

John Wright. Revised edition, 1993. $17.00. 704 pages. This is a comprehensive guide to the wages of hundreds of occupations in a wide variety of industries and organizations.

★3522★ **American Management Association (AMA)**

135 W. 50th St.
New York, NY 10020-1201
Ph: (212)586-8100   Fax: (212)903-8168

Members: American Management Association provides educational forums worldwide where members and their colleagues learn superior, practical business skills and explore best practices of world-class organizations through interaction with each other and expert faculty practitioners. **Purpose:** AMA's publishing program provides tools individuals use to extend learning beyond the classroom in a process of life-long professional growth and development through education.

★3523★ **Center for Creative Leadership (CCL)**

PO Box 26300
Greensboro, NC 27438-6300
Ph: (910)288-7210   Fax: (910)288-3999

Members: Upper- and middle-level managers in the fields of education, business, government, and public service. **Purpose:** Seeks to improve management practices. Sponsors management development programs; conducts research projects involving managerial jobs.

★3524★ **The International Alliance, An Association of Executive and Professional Women (TIA)**

8600 LaSalle Rd., Ste. 617
Baltimore, MD 21286
Ph: (410)472-4221   Fax: (410)472-2920

Members: Local networks comprising 7000 professional and executive women; individual businesswomen without a network affiliation are alliance associates. **Purpose:** To promote recognition of the achievements of women in business; encourage placement of women in senior executive positions; maintain high standards of professional competence among members. Facilitates communication on an international scale among professional women's networks and their members. Represents members' interests before policymakers in business and government. **Activities:** Sponsors programs that support equal opportunity and enhance members' business and professional skills.

★3525★ **National Association of Corporate Directors (NACD)**

1707 L St. NW, Ste. 560
Washington, DC 20036
Ph: (202)775-0509   Fax: (202)775-4857

Members: Corporate directors and boards of directors; chief executive officers, presidents, accountants, lawyers, consultants, and other executives are members. **Activities:** Conducts research, surveys, and seminars.

★3526★ **National Management Association (NMA)**

2210 Arbor Blvd.
Dayton, OH 45439
Ph: (513)294-0421   Fax: (513)294-2374

Members: Business and industrial management personnel; membership comes from supervisory level, with the remainder from middle management and above. **Purpose:** Seeks to develop and recognize management as a profession and to promote the free enterprise system. Prepares chapter programs on basic management, management policy and practice, communications, human behavior, industrial relations, economics, political education, and liberal education. Maintains speakers' bureau and hall of fame. Maintains educational, charitable, and research programs. Sponsors charitable programs.

★3527★ **Women in Management (WIM)**

30 N. Michigan Ave., Ste. 508
Chicago, IL 60602
Ph: (312)263-3636   Fax: (312)372-8738

Purpose: Support network of women in professional and management positions that facilitates the exchange of experience and ideas. Promotes self-growth in management; provides speakers who are successful in management; sponsors workshops and special interest groups to discuss problems and share job experiences.

Geographers

SOURCES OF HELP-WANTED ADS

★3528★ *Photogrammetric Engineering and Remote Sensing*

American Society for Photogrammetry and Remote Sensing (ASPRS)
5410 Grosvenor Ln., Ste. 210
Bethesda, MD 20814-2160
Ph: (301)493-0290   Fax: (301)493-0208

Monthly. Free to members; $120.00/year for nonmembers. Provides technical information about the applications of photogrammetry, remote sensing, and geographic information systems.

PLACEMENT AND JOB REFERRAL SERVICES

★3529★ African Studies Association (ASA)

Emory University
Credit Union Bldg.
Atlanta, GA 30322
Ph: (404)329-6410   Fax: (404)329-6433

Members: Persons specializing in teaching, writing, or research on Africa including political scientists, historians, geographers, anthropologists, economists, librarians, linguists, and government officials; persons who are studying African subjects; institutional members are universities, libraries, government agencies, and others interested in receiving information about Africa. **Purpose:** Seeks to foster communication and to stimulate research among scholars on Africa. **Activities:** Sponsors placement service; conducts panels and discussion groups; presents exhibits and films. **E-Mail:** africa@mony.edu

★3530★ Association of American Geographers (AAG)

1710 16th St. NW
Washington, DC 20009-3198
Ph: (202)234-1450   Fax: (202)234-2744

Members: Professional society of educators and scientists in the field of geography. **Purpose:** Seeks to further professional investigations in geography and to encourage the application of geographic research in education, government, and business. **Activities:** Conducts research; maintains placement service; compiles statistics. **E-Mail:** gala@aag.org

★3531★ Social Sciences Services and Resources

PO Box 153
Wasco, IL 60183
Ph: (708)897-5345

Members: Consulting associates in social sciences. **Purpose:** Established to advance the teaching, consulting, and practice of the social sciences basic disciplines including sociology, anthropology, political science, geography, history, economics, and their applied disciplines: social work, community development, planning, and public administration. Serves as: a center for dissemination of current and comprehensive social research findings. Provides consultants for citizen groups, community projects, and governmental units on written request. Upon request from colleges, school boards, and citizens groups, conducts in-service workshops on teaching, consulting, and new developments in the social sciences. Provides consultant evaluation services for small colleges throughout the U.S. **Activities:** Maintains speakers' bureau and placement information service. Conducts research programs.

EMPLOYER DIRECTORIES AND NETWORKING LISTS

★3532★ *AAG Geography Department Guide*

Association of American Geographers (AAG)
1710 16th St. NW
Washington, DC 20009-3198
Ph: (202)234-1450   Fax: (202)234-2744

Annual.

★3533★ *Association of American Geographers Directory*

Association of American Geographers (AAG)
1710 16th St. NW
Washington, DC 20009-3198
Ph: (202)234-1450   Fax: (202)234-2744

Annual.

HANDBOOKS AND MANUALS

★3534★ *Careers in Geography*

Association of American Geographers
1710 16th St., NW
Washington, DC 20009
Ph: (202)234-1450

Salvatore J. Natoli. Sixth edition, 1994. $3.00. Focuses on job opportunities in geography in many areas, including business, government, planning and teaching. Includes a membership directory which may be used for networking purposes.

★3535★ *Geographers*

Chronicle Guidance Publications, Inc.
66 Aurora St.
PO Box 1190
Moravia, NY 13118-1190
Ph: (315)497-0330   Fax: (315)497-3359
Fr: 800-622-7284

Chronicle Guidance Staff. 1992. $2.00. Provides concise career information and sources of additional information.

★3536★ Geography: Today's Career for Tomorrow

Chronicle Guidance Publications, Inc.
66 Aurora St.
PO Box 1190
Moravia, NY 13118-1190
Ph: (315)497-0330   Fax: (315)497-3359
Fr: 800-622-7284

Chronicle Guidance Staff. 1993. $2.00. Article reprint from current professional journal.

★3537★ Opportunities in Social Science Careers

VGM Career Horizons
4255 W. Touhy Ave.
Lincolnwood, IL 60646-1975
Ph: (847)679-5500   Fax: (847)679-2494
Fr: 800-323-4900

Rosanne J. Marek. 1990. $14.95; $11.95 (paper). 160 pages. Profiles job opportunities in education, government, and business, along with their salary levels and outlook in the years to come. Illustrated.

OTHER SOURCES

★3538★ AAG Newsletter

Association of American Geographers (AAG)
1710 16th St. NW
Washington, DC 20009-3198
Ph: (202)234-1450   Fax: (202)234-2744
Monthly.

★3539★ American Society for Photogrammetry and Remote Sensing (ASPRS)

5410 Grosvenor Ln., Ste. 210
Bethesda, MD 20814-2160
Ph: (301)493-0290   Fax: (301)493-0208

Members: Firms, individuals, government employees, and academicians engaged in photogrammetry, photointerpretation, remote sensing, and geographic information systems and their application to such fields as archaeology, geographic information systems, military reconnaissance, urban planning, engineering, traffic surveys, meteorological observations, medicine, geology, forestry, agriculture, construction, and topographic mapping. **Activities:** Offers voluntary certification program open to persons associated with one or more functional area of photogrammetry, remote sensing, and GIS. Surveys the profession of private firms in photogrammetry and remote sensing in the areas of products and services.

★3540★ Base Line

Map and Geography Round Table (MAGERT)
American Library Association (ALA)
50 E. Huron St.
Chicago, IL 60611
Ph: (312)280-3205   Fax: (312)280-3257
Fr: 800-545-2433

Bimonthly. Included in membership; $15.00/year for nonmembers and Canada; $20.00/year elsewhere. Provides current information on cartographic materials, publications of interest to map and geography librarians, related government activities, and map librarianship. Recurring features include conference and meeting information, news of research, job listings, and columns by the Division chair and the editor.

★3541★ National Council for Geographic Education (NCGE)

Indiana University of Pennsylvania
16A Leonard Hall
Indiana, PA 15705
Ph: (412)357-6290   Fax: (412)357-7708

Members: Teachers of geography and social studies in elementary and secondary schools, colleges, and universities; geographers in governmental agencies and private businesses. **Purpose:** Encourages the training of teachers in geographic concepts, practices, teaching methods, and techniques; works to develop effective geographic educational programs in schools and colleges and with adult groups; stimulates the production and use of accurate and understandable geographic teaching aids and materials.

★3542★ Professional Geographer

Association of American Geographers (AAG)
1710 16th St. NW
Washington, DC 20009-3198
Ph: (202)234-1450   Fax: (202)234-2744

Quarterly. $85.50/year. Geographic journal.

Geologists and Geophysicists

SOURCES OF HELP-WANTED ADS

★3543★ **AAPG Bulletin**

American Association of Petroleum
Geologists
1444 S. Bouider
PO Box 979
Tulsa, OK 74101-0979
Ph: (918)584-2555   Fax: (918)584-0469

Monthly. Journal on the application of geological and geophysical principles to exploration and production for the development of energy resources. Subjects include petroleum ecology, oil shale, coal, uranium, and geothermal energy.

★3544★ **AAPG Explorer**

American Association of Petroleum
Geologists
1444 S. Bouider
PO Box 979
Tulsa, OK 74101-0979
Ph: (918)584-2555   Fax: (918)584-0469

Monthly. Magazine containing articles about energy issues with an emphasis on exploration for hydrocarbons and energy minerals.

★3545★ **AEG News**

Association of Engineering Geologists
323 Boston Post Rd., Ste. 2D
Sudbury, MA 01776
Ph: (508)443-4639

Quarterly. Included in membership; $20.00/year for nonmembers. Covers news of the engineering geology profession.

★3546★ **Engineering and Mining Journal**

Intertec Publishing Co.
29 N. Wacker Dr.
Chicago, IL 60606
Ph: (312)435-2330   Fax: (312)726-4103
Fr: 800-621-9907

Monthly. Magazine focusing on metal and non-metallic mining.

★3547★ **Geology**

Geological Society of America
PO Box 9140
Boulder, CO 80301
Ph: (303)447-2020   Fax: (303)447-1133
Fr: 800-472-1988

Monthly. Geology journal.

★3548★ **Nature: International Weekly Journal of Science**

Nature Publishing Co.
65 Bleecker St.
New York, NY 10012-2467
Ph: (212)477-9600   Fax: (212)505-1364

Weekly. Magazine covering science and technology, including the fields of biology, biochemistry, genetics, medicine, earth sciences, physics, pharmacology, and behavioral sciences.

★3549★ **Oil and Gas Journal**

PennWell Publishing Co.
3050 Post Oak Blvd., Ste. 200
Houston, TX 77056
Ph: (713)621-9720   Fax: (713)963-6285

Weekly. Trade magazine serving engineers and managers in international petroleum operations.

★3550★ **Photogrammetric Engineering and Remote Sensing**

American Society for Photogrammetry and
Remote Sensing (ASPRS)
5410 Grosvenor Ln., Ste. 210
Bethesda, MD 20814-2160
Ph: (301)493-0290   Fax: (301)493-0208

Monthly. Free to members; $120.00/year for nonmembers. Provides technical information about the applications of photogrammetry, remote sensing, and geographic information systems.

★3551★ **The Scientist**

The Scientist, Inc.
3501 Market St.
Philadelphia, PA 19104
Ph: (215)386-0100   Fax: (215)387-7542

Biweekly. $58.00/year for individuals; $82.00/year for Canada and Mexico; $79.00/year for other countries. Newspaper (tabloid) for scientists featuring news, opinions, research, and professional section.

★3552★ **Water Well Journal**

Ground Water Publishing Co.
6375 Riverside Dr.
Dublin, OH 43017
Ph: (614)761-3222   Fax: (614)761-3446
Fr: 800-322-2104

Monthly. Water well contractors trade magazine.

PLACEMENT AND JOB REFERRAL SERVICES

★3553★ **American Geophysical Union (AGU)**

2000 Florida Ave. NW
Washington, DC 20009
Ph: (202)462-6900   Fax: (202)328-0566
Fr: 800-966-AGU1

Members: Individuals professionally associated with the field of geophysics; supporting members are companies and other organizations whose work involves geophysics. **Purpose:** Promotes the study of problems concerned with the figure and physics of the earth; initiates and coordinates research that depends upon national and international cooperation and provides for scientific discussion of research results. **Activities:** Sponsors placement service at semiannual meeting. **E-Mail:** custser@kosmos.agu.org **Website:** http://www.agu.org

★3554★ **Association of Ground Water Scientists and Engineers (AGWSE)**

6375 Riverside Dr.
Dublin, OH 43017
Ph: (614)761-1711   Fax: (614)761-3446
Fr: 800-551-7379

Members: A technical division of the National Ground Water Association. Hydrogeologists, geologists, hydrologists, civil and environmental engineers, geochemists, biologists, and scientists in related fields. **Purpose:** Seek to: provide leadership and guidance for scientific, economical, and beneficial groundwater development; promote the use, protection, and management of the world's groundwater resources. Conducts educational programs, seminars, short courses, symposia, and field research projects. **Activities:** Maintains speakers' bureau and museum; offers placement service; sponsors competitions; compiles statistics. Operates library of 40,000 volumes on groundwater science and water well technology.

★3555★ Association for Women Geoscientists (AWG)

4779 126th St. N
White Bear Lake, MN 55110-5910
Ph: (612)426-3316   Fax: (612)426-5449

Members: Men and women geologists, geophysicists, petroleum engineers, geological engineers, hydrogeologists, paleontologists, geochemists, and other geoscientists. **Purpose:** Aims to: encourage the participation of women in the geosciences; exchange educational, technical, and professional information; enhance the professional growth and advancement of women in the geosciences. **Activities:** Provides information on opportunities and careers available to women in the geosciences. Maintains career profiles of women geoscientists, and Association for Women Geoscientists Foundation (educational arm).

★3556★ Geological Society of America (GSA)

3300 Penrose Pl.
PO Box 9140
Boulder, CO 80301-9140
Ph: (303)447-2020   Fax: (303)447-1133
Fr: 800-472-1988

Members: Professional society of geologists. **Purpose:** Promotes the science of geology. **Activities:** Maintains placement service.

★3557★ Korean Scientists and Engineers Association in America (KSEA)

6261 Executive Blvd.
Rockville, MD 20852
Ph: (301)984-7048   Fax: (301)984-1231

Members: Scientists and engineers holding single or advanced degrees. **Purpose:** Goals are to: promote friendship and mutuality among Korean and American scientists and engineers; contribute to Korea's scientific, technological, industrial, and economic developments; strengthen the scientific, technological, and cultural bonds between Korea and the U.S. Sponsors symposium. **Activities:** Maintains speakers' bureau, placement service, and biographical archives. Compiles statistics. Maintains 100 volume library of scientific handbooks and yearbooks in Korean.

★3558★ National Association of Black Geologists and Geophysicists (NABGG)

PO Box 720157
Houston, TX 77272

Members: Black geologists and geophysicists. **Purpose:** Assists minority geologists and geophysicists in establishing professional and business relationships. Informs minority students of career opportunities in geology and geophysics. Seeks to motivate minority students to utilize existing programs, grants, and loans. Provides annual scholarships and oversees the educational careers of scholar-

ship recipients. **Activities:** Assists minority students in their pursuit for summer employment and members interested in obtaining employees for summer positions.

★3559★ National Ground Water Association (NGWA)

6375 Riverside Dr.
Dublin, OH 43017
Ph: (614)761-1711   Fax: (614)761-3446
Fr: 800-551-7379

Purpose: Ground water drilling contractors; manufacturers and suppliers of drilling equipment; ground water scientists such as geologists, engineers, public health officials, and others interested in the problems of locating, developing, preserving, and using ground water supplies. Conducts seminars, and continuing education programs. **Activities:** Encourages scientific education, research, and the development of standards; offers placement services; compiles market statistics. Maintains speakers' bureau. Offers charitable program. Maintains museum.

★3560★ National Network of Minority Women in Science (MWIS)

Directorate for Education and Human
  Resources Programs
1333 H St. NW
Washington, DC 20005
Ph: (202)326-6757   Fax: (202)371-9849

Members: Asian, Black, Mexican American, Native American, and Puerto Rican women involved in science related professions; other interested persons. **Purpose:** Promotes the advancement of minority women in science fields and the improvement of the science and mathematics education and career awareness of minorities. Supports public policies and programs in science and technology that benefit minorities. **Activities:** Maintains placement servce. Compiles statistics; serves as clearinghouse for identifying minority women scientists. Offers writing and conference presentations, seminars, and workshops on minority women in science and local career conferences for students. Local chapters maintain speakers' bureaus, and children's services. **E-Mail:** ggilbert@aaas.org

EMPLOYER DIRECTORIES AND NETWORKING LISTS

★3561★ American Men and Women of Science

R. R. Bowker Co.
Reed Reference Publishing
121 Chanlon Rd.
New Providence, NJ 07974
Ph: (908)464-6800   Fax: (908)665-6688
Fr: 800-521-8110

Triennial, latest edition January 1995. $106.00, per volume; $850.00, set. Covers over 123,000 U.S. and Canadian scientists active in the physical, biological, mathematical, computer science, and engineering fields; includes references to previous edition for deceased scientists and nonrespondents.

Entries include: Name, address, education, personal and career data, memberships, honors and awards, research interest. Arrangement: Alphabetical. Indexes: Discipline (in separate volume).

★3562★ Directory of Certified Petroleum Geologists

American Association of Petroleum
  Geologists
Box 979
Tulsa, OK 74101-0979
Ph: (918)584-2555   Fax: (918)584-0469

Biennial, February of even years. $25.00, postpaid. Covers about 3,900 members of the association. Entries include: Name, address; education and career data; whether available for consulting. Arrangement: Alphabetical. Indexes: Geographical.

★3563★ Directory of Foreign Manufacturers in the United States

Georgia State University Business Press
College of Business Administration
University Plaza
Atlanta, GA 30303-3093
Ph: (404)651-4253   Fax: (404)651-4256

Biennial, odd years. $195.00, payment must accompany orders from individuals. Covers over 7,300 United States manufacturing, mining, and petroleum companies, and the over 6,800 firms abroad that own them. Entries include: Company name, address, phone, fax, products or services, Standard Industrial Classification (SIC) codes, parent company name and address. Arrangement: Alphabetical by U.S. company name. Indexes: U.S. subsidiary location, foreign company name, geographical (foreign company location), product.

★3564★ Geophysical Directory

Geophysical Directory, Inc.
PO Box 130508
Houston, TX 77219
Ph: (713)529-8789   Fax: (713)529-3646
Fr: 800-929-2462

Annual, March. $50.00, postpaid. Covers about 3,600 companies that provide geophysical equipment, supplies, or services, and mining and petroleum companies that use geophysical techniques; international coverage. Entries include: Company name, address, phone, names of principal executives, operations, and sales personnel; similar information for branch locations. Arrangement: Classified by product or service. Indexes: Company name, personal name.

★3565★ Geophysicists: A Directory of AGU Members

American Geophysical Union
2000 Florida Ave. NW
Washington, DC 20009
Ph: (202)462-6900   Fax: (202)328-0566
Fr: 800-966-2481

Biennial, Fall of odd years. $28.00. Covers 31,000 member geophysicists. Entries include: Name, address, office and home phone numbers, fax, electronic mail address, type of membership, year joined, and division membership. Arrangement: Alphabetical.

★3566★ Geophysics: The Leading Edge of Exploration—Directory Issue

Society of Exploration Geophysicists
Box 702740
Tulsa, OK 74170
Ph: (918)493-3516   Fax: (918)493-2074

Annual, May. $25.00. Publication includes: Membership roster of nearly 14,500 geophysicists, corporations, and students. Entries include: Name, address, phone, fax, type of member; affiliation given for individuals. Arrangement: Alphabetical; geographical.

★3567★ Oil & Gas Directory

Geophysical Directory, Inc.
PO Box 130508
Houston, TX 77219
Ph: (713)529-8789   Fax: (713)529-3646
Fr: 800-929-2462

Annual, October. $65.00, postpaid. Covers about 5,200 companies worldwide involved in petroleum exploration, drilling, and production, and suppliers to the industry. Entries include: Company name, address, phone, telex, names of principal personnel, branch office addresses, phone numbers, and key personnel. Arrangement: Classified by activity. Indexes: Company name, personal name.

★3568★ Peterson's Job Opportunities in Engineering and Technology 1996

Peterson's
PO Box 2123
Princeton, NJ 08543-2123
Ph: (609)243-9111   Fax: (609)243-9150
Fr: 800-338-3282

Compiled by the Peterson's staff. Annual. $19.95 paperback. 432 pages. Profiles 2,000 high-tech companies looking primarily for technical personnel in such fields as biotechnology, telecommunications, software, computers and peripherals, defense, and aerospace. Contains job-search strategies and career options to help match education and expertise to the job market. Indexed geographically, by industry, and by hiring needs.

★3569★ Scientific and Technical Organizations and Agencies Directory

Gale Research
835 Penobscot Bldg.
Detroit, MI 48226-4094
Ph: (313)961-2242   Fax: (313)961-6083
Fr: 800-877-GALE

Irregular; latest edition December 1993. $195.00. Covers over 25,600 national and international organizations and agencies concerned with the physical and applied sciences, engineering, and technology, including associations, computer information services, consulting firms, educational institutions, foundations, government advisory organizations, federal government agencies, general grant and assistance programs, libraries and information centers, patent sources and services, research and development centers, scholarships, fellowships, and loans, science-technology centers, standards organizations, state academies of science, and state government agencies in the fields of aeronautics and space sciences, chemistry, computer science specialties, electronics, geography, geology, machinery, mathematics, metallurgy, meteorology, mineralogy, nu-

clear science, petroleum and gas, physics, plastics, transportation, water resources, and other areas. Entries include: Organization name, address, phone, and name of contact; additional descriptive text for most entries. Arrangement: Classified by type of organization. Indexes: Organization name/key word.

★3570★ Who's Who in Technology

Gale Research
835 Penobscot Bldg.
Detroit, MI 48226-4094
Ph: (313)961-2242   Fax: (313)961-6083
Fr: 800-877-GALE

Irregular, new edition expected June 1995. $380.00. Covers 38,000 engineers, scientists, inventors, and researchers. Entries include: Name, title, affiliation, address; personal, education, and career data; publications, patents; technical field of activity; area of expertise. Arrangement: Alphabetical. Indexes: Geographical, employer, technical discipline, expertise.

HANDBOOKS AND MANUALS

★3571★ The Best Resumes for Scientists and Engineers

John Wiley and Sons
605 3rd Ave.
New York, NY 10158
Ph: (212)850-6000   Fr: 800-225-5945

Adele Lewis. Second edition, 1993. $37.50; $14.95 (paper). Presents an extensive collection of scientific and engineering resumes, highlighting the important differences between these and resumes written for other occupations.

★3572★ Career Information Center

Macmillan Publishing Co.
200 Old Tappan Rd.
Old Tappan, NJ 07675
Ph: (609)461-6500   Fr: 800-223-2336

Visual Education Center Staff. Fifth edition, 1992. $229.00. This 13-volume set profiles over 600 occupations. Each occupational profile describes job duties, educational requirements, how to get the job, advancement possibilities, employment outlook, working conditions, earnings and benefits, and where to write for more information.

★3573★ Careers in Geophysics

American Geophysical Union (AGU)
2000 Florida Ave. NW
Washington, DC 20009
Ph: (202)462-6900

Booklet. Explains geophysics and describes career possibilities and major employers, employment with the federal government, and academic preparation. Lists colleges and universities that offer coursework in geophysics.

★3574★ Careers in the Maritime Industry: Naval Architecture, Marine Engineering, Ocean Engineering

Society of Naval Architects and Marine Engineers
601 Pavonia Ave.
Jersey City, NJ 07306

1993. Free. 24 pages. Includes section on employment and employers.

★3575★ Careers for Nature Lovers and Other Outdoor Types

VGM Career Horizons
4255 W. Touhy Ave.
Lincolnwood, IL 60646-1975
Ph: (847)679-5500   Fax: (847)679-2494
Fr: 800-323-4900

Louise Miller. 1992. $12.95; $9.95 (paper). Examines career opportunities in biology, agriculture, landscaping, forestry and conservation, geology, and waste management, and pollution control. Offers insight into preparing for and finding outdoor jobs in federal and state government, as well as private industry.

★3576★ Careers in Science

VGM Career Horizons
4255 W. Touhy Ave.
Lincolnwood, IL 60646-1975
Ph: (847)679-5500   Fax: (847)679-2494
Fr: 800-323-4900

Thomas Easton. Third edition, 1996. 192 pages. $17.95; $13.95 (paper). Discusses careers in life science, earth science, physical and space science, social science, engineering, mathematics, and computer science. Offers job hunting advice.

★3577★ Compensation & Benefits in Engineering Firms in the Geotechnical Field

Abbott, Langer & Associates
548 1st St.
Crete, IL 60417
Ph: (708)672-4200   Fax: (708)672-4674

Steven Langer. $395.00 (paper).

★3578★ Encyclopedia of Careers and Vocational Guidance

J. G. Ferguson Publishing Co.
200 W. Monroe, Ste. 250
Chicago, IL 60606
Ph: (312)580-5480

William E. Hopke. Ninth edition, 1993. $129.95; $199.95 (CD-ROM). Four-volume set that profiles 900 occupations and describes job trends in 71 industries. Includes career description, educational requirements, history of the job, methods of entry, advancement, employment outlook, earnings, conditions of work, social and psychological factors, and sources of further information. Contains career and employment information for this field.

★3579★ *Future Employment Opportunities in the Geological Sciences*

The Geological Society of America
PO Box 9140
3300 Penrose Pl.
Boulder, CO 80301
Ph: (303)447-2020   Fax: (303)447-1133

1994. Free. 28 pages. Outlines job opportunities in a variety of settings, including petroleum; mining; local, state, and federal government; consulting; and the academic community. Gives tips on resume writing and interviewing.

★3580★ *Guiding Your Career As a Professional Geologist*

American Association of Petroleum Geologists.
PO Box 979
Tulsa, OK 74101-0979
Ph: (918)584-2555   Fax: (918)584-0469
Fr: 800-364-2274

Peter R. Rose, editor. 1994. $5.00 (paper).

EMPLOYMENT AGENCIES AND SEARCH FIRMS

★3581★ **Accro Personnel Services**

1654 Foothill Park Cir.
Lafayette, CA 94549
Ph: (510)937-3387

Employment agency.

OTHER SOURCES

★3582★ *American Almanac of Jobs and Salaries 1994-95*

Avon Books
1350 Avenue of the Americas, 2nd Fl.
New York, NY 10019
Ph: (212)261-6800   Fr: 800-238-0658

John Wright. Revised edition, 1993. $17.00. 704 pages. This is a comprehensive guide to the wages of hundreds of occupations in a wide variety of industries and organizations.

★3583★ **American Geological Institute (AGI)**

4220 King St.
Alexandria, VA 22302
Ph: (703)379-2480   Fax: (703)379-7563

Members: Federation of national scientific and technical societies in the earth sciences. **Purpose:** Seeks to: stimulate public understanding of geological sciences; improve teaching of the geological sciences in schools, colleges, and universities; maintain high standards of professional training and conduct; work for the general welfare of members. **Activities:** Provides career guidance program.

★3584★ **American Institute of Professional Geologists (AIPG)**

7828 Vance Dr., Ste. 103
Arvada, CO 80003-2125
Ph: (303)431-0831   Fax: (303)431-1332

Members: Geologists. **Purpose:** Provides certification to geologists attesting to their competence and integrity. **E-Mail:** aipg@netcom.com

★3585★ **American Society for Photogrammetry and Remote Sensing (ASPRS)**

5410 Grosvenor Ln., Ste. 210
Bethesda, MD 20814-2160
Ph: (301)493-0290   Fax: (301)493-0208

Members: Firms, individuals, government employees, and academicians engaged in photogrammetry, photointerpretation, remote sensing, and geographic information systems and their application to such fields as archaeology, geographic information systems, military reconnaissance, urban planning, engineering, traffic surveys, meteorological observations, medicine, geology, forestry, agriculture, construction, and topographic mapping. **Activities:** Offers voluntary certification program open to persons associated with one or more functional area of photogrammetry, remote sensing, and GIS. Surveys the profession of private firms in photogrammetry and remote sensing in the areas of products and services.

★3586★ **Association of Engineering Geologists (AEG)**

323 Boston Post Rd., Ste. 2D
Sudbury, MA 01776
Ph: (508)443-4639   Fax: (508)443-2948

Members: Graduate geologists and geological engineers; full members must have five years experience in the field of engineering geology. **Purpose:** Seeks to: provide a forum for the discussion and dissemination of technical and scientific information; encourage the advancement of professional recognition, scientific research, and high ethical and professional standards. Has compiled information on engineering geology curricula of colleges and universities. Promotes public understanding, health, safety and welfare, and acceptance of the engineering geology profession. **Activities:** Conducts technical sessions, symposia, abstracts, and short courses; cosponsors seminars and conferences with other professional and technical societies and organizations.

★3587★ **Association for International Practical Training (AIPT)**

10400 Little Patuxent Pky. Ste. 250
Columbia, MD 21044
Ph: (410)997-2200   Fax: (410)992-3924

Purpose: Helps coordinate training around the world in fields such as travel, the culinary arts, and hotel management. **Activities:** Conducts programs in career development and hospitality/tourism exchanges. Operates a student exchange program. Provides reciprocal practical training experience for recent graduates from the U.S., Austria, Germany, Finland, France, Hungary, Ireland, Japan, Malaysia, Netherlands, Switzerland, and the United Kingdom. Arranges training programs in the U.S. and abroad. Serves as U.S. affiliate to IAESTE (International Association for the Exchange of Students for Technical Experience) and operates a Professional Visitors Program to arrange short-term educational and training visits to the U.S. **E-Mail:** aipt@aipt.org

★3588★ *Geoscience Employment and Hiring Surveys*

American Geological Institute (AGI)
c/o AGI Publications Center
PO Box 205
Annapolis Junction, MD 20701
Ph: (301)953-1744

Annual. Gives current and projected employment statistics and approximate starting salaries for graduates by degree level.

★3589★ **Marine Technology Society (MTS)**

1828 L St. NW, No. 906
Washington, DC 20036
Ph: (202)775-5966   Fax: (202)429-9417

Members: Scientists, engineers, educators, and others with professional interests in the marine sciences or related fields; includes institutional and corporate members. **Purpose:** Disseminates marine scientific and technical information, including institutional, environmental, physical, and biological aspects; fosters a deeper understanding of the world's seas and attendant technologies. Maintains 14 sections and 29 professional committees. Conducts tutorials.

★3590★ *New Careers Directory: Internships and Professional Opportunities in Technology and Social Change*

Student Pugwash USA
815 15th St. NW, Ste. 814
Washington, DC 20005
Ph: (202)393-6555   Fax: (202)393-6550
Fr: 800-WOW-A-PUG

Irregular; latest edition spring 1993. $13.00 for students; $21.00 for institutions, plus $3.00 shipping. Covers about 300 research institutes, think tanks, laboratories, government agencies, professional, science, and other non-profit organizations offering public policy, science, and technology internships and jobs. Entries include: Sponsoring organization name, description of organization, programs offered, work environment and application procedures, compensation offered. Arrangement: Alphabetical and classified by subject. Indexes: Geographical, subject.

★3591★ *Resumes for Scientific and Technical Careers*

VGM Career Horizons
NTC Publishing Group
4255 W. Touhy Ave.
Lincolnwood, IL 60646-1975
Ph: (847)679-5500   Fax: (847)679-2494
Fr: 800-323-4900

1994. $9.95. 160 pages. Provides resume advice for individuals interested in working in scientific and technical careers. Includes sample resumes and cover letters.

★3592★ Salaries of Scientists, Engineers, and Technicians: A Summary of Salary Surveys

Commission on Professionals in Science and Technology (CPST)
1500 Massachusetts Ave. NW, Ste. 831
Washington, DC 20005
Ph: (202)223-6995

1993.

★3593★ Society of Exploration Geophysicists (SEG)

PO Box 702740
Tulsa, OK 74170
Ph: (918)493-3516   Fax: (918)493-2074

Members: Individuals having eight years of education and experience in exploration geo-physics or geology. **Purpose:** Promotes the science of geophysics, especially as it applies to the exploration for petroleum and other minerals. Encourages high professional standards among members; supports the common interests of members. Maintains SEG Foundation, which receives contributions from companies and individuals and distributes them in the form of scholarships to students of geophysics and related subjects. **Activities:** Offers short continuing education courses to geophysicists and geologists. Maintains 37 committees including: Development and Production; Engineering and Groundwater Geophysics; Mining and Geothermal; Offshore Exploration and Oceanography.

★3594★ Summer Opportunities in Marine and Environmental Science

Summer Opportunities Guide
38 Litchfield Rd.
Londonderry, NH 03053

Herriott and Herrin. Second edition, 1994. $14.95. 60 pages. Subtitled: ''A Student's Guide to Jobs, Internships and Study, Camp and Travel Programs''. Prepared for both high school and college students.

Hazardous Waste Management Specialists

product news for decision makers in the municipal and industrial water and water pollution control industries.

PLACEMENT AND JOB REFERRAL SERVICES

★3610★ **American Academy of Environmental Engineers (AAEE)**

130 Holiday Ct., No. 100
Annapolis, MD 21401
Ph: (410)266-3311   Fax: (410)266-7653

Members: Environmentally oriented registered professional engineers certified by examination as diplomates of the academy. **Purpose:** Purposes are: to improve the standards of environmental engineering; to certify those with special knowledge of environmental engineering; to furnish lists of those certified to the public. **Activities:** Maintains speakers' bureau. Recognizes areas of specialization: Air Pollution Control; General Environmental; Hazardous Waste Management; Industrial Hygiene; Radiation Protection; Solid Waste Management; Water Supply and Wastewater. Requires written and oral examinations for certification. Works with other professional organizations on environmentally oriented activities. Identifies potential employment candidates through Talent Search Service.

★3611★ **Hazardous Waste Treatment Council (HWTC)**

915 15th St. NW, 5th Fl.
Washington, DC 20005
Ph: (202)783-0870   Fax: (202)737-2038

Purpose: Firms dedicated to the use of high technology treatment in the management of hazardous wastes and to the restricted use of land disposal facilities in the interests of protecting human health and the environment. Advocates minimization of hazardous wastes and the use of alternative technologies in their treatment, including chemical and biological treatments, fixation, neutralization, reclamation, recycling, and thermal treatments such as incineration. Encourages land disposal prohibitions. Promotes reductions in the volume of hazardous waste generated annually and expansion of EPA hazardous waste list. Advocates use of treatment technology as a more cost-effective approach to Superfund site cleanups. Works with state, national, and international officials and firms to assist in development of programs that utilize treatment and minimize land disposal. **Activities:** Provides technical and placement assistance to members; sponsors special studies, technical seminars, and workshops; participates in federal legislation, litigation, and regulatory development.

★3612★ **Spill Control Association of America (SCAA)**

400 Renaissance Center, Ste. 1900
Detroit, MI 48243
Ph: (313)259-1144   Fax: (313)259-8943

Members: Third party contractors; manufacturers or suppliers of pollution control and containment equipment; individuals in private or governmental capacities involved with spill clean-up and containment operations; associate companies. **Purpose:** To provide information on the oil and hazardous material emergency response and remediation industry's practices, trends, and achievements; to establish liaison with local, state, and federal government agencies responsible for laws and regulations regarding pollution caused by oil and hazardous materials; to cooperate in the development of industry programs and efforts so that pollutants are properly controlled and removed from land and water. **Activities:** Provides certification for hazardous material technicians. Maintains placement service.

EMPLOYER DIRECTORIES AND NETWORKING LISTS

★3613★ **Asbestos Removal Service Directory**

American Business Directories, Inc.
American Business Information, Inc.
5711 S. 86th Cir.
Omaha, NE 68127
Ph: (402)593-4600   Fax: (402)331-1505

Annual. $235.00, payment with order. Entries include: Name, address, phone (including area code), size of advertisement, year first in Yellow Pages, name of owner or manager, number of employees. Compiled from telephone company Yellow Pages, nationwide. Arrangement: Geographical.

★3614★ **Directory of Chemical Waste Transporters**

Chemical Waste Transportation Institute
4301 Connecticut Ave. NW, Ste. 300
Washington, DC 20008
Ph: (202)659-4613   Fax: (202)775-5917

Biennial, odd years. $5.00. Covers about 100 hazardous waste transportation companies; includes Canada. Entries include: Company name, address, phone, name of contact; area of operation, service offered (rail, truck). Arrangement: Geographical. Indexes: Product, Environmental Protection Agency DOT regions.

★3615★ **Directory of Hazardous Waste Services**

Corpus Information Services
Southam Business Communications Inc.
1450 Don Mills Rd.
Don Mills, ON, Canada M3B 2X7
Ph: (416)442-2122   Fax: (416)442-2200

Annual. $115.00. Covers about 1,300 companies supplying equipment or services related to hazardous waste disposal in Canada, including transportation, disposal, consulting, recycling, analysis, and spill cleanup; 400 federal and provincial environmental officials; 100 professional and business associations. Entries include: For companies: name, address, phone, name and title of contact, geographical area covered, subsidiary and branch names and locations, products and services. For officials and associations: name, address, phone. Arrangement: Alphabetical. Indexes: Product/service, Geographical.

★3616★ **El Environmental Services Directory**

Environmental Information Ltd.
4801 W. 81st St., Ste. 119
Bloomington, MN 55437
Ph: (612)831-2473   Fax: (612)831-6550

Biennial, December of even years. $495.00, postpaid; payment with order. Covers over 620 waste-handling facilities, 600 transportation firms, 500 spill response firms, 2,100 consultants, 470 laboratories, 450 soil boring/well drilling firms; also includes incineration services, polychlorinated biphenyl (PCB) detoxification and mobile solvent-recovery services, asbestos services and underground tank services, summaries of states' regulatory programs. Entries include: Company name, address, phone, service, regulatory status, on and off site processes used, type of waste handled. Arrangement: Geographical. Indexes: Service.

★3617★ **Environmental Industry Yearbook and Investment Guide**

Environmental Economics
PO Box 18853
Philadelphia, PA 19113
Ph: (215)844-5839   Fax: (215)923-1794

Semiannual, July and January. $75.00. Covers Approximately 80 publicly-traded companies, plus Fortune 500 firms involved in environmental services such as air pollution control, asbestos abatement, hazardous waste management, waste testing and analysis, nuclear waste handling, recycling, solid waste disposal, waste-related infrastructure work, waste-to-energy systems, and water treatment. Entries include: Company name, address, phone, names and titles of key personnel, number of employees, geographical area served, financial data, description of services, industry-related data. Arrangement: Alphabetical. Indexes: Service.

★3618★ **Hazardous Materials Advisory Council—Directory**

Hazardous Materials Advisory Council (HMAC)
1101 Vermont Ave. NW, Ste. 301
Washington, DC 20005-3521
Ph: (202)289-4550   Fax: (202)289-4074

Annual, July. Available to members only. Covers about 300 member shippers and carriers of hazardous materials; manufacturers of hazardous materials containers; and related organizations. Entries include: Company name, address, phone, fax, representative name. Arrangement: Classified by line of business.

★3619★ **Hazardous Waste Consultant—Directory of Commercial Hazardous Waste Management Facilities Issue**

Physical Sciences Group
Elsevier Science, Inc.
655 Ave. of the Americas
New York, NY 10010
Ph: (212)633-3827   Fax: (212)633-3795

Annual, March-April. $100.00. Publication includes: List of nearly 160 licensed commercial facilities that treat and/or dispose of hazardous waste material. Entries include: Facility name, address, phone, contact name, type of waste handled, methods of on-site treatment and/or disposal, Environmental Protection Agency permit status and identification number, restrictions, description of other services. Arrangement: Geographical. Indexes: Organization name.

★3620★ HWAC Directory: The Leading Engineering and Science Firms Practicing in Hazardous Waste Management

Hazardous Waste Action Coalition (HWAC)
c/o American Consulting Engineers Council
1015 15th St. NW, No. 802
Washington, DC 20005
Ph: (202)347-7474   Fax: (202)898-0076

Annual, November. $100.00. Covers HWAC's 100 member engineering firms responsible for designing cleanup solutions for hazardous waste sites. Entries include: Company name, address, phone, office locations, corporate data, firm activities. Arrangement: Geographical.

★3621★ ICWM Directory of Hazardous Waste Treatment and Disposal Facilities

Institute of Chemical Waste Management
Environmental Industries Association
4301 Connecticut Ave., NW, Ste. 300
Washington, DC 20008
Ph: (202)659-4613   Fax: (202)775-5917
Fr: 800-424-2869

Irregular, latest edition 1992. $7.00. Covers more than 20 commercial hazardous waste management firms in the United States and Canada. Entries include: Firm name, address, phone, types and locations of facilities, services offered. Arrangement: Geographical.

★3622★ Peterson's Job Opportunities in Engineering and Technology 1996

Peterson's
PO Box 2123
Princeton, NJ 08543-2123
Ph: (609)243-9111   Fax: (609)243-9150
Fr: 800-338-3282

Compiled by the Peterson's staff. Annual. $19.95 paperback. 432 pages. Profiles 2,000 high-tech companies looking primarily for technical personnel in such fields as biotechnology, telecommunications, software, computers and peripherals, defense, and aerospace. Contains job-search strategies and career options to help match education and expertise to the job market. Indexed geographically, by industry, and by hiring needs.

★3623★ Peterson's Job Opportunities in the Environment

Peterson's Guides, Inc.
202 Carnegie Ctr.
Box 2123
Princeton, NJ 08543-2123
Ph: (609)243-9111   Fax: (609)243-9150
Fr: 800-338-3282

Annual, August. $18.95. Covers Approximately 1,500 companies and government

agencies hiring environmental professionals, including waste-management companies, state and federal agencies, advocacy groups, and environmental design firms. Entries include: Organization name, address, phone, name and title of contact, type of organization, number of employees, Standard Industrial Classification (SIC) code; description of opportunities available including desciplines, level of education required, starting locations and salaries, level of experience accepted, benefits. Arrangement: Alphabetical. Indexes: Employer by type of organization, industry classification, number of employees, starting location, special interest area; education level, company.

★3624★ Waste Age—Waste Industry Yellow Pages

Waste Age Magazine
4301 Connecticut Ave., NW, Ste. 300
Washington, DC 20008
Ph: (202)244-4700   Fax: (202)966-4868
Fr: 800-424-2869

Annual, January. $15.00. Covers suppliers, consultants (legal, financial, environmental), and underwriters of waste industry services and equipment. Entries include: Company name, address, phone, product or services. Arrangement: Classified by product or service. Indexes: Company/name.

★3625★ Who's Who in Environmental Engineering

American Academy of Environmental Engineers
130 Holiday Ct., Ste. 100
Annapolis, MD 21401
Ph: (410)266-3311   Fax: (410)266-7653

Annual, April. $75.00, payment with order. Covers about 2,600 licensed professional environmental engineers that have been certified by examination in one or more of seven specialties: air pollution control, general environmental engineering, industrial hygiene, hazardous waste management, radiation protection, solid waste management, water supply and wastewater. Entries include: Name, affiliation, address, phone, area of specialization, biographical data. Arrangement: Alphabetical, geographical, area of specialization.

★3626★ World Directory of Radwaste Managers

American Nuclear Society
555 N. Kensington Ave.
La Grange Park, IL 60525
Ph: (708)352-6611   Fax: (708)352-6464

Biennial, next January 1996. $190.00. Covers Approximately 1,200 individuals in 376 agencies or offices that oversee, regulate, or handle radioactive waste. Entries include: Agency name, address, phone, names and titles of key personnel, geographical area served, subsidiary and branch names and locations. Arrangement: Geographical.

HANDBOOKS AND MANUALS

★3627★ The Best Resumes for Scientists and Engineers

John Wiley and Sons
605 3rd Ave.
New York, NY 10158
Ph: (212)850-6000   Fr: 800-225-5945

Adele Lewis. Second edition, 1993. $37.50; $14.95 (paper). Presents an extensive collection of scientific and engineering resumes, highlighting the important differences between these and resumes written for other occupations.

★3628★ Careers for Nature Lovers and Other Outdoor Types

VGM Career Horizons
4255 W. Touhy Ave.
Lincolnwood, IL 60646-1975
Ph: (847)679-5500   Fax: (847)679-2494
Fr: 800-323-4900

Louise Miller. 1992. $12.95; $9.95 (paper). Examines career opportunities in biology, agriculture, landscaping, forestry and conservation, geology, and waste management, and pollution control. Offers insight into preparing for and finding outdoor jobs in federal and state government, as well as private industry.

★3629★ Hazardous Materials & Waste Management: A Guide for the Professional Hazards Manager

Noyes Data Corp.
120 Mill Rd.
Park Ridge, NJ 07656
Ph: (201)391-8484   Fax: (201)391-6833

Nicholas P. Cheremisinoff. 1995. $54.00.

★3630★ Jobs from Recyclables Possibility Newsletter

Prosperity & Profits Unlimited Distribution Services
PO Box 416
Denver, CO 80201
Ph: (303)575-5676

Annual. $4.50. Describes employment options for environmentalists, waste management, and businesses.

★3631★ 100 Best Careers for the Year 2000

Prentice Hall General Reference
15 Columbus Cir.
New York, NY 10023
Ph: (212)373-8500   Fr: 800-223-2348

Shelly Field. 1992. $15.00 (paper). Covers 100 of the fastest growing jobs. The publication is divided into 11 general employment sections. Specific careers are covered within each section. Provides job description, responsibilities, employment opportunities, earnings, education and training, advancement opportunities, and experience and qualifications for each occupation.

★3632★ *Opportunities in Waste Management Careers*

VGM Career Horizons
4255 W. Touhy Ave.
Lincolnwood, IL 60646-1975
Ph: (847)679-5500   Fax: (847)679-2494
Fr: 800-323-4900

Mark Rowh. 1992. $13.95; $10.95 (paper). Outlines the diverse opportunities in waste management and examines the duties, working conditions, salaries, and future of a variety of positions. Profiles jobs and opportunities in solid waste and waste water management, environmental engineering, soil and wildlife conservation, and related career areas.

EMPLOYMENT AGENCIES AND SEARCH FIRMS

★3633★ **The Energists**
10260 Westheimer, Ste. 300
Houston, TX 77042
Ph: (713)781-6881   Fax: (713)781-2998
Executive search firm.

★3634★ **Environmental Professional Associates**
3857 Birch St., Ste. 186
Newport Beach, CA 92660
Ph: (310)273-5320

Executive search firm. Focuses on environmental positions.

★3635★ **Intech Summit Group, Inc.**
6540 Lusk Blvd., C-228
San Diego, CA 92121
Ph: (619)452-2100

Employment agency and executive recruiter.

★3636★ **LOR Personnel Division**
418 Wall St.
Princeton, NJ 08540
Ph: (609)921-6580

Employment agency. Executive search firm.

★3637★ **Lybrook Associates, Inc.**
PO Box 572
Newport, RI 02840
Ph: (401)683-6990

Executive search firm.

★3638★ **Search Consultants International, Inc.**
4545 Post Oak Pl., Ste. 208
Houston, TX 77027
Ph: (713)622-9188

Executive search firm.

OTHER SOURCES

★3639★ **Air and Waste Management Association (A&WMA)**
1 Gateway Ctr., 3rd Fl.
Pittsburgh, PA 15222
Ph: (412)232-3444   Fax: (412)232-3450
Fr: 800-270-3444

Purpose: Environmental, educational, and technical organization. Seeks to provide a neutral forum for the exchange of technical information on a wide variety of environmental topics.

★3640★ **Environmental Industry Associations**
4301 Connecticut Ave., NW, Ste. 300
Washington, DC 20008
Ph: (202)244-4700   Fax: (202)966-4818

Activities: Compiles statistics; conducts research and educational programs.

★3641★ **Water Environment Federation (WEF)**
601 Wythe St.
Alexandria, VA 22314-1994
Ph: (703)684-2400   Fax: (703)684-2492
Fr: 800-666-0206

Members: Technical societies representing chemists, biologists, ecologists, geologists, operators, educational and research personnel, industrial wastewater engineers, consultant engineers, municipal officials, equipment manufacturers, and university professors and students dedicated to the ehancement and preservation of water quality and resources. **Purpose:** Seeks to advance fundamental and practical knowledge concerning the nature, collection, treatment, and disposal of domestic and industrial wastewaters, and the design, construction, operation, and management of facilities for these purposes. Disseminates technical information; promotes good public relations and regulations that improve water quality and the status of individuals working in this field. **Activities:** Conducts educational and research programs.

Health Services Managers and Hospital Administrators

PLACEMENT AND JOB REFERRAL SERVICES

★3655★ Alliance for Healthcare Strategy and Marketing (The Allian)
11 S. LaSalle St., Ste. 2300
Chicago, IL 60603-1303
Ph: (312)704-9700   Fax: (312)704-9709
Members: Marketing professionals in the health care field; vice presidents and directors of hospitals, health maintenance organizations, nursing homes, and other health care institutions. **Purpose:** Promotes the marketing of health services; sponsors continuing education for and professional development of members to this end. **Activities:** Conducts seminars; offers placement service.

★3656★ American Academy of Medical Administrators (AAMA)
30555 Southfield Rd., Ste. 150
Southfield, MI 48076-7747
Ph: (810)540-4310   Fax: (810)645-0590
Members: Individuals involved in medical administration at the executive- or middle-management levels. **Purpose:** Promotes educational courses for the training of persons in medical administration. Conducts research. **Activities:** Offers placement service.

★3657★ American Academy of Medical Administrators Research and Educational Foundation (AAMA)
30555 Southfield Rd., Ste. 150
Southfield, MI 48076
Ph: (810)540-4310   Fax: (810)645-0590
Members: Individuals with health care backgrounds. **Activities:** Conducts research in the health care field and seminars geared toward professional development. Maintains placement services.

★3658★ American College Health Association (ACHA)
PO Box 28937
Baltimore, MD 21240-8937
Ph: (410)859-1500   Fax: (410)859-1510
Members: Institutions and individuals. **Purpose:** Provides an organization in which institutions of higher education and interested individuals may work together to promote health in its broadest aspects for students and all other members of the college community. **Activities:** Offers continuing education programs for health professionals. Maintains placement listings for physicians and other personnel seeking positions in college health.

★3659★ American College of Health Care Administrators (ACHCA)
325 S. Patrick St.
Alexandria, VA 22314
Ph: (703)739-7900   Fax: (703)739-7901
Members: Persons actively engaged in the administration of long-term care facilities, assisted-living facilities in medical administration, or activities designed to improve the quality of long-term administration. **Purpose:** Certifies members' ability to meet and maintain a standard of competence in nursing home and long-term care administration. Works to elevate the standards in the field and to develop and promote a code of ethics and standards of education and training. Seeks to inform allied professions and the public that good administration of long-term care facilities calls for special formal academic training and experience. Encourages research in all aspects of geriatrics, the chronically ill, and administration. **Activities:** Maintains placement service. Conducts research and special education programs.

★3660★ American College of Healthcare Executives (ACHE)
1 N. Franklin, Ste. 1700
Chicago, IL 60606-3491
Ph: (312)424-2800   Fax: (312)424-0023
Members: Professional society for hospital and health service executives. **Purpose:** Works to: keep members abreast of current and future trends, issues, and developments; shape productive and effective organizational strategies and professional performance; increase the visibility and recognition of the health care management profession; act as advocate for health care management in legislative activities and with government agencies; develop cooperation among professional societies and other health care associations in dealing with current issues; strengthen and encourage the profession's code of ethics; maintain professional standards. **Activities:** Maintains database of personal and career data on its membership. Holds educational seminars and training programs on health care management. Operates Healthcare Executives Career Resource Center.

★3661★ American College of Healthcare Information Administrators (ACHIA)
30555 Southfield Rd., Ste. 150
Southfield, MI 48076
Ph: (810)540-4310   Fax: (810)645-0590
Chapter of the American Academy of Medical Administrators. **Members:** Healthcare leaders serving in a management position in the information field. **Purpose:** Works to promote the advancement of members' knowledge, professional standing, credentialing, and personal achievements in information technology, management, and strategic planning. **Activities:** Conducts an employment referral and educational programs.

★3662★ American College of Managed Care Administrators (ACMCA)
30555 Southfield Rd., Ste. 150
Southfield, MI 48076
Ph: (810)540-4310   Fax: (810)645-0590
National chapter of the American Academy of Medical Administrators. **Members:** Managers of professionals who are directly or indirectly providing managed healthcare. **Purpose:** Works to promote the advancement of members' professional standing, education, and personal achievement and develop innovative concepts in managed care administration. **Activities:** Conducts an employment referral and educational programs.

★3663★ American College of Medical Quality (ACMQ)
9005 Congressional Ct.
Potomac, MD 20854
Ph: (301)365-3570   Fax: (301)365-3202
Members: Physicians, affiliates, and institutions. **Purpose:** Seeks to set standards of competence in the field of quality assurance and utilization review. Conducts educational seminars and workshops in quality assurance and utilization review. **Activities:** Offers placement service. Compiles statistics on numbers of physicians and allied health personnel working in quality assurance and utilization review.

★3664★ American Correctional Health Services Association (ACHSA)
PO Box 2307
Dayton, OH 45401-2307
Ph: (513)223-9630   Fax: (513)223-6307
Members: Health care providers, individuals, or organizations interested in improving the quality of correctional health services. **Purpose:** Aims are: to promote the provision of health services to incarcerated persons consistent in quality and quantity with acceptable health care practices; to promote and encourage continuing education and provide technical and professional guidance for correctional health care personnel; to establish a forum for the sharing and discussion of correctional health care issues. **Activities:** Conducts conferences on correctional health care management, nursing, mental health, juvenile corrections, dentistry, and related subjects. Maintains placement service.

★3665★ American Public Health Association (APHA)
1015 15th St. NW
Washington, DC 20005
Ph: (202)789-5600   Fax: (202)789-5681
Members: Professional organization of physicians, nurses, educators, academicians, environmentalists, epidemiologists, new professionals, social workers, health administrators, optometrists, podiatrists, pharmacists, dentists, nutritionists, health planners, other community and mental health specialists, and interested consumers. **Purpose:** Seeks to protect and promote personal, mental, and environmental health. **Activities:** Services include: promulgation of standards; establishment of uniform practices and procedures; development of the etiology of communicable diseases; research in public health; exploration of medical care programs and their relationships to public health. Sponsors job placement service.

★3666★ American Society for Healthcare Environmental Services of the American Hospital Association (ASHES)
Yvonne J. Cernick
840 N. Lake Shore Dr.
Chicago, IL 60611
Ph: (312)422-3860   Fax: (312)280-4152
Members: Managers and directors of hospital environmental services, laundry and linen services, housekeeping departments, and long-term care units. **Purpose:** Provides a forum for discussion among members of

common problems including educational opportunities, professional development, and career advancement. **Activities:** Operates technical assistance center and placement services. Offers legal advocacy; maintains liaison between members and governmental and code-writing bodies. Bestows Accolades Awards, Phoenix Award, Years of Service Award, Professional Recognition of Achievement – Actions for Professional Excellence Awards, and Scholarship Award. Compiles statistics; maintains library; conducts educational programs.

★3667★ **American Society of Ophthalmic Administrators (ASOA)**
4000 Legato Rd., No. 850
Fairfax, VA 22033
Ph: (703)591-2222   Fax: (703)591-0614
Fr: 800-451-1339

Members: A division of the American Society of Cataract and Refractive Surgery. Persons involved with the administration of an ophthalmic office or clinic. **Purpose:** Facilitates the exchange of ideas and information in order to improve management practices and working conditions. **Activities:** Offers placement services.

★3668★ **Association for the Advancement of Medical Instrumentation (AAMI)**
3330 Washington Blvd., Ste. 400
Arlington, VA 22201
Ph: (703)525-4890   Fax: (703)276-0793
Fr: 800-332-2264

Members: Clinical engineers, biomedical equipment technicians, physicians, hospital administrators, consultants, engineers, manufacturers of medical devices, nurses researchers and others interested in medical instrumentation. Purpose is to improve the quality of medical care through the application, development, and management of technology. **Activities:** Maintains placement service. Offers certification programs for biomedical equipment technicians and clinical engineers. Produces numerous standards and recommended practices on medical devices and procedures. Offers educational programs.

★3669★ **Association of Healthcare Internal Auditors (AHIA)**
1200 19th St. NW, Ste. 300
Washington, DC 20036
Ph: (202)429-5134   Fax: (202)223-4579

Members: Health care internal auditors and other interested individuals. **Purpose:** Promotes cost containment and increased productivity in health care institutions through internal auditing. Serves as a forum for the exchange of experience, ideas, and information among members; provides continuing professional education courses and informs members of developments in health care internal auditing. **Activities:** Offers employment clearinghouse services.

★3670★ **Group Health Association of America (GHAA)**
1129 20th St. NW, Ste. 600
Washington, DC 20036
Ph: (202)778-3200   Fax: (202)331-7487

Purpose: Supports the Health Maintenance Organization industry. **Activities:** Lobbies; conducts research programs and workshops; compiles statistics. Maintains placement service.

★3671★ **Medical Group Management Association (MGMA)**
104 Inverness Ter. E.
Englewood, CO 80112
Ph: (303)799-1111   Fax: (303)643-4427

Members: Persons actively engaged in the business management of medical groups consisting of three or more physicians in medical practice with centralized business functions. **Activities:** Sponsors educational training programs. Provides placement and information services. Compiles statistics.

★3672★ **National Executive Housekeepers Association (N.E.H.A.)**
1001 Eastwind Dr., Ste. 301
Westerville, OH 43081-3361
Ph: (614)895-7166   Fax: (614)895-1248
Fr: 800-200-NEHA

Members: Persons engaged in institutional housekeeping management in hospitals, hotels and motels, schools, and industrial establishments. **Activities:** Has established educational standards. Sponsors certificate and collegiate degree programs. Holds annual National Housekeepers Week celebration during the second week in September. Created the N.E.H.A. Educational Foundation to allocate financial awards to recognized schools to assist students in institutional housekeeping. Maintains referral service.

★3673★ **Radiology Business Management Association (RBMA)**
2755 Bristol St., Ste. 110
Costa Mesa, CA 92626
Ph: (714)833-1651   Fax: (714)546-6919

Members: Business managers for radiology groups; vendors of equipment, services, or supplies. **Purpose:** To improve business administration of radiologists' practices to better serve patients and the medical profession; and to provide opportunities for professional development and recognition. **Activities:** Offers informal placement service. Maintains information services.

★3674★ **Society for Radiation Oncology Administrators (SROA)**
2021 Spring Rd., Ste. 600
Oak Brook, IL 60521
Ph: (708)571-9065   Fax: (708)571-7837

Members: Individuals with managerial responsibilities in radiation oncology at the executive, divisional, or departmental level, and whose functions include personnel, budget, and development of operational procedures and guidelines for therapeutic radiology departments. **Purpose:** Strives to improve the administration of the business and nonmedical management aspects of therapeutic radiology, to promote the field of

therapeutic radiology administration, to provide a forum for communication among members, and to disseminate information among members. **Activities:** Maintains speakers' bureau; offers placement service.

EMPLOYER DIRECTORIES AND NETWORKING LISTS

★3675★ *AHA Guide to the Health Care Field*
Health Statistics Group
American Hospital Association (AHA)
1 N. Franklin
Chicago, IL 60606
Ph: (312)422-3501   Fax: (312)280-6015

Annual, July. $195.00, payment with order. Covers hospitals, multi-health care systems, freestanding ambulatory surgery centers, psychiatric facilities, long-term care facilities, substance abuse programs, hospices, Health Maintenance Organizations (HMOs), and other health-related organizations. Entries include: For hospitals: facility name, address, phone, administrator's name, number of beds, facilities and services, number of employees, expenses, other statistics. For other organizations: name, address, phone, name and title of contact. Arrangement: Geographical. Indexes: Hospital name.

★3676★ *American Group Practice Association—Directory*
American Group Practice Association
1422 Duke St.
Alexandria, VA 22314
Ph: (703)838-0033   Fax: (703)548-1890

Annual, February. $150.00. Covers about 250 private group medical practices and their professional staffs, totalling about 25,000 physicians and administrators. Entries include: Group member name, address, phone, names of administrator and other executives, names of physician listed by medical specialties. Arrangement: Alphabetical. Indexes: Group location, personal name.

★3677★ *Directory of Hospital Personnel*
Medical Economics
5 Paragon Dr.
Montvale, NJ 07645-1725
Ph: (201)358-7500   Fax: (201)573-4956
Fr: 800-222-3045

Annual, September. $325.00, plus 7.50 shipping. Covers 200,000 executives at 7,100 U.S. hospitals. Entries include: Name of hospital, address, phone, number of beds, type and JCAHO status of hospital, names and titles of key department heads and staff, medical and nursing school affiliations; number of residents, interns, and nursing students. Arrangement: Geographical. Indexes: Hospital name, personnel, hospital size.

★3678★ **Directory of Nursing Homes**

HCIA Inc.
300 E. Lombard St.
Baltimore, MD 21202
Ph: (410)576-9600   Fax: (410)539-5220
Fr: 800-568-3282

Annual. $249.00. Covers over 16,000 state-licensed long-term care facilities. Entries include: Facility name, address, phone, names and titles of key personnel, licensure status, number of beds; number of nursing, dietary, and auxiliary staff members; program/services; medicaid/medicare certification status; admission and referral requirements; age and gender restrictions; languages spoken; management or chain company name. Arrangement: Geographical. Indexes: Alphabetical, geographical (county) and by chain headquarters.

★3679★ **Hospital Blue Book**

Billian Publishing Co.
2100 Powers Ferry Rd., Ste. 300
Atlanta, GA 30339
Ph: (404)955-5656   Fax: (404)952-0669

Annual, spring. $154.50, national edition, plus $20.00 shipping. Covers more than 7,100 hospitals; some listings also appear in a separate southern edition of this publication. Entries include: Name of hospital, accreditation, mailing address, phone, fax, number of beds, type of facility (nonprofit, general, state, etc.); list of administrative personnel and chiefs of medical services, with specific titles. Arrangement: Geographical.

★3680★ **Hospital Market Atlas**

SMG Marketing Group, Inc.
1342 N. LaSalle Dr.
Chicago, IL 60610
Ph: (312)642-3026   Fax: (312)642-9729
Fr: 800-678-3026

Biennial, odd years. $495.00, payment with order. Covers over 7,000 hospitals, hospital systems and 480 group purchasing organizations. Entries include: Hospital or organization name, address, phone, county code, management, type of hospital service, number of beds, admissions, surgical operations, and emergency room visits. Arrangement: Geographical.

★3681★ **Hospitals Directory**

American Business Directories, Inc.
American Business Information, Inc.
5711 S. 86th Cir.
Omaha, NE 68127
Ph: (402)593-4600   Fax: (402)331-1505

Annual. $870.00, U.S. edition. Entries include: Name, address, phone (including area code), size of advertisement, year first in Yellow Pages, name of owner or manager, number of employees. Compiled from telephone company Yellow Pages, nationwide. Arrangement: Geographical.

★3682★ **Medical and Health Information Directory**

Gale Research
835 Penobscot Bldg.
Detroit, MI 48226-4094
Ph: (313)961-2242   Fax: (313)961-6083
Fr: 800-877-GALE

Approximately biennial; latest edition 1994. $195.00, per volume; $485.00, for the three-volume set. Covers in Volume 1, almost 18,600 medical and health oriented associations, organizations, institutions, and government agencies, including health maintenance organizations (HMOs), preferred provider organizations (PPOs), insurance companies, pharmaceutical companies, research centers, and medical and allied health schools. In Volume 2, nearly 11,800 medical book publishers; medical periodicals, directories, audiovisual producers and services, medical libraries and information centers, and electronic resources. In Volume 3, nearly 26,000 clinics, treatment centers, care programs, and counseling/diagnostic services for 30 subject areas. Entries include: Institution, service, or firm name, address, phone; many include names of key personnel and, when pertinent, descriptive annotation. Arrangement: Classified by organization activity, service, etc. Indexes: Each volume has a complete alphabetical name and keyword index.

★3683★ **Osteopathic Membership Directory—AOHA**

American Osteopathic Healthcare
Association
5301 Wisconsin Ave. NW, Ste. 630
Washington, DC 20015-2015
Ph: (202)686-1700   Fax: (202)686-7615

Annual, summer. $125.00, payment with order. Covers about 110 osteopathic hospitals. Includes list of individual and institutional members; also lists osteopathic colleges, and directors of medical education. Entries include: For hospitals: name of hospital, name of chief executive officer, address, phone, number of beds and other hospital data. Arrangement: Geographical. Indexes: Name, institution.

HANDBOOKS AND MANUALS

★3684★ **Encyclopedia of Careers and Vocational Guidance**

J. G. Ferguson Publishing Co.
200 W. Monroe, Ste. 250
Chicago, IL 60606
Ph: (312)580-5480

William E. Hopke. Ninth edition, 1993. $129.95; $199.95 (CD-ROM). Four-volume set that profiles 900 occupations and describes job trends in 71 industries. Includes career description, educational requirements, history of the job, methods of entry, advancement, employment outlook, earnings, conditions of work, social and psychological factors, and sources of further information. Contains career and employment information for this field.

★3685★ **Hospital and Health Services Administrators**

Chronicle Guidance Publications, Inc.
66 Aurora St.
PO Box 1190
Moravia, NY 13118-1190
Ph: (315)497-0330   Fax: (315)497-3359
Fr: 800-622-7284

Chronicle Guidance Staff. 1994. $2.00. Provides concise career information and sources of additional information.

★3686★ **Liberal Arts Jobs: What They Are and How to Get Them**

Peterson's
PO Box 2123
Princeton, NJ 08543-2123
Ph: (609)243-9111   Fax: (609)243-9150
Fr: 800-338-3282

Burton Jay Nadler. Second edition, 1989. $9.95. 153 pages. Presents a list of the top 20 fields for liberal arts majors, covering more than 300 job opportunities. Discusses strategies for going after those jobs, including guidance on the language of a successful job search, informational interviews, and making networking work.

★3687★ **100 Best Careers for the Year 2000**

Prentice Hall General Reference
15 Columbus Cir.
New York, NY 10023
Ph: (212)373-8500   Fr: 800-223-2348

Shelly Field. 1992. $15.00 (paper). Covers 100 of the fastest growing jobs. The publication is divided into 11 general employment sections. Specific careers are covered within each section. Provides job description, responsibilities, employment opportunities, earnings, education and training, advancement opportunities, and experience and qualifications for each occupation.

★3688★ **Opportunities in Health and Medical Careers**

VGM Career Horizons
4255 W. Touhy Ave.
Lincolnwood, IL 60646-1975
Ph: (847)679-5500   Fax: (847)679-2494
Fr: 800-323-4900

Donald Snook, Jr. and Leo D'Orazio. 1993. $14.95; $11.95 (paper). Covers the full range of medical and health occupations. Illustrated.

★3689★ **Opportunities in Hospital Administration Careers**

VGM Career Horizons
4255 W. Touhy Ave.
Lincolnwood, IL 60646-1975
Ph: (847)679-5500   Fax: (847)679-2494
Fr: 800-323-4900

I. Donald Snook. 1989. $14.95; $11.95 (paper). 160 pages. Discusses opportunities for administrators in a variety of management settings: hospital, department, clinic, group practice, HMO, mental health, and extended care facilities.

★3690★ Opportunities in Vocational and Technical Careers

VGM Career Horizons
4255 W. Touhy Ave.
Lincolnwood, IL 60646-1975
Ph: (847)679-5500   Fax: (847)679-2494
Fr: 800-323-4900

Adrian A. Paradis. 1992. $14.95; $11.95 (paper). 160 pages. Provides information on a variety of opportunities and advice on breaking into the field.

★3691★ Resumes for Health and Medical Careers

4255 W. Touhy Ave.
Lincolnwood, IL 60646-1975
Ph: (708)679-5500   Fax: (708)679-6375
Fr: 800-323-4900

Compiled by VGM Career Horizons Staff 1995. $9.95 (paper).

★3692★ Where the Jobs Are: The Hottest Careers for the '90s

The Career Press, Inc.
3 Tice Rd.
PO Box 687
Franklin Lakes, NJ 07417
Ph: (201)848-0310   Fax: (201)848-1727
Fr: 800-237-3371

Joyce Hadley. Second edition, 1995. $9.99. 300 pages. Describes careers in fifteen general fields, from accounting to travel and hospitality.

★3693★ Your Resume: Key to a Better Job

Prentice Hall General Reference and Travel
15 Columbus Cir.
New York, NY 10023
Ph: (212)373-8500

Leonard Corwen. Fifth edition, 1993. $11.00. Provides guidelines for resume writing; explains what employers look for in a resume, including contents and style. Includes model resumes for high-demand careers such as computer programmers, health administrators, and high-tech professionals. Notes basic job-getting information and strategies.

EMPLOYMENT AGENCIES AND SEARCH FIRMS

★3694★ Action Plus Employer Services

1211 W. Imperial Hwy., Ste. 100
Brea, CA 92621
Ph: (714)773-1506   Fax: (714)773-9201

Employment agency.

★3695★ CT Group

264 N. Elm St.
North Massapequa, NY 11758-2525
Ph: (516)797-3642   Fax: (516)795-4350

Executive search firm and employment agency.

★3696★ Executive Medical Recruiters

2350 W. 7th St.
St. Paul, MN 55116
Ph: (612)699-3020

Employment agency.

★3697★ JPM International

4665 MacArthur Ct., Ste. 100B
Newport Beach, CA 92660
Ph: (714)955-2545   Fax: (714)757-1320

Executive search firm and employment agency.

★3698★ Midwest Medical Consultants

8910 Purdue Rd., Ste. 200
Indianapolis, IN 46268-1155
Ph: (317)872-1053

Employment agency. Executive search firm.

★3699★ Weatherby Healthcare

25 Van Zant St.
Norwalk, CT 06855
Ph: (203)866-1144   Fax: (203)853-3154

Executive search firm. Branch office in Fairfax, VA.

OTHER SOURCES

★3700★ American Almanac of Jobs and Salaries 1994-95

Avon Books
1350 Avenue of the Americas, 2nd Fl.
New York, NY 10019
Ph: (212)261-6800   Fr: 800-238-0658

John Wright. Revised edition, 1993. $17.00. 704 pages. This is a comprehensive guide to the wages of hundreds of occupations in a wide variety of industries and organizations.

★3701★ American Health Care Association

1201 L St. NW
Washington, DC 20005
Ph: (202)842-4444   Fax: (202)842-3860

Members: Federation of state associations of long-term health care facilities. **Purpose:** Promotes standards for professionals in long-term health care delivery and quality care for patients and residents in a safe environment. Focuses on issues of availability, quality, affordability, and fair payment. Operates as a liaison with governmental agencies, Congress, and professional associations.

★3702★ American Hospital Association (AHA)

1 N. Franklin, Ste. 27
Chicago, IL 60606
Ph: (312)422-3000   Fax: (312)422-4796

Members: Individuals and health care institutions including hospitals, health care systems, and pre- and postacute health care delivery organizations. **Purpose:** Is dedicated to promoting the welfare of the public through its leadership and assistance to its members in the provision of better health services for all people. Conducts educational

programs furthering the in-service education of hospital personnel; collects and analyzes data; furnishes multimedia educational materials; maintains 44,000 volume health care administration library, and biographical archive.

★3703★ Hospice Administrators

Chronicle Guidance Publications, Inc.
66 Aurora St.
PO Box 1190
Moravia, NY 13118-1190
Ph: (315)497-0330   Fax: (315)497-3359
Fr: 800-622-7284

Chronicle Guidance Staff. 1994. $2.00. Provides concise career information and sources of additional information.

★3704★ Hospital Salary Survey Report

Hospital Compensation Service
John R. Zabka Associates, Inc.
69 Minnehaha Blvd.
PO Box 376
Oakland, NJ 07436
Ph: (201)405-0075

Annual. Reports salaries for management employees, registered nurses, and licensed practical nurses by hospital bed size, by profit and nonprofit status for governmental hospitals, and by geographic area.

★3705★ National Association of Health Services Executives (NAHSE)

10320 Little Patuxent Pky., Ste. 1106
Columbia, MD 21044
Ph: (301)628-3953   Fax: (301)588-0011

Members: Black health care executive managers, planners, educators, advocates, providers, organizers, researchers, and consumers participating in academic ventures, educational forums, seminars, workshops, systems design, legislation, and other activities. **Activities:** Conducts National Work-Study Program and sponsors educational programs.

★3706★ National Association for Healthcare Quality (NAHQ)

4700 W. Lake Ave.
Glenview, IL 60025-1485
Ph: (708)375-4700   Fax: (708)875-4777

Members: Healthcare professionals in quality assessment and improvement, utilization and risk management, case management, infection control, managed care, nursing, and medical records. **Purpose:** Objectives are: to encourage, develop, and provide continuing education for all persons involved in health care quality; to give the patient primary consideration in all actions affecting his or her health and welfare; to promote the sharing of knowledge and encourage a high degree of professional ethics in health care quality. Offers accredited certification in the field of healthcare quality, utilization, and risk management. Facilitates communication and cooperation among members, medical staff, and health care government agencies. Conducts educational seminars and conferences.

★3707★ **National Health Council (NHC)**
1730 M St. NW, Ste. 500
Washington, DC 20036
Ph: (202)785-3910   Fax: (202)785-5923

Members: National membership association of voluntary and professional societies in the health field; national organizations and business groups with strong health interests. **Purpose:** Seeks to improve the health of the nation. Holds annual National Health Forum. Distributes printed material on health careers and related subjects. Promotes standardization of financial reporting for voluntary health groups.

★3708★ **National Rural Health Association (NRHA)**
1 W. Armour Blvd., Ste. 301
Kansas City, MO 64111
Ph: (816)756-3140   Fax: (816)756-3144

Members: Administrators, physicians, nurses, physician assistants, health planners, academicians, and others interested or involved in rural health care. **Purpose:** To create a better understanding of health care problems unique to rural areas; utilize a collective approach in finding positive solutions; articulate and represent the health care needs of rural America; supply current information to rural health care providers; serve as a liaison between rural health care programs throughout the country. Offers continuing education credits for medical, dental, nursing, and management courses.

★3709★ **Society for Ambulatory Care Professionals (SACP)**
1 N. Franklin, 31st Fl.
Chicago, IL 60606
Ph: (312)422-3900   Fax: (312)422-4577

Purpose: Works to advance the development of ambulatory care and advocates issues that enhance the value, role, delivery, and management of ambulatory care services.

Heating, Air-Conditioning, and Refrigeration Mechanics

★3710★ Air Conditioning, Heating and Refrigeration News

Business News Publishing Co.
PO Box 2600
Troy, MI 48007
Ph: (810)362-3700   Fax: (810)362-0317

Weekly. $76.00/year for individuals. Tabloid for HVAC and commercial refrigeration contractors, wholesalers, manufacturers, engineers, and owners/managers.

★3711★ ASHRAE Journal

American Society of Heating, Refrigerating and Air-Conditioning Engineers
1791 Tullie Cir. NE
Atlanta, GA 30329
Ph: (404)636-8400   Fax: (404)321-4578

Monthly. $49.00/year for individuals; $6.00 for single issue. Magazine for the heating, refrigeration, and air conditioning trade.

★3712★ Contractor Magazine

Cahners Publishing Co.
1350 E. Touhy Ave.
Des Plaines, IL 60018
Ph: (708)635-8800   Fax: (708)390-2770

Monthly. Free to qualified subscribers; $70.00/year for individuals. Industry news and management how-to magazine for air conditioning, heating, plumbing and other mechanical specialties contracting firms.

★3713★ Heating/Piping/Air Conditioning

Peter Li
1100 Superior Ave.
Cleveland, OH 44114
Ph: (216)696-7000   Fax: (216)696-7670

Monthly. $60.00/year for individuals; $75.00/year for Canada; $95.00/year for other countries.

★3714★ HVAC

Cahner's Publishing
455 N. Michigan Ave.
Chicago, IL 60611-5503
Ph: (312)222-2000   Fax: (312)222-2026

Monthly. Heating, ventilating, and air conditioning magazine (tabloid).

★3715★ Industrial Heating

Business News Publishing Co.
1910 Cochran Rd., Ste. 630
Pittsburgh, PA 15220
Ph: (412)531-3370   Fax: (412)531-3375

Monthly. Magazine.

★3716★ Plumbing Heating Piping

Cahners Publishing
1350 W. Touhy Ave.
Des Plaines, IL 60018
Ph: (312)222-2000   Fax: (312)222-2026

Monthly. Magazine on the plumbing, piping, and hydronics industries.

★3717★ Reeves Journal: Plumbing Heating Cooling

Business News Publishing Co.
23187 La Cadena Dr., Ste. 101
PO Box 30700
Laguna Hills, CA 92653
Ph: (714)830-0881   Fax: (714)859-7845

Monthly. Free to qualified subscribers; $24.00/year for individuals. Regional plumbing, heating, and cooling magazine.

★3718★ RSC (Refrigeration Service and Contracting)

Business News Publishing Co.
PO Box 2600
Troy, MI 48007
Ph: (810)362-3700   Fax: (810)362-0317

Monthly. $36.00/year; $51.00/year for other countries. Official magazine of the Refrigeration Service Engineer's Society; reporting on service, repair, installation, and replacement articles.

★3719★ Service Reporter

Technical Reporting Co./Palmer Publishing Co.
651 W. Washington St., Ste. 300
Chicago, IL 60606
Ph: (312)993-0929   Fax: (312)993-0960

Monthly. $12.00/year for individuals; $30.00/year for Canada; $60.00/year for other countries; $2.00 for single issue. Magazine (tabloid) focusing on air conditioning and ventilation, heating, and refrigeration.

★3720★ Snips Magazine

1949 Cornell Ave.
Melrose Park, IL 60160-9953
Ph: (708)544-3870   Fax: (708)544-3884

Monthly. $12.00/year for individuals; $2.00 for single issue. Magazine for the sheet metal, warm-air heating, ventilating, and air conditioning industry.

★3721★ Southern Plumbing, Heating, Cooling Magazine

Southern Trade Publications, Inc.
Box 18343
Greensboro, NC 27419
Ph: (919)454-3516

Bimonthly. Trade magazine covering plumbing, heating, and air conditioning.

★3722★ Summer Jobs: Opportunities in the Federal Government

Office of Personnel Management
1900 E St. NW
Washington, DC 20415
Ph: (202)606-0950

Formerly annual; latest edition January 1993; suspended indefinitely. Free. Covers GS-1 through GS-4 clerical jobs and other jobs at GS-5 and above which are expected to be available in federal agencies and departments throughout the United States during the season. Most jobs are in Metropolitan Washington, D.C. Latest application date is generally April 15; many are earlier. Includes general information on applying for jobs in trades and labor occupations and summer employment for needy youth programs. Entries include: Agency name, filing deadline, titles of jobs available, brief information on qualifications needed, location, etc. Complete agency names and addresses are given in separate list. Publication is available from

Federal Employment Information Center offices and agency personnel offices. Arrangement: By job level, then alphabetical by agency name.

★3723★ Tradeswomen

Tradeswomen, Inc.
PO Box 2622
Berkeley, CA 94702
Ph: (510)649-6260

Bimonthly. $35.00/year. Subtitled: "A Quarterly Magazine for Women in Blue Collar Work". Reports activities of the organization and other events in the California Bay Area and of national interest to women working or wishing to work in nontraditional and blue collar jobs. Recurring features include announcements of apprenticeship opportunities and job openings, information on unions and government agencies, and U.S. Department of Labor statistics.

★3724★ Western HVACR News

Palatrom Publishing Co.
PO Box 42749
Los Angeles, CA 90050-0749
Ph: (213)225-8034

Monthly. $23.00 for two years. Western regional newspaper (tabloid) for the heating, ventilating, air conditioning, refrigeration, hydronics, sheet metal, solar, and allied industries.

PLACEMENT AND JOB REFERRAL SERVICES

★3725★ Associated Builders and Contractors (ABC)

1300 N. 17th St.
Rosslyn, VA 22209
Ph: (703)812-2000   Fax: (703)812-8200

Members: Construction contractors, subcontractors, suppliers, and associates. **Purpose:** Aim is to foster and perpetuate the principles of rewarding construction workers and management on the basis of merit. **Activities:** Maintains placement service. Sponsors management education programs and craft training; also sponsors apprenticeship and skill training programs. Disseminates technological and labor relations information. Compiles statistics.

★3726★ National Association of Home Builders of the U.S. (NAHB)

1201 15th St. NW
Washington, DC 20005
Ph: (202)822-0200   Fax: (202)822-0559

Members: Single and multifamily home builders, commercial builders, and others associated with the building industry. **Purpose:** Lobbies on behalf of the housing industry and conducts public affairs activities to increase public understanding of housing and the economy. Collects and disseminates data on current developments in home building and home builders' plans through its Economics Department and nationwide Metropolitan Housing Forecast. **Activities:** Maintains NAHB Research Center, which func-

tions as the research arm of the home building industry. Sponsors seminars and workshops on construction, mortgage credit, labor relations, cost reduction, land use, remodeling, and business management. Compiles statistics; offers charitable program, spokesman training, and placement service; maintains speakers' bureau, and hall of fame.

EMPLOYER DIRECTORIES AND NETWORKING LISTS

★3727★ ABC Today—Associated Builders and Contractors Membership Directory Issue

Associated Builders and Contractors
1300 N. 17th St.
Rosslyn, VA 22209
Ph: (703)812-2000   Fax: (703)812-8200

Annual, November. $150.00, plus $7.00 shipping. Publication includes: List of approximately 17,000 member construction contractors and suppliers. Entries include: Company name, address, phone, name of principal executive, code to volume of business, business specialty. Arrangement: Classified by chapter, then by work specialty.

★3728★ Air Conditioning Contractors of America—Membership Directory

Air Conditioning Contractors of America
1712 New Hampshire Ave., NW
Washington, DC 20009
Ph: (202)483-9370   Fax: (202)234-4721

Annual, Summer. Available to members only. Covers member air conditioning and heating contractors, manufacturers, vocational technical schools. Entries include: Company name, address, phone, fax, names and titles of key personnel, description of fields, and types of work performed. Arrangement: Geographical. Indexes: Alphabetical.

★3729★ Air Conditioning Equipment Repair Directory

American Business Directories, Inc.
American Business Information, Inc.
5711 S. 86th Cir.
Omaha, NE 68127
Ph: (402)593-4600   Fax: (402)331-1505

Annual. $810.00, payment with order. Covers approximately 11,351 companies that specialize in equipment for air conditioning repair. Entries include: Company name, address, phone (including area code), size of advertisement, year first in Yellow Pages, name of owner or manager, number of employees. Compiled from telephone company Yellow Pages, nationwide. Arrangement: Geographical.

★3730★ Air Conditioning, Heating and Refrigeration News—Directory Issue

Business News Publishing Co.
755 W. Big Beaver Rd., 10th Fl.
Troy, MI 48084
Ph: (810)362-3700   Fr: 800-837-7370

Annual, January. $230.00, plus $2.50 shipping. Publication includes: Lists of about

1,900 manufacturers, 5,300 wholesalers and factory outlets, 10,000 HVACR products, exporters specializing in the industry; related trade organizations; manufacturers representatives, consultants, services; videos and software. Entries include: For manufacturers Company name, address, phone, fax, names of key personnel, brand names, list of products; similar information for other categories. Arrangement: Manufacturers and exporters are alphabetical; wholesalers and representatives are geographical. Indexes: Product, trade name.

★3731★ Constructor—Directory of Membership and Services Issue

AGC Information, Inc.
Associated General Contractors of America
1957 E St. NW
Washington, DC 20006
Ph: (202)393-2040   Fax: (202)347-4004

Annual, July. $135.00. Publication includes: List of more than 8,500 member firms and 9,000 national associate member firms engaged in building, highway, heavy, industrial, municipal utilities, and railroad construction, listing of state and local chapter officers. Arrangement: Geographical. Indexes: Company name.

★3732★ ENR—Top 400 Construction Contractors Issue

McGraw-Hill, Inc.
1221 Ave. of the Americas
New York, NY 10020
Ph: (212)512-4635   Fax: (212)512-2820

Annual, May issue of Engineering News Record. $10.00, Reprint, payment with order. Publication includes: List of 400 United States contractors receiving largest dollar volumes of contracts in preceding calendar year. Separate lists of 50 largest design/construct management firms; 50 largest program and construction managers; 25 building contractors; 25 heavy contractors. Entries include: Company name, headquarters location, total value of contracts received in preceding year, value of foreign contracts, countries in which operated, construction specialities. Arrangement: By total value of contracts received.

★3733★ Heating Equipment Dealers & Contractors Directory

American Business Directories, Inc.
American Business Information, Inc.
5711 S. 86th Cir.
Omaha, NE 68127
Ph: (402)593-4600   Fax: (402)331-1505

Annual. $1,495.00, U.S. edition; $310.00, (Canadian edition); payment with order. Significant discounts offered for standing orders. Number of listings: 44,851 (U.S. edition); 6,523 (Canadian edition). Entries include: Name, address, phone (including area code), size of advertisement, year first in Yellow Pages, coding indicating brands carried, specialties, or franchises held. Regional editions available: Eastern, $1,090.00; Western, $555.00. Compiled from telephone company Yellow Pages, nationwide. Arrangement: Geographical.

★3734★ Mechanical Contractors Association of America—Membership Directory/Buyers Guide & Publications Catalog

Naylor Publications
Shawan Pl.
5 Shawan Rd.
Hunt Valley, MD 21030
Ph: (410)785-2445   Fax: (410)785-2459
Fr: 800-879-1107

Annual, March. Available only to members and advertisers. Covers 1,400 contractors who install piping and related equipment for heating, air conditioning, plumbing, and cooling systems in commercial and institutional buildings, and process piping in industrial facilities. Also includes list of state and local associations. Entries include: Company name, address, phone, and names of principal executives. Arrangement: Geographical. Indexes: Alphabetical.

★3735★ Mechanical Contractors Directory

American Business Directories, Inc.
American Business Information, Inc.
5711 S. 86th Cir.
Omaha, NE 68127
Ph: (402)593-4600   Fax: (402)331-1505

Annual. $420.00, U.S. edition. Number of listings: 4,659 (U.S. edition); 1,094 (Canadian edition). Entries include: Name, address, phone (including area code), size of advertisement, year first in Yellow Pages, name of owner or manager, number of employees. Compiled from telephone company Yellow Pages, nationwide. Arrangement: Geographical.

★3736★ Michigan Plumbing and Mechanical Contractors Association—Membership Directory

Michigan Plumbing and Mechanical
  Contractors Association (MPMCA)
400 N. Walnut St.
Lansing, MI 48933
Ph: (517)484-5500   Fax: (517)484-5225
Fr: 800-292-1044

Annual. Available to subscribers only. Covers member firms, industry and auxiliary associations, legislative and regulatory agencies in the plumbing and heating industry of Michigan. Entries include: Organization name, address, phone, names and titles of key personnel. Arrangement: Separate sections for members, industry associations, legislative and regulatory, and auxiliaries; members are geographical. Indexes: Company name (members), president name (members).

★3737★ Minnesota P-H-C Contractor—Membership Directory Issue

Minnesota Association of Plumbing-
  Heating-Cooling Contractors
8085 Wayzata Blvd., Ste. 109
Minneapolis, MN 55426
Ph: (612)546-4448   Fr: 800-328-4827

Annual, January. Available to members only. Publication includes: List of 450 member firms and associates. Entries include: Name of company, address, phone, fax, code indicating type of work, local association affiliation (chapter memberships and other), name and title of owner or officer, home address

and phone. Arrangement: Alphabetical. Indexes: Alphabetical by service/line of business.

★3738★ National Commercial Refrigeration Sales Association—Membership Directory

National Commercial Refrigeration Sales
  Association (NCRSA)
c/o Fernley & Fernley, Inc.
1900 Arch St.
Philadelphia, PA 19103
Ph: (215)564-3484   Fax: (215)564-2175

Annual, Spring. Free. Covers about 100 member refrigeration contracting companies. Entries include: Company name, address, phone, names and titles of key personnel, description of products or services provided, branch office or subsidiary names and addresses. Arrangement: Geographical. Indexes: Company name.

★3739★ Northamerican Heating, Refrigeration & Airconditioning Wholesalers Association—Membership Directory

Northamerican Heating, Refrigeration &
  Airconditioning Wholesalers Association
PO Box 16790
Columbus, OH 43216-6790
Ph: (614)488-1835   Fax: (614)488-0482

Annual, spring. Available to members only. Covers about 2,000 wholesalers and distributors. Entries include: Company name, address, phone and names of executives. Arrangement: Alphabetical.

★3740★ Refrigerating Equipment-Commercial Directory

American Business Directories, Inc.
American Business Information, Inc.
5711 S. 86th Cir.
Omaha, NE 68127
Ph: (402)593-4600   Fax: (402)331-1505

Annual. $185.00, payment with order. Number of listings: 2,059. Entries include: Name, address, phone (including area code), size of advertisement, year first in Yellow Pages, name of owner or manager, number of employees. Compiled from telephone company Yellow Pages, nationwide. Arrangement: Geographical.

★3741★ Who's Who in the Plumbing-Heating-Cooling Contracting Business

National Association of Plumbing-Heating-
  Cooling Contractors (NAPHCC)
180 S. Washington St.
Falls Church, VA 22046
Ph: (703)237-8100   Fax: (703)237-7442
Fr: 800-533-7694

Annual. $75.00. Covers About 6,000 professional plumbing/heating/cooling contractors and member firms. Entries include: Name, address, phone, contact, line of business. Arrangement: Geographical. Indexes: Individual member.

HANDBOOKS AND MANUALS

★3742★ Exploring Nontraditional Jobs for Women

Rosen Publishing Group, Inc.
29 E. 21st St.
New York, NY 10010
Ph: (212)777-3017   Fax: (212)777-0277
Fr: 800-237-9932

Rose Neufeld. 1989. $14.95. Describes occupations where few women are found. Covers job duties, training routes, where to apply for jobs, tools used, salary, and advantages and disadvantages of the job.

★3743★ Opportunities in Building Construction Trades

VGM Career Horizons
4255 W. Touhy Ave.
Lincolnwood, IL 60646-1975
Ph: (847)679-5500   Fax: (847)679-2494
Fr: 800-323-4900

Michael Sumichrast. 1993. $14.95; $11.95 (paper). From custom builder to rehabber, the many kinds of companies that employ craftspeople and contractors are explored. Includes job descriptions, requirements, and salaries for dozens of specialties within the construction industry. Contains a complete list of Bureau of Apprenticeship and Training state and area offices. Illustrated.

★3744★ Opportunities in Heating, Ventilating, Air Conditioning, and Refrigeration Occupations

VGM Career Horizons
4255 W. Touhy Ave.
Lincolnwood, IL 60646-1975
Ph: (847)679-5500   Fax: (847)679-2494
Fr: 800-323-4900

Richard Budzik. 1996. $11.95. 160 pages. Outlines jobs in the installation, operation, and service of refrigeration systems in homes, civic centers, office buildings, automobiles, trucks, and ships, and discusses how to identify opportunities.

★3745★ Opportunities in Plumbing and Pipefitting Careers

VGM Career Horizons
4255 W. Touhy Ave.
Lincolnwood, IL 60646-1975
Ph: (847)679-5500   Fax: (847)679-2494
Fr: 800-323-4900

Patrick J. Galvin. 1995. $14.95; $11.95 (paper). 160 pages. Provides information on getting into the trade, apprenticeship programs, and how to build a career in a variety of settings. Illustrated.

★3746★ Opportunities in Vocational and Technical Careers

VGM Career Horizons
4255 W. Touhy Ave.
Lincolnwood, IL 60646-1975
Ph: (847)679-5500   Fax: (847)679-2494
Fr: 800-323-4900

Adrian A. Paradis. 1992. $14.95; $11.95 (paper). 160 pages. Provides information on a variety of opportunities and advice on breaking into the field.

EMPLOYMENT AGENCIES AND SEARCH FIRMS

★3747★ Jobs, Training, and Services, Inc.

101 S. Moberly Ave.
Longview, TX 75602-1433
Ph: (903)757-3046

Employment agency. Another office is located in Henderson, TX.

OTHER SOURCES

★3748★ Air Conditioning Contractors of America (ACCA)

1712 New Hampshire Ave., NW
Washington, DC 20009
Ph: (202)483-9370   Fax: (202)234-4721
Members: Contractors involved in installation and service of heating, air conditioning, and refrigeration systems. Associate members are utilities, manufacturers, wholesalers, and other market-oriented businesses. **Purpose:** Monitors utility competition and operating practices of HVAC manufacturers and wholesalers. Provides consulting services, technical training, and instructor certification program; offers management seminars. Operates annual educational institute.

★3749★ Associated Specialty Contractors (ASC)

3 Bethesda Metro Ctr., Ste. 1100
Bethesda, MD 20814
Ph: (301)657-3110   Fax: (301)215-4500
Members: Subcontractor associations with a total of 25,000 members representing electrical, heating, piping, mechanical, air conditioning, sheet metal, plumbing, ventilating, masonry, painting and decorating, and roofing and insulation contractors. **Purpose:** Promotes liaison with general contractors, architects, and engineers on inter-industry matters, codes, bidding, and contracting procedures. Coordinates governmental affairs, research, and educational matters.

★3750★ Career Connections Video Series

Cambridge Career Products
PO Box 2153
Dept. CC15
Charleston, WV 25328-2153
Ph: (304)744-9323   Fax: (304)744-9351
Fr: 800-468-4227

Series of six videos. 1993. $219.95/set. $39.95/each. 15-20 minutes. Each video contains interviews with workers and on-the-job footage. Titles include Graphic Design, Welding, Electrician, Plumber, Pipefitter, and HVAC.

★3751★ Careers for Today and Tomorrow in HVACR

Air-Conditioning and Refrigeration Institute
Education Dept.
4301 N. Fairfax Dr., 4th Fl.
Arlington, VA 22203
Ph: (202)362-1117

Video. $16.50 (educational institutions); $26.50 (others). 10 minutes. Covers career options in the HVACR field.

★3752★ COIN Career Guidance System

COIN Educational Products
3361 Executive Pky., Ste. 302
Toledo, OH 43606
Ph: (419)536-5353   Fr: 800-274-8515

CD-ROM product; also available on diskette. Provides career information through seven cross-referenced files covering postsecondary schools, college majors, vocational programs, military service, apprenticeship programs, financial aid, and scholarships. Apprenticeship file describes national apprenticeship training programs, including information on how to apply, contact agencies, and program content. Military file describes more than 200 military occupations and training opportunities related to civilian employment.

★3753★ Mechanical Contractors Association of America (MCAA)

1385 Piccard Dr.
Rockville, MD 20850-4329
Ph: (301)869-5800   Fax: (301)990-9690
Members: Contractors who furnish, install, and service piping systems and related equipment for heating, cooling, refrigeration, ventilating, and air conditioning systems. **Purpose:** Works to standardize materials and methods used in the industry. Conducts business overhead, labor wage, and statistical surveys. Maintains dialogue with key officials in building trade unions. Promotes apprenticeship training programs. Conducts seminars on contracts, labor estimating, job cost control, project management, market-ing, collective bargaining, contractor insurance, and other management topics. Promotes methods to conserve energy in new and existing buildings. Sponsors Industrial Relations Council for the Plumbing and Pipe Fitting Industry.

★3754★ National Association of Plumbing-Heating-Cooling Contractors (NAPHCC)

180 S. Washington St.
PO Box 6808
Falls Church, VA 22040
Ph: (703)237-8100   Fax: (703)237-7442
Fr: 800-533-7694

Members: Federation of state and local associations of plumbing, heating, and cooling contractors. **Purpose:** Seeks to advance sanitation, encourage sanitary laws, and generally improve the plumbing, heating, ventilating, and air conditioning industries. **Activities:** Conducts apprenticeship training programs, workshops, and seminars; cooperates with Plumbing-Heating-Cooling Information Bureau. Maintains speakers' bureau and political action committee. Conducts educational and research programs.

★3755★ National Association of Women in Construction (NAWIC)

327 S. Adams St.
Fort Worth, TX 76104
Ph: (817)877-5551   Fax: (817)877-0324
Fr: 800-552-3506

Purpose: NAWIC is an international association of women employed in the construction industry which promotes that industry and supports the advancement of women within it.

★3756★ Refrigeration Service Engineers Society (RSES)

1666 Rand Rd.
Des Plaines, IL 60016-3552
Ph: (708)297-6464   Fax: (708)297-5038
Members: Persons engaged in refrigeration, air-conditioning and heating installation, service, sales, and maintenance. **Activities:** Conducts training courses and certification testing. Maintains a hall of fame and a speakers' bureau.

★3757★ WIT

Northern New England Tradeswomen
26 Railroad St.
St. Johnsbury, VT 05819
Ph: (802)748-3308   Fax: (802)748-1768
Quarterly. Included in membership; $10.00/year for nonmembers. Provides a network of support, information, and skill sharing for women in trade professions.

Historians

SOURCES OF HELP-WANTED ADS

★3758★ Historic Preservation News

National Trust for Historic Preservation
1785 Massachusetts Ave. NW
Washington, DC 20036
Ph: (202)673-4075

Monthly. $15.00/year for members only. Newspaper featuring historic preservation and architecture.

★3759★ History News

American Association for State and Local History
530 Church St., #600
Nashville, TN 37219-2325
Ph: (615)255-2971   Fax: (615)255-2979

Bimonthly. Magazine for employees of historic sites, museums, and public history agencies. Coverage includes museum education programs and techniques for working with volunteers.

★3760★ Perspectives—Employment Information Section

American Historical Association
400 A St. SE
Washington, DC 20003-3889
Ph: (202)544-2422   Fax: (202)544-8307

Nine issues per year. $65.00 for institutions. Publication includes: List of over 1000 job openings per year for historians; international coverage. Entries include: Institution or organization name, address, department name, name and title of contact, responsibilities, application deadline. Arrangement: Geographical.

PLACEMENT AND JOB REFERRAL SERVICES

★3761★ African Studies Association (ASA)

Emory University
Credit Union Bldg.
Atlanta, GA 30322
Ph: (404)329-6410   Fax: (404)329-6433

Members: Persons specializing in teaching, writing, or research on Africa including political scientists, historians, geographers, anthropologists, economists, librarians, linguists, and government officials; persons who are studying African subjects; institutional members are universities, libraries, government agencies, and others interested in receiving information about Africa. **Purpose:** Seeks to foster communication and to stimulate research among scholars on Africa. **Activities:** Sponsors placement service; conducts panels and discussion groups; presents exhibits and films. **E-Mail:** africa@mony.edu

★3762★ Flag Research Center (FRC)

PO Box 580
Winchester, MA 01890
Ph: (617)729-9410   Fax: (617)721-4817

Purpose: Professional and amateur vexillologists (flag historians) seeking to coordinate flag research activities and promote vexillology as a historical discipline and hobby and to increase knowledge of and appreciation for flags of all kinds. Provides data and gives lectures on flag history, etiquette, design, symbolism, and uses. **Activities:** Operates speakers' bureau; offers children's services and placement service.

★3763★ Organization of American Historians (OAH)

112 N. Bryan St.
Bloomington, IN 47408
Ph: (812)855-7311   Fax: (812)855-0696

Members: Professional historians, including college faculty members, secondary school teachers, graduate students, and other individuals in related fields; institutional subscribers are college, university, high school and public libraries, and historical agencies. **Purpose:** Promotes historical research and study. Sponsors 12 prize programs for historical writing; maintains speakers' bureau. **Activities:** Operates a professional job registry at annual meeting. Conducts educational programs. **E-Mail:** OAH@INDIANA.EDU

★3764★ Social Sciences Services and Resources

PO Box 153
Wasco, IL 60183
Ph: (708)897-5345

Members: Consulting associates in social sciences. **Purpose:** Established to advance the teaching, consulting, and practice of the social sciences basic disciplines including sociology, anthropology, political science, geography, history, economics, and their applied disciplines: social work, community development, planning, and public administration. Serves as: a center for dissemination of current and comprehensive social research findings. Provides consultants for citizen groups, community projects, and governmental units on written request. Upon request from colleges, school boards, and citizens groups, conducts in-service workshops on teaching, consulting, and new developments in the social sciences. Provides consultant evaluation services for small colleges throughout the U.S. **Activities:** Maintains speakers' bureau and placement information service. Conducts research programs.

EMPLOYER DIRECTORIES AND NETWORKING LISTS

★3765★ Directory of Federal Historical Programs and Activities

American Historical Association
400 A St. SE
Washington, DC 20003-3889
Ph: (202)544-2422

Triennial, latest edition December 1993. $10.00. Covers about 1,700 federally employed historians and federal government agencies operating historical programs. Entries include: For historians: name, phone, area of expertise, historical program. For programs: name, address, functions of historians.

★3766★ Historical Archaeology Newsletter—Society for Historical Archaeology Membership Directory Issue

Society for Historical Archaeology
Box 30446
Tucson, AZ 85751
Ph: (602)886-8006   Fax: (602)886-0182

Annual, June. Available to members only. Publication includes: List of about 2,100 member archaeologists, historians, anthropologists, and ethnohistorians, and other individuals and institutions having an interest in historical archeology or allied fields. Entries include: Name, address. Arrangement: Alphabetical.

HANDBOOKS AND MANUALS

★3767★ Career Choices for the 90's for Students of History

Walker and Company
435 Hudson St.
New York, NY 10014
Ph: (212)727-8300   Fax: (212)727-0984
Fr: 800-289-2553

Prepared by the Career Associates staff. 1990. $8.95. 166 pages. Discusses alternatives for students of history. Offers advice on how to break into the field and how to move up. Covers where and who the employers are, internship possibilities, and professional networking associations. Comprehensive guide to career and job search planning.

★3768★ Careers for History Buffs & Others Who Learn from the Past

NTC Publishing Group
4255 W. Touhy Ave.
Lincolnwood, IL 60646-1975
Ph: (708)679-5500   Fax: (708)679-6375
Fr: 800-323-4900

Blythe Camenson. 1994. $12.95; $9.95 (paper).

★3769★ Careers Information

American Association for State and Local History
530 Church St., Ste. 600
Nashville, TN 37219
Ph: (615)255-2971   Fax: (615)255-2979

Information chart. $5.00. Presents information on job prospects and the job market for historians.

★3770★ Historians

Chronicle Guidance Publications, Inc.
66 Aurora St.
PO Box 1190
Moravia, NY 13118-1190
Ph: (315)497-0330   Fax: (315)497-3359
Fr: 800-622-7284

Chronicle Guidance Staff. 1993. $2.00. Provides concise career information and sources of additional information.

★3771★ Opportunities in Social Science Careers

VGM Career Horizons
4255 W. Touhy Ave.
Lincolnwood, IL 60646-1975
Ph: (847)679-5500   Fax: (847)679-2494
Fr: 800-323-4900

Rosanne J. Marek. 1990. $14.95; $11.95 (paper). 160 pages. Profiles job opportunities in education, government, and business, along with their salary levels and outlook in the years to come. Illustrated.

OTHER SOURCES

★3772★ American Association for State and Local History (AASLH)

530 Church St., Ste. 600
Nashville, TN 37219
Ph: (615)255-2971   Fax: (615)255-2979

Purpose: Organization of educators, historians, writers, and other individuals; state and local historical societies; agencies and institutions interested in improving the study of state and local history in the United States and Canada, and assisting historical organizations in improving their public services.

★3773★ American Catholic Historical Association (ACHA)

Mullen Library, Rm. 318
Catholic University of America
Washington, DC 20064
Ph: (202)319-5079   Fax: (202)319-4967

Purpose: Professional society of historians, educators, students, and others interested in the history of the Catholic church in the United States and abroad and in the promotion of historical scholarship among Catholics. Has sponsored the publication of the papers of John Carroll, first Bishop and Archbishop of Baltimore, MD.

★3774★ American Historical Association (AHA)

400 A St. SE
Washington, DC 20003
Ph: (202)544-2422   Fax: (202)544-8307

Members: Professional historians, educators, and others interested in promoting historical studies and collecting and preserving historical manuscripts. **Activities:** Conducts research and educational programs.

★3775★ American Society for Eighteenth-Century Studies (ASECS)

Utah State University
USU CC108
Logan, UT 84322-3730
Ph: (801)797-4065   Fax: (801)797-4065

Members: Scholars and others interested in the cultural history of the 18th century. **Purpose:** Encourages and advances study and research in this area; promotes the interchange of information and ideas among scholars from different disciplines (such as librarianship and bibliography) who are interested in the 18th century. **Activities:** Cosponsors seven fellowship programs; sponsors Graduate Student Caucus.

★3776★ Grants, Fellowships, and Prizes of Interest to Historians

American Historical Association
400 A St. SE
Washington, DC 20003-3889
Ph: (202)544-2422   Fax: (202)544-8307

Annual, July. $10.00, plus $1.00 shipping, payment with order. Covers over 450 sources of funding (scholarships, fellowships, internships, awards, and book and essay prizes) in the United States and abroad for graduate students, postdoctoral researchers, and institutions in the humanities. Entries include: Name of source, institution name or contact, address, phone, eligibility and proposal requirements, award or stipend amount, location requirements for research, application deadlines. Arrangement: Alphabetical in three categories: support for individual research and teaching; grants for groups and organizations for research and education; and book, article, essay, and manuscript prizes.

★3777★ International Studies Association (ISA)

Brigham Young University
David M. Kennedy Center
216 HRCB
Provo, UT 84602
Ph: (801)378-5459   Fax: (801)378-7075

Members: Social scientists and other scholars from a wide variety of disciplines who are specialists in international affairs and cross-cultural studies; academicians; government officials; officials in international organizations; business executives; students. **Purpose:** Promotes research, improved teaching, and the orderly growth of knowledge in the field of international studies; emphasizes a multidisciplinary approach to problems. **Activities:** Holds conferences with government officials; conducts workshops and discussion groups; sponsors development of modular curriculum materials.

★3778★ National Coordinating Committee for the Promotion of History (NCC)

400 A St. SE
Washington, DC 20003
Ph: (202)544-2422   Fax: (202)544-8307

Members: Archival and historical organizations such as: American Historical Association; Organization of American Historians; Phi Alpha Theta; Society of American Archivists; Western History Association. **Purpose:** Monitors employment opportunities. Seeks to protect historians' interests with regard to federal policy. Serves as central advocacy office and information clearinghouse for government agencies, legislative aides, and professional history and archival associations; develops network of constituent contacts in districts and states; testifies before congressional committees.

★3779★ National Council on Public History (NCPH)
Indiana University - Purdue University at Indiana
327 Cavanaugh
425 University Blvd.
Indianapolis, IN 46202
Ph: (317)274-2716   Fax: (317)274-2347
Purpose: To encourage a broader interest in professional history and to stimulate national interest in public history by promoting its use at all levels of society. Serves as an information clearinghouse; sponsors training programs, local and regional colloquia, projects, and panels. **Activities:** Offers advice to departments of history, historical associations, and others seeking information on public history, professional standards, opportunities, and internships.

★3780★ Newcomen Society of the United States (NSUS)
412 Newcomen Rd.
Exton, PA 19341
Ph: (610)363-6600   Fax: (610)363-0612
Members: Business and professional people in education and industry in the United States and Canada. **Purpose:** Studies material history, as distinguished from political history, in terms of the beginnings, growth, and contributions of industry, transportation, communication, mining, agriculture, banking, insurance, medicine, education, invention, law, and related historical fields. Maintains Thomas Newcomen Memorial Museum in Steam Technology and Industrial History in Chester County, PA. Society named for Thomas Newcomen (1663-1729), British pioneer who invented the first atmospheric steam engine.

★3781★ United States Capitol Historical Society (USCHS)
200 Maryland Ave. NW
Washington, DC 20002
Ph: (202)543-8919   Fax: (202)544-8244
Members: Congressmen, organizations, and others interested in American history in general, and specifically the U.S. Capitol Building in Washington, DC. **Purpose:** Encourages understanding of the founding, growth, and significance of the Capitol as a tangible symbol of representative government; conducts research into the history of the Congress and the Capitol. **Activities:** Conducts research, pulbications and symposia.

Home Health Aides

SOURCES OF HELP-WANTED ADS

★3782★ *Homecare Magazine*

Miramar Communications, Inc.
23815 Stuart Ranch Rd.
PO Box 8987
Malibu, CA 90265-8987
Ph: (310)317-4522   Fax: (310)317-9644
Fr: 800-543-4116

Monthly. $48.00/year for individuals; $60.00/year for Canada; $75.00/year for other countries.

★3783★ *Journal of Gerontological Nursing*

Slack, Inc.
6900 Grove Rd.
Thorofare, NJ 08086-9447
Ph: (609)848-1000   Fax: (609)853-5991
Fr: 800-257-8290

Monthly. Gerontological nursing journal.

★3784★ *Modern Healthcare*

Crain Communications, Inc.
740 N. Rush St.
Chicago, IL 60611-2590
Ph: (312)649-5311   Fax: (312)280-3189

Weekly. $110.00/year. Business news magazine for Healthcare Management.

★3785★ *Provider*

American Health Care Association
1201 L St. NW
Washington, DC 20005
Ph: (202)842-4444   Fax: (202)842-3860

Monthly. $48.00/year for nonmembers. Magazine.

PLACEMENT AND JOB REFERRAL SERVICES

★3786★ **American Public Health Association (APHA)**

1015 15th St. NW
Washington, DC 20005
Ph: (202)789-5600   Fax: (202)789-5681

Members: Professional organization of physicians, nurses, educators, academicians, environmentalists, epidemiologists, new professionals, social workers, health administrators, optometrists, podiatrists, pharmacists, dentists, nutritionists, health planners, other community and mental health specialists, and interested consumers. **Purpose:** Seeks to protect and promote personal, mental, and environmental health. **Activities:** Services include: promulgation of standards; establishment of uniform practices and procedures; development of the etiology of communicable diseases; research in public health; exploration of medical care programs and their relationships to public health. Sponsors job placement service.

★3787★ **National Association of Professional Geriatric Care Managers (NAPGCM)**

1604 N. Country Club Rd.
Tucson, AZ 85716
Ph: (520)881-8008   Fax: (520)325-7925

Purpose: Promotes quality services and care for elderly citizens. Provides referral service and distributes information to individuals interested in geriatric care management. **Activities:** Maintains referral network.

EMPLOYER DIRECTORIES AND NETWORKING LISTS

★3788★ *American Journal of Nursing—Directory of Nursing Organizations Issue*

American Journal of Nursing Co.
555 W. 57th St.
New York, NY 10019
Ph: (212)582-8820   Fax: (212)586-5462
Fr: 800-627-0484

Annual, April. $5.00. Publication includes: List of nursing organizations and agencies. Entries include: Name, address, names of officers or nursing representative. Arrangement: Classified by type of organization.

★3789★ *Home Care Agency Report and Directory*

Find/SVP
625 Avenue of the Americas
New York, NY 10011
Ph: (212)645-4500   Fr: 800-346-3787

1992. $425.00. Directory covering more than 10,000 US medicare and nonmedicare home health agencies. Listings include company name, address, telephone number, type of agency, management control, number of employees, and types of services offered. Provides a statistical analysis of data.

★3790★ *Home Health Service Directory*

American Business Directories, Inc.
American Business Information, Inc.
5711 S. 86th Cir.
Omaha, NE 68127
Ph: (402)593-4600   Fax: (402)331-1505

Annual. $1,200.00. U.S. edition. Entries include: Name, address, phone (including area code), size of advertisement, year first in Yellow Pages, name of owl her or manager, number of employees. Compiled from telephone company Yellow Pages, nationwide. Arrangement: Geographical.

★3791★ Hospital Market Atlas

SMG Marketing Group, Inc.
1342 N. LaSalle Dr.
Chicago, IL 60610
Ph: (312)642-3026   Fax: (312)642-9729
Fr: 800-678-3026

Biennial, odd years. $495.00, payment with order. Covers over 7,000 hospitals, hospital systems and 480 group purchasing organizations. Entries include: Hospital or organization name, address, phone, county code, management, type of hospital service, number of beds, admissions, surgical operations, and emergency room visits. Arrangement: Geographical.

★3792★ Hospitals Directory

American Business Directories, Inc.
American Business Information, Inc.
5711 S. 86th Cir.
Omaha, NE 68127
Ph: (402)593-4600   Fax: (402)331-1505

Annual. $870.00, U.S. edition. Entries include: Name, address, phone (including area code), size of advertisement, year first in Yellow Pages, name of owner or manager, number of employees. Compiled from telephone company Yellow Pages, nationwide. Arrangement: Geographical.

★3793★ Medi-Pages

Medi-Pages, Inc.
757 Cayuga St.
Lewiston, NY 14092
Ph: (716)284-4277   Fax: (716)284-4401
Fr: 800-554-6661

Annual, March. $60.00 plus $5.00 shipping. Covers more than 100,000 listings of hospitals, nursing homes, clinics, home healthcare providers, HMO's, PPO's, CPO's, health associations, professional associations, national nursing associations, federal government agencies, international health organizations, scholarship funds, research grants, medical libraries, hospital management companys, case managers, HFCA offices, AT&T numbers. Entries include: Facility, association, company, library, or personal name, address, phone. Arrangement: Main listing of hospitals, physicians, and medical supply companies is classified by product or service, then geographical; others are geographical within section.

★3794★ Medical and Health Information Directory

Gale Research
835 Penobscot Bldg.
Detroit, MI 48226-4094
Ph: (313)961-2242   Fax: (313)961-6083
Fr: 800-877-GALE

Approximately biennial; latest edition 1994. $195.00, per volume; $485.00, for the three-volume set. Covers in Volume 1, almost 18,600 medical and health oriented associations, organizations, institutions, and government agencies, including health maintenance organizations (HMOs), preferred provider organizations (PPOs), insurance companies, pharmaceutical companies, research centers, and medical and allied health schools. In Volume 2, nearly 11,800 medical book publishers; medical periodicals, directories, audiovisual producers and services, medical li-

braries and information centers, and electronic resources. In Volume 3, nearly 26,000 clinics, treatment centers, care programs, and counseling/diagnostic services for 30 subject areas. Entries include: Institution, service, or firm name, address, phone; many include names of key personnel and, when pertinent, descriptive annotation. Arrangement: Classified by organization activity, service, etc. Indexes: Each volume has a complete alphabetical name and keyword index.

★3795★ National Home Care and Hospice Directory

National Association for Home Care
519 C St. NE
Washington, DC 20002-5809
Ph: (202)547-7424   Fax: (202)547-3540

Annual, January. $140.00. Covers Approximately 15,000 home care and hospice providers in the U.S. & Puerto Rico. Entries include: Agency name, address, phone, director's name, product/service provided, area served. Arrangement: Geographical by state and town. Indexes: Agency, personnel.

★3796★ Nurses and Nurses' Registries Directory

American Business Directories, Inc.
American Business Information, Inc.
5711 S. 86th Cir.
Omaha, NE 68127
Ph: (402)593-4600   Fax: (402)331-1505

Annual. $880.00, U.S. edition. Entries include: Name, address, phone (including area code), size of advertisement, year first in Yellow Pages, name of owner or manager, number of employees. Compiled from telephone company Yellow Pages, nationwide. Arrangement: Geographical.

★3797★ Peterson's Job Opportunities in Health Care

Peterson's Guides, Inc.
202 Carnegie Ctr.
Box 2123
Princeton, NJ 08543-2123
Ph: (609)243-9111   Fax: (609)243-9150
Fr: 800-338-3282

Annual, August. $18.95. Covers Over 1,500 companies hiring health-care professionals for skilled nursing care facilities, hospitals, medical laboratories, home health care, and pharmaceuticals. Entries include: Organization name, address, phone, name and title of contact, type of organization, number of employees, Standard Industrial Classification (SIC) code; description of opportunities available including disciplines, level of education required, starting locations and salaries, level of experience accepted, benefits. Arrangement: Alphabetical. Indexes: Employer by type of organization, industry classification, number of employees, starting location, special interest area; education level, company.

HANDBOOKS AND MANUALS

★3798★ America's 50 Fastest Growing Jobs

JIST Works, Inc.
720 N. Park Ave.
Indianapolis, IN 46202
Ph: (317)264-3720   Fr: 800-648-5478

Third edition, 1995. $14.95. 288 pages. Each job profile explains the nature of the work, skills and abilities required, employment outlook, average earnings, related occupations, education and training requirements, and employment opportunities. Also contains career planning information and job search tips.

★3799★ Becoming a Helper

Brooks/Cole Publishing Co.
511 Forest Lodge Rd.
Pacific Grove, CA 93950
Ph: (408)373-0728

Marianne S. Corey and Gerald Corey. Second edition, 1993. $28.95. 365 pages. Includes a bibliography and an index.

★3800★ Careers in Health Care

VGM Career Horizons
4255 W. Touhy Ave.
Lincolnwood, IL 60646-1975
Ph: (847)679-5500   Fax: (847)679-2494
Fr: 800-323-4900

Barbara M. Swanson. 1995. $17.95; $13.95 (paper). Describes job duties, work settings, salaries, licensing and certification requirements, educational preparation, and future outlook. Gives ideas on how to secure a job.

★3801★ Medical Technologists and Technicians Career Directory

Gale Research
835 Penobscot Bldg.
Detroit, MI 48226-4094
Ph: (313)961-2242   Fax: (313)961-6083
Fr: 800-877-GALE

Bradley Morgan. 1993. $39.00. 324 pages. Essays on specific careers provide an insider's perspective. Features extensive listings of contacts and entry-level job opportunities. Provides information on internships and sources of help-wanted ads.

★3802★ 100 Best Careers for the Year 2000

Prentice Hall General Reference
15 Columbus Cir.
New York, NY 10023
Ph: (212)373-8500   Fr: 800-223-2348

Shelly Field. 1992. $15.00 (paper). Covers 100 of the fastest growing jobs. The publication is divided into 11 general employment sections. Specific careers are covered within each section. Provides job description, responsibilities, employment opportunities, earnings, education and training, advancement opportunities, and experience and qualifications for each occupation.

★3803★ Opportunities in Health and Medical Careers

VGM Career Horizons
4255 W. Touhy Ave.
Lincolnwood, IL 60646-1975
Ph: (847)679-5500   Fax: (847)679-2494
Fr: 800-323-4900

Donald Snook, Jr. and Leo D'Orazio. 1993. $14.95; $11.95 (paper). Covers the full range of medical and health occupations. Illustrated.

★3804★ Resumes for Health and Medical Careers

4255 W. Touhy Ave.
Lincolnwood, IL 60646-1975
Ph: (708)679-5500   Fax: (708)679-6375
Fr: 800-323-4900

Compiled by VGM Career Horizons Staff 1995. $9.95 (paper).

★3805★ Where the Jobs Are: The Hottest Careers for the '90s

The Career Press, Inc.
3 Tice Rd.
PO Box 687
Franklin Lakes, NJ 07417
Ph: (201)848-0310   Fax: (201)848-1727
Fr: 800-237-3371

Joyce Hadley. Second edition, 1995. $9.99. 300 pages. Describes careers in fifteen general fields, from accounting to travel and hospitality.

EMPLOYMENT AGENCIES AND SEARCH FIRMS

★3806★ Academy Medical Personnel Services

571 High St.
Columbus, OH 43085-4132
Ph: (614)848-6011

Employment agency. Fills openings on a regular or temporary basis.

★3807★ CT Group

264 N. Elm St.
North Massapequa, NY 11758-2525
Ph: (516)797-3642   Fax: (516)795-4350

Executive search firm and employment agency.

★3808★ Eden Temporary Services

280 Madison Ave.
New York, NY 10016-0801
Ph: (212)685-4666

Employment agency. Places individuals in regular or temporary positions.

★3809★ Medical Personnel Pool

2901 S. Ridgewood Ave.
Daytona Beach, FL 32119-3542
Ph: (904)736-1648

Provides regular and temporary staffing assistance. Offices located in cities throughout United States.

★3810★ Medical Personnel Services, Inc.

1707 L St. NW, Ste. 700
Washington, DC 20036
Ph: (202)466-2955   Fax: (202)452-1818

Employment agency.

★3811★ Midwest Medical Consultants

8910 Purdue Rd., Ste. 200
Indianapolis, IN 46268-1155
Ph: (317)872-1053

Employment agency. Executive search firm.

★3812★ Poston Personnel

16 E. 79th St., Ste. G-4
New York, NY 10021
Ph: (212)535-4116   Fax: (212)988-7080

Employment agency.

★3813★ Professional Placement Associates, Inc.

11 Rye Ridge Plaza
Rye Brook, NY 10573
Ph: (914)251-1000   Fax: (914)939-1959

Employment agency.

OTHER SOURCES

★3814★ American Federation of Home Health Agencies (AFHHA)

1320 Fenwick Ln., Ste. 100
Silver Spring, MD 20910
Ph: (301)588-1454   Fax: (301)588-4732

Purpose: Agencies providing therapeutic services such as nursing, speech therapy, and physical therapy in the home; associate members are corporations and individuals that support the federation. Promotes home health by influencing public policy. Presents the concerns of home health agencies to Congress and the Health Care Financing Administration; helps members work with their fiscal intermediary.

★3815★ American Health Care Association

1201 L St. NW
Washington, DC 20005
Ph: (202)842-4444   Fax: (202)842-3860

Members: Federation of state associations of long-term health care facilities. **Purpose:** Promotes standards for professionals in long-term health care delivery and quality care for patients and residents in a safe environment. Focuses on issues of availability, quality, affordability, and fair payment. Operates as a liaison with governmental agencies, Congress, and professional associations.

★3816★ Day in a Career: Medical Home Health Aide

Cambridge Career Products
PO Box 2153
Dept. CC15
Charleston, WV 25328-2153
Ph: (304)744-9323   Fax: (304)744-9351
Fr: 800-468-4227

Video. 1994. $89.00. 15-22 minutes. Includes candid interviews and work situations, plus outlines of relevant career information.

★3817★ Home Economics Careers

Cambridge Career Products
PO Box 2153
Dept. CC15
Charleston, WV 25328-2153
Ph: (304)744-9323   Fax: (304)744-9351
Fr: 800-468-4227

Video. $79.95. 30 minutes. Presents a series of interviews with men and women working in different areas of home economics, including dietetics, foods and nutrition, child development, interior design, and fashion. Covers educational, personal, and professional requirements for each occupation.

★3818★ National Association for Home Care (NAHC)

519 C St. NE
Stanton Park
Washington, DC 20002
Ph: (202)547-7424   Fax: (202)547-3540

Members: Providers of home health care, hospice, and homemaker-home health aide services; interested individuals and organizations. **Purpose:** Develops and promotes high standards of patient care in home care services. Seeks to affect legislative and regulatory processes concerning home care services; gathers and disseminates home care industry data; develops public relations strategies; works to increase political visibility of home care services. Interprets home care services to governmental and private sector bodies affecting the delivery and financing of such services.

★3819★ National Rural Health Association (NRHA)

1 W. Armour Blvd., Ste. 301
Kansas City, MO 64111
Ph: (816)756-3140   Fax: (816)756-3144

Members: Administrators, physicians, nurses, physician assistants, health planners, academicians, and others interested or involved in rural health care. **Purpose:** To create a better understanding of health care problems unique to rural areas; utilize a collective approach in finding positive solutions; articulate and represent the health care needs of rural America; supply current information to rural health care providers; serve as a liaison between rural health care programs throughout the country. Offers continuing education credits for medical, dental, nursing, and management courses.

★3820★ Visiting Nurse Associations of America (VNAA)
3801 E. Florida, Ste. 900
Denver, CO 80210
Ph: (303)753-0218   Fax: (303)753-0258
Fr: 800-426-2547

Members: Voluntary, nonprofit home health care agencies. **Purpose:** Develops competitive strength among community-based nonprofit visiting nurse organizations; works to strengthen business resources and economic programs through contracting, marketing, governmental affairs and publications.

Hotel Managers and Assistants

SOURCES OF HELP-WANTED ADS

★3821★ **Hotel & Motel Management**
Advanstar Communications, Inc.
7600 Old Oak Blvd.
Cleveland, OH 44130
Ph: (216)243-8100   Fax: (216)891-2733
Magazine (tabloid) covering the global lodging industry.

★3822★ **Hotel & Resort Industry**
Coastal Communications Corp.
488 Madison Ave.
New York, NY 10022
Ph: (212)888-1500   Fax: (212)888-8008
Monthly. Magazine for headquarters executives, owners, operations management, specifiers, and purchasing directors in hotels, resorts, motels, and motor inns.

★3823★ **HOTELS**
Cahners Publishing Co.
1350 E. Touhy Ave.
Des Plaines, IL 60018
Ph: (708)635-8800   Fax: (708)390-2770
Monthly. $75.00/year for individuals. Magazine covering management and operations as well as foodservice and design in the hospitality industry.

★3824★ **Lodging Hospitality**
Peter Li
1100 Superior Ave.
Cleveland, OH 44114
Ph: (216)696-7000   Fax: (216)696-7670
Monthly. $60.00/year for individuals. Magazine serving managers of independent, franchise, chain-owned, and referral groups in the hospitality industry.

★3825★ **Restaurants & Institutions**
Cahners Publishing Co.
1350 E. Touhy Ave.
Des Plaines, IL 60018
Ph: (708)635-8800   Fax: (708)390-2770
Semimonthly. $99.95/year for individuals. Magazine focusing on foodservice and lodging management.

PLACEMENT AND JOB REFERRAL SERVICES

★3826★ **Association for Convention Operations Management (ACOM)**
William H. Just & Assoc., Inc.
1819 Peachtree St. NE, Ste. 620
Atlanta, GA 30309
Ph: (404)351-3220   Fax: (404)351-3348
Members: Convention service directors and managers of hotels, convention centers, and convention bureaus; suppliers of services and products to the convention and meetings industry are affiliate members. **Purpose:** Works to increase the effectiveness, productivity, and quality of meetings, conventions, and exhibitions. Works to establish high ethical standards, improve professional management techniques, and increase awareness of client, employer, and provider needs. **Activities:** Maintains speakers' bureau, resource center, and placement services; compiles statistics. Conducts research and educational programs.

★3827★ **Club Managers Association of America (CMAA)**
1733 King St.
Alexandria, VA 22314
Ph: (703)739-9500   Fax: (703)739-0124
Members: Professional managers and assistant managers of private golf, yacht, athletic, city, country, luncheon, university, and military clubs. **Purpose:** Encourages education and advancement of members and promotes efficient and successful club operations. **Activities:** Maintains management referral service. Provides reprints of articles on club management. Supports courses in club management. Compiles statistics.

★3828★ **National Association of Black Hospitality Professionals (NABHP)**
PO Box 8132
Columbus, GA 31908-8132
Ph: (334)298-4802
Purpose: Works to develop global educational and economic opportunities for the hospitality industry through the expansion and diversification of minority involvement in the industry. Encourages professional development and opportunity in the industry through the design and implementation of workshops and seminars. Seeks to increase the number, size, and capability of minority-owned businesses within the hospitality and tourism industries. **Activities:** Offers placement service; conducts research and educational programs; compiles statistics.

★3829★ **National Executive Housekeepers Association (N.E.H.A.)**
1001 Eastwind Dr., Ste. 301
Westerville, OH 43081-3361
Ph: (614)895-7166   Fax: (614)895-1248
Fr: 800-200-NEHA
Members: Persons engaged in institutional housekeeping management in hospitals, hotels and motels, schools, and industrial establishments. **Activities:** Has established educational standards. Sponsors certificate and collegiate degree programs. Holds annual National Housekeepers Week celebration during the second week in September. Created the N.E.H.A. Educational Foundation to allocate financial awards to recognized schools to assist students in institutional housekeeping. Maintains referral service.

EMPLOYER DIRECTORIES AND NETWORKING LISTS

★3830★ **Directory of Hotel & Motel Companies**
American Hotel Association Directory Corp.
1201 New York Ave. NW
Washington, DC 20005
Ph: (202)289-3157   Fax: (202)289-3110
Annual, March. $79.00, plus $3.50 shipping. Covers over 900 hotel, motel, and resort chain companies owning, managing, or operating worldwide. Entries include: Company name, address, phone, names of executives, properties owned and their locations, numbers of rooms, annual gross sales. Arrangement: Alphabetical.

★3831★ Lodging Hospitality—400 Top Performers Issue

Penton Publishing Co.
1100 Superior Ave.
Cleveland, OH 44114
Ph: (216)696-7000   Fax: (216)696-7932

Annual, August. $5.00. Publication includes: Top 400 hotels, motels, inns, and lodges based on total sales per room, and top 50 chains and franchises based on number of rooms. Arrangement: Hotels in separate sections for convention/commercial, resort, suburban, roadside, and airport units, then ranked by total sales per room; chains ranked by number of rooms.

★3832★ Official Hotel Guide

Reed Hotel Directories Network
500 Plaza Dr.
Secaucus, NJ 07096
Ph: (201)902-1800   Fax: (201)319-1797

Annual. $385.00, for 3 volume set. Covers in three volumes, 30,000 hotels, motels, and resorts worldwide. Volume 1 covers most of the U.S.; Volume 2 covers the rest of the U.S. and the Western Hemisphere; Volume 3 covers Europe, the Middle East, Asia, and Africa. Includes separate lists of golf resorts and tennis resorts; health spas, dude ranches, bed and breakfasts, theme and national parks, and marina hotels in the United States; also includes lists of hotels in the Caribbean with golf, tennis, scuba diving, casinos, marinas, and windsurfing. Arrangement: Geographical.

★3833★ Peterson's Job Opportunities in Business 1996

Peterson's
PO Box 2123
Princeton, NJ 08543-2123
Ph: (609)243-9111   Fax: (609)243-9150
Fr: 800-338-3282

Compiled by the Peterson's staff. Annual. $19.95 (paper). 416 pages. Profiles 2,000 companies that are hiring employees in a number of nontechnical fields, including financial services, management consulting, retailers, utilities, and consumer products companies. Contains job-search strategies and career options to help match education and expertise to the job market. Indexed geographically, by industry, and by hiring needs.

★3834★ Resorts Directory

American Business Directories, Inc.
American Business Information, Inc.
5711 S. 86th Cir.
Omaha, NE 68127
Ph: (402)593-4600   Fax: (402)331-1505

Annual. $760.00, U.S. edition. Entries include: Name, address, phone (including area code), size of advertisement, year first in Yellow Pages, name of owner or manager, number of employees. Compiled from telephone company Yellow Pages, nationwide. Arrangement: Geographical.

★3835★ Who's Who in the Lodging Industry

American Hotel and Motel Association
1201 New York Ave. NW
Washington, DC 20005
Ph: (202)289-3100   Fax: (202)289-3199

Annual, June. $45.00, plus $4.00 shipping. Covers Approximately 40,000 individuals at hotels, motels, suppliers, corporations, affiliated with the lodging industry. Entries include: For individuals, name, address, phone, name of affiliated company. For properties and corporations, name, address, phone, names and titles of key personnel. For suppliers, company name, address, phone, names and titles of key personnel, product or service provided. Arrangement: Classified by line of business, then alphabetical.

HANDBOOKS AND MANUALS

★3836★ Best Impressions in Hospitality: Your Professional Image for Excellence

Impact Publications
9104N Manassas Dr.
Manassas Park, VA 22111-5211
Ph: (703)361-7300   Fax: (703)335-9486

Angie Michaels. 1995. $14.95 (paper).

★3837★ Career Choices for the 90's for Students of Business

Walker and Company
435 Hudson St.
New York, NY 10014
Ph: (212)727-8300   Fax: (212)727-0984
Fr: 800-289-2553

Prepared by the Career Associates staff. 1990. $9.95. 166 pages. Discusses alternatives for students of business. Offers advice on how to break into the field and how to move up. Covers where and who the employers are, internship possibilities, and professional networking associations. Comprehensive guide to career and job search planning.

★3838★ Career Opportunities in Travel and Tourism

Facts on File, Inc.
11 Penn Plaza, 15th Fl.
New York, NY 10001-2006
Ph: (212)967-8800   Fax: 800-678-3633
Fr: 800-322-8755

John Hawks. 1995. $29.95; $15.95 (paper). 224 pages. Includes detailed job descriptions, educational requirements, salary ranges, and advancement prospects for 70 different job opportunities in this fast-paced industry. Contains index and bibliography.

★3839★ The Encyclopedia of Career Choices for the 1990s: Guide to Entry-Level Jobs

Perigree Books
The Berkley Publishing Group
PO Box 506
East Rutherford, NJ 07073
Ph: (201)933-9292   Fr: 800-223-0510

Career Associates Staff. 1992. $19.95. 862 pages. Describes 500 entry-level careers in a

variety of industries. Presents qualifications required, working conditions, salary, internships, and professional associations.

★3840★ Encyclopedia of Careers and Vocational Guidance

J. G. Ferguson Publishing Co.
200 W. Monroe, Ste. 250
Chicago, IL 60606
Ph: (312)580-5480

William E. Hopke. Ninth edition, 1993. $129.95; $199.95 (CD-ROM). Four-volume set that profiles 900 occupations and describes job trends in 71 industries. Includes career description, educational requirements, history of the job, methods of entry, advancement, employment outlook, earnings, conditions of work, social and psychological factors, and sources of further information. Contains career and employment information for this field.

★3841★ Flying High in Travel

John Wiley and Sons
605 3rd Ave.
New York, NY 10158
Ph: (212)850-6000   Fr: 800-225-5945

Karen Rubin. Second edition, 1992. $19.95. 336 pages. A guide to careers and job hunting in the travel industry. Describes the many job opportunities available, from writing to hotel management to law. Includes information on educational preparation, training, and job hunting.

★3842★ Hospitality Management: An Introduction to the Industry

Kendall Hunt Publishing Co.
4050 Westmark Dr.
PO Box 1840
Dubuque, IA 52004-1840
Ph: (319)589-1000   Fax: 800-772-9165
Fr: 800-228-0810

Robert Brymer. 1994. $28.95.

★3843★ Hotel Industry International Handbook

Rector Press, Ltd.
130 Rattlesnake
Leverett, MA 01054-9726
Ph: (413)548-9708   Fax: (413)367-2853
Fr: 800-247-3473

1994.

★3844★ Hotel and Motel Management

NTC Publishing Group
4255 W. Touhy Ave.
Lincolnwood, IL 60646-1975
Ph: (708)679-5500   Fax: (708)679-6375
Fr: 800-323-4900

Shepard Henkin. 1994. $13.95; $10.95 (paper).

★3845★ How to Get a Job with a Cruise Line

Ticket to Adventure, Inc.
PO Box 41005
St. Petersburg, FL 33743
Ph: (813)544-6440   Fr: 800-929-7447

Mary Fallon Miller. Third edition, 1994. $14.95. 224 pages. Explores jobs with cruise ships, describing duties, responsibilities, benefits, and training. Lists cruise ship lines and schools offering cruise line training. Offers job hunting advice.

★3846★ **Liberal Arts Jobs: What They Are and How to Get Them**

Peterson's
PO Box 2123
Princeton, NJ 08543-2123
Ph: (609)243-9111   Fax: (609)243-9150
Fr: 800-338-3282

Burton Jay Nadler. Second edition, 1989. $9.95. 153 pages. Presents a list of the top 20 fields for liberal arts majors, covering more than 300 job opportunities. Discusses strategies for going after those jobs, including guidance on the language of a successful job search, informational interviews, and making networking work.

★3847★ **100 Best Careers for the Year 2000**

Prentice Hall General Reference
15 Columbus Cir.
New York, NY 10023
Ph: (212)373-8500   Fr: 800-223-2348

Shelly Field. 1992. $15.00 (paper). Covers 100 of the fastest growing jobs. The publication is divided into 11 general employment sections. Specific careers are covered within each section. Provides job description, responsibilities, employment opportunities, earnings, education and training, advancement opportunities, and experience and qualifications for each occupation.

★3848★ **Opportunities in Hotel and Motel Careers**

VGM Career Horizons
4255 W. Touhy Ave.
Lincolnwood, IL 60646-1975
Ph: (847)679-5500   Fax: (847)679-2494
Fr: 800-323-4900

Shepard Henkin. 1992. $14.95; $11.95 (paper). 160 pages. A guide to planning for and seeking opportunities in this growing field. Illustrated.

★3849★ **Opportunities in Travel Careers**

VGM Career Horizons
4255 W. Touhy Ave.
Lincolnwood, IL 60646-1975
Ph: (847)679-5500   Fax: (847)679-2494
Fr: 800-323-4900

Robert Scott Milne. 1996. $14.95; $11.95 (paper). 160 pages. Discusses what the jobs are and where to find them in airlines, shipping lines, and railroads. Discusses related opportunities in hotels, motels, resorts, travel agencies, public relation firms, and recreation departments. Illustrated.

★3850★ **So–You Want to Be an Innkeeper**

Chronicle Books
275 5th St.
San Francisco, CA 94103
Ph: (415)777-7240   Fax: (415)777-8887
Fr: 800-722-6657

Mary E. Davies. 1996.

★3851★ **Travel and Hospitality Career Directory**

Gale Research
835 Penobscot Bldg.
Detroit, MI 48226-4094
Ph: (313)961-2242   Fax: (313)961-6083
Fr: 800-877-GALE

Bradley Morgan. Second edition, 1992. $39.00. 289 pages. Features a basic and comprehensive job search section, articles by top professionals in the field, and detailed listings of hundreds of top companies who hire individuals in this field. Aimed particularly at entry-level job hunters.

★3852★ **Working in Hotels and Catering**

Routledge
29 W. 35th St.
New York, NY 10001-2299
Ph: (212)244-3336   Fax: 800-248-4724

Roy C. Wood. 1992. $79.95.

EMPLOYMENT AGENCIES AND SEARCH FIRMS

★3853★ **Domenico/Bowman Associates**

23861 El Toro Rd., Ste. 700
Lake Forest, CA 92630
Ph: (714)588-2390

Executive search firm. Concentrates on placement to the food and lodging industry.

★3854★ **EHS and Associates, Inc.**

3033 Excelsior Blvd., Ste. 303
Minneapolis, MN 55416
Ph: (612)924-2366   Fax: (612)924-2367

Executive search firm and employment agency.

★3855★ **Employment Advisors**

526 Nicollet Mall
Minneapolis, MN 55402-0521
Ph: (612)339-0521

Employment agency. Also located in Bloomington, Minnesota. Places candidates in variety of fields.

★3856★ **Harper Associates**

29870 Middlebelt
Farmington Hills, MI 48334
Ph: (810)932-1170

Employment agency.

★3857★ **Hospitality International**

181 Port Watson St.
Cortland, NY 13045-2811

Executive search firm. Branch office in New York, NY.

★3858★ **HRI Services Inc.**

150 Wood Rd., Ste. 303
Braintree, MA 02184
Ph: (617)848-9110

Employment agency.

★3859★ **J.D. Hersey and Associates**

1685 Old Henderson Rd.
Columbus, OH 43220
Ph: (614)459-4555

Executive search firm.

★3860★ **The Personnel Network, Inc.**

1621 Lake Murray Blvd.
Columbia, SC 29212
Ph: (803)781-2087

Executive search firm.

★3861★ **Peter Barrett Associates, Inc.**

23201 Lake Center Dr., Ste. 301
Lake Forest, CA 92630

Executive search firm.

★3862★ **Ritt-Ritt and Associates**

424 Swan Blvd.
Deerfield, IL 60015
Ph: (708)520-9999

Employment agency.

★3863★ **Sales Consultants**

33 S. King St.
Honolulu, HI 96813-3206
Ph: (808)521-7828

Employment agency. Executive search firm. Main office located in Cleveland, OH.

OTHER SOURCES

★3864★ **American Almanac of Jobs and Salaries 1994-95**

Avon Books
1350 Avenue of the Americas, 2nd Fl.
New York, NY 10019
Ph: (212)261-6800   Fr: 800-238-0658

John Wright. Revised edition, 1993. $17.00. 704 pages. This is a comprehensive guide to the wages of hundreds of occupations in a wide variety of industries and organizations.

★3865★ **American Hotel & Motel Association (AH&MA)**

1201 New York Ave. NW, Ste. 600
Washington, DC 20005-3931
Ph: (202)289-3100   Fax: (202)289-3199

Members: Federation of 50 state and regional hotel associations, representing over 1.4 million hotel and motel rooms. **Purpose:** Promotes business of hotels and motels through publicity and promotion programs. Works to improve operating methods through dissemination of information on industry methods. Conducts educational institute for training at all levels, through home study, adult education, and colleges. Provides guidance on member and labor relations. Reviews proposed legislation affecting hotels. Sponsors study group programs. Maintains speakers' bureau and library; conducts research; compiles statistics; sponsors competitions.

★3866★ Association for International Practical Training (AIPT)

10400 Little Patuxent Pky. Ste. 250
Columbia, MD 21044
Ph: (410)997-2200   Fax: (410)992-3924

Purpose: Helps coordinate training around the world in fields such as travel, the culinary arts, and hotel management. **Activities:** Conducts programs in career development and hospitality/tourism exchanges. Operates a student exchange program. Provides reciprocal practical training experience for recent graduates from the U.S., Austria, Germany, Finland, France, Hungary, Ireland, Japan, Malaysia, Netherlands, Switzerland, and the United Kingdom. Arranges training programs in the U.S. and abroad. Serves as U.S. affiliate to IAESTE (International Association for the Exchange of Students for Technical Experience) and operates a Professional Visitors Program to arrange short-term educational and training visits to the U.S. **E-Mail:** aipt@aipt.org

★3867★ Council on Hotel, Restaurant, and Institutional Education (CHRIE)

1200 17th St. NW
Washington, DC 20036-3097
Ph: (202)331-5990   Fax: (202)785-2511

Purpose: Schools and colleges offering specialized education and training in cooking, baking, tourism and hotel, restaurant, and institutional administration; individuals, executives, and students. **Activities:** Provides networking opportunities and professional development. Sponsors competitions.

★3868★ Home Economics Careers

Cambridge Career Products
PO Box 2153
Dept. CC15
Charleston, WV 25328-2153
Ph: (304)744-9323   Fax: (304)744-9351
Fr: 800-468-4227

Video. $79.95. 30 minutes. Presents a series of interviews with men and women working in different areas of home economics, including dietetics, foods and nutrition, child development, interior design, and fashion. Covers educational, personal, and professional requirements for each occupation.

★3869★ Hospitality: A World of Opportunities

Educational Institute of the American Hotel and Motel Association
PO Box 1240
East Lansing, MI 48826

Video. $62.95. Describes the choices, opportunities, and rewards of a career in the hospitality industry.

★3870★ Hospitality Industry Compensation Survey

American Hotel & Motel Association
1201 New York Ave. NW, Ste. 600
Washington, DC 20005-3931
Ph: (202)289-3100

Reports the salaries of 17 managerial positions by region, property size, and revenue.

★3871★ Travel Agent

Prentice Hall
113 Sylvan Ave.
Rte. 9W
Englewood Cliffs, NJ 07632
Ph: (201)592-2000   Fr: 800-922-0579

Wilma Boyd. 1989. $14.95. 256 pages. Outlines entry-level positions in the airline, car rental, and hospitality industries as well as in travel agencies and related travel services. Explains travel agency operations, sales techniques, and the use of computers in travel services. Gives job hunting advice and sales tips.

Human Services Workers

SOURCES OF HELP-WANTED ADS

★3872★ Community Jobs: The Employment Newspaper for the Non-Profit Sector
ACCESS: Networking in the Public Interest
30 Irving Pl.
New York, NY 10003
Ph: (212)475-1001   Fax: (212)475-1199

Monthly. $69.00. Covers jobs and internships available with nonprofit organizations active in issues such as the environment, foreign policy, consumer advocacy, housing, education, etc. Entries include: Position title; name, address, and phone of contact; description, responsibilities; requirements; salary. Arrangement: Geographical.

★3873★ Journal of Jewish Communal Service
Jewish Communal Service Association
3084 State Hwy. 27, Ste. 9
Kendall Park, NJ 08824-1657
Ph: (201)821-1871   Fax: (201)821-5335

Quarterly. Journal covering Jewish communal service and social work.

★3874★ The Lutheran
Augsburg Fortress, Publishers
426 S. 5th St.
PO Box 1209
Minneapolis, MN 55440
Ph: (612)330-3246   Fax: (612)330-3455
Fr: 800-328-4648

Monthly. $11.90/year for individuals; $1.50 for single issue. Magazine of the Evangelical Lutheran Church in America.

★3875★ The NonProfit Times
The Davis Information Group, Inc.
190 Tamarack Cir.
Skillman, NJ 08558-9662
Ph: (609)466-4600

Monthly. $39.00/year.

★3876★ Social Service Jobs
10 Angelica Dr.
Framingham, MA 01701
Ph: (508)620-8644

Biweekly. $109.00/year.

PLACEMENT AND JOB REFERRAL SERVICES

★3877★ American Humanics (AH)
4601 Madison Ave.
Kansas City, MO 64112
Ph: (816)561-6415   Fax: (816)531-3527
Fr: 800-343-6466

Members: Individuals, corporations, and foundations supporting AH work in preparing young people for professional leadership in youth and human service agencies. **Purpose:** Provides leadership for co-curricular program on 14 campuses: Arizona State University; California State University-Los Angeles; College of the Ozarks; High Point University; Knoxville College; Lindenwood College; Missouri Valley College; Murray State University; Pepperdine University; Rockhurst College; Salem-Teikyo University; University of Houston; University of Northern Iowa; and University of San Diego. These colleges feature specialized professional courses that lead to B.A., B.S., or M.A. degrees and prepare graduates to serve professionally with groups such as Boy Scouts of America, Boys and Girls Clubs of America, American Red Cross, Big Brothers/Big Sisters of America, Camp Fire Boys and Girls, 4-H, Girl Scouts of the U.S.A., Junior Achievement, Young Men's Christian Associations of the United States of America, Young Women's Christian Association of the United States of America, and Girls, Inc. **Activities:** Offers counseling, loan assistance, and career placement services to students.

★3878★ American Public Health Association (APHA)
1015 15th St. NW
Washington, DC 20005
Ph: (202)789-5600   Fax: (202)789-5681

Members: Professional organization of physicians, nurses, educators, academicians, environmentalists, epidemiologists, new professionals, social workers, health administrators, optometrists, podiatrists, pharmacists, dentists, nutritionists, health planners, other community and mental health specialists, and interested consumers. **Purpose:** Seeks to protect and promote personal, mental, and environmental health. **Activities:** Services include: promulgation of standards; establishment of uniform practices and procedures; development of the etiology of communicable diseases; research in public health; exploration of medical care programs and their relationships to public health. Sponsors job placement service.

★3879★ Association on Higher Education and Disability (AHEAD)
PO Box 21192
Columbus, OH 43221-0192
Ph: (614)488-4972   Fax: (614)488-1174

Members: Individuals interested in promoting the equal rights and opportunities of disabled postsecondary students, staff, faculty, and graduates. **Purpose:** Provides an exchange of communication for those professionally involved with disabled students; collects, evaluates, and disseminates information; encourages and supports legislation for the benefit of disabled students. **Activities:** Conducts surveys on issues pertinent to college students with disabilities; offers resource referral system and employment exchange for positions in disability student services. Conducts research programs; compiles statistics.

★3880★ Child Life Council (CLC)
11820 Parklawn Dr., Ste. 202
Rockville, MD 20852-2529
Ph: (301)881-7090   Fax: (301)654-4964

Members: Professional organization representing child life personnel, patient activities specialists, and students in the field. **Purpose:** Promotes psychological well-being and optimum development of children, adolescents, and their families in health care settings. **Activities:** Works to minimize the stress and anxiety of illness and hospitalization. Addresses professional issues such as program standards, competencies, and core curriculum. Provides resources and conducts research and educational programs. Offers a

Job Bank Service listing employment openings.

★3881★ Council for Health and Human Services Ministries, United Church of Christ (CHHSM)

700 Prospect Ave.
Cleveland, OH 44115
Ph: (216)736-2250   Fax: (216)736-2251

Members: Health and human service institutions related to the United Church of Christ. **Purpose:** Seeks to study, plan, and implement a program in health and human services; assist members in developing and providing quality services and in financing institutional and noninstitutional health and human service ministries; stimulate awareness of and support for these programs; inform the UCC of policies that affect the needs, problems, and conditions of patients; cooperate with interdenominational agencies and others in the field. **Activities:** Maintains placement service and hall of fame. Compiles statistics; provides specialized education programs.

EMPLOYER DIRECTORIES AND NETWORKING LISTS

★3882★ Addiction & Recovery's National Treatment Resource Issue

Medquest Communications, Inc.
629 Euclid Ave., Ste. 500
Cleveland, OH 44114
Ph: (216)522-9700   Fax: (216)522-9707

Annual. Covers 3000 drug and alcohol treatment programs and facilities, addiction counselors, and physicians. Entries include institution name and address, addictions treated, type of facility, size.

★3883★ Child Welfare League of America—Directory of Member Agencies

Child Welfare League of America
440 1st St. NW, Ste. 310
Washington, DC 20001
Ph: (202)638-2952   Fax: (202)638-4004

Biennial. $14.00, payment with order. Covers accredited provisional, and general members, associates and supporting advocates. Includes member agencies of the Florence Crittenton Division. Entries include: Agency name, type of membership region, address, phone number, fax number, name of executive director, list of services. Arrangement: Geographical, then alphabetical.

★3884★ Directory of Catholic Charities Diocesan Agencies and Organizations

Catholic Charities USA
1731 King St., Ste. 200
Alexandria, VA 22314
Ph: (703)549-1390   Fax: (703)549-1656

Biennial, odd years. $20.00 for members; $35.00 for nonmembers; $10.00, update supplement. Covers nearly 1,200 Catholic community and social service agencies and residential and non-residential institutions and facilities. Listings include diocesan agencies, institutions for the elderly, handicapped, and youth, Catholic schools of social work, and state Catholic conferences. Entries include: Organization name, address, name and title of director, phone, fax, public relations contact. Arrangement: Geographical by diocese then classified by type of organization.

★3885★ Mental Health Directory

Office of Consumer, Family & Public Information
Center for Mental Health Services
U.S. Substance Abuse & Mental Health Services Administration
5600 Fishers Ln., Rm. 15-18
Rockville, MD 20857
Ph: (301)443-2792

Irregular, latest edition 1990. $23.00. Covers hospitals, treatment centers, outpatient clinics, day/night facilities, residential treatment centers for emotionally disturbed children, residential supportive programs such as halfway houses, and mental health centers offering mental health assistance; not included are substance abuse programs, Veteran's Administration programs, nursing homes, programs for the developmentally disabled, and organizations in which fees are retained by individual members. Entries include: Name, address, phone. Arrangement: Geographical.

★3886★ Mental Health Services Directory

American Business Directories, Inc.
American Business Information, Inc.
5711 S. 86th Cir.
Omaha, NE 68127
Ph: (402)593-4600   Fax: (402)331-1505

Annual. $1,095.00, payment with order. Entries include: Name, address, phone (including area code), size of advertisement, year first in Yellow Pages, name of owner or manager, number of employees. Compiled from telephone company Yellow Pages, nationwide. Arrangement: Geographical.

★3887★ National Directory of Children, Youth & Families Services

Marion L. Peterson, Publisher
PO Box 1837
Longmont, CO 80502-1837
Ph: (303)776-7539   Fax: 800-845-6452
Fr: 800-343-6681

Annual, July. $78.00, plus $6.00 shipping, postpaid. Covers child, youth, and family-oriented social services, health and mental health services, and juvenile/family court and youth advocacy services in state and private agencies, major cities, and 3,100 counties; also covers runaway youth centers, child abuse projects, congressional committees, clearinghouses, and national organizations concerned with family health and welfare; buyers' guide to specialized services and products. Entries include: Agency listings include agency name, address, phone, names of principal executives and staff, description of services. Arrangement: Geographical.

★3888★ National Directory of Private Social Agencies

Croner Publications, Inc.
34 Jericho Tpke.
Jericho, NY 11753
Ph: (516)333-9085   Fax: (516)338-4986
Fr: 800-441-4033

Base edition supplied upon order; monthly updates. $74.95, plus $4.95 shipping. Number of listings: Over 15,000. Entries include: Agency name, address, phone, name and title of contact, description of services. Arrangement: Geographical. Indexes: Service, agency type.

★3889★ Public Welfare Directory

American Public Welfare Association
810 1st St. NE, Ste. 500
Washington, DC 20002-4267
Ph: (202)682-0100   Fax: (202)289-6555

Annual, August. $70.00, postpaid, payment with order; $75.00, billed. Covers federal, state, territorial, county, and major municipal human service agencies; coverage includes Canadian federal and provincial agencies. Entries include: Agency name, address, phone, names of key personnel, type of service or clientele. Arrangement: Geographical.

★3890★ Who's Who Among Human Services Professionals

National Register Publishing
Reed Reference Publishing
121 Chanlon Rd.
New Providence, NJ 07974-1541
Ph: (908)464-6400   Fr: 800-621-9669

Latest edition February 1992; suspended indefinitely. $129.00. Covers nearly 20,000 human service professionals, in such fields as counseling, social work, psychology, audiology, and speech pathology. Entries include: Name, address, education, work experience, professional association memberships. Arrangement: Alphabetical.

HANDBOOKS AND MANUALS

★3891★ Becoming a Helper

Brooks/Cole Publishing Co.
511 Forest Lodge Rd.
Pacific Grove, CA 93950
Ph: (408)373-0728

Marianne S. Corey and Gerald Corey. Second edition, 1993. $28.95. 365 pages. Includes a bibliography and an index.

★3892★ Career Choices for the 90's for Students of Psychology

Walker and Company
435 Hudson St.
New York, NY 10014
Ph: (212)727-8300   Fax: (212)727-0984
Fr: 800-289-2553

Prepared by the Career Associates staff. 1990. $9.95. 166 pages. Discusses alternatives for students of psychology. Offers advice on how to break into the field and how to move up. Covers where and who the employers are, internship possibilities, and professional networking associations. Comprehensive guide to career and job search planning.

★3893★ Careers in Counseling & Human Services

Hemisphere Publishing Corp.
1900 Frost Rd., Ste. 101
Bristol, PA 19007
Ph: (215)785-5800   Fax: (215)785-5515
Fr: 800-821-8312

Brooke B. Collison, editor. 1995.

★3894★ Careers for Good Samaritans and Other Humanitarian Types

VGM Career Horizons
4255 W. Touhy Ave.
Lincolnwood, IL 60646-1975
Ph: (847)679-5500   Fax: (847)679-2494
Fr: 800-323-4900

Marjorie Eberts and Margaret Gisler. 1991. $12.95; $9.95 (paper). Contains hundreds of ideas for turning good work into paid work. Inventories opportunities in service organizations like the Red Cross, Goodwill, and the Salvation Army; religious groups, VISTA, the Peace Corps, and UNICEF; and agencies at all levels of the government.

★3895★ Careers in Health Care

VGM Career Horizons
4255 W. Touhy Ave.
Lincolnwood, IL 60646-1975
Ph: (847)679-5500   Fax: (847)679-2494
Fr: 800-323-4900

Barbara M. Swanson. 1995. $17.95; $13.95 (paper). Describes job duties, work settings, salaries, licensing and certification requirements, educational preparation, and future outlook. Gives ideas on how to secure a job.

★3896★ The Encyclopedia of Career Choices for the 1990s: Guide to Entry-Level Jobs

Perigree Books
The Berkley Publishing Group
PO Box 506
East Rutherford, NJ 07073
Ph: (201)933-9292   Fr: 800-223-0510

Career Associates Staff. 1992. $19.95. 862 pages. Describes 500 entry-level careers in a variety of industries. Presents qualifications required, working conditions, salary, internships, and professional associations.

★3897★ Interviewing in Health & Human Services

Nelson-Hall, Inc.
111 N. Canal St.
Chicago, IL 60606
Ph: (312)930-9446

Krishna Samantrai. 1996. $22.95 (paper).

★3898★ Non-Profits and Education Job Finder

Planning/Communications
7215 Oak Ave.
River Forest, IL 60305-1935
Ph: (708)366-5200   Fr: (888)366-5200

Daniel Lauber. 1996. $32.95; $16.95 (paper). 350 pages. Covers 1600 sources. Discusses how to use sources of non-profit sector job vacancies in a number of specialties and state-by-state, including job-matching services, job hotlines, specialty periodicals with job ads, salary surveys, and directories. Covers a variety of fields from education to religion. Includes chapters on resume and cover letter preparation and interviewing.

★3899★ Opportunities in Gerontology and Aging Services Careers

VGM Career Horizons
4255 W. Touhy Ave.
Lincolnwood, IL 60646-1975
Ph: (847)679-5500   Fax: (847)679-2494
Fr: 800-323-4900

Ellen Williams. 1995. $14.95; $11.95 (paper). 160 pages. Covers jobs in community, health and medical programs, financial, legal, residential, travel and tourism, and counseling, and how to go after them. Includes bibliography and illustrations.

EMPLOYMENT AGENCIES AND SEARCH FIRMS

★3900★ Arbor Associates, Inc.

15 Court Sq., Ste. 1050
Boston, MA 02108
Ph: (617)227-8829

Handles temporary placements.

OTHER SOURCES

★3901★ Child Welfare League of America (CWLA)

440 1st St. NW, Ste. 310
Washington, DC 20001
Ph: (202)638-2952   Fax: (202)638-4004

Purpose: Works to improve care and services for abused, dependent, or neglected children, youth, and their families. **Activities:** Provides consultation; conducts research; maintains information service; develops standards for child welfare practice; administers special projects.

★3902★ Home Economics Careers

Cambridge Career Products
PO Box 2153
Dept. CC15
Charleston, WV 25328-2153
Ph: (304)744-9323   Fax: (304)744-9351
Fr: 800-468-4227

Video. $79.95. 30 minutes. Presents a series of interviews with men and women working in different areas of home economics, including dietetics, foods and nutrition, child development, interior design, and fashion. Covers educational, personal, and professional requirements for each occupation.

★3903★ National Organization for Human Service Education (NOHSE)

Box 6257
Fitchburg State College
160 Pearl St.
Fitchburg, MA 01420
Ph: (508)345-2151

Members: Human service professionals, faculty, and students. **Purpose:** To foster excellence in teaching, research and curriculum planning in the human service area; to encourage and support the development of local, state, and national human services organizations; to aid faculty and professional members in their career development. Provides a medium for cooperation and communication among members; maintains registry of qualified consultants in human service education. Conducts professional development workshop; operates speakers' bureau.

★3904★ Personnel Resources (PR)

PO Box 4498
4131 N. Broad St.
Philadelphia, PA 19140
Ph: (215)324-3821

Purpose: Agency for upgrading human services careers "to an economic level of decency and dignity." Provides training and fieldwork in personal, professional, social, and skill development; provides medical screening and supervised follow-up remedial health care for trainees; acquaints trainees with varied community and cultural enrichment resources; offers educational seminars for employers and field work supervisors and postgraduate counseling for employees and employers. Has worked towards changing community attitudes about working conditions, job standards, personnel practices, compliance with Social Security laws, and salary upgrading. Future goals lie in the areas of legislation, day care group homes, solutions to transportation problems, union affiliation, group insurance coverage, and a national training center to provide training experiences for those interested in beginning similar programs. Offers guidance on other vocations such as caterers, pet and plant sitters, tour guides, and vacation parents.

Image Consultants

★3905★ American Consultants League—Consultants Directory

American Consultants League
1290 Palm Ave.
Sarasota, FL 34236
Ph: (813)952-9290   Fax: (813)925-3670

Annual, March. $30.00. Covers about 1,000 member consultants; international coverage. Entries include: Name, address, phone, specialty, description of expertise. Arrangement: Classified by specialty.

★3906★ Directory of Personal Image Consultants

Image Industry Publications
10 Bay St. Landing, Ste. 7F
Staten Island, NY 10301
Ph: (718)273-3229

Biennial, March of even years. $35.00, plus $4.00 shipping, postpaid; payment with order. Covers Approximately 300 firms that provide counseling in speech/presentation skills, dress, color, personal public relations, etiquette, and career advancement. Entries include: Company name, address, phone, specialty, teaching methods, fees, experience or background, staff size, principal corporate clients. Arrangement: Classified by specialty. Indexes: Alphabetical, geographical.

★3907★ The Woman's Consultants Directory

CAE Consultants, Inc.
41 Travers Ave.
Yonkers, NY 10705
Ph: (914)963-3695

Annual. $75.00. Covers About 3,000 women consultants in every line of business. Entries include: Consultant name, address, phone, fax, line of business, description. Arrangement: Classified by line of business.

★3908★ The Best Home-Based Businesses for the 90s

G.P. Putnam's Sons
Putnam Berkley Group
200 Madison Ave.
New York, NY 10016
Ph: (212)951-8400   Fr: 800-631-8571

Paul Edwards and Sarah Edwards. Second edition, 1994. $12.95. 400 pages. Profiles 95 businesses and careers that can be conducted from one's home. Lists sources of additional information.

★3909★ Career Portraits: Fashion

VGM Career Horizons
NTC Publishing Group
4255 W. Touhy Ave.
Lincolnwood, IL 60646-1975
Ph: (847)679-5500   Fax: (847)679-2494
Fr: 800-323-4900

Lucia Mauro. 1995. $13.95. 96 pages. Designed to capture the interest of middle school and reluctant readers.

★3910★ Careers for Fashion Plates and Other Trendsetters

VGM Career Horizons
NTC Publishing Group
4255 W. Touhy Ave.
Lincolnwood, IL 60646-1975
Ph: (847)679-5500   Fax: (847)679-2494
Fr: 800-323-4900

Lucia Mauro. 1996. $14.95; $9.95 (paper). 160 pages. Describes career opportunities in fashion, entertainment, retail, and promotion, with advice from fashion professionals.

★3911★ Consulting: Is Consulting for You?

Chronicle Guidance Publications, Inc.
66 Aurora St.
PO Box 1190
Moravia, NY 13118-1190
Ph: (315)497-0330   Fax: (315)497-3359
Fr: 800-622-7284

Chronicle Guidance Staff. 1995. $2.00. Reprint of a journal article.

★3912★ How to Start Your Own Fashion and Image Consulting Business

Academy of Fashion and Image
1903 Kirby Rd.
McLean, VA 22101
Ph: (703)442-0593   Fr: 800-450-5545

Brenda York. $9.95. Audiotape, $8.95.

★3913★ Image Consultants

Chronicle Guidance Publications, Inc.
66 Aurora St.
PO Box 1190
Moravia, NY 13118-1190
Ph: (315)497-0330   Fax: (315)497-3359
Fr: 800-622-7284

Chronicle Guidance Staff. 1994. $2.00. Provides concise career information and sources of additional information.

★3914★ Jumping the Job Track: Security, Satisfaction, and Success as an Independent Consultant

Crown Publishers
Covers issues related to establishing an independent consulting practice, with stories and advice from practicing consultants.

★3915★ 100 Best Careers for the Year 2000

Prentice Hall General Reference
15 Columbus Cir.
New York, NY 10023
Ph: (212)373-8500   Fr: 800-223-2348

Shelly Field. 1992. $15.00 (paper). Covers 100 of the fastest growing jobs. The publication is divided into 11 general employment sections. Specific careers are covered within each section. Provides job description, responsibilities, employment opportunities, earnings, education and training, advancement opportunities, and experience and qualifications for each occupation.

★3916★ The 10 Hottest Consulting Practices of the 1990s: What They Are, How to Get into Them

John Wiley & Sons, Inc.
605 3rd Ave.
New York, NY 10158-0012
Ph: (212)850-6000   Fr: 800-225-5945

Ron Tepper. 1995. $27.95.

OTHER SOURCES

★3917★ AICI Newsletter

Association of Image Consultants
International (AICI)
1000 Connecticut Ave. NW, Ste. 9
Washington, DC 20036-5032
Ph: (301)371-9021   Fax: (301)371-8847
Fr: 800-383-8831

Quarterly. $15.00/year. Contains shopping and consulting updates and chapter news; includes convention information.

★3918★ Association of Image Consultants International (AICI)

1000 Connecticut Ave. NW, Ste. 9
Washington, DC 20036-5032
Ph: (301)371-9021   Fax: (301)371-8847
Fr: 800-383-8831

Members: Personal color, style, wardrobe, and image planning consultants. **Purpose:** Promotes quality service for clients; aids in establishing working relations between retail stores and consultants; assists community colleges in offering accredited image consulting programs; maintains standards of professionalism for members in the image consulting industry. Provides continuing education and training; maintains speakers' bureau.

★3919★ Consultants' Network (CN)

57 W. 89th St.
New York, NY 10024
Ph: (212)799-5239

Purpose: Independent consultants and principals in small consulting firms in all areas of consulting. Operates a clearinghouse. Provides referral and market support services.
Website: http://www.consultants-mall.com/

★3920★ How to Become a Successful Consultant in Your Own Field

Prima Publishing
3875 Atherton Rd.
Rocklin, CA 95765
Ph: (916)632-4400

Hubert Bermont. Third edition, 1991. $21.95. 240 pages.

★3921★ How to Succeed as an Independent Consultant

John Wiley and Sons
605 3rd Ave.
New York, NY 10158
Ph: (212)850-6000   Fr: 800-225-5945

Herman Holtz. Third edition, 1993. $29.95. 416 pages. Presents information on launching a consulting venture, how to identify and secure clients, and how to build a practice.

★3922★ The Independent Consultant's Q&A Book

Bob Adams, Inc.
260 Center St.
Holbrook, MA 02343
Ph: (617)767-8100   Fax: (617)767-0994
Fr: 800-872-5627

Lawrence Tuller. 1992. $10.95. 300 pages. Directed at those considering entering consulting, consultants in the early stages of developing their practice, and experienced consultants in search of new ideas or directions. Designed in a question-and-answer format to enable the reader to scan and focus on particular topics of interest.

★3923★ Institute of Personal Image Consultants (IPIC)

c/o Image Industry Publications
10 Bay St. Landing, Ste. 7F
Staten Island, NY 10301
Ph: (718)273-3229   Fax: (718)727-3828

Purpose: Information clearinghouse serving the personal image consulting profession, comprised of practitioners engaged in speech and public appearance coaching, dress and color coordination, personal public relations counseling, and etiquette and motivational consulting. Sells books and audiocassettes providing information about the industry and its self-help services.

★3924★ Marketing Your Consulting and Professional Services

John Wiley and Sons, Inc.
605 3rd Ave.
New York, NY 10158
Ph: (212)850-6000   Fr: 800-225-5945

Richard A. Connor. Second edition, 1990. $29.95. Step-by-step guide to entering the consulting field including developing a marketing plan.

★3925★ San Francisco-Based Image Industry Council International

PO Box 422643
San Francisco, CA 94142
Ph: (415)863-2572

Activities: Maintains speakers' bureau. Conducts educational and research programs. Maintains library. Subjects covered include image management, color analysis, wardrobe strategies, grooming, etiquette.

Industrial Engineers

★3926★ **Applied Occupational & Environmental Hygiene**

Applied Industrial Hygiene, Inc.
1330 Kemper Meadow Dr., Ste. 600
Cincinnati, OH 45240
Ph: (513)742-2020   Fax: (513)742-3355

Monthly. $85.00/year for individuals; $155.00/year for institutions. Magazine presenting solutions in occupational and environmental hygiene.

★3927★ **Automotive Engineering**

Society of Automotive Engineers
400 Commonwealth Dr.
Warrendale, PA 15096
Ph: (412)776-4841   Fax: (412)776-4026

Monthly. $72.00/year for individuals; $126.00/year for other countries. Magazine for automotive engineers providing technical and design information.

★3928★ **Captsule Job Listings**

Publications and Communications, Inc.
12416 Hymeadow Dr.
Austin, TX 78750
Ph: (512)250-9023   Fax: (512)331-3900
Fr: 800-678-9724

Online database. Lists current job openings in the contract (temporary) technical services industry. Includes the Action Hot List, which provides information on job seekers. Includes employment opportunities in technical/professional engineering, computing, and design/drafting. Entries generally contain company name, address, and job opening.

★3929★ **Engineering Times**

National Society of Professional Engineers
1420 King St.
Alexandria, VA 22314
Ph: (703)684-2875   Fax: (703)836-4875

Monthly. Magazine (tabloid) covering professional, legislative, and techology issues for an engineering audience.

★3930★ **ENR: Engineering News Record**

New York Construction News
1221 Avenue of the Americas
New York, NY 10020
Ph: (212)512-4773   Fax: (212)512-4770

Weekly. $42.00/year; $2.00/issue.

★3931★ **High Technology Careers Magazine**

HTC
4701 Patrick Henry Dr., No. 1901
Santa Clara, CA 95054
Ph: (408)970-8800   Fax: (408)980-5103

Bimonthly. Magazine (tabloid) containing employment opportunity information for the engineering and technical community.

★3932★ **IIE Solutions**

Institute of Industrial Engineers
25 Technology Park/Atlanta
Norcross, GA 30092
Ph: (404)449-0461   Fax: (404)263-8532

Monthly. $49.00/year for individuals; $6.00 for single issue. Magazine covering industrial engineering, facilities design, systems integration, production control, and material handling management.

★3933★ **Managing Automation**

Thomas Publishing Co.
5 Penn Plaza
New York, NY 10001
Ph: (212)695-0500   Fax: (212)290-7362

Monthly. $60.00/year for individuals; $8.00 for single issue. Magazine serving manufacturing and non-manufacturing industries concerned with the planning and implementation of factory automation.

★3934★ **Minority Engineer**

Equal Opportunity Publications, Inc.
150 Motor Pkwy., Ste. 420
Hauppauge, NY 11788-5145
Ph: (516)273-0066   Fax: (516)273-8936

Affirmative-action recruitment magazine serving college graduating and professional minority engineers.

★3935★ **NSBE Magazine**

NSBE Publications
1454 Duke St.
Alexandria, VA 22314
Ph: (703)549-2207   Fax: (703)683-5312

$10.00/year for individuals; $2.00 for single issue. Journal providing information on engineering careers, self-development, and cultural issues for recent graduates with technical majors.

★3936★ **PEM Plant Engineering and Maintenance**

Clifford Elliot and Associates
277 Lakeshore Rd. E, Ste. 209
Oakville, ON, Canada L6J 6J3
Ph: (416)842-2884   Fax: (416)842-8226

Five issues/year.

★3937★ **Plant Engineering**

Cahners Publishing Co.
1350 E. Touhy Ave.
Des Plaines, IL 60018
Ph: (708)635-8800   Fax: (708)390-2770

Free to qualified subscribers; $50.00/year for institutions; $3.00 for single issue. Magazine focusing on engineering support and maintenance in industry.

★3938★ **Power**

New York Construction News
1221 Avenue of the Americas, 41st Fl.
New York, NY 10020
Ph: (212)512-4773   Fax: (212)512-4770

Monthly. Magazine for engineers in electric utilities, process and manufacturing plants, commercial and service establishments, and consulting, design, and construction engineering firms working in the power technology field.

★3939★ **Quality**

Chilton Publishing Co.
191 S. Gary Ave.
Carol Stream, IL 60188
Ph: (708)665-1000   Fax: (708)462-2225
Fr: 800-826-6270

Monthly. $70.00/year for individuals; $85.00/year for Canada and Mexico. Industrial and scientific magazine on continuous quality improvement.

★3940★ SWE

Society of Women Engineers
120 Wall St., 11th Fl.
New York, NY 10005-3902
Ph: (212)509-9577   Fax: (212)509-0224

Bimonthly. $30.00/year for nonmembers. Magazine for engineering students and for women and men working in the engineering and technology fields. Covers career guidance, continuing development and topical issues.

★3941★ Technology Review

The Tech
PO Box 397029
Cambridge, MA 02139
Ph: (617)253-1541   Fax: (617)258-8226

$30.00/year for individuals; $3.75 for single issue; $42.00/year for other countries. Magazine reviewing new developments in technology with an emphasis on economic, political, and social implications. Not a new product publication.

★3942★ Woman Engineer

Equal Opportunity Publications, Inc.
150 Motor Pkwy., Ste. 420
Hauppauge, NY 11788-5145
Ph: (516)273-0066   Fax: (516)273-8936

Engineer recruitment magazine.

PLACEMENT AND JOB REFERRAL SERVICES

★3943★ American Indian Science and Engineering Society (AISES)

1630 30th St., Ste. 301
Boulder, CO 80301
Ph: (303)492-8658   Fax: (303)492-3400

Members: American Indian and non-Indian students and professionals in science, technology, and engineering fields; corporations representing energy, mining, aerospace, electronic, and computer fields. **Purpose:** Seeks to motivate and encourage students to pursue undergraduate and graduate studies in science, engineering, and technology. **Activities:** Sponsors science fairs in grade schools, teacher training workshops, summer math/science sessions for 8th-12th graders, professional chapters, and student chapters in colleges. Offers scholarships. Adult members serve as role models, advisers, and mentors for students. Operates placement service. **E-Mail:** aise sha@spot.colorado.edu

★3944★ Association for Finishing Processes of the Society of Manufacturing Engineers (AFP/SME)

1 SME Dr.
PO Box 930
Dearborn, MI 48121-0930
Ph: (313)271-1500   Fax: (313)271-2861
Fr: 800-733-4SME

Purpose: Sponsored by Society of Manufacturing Engineers. Engineers, scientists, technicians, and students in 40 countries. Provides a network of communication for those involved in industrial finishes with specialization in liquid and powder coatings, radiation curing, waterborne, high solids, coating and finishing of plastics, pretreatment and surface preparation. Provides information on systems design, serves the continuing education needs of the manufacturing community by: following and assessing the trends and developments in industrial finishes; interpreting, publishing, and distributing such information; coordinating activities with other technical societies and trade organizations concerned with the dissemination of knowledge related to industrial finishing. Conducts clinics and expositions. Offers professional certification. **Activities:** Maintains placement service with free listings for members.

★3945★ Engineering Society of Detroit (ESD)

100 Farnsworth Ave.
Detroit, MI 48202
Ph: (313)832-5400   Fax: (313)832-5920

Members: Engineers from all disciplines; scientists and technologists. **Activities:** Offers placement services. Conducts technical programs and engineering refresher courses; sponsors conferences and expositions. Maintains speakers' bureau. Although based in Detroit, MI, society membership is international.

★3946★ Korean Scientists and Engineers Association in America (KSEA)

6261 Executive Blvd.
Rockville, MD 20852
Ph: (301)984-7048   Fax: (301)984-1231

Members: Scientists and engineers holding single or advanced degrees. **Purpose:** Goals are to: promote friendship and mutuality among Korean and American scientists and engineers; contribute to Korea's scientific, technological, industrial, and economic developments; strengthen the scientific, technological, and cultural bonds between Korea and the U.S. Sponsors symposium. **Activities:** Maintains speakers' bureau, placement service, and biographical archives. Compiles statistics. Maintains 100 volume library of scientific handbooks and yearbooks in Korean.

★3947★ Society of Hispanic Professional Engineers (SHPE)

5400 E. Olympic Blvd., Ste. 210
Los Angeles, CA 90022
Ph: (213)725-3970

Purpose: Engineers, student engineers, and scientists seeking to increase the number of Hispanic engineers by providing motivation and support to students. Sponsors competitions and educational programs. **Activities:** Maintains placement service and speakers' bureau; compiles statistics.

★3948★ Society of Logistics Engineers (SOLE)

8100 Professional Pl., Ste. 211
Hyattsville, MD 20785
Ph: (301)459-8446   Fax: (301)459-1522

Members: Corporate and individual management and technical practitioners in the field of logistics, including scientists, engineers, educators, managers, and other specialists in commerce, aerospace, and other industries, government, and the military. **Purpose:** Covers every logistics specialty, including maintainability, systems and equipment maintenance, maintenance support equipment, human factors, training and training equipment, spare parts, overhaul and repair, handbooks, field site activation and operation, field engineering, facilities, packaging, materials handling, and transportation. **Activities:** Sponsors job referral service; conducts specialized education programs; operates speakers' bureau. Sponsors the Logistics Education Foundation.

EMPLOYER DIRECTORIES AND NETWORKING LISTS

★3949★ American Men and Women of Science

R. R. Bowker Co.
Reed Reference Publishing
121 Chanlon Rd.
New Providence, NJ 07974
Ph: (908)464-6800   Fax: (908)665-6688
Fr: 800-521-8110

Triennial, latest edition January 1995. $106.00, per volume; $850.00, set. Covers over 123,000 U.S. and Canadian scientists active in the physical, biological, mathematical, computer science, and engineering fields; includes references to previous edition for deceased scientists and nonrespondents. Entries include: Name, address, education, personal and career data, memberships, honors and awards, research interest. Arrangement: Alphabetical. Indexes: Discipline (in separate volume).

★3950★ Directory of Contract Service Firms

C. E. Publications, Inc.
PO Box 97000
Kirkland, WA 98083
Ph: (206)823-2222   Fax: (206)821-0942

Annual, January. $10.00. Covers Approximately 900 contract firms actively engaged in the employment of engineering and technical personnel for temporary contract assignments throughout the world. Entries include: Company name, address, phone, name of contact. Arrangement: Alphabetical. Indexes: Geographical.

★3951★ Directory of Engineering Societies and Related Organizations

American Association of Engineering Societies
1111 19th St. NW, Ste. 608
Washington, DC 20036
Ph: (202)296-2237   Fax: (202)296-1151
Fr: 800-658-8897

1992. $185.00. Lists 1,000 national, regional, Canadian, and international organizations concerned with engineering and related fields.

★3952★ Directory of Engineers in Private Practice

National Society of Professional Engineers
1420 King St.
Alexandria, VA 22314
Ph: (703)684-2862   Fax: (703)836-4875

Annual. $85.00. Covers 600 consulting engineering firms and 7,200 individuals who are members of the society's Professional Engineers in Private Practice division. Entries include: For companies, name, address, phone, name of principal executive, list of services. For individuals, name, address; most listings include phone. Arrangement: Firms are geographic, then by specialty; individuals are alphabetical.

★3953★ Engineering Research Centres

Stockton Press
Groves Dictionaries
345 Park Ave. S., 10th Fl.
New York, NY 10010
Ph: (212)689-9200   Fr: 800-221-2123

Fourth edition, 1995. $515.00. 768 pages. Contains over 8,000 entries describing research and technology laboratories in over 70 countries. Provides details on industrial research centers and educational establishments with research and development activity. Indexes: Subject and title of establishments.

★3954★ Peterson's Job Opportunities in Engineering and Technology 1996

Peterson's
PO Box 2123
Princeton, NJ 08543-2123
Ph: (609)243-9111   Fax: (609)243-9150
Fr: 800-338-3282

Compiled by the Peterson's staff. Annual. $19.95 paperback. 432 pages. Profiles 2,000 high-tech companies looking primarily for technical personnel in such fields as biotechnology, telecommunications, software, computers and peripherals, defense, and aerospace. Contains job-search strategies and career options to help match education and expertise to the job market. Indexed geographically, by industry, and by hiring needs.

★3955★ Scientific and Technical Organizations and Agencies Directory

Gale Research
835 Penobscot Bldg.
Detroit, MI 48226-4094
Ph: (313)961-2242   Fax: (313)961-6083
Fr: 800-877-GALE

Irregular; latest edition December 1993. $195.00. Covers over 25,600 national and international organizations and agencies concerned with the physical and applied sciences, engineering, and technology, including associations, computer information services, consulting firms, educational institutions, foundations, government advisory organizations, federal government agencies, general grant and assistance programs, libraries and information centers, patent sources and services, research and development centers, scholarships, fellowships, and loans, science-technology centers, standards organizations, state academies of science, and state government agencies in the fields of aeronautics and space sciences, chemis-

try, computer science specialties, electronics, geography, geology, machinery, mathematics, metallurgy, meteorology, mineralogy, nuclear science, petroleum and gas, physics, plastics, transportation, water resources, and other areas. Entries include: Organization name, address, phone, and name of contact; additional descriptive text for most entries. Arrangement: Classified by type of organization. Indexes: Organization name/key word.

★3956★ Who's Who in Technology

Gale Research
835 Penobscot Bldg.
Detroit, MI 48226-4094
Ph: (313)961-2242   Fax: (313)961-6083
Fr: 800-877-GALE

Irregular, new edition expected June 1995. $380.00. Covers 38,000 engineers, scientists, inventors, and researchers. Entries include: Name, title, affiliation, address; personal, education, and career data; publications, patents; technical field of activity; area of expertise. Arrangement: Alphabetical. Indexes: Geographical, employer, technical discipline, expertise.

HANDBOOKS AND MANUALS

★3957★ The Best Resumes for Scientists and Engineers

John Wiley and Sons
605 3rd Ave.
New York, NY 10158
Ph: (212)850-6000   Fr: 800-225-5945

Adele Lewis. Second edition, 1993. $37.50; $14.95 (paper). Presents an extensive collection of scientific and engineering resumes, highlighting the important differences between these and resumes written for other occupations.

★3958★ Careers in Engineering

VGM Career Horizons
4255 W. Touhy Ave.
Lincolnwood, IL 60646-1975
Ph: (847)679-5500   Fax: (847)679-2494
Fr: 800-323-4900

Geraldine O. Gardner. 1994. $17.95; $13.95 (paper). Covers careers in the public or private sector, in industry, the university, or the military, from applications in computer architecture design to high temperature ceramics.

★3959★ Engineering Success

Kendall Hunt Publishing
4050 Westmark Dr.
PO Box 1840
Dubuque, IA 52004-1840
Ph: (319)589-1000   Fax: 800-772-9165
Fr: 800-228-0810

Bill Osher. 1994. $27.96.

★3960★ Engineering Your Job Search: A Job-Finding Resource for Engineering Professionals

Professional Publications, Inc.
1250 5th Ave.
Belmont, CA 94002
Ph: (415)593-9119   Fax: (415)592-4519
Fr: 800-426-1178

Compiled by Professional Publications editors. 1995. $12.95 (paper).

★3961★ Introduction to the Engineering Profession

HarperCollins Publishers, Inc.
10 E. 53rd. St.
New York, NY 10022-5299
Ph: (212)207-7000   Fax: (212)207-7145
Fr: 800-331-3761

David M. Burghardt. 1995. $30.00 (paper).

★3962★ Job Opportunities in Engineering and Technology

Peterson's Guides, Inc.
PO Box 2123
Princeton, NJ 08543-2123
Ph: (609)243-9111   Fax: (609)243-9150
Fr: 800-338-3282

1994. $18.95 (paper).

★3963★ Majoring in Engineering: How to Get from Your Freshman Year to Your First Job

Farrar, Straus & Giroux, Inc.
19 Union Sq., W
New York, NY 10003
Ph: (212)741-6900   Fr: 800-788-6262

John Garcia. 1995. $20.00; $10.00 (paper).

★3964★ Opportunities in Engineering Careers

VGM Career Horizons
4255 W. Touhy Ave.
Lincolnwood, IL 60646-1975
Ph: (847)679-5500   Fax: (847)679-2494
Fr: 800-323-4900

Nicholas Basta. 1995. $14.95; $11.95 (paper). Outlines typical job titles, salaries, career paths, and employment prospects.

★3965★ Opportunities in High Tech Careers

VGM Career Horizons
4255 W. Touhy Ave.
Lincolnwood, IL 60646-1975
Ph: (847)679-5500   Fax: (847)679-2494
Fr: 800-323-4900

Gary D. Golter and Deborah Yanuck. 1995. $14.95; $11.95 (paper). 160 pages. Explores high technology careers. Describes job opportunities, how to make a career decision, how to prepare for high technology jobs, job hunting techniques, and future trends.

★3966★ Problems and Solutions to the Principles and Practice of Engineering Examinations Industrial Engineers

Engineering & Management Press
25 Technology Pk.
Norcross, GA 30092
Ph: (770)449-0461   Fax: (770)263-8532

Donavon Young, editor. 1993. $24.95.

★3967★ *Resumes for Engineering Careers*

VGM Career Horizons
NTC Publishing Group
4255 W. Touhy Ave.
Lincolnwood, IL 60646-1975
Ph: (847)679-5500   Fax: (847)679-2494
Fr: 800-323-4900

1994. $9.95. 160 pages. Contains sample resumes and cover letters applicable to any engineering field.

★3968★ *Where the Jobs Are: The Hottest Careers for the '90s*

The Career Press, Inc.
3 Tice Rd.
PO Box 687
Franklin Lakes, NJ 07417
Ph: (201)848-0310   Fax: (201)848-1727
Fr: 800-237-3371

Joyce Hadley. Second edition, 1995. $9.99. 300 pages. Describes careers in fifteen general fields, from accounting to travel and hospitality.

EMPLOYMENT AGENCIES AND SEARCH FIRMS

★3969★ **ABC Employment Service**

25 S. Bemiston, Ste. 214
Clayton, MO 63105
Ph: (314)725-3140

Employment agency.

★3970★ **B and M Associates, Inc.**

199 Cambridge Rd.
Woburn, MA 01801-4705
Ph: (617)938-9120

Employment agency.

★3971★ **Bell Oaks Co.**

3390 Peachtree Rd., Ste. 1124
Atlanta, GA 30326
Ph: (404)261-2170

Personnel service firm.

★3972★ **Colli Associates of Tampa**

PO Box 2865
Tampa, FL 33601
Ph: (813)681-2145

Employment agency. Executive search firm.

★3973★ **Engineer One, Inc.**

10124 Dutchtown Rd.
Knoxville, TN 37932-2611
Ph: (615)690-2611   Fax: (615)690-2611

Employment agency.

★3974★ **Executive Recruiters Agency**

14 Office Park Dr.
PO Box 21810
Little Rock, AR 72221-1810
Ph: (501)224-7000   Fax: (501)224-8534

Personnel service firm.

★3975★ **Hayden and Associates, Inc.**

7825 Washington Ave. S., Ste. 120
Minneapolis, MN 55439-2431
Ph: (612)941-6300   Fax: (612)941-9602

Employment agency. Executive search firm. Fills openings in a variety of fields.

★3976★ **Industrial Recruiters Associates, Inc.**

630 Oakwood Ave., Ste. 318
West Hartford, CT 06110
Ph: (203)953-3643

Employment agency.

★3977★ **International Staffing Consultants**

500 Newport Center Dr., Ste. 300
Newport Beach, CA 92660-7003
Ph: (714)721-7990

Employment agency. Provides placement on regular or temporary basis. Affiliate office in London.

★3978★ **The Jobs Co.**

8900 E. Sprague Ave.
Spokane, WA 99212-2927
Ph: (509)928-3151   Fax: (509)928-3168

Employment agency. Has division specializing in engineering and scientific openings. Also operates division specializing in sales openings.

★3979★ **JR Professional Search**

PO Box 18356
Tucson, AZ 85731
Ph: (520)721-1855   Fax: (520)721-1855

Employment agency.

★3980★ **LOR Personnel Division**

418 Wall St.
Princeton, NJ 08540
Ph: (609)921-6580

Employment agency. Executive search firm.

★3981★ **Main Line Personnel Service, Inc.**

401 City Ave.
Bala Cynwyd, PA 19004-1122
Ph: (610)667-1820

Employment agency.

★3982★ **Mfg/Search, Inc.**

401 W. Colfax Ave., Ste. 600
South Bend, IN 46601
Ph: (219)282-2547   Fax: (219)289-0358

Executive search firm.

★3983★ **Rand Personnel Agency**

1200 Truxtun, Ste. 130
Bakersfield, CA 93301
Ph: (805)325-0751   Fax: (805)325-4120

Personnel service firm.

★3984★ **Search and Recruit International**

4455 South Blvd.
Virginia Beach, VA 23452
Ph: (804)490-3151

Employment agency. Headquartered in Virginia Beach. Other offices in Bremerton, WA; Charleston, SC; Jacksonville, FL; Memphis, TN; Pensacola, FL; Sacramento, CA; San Bernardino, CA; San Diego, CA.

★3985★ **Sierra Technology Corporation**

4150 Manzanita Ave., Ste. 100
Carmichael, CA 95608-1700
Ph: (916)488-4960   Fax: (916)488-7058

Employment agency. Provides placement on a temporary basis.

★3986★ **Software Services Corp.**

2850 S. Industrial Hwy., Ste. 300
Ann Arbor, MI 48104-6796
Ph: (313)971-2300

Employment agency.

★3987★ **Source Engineering**

5580 LBJ Fwy., Ste. 300
Dallas, TX 75240
Ph: (214)385-3002   Fax: (214)717-0075

Executive search firm. Many affiliate offices located throughout the U.S.

★3988★ **T.R. Employment Agency**

409 Wilshire Blvd.
Santa Monica, CA 90401
Ph: (310)393-4107

Employment agency.

★3989★ **Tri-Serv Inc.**

22 W. Padonia Rd., Ste. C53
Timonium, MD 21093
Ph: (301)561-1740

Employment agency.

OTHER SOURCES

★3990★ *Adventures in Manufacturing*

Society of Manufacturing Engineers (SME)
Education Dept.
1 SME Dr.
PO Box 930
Dearborn, MI 48121
Ph: (313)271-1500   Fr: 800-733-4SME

Video. Free. Comes with poster and brochure. Describes opportunities and preparation for careers in manufacturing.

★3991★ *American Almanac of Jobs and Salaries 1994-95*

Avon Books
1350 Avenue of the Americas, 2nd Fl.
New York, NY 10019
Ph: (212)261-6800   Fr: 800-238-0658

John Wright. Revised edition, 1993. $17.00. 704 pages. This is a comprehensive guide to the wages of hundreds of occupations in a wide variety of industries and organizations.

★3992★ *American Association of Engineering Societies (AAES)*

1111 19th St. NW, Ste. 608
Washington, DC 20036
Ph: (202)296-2237   Fax: (202)296-1151

Purpose: Seeks to promote leadership in public affairs for the engineering community, work in support of math and science education for young persons. Disseminates of information about the profession. Provides statistics about engineers.

★3993★ **American Supplier Institute (ASI)**

17333 Federal Dr., Ste. 220
Allen Park, MI 48101
Ph: (313)336-8877   Fax: (313)336-3187
Fr: 800-462-4500

Purpose: Seeks to encourage change in U.S. industry through development and implementation of advanced manufacturing and engineering technologies such as taguchi methods, quality function deployment, just-in-time manufacturing, statistical process control, and total quality management. **Activities:** Offers educational courses, training seminars, and workshops to improve quality, reduce cost, and enhance competitive position of U.S. products. Maintains international network of affiliates for developing training specialists and technologies curriculum. Has government contract to provide training services to government supplier companies.

★3994★ **Association for International Practical Training (AIPT)**

10400 Little Patuxent Pky. Ste. 250
Columbia, MD 21044
Ph: (410)997-2200   Fax: (410)992-3924

Purpose: Helps coordinate training around the world in fields such as travel, the culinary arts, and hotel management. **Activities:** Conducts programs in career development and hospitality/tourism exchanges. Operates a student exchange program. Provides reciprocal practical training experience for recent graduates from the U.S., Austria, Germany, Finland, France, Hungary, Ireland, Japan, Malaysia, Netherlands, Switzerland, and the United Kingdom. Arranges training programs in the U.S. and abroad. Serves as U.S. affiliate to IAESTE (International Association for the Exchange of Students for Technical Experience) and operates a Professional Visitors Program to arrange short-term educational and training visits to the U.S. **E-Mail:** aipt@aipt.org

★3995★ *Engineering Salary Survey*

Source Engineering
1290 Oakmead, Ste. 318
Sunnyvale, CA 94086
Ph: (408)738-8440

Annual. Discusses the structure of the engineering profession, trends, and compensation. Salaries are listed by job function, industry, and years of experience.

★3996★ *Graduating Engineer*

Peterson's/COG Publishing Group
16030 Ventura Blvd., No. 560
Encino, CA 91436
Ph: (818)789-5293

Eight issues/year. Magazine focusing on employment, education, and career development for entry-level engineers.

★3997★ **Institute of Industrial Engineers (IIE)**

25 Technology Park/Atlanta
Norcross, GA 30092
Ph: (770)449-0460   Fax: (770)263-8532

Members: Professional society of industrial engineers and student members. **Purpose:** Concerned with the design, improvement, and installation of integrated systems of people, materials, equipment, and energy. Draws upon specialized knowledge and skill in the mathematical, physical, and social sciences together with the principles and methods of engineering analysis and design, to specify, predict, and evaluate the results obtained from such systems. **Activities:** Maintains technical societies and divisions.

★3998★ **National Action Council for Minorities in Engineering (NACME)**

3 W. 35th St.
New York, NY 10001-2281
Ph: (212)279-2626   Fax: (212)629-5178

Purpose: Seeks to increase the number of African American, Latino, and Native American students enrolled in and graduating from engineering schools. Through the Corporate Scholars Program, offers comprehensive scholarships to engineering students that include leadership development, corporate mentors and summer internships. Works with local, regional, and national education organizations to motivate and encourage precollege students to engage in engineering careers. Conducts educational and research

programs; operates project to assist engineering schools in improving the retention and graduation rates of minority students. Maintains speakers' bureau; compiles statistics.

★3999★ **National Society of Professional Engineers (NSPE)**

1420 King St.
Alexandria, VA 22314
Ph: (703)684-2800   Fax: (703)836-4875

Members: Professional engineers and engineers-in-training in all fields registered in accordance with the laws of states or territories of the U.S. or provinces of Canada; qualified graduate engineers, student members, and registered land surveyors. **Purpose:** Is concerned with social, professional, ethical, and economic considerations of engineering as a profession; encompasses programs in public relations, employment practices, ethical considerations, education, and career guidance. Monitors legislative and regulatory actions of interest to the engineering profession. **Website:** http://www.hspc.org

★4000★ *Salaries of Scientists, Engineers, and Technicians: A Summary of Salary Surveys*

Commission on Professionals in Science and Technology (CPST)
1500 Massachusetts Ave. NW, Ste. 831
Washington, DC 20005
Ph: (202)223-6995

1993.

★4001★ **Society of Women Engineers (SWE)**

120 Wall St., 11th Fl.
New York, NY 10005
Ph: (212)509-9577   Fax: (212)509-0224

Members: Educational service society of women engineers; membership is also open to men. **Purpose:** Supplies information on the achievements of women engineers and the opportunities available to them; assists women engineers in preparing for return to active work following temporary retirement. Serves as an informational center on women in engineering. **Activities:** Administers several certificate and scholarship programs. Offers tours and career guidance; conducts surveys. Compiles statistics.

Inspectors and Compliance Officers, Except Construction

★4002★ **American City and County**
Communication Channels, Inc.
6255 Barfield Rd.
Atlanta, GA 30328
Ph: (404)955-9970   Fax: (404)256-3116

Monthly. $54.00/year for individuals. Municipal and county administration magazine.

★4003★ **American Industrial Hygiene Association Journal**
American Industrial Hygiene Association
2700 Prosperity, Ste. 250
Fairfax, VA 22031
Ph: (703)849-8888   Fax: (703)207-3561

Monthly. Journal providing a forum for peer-reviewed articles in the field of industrial hygiene.

★4004★ **Applied Occupational & Environmental Hygiene**
Applied Industrial Hygiene, Inc.
1330 Kemper Meadow Dr., Ste. 600
Cincinnati, OH 45240
Ph: (513)742-2020   Fax: (513)742-3355

Monthly. $85.00/year for individuals; $155.00/year for institutions. Magazine presenting solutions in occupational and environmental hygiene.

★4005★ **Federal Career Opportunities**
Federal Research Service, Inc.
243 Church St. NW
PO Box 1059
Vienna, VA 22183
Ph: (703)281-0200   Fax: (703)281-7639
Fr: 800-822-5627

Biweekly. $7.95, per copy; $39.00, 6 issues; $77.00, 12 issues; $175.00, 26 issues. Covers more than 4,000 current federal job vacancies in the United States and overseas; includes permanent, part-time, and temporary positions. Entries include: Position title, location, series and grade, job requirements, special forms, announcement number, closing date, application address. Arrangement: Classified by federal agency and occupation.

★4006★ **Federal Jobs Digest**
Federal Jobs Digest
325 Pennsylvania Ave. SE
Washington, DC 20003
Ph: (202)762-5111   Fax: (202)762-4818
Fr: 800-824-5000

Biweekly. $4.50, per issue; $29.00, for three months; $110.00, per year. Covers over 10,000 specific job openings in the federal government in each issue. Entries include: Position name, title, General Schedule (GS) grade, and Wage Grade (WG), closing date for applications, announcement number, application address, phone, and name of contact. Arrangement: By federal department or agency, then geographical.

★4007★ **Food Production Management**
CTI Publications, Inc.
2619 Maryland Ave.
Baltimore, MD 21218
Ph: (410)467-3338   Fax: (410)467-7434

Monthly. $25.00/year for individuals; $5.00 for single issue. Magazine on food processing and individual packing news for management, sales, and production personnel in the canning, glass packing, and frozen food industries.

★4008★ **Industrial Hygiene News**
Rimbach Publishing, Inc.
8650 Babcock Blvd.
Pittsburgh, PA 15237-5821
Ph: (412)364-5366   Fax: (412)369-9720
Fr: 800-245-3182

Bimonthly. Magazine covering industrial hygiene, occupational health, and safety.

★4009★ **Journal of Occupational and Environmental Medicine**
Williams & Wilkins
351 W. Camden St.
Baltimore, MD 21201-2436
Ph: (410)361-8004   Fax: (410)528-4312
Fr: 800-222-3790

Monthly. $77.00/year for individuals; $14.00 for single issue. Occupational and environmental medicine journal.

★4010★ **Occupational Health and Safety**
Stevens Publishing Corp.
PO Box 2573
Waco, TX 76702-2573
Ph: (817)776-9000   Fax: (817)662-7075
Fr: 800-727-7573

Monthly. Magazine covering federal and state regulation of occupational health and safety.

★4011★ **Pharmaceutical Technology**
Advanstar Communications
859 Willamette St.
PO Box 10460
Eugene, OR 97401
Ph: (503)343-1200   Fax: (503)344-3514

Monthly. Magazine on applied technology for pharmaceutical firms.

★4012★ **Safety Health**
National Safety Council
1121 Spring Lake Dr.
Itasca, IL 60143
Ph: (708)285-1121   Fax: (708)285-9114

Monthly. Publication focusing on safety and health issues.

★4013★ **American Public Health Association (APHA)**
1015 15th St. NW
Washington, DC 20005
Ph: (202)789-5600   Fax: (202)789-5681

Members: Professional organization of physicians, nurses, educators, academicians, environmentalists, epidemiologists, new professionals, social workers, health administrators, optometrists, podiatrists, pharmacists, dentists, nutritionists, health planners, other community and mental health specialists, and interested consumers. **Purpose:** Seeks to protect and promote personal, mental, and environmental health. **Activities:** Services include: promulgation of standards; establishment of uniform practices and procedures; development of the etiology of communicable diseases; research in public health; exploration of medical care programs and their relationships to public health. Sponsors job placement service.

★4014★ **American Society of Safety Engineers (ASSE)**

1800 E. Oakton St.
Des Plaines, IL 60018-2187
Ph: (708)692-4121   Fax: (708)296-3769

Members: Professional society of safety engineers, safety directors, and others concerned with accident prevention and safety, and health programs. **Activities:** Sponsors National Safety Week conducts research and educational programs. Compiles statistics; maintains job placement service.

★4015★ **National Environmental Health Association (NEHA)**

720 S. Colorado Blvd., Ste. 970, S. Tower
Denver, CO 80222
Ph: (303)756-9090   Fax: (303)691-9490

Purpose: Professional society of persons engaged in environmental health and protection for governmental agencies, public health and environmental protection agencies, industry, colleges, and universities. Conducts national professional registration program and continuing education programs. Provides self-paced learning modules for field professionals. **Activities:** Offers placement service; compiles statistics. Maintains speakers' bureau. Plans to offer an electronic bulletin board service.

EMPLOYER DIRECTORIES AND NETWORKING LISTS

★4016★ *American Industrial Hygiene Association—Directory*

American Industrial Hygiene Association
2700 Prosperity Ave., Ste. 250
Fairfax, VA 22031
Ph: (703)849-8888   Fax: (703)207-3561

Annual, September. Available to members only. Covers Approximately 11,000 members concerned with the study and control of environmental factors affecting people at work. Entries include: Name, address, phone, affiliation. Arrangement: Alphabetical. Indexes: Employer, geographical.

★4017★ *Carroll's State Directory*

Carroll Publishing
1058 Thomas Jefferson St. NW
Washington, DC 20007
Ph: (202)333-8620   Fax: (202)337-7020
Fr: 800-336-4240

Three times per year. $180.00, includes CD-ROM or diskette. Covers about 37,000 state government officials in all branches of government and members of authorities. Entries include: Name, address, phone, fax, title. Arrangement: Geographical; separate sections for state offices and legislatures. Indexes: Personal name (with phone), organizational, keyword.

★4018★ *Federal Staff Directory*

Staff Directories Ltd.
PO Box 62
Mount Vernon, VA 22121-0062
Ph: (703)739-0900   Fax: (703)739-0234

Semiannual, March and September. $79.00. Covers Approximately 33,000 persons in federal government offices and independent agencies, with biographies of 2,800 key executives; includes officials at policy level in agencies of the Office of the President, Cabinet-level departments, independent and regulatory agencies, military commands, federal information centers, and libraries, and United States attorneys, marshals, and ambassadors. Entries include: Name, title, location (indicating building, address, and/or room), phone, symbols indicating whether position is a presidential appointment and whether senate approval is required. Arrangement: Classified by department/agency. Indexes: Personal name, subject.

★4019★ *Municipal/County Directory Library Edition*

Carroll Publishing
1058 Thomas Jefferson St. NW
Washington, DC 20007
Ph: (202)333-8620   Fax: (202)337-7020
Fr: 800-336-4240

Annual, July. $137.00, plus $8.00 shipping; payment must accompany order. Covers officials of 1,400 county governments (with populations over 25,000) and 2,000 municipalities (with populations over 1,000); includes elected, appointed, and career office holders. Entries include: Name, title, agency, address, phone. Arrangement: County officials are geographical, then by agency; municipal officials are by city. Indexes: personal name (with phone), agency.

★4020★ *Municipal Year Book*

Newman Books Ltd.
32 Vauxhall Bridge Rd.
London SW1V 2SS, England
Ph: 71 9736400   Fax: 71 2335057

Annual, December. $140.00, postpaid. Covers local and central government agencies and officials of the United Kingdom; municipal art galleries, associations, development organizations, fairs, libraries, museums, airports, and other local authorities. Entries include: Name of authority or governing agency, address, phone, fax, names of elected councillors, officers, names and titles of key personnel, contacts, population, and pay. Arrangement: Geographical. Indexes: Subject, place names.

★4021★ *State Directory Library Edition*

Carroll Publishing
1058 Thomas Jefferson St. NW
Washington, DC 20007
Ph: (202)333-8620   Fax: (202)337-7020
Fr: 800-336-4240

Annual, July. $137.00, plus $8.00 shipping. Covers 37,000 state government officials in all branches of government and members of authorities. Entries include: Name, address, phone, fax, title. Arrangement: Geographical, then by agency within each state. Indexes: Personal name (with phone) organizational, keyword.

HANDBOOKS AND MANUALS

★4022★ *Encyclopedia of Careers and Vocational Guidance*

J. G. Ferguson Publishing Co.
200 W. Monroe, Ste. 250
Chicago, IL 60606
Ph: (312)580-5480

William E. Hopke. Ninth edition, 1993. $129.95; $199.95 (CD-ROM). Four-volume set that profiles 900 occupations and describes job trends in 71 industries. Includes career description, educational requirements, history of the job, methods of entry, advancement, employment outlook, earnings, conditions of work, social and psychological factors, and sources of further information. Contains career and employment information for this field.

★4023★ *Opportunities in State and Local Government Careers*

VGM Career Horizons
4255 W. Touhy Ave.
Lincolnwood, IL 60646-1975
Ph: (847)679-5500   Fax: (847)679-2494
Fr: 800-323-4900

Neale Baxter. 1993. $13.95; $10.95 (paper). 160 pages. Points out the incentives and drawbacks of a government career. Describes hiring procedures and provides tips on filling out applications, taking physical and aptitude tests, handling interviews, and finding jobs. Describes the jobs in which 75% of all state and local government workers are employed. For each occupation, covers the nature of the work and the training required.

EMPLOYMENT AGENCIES AND SEARCH FIRMS

★4024★ **Summit Executive Search Consultants, Inc.**

420 Lincoln Rd., Ste. 265
Miami Beach, FL 33139
Ph: (305)672-5008   Fax: (305)534-4327

Executive search firm.

Insurance Sales Agents

★4025★ Best's Review (Life/Health Edition)

A.M. Best Co.
Ambest Rd.
Oldwick, NJ 08858
Ph: (908)439-2200   Fax: (908)439-3363

Monthly. $21.00/year for individuals; $7.50/year for single issue. Magazine covering issues and trends for the management personnel of life/health insurers, the agents, and brokers who market their products.

★4026★ Business Insurance

Crain Communications, Inc.
740 N. Rush St.
Chicago, IL 60611-2590
Ph: (312)649-5311   Fax: (312)280-3189

Weekly. $80.00/year for individuals. Magazine for executives in the corporate risk, employee benefit, and finance fields.

★4027★ Insurance Journal

Wells Publishing
9191 Town Centre Dr., No. 550
San Diego, CA 92122
Ph: (619)455-7717   Fax: (619)546-1462

Biweekly. $78.00/year for nonmembers; $72.00/year for individuals; $3.00 for single issue. Property/Casualty Magazine of the West.

★4028★ InsuranceWeek

IW Publications
1001 4th Ave., Ste. 3029
Seattle, WA 98154
Ph: (206)624-6965   Fax: (206)624-5021

Weekly (Mon.). Magazine about multi-line insurance for agents and brokers in the western U.S.

★4029★ National Underwriter Property and Casualty/Risk and Benefits Management

National Underwriter Co.
505 Gest St.
Cincinnati, OH 45203-1716
Ph: (513)721-2140   Fax: (513)721-0126

Weekly (Mon.). Newsweekly for agents, brokers, executives, and managers in risk and benefit insurance.

★4030★ The Standard

155 Federal St.
Boston, MA 02110
Ph: (617)457-0600   Fax: (617)457-0608

Weekly (Fri.). $40.00/year for individuals. Trade newspaper covering insurance events, legislation, regulatory hearings, and court sessions for independent insurance agents.

★4031★ Today's Insurance Woman

National Association of Insurance Women International
PO Box 4410
Tulsa, OK 74159
Ph: (918)744-5195   Fax: (918)743-1968
Fr: 800-766-NAIW

Bimonthly. Magazine on insurance and professional development topics for men and women in the risk and insurance field.

PLACEMENT AND JOB REFERRAL SERVICES

★4032★ American Agents Association (AAA)

PO Box 7079
Hilton Head Island, SC 29938
Ph: (803)785-2808   Fax: (803)785-9068
Fr: 800-248-9288

Members: Licensed insurance agents. **Purpose:** Purpose is to provide programs to enhance the security of insurance agents and their families and to take advantage of programs designed for insurance agents. **Activities:** Offers placement services; compiles statistics. Plans to establish a scholarship program for members' children.

★4033★ American Association of Insurance Management Consultants (AAIMCO)

Roger Thomas
PO Box 1168
Livingston, TX 77351
Ph: (409)327-7623   Fax: (409)327-8866

Members: Insurance companies, agents, and brokers; professors of insurance; accountants and attorneys; personnel management specialists; and those with advanced degrees in management. **Purpose:** Advises and assists the insurance industry and seeks to achieve professional recognition for insurance management consultants. Mediates the exchange of ideas; sets standards of service and performance; maintains a code of ethics; offers a referral service and a series of educational conferences and seminars. **Activities:** Operates speakers' bureau; offers placement services; compiles statistics.

EMPLOYER DIRECTORIES AND NETWORKING LISTS

★4034★ Best's Agents Guide

A. M. Best Co.
Ambest Rd.
Oldwick, NJ 08858
Ph: (908)439-2200   Fax: (908)439-3296

Annual, August. $95.00. Covers over 1,700 life and health insurance companies nationwide. Entries include: Company name, address, names of president and secretary, phone, whether a stock or mutual company, states where licensed, Best's rating, current and historical financial data. Arrangement: Alphabetical.

★4035★ Best's Insurance Reports

A. M. Best Co.
Ambest Rd.
Oldwick, NJ 08858
Ph: (908)439-2200   Fax: (908)439-3296

Annual, August. $570.00, per edition; monthly publications included. Published in two editions: Life-health insurance, covering about 1,800 companies, and property-casualty insurance, covering over 2,000 companies; scope includes Canada. Each edition lists state insurance commissioners and related companies and agencies (mutual funds, worker compensation funds, underwriting agencies, etc.). Entries include: For each company, company name, address, phone; history; states in which licensed; names of officers and directors; financial data; editorial comment and rating. Arrangement: Alphabetical.

★4036★ **Business Insurance—Agent/ Broker Profiles Issue**

Crain Communications, Inc.
740 N. Rush St.
Chicago, IL 60611-2590
Ph: (312)649-5279   Fax: (312)280-3174

Annual, July. $10.00. Publication includes: List of more than 250 insurance agents and brokers specializing in commercial insurance. Entries include: Firm name, address, phone, fax, branch office locations, year established, names of subsidiaries, gross revenues, premium volume, number of employees, principal officers, percent of revenue generated by commercial retail brokerage, acquisitions, and states in which excess/surplus lines broker. Arrangement: Alphabetical.

★4037★ **General Insurance Register— Canada**

Stone & Cox Ltd.
111 Peter St., Ste. 202
Toronto, ON, Canada M5V 2H1
Ph: (416)599-0772   Fax: (416)599-0867

Annual, January. $40.66. Covers about 8,500 property and casualty insurance brokers and agencies in Canada; 250 insurance companies; 300 insurance adjusting offices. Entries include: Company name, address, phone, names and titles of key personnel. Insurance company listings also include assets, investment income, and other financial data. Arrangement: Alphabetical.

★4038★ **Insurance Agencies Directory**

American Business Directories, Inc.
American Business Information, Inc.
5711 S. 86th Cir.
Omaha, NE 68127
Ph: (402)593-4600   Fax: (402)331-1505

Annual. $5,480.00, U.S. edition. Entries include: Name, address, phone, size of advertisement, name of owner or manager, number of employees, year first in Yellow Pages. Regional editions available. Compiled from telephone company Yellow Pages, nationwide. Arrangement: Geographical.

★4039★ **Insurance Almanac**

Underwriter Printing and Publishing Co.
50 E. Palisade Ave.
Englewood, NJ 07631
Ph: (201)569-8808   Fr: 800-526-4700

Annual, July. $115.00. Covers over 3,000 insurance companies that write fire, casualty, accident and health, life, and Lloyd's policies; also lists mutual and reciprocal companies. Includes national, state, and local insurance associations; state insurance officials; and about 800 agents, brokers, actuaries, and adjusters. Arrangement: Classified by insurance lines, type of activity, etc. Indexes: Company name.

★4040★ **Insurance Consultants Directory**

American Business Directories, Inc.
American Business Information, Inc.
5711 S. 86th Cir.
Omaha, NE 68127
Ph: (402)593-4600   Fax: (402)331-1505

Annual. $910.00, U.S. edition. Entries include: Name, address, phone (including area code), size of advertisement, year first in Yellow Pages, name of owner or manager, number of employees. Compiled from telephone company Yellow Pages, nationwide. Arrangement: Geographical.

★4041★ **Insurance Phone Book and Directory**

U.S. Directory Service
Reed Reference Publishing
121 Chanlon Rd.
New Providence, NJ 07974
Ph: (908)464-6800   Fax: (908)665-6688
Fr: 800-521-8110

Annual. $89.95, plus $6.30 shipping. Covers about 4,000 life, accident and health, worker's compensation, auto, fire and casualty, marine, surety, and other insurance companies. Entries include: Company name, address, phone, fax, toll-free number, type of insurance provided. Arrangement: Alphabetical.

★4042★ **Kirschner's Insurance Directory**

Kirschner's Insurance Directories
Box 1087
Folsom, CA 95763
Ph: (916)983-7170   Fax: (916)983-1704

Semiannual. $14.95, each. Covers insurance companies, agents, brokers, surplus line brokers, and adjusters; separate editions for northern California, southern California, and Pacific Northwest. Associations and their members may also be listed. Entries include: Company name, address, phone, fax, names and titles of key personnel, risk placement. Arrangement: Classified by activity, then alphabetical. Indexes: Risk placement.

★4043★ **Moody's Bank and Finance Manual**

Moody's Investors Service, Inc.
99 Church St.
New York, NY 10007
Ph: (212)553-0300   Fax: (212)553-4700
Fr: 800-342-5647

Annual, July; supplements in *Moody's Bank & Finance News Reports*. $1,475.00, per year, including supplements. Covers in four volumes, over 20,000 national, state, and private banks, savings and loans, mutual funds, unit investment trusts, and insurance and real estate companies in the United States. Entries include: Company name, headquarters and branch offices, phones, names and titles of principal executives, directors, history, Moody's rating, and extensive financial and statistical data. Arrangement: Classified by type of business. Indexes: Company name.

★4044★ **National Insurance Association—Member Roster**

National Insurance Association
PO Box 53230
Chicago, IL 60653-0230
Ph: (312)924-3308   Fax: (312)285-0064

Annual, June. Available to members only. Covers about 18 insurance companies owned or controlled by African-Americans. Entries include: Company name, address, phone, date founded, states in which licensed, officers. Arrangement: Alphabetical.

★4045★ **National Underwriter Insurance Telephone Directory Series**

National Underwriter Co.
505 Gest St.
Cincinnati, OH 45203-1716
Ph: (513)721-2140   Fax: (513)721-0126
Fr: 800-543-0874

Approximately annual. $14.50. A series of eight directories published under the title (City or area name) Insurance Telephone Directory for Baltimore, Maryland, Washington, D.C., and northern Virginia; Boston, Massachusetts; Chicago, Illinois; Cleveland, Ohio; Detroit, Michigan; Philadelphia, Pennsylvania; Pittsburgh, Pennsylvania; and southern New Jersey and Delaware. Covers companies, brokers, and agents in each area handling all lines of insurance. Entries include: Firm and/or individual agent name, address, phone. Arrangement: Alphabetical.

★4046★ **New York Telephone Tickler**

Underwriter Printing & Publishing Co.
50 E. Palisade Ave.
Englewood, NJ 07631
Ph: (201)569-8808   Fr: 800-526-4700

Annual, November. $14.50. Covers about 10,000 insurance companies, brokers, agents, and related suppliers in the New York city area. Entries include: Company name, address, phone. Arrangement: Alphabetical. Indexes: Product/service.

★4047★ **North Jersey Telephone Tickler**

Underwriter Printing & Publishing Co.
50 E. Palisade Ave.
Englewood, NJ 07631
Ph: (201)569-8808   Fr: 800-526-4700

Annual, July. $7.00. Covers insurance companies, brokers, agents, and related suppliers in the northern New Jersey area. Entries include: Company name, address, phone. Arrangement: Alphabetical. Indexes: Product/service.

★4048★ **Ontario Insurance Directory**

Southam Magazine & Information Group
1450 Don Mills Rd.
Don Mills, ON, Canada M3B 2X7
Ph: (416)445-6641   Fax: (416)442-2213

Annual, January. $34.50. Covers brokers, insurance companies, adjusters, appraisers, lawyers, rehabilitation services, restoration services, and related associations in Ontario, Canada. Entries include: Company name, address, phone, telex, geographical area covered, subsidiary and branch names and locations. Arrangement: Geographical. Indexes: Product/service.

★4049★ **Society of Certified Insurance Counselors—National Membership Directory**

Society of Certified Insurance Counselors
3630 N. Hills Dr.
Austin, TX 78731
Ph: (512)345-7932   Fax: (512)343-2167

Biennial. Available to members only. Covers Approximately 17,000 insurance agents and practitioners who have qualified as Certified Insurance Counselors through training and examination. Entries include: Agent name; company name and address. Arrangement: Geographical.

★4050★ **Underwriters' Handbook Series**

National Underwriter Co.
505 Gest St.
Cincinnati, OH 45203-1716
Ph: (513)721-2140   Fax: (513)721-0126
Fr: 800-543-0874

Annual. $48.50, per state volume; 5th edition. Covers 142,000 insurance agents and agencies in 35 states and the District of Columbia; also names field representatives, managing general agents and general agents for both property/casualty and life/health insurance, adjusters, consultants, appraisers, audit and inspection services, and related insurance groups and associations and state departments of insurance. Published in 22 separate editions for Rocky Mountain States (Arizona, Colorado, Idaho, Montana, Nevada, New Mexico, Utah, and Wyoming); Georgia-Alabama; Missouri; Nebraska; North Dakota-South Dakota; Arkansas; Minnesota; Oklahoma; West Virginia; Maryland-Delaware-District of Columbia; Indiana; Florida-U.S. Caribbean; Pennsylvania; Iowa; Michigan; Illinois; Massachusetts; Ohio; Wisconsin; Connecticut-Rhode Island; Maine-New Hampshire-Vermont; and Kansas. Entries include: For companies Name, address, year established, divisions, key personnel (with addresses and phone numbers). Many list assets, liabilities, capital, and surplus. Arrangement: Separate alphabetical sections for insurance companies and field agents; other agents and activity are listed geographically, then by activity. Indexes: Type of insurance.

★4051★ **Who's Who in Insurance**

Underwriter Printing and Publishing Co.
50 E. Palisade Ave.
Englewood, NJ 07631
Ph: (201)569-8808   Fr: 800-526-4700

Annual, February. $115.00. Covers over 5,000 insurance officials, brokers, agents, and buyers. Entries include: Name, title, company name, address, home address, educational background, professional club and association memberships, personal and career data. Arrangement: Alphabetical.

★4052★ **Yearbook**

American Association of Managing
General Agents
9140 Ward Pkwy.
Kansas City, MO 64114
Ph: (816)444-3500   Fax: (816)444-0330

Annual, spring. Available to members only. Covers 250 managing general agents of insurance companies and their more than

500 branch offices; coverage includes Canada. Entries include: Name, address, names and titles of principal and contact, insurance companies represented. Arrangement: Geographical.

HANDBOOKS AND MANUALS

★4053★ **Business and Finance Career Directory**

Gale Research
835 Penobscot Bldg.
Detroit, MI 48226-4094
Ph: (313)961-2242   Fax: (313)961-6083
Fr: 800-877-GALE

Bradley Morgan. Second edition, 1992. $39.00. 413 pages. Features a basic and comprehensive job search section, articles by top professionals in the field, and detailed listings of hundreds of top companies who hire individuals in this field. Aimed particularly at entry-level job hunters.

★4054★ **Career Choices for the 90's for Students of Business**

Walker and Company
435 Hudson St.
New York, NY 10014
Ph: (212)727-8300   Fax: (212)727-0984
Fr: 800-289-2553

Prepared by the Career Associates staff. 1990. $9.95. 166 pages. Discusses alternatives for students of business. Offers advice on how to break into the field and how to move up. Covers where and who the employers are, internship possibilities, and professional networking associations. Comprehensive guide to career and job search planning.

★4055★ **Career Choices for the 90's for Students of Communications and Journalism**

Walker and Company
435 Hudson St.
New York, NY 10014
Ph: (212)727-8300   Fax: (212)727-0984
Fr: 800-289-2553

Prepared by the Career Associates staff. 1990. $8.95. 166 pages. Discusses alternatives for students of communications and journalism. Offers advice on how to break into the field and how to move up. Covers where and who the employers are, internship possibilities, and professional networking associations. Comprehensive guide to career and job search planning.

★4056★ **Career Choices for the 90's for Students of Economics**

Walker and Company
435 Hudson St.
New York, NY 10014
Ph: (212)727-8300   Fax: (212)727-0984
Fr: 800-289-2553

Prepared by the Career Associates staff. 1990. $8.95. 166 pages. Discusses alternatives for students of economics. Offers advice on how to break into the field and how to move up. Covers where and who the employers are, internship possibilities, and profes-

sional networking associations. Comprehensive guide to career and job search planning.

★4057★ **Career Choices for the 90's for Students of Mathematics**

Walker and Company
435 Hudson St.
New York, NY 10014
Ph: (212)727-8300   Fax: (212)727-0984
Fr: 800-289-2553

Prepared by the Career Associates staff. 1990. $8.95. 166 pages. Discusses alternatives for students of mathematics. Offers advice on how to break into the field and how to move up. Covers where and who the employers are, internship possibilities, and professional networking associations. Comprehensive guide to career and job search planning.

★4058★ **Career Choices for the 90's for Students of Political Science and Government**

Walker and Company
435 Hudson St.
New York, NY 10014
Ph: (212)727-8300   Fax: (212)727-0984
Fr: 800-289-2553

Prepared by the Career Associates staff. 1990. $8.95. 166 pages. Discusses alternatives for students of political science and government. Offers advice on how to break into the field and how to move up. Covers where and who the employers are, internship possibilities, and professional networking associations. Comprehensive guide to career and job search planning.

★4059★ **Career Choices for the 90's for Students of Psychology**

Walker and Company
435 Hudson St.
New York, NY 10014
Ph: (212)727-8300   Fax: (212)727-0984
Fr: 800-289-2553

Prepared by the Career Associates staff. 1990. $9.95. 166 pages. Discusses alternatives for students of psychology. Offers advice on how to break into the field and how to move up. Covers where and who the employers are, internship possibilities, and professional networking associations. Comprehensive guide to career and job search planning.

★4060★ **The Encyclopedia of Career Choices for the 1990s: Guide to Entry-Level Jobs**

Perigree Books
The Berkley Publishing Group
PO Box 506
East Rutherford, NJ 07073
Ph: (201)933-9292   Fr: 800-223-0510

Career Associates Staff. 1992. $19.95. 862 pages. Describes 500 entry-level careers in a variety of industries. Presents qualifications required, working conditions, salary, internships, and professional associations.

★4061★ Hot Tips, Sneaky Tricks and Last-Ditch Tactics

John Wiley and Sons, Inc.
605 3rd Ave.
New York, NY 10158
Ph: (212)850-6000   Fr: 800-225-5945

Jeff B. Speck. 1989. $12.95. Subtitled: "An Insider's Guide to Getting Your First Corporate Job". Gives an inside glimpse of the recruiting process and provides tips on using this knowledge to get the interview or the job.

★4062★ Jobs '90

Prentice Hall
113 Sylvan Ave.
Rte. 9W
Englewood Cliffs, NJ 07632
Ph: (201)592-2000   Fr: 800-922-0579

Kathryn Petras and Ross Petras. 1990. $14.95. 320 pages. Discusses employment prospects and trends. Lists leading companies, associations, directories, and magazines.

★4063★ 100 Best Careers for the Year 2000

Prentice Hall General Reference
15 Columbus Cir.
New York, NY 10023
Ph: (212)373-8500   Fr: 800-223-2348

Shelly Field. 1992. $15.00 (paper). Covers 100 of the fastest growing jobs. The publication is divided into 11 general employment sections. Specific careers are covered within each section. Provides job description, responsibilities, employment opportunities, earnings, education and training, advancement opportunities, and experience and qualifications for each occupation.

★4064★ Opportunities in Insurance Careers

VGM Career Horizons
4255 W. Touhy Ave.
Lincolnwood, IL 60646-1975
Ph: (847)679-5500   Fax: (847)679-2494
Fr: 800-323-4900

Robert Schrayer. 1994. $14.95; $11.95 (paper). A guide to planning for and seeking opportunities in the field. Contains bibliography and illustrations.

★4065★ Opportunities in Vocational and Technical Careers

VGM Career Horizons
4255 W. Touhy Ave.
Lincolnwood, IL 60646-1975
Ph: (847)679-5500   Fax: (847)679-2494
Fr: 800-323-4900

Adrian A. Paradis. 1992. $14.95; $11.95 (paper). 160 pages. Provides information on a variety of opportunities and advice on breaking into the field.

EMPLOYMENT AGENCIES AND SEARCH FIRMS

★4066★ Avery Crafts Associates, Ltd.

116 John St., Ste. 820
New York, NY 10038
Ph: (212)285-1074   Fax: (212)732-1039

Executive search firm.

★4067★ The Canon Group

27936 Lost Canyon Rd.
Santa Clarita, CA 91351
Ph: (805)252-7400

Employment agency and search firm.

★4068★ E.J. Ashton and Associates, Ltd.

3125 N. Wilke Rd.
Arlington Heights, IL 60004-1452
Ph: (708)577-7900

Employment agency. Executive search firm.

★4069★ Employment Advisors

526 Nicollet Mall
Minneapolis, MN 55402-0521
Ph: (612)339-0521

Employment agency. Also located in Bloomington, Minnesota. Places candidates in variety of fields.

★4070★ Godfrey Personnel Inc.

300 W. Adams, Ste. 612
Chicago, IL 60606-5194
Ph: (312)236-4455

Employment agency.

★4071★ Insurance Personnel

65 Franklin St.
Boston, MA 02110-1303
Ph: (617)357-5380   Fax: (617)482-6581

Employment agency.

★4072★ Insurance Personnel Service

120 Kearny St., Ste. 1480
San Francisco, CA 94108-4803
Ph: (415)391-5900

Employment agency.

★4073★ International Insurance Personnel, Inc.

PO Box 28408
Atlanta, GA 30358
Ph: (404)257-9685

★4074★ The Oxford Group

901 Waterfall Way
Richardson, TX 75080
Ph: (214)644-5544   Fax: (214)644-7134

Executive search firm.

★4075★ Questor Consultants, Inc.

2515 N. Broad St.
Colmar, PA 18915
Ph: (215)997-9262   Fax: (215)997-9226

Executive search firm.

OTHER SOURCES

★4076★ Alliance of American Insurers (ALLIANCE)

1501 Woodfield Rd., Ste. 400 W
Schaumburg, IL 60173-4980
Ph: (708)330-8500   Fax: (708)330-8602

Members: Property and casualty insurance companies.

★4077★ American Council of Life Insurance (ACLI)

1001 Pennsylvania Ave. NW
Washington, DC 20004-2599
Ph: (202)624-2000   Fax: (202)624-2319
Fr: 800-942-4242

Members: Legal reserve life insurance companies authorized to do business in the U.S. **Purpose:** Works to advance the interests of the life insurance industry and to provide effective government relations. **Activities:** Conducts investment and social research programs; compiles statistics. Maintains Insurance Industry's Citizen Action Network and Center for Corporate Public Involvement and Medical Research Fund.

★4078★ American Society of CLU and ChFC (ASCLU & Ch)

270 S. Bryn Mawr Ave.
Bryn Mawr, PA 19010
Ph: (610)526-2500   Fax: (610)527-4010

Members: Professional society of insurance agents and financial services professionals who hold Chartered Life Underwriter (CLU) or Chartered Financial Consultant (ChFC) designations. **Activities:** Conducts week-long graduate-level educational sessions (CLU Institutes); one-day seminars with experts lecturing on subjects such as law, taxation, estate planning, and business life insurance; symposia and clinics; research. Offers scholarship to society programs.

★4079★ APIW

PO Box 98, Church Street Sta.
New York, NY 10008
Ph: (212)361-5880   Fax: (212)361-5885

Members: Professional women and men from the insurance/reinsurance industry. **Purpose:** Promotes cooperation and understanding among members; maintains high professional standards in the insurance industry; provides a strong network of professional contacts and educational aid; recognizes the contributions of women to insurance; encourages women to seek employment in the insurance community.

★4080★ General Agents and Managers Association (GAMA)

1922 F St. NW
Washington, DC 20006
Ph: (202)331-6088   Fax: (202)785-5712
Fr: 800-345-2687

Members: Life insurance general agents and managers, assistant agency heads, home office officials, and others interested in life insurance field management. **Purpose:** Works to improve quality of management and of life insurance selling through educational programs, code of ethical practices, and research programs. Maintains hall of fame and speakers' bureau.

★4081★ **Independent Insurance Agents of America (IIAA)**

127 S. Peyton
Alexandria, VA 22314
Ph: (703)683-4422   Fax: (703)683-7556

Purpose: Sales agencies handling property, fire, casualty, and surety insurance. Organizes technical and sales courses for new and established agents. Sponsors Insurance Youth Golf Classic.

★4082★ **Insurance Information Institute (III)**

110 William St.
New York, NY 10038
Ph: (212)669-9200   Fax: (212)732-1916

Members: Property and liability insurance companies. **Purpose:** Provides information and educational services to mass media, educational institutions, trade associations, businesses, government agencies, and the public. Conducts public opinion surveys. Sponsors seminars and briefings on insurance, safety, research, public policy, and economic topics.

★4083★ **Life Office Management Association (LOMA)**

2300 Windy Ridge Pkwy., Ste. 600
Atlanta, GA 30339-8443
Ph: (404)951-1770   Fax: (404)984-0441

Members: Life and health insurance companies and financial services in the U.S. and Canada; and overseas in 45 countries; affiliate members are firms that provide professional support to member companies. **Purpose:** Provides research, information, training, and educational activities in areas of operations and systems, human resources, financial planning and employee development. Administers FLMI Insurance Education Program, which awards FLMI (Fellow, Life Management Institute) designation to those who complete the ten-examination program.

★4084★ **National Association of Health Underwriters (NAHU)**

1000 Connecticut Ave. NW, Ste. 810
Washington, DC 20037
Ph: (202)778-8767   Fax: (202)785-2274

Members: Insurance agencies and individuals engaged in the promotion, sale, and administration of disability income and health insurance. **Purpose:** Sponsors advanced health insurance underwriting and research seminars at universities. Testifies before federal and state committees on pending health insurance legislation. Sponsors leading producers roundtable awards and health insurance quality awards for leading salesmen.

Maintains a speakers' bureau and a political action committee.

★4085★ **National Association of Insurance Women - International (NAIW)**

1847 E. 15th
PO Box 4410
Tulsa, OK 74159
Ph: (918)744-5195   Fax: (918)743-1968
Fr: 800-766-6249

Members: Insurance industry professionals. **Purpose:** Promotes continuing education and networking for the professional advancement of its members. **Activities:** Offers education programs, meetings, services, and leadership opportunities.

★4086★ **National Association of Professional Insurance Agents (NAPIA)**

400 N. Washington St.
Alexandria, VA 22314
Ph: (703)836-9340   Fax: (703)836-1279

Members: Independent property and casualty agents. **Activities:** Activities are educational, representative, and service-oriented. Sponsors over 200 educational programs and seminars each year on all aspects of property and casualty insurance, ranging from the novice to specialist level. Compiles statistics; conducts research programs; develops products/services unique to independent agencies.

Interior Designers

★4087★ Accessory Merchandising

Commerce Publishing Co.
330 N. 4th St.
St. Louis, MO 63102
Ph: (314)421-5445   Fax: (314)421-1070

Magazine reporting on current trends in decorative accessories and home furnishings retailing.

★4088★ Cabinet Manufacturing & Fabricating

PTN Publications
2 University Plaza, Ste. 11
Hackensack, NJ 07601
Ph: (201)487-7800   Fax: (201)487-1061

Monthly.

★4089★ Captsule Job Listings

Publications and Communications, Inc.
12416 Hymeadow Dr.
Austin, TX 78750
Ph: (512)250-9023   Fax: (512)331-3900
Fr: 800-678-9724

Online database. Lists current job openings in the contract (temporary) technical services industry. Includes the Action Hot List, which provides information on job seekers. Includes employment opportunities in technical/professional engineering, computing, and design/drafting. Entries generally contain company name, address, and job opening.

★4090★ Custom Home

Hanley-Wood, Inc.
1 Thomas Cir., Ste. 600
Washington, DC 20005
Ph: (202)452-0800   Fax: (202)785-1974

Bimonthly. Trade publication.

★4091★ DISPLAY & DESIGN IDEAS

Shore Communications, Inc.
180 Allen Rd. NE, Bldg. N, Ste. 300
Atlanta, GA 30328
Ph: (404)252-8831   Fax: (404)252-4436

Magazine.

★4092★ Interior Design

Conners Publishing
245 W. 17th St.
New York, NY 10011
Ph: (212)463-6835   Fax: (212)463-6836

Monthly. Interior designing and furnishings magazine.

★4093★ Interior Landscape

American Nurseryman Publishing Co.
77 W. Washington St., Ste. 2100
Chicago, IL 60602-2904
Ph: (312)782-5505   Fax: (312)782-3232

Quarterly. $16.00/year for individuals; $5.00 for single issue. Provides in-depth coverage of business and technical topics of importance to interior landscape professionals.

★4094★ INTERIORS

BPI Communications
1515 Broadway, 11th Fl.
New York, NY 10036
Ph: (212)536-5167   Fax: (212)536-5351
Fr: 800-274-4100

Monthly. Magazine for interior designers and architects.

★4095★ Kitchen and Bath Design News

PTN Publications
2 University Plaza, Ste. 11
Hackensack, NJ 07601
Ph: (201)487-7800   Fax: (201)487-1061

Monthly.

★4096★ Progressive Architecture

600 Summer St.
PO Box 1361
Stamford, CT 06904
Ph: (203)348-7531

Monthly. $48.00/year; $7.50/issue. National magazine on architecture, interior designs, and planning.

★4097★ Qualified Remodeler

20 E. Jackson Blvd.
Chicago, IL 60604-2203

Free to qualified subscribers; $50.00/year for individuals. Magazine for remodeling contractor/distributors.

★4098★ Remodeling

Hanley-Wood, Inc.
1 Thomas Cir., Ste. 600
Washington, DC 20005
Ph: (202)452-0800   Fax: (202)785-1974

$24.95/year for individuals; $5.00 for single issue. Trade magazine for the professional remodeling industry.

★4099★ Tile World

Tradelink Publishing Co., Inc.
1 Kalisa Way, No. 205
Paramus, NJ 07652
Ph: (201)599-0136   Fax: (201)599-2378

Bimonthly. $38.00/year; $7.00/single issue.

★4100★ VM & SD: Visual Merchandising and Store Design

ST Publications
407 Gilbert Ave.
Cincinnati, OH 45202
Ph: (513)421-2050   Fax: (513)421-5144
Fr: 800-925-1110

Monthly. $36.00/year.

★4101★ Window Fashions

G & W McNamara Publishing, Inc.
4225 White Bear Pkwy., No. 400
St. Paul, MN 55110
Ph: (612)293-1544   Fax: (612)653-4308

Monthly. $32.00/year for individuals. Design and merchandizing magazine for specialty retailers, dealers and designers in the business of custom window treatments. Provides design, fashion, and color trend info as well as installation techniques and practical business information.

PLACEMENT AND JOB REFERRAL SERVICES

★4102★ American Society of Interior Designers (ASID)

608 Massachusetts Ave. NE
Washington, DC 20002
Ph: (202)546-3480   Fax: (202)546-3480

Members: Practicing professional interior designers and affiliate members in allied design fields. **Purpose:** ASID Educational Foundation sponsors scholarship competitions, finances educational research, and awards special grants. **Activities:** Maintains placement service.

★4103★ Council of Educational Facility Planners, International (CEFPI)

8687 E. Via de Ventura, Ste. 311
Scottsdale, AZ 85258-3347
Ph: (602)948-2337   Fax: (602)948-4420

Members: Individuals and firms who are responsible for planning, designing, creating, maintaining, and equipping the physical environment of education. **Purpose:** Sponsors an exchange of information, professional experiences, research results, and other investigative techniques concerning educational facility planning. **Activities:** Activities include publication and review of current and emerging practices in educational facility planning; identification and execution of needed research; development of professional training programs; strengthening of planning services on various levels of government and in institutions of higher learning; leadership in the development of higher standards for facility design and the physical environment of education. Operates speakers' bureau; sponsors placement service; compiles statistics.

★4104★ Institute of Store Planners (ISP)

25 N. Broadway
Tarrytown, NY 10591
Ph: (914)332-1806   Fax: (914)332-1541

Members: Persons active in store planning and design; visual merchandisers, students, and educators; contractors and suppliers to the industry. **Purpose:** Dedicated to the professional growth of members while providing service to the public through improvement of the retail environment. Provides forum for debate and discussion by store design experts, retailers, and public figures. **Activities:** Makes available speakers for store planning and design courses at the college level; develops programs for store planning courses. Sponsors student design competitions and annual international store design competition with awards in 7 categories. Maintains placement service.

★4105★ Interior Design Educators Council (IDEC)

14252 Culver Dr., Ste. A-311
Irvine, CA 92714
Ph: (714)551-1622

Members: Interior design educators at universities or schools that have at least a 2-year professional program; other interested individuals. **Purpose:** Seeks to develop and improve interior design education and the professional level of interior design practice. **Activities:** Offers placement services. Maintains Interior Design Education Foundation.

EMPLOYER DIRECTORIES AND NETWORKING LISTS

★4106★ Art Marketing Sourcebook
ArtNetwork
18757 Wildflower Dr.
Penn Valley, CA 95946-9717
Ph: (916)432-7630   Fax: (916)432-1633

Biennial, spring 1995. $22.95, plus 4.00 shipping; payment must accompany order; libraries, schools may send purchase orders. Covers over 2,000 representatives, consultants, galleries, critics, architects, interior designers, corporations, museum curators. Entries include: Company name, address, phone, description of services, style represented, mediums, years in business, types of companies dealt with, geographical limitations, number of clients, requirements for viewing slides. Arrangement: Classified by type of organization.

★4107★ Association of University Interior Designers—Membership List
Association of University Interior Designers
c/o Denise Beard
Ohio State University
The Office of the University Architect and Physical Planning
2009 Millikin Rd.
Columbus, OH 43210
Ph: (614)292-4458

Twice yearly, June and October. Available to members only. Covers nearly 100 in-house interior designers, landscape designers, architects, and purchasing agents associated with universities. Entries include: Name, title, affiliation, address, phone. Arrangement: Alphabetical.

★4108★ Design Firm Directory
Wefler & Associates, Inc.
PO Box 1167
Evanston, IL 60204
Ph: (708)475-1866

Annual, volume 1, April; volume 2, October. $57.00, volume 1; $47.00, volume 2; postpaid, payment with order. Covers more than 2,200 commercial and private design and consulting firms, including industrial, graphic, interior, landscape and environmental design; in two volumes: Design Firm Directory Graphic and Industrial Design Edition (volume 1), and Design Firm Directory Environmental and Interior Design Edition (volume 2). Entries include: Firm name, address, phone; year established; number of employees; locations of branches (if any); names and titles of key personnel; areas of specialization; clients. Arrangement: Geographical. Indexes: Alphabetical.

★4109★ Interior Decorators Directory
American Business Directories, Inc.
American Business Information, Inc.
5711 S. 86th Cir.
Omaha, NE 68127
Ph: (402)593-4600   Fax: (402)331-1505

Annual. $1,000.00 U.S. edition; $685.00 Eastern region; $515.00 Western region; $170.00 (Canad. ed.); payment with order.

Entries include: Name, address, phone (including area code), size of advertisement, year first in Yellow Pages, name of owner or manager, number of employees. Compiled from telephone company Yellow Pages, nationwide. Arrangement: Geographical.

★4110★ Saskatchewan Design Directory
Design Council of Saskatchewan, Inc.
642 Broadway Ave., Ste. 200
Saskatoon, SK, Canada S7N 1A9
Ph: (306)242-0733   Fax: (306)664-2598

Biennial, spring of odd years. $5.00. Covers members of the Saskatchewan Association of Architects, the Association of Professional Community Planners of Saskatchewan, the Saskatchewan Graphic Arts Association, the Interior Designers of Saskatchewan, Association of Consulting Engineers of Saskatchewan, Saskatchewan Society of Illustrators and Designers, and the Saskatchewan Association of Landscape Architects, which are members of the council; about 380 persons and firms listed. Entries include: Name, address, phone, fax, professional association with which affiliated. Arrangement: Classified by professional group.

★4111★ Who's Who in Interior Design
Baron's Who's Who
412 N. Coast Hwy., Ste. B-110
Laguna Beach, CA 92651
Ph: (714)497-8615   Fax: (714)786-8918

Biennial, January of even years. $175.00. Covers over 3,500 interior designers worldwide. Entries include: Name, address, phone, fax, biographical data. Arrangement: Alphabetical. Indexes: Geographical.

HANDBOOKS AND MANUALS

★4112★ Career Information Center
Macmillan Publishing Co.
200 Old Tappan Rd.
Old Tappan, NJ 07675
Ph: (609)461-6500   Fr: 800-223-2336

Visual Education Center Staff. Fifth edition, 1992. $229.00. This 13-volume set profiles over 600 occupations. Each occupational profile describes job duties, educational requirements, how to get the job, advancement possibilities, employment outlook, working conditions, earnings and benefits, and where to write for more information.

★4113★ Careers for Culture Lovers and Other Artsy Types
VGM Career Horizons
4255 W. Touhy Ave.
Lincolnwood, IL 60646-1975
Ph: (847)679-5500   Fax: (847)679-2494
Fr: 800-323-4900

Marjorie Eberts and Margaret Gisler. 1994. $14.95; $9.95 (paper). Describes how to get work in a variety of fields related to art and culture. Opportunities include picture framer, curator, art restorer, symphony manager, disk jockey, music reviewer, dance teacher, choreographer, costume designer, theater manager, light designer, drama teacher, bookstore owner, interior decorator, antique store owner, and others.

★4114★ Interior Design Career Guide

American Society of Interior Designers (ASID)
608 Massachusetts Ave. NE
Washington, DC 20002
Ph: (202)546-3480

Annual. Free (first copy). Booklet of basic information on the profession, including overview, educational requirements, employment prospects, and compensation. Lists three-, four-, and five-year design programs, with ASID student chapters and Foundation for Interior Design Education Research accreditation.

★4115★ The New Decorator's Handbook

HarperCollins Publishers, Inc.
10 E. 53rd St.
New York, NY 10022-5299
Ph: (212)207-7000   Fax: (212)207-7145
Fr: 800-331-3761

Jocasta Innes. 1996. $23.00.

★4116★ Opportunities in Interior Design and Decorating Careers

VGM Career Horizons
4255 W. Touhy Ave.
Lincolnwood, IL 60646-1975
Ph: (847)679-5500   Fax: (847)679-2494
Fr: 800-323-4900

Victoria Ball and David Stearns. 1995. $14.95; $11.95 (paper). 160 pages. Covers opportunities and job search techniques in interior design. Addresses working for a design house, contract work, and starting a business. Illustrated.

★4117★ Start Your Own Interior Design Business and Keep It Growing!

Touch of Design
475 College Blvd., Ste. 6290
Oceanside, CA 92057
Ph: (619)945-7909

Linda M. Ramsay. 1994. $39.99 (paper).

EMPLOYMENT AGENCIES AND SEARCH FIRMS

★4118★ Claremont-Branan, Inc.

2150 Parklake Dr., Ste. 212
Atlanta, GA 30345
Ph: (404)491-1292

Employment agency. Executive search firm.

★4119★ Connelly Search

PO Box 30926
Tucson, AZ 85751-0926
Ph: (602)327-7999

Executive search firm.

★4120★ Consultants and Designers Inc.

7240 Parkway Dr., Ste. 250
Hanover, MD 21076-1367
Ph: (410)712-0052

Places staff in temporary positions. West Coast office located in Santa Clara, CA.

★4121★ Randolph Associates, Inc.

950 Massachusetts Ave., Ste. 105
Cambridge, MA 02139-3174
Ph: (617)441-8777   Fax: (617)441-8778

Employment agency. Provides regular or temporary placement of staff.

★4122★ RitaSue Siegel Associates, Inc.

20 E. 46th St.
New York, NY 10017-2417
Ph: (212)682-2100

Executive search firm.

OTHER SOURCES

★4123★ Directory of Interior Design Programs Accredited by FIDER

Foundation for Interior Design Education Research (FIDER)
60 Monroe Center NW, Ste. 300
Grand Rapids, MI 49503-2920
Ph: (616)458-0400   Fax: (616)458-0460

Semiannual, April and August. Free. Covers 108 interior design programs in the United States and Canada in conformance with the accreditation standards of the foundation. Entries include: Type of program, name of institution, address, name of department chair or program head, phone, dates of last and next accreditation review, degrees offered. Arrangement: Geographical, degree level offered, then alphabetical by institution name.

★4124★ A Guide to FIDER Accredited Interior Design Programs in North America

Foundation for Interior Design Education Research (FIDER)
60 Monroe Center NW
Grand Rapids, MI 49503
Ph: (616)458-0400   Fax: (616)458-0460

Annual, October. $17.50. Covers 108 interior design programs in the United States and Canada accredited by FIDER. Entries include: Program title, sponsoring institution name, address, phone, names of faculty, fees, application dates, number of students, program description. Arrangement: Geographical.

★4125★ Home Economics Careers

Cambridge Career Products
PO Box 2153
Dept. CC15
Charleston, WV 25328-2153
Ph: (304)744-9323   Fax: (304)744-9351
Fr: 800-468-4227

Video. $79.95. 30 minutes. Presents a series of interviews with men and women working in different areas of home economics, including dietetics, foods and nutrition, child development, interior design, and fashion. Covers educational, personal, and professional requirements for each occupation.

★4126★ Interior Design Society (IDS)

PO Box 2396
High Point, NC 27261
Ph: 800-888-9590   Fax: (910)883-1195

Members: Retail designers, independent designers, design-oriented firms, and design service firms. Grants accreditation and recognition to qualified residential interior designers and retail home furnishing stores. **Activities:** Conducts educational courses in management, design, sales training, and marketing. Maintains extensive industry information center. Sponsors competitions.

★4127★ International Interior Design Association (IIDA)

341 Merchandise Mart
Chicago, IL 60654
Ph: (312)467-1950   Fax: (312)467-0779

Purpose: Professional interior designers, including designers of commerical, healthcare, hospitality, government, retail, residential facilities; educators; researchers; representatives of allied manufacturing sources. **Activities:** Conducts research, student programs, and continuing education programs for members. Has developed a code of ethics for the profesional design membership.

Jewelers

SOURCES OF HELP-WANTED ADS

★4128★ American Jewelry Manufacturer
Chilton Publications
825 7th Ave.
New York, NY 10019
Ph: (212)887-8400   Fax: (212)887-8484
Monthly. Trade magazine. Official publication of Manufacturing Jewelers and Silversmiths of America.

★4129★ Fashion Accessories
S.C.M. Publications, Inc.
65 W. Main St.
Bergenfield, NJ 07621
Ph: (201)384-3336   Fax: (201)384-6776
Monthly. $22.00/year.

★4130★ Modern Jeweler
Vance Publishing Corp.
10901 W. 84th Terr.
Lenexa, KS 66214
Ph: (913)438-8700   Fax: (913)438-0692
Fr: 800-255-5113
Monthly. $25.00/year for individuals; $4.00 for single issue; $100.00/year for other countries. Trade magazine for retail jewelers.

★4131★ National Jeweler
Miller Freeman, Inc.
1515 Broadway
New York, NY 10036
Ph: (212)626-2380   Fax: (212)944-7164
Fr: 800-950-1314
Semimonthly. Jewelry industry magazine.

PLACEMENT AND JOB REFERRAL SERVICES

★4132★ Gemological Institute of America (GIA)
1660 Stewart St.
Santa Monica, CA 90404
Ph: (310)829-2991   Fax: (310)453-7674
Fr: 800-421-7250
Purpose: Alumni are sustaining members. Conducts home study programs, resident courses, and traveling seminars in identification and quality analysis of diamonds and other gemstones and pearls, and in jewelry making and repair, jewelry designing, and jewelry sales. Through subsidiaries, manufactures and sells gem testing and diamond grading equipment and audiovisual gemstone presentations. **Activities:** Offers job placement service; organizes gemological study tours. Awards diplomas as Gemologist, Graduate Gemologist, Graduate Jeweler, and Graduate Jeweler Gemologist; also awards Diamonds Certificate, Colored Stones Certificate, Jewelry Display Certificate, Fine Jewelry Sales Certificate, Jewelry Design Certificate, and Pearls Certificate.

★4133★ Institute of Metal Repair (IMR)
1558 S. Redwood St.
Escondido, CA 92025
Ph: (619)432-8942
Members: Jewelers, platers, silversmiths, and individuals interested in metal restoration and repair. **Purpose:** Works to upgrade the metal repair trade; maintains high standards and quality workmanship in the field. Sponsors competitions; conducts training seminars and lectures. **Activities:** Compiles statistics; maintains biographical archives; offers placement service; conducts research and disseminates information. Maintains 150 volume library, including metalworking and restoration books, and a magazine article file.

★4134★ Jewelry Manufacturers Guild (JMG)
PO Box 46099
Los Angeles, CA 90046
Ph: (909)769-1820   Fax: (909)769-1920
Members: Jewelry manufacturers and associated product suppliers. **Purpose:** Seeks to improve conditions in the fine jewelry industry; promotes high standard of ethics in the business; provides a medium for communication within the field. **Activities:** Represents the industry at trade shows; lobbies for fine jewelry industry's concerns at all levels of government. Maintains sales reps and credit information network placement service.

★4135★ National Association of Jewelry Appraisers (NAJA)
PO Box 6558
Annapolis, MD 21401-0558
Ph: (301)261-8270
Members: Gem and jewelry appraisers, jewelers, importers, brokers, manufacturers, gemological students, and others professionally interested in jewelry appraisal. **Purpose:** Seeks to recognize and make available to the public the services of highly qualified, experienced, independent, and reliable jewelry appraisers. Conducts seminars on jewelry appraisal techniques, methods, and pricing for members and the public. Supports legislation to establish minimum standards of competency and licensing of jewelry appraisers; maintains code of professional ethics. **Activities:** Operates appraiser referral program; sponsors ongoing public relations campaign. Offers equipment discounts, new appraisal forms, travel discounts, insurance, and professional aids for members only. Compiles statistics.

★4136★ Women's Jewelry Association (WJA)
333 Rte. 46 West
Fairfield, NJ 07004
Ph: (201)575-7190   Fax: (201)575-1445
Members: Women involved in jewelry design, manufacture, retail, and advertising; men may join as associate members. **Purpose:** Aims to: enhance the status of women in the jewelry industry; make known the contribution of women to the industry; provide a network for women involved with fine

jewelry. **Activities:** Maintains hall of fame and offers placement services.

EMPLOYER DIRECTORIES AND NETWORKING LISTS

★4137★ Diamond Retailers Directory

American Business Directories, Inc.
American Business Information, Inc.
5711 S. 86th Cir.
Omaha, NE 68127
Ph: (402)593-4600   Fax: (402)331-1505

Updated continuously; printed on request. Please inquire. Entries include: Name, address, phone (including area code), size of advertisement, year first in Yellow Pages, name of owner or manager, number of employees. Compiled from telephone company Yellow Pages, nationwide. Arrangement: Geographical.

★4138★ Jewelers Board of Trade— Confidential Reference Book

Jewelers Board of Trade
70 Catamore Blvd.
East Providence, RI 02914
Ph: (401)438-0750

Semiannual, March and September. Available to members only. Covers about 45,000 jewelry manufacturers, importers, distributors, and retailers. Entries include: Company name, address, phone, whether a wholesaler, retailer, or manufacturer, credit rating. Arrangement: Geographical.

★4139★ Jewelers' Circular/Keystone— Almanac Issue

Chilton Co.
Chilton Way
Radnor, PA 19089
Ph: (215)964-4487   Fax: (215)964-4481

Annual, July. $10.00. Publication includes: List of jewelery associations. Entries include: Association name, address, phone. Principal content of publication is jewelry industry statistics as well as a complete listing of industry associations.

★4140★ Jewelers' Circular/Keystone— Jewelers' Directory Issue

Chilton Co.
Chilton Way
Radnor, PA 19089
Ph: (610)964-4470   Fax: (610)964-4481

Annual, December. $31.95, included in subscription. Publication includes: About 10,000 manufacturers, importers, and wholesale jewelers providing merchandise and supplies to the jewelry retailing industry; and related trade organizations. Entries include: For all companies Company name, address, phone, toll-free phone, fax, distribution methods. Arrangement: Classified by product/service, then alphabetical. Indexes: Alphabetical.

★4141★ Jewelers Retail Directory

American Business Directories, Inc.
American Business Information, Inc.
5711 S. 86th Cir.
Omaha, NE 68127
Ph: (402)593-4600   Fax: (402)331-1505

Annual. $1,495.00, U.S. edition; $265.00, (Canad. ed.); payment with order. Number of listings: 44,879 (U.S. edition); 5,238 (Canadian edition). Entries include: Name, address, phone (including area code), size of advertisement, year first in Yellow Pages, name of owner or manager, number of employees. Regional editions available: Eastern, $945.00; Western, $685.00. Compiled from telephone company Yellow Pages, nationwide. Arrangement: Geographical.

★4142★ Jewelers Wholesale Directory

American Business Directories, Inc.
American Business Information, Inc.
5711 S. 86th Cir.
Omaha, NE 68127
Ph: (402)593-4600   Fax: (402)331-1505

Annual. $520.00, U.S. edition. Number of listings: 7,292 (U.S. edition); 695 (Canadian edition). Entries include: Name, address, phone (including area code), size of advertisement, year first in Yellow Pages, name of owner or manager, number of employees. Compiled from telephone company Yellow Pages, nationwide. Arrangement: Geographical.

★4143★ Jewelry Industry Distributors Association—Directory of Members

Jewelry Industry Distributors Association
720 Light St.
Baltimore, MD 21230
Ph: (301)752-3318

Annual, April. $100.00. Covers 130 member firms and their suppliers. Entries include: Firm name, address, phone, name and title of chief executive, products or services. Arrangement: Distributors and suppliers are listed separately in alphabetical order. Indexes: Geographical, firm name.

HANDBOOKS AND MANUALS

★4144★ How to Be Successful in the Bead Jewelry Business

Nomad Press International
PO Box 1803
Bisbee, AZ 85603
Ph: (602)432-7117

Kate Drew-Wilkinson. 1994. $24.00 (paper).

★4145★ JCK's Jewelers' Management Series

Jewelers' Book Club
Chilton Way
Radnor, PA 19089
Ph: (610)964-4480

1993. $224.75.

★4146★ Opportunities in Metalworking Careers

VGM Career Horizons
4255 W. Touhy Ave.
Lincolnwood, IL 60646-1975
Ph: (847)679-5500   Fax: (847)679-2494
Fr: 800-323-4900

Mark Rowh. 1991. $14.95; $11.95 (paper). Includes jewelry-making among the metalworking occupations. Offers advice for breaking into the field.

★4147★ Opportunities in Vocational and Technical Careers

VGM Career Horizons
4255 W. Touhy Ave.
Lincolnwood, IL 60646-1975
Ph: (847)679-5500   Fax: (847)679-2494
Fr: 800-323-4900

Adrian A. Paradis. 1992. $14.95; $11.95 (paper). 160 pages. Provides information on a variety of opportunities and advice on breaking into the field.

★4148★ Retail Jewelers

Chronicle Guidance Publications, Inc.
66 Aurora St.
PO Box 1190
Moravia, NY 13118-1190
Ph: (315)497-0330   Fax: (315)497-3359
Fr: 800-622-7284

Chronicle Guidance Staff. 1991. $2.00. Provides concise career information and sources of additional information.

EMPLOYMENT AGENCIES AND SEARCH FIRMS

★4149★ Saxon Morse Associates

Burning Bush Ct.
Pomona, NY 10970
Ph: (914)362-1300

Executive search firm.

OTHER SOURCES

★4150★ American Watchmakers Institute (AWI)

701 Enterprise Dr.
Harrison, OH 45030
Ph: (513)367-9800   Fax: (513)367-1414

Members: Jewelers, watchmakers, clockmakers, watch and clock engineers, scientists, repairmen, and others in the watch, clock, and jewelry industry. **Purpose:** Examines and certifies master watchmakers and clockmakers. Maintains a museum displaying horological items, and the National Watch Mark Identification Bureau. Conducts home study course in clock repairing and bench courses for watchmakers in most major U.S. cities. Disseminates career information to vocational counselors in the form of brochures and filmstrips.

★4151★ Jewelers of America (JA)
1185 6th Ave., 30th Fl.
New York, NY 10036
Ph: (212)768-8777   Fax: (212)768-8087
Fr: 800-223-0673

Members: Retailers of jewelry, watches, silver, and allied merchandise. **Activities:** Conducts surveys and compiles statistics. Conducts educatinal programs. Provides information to consumers.

★4152★ Jewelry Manufacturers Directory

American Business Directories, Inc.
American Business Information, Inc.
5711 S. 86th Cir.
Omaha, NE 68127
Ph: (402)593-4600   Fax: (402)331-1505

Annual. $455.00, U.S. edition. Entries include: Name, address, phone (including area code), size of advertisement, year first in Yellow Pages, name of owner or manager, number of employees. Compiled from telephone company Yellow Pages, nationwide. Arrangement: Geographical.

★4153★ Manufacturing Jewelers and Silversmiths of America (MJSA)
1 State St., 6th Fl.
Providence, RI 02908-5035
Ph: (401)274-3840   Fax: (401)274-0265
Fr: 800-444-MJSA

Members: Manufacturers of jewelry, silverware, and allied items; suppliers to the industry; jewelry salesmen. **Purpose:** Conducts wage and company policy survey annually and the Export Development Assistance Program. Sponsors educational programs and competitions. Compiles statistics.

★4154★ National Association of Jewelry Appraisers—Membership Directory

National Association of Jewelry Appraisers (NAJA)
PO Box 6558
Annapolis, MD 21401-0558
Ph: (301)261-8270   Fax: (301)261-8270

Annual, January. Available to members only. Covers nearly 600 members. Entries include: Name, address, phone, business affiliation, area of specialization. Arrangement: Alphabetical, with seperate georgraphical listing. Indexes: Specialty.

★4155★ National Jeweler—Industry Yellow Pages

Miller Freeman Inc.
1515 Broadway
New York, NY 10036
Ph: (212)626-2380   Fax: (212)944-7164
Fr: 800-950-1314

Annual, December. $10.00. Covers Approximately 5,000 companies providing products and services in the jewelry and watch industries. Entries include: Company name, address, phone, fax, branch office or subsidiary names and addresses, description of product/service provided. Arrangement: Alphabetical by company name. Indexes: Product/service.

Kindergarten and Elementary School Teachers

★4169★ Opening List of Professional Openings in American Overseas & International Schools

Education Information Services
Instant Alert
PO Box 662
Newton, MA 02162-0002
Ph: (617)237-0887

Every 6 weeks. $9.00. Covers about 150 current professional openings for teachers, administrators, counselors, librarians, and educational specialists in American overseas schools and international schools at which the teaching language is primarily English. Also covers English as a Second/Foreign Language (ESL-EFL) at all age levels. Entries include: Institute name, address, names and titles of key personnel, positions available.

★4170★ Opening List in U.S. Colleges, Public & Private Schools

Education Information Services
PO Box 662
Newton, MA 02162-0002
Ph: (617)237-0887

Every 6 weeks. $9.00. Covers about 150 current professional openings in U.S. public schools, and private schools. Entries include: Institute name, address, names and titles of key personnel, available openings.

★4171★ Strategies

American Alliance for Health, Physical Education, Recreation, and Dance
1900 Association Dr.
Reston, VA 22091
Ph: (703)476-3495   Fax: (703)476-9527

$20.00/year for members; $40.00/year for individuals; $50.00/year for libraries. Journal providing practical, hands-on information to physical educators and coaches.

★4172★ Teacher Magazine

Editorial Projects in Education, Inc.
4301 Connecticut Ave. NW
Washington, DC 20008
Ph: (202)686-0800   Fax: (202)686-0797

Professional magazine for elementary and secondary teachers.

★4173★ Teaching Children Mathematics

National Council of Teachers of
  Mathematics
1906 Association Dr.
Reston, VA 22091-1593
Ph: (703)620-9840   Fax: (703)476-2970
Fr: 800-235-7566

$45.00/year for individuals; $50.00/year for institutions. Journal covering mathematics content and methods for pre-service and in-service teachers of grades pre-kindergarten through 6th.

★4174★ Teaching Exceptional Children

The Council for Exceptional Children
1920 Association Dr.
Reston, VA 22091-1589
Ph: (703)620-3660   Fax: (703)264-9494
Fr: 800-CEC-READ

Quarterly. $35.00/year for individuals. Journal exploring practical methods for teaching talented and gifted children who have disabilities.

★4175★ Teaching K-8

Early Years, Inc.
40 Richards Ave.
Norwalk, CT 06854-2509
Ph: (203)855-2650   Fax: (203)855-2656

$19.77/year for individuals. Magazine for elementary teachers.

PLACEMENT AND JOB REFERRAL SERVICES

★4176★ American Alliance for Health, Physical Education, Recreation and Dance (AAHPERD)

1900 Association Dr.
Reston, VA 22091
Ph: (703)476-3400   Fax: (703)476-9527

Members: Students and educators in physical education, dance, health, athletics, safety education, recreation, and outdoor education. **Purpose:** To improve its fields of education at all levels through such services as consultation, periodicals and special publications, leadership development, determination of standards, and research. **Activities:** Sponsors placement service. Operates Information and Resource Utilization Center devoted to physical education and recreation for the handicapped and programs for senior citizens.

★4177★ American Association of Christian Schools (AACS)

PO Box 2189
Independence, MO 64055
Ph: (816)795-7709   Fax: (816)795-7462

Activities: Maintains teacher/administrator certification program and placement service. Participates in school accreditation program. Sponsors National Academic Tournament and high school sports tournaments. Maintains American Christian Honor Society. Compiles statistics; maintains speakers' bureau and placement service.

★4178★ American Association of Teachers of French (AATF)

57 E. Armory Ave.
Champaign, IL 61820
Ph: (217)333-2842   Fax: (217)333-5850

Members: Teachers of French in public and private elementary and secondary schools, colleges, and universities. **Activities:** Maintains Pedagogical Aids Bureau, offering French maps, postcards, and medals, at cost; conducts annual French contest in elementary and secondary schools and awards prizes to the winners; maintains a placement bureau and a high school honor society. Furnishes traveling exhibits and provides a pen pal agency for exchange of letters between French and American boys and girls.

★4179★ American Association of Teachers of Spanish and Portuguese (AATSP)

University of Northern Colorado
106 Gunter Hall
Greeley, CO 80639
Ph: (303)351-1090   Fax: (303)351-1095

Members: Teachers of Spanish and Portuguese languages and literatures and others interested in Hispanic culture. **Activities:** Operates placement bureau and maintains pen pal registry. Sponsors honor society, Sociedad Honoraria Hispanica and National Spanish Examinations for secondary school students.

★4180★ American Montessori Society (AMS)

150 5th Ave., Ste. 203
New York, NY 10011-4384
Ph: (212)924-3209   Fax: (212)727-2254

Members: School affiliates and teacher training affiliates; heads of schools, teachers, parents, non-Montessori educators, and other interested individuals dedicated to stimulating the use of the Montessori teaching approach and promoting better education for all children. **Purpose:** Formed to meet demands of growing interest in the Montessori approach to early learning. Developed in Italy in 1907 by Dr. Maria Montessori, the system is based on the young child's instinctive love and need for purposeful work realized in an environment prepared with auto-educative, multi-sensory, manipulative learning devices for language, math, science, and practical life. **Activities:** Offers placement service. Assists in establishing schools; supplies information and limited services to member schools in other countries. Maintains school consultation and accreditation service.

★4181★ Association for Direct Instruction (ADI)

PO Box 10252
Eugene, OR 97440
Ph: (503)485-1293   Fax: (503)683-7543

Members: Public school regular and special education teachers and university instructors. **Purpose:** Encourages, promotes, and engages in research aimed at improving educational methods. Promotes dissemination of developmental information and skills that facilitate the education of adults and children. **Activities:** Maintains placement service. Administers a preschool for developmentally delayed children. Offers educational training workshops for instructors.

★4182★ Christian Schools International (CSI)

3350 E. Paris Ave. SE
Grand Rapids, MI 49512-3054
Ph: (616)957-1070   Fax: (616)957-5022

Members: Christian elementary and secondary schools enrolling 93,000 pupils and employing 6650 teachers. **Purpose:** To provide a medium for a united witness regarding the role of Christian schools in contemporary society; to promote the establishment of Christian schools; to help members function more effectively in areas of promotion, organization, administration, and curriculum; to help establish standards and criteria to guide the operation of its members; to foster high professional ideals and economic well-being among Christian school personnel; to establish and maintain communication with member schools, colleges, churches, government agencies, and the public. Encourages study, research, and writing that embodies Christian theories of education; conducts salary studies, research, and surveys on operating costs; offers expert and confidential analysis of member school programs and operation. **Activities:** Offers placement service. Administers the Christian School Pension and Trust Funds, Group Insurance Plans, and Life and Insurance Plans and Trust Funds.

★4183★ **Convention of American Instructors of the Deaf (CAID)**

PO Box 377
Bedford, TX 76095-0377
Ph: (817)354-8414

Members: Professional organization of teachers, administrators, and professionals in allied fields related to education of the deaf and hard-of-hearing. **Purpose:** Objectives are: to provide opportunities for a free interchange of views concerning methods and means of educating the deaf and hard-of-hearing; to promote such education by the publication of reports, essays, and other information; to develop more effective methods of teaching deaf and hard-of-hearing children. **Activities:** Maintains speakers' bureau; offers placement services.

★4184★ **Independent Educational Services (IES)**

353 Nassau St.
Princeton, NJ 08540
Ph: (609)921-6195   Fax: (609)921-0155
Fr: 800-257-5102

Purpose: Nonprofit consulting, head search, and teacher recruitment organization. Furnishes to independent (private) schools dossiers of qualified candidates for teaching and administrative positions. Offers to teachers and prospective teachers information concerning current requirements and qualifications for positions in the field of education and vacancies for which they qualify. Conducts searches for heads of schools. **Activities:** Offers specialized placement workshops, consulting, and in-service programs to independent schools.

★4185★ **International Educator's Institute (TIE)**

PO Box 513
Cummaquid, MA 02637
Ph: (508)362-1414

Purpose: Facilitates the placement of teachers and administrators in American, British, and international schools. Seeks to create a network that provides for professional development opportunities and improved financial security of members. Offers advice and information on international school news, recent educational developments, job placement, and investment, consumer, and professional development opportunities. Makes available insurance and travel benefits. Operates International Schools Internship Program. Sponsors competitions. Bestows awards.

★4186★ **Jewish Education Service of North America (JESNA)**

730 Broadway, 2nd Fl.
New York, NY 10003-9540
Ph: (212)529-2000

Members: National education organizations, bureaus of Jewish education, and individuals. **Purpose:** Service agency to coordinate, promote, and conduct research in North American Jewish education. Operates Mandell L. Berman Jewish Heritage Center for Research and Evaluation. Supports the Convenant Foundation, a joint venture with the Crown Family, which makes awards and grants for creativity in Jewish education. **Activities:** Maintains teachers placement service for Jewish schools.

★4187★ **Jewish Educators Assembly (JEA)**

106-06 Queens Blvd.
Flushing, NY 11375-4248
Ph: (718)268-9452   Fax: (718)520-4369

Members: Educational and supervisory personnel serving Jewish educational institutions. **Purpose:** Seeks to: advance the development of Jewish education in the congregation on all levels in consonance with the philosophy of the Conservative Movement; cooperate with the United Synagogue of America Commission on Jewish Education as the policy-making body of the educational enterprise; join in cooperative effort with other Jewish educational institutions and organizations; establish and maintain professional standards for Jewish educators; serve as a forum for the exchange of ideas; promote the values of Jewish education as a basis for the creative continuity of the Jewish people. **Activities:** Maintains placement service.

★4188★ **NAFSA/Association of International Educators (NAFSA)**

1875 Connecticut Ave. NW, Ste. 1000
Washington, DC 20009
Ph: (202)462-4811   Fax: (202)667-3419

Members: Individuals, organizations, and institutions dealing with international educational exchange, including foreign student advisers, overseas educational advisers, credentials and admissions officers, administrators and teachers of English as a second language, community support personnel, study-abroad administrators, and embassy cultural or educational personnel. **Purpose:** Promotes self-regulation standards and responsibilities in international educational exchange; offers professional development opportunities primarily through publications, workshops, grants, and regional and national conferences. Advocates for increased awareness and support of international education and exchange on campuses, in government, and in communities. **Activities:** Offers services including: a job registry for employers and professionals involved with international education; a consultant referral service. Sponsors joint liaison activities with a variety of other educational and government organizations to conduct a census of foreign student enrollment in the U.S.; conducts workshops about specific subjects and countries.

★4189★ **National Art Education Association (NAEA)**

1916 Association Dr.
Reston, VA 22091-1590
Ph: (703)860-8000   Fax: (703)860-2960

Members: Teachers of art at elementary, secondary, and college levels; colleges, libraries, museums, and other educational institutions. **Purpose:** Studies problems of teaching art; encourages research and experimentation. **Activities:** Maintains placement services. Serves as clearinghouse for information on art education programs, materials, and methods of instruction. Sponsors special institutes. Cooperates with other national organizations for the furtherance of creative art experiences for youth.

★4190★ **National Association of Episcopal Schools (NAES)**

815 2nd Ave.
New York, NY 10017-4594
Ph: (212)922-5173   Fax: (212)286-9366
Fr: 800-334-7626

Members: Episcopal church-related boarding and day schools. **Purpose:** Promotes the educational ministry of the Episcopal Church; helps strengthen programs, teaching, and pastoral roles of Episcopal schools; develops criteria and curriculum materials. Provides worship materials and resources geared specifically to the needs of Episcopal schools. Works to aid communication between the National Episcopal Church and its schools and among member schools. **Activities:** Celebrates Episcopal School Week annually. Maintains charitable program, world partnership programs, and placement service.

★4191★ **National Association for Sport and Physical Education (NASPE)**

1900 Association Dr.
Reston, VA 22091
Ph: (703)476-3410   Fax: (703)476-8316

Members: Men and women professionally involved with physical activity and sports. **Purpose:** Seeks to improve the total sport and physical activity experience in America. Conducts research and education programs in such areas as sport psychology, curriculum development, kinesiology, history, philosophy, sport sociology, and the biological and behavioral basis of human activity. Develops and distributes public information materials which explain the value of physical education programs. **Activities:** Maintains placement service, and media resource center for public information and professional preparation. Sponsors skills clinics and foreign coach exchange programs.

★4192★ **National Association of Teachers' Agencies (NATA)**

PO Box 223
Georgetown, MA 01833-0323
Ph: (508)352-8473   Fax: (508)352-8680

Purpose: Private employment agencies engaged primarily in the placement of teaching and administration personnel. Works to standardize records and promote a strong ethical sense in the placement field. Maintains speakers' bureau.

★4193★ Speech Communication Association (SCA)

5105 Backlick Rd., Bldg. E
Annandale, VA 22003
Ph: (703)750-0533   Fax: (703)914-9471

Members: Elementary, secondary, college, and university teachers, speech clinicians, media specialists, communication consultants, students, theater directors, and other interested persons; libraries and other institutions. **Purpose:** To promote study, criticism, research, teaching, and application of the artistic, humanistic, and scientific principles of communication, particularly speech communication. Sponsors the publication of scholarly volumes in speech. **Activities:** Maintains placement service.

★4194★ U.S.-China Education Foundation (USCEF)

5345 Light Circle
Norcross, GA 30071
Ph: (770)729-1779   Fax: (770)448-1859

A project of the Society for the Advancement of Global Education. **Purpose:** To promote the learning of the Chinese languages (including Mandarin, Cantonese, and minority languages such as Mongolian) by Americans, and the learning of English by Chinese. **Activities:** Operates teacher placement service. Conducts short-term travel-study program to prepare Americans and Chinese for stays of four, six, or eight months or one to four years in China or the U.S., respectively. A project of S.A.G.E. the Society for the Development of Global Education.

EMPLOYER DIRECTORIES AND NETWORKING LISTS

★4195★ Boarding Schools Directory

The Association of Boarding Schools (TABS)
National Association of Independent Schools (NAIS)
1620 L St. NW
Washington, DC 20036
Ph: (202)973-9700   Fax: (202)973-9790
Fr: 800-541-5908

Annual, August. Free. Covers 276 boarding schools that are members of the National Association of Independent Schools. Entries include: School name, address, phone, contact name, grades for which boarding students are accepted, enrollment, brief description. Arrangement: Classified by type of school. Indexes: Geographical; program.

★4196★ Christian Schools International—Directory

Christian Schools International
3350 E. Paris Ave. SE
Grand Rapids, MI 49512
Ph: (616)957-1070   Fax: (616)957-5022

Annual, November. $45.00. Covers nearly 450 Reformed Christian elementary and secondary schools; related associations; societies without schools. Entries include: School name, address, phone; name, title, and ad-

dress of officers; names of faculty members. Arrangement: Geographical.

★4197★ Directory of Day Schools in the United States and Canada

Torah Umesorah National Society for Hebrew Day Schools
5723 18th Ave.
Brooklyn, NY 11204
Ph: (718)259-1223   Fax: (718)259-1795

Irregular, latest edition January 1993, new edition expected 1996. $12.00. Covers approximately 500 elementary and secondary Hebrew day schools in the U.S. and Canada. Entries include: School name, address, phone, names of administrative personnel, grades taught, language of instruction, year established (when available). Arrangement: Geographical.

★4198★ Directory of Public Elementary and Secondary Education Agencies

U.S. National Center for Education Statistics
555 New Jersey Ave. NW
Washington, DC 20208-5651
Ph: (202)219-1335   Fax: (202)219-1728
Fr: 800-424-1616

Annual. $22.00. Covers about 17,000 local education agencies in the United States, the District of Columbia, and five territories which operate their own schools or pay tuition to other local education agencies. Also lists intermediate education agencies. Entries include: Agency name, address, phone, county, description of district, grade span, membership, special education students, metropolitan status, number of high school graduates, teachers, and schools. Also available from Superintendent of Documents, U.S. Government Printing Office. Arrangement: Geographical, then by type of agency.

★4199★ Directory of Public School Systems in the U.S.

Association for School, College and University Staffing
1600 Dodge Ave., S-330
Evanston, IL 60201-3451
Ph: (708)864-1999   Fax: (708)864-8303

Annual, August. $65.00. Covers about 14,500 public school systems in the United States and their administrative personnel. Entries include: System name, address, phone, name and title of personnel administrator. Arrangement: Geographical by state.

★4200★ The Directory of Schools, Colleges, and Universities Overseas

Overseas Employment Services
PO Box 460
Mount Royal, PQ, Canada H3P 3C7
Ph: (514)739-1108   Fax: (514)739-0795

Annual. $15.00, postpaid. Covers Approximately 300 educational institutions worldwide that hire teachers to teach various subjects in English.

★4201★ Education Career Directory

Gale Research
835 Penobscot Bldg.
Detroit, MI 48226-4094
Ph: (313)961-2242   Fax: (313)961-6083
Fr: 800-877-GALE

First edition March 1994. $34.00; $17.95(paper). Covers over 220 public school districts, universities, and colleges offering entry-level positions, internships, and student teaching opportunities in the U.S.; sources of help-wanted ads, professional associations, producers of videos, databases, career guides, and professional guides and handbooks. Entries include: For schools: Name, address, phone, fax, names and titles of key personnel, number of employees, average number of entry-level positions available, human resources contact, description of internship and student teaching opportunities including contact, type and number available, application procedures, qualifications, and duties. For others: Name or title, address, phone, description. Paperback edition is available from Visible Ink Press. Arrangement: Schools are alphabetical; others are classified by type of resource. Indexes: Name and keyword.

★4202★ Educators Hiring Guide for Alaska, Hawaii, Idaho, Nevada, Montana, Oregon, Utah, Washington, and Wyoming

Career Center
Boise State University
Boise, ID 83725
Ph: (208)385-1747   Fax: (208)385-3437
Fr: 800-824-7017

Annual, February. $48.00 plus 2.00 shipping. Covers about 1,300 public school districts and 1,200 private schools in Alaska, Hawaii, Idaho, Montana, Nevada, Oregon, Utah, Washington, and Wyoming; also includes colleges and universities that provide educational employment information as a service. Entries include: For districts and private schools: name, address, phone, names and titles of contacts, job application and interview information, enrollment, number of elementary, middle, and high schools, starting salary. For universities and colleges: name, address, phone, description of services and fees. Arrangement: Geographical by city within state sections. Indexes: Geographical by county within state.

★4203★ Employment Opportunities, USA

Washington Research Associates
1660 S. Albion, Ste. 390
Denver, CO 80222
Ph: (303)756-9038   Fax: (303)770-1945

Annual, quarterly updates. $184.00, includes quarterly updates. Publication includes: List of over 1,000 employment contacts in companies and agencies in the banking, arts, telecommunications, education, and 14 other industries and professions, including the federal government. Entries include: Company name, name of representative, address, description of products or services, hiring and recruiting practices, training programs, and year established. Principal content is industry overviews, carrer news, and employment opportunity information on 14 different job markets. Arrangement: Classified by industry. Indexes: Occupation.

★4204★ The Encyclopedia of Education Information

Grey House Publishing
Pocket Knife Sq.
PO Box 1866
Lakeville, CT 06039
Ph: (203)435-0868   Fax: (203)435-0867
Fr: 800-562-2139

$125.00. Covers Publishing opportunities, state by state information on enrollment, funding and grant resources, associations and conferences, teaching jobs abroad all geared toward elementary and secondary school professionals. Also covers online databases, textbook publishers, school suppliers, plus state and federal agencies. Entries include: Contact name, address, phone, fax, description, publications.

★4205★ 50 State Educational Directories

Career Guidance Foundation
8090 Engineer Rd.
San Diego, CA 92111
Ph: (619)560-8051   Fax: (619)278-8960
Fr: 800-854-2670

Annual, latest edition June 1996. $89.00. Microfiche. Collection consists of reproductions of the state educational directories published by the departments of education of individual states. Directory contents vary, but the majority contain listings of elementary and secondary schools, colleges and universities, and state education officials. Amount of detail in each also varies. Entries include: Usually, institution name, address, and name of one executive.

★4206★ Ganley's Catholic Schools in America—Elementary/Secondary

Fisher Publishing Co.
Box 1073
Montrose, CO 81402
Ph: (303)249-1303   Fax: (303)249-0348
Fr: 800-766-5151

Annual, spring. $40.00. Covers about 8,345 Catholic schools. Entries include: Name, address, phone, administrative personnel, statistics, enrollment, grade span.

★4207★ Handbook of Private Schools

Porter Sargent Publishers, Inc.
11 Beacon St., Ste. 1400
Boston, MA 02108
Ph: (617)523-1670   Fax: (617)523-1021

Annual, June. $85.00, plus $2.41 shipping: Covers 1,700 elementary and secondary boarding and day schools in the United States. Entries include: School name, address, phone, fax, type of school (boarding or day), sex and age range, names and titles of administrators, grades offered, academic orientation, curriculum, new admissions yearly, tests required for admission, enrollment and faculty, graduate record, number of alumni, tuition and scholarship figures, summer session, plant evaluation and endowment, date of establishment, calendar, association membership, description of school's offerings and history. Arrangement: Geo-

graphical. Indexes: Alphabetical by school name.

★4208★ How to Find Jobs Teaching Overseas

KSJ Publishing Co.
7600 Washington Ave.
Sebastopol, CA 95473
Ph: (707)829-9109   Fr: 800-356-9315

Latest edition 1992. $7.95. Publication includes: List of 200 schools and agencies in 65 counties providing information on teaching opportunities abroad. Principal content of publication is step-by-step guide on how to locate teaching positions outside the United States, including the author's personal experiences in locating teaching positions in England, Spain, Saudi Arabia, and Japan. Arrangement: Alphabetical.

★4209★ Independent School Guide for Washington DC and Surrounding Area

Independent School Guides
7315 Brookville Rd.
Chevy Chase, MD 20815
Ph: (301)986-5370   Fax: (301)718-4651

Biennial, summer of odd years. $12.95 plus $2.00 shipping. Covers over 300 independent schools (including parochial schools) in the Washington, DC area, including Maryland and Virginia. Entries include: School name, address, phone, name and title of contact, number of faculty, geographical area served, tuition, courses, admission procedures, summer programs, LD/ED programs, scholarships available. Arrangement: Alphabetical. Indexes: Geographical.

★4210★ Independent Schools Association of the Southwest—Membership List

Independent Schools Association of the Southwest
Box 52297
Tulsa, OK 74152-0297
Ph: (918)749-5927   Fax: (918)749-5937
Fr: 800-880-0527

Annual, August. Free. Covers over 60 independent elementary and secondary schools accredited by the association. Entries include: School name, address, phone, chief administrative officer, structure, and enrollment. Arrangement: Geographical. Indexes: Alphabetical.

★4211★ Jobs Clearing House

Association for Experiential Education
2885 Aurora Ave., Ste. 28
Boulder, CO 80303-2252
Ph: (303)440-8844   Fax: (303)440-9581

Monthly. $5.00 per issue; $40.00 per year. Covers organizations and firms offering jobs, apprenticeships, internships, and other positions in experiential education in schools and colleges, wilderness leadership, therapeutic adventure programming, environmental education, and experiential/outdoor education; coverage includes Canada. Entries include: Position title, organization name, address, name of contact, description of duties, requirements, pay, and benefits. Arrangement: Geographical by state.

★4212★ MDR's School Directories

Market Data Retrieval (MDR)
Dun & Bradstreet Corp.
16 Progress Dr.
Shelton, CT 06484-1117
Ph: (203)926-4800   Fax: (203)929-5253
Fr: 800-333-8802

Annual, October. $1,075.00 for 51-volume set (every state and D.C. area); $175.00 for regional sets of state volumes (per region); $36.00 for each state edition. Covers over 83,000 public, 8,300 Catholic, and 13,800 other private schools (grades K-12) in the United States; over 16,000 school district offices, and 72,000 school librarians. Includes names of over 160,000 school district administrators and staff members in county and state education administration. Entries include: Name of school or district office, address, phone, name of principal and librarian, special facilities, grade span, and enrollment figures. District entries also list superintendents; school board chairpersons; curriculum, personnel, and guidance directors; and other district-level administrators. Arrangement: Geographical. Indexes: District name, county/district name, school name, district personnel.

★4213★ National Association of Teachers' Agencies—Membership Directory

National Association of Teachers' Agencies
104 S. Central Ave., Ste. 12
Valley Stream, NY 11580
Ph: (516)568-8871   Fax: (516)872-1944

Annual, January. Free. Covers approximately 20 private employment agencies engaged primarily in the placement of teaching and administrative personnel in education. Entries include: Name, address, phone, names of key officials. Arrangement: Alphabetical.

★4214★ National Association for Women in Education—Member Handbook

National Association for Women in Education
1325 18th St. NW, Ste. 210
Washington, DC 20036
Ph: (202)659-9330   Fax: (202)457-0946

Annual. Available to members only. Covers 2,000 American and foreign members. Entries include: Name, institution, office and home addresses, phone, education, position, committee membership. Arrangement: Geographical. Indexes: Alphabetical.

★4215★ National Directory of Alternative Schools

National Coalition of Alternative Community Schools
PO Box 15036
Santa Fe, NM 87506
Ph: (505)474-4312

Biennial, even years. $15.00. Covers over 400 alternative education programs, including home schools, and state and regional coalitions of alternative schools and colleges; also lists organizations and networks offering services and resources to those working with children; international coverage. Entries include: Name, address, phone, name of contact; some also include descriptions of programs. Arrangement: Schools are geographical.

★4216★ **National Directory for Employment in Education**

Association for School, College and University Staffing
1600 Dodge Ave., S-330
Evanston, IL 60201-3451
Ph: (708)864-1999   Fax: (708)864-8303

Annual, winter. $20.00. Covers about 550 placement offices maintained by teacher-training institutions and 450 school district personnel officers and/or superintendents responsible for hiring professional staff. Entries include: Institution name, address, phone, contact name. Arrangement: Geographical. Indexes: Personal name, subject-field of teacher training, institutions which provide vacancy bulletins and placement services to non-enrolled students.

★4217★ **NCA Quarterly—Roster Issues**

North Central Association of Colleges and Schools
Arizona State University
PO Box 873011
Tempe, AZ 85287-3011
Ph: (602)965-8700   Fax: (602)965-9423
Fr: 800-525-9517

Annual, school issue, summer; college issue, spring. $7.00. Publication includes: Elementary schools and secondary schools (summer issue), and colleges (spring issue) accredited by the association in a 19-state region. Entries include: School name, address, year first accredited, staffing, enrollment, name of president or principal. Arrangement: Geographical.

★4218★ **Nursery Schools & Kindergartens Directory**

American Business Directories, Inc.
American Business Information, Inc.
5711 S. 86th Cir.
Omaha, NE 68127
Ph: (402)593-4600   Fax: (402)331-1505

Annual. $1,310, U.S. edition; $145.00, (Canad. ed.). Number of listings: 38,967 (U.S. edition); 1,574 (Canadian edition). Entries include: Name, address, phone (including area code), size of advertisement, year first in Yellow Pages, name of owner or manager, number of employees. Regional editions available: Eastern, $760.00; Western, $645.00. Compiled from telephone company Yellow Pages, nationwide. Arrangement: Geographical.

★4219★ **Opportunities Abroad for Educators**

Fulbright Teacher Exchange Program
600 Maryland Ave., SW, Rm. 235
Washington, DC 20024-2520
Ph: (202)382-8586   Fax: (202)426-0657
Fr: 800-726-0479

Annual, May. Free. Covers opportunities available for elementary and secondary teachers, college and university instructors and professors, and school administrators to attend seminars or to teach abroad under the Mutual Educational and Cultural Exchange Act of 1961. Entries include: Countries of

placement, dates, eligibility requirements, teaching assignments. Arrangement: Geographical.

★4220★ **Patterson's Elementary Education**

Educational Directories, Inc.
PO Box 199
Mount Prospect, IL 60056-0199
Ph: (708)459-0605   Fax: (708)459-0608

Annual, October. $75.00, plus $4.00 shipping. Covers over 13,000 public school districts; more than 71,000 public, private, and Catholic elementary and middle schools; 1,600 territorial schools; and 400 state department of education personnel. Entries include: County name, city, population, public school district name, enrollment, grade range; superintendent name, address, phone; names of public schools, address, phone, principal's name, enrollment; private ad Catholic school listings include school name, enrollment, grade ranges, principal's name, address, phone. Arrangement: Geographical by state, then alphabetical by city.

★4221★ **Private Independent Schools**

Bunting and Lyon, Inc.
238 N. Main St.
Wallingford, CT 06492
Ph: (203)269-3333   Fax: (203)269-5697

Annual, March. $96.00. Covers 1,200 English-speaking elementary and secondary private schools and summer programs in the U.S. and abroad. Entries include: School name, address, phone, enrollment, tuition and other fees, scholarship information, administrator's name and educational background, director of admissions, regional accreditation, description of programs, curriculum, activities. Arrangement: Geographical. Indexes: School name; geographical.

★4222★ **Private Schools of the United States**

Council for American Private Education
1726 M St. NW, Ste. 1102
Washington, DC 20036-4502
Ph: (202)659-0016   Fax: (202)659-0018
Fr: 800-333-8802

Irregular, latest edition 1992. $29.95. Covers Approximately 15,000 private elementary and secondary schools. Entries include: Institution name, address, phone, grades, enrollment, tuition, types of facilities and programs, association affiliations, name of principal, plans of graduates. Arrangement: Geographical. Indexes: Institution name; association affiliation.

★4223★ **Public School Districts**

Office of Educational Research and Improvement
U.S. Department of Education
555 New Jersey Ave. NW, Ste. 214
Washington, DC 20208-5641
Ph: (202)357-6528   Fax: (202)219-1817
Fr: 800-424-1616

Annual, From 1968-1969 to 1991-1992. $175.00, Magnetic tape; $120.00, diskette. Data files describing approximately 17,000 operating and nonoperating local public school systems. Database includes: System name, city, zip code, county, metropolitan

status, standard metropolitan statistical area (SMSA) number (if any), number of schools, grade span, whether operating or nonoperating, extent to which independent or unified, average daily attendance, fiscal status, selection process for board of education, and consolidation status, number of diplomas and other certificates of completion granted, number of students requiring individual education plans under the Disabilities Act.

★4224★ **Public Schools USA: A Comparative Guide to School Districts**

Peterson's Guides, Inc.
202 Carnegie Center
PO Box 2123
Princeton, NJ 08543-2123
Ph: (609)243-9111   Fax: (609)243-9150
Fr: 800-338-3282

Annual, November. $44.95. Covers over 400 school districts in 52 metropolitan areas throughout the United States. Entries include: School district name, central office address, Effective Schools Index (ESI) rating; appraisals of quality of school leadership, quality of instruction, and quality of school environment including total enrollment, average daily attendance, expense per student, student/teacher ratio, dropout rate, number of advanced placement subjects, starting and maximum teachers' salaries. Arrangement: Geographical. Indexes: School district name.

★4225★ **QED's State-by-State School Guides**

Quality Education Data (QED)
1600 Broadway, 12th Fl.
Denver, CO 80202-4912
Ph: (303)860-1832   Fax: (303)860-0238
Fr: 800-525-5811

Annual, November. $1,100.00 national set; individual state volumes available. Covers over 100,000 public and private elementary and secondary schools in 17,000 school districts; in 52 volumes (national set). Entries include: School district name, address, phone, district enrollment, number of teachers, number of schools, financial data, minority enrollment statistics, names and educational specializations of key personnel, list of member schools, including school name, address, phone, name of principal, name of librarian, grade levels taught, enrollment, number of VCR units, number and types of microcomputers used. Arrangement: Geographical. Indexes: School name, district name, geographical (county name), personal name.

★4226★ **Recruiting Fairs for Overseas Teaching**

Education Information Services
Instant Alert
865 Central Ave., Ste. L-504
Needham, MA 02192-1344
Ph: (617)433-0125

Covers recruiting fairs and sponsors in the U.S. and elsewhere for American educators who wish to teach outside the U.S. Entries include: Fair sponsor, name, address, and phone; fair dates and locations are given in a separate list.

HANDBOOKS AND MANUALS

★4227★ *Becoming a Teacher*
Taylor & Francis, Inc.
1900 Frost Rd., Ste. 101
Bristol, PA 19007-1598
Ph: (215)785-5800   Fax: (215)785-5515
Gary Borich. 1995. $75.00; $23.95 (paper).

★4228★ *Beginnings: Teaching &
Learning in the Kindergarten*
Richard C. Owen Publishers, Inc.
PO Box 585
Katonah, NY 10536
Ph: (914)232-3903   Fax: (914)232-3977
Fr: 800-336-5588
Ron Benson. 1993. $19.95 (paper).

★4229★ *Career Choices for the 90's
for Students of Art*
Walker and Company
435 Hudson St.
New York, NY 10014
Ph: (212)727-8300   Fax: (212)727-0984
Fr: 800-289-2553
Prepared by the Career Associates staff.
1990. $9.95. 166 pages. Discusses alterna-
tives for students of art. Offers advice on
how to break into the field and how to move
up. Covers where and who the employers
are, internship possibilities, and professional
networking associations. Comprehensive
guide to career and job search planning.

★4230★ *Career Choices for the 90's
for Students of Political Science and
Government*
Walker and Company
435 Hudson St.
New York, NY 10014
Ph: (212)727-8300   Fax: (212)727-0984
Fr: 800-289-2553
Prepared by the Career Associates staff.
1990. $8.95. 166 pages. Discusses alterna-
tives for students of political science and
government. Offers advice on how to break
into the field and how to move up. Covers
where and who the employers are, internship
possibilities, and professional networking associations. Comprehensive guide to career
and job search planning.

★4231★ *Career Information Center*
Macmillan Publishing Co.
200 Old Tappan Rd.
Old Tappan, NJ 07675
Ph: (609)461-6500   Fr: 800-223-2336
Visual Education Center Staff. Fifth edition,
1992. $229.00. This 13-volume set profiles
over 600 occupations. Each occupational
profile describes job duties, educational requirements, how to get the job, advancement
possibilities, employment outlook, working
conditions, earnings and benefits, and where
to write for more information.

★4232★ *Careers in Education*
VGM Career Horizons
4255 W. Touhy Ave.
Lincolnwood, IL 60646-1975
Ph: (847)679-5500   Fax: (847)679-2494
Fr: 800-323-4900
Roy A. Edelfeldt. 1993. $17.95; $13.95
(paper). 192 pages. Explores opportunities
for teachers, administrators, and specialists
in elementary and secondary schools, as well
as teaching, research, and administrative
positions in higher education. Additional focus on adult and continuing education and
industry opportunities for educators. Provides detailed background on careers in state
boards and state departments of education,
accrediting agencies, federal agencies, and
national associations and councils.

★4233★ *Customizing Your Resume for
Teaching Positions*
University Press of America
4720 Boston Way
Lanham, MD 20706
Ph: (301)459-3366   Fax: (301)459-2118
Fr: 800-462-6420
Edward G. Pultorak. 1993. $17.50 (paper).

★4234★ *Educator's Job Search: The
Ultimate Guide to Finding Positions in
Education*
National Education Association
1201 16th St., NW
Washington, DC 20036
Ph: (202)822-7252   Fax: (202)822-7206
Martin Kimeldorf. 1993. $15.95 (paper).

★4235★ *The Encyclopedia of Career
Choices for the 1990s: Guide to Entry-
Level Jobs*
Perigree Books
The Berkley Publishing Group
PO Box 506
East Rutherford, NJ 07073
Ph: (201)933-9292   Fr: 800-223-0510
Career Associates Staff. 1992. $19.95. 862
pages. Describes 500 entry-level careers in a
variety of industries. Presents qualifications
required, working conditions, salary, intern-
ships, and professional associations.

★4236★ *The First Year for Elementary
School Teachers*
Charles C. Thomas Publisher
2600 S. 1st St.
Springfield, IL 62794-9265
Ph: (217)789-8980   Fax: (217)789-9130
Fr: 800-258-8980
Karen Megay-Nespoli. 1993. $31.95; $16.95
(paper).

★4237★ *How to Get a Job in Education*
Bob Adams, Inc.
260 Center St.
Holbrook, MA 02343
Ph: (617)767-8100   Fax: (617)767-0994
Fr: 800-872-5627
Joel Levin. Second edition, 1995. $12.95.
320 pages. Prepared for recent college graduates, seasoned educators, and career-
changing professionals, this publication
guides the job-seeker through the necessary
steps to obtaining a job in education at the

elementary, secondary, and university levels.
Offers advice on how to prepare for state
and local examinations, how to locate teaching opportunities nationwide, and how to
obtain certification. Includes a nationwide
salary survey. Covers public, private, summer, and overseas opportunities.

★4238★ *How to Get the Teaching
Position You Want: Teacher Candidate
Guide*
Education Enterprises
PO Box 1836
Spring Valley, CA 91979
Ph: (619)660-7740
M. Phyllis Murton. 1993.

★4239★ *Liberal Arts Jobs: What They
Are and How to Get Them*
Peterson's
PO Box 2123
Princeton, NJ 08543-2123
Ph: (609)243-9111   Fax: (609)243-9150
Fr: 800-338-3282
Burton Jay Nadler. Second edition, 1989.
$9.95. 153 pages. Presents a list of the top
20 fields for liberal arts majors, covering
more than 300 job opportunities. Discusses
strategies for going after those jobs, includ-
ing guidance on the language of a successful
job search, informational interviews, and
making networking work.

★4240★ *Non-Profits and Education Job
Finder*
Planning/Communications
7215 Oak Ave.
River Forest, IL 60305-1935
Ph: (708)366-5200   Fr: (888)366-5200
Daniel Lauber. 1996. $32.95; $16.95 (paper).
350 pages. Covers 1600 sources. Discusses
how to use sources of non-profit sector job
vacancies in a number of specialties and
state-by-state, including job-matching services, job hotlines, specialty periodicals with
job ads, salary surveys, and directories.
Covers a variety of fields from education to
religion. Includes chapters on resume and
cover letter preparation and interviewing.

★4241★ *100 Best Careers for the Year
2000*
Prentice Hall General Reference
15 Columbus Cir.
New York, NY 10023
Ph: (212)373-8500   Fr: 800-223-2348
Shelly Field. 1992. $15.00 (paper). Covers
100 of the fastest growing jobs. The publication is divided into 11 general employment
sections. Specific careers are covered within
each section. Provides job description, responsibilities, employment opportunities,
earnings, education and training, advancement opportunities, and experience and qualifications for each occupation.

★4242★ Opportunities in State and Local Government Careers

VGM Career Horizons
4255 W. Touhy Ave.
Lincolnwood, IL 60646-1975
Ph: (847)679-5500   Fax: (847)679-2494
Fr: 800-323-4900

Neale Baxter. 1993. $13.95; $10.95 (paper). 160 pages. Points out the incentives and drawbacks of a government career. Describes hiring procedures and provides tips on filling out applications, taking physical and aptitude tests, handling interviews, and finding jobs. Describes the jobs in which 75% of all state and local government workers are employed. For each occupation, covers the nature of the work and the training required.

★4243★ Opportunities in Teaching Careers

VGM Career Horizons
4255 W. Touhy Ave.
Lincolnwood, IL 60646-1975
Ph: (847)679-5500   Fax: (847)679-2494
Fr: 800-323-4900

Janet Fine. 1995. $14.95; $11.95 (paper). 160 pages. Discusses licensing and accreditation programs, sources of placement information, job-seeking correspondence, selection procedures, and paths to advancement. Also covers professional associations, non-traditional teaching opportunities, and jobs abroad.

★4244★ The RNT Careers in Teaching Handbook

Recruting New Teachers, Inc.
385 Concord Ave.
Belmont, MA 02178
Ph: (617)489-6000   Fax: (617)489-6005
1993.

★4245★ Teaching

NTC Publishing Group
4255 W. Touhy Ave.
Lincolnwood, IL 60646-1975
Ph: (708)679-5500   Fax: (708)679-6375
Fr: 800-323-4900

1994. $13.95; $10.95 (paper).

★4246★ Where the Jobs Are: The Hottest Careers for the '90s

The Career Press, Inc.
3 Tice Rd.
PO Box 687
Franklin Lakes, NJ 07417
Ph: (201)848-0310   Fax: (201)848-1727
Fr: 800-237-3371

Joyce Hadley. Second edition, 1995. $9.99. 300 pages. Describes careers in fifteen general fields, from accounting to travel and hospitality.

EMPLOYMENT AGENCIES AND SEARCH FIRMS

★4247★ Educational Placement Service

5050 Poplar Ave., Ste. 1700
Memphis, TN 38157-1701
Ph: (901)767-1884

Employment agency. Focuses on teaching, administrative, and education-related openings.

OTHER SOURCES

★4248★ American Association of Teachers of German (AATG)

112 Haddontowne Ct., No. 104
Cherry Hill, NJ 08034
Ph: (609)795-5553   Fax: (609)795-9398

Members: Teachers of German at all levels; individuals interested in German language and culture. **Activities:** Offers in-service teacher-training workshops.

★4249★ American Federation of Teachers (AFT)

555 New Jersey Ave. NW
Washington, DC 20001
Ph: (202)879-4400   Fr: 800-238-1133

Purpose: AFL-CIO. Works with teachers and other educational employees at the state and local level in organizing, collective bargaining, research, educational issues, and public relations. Conducts research in areas such as educational reform, bilingual education, teacher certification, and evaluation and national assessments and standards. Represents members' concerns through legislative action; offers technical assistance. Seeks to serve professionals with concerns similar to those of teachers, including state employees, healthcare workers, and paraprofessionals.

★4250★ Association for the Advancement of Health Education (AAHE)

1900 Association Dr.
Reston, VA 22091
Ph: (703)476-3437   Fax: (703)476-6638

Members: Professionals who have responsibility for health education in schools, colleges, communities, hospitals and clinics, and industries. **Purpose:** Advancement of health education through program activities and federal legislation; encouragement of close working relationships between all health education and health service organizations; achievement of good health and well-being for all Americans automatically, without conscious thought and endeavor. Member of the American Alliance for Health, Physical Education, Recreation and Dance.

★4251★ Association of Christian Schools International (ACSI)

PO Box 35097
Colorado Springs, CO 80935-3509
Ph: (719)528-6906   Fax: (719)531-0631

Purpose: Service organization for Christian schools. Represents members in legislative efforts and First Amendment confrontations with the government. **Activities:** Sponsors student activities such as academic and speech meets, sports events, piano and choir festivals, and science fairs. Holds Christian Cheerleader Camp for high school students. Offers volume-reduced cost purchasing for school supplies and curriculum materials; recommends additional sources for purchasing. Sponsors ACSI Missionary Fund to send teams of Christian school educators throughout the world to conduct conventions, and in-service training programs. Provides speakers.

★4252★ Career Close-ups: School Teacher

AIMS Media
9710 DeSoto Ave.
Chatsworth, CA 91311
Fax: (818)341-6700   Fr: 800-367-2467

Video. 1994. $195.00. 27 minutes. Profiles of outstanding teachers.

★4253★ Career Encounters: Teaching

Cambridge Career Products
PO Box 2153
Dept. CC15
Charleston, WV 25328-2153
Ph: (304)744-9323   Fax: (304)744-9351
Fr: 800-468-4227

Video. $99.95. 25 minutes. Professionals shown in a variety of settings discuss different aspects of their careers.

★4254★ Educating Elementary School Teachers: The Struggle for Coherent Vision, 1909-1978

University Press of America
4720 Boston Way
Lanham, MD 20706
Ph: (301)459-3366   Fax: (301)459-2118
Fr: 800-462-6420

Robert A. Levin. 1993. $46.50; $17.50 (paper).

★4255★ Educational Placement Sources Abroad

Education Information Services (EIS)
PO Box 660662
Newton, MA 02162-0662
Ph: (617)443-0125

Annual, August. Includes about 150 organizations in the United States and abroad which place English-speaking teachers and education administrators in positions abroad. Provides organization name and address. Classified by type of organization.

★4256★ Educational Placement Sources—U.S.A.

Education Information Service
PO Box 662
4523 Andes Dr.
Newton, MA 02162-0002
Ph: (617)237-0887

Annual, fall. $4.95. Covers about 75 organizations in the United States that find positions for teachers, educational administrators, and counselors. Entries include: Organization name, address, phone. Arrangement: Alphabetical.

★4257★ Friends Council on Education (FCE)

1507 Cherry St.
Philadelphia, PA 19102
Ph: (215)241-7245

Members: Representatives appointed by Friends Yearly Meetings; heads of Quaker secondary and elementary schools and colleges; members-at-large. **Purpose:** Acts as a clearinghouse for information on Quaker schools and colleges. **Activities:** Holds meetings and conferences on education and provides in-service training for teachers, administrators, and trustees in Friends schools.

★4258★ International Reading Association (IRA)

800 Barksdale Rd.
PO Box 8139
Newark, DE 19714-8139
Ph: (302)731-1600   Fax: (302)731-1057

Members: Teachers, reading specialists, consultants, administrators, supervisors, researchers, psychologists, librarians, and parents interested in promoting literacy. **Purpose:** Seeks to improve the quality of reading instruction and promote literacy worldwide. Disseminates information pertaining to research on reading, including information on adult literacy, early childhood and literacy development, international education, literature for children and adolescents, and teacher education and professional development. **Activities:** Maintains over 40 special interest groups and over 70 committees. **E-Mail:** 74673.3646@compuserve.com.

★4259★ International Technology Education Association - Council for Supervisors (ITEA-CS)

George R. Willcox
Virginia Department of Education
PO Box 2120, 21st Fl.
Richmond, VA 23216-2120
Ph: (804)225-2020   Fax: (804)371-0249

Members: Technology education supervisors from the U.S. Office of Education; local school department chairpersons; state departments of education, local school districts, territories, provinces, and foreign countries. **Purpose:** To improve instruction and supervision of programs in technology education. **Activities:** Conducts research; compiles statistics. Sponsors competitions. Maintains speakers' bureau.

★4260★ National Association of Blind Teachers (NABT)

1155 15th St. NW, Ste. 720
Washington, DC 20005
Ph: (202)467-5081   Fr: 800-424-8666

Members: Public school teachers, college and university professors, and teachers in residential schools for the blind. **Purpose:** To promote employment and professional goals of blind persons entering the teaching profession or those established in their respective teaching fields. Serves as a vehicle for the dissemination of information and the exchange of ideas addressing special problems of members.

★4261★ National Association of Catholic School Teachers (NACST)

1700 Sansom St., Ste. 903
Philadelphia, PA 19103
Ph: (215)665-0993   Fax: (215)568-8270

Members: Catholic school teachers. **Purpose:** To unify, advise, and assist Catholic school teachers in matters of collective bargaining. Promotes the welfare and rights of Catholic schools and teaching; determines needs of Catholic schools and teachers. Monitors legislation, trends, and statistics concerning Catholic education; promotes legislation favorable to nonpublic schools and Catholic school teachers; offers legal advice and addresses issues such as unemployment compensation; assists teachers in organizing and negotiating contracts.

★4262★ National Association of Independent Schools (NAIS)

1620 L St. NW
Washington, DC 20036-5605
Ph: (202)973-9700   Fax: (202)973-9790

Members: Independent elementary and secondary school members; regional associations of independent schools and related associations. **Purpose:** Provides curricular and administrative research and services. Conducts educational programs; compiles statistics.

★4263★ National Association for Research in Science Teaching (NARST)

Dr. John R. Staver
Kansas State University
219 Bluemont Hall
Manhattan, KS 66506
Ph: (913)532-6294   Fax: (913)532-7304

Members: Science teachers, supervisors, and science educators specializing in research and teacher education. **Purpose:** Promotes and coordinates science education research and interprets and reports the results.

★4264★ National Association of State Directors of Special Education (NASDSE)

1800 Diagonal Rd., Ste. 320
Alexandria, VA 22314
Ph: (703)519-3800   Fax: (703)519-3808

Members: Professional society of state directors; consultants, supervisors, and administrators who have statewide responsibilities for administering special education programs. **Purpose:** Provides services to state agencies to facilitate their efforts to maximize educational outcomes for individuals with disabilities.

★4265★ National Community Education Association (NCEA)

3929 Old Lee Hwy., Ste. 91-A
Fairfax, VA 22032
Ph: (703)359-8973   Fax: (703)359-0972

Members: Community school directors, principals, superintendents, professors, teachers, students, and laypeople. **Purpose:** Promotes and establishes community schools as an integral part of the educational plan of every community. Serves as a clearinghouse for the exchange of ideas and information, and the sharing of efforts. **Activities:** Offers leadership training.

★4266★ National Council for Accreditation of Teacher Education (NCATE)

2010 Massachusetts Ave. NW, Ste. 500
Washington, DC 20036-1023
Ph: (202)466-7496   Fax: (202)296-6620

Members: Representatives from constituent colleges and universities, state departments of education, school boards, teacher, and other professional groups. **Purpose:** Voluntary accrediting body devoted exclusively to: evaluation and accreditation of institutions for preparation of elementary and secondary school teachers; preparation of school service personnel, including school principals, supervisors, superintendents, school psychologists, instructional technologists, and other specialists for school-oriented positions.

★4267★ National Council for Geographic Education (NCGE)

Indiana University of Pennsylvania
16A Leonard Hall
Indiana, PA 15705
Ph: (412)357-6290   Fax: (412)357-7708

Members: Teachers of geography and social studies in elementary and secondary schools, colleges, and universities; geographers in governmental agencies and private businesses. **Purpose:** Encourages the training of teachers in geographic concepts, practices, teaching methods, and techniques; works to develop effective geographic educational programs in schools and colleges and with adult groups; stimulates the production and use of accurate and understandable geographic teaching aids and materials.

★4268★ National Council of Teachers of Mathematics (NCTM)

1906 Association Dr.
Reston, VA 22091
Ph: (703)620-9840   Fax: (703)476-2970
Fr: 800-235-7566

Members: Teachers of mathematics in grades K-12, two-year colleges, and teacher education personnel on college campuses.

★4269★ *Overseas Employment Opportunities for Educators: Department of Defense Dependents Schools*

Diane Publishing Co.
600 Upland Ave.
Upland, PA 19015
Ph: (610)499-7415

1993. $29.95. 52 pages.

★4270★ *Requirements for Certification of Teachers, Counselors, Librarians, Administrators for Elementary and Secondary Schools*

University of Chicago Press
5801 Ellis Ave., 4th Fl.
Chicago, IL 60637
Ph: (312)702-7648   Fax: 800-621-8476
Fr: 800-621-2736

Annual, June. $34.00. Publication includes: List of state and local departments of education. Entries include: Office name, address, phone. Principal content of publication is summaries of each state's teaching and administrative certification requirements. Arrangement: Geographical.

★4271★ *Resumes for Education Careers*

VGM Career Horizons
4255 W. Touhy Ave.
Lincolnwood, IL 60646-1975
Ph: (847)679-5500   Fax: (847)679-2494
Fr: 800-323-4900

1992. $9.95. Sample resumes cover a variety of education careers and reflect education professionals at all levels of experience.

Landscape Architects

★4272★ Architectural Record

New York Construction News
1221 Avenue of the Americas, 41st Fl.
New York, NY 10020
Ph: (212)512-4773   Fax: (212)512-4770

Magazine focusing on architecture.

★4273★ Fabrics and Architecture

Industrial Fabrics Association Intl.
345 Cedar St., Ste. 800
St. Paul, MN 55101
Ph: (612)222-2508   Fax: (612)222-8215

Bimonthly. $21.00/year. Magazine specializing in interior and exterior design ideas for fabric applications in architecture.

★4274★ Interior Landscape

American Nurseryman Publishing Co.
77 W. Washington St., Ste. 2100
Chicago, IL 60602-2904
Ph: (312)782-5505   Fax: (312)782-3232

Quarterly. $16.00/year for individuals; $5.00 for single issue. Provides in-depth coverage of business and technical topics of importance to interior landscape professionals.

★4275★ Landscape Design

Adams Publishing Co.
68-860 Perez Rd., No. J
Cathedral City, CA 92234-7248
Ph: (619)770-4370   Fax: (619)770-4380

Bimonthly. Magazine for licensed landscape architects.

★4276★ Landscape Management

Advanstar Communications Inc.
7600 Old Oak Blvd.
Cleveland, OH 44130
Ph: (216)243-8100   Fax: (216)891-2733

Monthly. $40.00/year for individuals. Magazine for professionals in landscape and golf course design, construction, and maintenance.

★4277★ Nursery News

Cenflo, Inc.
120 S. Riverside Plz., Ste. 464
Chicago, IL 60606-3508
Ph: (312)236-8648   Fax: (312)236-8891

Monthly. Trade newspaper (tabloid) for nursery industry.

★4278★ Progressive Architecture

600 Summer St.
PO Box 1361
Stamford, CT 06904
Ph: (203)348-7531

Monthly. $48.00/year; $7.50/issue. National magazine on architecture, interior designs, and planning.

★4279★ Qualified Remodeler

20 E. Jackson Blvd.
Chicago, IL 60604-2203

Free to qualified subscribers; $50.00/year for individuals. Magazine for remodeling contractor/distributors.

★4280★ Remodeling

Hanley-Wood, Inc.
1 Thomas Cir., Ste. 600
Washington, DC 20005
Ph: (202)452-0800   Fax: (202)785-1974

$24.95/year for individuals; $5.00 for single issue. Trade magazine for the professional remodeling industry.

PLACEMENT AND JOB REFERRAL SERVICES

★4281★ American Society of Landscape Architects (ASLA)

4401 Connecticut Ave. NW, 5th Fl.
Washington, DC 20008
Ph: (202)686-2752   Fax: (202)686-1001

Members: Professional society of landscape architects. **Purpose:** To promote the advancement of education and skill in the art of landscape architecture as an instrument in service to the public welfare. As the official accrediting agency, seeks to strengthen existing and proposed university programs in landscape architecture. Offers counsel to new and emerging programs; encourages state registration of landscape architects. Sponsors annual educational exhibit. **Activities:** Offers placement service; conducts specialized education and research. **Website:** Internet: http://www.asla.org/asla/

EMPLOYER DIRECTORIES AND NETWORKING LISTS

★4282★ American Society of Landscape Architects—Members' Handbook

American Society of Landscape Architects
4401 Connecticut Ave. NW, Ste. 500
Washington, DC 20008-2302
Ph: (202)686-2752   Fax: (202)686-1001

Annual, November. $129.95 for individuals; $24.95 for libraries. Covers 11,000 member landscape architects. Entries include: Name, address, phone, chapter, membership category, year joined, type of practice. Arrangement: Alphabetical. Indexes: Geographical, affiliation.

★4283★ Association of University Interior Designers—Membership List

Association of University Interior Designers
c/o Denise Beard
Ohio State University
The Office of the University Architect and Physical Planning
2009 Millikin Rd.
Columbus, OH 43210
Ph: (614)292-4458

Twice yearly, June and October. Available to members only. Covers nearly 100 in-house interior designers, landscape designers, architects, and purchasing agents associated with universities. Entries include: Name, title, affiliation, address, phone. Arrangement: Alphabetical.

★4284★ **Directory of African American Design Firms**

San Francisco Redevelopment Agency
770 Golden Gate Ave.
San Francisco, CA 94102-3120
Ph: (415)749-2423   Fax: (415)749-2526

Annual, December. Free. Covers over 100 architectural, engineering, planning, and landscape design firms. Entries include: Firm name, address, phone names and titles of key personnel, particular type of work. Arrangement: Alphabetical.

★4285★ **Landscape Architects Directory**

American Business Directories, Inc.
American Business Information, Inc.
5711 S. 86th Cir.
Omaha, NE 68127
Ph: (402)593-4600   Fax: (402)331-1505

Annual. $710.00, U.S. edition. Entries include: Name, address, phone (including area code), size of advertisement, year first in Yellow Pages, name of owner or manager, number of employees. Compiled from telephone company Yellow Pages, nationwide. Arrangement: Geographical.

★4286★ **Landscape Contractors Directory**

American Business Directories, Inc.
American Business Information, Inc.
5711 S. 86th Cir.
Omaha, NE 68127
Ph: (402)593-4600   Fax: (402)331-1505

Annual. $1,250.00, U.S. edition; $290.00, (Canad. ed.); payment with order. Entries include: Name, address, phone (including area code), size of advertisement, year first in Yellow Pages, name of owner or manager, number of employees. Regional editions available: Compiled from telephone company Yellow Pages, nationwide. Arrangement: Geographical.

★4287★ **Landscape Designers Directory**

American Business Directories, Inc.
American Business Information, Inc.
5711 S. 86th Cir.
Omaha, NE 68127
Ph: (402)593-4600   Fax: (402)331-1505

Updated continuously; printed on request. Please inquire. Entries include: Name, address, phone (including area code), size of advertisement, year first in Yellow Pages, name of owner or manager, number of employees. Compiled from telephone company Yellow Pages, nationwide. Arrangement: Geographical.

★4288★ **ProFile/The Directory of U.S. Architectual Design Firms**

American Institute of Architects
1735 New York Ave. NW
Washington, DC 20006
Ph: (202)626-7300   Fr: 800-365-2724

Annual. $145.00, plus $8.00 shipping. Covers more than 14,500 architectural firms, one or more of whose principals is a member of the American Institute of Architects. Entries include: For firms, firm name, address, phone, fax, year established, parent organization, key staff and their primary responsibilities, branches, number of staff personnel by discipline, types of work, geographical area served, projects. Arrangement: Firms are geographical. Indexes: Firm name, key individuals, specialization by category.

★4289★ **Saskatchewan Design Directory**

Design Council of Saskatchewan, Inc.
642 Broadway Ave., Ste. 200
Saskatoon, SK, Canada S7N 1A9
Ph: (306)242-0733   Fax: (306)664-2598

Biennial, spring of odd years. $5.00. Covers members of the Saskatchewan Association of Architects, the Association of Professional Community Planners of Saskatchewan, the Saskatchewan Graphic Arts Association, the Interior Designers of Saskatchewan, Association of Consulting Engineers of Saskatchewan, Saskatchewan Society of Illustrators and Designers, and the Saskatchewan Association of Landscape Architects, which are members of the council; about 380 persons and firms listed. Entries include: Name, address, phone, fax, professional association with which affiliated. Arrangement: Classified by professional group.

HANDBOOKS AND MANUALS

★4290★ **Between People and Nature: The Profession of Landscape Architecture**

American Society of Landscape Architects (ASLA)
4401 Connecticut Ave. NW, 5th Fl.
Washington, DC 20008
Ph: (202)686-2752

Describes the field of landscape architecture, educational preparation, and employment and earnings.

★4291★ **Career Information Center**

Macmillan Publishing Co.
200 Old Tappan Rd.
Old Tappan, NJ 07675
Ph: (609)461-6500   Fr: 800-223-2336

Visual Education Center Staff. Fifth edition, 1992. $229.00. This 13-volume set profiles over 600 occupations. Each occupational profile describes job duties, educational requirements, how to get the job, advancement possibilities, employment outlook, working conditions, earnings and benefits, and where to write for more information.

★4292★ **Careers for Nature Lovers and Other Outdoor Types**

VGM Career Horizons
4255 W. Touhy Ave.
Lincolnwood, IL 60646-1975
Ph: (847)679-5500   Fax: (847)679-2494
Fr: 800-323-4900

Louise Miller. 1992. $12.95; $9.95 (paper). Examines career opportunities in biology, agriculture, landscaping, forestry and conservation, geology, and waste management, and pollution control. Offers insight into preparing for and finding outdoor jobs in federal and state government, as well as private industry.

★4293★ **Encyclopedia of Careers and Vocational Guidance**

J. G. Ferguson Publishing Co.
200 W. Monroe, Ste. 250
Chicago, IL 60606
Ph: (312)580-5480

William E. Hopke. Ninth edition, 1993. $129.95; $199.95 (CD-ROM). Four-volume set that profiles 900 occupations and describes job trends in 71 industries. Includes career description, educational requirements, history of the job, methods of entry, advancement, employment outlook, earnings, conditions of work, social and psychological factors, and sources of further information. Contains career and employment information for this field.

★4294★ **Opportunities in Environmental Careers**

VGM Career Horizons
4255 W. Touhy Ave.
Lincolnwood, IL 60646-1975
Ph: (847)679-5500   Fax: (847)679-2494
Fr: 800-323-4900

Odom Fanning. 1995. $14.95; $11.95 (paper). 160 pages. Describes a broad range of opportunities in fields such as environmental health, recreation, physics, and hygiene, and provides job search advice.

EMPLOYMENT AGENCIES AND SEARCH FIRMS

★4295★ **Blake and Associates Executive Search**

PO Box 1425
Pleasantville, NJ 08232
Ph: (609)645-3330   Fax: (609)383-0320

Executive search firm.

★4296★ **Claremont-Branan, Inc.**

2150 Parklake Dr., Ste. 212
Atlanta, GA 30345
Ph: (404)491-1292

Employment agency. Executive search firm.

★4297★ **Connelly Search**

PO Box 30926
Tucson, AZ 85751-0926
Ph: (602)327-7999

Executive search firm.

OTHER SOURCES

★4298★ **American Association of Botanical Gardens and Arboreta (AABGA)**

786 Church Rd.
Wayne, PA 19087
Ph: (610)688-1120   Fax: (610)293-0149

Members: Directors and staffs of botanical gardens, arboreta, institutions maintaining or conducting horticultural courses, and others.
Purpose: Seeks to serve North American

public gardens and horticultural organizations by promoting professional development through its publications and meetings, advocating the interests of public gardens in political, corporate, foundation, and community arenas, and encouraging gardens to adhere to professional standards in their programs and operations.

★4299★ How to Open and Operate a Home-Based Landscaping Business: An Unabridged Guide

Globe Pequot Press
PO Box 833
Old Saybrook, CT 06475
Ph: (203)395-0440   Fax: (203)395-0312
Fr: 800-243-0495

Owen E. Dell. 1994. $14.95 (paper).

★4300★ Internship Directory: Internships and Summer Jobs at Public Gardens

American Association of Botanical Gardens and Arboreta (AABGA)
786 Church Rd.
Wayne, PA 19087
Ph: (610)688-1120   Fax: (610)293-0149

Annual, October. $5.00. Covers over 130 gardens, arboreta, and other horticultural organizations that offer student internships and summer jobs. Entries include: Name of institution, address, name of contact, deadline for application, number of students hired, whether internships are available, employment period, hours, rate of pay, whether housing is available, other comments. Arrangement: Alphabetical.

★4301★ Landscape Architecture Foundation (LAF)

4401 Connecticut Ave. NW, 5th Fl.
Washington, DC 20008
Ph: (202)686-0068   Fax: (202)686-1001

Members: Education and research vehicle for the landscape architecture profession in the U.S. Combines the capabilities of landscape architects, interests of environmentalists, and needs of agencies and resource foundations. **Purpose:** To encourage development of environmental research; to support and disseminate information on landscape architecture. Provides for the preparation and dissemination of educational and scientific information through publications, exhibits, lectures, and seminars. Solicits and expends gifts, legacies, and grants; has established an endowment fund; finances new programs. Sponsors California Landscape Architectural Student Scholarship Fund; endows and establishes professorships at colleges and universities. Develops programmed teaching materials in landscape architectural planning and construction; encourages submittal of proposals for unique and/or interdisciplinary educational research projects. Prepares slide, film, and tape presentations; operates charitable program. Has conducted a study of the profession to establish goals in terms of education, research needs, practice, and formulation of public policy.

★4302★ Landscaping: Principles & Practice

Van Nostrand Reinhold
115 5th Ave.
New York, NY 10003
Ph: (212)254-3232   Fax: (212)254-9499
Fr: 800-842-3636

Ingels. 1996. $32.95.

Landscapers

★4318★ Western City

League of California Cities
1400 K St.
Sacramento, CA 95814
Ph: (916)444-5790   Fax: (916)658-8240

Monthly. $30.00/year for individuals; $49.00 for two years. Municipal interest magazine.

PLACEMENT AND JOB REFERRAL SERVICES

★4319★ American Landscape Horticulture Association (ALHA)

3124 Gray Fox Ln.
Paso Robles, CA 93446
Ph: (805)238-7921   Fr: 800-359-6647

Purpose: Promotes the landscape horticulture industry. Maintains the Landscape Horticulture Center for Personnel Development. Provides apprenticeship training, certification testing, and ongoing educational programs. **Activities:** Offers placement service. Maintains speakers' bureau and research programs.

★4320★ Professional Grounds Management Society (PGMS)

120 Cockeysville Rd., Ste. 104
Hunt Valley, MD 21031
Ph: (410)584-9754   Fax: (410)584-9756
Fr: 800-609-7467

Members: Professional society of grounds managers of large institutions of all sorts and independent landscape contractors. **Purpose:** Establishs grounds management as a profession; secures opportunities for professional advancement of well-qualified grounds managers; acquaints the public with the distinction between competent ground managers, equipped through practical experience and systematic study, and self-styled °maintenance' personnel, lacking these essentials. **Activities:** Provides employment referral service to members. Conducts research and surveys; sponsors certification program for professional grounds managers. Takes action with the legislative and executive branches of government on issues affecting grounds managers; keeps members informed on matters affecting the profession.

EMPLOYER DIRECTORIES AND NETWORKING LISTS

★4321★ California Landscape Contractors Association—Roster

California Landscape Contractors Association
2021 N. St., Ste. 300
Sacramento, CA 95814
Ph: (916)448-2522   Fax: (916)446-7692
Fr: 800-448-CLCA

Annual, January. $50.00. Covers about 2,000 member landscape contractors and suppliers of products and services to the landscape contracting industry. Entries include: Name of firm, address, phone, representative to the association, chapter, products and services offered. Arrangement: Geographical. Indexes: Product/service.

★4322★ Grounds Maintenance—Buyers' Guide Issue

Intertec Publishing Corp.
9800 Metcalf Ave.
Shawnee Mission, KS 66215-2215
Ph: (913)341-1300   Fax: (913)967-1898
Fr: 800-441-0294

Annual, December. $3.00. Publication includes: List of manufacturers, growers, and suppliers of materials for landscaping design, construction, and maintenance; landscaping associations. Entries include: Company name, address, phone. Arrangement: Alphabetical. Indexes: Product.

★4323★ Municipal/County Directory Library Edition

Carroll Publishing
1058 Thomas Jefferson St. NW
Washington, DC 20007
Ph: (202)333-8620   Fax: (202)337-7020
Fr: 800-336-4240

Annual, July. $137.00, plus $8.00 shipping; payment must accompany order. Covers officials of 1,400 county governments (with populations over 25,000) and 2,000 municipalities (with populations over 1,000); includes elected, appointed, and career office holders. Entries include: Name, title, agency, address, phone. Arrangement: County officials are geographical, then by agency; municipal officials are by city. Indexes: personal name (with phone), agency.

★4324★ Municipal Year Book

Newman Books Ltd.
32 Vauxhall Bridge Rd.
London SW1V 2SS, England
Ph: 71 9736400   Fax: 71 2335057

Annual, December. $140.00, postpaid. Covers local and central government agencies and officials of the United Kingdom; municipal art galleries, associations, development organizations, fairs, libraries, museums, airports, and other local authorities. Entries include: Name of authority or governing agency, address, phone, fax, names of elected councillors, officers, names and titles of key personnel, contacts, population, and pay. Arrangement: Geographical. Indexes: Subject, place names.

★4325★ New York State Nurserymen's Association—Directory

New York State Nurserymen's Association
PO Box 657
Baldwinsville, NY 13027

Annual, January. Covers over 350 member nursery, landscape, gardening, and lawn maintenance firms in New York. Entries include: Company name, address, phone, name. Arrangement: Alphabetical.

★4326★ Nurseries Directory

American Business Directories, Inc.
American Business Information, Inc.
5711 S. 86th Cir.
Omaha, NE 68127
Ph: (402)593-4600   Fax: (402)331-1505

Updated continuously; printed on request. Entries include: Name, address, phone (including area code), size of advertisement, year first in Yellow Pages, name of owner or manager, number of employees. Compiled from telephone company Yellow Pages, nationwide. Arrangement: Geographical.

★4327★ Roster of Licensed Landscaping Businesses and Licensed Landscape Contractors

State Landscape Contractors Board
700 Summer NE, Ste. 300
Salem, OR 97310
Ph: (503)378-4621   Fax: (503)373-2007

Monthly. $20.00. Covers nearly 2,000 licensed landscapers and landscape businesses in Oregon. Entries include: Name of firm or individual, address. Arrangement: Alphabetical. Indexes: Geographical.

★4328★ Who's Who in Landscape Contracting

Associated Landscape Contractors of America
12200 Sunrise Valley Dr.
Reston, VA 22091
Ph: (703)620-6363   Fax: (703)620-6365

Annual, spring. $25.00. Covers 1,400 member exterior and interior landscape contractors and related suppliers. Entries include: Company name, address, phone, names of key personnel, specialties. Arrangement: Alphabetical. Indexes: Interior contractor location, exterior contractor location, personal name.

HANDBOOKS AND MANUALS

★4329★ Careers in Arboriculture

National Arborist Association, Inc.
PO Box 1094
Amherst, NH 03031
Ph: (603)673-3311

1994. Up to two copies free. 14 pages. Covers types of careers in arboriculture, how to prepare for them, and employment opportunities.

★4330★ Careers in National Park Service

National Park Service
U.S. Department of the Interior
Public Information Office
PO Box 37127
Washington, DC 20013-7127
Ph: (202)208-5228

Booklet. Free. 20 pages. Information about the hiring process for park service opportunities.

★4331★ Careers for Nature Lovers and Other Outdoor Types

VGM Career Horizons
4255 W. Touhy Ave.
Lincolnwood, IL 60646-1975
Ph: (847)679-5500   Fax: (847)679-2494
Fr: 800-323-4900

Louise Miller. 1992. $12.95; $9.95 (paper). Examines career opportunities in biology, agriculture, landscaping, forestry and conservation, geology, and waste management, and pollution control. Offers insight into preparing for and finding outdoor jobs in federal and state government, as well as private industry.

EMPLOYMENT AGENCIES AND SEARCH FIRMS

★4332★ Grosse Pointe Employment

18514 Mack Ave
Grosse Pointe Farms, MI 48236
Ph: (313)885-4576

Employment agency.

OTHER SOURCES

★4333★ American Association of Botanical Gardens and Arboreta (AABGA)

786 Church Rd.
Wayne, PA 19087
Ph: (610)688-1120   Fax: (610)293-0149

Members: Directors and staffs of botanical gardens, arboreta, institutions maintaining or conducting horticultural courses, and others. **Purpose:** Seeks to serve North American public gardens and horticultural organizations by promoting professional development through its publications and meetings, advocating the interests of public gardens in political, corporate, foundation, and commu-nity arenas, and encouraging gardens to adhere to professional standards in their programs and operations.

★4334★ American Association of Nurserymen (AAN)

1250 Eye St. NW, Ste. 500
Washington, DC 20005
Ph: (202)789-2900   Fax: (202)789-1893

Members: Vertical organization of wholesale growers; landscape firms; garden centers; mail order nurseries; suppliers. **Purpose:** Promotes the industry and its products. Offers management and consulting services and insurance, uniform, and public relations programs. Provides government representation and bank card plan for members. Maintains hall of fame and library; sponsors landscape awards programs.

★4335★ Associated Landscape Contractors of America (ALCA)

12200 Sunrise Valley, Ste. 150
Reston, VA 22091
Ph: (703)620-6363   Fax: (703)620-6365

Members: Landscape contractors. **Purpose:** Works to represent, lead, and unify the interior and exterior landscape industry by working together on a national basis; addressing environmental and legislative issues; and creating increased opportunities in business. **Activities:** Provides forum to encourage members' profitability, personal growth, and professional advancement.

★4336★ International Society of Arboriculture (ISA)

PO Box GG
Savoy, IL 61874
Ph: (217)355-9411   Fax: (217)355-9516

Members: Individuals engaged in commercial, municipal, and utility arboriculture; city, state, and national government employees; municipal and commercial arborists; others interested in shade tree welfare. **Purpose:** Disseminates information on the care and preservation of shade and ornamental trees. Supports research projects at educational institutions.

★4337★ Internship Directory: Internships and Summer Jobs at Public Gardens

American Association of Botanical Gardens and Arboreta (AABGA)
786 Church Rd.
Wayne, PA 19087
Ph: (610)688-1120   Fax: (610)293-0149

Annual, October. $5.00. Covers over 130 gardens, arboreta, and other horticultural organizations that offer student internships and summer jobs. Entries include: Name of institution, address, name of contact, deadline for application, number of students hired, whether internships are available, employment period, hours, rate of pay, whether housing is available, other comments. Arrangement: Alphabetical.

★4338★ National Landscape Association (NLA)

1250 Eye St. NW, Ste. 500
Washington, DC 20005
Ph: (202)789-2900   Fax: (202)789-1893

Members: Landscape firms. **Purpose:** Works to: enhance the professionalism of its member firms in designing, building, and maintaining quality landscapes in a profitable and environmentally responsible manner; represent the landscape perspective within the industry. **Activities:** Sponsors annual landscape tour in conjunction with American Association of Nurserymen.

★4339★ Seasonal Employment

U.S. National Park Service
PO Box 37127
Washington, DC 20013-7127
Ph: (202)208-5074

Updated as needed. Free. Publication includes: List of 10 regional offices and branches of the National Park Service that accept applications for seasonal jobs. Entries include: Name, address, phone, geographical area served. Principal content of publication is information on seasonal jobs offered by the National Park Services, with description of duties, qualifications, and application procedures for each type of job offered. Arrangement: Geographical.

Law Enforcement Officers

SOURCES OF HELP-WANTED ADS

★4340★ ACJS Today
Academy of Criminal Justice Sciences
Northern Kentucky University
402 Nunn Hall
Highland Heights, KY 41099-5998
Ph: (606)572-5634   Fax: (606)572-6665
Fr: 800-757-ACJS

Four issues/year. Included in membership. Contains criminal justice information.

★4341★ American City and County
Communication Channels, Inc.
6255 Barfield Rd.
Atlanta, GA 30328
Ph: (404)955-9970   Fax: (404)256-3116

Monthly. $54.00/year for individuals. Municipal and county administration magazine.

★4342★ Law Enforcement Technology
PTN Publishing Co.
445 Broad Hollow Rd., Ste. 21
Melville, NY 11747
Ph: (516)845-2700   Fax: (516)845-7109

Magazine for police technology and management.

★4343★ Law and Order
1000 Skokie Blvd.
Wilmette, IL 60091
Ph: (708)256-8555   Fax: (708)256-8574

Monthly. $20.00/year for individuals. Law enforcement trade magazine.

★4344★ The Municipality
League of Wisconsin Municipalities
122 W. Washington Ave., Ste. 301
Madison, WI 53703-2757
Ph: (608)267-2380   Fax: (608)267-0645

Monthly. Magazine for officials of Wisconsin's local municipal governments.

★4345★ National Employment Listing Service Bulletin
Criminal Justice Center
Sam Houston State University
Huntsville, TX 77341
Ph: (409)294-1692   Fax: (409)294-1653

Free. Covers job openings in police departments, sheriff's departments, courts, and other law enforcement and security agencies; correctional agencies; community agencies; and universities and schools offering educational programs in criminal justice and related disciplines. Entries include: Name of position, qualifications sought, salary, name and address of office for contact. Arrangement: Geographical within field.

★4346★ Police & Security News
Days Communications
1690 Quarry Rd.
PO Box 330
Kulpsville, PA 19443
Ph: (215)538-1240   Fax: (215)538-1208

Bimonthly. $14.00/year by mail; $26.00/year for other countries. Tabloid for the law enforcement and private security industries. Includes articles on training, new products, and new technology.

★4347★ Western City
League of California Cities
1400 K St.
Sacramento, CA 95814
Ph: (916)444-5790   Fax: (916)658-8240

Monthly. $30.00/year for individuals; $49.00 for two years. Municipal interest magazine.

PLACEMENT AND JOB REFERRAL SERVICES

★4348★ American Federation of Police (AFP)
3801 Biscayne Blvd.
Miami, FL 33137
Ph: (305)573-0070   Fax: (305)573-9819

Purpose: Governmental and private law enforcement officers (paid, part-time, or volunteer) united for the prevention of crime and the apprehension of criminals. Offers death benefits and training programs to members. **Activities:** Sponsors American Police Academy. Maintains placement service and hall of fame. Conducts workshops.

★4349★ American Police Academy (APA)
1000 Conneticut Ave. NW, Ste. 9
Washington, DC 20036
Ph: (202)293-9088   Fax: (305)573-9819

Members: Educational arm of the American Federation of Police and National Association of Chiefs of Police. Law enforcement officers who have completed advanced training offered by the academy for on-duty police officers and security personnel. **Purpose:** Establishes professional certification standards for career officers. **Activities:** Conducts home study programs. Operates speakers' bureau and placement service; compiles statistics.

★4350★ American Society of Criminology (ASC)
1314 Kinnear Rd., Ste. 212
Columbus, OH 43212
Ph: (614)292-9207   Fax: (614)292-6767

Members: Professional and academic criminologists; students of criminology in accredited universities; psychiatrists, psychologists, and sociologists. **Purpose:** To develop criminology as a science and academic discipline; to aid in the construction of criminological curricula in accredited universities; to upgrade the practitioner in criminological fields (police, prisons, probation, parole, delinquency workers). Conducts research programs; sponsors three student paper competitions. **Activities:** Provides placement service at annual convention.

★4351★ Federal Investigators Association (FIA)
2200 Wilson Blvd.
Box 102-219
Arlington, VA 22201

Members: Persons currently or formerly engaged in investigations, enforcement, security, and related activities for the federal government. **Purpose:** Goal is to recognize and promote criminal investigation. Has established professional standards of work, education, and conduct. Serves as a vehicle for exchange of ideas and broadening of professional contacts; conducts specialized education programs. Addresses such topics as advanced white collar crime investigations, suitability investigations, terrorism, and adjudication standards. **Activities:** Supports charitable programs. Offers placement service.

★4352★ **International Security and Detective Alliance (ISDA)**
PO Box 6303
Corpus Christi, TX 78466-6303
Ph: (512)888-6164   Fax: (512)888-6164

Members: Private investigation, and security professionals, investigative reporters and writers, researchers, military personnel, and some interested laypersons. **Purpose:** Seeks to: maintain an international registry of investigators for purposese of referral; support a more positive and accurate media image of P.I.s and security officers; provide a professional association for freelance operators; provide continuing education courses and materials. **Activities:** Offers the vocational trade association degree of Graduate Investigative Specialist - G.I.S., which can be completed through correspondence courses provided by the alliance. Provides professional certification in numerous speciality areas of investigation and security.

★4353★ **National Association of Investigative Specialists (NAIS)**
PO Box 33244
Austin, TX 78764
Ph: (512)719-3595   Fax: (512)719-3594

Members: Private investigators, automobile repossessors, bounty hunters, and law enforcement officers. **Purpose:** Promotes professionalism and provides for information exchange among private investigators. Lobbies for investigative regulations. Offers training programs and issues certificates of completion. **Activities:** Sponsors charitable programs; compiles statistics; maintains speakers' bureau and placement service. Operates Investigators' Hall of Fame of Private Investigators. Offers seminars on cassette tape.

★4354★ **National Organization of Black Law Enforcement Executives (NOBLE)**
4609 Pinecrest Office Park Dr., Ste. 2-F
Alexandria, VA 22312
Ph: (703)658-1529   Fax: (703)658-9479

Members: Law enforcement executives above the rank of lieutenant; police educators; academy directors; interested individuals and organizations. **Purpose:** Goals are to: provide a platform from which the concerns and opinions of minority law enforcement executives and command-level officers can be expressed; to facilitate the exchange of programmatic information among minority law enforcement executives; to increase minority participation at all levels of law enforcement; to eliminate racism in the field of criminal justice; to secure increased cooperation from criminal justice agencies; to reduce urban crime and violence. Seeks to develop and maintain channels of communication between law enforcement agencies and the community; encourages coordinated

community efforts to prevent and abate crime and its causes. Offers on-site technical assistance and training to police departments; develops model policies, practices, and procedures designed to decrease racial and religious violence and harassment. **Activities:** Provides job referral services to organizations seeking minority executives. Conducts research and training and offers technical assistance in crime victim assistance, community oriented policing, domestic violence, use of deadly force, reduction of fear of crime, airport security assessment, and minority recruitment. Offers internships.

★4355★ **Nine Lives Associates (NLA)**
Arcadia Manor
Rte. 2, Box 3645
Berryville, VA 22611
Ph: (703)955-1128

Members: Law enforcement, correctional, military, and security professionals who have been granted Personal Protection Specialist certification through completion of the protective services program offered by the Executive Protection Institute; conducts research. EPI programs emphasize personal survival skills and techniques for the protection of others. **Purpose:** Provides professional recognition for qualified individuals engaged in executive protection assignments. **Activities:** Maintains placement service.

★4356★ **USCCCN National Clearinghouse on Satanic Crime in America**
PO Box 1092
South Orange, NJ 07079
Ph: (908)549-2599   Fax: (908)549-2599

Purpose: Educates the public on satanic and occult related crimes being committed against animals and humans. Disseminates information to law enforcement personnel and the public through publications, videos, seminars, workshops, lectures, and radio and televison programming. **Activities:** Sponsors speakers' bureau; operates referral service. Compiles statistics. Offers children's services and research and charitable programs. Maintains hall of fame.

EMPLOYER DIRECTORIES AND NETWORKING LISTS

★4357★ *Association of Former Agents of the U.S. Secret Service— Membership Directory*
Association of Former Agents of the U.S. Secret Service
PO Box 11681
Alexandria, VA 22312
Ph: (703)256-0188

Annual, March. Available to members only. Entries include: Name, home address. Arrangement: Alphabetical.

★4358★ *International Association of Chiefs of Police—World Membership Directory*
International Association of Chiefs of Police
515 N. Washington St., No. 400
Alexandria, VA 22314-2357
Ph: (703)836-6767   Fax: (703)836-4593
Fr: 800-THE-IACP

Annual, October. $50.00. Covers 14,200 members in command and administrative positions in federal, state, and local law enforcement and related fields; includes county police and sheriffs; international, national, and regional law enforcement agencies and related organizations. Entries include: For officers: name, title, name of law enforcement agency, address, phone. For agencies and organizations: name, address, names and titles of key personnel, publications. Arrangement: Geographical. Indexes: Product.

★4359★ *Jeffers Directory of Law Enforcement Officials*
Pace Publications
1900 L St. NW, No. 312
Washington, DC 20036
Ph: (202)835-0119

Irregular, latest edition June 1992. $198. Covers 38,000 officials in over 17,000 municipal, county, state, and federal law enforcement organizations. Entries include: Organization name, address, phone; names, titles, and phone numbers of administrative, patrol, and investigative personnel, arranged by department. Arrangement: Geographical.

★4360★ *Justice—Directory of Services*
Canadian Criminal Justice Association
383 Parkdale Ave., Ste. 304
Ottawa, ON, Canada K1Y 4R4
Ph: (613)725-3715   Fax: (613)725-3720

Annual, February. $25.00, payment with order. Covers nearly 2,000 police commissions, Royal Canadian Mounted Police divisions, human rights commissions, legal aid services, police colleges, courts, parole boards, correctional authorities, prisoner aid agencies, and professional and voluntary associations related to corrections and criminal justice. Entries include: Organization or agency name, address, phone, name and title of director or contact. Arrangement: Federal government services and voluntary organizations are listed separately; other listings are geographical.

★4361★ *Municipal/County Directory Library Edition*
Carroll Publishing
1058 Thomas Jefferson St. NW
Washington, DC 20007
Ph: (202)333-8620   Fax: (202)337-7020
Fr: 800-336-4240

Annual, July. $137.00, plus $8.00 shipping; payment must accompany order. Covers officials of 1,400 county governments (with populations over 25,000) and 2,000 municipalities (with populations over 1,000); includes elected, appointed, and career office holders. Entries include: Name, title, agency, address, phone. Arrangement: County officials are geographical, then by agency; municipal officials are by city. Indexes: personal name (with phone), agency.

★4362★ Municipal Year Book

Newman Books Ltd.
32 Vauxhall Bridge Rd.
London SW1V 2SS, England
Ph: 71 9736400   Fax: 71 2335057

Annual, December. $140.00, postpaid. Covers local and central government agencies and officials of the United Kingdom; municipal art galleries, associations, development organizations, fairs, libraries, museums, airports, and other local authorities. Entries include: Name of authority or governing agency, address, phone, fax, names of elected councillors, officers, names and titles of key personnel, contacts, population, and pay. Arrangement: Geographical. Indexes: Subject, place names.

★4363★ National Directory of Law Enforcement Administrators and Correctional Institutions

National Police Chiefs and Sheriffs
  Information Bureau
PO Box 365
Stevens Point, WI 54481
Ph: (715)345-2772   Fax: (715)345-7288
Fr: 800-647-7579

Annual, August. $64.95, postpaid. Covers police departments and police chiefs in cities and towns with populations of more than 1,600; sheriffs and criminal prosecutors in all counties in the nation; state law enforcement and criminal investigation agencies; federal criminal investigation and related agencies; state and federal correctional institutions; campus law enforcement departments; airport and harbor police, Bureau of Indian Affairs officials, and Canadian law enforcement personnel. Entries include: Name, address, phone, fax, names and titles of key personnel. Arrangement: Separate geographical sections for sheriffs and prosecutors, city police chiefs, and state criminal investigation agencies; also separate sections for federal agencies and miscellaneous law enforcement and related agencies.

★4364★ NSA Directory

National Sheriffs' Association
1450 Duke St.
Alexandria, VA 22314
Ph: (703)836-7827   Fax: (703)683-6541
Fr: 800-424-7827

Annual, February/March. $50.00. Covers 3,100 member sheriffs and others in criminal justice at the federal, state, or county levels, and some local chiefs of police. Entries include: Name, title, affiliation, address, phone, fax. Arrangement: Geographical. Indexes: Alphabetical.

★4365★ United States Probation and Pretrial Services Officers Directory

Probation Division
Administrative Office of the U.S. Courts
1 Columbus Cir. NE, Ste. 4-300
Washington, DC 20544
Ph: (202)273-1600   Fax: (202)273-1603

Annual, latest edition December, 1994. Free. Covers federal probation offices and pretrial services offices; federal prisons; members of

the United States Parole Commission and the Federal Bureau of Prisons. Entries include: For district offices: District name, address, phone, Federal Telephone System phone; names and titles of chief, other key officials, and probation officers and chiefs; home phone of chief; counties served. For prisons: name, address, phone; number of male and female inmates. For government agencies: name, address, phone, FTS phone; names, titles, and phone numbers of board members; regional offices with addresses, phone numbers, and names of commissioners. Arrangement: District offices are by district; prisons are by type of prison, then by city.

★4366★ Who's Who in American Law Enforcement

National Association of Chiefs of Police
3801 Biscayne Blvd.
Miami, FL 33137
Ph: (305)573-0070   Fax: (305)573-9819

Triennial, latest edition December 1992. $65.00. Covers persons in supervisory or command positions in law enforcement agencies; not limited to members. Entries include: Name, office address and phone, highest degree held, areas of occupational specialization, personal and career data, awards and honors; some entries include photos. Arrangement: Alphabetical.

HANDBOOKS AND MANUALS

★4367★ Career Planning in Criminal Justice

Anderson Publishing Co.
2035 Reading Rd.
Cincinnati, OH 45202
Ph: (513)421-4142

Robert C. DeLucia and Thomas J. Doyle. Second edition, 1993. 178 pages. Surveys a wide range of career and employment opportunities in law enforcement, the courts, corrections, forensic science, and private security. Contains career planning and job hunting advice.

★4368★ Careers in Law Enforcement: Interviewing for Results

The Graduate Group
86 Norwood Rd.
West Hartford, CT 06117-2236
Ph: (203)232-3100

Jim Nelson. 1995. $27.50 (paper).

★4369★ Careers in Law Enforcement and Security

Rosen Publishing Group, Inc.
29 E. 21st St.
New York, NY 10010
Ph: (212)777-3017   Fax: (212)777-0277
Fr: 800-237-9932

Paul Cohen and Shari Cohen. Revised edition, 1994. $14.95; $9.95 (paper). Describes jobs such as police, sheriff, detective, FBI, CIA, and Secret Service agents, parole and probation officers, security guards, and private investigators. Covers job duties, qualifi-

cations, education, training, income, and advancement possibilities. Offers advice about where and how to apply for jobs.

★4370★ Civil Service Handbook

Prentice Hall General Reference
15 Columbus Cir.
New York, NY 10023
Ph: (212)373-8500   Fr: 800-223-2348

Hy Hammer. Eleventh edition, 1994. $10.00. Subtitled: "How to Get a Civil Service Job." Comprehensive guide to working in state and federal government. Includes sample exams for postal clerks and police officers.

★4371★ Federal Jobs in Law Enforcement

Impact Publications
9104 N Manassas Dr.
Manassas Park, VA 22111-5211
Ph: (703)361-7300   Fax: (703)335-9486

Russ Smith. 1995. $14.95 (paper).

★4372★ Inside Jobs: A Realistic Guide to Criminal Justice Careers for College Graduates

Sheffield Publishing Co.
PO Box 359
Salem, WI 53168
Ph: (414)843-2281   Fax: (414)843-3683

Stuart Henry, editor. 1994. $13.95 (paper).

★4373★ Law Enforcement Employment Guide

Lawman Press
PO Box 1468
Mt. Shasta, CA 96067
Ph: (818)344-6146

Ron Stern. Second edition, 1990. $19.95. Directed toward law enforcement applicants, officers, and career changers. Lists requirements for the scores of law enforcement agencies, from very small departments to the largest federal agencies. Includes potential number of openings in the field.

★4374★ The Law Enforcement Manual

Princeton Educational Research Institute
239 Hillside Ave.
Cranford, NJ 07016
Ph: (908)276-5101   Fax: (908)931-0210

Mark Adamson. 1994. $39.95.

★4375★ 100 Best Careers for the Year 2000

Prentice Hall General Reference
15 Columbus Cir.
New York, NY 10023
Ph: (212)373-8500   Fr: 800-223-2348

Shelly Field. 1992. $15.00 (paper). Covers 100 of the fastest growing jobs. The publication is divided into 11 general employment sections. Specific careers are covered within each section. Provides job description, responsibilities, employment opportunities, earnings, education and training, advancement opportunities, and experience and qualifications for each occupation.

★4376★ *Opportunities in Law Enforcement and Criminal Justice*

VGM Career Horizons
4255 W. Touhy Ave.
Lincolnwood, IL 60646-1975
Ph: (847)679-5500   Fax: (847)679-2494
Fr: 800-323-4900

James Stinchcomb. 1994. $14.95; $11.95 (paper). Offers information on opportunities at the city, county, state, military, and federal levels. Contains bibliography and illustrations.

★4377★ *Opportunities in Vocational and Technical Careers*

VGM Career Horizons
4255 W. Touhy Ave.
Lincolnwood, IL 60646-1975
Ph: (847)679-5500   Fax: (847)679-2494
Fr: 800-323-4900

Adrian A. Paradis. 1992. $14.95; $11.95 (paper). 160 pages. Provides information on a variety of opportunities and advice on breaking into the field.

★4378★ *Your Opportunities in Law Enforcement*

Energeia Publishing, Inc.
PO Box 985
Salem, OR 97308
Ph: (503)362-1480   Fax: (503)362-2123

Victor D. Tognazzini. 1994. $2.00 (paper).

OTHER SOURCES

★4379★ **International Association of Campus Law Enforcement Administrators (IACLEA)**

638 Prospect Ave.
Hartford, CT 06105-4298
Ph: (203)586-7517   Fax: (203)586-7550

Members: Two-year or four-year colleges and universities with a full-time law enforcement or security agency. **Purpose:** Serves as a forum for exchange of information and ideas in an effort to improve administration, planning and development, and operation and maintenance of security, police, and public safety departments of institutions of higher education. **Activities:** Conducts workshops and specialized education.

★4380★ *Law Enforcement Exams Handbook*

Prentice Hall General Reference & Travel
15 Columbus Cir.
New York, NY 10023
Ph: (212)373-8500   Fax: 800-445-6991
Fr: 800-223-2348

E.P. Steinberg. 1993. $10.00 (paper).

★4381★ **National Disabled Law Officers Association (NDLOA)**

75 New St.
Nutley, NJ 07110
Ph: (201)667-9569

Members: Law officers disabled in the line of duty. **Purpose:** Seeks to help policemen who have suffered permanent, serious injuries find new jobs in the law enforcement field. Promotes legislation providing better benefits for disabled officers; helps members cope with being disabled; maintains file of information on benefits available to disabled policemen.

★4382★ **Society of Professional Investigators (SPI)**

80 8th Ave., Ste. 303
New York, NY 10011
Ph: (212)807-5658

Members: Persons with at least 5 years' investigative experience for an official federal, state, or local government agency or for a quasi-official agency formed for law enforcement or related activities. **Purpose:** Seeks to advance knowledge of the science and technology of professional investigation, law enforcement, and police science; maintains high standards and ethics; promotes efficiency of investigators in the services they perform.

Lawyers

SOURCES OF HELP-WANTED ADS

★4383★ The American Lawyer

600 3rd Ave.
New York, NY 10016
Ph: (212)973-2800   Fax: (212)972-6258

Monthly. Legal magazine.

★4384★ Armando Castro

Los Angeles County Bar Association
617 S. Olive St.
Los Angeles, CA 90014
Ph: (213)896-6503   Fax: (213)623-4328

Monthly. $28.00/year for individuals; $3.00 for single issue. Magazine featuring scholarly legal articles.

★4385★ California Lawyer

Daily Journal Corporation
915 E. 1st St.
Los Angeles, CA 90012-4042
Ph: (213)229-5300   Fax: (213)680-3682
Fr: 800-788-7840

Monthly. $36.00/year for individuals. Law magazine.

★4386★ Chicago Lawyer

Law Bulletin Publishing Co.
415 N. State St.
Chicago, IL 60610
Ph: (312)644-7800   Fax: (312)644-4255

Monthly. Free to qualified subscribers; $40.00/year for institutions. Legal magazine.

★4387★ Community Jobs: The Employment Newspaper for the Non-Profit Sector

ACCESS: Networking in the Public Interest
30 Irving Pl.
New York, NY 10003
Ph: (212)475-1001   Fax: (212)475-1199

Monthly. $69.00. Covers jobs and internships available with nonprofit organizations active in issues such as the environment, foreign policy, consumer advocacy, housing, education, etc. Entries include: Position title; name, address, and phone of contact; de-scription, responsibilities; requirements; salary. Arrangement: Geographical.

★4388★ The Florida Bar News

The Florida Bar
650 Apalachee Pkwy.
Tallahassee, FL 32399-2300
Ph: (904)561-5601   Fax: (904)681-3859
Fr: 800-342-8060

Semimonthly. $20.00/year for individuals. Legal newspaper covering Florida lawyers and courts.

★4389★ Job Announcements

National Center for State Courts
300 Newport Ave.
Williamsburg, VA 23187
Ph: (804)253-2000

Semimonthly. $30.00/year. Provides lists of court-related job openings in the United States and its territories.

★4390★ Journal of the Missouri Bar

The Missouri Bar
326 Monroe St.
PO Box 119
Jefferson City, MO 65102
Ph: (314)635-4128   Fax: (314)635-2811

Bimonthly. Magazine featuring short, practical articles on legal subjects for practicing attorneys.

★4391★ The Journal of Taxation

Warren, Gorham Lamont
1 Penn Plaza
New York, NY 10119
Ph: (212)971-5185   Fax: (212)971-5025
Fr: 800-950-1252

Monthly. $170.00/year for individuals. Journal for professional tax practitioners.

★4392★ Kentucky Bench and Bar Magazine

Kentucky Bar Association
514 W. Main St.
Frankfort, KY 40601-1883
Ph: (502)564-3795   Fax: (502)564-3225

Quarterly. $15.00/year for individuals. Kentucky law journal.

★4393★ Lawyers Job Bulletin Board

Federal Bar Association
1815 H St., No. 408
Washington, DC 20006-3697
Ph: (202)638-0252

Monthly. $30.00/year. Provides a list of job openings for attorneys, usually in the federal sector.

★4394★ Legal Times

American Lawyer Media, L.P.
1730 M St. NW
Washington, DC 20036
Ph: (202)457-0686   Fax: (202)457-0718

Weekly. $635.00/year for individuals; $475.00/year for institutions. Legal newspaper covering law, lobbying, and politics in the Nation's capital.

★4395★ Massachusetts Lawyers Weekly

Lawyers Weekly Publications
41 West St.
Boston, MA 02111
Ph: (617)451-7300   Fax: (617)451-7324

Weekly. $259.00/year for individuals. Newspaper (tabloid) reporting Massachusetts legal news.

★4396★ Michigan Bar Journal

State Bar of Michigan
306 Townsend St.
Lansing, MI 48933-2083
Ph: (517)372-9030   Fax: (517)482-6248

Monthly. Legal magazine.

★4397★ National and Federal Legal Employment Report

Federal Reports Inc.
1010 Vermont Ave. NW, Ste. 408
Washington, DC 20005
Ph: (202)393-3311   Fax: (202)393-1553
Fr: 800-296-9611

Monthly. $111.20 for individuals; $147.20 for institution. Publication includes: Listings of approximately 600 current attorney and law-related job opportunities with the U.S. government and other public and private employers in Washington D.C., nationwide, and abroad. Includes positions for contract specialists, attorney-advisors, legal assistants, investigators, court researchers, and public defenders. Arrangement: Geographical.

★4398★ *The National Law Journal*

The National Law Journal
345 Park Ave. S
New York, NY 10010
Ph: (212)779-9200   Fax: (212)481-8074
Fr: 800-888-8300

Weekly (Mon.). Tabloid focusing on the practice of law and trends in law.

★4399★ *New Jersey Law Journal*

American Lawyer Media, L.P.
238 Mulberry St.
PO Box 20081
Newark, NJ 07101-6081
Ph: (201)642-0075   Fax: (201)642-0920

Weekly (Mon.). $295.00/year for individuals; $7.50 for single issue. Journal containing digests of court opinions, notes, and orders to the bar from New Jersey Supreme Court and federal district court. Includes news articles on legal topics and commentary by legal specialists.

★4400★ *New York State Bar Journal*

New York State Bar Association
1 Marine Midland Plaza
PO Box 2039
Binghamton, NY 13902
Ph: (607)723-9511   Fax: (607)772-6093

Legal journal.

★4401★ *Pennsylvania Law Journal*

Legal Communications, Ltd.
1617 JFK Blvd. Ste. 960
Philadelphia, PA 19103
Ph: (215)557-2300   Fax: (215)557-2301
Fr: 800-722-7670

Weekly (Mon.). Newspaper covering law news including recent court decisions.

★4402★ *Public Interest Employment Service Job Alert*

Public Interest Clearing House
200 McAllister St.
San Francisco, CA 94102-4978
Ph: (415)255-1714

Semimonthly. $120.00/year for employed persons; $60.00/year for unemployed. Lists job openings in legal aid offices, public interest law firms, and nonprofit organizations.

★4403★ *The Recorder*

American Lawyer Media, L.P.
625 Polk St., Ste. 500
San Francisco, CA 94102-3368
Ph: (415)749-5400   Fax: (415)749-5449

Daily (morn.). $205.00/year for individuals. Legal newspaper.

★4404★ *Texas Bar Journal*

State Bar of Texas
PO Box 12487, Capitol Sta.
Austin, TX 78711-2487
Ph: (512)463-1463   Fax: (512)463-1475
Fr: 800-204-2222

Monthly. Legal news journal for the legal profession.

★4405★ *The Washington Lawyer*

The District of Columbia Bar
1707 L St. NW, Ste. 350
Washington, DC 20036
Ph: (202)331-7700   Fax: (202)331-7311

Bimonthly. Forum for articles and news items for the Washington legal community.

★4406★ *Wisconsin Lawyer*

State Bar of Wisconsin
402 W. Wilson St.
Madison, WI 53703
Ph: (608)257-3838   Fax: (608)257-5502
Fr: 800-728-7788

Monthly. $42.00/year for individuals. Magazine for Wisconsin legal professionals.

PLACEMENT AND JOB REFERRAL SERVICES

★4407★ American Association of Attorney-Certified Public Accountants (AAA-CPA)

24196 Alicia Pky., Ste. K
Mission Viejo, CA 92691
Ph: (714)768-0336

Members: Persons who are licensed both as attorneys and as certified public accountants (CPAs). **Purpose:** Promotes high professional and ethical standards; seeks to safeguard and defend the professional and legal rights of attorney-CPAs. **Activities:** Maintains placement service. Conducts research on dual licensing and dual practice; maintains speakers' bureau, and a collection of published and unpublished articles. Has compiled a list of attorney-CPAs in the United States; conducts biennial economic and practice survey. Maintains liaison with bar associations and accounting groups and offers referral service of potential clients. State groups conduct extensive self-education programs.

★4408★ The American Association of Nurse Attorneys (TAANA)

720 Light St.
Baltimore, MD 21230-3816
Ph: (410)752-3318   Fax: (410)752-8295

Members: Nurse attorneys, nurses in law school, and attorneys in nursing school. **Purpose:** Aims to better nurse attorneys and inform the public on matters of nursing, health care, and law. Goals are to facilitate communication and information sharing between professional groups; to establish an employment network; to assist new and potential nurse attorneys; to develop the profession; to promote the image of nurse attorneys as experts and consultants in nursing and law. **Activities:** Maintains educational foundation.

★4409★ American Board of Professional Liability Attorneys (ABPLA)

175 E. Shore Rd.
Great Neck, NY 11023
Ph: (516)487-1990   Fax: (516)487-4304
Fr: 800-633-6255

Members: Liability litigation attorneys who have satisfied requirements of litigation experience and who have passed the National Board of Trial Advocacy written civil litigation specialist examination and the oral ABPLA examination. **Purpose:** Promotes and improves ethical and technical standards of advocacy and litigation practice in product and professional liability litigation; establish basic standards for training, qualification, and recognition of specialists; foster efficient administration of justice. **Activities:** Provides graduated training program for licensed attorneys desiring certification as specialists in the field. Offers placement service; compiles statistics. Maintains file of abstracts and program transcripts.

★4410★ Association of American Law Schools (AALS)

1201 Connecticut Ave. NW, Ste. 800
Washington, DC 20036-2605
Ph: (202)296-8851   Fax: (202)296-8869

Members: Law schools. **Purpose:** Seeks to improve the legal profession through legal education. Cooperates with state and federal government, other legal education and professional associations, and other national higher education and learned society organizations. **Activities:** Compiles statistics; sponsors teacher placement service.

★4411★ Christian Management Association (CMA)

PO Box 4638
Diamond Bar, CA 91765
Ph: (909)861-8861   Fax: (909)860-8247
Fr: 800-727-4CMA

Members: Managers, lawyers, auditors, pastors, church administrators, and other individuals who serve Christian organizations. **Purpose:** To promote the general welfare of Christian nonprofit organizations by assisting those involved in management and administration. Emphasizes areas such as: accounting and finance; media; legal and tax issues; general, church, fundraising, financial, time, and personnel management; deferred giving; women in management; executive development; marketing and communications; public relations; information development. Maintains task forces that consider emerging and potentially troubling issues. **Activities:** Offers national and regional seminars in all areas of management through its annual national conference, the Christian Management Institute. Holds bimonthly fellowship meeting for training and information reports. Provides job referral and professional referral service to assist Christian managment personnel.

★4412★ Computer Law Association (CLA)

3028 Javier Rd., Ste. 402
Fairfax, VA 22031
Ph: (703)560-7747   Fax: (703)207-7028

Members: Lawyers, law students, and others interested in legal problems related to computer-communications technology. **Purpose:** Aids in: contracting for computer-communications goods and services; perfecting and protecting proprietary rights chiefly in software; taxing computer-communications goods, services, and transactions, and liability for acquisition and use of computer-communications goods and services. **Activities:** Provides specialized educational programs; offers limited placement service. Holds Annual Computer Law Update.

★4413★ Decalogue Society of Lawyers (DSL)

39 S. La Salle, No. 410
Chicago, IL 60603
Ph: (312)263-6493   Fax: (312)263-6512

Members: Lawyers of the Jewish faith. **Purpose:** Seeks to promote and cultivate social and professional relations among members of the legal profession. Conducts a forum on topics of general and Jewish interest. **Activities:** Maintains placement service to help members find employment and office facilities.

★4414★ Food and Drug Law Institute (FDLI)

1000 Vermont Ave., 12th Fl.
Washington, DC 20005
Ph: (202)371-1420   Fax: (202)371-0649

Members: Manufacturers and distributors of food, drugs, cosmetics, and devices are industrial members; law firms and others are associate members. **Purpose:** Promotes the development of essential knowledge about the laws that regulate the research for, production, and sale of food, drugs, medical devices, and cosmetics. Seeks to provide a forum for the discussion of issues pertaining to food and drug laws. **Activities:** Maintains placement service.

★4415★ Franchise Consultants International Association (FCIA)

5147 S. Angela Rd.
Memphis, TN 38117
Ph: (901)867-0800   Fax: (901)867-0010

Members: Individuals and corporations involved in franchising including attorneys, consultants, brokers, sales personnel, suppliers, Universities, consulatants, advertisers, and developers. **Purpose:** To provide standardized information for the franchise industry. Seeks to coordinate effective and professional franchise consulting and to educate members in franchise law and logistics. Serves as a clearinghouse of approved literature on franchising. **Activities:** Operates archive and hall of fame; compiles statistics. Provides placement service, charitable program, and speakers' bureau.

★4416★ National Association of Black Women Attorneys (NABWA)

724 9th St. NW, Ste. 206
Washington, DC 20001
Ph: (202)637-3570   Fax: (202)637-4892

Members: Black women who are members of the bar of any U.S. state or territory; associate members include law school graduates, paralegals, and law students. **Purpose:** Seeks to: advance jurisprudence and the administration of justice by increasing the opportunities of black and non-black women at all levels; aid in protecting the civil and human rights of all citizens and residents of the U.S.; expand opportunities for women lawyers through education; promote fellowship among women lawyers. **Activities:** Provides pre-law and student counseling; serves as job placement resource for firms, companies, and others interested in the field. Holds regional seminars. Maintains hall of fame; offers charitable program.

★4417★ National/Black Law Student Association (NBLSA)

1225 11th St. NW
Washington, DC 20001

Members: Black law students united to meet the needs of black people within the legal profession and to work for the benefit of the black community. **Purpose:** Objectives are to: articulate and promote professional competence, needs, and goals of black law students; focus on the relationship between black students and attorneys and the American legal system; instill in black law students and attorneys a greater commitment to the black community; encourage the legal community to bring about change to meet the needs of the black community. Supports black law students at Harvard University who recently called for a boycott of a course on racial discrimination to protest the law school's faculty-hiring practices. **Activities:** Sponsors the Frederick Douglass Moot Court Competition; offers placement service.

★4418★ National Conference of Black Lawyers (NCBL)

2 W. 125th St.
New York, NY 10027
Ph: (212)864-4000

Purpose: Attorneys throughout the U.S. and Canada united to use legal skills in the service of black and poor communities. Maintains projects in legal services to community organizations, voting rights, and international affairs; provides public education on legal issues affecting blacks and poor people. Researches racism in law schools and bar admissions. **Activities:** Conducts programs of continuing legal education for member attorneys. Maintains general law library. Compiles statistics; maintains lawyer referral and placement services. Provides speakers' bureau on criminal justice issues, international human rights law, and civil rights practice.

★4419★ Puerto Rican Legal Defense and Education Fund (PRLDEF)

99 Hudson St., 14th Fl.
New York, NY 10013
Ph: (212)219-3360   Fax: (212)431-4276
Fr: 800-328-2322

Purpose: Works to protect and promote the civil rights of Puerto Ricans and other Latinos, and to increase the number of minority lawyers who can serve their community. Conducts class action litigation on issues facing the Latino community such as education, employment, voting rights, and housing. Seeks to facilitate the pursuit of a legal career for Puerto Ricans and other minorities. **Activities:** Offers programs for pre-law students including law school admissions day, counseling, writing and financial aid workshops, employment listings, and scholarships. Refers legal questions from the Latino community to appropriate agencies.

★4420★ Scandanavian American Lawyers Association

4177 Garrick
Warren, MI 48091
Ph: (810)757-4177   Fax: (810)758-8173

Members: Professional association of Scandanavian-American attorneys. **Purpose:** Provides a forum to discuss and address issues of interest to members. **Activities:** Maintains a placement service.

EMPLOYER DIRECTORIES AND NETWORKING LISTS

★4421★ *American Bar Association—Directory*

American Bar Association (ABA)
750 N. Lake Shore Dr.
Chicago, IL 60611
Ph: (312)988-5000   Fax: (312)988-6389

Annual, October. $14.95. Covers Approximately 7,500 lawyers active in the affairs of the Association, including officers, members of Boards of Governors and House of Delegates, section officers and council members, committee chairpersons and members, headquarters staff, state and local bars, and affiliated organizations. Entries include: Section, council, or other unit name; names, addresses, and phone numbers of officers or chairpersons and members. Arrangement: Classified by position in ABA. Indexes: Alphabetical, Geographical committee.

★4422★ *The American Bar-The Canadian Bar-The International Bar*

Forster-Long, Inc.
3280 Ramos Cir.
Sacramento, CA 95827
Ph: (916)362-3276   Fax: (916)362-5643
Fr: 800-328-5091

Annual, March. $290.00. Covers over 91,500 lawyers in the United States and 105 other countries; selected state administrative offices. Entries include: Firm name, type of practice, address, phone, names, educational data, and memberships of partners and associates. State offices' listings include address, phone. A general law list. Arrangement: Geographical; separate sections for Canadian and international lawyers. Indexes: Personal name; firm name and location.

★4423★ American Lawyers Quarterly
The American Lawyers Co.
853 Westpoint Pkwy., Ste. 710
Cleveland, OH 44145-1595
Ph: (216)871-8700   Fax: (216)871-9997
Fr: 800-843-4000

Semiannual, January and July; monthly supplements. Available only to qualified subscribers. A commercial law list. See separate listing, Law Lists. Arrangement: Geographical.

★4424★ Attorneys Directory
American Business Directories, Inc.
American Business Information, Inc.
5711 S. 86th Cir.
Omaha, NE 68127
Ph: (402)593-4600   Fax: (402)331-1505

Annual. $12,725.00, U.S. edition; $1,155.00, (Canad. ed.); payment with order. Number of listings: 500,232 (U.S. edition); 32,391 (Canadian edition). Entries include: Name, address, phone (including area code), size of advertisement, year first in Yellow Pages, name of owner or manager, number of employees. Regional editions available. Compiled from telephone company Yellow Pages, nationwide. Arrangement: Geographical.

★4425★ Attorneys—Firms Directory
American Business Directories, Inc.
American Business Information, Inc.
5711 S. 86th Cir.
Omaha, NE 68127
Ph: (402)593-4600   Fax: (402)331-1505

Annual. $3,130.00. Entries include: Name, address, phone, size of advertisement, name of owner or manager, number of employees, year first in Yellow Pages. Regional editions available: Compiled from telephone company Yellow Pages, nationwide. Arrangement: Geographical.

★4426★ Attorneys' Service Bureaus Directory
American Business Directories, Inc.
American Business Information, Inc.
5711 S. 86th Cir.
Omaha, NE 68127
Ph: (402)593-4600   Fax: (402)331-1505

Updated continuously; printed on request. Please inquire. Entries include: Name, address, phone, size of advertisement, name of owner or manager, number of employees, year first in Yellow Pages. Compiled from telephone company Yellow Pages, nationwide. Arrangement: Geographical.

★4427★ Best Lawyers in America
Woodward/White, Inc.
129 1st Ave. SW
Aiken, SC 29801
Ph: (803)648-0300   Fax: (803)641-1709

Biennial, January of odd years. $110.00. Covers approximately 13,500 attorneys selected as the best in their specialties by a survey of about 15,000 lawyers. Entries include: Individual or firm name, address,

phone, and subspecialties of interest. Arrangement: Geographical, then classified by legal specialty.

★4428★ Canada Legal Directory
Carswell Publishers
Thompson Canada Ltd.
2075 Kennedy Rd.
Scarborough, ON, Canada M1T 3V4
Ph: (416)298-5141   Fax: (416)298-5094

Annual, January. $95.00. Covers about 45,000 lawyers, judges, and court officials in Canada. Entries include: Firm name, address, phone, telecommunications numbers, names of individual attorneys. Arrangement: Geographical by province, then by city. Indexes: Personal name.

★4429★ Canadian Law List
Canada Law Book, Inc.
240 Edward St.
Aurora, ON, Canada L4G 3S9
Ph: (905)841-6472   Fax: (905)841-5085

Annual, January. $99.00. Covers 55,000 legal firms and attorneys, courts, related government ministries, and law schools; primarily in Canada, with some international coverage. Entries include: For firms and organizations: company or organization name, address, phone, fax, names and titles of key personnel, number of employees, geographical area served, and branch office or subsidiary names and addresses. For individuals: name, address, phone, corporate affiliation (if any), biographical data. Arrangement: Geographical.

★4430★ Decalogue Society of Lawyers—Directory of Members
Decalogue Society of Lawyers
39 S. La Salle, No. 410
Chicago, IL 60603
Ph: (312)263-6493   Fax: (312)263-6512

Annual. Available only to members, law students, and advertisers. Covers about 1,500 lawyers of the Jewish faith. Entries include: Name, address, phone. Arrangement: Alphabetical.

★4431★ Directory of Opportunities in International Law
John Bassett Moore Society of
  International Law
School of Law
University of Virginia
Charlottesville, VA 22901
Ph: (804)296-1467

Irregular. Latest edition February 1992. $10.00, to students, payment with order.; $20.00, to others. Covers several hundred possible employers of specialists in international law, including United States and foreign law firms, United Nations agencies, governmental organizations and bodies; also includes lists of law schools which include international law in their programs, sponsors of fellowships, volunteer programs. Entries include: For law firms: name, address, phone, approximate number of attorneys hired per year, hiring prerequisites, branch offices. For other organizations: name, address, phone, branch offices, languages preferred, fellowships offered, hiring require-

ments. Arrangement: Law firms are geographical; others are by type of organization.

★4432★ Directory of Public Interest Law Centers
Alliance for Justice
1601 Connecticut Ave. NW, Ste. 601
Washington, DC 20009
Ph: (202)332-3224   Fax: (202)265-2150

Annual, November. $6.00. Covers about 200 nonprofit, groups that provide legal assistance and referral for under-represented interests in courts and agencies. Entries include: Name, address, phone, branch office locations, executive director. Arrangement: Alphabetical. Indexes: Geographical, program emphasis.

★4433★ District of Columbia Bar—Legal Services Sourcebook
District of Columbia Bar
1250 H St. NW
Washington, DC 20005
Ph: (202)737-4700   Fax: (202)626-3471

Irregular, latest edition spring 1994. $5.00, includes shipping. Covers about 300 lawyers in Washington, D.C.; all listings are paid. Entries include: Name, address, phone, fields of special interest or competency, fees for common legal procedures. Arrangement: Classified by legal specialty. Indexes: Alphabetical, language fluency, bar admissions.

★4434★ Federal Careers for Attorneys
Federal Reports Inc.
1010 Vermont Ave. NW, Ste. 408
Washington, DC 20005
Ph: (202)393-3311   Fax: (202)393-1553
Fr: 800-296-9611

Latest edition 1991. $23.95. Covers over 300 U.S. government general counsel and other legal offices throughout the Federal system. Entries include: Agency's name, address, mission, work of the office, divisions/structures, number of attorneys, hiring procedures, special recruitment programs, and locations of regional/field offices. Arrangement: Geographical. Indexes: Legal specialty and geographical.

★4435★ Insider's Guide to Law Firms
Mobius Press
PO Box 3339
Boulder, CO 80307
Ph: (303)543-9429   Fax: (303)499-5289
Fr: 800-LAW-JOBS

Annual, August. $28.95. Covers Over 200 major law firms throughout twelve major U.S. cities: Atlanta, Baltimore, Boston, Chicago, Dallas, Houston, Los Angeles, New York, Philadelphia, Pittsburgh, San Francisco/Palo Alto, and Washington. Entries include: Firm name, address, phone, name and title of contact, names and titles of key personnel, number of partners and associates, salary information, percentage of pro bono work, summer opportunities, area of practice, subsidiary and branch names and locations, description. Arrangement: Geographical. Indexes: Firm name.

★4436★ International Law and Practice—Leadership Directory

International Law and Practice Section
American Bar Association (ABA)
1800 M St. NW, Ste. 450-S.
Washington, DC 20036-5886
Ph: (202)331-2239

Annual. Available to members only. Covers over 12,800 member lawyers, judges, law students, and law clerks; international coverage. Entries include: Name, address, phone.

★4437★ Law & Business Directory of Litigation Attorneys

Prentice Hall Law & Business
270 Sylvan Ave.
Englewood Cliffs, NJ 07632-2521
Ph: (201)894-8484   Fax: (201)894-8666
Fr: 800-223-0231

Annual, October. $360.00. Covers more than 40,000 litigating attorneys and nearly 15,000 law firms with which the attorneys are affiliated; covers more than 100 subject fields. Entries include: For attorneys: Name, address, phone, fax, biographical data, firm and organization affiliations, date joined firm, areas of concentration, contingency fee acceptance, courts and percentage of time in each, recent cases and publications. For firms: company name, address, phone, fax, branch offices, concentrations, number of attorneys, number of litigation attorneys. Arrangement: Geographical by city and state. Indexes: Attorney name, law firm name, area of concentration.

★4438★ Law Firms Yellow Book

Leadership Directories, Inc.
104 5th Ave., 2nd Fl.
New York, NY 10011
Ph: (212)627-4140   Fax: (212)645-0931

Semiannual, winter and summer. $180.00 per year. Covers Approximately 700 large law firms and over 17,000 attorneys and administrators at more than 3,000 domestic and foreign offices, subsidiaries, and affiliates. Entries include: Firm name, address, phone, fax, telex, year founded, description of practice; officers' names, titles, phone numbers, and law schools attended, addresses, phone numbers, and principal officials at branch offices. Arrangement: Alphabetical by firm name. Indexes: Geographical, administrative, law school, individual name, specialty, law firm.

★4439★ Law and Legal Information Directory

Gale Research
835 Penobscot Bldg.
Detroit, MI 48226-4094
Ph: (313)961-2242   Fax: (313)961-6083
Fr: 800-877-GALE

Biennial, October of even years. $320.00. Covers more than 33,000 national and international organizations, bar associations, federal and highest state courts, federal regulatory agencies, law schools, firms and organizations offering continuing legal education, paralegal education, sources of scholarships and grants, awards and prizes, special libraries, information systems and services, research centers, publishers of legal periodicals, books, and audiovisual materials, lawyer referral services, legal aid offices, public defender offices, legislature manuals and registers, small claims courts, corporation departments of state, law enforcement agencies, state agencies, including disciplinary agencies, and state bar requirements. Entries include: All entries include institution or firm name, address, phone; many include names and titles of key personnel and, when pertinent, descriptive annotations. Arrangement: Classified by type of organization, activity, service, etc. Indexes: Individual sections have special indexes as required.

★4440★ Lawyers' List

Commercial Publishing Co., Inc.
20 W. Dover St.
Easton, MD 21601
Ph: (410)820-4494   Fax: (410)820-4474

Annual, April. $75.00. Covers about 2,500 lawyers in general, corporate, trial, patent, trademark, and copywrite practices in the United States. Entries include: Firm name, address, phone, type of practice, names of representative clients, names of partners and associates. Arrangement: Geographical.

★4441★ Lawyer's Register International by Specialties and Fields of Law Including a Directory of Corporate Counsel

Lawyer's Register Publishing Co.
28790 Chagrin Blvd., Ste. 140
Cleveland, OH 44122
Ph: (216)591-1492   Fax: (216)591-0265
Fr: 800-477-6345

Irregular, latest edition June 1994. $129.50. Covers corporate legal staffs worldwide; legal firms; independent practicing attorneys each identified as a specialist in one or more fields of law. Entries include: In corporate section Corporation, subsidiary, and department names; address, phone, fax; names and titles of legal staff, law schools attended, specialties. In fields of law sections Name, address, phone, fax, specialties. A general international/corporate law list. Incorporates Lawyer to Lawyer Consultation Panel. Arrangement: Separate sections for specializing lawyers and their firms and corporate counsel.

★4442★ Martindale-Hubbell Bar Register of Preeminent Lawyers

Martindale-Hubbell
Reed Reference Publishing
121 Chanlon Rd.
New Providence, NJ 07974
Ph: (908)464-6800   Fax: (908)464-3553
Fr: 800-526-4902

Annual. $159.55. Covers over 23,000 of today's most skilled attorneys and law partnerships and firms. Entries include: Firm name, telephone, fax, members, associate clients, and name and title of contact. Arrangement: Geographical.

★4443★ Martindale-Hubbell Canadian Law Directory

National Register Publishing
Reed Reference Publishing
121 Chanlon Rd.
New Providence, NJ 07974
Ph: (908)464-6800   Fax: (908)771-7704
Fr: 800-521-8110

$75.00. Covers Thousands of Canadian attorneys, law firms, and corporate law departments, as well as U.S. laywers interested in receiving referrals from Canada. Indexes: Alphabetical, Area of Practice.

★4444★ Martindale-Hubbell Law Directory

Martindale-Hubbell
Reed Reference Publishing
121 Chanlon Rd.
New Providence, NJ 07974
Ph: (908)464-6800   Fax: (908)464-3553
Fr: 800-526-4902

Annual, February. $660.00, plus $60.00 shipping. Covers lawyers and law firms in the United States, its possessions, and Canada, plus leading law firms worldwide; includes a biographical section by firm, and a separate list of patent lawyers, attorneys in government service, in-house counsel, and services, suppliers, and consultants to the legal profession. Entries include: For non-subscribing lawyers: name, year of birth and of first admission to bar, code indicating college and law school attended and first degree, firm name (or other affiliation, if any) and relationship to firm, whether practicing other than as individual or in partnership. For subscribing lawyers: above information plus complete address, phone, fax, type of practice, clients, plus additional personal details (education, certifications, etc.). Arrangement: Geographical. Indexes: Alphabetical, area of practice.

★4445★ National Association for Law Placement Directory of Legal Employers

National Association for Law Placement
1666 Connecticut Ave., Ste. 325
Washington, DC 20009
Ph: (202)667-1666   Fax: (202)265-6735

Annual. Database covers: Over 1,300 employers of legal professionals in the U.S., including law firms, corporate legal departments, local and federal government agencies, and public interest organizations. Entries include: Organization name, address, phone, practice specialties, organization and demographics, recruiting and promotion patterns, job opportunities.

★4446★ National Directory of Prosecuting Attorneys

National District Attorneys Association
99 Canal Center Plaza, Ste. 510
Alexandria, VA 22314
Ph: (703)549-9222   Fax: (703)836-3195

Biennial, spring of even years. $15.00, payment with order. Covers about 2,800 elected or appointed local prosecuting attorneys. Entries include: Name, address, phone, jurisdiction. Arrangement: Geographical. Indexes: Alphabetical.

★4447★ National Hispanic American Attorney Directory

Hispanic National Bar Association (HNBA)
c/o Carlos Ortiz
Goya Foods
100 Seaview Dr.
Secaucus, NJ 07096
Ph: (201)348-4900   Fax: (201)348-6609

Irregular, latest edition January 1994. Available to members only. Covers Approximately 8,000 Hispanic American lawyers. Entries include: Name, business address, phone, fax, home phone, area of practice. Arrangement: Alphabetical. Indexes: Geographical; area of practice.

★4448★ National Institute of Municipal Law Officers–Directory of Officers and Sections

National Institute of Municipal Law Officers (NIMLO)
1000 Connecticut Ave. NW, Ste. 902
Washington, DC 20036
Ph: (202)466-5424   Fax: (202)785-0152

Description: Annual, winter. Available to members only. Covers members of NIMLO committees. Entries include: Name and title of member, address, phone, fax. Arrangement: Classified by sections, officers, and membership department.

★4449★ Nelson's Law Office Directory

The Nelson Co.
PO Box 309
Hopkins, MN 55343

Annual, April. $23.00. Covers Top rated law offices in the United States chosen by peers on the basis of legal ability, integrity, and diligence. Most offices have a general practice. Entries include: Office name, address, phone, fax. See separate listing, Law Lists. Arrangement: Geographical.

★4450★ NLADA Directory of Legal Aid and Defender Offices in the United States and Territories

National Legal Aid and Defender Association (NLADA)
1625 K St. NW, Ste. 800
Washington, DC 20006
Ph: (202)452-0620   Fax: (202)872-1031

Biennial, August of odd years. $30.00, payment must accompany order. Covers about 3,600 civil legal aid and indigent defense organizations in the United States; includes programs for specific groups such as prisoners, senior citizens, the disabled, etc. Entries include: Agency name, address, phone, director's name. Arrangement: Geographical. Indexes: Type of service.

★4451★ Now Hiring: Government Jobs for Lawyers

American Bar Association (ABA)
750 N. Lake Shore Dr.
Chicago, IL 60611
Ph: (312)988-5555   Fax: (312)988-6281

Irregular, latest edition 1991. $14.95, plus $3.95 shipping. Covers over 100 offices of the federal government, quasi-government, and independent agencies. Entries include: Organization name, contact name and address, application deadline, number of attorneys employed and number of anticipated openings, location of positions, salaries and qualifications, nature of legal work performed by office, advancement opportunities. Arrangement: By government agency.

★4452★ Russell Law List

Commercial Publishing Co.
20 W. Dover St.
Easton, MD 21601
Ph: (410)820-8089   Fax: (410)820-4474

Annual, April. Restricted circulation. Covers law offices (limited one to a city) in general practice, worldwide. Entries include: Name, address, phone, telex, fax, cable address. A general law list. Arrangement: Geographical.

★4453★ United States Bar Directory

Attorneys' National Clearing House Co.
PO Box 8688
Naples, FL 33941
Ph: (813)263-0840

Annual, October. $19.95. Covers over 3,000 general and specialized practice attorneys employed through correspondence. Entries include: Firm name, address, phone, preferred fields of practice. Arrangement: Geographical.

★4454★ United States Lawyers Reference Directory

Legal Directories Publishing Co.
9111 Garland Rd.
PO Box 189000
Dallas, TX 75218-9000
Ph: (214)321-3238   Fr: 800-447-5375

Annual, latest edition 1994-1995. $150.00. Covers Subscribing attorneys and principal personnel of county, state, and federal governments, and court personnel.

★4455★ Who's Who in American Law

Marquis Who's Who
Reed Reference Publishing
121 Chanlon Rd.
New Providence, NJ 07974
Ph: (908)464-6800   Fax: (908)665-6688
Fr: 800-521-8110

Biennial, latest edition February 1994. $249.95 plus 17.50 shipping. Covers over 27,800 lawyers, judges, law school deans and professors, and other legal professionals. Entries include: Name, home and office addresses, place and date of birth, educational background, career history, civic positions, professional memberships, publications, awards, special achievements. Arrangement: Alphabetical.

★4456★ Wright-Holmes Law List

Wright-Holmes, Inc.
852 1st Ave., S
Naples, FL 33940
Ph: (813)434-8880   Fax: (813)434-5983

Annual, April. Covers about 2,000 commercial law firms. Entries include: Firm name, address, phone. A commercial law list. Arrangement: Geographical.

HANDBOOKS AND MANUALS

★4457★ Career Choices for the 90's for Students of History

Walker and Company
435 Hudson St.
New York, NY 10014
Ph: (212)727-8300   Fax: (212)727-0984
Fr: 800-289-2553

Prepared by the Career Associates staff. 1990. $8.95. 166 pages. Discusses alternatives for students of history. Offers advice on how to break into the field and how to move up. Covers where and who the employers are, internship possibilities, and professional networking associations. Comprehensive guide to career and job search planning.

★4458★ Career Choices for the 90's for Students of Law

Walker and Company
435 Hudson St.
New York, NY 10014
Ph: (212)727-8300   Fax: (212)727-0984
Fr: 800-289-2553

Prepared by the Career Associates staff. 1990. $8.95. 166 pages. Discusses career alternatives and offers advice on how to break in and move up. Covers where and who the employers are, internship possibilities, and professional networking associations. Comprehensive guide to career and job search planning.

★4459★ Career Choices for the 90's for Students of Political Science and Government

Walker and Company
435 Hudson St.
New York, NY 10014
Ph: (212)727-8300   Fax: (212)727-0984
Fr: 800-289-2553

Prepared by the Career Associates staff. 1990. $8.95. 166 pages. Discusses alternatives for students of political science and government. Offers advice on how to break into the field and how to move up. Covers where and who the employers are, internship possibilities, and professional networking associations. Comprehensive guide to career and job search planning.

★4460★ Career Information Center

Macmillan Publishing Co.
200 Old Tappan Rd.
Old Tappan, NJ 07675
Ph: (609)461-6500   Fr: 800-223-2336

Visual Education Center Staff. Fifth edition, 1992. $229.00. This 13-volume set profiles over 600 occupations. Each occupational profile describes job duties, educational requirements, how to get the job, advancement possibilities, employment outlook, working conditions, earnings and benefits, and where to write for more information.

★4461★ Careers in Law

VGM Career Horizons
4255 W. Touhy Ave.
Lincolnwood, IL 60646-1975
Ph: (847)679-5500   Fax: (847)679-2494
Fr: 800-323-4900

Gary Munneke. 1992. $17.95; $13.95 (paper). Overview of opportunities available to lawyers in private practice, corporate law, in federal, state, and local governments, and in teaching. Provides information on the typical law school curriculum plus opportunities in internships and clerkships.

★4462★ The Encyclopedia of Career Choices for the 1990s: Guide to Entry-Level Jobs

Perigree Books
The Berkley Publishing Group
PO Box 506
East Rutherford, NJ 07073
Ph: (201)933-9292   Fr: 800-223-0510

Career Associates Staff. 1992. $19.95. 862 pages. Describes 500 entry-level careers in a variety of industries. Presents qualifications required, working conditions, salary, internships, and professional associations.

★4463★ Flying High in Travel

John Wiley and Sons
605 3rd Ave.
New York, NY 10158
Ph: (212)850-6000   Fr: 800-225-5945

Karen Rubin. Second edition, 1992. $19.95. 336 pages. A guide to careers and job hunting in the travel industry. Describes the many job opportunities available, from writing to hotel management to law. Includes information on educational preparation, training, and job hunting.

★4464★ Guide to Careers in World Affairs

Impact Publications
9104-N Manassas Dr.
Manassas Park, VA 22111-5211
Ph: (703)361-7300   Fax: (703)335-9486

Foreign Policy Association. 1993. $14.95. 331 pages. Describes jobs in business, government, and nonprofit organizations. Explains the methods and credentials required to secure a job in many fields, including international law and journalism. Contains sections on internships and graduate programs.

★4465★ The Lawyer's Almanac, 1995

Aspen Law & Business
200 Orchard Ridge Dr.
Gaithersburg, MD 20878
Ph: (301)417-9075   Fax: 800-901-9075
Fr: 800-638-8437

1995. $116.00.

★4466★ Lawyer's Desk Book

Prentice Hall
113 Sylvan Ave., Rte. 9W
Englewood Cliffs, NJ 07632
Ph: (201)592-2000   Fax: 800-445-6991
Fr: 800-922-0579

1995.

★4467★ Liberal Arts Jobs: What They Are and How to Get Them

Peterson's
PO Box 2123
Princeton, NJ 08543-2123
Ph: (609)243-9111   Fax: (609)243-9150
Fr: 800-338-3282

Burton Jay Nadler. Second edition, 1989. $9.95. 153 pages. Presents a list of the top 20 fields for liberal arts majors, covering more than 300 job opportunities. Discusses strategies for going after those jobs, including guidance on the language of a successful job search, informational interviews, and making networking work.

★4468★ My First Year As a Lawyer: Real-World Stories from America's Lawyers

Walker & Co.
435 Hudson St.
New York, NY 10014
Ph: (212)727-8300   Fax: (212)727-0984
Fr: 800-289-2553

Mark Simenhoff, editor. 1994. $19.95.

★4469★ 100 Best Careers for the Year 2000

Prentice Hall General Reference
15 Columbus Cir.
New York, NY 10023
Ph: (212)373-8500   Fr: 800-223-2348

Shelly Field. 1992. $15.00 (paper). Covers 100 of the fastest growing jobs. The publication is divided into 11 general employment sections. Specific careers are covered within each section. Provides job description, responsibilities, employment opportunities, earnings, education and training, advancement opportunities, and experience and qualifications for each occupation.

★4470★ Opportunities in Gerontology and Aging Services Careers

VGM Career Horizons
4255 W. Touhy Ave.
Lincolnwood, IL 60646-1975
Ph: (847)679-5500   Fax: (847)679-2494
Fr: 800-323-4900

Ellen Williams. 1995. $14.95; $11.95 (paper). 160 pages. Covers jobs in community, health and medical programs, financial, legal, residential, travel and tourism, and counseling, and how to go after them. Includes bibliography and illustrations.

★4471★ Opportunities in Law Careers

VGM Career Horizons
4255 W. Touhy Ave.
Lincolnwood, IL 60646-1975
Ph: (847)679-5500   Fax: (847)679-2494
Fr: 800-323-4900

Gary A. Munneke. 1994. $14.95; $11.95 (paper). 160 pages. Covers the entire range of careers in law, from admission to law school to finding the job in private practice, corporate law, public interest law, or teaching.

★4472★ Opportunities in State and Local Government Careers

VGM Career Horizons
4255 W. Touhy Ave.
Lincolnwood, IL 60646-1975
Ph: (847)679-5500   Fax: (847)679-2494
Fr: 800-323-4900

Neale Baxter. 1993. $13.95; $10.95 (paper). 160 pages. Points out the incentives and drawbacks of a government career. Describes hiring procedures and provides tips on filling out applications, taking physical and aptitude tests, handling interviews, and finding jobs. Describes the jobs in which 75% of all state and local government workers are employed. For each occupation, covers the nature of the work and the training required.

★4473★ Professional Skills for Lawyers: A Student's Guide

Butterworth U.S., Legal Publishers, Inc.
8 Industrial Way., Bldg. C
Salem, NH 03079-2837
Ph: (603)890-6001   Fax: (603)898-9858
Fr: 800-548-4001

1994. $33.00 (paper).

★4474★ Where the Jobs Are: The Hottest Careers for the '90s

The Career Press, Inc.
3 Tice Rd.
PO Box 687
Franklin Lakes, NJ 07417
Ph: (201)848-0310   Fax: (201)848-1727
Fr: 800-237-3371

Joyce Hadley. Second edition, 1995. $9.99. 300 pages. Describes careers in fifteen general fields, from accounting to travel and hospitality.

EMPLOYMENT AGENCIES AND SEARCH FIRMS

★4475★ Attorney Resource, Inc.

2301 Cedar Springs Rd.
Dallas, TX 75201-6901
Ph: (214)922-8050

Employment agency. Offices in Fort Worth, TX, and Tulsa, OK. Provides staffing assistance on regular or temporary basis.

★4476★ Bader Research Corp.

6 E. 45th St.
New York, NY 10017
Ph: (212)682-4750   Fax: (212)682-4758

Executive search firm.

★4477★ Bellon and Associates, Inc.

1175 Peachtree St. NE
100 Colony Sq., Ste. 1920
Atlanta, GA 30361
Executive search firm.

★4478★ **Beverly Hills Bar Association Personnel Service**

300 S. Beverly Dr., Ste. 214
Beverly Hills, CA 90212
Ph: (213)553-4575

Employment agency.

★4479★ **Coleman Legal Search Consultants**

The Drexel Bldg.
1435 Walnut St.
Philadelphia, PA 19102-3222
Ph: (215)864-2700

Executive search firm.

★4480★ **Conaway Legal Search**

112 Hawthorn Rd.
Baltimore, MD 21210
Ph: (410)539-1234   Fax: (410)539-2734

Executive search firm.

★4481★ **Continental Field Service Corp.**

37 E. Main St.
Elmsford, NY 10523-2607
Ph: (914)592-7240

Employment agency.

★4482★ **E.J. Ashton and Associates, Ltd.**

3125 N. Wilke Rd.
Arlington Heights, IL 60004-1452
Ph: (708)577-7900

Employment agency. Executive search firm.

★4483★ **Gillard Associates Legal Search**

850 Providence Hwy., Ste. 305
Dedham, MA 02026
Ph: (617)329-4731   Fax: (617)329-1357

Employment agency.

★4484★ **Henry Labus Personnel**

820 Ford Bldg.
Detroit, MI 48226
Ph: (313)962-4461

Employment agency.

★4485★ **Legal Briefs, Inc.**

327 Merritt Dr.
Oradell, NJ 07649
Ph: (201)967-7073

Employment agency. Executive search firm.

★4486★ **Legal Placement Services, Inc.**

161 W. Wisconsin Ave., Ste. 3054
Milwaukee, WI 53203
Ph: (414)276-6689

Employment agency.

★4487★ **Major, Hagen, and Africa**

655 Commercial St.
San Francisco, CA 94111
Ph: (415)956-1010   Fax: (415)398-2425

Executive search firm. Affiliate offices in Atlanta, GA, Chicago, IL, and New York, NY.

★4488★ **Parks Associates**

342 Madison Ave., Ste. 1430
New York, NY 10173
Ph: (212)286-0777   Fax: (212)286-1973

Employment agency.

★4489★ **Phyllis Hawkins and Associates**

3550 N. Central Ave., Ste. 1400
Phoenix, AZ 85012
Ph: (602)263-0248   Fax: (602)263-1016

Executive search firm.

★4490★ **Raymond Smith and Associates**

Cary Oaks Executive Bldg.
8807 Cary-Algonquin Rd.
Cary, IL 60013
Ph: (708)639-8250

Executive search firm.

★4491★ **Wichita Bar and Legal Placement**

301 N. Main, Ste. 700
Wichita, KS 67202
Ph: (316)263-2469

Employment agency.

OTHER SOURCES

★4492★ *American Almanac of Jobs and Salaries 1994-95*

Avon Books
1350 Avenue of the Americas, 2nd Fl.
New York, NY 10019
Ph: (212)261-6800   Fr: 800-238-0658

John Wright. Revised edition, 1993. $17.00. 704 pages. This is a comprehensive guide to the wages of hundreds of occupations in a wide variety of industries and organizations.

★4493★ **American Bar Association (ABA)**

750 N. Lake Shore Dr.
Chicago, IL 60611
Ph: (312)988-5000   Fax: (312)988-6281
Fr: 800-285-2221

Members: Attorneys in good standing of the bar of any state. **Purpose:** Conducts research and educational projects and activities to: encourage professional improvement; provide public services; improve the administration of civil and criminal justice; increase the availability of legal services to the public. Sponsors Law Day USA. Administers numerous standing and special committees such as Committee on Soviet and East European Law, providing seminars and newsletters. **Activities:** Operates 25 sections, including Criminal Justice, Economics of Law Practice, and Family Law. Sponsors essay competitions. Maintains library.

★4494★ **American Blind Lawyers Association (ABLA)**

1155 15th St. NW, Ste. 720
Washington, DC 20005
Ph: (202)467-5081   Fr: 800-424-8666

Members: Blind lawyers and blind law students. **Purpose:** Seeks to: provide a forum for discussion of the special problems encountered by blind persons licensed to practice law and by blind students training for the legal profession; protect the interests of blind members of the legal profession; acquire, preserve, and maintain law libraries and periodicals of special interest to blind lawyers and blind law students; promote the production of and disseminate information concerning legal materials in braille or recorded form; advance the legal profession.

★4495★ **American Intellectual Property Law Association (AIPLA)**

2001 Jefferson Davis Hwy., Ste. 203
Arlington, VA 22202
Ph: (703)415-0780   Fax: (703)415-0786

Members: Voluntary bar association of lawyers practicing in the fields of patents, trademarks, and copyrights. **Purpose:** Aids in the operation and improvement of U.S. patent, trademark, and copyright systems, including the laws by which they are governed and rules and regulations under which federal agencies administer those laws. **Activities:** Sponsors moot court and legal writing competitions. Offers resume service. Compiles statistics.

★4496★ *Becoming a Lawyer: A Humanistic Perspective on Legal Education, Professionalism*

West Publishing Co., College & School Division
610 Opperman Dr.
PO Box 64526
St. Paul, MN 55164-0526
Ph: (612)687-8000   Fr: 800-328-9424

Elizabeth Dvorkin. 1993. $17.50 (paper).

★4497★ *Getting into Law School Today*

Prentice Hall General Reference & Travel
15 Columbus Cir.
New York, NY 10023
Ph: (212)373-8500   Fax: 800-445-6991
Fr: 800-223-2348

Thomas H. Martinson. 1994. $12.00 (paper).

★4498★ *Handy Hints on Legal Practice*

Gaunt, Inc.
3011 Gulf Dr.
Holmes Beach, FL 34218
Ph: (941)778-5211   Fax: (941)778-5252
Fr: 800-942-8683

Gordon D. Lewis. 1993. $45.00 (paper).

★4499★ **Libel Defense Resource Center (LDRC)**

404 Park Ave. S., 16th Fl.
New York, NY 10016
Ph: (212)889-2306   Fax: (212)689-3315

Purpose: Provides support for media defendants in libel and privacy cases, including development of statistical and empirical data, assistance in locating expert witnesses or consultants, and help in coordinating amicus curiae briefs by supporting organizations. Maintains a brief, pleading, and information bank; collects and disseminates information on pending libel and privacy cases for use in legal defense against claims. **Activities:** Compiles statistics on the incidence and cost of libel and privacy litigation. Provides employment for law student interns. Conducts educational and training workshops and programs; has established fellowship program in libel law. Operates LDRC Institute.

★4500★ National Association for Law Placement (NALP)

1666 Connecticut Ave., Ste. 325
Washington, DC 20009
Ph: (202)667-1666   Fax: (202)265-6735

Members: Law schools, legal employers, and bar associations actively engaged in the recruitment and placement of lawyers. **Purpose:** To: provide for the creation and maintenance of standards and ethical procedures to guide law schools and employers in career services and recruitment; promote the exchange of ideas, information, and experiences; develop resource materials and edu-cational programs; enlist employers and law schools in developing well-coordinated placement and recruiting services; provide means for member organizations to participate in an affirmative policy against discrimination in employment. **Activities:** Conducts annual survey of law school graduates and other research.

★4501★ National Association for Public Interest Law (NAPIL)

22nd St. NW, 3rd Fl.
Washington, DC 20037
Ph: (202)466-3686   Fax: (202)429-9766

Members: Coalition of law student public interest organizations. **Purpose:** Strives to educate and prepare future lawyers to redress inequities in the U.S. legal system and to dedicate their professional lives to the development of a more just society. Works to: create public interest legal employment and training opportunities; remove economic barriers confronting future public interest lawyers; provide resources for public service work. **Activities:** Serves as clearinghouse and public education and training center.

★4502★ Running from the Law

Ten Speed Press
PO Box 7123
Berkeley, CA 94707
Ph: (510)559-1600   Fax: (510)559-1629
Fr: 800-841-BOOK

Deborah Arron. 1991. $11.95. 208 pages. Offers career-changing suggestions and support for lawyers.

★4503★ U.S. Travel Data Center (USTDC)

1100 New York Ave., NW, Ste. 450
Washington, DC 20005
Ph: (202)408-1832   Fax: (202)408-1255

Purpose: Conducts statistical, economic, and market research concerning travel; encourages standardized travel research terminology and techniques. Program objectives include: monitoring trends in travel activity and the travel industry; measuring the economic impact of travel on geographic areas; evaluating the effect of government programs on travel and the travel industry; measuring the cost of travel in the U.S.

Legal Assistants

Sources of Help-Wanted Ads

★4504★ Job Announcements

National Center for State Courts
300 Newport Ave.
Williamsburg, VA 23187
Ph: (804)253-2000

Semimonthly. $30.00/year. Provides lists of court-related job openings in the United States and its territories.

★4505★ The Journal of Taxation

Warren, Gorham Lamont
1 Penn Plaza
New York, NY 10119
Ph: (212)971-5185   Fax: (212)971-5025
Fr: 800-950-1252

Monthly. $170.00/year for individuals. Journal for professional tax practitioners.

★4506★ National and Federal Legal Employment Report

Federal Reports Inc.
1010 Vermont Ave. NW, Ste. 408
Washington, DC 20005
Ph: (202)393-3311   Fax: (202)393-1553
Fr: 800-296-9611

Monthly. $111.20 for individuals; $147.20 for institution. Publication includes: Listings of approximately 600 current attorney and law-related job opportunities with the U.S. government and other public and private employers in Washington D.C., nationwide, and abroad. Includes positions for contract specialists, attorney-advisors, legal assistants, investigators, court researchers, and public defenders. Arrangement: Geographical.

★4507★ National Paralegal Reporter

National Federation of Paralegal
  Associations (NFPA)
PO Box 33108
Kansas City, MO 64114
Ph: (816)941-4000

Quarterly. $20.00/year.

★4508★ Public Interest Employment Service Job Alert

Public Interest Clearing House
200 McAllister St.
San Francisco, CA 94102-4978
Ph: (415)255-1714

Semimonthly. $120.00/year for employed persons; $60.00/year for unemployed. Lists job openings in legal aid offices, public interest law firms, and nonprofit organizations.

Placement and Job Referral Services

★4509★ National Association of Black Women Attorneys (NABWA)

724 9th St. NW, Ste. 206
Washington, DC 20001
Ph: (202)637-3570   Fax: (202)637-4892

Members: Black women who are members of the bar of any U.S. state or territory; associate members include law school graduates, paralegals, and law students. **Purpose:** Seeks to: advance jurisprudence and the administration of justice by increasing the opportunities of black and non-black women at all levels; aid in protecting the civil and human rights of all citizens and residents of the U.S.; expand opportunities for women lawyers through education; promote fellowship among women lawyers. **Activities:** Provides pre-law and student counseling; serves as job placement resource for firms, companies, and others interested in the field. Holds regional seminars. Maintains hall of fame; offers charitable program.

★4510★ National Association of Para-Legals Personnel (NAP-LP)

PO Box 8202
Northfield, IL 60093

Activities: Maintains registry of paralegal personnel in the profession. Conducts charitable program; operates hall of fame. Conducts educational program and placement service.

★4511★ National Paralegal Association (NPA)

Box 406
Solebury, PA 18963
Ph: (215)297-8333   Fax: (215)297-8358

Members: Paralegals, paralegal students, educators, supervisors, paralegal schools, administrators, law librarians, law clinics, and attorneys. **Purpose:** Objective is to advance the paralegal profession by promoting recognition, economic benefits, and high standards. **Activities:** Registers paralegals; maintains speakers' bureau, job bank, and placement service; offers resume preparation assistance. Sponsors commercial exhibits. Operates mail order bookstore and gift shop. Compiles statistics. Is developing promotion and public relations, insurance, certification, and computer bank programs.

Employer Directories and Networking Lists

★4512★ Directory of Opportunities in International Law

John Bassett Moore Society of
  International Law
School of Law
University of Virginia
Charlottesville, VA 22901
Ph: (804)296-1467

Irregular. Latest edition February 1992. $10.00, to students, payment with order.; $20.00, to others. Covers several hundred possible employers of specialists in international law, including United States and foreign law firms, United Nations agencies, governmental organizations and bodies; also includes lists of law schools which include international law in their programs, sponsors of fellowships, volunteer programs. Entries include: For law firms: name, address, phone, approximate number of attorneys hired per year, hiring prerequisites, branch offices. For other organizations: name, address, phone, branch offices, languages preferred, fellowships offered, hiring requirements. Arrangement: Law firms are geographical; others are by type of organization.

★4513★ Law and Legal Information Directory

Gale Research
835 Penobscot Bldg.
Detroit, MI 48226-4094
Ph: (313)961-2242   Fax: (313)961-6083
Fr: 800-877-GALE

Biennial, October of even years. $320.00. Covers more than 33,000 national and international organizations, bar associations, federal and highest state courts, federal regulatory agencies, law schools, firms and organizations offering continuing legal education, paralegal education, sources of scholarships and grants, awards and prizes, special libraries, information systems and services, research centers, publishers of legal periodicals, books, and audiovisual materials, lawyer referral services, legal aid offices, public defender offices, legislature manuals and registers, small claims courts, corporation departments of state, law enforcement agencies, state agencies, including disciplinary agencies, and state bar requirements. Entries include: All entries include institution or firm name, address, phone; many include names and titles of key personnel and, when pertinent, descriptive annotations. Arrangement: Classified by type of organization, activity, service, etc. Indexes: Individual sections have special indexes as required.

★4514★ Lawyer's Register International by Specialties and Fields of Law Including a Directory of Corporate Counsel

Lawyer's Register Publishing Co.
28790 Chagrin Blvd., Ste. 140
Cleveland, OH 44122
Ph: (216)591-1492   Fax: (216)591-0265
Fr: 800-477-6345

Irregular, latest edition June 1994. $129.50. Covers corporate legal staffs worldwide; legal firms; independent practicing attorneys each identified as a specialist in one or more fields of law. Entries include: In corporate section Corporation, subsidiary, and department names; address, phone, fax; names and titles of legal staff, law schools attended, specialties. In fields of law sections Name, address, phone, fax, specialties. A general international/corporate law list. Incorporates Lawyer to Lawyer Consultation Panel. Arrangement: Separate sections for specializing lawyers and their firms and corporate counsel.

★4515★ Martindale-Hubbell Law Directory

Martindale-Hubbell
Reed Reference Publishing
121 Chanlon Rd.
New Providence, NJ 07974
Ph: (908)464-6800   Fax: (908)464-3553
Fr: 800-526-4902

Annual, February. $660.00, plus $60.00 shipping. Covers lawyers and law firms in the United States, its possessions, and Canada, plus leading law firms worldwide; includes a biographical section by firm, and a separate list of patent lawyers, attorneys in government service, in-house counsel, and services, suppliers, and consultants to the legal profession. Entries include: For non-subscribing lawyers: name, year of birth and of first

admission to bar, code indicating college and law school attended and first degree, firm name (or other affiliation, if any) and relationship to firm, whether practicing other than as individual or in partnership. For subscribing lawyers: above information plus complete address, phone, fax, type of practice, clients, plus additional personal details (education, certifications, etc.). Arrangement: Geographical. Indexes: Alphabetical, area of practice.

★4516★ National Association for Law Placement Directory of Legal Employers

National Association for Law Placement
1666 Connecticut Ave., Ste. 325
Washington, DC 20009
Ph: (202)667-1666   Fax: (202)265-6735

Annual. Database covers: Over 1,300 employers of legal professionals in the U.S., including law firms, corporate legal departments, local and federal government agencies, and public interest organizations. Entries include: Organization name, address, phone, practice specialties, organization and demographics, recruiting and promotion patterns, job opportunities.

★4517★ Nelson's Law Office Directory

The Nelson Co.
PO Box 309
Hopkins, MN 55343

Annual, April. $23.00. Covers Top rated law offices in the United States chosen by peers on the basis of legal ability, integrity, and diligence. Most offices have a general practice. Entries include: Office name, address, phone, fax. See separate listing, Law Lists. Arrangement: Geographical.

HANDBOOKS AND MANUALS

★4518★ Career Choices for the 90's for Students of English

Walker and Company
435 Hudson St.
New York, NY 10014
Ph: (212)727-8300   Fax: (212)727-0984
Fr: 800-289-2553

Prepared by the Career Associates staff. 1990. $8.95. 166 pages. Discusses alternatives for students of English. Offers advice on how to break into the field and how to move up. Covers where and who the employers are, internship possibilities, and professional networking associations. Comprehensive guide to career and job search planning.

★4519★ Career Choices for the 90's for Students of History

Walker and Company
435 Hudson St.
New York, NY 10014
Ph: (212)727-8300   Fax: (212)727-0984
Fr: 800-289-2553

Prepared by the Career Associates staff. 1990. $8.95. 166 pages. Discusses alternatives for students of history. Offers advice on how to break into the field and how to move up. Covers where and who the employers

are, internship possibilities, and professional networking associations. Comprehensive guide to career and job search planning.

★4520★ Career Information Center

Macmillan Publishing Co.
200 Old Tappan Rd.
Old Tappan, NJ 07675
Ph: (609)461-6500   Fr: 800-223-2336

Visual Education Center Staff. Fifth edition, 1992. $229.00. This 13-volume set profiles over 600 occupations. Each occupational profile describes job duties, educational requirements, how to get the job, advancement possibilities, employment outlook, working conditions, earnings and benefits, and where to write for more information.

★4521★ Career Opportunities for Writers

Facts on File, Inc.
11 Penn Plaza, 15th Fl.
New York, NY 10001-2006
Ph: (212)967-8800   Fax: 800-678-3633
Fr: 800-322-8755

Rosemary Guiley. Third edition, 1995. $29.95; $15.95 (paper). Describes more than 100 jobs in eight major fields, offering such details as duties, salaries, perquisites, employment and advancement opportunities, organizations to join, and opportunities for women and minorities.

★4522★ Careers in Law

VGM Career Horizons
4255 W. Touhy Ave.
Lincolnwood, IL 60646-1975
Ph: (847)679-5500   Fax: (847)679-2494
Fr: 800-323-4900

Gary Munneke. 1992. $17.95; $13.95 (paper). Overview of opportunities available to lawyers in private practice, corporate law, in federal, state, and local governments, and in teaching. Provides information on the typical law school curriculum plus opportunities in internships and clerkships.

★4523★ CLA Review Manual: A Practical Guide to CLA Exam Preparation

West Publishing Co.
610 Opperman Dr.
PO Box 64526
St. Paul, MN 55164-0526
Ph: (612)687-8000   Fr: 800-328-9424

Compiled by National Association of Legal Assistants. 1993. $67.00 (paper).

★4524★ Effective Interviewing for Paralegals

Anderson Publishing Co.
PO Box 1576
Cincinnati, OH 45201-1576
Ph: (513)421-4142   Fr: (513)562-8180

Fred E. Jandt. 1994.

★4525★ The Encyclopedia of Career Choices for the 1990s: Guide to Entry-Level Jobs

Perigree Books
The Berkley Publishing Group
PO Box 506
East Rutherford, NJ 07073
Ph: (201)933-9292   Fr: 800-223-0510

Career Associates Staff. 1992. $19.95. 862 pages. Describes 500 entry-level careers in a variety of industries. Presents qualifications required, working conditions, salary, internships, and professional associations.

★4526★ Everything You Need to Know About Being a Legal Assistant

Delmar Publishers
3 Columbia Cir., Box 15015
Albany, NY 12212
Ph: (518)464-3500   Fax: (518)464-0358
Fr: 800-347-7707

Chere B. Estrin. 1995. $20.95. 224 p.

★4527★ The Independent Paralegal's Handbook

Nolo Press
950 Parker St.
Berkeley, CA 94710
Ph: (510)549-1976   Fax: 800-645-0895
Fr: 800-992-6656

Ralph E. Warner. 1994. $29.95 (paper).

★4528★ Life Outside the Law Firm: Non-Traditional Careers for Paralegals

Delmar Publishers
3 Columbia Cir., Box 15015
Albany, NY 12212
Ph: (518)464-3500   Fax: (518)464-0358
Fr: 800-347-7707

Karen Treffinger. 1995. $21.95 (paper).

★4529★ Mastering the CLA: The NALTT Review

National Association for Legal Testing and Training
17337 Ventura Blvd., Ste. 112
Encino, CA 91316
Ph: (818)386-1160   Fax: (818)789-7183
Fr: 800-316-2588

1993. $99.00 (paper).

★4530★ 100 Best Careers for the Year 2000

Prentice Hall General Reference
15 Columbus Cir.
New York, NY 10023
Ph: (212)373-8500   Fr: 800-223-2348

Shelly Field. 1992. $15.00 (paper). Covers 100 of the fastest growing jobs. The publication is divided into 11 general employment sections. Specific careers are covered within each section. Provides job description, responsibilities, employment opportunities, earnings, education and training, advancement opportunities, and experience and qualifications for each occupation.

★4531★ Opportunities in Paralegal Careers

VGM Career Horizons
4255 W. Touhy Ave.
Lincolnwood, IL 60646-1975
Ph: (847)679-5500   Fax: (847)679-2494
Fr: 800-323-4900

Alice Fins. 1990. $14.95; $11.95 (paper). 160 pages. Defines job opportunities and provides advice about identifying and obtaining positions. Includes bibliography and illustrations.

★4532★ Opportunities in Vocational and Technical Careers

VGM Career Horizons
4255 W. Touhy Ave.
Lincolnwood, IL 60646-1975
Ph: (847)679-5500   Fax: (847)679-2494
Fr: 800-323-4900

Adrian A. Paradis. 1992. $14.95; $11.95 (paper). 160 pages. Provides information on a variety of opportunities and advice on breaking into the field.

★4533★ Paralegal: An Insider's Guide to One of the Fastest-Growing Occupations of the 1990s

Peterson's Guides, Inc.
PO Box 2123
Princeton, NJ 08543-2123
Ph: (609)243-9111   Fax: (609)243-9150
Fr: 800-338-3282

Barbara Bernardo. 1993. $11.95 (paper).

★4534★ Paralegal Employment: Facts and Strategies for the 1990's

West Publishing Company
PO Box 64526
610 Opperman Dr.
St. Paul, MN 55164-0526
Ph: (612)687-8000   Fr: 800-328-9424

William P. Statsky. Second edition, 1993. $23.25. 200 pages. Contains index.

★4535★ Paralegal Internships Manual

Pearson Publications Co.
5910 N. Central Expy., Ste. 1070
Dallas, TX 75206
Ph: (214)891-6332   Fax: (214)891-6335

Charles P. Nemeth. 1995.

★4536★ Paralegal Practice and Procedure: A Practical Guide for The Legal Assistant

Prentice Hall
113 Sylvan Ave., Rte. 9W
Englewood Cliffs, NJ 07632
Ph: (201)592-2000   Fr: 800-922-0579

Deborah E. Larbales. 1994. $19.95 (paper).

★4537★ The Paralegal's Guide to U.S. Government Jobs: How to Land a Job in 70 Law-Related Career Fields

Federal Reports, Inc.
1010 Vermont Ave. NW, Ste. 408
Washington, DC 20005
Ph: (202)393-3311

Richard L. Hermann and Linda P. Sutherland. Sixth edition, 1993. $16.00. 132 pages. Explains U.S. Government procedures and describes 70 law-related federal careers for which paralegals may qualify. Includes a directory of several hundred Federal Agency personnel offices that hire the most paralegal and law-related talents.

★4538★ Starting and Managing Your Own Business: A Freelancing Guide for Paralegals

John Wiley & Sons, Inc.
605 3rd Ave.
New York, NY 10158-0012
Ph: (212)850-6000   Fr: 800-225-5945

Dorothy Secol. 1994. $68.00.

★4539★ Where the Jobs Are: The Hottest Careers for the '90s

The Career Press, Inc.
3 Tice Rd.
PO Box 687
Franklin Lakes, NJ 07417
Ph: (201)848-0310   Fax: (201)848-1727
Fr: 800-237-3371

Joyce Hadley. Second edition, 1995. $9.99. 300 pages. Describes careers in fifteen general fields, from accounting to travel and hospitality.

★4540★ Your Opportunities in Legal Support

Energeia Publishing, Inc.
PO Box 985
Salem, OR 97308
Ph: (503)362-1480   Fax: (503)362-2123

Laurie Bean. 1994. $2.00 (paper).

EMPLOYMENT AGENCIES AND SEARCH FIRMS

★4541★ Attorney Resource, Inc.

2301 Cedar Springs Rd.
Dallas, TX 75201-6901
Ph: (214)922-8050

Employment agency. Offices in Fort Worth, TX, and Tulsa, OK. Provides staffing assistance on regular or temporary basis.

★4542★ Beverly Hills Bar Association Personnel Service

300 S. Beverly Dr., Ste. 214
Beverly Hills, CA 90212
Ph: (213)553-4575

Employment agency.

★4543★ Bill Young and Associates

8550 Arlington Blvd., Ste. 202
Fairfax, VA 22031
Ph: (703)573-0200   Fax: (703)573-3612

Employment agency.

★4544★ Coleman Legal Search Consultants

The Drexel Bldg.
1435 Walnut St.
Philadelphia, PA 19102-3222
Ph: (215)864-2700

Executive search firm.

★4545★ Conaway Legal Search

112 Hawthorn Rd.
Baltimore, MD 21210
Ph: (410)539-1234   Fax: (410)539-2734

Executive search firm.

★4546★ Fergus Legal Search and Consulting, Inc.

350 5th Ave., Ste. 5809
New York, NY 10118
Ph: (212)947-1775   Fax: (212)594-9740

Employment agency.

★4547★ Gillard Associates Legal Search

850 Providence Hwy., Ste. 305
Dedham, MA 02026
Ph: (617)329-4731   Fax: (617)329-1357

Employment agency.

★4548★ Lawstaf, Inc.

1201 W. Peachtree St. NE, Ste. 4830
Atlanta, GA 30309
Ph: (404)872-6672   Fax: (404)892-3180

Employment agency.

★4549★ Legal Placement Services, Inc.

161 W. Wisconsin Ave., Ste. 3054
Milwaukee, WI 53203
Ph: (414)276-6689

Employment agency.

★4550★ Legal Staffing, Inc.

1100 Milam St., Ste. 2070
Houston, TX 77002-5505
Ph: (713)650-8195

Employment agency.

★4551★ Mark Associates

300 Montgomery St., Ste. 860
San Francisco, CA 94104-1910
Ph: (415)392-1835

Employment agency.

★4552★ Opportunities Unlimited

53 W. Jackson, Ste. 215
Chicago, IL 60604
Ph: (312)922-8898   Fax: (312)347-1206

Employment agency.

★4553★ Parks Associates

342 Madison Ave., Ste. 1430
New York, NY 10173
Ph: (212)286-0777   Fax: (212)286-1973

Employment agency.

★4554★ The Pathfinder Group

295 Danbury Rd.
Wilton, CT 06897-3095
Ph: (203)834-2467

Employment agency. Executive search firm. Recruits staff in a variety of fields.

★4555★ Staley/Adams and Associates Personnel Services Inc.

4615 Post Oak Pl.
Houston, TX 77027-9731
Ph: (713)965-0402

Employment agency.

★4556★ Wichita Bar and Legal Placement

301 N. Main, Ste. 700
Wichita, KS 67202
Ph: (316)263-2469

Employment agency.

OTHER SOURCES

★4557★ American Almanac of Jobs and Salaries 1994-95

Avon Books
1350 Avenue of the Americas, 2nd Fl.
New York, NY 10019
Ph: (212)261-6800   Fr: 800-238-0658

John Wright. Revised edition, 1993. $17.00. 704 pages. This is a comprehensive guide to the wages of hundreds of occupations in a wide variety of industries and organizations.

★4558★ Day in a Career: Paralegal

Cambridge Career Products
PO Box 2153
Dept. CC15
Charleston, WV 25328-2153
Ph: (304)744-9323   Fax: (304)744-9351
Fr: 800-468-4227

Video. 1994. $89.00. 15-22 minutes. Includes candid interviews and work situations, plus outlines of relevant career information.

★4559★ Federal Law-Related Careers Directory

Federal Reports Inc.
1010 Vermont Ave. NW, Ste. 408
Washington, DC 20005
Ph: (202)393-3311   Fax: (202)393-1553
Fr: 800-296-9611

Irregular. $16.95 postpaid. Publication includes: Listings of over 1,000 federal government recruiting offices. Entries include: Agency name, address, how to apply, and hiring procedure. Principal content of publication is the description of over 150 law-related careers in the U.S. government for which a law degree is an asset, but not a requirement, including contract specialist, criminal investigator, legal research analyst, and labor relations specialist. Arrangement: Classified by by subject.

★4560★ National Association of Legal Assistants (NALA)

1516 S. Boston, Ste. 200
Tulsa, OK 74119
Ph: (918)587-6828   Fax: (918)582-6772

Members: Professional paralegals employed for over six months; graduates or students of legal assistant training programs; attorneys. Members subscribe to and are bound by the NALA Code of Ethics and Professional Responsibility. **Purpose:** Cooperates with local, state, and national bar associations in setting standards and guidelines for legal assistants. Promotes the profession and attempts to broaden public understanding of the function of the legal assistant. **Activities:** Offers continuing education for legal assistants both nationwide and statewide, and professional certification on a national basis to members and nonmembers who meet certain criteria. Conducts regional seminars; publishes books and quarterly journal. **Website:** http://www.nala.org

★4561★ National Federation of Paralegal Associations (NFPA)

PO Box 33108
Kansas City, MO 64114-0108
Ph: (816)941-4000   Fax: (816)941-2725

Members: State and local paralegal associations and other organizations supporting the goals of the federation; individual paralegals. **Purpose:** To serve as a national voice of the paralegal profession; to advance, foster, and promote the paralegal concept; to monitor and participate in developments in the paralegal profession; to maintain a nationwide communications network among paralegal associations and other members of the legal community. **Activities:** Provides a resource center of books, publications, and literature of the field. Monitors activities of local, state, and national bar associations and legislative bodies; presents testimony on matters affecting the profession. Has established a 15-member advisory council of attorneys, paralegals, educators, paralegal administrators, and members of the public to advise on policy and issues of concern to the paralegal and legal professions. **E-Mail:** info@paralysis.org

★4562★ Now Hiring: Government Jobs for Lawyers

American Bar Association (ABA)
750 N. Lake Shore Dr.
Chicago, IL 60611
Ph: (312)988-5555   Fax: (312)988-6281

Irregular, latest edition 1991. $14.95, plus $3.95 shipping. Covers over 100 offices of the federal government, quasi-government, and independent agencies. Entries include: Organization name, contact name and address, application deadline, number of attorneys employed and number of anticipated openings, location of positions, salaries and qualifications, nature of legal work performed by office, advancement opportunities. Arrangement: By government agency.

Librarians

SOURCES OF HELP-WANTED ADS

★4563★ AJL Newsletter

Association of Jewish Libraries
15 E. 26th St., Rm. 1034
New York, NY 10010-1579
Ph: (212)678-8092   Fax: (212)678-8998

Quarterly. Focuses on activities related to the Judaica Library. Includes job listings.

★4564★ Base Line

Map and Geography Round Table
(MAGERT)
American Library Association (ALA)
50 E. Huron St.
Chicago, IL 60611
Ph: (312)280-3205   Fax: (312)280-3257
Fr: 800-545-2433

Bimonthly. Included in membership; $15.00/year for nonmembers and Canada; $20.00/year elsewhere. Provides current information on cartographic materials, publications of interest to map and geography librarians, related government activities, and map librarianship. Recurring features include conference and meeting information, news of research, job listings, and columns by the Division chair and the editor.

★4565★ The Chronicle of Higher Education

The Chronicle of Higher Education
1255 23rd St. NW, Ste. 700
Washington, DC 20037
Ph: (202)466-1000   Fax: (202)296-2691
Fr: 800-347-6969

Weekly. $67.50/year for individuals; $2.75 for single issue. Higher education magazine (tabloid).

★4566★ Computers in Libraries

VR World
20 Ketchum St.
Westport, CT 06880
Ph: (203)226-6967

Monthly. $87.00/year for individuals. Library science and computer magazine.

★4567★ Current Openings in Education in U.S.A.

Education Information Service
PO Box 660662
Newton, MA 02162-0662
Ph: (617)443-0125

Seven times/year. $8.00/issue. Publication is a booklet listing about 140 institutions or school systems, each with one to a dozen or more openings for teachers, librarians, counselors, administrators, and other personnel.

★4568★ Foreign Faculty and Administrative Openings

Education Information Service
Box 662
Newton, MA 02162
Ph: (617)237-0887

Approximately every six weeks. $9.00. Covers approximately 150 specific openings in administration, counseling, library, teaching and other disciplines for American teachers in American schools overseas and in international schools, both of which must teach English as a primarily language. Entries include: Institution name, address.

★4569★ Information Today

Information Today, Inc.
143 Old Marlton Pke.
Medford, NJ 08055-8707
Ph: (609)654-6266   Fax: (609)654-4309

Monthly. User and producer magazine (tabloid) covering electronic and optical information services.

★4570★ Library Journal

Conners Publishing
245 W. 17th St.
New York, NY 10011
Ph: (212)463-6835   Fax: (212)463-6836

$87.50/year for individuals. Library management and book selection journal.

★4571★ Opening List of Professional Openings in American Overseas & International Schools

Education Information Services
Instant Alert
PO Box 662
Newton, MA 02162-0002
Ph: (617)237-0887

Every 6 weeks. $9.00. Covers about 150 current professional openings for teachers, administrators, counselors, librarians, and educational specialists in American overseas schools and international schools at which the teaching language is primarily English. Also covers English as a Second/Foreign Language (ESL-EFL) at all age levels. Entries include: Institute name, address, names and titles of key personnel, positions available.

★4572★ School Library Journal

Conners Publishing
245 W. 17th St.
New York, NY 10011
Ph: (212)463-6835   Fax: (212)463-6836

$74.50/year for individuals; $99.00/year for Canada.

★4573★ TEST Engineering & Management

The Mattingley Publishing Co., Inc.
3756 Grand Ave., Ste. 205
Oakland, CA 94610
Ph: (510)839-0909   Fax: (510)839-2950

Bimonthly. $30.00/year for individuals; $40.00/year for other countries; $5.00 for single issue. Reliability/qualifications test engineering magazine.

★4574★ Wilson Library Bulletin

The H.W. Wilson Co.
950 University Ave.
Bronx, NY 10452
Ph: (718)588-8400   Fax: (718)681-1511
Fr: 800-367-6770

Monthly. Magazine for library professionals.

PLACEMENT AND JOB REFERRAL SERVICES

★4575★ African Studies Association (ASA)

Emory University
Credit Union Bldg.
Atlanta, GA 30322
Ph: (404)329-6410   Fax: (404)329-6433

Members: Persons specializing in teaching, writing, or research on Africa including political scientists, historians, geographers, anthropologists, economists, librarians, linguists, and government officials; persons who are studying African subjects; institutional members are universities, libraries, government agencies, and others interested in receiving information about Africa. **Purpose:** Seeks to foster communication and to stimulate research among scholars on Africa. **Activities:** Sponsors placement service; conducts panels and discussion groups; presents exhibits and films. **E-Mail:** africa@mony.edu

★4576★ American Association of Law Libraries (AALL)

53 W. Jackson Blvd., Ste. 940
Chicago, IL 60604
Ph: (312)939-4764   Fax: (312)431-1097

Members: Librarians who serve the legal profession in the courts, bar associations, law societies, law schools, private law firms, federal, state, and county governments, and business; associate members are legal publishers and other interested persons. **Purpose:** Sponsors institutes which are generally held in mid-winter and in the summer during the week preceding the annual meeting; directs procedure for exchange of duplicate materials among law libraries. **Activities:** Maintains placement service.

★4577★ American Library Association (ALA)

50 E. Huron St.
Chicago, IL 60611
Ph: (312)944-6780   Fax: (312)280-3255
Fr: 800-545-2433

Members: Librarians, libraries, trustees, friends of libraries, and others interested in the responsibilities of libraries in the educational, social, and cultural needs of society. **Purpose:** Promotes and improves library service and librarianship. Establishes standards of service, support, education, and welfare for libraries and library personnel; promotes the adoption of such standards in libraries of all kinds; safeguards the professional status of librarians; encourages the recruiting of competent personnel for professional careers in librarianship; promotes popular understanding and public acceptance of the value of library service and librarianship. **Activities:** Works in liaison with federal agencies to initiate the enactment and administration of legislation that will extend library services. Offers placement services.

★4578★ American Society for Information Science (ASIS)

8720 Georgia Ave., Ste. 501
Silver Spring, MD 20910-3602
Ph: (301)495-0900   Fax: (301)495-0810

Members: Information specialists, scientists, librarians, administrators, social scientists, and others interested in the use, organization, storage, retrieval, evaluation, and dissemination of recorded specialized information. **Purpose:** Seeks to improve the information transfer process through research, development, application, and education. Provides a forum for the discussion, publication, and critical analysis of work dealing with the theory, practice, research, and development of elements involved in communication of information. **Activities:** Maintains placement service. Members are engaged in a variety of activities and specialties including classification and coding systems, automatic and associative indexing, machine translation of languages, special librarianship and library systems analysis, and copyright issues. Sponsors National Auxiliary Publications Service, which provides reproduction services and a central depository for all types of information (operated for ASIS by Microfiche Publications). Sponsors numerous special interest groups. Conducts continuing education programs and professional development workshops. **E-Mail:** asis@cni.org

★4579★ Asian/Pacific American Librarians Association (APALA)

Michigan Initiative for Women's Health
University of Michigan
Rm. 4222, 400 NIB
Ann Arbor, MI 48109
Ph: (313)332-0390   Fax: (313)332-0390

Members: Librarians and information specialists of Asian Pacific descent working in the U.S.; interested persons. **Purpose:** Provides a forum for discussing problems and concerns; supports and encourages library services to Asian Pacific communities; recruits and supports Asian Pacific Americans in the library and information science professions. **Activities:** Offers placement service; compiles statistics. Conducts fundraising for scholarships. **E-Mail:** MLI@ZODIAC

★4580★ Association of College and Research Libraries (ACRL)

50 E. Huron St.
Chicago, IL 60611-2795
Ph: (312)280-3248   Fax: (312)280-2520
Fr: 800-545-2433

A division of the American Library Association. **Members:** Academic and research librarians. **Purpose:** Seeks to improve the quality of service in academic libraries; promotes the professional and career development of academic and research librarians; represents the interests and supports the programs of academic and research libraries. **Activities:** Operates placement services; sponsors specialized education and research grants and programs; gathers, compiles, and disseminates statistics. Establishes and adopts standards; maintains publishing program; offers professional development courses.

★4581★ Association of Jewish Libraries (AJL)

15 E. 26th St., Rm. 1034
New York, NY 10010-1579
Ph: (212)678-8092   Fax: (212)678-8998

Purpose: Works to advance the interests of Jewish libraries and promote publications of Jewish bibliographical interest. **Activities:** Provides placement and library consultant services.

★4582★ Association for Library and Information Science Education (ALISE)

4101 Lake Boone Trl., Ste. 201
Raleigh, NC 27607
Ph: (919)787-5181   Fax: (919)787-4916

Members: Graduate schools offering degree programs in library science and their faculties. **Purpose:** Seeks to: promote excellence in education for library and information science as a means of increasing the effectiveness of library and information services; provide a forum for the active interchange of ideas and information among library educators; promote research related to teaching and to library and information science; formulate and promulgate positions on matters related to library education. **Activities:** Offers employment program.

★4583★ Association of Seventh-Day Adventist Librarians (ASDAL)

Columbia Union College Library
Takoma Park, MD 20912-7796
Ph: (301)891-4222   Fax: (301)891-4204

Members: Librarians belonging to the Seventh-Day Adventist church. **Purpose:** To enhance communication among members; serve as a forum for discussion of mutual problems and professional concerns; promote librarianship and library services to Seventh-Day Adventist institutions. **Activities:** Sponsors D. Glenn Hilts Scholarship for graduate studies. Maintains placement service. Compiles statistics.

★4584★ Chinese American Librarians Association (CALA)

Sheila Lai
CSU, Sacramento
2000 Jed Smith Dr.
Sacramento, CA 95819-6039
Ph: (916)278-6201   Fax: (916)363-0868

Purpose: Promotes better communication among Chinese American librarians in the U.S., serves as a forum for the discussion of mutual problems, and supports the development and promotion of librarianship. **Activities:** Maintains placement referral service.

★4585★ Health Sciences Communications Association (HESCA)

1 Wedgewood Dr.
Jewett City, CT 06351
Ph: (203)376-5915   Fax: (203)376-6621

Members: Media managers, graphic artists, biomedical librarians, producers, faculty members of health science and veterinary medicine schools, health professional organizations, and industry representatives. **Purpose:** Acts as a clearinghouse for information used by professionals engaged in health science communications. Coordinates Media

Festivals Program which recognizes outstanding media productions in the health sciences. **Activities:** Offers placement service.

★4586★ Medical Library Association (MLA)

6 N. Michigan Ave., Ste. 300
Chicago, IL 60602
Ph: (312)419-9094   Fax: (312)419-8950

Members: Librarians and others engaged in professional library or bibliographical work in medical and allied scientific libraries. **Purpose:** To foster medical and allied scientific libraries, to promote the educational and professional growth of health science librarians, and to exchange medical literature among members. **Activities:** Offers continuing education courses, certification and recertification programs, and placement service. Compiles statistics.

★4587★ Music Library Association (MLA)

PO Box 487
Canton, MA 02021
Ph: (617)828-8450   Fax: (617)828-8915

Purpose: Promotes the establishment, growth, and use of music libraries and collection of music, musical instruments, musical literature, and audiovisual aids. **Activities:** Maintains placement service.

★4588★ Special Libraries Association (SLA)

1700 18th St. NW
Washington, DC 20009-2508
Ph: (202)234-4700   Fax: (202)265-9317

Members: International association of information professionals who work in special libraries serving business, research, government, universities, newspapers, museums, and institutions that use or produce specialized information. **Purpose:** Seeks to advance the leadership role of special librarians. Offers consulting services to organizations that wish to establish or expand a library or information services. Conducts continuing education courses, public relations, and government relations programs. **Activities:** Provides employment services. Operates Information Resources Center on topics pertaining to the development and management of special libraries. Maintains Hall of Fame. **E-Mail:** SLA@CAPON.NET

EMPLOYER DIRECTORIES AND NETWORKING LISTS

★4589★ American Library Directory

R. R. Bowker Co.
Reed Reference Publishing
121 Chanlon Rd.
New Providence, NJ 07974
Ph: (908)464-6800   Fax: (908)771-7704
Fr: 800-521-8110

Annual, June. $235.00. Covers over 35,000 U.S. and Canadian academic, public, county, provincial, and regional libraries; library systems; medical, law, and other special librar-

ies; and libraries for the blind and physically handicapped. Separate section lists over 350 library networks and consortia and 220 accredited and unaccredited library school programs. Entries include: For libraries: Name, supporting or affiliated institution or firm name, address, phone, fax, electronic mail address, Standard Address Number (SANs), names of librarian and department heads, income, collection size, special collections, computer hardware, automated functions, and type of catalog. For library systems: Name, location. For library schools: Name, address, phone, fax, electronic mail address, director, type of training and degrees, admission requirements, tuition, faculty size. For networks and consortia: Name, address, phone, names of affiliates, name of director, function. Arrangement: Geographical. Indexes: Institution name.

★4590★ Directory of Federal Libraries

Oryx Press
4041 N. Central, No. 700
Phoenix, AZ 85012-3397
Ph: (602)265-2651   Fax: 800-279-4663
Fr: 800-279-6799

Irregular. Latest edition January 1993. $97.50. Covers nearly 3,000 libraries serving branches of the federal government. Entries include: Library name, type, address, phone, fax, name of administrator and selected staff, special collections, database services available, depository status for documents from the Government Printing Office or other organizations, involvement with cooperative library organizations, electronic mail or cataloging networks, whether accessible to the public. Arrangement: Classified by federal establishment. Indexes: Library type, subject, geographical.

★4591★ Directory of Special Libraries and Information Centers

Gale Research
835 Penobscot Bldg.
Detroit, MI 48226-4094
Ph: (313)961-2242   Fax: (313)961-6083
Fr: 800-877-GALE

Annual. Three volumes: Volume 1, "Directory of Special Libraries and Information Centers", $475.00; Volume 2 "Geographic and Personnel Indexes", $395.00; Volume 3, "New Special Libraries", $390.00. Covers over 19,000 special libraries, information centers, documentation centers, etc., in the United States, Canada, and 80 other countries. Provides comprehensive information about the library or information center's services, facilities, holdings, availability, and staff.

★4592★ Employment Sources in the Library & Information Professions

Office for Library Personnel Resources (OLPR)
American Library Association (ALA)
50 E. Huron St.
Chicago, IL 60611
Ph: (312)280-4277   Fax: (312)280-3256

Annual, spring. Free. Covers library job sources, such as specialized and state and regional library associations, state library agencies, federal library agencies, and overseas exchange programs. Entries include:

Library, company, or organization name, address, phone; contact name, description of services, publications, etc. Arrangement: Classified by type of source.

★4593★ International Association of School Librarianship—Membership Directory

International Association of School Librarianship
PO Box 19586
Kalamazoo, MI 49019
Ph: (616)343-5728   Fax: (616)387-4079

Annual, October. $15.00. Covers 800 members engaged in some form of school library service; international coverage. Entries include: Name, address, institution. Arrangement: Geographical.

HANDBOOKS AND MANUALS

★4594★ Career Information Center

Macmillan Publishing Co.
200 Old Tappan Rd.
Old Tappan, NJ 07675
Ph: (609)461-6500   Fr: 800-223-2336

Visual Education Center Staff. Fifth edition, 1992. $229.00. This 13-volume set profiles over 600 occupations. Each occupational profile describes job duties, educational requirements, how to get the job, advancement possibilities, employment outlook, working conditions, earnings and benefits, and where to write for more information.

★4595★ Career Opportunities in Art

Facts on File, Inc.
11 Penn Plaza, 15th Fl.
New York, NY 10001-2006
Ph: (212)967-8800   Fax: 800-678-3633
Fr: 800-322-8755

Susan H. Haubenstock and David Joselit. Revised edition, 1994. $29.95; $15.95 (paper). 208 pages. This book profiles seventy-five jobs that can be found in the art field. Each profile includes a career description, career ladder, employment and advancement prospects, education, experience and skills required, salary range, and tips for entry into the field.

★4596★ Career Opportunities for Writers

Facts on File, Inc.
11 Penn Plaza, 15th Fl.
New York, NY 10001-2006
Ph: (212)967-8800   Fax: 800-678-3633
Fr: 800-322-8755

Rosemary Guiley. Third edition, 1995. $29.95; $15.95 (paper). Describes more than 100 jobs in eight major fields, offering such details as duties, salaries, perquisites, employment and advancement opportunities, organizations to join, and opportunities for women and minorities.

★4597★ Careers for Bookworms and Other Literary Types

VGM Career Horizons
4255 W. Touhy Ave.
Lincolnwood, IL 60646-1975
Ph: (847)679-5500   Fax: (847)679-2494
Fr: 800-323-4900

Marjorie Eberts and Margaret Gisler. Second edition, 1995. $14.95; $9.95 (paper). Details opportunities in education, publishing, libraries, journalism, think tanks, museums, film, broadcasting, the public sector, and other fields. Helps job seekers identify reading, writing, or research jobs.

★4598★ Careers in Health Care

VGM Career Horizons
4255 W. Touhy Ave.
Lincolnwood, IL 60646-1975
Ph: (847)679-5500   Fax: (847)679-2494
Fr: 800-323-4900

Barbara M. Swanson. 1995. $17.95; $13.95 (paper). Describes job duties, work settings, salaries, licensing and certification requirements, educational preparation, and future outlook. Gives ideas on how to secure a job.

★4599★ Extending the Librarian's Domain: A Survey of Emerging Occupational Opportunities for Librarians & Information Professionals

Special Libraries Association
1700 18th St. NW
Washington, DC 20009
Ph: (202)234-4700   Fax: (202)265-9317

1994. $29.00 (paper)

★4600★ How to Get a Job in Education

Bob Adams, Inc.
260 Center St.
Holbrook, MA 02343
Ph: (617)767-8100   Fax: (617)767-0994
Fr: 800-872-5627

Joel Levin. Second edition, 1995. $12.95. 320 pages. Prepared for recent college graduates, seasoned educators, and career-changing professionals, this publication guides the job-seeker through the necessary steps to obtaining a job in education at the elementary, secondary, and university levels. Offers advice on how to prepare for state and local examinations, how to locate teaching opportunities nationwide, and how to obtain certification. Includes a nationwide salary survey. Covers public, private, summer, and overseas opportunities.

★4601★ Librarianship & Information Work Worldwide: An Annual Survey

Reed Reference Publishing
121 Chanlon Rd.
New Providence, NJ 07974
Ph: (908)464-6800   Fax: (908)665-6707
Fr: 800-521-8110

Maurice B. Line. 1995. $100.00.

★4602★ Library Employment Within the Law

Neal-Schuman Publishers, Inc.
100 Varick St.
New York, NY 10013
Ph: (212)925-8650   Fax: (212)219-8916

Arlene C. Bielefield. 1993. $35.00.

★4603★ MLA Salary Survey

Medical Library Association
6 N. Michigan Ave., Ste. 300
Chicago, IL 60602-4805
Ph: (312)419-9094   Fax: (312)419-8950

1995. $60.00 (paper).

★4604★ Opportunities in Library and Information Science Careers

VGM Career Horizons
4255 W. Touhy Ave.
Lincolnwood, IL 60646-1975
Ph: (847)679-5500   Fax: (847)679-2494
Fr: 800-323-4900

Peggy Sullivan and Margaret Myers. 1992. $13.95; $10.95 (paper). 160 pages. A guide to planning for and seeking opportunities in this changing field. Includes bibliography and illustrations.

★4605★ Opportunities in State and Local Government Careers

VGM Career Horizons
4255 W. Touhy Ave.
Lincolnwood, IL 60646-1975
Ph: (847)679-5500   Fax: (847)679-2494
Fr: 800-323-4900

Neale Baxter. 1993. $13.95; $10.95 (paper). 160 pages. Points out the incentives and drawbacks of a government career. Describes hiring procedures and provides tips on filling out applications, taking physical and aptitude tests, handling interviews, and finding jobs. Describes the jobs in which 75% of all state and local government workers are employed. For each occupation, covers the nature of the work and the training required.

★4606★ Special Librarianship As a Career: An SLA Information Kit

Special Libraries Association
1700 18th St., NW
Washington, DC 20009
Ph: (202)234-4700   Fax: (202)265-9317

1995. $60.00 (paper).

EMPLOYMENT AGENCIES AND SEARCH FIRMS

★4607★ Advanced Information Management

444 Castro St., Ste. 320
Mountain View, CA 94041
Ph: (415)965-7799

Employment agency. Fills openings on a regular, temporary, or contractual basis.

★4608★ C. Berger and Company

327 E. Gundersen Dr.
Carol Stream, IL 60188
Ph: (708)653-1115   Fax: (708)653-1691

Employment agency. Executive search firm. Recruits staff on a regular, temporary, or contractual basis.

★4609★ C.F. Heller Associates, Inc.

2 W. 45th St.
New York, NY 10036
Ph: (212)819-1919   Fax: (212)819-9196

Employment agency.

★4610★ Gossage Regan Associates

25 W. 43rd St., Ste. 812
New York, NY 10036
Ph: (212)869-3348

Employment agency. Concentrates in placement of library and information professionals on permanent basis nationwide.

★4611★ Hunter Mac and Associates

139 Fulton St.
New York, NY 10038
Ph: (212)267-2790   Fax: (212)962-2339

Employment agency.

★4612★ Pro Libra Associates, Inc.

6 Inwood Pl.
Maplewood, NJ 07040-2529
Ph: (201)762-0070

Employment agency. Handles temporary or permanent placement of staff.

OTHER SOURCES

★4613★ American Almanac of Jobs and Salaries 1994-95

Avon Books
1350 Avenue of the Americas, 2nd Fl.
New York, NY 10019
Ph: (212)261-6800   Fr: 800-238-0658

John Wright. Revised edition, 1993. $17.00. 704 pages. This is a comprehensive guide to the wages of hundreds of occupations in a wide variety of industries and organizations.

★4614★ Art Libraries Society/North America (ARLIS/NA)

4101 Lake Boone Trl., Ste. 201
Raleigh, NC 27607-7506
Ph: (919)787-5181   Fax: (919)787-4916
Fr: 800-89-ARLIS

Members: Individuals and institutions interested in art librarianship and visual resources curatorship (in public libraries, museums, galleries, art schools, universities, colleges, and publishing houses). **Purpose:** Acts as forum for exchange of materials and information on documentation of the visual arts.

★4615★ Career Encounters: Information Science and Technology

Cambridge Career Products
PO Box 2153
Dept. CC15
Charleston, WV 25328-2153
Ph: (304)744-9323   Fax: (304)744-9351
Fr: 800-468-4227

Video. $99.95. 25 minutes. Professionals shown in a variety of settings discuss different aspects of their careers.

★4616★ *How to Run a Lending Library, a Book Store, or Both*

Mokelumne Hill Press
PO Box 70
Mokelumne Hill, CA 95245
Ph: (209)667-8876

Health Research Staff. 1994. $3.30.

★4617★ *Journal of Documentation*

Learned Information, Inc.
143 Old Marlton Pke.
Medford, NJ 08055-8750
Ph: (609)654-6266   Fax: (609)654-4309

Quarterly. $210.00/year. Reference magazine covering librarianship and information science.

★4618★ North American Serials Interest Group (NASIG)

2103 N. Decatur Rd., No. 214
Decatur, GA 30033

Members: Librarians; subscription vendors; publishers; serial automation experts; serials binders; library science educators; others involved in serials management. **Purpose:** Promotes educational and social networking among members. Participates in the prelimi-nary organization of standards and guidelines. **Activities:** Disseminates information.

★4619★ Online Hotline News Service

Information Intelligence, Inc.
PO Box 31098
Phoenix, AZ 85046
Ph: (602)996-2283   Fr: 800-228-9982

Online database containing five files, one of which is Joblines, which features listings of employment and resume services available in voice, print, and online throughout North America. Joblines focuses on the online, library automation, and information-related fields.

★4620★ *Recruiting, Educating & Training Librarians for Collection Development*

Greenwood Publishing Group, Inc.
88 Post Rd. W., Box 5007
Westport, CT 06881
Ph: (203)226-3571   Fax: (203)222-1502
Fr: 800-225-5800

Peggy Johnson. 1994. $55.00.

★4621★ *The Reference Librarian*

The Haworth Press, Inc.
10 Alice St.
Binghamton, NY 13904-1580
Ph: (607)722-5857   Fax: (607)722-5857
Fr: 800-342-9678

$60.00/year. Journal for librarians and students, providing information on the changing field of reference librarianship.

★4622★ *Requirements for Certification of Teachers, Counselors, Librarians, Administrators for Elementary and Secondary Schools*

University of Chicago Press
5801 Ellis Ave., 4th Fl.
Chicago, IL 60637
Ph: (312)702-7648   Fax: 800-621-8476
Fr: 800-621-2736

Annual, June. $34.00. Publication includes: List of state and local departments of education. Entries include: Office name, address, phone. Principal content of publication is summaries of each state's teaching and administrative certification requirements. Arrangement: Geographical.

Library Technicians

sponsors specialized education and research grants and programs; gathers, compiles, and disseminates statistics. Establishes and adopts standards; maintains publishing program; offers professional development courses.

★4633★ Special Libraries Association (SLA)

1700 18th St. NW
Washington, DC 20009-2508
Ph: (202)234-4700   Fax: (202)265-9317

Members: International association of information professionals who work in special libraries serving business, research, government, universities, newspapers, museums, and institutions that use or produce specialized information. **Purpose:** Seeks to advance the leadership role of special librarians. Offers consulting services to organizations that wish to establish or expand a library or information services. Conducts continuing education courses, public relations, and government relations programs. **Activities:** Provides employment services. Operates Information Resources Center on topics pertaining to the development and management of special libraries. Maintains Hall of Fame. **E-Mail:** SLA@CAPON.NET

EMPLOYER DIRECTORIES AND NETWORKING LISTS

★4634★ American Library Directory

R. R. Bowker Co.
Reed Reference Publishing
121 Chanlon Rd.
New Providence, NJ 07974
Ph: (908)464-6800   Fax: (908)771-7704
Fr: 800-521-8110

Annual, June. $235.00. Covers over 35,000 U.S. and Canadian academic, public, county, provincial, and regional libraries; library systems; medical, law, and other special libraries; and libraries for the blind and physically handicapped. Separate section lists over 350 library networks and consortia and 220 accredited and unaccredited library school programs. Entries include: For libraries: Name, supporting or affiliated institution or firm name, address, phone, fax, electronic mail address, Standard Address Number (SANs), names of librarian and department heads, income, collection size, special collections, computer hardware, automated functions, and type of catalog. For library systems: Name, location. For library schools: Name, address, phone, fax, electronic mail address, director, type of training and degrees, admission requirements, tuition, faculty size. For networks and consortia: Name, address, phone, names of affiliates, name of director, function. Arrangement: Geographical. Indexes: Institution name.

★4635★ Directory of Federal Libraries

Oryx Press
4041 N. Central, No. 700
Phoenix, AZ 85012-3397
Ph: (602)265-2651   Fax: 800-279-4663
Fr: 800-279-6799

Irregular. Latest edition January 1993. $97.50. Covers nearly 3,000 libraries serving branches of the federal government. Entries include: Library name, type, address, phone, fax, name of administrator and selected staff, special collections, database services available, depository status for documents from the Government Printing Office or other organizations, involvement with cooperative library organizations, electronic mail or cataloging networks, whether accessible to the public. Arrangement: Classified by federal establishment. Indexes: Library type, subject, geographical.

★4636★ Directory of Special Libraries and Information Centers

Gale Research
835 Penobscot Bldg.
Detroit, MI 48226-4094
Ph: (313)961-2242   Fax: (313)961-6083
Fr: 800-877-GALE

Annual. Three volumes: Volume 1, "Directory of Special Libraries and Information Centers", $475.00; Volume 2 "Geographic and Personnel Indexes", $395.00; Volume 3, "New Special Libraries", $390.00. Covers over 19,000 special libraries, information centers, documentation centers, etc., in the United States, Canada, and 80 other countries. Provides comprehensive information about the library or information center's services, facilities, holdings, availability, and staff.

★4637★ Employment Sources in the Library & Information Professions

Office for Library Personnel Resources (OLPR)
American Library Association (ALA)
50 E. Huron St.
Chicago, IL 60611
Ph: (312)280-4277   Fax: (312)280-3256

Annual, spring. Free. Covers library job sources, such as specialized and state and regional library associations, state library agencies, federal library agencies, and overseas exchange programs. Entries include: Library, company, or organization name, address, phone; contact name, description of services, publications, etc. Arrangement: Classified by type of source.

★4638★ International Association of School Librarianship—Membership Directory

International Association of School Librarianship
PO Box 19586
Kalamazoo, MI 49019
Ph: (616)343-5728   Fax: (616)387-4079

Annual, October. $15.00. Covers 800 members engaged in some form of school library service; international coverage. Entries include: Name, address, institution. Arrangement: Geographical.

HANDBOOKS AND MANUALS

★4639★ Careers for Bookworms and Other Literary Types

VGM Career Horizons
4255 W. Touhy Ave.
Lincolnwood, IL 60646-1975
Ph: (847)679-5500   Fax: (847)679-2494
Fr: 800-323-4900

Marjorie Eberts and Margaret Gisler. Second edition, 1995. $14.95; $9.95 (paper). Details opportunities in education, publishing, libraries, journalism, think tanks, museums, film, broadcasting, the public sector, and other fields. Helps job seekers identify reading, writing, or research jobs.

★4640★ How to Get a Job in Education

Bob Adams, Inc.
260 Center St.
Holbrook, MA 02343
Ph: (617)767-8100   Fax: (617)767-0994
Fr: 800-872-5627

Joel Levin. Second edition, 1995. $12.95. 320 pages. Prepared for recent college graduates, seasoned educators, and career-changing professionals, this publication guides the job-seeker through the necessary steps to obtaining a job in education at the elementary, secondary, and university levels. Offers advice on how to prepare for state and local examinations, how to locate teaching opportunities nationwide, and how to obtain certification. Includes a nationwide salary survey. Covers public, private, summer, and overseas opportunities.

★4641★ Opportunities in Library and Information Science Careers

VGM Career Horizons
4255 W. Touhy Ave.
Lincolnwood, IL 60646-1975
Ph: (847)679-5500   Fax: (847)679-2494
Fr: 800-323-4900

Peggy Sullivan and Margaret Myers. 1992. $13.95; $10.95 (paper). 160 pages. A guide to planning for and seeking opportunities in this changing field. Includes bibliography and illustrations.

★4642★ Opportunities in Vocational and Technical Careers

VGM Career Horizons
4255 W. Touhy Ave.
Lincolnwood, IL 60646-1975
Ph: (847)679-5500   Fax: (847)679-2494
Fr: 800-323-4900

Adrian A. Paradis. 1992. $14.95; $11.95 (paper). 160 pages. Provides information on a variety of opportunities and advice on breaking into the field.

EMPLOYMENT AGENCIES AND SEARCH FIRMS

★4643★ C.F. Heller Associates, Inc.
2 W. 45th St.
New York, NY 10036
Ph: (212)819-1919   Fax: (212)819-9196
Employment agency.

★4644★ Gossage Regan Associates
25 W. 43rd St., Ste. 812
New York, NY 10036
Ph: (212)869-3348
Employment agency. Concentrates in placement of library and information professionals on permanent basis nationwide.

OTHER SOURCES

★4645★ Council on Library-Media Technical-Assistants (COLT)
Margaret Barron
Cuyahoga Community College
Library/Media Technology Dept., SC 201
2900 Community College Ave.
Cleveland, OH 44115
Ph: (216)987-4296   Fax: (216)987-4404
Members: Persons involved in two-year associate degree programs for the training of library technical assistants (professional-support workers) and graduates of programs employed as library/media technical assistants (B.A. degree holders without M.L.S. degree). Membership includes junior college deans, librarians, curriculum directors, professors, employers, special libraries, university libraries, library schools, publishers, and library technical assistants. **Purpose:** Provides a channel of communication among the institutions and personnel that have developed such training programs; attempts to standardize curriculum offerings; develops educational standards; conducts research on graduates of the programs; represents the interests of library technical assistants and

support staff. The council's concerns also include development of clear job descriptions and criteria for employment of technicians and dissemination of information to the public and to prospective students.

★4646★ Requirements for Certification of Teachers, Counselors, Librarians, Administrators for Elementary and Secondary Schools
University of Chicago Press
5801 Ellis Ave., 4th Fl.
Chicago, IL 60637
Ph: (312)702-7648   Fax: 800-621-8476
Fr: 800-621-2736
Annual, June. $34.00. Publication includes: List of state and local departments of education. Entries include: Office name, address, phone. Principal content of publication is summaries of each state's teaching and administrative certification requirements. Arrangement: Geographical.

★4647★ Special Librarianship As a Career: An SLA Information Kit
Special Libraries Association
1700 18th St., NW
Washington, DC 20009
Ph: (202)234-4700   Fax: (202)265-9317
1995. $60.00 (paper).

Licensed Practical Nurses

★4648★ *AANA Journal*

AANA Publishing, Inc.
222 S. Prospect
Park Ridge, IL 60068
Ph: (708)692-7050   Fax: (708)692-6968

Bimonthly. $24.00/year for individuals; $5.00 for single issue. Nursing and anesthesia journal.

★4649★ *AAOHN Journal*

Slack, Inc.
6900 Grove Rd.
Thorofare, NJ 08086-9447
Ph: (609)848-1000   Fax: (609)853-5991
Fr: 800-257-8290

Monthly. $49.00/year; $62.00/year for institutions; $15.00 for single issue. Official journal of the American Association of Occupational Health Nurses.

★4650★ *Advances in Nursing Science*

Aspen Publishers, Inc.
200 Orchard Ridge Dr., Ste. 200
Gaithersburg, MD 20878
Ph: (301)417-7500   Fax: (301)417-7550
Fr: 800-638-8437

Quarterly. $68.00/year; $34.00/year for students; $17.00 for single issue. Academic medical journal.

★4651★ *ANNA Journal*

ANNA Journal East
E. Holly Ave., Box 56
Pitman, NJ 08071-0056
Ph: (609)256-2320   Fax: (609)589-7463

Bimonthly. $5.00 for single issue; $28.00/year; $40.00/year for institutions. Nursing journal.

★4652★ *Heart and Lung: The Journal of Acute and Critical Care*

Mosby Year Book
11830 Westline Industrial Dr.
St. Louis, MO 63146
Ph: (314)872-8370   Fax: 800-535-9935
Fr: 800-633-6699

Bimonthly. $39.00/year for individuals; $57.78.00/year for Canada; $54.00/year for other countries; $21.00/year for students. Journal offering articles prepared by nurse and physician members of the critical care team, recognizing the nurse's role in the care and management of major organ-system conditions in critically ill patients.

★4653★ *Homecare Magazine*

Miramar Communications, Inc.
23815 Stuart Ranch Rd.
PO Box 8987
Malibu, CA 90265-8987
Ph: (310)317-4522   Fax: (310)317-9644
Fr: 800-543-4116

Monthly. $48.00/year for individuals; $60.00/year for Canada; $75.00/year for other countries.

★4654★ *Imprint*

National Student Nurses Association
555 W. 57th St.
New York, NY 10019
Ph: (212)581-2211   Fax: (212)581-2368

Magazine for nursing students, focusing on issues and trends in nursing education.

★4655★ *Journal of the American Academy of Nurse Practitioners*

Pharmaceutical Media, Inc.
30 E. 33rd St.
New York, NY 10016
Ph: (212)685-5010   Fax: (212)685-5010

Quarterly. Journal for nurse practitioners and others involved in primary health care.

★4656★ *The Journal of Continuing Education in Nursing*

Slack, Inc.
6900 Grove Rd.
Thorofare, NJ 08086-9447
Ph: (609)848-1000   Fax: (609)853-5991
Fr: 800-257-8290

Bimonthly. Journal for nurses involved in planning and implementing educational programs for the practitioner and others in patient care.

★4657★ *Journal of Emergency Nursing*

Mosby Year Book
11830 Westline Industrial Dr.
St. Louis, MO 63146
Ph: (314)872-8370   Fax: 800-535-9935
Fr: 800-633-6699

Bimonthly. $52.00/year for individuals; $70.62/year for Canada; $66.00/year for other countries; $29.00/year for students. Journal containing peer-reviewed articles on clinical aspects of emergency care by, and for, emergency nurses. Presents information about professional, political, administrative, and educational aspects of emergency nursing and nursing in general.

★4658★ *Journal of Gerontological Nursing*

Slack, Inc.
6900 Grove Rd.
Thorofare, NJ 08086-9447
Ph: (609)848-1000   Fax: (609)853-5991
Fr: 800-257-8290

Monthly. Gerontological nursing journal.

★4659★ *Journal of Nurse-Midwifery*

Elsevier Science Inc.
655 Avenue of the Americas
New York, NY 10010
Ph: (212)989-5800   Fax: (212)633-3990

Bimonthly. $75.00/year for individuals; $150.00/year for institutions. Journal of the American College of Nurse-Midwives.

★4660★ *Journal of Nursing Education*

6900 Grove Rd.
Thorofare, NJ 08086-9447
Ph: (609)848-1000   Fax: (609)853-5991

Bimonthly. $44.00/year.

★4661★ *Journal of Obstetric, Gynecologic, and Neonatal Nursing*

Pharmaceutical Media Inc.
30 E. 33rd St.
New York, NY 10016
Ph: (212)685-5010

Bimonthly. $39.00/year; $17.00/single issue.

★4662★ Journal of Pediatric Health Care

Mosby Year Book
11830 Westline Industrial Dr.
St. Louis, MO 63146
Ph: (314)872-8370   Fax: 800-535-9935
Fr: 800-633-6699

Bimonthly. $49.00/year for individuals; $67.41/year for Canada; $63.00/year for other countries; $25.00/year for students. Official pubolication of the National Association of Pediatric Nurse Associates and Practitioners. Provides current information on pediatric clinical topics as well as research studies, health policy, and legislative issues applicable to pediatric clinical practice.

★4663★ Journal of Practical Nursing

National Association for Practical Nurse Education and Service
1400 Spring St., No. 310
Silver Spring, MD 20910
Ph: (301)588-2491   Fax: (301)588-3667

Quarterly. Journal providing information on licensed practical nursing for LPNs, PN educators, and students.

★4664★ Journal of Psychosocial Nursing and Mental Health Services

Slack, Inc.
6900 Grove Rd.
Thorofare, NJ 08086-9447
Ph: (609)848-1000   Fax: (609)853-5991
Fr: 800-257-8290

Monthly. Journal presenting original, peer-reviewed articles on psychiatric/mental health nursing.

★4665★ McKnight's Long-Term Care News

McKnight Medical Communications Co.
2 Northfield Plaza, Ste. 300
Northfield, IL 60093-1217
Ph: (708)441-3700   Fax: (708)441-3701
Fr: 800-451-7838

Monthly. $44.95/year; $5.00 for single issue. Professional magazine.

★4666★ MCN, The American Journal of Maternal/Child Nursing

American Journal of Nursing Co.
555 W. 57th St.
New York, NY 10019
Ph: (212)582-8820   Fax: (212)586-5462

Bimonthly. Journal focusing on maternal/child nursing and health.

★4667★ Military Medicine

Association of Military Surgeons of the U.S.
9320 Old Georgetown Rd.
Bethesda, MD 20814
Ph: (301)897-8800   Fax: (301)530-5446

Monthly. $35.00/year for individuals; $40.00/year for other countries; $4.50 for single issue. Journal for professional personnel affiliated with the Federal medical services.

★4668★ Modern Healthcare

Crain Communications, Inc.
740 N. Rush St.
Chicago, IL 60611-2590
Ph: (312)649-5311   Fax: (312)280-3189

Weekly. $110.00/year. Business news magazine for Healthcare Management.

★4669★ N&HC: Perspectives on Community

National League for Nursing
350 Hudson St.
New York, NY 10014
Ph: (212)989-9393   Fax: (212)989-3710

Bimonthly. Professional journal for nurses. Includes articles on health policy, and social and economic issues affecting health care, and nursing education and practice.

★4670★ Nurse Practitioner Forum

W.B. Saunders Co.
Periodical Dept.
6277 Sea Harbor Dr.
Orlando, FL 32887-4800
Fax: (407)363-9661   Fr: 800-654-2452

Quarterly. Journal for nurse practitioners.

★4671★ Nursing Management

SN Publications, Inc.
PO Box 908
Spring House, PA 19477-0903

Monthly. $25.00/year for individuals. Magazine focusing on nursing management.

★4672★ Nursing 95

Springhouse Corp.
1111 Bethlehem Pke.
PO Box 908
Spring House, PA 19477
Ph: (215)646-8700   Fax: (215)653-0826
Fr: 800-617-1717

Monthly. $42.00/year for individuals. Practical journal for nurses. Includes special sections for critical-care, continuing care, and nurse practitioners.

★4673★ Nursing Outlook

Mosby Year Book
11830 Westline Industrial Dr.
St. Louis, MO 63146
Ph: (314)872-8370   Fax: 800-535-9935
Fr: 800-633-6699

Bimonthly. $37.00/year for individuals. Official magazine of the American Academy of Nursing, reporting on trends and issues in nursing.

★4674★ Nursing Research

American Journal of Nursing Co.
555 W. 57th St.
New York, NY 10019-2961
Ph: (212)582-8820   Fax: (212)315-3187

Bimonthly. Magazine focusing on nursing research.

★4675★ Nursingworld Journal

Prime National Publishing Corp.
470 Boston Post Rd.
Weston, MA 02193
Ph: (617)899-2702   Fax: (617)899-4900

Monthly. Magazine for the nursing profession.

★4676★ Orthopaedic Nursing

ANNA Journal East
E. Holly Ave., Box 56
Pitman, NJ 08071-0056
Ph: (609)256-2320   Fax: (609)589-7463

Bimonthly. Nursing magazine.

★4677★ Ostomy/Wound Management

Health Management Publications, Inc.
550 American Ave.
King of Prussia, PA 19406
Ph: (610)337-4466   Fax: (610)337-0890
Fr: 800-237-7285

Medical journal.

★4678★ Pediatric Nursing

Jannetti Publications, Inc.
E. Holly Ave., Box 56
Pitman, NJ 08071-0056
Ph: (609)256-2300   Fax: (609)589-7463

Bimonthly. Professional nursing magazine.

★4679★ Perinatal Press–Newsletter

Perinatal Press, Inc.
PO Box 710698
San Diego, CA 92171
Ph: (619)541-6875

Bimonthly. $21.00/year.

★4680★ Perspectives in Psychiatric Care

Nursecom, Inc.
1211 Locust St.
Philadelphia, PA 19107
Ph: (215)545-7222   Fax: (215)545-8107
Fr: 800-242-6757

Quarterly. Journal covering psychiatric care and nursing.

★4681★ Provider

American Health Care Association
1201 L St. NW
Washington, DC 20005
Ph: (202)842-4444   Fax: (202)842-3860

Monthly. $48.00/year for nonmembers. Magazine.

★4682★ Rehabilitation Nursing

Association of Rehabilitation Nurses
5700 Old Orchard Rd., 1st Fl.
Skokie, IL 60077-1057
Ph: (708)966-3433   Fax: (708)966-9418

Bimonthly. $50.00/year for individuals; $75.00/year for institutions; $90.00/year for other countries; $13.00 for single issue. Magazine focusing on rehabilitation nursing involving clinical practice, research, education, and administration.

★4683★ Research in Nursing & Health

John Wiley and Sons, Inc.
605 3rd Ave.
New York, NY 10158
Ph: (212)850-6000   Fax: (212)850-8888
Fr: 800-225-5945

Bimonthly. Journal providing forum for research in the areas of nursing practice, education, and administration. Covers health issues relevant to nursing as well as investigations of the applications of research findings in clinical settings.

★4684★ Seminars in Oncology

W.B. Saunders Co.
The Curtis Center, 3rd Fl.
Philadelphia, PA 19106-3399
Ph: (215)238-7800   Fax: (215)238-8772
Fr: 800-654-2452

Bimonthly. $109.00/year for individuals; $154.00/year for institutions; $65.00/year for students; $36.00 for single issue. Journal reviewing current diagnostic and treatment techniques used in oncology patient care.

PLACEMENT AND JOB REFERRAL SERVICES

★4685★ American Association of Occupational Health Nurses (AAOHN)

50 Lenox Pointe
Atlanta, GA 30324
Ph: (404)262-1162   Fax: (404)262-1165

Members: Registered professional nurses employed by business and industrial firms; nurse educators, nurse editors, nurse writers, and others interested in occupational health nursing. **Purpose:** Promotes and sets standards for the profession. **Activities:** Provides and approves continuing education; maintains governmental affairs program; offers placement service.

★4686★ American Nurses in Business Association (ANBA)

PO Box 741384
Houston, TX 77274-1384
Ph: (713)771-5016   Fax: (713)771-6619

Members: Nursing students, companies, self-employed nurses, registered nurses, and licensed vocational nurses. **Purpose:** Serves as support group for nurses interested in seeking business opportunities. Provides business-related information. **Activities:** Sponsors speakers' bureau; offers placement service.

★4687★ American Public Health Association (APHA)

1015 15th St. NW
Washington, DC 20005
Ph: (202)789-5600   Fax: (202)789-5681

Members: Professional organization of physicians, nurses, educators, academicians, environmentalists, epidemiologists, new professionals, social workers, health administrators, optometrists, podiatrists, pharmacists, dentists, nutritionists, health planners, other community and mental health specialists, and

interested consumers. **Purpose:** Seeks to protect and promote personal, mental, and environmental health. **Activities:** Services include: promulgation of standards; establishment of uniform practices and procedures; development of the etiology of communicable diseases; research in public health; exploration of medical care programs and their relationships to public health. Sponsors job placement service.

★4688★ American School Health Association (ASHA)

7263 State Rte. 43
PO Box 708
Kent, OH 44240
Ph: (216)678-1601   Fax: (216)678-4526

Members: School physicians, school nurses, dentists, nurses, nutritionists, health educators, dental hygienists, school-based professionals, and public health workers. **Purpose:** Promotes comprehensive and constructive school health programs including the teaching of health, health services, and promotion of a healthful school environment. **Activities:** Offers a professional referral service, classroom teaching aids, and professional reference materials. Conducts research programs; maintains placement service; compiles statistics. Sponsors foreign travel study tour.

★4689★ Christian Medical Foundation International (CMF)

7522 N. Himes Ave.
PO Box 152136
Tampa, FL 33684-2136
Ph: (813)932-3688   Fax: (813)932-3767

Members: Physicians, nurses, clergy, and laity. **Purpose:** Seeks to: investigate and promote the Christian spiritual care of those who are ill; educate doctors, nurses, and medical students regarding Christian medical and ethical principles. **Activities:** Maintains speakers' bureau, placement service, biographical archives, and 2500 volume library; sponsors charitable programs.

★4690★ National Health Career Association

Empire State Bldg.
350 5th Ave., Ste. 3304
New York, NY 10118-0069
Ph: (212)259-9412

Activities: Conducts research and educational programs. Offers placement service.

EMPLOYER DIRECTORIES AND NETWORKING LISTS

★4691★ AHA Guide to the Health Care Field

Health Statistics Group
American Hospital Association (AHA)
1 N. Franklin
Chicago, IL 60606
Ph: (312)422-3501   Fax: (312)280-6015

Annual, July. $195.00, payment with order. Covers hospitals, multi-health care systems, freestanding ambulatory surgery centers,

psychiatric facilities, long-term care facilities, substance abuse programs, hospices, Health Maintenance Organizations (HMOs), and other health-related organizations. Entries include: For hospitals: facility name, address, phone, administrator's name, number of beds, facilities and services, number of employees, expenses, other statistics. For other organizations: name, address, phone, name and title of contact. Arrangement: Geographical. Indexes: Hospital name.

★4692★ American Group Practice Association—Directory

American Group Practice Association
1422 Duke St.
Alexandria, VA 22314
Ph: (703)838-0033   Fax: (703)548-1890

Annual, February. $150.00. Covers about 250 private group medical practices and their professional staffs, totalling about 25,000 physicians and administrators. Entries include: Group member name, address, phone, names of administrator and other executives, names of physician listed by medical specialties. Arrangement: Alphabetical. Indexes: Group location, personal name.

★4693★ American Journal of Nursing— Directory of Nursing Organizations Issue

American Journal of Nursing Co.
555 W. 57th St.
New York, NY 10019
Ph: (212)582-8820   Fax: (212)586-5462
Fr: 800-627-0484

Annual, April. $5.00. Publication includes: List of nursing organizations and agencies. Entries include: Name, address, names of officers or nursing representative. Arrangement: Classified by type of organization.

★4694★ Canada Nursing Job Guide Directory

Prime National Publishing Corporation
470 Boston Post Rd.
Weston, MA 02193
Ph: (617)899-2702

Martha J. Denney. 1989. $50.00. 166 pages. Directory of Canadian hospitals.

★4695★ Directory of Hospital Personnel

Medical Economics
5 Paragon Dr.
Montvale, NJ 07645-1725
Ph: (201)358-7500   Fax: (201)573-4956
Fr: 800-222-3045

Annual, September. $325.00, plus 7.50 shipping. Covers 200,000 executives at 7,100 U.S. hospitals. Entries include: Name of hospital, address, phone, number of beds, type and JCAHO status of hospital, names and titles of key department heads and staff, medical and nursing school affiliations; number of residents, interns, and nursing students. Arrangement: Geographical. Indexes: Hospital name, personnel, hospital size.

★4696★ Directory of Nursing Homes

HCIA Inc.
300 E. Lombard St.
Baltimore, MD 21202
Ph: (410)576-9600   Fax: (410)539-5220
Fr: 800-568-3282

Annual. $249.00. Covers over 16,000 state-licensed long-term care facilities. Entries include: Facility name, address, phone, names and titles of key personnel, licensure status, number of beds; number of nursing, dietary, and auxiliary staff members; program/services; medicaid/medicare certification status; admission and referral requirements; age and gender restrictions; languages spoken; management or chain company name. Arrangement: Geographical. Indexes: Alphabetical, geographical (county) and by chain headquarters.

★4697★ Hospital Blue Book

Billian Publishing Co.
2100 Powers Ferry Rd., Ste. 300
Atlanta, GA 30339
Ph: (404)955-5656   Fax: (404)952-0669

Annual, spring. $154.50, national edition, plus $20.00 shipping. Covers more than 7,100 hospitals; some listings also appear in a separate southern edition of this publication. Entries include: Name of hospital, accreditation, mailing address, phone, fax, number of beds, type of facility (nonprofit, general, state, etc.); list of administrative personnel and chiefs of medical services, with specific titles. Arrangement: Geographical.

★4698★ Hospital Market Atlas

SMG Marketing Group, Inc.
1342 N. LaSalle Dr.
Chicago, IL 60610
Ph: (312)642-3026   Fax: (312)642-9729
Fr: 800-678-3026

Biennial, odd years. $495.00, payment with order. Covers over 7,000 hospitals, hospital systems and 480 group purchasing organizations. Entries include: Hospital or organization name, address, phone, county code, management, type of hospital service, number of beds, admissions, surgical operations, and emergency room visits. Arrangement: Geographical.

★4699★ Hospitals Directory

American Business Directories, Inc.
American Business Information, Inc.
5711 S. 86th Cir.
Omaha, NE 68127
Ph: (402)593-4600   Fax: (402)331-1505

Annual. $870.00, U.S. edition. Entries include: Name, address, phone (including area code), size of advertisement, year first in Yellow Pages, name of owner or manager, number of employees. Compiled from telephone company Yellow Pages, nationwide. Arrangement: Geographical.

★4700★ Medical and Health Information Directory

Gale Research
835 Penobscot Bldg.
Detroit, MI 48226-4094
Ph: (313)961-2242   Fax: (313)961-6083
Fr: 800-877-GALE

Approximately biennial; latest edition 1994. $195.00, per volume; $485.00, for the three-volume set. Covers in Volume 1, almost 18,600 medical and health oriented associations, organizations, institutions, and government agencies, including health maintenance organizations (HMOs), preferred provider organizations (PPOs), insurance companies, pharmaceutical companies, research centers, and medical and allied health schools. In Volume 2, nearly 11,800 medical book publishers; medical periodicals, directories, audiovisual producers and services, medical libraries and information centers, and electronic resources. In Volume 3, nearly 26,000 clinics, treatment centers, care programs, and counseling/diagnostic services for 30 subject areas. Entries include: Institution, service, or firm name, address, phone; many include names of key personnel and, when pertinent, descriptive annotation. Arrangement: Classified by organization activity, service, etc. Indexes: Each volume has a complete alphabetical name and keyword index.

★4701★ Nurses and Nurses' Registries Directory

American Business Directories, Inc.
American Business Information, Inc.
5711 S. 86th Cir.
Omaha, NE 68127
Ph: (402)593-4600   Fax: (402)331-1505

Annual. $880.00, U.S. edition. Entries include: Name, address, phone (including area code), size of advertisement, year first in Yellow Pages, name of owner or manager, number of employees. Compiled from telephone company Yellow Pages, nationwide. Arrangement: Geographical.

★4702★ Nursing Career Directory

Springhouse Corp.
1111 Bethlehem Pke.
PO Box 908
Spring House, PA 19477-0908
Ph: (215)646-8700   Fax: (215)646-8700

Annual, January. Covers nonprofit and investor-owned hospitals and departments of the United States government which hire nurses. Does not report specific positions available. Entries include: Unit name, location, areas of nursing specialization, educational requirements for nurses, licensing, facilities, benefits, etc. Arrangement: Geographical.

★4703★ Nursingworld Journal—Nursing Job Guide Issue

Prime National Publishing Corp.
470 Boston Post Rd.
Weston, MA 02193
Ph: (617)899-2702   Fax: (617)899-4900
Fr: 800-869-2700

Annual, July. $75.00. Covers over 7,000 hospitals and medical centers, infirmaries, government hospitals, and other hospitals in the United States; in tabular format, provides information about each facility that would be of interest to nurses considering employment there, but does not list specific openings. Entries include: Hospital name, address, phone, name of nurse recruiter; number of beds, number of admissions, number of patient days, type of control, whether a teaching institution, nursing specialties utilized. Arrangement: Geographical.

★4704★ Osteopathic Membership Directory—AOHA

American Osteopathic Healthcare
  Association
5301 Wisconsin Ave. NW, Ste. 630
Washington, DC 20015-2015
Ph: (202)686-1700   Fax: (202)686-7615

Annual, summer. $125.00, payment with order. Covers about 110 osteopathic hospitals. Includes list of individual and institutional members; also lists osteopathic colleges, and directors of medical education. Entries include: For hospitals: name of hospital, name of chief executive officer, address, phone, number of beds and other hospital data. Arrangement: Geographical. Indexes: Name, institution.

★4705★ Peterson's Job Opportunities in Health Care

Peterson's Guides, Inc.
202 Carnegie Ctr.
Box 2123
Princeton, NJ 08543-2123
Ph: (609)243-9111   Fax: (609)243-9150
Fr: 800-338-3282

Annual, August. $18.95. Covers Over 1,500 companies hiring health-care professionals for skilled nursing care facilities, hospitals, medical laboratories, home health care, and pharmaceuticals. Entries include: Organization name, address, phone, name and title of contact, type of organization, number of employees, Standard Industrial Classification (SIC) code; description of opportunities available including disciplines, level of education required, starting locations and salaries, level of experience accepted, benefits. Arrangement: Alphabetical. Indexes: Employer by type of organization, industry classification, number of employees, starting location, special interest area; education level, company.

★4706★ Who's Who in American Nursing

Society of Nursing Professionals
Reed Reference Publishing
121 Chanlon Rd.
New Providence, NJ 07974-1541
Ph: (908)464-6800   Fax: (908)665-6688
Fr: 800-521-8110

Biennial, Odd years. $139.00, plus $9.73 shipping. Covers approximately 27,000 nursing professionals, including educators, administrators, deans of nursing, directors of nursing, nurse practitioners, clinical supervisors, and others. Entries include: Name, address, personal history, area of specialization, professional experience, education, professional organization membership, honors, publications, experience in public speaking. Arrangement: Alphabetical. Indexes: Geographical, specialization.

HANDBOOKS AND MANUALS

★4707★ Career Planning: Nurse's Guide to Career Advancement

National League for Nursing (NLN)
350 Hudson St.
New York, NY 10014
Ph: (212)989-9393   Fr: 800-669-1656

Patricia Winstead-Fry. 1990. $29.95. 256 pages. This is a guide to career planning and self assessment. Describes opportunities in nurse-midwifery, independent practice, community health, administration, research and education. Gives advice on getting into the field and acquiring the education needed.

★4708★ Careers in Health Care

VGM Career Horizons
4255 W. Touhy Ave.
Lincolnwood, IL 60646-1975
Ph: (847)679-5500   Fax: (847)679-2494
Fr: 800-323-4900

Barbara M. Swanson. 1995. $17.95; $13.95 (paper). Describes job duties, work settings, salaries, licensing and certification requirements, educational preparation, and future outlook. Gives ideas on how to secure a job.

★4709★ Comprehensive Review of Practical Nursing

Mosby-Year Book, Inc.
11830 Westline Industrial Dr.
St. Louis, MO 63146
Ph: (314)872-8370   Fax: (314)432-1380
Fr: 800-426-4545

Yannes. 1993. $25.95 (paper).

★4710★ Developing Your Career in Nursing

Cassell Publishing
215 Park Ave. S, 10th Fl.
New York, NY 10003
Ph: (212)598-5717   Fax: (212)598-5740

Robert Newell, editor. 1996.

★4711★ Exploring Careers in Nursing

Rosen Publishing Group, Inc.
29 E. 21st St.
New York, NY 10010
Ph: (212)777-3017   Fax: (212)777-0277
Fr: 800-237-9932

Jackie Heron. Revised edition, 1990. $14.95. 144 pages. Describes the job of nursing, what it takes to succeed in nursing, educational preparation, and professional opportunities in nursing. Gives job hunting advice for nurses including job hunting strategies, contacting employers, and writing resumes and cover letters.

★4712★ Federal Jobs in Nursing and Health Sciences

Impact Publications
9104 N. Manassas Dr.
Manassas Park, VA 22111-5211
Ph: (703)361-7300   Fax: (703)335-9486

Russ Smith. 1995. $14.95 (paper).

★4713★ Gerontological Nursing Certification Review Guide for the Generalist, Clinical Specialist & Nurse Practitioner

Health Leadership Associates, Inc
PO Box 59153
Potomac, MD 20859
Ph: (301)983-2405   Fax: (301)299-2341
Fr: 800-435-4775

Cacchione. 1993. $43.95 (paper).

★4714★ Healthcare Career Directory–Nurses and Physicians

Gale Research
835 Penobscot Bldg.
Detroit, MI 48226-4094
Ph: (313)961-2242   Fax: (313)961-6083
Fr: 800-877-GALE

Bradley Morgan. Second edition, 1993. $39.00. 327 pages. Essays on specific careers provide an insider's perspective. Features extensive listings of contacts and entry-level job opportunities. Provides information on internships and sources of help-wanted ads.

★4715★ Job Opportunities in Health Care 1995

Peterson's Guides, Inc.
PO Box 2123
Princeton, NJ 08543-2123
Ph: (609)243-9111   Fax: (609)243-9150
Fr: 800-338-3282

1994. $18.95 (paper).

★4716★ Licensed Practical Nurse

R & E Publishers Inc.
468 Auzerais Ave., Ste. A
San Jose, CA 95126
Ph: (408)977-0691   Fax: (408)977-0693

Ronald R. Smith. 1993. $1.95 (paper).

★4717★ Licensed Practical/Vocational Nurses in the Veterans Administration: Nationwide Opportunities

Veterans Health Administration
U.S. Veterans Administration
810 Vermont Ave. NW
Washington, DC 20420
Ph: (202)535-7528

This six-page pamphlet describes job opportunities and employee benefits for practical nurses. Gives a state-by-state listing of U.S. Veterans Administration Medical Centers.

★4718★ Long-Term Practice: Skills for the Certified Nursing Assistant

Little, Brown & Company
Time & Life Bldg.
1271 Avenue of the Americas
New York, NY 10020
Ph: (212)522-8700   Fax: (212)522-2067
Fr: 800-343-9204

Marjorie G. Frazier. 1995.

★4719★ Medical-Surgical Nursing

Skidmore-Roth Publishing, Inc.
7730 Trade Ctr. Dr.
El Paso, TX 79912
Ph: (915)877-4455   Fax: (915)544-4506
Fr: 800-825-3150

Brenda Goodner. 1994. $18.95 (paper).

★4720★ Mosby's Assestest: A Practice Exam for RN Licensure

Mosby-Year Book, Inc.
11830 Westline Industrial Dr.
St. Louis, MO 63146
Ph: (314)872-8370   Fax: (314)432-1380
Fr: 800-426-4545

Saxton. 1994. $28.95 (paper).

★4721★ Mosby's Review for NCLEX-RN

Mosby-Year Book, Inc.
11830 Westline Industrial Dr.
St. Louis, MO 63146
Ph: (314)872-8370   Fax: (314)432-1380
Fr: 800-426-4545

Dolores F. Saxton. 1994. $27.95.

★4722★ Mosby's Tour Guide to Nursing School: A Student's Road Survival Guide

Mosby-Year Book, Inc.
11830 Westline Industrial Dr.
St. Louis, MO 63146
Ph: (314)872-8370   Fax: (314)432-1380
Fr: 800-426-4545

Melodie Chenevert. 1994. $18.95.

★4723★ NSNA, NCLEX-RN Review

Delmar Publishers
3 Columbia Cir., Box 15015
Albany, NY 12212
Ph: (518)464-3500   Fax: (518)464-0358
Fr: 800-347-7707

Alice M. Stein. 1994. $29.95 (paper).

★4724★ Nurse Entrepeneur: Building the Bridge of Opportunity

Vista Publishing, Inc
473 Broadway
Long Branch, NJ 07740
Ph: (908)229-4545   Fax: (908)229-9647
Fr: 800-634-2498

Carolyn S. Zagury. 1993. $21.95 (paper).

★4725★ Nursing

NTC Publishing Group
4255 W. Touhy Ave.
Lincolnwood, IL 60646-1975
Ph: (708)679-5500   Fax: (708)679-6375
Fr: 800-323-4900

Blythe Camenson. 1995. $13.95.

★4726★ The Nursing Experience: Trends, Challenges & Transitions

Health Professions Division
McGraw Hill, Inc
1221 Avenue of the Americas, 28th Fl.
New York, NY 10020
Ph: (212)512-4484   Fr: 800-262-4729

Lucie Y. Kelly. 1996.

★4727★ Nursing Today: Transition and Trends

W.B. Saunders Co.
Curtis Ctr., Independence Sq., W.
Philadelphia, PA 19106-3399
Ph: (215)238-7800   Fax: (215)238-7883

JoAnn Zerwekh, editor. 1994. $23.50 (paper).

★4728★ *Obstetric Nursing*

Skidmore-Roth Publishing, Inc.
7730 Trade Ctr. Dr.
El Paso, TX 79912
Ph: (915)877-4455   Fax: (915)544-4506
Fr: 800-825-3150

Brenda Goodner. 1994. $18.95 (paper).

★4729★ *100 Best Careers for the Year 2000*

Prentice Hall General Reference
15 Columbus Cir.
New York, NY 10023
Ph: (212)373-8500   Fr: 800-223-2348

Shelly Field. 1992. $15.00 (paper). Covers 100 of the fastest growing jobs. The publication is divided into 11 general employment sections. Specific careers are covered within each section. Provides job description, responsibilities, employment opportunities, earnings, education and training, advancement opportunities, and experience and qualifications for each occupation.

★4730★ *101 Career Options for Nurses*

Mosby-Year Book, Inc.
11830 Westline Industrial Dr.
St. Louis, MO 63146
Ph: (314)872-8370   Fax: (314)432-1380
Fr: 800-426-4545

Walraven. $21.95 (paper).

★4731★ *Opportunities in Child Care Careers*

VGM Career Horizons
4255 W. Touhy Ave.
Lincolnwood, IL 60646-1975
Ph: (847)679-5500   Fax: (847)679-2494
Fr: 800-323-4900

Renee Wittenberg. 1995. $14.95; $11.95 (paper). 160 pages. Discusses various job opportunities and how to secure a position. Illustrated.

★4732★ *Opportunities in Environmental Careers*

VGM Career Horizons
4255 W. Touhy Ave.
Lincolnwood, IL 60646-1975
Ph: (847)679-5500   Fax: (847)679-2494
Fr: 800-323-4900

Odom Fanning. 1995. $14.95; $11.95 (paper). 160 pages. Describes a broad range of opportunities in fields such as environmental health, recreation, physics, and hygiene, and provides job search advice.

★4733★ *Opportunities in Health and Medical Careers*

VGM Career Horizons
4255 W. Touhy Ave.
Lincolnwood, IL 60646-1975
Ph: (847)679-5500   Fax: (847)679-2494
Fr: 800-323-4900

Donald Snook, Jr. and Leo D'Orazio. 1993. $14.95; $11.95 (paper). Covers the full range of medical and health occupations. Illustrated.

★4734★ *Opportunities in Nursing Careers*

VGM Career Horizons
4255 W. Touhy Ave.
Lincolnwood, IL 60646-1975
Ph: (847)679-5500   Fax: (847)679-2494
Fr: 800-323-4900

Keville Frederickson. 1995. $14.95; $11.95 (paper) Discusses the employment outlook and job-seeking techniques for LVN's, LPN's, RN's, nurse practitioners, nurse anesthetists, and other nurse members of the medical team. Includes a complete list of state nurses associations, state nursing boards, and specialty nursing organizations. Contains bibliography and illustrations.

★4735★ *Opportunities in Public Health Careers*

VGM Career Horizons
4255 W. Touhy Ave.
Lincolnwood, IL 60646-1975
Ph: (847)679-5500   Fax: (847)679-2494
Fr: 800-323-4900

George E. Pickett and Terry W. Pickett. 1995. $14.95; $11.95 (paper). 160 pages. Defines the public health field and describes a variety of health, science, and business opportunities as well as educational preparation and the future of the public health field. Offers job-hunting tips. The appendixes list public health organizations, state and federal public health agencies, and graduate schools offering public health programs.

★4736★ *Opportunities in State and Local Government Careers*

VGM Career Horizons
4255 W. Touhy Ave.
Lincolnwood, IL 60646-1975
Ph: (847)679-5500   Fax: (847)679-2494
Fr: 800-323-4900

Neale Baxter. 1993. $13.95; $10.95 (paper). 160 pages. Points out the incentives and drawbacks of a government career. Describes hiring procedures and provides tips on filling out applications, taking physical and aptitude tests, handling interviews, and finding jobs. Describes the jobs in which 75% of all state and local government workers are employed. For each occupation, covers the nature of the work and the training required.

★4737★ *Opportunities in Vocational and Technical Careers*

VGM Career Horizons
4255 W. Touhy Ave.
Lincolnwood, IL 60646-1975
Ph: (847)679-5500   Fax: (847)679-2494
Fr: 800-323-4900

Adrian A. Paradis. 1992. $14.95; $11.95 (paper). 160 pages. Provides information on a variety of opportunities and advice on breaking into the field.

★4738★ *Resume Writing for the Professional Nurse*

CES Associates
112 S. Grant St.
Hinsdale, IL 60521
Ph: (708)654-2596

Nancy Kuzmich. Revised edition, 1995. $39.95. 110 pages. Self-study guide written

for the professional nurse on how to set career goals, interview for a job, and select the best job offer. Includes sample resumes and cover letters.

★4739★ *Resumes for the Health Care Professional*

John Wiley & Sons, Inc.
605 3rd Ave.
New York, NY 10158-0012
Ph: (212)850-6000   Fr: 800-225-5945

Kim Marino. 1993. $14.95 (paper).

★4740★ *Self-Employment in Nursing: The Basics of Starting a Business*

American Nurses Association (ANA)
Publishing Distribution Ctr.
PO Box 2244
Waldorf, MD 20604
Fr: 800-637-0323

Lyndia Flanagan. 1993. $9.50. 32 pages. Defines options and qualifications as well as risks, responsibilities, and benefits of being self-employed in nursing.

★4741★ *To Be a Nurse*

Vista Publishing, Inc.
473 Broadway
Long Branch, NJ 07740
Ph: (908)229-4545   Fax: (908)229-9647
Fr: 800-634-2498

Linda Strangio. 1995. $12.95 (paper).

★4742★ *Vocational & Personal Adjustments in Practical Nursing*

Mosby-Year Book, Inc.
11830 Westline Industrial Dr.
St. Louis, MO 63146
Ph: (314)872-8370   Fax: (314)432-1380
Fr: 800-426-4545

Becker. 1990. $16.95 (paper).

★4743★ *Your Opportunities in Nursing*

Energeia Publishing, Inc.
860 Commercial St., S.
Salem, OR 97302
Ph: (503)362-1480   Fax: (503)362-2123

Margie Sherman. 1994. $2.00 (paper).

EMPLOYMENT AGENCIES AND SEARCH FIRMS

★4744★ *Academy Medical Personnel Services*

571 High St.
Columbus, OH 43085-4132
Ph: (614)848-6011

Employment agency. Fills openings on a regular or temporary basis.

★4745★ *Eden Temporary Services*

280 Madison Ave.
New York, NY 10016-0801
Ph: (212)685-4666

Employment agency. Places individuals in regular or temporary positions.

★4746★ Harper Associates

29870 Middlebelt
Farmington Hills, MI 48334
Ph: (810)932-1170

Employment agency.

★4747★ Health and Science Center

209 Hunter St.
Media, PA 19063-5726
Ph: (610)891-0714

Employment agency. Executive search firm.

★4748★ Medical Personnel Pool

2901 S. Ridgewood Ave.
Daytona Beach, FL 32119-3542
Ph: (904)736-1648

Provides regular and temporary staffing assistance. Offices located in cities throughout United States.

★4749★ Medical Personnel Services, Inc.

1707 L St. NW, Ste. 700
Washington, DC 20036
Ph: (202)466-2955   Fax: (202)452-1818

Employment agency.

★4750★ Midwest Medical Consultants

8910 Purdue Rd., Ste. 200
Indianapolis, IN 46268-1155
Ph: (317)872-1053

Employment agency. Executive search firm.

★4751★ Professional Placement Associates, Inc.

11 Rye Ridge Plaza
Rye Brook, NY 10573
Ph: (914)251-1000   Fax: (914)939-1959

Employment agency.

★4752★ Travcorps, Inc.

40 Eastern Ave.
Malden, MA 02148
Ph: (617)322-2600

Places staff in temporary assignments.

OTHER SOURCES

★4753★ American Almanac of Jobs and Salaries 1994-95

Avon Books
1350 Avenue of the Americas, 2nd Fl.
New York, NY 10019
Ph: (212)261-6800   Fr: 800-238-0658

John Wright. Revised edition, 1993. $17.00. 704 pages. This is a comprehensive guide to the wages of hundreds of occupations in a wide variety of industries and organizations.

★4754★ American Health Care Association

1201 L St. NW
Washington, DC 20005
Ph: (202)842-4444   Fax: (202)842-3860

Members: Federation of state associations of long-term health care facilities. **Purpose:** Promotes standards for professionals in long-term health care delivery and quality care for patients and residents in a safe environment. Focuses on issues of availability, quality, affordability, and fair payment. Operates as a liaison with governmental agencies, Congress, and professional associations.

★4755★ American Hospital Association (AHA)

1 N. Franklin, Ste. 27
Chicago, IL 60606
Ph: (312)422-3000   Fax: (312)422-4796

Members: Individuals and health care institutions including hospitals, health care systems, and pre- and postacute health care delivery organizations. **Purpose:** Is dedicated to promoting the welfare of the public through its leadership and assistance to its members in the provision of better health services for all people. Conducts educational programs furthering the in-service education of hospital personnel; collects and analyzes data; furnishes multimedia educational materials; maintains 44,000 volume health care administration library, and biographical archive.

★4756★ American Licensed Practical Nurses Association (ALPNA)

1090 Vermont Ave. NW, Ste. 1200
Washington, DC 20005
Ph: (202)682-5800   Fax: (202)682-0168

Members: Licensed practical nurses. **Purpose:** Promotes the practical nursing profession; lobbies and maintains relations with the government on issues and legislation that may have an impact on LPNs. **Activities:** Conducts continuing education classes. Facilitates discussion of issues affecting the nursing and health professions.

★4757★ Career Encounters: Nursing

Cambridge Career Products
PO Box 2153
Dept. CC15
Charleston, WV 25328-2153
Ph: (304)744-9323   Fax: (304)744-9351
Fr: 800-468-4227

Video. $99.95. 25 minutes. Professionals shown in a variety of settings discuss different aspects of their careers.

★4758★ Day in a Career: Nursing

Cambridge Career Products
PO Box 2153
Dept. CC15
Charleston, WV 25328-2153
Ph: (304)744-9323   Fax: (304)744-9351
Fr: 800-468-4227

Video. 1994. $89.00. 15-22 minutes. Includes candid interviews and work situations, plus outlines of relevant career information.

★4759★ Hospital Salary Survey Report

Hospital Compensation Service
John R. Zabka Associates, Inc.
69 Minnehaha Blvd.
PO Box 376
Oakland, NJ 07436
Ph: (201)405-0075

Annual. Reports salaries for management employees, registered nurses, and licensed practical nurses by hospital bed size, by profit and nonprofit status for governmental hospitals, and by geographic area.

★4760★ Interviewing Skills for Nurses & Other Health Care Professionals: A Structured Approach

Routledge
29 W. 35th St.
New York, NY 10001-2299
Ph: (212)244-3336   Fax: 800-248-4724

Robert Newell. 1994. $65.00; $18.95 (paper).

★4761★ National Association for Practical Nurse Education and Service (NAPNES)

1400 Spring St., Ste. 310
Silver Spring, MD 20910
Ph: (301)588-2491   Fax: (301)588-2839

Members: Licensed practical/vocational nurses, registered nurses, physicians, hospital and nursing home administrators, and interested others. **Purpose:** Provides consultation service to advise schools wishing to develop a practical/vocational nursing program on facilities, equipment, policies, curriculum, and staffing. Promotes recruitment of students through preparation and distribution of recruitment materials. Sponsors seminars for directors and instructors in schools of practical/vocational nursing and continuing education programs for LPNs/LVNs; approves continuing education programs and awards contact hours; holds national certification courses in pharmacology and gerontics.

★4762★ National Federation of Licensed Practical Nurses (NFLPN)

1418 Aversboro Rd.
Garner, NC 27529-4547
Ph: (919)779-0046   Fax: (919)779-5642

Members: Federation of state associations of licensed practical and vocational nurses. **Purpose:** Aims to: preserve and foster the ideal of comprehensive nursing care for the ill and aged; improve standards of practice; secure recognition and effective utilization of LPNs; further continued improvement in the education of LPNs. Acts as clearinghouse for information on practical nursing and cooperates with other groups concerned with better patient care. Maintains loan program.

★4763★ National League for Nursing (NLN)

350 Hudson St.
New York, NY 10014
Ph: (212)989-9393   Fax: (212)989-9256
Fr: 800-669-1656

Members: Individuals and leaders in nursing and other health professions, and community members interested in solving health care problems; agencies, nursing educational institutions, departments of nursing in hospitals and related facilities, and home and community health agencies. **Purpose:** Works to assess nursing needs, improve organized nursing services and nursing education, and foster collaboration between nursing and other health and community services. Provides tests used in selection of applicants to schools of nursing; also prepares tests for evaluating nursing student progress and nursing service tests. Nationally accredits nursing education programs and community health agencies. Collects and disseminates data on nursing services and nursing education. Conducts studies and demonstration projects on community planning for nursing and nursing service and education.

★4764★ **National Rural Health Association (NRHA)**

1 W. Armour Blvd., Ste. 301
Kansas City, MO 64111
Ph: (816)756-3140   Fax: (816)756-3144

Members: Administrators, physicians, nurses, physician assistants, health planners, academicians, and others interested or involved in rural health care. **Purpose:** To create a better understanding of health care problems unique to rural areas; utilize a collective approach in finding positive solutions; articulate and represent the health care needs of rural America; supply current information to rural health care providers; serve as a liaison between rural health care programs throughout the country. Offers continuing education credits for medical, dental, nursing, and management courses.

★4765★ *Nursing Home Salary and Benefits Report*

Hospital Compensation Service
John R. Zabka Associates, Inc.
69 Minnehaha Blvd.
PO Box 376
Oakland, NJ 07436
Ph: (201)405-0075

Annual. Gives salaries and fringe benefits for registered and licensed practical nurses. Lists salaries by the annual gross revenue of the nursing home, bed size, and profit and nonprofit status.

★4766★ *Nursing: The Challenge of a Lifetime*

National League for Nursing
Publications Order Unit
350 Hudson St.
New York, NY 10014
Ph: (212)989-9393   Fr: 800-669-1656

Video. $60.00 (10-day preview); $131.25 (purchase). 15 minutes.

★4767★ *Pediatric Nurse Practitioner Certification Review Guide*

Health Leadership Associates, Inc
PO Box 59153
Potomac, MD 20859
Ph: (301)983-2405   Fax: (301)299-2341
Fr: 800-435-4775

Edmonds. 1994. $47.75 (paper).

★4768★ *Peterson's Guide to Nursing Programs*

Peterson's Guides, Inc.
202 Carnegie Center
PO Box 2123
Princeton, NJ 08543-2123
Ph: (609)243-9111   Fax: (609)243-9150
Fr: 800-338-3282

$21.95. Covers Over 600 institutions offering approximately 1,500 accredited nursing programs in the U.S. and Canada. Entries include: Academic information, extracurricular issues, costs, financial aid.

★4769★ *Review for NCLEX-PN*

National Nursing Review, Inc.
342 State St., No. 6
Los Altos, CA 94022
Ph: (415)941-5784   Fax: (415)941-4354
Fr: 800-950-4095

Sandra Smith. 1994. $24.95 (paper).

★4770★ **Visiting Nurse Associations of America (VNAA)**

3801 E. Florida, Ste. 900
Denver, CO 80210
Ph: (303)753-0218   Fax: (303)753-0258
Fr: 800-426-2547

Members: Voluntary, nonprofit home health care agencies. **Purpose:** Develops competitive strength among community-based nonprofit visiting nurse organizations; works to strengthen business resources and economic programs through contracting, marketing, governmental affairs and publications.

Loan Officers

SOURCES OF HELP-WANTED ADS

★4771★ American Banker

American Banker, Inc.
1 State St. Plaza
New York, NY 10004
Ph: (212)943-6700   Fax: (212)943-2984

Daily (morn.). Newspaper for senior executives in banking and other financial services industries. Coverage includes news on the financial service industry, news analysis, statistical data ranking financial institutions, investigative pieces, and financial industry trend stories for decision-makers.

★4772★ Bankers Monthly

Hanover Publishers
200 W. 57th St.
New York, NY 10019
Ph: (212)399-1084   Fax: (212)245-1973

Monthly. Magazine covering current banking topics of interest to senior bank executives.

★4773★ Mortgage Banking

Mortgage Bankers Association of America
1125 15th St. NW
Washington, DC 20005
Ph: (202)861-6500   Fax: (202)872-0186

Monthly. $40.00/year for individuals. Magazine on the real estate finance industry.

★4774★ National Mortgage News

National News, Inc.
212 W. 35th St., 13th Fl.
New York, NY 10001
Ph: (212)563-4008   Fax: (212)564-8879

$199.00/year. Newspaper for mortgage lenders and investment bankers.

★4775★ Northwestern Financial Review

NFR Communications
2850 Metro Dr., Ste. 524
Minneapolis, MN 55425
Ph: (612)854-2177   Fax: (612)854-2627

Weekly. $65.00/year for individuals; $4.00. for single issue. Bank and financial magazine and newsletter.

★4776★ Servicing Management

LDJ Corp.
70 Edwin Ave.
PO Box 2330
Waterbury, CT 06722
Ph: (203)755-0158   Fax: (203)755-3480
Fr: 800-325-6745

Monthly. Trade magazine.

★4777★ United States Banker

Faulkner and Gray, Inc.
11 Penn Plaza, 17th Fl.
New York, NY 10001
Ph: (212)967-7000   Fax: (212)967-2162
Fr: 800-535-8403

Monthly. $59.00/year for individuals. Magazine serving the financial services industry.

PLACEMENT AND JOB REFERRAL SERVICES

★4778★ National Bankers Association (NBA)

1802 T St. NW
Washington, DC 20009
Ph: (202)588-5432   Fax: (202)588-5443

Members: Minority banking institutions owned by minority individuals and institutions. **Purpose:** Serves as an advocate for the minority banking industry. Organizes banking services, government relations, marketing, scholarship, and technical assistance programs. **Activities:** Offers placement services; compiles statistics.

EMPLOYER DIRECTORIES AND NETWORKING LISTS

★4779★ American Bank Directory

Thomson Financial Publishing Inc.
4709 W. Golf Rd.
Skokie, IL 60076-1253
Ph: (708)676-9600   Fax: (708)933-8101
Fr: 800-321-3373

Semiannual, April and October. $249.00, single issue of national edition; $26.00, for single state edition; $11.00, each additional state in same binder. Covers over 12,000 banks and registered multi-bank holding companies nationwide; also published in editions for individual states. Entries include: Bank name, address (including county and Federal Reserve District), phone, fax, fedwire number, year established, ABA number, names of officers, condensed statement of condition, principal correspondents, branches. Arrangement: Geographical.

★4780★ American Banker—Top Commercial Banks by Assets, Deposits

American Banker-Bond Buyer
International Thomson Publishing Corp.
1 State St. Plaza
New York, NY 10004
Ph: (212)943-5288   Fax: (212)480-0165
Fr: 800-367-3989

Semiannual, March and September. $25.00. Publication includes: List of the top 300 commercial banks. Entries include: Name of bank, headquarters, amount of deposits at the previous quarter, place in rank at quarter. Arrangement: Ranked by deposits and assets. Indexes: Geographical.

★4781★ American Banker—Top Finance Companies Issue

American Banker-Bond Buyer
International Thomson Publishing Corp.
1 State St. Plaza
New York, NY 10004
Ph: (212)943-5288   Fax: (212)480-0165
Fr: 800-367-3989

Annual, December. $25.00. Publication includes: List of top finance companies with $10 million or more in capital funds. Entries include: Finance company name, headquarters, city; rankings of net receivables by type, business, consumer, and other; total capital funds for two preceding years; capital and surplus, total assets, net receivables, net income, deferred income, receivables acquired, and amount of bank credit at end of the preceding year. Arrangement: Ranked by size of capital funds.

★4782★ American Banker—Top 300 Mortgage Companies Issue

American Banker-Bond Buyer
International Thomson Publishing Corp.
1 State St. Plaza
New York, NY 10004
Ph: (212)943-5288   Fax: (212)943-8815
Fr: 800-238-8422

Annual, October. $25.00. Entries include: Company name, headquarters city, rank; dollar value of mortgages serviced for current and prior year; prior year's rank and gain in rank; number of mortgages; number of investors. Arrangement: Ranked by total dollar value of mortgages.

★4783★ American Banker—Top 300 Thrifts by Deposits

American Banker-Bond Buyer
International Thomson Publishing Corp.
1 State St. Plaza
New York, NY 10004
Ph: (212)943-5288   Fax: (212)480-0165
Fr: 800-367-3989

Semiannual, May and November. $25.00. Publication includes: List of top 300 thrift institutions. Entries include: Name of institution, city, rank; total assets, deposits, and total capital. Arrangement: Ranked by deposits, assets, and risk-based capital ratios.

★4784★ American Banker—Top World Banks by Deposits and Assets

American Banker-Bond Buyer
International Thomson Publishing Corp.
1 State St. Plaza
New York, NY 10004
Ph: (212)943-5288   Fax: (212)480-0165
Fr: 800-367-3989

Annual, July. $25.00. Publication includes: List of 500 largest banks in the world by assets with total deposits and deposit rank; also, the risk-based capital position of the 100 largest banking companies in the world as measured by total assets. Entries include: Bank name, headquarters, rankings by assets and amount of deposits and assets for two previous years. Arrangement: Ranked by assets. Indexes: Geographic listing of largest banks outside United States.

★4785★ Branches of Your State: Banks, Savings and Loans, Credit Unions, & Savings Banks

Sheshunoff Information Services, Inc.
Box 13202, Capitol Sta.
Austin, TX 78711-3203
Ph: (512)472-2244   Fax: (512)476-1251
Fr: 800-456-2340

Annual, February. $345.00. Covers in separate state editions, banks, savings and loan branches, and credit unions. For those states without branch banking, individual banks, savings and loan institutions, and credit unions are listed. Entries include: Institution name, address, institution type, deposit totals, percent change over 12 months, percentage share of parent company's total deposits. Arrangement: Geographical.

★4786★ Directory of the Savings & Community Bankers of America

Savings & Community Bankers of America
900 19th St. NW
Washington, DC 20006
Ph: (202)857-3100   Fax: (202)659-4816

Annual, July. $55.00 for members; $95.00 for nonmembers. Covers about 2,000 community banks and savings and loan associations; related state and regional trade organizations; other affiliated members. Entries include: For savings banks and savings and loan associations Name, address, phone, fax, names and titles of key personnel, year established, type of charter, name of insuring agency, type of ownership, whether a member of the Federal Home Loan Board system; financial data of assets and deposits. Arrangement: Classified by type of membership; community banks and savings and loan associations are then geographical. Indexes: Alphabetical.

★4787★ Employment Opportunities, USA

Washington Research Associates
1660 S. Albion, Ste. 390
Denver, CO 80222
Ph: (303)756-9038   Fax: (303)770-1945

Annual, quarterly updates. $184.00, includes quarterly updates. Publication includes: List of over 1,000 employment contacts in companies and agencies in the banking, arts, telecommunications, education, and 14 other industries and professions, including the federal government. Entries include: Company name, name of representative, address, description of products or services, hiring and recruiting practices, training programs, and year established. Principal content is industry overviews, carrer news, and employment opportunity information on 14 different job markets. Arrangement: Classified by industry. Indexes: Occupation.

★4788★ Moody's Bank and Finance Manual

Moody's Investors Service, Inc.
99 Church St.
New York, NY 10007
Ph: (212)553-0300   Fax: (212)553-4700
Fr: 800-342-5647

Annual, July; supplements in *Moody's Bank & Finance News Reports*. $1,475.00, per year, including supplements. Covers in four volumes, over 20,000 national, state, and private banks, savings and loans, mutual funds, unit investment trusts, and insurance and real estate companies in the United States. Entries include: Company name, headquarters and branch offices, phones, names and titles of principal executives, directors, history, Moody's rating, and extensive financial and statistical data. Arrangement: Classified by type of business. Indexes: Company name.

★4789★ National Bankers Association— Roster of Minority Banking Institutions

National Bankers Association
1802 T St. NW
Washington, DC 20009
Ph: (202)588-5432   Fax: (202)588-5443

Annual, October. $5.00. Covers about 140 banks owned or controlled by minority group persons or women. Entries include: Bank name, address, phone, name of one executive. Arrangement: Geographical.

★4790★ Peterson's Job Opportunities in Business 1996

Peterson's
PO Box 2123
Princeton, NJ 08543-2123
Ph: (609)243-9111   Fax: (609)243-9150
Fr: 800-338-3282

Compiled by the Peterson's staff. Annual. $19.95 (paper). 416 pages. Profiles 2,000 companies that are hiring employees in a number of nontechnical fields, including financial services, management consulting, retailers, utilities, and consumer products companies. Contains job-search strategies and career options to help match education and expertise to the job market. Indexed geographically, by industry, and by hiring needs.

★4791★ Polk Financial Institutions Directory

R. L. Polk & Co.
PO Box 305100
Nashville, TN 37230-5100
Ph: (615)889-3350   Fax: (615)885-3081
Fr: 800-827-2265

Semiannual. $303.75. Covers 15,000 banks and their branches; over 2,000 head offices, and 15,500 branches of savings and loan associations; over 5,500 credit unions with assets over $5 million; Federal Reserve System and other U.S. government and state government banking agencies; bank holding, commercial finance, and leasing companies; ocverage includes the United States, Canada, Mexico, and Central America. Arrangement: Geographical. Indexes: Alphabetical.

★4792★ Roster of Minority Financial Institutions

U.S. Department of the Treasury
401 14th St. SW, Rm. 523-C
Washington, DC 20227
Ph: (202)874-6846   Fax: (202)874-6907

Biennial. Free. Covers about 170 commercial, minority-owned and controlled financial institutions participating in the Department of the Treasury's Minority Bank Deposit Program. Entries include: Name of institution, name and title of chief officer, address, phone, fax. Arrangement: Geographical.

★4793★ Thomson Bank Directory

Thomson Financial Publishing
4709 W. Golf Rd., 6th Fl.
Skokie, IL 60076-1253
Ph: (708)676-9600   Fax: (708)933-8101
Fr: 800-321-3373

Semiannual, May and November. $369.00, for 4-volume set. Covers in four volumes, about 11,000 banks and 50,000 branches of

United States banks, and 60,000 foreign banks and branches engaged in foreign banking; Federal Reserve system and other United States government and state government banking agencies; 500 largest North American and International commercial banks; paper and automated clearinghouses. Entries include: For domestic banks, bank name, address, phone, telex, cable, date established, routing number, charter type, bank holding company affiliation, memberships in Federal Reserve System and other banking organizations, principal officers by function performed, principal correspondent banks, and key financial data (deposits, etc.). For international banks, bank name, address, phone, fax, telex, cable, SWIFT address, transit or sort codes within home country, ownership, financial data, names and titles of key personnel, branch locations. For branches, bank name, address, phone, charter type, ownership and other details comparable to domestic bank listings. Arrangement: Geographical. Indexes: Alphabetical, geographical.

★4794★ Who's Who in Finance and Industry

Marquis Who's Who
Reed Reference Publishing
121 Chanlon Rd.
New Providence, NJ 07974
Ph: (908)464-6800   Fax: (908)665-6688
Fr: 800-521-8110

Biennial, July of odd years. $249.95, plus $17.50 shipping. Covers over 24,500 individuals. Entries include: Name, home and office addresses, personal, career, and family data; civic and political activities; memberships, publications, awards. Arrangement: Alphabetical.

HANDBOOKS AND MANUALS

★4795★ Business and Finance Career Directory

Gale Research
835 Penobscot Bldg.
Detroit, MI 48226-4094
Ph: (313)961-2242   Fax: (313)961-6083
Fr: 800-877-GALE

Bradley Morgan. Second edition, 1992. $39.00. 413 pages. Features a basic and comprehensive job search section, articles by top professionals in the field, and detailed listings of hundreds of top companies who hire individuals in this field. Aimed particularly at entry-level job hunters.

★4796★ Careers in Banking and Finance

Rosen Publishing Group, Inc.
29 E. 21st St.
New York, NY 10010
Ph: (212)777-3017   Fax: (212)777-0277
Fr: 800-237-9932

Patricia Haddock. 1990. $14.95. Offers advice on job hunting. Describes jobs at all levels in banking and finance. Contains information about the types of financial organiza-

tions where the jobs are found, educational requirements, job duties, and salaries.

★4797★ Encyclopedia of Careers and Vocational Guidance

J. G. Ferguson Publishing Co.
200 W. Monroe, Ste. 250
Chicago, IL 60606
Ph: (312)580-5480

William E. Hopke. Ninth edition, 1993. $129.95; $199.95 (CD-ROM). Four-volume set that profiles 900 occupations and describes job trends in 71 industries. Includes career description, educational requirements, history of the job, methods of entry, advancement, employment outlook, earnings, conditions of work, social and psychological factors, and sources of further information. Contains career and employment information for this field.

★4798★ Opportunities in Banking Careers

VGM Career Horizons
4255 W. Touhy Ave.
Lincolnwood, IL 60646-1975
Ph: (847)679-5500   Fax: (847)679-2494
Fr: 800-323-4900

Adrian A. Paradis. 1993. $14.95; $11.95 (paper). 160 pages. Discusses banking opportunities in a variety of settings: commercial banks, savings and loans, finance companies, and mortgage banks.

★4799★ Opportunities in Financial Careers

VGM Career Horizons
4255 W. Touhy Ave.
Lincolnwood, IL 60646-1975
Ph: (847)679-5500   Fax: (847)679-2494
Fr: 800-323-4900

Michael Sumichrast and Dean A. Christ. 1991. $14.95; $11.95 (paper). A guide to planning for and seeking opportunities in this challenging field.

★4800★ Where the Jobs Are: The Hottest Careers for the '90s

The Career Press, Inc.
3 Tice Rd.
PO Box 687
Franklin Lakes, NJ 07417
Ph: (201)848-0310   Fax: (201)848-1727
Fr: 800-237-3371

Joyce Hadley. Second edition, 1995. $9.99. 300 pages. Describes careers in fifteen general fields, from accounting to travel and hospitality.

EMPLOYMENT AGENCIES AND SEARCH FIRMS

★4801★ Addington Personnel Services
2401 Fountainview, Ste.104
Houston, TX 77057
Ph: (713)780-8810

Employment agency. Places individuals in regular or temporary positions.

★4802★ Cross Employment Agency
150 Broadway, Ste. 902
New York, NY 10038-4389
Ph: (212)227-6705

Employment agency. Temporary and regular placement of personnel.

★4803★ Financial Professionals
4100 Spring Valley Rd.
Farmers Branch, TX 75244-3618
Ph: (214)991-8999

Executive search consultants.

★4804★ J.B. Brown and Associates
Terminal Tower, Ste. 1114
Cleveland, OH 44113
Ph: (216)696-2525   Fax: (216)696-5825

Employment agency.

★4805★ Jim King and Associates
1301 Gulf Life Dr., Ste. 1901
Jacksonville, FL 32207-9062
Ph: (904)398-5464

Employment agency.

★4806★ Kanon Personnel Inc.
8 W. 40th St., 11th Fl.
New York, NY 10018-3994
Ph: (212)391-2610

Employment agency.

★4807★ The Murphy Group
1211 W. 22nd St., Ste. 221
Oak Brook, IL 60521-2115
Ph: (708)574-2840

Employment agency. Places personnel in a variety of positions.

★4808★ Romac International, Inc.
120 Hyde Park Pl., Ste. 200
Tampa, FL 33606
Fr: 800-341-0263

Executive search firm. More than 30 locations throughout the U.S.

★4809★ Source Finance
5580 LBJ Fwy., Ste. 300
Dallas, TX 75240
Ph: (214)385-3002   Fax: (214)717-0075

Executive search firm. Many affiliate offices located in most major cities throughout the U.S.

OTHER SOURCES

★4810★ American League of Financial Institutions (ALFI)
900 19th St. NW, Ste. 400
Washington, DC 20006
Ph: (202)857-3176   Fax: (202)296-8716

Members: Federal and state chartered minority savings and loan associations in 25 states and the District of Columbia. **Purpose:** Undertakes programs to increase the income of and savings flow into the associations including a direct solicitation effort; provides counseling and technical assistance for member associations; offers consultant services to assist individual associations and groups wishing to organize new associations or acquire existing associations with development potential; collects, organizes, and distributes materials that will aid member associations. **Activities:** Conducts research to improve investment capability, resolve common management problems, and evaluate statistical data on an industry-wide basis to develop and institute training programs for management personnel. Conducts research programs.

★4811★ Bank Administration Institute (BAI)

1 N. Franklin St.
Chicago, IL 60606
Ph: (312)553-4600   Fax: (312)683-2373
Fr: 800-323-8552

Purpose: Works to provide research, technical studies, publications, professional development programs, and advisory services to bank managers seeking to improve bank performance. **Activities:** Offers educational programs through conferences and research and technical studies in retail, payment systems, human resources, operations, lending, finance, executive education, audit, security, and compliance. Maintains The BAI School.

★4812★ Financial Managers Society (FMS)

8 S. Michigan Ave., Ste. 500
Chicago, IL 60603-3307
Ph: (312)578-1300   Fax: (312)578-1308

Purpose: Technical information exchange for financial managers of financial institutions.

★4813★ Robert Morris Associates - Association of Bank Loan and Credit Officers (RMA)

1 Liberty Pl.
1650 Market St., Ste. 2300
Philadelphia, PA 19103
Ph: (215)851-9100   Fax: (215)851-9206

Members: Commercial and savings banks and savings and loan institutions represented by more than 15,000 commercial loan and credit officers. **Activities:** Conducts research and professional development activities in areas of loan administration, asset management, and commercial lending and credit to increase professionalism. Named in honor of Robert Morris (1734-1806), a financier and politician. Provides Mentor training curriculum for commercial lending professionals. From more than 90,000 financial statements supplied by member institutions, annually compiles the Statement Studies containing average composite balance sheets for more than 360 different lines of business in manufacturing, wholesaling, retailing, and contracting.

Management Analysts and Consultants

SOURCES OF HELP-WANTED ADS

★4814★ Forbes

Forbes, Inc.
60 5th Ave.
New York, NY 10011
Ph: (212)620-2200   Fr: 800-888-9896

Biweekly. Magazine reporting on industry, business and finance management.

★4815★ National Business Employment Weekly

Dow Jones & Co., Inc.
PO Box 300
Princeton, NJ 08543
Ph: (609)520-4306   Fax: (609)520-4309
Fr: 800-323-NBEW

Weekly. $52.00/year. Magazine (tabloid) containing help-wanted advertising from the regional editions of the Wall Street Journal. Includes statistics and articles about employment opportunities and career advancement.

★4816★ Training & Development

American Society for Training and Development
1640 King St.
PO Box 1443
Alexandria, VA 22313
Ph: (703)683-8100   Fax: (703)683-8103

Monthly. $85.00/year for individuals. Magazine on training and development.

★4817★ Training Magazine

Adams Recreation Pub.
527 Marquette, Ste. 1300
Minneapolis, MN 55402
Ph: (612)342-2121   Fax: (612)342-2480
Fr: 800-923-2326

Monthly. $64.00/year for individuals; $74.00/year for Canada and Mexico; $85.00/year for other countries. Business magazine focusing on the impact of training on human performance and productivity in American organizations.

PLACEMENT AND JOB REFERRAL SERVICES

★4818★ Association of Management Consulting Firms (ACME)

521 5th Ave.
New York, NY 10175
Ph: (212)697-9693   Fax: (212)949-6571

Members: Division of Council of Consulting Organizations. Management consulting organizations that provide a broad range of managerial services to commercial, industrial, governmental, and other organizations and individuals. **Purpose:** Seeks to unite management consulting firms in order to develop and improve professional standards and practice in the field. **Activities:** Offers information and referral services on management consultants; administers public relations program. Conducts research.

★4819★ Franchise Consultants International Association (FCIA)

5147 S. Angela Rd.
Memphis, TN 38117
Ph: (901)867-0800   Fax: (901)867-0010

Members: Individuals and corporations involved in franchising including attorneys, consultants, brokers, sales personnel, suppliers, Universities, consulatants, advertisers, and developers. **Purpose:** To provide standardized information for the franchise industry. Seeks to coordinate effective and professional franchise consulting and to educate members in franchise law and logistics. Serves as a clearinghouse of approved literature on franchising. **Activities:** Operates archive and hall of fame; compiles statistics. Provides placement service, charitable program, and speakers' bureau.

★4820★ Organization Development Institute

11234 Walnut Ridge Rd.
Chesterland, OH 44026
Ph: (216)461-4333   Fax: (216)729-9319

Members: Professionals, students, and individuals interested in organization development. Disseminates information on and promotes a better understanding of organization development worldwide. **Purpose:** Conducts specialized education programs. Has developed a code of ethics and a competency test for individuals wishing to qualify as a Registered Organization Development Consultant. Has developed a statement on the knowledge and skill necessary to be competent in organization development and criteria for the accreditation of OD/OB academic programs. **Activities:** Maintains job and consultant information service. **E-Mail:** aa563@Cleveland.Freenet.edu

★4821★ Professional and Technical Consultants Association (PATCA)

PO Box 4143
Mountain View, CA 94040
Ph: (415)903-8305   Fax: (415)967-0995
Fr: 800-286-8703

Members: Independent consultants active in the support of business, industry, and government. **Activities:** Serves as a referral service to aid independent consultants in marketing their services as well as to assist those seeking their services. **E-Mail:** patca@ix.netcom.com **Website:** http://wwwpatca.org/patca

EMPLOYER DIRECTORIES AND NETWORKING LISTS

★4822★ ACME—The Association of Management Consulting Firms— Directory of Members

ACME
521 5th Ave., 35th Fl.
New York, NY 10175-3598
Ph: (212)697-9693   Fax: (212)949-6571

Biennial, latest edition October 1994. $50.00. Covers about 50 management consulting firms that are members of ACME. Entries include: Firm name, address, description of services offered, areas of expertise, locations of branch offices and affiliates. Arrangement: Alphabetical.

★4823★ American Consultants League—Consultants Directory

American Consultants League
1290 Palm Ave.
Sarasota, FL 34236
Ph: (813)952-9290   Fax: (813)925-3670

Annual, March. $30.00. Covers about 1,000 member consultants; international coverage. Entries include: Name, address, phone, specialty, description of expertise. Arrangement: Classified by specialty.

★4824★ Business Consultants Directory

American Business Directories, Inc.
American Business Information, Inc.
5711 S. 86th Cir.
Omaha, NE 68127
Ph: (402)593-4600   Fax: (402)331-1505

Annual. $910.00, U.S. edition. Entries include: Company or individual name, address, and phone (including area code), size of advertisement, year first in Yellow Pages, name of owner or manager, number of employees. Compiled from telephone company Yellow Pages, nationwide. Arrangement: Geographical.

★4825★ Business Management Consultants Directory

American Business Directories, Inc.
American Business Information, Inc.
5711 S. 86th Cir.
Omaha, NE 68127
Ph: (402)593-4600   Fax: (402)331-1505

Annual. $745.00, U.S. edition; $240.00, (Canad. ed.); payment with order. Entries include: Name, address, phone (including area code), size of advertisement, year first in Yellow Pages, name of owner or manager, number of employees. Compiled from telephone company Yellow Pages, nationwide. Arrangement: Geographical.

★4826★ Consultants and Consulting Organizations Directory

Gale Research
835 Penobscot Bldg.
Detroit, MI 48226-4094
Ph: (313)961-2242   Fax: (313)961-6083
Fr: 800-877-GALE

Annual, autumn; interedition supplement. $490.00; $400.00, supplement. Covers over 22,000 firms, individuals, and and organizations active in consulting. Entries include: Individual or organization name, address, phone, fax, telex, specialties, founding date, branch offices, names and titles of key personnel, number of employees, financial data, publications, conferences. Arrangement: By broad subject categories. Indexes: Subject, geographical, personal name, organization name.

★4827★ Consultants in the Midwest

Midwest Society of Professional
  Consultants
710 E. Ogden Ave., Ste. 113
Naperville, IL 60563
Ph: (312)201-0596

Annual. Covers members of the Midwest Society of Professional Consultants. Entries include: Individual member profiles, brief descriptions of each member's background,

experience, and expertise. Arrangement: Alphabetical. Indexes: Company name and area of specialization.

★4828★ Directory of Certified Business Counselors

Institute of Certified Business Counselors
PO Box 70326
Eugene, OR 97401
Ph: (503)345-8064   Fax: (503)726-2402

Irregular, updated as necessary. Available to members only. Covers 125 member counselors, brokers, and attorneys qualified to act as advisors for persons with business problems. Entries include: Name, address, phone, business specialty. Arrangement: Alphabetical.

★4829★ Directory of Management Consultants

Kennedy Publications
Templeton Rd.
Fitzwilliam, NH 03447
Ph: (603)585-6544   Fax: (603)585-9555
Fr: 800-531-0007

Biennial. $99.95, plus $7.00 shipping. Covers over 1,800 management consulting firms; coverage includes Canada and Mexico. Entries include: Firm name, address, phone, name of principal executive, date founded, number of employees, annual volume, services offered, SIC numbers of industries served, plus brief description of firm. Arrangement: Alphabetical. Indexes: Geographical, key principals, function, industry.

★4830★ Directory of Minority Management Consulting Firms

San Francisco Redevelopment Agency
770 Golden Gate Ave.
San Francisco, CA 94102
Ph: (415)749-2400

Annual. Free. Covers more than 60 management and tax consultants and appraisers. Entries include: Firm name, address, phone, name and title of contact, services, clients. Arrangement: Alphabetical.

★4831★ Dun & Bradstreet Reference Book of Corporate Managements

Dun & Bradstreet Information Services
Dun & Bradstreet Corp.
3 Sylvan Way
Parsippany, NJ 07054-3896
Ph: (201)605-6000   Fax: (201)605-6911
Fr: 800-526-0651

Annual, April. $785.00, lease basis; $635.00, for public libraries, lease basis. Covers nearly 200,000 presidents, directors, vice presidents, officers, and managers in 12,000 companies of greatest economic, marketing, and investment interests; those firms whose revenues are the highest in the United States. Arrangement: Alphabetical by company name. Indexes: Personal name (with abbreviated title and company affiliation), geographical, SIC code, advanced education institution, military affiliation.

★4832★ Dun's Consultants Directory

Dun & Bradstreet Information Services
Dun & Bradstreet Corp.
3 Sylvan Way
Parsippany, NJ 07054-3896
Ph: (201)605-6000   Fax: (201)605-6911
Fr: 800-526-0651

Annual, winter. $310.00, to public libraries; $415.00, to others (lease basis). Covers top 25,000 consulting firms in more than 200 areas of specialization. Entries include: Firm name, address, phone, sales, number of employees, year established, description of service, other locations, names and titles of key personnel, reference to parent company. Arrangement: Alphabetical. Indexes: Geographical, specialty, other location.

★4833★ Institute of Management Consultants—Directory of Members

Institute of Management Consultants
521 5th Ave., 35th Fl.
New York, NY 10175
Ph: (212)697-8262   Fax: (212)949-6571

Biennial, Periodic updates. $95.00, payment with order. Covers 2,400 individuals who practice management consulting as individuals or members of firms worldwide. Entries include: Name, firm, address, phone; areas of competence for certified management consultants. Arrangement: Classified by membership class, then alphabetical. Indexes: Geographical, industry specialization, consulting practice areas.

★4834★ Management Consulting: A Harvard Business School Career Guide

Harvard Business School Press
Harvard Business School
Gallatin E-115
Boston, MA 02163
Ph: (617)495-6700

Annual. $25.00. This book profiles management consulting firms that hire M.B.A. graduates. Describes companies, giving the name, address, contact person, and office locations. Explains what the company does and the recruiting process.

★4835★ MBA Employment Guide Report

Association of MBA Executives
5 Summit Pl.
Branford, CT 06405

Database covers: more than 4,000 firms that employ persons with Master of Business Administration degrees. More detailed profiles are given for 100 firms selected on the basis of their on-campus recruitment activity. Custom reports are issued upon request at $10.00 per report. Database includes: For companies covered in detail: name, headquarters location, description of business, current recruitment objectives, employment policies, benefits offered, name and address of employment representative, financial data. For others: name, location, contact person and telephone number, parent company (if any), code for primary line of business.

★4836★ Peterson's Job Opportunities in Business 1996

Peterson's
PO Box 2123
Princeton, NJ 08543-2123
Ph: (609)243-9111   Fax: (609)243-9150
Fr: 800-338-3282

Compiled by the Peterson's staff. Annual. $19.95 (paper). 416 pages. Profiles 2,000 companies that are hiring employees in a number of nontechnical fields, including financial services, management consulting, retailers, utilities, and consumer products companies. Contains job-search strategies and career options to help match education and expertise to the job market. Indexed geographically, by industry, and by hiring needs.

★4837★ Professional and Technical Consultants Association—Membership Directory

Professional and Technical Consultants Association
PO Box 4143
Mountain View, CA 94040
Ph: (415)903-8305   Fax: (415)967-0955
Fr: 800-286-8703

Annual, August. $15.00. Covers more than 350 consultants involved in computer technology, management, marketing, manufacturing, engineering, etc. Entries include: Individual or firm name, address, phone, specialties, degrees held. Arrangement: Alphabetical. Indexes: Specialty, geographical.

★4838★ The Woman's Consultants Directory

CAE Consultants, Inc.
41 Travers Ave.
Yonkers, NY 10705
Ph: (914)963-3695

Annual. $75.00. Covers About 3,000 women consultants in every line of business. Entries include: Consultant name, address, phone, fax, line of business, description. Arrangement: Classified by line of business.

HANDBOOKS AND MANUALS

★4839★ Become a Successful Consultant: Manage & Market Your Skills Effectively

Atrium Publishers Group
3356 Coffey Ln.
Santa Rosa, CA 95403
Ph: (707)542-5400   Fax: (707)542-5444
Fr: 800-275-2606

Raymond Hebson. 1995.

★4840★ Career Choices for the 90's for Students of Business

Walker and Company
435 Hudson St.
New York, NY 10014
Ph: (212)727-8300   Fax: (212)727-0984
Fr: 800-289-2553

Prepared by the Career Associates staff. 1990. $9.95. 166 pages. Discusses alternatives for students of business. Offers advice on how to break into the field and how to move up. Covers where and who the employers are, internship possibilities, and professional networking associations. Comprehensive guide to career and job search planning.

★4841★ Career Choices for the 90's for Students Considering an MBA

Walker and Company
435 Hudson St.
New York, NY 10014
Ph: (212)727-8300   Fax: (212)727-0984
Fr: 800-289-2553

Prepared by the Career Associates staff. 1990. $8.95. 166 pages. Discusses career alternatives and offers advice on how to break in and move up. Covers where and who the employers are, internship possibilities, and professional networking associations. Comprehensive guide to career and job search planning.

★4842★ Careers in Business

VGM Career Horizons
4255 W. Touhy Ave.
Lincolnwood, IL 60646-1975
Ph: (847)679-5500   Fax: (847)679-2494
Fr: 800-323-4900

Lila B. Stair and Dorothy Domkowski. 1992. $17.95; $13.95 (paper). 196 pages. Examines careers and job opportunities in business, including management and supervision. A separate chapter sketches the entrepreneurial opportunities of consulting or owning a small business.

★4843★ Developing a Consulting Practice

Sage Publications, Inc.
2455 Teller Rd.
Thousand Oaks, CA 91320
Ph: (805)499-0721   Fax: (805)499-0871

Robert O. Metzger. 1993. $27.50; $12.95 (paper).

★4844★ Jobs in Arts and Media Management: What They Are and How to Get One!

American Council for the Arts
1 E. 53rd St.
New York, NY 10022-4201
Ph: (212)223-2787   Fr: 800-321-4510

Stephen Langley and James Abruzzo. Revised edition, 1990. $21.95. 281 pages. Includes lists of about 150 sources of information on job opportunities in the arts, including organizations offering internships, job listings, graduate programs, and short-term study; professional groups concerned with theater, music, dance, opera, museum and gallery management, film, and telecommunication management. (Does not include popular music performing or music recording.) Entries include: For internships Organization name, address, phone, description, requirements. For job referral associations and periodicals - Association or publisher name, address, fields covered, services offered, turn-around time, average number of jobs, cost of subscription or dues, comments. Arrangement: Classified by type of source.

★4845★ Liberal Arts Jobs: What They Are and How to Get Them

Peterson's
PO Box 2123
Princeton, NJ 08543-2123
Ph: (609)243-9111   Fax: (609)243-9150
Fr: 800-338-3282

Burton Jay Nadler. Second edition, 1989. $9.95. 153 pages. Presents a list of the top 20 fields for liberal arts majors, covering more than 300 job opportunities. Discusses strategies for going after those jobs, including guidance on the language of a successful job search, informational interviews, and making networking work.

★4846★ Opportunities in Business Management Careers

VGM Career Horizons
4255 W. Touhy Ave.
Lincolnwood, IL 60646-1975
Ph: (847)679-5500   Fax: (847)679-2494
Fr: 800-323-4900

Irene Place. 1991. $14.95; $11.95 (paper). 160 pages. Provides guidance on the most effective channels to management positions.

★4847★ The Programmer's Survival Guide: Career Strategies for Computer Professionals

Prentice Hall
113 Sylvan Ave.
Rte. 9W
Englewood Cliffs, NJ 07632
Ph: (201)592-2000   Fr: 800-922-0579

Janet Lehrman Ruhl. 1989. $16.95. 280 pages. Contains information on career planning, job hunting, and job changing. Gives advice on the software packages needed in corporate America, how to interview, and when to change jobs.

★4848★ So You Want to Be a Consultant

Black Forrest Press
539 Telegraph Canyon Rd.
PO Box 521
Chula Vista, CA 91910-5704
Ph: (619)656-8048   Fax: (619)482-8704

Kabis. 1993. $59.95.

★4849★ The 10 Hottest Consulting Practices of the 1990s: What They Are, How to Get into Them

John Wiley & Sons, Inc.
605 3rd Ave.
New York, NY 10158-0012
Ph: (212)850-6000   Fr: 800-225-5945

Ron Tepper. 1995. $27.95.

EMPLOYMENT AGENCIES AND SEARCH FIRMS

★4850★ A.G. Fishkin and Associates, Inc.

PO Box 34413
Bethesda, MD 20827-0413
Ph: (301)770-4944

Employment agency.

★4851★ Boyden

375 Park Ave., Ste. 1008
New York, NY 10152
Ph: (212)980-6480

Executive search firm. Affiliate offices across the country and abroad.

★4852★ Conaway Legal Search

112 Hawthorn Rd.
Baltimore, MD 21210
Ph: (410)539-1234   Fax: (410)539-2734

Executive search firm.

★4853★ Don Richard Associates of Washington D.C.

1717 K St. NW, Ste. 1000
Washington, DC 20006-1587
Ph: (202)463-7210   Fax: (202)331-9743

Employment agency.

★4854★ Egon Zehnder International Inc.

55 E. 59th St., 14th Fl.
New York, NY 10022
Ph: (212)838-9199   Fax: (212)750-0574

Executive search firm. A number of U.S. and foreign affiliate offices.

★4855★ E.J. Ashton and Associates, Ltd.

3125 N. Wilke Rd.
Arlington Heights, IL 60004-1452
Ph: (708)577-7900

Employment agency. Executive search firm.

★4856★ Hawkes Peers

805 3rd Ave., 28th Fl.
New York, NY 10022
Ph: (212)593-3131   Fax: (212)593-3249

Executive search firm.

★4857★ Heidrick and Struggles, Inc.

125 S. Wacker Dr., Ste. 2800
Chicago, IL 60606-4590
Ph: (312)372-8811   Fax: (312)372-8641

Executive search firm. International organization with a variety of affiliate offices.

★4858★ Hintz Associates, Inc.

PO Box 442
Valhalla, NY 10595-1831
Ph: (914)761-4227

Executive search firm.

★4859★ Intech Summit Group, Inc.

6540 Lusk Blvd., C-228
San Diego, CA 92121
Ph: (619)452-2100

Employment agency and executive recruiter.

★4860★ Kenmore Executives Inc.

1 S. Ocean Blvd., Ste. 208
Boca Raton, FL 33432
Ph: (407)392-0700   Fax: (407)392-4748

Executive search firm.

★4861★ Korn/Ferry International

237 Park Ave.
New York, NY 10017
Ph: (212)687-1834   Fax: (212)986-5684

Executive search firm. International organization with a variety of affiliate offices.

★4862★ Protocol Inc.

300 N. Lake Ave., Ste. 208
Pasadena, CA 91101-4106
Ph: (818)449-2214   Fax: (818)577-0484

Executive search firm.

★4863★ Russell Reynolds Associates, Inc.

200 Park Ave.
New York, NY 10166-0002
Ph: (212)351-2000   Fax: (212)370-0896

Executive search firm. Affiliate offices across the country and abroad.

★4864★ SpencerStuart

277 Park Ave., 29th Fl.
New York, NY 10172
Ph: (212)336-0200

Executive search firm. A number of U.S. and foreign affiliate offices.

★4865★ Systems Careers

211 Sutter St., Ste. 607
San Francisco, CA 94108
Ph: (415)434-4770

Employment agency.

★4866★ Ward Howell International Inc.

99 Park Ave., 20th Fl.
New York, NY 10016-1699
Ph: (212)697-3730

Executive search firm. International organization with a variety of affiliate locations.

OTHER SOURCES

★4867★ American Almanac of Jobs and Salaries 1994-95

Avon Books
1350 Avenue of the Americas, 2nd Fl.
New York, NY 10019
Ph: (212)261-6800   Fr: 800-238-0658

John Wright. Revised edition, 1993. $17.00. 704 pages. This is a comprehensive guide to the wages of hundreds of occupations in a wide variety of industries and organizations.

★4868★ Consultants' Network (CN)

57 W. 89th St.
New York, NY 10024
Ph: (212)799-5239

Purpose: Independent consultants and principals in small consulting firms in all areas of consulting. Operates a clearinghouse. Provides referral and market support services.
Website: http://www.consultants-mall.com/

★4869★ Handbook of Management Consulting Services

McGraw-Hill, Inc.
1221 Avenue of the Americas
New York, NY 10020
Ph: (212)512-2000

Sam W. Barcus and Joseph W. Wilkinson. Second edition, 1995. $59.50. Practical guidebook that describes the management consulting profession and effective delivery and administration of management consulting services.

★4870★ How to Become a Successful Consultant in Your Own Field

Prima Publishing
3875 Atherton Rd.
Rocklin, CA 95765
Ph: (916)632-4400

Hubert Bermont. Third edition, 1991. $21.95. 240 pages.

★4871★ How to Make It Big as a Consultant

AMACOM
135 W. 50th St.
New York, NY 10020-1201
Ph: (212)903-8089   Fr: 800-262-9696

William A. Cohen. Second edition, 1990. Explains how to get clients and market consulting services. Gives advice on successfully negotiating contracts, writing a business proposal, and pricing the services offered.

★4872★ How to Succeed as an Independent Consultant

John Wiley and Sons
605 3rd Ave.
New York, NY 10158
Ph: (212)850-6000   Fr: 800-225-5945

Herman Holtz. Third edition, 1993. $29.95. 416 pages. Presents information on launching a consulting venture, how to identify and secure clients, and how to build a practice.

★4873★ The Independent Consultant's Q&A Book

Bob Adams, Inc.
260 Center St.
Holbrook, MA 02343
Ph: (617)767-8100   Fax: (617)767-0994
Fr: 800-872-5627

Lawrence Tuller. 1992. $10.95. 300 pages. Directed at those considering entering consulting, consultants in the early stages of developing their practice, and experienced consultants in search of new ideas or directions. Designed in a question-and-answer format to enable the reader to scan and focus on particular topics of interest.

★4874★ International Association of Career Consulting Firms (IACCF)

11250 Roger Bacon Dr., Ste. 8
Reston, VA 22090-5202
Ph: (703)525-1191   Fax: (703)276-8146

Members: Firms offering career counseling and outplacement services to business executives. (Outplacement services constitute training designed to prepare individuals for new careers while easing them out of their present jobs.) **Purpose:** Works to establish and advocate adherence to industry ethics; provides professional training and certification. Helps prepare legislation pertinent to the industry. Seeks to increase public acceptance of outplacement programs.

★4875★ *Marketing Your Consulting and Professional Services*

John Wiley and Sons, Inc.
605 3rd Ave.
New York, NY 10158
Ph: (212)850-6000   Fr: 800-225-5945

Richard A. Connor. Second edition, 1990. $29.95. Step-by-step guide to entering the consulting field including developing a marketing plan.

★4876★ **Organization Development Network (ODN)**

76 S. Orange Ave., Ste. 101
South Orange, NJ 07079-1923
Ph: (201)763-7337   Fax: (201)763-7488

Purpose: Practitioners, academics, managers, and students employed or interested in organization development. Works to enhance and provide opportunities for colleagueship and professional development.

Manufacturer's Sales Representatives

★4877★ Advertising Age's Business Marketing

Crain Communications, Inc.
740 N. Rush St.
Chicago, IL 60611
Ph: (312)649-5260   Fax: (312)649-5228

Monthly. $35.00/year for individuals. Trade magazine on business-to-business marketing news, strategy, and tactics.

★4878★ Agency Sales Magazine

Manufacturers' Agents National Association
23016 Mill Creek Rd.
PO Box 3467
Laguna Hills, CA 92654
Ph: (714)859-4040   Fax: (714)855-2973

Monthly. $37.50/year for individuals; $50.00/year for other countries. Magazine for manufacturers' agents and manufacturers. Includes tax developments and tips, management aids for manufacturers and agents, legal bulletins, trend-identifying market data, classified ads, industry trade show calendar, and new product information.

★4879★ American Bookseller

828 S. Broadway
Tarrytown, NY 10591
Ph: (914)631-7800   Fax: (914)631-8391
Fr: 800-637-0037

Monthly. Trade bookselling magazine.

★4880★ American Jewelry Manufacturer

Chilton Publications
825 7th Ave.
New York, NY 10019
Ph: (212)887-8400   Fax: (212)887-8484

Monthly. Trade magazine. Official publication of Manufacturing Jewelers and Silversmiths of America.

★4881★ American Metal Market

Chilton Publications
825 7th Ave., 7th Fl.
New York, NY 10019
Ph: (212)887-8550   Fax: (212)887-8520

Daily. $575.00/year. Newspaper of the metals industry, written for and read by executives and managers. Provides information for metal users, producers, distributors, and recyclers.

★4882★ American Papermaker

Roger's American Papermaker
57 Executive Park S, Ste. 310
Atlanta, GA 30329
Ph: (404)325-9153   Fax: (404)325-9581

Monthly. $30.00/year for individuals; $45.00/year for other countries. Magazine for paper manufacturing industry.

★4883★ BedTimes

International Sleep Products Association
333 Commerce St.
Alexandria, VA 22314
Ph: (703)683-8371   Fax: (703)683-4503

Monthly. $50.00/year; $65.00/year for other countries. Magazine covering trends and developments in the mattress industry.

★4884★ Bobbin

Bobbin Blenheim Media Corp.
1110 Shop Rd.
PO Box 1986
Columbia, SC 29202
Ph: (803)771-7500   Fax: (803)799-1461
Fr: 800-845-8820

Monthly. Trade magazine on sewn-products industry management and manufacturing. Reports on industry trends, technology, new products, etc.

★4885★ Building Supply Home Centers

Cahners Publishing Co.
1350 E. Touhy Ave.
Des Plaines, IL 60018
Ph: (708)635-8800   Fax: (708)390-2770

Monthly. Free to qualified subscribers; $60.00/year for individuals. Magazine for owners, executives, and managers responsible for product selection and purchase, merchandising, marketing, and management within the building supply retail and home center market.

★4886★ Chemical Business

Schnell Publishing Co., Inc.
80 Broad St.
New York, NY 10004-2203
Ph: (212)248-4177   Fax: (212)248-4901

Monthly. Magazine covering important aspects of chemical industry management.

★4887★ Chemical Marketing Reporter

Schnell Publishing Co., Inc.
80 Broad St.
New York, NY 10004-2203
Ph: (212)248-4177   Fax: (212)248-4901

Weekly (Mon.). $99.00/year. International tabloid newspaper for the chemical process industries. Includes analytical reports on developments in the chemical marketplace, plant expansions, new technology, corporate mergers, finance, current chemical prices, and regulatory matters.

★4888★ Concrete Products

Intertec Publishing Co.
29 N. Wacker Dr.
Chicago, IL 60606
Ph: (312)435-2330   Fax: (312)726-4103
Fr: 800-621-9907

Monthly. Magazine on concrete products and ready-mixed concrete.

★4889★ Cosmetics & Toiletries

Allured Publishing Corp.
362 S. Schmale Rd.
Carol Stream, IL 60188-2787
Ph: (708)653-2155   Fax: (708)653-2192

Monthly. $72.00/year for individuals; $100.00/year for Canada; $142.00/year for other countries. Trade magazine on cosmetic and toiletries manufacturing with an emphasis on product research and development issues.

★4890★ *Dealernews*

Advanstar Communications, Inc.
201 E. Sandpoint Ave., Ste. 600
Santa Ana, CA 92707-5761
Ph: (714)513-8400   Fax: (714)513-8414
Fr: 800-854-3112

Magazine covering motorcycles, watercraft, and other power sports.

★4891★ *Drug & Cosmetic Industry*

Advanstar Communications, Inc.
270 Madison Ave.
New York, NY 10016-0601
Ph: (212)951-6600   Fax: (212)481-6561

Monthly. $32.00/year; $5.00 for single issue. Trade magazine for manufacturers and merchandisers of personal products and health and beauty aids.

★4892★ *Earnshaw's Review*

Earnshaw Publications, Inc.
225 W. 34th St., Rm. 1212
New York, NY 10001
Ph: (212)563-2742   Fax: (212)629-3249

Monthly. Fashion and business magazine for retailers, manufacturers, licensees, and fiber companies in the children's apparel industry.

★4893★ *Electrical Wholesaling*

Intertec Publishing Corp.
9800 Metcalf
PO Box 12901
Overland Park, KS 66212-2215
Ph: (913)341-1300   Fax: (913)967-1898
Fr: 800-441-0294

Monthly. $20.00/year for individuals. Magazine focusing on electrical wholesaling.

★4894★ *Feedstuffs*

Miller Publishing Co.
12400 Whitewater Dr., Ste. 1600
Minnetonka, MN 55343
Ph: (612)931-0211   Fax: (612)938-1832

Weekly (Mon.). Magazine serving the grain and feed industries.

★4895★ *Food Production Management*

CTI Publications, Inc.
2619 Maryland Ave.
Baltimore, MD 21218
Ph: (410)467-3338   Fax: (410)467-7434

Monthly. $25.00/year for individuals; $5.00 for single issue. Magazine on food processing and individual packing news for management, sales, and production personnel in the canning, glass packing, and frozen food industries.

★4896★ *The Foodservice Distributor*

Peter Li
1100 Superior Ave.
Cleveland, OH 44114
Ph: (216)696-7000   Fax: (216)696-7670

Monthly. Trade magazine catering to food service distributor executives and sales representatives.

★4897★ *Furniture Today*

Cahners Publishing Company
7025 Albert Pick Rd., Ste.200
Greensboro, NC 27409
Ph: (910)605-0121   Fax: (910)605-1143

Weekly. $94.97/year for U.S., Canada, and Mexico. Furniture retailing and manufacturing magazine (tabloid).

★4898★ *Gases and Welding Distributor*

Peter Li
1100 Superior Ave.
Cleveland, OH 44114
Ph: (216)696-7000   Fax: (216)696-7670

Bimonthly. Distributors magazine featuring industrial, medical, specialty gases and welding supplies.

★4899★ *Health Foods Business*

PTN Publishing
445 Broad Hollow Rd.
Melville, NY 11747
Ph: (516)845-2700   Fax: (516)845-7109

Monthly. Health and nutrition magazine.

★4900★ *Implement and Tractor*

Freiberg Publishing
2302 W. 1st St.
Cedar Falls, IA 50613
Ph: (319)277-3599   Fax: (319)277-3783

Monthly. $25.00/year. Magazine on farm and industrial machinery.

★4901★ *Industrial Distribution*

Cahners Publishing Co.
275 Washington St.
Newton, MA 02158-1630
Ph: (617)964-3030   Fax: (617)558-4470

Monthly. Magazine covering industrial supplies marketing, management, sales, telecommunications, computers, inventory, and warehouse management.

★4902★ *Industrial Heating*

Business News Publishing Co.
1910 Cochran Rd., Ste. 630
Pittsburgh, PA 15220
Ph: (412)531-3370   Fax: (412)531-3375

Monthly. Magazine.

★4903★ *Institutional Distribution*

633 3rd Ave.
New York, NY 10010-1706
Ph: (212)986-4800   Fax: (212)983-3212

Monthly. $66.00/year; $7.00/single issue. Magazine for foodservice wholesalers and sales forces.

★4904★ *Kitchen & Bath Business*

Miller Freeman, Inc.
1515 Broadway
New York, NY 10036
Ph: (212)626-2380   Fax: (212)944-7164
Fr: 800-950-1314

Monthly. Trade magazine on kitchen and bath remodeling and construction.

★4905★ *Laser Focus World*

PennWell Publishing Co.
10 Tara Blvd., 5th Fl.
Nashua, NH 03062-2801
Ph: (603)891-0123   Fax: (603)891-0597

Monthly. $149.00/year for individuals; $10.00 for single issue. Magazine covering laser, optics, fiberoptics, detector imaging technology, and electro-optical equipment and systems.

★4906★ *LD+A*

Illuminating Engineering Society
120 Wall St. 7th Fl.
New York, NY 10005-4001

Monthly. $39.00/year for individuals; $54.00/year for other countries; $4.00 for single issue. Magazine presenting current lighting and energy news and applications.

★4907★ *LDB Interior Textiles Magazine*

Columbia Communications, Inc.
342 Madison Ave., Ste. 1901
New York, NY 10017
Ph: (212)661-1516   Fax: (212)661-1713

Monthly. Magazine for buyers of home fashions, including linens, domestics and bath products, window treatments, home fragrances, decorative pillows and accessories.

★4908★ *Manufacturers Representatives of America–Newsline*

Manufacturers Representatives of America
PO Box 150229
Arlington, TX 76015-6229
Ph: (817)465-5511

Quarterly. Included in membership. Published for member independent manufacturers' representatives handling sanitary supplies and paper and plastic disposable products. Carries articles to help improve agent sales skills, market coverage, and customer service, and to help establish more effective agent/principal communications. Recurring features include news of members, a calendar of events, job listings, notices of publications available, news of educational opportunities, and a column titled: President's Report.

★4909★ *Marketing Computers*

Billboard Magazine
33 Commercial St.
Gloucester, MA 01930
Ph: (508)281-3110   Fax: (508)281-0136

Monthly. $30.00/year for individuals. Marketing and advertising magazine.

★4910★ *Med Ad News*

Engel Publishing Ptrs.
820 Bear Tavern Rd., Ste. 302
West Trenton, NJ 08628
Ph: (609)530-0044   Fax: (609)530-0207

Monthly. Pharmaceutical business and marketing magazine.

★4911★ Medical Products Sales

McKnight Medical Communications Co.
2 Northfield Plaza, Ste. 300
Northfield, IL 60093-1217
Ph: (708)441-3700   Fax: (708)441-3701
Fr: 800-451-7838

Monthly. Tabloid on medical products distribution and health industry sales and marketing topics.

★4912★ Milling & Baking News

Sosland Publishing Co.
4800 Main St., Ste. 100
Kansas City, MO 64112
Ph: (816)756-1000   Fax: (816)756-0494

Weekly (Tues.). $89.00/year for individuals. Trade magazine covering the grain-based food industries.

★4913★ Modern Grocer

Grocers Publishing Co., Inc.
15 Emerald St.
Hackensack, NJ 07601
Ph: (201)488-1800

Semimonthly. Magazine for food retailers, wholesalers, distributors, brokers, manufacturers, and packers in the metro New York and New Jersey marketing area.

★4914★ Modern Jeweler

Vance Publishing Corp.
10901 W. 84th Terr.
Lenexa, KS 66214
Ph: (913)438-8700   Fax: (913)438-0692
Fr: 800-255-5113

Monthly. $25.00/year for individuals; $4.00 for single issue; $100.00/year for other countries. Trade magazine for retail jewelers.

★4915★ Modern Plastics

New York Construction News
1221 Avenue of the Americas, 41st Fl.
New York, NY 10020
Ph: (212)512-4773   Fax: (212)512-4770

Monthly. Magazine for the plastics industry.

★4916★ Money Making Opportunities

Success Publishing International
11071 Ventura Blvd.
Studio City, CA 91604
Ph: (818)980-9166

Monthly. Classified advertising magazine.

★4917★ Multi-Housing News

Miller Freeman, Inc.
1515 Broadway
New York, NY 10036
Ph: (212)626-2380   Fax: (212)944-7164
Fr: 800-950-1314

$30.00/year. Trade magazine (tabloid).

★4918★ National Home Center News

Lebhar-Friedman, Inc.
425 Park Ave.
New York, NY 10022
Ph: (212)756-5257   Fax: (212)756-5270

Semimonthly. $99.00/year for individuals; $119.00/year for Canada; $279.00/year for other countries. Business tabloid serving home center/building material retailers.

★4919★ Nursery Business Retailer

Brantwood Publications, Inc.
3023 Eastland Blvd., Ste. 103
Clearwater, FL 34621-4106
Ph: (813)796-3877   Fax: (813)791-4126

Bimonthly. $15.00/year for individuals; $3.00 for single issue. Wholesale and retail nursery operations magazine.

★4920★ Opportunity Magazine

73 Spring St., Ste. 303
New York, NY 10012
Ph: (212)925-3612

Monthly. $15.89/year; $2.00/issue.

★4921★ Packaging

Cahners Publishing Co.
1350 E. Touhy Ave. St.
Des Plaines, IL 60018
Ph: (708)635-8800

Thirteen issues/year. $84.95/year.

★4922★ Pharmaceutical Marketers Directory

CPS Communications, Inc.
7200 W. Camino Real, Ste. 215
Boca Raton, FL 33433
Ph: (407)368-9301   Fax: (407)368-7870

Annual. $155.00.

★4923★ Photo Marketing

Photo Marketing Association International
3000 Picture Pl.
Jackson, MI 49201
Ph: (517)788-8100   Fax: (517)788-8371

Monthly. $25.00/year for individuals; $30.00/year for Canada. Trade magazine for photo/video dealers and photo finishers.

★4924★ Profitable Craft Merchandising

PJS Publications, Inc.
2 News Plaza
PO Box 1790
Peoria, IL 61656
Ph: (309)682-6626   Fax: (309)682-7394

Monthly. $30.00/year for individuals. Magazine for retailers of craft, needlework, and sewing supplies.

★4925★ Rental Dealer News

2900 Bristol St., Ste. J101
Costa Mesa, CA 92626
Ph: (714)546-9501

Monthly.

★4926★ RV Business

TL Enterprises, Inc.
2575 Vista Del Mar Dr.
Ventura, CA 93001
Ph: (805)667-4100   Fax: (805)667-4484

Monthly. $48.00/year for individuals; $2.00 for single issue. Magazine about the business of manufacturing, distributing, and selling travel trailers, conversion vehicles, and motorhomes and related parts, accessories, and services.

★4927★ Sales & Marketing Management

Bill Communications, Inc.
355 Park Ave. S
New York, NY 10010-1789
Ph: (212)592-6200   Fax: (212)592-6309
Fr: 800-821-6897

Business magazine.

★4928★ Security Distributing and Marketing

Cahners Publishing Co.
1350 E. Touhy Ave.
Des Plaines, IL 60018
Ph: (708)635-8800   Fax: (708)390-2770

Monthly. Free to qualified subscribers. Trade magazine focusing on security, burglar, and fire alarm systems protection.

★4929★ Sporting Goods Dealer

Times Mirror Magazines, Inc.
2 Park Ave.
New York, NY 10016
Ph: (212)779-5285   Fax: (212)779-5465

Monthly. Magazine providing merchandising information, market data, and new product information to retailers of sporting goods.

★4930★ Textile Chemist and Colorist

American Association of Textile Chemists and Colorists
PO Box 12215
Research Triangle Park, NC 27709
Ph: (919)549-8141   Fax: (919)549-8933

Monthly. $40.00/year for U.S. and Canada; $55.00/year for other countries. Magazine focusing on dyeing, finishing of fibers and fabrics.

★4931★ Tile & Decorative Surfaces

Tile & Decorative Surfaces
6300 Variel Ave., Ste.I
Woodland Hills, CA 91367
Ph: (818)704-5555   Fax: (818)704-6500

Monthly. $50.00/year for individuals; $5.00 for single issue. International trade publication available to the hard surfaces industries: ceramic tile, natural stone tiles, terrazzo, cement tiles, glass tiles, and agglome rated marble and granite tiles.

★4932★ Timber Harvesting

Hatton-Brown Publishers, Inc.
225 Hanrick St.
Montgomery, AL 36104
Ph: (334)834-1170   Fax: (334)834-4525
Fr: 800-669-5613

Monthly. Free to qualified subscribers; $30.00/year for individuals. National magazine for the U.S. logging industry.

★4933★ TWICE

Cahners Publishing Co.
249 W. 17th St.
New York, NY 10010
Ph: (212)645-0067   Fax: (212)337-7066

Semiweekly. Trade tabloid covering consumer electronics, appliance, and camera industries for retailers, manufacturers, and distributors.

★4934★ UAMR Confidential Bulletin

United Association of Manufacturers'
Representatives
PO Box 986
Dana Point, CA 92629
Ph: (714)240-4966   Fax: (714)240-4966

Monthly. Included in membership. Covers product lines offered for representation in all fields. Provides details of the company and product, type of accounts to be serviced, and the areas open for representation. Subscription includes three newsletters and bulletin of lines for representatives.

★4935★ Undercar Digest

M D Publications, Inc.
PO Box 2210
Springfield, MO 65801-2210
Ph: (417)866-3917   Fax: (417)866-2781
Fr: 800-274-7890

Monthly. $34.00/year; $3.00 for single issue. Magazine for the undercar service and supply industry.

★4936★ Video Software

825 7th Ave., 6th Fl.
New York, NY 10019
Ph: (212)887-8400   Fax: (212)887-8384

Monthly. $60.00/year. Magazine for retailers and wholesalers of prerecorded video programming.

★4937★ The Wholesaler

Cahner's Publishing
455 N. Michigan Ave.
Chicago, IL 60611-5503
Ph: (312)222-2000   Fax: (312)222-2026

Monthly. $75.00/year for individuals; $10.00 for single issue. Tabloid featuring wholesale plumbing, heating, air conditioning, pipe, valves, and fittings.

★4938★ World Fence News

World Fence & Data Center
6101 W. Courtyard Dr.
Bldg. 3 Ste.115
Austin, TX 78730
Ph: (512)349-2536   Fax: (512)349-2567
Fr: 800-231-0275

Monthly. Trade magazine featuring news, technical articles, new products, and humor for fencing and access control industries.

★4939★ Yard and Garden

Johnson Hill Press, Inc.
1233 Jonesville Ave.
PO Box 803
Fort Atkinson, WI 53538-0803
Ph: (414)563-1619   Fax: (414)563-1702
Fr: 800-547-7377

$21.00/year for individuals; $28.00/year for Canada and Mexico. Yard and garden magazine featuring product news and retailer success stories.

PLACEMENT AND JOB REFERRAL SERVICES

★4940★ Automotive Booster Clubs International (ABCI)

1806 Johns Dr.
Glenview, IL 60025
Ph: (708)729-2227   Fax: (708)729-3670

Members: Sales executives or salespersons representing independent manufacturers and manufacturers' agents of replacement parts, supplies, accessories, and equipment in the automotive aftermarket or service industry. **Activities:** Maintains placement service for manufacturers' representatives who are members of a local booster club and an automotive career opportunity program. Sponsors ABCI Educational and Scholastic Foundation.

★4941★ National Association of Business and Industrial Saleswomen (NABIS)

5107 Mesa Dr.
Castle Rock, CO 80104
Ph: (303)660-3693   Fax: (303)660-5053

Members: An online virtual community of women. Women who sell business and industrial products or services. **Purpose:** Facilitates the exchange of ideas and experiences in an effort to further professional and personal development for women in business and industrial sales. Encourages women to enter the sales field and to move into sales/marketing management; seeks recognition of saleswomen's needs through trade publications and other media. **Activities:** Provides resource services to corporations and individuals. Maintains career counseling for individuals and search services for organizations. Fee schedule according to ability to pay. **E-Mail:** charlyjo@ix.netcom.com

★4942★ National Electrical Manufacturer's Representatives Association (NEMRA)

200 Business Park Dr., Ste. 301
Armonk, NY 10504
Ph: (914)273-6780   Fax: (914)273-6785

Purpose: North American trade association dedicated to promoting continuing education, professionalism, and the use of independent manufacturers representatives in the electrical industry. Offers professional development programs in business management and sales training, and offers a proprietary computer system for independent electrical representatives. Sponsors educational programs; compiles statistics; and holds an annual networking conference for its representative members and their manufacturers.

★4943★ National Marine Representatives Association (NMRA)

PO Box 660
Camden, TN 38320
Ph: (901)584-0203   Fax: (901)584-0420

Members: Independent sales representatives working on straight commission for firms producing boats, motors, and marine accessories. **Purpose:** Conducts employment clearinghouse for manufacturers seeking representatives. **Activities:** Participates in annual International Marine Trades Exhibit and Miami International Boat Show.

★4944★ National Shoe Traveler's Association (NSTA)

PO Box 456
Abington, MA 02351
Ph: 800-200-6782   Fax: (617)871-8033

Members: Traveling salespeople handling shoes and related products on the wholesale and retail levels. **Activities:** Holds seminars for members. Conducts certified footwear representative program. Compiles statistics; maintains placement service.

★4945★ Sporting Goods Agents Association (SGAA)

PO Box 998
Morton Grove, IL 60053
Ph: (708)296-3670   Fax: (708)827-0196

Members: Manufacturers' agents whose goal is to provide free legal counsel for members and additional product lines from manufacturers, and to improve the image of the independent agent. Maintains Sporting Goods Agents Hall of Fame. **Activities:** Offers placement service.

EMPLOYER DIRECTORIES AND NETWORKING LISTS

★4946★ Agricultural & Industrial Manufacturers Representatives Association—Membership Directory

Agricultural & Industrial Manufacturers Representatives Association
5818 Reeds Rd.
Shawnee Mission, KS 66202-2740
Ph: (913)262-4511   Fax: (913)262-0174

Annual, January. $25.00. Covers 135 members; coverage includes Canada. Entries include: Company name, address, phone, name of principal executive, territory covered. Arrangement: Alphabetical.

★4947★ American Hardware Manufacturers Association—Rep/Factory Contact Service Directory

American Hardware Manufacturers Association (AHMA)
801 N. Plaza Dr.
Schaumburg, IL 60173
Ph: (708)605-1025   Fax: (708)605-1093

Annual, April. $250.00. Covers over 280 manufacturer representatives in the hardware industry. Entries include: Firm name, address, number of years in business, number of salespeople, territory covered, manufacturers represented, products or service offered, type of accounts currently served, whether firm has a distribution network or warehouses, whether firm provides rack-jobber service. Arrangement: Geographical. Indexes: Product line, firm name.

★4948★ American Manufacturers Directory

American Business Directories, Inc.
American Business Information, Inc.
5711 S. 86th Cir.
Omaha, NE 68127
Ph: (402)593-4600   Fax: (402)331-5481

Annual, January. $495.00, lease basis. Covers more than 120,000 manufacturing companies with 25 or more employees. Entries include: Company name, address, phone, contact name, Standard Industrial Classification (SIC) codes, number of employees, sales volume code. Arrangement: Entries listed alphabetically, geographically, and by Standard Industrial Classification (SIC) code. Indexes: Geographical.

★4949★ American Salon's Green Book

Advanstar Communications, Inc.
270 Madison Ave.
New York, NY 10016
Ph: (212)951-6600

Annual, December. $80.00, plus $3.50 shipping. Covers about 1,300 manufacturers of supplies and equipment for barbers and cosmetologists; 130 manufacturers' representatives; 3,200 distributors; employment agencies, show management companies, and related trade organizations. Entries include: For manufacturers and agents: company name, address, phone, names of principal executives, products available. For distributors: company name, address, phone, branches, name of owner or president, number of sales representatives, trade association affiliation, Metropolitan Statistical Area (MSA) in which located. For representatives: company name, address, phone, territory covered. Arrangement: Manufacturers are alphabetical; agents, distributors, representatives are geographical. Indexes: Product, trade name.

★4950★ American Wholesalers and Distributors Directory

Gale Research
835 Penobscot Bldg.
Detroit, MI 48226-4094
Ph: (313)961-2242   Fax: (313)961-6083
Fr: 800-877-GALE

Third edition, 1994. $170.00. 2000 pages. Lists wholesalers and distributors on national, regional, state, and major local area levels. Includes statistical listing of the top 50 companies in each SIC area ranked by sales. Entries include: name, address, principal product lines, generic brands and private labels, territory and distribution area, total number of employees, estimated annual sales volume, means of distribution, and other details. Indexes: Geographic, brand name, product line, and SIC.

★4951★ Automotive Parts & Accessories Association— Manufacturers' Representatives Roster, Aftermarket Resource Bibliography

Automotive Parts & Accessories Association (APAA)
4600 East-West Hwy., Ste. 300
Bethesda, MD 20814-3415
Ph: (301)654-6664   Fax: (301)654-3299

Annual, fall. $30.00. Covers over 350 manufacturers' representatives (both firms and individuals) engaged in the automotive aftermarket. Representatives are grouped in two sections; alphabetical and state covered. Entries include: Company and individual names, address, phone, number of salespersons, products handled, state covered, and warehouse facilities. Arrangement: Alphabetical.

★4952★ Automotive Service Industry Association–Guide to Manufacturers' Representatives

Automotive Service Industry Association
25 Northwest Pt., No. 425
Elk Grove Village, IL 60007-1035
Ph: (708)228-1310   Fax: (708)228-1510

Biennial, June of odd years. $125.00. Covers 200 manufacturers' agents serving the automotive parts and equipment aftermarket industry. Entries include: Company name, address; name, business phone of owner; branch locations, services, territory covered, list of products handled. Arrangement: Geographical. Indexes: Geographical, product lines sold, alphabetical.

★4953★ Electrical Equipment Representatives Association— Membership Directory

Electrical Equipment Representatives Association
406 W. 34th St.
Kansas City, MO 64111
Ph: (816)753-0210   Fax: (816)753-1954

Annual, October. Covers more than 105 manufacturers' representatives of electrical equipment companies. Entries include: Company name, address, phone, names and titles of key personnel. Arrangement: Alphabetical.

★4954★ Electronic Industry Manufacturers' Representatives Locator

Electronics Representatives Association
20 E. Huron St.
Chicago, IL 60611
Ph: (312)649-1333   Fax: (312)649-9509

Annual, September. $50.00. Covers 2,000 member firms; international coverage. Entries include: Firm name, address, phone; names of owners; facilities; states in territory; association divisional memberships; number of employees; branch offices' addresses, phone numbers, fax, and names of managers. Type of product handled is shown in separate tabulation at beginning of each chapter section. Arrangement: Geographical, by chapter. Indexes: Key personnel name, company.

★4955★ Gift and Decorative Accessories Center Association— Directory

Gift and Decorative Accessories Center Association
59 Middlesex Tpke.
Bedford, MA 01730
Ph: (617)275-2775

Semiannual, January and July. Free. Covers about 100 individuals who are giftware manufacturers' representatives in New England; also lists their manufacturers and suppliers. Entries include: For representatives: name, address, phone, manufacturers and products represented. Arrangement: Alphabetical.

★4956★ Hardware Age Who's Who Verified Directory of Hardlines Distribution

Chilton Co.
Chilton Way
Randnor, PA 19089
Ph: (610)964-4269   Fax: (610)964-4284

Biennial, July of even years. $195.00, payment with order. Covers about 2,900 hardware wholesalers, specialty distributors, manufacturers' representatives, retailers (hardware, home center, building material, general retail, home and auto supply, specialty stores) and export management companies. Entries include: Generally, company name, address, phone, sales volume, territories covered, names of principal executives, area served, buyers of lines handled, special services (drop shipments, warehousing, etc.), if any, type of outlet, number of salesmen. Arrangement: Classified by type of company, then geographical.

★4957★ MacRae's Blue Book

MacRae's Blue Book, Inc.
Business Research Publications, Inc.
65 Bleecker St.
New York, NY 10012
Ph: (212)673-4700   Fax: (212)475-1790
Fr: 800-622-7237

Annual, March. $165.00, plus $5.00 shipping (1995 edition). Covers about 50,000 manufacturing firms. Entries include: Company name, address, products or services, phone, locations and phone numbers of branches and sales outlets. Arrangement: Alphabetical. Indexes: Corporate, Product/service (with address and financial key), trade name.

★4958★ Manufacturers' Agents National Association—Directory of Manufacturers' Sales Agencies

Manufacturers' Agents National Association
PO Box 3467
Laguna Hills, CA 92654
Ph: (714)859-4040   Fax: (714)855-2973

Annual, May/June. Covers 9,000 independent agents and firms representing manufacturers and other businesses in specified territories on a commission basis, including consultants and associate member firms interested in the manufacturer/agency method of marketing. Arrangement: Separate alphabetical sections for manufacturers and agencies. Indexes: Geographical, target industries.

★4959★ Manufacturers Agents & Representatives Directory

American Business Directories, Inc.
American Business Information, Inc.
5711 S. 86th Cir.
Omaha, NE 68127
Ph: (402)593-4600   Fax: (402)331-1505

Annual. $745.00, U.S. edition; $145.00, (Canad. ed.); payment with order. Number of listings: 20,385 (U.S. edition); 1,677 (Canadian edition). Entries include: Name, address, phone (including area code), size of advertisement, year first in Yellow Pages, name of owner or manager, number of employees. Compiled from telephone company Yellow Pages, nationwide. Arrangement: Geographical.

★4960★ Manufacturers Representatives of America—Yearbook and Directory of Members

Manufacturers Representatives of America
PO Box 150229
Arlington, TX 76017
Ph: (817)465-5511   Fax: (817)468-5757

Annual, fall. $250.00. Covers several hundred independent manufacturers' representatives in paper, plastic, packaging, and sanitary supplies. Entries include: Name, address, phone, distributors served, territory, number of persons in sales, branch offices, products handled, marketing services provided, warehouse locations and facilities. Arrangement: Geographical. Indexes: Organization, personal name.

★4961★ National Association of Specialty Food and Confection Brokers— Directory of Members

National Association of Specialty Food and Confection Brokers
c/o Judi Epstein, Chesapeake Sales
11044 Wood Elves Way
Columbia, MD 21044
Ph: (410)587-0923   Fax: (410)741-0328

Annual, summer; updated as needed. Free, request on company letterhead. Covers about 100 member brokerage companies dealing in specialty foods, confections, and candy. Entries include: Firm name, address, phone; geographical area covered; types of accounts solicited. Arrangement: Geographical.

★4962★ Office Products Representatives Alliance—Rep Locator

Office Products Representatives Association
330 S. Wells St., No. 1422
Chicago, IL 60606
Ph: (312)360-0386   Fax: (312)360-0388

Annual, January. $25.00. Covers about 105 member manufacturers' representative firms in the office products industry. Entries include: Firm name, address, phone, names of contacts, fax. Arrangement: Geographical.

★4963★ Pharmaceutical Products–Wholesalers & Manufacturers Directory

American Business Directories, Inc.
American Business Information, Inc.
5711 S. 86th Cir.
Omaha, NE 68127
Ph: (402)593-4600   Fax: (402)331-1505

Annual. $255.00, payment with order. Entries include: Name, address, phone (including area code), size of advertisement, year first in Yellow Pages, name of owner or manager, number of employees. Compiled from telephone company Yellow Pages, nationwide. Arrangement: Geographical.

★4964★ Wholesaler—Wholesaling 100 Issue

TMB Publishing Inc.
1838 Techny Ct.
Northbrook, IL 60062
Ph: (708)564-1127   Fax: (708)564-1264

Annual, July. $25.00. Publication includes: List of 100 leading wholesalers of plumbing, heating, air conditioning, refrigeration equipment, and supplies such as industrial pipe, valves and fittings. Entries include: Company name, address, phone, fax, names and titles of key personnel, number of employees, business breakdown (percentage). Arrangement: Ranked by sales.

★4965★ Who's Where? Sales and Marketing Management in the Computer Industry

Ex-IBM Corp.
2713 Foxboro Dr.
Garland, TX 75044
Ph: (214)414-0046

Updated continuously; printed on request. $95.00, base edition. Covers about 1,900 sales and marketing executives at about 1,000 firms in the computer industry. Entries include: Name, title, company name, address, phone. Arrangement: Alphabetical. Indexes: Company name, title, geographical by ZIP code; indexes are available as supplements to the base edition.

★4966★ Who's Who in Direct Selling

Direct Selling Association
1666 K St. NW, Ste. 1010
Washington, DC 20006-2808
Ph: (202)293-5760

Free with return postage for two ounces. 15 pages.

HANDBOOKS AND MANUALS

★4967★ America's Top Office, Management, & Sales Jobs

JIST Works, Inc.
720 N. Park Ave.
Indianapolis, IN 46202-3431
Ph: (317)264-3720   Fax: (317)264-3709
Fr: 800-648-5478

Compiled by Michael J. Farr. 1993. $11.95 (paper).

★4968★ Career Choices for the 90's for Students of Business

Walker and Company
435 Hudson St.
New York, NY 10014
Ph: (212)727-8300   Fax: (212)727-0984
Fr: 800-289-2553

Prepared by the Career Associates staff. 1990. $9.95. 166 pages. Discusses alternatives for students of business. Offers advice on how to break into the field and how to move up. Covers where and who the employers are, internship possibilities, and professional networking associations. Comprehensive guide to career and job search planning.

★4969★ Career Choices for the 90's for Students of Communications and Journalism

Walker and Company
435 Hudson St.
New York, NY 10014
Ph: (212)727-8300   Fax: (212)727-0984
Fr: 800-289-2553

Prepared by the Career Associates staff. 1990. $8.95. 166 pages. Discusses alternatives for students of communications and journalism. Offers advice on how to break into the field and how to move up. Covers where and who the employers are, internship possibilities, and professional networking associations. Comprehensive guide to career and job search planning.

★4970★ Career Choices for the 90's for Students of Political Science and Government

Walker and Company
435 Hudson St.
New York, NY 10014
Ph: (212)727-8300   Fax: (212)727-0984
Fr: 800-289-2553

Prepared by the Career Associates staff. 1990. $8.95. 166 pages. Discusses alternatives for students of political science and government. Offers advice on how to break into the field and how to move up. Covers where and who the employers are, internship possibilities, and professional networking associations. Comprehensive guide to career and job search planning.

★4971★ Career Choices for the 90's for Students of Psychology

Walker and Company
435 Hudson St.
New York, NY 10014
Ph: (212)727-8300   Fax: (212)727-0984
Fr: 800-289-2553

Prepared by the Career Associates staff. 1990. $9.95. 166 pages. Discusses alternatives for students of psychology. Offers advice on how to break into the field and how to move up. Covers where and who the employers are, internship possibilities, and professional networking associations. Comprehensive guide to career and job search planning.

★4972★ The Encyclopedia of Career Choices for the 1990s: Guide to Entry-Level Jobs

Perigree Books
The Berkley Publishing Group
PO Box 506
East Rutherford, NJ 07073
Ph: (201)933-9292   Fr: 800-223-0510

Career Associates Staff. 1992. $19.95. 862 pages. Describes 500 entry-level careers in a variety of industries. Presents qualifications required, working conditions, salary, internships, and professional associations.

★4973★ The Manufacturers' Agent

Manufacturers' Agents National
  Association
23016 Mill Creek Rd.
PO Box 3467
Laguna Hills, CA 92654-3467
Ph: (714)859-4040

Brochure. Free. 5 pages. Covers duties, qualifications, education, earnings, and employment outlook.

★4974★ Marketing and Sales Career Directory

Gale Research
835 Penobscot Bldg.
Detroit, MI 48226-4094
Ph: (313)961-2242   Fax: (313)961-6083
Fr: 800-877-GALE

Bradley Morgan. Fourth edition, 1992. $39.00. 341 pages. Features extensive listings of contacts and entry-level job opportunities at major corporations, research supplier firms, and major advertising and public relations agencies nationwide. Aimed at students looking for jobs in any area of marketing, advertising, or sales on the corporate side.

★4975★ 100 Best Careers for the Year 2000

Prentice Hall General Reference
15 Columbus Cir.
New York, NY 10023
Ph: (212)373-8500   Fr: 800-223-2348

Shelly Field. 1992. $15.00 (paper). Covers 100 of the fastest growing jobs. The publication is divided in 11 general employment sections. Specific careers are covered within each section. Provides job description, responsibilities, employment opportunities, earnings, education and training, advancement opportunities, and experience and qualifications for each occupation.

★4976★ Opportunities in Marketing Careers

VGM Career Horizons
4255 W. Touhy Ave.
Lincolnwood, IL 60646-1975
Ph: (847)679-5500   Fax: (847)679-2494
Fr: 800-323-4900

Margery Steinberg. 1994. $14.95; $11.95 (paper). 160 pages. Includes guidance on identifying and pursuing job opportunities. Illustrated.

★4977★ Opportunities in Pharmacy Careers

VGM Career Horizons
4255 W. Touhy Ave.
Lincolnwood, IL 60646-1975
Ph: (847)679-5500   Fax: (847)679-2494
Fr: 800-323-4900

Fred B. Gable. 1990. $14.95; $11.95 (paper). Identifies opportunities in a variety of settings, including retail chains, private ownership, clinics, hospitals, and other private, commercial, and industrial operations. Provides information on job-hunting techniques. Illustrated.

★4978★ Opportunities in Sales Careers

VGM Career Horizons
4255 W. Touhy Ave.
Lincolnwood, IL 60646-1975
Ph: (847)679-5500   Fax: (847)679-2494
Fr: 800-323-4900

James Briscoll and Ralph Dahm. 1995. $14.95; $11.95 (paper). Details sales in retail, wholesale and industrial sales, sales of services and intangibles, and sales management. Illustrated.

★4979★ Opportunities in Vocational and Technical Careers

VGM Career Horizons
4255 W. Touhy Ave.
Lincolnwood, IL 60646-1975
Ph: (847)679-5500   Fax: (847)679-2494
Fr: 800-323-4900

Adrian A. Paradis. 1992. $14.95; $11.95 (paper). 160 pages. Provides information on a variety of opportunities and advice on breaking into the field.

★4980★ Where the Jobs Are: The Hottest Careers for the '90s

The Career Press, Inc.
3 Tice Rd.
PO Box 687
Franklin Lakes, NJ 07417
Ph: (201)848-0310   Fax: (201)848-1727
Fr: 800-237-3371

Joyce Hadley. Second edition, 1995. $9.99. 300 pages. Describes careers in fifteen general fields, from accounting to travel and hospitality.

★4981★ Your Career in Direct Marketing and Direct Response Advertising

Direct Marketing Educational Foundation, Inc.
1120 Avenue of the Americas
New York, NY 10036
Ph: (212)689-4977

This free booklet explains direct marketing and lists the types of companies engaged in direct marketing. Lists career opportunities and offers advice on entry into the field.

★4982★ Your Career Opportunities in a Direct Marketing Agency

Direct Marketing Educational Foundation, Inc.
1120 Avenue of the Americas
New York, NY 10036
Ph: (212)689-4977

This free booklet describes career opportunities in agencies involved in direct marketing.

★4983★ Your Opportunities in Sales

Energeia Publishing, Inc.
PO Box 985
Salem, OR 97308
Ph: (503)362-1480   Fax: (503)362-2123

Shawn E. Strahan. 1994. $2.00 (paper).

EMPLOYMENT AGENCIES AND SEARCH FIRMS

★4984★ Amherst Personnel Group Inc.

PO Box 187
Hicksville, NY 11801
Ph: (516)433-7610   Fax: (516)433-7848

Employment agency. Executive search firm. Other offices in Milltown, NJ, and Rochelle Park, NJ.

★4985★ Arancio Associates

542 High Rock St.
Needham, MA 02192
Ph: (617)449-4436

Employment agency. Executive search firm.

★4986★ Don Waldron and Associates, Inc.

450 7th Ave., Ste. 501
New York, NY 10123-0101
Ph: (212)239-9110

Employment agency.

★4987★ Hansen Agri-Placement

PO Box 1172
Grand Island, NE 68802
Ph: (308)382-7350

Employment agency. Handles placements in a variety of fields on a regular or temporary basis.

★4988★ The Jobs Co.

8900 E. Sprague Ave.
Spokane, WA 99212-2927
Ph: (509)928-3151   Fax: (509)928-3168

Employment agency. Has division specializing in engineering and scientific openings. Also operates division specializing in sales openings.

★4989★ National Register, Inc.

2700 E. Dublin Granville Rd.
Columbus, OH 43231-4097
Ph: (614)890-1200

Employment agency. Offices in Akron and Toledo, OH.

★4990★ The Pathfinder Group

295 Danbury Rd.
Wilton, CT 06897-3095
Ph: (203)834-2467

Employment agency. Executive search firm. Recruits staff in a variety of fields.

★4991★ Peter Mann and Associates

250 S. IH 35 E.
Lewisville, TX 75067
Ph: (214)221-7516

Employment agency.

★4992★ Sales Consultants

33 S. King St.
Honolulu, HI 96813-3206
Ph: (808)521-7828

Employment agency. Executive search firm. Main office located in Cleveland, OH.

★4993★ Sales Consultants (Main Office)

1127 Euclid Ave., Ste. 1400
Cleveland, OH 44115-1638
Ph: (216)696-1122 Fax: (216)696-3221

Employment agency. Executive search firm. 150 branch offices across the country.

★4994★ Sales Executives Inc.

755 W. Big Beaver Rd., Ste. 2107
Troy, MI 48084
Ph: (810)362-1900

Employment agency. Executive search firm.

★4995★ Sales Recruiters International, Ltd.

660 White Plains Rd.
Tarrytown, NY 10591-5107
Ph: (914)631-0090

Employment agency.

★4996★ Salesworld Inc.

899 W. Cypress Creek Blvd.
Ft. Lauderdale, FL 33309-2072
Ph: (954)492-0088

Employment agency. National agency with offices in Annapolis, MD; Atlanta, GA; Baltimore, MD; Birmingham, AL; Boston, MA; Chicago, IL; Cincinnati, OH; Cleveland, OH; Dallas, TX; Detroit, MI; Ft. Worth, TX; Houston, TX; Irvine, CA; Jacksonville, FL; Los Angeles, CA; New York, NY; Philadelphia, PA; St. Louis, MO; San Francisco, CA; Washington, VA.

★4997★ Selected Executives Inc.

76 Winn St.
Woburn, MA 01801
Ph: (617)933-1500

Employment agency.

OTHER SOURCES

★4998★ American Wholesale Marketers Association (AWMA)

1128 16th St.
Washington, DC 20036
Ph: (202)463-2124 Fax: (202)467-0559
Fr: 800-482-2962

Members: Wholesalers of tobacco and confectionery products, health and beauty aids, and general merchandise; brokers and salespersons; manufacturers; retailers; individuals in allied industries. **Activities:** Conducts research and educational programs; offers industry resouce materials.

★4999★ Asian American Manufacturers Association (AAMA)

770 Menlo Ave., Ste. 227
Menlo Park, CA 94025
Ph: (415)321-2262 Fax: (415)325-5499

Members: Asian American manufacturers of technology products, such as computers, microprocessors, semiconductors, biotech, software and electronics equipment. **Purpose:** Seeks to enhance members' business opportunities. Sponsors educational programs in management and business operations.

★5000★ Association of Industry Manufacturer's Representatives (AIM/R)

222 Merchandise Mart Plz., Ste. 1360
Chicago, IL 60654
Ph: (312)464-0092 Fax: (312)464-0091

Members: Manufacturers' representative companies in the plumbing-heating-cooling-piping industry promoting the use of independent sales representatives. **Activities:** Conducts educational programs and establishes a code of ethics between members and customers.

★5001★ Automotive Parts and Accessories Association (APAA)

4600 East-West Hwy., Ste. 300
Bethesda, MD 20814
Ph: (301)654-6664 Fax: (301)654-3299

Members: Automotive parts and accessories retailers, distributors, manufacturers, and manufacturers' representatives. Conducts research and compiles statistics. **Activities:** Conducts seminars and provides specialized education program.

★5002★ Computing Technology Industry Association (CompTIA)

450 E. 22nd St., Ste. 230
Lombard, IL 60148
Ph: (708)268-1818 Fax: (708)268-1384

Members: Computer equipment resellers, computer equipment producers and software manufacturers, computer distributors, and other companies doing business with the computer industry. **Purpose:** Objectives are to: increase professional and ethical standards in the industry; protect consumers from inept or nonservicing dealers; help the consumer to easily identify better dealers and obtain an appropriate system for their needs; provide for the exchange of ideas for improvement within the reseller channel; promote a consistent level of service and ethical standards. Members are required to provide fully staffed service departments and offer customers maintenance contracts guaranteeing prompt response time. **Activities:** Conducts professional development and training programs in areas such as management, sales, and channel development. Serves as information clearinghouse for industry; makes available educational programs. Sponsors competitions; compiles statistics.

★5003★ Incentive—Directory Issue

Bill Communications, Inc.
355 Park Ave. S.
New York, NY 10010-1789
Ph: (212)592-6200 Fax: (212)592-6459

Annual, February. $5.00. Publication includes: List of approximately 1,000 suppliers of products used as promotional premiums and incentives, and services needed to conduct a premium or incentive campaign; includes trading stamp services and specialists in various forms of promotion (contests and sweepstakes, financial promotion, etc.), and manufacturers' representatives. Entries include: Company name, address, phone, name of contact, information on product or service. Arrangement: Classified by product or service.

★5004★ Manufacturers' Agents National Association (MANA)

23016 Mill Creek Rd.
PO Box 3467
Laguna Hills, CA 92654
Ph: (714)859-4040 Fax: (714)855-2973

Members: Manufacturers' agents in all fields representing two or more manufacturers on a commission basis; associate members are manufacturers and others interested in improving the agent-principal relationship. **Activities:** Maintains code of ethics and rules of business and professional conduct; maintains list of attorneys and accountants experienced in agency matters; issues model standard form of agreement.

★5005★ Resumes for Sales and Marketing Careers

VGM Career Horizons
4255 W. Touhy Ave.
Lincolnwood, IL 60646-1975
Ph: (847)679-5500 Fax: (847)679-2494
Fr: 800-323-4900

1991. $9.95. 128 pages. Sample resumes and cover letters from all levels of the sales and marketing field.

★5006★ Sales and Marketing Executives International (SMEI)

Statler Office Tower, No. 977
Cleveland, OH 44115
Ph: (216)771-6650 Fax: (216)771-6652

Members: Executives concerned with sales and marketing management, research, training, and other managerial aspects of distribution. Members control activities of 3,000,000 salespersons. **Purpose:** Undertakes studies in the field of selling and sales management; sponsors sales workshops, rallies, clinics, and seminars. Conducts career education programs, working with teachers, establishing sales clubs and fraternities, and cooperating with Junior Achievement and Distributive Education Clubs of America to interest young people in sales careers. Offers Graduate School of Sales Management and Marketing at Syracuse University, NY.

Market Research Analysts

★5007★ Advertising Age's Business Marketing

Crain Communications, Inc.
740 N. Rush St.
Chicago, IL 60611
Ph: (312)649-5260   Fax: (312)649-5228

Monthly. $35.00/year for individuals. Trade magazine on business-to-business marketing news, strategy, and tactics.

★5008★ Alert

Marketing Research Association
2189 Silas Deane Hwy., Ste. 5
Rocky Hill, CT 06067
Ph: (203)257-4008   Fax: (203)257-3990

Monthly. $30.00/year.

★5009★ Direct Marketing Magazine

Hoke Communications, Inc.
224 7th St.
Garden City, NY 11530
Ph: (516)746-6700   Fax: (516)294-8141
Fr: 800-229-6700

Monthly. Direct response advertising magazine.

★5010★ DM News

Mill Hollow Publications
19 W. 21st St.
New York, NY 10010
Ph: (212)741-2095   Fax: (212)633-9367

Weekly. Tabloid newspaper for publishers, fund raisers, financial marketers, catalogers, package goods advertisers and their agencies, and other marketers who use direct mail, mail order advertising, catalogs, or other direct response media to sell their products or services.

★5011★ Marketing News

American Marketing Association
250 S. Wacker Dr., Ste. 200
Chicago, IL 60606-5819
Ph: (312)648-0536   Fax: (312)993-7540

Biweekly. $30.00/year; $60.00/year for non-members; $110.00/year for libraries; $3.00 for single issue. Business magazine focusing on current marketing trends.

★5012★ POPAI News

Point-of-Purchase Advertising Institute
66 N. Van Brunt St.
Englewood, NJ 07631
Ph: (201)894-8899   Fax: (201)894-0529

Bimonthly. $35.00/year.

★5013★ Potentials in Marketing

Adams Recreation Pub.
527 Marquette, Ste.1300
Minneapolis, MN 55402
Ph: (612)342-2121   Fax: (612)342-2480
Fr: 800-923-2326

★5014★ Quirk's Marketing Research Review

Quirk Enterprises
PO Box 23536
Minneapolis, MN 55423
Ph: (612)861-8051

Ten times/year. $50.00/year.

★5015★ Sales & Marketing Management

Bill Communications, Inc.
355 Park Ave. S
New York, NY 10010-1789
Ph: (212)592-6200   Fax: (212)592-6309
Fr: 800-821-6897

Business magazine.

Placement and Job Referral Services

★5016★ Academy of Marketing Science (AMS)

University of Miami
School of Bus. Admin.
PO Box 248012
Coral Gables, FL 33124
Ph: (305)284-6673   Fax: (305)284-3762

Members: Marketing academicians and practitioners; individuals interested in fostering education in marketing science. **Purpose:** To promote the advancement of knowledge and the furthering of professional standards in the field of marketing. Explores the special application areas of marketing science and its responsibilities as an economic, ethical, and social force; promotes research and the widespread dissemination of findings. Facilitates exchange of information and experience among members, and the transfer of marketing knowledge and technology to developing countries; promotes marketing science on an international level. Encourages members to utilize their marketing talents to the fullest through redirection, reassignment, and relocation. **Activities:** Offers placement service; sponsors competitions.

★5017★ American Marketing Association (AMA)

250 S. Wacker Dr., Ste. 200
Chicago, IL 60606
Ph: (312)648-0536   Fax: (312)993-7542

Members: Professional society of marketing and market research executives, sales and promotion managers, advertising specialists, academics, and others interested in marketing. **Activities:** Fosters research; sponsors seminars, conferences, and student marketing clubs; provides educational placement service and doctoral consortium.

Employer Directories and Networking Lists

★5018★ Annual Directory of Marketing Information Companies

American Demographics, Inc.
PO Box 68
Ithaca, NY 14851
Ph: (607)273-6343   Fax: (607)273-3196
Fr: 800-828-1133

Annual, October. Free to subscribers (single issues only). Publication includes: List of firms offering demographic and research services, data retrieval and analysis, market evaluation and forecasting, media services, direct marketing expertise, and hardware/software/mapping services. Entries include: Company or organization name, address, phone, names and titles of key personnel, subsidiary and branch names and locations, description of products and services. Arrangement: Classified by product or service. Indexes: Product/service, company name, magazine.

★5019★ Bradford's Directory of Marketing Research Agencies and Management Consultants in the United States and the World

Bradford's Directory of Marketing
Research Agencies
9991 Caitland Ct.
Manassas, VA 22110
Ph: (703)367-0731   Fax: (703)830-5303

Biennial, January of odd years. $90.00. Covers over 2,400 marketing research agencies and management consultants in market research; associations concerned with market research; international coverage. Entries include: For agencies and consultants Individual or firm name, address, phone. For associations Name, address, phone, name of director, description of purpose, activities, and publications (if any). Arrangement: Agencies are geographical; associations are alphabetical. Indexes: Service, personal name, branch office location.

★5020★ Directory of Research Services Provided by Members of the Marketing Research Association

Marketing Research Association
2189 Silas Deane Hwy., Ste. 5
Rocky Hill, CT 06067
Ph: (203)257-4008   Fax: (203)257-3990

Annual, January. $100.00. Covers over 1,000 international marketing research companies and field interviewing services. Entries include: Company name, address, phone, names of executives, services, facilities, special interviewing capabilities. Arrangement: Geographical.

★5021★ European Directory of Marketing Information Sources

Euromonitor Publications Ltd.
87-88 Turnmill St.
London EC1M 5QU, England
Ph: 71 2518024   Fax: 71 6083149

Irregular, latest edition 1991. $255.00. Covers 2,500 market research organizations, libraries and information services, information databases, business and marketing associations, business and marketing journals, statistical offices, chambers of commerce, embassies, and foreign trade departments in Europe. Entries include: Organization, agency, or association name, contact name and address, type of data offered, publications. Arrangement: Classified by line of business. Indexes: Geographical, subject.

★5022★ International Directory of Market Research Organizations

Market Research Society
15 Northburgh St.
London EC1V 0AH, England
Ph: 71 4904911   Fax: 71 4900608

Biennial, odd years. $255.00. Covers nearly 1,700 market research firms in 70 countries worldwide. Entries include: Company name, address, phone, telegraph, telex, contact, date founded, affiliated companies, product specialties, services and facilities, sales,

number of staff, size of interviewer force, overseas expertise. Arrangement: Geographical. Indexes: Company name, service.

★5023★ International Directory of Marketing Research Companies and Services (The GreenBook)

New York Chapter
American Marketing Association
60 E. 42nd St., Ste. 1765
New York, NY 10165
Ph: (914)761-0199   Fax: (914)948-9466

Annual, March. $105.00, payment with order. Covers more than 1,500 marketing research consultants and suppliers (computer services, interviewing services, etc.) of marketing research needs; limited international coverage. Includes a list of computer programs for market research. Entries include: Company name, address, phone, name of principal executive, products and services, branch offices. Arrangement: Alphabetical. Indexes: Geographical, principal executive name, service, market/industry served, computer program name, trademark.

★5024★ Market Research and Analysis Directory

American Business Directories, Inc.
American Business Information, Inc.
5711 S. 86th Cir.
Omaha, NE 68127
Ph: (402)593-4600   Fax: (402)331-1505

Annual. $445.00, U.S. edition. Entries include: Name, address, phone (including area code), size of advertisement, year first in Yellow Pages, name of owner or manager, number of employees. Compiled from telephone company Yellow Pages, nationwide. Arrangement: Geographical.

★5025★ Quirk's Marketing Research Review—Researcher SourceBooks Issue

Quirk Enterprises, Inc.
6607 18th Ave. S.
Minneapolis, MN 55423
Ph: (612)861-8051   Fax: (612)861-1836

Annual, August. $35.00. Covers About 3,400 organizations providing marketing research products and services. Entries include: Name, address, phone, fax, contact, research specialties. Arrangement: Geographical.

HANDBOOKS AND MANUALS

★5026★ Career Choices for the 90's for Students of Economics

Walker and Company
435 Hudson St.
New York, NY 10014
Ph: (212)727-8300   Fax: (212)727-0984
Fr: 800-289-2553

Prepared by the Career Associates staff. 1990. $8.95. 166 pages. Discusses alternatives for students of economics. Offers advice on how to break into the field and how to move up. Covers where and who the employers are, internship possibilities, and profes-

sional networking associations. Comprehensive guide to career and job search planning.

★5027★ Careers in Marketing

VGM Career Horizons
4255 W. Touhy Ave.
Lincolnwood, IL 60646-1975
Ph: (847)679-5500   Fax: (847)679-2494
Fr: 800-323-4900

Lila B. Stair. Second edition, 1995. $17.95; $13.95 (paper). Surveys career opportunities in marketing and related areas such as marketing research, product development, and sales promotion. Includes a description of the work, places of employment, employment outlook, trends, and salaries. Offers job hunting advice.

★5028★ Careers for Number Crunchers and Other Quantitative Types

VGM Career Horizons
4255 W. Touhy Ave.
Lincolnwood, IL 60646-1975
Ph: (847)679-5500   Fax: (847)679-2494
Fr: 800-323-4900

Rebecca Burnett. 1993. $14.95; $9.95 (paper). Provides information to math-oriented job hunters on how to become statisticians, field researchers, computer programmers, stock analysts, investment managers, bankers, engineers, accountants, underwriters, economists, market analysts, mathematicians, systems analysts, and more.

★5029★ Encyclopedia of Careers and Vocational Guidance

J. G. Ferguson Publishing Co.
200 W. Monroe, Ste. 250
Chicago, IL 60606
Ph: (312)580-5480

William E. Hopke. Ninth edition, 1993. $129.95; $199.95 (CD-ROM). Four-volume set that profiles 900 occupations and describes job trends in 71 industries. Includes career description, educational requirements, history of the job, methods of entry, advancement, employment outlook, earnings, conditions of work, social and psychological factors, and sources of further information. Contains career and employment information for this field.

★5030★ Marketing and Sales Career Directory

Gale Research
835 Penobscot Bldg.
Detroit, MI 48226-4094
Ph: (313)961-2242   Fax: (313)961-6083
Fr: 800-877-GALE

Bradley Morgan. Fourth edition, 1992. $39.00. 341 pages. Features extensive listings of contacts and entry-level job opportunities at major corporations, research supplier firms, and major advertising and public relations agencies nationwide. Aimed at students looking for jobs in any area of marketing, advertising, or sales on the corporate side.

★5031★ Opportunities in Direct Marketing

VGM Career Horizons
4255 W. Touhy Ave.
Lincolnwood, IL 60646-1975
Ph: (847)679-5500   Fax: (847)679-2494
Fr: 800-323-4900

Anne Basye. 1994. $14.95; $11.95 (paper). Examines opportunities with direct marketers, catalog companies, direct marketing agencies, telemarketing firms, mailing list brokers, and database marketing companies. Describes how to prepare for a career in direct marketing and how to break into the field. Includes sources of short-term professional training.

★5032★ Opportunities in Marketing Careers

VGM Career Horizons
4255 W. Touhy Ave.
Lincolnwood, IL 60646-1975
Ph: (847)679-5500   Fax: (847)679-2494
Fr: 800-323-4900

Margery Steinberg. 1994. $14.95; $11.95 (paper). 160 pages. Includes guidance on identifying and pursuing job opportunities. Illustrated.

EMPLOYMENT AGENCIES AND SEARCH FIRMS

★5033★ The Personnel Institute

1000 Connecticut Ave. NW, Ste. 1108
Washington, DC 20036
Ph: (202)223-4911

Consulting firm.

OTHER SOURCES

★5034★ Marketing Research Association (MRA)

2189 Silas Deane Hwy., Ste. 5
PO Box 230
Rocky Hill, CT 06067-0230
Ph: (203)257-4008   Fax: (203)257-3990

Members: Companies and individuals involved in any area of marketing research, such as data collection, research, or as an end-user. **E-Mail:** mrahq@aol.com.

★5035★ Resumes for Sales and Marketing Careers

VGM Career Horizons
4255 W. Touhy Ave.
Lincolnwood, IL 60646-1975
Ph: (847)679-5500   Fax: (847)679-2494
Fr: 800-323-4900

1991. $9.95. 128 pages. Sample resumes and cover letters from all levels of the sales and marketing field.

Marketing, Advertising, and Public Relations Managers

★5051★ Marketing Computers

Billboard Magazine
33 Commercial St.
Gloucester, MA 01930
Ph: (508)281-3110   Fax: (508)281-0136

Monthly. $30.00/year for individuals. Marketing and advertising magazine.

★5052★ Marketing News

American Marketing Association
250 S. Wacker Dr., Ste. 200
Chicago, IL 60606-5819
Ph: (312)648-0536   Fax: (312)993-7540

Biweekly. $30.00/year; $60.00/year for nonmembers; $110.00/year for libraries; $3.00 for single issue. Business magazine focusing on current marketing trends.

★5053★ Petroleum Marketer

GCI Publishing Co., Inc.
1801 Rockville Pke., Ste. 330
Rockville, MD 20852
Ph: (301)984-7333   Fax: (301)984-7340

Bimonthly. $24.00/year for individuals; $30.00 for two years. Magazine for oil marketing equipment and merchandising industry.

★5054★ POPAI News

Point-of-Purchase Advertising Institute
66 N. Van Brunt St.
Englewood, NJ 07631
Ph: (201)894-8899   Fax: (201)894-0529

Bimonthly. $35.00/year.

★5055★ Potentials in Marketing

Adams Recreation Pub.
527 Marquette, Ste.1300
Minneapolis, MN 55402
Ph: (612)342-2121   Fax: (612)342-2480
Fr: 800-923-2326

★5056★ PR Marcom Jobs East

Rachel PR Services
208 E. 51st St., No. 1600
New York, NY 10022
Ph: (212)962-9100

Biweekly. Provides news of job openings in public relations, marketing, journalism, communications, public relations agencies and corporations, and freelance and temporary writing positions. Focuses on the New York City, Washingtion, DC, and Boston, and surrounding areas.

★5057★ PR Marcom Jobs West:
Northern California–Pacific Northwest

Rachel PR Services
298 4th Ave., No. 344
San Francisco, CA 94118
Ph: (415)334-7124

Biweekly. Provides information concerning job openings in public relations, journalism, marketing, communications, public relations agencies and corporations, and freelance and temporary writing positions. Focuses on opportunities in Northern California and Pacific Northwest areas.

★5058★ PR Marcom Jobs West:
Southern California

Rachel PR Services
1650 S. Pacific Coast Hwy., Ste. 200-C
Redondo Beach, CA 90277
Ph: (310)792-1313

Biweekly. Provides information concerning job openings in public relations, journalism, marketing, communications, public relations agencies and corporations, and freelance and temporary writing positions. Focuses on opportunities in Southern California.

★5059★ Print

R.C. Publications, Inc.
104 5th Ave., 19th Fl.
New York, NY 10011
Ph: (212)463-0600   Fax: (212)989-9891

Bimonthly. Covers all aspects of graphic design for visual communication.

★5060★ Profitable Craft Merchandising

PJS Publications, Inc.
2 News Plaza
PO Box 1790
Peoria, IL 61656
Ph: (309)682-6626   Fax: (309)682-7394

Monthly. $30.00/year for individuals. Magazine for retailers of craft, needlework, and sewing supplies.

★5061★ Public Relations Journal

Public Relations Society of America
33 Irving Pl.
New York, NY 10003-2376
Ph: (212)460-1413   Fax: (212)995-0757

$45.00/year for individuals. Public relations magazine containing articles on theory and practice for practitioners and those in related fields.

★5062★ Quirk's Marketing Research
Review

Quirk Enterprises
PO Box 23536
Minneapolis, MN 55423
Ph: (612)861-8051

Ten times/year. $50.00/year.

★5063★ Sales & Marketing
Management

Bill Communications, Inc.
355 Park Ave. S
New York, NY 10010-1789
Ph: (212)592-6200   Fax: (212)592-6309
Fr: 800-821-6897

Business magazine.

★5064★ Security Distributing and
Marketing

Cahners Publishing Co.
1350 E. Touhy Ave.
Des Plaines, IL 60018
Ph: (708)635-8800   Fax: (708)390-2770

Monthly. Free to qualified subscribers. Trade magazine focusing on security, burglar, and fire alarm systems protection.

★5065★ Southern Graphics

PTN Publishing Co.
445 Broad Hollow Rd., Ste. 21
Melville, NY 11747
Ph: (516)845-2700   Fax: (516)845-7109

Monthly. $22.00/year for individuals. Graphic arts magazine serving the printing and graphic arts industry in 14 southern states.

PLACEMENT AND JOB REFERRAL SERVICES

★5066★ Academy of Marketing Science
(AMS)

University of Miami
School of Bus. Admin.
PO Box 248012
Coral Gables, FL 33124
Ph: (305)284-6673   Fax: (305)284-3762

Members: Marketing academicians and practitioners; individuals interested in fostering education in marketing science. **Purpose:** To promote the advancement of knowledge and the furthering of professional standards in the field of marketing. Explores the special application areas of marketing science and its responsibilities as an economic, ethical, and social force; promotes research and the widespread dissemination of findings. Facilitates exchange of information and experience among members, and the transfer of marketing knowledge and technology to developing countries; promotes marketing science on an international level. Encourages members to utilize their marketing talents to the fullest through redirection, reassignment, and relocation. **Activities:** Offers placement service; sponsors competitions.

★5067★ Alliance for Healthcare
Strategy and Marketing (The Allian)

11 S. LaSalle St., Ste. 2300
Chicago, IL 60603-1303
Ph: (312)704-9700   Fax: (312)704-9709

Members: Marketing professionals in the health care field; vice presidents and directors of hospitals, health maintenance organizations, nursing homes, and other health care institutions. **Purpose:** Promotes the marketing of health services; sponsors continuing education for and professional development of members to this end. **Activities:** Conducts seminars; offers placement service.

★5068★ American Marketing
Association (AMA)

250 S. Wacker Dr., Ste. 200
Chicago, IL 60606
Ph: (312)648-0536   Fax: (312)993-7542

Members: Professional society of marketing and market research executives, sales and promotion managers, advertising specialists, academics, and others interested in marketing. **Activities:** Fosters research; sponsors seminars, conferences, and student marketing clubs; provides educational placement service and doctoral consortium.

★5069★ American Society of Association Executives (ASAE)

1575 Eye St. NW
Washington, DC 20005
Ph: (202)626-2723   Fax: (202)371-8825

Members: Professional society of paid executives of national, state, and local trade, professional, and philanthropic associations. **Purpose:** Seeks to educate association executives on effective management, including: the proper objectives, functions, and activities of associations; the basic principles of association organization; the legal aspects of association activity; policies relating to association management; efficient methods, procedures, and techniques of association management; the responsibilities and professional standards of association executives. **Activities:** Maintains central resource center. Conducts referral, resume, guidance, and consultation services; compiles statistics in the form of reports, surveys, and studies; carries out research and education. Offer executive search services and insurance programs. Provides CEO center for chief staff executives. Conducts Certified Association Executive (CAE) program. **E-Mail:** asac@asae.asaenet.org

★5070★ Direct Marketing Association (DMA)

1120 Avenue of the Americas
New York, NY 10036-6700
Ph: (212)768-7277   Fax: (212)768-4547

Members: Manufacturers, wholesalers, public utilities, retailers, mail order firms, publishers, schools, clubs, insurance companies, financial organizations, business equipment manufacturers, paper and envelope manufacturers, list brokers, compilers, managers, owners, computer service bureaus, advertising agencies, lettershops, research organizations, printers, lithographers, creators, and producers of direct mail and direct response advertising. **Purpose:** Studies consumer and business attitudes toward direct mail and related direct marketing statistics. **Activities:** Offers placement service. Offers Mail Preference Service for consumers who wish to receive less mail advertising, Mail Order Action Line to help resolve difficulties with mail order purchases, and Telephone Preference Service for people who wish to receive fewer telephone sales calls. Sponsors several three-day Basic Direct Marketing Institutes, Advanced Direct Marketing Institutes, and special interest seminars and workshops.

★5071★ Franchise Consultants International Association (FCIA)

5147 S. Angela Rd.
Memphis, TN 38117
Ph: (901)867-0800   Fax: (901)867-0010

Members: Individuals and corporations involved in franchising including attorneys, consultants, brokers, sales personnel, suppliers, Universities, consulatants, advertisers, and developers. **Purpose:** To provide standardized information for the franchise industry. Seeks to coordinate effective and professional franchise consulting and to educate members in franchise law and logistics. Serves as a clearinghouse of approved literature on franchising. **Activities:** Operates archive and hall of fame; compiles statistics. Provides placement service, charitable program, and speakers' bureau.

★5072★ International Exhibitors Association (IEA)

5501 Backlick Rd., Ste. 105
Springfield, VA 22151
Ph: (703)941-3725   Fax: (703)941-8275

Members: Exhibitors working to improve the effectiveness of trade shows as a marketing tool. **Purpose:** To promote the progress and development of trade show exhibiting; to collect and disseminate trade show information; conduct studies, surveys, and stated projects designed to improve trade shows; to foster good relations and communications with organizations representing others in the industry; to undertake other activities necessary to promote the welfare of member companies. Sponsors Exhibit Industry Education Foundation and professional exhibiting seminars; the forum series of educational programs on key issues affecting the industry. **Activities:** Maintains placement services; compiles statistics.

★5073★ Public Relations Society of America (PRSA)

33 Irving Pl., 3rd Fl.
New York, NY 10003
Ph: (212)995-2230   Fax: (212)995-0757
Fr: 800-WER-PRSA

Members: Professional society of public relations practitioners in business and industry, counseling firms, government, associations, hospitals, schools, and nonprofit organizations. **Activities:** Conducts professional development programs. Maintains job referral service, and research information center. Offers accreditation program.

★5074★ Publishers' Advertising and Marketing Association (PAMA)

John Wiley & Sons
605 3rd Ave.
New York, NY 10158
Ph: (212)850-6000   Fax: (212)850-6566

Members: Book publishing companies, book ad agencies, and media representatives. **Purpose:** Maintains placement service and provides scholarships.

★5075★ Sports Careers

PO Box 10129
Phoenix, AZ 85064
Fr: 800-776-7877

Career development firm for the sports industry. Provides career-related programs, conferences, seminars, educational products, and publications. Offers Career Enhancement Profile Program and Resume Development Kit. Maintains an electronic resume bank for members which is available to sports companies and organizations. Publishes newsletter listing job opportunities.

★5076★ Women in Advertising and Marketing (WAM)

4200 Wisconsin Ave. NW, Ste. 106-238
Washington, DC 20016
Ph: (202)369-7400

Members: Professional women in advertising and marketing. **Purpose:** Serves as a network to keep members abreast of developments in advertising and marketing. Fosters professional contact among members. **Activities:** Operates job bank.

EMPLOYER DIRECTORIES AND NETWORKING LISTS

★5077★ Ad Facs Directory—Upstate New York's Guide to Creative Resources, Production Facilities and Advertising Services

Ad Facs
Stuyvesant Plaza
Box 3933
Albany, NY 12203
Ph: (518)283-3923

Annual. $8.95. Covers about 3,000 advertising agencies, photographers, freelance writers, artists; film, video, and music production facilities; mail houses, and other companies, firms, and individuals involved in the advertising and marketing professions in New York. Entries include: Company, firm, or individual name, address, phone. Arrangement: Classified by type of service. Indexes: Name.

★5078★ Adcrafter—Roster Issue

Adcraft Club of Detroit
2630 Book Tower
Detroit, MI 48226
Ph: (313)962-7225   Fax: (313)962-3599

Annual, May. $12.00. Covers 3,900 executives of advertising agencies, advertising media, and advertising companies in the Detroit metropolitan area, and 500 out-of-state members. Entries include: Name, title, company name, office address and phone, business classification, membership code. Arrangement: Alphabetical and classified by line of business; identical information in both sections.

★5079★ Advertiser & Agency Red Books Plus

National Register Publishing
Reed Reference Publishing
121 Chanlon Rd.
New Providence, NJ 07974
Ph: (908)464-6800   Fax: (908)771-7704
Fr: 800-521-8110

$1,195.00. CD-ROM. Covers 26,000 of the world's top advertisers, their products and what media they use, as well as 11,000 U.S. and international ad agencies. Entries include: Company name, employees' names, job function/title, product/brand name, advertising expenditures by media.

★5080★ Advertising Age—Advertising Agency Income Report Issue

Crain Communications, Inc.
740 N. Rush St.
Chicago, IL 60611-2590
Ph: (312)649-5200   Fax: (312)649-5360
Fr: 800-992-9970

Annual, April. $5.00. Publication includes: Ranked lists of about 650 U.S advertising agencies, 1,000 foreign agencies, and the world's top 50 advertising organizations which reported billings and gross income, or whose billings and gross incomes were as-certained through research. Arrangement: Ranked by gross income.

★5081★ Advertising-Agencies Directory

American Business Directories, Inc.
American Business Information, Inc.
5711 S. 86th Cir.
Omaha, NE 68127
Ph: (402)593-4600   Fax: (402)331-1505

Annual. $845.00, U.S. edition; $150.00, (Canadian edition); payment with order. Number of listings: Approximately 24,777 (U.S. edition); 2,524 (Canadian edition); advertising agencies. Entries include: Name, address, phone (including area code), size of advertisement, year first in Yellow Pages, name of owner or manager, number of employees. Compiled from telephone company Yellow Pages, nationwide. Arrangement: Geographical.

★5082★ Advertising-Radio Directory

American Business Directories, Inc.
American Business Information, Inc.
5711 S. 86th Cir.
Omaha, NE 68127
Ph: (402)593-4600   Fax: (402)331-1505

Updated continuously; printed on request. Entries include: Name, address, phone (including area code), size of advertisement, year first in Yellow Pages, name of owner or manager, number of employees. Compiled from telephone company Yellow Pages, nationwide. Arrangement: Geographical.

★5083★ ADWEEK Agency Directory

ADWEEK Directories
1515 Broadway, 12th Fl.
New York, NY 10036
Ph: (212)536-6504   Fax: (212)536-5321

Annual, August. $250.00, plus $12.00 shipping. Covers over 4,000 U.S. advertising agencies, public relations firms, media buying services, direct marketing and related organizations. Entries include: Agency name, address, phone, fax; names and titles of key personnel; major accounts; headquarters location; major subsidiaries and other operating units; year founded; number of employees; fee income; billings; percentage of billings by medium. Arrangement: Alphabetical. Indexes: Geographical; parent company, subsidiary, division; fields served; ethnic sprcialities; organizations.

★5084★ Agri Marketing—The Top 50: Ag's Biggest Agencies Issue

Doane Agricultural Serices
11701 Borman Dr., Ste. 100
St. Louis, MO 63146
Ph: (314)569-2700   Fax: (314)569-1083

Annual, April or May. $5.00. Publication includes: List of the top 50 U.S. and Canadian advertising agencies and public relations firms, chosen on the basis of agricultural business income. Entries include: Agency name, location, income for agricultural accounts in most recent year, branch offices, major clients served. Arrangement: Alphabetical.

★5085★ American Association of Advertising Agencies—Roster and Organization

American Association of Advertising Agencies
666 3rd Ave.
New York, NY 10017-4056
Ph: (212)682-2500   Fax: (212)953-5665

Annual. Free. Covers 627 member advertising agencies. Entries include: Firm name, address, phone, branch offices. Arrangement: Alphabetical. Indexes: Geographical.

★5086★ American Marketing Association—Yellow Pages and International Membership Directory

American Marketing Association
250 S. Wacker Dr., Ste. 200
Chicago, IL 60606-5819
Ph: (312)648-0536

Annual, January. $125.00. Covers 26,000 individual members and about 1,000 paid listings for member research and service firms. Entries include: For individuals: member name, position, home and office address, and phone numbers. For advertisers: company name, address, phone, names of principal executives.

★5087★ Chicago Creative Directory

Chicago Creative Directory, Inc.
333 N. Michigan Ave., Ste. 810
Chicago, IL 60601
Ph: (312)236-7337   Fax: (312)236-6078

Annual, March. $40.00. Covers over 3,000 advertising agencies, photographers, sound studios, talent agencies, audiovisual services, and others offering creative and production services. Entries include: For most listings: company name, address, phone, list of officers, description of services. For free-lance listings: name, talent, address, phone. Arrangement: Classified by specialty.

★5088★ Creative Black Book

Black Book Marketing Group
866 3rd Ave.
New York, NY 10022
Ph: (212)702-9700   Fax: (212)605-4808

Annual, January. $140.00, plus $7.00 shipping. Publication includes: photographers and photographic services, design firms, advertising agencies, and other firms whose products or services are used in advertising. Entries include: Company name, address, phone. Principal content of publication is 4-color samples from the leading commercial photographers. Arrangement: Classified by product/service.

★5089★ Directory of Multicultural Public Relations Professionals

Public Relations Society of America
33 Irving Pl., 3rd Fl.
New York, NY 10003
Ph: (212)995-2230   Fax: (212)995-0757
Fr: 800-WER-PRSA

Irregular, latest edition 1993. $40.00, plus $3.00 shipping. Covers about 190 minority individuals in the field of public relations. Entries include: Individual name, title, company name, address, phone. Arrangement: Geographical.

★5090★ International Advertising Association—Membership Directory

International Advertising Association
521 5th Ave., Ste. 1807
New York, NY 10175
Ph: (212)557-1133   Fax: (212)983-0455

Annual, March. $350.00. Covers over 3,400 advertisers, advertising agencies, media, and other firms involved in advertising. Entries include: Company name, address, phone, fax. Arrangement: Geographical.

★5091★ Madison Avenue Handbook: The Image Makers Source

Peter Glenn Publications
42 W. 38th St., No. 802
New York, NY 10018
Ph: (212)869-2020   Fax: (212)869-3287
Fr: 800-223-1254

Annual, spring. $45.00. Covers advertising agencies and related services in the U.S. and Canada. Includes television, film, and music producers; photographers, agents, suppliers, sources of props and rentals, fashion houses, beauty services, locations, and film commissions. Entries include: Company name, address, phone; paid listings include description of products or services, key personnel. Arrangement: Classified by line of business.

★5092★ Medical Marketing and Media—Healthcare Agency Profiles Issue

CPS Communications, Inc.
7200 W. Camino Real, Ste. 215
Boca Raton, FL 33433
Ph: (407)368-9301   Fax: (407)368-7870

Annual, July. $7.00. Publication includes: List of about 130 health care advertising agencies. Entries include: Company name, address, phone, name and title of contact, financial revenue, percentages of regional markets, market breakdown, current accounts, new accounts and accounts lost, number of employees, year established, special services, divisions. Arrangement: Alphabetical.

★5093★ O'Dwyer's Directory of Corporate Communications

J. R. O'Dwyer Co., Inc.
271 Madison Ave.
New York, NY 10016
Ph: (212)679-2471   Fax: (212)683-2750

Annual, July. $110.00. Covers public relations departments of approximately 4,450 major United States companies (listed on the New York Stock Exchange and in the Fortune list of 1,000 largest firms); also includes similar information on over 1,300 large trade associations and foreign embassies in the United States. Arrangement: Alphabetical. Indexes: Geographical, product.

★5094★ O'Dwyer's Directory of Public Relations Executives

J. R. O'Dwyer Co. Inc.
271 Madison Ave.
New York, NY 10016
Ph: (212)679-2471   Fax: (212)683-2750

Annual, November/December. $70.00. Covers about 6,200 corporation and public relations agency executives and private counselors. Entries include: Name, business affiliation, address, phone; personal, education, and career data. Arrangement: Alphabetical.

★5095★ O'Dwyer's Directory of Public Relations Firms

J. R. O'Dwyer Co., Inc.
271 Madison Ave.
New York, NY 10016
Ph: (212)679-2471   Fax: (212)683-2750

Annual, April/May. $125.00. Covers over 2,200 public relations firms; international coverage. Entries include: Firm name, address, phone, principal executives, branch and overseas offices, billings, date founded, and clients. Arrangement: Geographical by country. Indexes: Specialty (beauty and fashions, finance/investor, etc.), geographical, client.

★5096★ Peterson's Job Opportunities in Business 1996

Peterson's
PO Box 2123
Princeton, NJ 08543-2123
Ph: (609)243-9111   Fax: (609)243-9150
Fr: 800-338-3282

Compiled by the Peterson's staff. Annual. $19.95 (paper). 416 pages. Profiles 2,000 companies that are hiring employees in a number of nontechnical fields, including financial services, management consulting, retailers, utilities, and consumer products companies. Contains job-search strategies and career options to help match education and expertise to the job market. Indexed geographically, by industry, and by hiring needs.

★5097★ Public Relations Journal— Register Issue

Public Relations Society of America (PRSA)
33 Irving Pl.
New York, NY 10003-2376
Ph: (212)460-1468   Fax: (212)995-0757

Annual, June. $120.00. Publication includes: About 15,475 public relations practitioners in business, government, education, etc., who are members. Entries include: Name, professional affiliation and title, address, phone, membership rank. Arrangement: Alphabetical. Indexes: Geographical, organizational.

★5098★ Sports Market Place Register

Sports Careers
PO Box 10129
Phoenix, AZ 85064
Fr: 800-776-7877

Annual $59.00. Resource guide for the sports industry. Lists over 24,000 national and international sports business contacts. Entries include: organization name, name of key executive, address, and phone and fax numbers. Provides listings for: Individual and Multiple Sports Organizations/Teams/Media; College Sports; Sponsorship/Marketing/ Event Management; Sports Agents/Lawyers; Manufacturers/Retailers. Indexes: Geographic and Alphabetical.

★5099★ Standard Directory of Advertising Agencies

National Register Publishing
Reed Reference Publishing
121 Chanlon Rd.
New Providence, NJ 07974
Ph: (908)464-6800   Fax: (908)665-6688
Fr: 800-521-8110

Semiannual, January and July; quarterly supplements. $575.00, per year, including supplements; $475.00, single copy, w/o supplements. Covers over 9,000 advertising agencies. Entries include: Agency name, address, phone, year founded, number of employees, association memberships, area of specialization, annual billing, breakdown of gross billings by media, clients, executives, special markets, and new agencies. Arrangement: Alphabetical. Indexes: Geographical (includes address), special market, agency responsibilities, and personnel.

★5100★ Standard Directory of International Advertisers and Agencies

National Register Publishing
Reed Reference Publishing Co.
121 Chanlon Rd.
New Providence, NJ 07974
Ph: (908)464-6800   Fax: (908)771-7704
Fr: 800-521-8110

Annual, January. $375.00, plus $22.54 shipping. Covers about 4,000 advertiser companies and advertising agencies; international coverage. Entries include: Company name, address, phone, fax, telex, annual sales or billings, number of employees, Standard Industrial Classification (SIC) code, names and titles of key personnel, line of business, subsidiary and branch office names, address, phone, telex, key officers; advertiser companies include their advertising agency's name, address, and description of advertising budget and strategies; advertising agencies include names of client companies and their lines of business. Arrangement: Separate alphabetical sections for advertiser companies and advertising agencies. Indexes: Geographical, company name, personal name, trade name, SIC.

★5101★ The Workbook

Scott & Daughters Publishing
940 N. Highland Ave.
Los Angeles, CA 90038
Ph: (213)856-0008   Fax: (213)856-4368
Fr: 800-547-2688

Annual, January. $95.00. Covers in four regional volumes, 25,000 advertising agencies, art directors, photographers, freelance illustrators and designers, artists' representatives, commercial production companies, printers, color separators, and typographers in the U.S. Entries include: Company or individual name, address, phone, specialty. Regional volumes are East, West, Midwest, and South. Arrangement: Classified by product or service.

★5102★ World Book of IABC Communicators

International Association of Business Communicators
1 Hallidie Plaza, Ste. 600
San Francisco, CA 94102
Ph: (415)433-3400   Fax: (415)362-8762

Annual, January. $100.00. Covers about 13,000 association members involved with organizational, corporate, and public relations and other communications fields. Entries include: Name, address, title, code indicating type of business or organization, phone. Arrangement: Alphabetical. Indexes: Geographical, then classified by type of business.

HANDBOOKS AND MANUALS

★5103★ Advertising Career Directory

Gale Research
835 Penobscot Bldg.
Detroit, MI 48226-4094
Ph: (313)961-2242   Fax: (313)961-6083
Fr: 800-877-GALE

Bradley Morgan. Fifth edition, 1992. $39.00. 256 pages. Presents detailed listings of thousands of entry-level jobs at most major agencies nationwide. Features articles and advice from top advertising professionals to provide an insider's view of the profession.

★5104★ Career Choices for the 90's for Students of Business

Walker and Company
435 Hudson St.
New York, NY 10014
Ph: (212)727-8300   Fax: (212)727-0984
Fr: 800-289-2553

Prepared by the Career Associates staff. 1990. $9.95. 166 pages. Discusses alternatives for students of business. Offers advice on how to break into the field and how to move up. Covers where and who the employers are, internship possibilities, and professional networking associations. Comprehensive guide to career and job search planning.

★5105★ Career Choices for the 90's for Students of Communications and Journalism

Walker and Company
435 Hudson St.
New York, NY 10014
Ph: (212)727-8300   Fax: (212)727-0984
Fr: 800-289-2553

Prepared by the Career Associates staff. 1990. $8.95. 166 pages. Discusses alternatives for students of communications and journalism. Offers advice on how to break into the field and how to move up. Covers where and who the employers are, internship possibilities, and professional networking associations. Comprehensive guide to career and job search planning.

★5106★ Career Choices for the 90's for Students of English

Walker and Company
435 Hudson St.
New York, NY 10014
Ph: (212)727-8300   Fax: (212)727-0984
Fr: 800-289-2553

Prepared by the Career Associates staff. 1990. $8.95. 166 pages. Discusses alternatives for students of English. Offers advice on how to break into the field and how to move up. Covers where and who the employers are, internship possibilities, and professional networking associations. Comprehensive guide to career and job search planning.

★5107★ Career Choices for the 90's for Students of Psychology

Walker and Company
435 Hudson St.
New York, NY 10014
Ph: (212)727-8300   Fax: (212)727-0984
Fr: 800-289-2553

Prepared by the Career Associates staff. 1990. $9.95. 166 pages. Discusses alternatives for students of psychology. Offers advice on how to break into the field and how to move up. Covers where and who the employers are, internship possibilities, and professional networking associations. Comprehensive guide to career and job search planning.

★5108★ Career Opportunities in Advertising and Public Relations

Facts on File, Inc.
11 Penn Plaza, 15th Fl.
New York, NY 10001-2006
Ph: (212)967-8800   Fax: 800-678-3633
Fr: 800-322-8755

Shelly Field. Revised edition, 1996. $29.95; $15.95 (paper). 320 pages. Provides the job seeker with information about locating and landing the right position. Includes detailed job descriptions for many specific positions and lists trade associations, recruiting organizations, and major agencies. Contains index and bibliography.

★5109★ Career Opportunities in Art

Facts on File, Inc.
11 Penn Plaza, 15th Fl.
New York, NY 10001-2006
Ph: (212)967-8800   Fax: 800-678-3633
Fr: 800-322-8755

Susan H. Haubenstock and David Joselit. Revised edition, 1994. $29.95; $15.95 (paper). 208 pages. This book profiles seventy-five jobs that can be found in the art field. Each profile includes a career description, career ladder, employment and advancement prospects, education, experience and skills required, salary range, and tips for entry into the field.

★5110★ Career Opportunities for Writers

Facts on File, Inc.
11 Penn Plaza, 15th Fl.
New York, NY 10001-2006
Ph: (212)967-8800   Fax: 800-678-3633
Fr: 800-322-8755

Rosemary Guiley. Third edition, 1995. $29.95; $15.95 (paper). Describes more than 100 jobs in eight major fields, offering such details as duties, salaries, perquisites, employment and advancement opportunities, organizations to join, and opportunities for women and minorities.

★5111★ Careers in Advertising

American Advertising Foundation (AAF)
1101 Vermont Ave. NW, Ste. 500
Washington, DC 20005-3521
Ph: (202)898-0089

Single copy free. 50 pages. Describes advertising job opportunities and educational preparation. Gives job-hunting tips.

★5112★ Careers in Advertising

VGM Career Horizons
4255 W. Touhy Ave.
Lincolnwood, IL 60646-1975
Ph: (847)679-5500   Fax: (847)679-2494
Fr: 800-323-4900

S. William Pattis. Second edition, 1996. $17.95; $13.95 (paper). 192 pages. Explains the role of the media in advertising, personal characteristics needed to succeed in this field, educational requirements, and related jobs. Covers copy writing, art, design, account management, media, and research. Gives job hunting tips.

★5113★ Careers in Communications

VGM Career Horizons
4255 W. Touhy Ave.
Lincolnwood, IL 60646-1975
Ph: (847)679-5500   Fax: (847)679-2494
Fr: 800-323-4900

Shonan Noronha. 1994. $17.95; $13.95 (paper). 176 pages. Examines the fields of journalism, photography, radio, television, film, public relations, and advertising. Gives concrete details on job locations and how to secure a job. Suggests many resources for job hunting.

★5114★ Careers in Marketing

VGM Career Horizons
4255 W. Touhy Ave.
Lincolnwood, IL 60646-1975
Ph: (847)679-5500   Fax: (847)679-2494
Fr: 800-323-4900

Lila B. Stair. Second edition, 1995. $17.95; $13.95 (paper). Surveys career opportunities in marketing and related areas such as marketing research, product development, and sales promotion. Includes a description of the work, places of employment, employment outlook, trends, and salaries. Offers job hunting advice.

★5115★ Careers in Public Relations

Public Relations Society of America
33 Irving Pl., 3rd Fl.
New York, NY 10003-2376
Ph: (212)995-2230

$2.00. This eight-page booklet describes the field of public relations, including salaries, nature of the work, and finding a job. Lists necessary personal qualifications, educational preparation, and work experience.

★5116★ Careers in the Visual Arts: A Guide to Jobs, Money, Opportunities, and an Artistic Life

Watson-Guptill Publications, Inc.
BPI Communications, Inc.
1515 Broadway
New York, NY 10036
Ph: (212)536-5121   Fr: 800-451-1741

Dee Ito. 1993. $14.95. 320 pages. Gives a broad overview of each field included, with educational requirements and employment opportunities. Includes ideas on how to get started.

★5117★ The Employment Kit and Careers in Marketing

American Marketing Association
Publications Order Dept.
250 S. Wacker Dr., Ste. 200
Chicago, IL 60606

Ginny Shipe. $10.00. The employment kit section details job search techniques. The 'Careers in Marketing' section includes information on how to pursue and land a job in marketing.

★5118★ Encyclopedia of Careers and Vocational Guidance

J. G. Ferguson Publishing Co.
200 W. Monroe, Ste. 250
Chicago, IL 60606
Ph: (312)580-5480

William E. Hopke. Ninth edition, 1993. $129.95; $199.95 (CD-ROM). Four-volume set that profiles 900 occupations and describes job trends in 71 industries. Includes career description, educational requirements, history of the job, methods of entry, advancement, employment outlook, earnings, conditions of work, social and psychological factors, and sources of further information. Contains career and employment information for this field.

★5119★ *The Harvard Guide to Careers in the Mass Media*

Bob Adams, Inc.
260 Center St.
Holbrook, MA 02343
Ph: (617)767-8100   Fax: (617)767-0994
Fr: 800-872-5627

John Noble. 1989. $7.95. 202 pages. Each section of the book evaluates one media profession in depth and contains an industry profile, a career profile that describes positions available in that area, information about current salary ranges, industry-specific job-hunting tips and strategies, and a case study outlining the methods that were used in a successful job hunt.

★5120★ *Jobs in Arts and Media Management: What They Are and How to Get One!*

American Council for the Arts
1 E. 53rd St.
New York, NY 10022-4201
Ph: (212)223-2787   Fr: 800-321-4510

Stephen Langley and James Abruzzo. Revised edition, 1990. $21.95. 281 pages. Includes lists of about 150 sources of information on job opportunities in the arts, including organizations offering internships, job listings, graduate programs, and short-term study; professional groups concerned with theater, music, dance, opera, museum and gallery management, film, and telecommunication management. (Does not include popular music performing or music recording.) Entries include: For internships Organization name, address, phone, description, requirements. For job referral associations and periodicals - Association or publisher name, address, fields covered, services offered, turn-around time, average number of jobs, cost of subscription or dues, comments. Arrangement: Classified by type of source.

★5121★ *Liberal Arts Jobs: What They Are and How to Get Them*

Peterson's
PO Box 2123
Princeton, NJ 08543-2123
Ph: (609)243-9111   Fax: (609)243-9150
Fr: 800-338-3282

Burton Jay Nadler. Second edition, 1989. $9.95. 153 pages. Presents a list of the top 20 fields for liberal arts majors, covering more than 300 job opportunities. Discusses strategies for going after those jobs, including guidance on the language of a successful job search, informational interviews, and making networking work.

★5122★ *Marketing and Sales Career Directory*

Gale Research
835 Penobscot Bldg.
Detroit, MI 48226-4094
Ph: (313)961-2242   Fax: (313)961-6083
Fr: 800-877-GALE

Bradley Morgan. Fourth edition, 1992. $39.00. 341 pages. Features extensive listings of contacts and entry-level job opportunities at major corporations, research supplier firms, and major advertising and public relations agencies nationwide. Aimed at students looking for jobs in any area of marketing, advertising, or sales on the corporate side.

★5123★ *100 Best Careers for the Year 2000*

Prentice Hall General Reference
15 Columbus Cir.
New York, NY 10023
Ph: (212)373-8500   Fr: 800-223-2348

Shelly Field. 1992. $15.00 (paper). Covers 100 of the fastest growing fields. The publication is divided into 11 general employment sections. Specific careers are covered within each section. Provides job description, responsibilities, employment opportunities, earnings, education and training, advancement opportunities, and experience and qualifications for each occupation.

★5124★ *Opportunities in Advertising Careers*

VGM Career Horizons
4255 W. Touhy Ave.
Lincolnwood, IL 60646-1975
Ph: (847)679-5500   Fax: (847)679-2494
Fr: 800-323-4900

S. William Pattis. 1995. $14.95; $11.95 (paper). 160 pages. A guide to planning for and seeking opportunities in this growing field. Illustrated.

★5125★ *Opportunities in Direct Marketing*

VGM Career Horizons
4255 W. Touhy Ave.
Lincolnwood, IL 60646-1975
Ph: (847)679-5500   Fax: (847)679-2494
Fr: 800-323-4900

Anne Basye. 1994. $14.95; $11.95 (paper). Examines opportunities with direct marketers, catalog companies, direct marketing agencies, telemarketing firms, mailing list brokers, and database marketing companies. Describes how to prepare for a career in direct marketing and how to break into the field. Includes sources of short-term professional training.

★5126★ *Opportunities in International Business Careers*

VGM Career Horizons
4255 W. Touhy Ave.
Lincolnwood, IL 60646-1975
Ph: (847)679-5500   Fax: (847)679-2494
Fr: 800-323-4900

Jeffrey Arpan. 1995. $14.95; $11.95 (paper). 160 pages. Describes what types of jobs exist in international business, where they are located, what challenges and rewards they bring, and how to prepare for and obtain jobs in international business.

★5127★ *Opportunities in Journalism Careers*

VGM Career Horizons
4255 W. Touhy Ave.
Lincolnwood, IL 60646-1975
Ph: (847)679-5500   Fax: (847)679-2494
Fr: 800-323-4900

Jim Patten and Donald L. Ferguson. 1993. $14.95; $11.95 (paper). 160 pages. Outlines opportunities in every field of journalism, including newspaper reporting and editing, magazine and book publishing, corporate communications, advertising and public relations, freelance writing, and teaching. Covers how to prepare for and enter each field, outlining responsibilities, salaries, benefits, and job outlook for each specialty. Illustrated.

★5128★ *Opportunities in Magazine Publishing Careers*

VGM Career Horizons
4255 W. Touhy Ave.
Lincolnwood, IL 60646-1975
Ph: (847)679-5500   Fax: (847)679-2494
Fr: 800-323-4900

S. William Pattis. 1992. $14.95; $11.95 (paper). 160 pages. Covers the scope of magazine publishing and addresses how to identify and pursue available positions. Illustrated.

★5129★ *Opportunities in Marketing Careers*

VGM Career Horizons
4255 W. Touhy Ave.
Lincolnwood, IL 60646-1975
Ph: (847)679-5500   Fax: (847)679-2494
Fr: 800-323-4900

Margery Steinberg. 1994. $14.95; $11.95 (paper). 160 pages. Includes guidance on identifying and pursuing job opportunities. Illustrated.

★5130★ *Opportunities in Public Relations Careers*

VGM Career Horizons
4255 W. Touhy Ave.
Lincolnwood, IL 60646-1975
Ph: (847)679-5500   Fax: (847)679-2494
Fr: 800-323-4900

Morris B. Rotman. 1995. $14.95; $11.95 (paper). 160 pages. Tells the reader how to enter the field and how to build a career. Contains bibliography and illustrations.

★5131★ *Opportunities in Publishing Careers*

VGM Career Horizons
4255 W. Touhy Ave.
Lincolnwood, IL 60646-1975
Ph: (847)679-5500   Fax: (847)679-2494
Fr: 800-323-4900

Robert A. Carter and S. William Pattis. 1995. $11.95 paperback. $14.95 hardcover. 160 pages. Covers all positions in book and magazine publishing, including new opportunities in multimedia publishing.

★5132★ *Public Relations Career Directory*

Gale Research
835 Penobscot Bldg.
Detroit, MI 48226-4094
Ph: (313)961-2242   Fax: (313)961-6083
Fr: 800-877-GALE

Bradley Morgan. Fifth edition, 1993. $39.00. 337 pages. Features extensive listings of contacts and entry-level job opportunities at major corporations and public relations agencies nationwide. Includes articles and advice from top public relations practitioners on such areas as corporate communications, international public relations, community affairs, and media relations.

★5133★ **★5133★ Where the Jobs Are: The Hottest Careers for the '90s**

The Career Press, Inc.
3 Tice Rd.
PO Box 687
Franklin Lakes, NJ 07417
Ph: (201)848-0310   Fax: (201)848-1727
Fr: 800-237-3371

Joyce Hadley. Second edition, 1995. $9.99. 300 pages. Describes careers in fifteen general fields, from accounting to travel and hospitality.

EMPLOYMENT AGENCIES AND SEARCH FIRMS

★5134★ Arancio Associates

542 High Rock St.
Needham, MA 02192
Ph: (617)449-4436

Employment agency. Executive search firm.

★5135★ Calvert Associates, Inc.

202 E. Washington St., Ste. 304
Ann Arbor, MI 48104
Ph: (313)769-5413

Employment agency.

★5136★ Chaloner Associates

PO Box 1097, Back Bay Station
Boston, MA 02117
Ph: (617)451-5170   Fax: (617)451-8160

Executive search firm.

★5137★ Dussick Management Associates

149 Durham Rd.
Madison, CT 06443
Ph: (203)245-9311   Fax: (203)245-9570

Executive search firm.

★5138★ Esquire Personnel Services, Inc.

222 S. Riverside Plaza, Ste. 320
Chicago, IL 60606-5804
Ph: (312)648-4600   Fax: (312)648-4637

Employment agency.

★5139★ Howard-Sloan Associates, Inc.

353 Lexington Ave., 11th Fl.
New York, NY 10016
Ph: (212)661-5250   Fax: (212)687-5760
Fr: 800-221-1326

Executive search firm.

★5140★ The Pathfinder Group

295 Danbury Rd.
Wilton, CT 06897-3095
Ph: (203)834-2467

Employment agency. Executive search firm. Recruits staff in a variety of fields.

★5141★ Remer-Ribolow and Associates

230 Park Ave., Ste. 222
New York, NY 10169
Ph: (212)808-0580

Employment agency.

★5142★ Sales Executives Inc.

755 W. Big Beaver Rd., Ste. 2107
Troy, MI 48084
Ph: (810)362-1900

Employment agency. Executive search firm.

★5143★ Sales Recruiters International, Ltd.

660 White Plains Rd.
Tarrytown, NY 10591-5107
Ph: (914)631-0090

Employment agency.

★5144★ Selected Executives Inc.

76 Winn St.
Woburn, MA 01801
Ph: (617)933-1500

Employment agency.

★5145★ The Wright Group

5902 Windmier Ct.
Dallas, TX 75252
Ph: (214)733-7245

Executive search firm.

OTHER SOURCES

★5146★ American Advertising Federation (AAF)

1101 Vermont Ave. NW, Ste. 500
Washington, DC 20005
Ph: (202)898-0089   Fax: (202)898-0159

Purpose: Works to advance the business of advertising as a vital and essential part of the American economy and culture through government and public relations; professional development and recognition; community service, social responsibility and high standards; and benefits and services to members. Operates Advertising Hall of Fame, Hall of Achievement, and National Student Advertising Competition.

★5147★ American Association of Advertising Agencies (AAAA)

405 Lexington Ave., 18th Fl.
New York, NY 10174-1801
Ph: (212)682-2500   Fax: (212)953-5665

Purpose: Fosters development of the advertising industry; assists member agencies to operate more efficiently and profitably. **Activities:** Sponsors member information and international services. Maintains 44 committees. Conducts government relations.

★5148★ Bank Marketing Association (BMA)

1120 Conneticut Ave. NW
Washington, DC 20036
Ph: (202)663-5268   Fax: (202)828-4540
Fr: 800-433-9013

Members: Marketing and public relations executives for commercial and savings banks, credit unions, and savings and loans associations, and related groups such as advertising agencies and research firms. **Purpose:** Provides marketing education, information, and services to the financial services industry. **Activities:** Conducts research; cosponsors summer sessions of fundamentals and advanced courses in marketing at the University of Colorado at Boulder; compiles statistics.

★5149★ Careers in Art

Cambridge Career Products
PO Box 2153
Dept. CC15
Charleston, WV 25328-2153
Ph: (304)744-9323   Fax: (304)744-9351
Fr: 800-468-4227

Video. $49.95. 21 minutes. Covers many professional options available in the world of art.

★5150★ Council of Sales Promotion Agencies (CSPA)

750 Summer St.
Stamford, CT 06901
Ph: (203)325-3911   Fax: (203)969-1499

Members: Agencies with a primary interest in promotion marketing. **Purpose:** Seeks to increase understanding, by management, of promotion marketing as a special component of the total marketing management and corporate communication function; will stimulate methods of scientific research and evaluation of marketing promotion effectiveness. **Activities:** Sponsors intern program; conducts research; maintains speakers' bureau and hall of fame. Plans to establish library.

★5151★ National School Public Relations Association (NSPRA)

1501 Lee Hwy., Ste. 201
Arlington, VA 22209
Ph: (703)528-5840   Fax: (703)528-7017

Members: School system public relations directors, school administrators, and others interested in furthering public understanding of the public schools. **Activities:** Has adopted standards for public relations professionals and programs and an accreditation program.

★5152★ PROMAX International

2029 Century Park East, Ste. 555
Los Angeles, CA 90067-3283
Ph: (310)788-7600   Fax: (310)788-7616

Members: Advertising, public relations, and promotion managers of cable, radio, and television stations, systems and networks; syndicators. **Purpose:** Seeks to: advance the role and increase the effectiveness of promotion and marketing within the industry, related industries, and educational communities. Conducts workshops and weekly fax service for members. **Activities:** Operates employment service. Maintains speakers' bureau, hall of fame, and resource center with print, audio, and visual materials.

★5153★ **Promotion Marketing Association of America (PMAA)**
257 Park Ave. S., 11th Fl.
New York, NY 10001
Ph: (212)420-1100   Fax: (212)533-7622

Members: Fortune 500 marketer companies, promotion agencies, and companies using promotion programs; supplier members are manufacturers of package goods, cosmetics, and pharmaceuticals, consultants, and advertising agencies. **Activities:** Conducts surveys and studies of industry issues.

★5154★ *Resumes for Advertising Careers*
VGM Career Horizons
4255 W. Touhy Ave.
Lincolnwood, IL 60646-1975
Ph: (847)679-5500   Fax: (847)679-2494
Fr: 800-323-4900

1993. $9.95. Aimed at job seekers trying to enter or advance in advertising. Provides sample resumes for copywriters, art directors, account managers, ad managers, and media perople at all levels of experience. Furnishes sample cover letters.

★5155★ *Resumes for Sales and Marketing Careers*
VGM Career Horizons
4255 W. Touhy Ave.
Lincolnwood, IL 60646-1975
Ph: (847)679-5500   Fax: (847)679-2494
Fr: 800-323-4900

1991. $9.95. 128 pages. Sample resumes and cover letters from all levels of the sales and marketing field.

★5156★ **Sales and Marketing Executives International (SMEI)**
Statler Office Tower, No. 977
Cleveland, OH 44115
Ph: (216)771-6650   Fax: (216)771-6652

Members: Executives concerned with sales and marketing management, research, train-ing, and other managerial aspects of distribution. Members control activities of 3,000,000 salespersons. **Purpose:** Undertakes studies in the field of selling and sales management; sponsors sales workshops, rallies, clinics, and seminars. Conducts career education programs, working with teachers, establishing sales clubs and fraternities, and cooperating with Junior Achievement and Distributive Education Clubs of America to interest young people in sales careers. Offers Graduate School of Sales Management and Marketing at Syracuse University, NY.

★5157★ **Society for Marketing Professional Services (SMPS)**
99 Canal Center Plz., Ste. 250
Alexandria, VA 22314
Ph: (703)549-6117   Fax: (703)549-2498

Members: Employees of architectural, engineering, planning, interior design, landscape architectural, and construction management firms who are responsible for the new business development of their companies. **Activities:** Compiles statistics. Offers local and national educational programs; maintains certification program.

★5158★ *The Source*
Rachel P.R. Services
1650 S. Pacific Coast Hwy., Ste. 200-C
Redondo Beach, CA 90277
Ph: (310)792-1313   Fax: (310)792-1309
Fr: 800-874-8577

Annual, November. $29.00. Covers Over 3,000 job banks, referral services, recruiters, employment agencies, schools/colleges, internships/mentors, trade groups, telephone hotlines, directories, trade journals, and other organizations in the U.S. offering information on employment opportunities in advertising, public relations, journalism, and marketing. Entries include: Contact name, address, phone, products or services, cost/details. Arrangement: Classified by product or ser-vice. Indexes: Product/service, organization name, subject, geographical.

★5159★ *Sports Careers Industry Audio Cassette Series*
Sports Careers
PO Box 10129
Phoenix, AZ 85064
Fr: 800-776-7877

Audiocassette series. Covers the top ten major career categories for the sports industry: Special Events; TV and Cable; Sporting Goods; Colleges/Universities; Facility Management; Corporate Sponsorship; Athletic Representation; Front Office; Print and Radio; Health and Fitness.

★5160★ *Student Guide to Mass Media Internships*
Intern Research Group
Box 52, Regent Hall
University of Colorado
Boulder, CO 80309
Ph: (303)442-8340

Annual, latest edition 1995. $35.00, payment with order; $40.00, billed. Covers about 10,000 internships offered by 2,700 newspapers, radio and television stations, cable television companies, magazines, advertising agencies, and other firms. Entries include: Organization name, address, type and number of internships offered, eligibility requirements, application deadline, salary or other stipend offered, name and title of contact; many listings also include description of intern's duties. Arrangement: Classified by type of medium, then geographical.

★5161★ **Women in Communications**
10605 Judicial Dr., Ste. A4
Fairfax, VA 22030-5167
Ph: (703)359-9000   Fax: (703)359-0603

Members: Professional association of journalism and communications.

Mathematicians

SOURCES OF HELP-WANTED ADS

★5162★ Employment Information in the Mathematical Sciences

American Mathematical Society
201 Charles St.
PO Box 6248
Providence, RI 02940
Ph: (401)455-4000   Fax: (401)331-3842
Fr: 800-321-4AMS

Five times a year. $160.00 for institutions, Included in subscription; $96.00 for individuals. $40.00 for students, or the unemployed; payment must accompany order. Covers colleges and universities with departments in the mathematical sciences, and non-academic and foreign organizations with employment openings. Entries include: For departments: name, address, name and title of contact; job title, job description, salary (if applicable). Arrangement: Classified as academic or non-academic, then geographical.

★5163★ Minority Engineer

Equal Opportunity Publications, Inc.
150 Motor Pkwy., Ste. 420
Hauppauge, NY 11788-5145
Ph: (516)273-0066   Fax: (516)273-8936

Affirmative-action recruitment magazine serving college graduating and professional minority engineers.

★5164★ Notices of the American Mathematical Society

American Mathematical Society
PO Box 6248
Providence, RI 02940
Ph: (401)455-4000   Fax: (401)331-3842
Fr: 800-321-4267

$146.00/year; $88.00/year for members. AMS journal publishing programs, meeting reports, new publications announcements, upcoming mathematical meetings, scientific development trends, computer software reviews, and federal funding reports.

PLACEMENT AND JOB REFERRAL SERVICES

★5165★ American Academy of Mechanics (AAM)

ESM Department
Blacksburg, VA 24061-0219
Ph: (703)231-6841   Fax: (703)231-4574

Members: Individuals recognized for their contributions to the science and profession of mechanics; affiliates are firms and companies interested in advancing the field of mechanics. Criteria for membership include authorship of at least two published articles in books or periodicals that are recognized by the board of directors as significant in the field of mechanics. **Purpose:** Promotes the science and profession of mechanics; provides a forum wherein engineers, mathematicians, scientists, and others active in mechanics can meet to pursue their common interests. **Activities:** Maintains placement service.

★5166★ American Geophysical Union (AGU)

2000 Florida Ave. NW
Washington, DC 20009
Ph: (202)462-6900   Fax: (202)328-0566
Fr: 800-966-AGU1

Members: Individuals professionally associated with the field of geophysics; supporting members are companies and other organizations whose work involves geophysics. **Purpose:** Promotes the study of problems concerned with the figure and physics of the earth; initiates and coordinates research that depends upon national and international cooperation and provides for scientific discussion of research results. **Activities:** Sponsors placement service at semiannual meeting. **E-Mail:** custser@kosmos.agu.org **Website:** http://www.agu.org

★5167★ American Mathematical Society (AMS)

PO Box 6248
Providence, RI 02940
Ph: (401)455-4000   Fax: (401)331-3842
Fr: 800-321-4AMS

Members: Professional society of mathematicians and educators. **Purpose:** Promotes the interests of mathematical scholarship and research. Holds institutes, seminars, short courses, and symposia to further mathematical research; awards prizes. **Activities:** Offers placement services; compiles statistics.

EMPLOYER DIRECTORIES AND NETWORKING LISTS

★5168★ American Men and Women of Science

R. R. Bowker Co.
Reed Reference Publishing
121 Chanlon Rd.
New Providence, NJ 07974
Ph: (908)464-6800   Fax: (908)665-6688
Fr: 800-521-8110

Triennial, latest edition January 1995. $106.00, per volume; $850.00, set. Covers over 123,000 U.S. and Canadian scientists active in the physical, biological, mathematical, computer science, and engineering fields; includes references to previous edition for deceased scientists and nonrespondents. Entries include: Name, address, education, personal and career data, memberships, honors and awards, research interest. Arrangement: Alphabetical. Indexes: Discipline (in separate volume).

★5169★ Assistantships and Graduate Fellowships in the Mathematical Sciences

American Mathematical Society
201 Charles St.
PO Box 6248
Providence, RI 02940
Ph: (401)455-4000   Fax: (401)331-3842

Annual, October. $17.00. Publication includes: List of assistantship and graduate fellowship opportunities in math, statistics, computer science and related fields in about 270 colleges and universities in the United States and Canada; sources of fellowship information. Entries include: For assistantships and fellowships: title, sponsoring organization name, address, name and title of contact; description of position, including stipend (if any), duties, deadline for application; number and type of degrees awarded for previous year. For fellowship information sources: name, address. Arrangement: Geographical. Indexes: Type of stipend.

★5170★ **Directory of Statisticians**

American Statistical Association
1429 Duke St.
Alexandria, VA 22314
Ph: (703)684-1221   Fax: (703)684-2037

Irregular. Latest edition 1994. $125.00. Covers more than 25,000 members of the American Statistical Association, the Eastern and Western North American Regions of the Biometric Society, the Statistical Society of Canada, the Institute of Mathematical Statistics and the Bernoulli Society. Entries include: Name, address, phone, fax, electronic mail number, degrees, work affiliation. Arrangement: Alphabetical. Indexes: Geographical.

★5171★ **Mathematical Sciences Professional Directory**

American Mathematical Society
201 Charles St.
PO Box 6248
Providence, RI 02940
Ph: (401)455-4000   Fax: (401)331-3842
Fr: 800-321-4AMS

Annual. $45.00, payment with order. Covers 37 professional organizations concerned with mathematics, government agencies, academic institutions with department in the mathematical sciences, nonacademic organizations, and individuals. Entries include: For professional organizations and government agencies Name, address, names and titles of key personnel. For institutions: name, address, name, title, and address of department chair. Arrangement: Classified by type of organization; institutions are geographical; others, alphabetical. Indexes: University or college name.

HANDBOOKS AND MANUALS

★5172★ **Career Choices for the 90's for Students of Mathematics**

Walker and Company
435 Hudson St.
New York, NY 10014
Ph: (212)727-8300   Fax: (212)727-0984
Fr: 800-289-2553

Prepared by the Career Associates staff. 1990. $8.95. 166 pages. Discusses alternatives for students of mathematics. Offers advice on how to break into the field and how to move up. Covers where and who the employers are, internship possibilities, and professional networking associations. Comprehensive guide to career and job search planning.

★5173★ **Career Information in the Mathematical Sciences**

Conference Board of the Mathematical Sciences (CBMS)
1529 18th St. NW
Washington, DC 20036

Single copy free. Resource guide lists career materials.

★5174★ **Careers for Number Crunchers and Other Quantitative Types**

VGM Career Horizons
4255 W. Touhy Ave.
Lincolnwood, IL 60646-1975
Ph: (847)679-5500   Fax: (847)679-2494
Fr: 800-323-4900

Rebecca Burnett. 1993. $14.95; $9.95 (paper). Provides information to math-oriented job hunters on how to become statisticians, field researchers, computer programmers, stock analysts, investment managers, bankers, engineers, accountants, underwriters, economists, market analysts, mathematicians, systems analysts, and more.

★5175★ **Careers for Number Lovers**

The Millbrook Press
2 Old New Milford Rd.
Brookfield, CT 06804
Ph: (203)740-2220   Fr: 800-462-4703

Andrew Kaplan. 1991. $14.40; $4.95 (paper). 64 pages. Contains interviews with people in math-related careers. Provides job descriptions, methods of entry into the field, educational preparation, and earnings.

★5176★ **Careers in Science**

VGM Career Horizons
4255 W. Touhy Ave.
Lincolnwood, IL 60646-1975
Ph: (847)679-5500   Fax: (847)679-2494
Fr: 800-323-4900

Thomas Easton. Third edition, 1996. 192 pages. $17.95; $13.95 (paper). Discusses careers in life science, earth science, physical and space science, social science, engineering, mathematics, and computer science. Offers job hunting advice.

★5177★ **Chronicle Math & Science Occupations Guidebook**

Chronicle Guidance Publications, Inc.
PO Box 1190
Moravia, NY 13118-1190
Ph: (315)497-0330   Fax: (315)497-3359
Fr: 800-622-7284

Paul Downes, editor. 1994. $109.25.

★5178★ **Encyclopedia of Careers and Vocational Guidance**

J. G. Ferguson Publishing Co.
200 W. Monroe, Ste. 250
Chicago, IL 60606
Ph: (312)580-5480

William E. Hopke. Ninth edition, 1993. $129.95; $199.95 (CD-ROM). Four-volume set that profiles 900 occupations and describes job trends in 71 industries. Includes career description, educational requirements, history of the job, methods of entry, advancement, employment outlook, earnings, conditions of work, social and psychological factors, and sources of further information.

Contains career and employment information for this field.

★5179★ **Prentice Hall Guide to Scholarships and Fellowships for Math and Science Students**

Prentice Hall
113 Sylvan Ave., Rte. 9W
Englewood Cliffs, NJ 07632
Ph: (201)592-2000   Fr: 800-922-0579

Mark Kantrowitz. 1993. $29.95; $19.95 (paper). Acts as a resource guide for those pursuing careers in mathematics, science, and engineering.

★5180★ **Project MASCOT Mathematics & Science Careers of Tomorrow**

American Counseling Association
5999 Stevenson Ave.
Alexandria, VA 22304-3300
Ph: (703)823-9800   Fax: 800-473-2329
1994. $14.99.

OTHER SOURCES

★5181★ **Association for International Practical Training (AIPT)**

10400 Little Patuxent Pky. Ste. 250
Columbia, MD 21044
Ph: (410)997-2200   Fax: (410)992-3924

Purpose: Helps coordinate training around the world in fields such as travel, the culinary arts, and hotel management. **Activities:** Conducts programs in career development and hospitality/tourism exchanges. Operates a student exchange program. Provides reciprocal practical training experience for recent graduates from the U.S., Austria, Germany, Finland, France, Hungary, Ireland, Japan, Malaysia, Netherlands, Switzerland, and the United Kingdom. Arranges training programs in the U.S. and abroad. Serves as U.S. affiliate to IAESTE (International Association for the Exchange of Students for Technical Experience) and operates a Professional Visitors Program to arrange short-term educational and training visits to the U.S. **E-Mail:** aipt@aipt.org

★5182★ **Institute of Mathematical Statistics (IMS)**

3401 Investment Blvd., Ste. 7
Hayward, CA 94545-3819
Ph: (510)783-8141   Fax: (510)783-4131

Members: Professional society of mathematicians and others interested in mathematical statistics and probability theory. **Purpose:** Seeks to further research in mathematical statistics and probability. **E-Mail:** ims@stat.berkeley.edu

★5183★ **Mathematical Association of America (MAA)**

1529 18th St. NW
Washington, DC 20036
Ph: (202)387-5200   Fax: (202)265-2384

Members: College mathematics teachers; individuals using mathematics as a tool in a business or profession. **Purpose:** Sponsors annual high school mathematics contests and W.L. Putnam Competition for college students. Conducts faculty enhancement workshops and promotes the use of computers through classroom training. **Activities:** Offers college placement test program; operates speakers' bureau. **E-Mail:** maahq@maa.org

★5184★ National Council of Teachers of Mathematics (NCTM)

1906 Association Dr.
Reston, VA 22091
Ph: (703)620-9840   Fax: (703)476-2970
Fr: 800-235-7566

Members: Teachers of mathematics in grades K-12, two-year colleges, and teacher education personnel on college campuses.

Mechanical Engineers

SOURCES OF HELP-WANTED ADS

★5185★ Advanced Materials & Processes

ASM International
9639 Kinsman Rd.
Materials Park, OH 44073-0002
Ph: (216)338-5151   Fax: (216)338-4634

Monthly. $68.00/year for members; $120.00/year for nonmembers. Magazine covering advances in materials technology.

★5186★ ASME News

American Society of Mechanical Engineers
345 E. 47th St.
New York, NY 10017-2392
Ph: (212)705-7723   Fax: (212)705-7841
Fr: 800-843-2763

Monthly. Engineering tabloid.

★5187★ Automotive Engineering

Society of Automotive Engineers
400 Commonwealth Dr.
Warrendale, PA 15096
Ph: (412)776-4841   Fax: (412)776-4026

Monthly. $72.00/year for individuals; $126.00/year for other countries. Magazine for automotive engineers providing technical and design information.

★5188★ Captsule Job Listings

Publications and Communications, Inc.
12416 Hymeadow Dr.
Austin, TX 78750
Ph: (512)250-9023   Fax: (512)331-3900
Fr: 800-678-9724

Online database. Lists current job openings in the contract (temporary) technical services industry. Includes the Action Hot List, which provides information on job seekers. Includes employment opportunities in technical/professional engineering, computing, and design/drafting. Entries generally contain company name, address, and job opening.

★5189★ Chemical Equipment

Curpier/ Group Publishing
301 Gibraltar Dr.
PO Box 231
Cooperstown, NY 13326
Ph: (607)547-2591   Fax: (607)547-2923
Fr: 800-733-1284

Monthly. Tabloid on the chemical process industry.

★5190★ Consulting-Specifying Engineer

Cahners Publishing Co.
1350 E. Touhy Ave.
Des Plaines, IL 60018
Ph: (708)635-8800   Fax: (708)390-2770

$74.95.00/year for individuals. The integrated engineering magazine of the building construction industry.

★5191★ Engineering Times

National Society of Professional Engineers
1420 King St.
Alexandria, VA 22314
Ph: (703)684-2875   Fax: (703)836-4875

Monthly. Magazine (tabloid) covering professional, legislative, and techology issues for an engineering audience.

★5192★ ENR: Engineering News Record

New York Construction News
1221 Avenue of the Americas
New York, NY 10020
Ph: (212)512-4773   Fax: (212)512-4770

Weekly. $42.00/year; $2.00/issue.

★5193★ High Technology Careers Magazine

HTC
4701 Patrick Henry Dr., No. 1901
Santa Clara, CA 95054
Ph: (408)970-8800   Fax: (408)980-5103

Bimonthly. Magazine (tabloid) containing employment opportunity information for the engineering and technical community.

★5194★ Hydraulics & Pneumatics

Peter Li
1100 Superior Ave.
Cleveland, OH 44114
Ph: (216)696-7000   Fax: (216)696-7670

Monthly. $50.00/year; $65.00/year for Canada; $85.00/year for other countries. Magazine of hydraulic and pneumatic systems and engineering.

★5195★ Machine Design

Peter Li
1100 Superior Ave.
Cleveland, OH 44114
Ph: (216)696-7000   Fax: (216)696-7670

$100.00/year. Magazine on design engineering function.

★5196★ Mechanical Engineering

American Society of Mechanical Engineers
345 E. 47th St.
New York, NY 10017-2392
Ph: (212)705-7723   Fax: (212)705-7841
Fr: 800-843-2763

Monthly. Mechanical engineering.

★5197★ Minority Engineer

Equal Opportunity Publications, Inc.
150 Motor Pkwy., Ste. 420
Hauppauge, NY 11788-5145
Ph: (516)273-0066   Fax: (516)273-8936

Affirmative-action recruitment magazine serving college graduating and professional minority engineers.

★5198★ Noise Control Engineer Journal

Institute of Noise Control Engineering
345 Ross Hall
Dept. of Mechanical Engineering
Auburn, AL 36849-3541
Ph: (205)844-3306   Fax: (205)844-3307

Bimonthly. $60.00/year for individuals. Refereed journal containing technical articles for professionals concerned with noise reduction in industry, buildings, transportation, products, and communities.

★5199★ NSBE Magazine

NSBE Publications
1454 Duke St.
Alexandria, VA 22314
Ph: (703)549-2207   Fax: (703)683-5312

$10.00/year for individuals; $2.00 for single issue. Journal providing information on engineering careers, self-development, and cultural issues for recent graduates with technical majors.

★5200★ Plumbing Engineer

TMB Publishing, Inc.
1850 Techny Ct.
Northbrook, IL 60062
Ph: (708)564-1127

Ten times/year. Trade journal for consulting engineering, mechanical engineering, architecture, and contracting professionals.

★5201★ Power

New York Construction News
1221 Avenue of the Americas, 41st Fl.
New York, NY 10020
Ph: (212)512-4773   Fax: (212)512-4770

Monthly. Magazine for engineers in electric utilities, process and manufacturing plants, commercial and service establishments, and consulting, design, and construction engineering firms working in the power technology field.

★5202★ Reeves Journal: Plumbing Heating Cooling

Business News Publishing Co.
23187 La Cadena Dr., Ste. 101
PO Box 30700
Laguna Hills, CA 92653
Ph: (714)830-0881   Fax: (714)859-7845

Monthly. Free to qualified subscribers; $24.00/year for individuals. Regional plumbing, heating, and cooling magazine.

★5203★ SWE

Society of Women Engineers
120 Wall St., 11th Fl.
New York, NY 10005-3902
Ph: (212)509-9577   Fax: (212)509-0224

Bimonthly. $30.00/year for nonmembers. Magazine for engineering students and for women and men working in the engineering and technology fields. Covers career guidance, continuing development and topical issues.

★5204★ Technology Review

The Tech
PO Box 397029
Cambridge, MA 02139
Ph: (617)253-1541   Fax: (617)258-8226

$30.00/year for individuals; $3.75 for single issue; $42.00/year for other countries. Magazine reviewing new developments in technology with an emphasis on economic, political, and social implications. Not a new product publication.

★5205★ Woman Engineer

Equal Opportunity Publications, Inc.
150 Motor Pkwy., Ste. 420
Hauppauge, NY 11788-5145
Ph: (516)273-0066   Fax: (516)273-8936

Engineer recruitment magazine.

PLACEMENT AND JOB REFERRAL SERVICES

★5206★ American Academy of Mechanics (AAM)

ESM Department
Blacksburg, VA 24061-0219
Ph: (703)231-6841   Fax: (703)231-4574

Members: Individuals recognized for their contributions to the science and profession of mechanics; affiliates are firms and companies interested in advancing the field of mechanics. Criteria for membership include authorship of at least two published articles in books or periodicals that are recognized by the board of directors as significant in the field of mechanics. **Purpose:** Promotes the science and profession of mechanics; provides a forum wherein engineers, mathematicians, scientists, and others active in mechanics can meet to pursue their common interests. **Activities:** Maintains placement service.

★5207★ American Indian Science and Engineering Society (AISES)

1630 30th St., Ste. 301
Boulder, CO 80301
Ph: (303)492-8658   Fax: (303)492-3400

Members: American Indian and non-Indian students and professionals in science, technology, and engineering fields; corporations representing energy, mining, aerospace, electronic, and computer fields. **Purpose:** Seeks to motivate and encourage students to pursue undergraduate and graduate studies in science, engineering, and technology. **Activities:** Sponsors science fairs in grade schools, teacher training workshops, summer math/science sessions for 8th-12th graders, professional chapters, and student chapters in colleges. Offers scholarships. Adult members serve as role models, advisers, and mentors for students. Operates placement service. **E-Mail:** aisesha@spot.colorado.edu

★5208★ Engineering Society of Detroit (ESD)

100 Farnsworth Ave.
Detroit, MI 48202
Ph: (313)832-5400   Fax: (313)832-5920

Members: Engineers from all disciplines; scientists and technologists. **Activities:** Offers placement services. Conducts technical programs and engineering refresher courses; sponsors conferences and expositions. Maintains speakers' bureau. Although based in Detroit, MI, society membership is international.

★5209★ ISA

PO Box 12277
67 Alexander Dr.
Research Triangle Park, NC 27709
Ph: (919)549-8411   Fax: (919)549-8288

Purpose: Educational organization dedicated to advancing knowledge and practice related to the theory, design, manufacture, and use of instruments and controls in science and industry. Operates training center for industry; conducts symposia; develops standards; recognizes individual achievement. **Activities:** Maintains speakers' bureau and placement service.

★5210★ Korean Scientists and Engineers Association in America (KSEA)

6261 Executive Blvd.
Rockville, MD 20852
Ph: (301)984-7048   Fax: (301)984-1231

Members: Scientists and engineers holding single or advanced degrees. **Purpose:** Goals are to: promote friendship and mutuality among Korean and American scientists and engineers; contribute to Korea's scientific, technological, industrial, and economic developments; strengthen the scientific, technological, and cultural bonds between Korea and the U.S. Sponsors symposium. **Activities:** Maintains speakers' bureau, placement service, and biographical archives. Compiles statistics. Maintains 100 volume library of scientific handbooks and yearbooks in Korean.

★5211★ Robotics International of the Society of Manufacturing Engineers (RI/SME)

1 SME Dr.
PO Box 0930
Dearborn, MI 48121-0930
Ph: (313)271-1500   Fax: (313)271-2861

Members: Engineers, managers, educators, and government officials in 50 countries working or interested in the field of robotics. **Purpose:** Promotes efficient and effective use of current and future robot technology. Serves as a clearinghouse for the industry trends and developments. Areas of interest include: aerospace; assembly systems; casting and forging; education and training; human factors and safety; human and food service; material handling; military systems; nontraditional systems; research and development; small shop applications; welding. Offers professional certification. **Activities:** Operates placement service; compiles statistics. Maintains speakers' bureau.

★5212★ Society of Hispanic Professional Engineers (SHPE)

5400 E. Olympic Blvd., Ste. 210
Los Angeles, CA 90022
Ph: (213)725-3970

Purpose: Engineers, student engineers, and scientists seeking to increase the number of Hispanic engineers by providing motivation and support to students. Sponsors competitions and educational programs. **Activities:** Maintains placement service and speakers' bureau; compiles statistics.

★5213★ SPIE–The International Society for Optical Engineering (SPIE)

PO Box 10
1000 20th St.
Bellingham, WA 98227
Ph: (206)676-3290   Fax: (206)647-1445

Purpose: Technical society dedicated to advancing engineering and scientific applications of optical, electro-optical, and photo-electronic instrumentation systems and technology. Fosters information exchange and technical communication among scientific, engineering, and user communities. Organizes educational programs; conducts annual Optics Education survey. **Activities:** Offers professional placement exchange.

EMPLOYER DIRECTORIES AND NETWORKING LISTS

★5214★ American Men and Women of Science

R. R. Bowker Co.
Reed Reference Publishing
121 Chanlon Rd.
New Providence, NJ 07974
Ph: (908)464-6800   Fax: (908)665-6688
Fr: 800-521-8110

Triennial, latest edition January 1995. $106.00, per volume; $850.00, set. Covers over 123,000 U.S. and Canadian scientists active in the physical, biological, mathematical, computer science, and engineering fields; includes references to previous edition for deceased scientists and nonrespondents. Entries include: Name, address, education, personal and career data, memberships, honors and awards, research interest. Arrangement: Alphabetical. Indexes: Discipline (in separate volume).

★5215★ Directory of Contract Service Firms

C. E. Publications, Inc.
PO Box 97000
Kirkland, WA 98083
Ph: (206)823-2222   Fax: (206)821-0942

Annual, January. $10.00. Covers Approximately 900 contract firms actively engaged in the employment of engineering and technical personnel for temporary contract assignments throughout the world. Entries include: Company name, address, phone, name of contact. Arrangement: Alphabetical. Indexes: Geographical.

★5216★ Directory of Engineering Societies and Related Organizations

American Association of Engineering Societies
1111 19th St. NW, Ste. 608
Washington, DC 20036
Ph: (202)296-2237   Fax: (202)296-1151
Fr: 800-658-8897

1992. $185.00. Lists 1,000 national, regional, Canadian, and international organizations concerned with engineering and related fields.

★5217★ Directory of Engineers in Private Practice

National Society of Professional Engineers
1420 King St.
Alexandria, VA 22314
Ph: (703)684-2862   Fax: (703)836-4875

Annual. $85.00. Covers 600 consulting engineering firms and 7,200 individuals who are members of the society's Professional Engineers in Private Practice division. Entries include: For companies, name, address, phone, name of principal executive, list of services. For individuals, name, address; most listings include phone. Arrangement: Firms are geographic, then by specialty; individuals are alphabetical.

★5218★ Engineering Research Centres

Stockton Press
Groves Dictionaries
345 Park Ave. S., 10th Fl.
New York, NY 10010
Ph: (212)689-9200   Fr: 800-221-2123

Fourth edition, 1995. $515.00. 768 pages. Contains over 8,000 entries describing research and technology laboratories in over 70 countries. Provides details on industrial research centers and educational establishments with research and development activity. Indexes: Subject and title of establishments.

★5219★ National Certified Pipe Welding Bureau—Membership Directory

National Certified Pipe Welding Bureau
1385 Piccard Dr.
Rockville, MD 20850
Ph: (301)869-5800   Fax: (301)990-9690

Annual, December. Available to members only. Covers about 600 mechanical contractors regularly engaged in the fabrication or erecting of piping systems, who employ certified pipe welders. Entries include: Firm name, address, phone, telex, fax, name of contact. Arrangement: By each chapter, then by firm name.

★5220★ Peterson's Job Opportunities in Engineering and Technology 1996

Peterson's
PO Box 2123
Princeton, NJ 08543-2123
Ph: (609)243-9111   Fax: (609)243-9150
Fr: 800-338-3282

Compiled by the Peterson's staff. Annual. $19.95 paperback. 432 pages. Profiles 2,000 high-tech companies looking primarily for technical personnel in such fields as biotechnology, telecommunications, software, computers and peripherals, defense, and aerospace. Contains job-search strategies and career options to help match education and expertise to the job market. Indexed geographically, by industry, and by hiring needs.

★5221★ Scientific and Technical Organizations and Agencies Directory

Gale Research
835 Penobscot Bldg.
Detroit, MI 48226-4094
Ph: (313)961-2242   Fax: (313)961-6083
Fr: 800-877-GALE

Irregular; latest edition December 1993. $195.00. Covers over 25,600 national and international organizations and agencies concerned with the physical and applied sciences, engineering, and technology, including associations, computer information services, consulting firms, educational institutions, foundations, government advisory organizations, federal government agencies, general grant and assistance programs, libraries and information centers, patent sources and services, research and development centers, scholarships, fellowships, and loans, science-technology centers, standards organizations, state academies of science, and state government agencies in the fields of aeronautics and space sciences, chemistry, computer science specialties, electronics, geography, geology, machinery, mathematics, metallurgy, meteorology, mineralogy, nuclear science, petroleum and gas, physics, plastics, transportation, water resources, and other areas. Entries include: Organization name, address, phone, and name of contact; additional descriptive text for most entries. Arrangement: Classified by type of organization. Indexes: Organization name/key word.

★5222★ Who's Who in Technology

Gale Research
835 Penobscot Bldg.
Detroit, MI 48226-4094
Ph: (313)961-2242   Fax: (313)961-6083
Fr: 800-877-GALE

Irregular, new edition expected June 1995. $380.00. Covers 38,000 engineers, scientists, inventors, and researchers. Entries include: Name, title, affiliation, address; personal, education, and career data; publications, patents; technical field of activity; area of expertise. Arrangement: Alphabetical. Indexes: Geographical, employer, technical discipline, expertise.

HANDBOOKS AND MANUALS

★5223★ The Best Resumes for Scientists and Engineers

John Wiley and Sons
605 3rd Ave.
New York, NY 10158
Ph: (212)850-6000   Fr: 800-225-5945

Adele Lewis. Second edition, 1993. $37.50; $14.95 (paper). Presents an extensive collection of scientific and engineering resumes, highlighting the important differences between these and resumes written for other occupations.

★5224★ Careers in Engineering

VGM Career Horizons
4255 W. Touhy Ave.
Lincolnwood, IL 60646-1975
Ph: (847)679-5500   Fax: (847)679-2494
Fr: 800-323-4900

Geraldine O. Gardner. 1994. $17.95; $13.95 (paper). Covers careers in the public or private sector, in industry, the university, or the military, from applications in computer architecture design to high temperature ceramics.

★5225★ Careers in Power Engineering and Boiler Operation: Your Guide to a Secure Future

Powerplant Press
PO Box 431219
Pontiac, MI 48343

Stanley D. Guiling. 1993. $39.95 (paper).

★5226★ Engineering Success

Kendall Hunt Publishing
4050 Westmark Dr.
PO Box 1840
Dubuque, IA 52004-1840
Ph: (319)589-1000   Fax: 800-772-9165
Fr: 800-228-0810

Bill Osher. 1994. $27.96.

★5227★ Engineering Your Job Search: A Job-Finding Resource for Engineering Professionals

Professional Publications, Inc.
1250 5th Ave.
Belmont, CA 94002
Ph: (415)593-9119   Fax: (415)592-4519
Fr: 800-426-1178

Compiled by Professional Publications editors. 1995. $12.95 (paper).

★5228★ Introduction to the Engineering Profession

HarperCollins Publishers, Inc.
10 E. 53rd. St.
New York, NY 10022-5299
Ph: (212)207-7000   Fax: (212)207-7145
Fr: 800-331-3761

David M. Burghardt. 1995. $30.00 (paper).

★5229★ Job Opportunities in Engineering and Technology

Peterson's Guides, Inc.
PO Box 2123
Princeton, NJ 08543-2123
Ph: (609)243-9111   Fax: (609)243-9150
Fr: 800-338-3282

1994. $18.95 (paper).

★5230★ Majoring in Engineering: How to Get from Your Freshman Year to Your First Job

Farrar, Straus & Giroux, Inc.
19 Union Sq., W
New York, NY 10003
Ph: (212)741-6900   Fr: 800-788-6262

John Garcia. 1995. $20.00; $10.00 (paper).

★5231★ 100 Best Careers for the Year 2000

Prentice Hall General Reference
15 Columbus Cir.
New York, NY 10023
Ph: (212)373-8500   Fr: 800-223-2348

Shelly Field. 1992. $15.00 (paper). Covers 100 of the fastest growing jobs. The publication is divided into 11 general employment sections. Specific careers are covered within each section. Provides job description, responsibilities, employment opportunities, earnings, education and training, advancement opportunities, and experience and qualifications for each occupation.

★5232★ Opportunities in Engineering Careers

VGM Career Horizons
4255 W. Touhy Ave.
Lincolnwood, IL 60646-1975
Ph: (847)679-5500   Fax: (847)679-2494
Fr: 800-323-4900

Nicholas Basta. 1995. $14.95; $11.95 (paper). Outlines typical job titles, salaries, career paths, and employment prospects.

★5233★ Opportunities in High Tech Careers

VGM Career Horizons
4255 W. Touhy Ave.
Lincolnwood, IL 60646-1975
Ph: (847)679-5500   Fax: (847)679-2494
Fr: 800-323-4900

Gary D. Golter and Deborah Yanuck. 1995. $14.95; $11.95 (paper). 160 pages. Explores high technology careers. Describes job opportunities, how to make a career decision, how to prepare for high technology jobs, job hunting techniques, and future trends.

★5234★ Resumes for Engineering Careers

VGM Career Horizons
NTC Publishing Group
4255 W. Touhy Ave.
Lincolnwood, IL 60646-1975
Ph: (847)679-5500   Fax: (847)679-2494
Fr: 800-323-4900

1994. $9.95. 160 pages. Contains sample resumes and cover letters applicable to any engineering field.

★5235★ Where the Jobs Are: The Hottest Careers for the '90s

The Career Press, Inc.
3 Tice Rd.
PO Box 687
Franklin Lakes, NJ 07417
Ph: (201)848-0310   Fax: (201)848-1727
Fr: 800-237-3371

Joyce Hadley. Second edition, 1995. $9.99. 300 pages. Describes careers in fifteen general fields, from accounting to travel and hospitality.

EMPLOYMENT AGENCIES AND SEARCH FIRMS

★5236★ ABC Employment Service

25 S. Bemiston, Ste. 214
Clayton, MO 63105
Ph: (314)725-3140

Employment agency.

★5237★ B and M Associates, Inc.

199 Cambridge Rd.
Woburn, MA 01801-4705
Ph: (617)938-9120

Employment agency.

★5238★ Bell Oaks Co.

3390 Peachtree Rd., Ste. 1124
Atlanta, GA 30326
Ph: (404)261-2170

Personnel service firm.

★5239★ Claremont-Branan, Inc.

2150 Parklake Dr., Ste. 212
Atlanta, GA 30345
Ph: (404)491-1292

Employment agency. Executive search firm.

★5240★ Colli Associates of Tampa

PO Box 2865
Tampa, FL 33601
Ph: (813)681-2145

Employment agency. Executive search firm.

★5241★ Engineer One, Inc.

10124 Dutchtown Rd.
Knoxville, TN 37932-2611
Ph: (615)690-2611   Fax: (615)690-2611

Employment agency.

★5242★ Executive Recruiters Agency

14 Office Park Dr.
PO Box 21810
Little Rock, AR 72221-1810
Ph: (501)224-7000   Fax: (501)224-8534

Personnel service firm.

★5243★ Hayden and Associates, Inc.

7825 Washington Ave. S., Ste. 120
Minneapolis, MN 55439-2431
Ph: (612)941-6300   Fax: (612)941-9602

Employment agency. Executive search firm. Fills openings in a variety of fields.

★5244★ Industrial Recruiters Associates, Inc.

630 Oakwood Ave., Ste. 318
West Hartford, CT 06110
Ph: (203)953-3643

Employment agency.

★5245★ The Jobs Co.

8900 E. Sprague Ave.
Spokane, WA 99212-2927
Ph: (509)928-3151   Fax: (509)928-3168

Employment agency. Has division specializing in engineering and scientific openings. Also operates division specializing in sales openings.

★5246★ JR Professional Search

PO Box 18356
Tucson, AZ 85731
Ph: (520)721-1855   Fax: (520)721-1855

Employment agency.

★5247★ LOR Personnel Division

418 Wall St.
Princeton, NJ 08540
Ph: (609)921-6580

Employment agency. Executive search firm.

★5248★ Main Line Personnel Service, Inc.
401 City Ave.
Bala Cynwyd, PA 19004-1122
Ph: (610)667-1820
Employment agency.

★5249★ Rand Personnel Agency
1200 Truxtun, Ste. 130
Bakersfield, CA 93301
Ph: (805)325-0751   Fax: (805)325-4120
Personnel service firm.

★5250★ Search and Recruit International
4455 South Blvd.
Virginia Beach, VA 23452
Ph: (804)490-3151
Employment agency. Headquartered in Virginia Beach. Other offices in Bremerton, WA; Charleston, SC; Jacksonville, FL; Memphis, TN; Pensacola, FL; Sacramento, CA; San Bernardino, CA; San Diego, CA.

★5251★ Sierra Technology Corporation
4150 Manzanita Ave., Ste. 100
Carmichael, CA 95608-1700
Ph: (916)488-4960   Fax: (916)488-7058
Employment agency. Provides placement on a temporary basis.

★5252★ Software Services Corp.
2850 S. Industrial Hwy, Ste. 300
Ann Arbor, MI 48104-6796
Ph: (313)971-2300
Employment agency.

★5253★ Source Engineering
5580 LBJ Fwy., Ste. 300
Dallas, TX 75240
Ph: (214)385-3002   Fax: (214)717-0075
Executive search firm. Many affiliate offices located throughout the U.S.

★5254★ T.R. Employment Agency
409 Wilshire Blvd.
Santa Monica, CA 90401
Ph: (310)393-4107
Employment agency.

★5255★ Tri-Serv Inc.
22 W. Padonia Rd., Ste. C53
Timonium, MD 21093
Ph: (301)561-1740
Employment agency.

OTHER SOURCES

★5256★ Adventures in Manufacturing
Society of Manufacturing Engineers (SME)
Education Dept.
1 SME Dr.
PO Box 930
Dearborn, MI 48121
Ph: (313)271-1500   Fr: 800-733-4SME
Video. Free. Comes with poster and brochure. Describes opportunities and preparation for careers in manufacturing.

★5257★ American Almanac of Jobs and Salaries 1994-95
Avon Books
1350 Avenue of the Americas, 2nd Fl.
New York, NY 10019
Ph: (212)261-6800   Fr: 800-238-0658
John Wright. Revised edition, 1993. $17.00. 704 pages. This is a comprehensive guide to the wages of hundreds of occupations in a wide variety of industries and organizations.

★5258★ American Association of Engineering Societies (AAES)
1111 19th St. NW, Ste. 608
Washington, DC 20036
Ph: (202)296-2237   Fax: (202)296-1151
Purpose: Seeks to promote leadership in public affairs for the engineering community, work in support of math and science education for young persons. Disseminates of information about the profession. Provides statistics about engineers.

★5259★ American Society of Mechanical Engineers (ASME)
345 E. 47th St.
New York, NY 10017
Ph: (212)705-7722   Fax: (212)705-7739
Fr: 800-THE-ASME
Members: Technical society of mechanical engineers and students. **Purpose:** Conducts research; develops boiler, pressure vessel, and power test codes. Develops safety codes and standards for equipment. Conducts short course programs, and Identifying Research Needs Program. Maintains 19 research committees and 38 divisions.

★5260★ Association for International Practical Training (AIPT)
10400 Little Patuxent Pky. Ste. 250
Columbia, MD 21044
Ph: (410)997-2200   Fax: (410)992-3924
Purpose: Helps coordinate training around the world in fields such as travel, the culinary arts, and hotel management. **Activities:** Conducts programs in career development and hospitality/tourism exchanges. Operates a student exchange program. Provides reciprocal practical training experience for recent graduates from the U.S., Austria, Germany, Finland, France, Hungary, Ireland, Japan, Malaysia, Netherlands, Switzerland, and the United Kingdom. Arranges training programs in the U.S. and abroad. Serves as U.S. affiliate to IAESTE (International Association for the Exchange of Students for Technical Experience) and operates a Professional Visitors Program to arrange short-term educational and training visits to the U.S. **E-Mail:** aipt@aipt.org

★5261★ Career Encounters: Mechanical Engineering
Cambridge Career Products
PO Box 2153
Dept. CC15
Charleston, WV 25328-2153
Ph: (304)744-9323   Fax: (304)744-9351
Fr: 800-468-4227
Video. $99.95. 25 minutes. Professionals shown in a variety of settings discuss different aspects of their careers.

★5262★ Career Encounters: Women in Engineering
Cambridge Career Products
PO Box 2153
Dept. CC15
Charleston, WV 25328-2153
Ph: (304)744-9323   Fax: (304)744-9351
Fr: 800-468-4227
Video. $99.95. 25 minutes. Professionals shown in a variety of settings discuss different aspects of their careers.

★5263★ Engineering Salary Survey
Source Engineering
1290 Oakmead, Ste. 318
Sunnyvale, CA 94086
Ph: (408)738-8440
Annual. Discusses the structure of the engineering profession, trends, and compensation. Salaries are listed by job function, industry, and years of experience.

★5264★ Graduating Engineer
Peterson's/COG Publishing Group
16030 Ventura Blvd., No. 560
Encino, CA 91436
Ph: (818)789-5293
Eight issues/year. Magazine focusing on employment, education, and career development for entry-level engineers.

★5265★ National Action Council for Minorities in Engineering (NACME)
3 W. 35th St.
New York, NY 10001-2281
Ph: (212)279-2626   Fax: (212)629-5178
Purpose: Seeks to increase the number of African American, Latino, and Native American students enrolled in and graduating from engineering schools. Through the Corporate Scholars Program, offers comprehensive scholarships to engineering students that include leadership development, corporate mentors and summer internships. Works with local, regional, and national education organizations to motivate and encourage precollege students to engage in engineering careers. Conducts educational and research programs; operates project to assist engineering schools in improving the retention and graduation rates of minority students. Maintains speakers' bureau; compiles statistics.

★5266★ National Society of Professional Engineers (NSPE)
1420 King St.
Alexandria, VA 22314
Ph: (703)684-2800   Fax: (703)836-4875
Members: Professional engineers and engineers-in-training in all fields registered in accordance with the laws of states or territories of the U.S. or provinces of Canada; qualified graduate engineers, student members, and registered land surveyors. **Purpose:** Is concerned with social, professional, ethical, and economic considerations of engineering as a profession; encompasses programs in public relations, employment practices, ethical considerations, education, and career guidance. Monitors legislative and regulatory actions of interest to the engineer-

ing profession. **Website:** http.//www.hspc.org

★5267★ *Salaries of Scientists, Engineers, and Technicians: A Summary of Salary Surveys*

Commission on Professionals in Science and Technology (CPST)
1500 Massachusetts Ave. NW, Ste. 831
Washington, DC 20005
Ph: (202)223-6995

1993.

★5268★ **Society of Women Engineers (SWE)**
120 Wall St., 11th Fl.
New York, NY 10005
Ph: (212)509-9577   Fax: (212)509-0224

Members: Educational service society of women engineers; membership is also open to men. **Purpose:** Supplies information on the achievements of women engineers and the opportunities available to them; assists women engineers in preparing for return to active work following temporary retirement.

Serves as an informational center on women in engineering. **Activities:** Administers several certificate and scholarship programs. Offers tours and career guidance; conducts surveys. Compiles statistics.

Medical Assistants

SOURCES OF HELP-WANTED ADS

★5269★ The PMA

American Association of Medical
Assistants
20 N. Wacker Dr., Ste. 1575
Chicago, IL 60606-2903
Ph: (312)899-1500   Fax: (312)899-1259

Bimonthly. $30.00/year for nonmembers.
Professional health journal.

PLACEMENT AND JOB REFERRAL SERVICES

**★5270★ American Medical
Technologists (AMT)**

710 Higgins Rd.
Park Ridge, IL 60068
Ph: (708)823-5169   Fax: (708)823-0458
Fr: 800-275-1268

Members: National professional registry of
medical laboratory technologists, technicians, medical assistants, dental assistants,
and phlebotomists. **Activities:** Maintains job
information service. Sponsors AMT Institute
for Education, which has developed continuing education programs.

EMPLOYER DIRECTORIES AND NETWORKING LISTS

**★5271★ AHA Guide to the Health Care
Field**

Health Statistics Group
American Hospital Association (AHA)
1 N. Franklin
Chicago, IL 60606
Ph: (312)422-3501   Fax: (312)280-6015

Annual, July. $195.00, payment with order.
Covers hospitals, multi-health care systems,
freestanding ambulatory surgery centers,

psychiatric facilities, long-term care facilities,
substance abuse programs, hospices, Health
Maintenance Organizations (HMOs), and other health-related organizations. Entries include: For hospitals: facility name, address,
phone, administrator's name, number of
beds, facilities and services, number of employees, expenses, other statistics. For other
organizations: name, address, phone, name
and title of contact. Arrangement: Geographical. Indexes: Hospital name.

**★5272★ American Group Practice
Association—Directory**

American Group Practice Association
1422 Duke St.
Alexandria, VA 22314
Ph: (703)838-0033   Fax: (703)548-1890

Annual, February. $150.00. Covers about
250 private group medical practices and their
professional staffs, totalling about 25,000
physicians and administrators. Entries include: Group member name, address, phone,
names of administrator and other executives,
names of physician listed by medical specialties. Arrangement: Alphabetical. Indexes:
Group location, personal name.

★5273★ Hospital Blue Book

Billian Publishing Co.
2100 Powers Ferry Rd., Ste. 300
Atlanta, GA 30339
Ph: (404)955-5656   Fax: (404)952-0669

Annual, spring. $154.50, national edition,
plus $20.00 shipping. Covers more than
7,100 hospitals; some listings also appear in
a separate southern edition of this publication. Entries include: Name of hospital, accreditation, mailing address, phone, fax,
number of beds, type of facility (nonprofit,
general, state, etc.); list of administrative
personnel and chiefs of medical services,
with specific titles. Arrangement: Geographical.

★5274★ Hospital Market Atlas

SMG Marketing Group, Inc.
1342 N. LaSalle Dr.
Chicago, IL 60610
Ph: (312)642-3026   Fax: (312)642-9729
Fr: 800-678-3026

Biennial, odd years. $495.00, payment with
order. Covers over 7,000 hospitals, hospital

systems and 480 group purchasing organizations. Entries include: Hospital or organization name, address, phone, county code,
management, type of hospital service, number of beds, admissions, surgical operations,
and emergency room visits. Arrangement:
Geographical.

★5275★ Hospitals Directory

American Business Directories, Inc.
American Business Information, Inc.
5711 S. 86th Cir.
Omaha, NE 68127
Ph: (402)593-4600   Fax: (402)331-1505

Annual. $870.00, U.S. edition. Entries in-
clude: Name, address, phone (including area
code), size of advertisement, year first in
Yellow Pages, name of owner or manager,
number of employees. Compiled from telephone company Yellow Pages, nationwide.
Arrangement: Geographical.

**★5276★ Medical and Health Information
Directory**

Gale Research
835 Penobscot Bldg.
Detroit, MI 48226-4094
Ph: (313)961-2242   Fax: (313)961-6083
Fr: 800-877-GALE

Approximately biennial; latest edition 1994.
$195.00, per volume; $485.00, for the three-
volume set. Covers in Volume 1, almost
18,600 medical and health oriented associations, organizations, institutions, and government agencies, including health maintenance
organizations (HMOs), preferred provider organizations (PPOs), insurance companies,
pharmaceutical companies, research centers,
and medical and allied health schools. In
Volume 2, nearly 11,800 medical book publishers; medical periodicals, directories, audiovisual producers and services, medical libraries and information centers, and electronic resources. In Volume 3, nearly 26,000
clinics, treatment centers, care programs,
and counseling/diagnostic services for 30
subject areas. Entries include: Institution,
service, or firm name, address, phone; many
include names of key personnel and, when
pertinent, descriptive annotation. Arrangement: Classified by organization activity, service, etc. Indexes: Each volume has a complete alphabetical name and keyword index.

★5277★ Osteopathic Membership Directory—AOHA

American Osteopathic Healthcare Association
5301 Wisconsin Ave. NW, Ste. 630
Washington, DC 20015-2015
Ph: (202)686-1700   Fax: (202)686-7615

Annual, summer. $125.00, payment with order. Covers about 110 osteopathic hospitals. Includes list of individual and institutional members; also lists osteopathic colleges, and directors of medical education. Entries include: For hospitals: name of hospital, name of chief executive officer, address, phone, number of beds and other hospital data. Arrangement: Geographical. Indexes: Name, institution.

★5278★ Peterson's Job Opportunities in Health Care

Peterson's Guides, Inc.
202 Carnegie Ctr.
Box 2123
Princeton, NJ 08543-2123
Ph: (609)243-9111   Fax: (609)243-9150
Fr: 800-338-3282

Annual, August. $18.95. Covers Over 1,500 companies hiring health-care professionals for skilled nursing care facilities, hospitals, medical laboratories, home health care, and pharmaceuticals. Entries include: Organization name, address, phone, name and title of contact, type of organization, number of employees, Standard Industrial Classification (SIC) code; description of opportunities available including disciplines, level of education required, starting locations and salaries, level of experience accepted, benefits. Arrangement: Alphabetical. Indexes: Employer by type of organization, industry classification, number of employees, starting location, special interest area; education level, company.

HANDBOOKS AND MANUALS

★5279★ America's 50 Fastest Growing Jobs

JIST Works, Inc.
720 N. Park Ave.
Indianapolis, IN 46202
Ph: (317)264-3720   Fr: 800-648-5478

Third edition, 1995. $14.95. 288 pages. Each job profile explains the nature of the work, skills and abilities required, employment outlook, average earnings, related occupations, education and training requirements, and employment opportunities. Also contains career planning information and job search tips.

★5280★ Careers in Health Care

VGM Career Horizons
4255 W. Touhy Ave.
Lincolnwood, IL 60646-1975
Ph: (847)679-5500   Fax: (847)679-2494
Fr: 800-323-4900

Barbara M. Swanson. 1995. $17.95; $13.95 (paper). Describes job duties, work settings, salaries, licensing and certification requirements, educational preparation, and future outlook. Gives ideas on how to secure a job.

★5281★ Chronicle Health Occupations Guidebook

Chronicle Guidance Publications
PO Box 1190
Moravia, NY 13118-1190
Ph: (315)497-0330   Fax: (315)497-3359
Fr: 800-622-7284

Paul Downes, editor. 1994. $100.65.

★5282★ Exploring Health Careers

Delmar Publishers
3 Columbia Cir., Box 15015
Albany, NY 12212
Ph: (518)464-3500   Fax: (518)464-0358
Fr: 800-347-7707

Maureen McCutcheon. 1993. $27.95.

★5283★ Health Care Job Explosion! Careers in the 90's

Bookhaven Press
401 Amherst Ave.
Coraopolis, PA 15108
Ph: (412)262-5578

Dennis Y. Damp. 1993. $14.95 (paper).

★5284★ Health Careers: Undergraduate Careers in the Health Profession

Kendall Hunt Publishing Co.
4050 Westmark Dr.
PO Box 1840
Dubuque, IA 52004-1840
Ph: (319)589-1000   Fax: 800-772-9165
Fr: 800-228-0810

Michael Beard. 1994. $11.95.

★5285★ Hot Health-Care Careers

MasterMedia Ltd.
17 E. 89th St., 7D
New York, NY 10128
Ph: (212)546-7650   Fax: (212)546-7638
Fr: 800-334-8232

Margaret McNally. 1993. $17.95; $10.95 (paper).

★5286★ Job Opportunities in Health Care 1995

Peterson's Guides, Inc.
PO Box 2123
Princeton, NJ 08543-2123
Ph: (609)243-9111   Fax: (609)243-9150
Fr: 800-338-3282

1994. $18.95 (paper).

★5287★ The Medical Assistant: Administrative and Clinical

W. B. Saunders Co.
Curtis Ctr., Independence Sq., W
Philadelphia, PA 19106-3399
Ph: (215)238-7800   Fax: (215)238-7883

Mary E. Kinn. 1993. $33.95.

★5288★ Medical Assisting Career Pack

American Association of Medical Assistants
20 N. Wacker Dr., Ste. 1575
Chicago, IL 60606-2903
Ph: (312)899-1500   Fr: 800-228-2262

Free. 20 pages. A collection of fact sheets on the medical assisting profession.

★5289★ Medical Technologists and Technicians Career Directory

Gale Research
835 Penobscot Bldg.
Detroit, MI 48226-4094
Ph: (313)961-2242   Fax: (313)961-6083
Fr: 800-877-GALE

Bradley Morgan. 1993. $39.00. 324 pages. Essays on specific careers provide an insider's perspective. Features extensive listings of contacts and entry-level job opportunities. Provides information on internships and sources of help-wanted ads.

★5290★ 150 Careers in Health Care

U.S. Directory Service
121 Chanlon Rd.
New Providence, NJ 07974
Ph: (908)464-6800   Fax: (908)665-3560
Fr: 800-521-8110

1993. $59.95.

★5291★ Opportunities in Health and Medical Careers

VGM Career Horizons
4255 W. Touhy Ave.
Lincolnwood, IL 60646-1975
Ph: (847)679-5500   Fax: (847)679-2494
Fr: 800-323-4900

Donald Snook, Jr. and Leo D'Orazio. 1993. $14.95; $11.95 (paper). Covers the full range of medical and health occupations. Illustrated.

★5292★ Opportunities in Paramedical Careers

VGM Career Horizons
4255 W. Touhy Ave.
Lincolnwood, IL 60646-1975
Ph: (847)679-5500   Fax: (847)679-2494
Fr: 800-323-4900

Alex Kacen. 1994. $14.95; 11.95 (paper). 160 pages. Discusses a variety of opportunities in this field and how to pursue them. Illustrated.

★5293★ Resumes for the Health Care Professional

John Wiley & Sons, Inc.
605 3rd Ave.
New York, NY 10158-0012
Ph: (212)850-6000   Fr: 800-225-5945

Kim Marino. 1993. $14.95 (paper).

★5294★ Resumes for Health and Medical Careers

4255 W. Touhy Ave.
Lincolnwood, IL 60646-1975
Ph: (708)679-5500   Fax: (708)679-6375
Fr: 800-323-4900

Compiled by VGM Career Horizons Staff 1995. $9.95 (paper).

★5295★ VGM's Handbook of Health Care Careers

4255 W. Touhy Ave.
Lincolnwood, IL 60646-1975
Ph: (708)679-5500   Fax: (708)679-6375
Fr: 800-323-4900

Annette Selden, editor. 1994. $12.95 (paper).

★5296★ **Where the Jobs Are: The Hottest Careers for the '90s**

The Career Press, Inc.
3 Tice Rd.
PO Box 687
Franklin Lakes, NJ 07417
Ph: (201)848-0310   Fax: (201)848-1727
Fr: 800-237-3371

Joyce Hadley. Second edition, 1995. $9.99. 300 pages. Describes careers in fifteen general fields, from accounting to travel and hospitality.

★5297★ **Your Opportunities in Medical Support**

Energeia Publishing, Inc.
PO Box 985
Salem, OR 97308
Ph: (503)362-1480   Fax: (503)362-2123

Margie Sherman. 1994. $2.00 (paper).

EMPLOYMENT AGENCIES AND SEARCH FIRMS

★5298★ **Academy Medical Personnel Services**

571 High St.
Columbus, OH 43085-4132
Ph: (614)848-6011

Employment agency. Fills openings on a regular or temporary basis.

★5299★ **Davis-Smith, Inc.**

24725 W. 12 Mile Rd., Ste. 302
Southfield, MI 48034
Ph: (810)354-4100

Employment agency. Executive search firm.

★5300★ **Eden Temporary Services**

280 Madison Ave.
New York, NY 10016-0801
Ph: (212)685-4666

Employment agency. Places individuals in regular or temporary positions.

★5301★ **Harper Associates**

29870 Middlebelt
Farmington Hills, MI 48334
Ph: (810)932-1170

Employment agency.

★5302★ **Medical Personnel Pool**

2901 S. Ridgewood Ave.
Daytona Beach, FL 32119-3542
Ph: (904)736-1648

Provides regular and temporary staffing assistance. Offices located in cities throughout United States.

★5303★ **Midwest Medical Consultants**

8910 Purdue Rd., Ste. 200
Indianapolis, IN 46268-1155
Ph: (317)872-1053

Employment agency. Executive search firm.

★5304★ **Professional Placement Associates, Inc.**

11 Rye Ridge Plaza
Rye Brook, NY 10573
Ph: (914)251-1000   Fax: (914)939-1959

Employment agency.

★5305★ **Staley/Adams and Associates Personnel Services Inc.**

4615 Post Oak Pl.
Houston, TX 77027-9731
Ph: (713)965-0402

Employment agency.

OTHER SOURCES

★5306★ **American Association of Medical Assistants (AAMA)**

20 N. Wacker Dr., Ste. 1575
Chicago, IL 60606-2903
Ph: (312)899-1500   Fax: (312)899-1259

Members: Assistants, receptionists, secretaries, bookkeepers, nurses, and laboratory personnel employed in the offices of physicians and other medical facilities. **Activities:** Activities include a certification program consisting of study and an examination, passage of which entitles the individual to a certificate as a Certified Medical Assistant. Conducts accreditation of one- and two-year programs in medical assisting in conjunction with the Committee on Allied Health Education and Accreditation of the American Medical Association. Provides assistance and information to institutions of higher learning desirous of initiating courses for medical assistants.

★5307★ **American Society of Podiatric Medical Assistants (ASPMA)**

2124 S. Austin Blvd.
Cicero, IL 60650
Ph: (708)863-6303   Fax: (708)863-5375

Members: Podiatric assistants. **Purpose:** To hold educational seminars and to administer certification examinations.

★5308★ **Registered Medical Assistants of American Medical Technologists (RMAAMT)**

710 Higgins Rd.
Park Ridge, IL 60068-5765
Ph: (708)823-5169   Fax: (708)823-0458
Fr: 800-275-1268

A program of the American Medical Technologists. **Members:** Certified assistants to physicians in office practice, clinics, hospitals, and private health care facilities. **Purpose:** Works to establish standards of training; provides continuing education and home study programs; promotes quality care in allied health. Works with the Accrediting Bureau of Health Education Schools in regard to certification examinations and student societies.

Medical Record Technicians

PLACEMENT AND JOB REFERRAL SERVICES

★5309★ Association of Records Managers and Administrators (ARMA Inter)

4200 Somerset, Ste. 215
Prairie Village, KS 66208
Ph: (913)341-3808   Fax: (913)341-3742

Members: Administrators, managers, supervisors, specialists, educators, and others interested in the study of efficient records-making and records-keeping. **Purpose:** Promotes a scientific interest in records and information management; provides a forum for research and the exchange of ideas and knowledge; furnishes a source of records and information management guidance. Conducts research in standardized alphabetical filing, shelf filing methods and equipment, machine-processed data control, microfilm systems, records protection, forms/reports management, and retention practices. **Activities:** Maintains speakers' bureau and placement service.

EMPLOYER DIRECTORIES AND NETWORKING LISTS

★5310★ AHA Guide to the Health Care Field

Health Statistics Group
American Hospital Association (AHA)
1 N. Franklin
Chicago, IL 60606
Ph: (312)422-3501   Fax: (312)280-6015

Annual, July. $195.00, payment with order. Covers hospitals, multi-health care systems, freestanding ambulatory surgery centers, psychiatric facilities, long-term care facilities, substance abuse programs, hospices, Health Maintenance Organizations (HMOs), and other health-related organizations. Entries include: For hospitals: facility name, address, phone, administrator's name, number of beds, facilities and services, number of employees, expenses, other statistics. For other

organizations: name, address, phone, name and title of contact. Arrangement: Geographical. Indexes: Hospital name.

★5311★ American Group Practice Association—Directory

American Group Practice Association
1422 Duke St.
Alexandria, VA 22314
Ph: (703)838-0033   Fax: (703)548-1890

Annual, February. $150.00. Covers about 250 private group medical practices and their professional staffs, totalling about 25,000 physicians and administrators. Entries include: Group member name, address, phone, names of administrator and other executives, names of physician listed by medical specialties. Arrangement: Alphabetical. Indexes: Group location, personal name.

★5312★ Directory of Hospital Personnel

Medical Economics
5 Paragon Dr.
Montvale, NJ 07645-1725
Ph: (201)358-7500   Fax: (201)573-4956
Fr: 800-222-3045

Annual, September. $325.00, plus 7.50 shipping. Covers 200,000 executives at 7,100 U.S. hospitals. Entries include: Name of hospital, address, phone, number of beds, type and JCAHO status of hospital, names and titles of key department heads and staff, medical and nursing school affiliations; number of residents, interns, and nursing students. Arrangement: Geographical. Indexes: Hospital name, personnel, hospital size.

★5313★ Hospital Blue Book

Billian Publishing Co.
2100 Powers Ferry Rd., Ste. 300
Atlanta, GA 30339
Ph: (404)955-5656   Fax: (404)952-0669

Annual, spring. $154.50, national edition, plus $20.00 shipping. Covers more than 7,100 hospitals; some listings also appear in a separate southern edition of this publication. Entries include: Name of hospital, accreditation, mailing address, phone, fax, number of beds, type of facility (nonprofit, general, state, etc.); list of administrative personnel and chiefs of medical services, with specific titles. Arrangement: Geographical.

★5314★ Hospital Market Atlas

SMG Marketing Group, Inc.
1342 N. LaSalle Dr.
Chicago, IL 60610
Ph: (312)642-3026   Fax: (312)642-9729
Fr: 800-678-3026

Biennial, odd years. $495.00, payment with order. Covers over 7,000 hospitals, hospital systems and 480 group purchasing organizations. Entries include: Hospital or organization name, address, phone, county code, management, type of hospital service, number of beds, admissions, surgical operations, and emergency room visits. Arrangement: Geographical.

★5315★ Hospitals Directory

American Business Directories, Inc.
American Business Information, Inc.
5711 S. 86th Cir.
Omaha, NE 68127
Ph: (402)593-4600   Fax: (402)331-1505

Annual. $870.00, U.S. edition. Entries include: Name, address, phone (including area code), size of advertisement, year first in Yellow Pages, name of owner or manager, number of employees. Compiled from telephone company Yellow Pages, nationwide. Arrangement: Geographical.

★5316★ Medical and Health Information Directory

Gale Research
835 Penobscot Bldg.
Detroit, MI 48226-4094
Ph: (313)961-2242   Fax: (313)961-6083
Fr: 800-877-GALE

Approximately biennial; latest edition 1994. $195.00, per volume; $485.00, for the three-volume set. Covers in Volume 1, almost 18,600 medical and health oriented associations, organizations, institutions, and government agencies, including health maintenance organizations (HMOs), preferred provider organizations (PPOs), insurance companies, pharmaceutical companies, research centers, and medical and allied health schools. In Volume 2, nearly 11,800 medical book publishers; medical periodicals, directories, audiovisual producers and services, medical libraries and information centers, and electronic resources. In Volume 3, nearly 26,000 clinics, treatment centers, care programs, and counseling/diagnostic services for 30 subject areas. Entries include: Institution, service, or firm name, address, phone; many include names of key personnel and, when pertinent, descriptive annotation. Arrangement: Classified by organization activity, service, etc. Indexes: Each volume has a complete alphabetical name and keyword index.

★5317★ *Osteopathic Membership Directory—AOHA*

American Osteopathic Healthcare Association
5301 Wisconsin Ave. NW, Ste. 630
Washington, DC 20015-2015
Ph: (202)686-1700   Fax: (202)686-7615

Annual, summer. $125.00, payment with order. Covers about 110 osteopathic hospitals. Includes list of individual and institutional members; also lists osteopathic colleges, and directors of medical education. Entries include: For hospitals: name of hospital, name of chief executive officer, address, phone, number of beds and other hospital data. Arrangement: Geographical. Indexes: Name, institution.

HANDBOOKS AND MANUALS

★5318★ *Careers in Health Care*

VGM Career Horizons
4255 W. Touhy Ave.
Lincolnwood, IL 60646-1975
Ph: (847)679-5500   Fax: (847)679-2494
Fr: 800-323-4900

Barbara M. Swanson. 1995. $17.95; $13.95 (paper). Describes job duties, work settings, salaries, licensing and certification requirements, educational preparation, and future outlook. Gives ideas on how to secure a job.

★5319★ *Medical Records Technician*

R & E Publishers, Inc.
468 Auzerais Ave., Ste. A
San Jose, CA 95126
Ph: (408)977-0691   Fax: (408)977-0693

Ronald R. Smith. 1993. $1.95 (paper).

★5320★ *100 Best Careers for the Year 2000*

Prentice Hall General Reference
15 Columbus Cir.
New York, NY 10023
Ph: (212)373-8500   Fr: 800-223-2348

Shelly Field. 1992. $15.00 (paper). Covers 100 of the fastest growing jobs. The publication is divided into 11 general employment sections. Specific careers are covered within each section. Provides job description, responsibilities, employment opportunities, earnings, education and training, advancement opportunities, and experience and qualifications for each occupation.

★5321★ *Opportunities in Health and Medical Careers*

VGM Career Horizons
4255 W. Touhy Ave.
Lincolnwood, IL 60646-1975
Ph: (847)679-5500   Fax: (847)679-2494
Fr: 800-323-4900

Donald Snook, Jr. and Leo D'Orazio. 1993. $14.95; $11.95 (paper). Covers the full range of medical and health occupations. Illustrated.

★5322★ *Opportunities in Vocational and Technical Careers*

VGM Career Horizons
4255 W. Touhy Ave.
Lincolnwood, IL 60646-1975
Ph: (847)679-5500   Fax: (847)679-2494
Fr: 800-323-4900

Adrian A. Paradis. 1992. $14.95; $11.95 (paper). 160 pages. Provides information on a variety of opportunities and advice on breaking into the field.

★5323★ *Resumes for Health and Medical Careers*

4255 W. Touhy Ave.
Lincolnwood, IL 60646-1975
Ph: (708)679-5500   Fax: (708)679-6375
Fr: 800-323-4900

Compiled by VGM Career Horizons Staff 1995. $9.95 (paper).

EMPLOYMENT AGENCIES AND SEARCH FIRMS

★5324★ **Academy Medical Personnel Services**

571 High St.
Columbus, OH 43085-4132
Ph: (614)848-6011

Employment agency. Fills openings on a regular or temporary basis.

★5325★ **Davis-Smith, Inc.**

24725 W. 12 Mile Rd., Ste. 302
Southfield, MI 48034
Ph: (810)354-4100

Employment agency. Executive search firm.

★5326★ **Eden Temporary Services**

280 Madison Ave.
New York, NY 10016-0801
Ph: (212)685-4666

Employment agency. Places individuals in regular or temporary positions.

★5327★ **Harper Associates**

29870 Middlebelt
Farmington Hills, MI 48334
Ph: (810)932-1170

Employment agency.

★5328★ **JPM International**

4665 MacArthur Ct., Ste. 100B
Newport Beach, CA 92660
Ph: (714)955-2545   Fax: (714)757-1320

Executive search firm and employment agency.

★5329★ **Professional Placement Associates, Inc.**

11 Rye Ridge Plaza
Rye Brook, NY 10573
Ph: (914)251-1000   Fax: (914)939-1959

Employment agency.

★5330★ **Sue Carroll Personnel, Inc.**

16 E. 79th St.
New York, NY 10021
Ph: (212)288-8866   Fax: (212)988-7191

Employment agency and executive search firm.

OTHER SOURCES

★5331★ **American Health Information Management Association (AMRA)**

919 N. Michigan Ave., Ste. 1400
Chicago, IL 60611-1683
Ph: (312)787-2672   Fax: (312)787-9793

Members: Registered record administrators; accredited record technicians with expertise in health information management, biostatistics, classification systems, and systems analysis. **Activities:** Sponsors Independent Study Programs in Medical Record Technology and coding. Conducts annual qualification examinations to credential medical record personnel as Registered Record Administrators (RRA), Accredited Record Technicians (ART) and Certified Coding Specialists (CCS). Maintains Foundation of Research and Education Library, Scholarships and loans. **Website:** http://www.ahima.org

★5332★ **National Association for Healthcare Quality (NAHQ)**

4700 W. Lake Ave.
Glenview, IL 60025-1485
Ph: (708)375-4700   Fax: (708)875-4777

Members: Healthcare professionals in quality assessment and improvement, utilization and risk management, case management, infection control, managed care, nursing, and medical records. **Purpose:** Objectives are: to encourage, develop, and provide continuing education for all persons involved in health care quality; to give the patient primary consideration in all actions affecting his or her health and welfare; to promote the sharing of knowledge and encourage a high degree of professional ethics in health care quality. Offers accredited certification in the field of healthcare quality, utilization, and risk management. Facilitates communication and cooperation among members, medical staff, and health care government agencies. Conducts educational seminars and conferences.

Metallurgical, Ceramic, and Materials Engineers

SOURCES OF HELP-WANTED ADS

★5333★ Advanced Materials & Processes

ASM International
9639 Kinsman Rd.
Materials Park, OH 44073-0002
Ph: (216)338-5151   Fax: (216)338-4634

Monthly. $68.00/year for members; $120.00/year for nonmembers. Magazine covering advances in materials technology.

★5334★ American Metal Market

Chilton Publications
825 7th Ave., 7th Fl.
New York, NY 10019
Ph: (212)887-8550   Fax: (212)887-8520

Daily. $575.00/year. Newspaper of the metals industry, written for and read by executives and managers. Provides information for metal users, producers, distributors, and recyclers.

★5335★ ASTM Standardization News

ASTM
1916 Race St.
Philadelphia, PA 19103
Ph: (215)299-5400   Fax: (215)299-5511

Monthly. Magazine publishing news on the testing and evaluation industry.

★5336★ Captsule Job Listings

Publications and Communications, Inc.
12416 Hymeadow Dr.
Austin, TX 78750
Ph: (512)250-9023   Fax: (512)331-3900
Fr: 800-678-9724

Online database. Lists current job openings in the contract (temporary) technical services industry. Includes the Action Hot List, which provides information on job seekers. Includes employment opportunities in technical/professional engineering, computing, and design/drafting. Entries generally contain company name, address, and job opening.

★5337★ Ceramic Industry

Business News Publishing Co.
5900 Harper Rd., Ste. 109
Solon, OH 44139-1835
Ph: (216)498-9214   Fax: (216)498-9121

Monthly. $59.00/year for individuals. Magazine covering glass, whiteware, porcelain, enamel, refractories, and advanced ceramics.

★5338★ Chemical and Engineering News

American Chemical Society
1155 16th St. NW
Washington, DC 20036
Ph: (202)872-4600   Fax: (202)872-6005
Fr: 800-227-5558

Weekly. Free to qualified subscribers; $105.00/year for individuals. Chemical process industries trade journal.

★5339★ Electrochemical Society Interface

The Electrochemical Society
10 S. Main St.
Pennington, NJ 08534
Ph: (609)737-1902   Fax: (609)737-2743

Quarterly. 40.00/year.

★5340★ Engineering Times

National Society of Professional Engineers
1420 King St.
Alexandria, VA 22314
Ph: (703)684-2875   Fax: (703)836-4875

Monthly. Magazine (tabloid) covering professional, legislative, and techology issues for an engineering audience.

★5341★ ENR: Engineering News Record

New York Construction News
1221 Avenue of the Americas
New York, NY 10020
Ph: (212)512-4773   Fax: (212)512-4770

Weekly. $42.00/year; $2.00/issue.

★5342★ High Technology Careers Magazine

HTC
4701 Patrick Henry Dr., No. 1901
Santa Clara, CA 95054
Ph: (408)970-8800   Fax: (408)980-5103

Bimonthly. Magazine (tabloid) containing employment opportunity information for the engineering and technical community.

★5343★ International Journal of Powder Metallurgy

American Powder Metallurgy Institute.
105 College Rd. E
Princeton, NJ 08540
Ph: (609)452-7700   Fax: (609)987-8523

Quarterly. $75.00/year for individuals. Powder metallurgy journal.

★5344★ Iron Age

Chilton Publishing
191 S. Gary Ave.
Carol Stream, IL 60188
Ph: (708)462-2282   Fax: (708)462-2862

Monthly. Management magazine for metal producers.

★5345★ Light Metal Age

Fellon Publishing Co.
170 S. Spruce Ave., Ste. 120
South San Francisco, CA 94080
Ph: (415)588-8832   Fax: (415)588-0901

Bimonthly. $32.00/year for individuals. Magazine serving primary and semi-fabrication metal plants that produce, semi-fabricate, process or manufacture the light metals: aluminum, magnesium, titanium, beryllium and their alloys, and/or the non-ferrous metals copper and zinc.

★5346★ Material Handling Engineering

Peter Li
1100 Superior Ave.
Cleveland, OH 44114
Ph: (216)696-7000   Fax: (216)696-7670

Monthly. Magazine for managers of material handling systems in warehouses and manufacturing plants.

★5347★ Materials Performance

National Association of Corrosion
  Engineers
PO Box 218340
Houston, TX 77218
Ph: (713)492-0535   Fax: (713)492-8254

Monthly. Magazine on performance and protection of materials in a corrosive environment.

★5348★ Metal Finishing

Elsevier Science Inc.
655 Avenue of the Americas
New York, NY 10010
Ph: (212)989-5800   Fax: (212)633-3990

Monthly. $45.00/year; $67.00/year for Canada and Mexico; $116.00/year for other countries. Magazine on surface treatment, plating, and painting.

★5349★ Metal Forming

Precision Metalforming Association
27027 Chardon Rd.
Richmond Heights, OH 44143
Ph: (216)585-8800   Fax: (216)585-3126

Monthly. $25.00/year for individuals; $75.00/year for other countries. Metal forming and metal trade magazine.

★5350★ Metlfax

Huebcore Communications, Inc.
29100 Aurora Rd., Ste. 200
Solon, OH 44139
Ph: (216)248-1125   Fax: (216)248-0187

Monthly. Metalworking magazine.

★5351★ Minority Engineer

Equal Opportunity Publications, Inc.
150 Motor Pkwy., Ste. 420
Hauppauge, NY 11788-5145
Ph: (516)273-0066   Fax: (516)273-8936

Affirmative-action recruitment magazine serving college graduating and professional minority engineers.

★5352★ Modern Metals

Trend Publishing
625 N. Michigan Ave.
Chicago, IL 60611-5503
Ph: (312)654-2300   Fax: (312)654-2323

Monthly. $70.00/year for individuals; $6.00 for single issue. Metals fabrication magazine.

★5353★ NSBE Magazine

NSBE Publications
1454 Duke St.
Alexandria, VA 22314
Ph: (703)549-2207   Fax: (703)683-5312

$10.00/year for individuals; $2.00 for single issue. Journal providing information on engineering careers, self-development, and cultural issues for recent graduates with technical majors.

★5354★ SWE

Society of Women Engineers
120 Wall St., 11th Fl.
New York, NY 10005-3902
Ph: (212)509-9577   Fax: (212)509-0224

Bimonthly. $30.00/year for nonmembers. Magazine for engineering students and for women and men working in the engineering and technology fields. Covers career guidance, continuing development and topical issues.

★5355★ Technology Review

The Tech
PO Box 397029
Cambridge, MA 02139
Ph: (617)253-1541   Fax: (617)258-8226

$30.00/year for individuals; $3.75 for single issue; $42.00/year for other countries. Magazine reviewing new developments in technology with an emphasis on economic, political, and social implications. Not a new product publication.

★5356★ 33 MetalProducing

Peter Li
1100 Superior Ave.
Cleveland, OH 44114
Ph: (216)696-7000   Fax: (216)696-7670

Monthly. $50.00/year for individuals. Magazine covering the metal-producing industry.

★5357★ Tooling and Production

Huebcore Communications, Inc.
29100 Aurora Rd., Ste. 200
Solon, OH 44139
Ph: (216)248-1125   Fax: (216)248-0187

Monthly. Magazine concerning metalworking.

★5358★ Woman Engineer

Equal Opportunity Publications, Inc.
150 Motor Pkwy., Ste. 420
Hauppauge, NY 11788-5145
Ph: (516)273-0066   Fax: (516)273-8936

Engineer recruitment magazine.

PLACEMENT AND JOB REFERRAL SERVICES

★5359★ American Ceramic Society (ACerS)

735 Ceramic Pl.
PO Box 6136
Westerville, OH 43086-6136
Ph: (614)890-4700   Fax: (614)899-6109

Members: Professional society of scientists, engineers, educators, plant operators, and others interested in the glass, cements, refractories, nuclear ceramics, whitewares, electronics, engineering, and structural clay products industries. **Purpose:** Disseminates scientific and technical information through its publications and technical meetings. Conducts continuing education courses and training such as the Precollege Education Program. Sponsors over 10 meetings yearly; encourages high school and college students' interest in ceramics. **Activities:** Maintains Ross C. Purdy Museum of Ceramics; offers placement service and speakers' bureau.

★5360★ American Indian Science and Engineering Society (AISES)

1630 30th St., Ste. 301
Boulder, CO 80301
Ph: (303)492-8658   Fax: (303)492-3400

Members: American Indian and non-Indian students and professionals in science, technology, and engineering fields; corporations representing energy, mining, aerospace, electronic, and computer fields. **Purpose:** Seeks to motivate and encourage students to pursue undergraduate and graduate studies in science, engineering, and technology. **Activities:** Sponsors science fairs in grade schools, teacher training workshops, summer math/science sessions for 8th-12th graders, professional chapters, and student chapters in colleges. Offers scholarships. Adult members serve as role models, advisers, and mentors for students. Operates placement service. **E-Mail:** aise sha@spot.colorado.edu

★5361★ APMI International

105 College Rd. E.
Princeton, NJ 08540
Ph: (609)452-7700   Fax: (609)987-8523

Members: Technical society for powder metallurgists and others interested in powder metallurgy and its applications. **Purpose:** Maintains speakers' bureau and placement service.

★5362★ Engineering Society of Detroit (ESD)

100 Farnsworth Ave.
Detroit, MI 48202
Ph: (313)832-5400   Fax: (313)832-5920

Members: Engineers from all disciplines; scientists and technologists. **Activities:** Offers placement services. Conducts technical programs and engineering refresher courses; sponsors conferences and expositions. Maintains speakers' bureau. Although based in Detroit, MI, society membership is international.

★5363★ ISA

PO Box 12277
67 Alexander Dr.
Research Triangle Park, NC 27709
Ph: (919)549-8411   Fax: (919)549-8288

Purpose: Educational organization dedicated to advancing knowledge and practice related to the theory, design, manufacture, and use of instruments and controls in science and industry. Operates training center for industry; conducts symposia; develops standards; recognizes individual achievement. **Activities:** Maintains speakers' bureau and placement service.

★5364★ Korean Scientists and Engineers Association in America (KSEA)

6261 Executive Blvd.
Rockville, MD 20852
Ph: (301)984-7048   Fax: (301)984-1231

Members: Scientists and engineers holding single or advanced degrees. **Purpose:** Goals are to: promote friendship and mutuality among Korean and American scientists and engineers; contribute to Korea's scientific, technological, industrial, and economic developments; strengthen the scientific, technological, and cultural bonds between Korea and the U.S. Sponsors symposium. **Activities:** Maintains speakers' bureau, placement service, and biographical archives. Compiles statistics. Maintains 100 volume library of scientific handbooks and yearbooks in Korean.

★5365★ Metal Powder Industries Federation (MPIF)

105 College Rd. E.
Princeton, NJ 08540-6692
Ph: (609)452-7700   Fax: (609)987-8523

Members: Manufacturers of metal powders, powder metallurgy processing equipment and tools, powder metallurgy products, and refractory and reactive metals. Member associations are: Metal Injection Molding Association; Metal Powder Producers Association; Metal Powder Technology Association; Powder Metallurgy Equipment Association; Powder Metallurgy Parts Association; Refractory Metals Association. **Purpose:** Promotes the science and industry of powder metallurgy and metal powder application through: sponsorship of technical meetings, seminars, and exhibits; establishment of standards; compilation of statistics; public relations; publications. **Activities:** Maintains speakers' bureau and placement service; conducts research.

★5366★ National Institute of Ceramic Engineers (NICE)

University of Florida
Dept. of Materials Science & Eng.
PO Box 116400, 136 MAE
Gainesville, FL 32611-6400
Ph: (904)392-3163   Fax: (904)846-2033

Purpose: Promotes the professional status of ceramic engineering, accreditation of educational programs in ceramic engineering and science, and high ethical engineering standards and practices. **Activities:** Sponsors continuing education courses. Offers employment service and promotes professional engineer registration. Responsible for Professional Engineering exams in Ceramic Engineering.

★5367★ Society for the Advancement of Material and Process Engineering (SAMPE)

PO Box 2459
Covina, CA 91722
Ph: (818)331-0616   Fax: (818)332-8929

Purpose: Material and process engineers, scientists, and other professionals engaged in development of materials and processing technology in airframe, missile, aerospace, propulsion, electronics, life sciences, management, and related industries. **Activities:** International and local chapters sponsor scholarships for science students seeking financial assistance. Provides placement service for members.

★5368★ Society of Hispanic Professional Engineers (SHPE)

5400 E. Olympic Blvd., Ste. 210
Los Angeles, CA 90022
Ph: (213)725-3970

Purpose: Engineers, student engineers, and scientists seeking to increase the number of Hispanic engineers by providing motivation and support to students. Sponsors competitions and educational programs. **Activities:** Maintains placement service and speakers' bureau; compiles statistics.

★5369★ Society for Mining, Metallurgy, and Exploration (SME)

PO Box 625002
Littleton, CO 80162-5002
Ph: (303)973-9550   Fax: (303)973-3845
Fr: 800-763-3132

Members: Member society of the American Institute of Mining, Metallurgical and Petroleum Engineers. Persons engaged in the finding, exploitation, treatment, and marketing of all classes of minerals (metal ores, industrial minerals, and solid fuels) except petroleum. **Purpose:** Promotes the arts and sciences connected with the production of useful minerals and metals. **Activities:** Provides placement service. Offers specialized education programs; compiles enrollment and graduation statistics from schools offering engineering degrees in mining, mineral, mineral processing/metallurgical, geological, geophysical, and mining technology. **E-Mail:** smeaime@aol.com

EMPLOYER DIRECTORIES AND NETWORKING LISTS

★5370★ American Men and Women of Science

R. R. Bowker Co.
Reed Reference Publishing
121 Chanlon Rd.
New Providence, NJ 07974
Ph: (908)464-6800   Fax: (908)665-6688
Fr: 800-521-8110

Triennial, latest edition January 1995. $106.00, per volume; $850.00, set. Covers over 123,000 U.S. and Canadian scientists active in the physical, biological, mathematical, computer science, and engineering fields; includes references to previous edition for deceased scientists and nonrespondents. Entries include: Name, address, education, personal and career data, memberships, honors and awards, research interest. Arrangement: Alphabetical. Indexes: Discipline (in separate volume).

★5371★ Directory of Contract Service Firms

C. E. Publications, Inc.
PO Box 97000
Kirkland, WA 98083
Ph: (206)823-2222   Fax: (206)821-0942

Annual, January. $10.00. Covers Approximately 900 contract firms actively engaged in the employment of engineering and technical personnel for temporary contract assign-

ments throughout the world. Entries include: Company name, address, phone, name of contact. Arrangement: Alphabetical. Indexes: Geographical.

★5372★ Directory of Engineering Societies and Related Organizations

American Association of Engineering Societies
1111 19th St. NW, Ste. 608
Washington, DC 20036
Ph: (202)296-2237   Fax: (202)296-1151
Fr: 800-658-8897

1992. $185.00. Lists 1,000 national, regional, Canadian, and international organizations concerned with engineering and related fields.

★5373★ Directory of Engineers in Private Practice

National Society of Professional Engineers
1420 King St.
Alexandria, VA 22314
Ph: (703)684-2862   Fax: (703)836-4875

Annual. $85.00. Covers 600 consulting engineering firms and 7,200 individuals who are members of the society's Professional Engineers in Private Practice division. Entries include: For companies, name, address, phone, name of principal executive, list of services. For individuals, name, address; most listings include phone. Arrangement: Firms are geographic, then by specialty; individuals are alphabetical.

★5374★ Engineering Research Centres

Stockton Press
Groves Dictionaries
345 Park Ave. S., 10th Fl.
New York, NY 10010
Ph: (212)689-9200   Fr: 800-221-2123

Fourth edition, 1995. $515.00. 768 pages. Contains over 8,000 entries describing research and technology laboratories in over 70 countries. Provides details on industrial research centers and educational establishments with research and development activity. Indexes: Subject and title of establishments.

★5375★ JOM—The Minerals, Metals & Materials Society Membership Directory Issue

American Institute of Mining, Metallurgical and Petroleum Engineers (AIME)
420 Commonwealth Dr.
Warrendale, PA 15086
Ph: (412)776-9000   Fax: (412)776-3770
Fr: 800-759-4867

Annual, July. Available to members only. Covers 9,700 metallurgists, metallurgical engineers, and materials scientists, worldwide. Entries include: Name, office address, career data. Arrangement: Alphabetical; geographical. Indexes: Geographical.

★5376★ *Peterson's Job Opportunities in Engineering and Technology 1996*

Peterson's
PO Box 2123
Princeton, NJ 08543-2123
Ph: (609)243-9111   Fax: (609)243-9150
Fr: 800-338-3282

Compiled by the Peterson's staff. Annual. $19.95 paperback. 432 pages. Profiles 2,000 high-tech companies looking primarily for technical personnel in such fields as biotechnology, telecommunications, software, computers and peripherals, defense, and aerospace. Contains job-search strategies and career options to help match education and expertise to the job market. Indexed geographically, by industry, and by hiring needs.

★5377★ *Scientific and Technical Organizations and Agencies Directory*

Gale Research
835 Penobscot Bldg.
Detroit, MI 48226-4094
Ph: (313)961-2242   Fax: (313)961-6083
Fr: 800-877-GALE

Irregular; latest edition December 1993. $195.00. Covers over 25,600 national and international organizations and agencies concerned with the physical and applied sciences, engineering, and technology, including associations, computer information services, consulting firms, educational institutions, foundations, government advisory organizations, federal government agencies, general grant and assistance programs, libraries and information centers, patent sources and services, research and development centers, scholarships, fellowships, and loans, science-technology centers, standards organizations, state academies of science, and state government agencies in the fields of aeronautics and space sciences, chemistry, computer science specialties, electronics, geography, geology, machinery, mathematics, metallurgy, meteorology, mineralogy, nuclear science, petroleum and gas, physics, plastics, transportation, water resources, and other areas. Entries include: Organization name, address, phone, and name of contact; additional descriptive text for most entries. Arrangement: Classified by type of organization. Indexes: Organization name/key word.

★5378★ *Who's Who in Technology*

Gale Research
835 Penobscot Bldg.
Detroit, MI 48226-4094
Ph: (313)961-2242   Fax: (313)961-6083
Fr: 800-877-GALE

Irregular, new edition expected June 1995. $380.00. Covers 38,000 engineers, scientists, inventors, and researchers. Entries include: Name, title, affiliation, address; personal, education, and career data; publications, patents; technical field of activity; area of expertise. Arrangement: Alphabetical. Indexes: Geographical, employer, technical discipline, expertise.

HANDBOOKS AND MANUALS

★5379★ *The Best Resumes for Scientists and Engineers*

John Wiley and Sons
605 3rd Ave.
New York, NY 10158
Ph: (212)850-6000   Fr: 800-225-5945

Adele Lewis. Second edition, 1993. $37.50; $14.95 (paper). Presents an extensive collection of scientific and engineering resumes, highlighting the important differences between these and resumes written for other occupations.

★5380★ *Careers in Engineering*

VGM Career Horizons
4255 W. Touhy Ave.
Lincolnwood, IL 60646-1975
Ph: (847)679-5500   Fax: (847)679-2494
Fr: 800-323-4900

Geraldine O. Gardner. 1994. $17.95; $13.95 (paper). Covers careers in the public or private sector, in industry, the university, or the military, from applications in computer architecture design to high temperature ceramics.

★5381★ *Encyclopedia of Careers and Vocational Guidance*

J. G. Ferguson Publishing Co.
200 W. Monroe, Ste. 250
Chicago, IL 60606
Ph: (312)580-5480

William E. Hopke. Ninth edition, 1993. $129.95; $199.95 (CD-ROM). Four-volume set that profiles 900 occupations and describes job trends in 71 industries. Includes career description, educational requirements, history of the job, methods of entry, advancement, employment outlook, earnings, conditions of work, social and psychological factors, and sources of further information. Contains career and employment information for this field.

★5382★ *Opportunities in Engineering Careers*

VGM Career Horizons
4255 W. Touhy Ave.
Lincolnwood, IL 60646-1975
Ph: (847)679-5500   Fax: (847)679-2494
Fr: 800-323-4900

Nicholas Basta. 1995. $14.95; $11.95 (paper). Outlines typical job titles, salaries, career paths, and employment prospects.

★5383★ *Opportunities in High Tech Careers*

VGM Career Horizons
4255 W. Touhy Ave.
Lincolnwood, IL 60646-1975
Ph: (847)679-5500   Fax: (847)679-2494
Fr: 800-323-4900

Gary D. Golter and Deborah Yanuck. 1995. $14.95; $11.95 (paper). 160 pages. Explores high technology careers. Describes job opportunities, how to make a career decision, how to prepare for high technology jobs, job hunting techniques, and future trends.

★5384★ *Resumes for Engineering Careers*

VGM Career Horizons
NTC Publishing Group
4255 W. Touhy Ave.
Lincolnwood, IL 60646-1975
Ph: (847)679-5500   Fax: (847)679-2494
Fr: 800-323-4900

1994. $9.95. 160 pages. Contains sample resumes and cover letters applicable to any engineering field.

EMPLOYMENT AGENCIES AND SEARCH FIRMS

★5385★ **ABC Employment Service**

25 S. Bemiston, Ste. 214
Clayton, MO 63105
Ph: (314)725-3140

Employment agency.

★5386★ **Colli Associates of Tampa**

PO Box 2865
Tampa, FL 33601
Ph: (813)681-2145

Employment agency. Executive search firm.

★5387★ **Engineer One, Inc.**

10124 Dutchtown Rd.
Knoxville, TN 37932-2611
Ph: (615)690-2611   Fax: (615)690-2611

Employment agency.

★5388★ **Hayden and Associates, Inc.**

7825 Washington Ave. S., Ste. 120
Minneapolis, MN 55439-2431
Ph: (612)941-6300   Fax: (612)941-9602

Employment agency. Executive search firm. Fills openings in a variety of fields.

★5389★ **Industrial Recruiters Associates, Inc.**

630 Oakwood Ave., Ste. 318
West Hartford, CT 06110
Ph: (203)953-3643

Employment agency.

★5390★ **International Staffing Consultants**

500 Newport Center Dr., Ste. 300
Newport Beach, CA 92660-7003
Ph: (714)721-7990

Employment agency. Provides placement on regular or temporary basis. Affiliate office in London.

★5391★ **The Jobs Co.**

8900 E. Sprague Ave.
Spokane, WA 99212-2927
Ph: (509)928-3151   Fax: (509)928-3168

Employment agency. Has division specializing in engineering and scientific openings. Also operates division specializing in sales openings.

★5392★ JR Professional Search

PO Box 18356
Tucson, AZ 85731
Ph: (520)721-1855   Fax: (520)721-1855

Employment agency.

★5393★ LOR Personnel Division

418 Wall St.
Princeton, NJ 08540
Ph: (609)921-6580

Employment agency. Executive search firm.

★5394★ Main Line Personnel Service, Inc.

401 City Ave.
Bala Cynwyd, PA 19004-1122
Ph: (610)667-1820

Employment agency.

★5395★ Search and Recruit International

4455 South Blvd.
Virginia Beach, VA 23452
Ph: (804)490-3151

Employment agency. Headquartered in Virginia Beach. Other offices in Bremerton, WA; Charleston, SC; Jacksonville, FL; Memphis, TN; Pensacola, FL; Sacramento, CA; San Bernardino, CA; San Diego, CA.

★5396★ Sierra Technology Corporation

4150 Manzanita Ave., Ste. 100
Carmichael, CA 95608-1700
Ph: (916)488-4960   Fax: (916)488-7058

Employment agency. Provides placement on a temporary basis.

★5397★ Software Services Corp.

2850 S. Industrial Hwy, Ste. 300
Ann Arbor, MI 48104-6796
Ph: (313)971-2300

Employment agency.

★5398★ Source Engineering

5580 LBJ Fwy., Ste. 300
Dallas, TX 75240
Ph: (214)385-3002   Fax: (214)717-0075

Executive search firm. Many affiliate offices located throughout the U.S.

OTHER SOURCES

★5399★ American Almanac of Jobs and Salaries 1994-95

Avon Books
1350 Avenue of the Americas, 2nd Fl.
New York, NY 10019
Ph: (212)261-6800   Fr: 800-238-0658

John Wright. Revised edition, 1993. $17.00. 704 pages. This is a comprehensive guide to the wages of hundreds of occupations in a wide variety of industries and organizations.

★5400★ American Association of Engineering Societies (AAES)

1111 19th St. NW, Ste. 608
Washington, DC 20036
Ph: (202)296-2237   Fax: (202)296-1151

Purpose: Seeks to promote leadership in public affairs for the engineering community, work in support of math and science education for young persons. Disseminates of information about the profession. Provides statistics about engineers.

★5401★ ASM International (ASM)

9639 Kinsman
Materials Park, OH 44073-0002
Ph: (216)338-5151   Fax: (216)338-4634
Fr: 800-336-5152

Members: Metallurgists, materials engineers, executives in materials producing and consuming industries; teachers and students. Disseminates technical information about the manufacture, use, and treatment of engineered materials. **Activities:** Offers in-plant, home study, and intensive courses through Materials Engineering Institute. Conducts career development program. Established ASM Foundation for Education and Research. Maintains library of 10,000 volumes on metals and other materials.

★5402★ Association for International Practical Training (AIPT)

10400 Little Patuxent Pky. Ste. 250
Columbia, MD 21044
Ph: (410)997-2200   Fax: (410)992-3924

Purpose: Helps coordinate training around the world in fields such as travel, the culinary arts, and hotel management. **Activities:** Conducts programs in career development and hospitality/tourism exchanges. Operates a student exchange program. Provides reciprocal practical training experience for recent graduates from the U.S., Austria, Germany, Finland, France, Hungary, Ireland, Japan, Malaysia, Netherlands, Switzerland, and the United Kingdom. Arranges training programs in the U.S. and abroad. Serves as U.S. affiliate to IAESTE (International Association for the Exchange of Students for Technical Experience) and operates a Professional Visitors Program to arrange short-term educational and training visits to the U.S. **E-Mail:** aipt@aipt.org

★5403★ Engineering Salary Survey

Source Engineering
1290 Oakmead, Ste. 318
Sunnyvale, CA 94086
Ph: (408)738-8440

Annual. Discusses the structure of the engineering profession, trends, and compensation. Salaries are listed by job function, industry, and years of experience.

★5404★ Graduating Engineer

Peterson's/COG Publishing Group
16030 Ventura Blvd., No. 560
Encino, CA 91436
Ph: (818)789-5293

Eight issues/year. Magazine focusing on employment, education, and career development for entry-level engineers.

★5405★ National Action Council for Minorities in Engineering (NACME)

3 W. 35th St.
New York, NY 10001-2281
Ph: (212)279-2626   Fax: (212)629-5178

Purpose: Seeks to increase the number of African American, Latino, and Native American students enrolled in and graduating from engineering schools. Through the Corporate Scholars Program, offers comprehensive scholarships to engineering students that include leadership development, corporate mentors and summer internships. Works with local, regional, and national education organizations to motivate and encourage precollege students to engage in engineering careers. Conducts educational and research programs; operates project to assist engineering schools in improving the retention and graduation rates of minority students. Maintains speakers' bureau; compiles statistics.

★5406★ National Society of Professional Engineers (NSPE)

1420 King St.
Alexandria, VA 22314
Ph: (703)684-2800   Fax: (703)836-4875

Members: Professional engineers and engineers-in-training in all fields registered in accordance with the laws of states or territories of the U.S. or provinces of Canada; qualified graduate engineers, student members, and registered land surveyors. **Purpose:** Is concerned with social, professional, ethical, and economic considerations of engineering as a profession; encompasses programs in public relations, employment practices, ethical considerations, education, and career guidance. Monitors legislative and regulatory actions of interest to the engineering profession. **Website:** http.// www.hspc.org

★5407★ Salaries of Scientists, Engineers, and Technicians: A Summary of Salary Surveys

Commission on Professionals in Science and Technology (CPST)
1500 Massachusetts Ave. NW, Ste. 831
Washington, DC 20005
Ph: (202)223-6995

1993.

★5408★ Society of Women Engineers (SWE)

120 Wall St., 11th Fl.
New York, NY 10005
Ph: (212)509-9577   Fax: (212)509-0224

Members: Educational service society of women engineers; membership is also open to men. **Purpose:** Supplies information on the achievements of women engineers and the opportunities available to them; assists women engineers in preparing for return to active work following temporary retirement. Serves as an informational center on women in engineering. **Activities:** Administers several certificate and scholarship programs. Offers tours and career guidance; conducts surveys. Compiles statistics.

Meteorologists

SOURCES OF HELP-WANTED ADS

★5409★ Nature: International Weekly Journal of Science

Nature Publishing Co.
65 Bleecker St.
New York, NY 10012-2467
Ph: (212)477-9600 Fax: (212)505-1364

Weekly. Magazine covering science and technology, including the fields of biology, biochemistry, genetics, medicine, earth sciences, physics, pharmacology, and behavioral sciences.

★5410★ Photogrammetric Engineering and Remote Sensing

American Society for Photogrammetry and Remote Sensing (ASPRS)
5410 Grosvenor Ln., Ste. 210
Bethesda, MD 20814-2160
Ph: (301)493-0290 Fax: (301)493-0208

Monthly. Free to members; $120.00/year for nonmembers. Provides technical information about the applications of photogrammetry, remote sensing, and geographic information systems.

★5411★ The Scientist

The Scientist, Inc.
3501 Market St.
Philadelphia, PA 19104
Ph: (215)386-0100 Fax: (215)387-7542

Biweekly. $58.00/year for individuals; $82.00/year for Canada and Mexico; $79.00/year for other countries. Newspaper (tabloid) for scientists featuring news, opinions, research, and professional section.

★5412★ Weatherwise

Heldref Publications
Helen Dwight Reid Educational Foundation
1319 18th St. NW
Washington, DC 20036-1802
Ph: (202)296-6267 Fax: (202)296-5149
Fr: 800-365-9753

Bimonthly. $33.00/year for individuals; $9.50/year for single issue; $57.00/year for institutions; $71.00/year for institutions, oth-er countries. Popular weather magazine for students, teachers, and professionals.

PLACEMENT AND JOB REFERRAL SERVICES

★5413★ American Meteorological Society (AMS)

45 Beacon St.
Boston, MA 02108
Ph: (617)227-2425 Fax: (617)742-8718

Members: Professional meteorologists, oceanographers, and hydrologists; interested students and nonprofessionals. **Purpose:** Develops and disseminates information on the atmospheric and related oceanic and hydrospheric sciences; seeks to advance professional applications. **Activities:** Activities include guidance service, scholarship programs, career information, certification of consulting meteorologists, and a seal of approval program to recognize competence in radio and television weathercasting. Issues statements of policy to assist public understanding on subjects such as weather modification, forecasting, tornadoes, hurricanes, flash floods, and meteorological satellites. Provides abstracting services. Has prepared educational films, filmstrips, and slides for a new curriculum in meteorology at the ninth grade level. Issues monthly announcements of job openings for meteorologists.

★5414★ Korean Scientists and Engineers Association in America (KSEA)

6261 Executive Blvd.
Rockville, MD 20852
Ph: (301)984-7048 Fax: (301)984-1231

Members: Scientists and engineers holding single or advanced degrees. **Purpose:** Goals are to: promote friendship and mutuality among Korean and American scientists and engineers; contribute to Korea's scientific, technological, industrial, and economic developments; strengthen the scientific, technological, and cultural bonds between Korea and the U.S. Sponsors symposium. **Activities:** Maintains speakers' bureau, placement service, and biographical archives. Compiles statistics. Maintains 100 volume library of scientific handbooks and yearbooks in Korean.

★5415★ National Network of Minority Women in Science (MWIS)

Directorate for Education and Human Resources Programs
1333 H St. NW
Washington, DC 20005
Ph: (202)326-6757 Fax: (202)371-9849

Members: Asian, Black, Mexican American, Native American, and Puerto Rican women involved in science related professions; other interested persons. **Purpose:** Promotes the advancement of minority women in science fields and the improvement of the science and mathematics education and career awareness of minorities. Supports public policies and programs in science and technology that benefit minorities. **Activities:** Maintains placement servce. Compiles statistics; serves as clearinghouse for identifying minority women scientists. Offers writing and conference presentations, seminars, and workshops on minority women in science and local career conferences for students. Local chapters maintain speakers' bureaus, and children's services. **E-Mail:** ggil bert@aaas.org

EMPLOYER DIRECTORIES AND NETWORKING LISTS

★5416★ American Men and Women of Science

R. R. Bowker Co.
Reed Reference Publishing
121 Chanlon Rd.
New Providence, NJ 07974
Ph: (908)464-6800 Fax: (908)665-6688
Fr: 800-521-8110

Triennial, latest edition January 1995. $106.00, per volume; $850.00, set. Covers over 123,000 U.S. and Canadian scientists active in the physical, biological, mathematical, computer science, and engineering fields; includes references to previous edition for deceased scientists and nonrespondents. Entries include: Name, address, education, personal and career data, memberships, honors and awards, research interest. Arrangement: Alphabetical. Indexes: Discipline (in separate volume).

★5417★ American Weather Observer Supplemental Observation Network Directory of Stations

American Weather Observer Supplemental Observation Network
401 Whitney Blvd.
Belvidere, IL 61008-3772
Ph: (815)544-5665   Fax: (815)544-6334

$5.95. Publication includes: List of member weather observers in North America. Entries include: Personal or organization name, address, phone. Arrangement: Geographical.

★5418★ National Weather Service Offices and Stations

U.S. National Weather Service
1325 East-West Hwy.
Silver Spring, MD 20910
Ph: (301)713-1698

Annual, September. Free. Covers offices and stations operated by or under the supervision of the National Weather Service in the United States, Mexico, the Caribbean, Central and South America, and Oceania. Entries include: Station and airport name, type of station, call letters, International Index Number, latitude, longitude, elevation; and number, type, and frequency of weather observations. Arrangement: Geographical.

★5419★ Peterson's Job Opportunities in Engineering and Technology 1996

Peterson's
PO Box 2123
Princeton, NJ 08543-2123
Ph: (609)243-9111   Fax: (609)243-9150
Fr: 800-338-3282

Compiled by the Peterson's staff. Annual. $19.95 paperback. 432 pages. Profiles 2,000 high-tech companies looking primarily for technical personnel in such fields as biotechnology, telecommunications, software, computers and peripherals, defense, and aerospace. Contains job-search strategies and career options to help match education and expertise to the job market. Indexed geographically, by industry, and by hiring needs.

★5420★ Scientific and Technical Organizations and Agencies Directory

Gale Research
835 Penobscot Bldg.
Detroit, MI 48226-4094
Ph: (313)961-2242   Fax: (313)961-6083
Fr: 800-877-GALE

Irregular; latest edition December 1993. $195.00. Covers over 25,600 national and international organizations and agencies concerned with the physical and applied sciences, engineering, and technology, including associations, computer information services, consulting firms, educational institutions, foundations, government advisory organizations, federal government agencies, general grant and assistance programs, libraries and information centers, patent sources and services, research and development centers, scholarships, fellowships, and loans, science-technology centers, standards

organizations, state academies of science, and state government agencies in the fields of aeronautics and space sciences, chemistry, computer science specialties, electronics, geography, geology, machinery, mathematics, metallurgy, meteorology, mineralogy, nuclear science, petroleum and gas, physics, plastics, transportation, water resources, and other areas. Entries include: Organization name, address, phone, and name of contact; additional descriptive text for most entries. Arrangement: Classified by type of organization. Indexes: Organization name/key word.

★5421★ Who's Who in Technology

Gale Research
835 Penobscot Bldg.
Detroit, MI 48226-4094
Ph: (313)961-2242   Fax: (313)961-6083
Fr: 800-877-GALE

Irregular, new edition expected June 1995. $380.00. Covers 38,000 engineers, scientists, inventors, and researchers. Entries include: Name, title, affiliation, address; personal, education, and career data; publications, patents; technical field of activity; area of expertise. Arrangement: Alphabetical. Indexes: Geographical, employer, technical discipline, expertise.

HANDBOOKS AND MANUALS

★5422★ The Best Resumes for Scientists and Engineers

John Wiley and Sons
605 3rd Ave.
New York, NY 10158
Ph: (212)850-6000   Fr: 800-225-5945

Adele Lewis. Second edition, 1993. $37.50; $14.95 (paper). Presents an extensive collection of scientific and engineering resumes, highlighting the important differences between these and resumes written for other occupations.

★5423★ Career Information Center

Macmillan Publishing Co.
200 Old Tappan Rd.
Old Tappan, NJ 07675
Ph: (609)461-6500   Fr: 800-223-2336

Visual Education Center Staff. Fifth edition, 1992. $229.00. This 13-volume set profiles over 600 occupations. Each occupational profile describes job duties, educational requirements, how to get the job, advancement possibilities, employment outlook, working conditions, earnings and benefits, and where to write for more information.

★5424★ Careers in Science

VGM Career Horizons
4255 W. Touhy Ave.
Lincolnwood, IL 60646-1975
Ph: (847)679-5500   Fax: (847)679-2494
Fr: 800-323-4900

Thomas Easton. Third edition, 1996. 192 pages. $17.95; $13.95 (paper). Discusses careers in life science, earth science, physical and space science, social science, engineer-

ing, mathematics, and computer science. Offers job hunting advice.

★5425★ Encyclopedia of Careers and Vocational Guidance

J. G. Ferguson Publishing Co.
200 W. Monroe, Ste. 250
Chicago, IL 60606
Ph: (312)580-5480

William E. Hopke. Ninth edition, 1993. $129.95; $199.95 (CD-ROM). Four-volume set that profiles 900 occupations and describes job trends in 71 industries. Includes career description, educational requirements, history of the job, methods of entry, advancement, employment outlook, earnings, conditions of work, social and psychological factors, and sources of further information. Contains career and employment information for this field.

★5426★ 100 Best Careers for the Year 2000

Prentice Hall General Reference
15 Columbus Cir.
New York, NY 10023
Ph: (212)373-8500   Fr: 800-223-2348

Shelly Field. 1992. $15.00 (paper). Covers 100 of the fastest growing jobs. The publication is divided into 11 general employment sections. Specific careers are covered within each section. Provides job description, responsibilities, employment opportunities, earnings, education and training, advancement opportunities, and experience and qualifications for each occupation.

OTHER SOURCES

★5427★ American Almanac of Jobs and Salaries 1994-95

Avon Books
1350 Avenue of the Americas, 2nd Fl.
New York, NY 10019
Ph: (212)261-6800   Fr: 800-238-0658

John Wright. Revised edition, 1993. $17.00. 704 pages. This is a comprehensive guide to the wages of hundreds of occupations in a wide variety of industries and organizations.

★5428★ American Society for Photogrammetry and Remote Sensing (ASPRS)

5410 Grosvenor Ln., Ste. 210
Bethesda, MD 20814-2160
Ph: (301)493-0290   Fax: (301)493-0208

Members: Firms, individuals, government employees, and academicians engaged in photogrammetry, photointerpretation, remote sensing, and geographic information systems and their application to such fields as archaeology, geographic information systems, military reconnaissance, urban planning, engineering, traffic surveys, meteorological observations, medicine, geology, forestry, agriculture, construction, and topographic mapping. **Activities:** Offers voluntary certification program open to persons associated with one or more functional area of photogrammetry, remote sensing, and GIS.

Surveys the profession of private firms in photogrammetry and remote sensing in the areas of products and services.

★5429★ Association for International Practical Training (AIPT)
10400 Little Patuxent Pky. Ste. 250
Columbia, MD 21044
Ph: (410)997-2200   Fax: (410)992-3924

Purpose: Helps coordinate training around the world in fields such as travel, the culinary arts, and hotel management. **Activities:** Conducts programs in career development and hospitality/tourism exchanges. Operates a student exchange program. Provides reciprocal practical training experience for recent graduates from the U.S., Austria, Germany, Finland, France, Hungary, Ireland, Japan, Malaysia, Netherlands, Switzerland, and the United Kingdom. Arranges training programs in the U.S. and abroad. Serves as U.S. affiliate to IAESTE (International Association for the Exchange of Students for Technical Experience) and operates a Professional Visitors Program to arrange short-term educational and training visits to the U.S. **E-Mail:** aipt@aipt.org

★5430★ *Salaries of Scientists, Engineers, and Technicians: A Summary of Salary Surveys*
Commission on Professionals in Science and Technology (CPST)
1500 Massachusetts Ave. NW, Ste. 831
Washington, DC 20005
Ph: (202)223-6995

1993.

Mining Engineers

SOURCES OF HELP-WANTED ADS

★5431★ AEG News

Association of Engineering Geologists
323 Boston Post Rd., Ste. 2D
Sudbury, MA 01776
Ph: (508)443-4639

Quarterly. Included in membership; $20.00/year for nonmembers. Covers news of the engineering geology profession.

★5432★ California Mining Journal

PO Box 2260
Aptos, CA 95001
Ph: (408)662-2899   Fax: (408)662-3014

Monthly. $21.95/year for individuals; $2.75 for single issue; $33.95/year for other countries. Mining trade magazine covering prospecting and mining throughout the world.

★5433★ Captsule Job Listings

Publications and Communications, Inc.
12416 Hymeadow Dr.
Austin, TX 78750
Ph: (512)250-9023   Fax: (512)331-3900
Fr: 800-678-9724

Online database. Lists current job openings in the contract (temporary) technical services industry. Includes the Action Hot List, which provides information on job seekers. Includes employment opportunities in technical/professional engineering, computing, and design/drafting. Entries generally contain company name, address, and job opening.

★5434★ Coal

Intertec Publishing Co.
29 N. Wacker Dr.
Chicago, IL 60606
Ph: (312)435-2330   Fax: (312)726-4103
Fr: 800-621-9907

Monthly. Coal production magazine.

★5435★ Energy User News

Chilton Publications
825 7th Ave.
New York, NY 10019
Ph: (212)887-8400   Fax: (212)887-8484

Monthly. Magazine exploring industrial and commercial energy efficiency markets and strategies.

★5436★ Engineering and Mining Journal

Intertec Publishing Co.
29 N. Wacker Dr.
Chicago, IL 60606
Ph: (312)435-2330   Fax: (312)726-4103
Fr: 800-621-9907

Monthly. Magazine focusing on metal and non-metallic mining.

★5437★ Engineering Times

National Society of Professional Engineers
1420 King St.
Alexandria, VA 22314
Ph: (703)684-2875   Fax: (703)836-4875

Monthly. Magazine (tabloid) covering professional, legislative, and techology issues for an engineering audience.

★5438★ ENR: Engineering News Record

New York Construction News
1221 Avenue of the Americas
New York, NY 10020
Ph: (212)512-4773   Fax: (212)512-4770

Weekly. $42.00/year; $2.00/issue.

★5439★ High Technology Careers Magazine

HTC
4701 Patrick Henry Dr., No. 1901
Santa Clara, CA 95054
Ph: (408)970-8800   Fax: (408)980-5103

Bimonthly. Magazine (tabloid) containing employment opportunity information for the engineering and technical community.

★5440★ The Mining Record

Mining Record Co.
PO Box 37510
Denver, CO 80237
Ph: (303)770-6791   Fax: (303)770-6796

Weekly (Wed.). $39.00/year for individuals. Mining industry newspaper for the western United States.

★5441★ Minority Engineer

Equal Opportunity Publications, Inc.
150 Motor Pkwy., Ste. 420
Hauppauge, NY 11788-5145
Ph: (516)273-0066   Fax: (516)273-8936

Affirmative-action recruitment magazine serving college graduating and professional minority engineers.

★5442★ National Engineer

National Association of Power Engineers
1 Springfield St.
Chicopee, MA 01013-2624
Ph: (413)592-6273   Fax: (413)592-1998

Monthly. $23.40/year for individuals; $2.50 for single issue.

★5443★ NSBE Magazine

NSBE Publications
1454 Duke St.
Alexandria, VA 22314
Ph: (703)549-2207   Fax: (703)683-5312

$10.00/year for individuals; $2.00 for single issue. Journal providing information on engineering careers, self-development, and cultural issues for recent graduates with technical majors.

★5444★ Southwestern Pay Dirt

Copper Queen Publishing Co., Inc.
Drawer 48
Bisbee, AZ 85603
Ph: (602)432-2244

Monthly. $25.00/year; $3.00/single issue.

★5445★ SWE

Society of Women Engineers
120 Wall St., 11th Fl.
New York, NY 10005-3902
Ph: (212)509-9577   Fax: (212)509-0224

Bimonthly. $30.00/year for nonmembers. Magazine for engineering students and for women and men working in the engineering and technology fields. Covers career guidance, continuing development and topical issues.

★5446★ **Technology Review**

The Tech
PO Box 397029
Cambridge, MA 02139
Ph: (617)253-1541   Fax: (617)258-8226

$30.00/year for individuals; $3.75 for single issue; $42.00/year for other countries. Magazine reviewing new developments in technology with an emphasis on economic, political, and social implications. Not a new product publication.

★5447★ **Woman Engineer**

Equal Opportunity Publications, Inc.
150 Motor Pkwy., Ste. 420
Hauppauge, NY 11788-5145
Ph: (516)273-0066   Fax: (516)273-8936

Engineer recruitment magazine.

PLACEMENT AND JOB REFERRAL SERVICES

★5448★ **American Association of Blacks in Energy (AABE)**

927 15th St. NW, Ste. 200
Washington, DC 20005
Ph: (202)371-9530   Fax: (202)371-9218

Members: Blacks in energy-related professions, including engineers, scientists, consultants, academicians, and entrepreneurs; government officials and public policymakers; interested students. **Purpose:** Represents blacks and other minorities in matters involving energy use and research, the formulation of energy policy, the ownership of energy resources, and the development of energy technologies. Seeks to increase the knowledge, understanding, and awareness of the minority community inenergy issues by serving as an energy information source for policymakers, recommending blacks and other minorities to appropriate energy officials and executives, encouraging students to pursue professional careers in the energy industry, and advocating the participation of blacks and other minorities in energy programs and policymaking activities. Updates members on key legislation and regulations being developed by the Department of Energy, the Department of Interior, the Department of Commerce, the Small Business Administration, and other federal and state agencies. **Activities:** Offers information on current job openings.

★5449★ **American Indian Science and Engineering Society (AISES)**

1630 30th St., Ste. 301
Boulder, CO 80301
Ph: (303)492-8658   Fax: (303)492-3400

Members: American Indian and non-Indian students and professionals in science, technology, and engineering fields; corporations representing energy, mining, aerospace, electronic, and computer fields. **Purpose:**

Seeks to motivate and encourage students to pursue undergraduate and graduate studies in science, engineering, and technology. **Activities:** Sponsors science fairs in grade schools, teacher training workshops, summer math/science sessions for 8th-12th graders, professional chapters, and student chapters in colleges. Offers scholarships. Adult members serve as role models, advisers, and mentors for students. Operates placement service. **E-Mail:** aise sha@spot.colorado.edu

★5450★ **Engineering Society of Detroit (ESD)**

100 Farnsworth Ave.
Detroit, MI 48202
Ph: (313)832-5400   Fax: (313)832-5920

Members: Engineers from all disciplines; scientists and technologists. **Activities:** Offers placement services. Conducts technical programs and engineering refresher courses; sponsors conferences and expositions. Maintains speakers' bureau. Although based in Detroit, MI, society membership is international.

★5451★ **Korean Scientists and Engineers Association in America (KSEA)**

6261 Executive Blvd.
Rockville, MD 20852
Ph: (301)984-7048   Fax: (301)984-1231

Members: Scientists and engineers holding single or advanced degrees. **Purpose:** Goals are to: promote friendship and mutuality among Korean and American scientists and engineers; contribute to Korea's scientific, technological, industrial, and economic developments; strengthen the scientific, technological, and cultural bonds between Korea and the U.S. Sponsors symposium. **Activities:** Maintains speakers' bureau, placement service, and biographical archives. Compiles statistics. Maintains 100 volume library of scientific handbooks and yearbooks in Korean.

★5452★ **Society of Hispanic Professional Engineers (SHPE)**

5400 E. Olympic Blvd., Ste. 210
Los Angeles, CA 90022
Ph: (213)725-3970

Purpose: Engineers, student engineers, and scientists seeking to increase the number of Hispanic engineers by providing motivation and support to students. Sponsors competitions and educational programs. **Activities:** Maintains placement service and speakers' bureau; compiles statistics.

★5453★ **Society for Mining, Metallurgy, and Exploration (SME)**

PO Box 625002
Littleton, CO 80162-5002
Ph: (303)973-9550   Fax: (303)973-3845
Fr: 800-763-3132

Members: Member society of the American Institute of Mining, Metallurgical and Petroleum Engineers. Persons engaged in the finding, exploitation, treatment, and marketing of all classes of minerals (metal ores, industrial minerals, and solid fuels) except petroleum. **Purpose:** Promotes the arts and sciences

connected with the production of useful minerals and metals. **Activities:** Provides placement service. Offers specialized education programs; compiles enrollment and graduation statistics from schools offering engineering degrees in mining, mineral, mineral processing/metallurgical, geological, geophysical, and mining technology. **E-Mail:** smeaime@aol.com

EMPLOYER DIRECTORIES AND NETWORKING LISTS

★5454★ **American Men and Women of Science**

R. R. Bowker Co.
Reed Reference Publishing
121 Chanlon Rd.
New Providence, NJ 07974
Ph: (908)464-6800   Fax: (908)665-6688
Fr: 800-521-8110

Triennial, latest edition January 1995. $106.00, per volume; $850.00, set. Covers over 123,000 U.S. and Canadian scientists active in the physical, biological, mathematical, computer science, and engineering fields; includes references to previous edition for deceased scientists and nonrespondents. Entries include: Name, address, education, personal and career data, memberships, honors and awards, research interest. Arrangement: Alphabetical. Indexes: Discipline (in separate volume).

★5455★ **Directory of Contract Service Firms**

C. E. Publications, Inc.
PO Box 97000
Kirkland, WA 98083
Ph: (206)823-2222   Fax: (206)821-0942

Annual, January. $10.00. Covers Approximately 900 contract firms actively engaged in the employment of engineering and technical personnel for temporary contract assignments throughout the world. Entries include: Company name, address, phone, name of contact. Arrangement: Alphabetical. Indexes: Geographical.

★5456★ **Directory of Engineering Societies and Related Organizations**

American Association of Engineering Societies
1111 19th St. NW, Ste. 608
Washington, DC 20036
Ph: (202)296-2237   Fax: (202)296-1151
Fr: 800-658-8897

1992. $185.00. Lists 1,000 national, regional, Canadian, and international organizations concerned with engineering and related fields.

★5457★ **Directory of Engineers in Private Practice**

National Society of Professional Engineers
1420 King St.
Alexandria, VA 22314
Ph: (703)684-2862   Fax: (703)836-4875

Annual. $85.00. Covers 600 consulting engineering firms and 7,200 individuals who are members of the society's Professional Engineers in Private Practice division. Entries include: For companies, name, address, phone, name of principal executive, list of services. For individuals, name, address; most listings include phone. Arrangement: Firms are geographic, then by specialty; individuals are alphabetical.

★5458★ **Directory of Foreign Manufacturers in the United States**

Georgia State University Business Press
College of Business Administration
University Plaza
Atlanta, GA 30303-3093
Ph: (404)651-4253   Fax: (404)651-4256

Biennial, odd years. $195.00, payment must accompany orders from individuals. Covers over 7,300 United States manufacturing, mining, and petroleum companies, and the over 6,800 firms abroad that own them. Entries include: Company name, address, phone, fax, products or services, Standard Industrial Classification (SIC) codes, parent company name and address. Arrangement: Alphabetical by U.S. company name. Indexes: U.S. subsidiary location, foreign company name, geographical (foreign company location), product.

★5459★ **Engineering and Mining Journal International Directory of Mining**

Maclean Hunter Publishing Co.
29 N. Wacker Dr.
Chicago, IL 60606
Ph: (312)726-2802   Fax: (312)726-4103
Fr: 800-621-9907

Annual, October. $130.00. Covers 1,500 companies and 2,000 mines and plants producing metals and nonmetallic minerals, worldwide. Also includes lists of ore buyers, consultants, contractors, and other service firms, and a directory of mining associations, government mine bureaus and geological surveys. Entries include: For company headquarters, company name, address, phone, names of executives, number of employees, general area explored, type of business and products. For mines and plants, company name, address, phone, minerals produced, amount produced, and names and titles of key personnel. Arrangement: Companies and consultants are alphabetical; mines and plants are geographical. Indexes: Personnel, type of ore or mineral.

★5460★ **Engineering Research Centres**

Stockton Press
Groves Dictionaries
345 Park Ave. S., 10th Fl.
New York, NY 10010
Ph: (212)689-9200   Fr: 800-221-2123

Fourth edition, 1995. $515.00. 768 pages. Contains over 8,000 entries describing research and technology laboratories in over 70 countries. Provides details on industrial research centers and educational establishments with research and development activity. Indexes: Subject and title of establishments.

★5461★ **Geophysical Directory**

Geophysical Directory, Inc.
PO Box 130508
Houston, TX 77219
Ph: (713)529-8789   Fax: (713)529-3646
Fr: 800-929-2462

Annual, March. $50.00, postpaid. Covers about 3,600 companies that provide geophysical equipment, supplies, or services, and mining and petroleum companies that use geophysical techniques; international coverage. Entries include: Company name, address, phone, names of principal executives, operations, and sales personnel; similar information for branch locations. Arrangement: Classified by product or service. Indexes: Company name, personal name.

★5462★ **Peterson's Job Opportunities in Engineering and Technology 1996**

Peterson's
PO Box 2123
Princeton, NJ 08543-2123
Ph: (609)243-9111   Fax: (609)243-9150
Fr: 800-338-3282

Compiled by the Peterson's staff. Annual. $19.95 paperback. 432 pages. Profiles 2,000 high-tech companies looking primarily for technical personnel in such fields as biotechnology, telecommunications, software, computers and peripherals, defense, and aerospace. Contains job-search strategies and career options to help match education and expertise to the job market. Indexed geographically, by industry, and by hiring needs.

★5463★ **Scientific and Technical Organizations and Agencies Directory**

Gale Research
835 Penobscot Bldg.
Detroit, MI 48226-4094
Ph: (313)961-2242   Fax: (313)961-6083
Fr: 800-877-GALE

Irregular; latest edition December 1993. $195.00. Covers over 25,600 national and international organizations and agencies concerned with the physical and applied sciences, engineering, and technology, including associations, computer information services, consulting firms, educational institutions, foundations, government advisory organizations, federal government agencies, general grant and assistance programs, libraries and information centers, patent sources and services, research and development centers, scholarships, fellowships, and loans, science-technology centers, standards organizations, state academies of science, and state government agencies in the fields of aeronautics and space sciences, chemistry, computer science specialties, electronics, geography, geology, machinery, mathematics, metallurgy, meteorology, mineralogy, nuclear science, petroleum and gas, physics, plastics, transportation, water resources, and other areas. Entries include: Organization name, address, phone, and name of contact; additional descriptive text for most entries. Arrangement: Classified by type of organization. Indexes: Organization name/key word.

★5464★ **Western Mining Directory**

Balfour-Howell International LLC
PO Box 37510
Denver, CO 80237
Ph: (303)770-6794   Fax: (303)770-6796

Annual, December. $46.00, plus $3.00 shipping. Covers about 700 mining firms and organizations in the mining industry of the western United States, including active hardrock and coal mines, uranium and vanadium mines, mining firms, active oil shale projects; consultants, contractors-developers, suppliers of equipment and services, exploration and drilling companies; educational institutions; mining associations; related government agencies; and mining exhibitions and conferences. Arrangement: Mines and mining firms are geographical; others are both alphabetical and by product or service. Indexes: Mining location.

★5465★ **Who's Who in Technology**

Gale Research
835 Penobscot Bldg.
Detroit, MI 48226-4094
Ph: (313)961-2242   Fax: (313)961-6083
Fr: 800-877-GALE

Irregular, new edition expected June 1995. $380.00. Covers 38,000 engineers, scientists, inventors, and researchers. Entries include: Name, title, affiliation, address; personal, education, and career data; publications, patents; technical field of activity; area of expertise. Arrangement: Alphabetical. Indexes: Geographical, employer, technical discipline, expertise.

★5466★ **Wyoming Directory of Manufacturing and Mining**

Wyoming Department of Commerce
Division of Economic & Community
  Development
Barrett Bldg., 4N
Cheyenne, WY 82002
Ph: (307)777-7284   Fax: (307)777-5840

Biennial, odd years. $15.00. Free, to nonprofit organizations. Covers About 790 companies in mining and manufacturing; state and local organizations and government agencies that provide business assistance. Entries include: For businesses: name of firm, address, phone, name of key executive, product or activity, parent company (if any), codes for number of employees and geographic scope, Standard Industrial Classification (SIC) code. For organizations and agencies: name of agency or organization, address, phone, contact name or official. Arrangement: Mining and manufacturing firms are in separate sections, then by SIC code; others are by area of expertise. Indexes: Alphabetical, geographical, product.

HANDBOOKS AND MANUALS

★5467★ The Best Resumes for Scientists and Engineers

John Wiley and Sons
605 3rd Ave.
New York, NY 10158
Ph: (212)850-6000   Fr: 800-225-5945

Adele Lewis. Second edition, 1993. $37.50; $14.95 (paper). Presents an extensive collection of scientific and engineering resumes, highlighting the important differences between these and resumes written for other occupations.

★5468★ Career Information Center

Macmillan Publishing Co.
200 Old Tappan Rd.
Old Tappan, NJ 07675
Ph: (609)461-6500   Fr: 800-223-2336

Visual Education Center Staff. Fifth edition, 1992. $229.00. This 13-volume set profiles over 600 occupations. Each occupational profile describes job duties, educational requirements, how to get the job, advancement possibilities, employment outlook, working conditions, earnings and benefits, and where to write for more information.

★5469★ Career Planning Workshop

Society for Mining, Metallurgy, and
   Exploration (SME)
Career Information
PO Box 625002
Littleton, CO 80162
Ph: (303)973-9550

Annual. $5.00. Contains papers prepared by presenters at the annual Career Planning Workshop. Topics covered vary each year.

★5470★ Careers in Engineering

VGM Career Horizons
4255 W. Touhy Ave.
Lincolnwood, IL 60646-1975
Ph: (847)679-5500   Fax: (847)679-2494
Fr: 800-323-4900

Geraldine O. Gardner. 1994. $17.95; $13.95 (paper). Covers careers in the public or private sector, in industry, the university, or the military, from applications in computer architecture design to high temperature ceramics.

★5471★ Encyclopedia of Careers and Vocational Guidance

J. G. Ferguson Publishing Co.
200 W. Monroe, Ste. 250
Chicago, IL 60606
Ph: (312)580-5480

William E. Hopke. Ninth edition, 1993. $129.95; $199.95 (CD-ROM). Four-volume set that profiles 900 occupations and describes job trends in 71 industries. Includes career description, educational requirements, history of the job, methods of entry, advancement, employment outlook, earnings, conditions of work, social and psychological factors, and sources of further information. Contains career and employment information for this field.

★5472★ Engineering Success

Kendall Hunt Publishing
4050 Westmark Dr.
PO Box 1840
Dubuque, IA 52004-1840
Ph: (319)589-1000   Fax: 800-772-9165
Fr: 800-228-0810

Bill Osher. 1994. $27.96.

★5473★ Engineering Your Job Search: A Job-Finding Resource for Engineering Professionals

Professional Publications, Inc.
1250 5th Ave.
Belmont, CA 94002
Ph: (415)593-9119   Fax: (415)592-4519
Fr: 800-426-1178

Compiled by Professional Publications editors. 1995. $12.95 (paper).

★5474★ Introduction to the Engineering Profession

HarperCollins Publishers, Inc.
10 E. 53rd. St.
New York, NY 10022-5299
Ph: (212)207-7000   Fax: (212)207-7145
Fr: 800-331-3761

David M. Burghardt. 1995. $30.00 (paper).

★5475★ Job Opportunities in Engineering and Technology

Peterson's Guides, Inc.
PO Box 2123
Princeton, NJ 08543-2123
Ph: (609)243-9111   Fax: (609)243-9150
Fr: 800-338-3282

1994. $18.95 (paper).

★5476★ Majoring in Engineering: How to Get from Your Freshman Year to Your First Job

Farrar, Straus & Giroux, Inc.
19 Union Sq., W
New York, NY 10003
Ph: (212)741-6900   Fr: 800-788-6262

John Garcia. 1995. $20.00; $10.00 (paper).

★5477★ Opportunities in Engineering Careers

VGM Career Horizons
4255 W. Touhy Ave.
Lincolnwood, IL 60646-1975
Ph: (847)679-5500   Fax: (847)679-2494
Fr: 800-323-4900

Nicholas Basta. 1995. $14.95; $11.95 (paper). Outlines typical job titles, salaries, career paths, and employment prospects.

★5478★ Resumes for Engineering Careers

VGM Career Horizons
NTC Publishing Group
4255 W. Touhy Ave.
Lincolnwood, IL 60646-1975
Ph: (847)679-5500   Fax: (847)679-2494
Fr: 800-323-4900

1994. $9.95. 160 pages. Contains sample resumes and cover letters applicable to any engineering field.

EMPLOYMENT AGENCIES AND SEARCH FIRMS

★5479★ ABC Employment Service

25 S. Bemiston, Ste. 214
Clayton, MO 63105
Ph: (314)725-3140

Employment agency.

★5480★ Engineer One, Inc.

10124 Dutchtown Rd.
Knoxville, TN 37932-2611
Ph: (615)690-2611   Fax: (615)690-2611

Employment agency.

★5481★ Hayden and Associates, Inc.

7825 Washington Ave. S., Ste. 120
Minneapolis, MN 55439-2431
Ph: (612)941-6300   Fax: (612)941-9602

Employment agency. Executive search firm. Fills openings in a variety of fields.

★5482★ Industrial Recruiters Associates, Inc.

630 Oakwood Ave., Ste. 318
West Hartford, CT 06110
Ph: (203)953-3643

Employment agency.

★5483★ The Jobs Co.

8900 E. Sprague Ave.
Spokane, WA 99212-2927
Ph: (509)928-3151   Fax: (509)928-3168

Employment agency. Has division specializing in engineering and scientific openings. Also operates division specializing in sales openings.

★5484★ JR Professional Search

PO Box 18356
Tucson, AZ 85731
Ph: (520)721-1855   Fax: (520)721-1855

Employment agency.

★5485★ Main Line Personnel Service, Inc.

401 City Ave.
Bala Cynwyd, PA 19004-1122
Ph: (610)667-1820

Employment agency.

★5486★ Search and Recruit International

4455 South Blvd.
Virginia Beach, VA 23452
Ph: (804)490-3151

Employment agency. Headquartered in Virginia Beach. Other offices in Bremerton, WA; Charleston, SC; Jacksonville, FL; Memphis, TN; Pensacola, FL; Sacramento, CA; San Bernardino, CA; San Diego, CA.

★5487★ Sierra Technology Corporation

4150 Manzanita Ave., Ste. 100
Carmichael, CA 95608-1700
Ph: (916)488-4960   Fax: (916)488-7058

Employment agency. Provides placement on a temporary basis.

★5488★ Source Engineering

5580 LBJ Fwy., Ste. 300
Dallas, TX 75240
Ph: (214)385-3002   Fax: (214)717-0075

Executive search firm. Many affiliate offices located throughout the U.S.

OTHER SOURCES

★5489★ *American Almanac of Jobs and Salaries 1994-95*

Avon Books
1350 Avenue of the Americas, 2nd Fl.
New York, NY 10019
Ph: (212)261-6800   Fr: 800-238-0658

John Wright. Revised edition, 1993. $17.00. 704 pages. This is a comprehensive guide to the wages of hundreds of occupations in a wide variety of industries and organizations.

★5490★ American Association of Engineering Societies (AAES)

1111 19th St. NW, Ste. 608
Washington, DC 20036
Ph: (202)296-2237   Fax: (202)296-1151

Purpose: Seeks to promote leadership in public affairs for the engineering community, work in support of math and science education for young persons. Disseminates of information about the profession. Provides statistics about engineers.

★5491★ Association for International Practical Training (AIPT)

10400 Little Patuxent Pky. Ste. 250
Columbia, MD 21044
Ph: (410)997-2200   Fax: (410)992-3924

Purpose: Helps coordinate training around the world in fields such as travel, the culinary arts, and hotel management. **Activities:** Conducts programs in career development and hospitality/tourism exchanges. Operates a student exchange program. Provides reciprocal practical training experience for recent graduates from the U.S., Austria, Germany, Finland, France, Hungary, Ireland, Japan, Malaysia, Netherlands, Switzerland, and the United Kingdom. Arranges training programs in the U.S. and abroad. Serves as U.S. affiliate to IAESTE (International Association for the Exchange of Students for Technical Experience) and operates a Professional Visitors Program to arrange short-term educational and training visits to the U.S. **E-Mail:** aipt@aipt.org

★5492★ *Engineering Salary Survey*

Source Engineering
1290 Oakmead, Ste. 318
Sunnyvale, CA 94086
Ph: (408)738-8440

Annual. Discusses the structure of the engineering profession, trends, and compensation. Salaries are listed by job function, industry, and years of experience.

★5493★ *Graduating Engineer*

Peterson's/COG Publishing Group
16030 Ventura Blvd., No. 560
Encino, CA 91436
Ph: (818)789-5293

Eight issues/year. Magazine focusing on employment, education, and career development for entry-level engineers.

★5494★ National Action Council for Minorities in Engineering (NACME)

3 W. 35th St.
New York, NY 10001-2281
Ph: (212)279-2626   Fax: (212)629-5178

Purpose: Seeks to increase the number of African American, Latino, and Native American students enrolled in and graduating from engineering schools. Through the Corporate Scholars Program, offers comprehensive scholarships to engineering students that include leadership development, corporate mentors and summer internships. Works with local, regional, and national education organizations to motivate and encourage precollege students to engage in engineering careers. Conducts educational and research programs; operates project to assist engineering schools in improving the retention and graduation rates of minority students. Maintains speakers' bureau; compiles statistics.

★5495★ National Society of Professional Engineers (NSPE)

1420 King St.
Alexandria, VA 22314
Ph: (703)684-2800   Fax: (703)836-4875

Members: Professional engineers and engineers-in-training in all fields registered in accordance with the laws of states or territories of the U.S. or provinces of Canada; qualified graduate engineers, student members, and registered land surveyors. **Purpose:** Is concerned with social, professional, ethical, and economic considerations of engineering as a profession; encompasses programs in public relations, employment practices, ethical considerations, education, and career guidance. Monitors legislative and regulatory actions of interest to the engineering profession. **Website:** http://www.hspc.org

★5496★ *Salaries of Scientists, Engineers, and Technicians: A Summary of Salary Surveys*

Commission on Professionals in Science and Technology (CPST)
1500 Massachusetts Ave. NW, Ste. 831
Washington, DC 20005
Ph: (202)223-6995

1993.

★5497★ Society of Women Engineers (SWE)

120 Wall St., 11th Fl.
New York, NY 10005
Ph: (212)509-9577   Fax: (212)509-0224

Members: Educational service society of women engineers; membership is also open to men. **Purpose:** Supplies information on the achievements of women engineers and the opportunities available to them; assists women engineers in preparing for return to active work following temporary retirement. Serves as an informational center on women in engineering. **Activities:** Administers several certificate and scholarship programs. Offers tours and career guidance; conducts surveys. Compiles statistics.

Ministers and Christian Religious Professionals

Sources of Help-Wanted Ads

★5498★ The Lutheran

Augsburg Fortress, Publishers
426 S. 5th St.
PO Box 1209
Minneapolis, MN 55440
Ph: (612)330-3246   Fax: (612)330-3455
Fr: 800-328-4648

Monthly. $11.90/year for individuals; $1.50 for single issue. Magazine of the Evangelical Lutheran Church in America.

★5499★ Sojourners

Sojurners
2401 15th St. NW
Washington, DC 20009
Ph: (202)328-8842   Fax: (202)328-8757

Bimonthly. Magazine endorsing the coming together of Christians in a movement of biblical faith and political conscience.

Placement and Job Referral Services

★5500★ American Association of Christian Schools (AACS)

PO Box 2189
Independence, MO 64055
Ph: (816)795-7709   Fax: (816)795-7462

Activities: Maintains teacher/administrator certification program and placement service. Participates in school accreditation program. Sponsors National Academic Tournament and high school sports tournaments. Maintains American Christian Honor Society. Compiles statistics; maintains speakers' bureau and placement service.

★5501★ American Association of Pastoral Counselors (AAPC)

9504A Lee Hwy.
Fairfax, VA 22031-2303
Ph: (703)385-6967   Fax: (703)352-7725

Members: Clergy and other religious professionals of all faiths with special training in counseling. **Purpose:** Works to: set standards and establish criteria for the operation of church-related counseling programs; provide certification for religious professionals engaged in specialized ministries of counseling; approve church-related counseling centers. **Activities:** Maintains placement service; compiles statistics. **E-Mail:** Internet: Info@AAPC.Org

★5502★ American Orff-Schulwerk Association (AOSA)

PO Box 391089
Cleveland, OH 44139-8089
Ph: (216)543-5366   Fax: (216)543-2687

Purpose: Music educators, music therapists, and church choir directors united to promote and encourage the philosophy of Carl Orff's (1895-1982, German composer) Schulwerk (Music for Children) in America. Distributes information on the activities and growth of Orff Schulwerk in America. **Activities:** Conducts research; offers information on teacher training. Operates clearinghouse. **E-Mail:** cleestew@peabody.jhu.edu

★5503★ Association of North American Missions (ANAM)

3859 Nottingham Dr
Sarasota, FL 34235
Ph: (813)955-8529   Fax: (813)951-0805

Members: Missions of more than five missionaries operating in North America. **Purpose:** To make missions more credible and visible; to promote unity and cooperation among members; to collect, organize, and disseminate information relating to missionary work to the public and to act as clearinghouse for members. **Activities:** Offers referral and placement service to qualified missionaries not serving with member missions. Provides information about missions to pastors and schools. Offers workshops and indepth seminars for mission leaders and missionaries.

★5504★ Association of Southern Baptist Campus Ministers (ASBCM)

1603 S. Lewis
Kirksville, MO 63501

Members: Full-time campus ministers with a graduate degree or five years experience in ministry; part-time and volunteer ministers, students, and interested individuals are affiliate members. **Purpose:** To strengthen the individual's commitment and expertise in the ministry through fellowship and programs; enhance the minister's view of campus and church; promote professional competence among campus ministers; develop and encourage fellowship among members; act as a liaison between campus ministers seeking employment or reassignment and employers seeking campus ministers; share knowledge, personnel, and material resources. Cooperates with seminaries in continuing education. Maintains collection of records available at the Dargan-Carver Library in Nashville, TN. **Activities:** Maintains placement registry for Southern Baptist campus ministers and applicants.

★5505★ Association of Unity Churches

PO Box 610
Lees Summit, MO 64063
Ph: (816)524-7414   Fax: (816)525-4020

Members: Ministers and interested members of Unity Churches and study groups. **Purpose:** Serves and supports member ministries by providing human resources, administrative and educational programs, and consultation in accordance with the teachings of the Unity School of Christianity founded by Charles and Myrtle Fillmore. **Activities:** Trains and licenses teachers, ministers, and youth advisors; offers continuing education programs and minister placement service. Holds skills development seminars and workshops; sponsors retreats. Offers media service consultation. Assists with the development of local groups. Maintains 30 committees.

★5506★ Catholic Campus Ministry Association (CCMA)

300 College Park Ave.
Dayton, OH 45469-2515
Ph: (513)229-4648   Fax: (513)229-4024

Purpose: To form a strong and coordinated voice for the church's ministry in higher education; to provide continuing education programs for members; to provide liaison with other individuals and agencies of the church interested in campus ministry and the role of the church in higher education; to advance ecumenical and interfaith understanding and cooperation; to provide guidelines for, and assistance in, developing effective campus ministries. **Activities:** Maintains placement service and speakers' bureau; offers colleague consultation service. Conducts biennial study weeks.

★5507★ **Catholic Press Association (CPA)**

3555 Veterans Hwy., Unit 10
Ronkonkoma, NY 11779
Ph: (516)471-4730   Fax: (516)471-4804

Members: Publishers of Catholic newspapers, magazines, pamphlets, and books; Catholic writers, illustrators, and teachers. **Purpose:** Sponsors research and specialized education programs. **Activities:** Maintains placement service. Maintains 25 committees, including Freedom of Information, News Service Liaison, and Research.

★5508★ **Chinese Christian Mission (CCM)**

PO Box 750759
Petaluma, CA 94975
Ph: (707)762-1314   Fax: (707)762-1713

Purpose: Serves as an evangelical faith mission dedicated to reaching Chinese people around the world with the gospel of Jesus Christ. Broadcasts radio programs to foster Christianity in China. **Activities:** Operates placement service providing ministers with churches. Sponsors short-term mission trips to Latin America and East Asia.

★5509★ **Christian Chiropractors Association (CCA)**

PO Box 9715
Fort Collins, CO 80525-0500
Ph: (303)482-1404   Fax: (303)482-1538
Fr: 800-999-1970

Members: Christian chiropractors organized to spread the gospel of Christ throughout the U.S. and abroad. **Purpose:** Works to unify Christian chiropractors around the essentials of Christianity, leaving Lesser Points of doctrine to the conscience of the individual believers. Focus is on world missions; seeks to expand the variety of mission fields. **Activities:** Aids in placement of Christian chiropractors as missionaries. Sponsors missions in Ecuador, Ethiopia, France, Kenya, Monaco, Peru, C.I.S., Philippines, the U.S., and Canada.

★5510★ **Christian Management Association (CMA)**

PO Box 4638
Diamond Bar, CA 91765
Ph: (909)861-8861   Fax: (909)860-8247
Fr: 800-727-4CMA

Members: Managers, lawyers, auditors, pastors, church administrators, and other individuals who serve Christian organizations. **Purpose:** To promote the general welfare of Christian nonprofit organizations by assisting those involved in management and administration. Emphasizes areas such as: account-ing and finance; media; legal and tax issues; general, church, fundraising, financial, time, and personnel management; deferred giving; women in management; executive development; marketing and communications; public relations; information development. Maintains task forces that consider emerging and potentially troubling issues. **Activities:** Offers national and regional seminars in all areas of management through its annual national conference, the Christian Management Institute. Holds bimonthly fellowship meeting for training and information reports. Provides job referral and professional referral service to assist Christian managment personnel.

★5511★ **A Christian Ministry in the National Parks (ACMNP)**

222 1/2 E. 49th St.
New York, NY 10017
Ph: (212)758-3450   Fax: (212)758-3451

Purpose: Recommends employment for seminary and college students with private concessionaires operating lodges, inns, restaurants, and stores within national parks; aims to offer students the opportunity to conduct worship services and Bible classes for park employees and visitors.

★5512★ **Christian Schools International (CSI)**

3350 E. Paris Ave. SE
Grand Rapids, MI 49512-3054
Ph: (616)957-1070   Fax: (616)957-5022

Members: Christian elementary and secondary schools enrolling 93,000 pupils and employing 6650 teachers. **Purpose:** To provide a medium for a united witness regarding the role of Christian schools in contemporary society; to promote the establishment of Christian schools; to help members function more effectively in areas of promotion, organization, administration, and curriculum; to help establish standards and criteria to guide the operation of its members; to foster high professional ideals and economic well-being among Christian school personnel; to establish and maintain communication with member schools, colleges, churches, government agencies, and the public. Encourages study, research, and writing that embodies Christian theories of education; conducts salary studies, research, and surveys on operating costs; offers expert and confidential analysis of member school programs and operation. **Activities:** Offers placement service. Administers the Christian School Pension and Trust Funds, Group Insurance Plans, and Life and Insurance Plans and Trust Funds.

★5513★ **Conservative Baptist Association of America**

PO Box 66
Wheaton, IL 60189
Ph: (708)653-5350   Fax: (708)653-5387

Members: Members of 1104 churches. **Purpose:** Provides leadership, fellowship, counseling services, and specialized support ministries to member churches in an effort "to advance the cause of Christ through worship, evangelism, instruction, and service throughout the world." **Activities:** Conducts charitable program; offers placement service, chaplaincy endorsement, clergy/missionary credit union, and ChurchMart.

★5514★ **Council for Health and Human Services Ministries, United Church of Christ (CHHSM)**

700 Prospect Ave.
Cleveland, OH 44115
Ph: (216)736-2250   Fax: (216)736-2251

Members: Health and human service institutions related to the United Church of Christ. **Purpose:** Seeks to study, plan, and implement a program in health and human services; assist members in developing and providing quality services and in financing institutional and noninstitutional health and human service ministries; stimulate awareness of and support for these programs; inform the UCC of policies that affect the needs, problems, and conditions of patients; cooperate with interdenominational agencies and others in the field. **Activities:** Maintains placement service and hall of fame. Compiles statistics; provides specialized education programs.

★5515★ **Episcopal Synod of America (ESA)**

6300 Ridglea Pl., Ste. 910
Fort Worth, TX 76116
Ph: (817)735-1675   Fax: (817)735-1351
Fr: 800-225-3661

Members: Dioceses, parishes, institutions, and societies of laity and clergy of the Episcopal Church of America who "embrace the Gospel of Jesus Christ and uphold the evangelical faith and order, laboring with zeal for the reform and renewal of the church." **Activities:** Maintains placement service. Promotes the establishment and implementation of cooperative programs.

★5516★ **Evangelical Press Association (EPA)**

485 Panorama Rd.
Earlysville, VA 22936
Ph: (804)973-5941   Fax: (804)973-2710

Members: Editors and publishers of Christian periodicals. **Activities:** Maintains placement service.

★5517★ **German Evangelical Lutheran Conference in North America (GELCINA)**

400 Lexington
Baltimore, MD 21202
Ph: (410)727-3939

Members: Pastors and congregations of the Evangelical Lutheran Church in America and the Evangelical Church In Canada who conduct or participate in worship services and other ministries in German. **Activities:** Assists congregations in finding bilingual pastors; offers fellowship; conducts missionary work. Maintains speakers' bureau, placement service, and biographical archives; compiles statistics.

★5518★ **Independent Fundamental Churches of America (IFCA)**

3520 Fairlanes Ave.
PO Box 810
Grandville, MI 49468
Ph: (616)531-1840   Fax: (616)531-1814
Fr: 800-347-1840

Members: Ministers, missionaries, youth

leaders, musicians, and ministerial students; churches and organizations. **Purpose:** Seeks to offer independent fundamentalist churches the benefits of unity, while allowing them to keep their autonomy. **Activities:** Maintains placement service for pastors. Supports active evangelism; encourages churches to extend their ministry into neighboring communities, the military, and other Christian churches, which the IFCA believes are in harmony with the Word of God. Serves to reinforce members' doctrinal beliefs; provides interchurch fellowship and the sharing of ministers; trains pastors and lay workers. Offers group insurance, retirement plans, investment programs, and counseling to local churches. Assists with ordinations; refers individuals who are traveling or moving to churches, Bible teachers, and evangelists.

★5519★ **Intercristo**

PO Box 33487
19303 Fremont Ave. N
Seattle, WA 98133
Ph: (206)546-7330   Fax: (206)546-7375
Fr: 800-251-7740

Members: Division of CRISTA Ministries. **Purpose:** Provides job exploration and job information service with computerized referrals on current openings with Christian organizations. **Activities:** Distributes Career Kit, a home study career-building program.

★5520★ **International Council of Community Churches (ICCC)**

21116 Washington Pkwy.
Frankfort, IL 60423-3112
Ph: (708)479-8400   Fax: (708)479-8402

Purpose: Promotes the fellowship of community churches internationally and provides an instrument through which community-minded and freedom-loving churches can cooperate in making a contribution toward a united church. **Activities:** Maintains placement bureau for ministers.

★5521★ **Jesuit Association of Student Personnel Administrators (JASPA)**

Creighton University
2500 California Plz.
Omaha, NE 68178
Ph: (402)280-2775   Fax: (402)280-3450
Fr: 800-426-7123

Members: Administrators of student personnel programs in 28 Jesuit colleges and universities in the United States. ACX Maintains placement service. Sponsors institutes and seminars for personnel in Jesuit colleges. Bestows Rev. Victor R. Yanitelli Award; compiles statistics. Cooperates with Catholic and non-Catholic educational associations in various projects. Conducts workshops. Operates organizational archives; compiles statistics.

★5522★ **National Association of Church Business Administration (NACBA)**

7001 Grapevine Hwy., Ste. 324
Fort Worth, TX 76180
Ph: (817)284-1732   Fax: (817)284-1762

Members: Business administrators and managers employed by local churches or institutions of the Christian church. **Purpose:** Provides a program of study, service, fellowship,

training, information exchange, and problem discussion. **Activities:** Offers placement service; conducts research programs; compiles statistics. Maintains hall of fame.

★5523★ **National Association of Congregational Christian Churches (NACCC)**

8473 S. Howell Ave.
PO Box 1620
Oak Creek, WI 53154
Ph: (414)764-1620   Fax: (414)764-0319
Fr: 800-262-1620

Purpose: Aims to provide a means whereby Congregational Christian churches may consult and exchange advise on spiritual and temporal matters of common concern; and to encourage the continuance of Christian purposes and practices that have been the historic and accepted characteristics of Congregational Christian churches. **Activities:** Supports the education of ministers through its Congregational Foundation for Theological Studies. Compiles statistics. Operates placement service and mission program.

★5524★ **National Association of Episcopal Schools (NAES)**

815 2nd Ave.
New York, NY 10017-4594
Ph: (212)922-5173   Fax: (212)286-9366
Fr: 800-334-7626

Members: Episcopal church-related boarding and day schools. **Purpose:** Promotes the educational ministry of the Episcopal Church; helps strengthen programs, teaching, and pastoral roles of Episcopal schools; develops criteria and curriculum materials. Provides worship materials and resources geared specifically to the needs of Episcopal schools. Works to aid communication between the National Episcopal Church and its schools and among member schools. **Activities:** Celebrates Episcopal School Week annually. Maintains charitable program, world partnership programs, and placement service.

★5525★ **National Association of Pastoral Musicians (NPM)**

225 Sheridan St. NW
Washington, DC 20011-1492
Ph: (202)723-5800   Fax: (202)723-2262

Members: Parish clergy, parish musicians, music teachers, and others engaged or interested in Catholic church music. **Purpose:** Goal is to improve music in an ordinary parish situation. Reviews current music; assists in parish music celebrations. **Activities:** Conducts research and specialized education programs. Operates Pastoral Press (publications division). Maintains speakers' bureau and placement service.

★5526★ **National Catholic Stewardship Council (NCSC)**

1275 K St. NW, Ste. 980
Washington, DC 20005
Ph: (202)289-1093   Fax: (202)682-9018

Purpose: Committed to promoting the right use of God's gifts of time, talent, and treasure through diocesan and parish leadership. Encourages the adoption of the wholistic stewardship concept which stresses that

everything is a gift from God, and that gratitude for gifts received is best expressed in right management and ministry to others. Fosters the exchange of ideas and materials among dioceses, parishes, and other church organizations. **Activities:** Maintains speakers' bureau and placement service. Compiles statistics.

★5527★ **National Conference of Diocesan Directors of Religious Education - CCD (NCDD-CCD)**

3021 4th St. NE
Washington, DC 20017-1102
Ph: (202)636-3826   Fax: (202)832-2712

Members: Diocesan directors of religious education and their staff; publishers, academics, Diocesan religious education, Associations, and individuals interested in religious education. **Purpose:** Fosters communication and unity among members. Addresses the special responsibility to provide lifelong religious education within the Catholic church; assists members with increasing religious education needs; coordinates religious education and helps to supply needed materials. **Activities:** Provides placement service. Aids in formal religious education for children, adults, and handicapped persons.

★5528★ **National Lutheran Outdoors Ministry Association (NLOMA)**

2016 Camp Lone Star Rd.
La Grange, TX 78945
Ph: (409)247-4128   Fax: (409)247-4120

Purpose: Individuals and camps joined to aid in the mission of the Lutheran church and to promote Christian camping and related experience. Provides support for all areas of outdoor ministry. Serves as resource base for camps in the areas of personnel development, site evaluation, program development, and staff recruitment. Conducts seminars and training sessions. **Activities:** Maintains placement service for individuals seeking employment at a member camp.

★5529★ **North American Association of Christians in Social Work (NACSW)**

Box 7090
St. Davids, PA 19087-7090
Ph: (610)687-5777   Fax: (610)687-5777

Members: Professional social workers and related professionals; students; interested individuals. **Purpose:** To provide opportunities for Christian fellowship, growth, learning, outreach, and witness. Promotes a Christian world view in social work and social welfare and encourages awareness within the Christian community of human need and of social work as a means for ministering to this need. Holds regional seminars, evening meetings, one-day conferences, and small study and support group meetings. **Activities:** Maintains employment service. Operates speakers' bureau.

★5530★ **North American Maritime Ministry Association (NAMMA)**

237 Thompson St.
New York, NY 10012
Ph: (212)533-6945   Fax: (212)533-6973

Members: Spiritual and social welfare agencies from the U.S., Canada, and the Caribbean providing facilities and services for merchant seafaring. **Activities:** Sponsors Chaplain Training School; operates placement service. Maintains archives; conducts research programs.

★5531★ Oblate Conference of the United States (OCUS)

8818 Cameron St.
Silver Spring, MD 20910-4113
Ph: (301)565-0060   Fax: (301)587-4575

Members: Members of a religious order of priests and brothers called Oblates of Mary Immaculate (OMI). **Activities:** Maintains placement service. Conducts research and advocacy on social and political issues from a Christian perspective. Acts as a network for exchange of information and experience. Offers research and educational programs to members. Sponsors charitable programs.

★5532★ Overseas Missionary Fellowship, U.S.A. Headquarters (OMF)

10 W. Dry Creek Cir.
Littleton, CO 80120-4413
Ph: (303)730-4160   Fax: (303)730-4165

Members: Protestant missionaries. **Purpose:** American office of international missionary society which originated in England in 1865 for work in inland China. **Activities:** Activities now carried out in 13 countries of East Asia. Through its publications, the group seeks to recruit new missionaries and supporters, and educate the public. Provides placement service.

★5533★ Presbyterian Association of Musicians (PAM)

100 Witherspoon St.
Louisville, KY 40202
Ph: (502)569-5288   Fax: (502)569-5018

Members: Organists, choir directors, singers, churches, clergy, directors of Christian education, and interested persons of all denominations. **Purpose:** Objective is to develop use of music and the arts in the life and worship of individual congregations. Offers assistance in the areas of worship, music, and the arts. **Activities:** Conducts continuing education. Acts as a clearinghouse for job referrals; promotes the professional status of church musicians and recommends salaries and benefits to churches; certifies church musicians.

★5534★ Presbyterians for Renewal

8134 New LaGrange Rd., Ste. 227
Louisville, KY 40222
Ph: (502)425-4630   Fax: (502)423-8324

Members: Supporters are individuals, congregations, and foundations. **Activities:** Provides placement services. Trains church officers. Conducts renewal weekends, officer retreats, and marriage enrichment programs. Bestows awards; compiles statistics. Operates charitable program and speakers' bureau.

★5535★ Society of Biblical Literature (SBL)

1201 Clairmont Ave., Ste. 300
Decatur, GA 30030
Ph: (404)636-4744   Fax: (404)248-0815

Members: Professors and persons interested in religious studies, especially as related to the study of the Bible. **Purpose:** Seeks to stimulate the critical investigation of classical biblical literature, together with other related literature, by the exchange of scholarly research both in published form and in public forum. Endeavors to support those disciplines and subdisciplines pertinent to the illumination of the literatures and religions of the ancient Near Eastern and Mediterranean regions, including the study of ancient languages, textual criticism, history, and archaeology. **Activities:** Offers placement services.

★5536★ Southern Baptist Women in Ministry/Folio (SBWM/FOLIO)

2800 Frankfort Ave.
Louisville, KY 40206
Ph: (502)896-4425

Members: Ordained and unordained female Baptist ministers; students of the Baptist ministry; interested individuals. **Purpose:** Promotes the image of women as ministers within the Southern Baptist Convention. Fosters support and communication among members. **Activities:** Conducts educational and research programs. Offers placement service; maintains speakers' bureau.

★5537★ Teen Missions International (TMI)

885 E. Hall Rd.
Merritt Island, FL 32953
Ph: (407)453-0350   Fax: (407)452-7988

Purpose: Organizes interdenominational evangelical missionary work projects in areas such as agriculture and community development; programs have operated in 60 countries, including Australia, Mexico, South Africa, and Zimbabwe. Trains teen and adult missionaries through camps and conferences; operates placement service. Promotes the Christian gospel through the production of films, videos, printed materials, and media presentations. Assists in establishing local teen mission clubs in an effort to encourage evangelical outreach.

★5538★ Youth for Christ/U.S.A. (YFC/USA)

PO Box 228822
Denver, CO 80222
Ph: (303)843-9000   Fax: (303)843-9002

Purpose: Interdenominational organization for the evangelization and discipling of teenagers. Fights juvenile delinquency through counseling and Youth Guidance programs for youth penal institutions. **Activities:** Maintain placement service. Programs for staff: area refreshers; college training; intern training; summer training. Programs for youth: camps; Campus Life Clubs; counseling; short-term missions and work projects overseas; Youth Guidance work with troubled teenagers.

EMPLOYER DIRECTORIES AND NETWORKING LISTS

★5539★ Christian Schools International—Directory

Christian Schools International
3350 E. Paris Ave. SE
Grand Rapids, MI 49512
Ph: (616)957-1070   Fax: (616)957-5022

Annual, November. $45.00. Covers nearly 450 Reformed Christian elementary and secondary schools; related associations; societies without schools. Entries include: School name, address, phone; name, title, and address of officers; names of faculty members. Arrangement: Geographical.

★5540★ Directory of Catholic Charities Diocesan Agencies and Organizations

Catholic Charities USA
1731 King St., Ste. 200
Alexandria, VA 22314
Ph: (703)549-1390   Fax: (703)549-1656

Biennial, odd years. $20.00 for members; $35.00 for nonmembers; $10.00, update supplement. Covers nearly 1,200 Catholic community and social service agencies and residential and non-residential institutions and facilities. Listings include diocesan agencies, institutions for the elderly, handicapped, and youth, Catholic schools of social work, and state Catholic conferences. Entries include: Organization name, address, name and title of director, phone, fax, public relations contact. Arrangement: Geographical by diocese then classified by type of organization.

★5541★ Ganley's Catholic Schools in America—Elementary/Secondary

Fisher Publishing Co.
Box 1073
Montrose, CO 81402
Ph: (303)249-1303   Fax: (303)249-0348
Fr: 800-766-5151

Annual, spring. $40.00. Covers about 8,345 Catholic schools. Entries include: Name, address, phone, administrative personnel, statistics, enrollment, grade span.

HANDBOOKS AND MANUALS

★5542★ Becoming a Minister

Baker Book House
PO Box 6287
Grand Rapids, MI 49516-6287
Ph: (616)676-9185   Fax: (616)676-9573
Fr: 800-877-2665

Thomas C. Oden. 1994. $10.99 (paper).

★5543★ **Jobs Rated Almanac: Ranks the Best and Worst Jobs by More Than a Dozen Vital Criteria**

John Wiley and Sons
605 Third Ave.
New York, NY 10158-0012
Ph: (212)850-6000   Fr: 800-225-5945

Les Krantz. Third edition, 1995. $16.95. 340 pages. Ranks 250 jobs by environment, salary, outlook, physical demands, stress, security, travel opportunities, and geographic location.

★5544★ **Non-Profits and Education Job Finder**

Planning/Communications
7215 Oak Ave.
River Forest, IL 60305-1935
Ph: (708)366-5200   Fr: (888)366-5200

Daniel Lauber. 1996. $32.95; $16.95 (paper). 350 pages. Covers 1600 sources. Discusses how to use sources of non-profit sector job vacancies in a number of specialties and state-by-state, including job-matching services, job hotlines, specialty periodicals with job ads, salary surveys, and directories. Covers a variety of fields from education to religion. Includes chapters on resume and cover letter preparation and interviewing.

★5545★ **Opportunities in Religious Service Careers**

NTC Publishing Group
4255 W. Touhy Ave.
Lincolnwood, IL 60646-1975
Ph: (708)679-5500   Fax: (708)679-6375
Fr: 800-323-4900

Oliver. 1992. $13.95; $10.95 (paper).

★5546★ **What Shall I Say? Discerning God's Call to Ministry**

Evangelical Lutheran Church in America
Division For Ministry
8765 W. Higgins Rd.
Chicago, IL 60631-4195
Ph: (312)380-2870   Fax: (312)380-1465
Fr: 800-638-3522

Walter R. Bouman. 1995. $5.95 (paper).

★5547★ **Who Will Go for Us?: An Invitation to Ordained Ministry**

Abingdon Press
PO Box 801
201 8th Ave., S.
Nashville, TN 37202-0801
Fax: (615)749-6512   Fr: 800-251-3320

Dennis M. Campbell. 1994. $6.95 (paper).

OTHER SOURCES

★5548★ **Association of Christian Schools International (ACSI)**

PO Box 35097
Colorado Springs, CO 80935-3509
Ph: (719)528-6906   Fax: (719)531-0631

Purpose: Service organization for Christian schools. Represents members in legislative efforts and First Amendment confrontations with the government. **Activities:** Sponsors student activities such as academic and speech meets, sports events, piano and choir festivals, and science fairs. Holds Christian Cheerleader Camp for high school students. Offers volume-reduced cost purchasing for school supplies and curriculum materials; recommends additional sources for purchasing. Sponsors ACSI Missionary Fund to send teams of Christian school educators throughout the world to conduct conventions, and in-service training programs. Provides speakers.

★5549★ **Commission for Racial Justice (MRSJ)**

700 Prospect Ave.
Cleveland, OH 44115-1110
Ph: (216)736-2161   Fax: (216)736-2171

Purpose: Ministers of United Church of Christ who work to maximize the impact of African American and other people of color constituencies within the UCC.

★5550★ **Division of Higher Education, Christian Church-Disciples of Christ**

11780 Borman Dr., Ste. 100
St. Louis, MO 63146-4159
Ph: (314)991-3000   Fax: (314)991-2957

Members: Elected administrative board working to advance the concerns of the Christian Church - Disciples of Christ in higher education and interpret issues in higher education to CCDC leadership. **Activities:** Maintains affiliation with 18 liberal arts colleges and 7 theological seminaries throughout the U.S.

★5551★ **Lutheran Deaconess Conference (LDC)**

Center for Diaconal Ministry
1304 La Porte Ave.
Valparaiso, IN 46383
Ph: (219)464-6925   Fax: (219)464-6928

Members: Consecrated deaconesses having completed the educational requirements of the Lutheran Deaconess Association; students in training. **Purpose:** Seeks to: develop sisterhood and community among deaconesses; present an opportunity for renewed inspiration and personal and professional growth; encourage women in the church to use their full potential and to shape, promote, and support the total deaconess program.

★5552★ **National Association of Parish Coordinators/Directors of Religious Education (NPCD)**

1077 30th St. NW, Ste. 100
Washington, DC 20007-3852
Ph: (202)337-6232   Fax: (202)333-6706

Members: A subdivision of the National Catholic Educational Association. Administrators, coordinators, and directors of religious education (DREs) programs in Roman Catholic parishes; students considering careers as DREs; clergy, laity, and others involved in the religious community. **Purpose:** Works to act as a representative and advocate for professionals who administer parish catechetical programs; foster cooperation and communication among organizations serving parish catechesis including other NCEA groups and independent associations; promote the spiritual, personal, and professional growth of parish DREs and encourage careers in catechetical ministry. **Activities:** Supports and develops the practice of family catechesis and encourages efforts in adult religious education; urges cooperation among parish leadership, especially parish staff members; promotes competency standards. Provides guidelines for members' contracts, salaries, benefits, and job descriptions. Disseminates information on members' jobs, educational background, salaries, and benefits; reports on parish program activities and surveys. Conducts research.

★5553★ **Presbyterian and Reformed Renewal Ministries International (PRRMI)**

PO Box 429
Black Mountain, NC 28711-0429
Ph: (704)669-7373   Fax: (704)669-4880

Purpose: Strives to ignite the church in the power of the Holy Spirit through prayer, leadership development, congregational renewal, and mission outreach. Seeks to call the church to prayer and teach the work of prayer, equip clergy and laity for Holy Spirit-empowered ministry, assist congregations in their renewal process and promote the Holy Spirit for the advancement of the Kingdom of God.

Musicians

SOURCES OF HELP-WANTED ADS

★5554★ ARTJOB

Western States Arts Federation
236 Montezuma Ave.
Santa Fe, NM 87501
Ph: (505)988-1166

Biweekly. $45.00, for 24-issue subscription. Covers national full- and part-time positions and temporary paid positions in visual, performing, and literary arts, arts education, and general arts administration, competitions, internships, conferences. Entries include: Job title, salary, description of responsibilities, qualifications, application procedure and deadline, name and address of contact. Arrangement: Classified by field.

★5555★ Billboard

BPI Communications
1515 Broadway, 11th Fl.
New York, NY 10036
Ph: (212)536-5167   Fax: (212)536-5351
Fr: 800-274-4100

Weekly. $229.00/year. International magazine of music and home entertainment geared toward professionals in the music and home video industries and related fields.

★5556★ Daily Variety

Cahners Business Newspapers
5700 Wilshire Blvd., Ste. 120
Los Angeles, CA 90036
Ph: (213)857-6600   Fax: (213)857-0494

Daily (morn.). Global entertainment newspaper (tabloid).

★5557★ Down Beat

Maher Publications, Inc.
102 N. Haven Rd.
Elmhurst, IL 60126
Ph: (708)941-2030   Fax: (708)941-3210
Fr: 800-535-7496

Monthly. $26.00/year for individuals; $2.50 for single issue. Magazine edited for the learning musician.

★5558★ International Musician

American Federation of Musicians
1501 Broadway, Ste. 600
New York, NY 10036
Ph: (212)869-1330   Fax: (212)302-4374

Monthly. Tabloid for labor union musicians.

★5559★ Music Educators Journal

Music Educators National Conference
1806 Robert Fulton Dr.
Reston, VA 22091-4348
Ph: (703)860-4000   Fax: (703)860-1531

Semimonthly. Journal covering all levels of music education.

★5560★ The Piano and Keyboard

The String Letter Press
412 Red Hill Ave., Ste. 1
San Anselmo, CA 94960-0767
Ph: (415)485-6946   Fax: (415)485-0831

Bimonthly. $36.00/year for individuals. Magazine providing a forum for pianists and piano teachers.

★5561★ SYMPHONY

American Symphony Orchestra League
1156 15th St. NW, Ste.800
Washington, DC 20005-1704
Ph: (202)628-0099   Fax: (202)783-7228

Bimonthly. $35.00/year for individuals. Magazine with news and articles for symphonic orchestra managers, trustees, volunteers, and musicians.

★5562★ Variety

Cahners Publishing Co.
249 W. 17th St.
New York, NY 10011
Ph: (212)645-0067   Fax: (212)463-6410

Weekly (Mon.). Newspaper (tabloid) reporting on theatre, television, radio, music, records, and movies.

PLACEMENT AND JOB REFERRAL SERVICES

★5563★ American Symphony Orchestra League

1156 15th St. NW, Ste. 800
Washington, DC 20005
Ph: (202)628-0099   Fax: (202)783-7228

Members: Symphony orchestras; associate members include educational institutions, arts councils, public libraries, business firms, orchestra professionals, and individuals interested in symphony orchestras. **Purpose:** Engages in extensive research on diverse facets of symphony orchestra operations and development. Provides consulting services for orchestras, their boards, and volunteer organizations. **Activities:** Sponsors management seminars and workshops for professional symphony orchestra administrative and artistic staff, volunteers, and prospective management personnel. Maintains employment services; collects and distributes resource materials, financial data, and statistical reports on many aspects of orchestra operations. Compiles statistics; sponsors educational programs; maintains resource center.

★5564★ Association of Anglican Musicians (AAM)

28 Ashton Rd.
Fort Mitchell, KY 41017
Ph: (606)344-9308   Fax: (606)344-9308

Members: Church musicians (laypersons or clergy) serving Episcopal and Anglican churches. **Purpose:** Seeks to promote excellence in church music by: fostering a relationship of mutual respect and trust between clergy and musicians actively encouraging and supporting composers and other artists to create works for the church; maintaining communication with and supporting the work of the Diocesan Standing Commission on Church Music and the Diocesan Standing Liturgical Commission. Encourages equitable compensation and benefits for professional church musicians. Works closely with seminaries toward the establishment and continuation of courses in music and the allied arts as they relate to worship and theology. **Activities:** Maintains placement service.

★5565★ Choreographers Theatre (CT)

94 Chambers St.
New York, NY 10007
Ph: (212)227-9067

Purpose: Provides a wide variety of production, administrative, management, and employment services to the dance and arts community. Serves as the in-residence Dance Department of the New School for Social Research in New York City.

★5566★ Country Music Showcase International (CMSI)

PO Box 368
Carlisle, IA 50047
Ph: (515)989-3748

Purpose: Helps songwriters and entertainers learn more about songwriting and the general music industry. **Activities:** Sponsors Song Evaluation and Critiques Service, songwriting seminars and workshops and songwriter showcases. Also operates a BMI Music Publishing Company for the benefit of members whose songs qualify for publishing.

★5567★ Guild of Temple Musicians (GTM)

Temple Beth El & Center
1435 W. 7th St.
San Pedro, CA 90732
Ph: (310)833-2467   Fax: (310)833-6504

Members: Individuals involved in Jewish temple music including music directors, organists, choir directors, singers, and teachers. Membership is concentrated in the U.S., Canada, and Israel. **Purpose:** Goals are to: preserve Jewish musical tradition through education and awareness of old and new available materials; share ideas and performances through concerts, workshops, and papers; keep members abreast of current developments and trends in the field. Conducts course in conjunction with School of Sacred Music, Hebrew Union College/Jewish Institute of Religion, in New York City, leading to certification. **Activities:** Offers placement service.

★5568★ Inter-American Music Council

1889 F St. NW, 220-L
Washington, DC 20006
Ph: (202)458-6194

Members: National music councils, music commissions, and musicians. **Purpose:** Promotes activity and study in musicology, folklore, and music education. Seeks to: establish centers for distribution of music by American composers; foster inter-American music festivals; support American activities in music by official and private organizations; solve problems related to copyrights and artistic property ownership. **Activities:** Sponsors competitions; maintains placement service.

★5569★ International Theatrical Arts Society (ITAA)

3101 N. Fitzhugh, Ste. 301
Dallas, TX 75204
Ph: (214)528-6112

Purpose: Theatrical agencies working to book entertainers and international acts into all live music venues. **Activities:** Provides placement service; conducts educational seminars.

★5570★ Jazz World Society (JWS)

Jan A. Byrczek
117 W. 58th St., Ste 12G
New York, NY 10019
Ph: (212)581-7188

Members: Professionals involved in jazz, including musicians, composers, record producers, distributors, collectors, and journalists; individuals actively supporting jazz music. **Purpose:** Promotes the development of jazz music in its various interpretations and fosters communication among jazz participants. **Activities:** Operates library of records, publications, books, and photographs. Organizes competitions; offers specialized education programs, seminars, and placement service.

★5571★ National Academy of Songwriters (NAS)

6381 Hollywood Blvd., Ste. 780
Hollywood, CA 90028
Ph: (213)463-7178   Fax: (213)463-2146
Fr: 800-826-7287

Members: Amateur and professional songwriters; others interested in the art, craft, and business of songwriting. **Purpose:** Objectives are: to provide education, protection, and other services to songwriters; to encourage expansion of social awareness through music. **Activities:** Offers ongoing, personalized counseling services; maintains legal panel and provides group legal services; operates bookstore of selected works and offers discounts; researches music-related questions for members; lobbies and testifies on legislative matters; conducts placement service. Operates Songbank, a registry that provides evidence of original authorship of songs and acts as an interim alternative until federal copyright is secured. Sponsors Songwriters Network, matching people who seek some type of collaboration; maintains lead sheet service for songwriters who cannot write down the music they create.

★5572★ National Association of Pastoral Musicians (NPM)

225 Sheridan St. NW
Washington, DC 20011-1492
Ph: (202)723-5800   Fax: (202)723-2262

Members: Parish clergy, parish musicians, music teachers, and others engaged or interested in Catholic church music. **Purpose:** Goal is to improve music in an ordinary parish situation. Reviews current music; assists in parish music celebrations. **Activities:** Conducts research and specialized education programs. Operates Pastoral Press (publications division). Maintains speakers' bureau and placement service.

★5573★ National Council for Culture and Art (NCCA)

1600 Broadway, Ste. 611C
New York, NY 10019
Ph: (212)757-7933

Members: Artists, civic and business leaders, professional performers, and visual arts organizations. **Purpose:** To provide exposure and employment opportunities for rural Americans, disabled Americans, and other minorities including blacks, Hispanics, American Indians, and European-Americans. Sponsors arts programs and spring and fall concert series. Operates Opening Night, a cable television show. Bestows annual Monarch Award and President's Award, and sponsors annual Monarch Scholarship Program. **Activities:** Offers children's and placement services; conducts charitable program; maintains hall of fame. Plans to conduct Minority Playwrights Forum, Dance Festival U.S.A., Vocal and Instrumental Competition, Film and Video Festival, and Concerts U.S.A.

★5574★ National Traditional Country Music Association (NTCMA)

PO Box 438
Walnut, IA 51577
Ph: (712)784-3001

Members: Individuals interested in the preservation, presentation, and perpetuation of traditional acoustic country, folk, honkytonk, ragtime, mountain, and bluegrass music celebrating contributions of U.S. settlers and pioneers; country music associations. **Purpose:** Supports what the association views as related, traditional values. **Activities:** Maintains placement service. Sponsors championship contests in numerous categories, including: Great Plains Story Telling; Hank Williams Songwriting; International Country Singer; Jimmie Rodgers Yodeling; Mid-West Horse Shoe Pitching; National Bluegrass Band; National Harmonica Playing.

★5575★ Presbyterian Association of Musicians (PAM)

100 Witherspoon St.
Louisville, KY 40202
Ph: (502)569-5288   Fax: (502)569-5018

Members: Organists, choir directors, singers, churches, clergy, directors of Christian education, and interested persons of all denominations. **Purpose:** Objective is to develop use of music and the arts in the life and worship of individual congregations. Offers assistance in the areas of worship, music, and the arts. **Activities:** Conducts continuing education. Acts as a clearinghouse for job referrals; promotes the professional status of church musicians and recommends salaries and benefits to churches; certifies church musicians.

★5576★ Professional Women Singers Association (PWSA)

PO Box 884, Planetarium Sta.
New York, NY 10024
Ph: (212)969-0590

Members: Professional women singers. **Purpose:** Promotes career advancement of women singers. **Activities:** Serves as a network for singers looking for employment opportunities. Participates in community concerts in hospitals for terminaly ill patients, senior homes, churches, synagogues, and opera companies. Conducts educational programs; operates placement service.

EMPLOYER DIRECTORIES AND NETWORKING LISTS

★5577★ Chamber Music America—Membership Directory

Chamber Music America
545 8th Ave.
New York, NY 10018
Ph: (212)244-2772   Fax: (212)244-2776

Annual, fall. $45.00, postpaid. Covers over 800 member ensembles, presenters, festivals, and training programs; over 4,000 associate members, including managers, publishers, arts organizations, instrument manufacturers, libraries and individuals. Entries include: For members: Name, address, phone, name of contact, activities, awards. For associates: Name, address, phone. Arrangement: Separate geographical sections for ensembles, presenters, festivals and training programs; associate members are classified by type of organization, then alphabetical. Indexes: General, ensemble format.

★5578★ Directory of Minority Arts Organizations

Civil Rights Division
National Endowment for the Arts
1100 Pennsylvania Ave. NW, Rm. 812
Washington, DC 20506
Ph: (202)682-5454   Fax: (202)682-5674

Irregular, latest edition February 1987. Free. Covers almost 1,000 performing groups, presenters, galleries, art and media centers, literary organizations, and community centers with significant arts programming that have leadership and constituency that is predominantly Asian-American, African-American, Hispanic, Native American, or multi-racial. Entries include: Organization name, address, phone, name and title of contact, description of activities. Arrangement: Geographical. Indexes: Organization name, activity.

★5579★ Directory of Summer Chamber Music Workshops, Schools & Festivals

Chamber Music America
545 8th Ave.
New York, NY 10018
Ph: (212)244-2772   Fax: (212)244-2776

Biennial, spring of even years. $12.00. Covers over 130 chamber music workshops and schools for students, young professionals, and adult amateurs; international listings. Entries include: Name, location or address, description of program and participants sought, procedure for auditions, type of accommodations and recreational facilities, dates, age requirements, and fees. Arrangement: Geographical.

★5580★ Employment Opportunities, USA

Washington Research Associates
1660 S. Albion, Ste. 390
Denver, CO 80222
Ph: (303)756-9038   Fax: (303)770-1945

Annual, quarterly updates. $184.00, includes quarterly updates. Publication includes: List of over 1,000 employment contacts in companies and agencies in the banking, arts, telecommunications, education, and 14 other industries and professions, including the federal government. Entries include: Company name, name of representative, address, description of products or services, hiring and recruiting practices, training programs, and year established. Principal content is industry overviews, carrer news, and employment opportunity information on 14 different job markets. Arrangement: Classified by industry. Indexes: Occupation.

★5581★ Gospel Music Association Official Resource Guide

Gospel Music Association
7 Music Cir. N.
Nashville, TN 37203
Ph: (615)242-0303   Fax: (615)254-9755

Annual, January. Covers gospel musicians, composers, and artists; recording companies, studios, and production companies; booking agencies; publishers; performing rights organizations; television and radio broadcasting stations; book stores, Bible supply stores, and other retailers/managers; publications; ministry organizations. All listings include name, address; some listings include phone. Broadcasting station listings include contact, program title, format. Arrangement: Broadcasting stations are geographical; others are alphabetical.

★5582★ Instrumentalist—Directory of Summer Music Camps, Clinics, and Workshops Issue

The Instrumentalist Co.
200 Northfield Rd.
Northfield, IL 60093
Ph: (708)446-5000   Fax: (708)446-6263

Annual, March. $2.50. Publication includes: List of nearly 250 summer music camps, clinics, and workshops in the United States; limited Canadian and foreign coverage. Entries include: Camp name, location, name of director, opening and closing dates, tuition fees, courses offered. Arrangement: Geographical.

★5583★ International Who's Who in Music and Musicians Directory

Taylor and Francis
1900 Frost Rd., Ste. 101
Bristol, PA 19007-1598
Ph: (215)785-5800

Biennial. $175.00. Covers almost all countries and represents a variety of musical interests. Contains approximately 10,000 biographical entries; includes data on orchestras, musical organizations, competitions, music libraries, and colleges and other educational establishments.

★5584★ Music Directory Canada

Norris-Whitney Communications, Inc.
23 Hannover Dr., No. 7
St. Catharines, ON, Canada L2W 1A3
Ph: (905)641-3471   Fax: (905)641-1648

Irregular, latest edition 1993. $29.95. Covers about 6,000 firms and organizations in the music industry, including associations, booking agencies, promoters, insurance companies, lawyers, music festivals, competitions, music libraries, music publishers, music camps, recording studios, radio stations, opera companies, and more. Entries include: Company name, address, phone, fax, trade names, products and services. Arrangement: Classified by product/service; some categories are then geographical, as appropriate. Indexes: Organization name.

★5585★ Musical America's International Directory of the Performing Arts

K-III Directory Corp.
424 W. 33rd St., 11th Fl.
New York, NY 10001
Ph: (212)714-3100   Fax: (212)714-3157
Fr: 800-221-5488

Annual, December. $90.00, (1992 ed.). Covers U.S., Canadian, and international orchestras, musicians, singers, performing arts series, dance and opera companies, festivals, contests, foundations and awards, publishers of music, artist managers, booking agents, music magazines, and service and professional music organizations. Entries include: Name of organization, institution, address, phone, fax, telex, key personnel; most entries include name of contact, manager, conductor, etc. For schools: Number of students and faculty. For orchestras: Number of concerts and seats. Arrangement: Geographical. Indexes: Alphabetical and by category.

★5586★ Nationwide Music Record Industry Toll Free Directory

CDE
PO Box 310551
Atlanta, GA 30331

Annual, January. $50.00 for individuals, payment with orders. Covers several hundred record companies, record services, record suppliers, wholesalers, music publishers, and videotape wholesalers, suppliers, and producers with toll-free 800- phone numbers. Entries include: Company name, address, toll-free phone number. Arrangement: Alphabetical.

★5587★ New York Casting and Survival Guide

Peter Glenn Publications
42 W. 38th St., Ste. 802
New York, NY 10018-6210
Ph: (212)869-2020   Fr: 800-223-1254

Annual, September. $15.95. Covers about 10,000 services and facilities for actors, models, and performers in the New York area, including agents in New York and Los Angeles, theaters, producers and casting agencies, casting personnel in advertising agencies, music clubs, typing services, schools, unions, health food stores, apartment and roommate referral agencies. Entries include: Company name, address, phone, and contact. Arrangement: Classified by service.

★5588★ **Radio and Records Ratings Report & Directory**

Radio and Records, Inc.
10100 Santa Monica Blvd., 5th Fl.
Los Angeles, CA 90067
Ph: (310)553-4330   Fax: (310)203-8450

Semiannual, April and September. $35.00. Covers nearly 2,700 radio group owners, equipment manufacturers, jingle producers, TV production houses and spot producers, record companies, representative firms, research companies, consulting firms, media brokers, networks, program suppliers, trade associations, and other organizations involved in the radio and record industry. Entries include: Organization name, address, phone, fax, name and title of chief executive officer, branch offices or subsidiary names and locations. Arrangement: Alphabetical; classified by subject.

★5589★ **Regional Theater Directory**

American Theatre Works, Inc.
PO Box 519
Dorset, VT 05251
Ph: (802)867-2223   Fax: (802)867-0144

Annual, May. $15.95. Covers regional theater companies with employment opportunities in acting, design, production, and management. Entries include: Company name, address, phone, name and title of contact; type of company, activities, and size of house; whether union affiliated, whether nonprofit or commercial; year established; hiring procedure and number of positions hired annually, season; description of stage; internships, description of artistic policy and audience. Arrangement: Geographical. Indexes: Company name, type of play produced.

★5590★ **Songwriter's Market: Where and How to Market Your Songs**

Writer's Digest Books
1507 Dana Ave.
Cincinnati, OH 45207
Ph: (513)531-2690   Fax: (513)531-4744
Fr: 800-289-0963

Annual, September. $21.99, plus 3.00 shipping. Covers 2,200 music publishers, jingle writers, advertising agencies, audiovisual firms, radio and television stations, booking agents, and other buyers of musical compositions and lyrics; also lists contests, competitions, and workshops. Entries include: Buyer's name and address, phone, payment rates, submission requirements, etc. Arrangement: Classified by type of market.

★5591★ **Summer Theater Directory**

American Theatre Works, Inc.
PO Box 519
Dorset, VT 05251
Ph: (802)867-2223   Fax: (802)867-0144

Annual, December. $15.95. Covers summer theater companies that offer employment opportunities in acting, design, production, and management; summer theater training programs. Entries include: Company name, address, phone, name and title of contact; type of company, activities and size of house; whether union affiliated, whether non-

profit or commercial; year established; hiring procedure and number of positions hired annually, season; description of stage; internships; description of company's artistic goals and audience. Arrangement: Geographical. Indexes: Company name.

★5592★ **Who's Who in Music**

Mid-South Management, Inc.
PO Box 1051
Vicksburg, MS 39181-1051
Ph: (601)631-7191

Irregular, latest edition 1987. $40.00, plus $2.00 shipping. Covers about 20,000 musicians, singers, music associations, broadcasting organizations, record companies, producers, representatives, and others in the Black music industry. Entries include: Individual, organization, or company name, address, phone, key personnel; listings for individuals include biographical data. Arrangement: Alphabetical. Indexes: Subject.

HANDBOOKS AND MANUALS

★5593★ **All You Need to Know About the Music Business**

Simon & Schuster, Inc.
1230 Avenue of the Americas
New York, NY 10020
Ph: (212)698-7000   Fr: 800-223-2348

Donald S. Passman. 1994. $25.00

★5594★ **Breakin' in...To the Music Business**

Cherry Lane Books
10 Midland Ave.
PO Box 430
Port Chester, NY 10573
Ph: (914)937-8601   Fr: 800-354-4004

Alan H. Siegel. 1993. $19.95. 276 pages. Describes the record deal; the artist-manager relationship; working with copyrights, demos, and the terminology used in the industry.

★5595★ **Career Information Center**

Macmillan Publishing Co.
200 Old Tappan Rd.
Old Tappan, NJ 07675
Ph: (609)461-6500   Fr: 800-223-2336

Visual Education Center Staff. Fifth edition, 1992. $229.00. This 13-volume set profiles over 600 occupations. Each occupational profile describes job duties, educational requirements, how to get the job, advancement possibilities, employment outlook, working conditions, earnings and benefits, and where to write for more information.

★5596★ **Career Opportunities in the Music Industry**

Facts on File, Inc.
460 Park Ave. S
New York, NY 10016
Ph: (212)683-2244   Fax: (212)213-4578
Fr: 800-322-8755

Shelly Field. 1995. $29.95.

★5597★ **Career Opportunities in Theater and the Performing Arts**

Facts on File, Inc.
11 Penn Plaza, 15th Fl.
New York, NY 10001-2006
Ph: (212)967-8800   Fax: 800-678-3633
Fr: 800-322-8755

Shelly Field. 1992. $29.95; $15.95 (paper). 256 pages. Offers a complete range of information about job opportunities in the performing arts.

★5598★ **Careers for Culture Lovers and Other Artsy Types**

VGM Career Horizons
4255 W. Touhy Ave.
Lincolnwood, IL 60646-1975
Ph: (847)679-5500   Fax: (847)679-2494
Fr: 800-323-4900

Marjorie Eberts and Margaret Gisler. 1994. $14.95; $9.95 (paper). Describes how to get work in a variety of fields related to art and culture. Opportunities include picture framer, curator, art restorer, symphony manager, disk jockey, music reviewer, dance teacher, choreographer, costume designer, theater manager, light designer, drama teacher, bookstore owner, interior decorator, antique store owner, and others.

★5599★ **The Essential Songwriter's Contract Handbook**

Nashville Songwriters Association International
15 Music Sq. W
Nashville, TN 37203
Ph: (615)256-3354   Fax: (615)256-0034
Fr: 800-321-6008

Compiled by NSAI Equity Committee staff. 1994. $12.95 (paper).

★5600★ **For the Working Artists: A Survival Guide for Performing, Visual and Media Artists Who Choose to Manage Their Own Careers**

National Network for Artist Placement
935 West Ave. 37
Los Angeles, CA 90065
Ph: (213)255-3096

Judith Luther. Second edition, 1991. $30.00. 338 pages.

★5601★ **The Harvard Guide to Careers in the Mass Media**

Bob Adams, Inc.
260 Center St.
Holbrook, MA 02343
Ph: (617)767-8100   Fax: (617)767-0994
Fr: 800-872-5627

John Noble. 1989. $7.95. 202 pages. Each section of the book evaluates one media profession in depth and contains an industry profile, a career profile that describes positions available in that area, information about current salary ranges, industry-specific job-hunting tips and strategies, and a case study outlining the methods that were used in a successful job hunt.

★5602★ How to Make a Living as a Musician: So You Never Have to Have a Day Job Again

Sonata Publishing
1277 S. Adams St.
Glendale, CA 91205
Ph: (818)242-7551   Fax: (818)242-5551

Marty Buttwinick. 1994. $29.95 (paper).

★5603★ In Concert: The Freelance Musician's Keys to Financial Success

Preludes Nouveaux, Ltd.
1506 E. Fox. Ln.
Milwaukee, WI 53217-2853
Ph: (414)241-9711

Gail Nelson. 1994. $16.95 (paper).

★5604★ Inside the Recording Studio: How to be Succesful in the Recording Studio

Frank Green Productions
395 Barrywood Dr.
Nashville, TN 37211
Ph: (615)834-5419

Frank Green. 1994. $9.95 (paper).

★5605★ Jobs in Arts and Media Management: What They Are and How to Get One!

American Council for the Arts
1 E. 53rd St.
New York, NY 10022-4201
Ph: (212)223-2787   Fr: 800-321-4510

Stephen Langley and James Abruzzo. Revised edition, 1990. $21.95. 281 pages. Includes lists of about 150 sources of information on job opportunities in the arts, including organizations offering internships, job listings, graduate programs, and short-term study; professional groups concerned with theater, music, dance, opera, museum and gallery management, film, and telecommunication management. (Does not include popular music performing or music recording.) Entries include: For internships Organization name, address, phone, description, requirements. For job referral associations and periodicals - Association or publisher name, address, fields covered, services offered, turn-around time, average number of jobs, cost of subscription or dues, comments. Arrangement: Classified by type of source.

★5606★ Making Money Teaching Music

Writer's Digest Books
1507 Dana Ave.
Cincinnati, OH 45207
Ph: (513)531-2690   Fax: (513)531-4082
Fr: 800-289-0963

Barbara Newsam. 1995. $18.95 (paper).

★5607★ More About This Business of Music

Watson-Guptill Publications, Inc.
1515 Broadway
New York, NY 10036
Ph: (212)536-5121   Fax: (212)536-5359
Fr: 800-451-1741

M. William Krasilovsky. 1994. $18.95

★5608★ Music: Careers in Music

Silver Burdett Press
250 James St.
Morristown, NJ 07960
Ph: (201)285-7900   Fax: (201)285-9241

Mary A. Marshall. 1994. $14.95.

★5609★ The New York Agent Book

Sweden Press
Box 1612
Studio City, CA 91604
Ph: (818)995-4250

Third edition, 1992. $15.95. 250 pages.

★5610★ Opportunities in Music Careers

VGM Career Horizons
4255 W. Touhy Ave.
Lincolnwood, IL 60646-1975
Ph: (847)679-5500   Fax: (847)679-2494
Fr: 800-323-4900

Robert Gerardi. $14.95; $11.95 (paper). Describes the job market and where to find work. Covers careers in performing, writing, musical directing, management, and technical areas. Illustrated.

★5611★ Opportunities in Performing Arts Careers

VGM Career Horizons
4255 W. Touhy Ave.
Lincolnwood, IL 60646-1975
Ph: (847)679-5500   Fax: (847)679-2494
Fr: 800-323-4900

Bonnie Bjorguine Bekken. 1991. $14.95; $11.95 (paper). Examines opportunities in classical and popular music; theater, television, and movie acting; classical and modern dance; performance art; and teaching and therapy careers. Assists aspiring performers with developing a portfolio and preparing for interviews, tests, and auditions.

OTHER SOURCES

★5612★ American Almanac of Jobs and Salaries 1994-95

Avon Books
1350 Avenue of the Americas, 2nd Fl.
New York, NY 10019
Ph: (212)261-6800   Fr: 800-238-0658

John Wright. Revised edition, 1993. $17.00. 704 pages. This is a comprehensive guide to the wages of hundreds of occupations in a wide variety of industries and organizations.

★5613★ American Federation of Musicians of the United States and Canada (AFM)

Paramount Bldg.
1501 Broadway, Ste. 600
New York, NY 10036
Ph: (212)869-1330   Fax: (212)764-6134
Fr: 800-762-3444

Members: AFL-CIO. Musicians interested in advancing the music industry. **Purpose:** Offers legal representation on issues dealing with breach of contract, job protection, and wage scale negotiations.

★5614★ American Guild of Musical Artists (AGMA)

1727 Broadway
New York, NY 10019
Ph: (212)265-3687

Members: AFL-CIO. Opera and classical concert singers, classical ballet and modern dance performers, and affiliated stage directors and stage managers.

★5615★ American Guild of Organists (AGO)

475 Riverside Dr., Ste. 1260
New York, NY 10115
Ph: (212)870-2310   Fax: (212)870-2163

Purpose: Educational and service organization organized to advance the cause of organ and choral music and to maintain standards of artistic excellence of organists and choral conductors. **Activities:** Offers professional certification in organ playing, choral and instrumental training, and theory and general knowledge of music.

★5616★ Music Educators National Conference (MENC)

1806 Robert Fulton Dr.
Reston, VA 22091
Ph: (703)860-4000   Fax: (703)860-1531
Fr: 800-336-3768

Members: Professional organization of music educators, administrators, supervisors, consultants, and music education majors in colleges.

★5617★ Music Teachers National Association (MTNA)

441 Vine St., Ste. 505
Cincinnati, OH 45202-2814
Ph: (513)421-1420   Fax: (513)421-2503

Purpose: Professional society of independent and collegiate music teachers committed to furthering the art of music through programs that encourage and support teaching, performance, composition, and scholarly research.

★5618★ National Association of Teachers of Singing (NATS)

2800 University Blvd. N
Jacksonville, FL 32211
Ph: (904)744-9022   Fax: (904)744-9033

Members: Professional society of vocal music teachers. **Purpose:** Establishes ethical principles in the profession of teaching singing and vocal arts. Encourages research on scientific vocal projects. Sponsors local study groups, chapter sessions, and student activities for extension of vocal education and improvement of teaching skills. **Activities:** Conducts surveys of conditions affecting vocal music teachers. Provides edited lists of new songs, text translations, and other material. **E-Mail:** wmvessels@aol.com

★5619★ National Directory of Arts Internships

National Network for Artist Placement
935 W. Ave. 37
Los Angeles, CA 90065
Ph: (213)222-4035   Fax: (213)222-4035

Biennial, odd years. $40.00, postpaid; payment with order. Covers Approximately

2,000 internship opportunities in dance, music, theater, art, design, film, and video. Entries include: Name of sponsoring organization, address, name of contact; description of positions available, eligibility requirements, stipend or salary (if any), application procedures. Arrangement: Classified by discipline, then geographical.

★5620★ National Jazz Service Organization (NJSO)
409 7th NW
Lower Level
Washington, DC 20004-0061
Ph: (202)347-2604 Fax: (202)638-3460

Members: Jazz artists, ensembles, orchestras, performing groups and organizations, record companies and retailers, and other individuals and groups. **Purpose:** Dedicated to the creation, instruction, performance, presentation, and preservation of jazz music. Provides information and education with the aim of enhancing the status and support of jazz music as an American art form; offers documentation on jazz; supports innovations in jazz. Promotes the development of new audiences and consumer markets for jazz; supports the entrepreneurial spirit of those involved in the field. Seeks to increase employment opportunities in the jazz field. **Activities:** Maintains the National Jazz Network.

★5621★ Organization of American Kodaly Educators (OAKE)
1457 S. 23rd St.
Fargo, ND 58103-3708
Ph: (701)235-0366 Fax: (701)241-7051

Members: Music educators, students, organizations, schools, and libraries interested in the Kodaly concept of music education. Zoltan Kodaly (1882-1967), Hungarian composer and educator, originated a concept of music education that seeks to develop the sensibilities, intellectual facilities, and skills of children, with the intention of creating a musically educated public. **Purpose:** Objectives are: to encourage communication and cooperation among Kodaly educators; to encourage musical and human growth; to provide a forum for comment on the impact of the Kodaly concept; to recognize, identify, and convey the multicultural musical heritage of American society; to contribute to and encourage the aesthetic education of the child. **Activities:** Conducts clinics and other small unit activities.

Nuclear Engineers

★5622★ **Captsule Job Listings**

Publications and Communications, Inc.
12416 Hymeadow Dr.
Austin, TX 78750
Ph: (512)250-9023   Fax: (512)331-3900
Fr: 800-678-9724

Online database. Lists current job openings in the contract (temporary) technical services industry. Includes the Action Hot List, which provides information on job seekers. Includes employment opportunities in technical/professional engineering, computing, and design/drafting. Entries generally contain company name, address, and job opening.

★5623★ *Energy User News*

Chilton Publications
825 7th Ave.
New York, NY 10019
Ph: (212)887-8400   Fax: (212)887-8484

Monthly. Magazine exploring industrial and commercial energy efficiency markets and strategies.

★5624★ *Engineering Times*

National Society of Professional Engineers
1420 King St.
Alexandria, VA 22314
Ph: (703)684-2875   Fax: (703)836-4875

Monthly. Magazine (tabloid) covering professional, legislative, and techology issues for an engineering audience.

★5625★ *ENR: Engineering News Record*

New York Construction News
1221 Avenue of the Americas
New York, NY 10020
Ph: (212)512-4773   Fax: (212)512-4770

Weekly. $42.00/year; $2.00/issue.

★5626★ *High Technology Careers Magazine*

HTC
4701 Patrick Henry Dr., No. 1901
Santa Clara, CA 95054
Ph: (408)970-8800   Fax: (408)980-5103

Bimonthly. Magazine (tabloid) containing employment opportunity information for the engineering and technical community.

★5627★ *Minority Engineer*

Equal Opportunity Publications, Inc.
150 Motor Pkwy., Ste. 420
Hauppauge, NY 11788-5145
Ph: (516)273-0066   Fax: (516)273-8936

Affirmative-action recruitment magazine serving college graduating and professional minority engineers.

★5628★ *National Engineer*

National Association of Power Engineers
1 Springfield St.
Chicopee, MA 01013-2624
Ph: (413)592-6273   Fax: (413)592-1998

Monthly. $23.40/year for individuals; $2.50 for single issue.

★5629★ *NSBE Magazine*

NSBE Publications
1454 Duke St.
Alexandria, VA 22314
Ph: (703)549-2207   Fax: (703)683-5312

$10.00/year for individuals; $2.00 for single issue. Journal providing information on engineering careers, self-development, and cultural issues for recent graduates with technical majors.

★5630★ *Nuclear Plant Journal*

Nuclear Plant Journal
799 Roosevelt Rd., Bldg. 6, Ste. 208
Glen Ellyn, IL 60137
Ph: (708)858-6161   Fax: (708)858-8787

$102.00/year for individuals; $17.00 for single issue. Magazine focusing on nuclear power plants.

★5631★ *Power*

New York Construction News
1221 Avenue of the Americas, 41st Fl.
New York, NY 10020
Ph: (212)512-4773   Fax: (212)512-4770

Monthly. Magazine for engineers in electric utilities, process and manufacturing plants, commercial and service establishments, and consulting, design, and construction engineering firms working in the power technology field.

★5632★ *Power Engineering*

PennWell Publishing Co.
1421 S. Sheridan
Tulsa, OK 74112
Ph: (918)835-3161   Fax: (918)831-9834
Fr: 800-331-4463

Monthly. $45.00/year for individuals. Magazine focusing on power generation.

★5633★ *SWE*

Society of Women Engineers
120 Wall St., 11th Fl.
New York, NY 10005-3902
Ph: (212)509-9577   Fax: (212)509-0224

Bimonthly. $30.00/year for nonmembers. Magazine for engineering students and for women and men working in the engineering and technology fields. Covers career guidance, continuing development and topical issues.

★5634★ *Technology Review*

The Tech
PO Box 397029
Cambridge, MA 02139
Ph: (617)253-1541   Fax: (617)258-8226

$30.00/year for individuals; $3.75 for single issue; $42.00/year for other countries. Magazine reviewing new developments in technology with an emphasis on economic, political, and social implications. Not a new product publication.

★5635★ *Woman Engineer*

Equal Opportunity Publications, Inc.
150 Motor Pkwy., Ste. 420
Hauppauge, NY 11788-5145
Ph: (516)273-0066   Fax: (516)273-8936

Engineer recruitment magazine.

PLACEMENT AND JOB REFERRAL SERVICES

★5636★ American Association of Blacks in Energy (AABE)
927 15th St. NW, Ste. 200
Washington, DC 20005
Ph: (202)371-9530   Fax: (202)371-9218

Members: Blacks in energy-related professions, including engineers, scientists, consultants, academicians, and entrepreneurs; government officials and public policymakers; interested students. **Purpose:** Represents blacks and other minorities in matters involving energy use and research, the formulation of energy policy, the ownership of energy resources, and the development of energy technologies. Seeks to increase the knowledge, understanding, and awareness of the minority community in energy issues by serving as an energy information source for policymakers, recommending blacks and other minorities to appropriate energy officials and executives, encouraging students to pursue professional careers in the energy industry, and advocating the participation of blacks and other minorities in energy programs and policymaking activities. Updates members on key legislation and regulations being developed by the Department of Energy, the Department of Interior, the Department of Commerce, the Small Business Administration, and other federal and state agencies. **Activities:** Offers information on current job openings.

★5637★ American Indian Science and Engineering Society (AISES)
1630 30th St., Ste. 301
Boulder, CO 80301
Ph: (303)492-8658   Fax: (303)492-3400

Members: American Indian and non-Indian students and professionals in science, technology, and engineering fields; corporations representing energy, mining, aerospace, electronic, and computer fields. **Purpose:** Seeks to motivate and encourage students to pursue undergraduate and graduate studies in science, engineering, and technology. **Activities:** Sponsors science fairs in grade schools, teacher training workshops, summer math/science sessions for 8th-12th graders, professional chapters, and student chapters in colleges. Offers scholarships. Adult members serve as role models, advisers, and mentors for students. Operates placement service. **E-Mail:** aise sha@spot.colorado.edu

★5638★ Engineering Society of Detroit (ESD)
100 Farnsworth Ave.
Detroit, MI 48202
Ph: (313)832-5400   Fax: (313)832-5920

Members: Engineers from all disciplines; scientists and technologists. **Activities:** Offers placement services. Conducts technical programs and engineering refresher courses; sponsors conferences and expositions. Maintains speakers' bureau. Although based in Detroit, MI, society membership is international.

★5639★ Korean Scientists and Engineers Association in America (KSEA)
6261 Executive Blvd.
Rockville, MD 20852
Ph: (301)984-7048   Fax: (301)984-1231

Members: Scientists and engineers holding single or advanced degrees. **Purpose:** Goals are to: promote friendship and mutuality among Korean and American scientists and engineers; contribute to Korea's scientific, technological, industrial, and economic developments; strengthen the scientific, technological, and cultural bonds between Korea and the U.S. Sponsors symposium. **Activities:** Maintains speakers' bureau, placement service, and biographical archives. Compiles statistics. Maintains 100 volume library of scientific handbooks and yearbooks in Korean.

★5640★ Society of Hispanic Professional Engineers (SHPE)
5400 E. Olympic Blvd., Ste. 210
Los Angeles, CA 90022
Ph: (213)725-3970

Purpose: Engineers, student engineers, and scientists seeking to increase the number of Hispanic engineers by providing motivation and support to students. Sponsors competitions and educational programs. **Activities:** Maintains placement service and speakers' bureau; compiles statistics.

EMPLOYER DIRECTORIES AND NETWORKING LISTS

★5641★ American Men and Women of Science
R. R. Bowker Co.
Reed Reference Publishing
121 Chanlon Rd.
New Providence, NJ 07974
Ph: (908)464-6800   Fax: (908)665-6688
Fr: 800-521-8110

Triennial, latest edition January 1995. $106.00, per volume; $850.00, set. Covers over 123,000 U.S. and Canadian scientists active in the physical, biological, mathematical, computer science, and engineering fields; includes references to previous edition for deceased scientists and nonrespondents. Entries include: Name, address, education, personal and career data, memberships, honors and awards, research interest. Arrangement: Alphabetical. Indexes: Discipline (in separate volume).

★5642★ Directory of Contract Service Firms
C. E. Publications, Inc.
PO Box 97000
Kirkland, WA 98083
Ph: (206)823-2222   Fax: (206)821-0942

Annual, January. $10.00. Covers Approximately 900 contract firms actively engaged in the employment of engineering and technical personnel for temporary contract assignments throughout the world. Entries include: Company name, address, phone, name of

contact. Arrangement: Alphabetical. Indexes: Geographical.

★5643★ Directory of Engineering Societies and Related Organizations
American Association of Engineering Societies
1111 19th St. NW, Ste. 608
Washington, DC 20036
Ph: (202)296-2237   Fax: (202)296-1151
Fr: 800-658-8897

1992. $185.00. Lists 1,000 national, regional, Canadian, and international organizations concerned with engineering and related fields.

★5644★ Directory of Engineers in Private Practice
National Society of Professional Engineers
1420 King St.
Alexandria, VA 22314
Ph: (703)684-2862   Fax: (703)836-4875

Annual. $85.00. Covers 600 consulting engineering firms and 7,200 individuals who are members of the society's Professional Engineers in Private Practice division. Entries include: For companies, name, address, phone, name of principal executive, list of services. For individuals, name, address; most listings include phone. Arrangement: Firms are geographic, then by specialty; individuals are alphabetical.

★5645★ Energy and Nuclear Sciences International Who's Who
Stockton Press
Groves Dictionaries
345 Park Ave. S., 10th Fl.
New York, NY 10010
Ph: (212)689-9200   Fr: 800-221-2123

Fourth edition, 1994. $550.00. 1312 pages. Provides personal, career, and professional data on more than 3,000 energy and nuclear scientists and engineers.

★5646★ Engineering Research Centres
Stockton Press
Groves Dictionaries
345 Park Ave. S., 10th Fl.
New York, NY 10010
Ph: (212)689-9200   Fr: 800-221-2123

Fourth edition, 1995. $515.00. 768 pages. Contains over 8,000 entries describing research and technology laboratories in over 70 countries. Provides details on industrial research centers and educational establishments with research and development activity. Indexes: Subject and title of establishments.

★5647★ Peterson's Job Opportunities in Engineering and Technology 1996
Peterson's
PO Box 2123
Princeton, NJ 08543-2123
Ph: (609)243-9111   Fax: (609)243-9150
Fr: 800-338-3282

Compiled by the Peterson's staff. Annual. $19.95 paperback. 432 pages. Profiles 2,000 high-tech companies looking primarily for technical personnel in such fields as biotechnology, telecommunications, software, computers and peripherals, defense, and aerospace. Contains job-search strategies and career options to help match education and expertise to the job market. Indexed geographically, by industry, and by hiring needs.

★5648★ **Scientific and Technical Organizations and Agencies Directory**
Gale Research
835 Penobscot Bldg.
Detroit, MI 48226-4094
Ph: (313)961-2242   Fax: (313)961-6083
Fr: 800-877-GALE

Irregular; latest edition December 1993. $195.00. Covers over 25,600 national and international organizations and agencies concerned with the physical and applied sciences, engineering, and technology, including associations, computer information services, consulting firms, educational institutions, foundations, government advisory organizations, federal government agencies, general grant and assistance programs, libraries and information centers, patent sources and services, research and development centers, scholarships, fellowships, and loans, science-technology centers, standards organizations, state academies of science, and state government agencies in the fields of aeronautics and space sciences, chemistry, computer science specialties, electronics, geography, geology, machinery, mathematics, metallurgy, meteorology, mineralogy, nuclear science, petroleum and gas, physics, plastics, transportation, water resources, and other areas. Entries include: Organization name, address, phone, and name of contact; additional descriptive text for most entries. Arrangement: Classified by type of organization. Indexes: Organization name/key word.

★5649★ **Who's Who in Technology**
Gale Research
835 Penobscot Bldg.
Detroit, MI 48226-4094
Ph: (313)961-2242   Fax: (313)961-6083
Fr: 800-877-GALE

Irregular, new edition expected June 1995. $380.00. Covers 38,000 engineers, scientists, inventors, and researchers. Entries include: Name, title, affiliation, address; personal, education, and career data; publications, patents; technical field of activity; area of expertise. Arrangement: Alphabetical. Indexes: Geographical, employer, technical discipline, expertise.

★5650★ **World Energy and Nuclear Directory**
Longman Publishing Group
The Longman Bldg.
10 Bank St.
White Plains, NY 10606-1951
Ph: (914)993-5000   Fr: 800-266-8855

Fifth edition, 1996. A worldwide guide to 2,000 organizations in over 60 countries that conduct, promote, and encourage research and development work in the field of energy. Includes nuclear research institutes, government departments, public corporations, industrial firms, and others.

HANDBOOKS AND MANUALS

★5651★ **The Best Resumes for Scientists and Engineers**
John Wiley and Sons
605 3rd Ave.
New York, NY 10158
Ph: (212)850-6000   Fr: 800-225-5945

Adele Lewis. Second edition, 1993. $37.50; $14.95 (paper). Presents an extensive collection of scientific and engineering resumes, highlighting the important differences between these and resumes written for other occupations.

★5652★ **Careers in Engineering**
VGM Career Horizons
4255 W. Touhy Ave.
Lincolnwood, IL 60646-1975
Ph: (847)679-5500   Fax: (847)679-2494
Fr: 800-323-4900

Geraldine O. Gardner. 1994. $17.95; $13.95 (paper). Covers careers in the public or private sector, in industry, the university, or the military, from applications in computer architecture design to high temperature ceramics.

★5653★ **Engineering Success**
Kendall Hunt Publishing
4050 Westmark Dr.
PO Box 1840
Dubuque, IA 52004-1840
Ph: (319)589-1000   Fax: 800-772-9165
Fr: 800-228-0810

Bill Osher. 1994. $27.96.

★5654★ **Engineering Your Job Search: A Job-Finding Resource for Engineering Professionals**
Professional Publications, Inc.
1250 5th Ave.
Belmont, CA 94002
Ph: (415)593-9119   Fax: (415)592-4519
Fr: 800-426-1178

Compiled by Professional Publications editors. 1995. $12.95 (paper).

★5655★ **Introduction to the Engineering Profession**
HarperCollins Publishers, Inc.
10 E. 53rd. St.
New York, NY 10022-5299
Ph: (212)207-7000   Fax: (212)207-7145
Fr: 800-331-3761

David M. Burghardt. 1995. $30.00 (paper).

★5656★ **Job Opportunities in Engineering and Technology**
Peterson's Guides, Inc.
PO Box 2123
Princeton, NJ 08543-2123
Ph: (609)243-9111   Fax: (609)243-9150
Fr: 800-338-3282

1994. $18.95 (paper).

★5657★ **Majoring in Engineering: How to Get from Your Freshman Year to Your First Job**
Farrar, Straus & Giroux, Inc.
19 Union Sq., W
New York, NY 10003
Ph: (212)741-6900   Fr: 800-788-6262

John Garcia. 1995. $20.00; $10.00 (paper).

★5658★ **Opportunities in Energy Careers**
VGM Career Horizons
4255 W. Touhy Ave.
Lincolnwood, IL 60646-1975
Ph: (847)679-5500   Fax: (847)679-2494
Fr: 800-323-4900

John Woodburn. 1992. $13.95; $10.95 (paper). 160 pages. Discusses opportunities in a variety of fields, including petroleum, nuclear, and thermal energy, and how to pursue employment. Illustrated.

★5659★ **Opportunities in Engineering Careers**
VGM Career Horizons
4255 W. Touhy Ave.
Lincolnwood, IL 60646-1975
Ph: (847)679-5500   Fax: (847)679-2494
Fr: 800-323-4900

Nicholas Basta. 1995. $14.95; $11.95 (paper). Outlines typical job titles, salaries, career paths, and employment prospects.

★5660★ **Opportunities in High Tech Careers**
VGM Career Horizons
4255 W. Touhy Ave.
Lincolnwood, IL 60646-1975
Ph: (847)679-5500   Fax: (847)679-2494
Fr: 800-323-4900

Gary D. Golter and Deborah Yanuck. 1995. $14.95; $11.95 (paper). 160 pages. Explores high technology careers. Describes job opportunities, how to make a career decision, how to prepare for high technology jobs, job hunting techniques, and future trends.

★5661★ **Resumes for Engineering Careers**
VGM Career Horizons
NTC Publishing Group
4255 W. Touhy Ave.
Lincolnwood, IL 60646-1975
Ph: (847)679-5500   Fax: (847)679-2494
Fr: 800-323-4900

1994. $9.95. 160 pages. Contains sample resumes and cover letters applicable to any engineering field.

EMPLOYMENT AGENCIES AND SEARCH FIRMS

★5662★ **ABC Employment Service**
25 S. Bemiston, Ste. 214
Clayton, MO 63105
Ph: (314)725-3140

Employment agency.

★5663★ **Engineer One, Inc.**

10124 Dutchtown Rd.
Knoxville, TN 37932-2611
Ph: (615)690-2611   Fax: (615)690-2611

Employment agency.

★5664★ **Hayden and Associates, Inc.**

7825 Washington Ave. S., Ste. 120
Minneapolis, MN 55439-2431
Ph: (612)941-6300   Fax: (612)941-9602

Employment agency. Executive search firm.
Fills openings in a variety of fields.

★5665★ **International Staffing
Consultants**

500 Newport Center Dr., Ste. 300
Newport Beach, CA 92660-7003
Ph: (714)721-7990

Employment agency. Provides placement on
regular or temporary basis. Affiliate office in
London.

★5666★ **The Jobs Co.**

8900 E. Sprague Ave.
Spokane, WA 99212-2927
Ph: (509)928-3151   Fax: (509)928-3168

Employment agency. Has division specializing in engineering and scientific openings.
Also operates division specializing in sales
openings.

★5667★ **JR Professional Search**

PO Box 18356
Tucson, AZ 85731
Ph: (520)721-1855   Fax: (520)721-1855

Employment agency.

★5668★ **LOR Personnel Division**

418 Wall St.
Princeton, NJ 08540
Ph: (609)921-6580

Employment agency. Executive search firm.

★5669★ **Main Line Personnel Service,
Inc.**

401 City Ave.
Bala Cynwyd, PA 19004-1122
Ph: (610)667-1820

Employment agency.

★5670★ **Search and Recruit
International**

4455 South Blvd.
Virginia Beach, VA 23452
Ph: (804)490-3151

Employment agency. Headquartered in Vir-
ginia Beach. Other offices in Bremerton, WA;
Charleston, SC; Jacksonville, FL; Memphis,
TN; Pensacola, FL; Sacramento, CA; San
Bernardino, CA; San Diego, CA.

★5671★ **Sierra Technology Corporation**

4150 Manzanita Ave., Ste. 100
Carmichael, CA 95608-1700
Ph: (916)488-4960   Fax: (916)488-7058

Employment agency. Provides placement on
a temporary basis.

★5672★ **Source Engineering**

5580 LBJ Fwy., Ste. 300
Dallas, TX 75240
Ph: (214)385-3002   Fax: (214)717-0075

Executive search firm. Many affiliate offices
located throughout the U.S.

OTHER SOURCES

★5673★ *American Almanac of Jobs and
Salaries 1994-95*

Avon Books
1350 Avenue of the Americas, 2nd Fl.
New York, NY 10019
Ph: (212)261-6800   Fr: 800-238-0658

John Wright. Revised edition, 1993. $17.00.
704 pages. This is a comprehensive guide to
the wages of hundreds of occupations in a
wide variety of industries and organizations.

★5674★ **American Association of
Engineering Societies (AAES)**

1111 19th St. NW, Ste. 608
Washington, DC 20036
Ph: (202)296-2237   Fax: (202)296-1151

Purpose: Seeks to promote leadership in
public affairs for the engineering community,
work in support of math and science education for young persons. Disseminates of
information about the profession. Provides
statistics about engineers.

★5675★ **American Nuclear Society
(ANS)**

555 N. Kensington Ave.
La Grange Park, IL 60525
Ph: (708)352-6611   Fax: (708)352-0499

Members: Physicists, chemists, educators,
mathematicians, life scientists, engineers,
metallurgists, managers, and administrators
with professional experience in nuclear science or nuclear engineering. **Purpose:**
Works to advance science and engineering in
the nuclear industry. Disseminates information; promotes research; conducts meetings
devoted to scientific and technical papers;
works with government agencies, educational institutions, and other organizations dealing with nuclear issues.

★5676★ **Association for International
Practical Training (AIPT)**

10400 Little Patuxent Pky. Ste. 250
Columbia, MD 21044
Ph: (410)997-2200   Fax: (410)992-3924

Purpose: Helps coordinate training around
the world in fields such as travel, the culinary
arts, and hotel management. **Activities:** Conducts programs in career development and
hospitality/tourism exchanges. Operates a
student exchange program. Provides reciprocal practical training experience for recent
graduates from the U.S., Austria, Germany,
Finland, France, Hungary, Ireland, Japan,
Malaysia, Netherlands, Switzerland, and the
United Kingdom. Arranges training programs
in the U.S. and abroad. Serves as U.S.
affiliate to IAESTE (International Association
for the Exchange of Students for Technical
Experience) and operates a Professional

Visitors Program to arrange short-term educational and training visits to the U.S. **E-Mail:**
aipt@aipt.org

★5677★ *Engineering Salary Survey*

Source Engineering
1290 Oakmead, Ste. 318
Sunnyvale, CA 94086
Ph: (408)738-8440

Annual. Discusses the structure of the engineering profession, trends, and compensation. Salaries are listed by job function,
industry, and years of experience.

★5678★ *Graduating Engineer*

Peterson's/COG Publishing Group
16030 Ventura Blvd., No. 560
Encino, CA 91436
Ph: (818)789-5293

Eight issues/year. Magazine focusing on
employment, education, and career development for entry-level engineers.

★5679★ **National Action Council for
Minorities in Engineering (NACME)**

3 W. 35th St.
New York, NY 10001-2281
Ph: (212)279-2626   Fax: (212)629-5178

Purpose: Seeks to increase the number of
African American, Latino, and Native American students enrolled in and graduating from
engineering schools. Through the Corporate
Scholars Program, offers comprehensive
scholarships to engineering students that
include leadership development, corporate
mentors and summer internships. Works
with local, regional, and national education
organizations to motivate and encourage
precollege students to engage in engineering
careers. Conducts educational and research
programs; operates project to assist engineering schools in improving the retention
and graduation rates of minority students.
Maintains speakers' bureau; compiles statistics.

★5680★ **National Society of
Professional Engineers (NSPE)**

1420 King St.
Alexandria, VA 22314
Ph: (703)684-2800   Fax: (703)836-4875

Members: Professional engineers and engineers-in-training in all fields registered in
accordance with the laws of states or territories of the U.S. or provinces of Canada;
qualified graduate engineers, student members, and registered land surveyors. **Purpose:** Is concerned with social, professional,
ethical, and economic considerations of engineering as a profession; encompasses programs in public relations, employment practices, ethical considerations, education, and
career guidance. Monitors legislative and
regulatory actions of interest to the engineering profession. **Website:** http://
www.hspc.org

★5681★ Salaries of Scientists, Engineers, and Technicians: A Summary of Salary Surveys

Commission on Professionals in Science and Technology (CPST)
1500 Massachusetts Ave. NW, Ste. 831
Washington, DC 20005
Ph: (202)223-6995
1993.

★5682★ Society of Women Engineers (SWE)

120 Wall St., 11th Fl.
New York, NY 10005
Ph: (212)509-9577   Fax: (212)509-0224

Members: Educational service society of women engineers; membership is also open to men. **Purpose:** Supplies information on the achievements of women engineers and the opportunities available to them; assists women engineers in preparing for return to active work following temporary retirement. Serves as an informational center on women in engineering. **Activities:** Administers several certificate and scholarship programs. Offers tours and career guidance; conducts surveys. Compiles statistics.

Nuclear Medicine Technologist

SOURCES OF HELP-WANTED ADS

★5683★ *Clinical Nuclear Medicine*
Pharmaceutical Media, Inc.
30 E. 33rd St.
New York, NY 10016
Ph: (212)685-5010   Fax: (212)685-5010

Monthly. $118.00/year for individuals; $152.00/year for other countries. Journal publishing original manuscripts about scanning, imaging, and related subjects.

★5684★ *Diagnostic Imaging*
Miller Freeman, Inc.
600 Harrison St.
San Francisco, CA 94107
Ph: (415)905-2200

Monthly. $70.00/year.

★5685★ *Radiology Today*
Slack, Inc.
6900 Grove Rd.
Thorofare, NJ 08086-9447
Ph: (609)848-1000   Fax: (609)853-5991
Fr: 800-257-8290

Monthly. Covering radiology technique and equipment innovations, related political activities, and daily practice.

EMPLOYER DIRECTORIES AND NETWORKING LISTS

★5686★ *AHA Guide to the Health Care Field*
Health Statistics Group
American Hospital Association (AHA)
1 N. Franklin
Chicago, IL 60606
Ph: (312)422-3501   Fax: (312)280-6015

Annual, July. $195.00, payment with order. Covers hospitals, multi-health care systems, freestanding ambulatory surgery centers, psychiatric facilities, long-term care facilities, substance abuse programs, hospices, Health Maintenance Organizations (HMOs), and oth-er health-related organizations. Entries include: For hospitals: facility name, address, phone, administrator's name, number of beds, facilities and services, number of employees, expenses, other statistics. For other organizations: name, address, phone, name and title of contact. Arrangement: Geographical. Indexes: Hospital name.

★5687★ *Directory of Hospital Personnel*
Medical Economics
5 Paragon Dr.
Montvale, NJ 07645-1725
Ph: (201)358-7500   Fax: (201)573-4956
Fr: 800-222-3045

Annual, September. $325.00, plus 7.50 shipping. Covers 200,000 executives at 7,100 U.S. hospitals. Entries include: Name of hospital, address, phone, number of beds, type and JCAHO status of hospital, names and titles of key department heads and staff, medical and nursing school affiliations; number of residents, interns, and nursing students. Arrangement: Geographical. Indexes: Hospital name, personnel, hospital size.

★5688★ *Hospital Blue Book*
Billian Publishing Co.
2100 Powers Ferry Rd., Ste. 300
Atlanta, GA 30339
Ph: (404)955-5656   Fax: (404)952-0669

Annual, spring. $154.50, national edition, plus $20.00 shipping. Covers more than 7,100 hospitals; some listings also appear in a separate southern edition of this publication. Entries include: Name of hospital, accreditation, mailing address, phone, fax, number of beds, type of facility (nonprofit, general, state, etc.); list of administrative personnel and chiefs of medical services, with specific titles. Arrangement: Geographical.

★5689★ *Hospital Market Atlas*
SMG Marketing Group, Inc.
1342 N. LaSalle Dr.
Chicago, IL 60610
Ph: (312)642-3026   Fax: (312)642-9729
Fr: 800-678-3026

Biennial, odd years. $495.00, payment with order. Covers over 7,000 hospitals, hospital systems and 480 group purchasing organizations. Entries include: Hospital or organiza-tion name, address, phone, county code, management, type of hospital service, number of beds, admissions, surgical operations, and emergency room visits. Arrangement: Geographical.

★5690★ *Hospitals Directory*
American Business Directories, Inc.
American Business Information, Inc.
5711 S. 86th Cir.
Omaha, NE 68127
Ph: (402)593-4600   Fax: (402)331-1505

Annual. $870.00, U.S. edition. Entries include: Name, address, phone (including area code), size of advertisement, year first in Yellow Pages, name of owner or manager, number of employees. Compiled from telephone company Yellow Pages, nationwide. Arrangement: Geographical.

★5691★ *Medical and Health Information Directory*
Gale Research
835 Penobscot Bldg.
Detroit, MI 48226-4094
Ph: (313)961-2242   Fax: (313)961-6083
Fr: 800-877-GALE

Approximately biennial; latest edition 1994. $195.00, per volume; $485.00, for the three-volume set. Covers in Volume 1, almost 18,600 medical and health oriented associations, organizations, institutions, and government agencies, including health maintenance organizations (HMOs), preferred provider organizations (PPOs), insurance companies, pharmaceutical companies, research centers, and medical and allied health schools. In Volume 2, nearly 11,800 medical book publishers; medical periodicals, directories, audiovisual producers and services, medical libraries and information centers, and electronic resources. In Volume 3, nearly 26,000 clinics, treatment centers, care programs, and counseling/diagnostic services for 30 subject areas. Entries include: Institution, service, or firm name, address, phone; many include names of key personnel and, when pertinent, descriptive annotation. Arrangement: Classified by organization activity, service, etc. Indexes: Each volume has a complete alphabetical name and keyword index.

★5692★ The Official American Board of Medical Specialties (ABMS)—Directory of Board Certified Nuclear Medicine Specialists

Marquis Who's Who
Reed Reference Publishing
121 Chanlon Rd.
New Providence, NJ 07974
Ph: (908)464-6800   Fax: (908)665-6688
Fr: 800-521-8110

Biennial. $119.95. Covers about 3,800 certified physicians specializing in the radioactive diagnosis and treatment of disease. Entries include: Name, address, phone, certification data, education, professional association membership. Arrangement: Alphabetical. Indexes: Geographical.

★5693★ Osteopathic Membership Directory—AOHA

American Osteopathic Healthcare Association
5301 Wisconsin Ave. NW, Ste. 630
Washington, DC 20015-2015
Ph: (202)686-1700   Fax: (202)686-7615

Annual, summer. $125.00, payment with order. Covers about 110 osteopathic hospitals. Includes list of individual and institutional members; also lists osteopathic colleges, and directors of medical education. Entries include: For hospitals: name of hospital, name of chief executive officer, address, phone, number of beds and other hospital data. Arrangement: Geographical. Indexes: Name, institution.

HANDBOOKS AND MANUALS

★5694★ Careers in Health Care

VGM Career Horizons
4255 W. Touhy Ave.
Lincolnwood, IL 60646-1975
Ph: (847)679-5500   Fax: (847)679-2494
Fr: 800-323-4900

Barbara M. Swanson. 1995. $17.95; $13.95 (paper). Describes job duties, work settings, salaries, licensing and certification requirements, educational preparation, and future outlook. Gives ideas on how to secure a job.

★5695★ Medical Technologists and Technicians Career Directory

Gale Research
835 Penobscot Bldg.
Detroit, MI 48226-4094
Ph: (313)961-2242   Fax: (313)961-6083
Fr: 800-877-GALE

Bradley Morgan. 1993. $39.00. 324 pages. Essays on specific careers provide an insider's perspective. Features extensive listings of contacts and entry-level job opportunities. Provides information on internships and sources of help-wanted ads.

★5696★ Opportunities in Health and Medical Careers

VGM Career Horizons
4255 W. Touhy Ave.
Lincolnwood, IL 60646-1975
Ph: (847)679-5500   Fax: (847)679-2494
Fr: 800-323-4900

Donald Snook, Jr. and Leo D'Orazio. 1993. $14.95; $11.95 (paper). Covers the full range of medical and health occupations. Illustrated.

★5697★ Opportunities in High Tech Careers

VGM Career Horizons
4255 W. Touhy Ave.
Lincolnwood, IL 60646-1975
Ph: (847)679-5500   Fax: (847)679-2494
Fr: 800-323-4900

Gary D. Golter and Deborah Yanuck. 1995. $14.95; $11.95 (paper). 160 pages. Explores high technology careers. Describes job opportunities, how to make a career decision, how to prepare for high technology jobs, job hunting techniques, and future trends.

★5698★ Opportunities in Medical Technology Careers

VGM Career Horizons
4255 W. Touhy Ave.
Lincolnwood, IL 60646-1975
Ph: (847)679-5500   Fax: (847)679-2494
Fr: 800-323-4900

Karen R. Karni and Sidney Oliver. 1990. $14.95; $11.95 (paper). Details opportunities for various technical medical personnel and supplies up-to-date information on salary levels and employment outlook. Appendices list associations and unions in each field. Illustrated.

★5699★ Resumes for Health and Medical Careers

4255 W. Touhy Ave.
Lincolnwood, IL 60646-1975
Ph: (708)679-5500   Fax: (708)679-6375
Fr: 800-323-4900

Compiled by VGM Career Horizons Staff 1995. $9.95 (paper).

EMPLOYMENT AGENCIES AND SEARCH FIRMS

★5700★ Blake and Associates Executive Search

PO Box 1425
Pleasantville, NJ 08232
Ph: (609)645-3330   Fax: (609)383-0320

Executive search firm.

★5701★ JPM International

4665 MacArthur Ct., Ste. 100B
Newport Beach, CA 92660
Ph: (714)955-2545   Fax: (714)757-1320

Executive search firm and employment agency.

★5702★ Sue Carroll Personnel, Inc.

16 E. 79th St.
New York, NY 10021
Ph: (212)288-8866   Fax: (212)988-7191

Employment agency and executive search firm.

OTHER SOURCES

★5703★ American Registry of Radiologic Technologists (ARRT)

1255 Northland Dr.
St. Paul, MN 55120
Ph: (612)687-0048

Purpose: Radiologic certification boards that administer examinations, issues certificates of registration to radiographers, nuclear medicine technologists, and radiation therapists, and investigates the qualifications of practicing radiologic technologists. Governed by trustees appointed from American College of Radiology and American Society of Radiologic Technologists.

★5704★ American Society of Radiologic Technologists (ASRT)

15000 Central Ave. SE
Albuquerque, NM 87123
Ph: (505)298-4500   Fax: (505)298-5063

Members: Professional society of diagnostic radiography, radiation therapy, ultrasound, and nuclear medicine technologists. **Purpose:** Advances the science of radiologic technology; establishes and maintains high standards of education; evaluates the quality of patient care; improves the welfare and socioeconomics of radiologic technologists. Operates ASRT Educational Foundation, which provides educational materials to radiologic technologists.

★5705★ Nuclear Medicine Technology: A Career with a Future

University of Alabama at Birmingham
Nuclear Medicine Technologist Program
UAB Sta., SHRP 333
Birmingham, AL 35294
Ph: (205)934-2004

Video. $28.00 (5-day preview); $100.00 (purchase). 14 minutes. Suitable for high school and college students. Describes career opportunities in nuclear medicine technology.

★5706★ Nuclear Medicine Technology Certification Board (NMTCB)

2970 Clairmont Rd., Ste. 610
Atlanta, GA 30329
Ph: (404)315-1739   Fax: (404)315-6502

Purpose: To provide for the certification of nuclear medical technologists and to develop, assess, and administer an examination relevant to nuclear medicine technology. Compiles statistics.

★5707★ Society of Nuclear Medicine (SNM)

1850 Samuel Morse Dr.
Reston, VA 22090
Ph: (703)708-9000   Fax: (703)708-9015

Members: Professional society of physicians, physicists, chemists, radiopharmacists, nuclear medicine technologists, and others interested in nuclear medicine, nuclear magnetic resonance, and the use of radioactive isotopes in clinical practice, research, and teaching. **Activities:** Disseminates information concerning the utilization of nuclear phenomena in the diagnosis and treatment of disease. Oversees the Technologist Section of the Society of Nuclear Medicine.

Nursing Aides and Psychiatric Aides

★5722★ *Rehabilitation Nursing*

Association of Rehabilitation Nurses
5700 Old Orchard Rd., 1st Fl.
Skokie, IL 60077-1057
Ph: (708)966-3433   Fax: (708)966-9418

Bimonthly. $50.00/year for individuals; $75.00/year for institutions; $90.00/year for other countries; $13.00 for single issue. Magazine focusing on rehabilitation nursing involving clinical practice, research, education, and administration.

PLACEMENT AND JOB REFERRAL SERVICES

★5723★ **American Association of Psychiatric Technicians (AAPT)**

PO Box 14014
Phoenix, AZ 85063
Ph: (602)873-1890   Fax: (602)873-4616
Fr: 800-391-7589

Members: Psychiatric technicians, behavioral health technicians, mental health workers, counselors, social workers, psychiatric nurses, psychologists, and other individuals and companies interested in mental health. **Purpose:** Promotes professionalism in mental health industry. Encourages further education of mental health workers and provides national certification of mental health workers. Works with colleges, schools, and mental health facilities to develop education and training. Awards accreditation to mental health worker training programs. **Activities:** Offers placement informations.

★5724★ **American Public Health Association (APHA)**

1015 15th St. NW
Washington, DC 20005
Ph: (202)789-5600   Fax: (202)789-5681

Members: Professional organization of physicians, nurses, educators, academicians, environmentalists, epidemiologists, new professionals, social workers, health administrators, optometrists, podiatrists, pharmacists, dentists, nutritionists, health planners, other community and mental health specialists, and interested consumers. **Purpose:** Seeks to protect and promote personal, mental, and environmental health. **Activities:** Services include: promulgation of standards; establishment of uniform practices and procedures; development of the etiology of communicable diseases; research in public health; exploration of medical care programs and their relationships to public health. Sponsors job placement service.

★5725★ **American School Health Association (ASHA)**

7263 State Rte. 43
PO Box 708
Kent, OH 44240
Ph: (216)678-1601   Fax: (216)678-4526

Members: School physicians, school nurses, dentists, nurses, nutritionists, health educators, dental hygienists, school-based professionals, and public health workers. **Purpose:** Promotes comprehensive and constructive school health programs including the teaching of health, health services, and promotion of a healthful school environment. **Activities:** Offers a professional referral service, classroom teaching aids, and professional reference materials. Conducts research programs; maintains placement service; compiles statistics. Sponsors foreign travel study tour.

EMPLOYER DIRECTORIES AND NETWORKING LISTS

★5726★ *AHA Guide to the Health Care Field*

Health Statistics Group
American Hospital Association (AHA)
1 N. Franklin
Chicago, IL 60606
Ph: (312)422-3501   Fax: (312)280-6015

Annual, July. $195.00, payment with order. Covers hospitals, multi-health care systems, freestanding ambulatory surgery centers, psychiatric facilities, long-term care facilities, substance abuse programs, hospices, Health Maintenance Organizations (HMOs), and other health-related organizations. Entries include: For hospitals: facility name, address, phone, administrator's name, number of beds, facilities and services, number of employees, expenses, other statistics. For other organizations: name, address, phone, name and title of contact. Arrangement: Geographical. Indexes: Hospital name.

★5727★ *American Journal of Nursing— Directory of Nursing Organizations Issue*

American Journal of Nursing Co.
555 W. 57th St.
New York, NY 10019
Ph: (212)582-8820   Fax: (212)586-5462
Fr: 800-627-0484

Annual, April. $5.00. Publication includes: List of nursing organizations and agencies. Entries include: Name, address, names of officers or nursing representative. Arrangement: Classified by type of organization.

★5728★ *Canada Nursing Job Guide Directory*

Prime National Publishing Corporation
470 Boston Post Rd.
Weston, MA 02193
Ph: (617)899-2702

Martha J. Denney. 1989. $50.00. 166 pages. Directory of Canadian hospitals.

★5729★ *Directory of Hospital Personnel*

Medical Economics
5 Paragon Dr.
Montvale, NJ 07645-1725
Ph: (201)358-7500   Fax: (201)573-4956
Fr: 800-222-3045

Annual, September. $325.00, plus 7.50 shipping. Covers 200,000 executives at 7,100 U.S. hospitals. Entries include: Name of hospital, address, phone, number of beds, type and JCAHO status of hospital, names and titles of key department heads and staff, medical and nursing school affiliations; number of residents, interns, and nursing students. Arrangement: Geographical. Indexes: Hospital name, personnel, hospital size.

★5730★ *Directory of Nursing Homes*

HCIA Inc.
300 E. Lombard St.
Baltimore, MD 21202
Ph: (410)576-9600   Fax: (410)539-5220
Fr: 800-568-3282

Annual. $249.00. Covers over 16,000 state-licensed long-term care facilities. Entries include: Facility name, address, phone, names and titles of key personnel, licensure status, number of beds; number of nursing, dietary, and auxiliary staff members; program/services; medicaid/medicare certification status; admission and referral requirements; age and gender restrictions; languages spoken; management or chain company name. Arrangement: Geographical. Indexes: Alphabetical, geographical (county) and by chain headquarters.

★5731★ *Hospital Blue Book*

Billian Publishing Co.
2100 Powers Ferry Rd., Ste. 300
Atlanta, GA 30339
Ph: (404)955-5656   Fax: (404)952-0669

Annual, spring. $154.50, national edition, plus $20.00 shipping. Covers more than 7,100 hospitals; some listings also appear in a separate southern edition of this publication. Entries include: Name of hospital, accreditation, mailing address, phone, fax, number of beds, type of facility (nonprofit, general, state, etc.); list of administrative personnel and chiefs of medical services, with specific titles. Arrangement: Geographical.

★5732★ *Hospital Market Atlas*

SMG Marketing Group, Inc.
1342 N. LaSalle Dr.
Chicago, IL 60610
Ph: (312)642-3026   Fax: (312)642-9729
Fr: 800-678-3026

Biennial, odd years. $495.00, payment with order. Covers over 7,000 hospitals, hospital systems and 480 group purchasing organizations. Entries include: Hospital or organization name, address, phone, county code, management, type of hospital service, number of beds, admissions, surgical operations, and emergency room visits. Arrangement: Geographical.

★5733★ *Hospitals Directory*

American Business Directories, Inc.
American Business Information, Inc.
5711 S. 86th Cir.
Omaha, NE 68127
Ph: (402)593-4600   Fax: (402)331-1505

Annual. $870.00, U.S. edition. Entries include: Name, address, phone (including area code), size of advertisement, year first in Yellow Pages, name of owner or manager, number of employees. Compiled from telephone company Yellow Pages, nationwide. Arrangement: Geographical.

★5734★ Medical and Health Information Directory

Gale Research
835 Penobscot Bldg.
Detroit, MI 48226-4094
Ph: (313)961-2242   Fax: (313)961-6083
Fr: 800-877-GALE

Approximately biennial; latest edition 1994. $195.00, per volume; $485.00, for the three-volume set. Covers in Volume 1, almost 18,600 medical and health oriented associations, organizations, institutions, and government agencies, including health maintenance organizations (HMOs), preferred provider organizations (PPOs), insurance companies, pharmaceutical companies, research centers, and medical and allied health schools. In Volume 2, nearly 11,800 medical book publishers; medical periodicals, directories, audiovisual producers and services, medical libraries and information centers, and electronic resources. In Volume 3, nearly 26,000 clinics, treatment centers, care programs, and counseling/diagnostic services for 30 subject areas. Entries include: Institution, service, or firm name, address, phone; many include names of key personnel and, when pertinent, descriptive annotation. Arrangement: Classified by organization activity, service, etc. Indexes: Each volume has a complete alphabetical name and keyword index.

★5735★ Mental Health Directory

Office of Consumer, Family & Public Information
Center for Mental Health Services
U.S. Substance Abuse & Mental Health Services Administration
5600 Fishers Ln., Rm. 15-18
Rockville, MD 20857
Ph: (301)443-2792

Irregular, latest edition 1990. $23.00. Covers hospitals, treatment centers, outpatient clinics, day/night facilities, residential treatment centers for emotionally disturbed children, residential supportive programs such as halfway houses, and mental health centers offering mental health assistance; not included are substance abuse programs, Veteran's Administration programs, nursing homes, programs for the developmentally disabled, and organizations in which fees are retained by individual members. Entries include: Name, address, phone. Arrangement: Geographical.

★5736★ Nurses and Nurses' Registries Directory

American Business Directories, Inc.
American Business Information, Inc.
5711 S. 86th Cir.
Omaha, NE 68127
Ph: (402)593-4600   Fax: (402)331-1505

Annual. $880.00, U.S. edition. Entries include: Name, address, phone (including area code), size of advertisement, year first in Yellow Pages, name of owner or manager, number of employees. Compiled from telephone company Yellow Pages, nationwide. Arrangement: Geographical.

★5737★ Nursing Career Directory

Springhouse Corp.
1111 Bethlehem Pke.
PO Box 908
Spring House, PA 19477-0908
Ph: (215)646-8700   Fax: (215)646-8700

Annual, January. Covers nonprofit and investor-owned hospitals and departments of the United States government which hire nurses. Does not report specific positions available. Entries include: Unit name, location, areas of nursing specialization, educational requirements for nurses, licensing, facilities, benefits, etc. Arrangement: Geographical.

★5738★ Nursingworld Journal—Nursing Job Guide Issue

Prime National Publishing Corp.
470 Boston Post Rd.
Weston, MA 02193
Ph: (617)899-2702   Fax: (617)899-4900
Fr: 800-869-2700

Annual, July. $75.00. Covers over 7,000 hospitals and medical centers, infirmaries, government hospitals, and other hospitals in the United States; in tabular format, provides information about each facility that would be of interest to nurses considering employment there, but does not list specific openings. Entries include: Hospital name, address, phone, name of nurse recruiter; number of beds, number of admissions, number of patient days, type of control, whether a teaching institution, nursing specialties utilized. Arrangement: Geographical.

★5739★ Osteopathic Membership Directory—AOHA

American Osteopathic Healthcare Association
5301 Wisconsin Ave. NW, Ste. 630
Washington, DC 20015-2015
Ph: (202)686-1700   Fax: (202)686-7615

Annual, summer. $125.00, payment with order. Covers about 110 osteopathic hospitals. Includes list of individual and institutional members; also lists osteopathic colleges, and directors of medical education. Entries include: For hospitals: name of hospital, name of chief executive officer, address, phone, number of beds and other hospital data. Arrangement: Geographical. Indexes: Name, institution.

★5740★ Peterson's Job Opportunities in Health Care

Peterson's Guides, Inc.
202 Carnegie Ctr.
Box 2123
Princeton, NJ 08543-2123
Ph: (609)243-9111   Fax: (609)243-9150
Fr: 800-338-3282

Annual, August. $18.95. Covers Over 1,500 companies hiring health-care professionals for skilled nursing care facilities, hospitals, medical laboratories, home health care, and pharmaceuticals. Entries include: Organization name, address, phone, name and title of contact, type of organization, number of employees, Standard Industrial Classification (SIC) code; description of opportunities available including disciplines, level of education required, starting locations and salaries, level of experience accepted, benefits. Arrange-

ment: Alphabetical. Indexes: Employer by type of organization, industry classification, number of employees, starting location, special interest area; education level, company.

★5741★ Who's Who in American Nursing

Society of Nursing Professionals
Reed Reference Publishing
121 Chanlon Rd.
New Providence, NJ 07974-1541
Ph: (908)464-6800   Fax: (908)665-6688
Fr: 800-521-8110

Biennial, Odd years. $139.00, plus $9.73 shipping. Covers approximately 27,000 nursing professionals, including educators, administrators, deans of nursing, directors of nursing, nurse practitioners, clinical supervisors, and others. Entries include: Name, address, personal history, area of specialization, professional experience, education, professional organization membership, honors, publications, experience in public speaking. Arrangement: Alphabetical. Indexes: Geographical, specialization.

HANDBOOKS AND MANUALS

★5742★ America's 50 Fastest Growing Jobs

JIST Works, Inc.
720 N. Park Ave.
Indianapolis, IN 46202
Ph: (317)264-3720   Fr: 800-648-5478

Third edition, 1995. $14.95. 288 pages. Each job profile explains the nature of the work, skills and abilities required, employment outlook, average earnings, related occupations, education and training requirements, and employment opportunities. Also contains career planning information and job search tips.

★5743★ Being a Long-Term Care Nursing Assistant

Prentice Hall
113 Sylvan Ave.
Rte. 9W
Englewood Cliffs, NJ 07632
Ph: (201)592-2000   Fr: 800-922-0579

Connie Will Black and Judith B. Eighmy. Fourth edition, 1995.

★5744★ Careers in Health Care

VGM Career Horizons
4255 W. Touhy Ave.
Lincolnwood, IL 60646-1975
Ph: (847)679-5500   Fax: (847)679-2494
Fr: 800-323-4900

Barbara M. Swanson. 1995. $17.95; $13.95 (paper). Describes job duties, work settings, salaries, licensing and certification requirements, educational preparation, and future outlook. Gives ideas on how to secure a job.

★5745★ Federal Jobs in Nursing and Health Sciences

Impact Publications
9104 N. Manassas Dr.
Manassas Park, VA 22111-5211
Ph: (703)361-7300   Fax: (703)335-9486

Russ Smith. 1995. $14.95 (paper).

★5746★ How to Be A Nurse Assistant: Career Training in Long Term Care

Mosby-Year Book, Inc.
11830 Westline Industrial Dr.
St. Louis, MO 63146
Ph: (314)872-8370   Fax: (314)432-1380
Fr: 800-426-4545

Margaret Casey, editor. 1994.

★5747★ Long-Term Practice: Skills for the Certified Nursing Assistant

Little, Brown & Company
Time & Life Bldg.
1271 Avenue of the Americas
New York, NY 10020
Ph: (212)522-8700   Fax: (212)522-2067
Fr: 800-343-9204

Marjorie G. Frazier. 1995.

★5748★ Nurse Assistant Test Preparation

Prentice Hall General Reference & Travel
15 Columbus Cir.
New York, NY 10023
Ph: (212)373-8500   Fax: 800-445-6991
Fr: 800-223-2348

Wanda Smith. 1994. $12.00 (paper).

★5749★ Nursing Attendants: Your Role Working in Psychiatry

Good Sign
3554 Carlisle Pl.
Bronx, NY 10467-6017
Ph: (718)519-7896

Gloria Elliott. 1994. $8.00 (paper).

★5750★ Nursing Today: Transition and Trends

W.B. Saunders Co.
Curtis Ctr., Independence Sq., W.
Philadelphia, PA 19106-3399
Ph: (215)238-7800   Fax: (215)238-7883

JoAnn Zerwekh, editor. 1994. $23.50 (paper).

★5751★ 100 Best Careers for the Year 2000

Prentice Hall General Reference
15 Columbus Cir.
New York, NY 10023
Ph: (212)373-8500   Fr: 800-223-2348

Shelly Field. 1992. $15.00 (paper). Covers 100 of the fastest growing jobs. The publication is divided into 11 general employment sections. Specific careers are covered within each section. Provides job description, responsibilities, employment opportunities, earnings, education and training, advancement opportunities, and experience and qualifications for each occupation.

★5752★ 101 Career Options for Nurses

Mosby-Year Book, Inc.
11830 Westline Industrial Dr.
St. Louis, MO 63146
Ph: (314)872-8370   Fax: (314)432-1380
Fr: 800-426-4545

Walraven. $21.95 (paper).

★5753★ Opportunities in Health and Medical Careers

VGM Career Horizons
4255 W. Touhy Ave.
Lincolnwood, IL 60646-1975
Ph: (847)679-5500   Fax: (847)679-2494
Fr: 800-323-4900

Donald Snook, Jr. and Leo D'Orazio. 1993. $14.95; $11.95 (paper). Covers the full range of medical and health occupations. Illustrated.

★5754★ Opportunities in Nursing Careers

VGM Career Horizons
4255 W. Touhy Ave.
Lincolnwood, IL 60646-1975
Ph: (847)679-5500   Fax: (847)679-2494
Fr: 800-323-4900

Keville Frederickson. 1995. $14.95; $11.95 (paper) Discusses the employment outlook and job-seeking techniques for LVN's, LPN's, RN's, nurse practitioners, nurse anesthetists, and other nurse members of the medical team. Includes a complete list of state nurses associations, state nursing boards, and specialty nursing organizations. Contains bibliography and illustrations.

★5755★ Resume Writing for the Professional Nurse

CES Associates
112 S. Grant St.
Hinsdale, IL 60521
Ph: (708)654-2596

Nancy Kuzmich. Revised edition, 1995. $39.95. 110 pages. Self-study guide written for the professional nurse on how to set career goals, interview for a job, and select the best job offer. Includes sample resumes and cover letters.

★5756★ Resumes for Health and Medical Careers

4255 W. Touhy Ave.
Lincolnwood, IL 60646-1975
Ph: (708)679-5500   Fax: (708)679-6375
Fr: 800-323-4900

Compiled by VGM Career Horizons Staff 1995. $9.95 (paper).

★5757★ To Be a Nurse

Vista Publishing, Inc.
473 Broadway
Long Branch, NJ 07740
Ph: (908)229-4545   Fax: (908)229-9647
Fr: 800-634-2498

Linda Strangio. 1995. $12.95 (paper).

★5758★ Your Opportunities in Nursing

Energeia Publishing, Inc.
860 Commercial St., S.
Salem, OR 97302
Ph: (503)362-1480   Fax: (503)362-2123

Margie Sherman. 1994. $2.00 (paper).

EMPLOYMENT AGENCIES AND SEARCH FIRMS

★5759★ Academy Medical Personnel Services

571 High St.
Columbus, OH 43085-4132
Ph: (614)848-6011

Employment agency. Fills openings on a regular or temporary basis.

★5760★ Davis-Smith, Inc.

24725 W. 12 Mile Rd., Ste. 302
Southfield, MI 48034
Ph: (810)354-4100

Employment agency. Executive search firm.

★5761★ Eden Temporary Services

280 Madison Ave.
New York, NY 10016-0801
Ph: (212)685-4666

Employment agency. Places individuals in regular or temporary positions.

★5762★ Harper Associates

29870 Middlebelt
Farmington Hills, MI 48334
Ph: (810)932-1170

Employment agency.

★5763★ Health and Science Center

209 Hunter St.
Media, PA 19063-5726
Ph: (610)891-0714

Employment agency. Executive search firm.

★5764★ Medical Personnel Pool

2901 S. Ridgewood Ave.
Daytona Beach, FL 32119-3542
Ph: (904)736-1648

Provides regular and temporary staffing assistance. Offices located in cities throughout United States.

★5765★ Medical Personnel Services, Inc.

1707 L St. NW, Ste. 700
Washington, DC 20036
Ph: (202)466-2955   Fax: (202)452-1818

Employment agency.

★5766★ Midwest Medical Consultants

8910 Purdue Rd., Ste. 200
Indianapolis, IN 46268-1155
Ph: (317)872-1053

Employment agency. Executive search firm.

★5767★ Poston Personnel

16 E. 79th St., Ste. G-4
New York, NY 10021
Ph: (212)535-4116   Fax: (212)988-7080

Employment agency.

★5768★ Professional Placement Associates, Inc.

11 Rye Ridge Plaza
Rye Brook, NY 10573
Ph: (914)251-1000   Fax: (914)939-1959

Employment agency.

★5769★ Staley/Adams and Associates Personnel Services Inc.

4615 Post Oak Pl.
Houston, TX 77027-9731
Ph: (713)965-0402

Employment agency.

★5770★ Travcorps, Inc.

40 Eastern Ave.
Malden, MA 02148
Ph: (617)322-2600

Places staff in temporary assignments.

OTHER SOURCES

★5771★ American Health Care Association

1201 L St. NW
Washington, DC 20005
Ph: (202)842-4444   Fax: (202)842-3860

Members: Federation of state associations of long-term health care facilities. **Purpose:** Promotes standards for professionals in long-term health care delivery and quality care for patients and residents in a safe environment. Focuses on issues of availabili-

ty, quality, affordability, and fair payment. Operates as a liaison with governmental agencies, Congress, and professional associations.

★5772★ American Hospital Association (AHA)

1 N. Franklin, Ste. 27
Chicago, IL 60606
Ph: (312)422-3000   Fax: (312)422-4796

Members: Individuals and health care institutions including hospitals, health care systems, and pre- and postacute health care delivery organizations. **Purpose:** Is dedicated to promoting the welfare of the public through its leadership and assistance to its members in the provision of better health services for all people. Conducts educational programs furthering the in-service education of hospital personnel; collects and analyzes data; furnishes multimedia educational materials; maintains 44,000 volume health care administration library, and biographical archive.

★5773★ American Nursing Assistant's Foundation (ANCF)

PO Box 2734
Fort Riley, KS 66442-0734

Members: Professional organization of certified nursing assistants and nurses' aides. **Purpose:** Represents the interests of members. **Activities:** Sponsors seminars.

★5774★ Career Encounters: Nursing

Cambridge Career Products
PO Box 2153
Dept. CC15
Charleston, WV 25328-2153
Ph: (304)744-9323   Fax: (304)744-9351
Fr: 800-468-4227

Video. $99.95. 25 minutes. Professionals shown in a variety of settings discuss different aspects of their careers.

★5775★ Day in a Career: Nursing

Cambridge Career Products
PO Box 2153
Dept. CC15
Charleston, WV 25328-2153
Ph: (304)744-9323   Fax: (304)744-9351
Fr: 800-468-4227

Video. 1994. $89.00. 15-22 minutes. Includes candid interviews and work situations, plus outlines of relevant career information.

★5776★ National Rural Health Association (NRHA)

1 W. Armour Blvd., Ste. 301
Kansas City, MO 64111
Ph: (816)756-3140   Fax: (816)756-3144

Members: Administrators, physicians, nurses, physician assistants, health planners, academicians, and others interested or involved in rural health care. **Purpose:** To create a better understanding of health care problems unique to rural areas; utilize a collective approach in finding positive solutions; articulate and represent the health care needs of rural America; supply current information to rural health care providers; serve as a liaison between rural health care programs throughout the country. Offers continuing education credits for medical, dental, nursing, and management courses.

★5777★ Visiting Nurse Associations of America (VNAA)

3801 E. Florida, Ste. 900
Denver, CO 80210
Ph: (303)753-0218   Fax: (303)753-0258
Fr: 800-426-2547

Members: Voluntary, nonprofit home health care agencies. **Purpose:** Develops competitive strength among community-based nonprofit visiting nurse organizations; works to strengthen business resources and economic programs through contracting, marketing, governmental affairs and publications.

Occupational Therapists

SOURCES OF HELP-WANTED ADS

★5778★ The American Journal of Occupational Therapy

American Occupational Therapy
Association, Inc.
4720 Montgomery Lane
PO Box 31220
Bethesda, MD 20824-1220
Ph: (301)652-2682   Fax: (301)652-7711
Fr: 800-877-1383

Monthly. $50.00/year for individuals; $12.00
for single issue. Journal providing a forum for
occupational therapy personnel to share research, case studies, and new theory.

★5779★ American Journal of Physical Medicine and Rehabilitation

Foot & Ankle International
7100 Lakewood Bldg., Ste. 112
5987 E. 71st St.
Indianapolis, IN 46220
Ph: (317)845-4200   Fax: (317)845-4200

Bimonthly. $65.00/year for individuals;
$85.00/year for other countries. Medical jour-
nal.

★5780★ Archives of Physical Medicine and Rehabilitation

American Congress of Rehabilitation
Medicine
78 E. Adams St., Ste. 1310
Chicago, IL 60603-6103
Ph: (312)922-9371   Fax: (312)922-6754

Monthly. $130.00/year

★5781★ Journal of Learning Disabilities

Pro-Ed Journals
8700 Shoal Creek Blvd.
Austin, TX 78757
Ph: (512)451-3246

Ten issues/year. $49.00/year. Special educa-
tion magazine.

★5782★ Teaching Exceptional Children

The Council for Exceptional Children
1920 Association Dr.
Reston, VA 22091-1589
Ph: (703)620-3660   Fax: (703)264-9494
Fr: 800-CEC-READ

Quarterly. $35.00/year for individuals. Jour-
nal exploring practical methods for teaching
talented and gifted children who have disabilities.

★5783★ TeamRehab Report

Miramar Publishing
6133 Bristol Pkwy.
Box 3640
Culver City, CA 90231-3640
Ph: (213)337-9717

Bimonthly.

PLACEMENT AND JOB REFERRAL SERVICES

★5784★ American Public Health Association (APHA)

1015 15th St. NW
Washington, DC 20005
Ph: (202)789-5600   Fax: (202)789-5681

Members: Professional organization of physicians, nurses, educators, academicians,
environmentalists, epidemiologists, new professionals, social workers, health administrators, optometrists, podiatrists, pharmacists,
dentists, nutritionists, health planners, other
community and mental health specialists, and
interested consumers. **Purpose:** Seeks to
protect and promote personal, mental, and
environmental health. **Activities:** Services
include: promulgation of standards; establishment of uniform practices and procedures; development of the etiology of communicable diseases; research in public
health; exploration of medical care programs
and their relationships to public health. Sponsors job placement service.

★5785★ Association on Higher Education and Disability (AHEAD)

PO Box 21192
Columbus, OH 43221-0192
Ph: (614)488-4972   Fax: (614)488-1174

Members: Individuals interested in promoting the equal rights and opportunities of
disabled postsecondary students, staff, faculty, and graduates. **Purpose:** Provides an
exchange of communication for those professionally involved with disabled students;
collects, evaluates, and disseminates information; encourages and supports legislation
for the benefit of disabled students. **Activities:** Conducts surveys on issues pertinent to
college students with disabilities; offers resource referral system and employment exchange for positions in disability student
services. Conducts research programs; compiles statistics.

EMPLOYER DIRECTORIES AND NETWORKING LISTS

★5786★ AHA Guide to the Health Care Field

Health Statistics Group
American Hospital Association (AHA)
1 N. Franklin
Chicago, IL 60606
Ph: (312)422-3501   Fax: (312)280-6015

Annual, July. $195.00, payment with order.
Covers hospitals, multi-health care systems,
freestanding ambulatory surgery centers,
psychiatric facilities, long-term care facilities,
substance abuse programs, hospices, Health
Maintenance Organizations (HMOs), and other health-related organizations. Entries include: For hospitals: facility name, address,
phone, administrator's name, number of
beds, facilities and services, number of employees, expenses, other statistics. For other
organizations: name, address, phone, name
and title of contact. Arrangement: Geographical. Indexes: Hospital name.

★5787★ Directory of Hospital Personnel

Medical Economics
5 Paragon Dr.
Montvale, NJ 07645-1725
Ph: (201)358-7500   Fax: (201)573-4956
Fr: 800-222-3045

Annual, September. $325.00, plus 7.50 shipping. Covers 200,000 executives at 7,100 U.S. hospitals. Entries include: Name of hospital, address, phone, number of beds, type and JCAHO status of hospital, names and titles of key department heads and staff, medical and nursing school affiliations; number of residents, interns, and nursing students. Arrangement: Geographical. Indexes: Hospital name, personnel, hospital size.

★5788★ Directory of Nursing Homes

HCIA Inc.
300 E. Lombard St.
Baltimore, MD 21202
Ph: (410)576-9600   Fax: (410)539-5220
Fr: 800-568-3282

Annual. $249.00. Covers over 16,000 state-licensed long-term care facilities. Entries include: Facility name, address, phone, names and titles of key personnel, licensure status, number of beds; number of nursing, dietary, and auxiliary staff members; program/services; medicaid/medicare certification status; admission and referral requirements; age and gender restrictions; languages spoken; management or chain company name. Arrangement: Geographical. Indexes: Alphabetical, geographical (county) and by chain headquarters.

★5789★ Home Health Service Directory

American Business Directories, Inc.
American Business Information, Inc.
5711 S. 86th Cir.
Omaha, NE 68127
Ph: (402)593-4600   Fax: (402)331-1505

Annual. $1,200.00, U.S. edition. Entries include: Name, address, phone (including area code), size of advertisement, year first in Yellow Pages, name of owl her or manager, number of employees. Compiled from telephone company Yellow Pages, nationwide. Arrangement: Geographical.

★5790★ Hospital Blue Book

Billian Publishing Co.
2100 Powers Ferry Rd., Ste. 300
Atlanta, GA 30339
Ph: (404)955-5656   Fax: (404)952-0669

Annual, spring. $154.50, national edition, plus $20.00 shipping. Covers more than 7,100 hospitals; some listings also appear in a separate southern edition of this publication. Entries include: Name of hospital, accreditation, mailing address, phone, fax, number of beds, type of facility (nonprofit, general, state, etc.); list of administrative personnel and chiefs of medical services, with specific titles. Arrangement: Geographical.

★5791★ Hospital Market Atlas

SMG Marketing Group, Inc.
1342 N. LaSalle Dr.
Chicago, IL 60610
Ph: (312)642-3026   Fax: (312)642-9729
Fr: 800-678-3026

Biennial, odd years. $495.00, payment with order. Covers over 7,000 hospitals, hospital systems and 480 group purchasing organizations. Entries include: Hospital or organization name, address, phone, county code, management, type of hospital service, number of beds, admissions, surgical operations, and emergency room visits. Arrangement: Geographical.

★5792★ Hospitals Directory

American Business Directories, Inc.
American Business Information, Inc.
5711 S. 86th Cir.
Omaha, NE 68127
Ph: (402)593-4600   Fax: (402)331-1505

Annual. $870.00, U.S. edition. Entries include: Name, address, phone (including area code), size of advertisement, year first in Yellow Pages, name of owner or manager, number of employees. Compiled from telephone company Yellow Pages, nationwide. Arrangement: Geographical.

★5793★ Medical and Health Information Directory

Gale Research
835 Penobscot Bldg.
Detroit, MI 48226-4094
Ph: (313)961-2242   Fax: (313)961-6083
Fr: 800-877-GALE

Approximately biennial; latest edition 1994. $195.00, per volume; $485.00, for the three-volume set. Covers in Volume 1, almost 18,600 medical and health oriented associations, organizations, institutions, and government agencies, including health maintenance organizations (HMOs), preferred provider organizations (PPOs), insurance companies, pharmaceutical companies, research centers, and medical and allied health schools. In Volume 2, nearly 11,800 medical book publishers; medical periodicals, directories, audiovisual producers and services, medical libraries and information centers, and electronic resources. In Volume 3, nearly 26,000 clinics, treatment centers, care programs, and counseling/diagnostic services for 30 subject areas. Entries include: Institution, service, or firm name, address, phone; many include names of key personnel and, when pertinent, descriptive annotation. Arrangement: Classified by organization activity, service, etc. Indexes: Each volume has a complete alphabetical name and keyword index.

★5794★ Osteopathic Membership Directory—AOHA

American Osteopathic Healthcare Association
5301 Wisconsin Ave. NW, Ste. 630
Washington, DC 20015-2015
Ph: (202)686-1700   Fax: (202)686-7615

Annual, summer. $125.00, payment with order. Covers about 110 osteopathic hospitals. Includes list of individual and institutional members; also lists osteopathic colleges, and directors of medical education. Entries in-

clude: For hospitals: name of hospital, name of chief executive officer, address, phone, number of beds and other hospital data. Arrangement: Geographical. Indexes: Name, institution.

HANDBOOKS AND MANUALS

★5795★ Careers in Health Care

VGM Career Horizons
4255 W. Touhy Ave.
Lincolnwood, IL 60646-1975
Ph: (847)679-5500   Fax: (847)679-2494
Fr: 800-323-4900

Barbara M. Swanson. 1995. $17.95; $13.95 (paper). Describes job duties, work settings, salaries, licensing and certification requirements, educational preparation, and future outlook. Gives ideas on how to secure a job.

★5796★ Developmental Disabilities Program Specialist

National Learning Corp.
212 Michael Dr.
Syosset, NY 11791
Ph: (516)921-8888   Fax: (516)921-8743
Fr: 800-645-6337

1994. $27.95 (paper).

★5797★ Occupational Roles and Career Exploration and Development

American Occupational Therapy Association, Inc.
PO Box 31220
Bethesda, MD 20824-1220
Ph: (301)652-2682   Fax: (301)652-7711
Fr: 800-377-8555

Compiled by Occupational Therapy Roles Task Force Staff. 1994.

★5798★ Opportunities in Fitness Careers

VGM Career Horizons
4255 W. Touhy Ave.
Lincolnwood, IL 60646-1975
Ph: (847)679-5500   Fax: (847)679-2494
Fr: 800-323-4900

Jean Rosenbaum. 1992. $14.95; $11.95 (paper). Surveys fitness related careers. Describes career opportunities, education and experience needed, how to get into entry-level jobs and what income to expect. Schools are listed in the appendix.

★5799★ Opportunities in Health and Medical Careers

VGM Career Horizons
4255 W. Touhy Ave.
Lincolnwood, IL 60646-1975
Ph: (847)679-5500   Fax: (847)679-2494
Fr: 800-323-4900

Donald Snook, Jr. and Leo D'Orazio. 1993. $14.95; $11.95 (paper). Covers the full range of medical and health occupations. Illustrated.

★5800★ Opportunities in Occupational Therapy Careers

VGM Career Horizons
4255 W. Touhy Ave.
Lincolnwood, IL 60646-1975
Ph: (847)679-5500   Fax: (847)679-2494
Fr: 800-323-4900

Zona R. Weeks. 1995. $14.95; $11.95 (paper). Provides an overview of opportunities in clinical positions, government and nonprofit agencies, rehabilitation centers, hospices, and other areas, and provides job-hunting guidance. Illustrated.

★5801★ Opportunities in Paramedical Careers

VGM Career Horizons
4255 W. Touhy Ave.
Lincolnwood, IL 60646-1975
Ph: (847)679-5500   Fax: (847)679-2494
Fr: 800-323-4900

Alex Kacen. 1994. $14.95; 11.95 (paper). 160 pages. Discusses a variety of opportunities in this field and how to pursue them. Illustrated.

★5802★ Opportunities in Vocational and Technical Careers

VGM Career Horizons
4255 W. Touhy Ave.
Lincolnwood, IL 60646-1975
Ph: (847)679-5500   Fax: (847)679-2494
Fr: 800-323-4900

Adrian A. Paradis. 1992. $14.95; $11.95 (paper). 160 pages. Provides information on a variety of opportunities and advice on breaking into the field.

★5803★ Therapists and Allied Health Professionals Career Directory

Gale Research
835 Penobscot Bldg.
Detroit, MI 48226-4094
Ph: (313)961-2242   Fax: (313)961-6083
Fr: 800-877-GALE

Bradley Morgan. 1993. $39.00. 326 pages. Essays on specific careers provide an insider's perspective. Also features extensive listings of contacts and entry-level job opportunities. Provides information on internships and sources of help-wanted ads.

★5804★ Where the Jobs Are: The Hottest Careers for the '90s

The Career Press, Inc.
3 Tice Rd.
PO Box 687
Franklin Lakes, NJ 07417
Ph: (201)848-0310   Fax: (201)848-1727
Fr: 800-237-3371

Joyce Hadley. Second edition, 1995. $9.99. 300 pages. Describes careers in fifteen general fields, from accounting to travel and hospitality.

★5805★ Your Opportunities as a Massage Therapist

Energeia Publishing, Inc.
PO Box 985
Salem, OR 97308
Ph: (503)362-1480   Fax: (503)362-2123

Laurie Bean. 1994. $2.00 (paper).

EMPLOYMENT AGENCIES AND SEARCH FIRMS

★5806★ Harper Associates

29870 Middlebelt
Farmington Hills, MI 48334
Ph: (810)932-1170

Employment agency.

★5807★ JPM International

4665 MacArthur Ct., Ste. 100B
Newport Beach, CA 92660
Ph: (714)955-2545   Fax: (714)757-1320

Executive search firm and employment agency.

★5808★ Medical Personnel Pool

2901 S. Ridgewood Ave.
Daytona Beach, FL 32119-3542
Ph: (904)736-1648

Provides regular and temporary staffing assistance. Offices located in cities throughout United States.

★5809★ Midwest Medical Consultants

8910 Purdue Rd., Ste. 200
Indianapolis, IN 46268-1155
Ph: (317)872-1053

Employment agency. Executive search firm.

★5810★ Professional Placement Associates, Inc.

11 Rye Ridge Plaza
Rye Brook, NY 10573
Ph: (914)251-1000   Fax: (914)939-1959

Employment agency.

★5811★ Sue Carroll Personnel, Inc.

16 E. 79th St.
New York, NY 10021
Ph: (212)288-8866   Fax: (212)988-7191

Employment agency and executive search firm.

★5812★ Travcorps, Inc.

40 Eastern Ave.
Malden, MA 02148
Ph: (617)322-2600

Places staff in temporary assignments.

OTHER SOURCES

★5813★ American Almanac of Jobs and Salaries 1994-95

Avon Books
1350 Avenue of the Americas, 2nd Fl.
New York, NY 10019
Ph: (212)261-6800   Fr: 800-238-0658

John Wright. Revised edition, 1993. $17.00. 704 pages. This is a comprehensive guide to the wages of hundreds of occupations in a wide variety of industries and organizations.

★5814★ American Health Care Association

1201 L St. NW
Washington, DC 20005
Ph: (202)842-4444   Fax: (202)842-3860

Members: Federation of state associations of long-term health care facilities. **Purpose:** Promotes standards for professionals in long-term health care delivery and quality care for patients and residents in a safe environment. Focuses on issues of availability, quality, affordability, and fair payment. Operates as a liaison with governmental agencies, Congress, and professional associations.

★5815★ American Kinesiotherapy Association (AKTA)

PO Box 614
Wheeling, IL 60090-0614
Fr: 800-296-AKTA

Members: Professional society of kinesiotherapists, and associate and student members with interest in physical and mental rehabilitation and adapted physical education. (Kinesiology is the study of human movement; kinesiotherapists use kinesiology to design and implement therapeutic exercise to meet the rehabilitative needs of persons with disease, injury, and/or physical disorders.) **Purpose:** Goal is to promote the profession of kinesiotherapy by working toward public recognition of kinesiotherapy and to pursue and support legislative concerns of the profession. Works to maintain and advance the standard of care through educational opportunities.

★5816★ American Occupational Therapy Association (AOTA)

4720 Montgomery Ln.
PO Box 31220
Bethesda, MD 20824-1220
Ph: (301)652-2682   Fax: (301)652-7711

Members: Registered occupational therapists and certified occupational therapy assistants who provide services to people whose lives have been disrupted by physical injury or illness, developmental problems, the aging process, or social or psychological difficulties. Occupational therapy focuses on the active involvement of the patient in specially designed therapeutic tasks and activities to improve function, performance capacity, and the ability to cope with demands of daily living. **Activities:** Conducts research and educational programs and compiles statistics. Supports the American Occupational Therapy Foundation, which administers a program of professional training and development in research and provides research information related to occupational therapy.

★5817★ American Society of Hand Therapists (ASHT)

401 N. Michigan Ave.
Chicago, IL 60611
Ph: (312)321-6866   Fax: (312)527-6636

Members: Registered and licensed occupational and physical therapists specializing in hand therapy and committed to excellence and professionalism in hand rehabilitation. **Purpose:** To promote research, publish information, improve treatment techniques, and standardize hand evaluation and care. Fosters education and communication between therapists in the U.S. and abroad. **Activities:** Compiles statistics; conducts research and education programs and continuing education seminars.

★5818★ *Day in a Career: Occupational Therapist*

Cambridge Career Products
PO Box 2153 .
Dept. CC15
Charleston, WV 25328-2153
Ph: (304)744-9323   Fax: (304)744-9351
Fr: 800-468-4227

Video. 1994. $89.00. 15-22 minutes. Includes candid interviews and work situations, plus outlines of relevant career information.

★5819★ National Rehabilitation Association (NRA)

633 S. Washington St.
Alexandria, VA 22314
Ph: (703)836-0850   Fax: (703)836-0848

Members: Administrators, instructors, placement specialists, secretaries, counselors, therapists, vocational evaluators, ADA specialists and others interested in rehabilitation of persons with disabilities. **Activities:** Conducts legislative activities; develops accessibility guidelines; offers specialized education.

Operations Research Analysts

★5820★ Operations Research Society of America (ORSA)

1314 Guilford Ave.
Baltimore, MD 21202
Ph: (410)528-4146   Fax: (410)528-8556
Members: Scientists, educators, and practitioners engaged or interested in methodological subjects such as optimization, probabilistic models, decision analysis, and game theory. Also involved in areas of public concern such as health, energy, urban issues, and defense systems through industrial applications including marketing, operations management, finance, and decision support systems. **Activities:** Operates a visiting lecturers program. Offers placement service; compiles statistics. **E-Mail:** out cmm@jhuvms

HANDBOOKS AND MANUALS

★5821★ Career Information Center

Macmillan Publishing Co.
200 Old Tappan Rd.
Old Tappan, NJ 07675
Ph: (609)461-6500   Fr: 800-223-2336
Visual Education Center Staff. Fifth edition, 1992. $229.00. This 13-volume set profiles over 600 occupations. Each occupational profile describes job duties, educational requirements, how to get the job, advancement possibilities, employment outlook, working conditions, earnings and benefits, and where to write for more information.

★5822★ Operations Research Analysts

Chronicle Guidance Publications, Inc.
66 Aurora St.
PO Box 1190
Moravia, NY 13118-1190
Ph: (315)497-0330   Fax: (315)497-3359
Fr: 800-622-7284

Chronicle Guidance Staff. 1993. $2.00. Provides concise career information and sources of additional information.

EMPLOYMENT AGENCIES AND SEARCH FIRMS

★5823★ Analytic Recruiting, Inc.

21 E. 40th St., Ste. 500
New York, NY 10016
Ph: (212)545-8511

Executive search firm.

★5824★ B and M Associates, Inc.

199 Cambridge Rd.
Woburn, MA 01801-4705
Ph: (617)938-9120

Employment agency.

★5825★ Colli Associates of Tampa

PO Box 2865
Tampa, FL 33601
Ph: (813)681-2145

Employment agency. Executive search firm.

★5826★ Computer Engineering Consortium

7353 McWhorten Pl., Ste. 212
Annandale, VA 22003-5648
Ph: (703)658-0016

Employment agency.

★5827★ Data Systems Search Consultants

1756 Lacassie Ave.
Walnut Creek, CA 94596-4015
Ph: (510)256-0635

Employment agency. Executive search firm.

★5828★ Hansen Agri-Placement

PO Box 1172
Grand Island, NE 68802
Ph: (308)382-7350

Employment agency. Handles placements in a variety of fields on a regular or temporary basis.

★5829★ Hayden and Associates, Inc.

7825 Washington Ave. S., Ste. 120
Minneapolis, MN 55439-2431
Ph: (612)941-6300   Fax: (612)941-9602

Employment agency. Executive search firm. Fills openings in a variety of fields.

★5830★ Mfg/Search, Inc.

401 W. Colfax Ave., Ste. 600
South Bend, IN 46601
Ph: (219)282-2547   Fax: (219)289-0358

Executive search firm.

★5831★ The Personnel Institute

1000 Connecticut Ave. NW, Ste. 1108
Washington, DC 20036
Ph: (202)223-4911

Consulting firm.

★5832★ Place Mart Personnel Service

5 Elm Row
New Brunswick, NJ 08901
Ph: (908)247-8844

Executive search firm.

★5833★ Professional Recruiters and Temporaries

220 E. 3900 S., #9
Salt Lake City, UT 84107
Ph: (801)268-9940

Employment agency.

★5834★ Sierra Technology Corporation

4150 Manzanita Ave., Ste. 100
Carmichael, CA 95608-1700
Ph: (916)488-4960   Fax: (916)488-7058

Employment agency. Provides placement on a temporary basis.

★5835★ Tri-Serv Inc.

22 W. Padonia Rd., Ste. C53
Timonium, MD 21093
Ph: (301)561-1740

Employment agency.

★5836★ Werbin Associates Executive Search, Inc.

521 5th Ave., Ste. 1749
New York, NY 10175
Ph: (212)953-0909

Employment agency. Executive search firm.

OTHER SOURCES

★5837★ American Supplier Institute (ASI)

17333 Federal Dr., Ste. 220
Allen Park, MI 48101
Ph: (313)336-8877   Fax: (313)336-3187
Fr: 800-462-4500

Purpose: Seeks to encourage change in U.S.
industry through development and implementation of advanced manufacturing and engineering technologies such as taguchi methods, quality function deployment, just-in-time manufacturing, statistical process control, and total quality management. **Activities:** Offers educational courses, training seminars, and workshops to improve quality, reduce cost, and enhance competitive position of U.S. products. Maintains international network of affiliates for developing training specialists and technologies curriculum. Has government contract to provide training services to government supplier companies.

★5838★ Military Operations Research Society (MORS)

Landmark Towers
101 S. Whiting St., Ste. 202
Alexandria, VA 22304
Ph: (703)751-7290   Fax: (703)751-8171

Purpose: Works to improve the quality and effectiveness of military operations research. Sponsors colloquia; facilitates exchange of information and peer criticism among students, theoreticians, practitioners, and users of military operations research. Does not make or advocate official policy nor does it attempt to influence policy formulation. **E-Mail:** morsoffice@aol.com

Ophthalmic Laboratory Technicians

SOURCES OF HELP-WANTED ADS

★5839★ *Review of Optometry*
Chilton Publications
825 7th Ave.
New York, NY 10019
Ph: (212)887-8400   Fax: (212)887-8484
Monthly. $42.00/year. Journal for the optometric profession and optical industry.

★5840★ *20/20*
Jobson Publishing Corp.
100 Avenue of the Americas, 9th Fl.
New York, NY 10013
Ph: (212)274-7000   Fax: (212)431-0500
Monthly. $80.00/year.

★5841★ *Vision Monday*
Jobson Publishing Corp.
100 Avenue of the Americas, 9th Fl.
New York, NY 10013
Ph: (212)274-7000   Fax: (212)431-0500
Fr: 800-ADS-LICK
Biweekly. Trade newspaper for the opticians, optometrists, opthalmologists, optical retailers.

PLACEMENT AND JOB REFERRAL SERVICES

★5842★ **Association of Technical Personnel in Ophthalmology (ATPO)**
306 Humboldt Rd.
Brisbane, CA 94005
Ph: (415)467-6304
Members: Certified and noncertified allied health personnel in ophthalmology. **Purpose:** Objectives are to: advance and preserve the vision and health of all persons through the improvement of medical eye care; support programs and activities leading to the promotion of allied health personnel in ophthalmology. Cosponsors, with the Joint Commission on Allied Health Personnel in Ophthalmology, a continuing education program for ophthalmic medical personnel. **Activities:** Provides placement services; compiles statistics; conducts educational programs.

EMPLOYER DIRECTORIES AND NETWORKING LISTS

★5843★ *Directory of Certified Ophthalmic Medical Personnel*
Joint Commission on Allied Health Personnel in Ophthalmology
2025 Woodlane Dr.
St. Paul, MN 55125-2995
Ph: (612)731-2944   Fax: (612)731-0410
Fr: 800-284-3937
Annual, February. Covers about 15,000 certified ophthalmic medical personnel trained to assist ophthalmologists in various medical procedures involving eye care. Entries include: Name, address, code indicating level of certification, codes indicating whether a member of the Association of Technical Personnel in Ophthalmology or American Association of Certified Orthoptists. Arrangement: Alphabetical. Indexes: Geographical.

HANDBOOKS AND MANUALS

★5844★ *Careers in Health Care*
VGM Career Horizons
4255 W. Touhy Ave.
Lincolnwood, IL 60646-1975
Ph: (847)679-5500   Fax: (847)679-2494
Fr: 800-323-4900
Barbara M. Swanson. 1995. $17.95; $13.95 (paper). Describes job duties, work settings, salaries, licensing and certification requirements, educational preparation, and future outlook. Gives ideas on how to secure a job.

★5845★ *Opportunities in Eye Care Careers*
VGM Career Horizons
4255 W. Touhy Ave.
Lincolnwood, IL 60646-1975
Ph: (847)679-5500   Fax: (847)679-2494
Fr: 800-323-4900
Kathleen M. Ahrens. 1994. $14.95; $11.95 (paper). Explores careers in ophthalmology, optometry, and support positions. Describes the work, salary, and employment outlook and opportunities.

★5846★ *Optometric Technicians & Assistants*
Chronicle Guidance Publications, Inc.
66 Aurora St.
PO Box 1190
Moravia, NY 13118-1190
Ph: (315)497-0330   Fax: (315)497-3359
Fr: 800-622-7284
Chronicle Guidance Staff. 1993. $2.00. Provides concise career information and sources of additional information.

★5847★ *Resumes for Health and Medical Careers*
4255 W. Touhy Ave.
Lincolnwood, IL 60646-1975
Ph: (708)679-5500   Fax: (708)679-6375
Fr: 800-323-4900
Compiled by VGM Career Horizons Staff 1995. $9.95 (paper).

EMPLOYMENT AGENCIES AND SEARCH FIRMS

★5848★ **Retail Recruiters/Spectrum Consultants, Inc.**
111 Presidential Blvd., Ste. 211
Bala Pointe
Bala Cynwyd, PA 19004
Ph: (610)667-6565   Fax: (610)667-5323
Employment agency. Affiliate offices in many locations across the country.

OTHER SOURCES

★5849★ *ATPO Placement*
Association of Technical Personnel in
  Ophthalmology (ATPO)
306 Humboldt Rd.
Brisbane, CA 94005
Ph: (415)467-6304

Monthly.

★5850★ *ATPO Viewpoints*
Association of Technical Personnel in
  Ophthalmology (ATPO)
306 Humboldt Rd.
Brisbane, CA 94005
Ph: (415)467-6304

Bimonthly. Newsletter.

**★5851★ Vision Educational Foundation
(VEF)**
PO Box 472305
Tulsa, OK 74147-2305
Ph: (918)762-3947   Fax: (918)451-9207

Members: Optometric doctors, ophthalmic
laboratories, manufacturers, related technicians, and other professionals in the field.
Purpose: To promote a long-range program
of support to optometric educational institutions; to allow practicing optometrists opportunities to update and expand their clinical
skills and keep abreast of new technology; to
expose students to pathology cases; to
provide access to the most advanced diagnostic equipment available. **Activities:** Provides referral services. Maintains VEF Educational and Diagnostic Center, which provides
practicing optometrists and senior professional students of optometric colleges with
clinical education of a diagnostic and therapeutic nature.

Optometrists

SOURCES OF HELP-WANTED ADS

★5852★ *Journal of Visual Impairment & Blindness*

American Foundation for the Blind
15 W. 16th St.
New York, NY 10011
Ph: (212)612-2000   Fax: (212)502-7777

Bimonthly. $45.00/year for individuals; $75.00/year for institutions. Journal of Visual Impairment & Blindness is the research and professional journal; JVIB News Service (Part Two of Journal of Visual Impairment and Blindness) is the newsletter. Both pieces mail in the same envelope, and both pieces are included in the subscription price.

★5853★ *OE Reports*

SPIE-The International Society for +Optical +Engineering
PO Box 10
Bellingham, WA 98227-0010
Ph: (360)676-3290   Fax: (360)647-1445

Monthly. $25.00/year for individuals; $35.00/year for other countries. Magazine (tabloid) publishing technical articles and interviews with recognized leaders in optical and optoelectronic applied science and engineering. Includes information about the industry, technological advances, upcoming symposia, and other news.

★5854★ *Optometric Management*

Viscom Publications
50 Washington St., 11th Fl.
Norwalk, CT 06854
Ph: (203)838-9100   Fax: (203)838-2550

Ten Issues/year.

★5855★ *RETINA*

Pharmaceutical Media, Inc.
30 E. 33rd St.
New York, NY 10016
Ph: (212)685-5010   Fax: (212)685-5010

Quarterly. $112.00/year for individuals; $63.00/year for students; $162.00/year for institutions. Journal publishing clinically oriented articles for the general ophthalmologist and vitreoretinal specialist.

★5856★ *Review of Optometry*

Chilton Publications
825 7th Ave.
New York, NY 10019
Ph: (212)887-8400   Fax: (212)887-8484

Monthly. $42.00/year. Journal for the optometric profession and optical industry.

★5857★ *20/20*

Jobson Publishing Corp.
100 Avenue of the Americas, 9th Fl.
New York, NY 10013
Ph: (212)274-7000   Fax: (212)431-0500

Monthly. $80.00/year.

★5858★ *Vision Monday*

Jobson Publishing Corp.
100 Avenue of the Americas, 9th Fl.
New York, NY 10013
Ph: (212)274-7000   Fax: (212)431-0500
Fr: 800-ADS-LICK

Biweekly. Trade newspaper for the opticians, optometrists, opthalmologists, optical retailers.

PLACEMENT AND JOB REFERRAL SERVICES

★5859★ **American Optometric Association (AOA)**

243 N. Lindbergh Blvd.
St. Louis, MO 63141
Ph: (314)991-4100   Fax: (314)991-4101

Members: Professional society of optometrists, students of optometry, and paraoptometric assistants and technicians. **Purpose:** To improve the quality, availability, and accessibility of eye and vision care; to represent the optometric profession; to help members conduct their practices; to promote the highest standards of patient care. **Activities:** Offers placement service. Monitors and promotes legislation concerning the scope of optometric practice, alternate health care delivery systems, health care cost containment, Medicare, and other issues relevant to eye/vision care. Supports the International Library, Archives and Museum of Optometry

which includes references on ophthalmic and related sciences with emphasis on the history and socieconomic aspects of optometry. Operates Vision U.S.A. program, which provides free eye care to the working poor. Conducts specialized education program and charitable programs; compiles statistics. Maintains museum. Conducts Seal of Certification and Acceptance Program.

★5860★ **American Public Health Association (APHA)**

1015 15th St. NW
Washington, DC 20005
Ph: (202)789-5600   Fax: (202)789-5681

Members: Professional organization of physicians, nurses, educators, academicians, environmentalists, epidemiologists, new professionals, social workers, health administrators, optometrists, podiatrists, pharmacists, dentists, nutritionists, health planners, other community and mental health specialists, and interested consumers. **Purpose:** Seeks to protect and promote personal, mental, and environmental health. **Activities:** Services include: promulgation of standards; establishment of uniform practices and procedures; development of the etiology of communicable diseases; research in public health; exploration of medical care programs and their relationships to public health. Sponsors job placement service.

EMPLOYER DIRECTORIES AND NETWORKING LISTS

★5861★ *Blue Book of Optometrists*

Butterworth-Heinemann
313 Washington St.
Newton, MA 02158
Ph: (617)928-2646   Fax: (617)279-4851
Fr: 800-366-2665

Annual, November. $70.00, postpaid, payment with order. Covers nearly 30,000 optometrists, optical supply houses, manufacturers and import firms, associations, national and state examining board members, colleges and programs concerned with optometry and para-optometry; coverage includes Canada. Entries include: For optometrists:

name, office address, phone; personal, education, and career data; specialty. Arrangement: Geographical. Indexes: Personal name.

★5862★ **College of Optometrists in Vision Development—Fellow Member Roster**

College of Optometrists in Vision Development
Box 285
Chula Vista, CA 91912
Ph: (619)425-6191

Annual, January. $1.50. Covers about 980 members. Entries include: Name, address, phone. Arrangement: Geographical.

★5863★ **HMO/PPO Directory**

Medical Economics Data
5 Paragon Dr.
Montvale, NJ 07645-1742
Ph: (201)358-7500   Fax: (201)573-4956
Fr: 800-222-3045

Annual, November. $225.00, plus $7.50 shipping. Covers over 700 health maintenance organizations (HMOs) and more than 900 preferred provider organizations (PPOs). Entries include: Name of organization, address, phone, number of members, names of officers, employer references, geographical area served, parent company, average fees and copayments, financial data, and cost control procedures. Arrangement: Geographical. Indexes: Organization name, personnel name, HMOs and PPOs by state, and number of members enrolled.

★5864★ **Medical and Health Information Directory**

Gale Research
835 Penobscot Bldg.
Detroit, MI 48226-4094
Ph: (313)961-2242   Fax: (313)961-6083
Fr: 800-877-GALE

Approximately biennial; latest edition 1994. $195.00, per volume; $485.00, for the three-volume set. Covers in Volume 1, almost 18,600 medical and health oriented associations, organizations, institutions, and government agencies, including health maintenance organizations (HMOs), preferred provider organizations (PPOs), insurance companies, pharmaceutical companies, research centers, and medical and allied health schools. In Volume 2, nearly 11,800 medical book publishers; medical periodicals, directories, audiovisual producers and services, medical libraries and information centers, and electronic resources. In Volume 3, nearly 26,000 clinics, treatment centers, care programs, and counseling/diagnostic services for 30 subject areas. Entries include: Institution, service, or firm name, address, phone; many include names of key personnel and, when pertinent, descriptive annotation. Arrangement: Classified by organization activity, service, etc. Indexes: Each volume has a complete alphabetical name and keyword index.

★5865★ **Optometrists Directory**

American Business Directories, Inc.
American Business Information, Inc.
5711 S. 86th Cir.
Omaha, NE 68127
Ph: (402)593-4600   Fax: (402)331-1505

Annual. $1,155.00, U.S. edition; $210.00, (Canad. ed.), payment with order. Entries include: Name, address, phone (including area code), size of advertisement, year first in Yellow Pages, name of owner or manager, number of employees. Regional editions available. Compiled from telephone company Yellow Pages, nationwide. Arrangement: Geographical.

★5866★ **Optometry and Vision Science—Geographical Directory, American Academy of Optometry Issue**

American Academy of Optometry
4330 East-West Hwy., Ste. 1117
Bethesda, MD 20814
Ph: (301)718-6500   Fax: (301)656-0989

Biennial, odd years. $25.00. Publication includes: List of 3,400 members; international coverage. Entries include: Name, title, affiliation; office address, phone, fax, email. Arrangement: Geographical and alphabetical. Indexes: Name, specialty.

HANDBOOKS AND MANUALS

★5867★ **Careers in Medicine: Traditional and Alternative Opportunities**

Garrett Park Press
PO Box 190 C
Garrett Park, MD 20896-0190
Ph: (301)946-2553

Donald T. Rucker and Martin D. Keller. 1990. $15.95. 346 pages. Cites training requirements, illustrative work activities, and a summary of the advantages and disadvantages in a variety of specialized areas. Includes hundreds of career alternatives and discusses ways to break into these fields for persons trained in medicine. Features contributions from over 40 professionals in all phases of medicine and provides 200 sources of information on specialties and subspecialties.

★5868★ **The Encyclopedia of Career Choices for the 1990s: Guide to Entry-Level Jobs**

Perigree Books
The Berkley Publishing Group
PO Box 506
East Rutherford, NJ 07073
Ph: (201)933-9292   Fr: 800-223-0510

Career Associates Staff. 1992. $19.95. 862 pages. Describes 500 entry-level careers in a variety of industries. Presents qualifications required, working conditions, salary, internships, and professional associations.

★5869★ **Opportunities in Eye Care Careers**

VGM Career Horizons
4255 W. Touhy Ave.
Lincolnwood, IL 60646-1975
Ph: (847)679-5500   Fax: (847)679-2494
Fr: 800-323-4900

Kathleen M. Ahrens. 1994. $14.95; $11.95 (paper). Explores careers in ophthalmology, optometry, and support positions. Describes the work, salary, and employment outlook and opportunities.

★5870★ **Opportunities in Paramedical Careers**

VGM Career Horizons
4255 W. Touhy Ave.
Lincolnwood, IL 60646-1975
Ph: (847)679-5500   Fax: (847)679-2494
Fr: 800-323-4900

Alex Kacen. 1994. $14.95; 11.95 (paper). 160 pages. Discusses a variety of opportunities in this field and how to pursue them. Illustrated.

★5871★ **Optometric Practice Management**

Appleton & Lange
25 Van Zant St.
East Norwalk, CT 06855
Ph: (203)838-4400   Fax: (203)854-9486
Fr: 800-423-1359

Richard J. Clompus. 1995. $65.00.

★5872★ **Optometry: A Career with Vision**

American Optometric Association
243 N. Lindbergh Blvd.
St. Louis, MO 63141
Ph: (314)991-4100   Fax: (314)991-4100

Annual, January; latest edition fall 1994. Free. Covers about 20 optometry schools. Entries include: School name, address, phone; name of contact; admission requirements; statistical profile of students in program. Arrangement: Alphabetical.

★5873★ **Resumes for Health and Medical Careers**

4255 W. Touhy Ave.
Lincolnwood, IL 60646-1975
Ph: (708)679-5500   Fax: (708)679-6375
Fr: 800-323-4900

Compiled by VGM Career Horizons Staff 1995. $9.95 (paper).

EMPLOYMENT AGENCIES AND SEARCH FIRMS

★5874★ **Retail Recruiters/Spectrum Consultants, Inc.**

111 Presidential Blvd., Ste. 211
Bala Pointe
Bala Cynwyd, PA 19004
Ph: (610)667-6565   Fax: (610)667-5323

Employment agency. Affiliate offices in many locations across the country.

OTHER SOURCES

★5875★ American Academy of Optometry (AAO)
4330 East West Hwy., Ste. 1117
Bethesda, MD 20814-4408
Ph: (301)718-6500   Fax: (301)656-0989

Members: Professional society of optometrists, educators, and scientists interested in clinical practice standards, optometric education, and experimental research in visual problems. **Purpose:** Conducts postgraduate education for optometrists and physicians. **Activities:** Sponsors annual two-day postgraduate courses and three-day research and clinical papers program. Confers Diplomate status in five fields of optometric practice.

★5876★ American Almanac of Jobs and Salaries 1994-95
Avon Books
1350 Avenue of the Americas, 2nd Fl.
New York, NY 10019
Ph: (212)261-6800   Fr: 800-238-0658

John Wright. Revised edition, 1993. $17.00. 704 pages. This is a comprehensive guide to the wages of hundreds of occupations in a wide variety of industries and organizations.

★5877★ American Optometric Student Association (AOSA)
243 N. Lindbergh
St. Louis, MO 63141
Ph: (314)991-4100   Fax: (314)991-4101

Members: Optometric students, state optometric associations, and family members of optometric students. **Activities:** Collects updated information on progress in the optometry field. Provides members with opportunities to work in areas of health care need such as local community health projects, school curriculum changes, and health manpower legislation.

★5878★ National Association of Optometrists and Opticians (NAOO)
18903 S. Miles Rd.
Cleveland, OH 44128
Ph: (216)475-8925   Fax: (216)475-8862

Members: Licensed optometrists, opticians, and corporations. **Activities:** Conducts public affairs programs of mutual importance to members; serves as an organizational center for special purpose programs; acts as a clearinghouse for information affecting the retail optical industry.

★5879★ National Optometric Association (NOA)
4426 Cambridge Ct.
Bloomington, IN 47401
Ph: (812)855-4475   Fax: (812)855-7045

Members: Optometrists dedicated to increasing minority optometric manpower. **Activities:** Conducts research programs and national recruiting program. Maintains speakers' bureau. Offers specialized education program.

★5880★ Vision Educational Foundation (VEF)
PO Box 472305
Tulsa, OK 74147-2305
Ph: (918)762-3947   Fax: (918)451-9207

Members: Optometric doctors, ophthalmic laboratories, manufacturers, related technicians, and other professionals in the field. **Purpose:** To promote a long-range program of support to optometric educational institutions; to allow practicing optometrists opportunities to update and expand their clinical skills and keep abreast of new technology; to expose students to pathology cases; to provide access to the most advanced diagnostic equipment available. **Activities:** Provides referral services. Maintains VEF Educational and Diagnostic Center, which provides practicing optometrists and senior professional students of optometric colleges with clinical education of a diagnostic and therapeutic nature.

Personnel, Training, and Labor Relations Specialists and Managers

SOURCES OF HELP-WANTED ADS

★5881★ Business Insurance

Crain Communications, Inc.
740 N. Rush St.
Chicago, IL 60611-2590
Ph: (312)649-5311   Fax: (312)280-3189

Weekly. $80.00/year for individuals. Magazine for executives in the corporate risk, employee benefit, and finance fields.

★5882★ EMAnet

Employment Management Association (EMA)
4101 Lake Boone Tr., Ste. 201
Raleigh, NC 27607
Ph: (919)787-6010   Fax: (919)787-4916

Online database. Contains the following: *EMA Journal*, a magazine published four times a year; and *EMA Reporter*, a newsletter published three times a year. Provides listings of job opportunities and scholarships, an EMA member directory, as well as access to databases from the American Compensation Association and the Society for Human Resource Management.

★5883★ Human Resource Executive

Axon Magazine Group
747 Dresher Rd., Ste. 500
PO Box 980
Horsham, PA 19044
Ph: (215)784-0860   Fax: (215)784-0870

Monthly. $64.95/year for individuals; $109.00/year for other countries. Business magazine (tabloid) for human resource executives in corporations, non-profit organizations, and government agencies.

★5884★ PENSION Management

Argus Business
6151 Powers Ferry Rd.
Atlanta, GA 30339
Ph: (404)955-9970   Fax: (404)256-3116

Monthly. $68.00/year for individuals. Magazine on pension investment and fund administration.

★5885★ Pensions and Investments

Crain Communications, Inc.
220 E. 42nd St.
New York, NY 10017
Ph: (212)210-0259   Fax: (212)210-0499

Biweekly. $180.00/year. Magazine containing news and features on investment management, pension management, corporate finance, and cash management.

★5886★ Personnel Journal

ACC Communications, Inc.
245 Fischer Ave., B-2
Costa Mesa, CA 92626
Ph: (714)751-1883   Fax: (714)751-4106

Monthly. $59.00/year for individuals; $6.00 for single issue.

★5887★ Training & Development

American Society for Training and Development
1640 King St.
PO Box 1443
Alexandria, VA 22313
Ph: (703)683-8100   Fax: (703)683-8103

Monthly. $85.00/year for individuals. Magazine on training and development.

★5888★ Training Magazine

Adams Recreation Pub.
527 Marquette, Ste. 1300
Minneapolis, MN 55402
Ph: (612)342-2121   Fax: (612)342-2480
Fr: 800-923-2326

Monthly. $64.00/year for individuals; $74.00/year for Canada and Mexico; $85.00/year for other countries. Business magazine focusing on the impact of training on human performance and productivity in American organizations.

PLACEMENT AND JOB REFERRAL SERVICES

★5889★ American Society for Healthcare Human Resources Administration (ASHHRA)

1 N. Franklin
Chicago, IL 60606
Ph: (312)280-6722   Fax: (312)280-4152

Purpose: To provide effective and continuous leadership in the field of health care human resources administration; to promote cooperation with hospitals and allied associations in matters pertaining to hospital human resources administration; to further the professional and educational development of members; to encourage and promote research; to encourage and assist local groups in chapter formation through regular programs and institutes on health care human resources issues. **Activities:** Offers placement service.

★5890★ Association of Human Resource Systems Professionals (HRSP)

PO Box 801646
Dallas, TX 75380-1646
Ph: (214)661-3727   Fax: (214)386-8180

Members: Human resource, payroll, and data processing professionals; others concerned with the development, maintenance, and operation of automated human resource systems. **Purpose:** Provides a forum for exchanging experiences, acquiring information, and discussing common needs and problems relating to human resource systems. Works to enhance capabilities for effective and efficient human resource management. Conducts activities on the local level. **Activities:** Offers programs and job referral services. Operates resource center, member referral network, and vendor fairs.

★5891★ Employment Management Association (EMA)

4101 Lake Boone Tr., Ste. 201
Raleigh, NC 27607
Ph: (919)787-6010   Fax: (919)787-5302

Members: Employment and personnel executives in business, education, and industry;

individuals in organizations servicing the employment community. **Purpose:** Seeks to: investigate and recommend solutions to the personnel and employment problems facing American business; provide a forum for the exchange of ideas and information on these matters among members. Topics of discussion include employment, advertising, work force planning, organization development, job posting, outplacement, college recruiting, professional placement, human resources, affirmative action, management development, and job enrichment. **Activities:** Conducts advisory programs, surveys, and panels; operates member placement service. Special projects have included: participation in civic, professional, and legislative conferences and panels as a voice on employment matters. Maintains placement services; compiles statistics; sponsors charitable programs.

★5892★ **International Registry of Organization Development Professionals (IRODP)**

781 Beta Dr., Ste. K
Cleveland, OH 44143
Ph: (216)461-4333   Fax: (216)729-9319

Members: Organization development professionals, students, and persons interested in improving the way organizations function. **Purpose:** Promotes a better understanding of and disseminates information about organization development. **Activities:** Maintains placement service. Conducts specialized education.   **E-Mail:** aa563%cleveland,Freenet.edu@cunyvm

★5893★ **Organization Development Institute**

11234 Walnut Ridge Rd.
Chesterland, OH 44026
Ph: (216)461-4333   Fax: (216)729-9319

Members: Professionals, students, and individuals interested in organization development. Disseminates information on and promotes a better understanding of organization development worldwide. **Purpose:** Conducts specialized education programs. Has developed a code of ethics and a competency test for individuals wishing to qualify as a Registered Organization Development Consultant. Has developed a statement on the knowledge and skill necessary to be competent in organization development and criteria for the accreditation of OD/OB academic programs. **Activities:** Maintains job and consultant information   service.   **E-Mail:** aa563@Cleveland.Freenet.edu

---

EMPLOYER DIRECTORIES AND NETWORKING LISTS

★5894★ **College and University Personnel Association—Membership Directory**

College and University Personnel Association
1233 20th St. NW, Ste. 301
Washington, DC 20036
Ph: (202)429-0311   Fax: (202)429-0149

Annual, November. $150.00. Covers about 5,500 members interested in college and university personnel administration; over 1,700 institutions. Entries include: For members: personal name, title, affiliation, address, fax, e-mail, phone. For institutions: organization name, address, phone, and names/titles of representatives. Arrangement: Members are alphabetical; institutions are geographical.

★5895★ **Dun & Bradstreet Reference Book of Corporate Managements**

Dun & Bradstreet Information Services
Dun & Bradstreet Corp.
3 Sylvan Way
Parsippany, NJ 07054-3896
Ph: (201)605-6000   Fax: (201)605-6911
Fr: 800-526-0651

Annual, April. $785.00, lease basis; $635.00, for public libraries, lease basis. Covers nearly 200,000 presidents, directors, vice presidents, officers, and managers in 12,000 companies of greatest economic, marketing, and investment interests; those firms whose revenues are the highest in the United States. Arrangement: Alphabetical by company name. Indexes: Personal name (with abbreviated title and company affiliation), geographical, SIC code, advanced education institution, military affiliation.

★5896★ **Employment Marketplace Resource Directory**

Employment Marketplace
PO Box 31112
St. Louis, MO 63131
Ph: (314)569-3095

Irregular, latest edition 1993. $40.00, plus $4.00 shipping; payment must accompany order. Covers over 1,500 firms and organizations supplying information, products, or services to the personnel and employment industry, including recruitment advertising agencies; trainers and training consultants; publishers of databases, newsletters, directories, periodicals, books, and computer software; associations; job fair coordinators; incentive merchandise suppliers; clipping services; speakers; insurance firms; and testing/assessment/evaluation firms. Entries include: Company name, address, phone, name and title of contact, publications (if any), description, field of activity. Arrangement: Alphabetical. Indexes: Business or service.

★5897★ **Executive Search Consultants Directory**

American Business Directories, Inc.
American Business Information, Inc.
5711 S. 86th Cir.
Omaha, NE 68127
Ph: (402)593-4600   Fax: (402)331-1505

Annual. $460.00, payment with order. Entries include: Name, address, phone (including area code), size of advertisement, year first in Yellow Pages, name of owner or manager, number of employees. Compiled from telephone company Yellow Pages, nationwide. Arrangement: Geographical.

★5898★ **Hoover's Directory of Human Resources Executives 1996**

The Reference Press, Inc.
PO Box 140375
Austin, TX 78714-0375
Fax: (512)454-9401   Fr: 800-486-8666

1996. $39.95 (paper). Lists names of key hiring executives for over 5,000 companies. Includes company profiles.

★5899★ **Peterson's Job Opportunities in Business 1996**

Peterson's
PO Box 2123
Princeton, NJ 08543-2123
Ph: (609)243-9111   Fax: (609)243-9150
Fr: 800-338-3282

Compiled by the Peterson's staff. Annual. $19.95 (paper). 416 pages. Profiles 2,000 companies that are hiring employees in a number of nontechnical fields, including financial services, management consulting, retailers, utilities, and consumer products companies. Contains job-search strategies and career options to help match education and expertise to the job market. Indexed geographically, by industry, and by hiring needs.

★5900★ **Training and Development Organizations Directory**

Gale Research
835 Penobscot Bldg.
Detroit, MI 48226-4094
Ph: (313)961-2242   Fax: (313)961-6083
Fr: 800-877-GALE

Biennial, latest edition July 1994. $375.00. Covers more than 2,600 companies, institutes, graduate schools, consulting groups, and other organizations which conduct managerial and supervisory training courses for business, government, and individuals. Entries include: Organization name, address, phone, date founded, staff size and names of director and principal staff, subject or functional specialties, packaged training programs, fees, and details concerning courses or training offered. Arrangement: Classified by subject, then alphabetical. Indexes: Geographical, subject, personal name, organization name.

HANDBOOKS AND MANUALS

★5901★ Career Choices for the 90's for Students of Business

Walker and Company
435 Hudson St.
New York, NY 10014
Ph: (212)727-8300   Fax: (212)727-0984
Fr: 800-289-2553

Prepared by the Career Associates staff. 1990. $9.95. 166 pages. Discusses alternatives for students of business. Offers advice on how to break into the field and how to move up. Covers where and who the employers are, internship possibilities, and professional networking associations. Comprehensive guide to career and job search planning.

★5902★ Career Choices for the 90's for Students of Psychology

Walker and Company
435 Hudson St.
New York, NY 10014
Ph: (212)727-8300   Fax: (212)727-0984
Fr: 800-289-2553

Prepared by the Career Associates staff. 1990. $9.95. 166 pages. Discusses alternatives for students of psychology. Offers advice on how to break into the field and how to move up. Covers where and who the employers are, internship possibilities, and professional networking associations. Comprehensive guide to career and job search planning.

★5903★ Encyclopedia of Careers and Vocational Guidance

J. G. Ferguson Publishing Co.
200 W. Monroe, Ste. 250
Chicago, IL 60606
Ph: (312)580-5480

William E. Hopke. Ninth edition, 1993. $129.95; $199.95 (CD-ROM). Four-volume set that profiles 900 occupations and describes job trends in 71 industries. Includes career description, educational requirements, history of the job, methods of entry, advancement, employment outlook, earnings, conditions of work, social and psychological factors, and sources of further information. Contains career and employment information for this field.

★5904★ Liberal Arts Jobs: What They Are and How to Get Them

Peterson's
PO Box 2123
Princeton, NJ 08543-2123
Ph: (609)243-9111   Fax: (609)243-9150
Fr: 800-338-3282

Burton Jay Nadler. Second edition, 1989. $9.95. 153 pages. Presents a list of the top 20 fields for liberal arts majors, covering more than 300 job opportunities. Discusses strategies for going after those jobs, including guidance on the language of a successful job search, informational interviews, and making networking work.

★5905★ Opportunities in Hospital Administration Careers

VGM Career Horizons
4255 W. Touhy Ave.
Lincolnwood, IL 60646-1975
Ph: (847)679-5500   Fax: (847)679-2494
Fr: 800-323-4900

I. Donald Snook. 1989. $14.95; $11.95 (paper). 160 pages. Discusses opportunities for administrators in a variety of management settings: hospital, department, clinic, group practice, HMO, mental health, and extended care facilities.

★5906★ Opportunities in Hotel and Motel Careers

VGM Career Horizons
4255 W. Touhy Ave.
Lincolnwood, IL 60646-1975
Ph: (847)679-5500   Fax: (847)679-2494
Fr: 800-323-4900

Shepard Henkin. 1992. $14.95; $11.95 (paper). 160 pages. A guide to planning for and seeking opportunities in this growing field. Illustrated.

★5907★ Opportunities in Human Resources Management Careers

VGM Career Horizons
4255 W. Touhy Ave.
Lincolnwood, IL 60646-1975
Ph: (847)679-5500   Fax: (847)679-2494
Fr: 800-323-4900

William Traynor and J. Steven McKenzie. 1994. $14.95; $11.95 (paper). 160 pages. A guide to planning for and seeking opportunities in this growing field. Contains bibliography and illustrations.

★5908★ Opportunities in Insurance Careers

VGM Career Horizons
4255 W. Touhy Ave.
Lincolnwood, IL 60646-1975
Ph: (847)679-5500   Fax: (847)679-2494
Fr: 800-323-4900

Robert Schrayer. 1994. $14.95; $11.95 (paper). A guide to planning for and seeking opportunities in the field. Contains bibliography and illustrations.

★5909★ Opportunities in International Business Careers

VGM Career Horizons
4255 W. Touhy Ave.
Lincolnwood, IL 60646-1975
Ph: (847)679-5500   Fax: (847)679-2494
Fr: 800-323-4900

Jeffrey Arpan. 1995. $14.95; $11.95 (paper). 160 pages. Describes what types of jobs exist in international business, where they are located, what challenges and rewards they bring, and how to prepare for and obtain jobs in international business.

★5910★ Opportunities in Public Health Careers

VGM Career Horizons
4255 W. Touhy Ave.
Lincolnwood, IL 60646-1975
Ph: (847)679-5500   Fax: (847)679-2494
Fr: 800-323-4900

George E. Pickett and Terry W. Pickett. 1995. $14.95; $11.95 (paper). 160 pages. Defines the public health field and describes a variety of health, science, and business opportunities as well as educational preparation and the future of the public health field. Offers job-hunting tips. The appendixes list public health organizations, state and federal public health agencies, and graduate schools offering public health programs.

★5911★ Where the Jobs Are: The Hottest Careers for the '90s

The Career Press, Inc.
3 Tice Rd.
PO Box 687
Franklin Lakes, NJ 07417
Ph: (201)848-0310   Fax: (201)848-1727
Fr: 800-237-3371

Joyce Hadley. Second edition, 1995. $9.99. 300 pages. Describes careers in fifteen general fields, from accounting to travel and hospitality.

EMPLOYMENT AGENCIES AND SEARCH FIRMS

★5912★ Abbott Smith Associates, Inc.

PO Box 318
Franklin Ave.
Millbrook, NY 12545
Ph: (914)677-5300   Fax: (914)677-3315

Executive search firm. Affiliate offices in Chicago and London.

★5913★ Addington Personnel Services

2401 Fountainview, Ste.104
Houston, TX 77057
Ph: (713)780-8810

Employment agency. Places individuals in regular or temporary positions.

★5914★ B and M Associates, Inc.

199 Cambridge Rd.
Woburn, MA 01801-4705
Ph: (617)938-9120

Employment agency.

★5915★ Dankowski and Associates, Inc.

842 Corporate Way, Ste. 820
Cleveland, OH 44145
Ph: (216)892-2800

Executive search firm.

★5916★ Esquire Personnel Services, Inc.

222 S. Riverside Plaza, Ste. 320
Chicago, IL 60606-5804
Ph: (312)648-4600   Fax: (312)648-4637

Employment agency.

★5917★ Hayden and Associates, Inc.

7825 Washington Ave. S., Ste. 120
Minneapolis, MN 55439-2431
Ph: (612)941-6300   Fax: (612)941-9602

Employment agency. Executive search firm. Fills openings in a variety of fields.

★5918★ Karras Personnel, Inc.
2 Central Ave.
Madison, NJ 07940
Ph: (201)966-6800
Executive search firm.

★5919★ The Morris Group
PO Box 188
Bryn Mawr, PA 19010
Ph: (610)520-0100
Executive search firm.

★5920★ The Pathfinder Group
295 Danbury Rd.
Wilton, CT 06897-3095
Ph: (203)834-2467
Employment agency. Executive search firm. Recruits staff in a variety of fields.

★5921★ Protocol Inc.
300 N. Lake Ave., Ste. 208
Pasadena, CA 91101-4106
Ph: (818)449-2214   Fax: (818)577-0484
Executive search firm.

★5922★ Willmott and Associates
922 Waltham St., Ste. 103
Lexington, MA 02173
Ph: (617)863-5400   Fax: (617)863-8000
Executive search firm.

OTHER SOURCES

★5923★ American Almanac of Jobs and Salaries 1994-95
Avon Books
1350 Avenue of the Americas, 2nd Fl.
New York, NY 10019
Ph: (212)261-6800   Fr: 800-238-0658
John Wright. Revised edition, 1993. $17.00. 704 pages. This is a comprehensive guide to the wages of hundreds of occupations in a wide variety of industries and organizations.

★5924★ American Compensation Association (ACA)
14040 N. Northsight Blvd.
Scottsdale, AZ 85260
Ph: (602)951-9191   Fax: (602)483-8352
Purpose: Managerial, professional, and executive level administrative personnel in business, industry, and government who are responsible for the design, establishment, execution, administration, or application of total compensation practices (including benefits) and policies in their organizations. **Activities:** Conducts surveys, research, and certification program; confers Certified Compensation Professional (CCP) designation and Certified Benefits Professional (CBP) designation. Furthers the exchange of information on current practice and research in all phases of employee compensation including wages, salaries, pensions, group insurance, and other related forms of employee remuneration.

★5925★ American Society for Training and Development (ASTD)
Box 1443
1640 King St.
Alexandria, VA 22313
Ph: (703)683-8100   Fax: (703)683-8103
Purpose: Professional association for persons engaged in the training and development of business, industry, education, and government employees. Undertakes special research projects and acts as clearinghouse. Operates 3000 volume information center on human resource development. Maintains 18 committees, 15 networks, and 30 industry groups.

★5926★ Association of Management (AoM)
Rte. 17, George Washington Hwy.
PO Box 1301
Grafton, VA 23692-1301
Ph: (804)479-5363   Fax: (804)479-0656
Members: Academics and practitioners of management. **Purpose:** Seeks to align theory and practice in the study of human resource management, information and technology management, computer science, organizational studies, information systems, global health and ecology, transportation, travel and related technology, educational studies and research, management functions and applications, and multidisciplinary related issues. Encourages research in the fields. **E-Mail:** 72430,3710@compuserve.COM

★5927★ Association for Quality and Participation (AQP)
801-B W. 8th St., Ste. 501
Cincinnati, OH 45203-1601
Ph: (513)381-1959   Fax: (513)381-0070
Fr: 800-733-3310
Members: Quality managers, manufacturing executives, professionals in personnel relations, organization presidents, and employee involvement professionals such as training directors, facilitators, and coordinators. **Purpose:** Promotes quality and participation in the workplace by providing education, an information center, conferences, in-house training, publications, and other resources.

★5928★ Association of Training and Employment Professionals (ATEP)
56 Main St.
PO Box 636
Windsor Locks, CT 06096
Members: Professionals in federally funded employment and training programs at city, county, state, and federal levels; organizations in vocational and career education, labor, and business; colleges and universities. **Purpose:** Provides a meeting ground for professionals in the manpower field. Allows members to become better acquainted with, and updated on, the regulations, practices, and ideas at work in the field.

★5929★ College and University Personnel Association (CUPA)
1233 20th St. NW, Ste. 301
Washington, DC 20036-1250
Ph: (202)429-0311   Fax: (202)429-0149
Members: Professional organization made up of colleges and universities interested in

the improvement of campus Human Resource administration. **Activities:** Carries out special research projects and surveys, including annual administrative compensation survey for higher education. Sponsors training seminars to meet members' technical, professional, and developmental needs in human resource management. Disseminates information to members regarding federal legislation and regulations affecting higher education institutions. Compiles statistics.

★5930★ Human Resource Certification Institute (HRCI)
606 N. Washington St.
Alexandria, VA 22314
Ph: (703)548-3440   Fax: (703)836-0367
Purpose: Promotes the establishment of standards for the profession. Recognizes human resource professionals who have met, through demonstrated professional experience and the passing of a comprehensive written examination, the Institute's requirements for mastering the codified HR body of knowledge.

★5931★ Human Resource Planning Society (HRPS)
317 Madison Ave., Ste. 1509
New York, NY 10017
Ph: (212)490-6387   Fax: (212)682-6851
Members: Human resource planning professionals representing 160 corporations and 2500 individual members, including strategic human resources planning and development specialists, staffing analysts, business planners, line managers, and others who function as business partners in the application of strategic human resource management practices. **Purpose:** Seeks to increase the impact of human resource planning and management on business and organizational performance. **Activities:** Sponsors program of professional development in human resource planning concepts, techniques, and practices. Offers networking opportunities.

★5932★ Industrial Relations Research Association (IRRA)
4233 Social Science Bldg.
1180 Observatory Dr.
Madison, WI 53706
Ph: (608)262-2762   Fax: (608)265-4591
Purpose: Businesspersons, union leaders, government officials, lawyers, arbitrators, academics, and others interested in research and exchange of ideas on social, political, economic, legal, and psychological aspects of labor, including employer and employee organization, labor relations, personnel administration, social security, and labor legislation. Disseminates research results.

★5933★ International Personnel Management Association (IPMA)
1617 Duke St.
Alexandria, VA 22314
Ph: (703)549-7100   Fax: (703)684-0948
Members: Public personnel agencies; individuals, including personnel workers, consultants, and professors. **Purpose:** Seeks to improve personnel practices in government through provision of testing services, advisory service, conferences, professional devel-

opment programs, research, and publications. Sponsors seminars and workshops on various phases of public personnel administration. Compiles statistics.

★5934★ Organization Development Network (ODN)

76 S. Orange Ave., Ste. 101
South Orange, NJ 07079-1923
Ph: (201)763-7337   Fax: (201)763-7488

Purpose: Practitioners, academics, managers, and students employed or interested in organization development. Works to enhance and provide opportunities for colleagueship and professional development.

★5935★ Society for Human Resource Management (SHRM)

606 N. Washington St.
Alexandria, VA 22314
Ph: (703)548-3440   Fax: (703)836-0367
Fr: 800-283-7476

Members: Professional organization of human resource, personnel, and industrial relations professionals and executives. **Purpose:** Promotes the advancement of human resource management. **Activities:** Sponsors SHRM Foundation. Offers certification through the Human Resource Certification Institute.

Petroleum Engineers

★5936★ *AEG News*

Association of Engineering Geologists
323 Boston Post Rd., Ste. 2D
Sudbury, MA 01776
Ph: (508)443-4639

Quarterly. Included in membership; $20.00/year for nonmembers. Covers news of the engineering geology profession.

★5937★ *Captsule Job Listings*

Publications and Communications, Inc.
12416 Hymeadow Dr.
Austin, TX 78750
Ph: (512)250-9023   Fax: (512)331-3900
Fr: 800-678-9724

Online database. Lists current job openings in the contract (temporary) technical services industry. Includes the Action Hot List, which provides information on job seekers. Includes employment opportunities in technical/professional engineering, computing, and design/drafting. Entries generally contain company name, address, and job opening.

★5938★ *Diesel and Gas Turbine Worldwide*

Diesel and Gas Turbine Publications
13555 Bishop's Ct.
Brookfield, WI 53005-6286
Ph: (414)784-9177   Fax: (414)784-8133
Fr: 800-558-4322

Monthly. International magazine covering the design, application, and operation of diesel, natural gas, and gas turbine engine systems.

★5939★ *Energy User News*

Chilton Publications
825 7th Ave.
New York, NY 10019
Ph: (212)887-8400   Fax: (212)887-8484

Monthly. Magazine exploring industrial and commercial energy efficiency markets and strategies.

★5940★ *Engineering Times*

National Society of Professional Engineers
1420 King St.
Alexandria, VA 22314
Ph: (703)684-2875   Fax: (703)836-4875

Monthly. Magazine (tabloid) covering professional, legislative, and techology issues for an engineering audience.

★5941★ *ENR: Engineering News Record*

New York Construction News
1221 Avenue of the Americas
New York, NY 10020
Ph: (212)512-4773   Fax: (212)512-4770

Weekly. $42.00/year; $2.00/issue.

★5942★ *Fueloil and Oil Heat Magazine*

SA Industry Publications
389 Passaic Ave.
Fairfield, NJ 07004
Ph: (201)227-5151   Fax: (201)227-9219

Free to qualified subscribers; $20.00/year for individuals; $30.00/year for Canada and Mexico; $75.00/year for other countries. Trade magazine covering energy systems and fueloil handling.

★5943★ *Gas Turbine World*

Pequot Publishing, Inc.
PO Box 447
Southport, CT 06490-0447
Ph: (203)259-1812

Bimonthly. Magazine containing technical and business information on the design application, operation, and maintenance of power plants for electrical generation, mechanical drive, oil and gas production and transmission, industrial process, CHP, and DHC applications.

★5944★ *High Technology Careers Magazine*

HTC
4701 Patrick Henry Dr., No. 1901
Santa Clara, CA 95054
Ph: (408)970-8800   Fax: (408)980-5103

Bimonthly. Magazine (tabloid) containing employment opportunity information for the engineering and technical community.

★5945★ *Minority Engineer*

Equal Opportunity Publications, Inc.
150 Motor Pkwy., Ste. 420
Hauppauge, NY 11788-5145
Ph: (516)273-0066   Fax: (516)273-8936

Affirmative-action recruitment magazine serving college graduating and professional minority engineers.

★5946★ *National Engineer*

National Association of Power Engineers
1 Springfield St.
Chicopee, MA 01013-2624
Ph: (413)592-6273   Fax: (413)592-1998

Monthly. $23.40/year for individuals; $2.50 for single issue.

★5947★ *NSBE Magazine*

NSBE Publications
1454 Duke St.
Alexandria, VA 22314
Ph: (703)549-2207   Fax: (703)683-5312

$10.00/year for individuals; $2.00 for single issue. Journal providing information on engineering careers, self-development, and cultural issues for recent graduates with technical majors.

★5948★ *Offshore*

PennWell Publishing Co.
3050 Post Oak Blvd., Ste. 200
Houston, TX 77056
Ph: (713)621-9720   Fax: (713)963-6285

Monthly. Magazine for petroleum industry covering marine operations, engineering, and technology.

★5949★ *Oil and Gas Journal*

PennWell Publishing Co.
3050 Post Oak Blvd., Ste. 200
Houston, TX 77056
Ph: (713)621-9720   Fax: (713)963-6285

Weekly. Trade magazine serving engineers and managers in international petroleum operations.

★5950★ Petroleum Engineer International

Hart's Oil and Gas World
4545 Post Oak Pl., Ste. 210
Houston, TX 77027
Ph: (713)993-9320   Fax: (713)840-8585

Trade magazine on drilling for oil and gas, on and offshore.

★5951★ Petroleum Management

Management Publishing Services
PO Box 55829
Houston, TX 77255-5829
Ph: (713)789-7887   Fax: (713)789-0742

Monthly. Trade magazine.

★5952★ SWE

Society of Women Engineers
120 Wall St., 11th Fl.
New York, NY 10005-3902
Ph: (212)509-9577   Fax: (212)509-0224

Bimonthly. $30.00/year for nonmembers. Magazine for engineering students and for women and men working in the engineering and technology fields. Covers career guidance, continuing development and topical issues.

★5953★ Technology Review

The Tech
PO Box 397029
Cambridge, MA 02139
Ph: (617)253-1541   Fax: (617)258-8226

$30.00/year for individuals; $3.75 for single issue; $42.00/year for other countries. Magazine reviewing new developments in technology with an emphasis on economic, political, and social implications. Not a new product publication.

★5954★ Woman Engineer

Equal Opportunity Publications, Inc.
150 Motor Pkwy., Ste. 420
Hauppauge, NY 11788-5145
Ph: (516)273-0066   Fax: (516)273-8936

Engineer recruitment magazine.

★5955★ World Oil

Gulf Publishing Co.
3301 Allen Pkwy.
PO Box 2608
Houston, TX 77252-2608
Ph: (713)529-4301   Fax: (713)520-4433

Monthly. Trade magazine on oil and gas exploration, drilling, and production.

PLACEMENT AND JOB REFERRAL SERVICES

★5956★ American Association of Blacks in Energy (AABE)

927 15th St. NW, Ste. 200
Washington, DC 20005
Ph: (202)371-9530   Fax: (202)371-9218

Members: Blacks in energy-related professions, including engineers, scientists, consultants, academicians, and entrepreneurs; government officials and public policymakers; interested students. **Purpose:** Represents blacks and other minorities in matters involving energy use and research, the formulation of energy policy, the ownership of energy resources, and the development of energy technologies. Seeks to increase the knowledge, understanding, and awareness of the minority community inenergy issues by serving as an energy information source for policymakers, recommending blacks and other minorities to appropriate energy officials and executives, encouraging students to pursue professional careers in the energy industry, and advocating the participation of blacks and other minorities in energy programs and policymaking activities. Updates members on key legislation and regulations being developed by the Department of Energy, the Department of Interior, the Department of Commerce, the Small Business Administration, and other federal and state agencies. **Activities:** Offers information on current job openings.

★5957★ American Indian Science and Engineering Society (AISES)

1630 30th St., Ste. 301
Boulder, CO 80301
Ph: (303)492-8658   Fax: (303)492-3400

Members: American Indian and non-Indian students and professionals in science, technology, and engineering fields; corporations representing energy, mining, aerospace, electronic, and computer fields. **Purpose:** Seeks to motivate and encourage students to pursue undergraduate and graduate studies in science, engineering, and technology. **Activities:** Sponsors science fairs in grade schools, teacher training workshops, summer math/science sessions for 8th-12th graders, professional chapters, and student chapters in colleges. Offers scholarships. Adult members serve as role models, advisers, and mentors for students. Operates placement service. **E-Mail:** aise sha@spot.colorado.edu

★5958★ Association for Women Geoscientists (AWG)

4779 126th St. N
White Bear Lake, MN 55110-5910
Ph: (612)426-3316   Fax: (612)426-5449

Members: Men and women geologists, geophysicists, petroleum engineers, geological engineers, hydrogeologists, paleontologists, geochemists, and other geoscientists. **Purpose:** Aims to: encourage the participation of women in the geosciences; exchange educational, technical, and professional information; enhance the professional growth and advancement of women in the geosciences. **Activities:** Provides information on opportunities and careers available to women in the geosciences. Maintains career profiles of women geoscientists, and Association for Women Geoscientists Foundation (educational arm).

★5959★ Engineering Society of Detroit (ESD)

100 Farnsworth Ave.
Detroit, MI 48202
Ph: (313)832-5400   Fax: (313)832-5920

Members: Engineers from all disciplines; scientists and technologists. **Activities:** Offers placement services. Conducts technical programs and engineering refresher courses; sponsors conferences and expositions. Maintains speakers' bureau. Although based in Detroit, MI, society membership is international.

★5960★ Korean Scientists and Engineers Association in America (KSEA)

6261 Executive Blvd.
Rockville, MD 20852
Ph: (301)984-7048   Fax: (301)984-1231

Members: Scientists and engineers holding single or advanced degrees. **Purpose:** Goals are to: promote friendship and mutuality among Korean and American scientists and engineers; contribute to Korea's scientific, technological, industrial, and economic developments; strengthen the scientific, technological, and cultural bonds between Korea and the U.S. Sponsors symposium. **Activities:** Maintains speakers' bureau, placement service, and biographical archives. Compiles statistics. Maintains 100 volume library of scientific handbooks and yearbooks in Korean.

★5961★ Society of Hispanic Professional Engineers (SHPE)

5400 E. Olympic Blvd., Ste. 210
Los Angeles, CA 90022
Ph: (213)725-3970

Purpose: Engineers, student engineers, and scientists seeking to increase the number of Hispanic engineers by providing motivation and support to students. Sponsors competitions and educational programs. **Activities:** Maintains placement service and speakers' bureau; compiles statistics.

★5962★ Society of Petroleum Engineers (SPE)

PO Box 833836
Richardson, TX 75083-3836
Ph: (214)952-9393   Fax: (214)952-9435

Members: Worldwide professional society of engineers in the field of petroleum engineering. **Activities:** Offers placement service. Conducts videotape courses, continuing education short courses, and distinguished lecturer program; sponsors contests.

EMPLOYER DIRECTORIES AND NETWORKING LISTS

★5963★ American Men and Women of Science

R. R. Bowker Co.
Reed Reference Publishing
121 Chanlon Rd.
New Providence, NJ 07974
Ph: (908)464-6800   Fax: (908)665-6688
Fr: 800-521-8110

Triennial, latest edition January 1995. $106.00, per volume; $850.00, set. Covers over 123,000 U.S. and Canadian scientists active in the physical, biological, mathematical, computer science, and engineering fields; includes references to previous edition for deceased scientists and nonrespondents. Entries include: Name, address, education, personal and career data, memberships, honors and awards, research interest. Arrangement: Alphabetical. Indexes: Discipline (in separate volume).

★5964★ **Directory of Certified Petroleum Geologists**
American Association of Petroleum Geologists
Box 979
Tulsa, OK 74101-0979
Ph: (918)584-2555   Fax: (918)584-0469

Biennial, February of even years. $25.00, postpaid. Covers about 3,900 members of the association. Entries include: Name, address; education and career data; whether available for consulting. Arrangement: Alphabetical. Indexes: Geographical.

★5965★ **Directory of Contract Service Firms**
C. E. Publications, Inc.
PO Box 97000
Kirkland, WA 98083
Ph: (206)823-2222   Fax: (206)821-0942

Annual, January. $10.00. Covers Approximately 900 contract firms actively engaged in the employment of engineering and technical personnel for temporary contract assignments throughout the world. Entries include: Company name, address, phone, name of contact. Arrangement: Alphabetical. Indexes: Geographical.

★5966★ **Directory of Engineering Societies and Related Organizations**
American Association of Engineering Societies
1111 19th St. NW, Ste. 608
Washington, DC 20036
Ph: (202)296-2237   Fax: (202)296-1151
Fr: 800-658-8897

1992. $185.00. Lists 1,000 national, regional, Canadian, and international organizations concerned with engineering and related fields.

★5967★ **Directory of Engineers in Private Practice**
National Society of Professional Engineers
1420 King St.
Alexandria, VA 22314
Ph: (703)684-2862   Fax: (703)836-4875

Annual. $85.00. Covers 600 consulting engineering firms and 7,200 individuals who are members of the society's Professional Engineers in Private Practice division. Entries include: For companies, name, address, phone, name of principal executive, list of services. For individuals, name, address; most listings include phone. Arrangement: Firms are geographic, then by specialty; individuals are alphabetical.

★5968★ **Directory of Foreign Manufacturers in the United States**
Georgia State University Business Press
College of Business Administration
University Plaza
Atlanta, GA 30303-3093
Ph: (404)651-4253   Fax: (404)651-4256

Biennial, odd years. $195.00, payment must accompany orders from individuals. Covers over 7,300 United States manufacturing, mining, and petroleum companies, and the over 6,800 firms abroad that own them. Entries include: Company name, address, phone, fax, products or services, Standard Industrial Classification (SIC) codes, parent company name and address. Arrangement: Alphabetical by U.S. company name. Indexes: U.S. subsidiary location, foreign company name, geographical (foreign company location), product.

★5969★ **Engineering Research Centres**
Stockton Press
Groves Dictionaries
345 Park Ave. S., 10th Fl.
New York, NY 10010
Ph: (212)689-9200   Fr: 800-221-2123

Fourth edition, 1995. $515.00. 768 pages. Contains over 8,000 entries describing research and technology laboratories in over 70 countries. Provides details on industrial research centers and educational establishments with research and development activity. Indexes: Subject and title of establishments.

★5970★ **Geophysical Directory**
Geophysical Directory, Inc.
PO Box 130508
Houston, TX 77219
Ph: (713)529-8789   Fax: (713)529-3646
Fr: 800-929-2462

Annual, March. $50.00, postpaid. Covers about 3,600 companies that provide geophysical equipment, supplies, or services, and mining and petroleum companies that use geophysical techniques; international coverage. Entries include: Company name, address, phone, names of principal executives, operations, and sales personnel; similar information for branch locations. Arrangement: Classified by product or service. Indexes: Company name, personal name.

★5971★ **Oil & Gas Directory**
Geophysical Directory, Inc.
PO Box 130508
Houston, TX 77219
Ph: (713)529-8789   Fax: (713)529-3646
Fr: 800-929-2462

Annual, October. $65.00, postpaid. Covers about 5,200 companies worldwide involved in petroleum exploration, drilling, and production, and suppliers to the industry. Entries include: Company name, address, phone, telex, names of principal personnel, branch office addresses, phone numbers, and key personnel. Arrangement: Classified by activity. Indexes: Company name, personal name.

★5972★ **Peterson's Job Opportunities in Engineering and Technology 1996**
Peterson's
PO Box 2123
Princeton, NJ 08543-2123
Ph: (609)243-9111   Fax: (609)243-9150
Fr: 800-338-3282

Compiled by the Peterson's staff. Annual. $19.95 paperback. 432 pages. Profiles 2,000 high-tech companies looking primarily for technical personnel in such fields as biotechnology, telecommunications, software, computers and peripherals, defense, and aerospace. Contains job-search strategies and career options to help match education and expertise to the job market. Indexed geographically, by industry, and by hiring needs.

★5973★ **Scientific and Technical Organizations and Agencies Directory**
Gale Research
835 Penobscot Bldg.
Detroit, MI 48226-4094
Ph: (313)961-2242   Fax: (313)961-6083
Fr: 800-877-GALE

Irregular; latest edition December 1993. $195.00. Covers over 25,600 national and international organizations and agencies concerned with the physical and applied sciences, engineering, and technology, including associations, computer information services, consulting firms, educational institutions, foundations, government advisory organizations, federal government agencies, general grant and assistance programs, libraries and information centers, patent sources and services, research and development centers, scholarships, fellowships, and loans, science-technology centers, standards organizations, state academies of science, and state government agencies in the fields of aeronautics and space sciences, chemistry, computer science specialties, electronics, geography, geology, machinery, mathematics, metallurgy, meteorology, mineralogy, nuclear science, petroleum and gas, physics, plastics, transportation, water resources, and other areas. Entries include: Organization name, address, phone, and name of contact; additional descriptive text for most entries. Arrangement: Classified by type of organization. Indexes: Organization name/key word.

★5974★ **Who's Who in Technology**
Gale Research
835 Penobscot Bldg.
Detroit, MI 48226-4094
Ph: (313)961-2242   Fax: (313)961-6083
Fr: 800-877-GALE

Irregular, new edition expected June 1995. $380.00. Covers 38,000 engineers, scientists, inventors, and researchers. Entries include: Name, title, affiliation, address; personal, education, and career data; publications, patents; technical field of activity; area of expertise. Arrangement: Alphabetical. Indexes: Geographical, employer, technical discipline, expertise.

HANDBOOKS AND MANUALS

★5975★ The Best Resumes for Scientists and Engineers

John Wiley and Sons
605 3rd Ave.
New York, NY 10158
Ph: (212)850-6000   Fr: 800-225-5945

Adele Lewis. Second edition, 1993. $37.50; $14.95 (paper). Presents an extensive collection of scientific and engineering resumes, highlighting the important differences between these and resumes written for other occupations.

★5976★ Career Information Center

Macmillan Publishing Co.
200 Old Tappan Rd.
Old Tappan, NJ 07675
Ph: (609)461-6500   Fr: 800-223-2336

Visual Education Center Staff. Fifth edition, 1992. $229.00. This 13-volume set profiles over 600 occupations. Each occupational profile describes job duties, educational requirements, how to get the job, advancement possibilities, employment outlook, working conditions, earnings and benefits, and where to write for more information.

★5977★ Careers in Engineering

VGM Career Horizons
4255 W. Touhy Ave.
Lincolnwood, IL 60646-1975
Ph: (847)679-5500   Fax: (847)679-2494
Fr: 800-323-4900

Geraldine O. Gardner. 1994. $17.95; $13.95 (paper). Covers careers in the public or private sector, in industry, the university, or the military, from applications in computer architecture design to high temperature ceramics.

★5978★ Encyclopedia of Careers and Vocational Guidance

J. G. Ferguson Publishing Co.
200 W. Monroe, Ste. 250
Chicago, IL 60606
Ph: (312)580-5480

William E. Hopke. Ninth edition, 1993. $129.95; $199.95 (CD-ROM). Four-volume set that profiles 900 occupations and describes job trends in 71 industries. Includes career description, educational requirements, history of the job, methods of entry, advancement, employment outlook, earnings, conditions of work, social and psychological factors, and sources of further information. Contains career and employment information for this field.

★5979★ Engineering Success

Kendall Hunt Publishing
4050 Westmark Dr.
PO Box 1840
Dubuque, IA 52004-1840
Ph: (319)589-1000   Fax: 800-772-9165
Fr: 800-228-0810

Bill Osher. 1994. $27.96.

★5980★ Engineering Your Job Search: A Job-Finding Resource for Engineering Professionals

Professional Publications, Inc.
1250 5th Ave.
Belmont, CA 94002
Ph: (415)593-9119   Fax: (415)592-4519
Fr: 800-426-1178

Compiled by Professional Publications editors. 1995. $12.95 (paper).

★5981★ Introduction to the Engineering Profession

HarperCollins Publishers, Inc.
10 E. 53rd. St.
New York, NY 10022-5299
Ph: (212)207-7000   Fax: (212)207-7145
Fr: 800-331-3761

David M. Burghardt. 1995. $30.00 (paper).

★5982★ Job Opportunities in Engineering and Technology

Peterson's Guides, Inc.
PO Box 2123
Princeton, NJ 08543-2123
Ph: (609)243-9111   Fax: (609)243-9150
Fr: 800-338-3282

1994. $18.95 (paper).

★5983★ Majoring in Engineering: How to Get from Your Freshman Year to Your First Job

Farrar, Straus & Giroux, Inc.
19 Union Sq., W
New York, NY 10003
Ph: (212)741-6900   Fr: 800-788-6262

John Garcia. 1995. $20.00; $10.00 (paper).

★5984★ Opportunities in Energy Careers

VGM Career Horizons
4255 W. Touhy Ave.
Lincolnwood, IL 60646-1975
Ph: (847)679-5500   Fax: (847)679-2494
Fr: 800-323-4900

John Woodburn. 1992. $13.95; $10.95 (paper). 160 pages. Discusses opportunities in a variety of fields, including petroleum, nuclear, and thermal energy, and how to pursue employment. Illustrated.

★5985★ Opportunities in Engineering Careers

VGM Career Horizons
4255 W. Touhy Ave.
Lincolnwood, IL 60646-1975
Ph: (847)679-5500   Fax: (847)679-2494
Fr: 800-323-4900

Nicholas Basta. 1995. $14.95; $11.95 (paper). Outlines typical job titles, salaries, career paths, and employment prospects.

★5986★ Opportunities in Petroleum Careers

VGM Career Horizons
4255 W. Touhy Ave.
Lincolnwood, IL 60646-1975
Ph: (847)679-5500   Fax: (847)679-2494
Fr: 800-323-4900

Gretchen Krueger. 1990. $14.95; $11.95 (paper). Outlines jobs in looking for oil; drilling and producing oil; and transporting, refining, and marketing oil. Discusses job seeking, opportunities for advancement, and employment outlook.

★5987★ Resumes for Engineering Careers

VGM Career Horizons
NTC Publishing Group
4255 W. Touhy Ave.
Lincolnwood, IL 60646-1975
Ph: (847)679-5500   Fax: (847)679-2494
Fr: 800-323-4900

1994. $9.95. 160 pages. Contains sample resumes and cover letters applicable to any engineering field.

EMPLOYMENT AGENCIES AND SEARCH FIRMS

★5988★ ABC Employment Service

25 S. Bemiston, Ste. 214
Clayton, MO 63105
Ph: (314)725-3140

Employment agency.

★5989★ B W and Associates, Inc.

4415 W. Harrison St.
Hillside, IL 60162-1910
Ph: (708)449-5400

Employment agency.

★5990★ Channel Personnel Services, Inc.

7007 Gulf Fwy., Ste. 214
Houston, TX 77087-2540
Ph: (713)643-8001

Executive search firm.

★5991★ Engineer One, Inc.

10124 Dutchtown Rd.
Knoxville, TN 37932-2611
Ph: (615)690-2611   Fax: (615)690-2611

Employment agency.

★5992★ Hayden and Associates, Inc.

7825 Washington Ave. S., Ste. 120
Minneapolis, MN 55439-2431
Ph: (612)941-6300   Fax: (612)941-9602

Employment agency. Executive search firm. Fills openings in a variety of fields.

★5993★ International Staffing Consultants

500 Newport Center Dr., Ste. 300
Newport Beach, CA 92660-7003
Ph: (714)721-7990

Employment agency. Provides placement on regular or temporary basis. Affiliate office in London.

★5994★ The Jobs Co.

8900 E. Sprague Ave.
Spokane, WA 99212-2927
Ph: (509)928-3151   Fax: (509)928-3168

Employment agency. Has division specializing in engineering and scientific openings.

Also operates division specializing in sales openings.

★5995★ JR Professional Search

PO Box 18356
Tucson, AZ 85731
Ph: (520)721-1855   Fax: (520)721-1855

Employment agency.

★5996★ Main Line Personnel Service, Inc.

401 City Ave.
Bala Cynwyd, PA 19004-1122
Ph: (610)667-1820

Employment agency.

★5997★ Search and Recruit International

4455 South Blvd.
Virginia Beach, VA 23452
Ph: (804)490-3151

Employment agency. Headquartered in Virginia Beach. Other offices in Bremerton, WA; Charleston, SC; Jacksonville, FL; Memphis, TN; Pensacola, FL; Sacramento, CA; San Bernardino, CA; San Diego, CA.

★5998★ Sierra Technology Corporation

4150 Manzanita Ave., Ste. 100
Carmichael, CA 95608-1700
Ph: (916)488-4960   Fax: (916)488-7058

Employment agency. Provides placement on a temporary basis.

★5999★ Source Engineering

5580 LBJ Fwy., Ste. 300
Dallas, TX 75240
Ph: (214)385-3002   Fax: (214)717-0075

Executive search firm. Many affiliate offices located throughout the U.S.

OTHER SOURCES

★6000★ American Association of Engineering Societies (AAES)

1111 19th St. NW, Ste. 608
Washington, DC 20036
Ph: (202)296-2237   Fax: (202)296-1151

Purpose: Seeks to promote leadership in public affairs for the engineering community, work in support of math and science education for young persons. Disseminates of information about the profession. Provides statistics about engineers.

★6001★ Association for International Practical Training (AIPT)

10400 Little Patuxent Pky. Ste. 250
Columbia, MD 21044
Ph: (410)997-2200   Fax: (410)992-3924

Purpose: Helps coordinate training around the world in fields such as travel, the culinary arts, and hotel management. **Activities:** Conducts programs in career development and hospitality/tourism exchanges. Operates a student exchange program. Provides reciprocal practical training experience for recent graduates from the U.S., Austria, Germany, Finland, France, Hungary, Ireland, Japan, Malaysia, Netherlands, Switzerland, and the United Kingdom. Arranges training programs in the U.S. and abroad. Serves as U.S. affiliate to IAESTE (International Association for the Exchange of Students for Technical Experience) and operates a Professional Visitors Program to arrange short-term educational and training visits to the U.S. **E-Mail:** aipt@aipt.org

★6002★ Engineering Salary Survey

Source Engineering
1290 Oakmead, Ste. 318
Sunnyvale, CA 94086
Ph: (408)738-8440

Annual. Discusses the structure of the engineering profession, trends, and compensation. Salaries are listed by job function, industry, and years of experience.

★6003★ Graduating Engineer

Peterson's/COG Publishing Group
16030 Ventura Blvd., No. 560
Encino, CA 91436
Ph: (818)789-5293

Eight issues/year. Magazine focusing on employment, education, and career development for entry-level engineers.

★6004★ National Action Council for Minorities in Engineering (NACME)

3 W. 35th St.
New York, NY 10001-2281
Ph: (212)279-2626   Fax: (212)629-5178

Purpose: Seeks to increase the number of African American, Latino, and Native American students enrolled in and graduating from engineering schools. Through the Corporate Scholars Program, offers comprehensive scholarships to engineering students that include leadership development, corporate mentors and summer internships. Works with local, regional, and national education organizations to motivate and encourage precollege students to engage in engineering careers. Conducts educational and research programs; operates project to assist engineering schools in improving the retention and graduation rates of minority students. Maintains speakers' bureau; compiles statistics.

★6005★ National Society of Professional Engineers (NSPE)

1420 King St.
Alexandria, VA 22314
Ph: (703)684-2800   Fax: (703)836-4875

Members: Professional engineers and engineers-in-training in all fields registered in accordance with the laws of states or territories of the U.S. or provinces of Canada; qualified graduate engineers, student members, and registered land surveyors. **Purpose:** Is concerned with social, professional, ethical, and economic considerations of engineering as a profession; encompasses programs in public relations, employment practices, ethical considerations, education, and career guidance. Monitors legislative and regulatory actions of interest to the engineering profession. **Website:** http://www.hspc.org

★6006★ Salaries of Scientists, Engineers, and Technicians: A Summary of Salary Surveys

Commission on Professionals in Science and Technology (CPST)
1500 Massachusetts Ave. NW, Ste. 831
Washington, DC 20005
Ph: (202)223-6995

1993.

★6007★ Society of Women Engineers (SWE)

120 Wall St., 11th Fl.
New York, NY 10005
Ph: (212)509-9577   Fax: (212)509-0224

Members: Educational service society of women engineers; membership is also open to men. **Purpose:** Supplies information on the achievements of women engineers and the opportunities available to them; assists women engineers in preparing for return to active work following temporary retirement. Serves as an informational center on women in engineering. **Activities:** Administers several certificate and scholarship programs. Offers tours and career guidance; conducts surveys. Compiles statistics.

Pharmacists

PLACEMENT AND JOB REFERRAL SERVICES

★6019★ American Academy of Clinical Toxicology (AACT)

Pittsburgh Poison Center
3705 5th Ave.
Pittsburgh, PA 15213
Ph: (412)692-6669   Fax: (412)692-7497

Members: Physicians, veterinarians, pharmacists, research scientists, and analytical chemists. **Purpose:** Objectives are to: unite medical scientists and facilitate the exchange of information; encourage the development of therapeutic methods and technology; establish a mechanism for the certification of medical scientists in clinical toxicology. **Activities:** Conducts professional training in poison information and emergency service personnel. Maintains placement services. **E-Mail:** Internet, krenzee@chplink.chp.edu

★6020★ American Association of Pharmaceutical Scientists (AAPS)

1650 King St.
Alexandria, VA 22314-2747
Ph: (703)548-3000   Fax: (703)684-7349

Members: Pharmaceutical scientists. **Purpose:** Provides a forum for exchange of scientific information; serves as a resource in forming public policies to regulate pharmaceutical sciences and related issues of public concern. Promotes pharmaceutical sciences and provides for recognition of individual achievement; works to foster career growth and the development of members. **Activities:** Offers placement service.

★6021★ **American College of Clinical Pharmacy (ACCP)**

3101 Broadway, Ste. 380
Kansas City, MO 64111
Ph: (816)531-2177   Fax: (816)531-4990

Members: Clinical pharmacists dedicated to: promoting rational use of drugs in society; advancing the practice of clinical pharmacy and interdisciplinary health care; assuring high quality clinical pharmacy by establishing and maintaining standards in education and training at advanced levels. **Purpose:** Encourages research and recognizes excellence in clinical pharmacy. Offers educational programs, symposia, research forums, fellowship training, and college-funded grants through competitions. **Activities:** Maintains placement service.

★6022★ **American Public Health Association (APHA)**

1015 15th St. NW
Washington, DC 20005
Ph: (202)789-5600   Fax: (202)789-5681

Members: Professional organization of physicians, nurses, educators, academicians, environmentalists, epidemiologists, new professionals, social workers, health administrators, optometrists, podiatrists, pharmacists, dentists, nutritionists, health planners, other community and mental health specialists, and interested consumers. **Purpose:** Seeks to protect and promote personal, mental, and environmental health. **Activities:** Services include: promulgation of standards; establishment of uniform practices and procedures; development of the etiology of communicable diseases; research in public health; exploration of medical care programs and their relationships to public health. Sponsors job placement service.

★6023★ **American Society of Consultant Pharmacists (ASCP)**

1321 Duke St.
Alexandria, VA 22314-3563
Ph: (703)739-1300   Fax: (703)739-1321

Members: Registered pharmacists and educators who are largely concerned with pharmaceutical procedures within nursing homes and related health facilities. **Purpose:** Works to: improve consultant pharmacist services to nursing homes and other long-term care facilities; define professional standards and to promote the certification of the profession; exchange information; sponsor and encourage the development of educational facilities and courses for the advancement of the profession; promote wider public information efforts; represent the interests of the profession before legislative and administrative branches of government. **Activities:** Operates placement service. Conducts surveys of long-term care pharmacy operations.

★6024★ **American Society of Hospital Pharmacists (ASHP)**

7272 Wisconsin Ave.
Bethesda, MD 20814
Ph: (301)657-3000   Fax: (301)652-8278

Members: Professional society of pharmacists employed by hospitals, HMOs, clinics, and other health systems. PUR Provides personnel placement service for members;

sponsors professional and personal liability program. Conducts educational and exhibit programs. Has 30 practice interest areas, special sections for home care practitioners and clinical specialists, and research and education foundation.

EMPLOYER DIRECTORIES AND NETWORKING LISTS

★6025★ *AHA Guide to the Health Care Field*

Health Statistics Group
American Hospital Association (AHA)
1 N. Franklin
Chicago, IL 60606
Ph: (312)422-3501   Fax: (312)280-6015

Annual, July. $195.00, payment with order. Covers hospitals, multi-health care systems, freestanding ambulatory surgery centers, psychiatric facilities, long-term care facilities, substance abuse programs, hospices, Health Maintenance Organizations (HMOs), and other health-related organizations. Entries include: For hospitals: facility name, address, phone, administrator's name, number of beds, facilities and services, number of employees, expenses, other statistics. For other organizations: name, address, phone, name and title of contact. Arrangement: Geographical. Indexes: Hospital name.

★6026★ *Directory of Drug Store & HBC Chains*

Chain Store Guide Information Services
3922 Coconut Palm Dr.
Tampa, FL 33619
Ph: (813)664-6868   Fax: (813)664-6810
Fr: 800-925-2288

Annual, November. $290.00. Covers drug store chains operating two or more units; mass merchants with pharmacies; and wholesale drug companies. Arrangement: Separate geographical sections for chains and wholesalers.

★6027★ *Directory of Hospital Personnel*

Medical Economics
5 Paragon Dr.
Montvale, NJ 07645-1725
Ph: (201)358-7500   Fax: (201)573-4956
Fr: 800-222-3045

Annual, September. $325.00, plus 7.50 shipping. Covers 200,000 executives at 7,100 U.S. hospitals. Entries include: Name of hospital, address, phone, number of beds, type and JCAHO status of hospital, names and titles of key department heads and staff, medical and nursing school affiliations; number of residents, interns, and nursing students. Arrangement: Geographical. Indexes: Hospital name, personnel, hospital size.

★6028★ *Federation of American Societies for Experimental Biology— Directory of Members*

Federation of American Societies for Experimental Biology (FASEB)
9650 Rockville Pke.
Bethesda, MD 20814
Ph: (301)530-7000   Fax: (301)571-1855

Annual, Fall. $50.00. Covers about 41,000 members of the American Physiological Society, American Society for Biochemistry and Molecular Biology, American Society for Pharmacology and Experimental Therapeutics, American Society for Investigative Pathology, American Institute of Nutrition, American Association of Immunologists, American Society for Cell Biology, Biophysical Society, and American Association of Anatomists. Entries include: Name, address, title, affiliation, memberships in federation societies, highest degree, year elected to membership, phone, fax and electronic mail address. Arrangement: Alphabetical. Indexes: Geographical.

★6029★ *Hospital Blue Book*

Billian Publishing Co.
2100 Powers Ferry Rd., Ste. 300
Atlanta, GA 30339
Ph: (404)955-5656   Fax: (404)952-0669

Annual, spring. $154.50, national edition, plus $20.00 shipping. Covers more than 7,100 hospitals; some listings also appear in a separate southern edition of this publication. Entries include: Name of hospital, accreditation, mailing address, phone, fax, number of beds, type of facility (nonprofit, general, state, etc.); list of administrative personnel and chiefs of medical services, with specific titles. Arrangement: Geographical.

★6030★ *Hospital Market Atlas*

SMG Marketing Group, Inc.
1342 N. LaSalle Dr.
Chicago, IL 60610
Ph: (312)642-3026   Fax: (312)642-9729
Fr: 800-678-3026

Biennial, odd years. $495.00, payment with order. Covers over 7,000 hospitals, hospital systems and 480 group purchasing organizations. Entries include: Hospital or organization name, address, phone, county code, management, type of hospital service, number of beds, admissions, surgical operations, and emergency room visits. Arrangement: Geographical.

★6031★ *Hospitals Directory*

American Business Directories, Inc.
American Business Information, Inc.
5711 S. 86th Cir.
Omaha, NE 68127
Ph: (402)593-4600   Fax: (402)331-1505

Annual. $870.00, U.S. edition. Entries include: Name, address, phone (including area code), size of advertisement, year first in Yellow Pages, name of owner or manager, number of employees. Compiled from telephone company Yellow Pages, nationwide. Arrangement: Geographical.

★6032★ Medical and Health Information Directory

Gale Research
835 Penobscot Bldg.
Detroit, MI 48226-4094
Ph: (313)961-2242   Fax: (313)961-6083
Fr: 800-877-GALE

Approximately biennial; latest edition 1994. $195.00, per volume; $485.00, for the three-volume set. Covers in Volume 1, almost 18,600 medical and health oriented associations, organizations, institutions, and government agencies, including health maintenance organizations (HMOs), preferred provider organizations (PPOs), insurance companies, pharmaceutical companies, research centers, and medical and allied health schools. In Volume 2, nearly 11,800 medical book publishers; medical periodicals, directories, audiovisual producers and services, medical libraries and information centers, and electronic resources. In Volume 3, nearly 26,000 clinics, treatment centers, care programs, and counseling/diagnostic services for 30 subject areas. Entries include: Institution, service, or firm name, address, phone; many include names of key personnel and, when pertinent, descriptive annotation. Arrangement: Classified by organization activity, service, etc. Indexes: Each volume has a complete alphabetical name and keyword index.

★6033★ Medical Research Centres

Stockton Press
Groves Dictionaries
345 Park Ave. S., 10th Fl.
New York, NY 10010
Ph: (212)689-9200   Fr: 800-221-2123

Eleventh edition, 1995. $595.00. 856 pages. Covers medical and biochemical research conducted in over 100 countries. Entries include information on industrial enterprises, research laboratories, universities, societies, and professional associations engaged in research in medicine and related subjects like dentistry, nursing, pharmacy, psychiatry, and surgery.

★6034★ National Wholesale Druggists' Association—Membership & Executive Directory

National Wholesle Druggists' Association
PO Box 2219
Reston, VA 22090-0219
Ph: (703)787-0000   Fax: (703)787-6930

Annual, January. $295.00. Covers wholesalers, manufacturers, national drug-trade associations, and colleges of pharmacy. Entries include: For industry: company name, address, phone, fax, names, of principal executives. For colleges: institution name, address. Arrangement: Classified by type of membership.

★6035★ Osteopathic Membership Directory—AOHA

American Osteopathic Healthcare
  Association
5301 Wisconsin Ave. NW, Ste. 630
Washington, DC 20015-2015
Ph: (202)686-1700   Fax: (202)686-7615

Annual, summer. $125.00, payment with order. Covers about 110 osteopathic hospitals. Includes list of individual and institutional

members; also lists osteopathic colleges, and directors of medical education. Entries include: For hospitals: name of hospital, name of chief executive officer, address, phone, number of beds and other hospital data. Arrangement: Geographical. Indexes: Name, institution.

★6036★ Peterson's Job Opportunities in Health Care

Peterson's Guides, Inc.
202 Carnegie Ctr.
Box 2123
Princeton, NJ 08543-2123
Ph: (609)243-9111   Fax: (609)243-9150
Fr: 800-338-3282

Annual, August. $18.95. Covers Over 1,500 companies hiring health-care professionals for skilled nursing care facilities, hospitals, medical laboratories, home health care, and pharmaceuticals. Entries include: Organization name, address, phone, name and title of contact, type of organization, number of employees, Standard Industrial Classification (SIC) code; description of opportunities available including disciplines, level of education required, starting locations and salaries, level of experience accepted, benefits. Arrangement: Alphabetical. Indexes: Employer by type of organization, industry classification, number of employees, starting location, special interest area; education level, company.

★6037★ Pharmaceutical Products–Wholesalers & Manufacturers Directory

American Business Directories, Inc.
American Business Information, Inc.
5711 S. 86th Cir.
Omaha, NE 68127
Ph: (402)593-4600   Fax: (402)331-1505

Annual. $255.00, payment with order. Entries include: Name, address, phone (including area code), size of advertisement, year first in Yellow Pages, name of owner or manager, number of employees. Compiled from telephone company Yellow Pages, nationwide. Arrangement: Geographical.

★6038★ Pharmacies Directory

American Business Directories, Inc.
American Business Information, Inc.
5711 S. 86th Cir.
Omaha, NE 68127
Ph: (402)593-4600   Fax: (402)331-1505

Annual. $1,835.00. Entries include: Name, address, phone, size of advertisement, name of owner or manager, number of employees, year first in Yellow Pages. Compiled from telephone company Yellow Pages, nationwide. Available in regional editions; please inquire. Arrangement: Geographical.

HANDBOOKS AND MANUALS

★6039★ Careers in Health Care

VGM Career Horizons
4255 W. Touhy Ave.
Lincolnwood, IL 60646-1975
Ph: (847)679-5500   Fax: (847)679-2494
Fr: 800-323-4900

Barbara M. Swanson. 1995. $17.95; $13.95 (paper). Describes job duties, work settings, salaries, licensing and certification requirements, educational preparation, and future outlook. Gives ideas on how to secure a job.

★6040★ Careers in Medicine: Traditional and Alternative Opportunities

Garrett Park Press
PO Box 190 C
Garrett Park, MD 20896-0190
Ph: (301)946-2553

Donald T. Rucker and Martin D. Keller. 1990. $15.95. 346 pages. Cites training requirements, illustrative work activities, and a summary of the advantages and disadvantages in a variety of specialized areas. Includes hundreds of career alternatives and discusses ways to break into these fields for persons trained in medicine. Features contributions from over 40 professionals in all phases of medicine and provides 200 sources of information on specialties and subspecialties.

★6041★ Discovering New Medicines: Careers in Pharmaceutical Research & Development

John Wiley & Sons, Inc.
605 3rd Ave.
New York, NY 10158-0012
Ph: (212)850-6000   Fr: 800-225-5945

P.D. Stonier, editor. 1995. $29.95 (paper).

★6042★ 100 Best Careers for the Year 2000

Prentice Hall General Reference
15 Columbus Cir.
New York, NY 10023
Ph: (212)373-8500   Fr: 800-223-2348

Shelly Field. 1992. $15.00 (paper). Covers 100 of the fastest growing jobs. The publication is divided into 11 general employment sections. Specific careers are covered within each section. Provides job description, responsibilities, employment opportunities, earnings, education and training, advancement opportunities, and experience and qualifications for each occupation.

★6043★ Opportunities in Health and Medical Careers

VGM Career Horizons
4255 W. Touhy Ave.
Lincolnwood, IL 60646-1975
Ph: (847)679-5500   Fax: (847)679-2494
Fr: 800-323-4900

Donald Snook, Jr. and Leo D'Orazio. 1993. $14.95; $11.95 (paper). Covers the full range of medical and health occupations. Illustrated.

★6044★ Opportunities in Pharmacy Careers

VGM Career Horizons
4255 W. Touhy Ave.
Lincolnwood, IL 60646-1975
Ph: (847)679-5500   Fax: (847)679-2494
Fr: 800-323-4900

Fred B. Gable. 1990. $14.95; $11.95 (paper). Identifies opportunities in a variety of settings, including retail chains, private ownership, clinics, hospitals, and other private, commercial, and industrial operations. Provides information on job-hunting techniques. Illustrated.

★6045★ The Pfizer Guide: Pharmacy Career Opportunities

Merritt Communications, Inc.
142 Ferry Rd., Ste. 13
Old Saybrook, CT 06475
Ph: (203)395-0528   Fax: (203)395-0889

John Frook, editor. 1994.

★6046★ Pharmacists

Rourke Book Co. Inc.
PO Box 3328
Vero Beach, FL 32964
Ph: (407)465-4575   Fax: (407)465-3132

Robert James. 1995.

★6047★ Resumes for Health and Medical Careers

4255 W. Touhy Ave.
Lincolnwood, IL 60646-1975
Ph: (708)679-5500   Fax: (708)679-6375
Fr: 800-323-4900

Compiled by VGM Career Horizons Staff 1995. $9.95 (paper).

★6048★ Therapists and Allied Health Professionals Career Directory

Gale Research
835 Penobscot Bldg.
Detroit, MI 48226-4094
Ph: (313)961-2242   Fax: (313)961-6083
Fr: 800-877-GALE

Bradley Morgan. 1993. $39.00. 326 pages. Essays on specific careers provide an insider's perspective. Also features extensive listings of contacts and entry-level job opportunities. Provides information on internships and sources of help-wanted ads.

Employment Agencies and Search Firms

★6049★ CT Group
264 N. Elm St.
North Massapequa, NY 11758-2525
Ph: (516)797-3642   Fax: (516)795-4350

Executive search firm and employment agency.

★6050★ EHS and Associates, Inc.
3033 Excelsior Blvd., Ste. 303
Minneapolis, MN 55416
Ph: (612)924-2366   Fax: (612)924-2367

Executive search firm and employment agency.

★6051★ JPM International
4665 MacArthur Ct., Ste. 100B
Newport Beach, CA 92660
Ph: (714)955-2545   Fax: (714)757-1320

Executive search firm and employment agency.

★6052★ Sue Carroll Personnel, Inc.
16 E. 79th St.
New York, NY 10021
Ph: (212)288-8866   Fax: (212)988-7191

Employment agency and executive search firm.

Other Sources

★6053★ American Almanac of Jobs and Salaries 1994-95

Avon Books
1350 Avenue of the Americas, 2nd Fl.
New York, NY 10019
Ph: (212)261-6800   Fr: 800-238-0658

John Wright. Revised edition, 1993. $17.00. 704 pages. This is a comprehensive guide to the wages of hundreds of occupations in a wide variety of industries and organizations.

★6054★ American Hospital Association (AHA)

1 N. Franklin, Ste. 27
Chicago, IL 60606
Ph: (312)422-3000   Fax: (312)422-4796

Members: Individuals and health care institutions including hospitals, health care systems, and pre- and postacute health care delivery organizations. **Purpose:** Is dedicated to promoting the welfare of the public through its leadership and assistance to its members in the provision of better health services for all people. Conducts educational programs furthering the in-service education of hospital personnel; collects and analyzes data; furnishes multimedia educational materials; maintains 44,000 volume health care administration library, and biographical archive.

★6055★ American Managed Care Pharmacy Association (AMCPA)

2300 9th St. S., Ste. 210
Arlington, VA 22204
Ph: (703)920-8480   Fax: (703)920-8491

Members: Preferred provider organizations that specialize in maintainence drug therapy in managed care environments and make available home-delivery pharmacy services. **Purpose:** Promotes managed care prescription services as suppliers of medication to home-delivery pharmacy services. Seeks to assist health plan officers and consumers in obtaining maximum value from prescription services; inform consumers and health care

organizations about members' efforts to improve prescription services through cost containment measures.

★6056★ American Pharmaceutical Association–Academy of Pharmacy Practice and Management (APPM)

2215 Constitution Ave. NW
Washington, DC 20037
Ph: (202)628-4410   Fax: (202)783-2351
Fr: 800-237-APHA

Members: Pharmacists concerned with rendering professional services directly to the public, without regard for status of employment or environment of practice. **Purpose:** To provide a forum and mechanism whereby pharmacists may meet to discuss and implement programs and activities relevant and helpful to the practitioner of pharmacy; to recommend programs and courses of action which should be undertaken or implemented by the profession; to coordinate academy efforts so as to be an asset to the progress of the profession. Provides and cosponsors continuing education meetings, seminars, and workshops; produces audiovisual materials.

★6057★ The Internship Experience–A Manual for Pharmacy Preceptors and Interns

National Association of Boards of Pharmacy
700 Bussey Hwy.
Park Ridge, IL 60068
Ph: (708)698-6227

1991.

★6058★ NACDS and Pharmacy Education: Programs for Progress

National Association of Chain Drug Stores (NACDS)
PO Box 1417-D49
Alexandria, VA 22313
Ph: (703)549-3001

Pamphlet. Describes internship, scholarship, and fellowship programs offered by the National Association of Chain Drug Stores.

★6059★ National Association of Boards of Pharmacy (NABP)

700 Busse Hwy.
Park Ridge, IL 60068
Ph: (708)698-6227   Fax: (708)698-0124

Members: Pharmacy boards of several states, District of Columbia, Puerto Rico, Virgin Islands, several Canadian provinces, and the states of Victoria, Australia, and New South Wales. **Purpose:** Provides for interstate reciprocity in pharmaceutic licensure based upon a uniform minimum standard of pharmaceutic education and uniform legislation; improves the standards of pharmaceutical education licensure and practice. **Activities:** Provides legislative information; sponsors uniform licensure examination; also provides information on accredited school and college requirements. Maintains pharmacy and drug law statistics.

★6060★ National Association of Chain Drug Stores (NACDS)

413 N. Lee St.
PO Box 1417-D49
Alexandria, VA 22313
Ph: (703)549-3001   Fax: (703)836-4869

Members: Chain drug members; associate members include manufacturers, suppliers, manufacturer's representatives, publishers, and advertising agencies. **Purpose:** Interprets actions by government agencies in such areas as drugs, public health, federal trade, labor, and excise taxes. **Activities:** Sponsors meetings and pharmacy student recruitment program.

★6061★ National Pharmaceutical Association (NPhA)

Howard University
College of Pharmacy and Pharmacal
  Sciences
P.O. Box 835332
Richardson, TX 75083
Ph: (214)806-6530   Fax: (214)235-4211

Members: State and local associations of professional minority pharmacists. **Purpose:** To provide a means whereby members may contribute to their common improvement, share their experiences, and contribute to the public good.

★6062★ Woman's Organization of the National Association of Retail Druggists (WONARD)

205 Daingerfield Rd.
Alexandria, VA 22314
Ph: (703)683-8200   Fax: (703)683-3619

Members: Women and female relatives of men in the pharmaceutical business. **Purpose:** Objective is to unite the families of persons interested in all aspects of the pharmaceutical profession. Promotes legislation for the betterment of the retail drug and pharmacy business. Conducts charitable program.

Pharmacy Assistants

organizations: name, address, phone, name and title of contact. Arrangement: Geographical. Indexes: Hospital name.

SOURCES OF HELP-WANTED ADS

★6063★ American Journal of Health-System Pharmacy

American Society of Health-System Pharmacists
7272 Wisconsin Ave.
Bethesda, MD 20814
Ph: (301)657-3000   Fax: (301)657-1258

Monthly. $137.00/year for individuals; $10.00 for single issue; $171.00/year for Canada; $162.00/year for other countries. Journal for directors and staffs of pharmaceutical departments in hospitals and health-care institutions.

★6064★ American Pharmacy

American Pharmaceutical Association
2215 Constitution Ave. NW
Washington, DC 20037
Ph: (202)628-4410   Fax: (202)783-2351
Fr: 800-237-2742

Monthly. $50.00/year for individuals. Journal for pharmacy professionals.

★6065★ Pharmacy Times

Romaine Pierson Publishers, Inc.
80 Shore Rd.
Port Washington, NY 11050
Ph: (516)883-6350   Fax: (516)883-6609

Monthly. Journal providing information on health items (including prescription and over-the-counter drugs and surgical supplies) to independent, chain, and hospital pharmacists.

★6066★ Southern Pharmacy Journal

333 W. Hampden Ave., Ste. 1050
Englewood, CO 80110-2340
Ph: (303)761-8818   Fax: (303)761-2440

Monthly. Free to qualified subscribers; $18.00/year for institutions; $3.00 for single issue. Magazine covering the pharmaceutical industry in the 14 southern states.

PLACEMENT AND JOB REFERRAL SERVICES

★6067★ American Public Health Association (APHA)

1015 15th St. NW
Washington, DC 20005
Ph: (202)789-5600   Fax: (202)789-5681

Members: Professional organization of physicians, nurses, educators, academicians, environmentalists, epidemiologists, new professionals, social workers, health administrators, optometrists, podiatrists, pharmacists, dentists, nutritionists, health planners, other community and mental health specialists, and interested consumers. **Purpose:** Seeks to protect and promote personal, mental, and environmental health. **Activities:** Services include: promulgation of standards; establishment of uniform practices and procedures; development of the etiology of communicable diseases; research in public health; exploration of medical care programs and their relationships to public health. Sponsors job placement service.

EMPLOYER DIRECTORIES AND NETWORKING LISTS

★6068★ AHA Guide to the Health Care Field

Health Statistics Group
American Hospital Association (AHA)
1 N. Franklin
Chicago, IL 60606
Ph: (312)422-3501   Fax: (312)280-6015

Annual, July. $195.00, payment with order. Covers hospitals, multi-health care systems, freestanding ambulatory surgery centers, psychiatric facilities, long-term care facilities, substance abuse programs, hospices, Health Maintenance Organizations (HMOs), and other health-related organizations. Entries include: For hospitals: facility name, address, phone, administrator's name, number of beds, facilities and services, number of employees, expenses, other statistics. For other

★6069★ Directory of Drug Store & HBC Chains

Chain Store Guide Information Services
3922 Coconut Palm Dr.
Tampa, FL 33619
Ph: (813)664-6868   Fax: (813)664-6810
Fr: 800-925-2288

Annual, November. $290.00. Covers drug store chains operating two or more units; mass merchants with pharmacies; and wholesale drug companies. Arrangement: Separate geographical sections for chains and wholesalers.

★6070★ Directory of Hospital Personnel

Medical Economics
5 Paragon Dr.
Montvale, NJ 07645-1725
Ph: (201)358-7500   Fax: (201)573-4956
Fr: 800-222-3045

Annual, September. $325.00, plus 7.50 shipping. Covers 200,000 executives at 7,100 U.S. hospitals. Entries include: Name of hospital, address, phone, number of beds, type and JCAHO status of hospital, names and titles of key department heads and staff, medical and nursing school affiliations; number of residents, interns, and nursing students. Arrangement: Geographical. Indexes: Hospital name, personnel, hospital size.

★6071★ Hospital Blue Book

Billian Publishing Co.
2100 Powers Ferry Rd., Ste. 300
Atlanta, GA 30339
Ph: (404)955-5656   Fax: (404)952-0669

Annual, spring. $154.50, national edition, plus $20.00 shipping. Covers more than 7,100 hospitals; some listings also appear in a separate southern edition of this publication. Entries include: Name of hospital, accreditation, mailing address, phone, fax, number of beds, type of facility (nonprofit, general, state, etc.); list of administrative personnel and chiefs of medical services, with specific titles. Arrangement: Geographical.

★6072★ Hospital Market Atlas

SMG Marketing Group, Inc.
1342 N. LaSalle Dr.
Chicago, IL 60610
Ph: (312)642-3026   Fax: (312)642-9729
Fr: 800-678-3026

Biennial, odd years. $495.00, payment with order. Covers over 7,000 hospitals, hospital systems and 480 group purchasing organizations. Entries include: Hospital or organization name, address, phone, county code, management, type of hospital service, number of beds, admissions, surgical operations, and emergency room visits. Arrangement: Geographical.

★6073★ Hospitals Directory

American Business Directories, Inc.
American Business Information, Inc.
5711 S. 86th Cir.
Omaha, NE 68127
Ph: (402)593-4600   Fax: (402)331-1505

Annual. $870.00, U.S. edition. Entries include: Name, address, phone (including area code), size of advertisement, year first in Yellow Pages, name of owner or manager, number of employees. Compiled from telephone company Yellow Pages, nationwide. Arrangement: Geographical.

★6074★ Medical and Health Information Directory

Gale Research
835 Penobscot Bldg.
Detroit, MI 48226-4094
Ph: (313)961-2242   Fax: (313)961-6083
Fr: 800-877-GALE

Approximately biennial; latest edition 1994. $195.00, per volume; $485.00, for the three-volume set. Covers in Volume 1, almost 18,600 medical and health oriented associations, organizations, institutions, and government agencies, including health maintenance organizations (HMOs), preferred provider organizations (PPOs), insurance companies, pharmaceutical companies, research centers, and medical and allied health schools. In Volume 2, nearly 11,800 medical book publishers; medical periodicals, directories, audiovisual producers and services, medical libraries and information centers, and electronic resources. In Volume 3, nearly 26,000 clinics, treatment centers, care programs, and counseling/diagnostic services for 30 subject areas. Entries include: Institution, service, or firm name, address, phone; many include names of key personnel and, when pertinent, descriptive annotation. Arrangement: Classified by organization activity, service, etc. Indexes: Each volume has a complete alphabetical name and keyword index.

★6075★ Peterson's Job Opportunities in Health Care

Peterson's Guides, Inc.
202 Carnegie Ctr.
Box 2123
Princeton, NJ 08543-2123
Ph: (609)243-9111   Fax: (609)243-9150
Fr: 800-338-3282

Annual, August. $18.95. Covers Over 1,500 companies hiring health-care professionals for skilled nursing care facilities, hospitals, medical laboratories, home health care, and pharmaceuticals. Entries include: Organization name, address, phone, name and title of contact, type of organization, number of employees, Standard Industrial Classification (SIC) code; description of opportunities available including disciplines, level of education required, starting locations and salaries, level of experience accepted, benefits. Arrangement: Alphabetical. Indexes: Employer by type of organization, industry classification, number of employees, starting location, special interest area; education level, company.

HANDBOOKS AND MANUALS

★6076★ Discovering New Medicines: Careers in Pharmaceutical Research & Development

John Wiley & Sons, Inc.
605 3rd Ave.
New York, NY 10158-0012
Ph: (212)850-6000   Fr: 800-225-5945

P.D. Stonier, editor. 1995. $29.95 (paper).

★6077★ Opportunities in Pharmacy Careers

VGM Career Horizons
4255 W. Touhy Ave.
Lincolnwood, IL 60646-1975
Ph: (847)679-5500   Fax: (847)679-2494
Fr: 800-323-4900

Fred B. Gable. 1990. $14.95; $11.95 (paper). Identifies opportunities in a variety of settings, including retail chains, private ownership, clinics, hospitals, and other private, commercial, and industrial operations. Provides information on job-hunting techniques. Illustrated.

★6078★ The Pfizer Guide: Pharmacy Career Opportunities

Merritt Communications, Inc.
142 Ferry Rd., Ste. 13
Old Saybrook, CT 06475
Ph: (203)395-0528   Fax: (203)395-0889

John Frook, editor. 1994.

★6079★ Pharmacists

Rourke Book Co. Inc.
PO Box 3328
Vero Beach, FL 32964
Ph: (407)465-4575   Fax: (407)465-3132

Robert James. 1995.

★6080★ Resumes for Health and Medical Careers

4255 W. Touhy Ave.
Lincolnwood, IL 60646-1975
Ph: (708)679-5500   Fax: (708)679-6375
Fr: 800-323-4900

Compiled by VGM Career Horizons Staff 1995. $9.95 (paper).

OTHER SOURCES

★6081★ American Managed Care Pharmacy Association (AMCPA)

2300 9th St. S., Ste. 210
Arlington, VA 22204
Ph: (703)920-8480   Fax: (703)920-8491

Members: Preferred provider organizations that specialize in maintainence drug therapy in managed care environments and make available home-delivery pharmacy services. **Purpose:** Promotes managed care prescription services as suppliers of medication to home-delivery pharmacy services. Seeks to assist health plan officers and consumers in obtaining maximum value from prescription services; inform consumers and health care organizations about members' efforts to improve prescription services through cost containment measures.

★6082★ NACDS and Pharmacy Education: Programs for Progress

National Association of Chain Drug Stores (NACDS)
PO Box 1417-D49
Alexandria, VA 22313
Ph: (703)549-3001

Pamphlet. Describes internship, scholarship, and fellowship programs offered by the National Association of Chain Drug Stores.

★6083★ National Association of Chain Drug Stores (NACDS)

413 N. Lee St.
PO Box 1417-D49
Alexandria, VA 22313
Ph: (703)549-3001   Fax: (703)836-4869

Members: Chain drug members; associate members include manufacturers, suppliers, manufacturer's representatives, publishers, and advertising agencies. **Purpose:** Interprets actions by government agencies in such areas as drugs, public health, federal trade, labor, and excise taxes. **Activities:** Sponsors meetings and pharmacy student recruitment program.

Photographers and Camera Operators

SOURCES OF HELP-WANTED ADS

★6084★ Advanced Imaging

PTN Publishing Co.
445 Broad Hollow Rd., Ste. 21
Melville, NY 11747
Ph: (516)845-2700   Fax: (516)845-7109

Monthly. Magazine covering the full range of electronic imaging technology and its uses.

★6085★ Adweek

Billboard Magazine
33 Commercial St.
Gloucester, MA 01930
Ph: (508)281-3110   Fax: (508)281-0136

Weekly (Mon.). $99.00/year for individuals. Advertising news magazine.

★6086★ American Cinematographer

ASC Holding Corp.
PO Box 2230
Los Angeles, CA 90078
Ph: (213)969-4333   Fax: (213)876-4973

Monthly. $24.00/year for individuals; $4.00 for single issue. Magazine of the American Society of Cinematographers; covering film and video production.

★6087★ Art Direction

Advertising Trade Publications, Inc.
10 E. 39th St., 6th Fl.
New York, NY 10016-0199
Ph: (212)889-6500   Fax: (212)889-6504

Monthly. Magazine on advertising art and photography.

★6088★ ARTJOB

Western States Arts Federation
236 Montezuma Ave.
Santa Fe, NM 87501
Ph: (505)988-1166

Biweekly. $45.00, for 24-issue subscription. Covers national full- and part-time positions and temporary paid positions in visual, performing, and literary arts, arts education, and general arts administration, competitions, internships, conferences. Entries include: Job title, salary, description of responsibilities, qualifications, application procedure and deadline, name and address of contact. Arrangement: Classified by field.

★6089★ AV Video

Knowledge Industry Publications, Inc.
701 Westchester Ave.
White Plains, NY 10604
Ph: (914)328-9157   Fax: (914)328-9093
Fr: 800-800-5474

Monthly. $48.00/year for individuals; $60.00/year for Canada and Mexico; $80.00/year for other countries. Magazine covering audio-visual and video production and presentation technology and techniques.

★6090★ Billboard

BPI Communications
1515 Broadway, 11th Fl.
New York, NY 10036
Ph: (212)536-5167   Fax: (212)536-5351
Fr: 800-274-4100

Weekly. $229.00/year. International magazine of music and home entertainment geared toward professionals in the music and home video industries and related fields.

★6091★ Broadcasting and Cable

Conners Publishing
245 W. 17th St.
New York, NY 10011
Ph: (212)463-6835   Fax: (212)463-6836

Weekly. $85.00/year for individuals; $3.00/year for single issue. News magazine covering "The Fifth Estate" (radio, TV, cable, and satellite), and the regulatory commissions involved.

★6092★ Columbia Journalism Review

Columbia Journalism Review
700 Journalism Bldg.
Columbia University
New York, NY 10027
Ph: (212)854-1881   Fax: (212)854-8580

Bimonthly. Magazine focusing on journalism.

★6093★ Communications Technology

Phillips Business Information, Inc.
1900 Grant St., Ste. 720
Denver, CO 80203-4307
Ph: (303)839-1565   Fax: (303)839-1564

Monthly. Free to qualified subscribers. Magazine catering to cable TV industry's technical community; written by industry engineers, technicians, managers, and professionals.

★6094★ Editor & Publisher

Editor & Publisher Co.
11 W. 19th St.
New York, NY 10011
Ph: (212)675-4380   Fax: (212)929-1259

Weekly (Sat.). Magazine focusing on journalism, advertising, and printing equipment.

★6095★ Electronic Media

Crain Communications, Inc.
740 N. Rush St.
Chicago, IL 60611
Ph: (312)649-5260   Fax: (312)649-5228

Weekly (Mon.). $69.00/year for individuals. Tabloid covering management, programing, syndication, technology, and trends in the television, radio, and electronic media industry.

★6096★ ETV Newsletter

Charles Tepfer, Publisher
PO Box 597
Ridgefield, CT 06877
Ph: (203)454-2618   Fax: (203)454-2618

Biweekly. $195.00/year for U.S. and Canada; $220.00/year for elsewhere. Offers inside information on what's happening in Public Television (PTV), Instructional Television (ITV), and Educational Television (ETV). Monitors government telecommunications policy changes; new marketing policies, grants and funding sources; and requests for bids on equipment, services, and programs. Recurring features include meetings and conference reports, a calendar of events, job listings, book reviews, and market studies.

★6097★ The Hollywood Reporter

Billboard Magazine
33 Commercial St.
Gloucester, MA 01930
Ph: (508)281-3110   Fax: (508)281-0136

Daily (morn.). $149.00/year for individuals. Film, TV, and entertainment trade newspaper.

★6098★ HOW

F&W Publications, Inc.
1507 Dana Ave.
Cincinnati, OH 45207
Ph: (513)531-2222   Fax: (513)531-1843

Bimonthly. $49.00/year for individuals. Instructional trade magazine.

★6099★ Industrial Photography

PTN Publishing Co.
445 Broad Hollow Rd., Ste. 21
Melville, NY 11747
Ph: (516)845-2700   Fax: (516)845-7109

Monthly. Magazine on industrial photography.

★6100★ News Photographer

National Press Photographers Association
1446 Conneaut Ave.
Bowling Green, OH 43402
Ph: (419)352-8175   Fax: (419)354-5435

Monthly. Magazine featuring still and television news photography.

★6101★ Print

R.C. Publications, Inc.
104 5th Ave., 19th Fl.
New York, NY 10011
Ph: (212)463-0600   Fax: (212)989-9891

Bimonthly. Covers all aspects of graphic design for visual communication.

★6102★ Producer's Masterguide

Producer's Masterguide
60 E. 8th St., 31st Fl.
New York, NY 10003-6514
Ph: (212)777-4002   Fax: (212)777-4101
Fr: 800-622-6111

Annual. $125.00/year for individuals; $145.00/year for out of country. Magazine for the professional motion picture, TV commercial, cable, and videotape industries in the U.S. Canada, the U.K., the Caribbean Islands, Mexico, Europe, Israel, the Far East and South America.

★6103★ Professional Photographer

Professional Photographers of America, Inc.
57 Forsyth St. NW, No. 1600
Atlanta, GA 30303
Ph: (404)522-8600   Fax: (404)614-6405

Monthly. $24.50/year for individuals; $40.00/year for Canada; $60.00/year for other countries.

★6104★ The RangeFinder

The RangeFinder Publishing Co., Inc.
1312 Lincoln Blvd.
PO Box 1703
Santa Monica, CA 90406
Ph: (310)451-8506

Monthly. $18.00/year for individuals. Trade publication for portrait, commercial and wedding photographers.

★6105★ Signature

South Wind Publishing Co.
PO Box 6808
Leawood, KS 66206-0808
Ph: (913)642-6611   Fax: (913)642-6676

Periodic. Free to qualified subscribers; $48.00/year for institutions; $58.00/year for Canada and Mexico. Publishing industry magazine and catalog.

★6106★ Video Systems

Intertec Publishing Corp.
9800 Metcalf
PO Box 12901
Overland Park, KS 66212-2215
Ph: (913)341-1300   Fax: (913)967-1898
Fr: 800-441-0294

Monthly. $45.00/year for individuals; $5.00 for single issue; $55.00/year for other countries; $110.00/year by mail. Magazine for users of professional video equipment.

PLACEMENT AND JOB REFERRAL SERVICES

★6107★ Broadcast Designers' Association International (BDA)

145 W. 45th St., Ste. 1100
New York, NY 10036-4008
Ph: (212)376-6222   Fax: (212)376-6202

Members: Designers, artists, art directors, illustrators, photographers, animators, and other professionals in the electronic media industry; educators and students; commercial and industrial companies that manufacture products related to design. **Purpose:** Objectives are to promote understanding between designers, clients, and management; to stimulate innovative ideas and techniques; to encourage and provide a resource for young talent; and to provide a forum for discussion on industry issues and concerns. **Activities:** Maintains placement service; conducts surveys and compiles statistics.

★6108★ Health Sciences Communications Association (HESCA)

1 Wedgewood Dr.
Jewett City, CT 06351
Ph: (203)376-5915   Fax: (203)376-6621

Members: Media managers, graphic artists, biomedical librarians, producers, faculty members of health science and veterinary medicine schools, health professional organizations, and industry representatives. **Purpose:** Acts as a clearinghouse for information used by professionals engaged in health science communications. Coordinates Media Festivals Program which recognizes outstanding media productions in the health sciences. **Activities:** Offers placement service.

★6109★ Institute of American Indian Arts (IAIA)

PO Box 20007
Santa Fe, NM 87504
Ph: (505)988-6463   Fax: (505)988-6446

Purpose: Federally chartered private institution. Offers learning opportunities in the arts and crafts to Native American youth (Indian, Eskimo, or Aleut). Emphasis is placed upon Indian traditions as the basis for creative expression in fine arts including painting, sculpture, museum studies, creative writing, printmaking, photography, communications, design, and dance, as well as training in metal crafts, jewelry, ceramics, textiles, and various traditional crafts. Students are encouraged to identify with their heritage and to be aware of themselves as members of a race rich in architecture, the fine arts, music, pageantry, and the humanities. All programs are based on elements of the Native American cultural heritage that emphasize differences between Native American and non-Native American cultures. **Activities:** Provides placement service. Sponsors Indian arts-oriented junior college offering Associate of Fine Arts degrees in various fields as well as seminars, an exhibition program, and traveling exhibits. Maintains extensive library, museum, and biographical archives.

★6110★ Media Alliance (MA)

814 Mission St., Ste. 205
San Francisco, CA 94103

Members: Writers, photographers, editors, broadcast workers, public relations people, and others who support free press and independent journalism. **Purpose:** Seeks to change what the alliance calls the characteristic cutthroat competitive attitude among its practitioners by encouraging contact and discussion and developing structures enabling members to assist each other and to mobilize the group's resources on behalf of mutually agreed-upon projects. **Activities:** Maintains job file. Conducts continuing professional education classes. Maintains speakers' bureau.

★6111★ National Association of Broadcasters (NAB)

1771 N St. NW
Washington, DC 20036
Ph: (202)429-5300   Fax: (202)429-5343

Members: Representatives of radio and television stations and networks; associate members include producers of equipment and programs. **Purpose:** Seeks to ensure the viability, strength, and success of free, over-the-air broadcasters; serves as an information resource to the industry. **Activities:** Offers minority placement service and employment clearinghouse. Monitors and reports on events regarding radio and television broadcasting. Maintains Broadcasting Hall of Fame.

★6112★ **University Photographers Association of America (UPAA)**

News Services
Western Michigan University
Kalamazoo, MI 49008
Ph: (616)387-4111   Fax: (616)387-4124

Members: College and university personnel engaged professionally in photography, teaching of photography, audiovisual work, or journalism for universities. **Purpose:** Seeks to advance applied photography and the profession through the exchange of thoughts and opinions among its members. **Activities:** Operates placement services. Awards fellowship for exceptional work in the advancement of photography. Provides a medium for exchange of ideas and technical information on photography, especially university photographic work.

EMPLOYER DIRECTORIES AND NETWORKING LISTS

★6113★ *American Photographers: An Illustrated Who's Who*

American References, Inc.
2210 N. Burling St.
Chicago, IL 60614-3712
Ph: (312)951-6200

Biennial, fall of odd years. $39.95. Covers well-known photographers working in the United States. Entries include: Name, address, phone. Arrangement: Alphabetical. Indexes: Working location (studio, locations, outdoors, etc.), subject matter, specialty (photojournalism, advertising, etc.), geographical.

★6114★ *American Society of Media Photographers—Membership Directory*

American Society of Media Photographers (ASMP)
14 Washington Rd., Ste. 502
Princeton Junction, NJ 08550-1033
Ph: (609)799-8300   Fax: (609)799-2233

Annual, January. $18.00. Covers 5,000 professional photographers for publications. Entries include: Name, address, phone, specialty. Arrangement: Alphabetical. Indexes: Geographical, specialty.

★6115★ *Artist's & Graphic Designer's Market: Where & How to Sell Your Illustrations, Fine Art, Graphic Design & Cartoons*

Writer's Digest Books
1507 Dana Ave.
Cincinnati, OH 45207
Ph: (513)531-2690   Fax: (513)531-4744
Fr: 800-289-0963

Annual, September. $23.99, plus 3.00 shipping. Covers 2,500 buyers of free-lance art work, including ad agencies, art studios, galleries, clip art firms, audiovisual firms, television film producers, periodicals, record companies, book publishers; coverage includes Canada. Entries include: Name of buyer, address, phone, payment rates, special submission requirements, reporting time,

how to break in. Arrangement: Classified by type of market.

★6116★ *Broadcasting & Cable Yearbook*

R. R. Bowker Co.
Reed Reference Publishing
121 Chanlon Rd.
New Providence, NJ 07974
Ph: (908)464-6800   Fax: (908)464-3553
Fr: 800-521-8110

Annual, March. $169.95. Covers all television and radio stations in the United States, its territories, and Canada; cable MSOs and their individual systems; television and radio networks, broadcast and cable group owners, station representatives, satellite networks and services, film companies, advertising agencies, government agencies, trade associations and schools. Entries include: Company name, address, phone, fax, names of executives. Station listings include broadcast power, other operating details. Arrangement: Stations and systems are geographical, others are alphabetical. Indexes: Alphabetical.

★6117★ *Burrelle's New York Media Directory*

Burrelle's Information Services
75 E. Northfield Rd.
Livingston, NJ 07039
Ph: (201)992-6600   Fr: 800-876-3342

Annual. $95.00. Includes information on radio and television stations, newspapers, and other media companies. Regional editions available for some Northeastern states.

★6118★ *Chicago Creative Directory*

Chicago Creative Directory, Inc.
333 N. Michigan Ave., Ste. 810
Chicago, IL 60601
Ph: (312)236-7337   Fax: (312)236-6078

Annual, March. $40.00. Covers over 3,000 advertising agencies, photographers, sound studios, talent agencies, audiovisual services, and others offering creative and production services. Entries include: For most listings: company name, address, phone, list of officers, description of services. For freelance listings: name, talent, address, phone. Arrangement: Classified by specialty.

★6119★ *Chicago Sourcebook*

Black Book Marketing Group
212 W. Superior St., Ste. 400
Chicago, IL 60610
Ph: (312)944-5115

Annual, November. Covers commercial artists and photographers and graphic designers in Chicago, Illinois area. Entries include: Firm name, address, phone; other details as provided by firm. Arrangement: Alphabetical.

★6120★ *CPB Public Broadcasting Directory*

Corporation for Public Broadcasting
901 E St. NW
Washington, DC 20004-2037
Ph: (202)879-9600   Fax: (202)783-1019

Annual, fall. $15.00. Covers public television and radio stations, national and regional public broadcasting organizations and net-

works, state government agencies and commissions, and other related organizations. Entries include: For radio and television stations: station call letters, frequency or channel, address, phone, licensee name, licensee type, date on air, antenna height, area covered, names and titles of key personnel. For organizations: name, address, phone, name and title of key personnel. Arrangement: National and regional listings are alphabetical; state groups and the public radio and television stations are each geographical; other organizations and agencies are alphabetical. Indexes: Geographical, personnel, call letter, licensee type (all in separate indexes for radio and television).

★6121★ *Creative Black Book*

Black Book Marketing Group
866 3rd Ave.
New York, NY 10022
Ph: (212)702-9700   Fax: (212)605-4808

Annual, January. $140.00, plus $7.00 shipping. Publication includes: photographers and photographic services, design firms, advertising agencies, and other firms whose products or services are used in advertising. Entries include: Company name, address, phone. Principal content of publication is 4-color samples from the leading commercial photographers. Arrangement: Classified by product/service.

★6122★ *International Television and Video Almanac*

Quigley Publishing Co., Inc.
159 W. 53rd St.
New York, NY 10019
Ph: (212)247-3100   Fax: (212)489-0871

Annual, January. $88.50, plus shipping. Covers Who's Who in Motion Pictures and Television and Home Video, television networks, major program producers, major group station owners, cable television companies, distributors, firms serving the television and home video industry, equipment manufacturers, casting agencies, literary agencies, advertising and publicity representatives, television stations, associations, list of feature films produced for television; statistics, industry's year in review, award winners. Entries include: Generally, company name, address, phone; manufacturer and service listings may include description of products and services and name of contact; producing, distributing, and station listings include additional detail. Arrangement: Classified by service or activity, then generally geographical.

★6123★ *Klik! Showcase Photography*

American Showcase, Inc.
915 Broadway
New York, NY 10010
Ph: (212)673-6600   Fax: (212)673-9795
Fr: 800-894-7469

Annual. $45.00. Covers 9,500 photographers, stock photographers, and related companies. Entries include: Name, address, phone, sample of work. Arrangement: Geographical. Indexes: Specialty.

★6124★ Madison Avenue Handbook: The Image Makers Source

Peter Glenn Publications
42 W. 38th St., No. 802
New York, NY 10018
Ph: (212)869-2020   Fax: (212)869-3287
Fr: 800-223-1254

Annual, spring. $45.00. Covers advertising agencies and related services in the U.S. and Canada. Includes television, film, and music producers; photographers, agents, suppliers, sources of props and rentals, fashion houses, beauty services, locations, and film commissions. Entries include: Company name, address, phone; paid listings include description of products or services, key personnel. Arrangement: Classified by line of business.

★6125★ National Directory of Magazines

Oxbridge Communications, Inc.
150 5th Ave., Ste. 301
New York, NY 10011
Ph: (212)741-0231

Annual. $445.00. Covers approximately 30,000 magazines.

★6126★ National Press Photographers Association—Membership Directory

National Press Photographers Association
3200 Croasdaile Dr., Ste. 306
Durham, NC 27705
Ph: (919)383-7246   Fax: (919)383-7261
Fr: 800-289-6772

Annual, August. $40.00. Covers 11,000 professional newspaper photographers, and television and motion picture photographers concerned with photojournalism. Entries include: Name, home address, employer name. Arrangement: Alphabetical. Indexes: Geographical.

★6127★ Photographers—Aerial Directory

American Business Directories, Inc.
American Business Information, Inc.
5711 S. 86th Cir.
Omaha, NE 68127
Ph: (402)593-4600   Fax: (402)331-1505

Updated continuously; printed on request. Please inquire. Entries include: Name, address, phone (including area code), size of advertisement, year first in Yellow Pages, name of owner or manager, number of employees. Compiled from telephone company Yellow Pages, nationwide. Arrangement: Geographical.

★6128★ Photographers—Commercial Directory

American Business Directories, Inc.
American Business Information, Inc.
5711 S. 86th Cir.
Omaha, NE 68127
Ph: (402)593-4600   Fax: (402)331-1505

Annual. $760.00, U.S. edition; $145.00, (Canad. ed.); payment with order. Number of listings: 20,399 (U.S. edition); 2,265 (Canadian edition). Entries include: Name, address, phone (including area code), size of advertisement, year first in Yellow Pages, name of owner or manager, number of employees. Compiled from telephone company Yellow

Pages, nationwide. Arrangement: Geographical.

★6129★ Photographer's Market: Where and How to Sell Your Photographers

Writer's Digest Books
1507 Dana Ave.
Cincinnati, OH 45207
Ph: (513)531-2690   Fax: (513)531-4744
Fr: 800-289-0963

Annual, September. $22.99 plus 3.00 shipping. Covers over 2,500 companies and publications that purchase original photographs, including advertising agencies, public relations agencies, book and periodical publishers, stock photo agencies, photographic workshops, galleries, and competitions. Entries include: Name of buyer, address, phone, payment rates, requirements, reporting time, how to break in. Arrangement: Classified by type of market.

★6130★ Photographers—Passport Directory

American Business Directories, Inc.
American Business Information, Inc.
5711 S. 86th Cir.
Omaha, NE 68127
Ph: (402)593-4600   Fax: (402)331-1505

Annual. $455.00, payment with order. Entries include: Name, address, phone (including area code), size of advertisement, year first in Yellow Pages, name of owner or manager, number of employees. Compiled from telephone company Yellow pages, nationwide. Arrangement: Geographical.

★6131★ Photographers—Portrait Directory

American Business Directories, Inc.
American Business Information, Inc.
5711 S. 86th Cir.
Omaha, NE 68127
Ph: (402)593-4600   Fax: (402)331-1505

Annual. $980.00, U.S. edition; $170.00, (Canad. ed.); payment with order. Number of listings: 29,611 (U.S. edition); 3,400 (Canadian edition). Entries include: Name, address, phone (including area code), size of advertisement, year first in Yellow Pages, name of owner or manager, number of employees. Regional editions available. Compiled from telephone company Yellow Pages, nationwide. Arrangement: Geographical.

★6132★ Photoletter

PhotoStockNotes
Pine Lake Farm
1910 35th Rd.
Osceola, WI 54020
Ph: (715)248-3800   Fax: (715)248-7394
Fr: 800-223-3860

Monthly. $9.00, per issue; $110.00. Covers magazine and book publishers, public relations firms, advertising and government agencies currently soliciting photographs for publication; 40-50 listings per issue. Entries include: Company name, name of contact, address, phone, project title, and nature of photos sought.

★6133★ Registry of Freelance Photographers

Publishers Network, Inc.
PO Box 3190
Vista, CA 92085
Ph: (619)941-4100   Fax: (619)941-0773

Semiannual, January and June. $15.00. Covers Approximately 1,000 photographers available for assignment in the cities in which they reside; coverage is mostly U.S. and Canada, with a few in Europe and Asia. Entries include: Name, geographical area served, phone, biographical data, qualifications, interests and experience. Arrangement: Geographical by ZIP code.

★6134★ Television & Cable Factbook

Warren Publishing, Inc.
2115 Ward Ct. NW
Washington, DC 20037
Ph: (202)872-9200   Fax: (202)293-3435

Annual, January. Weekly updates available. $405.00, plus $15.00 shipping. Covers commercial and noncommercial television stations and networks, including educational, low-power and instructional TV stations, and translators; United States cable television systems; cable and television group owners; national sales representatives of television stations; equipment manufacturers and distributors; program and service suppliers; brokerage and financing companies; consulting engineers; brokers; attorneys practicing before the Federal Communications Commission; cable system sales representatives; international coverage. Arrangement: Geographical by state, province, city, county, or country. Indexes: Call letters, product/service, name, general subject.

★6135★ Who's Who in Photographic Management

Photo Marketing Association International
3000 Picture Pl.
Jackson, MI 49201
Ph: (517)788-8100   Fr: 800-762-9287

Annual. $75.00. Covers over 15,500 members of the association and manufacturers and suppliers of photographic equipment; also members of the National Association of Photo Equipment Technicians and of the Professional School Photographers of America. Entries include: Name of firm, address, phone, name of contact. Arrangement: Separate alphabetical sections for each association and for the companies. Indexes: Geographical, product.

★6136★ Who's Who in Professional Imaging

Professional Photographers of America
57 Forsyth St. NW, Ste. 1600
Atlanta, GA 30303-2206
Ph: (404)522-8600   Fax: (404)614-6400
Fr: 800-786-6277

Annual, April. $110.00. Covers over 18,000 members, including portrait, commercial, wedding, and industrial photographers; also includes guide to photographic equipment and supply manufacturers and distributors. Entries include: For members: name, office address, phone, show specialties; listings for members available for assignments. For suppliers: company name, address, phone, product/service. Arrangement: Geographical.

★6137★ The Workbook

Scott & Daughters Publishing
940 N. Highland Ave.
Los Angeles, CA 90038
Ph: (213)856-0008   Fax: (213)856-4368
Fr: 800-547-2688

Annual, January. $95.00. Covers in four regional volumes, 25,000 advertising agencies, art directors, photographers, freelance illustrators and designers, artists' representatives, commercial production companies, printers, color separators, and typographers in the U.S. Entries include: Company or individual name, address, phone, specialty. Regional volumes are East, West, Midwest, and South. Arrangement: Classified by product or service.

★6138★ Working Press of the Nation

Reed Reference Publishing
121 Chanlon Rd.
New Providence, NJ 07974
Ph: (908)665-3561   Fax: (908)665-2894
Fr: 800-521-8110

Annual, September. $385.00, four-volume set; Covers in four separate volumes, syndicates and over 8,400 daily and weekly newspapers; 1,400 newsletters; over 14,900 radio and television stations; 10,600 magazines; 3,200 feature writers, photographers, and professional speakers; and 2,700 internal house organs. Entries include: All listings include name of publication or station, address, phone, names of executives, editors, writers, etc., as appropriate. Broadcasting and magazine volumes include data on kinds of material needed. Technical and mechanical requirements for publications are given. Arrangement: Magazines are classified by audience; newspapers and broadcasting stations are geographical.

HANDBOOKS AND MANUALS

★6139★ Career Choices for the 90's for Students of Art

Walker and Company
435 Hudson St.
New York, NY 10014
Ph: (212)727-8300   Fax: (212)727-0984
Fr: 800-289-2553

Prepared by the Career Associates staff. 1990. $9.95. 166 pages. Discusses alternatives for students of art. Offers advice on how to break into the field and how to move up. Covers where and who the employers are, internship possibilities, and professional networking associations. Comprehensive guide to career and job search planning.

★6140★ Career Information Center

Macmillan Publishing Co.
200 Old Tappan Rd.
Old Tappan, NJ 07675
Ph: (609)461-6500   Fr: 800-223-2336

Visual Education Center Staff. Fifth edition, 1992. $229.00. This 13-volume set profiles

over 600 occupations. Each occupational profile describes job duties, educational requirements, how to get the job, advancement possibilities, employment outlook, working conditions, earnings and benefits, and where to write for more information.

★6141★ Career Opportunities in Art

Facts on File, Inc.
11 Penn Plaza, 15th Fl.
New York, NY 10001-2006
Ph: (212)967-8800   Fax: 800-678-3633
Fr: 800-322-8755

Susan H. Haubenstock and David Joselit. Revised edition, 1994. $29.95; $15.95 (paper). 208 pages. This book profiles seventy-five jobs that can be found in the art field. Each profile includes a career description, career ladder, employment and advancement prospects, education, experience and skills required, salary range, and tips for entry into the field.

★6142★ Career Opportunities in Television, Cable and Video

Facts on File, Inc.
11 Penn Plaza, 15th Fl.
New York, NY 10001-2006
Ph: (212)967-8800   Fax: 800-678-3633
Fr: 800-322-8755

Maxine K. Reed and Robert M. Reed. Third edition, 1991. $29.95; $15.95 (paper). 272 pages.

★6143★ Careers in Communications

VGM Career Horizons
4255 W. Touhy Ave.
Lincolnwood, IL 60646-1975
Ph: (847)679-5500   Fax: (847)679-2494
Fr: 800-323-4900

Shonan Noronha. 1994. $17.95; $13.95 (paper). 176 pages. Examines the fields of journalism, photography, radio, television, film, public relations, and advertising. Gives concrete details on job locations and how to secure a job. Suggests many resources for job hunting.

★6144★ Careers in Health Care

VGM Career Horizons
4255 W. Touhy Ave.
Lincolnwood, IL 60646-1975
Ph: (847)679-5500   Fax: (847)679-2494
Fr: 800-323-4900

Barbara M. Swanson. 1995. $17.95; $13.95 (paper). Describes job duties, work settings, salaries, licensing and certification requirements, educational preparation, and future outlook. Gives ideas on how to secure a job.

★6145★ Careers in Health and Fitness

Rosen Publishing Group, Inc.
29 E. 21st St.
New York, NY 10010
Ph: (212)777-3017   Fax: (212)777-0277
Fr: 800-237-9932

Jackie Heron. Revised edition, 1990. $14.95. 160 pages. Contains occupational profiles for this field, including information on job duties, skills, advantages, basic equipment used, employment possibilities, certification, and salary.

★6146★ Careers for Shutterbugs: And Other Candid Types

NTC Publishing Group
4255 W. Touhy Ave.
Lincolnwood, IL 60646-1975
Ph: (708)679-5500   Fax: (708)679-6375
Fr: 800-323-4900

Cheryl McLean. 1994. $9.95 (paper).

★6147★ Careers for Sports Nuts and Other Athletic Types

VGM Career Horizons
4255 W. Touhy Ave.
Lincolnwood, IL 60646-1975
Ph: (847)679-5500   Fax: (847)679-2494
Fr: 800-323-4900

William Ray Heitzmann. 1994. Profiles sports enthusiasts who make their livings in a variety of ways in the world of sports. Explores opportunities in such sports-related fields as sports marketing, sports equipment sales, sports writing and photography, and sports management.

★6148★ Careers for Travel Buffs and Other Restless Types

VGM Career Horizons
4255 W. Touhy Ave.
Lincolnwood, IL 60646-1975
Ph: (847)679-5500   Fax: (847)679-2494
Fr: 800-323-4900

Paul Plawin. 1992. $14.95; $9.95 (paper). Includes a variety of travel and open-road careers, such as travel writers and photographers, tour bus drivers, entertainers, cruise line staff, travel agents, tour guides, sports writers, sales, the military, trucking, and meeting planning.

★6149★ Cinematographers, Production Designers, Editors and Costume Designers Guide

Lone Eagle Publishing Co.
2337 Roscomare Rd., Ste. 9
Los Angeles, CA 90077
Ph: (310)471-8066   Fax: (310)471-4969
Fr: 800-345-6257

Annual. $45.00, plus $6.00 shipping. Covers Approximately 2,500 motion picture and television cinematographers, editors, production designers, and costume designers. Entries include: Personal name; name, address, phone of agent or contact; chronological list of films or shows. Arrangement: Classified by line of business. Indexes: Film/show title, contact name, agents and managers.

★6150★ The Complete Photography Careers Handbook

The Consultant Press Ltd.
163 Amsterdam Ave., No. 201
New York, NY 10023
Ph: (212)838-8640

George Gilbert. Second edition, 1992. $19.95. 320 pages. Includes bibliography.

★6151★ The Encyclopedia of Career Choices for the 1990s: Guide to Entry-Level Jobs

Perigree Books
The Berkley Publishing Group
PO Box 506
East Rutherford, NJ 07073
Ph: (201)933-9292   Fr: 800-223-0510

Career Associates Staff. 1992. $19.95. 862 pages. Describes 500 entry-level careers in a variety of industries. Presents qualifications required, working conditions, salary, internships, and professional associations.

★6152★ Exploring Nontraditional Jobs for Women

Rosen Publishing Group, Inc.
29 E. 21st St.
New York, NY 10010
Ph: (212)777-3017   Fax: (212)777-0277
Fr: 800-237-9932

Rose Neufeld. 1989. $14.95. Describes occupations where few women are found. Covers job duties, training routes, where to apply for jobs, tools used, salary, and advantages and disadvantages of the job.

★6153★ Flying High in Travel

John Wiley and Sons
605 3rd Ave.
New York, NY 10158
Ph: (212)850-6000   Fr: 800-225-5945

Karen Rubin. Second edition, 1992. $19.95. 336 pages. A guide to careers and job hunting in the travel industry. Describes the many job opportunities available, from writing to hotel management to law. Includes information on educational preparation, training, and job hunting.

★6154★ The Harvard Guide to Careers in the Mass Media

Bob Adams, Inc.
260 Center St.
Holbrook, MA 02343
Ph: (617)767-8100   Fax: (617)767-0994
Fr: 800-872-5627

John Noble. 1989. $7.95. 202 pages. Each section of the book evaluates one media profession in depth and contains an industry profile, a career profile that describes positions available in that area, information about current salary ranges, industry-specific job-hunting tips and strategies, and a case study outlining the methods that were used in a successful job hunt.

★6155★ Magazines Career Directory

Gale Research
835 Penobscot Bldg.
Detroit, MI 48226-4094
Ph: (313)961-2242   Fax: (313)961-6083
Fr: 800-877-GALE

Bradley Morgan. Fifth edition, 1993. $39.00. Features extensive listings of contacts and entry-level job opportunities at many magazine publishing organizations. Includes articles by top professionals in the field on some of the industry's varied career paths: art, editorial, sales, and business management.

★6156★ Newspapers Career Directory

Gale Research
835 Penobscot Bldg.
Detroit, MI 48226-4094
Ph: (313)961-2242   Fax: (313)961-6083
Fr: 800-877-GALE

Bradley Morgan. Fourth edition, 1993. $39.00. 344 pages. Features extensive listings of contacts and entry-level job opportunities at many newspaper organizations. Focuses on each area of the business, from reporting and editorial to sales and marketing to promotion and production.

★6157★ 1996 Photographer's Market

Writer's Digest Books
1507 Dana Ave.
Cincinnati, OH 45207
Ph: (513)531-2690   Fax: (513)531-4082
Fr: 800-289-0963

Michael Willins, editor. 1995. $23.99 (cloth).

★6158★ Opportunities in Broadcasting Careers

VGM Career Horizons
4255 W. Touhy Ave.
Lincolnwood, IL 60646-1975
Ph: (847)679-5500   Fax: (847)679-2494
Fr: 800-323-4900

Elmo I. Ellis. 1994. $14.95; $11.95 (paper). Discusses opportunities and job search techniques in broadcasting, television, and radio. Illustrated.

★6159★ Opportunities in Cable Television Careers

VGM Career Horizons
4255 W. Touhy Ave.
Lincolnwood, IL 60646-1975
Ph: (847)679-5500   Fax: (847)679-2494
Fr: 800-323-4900

Jan Bone. 1993. $14.95; $11.95 (paper). 160 pages. Focuses on what the jobs are, where they are, and how to get them. Illustrated.

★6160★ Opportunities in Crafts Careers

VGM Career Horizons
4255 W. Touhy Ave.
Lincolnwood, IL 60646-1975
Ph: (847)679-5500   Fax: (847)679-2494
Fr: 800-323-4900

Marianne Munday. 1993. $14.95; $11.95 (paper). 160 pages. Provides information about careers and job opportunities in such areas as fine and applied arts, antiques and collectibles, ceramics, woodworking, sewing and needlecraft, and more. Illustrated.

★6161★ Opportunities in Film Careers

VGM Career Horizons
4255 W. Touhy Ave.
Lincolnwood, IL 60646-1975
Ph: (847)679-5500   Fax: (847)679-2494
Fr: 800-323-4900

Jan Bone. 1990. $14.95; $11.95 (paper). 160 pages. Provides advice on obtaining a job in film and in corporate non-broadcast film/video production. Illustrated.

★6162★ Opportunities in Journalism Careers

VGM Career Horizons
4255 W. Touhy Ave.
Lincolnwood, IL 60646-1975
Ph: (847)679-5500   Fax: (847)679-2494
Fr: 800-323-4900

Jim Patten and Donald L. Ferguson. 1993. $14.95; $11.95 (paper). 160 pages. Outlines opportunities in every field of journalism, including newspaper reporting and editing, magazine and book publishing, corporate communications, advertising and public relations, freelance writing, and teaching. Covers how to prepare for and enter each field, outlining responsibilities, salaries, benefits, and job outlook for each specialty. Illustrated.

★6163★ Opportunities in Magazine Publishing Careers

VGM Career Horizons
4255 W. Touhy Ave.
Lincolnwood, IL 60646-1975
Ph: (847)679-5500   Fax: (847)679-2494
Fr: 800-323-4900

S. William Pattis. 1992. $14.95; $11.95 (paper). 160 pages. Covers the scope of magazine publishing and addresses how to identify and pursue available positions. Illustrated.

★6164★ Opportunities in Newspaper Publishing Careers

VGM Career Horizons
4255 W. Touhy Ave.
Lincolnwood, IL 60646-1975
Ph: (847)679-5500   Fax: (847)679-2494
Fr: 800-323-4900

John Tebbel. 1989. $14.95; $11.95 (paper). 160 pages. Tells how to land a newspaper job, describing editorial and noneditorial positions at big city and small city papers and syndicated wire services. Career preparation chapters address the need to anticipate changing newspaper technology while acquiring fundamental news skills. Illustrated.

★6165★ Opportunities in Photography Careers

VGM Career Horizons
4255 W. Touhy Ave.
Lincolnwood, IL 60646-1975
Ph: (847)679-5500   Fax: (847)679-2494
Fr: 800-323-4900

Robert Mayer. 1994. $14.95; $11.95 (paper). Details opportunities in the field, including technical processing and sales, and how to pursue them. Contains bibliography and illustrations.

★6166★ Opportunities in Publishing Careers

VGM Career Horizons
4255 W. Touhy Ave.
Lincolnwood, IL 60646-1975
Ph: (847)679-5500   Fax: (847)679-2494
Fr: 800-323-4900

Robert A. Carter and S. William Pattis. 1995. $11.95 paperback. $14.95 hardcover. 160 pages. Covers all positions in book and magazine publishing, including new opportunities in multimedia publishing.

★6167★ Opportunities in Sports and Athletics

VGM Career Horizons
4255 W. Touhy Ave.
Lincolnwood, IL 60646-1975
Ph: (847)679-5500   Fax: (847)679-2494
Fr: 800-323-4900

William Ray Heitzmann. 1994. $14.95; $11.95 (paper). A guide to planning for and seeking opportunities in this growing field. Illustrated.

★6168★ Opportunities in Television and Video Careers

VGM Career Horizons
4255 W. Touhy Ave.
Lincolnwood, IL 60646-1975
Ph: (847)679-5500   Fax: (847)679-2494
Fr: 800-323-4900

Shonan Noronha. 1993. $14.95; $11.95 (paper). Details the employment opportunities open in television, cable, corporate video, institutional and government media, including independent production, and discusses how to land a job. Illustrated.

★6169★ Opportunities in Visual Arts Careers

VGM Career Horizons
4255 W. Touhy Ave.
Lincolnwood, IL 60646-1975
Ph: (847)679-5500   Fax: (847)679-2494
Fr: 800-323-4900

Mark Salmon. 1993. $14.95; $11.95 (paper). Points the way to a career in the visual arts, examining opportunities for designers, painters, sculptors, illustrators, animators, photographers, art therapists, educators, and others. Offers a view of the pros and cons of working for an art or design company or on your own.

★6170★ Radio and Television Career Directory

Gale Research
835 Penobscot Bldg.
Detroit, MI 48226-4094
Ph: (313)961-2242   Fax: (313)961-6083
Fr: 800-877-GALE

Bradley Morgan. Second edition, 1993. $39.00. 334 pages. Features extensive listings of contacts and entry-level job opportunities. Provides information on internships and sources of help-wanted ads.

OTHER SOURCES

★6171★ American Almanac of Jobs and Salaries 1994-95

Avon Books
1350 Avenue of the Americas, 2nd Fl.
New York, NY 10019
Ph: (212)261-6800   Fr: 800-238-0658

John Wright. Revised edition, 1993. $17.00. 704 pages. This is a comprehensive guide to the wages of hundreds of occupations in a wide variety of industries and organizations.

★6172★ American Society of Media Photographers (ASMP)

14 Washington Rd., Ste. 502
Princeton Junction, NJ 08550-1033
Ph: (609)799-8300   Fax: (609)799-2233

Members: Professional society of freelance photographers. Purpose: Works to evolve trade practices for photographers in communications fields. Provides business information to photographers and their potential clients; promotes ethics and rights of members. Activities: Holds educational programs and seminars. Compiles statistics.

★6173★ American Society of T.V. Cameramen and International Society of Videographers (ASTVC)

4314 Hilary St.
Las Vegas, NV 89117
Ph: (702)228-6704

Members: Professional cameramen, former cameramen, and persons in related jobs. Purpose: To bring together on a fraternal basis members of the industry with similar occupational interests and experiences, and to endeavor to promote the standards of professionalism within this segment of the industry. Activities: Conducts seminars. Maintains speakers' bureau.

★6174★ Biological Photographic Association (BPA)

1819 Peachtree Rd. NE, Ste. 620
Atlanta, GA 30309-1849
Ph: (404)351-6300   Fax: (404)351-3348

Members: Photographers, technicians, doctors, scientists, educators, and others concerned with photography in the health sciences and related fields. Purpose: Seeks to advance the techniques of biophotography and biomedical communications through meetings, seminars, and workshops. Activities: Has established Board of Registry to offer qualifying examinations for Registered Biological Photographer.

★6175★ Corporation for Public Broadcasting (CPB)

901 E St. NW
Washington, DC 20004-2037
Ph: (202)879-9600   Fax: (202)783-1019

A private, nonprofit corporation authorized under Public Broadcasting Act of 1967. Funded by U.S. government. Purpose: To promote and finance the growth and development of noncommercial radio and television. Makes grants to local public television and radio stations, program producers, and regional networks; studies emerging technologies; works to provide adequate long-range financing from the U.S. government and other sources for public broadcasting.

★6176★ Guide to Volunteer and Internship Programs in Public Broadcasting

Corporation for Public Broadcasting
Publications Dept.
901 E St. NW
Washington, DC 20004-2037
Ph: (202)879-9600

1991. Free.

★6177★ How You Can Make $25,000 a Year With Your Camera (No Matter Where You Live)

Writer's Digest Books
1507 Dana Ave.
Cincinnati, OH 45207
Ph: (513)531-2690   Fr: 800-289-0963

Larry Cribb. 1991. $12.95. 224 pages.

★6178★ International Museum Photographers Association (IMPA)

Lowell Anson Kenyon
5613 Johnson Ave.
Bethesda, MD 20817
Ph: (301)897-0083

Members: A division of the Council on Fine Art Photography. Practicing fine art still, film, and video photographers. Auditing and accrediting body for individuals using photography as part of their regular job assignment. Purpose: Seeks to: improve photographic quality; increase production; reduce operating costs; expand photographic services, flexibility, and turn-around time; enhance the photographer's position and his/her potential for advancement. Audits are designed to show the strengths and weaknesses of the individual. Ratings are primarily based on technical competence, and performance is indicated as not acceptable, acceptable, or excellent. Activities: Conducts correspondence courses designed to improve technical and administrative capabilities. Offers guest curatorial assistance and portfolio and resume evaluation and preparation.

★6179★ National Directory of Arts Internships

National Network for Artist Placement
935 W. Ave. 37
Los Angeles, CA 90065
Ph: (213)222-4035   Fax: (213)222-4035

Biennial, odd years. $40.00, postpaid; payment with order. Covers Approximately 2,000 internship opportunities in dance, music, theater, art, design, film, and video. Entries include: Name of sponsoring organization, address, name of contact; description of positions available, eligibility requirements, stipend or salary (if any), application procedures. Arrangement: Classified by discipline, then geographical.

★6180★ National Press Photographers Association (NPPA)

3200 Croasdaile Dr., Ste. 306
Durham, NC 27705
Ph: (919)383-7246   Fax: (919)383-7261

Purpose: Professional news photographers and others whose occupation has a direct professional relationship with photojournalism, the art of news communication by photographic image through publication, television film, or theater screen. Activities: Sponsors annual television-newsfilm workshop and annual cross-country (five locations) short course. Conducts annual competition for newsphotos and for television-newsfilm, and monthly contest for still clipping and television-newsfilm.

★6181★ The Photographer's Guide to Marketing and Self-Promotion

Writer's Digest Books
1507 Dana Ave.
Cincinnati, OH 45207
Ph: (513)531-2690   Fax: 800-543-4644
Fr: 800-289-0963

Maria Piscopo. Second edition, 1995. $18.95. 176 pages.

★6182★ Photomarket

PhotoStockNotes
Pine Lake Farm
1910 35th Rd.
Osceola, WI 54020
Ph: (715)248-3800   Fax: (715)248-7394
Fr: 800-223-3860

Semimonthly. $30.00 per month; $360.00 per year. Covers publishers and buyers of freelance photographs. Entries include: Company name, address, phone, contact person, publisher's requirements. Arrangement: Geographical.

★6183★ Professional Photographers of America (PP of A)

57 Forsyth St. NW, Ste. 1600
Atlanta, GA 30303
Ph: (404)522-8600   Fr: 800-742-7468

Members: Professional society of portrait, wedding, commercial, and industrial, and specialized photographers. **Activities:** Sponsors Winona International School of Professional Photography, Mt. Prospect, IL. Maintains speakers' bureau.

★6184★ Professional School Photographers of America (PSPA)

3000 Picture Pl.
Jackson, MI 49201
Ph: (517)788-8100   Fax: (517)788-8371

Members: A section of the Photo Marketing Association International. Firms engaged in the photographing and/or processing of school photographs. **Purpose:** To encourage the exchange of production ideas and econo-mies; to cooperate in the overall promotion of photography; to work for better relations and understanding with schools; to act as a group in making manufacturers of sensitized goods and photographic equipment aware of the specialized needs of school photography; to maintain a close watch on any legislation that may affect school photography; to promote career possibilities and personnel training and recruitment for school photography; to foster the well-being of the member firms by providing some of the advantages of a large-scale operation.

★6185★ Student Guide to Mass Media Internships

Intern Research Group
Box 52, Regent Hall
University of Colorado
Boulder, CO 80309
Ph: (303)442-8340

Annual, latest edition 1995. $35.00, payment with order; $40.00, billed. Covers about 10,000 internships offered by 2,700 newspapers, radio and television stations, cable television companies, magazines, advertising agencies, and other firms. Entries include: Organization name, address, type and number of internships offered, eligibility requirements, application deadline, salary or other stipend offered, name and title of contact; many listings also include description of intern's duties. Arrangement: Classified by type of medium, then geographical.

★6186★ TIPS: The International Photographic Sourcebook

L.A. Photogram
Box 2015
San Gabriel, CA 91778
Ph: (818)286-7510

Irregular, latest edition fall 1991; updated through *Photographic Digest*. $16.95. Covers over 2,000 manufacturers and distributors of photographic and audiovisual equipment, including speciality bookstores, retail stores, photographic laboratories, photochemical companies, photography organiza-tions; traveling, outdoor, and underwater photographers; colleges and universities offering photography programs, institutions housing largest photo collections; publishers of photography magazines, reference books, and supply catalogs; photo agencies that purchase photographs; limited international coverage. Entries include: Name, address, phone; entries for manufacturers and distributors also include description of products. Arrangement: Classified by line of business. Indexes: Product/service, trade name.

★6187★ Wedding Photographers International (WPI)

1312 Lincoln Blvd.
PO Box 1703
Santa Monica, CA 90406
Ph: (310)451-0090   Fax: (310)395-9058

Members: Wedding photographers and photographers employed at general photography studios. **Purpose:** Promotes high artistic and technical standards in wedding photography. Serves as a forum for the exchange of technical knowledge and experience; makes available the expertise of top professionals in the field of photographic arts and technology, advertising, sales promotion, marketing, public relations, accounting, business management, tax, and profit planning. Members are offered the opportunity to purchase special products and services. Compiles statistics.

★6188★ Women in Cable & Telecommunications (WIC)

230 W. Monroe St., Ste. 730
Chicago, IL 60606-4702
Ph: (312)634-2330   Fax: (312)634-2345
Fr: 800-628-WICT

Members: Individuals engaged in professional activity in cable and telecommunications. **Purpose:** Through leadership, education, and advocacy, works to empower women in cable and telecommunications to achieve their economic, professional, and personal goals while influencing the future of the industries they serve. **Activities:** Provides educational programs.

Physical Therapists

SOURCES OF HELP-WANTED ADS

★6189★ The American Journal of Orthopedics

Excerpta Medica, Inc.
105 Raider Blvd.
Belle Mead, NJ 08502
Ph: (908)874-8550   Fax: (908)874-8419

Monthly. $72.00/year; $95.00/year for institutions. Medical journal.

★6190★ American Journal of Physical Medicine and Rehabilitation

Foot & Ankle International
7100 Lakewood Bldg., Ste. 112
5987 E. 71st St.
Indianapolis, IN 46220
Ph: (317)845-4200   Fax: (317)845-4200

Bimonthly. $65.00/year for individuals; $85.00/year for other countries. Medical journal.

★6191★ Archives of Physical Medicine and Rehabilitation

American Congress of Rehabilitation
  Medicine
78 E. Adams St., Ste. 1310
Chicago, IL 60603-6103
Ph: (312)922-9371   Fax: (312)922-6754

Monthly. $130.00/year

★6192★ Journal of Applied Physiology

The American Physiological Society
9650 Rockville Pke.
Bethesda, MD 20814
Ph: (301)530-7071   Fax: (301)571-1814

Monthly. Journal covering respiratory, environmental, and exercise physiology.

★6193★ Journal of Learning Disabilities

Pro-Ed Journals
8700 Shoal Creek Blvd.
Austin, TX 78757
Ph: (512)451-3246

Ten issues/year. $49.00/year. Special education magazine.

★6194★ The Journal of Orthopaedic and Sports Physical Therapy

Foot & Ankle International
7100 Lakewood Bldg., Ste. 112
5987 E. 71st St.
Indianapolis, IN 46220
Ph: (317)845-4200   Fax: (317)845-4200

Monthly. $70.00/year for individuals; $100.00/year for other countries.

★6195★ Teaching Exceptional Children

The Council for Exceptional Children
1920 Association Dr.
Reston, VA 22091-1589
Ph: (703)620-3660   Fax: (703)264-9494
Fr: 800-CEC-READ

Quarterly. $35.00/year for individuals. Journal exploring practical methods for teaching talented and gifted children who have disabilities.

★6196★ TeamRehab Report

Miramar Publishing
6133 Bristol Pkwy.
Box 3640
Culver City, CA 90231-3640
Ph: (213)337-9717

Bimonthly.

PLACEMENT AND JOB REFERRAL SERVICES

★6197★ American Physical Therapy Association (APTA)

1111 N. Fairfax St.
Alexandria, VA 22314
Ph: (703)684-2782

Members: Professional organization of physical therapists and physical therapist assistants and students. **Purpose:** Fosters the development and improvement of physical therapy service, education, and research; evaluates the organization and administration of curricula; directs the maintenance of standards and promotes scientific research. Acts as an accrediting body for educational programs in physical therapy and is responsible for establishing standards. **Activities:** Offers advisory and consultation services to schools of physical therapy and facilities offering physical therapy services; provides placement services at conference.

★6198★ American Public Health Association (APHA)

1015 15th St. NW
Washington, DC 20005
Ph: (202)789-5600   Fax: (202)789-5681

Members: Professional organization of physicians, nurses, educators, academicians, environmentalists, epidemiologists, new professionals, social workers, health administrators, optometrists, podiatrists, pharmacists, dentists, nutritionists, health planners, other community and mental health specialists, and interested consumers. **Purpose:** Seeks to protect and promote personal, mental, and environmental health. **Activities:** Services include: promulgation of standards; establishment of uniform practices and procedures; development of the etiology of communicable diseases; research in public health; exploration of medical care programs and their relationships to public health. Sponsors job placement service.

★6199★ Association on Higher Education and Disability (AHEAD)

PO Box 21192
Columbus, OH 43221-0192
Ph: (614)488-4972   Fax: (614)488-1174

Members: Individuals interested in promoting the equal rights and opportunities of disabled postsecondary students, staff, faculty, and graduates. **Purpose:** Provides an exchange of communication for those professionally involved with disabled students; collects, evaluates, and disseminates information; encourages and supports legislation for the benefit of disabled students. **Activities:** Conducts surveys on issues pertinent to college students with disabilities; offers resource referral system and employment exchange for positions in disability student services. Conducts research programs; compiles statistics.

★6200★ U.S. Physical Therapy Association (USPTA)

1803 Avon Ln.
Arlington Heights, IL 60004

Members: Professional physical therapists and assistants. **Purpose:** Maintains U.S. Physical Therapy Academy which: conducts continuing education programs for members; sponsors workshops to acquaint personnel from other medical fields with physical therapy; accredits hospital and nursing home physical therapy departments, universities, and colleges of physical therapy; certifies physical therapists through board examinations. **Activities:** Promotes ethical standards; maintains placement service and charitable program; compiles statistics; conducts children's services.

EMPLOYER DIRECTORIES AND NETWORKING LISTS

★6201★ AHA Guide to the Health Care Field

Health Statistics Group
American Hospital Association (AHA)
1 N. Franklin
Chicago, IL 60606
Ph: (312)422-3501   Fax: (312)280-6015

Annual, July. $195.00, payment with order. Covers hospitals, multi-health care systems, freestanding ambulatory surgery centers, psychiatric facilities, long-term care facilities, substance abuse programs, hospices, Health Maintenance Organizations (HMOs), and other health-related organizations. Entries include: For hospitals: facility name, address, phone, administrator's name, number of beds, facilities and services, number of employees, expenses, other statistics. For other organizations: name, address, phone, name and title of contact. Arrangement: Geographical. Indexes: Hospital name.

★6202★ Directory of Hospital Personnel

Medical Economics
5 Paragon Dr.
Montvale, NJ 07645-1725
Ph: (201)358-7500   Fax: (201)573-4956
Fr: 800-222-3045

Annual, September. $325.00, plus 7.50 shipping. Covers 200,000 executives at 7,100 U.S. hospitals. Entries include: Name of hospital, address, phone, number of beds, type and JCAHO status of hospital, names and titles of key department heads and staff, medical and nursing school affiliations; number of residents, interns, and nursing students. Arrangement: Geographical. Indexes: Hospital name, personnel, hospital size.

★6203★ Directory of Nursing Homes

HCIA Inc.
300 E. Lombard St.
Baltimore, MD 21202
Ph: (410)576-9600   Fax: (410)539-5220
Fr: 800-568-3282

Annual. $249.00. Covers over 16,000 state-licensed long-term care facilities. Entries include: Facility name, address, phone, names and titles of key personnel, licensure status, number of beds; number of nursing, dietary, and auxiliary staff members; program/services; medicaid/medicare certification status; admission and referral requirements; age and gender restrictions; languages spoken; management or chain company name. Arrangement: Geographical. Indexes: Alphabetical, geographical (county) and by chain headquarters.

★6204★ Home Health Service Directory

American Business Directories, Inc.
American Business Information, Inc.
5711 S. 86th Cir.
Omaha, NE 68127
Ph: (402)593-4600   Fax: (402)331-1505

Annual. $1,200.00, U.S. edition. Entries include: Name, address, phone (including area code), size of advertisement, year first in Yellow Pages, name of owl her or manager, number of employees. Compiled from telephone company Yellow Pages, nationwide. Arrangement: Geographical.

★6205★ Hospital Blue Book

Billian Publishing Co.
2100 Powers Ferry Rd., Ste. 300
Atlanta, GA 30339
Ph: (404)955-5656   Fax: (404)952-0669

Annual, spring. $154.50, national edition, plus $20.00 shipping. Covers more than 7,100 hospitals; some listings also appear in a separate southern edition of this publication. Entries include: Name of hospital, accreditation, mailing address, phone, fax, number of beds, type of facility (nonprofit, general, state, etc.); list of administrative personnel and chiefs of medical services, with specific titles. Arrangement: Geographical.

★6206★ Hospital Market Atlas

SMG Marketing Group, Inc.
1342 N. LaSalle Dr.
Chicago, IL 60610
Ph: (312)642-3026   Fax: (312)642-9729
Fr: 800-678-3026

Biennial, odd years. $495.00, payment with order. Covers over 7,000 hospitals, hospital systems and 480 group purchasing organizations. Entries include: Hospital or organization name, address, phone, county code, management, type of hospital service, number of beds, admissions, surgical operations, and emergency room visits. Arrangement: Geographical.

★6207★ Hospitals Directory

American Business Directories, Inc.
American Business Information, Inc.
5711 S. 86th Cir.
Omaha, NE 68127
Ph: (402)593-4600   Fax: (402)331-1505

Annual. $870.00, U.S. edition. Entries include: Name, address, phone (including area code), size of advertisement, year first in Yellow Pages, name of owner or manager, number of employees. Compiled from telephone company Yellow Pages, nationwide. Arrangement: Geographical.

★6208★ Medical and Health Information Directory

Gale Research
835 Penobscot Bldg.
Detroit, MI 48226-4094
Ph: (313)961-2242   Fax: (313)961-6083
Fr: 800-877-GALE

Approximately biennial; latest edition 1994. $195.00, per volume; $485.00, for the three-volume set. Covers in Volume 1, almost 18,600 medical and health oriented associations, organizations, institutions, and government agencies, including health maintenance organizations (HMOs), preferred provider organizations (PPOs), insurance companies, pharmaceutical companies, research centers, and medical and allied health schools. In Volume 2, nearly 11,800 medical book publishers; medical periodicals, directories, audiovisual producers and services, medical libraries and information centers, and electronic resources. In Volume 3, nearly 26,000 clinics, treatment centers, care programs, and counseling/diagnostic services for 30 subject areas. Entries include: Institution, service, or firm name, address, phone; many include names of key personnel and, when pertinent, descriptive annotation. Arrangement: Classified by organization activity, service, etc. Indexes: Each volume has a complete alphabetical name and keyword index.

★6209★ Osteopathic Membership Directory—AOHA

American Osteopathic Healthcare Association
5301 Wisconsin Ave. NW, Ste. 630
Washington, DC 20015-2015
Ph: (202)686-1700   Fax: (202)686-7615

Annual, summer. $125.00, payment with order. Covers about 110 osteopathic hospitals. Includes list of individual and institutional members; also lists osteopathic colleges, and directors of medical education. Entries include: For hospitals: name of hospital, name of chief executive officer, address, phone, number of beds and other hospital data. Arrangement: Geographical. Indexes: Name, institution.

★6210★ Physical Therapists Directory

American Business Directories, Inc.
American Business Information, Inc.
5711 S. 86th Cir.
Omaha, NE 68127
Ph: (402)593-4600   Fax: (402)331-1505

Annual. $725.00, payment with order. Entries include: Name, address, phone (including area code), size of advertisement, year first in Yellow Pages, name of owner or manager, number of employees. Compiled from telephone company Yellow Pages, nationwide. Arrangement: Geographical.

★6211★ Private Practice Section of the American Physical Therapy Association—Membership Directory

Private Practice Section
American Physical Therapy Association
1101 17th St. NW, Ste. 1000
Washington, DC 20036
Ph: (202)457-1114   Fax: (202)457-9191

Biennial, March of even years. $250.00. Covers about 4,700 member physical therapists in private practice. Entries include: Firm name, home address, business address and phone, fax, names and titles of key personnel, specialty, type of practice, congressional district. Arrangement: Same information is listed alphabetically and geographically. Indexes: Geographical, personal name.

HANDBOOKS AND MANUALS

★6212★ Careers in Health Care

VGM Career Horizons
4255 W. Touhy Ave.
Lincolnwood,. IL 60646-1975
Ph: (847)679-5500   Fax: (847)679-2494
Fr: 800-323-4900

Barbara M. Swanson. 1995. $17.95; $13.95 (paper). Describes job duties, work settings, salaries, licensing and certification requirements, educational preparation, and future outlook. Gives ideas on how to secure a job.

★6213★ Careers in Health and Fitness

Rosen Publishing Group, Inc.
29 E. 21st St.
New York, NY 10010
Ph: (212)777-3017   Fax: (212)777-0277
Fr: 800-237-9932

Jackie Heron. Revised edition, 1990. $14.95. 160 pages. Contains occupational profiles for this field, including information on job duties, skills, advantages, basic equipment used, employment possibilities, certification, and salary.

★6214★ Occupational Therapy Careers

American Occupational Therapy
  Association
1383 Piccard Dr.
PO Box 1725
Rockville, MD 20849-1725
Ph: (301)948-9626

Brochure. Free. Describes employment outlook for occupational therapists, as well as education, places of employment, and earnings.

★6215★ 100 Best Careers for the Year 2000

Prentice Hall General Reference
15 Columbus Cir.
New York, NY 10023
Ph: (212)373-8500   Fr: 800-223-2348

Shelly Field. 1992. $15.00 (paper). Covers 100 of the fastest growing jobs. The publication is divided into 11 general employment sections. Specific careers are covered within each section. Provides job description, responsibilities, employment opportunities, earnings, education and training, advancement opportunities, and experience and qualifications for each occupation.

★6216★ Opportunities in Fitness Careers

VGM Career Horizons
4255 W. Touhy Ave.
Lincolnwood, IL 60646-1975
Ph: (847)679-5500   Fax: (847)679-2494
Fr: 800-323-4900

Jean Rosenbaum. 1992. $14.95; $11.95 (paper). Surveys fitness related careers. Describes career opportunities, education and experience needed, how to get into entry-level jobs and what income to expect. Schools are listed in the appendix.

★6217★ Opportunities in Health and Medical Careers

VGM Career Horizons
4255 W. Touhy Ave.
Lincolnwood, IL 60646-1975
Ph: (847)679-5500   Fax: (847)679-2494
Fr: 800-323-4900

Donald Snook, Jr. and Leo D'Orazio. 1993. $14.95; $11.95 (paper). Covers the full range of medical and health occupations. Illustrated.

★6218★ Opportunities in Paramedical Careers

VGM Career Horizons
4255 W. Touhy Ave.
Lincolnwood, IL 60646-1975
Ph: (847)679-5500   Fax: (847)679-2494
Fr: 800-323-4900

Alex Kacen. 1994. $14.95; 11.95 (paper). 160 pages. Discusses a variety of opportunities in this field and how to pursue them. Illustrated.

★6219★ Opportunities in Physical Therapy Careers

VGM Career Horizons
4255 W. Touhy Ave.
Lincolnwood, IL 60646-1975
Ph: (847)679-5500   Fax: (847)679-2494
Fr: 800-323-4900

Bernice R. Krumhansl. 1994. $14.95; $11.95 (paper). Defines what the jobs are, where they are, and how to pursue them. Contains bibliography and illustrations.

★6220★ Opportunities in Sports and Athletics

VGM Career Horizons
4255 W. Touhy Ave.
Lincolnwood, IL 60646-1975
Ph: (847)679-5500   Fax: (847)679-2494
Fr: 800-323-4900

William Ray Heitzmann. 1994. $14.95; $11.95 (paper). A guide to planning for and seeking opportunities in this growing field. Illustrated.

★6221★ Opportunities in Sports Medicine Careers

VGM Career Horizons
4255 W. Touhy Ave.
Lincolnwood, IL 60646-1975
Ph: (847)679-5500   Fax: (847)679-2494
Fr: 800-323-4900

William Ray Heitzmann. 1995. $14.95; $11.95 (paper). 160 pages. Discusses a variety of opportunities in this field and how

to pursue them. Contains bibliography and illustrations.

★6222★ Opportunities in Vocational and Technical Careers

VGM Career Horizons
4255 W. Touhy Ave.
Lincolnwood, IL 60646-1975
Ph: (847)679-5500   Fax: (847)679-2494
Fr: 800-323-4900

Adrian A. Paradis. 1992. $14.95; $11.95 (paper). 160 pages. Provides information on a variety of opportunities and advice on breaking into the field.

★6223★ Physical Therapists

Rourke Book Co., Inc.
PO Box 3328
Vero Beach, FL 32964
Ph: (407)465-4575   Fax: (407)465-3132

Robert James. 1995.

★6224★ Resumes for Health and Medical Careers

4255 W. Touhy Ave.
Lincolnwood, IL 60646-1975
Ph: (708)679-5500   Fax: (708)679-6375
Fr: 800-323-4900

Compiled by VGM Career Horizons Staff 1995. $9.95 (paper).

★6225★ Therapists and Allied Health Professionals Career Directory

Gale Research
835 Penobscot Bldg.
Detroit, MI 48226-4094
Ph: (313)961-2242   Fax: (313)961-6083
Fr: 800-877-GALE

Bradley Morgan. 1993. $39.00. 326 pages. Essays on specific careers provide an insider's perspective. Also features extensive listings of contacts and entry-level job opportunities. Provides information on internships and sources of help-wanted ads.

★6226★ Where the Jobs Are: The Hottest Careers for the '90s

The Career Press, Inc.
3 Tice Rd.
PO Box 687
Franklin Lakes, NJ 07417
Ph: (201)848-0310   Fax: (201)848-1727
Fr: 800-237-3371

Joyce Hadley. Second edition, 1995. $9.99. 300 pages. Describes careers in fifteen general fields, from accounting to travel and hospitality.

EMPLOYMENT AGENCIES AND SEARCH FIRMS

★6227★ EHS and Associates, Inc.

3033 Excelsior Blvd., Ste. 303
Minneapolis, MN 55416
Ph: (612)924-2366   Fax: (612)924-2367

Executive search firm and employment agency.

★6228★ Harper Associates

29870 Middlebelt
Farmington Hills, MI 48334
Ph: (810)932-1170

Employment agency.

★6229★ JPM International

4665 MacArthur Ct., Ste. 100B
Newport Beach, CA 92660
Ph: (714)955-2545   Fax: (714)757-1320

Executive search firm and employment agency.

★6230★ Medical Personnel Pool

2901 S. Ridgewood Ave.
Daytona Beach, FL 32119-3542
Ph: (904)736-1648

Provides regular and temporary staffing assistance. Offices located in cities throughout United States.

★6231★ Midwest Medical Consultants

8910 Purdue Rd., Ste. 200
Indianapolis, IN 46268-1155
Ph: (317)872-1053

Employment agency. Executive search firm.

★6232★ Professional Placement Associates, Inc.

11 Rye Ridge Plaza
Rye Brook, NY 10573
Ph: (914)251-1000   Fax: (914)939-1959

Employment agency.

★6233★ Sue Carroll Personnel, Inc.

16 E. 79th St.
New York, NY 10021
Ph: (212)288-8866   Fax: (212)988-7191

Employment agency and executive search firm.

★6234★ Travcorps, Inc.

40 Eastern Ave.
Malden, MA 02148
Ph: (617)322-2600

Places staff in temporary assignments.

OTHER SOURCES

★6235★ American Almanac of Jobs and Salaries 1994-95

Avon Books
1350 Avenue of the Americas, 2nd Fl.
New York, NY 10019
Ph: (212)261-6800   Fr: 800-238-0658

John Wright. Revised edition, 1993. $17.00. 704 pages. This is a comprehensive guide to the wages of hundreds of occupations in a wide variety of industries and organizations.

★6236★ American Health Care Association

1201 L St. NW
Washington, DC 20005
Ph: (202)842-4444   Fax: (202)842-3860

Members: Federation of state associations of long-term health care facilities. **Purpose:** Promotes standards for professionals in long-term health care delivery and quality care for patients and residents in a safe environment. Focuses on issues of availability, quality, affordability, and fair payment. Operates as a liaison with governmental agencies, Congress, and professional associations.

★6237★ American Kinesiotherapy Association (AKTA)

PO Box 614
Wheeling, IL 60090-0614
Fr: 800-296-AKTA

Members: Professional society of kinesiotherapists, and associate and student members with interest in physical and mental rehabilitation and adapted physical education. (Kinesiology is the study of human movement; kinesiotherapists use kinesiology to design and implement therapeutic exercise to meet the rehabilitative needs of persons with disease, injury, and/or physical disorders.) **Purpose:** Goal is to promote the profession of kinseotheraphy by working toward public recognition of kinesiotherapy and to pursue and support legislative concerns of the profession. Works to maintain and advance the standard of care through educational opportunities.

★6238★ American Society of Hand Therapists (ASHT)

401 N. Michigan Ave.
Chicago, IL 60611
Ph: (312)321-6866   Fax: (312)527-6636

Members: Registered and licensed occupational and physical therapists specializing in hand therapy and committed to excellence and professionalism in hand rehabilitation. **Purpose:** To promote research, publish information, improve treatment techniques, and standardize hand evaluation and care. Fosters education and communication between therapists in the U.S. and abroad. **Activities:** Compiles statistics; conducts research and education programs and continuing education seminars.

★6239★ Day in a Career: Physical Therapist

Cambridge Career Products
PO Box 2153
Dept. CC15
Charleston, WV 25328-2153
Ph: (304)744-9323   Fax: (304)744-9351
Fr: 800-468-4227

Video. 1994. $89.00. 15-22 minutes. Includes candid interviews and work situations, plus outlines of relevant career information.

★6240★ Holistic Dental Association (HDA)

c/o Dr. Paul Plowman
4801 Richmond Sq.
Oklahoma City, OK 73118
Ph: (405)840-5600   Fax: (405)843-0417

Members: Dentists, chiropractors, dental hygienists, physical therapists, and medical doctors. **Purpose:** Goals are: to provide a holistic approach to better dental care for patients; to expand techniques, medications, and philosophies that pertain to extractions, anesthetics, fillings, crowns, and orthodontics. Encourages use of homeopathic medications, acupuncture, cranial osteopathy, nutritional techniques, and physical therapy in treating patients in addition to conventional treatments. **Activities:** Classifies therapies; has developed a referral questionnaire for holistic practitioners. Sponsors training and educational seminars.

★6241★ National Rehabilitation Association (NRA)

633 S. Washington St.
Alexandria, VA 22314
Ph: (703)836-0850   Fax: (703)836-0848

Members: Administrators, instructors, placement specialists, secretaries, counselors, therapists, vocational evaluators, ADA specialists and others interested in rehabilitation of persons with disabilities. **Activities:** Conducts legislative activities; develops accessibility guidelines; offers specialized education.

★6242★ National Strength and Conditioning Association (NSCA)

530 Communication Cir., Ste. 204
Colorado Springs, CO 80905
Ph: (719)632-6722   Fax: (719)632-6367

Members: Professional coaches, athletic trainers, physical therapists, sports medicine physicians, and sports science researchers. **Purpose:** Promotes the total conditioning of athletes to a level of optimum performance, with the belief that a better conditioned athlete not only performs better but is less prone to injury. Conducts national, regional, state, and local clinics and workshops. Operates professional certification program.

Physician Assistants

SOURCES OF HELP-WANTED ADS

★6243★ *Physician Assistant*
105 Raider Blvd.
Belle Mead, NJ 08502
Ph: (908)874-8550
Monthly. $50.00/year.

PLACEMENT AND JOB REFERRAL SERVICES

★6244★ **American Association of Pathologists' Assistants (AAPA)**
183 Main St. E., No. 1200
Rochester, NY 14604-1617
Ph: (716)232-4030   Fax: (716)232-1669
Fr: 800-532-2272

Members: Pathologists' assistants and individuals qualified by academic and practical training to provide service in anatomic pathology under the direction of a qualified pathologist who is responsible for the performance of the assistant. **Purpose:** Promotes the mutual association of trained pathologists' assistants and informs the public and the medical profession concerning the goals of this profession. **Activities:** Compiles statistics on salaries, geographic distribution, and duties of pathologists' assistants. Sponsors a continuing medical education program; offers placement services for members only.

★6245★ **Association of Physician Assistant Programs (APAP)**
950 N. Washington St.
Alexandria, VA 22314
Ph: (703)548-5538

Members: Educational institutions with training programs for assistants to primary care and surgical physicians. **Purpose:** Assists in the development and organization of educational curricula for physician assistant (PA) programs to assure the public of competent PAs; contributes to defining the roles of PAs in the field of medicine to maximize their benefit to the public; serves as a public information center on the profession; coordinates program logistics such as admissions and career placements. Sponsors Annual Survey of Physician Assistant Educational Programs in the United States. Conducts research projects; compiles statistics.

EMPLOYER DIRECTORIES AND NETWORKING LISTS

★6246★ *AHA Guide to the Health Care Field*
Health Statistics Group
American Hospital Association (AHA)
1 N. Franklin
Chicago, IL 60606
Ph: (312)422-3501   Fax: (312)280-6015

Annual, July. $195.00, payment with order. Covers hospitals, multi-health care systems, freestanding ambulatory surgery centers, psychiatric facilities, long-term care facilities, substance abuse programs, hospices, Health Maintenance Organizations (HMOs), and other health-related organizations. Entries include: For hospitals: facility name, address, phone, administrator's name, number of beds, facilities and services, number of employees, expenses, other statistics. For other organizations: name, address, phone, name and title of contact. Arrangement: Geographical. Indexes: Hospital name.

★6247★ *American Group Practice Association—Directory*
American Group Practice Association
1422 Duke St.
Alexandria, VA 22314
Ph: (703)838-0033   Fax: (703)548-1890

Annual, February. $150.00. Covers about 250 private group medical practices and their professional staffs, totalling about 25,000 physicians and administrators. Entries include: Group member name, address, phone, names of administrator and other executives, names of physician listed by medical specialties. Arrangement: Alphabetical. Indexes: Group location, personal name.

★6248★ *Association of Physician's Assistants in Cardiovascular Surgery—Membership Directory*
Association of Physician's Assistants in Cardiovascular Surgery
2000 Tate Springs Rd.
Lynchburg, VA 24501
Ph: (804)847-8745   Fax: (804)528-1506

Annual. Available to members only. Covers about 800 physician's assistants who work with cardiovascular surgeons. Entries include: Name, address, phone. Arrangement: Alphabetical.

★6249★ *Directory of Hospital Personnel*
Medical Economics
5 Paragon Dr.
Montvale, NJ 07645-1725
Ph: (201)358-7500   Fax: (201)573-4956
Fr: 800-222-3045

Annual, September. $325.00, plus 7.50 shipping. Covers 200,000 executives at 7,100 U.S. hospitals. Entries include: Name of hospital, address, phone, number of beds, type and JCAHO status of hospital, names and titles of key department heads and staff, medical and nursing school affiliations; number of residents, interns, and nursing students. Arrangement: Geographical. Indexes: Hospital name, personnel, hospital size.

★6250★ *Hospital Blue Book*
Billian Publishing Co.
2100 Powers Ferry Rd., Ste. 300
Atlanta, GA 30339
Ph: (404)955-5656   Fax: (404)952-0669

Annual, spring. $154.50, national edition, plus $20.00 shipping. Covers more than 7,100 hospitals; some listings also appear in a separate southern edition of this publication. Entries include: Name of hospital, accreditation, mailing address, phone, fax, number of beds, type of facility (nonprofit, general, state, etc.); list of administrative personnel and chiefs of medical services, with specific titles. Arrangement: Geographical.

★6251★ Hospital Market Atlas

SMG Marketing Group, Inc.
1342 N. LaSalle Dr.
Chicago, IL 60610
Ph: (312)642-3026   Fax: (312)642-9729
Fr: 800-678-3026

Biennial, odd years. $495.00, payment with order. Covers over 7,000 hospitals, hospital systems and 480 group purchasing organizations. Entries include: Hospital or organization name, address, phone, county code, management, type of hospital service, number of beds, admissions, surgical operations, and emergency room visits. Arrangement: Geographical.

★6252★ Hospitals Directory

American Business Directories, Inc.
American Business Information, Inc.
5711 S. 86th Cir.
Omaha, NE 68127
Ph: (402)593-4600   Fax: (402)331-1505

Annual. $870.00, U.S. edition. Entries include: Name, address, phone (including area code), size of advertisement, year first in Yellow Pages, name of owner or manager, number of employees. Compiled from telephone company Yellow Pages, nationwide. Arrangement: Geographical.

★6253★ Medical and Health Information Directory

Gale Research
835 Penobscot Bldg.
Detroit, MI 48226-4094
Ph: (313)961-2242   Fax: (313)961-6083
Fr: 800-877-GALE

Approximately biennial; latest edition 1994. $195.00, per volume; $485.00, for the three-volume set. Covers in Volume 1, almost 18,600 medical and health oriented associations, organizations, institutions, and government agencies, including health maintenance organizations (HMOs), preferred provider organizations (PPOs), insurance companies, pharmaceutical companies, research centers, and medical and allied health schools. In Volume 2, nearly 11,800 medical book publishers; medical periodicals, directories, audiovisual producers and services, medical libraries and information centers, and electronic resources. In Volume 3, nearly 26,000 clinics, treatment centers, care programs, and counseling/diagnostic services for 30 subject areas. Entries include: Institution, service, or firm name, address, phone; many include names of key personnel and, when pertinent, descriptive annotation. Arrangement: Classified by organization activity, service, etc. Indexes: Each volume has a complete alphabetical name and keyword index.

★6254★ National Directory of Physician Assistant Programs

Association of Physician Assistant Programs
950 N. Washington St.
Alexandria, VA 22314
Ph: (703)836-2272   Fax: (703)684-1924

Annual. $25.00, payment must accompany order. Covers over 55 accredited programs that educate physician assistants. Entries include: Program name, institution name, address, phone; description of program, in-cluding curriculum, selection criteria, degrees of certificates offered. Arrangement: Geographical.

★6255★ Osteopathic Membership Directory—AOHA

American Osteopathic Healthcare Association
5301 Wisconsin Ave. NW, Ste. 630
Washington, DC 20015-2015
Ph: (202)686-1700   Fax: (202)686-7615

Annual, summer. $125.00, payment with order. Covers about 110 osteopathic hospitals. Includes list of individual and institutional members; also lists osteopathic colleges, and directors of medical education. Entries include: For hospitals: name of hospital, name of chief executive officer, address, phone, number of beds and other hospital data. Arrangement: Geographical. Indexes: Name, institution.

★6256★ Peterson's Job Opportunities in Health Care

Peterson's Guides, Inc.
202 Carnegie Ctr.
Box 2123
Princeton, NJ 08543-2123
Ph: (609)243-9111   Fax: (609)243-9150
Fr: 800-338-3282

Annual, August. $18.95. Covers Over 1,500 companies hiring health-care professionals for skilled nursing care facilities, hospitals, medical laboratories, home health care, and pharmaceuticals. Entries include: Organization name, address, phone, name and title of contact, type of organization, number of employees, Standard Industrial Classification (SIC) code; description of opportunities available including disciplines, level of education required, starting locations and salaries, level of experience accepted, benefits. Arrangement: Alphabetical. Indexes: Employer by type of organization, industry classification, number of employees, starting location, special interest area; education level, company.

HANDBOOKS AND MANUALS

★6257★ Careers in Health Care

VGM Career Horizons
4255 W. Touhy Ave.
Lincolnwood, IL 60646-1975
Ph: (847)679-5500   Fax: (847)679-2494
Fr: 800-323-4900

Barbara M. Swanson. 1995. $17.95; $13.95 (paper). Describes job duties, work settings, salaries, licensing and certification requirements, educational preparation, and future outlook. Gives ideas on how to secure a job.

★6258★ Careers in Medicine: Traditional and Alternative Opportunities

Garrett Park Press
PO Box 190 C
Garrett Park, MD 20896-0190
Ph: (301)946-2553

Donald T. Rucker and Martin D. Keller. 1990. $15.95. 346 pages. Cites training require-ments, illustrative work activities, and a summary of the advantages and disadvantages in a variety of specialized areas. Includes hundreds of career alternatives and discusses ways to break into these fields for persons trained in medicine. Features contributions from over 40 professionals in all phases of medicine and provides 200 sources of information on specialties and subspecialties.

★6259★ Federal Jobs in Nursing and Health Sciences

Impact Publications
9104 N. Manassas Dr.
Manassas Park, VA 22111-5211
Ph: (703)361-7300   Fax: (703)335-9486

Russ Smith. 1995. $14.95 (paper).

★6260★ Healthcare Career Directory–Nurses and Physicians

Gale Research
835 Penobscot Bldg.
Detroit, MI 48226-4094
Ph: (313)961-2242   Fax: (313)961-6083
Fr: 800-877-GALE

Bradley Morgan. Second edition, 1993. $39.00. 327 pages. Essays on specific careers provide an insider's perspective. Features extensive listings of contacts and entry-level job opportunities. Provides information on internships and sources of help-wanted ads.

★6261★ 100 Best Careers for the Year 2000

Prentice Hall General Reference
15 Columbus Cir.
New York, NY 10023
Ph: (212)373-8500   Fr: 800-223-2348

Shelly Field. 1992. $15.00 (paper). Covers 100 of the fastest growing jobs. The publication is divided into 11 general employment sections. Specific careers are covered within each section. Provides job description, responsibilities, employment opportunities, earnings, education and training, advancement opportunities, and experience and qualifications for each occupation.

★6262★ Opportunities in Health and Medical Careers

VGM Career Horizons
4255 W. Touhy Ave.
Lincolnwood, IL 60646-1975
Ph: (847)679-5500   Fax: (847)679-2494
Fr: 800-323-4900

Donald Snook, Jr. and Leo D'Orazio. 1993. $14.95; $11.95 (paper). Covers the full range of medical and health occupations. Illustrated.

★6263★ Opportunities in Paramedical Careers

VGM Career Horizons
4255 W. Touhy Ave.
Lincolnwood, IL 60646-1975
Ph: (847)679-5500   Fax: (847)679-2494
Fr: 800-323-4900

Alex Kacen. 1994. $14.95; 11.95 (paper). 160 pages. Discusses a variety of opportunities in this field and how to pursue them. Illustrated.

★6264★ *Opportunities in Vocational and Technical Careers*

VGM Career Horizons
4255 W. Touhy Ave.
Lincolnwood, IL 60646-1975
Ph: (847)679-5500   Fax: (847)679-2494
Fr: 800-323-4900

Adrian A. Paradis. 1992. $14.95; $11.95 (paper). 160 pages. Provides information on a variety of opportunities and advice on breaking into the field.

★6265★ *Resumes for the Health Care Professional*

John Wiley & Sons, Inc.
605 3rd Ave.
New York, NY 10158-0012
Ph: (212)850-6000   Fr: 800-225-5945

Kim Marino. 1993. $14.95 (paper).

★6266★ *Resumes for Health and Medical Careers*

4255 W. Touhy Ave.
Lincolnwood, IL 60646-1975
Ph: (708)679-5500   Fax: (708)679-6375
Fr: 800-323-4900

Compiled by VGM Career Horizons Staff 1995. $9.95 (paper).

★6267★ *Where the Jobs Are: The Hottest Careers for the '90s*

The Career Press, Inc.
3 Tice Rd.
PO Box 687
Franklin Lakes, NJ 07417
Ph: (201)848-0310   Fax: (201)848-1727
Fr: 800-237-3371

Joyce Hadley. Second edition, 1995. $9.99. 300 pages. Describes careers in fifteen general fields, from accounting to travel and hospitality.

EMPLOYMENT AGENCIES AND SEARCH FIRMS

★6268★ **Action Plus Employer Services**
1211 W. Imperial Hwy., Ste. 100
Brea, CA 92621
Ph: (714)773-1506   Fax: (714)773-9201
Employment agency.

★6269★ **Davis-Smith, Inc.**
24725 W. 12 Mile Rd., Ste. 302
Southfield, MI 48034
Ph: (810)354-4100

Employment agency. Executive search firm.

★6270★ **Midwest Medical Consultants**
8910 Purdue Rd., Ste. 200
Indianapolis, IN 46268-1155
Ph: (317)872-1053

Employment agency. Executive search firm.

★6271★ **Professional Placement Associates, Inc.**
11 Rye Ridge Plaza
Rye Brook, NY 10573
Ph: (914)251-1000   Fax: (914)939-1959
Employment agency.

OTHER SOURCES

★6272★ **American Academy of Physician Assistants (AAPA)**
950 N. Washington St.
Alexandria, VA 22314
Ph: (703)836-2272   Fax: (703)684-1924

Members: Physician assistants who have graduated from an American Medical Association accredited program and/or are certified by the National Commission on Certification of Physician Assistants; individuals who are enrolled in an accredited PA educational program. **Purpose:** To educate the public about the physician assistant profession; represent physician assistants' interests before Congress, government agencies, and health-related organizations; assure the competence of physician assistants through development of educational curricula and accreditation programs; provide services for members. **Activities:** Organizes annual National PA Day. Develops research and education programs; compiles statistics.

★6273★ *American Almanac of Jobs and Salaries 1994-95*

Avon Books
1350 Avenue of the Americas, 2nd Fl.
New York, NY 10019
Ph: (212)261-6800   Fr: 800-238-0658

John Wright. Revised edition, 1993. $17.00. 704 pages. This is a comprehensive guide to the wages of hundreds of occupations in a wide variety of industries and organizations.

★6274★ **Association of Physician Assistants in Cardiovascular Surgery (APACVS)**
11250 Rodger Bacon Dr. Ste., 8
Reston, VA 22090
Ph: (703)707-0476   Fax: (703)435-4390

Members: Physician assistants who work with cardiovascular surgeons. **Purpose:** Objective is to assist in defining the role of physician assistants in the field of cardiovascular surgery through educational forums.

★6275★ **Commission on Accreditation of Allied Health Education Programs (CAAHEP)**
515 N. State St., Ste. 7530
Chicago, IL 60610
Ph: (312)464-4636   Fax: (312)464-5830

Purpose: Serves as an nationally recognized accrediting agency for allied health programs in 19 occupational areas.

★6276★ **National Commission on Certification of Physician Assistants (NCCPA)**
2845 Henderson Mill Rd. NE
Atlanta, GA 30341
Ph: (404)493-9100   Fax: (404)493-7316

Purpose: Certifies physician assistants at the entry level and for continued competence. Has certified 22,750 physician assistants.

★6277★ **National Rural Health Association (NRHA)**
1 W. Armour Blvd., Ste. 301
Kansas City, MO 64111
Ph: (816)756-3140   Fax: (816)756-3144

Members: Administrators, physicians, nurses, physician assistants, health planners, academicians, and others interested or involved in rural health care. **Purpose:** To create a better understanding of health care problems unique to rural areas; utilize a collective approach in finding positive solutions; articulate and represent the health care needs of rural America; supply current information to rural health care providers; serve as a liaison between rural health care programs throughout the country. Offers continuing education credits for medical, dental, nursing, and management courses.

Physicians

★6293★ The American Surgeon

Pharmaceutical Media, Inc.
30 E. 33rd St.
New York, NY 10016
Ph: (212)685-5010   Fax: (212)685-5010

Monthly. Journal publishing original papers on the advancement of surgery.

★6294★ Anesthesia and Analgesia

Foot & Ankle International
7100 Lakewood Bldg., Ste. 112
5987 E. 71st St.
Indianapolis, IN 46220
Ph: (317)845-4200   Fax: (317)845-4200

Monthly. $157.00/year for individuals; $22.00 for single issue. Medical journal.

★6295★ Anesthesiology

Pharmaceutical Media Inc.
30 E. 33rd St.
New York, NY 10016
Ph: (212)685-5010   Fax: (212)685-5010

Monthly. $115.00/year for individuals. Medical journal publishing original manuscripts and brief abstracts from current literature on anesthesiology.

★6296★ Annals of Behavioral Medicine

Society of Behavioral Medicine
103 S. Adams St.
Rockville, MD 20850
Ph: (301)251-2790   Fax: (301)279-6749

Quarterly. $135.00/year; $160.00/year for other countries. Journal describing the interactions of behavior and health.

★6297★ Annals of Emergency Medicine

American College of Emergency
  Physicians
PO Box 619911
Dallas, TX 75261-9911
Ph: (214)550-0911   Fax: (214)580-2816

Monthly. $82.00/year for individuals; $116.63/year for Canada; $109.00/year for other countries. Medical journal for emergency physicians.

★6298★ Annals of Internal Medicine

American College of Physicians
Independence Mall W
6th St. at Race
Philadelphia, PA 19106-1572
Ph: (215)351-2651   Fax: (215)351-2644

Semimonthly. Medical journal.

★6299★ Annals of Neurology

Little, Brown and Co., Inc.
34 Beacon St.
Boston, MA 02108
Ph: (617)859-5607   Fax: (617)859-0629

Monthly. $119.00/year for individuals. Articles of scientific and clinical merit for neurologists.

★6300★ Annals of Plastic Surgery

Little, Brown and Co., Inc.
34 Beacon St.
Boston, MA 02108
Ph: (617)859-5607   Fax: (617)859-0629

Monthly. $127.00/year for individuals. Medical journal for the plastic surgeon.

★6301★ Annals of Surgery

Pharmaceutical Media, Inc.
30 E. 33rd St.
New York, NY 10016
Ph: (212)685-5010   Fax: (212)685-5010

Monthly. $88.00/year for individuals. Medical journal publishing original manuscripts promoting the advancement of surgical knowledge and practice.

★6302★ The Annals of Thoracic Surgery

Elsevier Science, Inc.
655 Avenue of the Americas
New York, NY 10010
Ph: (212)989-5800   Fax: (212)633-3990

Monthly. $125.00/year for individuals; $28.00 for single issue; $240.00/year for institutions. Presents original coverage of recent progress in chest and cardiovascular surgery related fields.

★6303★ Applied Radiology

Anderson Publishing Ltd.
80 Shore Rd.
Port Washington, NY 11050
Ph: (516)883-0164   Fax: (516)883-6609

Monthly. Free to qualified subscribers; $55.00/year for individuals; $6.00 for single issue. Magazine for radiologists, chief radiologic technologists, and radiology department administrators. Presents articles written by radiologic professionals on all aspects of general diagnostic radiology, the diagnostic radiologic subspecialties, and radiation therapy.

★6304★ Cancer

Pharmaceutical Media, Inc.
30 E. 33rd St.
New York, NY 10016
Ph: (212)685-5010   Fax: (212)685-5010

Semimonthly. Oncology journal publishing original articles on clinical aspects of cancer, surgical and medical therapy, and interdisciplinary research.

★6305★ CARDIO

Miller Freeman, Inc.
600 Harrison St.
San Francisco, CA 94107
Ph: (415)905-2200

Monthly. $85.00/year.

★6306★ Clinical Cardiology

Clinical Cardiology Publishing Co., Inc.
PO Box 832
Mahwah, NJ 07430-0832
Ph: (201)818-1010   Fax: (201)818-0086

Monthly. $80.00/year; $126.50/year for other countries. Medical journal.

★6307★ Clinical Pediatrics

Cortland Group
500 Executive Blvd.
Ossining, NY 10562
Ph: (914)762-0647   Fax: (914)762-8820

Monthly.

★6308★ Clinical Psychiatry News

International Medical News Group
51 John F. Kennedy Pky., 4th Fl.
Short Hills, NJ 07078-2702
Ph: (201)379-8766   Fax: (201)379-8765

Monthly. Medical and psychiatry tabloid.

★6309★ Contemporary OB/GYN

Medical Economics, Inc.
5 Paragon Dr.
Montvale, NJ 07645-1742
Ph: (201)358-7208   Fax: (201)358-7260

$89.00/year for individuals. Magazine covering clinical, investigative, and socioeconomic aspects of obstetrics and gynecology for specialists.

★6310★ Contemporary Pediatrics

Medical Economics
5 Paragon Dr.
Montvale, NJ 07645
Ph: (201)358-7500

Monthly. $79.00/year.

★6311★ Contemporary Urology

Medical Economics, Inc.
5 Paragon Dr.
Montvale, NJ 07645-1742
Ph: (201)358-7208   Fax: (201)358-7260

Clinical magazine for urologists.

★6312★ Critical Care Medicine

Foot & Ankle International
7100 Lakewood Bldg., Ste. 112
5987 E. 71st St.
Indianapolis, IN 46220
Ph: (317)845-4200   Fax: (317)845-4200

Monthly. $109.00/year for individuals; $169.00/year for institutions; $64.00/year for students; $214.00/year for out of country. Interdisciplinary journal for ICU and CCU specialists.

★6313★ Diabetes

660 S. Euclid Ave.
PO Box 8127
St. Louis, MO 63110
Ph: (314)362-7809

Monthly. $100.00/year.

★6314★ Diabetes Care

American Diabetes Association
National Center
PO Box 25757
1660 Duke St.
Alexandria, VA 22314
Ph: (703)549-1500

Monthly. $75.00/year.

★6315★ Diagnostic Imaging

Miller Freeman, Inc.
600 Harrison St.
San Francisco, CA 94107
Ph: (415)905-2200

Monthly. $70.00/year.

★6316★ Dialysis and Transplantation

Summer Communications, Inc.
7626 Densmore Ave.
Van Nuys, CA 91406-2042
Ph: (818)782-7328   Fax: (818)782-7450

Monthly. $35.00/year for individuals; $60.00/year for other countries. Medical magazine on dialysis and nephrology for medical personnel.

★6317★ Diseases of the Colon and Rectum

Williams & Wilkins
351 W. Camden St.
Baltimore, MD 21201-2436
Ph: (410)361-8004   Fax: (410)528-4312
Fr: 800-222-3790

Monthly. Medical journal.

★6318★ The DO

American Osteopathic Association
142 E. Ontario St.
Chicago, IL 60611-2864
Ph: (312)280-5870   Fax: (312)280-3860
Fr: 800-621-1773

Monthly. Free to qualified subscribers; $40.00/year by mail. Osteopathic magazine.

★6319★ Ear, Nose and Throat Journal

Medquest Communications
629 Euclid Ave., Ste. 500
Cleveland, OH 44114-3003
Ph: (216)522-9700   Fax: (216)522-9707

Monthly. $100.00/year for individuals; $50.00/year for students; $140.00/year for other countries; $12.00 for single issue. Journal on otorhinolaryugology, head and neck surgery, and allergies.

★6320★ Emergency Medical Services

Summer Communications, Inc.
7626 Densmore Ave.
Van Nuys, CA 91406-2042
Ph: (818)782-7328   Fax: (818)782-7450

Monthly. $18.95/year for individuals. Magazine covering emergency care, rescue and transportation.

★6321★ Family Practice News

International Medical News Group
51 John F. Kennedy Pky., 4th Fl.
Short Hills, NJ 07078-2702
Ph: (201)379-8766   Fax: (201)379-8765

Family physician medical tabloid.

★6322★ Head & Neck Surgery

John Wiley and Sons, Inc.
605 3rd Ave.
New York, NY 10158
Ph: (212)850-6000   Fax: (212)850-8888
Fr: 800-225-5945

Bimonthly. International, multidisciplinary publication of original contributions concerning diagnosis and surgical management of diseases of the head and neck. Publishes articles of interest to several medical and surgical specialists including general surgeons, neurosurgeons, otolaryngologists, and plastic surgeons.

★6323★ Heart and Lung: The Journal of Acute and Critical Care

Mosby Year Book
11830 Westline Industrial Dr.
St. Louis, MO 63146
Ph: (314)872-8370   Fax: 800-535-9935
Fr: 800-633-6699

Bimonthly. $39.00/year for individuals; $57.78 /year for Canada; $54.00/year for other countries; $21.00/year for students. Journal offering articles prepared by nurse and physician members of the critical care team, recognizing the nurse's role in the care and management of major organ-system conditions in critically ill patients.

★6324★ Infectious Disease News

Slack, Inc.
6900 Grove Rd.
Thorofare, NJ 08086-9447
Ph: (609)848-1000   Fax: (609)853-5991
Fr: 800-257-8290

Monthly. Newspaper for infectious disease specialists.

★6325★ Infectious Diseases in Children

Slack, Inc.
6900 Grove Rd.
Thorofare, NJ 08086-9447
Ph: (609)848-1000   Fax: (609)853-5991
Fr: 800-257-8290

Monthly. $160.00/year; $170.00/year for institutions. Professional journal.

★6326★ Internal Medicine News and Cardiology News

International Medical News Group
51 John F. Kennedy Pky., 4th Fl.
Short Hills, NJ 07078-2702
Ph: (201)379-8766   Fax: (201)379-8765

Semimonthly. Internal medicine tabloid distributed to internists, cardiologists, oncologists, nephrologists, and infectious disease specialists.

★6327★ International Journal of Dermatology

Decker Periodicals
1 James St. S
PO Box 620, LCD 1
Hamilton, ON, Canada L8N 3K7
Ph: (416)522-7017   Fax: (416)522-7839
Fr: 800-568-7281

Monthly. Journal covering news and developments in clinical dermatology.

★6328★ The Journal of Allergy and Clinical Immunology

Mosby Year Book
11830 Westline Industrial Dr.
St. Louis, MO 63146
Ph: (314)872-8370   Fax: 800-535-9935
Fr: 800-633-6699

Monthly. $115.00/year for individuals; $159.43/year for Canada; $149.00/year for other countries; $54.00/year for students. Journal for clinical allergists and immunologists, as well as dermatologists, internists, general practitioners, pediatricians, and otolaryngologists (ENT physicians) concerned with clinical manifestations of allergies in their practice.

★6329★ Journal of the American College of Surgeons

American College of Surgeons
54 E. Erie St.
Chicago, IL 60611
Ph: (312)787-9282   Fax: (312)440-7026
Fr: 800-440-5227

Monthly. $60.00/year for individuals; $70.00/year for institutions; $10.00 for single issue. Journal covering general surgery, surgical specialties, and experimental surgery.

★6330★ Journal of the American Medical Women's Association

American Medical Women's Association
801 N. Fairfax St.
Alexandria, VA 22314
Ph: (703)838-0500   Fax: (703)549-3864

Bimonthly. $50.00/year; $55.00/year for out of country; $5.00 for single issue. Medical journal.

★6331★ Journal of the American Osteopathic Association

American Osteopathic Association
142 E. Ontario St.
Chicago, IL 60611-2864
Ph: (312)280-5870   Fax: (312)280-3860
Fr: 800-621-1773

Monthly. Free to qualified subscribers; $40.00/year for institutions. Osteopathic clinical journal.

★6332★ Journal of the American Society of Echocardiography

Mosby Year Book
11830 Westline Industrial Dr.
St. Louis, MO 63146
Ph: (314)872-8370   Fax: 800-535-9935
Fr: 800-633-6699

Bimonthly. $83.00/year for individuals; $109.14/year for Canada; $102.00/year for other countries; $40.00/year for students. Official journal of the American Society of Echocardiography serving as a source of information on the technical basis and clinical application of echocardiography. Peer-reviewed publication featuring research, reviews, and case studies.

★6333★ Journal of Clinical Psychiatry

Physicians Postgraduate Press, Inc.
PO Box 240008
Memphis, TN 38124
Ph: (901)682-1001   Fax: (901)682-6992
Fr: 800-489-1001

Monthly. Journal containing original papers about practical and clinical psychiatry.

★6334★ The Journal of Family Practice

Appleton & Lange
PO Box 5630
Norwalk, CT 06856
Ph: (203)838-4400   Fax: (203)854-9486

Monthly. Free to qualified subscribers; $80.00/year for individuals; $106.00/year institutions. Journal covering clinical, family practice, and osteopathic medicine.

★6335★ *Journal of General Internal Medicine*

Hanley & Belfus, Inc.
210 S. 13th St.
Philadelphia, PA 19107
Ph: (215)546-0313   Fax: (215)790-9330

Bimonthly. Journal focusing on the development and excellence of primary care internal medicine practice and teaching.

★6336★ *Journal of Intensive Care Medicine*

21 N. Quinsiganmond Ave.
Shrewsbury, MA 01545
Ph: (508)756-1306   Fax: (508)754-5098

Bimonthly. $85.00/year for individuals. Medical journal for specialists working in intensive care units.

★6337★ *The Journal of Invasive Cardiology*

Health Management Publications, Inc.
550 American Ave.
King of Prussia, PA 19406
Ph: (215)337-4466   Fax: (215)337-0890

Journal for cardiologists, cardiovascular surgeons, and cath lab directors, featuring clinical papers, long-term case studies, product reports, and guest columns.

★6338★ *Journal of the National Medical Association*

Slack, Inc.
6900 Grove Rd.
Thorofare, NJ 08086-9447
Ph: (609)848-1000   Fax: (609)853-5991
Fr: 800-257-8290

Monthly. $76.00/year for individuals; $91.00/year for institutions; $15.00/year for single issue. Journal on specialized clinical research related to the health problems in the urban environment; recognizing significant contributions by black physicians and others towards inner city health care improvement.

★6339★ *Journal of Occupational and Environmental Medicine*

Williams & Wilkins
351 W. Camden St.
Baltimore, MD 21201-2436
Ph: (410)361-8004   Fax: (410)528-4312
Fr: 800-222-3790

Monthly. $77.00/year for individuals; $14.00 for single issue. Occupational and environmental medicine journal.

★6340★ *The Journal of Pediatrics*

Mosby Year Book
11830 Westline Industrial Dr.
St. Louis, MO 63146
Ph: (314)872-8370   Fax: 800-535-9935
Fr: 800-633-6699

Monthly. $113.00/year for individuals; $154.08 /year for Canada; $144 .00/year for other countries; $56.00/year for students. Journal for physicians who diagnose and treat disorders in infants and children.

★6341★ *Journal of Perinatology*

Mosby-Year Book, Inc.
11830 Westline Industrial Dr.
St. Louis, MO 63146
Ph: (314)872-8370   Fax: (314)872-9164

Bimonthly. $60.00/year. Official publication of the National Perinatal Association and the California Perinatal Association.

★6342★ *Journal of Trauma*

Foot & Ankle International
7100 Lakewood Bldg., Ste. 112
5987 E. 71st St.
Indianapolis, IN 46220
Ph: (317)845-4200   Fax: (317)845-4200

Monthly. $105.00/year for individuals; $145.00/year for other countries. Surgery journal.

★6343★ *Journal of Urology*

Foot & Ankle International
7100 Lakewood Bldg., Ste. 112
5987 E. 71st St.
Indianapolis, IN 46220
Ph: (317)845-4200   Fax: (317)845-4200

Monthly. $229.00/year for individuals. Journal.

★6344★ *The Lancet (North American Edition)*

Foot & Ankle International
7100 Lakewood Bldg., Ste. 112
5987 E. 71st St.
Indianapolis, IN 46220
Ph: (317)845-4200   Fax: (317)845-4200

Weekly. $98.00/year for individuals. Medical journal. Contents identical to British edition.

★6345★ *Medical Economics*

Medical Economics, Inc.
5 Paragon Dr.
Montvale, NJ 07645-1742
Ph: (201)358-7208   Fax: (201)358-7260

Semimonthly. Magazine covering physicians practice management, professional relations, and financial affairs.

★6346★ *Medical Electronics/Medical Electronic Products*

Measurements and Data Corp.
2994 W. Liberty Ave.
Pittsburgh, PA 15216
Ph: (412)343-9666   Fax: (412)343-9685

Bimonthly. Medical equipment magazine.

★6347★ *Medical Tribune*

Medical Tribune
257 Park Ave. S
New York, NY 10010
Ph: (212)460-1800   Fax: (212)505-6542

Semimonthly. Broadsheet reporting on health and medical sciences for office based physicians.

★6348★ *Military Medicine*

Association of Military Surgeons of the U.S.
9320 Old Georgetown Rd.
Bethesda, MD 20814
Ph: (301)897-8800   Fax: (301)530-5446

Monthly. $35.00/year for individuals; $40.00/year for other countries; $4.50 for single issue. Journal for professional personnel affiliated with the Federal medical services.

★6349★ *Neonatal Intensive Care*

Goldstein & Associates Publishing, Inc.
1150 Yale St., Ste. 12
Santa Monica, CA 90403
Ph: (310)828-1309   Fax: (310)829-1169

Bimonthly.

★6350★ *The New England Journal of Medicine*

Massachusetts Medical Society
1440 Main St.
Waltham, MA 02154-1649
Ph: (617)893-3800   Fax: (617)893-0413

Weekly (Thurs.). $99.00/year. Journal for the medical profession.

★6351★ *The New Physician*

American Medical Student Association
1890 Preston White Dr., 3rd Fl.
Reston, VA 22091
Ph: (703)620-6600   Fax: (703)620-5873

Magazine covering ethical, social, and economic issues of health care and medicine of interest to medical students, interns, and residents.

★6352★ *Ob Gyn News*

International Medical News Group
51 John F. Kennedy Pky., 4th Fl.
Short Hills, NJ 07078-2702
Ph: (201)379-8766   Fax: (201)379-8765

Semimonthly. Obstetrics and gynecology tabloid distributed to obstetricians and gynecologists.

★6353★ *Obstetrics and Gynecology*

Elsevier Science, Inc.
655 Avenue of the Americas
New York, NY 10010
Ph: (212)989-5800   Fax: (212)633-3990

Monthly. $134.00/year; $210.00/year for institutions. Professional journal focusing on medical and surgical treatment of female conditions, obstetrics management, and clinical evaluation of drugs and instruments.

★6354★ *Ocular Surgery News*

Slack, Inc.
6900 Grove Rd.
Thorofare, NJ 08086-9447
Ph: (609)848-1000   Fax: (609)853-5991
Fr: 800-257-8290

Semimonthly. Medical newspaper for ophthalmologists. Covering scientific meetings and events, with emphasis on cataract/IOL, glaucoma treatment, laser therapy, clinical anterior segment issues, and legislative and regulatory developments.

★6355★ Ophthalmic Surgery

Slack, Inc.
6900 Grove Rd.
Thorofare, NJ 08086-9447
Ph: (609)848-1000   Fax: (609)853-5991
Fr: 800-257-8290

Monthly. Journal publishing articles on ophthalmic surgery, research, and clinical approaches.

★6356★ Optometric Management

Viscom Publications, Inc.
50 Washington St., 11th Fl.
Norwalk, CT 06854
Ph: (203)838-9100   Fax: (203)838-2550

Medical professional journal.

★6357★ Orthopedics Today

Slack, Inc.
6900 Grove Rd.
Thorofare, NJ 08086-9447
Ph: (609)848-1000   Fax: (609)853-5991
Fr: 800-257-8290

Monthly. News tabloid; covering orthopedic meetings, courses, and symposia.

★6358★ Patient Care

Medical Economics, Inc.
5 Paragon Dr.
Montvale, NJ 07645-1742
Ph: (201)358-7208   Fax: (201)358-7260

Twenty issues/year. Journal for primary care physicians.

★6359★ Pediatric Annals

Slack, Inc.
6900 Grove Rd.
Thorofare, NJ 08086-9447
Ph: (609)848-1000   Fax: (609)853-5991
Fr: 800-257-8290

Monthly.

★6360★ Pediatric News

International Medical News Group
51 John F. Kennedy Pky., 4th Fl.
Short Hills, NJ 07078-2702
Ph: (201)379-8766   Fax: (201)379-8765

Monthly. Tabloid covering pediatric medicine and distributed to pediatricians.

★6361★ Pediatrics

American Academy of Pediatrics
141 NW Point Blvd.
PO Box 927
Elk Grove Village, IL 60007-0927
Ph: (708)228-5005   Fax: (708)228-5097

Monthly. $50.00/year for individuals; $60.00/year for other countries. Medical journal reporting on pediatrics.

★6362★ Physicians Career Opportunities

Physicians Career Resource
American Medical Association
515 N. State St.
Chicago, IL 60610
Ph: 800-955-3565   Fax: (312)464-4184

Monthly. $50.00, Free to AMA member physicians seeking positions. Covers employment or practice opportunities for physicians. Also has lists of practices for sale, state

medical societies, executive and professional recruiting firms, hospital or clinic management companies, medical schools, national medical specialty societies, health maintenance organizations, etc. Entries include: Medical specialty, location and type of practice, beginning financial arrangements, income range, size of community, physician population, date available. A companion volume, Physician Placement Register, lists key from registered physicians seeking positions. Arrangement: Opportunities listed geographically, then by medical specialty. Indexes: Medical specialty.

★6363★ Psychiatric Annals

Slack, Inc.
6900 Grove Rd.
Thorofare, NJ 08086-9447
Ph: (609)848-1000   Fax: (609)853-5991
Fr: 800-257-8290

Monthly. Journal analyzing concepts and practices in every area of psychiatry.

★6364★ Psychiatric News

American Psychiatric Press, Inc.
1400 K St. NW, Ste. 503
Washington, DC 20005
Ph: (202)682-6240   Fax: (202)692-6016
Fr: 800-368-5777

Semimonthly. $40.00/year for individuals. Professional magazine of the American Psychiatric Association.

★6365★ Psychiatric Services

American Psychiatric Press, Inc.
1400 K St. NW, Ste. 503
Washington, DC 20005
Ph: (202)682-6240   Fax: (202)692-6016
Fr: 800-368-5777

Monthly. $40.00/year for individuals; $60.00/year for institutions; $20 .00/year for students. Interdisciplinary mental health journal covering clinical, legal, and public policy issues.

★6366★ The Psychiatric Times

The Psychiatric Times
1924 E. Deere Ave., No. 100
Santa Ana, CA 92705-5723
Ph: (714)250-1008   Fax: (714)250-1245

Monthly. $120.00/year for individuals; $10.00 for single issue; $200.00/year for other countries. Newspaper (tabloid) serving psychiatrists, other mental health professionals, Neurologists and physicians interested in psychiatric disorders and issues.

★6367★ Radiology

Radiological Society of North America
2021 Spring Rd., Ste. 600
Oak Brook, IL 60521
Ph: (708)571-2670   Fax: (708)571-7837

Monthly. $195.00/year for individuals; $240.00/year for out of country. Journal focusing on radiology.

★6368★ Radiology Today

Slack, Inc.
6900 Grove Rd.
Thorofare, NJ 08086-9447
Ph: (609)848-1000   Fax: (609)853-5991
Fr: 800-257-8290

Monthly. Covering radiology technique and equipment innovations, related political activities, and daily practice.

★6369★ Rescue-EMS Magazine

Lifesaving Communications, Inc.
PO Box 100
Nassau, DE 19969-0100

Bimonthly. $15.00/year for individuals; $2.50 for single issue. Magazine (tabloid) serving the emergency medical services directors and field personnel.

★6370★ Resident and Staff Physician

Romaine Pierson Publishers, Inc.
80 Shore Rd.
Port Washington, NY 11050
Ph: (516)883-6350   Fax: (516)883-6609

Monthly. $55.00/year for individuals. Medical journal.

★6371★ RETINA

Pharmaceutical Media, Inc.
30 E. 33rd St.
New York, NY 10016
Ph: (212)685-5010   Fax: (212)685-5010

Quarterly. $112.00/year for individuals; $63.00/year for students; $162.00/year for institutions. Journal publishing clinically oriented articles for the general ophthalmologist and vitreoretinal specialist.

★6372★ Skin and Allergy News

International Medical News Group
51 John F. Kennedy Pky., 4th Fl.
Short Hills, NJ 07078-2702
Ph: (201)379-8766   Fax: (201)379-8765

Monthly. Dermatology/allergy tabloid.

★6373★ Southern Medical Journal

Southern Medical Association
35 Lakeshore Dr.
PO Box 190088
Birmingham, AL 35219-0088
Ph: (205)945-1840   Fax: (205)945-1548
Fr: 800-423-4992

Monthly. $55.00/year for individuals. Multispecialty medical journal.

★6374★ Surgical Rounds

Romaine Pierson Publishers, Inc.
80 Shore Rd.
Port Washington, NY 11050
Ph: (516)883-6350   Fax: (516)883-6609

Monthly. Medical and surgical magazine.

★6375★ TeamRehab Report

Miramar Publishing
6133 Bristol Pkwy.
Box 3640
Culver City, CA 90231-3640
Ph: (213)337-9717

Bimonthly.

★6376★ **The Western Journal of Medicine**

California Medical Association
221 Main St.
PO Box 7602
San Francisco, CA 94120-7602
Ph: (415)882-5177   Fax: (415)882-3379

Monthly. $40.00/year for institutions; $70.00/year for other countries; $7.50 for single issue. Journal featuring peer-reviewed articles for physicians and specialists on medical research, socioeconomics, and observation.

PLACEMENT AND JOB REFERRAL SERVICES

★6377★ **American Academy of Clinical Toxicology (AACT)**

Pittsburgh Poison Center
3705 5th Ave.
Pittsburgh, PA 15213
Ph: (412)692-6669   Fax: (412)692-7497

Members: Physicians, veterinarians, pharmacists, research scientists, and analytical chemists. **Purpose:** Objectives are to: unite medical scientists and facilitate the exchange of information; encourage the development of therapeutic methods and technology; establish a mechanism for the certification of medical scientists in clinical toxicology. **Activities:** Conducts professional training in poison information and emergency service personnel. Maintains placement services. **E-Mail:** Internet, krenzee@chplink.chp.edu

★6378★ **American Academy of Dermatology (AAD)**

930 N. Meacham Rd.
Schaumburg, IL 60172-4965
Ph: (708)330-0230   Fax: (708)330-0050

Members: Professional society of medical doctors specializing in skin diseases. **Activities:** Conducts educational programs. Provides placement service; compiles statistics.

★6379★ **American Academy of Family Physicians (AAFP)**

8880 Ward Pky.
Kansas City, MO 64114
Ph: (816)333-9700   Fax: (816)822-0580
Fr: 800-274-2237

Members: Professional society of family physicians who provide continuing comprehensive care to patients. **Activities:** Maintains placement service.

★6380★ **American Academy of Neurology (AAN)**

2221 University Ave. SE, Ste. 335
Minneapolis, MN 55414
Ph: (612)623-8115   Fax: (612)623-3504

Members: Professional society of medical doctors specializing in brain and nervous system diseases. **Activities:** Maintains placement service. Sponsors research and educational programs. Compiles statistics.

★6381★ **American Academy of Otolaryngology - Head and Neck Surgery (AAO-HNS)**

1 Prince St.
Alexandria, VA 22314-3357
Ph: (703)836-4444   Fax: (703)683-5100

Members: Professional society of medical doctors specializing in otolaryngology (diseases of the ear, nose, and throat) and head and neck surgery. **Purpose:** Represents otolaryngology in governmental and socioeconomic areas and provides high-quality medical education for otolaryngologists. Coordinates Combined Otolaryngological Spring Meetings for nine national otolaryngological societies. **Activities:** Operates job information exchange service and museum.

★6382★ **American Academy of Psychiatrists in Alcoholism and Addictions (aaPaa)**

PO Box 376
Greenbelt, MD 20768
Ph: (301)220-0951   Fax: (301)474-0219

Members: Psychiatrists and residents in training. **Purpose:** To provide a forum for discussion of issues related to substance abuse; further education, research, and clinical work in the field; assist in the development of appropriate standards of care for alcoholics and other drug-dependent persons. Facilitates worldwide communication among psychiatrists and others on issues and practices related to substance abuse and addiction. **Activities:** Maintains speakers' bureau; conducts placement service; compiles statistics.

★6383★ **American Academy of Tropical Medicine (AATM)**

16126 E. Warren
PO Box 24224
Detroit, MI 48224
Ph: (313)882-0641   Fax: (313)882-5110

Members: Physicians and allied health professionals interested in tropical medicine. **Purpose:** Provides postgraduate continuing medical education; confers certificates and diplomas. **Activities:** Maintains speakers' bureau; provides placement service. Conducts research and compiles statistics. Conducts educational programs; offers children's services.

★6384★ **American Association of Certified Orthoptists (AACO)**

MC 3-2700
6621 Fannin
Houston, TX 77030-2399
Ph: (713)770-3225   Fax: (713)796-8110

Members: Orthoptists certified by the American Orthoptic Council after completing a minimum of 24 months' special training, to treat defects in binocular function. **Activities:** Operates a placement listing. Assists in postgraduate instruction courses; conducts programs and courses at international, national, and regional meetings; helps individual orthoptists with special or unusual problem cases; trains new orthoptists.

★6385★ **American Association for Geriatric Psychiatry (AAGP)**

7910 Woodmont Ave., 7th Fl.
Bethesda, MD 20814
Ph: (301)654-7850   Fax: (301)654-4137

Purpose: Psychiatrists interested in promoting better mental health care for the elderly. **Activities:** Maintains placement service and speakers' bureau.

★6386★ **American Association of Neuropathologists (AANP)**

Jeannette J. Townsend, M.D.
Department of Pathology
University of Utah School of Medicine
50 N. Medical Dr.
Salt Lake City, UT 84132
Ph: (801)581-2507   Fax: (801)585-3831

Members: Professional society of physicians specializing in neuropathology. **Purpose:** Seeks to advance research and training in neuropathology. **Activities:** Offers placement service.

★6387★ **American Board of Neurological and Orthopaedic Medicine and Surgery (ABNOMS)**

522 Rossmore Dr.
Las Vegas, NV 89110-4123
Ph: (702)452-9538   Fax: (702)452-1031

Members: Individuals proficient in neurological and orthopaedic medicine and surgery who have previous board certification and proper preceptorship and have made significant contributions to the field. **Purpose:** Objective is to demonstrate expertise and capability in the field of neurological and orthopaedic medicine and surgery through written and oral certification examinations. Conducts research and educational programs on neuromusculoskeletal disorders of the limbs and spine. Maintains hall of fame. **Activities:** Operates charitable program and placement service.

★6388★ **American Board of Spinal Surgery (ABSS)**

522 Rossmore Dr.
Las Vegas, NV 89110-4123
Ph: (702)452-9538   Fax: (702)452-1031

Purpose: Spinal surgeons seeking to advance knowledge and provide education in the field of spinal surgery. **Activities:** Conducts charitable, education, and research programs; maintains hall of fame; offers placement service; compiles statistics; maintains speakers' bureau.

★6389★ **American College of Chest Physicians (ACCP)**

3300 Dundee Rd.
Northbrook, IL 60062
Ph: (708)498-1400   Fax: (708)498-5460
Fr: 800-343-ACCP

Members: Professional society of physicians and surgeons specializing in diseases of the chest (heart and lungs). **Purpose:** Promotes undergraduate and postgraduate medical education and research in the field. Sponsors forums. **Activities:** Maintains placement service; conducts educational programs.

★6390★ American College Health Association (ACHA)

PO Box 28937
Baltimore, MD 21240-8937
Ph: (410)859-1500   Fax: (410)859-1510

Members: Institutions and individuals. **Purpose:** Provides an organization in which institutions of higher education and interested individuals may work together to promote health in its broadest aspects for students and all other members of the college community. **Activities:** Offers continuing education programs for health professionals. Maintains placement listings for physicians and other personnel seeking positions in college health.

★6391★ American College of Medical Quality (ACMQ)

9005 Congressional Ct.
Potomac, MD 20854
Ph: (301)365-3570   Fax: (301)365-3202

Members: Physicians, affiliates, and institutions. **Purpose:** Seeks to set standards of competence in the field of quality assurance and utilization review. Conducts educational seminars and workshops in quality assurance and utilization review. **Activities:** Offers placement service. Compiles statistics on numbers of physicians and allied health personnel working in quality assurance and utilization review.

★6392★ American College of Occupational and Environmental Medicine (ACOEM)

55 W. Seegers Rd.
Arlington Heights, IL 60005
Ph: (708)228-6850   Fax: (708)228-1856

Members: Physicians specializing in occupational and environmental medicine. **Purpose:** Promotes maintenance and improvement of the health of workers; works to increase awareness of occupational medicine as a medical specialty. **Activities:** Sponsors educational programs; maintains placement service.

★6393★ American College of Osteopathic Internists (ACOI)

300 5th St. NE
Washington, DC 20002
Ph: (202)546-0095   Fax: (202)543-5584
Fr: 800-327-5183

Members: Osteopathic doctors who limit their practice to internal medicine and various subspecialties and who intend, through post-doctoral education, to qualify as certified specialists in the field. **Purpose:** Aims to provide educational programs and to improve educational standards in the field of osteopathic internal medicine. **Activities:** Sponsors competitions. Compiles statistics; offers placement service.

★6394★ American College of Osteopathic Surgeons (ACOS)

123 N. Henry St.
Alexandria, VA 22314-2903
Ph: (703)684-0416   Fax: (703)684-3280

Members: Professional society of osteopathic physicians specializing in surgery and surgical specialties. **Purpose:** Maintains

placement service; conducts postgraduate courses in continuing surgical education.

★6395★ American College of Physician Executives (ACPE)

4890 W. Kennedy Blvd., Ste. 200
Tampa, FL 33609
Ph: (813)287-2000   Fax: (813)287-8993
Fr: 800-562-8088

Members: Physicians whose primary professional responsibility is the management of health care organizations. **Purpose:** Provides for continuing education and certification of the physician executive and the advancement and recognition of the physician executive and the profession. **Activities:** Offers specialized career planning, counseling, recruitment and placement services, and research and information data on physician managers.

★6396★ American College of Radiology (ACR)

1891 Preston White Dr.
Reston, VA 22091
Ph: (703)648-8989   Fr: 800-ACR-LINE

Members: Professional society of physicians and radiologic physicists who specialize in the use of X-ray, ultrasound, nuclear medicine magnetic resonance, and other imaging modalities for the diagnosis of disease and treatment and management of cancer. **Activities:** Conducts research programs. Offers specialized education and placement service; provides insurance program.

★6397★ American Gastroenterological Association (AGA)

7910 Woodmont Ave., Ste. 914
Bethesda, MD 20814
Ph: (301)654-2055   Fax: (301)654-5920

Members: Physicians of internal medicine certified in gastroenterology; radiologists, pathologists, surgeons, and physiologists with special interest and competency in gastroenterology. **Purpose:** Studies normal and abnormal conditions of the digestive organs and problems connected with their metabolism. **Activities:** Conducts scientific research; offers placement services.

★6398★ American Managed Care and Review Association (AMCRA)

1200 19th St. NW, No. 200
Washington, DC 20036-2437
Ph: (202)728-0506   Fax: (202)728-0609

Members: Medical organizations from the managed health care industry, including health maintenance organizations (HMOs), preferred provider organizations (PPOs), independent practice/physician associations (IPAs), utilization review organizations (UROs), and physician hospital organizations (PHOs); represents over 250,000 practicing physicians and 25 million individuals with health insurance. **Purpose:** Seeks to provide better medical care at a reasonable cost, and to render the most appropriate and economical setting for its delivery. Conducts educational sessions and seminars. Maintains American Managed Care and Review Association Foundation. **Activities:** Sponsors job placement service.

★6399★ American Medical Association (AMA)

515 N. State St.
Chicago, IL 60610
Ph: (312)464-5000   Fax: (312)464-4184

Members: County medical societies and physicians. **Purpose:** Disseminates scientific information to members and the public. Informs members on significant medical and health legislation on state and national levels and represents the profession before Congress and governmental agencies. Cooperates in setting standards for medical schools, hospitals, residency programs, and continuing medical education courses. **Activities:** Offers physician placement service and counseling on practice management problems. Operates library which lends material and provides specific medical information to physicians. Ad-hoc committees are formed for such topics as health care planning and principles of medical ethics.

★6400★ American Medical Peer Review Association (AMPRA)

1140 Conneticut Ave. NE, Ste. 1050
Washington, DC 20036
Ph: (202)331-5790   Fax: (202)833-2047

Members: Institutions and individuals. **Purpose:** To develop communications programs for physicians, institutions, and others interested in peer review organizations (PROs). Provides a national forum for the interchange of ideas, techniques, and information relating to medical quality assessment. Conducts courses and on-site educational programs to increase physicians' involvement and leadership in PROs, improve practice patterns through review, understand and use PRO data to improve service delivery, pre-admission review, profile analysis, retrospective review, and organizational development. **Activities:** Sponsors placement service; maintains a speakers' bureau and a library.

★6401★ American Osteopathic Association (AOA)

142 E. Ontario St.
Chicago, IL 60611
Ph: (312)280-5800   Fax: (312)280-3860
Fr: 800-621-1773

Members: Osteopathic physicians, surgeons, and graduates of approved colleges of osteopathic medicine. Associate members include teaching, research, administrative, and executive employees of approved colleges, hospitals, divisional societies, and affiliated organizations. PUR Forms (with its affiliates) an officially recognized structure of the osteopathic profession. Promotes the public health, to encourage scientific research, and to maintain and improve high standards of medical education in osteopathic colleges. Inspects and accredits colleges and hospitals; conducts a specialty certification program; sponsors a national examining board satisfactory to state licensing agencies; maintains mandatory program of continuing medical education for members. Compiles statistics on location and type of practice of osteopathic physicians. Sponsors research activities through Bureau of Research in osteopathic colleges and hospitals. **Activities:** Maintains Physician Placement Service. Produces public service radio and television programs; maintains 2000 item library and biographical archives on osteopathic medicine and history. Offers speakers' bureau.

★6402★ American Osteopathic College of Pathologists (AOCP)

Joan Gross
12368 NW 13th Ct.
Pembroke Pines, FL 33026
Ph: (305)432-9640   Fax: (305)432-9640

Members: Osteopathic physicians who have completed residency training programs in pathology and clinical pathology; candidate members are in residency training in pathology. **Purpose:** Establishes guidelines for training programs in pathology and clinical pathology for osteopathic physicians; maintains standards in residency training programs. **Activities:** Offers placement service and midyear tutorial program. Maintains collection of slide study sets.

★6403★ American Public Health Association (APHA)

1015 15th St. NW
Washington, DC 20005
Ph: (202)789-5600   Fax: (202)789-5681

Members: Professional organization of physicians, nurses, educators, academicians, environmentalists, epidemiologists, new professionals, social workers, health administrators, optometrists, podiatrists, pharmacists, dentists, nutritionists, health planners, other community and mental health specialists, and interested consumers. **Purpose:** Seeks to protect and promote personal, mental, and environmental health. **Activities:** Services include: promulgation of standards; establishment of uniform practices and procedures; development of the etiology of communicable diseases; research in public health; exploration of medical care programs and their relationships to public health. Sponsors job placement service.

★6404★ American School Health Association (ASHA)

7263 State Rte. 43
PO Box 708
Kent, OH 44240
Ph: (216)678-1601   Fax: (216)678-4526

Members: School physicians, school nurses, dentists, nurses, nutritionists, health educators, dental hygienists, school-based professionals, and public health workers. **Purpose:** Promotes comprehensive and constructive school health programs including the teaching of health, health services, and promotion of a healthful school environment. **Activities:** Offers a professional referral service, classroom teaching aids, and professional reference materials. Conducts research programs; maintains placement service; compiles statistics. Sponsors foreign travel study tour.

★6405★ American Society of Anesthesiologists (ASA)

520 N. Northwest Hwy.
Park Ridge, IL 60068-2573
Ph: (708)825-5586   Fax: (708)825-1692

Members: Professional society of physicians specializing or interested in anesthesiology.

Purpose: Seeks to develop and further the specialty of anesthesiology for the general elevation of the standards of medical practice. Encourages education, research, and scientific progress in anesthesiology. **Activities:** Maintains placement service. Conducts refresher courses and other postgraduate educational activities.

★6406★ American Society of Colon and Rectal Surgeons (ASCRS)

85 W. Algonquin Rd., Ste. 550
Arlington Heights, IL 60005
Ph: (708)290-9184   Fax: (708)290-9203

Members: Professional society of surgeons specializing in the diagnosis and treatment of diseases of the colon, rectum, and anus. **Purpose:** Offers placement service; conducts research programs.

★6407★ American Society of Extra-Corporeal Technology (AmSECT)

11480 Sunset Hills Rd., No. 210E
Reston, VA 22090
Ph: (703)435-8556   Fax: (703)435-0056

Members: Perfusionists, technologists, doctors, nurses, and others actively employed and using the applied skills relating to the practice of extracorporeal technology (involving heart-lung machines); student members. **Purpose:** Disseminates information necessary to the proper practice of the technology. Conducts programs in continuing education and professional-public liaison and hands-on workshops. **Activities:** Maintains placement service.

★6408★ American Society of Handicapped Physicians (ASHP)

105 Morris Dr.
Bastrop, LA 71220
Ph: (318)281-4436

Members: Handicapped physicians and others concerned with the problems faced by handicapped physicians. **Purpose:** Acts as a forum to address the needs of physically disabled physicians. Works against discrimination of the handicapped and serves as a support group and legal and career counselor. Disseminates information about resources for handicapped physicians. Plans to offer rehabilitation services. **Activities:** Maintains speakers' bureau and placement service; compiles statistics; offers specialized education.

★6409★ American Society for Histocompatibility and Immunogenetics (ASHI)

PO Box 15804
Lenexa, KS 66285-5804
Ph: (913)541-0009   Fax: (913)541-0156

Members: Scientists, physicians, and technologists involved in research and clinical activities related to histocompatibility testing (a state of mutual tolerance that allows some tissues to be grafted effectively to others). **Activities:** Conducts proficiency testing and educational programs. Maintains liaison with regulatory agencies; offers placement services and laboratory accreditation. Has developed histocompatability specialist certification program.

★6410★ American Society of Nephrology (ASN)

1200 19th St. NW, Ste. 300
Washington, DC 20036
Ph: (202)857-1190   Fax: (202)223-4579

Members: Nephrologists united for the exchange of scientific information. **Purpose:** Seeks to contribute to the education of members and to improve the quality of patient care. **Activities:** Conducts educational courses. Maintains placement service.

★6411★ American Society for Reproductive Medicine (ASRM)

1209 Montgomery Hwy.
Birmingham, AL 35216-2809
Ph: (205)978-5000   Fax: (205)978-5005

Members: Gynecologists, obstetricians, urologists, reproductive endocrinologists, veterinarians, research workers, and others interested in reproductive health in humans and animals. **Purpose:** Seeks to extend knowledge of all aspects of fertility and problems of infertility and mammalian reproduction; provides a rostrum for the presentation of scientific studies dealing with these subjects. **Activities:** Offers patient resource information and placement service.

★6412★ American Urological Association (AUA)

1120 N. Charles St.
Baltimore, MD 21201
Ph: (410)727-1100   Fax: (410)625-2390

Members: Professional society of physicians specializing in urology. **Activities:** Provides placement service. Condusts educational programs; maintains museum.

★6413★ Association for Academic Surgery (AAS)

Box 242 UMHC
420 Delaware St. SE
Minneapolis, MN 55455
Ph: (612)626-1999   Fax: (612)625-8496

Members: Active and senior surgeons with backgrounds in all surgical specialties in academic surgical centers at chief resident level or above. **Purpose:** Encourages young surgeons to pursue careers in academic surgery; supports them in establishing themselves as investigators and educators by providing a forum in which senior surgical residents and junior faculty members may present papers on subjects of clinical or laboratory investigations; promotes interchange of ideas between senior surgical residents, junior faculty, and established academic surgeons; facilitates communication among academic surgeons in all surgical fields. **Activities:** Maintains placement service.

★6414★ Association for the Advancement of Medical Instrumentation (AAMI)

3330 Washington Blvd., Ste. 400
Arlington, VA 22201
Ph: (703)525-4890   Fax: (703)276-0793
Fr: 800-332-2264

Members: Clinical engineers, biomedical equipment technicians, physicians, hospital administrators, consultants, engineers, manufacturers of medical devices, nurses researchers and others interested in medical instrumentation. Purpose is to improve the quality of medical care through the application, development, and management of technology. **Activities:** Maintains placement service. Offers certification programs for biomedical equipment technicians and clinical engineers. Produces numerous standards and recommended practices on medical devices and procedures. Offers educational programs.

★6415★ **Association of Philippine Physicians in America (APPA)**

2717 W. Olive Ave., Ste. 200
Burbank, CA 91505
Ph: (818)843-8616

Members: Individuals from the Philippines who are licensed to practice medicine in the U.S. **Purpose:** Seeks to: render free medical care to indigent persons; establish a continuing medical education program for physicians; provide aid for education of physicians; support medical research. Sends medical missions to the Philippines. **Activities:** Provides medical residency program placement service. Maintains speakers' bureau; compiles statistics.

★6416★ **Association for Research in Vision and Ophthalmology (ARVO)**

9650 Rockville Pke.
Bethesda, MD 20814-3998
Ph: (301)571-1844   Fax: (301)571-8311

Members: Professional society of researchers in vision and ophthalmology. **Purpose:** To encourage ophthalmic research in the field of blinding eye disease. **Activities:** Administers Scientific Review Fight for Sight/Prevent Blindness America research program. Operates placement service. Maintains 13 scientific sections.

★6417★ **Black Psychiatrists of America (BPA)**

2730 Adeline St.
Oakland, CA 94607
Ph: (510)465-1800   Fax: (510)465-1508

Purpose: Black psychiatrists, either in practice or training, united to promote black behavioral science and foster high quality psychiatric care for blacks and minority group members. **Activities:** Offers placement service. Sponsors public information service. Maintains speakers' bureau and biographical archives; compiles statistics; conducts educational programs.

★6418★ **Chinese American Medical Society (CAMS)**

281 Edgewood Ave.
Teaneck, NJ 07666
Ph: (201)833-1506   Fax: (201)833-8252

Members: Physicians of Chinese origin residing in the U.S. and Canada. **Purpose:** Seeks to advance medical knowledge, scientific research, and interchange of information among members and to promote the health status of Chinese Americans. **Activities:** Conducts educational meetings; supports research. Maintains placement service. Sponsors limited charitable program.

★6419★ **Christian Medical Foundation International (CMF)**

7522 N. Himes Ave.
PO Box 152136
Tampa, FL 33684-2136
Ph: (813)932-3688   Fax: (813)932-3767

Members: Physicians, nurses, clergy, and laity. **Purpose:** Seeks to: investigate and promote the Christian spiritual care of those who are ill; educate doctors, nurses, and medical students regarding Christian medical and ethical principles. **Activities:** Maintains speakers' bureau, placement service, biographical archives, and 2500 volume library; sponsors charitable programs.

★6420★ **Clinical Ligand Assay Society (CLAS)**

3139 S. Wayne Rd.
Wayne, MI 48184
Ph: (313)722-6290   Fax: (313)722-7006

Members: Clinical laboratory directors and doctors, hospital technologists, private laboratories, industry, and other individuals interested in ligand. **Purpose:** Objectives are to establish and promote high standards in the science and application of ligand assay technology by encouraging research, educating practitioners, and fostering communication and cooperation among individuals in laboratories, medicine, academia, and industry. **Activities:** Sponsors job placement service.

★6421★ **College of American Pathologists (CAP)**

325 Waukegan Rd.
Northfield, IL 60093-2750
Ph: (708)446-8800   Fax: (708)446-8807
Fr: 800-323-4040

Members: Physicians practicing the specialty of pathology (diagnosis, treatment, observation, and understanding of the progress of disease or medical condition) obtained by morphologic, microscopic, chemical, microbiologic, serologic, or any other type of laboratory examination made on the patient. **Purpose:** Fosters improvement of education, research, and medical laboratory service to physicians, hospitals, and the public. Provides job placement information for members. Conducts laboratory accreditation program and laboratory proficiency testing surveys. Maintains spokepersons network; provides free health information to the public; compiles statistics; sponsors educational programs.

★6422★ **Congress of Neurological Surgeons (CNS)**

The Emory Clinic
1365 Clifton Rd. NE
Atlanta, GA 30322
Ph: (404)248-4369   Fax: (404)248-3791

Members: Professional society of neurological surgeons in the United States and 55 other countries who meet annually to express their views on various aspects of the principles and practice of neurological surgery; to exchange technical information and experience; to join study of the developments in scientific fields allied to neurological surgery. **Activities:** Promotes interest of neurological surgeons in their practice; provides placement service; honors a living

leader in the field of neurological surgery annually.

★6423★ **Emergency Medicine Residents' Association (EMRA)**

1125 Executive Cir.
Irving, TX 75038-2522
Ph: (214)550-0911   Fax: (214)580-2816
Fr: 800-798-1822

Members: Physicians enrolled in emergency medicine residency training programs; medical students. **Purpose:** To provide a unified voice for emergency medicine residents; encourage high standards in training and continuing education for emergency physicians; study socioeconomic aspects of emergency medical care; promote education of patients and the public. **Activities:** Sponsors educational programs: maintains placement service. Compiles statistics on graduate residents.

★6424★ **Endocrine Society (ES)**

4350 East West Hwy., Ste. 500
Bethesda, MD 20814-4410
Ph: (301)941-0200   Fax: (301)941-0259

Purpose: Promotes excellence in research, education, and clinical practice in endocrinology and related disciplines. **Activities:** Maintains placement service.

★6425★ **Institute on Psychiatric Services/American Psychiatric Association (IHCP)**

1400 K St. NW
Washington, DC 20005
Ph: (202)682-6237   Fax: (202)682-6345

Purpose: Open to employees of all psychiatric and related health and educational facilities. Includes lectures by experts in the field and workshops and accredited courses on problems, programs, and trends. **Activities:** Offers on-site Job Bank, which lists opportunities for mental health professionals. Organizes scientific exhibits.

★6426★ **International Oculoplastic Society, Inc. (IOSI)**

630 Park Ave.
New York, NY 10021
Ph: (212)734-1010   Fax: (212)871-8474

Members: Surgeons specializing in ophthalmology, otolaryngology, dermatology, and plastic surgery. **Purpose:** Sponsors professional education and clinically applied research in the prevention, diagnosis, and treatment of disorders of the eye, orbit, adnexa, face, and skin. Seeks to promote and establish successful forms of patient care and treatment through open discussions, seminars, and instructional courses on clinical research, surgery, and medical advances. Conducts educational and charitable programs. **Activities:** Maintains speakers' bureau and placement service. Compiles statistics.

★6427★ **Islamic Medical Association (IMA)**

4121 Fairview, Ste. 203
Downers Grove, IL 60515
Ph: (708)852-2122   Fax: (708)852-2151

Members: Muslim physicians and allied health professionals. **Purpose:** Unites Muslim physicians and allied health professionals in the U.S. and Canada for the improvement of professional and social contact; provides assistance to Muslim communities worldwide. Charitable programs include: donation of books, journals, and educational and research materials to medical institutions; donation of medical supplies and equipment to charity medical institutions in Muslim countries. **Activities:** Maintains speakers' bureau to present Islamic viewpoints on medical topics; sponsors placement service; offers assistance in orientation.

★6428★ **National Association of Managed Care Physicians (NAMCP)**

4435 Waterfront Dr.
PO Box 4765
Glen Allen, VA 23058-4765
Ph: (804)527-1905   Fax: (804)747-5316
Fr: 800-722-0376

Members: Licensed physicians and allied health professionals working in managed health care programs; medical residents and students interested in managed health care; corporations or agencies providing services or goods to the industry; interested others. **Purpose:** Enhances the ability of practicing physicians to proactively participate within the managed health care arena through research, communication, and education. Provides a forum for members to communicate their concerns about the changing health care environment, integrate into managed health care delivery systems, and assure continuous improvement in the quality of health care services provided. Develops practice criteria, quality assurance measures, and appropriate utilization management criteria. **Activities:** Offers placement service. Offers educational programs; maintains speakers; bureau; conducts research programs; developing informational clearinghouse.

★6429★ **National Medical Association (NMA)**

1012 10th St. NW
Washington, DC 20001
Ph: (202)347-1895   Fax: (202)842-3293

Members: Professional society of black physicians. **Purpose:** Maintains 24 scientific sections representing major specialties of medicine. **Activities:** Plans to establish library and physician placement service. Conducts symposia and workshops.

★6430★ **National Rural Health Association (NRHA)**

1 W. Armour Blvd., Ste. 301
Kansas City, MO 64111
Ph: (816)756-3140   Fax: (816)756-3144

Members: Administrators, physicians, nurses, physician assistants, health planners, academicians, and others interested or involved in rural health care. **Purpose:** To create a better understanding of health care

problems unique to rural areas; utilize a collective approach in finding positive solutions; articulate and represent the health care needs of rural America; supply current information to rural health care providers; serve as a liaison between rural health care programs throughout the country. Offers continuing education credits for medical, dental, nursing, and management courses.

★6431★ **Ruth Jackson Orthopaedic Society (RJS)**

c/o Carole Murphy
6300 North River Rd., Ste. 727
Rosemont, IL 60018
Ph: (708)698-1693   Fax: (708)823-0536

Members: Women orthopedic surgeons, residents, fellows, and medical students. **Purpose:** Seeks to advance the science of orthopedic surgery and to provide support for women orthopedic surgeons. Named for practicing orthopedic surgeon Dr. Ruth Jackson (1902-94), the first woman certified by the American Board of Orthopedic Surgery and the first female member of the American Academy of Orthopedic Surgeons. **Activities:** Conducts educational programs; operates placement service and speakers' bureau.

★6432★ **Ukrainian Medical Association of North America (UMANA)**

2247 W. Chicago Ave.
Chicago, IL 60622
Ph: (312)278-6262

Members: Physicians, surgeons, dentists, and persons in related professions who are of Ukrainian descent. **Purpose:** Provides assistance to members; sponsors lectures. **Activities:** Maintains placement service, museum, biographical and medical archives, and library of 1800 medical books and journals in Ukrainian.

EMPLOYER DIRECTORIES AND NETWORKING LISTS

★6433★ *AHA Guide to the Health Care Field*

Health Statistics Group
American Hospital Association (AHA)
1 N. Franklin
Chicago, IL 60606
Ph: (312)422-3501   Fax: (312)280-6015

Annual, July. $195.00, payment with order. Covers hospitals, multi-health care systems, freestanding ambulatory surgery centers, psychiatric facilities, long-term care facilities, substance abuse programs, hospices, Health Maintenance Organizations (HMOs), and other health-related organizations. Entries include: For hospitals: facility name, address, phone, administrator's name, number of beds, facilities and services, number of employees, expenses, other statistics. For other organizations: name, address, phone, name and title of contact. Arrangement: Geographical. Indexes: Hospital name.

★6434★ *American Academy of Pediatrics—Fellowship Directory*

American Academy of Pediatrics
141 Northwest Point Blvd.
Elk Grove Village, IL 60007
Ph: (708)228-5005   Fax: (708)228-5097
Fr: 800-433-9016

Annual, January. $95.00. Covers AAP staff, chapters, board of directors, councils and committees. Entries include: Name, address, phone, fax, year of graduation from medical school. Arrangement: Geographical.

★6435★ *American Association of Public Health Physicians—Membership Roster*

American Association of Public Health Physicians
Department of Family Medicine and Practice
University of Wisconsin Medical School
777 S. Mills St.
Madison, WI 53715
Ph: (608)263-1326   Fax: (608)263-5813

Annual. Covers 200 physicians. Entries include: Name, address, professional affiliation. Arrangement: Available in alphabetical or geographical arrangement.

★6436★ *American College of Chest Physicians—Membership Directory and Referral Guide*

American College of Chest Physicians
3300 Dundee Rd.
Northbrook, IL 60062-2303
Ph: (708)498-1400   Fax: (708)498-5460
Fr: 800-343-ACCP

Annual, spring. $100.00, payment must accompany order. Covers 15,000 physicians and surgeons specializing in diseases of the heart and lungs. Entries include: Name, personal and career data, address, certifications, specialty. Arrangement: Geographical. Indexes: Alphabetical, specialty.

★6437★ *American Group Practice Association—Directory*

American Group Practice Association
1422 Duke St.
Alexandria, VA 22314
Ph: (703)838-0033   Fax: (703)548-1890

Annual, February. $150.00. Covers about 250 private group medical practices and their professional staffs, totalling about 25,000 physicians and administrators. Entries include: Group member name, address, phone, names of administrator and other executives, names of physician listed by medical specialties. Arrangement: Alphabetical. Indexes: Group location, personal name.

★6438★ *American Group Psychotherapy Association—Membership Directory*

American Group Psychotherapy Association
25 E. 21st St., 6th Fl.
New York, NY 10010
Ph: (212)477-2677

Annual, fall. $45.00. Covers 3,700 physicians, psychologists, clinical social workers, psychiatric nurses, and other mental health professionals interested in treatment of emotional problems by group methods. Entries include: Name, office or home address, highest degree held, office or home phone number. Arrangement: Alphabetical. Indexes: Geographical.

★6439★ American Holistic Medical Association—Directory of Members

American Holistic Medical Association
4101 Lake Boone Trail, Ste. 201
Raleigh, NC 27607
Ph: (919)787-5146   Fax: (919)787-4916

Annual, spring. Covers Approximately 600 medical doctors, doctors of osteopathy, students, and health practitioners who are certified, registered, or licensed by their state and are interested in or practice holistic medicine. Entries include: Name, address, specialty. Arrangement: Alphabetical. Indexes: Geographical.

★6440★ American Osteopathic Association—Yearbook and Directory of Osteopathic Physicians

American Osteopathic Association
142 E. Ontario St.
Chicago, IL 60611
Ph: (312)280-5800

Annual, January. $75.00. Covers member and nonmember osteopathic physicians; also includes student and associate members. Entries include: Name, office or home address, specialty, type of practice, age, date and institution granting degree; code indicates whether member. Arrangement: Alphabetical. Indexes: Geographical, certifying board, field.

★6441★ Best Doctors in America

Woodward/White, Inc.
129 1st Ave. SW
Aiken, SC 29801
Ph: (803)648-0300   Fax: (803)641-1709

Biennial, January of even years. $65.00. Covers Approximately 3,800 doctors selected as the best in their specialties by a survey of about 5,500 doctors. Entries include: Name, address, phone, academic/hospital affiliations. Arrangement: Classified by medical speciality, then geographical.

★6442★ Directory of Hospital Personnel

Medical Economics
5 Paragon Dr.
Montvale, NJ 07645-1725
Ph: (201)358-7500   Fax: (201)573-4956
Fr: 800-222-3045

Annual, September. $325.00, plus 7.50 shipping. Covers 200,000 executives at 7,100 U.S. hospitals. Entries include: Name of hospital, address, phone, number of beds, type and JCAHO status of hospital, names and titles of key department heads and staff, medical and nursing school affiliations; number of residents, interns, and nursing students. Arrangement: Geographical. Indexes: Hospital name, personnel, hospital size.

★6443★ Directory of Physicians in the United States

American Medical Association
515 N. State St.
Chicago, IL 60610-4377
Ph: (312)464-5000   Fax: (312)464-5600
Fr: 800-621-8335

Biennial, September of even years. $545.00 per set. Covers in four volume set, more than 686,000 physicians in the United States, Puerto Rico, Virgin Islands, and certain Pacific Islands and United States physicians temporarily located in foreign countries. Entries include: Name, address, year licensed in mailing address state, medical school, type of practice, primary and secondary specialties, board certifications, and Physician's Recognition award status. Both print and CD-ROM versions are available only through a special licensing agreement with the American Medical Association. Arrangement: Geographical by city; federal service and United States physicians abroad in separate section. Indexes: Alphabetical (constitutes Volume 1 of set); geographical.

★6444★ Freestanding Outpatient Surgery Center Directory

SMG Marketing Group, Inc.
1342 N. LaSalle Dr.
Chicago, IL 60610
Ph: (312)642-3026   Fax: (312)642-9729
Fr: 800-678-3026

Annual, August. $425.00. Covers more than 1,600 ambulatory surgical centers. Entries include: Facility name, address, phone, medical director name, ownership; number of operating suites, number of surgeries performed each year, types of surgery performed. Arrangement: Geographical.

★6445★ Health & Medical Industry Directory

American Business Directories, Inc.
American Business Information, Inc.
5711 S. 86th Cir.
Omaha, NE 68127
Ph: (402)593-4600   Fax: (402)331-1505

Released 1993. $79.00. CD-ROM. Lists over 1.1 million physicians and surgeons, dentists, clinics, health clubs, and other health-related businesses in the U.S. and Canada. Entries include: Name, address, phone. IBM-compatible equipment required.

★6446★ HMO/PPO Directory

Medical Economics Data
5 Paragon Dr.
Montvale, NJ 07645-1742
Ph: (201)358-7500   Fax: (201)573-4956
Fr: 800-222-3045

Annual, November. $225.00, plus $7.50 shipping. Covers over 700 health maintenance organizations (HMOs) and more than 900 preferred provider organizations (PPOs). Entries include: Name of organization, address, phone, number of members, names of officers, employer references, geographical area served, parent company, average fees and copayments, financial data, and cost control procedures. Arrangement: Geographical. Indexes: Organization name, personnel name, HMOs and PPOs by state, and number of members enrolled.

★6447★ Hospital Blue Book

Billian Publishing Co.
2100 Powers Ferry Rd., Ste. 300
Atlanta, GA 30339
Ph: (404)955-5656   Fax: (404)952-0669

Annual, spring. $154.50, national edition, plus $20.00 shipping. Covers more than 7,100 hospitals; some listings also appear in a separate southern edition of this publication. Entries include: Name of hospital, accreditation, mailing address, phone, fax, number of beds, type of facility (nonprofit, general, state, etc.); list of administrative personnel and chiefs of medical services, with specific titles. Arrangement: Geographical.

★6448★ Hospital Market Atlas

SMG Marketing Group, Inc.
1342 N. LaSalle Dr.
Chicago, IL 60610
Ph: (312)642-3026   Fax: (312)642-9729
Fr: 800-678-3026

Biennial, odd years. $495.00, payment with order. Covers over 7,000 hospitals, hospital systems and 480 group purchasing organizations. Entries include: Hospital or organization name, address, phone, county code, management, type of hospital service, number of beds, admissions, surgical operations, and emergency room visits. Arrangement: Geographical.

★6449★ Hospitals Directory

American Business Directories, Inc.
American Business Information, Inc.
5711 S. 86th Cir.
Omaha, NE 68127
Ph: (402)593-4600   Fax: (402)331-1505

Annual. $870.00, U.S. edition. Entries include: Name, address, phone (including area code), size of advertisement, year first in Yellow Pages, name of owner or manager, number of employees. Compiled from telephone company Yellow Pages, nationwide. Arrangement: Geographical.

★6450★ Medi-Pages

Medi-Pages, Inc.
757 Cayuga St.
Lewiston, NY 14092
Ph: (716)284-4277   Fax: (716)284-4401
Fr: 800-554-6661

Annual, March. $60.00 plus $5.00 shipping. Covers more than 100,000 listings of hospitals, nursing homes, clinics, home healthcare providers, HMO's, PPO's, CPO's, health associations, professional associations, national nursing associations, federal government agencies, international health organizations, scholarship funds, research grants, medical libraries, hospital management companys, case managers, HFCA offices, AT&T numbers. Entries include: Facility, association, company, library, or personal name, address, phone. Arrangement: Main listing of hospitals, physicians, and medical supply companies is classified by product or service, then geographical; others are geographical within section.

★6451★ **Medical and Health Information Directory**

Gale Research
835 Penobscot Bldg.
Detroit, MI 48226-4094
Ph: (313)961-2242   Fax: (313)961-6083
Fr: 800-877-GALE

Approximately biennial; latest edition 1994. $195.00, per volume; $485.00, for the three-volume set. Covers in Volume 1, almost 18,600 medical and health oriented associations, organizations, institutions, and government agencies, including health maintenance organizations (HMOs), preferred provider organizations (PPOs), insurance companies, pharmaceutical companies, research centers, and medical and allied health schools. In Volume 2, nearly 11,800 medical book publishers; medical periodicals, directories, audiovisual producers and services, medical libraries and information centers, and electronic resources. In Volume 3, nearly 26,000 clinics, treatment centers, care programs, and counseling/diagnostic services for 30 subject areas. Entries include: Institution, service, or firm name, address, phone; many include names of key personnel and, when pertinent, descriptive annotation. Arrangement: Classified by organization activity, service, etc. Indexes: Each volume has a complete alphabetical name and keyword index.

★6452★ **Medical Research Centres**

Stockton Press
Groves Dictionaries
345 Park Ave. S., 10th Fl.
New York, NY 10010
Ph: (212)689-9200   Fr: 800-221-2123

Eleventh edition, 1995. $595.00. 856 pages. Covers medical and biochemical research conducted in over 100 countries. Entries include information on industrial enterprises, research laboratories, universities, societies, and professional associations engaged in research in medicine and related subjects like dentistry, nursing, pharmacy, psychiatry, and surgery.

★6453★ **The Official American Board of Medical Specialties–Directory of Board Certified Medical Specialists**

Marquis Who's Who
Reed Reference Publishing
121 Chanlon Rd.
New Providence, NJ 07974
Ph: (908)771-7730   Fax: (908)665-6688
Fr: 800-521-8110

Annual, November. $439.95, plus $29.75 shipping. Covers more than 465,000 board-certified specialists in 25 areas of medical practice from allergy to urology. Entries include: Name, certifications, office address, phone, date and place of birth, education, career date, date certified, type of practice, professional memberships. Arrangement: Classified by specialty, then geographical. Indexes: Alphabetical.

★6454★ **The Official American Board of Medical Specialties—Directory of Board Certified Pediatricians**

Marquis Who's Who
Reed Reference Publishing
121 Chanlon Rd.
New Providence, NJ 07974
Ph: (908)464-6800   Fax: (908)665-6688
Fr: 800-521-8110

Biennial. $99.95. Covers about 47,000 certified pediatricians. Entries include: Name, address, phone, certification data, education, professional association membership. Arrangement: Geographical. Indexes: Alphabetical.

★6455★ **Osteopathic Membership Directory—AOHA**

American Osteopathic Healthcare
  Association
5301 Wisconsin Ave. NW, Ste. 630
Washington, DC 20015-2015
Ph: (202)686-1700   Fax: (202)686-7615

Annual, summer. $125.00, payment with order. Covers about 110 osteopathic hospitals. Includes list of individual and institutional members; also lists osteopathic colleges, and directors of medical education. Entries include: For hospitals: name of hospital, name of chief executive officer, address, phone, number of beds and other hospital data. Arrangement: Geographical. Indexes: Name, institution.

★6456★ **Physicians and Dentists Database**

FIRSTMARK, Inc.
34 Juniper Ln.
Newton Center, MA 02159-2861
Ph: (617)965-7989   Fax: (617)965-8510
Fr: 800-729-2600

Updated continuously; printed on request. Please inquire. Database covers: More than 400,000 physicians and 160,000 dentists nationwide. Entries include: Individual name, address, phone, medical specialty, whether in single or group practice.

★6457★ **Physicians & Surgeons Directory**

American Business Directories, Inc.
American Business Information, Inc.
5711 S. 86th Cir.
Omaha, NE 68127
Ph: (402)593-4600   Fax: (402)331-1505

Annual. $11,695.00, U.S. edition; $1,090.00, Canad. ed. Entries include: Name, address, phone, size of advertisement, year first in Yellow Pages, name of owner or manager, number of employees. Regional and specialty editions available. Compiled from telephone company Yellow Pages nationwide. Arrangement: Geographical.

★6458★ **Physicians & Surgeons Information Bureaus Directory**

American Business Directories, Inc.
American Business Information, Inc.
5711 S. 86th Cir.
Omaha, NE 68127
Ph: (402)593-4600   Fax: (402)331-1505

Updated continuously; printed on request. Please inquire. Entries include: Name, address, phone (including area code), size of advertisement, year first in Yellow Pages, name of owner or manager, number of employees. Compiled from telephone company Yellow Pages, nationwide. Arrangement: Geographical.

HANDBOOKS AND MANUALS

★6459★ **Careers in Health Care**

VGM Career Horizons
4255 W. Touhy Ave.
Lincolnwood, IL 60646-1975
Ph: (847)679-5500   Fax: (847)679-2494
Fr: 800-323-4900

Barbara M. Swanson. 1995. $17.95; $13.95 (paper). Describes job duties, work settings, salaries, licensing and certification requirements, educational preparation, and future outlook. Gives ideas on how to secure a job.

★6460★ **Careers in Medicine**

VGM Career Horizons
4255 W. Touhy Ave.
Lincolnwood, IL 60646-1975
Ph: (847)679-5500   Fax: (847)679-2494
Fr: 800-323-4900

Terence J. Sacks. Second edition, 1996. $17.95; $13.95 (paper). 192 pages. Examines the many paths open to M.D.s, D.O.s, and M.D./Ph.D.s, including clinical private or group practice, hospitals, public health organizations, the armed forces, emergency rooms, research institutions, medical schools, pharmaceutical companies and private industry, and research/advocacy groups like the World Health Organization. A special chapter on osteopathy and chiropractic explores this branch of medicine.

★6461★ **Careers in Medicine: Traditional and Alternative Opportunities**

Garrett Park Press
PO Box 190 C
Garrett Park, MD 20896-0190
Ph: (301)946-2553

Donald T. Rucker and Martin D. Keller. 1990. $15.95. 346 pages. Cites training requirements, illustrative work activities, and a summary of the advantages and disadvantages in a variety of specialized areas. Includes hundreds of career alternatives and discusses ways to break into these fields for persons trained in medicine. Features contributions from over 40 professionals in all phases of medicine and provides 200 sources of information on specialties and subspecialties.

★6462★ **Chronicle Health Occupations Guidebook**

Chronicle Guidance Publications
PO Box 1190
Moravia, NY 13118-1190
Ph: (315)497-0330   Fax: (315)497-3359
Fr: 800-622-7284

Paul Downes, editor. 1994. $100.65.

★6463★ The Complete Medical Marketing Handbook: A Guide for Physicians & Managers

Practice Management Information Corp.
4727 Wilshire Blvd., Ste. 300
Los Angeles, CA 90010
Ph: (213)954-0224   Fax: (213)954-0253
Fr: 800-633-4215

Maryann Ricardo. 1994. $49.95.

★6464★ The Definitive Guide for the D.O. Trying to Get an M.D. Residency: D.O.'s Eat Their Young

Gotta Reach the Jam Publishing Co.
1074 Point Seaside Dr.
Crystal Beach, FL 34681
Ph: (813)785-6553

Jeremy S. Weiss. 1995. $24.95 (paper).

★6465★ Exploring Health Careers

Delmar Publishers
3 Columbia Cir., Box 15015
Albany, NY 12212
Ph: (518)464-3500   Fax: (518)464-0358
Fr: 800-347-7707

Maureen McCutcheon. 1993. $27.95.

★6466★ Health Care Job Explosion! Careers in the 90's

Bookhaven Press
401 Amherst Ave.
Coraopolis, PA 15108
Ph: (412)262-5578

Dennis Y. Damp. 1993. $14.95 (paper).

★6467★ Healthcare Career Directory–Nurses and Physicians

Gale Research
835 Penobscot Bldg.
Detroit, MI 48226-4094
Ph: (313)961-2242   Fax: (313)961-6083
Fr: 800-877-GALE

Bradley Morgan. Second edition, 1993. $39.00. 327 pages. Essays on specific careers provide an insider's perspective. Features extensive listings of contacts and entry-level job opportunities. Provides information on internships and sources of help-wanted ads.

★6468★ Hot Health-Care Careers

MasterMedia Ltd.
17 E. 89th St., 7D
New York, NY 10128
Ph: (212)546-7650   Fax: (212)546-7638
Fr: 800-334-8232

Margaret McNally. 1993. $17.95; $10.95 (paper).

★6469★ The International Medical Graduate Guide to U.S. Medicine: Negotiating the Maze

Galen Press, Ltd.
PO Box 64400
Tucson, AZ 85728-4400
Ph: (520)577-8363   Fax: (520)529-6459

Louise B. Ball. 1995.

★6470★ Job Opportunities in Health Care 1995

Peterson's Guides, Inc.
PO Box 2123
Princeton, NJ 08543-2123
Ph: (609)243-9111   Fax: (609)243-9150
Fr: 800-338-3282

1994. $18.95 (paper).

★6471★ The New Practice Handbook: A Guide to Establishing a Successful Medical Practice

Practice Management Information Corp.
4727 Wilshire Blvd.,Ste. 300
Los Angeles, CA 90010
Ph: (213)954-0224   Fax: (213)954-0253
Fr: 800-633-4215

Maryann Szostak-Ricardo. 1994. $49.95.

★6472★ 100 Best Careers for the Year 2000

Prentice Hall General Reference
15 Columbus Cir.
New York, NY 10023
Ph: (212)373-8500   Fr: 800-223-2348

Shelly Field. 1992. $15.00 (paper). Covers 100 of the fastest growing jobs. The publication is divided into 11 general employment sections. Specific careers are covered within each section. Provides job description, responsibilities, employment opportunities, earnings, education and training, advancement opportunities, and experience and qualifications for each occupation.

★6473★ Opportunities in Health and Medical Careers

VGM Career Horizons
4255 W. Touhy Ave.
Lincolnwood, IL 60646-1975
Ph: (847)679-5500   Fax: (847)679-2494
Fr: 800-323-4900

Donald Snook, Jr. and Leo D'Orazio. 1993. $14.95; $11.95 (paper). Covers the full range of medical and health occupations. Illustrated.

★6474★ Opportunities in Physician Careers

VGM Career Horizons
4255 W. Touhy Ave.
Lincolnwood, IL 60646-1975
Ph: (847)679-5500   Fax: (847)679-2494
Fr: 800-323-4900

Jan Sugar-Webb. 1991. $14.95; $11.95 (paper). Examines specialties like pediatrics, neurology, dermatology, and internal medicine and evaluates employment prospects and salary range for each specialty.

★6475★ Opportunities in Public Health Careers

VGM Career Horizons
4255 W. Touhy Ave.
Lincolnwood, IL 60646-1975
Ph: (847)679-5500   Fax: (847)679-2494
Fr: 800-323-4900

George E. Pickett and Terry W. Pickett. 1995. $14.95; $11.95 (paper). 160 pages. Defines the public health field and describes a variety of health, science, and business opportunities as well as educational preparation and the future of the public health field.

Offers job-hunting tips. The appendixes list public health organizations, state and federal public health agencies, and graduate schools offering public health programs.

★6476★ Opportunities in Sports and Athletics

VGM Career Horizons
4255 W. Touhy Ave.
Lincolnwood, IL 60646-1975
Ph: (847)679-5500   Fax: (847)679-2494
Fr: 800-323-4900

William Ray Heitzmann. 1994. $14.95; $11.95 (paper). A guide to planning for and seeking opportunities in this growing field. Illustrated.

★6477★ Opportunities in Sports Medicine Careers

VGM Career Horizons
4255 W. Touhy Ave.
Lincolnwood, IL 60646-1975
Ph: (847)679-5500   Fax: (847)679-2494
Fr: 800-323-4900

William Ray Heitzmann. 1995. $14.95; $11.95 (paper). 160 pages. Discusses a variety of opportunities in this field and how to pursue them. Contains bibliography and illustrations.

★6478★ Resumes for Health and Medical Careers

4255 W. Touhy Ave.
Lincolnwood, IL 60646-1975
Ph: (708)679-5500   Fax: (708)679-6375
Fr: 800-323-4900

Compiled by VGM Career Horizons Staff 1995. $9.95 (paper).

★6479★ Resumes & Personal Statements for Health Professionals

Galen Press, Ltd.
PO Box 64400
Tucson, AZ 85728-4400
Ph: (520)577-8363   Fax: (520)529-6459

James W. Tysinger. 1994. $15.95 (paper).

★6480★ Where the Jobs Are: The Hottest Careers for the '90s

The Career Press, Inc.
3 Tice Rd.
PO Box 687
Franklin Lakes, NJ 07417
Ph: (201)848-0310   Fax: (201)848-1727
Fr: 800-237-3371

Joyce Hadley. Second edition, 1995. $9.99. 300 pages. Describes careers in fifteen general fields, from accounting to travel and hospitality.

EMPLOYMENT AGENCIES AND SEARCH FIRMS

★6481★ Action Plus Employer Services
1211 W. Imperial Hwy., Ste. 100
Brea, CA 92621
Ph: (714)773-1506   Fax: (714)773-9201

Employment agency.

★6482★ **Consult One, Inc.**
10291 N. Meridan St., Ste. 325
Indianapolis, IN 46290-1078
Ph: (317)573-2025   Fax: (317)573-2035
Executive search firm.

★6483★ **EHS and Associates, Inc.**
3033 Excelsior Blvd., Ste. 303
Minneapolis, MN 55416
Ph: (612)924-2366   Fax: (612)924-2367
Executive search firm and employment agency.

★6484★ **The Energists**
10260 Westheimer, Ste. 300
Houston, TX 77042
Ph: (713)781-6881   Fax: (713)781-2998
Executive search firm.

★6485★ **Executive Medical Recruiters**
2350 W. 7th St.
St. Paul, MN 55116
Ph: (612)699-3020
Employment agency.

★6486★ **Harper Associates**
29870 Middlebelt
Farmington Hills, MI 48334
Ph: (810)932-1170
Employment agency.

★6487★ **Health and Science Center**
209 Hunter St.
Media, PA 19063-5726
Ph: (610)891-0714
Employment agency. Executive search firm.

★6488★ **Phyllis Hawkins and Associates**
3550 N. Central Ave., Ste. 1400
Phoenix, AZ 85012
Ph: (602)263-0248   Fax: (602)263-1016
Executive search firm.

★6489★ **Physicians Search, Inc.**
1224 E. KAtella Ave., Ste. 202
Orange, CA 92667-5045
Ph: (714)288-8350
Executive search firm. Affiliate office in Spokane, WA.

★6490★ **Professional Placement Associates, Inc.**
11 Rye Ridge Plaza
Rye Brook, NY 10573
Ph: (914)251-1000   Fax: (914)939-1959
Employment agency.

★6491★ **Putzek Medical Search**
4150 Falcon Dr.
Austell, GA 30001-3067
Ph: (404)941-3339
Employment agency. Executive search consultant.

★6492★ **Robert William James and Associates**
621 SW Morrison, Ste. 500
Portland, OR 97205
Ph: (503)224-5505
Employment agency.

★6493★ **Shiloh Careers International, Inc.**
7105 Peach Ct., Ste. 102
PO Box 831
Brentwood, TN 37024-0831
Ph: (615)373-3090
Employment agency.

★6494★ **Sue Carroll Personnel, Inc.**
16 E. 79th St.
New York, NY 10021
Ph: (212)288-8866   Fax: (212)988-7191
Employment agency and executive search firm.

★6495★ **Team Placement Service, Inc.**
5113 Leesburg Pike
Falls Church, VA 22041-3242
Ph: (703)820-8618   Fax: (703)820-3368
Employment agency.

★6496★ **Weatherby Healthcare**
25 Van Zant St.
Norwalk, CT 06855
Ph: (203)866-1144   Fax: (203)853-3154
Executive search firm. Branch office in Fairfax, VA.

OTHER SOURCES

★6497★ **American Academy of Head, Neck and Facial Pain (AAHNFP)**
520 W. Pipeline Rd.
Hurst, TX 76053-4924
Ph: (817)282-1501   Fax: (817)282-8012
Fr: 800-322-8651
Members: Health Care Practitioners who treat head, facial, and neck pain. **Purpose:** Functions as a referral service for patients suffering from head, facial, and neck pain worldwide. Plans to establish computerized medical procedures and insurance database.

★6498★ **American Academy of Sports Physicians (AASP)**
17445 Oak Creek Court
Encino, CA 91316
Ph: (818)501-4433   Fax: (818)501-8855
Members: Clinical physicians engaged in the practice of sports medicine who have made contributions in research, academics, or related fields. **Purpose:** To educate and inform physicians whose practices comprise mainly sports medicine and to register and recognize physicians who have expertise in sports medicine. Operates referral service for amateur and professional athletes. Conducts research; compiles statistics; sponsors seminars.

★6499★ **American Association of Immunologists (AAI)**
9650 Rockville Pike
Bethesda, MD 20814
Ph: (301)530-7178   Fax: (301)571-1816
Members: Scientists engaged in immunological research including aspects of virology, bacteriology, biochemistry, genetics, and related disciplines. **Purpose:** Goals are to advance knowledge of immunology and related disciplines and to facilitate the interchange of information among investigators in various fields. Promotes interaction between laboratory investigators and clinicians. Conducts training courses, symposia, workshop, and lectures. Compiles statistics.

★6500★ **American Association of Osteopathic Examiners (AAOE)**
300 5th St. NE
Washington, DC 20002
Ph: (202)544-5060   Fax: (202)544-3525
Members: Private physicians; state medical boards. **Purpose:** Works for adequate osteopathic representation on all physician licensing boards. Conducts examinations and offers certification of osteopathic physicians.

★6501★ **American Association of Physician Specialists (AAPS)**
804 Main St., Ste. D
Forest Park, GA 30050
Ph: (404)363-8263   Fax: (404)361-2285
Fr: 800-447-9397
Members: Osteopathic and allopathic physicians. **Purpose:** Formed for the benevolent, scientific, and educational purposes of improving the practice of the specialty disciplines. Promotes the study and education of specialty disciplines and high intellectual, moral, and ethical standards in specialty practice. Encourages improved quality of osteopathic medical and surgical patient care. Maintains continuing education programs: American Academy of Osteopathic Anesthesiologists; American Academy of Osteopathic Dermatologists; American Academy of Osteopathic Emergency Physicians; American Academy of Osteopathic Family Practitioners; American Academy of Osteopathic Internists; American Academy of Osteopathic Neurologists and Psychiatrists; American Academy of Osteopathic Obstetricians and Gynecologists; American Academy of Plastic and Reconstructive Surgeons; American Academy of Osteopathic Radiologists; American Academy of Osteopathic Orthopedic Surgeons. Provides certification programs in 26 different areas of specialization. Bestows degree of Fellow.

★6502★ **American College of Sports Medicine (ACSM)**
PO Box 1440
Indianapolis, IN 46206-1440
Ph: (317)637-9200   Fax: (317)634-7817
Purpose: Promotes and integrates scientific research, education, and practical applications of sports medicine and exercise science to maintain and enhance physical performance, fitness, health, and quality of life. **Activities:** Certifies fitness leaders, fitness instructors, exercise test technologists, exercise specialists, health/fitness program direc-

tors, and U.S. military fitness personnel. Grants continuing medical education (CME) and continuing education credits (CEC). Operates more than 50 committees.

★6503★ American Group Practice Association (AGPA)

1422 Duke St.
Alexandria, VA 22314-3430
Ph: (703)838-0033   Fax: (703)548-1890

Members: Private group practice medical and dental clinics representing more than 26,000 physicians. **Purpose:** Fosters accreditation of medical clinics; compiles statistics on group practice; sponsors research, patient education, and insurance programs. Conducts symposia; makes available consulting services.

★6504★ American Hospital Association (AHA)

1 N. Franklin, Ste. 27
Chicago, IL 60606
Ph: (312)422-3000   Fax: (312)422-4796

Members: Individuals and health care institutions including hospitals, health care systems, and pre- and postacute health care delivery organizations. **Purpose:** Is dedicated to promoting the welfare of the public through its leadership and assistance to its members in the provision of better health services for all people. Conducts educational programs furthering the in-service education of hospital personnel; collects and analyzes data; furnishes multimedia educational materials; maintains 44,000 volume health care administration library, and biographical archive.

★6505★ *Career Encounters: Physician*

Cambridge Career Products
PO Box 2153
Dept. CC15
Charleston, WV 25328-2153
Ph: (304)744-9323   Fax: (304)744-9351
Fr: 800-468-4227

Video. $99.95. 25 minutes. Professionals shown in a variety of settings discuss different aspects of their careers.

★6506★ *Directory of Child Life Programs*

Child Life Council
7910 Woodmont Ave., Ste. 310
Bethesda, MD 20814
Ph: (301)654-1343   Fax: (301)654-4964

Irregular. $22.00, plus $3.00 shipping. Covers Nearly 150 internships, fellowships, and other practical teaching experiences in hospitals for students of child life activity. Entries include: Facility name, address, phone, name of individual in charge of the practicum; number of hours and number of weeks for practicum; beginning dates, if specified; number of students accepted each term; total number of students accepted for the year; colleges from which students are generally referred; areas of study from which students generally come; fees; stipend and other benefits; prerequisites; whether application is to be made to college or hospital; level of student generally accepted; practicum experiences available; form of evaluation. Arrangement: Geographical.

★6507★ Holistic Dental Association (HDA)

c/o Dr. Paul Plowman
4801 Richmond Sq.
Oklahoma City, OK 73118
Ph: (405)840-5600   Fax: (405)843-0417

Members: Dentists, chiropractors, dental hygienists, physical therapists, and medical doctors. **Purpose:** Goals are: to provide a holistic approach to better dental care for patients; to expand techniques, medications, and philosophies that pertain to extractions, anesthetics, fillings, crowns, and orthodontics. Encourages use of homeopathic medications, acupuncture, cranial osteopathy, nutritional techniques, and physical therapy in treating patients in addition to conventional treatments. **Activities:** Classifies therapies; has developed a referral questionnaire for holistic practitioners. Sponsors training and educational seminars.

★6508★ International Association of Hygienic Physicians (IAHP)

204 Stambaugh Bldg.
Youngstown, OH 44503
Ph: (216)746-5000   Fax: (216)746-1836

Members: Doctors of medicine, osteopathy, chiropractic, and naturopathy who specialize in the supervision of therapeutic fasting as part of a natural hygiene regimen. **Purpose:** Promotes clinical advancement and ethical responsibility. Works for the health freedom of members. **Activities:** Provides certification for professionals and accreditation for schools and training programs; offers internship programs. Funds research.

★6509★ Joint Council of Allergy, Asthma and Immunology (JCAI)

PO Box 4620
Arlington Heights, IL 60006
Ph: (708)934-1918

Members: Physicians specializing in allergy or clinical immunology. Members must belong to the American Academy of Allergy and Immunology or the American College of Allergy and Immunology. Serves as political and socioeconomic arm for these organizations.

★6510★ *Journal of the American Medical Association—Physician Service Opportunities Overseas Section*

American Medical Association
515 N. State St.
Chicago, IL 60610-4377
Ph: (312)464-2446

Triennial, latest edition August 1993. Lists more than 170 organizations that provide assignments overseas for physicians from the United States. Entries include: Organization name, address, phone, contact person, countries served, medical specialties sought, length of assignment, stipend or salary (if provided), whether facilities or equipment, housing, and transportation are provided, and additional requirements. Arrangement: Alphabetical.

★6511★ National Rehabilitation Association (NRA)

633 S. Washington St.
Alexandria, VA 22314
Ph: (703)836-0850   Fax: (703)836-0848

Members: Administrators, instructors, placement specialists, secretaries, counselors, therapists, vocational evaluators, ADA specialists and others interested in rehabilitation of persons with disabilities. **Activities:** Conducts legislative activities; develops accessibility guidelines; offers specialized education.

★6512★ *The Overnight Resume*

Ten Speed Press
PO Box 7123
Berkeley, CA 94707
Ph: (510)559-1600   Fax: (510)559-1629
Fr: 800-841-BOOK

Donald Asher. 1990. $7.95. Discusses how to write aggressive business resumes, with additional information on special styles for technical, legal, and advertising personnel, actors, speakers, and students with no experience. Covers medical curricula vitae.

★6513★ Physicians Education Network (P.E.N.)

3944 Shore Acres Blvd. NE
St. Petersburg, FL 33703

Members: Ophthalmologists, other physicians, and concerned individuals whose current focus is on eye health care. **Purpose:** Encourages high standards of health care. Sponsors National Eye Health Care Month. Promotes consumer safety legislation; opposes legislation that could allow lower medical standards. Seeks requirement of an M.D. or D.O. degree as the minimum standard for persons delivering health care. Prepares speeches, position papers, and news releases; sponsors workshops on promotion of needed reforms; offers advice and counsel to members; provides speakers. Compiles statistics.

★6514★ Vision Educational Foundation (VEF)

PO Box 472305
Tulsa, OK 74147-2305
Ph: (918)762-3947   Fax: (918)451-9207

Members: Optometric doctors, ophthalmic laboratories, manufacturers, related technicians, and other professionals in the field. **Purpose:** To promote a long-range program of support to optometric educational institutions; to allow practicing optometrists opportunities to update and expand their clinical skills and keep abreast of new technology; to expose students to pathology cases; to provide access to the most advanced diagnostic equipment available. **Activities:** Provides referral services. Maintains VEF Educational and Diagnostic Center, which provides practicing optometrists and senior professional students of optometric colleges with clinical education of a diagnostic and therapeutic nature.

Physicists and Astronomers

Sources of Help-Wanted Ads

★6515★ Astronomy

Kalmbach Publishing Co.
PO Box 1612
Waukesha, WI 53187
Ph: (414)796-8776   Fax: (414)796-0126
Fr: 800-558-1544

Monthly. Magazine for amateur astronomers.

★6516★ Electrochemical Society Interface

The Electrochemical Society
10 S. Main St.
Pennington, NJ 08534
Ph: (609)737-1902   Fax: (609)737-2743

Quarterly. 40.00/year.

★6517★ Journal of Vacuum Science and Technology A & B

American Institute of Physics
500 Sunnyside Blvd.
Woodbury, NY 11797-2999
Ph: (516)576-2440   Fax: (516)576-2481

Monthly. Journal containing research review articles in all areas of vacuum science.

★6518★ Laser Focus World

PennWell Publishing Co.
10 Tara Blvd., 5th Fl.
Nashua, NH 03062-2801
Ph: (603)891-0123   Fax: (603)891-0597

Monthly. $149.00/year for individuals; $10.00 for single issue. Magazine covering laser, optics, fiberoptics, detector imaging technology, and electro-optical equipment and systems.

★6519★ Lasers & Optronics

Curpier/ Group Publishing
301 Gibraltar Dr.
PO Box 231
Cooperstown, NY 13326
Ph: (607)547-2591   Fax: (607)547-2923
Fr: 800-733-1284

Monthly. $55.00/year for individuals. Magazine serving the laser and optoelectronic market.

★6520★ Microwaves & RF

Penton Publishing
611 Rte. 46 W
Hasbrouck Heights, NJ 07604
Ph: (201)393-6060   Fax: (201)393-6297

Monthly. Magazine serving microwave and radio frequency specialists in the electronic manufacturing industry. Concerns research, design, development, application, production, purchasing and use functions, with information on news, marketing, products and technical design.

★6521★ Nature: International Weekly Journal of Science

Nature Publishing Co.
65 Bleecker St.
New York, NY 10012-2467
Ph: (212)477-9600   Fax: (212)505-1364

Weekly. Magazine covering science and technology, including the fields of biology, biochemistry, genetics, medicine, earth sciences, physics, pharmacology, and behavioral sciences.

★6522★ Photogrammetric Engineering and Remote Sensing

American Society for Photogrammetry and Remote Sensing (ASPRS)
5410 Grosvenor Ln., Ste. 210
Bethesda, MD 20814-2160
Ph: (301)493-0290   Fax: (301)493-0208

Monthly. Free to members; $120.00/year for nonmembers. Provides technical information about the applications of photogrammetry, remote sensing, and geographic information systems.

★6523★ The Physics Teacher

American Association of Physics Teachers
1 Physics Ellipse
College Park, MD 20740-3845
Ph: (301)209-3300   Fax: (301)209-0845

Scientific education magazine.

★6524★ Physics Today

American Institute of Physics
500 Sunnyside Blvd.
Woodbury, NY 11797-2999
Ph: (516)576-2440   Fax: (516)576-2481

Monthly. Journal covering news of physics research and activities that affect physics.

★6525★ The Scientist

The Scientist, Inc.
3501 Market St.
Philadelphia, PA 19104
Ph: (215)386-0100   Fax: (215)387-7542

Biweekly. $58.00/year for individuals; $82.00/year for Canada and Mexico; $79.00/year for other countries. Newspaper (tabloid) for scientists featuring news, opinions, research, and professional section.

★6526★ Sky & Telescope

Sky Publishing Corp.
PO Box 9111
Belmont, MA 02178-9111
Ph: (617)864-7360   Fax: (617)864-6117

Monthly. $33.00/year for individuals; $24.00/year for students; $3.95 for single issue. Magazine on astronomy and space science.

Placement and Job Referral Services

★6527★ American Association of Physicists in Medicine (AAPM)

One Physics Ellipse
College Park, MD 20740-3846
Ph: (301)209-3350   Fax: (301)209-0862

Members: Persons professionally engaged in application of physics to medicine and biology in medical research; educational institutions. **Purpose:** Encourages interest and training in medical physics and related fields; promotes high professional standards; disseminates technical information. **Activities:** Maintains placement service. Conducts research programs.

★6528★ American Astronomical Society (AAS)

2000 Florida Ave. NW, Ste. 400
Washington, DC 20009
Ph: (202)328-2010   Fax: (202)234-2560

Members: Astronomers, physicists, and scientists in related fields. **Purpose:** Conducts Visiting Professor in Astronomy Program. **Activities:** Maintains placement service.

★6529★ American Crystallographic Association (ACA)

PO Box 96, Ellicott Sta.
Buffalo, NY 14205-0096
Ph: (716)856-9600   Fax: (716)852-4846

Members: Chemists, biochemists, physicists, mineralogists, and metallurgists interested in crystallography and in the application of X-ray, electron, and neutron diffraction. **Purpose:** Promotes the study of the arrangement of atoms in matter, its causes, its nature, and its consequences, and of the tools and methods used in such studies. **Activities:** Maintains employment clearinghouse for members and employers.

★6530★ American Institute of Physics (AIP)

1 Physics Ellipse
College Park, MD 20740-3843
Ph: (301)209-3100

Members: Corporation of ten national societies in the field of physics with a total of 100,000 members, 17 affiliated societies, 68 corporate associates, and 7500 student members. **Purpose:** Seeks to assist in the advancement and diffusion of the knowledge of physics and its application to human welfare. To this end the institute publishes scientific journals devoted to physics and related sciences; provides secondary information services; conducts research in information systems; serves the public by making available to the press and other channels of public information reliable communications on physics and its progress; carries on extensive career placement activities; maintains projects directed toward providing information about physics education to students, physics teachers, and physics departments; encourages and assists in the documentation and study of the history of recent physics; cooperates with local, national, and international organizations devoted to physics; and fosters the relations of the science of physics to other sciences and to the arts and industry. **Activities:** Provides placement service; compiles statistics; maintains biographical archives and Niels Bohr Library of History of Physics.

★6531★ Health Physics Society (HPS)

1313 Dolley Madison Blvd., Ste. 402
McLean, VA 22101-3926
Ph: (703)790-1745   Fax: (703)790-9063

Members: Persons engaged in some form of activity in the field of health physics (the profession devoted to radiation protection). **Purpose:** To improve public understanding of the problems and needs in radiation protection; to promote health physics as a profession. Maintains Elda E. Anderson Memorial Fund to be used for teachers, researchers, and others. **Activities:** Provides placement service at annual meeting. Cosponsors American Board of Health Physics for certification of health physicists.

★6532★ International Planetarium Society (IPS)

Hansen Planetarium
15 S. State St.
Salt Lake City, UT 84111
Ph: (801)538-2104   Fax: (801)538-2059

Members: Planetarium staff members; planetarium equipment suppliers; students in planetarium education and astronomy. **Purpose:** Encourages exchange of ideas relating to planetariums and the profession. **Activities:** Operates placement service.

★6533★ Korean Scientists and Engineers Association in America (KSEA)

6261 Executive Blvd.
Rockville, MD 20852
Ph: (301)984-7048   Fax: (301)984-1231

Members: Scientists and engineers holding single or advanced degrees. **Purpose:** Goals are to: promote friendship and mutuality among Korean and American scientists and engineers; contribute to Korea's scientific, technological, industrial, and economic developments; strengthen the scientific, technological, and cultural bonds between Korea and the U.S. Sponsors symposium. **Activities:** Maintains speakers' bureau, placement service, and biographical archives. Compiles statistics. Maintains 100 volume library of scientific handbooks and yearbooks in Korean.

★6534★ National Network of Minority Women in Science (MWIS)

Directorate for Education and Human
  Resources Programs
1333 H St. NW
Washington, DC 20005
Ph: (202)326-6757   Fax: (202)371-9849

Members: Asian, Black, Mexican American, Native American, and Puerto Rican women involved in science related professions; other interested persons. **Purpose:** Promotes the advancement of minority women in science fields and the improvement of the science and mathematics education and career awareness of minorities. Supports public policies and programs in science and technology that benefit minorities. **Activities:** Maintains placement servce. Compiles statistics; serves as clearinghouse for identifying minority women scientists. Offers writing and conference presentations, seminars, and workshops on minority women in science and local career conferences for students. Local chapters maintain speakers' bureaus, and children's services. **E-Mail:** ggilbert@aaas.org

★6535★ Society for In Vitro Biology (SIVB)

8815 Centre Park Dr., Ste. 210
Columbia, MD 21045
Ph: (410)992-0946   Fax: (410)992-0949
Fr: 800-741-7476

Members: Professional society of individuals using mammalian, invertebrate, plant cell tissue, and organ cultures as research tools in chemistry, physics, radiation, medicine, physiology, nutrition, and cytogenetics. **Purpose:** Aims are to foster collection and dissemination of information concerning the

maintenance and experimental use of tissue cells in vitro and to establish evaluation and development procedures. **Activities:** Operates placement service.

EMPLOYER DIRECTORIES AND NETWORKING LISTS

★6536★ American Men and Women of Science

R. R. Bowker Co.
Reed Reference Publishing
121 Chanlon Rd.
New Providence, NJ 07974
Ph: (908)464-6800   Fax: (908)665-6688
Fr: 800-521-8110

Triennial, latest edition January 1995. $106.00, per volume; $850.00, set. Covers over 123,000 U.S. and Canadian scientists active in the physical, biological, mathematical, computer science, and engineering fields; includes references to previous edition for deceased scientists and nonrespondents. Entries include: Name, address, education, personal and career data, memberships, honors and awards, research interest. Arrangement: Alphabetical. Indexes: Discipline (in separate volume).

★6537★ APS News—American Physical Society Membership Directory Issue

American Institute of Physics
1 Physics Ellipse
College Park, MD 20740-3844
Ph: (301)209-3280   Fax: (301)209-0867

Biennial, December of odd years. $50.00. Publication includes: List of over 43,000 members in U.S., Canada, and other countries. Entries include: Name, office or home address, daytime phone, electronic mail address, fax. Arrangement: Alphabetical. Indexes: Geographical, specialty.

★6538★ Directory of Physics and Astronomy Staff

American Institute of Physics
500 Sunnyside Blvd.
Woodbury, NY 11797
Ph: (516)576-2205   Fax: (516)576-2450
Fr: 800-809-2247

Biennial, September of odd years. $60.00. Covers 38,000 staff members at 3,100 colleges, universities, and laboratories throughout North America that employ physicists and astronomers; list of foreign organizations. Entries include: Name, address, phone, electronic mail address. Arrangement: Separate alphabetical sections for individuals, academic institutions, and laboratories. Indexes: Academic institution location, type of laboratory.

★6539★ Life Sciences Organizations and Agencies Directory

Gale Research
835 Penobscot Bldg.
Detroit, MI 48226-4094
Ph: (313)961-2242   Fax: (313)961-6083
Fr: 800-877-GALE

$175.00. Covers about 7,500 associations,

government agencies, research centers, educational institutions, libraries and information centers, museums, consultants, electronic information services, and other organizations and agencies active in agriculture, biology, ecology, forestry, marine science, nutrition, wildlife and animal sciences, and other natural and life sciences. Entries include: Organization or agency name, address, phone, name and title of contact, description. Arrangement: Classified by type of organization. Indexes: Organization/agency name and keyword.

★6540★ *Peterson's Job Opportunities in Engineering and Technology 1996*

Peterson's
PO Box 2123
Princeton, NJ 08543-2123
Ph: (609)243-9111   Fax: (609)243-9150
Fr: 800-338-3282

Compiled by the Peterson's staff. Annual. $19.95 paperback. 432 pages. Profiles 2,000 high-tech companies looking primarily for technical personnel in such fields as biotechnology, telecommunications, software, computers and peripherals, defense, and aerospace. Contains job-search strategies and career options to help match education and expertise to the job market. Indexed geographically, by industry, and by hiring needs.

★6541★ *Scientific and Technical Organizations and Agencies Directory*

Gale Research
835 Penobscot Bldg.
Detroit, MI 48226-4094
Ph: (313)961-2242   Fax: (313)961-6083
Fr: 800-877-GALE

Irregular; latest edition December 1993. $195.00. Covers over 25,600 national and international organizations and agencies concerned with the physical and applied sciences, engineering, and technology, including associations, computer information services, consulting firms, educational institutions, foundations, government advisory organizations, federal government agencies, general grant and assistance programs, libraries and information centers, patent sources and services, research and development centers, scholarships, fellowships, and loans, science-technology centers, standards organizations, state academies of science, and state government agencies in the fields of aeronautics and space sciences, chemistry, computer science specialties, electronics, geography, geology, machinery, mathematics, metallurgy, meteorology, mineralogy, nuclear science, petroleum and gas, physics, plastics, transportation, water resources, and other areas. Entries include: Organization name, address, phone, and name of contact; additional descriptive text for most entries. Arrangement: Classified by type of organization. Indexes: Organization name/key word.

★6542★ *Who's Who in Technology*

Gale Research
835 Penobscot Bldg.
Detroit, MI 48226-4094
Ph: (313)961-2242   Fax: (313)961-6083
Fr: 800-877-GALE

Irregular, new edition expected June 1995.

$380.00. Covers 38,000 engineers, scientists, inventors, and researchers. Entries include: Name, title, affiliation, address; personal, education, and career data; publications, patents; technical field of activity; area of expertise. Arrangement: Alphabetical. Indexes: Geographical, employer, technical discipline, expertise.

HANDBOOKS AND MANUALS

★6543★ *The Best Resumes for Scientists and Engineers*

John Wiley and Sons
605 3rd Ave.
New York, NY 10158
Ph: (212)850-6000   Fr: 800-225-5945

Adele Lewis. Second edition, 1993. $37.50; $14.95 (paper). Presents an extensive collection of scientific and engineering resumes, highlighting the important differences between these and resumes written for other occupations.

★6544★ *A Career in Theoretical Physics*

World Scientific Publishing Company, Inc.
1060 Main St.
River Edge, NJ 07661
Ph: (201)487-9655   Fax: (201)487-9656
Fr: 800-227-7562

Philip Anderson. 1994. $99.00; $48.00 (paper).

★6545★ *Careers in Science*

VGM Career Horizons
4255 W. Touhy Ave.
Lincolnwood, IL 60646-1975
Ph: (847)679-5500   Fax: (847)679-2494
Fr: 800-323-4900

Thomas Easton. Third edition, 1996. 192 pages. $17.95; $13.95 (paper). Discusses careers in life science, earth science, physical and space science, social science, engineering, mathematics, and computer science. Offers job hunting advice.

★6546★ *Opportunities in Environmental Careers*

VGM Career Horizons
4255 W. Touhy Ave.
Lincolnwood, IL 60646-1975
Ph: (847)679-5500   Fax: (847)679-2494
Fr: 800-323-4900

Odom Fanning. 1995. $14.95; $11.95 (paper). 160 pages. Describes a broad range of opportunities in fields such as environmental health, recreation, physics, and hygiene, and provides job search advice.

★6547★ *Opportunities in High Tech Careers*

VGM Career Horizons
4255 W. Touhy Ave.
Lincolnwood, IL 60646-1975
Ph: (847)679-5500   Fax: (847)679-2494
Fr: 800-323-4900

Gary D. Golter and Deborah Yanuck. 1995. $14.95; $11.95 (paper). 160 pages. Explores high technology careers. Describes job op-

portunities, how to make a career decision, how to prepare for high technology jobs, job hunting techniques, and future trends.

EMPLOYMENT AGENCIES AND SEARCH FIRMS

★6548★ **ABC Employment Service**
25 S. Bemiston, Ste. 214
Clayton, MO 63105
Ph: (314)725-3140

Employment agency.

★6549★ **Erspamer Associates**
7300 France Ave. S., Ste. 402
Edina, MN 55435
Ph: (612)831-5564   Fax: (612)831-5981

Executive search firm.

★6550★ **Health and Science Center**
209 Hunter St.
Media, PA 19063-5726
Ph: (610)891-0714

Employment agency. Executive search firm.

★6551★ **Industrial Recruiters Associates, Inc.**
630 Oakwood Ave., Ste. 318
West Hartford, CT 06110
Ph: (203)953-3643

Employment agency.

★6552★ **International Staffing Consultants**
500 Newport Center Dr., Ste. 300
Newport Beach, CA 92660-7003
Ph: (714)721-7990

Employment agency. Provides placement on regular or temporary basis. Affiliate office in London.

★6553★ **The Jobs Co.**
8900 E. Sprague Ave.
Spokane, WA 99212-2927
Ph: (509)928-3151   Fax: (509)928-3168

Employment agency. Has division specializing in engineering and scientific openings. Also operates division specializing in sales openings.

★6554★ **The Personnel Institute**
1000 Connecticut Ave. NW, Ste. 1108
Washington, DC 20036
Ph: (202)223-4911

Consulting firm.

OTHER SOURCES

★6555★ American Almanac of Jobs and Salaries 1994-95

Avon Books
1350 Avenue of the Americas, 2nd Fl.
New York, NY 10019
Ph: (212)261-6800   Fr: 800-238-0658

John Wright. Revised edition, 1993. $17.00. 704 pages. This is a comprehensive guide to the wages of hundreds of occupations in a wide variety of industries and organizations.

★6556★ American Physical Society (APS)

1 Physics Ellipse
College Park, MD 20740-3844
Ph: (301)209-3200   Fax: (301)209-0865

Members: Educators, industrial and government research workers, and students of physics and related fields such as mathematics, astronomy, chemistry, and engineering. **Purpose:** Promotes international cooperation. Sponsors studies of the physics aspect of topics of public concern such as reactor safety, energy use, and plutonium recycling. **Activities:** Maintains education and outreach programs. **Website:** http://aps.org

★6557★ American Society for Photogrammetry and Remote Sensing (ASPRS)

5410 Grosvenor Ln., Ste. 210
Bethesda, MD 20814-2160
Ph: (301)493-0290   Fax: (301)493-0208

Members: Firms, individuals, government employees, and academicians engaged in photogrammetry, photointerpretation, remote sensing, and geographic information systems and their application to such fields as archaeology, geographic information systems, military reconnaissance, urban planning, engineering, traffic surveys, meteorological observations, medicine, geology, forestry, agriculture, construction, and topographic mapping. **Activities:** Offers voluntary certification program open to persons associated with one or more functional area of photogrammetry, remote sensing, and GIS. Surveys the profession of private firms in

photogrammetry and remote sensing in the areas of products and services.

★6558★ Association for International Practical Training (AIPT)

10400 Little Patuxent Pky. Ste. 250
Columbia, MD 21044
Ph: (410)997-2200   Fax: (410)992-3924

Purpose: Helps coordinate training around the world in fields such as travel, the culinary arts, and hotel management. **Activities:** Conducts programs in career development and hospitality/tourism exchanges. Operates a student exchange program. Provides reciprocal practical training experience for recent graduates from the U.S., Austria, Germany, Finland, France, Hungary, Ireland, Japan, Malaysia, Netherlands, Switzerland, and the United Kingdom. Arranges training programs in the U.S. and abroad. Serves as U.S. affiliate to IAESTE (International Association for the Exchange of Students for Technical Experience) and operates a Professional Visitors Program to arrange short-term educational and training visits to the U.S. **E-Mail:** aipt@aipt.org

★6559★ Astronomical League (AL)

2112 Kingfisher Ln. E
Rolling Meadows, IL 60008
Ph: (847)398-0562

Members: Members of 203 astronomical societies and other interested individuals. **Purpose:** Promotes the science of astronomy; encourages and coordinates activities of amateur astronomical societies; fosters observational and computational work and craftsmanship in various fields of astronomy; correlates amateur activities with professional research. **Activities:** Operates children's services; sponsors educational programs.

★6560★ New Careers Directory: Internships and Professional Opportunities in Technology and Social Change

Student Pugwash USA
815 15th St. NW, Ste. 814
Washington, DC 20005
Ph: (202)393-6555   Fax: (202)393-6550
Fr: 800-WOW-A-PUG

Irregular; latest edition spring 1993. $13.00 for students; $21.00 for institutions, plus

$3.00 shipping. Covers about 300 research institutes, think tanks, laboratories, government agencies, professional, science, and other non-profit organizations offering public policy, science, and technology internships and jobs. Entries include: Sponsoring organization name, description of organization, programs offered, work environment and application procedures, compensation offered. Arrangement: Alphabetical and classified by subject. Indexes: Geographical, subject.

★6561★ Radiation Research Society (RRS)

2021 Spring Rd., Ste. 600
Oak Brook, IL 60521
Ph: (708)571-2881   Fax: (708)571-7837

Members: Professional society of biologists, physicists, chemists, and physicians contributing to knowledge of radiation and its effects. **Purpose:** Promotes original research in the natural sciences relating to radiation; facilitates integration of different disciplines in the study of radiation effects.

★6562★ Resumes for Scientific and Technical Careers

VGM Career Horizons
NTC Publishing Group
4255 W. Touhy Ave.
Lincolnwood, IL 60646-1975
Ph: (847)679-5500   Fax: (847)679-2494
Fr: 800-323-4900

1994. $9.95. 160 pages. Provides resume advice for individuals interested in working in scientific and technical careers. Includes sample resumes and cover letters.

★6563★ Salaries of Scientists, Engineers, and Technicians: A Summary of Salary Surveys

Commission on Professionals in Science and Technology (CPST)
1500 Massachusetts Ave. NW, Ste. 831
Washington, DC 20005
Ph: (202)223-6995

1993.

Plumbers

★6564★ Builder

Hanley-Wood, Inc.
1 Thomas Cir., Ste. 600
Washington, DC 20005
Ph: (202)452-0800   Fax: (202)785-1974

Monthly. $29.95/year for individuals. Magazine covering housing, commercial, and industrial building.

★6565★ Construction Digest

Construction Magazine Group, Inc.
PO Box 6132
Indianapolis, IN 46206-6132
Ph: (317)329-3100   Fax: (317)329-3110
Fr: 800-860-3105

Semimonthly. $3.00 for single issue. Magazine for the public works and construction engineering industries.

★6566★ CONSTRUCTOR

Associated General Contractors Information
1957 E St. NW
Washington, DC 20006-5199
Ph: (202)393-2040   Fax: (202)628-7369

Monthly. $15.00/year for members; $4.00 for single issue.

★6567★ Contractor Magazine

Cahners Publishing Co.
1350 E. Touhy Ave.
Des Plaines, IL 60018
Ph: (708)635-8800   Fax: (708)390-2770

Monthly. Free to qualified subscribers; $70.00/year for individuals. Industry news and management how-to magazine for air conditioning, heating, plumbing and other mechanical specialties contracting firms.

★6568★ Plumbing Engineer

TMB Publishing, Inc.
1850 Techny Ct.
Northbrook, IL 60062
Ph: (708)564-1127

Ten times/year. Trade journal for consulting engineering, mechanical engineering, architecture, and contracting professionals.

★6569★ Plumbing Heating Piping

Cahners Publishing
1350 W. Touhy Ave.
Des Plaines, IL 60018
Ph: (312)222-2000   Fax: (312)222-2026

Monthly. Magazine on the plumbing, piping, and hydronics industries.

★6570★ Professional Builder

Cahners Publishing Co.
1350 E. Touhy Ave.
PO Box 5080
Des Plaines, IL 60018-5080
Ph: (708)635-8800   Fax: (708)635-9950

Monthly. $10.00 for single issue; $139.95/year by mail.

★6571★ Reeves Journal: Plumbing Heating Cooling

Business News Publishing Co.
23187 La Cadena Dr., Ste. 101
PO Box 30700
Laguna Hills, CA 92653
Ph: (714)830-0881   Fax: (714)859-7845

Monthly. Free to qualified subscribers; $24.00/year for individuals. Regional plumbing, heating, and cooling magazine.

★6572★ Southern Plumbing, Heating, Cooling Magazine

Southern Trade Publications, Inc.
Box 18343
Greensboro, NC 27419
Ph: (919)454-3516

Bimonthly. Trade magazine covering plumbing, heating, and air conditioning.

★6573★ Summer Jobs: Opportunities in the Federal Government

Office of Personnel Management
1900 E St. NW
Washington, DC 20415
Ph: (202)606-0950

Formerly annual; latest edition January 1993; suspended indefinitely. Free. Covers GS-1 through GS-4 clerical jobs and other jobs at GS-5 and above which are expected to be available in federal agencies and departments throughout the United States during the season. Most jobs are in Metropolitan Washington, D.C. Latest application date is generally April 15; many are earlier. Includes general information on applying for jobs in trades and labor occupations and summer employment for needy youth programs. Entries include: Agency name, filing deadline, titles of jobs available, brief information on qualifications needed, location, etc. Complete agency names and addresses are given in separate list. Publication is available from Federal Employment Information Center offices and agency personnel offices. Arrangement: By job level, then alphabetical by agency name.

★6574★ Tradeswomen

Tradeswomen, Inc.
PO Box 2622
Berkeley, CA 94702
Ph: (510)649-6260

Bimonthly. $35.00/year. Subtitled: "A Quarterly Magazine for Women in Blue Collar Work". Reports activities of the organization and other events in the California Bay Area and of national interest to women working or wishing to work in nontraditional and blue collar jobs. Recurring features include announcements of apprenticeship opportunities and job openings, information on unions and government agencies, and U.S. Department of Labor statistics.

PLACEMENT AND JOB REFERRAL SERVICES

★6575★ Associated Builders and Contractors (ABC)
1300 N. 17th St.
Rosslyn, VA 22209
Ph: (703)812-2000   Fax: (703)812-8200
Members: Construction contractors, subcontractors, suppliers, and associates. **Purpose:** Aim is to foster and perpetuate the principles of rewarding construction workers and management on the basis of merit. **Activities:** Maintains placement service. Sponsors management education programs and craft training; also sponsors apprenticeship and skill training programs. Disseminates technological and labor relations information. Compiles statistics.

★6576★ National Association of Home Builders of the U.S. (NAHB)
1201 15th St. NW
Washington, DC 20005
Ph: (202)822-0200   Fax: (202)822-0559
Members: Single and multifamily home builders, commercial builders, and others associated with the building industry. **Purpose:** Lobbies on behalf of the housing industry and conducts public affairs activities to increase public understanding of housing and the economy. Collects and disseminates data on current developments in home building and home builders' plans through its Economics Department and nationwide Metropolitan Housing Forecast. **Activities:** Maintains NAHB Research Center, which functions as the research arm of the home building industry. Sponsors seminars and workshops on construction, mortgage credit, labor relations, cost reduction, land use, remodeling, and business management. Compiles statistics; offers charitable program, spokesman training, and placement service; maintains speakers' bureau, and hall of fame.

EMPLOYER DIRECTORIES AND NETWORKING LISTS

★6577★ ABC Today—Associated Builders and Contractors Membership Directory Issue
Associated Builders and Contractors
1300 N. 17th St.
Rosslyn, VA 22209
Ph: (703)812-2000   Fax: (703)812-8200
Annual, November. $150.00, plus $7.00 shipping. Publication includes: List of approximately 17,000 member construction contractors and suppliers. Entries include: Company name, address, phone, name of principal executive, code to volume of business, business specialty. Arrangement: Classified by chapter, then by work specialty.

★6578★ Constructor—Directory of Membership and Services Issue
AGC Information, Inc.
Associated General Contractors of America
1957 E St. NW
Washington, DC 20006
Ph: (202)393-2040   Fax: (202)347-4004
Annual, July. $135.00. Publication includes: List of more than 8,500 member firms and 9,000 national associate member firms engaged in building, highway, heavy, industrial, municipal utilities, and railroad construction, listing of state and local chapter officers. Arrangement: Geographical. Indexes: Company name.

★6579★ ENR—Top 400 Construction Contractors Issue
McGraw-Hill, Inc.
1221 Ave. of the Americas
New York, NY 10020
Ph: (212)512-4635   Fax: (212)512-2820
Annual, May issue of Engineering News Record. $10.00, Reprint, payment with order. Publication includes: List of 400 United States contractors receiving largest dollar volumes of contracts in preceding calendar year. Separate lists of 50 largest design/construct management firms; 50 largest program and construction managers; 25 building contractors; 25 heavy contractors. Entries include: Company name, headquarters location, total value of contracts received in preceding year, value of foreign contracts, countries in which operated, construction specialities. Arrangement: By total value of contracts received.

★6580★ Mechanical Contractors Association of America—Membership Directory/Buyers Guide & Publications Catalog
Naylor Publications
Shawan Pl.
5 Shawan Rd.
Hunt Valley, MD 21030
Ph: (410)785-2445   Fax: (410)785-2459
Fr: 800-879-1107
Annual, March. Available only to members and advertisers. Covers 1,400 contractors who install piping and related equipment for heating, air conditioning, plumbing, and cooling systems in commercial and institutional buildings, and process piping in industrial facilities. Also includes list of state and local associations. Entries include: Company name, address, phone, and names of principal executives. Arrangement: Geographical. Indexes: Alphabetical.

★6581★ Mechanical Contractors Directory
American Business Directories, Inc.
American Business Information, Inc.
5711 S. 86th Cir.
Omaha, NE 68127
Ph: (402)593-4600   Fax: (402)331-1505
Annual. $420.00, U.S. edition. Number of listings: 4,659 (U.S. edition); 1,094 (Canadian edition). Entries include: Name, address, phone (including area code), size of advertisement, year first in Yellow Pages, name of owner or manager, number of employees.

Compiled from telephone company Yellow Pages, nationwide. Arrangement: Geographical.

★6582★ Michigan Plumbing and Mechanical Contractors Association—Membership Directory
Michigan Plumbing and Mechanical Contractors Association (MPMCA)
400 N. Walnut St.
Lansing, MI 48933
Ph: (517)484-5500   Fax: (517)484-5225
Fr: 800-292-1044
Annual. Available to subscribers only. Covers member firms, industry and auxiliary associations, legislative and regulatory agencies in the plumbing and heating industry of Michigan. Entries include: Organization name, address, phone, names and titles of key personnel. Arrangement: Separate sections for members, industry associations, legislative and regulatory, and auxiliaries; members are geographical. Indexes: Company name (members), president name (members).

★6583★ Minnesota P-H-C Contractor—Membership Directory Issue
Minnesota Association of Plumbing-Heating-Cooling Contractors
8085 Wayzata Blvd., Ste. 109
Minneapolis, MN 55426
Ph: (612)546-4448   Fr: 800-328-4827
Annual, January. Available to members only. Publication includes: List of 450 member firms and associates. Entries include: Name of company, address, phone, fax, code indicating type of work, local association affiliation (chapter memberships and other), name and title of owner or officer, home address and phone. Arrangement: Alphabetical. Indexes: Alphabetical by service/line of business.

★6584★ Plumbing Contractors Directory
American Business Directories, Inc.
American Business Information, Inc.
5711 S. 86th Cir.
Omaha, NE 68127
Ph: (402)593-4600   Fax: (402)331-1505
Annual. $1,850.00, U.S. edition; $310.00, (Canadian edition); payment with order. Number of listings: 54,637 (U.S. edition); 6,816 (Canadian edition). Entries includes: name, address, phone (including area code), size of advertisement, year first in Yellow Pages, name of owner or manager, number of employees. Regional editions available. Compiled from telephone company Yellow Pages, nationwide. Arrangement: Geographical.

★6585★ Plumbing-Drain & Sewer Directory
American Business Directories, Inc.
American Business Information, Inc.
5711 S. 86th Cir.
Omaha, NE 68127
Ph: (402)593-4600   Fax: (402)331-1505
Latest edition September 1986. $770.00, payment with order. Entries include: Name, address, phone (including area code), size of advertisement, year first in Yellow Pages, name of owner or manager, number of employees. Compiled from telephone com-

pany Yellow Pages, nationwide. Arrangement: Geographical.

★6586★ Who's Who in the Plumbing-Heating-Cooling Contracting Business

National Association of Plumbing-Heating-Cooling Contractors (NAPHCC)
180 S. Washington St.
Falls Church, VA 22046
Ph: (703)237-8100   Fax: (703)237-7442
Fr: 800-533-7694

Annual. $75.00. Covers About 6,000 professional plumbing/heating/cooling contractors and member firms. Entries include: Name, address, phone, contact, line of business. Arrangement: Geographical. Indexes: Individual member.

HANDBOOKS AND MANUALS

★6587★ Exploring Careers in the Construction Industry

Rosen Publishing Group
29 E. 21st St.
New York, NY 10010
Ph: (212)777-3017   Fax: (212)777-0277
Fr: 800-237-9932

Elizabeth Stewart Lytle. 1992. $14.95.

★6588★ Journeyman Plumber's Licensing Exam Guide

The McGraw-Hill Companies
1221 Avenue of the Americas
New York, NY 10020
Ph: (212)521-2000   Fr: 800-722-4726

R. Dodge Woodson. 1995. $34.95; $24.95 (paper).

★6589★ Opportunities in Building Construction Trades

VGM Career Horizons
4255 W. Touhy Ave.
Lincolnwood, IL 60646-1975
Ph: (847)679-5500   Fax: (847)679-2494
Fr: 800-323-4900

Michael Sumichrast. 1993. $14.95; $11.95 (paper). From custom builder to rehabber, the many kinds of companies that employ craftspeople and contractors are explored. Includes job descriptions, requirements, and salaries for dozens of specialties within the construction industry. Contains a complete list of Bureau of Apprenticeship and Training state and area offices. Illustrated.

★6590★ Opportunities in Plumbing and Pipefitting Careers

VGM Career Horizons
4255 W. Touhy Ave.
Lincolnwood, IL 60646-1975
Ph: (847)679-5500   Fax: (847)679-2494
Fr: 800-323-4900

Patrick J. Galvin. 1995. $14.95; $11.95 (paper). 160 pages. Provides information on getting into the trade, apprenticeship programs, and how to build a career in a variety of settings. Illustrated.

★6591★ Plumbing Contractor: Start & Run a Money Making Business

TAB Books
PO Box 40
Blue Ridge Summit, PA 17294-0850
Ph: (717)794-2191   Fax: (717)794-2080
Fr: 800-233-1128

R. Dodge Woodson. 1993. $17.95 (paper).

OTHER SOURCES

★6592★ American Society of Plumbing Engineers (ASPE)

3617 Thousand Oaks Blvd., No. 210
Westlake Village, CA 91362-3649
Ph: (805)495-7120   Fax: (805)495-4861

Members: Consulting engineers involved in the design and specification of plumbing systems; manufacturers, governmental officials, contractors, and publishers related to the industry may become members on a limited basis. Purpose: Seeks to resolve professional problems in plumbing engineering; advocates greater cooperation among members and plumbing officials, contractors, laborers, and the public. Code committees examine regulatory codes pertaining to the industry and submit proposed revisions to code writing authorities to simplify, standardize, and modernize all codes. Activities: Sponsors American Society of Plumbing Engineers Research Foundation; operates certification program.

★6593★ American Society of Sanitary Engineering (ASSE)

PO Box 40362
Bay Village, OH 44140
Ph: (216)835-3040   Fax: (216)835-3488

Members: Plumbing officials, sanitary engineers, plumbers, plumbing contractors, building officials, architects, engineers, designing engineers, physicians, and others interested in health. Purpose: Conducts research on plumbing and sanitation and develops performance standards for components of the plumbing system. Sponsors disease research program and other studies of waterborne epidemics.

★6594★ Associated General Contractors of America (AGC)

1957 E St. NW
Washington, DC 20006
Ph: (202)393-2040   Fax: (202)347-4004

Members: General construction contractors; subcontractors; industry suppliers; service firms. Purpose: Provides market services through its divisions. Conducts special conferences and seminars designed specifically for construction firms. Compiles statistics on job accidents reported by member firms. Maintains 65 committees, including joint cooperative committees with other associations and liaison committees with federal agencies.

★6595★ Associated Specialty Contractors (ASC)

3 Bethesda Metro Ctr., Ste. 1100
Bethesda, MD 20814
Ph: (301)657-3110   Fax: (301)215-4500

Members: Subcontractor associations with a total of 25,000 members representing electrical, heating, piping, mechanical, air conditioning, sheet metal, plumbing, ventilating, masonry, painting and decorating, and roofing and insulation contractors. Purpose: Promotes liaison with general contractors, architects, and engineers on inter-industry matters, codes, bidding, and contracting procedures. Coordinates governmental affairs, research, and educational matters.

★6596★ Career Connections Video Series

Cambridge Career Products
PO Box 2153
Dept. CC15
Charleston, WV 25328-2153
Ph: (304)744-9323   Fax: (304)744-9351
Fr: 800-468-4227

Series of six videos. 1993. $219.95/set. $39.95/each. 15-20 minutes. Each video contains interviews with workers and on-the-job footage. Titles include Graphic Design, Welding, Electrician, Plumber, Pipefitter, and HVAC.

★6597★ COIN Career Guidance System

COIN Educational Products
3361 Executive Pky., Ste. 302
Toledo, OH 43606
Ph: (419)536-5353   Fr: 800-274-8515

CD-ROM product; also available on diskette. Provides career information through seven cross-referenced files covering postsecondary schools, college majors, vocational programs, military service, apprenticeship programs, financial aid, and scholarships. Apprenticeship file describes national apprenticeship training programs, including information on how to apply, contact agencies, and program content. Military file describes more than 200 military occupations and training opportunities related to civilian employment.

★6598★ Mechanical Contractors Association of America (MCAA)

1385 Piccard Dr.
Rockville, MD 20850-4329
Ph: (301)869-5800   Fax: (301)990-9690

Members: Contractors who furnish, install, and service piping systems and related equipment for heating, cooling, refrigeration, ventilating, and air conditioning systems. Purpose: Works to standardize materials and methods used in the industry. Conducts business overhead, labor wage, and statistical surveys. Maintains dialogue with key officials in building trade unions. Promotes apprenticeship training programs. Conducts seminars on contracts, labor estimating, job cost control, project management, marketing, collective bargaining, contractor insurance, and other management topics. Promotes methods to conserve energy in new and existing buildings. Sponsors Industrial Relations Council for the Plumbing and Pipe Fitting Industry.

★6599★ National Association of Plumbing-Heating-Cooling Contractors (NAPHCC)

180 S. Washington St.
PO Box 6808
Falls Church, VA 22040
Ph: (703)237-8100   Fax: (703)237-7442
Fr: 800-533-7694

Members: Federation of state and local associations of plumbing, heating, and cooling contractors. **Purpose:** Seeks to advance sanitation, encourage sanitary laws, and generally improve the plumbing, heating, ventilating, and air conditioning industries. **Activities:** Conducts apprenticeship training programs, workshops, and seminars; cooperates with Plumbing-Heating-Cooling Information Bureau. Maintains speakers' bureau and political action committee. Conducts educational and research programs.

★6600★ National Association of Women in Construction (NAWIC)

327 S. Adams St.
Fort Worth, TX 76104
Ph: (817)877-5551   Fax: (817)877-0324
Fr: 800-552-3506

Purpose: NAWIC is an international association of women employed in the construction industry which promotes that industry and supports the advancement of women within it.

★6601★ Tradeswomen, Inc.

PO Box 40664 B
San Francisco, CA 94140
Ph: (415)821-7334   Fax: (415)861-8969

Members: Women who work in nontraditional, blue-collar occupations including construction, transportation, and industrial work; women who seek to enter these fields or who support the right of others to do so. **Purpose:** Serves as a network for women in the trades. Conducts social gatherings and local and regional forums on topics such as: health and safety on the job; racism and sexism in the trades; sexual harassment; working within unions. Makes available children's services; maintains speakers' bureau. Compiles statistics.

★6602★ WIT

Northern New England Tradeswomen
26 Railroad St.
St. Johnsbury, VT 05819
Ph: (802)748-3308   Fax: (802)748-1768

Quarterly. Included in membership; $10.00/year for nonmembers. Provides a network of support, information, and skill sharing for women in trade professions.

Podiatrists

EMPLOYER DIRECTORIES AND NETWORKING LISTS

★6612★ AHA Guide to the Health Care Field

Health Statistics Group
American Hospital Association (AHA)
1 N. Franklin
Chicago, IL 60606
Ph: (312)422-3501   Fax: (312)280-6015

Annual, July. $195.00, payment with order. Covers hospitals, multi-health care systems, freestanding ambulatory surgery centers, psychiatric facilities, long-term care facilities, substance abuse programs, hospices, Health Maintenance Organizations (HMOs), and other health-related organizations. Entries include: For hospitals: facility name, address, phone, administrator's name, number of beds, facilities and services, number of employees, expenses, other statistics. For other organizations: name, address, phone, name and title of contact. Arrangement: Geographical. Indexes: Hospital name.

★6613★ American Group Practice Association—Directory

American Group Practice Association
1422 Duke St.
Alexandria, VA 22314
Ph: (703)838-0033   Fax: (703)548-1890

Annual, February. $150.00. Covers about 250 private group medical practices and their professional staffs, totalling about 25,000 physicians and administrators. Entries include: Group member name, address, phone, names of administrator and other executives, names of physician listed by medical specialties. Arrangement: Alphabetical. Indexes: Group location, personal name.

★6614★ Directory of Hospital Personnel

Medical Economics
5 Paragon Dr.
Montvale, NJ 07645-1725
Ph: (201)358-7500   Fax: (201)573-4956
Fr: 800-222-3045

Annual, September. $325.00, plus 7.50 shipping. Covers 200,000 executives at 7,100 U.S. hospitals. Entries include: Name of hospital, address, phone, number of beds, type and JCAHO status of hospital, names and titles of key department heads and staff, medical and nursing school affiliations; number of residents, interns, and nursing students. Arrangement: Geographical. Indexes: Hospital name, personnel, hospital size.

★6615★ HMO/PPO Directory

Medical Economics Data
5 Paragon Dr.
Montvale, NJ 07645-1742
Ph: (201)358-7500   Fax: (201)573-4956
Fr: 800-222-3045

Annual, November. $225.00, plus $7.50 shipping. Covers over 700 health maintenance organizations (HMOs) and more than 900 preferred provider organizations (PPOs). Entries include: Name of organization, address, phone, number of members, names of officers, employer references, geographical area served, parent company, average fees and copayments, financial data, and cost control procedures. Arrangement: Geographical. Indexes: Organization name, personnel name, HMOs and PPOs by state, and number of members enrolled.

★6616★ Hospital Blue Book

Billian Publishing Co.
2100 Powers Ferry Rd., Ste. 300
Atlanta, GA 30339
Ph: (404)955-5656   Fax: (404)952-0669

Annual, spring. $154.50, national edition, plus $20.00 shipping. Covers more than 7,100 hospitals; some listings also appear in a separate southern edition of this publication. Entries include: Name of hospital, accreditation, mailing address, phone, fax, number of beds, type of facility (nonprofit, general, state, etc.); list of administrative personnel and chiefs of medical services, with specific titles. Arrangement: Geographical.

★6617★ Hospital Market Atlas

SMG Marketing Group, Inc.
1342 N. LaSalle Dr.
Chicago, IL 60610
Ph: (312)642-3026   Fax: (312)642-9729
Fr: 800-678-3026

Biennial, odd years. $495.00, payment with order. Covers over 7,000 hospitals, hospital systems and 480 group purchasing organizations. Entries include: Hospital or organization name, address, phone, county code, management, type of hospital service, number of beds, admissions, surgical operations, and emergency room visits. Arrangement: Geographical.

★6618★ Hospitals Directory

American Business Directories, Inc.
American Business Information, Inc.
5711 S. 86th Cir.
Omaha, NE 68127
Ph: (402)593-4600   Fax: (402)331-1505

Annual. $870.00, U.S. edition. Entries include: Name, address, phone (including area code), size of advertisement, year first in Yellow Pages, name of owner or manager, number of employees. Compiled from telephone company Yellow Pages, nationwide. Arrangement: Geographical.

★6619★ Medical and Health Information Directory

Gale Research
835 Penobscot Bldg.
Detroit, MI 48226-4094
Ph: (313)961-2242   Fax: (313)961-6083
Fr: 800-877-GALE

Approximately biennial; latest edition 1994. $195.00, per volume; $485.00, for the three-volume set. Covers in Volume 1, almost 18,600 medical and health oriented associations, organizations, institutions, and government agencies, including health maintenance organizations (HMOs), preferred provider organizations (PPOs), insurance companies, pharmaceutical companies, research centers, and medical and allied health schools. In Volume 2, nearly 11,800 medical book publishers; medical periodicals, directories, audiovisual producers and services, medical libraries and information centers, and electronic resources. In Volume 3, nearly 26,000 clinics, treatment centers, care programs, and counseling/diagnostic services for 30 subject areas. Entries include: Institution, service, or firm name, address, phone; many include names of key personnel and, when pertinent, descriptive annotation. Arrangement: Classified by organization activity, service, etc. Indexes: Each volume has a complete alphabetical name and keyword index.

★6620★ Podiatrists Directory

American Business Directories, Inc.
American Business Information, Inc.
5711 S. 86th Cir.
Omaha, NE 68127
Ph: (402)593-4600   Fax: (402)331-1505

Annual. $1,300.00, U.S. edition. Entries include: Name, address, phone (including area code), size of advertisement, year first in Yellow Pages, name of owner or manager, number of employees. Compiled from telephone company Yellow Pages, nationwide. Arrangement: Geographical.

HANDBOOKS AND MANUALS

★6621★ Careers in Health and Fitness

Rosen Publishing Group, Inc.
29 E. 21st St.
New York, NY 10010
Ph: (212)777-3017   Fax: (212)777-0277
Fr: 800-237-9932

Jackie Heron. Revised edition, 1990. $14.95. 160 pages. Contains occupational profiles for this field, including information on job duties, skills, advantages, basic equipment used, employment possibilities, certification, and salary.

★6622★ Careers in Medicine: Traditional and Alternative Opportunities

Garrett Park Press
PO Box 190 C
Garrett Park, MD 20896-0190
Ph: (301)946-2553

Donald T. Rucker and Martin D. Keller. 1990. $15.95. 346 pages. Cites training requirements, illustrative work activities, and a summary of the advantages and disadvantages in a variety of specialized areas. Includes hundreds of career alternatives and discusses ways to break into these fields for persons trained in medicine. Features contributions from over 40 professionals in all phases of medicine and provides 200 sources of information on specialties and subspecialties.

★6623★ 100 Best Careers for the Year 2000

Prentice Hall General Reference
15 Columbus Cir.
New York, NY 10023
Ph: (212)373-8500   Fr: 800-223-2348

Shelly Field. 1992. $15.00 (paper). Covers 100 of the fastest growing jobs. The publication is divided into 11 general employment sections. Specific careers are covered within each section. Provides job description, responsibilities, employment opportunities, earnings, education and training, advancement opportunities, and experience and qualifications for each occupation.

★6624★ Opportunities in Health and Medical Careers

VGM Career Horizons
4255 W. Touhy Ave.
Lincolnwood, IL 60646-1975
Ph: (847)679-5500   Fax: (847)679-2494
Fr: 800-323-4900

Donald Snook, Jr. and Leo D'Orazio. 1993. $14.95; $11.95 (paper). Covers the full range of medical and health occupations. Illustrated.

★6625★ Opportunities in Paramedical Careers

VGM Career Horizons
4255 W. Touhy Ave.
Lincolnwood, IL 60646-1975
Ph: (847)679-5500   Fax: (847)679-2494
Fr: 800-323-4900

Alex Kacen. 1994. $14.95; 11.95 (paper). 160 pages. Discusses a variety of opportunities in this field and how to pursue them. Illustrated.

★6626★ Opportunities in Sports Medicine Careers

VGM Career Horizons
4255 W. Touhy Ave.
Lincolnwood, IL 60646-1975
Ph: (847)679-5500   Fax: (847)679-2494
Fr: 800-323-4900

William Ray Heitzmann. 1995. $14.95; $11.95 (paper). 160 pages. Discusses a variety of opportunities in this field and how to pursue them. Contains bibliography and illustrations.

★6627★ Resumes for Health and Medical Careers

4255 W. Touhy Ave.
Lincolnwood, IL 60646-1975
Ph: (708)679-5500   Fax: (708)679-6375
Fr: 800-323-4900

Compiled by VGM Career Horizons Staff 1995. $9.95 (paper).

EMPLOYMENT AGENCIES AND SEARCH FIRMS

★6628★ Consult One, Inc.

10291 N. Meridan St., Ste. 325
Indianapolis, IN 46290-1078
Ph: (317)573-2025   Fax: (317)573-2035

Executive search firm.

★6629★ Executive Medical Recruiters

2350 W. 7th St.
St. Paul, MN 55116
Ph: (612)699-3020

Employment agency.

★6630★ Harper Associates

29870 Middlebelt
Farmington Hills, MI 48334
Ph: (810)932-1170

Employment agency.

★6631★ Phyllis Hawkins and Associates

3550 N. Central Ave., Ste. 1400
Phoenix, AZ 85012
Ph: (602)263-0248   Fax: (602)263-1016

Executive search firm.

★6632★ Physicians Search, Inc.

1224 E. KAtella Ave., Ste. 202
Orange, CA 92667-5045
Ph: (714)288-8350

Executive search firm. Affiliate office in Spokane, WA.

★6633★ Professional Placement Associates, Inc.

11 Rye Ridge Plaza
Rye Brook, NY 10573
Ph: (914)251-1000   Fax: (914)939-1959

Employment agency.

★6634★ Putzek Medical Search

4150 Falcon Dr.
Austell, GA 30001-3067
Ph: (404)941-3339

Employment agency. Executive search consultant.

★6635★ Robert William James and Associates

621 SW Morrison, Ste. 500
Portland, OR 97205
Ph: (503)224-5505

Employment agency.

★6636★ Shiloh Careers International, Inc.

7105 Peach Ct., Ste. 102
PO Box 831
Brentwood, TN 37024-0831
Ph: (615)373-3090

Employment agency.

★6637★ Team Placement Service, Inc.

5113 Leesburg Pike
Falls Church, VA 22041-3242
Ph: (703)820-8618   Fax: (703)820-3368

Employment agency.

★6638★ Weatherby Healthcare

25 Van Zant St.
Norwalk, CT 06855
Ph: (203)866-1144   Fax: (203)853-3154

Executive search firm. Branch office in Fairfax, VA.

OTHER SOURCES

★6639★ American Almanac of Jobs and Salaries 1994-95

Avon Books
1350 Avenue of the Americas, 2nd Fl.
New York, NY 10019
Ph: (212)261-6800   Fr: 800-238-0658

John Wright. Revised edition, 1993. $17.00. 704 pages. This is a comprehensive guide to the wages of hundreds of occupations in a wide variety of industries and organizations.

★6640★ American Association of Hospital Podiatrists (AAHP)

420 74th St.
Brooklyn, NY 11209
Ph: (718)836-1017

Members: A general specialty group of the American Podiatric Medical Association. Podiatrists (trained and certified persons dealing in the care and diseases of the foot) who are affiliated with hospitals. **Purpose:** Seeks to: elevate the standards of podiatry practices in hospitals and health institutions; standardize hospital podiatry procedures, charting, recording forms, and methods; promote understanding among personnel in podiatry, medicine, and allied health professions; aid podiatrists in attaining institutional affiliations; assist in the educational and teaching programs of health institutions and hospitals; foster the development of podiatric internships and residencies in hospitals and institutions.

★6641★ American Board of Podiatric Orthopedics and Primary Medicine (ABPOPPM)

401 N. Michigan Ave.
Chicago, IL 60611-4267
Ph: (312)321-5139   Fax: (312)644-1815

Members: Podiatrists who have taken a competency exam prepared by the board. **Purpose:** Offers certifying examinations in foot orthopedics primary podiatric medicine for podiatrists; aims at improving public health by encouraging and elevating standards for practicing podiatrics.

★6642★ American Board of Podiatric Surgery (ABPS)

1601 Dolores St.
San Francisco, CA 94110-4906
Ph: (415)826-3200   Fax: (415)826-4640

Members: Podiatrists certified as diplomates. **Purpose:** Objectives are: to protect and improve public health by advancing the science of foot surgery and by encouraging the study and evaluation of standards of foot surgery; to act upon application for certification of legally licensed podiatrists to ascertain their competency in foot surgery; to grant certificates to candidates who have met all qualifications.

★6643★ American Hospital Association (AHA)

1 N. Franklin, Ste. 27
Chicago, IL 60606
Ph: (312)422-3000   Fax: (312)422-4796

Members: Individuals and health care institutions including hospitals, health care systems, and pre- and postacute health care delivery organizations. **Purpose:** Is dedicated to promoting the welfare of the public through its leadership and assistance to its members in the provision of better health services for all people. Conducts educational programs furthering the in-service education of hospital personnel; collects and analyzes data; furnishes multimedia educational materials; maintains 44,000 volume health care administration library, and biographical archive.

★6644★ American Podiatric Medical Association (APMA)

9312 Old Georgetown Rd.
Bethesda, MD 20814
Ph: (301)571-9200   Fax: (301)530-2752

Members: Professional society of podiatrists.

★6645★ Career Encounters: Podiatric Medicine

Cambridge Career Products
PO Box 2153
Dept. CC15
Charleston, WV 25328-2153
Ph: (304)744-9323   Fax: (304)744-9351
Fr: 800-468-4227

Video. $99.95. 25 minutes. Professionals shown in a variety of settings discuss different aspects of their careers.

★6646★ Journal of the American Medical Association—Physician Service Opportunities Overseas Section

American Medical Association
515 N. State St.
Chicago, IL 60610-4377
Ph: (312)464-2446

Triennial, latest edition August 1993. Lists more than 170 organizations that provide assignments overseas for physicians from the United States. Entries include: Organization name, address, phone, contact person, countries served, medical specialties sought, length of assignment, stipend or salary (if provided), whether facilities or equipment, housing, and transportation are provided, and additional requirements. Arrangement: Alphabetical.

Political and Legislative Aides

PLACEMENT AND JOB REFERRAL SERVICES

★6647★ Administrative Assistants Association of the United States House of Representatives

Longworth House Office Bldg., Rm. 1526
Washington, DC 20515
Ph: (202)225-3831

Members: Chiefs of staff of members of the House of Representatives; government officials. **Purpose:** Sponsors social and professional programs to upgrade and enhance the profession; facilitates the exchange of ideas and information. **Activities:** Operates charitable program, speakers' bureau, and placement service. Maintains biographical archives. Sponsors semiannual seminar.

★6648★ American Political Science Association (APSA)

1527 New Hampshire Ave. NW
Washington, DC 20036
Ph: (202)483-2512   Fax: (202)483-2657

Members: College and university teachers of political science, public officials, research workers, and businessmen. **Purpose:** Encourages the impartial study and promotes the development of the art and science of government. Develops research projects of public interest and educational programs for political scientists and journalists; seeks to improve the knowledge of and increase citizen participation in political and governmental affairs. **Activities:** Serves as clearinghouse for teaching and research positions in colleges, universities, and research bureaus in the U.S. and abroad and for positions open to political scientists in government and private business. Offers placement service.

EMPLOYER DIRECTORIES AND NETWORKING LISTS

★6649★ Congressional Directory

Capitol Advantage
PO Box 1223
Order Department
McLean, VA 22101
Ph: (703)734-3266   Fax: (703)847-0573
Fr: 800-659-8708

Annual. $8.95, spiral or perfect bound. Covers 100 current senators and 395 House of Representative members. Entries include: Name, district office address, phone, fax; names and titles of key staff; committee and subcommittee assignments; photo. Arrangement: Available in separate alphabetical or geographical editions. Indexes: Name.

★6650★ Congressional Yellow Book

Leadership Directories, Inc.
104 5th Ave., 2nd Fl.
New York, NY 10011
Ph: (212)627-4140   Fax: (212)645-0931

Quarterly. $235.00, per year. Covers about 540 members of Congress and their principal aides, Congressional committees, leadership, and congressional support arms. Entries include: For members of Congress, name, Washington office address, party affiliation, state or district represented, year began service, reelection year (House members only); names, titles, and legislative responsibilities of principal aides, member's committee assignments and other responsibilities; photograph, biographical data, fax, and map of district; state and district office addresses and phone; ZIP codes by congressional district. For committees, committee name, office address, phone, members' names and parties, description of committee jurisdiction, fax, key staff for full and subcommittees. Subscription includes roster of new members and committee and leadership changes, published January of election years. Arrangement: Alphabetical by member of Congress or committee name.

★6651★ 50 State Legislative Directory

State Net
2101 K St.
Sacramento, CA 95816
Ph: (916)444-2840   Fax: (916)446-5369

Annual, January. $95.00. Covers roster of 7,424 state legislators and 535 members of Congress. Entries include: Name, address, phone, party affiliation, committee assignments, district numbers. Arrangement: Geographical.

★6652★ Washington Information Directory

Congressional Quarterly Inc.
1414 22nd St. NW
Washington, DC 20037
Ph: (202)887-8500   Fr: 800-638-1710

Annual. $99.95. 1,100 pages. Guide to the people and activities of government agencies and committees.

HANDBOOKS AND MANUALS

★6653★ Internships and Fellowships Information Pack

U.S. Capitol
Washington, DC 20510
Ph: (202)224-3121

Congressional Research Service. Ask for Report No. IPO631. Request from your representative in Congress at the address given above.

★6654★ Washington Job Source: Everything You Need to Land the Internship, Entry-Level or Middle Management Job of Your Choice

Metcom, Inc.
1708 Surrey Ln., NW
Washington, DC 20007
Ph: (202)337-7800   Fax: (202)337-3121

Benjamin S. Psillas. 1995. $15.95 (paper).

OTHER SOURCES

★6655★ Congressional Black Caucus (CBC)
2244 Rayburn
Washington, DC 20515
Ph: (202)225-3436

Members: Black members of the U.S. House of Representatives. **Purpose:** To address the legislative concerns of black and other under-represented citizens and to formalize and strengthen the efforts of its members. Works to implement these objectives through personal contact with other House members, through the dissemination of information to individual black constituents, and by working closely with black elected officials in other levels of government. **Activities:** Establishes a yearly legislative agenda setting forth the issues which it supports: full employment, national health development, welfare reform, and international affairs.

★6656★ Convention II (CII)
PO Box 1987
Washington, DC 20013
Ph: (202)544-1789

Members: High school participants in the annual model Constitutional Convention that convenes in the Halls of the U.S. Congress. **Purpose:** A national political/citizenship education program aimed at teaching American youth about the rule of law and politics. Delegates propose, debate, and vote on amendments to the Constitution as possible solutions to major challenges confronting the nation. Findings are presented at the White House and Congress, and sent to other American leaders. Sponsors internship program, placing former delegates in jobs on Capitol Hill, with the goal of increasing congressional support for the organization. Facilitates interaction between members and members of Congress. Communicates and collaborates with individuals, institutions, and organizations involved with business, education, government, humanities, politics, and youth.

★6657★ *Political Scientists*
Chronicle Guidance Publications, Inc.
66 Aurora St.
PO Box 1190
Moravia, NY 13118-1190
Ph: (315)497-0330   Fax: (315)497-3359
Fr: 800-622-7284

Chronicle Guidance Staff. 1993. $2.00. Provides concise career information and sources of additional information.

Political Scientists

SOURCES OF HELP-WANTED ADS

★6658★ Community Jobs: The Employment Newspaper for the Non-Profit Sector
ACCESS: Networking in the Public Interest
30 Irving Pl.
New York, NY 10003
Ph: (212)475-1001   Fax: (212)475-1199

Monthly. $69.00. Covers jobs and internships available with nonprofit organizations active in issues such as the environment, foreign policy, consumer advocacy, housing, education, etc. Entries include: Position title; name, address, and phone of contact; description, responsibilities; requirements; salary. Arrangement: Geographical.

★6659★ Federal Times
Times-Journal Co.
6883 Commercial Dr.
Springfield, VA 22159
Ph: (703)750-2000   Fax: (703)750-8622

Weekly (Mon.). Federal bureaucracy; technology in government.

★6660★ In These Times
Institute for Public Affairs Inc.
2040 N. Milwaukee Ave., 2nd Fl.
Chicago, IL 60647-4002
Ph: (312)772-0100   Fax: (312)772-4180

Biweekly. $34.95/year for individuals. National political newsmagazine.

★6661★ Personnel Service Newsletter
American Political Science Association
1527 New Hampshire Ave. NW
Washington, DC 20036
Ph: (202)483-2512

Monthly. Available to members only. Covers academic, governmental, and other positions currently open for political scientists, and opportunities for graduate research, study, travel, scholarly exchange abroad. Entries include: For professional openings; employer name, address, name of contact, description of position; some listings include phone. Arrangement: Classified by type of position

(administrative, academic, fellowship, late notice); academic positions are by subject area.

PLACEMENT AND JOB REFERRAL SERVICES

★6662★ African Studies Association (ASA)
Emory University
Credit Union Bldg.
Atlanta, GA 30322
Ph: (404)329-6410   Fax: (404)329-6433

Members: Persons specializing in teaching, writing, or research on Africa including political scientists, historians, geographers, anthropologists, economists, librarians, linguists, and government officials; persons who are studying African subjects; institutional members are universities, libraries, government agencies, and others interested in receiving information about Africa. **Purpose:** Seeks to foster communication and to stimulate research among scholars on Africa. **Activities:** Sponsors placement service; conducts panels and discussion groups; presents exhibits and films. **E-Mail:** africa@mony.edu

★6663★ American Political Science Association (APSA)
1527 New Hampshire Ave. NW
Washington, DC 20036
Ph: (202)483-2512   Fax: (202)483-2657

Members: College and university teachers of political science, public officials, research workers, and businessmen. **Purpose:** Encourages the impartial study and promotes the development of the art and science of government. Develops research projects of public interest and educational programs for political scientists and journalists; seeks to improve the knowledge of and increase citizen participation in political and governmental affairs. **Activities:** Serves as clearinghouse for teaching and research positions in colleges, universities, and research bureaus in the U.S. and abroad and for positions open to political scientists in government and private business. Offers placement service.

★6664★ Asian Political Scientists Group in U.S.A. (APSGUSA)
Huang Hsing Foundation
14017 Wagon Way
Silver Spring, MD 20906

Members: Political scientists of Asian descent in the U.S. **Purpose:** Promotes the professional and ethnic interests of the group. **Activities:** Activities include organization of panels for the annual meeting of the American Political Science Association. Maintains placement service.

★6665★ Foundation for International Human Relations (FIHR)
2020 Pennsylvania Ave., NW
Box 806
Washington, DC 20006
Ph: (202)429-2851   Fax: (202)429-2852

Purpose: Provides internships, fellowships, and other forms of professional experience to college students and future professionals in the fields of political science, public affairs, and international relations and business. Promotes education in leadership skills and cross-cultural and international communication. **Activities:** Conducts workshops, seminars, symposia, and programs on public relations, political psychology, and international media; provides consultation in community development and international health care. Sponsors research in agnihotra farming. Operates speakers' bureau and placement service.

★6666★ Social Sciences Services and Resources
PO Box 153
Wasco, IL 60183
Ph: (708)897-5345

Members: Consulting associates in social sciences. **Purpose:** Established to advance the teaching, consulting, and practice of the social sciences basic disciplines including sociology, anthropology, political science, geography, history, economics, and their applied disciplines: social work, community development, planning, and public administration. Serves as: a center for dissemination of current and comprehensive social research findings. Provides consultants for citizen groups, community projects, and governmental units on written request. Upon request from colleges, school boards, and citizens groups, conducts in-service workshops on teaching, consulting, and new developments in the social sciences. Provides consultant evaluation services for small colleges throughout the U.S. **Activities:** Maintains speakers' bureau and placement information service. Conducts research programs.

★6667★ U.S. Public Interest Research Group (USPIRG)

218 D. St. SE
Washington, DC 20003
Ph: (202)546-9707   Fax: (202)546-2461

Members: Individuals who contribute time, effort, or funds toward public interest research and advocacy. **Activities:** Conducts research, monitors corporate and government actions, and lobbies for reforms on consumer, environmental, energy, and governmental issues. Current efforts include support for: laws to protect consumers from unsafe products and unfair banking practices; laws to reduce the use of toxic chemicals; renewal of the Clean Air Act; efforts to reduce global warming and ozone depletion; energy conservation and use of safe, renewable energy sources. Sponsors internships for college students; provides opportunities for students to receive academic credit for activities such as investigative journalism, legislative research, lobbying, and public education and organizing. Offers summer jobs.

EMPLOYER DIRECTORIES AND NETWORKING LISTS

★6668★ American Political Science Association—Biographical Directory

American Political Science Association
1527 New Hampshire Ave. NW
Washington, DC 20036
Ph: (202)483-2512   Fax: (202)483-2657

Irregular, latest edition 1988; new edition expected 1996. $20.00 plus $4.00 shipping. Covers Approximately 9,500 members of the American Political Science Association including foreign members. Entries include: Personal name, address, phone, biographical data, education, awards and honors received, employment history, present title and affiliation, fields of specialization. Arrangement: Alphabetical. Indexes: Geographical, minorities.

★6669★ American Political Science Association—Membership Directory

American Political Science Association (APSA)
1527 New Hampshire Ave. NW
Washington, DC 20036
Ph: (202)483-2512   Fax: (202)483-2657

Usually triennial; latest edition March 1994. $55.00, plus $6.00 shipping. Number of listings: 13,000. Entries include: Name, address, title, affiliation, highest degree, specialties, fax, and e-mail. Arrangement: Alphabetical. Indexes: Women members, African American members, Latino members, Native

American members, fields of interest, geographical.

★6670★ Carroll's Federal Directory

Carroll Publishing
1058 Thomas Jefferson St. NW
Washington, DC 20007
Ph: (202)333-8620   Fax: (202)337-7020
Fr: 800-336-4240

Bimonthly. $197.00, includes CD-ROM or diskette in subscription. Covers about 35,000 executive managers in federal government offices in Washington, DC, including executive, congressional and judicial branches; members of Congress and Congressional committees and staff. Entries include: Agency names, titles, office address (including room numbers), e-mail addresses, and telephone and fax numbers. Available as part of a library edition titled, *Federal Executive Directory Annual*. Arrangement: By cabinet department or administrative agency. Indexes: Keyword, personal name (with phone).

★6671★ Complete Guide to Public Employment

Impact Publications
9104-N Manassas Dr.
Manassas Park, VA 22111-5211
Ph: (703)361-7300   Fax: (703)335-9486

Ron and Caryl Krannich. Third edition, 1995. $19.95 (paper). List of federal, state, and local government agencies and departments, trade and professional associations, contracting and consulting firms, nonprofit organizations, foundations, research organizations, political support groups, and other organizations offering public service career opportunities. Entries include: Organization name, address, phone, name and title of contact. Arrangement: Classified by type of service. Indexes: Subject.

★6672★ Directory of Black Americans in Political Science

American Political Science Association
1527 New Hampshire Ave. NW
Washington, DC 20036
Ph: (202)483-2512   Fax: (202)483-2657

$5.00. Covers over 500 Black advanced graduate students, academics, and professionals in the field of political science. A list of about 75 predominantly Black colleges and universities with political science programs is included. Entries include: For individuals: Name, title, affiliation, address, degree, fields of specialization, publications. For colleges: Name, address; many listings also include phone. Arrangement: Alphabetical. Indexes: Field of interest.

★6673★ Encyclopedia of Governmental Advisory Organizations

Gale Research
835 Penobscot Bldg.
Detroit, MI 48226-4094
Ph: (313)961-2242   Fax: (313)961-6083
Fr: 800-877-GALE

Biennial, odd years. $505.00, base edition; $375.00, supplement. Covers Approximately 7,000 boards, panels, commissions, committees, presidential conferences, and other groups that advise the President, Congress,

and departments and agencies of federal government; includes interagency committees and federally sponsored conferences. Also includes historically significant organizations. Entries include: Unit name, address (if active), name of principal executive, legal basis for the unit, purpose, reports and publications, findings and recommendations, description of activities, members. Arrangement: Classified by general subject. Indexes: Alphabetical/keyword, personnel, publication, federal department/agency, presidential administration.

★6674★ Federal Yellow Book

Leadership Directories, Inc.
104 5th Ave., 2nd Fl.
New York, NY 10011
Ph: (212)627-4140   Fax: (212)645-0931

Quarterly. $235.00. Covers federal departments, including the Executive Office of the President, the Office of the Vice President, the Office of Management and Budget, the Cabinet, and the National Security Council, and over 35,000 key personnel; over 70 independent federal agencies. Entries include: For personnel: name, address, phone, fax, titles. For departments and agencies. office, or branch name and address; names and titles of principal personnel, with their room numbers and direct-dial phone numbers. Arrangement: Classified by by department or agency.

★6675★ State Directory Library Edition

Carroll Publishing
1058 Thomas Jefferson St. NW
Washington, DC 20007
Ph: (202)333-8620   Fax: (202)337-7020
Fr: 800-336-4240

Annual, July. $137.00, plus $8.00 shipping. Covers 37,000 state government officials in all branches of government and members of authorities. Entries include: Name, address, phone, fax, title. Arrangement: Geographical, then by agency within each state. Indexes: Personal name (with phone) organizational, keyword.

★6676★ United States Government Manual

Office of the Federal Register
National Archives and Records Administration
Washington, DC 20408
Ph: (202)523-5230

Annual, September. $30.00. The manual is the official handbook of the United States government, and includes descriptions and lists of principal personnel of agencies and other bodies in the legislative, judicial, and executive branches; the executive branch is covered in greatest depth. The Congressional Directory and the Manual comprise the database for principal federal government organizations and personnel. Entries include: For each cabinet department and independent agency or other unit, titles of major administrative posts and the names of incumbents are given, along with a description of the unit's responsibilities. Additional listings of subordinate offices and bureaus give similar information. Addresses and phone numbers are provided for units at most levels. Arrangement: Classified by department and agency. Indexes: Personal name, agency/subject.

★6677★ Washington: A Comprehensive Directory of the Key Institutions and Leaders of the National Capital Area

Columbia Books, Inc.
1212 New York Ave. NW, Ste. 330
Washington, DC 20005
Ph: (202)737-3777   Fax: (202)898-0775

Annual. $75.00 prepaid. A subject-classified listing of about 4,500 federal and district government offices, business associations, publications, radio and television stations, and other organizations and offices in the District of Columbia area.

★6678★ Washington Information Directory

Congressional Quarterly Inc.
1414 22nd St. NW
Washington, DC 20037
Ph: (202)887-8500   Fr: 800-638-1710

Annual. $99.95. 1,100 pages. Guide to the people and activities of government agencies and committees.

HANDBOOKS AND MANUALS

★6679★ Career Choices for the 90's for Students of Political Science and Government

Walker and Company
435 Hudson St.
New York, NY 10014
Ph: (212)727-8300   Fax: (212)727-0984
Fr: 800-289-2553

Prepared by the Career Associates staff. 1990. $8.95. 166 pages. Discusses alternatives for students of political science and government. Offers advice on how to break into the field and how to move up. Covers where and who the employers are, internship possibilities, and professional networking associations. Comprehensive guide to career and job search planning.

★6680★ Careers in International Affairs

Georgetown University
Institute for the Study of Diplomacy
423 Intercultural Ctr.
Washington, DC 20057-1052
Ph: (202)687-8971

Mario Pinto Carland and Daniel H. Spatz, Jr. 1991. $15.00. 307 pages. Includes index and bibliography.

★6681★ Careers & the Study of Political Science: A Guide for Undergraduates

American Political Science Association
1527 New Hampshire Ave., NW
Washington, DC 20036
Ph: (202)483-2512   Fax: (202)462-7849

M.Hepburn. 1994. $3.50 (paper).

★6682★ Guide to Careers in World Affairs

Impact Publications
9104-N Manassas Dr.
Manassas Park, VA 22111-5211
Ph: (703)361-7300   Fax: (703)335-9486

Foreign Policy Association. 1993. $14.95. 331 pages. Describes jobs in business, government, and nonprofit organizations. Explains the methods and credentials required to secure a job in many fields, including international law and journalism. Contains sections on internships and graduate programs.

★6683★ Internships and Fellowships Information Pack

U.S. Capitol
Washington, DC 20510
Ph: (202)224-3121

Congressional Research Service. Ask for Report No. IPO631. Request from your representative in Congress at the address given above.

★6684★ Opportunities in Social Science Careers

VGM Career Horizons
4255 W. Touhy Ave.
Lincolnwood, IL 60646-1975
Ph: (847)679-5500   Fax: (847)679-2494
Fr: 800-323-4900

Rosanne J. Marek. 1990. $14.95; $11.95 (paper). 160 pages. Profiles job opportunities in education, government, and business, along with their salary levels and outlook in the years to come. Illustrated.

★6685★ Political Scientists

Chronicle Guidance Publications, Inc.
66 Aurora St.
PO Box 1190
Moravia, NY 13118-1190
Ph: (315)497-0330   Fax: (315)497-3359
Fr: 800-622-7284

Chronicle Guidance Staff. 1993. $2.00. Provides concise career information and sources of additional information.

OTHER SOURCES

★6686★ Academy of Political Science (APS)

475 Riverside Dr., Ste. 1274
New York, NY 10115-1274
Ph: (212)870-2500   Fax: (212)870-2202

Members: Individual members, libraries and institutions. Purpose: Promotes the cultivation of political science and its application to the solution of political, social, and economic problems.

★6687★ American Academy of Political and Social Science (AAPSS)

3937 Chestnut St.
Philadelphia, PA 19104
Ph: (215)386-4594   Fax: (215)386-4630

Members: Professionals and laymen concerned with the political and social sciences

and related fields. Purpose: Promotes the progress of political and social science through publications and meetings. The academy does not take sides in controversial issues, but seeks to gather and present reliable information to assist the public in forming an intelligent and accurate judgment.

★6688★ American Association of Political Consultants (AAPC)

900 2nd St. NE, No. 204
Washington, DC 20002
Ph: (202)371-9585   Fax: (202)371-6751

Members: Regular members are corporations and individuals who devote a major portion of their time to or earn a major portion of their livelihood from political counseling and related activities; associate members are persons who devote part of their time to or earn part of their living from political counseling, have an interest in the political process, are teachers or students of political science, or intend to become actively involved in political activities. Purpose: Provides a vehicle for the exchange of information, resources, and ideas among persons involved in political activity. Arranges seminars and holds biennial updates on campaign techniques and professional advances.

★6689★ International Directory for Youth Internships

Council on International & Public Affairs
777 United Nations Plaza
New York, NY 10017
Ph: (212)972-9877   Fr: 800-316-2739

Latest edition 1993. $7.50, plus $3.00 shipping. Covers United Nations agencies and nongovernmental organizations offering intern and volunteer opportunities. Entries include: Agency, organization, or office name, address, description of internship. Arrangement: Classified by type of organization.

★6690★ International Studies Association (ISA)

Brigham Young University
David M. Kennedy Center
216 HRCB
Provo, UT 84602
Ph: (801)378-5459   Fax: (801)378-7075

Members: Social scientists and other scholars from a wide variety of disciplines who are specialists in international affairs and cross-cultural studies; academicians; government officials; officials in international organizations; business executives; students. Purpose: Promotes research, improved teaching, and the orderly growth of knowledge in the field of international studies; emphasizes a multidisciplinary approach to problems. Activities: Holds conferences with government officials; conducts workshops and discussion groups; sponsors development of modular curriculum materials.

★6691★ New Careers Directory: Internships and Professional Opportunities in Technology and Social Change

Student Pugwash USA
815 15th St. NW, Ste. 814
Washington, DC 20005
Ph: (202)393-6555   Fax: (202)393-6550
Fr: 800-WOW-A-PUG

Irregular; latest edition spring 1993. $13.00 for students; $21.00 for institutions, plus $3.00 shipping. Covers about 300 research institutes, think tanks, laboratories, government agencies, professional, science, and other non-profit organizations offering public policy, science, and technology internships and jobs. Entries include: Sponsoring organization name, description of organization, programs offered, work environment and application procedures, compensation offered. Arrangement: Alphabetical and classified by subject. Indexes: Geographical, subject.

★6692★ Storming Washington: An Intern's Guide to National Government

American Political Science Association
1527 New Hampshire Ave., NW
Washington, DC 20036
Ph: (202)483-2512

Stephen E. Frantzich. Fourth edition, 1994. $3.00. 63 pages.

★6693★ Women's Caucus for Political Science (WCPS)

Dept. of Political Science
George Mason University
Fairfax, VA 22030
Ph: (703)727-6572   Fax: (703)874-6925

Members: Women professionally trained in political science. **Purpose:** To upgrade the status of women in the profession of political science; promote equal opportunities for women political scientists for graduate admission, financial assistance in such schools, and in employment, promotion, and tenure. **Activities:** Advances candidates for consideration for APSA offices and committees.

Preschool Teachers

SOURCES OF HELP-WANTED ADS

★6694★ *ASCUS Annual: Job Search Handbook for Educators*

Association for School, College and
  University Staffing (ASCUS)
820 Davis St., Ste. 222
Evanston, IL 60201
Ph: (708)864-1999

Annual. Includes employment notices from public school systems. Contains articles for educators seeking employment. Also includes "Directory of State Teacher Certification Offices."

★6695★ *Community Jobs: The Employment Newspaper for the Non-Profit Sector*

ACCESS: Networking in the Public
  Interest
30 Irving Pl.
New York, NY 10003
Ph: (212)475-1001   Fax: (212)475-1199

Monthly. $69.00. Covers jobs and internships available with nonprofit organizations active in issues such as the environment, foreign policy, consumer advocacy, housing, education, etc. Entries include: Position title; name, address, and phone of contact; description, responsibilities; requirements; salary. Arrangement: Geographical.

★6696★ *EIS Preschool Openings Overseas*

Education Information Services (EIS)
PO Box 660662
Newton, MA 02162-0662
Ph: (617)443-0125

$8.95. List providing names and addresses of American overseas and international schools which offer preschool classes.

★6697★ *Teaching K-8*

Early Years, Inc.
40 Richards Ave.
Norwalk, CT 06854-2509
Ph: (203)855-2650   Fax: (203)855-2656

$19.77/year for individuals. Magazine for elementary teachers.

PLACEMENT AND JOB REFERRAL SERVICES

★6698★ **American Montessori Society (AMS)**

150 5th Ave., Ste. 203
New York, NY 10011-4384
Ph: (212)924-3209   Fax: (212)727-2254

Members: School affiliates and teacher training affiliates; heads of schools, teachers, parents, non-Montessori educators, and other interested individuals dedicated to stimulating the use of the Montessori teaching approach and promoting better education for all children. **Purpose:** Formed to meet demands of growing interest in the Montessori approach to early learning. Developed in Italy in 1907 by Dr. Maria Montessori, the system is based on the young child's instinctive love and need for purposeful work realized in an environment prepared with auto-educative, multi-sensory, manipulative learning devices for language, math, science, and practical life. **Activities:** Offers placement service. Assists in establishing schools; supplies information and limited services to member schools in other countries. Maintains school consultation and accreditation service.

★6699★ **Association for Direct Instruction (ADI)**

PO Box 10252
Eugene, OR 97440
Ph: (503)485-1293   Fax: (503)683-7543

Members: Public school regular and special education teachers and university instructors. **Purpose:** Encourages, promotes, and engages in research aimed at improving educational methods. Promotes dissemination of developmental information and skills that facilitate the education of adults and children. **Activities:** Maintains placement service. Administers a preschool for developmentally delayed children. Offers educational training workshops for instructors.

EMPLOYER DIRECTORIES AND NETWORKING LISTS

★6700★ *National Directory of Alternative Schools*

National Coalition of Alternative
  Community Schools
PO Box 15036
Santa Fe, NM 87506
Ph: (505)474-4312

Biennial, even years. $15.00. Covers over 400 alternative education programs, including home schools, and state and regional coalitions of alternative schools and colleges; also lists organizations and networks offering services and resources to those working with children; international coverage. Entries include: Name, address, phone, name of contact; some also include descriptions of programs. Arrangement: Schools are geographical.

★6701★ *Nursery Schools & Kindergartens Directory*

American Business Directories, Inc.
American Business Information, Inc.
5711 S. 86th Cir.
Omaha, NE 68127
Ph: (402)593-4600   Fax: (402)331-1505

Annual. $1,310, U.S. edition; $145.00, (Canad. ed.). Number of listings: 38,967 (U.S. edition); 1,574 (Canadian edition). Entries include: Name, address, phone (including area code), size of advertisement, year first in Yellow Pages, name of owner or manager, number of employees. Regional editions available: Eastern, $760.00; Western, $645.00. Compiled from telephone company Yellow Pages, nationwide. Arrangement: Geographical.

HANDBOOKS AND MANUALS

★6702★ Career Information Center

Macmillan Publishing Co.
200 Old Tappan Rd.
Old Tappan, NJ 07675
Ph: (609)461-6500   Fr: 800-223-2336

Visual Education Center Staff. Fifth edition, 1992. $229.00. This 13-volume set profiles over 600 occupations. Each occupational profile describes job duties, educational requirements, how to get the job, advancement possibilities, employment outlook, working conditions, earnings and benefits, and where to write for more information.

★6703★ Careers in Child Care

Child Care Action Campaign
330 7th Ave., 17th Fl.
New York, NY 10001
Ph: (212)239-0138

Pamphlet. 2 pages. Addresses job opportunities in day care.

★6704★ Careers in Child Care

NTC Publishing Group
4255 W. Touhy Ave
Lincolnwood, IL 60646-1975
Ph: (708)679-5500   Fax: (708)679-6375
Fr: 800-323-4900

Marjorie Eberts. 1994. $16.95; $12.95 (paper).

★6705★ Careers in Education

VGM Career Horizons
4255 W. Touhy Ave.
Lincolnwood, IL 60646-1975
Ph: (847)679-5500   Fax: (847)679-2494
Fr: 800-323-4900

Roy A. Edelfeldt. 1993. $17.95; $13.95 (paper). 192 pages. Explores opportunities for teachers, administrators, and specialists in elementary and secondary schools, as well as teaching, research, and administrative positions in higher education. Additional focus on adult and continuing education and industry opportunities for educators. Provides detailed background on careers in state boards and state departments of education, accrediting agencies, federal agencies, and national associations and councils.

★6706★ How to Get the Teaching Position You Want: Teacher Candidate Guide

Education Enterprises
PO Box 1836
Spring Valley, CA 91979
Ph: (619)660-7740

M. Phyllis Murton. 1993.

★6707★ Opportunities in Child Care Careers

VGM Career Horizons
4255 W. Touhy Ave.
Lincolnwood, IL 60646-1975
Ph: (847)679-5500   Fax: (847)679-2494
Fr: 800-323-4900

Renee Wittenberg. 1995. $14.95; $11.95 (paper). 160 pages. Discusses various job opportunities and how to secure a position. Illustrated.

★6708★ The RNT Careers in Teaching Handbook

Recruting New Teachers, Inc.
385 Concord Ave.
Belmont, MA 02178
Ph: (617)489-6000   Fax: (617)489-6005
1993.

★6709★ Teaching

NTC Publishing Group
4255 W. Touhy Ave.
Lincolnwood, IL 60646-1975
Ph: (708)679-5500   Fax: (708)679-6375
Fr: 800-323-4900

1994. $13.95; $10.95 (paper).

★6710★ Where the Jobs Are: The Hottest Careers for the '90s

The Career Press, Inc.
3 Tice Rd.
PO Box 687
Franklin Lakes, NJ 07417
Ph: (201)848-0310   Fax: (201)848-1727
Fr: 800-237-3371

Joyce Hadley. Second edition, 1995. $9.99. 300 pages. Describes careers in fifteen general fields, from accounting to travel and hospitality.

EMPLOYMENT AGENCIES AND SEARCH FIRMS

★6711★ Arbor Associates, Inc.

15 Court Sq., Ste. 1050
Boston, MA 02108
Ph: (617)227-8829

Handles temporary placements.

★6712★ Educational Placement Service

5050 Poplar Ave., Ste. 1700
Memphis, TN 38157-1701
Ph: (901)767-1884

Employment agency. Focuses on teaching, administrative, and education-related openings.

OTHER SOURCES

★6713★ National Association for the Education of Young Children (NAEYC)

1509 16th St. NW
Washington, DC 20036
Ph: (202)232-8777   Fax: (202)328-1846
Fr: 800-424-2460

Members: Teachers and directors of pre-school and primary schools, kindergartens, child care centers, cooperatives, church schools, and groups having similar programs for young children; early childhood education and child development professors, trainers, and researchers. **Activities:** Offers voluntary accreditation for early childhood schools and centers through the National Academy of Early Childhood Programs.

★6714★ Overseas Employment Opportunities for Educators: Department of Defense Dependents Schools

Diane Publishing Co.
600 Upland Ave.
Upland, PA 19015
Ph: (610)499-7415

1993. $29.95. 52 pages.

★6715★ Resumes for Education Careers

VGM Career Horizons
4255 W. Touhy Ave.
Lincolnwood, IL 60646-1975
Ph: (847)679-5500   Fax: (847)679-2494
Fr: 800-323-4900

1992. $9.95. Sample resumes cover a variety of education careers and reflect education professionals at all levels of experience.

Printers and Bookbinders

★6731★ Printing Journal

East-West Communications
1432 Duke St.
Alexandria, VA 22314-3436
Ph: (703)683-8800   Fax: (703)683-8801

Monthly. Free to qualified subscribers; $39.00 for individuals; $3.00/year for single issue. Trade newspaper.

★6732★ Printing News Midwest

Quoin Research Inc.
800 W. Huron St., 3rd Fl.
Chicago, IL 60622
Ph: (312)226-5600   Fax: (312)226-4640
Fr: 800-783-6242

Monthly. $36.00/year for individuals; $56.00/year for Canada; $80.00/year for other countries. Magazine containing printing news for the Midwest.

★6733★ Quick Printing

PTN Publishing Co.
445 Broad Hollow Rd., Ste. 21
Melville, NY 11747
Ph: (516)845-2700   Fax: (516)845-7109

Monthly. $22.00/year for individuals; $3.00 for single issue.

★6734★ Signature

South Wind Publishing Co.
PO Box 6808
Leawood, KS 66206-0808
Ph: (913)642-6611   Fax: (913)642-6676

Periodic. Free to qualified subscribers; $48.00/year for institutions; $58.00/year for Canada and Mexico. Publishing industry magazine and catalog.

★6735★ Southern Graphics

PTN Publishing Co.
445 Broad Hollow Rd., Ste. 21
Melville, NY 11747
Ph: (516)845-2700   Fax: (516)845-7109

Monthly. $22.00/year for individuals. Graphic arts magazine serving the printing and graphic arts industry in 14 southern states.

PLACEMENT AND JOB REFERRAL SERVICES

★6736★ Printing Brokerage/Buyers Association (PB/BA)

1500 NW 49th St., Ste. 550
Fort Lauderdale, FL 33309
Ph: (305)771-5554   Fax: (305)771-5991
Fr: 800-448-8952

Members: Printing buyers/brokers/distributors, printers, typographers, binders, envelope and book manufacturers, packagers, color separation houses, pre-press service organizations, and related companies in the graphic arts industry. **Purpose:** Promotes understanding, cooperation, and interaction among members while obtaining the highest standard of professionalism in the graphic arts industry. Gathers information on current technology in the graphic communications industry. Sponsors seminars for members to learn how to work with buyers, brokers and printers; also conducts technical and management seminars. **Activities:** Maintains referral service; compiles statistics. Conducts charitable programs.

★6737★ Women in Production (WIP)

347 5th Ave., No. 1406
New York, NY 10016-5010
Ph: (212)481-7793   Fax: (212)481-7969

Members: Persons involved in all phases of print and graphics, including those working in magazine and book publishing, agency production and print manufacturing, print-related vending and buying, and advertising production. **Purpose:** To improve job performance by sharing information with each other and with suppliers of printing services. Acts as a network of contacts for those in the printing professions; offers assistance to persons with production problems. Membership is concentrated in the New York City area. **Activities:** Sponsors placement service; maintains speakers' bureau.

EMPLOYER DIRECTORIES AND NETWORKING LISTS

★6738★ Directory of Printers

Ad-Lib Publications
51 1/2 W. Adams
PO Box 1102
Fairfield, IA 52556-1102
Ph: (515)472-6617   Fax: (515)472-3186
Fr: 800-669-0773

Biennial, latest edition 1994. $14.95, plus $4.50 shipping. Covers about 1,000 book, catalog, magazine, and specialized printers; including about 100 Canadian and overseas printers. Entries include: Company name, address, phone, contact name, subsidiary and branch names and locations, annual sales, number of employees, products and services provided, specialization, whether unionized, type of print runs. Arrangement: Alphabetical. Indexes: Product/service, geographical, foreign, Canadian, type of print runs, binding capabilities, subject.

★6739★ Graphic Arts Blue Book

A. F. Lewis & Co., Inc.
245 5th Ave.
New York, NY 10016
Ph: (212)679-0770   Fax: (212)545-7963

Covers printing plants, bookbinders, typesetters, platemakers, paper merchants, paper manufacturers, printing machinery manufacturers and dealers, and others serving the graphic arts industry in six regional editions: New York; Southeastern; Northeastern; Delaware Valley-Ohio; Midwestern; and West Coast. Entries include: Company name, address, phone, names and titles of executives, name of buyer, list of products or services, year established. Arrangement: Same information given geographically, classified by product/service, and classified by paper brand name/watermark. Indexes: Alphabetical.

★6740★ International Directory of Private Presses

Educators Research Service
2443 Fair Oaks Blvd., Ste. 316
Sacramento, CA 95825
Ph: (916)924-1151   Fax: (916)924-9618

Annual, April. $50.00. Covers about 1,200 private presses and hobbyist printers worldwide who use the letterpress process of reproduction. Entries include: Press name, address, phone, information on press and types, kinds of work produced, whether samples will be exchanged, brief statement on goals, printing philosophy, etc. Arrangement: Alphabetical. Indexes: Proprietor name, geographical.

★6741★ International Literary Market Place

R. R. Bowker Co.
Reed Reference Publishing
121 Chanlon Rd.
New Providence, NJ 07974
Ph: (908)464-6800   Fax: (908)771-7704
Fr: 800-521-8110

Annual, Fall. $179.95. Covers more than 9,200 publishers in over 170 countries outside the United States and Canada, and about 1,150 trade and professional organizations related to publishing abroad; includes major printers, binders, typesetters, book manufacturers, book dealers, libraries, literary agencies, translators, book clubs, reference books and journals, periodicals, prizes, and international reference section. Entries include: For publishers Name, address, phone, fax, telex, names and titles of key personnel, branches, type of publications, subjects, ISBN prefix. Arrangement: Classified by business activities, then geographical. Indexes: Company name, subject, type of publication.

★6742★ Literary Market Place

R. R. Bowker Co.
Reed Reference Publishing
121 Chanlon Rd.
New Providence, NJ 07974
Ph: (908)464-6800   Fax: (908)771-7704
Fr: 800-521-8110

Annual, September. $165.00. Covers over 15,000 firms or organizations offering services related to the publishing industry, including 3,800 book publishers in the United States and Canada who issued three or more books during the preceding year, plus a small press section of publishers who publish less than three titles per year or those who are self-published. Also included: book printers and binders; book clubs; book trade and literary associations; selected syndicates, newspapers, periodicals, and radio and TV programs that use book reviews or book publishing news; translators and literary agents. Arrangement: Classified by line of business. Indexes: Principal index is 35,000-item combined index of publishers, publications, and personnel; several sections have geographical and/or subject indexes; translators are indexed by source and target language.

★6743★ *Printers Directory*

American Business Directories, Inc.
American Business Information, Inc.
5711 S. 86th Cir.
Omaha, NE 68127
Ph: (402)593-4600   Fax: (402)331-1505

Annual. $1,970.00, U.S. edition; $335.00, (Canadian edition); payment with order. Significant discounts offered for standing orders. Number of listings: 57,738 (U.S. edition); 7,009 (Canadian edition). Entries include: Name, address, phone (including area code), size of advertisement, year first in Yellow Pages, coding indicates brands carried, specialties, or franchises held. Regional editions available. Compiled from telephone company Yellow Pages, nationwide. Arrangement: Geographical.

★6744★ *Publishers Directory*

Gale Research
835 Penobscot Bldg.
Detroit, MI 48226-4094
Ph: (313)961-2242   Fax: (313)961-6083
Fr: 800-877-GALE

Annual, fall. $275.00. Covers approximately 20,000 new and established, commercial and nonprofit, private and alternative, corporate and association, government and institution publishing programs and their distributors; includes producers of books, classroom materials, prints, reports, and databases. Entries include: Firm name, address, phone, fax, year founded, ISBN prefix, Standard Address Number, whether firm participates in the Cataloging in Publication program of the Library of Congress, names of principal executives, number of titles in print, description of firm and its main subject interests, discount and returns policies, affiliated and parent companies, mergers and amalgamations, principal markets, imprints and divisions; distributors also list firms for which they distribute, special services, terms to publishers and regional offices. Arrangement: Alphabetical; distributors listed separately. Indexes: Subject, geographical, publisher name (including imprints).

★6745★ *Who's Who in Screen Printing*

Screenprinting and Graphic Imaging
  Association International
10015 Main St.
Fairfax, VA 22031
Ph: (703)385-1335   Fax: (703)273-0456

Annual, August. Available to members only. Covers about 3,200 screen printers, suppliers of screen printing equipment and materials, and donors to the Screen Printing Technical Foundation. Entries include: Company name, address, phone, fax, telex, name of contact, products or services, divisional memberships. Arrangement: Classified by type of business, then geographical.

★6746★ *The Workbook*

Scott & Daughters Publishing
940 N. Highland Ave.
Los Angeles, CA 90038
Ph: (213)856-0008   Fax: (213)856-4368
Fr: 800-547-2688

Annual, January. $95.00. Covers in four regional volumes, 25,000 advertising agencies, art directors, photographers, freelance illustrators and designers, artists' representatives, commercial production companies, printers, color separators, and typographers in the U.S. Entries include: Company or individual name, address, phone, specialty. Regional volumes are East, West, Midwest, and South. Arrangement: Classified by product or service.

HANDBOOKS AND MANUALS

★6747★ *Opportunities in Newspaper Publishing Careers*

VGM Career Horizons
4255 W. Touhy Ave.
Lincolnwood, IL 60646-1975
Ph: (847)679-5500   Fax: (847)679-2494
Fr: 800-323-4900

John Tebbel. 1989. $14.95; $11.95 (paper). 160 pages. Tells how to land a newspaper job, describing editorial and noneditorial positions at big city and small city papers and syndicated wire services. Career preparation chapters address the need to anticipate changing newspaper technology while acquiring fundamental news skills. Illustrated.

★6748★ *Opportunities in Printing Careers*

VGM Career Horizons
4255 W. Touhy Ave.
Lincolnwood, IL 60646-1975
Ph: (847)679-5500   Fax: (847)679-2494
Fr: 800-323-4900

Irvin J. Borowsky. 1992. $14.95; $11.95 (paper). 160 pages. Offers detailed information on the variety of pre-press, press, and post-press jobs available. Covers apprenticeships, unions, salaries, and how to get ahead. Illustrated.

★6749★ *Opportunities in Vocational and Technical Careers*

VGM Career Horizons
4255 W. Touhy Ave.
Lincolnwood, IL 60646-1975
Ph: (847)679-5500   Fax: (847)679-2494
Fr: 800-323-4900

Adrian A. Paradis. 1992. $14.95; $11.95 (paper). 160 pages. Provides information on a variety of opportunities and advice on breaking into the field.

★6750★ *Your Opportunities in the Printing Industry*

Energeia Publishing, Inc.
860 Commercial St., S.
Salem, OR 97302
Ph: (503)362-1480   Fax: (503)362-2123

Laurie Bean. 1994. $2.00 (paper).

EMPLOYMENT AGENCIES AND SEARCH FIRMS

★6751★ **Graphic Arts Employment Service, Inc.**

2530 Central Pkwy.
Cincinnati, OH 45214
Ph: (513)241-2201

Employment agency.

★6752★ **Graphic Search Associates Inc.**

PO Box 373
Newtown Square, PA 19073
Ph: (610)359-1234   Fax: (610)353-8120

Executive search firm.

★6753★ **Stewart Associates**

245 Butler Ave.
The Executive Offices
Lancaster, PA 17601
Ph: (717)299-9242   Fax: (717)299-4879

Executive search firm.

OTHER SOURCES

★6754★ **Amalgamated Printers' Association (APA)**

6906 Colony Loop Dr.
Austin, TX 78724

Purpose: Active printers interested in the furtherance of the art and craft of printing. Encourages excellence of printing content, design, and techniques among members. Sponsors competitions.

★6755★ **American Institute of Graphic Arts (AIGA)**

164 5th Ave.
New York, NY 10010
Ph: (212)807-1990   Fax: (212)807-1799
Fr: 800-548-1634

Purpose: Graphic designers, art directors, art directors, illustrators, packaging designers, and craftsmen involved in printing and allied graphic fields. Sponsors exhibits and projects in the public interest. Sponsors traveling exhibitions. Operates gallery. Maintains library of design books and periodicals; offers slide archives.

★6756★ **Binding Industries of America (BIA)**

70 E. Lake St.
Chicago, IL 60601
Ph: (312)372-7606   Fax: (312)704-5025

Members: Trade binders and loose-leaf manufacturers united to conduct seminars, hold conventions, and formulate and maintain standards.

★6757★ Graphic Arts Technical Foundation (GATF)

4615 Forbes Ave.
Pittsburgh, PA 15213
Ph: (412)621-6941   Fax: (412)621-3049

Members: Scientific, research, technical, and educational organization serving the international graphic communications industries. **Purpose:** Conducts research in all graphic processes and their commercial applications. Conducts seminars, workshops, and forums on graphic arts and environmental subjects. Conducts educational programs, including the publishing of graphic arts textbooks and learning modules, audiovisuals, videotapes, aptitude testing, in-plant and school counseling, and national career and manpower recruitment program. Conducts the GATF training and certification program in sheet-fed offset press operating, Web Offset press operating, Image Assembly, and desktop publishing. Produces test images and quality control devices for the industry. Performs technical services for the graphic arts industry, including problem-solving, material evaluation, and plant audits. Compiles statistics.

★6758★ Master Printers of America (MPA)

100 Daingerfield Rd.
Alexandria, VA 22314
Ph: (703)519-8130   Fax: (703)548-4165
Fr: 800-MPA-2227

Members: Open-shop establishments in the commercial printing industry. A division of Printing Industries of America. **Purpose:** Supports pro-business labor law reform and modern industrial relations in plants. Conducts institutes for industrial relations directors and managers of local associations. Sponsors ongoing employee recognition program.

★6759★ National Association of Printers and Lithographers (NAPL)

780 Palisade Ave.
Teaneck, NJ 07666
Ph: (201)342-0700   Fax: (201)692-0286
Fr: 800-642-NAPL

Purpose: Firms engaged in printing. Presents over 50 conferences, seminars, and workshops per year on management topics. Offers on-site cost, production control, marketing, and financial consulting services for members. **Activities:** Maintains Management Institute, which conducts Executive Certification Program. Compiles statistics.

★6760★ Printing Industries of America (PIA)

100 Daingerfield Rd.
Alexandria, VA 22314
Ph: (703)519-8100   Fax: (703)548-3227
Fr: 800-742-2666

Members: Commercial printing firms (lithography, letterpress, gravure, platemakers, typographic houses); allied firms in the graphic arts. **Purpose:** Provides extensive management services for member companies, including government relations, industry research and statistical information, technology information and assistance, and management education and publications. Compiles statistical and economic data, including annual ratio study which provides a benchmark for printers to compare profits as a basis for improving individual member company and industry profits. Provides reporting system on provisions, rates, and other matters relating to union contracts in effect throughout the industry. Sponsors annual Premier Print Awards Competition.

★6761★ Teams and Tools

Printing Industries of America
100 Daingerfield Rd.
Alexandria, VA 22314
Ph: (703)519-8100   Fax: (703)548-3227

Video. 1993. $24.95. 14 minutes. Illustrates career opportunities in the graphic arts industry, from management to prepress through postpress.

★6762★ "Typesetting and Graphic Arts" in *Small Businesses That Grow and Grow and Grow*

Divison of F&M Publications
1507 Dana Ave.
Cincinnati, OH 45207
Ph: (513)531-2222   Fr: 800-289-0963

Patricia A. Woy. 1989. $9.95 (paper). Contains a chapter about establishing businesses in the printing, typesetting, and graphic arts fields.

Property and Real Estate Managers

SOURCES OF HELP-WANTED ADS

★6763★ Buildings

Stamats Communications, Inc.
427 6th Ave. SE
PO Box 1888
Cedar Rapids, IA 52406
Ph: (319)364-6167   Fax: (319)364-4278

Monthly. $60.00/year for individuals; $75.00/year for Canada; $6.00 for single issue. Publication featuring management techniques, development, and ownership of facilities.

★6764★ Journal of Property Management

Institute of Real Estate Management
430 N. Michigan Ave.
Chicago, IL 60611
Ph: (312)661-1930   Fax: (312)661-0217

Bimonthly. $40.95/year for individuals; $7.00 for single issue. Magazine serving real estate managers.

★6765★ New England Real Estate Journal

East Coast Publications
PO Box 55
Accord, MA 02018
Ph: (617)878-4540   Fax: (617)871-1853

Weekly (Fri.). $139.00/year for individuals. Newspaper publishing commercial, industrial, and investment real estate news.

★6766★ Property Management Association-Bulletin

Property Management Association
8811 Colesville Rd., Ste. G106
Silver Spring, MD 20910
Ph: (301)587-6543

Monthly. Free to members. Reports information related to property management Includes job listings.

★6767★ Realtor News (All Member Issue)

National Association of Realtors
700 11th St.
Washington, DC 20001
Ph: (202)383-1193   Fax: (202)383-1231

Monthly. $12.00/year for individuals. Real estate newspaper.

PLACEMENT AND JOB REFERRAL SERVICES

★6768★ Building Owners and Managers Association International (BOMA)

1201 New York Ave. NW, Ste. 300
Washington, DC 20005
Ph: (202)408-2662   Fax: (202)371-0181

Members: Owners, managers, investors, and developers of commercial office buildings. **Purpose:** To promote the office building industry as a business enterprise through mutual discussion and cooperation, education, dissemination of information, and establishment of standards of practice and performance. The Building Owners and Managers Institute, BOMA's educational arm, provides courses leading to RPA (Real Property Administrator), SMA (Systems Maintenance Administrator), and FMA (Facilities Maintenance Administrator) certifications. **Activities:** Conducts research programs. Operates placement service; maintains speakers' bureau; compiles statistics.

★6769★ Institute of Real Estate Management (IREM)

430 N. Michigan Ave.
Chicago, IL 60611-4090
Ph: (312)329-6000   Fax: (312)661-0217
Fr: 800-837-0706

Members: Professional organization of real property and asset managers. **Purpose:** Awards professional designation Certified Property Manager (CPM) to qualifying individuals and Accredited Management Organization (AMO) to qualifying management firms. Also awards Accredited Residential Manager which recognizes outstanding residential site managers. Monitors legislation affecting real estate management. **Activities:** Maintains software vendor certification program. Offers management courses and seminars; conducts research and educational programs; maintains formal code of ethics; compiles statistics; maintains speakers' bureau and job referral service, and computer bulletin board. Administers IREM Smart Partners Safety Awareness and crime prevention program.

★6770★ International College of Real Estate Consulting Professionals (RECP)

297 Dakota St.
Le Sueur, MN 56058
Ph: (612)665-6280   Fax: (612)665-6280

Members: Individuals in 6 countries proficient in fields related to the real estate profession, including sales, accounting, law, consultation, education, finance, and government. **Activities:** Compiles statistics; provides referral and placement services.

★6771★ International Development Research Council (IDRC)

35 Technology Park/Atlanta, Ste. 150
Norcross, GA 30092
Ph: (770)446-8955   Fax: (770)662-8950

Members: Corporate executives whose duties involve corporate real estate and facility planning, including such fields as site selection, real estate management, financing, community comparison, site analysis, industrial zoning, and economic geography. **Purpose:** Seeks to increase public knowledge of the field of corporate real estate and industrial expansion planning. **Activities:** Conducts research through the International Development Research Foundation, focusing on issues critical to corporate real estate asset management and geoeconomics. Provides professional certification. Sponsors quarterly regional workshops; maintains placement service and research programs. **Website:** http://www.conway.com

★6772★ Nacore International (NACORE)

440 Columbia Dr., Ste. 100
West Palm Beach, FL 33409
Ph: (407)683-8111   Fax: (407)697-4853

Members: Executives, attorneys, real estate department heads, architects, engineers, analysts, researchers, and anyone responsible for the management, administration, and operation of national and regional real estate departments of national and international corporations. **Purpose:** Provides a meeting ground for the exchange of ideas, experience, and problems among members; encourages professionalism within corporate real estate through education and communication; protects the interests of corporate realty in dealing with adversaries, public or private; maintains contact with other real estate organizations; publicizes the availability of fully qualified members to the job market. Maintains Institute for Corporate Real Estate as educational arm. **Activities:** Maintains placement service.

★6773★ National Property Management Association (NPMA)

380 Main St., Ste. 290
Dunedin, FL 34698
Ph: (813)736-3788   Fax: (813)736-6707

Members: Individuals interested in professional asset management, primarily working with assets provided by government entities to contractors. **Purpose:** Objective is to provide a continuing forum for discussion, problem solving, standardized application of government regulations, and design and implementation of effective, efficient property systems. Provides educational methods, programs, materials and opportunities that enable members to learn and apply the principles and techniques of effective contractor property and facilities management and related subjects. Awards designations of Certified Professional Property Administrator, Certified Professional Property Managers, Certified Professional Property Specialist, and Consulting Fellows to qualified individuals. **Activities:** Offers placement services; sponsors educational programs.

EMPLOYER DIRECTORIES AND NETWORKING LISTS

★6774★ Executive Guide to Specialists in Industrial and Office Real Estate

Society of Industrial and Office Realtors
700 11th St. NW, Ste. 510
Washington, DC 20001-4511
Ph: (202)737-1150   Fax: (202)737-8796
Fr: 800-967-0085

Annual, June. $60.00. Covers approximately 1,800 specialists in industrial real estate. Entries include: Company name, address, phone, fax, name of individual member. Arrangement: Geographical. Indexes: Personal name.

★6775★ National Association of Real Estate Companies—Membership Directory

National Association of Real Estate Companies
Box 958
Columbia, MD 21044
Ph: (410)821-1614   Fax: (410)992-6363

Quarterly. Available to members only. Covers about 200 real estate development companies. Entries include: Company name, address, phone, name of contact.

★6776★ National Real Estate Investor Sourcebook

Argus Business
6151 Powers Ferry Rd. NW
Atlanta, GA 30339-2941
Ph: (404)955-2500   Fax: (404)955-0400

Annual, summer. $76.95, payment must accompany order. Publication includes: List of about 7,000 companies and individuals in 22 real estate fields, including appraisers; architects; asset managers; builders and contractors; business/office parks; computer services; corporate real estate managers; developers; economic and industrial development authorities; environmental consultants; equity investors; executive search firms; financial services; hospitality services; hotel franchisers; institutional and pension fund advisors; limited partnerships; property managers; real estate brokers, agents, consultants, and counselors; title insurance companies; related associations; and others. Arrangement: Classified by field or type of activity, then geographical.

HANDBOOKS AND MANUALS

★6777★ Becoming a Real Estate Professional

Vantage Press, Inc.
516 W. 34th St.
New York, NY 10001
Ph: (212)736-1767   Fax: (212)736-2273
Fr: 800-882-3273

Shawn J. Murphy. 1995. $19.95 (paper).

★6778★ Career Choices for the 90's for Students of Business

Walker and Company
435 Hudson St.
New York, NY 10014
Ph: (212)727-8300   Fax: (212)727-0984
Fr: 800-289-2553

Prepared by the Career Associates staff. 1990. $9.95. 166 pages. Discusses alternatives for students of business. Offers advice on how to break into the field and how to move up. Covers where and who the employers are, internship possibilities, and professional networking associations. Comprehensive guide to career and job search planning.

★6779★ Career Choices for the 90's for Students of Psychology

Walker and Company
435 Hudson St.
New York, NY 10014
Ph: (212)727-8300   Fax: (212)727-0984
Fr: 800-289-2553

Prepared by the Career Associates staff. 1990. $9.95. 166 pages. Discusses alternatives for students of psychology. Offers advice on how to break into the field and how to move up. Covers where and who the employers are, internship possibilities, and professional networking associations. Com-

prehensive guide to career and job search planning.

★6780★ Careers in Real Estate Management

Institute of Real Estate Management
PO Box 109025
Chicago, IL 60610-9025
Ph: (312)329-6000   Fax: (312)661-0217

1994. $30.00.

★6781★ The Encyclopedia of Career Choices for the 1990s: Guide to Entry-Level Jobs

Perigree Books
The Berkley Publishing Group
PO Box 506
East Rutherford, NJ 07073
Ph: (201)933-9292   Fr: 800-223-0510

Career Associates Staff. 1992. $19.95. 862 pages. Describes 500 entry-level careers in a variety of industries. Presents qualifications required, working conditions, salary, internships, and professional associations.

★6782★ Encyclopedia of Careers and Vocational Guidance

J. G. Ferguson Publishing Co.
200 W. Monroe, Ste. 250
Chicago, IL 60606
Ph: (312)580-5480

William E. Hopke. Ninth edition, 1993. $129.95; $199.95 (CD-ROM). Four-volume set that profiles 900 occupations and describes job trends in 71 industries. Includes career description, educational requirements, history of the job, methods of entry, advancement, employment outlook, earnings, conditions of work, social and psychological factors, and sources of further information. Contains career and employment information for this field.

★6783★ How About a Career in Real Estate?

Dearborn Financial Publishing, Inc.
155 N. Wacker Dr.
Chicago, IL 60606-1719
Ph: (312)836-4400   Fax: (312)836-1021

Carla Cross. 1993. $14.95 (paper).

★6784★ How to Become an Apartment Manager (Fast) & Live Rent Free

Pro-Guides, Publishing
PO Box 2071
Davis, CA 95617-2071

R. Robert Stuart, editor. 1994. $16.95 (paper).

★6785★ Opportunities in Property Management Careers

VGM Career Horizons
4255 W. Touhy Ave.
Lincolnwood, IL 60646-1975
Ph: (847)679-5500   Fax: (847)679-2494
Fr: 800-323-4900

Mariwyn Evans. 1990. $14.95; $11.95 (paper). 160 pages. Traces typical career paths and outlines job opportunities in this rapidly expanding field.

★6786★ *Real Estate Careers: Twenty-Five Growing Opportunities for Good Times & Bad*

John Wiley & Sons, Inc.
605 3rd Ave.
New York, NY 10158-0012
Ph: (212)850-6000   Fr: 800-225-5945

Carolyn Janik. 1994. $42.50; $16.95 (paper).

★6787★ *Your Opportunities in Real Estate*

Energeia Publishing, Inc.
860 Commercial St., S.
Salem, OR 97302
Ph: (503)362-1480   Fax: (503)362-2123

Laurie Bean. 1994. $2.00 (paper).

★6788★ *Your Successful Real Estate Career: Building a Future in Real Estate Sales*

AMACOM
135 W. 50th St., 15th Fl.
New York, NY 10020
Ph: (212)903-8315   Fr: 800-262-9699

Kenneth W. Edwards. 1992. $14.95. 192 pages. Provides an overview of career opportunities in real estate related careers.

EMPLOYMENT AGENCIES AND SEARCH FIRMS

★6789★ **The Ahrens Agency, Inc.**
3285 Wolfson Dr.
Baldwin, NY 11510
Ph: (516)223-5627

Employment agency. Fills positions in real estate and other fields.

★6790★ **Alzed Enterprises Ltd.**
4 Gateway Center, Ste. 205
Pittsburgh, PA 15222-1260
Ph: (412)261-7200   Fax: (412)392-2365

Executive search firm.

★6791★ **Consultants to Executive Management**
20 S. Clark St., Ste. 610
Chicago, IL 60603
Ph: (312)855-1500

Employment agency.

★6792★ **Continental Field Service Corp.**
37 E. Main St.
Elmsford, NY 10523-2607
Ph: (914)592-7240

Employment agency.

★6793★ **Kimmel and Associates**
25 Page Ave.
Asheville, NC 28801
Ph: (704)251-9900   Fax: (704)251-9955

Employment agency.

★6794★ **Preferred Leads, Inc.**
1660 S. Albion St., Ste. 812
Denver, CO 80222
Ph: (303)782-5447   Fax: (303)782-5649

Employment agency.

★6795★ **Real Estate Executive Search, Inc.**
PO Box 40
Santa Rosa, CA 95402-0040
Ph: (707)525-4591

Executive search firm.

★6796★ **Realty Recruiters, Inc.**
3510 Habersham Rd. NW
Atlanta, GA 30305
Ph: (404)239-0822

Employment agency.

★6797★ **Tina Morbitzer and Associates**
668 N. Orlando Ave., Ste. 105
Maitland, FL 32751
Ph: (407)539-1000   Fax: (407)539-0328

Executive search firm.

★6798★ **Webster Personnel**
131 State St.
Boston, MA 02109-3201
Ph: (617)742-2030

Employment agency.

OTHER SOURCES

★6799★ **Apartment Owners and Managers Association of America (AOMA)**
65 Cherry Plz.
Watertown, CT 06795-0238
Ph: (203)274-2589   Fax: (203)274-2580

Members: Builders, developers, owners, investors, or managers of multi-family housing; most members operate garden-type and mid-rise buildings constructed within the past two decades.

★6800★ *Compensation and Benefit Survey for Corporate Real Estate Executives*

NACORE International
471 Spencer Dr. S, Ste. 8
West Palm Beach, FL 33409-6685
Ph: (407)683-8111

Annual. Results of a survey of 900 corporate real estate executives representing 29 positions. Gives the type of company, annual sales, geographic area, education, age, and salary (overall average, overall medium, medium lower third, medium upper third) for 29 different job titles.

★6801★ **National Apartment Association (NAA)**
201 N. Union St., Ste. 200
Alexandria, VA 22314
Ph: (703)513-6141   Fax: (703)513-6191

Members: Federation of 150 state and local associations of industry professionals engaged in all aspects of the multifamily housing industry, including owners, builders, investors, developers, managers, and allied service representatives. **Purpose:** Provides education and certification for property management executives, on-site property managers, maintenance personnel, property supervisors, and leasing agents. Offers a nationwide legislative network concerned with governmental decisions at the federal, state, and local levels.

★6802★ **National Association of Realtors (NAR)**
430 N. Michigan Ave.
Chicago, IL 60611
Ph: (312)329-8200   Fax: (312)329-8576

Members: Federation of 54 state and territory associations and 1860 local real estate boards whose members are real estate brokers and agents. Terms are registered by the association in the U.S. Patent and Trademark Office and in the states. **Purpose:** Promotes education, high professional standards, and modern techniques in specialized real estate work such as brokerage, appraisal, property management, land development, industrial real estate, farm brokerage, and counseling. Conducts research programs.

★6803★ *National Real Estate Directory*

Real Estate Publications, Inc.
322 W. Rio Vista Ct.
Tampa, FL 33604-6941
Ph: (813)237-0484   Fr: 800-356-2317

Biennial. $29.95. Covers about 22,500 federal and state agencies, offices, and departments related to the regulation of real estate; real estate associations, publications, and organizations. Entries include: Agency, association, department, or publication name, address, phone. Arrangement: Classified by type of organization, then geographical.

★6804★ **Realtors Land Institute (RLI)**
430 N. Michigan Ave.
Chicago, IL 60611
Ph: (312)329-8440   Fr: 800-441-LAND

Members: Real estate brokers and salespersons selling, managing, appraising, or developing all types of land. **Purpose:** Maintains educational programs for real estate brokers; promotes competence and accredits members. **Activities:** Sponsors courses for realtors and others seeking professional excellence on Land Brokerage, Agricultural Land Brokerage, Exchanging Properties, Estate Planning, Subdivision Development, and Financial Analysis of Land Investment.

Psychologists

★6805★ **Alcoholism: Clinical and Experimental Research**

Williams & Wilkins
351 W. Camden St.
Baltimore, MD 21201-2436
Ph: (410)361-8004   Fax: (410)528-4312
Fr: 800-222-3790

Bimonthly. $155.00/year for individuals; $300.00/year for institutions. Publishing original clinical and research studies on alcoholism and alcohol-induced organ damage.

★6806★ **American Journal of Art Therapy**

American Journal of Art Therapy
Vermont College of Norwich University
Montpelier, VT 05602
Ph: (802)828-8540   Fax: (802)828-8855

Quarterly. $27.00/year for individuals; $48.00/year for institutions. Journal focusing on visual arts that contribute to human understanding and mental health.

★6807★ **American Journal of Psychology**

University of Illinois Press
1325 S. Oak St.
Champaign, IL 61820
Ph: (217)244-4682   Fax: (217)244-8082

Quarterly. $35.00/year for individuals. Journal dealing with experimental psychology and basic principles of psychology.

★6808★ **American Psychologist**

American Psychological Association
750 1st St. NE
Washington, DC 20002-4242
Ph: (202)336-6010   Fr: 800-374-2721

Monthly. Free to qualified subscribers; $131.00/year for nonmembers; $262.00/year for institutions. Official journal of the Association. Publishes empirical, theoretical, and professional articles.

★6809★ **Annals of Behavioral Medicine**

Society of Behavioral Medicine
103 S. Adams St.
Rockville, MD 20850
Ph: (301)251-2790   Fax: (301)279-6749

Quarterly. $135.00/year; $160.00/year for other countries. Journal describing the interactions of behavior and health.

★6810★ **Contemporary Psychology**

American Psychological Association
750 1st St. NE
Washington, DC 20002-4242
Ph: (202)336-6010   Fr: 800-374-2721

Monthly. $59.00/year for members; $122.00/year for nonmembers; $238.00/year for institutions. Journal presenting critical reviews of books, films, tapes, and other media representing a cross section of psychological literature.

★6811★ **EAP Digest**

Performance Resource Press
1863 Technology Dr.
Troy, MI 48083
Ph: (810)588-7733   Fax: (810)588-6633

Bimonthly. $8.00 for single issue; $46.00/year, $55.00/year for Canada; $64.00/year for other countries. Magazine covering planning, development, and administration of employee assistance programs.

★6812★ **Family Therapy News**

American Association for Marriage & Family Therapy
1100 17th St. NW, 10th Fl.
Washington, DC 20036
Ph: (202)452-0109   Fax: (202)223-2329

Bimonthly. $25.00/year for individuals; $40.00/year for institutions, Canada; $35.00/year for other countries; $4.00 for single issue. Newspaper on family therapy.

★6813★ **Journal of Behavioral Medicine**

Plenum Publishing Corp.
233 Spring St.
New York, NY 10013
Ph: (212)620-8000   Fax: (212)463-0742

Bimonthly. Journal focusing on behavioral science.

★6814★ **The Journal of Psychology: Interdisciplinary and Applied**

Heldref Publications
Helen Dwight Reid Educational Foundation
1319 18th St. NW
Washington, DC 20036-1802
Ph: (202)296-6267   Fax: (202)296-5149
Fr: 800-365-9753

Bimonthly. $110.00/year for individuals; $110.00/year for institutions; $18.50/year for single issue. Psychology journal which publishes a variety of research and theoretical articles.

★6815★ **Medical Economics**

Medical Economics, Inc.
5 Paragon Dr.
Montvale, NJ 07645-1742
Ph: (201)358-7208   Fax: (201)358-7260

Semimonthly. Magazine covering physicians practice management, professional relations, and financial affairs.

★6816★ **Mental Retardation**

American Association of Mental Retardation
444 N. Capitol St. NW, Ste. 846
Washington, DC 20001
Ph: (202)387-1968

Bimonthly. $75.00/year.

★6817★ **Pediatrics**

American Academy of Pediatrics
141 NW Point Blvd.
PO Box 927
Elk Grove Village, IL 60007-0927
Ph: (708)228-5005   Fax: (708)228-5097

Monthly. $50.00/year for individuals; $60.00/year for other countries. Medical journal reporting on pediatrics.

★6818★ **Psychiatric Annals**

Slack, Inc.
6900 Grove Rd.
Thorofare, NJ 08086-9447
Ph: (609)848-1000   Fax: (609)853-5991
Fr: 800-257-8290

Monthly. Journal analyzing concepts and practices in every area of psychiatry.

★6819★ *Psychiatric News*

American Psychiatric Press, Inc.
1400 K St. NW, Ste. 503
Washington, DC 20005
Ph: (202)682-6240   Fax: (202)692-6016
Fr: 800-368-5777

Semimonthly. $40.00/year for individuals. Professional magazine of the American Psychiatric Association.

★6820★ *Psychiatric Services*

American Psychiatric Press, Inc.
1400 K St. NW, Ste. 503
Washington, DC 20005
Ph: (202)682-6240   Fax: (202)692-6016
Fr: 800-368-5777

Monthly. $40.00/year for individuals; $60.00/year for institutions; $20 .00/year for students. Interdisciplinary mental health journal covering clinical, legal, and public policy issues.

★6821★ *Psychological Bulletin*

American Psychological Association
750 1st St. NE
Washington, DC 20002-4242
Ph: (202)336-6010   Fr: 800-374-2721

Bimonthly. $59.00/year for members; $126.00/year for nonmembers; $251 .00/year for institutions. Journal presenting comprehensive and integrative reviews and interpretations of critical substantive and methodological issues and practical problems from all the diverse areas of psychology.

★6822★ *The Psychotherapy Bulletin*

3900 E. Camelback, No. 200
Phoenix, AZ 85018
Ph: (602)952-8656

Quarterly. $8.00/year.

★6823★ *Social Service Jobs*

10 Angelica Dr.
Framingham, MA 01701
Ph: (508)620-8644

Biweekly. $109.00/year.

★6824★ *Teaching Exceptional Children*

The Council for Exceptional Children
1920 Association Dr.
Reston, VA 22091-1589
Ph: (703)620-3660   Fax: (703)264-9494
Fr: 800-CEC-READ

Quarterly. $35.00/year for individuals. Journal exploring practical methods for teaching talented and gifted children who have disabilities.

PLACEMENT AND JOB REFERRAL SERVICES

★6825★ **American Association of Psychiatric Technicians (AAPT)**

PO Box 14014
Phoenix, AZ 85063
Ph: (602)873-1890   Fax: (602)873-4616
Fr: 800-391-7589

Members: Psychiatric technicians, behavioral health technicians, mental health workers, counselors, social workers, psychiatric nurses, psychologists, and other individuals and companies interested in mental health. **Purpose:** Promotes professionalism in mental health industry. Encourages further education of mental health workers and provides national certification of mental health workers. Works with colleges, schools, and mental health facilities to develop education and training. Awards accreditation to mental health worker training programs. **Activities:** Offers placement informations.

★6826★ **American Public Health Association (APHA)**

1015 15th St. NW
Washington, DC 20005
Ph: (202)789-5600   Fax: (202)789-5681

Members: Professional organization of physicians, nurses, educators, academicians, environmentalists, epidemiologists, new professionals, social workers, health administrators, optometrists, podiatrists, pharmacists, dentists, nutritionists, health planners, other community and mental health specialists, and interested consumers. **Purpose:** Seeks to protect and promote personal, mental, and environmental health. **Activities:** Services include: promulgation of standards; establishment of uniform practices and procedures; development of the etiology of communicable diseases; research in public health; exploration of medical care programs and their relationships to public health. Sponsors job placement service.

★6827★ **American Society of Criminology (ASC)**

1314 Kinnear Rd., Ste. 212
Columbus, OH 43212
Ph: (614)292-9207   Fax: (614)292-6767

Members: Professional and academic criminologists; students of criminology in accredited universities; psychiatrists, psychologists, and sociologists. **Purpose:** To develop criminology as a science and academic discipline; to aid in the construction of criminological curricula in accredited universities; to upgrade the practitioner in criminological fields (police, prisons, probation, parole, delinquency workers). Conducts research programs; sponsors three student paper competitions. **Activities:** Provides placement service at annual convention.

★6828★ **Association for Behavior Analysis (ABA)**

Western Michigan University
258 Wood Hall
Kalamazoo, MI 49008
Ph: (616)387-4494   Fax: (616)387-4457

Members: Professionals, paraprofessionals, and students interested in the applied, experimental, and theoretical analysis of behavior. **Purpose:** Promotes the development of behavior analysis as a profession and science. Provides a forum for the discussion of issues; disseminates information on behavior analysis. Conducts workshops and seminars in 16 specialty areas including: Behavioral Pharmacology and Toxicology; Developmental Disabilities; Organizational Behavior Analysis. Offers continuing education credits for psychologists. **Activities:** Maintains archives of the association's publications; offers placement service.

★6829★ **Association for Chemoreception Sciences (AChemS)**

Panacea Associates
229 Westridge Dr.
Tallahassee, FL 32304
Ph: (904)576-5530   Fax: (904)898-2084

Members: Research scientists, experimental psychologists, and industrial researchers. **Purpose:** To study chemoreception (the physiological reception of chemical stimuli) by the senses of taste and smell. Conducts research on the differences in human and animal perception of chemical stimuli in taste and smell. Offers seminars, fellowships, and workshops. **Activities:** Maintains placement service. Bestows annual Best Student Presentation at conference.

★6830★ **International Association of Counselors and Therapists (IACT)**

10915 Bonita Beach Rd., Ste. 2142
Bonita Springs, FL 33923
Ph: (941)498-9710

Members: Mental health professionals, medical professionals, social workers, clergy, philosophers, educators, hypnotherapists, counselors, and individuals interested in the helping professions. **Purpose:** Promotes enhanced professional image and prestige for hypnotherapists. Provides a forum for exchange of information and ideas among practitioners of traditional and nontraditional therapies and methodologies; fosters unity among "grassroots" practitioners and those with advanced academic credentials. Facilitates the development of new therapy programs. **Activities:** Operates referral and placement services.

★6831★ **Psychology Society (PS)**

100 Beekman St.
New York, NY 10038-1810
Ph: (212)285-1872

Members: Professional membership is limited to psychologists who have a doctorate and are certified/licensed as such in the state where they practice. Associate membership is intended for teachers and researchers as well as persons who will attain professional status shortly. **Purpose:** Seeks to further the use of psychology in therapy, family and social problems, behavior modification, and treatment of drug abusers and prisoners. Encourages the use of psychology in the solution of social and political conflicts. Has established a referral service for laypeople and operates an information bureau to answer inquiries of authors, media, and students. Sponsors biennial overseas trip to enable members and their spouses to observe other programs and institutions. Collaborates with other associations. Evaluates programs in the use of psychology. Recommends legislation. **Activities:** Maintains placement service for members and recent graduates.

EMPLOYER DIRECTORIES AND NETWORKING LISTS

★6832★ Addiction & Recovery's National Treatment Resource Issue

Medquest Communications, Inc.
629 Euclid Ave., Ste. 500
Cleveland, OH 44114
Ph: (216)522-9700   Fax: (216)522-9707

Annual. Covers 3000 drug and alcohol treatment programs and facilities, addiction counselors, and physicians. Entries include institution name and address, addictions treated, type of facility, size.

★6833★ AHA Guide to the Health Care Field

Health Statistics Group
American Hospital Association (AHA)
1 N. Franklin
Chicago, IL 60606
Ph: (312)422-3501   Fax: (312)280-6015

Annual, July. $195.00, payment with order. Covers hospitals, multi-health care systems, freestanding ambulatory surgery centers, psychiatric facilities, long-term care facilities, substance abuse programs, hospices, Health Maintenance Organizations (HMOs), and other health-related organizations. Entries include: For hospitals: facility name, address, phone, administrator's name, number of beds, facilities and services, number of employees, expenses, other statistics. For other organizations: name, address, phone, name and title of contact. Arrangement: Geographical. Indexes: Hospital name.

★6834★ American Academy of Forensic Psychology—Directory of Diplomates

American Board of Forensic Psychology
Park Plaza
128 N. Craig St.
Pittsburgh, PA 15213
Ph: (412)681-3000   Fax: (412)681-1471

Irregular, latest edition spring 1995. $5.00. Covers Approximately 140 forensic psychologists. Entries include: Personal name, home and office addresses and phone numbers, biographical data, services. Arrangement: Alphabetical. Indexes: Geographical, specialty field.

★6835★ American Association for Correctional Psychology—Directory

American Association for Correctional Psychology
c/o Robert R. Smith
Counseling Program
West Virginia Graduate College
PO Box 1003
Institute, WV 25112-1003
Ph: (304)766-1929   Fax: (304)766-1942

Continuously updated. Free to members only. Covers 400 mental health professionals engaged in correctional and rehabilitative work in prisons, reformatories, juvenile institutions, probation and parole agencies, and in other aspects of criminal justice. Entries include: Name, affiliation, address, phone. Arrangement: Alphabetical.

★6836★ American Board of Professional Psychology—Directory of Diplomates

American Board of Professional Psychology
2100 E. Broadway, Ste. 313
Columbia, MO 65201
Ph: (314)875-1267   Fax: (314)443-1199

Biennial, even years. $25.00. Covers 3,200 psychologists who have passed the board's examination. Entries include: Name, office address, highest degree held, date of certification, practice areas. Arrangement: Alphabetical. Indexes: Geographical; speciality.

★6837★ American Group Psychotherapy Association—Membership Directory

American Group Psychotherapy Association
25 E. 21st St., 6th Fl.
New York, NY 10010
Ph: (212)477-2677

Annual, fall. $45.00. Covers 3,700 physicians, psychologists, clinical social workers, psychiatric nurses, and other mental health professionals interested in treatment of emotional problems by group methods. Entries include: Name, office or home address, highest degree held, office or home phone number. Arrangement: Alphabetical. Indexes: Geographical.

★6838★ American Psychological Association—APA Membership Register

American Psychological Association (APA)
750 1st St. NE
Washington, DC 20002-4242
Ph: (202)336-5500   Fax: (202)336-5502
Fr: 800-374-2721

Annual, April; except when APA Directory is published. $35.00, plus $3.50 shipping. Covers over 73,000 members in the United States, Canada, and abroad; also includes membership rosters of American Board of Professional Psychology and American Board of Psychological Hypnosis. Entries include: Name, office or home address, phone, fax, degrees and universities where obtained, election date, membership and divisional affiliations. Arrangement: Alphabetical. Indexes: Association division.

★6839★ Christian Association for Psychological Studies International—Membership Directory

Christian Association for Psychological Studies
PO Box 310400
New Braunfels, TX 78131-0400
Ph: (210)629-2277   Fax: (210)629-2342

Biennial, May, even years. $10.00. Covers 2,300 Christians involved in psychology, psychiatry, counseling, sociology, social work, ministry, and nursing. Entries include: Name, office address and phone number, highest degree held, area of occupational specialization, and career data. Arrangement: Geographical. Indexes: Alphabetical.

★6840★ Directory of the American Psychological Association

American Psychological Association (APA)
750 1st St. NE
Washington, DC 20002-4242
Ph: (202)336-5500   Fax: (202)336-5502
Fr: 800-374-2721

Quadrennial, latest edition July 1993. $70.00. Covers over 124,000 members, fellows, associate members, and affiliates in the United States, Canada, and abroad. Entries include: Name, office or home address, office and/or home phone, fax, e-mail address, major field of study, areas of specialization, highest academic degree (year, field, and institution), present position(s) and immediate past positions, state licensure/certification as a psychologist, U.S. state and Canadian provincial association memberships, and membership and divisional affiliations. Arrangement: Alphabetical. Indexes: Geographical, divisional.

★6841★ Directory of Counseling Services

International Association of Counseling Services
101 S. Whiting St., Ste. 211
Alexandria, VA 22304-3416
Ph: (703)823-9840   Fax: (703)823-9843

Annual, September. $50.00, payment with order. Covers about 200 accredited services in the United States and Canada concerned with psychological, educational, and vocational counseling, including those at colleges and universities, community and technical colleges, and public and private agencies. Entries include: Name, address, phone, hours of operation, director's name, service, clientele served. Arrangement: Geographical.

★6842★ Directory of Hospital Personnel

Medical Economics
5 Paragon Dr.
Montvale, NJ 07645-1725
Ph: (201)358-7500   Fax: (201)573-4956
Fr: 800-222-3045

Annual, September. $325.00, plus 7.50 shipping. Covers 200,000 executives at 7,100 U.S. hospitals. Entries include: Name of hospital, address, phone, number of beds, type and JCAHO status of hospital, names and titles of key department heads and staff, medical and nursing school affiliations; number of residents, interns, and nursing students. Arrangement: Geographical. Indexes: Hospital name, personnel, hospital size.

★6843★ Directory of Nationally Certified School Psychologists

National Association of School Psychologists
8455 Colesville Rd., Ste. 1000
Silver Spring, MD 20910
Ph: (301)608-0500

Triennial, latest edition December 1992. Cover nearly 12,000 psychologists who have been accredited by the NASP's National School Psychology Certification System and have been awarded the certificate of Nationally Certified School Psychologist (NCSP); limited international coverage. Entries include: Name, address, phone, position/title, employer, degree level, state certificates and licenses held, language fluency. Arrangement: Alphabetical. Indexes: Geographical.

★6844★ **Directory of Refugee Mental Health Professionals and Paraprofessionals**

Refugee Assistance Program–Mental Health Technical Assistance Center
University of Minnesota
Box 85
Mayo
Minneapolis, MN 55455

Covers Professionals who specialize in refugee mental health. Entries include: Name, address, phone, geographical area served and area of specialty. Arrangement: Geographical.

★6845★ **Hospital Blue Book**

Billian Publishing Co.
2100 Powers Ferry Rd., Ste. 300
Atlanta, GA 30339
Ph: (404)955-5656   Fax: (404)952-0669

Annual, spring. $154.50, national edition, plus $20.00 shipping. Covers more than 7,100 hospitals; some listings also appear in a separate southern edition of this publication. Entries include: Name of hospital, accreditation, mailing address, phone, fax, number of beds, type of facility (nonprofit, general, state, etc.); list of administrative personnel and chiefs of medical services, with specific titles. Arrangement: Geographical.

★6846★ **Hospital Market Atlas**

SMG Marketing Group, Inc.
1342 N. LaSalle Dr.
Chicago, IL 60610
Ph: (312)642-3026   Fax: (312)642-9729
Fr: 800-678-3026

Biennial, odd years. $495.00, payment with order. Covers over 7,000 hospitals, hospital systems and 480 group purchasing organizations. Entries include: Hospital or organization name, address, phone, county code, management, type of hospital service, number of beds, admissions, surgical operations, and emergency room visits. Arrangement: Geographical.

★6847★ **Hospitals Directory**

American Business Directories, Inc.
American Business Information, Inc.
5711 S. 86th Cir.
Omaha, NE 68127
Ph: (402)593-4600   Fax: (402)331-1505

Annual. $870.00, U.S. edition. Entries include: Name, address, phone (including area code), size of advertisement, year first in Yellow Pages, name of owner or manager, number of employees. Compiled from telephone company Yellow Pages, nationwide. Arrangement: Geographical.

★6848★ **International Council of Psychologists—Yearbook**

International Council of Psychologists
PO Box 62
Hopkinton, RI 02833-0062
Ph: (401)377-3092   Fax: (401)377-6013

Biennial, November of even years. Available to members only. Covers about 1,800 psy-

chologists and related mental health professionals. Entries include: Name, office and home address, career data, languages spoken and written, highest degree, fields of interest. Arrangement: Alphabetical. Indexes: Geographical, major field of interest.

★6849★ **Medical and Health Information Directory**

Gale Research
835 Penobscot Bldg.
Detroit, MI 48226-4094
Ph: (313)961-2242   Fax: (313)961-6083
Fr: 800-877-GALE

Approximately biennial; latest edition 1994. $195.00, per volume; $485.00, for the three-volume set. Covers in Volume 1, almost 18,600 medical and health oriented associations, organizations, institutions, and government agencies, including health maintenance organizations (HMOs), preferred provider organizations (PPOs), insurance companies, pharmaceutical companies, research centers, and medical and allied health schools. In Volume 2, nearly 11,800 medical book publishers; medical periodicals, directories, audiovisual producers and services, medical libraries and information centers, and electronic resources. In Volume 3, nearly 26,000 clinics, treatment centers, care programs, and counseling/diagnostic services for 30 subject areas. Entries include: Institution, service, or firm name, address, phone; many include names of key personnel and, when pertinent, descriptive annotation. Arrangement: Classified by organization activity, service, etc. Indexes: Each volume has a complete alphabetical name and keyword index.

★6850★ **Mental Health Directory**

Office of Consumer, Family & Public Information
Center for Mental Health Services
U.S. Substance Abuse & Mental Health Services Administration
5600 Fishers Ln., Rm. 15-18
Rockville, MD 20857
Ph: (301)443-2792

Irregular, latest edition 1990. $23.00. Covers hospitals, treatment centers, outpatient clinics, day/night facilities, residential treatment centers for emotionally disturbed children, residential supportive programs such as halfway houses, and mental health centers offering mental health assistance; not included are substance abuse programs, Veteran's Administration programs, nursing homes, programs for the developmentally disabled, and organizations in which fees are retained by individual members. Entries include: Name, address, phone. Arrangement: Geographical.

★6851★ **Mental Health Services Directory**

American Business Directories, Inc.
American Business Information, Inc.
5711 S. 86th Cir.
Omaha, NE 68127
Ph: (402)593-4600   Fax: (402)331-1505

Annual. $1,095.00, payment with order. Entries include: Name, address, phone (including area code), size of advertisement, year first in Yellow Pages, name of owner or manager, number of employees. Compiled

from telephone company Yellow Pages, nationwide. Arrangement: Geographical.

★6852★ **Mental Health and Social Work Career Directory**

Gale Research
835 Penobscot Bldg.
Detroit, MI 48226-4094
Ph: (313)961-2242   Fax: (313)961-6083
Fr: 800-877-GALE

Latest edition 1993. $34.00; $17.95 (paper). Covers over 300 agencies, organizations, and companies offering entry-level positions in mental health, social work, counseling, psychology, etc.; sources of help-wanted ads, professional associations, producers of videos, databases, career guides, and professional guides and handbooks. Entries include: For organizations offering positions: name, address, phone, description, names and titles of key personnel, number of employees, average number of entry-level positions available, human resources contact, description of internship opportunities including contact, type and number available, application procedures, qualifications, and duties. For others: name or title, address, phone, description. Paperback edition is available from Visible Ink Press. Arrangement: Organizations offering positions are alphabetical; others are classified by type of resource. Indexes: Name, keyword.

★6853★ **National Directory of Children, Youth & Families Services**

Marion L. Peterson, Publisher
PO Box 1837
Longmont, CO 80502-1837
Ph: (303)776-7539   Fax: 800-845-6452
Fr: 800-343-6681

Annual, July. $78.00, plus $6.00 shipping, postpaid. Covers child, youth, and family-oriented social services, health and mental health services, and juvenile/family court and youth advocacy services in state and private agencies, major cities, and 3,100 counties; also covers runaway youth centers, child abuse projects, congressional committees, clearinghouses, and national organizations concerned with family health and welfare; buyers' guide to specialized services and products. Entries include: Agency listings include agency name, address, phone, names of principal executives and staff, description of services. Arrangement: Geographical.

★6854★ **National Directory of Private Social Agencies**

Croner Publications, Inc.
34 Jericho Tpke.
Jericho, NY 11753
Ph: (516)333-9085   Fax: (516)338-4986
Fr: 800-441-4033

Base edition supplied upon order; monthly updates. $74.95, plus $4.95 shipping. Number of listings: Over 15,000. Entries include: Agency name, address, phone, name and title of contact, description of services. Arrangement: Geographical. Indexes: Service, agency type.

★6855★ Psychologists Directory

American Business Directories, Inc.
American Business Information, Inc.
5711 S. 86th Cir.
Omaha, NE 68127
Ph: (402)593-4600   Fax: (402)331-1505

Annual. $1,310.00. Entries include: Name, address, phone (including area code), size of advertisement, year first in Yellow Pages, name of owner or manager, number of employees. Regional editions available. Compiled from telephone company Yellow Pages, nationwide. Arrangement: Geographical.

★6856★ Psychotherapists Directory

American Business Directories, Inc.
American Business Information, Inc.
5711 S. 86th Cir.
Omaha, NE 68127
Ph: (402)593-4600   Fax: (402)331-1505

Annual. $790.00, U.S. edition. Entries include: Name, address, phone (including area code), size of advertisement, year first in Yellow Pages, name of owner or manager, number of employees. Compiled from telephone company Yellow Pages, nationwide. Arrangement: Geographical.

★6857★ Who's Who Among Human Services Professionals

National Register Publishing
Reed Reference Publishing
121 Chanlon Rd.
New Providence, NJ 07974-1541
Ph: (908)464-6400   Fr: 800-621-9669

Latest edition February 1992; suspended indefinitely. $129.00. Covers nearly 20,000 human service professionals, in such fields as counseling, social work, psychology, audiology, and speech pathology. Entries include: Name, address, education, work experience, professional association memberships. Arrangement: Alphabetical.

★6858★ World Sport Psychology Sourcebook

Human Kinetics
1607 N. Market St.
Box 5076
Champaign, IL 61825-5076
Ph: (217)351-5076   Fax: (217)351-2674
Fr: 800-747-4457

Irregular. previous edition 1981. latest edition 1992. $32.00. Covers Approximately 1,800 sport psychologists worldwide. Entries include: Name, address, phone, biographical data, academic interests; languages spoken, written, or read. Arrangement: Geographical. Indexes: Name.

HANDBOOKS AND MANUALS

★6859★ Career Choices for the 90's for Students of Psychology

Walker and Company
435 Hudson St.
New York, NY 10014
Ph: (212)727-8300   Fax: (212)727-0984
Fr: 800-289-2553

Prepared by the Career Associates staff.

1990. $9.95. 166 pages. Discusses alternatives for students of psychology. Offers advice on how to break into the field and how to move up. Covers where and who the employers are, internship possibilities, and professional networking associations. Comprehensive guide to career and job search planning.

★6860★ Encyclopedia of Careers and Vocational Guidance

J. G. Ferguson Publishing Co.
200 W. Monroe, Ste. 250
Chicago, IL 60606
Ph: (312)580-5480

William E. Hopke. Ninth edition, 1993. $129.95; $199.95 (CD-ROM). Four-volume set that profiles 900 occupations and describes job trends in 71 industries. Includes career description, educational requirements, history of the job, methods of entry, advancement, employment outlook, earnings, conditions of work, social and psychological factors, and sources of further information. Contains career and employment information for this field.

★6861★ Opportunities in Child Care Careers

VGM Career Horizons
4255 W. Touhy Ave.
Lincolnwood, IL 60646-1975
Ph: (847)679-5500   Fax: (847)679-2494
Fr: 800-323-4900

Renee Wittenberg. 1995. $14.95; $11.95 (paper). 160 pages. Discusses various job opportunities and how to secure a position. Illustrated.

★6862★ Opportunities in Health and Medical Careers

VGM Career Horizons
4255 W. Touhy Ave.
Lincolnwood, IL 60646-1975
Ph: (847)679-5500   Fax: (847)679-2494
Fr: 800-323-4900

Donald Snook, Jr. and Leo D'Orazio. 1993. $14.95; $11.95 (paper). Covers the full range of medical and health occupations. Illustrated.

★6863★ Opportunities in Psychology Careers

VGM Career Horizons
4255 W. Touhy Ave.
Lincolnwood, IL 60646-1975
Ph: (847)679-5500   Fax: (847)679-2494
Fr: 800-323-4900

Donald E. Super and Charles McAfee Super. 1994. $14.95; $11.95 (paper). A guide to planning for and building a career in the field. Includes bibliography and illustrations.

★6864★ Opportunities in Social Science Careers

VGM Career Horizons
4255 W. Touhy Ave.
Lincolnwood, IL 60646-1975
Ph: (847)679-5500   Fax: (847)679-2494
Fr: 800-323-4900

Rosanne J. Marek. 1990. $14.95; $11.95 (paper). 160 pages. Profiles job opportunities in education, government, and business,

along with their salary levels and outlook in the years to come. Illustrated.

★6865★ Opportunities in Sports and Athletics

VGM Career Horizons
4255 W. Touhy Ave.
Lincolnwood, IL 60646-1975
Ph: (847)679-5500   Fax: (847)679-2494
Fr: 800-323-4900

William Ray Heitzmann. 1994. $14.95; $11.95 (paper). A guide to planning for and seeking opportunities in this growing field. Illustrated.

★6866★ Opportunities in Sports Medicine Careers

VGM Career Horizons
4255 W. Touhy Ave.
Lincolnwood, IL 60646-1975
Ph: (847)679-5500   Fax: (847)679-2494
Fr: 800-323-4900

William Ray Heitzmann. 1995. $14.95; $11.95 (paper). 160 pages. Discusses a variety of opportunities in this field and how to pursue them. Contains bibliography and illustrations.

★6867★ Psychology as a Health Care Profession

American Psychological Association (APA)
750 First St. NE
Washington, DC 20002-4242
Ph: (202)955-7600   Fr: 800-374-2721

Pamphlet. 20 pages. Discusses the psychologist's role in the health-care field and describes places of employment.

OTHER SOURCES

★6868★ American Almanac of Jobs and Salaries 1994-95

Avon Books
1350 Avenue of the Americas, 2nd Fl.
New York, NY 10019
Ph: (212)261-6800   Fr: 800-238-0658

John Wright. Revised edition, 1993. $17.00. 704 pages. This is a comprehensive guide to the wages of hundreds of occupations in a wide variety of industries and organizations.

★6869★ American Association of Mental Health Professionals in Corrections (AAMHPC)

John S. Zil, M.D., J.D.
PO Box 163359
Sacramento, CA 95816-9359
Ph: (707)864-0910   Fax: (707)864-0910

Members: Psychiatrists, psychologists, social workers, nurses, and other mental health professionals; individuals working in correctional settings. **Purpose:** Fosters the progress of behavioral sciences related to corrections. Goals are: to improve the treatment, rehabilitation, and care of the mentally ill, mentally retarded, and emotionally disturbed; to promote research and professional education in psychiatry and allied fields in corrections; to advance standards of correctional services and facilities; to foster cooperation between individuals concerned with the medical, psychological, social, and legal aspects of corrections; to share knowledge with other medical practitioners, scientists, and the public.

★6870★ American Psychological Association (APA)

750 First St. NE
Washington, DC 20002-4242
Ph: (202)336-5500

Members: Scientific and professional society of psychologists. Students participate as affiliates. **Purpose:** Works to advance psychology as a science, a profession, and as a means of promoting human welfare.

★6871★ Association of Black Psychologists (ABPsi)

PO Box 55999
Washington, DC 20040-5999
Ph: (202)722-0808   Fax: (202)722-5941

Members: Professional psychologists and others in associated disciplines. **Purpose:** Aims to: enhance the psychological well-being of black people in America; define mental health in consonance with newly established psychological concepts and standards; develop policies for local, state, and national decision-making that have impact on the mental health of the black community; support established black sister organizations and aid in the development of new, independent black institutions to enhance the psychological, educational, cultural, and economic situation. **Activities:** Offers training and information on AIDS. Conducts seminars, workshops, and research.

★6872★ Association for Humanistic Education and Development (AHEAD)

5999 Stevenson Ave.
Alexandria, VA 22304
Ph: (703)823-9800   Fax: (703)823-0252
Fr: 800-347-6647

Members: A division of the American Counseling Association. Teachers, educational administrators, community agency workers, counselors, school social workers, and psychologists; others interested in the area of human development. **Purpose:** Aims to assist individuals in improving their quality of life. Provides forum for the exchange of information about humanistically-oriented administrative and instructional practices. Supports humanistic practices and research on instructional and organizational methods for facilitating humanistic education; encourages cooperation among related professional groups.

★6873★ Association of Psychology Postdoctoral and Internship Centers (APPIC)

733 15th St. NW, Ste. 717
Washington, DC 20005
Ph: (202)347-0022   Fax: (202)347-8480

Members: Veterans Administration hospitals, medical centers, state hospitals, university counseling centers, and other facilities that provide internship and postdoctoral programs in professional psychology. **Purpose:** Promotes activities that assist in the development of professional psychology training programs. **Activities:** Serves as a clearinghouse to provide college students with internship placement assistance at member facilities. Conducts workshops and seminars on training procedures in professional psychology.

★6874★ *Career Encounters: Psychology*

Cambridge Career Products
PO Box 2153
Dept. CC15
Charleston, WV 25328-2153
Ph: (304)744-9323   Fax: (304)744-9351
Fr: 800-468-4227

Video. $99.95. 25 minutes. Professionals shown in a variety of settings discuss different aspects of their careers.

★6875★ *Directory of Child Life Programs*

Child Life Council
7910 Woodmont Ave., Ste. 310
Bethesda, MD 20814
Ph: (301)654-1343   Fax: (301)654-4964

Irregular. $22.00, plus $3.00 shipping. Covers Nearly 150 internships, fellowships, and other practical teaching experiences in hospitals for students of child life activity. Entries include: Facility name, address, phone, name of individual in charge of the practicum; number of hours and number of weeks for practicum; beginning dates, if specified; number of students accepted each term; total number of students accepted for the year; colleges from which students are generally referred; areas of study from which students generally come; fees; stipend and other benefits; prerequisites; whether application is to be made to college or hospital; level of student generally accepted; practicum experiences available; form of evaluation. Arrangement: Geographical.

★6876★ Employee Assistance Society of North America (EASNA)

2728 Phillips
Berkley, MI 48072
Ph: (810)545-3888   Fax: (810)545-5528

Members: Individuals in the field of employee assistance, including psychiatrists, psychologists, and managers. **Purpose:** Facilitates

communication among members; provides resource information; serves as a network for employee assistance programs nationwide. Conducts research.

★6877★ International Council of Psychologists (ICP)

Psych Department
San Marcos, TX 78666-4601
Ph: (512)245-7605   Fax: (512)245-3153

Members: Psychologists and individuals professionally active in fields allied to psychology. **Purpose:** Seeks to advance psychology and further the application of its scientific findings. Conducts continuing education workshops and educational programs.

★6878★ *Internship Programs in Professional Psychology, Including Post-Doctoral Training Programs*

Association of Psychology Postdoctoral and Internship Centers
733 15th St. NW, Ste. 719
Washington, DC 20005
Ph: (202)347-0022   Fax: (202)347-8480

Annual, September. $30.00. Covers institutions offering PhD internship programs in professional psychology. Entries include: Institution name, name and address of contact, description of program including percentage of time spent in supervision and in seminar attendance, theoretical orientation, number of interns, stipend, admission requirements. Arrangement: Geographical.

★6879★ National Association of School Psychologists (NASP)

4340 East-West Hwy., Ste. 402
Bethesda, MD 20814-4411
Ph: (301)657-0270   Fax: (301)657-0275

Members: School psychologists. **Purpose:** Serves the mental health and educational needs of all children and youth. Encourages and provides opportunities for professional growth of individual members. Informs the public on the services and practice of school psychology, and advances the standards of the profession. **Activities:** Operates national school psychologist certification system. Sponsors children's services.

★6880★ Society for the Advancement of Social Psychology (SASP)

Department of Psychology
Mercer University
Macon, GA 31207
Ph: (912)752-2972   Fax: (912)752-2956

Members: Social psychologists and students in social psychology. **Purpose:** Advances social psychology as a profession by facilitating communication among social psychologists and improving dissemination and utilization of social psychological knowledge.

Public Relations Specialists

SOURCES OF HELP-WANTED ADS

★6881★ *Editor & Publisher*

Editor & Publisher Co.
11 W. 19th St.
New York, NY 10011
Ph: (212)675-4380   Fax: (212)929-1259
Weekly (Sat.). Magazine focusing on journalism, advertising, and printing equipment.

★6882★ *The Insider Newsletter*

Sports Careers
PO Box 10129
Phoenix, AZ 85064
Fr: 800-776-7877

Semimonthly. Subscription free to members; $99.00/six months for nonmembers. Provides articles on career development, salaries, and trends for the sports industry. Includes "Career Connections," an insert listing 60-75 job opportunities and internships within each issue.

★6883★ *PR Marcom Jobs East*

Rachel PR Services
208 E. 51st St., No. 1600
New York, NY 10022
Ph: (212)962-9100

Biweekly. Provides news of job openings in public relations, marketing, journalism, communications, public relations agencies and corporations, and freelance and temporary writing positions. Focuses on the New York City, Washingtion, DC, and Boston, and surrounding areas.

★6884★ *PR Marcom Jobs West: Northern California–Pacific Northwest*

Rachel PR Services
298 4th Ave., No. 344
San Francisco, CA 94118
Ph: (415)334-7124

Biweekly. Provides information concerning job openings in public relations, journalism, marketing, communications, public relations agencies and corporations, and freelance and temporary writing positions. Focuses on opportunities in Northern California and Pacific Northwest areas.

★6885★ *PR Marcom Jobs West: Southern California*

Rachel PR Services
1650 S. Pacific Coast Hwy., Ste. 200-C
Redondo Beach, CA 90277
Ph: (310)792-1313

Biweekly. Provides information concerning job openings in public relations, journalism, marketing, communications, public relations agencies and corporations, and freelance and temporary writing positions. Focuses on opportunities in Southern California.

★6886★ *The Professional Communicator*

Women in Communications, Inc.
10605 Judicial Dr., Ste. A4
Fairfax, VA 22030-5167
Ph: (703)920-5555   Fax: (703)920-5556

Magazine covering communications issues, trends and news.

★6887★ *Public Relations Journal*

Public Relations Society of America
33 Irving Pl.
New York, NY 10003-2376
Ph: (212)460-1413   Fax: (212)995-0757

$45.00/year for individuals. Public relations magazine containing articles on theory and practice for practitioners and those in related fields.

PLACEMENT AND JOB REFERRAL SERVICES

★6888★ Agricultural Relations Council (ARC)

1629 K St. NW, Ste. 1100
Washington, DC 20006
Ph: (202)785-6710   Fax: (202)331-4212

Members: Professional society of agricultural public relations executives employed by private business firms, associations, publications, and government agencies. **Activities:** Operates placement service.

★6889★ Media Alliance (MA)

814 Mission St., Ste. 205
San Francisco, CA 94103

Members: Writers, photographers, editors, broadcast workers, public relations people, and others who support free press and independent journalism. **Purpose:** Seeks to change what the alliance calls the characteristic cutthroat competitive attitude among its practitioners by encouraging contact and discussion and developing structures enabling members to assist each other and to mobilize the group's resources on behalf of mutually agreed-upon projects. **Activities:** Maintains job file. Conducts continuing professional education classes. Maintains speakers' bureau.

★6890★ Public Relations Society of America (PRSA)

33 Irving Pl., 3rd Fl.
New York, NY 10003
Ph: (212)995-2230   Fax: (212)995-0757
Fr: 800-WER-PRSA

Members: Professional society of public relations practitioners in business and industry, counseling firms, government, associations, hospitals, schools, and nonprofit organizations. **Activities:** Conducts professional development programs. Maintains job referral service, and research information center. Offers accreditation program.

★6891★ Sports Careers

PO Box 10129
Phoenix, AZ 85064
Fr: 800-776-7877

Career development firm for the sports industry. Provides career-related programs, conferences, seminars, educational products, and publications. Offers Career Enhancement Profile Program and Resume Development Kit. Maintains an electronic resume bank for members which is available to sports companies and organizations. Publishes newsletter listing job opportunities.

EMPLOYER DIRECTORIES AND NETWORKING LISTS

★6892★ **ADWEEK Agency Directory**

ADWEEK Directories
1515 Broadway, 12th Fl.
New York, NY 10036
Ph: (212)536-6504   Fax: (212)536-5321

Annual, August. $250.00, plus $12.00 shipping. Covers over 4,000 U.S. advertising agencies, public relations firms, media buying services, direct marketing and related organizations. Entries include: Agency name, address, phone, fax; names and titles of key personnel; major accounts; headquarters location; major subsidiaries and other operating units; year founded; number of employees; fee income; billings; percentage of billings by medium. Arrangement: Alphabetical. Indexes: Geographical; parent company, subsidiary, division; fields served; ethnic sprcialities; organizations.

★6893★ **ADWEEK/New England Edition—Guide to New England Advertising, Public Relations, and Direct Marketing Agencies Issue**

Adweek New England
100 Boylston St.
Boston, MA 02116
Ph: (617)482-0876   Fax: (617)482-2921

Annual, November. $35.00. Covers about 500 advertising, public relations, and direct marketing firms in New England. Entries include: Firm name, address, phone, year founded, number of full-time employees and free-lancers, names and titles of key personnel, specialties, clients. Arrangement: Alphabetical.

★6894★ **Communications Consultants Directory**

American Business Directories, Inc.
American Business Information, Inc.
5711 S. 86th Cir.
Omaha, NE 68127
Ph: (402)593-4600   Fax: (402)331-1505

Annual. $385.00, U.S. edition. Entries include: Name, address, phone (including area code), size of advertisement, year first in Yellow Pages, name of owner or manager, number of employees. Compiled from telephone company Yellow Pages, nationwide. Arrangement: Geographical.

★6895★ **Directory of Multicultural Public Relations Professionals**

Public Relations Society of America
33 Irving Pl., 3rd Fl.
New York, NY 10003
Ph: (212)995-2230   Fax: (212)995-0757
Fr: 800-WER-PRSA

Irregular, latest edition 1993. $40.00, plus $3.00 shipping. Covers about 190 minority individuals in the field of public relations. Entries include: Individual name, title, company name, address, phone. Arrangement: Geographical.

★6896★ **National School Public Relations Association—Directory**

National School Public Relations Association
1501 Lee Hwy.
Arlington, VA 22209
Ph: (703)528-6713   Fax: (703)528-7017
Fr: 800-48-NSPRA

Annual, January. Available to members only. Covers approximately 2,800 school system public relations directors, school administrators, principals, and others who are members of the National School Public Relations Association. Entries include: Name, affiliation, address, phone. Arrangement: Geographical.

★6897★ **O'Dwyer's Directory of Corporate Communications**

J. R. O'Dwyer Co., Inc.
271 Madison Ave.
New York, NY 10016
Ph: (212)679-2471   Fax: (212)683-2750

Annual, July. $110.00. Covers public relations departments of approximately 4,450 major United States companies (listed on the New York Stock Exchange and in the Fortune list of 1,000 largest firms); also includes similar information on over 1,300 large trade associations and foreign embassies in the United States. Arrangement: Alphabetical. Indexes: Geographical, product.

★6898★ **O'Dwyer's Directory of Public Relations Executives**

J. R. O'Dwyer Co. Inc.
271 Madison Ave.
New York, NY 10016
Ph: (212)679-2471   Fax: (212)683-2750

Annual, November/December. $70.00. Covers about 6,200 corporation and public relations agency executives and private counselors. Entries include: Name, business affiliation, address, phone; personal, education, and career data. Arrangement: Alphabetical.

★6899★ **O'Dwyer's Directory of Public Relations Firms**

J. R. O'Dwyer Co., Inc.
271 Madison Ave.
New York, NY 10016
Ph: (212)679-2471   Fax: (212)683-2750

Annual, April/May. $125.00. Covers over 2,200 public relations firms; international coverage. Entries include: Firm name, address, phone, principal executives, branch and overseas offices, billings, date founded, and clients. Arrangement: Geographical by country. Indexes: Specialty (beauty and fashions, finance/investor, etc.), geographical, client.

★6900★ **PR Agency Yellow Pages**

Inside PR
235 W. 48th St., No. 34A
New York, NY 10036
Ph: (212)245-8680   Fax: (212)245-8699

Annual. $50.00. Covers public relations firms in the U.S. and Canada. Entries include: Company name, address, phone. Arrangement: Alphabetical. Indexes: Geographical, firm specialty.

★6901★ **Public Relations Consultants Directory**

American Business Directories, Inc.
American Business Information, Inc.
5711 S. 86th Cir.
Omaha, NE 68127
Ph: (402)593-4600   Fax: (402)331-1505

$560.00, payment with order. Entries include: Name, address, phone (including area code). Compiled from telephone company Yellow Pages, nationwide. Arrangement: Geographical.

★6902★ **Public Relations Journal— Register Issue**

Public Relations Society of America (PRSA)
33 Irving Pl.
New York, NY 10003-2376
Ph: (212)460-1468   Fax: (212)995-0757

Annual, June. $120.00. Publication includes: About 15,475 public relations practitioners in business, government, education, etc., who are members. Entries include: Name, professional affiliation and title, address, phone, membership rank. Arrangement: Alphabetical. Indexes: Geographical, organizational.

★6903★ **Public Relations Society of America, Chicago Chapter— Membership Directory**

Public Relations Society of America, Chicago Chapter
30 N. Michigan Ave., Ste. 508
Chicago, IL 60602
Ph: (312)372-7744

Annual, October. $50.00. Covers about 550 individuals engaged in public relations and related occupations in Chicago. Entries include: Name, title, affiliation, address, phone, type of membership, year joined, employment history. Arrangement: Alphabetical. Indexes: Firm name.

★6904★ **Reed's Worldwide Directory of Public Relations Organizations**

Pigafetta Press
PO Box 39244
Washington, DC 20016
Ph: (202)244-2580   Fax: (202)244-2581

Annual, May. $85.00, plus $5.00 shipping. Covers Approximately 225 professional public relations associations in 75 countries. Entries include: Association name, address, phone, publications, current officers, activities, and history of the organization. Arrangement: Geographical; separate section for international organizations.

★6905★ **Sports Market Place Register**

Sports Careers
PO Box 10129
Phoenix, AZ 85064
Fr: 800-776-7877

Annual $59.00. Resource guide for the sports industry. Lists over 24,000 national and international sports business contacts. Entries include: organization name, name of key executive, address, and phone and fax numbers. Provides listings for: Individual and Multiple Sports Organizations/Teams/Media; College Sports; Sponsorship/Marketing/ Event Management; Sports Agents/Lawyers;

Manufacturers/Retailers. Indexes: Geographic and Alphabetical.

★6906★ World Book of IABC Communicators

International Association of Business
  Communicators
1 Hallidie Plaza, Ste. 600
San Francisco, CA 94102
Ph: (415)433-3400   Fax: (415)362-8762

Annual, January. $100.00. Covers about 13,000 association members involved with organizational, corporate, and public relations and other communications fields. Entries include: Name, address, title, code indicating type of business or organization, phone. Arrangement: Alphabetical. Indexes: Geographical, then classified by type of business.

HANDBOOKS AND MANUALS

★6907★ Career Choices for the 90's for Students of Business

Walker and Company
435 Hudson St.
New York, NY 10014
Ph: (212)727-8300   Fax: (212)727-0984
Fr: 800-289-2553

Prepared by the Career Associates staff. 1990. $9.95. 166 pages. Discusses alternatives for students of business. Offers advice on how to break into the field and how to move up. Covers where and who the employers are, internship possibilities, and professional networking associations. Comprehensive guide to career and job search planning.

★6908★ Career Choices for the 90's for Students of Communications and Journalism

Walker and Company
435 Hudson St.
New York, NY 10014
Ph: (212)727-8300   Fax: (212)727-0984
Fr: 800-289-2553

Prepared by the Career Associates staff. 1990. $8.95. 166 pages. Discusses alternatives for students of communications and journalism. Offers advice on how to break into the field and how to move up. Covers where and who the employers are, internship possibilities, and professional networking associations. Comprehensive guide to career and job search planning.

★6909★ Career Choices for the 90's for Students of Psychology

Walker and Company
435 Hudson St.
New York, NY 10014
Ph: (212)727-8300   Fax: (212)727-0984
Fr: 800-289-2553

Prepared by the Career Associates staff. 1990. $9.95. 166 pages. Discusses alternatives for students of psychology. Offers advice on how to break into the field and how to move up. Covers where and who the employers are, internship possibilities, and professional networking associations. Com-

prehensive guide to career and job search planning.

★6910★ Career Information Center

Macmillan Publishing Co.
200 Old Tappan Rd.
Old Tappan, NJ 07675
Ph: (609)461-6500   Fr: 800-223-2336

Visual Education Center Staff. Fifth edition, 1992. $229.00. This 13-volume set profiles over 600 occupations. Each occupational profile describes job duties, educational requirements, how to get the job, advancement possibilities, employment outlook, working conditions, earnings and benefits, and where to write for more information.

★6911★ Career Opportunities in Advertising and Public Relations

Facts on File, Inc.
11 Penn Plaza, 15th Fl.
New York, NY 10001-2006
Ph: (212)967-8800   Fax: 800-678-3633
Fr: 800-322-8755

Shelly Field. Revised edition, 1996. $29.95; $15.95 (paper). 320 pages. Provides the job seeker with information about locating and landing the right position. Includes detailed job descriptions for many specific positions and lists trade associations, recruiting organizations, and major agencies. Contains index and bibliography.

★6912★ Career Opportunities in Art

Facts on File, Inc.
11 Penn Plaza, 15th Fl.
New York, NY 10001-2006
Ph: (212)967-8800   Fax: 800-678-3633
Fr: 800-322-8755

Susan H. Haubenstock and David Joselit. Revised edition, 1994. $29.95; $15.95 (paper). 208 pages. This book profiles seventy-five jobs that can be found in the art field. Each profile includes a career description, career ladder, employment and advancement prospects, education, experience and skills required, salary range, and tips for entry into the field.

★6913★ Career Opportunities for Writers

Facts on File, Inc.
11 Penn Plaza, 15th Fl.
New York, NY 10001-2006
Ph: (212)967-8800   Fax: 800-678-3633
Fr: 800-322-8755

Rosemary Guiley. Third edition, 1995. $29.95; $15.95 (paper). Describes more than 100 jobs in eight major fields, offering such details as duties, salaries, perquisites, employment and advancement opportunities, organizations to join, and opportunities for women and minorities.

★6914★ Careers in Communications

VGM Career Horizons
4255 W. Touhy Ave.
Lincolnwood, IL 60646-1975
Ph: (847)679-5500   Fax: (847)679-2494
Fr: 800-323-4900

Shonan Noronha. 1994. $17.95; $13.95 (paper). 176 pages. Examines the fields of journalism, photography, radio, television,

film, public relations, and advertising. Gives concrete details on job locations and how to secure a job. Suggests many resources for job hunting.

★6915★ Careers in Health and Fitness

Rosen Publishing Group, Inc.
29 E. 21st St.
New York, NY 10010
Ph: (212)777-3017   Fax: (212)777-0277
Fr: 800-237-9932

Jackie Heron. Revised edition, 1990. $14.95. 160 pages. Contains occupational profiles for this field, including information on job duties, skills, advantages, basic equipment used, employment possibilities, certification, and salary.

★6916★ Careers in Public Relations

Public Relations Society of America
33 Irving Pl., 3rd Fl.
New York, NY 10003-2376
Ph: (212)995-2230

$2.00. This eight-page booklet describes the field of public relations, including salaries, nature of the work, and finding a job. Lists necessary personal qualifications, educational preparation, and work experience.

★6917★ The Encyclopedia of Career Choices for the 1990s: Guide to Entry-Level Jobs

Perigree Books
The Berkley Publishing Group
PO Box 506
East Rutherford, NJ 07073
Ph: (201)933-9292   Fr: 800-223-0510

Career Associates Staff. 1992. $19.95. 862 pages. Describes 500 entry-level careers in a variety of industries. Presents qualifications required, working conditions, salary, internships, and professional associations.

★6918★ Flying High in Travel

John Wiley and Sons
605 3rd Ave.
New York, NY 10158
Ph: (212)850-6000   Fr: 800-225-5945

Karen Rubin. Second edition, 1992. $19.95. 336 pages. A guide to careers and job hunting in the travel industry. Describes the many job opportunities available, from writing to hotel management to law. Includes information on educational preparation, training, and job hunting.

★6919★ The Harvard Guide to Careers in the Mass Media

Bob Adams, Inc.
260 Center St.
Holbrook, MA 02343
Ph: (617)767-8100   Fax: (617)767-0994
Fr: 800-872-5627

John Noble. 1989. $7.95. 202 pages. Each section of the book evaluates one media profession in depth and contains an industry profile, a career profile that describes positions available in that area, information about current salary ranges, industry-specific job-hunting tips and strategies, and a case study outlining the methods that were used in a successful job hunt.

★6920★ Jobs for English Majors and Other Smart People

Peterson's
PO Box 2123
Princeton, NJ 08543-2123
Ph: (609)243-9111   Fax: (609)243-9150
Fr: 800-338-3282

John L. Munschauer. Third edition, 1991. $11.95. 174 pages. Shows job seekers how to position themselves in the marketplace and how to demonstrate the ability to meet the needs of prospective employers.

★6921★ Liberal Arts Jobs: What They Are and How to Get Them

Peterson's
PO Box 2123
Princeton, NJ 08543-2123
Ph: (609)243-9111   Fax: (609)243-9150
Fr: 800-338-3282

Burton Jay Nadler. Second edition, 1989. $9.95. 153 pages. Presents a list of the top 20 fields for liberal arts majors, covering more than 300 job opportunities. Discusses strategies for going after those jobs, including guidance on the language of a successful job search, informational interviews, and making networking work.

★6922★ Marketing and Sales Career Directory

Gale Research
835 Penobscot Bldg.
Detroit, MI 48226-4094
Ph: (313)961-2242   Fax: (313)961-6083
Fr: 800-877-GALE

Bradley Morgan. Fourth edition, 1992. $39.00. 341 pages. Features extensive listings of contacts and entry-level job opportunities at major corporations, research supplier firms, and major advertising and public relations agencies nationwide. Aimed at students looking for jobs in any area of marketing, advertising, or sales on the corporate side.

★6923★ 100 Best Careers for the Year 2000

Prentice Hall General Reference
15 Columbus Cir.
New York, NY 10023
Ph: (212)373-8500   Fr: 800-223-2348

Shelly Field. 1992. $15.00 (paper). Covers 100 of the fastest growing jobs. The publication is divided into 11 general employment sections. Specific careers are covered within each section. Provides job description, responsibilities, employment opportunities, earnings, education and training, advancement opportunities, and experience and qualifications for each occupation.

★6924★ Opportunities in Insurance Careers

VGM Career Horizons
4255 W. Touhy Ave.
Lincolnwood, IL 60646-1975
Ph: (847)679-5500   Fax: (847)679-2494
Fr: 800-323-4900

Robert Schrayer. 1994. $14.95; $11.95 (paper). A guide to planning for and seeking opportunities in the field. Contains bibliography and illustrations.

★6925★ Opportunities in Journalism Careers

VGM Career Horizons
4255 W. Touhy Ave.
Lincolnwood, IL 60646-1975
Ph: (847)679-5500   Fax: (847)679-2494
Fr: 800-323-4900

Jim Patten and Donald L. Ferguson. 1993. $14.95; $11.95 (paper). 160 pages. Outlines opportunities in every field of journalism, including newspaper reporting and editing, magazine and book publishing, corporate communications, advertising and public relations, freelance writing, and teaching. Covers how to prepare for and enter each field, outlining responsibilities, salaries, benefits, and job outlook for each specialty. Illustrated.

★6926★ Opportunities in Marketing Careers

VGM Career Horizons
4255 W. Touhy Ave.
Lincolnwood, IL 60646-1975
Ph: (847)679-5500   Fax: (847)679-2494
Fr: 800-323-4900

Margery Steinberg. 1994. $14.95; $11.95 (paper). 160 pages. Includes guidance on identifying and pursuing job opportunities. Illustrated.

★6927★ Opportunities in Public Relations Careers

VGM Career Horizons
4255 W. Touhy Ave.
Lincolnwood, IL 60646-1975
Ph: (847)679-5500   Fax: (847)679-2494
Fr: 800-323-4900

Morris B. Rotman. 1995. $14.95; $11.95 (paper). 160 pages. Tells the reader how to enter the field and how to build a career. Contains bibliography and illustrations.

★6928★ Opportunities in Sports and Athletics

VGM Career Horizons
4255 W. Touhy Ave.
Lincolnwood, IL 60646-1975
Ph: (847)679-5500   Fax: (847)679-2494
Fr: 800-323-4900

William Ray Heitzmann. 1994. $14.95; $11.95 (paper). A guide to planning for and seeking opportunities in this growing field. Illustrated.

★6929★ Opportunities in Writing Careers

VGM Career Horizons
4255 W. Touhy Ave.
Lincolnwood, IL 60646-1975
Ph: (847)679-5500   Fax: (847)679-2494
Fr: 800-323-4900

Elizabeth Foote-Smith. 1989. $14.95; $11.95 (paper). 160 pages. Discusses opportunities in the print media, broadcasting, advertising or publishing. Business writing, public relations, and technical writing are among the careers covered. Contains bibliography and illustrations.

★6930★ Public Relations Career Directory

Gale Research
835 Penobscot Bldg.
Detroit, MI 48226-4094
Ph: (313)961-2242   Fax: (313)961-6083
Fr: 800-877-GALE

Bradley Morgan. Fifth edition, 1993. $39.00. 337 pages. Features extensive listings of contacts and entry-level job opportunities at major corporations and public relations agencies nationwide. Includes articles and advice from top public relations practitioners on such areas as corporate communications, international public relations, community affairs, and media relations.

★6931★ Where the Jobs Are: The Hottest Careers for the '90s

The Career Press, Inc.
3 Tice Rd.
PO Box 687
Franklin Lakes, NJ 07417
Ph: (201)848-0310   Fax: (201)848-1727
Fr: 800-237-3371

Joyce Hadley. Second edition, 1995. $9.99. 300 pages. Describes careers in fifteen general fields, from accounting to travel and hospitality.

EMPLOYMENT AGENCIES AND SEARCH FIRMS

★6932★ Blair Personnel of Parsippany, Inc.

1130 U.S. Hwy 46
Parsippany, NJ 07054-2158
Ph: (201)335-6150   Fax: (201)335-4657

Employment agency. Focuses on regular and temporary placement.

★6933★ Calvert Associates, Inc.

202 E. Washington St., Ste. 304
Ann Arbor, MI 48104
Ph: (313)769-5413

Employment agency.

★6934★ Chaloner Associates

PO Box 1097, Back Bay Station
Boston, MA 02117
Ph: (617)451-5170   Fax: (617)451-8160

Executive search firm.

★6935★ Esquire Personnel Services, Inc.

222 S. Riverside Plaza, Ste. 320
Chicago, IL 60606-5804
Ph: (312)648-4600   Fax: (312)648-4637

Employment agency.

★6936★ Howard-Sloan Associates, Inc.

353 Lexington Ave., 11th Fl.
New York, NY 10016
Ph: (212)661-5250   Fax: (212)687-5760
Fr: 800-221-1326

Executive search firm.

★6937★ The Pathfinder Group

295 Danbury Rd.
Wilton, CT 06897-3095
Ph: (203)834-2467

Employment agency. Executive search firm. Recruits staff in a variety of fields.

OTHER SOURCES

★6938★ American Almanac of Jobs and Salaries 1994-95

Avon Books
1350 Avenue of the Americas, 2nd Fl.
New York, NY 10019
Ph: (212)261-6800   Fr: 800-238-0658

John Wright. Revised edition, 1993. $17.00. 704 pages. This is a comprehensive guide to the wages of hundreds of occupations in a wide variety of industries and organizations.

★6939★ Bank Marketing Association (BMA)

1120 Conneticut Ave. NW
Washington, DC 20036
Ph: (202)663-5268   Fax: (202)828-4540
Fr: 800-433-9013

Members: Marketing and public relations executives for commercial and savings banks, credit unions, and savings and loans associations, and related groups such as advertising agencies and research firms. **Purpose:** Provides marketing education, information, and services to the financial services industry. **Activities:** Conducts research; cosponsors summer sessions of fundamentals and advanced courses in marketing at the University of Colorado at Boulder; compiles statistics.

★6940★ Becoming a Public Relations Writer: A Writing Process Workbook for the Profession

HarperCollins Publishers, Inc.
10 E. 53rd St.
New York, NY 10022-5299
Ph: (212)207-7000   Fax: (212)207-7145
Fr: 800-331-3761

Ronald D. Smith. 1995.

★6941★ National School Public Relations Association (NSPRA)

1501 Lee Hwy., Ste. 201
Arlington, VA 22209
Ph: (703)528-5840   Fax: (703)528-7017

Members: School system public relations directors, school administrators, and others interested in furthering public understanding of the public schools. **Activities:** Has adopted standards for public relations professionals and programs and an accreditation program.

★6942★ PROMAX International

2029 Century Park East, Ste. 555
Los Angeles, CA 90067-3283
Ph: (310)788-7600   Fax: (310)788-7616

Members: Advertising, public relations, and promotion managers of cable, radio, and television stations, systems and networks; syndicators. **Purpose:** Seeks to: advance the role and increase the effectiveness of promotion and marketing within the industry, related industries, and educational communities. Conducts workshops and weekly fax service for members. **Activities:** Operates employment service. Maintains speakers' bureau, hall of fame, and resource center with print, audio, and visual materials.

★6943★ Resumes for Communications Careers

VGM Career Horizons
4255 W. Touhy Ave.
Lincolnwood, IL 60646-1975
Ph: (847)679-5500   Fax: (847)679-2494
Fr: 800-323-4900

1991. $9.95. 160 pages. Includes sample resumes representing journalists, writers, publicists, and other communications specialists.

★6944★ The Source

Rachel P.R. Services
1650 S. Pacific Coast Hwy., Ste. 200-C
Redondo Beach, CA 90277
Ph: (310)792-1313   Fax: (310)792-1309
Fr: 800-874-8577

Annual, November. $29.00. Covers Over 3,000 job banks, referral services, recruiters, employment agencies, schools/colleges, internships/mentors, trade groups, telephone hotlines, directories, trade journals, and other organizations in the U.S. offering information on employment opportunities in advertising, public relations, journalism, and marketing. Entries include: Contact name, address, phone, products or services, cost/details. Arrangement: Classified by product or service. Indexes: Product/service, organization name, subject, geographical.

★6945★ Sports Careers Industry Audio Cassette Series

Sports Careers
PO Box 10129
Phoenix, AZ 85064
Fr: 800-776-7877

Audiocassette series. Covers the top ten major career categories for the sports industry: Special Events; TV and Cable; Sporting Goods; Colleges/Universities; Facility Management; Corporate Sponsorship; Athletic Representation; Front Office; Print and Radio; Health and Fitness.

★6946★ Women in Communications

10605 Judicial Dr., Ste. A4
Fairfax, VA 22030-5167
Ph: (703)359-9000   Fax: (703)359-0603

Members: Professional association of journalism and communications.

Purchasing Agents and Managers

★6947★ Electronic Business Buyer

Cahners Publishing Co.
275 Washington St.
Newton, MA 02158-1630
Ph: (617)964-3030   Fax: (617)558-4470

Monthly. Magazine for purchasing managers and buyers of electronic components and materials used in end product manufacture.

★6948★ Hospital Purchasing News

McKnight Medical Communications Co.
2 Northfield Plaza, Ste. 300
Northfield, IL 60093-1217
Ph: (708)441-3700   Fax: (708)441-3701
Fr: 800-451-7838

Monthly. Free to qualified subscribers; $49.95/year for individuals; $5.00 for single issue. Magazine for hospital material managers and central service personnel.

★6949★ Purchasing

Cahners Publishing Co.
275 Washington St.
Newton, MA 02158-1630
Ph: (617)964-3030   Fax: (617)558-4470

Semimonthly. Magazine for buying professionals.

★6950★ American Purchasing Society (APS)

11910 Oak Trail Way
Port Richey, FL 34668
Ph: (813)862-7998   Fax: (813)862-8199

Purpose: Seeks to certify qualified purchasing personnel. **Activities:** Maintains speakers' bureau and placement service. Conducts research programs; compiles statistics including salary surveys. Provides consulting service for purchasing, materials management, and marketing.

★6951★ National Association of Purchasing Management (NAPM)

2055 E. Centennial Cir.
PO Box 22160
Tempe, AZ 85285-2160
Ph: (602)752-6276   Fax: (602)752-7890
Fr: 800-888-6276

Members: Purchasing and materials managers for industrial, commercial, and utility firms; educational institutions and government agencies. **Purpose:** Disseminates information on procurement. Works to develop more efficient purchasing methods. **Activities:** Maintains reference service. Conducts program for certification as a purchasing manager.

★6952★ National Contract Management Association (NCMA)

1912 Woodford Rd.
Vienna, VA 22182
Ph: (703)448-9231   Fax: (703)448-0939
Fr: 800-344-8096

Members: Individuals concerned with administration, procurement, acquisition, negotiation, and management of government contracts and subcontracts. **Purpose:** Works for the education, improvement, and professional development of members and nonmembers through national and chapter programs, symposia, and workshops. Develops training materials to serve the procurement field. Offers certification in Contract Management (CPCM and CACM) designations. **Activities:** Conducts annual education seminar in 80 locations throughout the U.S. Operates speakers' bureau; maintains job listing service.

★6953★ Multi-Hospital Systems and Group Purchasing Organizations Directory

SMG Marketing Group, Inc.
1342 N. LaSalle
Chicago, IL 60610
Ph: (312)642-3026   Fax: (312)642-9729
Fr: 800-678-3026

Quarterly. $495.00, single issue; $795.00, yearly subscription. Covers over 480 multi-hospital systems and group purchasing organizations. Entries include: Company name, address, phone; hospital name, address, phone, type of hospital service, licensed number of beds, number of staffed beds, annual admission data, annual surgical information, status of hospital, activity in recent quarter, date and length of management contract with the hospital. Arrangement: Geographical. Indexes: Company name.

★6954★ Business and Finance Career Directory

Gale Research
835 Penobscot Bldg.
Detroit, MI 48226-4094
Ph: (313)961-2242   Fax: (313)961-6083
Fr: 800-877-GALE

Bradley Morgan. Second edition, 1992. $39.00. 413 pages. Features a basic and comprehensive job search section, articles by top professionals in the field, and detailed listings of hundreds of top companies who hire individuals in this field. Aimed particularly at entry-level job hunters.

★6955★ Encyclopedia of Careers and Vocational Guidance

J. G. Ferguson Publishing Co.
200 W. Monroe, Ste. 250
Chicago, IL 60606
Ph: (312)580-5480

William E. Hopke. Ninth edition, 1993. $129.95; $199.95 (CD-ROM). Four-volume set that profiles 900 occupations and describes job trends in 71 industries. Includes career description, educational requirements, history of the job, methods of entry, advancement, employment outlook, earnings, conditions of work, social and psychological factors, and sources of further information. Contains career and employment information for this field.

★6956★ Federal Contracting Careers

Federal Acquisition Institute
General Services Administration
18th & F Sts. NW, Rm. 4019
Washington, DC 20405
Ph: (202)501-0964

This nine-page booklet describes working for the federal government as a contract specialist; explains intern programs, advancement, and career development and training, as well as how to apply for programs.

★6957★ Opportunities in Hospital Administration Careers

VGM Career Horizons
4255 W. Touhy Ave.
Lincolnwood, IL 60646-1975
Ph: (847)679-5500   Fax: (847)679-2494
Fr: 800-323-4900

I. Donald Snook. 1989. $14.95; $11.95 (paper). 160 pages. Discusses opportunities for administrators in a variety of management settings: hospital, department, clinic, group practice, HMO, mental health, and extended care facilities.

★6958★ Opportunities in International Business Careers

VGM Career Horizons
4255 W. Touhy Ave.
Lincolnwood, IL 60646-1975
Ph: (847)679-5500   Fax: (847)679-2494
Fr: 800-323-4900

Jeffrey Arpan. 1995. $14.95; $11.95 (paper). 160 pages. Describes what types of jobs exist in international business, where they are located, what challenges and rewards they bring, and how to prepare for and obtain jobs in international business.

★6959★ Opportunities in Purchasing Careers

VGM Career Horizons
4255 W. Touhy Ave.
Lincolnwood, IL 60646-1975
Ph: (847)679-5500   Fax: (847)679-2494
Fr: 800-323-4900

Kent Banning. 1990. $14.95; $11.95 (paper). 160 pages. Tells how to start and advance in purchasing, detailing job requirements, sala-

ries, and benefits for beginning and experienced agents. Illustrated.

EMPLOYMENT AGENCIES AND SEARCH FIRMS

★6960★ Accountants Overload Group

10990 Wilshire Blvd.
Los Angeles, CA 90024-3913
Ph: (213)629-2800

Employment agency.

★6961★ B and M Associates, Inc.

199 Cambridge Rd.
Woburn, MA 01801-4705
Ph: (617)938-9120

Employment agency.

★6962★ Britt Associates Inc.

2709 Black Rd.
Joliet, IL 60435
Ph: (815)744-7200

Employment agency.

★6963★ Colli Associates of Tampa

PO Box 2865
Tampa, FL 33601
Ph: (813)681-2145

Employment agency. Executive search firm.

★6964★ Esquire Personnel Services, Inc.

222 S. Riverside Plaza, Ste. 320
Chicago, IL 60606-5804
Ph: (312)648-4600   Fax: (312)648-4637

Employment agency.

★6965★ Financial Search Corp.

2720 Des Plaines Ave., Ste. 154
Des Plaines, IL 60018
Ph: (708)297-4900   Fax: (708)297-0294

Executive search firm.

★6966★ Hayden and Associates, Inc.

7825 Washington Ave. S., Ste. 120
Minneapolis, MN 55439-2431
Ph: (612)941-6300   Fax: (612)941-9602

Employment agency. Executive search firm. Fills openings in a variety of fields.

★6967★ Industrial Recruiters Associates, Inc.

630 Oakwood Ave., Ste. 318
West Hartford, CT 06110
Ph: (203)953-3643

Employment agency.

★6968★ Rocky Mountain Recruiters, Inc.

1801 Broadway, Ste. 810
Denver, CO 80202
Ph: (303)296-2000

Executive search firm.

★6969★ Romac International, Inc.

120 Hyde Park Pl., Ste. 200
Tampa, FL 33606
Fr: 800-341-0263

Executive search firm. More than 30 locations throughout the U.S.

★6970★ Sierra Technology Corporation

4150 Manzanita Ave., Ste. 100
Carmichael, CA 95608-1700
Ph: (916)488-4960   Fax: (916)488-7058

Employment agency. Provides placement on a temporary basis.

★6971★ Source Finance

5580 LBJ Fwy., Ste. 300
Dallas, TX 75240
Ph: (214)385-3002   Fax: (214)717-0075

Executive search firm. Many affiliate offices located in most major cities throughout the U.S.

★6972★ T.R. Employment Agency

409 Wilshire Blvd.
Santa Monica, CA 90401
Ph: (310)393-4107

Employment agency.

OTHER SOURCES

★6973★ American Almanac of Jobs and Salaries 1994-95

Avon Books
1350 Avenue of the Americas, 2nd Fl.
New York, NY 10019
Ph: (212)261-6800   Fr: 800-238-0658

John Wright. Revised edition, 1993. $17.00. 704 pages. This is a comprehensive guide to the wages of hundreds of occupations in a wide variety of industries and organizations.

★6974★ National Institute of Governmental Purchasing (NIGP)

11800 Sunrise Valley Dr., Ste. 1050
Reston, VA 22091-5302
Ph: (703)715-9400   Fax: (703)715-9897
Fr: 800-FOR-NIGP

Members: Federal, state, provincial, county, and local government buying agencies; hospital, school, prison, and public utility purchasing agencies in the U.S. and Canada. **Purpose:** Develops standards and specifications for governmental buying; promotes uniform purchasing laws and procedures; conducts specialized education and research programs. **Activities:** Conducts certification program for Certified Professional Public Buyer (CPPB) and Certified Public Purchasing Officer (CPPO); offers consulting services and cost-saving programs and tools for governmental agencies, including product commodity code to computerized purchasing. Maintains speakers' bureau; compiles statistics.

Rabbis and Jewish Religious Professionals

★6975★ JCC Association Personnel Reporter

Jewish Community Center Association
15 E. 26th St.
New York, NY 10010-1579

Quarterly. Free. Covers opportunities in Jewish community centers and camps.

PLACEMENT AND JOB REFERRAL SERVICES

★6976★ American Association of Rabbis (AAR)

350 5th Ave., Ste. 3304
New York, NY 10118
Ph: (212)244-3350   Fax: (516)377-0449

Members: Fraternal organization of rabbis serving in pulpits, education, social work, and Hillel activities. **Activities:** Provides placement services. Assist congregations.

★6977★ Association for the Study of Jewish Languages (ASJL)

67-07 215 St.
Oakland Gardens, NY 11364-2523

Purpose: Institutions and individuals in 25 countries interested in encouraging research on the linguistic history of Jews and related groups. Traces origin and meaning of Jewish family names. **Activities:** Operates placement services. Offers advice on proper romanization of Hebrew and Yiddish words. Maintains speakers' bureau; collects Jewish genealogies.

★6978★ Central Conference of American Rabbis (CCAR)

192 Lexington Ave.
New York, NY 10016
Ph: (212)684-4990   Fax: (212)689-1649

Members: National organization of Reform rabbis. **Activities:** Offers placement service; compiles statistics. Maintains 38 committees.

★6979★ Council for Jewish Education (CJE)

730 Broadway
New York, NY 10003
Ph: (212)529-2000   Fax: (212)529-2009

Members: Teachers of Hebrew in universities; heads of Bureaus of Jewish Education and their administrative departments; faculty members of Jewish teacher training schools. **Purpose:** Seeks to: further the cause of Jewish education in America; raise professional standards and practices; promote the welfare and growth of Jewish educational workers; improve and strengthen Jewish life. **Activities:** Conducts educational programs; cosponsors a Personnel Placement Committee with Jewish Education Service of North America.

★6980★ Council of Young Israel Rabbis (CYIR)

National Council of Young Israel
3 W. 16th St.
New York, NY 10011
Ph: (212)929-1525   Fax: (212)727-9526

Members: Rabbis serving 200 Young Israel congregations in the U.S., Canada, and Israel. **Purpose:** Encourages study and observance of Judaism and provides spiritual leadership to the Young Israel Movement. Adjudicates issues relating to the Young Israel Synagogues. **Activities:** Provides placement service. Is concerned with welfare of rabbis.

★6981★ Federation of Reconstructionist Congregations and Havurot (FRCH)

Church Rd. & Greenwood Ave.
Wyncote, PA 19095
Ph: (215)887-1988   Fax: (215)887-5348

Purpose: Federation of synagogues and fellowships committed to the philosophy and program of the Jewish Reconstructionist Movement. Coordinates rabbinical and educational training. **Activities:** Maintains placement service and speakers' bureau.

★6982★ Guild of Temple Musicians (GTM)

Temple Beth El & Center
1435 W. 7th St.
San Pedro, CA 90732
Ph: (310)833-2467   Fax: (310)833-6504

Members: Individuals involved in Jewish temple music including music directors, organists, choir directors, singers, and teachers. Membership is concentrated in the U.S., Canada, and Israel. **Purpose:** Goals are to: preserve Jewish musical tradition through education and awareness of old and new available materials; share ideas and performances through concerts, workshops, and papers; keep members abreast of current developments and trends in the field. Conducts course in conjunction with School of Sacred Music, Hebrew Union College/Jewish Institute of Religion, in New York City, leading to certification. **Activities:** Offers placement service.

★6983★ Jewish Community Centers Association of North America (JCCANA)

15 E. 26th St.
New York, NY 10010
Ph: (212)532-4949   Fax: (212)481-4174

Members: Affiliated Jewish Community Centers including The 92nd Street Young Men's and Young Women's Hebrew Association and their branches and camps in the U.S. and Canada which have a combined membership of more than 1,000,000; local Armed Services committees; full- and part-time Jewish chaplains and lay leaders in all branches of the Armed Forces. **Purpose:** Through community consultants and program specialists, aids Jewish community centers in planning programs, personnel recruitment, building construction, camping, health and physical education, administration, research publications, and public relations. Acts as U.S. government-authorized agency for serving religious and welfare needs of Jewish military personnel and their dependents in the U.S. Armed Forces and Veterans Administration Hospitals through the JWB Jewish Chaplains Council. **Activities:** Maintains placement services for professional Jewish community center and YM and YWHA workers.

★6984★ Jewish Education Service of North America (JESNA)

730 Broadway, 2nd Fl.
New York, NY 10003-9540
Ph: (212)529-2000

Members: National education organizations, bureaus of Jewish education, and individuals. **Purpose:** Service agency to coordinate, promote, and conduct research in North American Jewish education. Operates Mandell L. Berman Jewish Heritage Center for Research and Evaluation. Supports the Convenant Foundation, a joint venture with the Crown Family, which makes awards and grants for creativity in Jewish education. **Activities:** Maintains teachers placement service for Jewish schools.

★6985★ Jewish Educators Assembly (JEA)

106-06 Queens Blvd.
Flushing, NY 11375-4248
Ph: (718)268-9452   Fax: (718)520-4369

Members: Educational and supervisory personnel serving Jewish educational institutions. **Purpose:** Seeks to: advance the development of Jewish education in the congregation on all levels in consonance with the philosophy of the Conservative Movement; cooperate with the United Synagogue of America Commission on Jewish Education as the policy-making body of the educational enterprise; join in cooperative effort with other Jewish educational institutions and organizations; establish and maintain professional standards for Jewish educators; serve as a forum for the exchange of ideas; promote the values of Jewish education as a basis for the creative continuity of the Jewish people. **Activities:** Maintains placement service.

★6986★ Jewish Ministers and Cantors' Association of America (JMCA)

3 W. 16th St.
New York, NY 10011
Ph: (212)633-0051   Fr: 800-727-8567

Members: Jewish ministers and cantors. **Purpose:** Perpetuates the rabbinate and cantorial profession in its traditional form. Holds classes for rabbis and cantors; maintains a library of cantorial recitations and Hebrew music; assists needy rabbis and cantors. **Activities:** Bestows awards; maintains speakers' bureau and placement service.

★6987★ National Association for the Advancement of Orthodox Judaism (NAAOJ)

132 Nassau St.
New York, NY 10038
Ph: (212)513-0100   Fax: (718)436-0888

Purpose: To provide, through publications and oral representations by member rabbis and scholars, the teaching of true Judaism; to provide rabbinical guidance to the public; to promote interest in Jewish education; to give advisory assistance to member rabbis; to assist in placement of foreign-born rabbis and others seeking help.

★6988★ National Association of Synagogue Administrators (NASA)

Adath Jesaurun
10500 Hillside Ln., W
Minnetonka, MN 55305
Ph: (612)361-2990

Members: Professional society of synagogue administrators. **Purpose:** "To foster the advancement of conservative Judaism and further the development of the profession of synagogue administration." **Activities:** Maintains placement service and speakers' bureau; compiles statistics. Sponsors educational programs.

★6989★ National Association of Temple Administrators (NATA)

Wilshire Blvd. Temple
3663 Wilshire Blvd.
Los Angeles, CA 90010
Ph: (213)388-2401   Fax: (213)388-2595

Members: Full-time administrators of Jewish synagogues affiliated with the Union of American Hebrew Congregations. **Purpose:** Conducts educational programs; has established code of standards and ethics. Offers congregational survey service and compiles synagogue research reports and salary reports. **Activities:** Conducts placement service.

★6990★ National Association of Temple Educators (NATE)

Richard Morin
707 Summerly Dr.
Nashville, TN 37209-4253
Ph: (615)352-6800   Fax: (615)352-7800

Members: Directors of education in Reform Jewish religious schools, principals, heads of departments, supervisors, educational consultants, students, and authors. **Purpose:** To assist in the growth and development of Jewish religious education consistent with the aims of Reform Judaism; stimulate communal interest in Jewish religious education; represent and encourage the profession of temple educator. **Activities:** Maintains placement service. Conducts surveys on personnel practices, confirmation practices, religious school organization and administration, curricular practices, and other aspects of religious education. Sponsors institutes for principals and educational directors. **E-Mail:** nateoff@aol.com

★6991★ Rabbinical Alliance of America (RAA)

3 W. 16th St., 4th Fl.
New York, NY 10011
Ph: (212)242-6420   Fax: (212)255-8313

Members: Orthodox rabbis who serve in pulpits and as principals of Jewish day schools and Hebrew schools throughout the world. **Purpose:** Supervises Hebrew Schools Program for Adult Studies. **Activities:** Provides placement service aid for indigent Torah scholars; contributes to Jewish charitable causes. Maintains the Rabbinical Court which handles orthodox Jewish divorces, court of arbitration, Dinei Torahs, and family and marriage counseling.

★6992★ Rabbinical Assembly (RA)

3080 Broadway
New York, NY 10027
Ph: (212)678-8060   Fax: (212)749-9166

Members: Rabbis serving Conservative Jewish congregations; chaplains in the Armed Forces and in educational or communal organizations. **Purpose:** To promote Conservative Judaism; to cooperate with the Jewish Theological Seminary of America; to advance the cause of Jewish learning; to promote the welfare of the members; and to foster the spirit of fellowship and cooperation among the rabbis and other Jewish scholars. **Activities:** Offers placement service.

★6993★ Solomon Schecher Day School Association (SSDSA)

155 5th Ave.
New York, NY 10010
Ph: (212)260-8450   Fax: (212)353-9439

Members: A division of the United Synagogue of America Commission on Jewish Education. Jewish elementary day schools and high schools with a total of over 17,000 students. Named for Solomon Schecher (1850-1915), reader of Talmud and rabbinical literature and founder of the United Synagogue of America and the Jewish Theological Seminary. **Purpose:** Provides educational consultation via telephone, mail, and personal visits to the school. Encourages maintenance of high standards for members; coordinates accreditation visits to each school. **Activities:** Cosponsors Master Program to Prepare Principals for Jewish Day Schools with the graduate school of the Jewish Theological Seminary of America, New York City; develops curriculum for day schools. Offers seminars, workshops, and consulting service. Provides educational services, materials, and statistics.

★6994★ Union of Sephardic Congregations (USC)

8 W. 70th St.
New York, NY 10023
Ph: (212)873-0300   Fax: (212)724-6165

Members: Affiliated congregations practicing Sephardic (Spanish, Portuguese, or Greek) Judaism. **Activities:** Assists in the placement of rabbis in Sephardic congregations.

EMPLOYER DIRECTORIES AND NETWORKING LISTS

★6995★ Directory of Day Schools in the United States and Canada

Torah Umesorah National Society for Hebrew Day Schools
5723 18th Ave.
Brooklyn, NY 11204
Ph: (718)259-1223   Fax: (718)259-1795

Irregular, latest edition January 1993, new edition expected 1996. $12.00. Covers approximately 500 elementary and secondary Hebrew day schools in the U.S. and Canada. Entries include: School name, address, phone, names of administrative personnel, grades taught, language of instruction, year established (when available). Arrangement: Geographical.

HANDBOOKS AND MANUALS

★6996★ Jobs Rated Almanac: Ranks the Best and Worst Jobs by More Than a Dozen Vital Criteria

John Wiley and Sons
605 Third Ave.
New York, NY 10158-0012
Ph: (212)850-6000   Fr: 800-225-5945

Les Krantz. Third edition, 1995. $16.95. 340 pages. Ranks 250 jobs by environment, salary, outlook, physical demands, stress, security, travel opportunities, and geographic location.

★6997★ Non-Profits and Education Job Finder

Planning/Communications
7215 Oak Ave.
River Forest, IL 60305-1935
Ph: (708)366-5200   Fr: (888)366-5200

Daniel Lauber. 1996. $32.95; $16.95 (paper). 350 pages. Covers 1600 sources. Discusses how to use sources of non-profit sector job vacancies in a number of specialties and state-by-state, including job-matching services, job hotlines, specialty periodicals with job ads, salary surveys, and directories. Covers a variety of fields from education to religion. Includes chapters on resume and cover letter preparation and interviewing.

★6998★ Opportunities in Religious Service Careers

NTC Publishing Group
4255 W. Touhy Ave.
Lincolnwood, IL 60646-1975
Ph: (708)679-5500   Fax: (708)679-6375
Fr: 800-323-4900

Oliver. 1992. $13.95; $10.95 (paper).

★6999★ Rabbinate as Calling and Vocation: Models of Rabbinic Leadership

Jason Aronson, Inc.
230 Livingston St.
Northvale, NJ 07647
Ph: (201)767-4093

Basil Herring. 1991. $40.00. 320 pages.

OTHER SOURCES

★7000★ National Council of Young Israel (NCYI)

3 W. 16th St.
New York, NY 10011
Ph: (212)929-1525   Fax: (212)727-9526
Fr: 800-617-NCYI

Members: Families of traditional Jewish faith in the U.S., Canada, Mexico, and Israel. **Purpose:** Seeks to perpetuate traditional Judaism; instill a love for Americanism and the principles of democracy; bring Jewish youth back to the synagogue; educate the youth and adults in the heritage and culture of the Jewish people. **Activities:** Sponsors Institute for Jewish Studies, which provides specialized programs in Jewish education. Sponsors children's services, charitable program, and competitions. Maintains speakers' bureau; compiles statistics.

Radio and Television Announcers and Newscasters

★7001★ *Broadcasting and Cable*

Conners Publishing
245 W. 17th St.
New York, NY 10011
Ph: (212)463-6835   Fax: (212)463-6836

Weekly. $85.00/year for individuals; $3.00/year for single issue. News magazine covering "The Fifth Estate" (radio, TV, cable, and satellite), and the regulatory commissions involved.

★7002★ *College Broadcaster*

National Association of College
  Broadcasters
71 George St.
PO Box 1824
Providence, RI 02912-1824
Ph: (401)863-2225   Fax: (401)863-2221

Quarterly.

★7003★ *Current*

Heldref Publications
Helen Dwight Reid Educational Foundation
1319 18th St. NW
Washington, DC 20036-1802
Ph: (202)296-6267   Fax: (202)296-5149
Fr: 800-365-9753

$32.00/year for individuals; $6.00 for single issue; $60.00/year for institutions; $76.00/year for institutions, other countries. Journal that reprints articles on education, politics, and other social issues.

★7004★ *Daily Variety*

Cahners Business Newspapers
5700 Wilshire Blvd., Ste. 120
Los Angeles, CA 90036
Ph: (213)857-6600   Fax: (213)857-0494

Daily (morn.). Global entertainment newspaper (tabloid).

★7005★ *Editor & Publisher*

Editor & Publisher Co.
11 W. 19th St.
New York, NY 10011
Ph: (212)675-4380   Fax: (212)929-1259

Weekly (Sat.). Magazine focusing on journalism, advertising, and printing equipment.

★7006★ *Electronic Media*

Crain Communications, Inc.
740 N. Rush St.
Chicago, IL 60611
Ph: (312)649-5260   Fax: (312)649-5228

Weekly (Mon.). $69.00/year for individuals. Tabloid covering management, programing, syndication, technology, and trends in the television, radio, and electronic media industry.

★7007★ *ETV Newsletter*

Charles Tepfer, Publisher
PO Box 597
Ridgefield, CT 06877
Ph: (203)454-2618   Fax: (203)454-2618

Biweekly. $195.00/year for U.S. and Canada; $220.00/year for elsewhere. Offers inside information on what's happening in Public Television (PTV), Instructional Television (ITV), and Educational Television (ETV). Monitors government telecommunications policy changes; new marketing policies, grants and funding sources; and requests for bids on equipment, services, and programs. Recurring features include meetings and conference reports, a calendar of events, job listings, book reviews, and market studies.

★7008★ *The Hollywood Reporter*

Billboard Magazine
33 Commercial St.
Gloucester, MA 01930
Ph: (508)281-3110   Fax: (508)281-0136

Daily (morn.). $149.00/year for individuals. Film, TV, and entertainment trade newspaper.

★7009★ *The Insider Newsletter*

Sports Careers
PO Box 10129
Phoenix, AZ 85064
Fr: 800-776-7877

Semimonthly. Subscription free to members; $99.00/six months for nonmembers. Provides articles on career development, salaries, and trends for the sports industry. Includes "Career Connections," an insert listing 60-75 job opportunities and internships within each issue.

★7010★ *Multichannel News*

Capital Cities/ABC, Inc.
825 7th Ave., 6th Fl.
New York, NY 10019
Ph: (212)887-8400   Fax: (212)887-8384

Weekly (Mon.). $84.00/year for individuals. Cable and pay TV magazine.

★7011★ *The Quill*

Russell Sage College
Box 2134
Troy, NY 12180
Ph: (518)270-2259

Weekly (Thurs.). Collegiate newspaper.

★7012★ *Religious Broadcasting*

National Religious Broadcasters
7839 Ashton Ave.
Manassas, VA 22110
Ph: (703)330-7000

Monthly. $24.00/year.

★7013★ *Weatherwise*

Heldref Publications
Helen Dwight Reid Educational Foundation
1319 18th St. NW
Washington, DC 20036-1802
Ph: (202)296-6267   Fax: (202)296-5149
Fr: 800-365-9753

Bimonthly. $33.00/year for individuals; $9.50/year for single issue; $57.00/year for institutions; $71.00/year for institutions, other countries. Popular weather magazine for students, teachers, and professionals.

PLACEMENT AND JOB REFERRAL SERVICES

★7014★ American Sportscasters Association (ASA)

5 Beekman St., Ste. 814
New York, NY 10038
Ph: (212)227-8080   Fax: (212)571-0556

Members: Radio and television sportscasters. **Activities:** Operates placement service, hall of fame, and biographical archives. Maintains American Sportscaster Charitable Trust. Is currently implementing an antidrug program. Sponsors seminars, clinics, and symposia for aspiring announcers and sportscasters. Compiles statistics.

★7015★ Armed Forces Broadcasters Association (AFBA)

PO Box 335
Sun Valley, CA 91353-0335
Ph: (213)256-3482   Fax: (213)256-3482

Members: Former and current military and commercial broadcasters. **Purpose:** Provides an opportunity for military broadcasters and supporters to meet and socialize. Assists broadcasters returning to the U.S. from overseas. **Activities:** Provides job information center.

★7016★ Broadcast Education Association (BEA)

1771 N St. NW
Washington, DC 20036-2891
Ph: (202)429-5354   Fax: (202)429-5343

Members: Universities and colleges; faculty and students; radio and television stations that belong to the National Association of Broadcasters. **Purpose:** Promotes improvement of curriculum and teaching methods, broadcasting research, television and radio production, and programming teaching. **Activities:** Offers placement services.

★7017★ Broadcast Foundation of College/University Students (BROADCAST)

89 Longview Rd.
Port Washington, NY 11050
Ph: (516)883-2897   Fax: (516)883-7460

Members: College students interested in broadcasting and professional broadcasters interested in encouraging practical broadcasting experience in colleges and universities. **Activities:** Conducts annual survey of all professional broadcasting stations for part-time and summer employment for college students. Sponsors job advisory and placement service.

★7018★ National Association of African-American Sportswriters and Broadcasters

21 Bedford St.
Wyandanch, NY 11798
Ph: (516)491-7774

Members: African-American men and women involved in the sports industry. **Purpose:** Provides job information in the areas of sports medicine, sports law, and sports management. **Activities:** Offers children's

services; sponsors research and educational programs.

★7019★ National Association of Broadcasters (NAB)

1771 N St. NW
Washington, DC 20036
Ph: (202)429-5300   Fax: (202)429-5343

Members: Representatives of radio and television stations and networks; associate members include producers of equipment and programs. **Purpose:** Seeks to ensure the viability, strength, and success of free, over-the-air broadcasters; serves as an information resource to the industry. **Activities:** Offers minority placement service and employment clearinghouse. Monitors and reports on events regarding radio and television broadcasting. Maintains Broadcasting Hall of Fame.

★7020★ National Association of College Broadcasters (NACB)

71 George St., Box 1824
Providence, RI 02912-1824
Ph: (401)863-2225   Fax: (401)863-2221

Purpose: Created to fulfill perceived needs in the student broadcasting community by opening channels of communication between college and school radio and TV stations. Maintains reference library containing books, periodicals, clippings, audio visual material, and archival holdings pertaining to student radio and TV broadcasting. **Activities:** Compiles statistics; maintains placement service and speakers' bureau. **E-Mail:** NACB@AOL.COM

★7021★ National Association of Farm Broadcasters (NAFB)

26 E. Exchange St., No. 307
St. Paul, MN 55101
Ph: (612)224-0508   Fax: (612)224-1956

Members: Radio and television farm directors actively engaged in broadcasting or telecasting farm news and information; associate members are persons with agricultural interests who are affiliated with advertising agencies, government agencies, farm organizations, and commercial firms. **Purpose:** Works to improve quantity and quality of farm programming and serve as a clearinghouse for new ideas in farm broadcasting. **Activities:** Provides placement information.

★7022★ National Religious Broadcasters (NRB)

7839 Ashton Ave.
Manassas, VA 22110
Ph: (703)330-7000   Fax: (703)330-7100

Members: Religious radio and television program producers; religious radio and television station owners and operators within the U.S. and Canada; foreign broadcasters interested in religious broadcasting throughout the world. **Purpose:** Seeks to support those providing programming for radio and television and those engaging in the operation of religious radio and television stations. Is dedicated to the communication of the gospel and complete access to broadcast media for religious broadcasting. Serves as a central source of information concerning Christian radio and television. Sponsors seven

regional conventions, international tours, and professional training courses. **Activities:** Compiles statistics; provides placement service; maintains hall of fame.

★7023★ Radio-Television News Directors Association (RTNDA)

1000 Connecticut Ave. NW, Ste. 615
Washington, DC 20036
Ph: (202)659-6510   Fax: (202)223-4007
Fr: 800-80-RTNDA

Members: Professional society of heads of news departments for broadcast and cable stations and networks; associate members are journalists engaged in the preparation and presentation of broadcast news and teachers of electronic journalism; other members represent industry services, public relations departments of business firms, public relations firms, and networks. **Purpose:** Works to improve standards of electronic journalism; defends rights of journalists to access news; promotes journalism training to meet specific needs of the industry. **Activities:** Operates placement service and speakers' bureau.

★7024★ Sports Careers

PO Box 10129
Phoenix, AZ 85064
Fr: 800-776-7877

Career development firm for the sports industry. Provides career-related programs, conferences, seminars, educational products, and publications. Offers Career Enhancement Profile Program and Resume Development Kit. Maintains an electronic resume bank for members which is available to sports companies and organizations. Publishes newsletter listing job opportunities.

EMPLOYER DIRECTORIES AND NETWORKING LISTS

★7025★ Advertising-Radio Directory

American Business Directories, Inc.
American Business Information, Inc.
5711 S. 86th Cir.
Omaha, NE 68127
Ph: (402)593-4600   Fax: (402)331-1505

Updated continuously; printed on request. Entries include: Name, address, phone (including area code), size of advertisement, year first in Yellow Pages, name of owner or manager, number of employees. Compiled from telephone company Yellow Pages, nationwide. Arrangement: Geographical.

★7026★ Bacon's Radio/TV/Cable Directory, Volume 1

Bacon's Publishing Co.
332 S. Michigan Ave., Ste. 900
Chicago, IL 60604
Ph: (312)922-2400   Fax: (312)922-3127
Fr: 800-621-0561

Annual, November; interedition supplement. $270.00 postpaid; includes updates. Covers over 10,300 radio and television stations, including college radio and public television stations, and cable companies. Entries include: For radio and television stations: call letters, address, phone, names and titles of key personnel, programs, times broadcast, name of contact, network affiliation, frequency or channel number, target audience data. For cable companies: name, address, phone, description of activities. Arrangement: Geographical.

★7027★ Broadcasting & Cable Yearbook

R. R. Bowker Co.
Reed Reference Publishing
121 Chanlon Rd.
New Providence, NJ 07974
Ph: (908)464-6800   Fax: (908)464-3553
Fr: 800-521-8110

Annual, March. $169.95. Covers all television and radio stations in the United States, its territories, and Canada; cable MSOs and their individual systems; television and radio networks, broadcast and cable group owners, station representatives, satellite networks and services, film companies, advertising agencies, government agencies, trade associations and schools. Entries include: Company name, address, phone, fax, names of executives. Station listings include broadcast power, other operating details. Arrangement: Stations and systems are geographical, others are alphabetical. Indexes: Alphabetical.

★7028★ Burrelle's New York Media Directory

Burrelle's Information Services
75 E. Northfield Rd.
Livingston, NJ 07039
Ph: (201)992-6600   Fr: 800-876-3342

Annual. $95.00. Includes information on radio and television stations, newspapers, and other media companies. Regional editions available for some Northeastern states.

★7029★ Cash Box—Directory Issue

Cash Box Publishing Co., Inc.
345 W. 58th St., 15W
New York, NY 10019
Ph: (212)245-4224   Fax: (212)245-4226

Annual, August. $15.00 postpaid. Publication includes: Lists of record manufacturers, pressers, importers, exporters, distributors, music publishers, producers, radio stations, radio chains, one stops, rack jobbers, personal managers, performance facilities, recording studios, concert and record promotion and publicity offices, jacket and label manufacturers, independent record promoters, and manufacturers and distributors of juke boxes, pinball machines, and similar coin machines. Coverage of manufacturers, music publishers, and some radio stations includes Europe, Australia, Japan, Central America, and South America. Entries include: All listings include company name or call letters, address, and phone. Record manufacturers include labels; producers include performer and title of top record; facilities include capacity and names and titles of key personnel; radio stations include names and titles of key personnel, format, and cost of one-time advertising spot; radio chains include names of chief executives, call letters, city, format, and key personnel for each station in chain. Arrangement: Classified by

line of business in separate sections for domestic, international, and coin machine listings.

★7030★ Chicago Media Directory

Chicago Convention and Tourism Bureau
McCormick Place-on-the-Lake
Chicago, IL 60616
Ph: (312)567-8500   Fax: (312)567-8533

Quarterly. $5.00. Covers executive and editorial personnel at Chicago's major daily newspapers, downtown weeklies, and wire services, as well as radio and television station personnel. Entries include: For newspapers: publication name, address, phone, names and titles of key personnel. For radio and TV Station: name, address, phone, names and titles of key personnel. Arrangement: Classified by type of medium or outlet.

★7031★ Country Radio Broadcasters—Program Book and Directory

Country Radio Broadcasters
50 Music Sq. W, No. 702
Nashville, TN 37203-3228
Ph: (615)327-4487   Fax: (615)329-4492

Annual, March. Covers Approximately 10,000 country radio professionals, including station owners, music and program directors, managers, and broadcasters. Entries include: Name, address, phone. Arrangement: Alphabetical.

★7032★ CPB Public Broadcasting Directory

Corporation for Public Broadcasting
901 E St. NW
Washington, DC 20004-2037
Ph: (202)879-9600   Fax: (202)783-1019

Annual, fall. $15.00. Covers public television and radio stations, national and regional public broadcasting organizations and networks, state government agencies and commissions, and other related organizations. Entries include: For radio and television stations: station call letters, frequency or channel, address, phone, licensee name, licensee type, date on air, antenna height, area covered, names and titles of key personnel. For organizations: name, address, phone, name and title of key personnel. Arrangement: National and regional listings are alphabetical; state groups and the public radio and television stations are each geographical; other organizations and agencies are alphabetical. Indexes: Geographical, personnel, call letter, licensee type (all in separate indexes for radio and television).

★7033★ FM Atlas

FM Atlas Publishing and Electronics
PO Box 24
Adolph, MN 55701
Ph: (218)879-7676   Fax: (218)879-8333

Irregular, previous edition December 1993; latest edition 1995. $14.95, plus $1.05 shipping. Covers approximately 7,000 FM stations located in North America. Entries include: Call letters, location, musical format, transmitting radius in kilometers, whether stereo or monaural, FM subcarriers, etc. Arrangement: Geographical, then by frequency.

★7034★ Gebbie Press All-in-One Directory

Gebbie Press, Inc.
Box 1000
New Paltz, NY 12561
Ph: (914)255-7560

Annual, November. $80.00, payment with order. Covers 1,577 daily newspapers, 6,000 weekly newspapers, 7,600 radio stations, 1,260 television stations, 250 general-consumer magazines, 430 professional business publications, 2,900 trade magazines, 320 farm publications, list of the Black press and radio, Hispanic press and radio, and a list of news syndicates. Entries include: For periodicals: name, address, phone, fax, frequency, editor, circulation, readership. For newspapers: name, address, phone, circulation. For radio and television stations: call letters, address, phone, format. Arrangement: Classified by type of media.

★7035★ Hudson's State Capitals News Media Contacts Directory

Howard Penn Hudson Associates, Inc.
44 W. Market St.
PO Box 311
Rhinebeck, NY 12572
Ph: (914)876-2081   Fax: (914)876-2561

Annual. $108.00. Covers about 1,500 media outlets located in or near the state capitals; includes wire services, radio and television broadcasting stations, newspapers, magazine and newsletter publishers. Entries include: Name, address, phone, name of editorial contact. Arrangement: Alphabetical.

★7036★ International Radio and Television Society Foundation–Roster Yearbook

International Radio and Television Society Foundation
420 Lexington Ave.
New York, NY 10170
Ph: (212)867-6650   Fax: (212)867-6653

Annual, April. Available to members only. Covers Approximately 1,600 professionals in the communications industry. Entries include: Name, title (where applicable), business address, phone. Arrangement: Alphabetical.

★7037★ International Television and Video Almanac

Quigley Publishing Co., Inc.
159 W. 53rd St.
New York, NY 10019
Ph: (212)247-3100   Fax: (212)489-0871

Annual, January. $88.50, plus shipping. Covers Who's Who in Motion Pictures and Television and Home Video, television networks, major program producers, major group station owners, cable television companies, distributors, firms serving the television and home video industry, equipment manufacturers, casting agencies, literary agencies, advertising and publicity representatives, television stations, associations, list of feature films produced for television; statistics, industry's year in review, award winners. Entries include: Generally, company name, address, phone; manufacturer and service listings may include description of products and services and name of contact; producing, distributing, and station listings include additional detail. Arrangement: Classified by service or activity, then generally geographical.

★7038★ M Street Radio Directory

M Street Corp.
304 Park Ave. S, 7th Fl.
New York, NY 10010
Ph: (212)473-4668   Fax: (212)473-4626
Fr: 800-248-4242

Annual, fall. $42.00. Covers Approximately 14,000 AM and FM radio stations in the U.S. and Canada. Entries include: Company name, address, phone, fax, personnel, geographical area served, format, audience ratings, markets served, technical and market information. Arrangement: Geographical. Indexes: Geographical, call letters, station frequency.

★7039★ Media Directory San Diego County

San Diego Chamber of Commerce
402 W. Broadway, Ste. 1000
San Diego, CA 92101
Ph: (619)232-0124

Annual. $5.00. Covers San Diego county newspapers, magazines, news bureaus, radio and television stations. Entries include: For publications: name of publication, address, phone. For radio and television stations: call letters, frequency, address, mailing address, phone. Arrangement: Classified by type of media.

★7040★ Metro California Media

Public Relations Plus, Inc.
Box 1197
New Milford, CT 06776
Ph: (203)354-9361   Fax: (203)355-8048
Fr: 800-999-8448

Semiannual, May and November. $149.50.00, per year. Covers newspapers, radio and television stations, magazines, and broadcast programs in California. Entries include: Name, address, phone, names of editors and creative staff, with titles or indication of assignments. Arrangement: Geographical. Indexes: Alphabetical.

★7041★ Minority Employment Report

Federal Communications Commission
1919 M St. NW
Washington, DC 20554
Ph: (202)632-7000   Fax: (202)418-0200

Annual, December. Free. Covers television and radio stations with ten or more full-time employees. Entries include: Station name (call letters or channel), city and state, class of station; total, female, and minority full-time employment in higher and lower pay occupations, and part-time employment for previous five years. Arrangement: By state and community.

★7042★ National Radio Publicity Outlets

Morgan-Rand Media Group
800 Masons Mill Business Park
1800 Byberry Rd.
Huntingdon Valley, PA 19006
Ph: (215)938-5511   Fax: (215)938-5549
Fr: 800-677-3839

Annual, Spring. $99.00. Covers over 7,000

stations in all major U.S. and Canadian markets; network and syndicated talk shows; non-commercial and educational radio stations. Entries include: For stations: call letters, address, phone, fax, AM/FM dial positions, network affiliation, watts, coverage, format, names and titles of key personnel. For local talk shows: name of show, host name; name, address and phone of contact; topics, days and times aired, sister station airtime, show requirements, audience size, source of survey. Arrangement: Geographical. Indexes: Network program name, syndicated program name, station name, topic, ADI (Area of Dominant Influence).

★7043★ North Carolina News Media Directory

Gail E. West, Publisher
Box 316
Mount Dora, FL 32757
Ph: (904)383-3023   Fax: (904)383-3023
Fr: 800-749-6399

Annual, April. $45.00. Covers about 730 newspapers, periodicals, radio and television broadcasting stations, and press services operating in North Carolina. Entries include: Publisher or company name, address, phone, names and titles of key personnel, publication title, call letters, hours of operation, and frequency. Arrangement: Classified by type of media. Indexes: Title, call letters, county index.

★7044★ Pocket Media Guide

Media Distribution Services
307 W. 36th St., Dept. P
New York, NY 10018
Ph: (212)279-4800   Fax: (212)239-8208

Annual, November. Free to public relations professionals. Covers about 725 major market newspapers, radio and television stations and networks, foreign and national wire services, and trade and general interest publications in major United States cities and Canada. Entries include: Publication or call name, address, phone. Arrangement: Classified by line of business.

★7045★ PR Profitcenter

Ad-Lib Publications
51 1/2 W. Adams
PO Box 1102
Fairfield, IA 52556-1102
Ph: (515)472-6617   Fax: (515)472-3186
Fr: 800-669-0773

Monthly. $150.00. Diskette. Covers over 13,500 media, including 4,100 magazine editors, 5,500 newspaper editors, 2,300 radio shows, 975 TV shows, and 703 syndicated columnists. Database includes: Name of newspaper, magazine, station, or network; name and title of editor, columnist, or contact person; address, phone, audience in subject and categories covered. Additional details may include show host, format, circulation, frequency.

★7046★ Programming Radio

Mid-South Management, Inc.
PO Box 1051
Vicksburg, MS 39181-1051
Ph: (601)631-7191

Irregular, latest edition November 1993. $20.00. Covers Approximately 40,000 radio broadcasting companies in the United States. Entries include: Company name, address, phone; names, titles, and biographical data for key personnel. Arrangement: Classified by type of programming.

★7047★ Radio Advertising Source

SRDS
3004 Glenview Rd.
Wilmette, IL 60091
Ph: (708)441-2243   Fax: (708)441-2264
Fr: 800-323-4601

Monthly. $173.00 single copy; $1,396 year subscription. Covers over 10,500 AM and FM stations, networks, syndicators, group owners, and representative firms. Entries include: Call letters, name of owning company, address, phone; names of representatives and station personnel; demostration detail, station format, signal strength, programming opportunities, special features. Arrangement: Geographical by state, then Arbitron metro and nonmetro area.

★7048★ Radio Programming Profile

BF/Communication Services, Inc.
66 Chestnut Ln.
Woodbury, NY 11797
Ph: (516)364-2593

Three times yearly. $310.00, per vol.; no single copies sold. Covers about 3,000 AM and FM radio stations in top 200 markets, with hour-by-hour format information. Entries include: Station call letters, address, phone, names of executives, hour-by-hour format information. Arrangement: Alphabetical by market and call letters. Volume 1 has top 70 ranking markets; volume 2 has markets 71-200.

★7049★ Radio and Records Ratings Report & Directory

Radio and Records, Inc.
10100 Santa Monica Blvd., 5th Fl.
Los Angeles, CA 90067
Ph: (310)553-4330   Fax: (310)203-8450

Semiannual, April and September. $35.00. Covers nearly 2,700 radio group owners, equipment manufacturers, jingle producers, TV production houses and spot producers, record companies, representative firms, research companies, consulting firms, media brokers, networks, program suppliers, trade associations, and other organizations involved in the radio and record industry. Entries include: Organization name, address, phone, fax, name and title of chief executive officer, branch offices or subsidiary names and locations. Arrangement: Alphabetical; classified by subject.

★7050★ Radio Stations and Broadcasting Companies Directory

American Business Directories, Inc.
American Business Information, Inc.
5711 S. 86th Cir.
Omaha, NE 68127
Ph: (402)593-4600   Fax: (402)331-1505

Annual. $765.00 U.S. edition. Entries include: Name, address, phone (including area code), size of advertisement, year first in Yellow Pages, name of owner or manager, number of employees. Franchise editions available: AM Stations, $245.00; FM Stations, $430.00. Compiled from telephone company Yellow Pages, nationwide. Arrangement: Geographical.

★7051★ RTNDA Communicator— Directory Issues

Radio-Television News Directors
  Association (RTNDA)
1000 Connecticut Ave. NW, Ste. 615
Washington, DC 20036
Ph: (202)659-6510   Fax: (202)223-4007

Semiannual, January and July. Available to members only. Number of listings: 3,000; membership includes Canada and some foreign countries. Entries include: Member name, address, phone; and name of radio or television station, network, or other news organization with which affiliated. Arrangement: Same information given in alphabetical and geographical arrangements.

★7052★ Sports Market Place Register

Sports Careers
PO Box 10129
Phoenix, AZ 85064
Fr: 800-776-7877

Annual $59.00. Resource guide for the sports industry. Lists over 24,000 national and international sports business contacts. Entries include: organization name, name of key executive, address, and phone and fax numbers. Provides listings for: Individual and Multiple Sports Organizations/Teams/Media; College Sports; Sponsorship/Marketing/ Event Management; Sports Agents/Lawyers; Manufacturers/Retailers. Indexes: Geographic and Alphabetical.

★7053★ Television & Cable Factbook

Warren Publishing, Inc.
2115 Ward Ct. NW
Washington, DC 20037
Ph: (202)872-9200   Fax: (202)293-3435

Annual, January. Weekly updates available. $405.00, plus $15.00 shipping. Covers commercial and noncommercial television stations and networks, including educational, low-power and instructional TV stations, and translators; United States cable television systems; cable and television group owners; national sales representatives of television stations; equipment manufacturers and distributors; program and service suppliers; brokerage and financing companies; consulting engineers; brokers; attorneys practicing before the Federal Communications Commission; cable system sales representatives; international coverage. Arrangement: Geographical by state, province, city, county, or country. Indexes: Call letters, product/service, name, general subject.

★7054★ The Television Yearbook

BIA Publications
14595 Avion Pkwy., Ste. 500
Chantilly, VA 22021
Ph: (703)818-2425   Fax: (703)803-3299

Annual, March. $84.00. Covers U.S. television markets and their inclusive stations, television equipment manufacturers, and related service providers and trade associations. Entries include: For stations: Call letters, address; name and phone of general manager, owner, and other key personnel; technical attributes, rep firm, network affiliation, last acquistion date and price and ratings for total day and prime time. For others: Company or organization name, address, phone, description. Arrangement: Classified by market. Indexes: Numerical by market rank; call letters.

★7055★ Working Press of the Nation

Reed Reference Publishing
121 Chanlon Rd.
New Providence, NJ 07974
Ph: (908)665-3561   Fax: (908)665-2894
Fr: 800-521-8110

Annual, September. $385.00, four-volume set; Covers in four separate volumes, syndicates and over 8,400 daily and weekly newspapers; 1,400 newsletters; over 14,900 radio and television stations; 10,600 magazines; 3,200 feature writers, photographers, and professional speakers; and 2,700 internal house organs. Entries include: All listings include name of publication or station, address, phone, names of executives, editors, writers, etc., as appropriate. Broadcasting and magazine volumes include data on kinds of material needed. Technical and mechanical requirements for publications are given. Arrangement: Magazines are classified by audience; newspapers and broadcasting stations are geographical.

★7056★ World Radio TV Handbook

BPI Communications, Inc.
Affiliated Publications, Inc.
1515 Broadway, 39th Fl.
New York, NY 10036
Ph: (212)764-7300

Annual, January. $19.95, plus $2.50 shipping. Covers 25,000 radio and television stations worldwide; national regulatory bodies. Entries include: For stations: name, frequency, address, phone, telex, name and title of contact and key personnel, description of programming. For agencies: name, address, phone. Arrangement: Separate geographical sections for radio and television stations. Indexes: Station name and geographical.

HANDBOOKS AND MANUALS

★7057★ Announcers and Disc Jockeys

Chronicle Guidance Publications, Inc.
66 Aurora St.
PO Box 1190
Moravia, NY 13118-1190
Ph: (315)497-0330   Fax: (315)497-3359
Fr: 800-622-7284

Chronicle Guidance Staff. 1994. $2.00. Provides concise career information and sources of additional information.

★7058★ Announcing: Broadcast Communications Today

Wadsworth Publishing Co.
10 Davis Dr.
Belmont, CA 94002
Ph: (415)595-2350   Fax: (606)525-0978

Lewis B. O'Donnell. 1992. $55.95.

★7059★ Broadcasters

Rourke Press, Inc.
PO Box 3328
Vero Beach, FL 32964
Ph: (407)465-4575   Fax: (407)465-3132

William Russell. 1994.

★7060★ Career Choices for the 90's for Students of Communications and Journalism

Walker and Company
435 Hudson St.
New York, NY 10014
Ph: (212)727-8300   Fax: (212)727-0984
Fr: 800-289-2553

Prepared by the Career Associates staff. 1990. $8.95. 166 pages. Discusses alternatives for students of communications and journalism. Offers advice on how to break into the field and how to move up. Covers where and who the employers are, internship possibilities, and professional networking associations. Comprehensive guide to career and job search planning.

★7061★ Career Choices for the 90's for Students of History

Walker and Company
435 Hudson St.
New York, NY 10014
Ph: (212)727-8300   Fax: (212)727-0984
Fr: 800-289-2553

Prepared by the Career Associates staff. 1990. $8.95. 166 pages. Discusses alternatives for students of history. Offers advice on how to break into the field and how to move up. Covers where and who the employers are, internship possibilities, and professional networking associations. Comprehensive guide to career and job search planning.

★7062★ Career Information Center

Macmillan Publishing Co.
200 Old Tappan Rd.
Old Tappan, NJ 07675
Ph: (609)461-6500   Fr: 800-223-2336

Visual Education Center Staff. Fifth edition, 1992. $229.00. This 13-volume set profiles over 600 occupations. Each occupational profile describes job duties, educational requirements, how to get the job, advancement possibilities, employment outlook, working conditions, earnings and benefits, and where to write for more information.

★7063★ *Career Opportunities in the Sports Industry*

Facts on File, Inc.
11 Penn Plaza, 15th Fl.
New York, NY 10001-2006
Ph: (212)967-8800   Fax: 800-678-3633
Fr: 800-322-8755

Shelly Field. 1991. $29.95; $15.95 (paper). 272 pages. Describes various jobs in the sports industry. Each occupational profile covers job duties, employment outlook, career paths, salaries, skills, and education preparation. Offers tips for entering the field. Fields covered include professional sports teams, sports and business administration, coaching, sports officiating, sports journalism, fitness and recreation, and sports medicine and therapy, among others.

★7064★ *Career Opportunities in Television, Cable and Video*

Facts on File, Inc.
11 Penn Plaza, 15th Fl.
New York, NY 10001-2006
Ph: (212)967-8800   Fax: 800-678-3633
Fr: 800-322-8755

Maxine K. Reed and Robert M. Reed. Third edition, 1991. $29.95; $15.95 (paper). 272 pages.

★7065★ *Careers in Communications*

VGM Career Horizons
4255 W. Touhy Ave.
Lincolnwood, IL 60646-1975
Ph: (847)679-5500   Fax: (847)679-2494
Fr: 800-323-4900

Shonan Noronha. 1994. $17.95; $13.95 (paper). 176 pages. Examines the fields of journalism, photography, radio, television, film, public relations, and advertising. Gives concrete details on job locations and how to secure a job. Suggests many resources for job hunting.

★7066★ *Careers in Radio*

National Association of Broadcasters (NAB)
1771 N. St., NW
Washington, DC 20036
Fr: 800-368-5644

Compiled by NAB Staff. 1991. $3.50.

★7067★ *Careers in Radio and Television News*

Radio-Television News Directors Association
1000 Connecticut Ave. NW, Ste. 615
Washington, DC 20036
Ph: (202)659-6510

$5.00. Booklet describes careers in radio and television, job locations, salaries, opportunities for women and minorities, and how to get started in the field.

★7068★ *Careers in Television & Radio*

Taylor & Francis, Inc.
1900 Frost Rd., Ste. 101
Bristol, PA 19007-1598
Ph: (215)785-5800   Fax: (215)785-5515
Julia Allen.

★7069★ *The Harvard Guide to Careers in the Mass Media*

Bob Adams, Inc.
260 Center St.
Holbrook, MA 02343
Ph: (617)767-8100   Fax: (617)767-0994
Fr: 800-872-5627

John Noble. 1989. $7.95. 202 pages. Each section of the book evaluates one media profession in depth and contains an industry profile, a career profile that describes positions available in that area, information about current salary ranges, industry-specific job-hunting tips and strategies, and a case study outlining the methods that were used in a successful job hunt.

★7070★ *How to Land a Job in TV News: The Insider's Guide*

Mustang Publishing
PO Box 3004
Memphis, TN 38173
Ph: (901)521-1406   Fax: (901)521-1412

Carl Filoreto. 1995. $14.95 (paper).

★7071★ *How to Launch Your Career in TV News*

NTC Publishing Group
4255 W. Touhy Ave.
Lincolnwood, IL 60646-1975
Ph: (708)679-5500   Fax: (708)679-6375
Fr: 800-323-4900

Jeff Leshay. 1994. $14.95 (paper).

★7072★ *Making it in Broadcasting: An Insider's Guide to Career Opportunities*

Macmillan Publishing Co.
200 Old Tappan Rd.
Old Tappan, NJ 07675
Fax: 800-223-2336   Fr: 800-445-6991

Leonard Mogel. 1994. $15.00 (paper).

★7073★ *100 Best Careers in Entertainment*

Prentice Hall General Reference & Travel
15 Columbus Cir.
New York, NY 10023
Ph: (212)373-8500   Fr: 800-223-2348

Shelly Field. 1994. $15.00 (paper).

★7074★ *Opportunities in Broadcasting Careers*

VGM Career Horizons
4255 W. Touhy Ave.
Lincolnwood, IL 60646-1975
Ph: (847)679-5500   Fax: (847)679-2494
Fr: 800-323-4900

Elmo I. Ellis. 1994. $14.95; $11.95 (paper). Discusses opportunities and job search techniques in broadcasting, television, and radio. Illustrated.

★7075★ *Opportunities in Cable Television Careers*

VGM Career Horizons
4255 W. Touhy Ave.
Lincolnwood, IL 60646-1975
Ph: (847)679-5500   Fax: (847)679-2494
Fr: 800-323-4900

Jan Bone. 1993. $14.95; $11.95 (paper). 160 pages. Focuses on what the jobs are, where they are, and how to get them. Illustrated.

★7076★ *Opportunities in Journalism Careers*

VGM Career Horizons
4255 W. Touhy Ave.
Lincolnwood, IL 60646-1975
Ph: (847)679-5500   Fax: (847)679-2494
Fr: 800-323-4900

Jim Patten and Donald L. Ferguson. 1993. $14.95; $11.95 (paper). 160 pages. Outlines opportunities in every field of journalism, including newspaper reporting and editing, magazine and book publishing, corporate communications, advertising and public relations, freelance writing, and teaching. Covers how to prepare for and enter each field, outlining responsibilities, salaries, benefits, and job outlook for each specialty. Illustrated.

★7077★ *Opportunities in Sports and Athletics*

VGM Career Horizons
4255 W. Touhy Ave.
Lincolnwood, IL 60646-1975
Ph: (847)679-5500   Fax: (847)679-2494
Fr: 800-323-4900

William Ray Heitzmann. 1994. $14.95; $11.95 (paper). A guide to planning for and seeking opportunities in this growing field. Illustrated.

★7078★ *Opportunities in Television and Video Careers*

VGM Career Horizons
4255 W. Touhy Ave.
Lincolnwood, IL 60646-1975
Ph: (847)679-5500   Fax: (847)679-2494
Fr: 800-323-4900

Shonan Noronha. 1993. $14.95; $11.95 (paper). Details the employment opportunities open in television, cable, corporate video, institutional and government media, including independent production, and discusses how to land a job. Illustrated.

★7079★ *Opportunities in Writing Careers*

VGM Career Horizons
4255 W. Touhy Ave.
Lincolnwood, IL 60646-1975
Ph: (847)679-5500   Fax: (847)679-2494
Fr: 800-323-4900

Elizabeth Foote-Smith. 1989. $14.95; $11.95 (paper). 160 pages. Discusses opportunities in the print media, broadcasting, advertising or publishing. Business writing, public relations, and technical writing are among the careers covered. Contains bibliography and illustrations.

★7080★ Radio & Television Broadcasting Workers

Chronicle Guidance Publications, Inc.
66 Aurora St.
PO Box 1190
Moravia, NY 13118-1190
Ph: (315)497-0330   Fax: (315)497-3359
Fr: 800-622-7284

Chronicle Guidance Staff. 1992. $2.00. Provides concise career information and sources of additional information.

★7081★ Radio and Television Career Directory

Gale Research
835 Penobscot Bldg.
Detroit, MI 48226-4094
Ph: (313)961-2242   Fax: (313)961-6083
Fr: 800-877-GALE

Bradley Morgan. Second edition, 1993. $39.00. 334 pages. Features extensive listings of contacts and entry-level job opportunities. Provides information on internships and sources of help-wanted ads.

★7082★ Working in TV News: The Insider's Guide

Mustang Publishing
PO Box 3004
Memphis, TN 38173
Ph: (901)521-1406   Fax: (901)521-1412

Carl Filoreto. 1993. $12.95 (paper).

EMPLOYMENT AGENCIES AND SEARCH FIRMS

★7083★ Joe Sullivan and Associates, Inc.

44210 County Rd. 48
PO Box 612
Southold, NY 11971
Ph: (516)765-5050

Executive search firm. Recruits for the broadcasting and media industries.

★7084★ Search Source, Inc.

2019B Johnson Rd.
PO Box 1161
Granite City, IL 62040
Ph: (618)876-6060   Fax: (618)876-6071

Executive search firm. Concentrates on placement to broadcasting industry.

OTHER SOURCES

★7085★ ADWEEK Marketer's Guide to Media

ADWEEK Directories
1515 Broadway, 12th Fl.
New York, NY 10036
Ph: (212)536-5336   Fr: 800-468-2395

Semiannual, May and November. $60.00 per issue; $100.00. Covers television, radio, cable, magazines, newspapers, out-of-home and promotion media. Entries include: Publication, organization, or station name, address, phone, key personnel, current rates and audience demographics. Arrangement: Classified by type of media.

★7086★ American Almanac of Jobs and Salaries 1994-95

Avon Books
1350 Avenue of the Americas, 2nd Fl.
New York, NY 10019
Ph: (212)261-6800   Fr: 800-238-0658

John Wright. Revised edition, 1993. $17.00. 704 pages. This is a comprehensive guide to the wages of hundreds of occupations in a wide variety of industries and organizations.

★7087★ Corporation for Public Broadcasting (CPB)

901 E St. NW
Washington, DC 20004-2037
Ph: (202)879-9600   Fax: (202)783-1019

A private, nonprofit corporation authorized under Public Broadcasting Act of 1967. Funded by U.S. government. **Purpose:** To promote and finance the growth and development of noncommercial radio and television. Makes grants to local public television and radio stations, program producers, and regional networks; studies emerging technologies; works to provide adequate long-range financing from the U.S. government and other sources for public broadcasting.

★7088★ Country Radio Broadcasters (CRB)

PO Box 120429
Nashville, TN 37212
Ph: (615)327-4487   Fax: (615)329-4492

Members: Country radio station owners, managers, and program and music directors. **Activities:** Conducts charitable and educational programs.

★7089★ Guide to Volunteer and Internship Programs in Public Broadcasting

Corporation for Public Broadcasting
Publications Dept.
901 E St. NW
Washington, DC 20004-2037
Ph: (202)879-9600

1991. Free.

★7090★ National Association of Black Owned Broadcasters (NABOB)

1333 New Hampshire Ave., N.W., Ste. 1000
Washington, DC 20036
Ph: (202)463-8970   Fax: (202)429-0657

Members: Black broadcast station owners; black formatted stations not currently owned or controlled by blacks; organizations having an interest in the black consumer market or black broadcast industry; individuals interested in becoming owners; and communications schools, departments, and professional groups and associations. **Purpose:** Represents the interests of existing and potential black radio and television stations. Is currently working with the Office of Federal Procurement Policy to determine which government contracting major advertisers and advertising agencies are complying with government initiatives to increase the amount of advertising dollars received by minority-owned firms. Conducts lobbying activities; provides legal representation for the protection of minority ownership policies. Participates in the reorganization of the Advisory Committee on Radio Broadcasting. Sponsors annual Communications Awards Dinner each March. Conducts workshops; compiles statistics.

★7091★ Sports Careers Industry Audio Cassette Series

Sports Careers
PO Box 10129
Phoenix, AZ 85064
Fr: 800-776-7877

Audiocassette series. Covers the top ten major career categories for the sports industry: Special Events; TV and Cable; Sporting Goods; Colleges/Universities; Facility Management; Corporate Sponsorship; Athletic Representation; Front Office; Print and Radio; Health and Fitness.

★7092★ Student Guide to Mass Media Internships

Intern Research Group
Box 52, Regent Hall
University of Colorado
Boulder, CO 80309
Ph: (303)442-8340

Annual, latest edition 1995. $35.00, payment with order; $40.00, billed. Covers about 10,000 internships offered by 2,700 newspapers, radio and television stations, cable television companies, magazines, advertising agencies, and other firms. Entries include: Organization name, address, type and number of internships offered, eligibility requirements, application deadline, salary or other stipend offered, name and title of contact; many listings also include description of intern's duties. Arrangement: Classified by type of medium, then geographical.

Radiologic Technologists

SOURCES OF HELP-WANTED ADS

★7093★ Applied Radiology

Anderson Publishing Ltd.
80 Shore Rd.
Port Washington, NY 11050
Ph: (516)883-0164   Fax: (516)883-6609

Monthly. Free to qualified subscribers; $55.00/year for individuals; $6.00 for single issue. Magazine for radiologists, chief radiologic technologists, and radiology department administrators. Presents articles written by radiologic professionals on all aspects of general diagnostic radiology, the diagnostic radiologic subspecialties, and radiation therapy.

★7094★ Clinical Imaging

Elsevier Science, Inc.
655 Avenue of the Americas
New York, NY 10010
Ph: (212)989-5800   Fax: (212)633-3990

Quarterly. Radiology journal.

★7095★ Computerized Medical Imaging and Graphics

Elsevier Science
660 White Plains Rd.
Tarrytown, NY 10591-5153
Ph: (914)524-9200   Fax: (914)333-2444

Bimonthly. Journal focusing on new developments in medical imaging and graphics and the medical application of these to patient care.

★7096★ Diagnostic Imaging

Miller Freeman, Inc.
600 Harrison St.
San Francisco, CA 94107
Ph: (415)905-2200

Monthly. $70.00/year.

★7097★ Investigative Radiology

Pharmaceutical Media, Inc.
30 E. 33rd St.
New York, NY 10016
Ph: (212)685-5010   Fax: (212)685-5010

Monthly. $179.00/year for individuals; $64.00/year for students; $239.00/year for Canada and Mexico. Journal covering clinical and laboratory investigations in diagnostic imaging.

★7098★ Journal of Clinical Ultrasound

John Wiley and Sons, Inc.
605 3rd Ave.
New York, NY 10158
Ph: (212)850-6000   Fax: (212)850-8888
Fr: 800-225-5945

International journal devoted to the clinical applications of ultrasound in medicine. Features include scholarly, peer-reviewed articles on research procedures and techniques encompassing all phases of diagnostic ultrasound.

★7099★ Journal of Computer-Assisted Tomography

Liptencoct-Raven
1185 Avenue of the Americas
Mail Stop 3B
New York, NY 10036
Ph: (212)930-9500   Fax: (212)575-1160

Bimonthly. Radiology journal.

★7100★ Magnetic Resonance Quarterly

Liptencoct-Raven
1185 Avenue of the Americas
Mail Stop 3B
New York, NY 10036
Ph: (212)930-9500   Fax: (212)575-1160

Quarterly. Journal presenting international advances in MRI.

★7101★ Radio Graphics

Radiological Society of North America
2021 Spring Rd., Ste. 600
Oak Brook, IL 60521-1860
Ph: (708)571-2670   Fax: (708)571-7837

Bimonthly. $90.00/year for individuals; $105.00/year for other countries. Scientific publication for radiologists.

★7102★ Radiology

Radiological Society of North America
2021 Spring Rd., Ste. 600
Oak Brook, IL 60521
Ph: (708)571-2670   Fax: (708)571-7837

Monthly. $195.00/year for individuals; $240.00/year for out of country. Journal focusing on radiology.

★7103★ Radiology Today

Slack, Inc.
6900 Grove Rd.
Thorofare, NJ 08086-9447
Ph: (609)848-1000   Fax: (609)853-5991
Fr: 800-257-8290

Monthly. Covering radiology technique and equipment innovations, related political activities, and daily practice.

PLACEMENT AND JOB REFERRAL SERVICES

★7104★ American Institute of Ultrasound in Medicine (AIUM)

14750 Sweetzer Ln., Ste. 100
Laurel, MD 20707-5906
Ph: (301)498-4100   Fax: (301)498-4450
Fr: 800-638-5352

Members: Physicians, engineers, scientists, sonographers, and other professionals involved with diagnostic medical ultrasound. **Purpose:** Promotes the application of ultrasound in clinical medicine, diagnostically, and in research; studies its effects on tissue and recommend standards for its applications. Promotes education in the use of ultrasonics for medical purposes. **Activities:** Administers educational programs and placement service. Maintains hall of fame; operates speakers' bureau.

★7105★ Society of Diagnostic Medical Sonographers (SDMS)

12770 Coit Rd., Ste. 508
Dallas, TX 75251
Ph: (214)239-7367   Fax: (214)239-7378

Members: Sonographers, physician sonologists, and those in medical specialties utilizing high frequency sound for diagnostic purposes. **Purpose:** Works to advance the science of diagnostic medical sonography to establish and maintain high standards of education, to provide an identity and sense of direction for members. **Activities:** Collects information concerning educational programs and informs schools of minimum standards currently being proposed. Has developed American Registry of Diagnostic Medical Sonographers , the first registering body for the field of diagnostic ultrasound. Maintains list of job openings.

EMPLOYER DIRECTORIES AND NETWORKING LISTS

★7106★ AHA Guide to the Health Care Field

Health Statistics Group
American Hospital Association (AHA)
1 N. Franklin
Chicago, IL 60606
Ph: (312)422-3501   Fax: (312)280-6015

Annual, July. $195.00, payment with order. Covers hospitals, multi-health care systems, freestanding ambulatory surgery centers, psychiatric facilities, long-term care facilities, substance abuse programs, hospices, Health Maintenance Organizations (HMOs), and other health-related organizations. Entries include: For hospitals: facility name, address, phone, administrator's name, number of beds, facilities and services, number of employees, expenses, other statistics. For other organizations: name, address, phone, name and title of contact. Arrangement: Geographical. Indexes: Hospital name.

★7107★ Directory of Hospital Personnel

Medical Economics
5 Paragon Dr.
Montvale, NJ 07645-1725
Ph: (201)358-7500   Fax: (201)573-4956
Fr: 800-222-3045

Annual, September. $325.00, plus 7.50 shipping. Covers 200,000 executives at 7,100 U.S. hospitals. Entries include: Name of hospital, address, phone, number of beds, type and JCAHO status of hospital, names and titles of key department heads and staff, medical and nursing school affiliations; number of residents, interns, and nursing students. Arrangement: Geographical. Indexes: Hospital name, personnel, hospital size.

★7108★ Directory of Personnel Responsible for Radiological Health Programs

Conference of Radiation Control Program Directors
205 Capital Ave.
Frankfort, KY 40601-2832
Ph: (502)227-4543   Fax: (502)227-7862

Annual, January. $30.00, payment must accompany order. Covers about 350 individuals who conduct radiological health program activities in federal, state, and local government agencies; members of the conferences. Arrangement: Directors are by level of agen-

cy and geographical. Indexes: Personal name, agency, state.

★7109★ Hospital Blue Book

Billian Publishing Co.
2100 Powers Ferry Rd., Ste. 300
Atlanta, GA 30339
Ph: (404)955-5656   Fax: (404)952-0669

Annual, spring. $154.50, national edition, plus $20.00 shipping. Covers more than 7,100 hospitals; some listings also appear in a separate southern edition of this publication. Entries include: Name of hospital, accreditation, mailing address, phone, fax, number of beds, type of facility (nonprofit, general, state, etc.); list of administrative personnel and chiefs of medical services, with specific titles. Arrangement: Geographical.

★7110★ Hospital Market Atlas

SMG Marketing Group, Inc.
1342 N. LaSalle Dr.
Chicago, IL 60610
Ph: (312)642-3026   Fax: (312)642-9729
Fr: 800-678-3026

Biennial, odd years. $495.00, payment with order. Covers over 7,000 hospitals, hospital systems and 480 group purchasing organizations. Entries include: Hospital or organization name, address, phone, county code, management, type of hospital service, number of beds, admissions, surgical operations, and emergency room visits. Arrangement: Geographical.

★7111★ Hospitals Directory

American Business Directories, Inc.
American Business Information, Inc.
5711 S. 86th Cir.
Omaha, NE 68127
Ph: (402)593-4600   Fax: (402)331-1505

Annual. $870.00, U.S. edition. Entries include: Name, address, phone (including area code), size of advertisement, year first in Yellow Pages, name of owner or manager, number of employees. Compiled from telephone company Yellow Pages, nationwide. Arrangement: Geographical.

★7112★ Medical and Health Information Directory

Gale Research
835 Penobscot Bldg.
Detroit, MI 48226-4094
Ph: (313)961-2242   Fax: (313)961-6083
Fr: 800-877-GALE

Approximately biennial; latest edition 1994. $195.00, per volume; $485.00, for the three-volume set. Covers in Volume 1, almost 18,600 medical and health oriented associations, organizations, institutions, and government agencies, including health maintenance organizations (HMOs), preferred provider organizations (PPOs), insurance companies, pharmaceutical companies, research centers, and medical and allied health schools. In Volume 2, nearly 11,800 medical book publishers; medical periodicals, directories, audiovisual producers and services, medical libraries and information centers, and electronic resources. In Volume 3, nearly 26,000 clinics, treatment centers, care programs, and counseling/diagnostic services for 30

subject areas. Entries include: Institution, service, or firm name, address, phone; many include names of key personnel and, when pertinent, descriptive annotation. Arrangement: Classified by organization activity, service, etc. Indexes: Each volume has a complete alphabetical name and keyword index.

★7113★ Osteopathic Membership Directory—AOHA

American Osteopathic Healthcare Association
5301 Wisconsin Ave. NW, Ste. 630
Washington, DC 20015-2015
Ph: (202)686-1700   Fax: (202)686-7615

Annual, summer. $125.00, payment with order. Covers about 110 osteopathic hospitals. Includes list of individual and institutional members; also lists osteopathic colleges, and directors of medical education. Entries include: For hospitals: name of hospital, name of chief executive officer, address, phone, number of beds and other hospital data. Arrangement: Geographical. Indexes: Name, institution.

★7114★ X-Ray Laboratories Medical Directory

American Business Directories, Inc.
American Business Information, Inc.
5711 S. 86th Cir.
Omaha, NE 68127
Ph: (402)593-4600   Fax: (402)331-1505

Updated continuously; printed on request. Please inquire. Entries include: Name, address, phone, size of advertisement, name of owner or manager, number of employees, year first in Yellow Pages. Compiled from telephone company Yellow Pages, nationwide. Arrangement: Geographical.

HANDBOOKS AND MANUALS

★7115★ Careers in Health Care

VGM Career Horizons
4255 W. Touhy Ave.
Lincolnwood, IL 60646-1975
Ph: (847)679-5500   Fax: (847)679-2494
Fr: 800-323-4900

Barbara M. Swanson. 1995. $17.95; $13.95 (paper). Describes job duties, work settings, salaries, licensing and certification requirements, educational preparation, and future outlook. Gives ideas on how to secure a job.

★7116★ Medical Technologists and Technicians Career Directory

Gale Research
835 Penobscot Bldg.
Detroit, MI 48226-4094
Ph: (313)961-2242   Fax: (313)961-6083
Fr: 800-877-GALE

Bradley Morgan. 1993. $39.00. 324 pages. Essays on specific careers provide an insider's perspective. Features extensive listings of contacts and entry-level job opportunities. Provides information on internships and sources of help-wanted ads.

★7117★ 100 Best Careers for the Year 2000

Prentice Hall General Reference
15 Columbus Cir.
New York, NY 10023
Ph: (212)373-8500   Fr: 800-223-2348

Shelly Field. 1992. $15.00 (paper). Covers 100 of the fastest growing jobs. The publication is divided into 11 general employment sections. Specific careers are covered within each section. Provides job description, responsibilities, employment opportunities, earnings, education and training, advancement opportunities, and experience and qualifications for each occupation.

★7118★ Opportunities in Health and Medical Careers

VGM Career Horizons
4255 W. Touhy Ave.
Lincolnwood, IL 60646-1975
Ph: (847)679-5500   Fax: (847)679-2494
Fr: 800-323-4900

Donald Snook, Jr. and Leo D'Orazio. 1993. $14.95; $11.95 (paper). Covers the full range of medical and health occupations. Illustrated.

★7119★ Opportunities in Medical Imaging Careers

VCH Publishers, Inc.
220 E. 23rd St., Ste. 909
New York, NY 10010-4606
Ph: (212)683-8333   Fax: (212)481-0897

Clifford J. Sherry. 1993.

★7120★ Opportunities in Medical Technology Careers

VGM Career Horizons
4255 W. Touhy Ave.
Lincolnwood, IL 60646-1975
Ph: (847)679-5500   Fax: (847)679-2494
Fr: 800-323-4900

Karen R. Karni and Sidney Oliver. 1990. $14.95; $11.95 (paper). Details opportunities for various technical medical personnel and supplies up-to-date information on salary levels and employment outlook. Appendices list associations and unions in each field. Illustrated.

★7121★ Opportunities in Vocational and Technical Careers

VGM Career Horizons
4255 W. Touhy Ave.
Lincolnwood, IL 60646-1975
Ph: (847)679-5500   Fax: (847)679-2494
Fr: 800-323-4900

Adrian A. Paradis. 1992. $14.95; $11.95 (paper). 160 pages. Provides information on a variety of opportunities and advice on breaking into the field.

EMPLOYMENT AGENCIES AND SEARCH FIRMS

★7122★ Action Plus Employer Services

1211 W. Imperial Hwy., Ste. 100
Brea, CA 92621
Ph: (714)773-1506   Fax: (714)773-9201

Employment agency.

★7123★ Blake and Associates Executive Search

PO Box 1425
Pleasantville, NJ 08232
Ph: (609)645-3330   Fax: (609)383-0320

Executive search firm.

★7124★ Harper Associates

29870 Middlebelt
Farmington Hills, MI 48334
Ph: (810)932-1170

Employment agency.

★7125★ JPM International

4665 MacArthur Ct., Ste. 100B
Newport Beach, CA 92660
Ph: (714)955-2545   Fax: (714)757-1320

Executive search firm and employment agency.

★7126★ Midwest Medical Consultants

8910 Purdue Rd., Ste. 200
Indianapolis, IN 46268-1155
Ph: (317)872-1053

Employment agency. Executive search firm.

★7127★ Professional Placement Associates, Inc.

11 Rye Ridge Plaza
Rye Brook, NY 10573
Ph: (914)251-1000   Fax: (914)939-1959

Employment agency.

★7128★ Shiloh Careers International, Inc.

7105 Peach Ct., Ste. 102
PO Box 831
Brentwood, TN 37024-0831
Ph: (615)373-3090

Employment agency.

★7129★ Sue Carroll Personnel, Inc.

16 E. 79th St.
New York, NY 10021
Ph: (212)288-8866   Fax: (212)988-7191

Employment agency and executive search firm.

★7130★ Travcorps, Inc.

40 Eastern Ave.
Malden, MA 02148
Ph: (617)322-2600

Places staff in temporary assignments.

OTHER SOURCES

★7131★ American Registry of Diagnostic Medical Sonographers (ARDMS)

600 Jefferson Plz., Ste. 360
Rockville, MD 20852-1150
Ph: (301)738-8401   Fax: (301)738-0312
Fr: 800-541-9754

Members: Administers examinations in the field of diagnostic medical sonography and vascular technology throughout the U.S. and Canada and registers candidates passing those exams in the specialties of their expertise. **Activities:** Maintains central office for administering examination plans and schedules and assisting registered candidates and those interested in becoming registered.

★7132★ American Registry of Radiologic Technologists (ARRT)

1255 Northland Dr.
St. Paul, MN 55120
Ph: (612)687-0048

Purpose: Radiologic certification boards that administer examinations, issues certificates of registration to radiographers, nuclear medicine technologists, and radiation therapists, and investigates the qualifications of practicing radiologic technologists. Governed by trustees appointed from American College of Radiology and American Society of Radiologic Technologists.

★7133★ American Society of Radiologic Technologists (ASRT)

15000 Central Ave. SE
Albuquerque, NM 87123
Ph: (505)298-4500   Fax: (505)298-5063

Members: Professional society of diagnostic radiography, radiation therapy, ultrasound, and nuclear medicine technologists. **Purpose:** Advances the science of radiologic technology; establishes and maintains high standards of education; evaluates the quality of patient care; improves the welfare and socioeconomics of radiologic technologists. Operates ASRT Educational Foundation, which provides educational materials to radiologic technologists.

★7134★ Career Encounters: Radiology

Cambridge Career Products
PO Box 2153
Dept. CC15
Charleston, WV 25328-2153
Ph: (304)744-9323   Fax: (304)744-9351
Fr: 800-468-4227

Video. $99.95. 25 minutes. Professionals shown in a variety of settings discuss different aspects of their careers.

★7135★ Day in a Career: X-Ray Technologist

Cambridge Career Products
PO Box 2153
Dept. CC15
Charleston, WV 25328-2153
Ph: (304)744-9323   Fax: (304)744-9351
Fr: 800-468-4227

Video. 1994. $89.00. 15-22 minutes. Includes candid interviews and work situations, plus outlines of relevant career information.

Real Estate Agents

★7136★ New England Real Estate Journal

East Coast Publications
PO Box 55
Accord, MA 02018
Ph: (617)878-4540   Fax: (617)871-1853

Weekly (Fri.). $139.00/year for individuals. Newspaper publishing commercial, industrial, and investment real estate news.

★7137★ Realtor News (All Member Issue)

National Association of Realtors
700 11th St.
Washington, DC 20001
Ph: (202)383-1193   Fax: (202)383-1231

Monthly. $12.00/year for individuals. Real estate newspaper.

PLACEMENT AND JOB REFERRAL SERVICES

★7138★ The Counselors of Real Estate (American Society of Real Estate Counselors)

430 N. Michigan Ave.
Chicago, IL 60611-4089
Ph: (312)329-8427   Fax: (312)329-8881

Members: Professional society of individuals with extensive experience in all phases of real estate who provide a counseling service for which they are compensated by a pre-agreed fee or salary for services, as opposed to a commission or a contingent fee. Members are entitled to use the professional designation CRE (Counselor of Real Estate). **Activities:** Conducts educational programs; maintains speakers' bureau; operates placement service and research programs.

★7139★ International College of Real Estate Consulting Professionals (RECP)

297 Dakota St.
Le Sueur, MN 56058
Ph: (612)665-6280   Fax: (612)665-6280

Members: Individuals in 6 countries proficient in fields related to the real estate profession, including sales, accounting, law, consultation, education, finance, and government. **Activities:** Compiles statistics; provides referral and placement services.

★7140★ Women's Direct Marketing International (WDRG)

224 7th St.
Garden City, NY 11530
Ph: (516)746-6700

Members: Direct marketing professionals. **Purpose:** Seeks to: advance the interests and influence of women in the direct response industry; provide for communication and career education; assist in advancement of personal career objectives; serve as professional network to develop business contacts and foster mutual goals. **Activities:** Maintains career talent bank. Distributes information nationally; maintains other chapters in Chicago, IL, Los Angeles, CA, and Dallas, TX.

EMPLOYER DIRECTORIES AND NETWORKING LISTS

★7141★ American Real Estate Guide

LL & IL Publishing, Inc.
125A S. Service Rd.
Jericho, NY 11753
Fax: (516)829-7416

Annual. $100.00, per volume. Covers Approximately 10,000 key officials at real estate companies and related businesses. Published in a national edition and four regional editions. Entries include: Executive name, title, company name, address, phone, product/service. Arrangement: Alphabetical. Indexes: Company name, line of business.

★7142★ Buyers Broker Registry

Who's Who in Creative Real Estate
PO Box 23275
Ventura, CA 93002
Ph: (805)492-8120

Annual, March. $25.00. Covers 700 real agents in the U.S. who have met certain performance criteria as set forth by the publisher. Entries include: Name, address, phone, location, telex, geographical area served, description. Arrangement: Geographical. Indexes: Name.

★7143★ CRB-CRS Referral Directory

Realtors National Marketing Institute
430 N. Michigan Ave., Ste. 500
Chicago, IL 60611-4092
Ph: (312)670-3780   Fax: (312)329-8882

Annual, October. Free. Covers 27,000 Certified Real Estate Brokerage Managers (CRB) and Certified Residential Specialists (CRS). Entries include: Member name, firm name, address, phone, fax; designations held, real estate board with which affiliated, areas of specialization, housing information. Arrangement: Geographical. Indexes: Alphabetical.

★7144★ Directory of Real Estate Development & Related Education Programs

Urban Land Institute
625 Indiana Ave. NW
Washington, DC 20004
Ph: (202)624-7000   Fax: 800-248-4585
Fr: 800-321-5011

Biennial, May of even years. $19.00. Covers over 60 real estate development education programs currently being offered at colleges and universities. Entries include: College or university name, address, list of faculty members, curriculum, tuition, length of program, degrees offered, financial aid information, job placement services.

★7145★ E-R-C Directory of Real Estate Appraisers and Brokers

Employee Relocation Council
1720 N St. NW
Washington, DC 20036
Ph: (202)857-0857   Fax: (202)467-4012

Annual, March. $35.00, payment with order. Covers about 10,000 member brokers and appraisers worldwide, equipped to handle the relocation of employees. Entries include: For brokers, firm name, address, phone, number of offices, median price, code indicating services offered, list of corporations served, code indicating means of working with other brokers. For appraisers name, firm affiliation (if any), address, phone, code indicating professional designations, names of corporations served. Arrangement: Appraisers and brokers are geographical.

★7146★ **Executive Guide to Specialists in Industrial and Office Real Estate**

Society of Industrial and Office Realtors
700 11th St. NW, Ste. 510
Washington, DC 20001-4511
Ph: (202)737-1150   Fax: (202)737-8796
Fr: 800-967-0085

Annual, June. $60.00. Covers approximately 1,800 specialists in industrial real estate. Entries include: Company name, address, phone, fax, name of individual member. Arrangement: Geographical. Indexes: Personal name.

★7147★ **National Association of Real Estate Companies—Membership Directory**

National Association of Real Estate
  Companies
Box 958
Columbia, MD 21044
Ph: (410)821-1614   Fax: (410)992-6363

Quarterly. Available to members only. Covers about 200 real estate development companies. Entries include: Company name, address, phone, name of contact.

★7148★ **National Real Estate Investor Sourcebook**

Argus Business
6151 Powers Ferry Rd. NW
Atlanta, GA 30339-2941
Ph: (404)955-2500   Fax: (404)955-0400

Annual, summer. $76.95, payment must accompany order. Publication includes: List of about 7,000 companies and individuals in 22 real estate fields, including appraisers; architects; asset managers; builders and contractors; business/office parks; computer services; corporate real estate managers; developers; economic and industrial development authorities; environmental consultants; equity investors; executive search firms; financial services; hospitality services; hotel franchisers; institutional and pension fund advisors; limited partnerships; property managers; real estate brokers, agents, consultants, and counselors; title insurance companies; related associations; and others. Arrangement: Classified by field or type of activity, then geographical.

★7149★ **National Referral Roster**

Stamats Communications, Inc.
427 6th Ave. SE
Cedar Rapids, IA 52401
Ph: (319)364-6167   Fax: (319)365-5421
Fr: 800-553-8878

Annual, February. $75.00. Covers 130,000 residential real estate firms. Entries include: Firm name, address, phone, fax, name and title of contact. Arrangement: Geographical.

★7150★ **Nelson's Directory of Institutional Real Estate**

Nelson Publications
1 Gateway Plaza
PO Box 591
Port Chester, NY 10573
Ph: (914)937-8400   Fax: (914)937-8908
Fr: 800-333-6357

Annual, August. $295.00. Covers real estate firms, insurance companies, and plan sponsors providing specialized real estate services. Entries include: Company name, address, phone, fax, description, key executives. Arrangement: Separate sections for real estate investment managers, plan sponsors, consultants, insurance companies, and real estate service providers. Indexes: Geographical, product/service.

★7151★ **Real Estate Consultants Directory**

American Business Directories, Inc.
American Business Information, Inc.
5711 S. 86th Cir.
Omaha, NE 68127
Ph: (402)593-4600   Fax: (402)331-1505

Annual. $800.00, U.S. edition. Entries include: Name, address, phone (including area code), size of advertisement, year first in Yellow Pages, name of owner or manager, number of employees. Compiled from telephone company Yellow Pages, nationwide. Arrangement: Geographical.

★7152★ **U.S. Real Estate Register**

Barry, Inc.
PO Box 551
Wilmington, MA 01887
Ph: (508)658-0441   Fax: (508)657-8691
Fr: 800-752-1269

Annual, July. $62.50, postpaid. Covers real estate departments of large national companies, industrial economic/development organizations, chambers of commerce, utilities, real estate brokers, and railroads involved in commercial and industrial real estate development. Entries include: Company or organization name, address; many listings include name of contact. Arrangement: Companies are alphabetical; others are geographical.

★7153★ **Who's Who in Creative Real Estate**

Who's Who in Creative Real Estate, Inc.
Box 23275
Ventura, CA 93002
Ph: (805)492-8120   Fax: (805)492-5802
Fr: 800-729-5147

Annual, February. $25.00, plus $2.90 shipping. Covers about 700 licensed real estate salespersons and brokers who have completed 3-5 specified 2-6 day seminars in real estate subjects; Buyer's Broker Registry section of about 330 real estate agents who have completed two transactions acting as a buyer's agent and completed specified seminars (agents can appear in both sections); about 35 individuals or firms that conduct real estate seminars; state real estate licensing agencies. Arrangement: Geographical. Indexes: Alphabetical.

★7154★ **Who's Who in Luxury Real Estate**

JBL, Inc.
2110 Western Ave.
Seattle, WA 98121
Ph: (206)441-7900   Fax: (206)441-5297
Fr: 800-488-4066

Annual, January. $19.95. Covers Approximately 500 international luxury real estate brokers. Entries include: Company name, address, phone, names and titles of key personnel, description, number of employees, geographical area served, number of offices, area price range, referral, logo. Arrangement: Geographical. Indexes: Geographical, trade name.

HANDBOOKS AND MANUALS

★7155★ **Becoming a Real Estate Professional**

Vantage Press, Inc.
516 W. 34th St.
New York, NY 10001
Ph: (212)736-1767   Fax: (212)736-2273
Fr: 800-882-3273

Shawn J. Murphy. 1995. $19.95 (paper).

★7156★ **Career Choices for the 90's for Students of Business**

Walker and Company
435 Hudson St.
New York, NY 10014
Ph: (212)727-8300   Fax: (212)727-0984
Fr: 800-289-2553

Prepared by the Career Associates staff. 1990. $9.95. 166 pages. Discusses alternatives for students of business. Offers advice on how to break into the field and how to move up. Covers where and who the employers are, internship possibilities, and professional networking associations. Comprehensive guide to career and job search planning.

★7157★ **Career Choices for the 90's for Students of Communications and Journalism**

Walker and Company
435 Hudson St.
New York, NY 10014
Ph: (212)727-8300   Fax: (212)727-0984
Fr: 800-289-2553

Prepared by the Career Associates staff. 1990. $8.95. 166 pages. Discusses alternatives for students of communications and journalism. Offers advice on how to break into the field and how to move up. Covers where and who the employers are, internship possibilities, and professional networking associations. Comprehensive guide to career and job search planning.

★7158★ **Career Choices for the 90's for Students of Economics**

Walker and Company
435 Hudson St.
New York, NY 10014
Ph: (212)727-8300   Fax: (212)727-0984
Fr: 800-289-2553

Prepared by the Career Associates staff.

1990. $8.95. 166 pages. Discusses alternatives for students of economics. Offers advice on how to break into the field and how to move up. Covers where and who the employers are, internship possibilities, and professional networking associations. Comprehensive guide to career and job search planning.

★7159★ **Career Choices for the 90's for Students of Mathematics**

Walker and Company
435 Hudson St.
New York, NY 10014
Ph: (212)727-8300   Fax: (212)727-0984
Fr: 800-289-2553

Prepared by the Career Associates staff. 1990. $8.95. 166 pages. Discusses alternatives for students of mathematics. Offers advice on how to break into the field and how to move up. Covers where and who the employers are, internship possibilities, and professional networking associations. Comprehensive guide to career and job search planning.

★7160★ **Careers in Real Estate**

National Association of Realtors
430 N. Michigan Ave., Rm. 251
Chicago, IL 60611-4087
Ph: (312)329-8292

Booklet exploring the varied opportunities in real estate sales.

★7161★ **The Encyclopedia of Career Choices for the 1990s: Guide to Entry-Level Jobs**

Perigree Books
The Berkley Publishing Group
PO Box 506
East Rutherford, NJ 07073
Ph: (201)933-9292   Fr: 800-223-0510

Career Associates Staff. 1992. $19.95. 862 pages. Describes 500 entry-level careers in a variety of industries. Presents qualifications required, working conditions, salary, internships, and professional associations.

★7162★ **Encyclopedia of Careers and Vocational Guidance**

J. G. Ferguson Publishing Co.
200 W. Monroe, Ste. 250
Chicago, IL 60606
Ph: (312)580-5480

William E. Hopke. Ninth edition, 1993. $129.95; $199.95 (CD-ROM). Four-volume set that profiles 900 occupations and describes job trends in 71 industries. Includes career description, educational requirements, history of the job, methods of entry, advancement, employment outlook, earnings, conditions of work, social and psychological factors, and sources of further information. Contains career and employment information for this field.

★7163★ **Fast Start in Real Estate: A Survival Guide for New Agents**

Dearborn Financial Publishing, Inc.
155 N. Wacker Dr.
Chicago, IL 60606-1719
Ph: (312)836-4400   Fax: (312)836-1021

Karl Breckenridge. 1991. $12.95 (paper).

★7164★ **Hot Tips, Sneaky Tricks and Last-Ditch Tactics**

John Wiley and Sons, Inc.
605 3rd Ave.
New York, NY 10158
Ph: (212)850-6000   Fr: 800-225-5945

Jeff B. Speck. 1989. $12.95. Subtitled: ''An Insider's Guide to Getting Your First Corporate Job''. Gives an inside glimpse of the recruiting process and provides tips on using this knowledge to get the interview or the job.

★7165★ **How About a Career in Real Estate?**

Dearborn Financial Publishing, Inc.
155 N. Wacker Dr.
Chicago, IL 60606-1719
Ph: (312)836-4400   Fax: (312)836-1021

Carla Cross. 1993. $14.95 (paper).

★7166★ **Jobs '90**

Prentice Hall
113 Sylvan Ave.
Rte. 9W
Englewood Cliffs, NJ 07632
Ph: (201)592-2000   Fr: 800-922-0579

Kathryn Petras and Ross Petras. 1990. $14.95. 320 pages. Discusses employment prospects and trends. Lists leading companies, associations, directories, and magazines.

★7167★ **100 Best Careers for the Year 2000**

Prentice Hall General Reference
15 Columbus Cir.
New York, NY 10023
Ph: (212)373-8500   Fr: 800-223-2348

Shelly Field. 1992. $15.00 (paper). Covers 100 of the fastest growing jobs. The publication is divided into 11 general employment sections. Specific careers are covered within each section. Provides job description, responsibilities, employment opportunities, earnings, education and training, advancement opportunities, and experience and qualifications for each occupation.

★7168★ **Real Estate Careers: Twenty-Five Growing Opportunities for Good Times & Bad**

John Wiley & Sons, Inc.
605 3rd Ave.
New York, NY 10158-0012
Ph: (212)850-6000   Fr: 800-225-5945

Carolyn Janik. 1994. $42.50; $16.95 (paper).

★7169★ **Success in New Home Sales: Developing the Right Mentality & Techniques**

Tiller Marketing Services
1373 Butter Churn Dr.
Herndon, VA 22070
Ph: (703)450-5214

Richard Tiller. 1991. $19.95 (paper).

★7170★ **Where the Jobs Are: The Hottest Careers for the '90s**

The Career Press, Inc.
3 Tice Rd.
PO Box 687
Franklin Lakes, NJ 07417
Ph: (201)848-0310   Fax: (201)848-1727
Fr: 800-237-3371

Joyce Hadley. Second edition, 1995. $9.99. 300 pages. Describes careers in fifteen general fields, from accounting to travel and hospitality.

★7171★ **Your Opportunities in Real Estate**

Energeia Publishing, Inc.
860 Commercial St., S.
Salem, OR 97302
Ph: (503)362-1480   Fax: (503)362-2123

Laurie Bean. 1994. $2.00 (paper).

★7172★ **Your Successful Real Estate Career: Building a Future in Real Estate Sales**

AMACOM
135 W. 50th St., 15th Fl.
New York, NY 10020
Ph: (212)903-8315   Fr: 800-262-9699

Kenneth W. Edwards. 1992. $14.95. 192 pages. Provides an overview of career opportunities in real estate related careers.

EMPLOYMENT AGENCIES AND SEARCH FIRMS

★7173★ **Alzed Enterprises Ltd.**

4 Gateway Center, Ste. 205
Pittsburgh, PA 15222-1260
Ph: (412)261-7200   Fax: (412)392-2365

Executive search firm.

★7174★ **Consultants to Executive Management**

20 S. Clark St., Ste. 610
Chicago, IL 60603
Ph: (312)855-1500

Employment agency.

★7175★ **Kimmel and Associates**

25 Page Ave.
Asheville, NC 28801
Ph: (704)251-9900   Fax: (704)251-9955

Employment agency.

★7176★ **Preferred Leads, Inc.**

1660 S. Albion St., Ste. 812
Denver, CO 80222
Ph: (303)782-5447   Fax: (303)782-5649

Employment agency.

★7177★ **Real Estate Executive Search, Inc.**

PO Box 40
Santa Rosa, CA 95402-0040
Ph: (707)525-4591

Executive search firm.

★7178★ Tina Morbitzer and Associates

668 N. Orlando Ave., Ste. 105
Maitland, FL 32751
Ph: (407)539-1000   Fax: (407)539-0328
Executive search firm.

OTHER SOURCES

★7179★ CRE Member Directory

The Counselors of Real Estate
430 N. Michigan Ave.
Chicago, IL 60611
Ph: (312)329-8427   Fax: (312)329-8881

Annual, March. Free. Covers nearly 1,000 Counselors of Real Estate (CRE), including 50 counselors in Canada, Great Britain, Japan, and Australia. Entries include: Name, title, office address and phone, home address and phone, fax, areas of counseling specialty. Arrangement: Geographical. Indexes: Alphabetical, type of property counseled, counseling specialization.

★7180★ Home Economics Careers

Cambridge Career Products
PO Box 2153
Dept. CC15
Charleston, WV 25328-2153
Ph: (304)744-9323   Fax: (304)744-9351
Fr: 800-468-4227

Video. $79.95. 30 minutes. Presents a series of interviews with men and women working in different areas of home economics, including dietetics, foods and nutrition, child development, interior design, and fashion. Covers educational, personal, and professional requirements for each occupation.

★7181★ National Association of Realtors (NAR)

430 N. Michigan Ave.
Chicago, IL 60611
Ph: (312)329-8200   Fax: (312)329-8576

Members: Federation of 54 state and territory associations and 1860 local real estate boards whose members are real estate brokers and agents. Terms are registered by the association in the U.S. Patent and Trademark Office and in the states. **Purpose:** Promotes education, high professional standards, and modern techniques in specialized real estate work such as brokerage, appraisal, property management, land development, industrial real estate, farm brokerage, and counseling. Conducts research programs.

★7182★ National Directory of 420 Current Real Estate Periodicals and Professional Real Estate Associations, Institutes, Councils & Societies

Real Estate Publishing Co.
Box 41177
Sacramento, CA 95841
Ph: (916)677-3864

Biennial, August of even years. $14.95. Covers about 420 real estate resource publications and institutions. Entries include: Publisher, organization, or institute name, address, phone, publication name, product or services provided. Arrangement: Alphabetical. Indexes: Name, subject.

★7183★ National Real Estate Directory

Real Estate Publications, Inc.
322 W. Rio Vista Ct.
Tampa, FL 33604-6941
Ph: (813)237-0484   Fr: 800-356-2317

Biennial. $29.95. Covers about 22,500 federal and state agencies, offices, and departments related to the regulation of real estate; real estate associations, publications, and organizations. Entries include: Agency, association, department, or publication name, address, phone. Arrangement: Classified by type of organization, then geographical.

★7184★ Real Estate Books and Periodicals in Print

Real Estate Publishing Co.
Box 41177
Sacramento, CA 95841
Ph: (916)677-3864

Biennial, August of odd years. $29.95. Covers about 400 publishers of real estate books and periodicals; sources of audiocassette tapes, training films, and videotapes on real estate; real estate associations. Entries include: Organization name, address, phone, ordering information; description of publications or audiovisual materials. Arrangement: Alphabetical. Indexes: Subject.

★7185★ Real Estate Schools Directory

American Business Directories, Inc.
American Business Information, Inc.
5711 S. 86th Cir.
Omaha, NE 68127
Ph: (402)593-4600   Fax: (402)331-1505

Updated continuously; printed on request. Entries include: Name, address, phone, size of advertisement, name of owner or manager, number of employees, year first in Yellow Pages. Compiled from telephone company Yellow Pages, nationwide. Arrangement: Geographical.

★7186★ Realtors Land Institute (RLI)

430 N. Michigan Ave.
Chicago, IL 60611
Ph: (312)329-8440   Fr: 800-441-LAND

Members: Real estate brokers and salespersons selling, managing, appraising, or developing all types of land. **Purpose:** Maintains educational programs for real estate brokers; promotes competence and accredits members. **Activities:** Sponsors courses for realtors and others seeking professional excellence on Land Brokerage, Agricultural Land Brokerage, Exchanging Properties, Estate Planning, Subdivision Development, and Financial Analysis of Land Investment.

★7187★ Women's Council of Realtors (WCR)

430 N. Michigan Ave.
Chicago, IL 60611
Ph: (312)329-8483   Fax: (312)329-3290

Members: Women real estate brokers and salespeople. **Purpose:** Provides opportunity for real estate professionals to participate at local, state, and national levels. Makes programs available for personal and career growth. Encourages increased productivity, financial security, and the development of leadership skills among members. Offers courses in leadership training, and referral and relocation business.

Real Estate Appraisers

★7188★ Realtor News (All Member Issue)

National Association of Realtors
700 11th St.
Washington, DC 20001
Ph: (202)383-1193   Fax: (202)383-1231
Monthly. $12.00/year for individuals. Real estate newspaper.

PLACEMENT AND JOB REFERRAL SERVICES

★7189★ American Society of Farm Managers and Rural Appraisers (ASFMRA)

950 S. Cherry St., Ste. 508
Denver, CO 80222
Ph: (303)758-3513   Fax: (303)758-0190
Members: Professional farm managers, appraisers, lenders, and researchers in farm and ranch management and/or rural appraisal. **Activities:** Bestows registered ARA (Accredited Rural Appraiser) and AFM (Accredited Farm Manager) designations. Operates managing and appraisal schools, seminars, and conferences. Maintains placement service.

★7190★ International College of Real Estate Consulting Professionals (RECP)

297 Dakota St.
Le Sueur, MN 56058
Ph: (612)665-6280   Fax: (612)665-6280
Members: Individuals in 6 countries proficient in fields related to the real estate profession, including sales, accounting, law, consultation, education, finance, and government. **Activities:** Compiles statistics; provides referral and placement services.

★7191★ International Real Estate Institute (IREI)

8383 E. Evans Rd.
Scottsdale, AZ 85260
Ph: (602)998-8267   Fax: (602)998-8022
Members: Professionals in 120 countries specializing in the development, finance, investment, and valuation of real estate. **Activities:** Conducts educational seminars and regional programs; operates speakers' bureau and placement service. Compiles statistics, consults United Nations on property issues.

★7192★ National Association of Master Appraisers (NAMA)

303 W. Cypress St.
PO Box 12617
San Antonio, TX 78212-0617
Ph: (210)271-0781   Fax: (210)225-8450
Fr: 800-229-6262
Members: Appraisers, analysts, assessors, brokers, salespersons, and others involved in real estate appraisal. **Purpose:** Works to enhance competency in the appraisal industry through education. Provides basic and advanced courses and educational meetings in techniques, management practices, and marketing strategies. **Activities:** Sponsors Lender Awareness Program to increase awareness among banks and savings association officers. Provides referral services and speakers' bureau.

★7193★ National Association of Review Appraisers and Mortgage Underwriters (NARA/MU)

8383 E. Evans Rd.
Scottsdale, AZ 85260
Ph: (602)998-3000   Fax: (602)998-8022
Members: Real estate professionals and mortgage underwriters who aid in determining value of property. **Purpose:** Acts as umbrella group for real estate appraisers. **Activities:** Conducts educational seminars; maintains speakers' bureau; operates placement service.

EMPLOYER DIRECTORIES AND NETWORKING LISTS

★7194★ Appraisal Institute—Directory of Designated Members

Appraisal Institute
875 N. Michigan Ave., Ste. 2400
Chicago, IL 60611-1980
Ph: (312)335-4100   Fax: (312)335-4400
Annual, March. Free; request on company letterhead. Covers over 12,000 real estate appraisers of all types of real property in the United States and Canada who hold the MAI, SRA, or SREA general appraisal, and/or SRPA or RM residential appraisal membership designations of the Appraisal Institute; includes limited overseas listings. Entries include: Name of individual member, company name, address, phone. Arrangement: Geographical.

★7195★ Directory of Accredited Real Property Appraisers

American Society of Appraisers
PO Box 17265
Washington, DC 20041
Ph: (202)478-2228   Fax: (202)742-8471
Fr: 800-272-8258
Annual, January. Free. Covers Approximately 1,700 urban, residential, rural, ad valorem, and timberland appraisers; limited international coverage. Entries include: Personal and company name, address, phone, fax. Arrangement: Geographical. Indexes: Specialty.

★7196★ E-R-C Directory of Real Estate Appraisers and Brokers

Employee Relocation Council
1720 N St. NW
Washington, DC 20036
Ph: (202)857-0857   Fax: (202)467-4012
Annual, March. $35.00, payment with order. Covers about 10,000 member brokers and appraisers worldwide, equipped to handle the relocation of employees. Entries include: For brokers, firm name, address, phone, number of offices, median price, code indicating services offered, list of corporations served, code indicating means of working

with other brokers. For appraisers name, firm affiliation (if any), address, phone, code indicating professional designations, names of corporations served. Arrangement: Appraisers and brokers are geographical.

★7197★ National Association of Independent Fee Appraisers—National Membership Directory

National Association of Independent Fee Appraisers
7501 Murdoch Ave.
St. Louis, MO 63119
Ph: (314)781-6688   Fax: (314)781-2872

Annual, January. Free. Covers 5,500 independent real estate appraisers. Entries include: Name, address, phone, level of membership. Arrangement: Geographical.

★7198★ National Association of Master Appraisers—Membership Directory

National Association of Master Appraisers (NAMA)
303 W. Cypress St.
San Antonio, TX 78212
Ph: (512)271-0781   Fax: (512)225-8450
Fr: 800-229-6262

Annual, January. Free. Covers Approximately 3,500 real estate appraisers. Entries include: Personal name, address, phone, field of specialty. Arrangement: Geographical. Indexes: Name.

★7199★ National Association of Real Estate Companies—Membership Directory

National Association of Real Estate Companies
Box 958
Columbia, MD 21044
Ph: (410)821-1614   Fax: (410)992-6363

Quarterly. Available to members only. Covers about 200 real estate development companies. Entries include: Company name, address, phone, name of contact.

★7200★ National Real Estate Investor Sourcebook

Argus Business
6151 Powers Ferry Rd. NW
Atlanta, GA 30339-2941
Ph: (404)955-2500   Fax: (404)955-0400

Annual, summer. $76.95, payment must accompany order. Publication includes: List of about 7,000 companies and individuals in 22 real estate fields, including appraisers; architects; asset managers; builders and contractors; business/office parks; computer services; corporate real estate managers; developers; economic and industrial development authorities; environmental consultants; equity investors; executive search firms; financial services; hospitality services; hotel franchisers; institutional and pension fund advisors; limited partnerships; property managers; real estate brokers, agents, consultants, and counselors; title insurance companies; related associations; and others. Arrangement: Classified by field or type of activity, then geographical.

★7201★ National Referral Roster

Stamats Communications, Inc.
427 6th Ave. SE
Cedar Rapids, IA 52401
Ph: (319)364-6167   Fax: (319)365-5421
Fr: 800-553-8878

Annual, February. $75.00. Covers 130,000 residential real estate firms. Entries include: Firm name, address, phone, fax, name and title of contact. Arrangement: Geographical.

★7202★ Real Estate Appraisers Directory

American Business Directories, Inc.
American Business Information, Inc.
5711 S. 86th Cir.
Omaha, NE 68127
Ph: (402)593-4600   Fax: (402)331-1505

Annual. $980.00, U.S. edition; $145.00, Canad. ed.; payment with order. Number of listings: 29,233 (U.S. edition); 1,852 (Canadian edition). Entries include: Name, address, phone (including area code), size of advertisement, year first in Yellow Pages, name of owner or manager, number of employees. Regional editions available. Compiled from telephone company Yellow Pages, nationwide. Arrangement: Geographical.

Handbooks and Manuals

★7203★ Becoming a Real Estate Professional

Vantage Press, Inc.
516 W. 34th St.
New York, NY 10001
Ph: (212)736-1767   Fax: (212)736-2273
Fr: 800-882-3273

Shawn J. Murphy. 1995. $19.95 (paper).

★7204★ Career Choices for the 90's for Students of Business

Walker and Company
435 Hudson St.
New York, NY 10014
Ph: (212)727-8300   Fax: (212)727-0984
Fr: 800-289-2553

Prepared by the Career Associates staff. 1990. $9.95. 166 pages. Discusses alternatives for students of business. Offers advice on how to break into the field and how to move up. Covers where and who the employers are, internship possibilities, and professional networking associations. Comprehensive guide to career and job search planning.

★7205★ Career Choices for the 90's for Students of Economics

Walker and Company
435 Hudson St.
New York, NY 10014
Ph: (212)727-8300   Fax: (212)727-0984
Fr: 800-289-2553

Prepared by the Career Associates staff. 1990. $8.95. 166 pages. Discusses alternatives for students of economics. Offers advice on how to break into the field and how to move up. Covers where and who the employers are, internship possibilities, and profes-

sional networking associations. Comprehensive guide to career and job search planning.

★7206★ Career Choices for the 90's for Students of Mathematics

Walker and Company
435 Hudson St.
New York, NY 10014
Ph: (212)727-8300   Fax: (212)727-0984
Fr: 800-289-2553

Prepared by the Career Associates staff. 1990. $8.95. 166 pages. Discusses alternatives for students of mathematics. Offers advice on how to break into the field and how to move up. Covers where and who the employers are, internship possibilities, and professional networking associations. Comprehensive guide to career and job search planning.

★7207★ The Encyclopedia of Career Choices for the 1990s: Guide to Entry-Level Jobs

Perigree Books
The Berkley Publishing Group
PO Box 506
East Rutherford, NJ 07073
Ph: (201)933-9292   Fr: 800-223-0510

Career Associates Staff. 1992. $19.95. 862 pages. Describes 500 entry-level careers in a variety of industries. Presents qualifications required, working conditions, salary, internships, and professional associations.

★7208★ Encyclopedia of Careers and Vocational Guidance

J. G. Ferguson Publishing Co.
200 W. Monroe, Ste. 250
Chicago, IL 60606
Ph: (312)580-5480

William E. Hopke. Ninth edition, 1993. $129.95; $199.95 (CD-ROM). Four-volume set that profiles 900 occupations and describes job trends in 71 industries. Includes career description, educational requirements, history of the job, methods of entry, advancement, employment outlook, earnings, conditions of work, social and psychological factors, and sources of further information. Contains career and employment information for this field.

★7209★ Fast Start in Real Estate: A Survival Guide for New Agents

Dearborn Financial Publishing, Inc.
155 N. Wacker Dr.
Chicago, IL 60606-1719
Ph: (312)836-4400   Fax: (312)836-1021

Karl Breckenridge. 1991. $12.95 (paper).

★7210★ How About a Career in Real Estate?

Dearborn Financial Publishing, Inc.
155 N. Wacker Dr.
Chicago, IL 60606-1719
Ph: (312)836-4400   Fax: (312)836-1021

Carla Cross. 1993. $14.95 (paper).

★7211★ Real Estate Careers: Twenty-Five Growing Opportunities for Good Times & Bad

John Wiley & Sons, Inc.
605 3rd Ave.
New York, NY 10158-0012
Ph: (212)850-6000   Fr: 800-225-5945

Carolyn Janik. 1994. $42.50; $16.95 (paper).

★7212★ Your Opportunities in Real Estate

Energeia Publishing, Inc.
860 Commercial St., S.
Salem, OR 97302
Ph: (503)362-1480   Fax: (503)362-2123

Laurie Bean. 1994. $2.00 (paper).

★7213★ Your Successful Real Estate Career: Building a Future in Real Estate Sales

AMACOM
135 W. 50th St., 15th Fl.
New York, NY 10020
Ph: (212)903-8315   Fr: 800-262-9699

Kenneth W. Edwards. 1992. $14.95. 192 pages. Provides an overview of career opportunities in real estate related careers.

EMPLOYMENT AGENCIES AND SEARCH FIRMS

★7214★ The Ahrens Agency, Inc.

3285 Wolfson Dr.
Baldwin, NY 11510
Ph: (516)223-5627

Employment agency. Fills positions in real estate and other fields.

★7215★ Alzed Enterprises Ltd.

4 Gateway Center, Ste. 205
Pittsburgh, PA 15222-1260
Ph: (412)261-7200   Fax: (412)392-2365

Executive search firm.

★7216★ Continental Field Service Corp.

37 E. Main St.
Elmsford, NY 10523-2607
Ph: (914)592-7240

Employment agency.

★7217★ Culver Personnel Service

1555 Old Bayshore Hwy., Ste. 100
Burlingame, CA 94010
Ph: (415)692-9090   Fax: (415)692-6618

Employment agency.

★7218★ Real Estate Executive Search, Inc.

PO Box 40
Santa Rosa, CA 95402-0040
Ph: (707)525-4591

Executive search firm.

★7219★ Tina Morbitzer and Associates

668 N. Orlando Ave., Ste. 105
Maitland, FL 32751
Ph: (407)539-1000   Fax: (407)539-0328

Executive search firm.

OTHER SOURCES

★7220★ Appraisal Institute (AI)

875 N. Michigan Ave., Ste. 2400
Chicago, IL 60611-1980
Ph: (312)335-4100   Fax: (312)335-4400

Members: General appraisers who hold the MAI, SRPA, or SREA designations, and residential members who hold the SRA or RM designations. **Purpose:** Enforces Code of Professional Ethics and Standards of Professional Appraisal Practice. Confers one general designation, the MAI, and one residential designation, the SRA. Provides training in valuation of residential and income properties, market analysis, and standards of professional appraisal practice. Sponsors courses in preparation for state certification and licensing; offers continuing education programs for members.

★7221★ Compensation and Benefit Survey for Corporate Real Estate Executives

NACORE International
471 Spencer Dr. S, Ste. 8
West Palm Beach, FL 33409-6685
Ph: (407)683-8111

Annual. Results of a survey of 900 corporate real estate executives representing 29 positions. Gives the type of company, annual sales, geographic area, education, age, and salary (overall average, overall medium, medium lower third, medium upper third) for 29 different job titles.

★7222★ National Association of Real Estate Appraisers (NAREA)

8383 E. Evans Rd.
Scottsdale, AZ 85260
Ph: (602)948-8000   Fax: (602)998-8022

Members: Real estate appraisers. **Purpose:** To make available the services of the most highly qualified real estate appraisers. **Activities:** Offers certification to members.

★7223★ National Association of Realtors (NAR)

430 N. Michigan Ave.
Chicago, IL 60611
Ph: (312)329-8200   Fax: (312)329-8576

Members: Federation of 54 state and territory associations and 1860 local real estate boards whose members are real estate brokers and agents. Terms are registered by the association in the U.S. Patent and Trademark Office and in the states. **Purpose:** Promotes education, high professional standards, and modern techniques in specialized real estate

work such as brokerage, appraisal, property management, land development, industrial real estate, farm brokerage, and counseling. Conducts research programs.

★7224★ National Directory of 420 Current Real Estate Periodicals and Professional Real Estate Associations, Institutes, Councils & Societies

Real Estate Publishing Co.
Box 41177
Sacramento, CA 95841
Ph: (916)677-3864

Biennial, August of even years. $14.95. Covers about 420 real estate resource publications and institutions. Entries include: Publisher, organization, or institute name, address, phone, publication name, product or services provided. Arrangement: Alphabetical. Indexes: Name, subject.

★7225★ National Real Estate Directory

Real Estate Publications, Inc.
322 W. Rio Vista Ct.
Tampa, FL 33604-6941
Ph: (813)237-0484   Fr: 800-356-2317

Biennial. $29.95. Covers about 22,500 federal and state agencies, offices, and departments related to the regulation of real estate; real estate associations, publications, and organizations. Entries include: Agency, association, department, or publication name, address, phone. Arrangement: Classified by type of organization, then geographical.

★7226★ Real Estate Schools Directory

American Business Directories, Inc.
American Business Information, Inc.
5711 S. 86th Cir.
Omaha, NE 68127
Ph: (402)593-4600   Fax: (402)331-1505

Updated continuously; printed on request. Entries include: Name, address, phone, size of advertisement, name of owner or manager, number of employees, year first in Yellow Pages. Compiled from telephone company Yellow Pages, nationwide. Arrangement: Geographical.

★7227★ Realtors Land Institute (RLI)

430 N. Michigan Ave.
Chicago, IL 60611
Ph: (312)329-8440   Fr: 800-441-LAND

Members: Real estate brokers and salespersons selling, managing, appraising, or developing all types of land. **Purpose:** Maintains educational programs for real estate brokers; promotes competence and accredits members. **Activities:** Sponsors courses for realtors and others seeking professional excellence on Land Brokerage, Agricultural Land Brokerage, Exchanging Properties, Estate Planning, Subdivision Development, and Financial Analysis of Land Investment.

Recreation Workers

SOURCES OF HELP-WANTED ADS

★7228★ American City and County

Communication Channels, Inc.
6255 Barfield Rd.
Atlanta, GA 30328
Ph: (404)955-9970   Fax: (404)256-3116

Monthly. $54.00/year for individuals. Municipal and county administration magazine.

★7229★ Amusement Business

BPI Communications
1515 Broadway, 39th Fl.
New York, NY 10036
Ph: (212)536-5025   Fax: (212)525-5055
Fr: 800-344-7119

Weekly. $115.00/year for individuals. Trade newspaper covering mass entertainment management including events, attendance, and spending at arenas, stadiums, amusement and theme parks, fairs, festivals, carnivals, and touring shows. Live entertainment, sports business, merchandise, and food and drink are also covered.

★7230★ Camping Magazine

American Camping Association
5000 State Rd. 67 N
Martinsville, IN 46151-7902
Ph: (317)342-8456   Fax: (317)342-2065

Bimonthly. $23.95/year for individuals; $30.50/year for institutions; $4.00 for single issue. Magazine on organized camp management.

★7231★ Job Opportunities Bulletin

National Recreation and Park Association (NRPA)
2775 S. Quincy St., Ste. 300
Arlington, VA 22206
Ph: (703)820-4940   Fr: 800-626-6772

Bimonthly $30.00/year.

★7232★ The Municipality

League of Wisconsin Municipalities
122 W. Washington Ave., Ste. 301
Madison, WI 53703-2757
Ph: (608)267-2380   Fax: (608)267-0645

Monthly. Magazine for officials of Wisconsin's local municipal governments.

★7233★ Ski Area Management

Beardsley Publishing Corp.
45 Main St. N
PO Box 644
Woodbury, CT 06798
Ph: (203)263-0888

Bimonthly. $26.00/year; $4.25/single issue.

★7234★ Skiing Trade News

Times Mirror Magazines, Inc.
2 Park Ave.
New York, NY 10016
Ph: (212)779-5285   Fax: (212)779-5465

$15.00/year for individuals. Trade newspaper for the ski industry. Includes trade show previews, company news, retail trends, personnel changes, and miscellaneous news.

★7235★ Strategies

American Alliance for Health, Physical Education, Recreation, and Dance
1900 Association Dr.
Reston, VA 22091
Ph: (703)476-3495   Fax: (703)476-9527

$20.00/year for members; $40.00/year for individuals; $50.00/year for libraries. Journal providing practical, hands-on information to physical educators and coaches.

★7236★ Western City

League of California Cities
1400 K St.
Sacramento, CA 95814
Ph: (916)444-5790   Fax: (916)658-8240

Monthly. $30.00/year for individuals; $49.00 for two years. Municipal interest magazine.

★7237★ Woodall's Campground Management

Woodall Publications Corp.
PO Box 5000
Lake Forest, IL 60045-5000
Ph: (708)362-6700   Fax: (708)362-8776

Monthly. $24.95/year for individuals; $34.95/year for Canada. Magazine focusing on operating and maintaining recreation vehicle parks.

PLACEMENT AND JOB REFERRAL SERVICES

★7238★ American Alliance for Health, Physical Education, Recreation and Dance (AAHPERD)

1900 Association Dr.
Reston, VA 22091
Ph: (703)476-3400   Fax: (703)476-9527

Members: Students and educators in physical education, dance, health, athletics, safety education, recreation, and outdoor education. **Purpose:** To improve its fields of education at all levels through such services as consultation, periodicals and special publications, leadership development, determination of standards, and research. **Activities:** Sponsors placement service. Operates Information and Resource Utilization Center devoted to physical education and recreation for the handicapped and programs for senior citizens.

★7239★ American Association for Leisure and Recreation (AALR)

1900 Association Dr.
Reston, VA 22091
Ph: (703)476-3472   Fax: (703)476-9527

Members: Teachers of recreation and park administration, leisure studies, and recreation programming in colleges and universities; professional recreation and park practitioners; people involved in other areas of health, physical education, and recreation with an interest in recreation. **Purpose:** Goals are to: encourage professional involvement and exchange; monitor recreation legislation and render consultation at the request of legislators; disseminate information on topics of current interest in leisure and recreation; maintain liaison with organizations having allied interests in leisure and recreation; support, encourage, and provide guidance to members in the development of programs of leisure services; aid in the development of quality educational/recreational programs in the schools; facilitate communication between professionals and lay people and between the schools and the community; create opportunity for professional growth and development. **Activities:** Maintains placement service. **E-Mail:** Internet, aalr@aahpend.org

★7240★ **American Sail Training Association (ASTA)**

PO Box 1459
Newport, RI 02840
Ph: (401)846-1775   Fax: (401)849-5400

Members: Organizations operating sail training programs; corporations and educational institutions supporting sail training; private citizens with an interest in sailing and sail training. **Purpose:** Promotes sail training as an educational and character-building experience for youth of all ages. Seeks to bring together the sail training ships of the world in a spirit of friendship and international goodwill. **Activities:** Sponsors Tall Ship events including sail training rallies. Maintains placement service; compiles statistics. **E-Mail:** ASTANPT$.com

★7241★ **Exer-Safety Association (ESA)**

10151 University Blvd., No. 138
Orlando, FL 32817-1981
Ph: (407)677-9501

Members: Fitness instructors, personal trainers, health spas, YMCAs, community recreation departments, and hospital wellness programs. **Purpose:** To improve the qualifications of exercise instructors; to train instructors to develop safe exercise routines that will help people avoid injury while exercising; to prepare instructors for national certification. **Activities:** Offers training in aerobics and exercise and on the physiological aspects of exercise. Conducts exercise safety and research programs. Sponsors charitable program; maintains speakers' bureau. Offers placement and children's services.

★7242★ **Horsemanship Safety Association (HSA)**

517 Bear Rd.
Lake Placid, FL 33852-9726
Fr: 800-798-8106

Members: Schools of horsemanship; equine programs at colleges and technical schools; riding instructors and students; medical personnel. **Purpose:** To educate equestrians and instructors in safe horsemanship practices. Trains instructors in leadership techniques; conducts group and private lessons for children and adults; sponsors seminars and speaking engagements by certified clinicians. Conducts riding instructor clinics for adults. Certifies instructors at 4 levels: assistant riding instructor, horsemanship safety instructor, associate instructor, and clinic instructor. **Activities:** Operates job placement services. Compiles statistics; maintains

library of instructor training manuals, speakers bureau, and placement service.

★7243★ **Jackie Robinson Foundation (JRF)**

3 W. 35th St.
New York, NY 10001
Ph: (212)290-8600   Fax: (212)290-8081

Purpose: Seeks to develop the leadership and achievement potential of minority and urban youth. Founded by the friends and family of Jackie Robinson (1919-72), the first black athlete to play major league baseball. Trains minority and poor youths for sports management careers. **Activities:** Provides counseling, support, and placement services. Awards full college scholarships to promising minority students. Maintains collection of Jackie Robinson memorabilia; has produced a national touring exhibit of archival materials pertaining to Robinson.

★7244★ **Resort and Commercial Recreation Association (RCRA)**

PO Box 1208
New Port Richey, FL 34656
Ph: (813)845-7373

Members: Professionals, agencies, vendors, educators, and students involved in the resort and commercial recreation field. **Purpose:** Seeks to advance the resort and commercial recreation industries; increase the profitability of commercial recreation enterprises; foster communication among members; promote professionalism within the industry; provide opportunities for continuing education. **Activities:** Acts as a vehicle for networking; offers program exchange and job placement services. Holds specialized educational presentations; operates student chapters; encourages and facilitates internships.

★7245★ **Society of Recreation Executives (SRE)**

Box 520
Gonzalez, FL 32560-0520
Ph: (904)477-7992   Fax: (904)479-8393

Members: Corporate executives in the recreation, leisure, and travel industry. **Purpose:** To obtain individual and collective recognition for recreation executives. Works to: provide a perspective on needs, trends, and changes within the industry; provide opportunities for the exchange of ideas and expertise among members; inform, train, and instruct members in industry principles and practices. **Activities:** Operates placement service and speakers bureau.

★7246★ **YMCA International Camp Counselor Program (ICCP)**

71 W. 23rd St., Ste. 1904
New York, NY 10010
Ph: (212)727-8800   Fax: (212)727-8814

Purpose: A work-travel program designed to introduce international university students and teachers and social workers aged 19-30 to life in America. The students spend 8 to 9 weeks counseling in children's camps across the country, followed by a period of independent or group travel. Also sponsors ICCP-Abroad placement service for American university students aged 18-25 wishing to serve

as camp counselors in Africa, Asia, Australia, Hungary, New Zealand, and South America.

EMPLOYER DIRECTORIES AND NETWORKING LISTS

★7247★ *Camps Directory*

American Business Directories, Inc.
American Business Information, Inc.
5711 S. 86th Cir.
Omaha, NE 68127
Ph: (402)593-4600   Fax: (402)331-1505

Annual. $470.00, U.S. edition. Entries include: Name, address, phone (including area code), size of advertisement, year first in Yellow Pages, name of owner or manager, number of employees. Compiled from telephone company Yellow Pages, nationwide. Arrangement: Geographical.

★7248★ *Exercise and Physical Fitness Programs Directory*

American Business Directories, Inc.
American Business Information, Inc.
5711 S. 86th Cir.
Omaha, NE 68127
Ph: (402)593-4600   Fax: (402)331-1505

Annual. $560.00, payment with order. Number of listings: 7,843. Entries include: Name, address, phone (including area code), size of advertisement, year first in Yellow Pages, name of owner or manager, number of employees. Compiled from telephone company Yellow Pages, nationwide. Arrangement: Geographical.

★7249★ *Guide to Accredited Camps*

American Camping Association
5000 State Rd., 67 N
Martinsville, IN 46151-7902
Ph: (317)342-8456   Fax: (317)342-2065
Fr: 800-428-2267

Annual, January. $10.95, postpaid. Covers approximately 2,100 summer camps. Entries include: Name of camp, address, phone, name and permanent address of owner or director, age and sex of children accepted, rates, season, capacity, facilities, programs. Arrangement: Geographical, then by day or resident camp. Indexes: Activity, special clientele, camp name, specific disabilities.

★7250★ *Health Clubs Directory*

American Business Directories, Inc.
American Business Information, Inc.
5711 S. 86th Cir.
Omaha, NE 68127
Ph: (402)593-4600   Fax: (402)331-1505

Updated continuously; printed on request. $875.00, U.S. edition. Entries include: Name, address, phone (including area code). Compiled from telephone company Yellow Pages, nationwide. Arrangement: Geographical.

★7251★ Health & Fitness Program Consultants Directory

American Business Directories, Inc.
American Business Information, Inc.
5711 S. 86th Cir.
Omaha, NE 68127
Ph: (402)593-4600   Fax: (402)331-1505

Annual. $265.00, U.S. edition. Entries include: Name, address, phone (including area code), size of advertisement, year first in Yellow Pages, name of owner or manager, number of employees. Compiled from telephone company Yellow Pages, nationwide. Arrangement: Geographical.

★7252★ Membership and Peer Network Directory

National Employee Services & Recreation Association
2211 York Rd., Ste. 207
Oak Brook, IL 60521-2371
Ph: (708)368-1280   Fax: (708)368-1286

Annual, April. Available to members only. Covers over 4,500 personnel managers, recreation directors, suppliers, and certified administrators in employee recreation, fitness, and services. Entries include: Name, address, phone. Arrangement: Alphabetical.

★7253★ Municipal/County Directory Library Edition

Carroll Publishing
1058 Thomas Jefferson St. NW
Washington, DC 20007
Ph: (202)333-8620   Fax: (202)337-7020
Fr: 800-336-4240

Annual, July. $137.00, plus $8.00 shipping; payment must accompany order. Covers officials of 1,400 county governments (with populations over 25,000) and 2,000 municipalities (with populations over 1,000); includes elected, appointed, and career office holders. Entries include: Name, title, agency, address, phone. Arrangement: County officials are geographical, then by agency; municipal officials are by city. Indexes: personal name (with phone), agency.

★7254★ Municipal Year Book

Newman Books Ltd.
32 Vauxhall Bridge Rd.
London SW1V 2SS, England
Ph: 71 9736400   Fax: 71 2335057

Annual, December. $140.00, postpaid. Covers local and central government agencies and officials of the United Kingdom; municipal art galleries, associations, development organizations, fairs, libraries, museums, airports, and other local authorities. Entries include: Name of authority or governing agency, address, phone, fax, names of elected councillors, officers, names and titles of key personnel, contacts, population, and pay. Arrangement: Geographical. Indexes: Subject, place names.

★7255★ Recreation Centers Directory

American Business Directories, Inc.
American Business Information, Inc.
5711 S. 86th Cir.
Omaha, NE 68127
Ph: (402)593-4600   Fax: (402)331-1505

Annual. $375.00, U.S. edition. Entries include: Name, address, phone (including area code), size of advertisement, year first in Yellow Pages, name of owner or manager, number of employees. Compiled from telephone company Yellow Pages, nationwide. Arrangement: Geographical.

★7256★ Recreational Sports Directory

National Intramural Recreational Sports Association
850 SW 15th St.
Corvallis, OR 97333-4145
Ph: (503)737-2088   Fax: (503)737-2026

Annual, October. $69.95, to corporations; $25.95, to members. Covers recreational sports programs in approximately 1,300 four-year colleges and universities, nearly 700 junior and community colleges, Canadian colleges and universities, and over 350 military installations. Entries include: Institution name and address; institution enrollment; name of president; names, phone numbers, fax numbers, Internet access, and job titles of recreational directors and staff; existing sports clubs; degrees offered in physical education and recreation; whether graduate assistantships or internships are available. Arrangement: Classified by institution type, then alphabetical. Indexes: Alphabetical, geographical, personal name, recreational sports program.

★7257★ YMCA Resident Camp Directory

Camping Programs
YMCA of the U.S.A.
101 N. Wacker Dr.
Chicago, IL 60606
Ph: (312)269-0502

Irregular. $5.00. Covers over 235 resident camps and conference and retreat centers operated by local YMCA associations in the United States. Entries include: Association name, camp name, address and phone of winter office, camp location and summer address and phone, name of director, seasons of operation, capacity; whether coed or restricted to boys or girls, or available for family and adult camping; special programs offered. Arrangement: Classified by type of camp (resident, family, conference centers).

HANDBOOKS AND MANUALS

★7258★ Career Opportunities in the Sports Industry

Facts on File, Inc.
11 Penn Plaza, 15th Fl.
New York, NY 10001-2006
Ph: (212)967-8800   Fax: 800-678-3633
Fr: 800-322-8755

Shelly Field. 1991. $29.95; $15.95 (paper). 272 pages. Describes various jobs in the sports industry. Each occupational profile covers job duties, employment outlook, career paths, salaries, skills, and education preparation. Offers tips for entering the field. Fields covered include professional sports teams, sports and business administration, coaching, sports officiating, sports journalism, fitness and recreation, and sports medicine and therapy, among others.

★7259★ Careers in Camping

American Camping Association (ACA)
Bradford Woods
5000 State Rd. 67 N.
Martinsville, IN 46151-7902
Ph: (317)342-8456

Brochure. Free. 8 pages. Describes camping careers, job duties, qualifications, salaries, educational preparation, and employment opportunities.

★7260★ Careers for Nature Lovers and Other Outdoor Types

VGM Career Horizons
4255 W. Touhy Ave.
Lincolnwood, IL 60646-1975
Ph: (847)679-5500   Fax: (847)679-2494
Fr: 800-323-4900

Louise Miller. 1992. $12.95; $9.95 (paper). Examines career opportunities in biology, agriculture, landscaping, forestry and conservation, geology, and waste management, and pollution control. Offers insight into preparing for and finding outdoor jobs in federal and state government, as well as private industry.

★7261★ Careers for Travel Buffs and Other Restless Types

VGM Career Horizons
4255 W. Touhy Ave.
Lincolnwood, IL 60646-1975
Ph: (847)679-5500   Fax: (847)679-2494
Fr: 800-323-4900

Paul Plawin. 1992. $14.95; $9.95 (paper). Includes a variety of travel and open-road careers, such as travel writers and photographers, tour bus drivers, entertainers, cruise line staff, travel agents, tour guides, sports writers, sales, the military, trucking, and meeting planning.

★7262★ Encyclopedia of Careers and Vocational Guidance

J. G. Ferguson Publishing Co.
200 W. Monroe, Ste. 250
Chicago, IL 60606
Ph: (312)580-5480

William E. Hopke. Ninth edition, 1993. $129.95; $199.95 (CD-ROM). Four-volume set that profiles 900 occupations and describes job trends in 71 industries. Includes career description, educational requirements, history of the job, methods of entry, advancement, employment outlook, earnings, conditions of work, social and psychological factors, and sources of further information. Contains career and employment information for this field.

★7263★ Great Careers for People Who Like Being Outdoors

Gale Research
835 Penobscot Bldg.
Detroit, MI 48226-4094
Ph: (313)961-2242   Fax: (313)961-6083
Fr: 800-877-GALE

Helen Mason. 1993. $17.95.

★7264★ How to Get a Job with a Cruise Line

Ticket to Adventure, Inc.
PO Box 41005
St. Petersburg, FL 33743
Ph: (813)544-6440   Fr: 800-929-7447

Mary Fallon Miller. Third edition, 1994. $14.95. 224 pages. Explores jobs with cruise ships, describing duties, responsibilities, benefits, and training. Lists cruise ship lines and schools offering cruise line training. Offers job hunting advice.

★7265★ Now Hiring! Outdoor Jobs: The Insider's Guide to Gaining Seasonal & Year-Round Employment in America's National Parks and Forests

Progressive Media, Inc.
4556 University Way NE., STE. 2222
Seattle, WA 98105
Ph: (206)545-7950   Fax: (206)545-7951

Kevin Lustgarten. 1993. $17.95 (paper).

★7266★ Opportunities in Child Care Careers

VGM Career Horizons
4255 W. Touhy Ave.
Lincolnwood, IL 60646-1975
Ph: (847)679-5500   Fax: (847)679-2494
Fr: 800-323-4900

Renee Wittenberg. 1995. $14.95; $11.95 (paper). 160 pages. Discusses various job opportunities and how to secure a position. Illustrated.

★7267★ Opportunities in Recreation and Leisure

VGM Career Horizons
4255 W. Touhy Ave.
Lincolnwood, IL 60646-1975
Ph: (847)679-5500   Fax: (847)679-2494
Fr: 800-323-4900

Clayne R. Jensen and Jay H. Naylor. 1990. $14.95; $11.95 (paper). 160 pages. Presents information on pursuing a position in a variety of fields, including senior citizen recreation, corporate employee recreation programs, and urban fitness centers. Illustrated.

★7268★ Opportunities in Travel Careers

VGM Career Horizons
4255 W. Touhy Ave.
Lincolnwood, IL 60646-1975
Ph: (847)679-5500   Fax: (847)679-2494
Fr: 800-323-4900

Robert Scott Milne. 1996. $14.95; $11.95 (paper). 160 pages. Discusses what the jobs are and where to find them in airlines, shipping lines, and railroads. Discusses related opportunities in hotels, motels, resorts, travel agencies, public relation firms, and recreation departments. Illustrated.

★7269★ Outdoor Careers: Exploring Occupations in Outdoor Fields

Stackpole Books
5067 Ritter Rd.
Mechanicsburg, PA 17055
Ph: (717)796-0411   Fax: (717)796-0412
Fr: 800-732-3669

Ellen Shenk. 1992. $16.95 (Paper).

OTHER SOURCES

★7270★ American Camping Association (ACA)

5000 State Rd. 67 N.
Martinsville, IN 46151-7902
Ph: (317)342-8456   Fax: (317)342-2065

Members: Camp owners, directors, program directors, businesses, and students interested in resident and daycamp programming for youth and adults. **Activities:** Conducts camp standards. Offers educational programs in areas of administration, staffing, child development, promotion, and programming.

★7271★ Association for Worksite Health Promotion (AWHP)

60 Revere Dr., Ste. 500
Northbrook, IL 60062-1577
Ph: (847)480-9574   Fax: (847)480-9282

Members: Health and fitness professionals employed by major companies (some smaller companies and businesses are also represented) and conducting wellness fitness programs for employees; interested persons in personnel and sales to fitness facilities; health educators and other health professionals; students interested in the field. **Purpose:** Supports and assists in the development of quality programs of health and fitness in business and industry. Seeks to create an awareness of the importance of physical, emotional, and mental health among employees. **Activities:** Stimulates active research and serves as a clearinghouse on employee health and fitness. Sponsors seminars and an educational committee that studies effectiveness of preparation, training programs, and certification. Conducts open discussions and workshops on health and nutrition. Compiles statistics.

★7272★ IDEA: International Association of Fitness Professionals (IDEA)

6190 Cornerstone Ct. E., Ste. 204
San Diego, CA 92121
Ph: (619)535-8979   Fax: (619)535-8234
Fr: 800-999-IDEA

Purpose: Provides continuing education for fitness professionals including; fitness instructors, personal trainers, program directors, and club/studio owners. **Activities:** Offers workshops for continuing education credits.

★7273★ Internship Directory: Internships and Summer Jobs at Public Gardens

American Association of Botanical
  Gardens and Arboreta (AABGA)
786 Church Rd.
Wayne, PA 19087
Ph: (610)688-1120   Fax: (610)293-0149

Annual, October. $5.00. Covers over 130 gardens, arboreta, and other horticultural organizations that offer student internships and summer jobs. Entries include: Name of institution, address, name of contact, deadline for application, number of students hired, whether internships are available, employment period, hours, rate of pay, whether housing is available, other comments. Arrangement: Alphabetical.

★7274★ National Employee Services and Recreation Association (NESRA)

2211 York Rd., Ste. 207
Oak Brook, IL 60521-2371
Ph: (708)368-1280   Fax: (708)368-1286

Purpose: Corporations and governmental agencies that sponsor recreation, fitness, and service programs for their employees; associate members are manufacturers and suppliers in the employee recreation market and distributors of consumer products and services. Helps members contact manufacturers and suppliers who will assist them in meeting their program objectives and employee needs. **Activities:** Provides associate members with advertising services and direct mail and market research assistance.

★7275★ National Recreation and Park Association (NRPA)

2775 S. Quincy St., Ste. 300
Arlington, VA 22206-2204
Ph: (703)820-4940   Fax: (703)671-6772
Fr: 800-626-6772

Purpose: Public interest organization dedicated to improving the human environment through improved park, recreation, and leisure opportunities. Activities include: programs for the development and upgrading of professional and citizen leadership in the park, recreation, and leisure field; dissemination of innovations and research results; technical assistance to affiliated organizations, local communities, and members; providing information on public policy; public education; extensive publications program.

★7276★ Seasonal Employment

U.S. National Park Service
PO Box 37127
Washington, DC 20013-7127
Ph: (202)208-5074

Updated as needed. Free. Publication includes: List of 10 regional offices and branches of the National Park Service that accept applications for seasonal jobs. Entries include: Name, address, phone, geographical area served. Principal content of publication is information on seasonal jobs offered by the National Park Services, with description of duties, qualifications, and application procedures for each type of job offered. Arrangement: Geographical.

★7277★ *Summer Jobs USA*

Peterson's Guides, Inc.
202 Carnegie Center
PO Box 2123
Princeton, NJ 08543-2123
Ph: (609)243-9111   Fax: (609)243-9150
Fr: 800-338-3282

Annual, October. $16.95. Covers over 488 camps, resorts, amusement parks, hotels, businesses, national parks, conference and training centers, ranches, and restaurants offering about 20,000 temporary summer jobs; listings are paid. Entries include: Name and address, length of employment, pay rate, fringe benefits, duties, qualifications, application deadline and procedure. Arrangement: Geographical, then type of job. Indexes: Job title.

Recreational Therapists

SOURCES OF HELP-WANTED ADS

★7278★ Archives of Physical Medicine and Rehabilitation

American Congress of Rehabilitation Medicine
78 E. Adams St., Ste. 1310
Chicago, IL 60603-6103
Ph: (312)922-9371   Fax: (312)922-6754
Monthly. $130.00/year

PLACEMENT AND JOB REFERRAL SERVICES

★7279★ American Association for Leisure and Recreation (AALR)

1900 Association Dr.
Reston, VA 22091
Ph: (703)476-3472   Fax: (703)476-9527
Members: Teachers of recreation and park administration, leisure studies, and recreation programming in colleges and universities; professional recreation and park practitioners; people involved in other areas of health, physical education, and recreation with an interest in recreation. **Purpose:** Goals are to: encourage professional involvement and exchange; monitor recreation legislation and render consultation at the request of legislators; disseminate information on topics of current interest in leisure and recreation; maintain liaison with organizations having allied interests in leisure and recreation; support, encourage, and provide guidance to members in the development of programs of leisure services; aid in the development of quality educational/recreational programs in the schools; facilitate communication between professionals and lay people and between the schools and the community; create opportunity for professional growth and development. **Activities:** Maintains placement service. **E-Mail:** Internet, aalr@aahpend.org

★7280★ Association on Higher Education and Disability (AHEAD)

PO Box 21192
Columbus, OH 43221-0192
Ph: (614)488-4972   Fax: (614)488-1174
Members: Individuals interested in promoting the equal rights and opportunities of disabled postsecondary students, staff, faculty, and graduates. **Purpose:** Provides an exchange of communication for those professionally involved with disabled students; collects, evaluates, and disseminates information; encourages and supports legislation for the benefit of disabled students. **Activities:** Conducts surveys on issues pertinent to college students with disabilities; offers resource referral system and employment exchange for positions in disability student services. Conducts research programs; compiles statistics.

★7281★ Child Life Council (CLC)

11820 Parklawn Dr., Ste. 202
Rockville, MD 20852-2529
Ph: (301)881-7090   Fax: (301)654-4964
Members: Professional organization representing child life personnel, patient activities specialists, and students in the field. **Purpose:** Promotes psychological well-being and optimum development of children, adolescents, and their families in health care settings. **Activities:** Works to minimize the stress and anxiety of illness and hospitalization. Addresses professional issues such as program standards, competencies, and core curriculum. Provides resources and conducts research and educational programs. Offers a Job Bank Service listing employment openings.

★7282★ National Association of Activity Professionals (NAAP)

1225 Eye St. NW, Ste. 300
Washington, DC 20005
Ph: (202)289-0722   Fax: (202)842-0621
Members: Those who are or have been therapists, activity directors, and activity consultants in nursing homes, senior centers, retirement housing, or adult day care programs; other interested individuals. **Purpose:** To promote quality care and services for elderly and/or handicapped persons; to assist in the delivery of activity services; to foster research and the production of relevant literature; to upgrade educational programs. Sets standards and has established a certification process. **Activities:** Compiles statistics; maintains speakers' bureau, placement service, and resource review; sponsors National Activity Professional Day. Offers correspondence courses.

★7283★ Special Recreation, Inc. (SRI)

362 Koser Ave.
Iowa City, IA 52246
Ph: (319)337-7578
Members: Disabled consumers, parents of the disabled, rehabilitation professionals, and volunteers. **Purpose:** Promotes self-determination, equal opportunity, consumerism, and normalization in recreation and leisure for disabled individuals; works to advance the national and international policy and philosophy of special recreation; provides national information services on federal, state, and local laws, regulations, and public programs for special recreation. Sponsors the International Center on Special Recreation that works to: collect and disseminate international information on special recreation services for disabled persons, special recreation programs, and personnel training; conduct, provide, and support international exchange of technical, professional, and general information on special recreation for the disabled; cooperate with both governmental and voluntary organizations on national and international levels. **Activities:** Offers career guidance and placement service. Maintains speakers' bureau; compiles statistics.

EMPLOYER DIRECTORIES AND NETWORKING LISTS

★7284★ AHA Guide to the Health Care Field

Health Statistics Group
American Hospital Association (AHA)
1 N. Franklin
Chicago, IL 60606
Ph: (312)422-3501   Fax: (312)280-6015
Annual, July. $195.00, payment with order. Covers hospitals, multi-health care systems,

freestanding ambulatory surgery centers, psychiatric facilities, long-term care facilities, substance abuse programs, hospices, Health Maintenance Organizations (HMOs), and other health-related organizations. Entries include: For hospitals: facility name, address, phone, administrator's name, number of beds, facilities and services, number of employees, expenses, other statistics. For other organizations: name, address, phone, name and title of contact. Arrangement: Geographical. Indexes: Hospital name.

★7285★ Directory of Hospital Personnel

Medical Economics
5 Paragon Dr.
Montvale, NJ 07645-1725
Ph: (201)358-7500   Fax: (201)573-4956
Fr: 800-222-3045

Annual, September. $325.00, plus 7.50 shipping. Covers 200,000 executives at 7,100 U.S. hospitals. Entries include: Name of hospital, address, phone, number of beds, type and JCAHO status of hospital, names and titles of key department heads and staff, medical and nursing school affiliations; number of residents, interns, and nursing students. Arrangement: Geographical. Indexes: Hospital name, personnel, hospital size.

★7286★ Directory of Nursing Homes

HCIA Inc.
300 E. Lombard St.
Baltimore, MD 21202
Ph: (410)576-9600   Fax: (410)539-5220
Fr: 800-568-3282

Annual. $249.00. Covers over 16,000 state-licensed long-term care facilities. Entries include: Facility name, address, phone, names and titles of key personnel, licensure status, number of beds; number of nursing, dietary, and auxiliary staff members; program/services; medicaid/medicare certification status; admission and referral requirements; age and gender restrictions; languages spoken; management or chain company name. Arrangement: Geographical. Indexes: Alphabetical, geographical (county) and by chain headquarters.

★7287★ Hospital Blue Book

Billian Publishing Co.
2100 Powers Ferry Rd., Ste. 300
Atlanta, GA 30339
Ph: (404)955-5656   Fax: (404)952-0669

Annual, spring. $154.50, national edition, plus $20.00 shipping. Covers more than 7,100 hospitals; some listings also appear in a separate southern edition of this publication. Entries include: Name of hospital, accreditation, mailing address, phone, fax, number of beds, type of facility (nonprofit, general, state, etc.); list of administrative personnel and chiefs of medical services, with specific titles. Arrangement: Geographical.

★7288★ Hospital Market Atlas

SMG Marketing Group, Inc.
1342 N. LaSalle Dr.
Chicago, IL 60610
Ph: (312)642-3026   Fax: (312)642-9729
Fr: 800-678-3026

Biennial, odd years. $495.00, payment with

order. Covers over 7,000 hospitals, hospital systems and 480 group purchasing organizations. Entries include: Hospital or organization name, address, phone, county code, management, type of hospital service, number of beds, admissions, surgical operations, and emergency room visits. Arrangement: Geographical.

★7289★ Hospitals Directory

American Business Directories, Inc.
American Business Information, Inc.
5711 S. 86th Cir.
Omaha, NE 68127
Ph: (402)593-4600   Fax: (402)331-1505

Annual. $870.00, U.S. edition. Entries include: Name, address, phone (including area code), size of advertisement, year first in Yellow Pages, name of owner or manager, number of employees. Compiled from telephone company Yellow Pages, nationwide. Arrangement: Geographical.

★7290★ Medical and Health Information Directory

Gale Research
835 Penobscot Bldg.
Detroit, MI 48226-4094
Ph: (313)961-2242   Fax: (313)961-6083
Fr: 800-877-GALE

Approximately biennial; latest edition 1994. $195.00, per volume; $485.00, for the three-volume set. Covers in Volume 1, almost 18,600 medical and health oriented associations, organizations, institutions, and government agencies, including health maintenance organizations (HMOs), preferred provider organizations (PPOs), insurance companies, pharmaceutical companies, research centers, and medical and allied health schools. In Volume 2, nearly 11,800 medical book publishers; medical periodicals, directories, audiovisual producers and services, medical libraries and information centers, and electronic resources. In Volume 3, nearly 26,000 clinics, treatment centers, care programs, and counseling/diagnostic services for 30 subject areas. Entries include: Institution, service, or firm name, address, phone; many include names of key personnel and, when pertinent, descriptive annotation. Arrangement: Classified by organization activity, service, etc. Indexes: Each volume has a complete alphabetical name and keyword index.

★7291★ Osteopathic Membership Directory—AOHA

American Osteopathic Healthcare Association
5301 Wisconsin Ave. NW, Ste. 630
Washington, DC 20015-2015
Ph: (202)686-1700   Fax: (202)686-7615

Annual, summer. $125.00, payment with order. Covers about 110 osteopathic hospitals. Includes list of individual and institutional members; also lists osteopathic colleges, and directors of medical education. Entries include: For hospitals: name of hospital, name of chief executive officer, address, phone, number of beds and other hospital data. Arrangement: Geographical. Indexes: Name, institution.

HANDBOOKS AND MANUALS

★7292★ Career Opportunities in the Sports Industry

Facts on File, Inc.
11 Penn Plaza, 15th Fl.
New York, NY 10001-2006
Ph: (212)967-8800   Fax: 800-678-3633
Fr: 800-322-8755

Shelly Field. 1991. $29.95; $15.95 (paper). 272 pages. Describes various jobs in the sports industry. Each occupational profile covers job duties, employment outlook, career paths, salaries, skills, and education preparation. Offers tips for entering the field. Fields covered include professional sports teams, sports and business administration, coaching, sports officiating, sports journalism, fitness and recreation, and sports medicine and therapy, among others.

★7293★ Careers in Health Care

VGM Career Horizons
4255 W. Touhy Ave.
Lincolnwood, IL 60646-1975
Ph: (847)679-5500   Fax: (847)679-2494
Fr: 800-323-4900

Barbara M. Swanson. 1995. $17.95; $13.95 (paper). Describes job duties, work settings, salaries, licensing and certification requirements, educational preparation, and future outlook. Gives ideas on how to secure a job.

★7294★ 100 Best Careers for the Year 2000

Prentice Hall General Reference
15 Columbus Cir.
New York, NY 10023
Ph: (212)373-8500   Fr: 800-223-2348

Shelly Field. 1992. $15.00 (paper). Covers 100 of the fastest growing jobs. The publication is divided into 11 general employment sections. Specific careers are covered within each section. Provides job description, responsibilities, employment opportunities, earnings, education and training, advancement opportunities, and experience and qualifications for each occupation.

★7295★ Opportunities in Gerontology and Aging Services Careers

VGM Career Horizons
4255 W. Touhy Ave.
Lincolnwood, IL 60646-1975
Ph: (847)679-5500   Fax: (847)679-2494
Fr: 800-323-4900

Ellen Williams. 1995. $14.95; $11.95 (paper). 160 pages. Covers jobs in community, health and medical programs, financial, legal, residential, travel and tourism, and counseling, and how to go after them. Includes bibliography and illustrations.

★7296★ Opportunities in Health and Medical Careers

VGM Career Horizons
4255 W. Touhy Ave.
Lincolnwood, IL 60646-1975
Ph: (847)679-5500   Fax: (847)679-2494
Fr: 800-323-4900

Donald Snook, Jr. and Leo D'Orazio. 1993.

$14.95; $11.95 (paper). Covers the full range of medical and health occupations. Illustrated.

★7297★ Opportunities in Recreation and Leisure

VGM Career Horizons
4255 W. Touhy Ave.
Lincolnwood, IL 60646-1975
Ph: (847)679-5500   Fax: (847)679-2494
Fr: 800-323-4900

Clayne R. Jensen and Jay H. Naylor. 1990. $14.95; $11.95 (paper). 160 pages. Presents information on pursuing a position in a variety of fields, including senior citizen recreation, corporate employee recreation programs, and urban fitness centers. Illustrated.

★7298★ Resumes for Health and Medical Careers

4255 W. Touhy Ave.
Lincolnwood, IL 60646-1975
Ph: (708)679-5500   Fax: (708)679-6375
Fr: 800-323-4900

Compiled by VGM Career Horizons Staff 1995. $9.95 (paper).

★7299★ Therapists and Allied Health Professionals Career Directory

Gale Research
835 Penobscot Bldg.
Detroit, MI 48226-4094
Ph: (313)961-2242   Fax: (313)961-6083
Fr: 800-877-GALE

Bradley Morgan. 1993. $39.00. 326 pages. Essays on specific careers provide an insider's perspective. Also features extensive listings of contacts and entry-level job opportunities. Provides information on internships and sources of help-wanted ads.

EMPLOYMENT AGENCIES AND SEARCH FIRMS

★7300★ Harper Associates

29870 Middlebelt
Farmington Hills, MI 48334
Ph: (810)932-1170

Employment agency.

★7301★ Medical Personnel Pool

2901 S. Ridgewood Ave.
Daytona Beach, FL 32119-3542
Ph: (904)736-1648

Provides regular and temporary staffing assistance. Offices located in cities throughout United States.

★7302★ Professional Placement Associates, Inc.

11 Rye Ridge Plaza
Rye Brook, NY 10573
Ph: (914)251-1000   Fax: (914)939-1959

Employment agency.

★7303★ Sue Carroll Personnel, Inc.

16 E. 79th St.
New York, NY 10021
Ph: (212)288-8866   Fax: (212)988-7191

Employment agency and executive search firm.

★7304★ Travcorps, Inc.

40 Eastern Ave.
Malden, MA 02148
Ph: (617)322-2600

Places staff in temporary assignments.

OTHER SOURCES

★7305★ American Health Care Association

1201 L St. NW
Washington, DC 20005
Ph: (202)842-4444   Fax: (202)842-3860

Members: Federation of state associations of long-term health care facilities. **Purpose:** Promotes standards for professionals in long-term health care delivery and quality care for patients and residents in a safe environment. Focuses on issues of availability, quality, affordability, and fair payment. Operates as a liaison with governmental agencies, Congress, and professional associations.

★7306★ American Kinesiotherapy Association (AKTA)

PO Box 614
Wheeling, IL 60090-0614
Fr: 800-296-AKTA

Members: Professional society of kinesiotherapists, and associate and student members with interest in physical and mental rehabilitation and adapted physical education. (Kinesiology is the study of human movement; kinesiotherapists use kinesiology to design and implement therapeutic exercise to meet the rehabilitative needs of persons with disease, injury, and/or physical disorders.) **Purpose:** Goal is to promote the profession of kinseotheraphy by working toward public recognition of kinesiotherapy and to pursue and support legislative concerns of the profession. Works to maintain and advance the standard of care through educational opportunities.

★7307★ American Therapeutic Recreation Association (ATRA)

PO Box 15215
Hattiesburg, MS 39404
Ph: (601)264-3413   Fax: (601)264-3337
Fr: 800-553-0304

Members: Therapeutic recreation professionals and students; interested others. (Therapeutic recreation is often referred to as recreational therapy and uses treatment modalities to improve the physical, mental, and emotional functions of persons with illnesses or disabling conditions.) **Purpose:** Promotes the use of therapeutic recreation in hospitals, mental rehabilitation centers, physical rehabilitation centers, senior citizen treatment centers, and other public health facilities. **Activities:** Conducts discussions on certification and legislative and regulatory concerns that affect the industry. Sponsors seminars and workshops; conducts research.

★7308★ National Council for Therapeutic Recreation Certification (NCTRC)

PO Box 479
Thiells, NY 10984
Ph: (914)947-4346

Purpose: Objectives are to: establish national evaluative standards for certification and recertification of individuals who work in the therapeutic recreation field; grant recognition to individuals who voluntarily apply and meet established standards; monitor adherence to standards by certified personnel.

★7309★ National Rehabilitation Association (NRA)

633 S. Washington St.
Alexandria, VA 22314
Ph: (703)836-0850   Fax: (703)836-0848

Members: Administrators, instructors, placement specialists, secretaries, counselors, therapists, vocational evaluators, ADA specialists and others interested in rehabilitation of persons with disabilities. **Activities:** Conducts legislative activities; develops accessibility guidelines; offers specialized education.

★7310★ National Therapeutic Recreation Society (NTRS)

2775 S. Quincy St., Ste. 300
Arlington, VA 22206
Ph: (703)578-5548   Fax: (703)671-6772
Fr: 800-626-6772

Members: Professionals, educators, and students involved in the provision of therapeutic recreation services for persons with disabilities in clinical facilities and in the community. **Purpose:** Offers technical assistance services to agencies, institutions, and individuals on matters related to the field. **Activities:** Encourages professional growth through research, training, and workshops.

Registered Nurses

SOURCES OF HELP-WANTED ADS

★7311★ AANA Journal

AANA Publishing, Inc.
222 S. Prospect
Park Ridge, IL 60068
Ph: (708)692-7050   Fax: (708)692-6968

Bimonthly. $24.00/year for individuals; $5.00 for single issue. Nursing and anesthesia journal.

★7312★ AAOHN Journal

Slack, Inc.
6900 Grove Rd.
Thorofare, NJ 08086-9447
Ph: (609)848-1000   Fax: (609)853-5991
Fr: 800-257-8290

Monthly. $49.00/year; $62.00/year for institutions; $15.00 for single issue. Official journal of the American Association of Occupational Health Nurses.

★7313★ Advances in Nursing Science

Aspen Publishers, Inc.
200 Orchard Ridge Dr., Ste. 200
Gaithersburg, MD 20878
Ph: (301)417-7500   Fax: (301)417-7550
Fr: 800-638-8437

Quarterly. $68.00/year; $34.00/year for students; $17.00 for single issue. Academic medical journal.

★7314★ ANNA Journal

ANNA Journal East
E. Holly Ave., Box 56
Pitman, NJ 08071-0056
Ph: (609)256-2320   Fax: (609)589-7463

Bimonthly. $5.00 for single issue; $28.00/year; $40.00/year for institutions. Nursing journal.

★7315★ AORN Journal

Association of Operating Room Nurses
2170 S. Parker Rd., Ste. 300
Denver, CO 80231-5711
Ph: (303)755-6300   Fax: (303)750-3441
Fr: 800-755-AORN

Monthly. $50.00/year for individuals. Journal for perioperative nurses.

★7316★ Cancer

Pharmaceutical Media, Inc.
30 E. 33rd St.
New York, NY 10016
Ph: (212)685-5010   Fax: (212)685-5010

Semimonthly. Oncology journal publishing original articles on clinical aspects of cancer, surgical and medical therapy, and interdisciplinary research.

★7317★ Clinical Nurse Specialist

Williams & Wilkins
351 W. Camden St.
Baltimore, MD 21201-2436
Ph: (410)361-8004   Fax: (410)528-4312
Fr: 800-222-3790

Quarterly. Nursing journal.

★7318★ Critical Care Nurse

101 Columbia
Aliso Viejo, CA 92656
Ph: (714)362-2000   Fax: (714)362-2020
Fr: 800-809-2273

Bimonthly. Nursing magazine.

★7319★ Dialysis and Transplantation

Summer Communications, Inc.
7626 Densmore Ave.
Van Nuys, CA 91406-2042
Ph: (818)782-7328   Fax: (818)782-7450

Monthly. $35.00/year for individuals; $60.00/year for other countries. Medical magazine on dialysis and nephrology for medical personnel.

★7320★ Emergency Medical Services

Summer Communications, Inc.
7626 Densmore Ave.
Van Nuys, CA 91406-2042
Ph: (818)782-7328   Fax: (818)782-7450

Monthly. $18.95/year for individuals. Magazine covering emergency care, rescue and transportation.

★7321★ Geriatric Nursing

Mosby Year Book
11830 Westline Industrial Dr.
St. Louis, MO 63146
Ph: (314)872-8370   Fax: 800-535-9935
Fr: 800-633-6699

Bimonthly. $34.00/year for individuals; $51.36/year for Canada; $48.00/year for other countries. Magazine for nurses in geriatric and gerontologic nursing practice, the primary professional providers of care for the aging. Provides news on issues affecting elders and clinical information on techniques and procedures.

★7322★ Health Progress

Catholic Health Association of the U.S.
4455 Woodson Rd.
St. Louis, MO 63134
Ph: (314)427-2500   Fax: (314)427-0029

Free to qualified subscribers; $40.00/year for individuals; $45.00/year for other countries; $6.00 for single issue. Magazine for administrative-level and other managerial personnel in Catholic healthcare and related organizations. Featured are articles on management concepts, legislative and regulatory trends, and theological, sociological, ethical, legal, and technical issues.

★7323★ Heart and Lung: The Journal of Acute and Critical Care

Mosby Year Book
11830 Westline Industrial Dr.
St. Louis, MO 63146
Ph: (314)872-8370   Fax: 800-535-9935
Fr: 800-633-6699

Bimonthly. $39.00/year for individuals; $57.78 /year for Canada; $54.00/year for other countries; $21.00/year for students. Journal offering articles prepared by nurse and physician members of the critical care team, recognizing the nurse's role in the care and management of major organ-system conditions in critically ill patients.

★7324★ **Homecare Magazine**

Miramar Communications, Inc.
23815 Stuart Ranch Rd.
PO Box 8987
Malibu, CA 90265-8987
Ph: (310)317-4522   Fax: (310)317-9644
Fr: 800-543-4116

Monthly. $48.00/year for individuals; $60.00/year for Canada; $75.00/year for other countries.

★7325★ **Imprint**

National Student Nurses Association
555 W. 57th St.
New York, NY 10019
Ph: (212)581-2211   Fax: (212)581-2368

Magazine for nursing students, focusing on issues and trends in nursing education.

★7326★ **Journal of the American Academy of Nurse Practitioners**

Pharmaceutical Media, Inc.
30 E. 33rd St.
New York, NY 10016
Ph: (212)685-5010   Fax: (212)685-5010

Quarterly. Journal for nurse practitioners and others involved in primary health care.

★7327★ **The Journal of Continuing Education in Nursing**

Slack, Inc.
6900 Grove Rd.
Thorofare, NJ 08086-9447
Ph: (609)848-1000   Fax: (609)853-5991
Fr: 800-257-8290

Bimonthly. Journal for nurses involved in planning and implementing educational programs for the practitioner and others in patient care.

★7328★ **Journal of Emergency Nursing**

Mosby Year Book
11830 Westline Industrial Dr.
St. Louis, MO 63146
Ph: (314)872-8370   Fax: 800-535-9935
Fr: 800-633-6699

Bimonthly. $52.00/year for individuals; $70.62/year for Canada; $66.00/year for other countries; $29.00/year for students. Journal containing peer-reviewed articles on clinical aspects of emergency care by, and for, emergency nurses. Presents information about professional, political, administrative, and educational aspects of emergency nursing and nursing in general.

★7329★ **Journal of Gerontological Nursing**

Slack, Inc.
6900 Grove Rd.
Thorofare, NJ 08086-9447
Ph: (609)848-1000   Fax: (609)853-5991
Fr: 800-257-8290

Monthly. Gerontological nursing journal.

★7330★ **Journal of Intravenous Nursing**

Pharmaceutical Media, Inc.
30 E. 33rd St.
New York, NY 10016
Ph: (212)685-5010   Fax: (212)685-5010

Bimonthly. Journal publishing I.V.-related articles, studies, reports, and reviews fro the continuing education of professionals in I.V. therapy. Includes correspondence, book reviews, and news of the Intravenous Nurse Society.

★7331★ **Journal of Nurse-Midwifery**

Elsevier Science Inc.
655 Avenue of the Americas
New York, NY 10010
Ph: (212)989-5800   Fax: (212)633-3990

Bimonthly. $75.00/year for individuals; $150.00/year for institutions. Journal of the American College of Nurse-Midwives.

★7332★ **Journal of Nursing Administration**

Pharmaceutical Media, Inc.
30 E. 33rd St.
New York, NY 10016
Ph: (212)685-5010   Fax: (212)685-5010

Journal covering developments and advances in nursing administration and management.

★7333★ **Journal of Nursing Education**

6900 Grove Rd.
Thorofare, NJ 08086-9447
Ph: (609)848-1000   Fax: (609)853-5991

Bimonthly. $44.00/year.

★7334★ **Journal of Obstetric, Gynecologic, and Neonatal Nursing**

Pharmaceutical Media Inc.
30 E. 33rd St.
New York, NY 10016
Ph: (212)685-5010

Bimonthly. $39.00/year; $17.00/single issue.

★7335★ **Journal of Pediatric Health Care**

Mosby Year Book
11830 Westline Industrial Dr.
St. Louis, MO 63146
Ph: (314)872-8370   Fax: 800-535-9935
Fr: 800-633-6699

Bimonthly. $49.00/year for individuals; $67.41/year for Canada; $63.00/year for other countries; $25.00/year for students. Official pubolication of the National Association of Pediatric Nurse Associates and Practitioners. Provides current information on pediatric clinical topics as well as research studies, health policy, and legislative issues applicable to pediatric clinical practice.

★7336★ **Journal of Psychosocial Nursing and Mental Health Services**

Slack, Inc.
6900 Grove Rd.
Thorofare, NJ 08086-9447
Ph: (609)848-1000   Fax: (609)853-5991
Fr: 800-257-8290

Monthly. Journal presenting original, peer-reviewed articles on psychiatric/mental health nursing.

★7337★ **McKnight's Long-Term Care News**

McKnight Medical Communications Co.
2 Northfield Plaza, Ste. 300
Northfield, IL 60093-1217
Ph: (708)441-3700   Fax: (708)441-3701
Fr: 800-451-7838

Monthly. $44.95/year; $5.00 for single issue. Professional magazine.

★7338★ **MCN, The American Journal of Maternal/Child Nursing**

American Journal of Nursing Co.
555 W. 57th St.
New York, NY 10019
Ph: (212)582-8820   Fax: (212)586-5462

Bimonthly. Journal focusing on maternal/child nursing and health.

★7339★ **Military Medicine**

Association of Military Surgeons of the U.S.
9320 Old Georgetown Rd.
Bethesda, MD 20814
Ph: (301)897-8800   Fax: (301)530-5446

Monthly. $35.00/year for individuals; $40.00/year for other countries; $4.50 for single issue. Journal for professional personnel affiliated with the Federal medical services.

★7340★ **Modern Healthcare**

Crain Communications, Inc.
740 N. Rush St.
Chicago, IL 60611-2590
Ph: (312)649-5311   Fax: (312)280-3189

Weekly. $110.00/year. Business news magazine for Healthcare Management.

★7341★ **N&HC: Perspectives on Community**

National League for Nursing
350 Hudson St.
New York, NY 10014
Ph: (212)989-9393   Fax: (212)989-3710

Bimonthly. Professional journal for nurses. Includes articles on health policy, and social and economic issues affecting health care, and nursing education and practice.

★7342★ **The New England Journal of Medicine**

Massachusetts Medical Society
1440 Main St.
Waltham, MA 02154-1649
Ph: (617)893-3800   Fax: (617)893-0413

Weekly (Thurs.). $99.00/year. Journal for the medical profession.

★7343★ **Nurse Educator**

Pharmaceutical Media, Inc.
30 E. 33rd St.
New York, NY 10016
Ph: (212)685-5010   Fax: (212)685-5010

Bimonthly. Journal for nursing educators.

★7344★ The Nurse Practitioner

Elsevier Science, Inc.
655 Avenue of the Americas
New York, NY 10010
Ph: (212)633-3875

Monthly. $45.00/year; $75.00/year for institutions. Magazine presenting clinical information to nurses in advanced primary care practice. Also covers legal, business, economic, ethical, research, pharmaceutical, and theoretical issues.

★7345★ Nurse Practitioner Forum

W.B. Saunders Co.
Periodical Dept.
6277 Sea Harbor Dr.
Orlando, FL 32887-4800
Fax: (407)363-9661   Fr: 800-654-2452

Quarterly. Journal for nurse practitioners.

★7346★ Nursing Economic$

Jannetti Publications, Inc.
E. Holly Ave., Box 56
Pitman, NJ 08071-0056
Ph: (609)256-2300   Fax: (609)589-7463

Bimonthly. Business magazine for nursing administrators.

★7347★ Nursing Management

SN Publications, Inc.
PO Box 908
Spring House, PA 19477-0903

Monthly. $25.00/year for individuals. Magazine focusing on nursing management.

★7348★ Nursing 95

Springhouse Corp.
1111 Bethlehem Pke.
PO Box 908
Spring House, PA 19477
Ph: (215)646-8700   Fax: (215)653-0826
Fr: 800-617-1717

Monthly. $42.00/year for individuals. Practical journal for nurses. Includes special sections for critical-care, continuing care, and nurse practitioners.

★7349★ Nursing Outlook

Mosby Year Book
11830 Westline Industrial Dr.
St. Louis, MO 63146
Ph: (314)872-8370   Fax: 800-535-9935
Fr: 800-633-6699

Bimonthly. $37.00/year for individuals. Official magazine of the American Academy of Nursing, reporting on trends and issues in nursing.

★7350★ Nursing Research

American Journal of Nursing Co.
555 W. 57th St.
New York, NY 10019-2961
Ph: (212)582-8820   Fax: (212)315-3187

Bimonthly. Magazine focusing on nursing research.

★7351★ Nursingworld Journal

Prime National Publishing Corp.
470 Boston Post Rd.
Weston, MA 02193
Ph: (617)899-2702   Fax: (617)899-4900

Monthly. Magazine for the nursing profession.

★7352★ Oncology

S. Karger Publishers, Inc.
26 W. Avon Rd.
PO Box 529
Farmington, CT 06085
Ph: (203)675-7834   Fax: (203)675-7302

Bimonthly. $567.00/year. Medical journal presenting experimental and clinical findings.

★7353★ Orthopaedic Nursing

ANNA Journal East
E. Holly Ave., Box 56
Pitman, NJ 08071-0056
Ph: (609)256-2320   Fax: (609)589-7463

Bimonthly. Nursing magazine.

★7354★ Ostomy/Wound Management

Health Management Publications, Inc.
550 American Ave.
King of Prussia, PA 19406
Ph: (610)337-4466   Fax: (610)337-0890
Fr: 800-237-7285

Medical journal.

★7355★ Pediatric Nursing

Jannetti Publications, Inc.
E. Holly Ave., Box 56
Pitman, NJ 08071-0056
Ph: (609)256-2300   Fax: (609)589-7463

Bimonthly. Professional nursing magazine.

★7356★ Perinatal Press–Newsletter

Perinatal Press, Inc.
PO Box 710698
San Diego, CA 92171
Ph: (619)541-6875

Bimonthly. $21.00/year.

★7357★ Perspectives in Psychiatric Care

Nursecom, Inc.
1211 Locust St.
Philadelphia, PA 19107
Ph: (215)545-7222   Fax: (215)545-8107
Fr: 800-242-6757

Quarterly. Journal covering psychiatric care and nursing.

★7358★ Physician Assistant

105 Raider Blvd.
Belle Mead, NJ 08502
Ph: (908)874-8550

Monthly. $50.00/year.

★7359★ Provider

American Health Care Association
1201 L St. NW
Washington, DC 20005
Ph: (202)842-4444   Fax: (202)842-3860

Monthly. $48.00/year for nonmembers. Magazine.

★7360★ Rehabilitation Nursing

Association of Rehabilitation Nurses
5700 Old Orchard Rd., 1st Fl.
Skokie, IL 60077-1057
Ph: (708)966-3433   Fax: (708)966-9418

Bimonthly. $50.00/year for individuals; $75.00/year for institutions; $90.00/year for other countries; $13.00 for single issue. Magazine focusing on rehabilitation nursing involving clinical practice, research, education, and administration.

★7361★ Research in Nursing & Health

John Wiley and Sons, Inc.
605 3rd Ave.
New York, NY 10158
Ph: (212)850-6000   Fax: (212)850-8888
Fr: 800-225-5945

Bimonthly. Journal providing forum for research in the areas of nursing practice, education, and administration. Covers health issues relevant to nursing as well as investigations of the applications of research findings in clinical settings.

★7362★ RN Magazine

Medical Economics, Inc.
5 Paragon Dr.
Montvale, NJ 07645-1742
Ph: (201)358-7208   Fax: (201)358-7260

Monthly. Clinical journal for registered nurses.

★7363★ Seminars in Oncology

W.B. Saunders Co.
The Curtis Center, 3rd Fl.
Philadelphia, PA 19106-3399
Ph: (215)238-7800   Fax: (215)238-8772
Fr: 800-654-2452

Bimonthly. $109.00/year for individuals; $154.00/year for institutions; $65.00/year for students; $36.00 for single issue. Journal reviewing current diagnostic and treatment techniques used in oncology patient care.

★7364★ Today's OR Nurse

Slack, Inc.
6900 Grove Rd.
Thorofare, NJ 08086-9447
Ph: (609)848-1000   Fax: (609)853-5991
Fr: 800-257-8290

Bimonthly. $39.05/year. Journal for the operating room nurse. Contains articles on clinical/procedural techniques, management, and education.

PLACEMENT AND JOB REFERRAL SERVICES

★7365★ The American Association of Nurse Attorneys (TAANA)

720 Light St.
Baltimore, MD 21230-3816
Ph: (410)752-3318   Fax: (410)752-8295

Members: Nurse attorneys, nurses in law school, and attorneys in nursing school. **Purpose:** Aims to better nurse attorneys and inform the public on matters of nursing, health care, and law. Goals are to facilitate communication and information sharing between professional groups; to establish an employment network; to assist new and potential nurse attorneys; to develop the profession; to promote the image of nurse attorneys as experts and consultants in nursing and law. **Activities:** Maintains educational foundation.

★7366★ American Association of Occupational Health Nurses (AAOHN)

50 Lenox Pointe
Atlanta, GA 30324
Ph: (404)262-1162   Fax: (404)262-1165

Members: Registered professional nurses employed by business and industrial firms; nurse educators, nurse editors, nurse writers, and others interested in occupational health nursing. **Purpose:** Promotes and sets standards for the profession. **Activities:** Provides and approves continuing education; maintains governmental affairs program; offers placement service.

★7367★ American College of Nurse-Midwives (ACNM)

1522 K St. NW, Ste. 1000
Washington, DC 20005
Ph: (202)728-9860   Fax: (202)289-4395

Members: Registered nurses certified to extend their practice into providing gynecological services and care of mothers and babies throughout the maternity cycle; members have completed an ACNM accredited program of study and clinical experience in midwifery and passed a national certification exam. **Purpose:** Cooperates with allied groups to enable nurse-midwives to concentrate their efforts in the improvement of services for mothers and newborn babies. Seeks to identify areas of nurse-midwifery practices as they relate to the total service and educational aspects of maternal and newborn care. Studies and evaluates activities of nurse-midwives in order to establish qualifications; cooperates in planning and developing educational programs; conducts research and continuing education workshops. **Activities:** Offers placement service.

★7368★ American Nurses in Business Association (ANBA)

PO Box 741384
Houston, TX 77274-1384
Ph: (713)771-5016   Fax: (713)771-6619

Members: Nursing students, companies, self-employed nurses, registered nurses, and licensed vocational nurses. **Purpose:** Serves as support group for nurses interested in seeking business opportunities. Provides business-related information. **Activities:** Sponsors speakers' bureau; offers placement service.

★7369★ American Organization of Nurse Executives (AONE)

One N. Franklin, 34th Fl.
Chicago, IL 60606
Ph: (312)422-2800   Fax: (312)422-4503

Purpose: Provides leadership, professional development, advocacy, and research to advance nursing practice and patient care, promote nursing leadership and excellence,

and shape healthcare public policy. Supports and enhances the management, leadership, educational, and professional development of nursing leaders. **Activities:** Offers placement service through Career Development and Referral Center.

★7370★ American Public Health Association (APHA)

1015 15th St. NW
Washington, DC 20005
Ph: (202)789-5600   Fax: (202)789-5681

Members: Professional organization of physicians, nurses, educators, academicians, environmentalists, epidemiologists, new professionals, social workers, health administrators, optometrists, podiatrists, pharmacists, dentists, nutritionists, health planners, other community and mental health specialists, and interested consumers. **Purpose:** Seeks to protect and promote personal, mental, and environmental health. **Activities:** Services include: promulgation of standards; establishment of uniform practices and procedures; development of the etiology of communicable diseases; research in public health; exploration of medical care programs and their relationships to public health. Sponsors job placement service.

★7371★ American School Health Association (ASHA)

7263 State Rte. 43
PO Box 708
Kent, OH 44240
Ph: (216)678-1601   Fax: (216)678-4526

Members: School physicians, school nurses, dentists, nurses, nutritionists, health educators, dental hygienists, school-based professionals, and public health workers. **Purpose:** Promotes comprehensive and constructive school health programs including the teaching of health, health services, and promotion of a healthful school environment. **Activities:** Offers a professional referral service, classroom teaching aids, and professional reference materials. Conducts research programs; maintains placement service; compiles statistics. Sponsors foreign travel study tour.

★7372★ American Society of Extra-Corporeal Technology (AmSECT)

11480 Sunset Hills Rd., No. 210E
Reston, VA 22090
Ph: (703)435-8556   Fax: (703)435-0056

Members: Perfusionists, technologists, doctors, nurses, and others actively employed and using the applied skills relating to the practice of extracorporeal technology (involving heart-lung machines); student members. **Purpose:** Disseminates information necessary to the proper practice of the technology. Conducts programs in continuing education and professional-public liaison and hands-on workshops. **Activities:** Maintains placement service.

★7373★ Association of Black Nursing Faculty (ABNF)

5823 Queens Cove
Lisle, IL 60532
Ph: (708)969-3809   Fax: (708)969-3895

Members: Black nursing faculty teaching in nursing programs accredited by the National League for Nursing. **Purpose:** Works to promote health-related issues and educational concerns of interest to the black community and ABNF. **Activities:** Serves as a forum for communication and the exchange of information among members; develops strategies for expressing concerns to other individuals, institutions, and communities. Assists members in professional development; develops and sponsors continuing education activities; fosters networking and guidance in employment and recruitment activities. Promotes health-related issues of legislation, government programs, and community activities. Supports black consumer advocacy issues. Encourages research. Maintains speakers' bureau and hall of fame. Offers charitable program and placement services. Compiles statistics. Is establishing a computer-assisted job bank; plans to develop bibliographies related to research groups.

★7374★ Christian Medical Foundation International (CMF)

7522 N. Himes Ave.
PO Box 152136
Tampa, FL 33684-2136
Ph: (813)932-3688   Fax: (813)932-3767

Members: Physicians, nurses, clergy, and laity. **Purpose:** Seeks to: investigate and promote the Christian spiritual care of those who are ill; educate doctors, nurses, and medical students regarding Christian medical and ethical principles. **Activities:** Maintains speakers' bureau, placement service, biographical archives, and 2500 volume library; sponsors charitable programs.

★7375★ National Association of Pediatric Nurse Associates and Practitioners (NAPNAP)

1101 Kings Hwy. N., No. 206
Cherry Hill, NJ 08034-1912
Ph: (609)667-1773   Fax: (609)667-7187

Members: Pediatric, school, and family nurse practitioners and interested persons. **Purpose:** Seeks to improve the quality of infant, child, and adolescent health care by making health care services accessible and providing a forum for continuing education of members. **Activities:** Facilitates and supports legislation designed to promote the role of pediatric nurse practitioners and associates; promotes salary ranges commensurate with practitioners' and associates' responsibilities; facilitates exchange of information between prospective employers and job seekers in the field. Participates in the implementation of certification and certification maintenance of practitioners and associates, in cooperation with the National Certification Board of Pediatric Nurse Practitioners and Nurses . Supports research programs; compiles statistics. **E-Mail:** 74224.51@compuserve.com

★7376★ Nurses' House

350 Hudson St.
New York, NY 10014
Ph: (212)989-9393   Fax: (212)989-3710

Members: Registered nurses and interested individuals united to assist registered nurses in financial and other crises. **Purpose:** Provides short-term financial aid for shelter, food, and utilities until nurses obtain entitlements or jobs. Offers counseling and referrals. Encourages homebound or retired nurses through a volunteer corps. **Activities:** Participates in the American Nurses Association and the National League for Nursing conventions.

EMPLOYER DIRECTORIES AND NETWORKING LISTS

★7377★ AHA Guide to the Health Care Field

Health Statistics Group
American Hospital Association (AHA)
1 N. Franklin
Chicago, IL 60606
Ph: (312)422-3501   Fax: (312)280-6015

Annual, July. $195.00, payment with order. Covers hospitals, multi-health care systems, freestanding ambulatory surgery centers, psychiatric facilities, long-term care facilities, substance abuse programs, hospices, Health Maintenance Organizations (HMOs), and other health-related organizations. Entries include: For hospitals: facility name, address, phone, administrator's name, number of beds, facilities and services, number of employees, expenses, other statistics. For other organizations: name, address, phone, name and title of contact. Arrangement: Geographical. Indexes: Hospital name.

★7378★ American Group Practice Association—Directory

American Group Practice Association
1422 Duke St.
Alexandria, VA 22314
Ph: (703)838-0033   Fax: (703)548-1890

Annual, February. $150.00. Covers about 250 private group medical practices and their professional staffs, totalling about 25,000 physicians and administrators. Entries include: Group member name, address, phone, names of administrator and other executives, names of physician listed by medical specialties. Arrangement: Alphabetical. Indexes: Group location, personal name.

★7379★ American Journal of Nursing—Directory of Nursing Organizations Issue

American Journal of Nursing Co.
555 W. 57th St.
New York, NY 10019
Ph: (212)582-8820   Fax: (212)586-5462
Fr: 800-627-0484

Annual, April. $5.00. Publication includes: List of nursing organizations and agencies. Entries include: Name, address, names of officers or nursing representative. Arrangement: Classified by type of organization.

★7380★ Canada Nursing Job Guide Directory

Prime National Publishing Corporation
470 Boston Post Rd.
Weston, MA 02193
Ph: (617)899-2702

Martha J. Denney. 1989. $50.00. 166 pages. Directory of Canadian hospitals.

★7381★ Critical Care Choices

Springhouse Corp.
1111 Bethlehem Pke.
PO Box 908
Spring House, PA 19477
Ph: (215)646-8700   Fax: (215)646-4399
Fr: 800-346-7844

Annual, May. Free. Covers non-profit and investor-owned hospitals and departments of the United States government that hire critical care nurses. Does not report specific positions available. Entries include: Unit name, location, areas of nursing specialization, educational requirements for nurses, licensing, facilities, benefits. Arrangement: Geographical. Indexes: Geographical.

★7382★ Directory of Hospital Personnel

Medical Economics
5 Paragon Dr.
Montvale, NJ 07645-1725
Ph: (201)358-7500   Fax: (201)573-4956
Fr: 800-222-3045

Annual, September. $325.00, plus 7.50 shipping. Covers 200,000 executives at 7,100 U.S. hospitals. Entries include: Name of hospital, address, phone, number of beds, type and JCAHO status of hospital, names and titles of key department heads and staff, medical and nursing school affiliations; number of residents, interns, and nursing students. Arrangement: Geographical. Indexes: Hospital name, personnel, hospital size.

★7383★ Directory of Nursing Homes

HCIA Inc.
300 E. Lombard St.
Baltimore, MD 21202
Ph: (410)576-9600   Fax: (410)539-5220
Fr: 800-568-3282

Annual. $249.00. Covers over 16,000 state-licensed long-term care facilities. Entries include: Facility name, address, phone, names and titles of key personnel, licensure status, number of beds; number of nursing, dietary, and auxiliary staff members; program/services; medicaid/medicare certification status; admission and referral requirements; age and gender restrictions; languages spoken; management or chain company name. Arrangement: Geographical. Indexes: Alphabetical, geographical (county) and by chain headquarters.

★7384★ Freestanding Outpatient Surgery Center Directory

SMG Marketing Group, Inc.
1342 N. LaSalle Dr.
Chicago, IL 60610
Ph: (312)642-3026   Fax: (312)642-9729
Fr: 800-678-3026

Annual, August. $425.00. Covers more than 1,600 ambulatory surgical centers. Entries include: Facility name, address, phone, medi-

cal director name, ownership; number of operating suites, number of surgeries performed each year, types of surgery performed. Arrangement: Geographical.

★7385★ Hospital Blue Book

Billian Publishing Co.
2100 Powers Ferry Rd., Ste. 300
Atlanta, GA 30339
Ph: (404)955-5656   Fax: (404)952-0669

Annual, spring. $154.50, national edition, plus $20.00 shipping. Covers more than 7,100 hospitals; some listings also appear in a separate southern edition of this publication. Entries include: Name of hospital, accreditation, mailing address, phone, fax, number of beds, type of facility (nonprofit, general, state, etc.); list of administrative personnel and chiefs of medical services, with specific titles. Arrangement: Geographical.

★7386★ Hospital Market Atlas

SMG Marketing Group, Inc.
1342 N. LaSalle Dr.
Chicago, IL 60610
Ph: (312)642-3026   Fax: (312)642-9729
Fr: 800-678-3026

Biennial, odd years. $495.00, payment with order. Covers over 7,000 hospitals, hospital systems and 480 group purchasing organizations. Entries include: Hospital or organization name, address, phone, county code, management, type of hospital service, number of beds, admissions, surgical operations, and emergency room visits. Arrangement: Geographical.

★7387★ Hospitals Directory

American Business Directories, Inc.
American Business Information, Inc.
5711 S. 86th Cir.
Omaha, NE 68127
Ph: (402)593-4600   Fax: (402)331-1505

Annual. $870.00, U.S. edition. Entries include: Name, address, phone (including area code), size of advertisement, year first in Yellow Pages, name of owner or manager, number of employees. Compiled from telephone company Yellow Pages, nationwide. Arrangement: Geographical.

★7388★ Medical and Health Information Directory

Gale Research
835 Penobscot Bldg.
Detroit, MI 48226-4094
Ph: (313)961-2242   Fax: (313)961-6083
Fr: 800-877-GALE

Approximately biennial; latest edition 1994. $195.00, per volume; $485.00, for the three-volume set. Covers in Volume 1, almost 18,600 medical and health oriented associations, organizations, institutions, and government agencies, including health maintenance organizations (HMOs), preferred provider organizations (PPOs), insurance companies, pharmaceutical companies, research centers, and medical and allied health schools. In Volume 2, nearly 11,800 medical book publishers; medical periodicals, directories, audiovisual producers and services, medical libraries and information centers, and electronic resources. In Volume 3, nearly 26,000 clinics, treatment centers, care programs, and counseling/diagnostic services for 30 subject areas. Entries include: Institution, service, or firm name, address, phone; many include names of key personnel and, when pertinent, descriptive annotation. Arrangement: Classified by organization activity, service, etc. Indexes: Each volume has a complete alphabetical name and keyword index.

★7389★ Nurses and Nurses' Registries Directory

American Business Directories, Inc.
American Business Information, Inc.
5711 S. 86th Cir.
Omaha, NE 68127
Ph: (402)593-4600   Fax: (402)331-1505

Annual. $880.00, U.S. edition. Entries include: Name, address, phone (including area code), size of advertisement, year first in Yellow Pages, name of owner or manager, number of employees. Compiled from telephone company Yellow Pages, nationwide. Arrangement: Geographical.

★7390★ Nursing Career Directory

Springhouse Corp.
1111 Bethlehem Pke.
PO Box 908
Spring House, PA 19477-0908
Ph: (215)646-8700   Fax: (215)646-8700

Annual, January. Covers nonprofit and investor-owned hospitals and departments of the United States government which hire nurses. Does not report specific positions available. Entries include: Unit name, location, areas of nursing specialization, educational requirements for nurses, licensing, facilities, benefits, etc. Arrangement: Geographical.

★7391★ Nursingworld Journal—Nursing Job Guide Issue

Prime National Publishing Corp.
470 Boston Post Rd.
Weston, MA 02193
Ph: (617)899-2702   Fax: (617)899-4900
Fr: 800-869-2700

Annual, July. $75.00. Covers over 7,000 hospitals and medical centers, infirmaries, government hospitals, and other hospitals in the United States; in tabular format, provides information about each facility that would be of interest to nurses considering employment there, but does not list specific openings. Entries include: Hospital name, address, phone, name of nurse recruiter; number of beds, number of admissions, number of patient days, type of control, whether a teaching institution, nursing specialties utilized. Arrangement: Geographical.

★7392★ Osteopathic Membership Directory—AOHA

American Osteopathic Healthcare Association
5301 Wisconsin Ave. NW, Ste. 630
Washington, DC 20015-2015
Ph: (202)686-1700   Fax: (202)686-7615

Annual, summer. $125.00, payment with order. Covers about 110 osteopathic hospitals. Includes list of individual and institutional members; also lists osteopathic colleges, and directors of medical education. Entries include: For hospitals: name of hospital, name of chief executive officer, address, phone, number of beds and other hospital data. Arrangement: Geographical. Indexes: Name, institution.

★7393★ Peterson's Job Opportunities in Health Care

Peterson's Guides, Inc.
202 Carnegie Ctr.
Box 2123
Princeton, NJ 08543-2123
Ph: (609)243-9111   Fax: (609)243-9150
Fr: 800-338-3282

Annual, August. $18.95. Covers Over 1,500 companies hiring health-care professionals for skilled nursing care facilities, hospitals, medical laboratories, home health care, and pharmaceuticals. Entries include: Organization name, address, phone, name and title of contact, type of organization, number of employees, Standard Industrial Classification (SIC) code; description of opportunities available including disciplines, level of education required, starting locations and salaries, level of experience accepted, benefits. Arrangement: Alphabetical. Indexes: Employer by type of organization, industry classification, number of employees, starting location, special interest area; education level, company.

★7394★ Who's Who in American Nursing

Society of Nursing Professionals
Reed Reference Publishing
121 Chanlon Rd.
New Providence, NJ 07974-1541
Ph: (908)464-6800   Fax: (908)665-6688
Fr: 800-521-8110

Biennial, Odd years. $139.00, plus $9.73 shipping. Covers approximately 27,000 nursing professionals, including educators, administrators, deans of nursing, directors of nursing, nurse practitioners, clinical supervisors, and others. Entries include: Name, address, personal history, area of specialization, professional experience, education, professional organization membership, honors, publications, experience in public speaking. Arrangement: Alphabetical. Indexes: Geographical, specialization.

★7395★ Who's Who Among Human Services Professionals

National Register Publishing
Reed Reference Publishing
121 Chanlon Rd.
New Providence, NJ 07974-1541
Ph: (908)464-6400   Fr: 800-621-9669

Latest edition February 1992; suspended indefinitely. $129.00. Covers nearly 20,000 human service professionals, in such fields as counseling, social work, psychology, audiology, and speech pathology. Entries include: Name, address, education, work experience, professional association memberships. Arrangement: Alphabetical.

HANDBOOKS AND MANUALS

★7396★ Career Planning: Nurse's Guide to Career Advancement

National League for Nursing (NLN)
350 Hudson St.
New York, NY 10014
Ph: (212)989-9393   Fr: 800-669-1656

Patricia Winstead-Fry. 1990. $29.95. 256 pages. This is a guide to career planning and self assessment. Describes opportunities in nurse-midwifery, independent practice, community health, administration, research and education. Gives advice on getting into the field and acquiring the education needed.

★7397★ Careers in Health Care

VGM Career Horizons
4255 W. Touhy Ave.
Lincolnwood, IL 60646-1975
Ph: (847)679-5500   Fax: (847)679-2494
Fr: 800-323-4900

Barbara M. Swanson. 1995. $17.95; $13.95 (paper). Describes job duties, work settings, salaries, licensing and certification requirements, educational preparation, and future outlook. Gives ideas on how to secure a job.

★7398★ Careers in Medicine: Traditional and Alternative Opportunities

Garrett Park Press
PO Box 190 C
Garrett Park, MD 20896-0190
Ph: (301)946-2553

Donald T. Rucker and Martin D. Keller. 1990. $15.95. 346 pages. Cites training requirements, illustrative work activities, and a summary of the advantages and disadvantages in a variety of specialized areas. Includes hundreds of career alternatives and discusses ways to break into these fields for persons trained in medicine. Features contributions from over 40 professionals in all phases of medicine and provides 200 sources of information on specialties and subspecialties.

★7399★ Developing Your Career in Nursing

Cassell Publishing
215 Park Ave. S, 10th Fl.
New York, NY 10003
Ph: (212)598-5717   Fax: (212)598-5740

Robert Newell, editor. 1996.

★7400★ Exploring Careers in Nursing

Rosen Publishing Group, Inc.
29 E. 21st St.
New York, NY 10010
Ph: (212)777-3017   Fax: (212)777-0277
Fr: 800-237-9932

Jackie Heron. Revised edition, 1990. $14.95. 144 pages. Describes the job of nursing, what it takes to succeed in nursing, educational preparation, and professional opportunities in nursing. Gives job hunting advice for nurses including job hunting strategies, contacting employers, and writing resumes and cover letters.

★7401★ Federal Jobs in Nursing and Health Sciences

Impact Publications
9104 N. Manassas Dr.
Manassas Park, VA 22111-5211
Ph: (703)361-7300   Fax: (703)335-9486

Russ Smith. 1995. $14.95 (paper).

★7402★ Healthcare Career Directory–Nurses and Physicians

Gale Research
835 Penobscot Bldg.
Detroit, MI 48226-4094
Ph: (313)961-2242   Fax: (313)961-6083
Fr: 800-877-GALE

Bradley Morgan. Second edition, 1993. $39.00. 327 pages. Essays on specific careers provide an insider's perspective. Features extensive listings of contacts and entry-level job opportunities. Provides information on internships and sources of help-wanted ads.

★7403★ Job Opportunities in Health Care 1995

Peterson's Guides, Inc.
PO Box 2123
Princeton, NJ 08543-2123
Ph: (609)243-9111   Fax: (609)243-9150
Fr: 800-338-3282

1994. $18.95 (paper).

★7404★ Mosby's Tour Guide to Nursing School: A Student's Road Survival Guide

Mosby-Year Book, Inc.
11830 Westline Industrial Dr.
St. Louis, MO 63146
Ph: (314)872-8370   Fax: (314)432-1380
Fr: 800-426-4545

Melodie Chenevert. 1994. $18.95.

★7405★ Nurse Entrepeneur: Building the Bridge of Opportunity

Vista Publishing, Inc
473 Broadway
Long Branch, NJ 07740
Ph: (908)229-4545   Fax: (908)229-9647
Fr: 800-634-2498

Carolyn S. Zagury. 1993. $21.95 (paper).

★7406★ Nursing

NTC Publishing Group
4255 W. Touhy Ave.
Lincolnwood, IL 60646-1975
Ph: (708)679-5500   Fax: (708)679-6375
Fr: 800-323-4900

Blythe Camenson. 1995. $13.95.

★7407★ Nursing Today: Transition and Trends

W.B. Saunders Co.
Curtis Ctr., Independence Sq., W.
Philadelphia, PA 19106-3399
Ph: (215)238-7800   Fax: (215)238-7883

JoAnn Zerwekh, editor. 1994. $23.50 (paper).

★7408★ Obstetric Nursing

Skidmore-Roth Publishing, Inc.
7730 Trade Ctr. Dr.
El Paso, TX 79912
Ph: (915)877-4455   Fax: (915)544-4506
Fr: 800-825-3150

Brenda Goodner. 1994. $18.95 (paper).

★7409★ 100 Best Careers for the Year 2000

Prentice Hall General Reference
15 Columbus Cir.
New York, NY 10023
Ph: (212)373-8500   Fr: 800-223-2348

Shelly Field. 1992. $15.00 (paper). Covers 100 of the fastest growing jobs. The publication is divided into 11 general employment sections. Specific careers are covered within each section. Provides job description, responsibilities, employment opportunities, earnings, education and training, advancement opportunities, and experience and qualifications for each occupation.

★7410★ 101 Career Options for Nurses

Mosby-Year Book, Inc.
11830 Westline Industrial Dr.
St. Louis, MO 63146
Ph: (314)872-8370   Fax: (314)432-1380
Fr: 800-426-4545

Walraven. $21.95 (paper).

★7411★ Opportunities in Environmental Careers

VGM Career Horizons
4255 W. Touhy Ave.
Lincolnwood, IL 60646-1975
Ph: (847)679-5500   Fax: (847)679-2494
Fr: 800-323-4900

Odom Fanning. 1995. $14.95; $11.95 (paper). 160 pages. Describes a broad range of opportunities in fields such as environmental health, recreation, physics, and hygiene, and provides job search advice.

★7412★ Opportunities in Health and Medical Careers

VGM Career Horizons
4255 W. Touhy Ave.
Lincolnwood, IL 60646-1975
Ph: (847)679-5500   Fax: (847)679-2494
Fr: 800-323-4900

Donald Snook, Jr. and Leo D'Orazio. 1993. $14.95; $11.95 (paper). Covers the full range of medical and health occupations. Illustrated.

★7413★ Opportunities in Nursing Careers

VGM Career Horizons
4255 W. Touhy Ave.
Lincolnwood, IL 60646-1975
Ph: (847)679-5500   Fax: (847)679-2494
Fr: 800-323-4900

Keville Frederickson. 1995. $14.95; $11.95 (paper) Discusses the employment outlook and job-seeking techniques for LVN's, LPN's, RN's, nurse practitioners, nurse anesthetists, and other nurse members of the medical team. Includes a complete list of state nurses associations, state nursing boards, and specialty nursing organizations. Contains bibliography and illustrations.

★7414★ Opportunities in Paramedical Careers

VGM Career Horizons
4255 W. Touhy Ave.
Lincolnwood, IL 60646-1975
Ph: (847)679-5500   Fax: (847)679-2494
Fr: 800-323-4900

Alex Kacen. 1994. $14.95; 11.95 (paper). 160 pages. Discusses a variety of opportunities in this field and how to pursue them. Illustrated.

★7415★ Opportunities in Public Health Careers

VGM Career Horizons
4255 W. Touhy Ave.
Lincolnwood, IL 60646-1975
Ph: (847)679-5500   Fax: (847)679-2494
Fr: 800-323-4900

George E. Pickett and Terry W. Pickett. 1995. $14.95; $11.95 (paper). 160 pages. Defines the public health field and describes a variety of health, science, and business opportunities as well as educational preparation and the future of the public health field. Offers job-hunting tips. The appendixes list public health organizations, state and federal public health agencies, and graduate schools offering public health programs.

★7416★ Opportunities in State and Local Government Careers

VGM Career Horizons
4255 W. Touhy Ave.
Lincolnwood, IL 60646-1975
Ph: (847)679-5500   Fax: (847)679-2494
Fr: 800-323-4900

Neale Baxter. 1993. $13.95; $10.95 (paper). 160 pages. Points out the incentives and drawbacks of a government career. Describes hiring procedures and provides tips on filling out applications, taking physical and aptitude tests, handling interviews, and finding jobs. Describes the jobs in which 75% of all state and local government workers are employed. For each occupation, covers the nature of the work and the training required.

★7417★ Opportunities in Vocational and Technical Careers

VGM Career Horizons
4255 W. Touhy Ave.
Lincolnwood, IL 60646-1975
Ph: (847)679-5500   Fax: (847)679-2494
Fr: 800-323-4900

Adrian A. Paradis. 1992. $14.95; $11.95 (paper). 160 pages. Provides information on a variety of opportunities and advice on breaking into the field.

★7418★ Resume Writing for the Professional Nurse

CES Associates
112 S. Grant St.
Hinsdale, IL 60521
Ph: (708)654-2596

Nancy Kuzmich. Revised edition, 1995. $39.95. 110 pages. Self-study guide written for the professional nurse on how to set career goals, interview for a job, and select the best job offer. Includes sample resumes and cover letters.

★7419★ **Resumes for the Health Care Professional**

John Wiley & Sons, Inc.
605 3rd Ave.
New York, NY 10158-0012
Ph: (212)850-6000   Fr: 800-225-5945

Kim Marino. 1993. $14.95 (paper).

★7420★ **Resumes for Health and Medical Careers**

4255 W. Touhy Ave.
Lincolnwood, IL 60646-1975
Ph: (708)679-5500   Fax: (708)679-6375
Fr: 800-323-4900

Compiled by VGM Career Horizons Staff
1995. $9.95 (paper).

★7421★ **Self-Employment in Nursing: The Basics of Starting a Business**

American Nurses Association (ANA)
Publishing Distribution Ctr.
PO Box 2244
Waldorf, MD 20604
Fr: 800-637-0323

Lyndia Flanagan. 1993. $9.50. 32 pages.
Defines options and qualifications as well as risks, responsibilities, and benefits of being self-employed in nursing.

★7422★ **To Be a Nurse**

Vista Publishing, Inc.
473 Broadway
Long Branch, NJ 07740
Ph: (908)229-4545   Fax: (908)229-9647
Fr: 800-634-2498

Linda Strangio. 1995. $12.95 (paper).

★7423★ **Vocational & Personal Adjustments in Practical Nursing**

Mosby-Year Book, Inc.
11830 Westline Industrial Dr.
St. Louis, MO 63146
Ph: (314)872-8370   Fax: (314)432-1380
Fr: 800-426-4545

Becker. 1990. $16.95 (paper).

★7424★ **Where the Jobs Are: The Hottest Careers for the '90s**

The Career Press, Inc.
3 Tice Rd.
PO Box 687
Franklin Lakes, NJ 07417
Ph: (201)848-0310   Fax: (201)848-1727
Fr: 800-237-3371

Joyce Hadley. Second edition, 1995. $9.99.
300 pages. Describes careers in fifteen general fields, from accounting to travel and hospitality.

★7425★ **Your Opportunities in Nursing**

Energeia Publishing, Inc.
860 Commercial St., S.
Salem, OR 97302
Ph: (503)362-1480   Fax: (503)362-2123

Margie Sherman. 1994. $2.00 (paper).

EMPLOYMENT AGENCIES AND SEARCH FIRMS

★7426★ **Academy Medical Personnel Services**

571 High St.
Columbus, OH 43085-4132
Ph: (614)848-6011

Employment agency. Fills openings on a regular or temporary basis.

★7427★ **Eden Temporary Services**

280 Madison Ave.
New York, NY 10016-0801
Ph: (212)685-4666

Employment agency. Places individuals in regular or temporary positions.

★7428★ **Harper Associates**

29870 Middlebelt
Farmington Hills, MI 48334
Ph: (810)932-1170

Employment agency.

★7429★ **Health and Science Center**

209 Hunter St.
Media, PA 19063-5726
Ph: (610)891-0714

Employment agency. Executive search firm.

★7430★ **Medical Personnel Pool**

2901 S. Ridgewood Ave.
Daytona Beach, FL 32119-3542
Ph: (904)736-1648

Provides regular and temporary staffing assistance. Offices located in cities throughout United States.

★7431★ **Medical Personnel Services, Inc.**

1707 L St. NW, Ste. 700
Washington, DC 20036
Ph: (202)466-2955   Fax: (202)452-1818

Employment agency.

★7432★ **Midwest Medical Consultants**

8910 Purdue Rd., Ste. 200
Indianapolis, IN 46268-1155
Ph: (317)872-1053

Employment agency. Executive search firm.

★7433★ **Professional Placement Associates, Inc.**

11 Rye Ridge Plaza
Rye Brook, NY 10573
Ph: (914)251-1000   Fax: (914)939-1959

Employment agency.

★7434★ **Travcorps, Inc.**

40 Eastern Ave.
Malden, MA 02148
Ph: (617)322-2600

Places staff in temporary assignments.

OTHER SOURCES

★7435★ **American Almanac of Jobs and Salaries 1994-95**

Avon Books
1350 Avenue of the Americas, 2nd Fl.
New York, NY 10019
Ph: (212)261-6800   Fr: 800-238-0658

John Wright. Revised edition, 1993. $17.00.
704 pages. This is a comprehensive guide to the wages of hundreds of occupations in a wide variety of industries and organizations.

★7436★ **American Assembly for Men in Nursing (AAMN)**

437 Twin Bay Dr.
Pensacola, FL 32534-1350

Members: Registered nurses. **Purpose:** Works to: help eliminate prejudice in nursing; interest men in the nursing profession; provide opportunities for the discussion of common problems; encourage education and promote further professional growth; advise and assist in areas of professional inequity; help develop sensitivities to various social needs; promote the principles and practices of positive health care. **Activities:** Acts as a clearinghouse for information on men in nursing. Conducts educational programs.

★7437★ **American Health Care Association**

1201 L St. NW
Washington, DC 20005
Ph: (202)842-4444   Fax: (202)842-3860

Members: Federation of state associations of long-term health care facilities. **Purpose:** Promotes standards for professionals in long-term health care delivery and quality care for patients and residents in a safe environment. Focuses on issues of availability, quality, affordability, and fair payment. Operates as a liaison with governmental agencies, Congress, and professional associations.

★7438★ **American Hospital Association (AHA)**

1 N. Franklin, Ste. 27
Chicago, IL 60606
Ph: (312)422-3000   Fax: (312)422-4796

Members: Individuals and health care institutions including hospitals, health care systems, and pre- and postacute health care delivery organizations. **Purpose:** Is dedicated to promoting the welfare of the public through its leadership and assistance to its members in the provision of better health services for all people. Conducts educational programs furthering the in-service education of hospital personnel; collects and analyzes data; furnishes multimedia educational materials; maintains 44,000 volume health care administration library, and biographical archive.

★7439★ American Nurses Association (ANA)

600 Maryland Ave. SW, Ste. 100 W.
Washington, DC 20024-2571
Ph: (202)651-7000   Fax: (202)651-7001

Members: Member associations representing registered nurses. **Activities:** Sponsors American Nurses Foundation (for research), American Academy of Nursing, Center for Ethics and Human Rights, International Nursing Center, Ethnic/Racial Minority Fellowship Programs, and American Nurses Credentialing Center. Maintains hall of fame.

★7440★ Career Encounters: Advanced Practice Nursing

National League for Nursing
Publications Order Unit
350 Hudson St.
New York, NY 10014
Ph: (212)989-9393   Fr: 800-669-1656

Video. $100.00 (10-day preview); $250.00 (purchase). 30 minutes.

★7441★ Career Encounters: Nursing

Cambridge Career Products
PO Box 2153
Dept. CC15
Charleston, WV 25328-2153
Ph: (304)744-9323   Fax: (304)744-9351
Fr: 800-468-4227

Video. $99.95. 25 minutes. Professionals shown in a variety of settings discuss different aspects of their careers.

★7442★ Day in a Career: Nursing

Cambridge Career Products
PO Box 2153
Dept. CC15
Charleston, WV 25328-2153
Ph: (304)744-9323   Fax: (304)744-9351
Fr: 800-468-4227

Video. 1994. $89.00. 15-22 minutes. Includes candid interviews and work situations, plus outlines of relevant career information.

★7443★ Directory of Child Life Programs

Child Life Council
7910 Woodmont Ave., Ste. 310
Bethesda, MD 20814
Ph: (301)654-1343   Fax: (301)654-4964

Irregular. $22.00, plus $3.00 shipping. Covers Nearly 150 internships, fellowships, and other practical teaching experiences in hospitals for students of child life activity. Entries include: Facility name, address, phone, name of individual in charge of the practicum; number of hours and number of weeks for practicum; beginning dates, if specified; number of students accepted each term; total number of students accepted for the year; colleges from which students are generally referred; areas of study from which students generally come; fees; stipend and other benefits; prerequisites; whether application is to be made to college or hospital; level of student generally accepted; practicum experiences available; form of evaluation. Arrangement: Geographical.

★7444★ Hospital Salary Survey Report

Hospital Compensation Service
John R. Zabka Associates, Inc.
69 Minnehaha Blvd.
PO Box 376
Oakland, NJ 07436
Ph: (201)405-0075

Annual. Reports salaries for management employees, registered nurses, and licensed practical nurses by hospital bed size, by profit and nonprofit status for governmental hospitals, and by geographic area.

★7445★ Interviewing Skills for Nurses & Other Health Care Professionals: A Structured Approach

Routledge
29 W. 35th St.
New York, NY 10001-2299
Ph: (212)244-3336   Fax: 800-248-4724

Robert Newell. 1994. $65.00; $18.95 (paper).

★7446★ National Federation for Specialty Nursing Organizations (NFSNO)

E. Holly Ave., Box 56
Pitman, NJ 08071
Ph: (609)256-2333   Fax: (609)589-7463

Members: Nursing specialty organizations representing approximately 370,000 individuals. **Purpose:** Provides a forum for the discussion of issues of mutual concern to members; attempts to gain more input in the establishment of nursing standards. **Activities:** Sponsors Nurse in Washington Internship.

★7447★ National League for Nursing (NLN)

350 Hudson St.
New York, NY 10014
Ph: (212)989-9393   Fax: (212)989-9256
Fr: 800-669-1656

Members: Individuals and leaders in nursing and other health professions, and community members interested in solving health care problems; agencies, nursing educational institutions, departments of nursing in hospitals and related facilities, and home and community health agencies. **Purpose:** Works to assess nursing needs, improve organized nursing services and nursing education, and foster collaboration between nursing and other health and community services. Provides tests used in selection of applicants to schools of nursing; also prepares tests for evaluating nursing student progress and nursing service tests. Nationally accredits nursing education programs and community health agencies. Collects and disseminates data on nursing services and nursing education. Conducts studies and demonstration projects on community planning for nursing and nursing service and education.

★7448★ National Rural Health Association (NRHA)

1 W. Armour Blvd., Ste. 301
Kansas City, MO 64111
Ph: (816)756-3140   Fax: (816)756-3144

Members: Administrators, physicians, nurses, physician assistants, health planners, academicians, and others interested or involved in rural health care. **Purpose:** To create a better understanding of health care problems unique to rural areas; utilize a collective approach in finding positive solutions; articulate and represent the health care needs of rural America; supply current information to rural health care providers; serve as a liaison between rural health care programs throughout the country. Offers continuing education credits for medical, dental, nursing, and management courses.

★7449★ National Student Nurses' Association (NSNA)

555 W. 57th St., Ste. 1327
New York, NY 10019
Ph: (212)581-2211   Fax: (212)581-2368

Members: Students enrolled in state-approved schools for the preparation of registered nurses. **Purpose:** Seeks to aid in the development of the individual nursing student and to urge students of nursing, as future health professionals, to be aware of and to contribute to improving the health care of all people. Encourages programs and activities in state groups concerning nursing, health, and the community. Provides assistance for state board review, as well as materials for preparation for state RN licensing examination. Cooperates with nursing organizations in recruitment of nurses and in professional, community, and civic programs. **Activities:** Sponsors essay writing contest for members. Sponsors Foundation of the National Student Nurses' Association in Honor of Frances Tompkins to award scholarships to student nurses.

★7450★ Nursing Home Salary and Benefits Report

Hospital Compensation Service
John R. Zabka Associates, Inc.
69 Minnehaha Blvd.
PO Box 376
Oakland, NJ 07436
Ph: (201)405-0075

Annual. Gives salaries and fringe benefits for registered and licensed practical nurses. Lists salaries by the annual gross revenue of the nursing home, bed size, and profit and nonprofit status.

★7451★ Nursing: The Challenge of a Lifetime

National League for Nursing
Publications Order Unit
350 Hudson St.
New York, NY 10014
Ph: (212)989-9393   Fr: 800-669-1656

Video. $60.00 (10-day preview); $131.50 (purchase). 15 minutes.

★7452★ Peterson's Guide to Nursing Programs

Peterson's Guides, Inc.
202 Carnegie Center
PO Box 2123
Princeton, NJ 08543-2123
Ph: (609)243-9111   Fax: (609)243-9150
Fr: 800-338-3282

$21.95. Covers Over 600 institutions offering approximately 1,500 accredited nursing programs in the U.S. and Canada. Entries include: Academic information, extracurricular issues, costs, financial aid.

★7453★ Visiting Nurse Associations of America (VNAA)
3801 E. Florida, Ste. 900
Denver, CO 80210
Ph: (303)753-0218   Fax: (303)753-0258
Fr: 800-426-2547

Members: Voluntary, nonprofit home health care agencies. **Purpose:** Develops competitive strength among community-based nonprofit visiting nurse organizations; works to strengthen business resources and economic programs through contracting, marketing, governmental affairs and publications.

Reporters and Correspondents

SOURCES OF HELP-WANTED ADS

★7454★ Broadcasting and Cable

Conners Publishing
245 W. 17th St.
New York, NY 10011
Ph: (212)463-6835   Fax: (212)463-6836

Weekly. $85.00/year for individuals; $3.00/year for single issue. News magazine covering "The Fifth Estate" (radio, TV, cable, and satellite), and the regulatory commissions involved.

★7455★ Columbia Journalism Review

Columbia Journalism Review
700 Journalism Bldg.
Columbia University
New York, NY 10027
Ph: (212)854-1881   Fax: (212)854-8580

Bimonthly. Magazine focusing on journalism.

★7456★ Current

Heldref Publications
Helen Dwight Reid Educational Foundation
1319 18th St. NW
Washington, DC 20036-1802
Ph: (202)296-6267   Fax: (202)296-5149
Fr: 800-365-9753

$32.00/year for individuals; $6.00 for single issue; $60.00/year for institutions; $76.00/year for institutions, other countries. Journal that reprints articles on education, politics, and other social issues.

★7457★ Editor & Publisher

Editor & Publisher Co.
11 W. 19th St.
New York, NY 10011
Ph: (212)675-4380   Fax: (212)929-1259

Weekly (Sat.). Magazine focusing on journalism, advertising, and printing equipment.

★7458★ Electronic Media

Crain Communications, Inc.
740 N. Rush St.
Chicago, IL 60611
Ph: (312)649-5260   Fax: (312)649-5228

Weekly (Mon.). $69.00/year for individuals. Tabloid covering management, programing, syndication, technology, and trends in the television, radio, and electronic media industry.

★7459★ The Hollywood Reporter

Billboard Magazine
33 Commercial St.
Gloucester, MA 01930
Ph: (508)281-3110   Fax: (508)281-0136

Daily (morn.). $149.00/year for individuals. Film, TV, and entertainment trade newspaper.

★7460★ The Insider Newsletter

Sports Careers
PO Box 10129
Phoenix, AZ 85064
Fr: 800-776-7877

Semimonthly. Subscription free to members; $99.00/six months for nonmembers. Provides articles on career development, salaries, and trends for the sports industry. Includes "Career Connections," an insert listing 60-75 job opportunities and internships within each issue.

★7461★ Metro Magazine

Bobit Publishing
2512 Artesia Blvd.
Redondo Beach, CA 90278
Ph: (310)376-8788   Fax: (310)374-7878

$25.00/year for individuals; $4.00 for single issue. Magazine on public transportation.

★7462★ Multichannel News

Capital Cities/ABC, Inc.
825 7th Ave., 6th Fl.
New York, NY 10019
Ph: (212)887-8400   Fax: (212)887-8384

Weekly (Mon.). $84.00/year for individuals. Cable and pay TV magazine.

★7463★ The New Republic

New Republic, Inc.
1220 19th St. NW, 600
Washington, DC 20036
Ph: (202)331-7494   Fax: (202)331-0275

Weekly (Mon.). $69.67/year for individuals; $84.97/year for Canada; $99.97/year for other countries; $2.95 for single issue.

★7464★ Publishers Weekly

Publisher's Weekly
249 W. 17th St.
New York, NY 10011
Ph: (212)463-6758   Fax: (212)463-6631

Weekly (Mon.).

★7465★ The Quill

Russell Sage College
Box 2134
Troy, NY 12180
Ph: (518)270-2259

Weekly (Thurs.). Collegiate newspaper.

★7466★ Signature

South Wind Publishing Co.
PO Box 6808
Leawood, KS 66206-0808
Ph: (913)642-6611   Fax: (913)642-6676

Periodic. Free to qualified subscribers; $48.00/year for institutions; $58.00/year for Canada and Mexico. Publishing industry magazine and catalog.

★7467★ Writer's Digest

F&W Publications, Inc.
1507 Dana Ave.
Cincinnati, OH 45207
Ph: (513)531-2222   Fax: (513)531-1843

Monthly. $27.00/year for individuals. Professional magazine for writers.

PLACEMENT AND JOB REFERRAL SERVICES

★7468★ American Sportscasters Association (ASA)

5 Beekman St., Ste. 814
New York, NY 10038
Ph: (212)227-8080   Fax: (212)571-0556

Members: Radio and television sportscasters. **Activities:** Operates placement service, hall of fame, and biographical archives. Maintains American Sportscaster Charitable Trust. Is currently implementing an antidrug program. Sponsors seminars, clinics, and symposia for aspiring announcers and sportscasters. Compiles statistics.

★7469★ Asian American Journalists Association (AAJA)

1765 Sutter St., Ste. 1000
San Francisco, CA 94115
Ph: (415)346-2051   Fax: (415)931-4671

Members: Journalists, educator, employees of news organizations, public relations specialists, and students. **Purpose:** Seeks to increase employment of Asian Pacific American journalists; provides journalism students with career advice and aid; encourages fair and accurate news coverage of Asian and Asian Pacific American issues; provides support and fellowship for Asian Pacific American journalists. **Activities:** Maintains resource file of resumes for potential employers. Compiles statistics; operates speakers' bureau.

★7470★ Aviation/Space Writers Association (AWA)

6540 50th St. N.
Oakdale, MN 55128
Ph: (612)779-9390

Members: Aviation/space writers and editors of newspapers, magazines, books, radio, television, and press services; public relations representatives and other writers associated with the aviation/space industry. **Activities:** Operates placement service.

★7471★ Broadcast Foundation of College/University Students (BROADCAST)

89 Longview Rd.
Port Washington, NY 11050
Ph: (516)883-2897   Fax: (516)883-7460

Members: College students interested in broadcasting and professional broadcasters interested in encouraging practical broadcasting experience in colleges and universities. **Activities:** Conducts annual survey of all professional broadcasting stations for part-time and summer employment for college students. Sponsors job advisory and placement service.

★7472★ Computer Press Association (CPA)

3661 W. 4th Ave., No. 8
Vancouver, BC, Canada V6R 1P2
Ph: (604)733-5596   Fax: (604)732-4280

Members: Journalists and other individuals who write or report regularly about the computer industry. **Purpose:** Established to provide a forum for professional communication. **Activities:** Operates job listings service.

★7473★ Dow Jones Newspaper Fund (DJNF)

PO Box 300
Princeton, NJ 08543
Ph: (609)452-2820   Fax: (609)520-5804

Purpose: Established by Dow Jones and Company to encourage careers in journalism among young people. Operates Editing Internship Program for all junior, senior, and graduate level college students interested in journalism. Also offers On-Line Newspaper Program; Part-Time Information Intern Program; and Business Intern Program. Students work as copy editors during the summer for a daily newspaper or wire service and receive monetary scholarships to return to school in the fall. Offers information on careers in print journalism.

★7474★ Editorial Freelancers Association (EFA)

71 W. 23rd St., Ste. 1504
New York, NY 10010
Ph: (212)929-5400   Fax: (212)929-5439

Members: Persons who work full- or part-time as editorial freelancers. **Purpose:** Promotes professionalism and facilitates the exchange of information and support. **Activities:** Conducts professional training seminars; offers job phone. Compiles statistics.

★7475★ Education and Research Institute (ERI)

800 Maryland Ave. NE
Washington, DC 20002
Ph: (202)546-1710   Fax: (202)546-1638

Purpose: Organization dedicated to advancing awareness and understanding of America's traditional values and free enterprise system through the publication and distribution of studies on major issues of public policy. Conducts educational programs for youth. Founded and maintains the National Journalism Center to train college students in journalistic skills. **Activities:** Sponsors internship program that features research projects, writing assignments, and weekly seminars with professional journalists. Operates a job bank to match potential candidates with media-related jobs.

★7476★ Education Writers Association (EWA)

1001 Connecticut Ave. NW, Ste. 310
Washington, DC 20036
Ph: (202)429-9680   Fax: (202)872-4016

Members: Education writers and reporters of daily and weekly newspapers, national magazines of general circulation, and radio and television stations; associate members are school and college public relations personnel and others with a serious interest in education writing. **Purpose:** Improves the quality of education reporting and interpretation; encourages the development of education coverage by the press; to help attract top-notch writers and reporters to the education field. **Activities:** Sponsors regional and special workshops. Provides job referral/bank services.

★7477★ National Association of Broadcasters (NAB)

1771 N St. NW
Washington, DC 20036
Ph: (202)429-5300   Fax: (202)429-5343

Members: Representatives of radio and television stations and networks; associate members include producers of equipment and programs. **Purpose:** Seeks to ensure the viability, strength, and success of free, over-the-air broadcasters; serves as an information resource to the industry. **Activities:** Offers minority placement service and employment clearinghouse. Monitors and reports on events regarding radio and television broadcasting. Maintains Broadcasting Hall of Fame.

★7478★ National Association of Hispanic Journalists (NAHJ)

Natl. Press Bldg., Ste. 1193
529 14th St. NW
Washington, DC 20045
Ph: (202)662-7145   Fax: (202)662-7144
Fr: 800-708-2774

Purpose: To organize and support Hispanics involved in news gathering and dissemination. Encourages journalism and communications study and practice by Hispanics. Seeks recognition for Hispanic members of the profession regarding their skills and achievements. Promotes fair and accurate media treatment of Hispanics; opposes job discrimination and demeaning stereotypes. Works to increase educational and career opportunities and development for Hispanics in the field. Seeks to foster greater awareness of members' cultural identity, interests, and concerns. Provides a united voice for Hispanic journalists with the aim of achieving national visibility. **Activities:** Offers placement services to Hispanic students.

★7479★ Radio-Television News Directors Association (RTNDA)

1000 Connecticut Ave. NW, Ste. 615
Washington, DC 20036
Ph: (202)659-6510   Fax: (202)223-4007
Fr: 800-80-RTNDA

Members: Professional society of heads of news departments for broadcast and cable stations and networks; associate members are journalists engaged in the preparation and presentation of broadcast news and teachers of electronic journalism; other members represent industry services, public relations departments of business firms, public relations firms, and networks. **Purpose:** Works to improve standards of electronic journalism; defends rights of journalists to access news; promotes journalism training to meet specific needs of the industry. **Activities:** Operates placement service and speakers' bureau.

★7480★ Sports Careers

PO Box 10129
Phoenix, AZ 85064
Fr: 800-776-7877

Career development firm for the sports industry. Provides career-related programs, conferences, seminars, educational products, and publications. Offers Career Enhancement Profile Program and Resume

Development Kit. Maintains an electronic resume bank for members which is available to sports companies and organizations. Publishes newsletter listing job opportunities.

EMPLOYER DIRECTORIES AND NETWORKING LISTS

★7481★ Broadcasting & Cable Yearbook

R. R. Bowker Co.
Reed Reference Publishing
121 Chanlon Rd.
New Providence, NJ 07974
Ph: (908)464-6800   Fax: (908)464-3553
Fr: 800-521-8110

Annual, March. $169.95. Covers all television and radio stations in the United States, its territories, and Canada; cable MSOs and their individual systems; television and radio networks, broadcast and cable group owners, station representatives, satellite networks and services, film companies, advertising agencies, government agencies, trade associations and schools. Entries include: Company name, address, phone, fax, names of executives. Station listings include broadcast power, other operating details. Arrangement: Stations and systems are geographical, others are alphabetical. Indexes: Alphabetical.

★7482★ Burrelle's New York Media Directory

Burrelle's Information Services
75 E. Northfield Rd.
Livingston, NJ 07039
Ph: (201)992-6600   Fr: 800-876-3342

Annual. $95.00. Includes information on radio and television stations, newspapers, and other media companies. Regional editions available for some Northeastern states.

★7483★ CPB Public Broadcasting Directory

Corporation for Public Broadcasting
901 E St. NW
Washington, DC 20004-2037
Ph: (202)879-9600   Fax: (202)783-1019

Annual, fall. $15.00. Covers public television and radio stations, national and regional public broadcasting organizations and networks, state government agencies and commissions, and other related organizations. Entries include: For radio and television stations: station call letters, frequency or channel, address, phone, licensee name, licensee type, date on air, antenna height, area covered, names and titles of key personnel. For organizations: name, address, phone, name and title of key personnel. Arrangement: National and regional listings are alphabetical; state groups and the public radio and television stations are each geographical; other organizations and agencies are alphabetical. Indexes: Geographical, personnel, call letter, licensee type (all in separate indexes for radio and television).

★7484★ Directory of Leading Magazines and Newspapers

Publisher Media
1136 Broadway
El Cajon, CA 92021
Ph: (619)469-2610

Annual, January. $12.95. Covers over 300 newspapers and 700 consumer and trade magazines; coverage also includes Canada. Entries include: Company name, address, description of services, circulation figures advertising information. Arrangement: Classified by subject.

★7485★ Directory of Small Magazine—Press Editors and Publishers

Dustbooks
PO Box 100
Paradise, CA 95967
Ph: (916)877-6110   Fax: (916)877-0222
Fr: 800-477-6110

Annual, September. $23.95. Covers about 5,000 publishers and editors. Entries include: Individual name, title of press or magazine, address and phone number. Arrangement: Alphabetical.

★7486★ Editor & Publisher—Directory of Syndicated Services Issue

Editor & Publisher Co., Inc.
11 W. 19th St., 10th Fl.
New York, NY 10011
Ph: (212)675-4380   Fax: (212)691-6939

Annual, July. $8.00. Publication includes: Directory of several hundred syndicates serving newspapers in the United States and abroad with news, columns, features, comic strips, editorial cartoons, etc. Entries include: Syndicate name, address, phone, names of executives. Arrangement: Alphabetical. Indexes: Personnel, feature title.

★7487★ Editor & Publisher International Year Book

Editor & Publisher Co., Inc.
11 W. 19th St., 10th Fl.
New York, NY 10011
Ph: (212)675-4380   Fax: (212)691-6939

Annual, April. $100.00. Covers daily and Sunday newspapers in the United States and Canada; weekly newspapers; foreign daily newspapers; special service newspapers; newspaper syndicates; news services; journalism schools; foreign language and Black newspapers in the United States; news, picture, and press services; feature and news syndicates; comic and magazine services; advertising clubs; trade associations; clipping bureaus; house organs; journalism awards; also lists manufacturers of equipment and supplies. Arrangement: Publications and schools are geographical; most other lists are alphabetical.

★7488★ Editorial Freelancers Association—Membership Directory

Editorial Freelancers Association
71 W. 23 St.
New York, NY 10011
Ph: (212)929-5400   Fax: (212)929-5439

Annual, spring. $25.00, plus $3.00 shipping. Covers 1,100 member editorial freelancers. Entries include: Personal name, address,

phone, services provided, specialties. Arrangement: Alphabetical. Indexes: Product/service, special interest, geographical, computer skills.

★7489★ International Directory of Little Magazines and Small Presses

Dustbooks
PO Box 100
Paradise, CA 95967
Ph: (916)877-6110   Fax: (916)877-0222
Fr: 800-477-6110

Annual, September. $44.95. Covers over 5,000 small, independent magazines, presses, and papers. Entries include: Name, address, size, circulation, frequency, price, type of material used, number of issues or books published annually, and other pertinent data. Arrangement: Alphabetical. Indexes: Subject, regional.

★7490★ International Media Guide: Newspapers Worldwide

International Media Guides, Inc.
Macair Bldg.
85 Perimeter Rd.
Nashua, NH 03063
Ph: (603)882-9576   Fax: (603)595-0437
Fr: 800-964-6334

Annual. $150.00. Covers newspapers and color newspaper magazines/supplements from 200 countries, including the United States. Entries include: Publication name; publisher name, address, phone, fax, names of editor, advertising manager, and representatives in the United States and worldwide; advertising rates in U.S. dollars and/or local currency, circulation, mechanical data, ad closing, readership description, etc. Arrangement: Geographical.

★7491★ International Television and Video Almanac

Quigley Publishing Co., Inc.
159 W. 53rd St.
New York, NY 10019
Ph: (212)247-3100   Fax: (212)489-0871

Annual, January. $88.50, plus shipping. Covers Who's Who in Motion Pictures and Television and Home Video, television networks, major program producers, major group station owners, cable television companies, distributors, firms serving the television and home video industry, equipment manufacturers, casting agencies, literary agencies, advertising and publicity representatives, television stations, associations, list of feature films produced for television; statistics, industry's year in review, award winners. Entries include: Generally, company name, address, phone; manufacturer and service listings may include description of products and services and name of contact; producing, distributing, and station listings include additional detail. Arrangement: Classified by service or activity, then generally geographical.

★7492★ National Directory of Community Newspapers

American Newspaper Representatives, Inc.
1000 Shelard Pkwy., Ste. 360
Minneapolis, MN 55426
Ph: (612)545-1116   Fax: (612)545-1481
Fr: 800-752-6237

Annual, March. $75.00, postpaid, payment with order. Number of listings: 7,000. Entries include: Name of newspaper, address, county, type of area, circulation, day published, name of publisher, and information on advertising and production. Arrangement: Geographical.

★7493★ National Directory of Magazines

Oxbridge Communications, Inc.
150 5th Ave., Ste. 301
New York, NY 10011
Ph: (212)741-0231

Annual. $445.00. Covers approximately 30,000 magazines.

★7494★ Sports Market Place Register

Sports Careers
PO Box 10129
Phoenix, AZ 85064
Fr: 800-776-7877

Annual $59.00. Resource guide for the sports industry. Lists over 24,000 national and international sports business contacts. Entries include: organization name, name of key executive, address, and phone and fax numbers. Provides listings for: Individual and Multiple Sports Organizations/Teams/Media; College Sports; Sponsorship/Marketing/Event Management; Sports Agents/Lawyers; Manufacturers/Retailers. Indexes: Geographic and Alphabetical.

★7495★ Ulrich's International Periodicals Directory

R. R. Bowker Co.
Reed Reference Publishing
121 Chanlon Rd.
New Providence, NJ 07974
Ph: (908)665-2847   Fax: (908)771-7725
Fr: 800-521-8110

Annual, updates three times per year under. $415.00, includes updates. Covers nearly 126,000 current periodicals published worldwide; 7,000 newspapers published in the U.S. Entries include: In main list: publication title; Dewey Decimal Classification number, Library of Congress Classification Number (where applicable), CODEN designation (for sci-tech serials), British Library Document Supply Centre shelfmark number, country code, ISSN; subtitle, language(s) of text, year first published, frequency, subscription price in country of origin and U.S. rate, sponsoring organization, publisher name and address, editor; regular features (reviews, advertising, abstracts, bibliographies, trade literature, etc.), indexes, circulation, format, brief description of content; availability of microforms and reprints; whether refereed; CD-ROM availability with vendor name; online availability with host name; services that index or abstract the periodical, with years covered; advertising rates and contact; availability through document delivery services; Copyright Clearance Center participation; docu-

ment type; former title. Arrangement: Main listing is classified by subject; newspapers are listed in a separate volume; lists of cessations, online hosts, and CD-ROM vendors are alphabetical. Indexes: International organization publication title, online periodical title, ISSN, periodicals available on CD-ROM refereed serial, controlled circulation serial, cumulative title changes.

HANDBOOKS AND MANUALS

★7496★ Career Choices for the 90's for Students of Communications and Journalism

Walker and Company
435 Hudson St.
New York, NY 10014
Ph: (212)727-8300   Fax: (212)727-0984
Fr: 800-289-2553

Prepared by the Career Associates staff. 1990. $8.95. 166 pages. Discusses alternatives for students of communications and journalism. Offers advice on how to break into the field and how to move up. Covers where and who the employers are, internship possibilities, and professional networking associations. Comprehensive guide to career and job search planning.

★7497★ Career Choices for the 90's for Students of Political Science and Government

Walker and Company
435 Hudson St.
New York, NY 10014
Ph: (212)727-8300   Fax: (212)727-0984
Fr: 800-289-2553

Prepared by the Career Associates staff. 1990. $8.95. 166 pages. Discusses alternatives for students of political science and government. Offers advice on how to break into the field and how to move up. Covers where and who the employers are, internship possibilities, and professional networking associations. Comprehensive guide to career and job search planning.

★7498★ Career Information Center

Macmillan Publishing Co.
200 Old Tappan Rd.
Old Tappan, NJ 07675
Ph: (609)461-6500   Fr: 800-223-2336

Visual Education Center Staff. Fifth edition, 1992. $229.00. This 13-volume set profiles over 600 occupations. Each occupational profile describes job duties, educational requirements, how to get the job, advancement possibilities, employment outlook, working conditions, earnings and benefits, and where to write for more information.

★7499★ Career Opportunities in Art

Facts on File, Inc.
11 Penn Plaza, 15th Fl.
New York, NY 10001-2006
Ph: (212)967-8800   Fax: 800-678-3633
Fr: 800-322-8755

Susan H. Haubenstock and David Joselit. Revised edition, 1994. $29.95. $15.95 (pa-

per). 208 pages. This book profiles seventy-five jobs that can be found in the art field. Each profile includes a career description, career ladder, employment and advancement prospects, education, experience and skills required, salary range, and tips for entry into the field.

★7500★ Career Opportunities in the Sports Industry

Facts on File, Inc.
11 Penn Plaza, 15th Fl.
New York, NY 10001-2006
Ph: (212)967-8800   Fax: 800-678-3633
Fr: 800-322-8755

Shelly Field. 1991. $29.95; $15.95 (paper). 272 pages. Describes various jobs in the sports industry. Each occupational profile covers job duties, employment outlook, career paths, salaries, skills, and education preparation. Offers tips for entering the field. Fields covered include professional sports teams, sports and business administration, coaching, sports officiating, sports journalism, fitness and recreation, and sports medicine and therapy, among others.

★7501★ Career Opportunities for Writers

Facts on File, Inc.
11 Penn Plaza, 15th Fl.
New York, NY 10001-2006
Ph: (212)967-8800   Fax: 800-678-3633
Fr: 800-322-8755

Rosemary Guiley. Third edition, 1995. $29.95; $15.95 (paper). Describes more than 100 jobs in eight major fields, offering such details as duties, salaries, perquisites, employment and advancement opportunities, organizations to join, and opportunities for women and minorities.

★7502★ Careers for Bookworms and Other Literary Types

VGM Career Horizons
4255 W. Touhy Ave.
Lincolnwood, IL 60646-1975
Ph: (847)679-5500   Fax: (847)679-2494
Fr: 800-323-4900

Marjorie Eberts and Margaret Gisler. Second edition, 1995. $14.95; $9.95 (paper). Details opportunities in education, publishing, libraries, journalism, think tanks, museums, film, broadcasting, the public sector, and other fields. Helps job seekers identify reading, writing, or research jobs.

★7503★ Careers in Communications

VGM Career Horizons
4255 W. Touhy Ave.
Lincolnwood, IL 60646-1975
Ph: (847)679-5500   Fax: (847)679-2494
Fr: 800-323-4900

Shonan Noronha. 1994. $17.95; $13.95 (paper). 176 pages. Examines the fields of journalism, photography, radio, television, film, public relations, and advertising. Gives concrete details on job locations and how to secure a job. Suggests many resources for job hunting.

★7504★ Careers for Travel Buffs and Other Restless Types

VGM Career Horizons
4255 W. Touhy Ave.
Lincolnwood, IL 60646-1975
Ph: (847)679-5500   Fax: (847)679-2494
Fr: 800-323-4900

Paul Plawin. 1992. $14.95; $9.95 (paper). Includes a variety of travel and open-road careers, such as travel writers and photographers, tour bus drivers, entertainers, cruise line staff, travel agents, tour guides, sports writers, sales, the military, trucking, and meeting planning.

★7505★ Editorial Freelancing: A Practical Guide

Aletheia Publications
38-15 Corporal Kennedy St.
Bayside, NY 11361
Ph: (718)281-0403

Trumbull Rogers. 1995.

★7506★ The Encyclopedia of Career Choices for the 1990s: Guide to Entry-Level Jobs

Perigree Books
The Berkley Publishing Group
PO Box 506
East Rutherford, NJ 07073
Ph: (201)933-9292   Fr: 800-223-0510

Career Associates Staff. 1992. $19.95. 862 pages. Describes 500 entry-level careers in a variety of industries. Presents qualifications required, working conditions, salary, internships, and professional associations.

★7507★ Guide to Careers in World Affairs

Impact Publications
9104-N Manassas Dr.
Manassas Park, VA 22111-5211
Ph: (703)361-7300   Fax: (703)335-9486

Foreign Policy Association. 1993. $14.95. 331 pages. Describes jobs in business, government, and nonprofit organizations. Explains the methods and credentials required to secure a job in many fields, including international law and journalism. Contains sections on internships and graduate programs.

★7508★ The Harvard Guide to Careers in the Mass Media

Bob Adams, Inc.
260 Center St.
Holbrook, MA 02343
Ph: (617)767-8100   Fax: (617)767-0994
Fr: 800-872-5627

John Noble. 1989. $7.95. 202 pages. Each section of the book evaluates one media profession in depth and contains an industry profile, a career profile that describes positions available in that area, information about current salary ranges, industry-specific job-hunting tips and strategies, and a case study outlining the methods that were used in a successful job hunt.

★7509★ Jobs for English Majors and Other Smart People

Peterson's
PO Box 2123
Princeton, NJ 08543-2123
Ph: (609)243-9111   Fax: (609)243-9150
Fr: 800-338-3282

John L. Munschauer. Third edition, 1991. $11.95. 174 pages. Shows job seekers how to position themselves in the marketplace and how to demonstrate the ability to meet the needs of prospective employers.

★7510★ The Journalist's Road to Success

Dow Jones Newspaper Fund
PO Box 300
Princeton, NJ 08543-0300
Ph: (609)452-2820   Fr: 800-369-3863

Annual. 148 pages. $3.00. Provides information on newspaper careers and salaries, and how to apply for a newspaper job. Explains how to choose a journalism school and lists colleges and universities offering journalism majors; describes undergraduate and graduate financial aid programs. Lists scholarships, fellowships, internships, and continuing education opportunities.

★7511★ Liberal Arts Jobs: What They Are and How to Get Them

Peterson's
PO Box 2123
Princeton, NJ 08543-2123
Ph: (609)243-9111   Fax: (609)243-9150
Fr: 800-338-3282

Burton Jay Nadler. Second edition, 1989. $9.95. 153 pages. Presents a list of the top 20 fields for liberal arts majors, covering more than 300 job opportunities. Discusses strategies for going after those jobs, including guidance on the language of a successful job search, informational interviews, and making networking work.

★7512★ Magazines Career Directory

Gale Research
835 Penobscot Bldg.
Detroit, MI 48226-4094
Ph: (313)961-2242   Fax: (313)961-6083
Fr: 800-877-GALE

Bradley Morgan. Fifth edition, 1993. $39.00. Features extensive listings of contacts and entry-level job opportunities at many magazine publishing organizations. Includes articles by top professionals in the field on some of the industry's varied career paths: art, editorial, sales, and business management.

★7513★ Newspapers Career Directory

Gale Research
835 Penobscot Bldg.
Detroit, MI 48226-4094
Ph: (313)961-2242   Fax: (313)961-6083
Fr: 800-877-GALE

Bradley Morgan. Fourth edition, 1993. $39.00. 344 pages. Features extensive listings of contacts and entry-level job opportunities at many newspaper organizations. Focuses on each area of the business, from reporting and editorial to sales and marketing to promotion and production.

★7514★ Newspapers, Diversity, and You

Dow Jones Newspaper Fund
PO Box 300
Princeton, NJ 08543-0300
Ph: (609)452-2820   Fr: 800-369-3863

Updated biennially. Free. 71 pages. Provides information to minorities on how to prepare for a career in journalism. Includes list of newspaper groups that actively recruit minorities.

★7515★ 100 Best Careers for the Year 2000

Prentice Hall General Reference
15 Columbus Cir.
New York, NY 10023
Ph: (212)373-8500   Fr: 800-223-2348

Shelly Field. 1992. $15.00 (paper). Covers 100 of the fastest growing jobs. The publication is divided into 11 general employment sections. Specific careers are covered within each section. Provides job description, responsibilities, employment opportunities, earnings, education and training, advancement opportunities, and experience and qualifications for each occupation.

★7516★ Opportunities in Journalism Careers

VGM Career Horizons
4255 W. Touhy Ave.
Lincolnwood, IL 60646-1975
Ph: (847)679-5500   Fax: (847)679-2494
Fr: 800-323-4900

Jim Patten and Donald L. Ferguson. 1993. $14.95; $11.95 (paper). 160 pages. Outlines opportunities in every field of journalism, including newspaper reporting and editing, magazine and book publishing, corporate communications, advertising and public relations, freelance writing, and teaching. Covers how to prepare for and enter each field, outlining responsibilities, salaries, benefits, and job outlook for each specialty. Illustrated.

★7517★ Opportunities in Newspaper Publishing Careers

VGM Career Horizons
4255 W. Touhy Ave.
Lincolnwood, IL 60646-1975
Ph: (847)679-5500   Fax: (847)679-2494
Fr: 800-323-4900

John Tebbel. 1989. $14.95; $11.95 (paper). 160 pages. Tells how to land a newspaper job, describing editorial and noneditorial positions at big city and small city papers and syndicated wire services. Career preparation chapters address the need to anticipate changing newspaper technology while acquiring fundamental news skills. Illustrated.

★7518★ Opportunities in Sports and Athletics

VGM Career Horizons
4255 W. Touhy Ave.
Lincolnwood, IL 60646-1975
Ph: (847)679-5500   Fax: (847)679-2494
Fr: 800-323-4900

William Ray Heitzmann. 1994. $14.95; $11.95 (paper). A guide to planning for and seeking opportunities in this growing field. Illustrated.

★7519★ Opportunities in Technical Writing and Communications Careers

VGM Career Horizons
4255 W. Touhy Ave.
Lincolnwood, IL 60646-1975
Ph: (847)679-5500   Fax: (847)679-2494
Fr: 800-323-4900

Jay Gould and Wayne Losano. 1994. $14.95; $11.95 (paper). 160 pages. Provides advice on acquiring a position in medical, engineering, pharmaceutical, and other technical fields. Illustrated.

★7520★ Opportunities in Writing Careers

VGM Career Horizons
4255 W. Touhy Ave.
Lincolnwood, IL 60646-1975
Ph: (847)679-5500   Fax: (847)679-2494
Fr: 800-323-4900

Elizabeth Foote-Smith. 1989. $14.95; $11.95 (paper). 160 pages. Discusses opportunities in the print media, broadcasting, advertising or publishing. Business writing, public relations, and technical writing are among the careers covered. Contains bibliography and illustrations.

★7521★ Radio and Television Career Directory

Gale Research
835 Penobscot Bldg.
Detroit, MI 48226-4094
Ph: (313)961-2242   Fax: (313)961-6083
Fr: 800-877-GALE

Bradley Morgan. Second edition, 1993. $39.00. 334 pages. Features extensive listings of contacts and entry-level job opportunities. Provides information on internships and sources of help-wanted ads.

EMPLOYMENT AGENCIES AND SEARCH FIRMS

★7522★ Blair Personnel of Parsippany, Inc.

1130 U.S. Hwy 46
Parsippany, NJ 07054-2158
Ph: (201)335-6150   Fax: (201)335-4657

Employment agency. Focuses on regular and temporary placement.

★7523★ Joe Sullivan and Associates, Inc.

44210 County Rd. 48
PO Box 612
Southold, NY 11971
Ph: (516)765-5050

Executive search firm. Recruits for the broadcasting and media industries.

★7524★ The Pathfinder Group

295 Danbury Rd.
Wilton, CT 06897-3095
Ph: (203)834-2467

Employment agency. Executive search firm. Recruits staff in a variety of fields.

★7525★ Remer-Ribolow and Associates

230 Park Ave., Ste. 222
New York, NY 10169
Ph: (212)808-0580

Employment agency.

★7526★ Search Source, Inc.

2019B Johnson Rd.
PO Box 1161
Granite City, IL 62040
Ph: (618)876-6060   Fax: (618)876-6071

Executive search firm. Concentrates on placement to broadcasting industry.

OTHER SOURCES

★7527★ Interviewing Techniques for Newspapers

State Mutual Book & Periodical Service, Ltd.
521 5th Ave., 17th Fl.
New York, NY 10175
Ph: (718)261-1704   Fax: (516)537-0412

Maurice Dunlevy. 1995. $20.00 (paper).

★7528★ Newsletter Association of American Foundation (NAA)

The Newspaper Center
11600 Sunrise Valley Dr.
Reston, VA 22091
Ph: (703)648-1000   Fax: (703)620-4557

Members: Daily and nondaily newspapers in the Western Hemisphere, Europe, and the Pacific region. **Purpose:** Goals are to advance the cause of a free press, and to ensure that it has the economic strength essential to serve the American people. Provides services for member newspapers on all phases of the newspaper business. Compiles information and publishes materials on advertising and marketing, circulation and readership, general management, labor and personnel relations, legislation, technical services and research, telecommunications, newsprint, literacy, and workforce diversity. **Activities:** Operates technical services and research facility in Reston, VA; maintains library of 5000 volumes on journalism, the newspaper business, and mass communications. Maintains 44 committees/councils.

★7529★ Resumes for Communications Careers

VGM Career Horizons
4255 W. Touhy Ave.
Lincolnwood, IL 60646-1975
Ph: (847)679-5500   Fax: (847)679-2494
Fr: 800-323-4900

1991. $9.95. 160 pages. Includes sample resumes representing journalists, writers, publicists, and other communications specialists.

★7530★ Society of Professional Journalists (SPJ)

16 S. Jackson
Greencastle, IN 46135
Ph: (317)653-3333   Fax: (317)653-4631

Members: Professional society - journalism. **Purpose:** Promotes a free and unfettered press; high professional standards and ethical behavior; journalism as a career. Conducts lobbying activities; maintains legal defense fund. Sponsors Barney/Kilgore Freedom of Information Internships in Washington, DC. **Activities:** Holds forums on the free press. Maintains placement service. **E-Mail:** address spj@internetmci.com

★7531★ Sports Careers Industry Audio Cassette Series

Sports Careers
PO Box 10129
Phoenix, AZ 85064
Fr: 800-776-7877

Audiocassette series. Covers the top ten major career categories for the sports industry: Special Events; TV and Cable; Sporting Goods; Colleges/Universities; Facility Management; Corporate Sponsorship; Athletic Representation; Front Office; Print and Radio; Health and Fitness.

★7532★ Student Guide to Mass Media Internships

Intern Research Group
Box 52, Regent Hall
University of Colorado
Boulder, CO 80309
Ph: (303)442-8340

Annual, latest edition 1995. $35.00, payment with order; $40.00, billed. Covers about 10,000 internships offered by 2,700 newspapers, radio and television stations, cable television companies, magazines, advertising agencies, and other firms. Entries include: Organization name, address, type and number of internships offered, eligibility requirements, application deadline, salary or other stipend offered, name and title of contact; many listings also include description of intern's duties. Arrangement: Classified by type of medium, then geographical.

★7533★ Women in Communications

10605 Judicial Dr., Ste. A4
Fairfax, VA 22030-5167
Ph: (703)359-9000   Fax: (703)359-0603

Members: Professional association of journalism and communications.

Respiratory Therapists

SOURCES OF HELP-WANTED ADS

★7534★ American Review of Respiratory Disease

American Lung Association
1740 Broadway
New York, NY 10019
Ph: (212)315-8700   Fax: (212)265-5642

Monthly. Medical journal focusing on lung diseases.

★7535★ Heart and Lung: The Journal of Acute and Critical Care

Mosby Year Book
11830 Westline Industrial Dr.
St. Louis, MO 63146
Ph: (314)872-8370   Fax: 800-535-9935
Fr: 800-633-6699

Bimonthly. $39.00/year for individuals; $57.78 /year for Canada; $54.00/year for other countries; $21.00/year for students. Journal offering articles prepared by nurse and physician members of the critical care team, recognizing the nurse's role in the care and management of major organ-system conditions in critically ill patients.

★7536★ Journal of Cardiopulmonary Rehabilitation

Pharmaceutical Media, Inc.
30 E. 33rd St.
New York, NY 10016
Ph: (212)685-5010   Fax: (212)685-5010

Bimonthly. Medical journal.

★7537★ Respiratory Care

Daedalus Enterprises, Inc.
11030 Ables Ln.
Dallas, TX 75229
Ph: (214)243-2272   Fax: (214)484-6010

Monthly. Science journal about cardiorespiratory care.

PLACEMENT AND JOB REFERRAL SERVICES

★7538★ American Public Health Association (APHA)

1015 15th St. NW
Washington, DC 20005
Ph: (202)789-5600   Fax: (202)789-5681

Members: Professional organization of physicians, nurses, educators, academicians, environmentalists, epidemiologists, new professionals, social workers, health administrators, optometrists, podiatrists, pharmacists, dentists, nutritionists, health planners, other community and mental health specialists, and interested consumers. **Purpose:** Seeks to protect and promote personal, mental, and environmental health. **Activities:** Services include: promulgation of standards; establishment of uniform practices and procedures; development of the etiology of communicable diseases; research in public health; exploration of medical care programs and their relationships to public health. Sponsors job placement service.

EMPLOYER DIRECTORIES AND NETWORKING LISTS

★7539★ AHA Guide to the Health Care Field

Health Statistics Group
American Hospital Association (AHA)
1 N. Franklin
Chicago, IL 60606
Ph: (312)422-3501   Fax: (312)280-6015

Annual, July. $195.00, payment with order. Covers hospitals, multi-health care systems, freestanding ambulatory surgery centers, psychiatric facilities, long-term care facilities, substance abuse programs, hospices, Health Maintenance Organizations (HMOs), and other health-related organizations. Entries include: For hospitals: facility name, address, phone, administrator's name, number of beds, facilities and services, number of employees, expenses, other statistics. For other organizations: name, address, phone, name and title of contact. Arrangement: Geographical. Indexes: Hospital name.

★7540★ Directory of Hospital Personnel

Medical Economics
5 Paragon Dr.
Montvale, NJ 07645-1725
Ph: (201)358-7500   Fax: (201)573-4956
Fr: 800-222-3045

Annual, September. $325.00, plus 7.50 shipping. Covers 200,000 executives at 7,100 U.S. hospitals. Entries include: Name of hospital, address, phone, number of beds, type and JCAHO status of hospital, names and titles of key department heads and staff, medical and nursing school affiliations; number of residents, interns, and nursing students. Arrangement: Geographical. Indexes: Hospital name, personnel, hospital size.

★7541★ Home Health Service Directory

American Business Directories, Inc.
American Business Information, Inc.
5711 S. 86th Cir.
Omaha, NE 68127
Ph: (402)593-4600   Fax: (402)331-1505

Annual. $1,200.00, U.S. edition. Entries include: Name, address, phone (including area code), size of advertisement, year first in Yellow Pages, name of owl her or manager, number of employees. Compiled from telephone company Yellow Pages, nationwide. Arrangement: Geographical.

★7542★ Hospital Blue Book

Billian Publishing Co.
2100 Powers Ferry Rd., Ste. 300
Atlanta, GA 30339
Ph: (404)955-5656   Fax: (404)952-0669

Annual, spring. $154.50, national edition, plus $20.00 shipping. Covers more than 7,100 hospitals; some listings also appear in a separate southern edition of this publication. Entries include: Name of hospital, accreditation, mailing address, phone, fax, number of beds, type of facility (nonprofit, general, state, etc.); list of administrative personnel and chiefs of medical services, with specific titles. Arrangement: Geographical.

★7543★ Hospital Market Atlas

SMG Marketing Group, Inc.
1342 N. LaSalle Dr.
Chicago, IL 60610
Ph: (312)642-3026   Fax: (312)642-9729
Fr: 800-678-3026

Biennial, odd years. $495.00, payment with order. Covers over 7,000 hospitals, hospital systems and 480 group purchasing organizations. Entries include: Hospital or organization name, address, phone, county code, management, type of hospital service, number of beds, admissions, surgical operations, and emergency room visits. Arrangement: Geographical.

★7544★ Hospitals Directory

American Business Directories, Inc.
American Business Information, Inc.
5711 S. 86th Cir.
Omaha, NE 68127
Ph: (402)593-4600   Fax: (402)331-1505

Annual. $870.00, U.S. edition. Entries include: Name, address, phone (including area code), size of advertisement, year first in Yellow Pages, name of owner or manager, number of employees. Compiled from telephone company Yellow Pages, nationwide. Arrangement: Geographical.

★7545★ Medical and Health Information Directory

Gale Research
835 Penobscot Bldg.
Detroit, MI 48226-4094
Ph: (313)961-2242   Fax: (313)961-6083
Fr: 800-877-GALE

Approximately biennial; latest edition 1994. $195.00, per volume; $485.00, for the three-volume set. Covers in Volume 1, almost 18,600 medical and health oriented associations, organizations, institutions, and government agencies, including health maintenance organizations (HMOs), preferred provider organizations (PPOs), insurance companies, pharmaceutical companies, research centers, and medical and allied health schools. In Volume 2, nearly 11,800 medical book publishers; medical periodicals, directories, audiovisual producers and services, medical libraries and information centers, and electronic resources. In Volume 3, nearly 26,000 clinics, treatment centers, care programs, and counseling/diagnostic services for 30 subject areas. Entries include: Institution, service, or firm name, address, phone; many include names of key personnel and, when pertinent, descriptive annotation. Arrangement: Classified by organization activity, service, etc. Indexes: Each volume has a complete alphabetical name and keyword index.

★7546★ Osteopathic Membership Directory—AOHA

American Osteopathic Healthcare Association
5301 Wisconsin Ave. NW, Ste. 630
Washington, DC 20015-2015
Ph: (202)686-1700   Fax: (202)686-7615

Annual, summer. $125.00, payment with order. Covers about 110 osteopathic hospitals. Includes list of individual and institutional members; also lists osteopathic colleges, and

directors of medical education. Entries include: For hospitals: name of hospital, name of chief executive officer, address, phone, number of beds and other hospital data. Arrangement: Geographical. Indexes: Name, institution.

HANDBOOKS AND MANUALS

★7547★ Careers in Health Care

VGM Career Horizons
4255 W. Touhy Ave.
Lincolnwood, IL 60646-1975
Ph: (847)679-5500   Fax: (847)679-2494
Fr: 800-323-4900

Barbara M. Swanson. 1995. $17.95; $13.95 (paper). Describes job duties, work settings, salaries, licensing and certification requirements, educational preparation, and future outlook. Gives ideas on how to secure a job.

★7548★ Opportunities in Health and Medical Careers

VGM Career Horizons
4255 W. Touhy Ave.
Lincolnwood, IL 60646-1975
Ph: (847)679-5500   Fax: (847)679-2494
Fr: 800-323-4900

Donald Snook, Jr. and Leo D'Orazio. 1993. $14.95; $11.95 (paper). Covers the full range of medical and health occupations. Illustrated.

★7549★ Resumes for Health and Medical Careers

4255 W. Touhy Ave.
Lincolnwood, IL 60646-1975
Ph: (708)679-5500   Fax: (708)679-6375
Fr: 800-323-4900

Compiled by VGM Career Horizons Staff. 1995. $9.95 (paper).

★7550★ Therapists and Allied Health Professionals Career Directory

Gale Research
835 Penobscot Bldg.
Detroit, MI 48226-4094
Ph: (313)961-2242   Fax: (313)961-6083
Fr: 800-877-GALE

Bradley Morgan. 1993. $39.00. 326 pages. Essays on specific careers provide an insider's perspective. Also features extensive listings of contacts and entry-level job opportunities. Provides information on internships and sources of help-wanted ads.

EMPLOYMENT AGENCIES AND SEARCH FIRMS

★7551★ JPM International

4665 MacArthur Ct., Ste. 100B
Newport Beach, CA 92660
Ph: (714)955-2545   Fax: (714)757-1320

Executive search firm and employment agency.

★7552★ Professional Placement Associates, Inc.

11 Rye Ridge Plaza
Rye Brook, NY 10573
Ph: (914)251-1000   Fax: (914)939-1959

Employment agency.

★7553★ Sue Carroll Personnel, Inc.

16 E. 79th St.
New York, NY 10021
Ph: (212)288-8866   Fax: (212)988-7191

Employment agency and executive search firm.

★7554★ Travcorps, Inc.

40 Eastern Ave.
Malden, MA 02148
Ph: (617)322-2600

Places staff in temporary assignments.

OTHER SOURCES

★7555★ American Association for Respiratory Care (AARC)

11030 Ables Ln.
Dallas, TX 75229-4593
Ph: (214)243-2272   Fax: (214)484-2720

Members: Allied health society of respiratory care technicians and therapists employed by hospitals, skilled nursing facilities, home care companies, group practices, educational institutions, and municipal organizations. **Purpose:** To encourage, develop, and provide educational programs for persons interested in the profession of respiratory care; and to advance the science of respiratory care.

★7556★ Joint Review Committee for Respiratory Therapy Education (JRCRTE)

1701 W. Euless Blvd., Ste. 300
Euless, TX 76040
Ph: (817)283-2835   Fax: (817)354-8519
Fr: 800-874-5615

Members: Physicians; respiratory therapists; public representatives. **Purpose:** To develop standards and requirements for accredited educational programs of respiratory therapy for recommendation to the American Medical Association ; to conduct evaluations of educational programs that have applied for accreditation of the AMA and to make recommendations to the AMA's Committee on Allied Health Education and Accreditation; to maintain a working liaison with other organizations interested in respiratory therapy education and evaluation.

★7557★ National Board for Respiratory Care (NBRC)

8310 Nieman Rd.
Lenexa, KS 66214
Ph: (913)599-4200   Fax: (913)541-0156

Purpose: Offers credentialing examinations for respiratory therapists, respiratory therapy technicians, pulmonary technologists, and perinatal/pediatric respiratory care specialists.

Restaurant and Food Service Managers

★7558★ **Airport Press**
P.A.T.I., Inc.
PO Box 879, JFK Sta.
Jamaica, NY 11430-0879
Ph: (718)244-6788   Fax: (718)995-3432
Fr: 800-982-5832

Monthly. $32.00/year for individuals. Newspaper for the air transport industry.

★7559★ **Chef**
Talcott Communications Corp.
20 N. Wacker Dr., Ste. 3230
Chicago, IL 60606
Ph: (312)849-2220   Fax: (312)849-2174
Fr: 800-229-1967

$20.00/year for individuals; $2.95 for single issue. Covers the food service field for executive chefs.

★7560★ **Food Management**
Peter Li
1100 Superior Ave.
Cleveland, OH 44114
Ph: (216)696-7000   Fax: (216)696-7670

Monthly. $50.00/year. Professional magazine for foodservice directors.

★7561★ **FoodService Director**
Bill Communications, Inc.
355 Park Ave. S.
New York, NY 10010
Ph: (212)592-6200   Fax: (212)592-6539

Monthly. Tabloid newspaper of the noncommercial foodservice market.

★7562★ **Foodservice East**
The Newbury Street Group, Inc.
76 Summer St.
Boston, MA 02110
Ph: (617)695-9080   Fr: 800-852-5212

$20.00/year for individuals. Tabloid covering restaurant, hotel, school, college, and hospital food service in the Northeast.

★7563★ **Hotel & Motel Management**
Advanstar Communications, Inc.
7600 Old Oak Blvd.
Cleveland, OH 44130
Ph: (216)243-8100   Fax: (216)891-2733

Magazine (tabloid) covering the global lodging industry.

★7564★ **Journal of the American Dietetic Association**
American Dietetic Association
216 W. Jackson Blvd.
Chicago, IL 60606-6695
Ph: (312)899-0040   Fax: (312)899-1757

Monthly. $100.00/year; $9.75/issue. Magazine reporting original research on nutrition, diet therapy, education, and administration.

★7565★ **Midwest Foodservice News**
Metropolitan Publishing Services
PO Box 596
Worthington, OH 43085
Ph: (614)848-6151   Fax: (614)888-7695

Bimonthly. Restaurant trade newspaper featuring new products and suppliers and other industry news including food news, restaurant association updates, news of chefs, restaurant concepts, earnings, and openings and closings.

★7566★ **Modern Food Service News**
Grocers Publishing Co., Inc.
15 Emerald St.
Hackensack, NJ 07601
Ph: (201)488-1800

Monthly. Magazine for restaurateurs, chefs, caterers, purchasing agents in the food service industry.

★7567★ **Nation's Restaurant News**
Lebhar-Friedman, Inc.
425 Park Ave.
New York, NY 10022
Ph: (212)756-5257   Fax: (212)756-5270

Weekly (Mon.). $34.50/year for individuals.

★7568★ **Night Club and Bar Magazine**
Oxford Publishing, Inc.
307 W. Jackson Ave.
Oxford, MS 38655
Ph: (601)236-5510   Fax: (601)236-5541
Fr: 800-247-3881

Monthly. Trade magazine covering management, lighting, sound, food, beverage, promotions, current trends, and other bar industry news.

★7569★ **Restaurant Business**
Bill Communications, Inc.
355 Park Ave. S
New York, NY 10010-1789
Ph: (212)592-6200   Fax: (212)592-6309
Fr: 800-821-6897

Trade magazine for restaurants and commercial food service.

★7570★ **Restaurant Hospitality**
1100 Superior Ave.
Cleveland, OH 44114
Ph: (216)696-7000

Monthly. $60.00/year; $5.25/issue.

★7571★ **Restaurants & Institutions**
Cahners Publishing Co.
1350 E. Touhy Ave.
Des Plaines, IL 60018
Ph: (708)635-8800   Fax: (708)390-2770

Semimonthly. $99.95/year for individuals. Magazine focusing on foodservice and lodging management.

★7572★ **Southeast Food Service News**
Southeast Publishing Co., Inc.
PO Box 47719
Atlanta, GA 30362
Ph: (404)452-1807   Fax: (404)457-3829

Monthly. $23.00/year for individuals. Magazine (tabloid) serving the food industry.

★7573★ **Special Events**
9560 SW Nimbus Ave.
Beaverton, OR 97005
Ph: (503)520-1955   Fax: (503)520-1032

Monthly. Free. Magazine providing ideas for putting on special events and showing how specific events were planned and coordinated.

★7574★ Sunbelt Foodservice

Shelby Publishing Co., Inc.
517 Green St.
Gainesville, GA 30501
Ph: (404)534-8380   Fax: (404)535-0110

Monthly. $25.00/year for individuals. Trade newspaper (tabloid) covering the food industry geared toward restaurant operators.

★7575★ Yankee Food Service

Griffin Publishing Co., Inc.
1099 Hingham St.
Rockland, MA 02370
Ph: (617)878-5300   Fax: (617)871-4721

Monthly. $40.00/year for individuals. Newspaper (tabloid) covering business news, personnel changes, food trends, and trade events of the New England food service industry.

PLACEMENT AND JOB REFERRAL SERVICES

★7576★ Club Managers Association of America (CMAA)

1733 King St.
Alexandria, VA 22314
Ph: (703)739-9500   Fax: (703)739-0124

Members: Professional managers and assistant managers of private golf, yacht, athletic, city, country, luncheon, university, and military clubs. **Purpose:** Encourages education and advancement of members and promotes efficient and successful club operations. **Activities:** Maintains management referral service. Provides reprints of articles on club management. Supports courses in club management. Compiles statistics.

★7577★ Foodservice Consultants Society International (FCSI)

304 W. Liberty St., Ste. 201
Louisville, KY 40202
Ph: (502)583-3783   Fax: (502)589-3602

Purpose: Professional society of persons who design and layout foodservice facilities and advise on management and other aspects of food operations. Distributes business information; sponsors public relations programs; offers educational and training opportunities; maintains speakers' bureau; provides referral services.

★7578★ International Foodservice Distributors Association (IFDA)

201 Park Washington Ct.
Falls Church, VA 22046
Ph: (703)532-9400   Fax: (703)538-4673

Members: Wholesale distribution companies engaged in the distribution of food to the foodservice industry, including restaurants, hotels, hospitals, schools, and in-plant and in-office feeders. **Purpose:** Goal is to educate and inform members on industry events, government actions, and technological changes that may affect them. **Activities:** Activities include legislative and interindustry representation and research programs conducted in conjunction with other foodservice

industry associations. Operates placement service; compiles statistics; conducts executive compensation survey annually. Operates as foodservice arm of the National-American Wholesale Grocers' Association.

★7579★ Les Amis d'Escoffier

1230 Main St.
Leicester, MA 01524
Ph: (508)892-8000

Members: An educational organization of professionals in the food and wine industries. **Activities:** Maintains museum, speakers' bureau, hall of fame, and placement service. Sponsors charitable programs.

★7580★ Society for Foodservice Management (SFM)

304 W. Liberty St., Ste. 201
Louisville, KY 40202
Ph: (502)583-3783   Fax: (502)589-3602

Members: Companies that operate or maintain food service and vending facilities in businesses and industrial plants, or supply food products, equipment, or other essential industry services. **Purpose:** To serve the needs and interests of business and industry employee food service executives and management. Provides an opportunity for the exchange of experiences and opinions through study, discussion, and publications; develops greater efficiency and more economical methods of providing high-quality food and service at a reasonable cost. Develops and encourages the practice of high standards and professional conduct among management and executive personnel. **Activities:** Provides job placement and management personnel recruiting service; sends representative to the U.S. Air Force Hennessey Award Team, which selects the Air Force base having the most superior food service.

EMPLOYER DIRECTORIES AND NETWORKING LISTS

★7581★ AHA Guide to the Health Care Field

Health Statistics Group
American Hospital Association (AHA)
1 N. Franklin
Chicago, IL 60606
Ph: (312)422-3501   Fax: (312)280-6015

Annual, July. $195.00, payment with order. Covers hospitals, multi-health care systems, freestanding ambulatory surgery centers, psychiatric facilities, long-term care facilities, substance abuse programs, hospices, Health Maintenance Organizations (HMOs), and other health-related organizations. Entries include: For hospitals: facility name, address, phone, administrator's name, number of beds, facilities and services, number of employees, expenses, other statistics. For other organizations: name, address, phone, name and title of contact. Arrangement: Geographical. Indexes: Hospital name.

★7582★ College/University Foodservice Who's Who

Information Central, Inc.
Box 3900
Prescott, AZ 86302
Ph: (602)778-1513   Fax: (602)445-6407

Triennial, latest edition January 1993; $255.00. Covers over 2,200 food service programs in colleges and universities. Entries include: Institution name, address, phone, enrollment, total annual food purchases, number of meals served per day; name of management company, principal food service official, services, fast food chains on campus. Arrangement: Geographical. Indexes: Alphabetical.

★7583★ Directory of Chain Restaurant Operators

Chain Store Guide Information Services
3922 Coconut Palm Dr.
Tampa, FL 33619
Ph: (813)664-6700   Fax: 800-846-8047
Fr: 800-927-9292

Annual, June. $290.00. Covers over 4,000 3-or-more unit chain restaurant firms operating or franchising over nearly 200,000 restaurants, drive-ins, cafeterias, restaurants in hotels and motels, contract feeders, industrial caterers, and leased units in retail stores; includes hotel and motel chains operating food service units. Entries include: Company name, address, phone, fax, numbers of units company-owned and franchised, store names, whether private or public ownership, executive names, type of menus, type of food service, sales, territory, ownership, whether alcoholic beverages are served, year established. Also available in state editions. Arrangement: Geographical. Indexes: Type of menu, type of food service; top 100 ranked by sales, standard complete file index.

★7584★ Directory of Hospital Personnel

Medical Economics
5 Paragon Dr.
Montvale, NJ 07645-1725
Ph: (201)358-7500   Fax: (201)573-4956
Fr: 800-222-3045

Annual, September. $325.00, plus 7.50 shipping. Covers 200,000 executives at 7,100 U.S. hospitals. Entries include: Name of hospital, address, phone, number of beds, type and JCAHO status of hospital, names and titles of key department heads and staff, medical and nursing school affiliations; number of residents, interns, and nursing students. Arrangement: Geographical. Indexes: Hospital name, personnel, hospital size.

★7585★ Directory of Public School Systems in the U.S.

Association for School, College and University Staffing
1600 Dodge Ave., S-330
Evanston, IL 60201-3451
Ph: (708)864-1999   Fax: (708)864-8303

Annual, August. $65.00. Covers about 14,500 public school systems in the United States and their administrative personnel. Entries include: System name, address, phone, name and title of personnel administrator. Arrangement: Geographical by state.

★7586★ Healthcare Foodservice Who's Who

Information Central, Inc.
Box 3900
Prescott, AZ 86302
Ph: (602)778-1513   Fax: (602)445-6407

Triennial, latest edition January 1994. $275.00, per volume. Covers 4,500 hospitals, nursing homes, retirement facilities, homes for the aged, and other health care institutions; all institutions listed have at least 150 beds; food management companies. Entries include: Facility name, type of institution, address, phone, food service director, number of beds, annual food purchases, number of meals served per day, types of food service offered, name of food management company, cooperative buying organization, and fast food chains on premises. Arrangement: Geographical. Indexes: Alphabetical.

★7587★ Hospital Market Atlas

SMG Marketing Group, Inc.
1342 N. LaSalle Dr.
Chicago, IL 60610
Ph: (312)642-3026   Fax: (312)642-9729
Fr: 800-678-3026

Biennial, odd years. $495.00, payment with order. Covers over 7,000 hospitals, hospital systems and 480 group purchasing organizations. Entries include: Hospital or organization name, address, phone, county code, management, type of hospital service, number of beds, admissions, surgical operations, and emergency room visits. Arrangement: Geographical.

★7588★ Hospitals Directory

American Business Directories, Inc.
American Business Information, Inc.
5711 S. 86th Cir.
Omaha, NE 68127
Ph: (402)593-4600   Fax: (402)331-1505

Annual. $870.00, U.S. edition. Entries include: Name, address, phone (including area code), size of advertisement, year first in Yellow Pages, name of owner or manager, number of employees. Compiled from telephone company Yellow Pages, nationwide. Arrangement: Geographical.

★7589★ Osteopathic Membership Directory—AOHA

American Osteopathic Healthcare Association
5301 Wisconsin Ave. NW, Ste. 630
Washington, DC 20015-2015
Ph: (202)686-1700   Fax: (202)686-7615

Annual, summer. $125.00, payment with order. Covers about 110 osteopathic hospitals. Includes list of individual and institutional members; also lists osteopathic colleges, and directors of medical education. Entries include: For hospitals: name of hospital, name of chief executive officer, address, phone, number of beds and other hospital data. Arrangement: Geographical. Indexes: Name, institution.

★7590★ Restaurant Hospitality— Hospitality 500 Issue

Penton Publishing Co.
1100 Superior Ave.
Cleveland, OH 44114
Ph: (216)696-7000   Fax: (216)696-0836

Annual, June. $25.00. Publication includes: 500 independent restaurants selected on basis of sales. Entries include: Restaurant name, city and state, total sales, cost of food sales, cost of beverage sales, cost of labor, number of employees, number of seats, average dinner check. Arrangement: Ranked by total sales. Indexes: Restaurant name.

★7591★ Restaurants & Institutions–Annual 400 Issue

Cahners Publishing Co.
1350 E. Touhy Ave.
PO Box 5080
Des Plaines, IL 60017-5080
Ph: (708)635-8800   Fax: (708)635-6856

Annual, July. $25.00. Publication includes: List of 400 largest away-from-home food service companies. Entries include: Company name, location, rank, food service volume and number of units for two preceding years, brief summary of activities and prospects. Arrangement: Ranked by sales volume. Indexes: Alphabetical, segment of industry.

★7592★ School Foodservice Who's Who

Information Central, Inc.
Box 3900
Prescott, AZ 86302
Ph: (602)778-1513   Fax: (602)445-6407

Triennial, latest edition January 1995. $285.00, per volume; $500.00, per two-volume set. Covers about 5,500 food service programs in public and Catholic school systems with enrollments in excess of 1,500 students. Separate listings of the biggest buyers (school districts reporting over $1.5 million in foodservice purchases), state school foodservice officials, and co-op buying groups and food management companies involved in food service. Entries include: School district name, address, phone, fax; food service budget, key food service executive, number of meals served daily, types of food and services, food management company, fast food brands. Arrangement: Geographical.

HANDBOOKS AND MANUALS

★7593★ Career Choices for the 90's for Students of Business

Walker and Company
435 Hudson St.
New York, NY 10014
Ph: (212)727-8300   Fax: (212)727-0984
Fr: 800-289-2553

Prepared by the Career Associates staff. 1990. $9.95. 166 pages. Discusses alternatives for students of business. Offers advice on how to break into the field and how to move up. Covers where and who the employers are, internship possibilities, and profes-

sional networking associations. Comprehensive guide to career and job search planning.

★7594★ Career Opportunities in the Food and Beverage Industry

Facts on File, Inc.
11 Penn Plaza, 15th Fl.
New York, NY 10001-2006
Ph: (212)967-8800   Fax: 800-678-3633
Fr: 800-322-8755

Barbara Sims-Bell. 1994. $29.95; $15.95 (paper). 256 pages. Provides the job seeker with information about locating and landing 80 skilled and unskilled jobs in the industry. Includes detailed job descriptions for many specific positions and lists trade associations, recruiting organizations, and major agencies. Contains index and bibliography.

★7595★ Career Opportunities in Travel and Tourism

Facts on File, Inc.
11 Penn Plaza, 15th Fl.
New York, NY 10001-2006
Ph: (212)967-8800   Fax: 800-678-3633
Fr: 800-322-8755

John Hawks. 1995. $29.95; $15.95 (paper). 224 pages. Includes detailed job descriptions, educational requirements, salary ranges, and advancement prospects for 70 different job opportunities in this fast-paced industry. Contains index and bibliography.

★7596★ Careers for Gourmets and Others Who Relish Food

VGM Career Horizons
4255 W. Touhy Ave.
Lincolnwood, IL 60646-1975
Ph: (847)679-5500   Fax: (847)679-2494
Fr: 800-323-4900

Mary Donovan. 1993. $14.95; $9.95 (paper). 158 pages. Discusses such job prospects as foods columnist, cookbook writer, test kitchen worker, pastry chef, recipe developer, food festival organizer, restaurant manager, and food stylist.

★7597★ Careers in the Restaurant Industry

Rosen Publishing Group, Inc.
29 E. 21st St.
New York, NY 10010
Ph: (212)777-3017   Fax: (212)777-0277
Fr: 800-237-9932

Richard S. Lee and Mary Price Lee. 1990. $14.95. 160 pages. Explores various jobs in the restaurant industry. Describes job duties, salaries, educational preparation, and job hunting. Contains information about fast food, catering, and small businesses.

★7598★ Encyclopedia of Careers and Vocational Guidance

J. G. Ferguson Publishing Co.
200 W. Monroe, Ste. 250
Chicago, IL 60606
Ph: (312)580-5480

William E. Hopke. Ninth edition, 1993. $129.95; $199.95 (CD-ROM). Four-volume set that profiles 900 occupations and describes job trends in 71 industries. Includes career description, educational requirements, history of the job, methods of entry, advancement, employment outlook, earnings, conditions of work, social and psychological factors, and sources of further information. Contains career and employment information for this field.

★7599★ *Flying High in Travel*

John Wiley and Sons
605 3rd Ave.
New York, NY 10158
Ph: (212)850-6000   Fr: 800-225-5945

Karen Rubin. Second edition, 1992. $19.95. 336 pages. A guide to careers and job hunting in the travel industry. Describes the many job opportunities available, from writing to hotel management to law. Includes information on educational preparation, training, and job hunting.

★7600★ *How to Get a Job with a Cruise Line*

Ticket to Adventure, Inc.
PO Box 41005
St. Petersburg, FL 33743
Ph: (813)544-6440   Fr: 800-929-7447

Mary Fallon Miller. Third edition, 1994. $14.95. 224 pages. Explores jobs with cruise ships, describing duties, responsibilities, benefits, and training. Lists cruise ship lines and schools offering cruise line training. Offers job hunting advice.

★7601★ *100 Best Careers for the Year 2000*

Prentice Hall General Reference
15 Columbus Cir.
New York, NY 10023
Ph: (212)373-8500   Fr: 800-223-2348

Shelly Field. 1992. $15.00 (paper). Covers 100 of the fastest growing jobs. The publication is divided into 11 general employment sections. Specific careers are covered within each section. Provides job description, responsibilities, employment opportunities, earnings, education and training, advancement opportunities, and experience and qualifications for each occupation.

★7602★ *Opportunities in Culinary Careers*

VGM Career Horizons
4255 W. Touhy Ave.
Lincolnwood, IL 60646-1975
Ph: (847)679-5500   Fax: (847)679-2494
Fr: 800-323-4900

Mary Deirdre Donovan. 1990. $14.95; $11.95 (paper). 160 pages. Describes the educational preparation and training of chefs and cooks and explores a variety of food service jobs in restaurants, institutions, and research and development. Lists major culinary professional associations and schools. Offers guidance on landing a first job in cooking and related fields.

★7603★ *Opportunities in Fast Food Careers*

VGM Career Horizons
4255 W. Touhy Ave.
Lincolnwood, IL 60646-1975
Ph: (847)679-5500   Fax: (847)679-2494
Fr: 800-323-4900

Marjorie Eberts and Margaret Gisler. 1989.

$14.95; $11.95 (paper). 160 pages. Details opportunities at local restaurants, restaurant chains, and in related support areas. Also contains information on acquiring and operating a franchise. Illustrated.

★7604★ *Opportunities in Food Service Careers*

VGM Career Horizons
4255 W. Touhy Ave.
Lincolnwood, IL 60646-1975
Ph: (847)679-5500   Fax: (847)679-2494
Fr: 800-323-4900

Carol Caprione. 1992. $14.95; $11.95 (paper). 160 pages. Discusses how to secure employment and provides information on identifying openings, resume writing, and interviewing. Lists recruiters and associations to contact for further information and leads. Illustrated.

★7605★ *Opportunities in Hospital Administration Careers*

VGM Career Horizons
4255 W. Touhy Ave.
Lincolnwood, IL 60646-1975
Ph: (847)679-5500   Fax: (847)679-2494
Fr: 800-323-4900

I. Donald Snook. 1989. $14.95; $11.95 (paper). 160 pages. Discusses opportunities for administrators in a variety of management settings: hospital, department, clinic, group practice, HMO, mental health, and extended care facilities.

★7606★ *Opportunities in Hotel and Motel Careers*

VGM Career Horizons
4255 W. Touhy Ave.
Lincolnwood, IL 60646-1975
Ph: (847)679-5500   Fax: (847)679-2494
Fr: 800-323-4900

Shepard Henkin. 1992. $14.95; $11.95 (paper). 160 pages. A guide to planning for and seeking opportunities in this growing field. Illustrated.

★7607★ *Opportunities in Restaurant Careers*

VGM Career Horizons
4255 W. Touhy Ave.
Lincolnwood, IL 60646-1975
Ph: (847)679-5500   Fax: (847)679-2494
Fr: 800-323-4900

Carol Caprione Chmelynski. 1992. $14.95; $11.95 (paper). Covers opportunities in the food service industry and details salaries, benefits, training opportunities, and professional associations. Special emphasis is put on becoming a successful restaurant manager by working up through the ranks. Illustrated.

★7608★ *Travel and Hospitality Career Directory*

Gale Research
835 Penobscot Bldg.
Detroit, MI 48226-4094
Ph: (313)961-2242   Fax: (313)961-6083
Fr: 800-877-GALE

Bradley Morgan. Second edition, 1992. $39.00. 289 pages. Features a basic and comprehensive job search section, articles

by top professionals in the field, and detailed listings of hundreds of top companies who hire individuals in this field. Aimed particularly at entry-level job hunters.

EMPLOYMENT AGENCIES AND SEARCH FIRMS

★7609★ **Domenico/Bowman Associates**

23861 El Toro Rd., Ste. 700
Lake Forest, CA 92630
Ph: (714)588-2390

Executive search firm. Concentrates on placement to the food and lodging industry.

★7610★ **Employment Advisors**

526 Nicollet Mall
Minneapolis, MN 55402-0521
Ph: (612)339-0521

Employment agency. Also located in Bloomington, Minnesota. Places candidates in variety of fields.

★7611★ **Hospitality International**

181 Port Watson St.
Cortland, NY 13045-2811

Executive search firm. Branch office in New York, NY.

★7612★ **HRI Services Inc.**

150 Wood Rd., Ste. 303
Braintree, MA 02184
Ph: (617)848-9110

Employment agency.

★7613★ **J.D. Hersey and Associates**

1685 Old Henderson Rd.
Columbus, OH 43220
Ph: (614)459-4555

Executive search firm.

★7614★ **The Personnel Network, Inc.**

1621 Lake Murray Blvd.
Columbia, SC 29212
Ph: (803)781-2087

Executive search firm.

★7615★ **Peter Barrett Associates, Inc.**

23201 Lake Center Dr., Ste. 301
Lake Forest, CA 92630

Executive search firm.

★7616★ **Ritt-Ritt and Associates**

424 Swan Blvd.
Deerfield, IL 60015
Ph: (708)520-9999

Employment agency.

OTHER SOURCES

★7617★ American Correctional Food Service Association (ACFSA)

2040 Chestnut St.
Harrisburg, PA 17104
Ph: (717)233-2301   Fax: (717)233-2790

Members: Employees in the food services of federal, state, county, and city correctional and detention institutions. **Purpose:** Works to professionalize and improve correctional food service through on-the-job training.

★7618★ Association for International Practical Training (AIPT)

10400 Little Patuxent Pky. Ste. 250
Columbia, MD 21044
Ph: (410)997-2200   Fax: (410)992-3924

Purpose: Helps coordinate training around the world in fields such as travel, the culinary arts, and hotel management. **Activities:** Conducts programs in career development and hospitality/tourism exchanges. Operates a student exchange program. Provides reciprocal practical training experience for recent graduates from the U.S., Austria, Germany, Finland, France, Hungary, Ireland, Japan, Malaysia, Netherlands, Switzerland, and the United Kingdom. Arranges training programs in the U.S. and abroad. Serves as U.S. affiliate to IAESTE (International Association for the Exchange of Students for Technical Experience) and operates a Professional Visitors Program to arrange short-term educational and training visits to the U.S. **E-Mail:** aipt@aipt.org

★7619★ Council on Hotel, Restaurant, and Institutional Education (CHRIE)

1200 17th St. NW
Washington, DC 20036-3097
Ph: (202)331-5990   Fax: (202)785-2511

Purpose: Schools and colleges offering specialized education and training in cooking,

baking, tourism and hotel, restaurant, and institutional administration; individuals, executives, and students. **Activities:** Provides networking opportunities and professional development. Sponsors competitions.

★7620★ Educational Foundation of the National Restaurant Association (EFNRA)

250 S. Wacker Dr., No. 1400
Chicago, IL 60606
Ph: (312)715-1010   Fax: (312)715-0807
Fr: 800-765-2122

Members: Educational foundation supported by the National Restaurant Association and all segments of the foodservice industry including restaurateurs, foodservice companies, food and equipment manufacturers, distributors, and trade associations. **Purpose:** Dedicated to the advancement of professional standards in the industry through education and research. Offers video training programs, management courses, and careers information. Conducts research. Maintains hall of fame.

★7621★ A Guide to College Programs in Hospitality & Tourism

John Wiley & Sons, Inc.
605 3rd Ave.
New York, NY 10158-0012
Ph: (212)850-6000   Fr: 800-225-5945

Compiled by th Council of Hotel, Restaurant & Institutional Education staff. 1995. $24.95 (paper).

★7622★ Home Economics Careers

Cambridge Career Products
PO Box 2153
Dept. CC15
Charleston, WV 25328-2153
Ph: (304)744-9323   Fax: (304)744-9351
Fr: 800-468-4227

Video. $79.95. 30 minutes. Presents a series of interviews with men and women working in different areas of home economics, includ-

ing dietetics, foods and nutrition, child development, interior design, and fashion. Covers educational, personal, and professional requirements for each occupation.

★7623★ National Restaurant Association (NRA)

1200 17th St. NW
Washington, DC 20036
Ph: (202)331-5900   Fax: (202)331-2429

Members: Restaurants, cafeterias, clubs, contract foodservice management, drive-ins, caterers, institutional food services, and other members of the foodservice industry; also represents establishments belonging to nonaffiliated state and local restaurant associations in governmental affairs. **Purpose:** Supports foodservice education and research in several educational institutions; conducts traveling management courses and seminars for restaurant personnel. Affiliated with the Educational Foundation of the National Restaurant Association to provide training and education for operators, food and equipment manufacturers, distributors, and educators. Offers waiter/waitress training programs. Conducts the Great Menu Contest.

★7624★ Restaurant Business Guide

Entrepreneur, Inc.
2392 Morse Ave.
Box 19787
Irvine, CA 92713-9787
Fax: (714)851-9088   Fr: 800-421-2300

$79.50 (includes business guide and software). Presents data on profits and costs, location, financing, promotion and advertising, and other topics pertinent to the establishment of a restaurant.

Retail Sales Representatives

SOURCES OF HELP-WANTED ADS

★7625★ Building Supply Home Centers

Cahners Publishing Co.
1350 E. Touhy Ave.
Des Plaines, IL 60018
Ph: (708)635-8800   Fax: (708)390-2770

Monthly. Free to qualified subscribers; $60.00/year for individuals. Magazine for owners, executives, and managers responsible for product selection and purchase, merchandising, marketing, and management within the building supply retail and home center market.

★7626★ Chain Store Age Executive

Lebhar-Friedman, Inc.
425 Park Ave.
New York, NY 10022
Ph: (212)756-5257   Fax: (212)756-5270

Monthly. $79.00/year for individuals. Magazine for management of retail chain headquarters. Reports on marketing, merchandising, strategic planning, physical supports, and shopping center developments.

★7627★ The College Store

500 E. Lorain St.
Oberlin, OH 44074-1294
Ph: (216)775-7777   Fax: (216)775-4769

Bimonthly. Books and college supplies magazine.

★7628★ Counterman

Babcox Publications
11 S. Forge St.
Akron, OH 44304
Ph: (216)535-7011   Fax: (216)535-0874

Monthly. Free to qualified subscribers; $49.00/year for individuals; $83.00 for two years. Magazine devoted to improving the effectiveness of professional automotive parts counter-sales personnel.

★7629★ Daily News Record

Fairchild Publications
7 W. 34th St.
New York, NY 10001
Ph: (212)630-4580   Fax: (212)630-4879
Fr: 800-360-1700

Daily (morn.). $62.00/year. Newspaper reporting on men's and boys' clothing and textiles.

★7630★ Discount Store News

Lebhar-Friedman, Inc.
425 Park Ave.
New York, NY 10022
Ph: (212)756-5257   Fax: (212)756-5270

Semimonthly. $99.00/year.

★7631★ Gifts and Decorative Accessories

Geyer-McAllister Publications, Inc.
51 Madison Ave.
New York, NY 10010
Ph: (212)689-7929

Monthly. $37.00/year.

★7632★ Modern Grocer

Grocers Publishing Co., Inc.
15 Emerald St.
Hackensack, NJ 07601
Ph: (201)488-1800

Semimonthly. Magazine for food retailers, wholesalers, distributors, brokers, manufacturers, and packers in the metro New York and New Jersey marketing area.

★7633★ Money Making Opportunities

Success Publishing International
11071 Ventura Blvd.
Studio City, CA 91604
Ph: (818)980-9166

Monthly. Classified advertising magazine.

★7634★ Music, Inc.

Maher Publications
102 N. Haven Rd.
Elmhurst, IL 60126
Ph: (708)941-2030   Fax: (708)941-3210

Eleven times/year. $16.50/year.

★7635★ National Jeweler

Miller Freeman, Inc.
1515 Broadway
New York, NY 10036
Ph: (212)626-2380   Fax: (212)944-7164
Fr: 800-950-1314

Semimonthly. Jewelry industry magazine.

★7636★ Photo Marketing

Photo Marketing Association International
3000 Picture Pl.
Jackson, MI 49201
Ph: (517)788-8100   Fax: (517)788-8371

Monthly. $25.00/year for individuals; $30.00/year for Canada. Trade magazine for photo/video dealers and photo finishers.

★7637★ Profitable Craft Merchandising

PJS Publications, Inc.
2 News Plaza
PO Box 1790
Peoria, IL 61656
Ph: (309)682-6626   Fax: (309)682-7394

Monthly. $30.00/year for individuals. Magazine for retailers of craft, needlework, and sewing supplies.

★7638★ Sales & Marketing Management

Bill Communications, Inc.
355 Park Ave. S
New York, NY 10010-1789
Ph: (212)592-6200   Fax: (212)592-6309
Fr: 800-821-6897

Business magazine.

★7639★ Sporting Goods Dealer

Times Mirror Magazines, Inc.
2 Park Ave.
New York, NY 10016
Ph: (212)779-5285   Fax: (212)779-5465

Monthly. Magazine providing merchandising information, market data, and new product information to retailers of sporting goods.

★7640★ Tire Business

Crain Communications Inc
1725 Merriman Rd., Ste. 300
Akron, OH 44313-5251
Ph: (216)836-9180   Fax: (216)836-2831

Semimonthly. $50.00/year for individuals; $92.00. for two years. Newspaper (tabloid) serving independent tire dealers.

★7641★ VM & SD: Visual Merchandising and Store Design

ST Publications
407 Gilbert Ave.
Cincinnati, OH 45202
Ph: (513)421-2050   Fax: (513)421-5144
Fr: 800-925-1110

Monthly. $36.00/year.

PLACEMENT AND JOB REFERRAL SERVICES

★7642★ National Association of College Stores (NACS)

500 E. Lorain St.
Oberlin, OH 44074
Ph: (216)775-7777   Fax: (216)775-4769
Fr: 800-622-7498

Members: Institutional, private, leased, and cooperative college stores selling books, supplies, and other merchandise to college students, faculty, and staff; associate members include publishers and suppliers. **Purpose:** Seeks to effectively serve higher education by providing educational opportunities, services, and products to college stores and their suppliers. **Activities:** Maintains NACSCORP, Inc., a wholly owned subsidiary corporation, which distributes trade and mass market books and educational software. Operates placement service. Maintains College Stores Research and Educational Foundation which provides grants for NACS educational programs and conducts research.

★7643★ National Shoe Traveler's Association (NSTA)

PO Box 456
Abington, MA 02351
Ph: 800-200-6782   Fax: (617)871-8033

Members: Traveling salespeople handling shoes and related products on the wholesale and retail levels. **Activities:** Holds seminars for members. Conducts certified footwear representative program. Compiles statistics; maintains placement service.

★7644★ Women in Sales Association (WIS)

8 Madison Ave.
PO Box M
Valhalla, NY 10595
Ph: (914)946-3802   Fax: (914)946-7624

Members: Professional saleswomen. **Purpose:** Promotes professional development of women in sales. Provides opportunity to establish business contacts, and to share information and ideas. **Activities:** Conducts work sessions on topics including personal communication skills and use of audiovisual aids in sales presentations; provides speakers on topics fundamental to sales skills; sponsors career guidance workshops and position referral service. Provides discounts to members on relevant publications.

EMPLOYER DIRECTORIES AND NETWORKING LISTS

★7645★ Directory of Department Stores

Chain Store Guide Information Services
3922 Coconut Palm Dr.
Tampa, FL 33619
Ph: (813)664-6700   Fax: 800-846-8047
Fr: 800-925-2288

Updated continuously; printed on request. $260.00. Covers over 600 department store companies operating over 6,800 stores; over 900 mail order firms; resident buying organizations; and major industry trade shows. Entries include: For department store companies, company name, address, phone, fax, number of stores, sales, total square feet, resident buyer, store locations; private labels, leased departments; names and titles of executives, merchandise managers, and buyers. For mail order firms, company name, address, phone, sales, product lines, year established, catalog name(s), whether company also operates retail stores, names and titles of executives. For resident buyers, company name, address, phone, department store companies represented. For shows, name, location, dates, contact phone. Arrangement: Separate geographical sections for department stores, mail order firms, and resident buyers; shows are chronological. Indexes: Company/resident buyer name; top 75 department stores and top 100 mail order companies ranked by sales (with number of stores).

★7646★ Directory of Drug Store & HBC Chains

Chain Store Guide Information Services
3922 Coconut Palm Dr.
Tampa, FL 33619
Ph: (813)664-6868   Fax: (813)664-6810
Fr: 800-925-2288

Annual, November. $290.00. Covers drug store chains operating two or more units; mass merchants with pharmacies; and wholesale drug companies. Arrangement: Separate geographical sections for chains and wholesalers.

★7647★ Directory of General Merchandise/Variety & Specialty Stores

Chain Store Guide Information Services
3922 Coconut Palm Dr.
Tampa, FL 33619
Ph: (813)664-6700   Fax: (813)664-6810
Fr: 800-925-2288

Updated continuously; printed on request. $245.00, plus $5.00 shipping. Covers about 700 general merchandise and variety store companies; approximately 1,400 housewares and giftwares chains; over 2,200 novelty card and gift shop companies; over 1,422 toy, hobby, and craft retail operations and 500 wholesalers; and nearly 2,600 stationery and office products store companies. Entries include: Company name, headquarters address, phone, fax, number of units, store names, names and titles of key personnel, sales volume, products, year founded, ownership. Arrangement: Classified by line of business, then geographical. Indexes: Product, alphabetical.

★7648★ Discount Store News—Top Chains Issue

Chain Store Guides, Inc.
Lebhar-Friedman, Inc.
425 Park Ave.
New York, NY 10022
Ph: (212)756-5000

Annual, July. $79.00. Entries include: Chain name, location, sales and earnings for the past two years, number of stores, net store square footage. Arrangement: Ranked by sales volume.

★7649★ Stores—Top 100 Issue

National Retail Federation
100 W. 31st St.
New York, NY 10001
Ph: (212)244-8780   Fax: (212)594-0487

Annual, July. $5.00, pre-paid. Publication includes: 100 U.S. retail companies having largest estimated sales during preceding year. Entries include: Name of store, city, number of stores included, and total sales. Arrangement: Ranked by sales.

★7650★ Variety Stores Directory

American Business Directories, Inc.
American Business Information, Inc.
5711 S. 86th Cir.
Omaha, NE 68127
Ph: (402)593-4600   Fax: (402)331-1505

Annual. $760.00, U.S. edition. Number of listings: 10,682 (U.S. edition); 3,545 (Canadian edition). Entries include: Name, address, phone (including area code), size of advertisement, year first in Yellow Pages, name of owner or manager, number of employees. Compiled from telephone company Yellow Pages, nationwide. Arrangement: Geographical.

HANDBOOKS AND MANUALS

★7651★ Career Opportunities in Art

Facts on File, Inc.
11 Penn Plaza, 15th Fl.
New York, NY 10001-2006
Ph: (212)967-8800   Fax: 800-678-3633
Fr: 800-322-8755

Susan H. Haubenstock and David Joselit. Revised edition, 1994. $29.95; $15.95 (paper). 208 pages. This book profiles seventy-five jobs that can be found in the art field. Each profile includes a career description, career ladder, employment and advancement prospects, education, experience and skills required, salary range, and tips for entry into the field.

★7652★ Career Opportunities in Television, Cable and Video

Facts on File, Inc.
11 Penn Plaza, 15th Fl.
New York, NY 10001-2006
Ph: (212)967-8800   Fax: 800-678-3633
Fr: 800-322-8755

Maxine K. Reed and Robert M. Reed. Third edition, 1991. $29.95; $15.95 (paper). 272 pages.

★7653★ Careers in Health and Fitness

Rosen Publishing Group, Inc.
29 E. 21st St.
New York, NY 10010
Ph: (212)777-3017   Fax: (212)777-0277
Fr: 800-237-9932

Jackie Heron. Revised edition, 1990. $14.95. 160 pages. Contains occupational profiles for this field, including information on job duties, skills, advantages, basic equipment used, employment possibilities, certification, and salary.

★7654★ Careers Inside the World of Sales

Rosen Publishing Group, Inc.
29 E. 21st St.
New York, NY 10010
Ph: (212)777-3017   Fax: (212)777-0277
Fr: 800-237-9932

Carlienne Frisch. 1994. $14.95.

★7655★ The Encyclopedia of Career Choices for the 1990s: Guide to Entry-Level Jobs

Perigree Books
The Berkley Publishing Group
PO Box 506
East Rutherford, NJ 07073
Ph: (201)933-9292   Fr: 800-223-0510

Career Associates Staff. 1992. $19.95. 862 pages. Describes 500 entry-level careers in a variety of industries. Presents qualifications required, working conditions, salary, internships, and professional associations.

★7656★ Exploring Careers in the Computer Field

Rosen Publishing Group, Inc.
29 E. 21st St.
New York, NY 10010
Ph: (212)777-3017   Fax: (212)777-0277
Fr: 800-237-9932

Joseph Weintraub. Revised edition, 1993. Discusses entry into the field, salaries, future trends, and offers job search advice. Surveys the newest growth areas in the computer industry including artificial intelligence, desktop publishing, and personal computers.

★7657★ Exploring Careers in Computer Sales

Rosen Publishing Group, Inc.
29 E. 21st St.
New York, NY 10010
Ph: (212)777-3017   Fax: (212)777-0277
Fr: 800-237-9932

Lawrence Epstein. 1990. $14.95. Offers job hunting advice and lists computers, computer-related products, magazines, and companies. Describes working in computer hardware and software sales, the skills needed,

educational preparation, work environments, and salaries.

★7658★ 100 Best Careers for the Year 2000

Prentice Hall General Reference
15 Columbus Cir.
New York, NY 10023
Ph: (212)373-8500   Fr: 800-223-2348

Shelly Field. 1992. $15.00 (paper). Covers 100 of the fastest growing jobs. The publication is divided into 11 general employment sections. Specific careers are covered within each section. Provides job description, responsibilities, employment opportunities, earnings, education and training, advancement opportunities, and experience and qualifications for each occupation.

★7659★ Opportunities in Retailing Careers

VGM Career Horizons
4255 W. Touhy Ave.
Lincolnwood, IL 60646-1975
Ph: (847)679-5500   Fax: (847)679-2494
Fr: 800-323-4900

Roslyn Dolber. 1994. $14.95; $11.95 (paper). Discusses a number of opportunities in retailing, from entry-level to retail management.

★7660★ Opportunities in Sales Careers

VGM Career Horizons
4255 W. Touhy Ave.
Lincolnwood, IL 60646-1975
Ph: (847)679-5500   Fax: (847)679-2494
Fr: 800-323-4900

James Briscoll and Ralph Dahm. 1995. $14.95; $11.95 (paper). Details sales in retail, wholesale and industrial sales, sales of services and intangibles, and sales management. Illustrated.

★7661★ Opportunities in Vocational and Technical Careers

VGM Career Horizons
4255 W. Touhy Ave.
Lincolnwood, IL 60646-1975
Ph: (847)679-5500   Fax: (847)679-2494
Fr: 800-323-4900

Adrian A. Paradis. 1992. $14.95; $11.95 (paper). 160 pages. Provides information on a variety of opportunities and advice on breaking into the field.

★7662★ Real People Working in Sales and Marketing

VGM Career Horizons
NTC Publishing Group
4255 W. Touhy Ave.
Lincolnwood, IL 60646-1975
Ph: (847)679-5500   Fax: (847)679-2494
Fr: 800-323-4900

1996. $17.95; $12.95 (paper). 192 pages. Interviews and profiles of working sales and marketing professionals capture a range of opportunities in this field.

★7663★ Retailing

Prentice Hall
113 Sylvan Ave.
Rte. 9W
Englewood Cliffs, NJ 07632
Ph: (201)592-2000   Fr: 800-922-0579

Gerald Pintel and Jay Diamond. Fifth edition, 1991. $72.00. 544 pages. Includes an index.

★7664★ Where the Jobs Are: The Hottest Careers for the '90s

The Career Press, Inc.
3 Tice Rd.
PO Box 687
Franklin Lakes, NJ 07417
Ph: (201)848-0310   Fax: (201)848-1727
Fr: 800-237-3371

Joyce Hadley. Second edition, 1995. $9.99. 300 pages. Describes careers in fifteen general fields, from accounting to travel and hospitality.

★7665★ Your Career in Direct Marketing and Direct Response Advertising

Direct Marketing Educational Foundation, Inc.
1120 Avenue of the Americas
New York, NY 10036
Ph: (212)689-4977

This free booklet explains direct marketing and lists the types of companies engaged in direct marketing. Lists career opportunities and offers advice on entry into the field.

★7666★ Your Career Opportunities in a Direct Marketing Agency

Direct Marketing Educational Foundation, Inc.
1120 Avenue of the Americas
New York, NY 10036
Ph: (212)689-4977

This free booklet describes career opportunities in agencies involved in direct marketing.

★7667★ Your Opportunities in Retail

Energeia Publishing, Inc.
PO Box 985
Salem, OR 97308
Ph: (503)362-1480   Fax: (503)362-2123

Shawn E. Strahan. 1994. $2.00 (paper).

EMPLOYMENT AGENCIES AND SEARCH FIRMS

★7668★ Alan Lerner Associates

6 Eastgate Dr., #C
Boynton Beach, FL 33436
Ph: (407)735-3550

Nationwide executive search firm specializing in retail. Branch locations in Annapolis, MD; Braintree, MA; and Gibbsboro, NJ.

★7669★ Amherst Personnel Group Inc.

PO Box 187
Hicksville, NY 11801
Ph: (516)433-7610   Fax: (516)433-7848

Employment agency. Executive search firm. Other offices in Milltown, NJ, and Rochelle Park, NJ.

★7670★ Career Search Associates

284 E. Main St.
Oceanport, NJ 07757
Ph: (908)935-7111

Employment agency. Executive search firm specializing in retail industry.

★7671★ Don Waldron and Associates, Inc.

450 7th Ave., Ste. 501
New York, NY 10123-0101
Ph: (212)239-9110

Employment agency.

★7672★ Employment Advisors

526 Nicollet Mall
Minneapolis, MN 55402-0521
Ph: (612)339-0521

Employment agency. Also located in Bloomington, Minnesota. Places candidates in variety of fields.

★7673★ Fairfield Resources, Ltd.

Empire State Bldg.
350 5th Ave., Rm. 7605
New York, NY 10118
Ph: (212)268-0220   Fax: (212)268-8849

Employment agency.

★7674★ J.D. Hersey and Associates

1685 Old Henderson Rd.
Columbus, OH 43220
Ph: (614)459-4555

Executive search firm.

★7675★ The Jobs Co.

8900 E. Sprague Ave.
Spokane, WA 99212-2927
Ph: (509)928-3151   Fax: (509)928-3168

Employment agency. Has division specializing in engineering and scientific openings. Also operates division specializing in sales openings.

★7676★ Joel H. Wilensky Associates, Inc.

22 Union Ave.
PO Box 155
Sudbury, MA 01776
Ph: (508)443-5176   Fax: (508)443-3009

Executive search firm.

★7677★ National Register, Inc.

2700 E. Dublin Granville Rd.
Columbus, OH 43231-4097
Ph: (614)890-1200

Employment agency. Offices in Akron and Toledo, OH.

★7678★ The Personnel Network, Inc.

1621 Lake Murray Blvd.
Columbia, SC 29212
Ph: (803)781-2087

Executive search firm.

★7679★ Retail Pacesetters, Inc.

271 Rte. 46 W., Ste. D105
Fairfield, NJ 07004
Ph: (201)882-0303

Executive search firm.

★7680★ Retail Placement Associates

6110 Executive Blvd., Ste. 835
Rockville, MD 20852
Ph: (301)231-8150

Employment agency.

★7681★ Retail Recruiters/Spectrum Consultants, Inc.

111 Presidential Blvd., Ste. 211
Bala Pointe
Bala Cynwyd, PA 19004
Ph: (610)667-6565   Fax: (610)667-5323

Employment agency. Affiliate offices in many locations across the country.

★7682★ Youth Employment Project, Inc.

208 City Hall
Rochester, MN 55902
Ph: (507)287-2345

Employment agency. Provides regular and temporary employment assistance.

OTHER SOURCES

★7683★ Automotive Parts and Accessories Association (APAA)

4600 East-West Hwy., Ste. 300
Bethesda, MD 20814
Ph: (301)654-6664   Fax: (301)654-3299

Members: Automotive parts and accessories retailers, distributors, manufacturers, and manufacturers' representatives. Conducts research and compiles statistics. **Activities:** Conducts seminars and provides specialized education program.

★7684★ Christian Booksellers Association (CBA)

PO Box 200
Colorado Springs, CO 80901
Ph: (719)576-7880   Fax: (719)576-0795
Fr: 800-252-1950

Purpose: Trade Association for Retail book-

stores selling religious books, Bibles, gifts, and Sunday school and church supplies. Compiles statistics; conducts specialized education programs.

★7685★ Computing Technology Industry Association (CompTIA)

450 E. 22nd St., Ste. 230
Lombard, IL 60148
Ph: (708)268-1818   Fax: (708)268-1384

Members: Computer equipment resellers, computer equipment producers and software manufacturers, computer distributors, and other companies doing business with the computer industry. **Purpose:** Objectives are to: increase professional and ethical standards in the industry; protect consumers from inept or nonservicing dealers; help the consumer to easily identify better dealers and obtain an appropriate system for their needs; provide for the exchange of ideas for improvement within the reseller channel; promote a consistent level of service and ethical standards. Members are required to provide fully staffed service departments and offer customers maintenance contracts guaranteeing prompt response time. **Activities:** Conducts professional development and training programs in areas such as management, sales, and channel development. Serves as information clearinghouse for industry; makes available educational programs. Sponsors competitions; compiles statistics.

★7686★ National Retail Federation (NRF)

325 7th St. NW, Ste. 1000
Washington, DC 20004-2802
Ph: (202)783-7971   Fax: (202)737-2849

Purpose: Represents 50 state retail association, several dozen national retail associations as well as large and small corporate members representing the breadth and diversity of the retail industry's establishment and employees. **Activities:** Conducts informational and educational conferences related to all phases of retailing including financial planning and cash management, taxation, economic forecasting, expense planning, shortage control, credit, electronic data processing, telecommunications, merchandise management, buying, traffic, security, supply, materials handling, store planning and construction, personnel administration, recruitment and training, and advertising and display.

★7687★ Resume Writing, Interviewing and Role-playing Skills for Salespeople Looking for New Jobs

J B & Me
PO Box 3879
Manhattan Beach, CA 90266
Ph: (310)546-1255

Jack Bernstein. 1993. $12.50.

Roofers

SOURCES OF HELP-WANTED ADS

★7688★ Builder

Hanley-Wood, Inc.
1 Thomas Cir., Ste. 600
Washington, DC 20005
Ph: (202)452-0800   Fax: (202)785-1974

Monthly. $29.95/year for individuals. Magazine covering housing, commercial, and industrial building.

★7689★ Construction Digest

Construction Magazine Group, Inc.
PO Box 6132
Indianapolis, IN 46206-6132
Ph: (317)329-3100   Fax: (317)329-3110
Fr: 800-860-3105

Semimonthly. $3.00 for single issue. Magazine for the public works and construction engineering industries.

★7690★ CONSTRUCTOR

Associated General Contractors
  Information
1957 E St. NW
Washington, DC 20006-5199
Ph: (202)393-2040   Fax: (202)628-7369

Monthly. $15.00/year for members; $4.00 for single issue.

★7691★ Contractors Guide

Century Publishing Co.
990 Grove St.
Evanston, IL 60201-4370
Ph: (708)491-6440   Fax: (708)491-0867

Monthly. Free to qualified subscribers; $25.00/year for individuals; $5.00 for single issue. Trade magazine on roofing and insulation.

★7692★ Metal Construction News

Modern Trade Communications, Inc.
7450 N. Skokie Blvd.
Skokie, IL 60077
Ph: (708)674-2200   Fax: (708)674-3676

Monthly. $35.00/year for individuals. Magazine focusing on metal building, metal roof, and sidewall news.

★7693★ Professional Builder

Cahners Publishing Co.
1350 E. Touhy Ave.
PO Box 5080
Des Plaines, IL 60018-5080
Ph: (708)635-8800   Fax: (708)635-9950

Monthly. $10.00 for single issue; $139.95/year by mail.

★7694★ Professional Roofing

National Roofing Contractors Association
10255 W. Higgins Rd., Ste. 600
Rosemont, IL 60018
Ph: (708)299-9070   Fax: (708)299-1183

Monthly. $25.00/year for individuals; $65.00/year for other countries. Roofing industry magazine.

★7695★ Summer Jobs: Opportunities in the Federal Government

Office of Personnel Management
1900 E St. NW
Washington, DC 20415
Ph: (202)606-0950

Formerly annual; latest edition January 1993; suspended indefinitely. Free. Covers GS-1 through GS-4 clerical jobs and other jobs at GS-5 and above which are expected to be available in federal agencies and departments throughout the United States during the season. Most jobs are in Metropolitan Washington, D.C. Latest application date is generally April 15; many are earlier. Includes general information on applying for jobs in trades and labor occupations and summer employment for needy youth programs. Entries include: Agency name, filing deadline, titles of jobs available, brief information on qualifications needed, location, etc. Complete agency names and addresses are given in separate list. Publication is available from Federal Employment Information Center offices and agency personnel offices. Arrangement: By job level, then alphabetical by agency name.

★7696★ Tradeswomen

Tradeswomen, Inc.
PO Box 2622
Berkeley, CA 94702
Ph: (510)649-6260

Bimonthly. $35.00/year. Subtitled: "A Quarterly Magazine for Women in Blue Collar Work". Reports activities of the organization and other events in the California Bay Area and of national interest to women working or wishing to work in nontraditional and blue collar jobs. Recurring features include announcements of apprenticeship opportunities and job openings, information on unions and government agencies, and U.S. Department of Labor statistics.

PLACEMENT AND JOB REFERRAL SERVICES

★7697★ Associated Builders and Contractors (ABC)

1300 N. 17th St.
Rosslyn, VA 22209
Ph: (703)812-2000   Fax: (703)812-8200

Members: Construction contractors, subcontractors, suppliers, and associates. **Purpose:** Aim is to foster and perpetuate the principles of rewarding construction workers and management on the basis of merit. **Activities:** Maintains placement service. Sponsors management education programs and craft training; also sponsors apprenticeship and skill training programs. Disseminates technological and labor relations information. Compiles statistics.

★7698★ National Association of Home Builders of the U.S. (NAHB)

1201 15th St. NW
Washington, DC 20005
Ph: (202)822-0200   Fax: (202)822-0559

Members: Single and multifamily home builders, commercial builders, and others associated with the building industry. **Purpose:** Lobbies on behalf of the housing industry and conducts public affairs activities to increase public understanding of housing and the economy. Collects and disseminates data on current developments in home building and home builders' plans through its Economics Department and nationwide Metropolitan Housing Forecast. **Activities:** Maintains NAHB Research Center, which functions as the research arm of the home building industry. Sponsors seminars and workshops on construction, mortgage credit, labor relations, cost reduction, land use, remodeling, and business management. Compiles statistics; offers charitable program, spokesman training, and placement service; maintains speakers' bureau, and hall of fame.

★7699★ Roofing Industry Educational Institute (RIEI)
Bldg. H, Ste. 110
14 Inverness Dr. E
Englewood, CO 80112-5608
Ph: (303)790-7200   Fax: (303)790-9006

Members: Participants are contractors, architects, specifiers, owners, consultants, and others involved in the roofing industry. **Activities:** Conducts seminars and educational programs covering all aspects of roofing, highlighting design, installation, and maintenance including topics such as thermal insulation, vapors and condensation, and fire and codes. Provides referral service; presents diplomas; awards credits in continuing education.

EMPLOYER DIRECTORIES AND NETWORKING LISTS

★7700★ ABC Today—Associated Builders and Contractors Membership Directory Issue
Associated Builders and Contractors
1300 N. 17th St.
Rosslyn, VA 22209
Ph: (703)812-2000   Fax: (703)812-8200

Annual, November. $150.00, plus $7.00 shipping. Publication includes: List of approximately 17,000 member construction contractors and suppliers. Entries include: Company name, address, phone, name of principal executive, code to volume of business, business specialty. Arrangement: Classified by chapter, then by work specialty.

★7701★ Constructor—Directory of Membership and Services Issue
AGC Information, Inc.
Associated General Contractors of America
1957 E St. NW
Washington, DC 20006
Ph: (202)393-2040   Fax: (202)347-4004

Annual, July. $135.00. Publication includes: List of more than 8,500 member firms and 9,000 national associate member firms engaged in building, highway, heavy, industrial, municipal utilities, and railroad construction, listing of state and local chapter officers. Arrangement: Geographical. Indexes: Company name.

★7702★ ENR—Top 400 Construction Contractors Issue
McGraw-Hill, Inc.
1221 Ave. of the Americas
New York, NY 10020
Ph: (212)512-4635   Fax: (212)512-2820

Annual, May issue of *Engineering News Record*. $10.00, Reprint, payment with order. Publication includes: List of 400 United

States contractors receiving largest dollar volumes of contracts in preceding calendar year. Separate lists of 50 largest design/construct management firms; 50 largest program and construction managers; 25 building contractors; 25 heavy contractors. Entries include: Company name, headquarters location, total value of contracts received in preceding year, value of foreign contracts, countries in which operated, construction specialities. Arrangement: By total value of contracts received.

★7703★ Roofing Contractors Directory
American Business Directories, Inc.
American Business Information, Inc.
5711 S. 86th Cir.
Omaha, NE 68127
Ph: (402)593-4600   Fax: (402)331-1505

Annual. $1,155.00, U.S. edition; $190.00, (Canadian edition); payment with order. Significant discounts offered for standing orders. Number of listings: 33,946 (U.S. edition); 3,937 (Canadian edition). Entries includes: name, address, phone (including area code), size of advertisement, year first in Yellow Pages, name of owner or manager, number of employees. Regional editions available: Eastern, $760.00; Western, $515.00. Compiled from telephone company Yellow Pages, nationwide. Arrangement: Geographical.

HANDBOOKS AND MANUALS

★7704★ Exploring Careers in the Construction Industry
Rosen Publishing Group
29 E. 21st St.
New York, NY 10010
Ph: (212)777-3017   Fax: (212)777-0277
Fr: 800-237-9932

Elizabeth Stewart Lytle. 1992. $14.95.

★7705★ Opportunities in Building Construction Trades
VGM Career Horizons
4255 W. Touhy Ave.
Lincolnwood, IL 60646-1975
Ph: (847)679-5500   Fax: (847)679-2494
Fr: 800-323-4900

Michael Sumichrast. 1993. $14.95; $11.95 (paper). From custom builder to rehabber, the many kinds of companies that employ craftspeople and contractors are explored. Includes job descriptions, requirements, and salaries for dozens of specialties within the construction industry. Contains a complete list of Bureau of Apprenticeship and Training state and area offices. Illustrated.

★7706★ Roofing and Waterproofing: A Trade Worth Learning through Apprenticeship
United Union of Roofers, Waterproofers and Allied Workers
1125 17th St. NW
Washington, DC 20036
Ph: (202)638-3228

Free. This brochure describes the apprentice roofer program, including earnings, the work, and qualifications needed.

OTHER SOURCES

★7707★ Associated General Contractors of America (AGC)
1957 E St. NW
Washington, DC 20006
Ph: (202)393-2040   Fax: (202)347-4004

Members: General construction contractors; subcontractors; industry suppliers; service firms. **Purpose:** Provides market services through its divisions. Conducts special conferences and seminars designed specifically for construction firms. Compiles statistics on job accidents reported by member firms. Maintains 65 committees, including joint cooperative committees with other associations and liaison committees with federal agencies.

★7708★ Associated Specialty Contractors (ASC)
3 Bethesda Metro Ctr., Ste. 1100
Bethesda, MD 20814
Ph: (301)657-3110   Fax: (301)215-4500

Members: Subcontractor associations with a total of 25,000 members representing electrical, heating, piping, mechanical, air conditioning, sheet metal, plumbing, ventilating, masonry, painting and decorating, and roofing and insulation contractors. **Purpose:** Promotes liaison with general contractors, architects, and engineers on inter-industry matters, codes, bidding, and contracting procedures. Coordinates governmental affairs, research, and educational matters.

★7709★ COIN Career Guidance System
COIN Educational Products
3361 Executive Pky., Ste. 302
Toledo, OH 43606
Ph: (419)536-5353   Fr: 800-274-8515

CD-ROM product; also available on diskette. Provides career information through seven cross-referenced files covering postsecondary schools, college majors, vocational programs, military service, apprenticeship programs, financial aid, and scholarships. Apprenticeship file describes national apprenticeship training programs, including information on how to apply, contact agencies, and program content. Military file describes more than 200 military occupations and training opportunities related to civilian employment.

★7710★ **National Association of Women in Construction (NAWIC)**

327 S. Adams St.
Fort Worth, TX 76104
Ph: (817)877-5551   Fax: (817)877-0324
Fr: 800-552-3506

Purpose: NAWIC is an international association of women employed in the construction industry which promotes that industry and supports the advancement of women within it.

★7711★ *National Roofing Contractors Association—Directory*

National Roofing Contractors Association
O'Hare International Center
10255 W. Higgins, Ste. 600
Rosemont, IL 60018
Ph: (708)299-9070   Fax: (708)299-1183

Annual, July. $55.00, plus $2.00 shipping. Covers 2,400 contractors applying all types of commercial and residential roofing; 300 associate member manufacturers, suppliers, and distributors; 250 foreign members; and 82 institutions and related industries. Entries include: Company name, address, phone, and names of voting representatives. Arrangement: Alphabetical. Indexes: Geographical, voting representative.

★7712★ **Tradeswomen, Inc.**

PO Box 40664 B
San Francisco, CA 94140
Ph: (415)821-7334   Fax: (415)861-8969

Members: Women who work in nontraditional, blue-collar occupations including construction, transportation, and industrial work; women who seek to enter these fields or who support the right of others to do so.
Purpose: Serves as a network for women in the trades. Conducts social gatherings and local and regional forums on topics such as: health and safety on the job; racism and sexism in the trades; sexual harassment; working within unions. Makes available children's services; maintains speakers' bureau. Compiles statistics.

★7713★ *WIT*

Northern New England Tradeswomen
26 Railroad St.
St. Johnsbury, VT 05819
Ph: (802)748-3308   Fax: (802)748-1768

Quarterly. Included in membership; $10.00/year for nonmembers. Provides a network of support, information, and skill sharing for women in trade professions.

Science Technicians

Sources of Help-Wanted Ads

★7714★ American Biotechnology Laboratory

International Scientific Communications, Inc.
30 Controls Dr.
PO Box 870
Shelton, CT 06484-0870
Ph: (203)926-9300   Fax: (203)926-9310

$128.00/year for individuals. Biotechnology magazine.

★7715★ Analytical Chemistry

American Chemical Society
1155 16th St. NW
Washington, DC 20036
Ph: (202)872-4600   Fax: (202)872-6005
Fr: 800-227-5558

Biweekly. $33.00/year for members; $76.00/year for nonmembers. Journal covering measurement science.

★7716★ Bio/Technology

Nature Publishing Co.
345 Park Ave. S, 10th Fl.
New York, NY 10010-1707
Ph: (212)726-9200   Fax: (212)696-9006

Monthly. $59.00/year for individuals. Scientific research journal.

★7717★ Chemical and Engineering News

American Chemical Society
1155 16th St. NW
Washington, DC 20036
Ph: (202)872-4600   Fax: (202)872-6005
Fr: 800-227-5558

Weekly. Free to qualified subscribers; $105.00/year for individuals. Chemical process industries trade journal.

★7718★ Chemical Equipment

Curpier/ Group Publishing
301 Gibraltar Dr.
PO Box 231
Cooperstown, NY 13326
Ph: (607)547-2591   Fax: (607)547-2923
Fr: 800-733-1284

Monthly. Tabloid on the chemical process industry.

★7719★ Nature: International Weekly Journal of Science

Nature Publishing Co.
65 Bleecker St.
New York, NY 10012-2467
Ph: (212)477-9600   Fax: (212)505-1364

Weekly. Magazine covering science and technology, including the fields of biology, biochemistry, genetics, medicine, earth sciences, physics, pharmacology, and behavioral sciences.

★7720★ Popular Science

Times Mirror Magazines, Inc.
2 Park Ave.
New York, NY 10016
Ph: (212)779-5285   Fax: (212)779-5465

Monthly. General interest science magazine.

★7721★ Science

American Association for the Advancement of Science
1333 H St. NW
Washington, DC 20005
Ph: (202)326-6500   Fax: (202)682-0816

Weekly (Fri.). $87.00/year for individuals; $6.00 for single issue. Magazine devoted to science, scientific research, and public policy.

★7722★ The Scientist

The Scientist, Inc.
3501 Market St.
Philadelphia, PA 19104
Ph: (215)386-0100   Fax: (215)387-7542

Biweekly. $58.00/year for individuals; $82.00/year for Canada and Mexico; $79.00/year for other countries. Newspaper (tabloid) for scientists featuring news, opinions, research, and professional section.

Placement and Job Referral Services

★7723★ American Chemical Society (ACS)

1155 16th St. NW
Washington, DC 20036
Ph: (202)872-4600   Fax: (202)872-4615
Fr: 800-227-5558

Members: Scientific and educational society of chemists and chemical engineers. **Activities:** Conducts: studies and surveys; special programs for disadvantaged persons; legislation monitoring, analysis, and reporting; courses for graduate chemists and chemical engineers; radio and television programming. Offers career guidance counseling; administers the Petroleum Research Fund and other grants and fellowship programs. Operates Employment Clearing Houses. Compiles statistics. Maintains 33 divisions. **E-Mail:** mem info@acs.org

★7724★ American Society of Agronomy (ASA)

677 S. Segoe Rd.
Madison, WI 53711
Ph: (608)273-8080   Fax: (608)273-2021

Members: Professional society of agronomists, plant breeders, physiologists, soil scientists, chemists, educators, technicians, and others concerned with crop production and soil management, and conditions affecting them. **Activities:** Sponsors fellowship program and student essay and speech contests. Provides placement service.

★7725★ American Society for Histocompatibility and Immunogenetics (ASHI)

PO Box 15804
Lenexa, KS 66285-5804
Ph: (913)541-0009   Fax: (913)541-0156

Members: Scientists, physicians, and technologists involved in research and clinical activities related to histocompatibility testing (a state of mutual tolerance that allows some tissues to be grafted effectively to others). **Activities:** Conducts proficiency testing and educational programs. Maintains liaison with regulatory agencies; offers placement services and laboratory accreditation. Has developed histocompatability specialist certification program.

★7726★ Korean Scientists and Engineers Association in America (KSEA)

6261 Executive Blvd.
Rockville, MD 20852
Ph: (301)984-7048   Fax: (301)984-1231

Members: Scientists and engineers holding single or advanced degrees. **Purpose:** Goals are to: promote friendship and mutuality among Korean and American scientists and engineers; contribute to Korea's scientific, technological, industrial, and economic developments; strengthen the scientific, technological, and cultural bonds between Korea and the U.S. Sponsors symposium. **Activities:** Maintains speakers' bureau, placement service, and biographical archives. Compiles statistics. Maintains 100 volume library of scientific handbooks and yearbooks in Korean.

★7727★ National Network of Minority Women in Science (MWIS)

Directorate for Education and Human Resources Programs
1333 H St. NW
Washington, DC 20005
Ph: (202)326-6757   Fax: (202)371-9849

Members: Asian, Black, Mexican American, Native American, and Puerto Rican women involved in science related professions; other interested persons. **Purpose:** Promotes the advancement of minority women in science fields and the improvement of the science and mathematics education and career awareness of minorities. Supports public policies and programs in science and technology that benefit minorities. **Activities:** Maintains placement servce. Compiles statistics; serves as clearinghouse for identifying minority women scientists. Offers writing and conference presentations, seminars, and workshops on minority women in science and local career conferences for students. Local chapters maintain speakers' bureaus, and children's services. **E-Mail:** ggil bert@aaas.org

★7728★ Society for Range Management (SRM)

1839 York St.
Denver, CO 80206
Ph: (303)355-7070   Fax: (303)355-5059

Members: Professional international society of scientists, technicians, ranchers, administrators, teachers, and students interested in the study, use, and management of rangeland resources for livestock, wildlife, watershed, and recreation. **Activities:** Sponsors placement service.

EMPLOYER DIRECTORIES AND NETWORKING LISTS

★7729★ Life Sciences Organizations and Agencies Directory

Gale Research
835 Penobscot Bldg.
Detroit, MI 48226-4094
Ph: (313)961-2242   Fax: (313)961-6083
Fr: 800-877-GALE

$175.00. Covers about 7,500 associations, government agencies, research centers, educational institutions, libraries and information centers, museums, consultants, electronic information services, and other organizations and agencies active in agriculture, biology, ecology, forestry, marine science, nutrition, wildlife and animal sciences, and other natural and life sciences. Entries include: Organization or agency name, address, phone, name and title of contact, description. Arrangement: Classified by type of organization. Indexes: Organization/agency name and keyword.

★7730★ Peterson's Job Opportunities in Engineering and Technology 1996

Peterson's
PO Box 2123
Princeton, NJ 08543-2123
Ph: (609)243-9111   Fax: (609)243-9150
Fr: 800-338-3282

Compiled by the Peterson's staff. Annual. $19.95 paperback. 432 pages. Profiles 2,000 high-tech companies looking primarily for technical personnel in such fields as biotechnology, telecommunications, software, computers and peripherals, defense, and aerospace. Contains job-search strategies and career options to help match education and expertise to the job market. Indexed geographically, by industry, and by hiring needs.

★7731★ Scientific and Technical Organizations and Agencies Directory

Gale Research
835 Penobscot Bldg.
Detroit, MI 48226-4094
Ph: (313)961-2242   Fax: (313)961-6083
Fr: 800-877-GALE

Irregular; latest edition December 1993. $195.00. Covers over 25,600 national and international organizations and agencies concerned with the physical and applied sciences, engineering, and technology, including associations, computer information services, consulting firms, educational institutions, foundations, government advisory organizations, federal government agencies, general grant and assistance programs, libraries and information centers, patent sources and services, research and development centers, scholarships, fellowships, and loans, science-technology centers, standards organizations, state academies of science, and state government agencies in the fields of aeronautics and space sciences, chemistry, computer science specialties, electronics, geography, geology, machinery, mathematics, metallurgy, meteorology, mineralogy, nuclear science, petroleum and gas, physics, plastics, transportation, water resources,

and other areas. Entries include: Organization name, address, phone, and name of contact; additional descriptive text for most entries. Arrangement: Classified by type of organization. Indexes: Organization name/ key word.

HANDBOOKS AND MANUALS

★7732★ The Best Resumes for Scientists and Engineers

John Wiley and Sons
605 3rd Ave.
New York, NY 10158
Ph: (212)850-6000   Fr: 800-225-5945

Adele Lewis. Second edition, 1993. $37.50; $14.95 (paper). Presents an extensive collection of scientific and engineering resumes, highlighting the important differences between these and resumes written for other occupations.

★7733★ Careers in Science

VGM Career Horizons
4255 W. Touhy Ave.
Lincolnwood, IL 60646-1975
Ph: (847)679-5500   Fax: (847)679-2494
Fr: 800-323-4900

Thomas Easton. Third edition, 1996. 192 pages. $17.95; $13.95 (paper). Discusses careers in life science, earth science, physical and space science, social science, engineering, mathematics, and computer science. Offers job hunting advice.

★7734★ Opportunities in Biological Sciences

VGM Career Horizons
4255 W. Touhy Ave.
Lincolnwood, IL 60646-1975
Ph: (847)679-5500   Fax: (847)679-2494
Fr: 800-323-4900

Charles A. Winter. 1993. $14.95; $11.95 (paper). Identifies employers and outlines opportunities in plant and animal biology, biological specialties, biomedical sciences, applied biology, and other areas. Illustrated.

★7735★ Opportunities in High Tech Careers

VGM Career Horizons
4255 W. Touhy Ave.
Lincolnwood, IL 60646-1975
Ph: (847)679-5500   Fax: (847)679-2494
Fr: 800-323-4900

Gary D. Golter and Deborah Yanuck. 1995. $14.95; $11.95 (paper). 160 pages. Explores high technology careers. Describes job opportunities, how to make a career decision, how to prepare for high technology jobs, job hunting techniques, and future trends.

EMPLOYMENT AGENCIES AND SEARCH FIRMS

★7736★ ABC Employment Service

25 S. Bemiston, Ste. 214
Clayton, MO 63105
Ph: (314)725-3140

Employment agency.

★7737★ Banner Personnel Service

122 S. Michigan, Ste. 1510
Chicago, IL 60603
Ph: (312)704-6000   Fax: (312)580-2515

Employment agency. Executive search firm. Branch offices in Oak Brook and Schaumburg, IL.

★7738★ Health and Science Center

209 Hunter St.
Media, PA 19063-5726
Ph: (610)891-0714

Employment agency. Executive search firm.

★7739★ Intech Summit Group, Inc.

6540 Lusk Blvd., C-228
San Diego, CA 92121
Ph: (619)452-2100

Employment agency and executive recruiter.

★7740★ The Jobs Co.

8900 E. Sprague Ave.
Spokane, WA 99212-2927
Ph: (509)928-3151   Fax: (509)928-3168

Employment agency. Has division specializing in engineering and scientific openings. Also operates division specializing in sales openings.

★7741★ LOR Personnel Division

418 Wall St.
Princeton, NJ 08540
Ph: (609)921-6580

Employment agency. Executive search firm.

★7742★ National Career Centers

PO Box 447
Fayetteville, NC 28302
Ph: (919)487-0298   Fax: (919)486-7851

Employment agency. Fills openings in a variety of fields.

OTHER SOURCES

★7743★ American Institute of Biological Sciences (AIBS)

730 11th St. NW
Washington, DC 20001-4521
Ph: (202)628-1500   Fax: (202)628-1509
Fr: 800-992-AIBS

Members: Professional biological associations and laboratories whose members have an interest in the life sciences. **Purpose:** Promotes unity and effectiveness of effort among persons engaged in biological research, education, and application of biological sciences, including agriculture, environment, and medicine. Seeks to further the relationships of biological sciences to other sciences, the arts, and industries. **Activities:** Conducts symposium series; provides names of prominent biologists who are willing to serve as speakers and curriculum consultants; provides advisory committees and other services to the Department of Energy, Environmental Protection Agency, National Science Foundation, Department of Defense, and National Aeronautics and Space Administration. Maintains educational consultant panel.

★7744★ Association for International Practical Training (AIPT)

10400 Little Patuxent Pky. Ste. 250
Columbia, MD 21044
Ph: (410)997-2200   Fax: (410)992-3924

Purpose: Helps coordinate training around the world in fields such as travel, the culinary arts, and hotel management. **Activities:** Conducts programs in career development and hospitality/tourism exchanges. Operates a student exchange program. Provides reciprocal practical training experience for recent graduates from the U.S., Austria, Germany, Finland, France, Hungary, Ireland, Japan, Malaysia, Netherlands, Switzerland, and the United Kingdom. Arranges training programs in the U.S. and abroad. Serves as U.S. affiliate to IAESTE (International Association for the Exchange of Students for Technical Experience) and operates a Professional Visitors Program to arrange short-term educational and training visits to the U.S. **E-Mail:** aipt@aipt.org

★7745★ New Careers Directory: Internships and Professional Opportunities in Technology and Social Change

Student Pugwash USA
815 15th St. NW, Ste. 814
Washington, DC 20005
Ph: (202)393-6555   Fax: (202)393-6550
Fr: 800-WOW-A-PUG

Irregular; latest edition spring 1993. $13.00 for students; $21.00 for institutions, plus $3.00 shipping. Covers about 300 research institutes, think tanks, laboratories, government agencies, professional, science, and other non-profit organizations offering public policy, science, and technology internships and jobs. Entries include: Sponsoring organization name, description of organization, programs offered, work environment and application procedures, compensation offered. Arrangement: Alphabetical and classified by subject. Indexes: Geographical, subject.

★7746★ Salaries of Scientists, Engineers, and Technicians: A Summary of Salary Surveys

Commission on Professionals in Science and Technology (CPST)
1500 Massachusetts Ave. NW, Ste. 831
Washington, DC 20005
Ph: (202)223-6995

1993.

Secondary School Teachers

SOURCES OF HELP-WANTED ADS

★7747★ The American Biology Teacher

National Association of Biology Teachers
11250 Roger Bacon Dr., No. 19
Reston, VA 22090
Ph: (703)471-1134   Fax: (703)435-5582

$50.00/year; $65.00/year for other countries. Journal featuring articles on biology, science, and education for elementary, high school and college level biology teachers. Includes audio-visual, book, computer, and research reviews.

★7748★ ASCUS Annual: Job Search Handbook for Educators

Association for School, College and
  University Staffing (ASCUS)
820 Davis St., Ste. 222
Evanston, IL 60201
Ph: (708)864-1999

Annual. Includes employment notices from public school systems. Contains articles for educators seeking employment. Also includes "Directory of State Teacher Certification Offices."

★7749★ Community Jobs: The Employment Newspaper for the Non-Profit Sector

ACCESS: Networking in the Public
  Interest
30 Irving Pl.
New York, NY 10003
Ph: (212)475-1001   Fax: (212)475-1199

Monthly. $69.00. Covers jobs and internships available with nonprofit organizations active in issues such as the environment, foreign policy, consumer advocacy, housing, education, etc. Entries include: Position title; name, address, and phone of contact; description, responsibilities; requirements; salary. Arrangement: Geographical.

★7750★ Current Openings in Education in U.S.A.

Education Information Service
PO Box 660662
Newton, MA 02162-0662
Ph: (617)443-0125

Seven times/year. $8.00/issue. Publication is a booklet listing about 140 institutions or school systems, each with one to a dozen or more openings for teachers, librarians, counselors, administrators, and other personnel.

★7751★ Education Week

Editorial Projects in Education, Inc.
4301 Connecticut Ave. NW
Washington, DC 20008
Ph: (202)686-0800   Fax: (202)686-0797

Weekly. $59.94/year for individuals. Professional newspaper for elementary and secondary school educators.

★7752★ Educational Researcher

American Educational Research
  Association
1230 17th St. NW
Washington, DC 20036-3078
Ph: (202)223-9485   Fax: (202)775-1824

$39.00/year for individuals; $7.00 for single issue; $51.00/year for institutions; $48.00/year for out of country. Educational research journal.

★7753★ EIS Current Openings in Education Abroad

Education Information Services (EIS)
PO Box 660662
Newton, MA 02162-0662
Ph: (617)443-0125

$10.95. Monthly. List providing teaching and other professional education openings in American overseas schools and international schools.

★7754★ Foreign Faculty and Administrative Openings

Education Information Service
Box 662
Newton, MA 02162
Ph: (617)237-0887

Approximately every six weeks. $9.00. Covers approximately 150 specific openings in administration, counseling, library, teaching and other disciplines for American teachers in American schools overseas and in international schools, both of which must teach English as a primarily language. Entries include: Institution name, address.

★7755★ Journal of Chemical Education

Centcom Ltd.
1599 Post Rd. E
PO Box 231
Westport, CT 06881-0231
Ph: (203)256-8211   Fax: (203)256-8175

Monthly. $17.00/year for individuals. Magazine on chemical research and education.

★7756★ Journal of Learning Disabilities

Pro-Ed Journals
8700 Shoal Creek Blvd.
Austin, TX 78757
Ph: (512)451-3246

Ten issues/year. $49.00/year. Special education magazine.

★7757★ Journal of Teacher Education

American Association of Colleges for
  Teacher Education
1 Dupont Cir., Ste. 610
Washington, DC 20036-1186
Ph: (202)293-2450   Fax: (202)457-8095

$20.00/year for students; $45.00/year for individuals; $55.00/year for individuals; $75.00/year for institutions. Magazine of interest to educators.

★7758★ Music Educators Journal

Music Educators National Conference
1806 Robert Fulton Dr.
Reston, VA 22091-4348
Ph: (703)860-4000   Fax: (703)860-1531

Semimonthly. Journal covering all levels of music education.

★7759★ NABE News

National Association for Bilingual
  Education (NABE)
1220 L St. NW, Ste. 605
Washington, DC 20005-4018
Ph: (202)898-1829

Eight issues/year.

★7760★ NJEA Review

New Jersey Education Association
180 W. State St.
Box 1211
Trenton, NJ 08607
Ph: (609)599-4561   Fax: (609)392-6321

Educational journal for public school employees.

★7761★ Opening List of Professional Openings in American Overseas & International Schools

Education Information Services
Instant Alert
PO Box 662
Newton, MA 02162-0002
Ph: (617)237-0887

Every 6 weeks. $9.00. Covers about 150 current professional openings for teachers, administrators, counselors, librarians, and educational specialists in American overseas schools and international schools at which the teaching language is primarily English. Also covers English as a Second/Foreign Language (ESL-EFL) at all age levels. Entries include: Institute name, address, names and titles of key personnel, positions available.

★7762★ Opening List in U.S. Colleges, Public & Private Schools

Education Information Services
PO Box 662
Newton, MA 02162-0002
Ph: (617)237-0887

Every 6 weeks. $9.00. Covers about 150 current professional openings in U.S. public schools, and private schools. Entries include: Institute name, address, names and titles of key personnel, available openings.

★7763★ Scholastic Coach

Scholastic, Inc.
555 Broadway
New York, NY 10003
Ph: (212)343-6100

Monthly. Magazine on high school and college athletics.

★7764★ The Science Teacher

National Science Teachers Association
1840 Wilson Blvd.
Arlington, VA 22201
Ph: (703)312-9232   Fax: (703)243-7177

$52.00/year for individuals. Magazine on science education.

★7765★ Strategies

American Alliance for Health, Physical Education, Recreation, and Dance
1900 Association Dr.
Reston, VA 22091
Ph: (703)476-3495   Fax: (703)476-9527

$20.00/year for members; $40.00/year for individuals; $50.00/year for libraries. Journal providing practical, hands-on information to physical educators and coaches.

★7766★ Teacher Magazine

Editorial Projects in Education, Inc.
4301 Connecticut Ave. NW
Washington, DC 20008
Ph: (202)686-0800   Fax: (202)686-0797

Professional magazine for elementary and secondary teachers.

★7767★ Teaching Exceptional Children

The Council for Exceptional Children
1920 Association Dr.
Reston, VA 22091-1589
Ph: (703)620-3660   Fax: (703)264-9494
Fr: 800-CEC-READ

Quarterly. $35.00/year for individuals. Journal exploring practical methods for teaching talented and gifted children who have disabilities.

★7768★ Tech Directions

Prakken Publications, Inc.
275 Metty Dr., Ste. 1
Box 8623
Ann Arbor, MI 48107
Ph: (313)769-1211   Fax: (313)769-8383
Fr: 800-530-9673

Free to qualified subscribers; $30.00/year for individuals. Magazine covering industrial education, technology education, trade and industry, and vocational-technical education. Articles are geared for teacher use and reference from middle school through post-secondary levels.

★7769★ The Technology Teacher

International Technology Education Association
1914 Association Dr.
Reston, VA 22091
Ph: (703)860-2100

Magazine on technology education.

PLACEMENT AND JOB REFERRAL SERVICES

★7770★ American Alliance for Health, Physical Education, Recreation and Dance (AAHPERD)

1900 Association Dr.
Reston, VA 22091
Ph: (703)476-3400   Fax: (703)476-9527

Members: Students and educators in physical education, dance, health, athletics, safety education, recreation, and outdoor education. **Purpose:** To improve its fields of education at all levels through such services as consultation, periodicals and special publications, leadership development, determination of standards, and research. **Activities:** Sponsors placement service. Operates Information and Resource Utilization Center devoted to physical education and recreation for the handicapped and programs for senior citizens.

★7771★ American Association of Christian Schools (AACS)

PO Box 2189
Independence, MO 64055
Ph: (816)795-7709   Fax: (816)795-7462

Activities: Maintains teacher/administrator certification program and placement service. Participates in school accreditation program. Sponsors National Academic Tournament and high school sports tournaments. Maintains American Christian Honor Society. Compiles statistics; maintains speakers' bureau and placement service.

★7772★ American Association of Teachers of French (AATF)

57 E. Armory Ave.
Champaign, IL 61820
Ph: (217)333-2842   Fax: (217)333-5850

Members: Teachers of French in public and private elementary and secondary schools, colleges, and universities. **Activities:** Maintains Pedagogical Aids Bureau, offering French maps, postcards, and medals, at cost; conducts annual French contest in elementary and secondary schools and awards prizes to the winners; maintains a placement bureau and a high school honor society. Furnishes traveling exhibits and provides a pen pal agency for exchange of letters between French and American boys and girls.

★7773★ American Association of Teachers of Spanish and Portuguese (AATSP)

University of Northern Colorado
106 Gunter Hall
Greeley, CO 80639
Ph: (303)351-1090   Fax: (303)351-1095

Members: Teachers of Spanish and Portuguese languages and literatures and others interested in Hispanic culture. **Activities:** Operates placement bureau and maintains pen pal registry. Sponsors honor society, Sociedad Honoraria Hispanica and National Spanish Examinations for secondary school students.

★7774★ American Classical League (ACL)

Miami University
Oxford, OH 45056
Ph: (513)529-7741   Fax: (513)529-7742

Members: Teachers of classical languages in high schools and colleges. **Purpose:** To promote the teaching of Latin and other classical languages. Presents scholarship. **Activities:** Maintains placement service, teaching materials, and resource center at Miami University in Oxford, OH to sell teaching aids to Latin and Greek teachers.

★7775★ American Orff-Schulwerk Association (AOSA)

PO Box 391089
Cleveland, OH 44139-8089
Ph: (216)543-5366   Fax: (216)543-2687

Purpose: Music educators, music therapists, and church choir directors united to promote and encourage the philosophy of Carl Orff's (1895-1982, German composer) Schulwerk (Music for Children) in America. Distributes information on the activities and growth of Orff Schulwerk in America. **Activities:** Conducts research; offers information on teacher training. Operates clearinghouse. **E-Mail:** cleestew@peabody.jhu.edu

★7776★ Association for Direct Instruction (ADI)

PO Box 10252
Eugene, OR 97440
Ph: (503)485-1293   Fax: (503)683-7543

Members: Public school regular and special education teachers and university instructors. **Purpose:** Encourages, promotes, and engages in research aimed at improving educational methods. Promotes dissemination of developmental information and skills that facilitate the education of adults and children. **Activities:** Maintains placement service. Administers a preschool for developmentally delayed children. Offers educational training workshops for instructors.

★7777★ Association of Southern Baptist Colleges and Schools (ASBCS)

901 Commerce, Ste. 600
Nashville, TN 37203
Ph: (615)244-2362   Fax: (615)242-2153

Members: Southern Baptist seminaries, senior colleges, universities, junior colleges, academies, and Bible schools. **Purpose:** Promotes Christian education through literature, faculty workshops, student recruitment, teacher placement, trustee orientation, statistical information, and other assistance to members. Emphasizes Baptist Seminary, College, and School Day throughout the Southern Baptist Convention.

★7778★ Christian Schools International (CSI)

3350 E. Paris Ave. SE
Grand Rapids, MI 49512-3054
Ph: (616)957-1070   Fax: (616)957-5022

Members: Christian elementary and secondary schools enrolling 93,000 pupils and employing 6650 teachers. **Purpose:** To provide a medium for a united witness regarding the role of Christian schools in contemporary society; to promote the establishment of Christian schools; to help members function more effectively in areas of promotion, organization, administration, and curriculum; to help establish standards and criteria to guide the operation of its members; to foster high professional ideals and economic well-being among Christian school personnel; to establish and maintain communication with member schools, colleges, churches, government agencies, and the public. Encourages study, research, and writing that embodies Christian theories of education; conducts salary studies, research, and surveys on operating costs; offers expert and confidential analysis of member school programs and operation. **Activities:** Offers placement service. Administers the Christian School Pension and Trust Funds, Group Insurance Plans, and Life and Insurance Plans and Trust Funds.

★7779★ Convention of American Instructors of the Deaf (CAID)

PO Box 377
Bedford, TX 76095-0377
Ph: (817)354-8414

Members: Professional organization of teachers, administrators, and professionals in allied fields related to education of the deaf and hard-of-hearing. **Purpose:** Objectives are: to provide opportunities for a free interchange of views concerning methods and means of educating the deaf and hard-of-hearing; to promote such education by the publication of reports, essays, and other information; to develop more effective methods of teaching deaf and hard-of-hearing children. **Activities:** Maintains speakers' bureau; offers placement services.

★7780★ Independent Educational Services (IES)

353 Nassau St.
Princeton, NJ 08540
Ph: (609)921-6195   Fax: (609)921-0155
Fr: 800-257-5102

Purpose: Nonprofit consulting, head search, and teacher recruitment organization. Furnishes to independent (private) schools dossiers of qualified candidates for teaching and administrative positions. Offers to teachers and prospective teachers information concerning current requirements and qualifications for positions in the field of education and vacancies for which they qualify. Conducts searches for heads of schools. **Activities:** Offers specialized placement workshops, consulting, and in-service programs to independent schools.

★7781★ International Educator's Institute (TIE)

PO Box 513
Cummaquid, MA 02637
Ph: (508)362-1414

Purpose: Facilitates the placement of teachers and administrators in American, British, and international schools. Seeks to create a network that provides for professional development opportunities and improved financial security of members. Offers advice and information on international school news, recent educational developments, job placement, and investment, consumer, and professional development opportunities. Makes available insurance and travel benefits. Operates International Schools Internship Program. Sponsors competitions. Bestows awards.

★7782★ Jewish Education Service of North America (JESNA)

730 Broadway, 2nd Fl.
New York, NY 10003-9540
Ph: (212)529-2000

Members: National education organizations, bureaus of Jewish education, and individuals. **Purpose:** Service agency to coordinate, promote, and conduct research in North American Jewish education. Operates Mandell L. Berman Jewish Heritage Center for Research and Evaluation. Supports the Convenant Foundation, a joint venture with the Crown Family, which makes awards and grants for creativity in Jewish education.

Activities: Maintains teachers placement service for Jewish schools.

★7783★ Jewish Educators Assembly (JEA)

106-06 Queens Blvd.
Flushing, NY 11375-4248
Ph: (718)268-9452   Fax: (718)520-4369

Members: Educational and supervisory personnel serving Jewish educational institutions. **Purpose:** Seeks to: advance the development of Jewish education in the congregation on all levels in consonance with the philosophy of the Conservative Movement; cooperate with the United Synagogue of America Commission on Jewish Education as the policy-making body of the educational enterprise; join in cooperative effort with other Jewish educational institutions and organizations; establish and maintain professional standards for Jewish educators; serve as a forum for the exchange of ideas; promote the values of Jewish education as a basis for the creative continuity of the Jewish people. **Activities:** Maintains placement service.

★7784★ NAFSA/Association of International Educators (NAFSA)

1875 Connecticut Ave. NW, Ste. 1000
Washington, DC 20009
Ph: (202)462-4811   Fax: (202)667-3419

Members: Individuals, organizations, and institutions dealing with international educational exchange, including foreign student advisers, overseas educational advisers, credentials and admissions officers, administrators and teachers of English as a second language, community support personnel, study-abroad administrators, and embassy cultural or educational personnel. **Purpose:** Promotes self-regulation standards and responsibilities in international educational exchange; offers professional development opportunities primarily through publications, workshops, grants, and regional and national conferences. Advocates for increased awareness and support of international education and exchange on campuses, in government, and in communities. **Activities:** Offers services including: a job registry for employers and professionals involved with international education; a consultant referral service. Sponsors joint liaison activities with a variety of other educational and government organizations to conduct a census of foreign student enrollment in the U.S.; conducts workshops about specific subjects and countries.

★7785★ National Art Education Association (NAEA)

1916 Association Dr.
Reston, VA 22091-1590
Ph: (703)860-8000   Fax: (703)860-2960

Members: Teachers of art at elementary, secondary, and college levels; colleges, libraries, museums, and other educational institutions. **Purpose:** Studies problems of teaching art; encourages research and experimentation. **Activities:** Maintains placement services. Serves as clearinghouse for information on art education programs, materials, and methods of instruction. Sponsors special institutes. Cooperates with other national organizations for the furtherance of creative art experiences for youth.

★7786★ **National Association of Episcopal Schools (NAES)**

815 2nd Ave.
New York, NY 10017-4594
Ph: (212)922-5173   Fax: (212)286-9366
Fr: 800-334-7626

Members: Episcopal church-related boarding and day schools. **Purpose:** Promotes the educational ministry of the Episcopal Church; helps strengthen programs, teaching, and pastoral roles of Episcopal schools; develops criteria and curriculum materials. Provides worship materials and resources geared specifically to the needs of Episcopal schools. Works to aid communication between the National Episcopal Church and its schools and among member schools. **Activities:** Celebrates Episcopal School Week annually. Maintains charitable program, world partnership programs, and placement service.

★7787★ **National Association for Sport and Physical Education (NASPE)**

1900 Association Dr.
Reston, VA 22091
Ph: (703)476-3410   Fax: (703)476-8316

Members: Men and women professionally involved with physical activity and sports. **Purpose:** Seeks to improve the total sport and physical activity experience in America. Conducts research and education programs in such areas as sport psychology, curriculum development, kinesiology, history, philosophy, sport sociology, and the biological and behavioral basis of human activity. Develops and distributes public information materials which explain the value of physical education programs. **Activities:** Maintains placement service, and media resource center for public information and professional preparation. Sponsors skills clinics and foreign coach exchange programs.

★7788★ **National Association of Teachers' Agencies (NATA)**

PO Box 223
Georgetown, MA 01833-0323
Ph: (508)352-8473   Fax: (508)352-8680

Purpose: Private employment agencies engaged primarily in the placement of teaching and administration personnel. Works to standardize records and promote a strong ethical sense in the placement field. Maintains speakers' bureau.

★7789★ **Organization of American Historians (OAH)**

112 N. Bryan St.
Bloomington, IN 47408
Ph: (812)855-7311   Fax: (812)855-0696

Members: Professional historians, including college faculty members, secondary school teachers, graduate students, and other individuals in related fields; institutional subscribers are college, university, high school and public libraries, and historical agencies. **Purpose:** Promotes historical research and study. Sponsors 12 prize programs for historical writing; maintains speakers' bureau. **Activities:** Operates a professional job registry at annual meeting. Conducts educational programs. **E-Mail:** OAH@INDIANA.EDU.

★7790★ **Speech Communication Association (SCA)**

5105 Backlick Rd., Bldg. E
Annandale, VA 22003
Ph: (703)750-0533   Fax: (703)914-9471

Members: Elementary, secondary, college, and university teachers, speech clinicians, media specialists, communication consultants, students, theater directors, and other interested persons; libraries and other institutions. **Purpose:** To promote study, criticism, research, teaching, and application of the artistic, humanistic, and scientific principles of communication, particularly speech communication. Sponsors the publication of scholarly volumes in speech. **Activities:** Maintains placement service.

★7791★ **U.S.-China Education Foundation (USCEF)**

5345 Light Circle
Norcross, GA 30071
Ph: (770)729-1779   Fax: (770)448-1859

A project of the Society for the Advancement of Global Education. **Purpose:** To promote the learning of the Chinese languages (including Mandarin, Cantonese, and minority languages such as Mongolian) by Americans, and the learning of English by Chinese. **Activities:** Operates teacher placement service. Conducts short-term travel-study program to prepare Americans and Chinese for stays of four, six, or eight months or one to four years in China or the U.S., respectively. A project of S.A.G.E. the Society for the Development of Global Education.

EMPLOYER DIRECTORIES AND NETWORKING LISTS

★7792★ *Boarding Schools Directory*

The Association of Boarding Schools (TABS)
National Association of Independent Schools (NAIS)
1620 L St. NW
Washington, DC 20036
Ph: (202)973-9700   Fax: (202)973-9790
Fr: 800-541-5908

Annual, August. Free. Covers 276 boarding schools that are members of the National Association of Independent Schools. Entries include: School name, address, phone, contact name, grades for which boarding students are accepted, enrollment, brief description. Arrangement: Classified by type of school. Indexes: Geographical; program.

★7793★ *Christian Schools International—Directory*

Christian Schools International
3350 E. Paris Ave. SE
Grand Rapids, MI 49512
Ph: (616)957-1070   Fax: (616)957-5022

Annual, November. $45.00. Covers nearly 450 Reformed Christian elementary and secondary schools; related associations; socie-

ties without schools. Entries include: School name, address, phone; name, title, and address of officers; names of faculty members. Arrangement: Geographical.

★7794★ *Directory of Day Schools in the United States and Canada*

Torah Umesorah National Society for Hebrew Day Schools
5723 18th Ave.
Brooklyn, NY 11204
Ph: (718)259-1223   Fax: (718)259-1795

Irregular, latest edition January 1993, new edition expected 1996. $12.00. Covers approximately 500 elementary and secondary Hebrew day schools in the U.S. and Canada. Entries include: School name, address, phone, names of administrative personnel, grades taught, language of instruction, year established (when available). Arrangement: Geographical.

★7795★ *Directory of Public Elementary and Secondary Education Agencies*

U.S. National Center for Education Statistics
555 New Jersey Ave. NW
Washington, DC 20208-5651
Ph: (202)219-1335   Fax: (202)219-1728
Fr: 800-424-1616

Annual. $22.00. Covers about 17,000 local education agencies in the United States, the District of Columbia, and five territories which operate their own schools or pay tuition to other local education agencies. Also lists intermediate education agencies. Entries include: Agency name, address, phone, county, description of district, grade span, membership, special education students, metropolitan status, number of high school graduates, teachers, and schools. Also available from Superintendent of Documents, U.S. Government Printing Office. Arrangement: Geographical, then by type of agency.

★7796★ *Directory of Public School Systems in the U.S.*

Association for School, College and University Staffing
1600 Dodge Ave., S-330
Evanston, IL 60201-3451
Ph: (708)864-1999   Fax: (708)864-8303

Annual, August. $65.00. Covers about 14,500 public school systems in the United States and their administrative personnel. Entries include: System name, address, phone, name and title of personnel administrator. Arrangement: Geographical by state.

★7797★ *The Directory of Schools, Colleges, and Universities Overseas*

Overseas Employment Services
PO Box 460
Mount Royal, PQ, Canada H3P 3C7
Ph: (514)739-1108   Fax: (514)739-0795

Annual. $15.00, postpaid. Covers Approximately 300 educational institutions worldwide that hire teachers to teach various subjects in English.

★7798★ *Education Career Directory*

Gale Research
835 Penobscot Bldg.
Detroit, MI 48226-4094
Ph: (313)961-2242   Fax: (313)961-6083
Fr: 800-877-GALE

First edition March 1994. $34.00; $17.95(paper). Covers over 220 public school districts, universities, and colleges offering entry-level positions, internships, and student teaching opportunities in the U.S.; sources of help-wanted ads, professional associations, producers of videos, databases, career guides, and professional guides and handbooks. Entries include: For schools: Name, address, phone, fax, names and titles of key personnel, number of employees, average number of entry-level positions available, human resources contact, description of internship and student teaching opportunities including contact, type and number available, application procedures, qualifications, and duties. For others: Name or title, address, phone, description. Paperback edition is available from Visible Ink Press. Arrangement: Schools are alphabetical; others are classified by type of resource. Indexes: Name and keyword.

★7799★ *Educators Hiring Guide for Alaska, Hawaii, Idaho, Nevada, Montana, Oregon, Utah, Washington, and Wyoming*

Career Center
Boise State University
Boise, ID 83725
Ph: (208)385-1747   Fax: (208)385-3437
Fr: 800-824-7017

Annual, February. $48.00 plus 2.00 shipping. Covers about 1,300 public school districts and 1,200 private schools in Alaska, Hawaii, Idaho, Montana, Nevada, Oregon, Utah, Washington, and Wyoming; also includes colleges and universities that provide educational employment information as a service. Entries include: For districts and private schools: name, address, phone, names and titles of contacts, job application and interview information, enrollment, number of elementary, middle, and high schools, starting salary. For universities and colleges: name, address, phone, description of services and fees. Arrangement: Geographical by city within state sections. Indexes: Geographical by county within state.

★7800★ *Employment Opportunities, USA*

Washington Research Associates
1660 S. Albion, Ste. 390
Denver, CO 80222
Ph: (303)756-9038   Fax: (303)770-1945

Annual, quarterly updates. $184.00, includes quarterly updates. Publication includes: List of over 1,000 employment contacts in companies and agencies in the banking, arts, telecommunications, education, and 14 other industries and professions, including the federal government. Entries include: Company name, name of representative, address, description of products or services, hiring and recruiting practices, training programs, and year established. Principal content is industry overviews, carrer news, and employment opportunity information on 14 different job markets. Arrangement: Classified by industry. Indexes: Occupation.

★7801★ *The Encyclopedia of Education Information*

Grey House Publishing
Pocket Knife Sq.
PO Box 1866
Lakeville, CT 06039
Ph: (203)435-0868   Fax: (203)435-0867
Fr: 800-562-2139

$125.00. Covers Publishing opportunities, state by state information on enrollment, funding and grant resources, associations and conferences, teaching jobs abroad all geared toward elementary and secondary school professionals. Also covers online databases, textbook publishers, school suppliers, plus state and federal agencies. Entries include: Contact name, address, phone, fax, description, publications.

★7802★ *English in Asia: Teaching Tactics for New English Teachers*

Global Press
697 College Pkwy.
Rockville, MD 20850-1135
Ph: (202)466-1663

Irregular, latest edition 1992. $12.95. Publication includes: Directory covering over 1,000 private English-language schools in Asia to which applications can be made to teach. Entries include: School name, address, phone, contact.

★7803★ *50 State Educational Directories*

Career Guidance Foundation
8090 Engineer Rd.
San Diego, CA 92111
Ph: (619)560-8051   Fax: (619)278-8960
Fr: 800-854-2670

Annual, latest edition June 1996. $89.00. Microfiche. Collection consists of reproductions of the state educational directories published by the departments of education of individual states. Directory contents vary, but the majority contain listings of elementary and secondary schools, colleges and universities, and state education officials. Amount of detail in each also varies. Entries include: Usually, institution name, address, and name of one executive.

★7804★ *Ganley's Catholic Schools in America—Elementary/Secondary*

Fisher Publishing Co.
Box 1073
Montrose, CO 81402
Ph: (303)249-1303   Fax: (303)249-0348
Fr: 800-766-5151

Annual, spring. $40.00. Covers about 8,345 Catholic schools. Entries include: Name, address, phone, administrative personnel, statistics, enrollment, grade span.

★7805★ *Handbook of Private Schools*

Porter Sargent Publishers, Inc.
11 Beacon St., Ste. 1400
Boston, MA 02108
Ph: (617)523-1670   Fax: (617)523-1021

Annual, June. $85.00, plus $2.41 shipping. Covers 1,700 elementary and secondary boarding and day schools in the United States. Entries include: School name, address, phone, fax, type of school (boarding or day), sex and age range, names and titles of administrators, grades offered, academic orientation, curriculum, new admissions yearly, tests required for admission, enrollment and faculty, graduate record, number of alumni, tuition and scholarship figures, summer session, plant evaluation and endowment, date of establishment, calendar, association membership, description of school's offerings and history. Arrangement: Geographical. Indexes: Alphabetical by school name.

★7806★ *How to Find Jobs Teaching Overseas*

KSJ Publishing Co.
7600 Washington Ave.
Sebastopol, CA 95473
Ph: (707)829-9109   Fr: 800-356-9315

Latest edition 1992. $7.95. Publication includes: List of 200 schools and agencies in 65 counties providing information on teaching opportunities abroad. Principal content of publication is step-by-step guide on how to locate teaching positions outside the United States, including the author's personal experiences in locating teaching positions in England, Spain, Saudi Arabia, and Japan. Arrangement: Alphabetical.

★7807★ *Independent School Guide for Washington DC and Surrounding Area*

Independent School Guides
7315 Brookville Rd.
Chevy Chase, MD 20815
Ph: (301)986-5370   Fax: (301)718-4651

Biennial, summer of odd years. $12.95 plus $2.00 shipping. Covers over 300 independent schools (including parochial schools) in the Washington, DC area, including Maryland and Virginia. Entries include: School name, address, phone, name and title of contact, number of faculty, geographical area served, tuition, courses, admission procedures, summer programs, LD/ED programs, scholarships available. Arrangement: Alphabetical. Indexes: Geographical.

★7808★ *Independent Schools Association of the Southwest—Membership List*

Independent Schools Association of the Southwest
Box 52297
Tulsa, OK 74152-0297
Ph: (918)749-5927   Fax: (918)749-5937
Fr: 800-880-0527

Annual, August. Free. Covers over 60 independent elementary and secondary schools accredited by the association. Entries include: School name, address, phone, chief administrative officer, structure, and enrollment. Arrangement: Geographical. Indexes: Alphabetical.

★7809★ Jobs Clearing House

Association for Experiential Education
2885 Aurora Ave., Ste. 28
Boulder, CO 80303-2252
Ph: (303)440-8844   Fax: (303)440-9581

Monthly. $5.00 per issue; $40.00 per year. Covers organizations and firms offering jobs, apprenticeships, internships, and other positions in experiential education in schools and colleges, wilderness leadership, therapeutic adventure programming, environmental education, and experiential/outdoor education; coverage includes Canada. Entries include: Position title, organization name, address, name of contact, description of duties, requirements, pay, and benefits. Arrangement: Geographical by state.

★7810★ National Association of Teachers' Agencies—Membership Directory

National Association of Teachers'
Agencies
104 S. Central Ave., Ste. 12
Valley Stream, NY 11580
Ph: (516)568-8871   Fax: (516)872-1944

Annual, January. Free. Covers approximately 20 private employment agencies engaged primarily in the placement of teaching and administrative personnel in education. Entries include: Name, address, phone, names of key officials. Arrangement: Alphabetical.

★7811★ National Association for Women in Education—Member Handbook

National Association for Women in
Education
1325 18th St. NW, Ste. 210
Washington, DC 20036
Ph: (202)659-9330   Fax: (202)457-0946

Annual. Available to members only. Covers 2,000 American and foreign members. Entries include: Name, institution, office and home addresses, phone, education, position, committee membership. Arrangement: Geographical. Indexes: Alphabetical.

★7812★ National Directory of Alternative Schools

National Coalition of Alternative
Community Schools
PO Box 15036
Santa Fe, NM 87506
Ph: (505)474-4312

Biennial, even years. $15.00. Covers over 400 alternative education programs, including home schools, and state and regional coalitions of alternative schools and colleges; also lists organizations and networks offering services and resources to those working with children; international coverage. Entries include: Name, address, phone, name of contact; some also include descriptions of programs. Arrangement: Schools are geographical.

★7813★ National Directory for Employment in Education

Association for School, College and
University Staffing
1600 Dodge Ave., S-330
Evanston, IL 60201-3451
Ph: (708)864-1999   Fax: (708)864-8303

Annual, winter. $20.00. Covers about 550 placement offices maintained by teacher-training institutions and 450 school district personnel officers and/or superintendents responsible for hiring professional staff. Entries include: Institution name, address, phone, contact name. Arrangement: Geographical. Indexes: Personal name, subject-field of teacher training, institutions which provide vacancy bulletins and placement services to non-enrolled students.

★7814★ NCA Quarterly—Roster Issues

North Central Association of Colleges and
Schools
Arizona State University
PO Box 873011
Tempe, AZ 85287-3011
Ph: (602)965-8700   Fax: (602)965-9423
Fr: 800-525-9517

Annual, school issue, summer; college issue, spring. $7.00. Publication includes: Elementary schools and secondary schools (summer issue), and colleges (spring issue) accredited by the association in a 19-state region. Entries include: School name, address, year first accredited, staffing, enrollment, name of president or principal. Arrangement: Geographical.

★7815★ Opportunities Abroad for Educators

Fulbright Teacher Exchange Program
600 Maryland Ave., SW, Rm. 235
Washington, DC 20024-2520
Ph: (202)382-8586   Fax: (202)426-0657
Fr: 800-726-0479

Annual, May. Free. Covers opportunities available for elementary and secondary teachers, college and university instructors and professors, and school administrators to attend seminars or to teach abroad under the Mutual Educational and Cultural Exchange Act of 1961. Entries include: Countries of placement, dates, eligibility requirements, teaching assignments. Arrangement: Geographical.

★7816★ Patterson's American Education

Educational Directories, Inc.
PO Box 199
Mount Prospect, IL 60056-0199
Ph: (708)459-0605   Fax: (708)459-0608

Annual, October. $75.00, plus $4.00 shipping. Covers over 11,400 school districts in the United States; more than 34,000 public, private, and Catholic high schools, middle schools, and junior high schools; approximately 300 parochial superintendents; 400 territorial schools; 400 state department of education personnel; 400 educational associations. Entries include: For school districts and schools: district and superintendent name, address, phone, grade ranges, enrollment (for district and individual schools), school names, addresses, phone numbers, grade ranges, enrollment, names of princi-

pals. For postsecondary schools: school name, address, names of administrator or director of admissions. For private and Catholic high schools: name, address, phone, enrollment, grades offered, name of principal. Arrangement: Geographical. Indexes: Type of school, school name.

★7817★ Private Independent Schools

Bunting and Lyon, Inc.
238 N. Main St.
Wallingford, CT 06492
Ph: (203)269-3333   Fax: (203)269-5697

Annual, March. $96.00. Covers 1,200 English-speaking elementary and secondary private schools and summer programs in the U.S. and abroad. Entries include: School name, address, phone, enrollment, tuition and other fees, scholarship information, administrator's name and educational background, director of admissions, regional accreditation, description of programs, curriculum, activities. Arrangement: Geographical. Indexes: School name; geographical.

★7818★ Private Schools of the United States

Council for American Private Education
1726 M St. NW, Ste. 1102
Washington, DC 20036-4502
Ph: (202)659-0016   Fax: (202)659-0018
Fr: 800-333-8802

Irregular, latest edition 1992. $29.95. Covers Approximately 15,000 private elementary and secondary schools. Entries include: Institution name, address, phone, grades, enrollment, tuition, types of facilities and programs, association affiliations, name of principal, plans of graduates. Arrangement: Geographical. Indexes: Institution name; association affiliation.

★7819★ Public School Districts

Office of Educational Research and
Improvement
U.S. Department of Education
555 New Jersey Ave. NW, Ste. 214
Washington, DC 20208-5641
Ph: (202)357-6528   Fax: (202)219-1817
Fr: 800-424-1616

Annual, From 1968-1969 to 1991-1992. $175.00, Magnetic tape; $120.00, diskette. Data files describing approximately 17,000 operating and nonoperating local public school systems. Database includes: System name, city, zip code, county, metropolitan status, standard metropolitan statistical area (SMSA) number (if any), number of schools, grade span, whether operating or nonoperating, extent to which independent or unified, average daily attendance, fiscal status, selection process for board of education, and consolidation status, number of diplomas and other certificates of completion granted, number of students requiring individual education plans under the Disabilities Act.

★7820★ QED's State-by-State School Guides

Quality Education Data (QED)
1600 Broadway, 12th Fl.
Denver, CO 80202-4912
Ph: (303)860-1832   Fax: (303)860-0238
Fr: 800-525-5811

Annual, November. $1,100.00 national set; individual state volumes available. Covers over 100,000 public and private elementary and secondary schools in 17,000 school districts; in 52 volumes (national set). Entries include: School district name, address, phone, district enrollment, number of teachers, number of schools, financial data, minority enrollment statistics, names and educational specializations of key personnel, list of member schools, including school name, address, phone, name of principal, name of librarian, grade levels taught, enrollment, number of VCR units, number and types of microcomputers used. Arrangement: Geographical. Indexes: School name, district name, geographical (county name), personal name.

★7821★ Recruiting Fairs for Overseas Teaching

Education Information Services
Instant Alert
865 Central Ave., Ste. L-504
Needham, MA 02192-1344
Ph: (617)433-0125

Covers recruiting fairs and sponsors in the U.S. and elsewhere for American educators who wish to teach outside the U.S. Entries include: Fair sponsor, name, address, and phone; fair dates and locations are given in a separate list.

HANDBOOKS AND MANUALS

★7822★ Becoming a Secondary School Science Teacher

Macmillan Publishing Company, Inc.
200 Old Tappan Rd.
Old Tappan, NJ 07675
Fax: 800-445-6991   Fr: 800-223-2336

Leslie W. Trowbridge. 1990.

★7823★ Becoming a Teacher

Taylor & Francis, Inc.
1900 Frost Rd., Ste. 101
Bristol, PA 19007-1598
Ph: (215)785-5800   Fax: (215)785-5515

Gary Borich. 1995. $75.00; $23.95 (paper).

★7824★ Career Choices for the 90's for Students of Art

Walker and Company
435 Hudson St.
New York, NY 10014
Ph: (212)727-8300   Fax: (212)727-0984
Fr: 800-289-2553

Prepared by the Career Associates staff. 1990. $9.95. 166 pages. Discusses alternatives for students of art. Offers advice on how to break into the field and how to move up. Covers where and who the employers are, internship possibilities, and professional networking associations. Comprehensive guide to career and job search planning.

★7825★ Career Choices for the 90's for Students of Political Science and Government

Walker and Company
435 Hudson St.
New York, NY 10014
Ph: (212)727-8300   Fax: (212)727-0984
Fr: 800-289-2553

Prepared by the Career Associates staff. 1990. $8.95. 166 pages. Discusses alternatives for students of political science and government. Offers advice on how to break into the field and how to move up. Covers where and who the employers are, internship possibilities, and professional networking associations. Comprehensive guide to career and job search planning.

★7826★ Career Information Center

Macmillan Publishing Co.
200 Old Tappan Rd.
Old Tappan, NJ 07675
Ph: (609)461-6500   Fr: 800-223-2336

Visual Education Center Staff. Fifth edition, 1992. $229.00. This 13-volume set profiles over 600 occupations. Each occupational profile describes job duties, educational requirements, how to get the job, advancement possibilities, employment outlook, working conditions, earnings and benefits, and where to write for more information.

★7827★ Careers in Education

VGM Career Horizons
4255 W. Touhy Ave.
Lincolnwood, IL 60646-1975
Ph: (847)679-5500   Fax: (847)679-2494
Fr: 800-323-4900

Roy A. Edelfeldt. 1993. $17.95; $13.95 (paper). 192 pages. Explores opportunities for teachers, administrators, and specialists in elementary and secondary schools, as well as teaching, research, and administrative positions in higher education. Additional focus on adult and continuing education and industry opportunities for educators. Provides detailed background on careers in state boards and state departments of education, accrediting agencies, federal agencies, and national associations and councils.

★7828★ Customizing Your Resume for Teaching Positions

University Press of America
4720 Boston Way
Lanham, MD 20706
Ph: (301)459-3366   Fax: (301)459-2118
Fr: 800-462-6420

Edward G. Pultorak. 1993. $17.50 (paper).

★7829★ Educator's Job Search: The Ultimate Guide to Finding Positions in Education

National Education Association
1201 16th St., NW
Washington, DC 20036
Ph: (202)822-7252   Fax: (202)822-7206

Martin Kimeldorf. 1993. $15.95 (paper).

★7830★ The Encyclopedia of Career Choices for the 1990s: Guide to Entry-Level Jobs

Perigree Books
The Berkley Publishing Group
PO Box 506
East Rutherford, NJ 07073
Ph: (201)933-9292   Fr: 800-223-0510

Career Associates Staff. 1992. $19.95. 862 pages. Describes 500 entry-level careers in a variety of industries. Presents qualifications required, working conditions, salary, internships, and professional associations.

★7831★ How to Get a Job in Education

Bob Adams, Inc.
260 Center St.
Holbrook, MA 02343
Ph: (617)767-8100   Fax: (617)767-0994
Fr: 800-872-5627

Joel Levin. Second edition, 1995. $12.95. 320 pages. Prepared for recent college graduates, seasoned educators, and career-changing professionals, this publication guides the job-seeker through the necessary steps to obtaining a job in education at the elementary, secondary, and university levels. Offers advice on how to prepare for state and local examinations, how to locate teaching opportunities nationwide, and how to obtain certification. Includes a nationwide salary survey. Covers public, private, summer, and overseas opportunities.

★7832★ How to Get the Teaching Position You Want: Teacher Candidate Guide

Education Enterprises
PO Box 1836
Spring Valley, CA 91979
Ph: (619)660-7740

M. Phyllis Murton. 1993.

★7833★ Liberal Arts Jobs: What They Are and How to Get Them

Peterson's
PO Box 2123
Princeton, NJ 08543-2123
Ph: (609)243-9111   Fax: (609)243-9150
Fr: 800-338-3282

Burton Jay Nadler. Second edition, 1989. $9.95. 153 pages. Presents a list of the top 20 fields for liberal arts majors, covering more than 300 job opportunities. Discusses strategies for going after those jobs, including guidance on the language of a successful job search, informational interviews, and making networking work.

★7834★ Non-Profits and Education Job Finder

Planning/Communications
7215 Oak Ave.
River Forest, IL 60305-1935
Ph: (708)366-5200   Fr: (888)366-5200

Daniel Lauber. 1996. $32.95; $16.95 (paper). 350 pages. Covers 1600 sources. Discusses how to use sources of non-profit sector job vacancies in a number of specialties and state-by-state, including job-matching services, job hotlines, specialty periodicals with job ads, salary surveys, and directories. Covers a variety of fields from education to religion. Includes chapters on resume and cover letter preparation and interviewing.

★7835★ 100 Best Careers for the Year 2000

Prentice Hall General Reference
15 Columbus Cir.
New York, NY 10023
Ph: (212)373-8500   Fr: 800-223-2348

Shelly Field. 1992. $15.00 (paper). Covers 100 of the fastest growing jobs. The publication is divided into 11 general employment sections. Specific careers are covered within each section. Provides job description, responsibilities, employment opportunities, earnings, education and training, advancement opportunities, and experience and qualifications for each occupation.

★7836★ Opportunities in State and Local Government Careers

VGM Career Horizons
4255 W. Touhy Ave.
Lincolnwood, IL 60646-1975
Ph: (847)679-5500   Fax: (847)679-2494
Fr: 800-323-4900

Neale Baxter. 1993. $13.95; $10.95 (paper). 160 pages. Points out the incentives and drawbacks of a government career. Describes hiring procedures and provides tips on filling out applications, taking physical and aptitude tests, handling interviews, and finding jobs. Describes the jobs in which 75% of all state and local government workers are employed. For each occupation, covers the nature of the work and the training required.

★7837★ Opportunities in Teaching Careers

VGM Career Horizons
4255 W. Touhy Ave.
Lincolnwood, IL 60646-1975
Ph: (847)679-5500   Fax: (847)679-2494
Fr: 800-323-4900

Janet Fine. 1995. $14.95; $11.95 (paper). 160 pages. Discusses licensing and accreditation programs, sources of placement information, job-seeking correspondence, selection procedures, and paths to advancement. Also covers professional associations, non-traditional teaching opportunities, and jobs abroad.

★7838★ The RNT Careers in Teaching Handbook

Recruiting New Teachers, Inc.
385 Concord Ave.
Belmont, MA 02178
Ph: (617)489-6000   Fax: (617)489-6005
1993.

★7839★ Teaching

NTC Publishing Group
4255 W. Touhy Ave.
Lincolnwood, IL 60646-1975
Ph: (708)679-5500   Fax: (708)679-6375
Fr: 800-323-4900

1994. $13.95; $10.95 (paper).

★7840★ Teaching in the Middle and Secondary Schools

Macmillan Publishing Co., Inc.
200 Old Tappan Rd.
Old Tappan, NJ 07675
Fr: 800-223-2336

Leonard H. Clark. 1992.

★7841★ Where the Jobs Are: The Hottest Careers for the '90s

The Career Press, Inc.
3 Tice Rd.
PO Box 687
Franklin Lakes, NJ 07417
Ph: (201)848-0310   Fax: (201)848-1727
Fr: 800-237-3371

Joyce Hadley. Second edition, 1995. $9.99. 300 pages. Describes careers in fifteen general fields, from accounting to travel and hospitality.

EMPLOYMENT AGENCIES AND SEARCH FIRMS

★7842★ Educational Placement Service

5050 Poplar Ave., Ste. 1700
Memphis, TN 38157-1701
Ph: (901)767-1884

Employment agency. Focuses on teaching, administrative, and education-related openings.

OTHER SOURCES

★7843★ American Association of Teachers of German (AATG)

112 Haddontowne Ct., No. 104
Cherry Hill, NJ 08034
Ph: (609)795-5553   Fax: (609)795-9398

Members: Teachers of German at all levels; individuals interested in German language and culture. **Activities:** Offers in-service teacher-training workshops.

★7844★ American Federation of Teachers (AFT)

555 New Jersey Ave. NW
Washington, DC 20001
Ph: (202)879-4400   Fr: 800-238-1133

Purpose: AFL-CIO. Works with teachers and other educational employees at the state and local level in organizing, collective bargaining, research, educational issues, and public relations. Conducts research in areas such as educational reform, bilingual education, teacher certification, and evaluation and national assessments and standards. Represents members' concerns through legislative action; offers technical assistance. Seeks to serve professionals with concerns similar to those of teachers, including state employees, healthcare workers, and paraprofessionals.

★7845★ Association for the Advancement of Health Education (AAHE)

1900 Association Dr.
Reston, VA 22091
Ph: (703)476-3437   Fax: (703)476-6638

Members: Professionals who have responsibility for health education in schools, colleges, communities, hospitals and clinics, and industries. **Purpose:** Advancement of health education through program activities and federal legislation; encouragement of close working relationships between all health education and health service organizations; achievement of good health and well-being for all Americans automatically, without conscious thought and endeavor. Member of the American Alliance for Health, Physical Education, Recreation and Dance.

★7846★ Association of Christian Schools International (ACSI)

PO Box 35097
Colorado Springs, CO 80935-3509
Ph: (719)528-6906   Fax: (719)531-0631

Purpose: Service organization for Christian schools. Represents members in legislative efforts and First Amendment confrontations with the government. **Activities:** Sponsors student activities such as academic and speech meets, sports events, piano and choir festivals, and science fairs. Holds Christian Cheerleader Camp for high school students. Offers volume-reduced cost purchasing for school supplies and curriculum materials; recommends additional sources for purchasing. Sponsors ACSI Missionary Fund to send teams of Christian school educators throughout the world to conduct conventions, and in-service training programs. Provides speakers.

★7847★ Career Close-ups: School Teacher

AIMS Media
9710 DeSoto Ave.
Chatsworth, CA 91311
Fax: (818)341-6700   Fr: 800-367-2467

Video. 1994. $195.00. 27 minutes. Profiles of outstanding teachers.

★7848★ Career Encounters: Teaching

Cambridge Career Products
PO Box 2153
Dept. CC15
Charleston, WV 25328-2153
Ph: (304)744-9323   Fax: (304)744-9351
Fr: 800-468-4227

Video. $99.95. 25 minutes. Professionals shown in a variety of settings discuss different aspects of their careers.

★7849★ The Council Chronicle

National Council of Teachers of English
1111 Kenyon Rd.
Urbana, IL 61801
Ph: (217)328-3870   Fax: (217)328-0977
Fr: 800-369-6283

Newspaper for teachers of English or language arts at all levels.

★7850★ **Educational Placement Sources Abroad**

Education Information Services (EIS)
PO Box 660662
Newton, MA 02162-0662
Ph: (617)443-0125

Annual, August. Includes about 150 organizations in the United States and abroad which place English-speaking teachers and education administrators in positions abroad. Provides organization name and address. Classified by type of organization.

★7851★ **Educational Placement Sources—U.S.A.**

Education Information Service
PO Box 662
4523 Andes Dr.
Newton, MA 02162-0002
Ph: (617)237-0887

Annual, fall. $4.95. Covers about 75 organizations in the United States that find positions for teachers, educational administrators, and counselors. Entries include: Organization name, address, phone. Arrangement: Alphabetical.

★7852★ **Friends Council on Education (FCE)**

1507 Cherry St.
Philadelphia, PA 19102
Ph: (215)241-7245

Members: Representatives appointed by Friends Yearly Meetings; heads of Quaker secondary and elementary schools and colleges; members-at-large. **Purpose:** Acts as a clearinghouse for information on Quaker schools and colleges. **Activities:** Holds meetings and conferences on education and provides in-service training for teachers, administrators, and trustees in Friends schools.

★7853★ **International Reading Association (IRA)**

800 Barksdale Rd.
PO Box 8139
Newark, DE 19714-8139
Ph: (302)731-1600   Fax: (302)731-1057

Members: Teachers, reading specialists, consultants, administrators, supervisors, researchers, psychologists, librarians, and parents interested in promoting literacy. **Purpose:** Seeks to improve the quality of reading instruction and promote literacy worldwide. Disseminates information pertaining to research on reading, including information on adult literacy, early childhood and literacy development, international education, literature for children and adolescents, and teacher education and professional development. **Activities:** Maintains over 40 special interest groups and over 70 committees. **E-Mail:** 74673.3646@compuserve.com

★7854★ **International Technology Education Association - Council for Supervisors (ITEA-CS)**

George R. Willcox
Virginia Department of Education
PO Box 2120, 21st Fl.
Richmond, VA 23216-2120
Ph: (804)225-2020   Fax: (804)371-0249

Members: Technology education supervisors from the U.S. Office of Education; local school department chairpersons; state departments of education, local school districts, territories, provinces, and foreign countries. **Purpose:** To improve instruction and supervision of programs in technology education. **Activities:** Conducts research; compiles statistics. Sponsors competitions. Maintains speakers' bureau.

★7855★ **National Association of Blind Teachers (NABT)**

1155 15th St. NW, Ste. 720
Washington, DC 20005
Ph: (202)467-5081   Fr: 800-424-8666

Members: Public school teachers, college and university professors, and teachers in residential schools for the blind. **Purpose:** To promote employment and professional goals of blind persons entering the teaching profession or those established in their respective teaching fields. Serves as a vehicle for the dissemination of information and the exchange of ideas addressing special problems of members.

★7856★ **National Association of Catholic School Teachers (NACST)**

1700 Sansom St., Ste. 903
Philadelphia, PA 19103
Ph: (215)665-0993   Fax: (215)568-8270

Members: Catholic school teachers. **Purpose:** To unify, advise, and assist Catholic school teachers in matters of collective bargaining. Promotes the welfare and rights of Catholic schools and teaching; determines needs of Catholic schools and teachers. Monitors legislation, trends, and statistics concerning Catholic education; promotes legislation favorable to nonpublic schools and Catholic school teachers; offers legal advice and addresses issues such as unemployment compensation; assists teachers in organizing and negotiating contracts.

★7857★ **National Association of Independent Schools (NAIS)**

1620 L St. NW
Washington, DC 20036-5605
Ph: (202)973-9700   Fax: (202)973-9790

Members: Independent elementary and secondary school members; regional associations of independent schools and related associations. **Purpose:** Provides curricular and administrative research and services. Conducts educational programs; compiles statistics.

★7858★ **National Association for Research in Science Teaching (NARST)**

Dr. John R. Staver
Kansas State University
219 Bluemont Hall
Manhattan, KS 66506
Ph: (913)532-6294   Fax: (913)532-7304

Members: Science teachers, supervisors, and science educators specializing in research and teacher education. **Purpose:** Promotes and coordinates science education research and interprets and reports the results.

★7859★ **National Association of State Directors of Special Education (NASDSE)**

1800 Diagonal Rd., Ste. 320
Alexandria, VA 22314
Ph: (703)519-3800   Fax: (703)519-3808

Members: Professional society of state directors; consultants, supervisors, and administrators who have statewide responsibilities for administering special education programs. **Purpose:** Provides services to state agencies to facilitate their efforts to maximize educational outcomes for individuals with disabilities.

★7860★ **National Community Education Association (NCEA)**

3929 Old Lee Hwy., Ste. 91-A
Fairfax, VA 22032
Ph: (703)359-8973   Fax: (703)359-0972

Members: Community school directors, principals, superintendents, professors, teachers, students, and laypeople. **Purpose:** Promotes and establishes community schools as an integral part of the educational plan of every community. Serves as a clearinghouse for the exchange of ideas and information, and the sharing of efforts. **Activities:** Offers leadership training.

★7861★ **National Council for Accreditation of Teacher Education (NCATE)**

2010 Massachusetts Ave. NW, Ste. 500
Washington, DC 20036-1023
Ph: (202)466-7496   Fax: (202)296-6620

Members: Representatives from constituent colleges and universities, state departments of education, school boards, teacher, and other professional groups. **Purpose:** Voluntary accrediting body devoted exclusively to: evaluation and accreditation of institutions for preparation of elementary and secondary school teachers; preparation of school service personnel, including school principals, supervisors, superintendents, school psychologists, instructional technologists, and other specialists for school-oriented positions.

★7862★ **National Council for Geographic Education (NCGE)**

Indiana University of Pennsylvania
16A Leonard Hall
Indiana, PA 15705
Ph: (412)357-6290   Fax: (412)357-7708

Members: Teachers of geography and social studies in elementary and secondary schools, colleges, and universities; geographers in governmental agencies and private businesses. **Purpose:** Encourages the training of teachers in geographic concepts, practices, teaching methods, and techniques; works to develop effective geographic educational programs in schools and colleges and with adult groups; stimulates the production and use of accurate and understandable geographic teaching aids and materials.

★7863★ National Council of Teachers of Mathematics (NCTM)

1906 Association Dr.
Reston, VA 22091
Ph: (703)620-9840   Fax: (703)476-2970
Fr: 800-235-7566

Members: Teachers of mathematics in grades K-12, two-year colleges, and teacher education personnel on college campuses.

★7864★ Overseas Employment Opportunities for Educators: Department of Defense Dependents Schools

Diane Publishing Co.
600 Upland Ave.
Upland, PA 19015
Ph: (610)499-7415

1993. $29.95. 52 pages.

★7865★ Requirements for Certification of Teachers, Counselors, Librarians, Administrators for Elementary and Secondary Schools

University of Chicago Press
5801 Ellis Ave., 4th Fl.
Chicago, IL 60637
Ph: (312)702-7648   Fax: 800-621-8476
Fr: 800-621-2736

Annual, June. $34.00. Publication includes: List of state and local departments of education. Entries include: Office name, address, phone. Principal content of publication is summaries of each state's teaching and administrative certification requirements. Arrangement: Geographical.

★7866★ Resumes for Education Careers

VGM Career Horizons
4255 W. Touhy Ave.
Lincolnwood, IL 60646-1975
Ph: (847)679-5500   Fax: (847)679-2494
Fr: 800-323-4900

1992. $9.95. Sample resumes cover a variety of education careers and reflect education professionals at all levels of experience.

Security Professionals and Investigators

SOURCES OF HELP-WANTED ADS

★7867★ ACJS Today

Academy of Criminal Justice Sciences
Northern Kentucky University
402 Nunn Hall
Highland Heights, KY 41099-5998
Ph: (606)572-5634   Fax: (606)572-6665
Fr: 800-757-ACJS

Four issues/year. Included in membership. Contains criminal justice information.

★7868★ Locksmith Ledger International

Locksmith Publishing Corp.
850 Busse Hwy.
Park Ridge, IL 60068
Ph: (708)692-5940   Fax: (708)692-4604

Monthly. $38.00/year for individuals; $5.00 for single issue. Physical and electronic security.

★7869★ National Employment Listing Service Bulletin

Criminal Justice Center
Sam Houston State University
Huntsville, TX 77341
Ph: (409)294-1692   Fax: (409)294-1653

Free. Covers job openings in police departments, sheriff's departments, courts, and other law enforcement and security agencies; correctional agencies; community agencies; and universities and schools offering educational programs in criminal justice and related disciplines. Entries include: Name of position, qualifications sought, salary, name and address of office for contact. Arrangement: Geographical within field.

★7870★ National Locksmith

National Publishing Co., Inc.
1533 Burgundy Pkwy.
Streamwood, IL 60107
Ph: (708)837-2044   Fax: (708)837-1210

Monthly. $36.00/year for individuals; $5.00 for single issue. Magazine focusing on security and locksmithing.

★7871★ Occupational Hazards

Peter Li
1100 Superior Ave.
Cleveland, OH 44114
Ph: (216)696-7000   Fax: (216)696-7670

Monthly. Magazine serving health and safety officials in industrial establishments and governmental installations.

★7872★ Police & Security News

Days Communications
1690 Quarry Rd.
PO Box 330
Kulpsville, PA 19443
Ph: (215)538-1240   Fax: (215)538-1208

Bimonthly. $14.00/year by mail; $26.00/year for other countries. Tabloid for the law enforcement and private security industries. Includes articles on training, new products, and new technology.

★7873★ Safety Health

National Safety Council
1121 Spring Lake Dr.
Itasca, IL 60143
Ph: (708)285-1121   Fax: (708)285-9114

Monthly. Publication focusing on safety and health issues.

★7874★ SECURITY

Cahners Publishing Co.
1350 E. Touhy Ave.
PO Box 5080
Des Plaines, IL 60018
Ph: (708)635-8800   Fax: (708)635-9950

Monthly. $70.00/year for individuals; $10.00 for single issue. Magazine presenting news and technology for loss prevention and asset protection.

★7875★ Security Distributing and Marketing

Cahners Publishing Co.
1350 E. Touhy Ave.
Des Plaines, IL 60018
Ph: (708)635-8800   Fax: (708)390-2770

Monthly. Free to qualified subscribers. Trade magazine focusing on security, burglar, and fire alarm systems protection.

★7876★ Security Industry Buyers Guide

1201 7 Locks Rd., Ste. 300
Potomac, MD 20854
Ph: (301)340-1520   Fax: (301)309-9473
Annual. $169.00.

★7877★ Security Sales

Bobit Publishing
2512 Artesia Blvd.
Redondo Beach, CA 90278
Ph: (310)376-8788   Fax: (310)374-7878

Monthly. $35.00/year for individuals; $42.00/year for Canada; $53.00/year for other countries. Magazine covering the alarm manufacturing industry.

★7878★ Seed World

Scranton Gillette Communications, Inc.
380 E. Northwest Hwy.
Des Plaines, IL 60016-2282
Ph: (708)298-6622   Fax: (708)390-0408

Monthly. $25.00/year for individuals; $35.00/year for other countries. Magazine for breeders, retailers, wholesalers, brokers, conditioners and growers of flower, vegetable, grain, forage and turf seeds.

PLACEMENT AND JOB REFERRAL SERVICES

★7879★ American Society for Industrial Security (ASIS)

1655 N. Ft. Myer Dr., Ste. 1200
Arlington, VA 22209
Ph: (703)522-5800   Fax: (703)243-4954

Members: Security managers and directors responsible for loss prevention and security for private and public organizations. **Activities:** Sponsors workshops, roundtable, and educational courses on basic and special security principles and skills. Maintains professional certification program and placement service. Operates 35 committees and councils.

★7880★ Associated Locksmiths of America (ALOA)

3003 Live Oak St.
Dallas, TX 75204
Ph: (214)827-1701   Fax: (214)827-1810

Members: Retail locksmiths; associate members are manufacturers and distributors of locks, keys, safes, and burglar alarms. **Purpose:** Objective is to educate and provide current information to individuals in the physical security industry. **Activities:** Maintains information and referral services for members; offers insurance and bonding programs. Holds annual five-day technical training classes and 3-day technical exhibit. Maintains museum.

★7881★ Federal Investigators Association (FIA)

2200 Wilson Blvd.
Box 102-219
Arlington, VA 22201

Members: Persons currently or formerly engaged in investigations, enforcement, security, and related activities for the federal government. **Purpose:** Goal is to recognize and promote criminal investigation. Has established professional standards of work, education, and conduct. Serves as a vehicle for exchange of ideas and broadening of professional contacts; conducts specialized education programs. Addresses such topics as advanced white collar crime investigations, suitability investigations, terrorism, and adjudication standards. **Activities:** Supports charitable programs. Offers placement service.

★7882★ International Association for Healthcare Security and Safety (IAHSS)

PO Box 637
Lombard, IL 60148
Ph: (708)953-0990   Fax: (708)957-1786

Members: Administrative and supervisory personnel in the field of hospital security and safety. **Purpose:** To develop, promote, and coordinate better security/safety systems in medical care facilities. **Activities:** Offers placement services; conducts specialized education programs.

★7883★ International Association of Professional Security Consultants (IAPSC)

808 17th St. NW, Ste. 200
Washington, DC 20006
Ph: (202)466-7212   Fax: (202)223-9569

Members: Security management, technical, training, and forensic consultants. **Purpose:** Promotes understanding and cooperation among members and industries or individuals requiring such services. Seeks to enhance members' knowledge through seminars, training programs, and educational materials. Works to foster public awareness of the security consulting industry; serves as a clearinghouse for consultants requirements. **Activities:** Offers consultant referral service.

★7884★ International Security and Detective Alliance (ISDA)

PO Box 6303
Corpus Christi, TX 78466-6303
Ph: (512)888-6164   Fax: (512)888-6164

Members: Private investigation, and security professionals, investigative reporters and writers, researchers, military personnel, and some interested laypersons. **Purpose:** Seeks to: maintain an international registry of investigators for purposese of referral; support a more positive and accurate media image of P.I.s and security officers; provide a professional association for freelance operators; provide continuing education courses and materials. **Activities:** Offers the vocational trade association degree of Graduate Investigative Specialist - G.I.S., which can be completed through correspondence courses provided by the alliance. Provides professional certification in numerous speciality areas of investigation and security.

★7885★ National Association of Investigative Specialists (NAIS)

PO Box 33244
Austin, TX 78764
Ph: (512)719-3595   Fax: (512)719-3594

Members: Private investigators, automobile repossessors, bounty hunters, and law enforcement officers. **Purpose:** Promotes professionalism and provides for information exchange among private investigators. Lobbies for investigative regulations. Offers training programs and issues certificates of completion. **Activities:** Sponsors charitable programs; compiles statistics; maintains speakers' bureau and placement service. Operates Investigators' Hall of Fame of Private Investigators. Offers seminars on cassette tape.

★7886★ Nine Lives Associates (NLA)

Arcadia Manor
Rte. 2, Box 3645
Berryville, VA 22611
Ph: (703)955-1128

Members: Law enforcement, correctional, military, and security professionals who have been granted Personal Protection Specialist certification through completion of the protective services program offered by the Executive Protection Institute; conducts research. EPI programs emphasize personal survival skills and techniques for the protection of others. **Purpose:** Provides professional recognition for qualified individuals engaged in executive protection assignments. **Activities:** Maintains placement service.

★7887★ USCCCN National Clearinghouse on Satanic Crime in America

PO Box 1092
South Orange, NJ 07079
Ph: (908)549-2599   Fax: (908)549-2599

Purpose: Educates the public on satanic and occult related crimes being committed against animals and humans. Disseminates information to law enforcement personnel and the public through publications, videos, seminars, workshops, lectures, and radio and televison programming. **Activities:** Sponsors speakers' bureau; operates refer-

ral service. Compiles statistics. Offers children's services and research and charitable programs. Maintains hall of fame.

★7888★ World Association of Document Examiners (WADE)

111 N. Canal St.
Chicago, IL 60606
Ph: (312)930-9446

Members: Professional examiners of questioned documents. **Purpose:** Works to: encourage the enlargement and improvement of the standards in procedures, tests, and criteria practiced in the profession; keep members apprised of the latest techniques and discoveries in document work. Conducts research. Maintains 6000 volume library on crime detection, law enforcement, document examination, and psychology. Compiles statistics. Maintains placement service. **Activities:** Conducts quarterly seminar.

EMPLOYER DIRECTORIES AND NETWORKING LISTS

★7889★ Associated Locksmiths of America—Membership Directory

Associated Locksmiths of America
3003 Live Oak St.
Dallas, TX 75204
Ph: (214)827-1701   Fax: (214)827-1810

Annual, March. Publication includes: Roster of about 9,500 members of the association. Entries include: Name, address, phone. Arrangement: Alphabetical. Indexes: Geographical.

★7890★ Burglar Alarm Systems Directory

American Business Directories, Inc.
American Business Information, Inc.
5711 S. 86th Cir.
Omaha, NE 68127
Ph: (402)593-4600   Fax: (402)331-1505

Annual, January. $980.00, U.S. edition. Entries include: Name, address, phone (including area code), size of advertisement, year first in Yellow Pages, name of owner or manager, number of employees. Compiled from telephone company Yellow Pages, nationwide. Arrangement: Geographical.

★7891★ Detective Agencies Directory

American Business Directories, Inc.
American Business Information, Inc.
5711 S. 86th Cir.
Omaha, NE 68127
Ph: (402)593-4600   Fax: (402)331-1505

Annual. $430.00, payment with order. Entries include: Name, address, phone (including area code), size of advertisement, year first in Yellow Pages, name of owner or manager, number of employees. Compiled from telephone company Yellow Pages, nationwide. Arrangement: Geographical.

★7892★ **International Association of Professional Security Consultants—Directory**

International Association of Professional Security Consultants
13819-G Walsingham Rd.
Largo, FL 34644
Ph: (813)596-6696   Fax: (813)596-6696

Irregular, latest edition February 1992. Free. Covers Approximately 70 member security consultants. Entries include: Personal name and title; business address, phone, and year established; services offered; professional background; society affiliations; photo. Arrangement: Alphabetical.

★7893★ **International Security Management Association—Membership Directory**

International Security Management Association
66 Charles St., Ste. 280
Boston, MA 02114
Fr: 800-368-1894

; Available to members only. Covers member senior security officers of multinational firms and chief executive officers of security consultation services.

★7894★ **Investigators Directory**

American Business Directories, Inc.
American Business Information, Inc.
5711 S. 86th Cir.
Omaha, NE 68127
Ph: (402)593-4600   Fax: (402)331-1505

Annual. $545.00, U.S. edition. Number of listings: 7,645 (U.S. edition); 639 (Canadian edition). Entries include: Name, address, phone (including area code), size of advertisement, year first in Yellow Pages, name of owner or manager, number of employees. Compiled from telephone company Yellow Pages, nationwide. Arrangement: Geographical.

★7895★ **Investigator's Information Access Directory**

National Association of Investigative Specialists
PO Box 33244
Austin, TX 78764
Ph: (512)719-3595   Fax: (512)719-3594

Annual. $68.00. Covers state records sources, automobile tag sources, drivers record sources, and private information vendors. Arrangement: Geographical.

★7896★ **Security Guard & Patrol Service Directory**

American Business Directories, Inc.
American Business Information, Inc.
5711 S. 86th Cir.
Omaha, NE 68127
Ph: (402)593-4600   Fax: (402)331-1505

Annual. $490.00, U.S. edition. Number of listings: 6,876 (U.S. edition); 696 (Canadian edition). Entries include: Name, address, phone (including area code), size of advertisement, year first in Yellow Pages, name of owner or manager, number of employees. Compiled from telephone company Yellow Pages, nationwide. Arrangement: Geographical.

★7897★ **Security Letter Source Book**

Security Letter
166 E. 96th St.
New York, NY 10128
Ph: (212)348-1553

Biennial, March of odd years. $75.00, postpaid. Covers over 3,000 companies and individuals that supply security services, equipment, and products, including armored car carriers and vehicle manufacturers, central alarm stations, consultants, guard companies, investigators, risk management and insurance services, polygraph and pre-employment screening services, and art theft specialists. Entries include: Company name, address, phone, fax, names of executives, number of employees, brand names, financial keys, services and products, major clients. Arrangement: Classified by type of service or product.

★7898★ **Security Systems Consultants Directory**

American Business Directories, Inc.
American Business Information, Inc.
5711 S. 86th Cir.
Omaha, NE 68127
Ph: (402)593-4600   Fax: (402)331-1505

Updated continuously; printed on request. Please inquire. Entries include: Name, address, phone (including area code), size of advertisement, year first in Yellow Pages, name of owner or manager, number of employees. Compiled from telephone company Yellow Pages, nationwide. Arrangement: Geographical.

HANDBOOKS AND MANUALS

★7899★ **America's 50 Fastest Growing Jobs**

JIST Works, Inc.
720 N. Park Ave.
Indianapolis, IN 46202
Ph: (317)264-3720   Fr: 800-648-5478

Third edition, 1995. $14.95. 288 pages. Each job profile explains the nature of the work, skills and abilities required, employment outlook, average earnings, related occupations, education and training requirements, and employment opportunities. Also contains career planning information and job search tips.

★7900★ **Career Imaging**

Black Forrest Press
539 Telegraph Canyon Rd.
PO Box 521
Chula Vista, CA 91910-5704
Ph: (619)656-8048   Fax: (619)482-8704

Dahk Knox. 1993. $14.95 (paper).

★7901★ **Career Opportunities in Art**

Facts on File, Inc.
11 Penn Plaza, 15th Fl.
New York, NY 10001-2006
Ph: (212)967-8800   Fax: 800-678-3633
Fr: 800-322-8755

Susan H. Haubenstock and David Joselit. Revised edition, 1994. $29.95; $15.95 (paper). 208 pages. This book profiles seventy-five jobs that can be found in the art field. Each profile includes a career description, career ladder, employment and advancement prospects, education, experience and skills required, salary range, and tips for entry into the field.

★7902★ **Career Planning in Criminal Justice**

Anderson Publishing Co.
2035 Reading Rd.
Cincinnati, OH 45202
Ph: (513)421-4142

Robert C. DeLucia and Thomas J. Doyle. Second edition, 1993. 178 pages. Surveys a wide range of career and employment opportunities in law enforcement, the courts, corrections, forensic science, and private security. Contains career planning and job hunting advice.

★7903★ **Careers in Law Enforcement and Security**

Rosen Publishing Group, Inc.
29 E. 21st St.
New York, NY 10010
Ph: (212)777-3017   Fax: (212)777-0277
Fr: 800-237-9932

Paul Cohen and Shari Cohen. Revised edition, 1994. $14.95; $9.95 (paper). Describes jobs such as police, sheriff, detective, FBI, CIA, and Secret Service agents, parole and probation officers, security guards, and private investigators. Covers job duties, qualifications, education, training, income, and advancement possibilities. Offers advice about where and how to apply for jobs.

★7904★ **The Complete Security Officers Handbook & Career Guide**

Tecstor Corp./Terra Block Worldwide
315 E. Robinson St., Ste. 660
Orlando, FL 32801
Ph: (407)649-8335   Fax: (407)649-8704
Fr: 800-345-8625

John Francis. 1991. $12.00 (paper).

★7905★ **How to Be Your Own Private Investigator**

Gordon Press Publishers
PO Box 459, Bowling Green Sta.
New York, NY 10004
Ph: (718)624-8419

1991. $79.95.

★7906★ **Introduction to Private Investigation: Essential Knowledge & Procedures for the Private Investigator**

Charles C. Thomas Publisher
2600 S. 1st St.
Springfield, IL 62794-9265
Ph: (217)789-8980   Fax: (217)789-9130
Fr: 800-258-8980

Joseph A. Travers. 1995. $48.95; $29.95 (paper).

**★7907★ Opportunities in Law
Enforcement and Criminal Justice**

VGM Career Horizons
4255 W. Touhy Ave.
Lincolnwood, IL 60646-1975
Ph: (847)679-5500   Fax: (847)679-2494
Fr: 800-323-4900

James Stinchcomb. 1994. $14.95; $11.95
(paper). Offers information on opportunities
at the city, county, state, military, and federal
levels. Contains bibliography and illustrations.

**★7908★ Requirements to Become a P.I.
in the Fifty States & Elsewhere**

Research Investigative Services
4995 NW 79th St., Ste. 115
Miami, FL 33166
Ph: (305)599-9014

Joseph J. Culligan. 1994. $19.95 (paper).

EMPLOYMENT AGENCIES AND
SEARCH FIRMS

★7909★ Bill Young and Associates

8550 Arlington Blvd., Ste. 202
Fairfax, VA 22031
Ph: (703)573-0200   Fax: (703)573-3612

Employment agency.

★7910★ Supreme Associates

522 N. Maple Ave.
Ridgewood, NJ 07450
Ph: (201)444-6000

Executive search firm.

OTHER SOURCES

**★7911★ International Association of
Campus Law Enforcement
Administrators (IACLEA)**

638 Prospect Ave.
Hartford, CT 06105-4298
Ph: (203)586-7517   Fax: (203)586-7550

Members: Two-year or four-year colleges
and universities with a full-time law enforcement or security agency. **Purpose:** Serves as
a forum for exchange of information and
ideas in an effort to improve administration,
planning and development, and operation
and maintenance of security, police, and
public safety departments of institutions of
higher education. **Activities:** Conducts workshops and specialized education.

**★7912★ International Security
Management Association (ISMA)**

66 Charles St., Ste. 280
Boston, MA 02114
Ph: (617)381-4008   Fax: (617)381-4283

Members: Senior security executives of multinational business firms and chief executive
officers of full service security services companies. **Purpose:** To assist senior security
executives in coordinating and exchanging
information about security management and
to establish high business and professional
standards.

**★7913★ National Association of Legal
Investigators (NALI)**

Alan Hart
Alan Hart Assoc., Inc.
PO Box 286
Haddonfield, NJ 08033-0276
Ph: (609)465-4400

Members: Legal investigators, both independent and law firm staff, who specialize in

investigation of personal injury matters for
the plaintiff and criminal defense. **Purpose:**
Goal is the professionalization of the legal
investigator, accomplished by seminars and
a professional certification program. **Activities:** Provides nationwide network of contact
among members. Compiles statistics. Conducts regional seminars annually.

**★7914★ Society of Professional
Investigators (SPI)**

80 8th Ave., Ste. 303
New York, NY 10011
Ph: (212)807-5658

Members: Persons with at least 5 years'
investigative experience for an official federal, state, or local government agency or for a
quasi-official agency formed for law enforcement or related activities. **Purpose:** Seeks to
advance knowledge of the science and technology of professional investigation, law enforcement, and police science; maintains high
standards and ethics; promotes efficiency of
investigators in the services they perform.

**★7915★ World Association of
Detectives (WAD)**

PO Box 1049
Severna Park, MD 21146
Ph: (410)544-0119   Fax: (410)544-6181
Fr: 800-962-0516

Members: Executives of private investigation and security agencies. **Purpose:** Promotes high ethical practices and seeks to
imbue members with attitudes of efficiency
and responsibility. **Activities:** Provides members with referral work.

Services Sales Representatives

SOURCES OF HELP-WANTED ADS

★7916★ Advertising Age
Crain Communications, Inc.
740 N. Rush St.
Chicago, IL 60611
Ph: (312)649-5260   Fax: (312)649-5228
Weekly (Mon.). Advertising trade publication covering agency, media, and advertiser news and trends.

★7917★ Advertising Age's Business Marketing
Crain Communications, Inc.
740 N. Rush St.
Chicago, IL 60611
Ph: (312)649-5260   Fax: (312)649-5228
Monthly. $35.00/year for individuals. Trade magazine on business-to-business marketing news, strategy, and tactics.

★7918★ Money Making Opportunities
Success Publishing International
11071 Ventura Blvd.
Studio City, CA 91604
Ph: (818)980-9166
Monthly. Classified advertising magazine.

★7919★ Opportunity Magazine
73 Spring St., Ste. 303
New York, NY 10012
Ph: (212)925-3612
Monthly. $15.89/year; $2.00/issue.

★7920★ Sales & Marketing Management
Bill Communications, Inc.
355 Park Ave. S
New York, NY 10010-1789
Ph: (212)592-6200   Fax: (212)592-6309
Fr: 800-821-6897
Business magazine.

PLACEMENT AND JOB REFERRAL SERVICES

★7921★ National Association of Business and Industrial Saleswomen (NABIS)
5107 Mesa Dr.
Castle Rock, CO 80104
Ph: (303)660-3693   Fax: (303)660-5053
Members: An online virtual community of women. Women who sell business and industrial products or services. **Purpose:** Facilitates the exchange of ideas and experiences in an effort to further professional and personal development for women in business and industrial sales. Encourages women to enter the sales field and to move into sales/marketing management; seeks recognition of saleswomen's needs through trade publications and other media. **Activities:** Provides resource services to corporations and individuals. Maintains career counseling for individuals and search services for organizations. Fee schedule according to ability to pay. **E-Mail:** charlyjo@ix.netcom.com

EMPLOYER DIRECTORIES AND NETWORKING LISTS

★7922★ Who's Who in Direct Selling
Direct Selling Association
1666 K St. NW, Ste. 1010
Washington, DC 20006-2808
Ph: (202)293-5760
Free with return postage for two ounces. 15 pages.

HANDBOOKS AND MANUALS

★7923★ Advertising Career Directory
Gale Research
835 Penobscot Bldg.
Detroit, MI 48226-4094
Ph: (313)961-2242   Fax: (313)961-6083
Fr: 800-877-GALE
Bradley Morgan. Fifth edition, 1992. $39.00. 256 pages. Presents detailed listings of thousands of entry-level jobs at most major agencies nationwide. Features articles and advice from top advertising professionals to provide an insider's view of the profession.

★7924★ America's 50 Fastest Growing Jobs
JIST Works, Inc.
720 N. Park Ave.
Indianapolis, IN 46202
Ph: (317)264-3720   Fr: 800-648-5478
Third edition, 1995. $14.95. 288 pages. Each job profile explains the nature of the work, skills and abilities required, employment outlook, average earnings, related occupations, education and training requirements, and employment opportunities. Also contains career planning information and job search tips.

★7925★ Career Choices for the 90's for Students of Business
Walker and Company
435 Hudson St.
New York, NY 10014
Ph: (212)727-8300   Fax: (212)727-0984
Fr: 800-289-2553
Prepared by the Career Associates staff. 1990. $9.95. 166 pages. Discusses alternatives for students of business. Offers advice on how to break into the field and how to move up. Covers where and who the employers are, internship possibilities, and professional networking associations. Comprehensive guide to career and job search planning.

★7926★ Career Choices for the 90's for Students of Communications and Journalism

Walker and Company
435 Hudson St.
New York, NY 10014
Ph: (212)727-8300   Fax: (212)727-0984
Fr: 800-289-2553

Prepared by the Career Associates staff. 1990. $8.95. 166 pages. Discusses alternatives for students of communications and journalism. Offers advice on how to break into the field and how to move up. Covers where and who the employers are, internship possibilities, and professional networking associations. Comprehensive guide to career and job search planning.

★7927★ Career Choices for the 90's for Students of Political Science and Government

Walker and Company
435 Hudson St.
New York, NY 10014
Ph: (212)727-8300   Fax: (212)727-0984
Fr: 800-289-2553

Prepared by the Career Associates staff. 1990. $8.95. 166 pages. Discusses alternatives for students of political science and government. Offers advice on how to break into the field and how to move up. Covers where and who the employers are, internship possibilities, and professional networking associations. Comprehensive guide to career and job search planning.

★7928★ Career Choices for the 90's for Students of Psychology

Walker and Company
435 Hudson St.
New York, NY 10014
Ph: (212)727-8300   Fax: (212)727-0984
Fr: 800-289-2553

Prepared by the Career Associates staff. 1990. $9.95. 166 pages. Discusses alternatives for students of psychology. Offers advice on how to break into the field and how to move up. Covers where and who the employers are, internship possibilities, and professional networking associations. Comprehensive guide to career and job search planning.

★7929★ Career Opportunities in Advertising and Public Relations

Facts on File, Inc.
11 Penn Plaza, 15th Fl.
New York, NY 10001-2006
Ph: (212)967-8800   Fax: 800-678-3633
Fr: 800-322-8755

Shelly Field. Revised edition, 1996. $29.95; $15.95 (paper). 320 pages. Provides the job seeker with information about locating and landing the right position. Includes detailed job descriptions for many specific positions and lists trade associations, recruiting organizations, and major agencies. Contains index and bibliography.

★7930★ Career Opportunities in Television, Cable and Video

Facts on File, Inc.
11 Penn Plaza, 15th Fl.
New York, NY 10001-2006
Ph: (212)967-8800   Fax: 800-678-3633
Fr: 800-322-8755

Maxine K. Reed and Robert M. Reed. Third edition, 1991. $29.95; $15.95 (paper). 272 pages.

★7931★ Career Opportunities in Travel and Tourism

Facts on File, Inc.
11 Penn Plaza, 15th Fl.
New York, NY 10001-2006
Ph: (212)967-8800   Fax: 800-678-3633
Fr: 800-322-8755

John Hawks. 1995. $29.95; $15.95 (paper). 224 pages. Includes detailed job descriptions, educational requirements, salary ranges, and advancement prospects for 70 different job opportunities in this fast-paced industry. Contains index and bibliography.

★7932★ The Encyclopedia of Career Choices for the 1990s: Guide to Entry-Level Jobs

Perigree Books
The Berkley Publishing Group
PO Box 506
East Rutherford, NJ 07073
Ph: (201)933-9292   Fr: 800-223-0510

Career Associates Staff. 1992. $19.95. 862 pages. Describes 500 entry-level careers in a variety of industries. Presents qualifications required, working conditions, salary, internships, and professional associations.

★7933★ Marketing and Sales Career Directory

Gale Research
835 Penobscot Bldg.
Detroit, MI 48226-4094
Ph: (313)961-2242   Fax: (313)961-6083
Fr: 800-877-GALE

Bradley Morgan. Fourth edition, 1992. $39.00. 341 pages. Features extensive listings of contacts and entry-level job opportunities at major corporations, research supplier firms, and major advertising and public relations agencies nationwide. Aimed at students looking for jobs in any area of marketing, advertising, or sales on the corporate side.

★7934★ Newspapers Career Directory

Gale Research
835 Penobscot Bldg.
Detroit, MI 48226-4094
Ph: (313)961-2242   Fax: (313)961-6083
Fr: 800-877-GALE

Bradley Morgan. Fourth edition, 1993. $39.00. 344 pages. Features extensive listings of contacts and entry-level job opportunities at many newspaper organizations. Focuses on each area of the business, from reporting and editorial to sales and marketing to promotion and production.

★7935★ Opportunities in Sales Careers

VGM Career Horizons
4255 W. Touhy Ave.
Lincolnwood, IL 60646-1975
Ph: (847)679-5500   Fax: (847)679-2494
Fr: 800-323-4900

James Briscoll and Ralph Dahm. 1995. $14.95; $11.95 (paper). Details sales in retail, wholesale and industrial sales, sales of services and intangibles, and sales management. Illustrated.

★7936★ Travel and Hospitality Career Directory

Gale Research
835 Penobscot Bldg.
Detroit, MI 48226-4094
Ph: (313)961-2242   Fax: (313)961-6083
Fr: 800-877-GALE

Bradley Morgan. Second edition, 1992. $39.00. 289 pages. Features a basic and comprehensive job search section, articles by top professionals in the field, and detailed listings of hundreds of top companies who hire individuals in this field. Aimed particularly at entry-level job hunters.

★7937★ Where the Jobs Are: The Hottest Careers for the '90s

The Career Press, Inc.
3 Tice Rd.
PO Box 687
Franklin Lakes, NJ 07417
Ph: (201)848-0310   Fax: (201)848-1727
Fr: 800-237-3371

Joyce Hadley. Second edition, 1995. $9.99. 300 pages. Describes careers in fifteen general fields, from accounting to travel and hospitality.

★7938★ Your Career in Direct Marketing and Direct Response Advertising

Direct Marketing Educational Foundation, Inc.
1120 Avenue of the Americas
New York, NY 10036
Ph: (212)689-4977

This free booklet explains direct marketing and lists the types of companies engaged in direct marketing. Lists career opportunities and offers advice on entry into the field.

★7939★ Your Career Opportunities in a Direct Marketing Agency

Direct Marketing Educational Foundation, Inc.
1120 Avenue of the Americas
New York, NY 10036
Ph: (212)689-4977

This free booklet describes career opportunities in agencies involved in direct marketing.

EMPLOYMENT AGENCIES AND SEARCH FIRMS

★7940★ **Amherst Personnel Group Inc.**
PO Box 187
Hicksville, NY 11801
Ph: (516)433-7610   Fax: (516)433-7848

Employment agency. Executive search firm. Other offices in Milltown, NJ, and Rochelle Park, NJ.

★7941★ **Arancio Associates**
542 High Rock St.
Needham, MA 02192
Ph: (617)449-4436

Employment agency. Executive search firm.

★7942★ **Don Waldron and Associates, Inc.**
450 7th Ave., Ste. 501
New York, NY 10123-0101
Ph: (212)239-9110

Employment agency.

★7943★ **Hansen Agri-Placement**
PO Box 1172
Grand Island, NE 68802
Ph: (308)382-7350

Employment agency. Handles placements in a variety of fields on a regular or temporary basis.

★7944★ **The Jobs Co.**
8900 E. Sprague Ave.
Spokane, WA 99212-2927
Ph: (509)928-3151   Fax: (509)928-3168

Employment agency. Has division specializing in engineering and scientific openings. Also operates division specializing in sales openings.

★7945★ **National Register, Inc.**
2700 E. Dublin Granville Rd.
Columbus, OH 43231-4097
Ph: (614)890-1200

Employment agency. Offices in Akron and Toledo, OH.

★7946★ **The Pathfinder Group**
295 Danbury Rd.
Wilton, CT 06897-3095
Ph: (203)834-2467

Employment agency. Executive search firm. Recruits staff in a variety of fields.

★7947★ **Peter Mann and Associates**
250 S. IH 35 E.
Lewisville, TX 75067
Ph: (214)221-7516

Employment agency.

★7948★ **Phillip Thomas Personnel, Inc.**
545 5th Ave., Ste., 606
New York, NY 10017
Ph: (212)867-0860

Employment agency.

★7949★ **Sales Consultants**
33 S. King St.
Honolulu, HI 96813-3206
Ph: (808)521-7828

Employment agency. Executive search firm. Main office located in Cleveland, OH.

★7950★ **Sales Consultants (Main Office)**
1127 Euclid Ave., Ste. 1400
Cleveland, OH 44115-1638
Ph: (216)696-1122   Fax: (216)696-3221

Employment agency. Executive search firm. 150 branch offices across the country.

★7951★ **Sales Executives Inc.**
755 W. Big Beaver Rd., Ste. 2107
Troy, MI 48084
Ph: (810)362-1900

Employment agency. Executive search firm.

★7952★ **Sales Recruiters International, Ltd.**
660 White Plains Rd.
Tarrytown, NY 10591-5107
Ph: (914)631-0090

Employment agency.

★7953★ **Salesworld Inc.**
899 W. Cypress Creek Blvd.
Ft. Lauderdale, FL 33309-2072
Ph: (954)492-0088

Employment agency. National agency with offices in Annapolis, MD; Atlanta, GA; Balti-

more, MD; Birmingham, AL; Boston, MA; Chicago, IL; Cincinnati, OH; Cleveland, OH; Dallas, TX; Detroit, MI; Ft. Worth, TX; Houston, TX; Irvine, CA; Jacksonville, FL; Los Angeles, CA; New York, NY; Philadelphia, PA; St. Louis, MO; San Francisco, CA; Washington, VA.

★7954★ **Selected Executives Inc.**
76 Winn St.
Woburn, MA 01801
Ph: (617)933-1500

Employment agency.

OTHER SOURCES

★7955★ *Resumes for Sales and Marketing Careers*
VGM Career Horizons
4255 W. Touhy Ave.
Lincolnwood, IL 60646-1975
Ph: (847)679-5500   Fax: (847)679-2494
Fr: 800-323-4900

1991. $9.95. 128 pages. Sample resumes and cover letters from all levels of the sales and marketing field.

★7956★ **Sales and Marketing Executives International (SMEI)**
Statler Office Tower, No. 977
Cleveland, OH 44115
Ph: (216)771-6650   Fax: (216)771-6652

Members: Executives concerned with sales and marketing management, research, training, and other managerial aspects of distribution. Members control activities of 3,000,000 salespersons. **Purpose:** Undertakes studies in the field of selling and sales management; sponsors sales workshops, rallies, clinics, and seminars. Conducts career education programs, working with teachers, establishing sales clubs and fraternities, and cooperating with Junior Achievement and Distributive Education Clubs of America to interest young people in sales careers. Offers Graduate School of Sales Management and Marketing at Syracuse University, NY.

Social Workers

★7957★ American City and County

Communication Channels, Inc.
6255 Barfield Rd.
Atlanta, GA 30328
Ph: (404)955-9970   Fax: (404)256-3116

Monthly. $54.00/year for individuals. Municipal and county administration magazine.

★7958★ Community Jobs: The Employment Newspaper for the Non-Profit Sector

ACCESS: Networking in the Public
Interest
30 Irving Pl.
New York, NY 10003
Ph: (212)475-1001   Fax: (212)475-1199

Monthly. $69.00. Covers jobs and internships available with nonprofit organizations active in issues such as the environment, foreign policy, consumer advocacy, housing, education, etc. Entries include: Position title; name, address, and phone of contact; description, responsibilities; requirements; salary. Arrangement: Geographical.

★7959★ EAP Digest

Performance Resource Press
1863 Technology Dr.
Troy, MI 48083
Ph: (810)588-7733   Fax: (810)588-6633

Bimonthly. $8.00 for single issue; $46.00/year, $55.00/year for Canada; $64.00/year for other countries. Magazine covering planning, development, and administration of employee assistance programs.

★7960★ Family Therapy News

American Association for Marriage &
Family Therapy
1100 17th St. NW, 10th Fl.
Washington, DC 20036
Ph: (202)452-0109   Fax: (202)223-2329

Bimonthly. $25.00/year for individuals; $40.00/year for institutions, Canada; $35.00/year for other countries; $4.00 for single issue. Newspaper on family therapy.

★7961★ Journal of Jewish Communal Service

Jewish Communal Service Association
3084 State Hwy. 27, Ste. 9
Kendall Park, NJ 08824-1657
Ph: (201)821-1871   Fax: (201)821-5335

Quarterly. Journal covering Jewish communal service and social work.

★7962★ The Lutheran

Augsburg Fortress, Publishers
426 S. 5th St.
PO Box 1209
Minneapolis, MN 55440
Ph: (612)330-3246   Fax: (612)330-3455
Fr: 800-328-4648

Monthly. $11.90/year for individuals; $1.50 for single issue. Magazine of the Evangelical Lutheran Church in America.

★7963★ Mental Retardation

American Association of Mental
Retardation
444 N. Capitol St. NW, Ste. 846
Washington, DC 20001
Ph: (202)387-1968

Bimonthly. $75.00/year.

★7964★ Modern Healthcare

Crain Communications, Inc.
740 N. Rush St.
Chicago, IL 60611-2590
Ph: (312)649-5311   Fax: (312)280-3189

Weekly. $110.00/year. Business news magazine for Healthcare Management.

★7965★ National Employment Listing Service Bulletin

Criminal Justice Center
Sam Houston State University
Huntsville, TX 77341
Ph: (409)294-1692   Fax: (409)294-1653

Free. Covers job openings in police departments, sheriff's departments, courts, and other law enforcement and security agencies; correctional agencies; community agencies; and universities and schools offering educational programs in criminal justice and related disciplines. Entries include: Name of position, qualifications sought, salary, name and address of office for contact. Arrangement: Geographical within field.

★7966★ The New Social Worker

White Hat Communications
PO Box 5390
Harrisburg, PA 17110-0390
Ph: (717)238-3787

$13.25/year. Publication offering career guidance for social work students.

★7967★ The NonProfit Times

The Davis Information Group, Inc.
190 Tamarack Cir.
Skillman, NJ 08558-9662
Ph: (609)466-4600

Monthly. $39.00/year.

★7968★ Psychiatric Services

American Psychiatric Press, Inc.
1400 K St. NW, Ste. 503
Washington, DC 20005
Ph: (202)682-6240   Fax: (202)692-6016
Fr: 800-368-5777

Monthly. $40.00/year for individuals; $60.00/year for institutions; $20 .00/year for students. Interdisciplinary mental health journal covering clinical, legal, and public policy issues.

★7969★ Social Service Jobs

10 Angelica Dr.
Framingham, MA 01701
Ph: (508)620-8644

Biweekly. $109.00/year.

★7970★ Social Work

National Association of Social Workers
750 1st St. NE, Ste. 700
Washington, DC 20002-4241
Ph: (202)408-8600   Fax: (202)336-8312
Fr: 800-638-8799

Bimonthly. $67.00/year for individuals; $93.00/year for institutions; $12.00 for single issue. Magazine for social workers.

★7971★ Social Work in Education

National Association of Social Workers
750 1st St. NE, Ste. 700
Washington, DC 20002-4241
Ph: (202)408-8600   Fax: (202)336-8312
Fr: 800-638-8799

Quarterly. $58.00/year for individuals; $11.00

for single issue; $81.00/year for institutions. Journal.

★7972★ Teaching Exceptional Children
The Council for Exceptional Children
1920 Association Dr.
Reston, VA 22091-1589
Ph: (703)620-3660   Fax: (703)264-9494
Fr: 800-CEC-READ

Quarterly. $35.00/year for individuals. Journal exploring practical methods for teaching talented and gifted children who have disabilities.

PLACEMENT AND JOB REFERRAL SERVICES

★7973★ American Association of Psychiatric Technicians (AAPT)
PO Box 14014
Phoenix, AZ 85063
Ph: (602)873-1890   Fax: (602)873-4616
Fr: 800-391-7589

Members: Psychiatric technicians, behavioral health technicians, mental health workers, counselors, social workers, psychiatric nurses, psychologists, and other individuals and companies interested in mental health. **Purpose:** Promotes professionalism in mental health industry. Encourages further education of mental health workers and provides national certification of mental health workers. Works with colleges, schools, and mental health facilities to develop education and training. Awards accreditation to mental health worker training programs. **Activities:** Offers placement informations.

★7974★ American Public Health Association (APHA)
1015 15th St. NW
Washington, DC 20005
Ph: (202)789-5600   Fax: (202)789-5681

Members: Professional organization of physicians, nurses, educators, academicians, environmentalists, epidemiologists, new professionals, social workers, health administrators, optometrists, podiatrists, pharmacists, dentists, nutritionists, health planners, other community and mental health specialists, and interested consumers. **Purpose:** Seeks to protect and promote personal, mental, and environmental health. **Activities:** Services include: promulgation of standards; establishment of uniform practices and procedures; development of the etiology of communicable diseases; research in public health; exploration of medical care programs and their relationships to public health. Sponsors job placement service.

★7975★ Association on Higher Education and Disability (AHEAD)
PO Box 21192
Columbus, OH 43221-0192
Ph: (614)488-4972   Fax: (614)488-1174

Members: Individuals interested in promoting the equal rights and opportunities of disabled postsecondary students, staff, faculty, and graduates. **Purpose:** Provides an

exchange of communication for those professionally involved with disabled students; collects, evaluates, and disseminates information; encourages and supports legislation for the benefit of disabled students. **Activities:** Conducts surveys on issues pertinent to college students with disabilities; offers resource referral system and employment exchange for positions in disability student services. Conducts research programs; compiles statistics.

★7976★ Family Service America (FSA)
11700 W. Lake Park Dr.
Milwaukee, WI 53224
Ph: (414)359-1040   Fax: (414)359-1074
Fr: 800-221-3726

Purpose: Federation of local agencies in more than 1000 communities providing family counseling, family life education and family advocacy services, and other programs to help families with parent-child, marital, mental health, and other problems of family living. Assists member agencies in developing and providing effective family services. Works with the media, government, and corporations to promote strong family life. Compiles statistics; conducts research. Maintains extensive files of unpublished materials from member agencies. **Activities:** Offers placement services.

★7977★ International Association of Counselors and Therapists (IACT)
10915 Bonita Beach Rd., Ste. 2142
Bonita Springs, FL 33923
Ph: (941)498-9710

Members: Mental health professionals, medical professionals, social workers, clergy, philosophers, educators, hypnotherapists, counselors, and individuals interested in the helping professions. **Purpose:** Promotes enhanced professional image and prestige for hypnotherapists. Provides a forum for exchange of information and ideas among practitioners of traditional and nontraditional therapies and methodologies; fosters unity among "grassroots" practitioners and those with advanced academic credentials. Facilitates the development of new therapy programs. **Activities:** Operates referral and placement services.

★7978★ National Staff Development and Training Association (NSDTA)
810 1st St. NE, Ste. 500
Washington, DC 20002-4267
Ph: (202)682-0100

Members: Social welfare workers engaged in staff development and training. **Purpose:** Attempts to: support people in the field; influence welfare policy-making on the national level; form a network of contacts for members. Provides technical assistance. **Activities:** Maintains speakers' bureau; offers placement services.

★7979★ North American Association of Christians in Social Work (NACSW)
Box 7090
St. Davids, PA 19087-7090
Ph: (610)687-5777   Fax: (610)687-5777

Members: Professional social workers and related professionals; students; interested

individuals. **Purpose:** To provide opportunities for Christian fellowship, growth, learning, outreach, and witness. Promotes a Christian world view in social work and social welfare and encourages awareness within the Christian community of human need and of social work as a means for ministering to this need. Holds regional seminars, evening meetings, one-day conferences, and small study and support group meetings. **Activities:** Maintains employment service. Operates speakers' bureau.

EMPLOYER DIRECTORIES AND NETWORKING LISTS

★7980★ Addiction & Recovery's National Treatment Resource Issue
Medquest Communications, Inc.
629 Euclid Ave., Ste. 500
Cleveland, OH 44114
Ph: (216)522-9700   Fax: (216)522-9707

Annual. Covers 3000 drug and alcohol treatment programs and facilities, addiction counselors, and physicians. Entries include institution name and address, addictions treated, type of facility, size.

★7981★ Child Welfare League of America—Directory of Member Agencies
Child Welfare League of America
440 1st St. NW, Ste. 310
Washington, DC 20001
Ph: (202)638-2952   Fax: (202)638-4004

Biennial. $14.00, payment with order. Covers accredited provisional, and general members, associates and supporting advocates. Includes member agencies of the Florence Crittenton Division. Entries include: Agency name, type of membership region, address, phone number, fax number, name of executive director, list of services. Arrangement: Geographical, then alphabetical.

★7982★ Christian Association for Psychological Studies International—Membership Directory
Christian Association for Psychological Studies
PO Box 310400
New Braunfels, TX 78131-0400
Ph: (210)629-2277   Fax: (210)629-2342

Biennial, May, even years. $10.00. Covers 2,300 Christians involved in psychology, psychiatry, counseling, sociology, social work, ministry, and nursing. Entries include: Name, office address and phone number, highest degree held, area of occupational specialization, and career data. Arrangement: Geographical. Indexes: Alphabetical.

★7983★ Directory of Catholic Charities Diocesan Agencies and Organizations
Catholic Charities USA
1731 King St., Ste. 200
Alexandria, VA 22314
Ph: (703)549-1390   Fax: (703)549-1656

Biennial, odd years. $20.00 for members; $35.00 for nonmembers; $10.00, update supplement. Covers nearly 1,200 Catholic community and social service agencies and residential and non-residential institutions and facilities. Listings include diocesan agencies, institutions for the elderly, handicapped, and youth, Catholic schools of social work, and state Catholic conferences. Entries include: Organization name, address, name and title of director, phone, fax, public relations contact. Arrangement: Geographical by diocese then classified by type of organization.

★7984★ Mental Health Directory

Office of Consumer, Family & Public
  Information
Center for Mental Health Services
U.S. Substance Abuse & Mental Health
  Services Administration
5600 Fishers Ln., Rm. 15-18
Rockville, MD 20857
Ph: (301)443-2792

Irregular, latest edition 1990. $23.00. Covers hospitals, treatment centers, outpatient clinics, day/night facilities, residential treatment centers for emotionally disturbed children, residential supportive programs such as halfway houses, and mental health centers offering mental health assistance; not included are substance abuse programs, Veteran's Administration programs, nursing homes, programs for the developmentally disabled, and organizations in which fees are retained by individual members. Entries include: Name, address, phone. Arrangement: Geographical.

★7985★ Mental Health Services Directory

American Business Directories, Inc.
American Business Information, Inc.
5711 S. 86th Cir.
Omaha, NE 68127
Ph: (402)593-4600   Fax: (402)331-1505

Annual. $1,095.00, payment with order. Entries include: Name, address, phone (including area code), size of advertisement, year first in Yellow Pages, name of owner or manager, number of employees. Compiled from telephone company Yellow Pages, nationwide. Arrangement: Geographical.

★7986★ Mental Health and Social Work Career Directory

Gale Research
835 Penobscot Bldg.
Detroit, MI 48226-4094
Ph: (313)961-2242   Fax: (313)961-6083
Fr: 800-877-GALE

Latest edition 1993. $34.00; $17.95 (paper). Covers over 300 agencies, organizations, and companies offering entry-level positions in mental health, social work, counseling, psychology, etc.; sources of help-wanted ads, professional associations, producers of videos, databases, career guides, and professional guides and handbooks. Entries include: For organizations offering positions: name, address, phone, description, names and titles of key personnel, number of employees, average number of entry-level positions available, human resources contact, description of internship opportunities including contact, type and number available, application procedures, qualifications, and duties.

For others: name or title, address, phone, description. Paperback edition is available from Visible Ink Press. Arrangement: Organizations offering positions are alphabetical; others are classified by type of resource. Indexes: Name, keyword.

★7987★ National Directory of Children, Youth & Families Services

Marion L. Peterson, Publisher
PO Box 1837
Longmont, CO 80502-1837
Ph: (303)776-7539   Fax: 800-845-6452
Fr: 800-343-6681

Annual, July. $78.00, plus $6.00 shipping, postpaid. Covers child, youth, and family-oriented social services, health and mental health services, and juvenile/family court and youth advocacy services in state and private agencies, major cities, and 3,100 counties; also covers runaway youth centers, child abuse projects, congressional committees, clearinghouses, and national organizations concerned with family health and welfare; buyers' guide to specialized services and products. Entries include: Agency listings include agency name, address, phone, names of principal executives and staff, description of services. Arrangement: Geographical.

★7988★ National Directory of Private Social Agencies

Croner Publications, Inc.
34 Jericho Tpke.
Jericho, NY 11753
Ph: (516)333-9085   Fax: (516)338-4986
Fr: 800-441-4033

Base edition supplied upon order; monthly updates. $74.95, plus $4.95 shipping. Number of listings: Over 15,000. Entries include: Agency name, address, phone, name and title of contact, description of services. Arrangement: Geographical. Indexes: Service, agency type.

★7989★ Public Welfare Directory

American Public Welfare Association
810 1st St. NE, Ste. 500
Washington, DC 20002-4267
Ph: (202)682-0100   Fax: (202)289-6555

Annual, August. $70.00, postpaid, payment with order; $75.00, billed. Covers federal, state, territorial, county, and major municipal human service agencies; coverage includes Canadian federal and provincial agencies. Entries include: Agency name, address, phone, names of key personnel, type of service or clientele. Arrangement: Geographical.

★7990★ Social Workers Directory

American Business Directories, Inc.
American Business Information, Inc.
5711 S. 86th Cir.
Omaha, NE 68127
Ph: (402)593-4600   Fax: (402)331-1505

Annual. $455.00, payment with order. Entries include: Name, address, phone (including area code), size of advertisement, year first in Yellow Pages, name of owner or manager, number of employees. Compiled from telephone company Yellow Pages, nationwide. Arrangement: Geographical.

★7991★ Who's Who Among Human Services Professionals

National Register Publishing
Reed Reference Publishing
121 Chanlon Rd.
New Providence, NJ 07974-1541
Ph: (908)464-6400   Fr: 800-621-9669

Latest edition February 1992; suspended indefinitely. $129.00. Covers nearly 20,000 human service professionals, in such fields as counseling, social work, psychology, audiology, and speech pathology. Entries include: Name, address, education, work experience, professional association memberships. Arrangement: Alphabetical.

HANDBOOKS AND MANUALS

★7992★ Career Information Center

Macmillan Publishing Co.
200 Old Tappan Rd.
Old Tappan, NJ 07675
Ph: (609)461-6500   Fr: 800-223-2336

Visual Education Center Staff. Fifth edition, 1992. $229.00. This 13-volume set profiles over 600 occupations. Each occupational profile describes job duties, educational requirements, how to get the job, advancement possibilities, employment outlook, working conditions, earnings and benefits, and where to write for more information.

★7993★ Careers for Good Samaritans and Other Humanitarian Types

VGM Career Horizons
4255 W. Touhy Ave.
Lincolnwood, IL 60646-1975
Ph: (847)679-5500   Fax: (847)679-2494
Fr: 800-323-4900

Marjorie Eberts and Margaret Gisler. 1991. $12.95; $9.95 (paper). Contains hundreds of ideas for turning good work into paid work. Inventories opportunities in service organizations like the Red Cross, Goodwill, and the Salvation Army; religious groups, VISTA, the Peace Corps, and UNICEF; and agencies at all levels of the government.

★7994★ Careers in Health Care

VGM Career Horizons
4255 W. Touhy Ave.
Lincolnwood, IL 60646-1975
Ph: (847)679-5500   Fax: (847)679-2494
Fr: 800-323-4900

Barbara M. Swanson. 1995. $17.95; $13.95 (paper). Describes job duties, work settings, salaries, licensing and certification requirements, educational preparation, and future outlook. Gives ideas on how to secure a job.

★7995★ Careers in Social Work

National Association of Social Workers
  (NASW)
NASW Press
750 First St., Ste. 700
Washington, DC 20002-4241

Brochure. Describes career opportunities in mental health, child welfare, health care, public welfare, schools, family service, services to the aged, industry, business, labor, and corrections. Includes information on how to enter the profession, and educational preparation.

★7996★ **Encyclopedia of Careers and Vocational Guidance**

J. G. Ferguson Publishing Co.
200 W. Monroe, Ste. 250
Chicago, IL 60606
Ph: (312)580-5480

William E. Hopke. Ninth edition, 1993. $129.95; $199.95 (CD-ROM). Four-volume set that profiles 900 occupations and describes job trends in 71 industries. Includes career description, educational requirements, history of the job, methods of entry, advancement, employment outlook, earnings, conditions of work, social and psychological factors, and sources of further information. Contains career and employment information for this field.

★7997★ **Non-Profits and Education Job Finder**

Planning/Communications
7215 Oak Ave.
River Forest, IL 60305-1935
Ph: (708)366-5200   Fr: (888)366-5200

Daniel Lauber. 1996. $32.95; $16.95 (paper). 350 pages. Covers 1600 sources. Discusses how to use sources of non-profit sector job vacancies in a number of specialties and state-by-state, including job-matching services, job hotlines, specialty periodicals with job ads, salary surveys, and directories. Covers a variety of fields from education to religion. Includes chapters on resume and cover letter preparation and interviewing.

★7998★ **100 Best Careers for the Year 2000**

Prentice Hall General Reference
15 Columbus Cir.
New York, NY 10023
Ph: (212)373-8500   Fr: 800-223-2348

Shelly Field. 1992. $15.00 (paper). Covers 100 of the fastest growing jobs. The publication is divided into 11 general employment sections. Specific careers are covered within each section. Provides job description, responsibilities, employment opportunities, earnings, education and training, advancement opportunities, and experience and qualifications for each occupation.

★7999★ **Opportunities in Child Care Careers**

VGM Career Horizons
4255 W. Touhy Ave.
Lincolnwood, IL 60646-1975
Ph: (847)679-5500   Fax: (847)679-2494
Fr: 800-323-4900

Renee Wittenberg. 1995. $14.95; $11.95 (paper). 160 pages. Discusses various job opportunities and how to secure a position. Illustrated.

★8000★ **Opportunities in Gerontology and Aging Services Careers**

VGM Career Horizons
4255 W. Touhy Ave.
Lincolnwood, IL 60646-1975
Ph: (847)679-5500   Fax: (847)679-2494
Fr: 800-323-4900

Ellen Williams. 1995. $14.95; $11.95 (paper). 160 pages. Covers jobs in community, health and medical programs, financial, legal, residential, travel and tourism, and counseling, and how to go after them. Includes bibliography and illustrations.

★8001★ **Opportunities in Health and Medical Careers**

VGM Career Horizons
4255 W. Touhy Ave.
Lincolnwood, IL 60646-1975
Ph: (847)679-5500   Fax: (847)679-2494
Fr: 800-323-4900

Donald Snook, Jr. and Leo D'Orazio. 1993. $14.95; $11.95 (paper). Covers the full range of medical and health occupations. Illustrated.

★8002★ **Opportunities in Public Health Careers**

VGM Career Horizons
4255 W. Touhy Ave.
Lincolnwood, IL 60646-1975
Ph: (847)679-5500   Fax: (847)679-2494
Fr: 800-323-4900

George E. Pickett and Terry W. Pickett. 1995. $14.95; $11.95 (paper). 160 pages. Defines the public health field and describes a variety of health, science, and business opportunities as well as educational preparation and the future of the public health field. Offers job-hunting tips. The appendixes list public health organizations, state and federal public health agencies, and graduate schools offering public health programs.

★8003★ **Opportunities in State and Local Government Careers**

VGM Career Horizons
4255 W. Touhy Ave.
Lincolnwood, IL 60646-1975
Ph: (847)679-5500   Fax: (847)679-2494
Fr: 800-323-4900

Neale Baxter. 1993. $13.95; $10.95 (paper). 160 pages. Points out the incentives and drawbacks of a government career. Describes hiring procedures and provides tips on filling out applications, taking physical and aptitude tests, handling interviews, and finding jobs. Describes the jobs in which 75% of all state and local government workers are employed. For each occupation, covers the nature of the work and the training required.

★8004★ **The Quest for a Radical Profession: Social Service Careers & Political Ideology**

University Press of America
4720 Boston Way
Lanham, MD 20706
Ph: (301)459-3366   Fax: (301)459-2118
Fr: 800-462-6420

David Wagner. 1990. $45.00; $24.00 (paper).

EMPLOYMENT AGENCIES AND SEARCH FIRMS

★8005★ **Arbor Associates, Inc.**
15 Court Sq., Ste. 1050
Boston, MA 02108
Ph: (617)227-8829

Handles temporary placements.

OTHER SOURCES

★8006★ **American Almanac of Jobs and Salaries 1994-95**
Avon Books
1350 Avenue of the Americas, 2nd Fl.
New York, NY 10019
Ph: (212)261-6800   Fr: 800-238-0658

John Wright. Revised edition, 1993. $17.00. 704 pages. This is a comprehensive guide to the wages of hundreds of occupations in a wide variety of industries and organizations.

★8007★ **American Association of Mental Health Professionals in Corrections (AAMHPC)**
John S. Zil, M.D., J.D.
PO Box 163359
Sacramento, CA 95816-9359
Ph: (707)864-0910   Fax: (707)864-0910

Members: Psychiatrists, psychologists, social workers, nurses, and other mental health professionals; individuals working in correctional settings. **Purpose:** Fosters the progress of behavioral sciences related to corrections. Goals are: to improve the treatment, rehabilitation, and care of the mentally ill, mentally retarded, and emotionally disturbed; to promote research and professional education in psychiatry and allied fields in corrections; to advance standards of correctional services and facilities; to foster cooperation between individuals concerned with the medical, psychological, social, and legal aspects of corrections; to share knowledge with other medical practitioners, scientists, and the public.

★8008★ **Association for Humanistic Education and Development (AHEAD)**
5999 Stevenson Ave.
Alexandria, VA 22304
Ph: (703)823-9800   Fax: (703)823-0252
Fr: 800-347-6647

Members: A division of the American Counseling Association. Teachers, educational administrators, community agency workers, counselors, school social workers, and psychologists; others interested in the area of human development. **Purpose:** Aims to assist individuals in improving their quality of life. Provides forum for the exchange of information about humanistically-oriented administrative and instructional practices. Supports humanistic practices and research on instructional and organizational methods for facilitating humanistic education; encourages cooperation among related professional groups.

★8009★ Child Welfare League of America (CWLA)

440 1st St. NW, Ste. 310
Washington, DC 20001
Ph: (202)638-2952   Fax: (202)638-4004

Purpose: Works to improve care and services for abused, dependent, or neglected children, youth, and their families. **Activities:** Provides consultation; conducts research; maintains information service; develops standards for child welfare practice; administers special projects.

★8010★ *Day in a Career: Social Worker*

Cambridge Career Products
PO Box 2153
Dept. CC15
Charleston, WV 25328-2153
Ph: (304)744-9323   Fax: (304)744-9351
Fr: 800-468-4227

Video. 1994. $89.00. 15-22 minutes. Includes candid interviews and work situations, plus outlines of relevant career information.

★8011★ *Directory of Child Life Programs*

Child Life Council
7910 Woodmont Ave., Ste. 310
Bethesda, MD 20814
Ph: (301)654-1343   Fax: (301)654-4964

Irregular. $22.00, plus $3.00 shipping. Covers Nearly 150 internships, fellowships, and other practical teaching experiences in hospitals for students of child life activity. Entries include: Facility name, address, phone, name of individual in charge of the practicum; number of hours and number of weeks for practicum; beginning dates, if specified; number of students accepted each term; total number of students accepted for the year; colleges from which students are generally referred; areas of study from which students generally come; fees; stipend and other benefits; prerequisites; whether application is to be made to college or hospital; level of student generally accepted; practicum experiences available; form of evaluation. Arrangement: Geographical.

★8012★ Employee Assistance Society of North America (EASNA)

2728 Phillips
Berkley, MI 48072
Ph: (810)545-3888   Fax: (810)545-5528

Members: Individuals in the field of employee assistance, including psychiatrists, psychologists, and managers. **Purpose:** Facilitates

communication among members; provides resource information; serves as a network for employee assistance programs nationwide. Conducts research.

★8013★ National Association of Social Workers (NASW)

750 First St. NE, Ste. 700
Washington, DC 20002-4241
Ph: (202)408-8600   Fax: (202)336-8312
Fr: 800-638-8799

Members: Regular members are persons who hold a minimum of a baccalaureate degree in social work. Associate members are persons engaged in social work who have a baccalaureate degree in another field. Student members are persons enrolled in accredited graduate or undergraduate social work programs. **Purpose:** Purposes are to: create professional standards for social work practice; advocate sound public social policies through political and legislative action; provide a wide range of membership services, including continuing education opportunities and an extensive professional program.

★8014★ *What Do Social Workers Do?*

National Association of Social Workers
NASW Press
750 First St. NE, Ste. 700
Washington, DC 20002-4241
Ph: (202)408-8600

Video. $50.00.

Sociologists

SOURCES OF HELP-WANTED ADS

★8015★ The Gerontologist

Gerontological Society of America
1275 K St. NW, Ste. 350
Washington, DC 20005-4006
Ph: (202)842-1275   Fax: (202)842-1150

Bimonthly. $55.00/year for individuals. Journal presenting new concepts, clinical ideas, and applied research in gerntology. Includes book and audiovisual reviews.

★8016★ Perspective on Aging

National Council of the Aging
409 3rd St. SW, 2nd Fl.
Washington, DC 20024
Ph: (202)479-1200

Quarterly. $90.00/year.

PLACEMENT AND JOB REFERRAL SERVICES

★8017★ American Society of Criminology (ASC)

1314 Kinnear Rd., Ste. 212
Columbus, OH 43212
Ph: (614)292-9207   Fax: (614)292-6767

Members: Professional and academic criminologists; students of criminology in accredited universities; psychiatrists, psychologists, and sociologists. **Purpose:** To develop criminology as a science and academic discipline; to aid in the construction of criminological curricula in accredited universities; to upgrade the practitioner in criminological fields (police, prisons, probation, parole, delinquency workers). Conducts research programs; sponsors three student paper competitions. **Activities:** Provides placement service at annual convention.

★8018★ Social Sciences Services and Resources

PO Box 153
Wasco, IL 60183
Ph: (708)897-5345

Members: Consulting associates in social sciences. **Purpose:** Established to advance the teaching, consulting, and practice of the social sciences basic disciplines including sociology, anthropology, political science, geography, history, economics, and their applied disciplines: social work, community development, planning, and public administration. Serves as: a center for dissemination of current and comprehensive social research findings. Provides consultants for citizen groups, community projects, and governmental units on written request. Upon request from colleges, school boards, and citizens groups, conducts in-service workshops on teaching, consulting, and new developments in the social sciences. Provides consultant evaluation services for small colleges throughout the U.S. **Activities:** Maintains speakers' bureau and placement information service. Conducts research programs.

★8019★ Sociological Practice Association (SPA)

Department of Pediatrics/Human
  Development
Michigan State University
B140 Life Sciences
East Lansing, MI 48824
Ph: (517)353-0709   Fax: (517)355-1679

Purpose: Promotes the application of sociology to individual and social change and advances theory, research, and methods to this end; develops opportunities for the employment and use of clinically trained sociologists; provides a common ground for sociological practitioners, allied professionals, and interested scholars and students. Promotes training and educational opportunities to further sociological practice. **Activities:** Sponsors sessions and programs in clinical and applied sociology at national and regional meetings of other sociological associations. Has conducted a survey on skills, licenses, education, and experience of members. Conducts national certification program. **E-Mail:** 13642kal@msu.edu

★8020★ Sociologists for Women in Society (SWS)

Department of Soc.
Raleigh, NC 27695
Ph: (919)873-4950   Fax: (919)873-3301

Members: Members are mainly female professional sociologists and female students of sociology, though membership is open to any woman or man interested in the purposes of the organization. **Purpose:** Dedicated to: maximizing the effectiveness of and professional opportunities for women in sociology; exploring the contributions which sociology can, does, and should make to the investigation of and improvement in the status of women in society. Acts as watchdog of the American Sociological Association to ensure that it does not ignore the special needs of women in the profession. **Activities:** Has organized a job market service to bring potential jobs and applicants together; established a discrimination committee offering advice and organzational support for women who pursue cases charging sex discrimination; has aided women to establish social, professional, and intellectual contacts with each other. Conducts meetings of sociological societies.

EMPLOYER DIRECTORIES AND NETWORKING LISTS

★8021★ American Sociological Association—Biographical Directory of Members

American Sociological Association
1722 N St. NW
Washington, DC 20036
Ph: (202)833-3410   Fax: (202)785-0146
Fr: 800-877-2693

Biennial, May of even years. $48.00, payment with order. Covers 13,858 sociologists, worldwide. Entries include: Member name, preferred mailing address, educational background, and section memberships. Only the 1990 issue is biographical, others are cited as American Sociological Association Directory of Members. Arrangement: Alphabetical. Indexes: Geographical.

★8022★ Christian Association for Psychological Studies International— Membership Directory

Christian Association for Psychological Studies
PO Box 310400
New Braunfels, TX 78131-0400
Ph: (210)629-2277   Fax: (210)629-2342

Biennial, May, even years. $10.00. Covers 2,300 Christians involved in psychology, psychiatry, counseling, sociology, social work, ministry, and nursing. Entries include: Name, office address and phone number, highest degree held, area of occupational specialization, and career data. Arrangement: Geographical. Indexes: Alphabetical.

HANDBOOKS AND MANUALS

★8023★ Career Information Center

Macmillan Publishing Co.
200 Old Tappan Rd.
Old Tappan, NJ 07675
Ph: (609)461-6500   Fr: 800-223-2336

Visual Education Center Staff. Fifth edition, 1992. $229.00. This 13-volume set profiles over 600 occupations. Each occupational profile describes job duties, educational requirements, how to get the job, advancement possibilities, employment outlook, working conditions, earnings and benefits, and where to write for more information.

★8024★ Careers in Health Care

VGM Career Horizons
4255 W. Touhy Ave.
Lincolnwood, IL 60646-1975
Ph: (847)679-5500   Fax: (847)679-2494
Fr: 800-323-4900

Barbara M. Swanson. 1995. $17.95; $13.95 (paper). Describes job duties, work settings, salaries, licensing and certification requirements, educational preparation, and future outlook. Gives ideas on how to secure a job.

★8025★ Careers in Health and Fitness

Rosen Publishing Group, Inc.
29 E. 21st St.
New York, NY 10010
Ph: (212)777-3017   Fax: (212)777-0277
Fr: 800-237-9932

Jackie Heron. Revised edition, 1990. $14.95. 160 pages. Contains occupational profiles for this field, including information on job duties, skills, advantages, basic equipment used, employment possibilities, certification, and salary.

★8026★ Careers in Sociology

American Sociological Association
1722 N St. NW
Washington, DC 20036

1995. Single copy free. 25 pages. Covers scope of sociology and areas of specializa-

tion. Lists career opportunities available to B.A.'s, M.A.'s, and Ph.D.'s.

★8027★ Careers in Sociology: Yes, You Can Get a Job with a Degree in Sociology

Allyn & Bacon, Inc.
160 Gould St.
Needham Heights, MA 02194-2310
Ph: (617)455-1200   Fax: (617)455-1294

W. Richard Stephens. 1994.

★8028★ Embarking upon a Career with an Undergraduate Sociology Major

American Sociological Association
1722 N St., NW
Washington, DC 20036

Billson and Huber. 1993. $6.00. 65 pages. Aimed at the new college graduate with a sociology major. Reviews job search strategies.

★8029★ Encyclopedia of Careers and Vocational Guidance

J. G. Ferguson Publishing Co.
200 W. Monroe, Ste. 250
Chicago, IL 60606
Ph: (312)580-5480

William E. Hopke. Ninth edition, 1993. $129.95; $199.95 (CD-ROM). Four-volume set that profiles 900 occupations and describes job trends in 71 industries. Includes career description, educational requirements, history of the job, methods of entry, advancement, employment outlook, earnings, conditions of work, social and psychological factors, and sources of further information. Contains career and employment information for this field.

★8030★ Opportunities in Gerontology and Aging Services Careers

VGM Career Horizons
4255 W. Touhy Ave.
Lincolnwood, IL 60646-1975
Ph: (847)679-5500   Fax: (847)679-2494
Fr: 800-323-4900

Ellen Williams. 1995. $14.95; $11.95 (paper). 160 pages. Covers jobs in community, health and medical programs, financial, legal, residential, travel and tourism, and counseling, and how to go after them. Includes bibliography and illustrations.

★8031★ Opportunities in Social Science Careers

VGM Career Horizons
4255 W. Touhy Ave.
Lincolnwood, IL 60646-1975
Ph: (847)679-5500   Fax: (847)679-2494
Fr: 800-323-4900

Rosanne J. Marek. 1990. $14.95; $11.95 (paper). 160 pages. Profiles job opportunities in education, government, and business, along with their salary levels and outlook in the years to come. Illustrated.

OTHER SOURCES

★8032★ American Sociological Association (ASA)

1722 N St. NW
Washington, DC 20036
Ph: (202)833-3410   Fax: (202)785-0146

Members: Sociologists, social scientists, and others interested in research, teaching, and application of sociology; graduate and undergraduate sociology students. **Activities:** Compiles statistics. Operates the ASA Teaching Resources Center, which develops a variety of materials useful in teaching sociology. Sponsors Minority Fellowship and Professional Development Programs and Teaching Project. Maintains 37 sections including: Aging; Criminology; Medical; Population.

★8033★ Population Association of America (PAA)

1722 N St. NW
Washington, DC 20036
Ph: (202)429-0891   Fax: (202)785-0146

Purpose: Professional society of individuals interested in demography and its scientific aspects.

★8034★ Rural Sociological Society (RSS)

Institute for Environmental Studies
1101 W. Peabody Dr.
Urbana, IL 61801-4723
Ph: (217)333-2916   Fax: (217)333-8046

Members: Educators and others employed in the field of rural sociology. **Purpose:** Promotes the development of rural sociology through research, teaching, and extension work. **E-Mail:** burdge@ux1.cso.uiuc.edu

★8035★ Sociological Research Association (SRA)

1722 N St. NW
Washington, DC 20036
Ph: (202)833-3410   Fax: (202)785-0146

Members: Persons, elected from membership of the American Sociological Association, who have made significant contributions to sociological research, other than a doctoral dissertation, and who maintain an active interest in the advancement of sociological knowledge.

Software Engineers

SOURCES OF HELP-WANTED ADS

★8036★ BYTE

McGraw-Hill, Inc.
1 Phoenix Mill Ln.
Peterborough, NH 03458
Ph: (603)924-9281   Fax: (603)924-2550
Fr: 800-232-2983

Monthly. Magazine covering microcomputing for major brands of hardware and software. Includes reviews, features, and technology news for experienced and knowledgeable purchasers and users of microcomputers.

★8037★ Captsule Job Listings

Publications and Communications, Inc.
12416 Hymeadow Dr.
Austin, TX 78750
Ph: (512)250-9023   Fax: (512)331-3900
Fr: 800-678-9724

Online database. Lists current job openings in the contract (temporary) technical services industry. Includes the Action Hot List, which provides information on job seekers. Includes employment opportunities in technical/professional engineering, computing, and design/drafting. Entries generally contain company name, address, and job opening.

★8038★ Computer

IEEE Computer Society
1730 Massachusetts Ave. NW
Washington, DC 20036
Ph: (202)371-0101

Monthly. Covers major trends in computer science and engineering.

★8039★ Computerworld

500 Old Connecticut Path
Framingham, MA 01701-9208
Ph: (508)872-0080   Fax: (508)879-7784
Fr: 800-669-1002

Weekly. $48.00/year; $6.00/issue. Newspaper for information systems management professionals.

★8040★ Data Based Advisor

Data Based Solutions, Inc.
4010 Morena Blvd., Ste. 200
San Diego, CA 92117
Ph: (619)483-6400   Fax: (619)483-9851

Monthly. $35.00/year for individuals. Magazine covering microcomputer database management system topics; offering software reviews and programming tips and techniques.

★8041★ Database Programming and Design

Miller Freeman, Inc.
600 Harrison St.
San Francisco, CA 94107
Ph: (415)905-2200

Monthly. Computer magazine.

★8042★ High Technology Careers Magazine

HTC
4701 Patrick Henry Dr., No. 1901
Santa Clara, CA 95054
Ph: (408)970-8800   Fax: (408)980-5103

Bimonthly. Magazine (tabloid) containing employment opportunity information for the engineering and technical community.

★8043★ IEEE Software

IEEE Computer Society
10662 Los Vaqueros Cir.
PO Box 3014
Los Alamitos, CA 90720-3014
Ph: (714)821-8380   Fax: (714)821-4010
Fr: 800-272-6657

Bimonthly. $25.00/year for individuals. Magazine covering the computer software industry.

★8044★ Minority Engineer

Equal Opportunity Publications, Inc.
150 Motor Pkwy., Ste. 420
Hauppauge, NY 11788-5145
Ph: (516)273-0066   Fax: (516)273-8936

Affirmative-action recruitment magazine serving college graduating and professional minority engineers.

★8045★ Software

John Wiley and Sons, Inc.
605 3rd Ave.
New York, NY 10158
Ph: (212)850-6000   Fax: (212)850-6799

Monthly. $825.00/year. Journal for those who design, implement, or maintain computer software.

★8046★ SWE

Society of Women Engineers
120 Wall St., 11th Fl.
New York, NY 10005-3902
Ph: (212)509-9577   Fax: (212)509-0224

Bimonthly. $30.00/year for nonmembers. Magazine for engineering students and for women and men working in the engineering and technology fields. Covers career guidance, continuing development and topical issues.

★8047★ Woman Engineer

Equal Opportunity Publications, Inc.
150 Motor Pkwy., Ste. 420
Hauppauge, NY 11788-5145
Ph: (516)273-0066   Fax: (516)273-8936

Engineer recruitment magazine.

PLACEMENT AND JOB REFERRAL SERVICES

★8048★ American Indian Science and Engineering Society (AISES)

1630 30th St., Ste. 301
Boulder, CO 80301
Ph: (303)492-8658   Fax: (303)492-3400

Members: American Indian and non-Indian students and professionals in science, technology, and engineering fields; corporations representing energy, mining, aerospace, electronic, and computer fields. **Purpose:** Seeks to motivate and encourage students to pursue undergraduate and graduate studies in science, engineering, and technology. **Activities:** Sponsors science fairs in grade schools, teacher training workshops, summer math/science sessions for 8th-12th graders, professional chapters, and student chapters in colleges. Offers scholarships. Adult members serve as role models, advisers, and mentors for students. Operates placement service. **E-Mail:** aise sha@spot.colorado.edu

★8049★ Engineering Society of Detroit (ESD)

100 Farnsworth Ave.
Detroit, MI 48202
Ph: (313)832-5400   Fax: (313)832-5920

Members: Engineers from all disciplines; scientists and technologists. **Activities:** Offers placement services. Conducts technical programs and engineering refresher courses; sponsors conferences and expositions. Maintains speakers' bureau. Although based in Detroit, MI, society membership is international.

★8050★ Korean Scientists and Engineers Association in America (KSEA)

6261 Executive Blvd.
Rockville, MD 20852
Ph: (301)984-7048   Fax: (301)984-1231

Members: Scientists and engineers holding single or advanced degrees. **Purpose:** Goals are to: promote friendship and mutuality among Korean and American scientists and engineers; contribute to Korea's scientific, technological, industrial, and economic developments; strengthen the scientific, technological, and cultural bonds between Korea and the U.S. Sponsors symposium. **Activities:** Maintains speakers' bureau, placement service, and biographical archives. Compiles statistics. Maintains 100 volume library of scientific handbooks and yearbooks in Korean.

★8051★ Society of Hispanic Professional Engineers (SHPE)

5400 E. Olympic Blvd., Ste. 210
Los Angeles, CA 90022
Ph: (213)725-3970

Purpose: Engineers, student engineers, and scientists seeking to increase the number of Hispanic engineers by providing motivation and support to students. Sponsors competitions and educational programs. **Activities:** Maintains placement service and speakers' bureau; compiles statistics.

EMPLOYER DIRECTORIES AND NETWORKING LISTS

★8052★ American Men and Women of Science

R. R. Bowker Co.
Reed Reference Publishing
121 Chanlon Rd.
New Providence, NJ 07974
Ph: (908)464-6800   Fax: (908)665-6688
Fr: 800-521-8110

Triennial, latest edition January 1995. $106.00, per volume; $850.00, set. Covers over 123,000 U.S. and Canadian scientists active in the physical, biological, mathematical, computer science, and engineering fields; includes references to previous edition for deceased scientists and nonrespondents. Entries include: Name, address, education, personal and career data, memberships, honors and awards, research interest. Arrangement: Alphabetical. Indexes: Discipline (in separate volume).

★8053★ CD-ROM Information Products: An Evaluative Guide & Directory

Ashgate Publishing Co.
Old Post Rd.
Brookfield, VT 05036
Ph: (802)276-3162   Fax: (802)276-3837
Fr: 800-535-9544

Quarterly. $35.00, per issue; $110.00. Publication includes: List of CD-ROM publishers, producers, and distributors. Entries include: Publisher or distributor name, address, phone, database type, pricing information, product evaluation. Indexes: Title.

★8054★ Computer Directory

Computer Directories, Inc.
13205 Cypress N. Houston Rd.
Cypress, TX 77429-3606
Ph: (713)955-9791   Fax: (713)955-9793
Fr: 800-234-4353

Annual, fall. Covers Approximately 130,000 computer installations; 19 separate volumes for Alaska/Hawaii, Connecticut/New Jersey, Dallas/Ft. Worth, Eastern Seaboard, Far Midwest, Houston, Illinois, Midatlantic, Midcentral, Mideast, Minnesota/Wisconsin, North Central, New England, New York Metro, Northwest, Ohio, Pennsylvania/West Virginia, Southeast, and Southwest Texas. Entries include: Company name, address, phone, fax, name and title of contact, hardware used, software application, operating system, programming language, computer graphics, networking system. Arrangement: Geographical. Indexes: Alphabetical, industry, hardware.

★8055★ The Computer Industry Directory

Mentor Market Research
6214 Meridian Ave.
San Jose, CA 95120
Ph: (408)268-6333

Published June 1991. $49.95. Covers over 6,400 companies producing or distributing computer hardware or software products in the U.S. Entries include: Company name, address, phone, line of business, products and services, names and titles of key personnel. Arrangement: Alphabetical. Indexes: Product, geographical.

★8056★ Computers and People— Computer Directory and Buyers' Guide Issue

Berkeley Enterprises, Inc.
368 Crescent St., No. 2
Waltham, MA 02154-3804

Annual, October. $24.50, plus $1.00 shipping. Publication includes: List of over 3,600 companies offering hardware, software, and computing or data processing services; societies and associations in computer fields. Entries include: For companies: name, address, phone, products or services; some have name of principal executive or contact person, number of employees, year established, year information was verified. For organizations: name, address, phone, name of president or secretary. Arrangement: Alphabetical. Indexes: Product or service.

★8057★ Computing and Software Design Career Directory

Gale Research
835 Penobscot Bldg.
Detroit, MI 48226-4094
Ph: (313)961-2242   Fax: (313)961-6083
Fr: 800-877-GALE

Latest edition 1993. $34.00; $17.95 (paper). Covers over 200 companies and organizations with entry-level opportunities as computer programmers, software engineers, technical writers, information center analysts, and similar positions; sources of help-wanted ads, professional associations, producers of videos, databases, career guides, and professional guides and handbooks. Entries include: For companies and organizations: name, address, phone, business description, names and titles of key personnel, number of employees, average number of entry-level positions available, human resources contact, description of internship opportunities including contact, type and number available, application procedures, qualifications, and duties. For others: name or title, address, phone, description. Paperback edition is available from Visible Ink Press. Arrangement: Companies and organizations are alphabetical; others are classified by type of resource. Indexes: Name, keyword.

★8058★ Directory of Contract Service Firms

C. E. Publications, Inc.
PO Box 97000
Kirkland, WA 98083
Ph: (206)823-2222   Fax: (206)821-0942

Annual, January. $10.00. Covers Approximately 900 contract firms actively engaged in the employment of engineering and technical personnel for temporary contract assignments throughout the world. Entries include: Company name, address, phone, name of contact. Arrangement: Alphabetical. Indexes: Geographical.

★8059★ Directory of Engineers in Private Practice

National Society of Professional Engineers
1420 King St.
Alexandria, VA 22314
Ph: (703)684-2862   Fax: (703)836-4875

Annual. $85.00. Covers 600 consulting engineering firms and 7,200 individuals who are members of the society's Professional Engineers in Private Practice division. Entries include: For companies, name, address, phone, name of principal executive, list of services. For individuals, name, address; most listings include phone. Arrangement: Firms are geographic, then by specialty; individuals are alphabetical.

★8060★ Directory of Multi-Media Systems and Software

International Management Services, Inc.
363 E. Central St.
Franklin, MA 02038-1300
Ph: (508)520-1555   Fax: (508)520-1558

Annual, March. $135.00. Covers Approximately 200 companies that manufacture or service products used in building and presenting multi-media programs; international coverage. Entries include: Company name, address, phone, descriptions of services, product/service. Arrangement: Classified by product/service. Indexes: Alphabetical.

★8061★ Directory of Software Data Sources

ERIC Document Reproduction Service
7420 Fullerton Rd. Ste. 110
Springfield, VA 22153-2852
Ph: (703)440-1400   Fax: (703)440-1408
Fr: 800-443-ERIC

Covers Companys that provide databases that describe software and other technological products designed for use in special education. Entries include: Name, address, phone of companys, description of product/service, name and title of contact. Arrangement: Alphabetical.

★8062★ GIS Markets and Opportunities

Daratech, Inc.
140 6th St.
Cambridge, MA 02142-1048
Ph: (617)354-2339   Fax: (617)354-7822

Annual, September. $2,850.00. Covers over 250 geographic information system software vendors and products. Entries include: Company name, address, phone, names and titles of key personnel, number of employees, geographical area served, financial data, subsidiary and branch names and locations, description of software. Arrangement: Alphabetical. Indexes: Name, product.

★8063★ The Hidden Job Market: A Job Seeker's Guide to America's 2,000 Little-Known, Fastest-Growing High-Tech Companies

Peterson's Guides, Inc.
202 Carnegie Center
PO Box 2123
Princeton, NJ 08543-2123
Ph: (609)243-9111   Fax: (609)243-9150
Fr: 800-338-3282

Annual, October. $16.95. Covers Approximately 2,000 technology firms with under 1,000 employees, which have added the most employees in the survey year. Entries include: Company name, address, phone, fax, name and title of contact, number of employees, year founded, number of employees added in last year, percentage of growth, line of business. Arrangement: Geographical by state, then by area code. Indexes: Alphabetical by industry.

★8064★ How and Where to Get the Best Computer Jobs

Information Resource Group
50495 Corporate Dr., Ste. 112
Shelby Township, MI 48315
Ph: (810)254-8500   Fax: (810)254-8500

Annual. $69.95. per directory. Publication includes: Listing of the top dataprocessing employers in United States and Canada. Information divided among 67 editions, according to state/province. Principal content of publication is hiring/interview tips, salary surveys. Entries include: Company name, address, phone, name and title of contact. Arrangement: Geographical.

★8065★ Information Sources: The IIA Annual Directory

Information Industry Association (IIA)
555 New Jersey Ave. NW, Ste. 800
Washington, DC 20001
Ph: (202)639-8262   Fax: (202)638-4403

Annual, November. $95.00. Covers more than 500 companies involved in the creation, distribution, and use of information products, services, and technology. Entries are prepared by companies described. Entries include: Company name, address, phone, names of executives, international partners, regional offices, trade and brand names, and description of products and services. Arrangement: Alphabetical. Indexes: Product, personal name, trade name, geographical, corporate parents, international and niche markets.

★8066★ ISDN (Integrated Services Digital Network) Directory and Sourcebook

Phillips Business Information, Inc.
1201 Seven Locks Rd., Ste. 300
Potomac, MD 20854
Ph: (301)424-3338   Fax: (301)424-4297
Fr: 800-777-5006

Annual. $167.00. Covers hardware and software providers and technical services of the integrated services digital network.

★8067★ Manitoba Directory of Software Capabilities

Electronics & Information Association of Manitoba
Unit 68-1313 Border St.
Winnipeg, MB, Canada R3H 0X4
Ph: (204)697-6020   Fax: (204)697-6025

Annual. $15.00. Covers Approximately 100 software development companies in Manitoba. Entries include: Company name, address, phone, fax, telex, name and title of contact, names and titles of key personnel, number of employees, geographical area served, description of product/service. Arrangement: Alphabetical. Indexes: Product/service, company name, product name.

★8068★ Microsearch

Information, Inc.
7700 Old Georgetown Rd., 7th Fl.
Bethesda, MD 20814
Ph: (301)215-4688   Fax: (301)215-4600

Since 1981. 500 records biweekly. Database covers: Directory of about 8,500 computer hardware manufacturers and software publishers. Database includes: Company name, address, phone.

★8069★ Northwest High Tech: Fast Facts on the $7 Billion Computer Industry of Washington, Oregon, Idaho, British Columbia, and Alberta

Resolution Business Press
11101 NE 8th St., Ste. 208
Bellevue, WA 98004
Ph: (206)455-4611   Fax: (206)455-9143

Annual. $34.95. Covers over 1,800 computer-related companies in Washington, Oregon, and Idaho, and British Columbia and Alberta, Canada. Entries include: Company; name, address, phone, fax; toll-free number; names and titles of key personnel; product/service, programming languages, financial data, names and titles of key personnel, number of employees, operating systems, expansion plans (including hiring and site expansion plans), company market information, Standard Industrial Classification (SIC) code. Arrangement: Geographical, industry sector. Indexes: Company name, SIC.

★8070★ Saskatchewan Software Directory

Communications Branch
Saskatchewan Economic Development
1919 Saskatchewan Dr.
Regina, SK, Canada S4P 3V7
Ph: (306)787-1619   Fax: (306)787-8447

Latest edition March 1992. Free. Covers over 80 software developers in Saskatchewan, Canada. Entries include: Company name, address, phone, fax, names and titles of key personnel, subsidiary and branch names and locations, programming environments, work experience, principal sectors, description of products. Arrangement: Alphabetical. Indexes: Name, market sector.

★8071★ Scientific and Technical Organizations and Agencies Directory

Gale Research
835 Penobscot Bldg.
Detroit, MI 48226-4094
Ph: (313)961-2242   Fax: (313)961-6083
Fr: 800-877-GALE

Irregular; latest edition December 1993. $195.00. Covers over 25,600 national and international organizations and agencies concerned with the physical and applied sciences, engineering, and technology, including associations, computer information services, consulting firms, educational institutions, foundations, government advisory organizations, federal government agencies, general grant and assistance programs, libraries and information centers, patent sources and services, research and development centers, scholarships, fellowships, and loans, science-technology centers, standards organizations, state academies of science, and state government agencies in the fields of aeronautics and space sciences, chemistry, computer science specialties, electronics, geography, geology, machinery, mathematics, metallurgy, meteorology, mineralogy, nuclear science, petroleum and gas, physics, plastics, transportation, water resources, and other areas. Entries include: Organization name, address, phone, and name of contact; additional descriptive text for most entries. Arrangement: Classified by type of organization. Indexes: Organization name/ key word.

HANDBOOKS AND MANUALS

★8072★ ASIS Jobline

American Society for Information Science (ASIS)
8720 Georgia Ave., Ste. 501
Silver Spring, MD 20910
Ph: (301)495-0900

Monthly periodical provides job listings in information science.

★8073★ The Best Home-Based Businesses for the 90s

G.P. Putnam's Sons
Putnam Berkley Group
200 Madison Ave.
New York, NY 10016
Ph: (212)951-8400   Fr: 800-631-8571

Paul Edwards and Sarah Edwards. Second edition, 1994. $12.95. 400 pages. Profiles 95 businesses and careers that can be conducted from one's home. Lists sources of additional information.

★8074★ Career Choices for the 90's for Students of Computer Science

Walker and Company
435 Hudson St.
New York, NY 10014
Ph: (212)727-8300   Fax: (212)727-0984
Fr: 800-289-2553

Prepared by the Career Associates staff. 1990. $8.95. 166 pages. Discusses alternatives for students of computer science. Offers advice on how to break into the field and how to move up. Covers where and who the employers are, internship possibilities, and professional networking associations. Comprehensive guide to career and job search planning.

★8075★ Career Portraits: Computers

VGM Career Horizons
NTC Publishing Group
4255 W. Touhy Ave.
Lincolnwood, IL 60646-1975
Ph: (847)679-5500   Fax: (847)679-2494
Fr: 800-323-4900

Marjorie Eberts and Margaret Gisler. 1995. $13.95. 96 pages. Designed to capture the interest of middle school and reluctant readers.

★8076★ Careers for Computer Buffs and Other Technological Types

NTC Publishing Group
4255 W. Touhy Ave.
Lincolnwood, IL 60646-1975
Ph: (708)679-5500   Fax: (708)679-6375
Fr: 800-323-4900

Marjorie Eberts. 1994. $12.95; $9.95 (paper).

★8077★ Careers in Computers

VGM Career Horizons
4255 W. Touhy Ave.
Lincolnwood, IL 60646-1975
Ph: (847)679-5500   Fax: (847)679-2494
Fr: 800-323-4900

Lila B. Stair. Second edition, 1995. $17.95; $13.95 (paper). Describes trends affecting computer careers and explores a wide range of job opportunities from programming to consulting. Provides job qualifications, salary data, job market information, personal and educational requirements, career paths, and the place of the job in the organizational structure. Offers advice on education, certification, and job search.

★8078★ Careers in High Tech

VGM Career Horizons
NTC Publishing Group
4255 W. Touhy Ave.
Lincolnwood, IL 60646-1975
Ph: (847)679-5500   Fax: (847)679-2494
Fr: 800-323-4900

Nick Basta. 1994. $17.95; $13.95 (paper). 160 pages. Examines new career opportunities in such fields as biotechnology, computers, aerospace, telecommunications, and others.

★8079★ Careers in Information Science

American Society for Information Science (ASIS)
8720 Georgia Ave., Ste. 501
Silver Spring, MD 20910
Ph: (301)495-0900

Free brochure describes career opportunities in information science, communications, computer science, and research.

★8080★ Careers Inside the World of Technology

Rosen Publishing Group, Inc.
29 E. 21st St.
New York, NY 10010
Ph: (212)777-3017   Fax: (212)777-0277
Fr: 800-237-9932

Jean Spencer. 1995. $14.95. 64 pages. Describes computerrelated careers for reluctant readers.

★8081★ Careers for Number Crunchers and Other Quantitative Types

VGM Career Horizons
4255 W. Touhy Ave.
Lincolnwood, IL 60646-1975
Ph: (847)679-5500   Fax: (847)679-2494
Fr: 800-323-4900

Rebecca Burnett. 1993. $14.95; $9.95 (paper). Provides information to math-oriented job hunters on how to become statisticians, field researchers, computer programmers, stock analysts, investment managers, bankers, engineers, accountants, underwriters, economists, market analysts, mathematicians, systems analysts, and more.

★8082★ Careers in Science

VGM Career Horizons
4255 W. Touhy Ave.
Lincolnwood, IL 60646-1975
Ph: (847)679-5500   Fax: (847)679-2494
Fr: 800-323-4900

Thomas Easton. Third edition, 1996. 192 pages. $17.95; $13.95 (paper). Discusses careers in life science, earth science, physical and space science, social science, engineering, mathematics, and computer science. Offers job hunting advice.

★8083★ Computer Careers

Data Processing Management Association
505 Busse Hwy.
PArk Ridge, IL 60068
Ph: (708)825-8124

Free booklet.

★8084★ Computer Science and Related Fields

AMIDEAST
1100 17th St. NW
Washington, DC 20036-4601
Ph: (202)776-9600

$1.15. 4 pages. Describes career opportunities, educational programs, and additional sources of information.

★8085★ Covin's Mid-West Computer Job Guide

Vandamere Press
PO Box 5243
Arlington, VA 22205
Ph: (703)525-5488   Fax: (703)524-4105

Carol L. Covin. 1994. $13.95 (paper).

★8086★ Encyclopedia of Careers and Vocational Guidance

J. G. Ferguson Publishing Co.
200 W. Monroe, Ste. 250
Chicago, IL 60606
Ph: (312)580-5480

William E. Hopke. Ninth edition, 1993. $129.95; $199.95 (CD-ROM). Four-volume set that profiles 900 occupations and describes job trends in 71 industries. Includes career description, educational requirements, history of the job, methods of entry, advancement, employment outlook, earnings, conditions of work, social and psychological factors, and sources of further information. Contains career and employment information for this field.

★8087★ Engineering Success

Kendall Hunt Publishing
4050 Westmark Dr.
PO Box 1840
Dubuque, IA 52004-1840
Ph: (319)589-1000   Fax: 800-772-9165
Fr: 800-228-0810

Bill Osher. 1994. $27.96.

★8088★ **Engineering Your Job Search: A Job-Finding Resource for Engineering Professionals**
Professional Publications, Inc.
1250 5th Ave.
Belmont, CA 94002
Ph: (415)593-9119   Fax: (415)592-4519
Fr: 800-426-1178

Compiled by Professional Publications editors. 1995. $12.95 (paper).

★8089★ **Exploring Careers in the Computer Field**
Rosen Publishing Group, Inc.
29 E. 21st St.
New York, NY 10010
Ph: (212)777-3017   Fax: (212)777-0277
Fr: 800-237-9932

Joseph Weintraub. Revised edition, 1993. Discusses entry into the field, salaries, future trends, and offers job search advice. Surveys the newest growth areas in the computer industry including artificial intelligence, desktop publishing, and personal computers.

★8090★ **Exploring High-Tech Careers**
Rosen Publishing Group, Inc.
29 E. 21st St.
New York, NY 10010
Ph: (212)777-3017   Fax: (212)777-0277
Fr: 800-237-9932

Scott Southworth. Revised edition, 1993. $14.95; $9.95 (paper). 118 pages. Gives an orientation to the field of high technology and high-tech jobs. Describes educational preparation and job hunting. Includes a glossary and bibliography.

★8091★ **Job Opportunities in Engineering and Technology**
Peterson's Guides, Inc.
PO Box 2123
Princeton, NJ 08543-2123
Ph: (609)243-9111   Fax: (609)243-9150
Fr: 800-338-3282

1994. $18.95 (paper).

★8092★ **Jobs Rated Almanac: Ranks the Best and Worst Jobs by More Than a Dozen Vital Criteria**
John Wiley and Sons
605 Third Ave.
New York, NY 10158-0012
Ph: (212)850-6000   Fr: 800-225-5945

Les Krantz. Third edition, 1995. $16.95. 340 pages. Ranks 250 jobs by environment, salary, outlook, physical demands, stress, security, travel opportunities, and geographic location.

★8093★ **Majoring in Engineering: How to Get from Your Freshman Year to Your First Job**
Farrar, Straus & Giroux, Inc.
19 Union Sq., W
New York, NY 10003
Ph: (212)741-6900   Fr: 800-788-6262

John Garcia. 1995. $20.00; $10.00 (paper).

★8094★ **The 100 Best Jobs for the 1990s and Beyond**
Berkley Publishing Group
PO Box 506
East Rutherford, NJ 07073
Ph: (201)933-9292   Fr: 800-223-0510

Carol Kleiman. 1994. $5.50. 300 pages.

★8095★ **Opportunities in Computer Science Careers**
VGM Career Horizons
4255 W. Touhy Ave.
Lincolnwood, IL 60646-1975
Ph: (847)679-5500   Fax: (847)679-2494
Fr: 800-323-4900

Julie Lepick Kling. 1995. $14.95; $11.95 (paper). Discusses how to enter the field and build a career. Illustrated.

★8096★ **Opportunities in Engineering Careers**
VGM Career Horizons
4255 W. Touhy Ave.
Lincolnwood, IL 60646-1975
Ph: (847)679-5500   Fax: (847)679-2494
Fr: 800-323-4900

Nicholas Basta. 1995. $14.95; $11.95 (paper). Outlines typical job titles, salaries, career paths, and employment prospects.

★8097★ **Opportunities in High Tech Careers**
VGM Career Horizons
4255 W. Touhy Ave.
Lincolnwood, IL 60646-1975
Ph: (847)679-5500   Fax: (847)679-2494
Fr: 800-323-4900

Gary D. Golter and Deborah Yanuck. 1995. $14.95; $11.95 (paper). 160 pages. Explores high technology careers. Describes job opportunities, how to make a career decision, how to prepare for high technology jobs, job hunting techniques, and future trends.

★8098★ **Peterson's Hidden Job Market 1996**
Peterson's
PO Box 2123
Princeton, NJ 08543-2123
Ph: (609)243-9111   Fax: (609)243-9150
Fr: 800-338-3282

Fifth edition, 1995. $17.95. Guide to 2,000 fast-growing companies that are hiring now. Focuses on high technology companies in such fields as environmental consulting, genetic engineering, home health care, telecommunications, alternative energy systems, and others.

★8099★ **Peterson's Job Opportunities in Engineering and Technology 1996**
Peterson's
PO Box 2123
Princeton, NJ 08543-2123
Ph: (609)243-9111   Fax: (609)243-9150
Fr: 800-338-3282

Compiled by the Peterson's staff. Annual. $19.95 paperback. 432 pages. Profiles 2,000 high-tech companies looking primarily for technical personnel in such fields as biotechnology, telecommunications, software, computers and peripherals, defense, and aerospace. Contains job-search strategies and

career options to help match education and expertise to the job market. Indexed geographically, by industry, and by hiring needs.

★8100★ **Professional Awareness in Software Engineering: Or Should a Software Engineer Wear a Suit?**
The McGraw-Hill Companies
1221 Avenue of the Americas
New York, NY 10020
Ph: (212)512-2000   Fr: 800-262-4729

Colin Myers, editor. 1995.

★8101★ **Software Engineer's Reference Book**
CRC Press, Inc.
2000 Corporate Blvd. NW
Boca Raton, FL 33431
Ph: (407)997-0555   Fax: (407)997-0949
Fr: 800-272-7737

John A. McDermid, editor. 1993. $86.00.

★8102★ **Where the Jobs Are: The Hottest Careers for the '90s**
The Career Press, Inc.
3 Tice Rd.
PO Box 687
Franklin Lakes, NJ 07417
Ph: (201)848-0310   Fax: (201)848-1727
Fr: 800-237-3371

Joyce Hadley. Second edition, 1995. $9.99. 300 pages. Describes careers in fifteen general fields, from accounting to travel and hospitality.

★8103★ **Your Opportunities in Computers**
Energeia Publishing, Inc.
PO Box 985
Salem, OR 97308
Ph: (503)362-1480   Fax: (503)362-2123

John Tribbett. 1994. $2.00 (paper).

EMPLOYMENT AGENCIES AND SEARCH FIRMS

★8104★ **Amtec Engineering Corp.**
2749 Saturn St.
Brea, CA 92621
Ph: (714)993-1900   Fax: (714)993-2419
Employment agency.

★8105★ **Beard Management, Inc.**
245 Fifth Ave.
New York, NY 10016
Ph: (212)545-7777   Fax: (212)545-7796
Executive search firm.

★8106★ **Blake and Associates Executive Search**
PO Box 1425
Pleasantville, NJ 08232
Ph: (609)645-3330   Fax: (609)383-0320
Executive search firm.

★8107★ Career Development Services
14 Franklin St., Ste. 1200
Rochester, NY 14604
Ph: (716)325-2275   Fax: (716)325-2133
Employment agency.

★8108★ Cavan Systems Ltd.
10 Cuttermill Rd.
Great Neck, NY 11021
Ph: (516)487-7777   Fax: (516)487-7857
Executive search firm.

★8109★ Data Careers Personnel Services, Inc.
3320 4th Ave.
San Diego, CA 92103
Ph: (619)291-9994
Employment agency. Places staff on a regular or temporary basis.

★8110★ The Datafinders Group, Inc.
25 Spring Valley Ave.
Maywood, NJ 07607
Ph: (201)845-7700   Fax: (201)845-7365
Executive search firm.

★8111★ EHS and Associates, Inc.
3033 Excelsior Blvd., Ste. 303
Minneapolis, MN 55416
Ph: (612)924-2366   Fax: (612)924-2367
Executive search firm and employment agency.

★8112★ Erspamer Associates
7300 France Ave. S., Ste. 402
Edina, MN 55435
Ph: (612)831-5564   Fax: (612)831-5981
Executive search firm.

★8113★ Huntington Personnel Consultants, Inc.
PO Box 1077
Huntington, NY 11743-0640
Ph: (516)549-8888   Fax: (516)549-3012
Employment agency.

★8114★ JPM International
4665 MacArthur Ct., Ste. 100B
Newport Beach, CA 92660
Ph: (714)955-2545   Fax: (714)757-1320
Executive search firm and employment agency.

★8115★ JR Professional Search
PO Box 18356
Tucson, AZ 85731
Ph: (520)721-1855   Fax: (520)721-1855
Employment agency.

★8116★ Sue Carroll Personnel, Inc.
16 E. 79th St.
New York, NY 10021
Ph: (212)288-8866   Fax: (212)988-7191
Employment agency and executive search firm.

★8117★ Technical Talent Locators Ltd.
8850 Stanford Blvd., Ste. 3400
Columbia, MD 21045
Ph: (410)995-6051   Fax: (410)995-6281
Executive search firm.

★8118★ Version 2.0 Corp.
303 Congress St.
Boston, MA 02210
Ph: (617)439-0321
Executive search firm.

OTHER SOURCES

★8119★ American Association of Engineering Societies (AAES)
1111 19th St. NW, Ste. 608
Washington, DC 20036
Ph: (202)296-2237   Fax: (202)296-1151
Purpose: Seeks to promote leadership in public affairs for the engineering community, work in support of math and science education for young persons. Disseminates of information about the profession. Provides statistics about engineers.

★8120★ Association for Women in Computing (AWC)
41 Sutter St., Ste. 1006
San Francisco, CA 94104
Ph: (415)905-4663
Purpose: Individuals interested in promoting the education, professional development, and advancement of women in computing. E-Mail: awc@acm.org

★8121★ *Building a Successful Software Business*
New Careers Center
1515 23rd St.
Box 339-CT
Boulder, CO 80306
Ph: (303)447-1087
Radin. 1994. $19.95. Thorough treatment of the software development business.

★8122★ *Career Encounters: Information Science and Technology*
Cambridge Career Products
PO Box 2153
Dept. CC15
Charleston, WV 25328-2153
Ph: (304)744-9323   Fax: (304)744-9351
Fr: 800-468-4227
Video. $99.95. 25 minutes. Professionals shown in a variety of settings discuss different aspects of their careers.

★8123★ *The Computer Industry Almanac*
Computer Industry Almanac
225 Allen Way
Incline Village, NV 89451
Ph: (702)831-2288
Annual. $63.00. Also available on CD-ROM, $63.00. A compendium of information on the computer industry compiled from newsletters, reports, and magazines.

★8124★ *Computer Software Directory*
American Business Directories, Inc.
American Business Information, Inc.
5711 S. 86th Cir.
Omaha, NE 68127
Ph: (402)593-4600   Fax: (402)331-1505
Annual. $1,155.00, U.S. edition; $170.00, (Canad. ed.); payment with order. Entries include: Name, address, phone (including area code), size of advertisement, year first in Yellow Pages, name of owner or manager, number of employees. Regional editions available: Eastern, $685.00; Western, $610.00. Compiled from telephone company Yellow Pages, nationwide. Arrangement: Geographical.

★8125★ *Day in a Career: Computer Programmer*
Cambridge Career Products
PO Box 2153
Dept. CC15
Charleston, WV 25328-2153
Ph: (304)744-9323   Fax: (304)744-9351
Fr: 800-468-4227
Video. $89.00. About 20 minutes. Profile of a day in the life includes candid interviews and work situations, along with information on educational requirements, credentials, job outlook, salaries, contacts, and other aspects of the job.

★8126★ *Engineering Salary Survey*
Source Engineering
1290 Oakmead, Ste. 318
Sunnyvale, CA 94086
Ph: (408)738-8440
Annual. Discusses the structure of the engineering profession, trends, and compensation. Salaries are listed by job function, industry, and years of experience.

★8127★ *Entrepreneurial Software Engineering: A Practical Guide to Developing and Marketing Computer Software*
Ipser Publishing Co.
2616 Stadium Dr., Ste. 200
Fort Worth, TX 76109-1371
Ph: (817)927-2838   Fax: (817)927-0032
Edward A. Ipser, Jr. 1993. $24.95 (paper).

★8128★ *Graduating Engineer*
Peterson's/COG Publishing Group
16030 Ventura Blvd., No. 560
Encino, CA 91436
Ph: (818)789-5293
Eight issues/year. Magazine focusing on employment, education, and career development for entry-level engineers.

★8129★ *How to Start and Manage a Software Design Business: Step-by-Step Guide to Business Success*
Lewis & Renn Associates
10315 Harmony Dr.
Interlochen, MI 49643
Ph: (616)275-7287
Jerre G. Lewis. 1995. $9.95 (paper).

★8130★ International Journal of Software Engineering and Knowledge Engineering

World Scientific Publishing
1060 Main St., Ste. 1B
River Edge, NJ 07661
Ph: (201)487-9655   Fax: (201)487-9656
Fr: 800-227-7562

Quarterly. $198.00/year. Journal focusing on the interplay between software engineering and knowledge engineering.

★8131★ Journal of Software Maintenance

John Wiley and Sons, Inc.
605 3rd Ave.
New York, NY 10158
Ph: (212)850-6000   Fax: (212)850-6799

Bimonthly. $575.00/year. Journal devoted to maintaining the viability of software through swift software evolution cycles.

★8132★ Link-Up—New Lines Section

Learned Information, Inc.
143 Old Marlton Pike
Medford, NJ 08055-8750
Ph: (609)654-6266   Fax: (609)654-4309

Bimonthly. $3.00, per issue. Publication includes: List of companies offering new online services, databases, and computer software and hardware. Entries include: Company name, address, phone, description of product, price. Arrangement: Classified by product.

★8133★ Microsoft Systems Journal Buyers Guide

Miller Freeman Publications
600 Harrison St.
San Francisco, CA 94107
Ph: (415)206-0239   Fax: (415)905-2231

Annual. $10.00. Publication includes: List of companies that produce or distribute hardware and software compatible with Microsoft products. Arrangement: Alphabetical. Indexes: Company, product.

★8134★ National Action Council for Minorities in Engineering (NACME)

3 W. 35th St.
New York, NY 10001-2281
Ph: (212)279-2626   Fax: (212)629-5178

Purpose: Seeks to increase the number of African American, Latino, and Native American students enrolled in and graduating from engineering schools. Through the Corporate Scholars Program, offers comprehensive scholarships to engineering students that include leadership development, corporate mentors and summer internships. Works with local, regional, and national education organizations to motivate and encourage precollege students to engage in engineering careers. Conducts educational and research programs; operates project to assist engineering schools in improving the retention and graduation rates of minority students. Maintains speakers' bureau; compiles statistics.

★8135★ National Society of Professional Engineers (NSPE)

1420 King St.
Alexandria, VA 22314
Ph: (703)684-2800   Fax: (703)836-4875

Members: Professional engineers and engineers-in-training in all fields registered in accordance with the laws of states or territories of the U.S. or provinces of Canada; qualified graduate engineers, student members, and registered land surveyors. **Purpose:** Is concerned with social, professional, ethical, and economic considerations of engineering as a profession; encompasses programs in public relations, employment practices, ethical considerations, education, and career guidance. Monitors legislative and regulatory actions of interest to the engineering profession. **Website:** http://www.hspc.org

★8136★ Resumes for Computer Careers

VGM Career Horizons
NTC Publishing Group
4255 W. Touhy Ave.
Lincolnwood, IL 60646-1975
Ph: (847)679-5500   Fax: (847)679-2494
Fr: 800-323-4900

1996. $9.95. 160 pages. Offers complete instructions on producing quality resumes and cover letters for all areas and levels of the computer industry.

★8137★ Resumes for High Tech Careers

VGM Career Horizons
4255 W. Touhy Ave.
Lincolnwood, IL 60646-1975
Ph: (847)679-5500   Fax: (847)679-2494
Fr: 800-323-4900

1992. $9.95. 160 pages. Demonstrates how to tailor a resume that catches a high tech employer's attention.

★8138★ Resumes for Scientific and Technical Careers

VGM Career Horizons
NTC Publishing Group
4255 W. Touhy Ave.
Lincolnwood, IL 60646-1975
Ph: (847)679-5500   Fax: (847)679-2494
Fr: 800-323-4900

1994. $9.95. 160 pages. Provides resume advice for individuals interested in working in scientific and technical careers. Includes sample resumes and cover letters.

★8139★ Scientific Programming: Tools & Techniques

John Wiley and Sons, Inc.
605 3rd Ave.
New York, NY 10158
Ph: (212)850-6000   Fax: (212)850-8888
Fr: 800-225-5945

Quarterly. $180.00/year. Journal containing information on the practical experience of software engineering and scientific computing.

★8140★ Society of Women Engineers (SWE)

120 Wall St., 11th Fl.
New York, NY 10005
Ph: (212)509-9577   Fax: (212)509-0224

Members: Educational service society of women engineers; membership is also open to men. **Purpose:** Supplies information on the achievements of women engineers and the opportunities available to them; assists women engineers in preparing for return to active work following temporary retirement. Serves as an informational center on women in engineering. **Activities:** Administers several certificate and scholarship programs. Offers tours and career guidance; conducts surveys. Compiles statistics.

★8141★ The Software Encyclopedia

R. R. Bowker Co.
Reed Reference Publishing
121 Chanlon Rd.
New Providence, NJ 07974
Ph: (908)665-2848   Fax: (908)665-3502
Fr: 800-521-8110

Annual, February. $229.95. Covers over 16,000 software programs from over 3,000 publishers. Entries include: For software: title, version, release date, system requirements, price, ISBN, order number, description, publisher name. For publishers: company name, address, phone, toll-free phone, fax, ISBN prefix, titles. Arrangement: Two alphabetical sections for software, one by title, the other by system/application; also, one alphabetical section for publishers. Indexes: Title, system/application.

★8142★ Software Engineering Bibliography

Data & Analysis Center for Software
Kaman Sciences Corp.
PO Box 120
Utica, NY 13503
Ph: (315)734-3696   Fax: (315)734-3699

Annual, March. $30.00, postpaid, payment with order. Covers citation for over 533 technical reports, articles, theses, papers, and books concerned with software development and engineering. Entries include: Title, author name, publisher name and address, number of pages, other bibliographic information, and abstract. Arrangement: By document accession number. Indexes: Author, subject, keyword in context.

★8143★ Software Engineering Strategies

Auerbach Publishers
1 Penn Plaza
New York, NY 10119
Ph: (212)971-5000   Fax: (212)971-5025

$125.00/year. Journal covering software development.

★8144★ Software Process

John Wiley and Sons, Inc.
605 3rd Ave.
New York, NY 10158
Ph: (212)850-6000   Fax: (212)850-6799

$75.00/year. Journal for those involved in the software development process. Features experience reports, research papers, and critical discussion.

★8145★ Special Interest Group for Computers and the Physically Handicapped (SISCAPH)

Association for Computing Machinery
1515 Broadway, 17th Fl.
New York, NY 10036
Ph: (212)626-0613   Fax: (212)302-5826

Members: A special interest group of the Association of Computing Machinery. Physically disabled computer professionals; persons involved in the application of computers to aid the disabled; persons involved in the training or employment of physically disabled computer professionals; others interested in aiding the disabled. **Purpose:** To promote application of computer technology to aid the physically disabled; to educate the public about disabled computer professionals. **Activities:** Sponsors lectures and sessions at computer conferences on hiring and training disabled computer professionals. Compiles statistics.

Speech-Language Pathologists and Audiologists

SOURCES OF HELP-WANTED ADS

★8146★ American Annals of the Deaf
Conference of Educational Administrators
  Serving the Deaf
KDES, PAS-6
800 Florida Ave. NE
Washington, DC 20002-3625
Ph: (202)651-5340   Fax: (202)651-5708

$50.00/year for individuals; $55.00/year for Canada; $65.00/year for other countries. Magazine focusing on education of the deaf.

★8147★ Hearing Instruments
Advanstar Communications
7500 Old Oak Blvd.
Cleveland, OH 44130
Ph: (216)891-2604   Fax: (216)891-2675

Monthly. $50.00/year. Hearing instruments magazine.

★8148★ Hearing Journal
Williams & Wilkins
428 E. Preston St.
Baltimore, MD 21202-3993
Ph: (410)528-4000   Fax: (410)528-4312

Monthly. $45.00/year for individuals; $9.00 for single issue; $89.00/year for by mail. Magazine on hearing, health care, and technology.

★8149★ TeamRehab Report
Miramar Publishing
6133 Bristol Pkwy.
Box 3640
Culver City, CA 90231-3640
Ph: (213)337-9717

Bimonthly.

★8150★ Topics in Language Disorders
Aspen Publishers, Inc.
200 Orchard Ridge Dr., Ste. 200
Gaithersburg, MD 20878
Ph: (301)417-7500   Fax: (301)417-7550
Fr: 800-638-8437

Quarterly. $66.00/year for individuals; $79.00/year for other countries. Journal intending to clarify the application of theory to practice in the treatment, rehabilitation, and education of language disordered individuals.

★8151★ The Volta Review
Alexander Graham Bell Association for the
  Deaf
3417 Volta Pl. NW
Washington, DC 20007-2778
Ph: (202)337-5220   Fax: (202)337-8314

$42.00/year for individuals. Journal on educating the deaf.

PLACEMENT AND JOB REFERRAL SERVICES

★8152★ Association on Higher Education and Disability (AHEAD)
PO Box 21192
Columbus, OH 43221-0192
Ph: (614)488-4972   Fax: (614)488-1174

Members: Individuals interested in promoting the equal rights and opportunities of disabled postsecondary students, staff, faculty, and graduates. **Purpose:** Provides an exchange of communication for those professionally involved with disabled students; collects, evaluates, and disseminates information; encourages and supports legislation for the benefit of disabled students. **Activities:** Conducts surveys on issues pertinent to college students with disabilities; offers resource referral system and employment exchange for positions in disability student services. Conducts research programs; compiles statistics.

★8153★ Convention of American Instructors of the Deaf (CAID)
PO Box 377
Bedford, TX 76095-0377
Ph: (817)354-8414

Members: Professional organization of teachers, administrators, and professionals in allied fields related to education of the deaf and hard-of-hearing. **Purpose:** Objectives are: to provide opportunities for a free interchange of views concerning methods and means of educating the deaf and hard-of-hearing; to promote such education by the publication of reports, essays, and other information; to develop more effective methods of teaching deaf and hard-of-hearing children. **Activities:** Maintains speakers' bureau; offers placement services.

★8154★ Speech Communication Association (SCA)
5105 Backlick Rd., Bldg. E
Annandale, VA 22003
Ph: (703)750-0533   Fax: (703)914-9471

Members: Elementary, secondary, college, and university teachers, speech clinicians, media specialists, communication consultants, students, theater directors, and other interested persons; libraries and other institutions. **Purpose:** To promote study, criticism, research, teaching, and application of the artistic, humanistic, and scientific principles of communication, particularly speech communication. Sponsors the publication of scholarly volumes in speech. **Activities:** Maintains placement service.

EMPLOYER DIRECTORIES AND NETWORKING LISTS

★8155★ AHA Guide to the Health Care Field
Health Statistics Group
American Hospital Association (AHA)
1 N. Franklin
Chicago, IL 60606
Ph: (312)422-3501   Fax: (312)280-6015

Annual, July. $195.00, payment with order. Covers hospitals, multi-health care systems, freestanding ambulatory surgery centers, psychiatric facilities, long-term care facilities, substance abuse programs, hospices, Health Maintenance Organizations (HMOs), and other health-related organizations. Entries include: For hospitals: facility name, address, phone, administrator's name, number of beds, facilities and services, number of employees, expenses, other statistics. For other organizations: name, address, phone, name and title of contact. Arrangement: Geographical. Indexes: Hospital name.

★8156★ Directory of Hospital Personnel

Medical Economics
5 Paragon Dr.
Montvale, NJ 07645-1725
Ph: (201)358-7500　　Fax: (201)573-4956
Fr: 800-222-3045

Annual, September. $325.00, plus 7.50 shipping. Covers 200,000 executives at 7,100 U.S. hospitals. Entries include: Name of hospital, address, phone, number of beds, type and JCAHO status of hospital, names and titles of key department heads and staff, medical and nursing school affiliations; number of residents, interns, and nursing students. Arrangement: Geographical. Indexes: Hospital name, personnel, hospital size.

★8157★ Home Health Service Directory

American Business Directories, Inc.
American Business Information, Inc.
5711 S. 86th Cir.
Omaha, NE 68127
Ph: (402)593-4600　　Fax: (402)331-1505

Annual. $1,200.00, U.S. edition. Entries include: Name, address, phone (including area code), size of advertisement, year first in Yellow Pages, name of owl her or manager, number of employees. Compiled from telephone company Yellow Pages, nationwide. Arrangement: Geographical.

★8158★ Hospital Blue Book

Billian Publishing Co.
2100 Powers Ferry Rd., Ste. 300
Atlanta, GA 30339
Ph: (404)955-5656　　Fax: (404)952-0669

Annual, spring. $154.50, national edition, plus $20.00 shipping. Covers more than 7,100 hospitals; some listings also appear in a separate southern edition of this publication. Entries include: Name of hospital, accreditation, mailing address, phone, fax, number of beds, type of facility (nonprofit, general, state, etc.); list of administrative personnel and chiefs of medical services, with specific titles. Arrangement: Geographical.

★8159★ Hospital Market Atlas

SMG Marketing Group, Inc.
1342 N. LaSalle Dr.
Chicago, IL 60610
Ph: (312)642-3026　　Fax: (312)642-9729
Fr: 800-678-3026

Biennial, odd years. $495.00, payment with order. Covers over 7,000 hospitals, hospital systems and 480 group purchasing organizations. Entries include: Hospital or organization name, address, phone, county code, management, type of hospital service, number of beds, admissions, surgical operations, and emergency room visits. Arrangement: Geographical.

★8160★ Hospitals Directory

American Business Directories, Inc.
American Business Information, Inc.
5711 S. 86th Cir.
Omaha, NE 68127
Ph: (402)593-4600　　Fax: (402)331-1505

Annual. $870.00, U.S. edition. Entries include: Name, address, phone (including area code), size of advertisement, year first in Yellow Pages, name of owner or manager, number of employees. Compiled from telephone company Yellow Pages, nationwide. Arrangement: Geographical.

★8161★ Medical and Health Information Directory

Gale Research
835 Penobscot Bldg.
Detroit, MI 48226-4094
Ph: (313)961-2242　　Fax: (313)961-6083
Fr: 800-877-GALE

Approximately biennial; latest edition 1994. $195.00, per volume; $485.00, for the three-volume set. Covers in Volume 1, almost 18,600 medical and health oriented associations, organizations, institutions, and government agencies, including health maintenance organizations (HMOs), preferred provider organizations (PPOs), insurance companies, pharmaceutical companies, research centers, and medical and allied health schools. In Volume 2, nearly 11,800 medical book publishers; medical periodicals, directories, audiovisual producers and services, medical libraries and information centers, and electronic resources. In Volume 3, nearly 26,000 clinics, treatment centers, care programs, and counseling/diagnostic services for 30 subject areas. Entries include: Institution, service, or firm name, address, phone; many include names of key personnel and, when pertinent, descriptive annotation. Arrangement: Classified by organization activity, service, etc. Indexes: Each volume has a complete alphabetical name and keyword index.

★8162★ National Directory of Services in Audiology and Speech-Language Pathology

American Speech-Language-Hearing
Association
10801 Rockville Pke.
Rockville, MD 20852
Ph: (301)897-5700　　Fax: (301)571-0457
Fr: 800-638-8255

Irregular, latest edition 1993. $25.00, plus shipping. Covers accredited and nonaccredited clinical audiology and speech-language pathology services in the United States and other countries. Entries include: Program name, address, phone, director name; accredited programs are bolded. TTY/TDD telephone service is also available. Arrangement: Separate sections for audiology programs and speech-language pathology programs are geographical by state, then listed by zip code.

★8163★ Osteopathic Membership Directory—AOHA

American Osteopathic Healthcare
Association
5301 Wisconsin Ave. NW, Ste. 630
Washington, DC 20015-2015
Ph: (202)686-1700　　Fax: (202)686-7615

Annual, summer. $125.00, payment with order. Covers about 110 osteopathic hospitals. Includes list of individual and institutional members; also lists osteopathic colleges, and directors of medical education. Entries include: For hospitals: name of hospital, name of chief executive officer, address, phone, number of beds and other hospital data.

Arrangement: Geographical. Indexes: Name, institution.

★8164★ Who's Who Among Human Services Professionals

National Register Publishing
Reed Reference Publishing
121 Chanlon Rd.
New Providence, NJ 07974-1541
Ph: (908)464-6400　　Fr: 800-621-9669

Latest edition February 1992; suspended indefinitely. $129.00. Covers nearly 20,000 human service professionals, in such fields as counseling, social work, psychology, audiology, and speech pathology. Entries include: Name, address, education, work experience, professional association memberships. Arrangement: Alphabetical.

HANDBOOKS AND MANUALS

★8165★ Careers in Health Care

VGM Career Horizons
4255 W. Touhy Ave.
Lincolnwood, IL 60646-1975
Ph: (847)679-5500　　Fax: (847)679-2494
Fr: 800-323-4900

Barbara M. Swanson. 1995. $17.95; $13.95 (paper). Describes job duties, work settings, salaries, licensing and certification requirements, educational preparation, and future outlook. Gives ideas on how to secure a job.

★8166★ Clinical Administration in Audiology and Speech-Language Pathology

Singular Publishing Group, Inc.
4284 41st. St.
San Diego, CA 92105
Ph: (619)521-8000　　Fax: (619)563-9008
Fr: 800-521-8545

Stephen R. Rizzo. 1993. $59.95 (paper).

★8167★ Liberal Arts Jobs: What They Are and How to Get Them

Peterson's
PO Box 2123
Princeton, NJ 08543-2123
Ph: (609)243-9111　　Fax: (609)243-9150
Fr: 800-338-3282

Burton Jay Nadler. Second edition, 1989. $9.95. 153 pages. Presents a list of the top 20 fields for liberal arts majors, covering more than 300 job opportunities. Discusses strategies for going after those jobs, including guidance on the language of a successful job search, informational interviews, and making networking work.

★8168★ Opportunities in Health and Medical Careers

VGM Career Horizons
4255 W. Touhy Ave.
Lincolnwood, IL 60646-1975
Ph: (847)679-5500　　Fax: (847)679-2494
Fr: 800-323-4900

Donald Snook, Jr. and Leo D'Orazio. 1993. $14.95; $11.95 (paper). Covers the full range of medical and health occupations. Illustrated.

★8169★ Opportunities in Speech-Language Pathology Careers

VGM Career Horizons
4255 W. Touhy Ave.
Lincolnwood, IL 60646-1975
Ph: (847)679-5500   Fax: (847)679-2494
Fr: 800-323-4900

Patricia Larkins Hick. 1995. $14.95; $11.95 (paper). 160 pages. Provides information on opportunities in school systems, community and rehabilitation centers, hospitals, research, and other areas, and offers job-hunting guidance. Illustrated.

★8170★ Resumes for Health and Medical Careers

4255 W. Touhy Ave.
Lincolnwood, IL 60646-1975
Ph: (708)679-5500   Fax: (708)679-6375
Fr: 800-323-4900

Compiled by VGM Career Horizons Staff 1995. $9.95 (paper).

EMPLOYMENT AGENCIES AND SEARCH FIRMS

★8171★ Sue Carroll Personnel, Inc.

16 E. 79th St.
New York, NY 10021
Ph: (212)288-8866   Fax: (212)988-7191

Employment agency and executive search firm.

OTHER SOURCES

★8172★ American Almanac of Jobs and Salaries 1994-95

Avon Books
1350 Avenue of the Americas, 2nd Fl.
New York, NY 10019
Ph: (212)261-6800   Fr: 800-238-0658

John Wright. Revised edition, 1993. $17.00. 704 pages. This is a comprehensive guide to the wages of hundreds of occupations in a wide variety of industries and organizations.

★8173★ American Health Care Association

1201 L St. NW
Washington, DC 20005
Ph: (202)842-4444   Fax: (202)842-3860

Members: Federation of state associations of long-term health care facilities. **Purpose:** Promotes standards for professionals in long-term health care delivery and quality care for patients and residents in a safe environment. Focuses on issues of availability, quality, affordability, and fair payment. Operates as a liaison with governmental agencies, Congress, and professional associations.

★8174★ American Speech-Language-Hearing Association (ASHA)

10801 Rockville Pke.
Rockville, MD 20852
Ph: (301)897-5700   Fax: (301)571-0457
Fr: 800-638-8255

Members: Professional association for speech-language pathologists and audiologists. **Purpose:** Acts as an accrediting agency for college and university graduate school programs and clinic and hospital programs and as a certifying body for professionals providing speech, language, and hearing therapy to the public. **Activities:** Offers career information, listing of university training programs, and certification requirements. Conducts research on communication disorders and community needs.

★8175★ National Rehabilitation Association (NRA)

633 S. Washington St.
Alexandria, VA 22314
Ph: (703)836-0850   Fax: (703)836-0848

Members: Administrators, instructors, placement specialists, secretaries, counselors, therapists, vocational evaluators, ADA specialists and others interested in rehabilitation of persons with disabilities. **Activities:** Conducts legislative activities; develops accessibility guidelines; offers specialized education.

Sports Officials, Coaches, and Instructors

SOURCES OF HELP-WANTED ADS

★8176★ *Hang Gliding*

U.S. Hang Gliding Association, Inc.
559 E. Pikes Peak, Ste. 101
PO Box 8300
Colorado Springs, CO 80933
Ph: (719)632-8300   Fax: (719)632-6417

Monthly. $35.00/year for individuals; $3.95 for single issue. Magazine on hang gliding flight.

★8177★ *The Insider Newsletter*

Sports Careers
PO Box 10129
Phoenix, AZ 85064
Fr: 800-776-7877

Semimonthly. Subscription free to members; $99.00/six months for nonmembers. Provides articles on career development, salaries, and trends for the sports industry. Includes "Career Connections," an insert listing 60-75 job opportunities and internships within each issue.

★8178★ *Physical Education Digest*

111 Kingsmount Blvd.
Sudbury, ON, Canada P3E 1K8
Ph: (705)675-7055   Fax: (705)675-5539

Quarterly. $24.00/year; $6.00/single issue. Trade magazine featuring health, sports, and fitness topics.

★8179★ *Sailing World*

Cruising World Publications, Inc.
5 John Clarke Rd.
Newport, RI 02840
Ph: (401)847-1588   Fax: (401)848-5048

Monthly. $24.00/year for individuals. Magazine on sailboat racing and performance cruising.

★8180★ *Scholastic Coach*

Scholastic, Inc.
555 Broadway
New York, NY 10003
Ph: (212)343-6100

Monthly. Magazine on high school and college athletics.

★8181★ *Skiing Trade News*

Times Mirror Magazines, Inc.
2 Park Ave.
New York, NY 10016
Ph: (212)779-5285   Fax: (212)779-5465

$15.00/year for individuals. Trade newspaper for the ski industry. Includes trade show previews, company news, retail trends, personnel changes, and miscellaneous news.

★8182★ *Swimming World and Junior Swimmer*

Sports Publications, Inc.
228 Nevada St.
El Segundo, CA 90245
Ph: (310)607-9956   Fax: (310)607-9963

Monthly. $19.00/year for individuals; $2.50 for single issue. Magazine on competitive swimming, diving and water polo.

★8183★ *TennisPro*

U.S. Professional Tennis Registry
PO Box 4739
Hilton Head Island, SC 29938
Ph: (803)686-8732   Fax: (803)686-2033

Bimonthly. Included in membership. Focuses on programs and techniques for teaching tennis. Contains profiles of tennis teaching pros, and information about new equipment. Recurring features include columns titled Sport Science, New Drills, New Products, Sports Medicine, and Sport Psychology.

PLACEMENT AND JOB REFERRAL SERVICES

★8184★ **Affiliated National Riding Commission (ANRC)**

1900 Association Dr.
Reston, VA 22091
Ph: (703)476-3450   Fax: (703)476-9527

Members: Persons who have passed the rating test for riders as established by the Commission. **Purpose:** Encourages educated horseback riding through clinics, centers for ratings, seminars, and competitions. **Activities:** Maintains job placement service for rated riders.

★8185★ **American Athletic Trainers Association and Certification Board (AATA)**

660 W. Duarte Rd.
Arcadia, CA 91007
Ph: (818)445-1978

Purpose: To qualify and certify active athletic trainers; to establish minimum competence standards for individuals participating in the prevention and care of athletic injuries; to inform communities nationwide of the importance of having competent leadership in the area of athletic training. **Activities:** Conducts continuing education and charitable programs; maintains placement service.

★8186★ **American Sail Training Association (ASTA)**

PO Box 1459
Newport, RI 02840
Ph: (401)846-1775   Fax: (401)849-5400

Members: Organizations operating sail training programs; corporations and educational institutions supporting sail training; private citizens with an interest in sailing and sail training. **Purpose:** Promotes sail training as an educational and character-building experience for youth of all ages. Seeks to bring together the sail training ships of the world in a spirit of friendship and international goodwill. **Activities:** Sponsors Tall Ship events including sail training rallies. Maintains placement service; compiles statistics. **E-Mail:** ASTANPT$.com

★8187★ American Swimming Coaches Association (ASCA)

301 SE 20th St.
Fort Lauderdale, FL 33316
Ph: (305)462-6267   Fax: (305)462-6280
Fr: 800-356-2722

Members: Swimming coaches united for informational and educational purposes. **Activities:** Operates Swim America, a learn-to-swim program. Maintains placement service; conducts research programs; compiles statistics.

★8188★ Athletic Equipment Managers Association (AEMA)

6224 Hester Rd.
Oxford, OH 45056
Ph: (513)523-2362

Members: Athletic equipment managers and others who handle sports equipment for junior high and high schools, colleges, recreation centers, and professional sports; individuals involved in athletic management and coaching or the handling or purchasing of athletic, physical education, or recreational equipment. **Purpose:** Aims to improve the profession of equipment management and promote a better working relationship among those interested in problems of management. Works collectively to facilitate equipment improvement for greater safety among participants in all sports. **Activities:** Conducts workshops and clinics. Maintains job placement service.

★8189★ College Swimming Coaches Association of America (CSCAA)

Donald Megerle
Tufts University
College Ave.
Sports Ave.
Medford, MA 02155
Ph: (617)628-5000   Fax: (617)627-3516

Members: College and university swimming and diving coaches organized to promote college swimming. **Activities:** Disseminates information; maintains placement service and hall of fame.

★8190★ Exer-Safety Association (ESA)

10151 University Blvd., No. 138
Orlando, FL 32817-1981
Ph: (407)677-9501

Members: Fitness instructors, personal trainers, health spas, YMCAs, community recreation departments, and hospital wellness programs. **Purpose:** To improve the qualifications of exercise instructors; to train instructors to develop safe exercise routines that will help people avoid injury while exercising; to prepare instructors for national certification. **Activities:** Offers training in aerobics and exercise and on the physiological aspects of exercise. Conducts exercise safety and research programs. Sponsors charitable program; maintains speakers' bureau. Offers placement and children's services.

★8191★ Jackie Robinson Foundation (JRF)

3 W. 35th St.
New York, NY 10001
Ph: (212)290-8600   Fax: (212)290-8081

Purpose: Seeks to develop the leadership and achievement potential of minority and urban youth. Founded by the friends and family of Jackie Robinson (1919-72), the first black athlete to play major league baseball. Trains minority and poor youths for sports management careers. **Activities:** Provides counseling, support, and placement services. Awards full college scholarships to promising minority students. Maintains collection of Jackie Robinson memorabilia; has produced a national touring exhibit of archival materials pertaining to Robinson.

★8192★ National Association for Sport and Physical Education (NASPE)

1900 Association Dr.
Reston, VA 22091
Ph: (703)476-3410   Fax: (703)476-8316

Members: Men and women professionally involved with physical activity and sports. **Purpose:** Seeks to improve the total sport and physical activity experience in America. Conducts research and education programs in such areas as sport psychology, curriculum development, kinesiology, history, philosophy, sport sociology, and the biological and behavioral basis of human activity. Develops and distributes public information materials which explain the value of physical education programs. **Activities:** Maintains placement service, and media resource center for public information and professional preparation. Sponsors skills clinics and foreign coach exchange programs.

★8193★ National Association of Underwater Instructors (NAUI)

PO Box 14650
Montclair, CA 91763
Ph: (714)621-5801   Fax: (714)621-6405
Fr: 800-553-6284

Members: Certified instructors of basic, advanced, and specialized courses in underwater diving. **Activities:** Maintains placement service. Offers instructor certification programs and training programs. Conducts seminars, workshops, and symposia. Sells diving education books.

★8194★ National Athletic Trainers Association (NATA)

2952 Stemmons Fwy., Ste. 200
Dallas, TX 75247-6103
Ph: (214)637-6282   Fax: (214)637-2206
Fr: 800-879-6282

Members: Athletic trainers from universities, colleges, and junior colleges; professional football, baseball, basketball, and ice hockey; high schools, preparatory schools, military establishments, sports medicine clinics, and business/industrial health programs. **Activities:** Maintains hall of fame and placement service. Conducts research programs; compiles statistics.

★8195★ National Christian College Athletic Association (NCCAA)

PO Box 1312
Marion, IN 46952
Ph: (317)674-8401   Fax: (317)674-8487

Members: Evangelical Christian colleges. **Purpose:** Provides national competition for the Christian college movement in baseball, basketball, cross-country, golf, soccer, wrestling, women's volleyball, track and field, and softball. **Activities:** Maintains placement service; compiles statistics.

★8196★ Professional Association of Diving Instructors (PADI)

1251 E. Dyer Rd., No. 100
Santa Ana, CA 92705
Ph: (714)540-7234   Fax: (714)540-2609
Fr: 800-729-7234

Purpose: Educates and certifies underwater scuba instructors. Sanctions instructor training courses nationwide and in 175 foreign countries. Provides training course criteria, training aids, and national requirements for all aspects of diving instruction. Instructor training courses are held at geographically central locations. **Activities:** Sponsors PADI Travel Network and a retail dive store program. Offers courses in diving specialties; conducts educational programs. Offers placement service; compiles statistics.

★8197★ Professional Golfers' Association of America (PGA)

100 Ave. of Champions
Palm Beach Gardens, FL 33418
Ph: (407)624-8400   Fax: (407)624-8430

Members: Golf professionals and apprentices associated with golf clubs, courses, and tournaments. **Activities:** Offers employment counseling. Sponsors PGA Championship, PGA Seniors' Championship, Ryder Cup Matches, PGA Grand Slam of Golf, Club Professional Championship, National Golf Month Charities Event, and Senior Club Professional Championship; PGA Junior Championship; PGA Assistants Championship. Conducts Golf Professional Training Program; certifies college programs in golf management. Sponsors winter tournament program for club professionals including tournaments held in south Florida.

★8198★ Professional Skaters Association (PSA)

PO Box 5904
Rochester, MN 55903
Ph: (507)281-5122   Fax: (507)281-5491

Members: Professional ice skaters engaged in the teaching coaching and performing of ice skating. **Purpose:** Strives to form a cohesive body of all professional ice skaters for the benefit of the profession, to protect the interests of members' pupils, to advance all aspects of both ice figure skating and recreational skating, and to promote high ethical and professional standards in the field. **Activities:** Grades teachers on the basis of on-ice proficiency and oral examination, according to the official PSA Rating System. Operates placement service. **E-Mail:** skatepsa@aol.com

★8199★ Sports Careers

PO Box 10129
Phoenix, AZ 85064
Fr: 800-776-7877

Career development firm for the sports industry. Provides career-related programs, conferences, seminars, educational products, and publications. Offers Career Enhancement Profile Program and Resume Development Kit. Maintains an electronic resume bank for members which is available to sports companies and organizations. Publishes newsletter listing job opportunities.

★8200★ United States Association of Independent Gymnastic Clubs (USAIGC)

235 Pinehurst Rd.
Wilmington, DE 19803
Ph: (302)656-3706

Members: Gymnastic clubs and independent gymnastic club businesses offering professional class instruction and coaching; manufacturers of gymnastic equipment, apparel, and supplies. **Purpose:** Objectives are to: provide services, programs, and business advice to help gymnastic businesses to grow and prosper; locate organizations and individuals that will provide needed services for members' clientele; further coaching knowledge; advance the U.S. in gymnastic competitions throughout the world. Offers certification for coaches and developmental-training programs for gymnasts to prepare for international competitions. **Activities:** Provides placement service; conducts research programs. Maintains Medical Advisory Board and hall of fame.

★8201★ United States Judo (USJ)

PO Box 10013
El Paso, TX 79991
Ph: (915)565-8754   Fax: (915)566-1668

Members: Judo groups and athletes, referees, judges, and interested individuals. **Purpose:** Serves as national governing body for amateur judo in the United States. Promotes the sport of judo and trains athletes for competition. Develops eligibility and safety standards; conducts training courses for referees, coaches, and athletes. **Activities:** Sanctions and sponsors national amateur judo competitions; bestows awards. Maintains placement service; compiles statistics.

★8202★ United States Lacrosse Coaches' Association (USLCA)

20 Tower Pkwy.
New Haven, CT 06511
Ph: (203)432-1494   Fax: (203)432-7772

Members: Lacrosse coaches at schools, colleges, universities, and clubs; associate members are men interested in lacrosse. **Activities:** Conducts equipment research and educational programs; supports statistical services during lacrosse competition season. Offers placement service; maintains speakers' bureau.

★8203★ United States Professional Diving Coaches Association (PDCA)

Rick Schavone
189 Buckthorn Way
Menlo Park, CA 94025
Ph: (415)723-9159

Activities: Conducts educational programs; offers placement services. Maintains videotape library; bestows awards.

★8204★ United States Professional Tennis Association (USPTA)

1 USPTA Centre
3535 Briarpark Dr.
Houston, TX 77042
Ph: (713)97-USPTA   Fax: (713)978-7780

Members: Professional tennis instructors and college coaches. **Purpose:** Seeks to improve tennis instruction in the United States; maintains placement bureau and library. Offers specialized education; sponsors competitions; administrates an adult tennis league.

★8205★ United States Professional Tennis Registry (USPTR)

PO Box 4739
Hilton Head Island, SC 29938
Ph: 800-421-6289   Fax: (803)686-2033

Purpose: Tests, certifies, and registers international tennis teaching professionals. Certification requires successful completion of a written and on-court examination. **Activities:** Sponsors workshops, tennis clinics, and charitable program. Holds competitions; compiles statistics; maintains placement service.

★8206★ U.S. Ski Coaches Association (USSCA)

PO Box 100
Park City, UT 84060
Ph: (801)649-9090   Fax: (801)649-3613

Members: Alpine, Nordic, and Freestyle ski coaches and ski instructors; persons interested in sports medicine. **Purpose:** Promotes the highest standards of Alpine, Nordic, and Freestyle ski coaching. Provides educational and technical materials, supplies, and equipment necessary to the function of the ski coach. **Activities:** Offers courses, clinics, films, and placement service. Provides high standards of certification, recertification, accreditation, and coaching ethics; handles problems of common concern to the ski coaching profession.

EMPLOYER DIRECTORIES AND NETWORKING LISTS

★8207★ *Blue Book of College Athletics for Senior, Junior & Community Colleges*

Athletic Publishing Co. Inc.
PO Box 931
Montgomery, AL 36101-0931
Ph: (205)263-4436   Fax: (205)263-4437

Annual, September. $29.95, plus $3.00 shipping. Covers over 2,600 colleges and universities that have athletic programs, conferences, and related associations; coverage includes the U.S.; Canada and Puerto Rico. Arrangement: Classified by type of college, conference, or association, then alphabetical. Indexes: Senior colleges and universities in the U.S.; colleges of Canada, and Puerto Rico; senior conferences and associations, senior related associations and organizations; junior and community colleges; junior and community college conferences and associations.

★8208★ *Clell Wade Coaches Directory*

Clell Wade Coaches Directory, Inc.
PO Box 177
Cassville, MO 65625
Ph: (417)847-2783   Fax: (417)847-5920

Annual, August. $9.95, per edition; specify state of interest. Published in 50 state and/or regional editions as well as 10 Canadian province editions, this series covers high school and college athletic programs and their personnel. Entries include: For each school Name and titles of athletic director, superintendent, principal, cheerleader sponsor, band director, and trainer; school name, address, phone; enrollment; conference memberships; school colors, nickname; interscholastic sports, name of coach. College listings include name and seating capacity of the football stadium and basketball fieldhouse. Arrangement: Geographical.

★8209★ *Exercise and Physical Fitness Programs Directory*

American Business Directories, Inc.
American Business Information, Inc.
5711 S. 86th Cir.
Omaha, NE 68127
Ph: (402)593-4600   Fax: (402)331-1505

Annual. $560.00, payment with order. Number of listings: 7,843. Entries include: Name, address, phone (including area code), size of advertisement, year first in Yellow Pages, name of owner or manager, number of employees. Compiled from telephone company Yellow Pages, nationwide. Arrangement: Geographical.

★8210★ *Health Clubs Directory*

American Business Directories, Inc.
American Business Information, Inc.
5711 S. 86th Cir.
Omaha, NE 68127
Ph: (402)593-4600   Fax: (402)331-1505

Updated continuously; printed on request. $875.00, U.S. edition. Entries include: Name, address, phone (including area code). Compiled from telephone company Yellow Pages, nationwide. Arrangement: Geographical.

★8211★ *Health & Fitness Program Consultants Directory*

American Business Directories, Inc.
American Business Information, Inc.
5711 S. 86th Cir.
Omaha, NE 68127
Ph: (402)593-4600   Fax: (402)331-1505

Annual. $265.00, U.S. edition. Entries include: Name, address, phone (including area code), size of advertisement, year first in Yellow Pages, name of owner or manager, number of employees. Compiled from telephone company Yellow Pages, nationwide. Arrangement: Geographical.

★8212★ **The Insider's Guide to the Best Skiing in the USA**

Fodor's Travel Publications, Inc.
Random House, Inc.
201 E. 50th St.
New York, NY 10022
Ph: (212)572-8709   Fax: (212)572-2248

Biennial, even years. $16.00. Covers 30 top ski resorts in the U.S. Entries include: Resort name, address, phone; type of lifts, number of trails, snowmaking capabilities, length of season, hotels, restaurants, available transportation, other activities, and recommendations on the best trails for all levels. Arrangement: Geographical. Indexes: Resort name.

★8213★ **National Collegiate Athletic Association—Directory**

National Collegiate Athletic Association
Box 7347
Overland Park, KS 66207-0347
Ph: (913)339-1900

Annual, October. $6.00, pre-paid. Covers about 1,000 member institutions. Entries include: Name of institution, conference, address, phone, names and titles of key personnel. Arrangement: Alphabetical.

★8214★ **National Directory of College Athletics**

Collegiate Directories, Inc.
PO Box 450640
Cleveland, OH 44145
Ph: (216)835-1172   Fax: (216)835-8835
Fr: 800-42-NACDA

Annual, August. $14.95. Covers women's athletic departments at 2,000 senior and junior colleges. Entries include: School name, address; enrollment, colors, stadium and/or gym capacity, team nicknames; names of president, women's athletic director and physical education director, and coaches for each sport; athletic department phone number; and association affiliations. Arrangement: Alphabetical.

★8215★ **National Directory of College Athletics**

Collegiate Directories, Inc.
PO Box 450640
Cleveland, OH 44145
Ph: (216)835-1172   Fax: (216)835-8835
Fr: 800-42-NACDA

Annual, August. $19.95. Covers men's athletic departments of 2,100 senior and junior colleges in the United States and Canada. Entries include: School name, address, enrollment, colors, team nicknames, stadium and/or gym capacity; names of president, men's athletic director and physical education director and coaches for each sport; athletic department phone; association affiliations. Arrangement: Alphabetical.

★8216★ **National Directory of High School Coaches**

Athletic Publishing Co. Inc.
PO Box 931
Montgomery, AL 36101-0931
Ph: (205)263-4436   Fax: (205)263-4437

Annual, September. $49.95, plus $3.00 shipping. Covers more than 188,000 high school coaches at over 22,300 high schools. Entries include: School name, address, phone, names of coaches and codes for sports coached. Arrangement: Geographical.

★8217★ **Sports Market Place Register**

Sports Careers
PO Box 10129
Phoenix, AZ 85064
Fr: 800-776-7877

Annual $59.00. Resource guide for the sports industry. Lists over 24,000 national and international sports business contacts. Entries include: organization name, name of key executive, address, and phone and fax numbers. Provides listings for: Individual and Multiple Sports Organizations/Teams/Media; College Sports; Sponsorship/Marketing/Event Management; Sports Agents/Lawyers; Manufacturers/Retailers. Indexes: Geographic and Alphabetical.

★8218★ **White Book of Ski Areas: U.S., Canada**

Inter-Ski Services, Inc.
PO Box 9595
Washington, DC 20016
Ph: (202)342-0886   Fax: (202)338-1940

Annual, November. $16.95, plus $2.55 shipping. Covers about 700 lift-equipped ski areas and resorts. Entries include: Name of ski area, location, phone; snow condition phone numbers; ski statistics; season and rates; equipment and schooling available; lodging availability and phone, restaurants, apres-ski, and other recreational facilities in vicinity; shops; travel instructions. Arrangement: Geographical within four regions West, North Central, South, and Northeast. Indexes: Geographical.

HANDBOOKS AND MANUALS

★8219★ **Career Opportunities in the Sports Industry**

Facts on File, Inc.
11 Penn Plaza, 15th Fl.
New York, NY 10001-2006
Ph: (212)967-8800   Fax: 800-678-3633
Fr: 800-322-8755

Shelly Field. 1991. $29.95; $15.95 (paper). 272 pages. Describes various jobs in the sports industry. Each occupational profile covers job duties, employment outlook, career paths, salaries, skills, and education preparation. Offers tips for entering the field. Fields covered include professional sports teams, sports and business administration, coaching, sports officiating, sports journalism, fitness and recreation, and sports medicine and therapy, among others.

★8220★ **Careers Inside the World of Sports and Entertainment**

Rosen Publishing Group, Inc.
29 E. 21st St.
New York, NY 10010
Ph: (212)777-3017   Fax: (212)777-0277
Fr: 800-237-9932

Bruce McGlothlin. 1995. $14.95.

★8221★ **Careers in Sports**

Taylor & Francis, Inc.
1900 Frost Rd., Ste. 101
Bristol, PA 19007-1598
Ph: (215)785-5800   Fax: (215)785-5515

Louise Fyfe. Revised edition.

★8222★ **Careers for Sports Nuts and Other Athletic Types**

VGM Career Horizons
4255 W. Touhy Ave.
Lincolnwood, IL 60646-1975
Ph: (847)679-5500   Fax: (847)679-2494
Fr: 800-323-4900

William Ray Heitzmann. 1994. Profiles sports enthusiasts who make their livings in a variety of ways in the world of sports. Explores opportunities in such sports-related fields as sports marketing, sports equipment sales, sports writing and photography, and sports management.

★8223★ **Chronicle of Sports Careers**

Chronicle Guidance Publications, Inc.
PO Box 1190
Moravia, NY 13118-1190
Ph: (315)497-0330   Fax: (315)497-3359
Fr: 800-622-7284

Paul Downes, editor. 1994. $24.00.

★8224★ **Developing a Lifelong Contract in the Sports Marketplace**

Athletic Achievements
3036 Ontario Rd.
Little Canada, MN 55117
Ph: (612)484-8299

Greg J. Cylkowski. Second edition, 1991. $20.95. 400 pages. A guide to seeking opportunities in a variety of sports positions.

★8225★ **Developing a Sports Career in the Sports Marketplace: The Sports Career Development Handbook**

Global Sports Productions, Inc.
1223 Broadway, Ste. 102
Santa Monica, CA 90404
Ph: (310)454-9480   Fax: (310)454-6590

Ed Kobak, Jr. 1995. $21.95 (paper).

★8226★ **How to Get a Job in Sports: The Guide to Finding the Right Sports Career**

Macmillan Publishing Co.
200 Old Tappan Rd.
Old Tappan, NJ 07675
Fax: 800-445-6991   Fr: 800-223-2336

John Taylor. 1992. $10.00 (paper).

★8227★ Making It As a Sports Official

American Alliance for Health, Physical
  Education, Recreation and Dance
PO Box 385
Oxon Hill, MD 20750-0385
Ph: (301)476-3481   Fax: (301)567-9553
Fr: 800-321-0789

M.C. O'Bryant. 1991. $19.95 (paper).

**★8228★ Modern Sports Officiating: A
Practical Guide**

Brown & Benchmark
25 Kessel Ct.
Madison, WI 53711
Ph: (608)273-0040   Fax: 800-346-2377
Fr: 800-338-5578

Richard Clegg. 1992.

**★8229★ Opportunities in Sports and
Athletics**

VGM Career Horizons
4255 W. Touhy Ave.
Lincolnwood, IL 60646-1975
Ph: (847)679-5500   Fax: (847)679-2494
Fr: 800-323-4900

William Ray Heitzmann. 1994. $14.95;
$11.95 (paper). A guide to planning for and
seeking opportunities in this growing field.
Illustrated.

**★8230★ Opportunities in Sports
Medicine Careers**

VGM Career Horizons
4255 W. Touhy Ave.
Lincolnwood, IL 60646-1975
Ph: (847)679-5500   Fax: (847)679-2494
Fr: 800-323-4900

William Ray Heitzmann. 1995. $14.95;
$11.95 (paper). 160 pages. Discusses a
variety of opportunities in this field and how
to pursue them. Contains bibliography and
illustrations.

★8231★ A Woman's Guide to Coaching

Women's Sports Foundation
Eisenhower Park
East Meadow, NY 11554
Ph: (516)542-4700   Fax: (516)542-4716
Fr: 800-227-3988

Booklet. Free. 20 pages.

OTHER SOURCES

**★8232★ American Hockey Coaches
Association (AHCA)**

Bruce Delventhal
Union College
Achilles Rink
Schenectady, NY 12308
Ph: (518)388-6134   Fax: (518)388-6323

Members: University, college, and secondary
school ice hockey coaches. **Activities:** Conducts coaches' clinics throughout the U.S.

**★8233★ Association for Worksite Health
Promotion (AWHP)**

60 Revere Dr., Ste. 500
Northbrook, IL 60062-1577
Ph: (847)480-9574   Fax: (847)480-9282

Members: Health and fitness professionals
employed by major companies (some smaller
companies and businesses are also represented) and conducting wellness fitness programs for employees; interested persons in
personnel and sales to fitness facilities;
health educators and other health professionals; students interested in the field. **Purpose:** Supports and assists in the development of quality programs of health and
fitness in business and industry. Seeks to
create an awareness of the importance of
physical, emotional, and mental health
among employees. **Activities:** Stimulates active research and serves as a clearinghouse
on employee health and fitness. Sponsors
seminars and an educational committee that
studies effectiveness of preparation, training
programs, and certification. Conducts open
discussions and workshops on health and
nutrition. Compiles statistics.

**★8234★ Black Coaches Association
(BCA)**

PO Box J
Des Moines, IA 50311
Ph: (515)271-3010   Fax: (515)271-4542

Members: Blacks and other minorities in the
coaching profession. **Purpose:** Promotes the
creation of a positive environment in which
issues such as stereotyping, lack of significant media coverage, and discrimination can
be exposed, discussed, and resolved. Provides member services. Petitions the NCAA
legislative bodies to design, enact, and en-
force diligent guidelines and policies to improve professional mobility for minorities.

**★8235★ IDEA: International Association
of Fitness Professionals (IDEA)**

6190 Cornerstone Ct. E., Ste. 204
San Diego, CA 92121
Ph: (619)535-8979   Fax: (619)535-8234
Fr: 800-999-IDEA

Purpose: Provides continuing education for
fitness professionals including; fitness instructors, personal trainers, program directors, and club/studio owners. **Activities:** Offers workshops for continuing education
credits.

**★8236★ National Association for Girls
and Women in Sport (NAGWS)**

1900 Association Dr.
Reston, VA 22091
Ph: (703)476-3450   Fax: (703)476-9527

Members: An Association of the American
Alliance for Health, Physical Education, Recreation, and Dance. Teachers, coaches, athletic trainers, officials, athletic administrators,
and students. **Purpose:** Supports and fosters the development of quality sports programs that will enrich the lives of all participants. **Activities:** Holds training sessions for
leadership development.

**★8237★ National Association of Sailing
Instructors and Sailing Schools
(NASISS)**

15 Renier Ct.
Middletown, NJ 07748-1612
Ph: (908)671-6190

Members: Sailing schools and sailing instructors united to develop and institute national
programs that will set standards for the
entire sailing community, both commercial
and noncommercial, and achieve recognition
with the U.S. Coast Guard, insurance companies, and the public. **Purpose:** Provides
services to sailing schools and instructors;
works to form and amend legislation affecting sailing schools. **Activities:** Accredits sailing schools; certifies instructors and students.

**★8238★ National Association of Sports
Officials (NASO)**

2017 Lathrop Ave.
Racine, WI 53405
Ph: (414)632-5448   Fax: (414)632-5460

Members: Active sports officials, umpires,
companies, and individuals interested in
sports. **Purpose:** Develops programs to assist in the education of sports officials;
engages in programs to instruct fans,
coaches, players, and the media on the role
of sports officials. Conducts clinics and
camps; sponsors public service ads.

**★8239★ National Federation
Interscholastic Coaches Association
(NFICA)**

PO Box 20626
11724 NW Plaza Cir.
Kansas City, MO 64195
Ph: (816)464-5400   Fax: (816)464-5571

Members: High school athletic coaches.
Purpose: Promotes professional growth and
image of interscholastic sports coaches; provides a forum for coaches to make suggestions on rules and procedures in high school
sports in the U.S. Cooperates with state high
school athletic associations and uses extensive committee structure to ensure grass
roots involvement and input from the local,
state, and national levels. Maintains hall of
fame.

**★8240★ National High School Athletic
Coaches Association (NHSACA)**

PO Box 5020
Winter Park, FL 32793-5020
Ph: (407)679-1414

Members: High school coaches and athletic
directors; athletic directors for school systems; executive secretaries of state high
school coaches; state high school coaches
associations. Public members are college
coaches, former high school coaches, adult
athletic trainers, principals, officials, and
sporting goods salesmen. **Purpose:** Formed
to give greater national prestige and professional status to high school coaching and to
promote cooperation among coaches, school
administrators, the press, game officials, and
the public. Promotes drug and alcohol abuse
prevention through National Training Seminars in Drug Prevention in conjunction with
the Drug Enforcement Administration, Washington, DC. Conducts Sportsmedicine/Medi-

cal Aspects of Sports seminars in conjunction with national sports and medical groups, and National College Credit Program for coaches and athletic directors. Maintains National Awards Program to recognize outstanding high school athletic directors, coaches, and players.

★8241★ National Strength and Conditioning Association (NSCA)
530 Communication Cir., Ste. 204
Colorado Springs, CO 80905
Ph: (719)632-6722   Fax: (719)632-6367
Members: Professional coaches, athletic trainers, physical therapists, sports medicine physicians, and sports science researchers. **Purpose:** Promotes the total conditioning of athletes to a level of optimum performance, with the belief that a better conditioned athlete not only performs better but is less prone to injury. Conducts national, regional, state, and local clinics and workshops. Operates professional certification program.

★8242★ Sports Careers Industry Audio Cassette Series
Sports Careers
PO Box 10129
Phoenix, AZ 85064
Fr: 800-776-7877

Audiocassette series. Covers the top ten major career categories for the sports industry: Special Events; TV and Cable; Sporting Goods; Colleges/Universities; Facility Management; Corporate Sponsorship; Athletic Representation; Front Office; Print and Radio; Health and Fitness.

Statisticians

Sources of Help-Wanted Ads

★8243★ Journal of Financial and Quantitative Analysis

Journal of Financial and Quantitative Analysis
University of Washington
Graduate School of Business Administration
326 Lewis Hall, DJ-10
Seattle, WA 98195
Ph: (206)543-4598   Fax: (206)543-6872

Quarterly. Journal on research in finance.

★8244★ Minority Engineer

Equal Opportunity Publications, Inc.
150 Motor Pkwy., Ste. 420
Hauppauge, NY 11788-5145
Ph: (516)273-0066   Fax: (516)273-8936

Affirmative-action recruitment magazine serving college graduating and professional minority engineers.

Placement and Job Referral Services

★8245★ International Society of Parametric Analysts (ISPA)

PO Box 6402
Town & Country Branch
Chesterfield, MO 63006-6402
Ph: (314)527-2955   Fax: (314)256-8358

Members: Engineers, designers, statisticians, estimators, and managers in industry, the military, and government who develop and use computerized, parametric cost-estimating models. **Activities:** Conducts educational activities aimed at promoting usage of parametric modeling techniques for purposes of cost estimating, risk analysis, and technology forecasting. Sponsors placement service.

Employer Directories and Networking Lists

★8246★ American Men and Women of Science

R. R. Bowker Co.
Reed Reference Publishing
121 Chanlon Rd.
New Providence, NJ 07974
Ph: (908)464-6800   Fax: (908)665-6688
Fr: 800-521-8110

Triennial, latest edition January 1995. $106.00, per volume; $850.00, set. Covers over 123,000 U.S. and Canadian scientists active in the physical, biological, mathematical, computer science, and engineering fields; includes references to previous edition for deceased scientists and nonrespondents. Entries include: Name, address, education, personal and career data, memberships, honors and awards, research interest. Arrangement: Alphabetical. Indexes: Discipline (in separate volume).

★8247★ Directory of Statisticians

American Statistical Association
1429 Duke St.
Alexandria, VA 22314
Ph: (703)684-1221   Fax: (703)684-2037

Irregular. Latest edition 1994. $125.00. Covers more than 25,000 members of the American Statistical Association, the Eastern and Western North American Regions of the Biometric Society, the Statistical Society of Canada, the Institute of Mathematical Statistics and the Bernoulli Society. Entries include: Name, address, phone, fax, electronic mail number, degrees, work affiliation. Arrangement: Alphabetical. Indexes: Geographical.

Handbooks and Manuals

★8248★ Careers in Health and Fitness

Rosen Publishing Group, Inc.
29 E. 21st St.
New York, NY 10010
Ph: (212)777-3017   Fax: (212)777-0277
Fr: 800-237-9932

Jackie Heron. Revised edition, 1990. $14.95. 160 pages. Contains occupational profiles for this field, including information on job duties, skills, advantages, basic equipment used, employment possibilities, certification, and salary.

★8249★ Careers for Number Crunchers and Other Quantitative Types

VGM Career Horizons
4255 W. Touhy Ave.
Lincolnwood, IL 60646-1975
Ph: (847)679-5500   Fax: (847)679-2494
Fr: 800-323-4900

Rebecca Burnett. 1993. $14.95; $9.95 (paper). Provides information to math-oriented job hunters on how to become statisticians, field researchers, computer programmers, stock analysts, investment managers, bankers, engineers, accountants, underwriters, economists, market analysts, mathematicians, systems analysts, and more.

★8250★ Careers for Number Lovers

The Millbrook Press
2 Old New Milford Rd.
Brookfield, CT 06804
Ph: (203)740-2220   Fr: 800-462-4703

Andrew Kaplan. 1991. $14.40; $4.95 (paper). 64 pages. Contains interviews with people in math-related careers. Provides job descriptions, methods of entry into the field, educational preparation, and earnings.

★8251★ Careers in Statistics

American Statistical Association (ASA)
1429 Duke St.
Alexandria, VA 22314-3402
Ph: (703)684-1221

Brochure describes what statisticians do, opportunities for future employment, education required, and sources of additional information. Lists U.S. and Canadian schools offering degrees in statistics.

★8252★ Encyclopedia of Careers and Vocational Guidance

J. G. Ferguson Publishing Co.
200 W. Monroe, Ste. 250
Chicago, IL 60606
Ph: (312)580-5480

William E. Hopke. Ninth edition, 1993. $129.95; $199.95 (CD-ROM). Four-volume set that profiles 900 occupations and describes job trends in 71 industries. Includes career description, educational requirements, history of the job, methods of entry, advancement, employment outlook, earnings, conditions of work, social and psychological factors, and sources of further information. Contains career and employment information for this field.

★8253★ Opportunities in High Tech Careers

VGM Career Horizons
4255 W. Touhy Ave.
Lincolnwood, IL 60646-1975
Ph: (847)679-5500   Fax: (847)679-2494
Fr: 800-323-4900

Gary D. Golter and Deborah Yanuck. 1995. $14.95; $11.95 (paper). 160 pages. Explores high technology careers. Describes job opportunities, how to make a career decision, how to prepare for high technology jobs, job hunting techniques, and future trends.

★8254★ Opportunities in Social Science Careers

VGM Career Horizons
4255 W. Touhy Ave.
Lincolnwood, IL 60646-1975
Ph: (847)679-5500   Fax: (847)679-2494
Fr: 800-323-4900

Rosanne J. Marek. 1990. $14.95; $11.95 (paper). 160 pages. Profiles job opportunities in education, government, and business, along with their salary levels and outlook in the years to come. Illustrated.

★8255★ Opportunities in Sports and Athletics

VGM Career Horizons
4255 W. Touhy Ave.
Lincolnwood, IL 60646-1975
Ph: (847)679-5500   Fax: (847)679-2494
Fr: 800-323-4900

William Ray Heitzmann. 1994. $14.95; $11.95 (paper). A guide to planning for and seeking opportunities in this growing field. Illustrated.

EMPLOYMENT AGENCIES AND SEARCH FIRMS

★8256★ Analytic Recruiting, Inc.

21 E. 40th St., Ste. 500
New York, NY 10016
Ph: (212)545-8511

Executive search firm.

★8257★ Biomedical Search Consultants

PO Box 1070
Danbury, CT 06813
Ph: (203)744-4027   Fax: (203)748-2122

Employment agency.

★8258★ E.J. Ashton and Associates, Ltd.

3125 N. Wilke Rd.
Arlington Heights, IL 60004-1452
Ph: (708)577-7900

Employment agency. Executive search firm.

★8259★ Place Mart Personnel Service

5 Elm Row
New Brunswick, NJ 08901
Ph: (908)247-8844

Executive search firm.

★8260★ T.R. Employment Agency

409 Wilshire Blvd.
Santa Monica, CA 90401
Ph: (310)393-4107

Employment agency.

OTHER SOURCES

★8261★ American Statistical Association (ASA)

1429 Duke St.
Alexandria, VA 22314-3402
Ph: (703)684-1221   Fax: (703)684-2037

Members: Professional society of persons interested in the theory, methodology, and application of statistics to all fields of human endeavor.

★8262★ Caucus for Women in Statistics (CWS)

Cyntha Struthers
St. Jerome's College
Waterloo, ON, Canada N2L 3G3
Ph: (519)888-4801   Fax: (519)746-6530

Members: Individuals, primarily statisticians, united to improve employment and professional opportunities for women in statistics. **Activities:** Conducts technical sessions concerning statistical studies related to women. Maintains biographical archives.

★8263★ Institute of Mathematical Statistics (IMS)

3401 Investment Blvd., Ste. 7
Hayward, CA 94545-3819
Ph: (510)783-8141   Fax: (510)783-4131

Members: Professional society of mathematicians and others interested in mathematical statistics and probability theory. **Purpose:** Seeks to further research in mathematical statistics and probability. **E-Mail:** ims@stat.berkeley.edu

Stenographers and Court Reporters

SOURCES OF HELP-WANTED ADS

★8264★ Pennsylvania Law Journal

Legal Communications, Ltd.
1617 JFK Blvd. Ste. 960
Philadelphia, PA 19103
Ph: (215)557-2300   Fax: (215)557-2301
Fr: 800-722-7670

Weekly (Mon.). Newspaper covering law news including recent court decisions.

★8265★ Public Interest Employment Service Job Alert

Public Interest Clearing House
200 McAllister St.
San Francisco, CA 94102-4978
Ph: (415)255-1714

Semimonthly. $120.00/year for employed persons; $60.00/year for unemployed. Lists job openings in legal aid offices, public interest law firms, and nonprofit organizations.

EMPLOYER DIRECTORIES AND NETWORKING LISTS

★8266★ Court Reporters Directory

American Business Directories, Inc.
American Business Information, Inc.
5711 S. 86th Cir.
Omaha, NE 68127
Ph: (402)593-4600   Fax: (402)331-1505

Annual. $460.00, payment with order. Entries include: Name, address, phone (including area code), size of advertisement, year first in Yellow Pages, name of owner or manager, number of employees. Compiled from telephone company Yellow Pages, nationwide. Arrangement: Geographical.

★8267★ Law and Legal Information Directory

Gale Research
835 Penobscot Bldg.
Detroit, MI 48226-4094
Ph: (313)961-2242   Fax: (313)961-6083
Fr: 800-877-GALE

Biennial, October of even years. $320.00. Covers more than 33,000 national and international organizations, bar associations, federal and highest state courts, federal regulatory agencies, law schools, firms and organizations offering continuing legal education, paralegal education, sources of scholarships and grants, awards and prizes, special libraries, information systems and services, research centers, publishers of legal periodicals, books, and audiovisual materials, lawyer referral services, legal aid offices, public defender offices, legislature manuals and registers, small claims courts, corporation departments of state, law enforcement agencies, state agencies, including disciplinary agencies, and state bar requirements. Entries include: All entries include institution or firm name, address, phone; many include names and titles of key personnel and, when pertinent, descriptive annotations. Arrangement: Classified by type of organization, activity, service, etc. Indexes: Individual sections have special indexes as required.

HANDBOOKS AND MANUALS

★8268★ Career Planning in Criminal Justice

Anderson Publishing Co.
2035 Reading Rd.
Cincinnati, OH 45202
Ph: (513)421-4142

Robert C. DeLucia and Thomas J. Doyle. Second edition, 1993. 178 pages. Surveys a wide range of career and employment opportunities in law enforcement, the courts, corrections, forensic science, and private security. Contains career planning and job hunting advice.

★8269★ Court Reporters (Shorthand Reporters)

Chronicle Guidance Publications, Inc.
66 Aurora St.
PO Box 1190
Moravia, NY 13118-1190
Ph: (315)497-0330   Fax: (315)497-3359
Fr: 800-622-7284

Chronicle Guidance Staff. 1992. $2.00. Provides concise career information and sources of additional information.

★8270★ Court Reporting: It's Your Move

National Court Reporters Association
8224 Old Courthouse Rd.
Vienna, VA 22182
Ph: (703)556-NCRA

This brochure describes qualifications, work, future outlook, places of employment, and educational preparation of court reporters.

EMPLOYMENT AGENCIES AND SEARCH FIRMS

★8271★ Attorney Resource, Inc.

2301 Cedar Springs Rd.
Dallas, TX 75201-6901
Ph: (214)922-8050

Employment agency. Offices in Fort Worth, TX, and Tulsa, OK. Provides staffing assistance on regular or temporary basis.

★8272★ Beverly Hills Bar Association Personnel Service

300 S. Beverly Dr., Ste. 214
Beverly Hills, CA 90212
Ph: (213)553-4575

Employment agency.

★8273★ Hallmark Services

520 Pike St., Ste. 1450
Seattle, WA 98101-4001
Ph: (206)587-5360

Employment agency. Fills openings on a regular or temporary basis.

★8274★ **Legal Placement Services, Inc.**
161 W. Wisconsin Ave., Ste. 3054
Milwaukee, WI 53203
Ph: (414)276-6689

Employment agency.

★8275★ **Parks Associates**
342 Madison Ave., Ste. 1430
New York, NY 10173
Ph: (212)286-0777   Fax: (212)286-1973

Employment agency.

★8276★ **Pathfinders, Inc.**
229 Peachtree St. NE
Atlanta, GA 30303-1601
Ph: (404)688-5940

Employment agency.

★8277★ **Wichita Bar and Legal Placement**
301 N. Main, Ste. 700
Wichita, KS 67202
Ph: (316)263-2469

Employment agency.

OTHER SOURCES

★8278★ **National Court Reporters Association (NCRA)**
8224 Old Courthouse Rd.
Vienna, VA 22182
Ph: (703)556-6272   Fax: (703)556-6291

Members: Independent state, regional, and local associations. Verbatim shorthand reporters who work as official reporters for courts and government agencies, as freelance reporters for independent contractors, and as captioners for television programmings; retired reporters, teachers of shorthand reporting, and school officials; student shorthand reporters. **Activities:** Conducts research; compiles statistics; offers several certification programs.

Stockbrokers and Securities Analysts

week); Investment Management Workshop (one week). **Activities:** Operates Jobline Placement Service. Maintains Research Foundation of ICFA.

SOURCES OF HELP-WANTED ADS

★8279★ Investment Dealers' Digest

Investment Dealer's Digest
2 World Trade Center, 18th Fl.
New York, NY 10048
Ph: (212)227-1200   Fax: (212)321-3805

Weekly. Magazine focusing on securities and finance.

★8280★ Registered Representative

Plaza Communications, Inc.
18818 Teller Ave., Ste. 280
Irvine, CA 92715
Ph: (714)851-2220   Fax: (714)851-1636
Fr: 800-621-0720

Monthly. $21.00/year for individuals; $4.00 for single issue; $33 .00/year for out of country. Magazine providing comprehensive coverage of securities industry trends directly affecting the job performance and productivity of retail stockbrokers.

PLACEMENT AND JOB REFERRAL SERVICES

★8281★ Association for Investment Management and Research (AIMR)

5 Boar's Head Ln.
PO Box 3668
Charlottesville, VA 22903
Ph: (804)977-6600   Fax: (804)977-1103

Members: Security and financial analyst association whose members are practicing investment analysts. Includes private, voluntary self-regulation program in which AIMR members are enrolled. **Purpose:** Promotes education, uniform performance presentation standards, improved accounting and disclosure of corporate information, and development of improved standards of investment research and portfolio management. Educational programs include: Chartered Financial Analyst; Candidate Study and Examination Program; Financial Analysts Seminar (one

★8282★ Financial Women's Association of New York (FWA)

215 Park Ave. S, Ste. 2010
New York, NY 10003
Ph: (212)533-2141   Fax: (212)982-3008

Members: Persons of professional status in the field of finance in the New York metropolitan area. **Purpose:** Works to promote and maintain high professional standards in the financial and business communities; provide an opportunity for members to enhance one another's professional contacts; achieve recognition of the contribution of women to the financial and business communities; encourage other women to seek professional positions within the financial and business communities. **Activities:** Activities include educational trips to foreign countries; college internship program including foreign student exchange; high school mentorship program; Washington and international briefings; placement service for members. Maintains speakers' bureau.

★8283★ New York Society of Security Analysts (NYSSA)

1 World Trade Center, Ste. 4447
New York, NY 10048
Ph: (212)912-9249   Fax: (212)912-9310
Fr: 800-248-0108

Members: A member of the Financial Analysts Federation, a subsidiary of the Association for Investment Management and Research. Security analysts and portfolio managers employed in New York by brokerage houses, banks, insurance companies, mutual funds, and other financial institutions. **Activities:** Conducts educational forums on topics relating to the securities markets. Maintains placement service. **E-Mail:** staff@nyssa.org. **Website:** http://www.nyssa.org

EMPLOYER DIRECTORIES AND NETWORKING LISTS

★8284★ Bonds-Surety & Fidelity Directory

American Business Directories, Inc.
American Business Information, Inc.
5711 S. 86th Cir.
Omaha, NE 68127
Ph: (402)593-4600   Fax: (402)331-1505

Annual. $465.00, payment with order. Number of listings: 6,317. Entries include: Name, address, phone (including area code), size of advertisement, year first in Yellow Pages, name of owner or manager, number of employees. Compiled from telephone company Yellow Pages, nationwide. Arrangement: Geographical.

★8285★ Directory of Security Analysts Societies, Analyst Splinter Groups, and Stockbroker Clubs

National Investor Relations Institute
8045 Leesburg Pke., Ste. 600
Vienna, VA 22182
Ph: (703)506-3570   Fax: (703)506-3571

Annual. $50.00. Covers about 120 groups of security analysts, stockbrokers, and splinter groups (i.e., specialists in a single industry). Entries include: Group name; affiliations, business addresses and phone numbers of president and program chairman; time, location, and length of meetings; number of members; specific interests; speaker policy; average attendance at meetings; procedure for speaking at meetings; group events; costs to guest. Arrangement: Alphabetical within type of group.

★8286★ Institutional Investor—Ranking America's Biggest Brokers Issue

Institutional Investor, Inc.
488 Madison Ave.
New York, NY 10022
Ph: (212)303-3570   Fax: (212)303-3592
Fr: 800-437-9997

Annual, April. $45.00. Publication includes: Top 100 brokerage firms selected on the basis of total capital. Entries include: Company name, total capital, excess net capital, number of employees, officers, and registered representatives. Arrangement: Ranked by total capital.

★8287★ *Investment Securities Directory*

American Business Directories, Inc.
American Business Information, Inc.
5711 S. 86th Cir.
Omaha, NE 68127
Ph: (402)593-4600   Fax: (402)331-1505

Updated continuously; printed on request. Please inquire. Entries include: Name, address, phone (including area code), size of advertisement, year first in Yellow Pages, name of owner or manager, number of employees. Compiled from telephone company Yellow Pages, nationwide. Arrangement: Geographical.

★8288★ *National Association of Securities Dealers—Manual*

Commerce Clearing House, Inc.
4025 W. Peterson Ave.
Chicago, IL 60646
Ph: (312)382-3450   Fax: (312)382-1340
Fr: 800-TELL-CCH

$310.00, per year, including periodic reports. Publication includes: List of about 2,900 members of the National Association of Securities Dealers. Entries include: Company name, address. Principal contents of the manual are association by-laws and industry rules, arbitration code and code of procedure, and association's rules of fair practice. Arrangement: Alphabetical.

★8289★ *Securities Industry Yearbook*

Securities Industry Association
120 Broadway
New York, NY 10271
Ph: (212)608-1500   Fax: (212)608-1604

Annual, August. $115.00, payment must accompany order. Covers over 750 member securities firms, with about 480 of them covered in detail. Arrangement: Alphabetical. Indexes: National firms ranked by capital with capital and rank for prior year, number of offices and rank, number of employees and rank, and number of registered representatives and rank. Same data given in separate ranked list for regional firms.

★8290★ *Standard & Poor's Security Dealers of North America*

Standard & Poor's
25 Broadway, 14th Fl.
New York, NY 10004
Ph: (212)208-8000   Fax: (212)412-0305

Semiannual, March and September; supplements available every 6 weeks. $515.00, per set. Covers over 12,000 security dealers; includes over 300 offices outside North America. Entries include: Company name, address, phone, main and branch offices, departments, names and titles of principal personnel, exchange memberships, teletype, wire systems, clearing facilities, employer identification number, and date established. Arrangement: Geographical.

★8291★ *Who's Who in the Securities Industry*

Economist Publishing Co.
11 E. Hubbard St., No. 3A
Chicago, IL 60611-3536
Ph: (312)467-1888   Fax: (312)467-0225
Fr: 800-THE-ECON

Annual, December. $15.00. Covers about 1,000 investment bankers. Entries include: Name, company affiliation, city, position, birth date, educational and business background, directorships, club memberships, interests and hobbies. Arrangement: Alphabetical.

HANDBOOKS AND MANUALS

★8292★ *America's 50 Fastest Growing Jobs*

JIST Works, Inc.
720 N. Park Ave.
Indianapolis, IN 46202
Ph: (317)264-3720   Fr: 800-648-5478

Third edition, 1995. $14.95. 288 pages. Each job profile explains the nature of the work, skills and abilities required, employment outlook, average earnings, related occupations, education and training requirements, and employment opportunities. Also contains career planning information and job search tips.

★8293★ *Business and Finance Career Directory*

Gale Research
835 Penobscot Bldg.
Detroit, MI 48226-4094
Ph: (313)961-2242   Fax: (313)961-6083
Fr: 800-877-GALE

Bradley Morgan. Second edition, 1992. $39.00. 413 pages. Features a basic and comprehensive job search section, articles by top professionals in the field, and detailed listings of hundreds of top companies who hire individuals in this field. Aimed particularly at entry-level job hunters.

★8294★ *Career Choices for the 90's for Students of Business*

Walker and Company
435 Hudson St.
New York, NY 10014
Ph: (212)727-8300   Fax: (212)727-0984
Fr: 800-289-2553

Prepared by the Career Associates staff. 1990. $9.95. 166 pages. Discusses alternatives for students of business. Offers advice on how to break into the field and how to move up. Covers where and who the employers are, internship possibilities, and professional networking associations. Comprehensive guide to career and job search planning.

★8295★ *Career Choices for the 90's for Students Considering an MBA*

Walker and Company
435 Hudson St.
New York, NY 10014
Ph: (212)727-8300   Fax: (212)727-0984
Fr: 800-289-2553

Prepared by the Career Associates staff.

1990. $8.95. 166 pages. Discusses career alternatives and offers advice on how to break in and move up. Covers where and who the employers are, internship possibilities, and professional networking associations. Comprehensive guide to career and job search planning.

★8296★ *Career Choices for the 90's for Students of Economics*

Walker and Company
435 Hudson St.
New York, NY 10014
Ph: (212)727-8300   Fax: (212)727-0984
Fr: 800-289-2553

Prepared by the Career Associates staff. 1990. $8.95. 166 pages. Discusses alternatives for students of economics. Offers advice on how to break into the field and how to move up. Covers where and who the employers are, internship possibilities, and professional networking associations. Comprehensive guide to career and job search planning.

★8297★ *Career Choices for the 90's for Students of Law*

Walker and Company
435 Hudson St.
New York, NY 10014
Ph: (212)727-8300   Fax: (212)727-0984
Fr: 800-289-2553

Prepared by the Career Associates staff. 1990. $8.95. 166 pages. Discusses career alternatives and offers advice on how to break in and move up. Covers where and who the employers are, internship possibilities, and professional networking associations. Comprehensive guide to career and job search planning.

★8298★ *Career Choices for the 90's for Students of Mathematics*

Walker and Company
435 Hudson St.
New York, NY 10014
Ph: (212)727-8300   Fax: (212)727-0984
Fr: 800-289-2553

Prepared by the Career Associates staff. 1990. $8.95. 166 pages. Discusses alternatives for students of mathematics. Offers advice on how to break into the field and how to move up. Covers where and who the employers are, internship possibilities, and professional networking associations. Comprehensive guide to career and job search planning.

★8299★ *Career Choices for the 90's for Students of Political Science and Government*

Walker and Company
435 Hudson St.
New York, NY 10014
Ph: (212)727-8300   Fax: (212)727-0984
Fr: 800-289-2553

Prepared by the Career Associates staff. 1990. $8.95. 166 pages. Discusses alternatives for students of political science and government. Offers advice on how to break into the field and how to move up. Covers where and who the employers are, internship possibilities, and professional networking associations. Comprehensive guide to career and job search planning.

★8300★ Career Choices for the 90's for Students of Psychology

Walker and Company
435 Hudson St.
New York, NY 10014
Ph: (212)727-8300   Fax: (212)727-0984
Fr: 800-289-2553

Prepared by the Career Associates staff. 1990. $9.95. 166 pages. Discusses alternatives for students of psychology. Offers advice on how to break into the field and how to move up. Covers where and who the employers are, internship possibilities, and professional networking associations. Comprehensive guide to career and job search planning.

★8301★ Careers in Banking and Finance

Rosen Publishing Group, Inc.
29 E. 21st St.
New York, NY 10010
Ph: (212)777-3017   Fax: (212)777-0277
Fr: 800-237-9932

Patricia Haddock. 1990. $14.95. Offers advice on job hunting. Describes jobs at all levels in banking and finance. Contains information about the types of financial organizations where the jobs are found, educational requirements, job duties, and salaries.

★8302★ Careers for Number Crunchers and Other Quantitative Types

VGM Career Horizons
4255 W. Touhy Ave.
Lincolnwood, IL 60646-1975
Ph: (847)679-5500   Fax: (847)679-2494
Fr: 800-323-4900

Rebecca Burnett. 1993. $14.95; $9.95 (paper). Provides information to math-oriented job hunters on how to become statisticians, field researchers, computer programmers, stock analysts, investment managers, bankers, engineers, accountants, underwriters, economists, market analysts, mathematicians, systems analysts, and more.

★8303★ The Encyclopedia of Career Choices for the 1990s: Guide to Entry-Level Jobs

Perigree Books
The Berkley Publishing Group
PO Box 506
East Rutherford, NJ 07073
Ph: (201)933-9292   Fr: 800-223-0510

Career Associates Staff. 1992. $19.95. 862 pages. Describes 500 entry-level careers in a variety of industries. Presents qualifications required, working conditions, salary, internships, and professional associations.

★8304★ Jobs '90

Prentice Hall
113 Sylvan Ave.
Rte. 9W
Englewood Cliffs, NJ 07632
Ph: (201)592-2000   Fr: 800-922-0579

Kathryn Petras and Ross Petras. 1990. $14.95. 320 pages. Discusses employment prospects and trends. Lists leading companies, associations, directories, and magazines.

★8305★ Opportunities in Financial Careers

VGM Career Horizons
4255 W. Touhy Ave.
Lincolnwood, IL 60646-1975
Ph: (847)679-5500   Fax: (847)679-2494
Fr: 800-323-4900

Michael Sumichrast and Dean A. Christ. 1991. $14.95; $11.95 (paper). A guide to planning for and seeking opportunities in this challenging field.

★8306★ Traders: The Jobs, the Products, the Markets

New York Institute of Finance
2 Broadway
New York, NY 10004
Ph: (212)344-2900

David M. Weiss. 1990. $19.95. Describes the work and procedures of many different types of traders in many different marketplaces.

Employment Agencies and Search Firms

★8307★ Baker Scott and Co.

1259 Rte. 46
Parsippany, NJ 07054
Ph: (201)263-3355   Fax: (201)263-9255

Executive search firm.

★8308★ Cross Employment Agency

150 Broadway, Ste. 902
New York, NY 10038-4389
Ph: (212)227-6705

Employment agency. Temporary and regular placement of personnel.

★8309★ Hunter Mac and Associates

139 Fulton St.
New York, NY 10038
Ph: (212)267-2790   Fax: (212)962-2339

Employment agency.

★8310★ J.R. Scott and Associates

222 S. Riverside Plaza, Ste. 320
Chicago, IL 60606
Ph: (312)648-4630

Executive search firm specializing in retail securities sales, investment banking, and equity and debt trading.

★8311★ Mark Elzweig Co. Ltd.

101 Fifth Ave., Ste. 10A
New York, NY 10003
Ph: (212)243-0539

Executive search firm.

★8312★ Phillip Thomas Personnel, Inc.

545 5th Ave., Ste., 606
New York, NY 10017
Ph: (212)867-0860

Employment agency.

★8313★ Scan Management Inc.

Drawer 4835
Gettysburg, PA 17325-4835
Ph: (717)359-7473   Fax: (717)359-7082

Executive search firm.

★8314★ Straight and Company

3415 Merganser Ln.
Alpharetta, GA 30202
Ph: (770)663-0448

Executive search firm.

Other Sources

★8315★ Institutional Investor—All America Research Team Issue

Institutional Investor, Inc.
488 Madison Ave.
New York, NY 10022
Ph: (212)303-3570   Fax: (212)303-3592
Fr: 800-437-9997

Annual, October. $45.00. Publication includes: List of about 400 analysts at 35 firms judged to have been outstanding in their recommendations concerning stock transactions. Entries include: Analyst name, firm, ranking, comments by colleagues and clients. Arrangement: Classified by line of business.

★8316★ Securities Industry Association (SIA)

120 Broadway
New York, NY 10271
Ph: (212)608-1500   Fax: (212)608-1604

Members: Investment bankers, securities underwriters, and dealers in stocks and bonds. **Purpose:** To represent and serve all segments of the securities industry and provide a unified voice in legislation, regulation, and public information. **Activities:** Conducts studies and compiles statistics on investment, securities markets, and related matters. Sponsors management development programs; conducts roundtables. Maintains offices in New York City, and Washington, DC.

Surgical Technicians

★8317★ American Journal of Surgery

Conners Publishing
245 W. 17th St.
New York, NY 10011
Ph: (212)463-6835   Fax: (212)463-6836

Monthly. Surgical journal.

★8318★ Annals of Surgery

Pharmaceutical Media, Inc.
30 E. 33rd St.
New York, NY 10016
Ph: (212)685-5010   Fax: (212)685-5010

Monthly. $88.00/year for individuals. Medical journal publishing original manuscripts promoting the advancement of surgical knowledge and practice.

★8319★ Surgical Rounds

Romaine Pierson Publishers, Inc.
80 Shore Rd.
Port Washington, NY 11050
Ph: (516)883-6350   Fax: (516)883-6609

Monthly. Medical and surgical magazine.

EMPLOYER DIRECTORIES AND NETWORKING LISTS

★8320★ AHA Guide to the Health Care Field

Health Statistics Group
American Hospital Association (AHA)
1 N. Franklin
Chicago, IL 60606
Ph: (312)422-3501   Fax: (312)280-6015

Annual, July. $195.00, payment with order. Covers hospitals, multi-health care systems, freestanding ambulatory surgery centers, psychiatric facilities, long-term care facilities, substance abuse programs, hospices, Health Maintenance Organizations (HMOs), and other health-related organizations. Entries include: For hospitals: facility name, address, phone, administrator's name, number of

beds, facilities and services, number of employees, expenses, other statistics. For other organizations: name, address, phone, name and title of contact. Arrangement: Geographical. Indexes: Hospital name.

★8321★ Directory of Hospital Personnel

Medical Economics
5 Paragon Dr.
Montvale, NJ 07645-1725
Ph: (201)358-7500   Fax: (201)573-4956
Fr: 800-222-3045

Annual, September. $325.00, plus 7.50 shipping. Covers 200,000 executives at 7,100 U.S. hospitals. Entries include: Name of hospital, address, phone, number of beds, type and JCAHO status of hospital, names and titles of key department heads and staff, medical and nursing school affiliations; number of residents, interns, and nursing students. Arrangement: Geographical. Indexes: Hospital name, personnel, hospital size.

★8322★ Freestanding Outpatient Surgery Center Directory

SMG Marketing Group, Inc.
1342 N. LaSalle Dr.
Chicago, IL 60610
Ph: (312)642-3026   Fax: (312)642-9729
Fr: 800-678-3026

Annual, August. $425.00. Covers more than 1,600 ambulatory surgical centers. Entries include: Facility name, address, phone, medical director name, ownership; number of operating suites, number of surgeries performed each year, types of surgery performed. Arrangement: Geographical.

★8323★ Hospital Blue Book

Billian Publishing Co.
2100 Powers Ferry Rd., Ste. 300
Atlanta, GA 30339
Ph: (404)955-5656   Fax: (404)952-0669

Annual, spring. $154.50, national edition, plus $20.00 shipping. Covers more than 7,100 hospitals; some listings also appear in a separate southern edition of this publication. Entries include: Name of hospital, accreditation, mailing address, phone, fax, number of beds, type of facility (nonprofit, general, state, etc.); list of administrative personnel and chiefs of medical services,

with specific titles. Arrangement: Geographical.

★8324★ Hospital Market Atlas

SMG Marketing Group, Inc.
1342 N. LaSalle Dr.
Chicago, IL 60610
Ph: (312)642-3026   Fax: (312)642-9729
Fr: 800-678-3026

Biennial, odd years. $495.00, payment with order. Covers over 7,000 hospitals, hospital systems and 480 group purchasing organizations. Entries include: Hospital or organization name, address, phone, county code, management, type of hospital service, number of beds, admissions, surgical operations, and emergency room visits. Arrangement: Geographical.

★8325★ Hospitals Directory

American Business Directories, Inc.
American Business Information, Inc.
5711 S. 86th Cir.
Omaha, NE 68127
Ph: (402)593-4600   Fax: (402)331-1505

Annual. $870.00, U.S. edition. Entries include: Name, address, phone (including area code), size of advertisement, year first in Yellow Pages, name of owner or manager, number of employees. Compiled from telephone company Yellow Pages, nationwide. Arrangement: Geographical.

★8326★ Medical and Health Information Directory

Gale Research
835 Penobscot Bldg.
Detroit, MI 48226-4094
Ph: (313)961-2242   Fax: (313)961-6083
Fr: 800-877-GALE

Approximately biennial; latest edition 1994. $195.00, per volume; $485.00, for the three-volume set. Covers in Volume 1, almost 18,600 medical and health oriented associations, organizations, institutions, and government agencies, including health maintenance organizations (HMOs), preferred provider organizations (PPOs), insurance companies, pharmaceutical companies, research centers, and medical and allied health schools. In Volume 2, nearly 11,800 medical book publishers; medical periodicals, directories, audiovisual producers and services, medical libraries and information centers, and electronic resources. In Volume 3, nearly 26,000 clinics, treatment centers, care programs, and counseling/diagnostic services for 30 subject areas. Entries include: Institution, service, or firm name, address, phone; many include names of key personnel and, when pertinent, descriptive annotation. Arrangement: Classified by organization activity, service, etc. Indexes: Each volume has a complete alphabetical name and keyword index.

★8327★ Osteopathic Membership Directory—AOHA

American Osteopathic Healthcare Association
5301 Wisconsin Ave. NW, Ste. 630
Washington, DC 20015-2015
Ph: (202)686-1700   Fax: (202)686-7615

Annual, summer. $125.00, payment with order. Covers about 110 osteopathic hospitals. Includes list of individual and institutional members; also lists osteopathic colleges, and directors of medical education. Entries include: For hospitals: name of hospital, name of chief executive officer, address, phone, number of beds and other hospital data. Arrangement: Geographical. Indexes: Name, institution.

HANDBOOKS AND MANUALS

★8328★ Careers in Health Care

VGM Career Horizons
4255 W. Touhy Ave.
Lincolnwood, IL 60646-1975
Ph: (847)679-5500   Fax: (847)679-2494
Fr: 800-323-4900

Barbara M. Swanson. 1995. $17.95; $13.95 (paper). Describes job duties, work settings, salaries, licensing and certification requirements, educational preparation, and future outlook. Gives ideas on how to secure a job.

★8329★ Medical Technologists and Technicians Career Directory

Gale Research
835 Penobscot Bldg.
Detroit, MI 48226-4094
Ph: (313)961-2242   Fax: (313)961-6083
Fr: 800-877-GALE

Bradley Morgan. 1993. $39.00. 324 pages.

Essays on specific careers provide an insider's perspective. Features extensive listings of contacts and entry-level job opportunities. Provides information on internships and sources of help-wanted ads.

★8330★ Opportunities in Health and Medical Careers

VGM Career Horizons
4255 W. Touhy Ave.
Lincolnwood, IL 60646-1975
Ph: (847)679-5500   Fax: (847)679-2494
Fr: 800-323-4900

Donald Snook, Jr. and Leo D'Orazio. 1993. $14.95; $11.95 (paper). Covers the full range of medical and health occupations. Illustrated.

★8331★ Opportunities in Paramedical Careers

VGM Career Horizons
4255 W. Touhy Ave.
Lincolnwood, IL 60646-1975
Ph: (847)679-5500   Fax: (847)679-2494
Fr: 800-323-4900

Alex Kacen. 1994. $14.95; 11.95 (paper). 160 pages. Discusses a variety of opportunities in this field and how to pursue them. Illustrated.

★8332★ Opportunities in Vocational and Technical Careers

VGM Career Horizons
4255 W. Touhy Ave.
Lincolnwood, IL 60646-1975
Ph: (847)679-5500   Fax: (847)679-2494
Fr: 800-323-4900

Adrian A. Paradis. 1992. $14.95; $11.95 (paper). 160 pages. Provides information on a variety of opportunities and advice on breaking into the field.

★8333★ Resumes for Health and Medical Careers

4255 W. Touhy Ave.
Lincolnwood, IL 60646-1975
Ph: (708)679-5500   Fax: (708)679-6375
Fr: 800-323-4900

Compiled by VGM Career Horizons Staff 1995. $9.95 (paper).

★8334★ Surgical Technologist

R & E Publishers, Inc.
468 Auzerais Ave., Ste. A
San Jose, CA 95126
Ph: (408)977-0691   Fax: (408)977-0693

Ronald R. Smith. 1993. $1.95 (paper).

EMPLOYMENT AGENCIES AND SEARCH FIRMS

★8335★ Action Plus Employer Services

1211 W. Imperial Hwy., Ste. 100
Brea, CA 92621
Ph: (714)773-1506   Fax: (714)773-9201

Employment agency.

★8336★ Sue Carroll Personnel, Inc.

16 E. 79th St.
New York, NY 10021
Ph: (212)288-8866   Fax: (212)988-7191

Employment agency and executive search firm.

OTHER SOURCES

★8337★ Association of Surgical Technologists (AST)

7108-C S. Alton Way
Englewood, CO 80112
Ph: (303)694-9130   Fax: (303)694-9169

Members: Individuals who have received specific education and training to deliver surgical patient care in the operating room. Membership categories are available for both certified and uncertified technologists. Emphasis is placed on encouraging members to participate actively in a continuing education program. **Purpose:** Aims are: to study, discuss, and exchange knowledge, experience, and ideas in the field of surgical technology; to promote a high standard of surgical technology performance in the community for quality patient care; to stimulate interest in continuing education.

Surveyors

Sources of Help-Wanted Ads

★8338★ American City and County

Communication Channels, Inc.
6255 Barfield Rd.
Atlanta, GA 30328
Ph: (404)955-9970   Fax: (404)256-3116

Monthly. $54.00/year for individuals. Municipal and county administration magazine.

★8339★ APWA Reporter

American Public Works Association
1313 E. 60th St.
Chicago, IL 60637-2881
Ph: (312)667-2200   Fax: (312)667-2304

Monthly. $1.00 for single issue. Magazine reporting on public works.

★8340★ Architectural Record

New York Construction News
1221 Avenue of the Americas, 41st Fl.
New York, NY 10020
Ph: (212)512-4773   Fax: (212)512-4770

Magazine focusing on architecture.

★8341★ Builder

Hanley-Wood, Inc.
1 Thomas Cir., Ste. 600
Washington, DC 20005
Ph: (202)452-0800   Fax: (202)785-1974

Monthly. $29.95/year for individuals. Magazine covering housing, commercial, and industrial building.

★8342★ The Municipality

League of Wisconsin Municipalities
122 W. Washington Ave., Ste. 301
Madison, WI 53703-2757
Ph: (608)267-2380   Fax: (608)267-0645

Monthly. Magazine for officials of Wisconsin's local municipal governments.

★8343★ NAHRO Monitor

National Association of Housing and Redevelopment Officials
1320 18th St. NW
Washington, DC 20036
Ph: (202)429-2960

Semimonthly.

★8344★ Photogrammetric Engineering and Remote Sensing

American Society for Photogrammetry and Remote Sensing (ASPRS)
5410 Grosvenor Ln., Ste. 210
Bethesda, MD 20814-2160
Ph: (301)493-0290   Fax: (301)493-0208

Monthly. Free to members; $120.00/year for nonmembers. Provides technical information about the applications of photogrammetry, remote sensing, and geographic information systems.

★8345★ Western City

League of California Cities
1400 K St.
Sacramento, CA 95814
Ph: (916)444-5790   Fax: (916)658-8240

Monthly. $30.00/year for individuals; $49.00 for two years. Municipal interest magazine.

Placement and Job Referral Services

★8346★ Associated Builders and Contractors (ABC)

1300 N. 17th St.
Rosslyn, VA 22209
Ph: (703)812-2000   Fax: (703)812-8200

Members: Construction contractors, subcontractors, suppliers, and associates. **Purpose:** Aim is to foster and perpetuate the principles of rewarding construction workers and management on the basis of merit. **Activities:** Maintains placement service. Sponsors management education programs and craft training; also sponsors apprenticeship and skill training programs. Disseminates technological and labor relations information. Compiles statistics.

★8347★ National Association of Home Builders of the U.S. (NAHB)

1201 15th St. NW
Washington, DC 20005
Ph: (202)822-0200   Fax: (202)822-0559

Members: Single and multifamily home builders, commercial builders, and others associated with the building industry. **Purpose:** Lobbies on behalf of the housing industry and conducts public affairs activities to increase public understanding of housing and the economy. Collects and disseminates data on current developments in home building and home builders' plans through its Economics Department and nationwide Metropolitan Housing Forecast. **Activities:** Maintains NAHB Research Center, which functions as the research arm of the home building industry. Sponsors seminars and workshops on construction, mortgage credit, labor relations, cost reduction, land use, remodeling, and business management. Compiles statistics; offers charitable program, spokesman training, and placement service; maintains speakers' bureau, and hall of fame.

★8348★ Professional Women in Construction (PWC)

342 Madison Ave., Rm. 451
New York, NY 10173
Ph: (212)687-0610   Fax: (212)490-1213

Members: Management-level women and men in construction and allied industries; owners, suppliers, architects, engineers, field personnel, office personnel, and bonding/surety personnel. **Purpose:** Provides a forum for exchange of ideas and promotion of political and legislative action, education, and job opportunities for women in construction and related fields; forms liaisons with other trade and professional groups; develops research programs. Strives to reform abuses and to assure justice and equity within the construction industry. Sponsors mini-workshops. **Activities:** Maintains Action Line which provides members with current information on pertinent legislation and on the association's activities and job referrals.

EMPLOYER DIRECTORIES AND NETWORKING LISTS

★8349★ ABC Today—Associated Builders and Contractors Membership Directory Issue

Associated Builders and Contractors
1300 N. 17th St.
Rosslyn, VA 22209
Ph: (703)812-2000   Fax: (703)812-8200

Annual, November. $150.00, plus $7.00 shipping. Publication includes: List of approximately 17,000 member construction contractors and suppliers. Entries include: Company name, address, phone, name of principal executive, code to volume of business, business specialty. Arrangement: Classified by chapter, then by work specialty.

★8350★ Constructor—Directory of Membership and Services Issue

AGC Information, Inc.
Associated General Contractors of America
1957 E St. NW
Washington, DC 20006
Ph: (202)393-2040   Fax: (202)347-4004

Annual, July. $135.00. Publication includes: List of more than 8,500 member firms and 9,000 national associate member firms engaged in building, highway, heavy, industrial, municipal utilities, and railroad construction, listing of state and local chapter officers. Arrangement: Geographical. Indexes: Company name.

★8351★ Indiana Society of Professional Engineers—Directory

Indiana Society of Professional Engineers
Box 20806
Indianapolis, IN 46220
Ph: (317)255-2267

Annual, fall. $25.00. Covers member registered engineers, land surveyors, engineering students, and engineers in training. Entries include: Member name, address, phone, type of membership, business information. Arrangement: Geographical by city. Indexes: Personal name.

★8352★ Municipal/County Directory Library Edition

Carroll Publishing
1058 Thomas Jefferson St. NW
Washington, DC 20007
Ph: (202)333-8620   Fax: (202)337-7020
Fr: 800-336-4240

Annual, July. $137.00, plus $8.00 shipping; payment must accompany order. Covers officials of 1,400 county governments (with populations over 25,000) and 2,000 municipalities (with populations over 1,000); includes elected, appointed, and career office holders. Entries include: Name, title, agency, address, phone. Arrangement: County officials are geographical, then by agency; municipal officials are by city. Indexes: personal name (with phone), agency.

★8353★ Municipal Year Book

Newman Books Ltd.
32 Vauxhall Bridge Rd.
London SW1V 2SS, England
Ph: 71 9736400   Fax: 71 2335057

Annual, December. $140.00, postpaid. Covers local and central government agencies and officials of the United Kingdom; municipal art galleries, associations, development organizations, fairs, libraries, museums, airports, and other local authorities. Entries include: Name of authority or governing agency, address, phone, fax, names of elected councillors, officers, names and titles of key personnel, contacts, population, and pay. Arrangement: Geographical. Indexes: Subject, place names.

★8354★ Surveyors-Land Directory

American Business Directories, Inc.
American Business Information, Inc.
5711 S. 86th Cir.
Omaha, NE 68127
Ph: (402)593-4600   Fax: (402)331-1505

Annual. $1,025.00, U.S. edition. Entries include: Name, address, phone (including area code), size of advertisement, year first in Yellow Pages, name of owner or manager, number of employees. Compiled from telephone company Yellow Pages, nationwide. Arrangement: Geographical.

HANDBOOKS AND MANUALS

★8355★ Career Information Center

Macmillan Publishing Co.
200 Old Tappan Rd.
Old Tappan, NJ 07675
Ph: (609)461-6500   Fr: 800-223-2336

Visual Education Center Staff. Fifth edition, 1992. $229.00. This 13-volume set profiles over 600 occupations. Each occupational profile describes job duties, educational requirements, how to get the job, advancement possibilities, employment outlook, working conditions, earnings and benefits, and where to write for more information.

★8356★ Encyclopedia of Careers and Vocational Guidance

J. G. Ferguson Publishing Co.
200 W. Monroe, Ste. 250
Chicago, IL 60606
Ph: (312)580-5480

William E. Hopke. Ninth edition, 1993. $129.95; $199.95 (CD-ROM). Four-volume set that profiles 900 occupations and describes job trends in 71 industries. Includes career description, educational requirements, history of the job, methods of entry, advancement, employment outlook, earnings, conditions of work, social and psychological factors, and sources of further information. Contains career and employment information for this field.

EMPLOYMENT AGENCIES AND SEARCH FIRMS

★8357★ B W and Associates, Inc.

4415 W. Harrison St.
Hillside, IL 60162-1910
Ph: (708)449-5400

Employment agency.

★8358★ Construction Personnel Service

14697 E. Easter Ave., Ste. B
Englewood, CO 80112-4207
Ph: (303)766-0509

Employment agency. Provides temporary staffing services.

★8359★ Roper Personnel Services

220 Executive Center Dr., Ste. 110
Columbia, SC 29210-8421
Ph: (803)798-8500

Employment agency. Fills openings on temporary or regular basis.

OTHER SOURCES

★8360★ American Congress on Surveying and Mapping (ACSM)

5410 Grosvenor Ln.
Bethesda, MD 20814-2122
Ph: (301)493-0200   Fax: (301)493-8245

Members: Professionals, technicians, and students in the field of surveying and mapping including surveying of all disciplines, land and geographic information systems, cartography, geodesy, photogrammetry, engineering, geophysics, geography, and computer graphics; American Association for Geodetic Surveying, American Cartographic Association, and National Society of Professional Surveyors. **Purpose:** Objectives are to: advance the sciences of surveying and mapping; promote public understanding and use of surveying and mapping; speak on the national level as the collective voice of the profession; provide publications to serve the surveying and mapping community. Member organizations encourage improvement of university and college curricula for surveying and mapping.

★8361★ American Society for Photogrammetry and Remote Sensing (ASPRS)

5410 Grosvenor Ln., Ste. 210
Bethesda, MD 20814-2160
Ph: (301)493-0290   Fax: (301)493-0208

Members: Firms, individuals, government employees, and academicians engaged in photogrammetry, photointerpretation, remote sensing, and geographic information systems and their application to such fields as archaeology, geographic information systems, military reconnaissance, urban planning, engineering, traffic surveys, meteorological observations, medicine, geology, forestry, agriculture, construction, and topographic mapping. **Activities:** Offers voluntary certification program open to persons associated with one or more functional area of photogrammetry, remote sensing, and GIS. Surveys the profession of private firms in photogrammetry and remote sensing in the areas of products and services.

★8362★ **Associated General Contractors of America (AGC)**
1957 E St. NW
Washington, DC 20006
Ph: (202)393-2040   Fax: (202)347-4004
Members: General construction contractors; subcontractors; industry suppliers; service firms.**Purpose:** Provides market services through its divisions. Conducts special conferences and seminars designed specifically for construction firms. Compiles statistics on job accidents reported by member firms. Maintains 65 committees, including joint cooperative committees with other associations and liaison committees with federal agencies.

★8363★ **Construction Education Foundation (MSF)**
1300 N. 17th St.
Rosslyn, VA 22209
Ph: (703)812-2000   Fax: (703)812-8235
Purpose: Works to promote the merit shop for the benefit of the construction industry. (A merit shop is an open, nonunion shop that competes for business on the basis of price and quality rather than union status.) Conducts annual grants program to fund research and education projects aimed at improving the technology and environment of the construction industry and to promote the merit shop philosophy. Sponsors college programs and activities including: informational mailings to construction programs; financial aid for construction students; assistance to educators traveling to merit shop meetings; merit shop nights. Provides grants for publications and research studies to forecast trends in open shop construction, to compile information on the economic impact

of wage laws, and to create an awareness of merit shop principles among students. Distributes study summaries, reports, and information about merit shop construction to public officials, contractors, educators, and students. Sponsors Wheels of Learning to provide apprenticeship and task training in 15 trade areas. Holds annual Job Fair for construction management, engineering, architecture, and building science students.

★8364★ **National Association of Women in Construction (NAWIC)**
327 S. Adams St.
Fort Worth, TX 76104
Ph: (817)877-5551   Fax: (817)877-0324
Fr: 800-552-3506
Purpose: NAWIC is an international association of women employed in the construction industry which promotes that industry and supports the advancement of women within it.

Teacher Aides

★8365★ Community Jobs: The Employment Newspaper for the Non-Profit Sector
ACCESS: Networking in the Public Interest
30 Irving Pl.
New York, NY 10003
Ph: (212)475-1001   Fax: (212)475-1199

Monthly. $69.00. Covers jobs and internships available with nonprofit organizations active in issues such as the environment, foreign policy, consumer advocacy, housing, education, etc. Entries include: Position title; name, address, and phone of contact; description, responsibilities; requirements; salary. Arrangement: Geographical.

★8366★ Current Openings in Education in U.S.A.
Education Information Service
PO Box 660662
Newton, MA 02162-0662
Ph: (617)443-0125

Seven times/year. $8.00/issue. Publication is a booklet listing about 140 institutions or school systems, each with one to a dozen or more openings for teachers, librarians, counselors, administrators, and other personnel.

★8367★ Education Week
Editorial Projects in Education, Inc.
4301 Connecticut Ave. NW
Washington, DC 20008
Ph: (202)686-0800   Fax: (202)686-0797

Weekly. $59.94/year for individuals. Professional newspaper for elementary and secondary school educators.

★8368★ Journal of Learning Disabilities
Pro-Ed Journals
8700 Shoal Creek Blvd.
Austin, TX 78757
Ph: (512)451-3246

Ten issues/year. $49.00/year. Special education magazine.

★8369★ Journal of Teacher Education
American Association of Colleges for Teacher Education
1 Dupont Cir., Ste. 610
Washington, DC 20036-1186
Ph: (202)293-2450   Fax: (202)457-8095

$20.00/year for students; $45.00/year for individuals; $55.00/year for individuals; $75.00/year for institutions. Magazine of interest to educators.

★8370★ NJEA Review
New Jersey Education Association
180 W. State St.
Box 1211
Trenton, NJ 08607
Ph: (609)599-4561   Fax: (609)392-6321

Educational journal for public school employees.

★8371★ Strategies
American Alliance for Health, Physical Education, Recreation, and Dance
1900 Association Dr.
Reston, VA 22091
Ph: (703)476-3495   Fax: (703)476-9527

$20.00/year for members; $40.00/year for individuals; $50.00/year for libraries. Journal providing practical, hands-on information to physical educators and coaches.

★8372★ Teaching Exceptional Children
The Council for Exceptional Children
1920 Association Dr.
Reston, VA 22091-1589
Ph: (703)620-3660   Fax: (703)264-9494
Fr: 800-CEC-READ

Quarterly. $35.00/year for individuals. Journal exploring practical methods for teaching talented and gifted children who have disabilities.

★8373★ Teaching K-8
Early Years, Inc.
40 Richards Ave.
Norwalk, CT 06854-2509
Ph: (203)855-2650   Fax: (203)855-2656

$19.77/year for individuals. Magazine for elementary teachers.

★8374★ Tech Directions
Prakken Publications, Inc.
275 Metty Dr., Ste. 1
Box 8623
Ann Arbor, MI 48107
Ph: (313)769-1211   Fax: (313)769-8383
Fr: 800-530-9673

Free to qualified subscribers; $30.00/year for individuals. Magazine covering industrial education, technology education, trade and industry, and vocational-technical education. Articles are geared for teacher use and reference from middle school through post-secondary levels.

★8375★ American Montessori Society (AMS)
150 5th Ave., Ste. 203
New York, NY 10011-4384
Ph: (212)924-3209   Fax: (212)727-2254

Members: School affiliates and teacher training affiliates; heads of schools, teachers, parents, non-Montessori educators, and other interested individuals dedicated to stimulating the use of the Montessori teaching approach and promoting better education for all children. **Purpose:** Formed to meet demands of growing interest in the Montessori approach to early learning. Developed in Italy in 1907 by Dr. Maria Montessori, the system is based on the young child's instinctive love and need for purposeful work realized in an environment prepared with auto-educative, multi-sensory, manipulative learning devices for language, math, science, and practical life. **Activities:** Offers placement service. Assists in establishing schools; supplies information and limited services to member schools in other countries. Maintains school consultation and accreditation service.

EMPLOYER DIRECTORIES AND NETWORKING LISTS

★8376★ Christian Schools International—Directory

Christian Schools International
3350 E. Paris Ave. SE
Grand Rapids, MI 49512
Ph: (616)957-1070   Fax: (616)957-5022

Annual, November. $45.00. Covers nearly 450 Reformed Christian elementary and secondary schools; related associations; societies without schools. Entries include: School name, address, phone; name, title, and address of officers; names of faculty members. Arrangement: Geographical.

★8377★ Directory of Public School Systems in the U.S.

Association for School, College and
    University Staffing
1600 Dodge Ave., S-330
Evanston, IL 60201-3451
Ph: (708)864-1999   Fax: (708)864-8303

Annual, August. $65.00. Covers about 14,500 public school systems in the United States and their administrative personnel. Entries include: System name, address, phone, name and title of personnel administrator. Arrangement: Geographical by state.

★8378★ Employment Opportunities, USA

Washington Research Associates
1660 S. Albion, Ste. 390
Denver, CO 80222
Ph: (303)756-9038   Fax: (303)770-1945

Annual, quarterly updates. $184.00, includes quarterly updates. Publication includes: List of over 1,000 employment contacts in companies and agencies in the banking, arts, telecommunications, education, and 14 other industries and professions, including the federal government. Entries include: Company name, name of representative, address, description of products or services, hiring and recruiting practices, training programs, and year established. Principal content is industry overviews, carrer news, and employment opportunity information on 14 different job markets. Arrangement: Classified by industry. Indexes: Occupation.

★8379★ Ganley's Catholic Schools in America—Elementary/Secondary

Fisher Publishing Co.
Box 1073
Montrose, CO 81402
Ph: (303)249-1303   Fax: (303)249-0348
Fr: 800-766-5151

Annual, spring. $40.00. Covers about 8,345 Catholic schools. Entries include: Name, address, phone, administrative personnel, statistics, enrollment, grade span.

★8380★ Handbook of Private Schools

Porter Sargent Publishers, Inc.
11 Beacon St., Ste. 1400
Boston, MA 02108
Ph: (617)523-1670   Fax: (617)523-1021

Annual, June. $85.00, plus $2.41 shipping: Covers 1,700 elementary and secondary boarding and day schools in the United States. Entries include: School name, address, phone, fax, type of school (boarding or day), sex and age range, names and titles of administrators, grades offered, academic orientation, curriculum, new admissions yearly, tests required for admission, enrollment and faculty, graduate record, number of alumni, tuition and scholarship figures, summer session, plant evaluation and endowment, date of establishment, calendar, association membership, description of school's offerings and history. Arrangement: Geographical. Indexes: Alphabetical by school name.

★8381★ National Directory of Alternative Schools

National Coalition of Alternative
    Community Schools
PO Box 15036
Santa Fe, NM 87506
Ph: (505)474-4312

Biennial, even years. $15.00. Covers over 400 alternative education programs, including home schools, and state and regional coalitions of alternative schools and colleges; also lists organizations and networks offering services and resources to those working with children; international coverage. Entries include: Name, address, phone, name of contact; some also include descriptions of programs. Arrangement: Schools are geographical.

★8382★ National Directory for Employment in Education

Association for School, College and
    University Staffing
1600 Dodge Ave., S-330
Evanston, IL 60201-3451
Ph: (708)864-1999   Fax: (708)864-8303

Annual, winter. $20.00. Covers about 550 placement offices maintained by teacher-training institutions and 450 school district personnel officers and/or superintendents responsible for hiring professional staff. Entries include: Institution name, address, phone, contact name. Arrangement: Geographical. Indexes: Personal name, subject-field of teacher training, institutions which provide vacancy bulletins and placement services to non-enrolled students.

★8383★ Private Independent Schools

Bunting and Lyon, Inc.
238 N. Main St.
Wallingford, CT 06492
Ph: (203)269-3333   Fax: (203)269-5697

Annual, March. $96.00. Covers 1,200 English-speaking elementary and secondary private schools and summer programs in the U.S. and abroad. Entries include: School name, address, phone, enrollment, tuition and other fees, scholarship information, administrator's name and educational background, director of admissions, regional accreditation, description of programs, curriculum, activities. Arrangement: Geographical. Indexes: School name; geographical.

HANDBOOKS AND MANUALS

★8384★ Careers in Education

VGM Career Horizons
4255 W. Touhy Ave.
Lincolnwood, IL 60646-1975
Ph: (847)679-5500   Fax: (847)679-2494
Fr: 800-323-4900

Roy A. Edelfeldt. 1993. $17.95; $13.95 (paper). 192 pages. Explores opportunities for teachers, administrators, and specialists in elementary and secondary schools, as well as teaching, research, and administrative positions in higher education. Additional focus on adult and continuing education and industry opportunities for educators. Provides detailed background on careers in state boards and state departments of education, accrediting agencies, federal agencies, and national associations and councils.

★8385★ How to Get a Job in Education

Bob Adams, Inc.
260 Center St.
Holbrook, MA 02343
Ph: (617)767-8100   Fax: (617)767-0994
Fr: 800-872-5627

Joel Levin. Second edition, 1995. $12.95. 320 pages. Prepared for recent college graduates, seasoned educators, and career-changing professionals, this publication guides the job-seeker through the necessary steps to obtaining a job in education at the elementary, secondary, and university levels. Offers advice on how to prepare for state and local examinations, how to locate teaching opportunities nationwide, and how to obtain certification. Includes a nationwide salary survey. Covers public, private, summer, and overseas opportunities.

★8386★ Liberal Arts Jobs: What They Are and How to Get Them

Peterson's
PO Box 2123
Princeton, NJ 08543-2123
Ph: (609)243-9111   Fax: (609)243-9150
Fr: 800-338-3282

Burton Jay Nadler. Second edition, 1989. $9.95. 153 pages. Presents a list of the top 20 fields for liberal arts majors, covering more than 300 job opportunities. Discusses strategies for going after those jobs, including guidance on the language of a successful job search, informational interviews, and making networking work.

★8387★ Opportunities in Child Care Careers

VGM Career Horizons
4255 W. Touhy Ave.
Lincolnwood, IL 60646-1975
Ph: (847)679-5500   Fax: (847)679-2494
Fr: 800-323-4900

Renee Wittenberg. 1995. $14.95; $11.95 (paper). 160 pages. Discusses various job opportunities and how to secure a position. Illustrated.

★8388★ Opportunities in Teaching Careers

VGM Career Horizons
4255 W. Touhy Ave.
Lincolnwood, IL 60646-1975
Ph: (847)679-5500   Fax: (847)679-2494
Fr: 800-323-4900

Janet Fine. 1995. $14.95; $11.95 (paper). 160 pages. Discusses licensing and accreditation programs, sources of placement information, job-seeking correspondence, selection procedures, and paths to advancement. Also covers professional associations, nontraditional teaching opportunities, and jobs abroad.

EMPLOYMENT AGENCIES AND SEARCH FIRMS

★8389★ Arbor Associates, Inc.

15 Court Sq., Ste. 1050
Boston, MA 02108
Ph: (617)227-8829

Handles temporary placements.

★8390★ Educational Placement Service

5050 Poplar Ave., Ste. 1700
Memphis, TN 38157-1701
Ph: (901)767-1884

Employment agency. Focuses on teaching, administrative, and education-related openings.

OTHER SOURCES

★8391★ National Association of Independent Schools (NAIS)

1620 L St. NW
Washington, DC 20036-5605
Ph: (202)973-9700   Fax: (202)973-9790

Members: Independent elementary and secondary school members; regional associations of independent schools and related associations. **Purpose:** Provides curricular and administrative research and services. Conducts educational programs; compiles statistics.

★8392★ National Community Education Association (NCEA)

3929 Old Lee Hwy., Ste. 91-A
Fairfax, VA 22032
Ph: (703)359-8973   Fax: (703)359-0972

Members: Community school directors, principals, superintendents, professors, teachers, students, and laypeople. **Purpose:** Promotes and establishes community schools as an integral part of the educational plan of every community. Serves as a clearinghouse for the exchange of ideas and information, and the sharing of efforts. **Activities:** Offers leadership training.

★8393★ Overseas Employment Opportunities for Educators: Department of Defense Dependents Schools

Diane Publishing Co.
600 Upland Ave.
Upland, PA 19015
Ph: (610)499-7415

1993. $29.95. 52 pages.

★8394★ Resumes for Education Careers

VGM Career Horizons
4255 W. Touhy Ave.
Lincolnwood, IL 60646-1975
Ph: (847)679-5500   Fax: (847)679-2494
Fr: 800-323-4900

1992. $9.95. Sample resumes cover a variety of education careers and reflect education professionals at all levels of experience.

Telemarketing Representatives

PLACEMENT AND JOB REFERRAL SERVICES

★8395★ International Customer Service Association (ICSA)

401 N. Michigan Ave.
Chicago, IL 60611-4267
Ph: (312)321-6800   Fax: (312)321-6869
Members: Customer service professionals in public and private sectors united to develop the theory and understanding of customer service and management. **Purpose:** Goals are to: promote professional development; standardize terminology and phrases; provide career counseling and placement services; establish hiring guidelines, performance standards, and job descriptions. Provides a forum for shared problems and solutions. Compiles statistics.

EMPLOYER DIRECTORIES AND NETWORKING LISTS

★8396★ Annual Guide to Telemarketing

Marketing Logistics, Inc.
1460 Cloverdale Ave.
Highland Park, IL 60035
Ph: (708)831-1575

Irregular, latest edition April 1992. $475.00. Covers about 400 telemarketing service bureaus in the United States. Entries include: Company name, address, phone, description of products or services. Arrangement: Classified by service.

★8397★ Quirk's Marketing Research Review—Telephone Interviewing Facilities Directory Issue

Quirk's Enterprises, Inc.
6607 18th Ave. S
Richfield, MN 55423
Ph: (612)861-8051   Fax: (612)861-1836

Annual, May. $10.00. Publication includes: List of more than 550 telephone interviewing facilities that conduct marketing research projects. Entries include: Company name,

address, phone, fax, description of interviewing stations. Arrangement: Geographical. Indexes: Geographical.

★8398★ Telemarketing Service Directory

American Business Directories, Inc.
American Business Information, Inc.
5711 S. 86th Cir.
Omaha, NE 68127
Ph: (402)593-4600   Fax: (402)331-1505

Updated continuously; printed on request. Please inquire. Entries include: Name, address, phone, size of advertisement, name of owner or manager, number of employees, year first in Yellow Pages. Compiled from telephone company Yellow Pages, nationwide. Arrangement: Geographical.

★8399★ Telemarketing—Who's Who Directory to TSAs Issue

Technology Marketing Corp.
1 Technology Plaza
Norwalk, CT 06854
Ph: (203)852-6800   Fax: (203)853-2845
Fr: 800-243-6002

Annual, October. $7.00. Publication includes: List of more than 250 telemarketing and telecommunications companies that provide inbound, outbound, business-to-business, and business-to-consumer and/or interactive telemarketing services. Entries include: Company name, address, phone, services. Arrangement: Alphabetical. Indexes: Service.

HANDBOOKS AND MANUALS

★8400★ Careers Inside the World of Sales

Rosen Publishing Group, Inc.
29 E. 21st St.
New York, NY 10010
Ph: (212)777-3017   Fax: (212)777-0277
Fr: 800-237-9932

Carlienne Frisch. 1995. $14.95. 64 pages. Describes different sales careers for reluctant readers.

★8401★ Careers in Marketing

VGM Career Horizons
4255 W. Touhy Ave.
Lincolnwood, IL 60646-1975
Ph: (847)679-5500   Fax: (847)679-2494
Fr: 800-323-4900

Lila B. Stair. Second edition, 1995. $17.95; $13.95 (paper). Surveys career opportunities in marketing and related areas such as marketing research, product development, and sales promotion. Includes a description of the work, places of employment, employment outlook, trends, and salaries. Offers job hunting advice.

★8402★ Careers Without College: Office Careers

New Careers Center
1515 23rd St.
Box 339-CT
Boulder, CO 80306
Ph: (303)447-1087

$7.95.

★8403★ The Complete Job-Finding Guide for Secretaries and Administrative Support Staff

New Careers Center
1515 23rd St.
Box 339-CT
Boulder, CO 80306
Ph: (303)447-1087

Paul Falcone. 1995. $16.95. 258 pages. Covers several secretarial and administrative staff support positions and includes tips on resume writing, interview preparation, and other aspects of the job search.

★8404★ Encyclopedia of Careers and Vocational Guidance

J. G. Ferguson Publishing Co.
200 W. Monroe, Ste. 250
Chicago, IL 60606
Ph: (312)580-5480

William E. Hopke. Ninth edition, 1993. $129.95; $199.95 (CD-ROM). Four-volume set that profiles 900 occupations and describes job trends in 71 industries. Includes career description, educational requirements, history of the job, methods of entry, advancement, employment outlook, earnings, conditions of work, social and psychological factors, and sources of further information.

Contains career and employment information for this field.

★8405★ Marketing and Sales Career Directory

Gale Research
835 Penobscot Bldg.
Detroit, MI 48226-4094
Ph: (313)961-2242   Fax: (313)961-6083
Fr: 800-877-GALE

Bradley Morgan. Fourth edition, 1992. $39.00. 341 pages. Features extensive listings of contacts and entry-level job opportunities at major corporations, research supplier firms, and major advertising and public relations agencies nationwide. Aimed at students looking for jobs in any area of marketing, advertising, or sales on the corporate side.

★8406★ Opportunities in Customer Service Careers

VGM Career Horizons
NTC Publishing Group
4255 W. Touhy Ave.
Lincolnwood, IL 60646-1975
Ph: (847)679-5500   Fax: (847)679-2494
Fr: 800-323-4900

Blanche Ettinger. 1992. $14.95; $11.95 (paper). 160 pages. Describes the duties, salaries, and benefits associated with different positions in customer service. Includes advice on how to prepare for and find a job in this field.

★8407★ Opportunities in Direct Marketing

VGM Career Horizons
4255 W. Touhy Ave.
Lincolnwood, IL 60646-1975
Ph: (847)679-5500   Fax: (847)679-2494
Fr: 800-323-4900

Anne Basye. 1994. $14.95; $11.95 (paper). Examines opportunities with direct marketers, catalog companies, direct marketing agencies, telemarketing firms, mailing list brokers, and database marketing companies. Describes how to prepare for a career in direct marketing and how to break into the field. Includes sources of short-term professional training.

★8408★ Opportunities in Sales Careers

VGM Career Horizons
4255 W. Touhy Ave.
Lincolnwood, IL 60646-1975
Ph: (847)679-5500   Fax: (847)679-2494
Fr: 800-323-4900

James Briscoll and Ralph Dahm. 1995. $14.95; $11.95 (paper). Details sales in retail, wholesale and industrial sales, sales of services and intangibles, and sales management. Illustrated.

★8409★ Opportunities in Telemarketing Careers

VGM Career Horizons
NTC Publishing Group
4255 W. Touhy Ave.
Lincolnwood, IL 60646-1975
Ph: (847)679-5500   Fax: (847)679-2494
Fr: 800-323-4900

Anne Basye. 1994. $14.95; $11.95 (paper).

160 pages. Discusses opportunities in inside sales, customer service, telesearch, multilingual marketing, and more.

★8410★ Real People Working in Sales and Marketing

VGM Career Horizons
NTC Publishing Group
4255 W. Touhy Ave.
Lincolnwood, IL 60646-1975
Ph: (847)679-5500   Fax: (847)679-2494
Fr: 800-323-4900

1996. $17.95; $12.95 (paper). 192 pages. Interviews and profiles of working sales and marketing professionals capture a range of opportunities in this field.

★8411★ Telemarketer's Handbook

Sterling Publishing Co., Inc.
387 Park Ave. S
New York, NY 10016-8810
Ph: (212)532-7160   Fax: (212)213-2495
Fr: 800-367-9692

Darlene Maciuba-Koppel. 1992. $12.95 (paper).

★8412★ Telephone Salespeople (Telemarketers)

Chronicle Guidance Publications, Inc.
66 Aurora St.
PO Box 1190
Moravia, NY 13118-1190
Ph: (315)497-0330   Fax: (315)497-3359
Fr: 800-622-7284

Chronicle Guidance Staff. 1992. $2.00. Provides concise career information and sources of additional information.

★8413★ Your Career in Direct Marketing and Direct Response Advertising

Direct Marketing Educational Foundation, Inc.
1120 Avenue of the Americas
New York, NY 10036
Ph: (212)689-4977

This free booklet explains direct marketing and lists the types of companies engaged in direct marketing. Lists career opportunities and offers advice on entry into the field.

★8414★ Your Career Opportunities in a Direct Marketing Agency

Direct Marketing Educational Foundation, Inc.
1120 Avenue of the Americas
New York, NY 10036
Ph: (212)689-4977

This free booklet describes career opportunities in agencies involved in direct marketing.

EMPLOYMENT AGENCIES AND SEARCH FIRMS

★8415★ ABA Placements

1526 Miner St.
Des Plaines, IL 60016
Ph: (708)297-1526   Fax: (708)297-4545

Employment agency.

★8416★ Addison Personnel

3540 Wilshire Blvd., Ste. 515
Los Angeles, CA 90010
Ph: (213)386-6238   Fax: (213)386-2358

Employment agency.

★8417★ Blake and Associates Executive Search

PO Box 1425
Pleasantville, NJ 08232
Ph: (609)645-3330   Fax: (609)383-0320

Executive search firm.

★8418★ Career Development Services

14 Franklin St., Ste. 1200
Rochester, NY 14604
Ph: (716)325-2275   Fax: (716)325-2133

Employment agency.

★8419★ Citizens Employment Services, Inc.

1 Magnolia Ave.
Montvale, NJ 07645
Ph: (201)391-5144

Employment agency.

★8420★ Culver Personnel Service

1555 Old Bayshore Hwy., Ste. 100
Burlingame, CA 94010
Ph: (415)692-9090   Fax: (415)692-6618

Employment agency.

★8421★ Dial Personnel Associates

1033 E. Imperial Hwy., Ste. E-10
Brea, CA 92621
Ph: (714)671-1726

Employment agency.

★8422★ Esquire Personnel Services, Inc.

222 S. Riverside Plaza, Ste. 320
Chicago, IL 60606-5804
Ph: (312)648-4600   Fax: (312)648-4637

Employment agency.

★8423★ Group Agency, Inc.

1419 Avenue J
Brooklyn, NY 11230
Ph: (718)258-9202

Employment agency.

★8424★ Winters and Ross

442 Main St.
Fort Lee, NJ 07024
Ph: (201)947-8400

OTHER SOURCES

★8425★ American Telemarketing Association—Membership Services Referral Directory

American Telemarketing Association
444 N. Larchmont Blvd., Ste. 200
Los Angeles, CA 90004
Ph: (213)463-2330   Fax: (213)462-3372
Fr: 800-441-3335

Annual, July. $150.00. Covers member companies that supply telemarketing products and services. Entries include: Company name, address, phone, name and title of contact, product or service provided, branch office location. Arrangement: Alphabetical. Indexes: Product/service.

★8426★ *Resumes for Sales and Marketing Careers*
VGM Career Horizons
4255 W. Touhy Ave.
Lincolnwood, IL 60646-1975
Ph: (847)679-5500   Fax: (847)679-2494
Fr: 800-323-4900

1991. $9.95. 128 pages. Sample resumes and cover letters from all levels of the sales and marketing field.

★8427★ *Telemarketing at Home–Finding Opportunities Workbook*
Prosperity & Profits Unlimited Distribution Services
PO Box 416
Denver, CO 80201
Ph: (303)575-5676

Frieda Carrol. 1991. $25.95 (ringbound).

★8428★ *Video Career Library: Marketing and Sales*
Chronicle Guidance Publications, Inc.
66 Aurora St.
PO Box 1190
Moravia, NY 13118-1190
Ph: (315)497-0330   Fax: (315)497-3359
Fr: 800-622-7284

Video. $79.95. 21 minutes. Full-color video shows workers performing tasks and provides information on job duties, working conditions, salaries, outlook, education, training, and other aspects of the job.

Tool Programmers, Numerical Control

SOURCES OF HELP-WANTED ADS

★8429★ American Machinist

Peter Li
1100 Superior Ave.
Cleveland, OH 44114
Ph: (216)696-7000   Fax: (216)696-7670

Monthly. Magazine.

★8430★ Automatic Machining

Automatic Machine
100 Seneca Ave.
Rochester, NY 14621
Ph: (716)338-1522   Fax: (716)338-2625

Monthly. Metalworking magazine.

★8431★ Captsule Job Listings

Publications and Communications, Inc.
12416 Hymeadow Dr.
Austin, TX 78750
Ph: (512)250-9023   Fax: (512)331-3900
Fr: 800-678-9724

Online database. Lists current job openings in the contract (temporary) technical services industry. Includes the Action Hot List, which provides information on job seekers. Includes employment opportunities in technical/professional engineering, computing, and design/drafting. Entries generally contain company name, address, and job opening.

★8432★ Tooling and Production

Huebcore Communications, Inc.
29100 Aurora Rd., Ste. 200
Solon, OH 44139
Ph: (216)248-1125   Fax: (216)248-0187

Monthly. Magazine concerning metalworking.

PLACEMENT AND JOB REFERRAL SERVICES

★8433★ American Indian Science and Engineering Society (AISES)

1630 30th St., Ste. 301
Boulder, CO 80301
Ph: (303)492-8658   Fax: (303)492-3400

Members: American Indian and non-Indian students and professionals in science, technology, and engineering fields; corporations representing energy, mining, aerospace, electronic, and computer fields. **Purpose:** Seeks to motivate and encourage students to pursue undergraduate and graduate studies in science, engineering, and technology. **Activities:** Sponsors science fairs in grade schools, teacher training workshops, summer math/science sessions for 8th-12th graders, professional chapters, and student chapters in colleges. Offers scholarships. Adult members serve as role models, advisers, and mentors for students. Operates placement service. **E-Mail:** aisesha@spot.colorado.edu

★8434★ Composites Manufacturing Association of the Society of Manufacturing Engineers (CMA/SME)

1 SME Dr.
PO Box 930
Dearborn, MI 48121-0930
Ph: (313)271-1500   Fax: (313)271-2861
Fr: 800-743-4SME

Members: A division of the Society of Manufacturing Engineers. Composites manufacturing professionals and students in 21 countries. **Purpose:** Addresses design, tooling, assembly, producibility, supportability, and future trends of composites materials and hardware; promotes advanced composites technology. Analyzes industry trends; evaluates composites usage. **Activities:** Operates placement service. Conducts educational programs; facilitates exchange of information among members.

HANDBOOKS AND MANUALS

★8435★ Career Choices for the 90's for Students of Computer Science

Walker and Company
435 Hudson St.
New York, NY 10014
Ph: (212)727-8300   Fax: (212)727-0984
Fr: 800-289-2553

Prepared by the Career Associates staff. 1990. $8.95. 166 pages. Discusses alternatives for students of computer science. Offers advice on how to break into the field and how to move up. Covers where and who the employers are, internship possibilities, and professional networking associations. Comprehensive guide to career and job search planning.

★8436★ Careers in Computers

VGM Career Horizons
4255 W. Touhy Ave.
Lincolnwood, IL 60646-1975
Ph: (847)679-5500   Fax: (847)679-2494
Fr: 800-323-4900

Lila B. Stair. Second edition, 1995. $17.95; $13.95 (paper). Describes trends affecting computer careers and explores a wide range of job opportunities from programming to consulting. Provides job qualifications, salary data, job market information, personal and educational requirements, career paths, and the place of the job in the organizational structure. Offers advice on education, certification, and job search.

★8437★ Careers for Number Crunchers and Other Quantitative Types

VGM Career Horizons
4255 W. Touhy Ave.
Lincolnwood, IL 60646-1975
Ph: (847)679-5500   Fax: (847)679-2494
Fr: 800-323-4900

Rebecca Burnett. 1993. $14.95; $9.95 (paper). Provides information to math-oriented job hunters on how to become statisticians, field researchers, computer programmers, stock analysts, investment managers, bankers, engineers, accountants, underwriters, economists, market analysts, mathematicians, systems analysts, and more.

★8438★ Opportunities in Computer-Aided Design and Computer-Aided Manufacturing

VGM Career Horizons
4255 W. Touhy Ave.
Lincolnwood, IL 60646-1975
Ph: (847)679-5500   Fax: (847)679-2494
Fr: 800-323-4900

Jan Bone. 1994. $14.95; $11.95 (paper). 160 pages. Defines cad (computer-aided design), cam (computer-aided manufacturing), and map (manufacturing automation protocol). Explains career opportunities in the cad/cam field, and education and training needed. Gives job-hunting tips.

★8439★ Opportunities in Computer Science Careers

VGM Career Horizons
4255 W. Touhy Ave.
Lincolnwood, IL 60646-1975
Ph: (847)679-5500   Fax: (847)679-2494
Fr: 800-323-4900

Julie Lepick Kling. 1995. $14.95; $11.95 (paper). Discusses how to enter the field and build a career. Illustrated.

★8440★ Opportunities in Vocational and Technical Careers

VGM Career Horizons
4255 W. Touhy Ave.
Lincolnwood, IL 60646-1975
Ph: (847)679-5500   Fax: (847)679-2494
Fr: 800-323-4900

Adrian A. Paradis. 1992. $14.95; $11.95 (paper). 160 pages. Provides information on a variety of opportunities and advice on breaking into the field.

EMPLOYMENT AGENCIES AND SEARCH FIRMS

★8441★ Computer Network Resources Inc.

7000 Central Pkwy. NE
Atlanta, GA 30328-4579
Ph: (404)391-9009

Employment agency.

★8442★ LOR Personnel Division

418 Wall St.
Princeton, NJ 08540
Ph: (609)921-6580

Employment agency. Executive search firm.

★8443★ Mfg/Search, Inc.

401 W. Colfax Ave., Ste. 600
South Bend, IN 46601
Ph: (219)282-2547   Fax: (219)289-0358

Executive search firm.

★8444★ Romac International, Inc.

120 Hyde Park Pl., Ste. 200
Tampa, FL 33606
Fr: 800-341-0263

Executive search firm. More than 30 locations throughout the U.S.

★8445★ Source EDP

5580 LBJ Fwy., Ste. 300
Dallas, TX 75240
Ph: (214)385-3002

Executive search firm. Many affiliate offices located in most major cities in the U.S.

OTHER SOURCES

★8446★ AMT–The Association For Manufacturing Technology

7901 Westpark Dr.
McLean, VA 22102
Ph: (703)893-2900   Fax: (703)893-1151
Fr: 800-544-3597

Members: Makers of power driven machines used in the process of transforming man-made materials into durable goods, including machine tools, assembly machines, inspection and testing machinery, robots, parts loaders, and plastics molding machines; associate members are producers of tools and tooling parts and components, attachments and accessories, controls and software, and engineering and systems design services. **Purpose:** Seeks to improve methods of producing and marketing machine tools; promotes research and development in the industry. Sponsors: seminars for training production supervisors, accident prevention and safety, and advertising management; industry standards and technical aspects of the industry. Serves as a clearinghouse for technical aspects of the industry. Promotes

orderly disposal of government-owned surplus machine tools.

★8447★ National Tooling and Machining Association (NTMA)

9300 Livingston Rd.
Fort Washington, MD 20744
Ph: (301)248-6200   Fax: (301)248-7104
Fr: 800-248-NTMA

Members: Manufacturers of tools, dies, jigs, fixtures, molds, gages, or special machinery; companies that do precision machining on a contract basis; past service and associate members. **Purpose:** Provides management services; represents members in legislative matters. Promotes apprenticeship programs. Compiles management surveys; conducts management training workshops; maintains speakers' bureau. Has produced motion pictures and videocassettes on tool, die, and precision machining for educational showings.

★8448★ Precision Machined Products Association (PMPA)

6700 W. Snowville Rd.
Brecksville, OH 44141
Ph: (216)526-0300   Fax: (216)526-5803

Purpose: Manages the information, training, and technical needs of manufacturers of component parts to customer's order, machined from rod, bar, or tube stock, of metal, fiber, plastic, or other material, using automatic or hand screw machines, automatic bar machines, and CNC machines.

★8449★ Special Interest Group for Computers and the Physically Handicapped (SISCAPH)

Association for Computing Machinery
1515 Broadway, 17th Fl.
New York, NY 10036
Ph: (212)626-0613   Fax: (212)302-5826

Members: A special interest group of the Association of Computing Machinery. Physically disabled computer professionals; persons involved in the application of computers to aid the disabled; persons involved in the training or employment of physically disabled computer professionals; others interested in aiding the disabled. **Purpose:** To promote application of computer technology to aid the physically disabled; to educate the public about disabled computer professionals. **Activities:** Sponsors lectures and sessions at computer conferences on hiring and training disabled computer professionals. Compiles statistics.

Tour Guides and Operators

SOURCES OF HELP-WANTED ADS

★8450★ Corporate Travel

Miller Freeman, Inc.
1515 Broadway
New York, NY 10036
Ph: (212)626-2380   Fax: (212)944-7164
Fr: 800-950-1314

Monthly. Tabloid reporting on international business travel and corporate meetings.

★8451★ Meeting News

Miller Freeman, Inc.
1515 Broadway
New York, NY 10036
Ph: (212)626-2380   Fax: (212)944-7164
Fr: 800-950-1314

Monthly. News, education, and ideas for better meetings.

★8452★ Southeast Travel Professional

Southern Travel Professional
1200 NW 78th Ave., Ste. 201
Miami, FL 33126
Ph: (305)592-6133   Fax: (305)592-9741

Monthly. Travel newspaper (tabloid).

★8453★ Tour and Travel News

CMP Publications, Inc.
600 Community Dr.
Manhasset, NY 11030
Ph: (516)562-5000   Fax: (516)562-5055

Weekly. Magazine for the travel industry, covering issues of interest to travel agents.

★8454★ Travel Agent

Universal Media, Inc.
801 2nd Ave., 12th Fl.
New York, NY 10017
Ph: (212)370-5050   Fax: (212)370-4491

Semiweekly. Travel industry magazine.

★8455★ Travel Trade

Travel Trade
15 W. 44th St.
New York, NY 10036
Ph: (212)730-6600   Fax: (212)730-7137

Weekly. Travel industry magazine.

★8456★ Travel Weekly

Reed Travel Group
500 Plaza Dr.
Secaucus, NJ 07096
Ph: (201)902-2000   Fax: (201)319-1947

Semiweekly (Mon. and Thurs.). Travel industry magazine.

★8457★ TravelAge MidAmerica

Reed Travel Group
500 Plaza Dr.
Secaucus, NJ 07094-3626
Ph: (201)902-1600   Fax: (201)319-1628

Weekly. $28.00/year for individuals. Magazine for travel counselors.

★8458★ TravelAge West

Reed Travel Group
500 Plaza Dr.
Secaucus, NJ 07096
Ph: (201)902-2000   Fax: (201)319-1947

Weekly (Mon.). Free to qualified subscribers; $25.00/year for individuals. Magazine for retail travel agents in western U.S. and western Canada.

PLACEMENT AND JOB REFERRAL SERVICES

★8459★ International Association of Tour Managers - North American Region (IATM-NAR)

65 Charnes Dr.
East Haven, CT 06513-1225
Ph: (203)466-0425   Fax: (203)787-6384

Members: Travel agents, travel wholesalers, airlines, hotel associations, shipping lines, tourist organizations, restaurants, shops, and entertainment organizations. **Purpose:** Works to maintain the highest possible standards of tour management; guarantee excellence of performance; educate the travel world on the role of the tour manager (also referred to as tour director, tour escort, or tour leader) in the successful completion of the tour itinerary and in bringing business to related industries. **Activities:** Operates placement service. Offers courses in tour management, travel marketing, and sales promotion through New York University in New York City and Metropolitan State College in Denver, CO. Conducts Professional Tour Management, U.S.A. Certificate Program.

★8460★ International Institute of Convention Management

9200 Bayard Pl.
Fairfax, VA 22032
Ph: (703)978-6287   Fax: (703)978-5524

Members: Meeting planners, travel agents, tour operators, and seminar organizers in 42 countries. **Purpose:** Works to improve the skills of professional conference and convention planners. Serves as a clearinghouse of information on new travel destinations and planning technologies, techniques, and strategies. **Activities:** Conducts research programs and placement service. **E-Mail:** 7417.351@compuserve.com

★8461★ Travel Professionals Association (TPA)

216 S. Bungalow Park Ave.
Tampa, FL 33609
Ph: (813)876-0286   Fax: (813)876-0286

Members: Travel industry personnel seeking career advancement. **Purpose:** Fosters professionalism by providing marketing assistance, research opportunities, and a forum for exchange and discussion of ideas and issues. Works to bridge the gap between the travel industry and the public's awareness of and access to travel professionals. Sponsors technical, civic, social, and cultural programs. Conducts surveys and questionnaires and disseminates results. **Activities:** Maintains charitable program, speakers' bureau, and placement services. Plans to extend advertising and referral services and insurance benefits. Candidates for membership must pass a four-part exam composed of destination information, travel terminology, identification of cities , states, and countries, and a written essay. Holds 6 exams/year.

EMPLOYER DIRECTORIES AND NETWORKING LISTS

★8462★ Institute of Certified Travel Agents—Directory

Institute of Certified Travel Agents
148 Linden St.
PO Box 812059
Wellesley, MA 02181-0012
Ph: (617)237-0280   Fax: (617)237-3860
Fr: 800-542-4282

Annual, suspended indefinitely. Available to members only. Covers about 8,000 member certified travel counselors, and 108 fellows. Entries include: Name, office address and phone. Arrangement: Geographical within membership categories. Indexes: Member name.

★8463★ Reed's Travel Group's Travel Agent Database

Reed Travel Group
2000 Clearwater Dr.
Oak Brook, IL 60521
Ph: (708)902-1859   Fax: (708)574-6284

Annual, winter. $270.00, per thousand listings. Database covers: about 75,500 wholesale, retail, and co-operative travel agencies worldwide, including tour operators. Database includes: Generally, company name, address, phone, telex, number of employees, subsidiary and branch names and locations, key personnel, services available, date established. Indexes: Geographic location/specialization, special interest tours.

★8464★ Specialty Travel Index: The Directory of Special Interest Travel

Alpine Hansen, Publishers
305 San Anselmo Ave., Ste. 313
San Anselmo, CA 94960
Ph: (415)459-4900   Fax: (415)459-4974
Fr: 800-442-4922

Semiannual, January and August. Covers over 600 special interest tour operators, worldwide; all listings are paid. Entries include: Firm name, address, phone; description of tours offered, including nature of trip, destinations, sample cost and duration of trip. Arrangement: Alphabetical. Indexes: Special interest activity (with location of activity), Geographical (and the special interest activities possible).

★8465★ Tours-Operators & Promoters Directory

American Business Directories, Inc.
American Business Information, Inc.
5711 S. 86th Cir.
Omaha, NE 68127
Ph: (402)593-4600   Fax: (402)331-1505

Annual. $465.00, U.S. edition. Entries include: Name, address, phone (including area code), size of advertisement, year first in Yellow Pages, name of owner or manager, number of employees. Compiled from telephone company Yellow Pages, nationwide. Arrangement: Geographical.

★8466★ Travel Agency Reference & Profile Directory

World Travel Communications, Inc.
7380 S. Eastern Ave. 124-142
Las Vegas, NV 89123
Ph: (702)795-2411

Annual, June. $80.00. Covers travel agents and wholesale tour operators in North America. Entries include: Company name, address, phone, fax, cable address, names of owner, number of employees, association memberships, head office location, year established, specialty, conference appointments, business volume. Arrangement: Classified by type of business. Indexes: Travel agency name, geographical.

★8467★ Travel Industry Personnel Directory

Fairchild Books
Fairchild Publications, Inc.
7 W. 34th St.
New York, NY 10001
Ph: (212)630-3880   Fax: (212)630-3862
Fr: 800-247-6622

Annual, April. $30.00, plus 4.95 shipping. Covers air and steamship lines, tour operators, bus lines, hotel representatives, foreign and domestic railroads, foreign and domestic tourist information offices, travel trade associations, etc. Entries include: Agency or company name, address, phone, names of principal personnel. Arrangement: Classified by companies or agencies within functional or service categories (airlines, information offices, etc.).

★8468★ Worldwide Travel Information Contact Book

Gale Research
835 Penobscot Bldg.
Detroit, MI 48226-4094
Ph: (313)961-2242   Fax: (313)961-6083
Fr: 800-877-GALE

Second edition, 1992. $175.00. Guide to travel information for tourism professionals, the travel trade press, individuals and business travelers, researchers, and students. Includes information on travel agencies/tour operators; hotel, travel, and transportation associations; tourism and automobile clubs; national and international ministries, departments, and boards of tourism; local tourist sources; and other travel organizations and sources. Arranged on a country-by-country basis. Indexes: Alphabetical and keyword.

HANDBOOKS AND MANUALS

★8469★ Career Opportunities in Travel and Tourism

Facts on File, Inc.
11 Penn Plaza, 15th Fl.
New York, NY 10001-2006
Ph: (212)967-8800   Fax: 800-678-3633
Fr: 800-322-8755

John Hawks. 1995. $29.95; $15.95 (paper). 224 pages. Includes detailed job descriptions, educational requirements, salary ranges, and advancement prospects for 70 different job opportunities in this fast-paced industry. Contains index and bibliography.

★8470★ Careers for Foreign Language Aficionados and Other Multilingual Types

VGM Career Horizons
4255 W. Touhy Ave.
Lincolnwood, IL 60646-1975
Ph: (847)679-5500   Fax: (847)679-2494
Fr: 800-323-4900

Ned H. Seelye and J. Laurence Day. 1992. $14.95; $9.95 (paper). Outlines mainstream and unusual jobs for teachers, translators, tour guides, and others who want to use a foreign language on the job.

★8471★ Careers for Travel Buffs and Other Restless Types

VGM Career Horizons
4255 W. Touhy Ave.
Lincolnwood, IL 60646-1975
Ph: (847)679-5500   Fax: (847)679-2494
Fr: 800-323-4900

Paul Plawin. 1992. $14.95; $9.95 (paper). Includes a variety of travel and open-road careers, such as travel writers and photographers, tour bus drivers, entertainers, cruise line staff, travel agents, tour guides, sports writers, sales, the military, trucking, and meeting planning.

★8472★ Exploring Careers in the Travel Industry

Rosen Publishing Group, Inc.
29 E. 21st St.
New York, NY 10010
Ph: (212)777-3017   Fax: (212)777-0277
Fr: 800-237-9932

Edgar Grant. Revised edition, 1989. $14.95. Provides an overview of the travel and tourism industries. Describes the work of the travel agent, skills, training, pay, and employment outlook. Offers job hunting advice.

★8473★ First Class: An Introduction to Travel and Tourism

Glencoe
936 Eastwind Dr.
Westerville, OH 43081
Ph: (614)890-1111   Fax: (614)899-4304
Fr: 800-848-1567

Dennis L. Foster. 1993.

★8474★ Flying High in Travel

John Wiley and Sons
605 3rd Ave.
New York, NY 10158
Ph: (212)850-6000   Fr: 800-225-5945

Karen Rubin. Second edition, 1992. $19.95. 336 pages. A guide to careers and job hunting in the travel industry. Describes the many job opportunities available, from writing to hotel management to law. Includes information on educational preparation, training, and job hunting.

★8475★ Handbook of Professional Tour Management

Delmar Publishers
3 Columbia Cir., Box 15015
Albany, NY 12212
Ph: (518)464-3500   Fax: (518)464-0358
Fr: 800-347-7707

Robert T. Reilly. 1991. $29.95.

★8476★ How to Be a Cruise Consultant

GE Mitchell & Associates, Inc.
PO Box 159
Sullivans Island, SC 29482-0159
Ph: (803)723-7400   Fax: (803)853-2822
Fr: 800-209-0019

Gerald E. Mitchell. 1992. $49.95.

★8477★ How to Be an International Tour Director

G.E. Mitchell & Associates, Inc.
PO Box 159
Sullivans Island, SC 29482-0159
Ph: (803)723-7400   Fax: (803)853-2822
Fr: 800-209-0019

Gerald E. Mitchell. 1992. $49.95.

★8478★ How to Be a Tour Guide

G.E. Mitchell & Associates, Inc.
PO Box 159
Sullivans Island, SC 29482-0159
Ph: (803)723-7400   Fax: (803)853-2822
Fr: 800-209-0019

Gerald E. Mitchell. 1992. $49.95.

★8479★ How to Get a Job with a Cruise Line

Ticket to Adventure, Inc.
PO Box 41005
St. Petersburg, FL 33743
Ph: (813)544-6440   Fr: 800-929-7447

Mary Fallon Miller. Third edition, 1994. $14.95. 224 pages. Explores jobs with cruise ships, describing duties, responsibilities, benefits, and training. Lists cruise ship lines and schools offering cruise line training. Offers job hunting advice.

★8480★ Managing Group Tours: Your Complete Reference Guide to Successful Tour Management

Shoreline Creations, Ltd.
143 Douglas Ave., Ste. 8
Holland, MI 49424
Ph: (616)393-2077   Fax: (616)393-0085
Fr: 800-767-3489

Anita L. Fielder. 1995. $19.95 (paper).

★8481★ Now Hiring: Travel and Tourism

Zinks International Career Guidance
PO Box 585
Dearborn, MI 48121-0585
Ph: (313)584-7529

Richard M. Zink. 1994. $14.95 (paper).

★8482★ Opportunities in Recreation and Leisure

VGM Career Horizons
4255 W. Touhy Ave.
Lincolnwood, IL 60646-1975
Ph: (847)679-5500   Fax: (847)679-2494
Fr: 800-323-4900

Clayne R. Jensen and Jay H. Naylor. 1990. $14.95; $11.95 (paper). 160 pages. Presents information on pursuing a position in a variety of fields, including senior citizen recreation, corporate employee recreation programs, and urban fitness centers. Illustrated.

★8483★ Opportunities in Travel Careers

VGM Career Horizons
4255 W. Touhy Ave.
Lincolnwood, IL 60646-1975
Ph: (847)679-5500   Fax: (847)679-2494
Fr: 800-323-4900

Robert Scott Milne. 1996. $14.95; $11.95 (paper). 160 pages. Discusses what the jobs are and where to find them in airlines, shipping lines, and railroads. Discusses related opportunities in hotels, motels, resorts, travel agencies, public relation firms, and recreation departments. Illustrated.

★8484★ Part-Time Travel Agent: How to Cash in on the Exciting New World of Travel Marketing

The Intrepid Traveler
PO Box 438
New York, NY 10034-0438
Ph: (212)569-1081   Fax: (212)942-6687

Kelly Monaghan. 1994. $24.95 (paper).

★8485★ Passport: An Introduction to the Travel and Tourism Industry

South-Western Publishing Company
5101 Madison Rd.
Cincinnati, OH 45227
Ph: (513)271-8811   Fax: (513)527-6194
Fr: 800-543-0487

David W. Howell. 1993. $38.95 (paper).

★8486★ Travel Agent

Prentice Hall
113 Sylvan Ave.
Rte. 9W
Englewood Cliffs, NJ 07632
Ph: (201)592-2000   Fr: 800-922-0579

Wilma Boyd. 1989. $14.95. 256 pages. Outlines entry-level positions in the airline, car rental, and hospitality industries as well as in travel agencies and related travel services. Explains travel agency operations, sales techniques, and the use of computers in travel services. Gives job hunting advice and sales tips.

★8487★ The Travel Agent: Dealer in Dreams

Prentice Hall
113 Sylvan Ave.
Rte. 9W
Englewood Cliffs, NJ 07632
Ph: (201)592-2000   Fr: 800-922-0579

Gregory Aryear. Fourth edition, 1992. $44.00. 375 pages. Comprehensive guide for those interested in the travel industry. Covers various jobs within the travel industry including travel consultant, agency manager, and tour operators.

★8488★ Travel and Hospitality Career Directory

Gale Research
835 Penobscot Bldg.
Detroit, MI 48226-4094
Ph: (313)961-2242   Fax: (313)961-6083
Fr: 800-877-GALE

Bradley Morgan. Second edition, 1992. $39.00. 289 pages. Features a basic and comprehensive job search section, articles by top professionals in the field, and detailed listings of hundreds of top companies who hire individuals in this field. Aimed particularly at entry-level job hunters.

★8489★ Travel Industry Guidelines for Employment

Travel Text Associates
42883 Heydenreich Rd.
Clinton Township, MI 48038
Ph: (810)799-4018

Chris Hoosen and Francis Dix. 1990. $20.00.

★8490★ Travel and Tourism

Franklin Watts, Inc.
Sherman Turnpike
Danbury, CT 06810

Marjorie Rittenberg Schulz. 1990. Surveys employment opportunities in the travel and tourism industry. Provides salaries and employment outlook. Offers job hunting advice.

★8491★ Travel the World Free as an International Tour Director: How to Be an International Tour Director

G.E. Mitchell & Associates, Inc.
PO Box 159
Sullivans Island, SC 29482-0159
Ph: (803)723-7400   Fax: (803)853-2822
Fr: 800-209-0019

Gerald E. Mitchell. 1995. $59.95.

★8492★ Your Opportunities in Recreation, Travel and Tourism

Energeia Publishing, Inc.
860 Commercial St.
PO Box 985
Salem, OR 97308
Ph: (503)362-1480   Fax: (503)362-2123

Laurie Bean. 1994. $2.00 (paper).

EMPLOYMENT AGENCIES AND SEARCH FIRMS

★8493★ The Pathfinder Group

295 Danbury Rd.
Wilton, CT 06897-3095
Ph: (203)834-2467

Employment agency. Executive search firm. Recruits staff in a variety of fields.

★8494★ **Travel Executive Search**

5 Rose Ave.
Great Neck, NY 11021
Ph: (516)829-8829

Executive search firm.

OTHER SOURCES

★8495★ *Interpersonal Skills for Travel and Tourism*

Trans-Atlantic Publications, Inc.
311 Bainbridge St.
Philadelphia, PA 19147
Ph: (215)925-5083   Fax: (215)925-1912

Lisa Burton. 1994. $47.50 (paper).

★8496★ **United States Tour Operators Association (USTOA)**

211 E. 51st St., Ste. 12B
New York, NY 10022
Ph: (212)750-7371   Fax: (212)421-1285

Members: Wholesale tour operators, common carriers, associations, government agencies, suppliers, purveyors of travel services, trade press, communications media, and public relations and advertising representatives. **Purpose:** Encourages and supports professional and financial integrity in tourism. Protects the legitimate interests of the consumer and the retail agent from financial loss from business conducted with members. Informs the travel trade, government agencies, and the public concerning the activities and objectives of tour operators, focusing attention on their contributions in furthering worldwide travel. Provides tour operators with an opportunity to formulate and express an independent industry voice on matters of common interest and self-regulation; works with other trade organizations and government agencies.

Translators and Interpreters

SOURCES OF HELP-WANTED ADS

★8497★ NABE News

National Association for Bilingual Education (NABE)
1220 L St. NW, Ste. 605
Washington, DC 20005-4018
Ph: (202)898-1829

Eight issues/year.

PLACEMENT AND JOB REFERRAL SERVICES

★8498★ African Studies Association (ASA)

Emory University
Credit Union Bldg.
Atlanta, GA 30322
Ph: (404)329-6410   Fax: (404)329-6433

Members: Persons specializing in teaching, writing, or research on Africa including political scientists, historians, geographers, anthropologists, economists, librarians, linguists, and government officials; persons who are studying African subjects; institutional members are universities, libraries, government agencies, and others interested in receiving information about Africa. **Purpose:** Seeks to foster communication and to stimulate research among scholars on Africa. **Activities:** Sponsors placement service; conducts panels and discussion groups; presents exhibits and films. **E-Mail:** africa@mony.edu

★8499★ American Society of Interpreters (ASI)

PO Box 9603
Washington, DC 20016
Ph: (202)883-0611

Purpose: Professional interpreters united to foster a high code of ethics among interpreters, improve working practices and recommend professional standards, and keep members informed of new developments in the profession. **Activities:** Offers member referrals and advice to meeting organizers; recommends experienced chief interpreters and specialized organizations to prospective meeting organizers. Disseminates information on interpretation systems and related conference services.

★8500★ Foundation for International Human Relations (FIHR)

2020 Pennsylvania Ave., NW
Box 806
Washington, DC 20006
Ph: (202)429-2851   Fax: (202)429-2852

Purpose: Provides internships, fellowships, and other forms of professional experience to college students and future professionals in the fields of political science, public affairs, and international relations and business. Promotes education in leadership skills and cross-cultural and international communication. **Activities:** Conducts workshops, seminars, symposia, and programs on public relations, political psychology, and international media; provides consultation in community development and international health care. Sponsors research in agnihotra farming. Operates speakers' bureau and placement service.

EMPLOYER DIRECTORIES AND NETWORKING LISTS

★8501★ American Society of Interpreters—Membership List

American Society of Interpreters
PO Box 9603
Washington, DC 20016
Ph: (202)883-0611

Annual, April. Free. Covers about 80 foreign-language conference interpreters and certified court interpreters. Entries include: Name, address, and language combinations. Arrangement: Alphabetical.

★8502★ American Translators Association—Membership Directory

American Translators Association
1735 Jefferson Davis Hwy., Ste. 903
Arlington, VA 22202-3413
Ph: (703)412-1500   Fax: (703)412-1501

Annual, summer. $75.00 for members. Includes more than 5,300 member translators, interpreters, and linguists in the United States, Canada, Mexico, Central and South America, Europe, and Asia. Entries include: Name, address, phone, languages in which member has ATA accreditation. Arrangement: Alphabetical.

★8503★ ATA Translation Services Directory

American Translators Association
1735 Jefferson Davis Hwy., Ste. 903
Arlington, VA 22202-3413
Ph: (703)412-1500   Fax: (703)412-1501

Annual, Fall. $75.00. Covers over 1,200 member translators and interpreters. Entries include: Name, address, languages in which proficient, subject competencies, professional background. Arrangement: Alphabetical, area of specialization, language. Indexes: Language-subject competency (with state).

★8504★ Career Opportunities for Bilinguals and Multilinguals

Scarecrow Press
PO Box 4167
Metuchen, NJ 08840
Ph: (908)548-8600   Fax: (908)548-5767
Fr: 800-537-7107

Published 1994. $35.00. Covers 3,800 companies and organizations that hire people who are fluent in languages other than English; colleges and universities, libraries, books, and other educational resources for those wishing to learn other languages. Entries include: For employers: name, address, phone, description of work, languages sought. For educational resources: name, address, phone, languages. Arrangement: Separate sections for educational resources, U.S. opportunities, and overseas opportunities. Indexes: Language, educational background, geographical.

★8505★ International Literary Market Place

R. R. Bowker Co.
Reed Reference Publishing
121 Chanlon Rd.
New Providence, NJ 07974
Ph: (908)464-6800 Fax: (908)771-7704
Fr: 800-521-8110

Annual, Fall. $179.95. Covers more than 9,200 publishers in over 170 countries outside the United States and Canada, and about 1,150 trade and professional organizations related to publishing abroad; includes major printers, binders, typesetters, book manufacturers, book dealers, libraries, literary agencies, translators, book clubs, reference books and journals, periodicals, prizes, and international reference section. Entries include: For publishers Name, address, phone, fax, telex, names and titles of key personnel, branches, type of publications, subjects, ISBN prefix. Arrangement: Classified by business activities, then geographical. Indexes: Company name, subject, type of publication.

★8506★ Literary Market Place

R. R. Bowker Co.
Reed Reference Publishing
121 Chanlon Rd.
New Providence, NJ 07974
Ph: (908)464-6800 Fax: (908)771-7704
Fr: 800-521-8110

Annual, September. $165.00. Covers over 15,000 firms or organizations offering services related to the publishing industry, including 3,800 book publishers in the United States and Canada who issued three or more books during the preceding year, plus a small press section of publishers who publish less than three titles per year or those who are self-published. Also included: book printers and binders; book clubs; book trade and literary associations; selected syndicates, newspapers, periodicals, and radio and TV programs that use book reviews or book publishing news; translators and literary agents. Arrangement: Classified by line of business. Indexes: Principal index is 35,000-item combined index of publishers, publications, and personnel; several sections have geographical and/or subject indexes; translators are indexed by source and target language.

★8507★ Translators & Interpretors Directory

American Business Directories, Inc.
American Business Information, Inc.
5711 S. 86th Cir.
Omaha, NE 68127
Ph: (402)593-4600 Fax: (402)331-1505

Updated continuously; printed on request. Please inquire. Entries include: Name, address, phone, size of advertisement, name of owner or manager, number of employees, year first in Yellow Pages. Compiled from telephone company Yellow Pages, nationwide. Arrangement: Geographical.

HANDBOOKS AND MANUALS

★8508★ Careers for Foreign Language Aficionados and Other Multilingual Types

VGM Career Horizons
4255 W. Touhy Ave.
Lincolnwood, IL 60646-1975
Ph: (847)679-5500 Fax: (847)679-2494
Fr: 800-323-4900

Ned H. Seelye and J. Laurence Day. 1992. $14.95; $9.95 (paper). Outlines mainstream and unusual jobs for teachers, translators, tour guides, and others who want to use a foreign language on the job.

★8509★ Careers in International Affairs

Georgetown University
Institute for the Study of Diplomacy
423 Intercultural Ctr.
Washington, DC 20057-1052
Ph: (202)687-8971

Mario Pinto Carland and Daniel H. Spatz, Jr. 1991. $15.00. 307 pages. Includes index and bibliography.

★8510★ Exploring Careers Using Foreign Languages

Rosen Publishing Group, Inc.
29 E. 21st St.
New York, NY 10010
Ph: (212)777-3017 Fax: (212)777-0277
Fr: 800-237-9932

E.W. Edwards. Revised edition, 1990. $14.95. Explores careers in teaching, translating, interpreting, business and finance, government, the military, communications, and the media. Covers employment ideas, salaries, job duties, and educational preparation. Contains information on accreditation and job hunting.

★8511★ Foreign Languages and Your Career

Audio-Forum
96 Broad St.
Guilford, CT 06437-2635
Ph: (203)453-9794 Fr: 800-243-1234

Edward Bourgoin. Fourth edition, 1993. 120 pages. $8.95. Includes index and bibliography.

★8512★ Great Jobs for Foreign Language Majors

NTC Publishing Group
4255 W. Touhy Ave.
Lincolnwood, IL 60646-1975
Ph: (708)679-5500 Fax: (708)679-6375
Fr: 800-323-4900

Julie DeGalan. 1994. $11.95 (paper).

★8513★ Guide to Careers in World Affairs

Impact Publications
9104-N Manassas Dr.
Manassas Park, VA 22111-5211
Ph: (703)361-7300 Fax: (703)335-9486

Foreign Policy Association. 1993. $14.95. 331 pages. Describes jobs in business, government, and nonprofit organizations. Explains the methods and credentials required to secure a job in many fields, including international law and journalism. Contains sections on internships and graduate programs.

★8514★ Interpreter (Spanish)

National Learning Corp.
212 Michael Dr.
Syosset, NY 11791
Ph: (516)921-8888 Fax: (516)921-8743
Fr: 800-645-6337

★8515★ Interpreters and Translators

Chronicle Guidance Publications, Inc.
66 Aurora St.
PO Box 1190
Moravia, NY 13118-1190
Ph: (315)497-0330 Fax: (315)497-3359
Fr: 800-622-7284

Chronicle Guidance Staff. 1991. $2.00. Provides concise career information and sources of additional information.

★8516★ Opportunities in Foreign Language Careers

VGM Career Horizons
4255 W. Touhy Ave.
Lincolnwood, IL 60646-1975
Ph: (847)679-5500 Fax: (847)679-2494
Fr: 800-323-4900

Wilga Rivers. 1993. $14.95; $11.95 (paper). Explores a variety of foreign language careers and discusses how to pursue them. Contains bibliography and illustrations.

EMPLOYMENT AGENCIES AND SEARCH FIRMS

★8517★ Bilingual Agency, Ltd.

780 Third Ave., Ste. 4203
New York, NY 10017
Ph: (212)755-1090

Employment agency. Focuses on placement to openings requiring bi-lingual skills.

OTHER SOURCES

★8518★ Alternative Careers for Ph.D.'s in the Humanities: A Selected Bibliography

Books on Demand
300 N. Zeeb Rd.
Ann Arbor, MI 48106-1346
Ph: (313)761-4700 Fr: 800-521-0600

Christine F. Donaldson and Elizabeth A. Flynn. Reprint edition (originally published by Modern Language Association). $25.00. 48 pages. Bibliography of job-hunting resources and alternative occupations for Ph.D.'s in the humanities. Includes information on foreign language careers.

★8519★ Society of Federal Linguists (SFL)
PO Box 7765
Washington, DC 20044
Ph: (202)707-5397

Members: Translators, interpreters, and others employed by the U.S. government who use foreign language in their work; nongovernment individuals working at language-related jobs (teachers, abstractors, editors, cataloguers, and librarians).

Travel Agents and Managers

SOURCES OF HELP-WANTED ADS

★8520★ Business Travel News

Miller-Freeman, Inc.
1515 Broadway, 32nd Fl.
Manhasset, NY 11030
Ph: (212)869-1300   Fax: (212)768-0917

Tabloid newspaper covering business travel.

★8521★ Corporate Travel

Miller Freeman, Inc.
1515 Broadway
New York, NY 10036
Ph: (212)626-2380   Fax: (212)944-7164
Fr: 800-950-1314

Monthly. Tabloid reporting on international business travel and corporate meetings.

★8522★ Meeting News

Miller Freeman, Inc.
1515 Broadway
New York, NY 10036
Ph: (212)626-2380   Fax: (212)944-7164
Fr: 800-950-1314

Monthly. News, education, and ideas for better meetings.

★8523★ Southeast Travel Professional

Southern Travel Professional
1200 NW 78th Ave., Ste. 201
Miami, FL 33126
Ph: (305)592-6133   Fax: (305)592-9741

Monthly. Travel newspaper (tabloid).

★8524★ Tour and Travel News

CMP Publications, Inc.
600 Community Dr.
Manhasset, NY 11030
Ph: (516)562-5000   Fax: (516)562-5055

Weekly. Magazine for the travel industry, covering issues of interest to travel agents.

★8525★ Travel Agent

Universal Media, Inc.
801 2nd Ave., 12th Fl.
New York, NY 10017
Ph: (212)370-5050   Fax: (212)370-4491

Semiweekly. Travel industry magazine.

★8526★ Travel Trade

Travel Trade
15 W. 44th St.
New York, NY 10036
Ph: (212)730-6600   Fax: (212)730-7137

Weekly. Travel industry magazine.

★8527★ Travel Weekly

Reed Travel Group
500 Plaza Dr.
Secaucus, NJ 07096
Ph: (201)902-2000   Fax: (201)319-1947

Semiweekly (Mon. and Thurs.). Travel industry magazine.

★8528★ TravelAge MidAmerica

Reed Travel Group
500 Plaza Dr.
Secaucus, NJ 07094-3626
Ph: (201)902-1600   Fax: (201)319-1628

Weekly. $28.00/year for individuals. Magazine for travel counselors.

★8529★ TravelAge West

Reed Travel Group
500 Plaza Dr.
Secaucus, NJ 07096
Ph: (201)902-2000   Fax: (201)319-1947

Weekly (Mon.). Free to qualified subscribers; $25.00/year for individuals. Magazine for retail travel agents in western U.S. and western Canada.

PLACEMENT AND JOB REFERRAL SERVICES

★8530★ International Association of Tour Managers - North American Region (IATM-NAR)

65 Charnes Dr.
East Haven, CT 06513-1225
Ph: (203)466-0425   Fax: (203)787-6384

Members: Travel agents, travel wholesalers, airlines, hotel associations, shipping lines, tourist organizations, restaurants, shops, and entertainment organizations. **Purpose:** Works to maintain the highest possible standards of tour management; guarantee excellence of performance; educate the travel world on the role of the tour manager (also referred to as tour director, tour escort, or tour leader) in the successful completion of the tour itinerary and in bringing business to related industries. **Activities:** Operates placement service. Offers courses in tour management, travel marketing, and sales promotion through New York University in New York City and Metropolitan State College in Denver, CO. Conducts Professional Tour Management, U.S.A. Certificate Program.

★8531★ International Institute of Convention Management

9200 Bayard Pl.
Fairfax, VA 22032
Ph: (703)978-6287   Fax: (703)978-5524

Members: Meeting planners, travel agents, tour operators, and seminar organizers in 42 countries. **Purpose:** Works to improve the skills of professional conference and convention planners. Serves as a clearinghouse of information on new travel destinations and planning technologies, techniques, and strategies. **Activities:** Conducts research programs and placement service. **E-Mail:** 7417.351@compuserve.com

★8532★ Society of Incentive Travel Executives (SITE)

21 W. 38th St., 10th Fl.
New York, NY 10018
Ph: (212)575-0910   Fax: (212)575-1838

Members: Individuals responsible for the administration or sale of incentive travel including corporate users, incentive travel houses, cruise lines, hotel chains, resort operators, airlines, and tourist boards. **Purpose:** Unites individuals in the incentive travel industry and facilitates information exchange and problem solving on a personal and professional basis. Supports expansion of incentive travel through public relations, promotion, and speakers' bureau activities. **Activities:** Contributes to the continuing professional education of members through meetings, publications, and research services. Helps upgrade standards through educational services to nonmembers. Bestows Certified Incentive Travel Executive designation. Compiles statistics; provides placement service.

★8533★ Travel Professionals Association (TPA)

216 S. Bungalow Park Ave.
Tampa, FL 33609
Ph: (813)876-0286   Fax: (813)876-0286

Members: Travel industry personnel seeking career advancement. **Purpose:** Fosters professionalism by providing marketing assistance, research opportunities, and a forum for exchange and discussion of ideas and issues. Works to bridge the gap between the travel industry and the public's awareness of and access to travel professionals. Sponsors technical, civic, social, and cultural programs. Conducts surveys and questionnaires and disseminates results. **Activities:** Maintains charitable program, speakers' bureau, and placement services. Plans to extend advertising and referral services and insurance benefits. Candidates for membership must pass a four-part exam composed of destination information, travel terminology, identification of cities, states, and countries, and a written essay. Holds 6 exams/year.

EMPLOYER DIRECTORIES AND NETWORKING LISTS

★8534★ American Society of Travel Agents—Membership Directory

American Society of Travel Agents
1101 King St.
Alexandria, VA 22314
Ph: (703)739-2782   Fax: (703)684-8319

Annual, January. $125.00. Covers about 13,500 travel agents representing over 25,600 members in 130 countries. Entries include: Company name, address, phone, fax, telex, name of principal executive and other officials, services. Arrangement: Classified by membership category, then geographical. Indexes: Personal name, company name.

★8535★ Corporate Travel's Black Book

Miller Freeman, Inc.
1515 Broadway
New York, NY 10036
Ph: (212)869-1300   Fax: (212)768-3481

Annual, October. $15.00. Covers Approximately 2,000 airlines, hotels, car rentals, corporate charge cards, travel agencies, and other businesses offering travel packages to corporations. Entries include: Company name, address, phone, fax, name and title of contact. Arrangement: Classified by industry.

★8536★ Directory of Travel Agencies for the Disabled

Twin Peaks Press
Box 129
Vancouver, WA 98666
Ph: (206)694-2462   Fax: (206)696-3210
Fr: 800-637-2256

Quarterly. $19.95, plus $2.00 shipping. Number of listings: 370. Entries include: Company name, address, phone, fax, names and titles of key personnel, subsidiary and branch names and locations, description of services. Arrangement: Geographical.

★8537★ Institute of Certified Travel Agents—Directory

Institute of Certified Travel Agents
148 Linden St.
PO Box 812059
Wellesley, MA 02181-0012
Ph: (617)237-0280   Fax: (617)237-3860
Fr: 800-542-4282

Annual, suspended indefinitely. Available to members only. Covers about 8,000 member certified travel counselors, and 108 fellows. Entries include: Name, office address and phone. Arrangement: Geographical within membership categories. Indexes: Member name.

★8538★ National Business Travel Association—Membership Directory

National Business Travel Association
1650 King St., No. 301
Alexandria, VA 22314
Ph: (703)684-0836   Fax: (703)684-0263

Annual. Available to members only. Covers 1,500 corporate travel managers and allied members in the United States and Canada. Entries include: Individual name, corporate name, type of membership, office address, phone, and fax. Arrangement: Alphabetical by individual/company name. Indexes: Geographical, member type, advertiser.

★8539★ Personnel Guide to Canada's Travel Industry

Baxter Publishing Co.
310 Dupont St.
Toronto, ON, Canada M5R 1V9
Ph: (416)968-7252   Fax: (416)968-2377

Semiannual, spring and fall. $45.00, per copy, payment with order. Covers 8,000 tour operators, travel agencies, tourist boards, airlines, car rentals, cruise lines, hotels, etc., primarily in Canada. Entries include: Company name, address, phone, names and titles of key personnel, number of employees. Arrangement: Classified by line of business.

★8540★ Reed's Travel Group's Travel Agent Database

Reed Travel Group
2000 Clearwater Dr.
Oak Brook, IL 60521
Ph: (708)902-1859   Fax: (708)574-6284

Annual, winter. $270.00, per thousand listings. Database covers: about 75,500 wholesale, retail, and co-operative travel agencies worldwide, including tour operators. Database includes: Generally, company name, address, phone, telex, number of employees, subsidiary and branch names and locations, key personnel, services available, date established. Indexes: Geographic location/specialization, special interest tours.

★8541★ Survey of State Travel Offices

United States Travel Data Center
1100 New York Ave., NW, Ste. 450
Washington, DC 20005-3934
Ph: (202)408-1832   Fax: (202)408-1255

Annual, March. $475.00, payment with order. Covers state and territorial government agencies responsible for travel and travel promotion in their states. Entries include: Agency name, address, phone, number of full- and part-time staff, number of professional staff directly involved in travel; name and title of state travel director, and length of service as director, length of service in agency, and whether employed under the Civil Service program; advertising director and agency and public relations director in separate sections. Although addresses are not given, some listings do include name, title, and department of contact. Arrangement: By function (administration, advertising, etc.), then geographical.

★8542★ Travel Agencies Directory

American Business Directories, Inc.
American Business Information, Inc.
5711 S. 86th Cir.
Omaha, NE 68127
Ph: (402)593-4600   Fax: (402)331-1505

Annual. $1,310.00, U.S. edition; $290.00, (Canadian edition); payment with order. Number of listings: 42,039 (U.S. edition); 6,136 (Canadian edition). Entries include: Name, address, phone (including area code), size of advertisement, year first in Yellow Pages, name of owner or manager, number of employees. Regional editions available: Eastern, $845.00; Western, $645.00. Compiled from telephone company Yellow Pages, nationwide. Arrangement: Geographical.

★8543★ Travel Agency Reference & Profile Directory

World Travel Communications, Inc.
7380 S. Eastern Ave. 124-142
Las Vegas, NV 89123
Ph: (702)795-2411

Annual, June. $80.00. Covers travel agents and wholesale tour operators in North America. Entries include: Company name, address, phone, fax, cable address, names of owner, number of employees, association memberships, head office location, year established, specialty, conference appointments, business volume. Arrangement: Classified by type of business. Indexes: Travel agency name, geographical.

★8544★ Travel Industry Personnel Directory

Fairchild Books
Fairchild Publications, Inc.
7 W. 34th St.
New York, NY 10001
Ph: (212)630-3880   Fax: (212)630-3862
Fr: 800-247-6622

Annual, April. $30.00, plus 4.95 shipping. Covers air and steamship lines, tour operators, bus lines, hotel representatives, foreign and domestic railroads, foreign and domestic tourist information offices, travel trade associations, etc. Entries include: Agency or company name, address, phone, names of principal personnel. Arrangement: Classified by companies or agencies within functional or service categories (airlines, information offices, etc.).

★8545★ Travel and Tourism Research Association—Membership Directory

Travel & Tourism Research Association
10200 W. 44th Ave., No. 304
Wheat Ridge, CO 80033
Ph: (303)940-6557   Fax: (303)422-8894

Annual, June. $50.00, payment with order; controlled circulation. Covers over 750 state and local tourism bureaus and other federal and provincial government agencies, airlines, media, hotels, university bureaus of business research, and other university departments, and research and consulting firms concerned with travel research, marketing, and promotion. Entries include: Firm or individual name, address, phone; company listings also include name and title of representative or alternate. Arrangement: Alphabetical. Indexes: Personal name, geographical, industry category.

★8546★ Worldwide Travel Information Contact Book

Gale Research
835 Penobscot Bldg.
Detroit, MI 48226-4094
Ph: (313)961-2242   Fax: (313)961-6083
Fr: 800-877-GALE

Second edition, 1992. $175.00. Guide to travel information for tourism professionals, the travel trade press, individuals and business travelers, researchers, and students. Includes information on travel agencies/tour operators; hotel, travel, and transportation associations; tourism and automobile clubs; national and international ministries, departments, and boards of tourism; local tourist sources; and other travel organizations and sources. Arranged on a country-by-country basis. Indexes: Alphabetical and keyword.

HANDBOOKS AND MANUALS

★8547★ America's 50 Fastest Growing Jobs

JIST Works, Inc.
720 N. Park Ave.
Indianapolis, IN 46202
Ph: (317)264-3720   Fr: 800-648-5478

Third edition, 1995. $14.95. 288 pages. Each job profile explains the nature of the work, skills and abilities required, employment outlook, average earnings, related occupations, education and training requirements, and employment opportunities. Also contains career planning information and job search tips.

★8548★ Career Opportunities in Travel and Tourism

Facts on File, Inc.
11 Penn Plaza, 15th Fl.
New York, NY 10001-2006
Ph: (212)967-8800   Fax: 800-678-3633
Fr: 800-322-8755

John Hawks. 1995. $29.95; $15.95 (paper). 224 pages. Includes detailed job descriptions, educational requirements, salary ranges, and advancement prospects for 70 different job opportunities in this fast-paced industry. Contains index and bibliography.

★8549★ Careers for Travel Buffs and Other Restless Types

VGM Career Horizons
4255 W. Touhy Ave.
Lincolnwood, IL 60646-1975
Ph: (847)679-5500   Fax: (847)679-2494
Fr: 800-323-4900

Paul Plawin. 1992. $14.95; $9.95 (paper). Includes a variety of travel and open-road careers, such as travel writers and photographers, tour bus drivers, entertainers, cruise line staff, travel agents, tour guides, sports writers, sales, the military, trucking, and meeting planning.

★8550★ Exploring Careers in the Travel Industry

Rosen Publishing Group, Inc.
29 E. 21st St.
New York, NY 10010
Ph: (212)777-3017   Fax: (212)777-0277
Fr: 800-237-9932

Edgar Grant. Revised edition, 1989. $14.95. Provides an overview of the travel and tourism industries. Describes the work of the travel agent, skills, training, pay, and employment outlook. Offers job hunting advice.

★8551★ First Class: An Introduction to Travel and Tourism

Glencoe
936 Eastwind Dr.
Westerville, OH 43081
Ph: (614)890-1111   Fax: (614)899-4304
Fr: 800-848-1567

Dennis L. Foster. 1993.

★8552★ Flying High in Travel

John Wiley and Sons
605 3rd Ave.
New York, NY 10158
Ph: (212)850-6000   Fr: 800-225-5945

Karen Rubin. Second edition, 1992. $19.95. 336 pages. A guide to careers and job hunting in the travel industry. Describes the many job opportunities available, from writing to hotel management to law. Includes information on educational preparation, training, and job hunting.

★8553★ How to Get a Job with a Cruise Line

Ticket to Adventure, Inc.
PO Box 41005
St. Petersburg, FL 33743
Ph: (813)544-6440   Fr: 800-929-7447

Mary Fallon Miller. Third edition, 1994. $14.95. 224 pages. Explores jobs with cruise ships, describing duties, responsibilities, benefits, and training. Lists cruise ship lines and schools offering cruise line training. Offers job hunting advice.

★8554★ Managing Group Tours: Your Complete Reference Guide to Successful Tour Management

Shoreline Creations, Ltd.
143 Douglas Ave., Ste. 8
Holland, MI 49424
Ph: (616)393-2077   Fax: (616)393-0085
Fr: 800-767-3489

Anita L. Fielder. 1995. $19.95 (paper).

★8555★ Now Hiring: Travel and Tourism

Zinks International Career Guidance
PO Box 585
Dearborn, MI 48121-0585
Ph: (313)584-7529

Richard M. Zink. 1994. $14.95 (paper).

★8556★ 100 Best Careers for the Year 2000

Prentice Hall General Reference
15 Columbus Cir.
New York, NY 10023
Ph: (212)373-8500   Fr: 800-223-2348

Shelly Field. 1992. $15.00 (paper). Covers 100 of the fastest growing jobs. The publication is divided into 11 general employment sections. Specific careers are covered within each section. Provides job description, responsibilities, employment opportunities, earnings, education and training, advancement opportunities, and experience and qualifications for each occupation.

★8557★ Opportunities in Travel Careers

VGM Career Horizons
4255 W. Touhy Ave.
Lincolnwood, IL 60646-1975
Ph: (847)679-5500   Fax: (847)679-2494
Fr: 800-323-4900

Robert Scott Milne. 1996. $14.95; $11.95 (paper). 160 pages. Discusses what the jobs are and where to find them in airlines, shipping lines, and railroads. Discusses related opportunities in hotels, motels, resorts, travel agencies, public relation firms, and recreation departments. Illustrated.

★8558★ Part-Time Travel Agent: How to Cash in on the Exciting New World of Travel Marketing

The Intrepid Traveler
PO Box 438
New York, NY 10034-0438
Ph: (212)569-1081   Fax: (212)942-6687

Kelly Monaghan. 1994. $24.95 (paper).

★8559★ Passport: An Introduction to the Travel and Tourism Industry

South-Western Publishing Company
5101 Madison Rd.
Cincinnati, OH 45227
Ph: (513)271-8811   Fax: (513)527-6194
Fr: 800-543-0487

David W. Howell. 1993. $38.95 (paper).

★8560★ So–You Want to Be a Travel Agent: An Introduction to Domestic Travel

Prentice Hall
113 Sylvan Ave., Rte. 9W
Englewood Cliffs, NJ 07632
Ph: (201)592-2000   Fr: 800-922-0579

Douglas A. Payette. 1994. $34.80 (paper).

★8561★ Travel Agent

Prentice Hall
113 Sylvan Ave.
Rte. 9W
Englewood Cliffs, NJ 07632
Ph: (201)592-2000   Fr: 800-922-0579

Wilma Boyd. 1989. $14.95. 256 pages. Outlines entry-level positions in the airline, car rental, and hospitality industries as well as in travel agencies and related travel services. Explains travel agency operations, sales techniques, and the use of computers in travel services. Gives job hunting advice and sales tips.

★8562★ The Travel Agent: Dealer in Dreams

Prentice Hall
113 Sylvan Ave.
Rte. 9W
Englewood Cliffs, NJ 07632
Ph: (201)592-2000   Fr: 800-922-0579

Gregory Aryear. Fourth edition, 1992. $44.00. 375 pages. Comprehensive guide for those interested in the travel industry. Covers various jobs within the travel industry including travel consultant, agency manager, and tour operators.

★8563★ Travel and Hospitality Career Directory

Gale Research
835 Penobscot Bldg.
Detroit, MI 48226-4094
Ph: (313)961-2242   Fax: (313)961-6083
Fr: 800-877-GALE

Bradley Morgan. Second edition, 1992. $39.00. 289 pages. Features a basic and comprehensive job search section, articles by top professionals in the field, and detailed listings of hundreds of top companies who hire individuals in this field. Aimed particularly at entry-level job hunters.

★8564★ Travel Industry Guidelines for Employment

Travel Text Associates
42883 Heydenreich Rd.
Clinton Township, MI 48038
Ph: (810)799-4018

Chris Hoosen and Francis Dix. 1990. $20.00.

★8565★ Travel Perspectives: A Guide to Becoming a Travel Agent

Delmar Publishers
3 Columbia Cir.
Box 15015
Albany, NY 12212
Ph: (518)464-3500   Fax: (518)464-0358
Fr: 800-347-7707

Ginger Todd. 1996. $34.95 (paper).

★8566★ Travel and Tourism

Franklin Watts, Inc.
Sherman Turnpike
Danbury, CT 06810

Marjorie Rittenberg Schulz. 1990. Surveys employment opportunities in the travel and tourism industry. Provides salaries and employment outlook. Offers job hunting advice.

★8567★ Travel the World Free as an International Tour Director: How to Be an International Tour Director

G.E. Mitchell & Associates, Inc.
PO Box 159
Sullivans Island, SC 29482-0159
Ph: (803)723-7400   Fax: (803)853-2822
Fr: 800-209-0019

Gerald E. Mitchell. 1995. $59.95.

★8568★ Where the Jobs Are: The Hottest Careers for the '90s

The Career Press, Inc.
3 Tice Rd.
PO Box 687
Franklin Lakes, NJ 07417
Ph: (201)848-0310   Fax: (201)848-1727
Fr: 800-237-3371

Joyce Hadley. Second edition, 1995. $9.99. 300 pages. Describes careers in fifteen general fields, from accounting to travel and hospitality.

★8569★ Your Opportunities in Recreation, Travel and Tourism

Energeia Publishing, Inc.
860 Commercial St.
PO Box 985
Salem, OR 97308
Ph: (503)362-1480   Fax: (503)362-2123

Laurie Bean. 1994. $2.00 (paper).

EMPLOYMENT AGENCIES AND SEARCH FIRMS

★8570★ The Pathfinder Group

295 Danbury Rd.
Wilton, CT 06897-3095
Ph: (203)834-2467

Employment agency. Executive search firm. Recruits staff in a variety of fields.

★8571★ Travel Executive Search

5 Rose Ave.
Great Neck, NY 11021
Ph: (516)829-8829

Executive search firm.

OTHER SOURCES

★8572★ American Society of Travel Agents (ASTA)

1101 King St.
Alexandria, VA 22314
Ph: (703)739-2782   Fax: (703)684-8319

Members: Travel agents; allied members are representatives of carriers, hotels, resorts, sightseeing and car rental companies, official tourist organizations, and other travel interests. **Purpose:** To Promote and encourage travel among people of all nations; to promote the image and encourage the use of professional travel agents worldwide; serve as an information resource for the travel industry worldwide; promote and represent the views and interests of travel agents to all levels of government and industry; promote professional and ethical conduct in the travel agency industry worldwide; facilitate consumer protection and safety for the traveling public. **Activities:** Maintains biographical archives and travel hall of fame. Conducts research and education programs.

★8573★ Corporate Meetings & Incentives' Directory of Incentive Facilities & Services

The Laux Co., Inc.
63 Great Rd.
Maynard, MA 01754
Ph: (508)897-5552   Fax: (508)897-6824

Annual, November. $20.00. Covers hotels, convention bureaus, tourist boards, resorts, cruise lines, airlines, that regularly do business in incentive travel. Entries include: Company name, address, phone, names of sales contacts, description of facilities or services. Arrangement: Classified by line of business.

★8574★ Institute of Certified Travel Agents (ICTA)

148 Linden St.
PO Box 812059
Wellesley, MA 02181-0012
Ph: (617)237-0280   Fax: (617)237-3860
Fr: 800-542-4282

Members: Individuals who have been accredited as Certified Travel Counselors (CTC) after meeting the institute's requirements (5 years' travel industry experience, 5 travel management courses, 4 examinations, an original research project, and a presentation). **Purpose:** Seeks to increase the level of competence in the travel industry. Provides continuing education, and examination and certification programs; conducts workshops and professional management seminars. **Activities:** Operates Travel Career Development Program to increase professional skills and Destination Specialist Programs to enhance the geographical knowledge of sales agents. Organizes study groups of instruction with enrolled student bodies in most major cities.

★8575★ *Interpersonal Skills for Travel and Tourism*
Trans-Atlantic Publications, Inc.
311 Bainbridge St.
Philadelphia, PA 19147
Ph: (215)925-5083   Fax: (215)925-1912
Lisa Burton. 1994. $47.50 (paper).

★8576★ *Travel Agency Business Guide*
Entrepreneur, Inc.
2392 Morse Ave.
Box 19787
Irvine, CA 92713-9787
Fax: (714)851-9088   Fr: 800-421-2300
$79.50 (includes business guide and soft-

ware). Contains step-by-step instructions on how to start a travel agency. Includes information on profits and costs, location, financing, promotion and advertising, and related topics.

Typesetters and Compositors

★8577★ American Printer

Intertec Publishing Co.
29 N. Wacker Dr.
Chicago, IL 60606
Ph: (312)435-2330   Fax: (312)726-4103
Fr: 800-621-9907

Monthly. $50.00/year for individuals. Magazine covering the printing and publishing market.

★8578★ Electronic Publishing & Typeworld

PennWell Publishing Co.
10 Tara Blvd., 5th Fl.
Nashua, NH 03062-2801
Ph: (603)891-0123   Fax: (603)891-0597

Eighteen issues/year. $30.00/year. Newspaper for digital publishing professionals.

★8579★ Graphic Arts Monthly

Cahners Publishing Co.
249 W. 17th St.
New York, NY 10011
Ph: (212)463-6836

Monthly. $85.00/year. Magazine featuring commercial printing and graphic arts, including digital technologies and quick printing.

★8580★ IN-PLANT Reproductions

Intertec Publishing
9800 Metcalf
Overland Park, KS 66212
Ph: (913)341-1300   Fax: (913)967-1905

Eleven issues/year. $65.00/year.

★8581★ Print

R.C. Publications, Inc.
104 5th Ave., 19th Fl.
New York, NY 10011
Ph: (212)463-0600   Fax: (212)989-9891

Bimonthly. Covers all aspects of graphic design for visual communication.

★8582★ Print and Graphics

East-West Communications
1432 Duke St.
Alexandria, VA 22314-3436
Ph: (703)683-8800   Fax: (703)683-8801

Monthly. Magazine (tabloid).

★8583★ Printing Impressions

Intertec Publishing
9800 Metcalf
Overland Park, KS 66212
Ph: (913)341-1300   Fax: (913)967-1905

Monthly. $75.00/year for individuals. Trade magazine.

★8584★ Signature

South Wind Publishing Co.
PO Box 6808
Leawood, KS 66206-0808
Ph: (913)642-6611   Fax: (913)642-6676

Periodic. Free to qualified subscribers; $48.00/year for institutions; $58.00/year for Canada and Mexico. Publishing industry magazine and catalog.

★8585★ Southern Graphics

PTN Publishing Co.
445 Broad Hollow Rd., Ste. 21
Melville, NY 11747
Ph: (516)845-2700   Fax: (516)845-7109

Monthly. $22.00/year for individuals. Graphic arts magazine serving the printing and graphic arts industry in 14 southern states.

PLACEMENT AND JOB REFERRAL SERVICES

★8586★ Printing Brokerage/Buyers Association (PB/BA)

1500 NW 49th St., Ste. 550
Fort Lauderdale, FL 33309
Ph: (305)771-5554   Fax: (305)771-5991
Fr: 800-448-8952

Members: Printing buyers/brokers/distributors, printers, typographers, binders, envelope and book manufacturers, packagers, color separation houses, pre-press service organizations, and related companies in the graphic arts industry. **Purpose:** Promotes understanding, cooperation, and interaction among members while obtaining the highest standard of professionalism in the graphic arts industry. Gathers information on current technology in the graphic communications industry. Sponsors seminars for members to learn how to work with buyers, brokers and printers; also conducts technical and management seminars. **Activities:** Maintains referral service; compiles statistics. Conducts charitable programs.

★8587★ Women in Production (WIP)

347 5th Ave., No. 1406
New York, NY 10016-5010
Ph: (212)481-7793   Fax: (212)481-7969

Members: Persons involved in all phases of print and graphics, including those working in magazine and book publishing, agency production and print manufacturing, print-related vending and buying, and advertising production. **Purpose:** To improve job performance by sharing information with each other and with suppliers of printing services. Acts as a network of contacts for those in the printing professions; offers assistance to persons with production problems. Membership is concentrated in the New York City area. **Activities:** Sponsors placement service; maintains speakers' bureau.

EMPLOYER DIRECTORIES AND NETWORKING LISTS

★8588★ Graphic Arts Blue Book

A. F. Lewis & Co., Inc.
245 5th Ave.
New York, NY 10016
Ph: (212)679-0770   Fax: (212)545-7963

Covers printing plants, bookbinders, typesetters, platemakers, paper merchants, paper manufacturers, printing machinery manufacturers and dealers, and others serving the graphic arts industry in six regional editions: New York; Southeastern; Northeastern; Delaware Valley-Ohio; Midwestern; and West Coast. Entries include: Company name, address, phone, names and titles of executives, name of buyer, list of products or services, year established. Arrangement: Same information given geographically, classified by product/service, and classified by paper brand name/watermark. Indexes: Alphabetical.

★8589★ **International Literary Market Place**

R. R. Bowker Co.
Reed Reference Publishing
121 Chanlon Rd.
New Providence, NJ 07974
Ph: (908)464-6800   Fax: (908)771-7704
Fr: 800-521-8110

Annual, Fall. $179.95. Covers more than 9,200 publishers in over 170 countries outside the United States and Canada, and about 1,150 trade and professional organizations related to publishing abroad; includes major printers, binders, typesetters, book manufacturers, book dealers, libraries, literary agencies, translators, book clubs, reference books and journals, periodicals, prizes, and international reference section. Entries include: For publishers Name, address, phone, fax, telex, names and titles of key personnel, branches, type of publications, subjects, ISBN prefix. Arrangement: Classified by business activities, then geographical. Indexes: Company name, subject, type of publication.

★8590★ **Literary Market Place**

R. R. Bowker Co.
Reed Reference Publishing
121 Chanlon Rd.
New Providence, NJ 07974
Ph: (908)464-6800   Fax: (908)771-7704
Fr: 800-521-8110

Annual, September. $165.00. Covers over 15,000 firms or organizations offering services related to the publishing industry, including 3,800 book publishers in the United States and Canada who issued three or more books during the preceding year, plus a small press section of publishers who publish less than three titles per year or those who are self-published. Also included: book printers and binders; book clubs; book trade and literary associations; selected syndicates, newspapers, periodicals, and radio and TV programs that use book reviews or book publishing news; translators and literary agents. Arrangement: Classified by line of business. Indexes: Principal index is 35,000-item combined index of publishers, publications, and personnel; several sections have geographical and/or subject indexes; translators are indexed by source and target language.

★8591★ **Publishers Directory**

Gale Research
835 Penobscot Bldg.
Detroit, MI 48226-4094
Ph: (313)961-2242   Fax: (313)961-6083
Fr: 800-877-GALE

Annual, fall. $275.00. Covers approximately 20,000 new and established, commercial and nonprofit, private and alternative, corporate and association, government and institution publishing programs and their distributors; includes producers of books, classroom materials, prints, reports, and databases. Entries include: Firm name, address, phone,

fax, year founded, ISBN prefix, Standard Address Number, whether firm participates in the Cataloging in Publication program of the Library of Congress, names of principal executives, number of titles in print, description of firm and its main subject interests, discount and returns policies, affiliated and parent companies, mergers and amalgamations, principal markets, imprints and divisions; distributors also list firms for which they distribute, special services, terms to publishers and regional offices. Arrangement: Alphabetical; distributors listed separately. Indexes: Subject, geographical, publisher name (including imprints).

★8592★ **Typesetting Services Directory**

American Business Directories, Inc.
American Business Information, Inc.
5711 S. 86th Cir.
Omaha, NE 68127
Ph: (402)593-4600   Fax: (402)331-1505

Annual. $855.00, U.S. edition. Number of listings: 11,935 (U.S. edition); 938 (Canadian edition). Entries include: Name, address, phone (including area code), size of advertisement, year first in Yellow Pages, name of owner or manager, number of employees. Compiled from telephone company Yellow Pages, nationwide. Arrangement: Geographical.

★8593★ **The Workbook**

Scott & Daughters Publishing
940 N. Highland Ave.
Los Angeles, CA 90038
Ph: (213)856-0008   Fax: (213)856-4368
Fr: 800-547-2688

Annual, January. $95.00. Covers in four regional volumes, 25,000 advertising agencies, art directors, photographers, freelance illustrators and designers, artists' representatives, commercial production companies, printers, color separators, and typographers in the U.S. Entries include: Company or individual name, address, phone, specialty. Regional volumes are East, West, Midwest, and South. Arrangement: Classified by product or service.

HANDBOOKS AND MANUALS

★8594★ **Opportunities in Newspaper Publishing Careers**

VGM Career Horizons
4255 W. Touhy Ave.
Lincolnwood, IL 60646-1975
Ph: (847)679-5500   Fax: (847)679-2494
Fr: 800-323-4900

John Tebbel. 1989. $14.95; $11.95 (paper). 160 pages. Tells how to land a newspaper job, describing editorial and noneditorial positions at big city and small city papers and syndicated wire services. Career preparation chapters address the need to anticipate changing newspaper technology while acquiring fundamental news skills. Illustrated.

★8595★ **Opportunities in Printing Careers**

VGM Career Horizons
4255 W. Touhy Ave.
Lincolnwood, IL 60646-1975
Ph: (847)679-5500   Fax: (847)679-2494
Fr: 800-323-4900

Irvin J. Borowsky. 1992. $14.95; $11.95 (paper). 160 pages. Offers detailed information on the variety of pre-press, press, and post-press jobs available. Covers apprenticeships, unions, salaries, and how to get ahead. Illustrated.

★8596★ **Opportunities in Vocational and Technical Careers**

VGM Career Horizons
4255 W. Touhy Ave.
Lincolnwood, IL 60646-1975
Ph: (847)679-5500   Fax: (847)679-2494
Fr: 800-323-4900

Adrian A. Paradis. 1992. $14.95; $11.95 (paper). 160 pages. Provides information on a variety of opportunities and advice on breaking into the field.

★8597★ **Your Opportunities in the Printing Industry**

Energeia Publishing, Inc.
860 Commercial St., S.
Salem, OR 97302
Ph: (503)362-1480   Fax: (503)362-2123

Laurie Bean. 1994. $2.00 (paper).

EMPLOYMENT AGENCIES AND SEARCH FIRMS

★8598★ **Alden and Clark, Inc.**

PO Box 180177
Boston, MA 02118
Ph: (617)247-1147

★8599★ **Graphic Arts Employment Service, Inc.**

2530 Central Pkwy.
Cincinnati, OH 45214
Ph: (513)241-2201

Employment agency.

★8600★ **Graphic Search Associates Inc.**

PO Box 373
Newtown Square, PA 19073
Ph: (610)359-1234   Fax: (610)353-8120

Executive search firm.

★8601★ **Stewart Associates**

245 Butler Ave.
The Executive Offices
Lancaster, PA 17601
Ph: (717)299-9242   Fax: (717)299-4879

Executive search firm.

OTHER SOURCES

★8602★ American Institute of Graphic Arts (AIGA)

164 5th Ave.
New York, NY 10010
Ph: (212)807-1990   Fax: (212)807-1799
Fr: 800-548-1634

Purpose: Graphic designers, art directors, art directors, illustrators, packaging designers, and craftsmen involved in printing and allied graphic fields. Sponsors exhibits and projects in the public interest. Sponsors traveling exhibitions. Operates gallery. Maintains library of design books and periodicals; offers slide archives.

★8603★ Graphic Arts Technical Foundation (GATF)

4615 Forbes Ave.
Pittsburgh, PA 15213
Ph: (412)621-6941   Fax: (412)621-3049

Members: Scientific, research, technical, and educational organization serving the international graphic communications industries. **Purpose:** Conducts research in all graphic processes and their commercial applications. Conducts seminars, workshops, and forums on graphic arts and environmental subjects. Conducts educational programs, including the publishing of graphic arts textbooks and learning modules, audiovisuals, videotapes, aptitude testing, in-plant and school counseling, and national career and manpower recruitment program. Conducts the GATF

training and certification program in sheet-fed offset press operating, Web Offset press operating, Image Assembly, and desktop publishing. Produces test images and quality control devices for the industry. Performs technical services for the graphic arts industry, including problem-solving, material evaluation, and plant audits. Compiles statistics.

★8604★ Printing Industries of America (PIA)

100 Daingerfield Rd.
Alexandria, VA 22314
Ph: (703)519-8100   Fax: (703)548-3227
Fr: 800-742-2666

Members: Commercial printing firms (lithography, letterpress, gravure, platemakers, typographic houses); allied firms in the graphic arts. **Purpose:** Provides extensive management services for member companies, including government relations, industry research and statistical information, technology information and assistance, and management education and publications. Compiles statistical and economic data, including annual ratio study which provides a benchmark for printers to compare profits as a basis for improving individual member company and industry profits. Provides reporting system on provisions, rates, and other matters relating to union contracts in effect throughout the industry. Sponsors annual Premier Print Awards Competition.

★8605★ Type Directors Club (TDC)

60 E. 42nd St., Ste. 721
New York, NY 10165
Ph: (212)983-6042   Fax: (212)983-6043

Members: Professional society of typographic designers, type directors, and teachers of typography; sustaining members are individuals with interests in typographic education. **Purpose:** Seeks to stimulate research and disseminate information. Provides speakers and offers presentations on new developments in typography.

★8606★ "Typesetting and Graphic Arts" in *Small Businesses That Grow and Grow and Grow*

Divison of F&M Publications
1507 Dana Ave.
Cincinnati, OH 45207
Ph: (513)531-2222   Fr: 800-289-0963

Patricia A. Woy. 1989. $9.95 (paper). Contains a chapter about establishing businesses in the printing, typesetting, and graphic arts fields.

★8607★ Typographers International Association (TIA)

84 Park Ave.
Flemington, NJ 08822
Ph: (908)782-4635   Fax: (908)782-4671

Members: Pre-press firms made up of suppliers of graphic arts services. **Purpose:** Reports on business and technological developments; monitors and participates in related legislative activities; provides management expertise; operates sales support system. Compiles statistics.

Typists, Word Processors, and Data Entry Keyers

SOURCES OF HELP-WANTED ADS

★8608★ *The Secretary*

Stratton Publishing and Marketing, Inc.
2800 Shirlington Rd., Ste. 706
Arlington, VA 22206
Ph: (703)998-2534   Fax: (703)379-4561

$19.00/year for individuals; $2.00 for single issue. Magazine for secretaries, administrative assistants, and office managers featuring information on trends in business, technology, career development, and management.

PLACEMENT AND JOB REFERRAL SERVICES

★8609★ **Association for Corporate Computing Technical Professionals (NaSPA)**

7040 S. 13th St.
Milwaukee, WI 53154
Ph: (414)768-8000   Fax: (414)423-2433

Members: Technicians and technical management personnel in 60 countries who work in corporate data processing. **Purpose:** Dedicated to enhancing the level of technical education among members through publications, public domain software, electronic information sharing, job and career assistance, and scholarships and grants. **Activities:** Conducts charitable and educational programs; maintains speakers' bureau and placement service; compiles statistics.

EMPLOYER DIRECTORIES AND NETWORKING LISTS

★8610★ *Northwest High Tech: Fast Facts on the $7 Billion Computer Industry of Washington, Oregon, Idaho, British Columbia, and Alberta*

Resolution Business Press
11101 NE 8th St., Ste. 208
Bellevue, WA 98004
Ph: (206)455-4611   Fax: (206)455-9143

Annual. $34.95. Covers over 1,800 computer-related companies in Washington, Oregon, and Idaho, and British Columbia and Alberta, Canada. Entries include: Company; name, address, phone, fax; toll-free number; names and titles of key personnel; product/service, programming languages, financial data, names and titles of key personnel, number of employees, operating systems, expansion plans (including hiring and site expansion plans), company market information, Standard Industrial Classification (SIC) code. Arrangement: Geographical, industry sector. Indexes: Company name, SIC.

HANDBOOKS AND MANUALS

★8611★ *Career Opportunities in Television, Cable and Video*

Facts on File, Inc.
11 Penn Plaza, 15th Fl.
New York, NY 10001-2006
Ph: (212)967-8800   Fax: 800-678-3633
Fr: 800-322-8755

Maxine K. Reed and Robert M. Reed. Third edition, 1991. $29.95; $15.95 (paper). 272 pages.

★8612★ *Exploring Careers in Word Processing and Desktop Publishing*

Rosen Publishing Group, Inc.
29 E. 21st St.
New York, NY 10010
Ph: (212)777-3017   Fax: (212)777-0277
Fr: 800-237-9932

Jean W. Spencer. 1990. $14.95. Covers the secretarial, information processing, and desktop publishing fields.

★8613★ *Exploring High-Tech Careers*

Rosen Publishing Group, Inc.
29 E. 21st St.
New York, NY 10010
Ph: (212)777-3017   Fax: (212)777-0277
Fr: 800-237-9932

Scott Southworth. Revised edition, 1993. $14.95; $9.95 (paper). 118 pages. Gives an orientation to the field of high technology and high-tech jobs. Describes educational preparation and job hunting. Includes a glossary and bibliography.

★8614★ *How to Prepare for the Civil Service Examinations for Stenographer, Typist, Clerk, and Office Machine Operator*

Barron's Educational Series, Inc.
250 Wireless Blvd.
Hauppauge, NY 11788-3917
Ph: (516)434-3311   Fax: (516)434-3723
Fr: 800-645-3476

Jerry Bobrow. 1994. $11.95 (paper).

★8615★ *100 Best Careers for the Year 2000*

Prentice Hall General Reference
15 Columbus Cir.
New York, NY 10023
Ph: (212)373-8500   Fr: 800-223-2348

Shelly Field. 1992. $15.00 (paper). Covers 100 of the fastest growing jobs. The publication is divided into 11 general employment sections. Specific careers are covered within each section. Provides job description, responsibilities, employment opportunities, earnings, education and training, advancement opportunities, and experience and qualifications for each occupation.

★8616★ *Opportunities in Data Processing Careers*

VGM Career Horizons
4255 W. Touhy Ave.
Lincolnwood, IL 60646-1975
Ph: (847)679-5500   Fax: (847)679-2494
Fr: 800-323-4900

Norman Noerper. 1989. $14.95; $11.95 (paper). 160 pages. Extensive information on education, training, and job prospecting make this a useful guide to an important career field. Illustrated.

★8617★ **Opportunities in High Tech Careers**

VGM Career Horizons
4255 W. Touhy Ave.
Lincolnwood, IL 60646-1975
Ph: (847)679-5500   Fax: (847)679-2494
Fr: 800-323-4900

Gary D. Golter and Deborah Yanuck. 1995. $14.95; $11.95 (paper). 160 pages. Explores high technology careers. Describes job opportunities, how to make a career decision, how to prepare for high technology jobs, job hunting techniques, and future trends.

★8618★ **Opportunities in Office Occupations**

VGM Career Horizons
4255 W. Touhy Ave.
Lincolnwood, IL 60646-1975
Ph: (847)679-5500   Fax: (847)679-2494
Fr: 800-323-4900

Blanche Ettinger. 1995. $14.95; $11.95 (paper). Covers a variety of office positions and discusses trends for the next decade. Describes the job market, opportunities, job duties, educational preparation, the work environment, and earnings.

★8619★ **Opportunities in Secretarial Careers**

VGM Career Horizons
4255 W. Touhy Ave.
Lincolnwood, IL 60646-1975
Ph: (847)679-5500   Fax: (847)679-2494
Fr: 800-323-4900

Blanche Ettinger. 1992. $14.95; $11.95 (paper). Includes a chapter on finding a secretarial job with sample resumes and interview questions.

★8620★ **Opportunities in State and Local Government Careers**

VGM Career Horizons
4255 W. Touhy Ave.
Lincolnwood, IL 60646-1975
Ph: (847)679-5500   Fax: (847)679-2494
Fr: 800-323-4900

Neale Baxter. 1993. $13.95; $10.95 (paper). 160 pages. Points out the incentives and drawbacks of a government career. Describes hiring procedures and provides tips on filling out applications, taking physical and aptitude tests, handling interviews, and finding jobs. Describes the jobs in which 75% of all state and local government workers are employed. For each occupation, covers the nature of the work and the training required.

★8621★ **Opportunities in Vocational and Technical Careers**

VGM Career Horizons
4255 W. Touhy Ave.
Lincolnwood, IL 60646-1975
Ph: (847)679-5500   Fax: (847)679-2494
Fr: 800-323-4900

Adrian A. Paradis. 1992. $14.95; $11.95 (paper). 160 pages. Provides information on a variety of opportunities and advice on breaking into the field.

★8622★ **Opportunities in Word Processing Careers**

VGM Career Horizons
4255 W. Touhy Ave.
Lincolnwood, IL 60646-1975
Ph: (847)679-5500   Fax: (847)679-2494
Fr: 800-323-4900

Marianne Munday. 1991. $14.95; $11.95 (paper). 160 pages. Identifies major employers, describes a variety of jobs as well as spin-off careers, and talks about how to pursue them. Illustrated.

EMPLOYMENT AGENCIES AND SEARCH FIRMS

★8623★ **Accountants Overload Group**

10990 Wilshire Blvd.
Los Angeles, CA 90024-3913
Ph: (213)629-2800

Employment agency.

★8624★ **Addington Personnel Services**

2401 Fountainview, Ste.104
Houston, TX 77057
Ph: (713)780-8810

Employment agency. Places individuals in regular or temporary positions.

★8625★ **B and M Associates, Inc.**

199 Cambridge Rd.
Woburn, MA 01801-4705
Ph: (617)938-9120

Employment agency.

★8626★ **Best Personnel Services**

8901 State Line Rd.
Kansas City, MO 64114-3200
Ph: (816)361-3100

Employment agency. Fills openings on a regular or temporary basis. Office also located in Independence, MO.

★8627★ **Beverly Hills Bar Association Personnel Service**

300 S. Beverly Dr., Ste. 214
Beverly Hills, CA 90212
Ph: (213)553-4575

Employment agency.

★8628★ **Consultants and Designers Inc.**

7240 Parkway Dr., Ste. 250
Hanover, MD 21076-1367
Ph: (410)712-0052

Places staff in temporary positions. West Coast office located in Santa Clara, CA.

★8629★ **Cross Employment Agency**

150 Broadway, Ste. 902
New York, NY 10038-4389
Ph: (212)227-6705

Employment agency. Temporary and regular placement of personnel.

★8630★ **Data Careers Personnel Services, Inc.**

3320 4th Ave.
San Diego, CA 92103
Ph: (619)291-9994

Employment agency. Places staff on a regular or temporary basis.

★8631★ **Davis-Smith, Inc.**

24725 W. 12 Mile Rd., Ste. 302
Southfield, MI 48034
Ph: (810)354-4100

Employment agency. Executive search firm.

★8632★ **Electronic Systems Personnel**

701 Fourth Ave. S., Ste. 1800
Minneapolis, MN 55415
Ph: (612)337-3000

Employment agency.

★8633★ **Esquire Personnel Services, Inc.**

222 S. Riverside Plaza, Ste. 320
Chicago, IL 60606-5804
Ph: (312)648-4600   Fax: (312)648-4637

Employment agency.

★8634★ **Hallmark Services**

520 Pike St., Ste. 1450
Seattle, WA 98101-4001
Ph: (206)587-5360

Employment agency. Fills openings on a regular or temporary basis.

★8635★ **Jobs, Training, and Services, Inc.**

101 S. Moberly Ave.
Longview, TX 75602-1433
Ph: (903)757-3046

Employment agency. Another office is located in Henderson, TX.

★8636★ **Pathfinders, Inc.**

229 Peachtree St. NE
Atlanta, GA 30303-1601
Ph: (404)688-5940

Employment agency.

★8637★ **Webster Personnel**

131 State St.
Boston, MA 02109-3201
Ph: (617)742-2030

Employment agency.

OTHER SOURCES

★8638★ **Black Data Processing Associates (BDPA)**

1250 Connecticut Ave. NW, Ste. 700
Washington, DC 20036-2603
Ph: (202)775-4301   Fax: (202)775-1344
Fr: 800-727-BDPA

Members: Persons employed in the information processing industry, including electronic data processing, electronic word processing, and data communications; others interested in information processing. **Purpose:** Seeks to accumulate and share information processing knowledge and business expertise in order to increase the career and business potential of minorities in the information processing field. **Activities:** Conducts professional seminars, workshops, tutoring services, and community introductions to data processing. Makes annual donation to the United Negro College Fund.

★8639★ Data Processing Management Association (DPMA)

505 Busse Hwy.
Park Ridge, IL 60068
Ph: (708)825-8124   Fax: (708)825-1693

Members: Managerial personnel, staff, educators, and individuals interested in the management of information resources. Founder of the Certificate in Data Processing examination program, now administered by an intersociety organization. **Purpose:** Maintains Legislative Communications Network. Professional education programs include EDP-oriented business and management principles self-study courses and a series of videotaped management development seminars. Sponsors student organizations around the country interested in data processing and encourages members to serve as counselors

for the Scout computer merit badge. Conducts research projects, including a business information systems curriculum for two- and four-year colleges.

★8640★ How to Start and Operate a Home-Based Word Processing or Desktop Publishing Business

Bob Adams, Inc.
260 Center St.
Holbrook, MA 02343
Ph: (617)767-8100   Fax: (617)767-0994
Fr: 800-872-5627

Michele Loftus. 1990. $9.95. 192 pages. Offers advice on making advertising decisions, obtaining clients, developing a business identity, setting prices, keeping the books, rating and selecting software and equipment, and keeping client relationships strong.

★8641★ National Association of Professional Word Processing Technicians (NAPWPT)

110 W. Byberry Rd., Ste. E2
Philadelphia, PA 19116

Members: Word processors and computer operators. **Purpose:** Purpose is to elevate

the professional status of word processors. **Activities:** Offers consulting and resume/portfolio services; conducts research on hardware and software; provides product endorsements.

★8642★ Visually Impaired Data Processors International (VIDPI)

1155 15th St. NW, Ste. 720
Washington, DC 20005
Ph: (202)467-5081   Fr: 800-424-8666

Members: Visually impaired electronic data processing employees; those seeking employment; employers, instructors, manufacturers, and students in the electronic data processing field. **Purpose:** Advocates high standards in training visually impaired students. Seeks to increase employment opportunities; encourages the exchange of work technique ideas and the development of new equipment. Works with agencies to increase the availability of braille and recorded materials. Supports a speakers' bureau.

Underwriters

SOURCES OF HELP-WANTED ADS

★8643★ Best's Review (Life/Health Edition)

A.M. Best Co.
Ambest Rd.
Oldwick, NJ 08858
Ph: (908)439-2200   Fax: (908)439-3363

Monthly. $21.00/year for individuals; $7.50/year for single issue. Magazine covering issues and trends for the management personnel of life/health insurers, the agents, and brokers who market their products.

★8644★ Business Insurance

Crain Communications, Inc.
740 N. Rush St.
Chicago, IL 60611-2590
Ph: (312)649-5311   Fax: (312)280-3189

Weekly. $80.00/year for individuals. Magazine for executives in the corporate risk, employee benefit, and finance fields.

★8645★ Insurance Journal

Wells Publishing
9191 Town Centre Dr., No. 550
San Diego, CA 92122
Ph: (619)455-7717   Fax: (619)546-1462

Biweekly. $78.00/year for nonmembers; $72.00/year for individuals; $3.00 for single issue. Property/Casualty Magazine of the West.

★8646★ InsuranceWeek

IW Publications
1001 4th Ave., Ste. 3029
Seattle, WA 98154
Ph: (206)624-6965   Fax: (206)624-5021

Weekly (Mon.). Magazine about multi-line insurance for agents and brokers in the western U.S.

★8647★ National Underwriter Property and Casualty/Risk and Benefits Management

National Underwriter Co.
505 Gest St.
Cincinnati, OH 45203-1716
Ph: (513)721-2140   Fax: (513)721-0126

Weekly (Mon.). Newsweekly for agents, brokers, executives, and managers in risk and benefit insurance.

★8648★ The Standard

155 Federal St.
Boston, MA 02110
Ph: (617)457-0600   Fax: (617)457-0608

Weekly (Fri.). $40.00/year for individuals. Trade newspaper covering insurance events, legislation, regulatory hearings, and court sessions for independent insurance agents.

EMPLOYER DIRECTORIES AND NETWORKING LISTS

★8649★ Best's Agents Guide

A. M. Best Co.
Ambest Rd.
Oldwick, NJ 08858
Ph: (908)439-2200   Fax: (908)439-3296

Annual, August. $95.00. Covers over 1,700 life and health insurance companies nationwide. Entries include: Company name, address, names of president and secretary, phone, whether a stock or mutual company, states where licensed, Best's rating, current and historical financial data. Arrangement: Alphabetical.

★8650★ Best's Insurance Reports

A. M. Best Co.
Ambest Rd.
Oldwick, NJ 08858
Ph: (908)439-2200   Fax: (908)439-3296

Annual, August. $570.00, per edition; monthly publications included. Published in two editions: Life-health insurance, covering about 1,800 companies, and property-casualty insurance, covering over 2,000 companies; scope includes Canada. Each edition lists state insurance commissioners and related companies and agencies (mutual funds, worker compensation funds, underwriting agencies, etc.). Entries include: For each company, company name, address, phone; history; states in which licensed; names of officers and directors; financial data; editorial comment and rating. Arrangement: Alphabetical.

★8651★ Business Insurance—Agent/Broker Profiles Issue

Crain Communications, Inc.
740 N. Rush St.
Chicago, IL 60611-2590
Ph: (312)649-5279   Fax: (312)280-3174

Annual, July. $10.00. Publication includes: List of more than 250 insurance agents and brokers specializing in commercial insurance. Entries include: Firm name, address, phone, fax, branch office locations, year established, names of subsidiaries, gross revenues, premium volume, number of employees, principal officers, percent of revenue generated by commercial retail brokerage, acquisitions, and states in which excess/surplus lines broker. Arrangement: Alphabetical.

★8652★ Insurance Almanac

Underwriter Printing and Publishing Co.
50 E. Palisade Ave.
Englewood, NJ 07631
Ph: (201)569-8808   Fr: 800-526-4700

Annual, July. $115.00. Covers over 3,000 insurance companies that write fire, casualty, accident and health, life, and Lloyd's policies; also lists mutual and reciprocal companies. Includes national, state, and local insurance associations; state insurance officials; and about 800 agents, brokers, actuaries, and adjusters. Arrangement: Classified by insurance lines, type of activity, etc. Indexes: Company name.

★8653★ Insurance Phone Book and Directory

U.S. Directory Service
Reed Reference Publishing
121 Chanlon Rd.
New Providence, NJ 07974
Ph: (908)464-6800   Fax: (908)665-6688
Fr: 800-521-8110

Annual. $89.95, plus $6.30 shipping. Covers

about 4,000 life, accident and health, worker's compensation, auto, fire and casualty, marine, surety, and other insurance companies. Entries include: Company name, address, phone, fax, toll-free number, type of insurance provided. Arrangement: Alphabetical.

★8654★ Moody's Bank and Finance Manual

Moody's Investors Service, Inc.
99 Church St.
New York, NY 10007
Ph: (212)553-0300   Fax: (212)553-4700
Fr: 800-342-5647

Annual, July; supplements in *Moody's Bank & Finance News Reports*. $1,475.00, per year, including supplements. Covers in four volumes, over 20,000 national, state, and private banks, savings and loans, mutual funds, unit investment trusts, and insurance and real estate companies in the United States. Entries include: Company name, headquarters and branch offices, phones, names and titles of principal executives, directors, history, Moody's rating, and extensive financial and statistical data. Arrangement: Classified by type of business. Indexes: Company name.

★8655★ Underwriters' Handbook Series

National Underwriter Co.
505 Gest St.
Cincinnati, OH 45203-1716
Ph: (513)721-2140   Fax: (513)721-0126
Fr: 800-543-0874

Annual. $48.50, per state volume; 5th edition. Covers 142,000 insurance agents and agencies in 35 states and the District of Columbia; also names field representatives, managing general agents and general agents for both property/casualty and life/health insurance, adjusters, consultants, appraisers, audit and inspection services, and related insurance groups and associations and state departments of insurance. Published in 22 separate editions for Rocky Mountain States (Arizona, Colorado, Idaho, Montana, Nevada, New Mexico, Utah, and Wyoming); Georgia-Alabama; Missouri; Nebraska; North Dakota-South Dakota; Arkansas; Minnesota; Oklahoma; West Virginia; Maryland-Delaware-District of Columbia; Indiana; Florida-U.S. Caribbean; Pennsylvania; Iowa; Michigan; Illinois; Massachusetts; Ohio; Wisconsin; Connecticut-Rhode Island; Maine-New Hampshire-Vermont; and Kansas. Entries include: For companies Name, address, year established, divisions, key personnel (with addresses and phone numbers). Many list assets, liabilities, capital, and surplus. Arrangement: Separate alphabetical sections for insurance companies and field agents; other agents and activity are listed geographically, then by activity. Indexes: Type of insurance.

★8656★ Who's Who in Insurance

Underwriter Printing and Publishing Co.
50 E. Palisade Ave.
Englewood, NJ 07631
Ph: (201)569-8808   Fr: 800-526-4700

Annual, February. $115.00. Covers over 5,000 insurance officials, brokers, agents, and buyers. Entries include: Name, title, company name, address, home address, educational background, professional club and association memberships, personal and career data. Arrangement: Alphabetical.

HANDBOOKS AND MANUALS

★8657★ Business and Finance Career Directory

Gale Research
835 Penobscot Bldg.
Detroit, MI 48226-4094
Ph: (313)961-2242   Fax: (313)961-6083
Fr: 800-877-GALE

Bradley Morgan. Second edition, 1992. $39.00. 413 pages. Features a basic and comprehensive job search section, articles by top professionals in the field, and detailed listings of hundreds of top companies who hire individuals in this field. Aimed particularly at entry-level job hunters.

★8658★ Career Choices for the 90's for Students of Business

Walker and Company
435 Hudson St.
New York, NY 10014
Ph: (212)727-8300   Fax: (212)727-0984
Fr: 800-289-2553

Prepared by the Career Associates staff. 1990. $9.95. 166 pages. Discusses alternatives for students of business. Offers advice on how to break into the field and how to move up. Covers where and who the employers are, internship possibilities, and professional networking associations. Comprehensive guide to career and job search planning.

★8659★ Career Choices for the 90's for Students of Economics

Walker and Company
435 Hudson St.
New York, NY 10014
Ph: (212)727-8300   Fax: (212)727-0984
Fr: 800-289-2553

Prepared by the Career Associates staff. 1990. $8.95. 166 pages. Discusses alternatives for students of economics. Offers advice on how to break into the field and how to move up. Covers where and who the employers are, internship possibilities, and professional networking associations. Comprehensive guide to career and job search planning.

★8660★ Career Choices for the 90's for Students of Mathematics

Walker and Company
435 Hudson St.
New York, NY 10014
Ph: (212)727-8300   Fax: (212)727-0984
Fr: 800-289-2553

Prepared by the Career Associates staff. 1990. $8.95. 166 pages. Discusses alternatives for students of mathematics. Offers advice on how to break into the field and how to move up. Covers where and who the employers are, internship possibilities, and professional networking associations. Comprehensive guide to career and job search planning.

★8661★ Careers for Number Crunchers and Other Quantitative Types

VGM Career Horizons
4255 W. Touhy Ave.
Lincolnwood, IL 60646-1975
Ph: (847)679-5500   Fax: (847)679-2494
Fr: 800-323-4900

Rebecca Burnett. 1993. $14.95; $9.95 (paper). Provides information to math-oriented job hunters on how to become statisticians, field researchers, computer programmers, stock analysts, investment managers, bankers, engineers, accountants, underwriters, economists, market analysts, mathematicians, systems analysts, and more.

★8662★ The Encyclopedia of Career Choices for the 1990s: Guide to Entry-Level Jobs

Perigree Books
The Berkley Publishing Group
PO Box 506
East Rutherford, NJ 07073
Ph: (201)933-9292   Fr: 800-223-0510

Career Associates Staff. 1992. $19.95. 862 pages. Describes 500 entry-level careers in a variety of industries. Presents qualifications required, working conditions, salary, internships, and professional associations.

★8663★ Encyclopedia of Careers and Vocational Guidance

J. G. Ferguson Publishing Co.
200 W. Monroe, Ste. 250
Chicago, IL 60606
Ph: (312)580-5480

William E. Hopke. Ninth edition, 1993. $129.95; $199.95 (CD-ROM). Four-volume set that profiles 900 occupations and describes job trends in 71 industries. Includes career description, educational requirements, history of the job, methods of entry, advancement, employment outlook, earnings, conditions of work, social and psychological factors, and sources of further information. Contains career and employment information for this field.

★8664★ Opportunities in Insurance Careers

VGM Career Horizons
4255 W. Touhy Ave.
Lincolnwood, IL 60646-1975
Ph: (847)679-5500   Fax: (847)679-2494
Fr: 800-323-4900

Robert Schrayer. 1994. $14.95; $11.95 (paper). A guide to planning for and seeking opportunities in the field. Contains bibliography and illustrations.

★8665★ Successful Life Insurance Selling

Dearborn Financial Publishing, Inc.
155 N. Wacker Dr.
Chicago, IL 60606-1719
Ph: (312)836-1021   Fax: (312)836-1021

Gary Schulte. 1994. $24.95.

EMPLOYMENT AGENCIES AND SEARCH FIRMS

★8666★ Avery Crafts Associates, Ltd.
116 John St., Ste. 820
New York, NY 10038
Ph: (212)285-1074   Fax: (212)732-1039
Executive search firm.

★8667★ Best Personnel Services
8901 State Line Rd.
Kansas City, MO 64114-3200
Ph: (816)361-3100
Employment agency. Fills openings on a regular or temporary basis. Office also located in Independence, MO.

★8668★ The Canon Group
27936 Lost Canyon Rd.
Santa Clarita, CA 91351
Ph: (805)252-7400
Employment agency and search firm.

★8669★ Culver Personnel Service
1555 Old Bayshore Hwy., Ste. 100
Burlingame, CA 94010
Ph: (415)692-9090   Fax: (415)692-6618
Employment agency.

★8670★ Employment Advisors
526 Nicollet Mall
Minneapolis, MN 55402-0521
Ph: (612)339-0521
Employment agency. Also located in Bloomington, Minnesota. Places candidates in variety of fields.

★8671★ Godfrey Personnel Inc.
300 W. Adams, Ste. 612
Chicago, IL 60606-5194
Ph: (312)236-4455
Employment agency.

★8672★ Insurance Personnel
65 Franklin St.
Boston, MA 02110-1303
Ph: (617)357-5380   Fax: (617)482-6581
Employment agency.

★8673★ Insurance Personnel Service
120 Kearny St., Ste. 1480
San Francisco, CA 94108-4803
Ph: (415)391-5900
Employment agency.

★8674★ International Insurance Personnel, Inc.
PO Box 28408
Atlanta, GA 30358
Ph: (404)257-9685

★8675★ The Oxford Group
901 Waterfall Way
Richardson, TX 75080
Ph: (214)644-5544   Fax: (214)644-7134
Executive search firm.

★8676★ Questor Consultants, Inc.
2515 N. Broad St.
Colmar, PA 18915
Ph: (215)997-9262   Fax: (215)997-9226
Executive search firm.

OTHER SOURCES

★8677★ Alliance of American Insurers (ALLIANCE)
1501 Woodfield Rd., Ste. 400 W
Schaumburg, IL 60173-4980
Ph: (708)330-8500   Fax: (708)330-8602
Members: Property and casualty insurance companies.

★8678★ American Almanac of Jobs and Salaries 1994-95
Avon Books
1350 Avenue of the Americas, 2nd Fl.
New York, NY 10019
Ph: (212)261-6800   Fr: 800-238-0658
John Wright. Revised edition, 1993. $17.00. 704 pages. This is a comprehensive guide to the wages of hundreds of occupations in a wide variety of industries and organizations.

★8679★ American Council of Life Insurance (ACLI)
1001 Pennsylvania Ave. NW
Washington, DC 20004-2599
Ph: (202)624-2000   Fax: (202)624-2319
Fr: 800-942-4242
Members: Legal reserve life insurance companies authorized to do business in the U.S. **Purpose:** Works to advance the interests of the life insurance industry and to provide effective government relations. **Activities:** Conducts investment and social research programs; compiles statistics. Maintains Insurance Industry's Citizen Action Network and Center for Corporate Public Involvement and Medical Research Fund.

★8680★ American Institute for Chartered Property Casualty Underwriters (AICPCU)
720 Providence Rd.
PO Box 3016
Malvern, PA 19355-0716
Ph: (610)644-2100   Fax: (610)251-9995
Fr: 800-644-2101
Purpose: Determines qualifications for professional certification of insurance personnel; conducts examinations and awards designation of Chartered Property Casualty Underwriter (CPCU).

★8681★ American Society of CLU and ChFC (ASCLU & Ch)
270 S. Bryn Mawr Ave.
Bryn Mawr, PA 19010
Ph: (610)526-2500   Fax: (610)527-4010
Members: Professional society of insurance agents and financial services professionals who hold Chartered Life Underwriter (CLU) or Chartered Financial Consultant (ChFC) designations. **Activities:** Conducts week-long graduate-level educational sessions (CLU Institutes); one-day seminars with experts lecturing on subjects such as law, taxation, estate planning, and business life insurance; symposia and clinics; research. Offers scholarship to society programs.

★8682★ CPCU Society
720 Providence Rd.
PO Box 3009
Malvern, PA 19355
Ph: (610)251-CPCU   Fax: (215)251-2761
Members: Professional society of individuals who have passed ten national examinations of the American Institute for Chartered Property Casualty Underwriters , have 3 years of work experience, have agreed to be bound by a code of ethics, and have been awarded CPCU designation. **Purpose:** Promotes education, research, social responsibility, and professionalism in the field. Holds seminars, symposia, videoconferences, and workshops; conducts research projects. Operates speakers' bureau.

★8683★ Insurance Information Institute (III)
110 William St.
New York, NY 10038
Ph: (212)669-9200   Fax: (212)732-1916
Members: Property and liability insurance companies. **Purpose:** Provides information and educational services to mass media, educational institutions, trade associations, businesses, government agencies, and the public. Conducts public opinion surveys. Sponsors seminars and briefings on insurance, safety, research, public policy, and economic topics.

★8684★ Life Office Management Association (LOMA)
2300 Windy Ridge Pkwy., Ste. 600
Atlanta, GA 30339-8443
Ph: (404)951-1770   Fax: (404)984-0441
Members: Life and health insurance companies and financial services in the U.S. and Canada; and overseas in 45 countries; affiliate members are firms that provide professional support to member companies. **Purpose:** Provides research, information, training, and educational activities in areas of operations and systems, human resources, financial planning and employee development. Administers FLMI Insurance Education Program, which awards FLMI (Fellow, Life Management Institute) designation to those who complete the ten-examination program.

★8685★ National Association of Health Underwriters (NAHU)
1000 Connecticut Ave. NW, Ste. 810
Washington, DC 20037
Ph: (202)778-8767   Fax: (202)785-2274
Members: Insurance agencies and individuals engaged in the promotion, sale, and administration of disability income and health insurance. **Purpose:** Sponsors advanced health insurance underwriting and research seminars at universities. Testifies before federal and state committees on pending health insurance legislation. Sponsors leading producers roundtable awards and health insurance quality awards for leading salesmen.

Maintains a speakers' bureau and a political action committee.

★8686★ **National Association of Insurance Women - International (NAIW)**

1847 E. 15th
PO Box 4410
Tulsa, OK 74159
Ph: (918)744-5195   Fax: (918)743-1968
Fr: 800-766-6249

Members: Insurance industry professionals. **Purpose:** Promotes continuing education and networking for the professional advancement of its members. **Activities:** Offers education programs, meetings, services, and leadership opportunities.

Urban and Regional Planners

SOURCES OF HELP-WANTED ADS

★8687★ American City and County
Communication Channels, Inc.
6255 Barfield Rd.
Atlanta, GA 30328
Ph: (404)955-9970 Fax: (404)256-3116

Monthly. $54.00/year for individuals. Municipal and county administration magazine.

★8688★ APWA Reporter
American Public Works Association
1313 E. 60th St.
Chicago, IL 60637-2881
Ph: (312)667-2200 Fax: (312)667-2304

Monthly. $1.00 for single issue. Magazine reporting on public works.

★8689★ Architectural Record
New York Construction News
1221 Avenue of the Americas, 41st Fl.
New York, NY 10020
Ph: (212)512-4773 Fax: (212)512-4770

Magazine focusing on architecture.

★8690★ Builder
Hanley-Wood, Inc.
1 Thomas Cir., Ste. 600
Washington, DC 20005
Ph: (202)452-0800 Fax: (202)785-1974

Monthly. $29.95/year for individuals. Magazine covering housing, commercial, and industrial building.

★8691★ ITE Journal
Institute of Transportation Engineers
525 School St. SW, Ste. 410
Washington, DC 20024-2729
Ph: (202)554-8050 Fax: (202)863-5486

Monthly. $50.00/year; $65.00/year for other countries. Technical magazine focusing on the plan, design, and operation of surface transportation systems.

★8692★ JobMart
American Planning Association
1313 E. 60th St.
Chicago, IL 60637
Ph: (312)955-9100

Semimonthly. $27.00/year. Reports on jobs in the planning field, covering urban and regional opportunities and related jobs in community development and transportation.

★8693★ The Municipality
League of Wisconsin Municipalities
122 W. Washington Ave., Ste. 301
Madison, WI 53703-2757
Ph: (608)267-2380 Fax: (608)267-0645

Monthly. Magazine for officials of Wisconsin's local municipal governments.

★8694★ NAHRO Monitor
National Association of Housing and
 Redevelopment Officials
1320 18th St. NW
Washington, DC 20036
Ph: (202)429-2960

Semimonthly.

★8695★ Passenger Transport
American Public Transit Association
1201 New York Ave. NW, Ste. 400
Washington, DC 20005
Ph: (202)898-4119 Fax: (202)898-4095

Weekly (Mon.). $65.00/year for individuals; $2.00 for single issue. Magazine covering the public transit industry in the U.S. and Canada.

**★8696★ Photogrammetric Engineering
and Remote Sensing**
American Society for Photogrammetry and
 Remote Sensing (ASPRS)
5410 Grosvenor Ln., Ste. 210
Bethesda, MD 20814-2160
Ph: (301)493-0290 Fax: (301)493-0208

Monthly. Free to members; $120.00/year for nonmembers. Provides technical information about the applications of photogrammetry, remote sensing, and geographic information systems.

★8697★ Planning
American Planning Association
1313 E. 60th St.
Chicago, IL 60637-2891
Ph: (312)955-9100 Fax: (312)955-8312

Monthly. $40.00/year. Urban planning magazine.

★8698★ Roads & Bridges Magazine
Scranton Gillette Communications, Inc.
380 E. Northwest Hwy.
Des Plaines, IL 60016-2282
Ph: (708)298-6622 Fax: (708)390-0408

Monthly. Free to qualified subscribers. Magazine containing information on highway, road, and bridge design, construction, and maintenance for government agencies, contractors, and consulting engineers.

★8699★ Western City
League of California Cities
1400 K St.
Sacramento, CA 95814
Ph: (916)444-5790 Fax: (916)658-8240

Monthly. $30.00/year for individuals; $49.00 for two years. Municipal interest magazine.

PLACEMENT AND JOB REFERRAL SERVICES

★8700★ American Planning Association (APA)

122 S. Michigan Ave., Ste. 1600
Chicago, IL 60603-9604
Ph: (312)431-9100 Fax: (312)431-9985

Members: Public and private planning agency officials, professional planners, planning educators, elected and appointed officials, and other persons involved in urban and rural development. **Purpose:** Works to foster the best techniques and decisions for the planned development of communities and regions. Provides extensive professional services and publications to professionals and laypeople in planning and related fields; serves as a clearinghouse for information. Through Planning Advisory Service, a research and inquiry-answering service, provides, on an annual subscription basis, advice on specific inquiries and a series of research reports on planning, zoning, and environmental regulations. **Activities:** Supplies information on job openings and makes definitive studies on salaries and recruitment of professional planners. Conducts research; collaborates in joint projects with local, national, and international organizations.

★8701★ Social Sciences Services and Resources

PO Box 153
Wasco, IL 60183
Ph: (708)897-5345

Members: Consulting associates in social sciences. **Purpose:** Established to advance the teaching, consulting, and practice of the social sciences basic disciplines including sociology, anthropology, political science, geography, history, economics, and their applied disciplines: social work, community development, planning, and public administration. Serves as: a center for dissemination of current and comprehensive social research findings. Provides consultants for citizen groups, community projects, and governmental units on written request. Upon request from colleges, school boards, and citizens groups, conducts in-service workshops on teaching, consulting, and new developments in the social sciences. Provides consultant evaluation services for small colleges throughout the U.S. **Activities:** Maintains speakers' bureau and placement information service. Conducts research programs.

EMPLOYER DIRECTORIES AND NETWORKING LISTS

★8702★ City & Regional Planners Directory

American Business Directories, Inc.
American Business Information, Inc.
5711 S. 86th Cir.
Omaha, NE 68127
Ph: (402)593-4600   Fax: (402)331-1505

Updated continuously; printed on request. Entries include: Name, address, phone (including area code), size of advertisement, year first in Yellow Pages, name of owner or manager, number of employees. Compiled from telephone company Yellow Pages, nationwide. Arrangement: Geographical.

★8703★ ENR Directory of Design Firms

McGraw-Hill, Inc.
1221 Ave. of the Americas
New York, NY 10020
Ph: (212)512-2534   Fax: (212)512-4178

Biennial, fall of even years; issue of *Engineering News Record*. $85.00. Covers 133 architects, architectural engineers, consultants, and other design firms; limited to advertisers. Mini-profiles on about 3,400 U.S. firms and 500 foreign firms or foreign offices of U.S. firms. Also includes lists of top 500 design firms in the United States, top 200 international design firms, top 50 United States

design-construction firms, and top 50 international design-construction firms, based on total amount of billings. Entries include: For advertisers: company name, address, branch locations, subsidiaries, list of key personnel, territory served, capabilities. In ranked lists: company name, address, phone; international firms include telex. Arrangement: Alphabetical (profiles); geographical (mini-profiles).

★8704★ ENR—Top 500 Design Firms Issue

McGraw-Hill, Inc.
1221 Ave. of the Americas
New York, NY 10020
Ph: (212)512-4635   Fax: (212)512-2820

Annual, April. $10.00, reprint, payment must accompany order. Publication includes: List of 500 leading architectural, engineering, and specialty design firms selected on basis of annual billings. Entries include: Company name, headquarters location, type of firm, current and prior year rank in billings, types of services, countries in which operated in preceding year. Arrangement: Ranked by billings.

★8705★ ENR—Top International Design Firms Issue

McGraw-Hill, Inc.
1221 Ave. of the Americas, Rm. 4188
New York, NY 10020
Ph: (212)512-4635

Annual, July. $10.00, reprint, payment with order. Publication includes: List of 200 design firms (including United States firms) competing outside their own national borders who received largest dollar volume of foreign contracts in preceding calendar year. Entries include: Company name, headquarters location, type of firm, current and previous year rankings in total billings, types of services, countries in which operated in preceding year. Arrangement: By amount billed to international clients in previous year.

★8706★ Municipal/County Directory Library Edition

Carroll Publishing
1058 Thomas Jefferson St. NW
Washington, DC 20007
Ph: (202)333-8620   Fax: (202)337-7020
Fr: 800-336-4240

Annual, July. $137.00, plus $8.00 shipping; payment must accompany order. Covers officials of 1,400 county governments (with populations over 25,000) and 2,000 municipalities (with populations over 1,000); includes elected, appointed, and career office holders. Entries include: Name, title, agency, address, phone. Arrangement: County officials are geographical, then by agency; municipal officials are by city. Indexes: personal name (with phone), agency.

★8707★ Municipal Year Book

Newman Books Ltd.
32 Vauxhall Bridge Rd.
London SW1V 2SS, England
Ph: 71 9736400   Fax: 71 2335057

Annual, December. $140.00, postpaid. Covers local and central government agencies and officials of the United Kingdom; municipal art galleries, associations, development

organizations, fairs, libraries, museums, airports, and other local authorities. Entries include: Name of authority or governing agency, address, phone, fax, names of elected councillors, officers, names and titles of key personnel, contacts, population, and pay. Arrangement: Geographical. Indexes: Subject, place names.

HANDBOOKS AND MANUALS

★8708★ Career Information Center

Macmillan Publishing Co.
200 Old Tappan Rd.
Old Tappan, NJ 07675
Ph: (609)461-6500   Fr: 800-223-2336

Visual Education Center Staff. Fifth edition, 1992. $229.00. This 13-volume set profiles over 600 occupations. Each occupational profile describes job duties, educational requirements, how to get the job, advancement possibilities, employment outlook, working conditions, earnings and benefits, and where to write for more information.

★8709★ Encyclopedia of Careers and Vocational Guidance

J. G. Ferguson Publishing Co.
200 W. Monroe, Ste. 250
Chicago, IL 60606
Ph: (312)580-5480

William E. Hopke. Ninth edition, 1993. $129.95; $199.95 (CD-ROM). Four-volume set that profiles 900 occupations and describes job trends in 71 industries. Includes career description, educational requirements, history of the job, methods of entry, advancement, employment outlook, earnings, conditions of work, social and psychological factors, and sources of further information. Contains career and employment information for this field.

★8710★ Liberal Arts Jobs: What They Are and How to Get Them

Peterson's
PO Box 2123
Princeton, NJ 08543-2123
Ph: (609)243-9111   Fax: (609)243-9150
Fr: 800-338-3282

Burton Jay Nadler. Second edition, 1989. $9.95. 153 pages. Presents a list of the top 20 fields for liberal arts majors, covering more than 300 job opportunities. Discusses strategies for going after those jobs, including guidance on the language of a successful job search, informational interviews, and making networking work.

★8711★ Opportunities in Environmental Careers

VGM Career Horizons
4255 W. Touhy Ave.
Lincolnwood, IL 60646-1975
Ph: (847)679-5500   Fax: (847)679-2494
Fr: 800-323-4900

Odom Fanning. 1995. $14.95; $11.95 (paper). 160 pages. Describes a broad range of opportunities in fields such as environmental health, recreation, physics, and hygiene, and provides job search advice.

★8712★ Opportunities in Social Science Careers

VGM Career Horizons
4255 W. Touhy Ave.
Lincolnwood, IL 60646-1975
Ph: (847)679-5500   Fax: (847)679-2494
Fr: 800-323-4900

Rosanne J. Marek. 1990. $14.95; $11.95 (paper). 160 pages. Profiles job opportunities in education, government, and business, along with their salary levels and outlook in the years to come. Illustrated.

OTHER SOURCES

★8713★ American Institute of Certified Planners (AICP)

1776 Massachusetts Ave. NW, Ste. 400
Washington, DC 20036
Ph: (202)872-0611   Fax: (202)872-0643

A subsidiary of the American Planning Association. **Members:** Members of the APA who have met the requirements of education, practice, and examination established for the professional practice of public planning. Provides continuing education and a written professional examination. Maintains code of ethics; conducts research.

★8714★ American Society for Photogrammetry and Remote Sensing (ASPRS)

5410 Grosvenor Ln., Ste. 210
Bethesda, MD 20814-2160
Ph: (301)493-0290   Fax: (301)493-0208

Members: Firms, individuals, government employees, and academicians engaged in photogrammetry, photointerpretation, remote sensing, and geographic information systems and their application to such fields as archaeology, geographic information systems, military reconnaissance, urban planning, engineering, traffic surveys, meteorological observations, medicine, geology, forestry, agriculture, construction, and topographic mapping. **Activities:** Offers voluntary certification program open to persons associated with one or more functional area of photogrammetry, remote sensing, and GIS. Surveys the profession of private firms in photogrammetry and remote sensing in the areas of products and services.

★8715★ National Urban/Rural Fellows (NU/RF)

55 W. 44th St., Ste. 600
New York, NY 10036
Ph: (212)921-9400   Fax: (212)921-9572

Purpose: Program designed to make top leadership opportunities in government and rural development available to minority group members. Recipients of the 14-month fellowships are selected competitively and must be U.S. citizens who: have a bachelor's degree, have experience in solving urban or rural problems; have three-five years of employment experience in an administrative or economic development capacity; have demonstrated ability, leadership qualities, and a commitment to the solution of urban or rural problems. Program is aimed at meeting the need for competent urban and rural administrators, particularly minority group members and women, by combining a nine month, on-the-job assignment as special assistant to an experienced practitioner with several kinds of academic work. A master's degree in public administration is awarded to qualified fellows at the end of the fellowship.

★8716★ Planners' Salaries and Employment Trends

American Planning Association (APA)
1313 E. 60th St.
Chicago, IL 60637
Ph: (312)955-9100

Annual. Describes the salaries of planners working in the federal government as consultants and in business. Surveys the average age of planners, percentage of women and minorities in planning, and the differences in salary by geographic area.

Veterinarians

SOURCES OF HELP-WANTED ADS

★8717★ American Journal of Veterinary Research

American Veterinary Medical Association
1931 N. Meacham Rd, Ste. 100
Schaumburg, IL 60173-4360
Ph: (708)925-8070   Fax: (708)925-1329

Monthly. $150.00/year for individuals. Veterinary research journal reporting on nutrition and diseases of domestic, wild, and furbearing animals.

★8718★ Dog World

Intertec Publishing Co.
29 N. Wacker Dr.
Chicago, IL 60606
Ph: (312)435-2330   Fax: (312)726-4103
Fr: 800-621-9907

Monthly. $28.00/year for individuals; $3.75 for single issue. Magazine serving breeders, exhibitors, hobbyists and professionals in kennel operations, groomers, veterinarians, animal hospitals/clinics and pet suppliers.

★8719★ DVM Newsmagazine

Advanstar Communications, Inc.
7600 Old Oak Blvd.
Cleveland, OH 44130
Ph: (216)243-8100   Fax: (216)891-2733

Monthly. $38.00/year; $3.00 for single issue. Recipients are veternarians in private practices in the U.S.

★8720★ Journal of the American Veterinary Medical Association

American Veterinary Medical Association
1931 N. Meacham Rd., Ste. 100
Schaumburg, IL 60173
Ph: (708)925-8070

Semimonthly.

★8721★ Lab Animal

Nature Publishing Co.
345 Park Ave. S, 10th Fl.
New York, NY 10010-1707
Ph: (212)726-9200   Fax: (212)696-9006

Life science magazine.

★8722★ Large Animal Veterinarian

Watt Publishing Co.
122 S. Wesley Ave.
Mount Morris, IL 61054-1497
Ph: (815)734-4171   Fax: (815)734-4201

Bimonthly. $36.00/year for individuals; $8.00 for single issue. Magazine for veterinarians of cattle, horses, and other large animals.

★8723★ Trends Magazine

American Animal Hospital Association
12575 W. Bayaud Ave.
Lakewood, CO 80228
Ph: (303)986-2800

Bimonthly. $60.00/year. Covers the management of small animal veterinary practices.

★8724★ Veterinary Economics

Veterinary Medicine Publishing Co.
9073 Lenexa Dr.
Lenexa, KS 66215
Ph: (913)492-4300   Fax: (913)492-4157
Fr: 800-255-6864

Monthly. Free to qualified subscribers; $35.00/year for institutions. Trade magazine on veterinary practice management.

★8725★ Veterinary and Human Toxicology

Comparative Toxicology Laboratories
Kansas State University
Manhattan, KS 66506
Ph: (913)532-4334   Fax: (913)532-4481

Bimonthly. $50.00/year for individuals; $60.00/year for Canada; $70.00/year for other countries. Professional journal containing refereed scientific articles, news, and reports from the field of toxicology. Includes reports of past meetings, announcements of forthcoming meetings, book reviews, job opportunities, membership, and other news from the several organizations in toxicology that sponsor this publication.

★8726★ Veterinary Surgery

Pharmaceutical Media Inc.
30 E. 33rd St.
New York, NY 10016
Ph: (212)685-5010   Fax: (212)685-5010

Bimonthly. Journal publishing reports on clinical and research topics for veterinary surgeons and anesthesiologists.

PLACEMENT AND JOB REFERRAL SERVICES

★8727★ American Academy of Clinical Toxicology (AACT)

Pittsburgh Poison Center
3705 5th Ave.
Pittsburgh, PA 15213
Ph: (412)692-6669   Fax: (412)692-7497

Members: Physicians, veterinarians, pharmacists, research scientists, and analytical chemists. **Purpose:** Objectives are to: unite medical scientists and facilitate the exchange of information; encourage the development of therapeutic methods and technology; establish a mechanism for the certification of medical scientists in clinical toxicology. **Activities:** Conducts professional training in poison information and emergency service personnel. Maintains placement services. **E-Mail:** Internet, krenzee@chplink.chp.edu

★8728★ American Veterinary Medical Association (AVMA)

1931 N. Meacham Rd., Ste. 100
Schaumburg, IL 60173-4360
Ph: (708)925-8070   Fax: (708)925-1329
Fr: 800-248-2862

Members: Professional society of veterinarians. **Activities:** Conducts educational and research programs. Provides placement service. Maintains the American Society of Laboratory Animal Practitioners. Sponsors American Veterinary Medical Association Foundation (also known as AVMA Foundation) and Educational Commission for Foreign Veterinary Graduates. Compiles statistics.

EMPLOYER DIRECTORIES AND NETWORKING LISTS

★8729★ Agricultural Research Centres

Stockton Press
Groves Dictionaries
345 Park Ave. S., 10th Fl.
New York, NY 10010
Ph: (212)689-9200   Fr: 800-221-2123

Twelfth edition, 1995. $595.00. 1000 pages. Covers 2,000 main organizations controlling over 7,500 departments engaged in research in agriculture, fisheries, food, forestry, horticulture, and the veterinary sciences.

★8730★ Agricultural and Veterinary Sciences International Who's Who

Stockton Press
Groves Dictionaries
345 Park Ave. S., 10th Fl.
New York, NY 10010
Ph: (212)689-9200   Fr: 800-221-2123

Fifth edition, 1994. $595.00. 1248 pages. Provides biographical profiles of about 7,500 senior agricultural and veterinary scientists from approximately 100 countries.

★8731★ American Association of Bovine Practitioners—Directory

American Association of Bovine Practitioners
c/o Dr. H.E. Amstutz
PO Box 2319
West Lafayette, IN 47906
Ph: (317)494-8560   Fax: (317)494-9353

Triennial, latest edition June 1991; annual supplements. Available only to members. Covers 5,000 member veterinarians who have a special interest in treatment of dairy and beef cattle. Entries include: Name, office address and phone. Arrangement: Alphabetical. Indexes: Alphabetical.

★8732★ American College of Veterinary Pathologists—Membership Directory

American College of Veterinary Pathologists
875 Kings Hwy., Ste. 200
Woodbury, NJ 08096
Ph: (609)848-7784   Fax: (609)853-0411

Annual, March. $350.00. Covers about 1,200 veterinary and veterinary clinical pathologists. Entries include: Name, office address, phone. Arrangement: Alphabetical.

★8733★ American Society of Veterinary Ophthalmology—Directory

American Society of Veterinary Ophthalmology
1528 Shalamar
Stillwater, OK 74074
Ph: (405)377-2134

Annual, December. Available to members only. Covers 250 member veterinarians interested in animal ophthalmology. Entries include: Name, address, office and home phone numbers, and year of graduation. Arrangement: Geographical. Indexes: Alphabetical, chronological.

★8734★ American Veterinary Medical Association—Directory

American Veterinary Medical Association (AVMA)
1931 N. Meacham Rd., Ste. 100
Schaumburg, IL 60173-4360
Ph: (708)925-8070   Fax: (708)925-1329
Fr: 800-248-2862

Annual, January. $90.00, payment with order. Covers 55,000 veterinarians; not limited to AVMA members. Entries include: Name, spouse's name, address, and codes for practice activity, type of employer, institution granting degree, and year received. Arrangement: Geographical. Indexes: Alphabetical.

★8735★ Animal Hospitals Directory

American Business Directories, Inc.
American Business Information, Inc.
5711 S. 86th Cir.
Omaha, NE 68127
Ph: (402)593-4600   Fax: (402)331-1505

Annual. $965.00, payment with order. Entries include: Name, address, phone (including area code), size of advertisement, year first in Yellow Pages, name of owner or manager, number of employees. Compiled from telephone company Yellow Pages nationwide. Arrangement: Geographical.

★8736★ Directory of Animal Care and Control Agencies

American Humane Association
63 Iverness Dr. E.
Englewood, CO 80112
Ph: (303)792-9900   Fax: (303)792-5333
Fr: 800-227-4645

Updated continuously; printed on request. $75.00, Base edition, to nonprofit organizations; $500.00, Base edition, to others. Covers over 4,500 animal protection agencies; Canadian and some other foreign agencies are available; national and individual state editions are available. Entries include: Agency name, address, phone, contact. Arrangement: Geographical.

★8737★ Life Sciences Organizations and Agencies Directory

Gale Research
835 Penobscot Bldg.
Detroit, MI 48226-4094
Ph: (313)961-2242   Fax: (313)961-6083
Fr: 800-877-GALE

$175.00. Covers about 7,500 associations, government agencies, research centers, educational institutions, libraries and information centers, museums, consultants, electronic information services, and other organizations and agencies active in agriculture, biology, ecology, forestry, marine science, nutrition, wildlife and animal sciences, and other natural and life sciences. Entries include: Organization or agency name, address, phone, name and title of contact, description. Arrangement: Classified by type of organization. Indexes: Organization/agency name and keyword.

★8738★ Programs in Veterinary Technology

American Veterinary Medical Association (AVMA)
1931 N. Meacham Rd., Ste. 100
Schaumburg, IL 60173-4360
Ph: (708)925-8070   Fr: 800-248-2862

Semiannual, June and December. Free. Covers more than 65 colleges and universities that offer accredited veterinary technician programs. Entries include: Institution name, address; department name, address, phone, name of departmental contact, degree offered, length of program, type of accreditation. Arrangement: Geographical.

★8739★ Veterinarian Clinics Directory

American Business Directories, Inc.
American Business Information, Inc.
5711 S. 86th Cir.
Omaha, NE 68127
Ph: (402)593-4600   Fax: (402)331-1505

Annual. $780.00. Entries include: Name, address, phone, size of advertisement, name of owner or manager, number of employees, year first in Yellow Pages. Compiled from telephone company Yellow Pages, nationwide. Arrangement: Geographical.

★8740★ Veterinarians Directory

American Business Directories, Inc.
American Business Information, Inc.
5711 S. 86th Cir.
Omaha, NE 68127
Ph: (402)593-4600   Fax: (402)331-1505

Annual. $1,310.00, (U.S. edition); $280.00, (Canad. ed.); payment with order. Entries include: Name, address, phone (including area code), size of advertisement, year first in Yellow Pages, name of owner or manager, number of employees. Regional editions available. Compiled from telephone company Yellow Pages nationwide. Arrangement: Geographical.

HANDBOOKS AND MANUALS

★8741★ The Advancement of Veterinary Science, Vol. 1: Veterinary Medicine Beyond 2000

CAB International North America
1230 N. Park Ave., No. 102
Tucson, AZ 85719
Ph: (602)621-1441   Fax: (602)621-8899
Fr: 800-426-3797

A.R. Michell. 1993. $81.00.

★8742★ Career Information Center

Macmillan Publishing Co.
200 Old Tappan Rd.
Old Tappan, NJ 07675
Ph: (609)461-6500   Fr: 800-223-2336

Visual Education Center Staff. Fifth edition, 1992. $229.00. This 13-volume set profiles over 600 occupations. Each occupational profile describes job duties, educational requirements, how to get the job, advancement possibilities, employment outlook, working conditions, earnings and benefits, and where to write for more information.

★8743★ *Career Portraits: Animals*

NTC Publishing Group
4255 W. Touhy Ave.
Lincolnwood, IL 60646-1975
Ph: (708)679-5500   Fax: (708)679-6375
Fr: 800-323-4900

Louise Miller. 1994. $13.95.

★8744★ *Careers for Animal Lovers and Other Zoological Types*

VGM Career Horizons
4255 W. Touhy Ave.
Lincolnwood, IL 60646-1975
Ph: (847)679-5500   Fax: (847)679-2494
Fr: 800-323-4900

Louise Miller. 1995. $14.95; $9.95 (paper). Surveys a range of opportunities working with animals in both the public and profit sectors. Includes such possibilities as groomers, trainers, zookeepers, researchers, veterinarians, pet psychologists, pet shelter operators, wildlife biologists, and animal writers, photographers, and illustrators.

★8745★ *Careers in Veterinary Medicine*

Rosen Publishing Group, Inc.
29 E. 21st St.
New York, NY 10010
Ph: (212)777-3017   Fax: (212)777-0277
Fr: 800-237-9932

Jane Caryl Duncan. Revised edition, 1994. $13.95; $9.95 (paper). Surveys job opportunities in teaching, private practice, private industry, and zoos.

★8746★ *100 Best Careers for the Year 2000*

Prentice Hall General Reference
15 Columbus Cir.
New York, NY 10023
Ph: (212)373-8500   Fr: 800-223-2348

Shelly Field. 1992. $15.00 (paper). Covers 100 of the fastest growing jobs. The publication is divided into 11 general employment sections. Specific careers are covered within each section. Provides job description, responsibilities, employment opportunities, earnings, education and training, advancement opportunities, and experience and qualifications for each occupation.

★8747★ *Opportunities in Animal and Pet Care Careers*

VGM Career Horizons
4255 W. Touhy Ave.
Lincolnwood, IL 60646-1975
Ph: (847)679-5500   Fax: (847)679-2494
Fr: 800-323-4900

Mary Price Lee and Richard S. Lee. 1994. $14.95; $11.95 (paper). 160 pages. Covers the field from small animal medicine to large animal medicine, and provides job-hunting advice. Illustrated.

★8748★ *Opportunities in Environmental Careers*

VGM Career Horizons
4255 W. Touhy Ave.
Lincolnwood, IL 60646-1975
Ph: (847)679-5500   Fax: (847)679-2494
Fr: 800-323-4900

Odom Fanning. 1995. $14.95; $11.95 (paper). 160 pages. Describes a broad range of opportunities in fields such as environmental health, recreation, physics, and hygiene, and provides job search advice.

★8749★ *Opportunities in Health and Medical Careers*

VGM Career Horizons
4255 W. Touhy Ave.
Lincolnwood, IL 60646-1975
Ph: (847)679-5500   Fax: (847)679-2494
Fr: 800-323-4900

Donald Snook, Jr. and Leo D'Orazio. 1993. $14.95; $11.95 (paper). Covers the full range of medical and health occupations. Illustrated.

★8750★ *Opportunities in Public Health Careers*

VGM Career Horizons
4255 W. Touhy Ave.
Lincolnwood, IL 60646-1975
Ph: (847)679-5500   Fax: (847)679-2494
Fr: 800-323-4900

George E. Pickett and Terry W. Pickett. 1995. $14.95; $11.95 (paper). 160 pages. Defines the public health field and describes a variety of health, science, and business opportunities as well as educational preparation and the future of the public health field. Offers job-hunting tips. The appendixes list public health organizations, state and federal public health agencies, and graduate schools offering public health programs.

★8751★ *Opportunities in Veterinary Medicine*

VGM Career Horizons
4255 W. Touhy Ave.
Lincolnwood, IL 60646-1975
Ph: (847)679-5500   Fax: (847)679-2494
Fr: 800-323-4900

Robert E. Swope. 1993. $14.95; $11.95 (paper). Covers all types of today's practice opportunities, including research, zoological careers, government agency positions at local, state, national, and world levels, and private practice. Illustrated.

★8752★ *So You Want to Be a Veterinarian*

Benjamin Publishing Co., Inc.
1862 Akron-Peninsula Rd.
Akron, OH 44313
Ph: (216)928-3674   Fax: (216)928-9124
Fr: 800-466-1464

Melvin S. Wolfman. 1993. $15.00 (paper).

★8753★ *Today's Veterinarian*

American Veterinary Medical Association
1931 N. Meacham Rd.
Schaumburg, IL 60173

22 pages. Free booklet answers questions most often asked about veterinarians, outlines job opportunities in a variety of settings, and includes a list of accredited colleges of veterinary medicine.

EMPLOYMENT AGENCIES AND SEARCH FIRMS

★8754★ **Management Search, Inc.**
2800 W. Country Club Dr.
Oklahoma City, OK 73116
Ph: (405)842-3173

Executive search firm.

OTHER SOURCES

★8755★ **American Association of Zoo Veterinarians (AAZV)**
3400 W. Girard Ave.
Philadelphia, PA 19104-1196
Ph: (215)387-9094   Fax: (215)387-2165

Members: Veterinarians actively engaged in the practice of zoo and wildlife medicine for at least four years; veterinarians who do not qualify for active membership; persons interested in diseases of wildlife; students of veterinary medicine in any accredited veterinary school. **Purpose:** To advance programs for preventive medicine, husbandry, and scientific research dealing with captive and free-ranging wild animals; provide a forum for the presentation and discussion of problems related to the field; enhance and uphold the professional ethics of veterinary medicine.

★8756★ **Association for Women Veterinarians (AWV)**
Chris Stone Payne, D.V.M.
32205 Allison Dr.
Union City, CA 94587
Ph: (510)471-8379   Fax: (510)471-8379

Members: Women veterinarians; students of veterinary medicine.

★8757★ *Career Encounters: Veterinary Medicine*

Cambridge Career Products
PO Box 2153
Dept. CC15
Charleston, WV 25328-2153
Ph: (304)744-9323   Fax: (304)744-9351
Fr: 800-468-4227

Video. $99.95. 25 minutes. Professionals shown in a variety of settings discuss different aspects of their careers.

★8758★ **National Association of Federal Veterinarians (NAFV)**
1101 Vermont Ave. NW, Ste. 710
Washington, DC 20005-3521
Ph: (202)289-6334

Members: Professional society of veterinarians employed by the U.S. Government. Maintains speakers' bureau.

Visual Artists

SOURCES OF HELP-WANTED ADS

★8759★ Adweek

Billboard Magazine
33 Commercial St.
Gloucester, MA 01930
Ph: (508)281-3110   Fax: (508)281-0136

Weekly (Mon.). $99.00/year for individuals. Advertising news magazine.

★8760★ American Artist

BPI Communications
1515 Broadway, 11th Fl.
New York, NY 10036
Ph: (212)536-5167   Fax: (212)536-5351
Fr: 800-274-4100

Monthly. $25.00/year for individuals; $3.00 for single issue. Art and educational journal.

★8761★ Art in America

Brant Publications, Inc.
575 Broadway
New York, NY 10012
Ph: (212)941-2800   Fax: (212)941-2937
Fr: 800-925-8055

Art magazine.

★8762★ Art Direction

Advertising Trade Publications, Inc.
10 E. 39th St., 6th Fl.
New York, NY 10016-0199
Ph: (212)889-6500   Fax: (212)889-6504

Monthly. Magazine on advertising art and photography.

★8763★ The Artist's Magazine

F&W Publications, Inc.
1507 Dana Ave.
Cincinnati, OH 45207
Ph: (513)531-2222   Fax: (513)531-1843

Monthly. $24.00/year for individuals. Magazine by artists for artists. Covers today's artwork, working methods, tools, materials, and markets.

★8764★ ARTJOB

Western States Arts Federation
236 Montezuma Ave.
Santa Fe, NM 87501
Ph: (505)988-1166

Biweekly. $45.00, for 24-issue subscription. Covers national full- and part-time positions and temporary paid positions in visual, performing, and literary arts, arts education, and general arts administration, competitions, internships, conferences. Entries include: Job title, salary, description of responsibilities, qualifications, application procedure and deadline, name and address of contact. Arrangement: Classified by field.

★8765★ ARTnews Magazine

48 W. 38th St.
New York, NY 10018
Ph: (212)398-1690

Monthly. $32.95/year

★8766★ Confetti

Randall Publishing, Inc.
1425 Lunt Ave.
Elk Grove Village, IL 60007
Ph: (708)437-6604   Fax: (708)437-6618

Bimonthly. Magazine for graphic artists.

★8767★ DM News

Mill Hollow Publications
19 W. 21st St.
New York, NY 10010
Ph: (212)741-2095   Fax: (212)633-9367

Weekly. Tabloid newspaper for publishers, fund raisers, financial marketers, catalogers, package goods advertisers and their agencies, and other marketers who use direct mail, mail order advertising, catalogs, or other direct response media to sell their products or services.

★8768★ Editor & Publisher

Editor & Publisher Co.
11 W. 19th St.
New York, NY 10011
Ph: (212)675-4380   Fax: (212)929-1259

Weekly (Sat.). Magazine focusing on journalism, advertising, and printing equipment.

★8769★ FIBERARTS, The Magazine of Textiles

Altamont Press
50 College St.
Asheville, NC 28801
Ph: (704)253-0467   Fax: (704)253-7952

$22.00/year. Art magazine.

★8770★ Graphic Arts Monthly

Cahners Publishing Co.
249 W. 17th St.
New York, NY 10011
Ph: (212)463-6836

Monthly. $85.00/year. Magazine featuring commercial printing and graphic arts, including digital technologies and quick printing.

★8771★ HOW

F&W Publications, Inc.
1507 Dana Ave.
Cincinnati, OH 45207
Ph: (513)531-2222   Fax: (513)531-1843

Bimonthly. $49.00/year for individuals. Instructional trade magazine.

★8772★ Jobline News

Graphic Artists Guide of New York
11 W. 20th St., 8th Fl.
New York, NY 10011-3704
Ph: (212)463-7759

Weekly. $100.00/year for nonmembers. Lists jobs for freelance artists in such areas as graphic design, illustration, art education. Most jobs listed are in the New York area.

★8773★ Modern Jeweler

Vance Publishing Corp.
10901 W. 84th Terr.
Lenexa, KS 66214
Ph: (913)438-8700   Fax: (913)438-0692
Fr: 800-255-5113

Monthly. $25.00/year for individuals; $4.00 for single issue; $100.00/year for other countries. Trade magazine for retail jewelers.

★8774★ *Ornament Magazine*

1230 Keystone Way
PO Box 2349
Vista, CA 92083
Ph: (619)599-0222   Fax: (619)599-0228

Quarterly. $25.00/year for individuals; $6.50.00/year for single issue;Jewelry and wearables magazine.

★8775★ *Paperboard Packaging*

Advanstar Communications, Inc.
7600 Old Oak Blvd.
Cleveland, OH 44130
Ph: (216)243-8100

Monthly. $30.00/year.

★8776★ *Print*

R.C. Publications, Inc.
104 5th Ave., 19th Fl.
New York, NY 10011
Ph: (212)463-0600   Fax: (212)989-9891

Bimonthly. Covers all aspects of graphic design for visual communication.

★8777★ *Producer's Masterguide*

Producer's Masterguide
60 E. 8th St., 31st Fl.
New York, NY 10003-6514
Ph: (212)777-4002   Fax: (212)777-4101
Fr: 800-622-6111

Annual. $125.00/year for individuals; $145.00/year for out of country. Magazine for the professional motion picture, TV commercial, cable, and videotape industries in the U.S. Canada, the U.K., the Caribbean Islands, Mexico, Europe, Israel, the Far East and South America.

★8778★ *Publishers Weekly*

Publisher's Weekly
249 W. 17th St.
New York, NY 10011
Ph: (212)463-6758   Fax: (212)463-6631

Weekly (Mon.).

★8779★ *Sculpture*

International Sculpture Center
1050 17th St. NW, Ste. 250
Washington, DC 20036
Ph: (202)965-6066   Fax: (202)965-7318

Bimonthly. $55.00/year; $5.00/issue. Magazine for sculptors, artists, contemporary sculpture experts, and arts professionals.

★8780★ *Signature*

South Wind Publishing Co.
PO Box 6808
Leawood, KS 66206-0808
Ph: (913)642-6611   Fax: (913)642-6676

Periodic. Free to qualified subscribers; $48.00/year for institutions; $58.00/year for Canada and Mexico. Publishing industry magazine and catalog.

★8781★ *SignCraft*

Signcraft Publishing Co., Inc.
PO Box 60031
Fort Myers, FL 33906
Ph: (813)939-4644   Fax: (813)939-0607
Fr: 800-204-0204

Bimonthly. $25.00/year for individuals; $4.95/year for single issue. Trade magazine.

★8782★ *Southern Graphics*

PTN Publishing Co.
445 Broad Hollow Rd., Ste. 21
Melville, NY 11747
Ph: (516)845-2700   Fax: (516)845-7109

Monthly. $22.00/year for individuals. Graphic arts magazine serving the printing and graphic arts industry in 14 southern states.

PLACEMENT AND JOB REFERRAL SERVICES

★8783★ **Association of Medical Illustrators (AMI)**

1819 Peachtree St. NE, Ste. 620
Atlanta, GA 30309
Ph: (404)350-7900   Fax: (404)351-3348

Members: Medical illustrators and individuals engaged in related pursuits. **Purpose:** Promotes the study and encourages the advancement of medical illustration and allied fields of visual education. Works to advance medical education and to promote understanding and cooperation with medical and related professions. **Activities:** Offers placement services. Maintains speakers' bureau; accredits six postgraduate medical illustration programs. Offers continuing education program; provides professional certification.

★8784★ **Broadcast Designers' Association International (BDA)**

145 W. 45th St., Ste. 1100
New York, NY 10036-4008
Ph: (212)376-6222   Fax: (212)376-6202

Members: Designers, artists, art directors, illustrators, photographers, animators, and other professionals in the electronic media industry; educators and students; commercial and industrial companies that manufacture products related to design. **Purpose:** Objectives are to promote understanding between designers, clients, and management; to stimulate innovative ideas and techniques; to encourage and provide a resource for young talent; and to provide a forum for discussion on industry issues and concerns. **Activities:** Maintains placement service; conducts surveys and compiles statistics.

★8785★ **Cartoonists Northwest**

PO Box 31122
Seattle, WA 98103
Ph: (206)226-7623   Fax: (206)227-0511

Members: Cartoonists, writers, publishers, illustrators, agents, and others interested in cartooning. Members are accepted nationwide and internationally. **Purpose:** Provides information on all aspects of the cartooning profession to amateur, aspiring, and practic-

ing cartoonists. Promotes cartooning as an art form. **Activities:** Provides networking opportunities and referral services. Conducts educational programs. **E-Mail:** motooner@aol.com

★8786★ **Graphic Artists Guild (GAG)**

11 W. 20th St., 8th Fl.
New York, NY 10011
Ph: (212)463-7730   Fax: (212)463-8779

Members: Graphic, textile, and needleart designers; cartoonists, computer artists, production artists, and illustrators. **Purpose:** Promotes professional and economic interests of graphic artists. Seeks to establish standards for ownership rights, reproduction rights, business practices, and copyrights. Has grievance procedure for members in disputes. Maintains artist-to-artist hot line, placement service, and speakers' bureau. Provides legal and accounting referrals and discount program for products and services. Offers specialized education in business school courses and seminars.

★8787★ **Graphic Artists Guild of New York**

11 W. 20th St.
New York, NY 10011
Ph: (212)463-7730   Fax: (212)463-8779

Members: New York Chapter of the Graphic Artists Guild. Professional artists who work in the disciplines of illustration, graphic design, surface design, computer graphics, and cartoons, and create work for national magazines, newspaper syndicates, books, television, advertising, and promotional materials. **Purpose:** Objectives are: to raise the business and ethical standards in the industry; to provide legal and educational services to members; to increase public appreciation of artists as professionals. **Activities:** Maintains professional discipline meetings, including grievance committee meetings; provides professional education services; publishes job listing newsletter (subscription fees vary).

★8788★ **Health Sciences Communications Association (HESCA)**

1 Wedgewood Dr.
Jewett City, CT 06351
Ph: (203)376-5915   Fax: (203)376-6621

Members: Media managers, graphic artists, biomedical librarians, producers, faculty members of health science and veterinary medicine schools, health professional organizations, and industry representatives. **Purpose:** Acts as a clearinghouse for information used by professionals engaged in health science communications. Coordinates Media Festivals Program which recognizes outstanding media productions in the health sciences. **Activities:** Offers placement service.

★8789★ **Institute of American Indian Arts (IAIA)**

PO Box 20007
Santa Fe, NM 87504
Ph: (505)988-6463   Fax: (505)988-6446

Purpose: Federally chartered private institution. Offers learning opportunities in the arts and crafts to Native American youth (Indian, Eskimo, or Aleut). Emphasis is placed upon

Indian traditions as the basis for creative expression in fine arts including painting, sculpture, museum studies, creative writing, printmaking, photography, communications, design, and dance, as well as training in metal crafts, jewelry, ceramics, textiles, and various traditional crafts. Students are encouraged to identify with their heritage and to be aware of themselves as members of a race rich in architecture, the fine arts, music, pageantry, and the humanities. All programs are based on elements of the Native American cultural heritage that emphasize differences between Native American and non-Native American cultures. **Activities:** Provides placement service. Sponsors Indian arts-oriented junior college offering Associate of Fine Arts degrees in various fields as well as seminars, an exhibition program, and traveling exhibits. Maintains extensive library, museum, and biographical archives.

★8790★ National Council for Culture and Art (NCCA)
1600 Broadway, Ste. 611C
New York, NY 10019
Ph: (212)757-7933

Members: Artists, civic and business leaders, professional performers, and visual arts organizations. **Purpose:** To provide exposure and employment opportunities for rural Americans, disabled Americans, and other minorities including blacks, Hispanics, American Indians, and European-Americans. Sponsors arts programs and spring and fall concert series. Operates Opening Night, a cable television show. Bestows annual Monarch Award and President's Award, and sponsors annual Monarch Scholarship Program. **Activities:** Offers children's and placement services; conducts charitable program; maintains hall of fame. Plans to conduct Minority Playwrights Forum, Dance Festival U.S.A., Vocal and Instrumental Competition, Film and Video Festival, and Concerts U.S.A.

★8791★ Southeastern Theatre Conference (SETC)
PO Box 9868
Greensboro, NC 27429-0868
Ph: (919)272-3645   Fax: (919)272-8810

Members: Individuals and theatre organizations involved in university, college, community, professional, children's, and secondary school theatres. **Purpose:** Purpose is to bring together people interested in theatre and theatre artists and craftsmen from 10 southeastern states of the U.S. in order to promote high standards and to stimulate creativity in all phases of theatrical endeavor. **Activities:** Services include: central office for business and communication; job contact service; new play project; annual auditions for summer indoor and outdoor theatres; fall auditions for professional theatres. Compiles statistics.

EMPLOYER DIRECTORIES AND NETWORKING LISTS

★8792★ American Art Directory
R. R. Bowker Co.
Reed Reference Publishing
121 Chanlon Rd.
New Providence, NJ 07974
Ph: (908)464-6800   Fax: (908)771-7704
Fr: 800-521-8110

Approximately biennial. $186.00. Covers over 7,000 museums, art libraries, and art organizations, and 1,700 art schools; also includes lists of state directors and supervisors of art education in schools, traveling exhibition booking agencies, corporations having art holdings for public viewing, newspapers that carry art notes, art scholarships and fellowships; and 190 national, regional, and state open art exhibitions. Arrangement: Geographical. Indexes: Geographical, collection/subject/name, personal name, institution name.

★8793★ American Showcase Illustration
American Showcase, Inc.
915 Broadway
New York, NY 10010
Ph: (212)673-6600   Fax: (212)673-9795
Fr: 800-894-7469

Annual. $75.00. Covers illustrators and graphic designers. Entries include: Name, address, phone, sample of work. Arrangement: Geographical.

★8794★ Art Marketing Sourcebook
ArtNetwork
18757 Wildflower Dr.
Penn Valley, CA 95946-9717
Ph: (916)432-7630   Fax: (916)432-1633

Biennial, spring 1995. $22.95, plus 4.00 shipping; payment must accompany order; libraries, schools may send purchase orders. Covers over 2,000 representatives, consultants, galleries, critics, architects, interior designers, corporations, museum curators. Entries include: Company name, address, phone, description of services, style represented, mediums, years in business, types of companies dealt with, geographical limitations, number of clients, requirements for viewing slides. Arrangement: Classified by type of organization.

★8795★ Art Sources Directory
Art Marketing Institute
PO Box 4564
North Hollywood, CA 91607
Ph: (818)879-0339   Fax: (818)879-9326

Biennial, even years; latest edition 1994. $95.00, includes Art Marketing Manual. Covers several hundred suppliers and outlets for artists and craftpersons; includes suppliers of art materials, sources of grants for artists, competitions and art and craft shows, publishers of newsletters, directories, and other periodicals, state art councils, trade and professional associations related to art, conventions and trade shows, American chambers of commerce worldwide, advertising agencies, corporate art buyers, mail order firms, art galleries, department stores, college stores, and resident buying offices. Entries include: Name, address, product or service provided. Offered as part of a course on art marketing given by author. Arrangement: Classified by product or service.

★8796★ Artists—Commercial Directory
American Business Directories, Inc.
American Business Information, Inc.
5711 S. 86th Cir.
Omaha, NE 68127
Ph: (402)593-4600   Fax: (402)331-1505

Annual. $505.00, U.S. edition. Number of listings: 7,068 (U.S. edition); 637 (Canadian edition). Entries include: Name, address, phone (including area code), size of advertisement, year first in Yellow Pages, name of owner or manager, number of employees. Compiled from telephone company Yellow Pages, nationwide. Arrangement: Geographical.

★8797★ Artists—Fine Arts Directory
American Business Directories, Inc.
American Business Information, Inc.
5711 S. 86th Cir.
Omaha, NE 68127
Ph: (402)593-4600   Fax: (402)331-1505

Annual. $315.00, payment with order. Number of listings: 3,526. Entries include: Name, address, phone (including area code), size of advertisement, year first in Yellow Pages, name of owner or manager, number of employees. Compiled from telephone company Yellow Pages, nationwide. Arrangement: Geographical.

★8798★ Artist's & Graphic Designer's Market: Where & How to Sell Your Illustrations, Fine Art, Graphic Design & Cartoons
Writer's Digest Books
1507 Dana Ave.
Cincinnati, OH 45207
Ph: (513)531-2690   Fax: (513)531-4744
Fr: 800-289-0963

Annual, September. $23.99, plus 3.00 shipping. Covers 2,500 buyers of free-lance art work, including ad agencies, art studios, galleries, clip art firms, audiovisual firms, television film producers, periodicals, record companies, book publishers; coverage includes Canada. Entries include: Name of buyer, address, phone, payment rates, special submission requirements, reporting time, how to break in. Arrangement: Classified by type of market.

★8799★ Chicago Sourcebook
Black Book Marketing Group
212 W. Superior St., Ste. 400
Chicago, IL 60610
Ph: (312)944-5115

Annual, November. Covers commercial artists and photographers and graphic designers in Chicago, Illinois area. Entries include: Firm name, address, phone; other details as provided by firm. Arrangement: Alphabetical.

★8800★ Creative Black Book

Black Book Marketing Group
866 3rd Ave.
New York, NY 10022
Ph: (212)702-9700   Fax: (212)605-4808

Annual, January. $140.00, plus $7.00 shipping. Publication includes: photographers and photographic services, design firms, advertising agencies, and other firms whose products or services are used in advertising. Entries include: Company name, address, phone. Principal content of publication is 4-color samples from the leading commercial photographers. Arrangement: Classified by product/service.

★8801★ Design Firm Directory

Wefler & Associates, Inc.
PO Box 1167
Evanston, IL 60204
Ph: (708)475-1866

Annual, volume 1, April; volume 2, October. $57.00, volume 1; $47.00, volume 2; postpaid, payment with order. Covers more than 2,200 commercial and private design and consulting firms, including industrial, graphic, interior, landscape and environmental design; in two volumes: Design Firm Directory Graphic and Industrial Design Edition (volume 1), and Design Firm Directory Environmental and Interior Design Edition (volume 2). Entries include: Firm name, address, phone; year established; number of employees; locations of branches (if any); names and titles of key personnel; areas of specialization; clients. Arrangement: Geographical. Indexes: Alphabetical.

★8802★ Directory of American Professional Artists & Craftspeople

American Society of Artists
PO Box 1326
Palatine, IL 60078
Ph: (312)751-2500

Annual, March. Available only to working members. Covers about 10,000 artists and craftspeople. Entries include: Name, address, art medium; members' listings may also include works available, slides or photos on file, shows in which participated. Arrangement: Geographical by state, then by ZIP code.

★8803★ Directory of Minority Arts Organizations

Civil Rights Division
National Endowment for the Arts
1100 Pennsylvania Ave. NW, Rm. 812
Washington, DC 20506
Ph: (202)682-5454   Fax: (202)682-5674

Irregular, latest edition February 1987. Free. Covers almost 1,000 performing groups, presenters, galleries, art and media centers, literary organizations, and community centers with significant arts programming that have leadership and constituency that is predominantly Asian-American, African-American, Hispanic, Native American, or multi-racial. Entries include: Organization name, address, phone, name and title of contact, description of activities. Arrangement: Geographical. Indexes: Organization name, activity.

★8804★ Employment Opportunities, USA

Washington Research Associates
1660 S. Albion, Ste. 390
Denver, CO 80222
Ph: (303)756-9038   Fax: (303)770-1945

Annual, quarterly updates. $184.00, includes quarterly updates. Publication includes: List of over 1,000 employment contacts in companies and agencies in the banking, arts, telecommunications, education, and 14 other industries and professions, including the federal government. Entries include: Company name, name of representative, address, description of products or services, hiring and recruiting practices, training programs, and year established. Principal content is industry overviews, carrer news, and employment opportunity information on 14 different job markets. Arrangement: Classified by industry. Indexes: Occupation.

★8805★ International Directory of Arts

K.G. Saur
121 Chanlon Rd.
New Providence, NJ 07974
Ph: (908)464-6800   Fr: 800-521-8110

Annual. Two volumes. $225.00/set. Guide to art sources and markets in 137 countries. Contains over 130,000 names and addresses, including working artists, individual collectors, and art dealers and galleries, art museums, and more.

★8806★ National Directory of Magazines

Oxbridge Communications, Inc.
150 5th Ave., Ste. 301
New York, NY 10011
Ph: (212)741-0231

Annual. $445.00. Covers approximately 30,000 magazines.

★8807★ RSVP: The Directory of Illustrations and Design

RSVP
PO Box 050314
Brooklyn, NY 11205
Ph: (718)857-9267   Fax: (718)783-2376

Annual, January/February. $24.00, postpaid. Covers about 250 illustrators and designers in the graphic arts industry. All listings are paid. Entries include: Name, address, phone, sample of work. Arrangement: Separate sections for illustrators and designers; each subdivided into color and black and white. Indexes: Specialty (with phone), geographical, alphabetical.

★8808★ Society of Illustrators–Annual of American Illustration

Society of Illustrators
128 E. 63rd St.
New York, NY 10021
Ph: (212)838-2560   Fax: (212)838-2561

Annual, January. $57.50   plus $3.50 shipping. Covers 800 illustrators and art directors. Entries include: Personal or firm name, address, clients. Arrangement: Alphabetical.

★8809★ Who's Who in American Art

R. R. Bowker Co.
Reed Reference Publishing
121 Chanlon Rd.
New Providence, NJ 07974
Ph: (908)464-6800   Fax: (908)771-7704
Fr: 800-521-8110

Biennial, May of odd years. $189.00, plus $13.23 shipping. Covers about 11,800 people active in visual arts, including sculptors, painters, illustrators, printmakers, collectors, curators, writers, educators, dealers, critics, patrons, and museum executives. Also includes cumulative necrology from 1953. Entries include: Name, professional classification, address; artists' listings include dealer's name and address, preferred media, works in public collections, awards, publications, teaching positions, etc. Arrangement: Alphabetical. Indexes: Geographical, professional classification.

★8810★ The Workbook

Scott & Daughters Publishing
940 N. Highland Ave.
Los Angeles, CA 90038
Ph: (213)856-0008   Fax: (213)856-4368
Fr: 800-547-2688

Annual, January. $95.00. Covers in four regional volumes, 25,000 advertising agencies, art directors, photographers, freelance illustrators and designers, artists' representatives, commercial production companies, printers, color separators, and typographers in the U.S. Entries include: Company or individual name, address, phone, specialty. Regional volumes are East, West, Midwest, and South. Arrangement: Classified by product or service.

HANDBOOKS AND MANUALS

★8811★ The Art Business Encyclopedia

Allworth Press
10 E. 23rd St., Ste. 400
New York, NY 10010
Ph: (212)777-8395   Fax: (212)777-8261

Leonard DuBoff. 1994. $29.95; $18.95 (paper).

★8812★ Book Publishing Career Directory

Gale Research
835 Penobscot Bldg.
Detroit, MI 48226-4094
Ph: (313)961-2242   Fax: (313)961-6083
Fr: 800-877-GALE

Bradley Morgan. Fifth edition, 1992. $39.00. 292 pages. Features extensive listings of contacts and entry-level job opportunities at many book publishing firms. Includes articles by top professionals in the field and covers every area of book publishing, from editorial and sales to production and publicity.

★8813★ Career Choices for the 90's for Students of Art

Walker and Company
435 Hudson St.
New York, NY 10014
Ph: (212)727-8300   Fax: (212)727-0984
Fr: 800-289-2553

Prepared by the Career Associates staff. 1990. $9.95. 166 pages. Discusses alternatives for students of art. Offers advice on how to break into the field and how to move up. Covers where and who the employers are, internship possibilities, and professional networking associations. Comprehensive guide to career and job search planning.

★8814★ Career Information Center

Macmillan Publishing Co.
200 Old Tappan Rd.
Old Tappan, NJ 07675
Ph: (609)461-6500   Fr: 800-223-2336

Visual Education Center Staff. Fifth edition, 1992. $229.00. This 13-volume set profiles over 600 occupations. Each occupational profile describes job duties, educational requirements, how to get the job, advancement possibilities, employment outlook, working conditions, earnings and benefits, and where to write for more information.

★8815★ Career Opportunities in Art

Facts on File, Inc.
11 Penn Plaza, 15th Fl.
New York, NY 10001-2006
Ph: (212)967-8800   Fax: 800-678-3633
Fr: 800-322-8755

Susan H. Haubenstock and David Joselit. Revised edition, 1994. $29.95; $15.95 (paper). 208 pages. This book profiles seventy-five jobs that can be found in the art field. Each profile includes a career description, career ladder, employment and advancement prospects, education, experience and skills required, salary range, and tips for entry into the field.

★8816★ Career Opportunities in Theater and the Performing Arts

Facts on File, Inc.
11 Penn Plaza, 15th Fl.
New York, NY 10001-2006
Ph: (212)967-8800   Fax: 800-678-3633
Fr: 800-322-8755

Shelly Field. 1992. $29.95; $15.95 (paper). 256 pages. Offers a complete range of information about job opportunities in the performing arts.

★8817★ Careers in Advertising

American Advertising Foundation (AAF)
1101 Vermont Ave. NW, Ste. 500
Washington, DC 20005-3521
Ph: (202)898-0089

Single copy free. 50 pages. Describes advertising job opportunities and educational preparation. Gives job-hunting tips.

★8818★ Careers in Advertising

VGM Career Horizons
4255 W. Touhy Ave.
Lincolnwood, IL 60646-1975
Ph: (847)679-5500   Fax: (847)679-2494
Fr: 800-323-4900

S. William Pattis. Second edition, 1996. $17.95; $13.95 (paper). 192 pages. Explains the role of the media in advertising, personal characteristics needed to succeed in this field, educational requirements, and related jobs. Covers copy writing, art, design, account management, media, and research. Gives job hunting tips.

★8819★ Careers for Culture Lovers and Other Artsy Types

VGM Career Horizons
4255 W. Touhy Ave.
Lincolnwood, IL 60646-1975
Ph: (847)679-5500   Fax: (847)679-2494
Fr: 800-323-4900

Marjorie Eberts and Margaret Gisler. 1994. $14.95; $9.95 (paper). Describes how to get work in a variety of fields related to art and culture. Opportunities include picture framer, curator, art restorer, symphony manager, disk jockey, music reviewer, dance teacher, choreographer, costume designer, theater manager, light designer, drama teacher, bookstore owner, interior decorator, antique store owner, and others.

★8820★ Careers in the Graphic Arts

Rosen Publishing Group, Inc.
29 E. 21st St.
New York, NY 10010
Ph: (212)777-3017   Fax: (212)777-0277
Fr: 800-237-9932

Virginia Lee Roberson. Revised edition, 1995. $14.95; $9.95 (paper). Discusses a career in graphic arts; outlines educational requirements, training, and skills needed to become an illustrator, layout artist, designer, and paste-up artist. Gives job hunting advice, describes how to write a resume, prepare a portfolio, and interview preparation. Gives a state-by-state listing of schools offering graphic arts.

★8821★ Careers in Health Care

VGM Career Horizons
4255 W. Touhy Ave.
Lincolnwood, IL 60646-1975
Ph: (847)679-5500   Fax: (847)679-2494
Fr: 800-323-4900

Barbara M. Swanson. 1995. $17.95; $13.95 (paper). Describes job duties, work settings, salaries, licensing and certification requirements, educational preparation, and future outlook. Gives ideas on how to secure a job.

★8822★ Careers in the Visual Arts: A Guide to Jobs, Money, Opportunities, and an Artistic Life

Watson-Guptill Publications, Inc.
BPI Communications, Inc.
1515 Broadway
New York, NY 10036
Ph: (212)536-5121   Fr: 800-451-1741

Dee Ito. 1993. $14.95. 320 pages. Gives a broad overview of each field included, with educational requirements and employment opportunities. Includes ideas on how to get started.

★8823★ Chronicle Artistic Occupations Guidebook

Chronicle Guidance Publications, Inc.
PO Box 1190
Moravia, NY 13118-1190
Ph: (315)497-0330   Fax: (315)497-3359
Fr: 800-622-7284

Paul Downes, editor. 1994. $81.80.

★8824★ Cinematographers, Production Designers, Editors and Costume Designers Guide

Lone Eagle Publishing Co.
2337 Roscomare Rd., Ste. 9
Los Angeles, CA 90077
Ph: (310)471-8066   Fax: (310)471-4969
Fr: 800-345-6257

Annual. $45.00, plus $6.00 shipping. Covers Approximately 2,500 motion picture and television cinematographers, editors, production designers, and costume designers. Entries include: Personal name; name, address, phone of agent or contact; chronological list of films or shows. Arrangement: Classified by line of business. Indexes: Film/show title, contact name, agents and managers.

★8825★ The Encyclopedia of Career Choices for the 1990s: Guide to Entry-Level Jobs

Perigree Books
The Berkley Publishing Group
PO Box 506
East Rutherford, NJ 07073
Ph: (201)933-9292   Fr: 800-223-0510

Career Associates Staff. 1992. $19.95. 862 pages. Describes 500 entry-level careers in a variety of industries. Presents qualifications required, working conditions, salary, internships, and professional associations.

★8826★ Exploring High-Tech Careers

Rosen Publishing Group, Inc.
29 E. 21st St.
New York, NY 10010
Ph: (212)777-3017   Fax: (212)777-0277
Fr: 800-237-9932

Scott Southworth. Revised edition, 1993. $14.95; $9.95 (paper). 118 pages. Gives an orientation to the field of high technology and high-tech jobs. Describes educational preparation and job hunting. Includes a glossary and bibliography.

★8827★ For the Working Artists: A Survival Guide for Performing, Visual and Media Artists Who Choose to Manage Their Own Careers

National Network for Artist Placement
935 West Ave. 37
Los Angeles, CA 90065
Ph: (213)255-3096

Judith Luther. Second edition, 1991. $30.00. 338 pages.

★8828★ Graphic Design Career Guide

Watson-Guptill Publications
1515 Broadway
New York, NY 10036
Ph: (212)764-7300

James Craig. Revised edition, 1992. $19.95. 160 pages. Includes advice on the job-hunting process. Contains index, bibliography, and illustrations.

★8829★ The Harvard Guide to Careers in the Mass Media

Bob Adams, Inc.
260 Center St.
Holbrook, MA 02343
Ph: (617)767-8100   Fax: (617)767-0994
Fr: 800-872-5627

John Noble. 1989. $7.95. 202 pages. Each section of the book evaluates one media profession in depth and contains an industry profile, a career profile that describes positions available in that area, information about current salary ranges, industry-specific job-hunting tips and strategies, and a case study outlining the methods that were used in a successful job hunt.

★8830★ How to Survive and Prosper as an Artist: A Complete Guide to Career Management

Henry Holt and Co., Inc.
115 W. 18th St.
New York, NY 10011
Ph: (212)886-9200   Fr: 800-488-5233

Caroll Michels. Third edition, 1992. $11.95. 288 pages. Includes index and bibliographical references.

★8831★ Jobs in Arts and Media Management: What They Are and How to Get One!

American Council for the Arts
1 E. 53rd St.
New York, NY 10022-4201
Ph: (212)223-2787   Fr: 800-321-4510

Stephen Langley and James Abruzzo. Revised edition, 1990. $21.95. 281 pages. Includes lists of about 150 sources of information on job opportunities in the arts, including organizations offering internships, job listings, graduate programs, and short-term study; professional groups concerned with theater, music, dance, opera, museum and gallery management, film, and telecommunication management. (Does not include popular music performing or music recording.) Entries include: For internships Organization name, address, phone, description, requirements. For job referral associations and periodicals - Association or publisher name, address, fields covered, services offered, turn-around time, average number of jobs, cost of subscription or dues, comments. Arrangement: Classified by type of source.

★8832★ Liberal Arts Jobs: What They Are and How to Get Them

Peterson's
PO Box 2123
Princeton, NJ 08543-2123
Ph: (609)243-9111   Fax: (609)243-9150
Fr: 800-338-3282

Burton Jay Nadler. Second edition, 1989. $9.95. 153 pages. Presents a list of the top 20 fields for liberal arts majors, covering more than 300 job opportunities. Discusses strategies for going after those jobs, including guidance on the language of a successful job search, informational interviews, and making networking work.

★8833★ Magazines Career Directory

Gale Research
835 Penobscot Bldg.
Detroit, MI 48226-4094
Ph: (313)961-2242   Fax: (313)961-6083
Fr: 800-877-GALE

Bradley Morgan. Fifth edition, 1993. $39.00. Features extensive listings of contacts and entry-level job opportunities at many magazine publishing organizations. Includes articles by top professionals in the field on some of the industry's varied career paths: art, editorial, sales, and business management.

★8834★ Newspapers Career Directory

Gale Research
835 Penobscot Bldg.
Detroit, MI 48226-4094
Ph: (313)961-2242   Fax: (313)961-6083
Fr: 800-877-GALE

Bradley Morgan. Fourth edition, 1993. $39.00. 344 pages. Features extensive listings of contacts and entry-level job opportunities at many newspaper organizations. Focuses on each area of the business, from reporting and editorial to sales and marketing to promotion and production.

★8835★ 1996 Artist's & Graphic Designer's Market

Writer's Digest Books
1507 Dana Ave.
Cincinnati, OH 45207
Ph: (513)531-2690   Fax: (513)531-4082
Fr: 800-289-0963

Mary Cox, editor. 1995. $23.99.

★8836★ On Becoming an Artist

Allworth Press
10 E. 23rd St., Ste. 400
New York, NY 10010
Ph: (212)777-8395   Fax: (212)777-8261

Daniel Grant. 1993. $12.95 (paper).

★8837★ 100 Best Careers for the Year 2000

Prentice Hall General Reference
15 Columbus Cir.
New York, NY 10023
Ph: (212)373-8500   Fr: 800-223-2348

Shelly Field. 1992. $15.00 (paper). Covers 100 of the fastest growing jobs. The publication is divided into 11 general employment sections. Specific careers are covered within each section. Provides job description, responsibilities, employment opportunities, earnings, education and training, advance-ment opportunities, and experience and qualifications for each occupation.

★8838★ Opportunities in Commercial Art and Graphic Design Careers

VGM Career Horizons
4255 W. Touhy Ave.
Lincolnwood, IL 60646-1975
Ph: (847)679-5500   Fax: (847)679-2494
Fr: 800-323-4900

Barbara Gordon. Second edition, 1992. $14.95; $11.95 (paper). 160 pages. Provides a survey of job opportunities in advertising and public relations, publishing, fashion, architecture, and newspapers, as well as in a variety of specialty markets. Illustrated.

★8839★ Opportunities in Crafts Careers

VGM Career Horizons
4255 W. Touhy Ave.
Lincolnwood, IL 60646-1975
Ph: (847)679-5500   Fax: (847)679-2494
Fr: 800-323-4900

Marianne Munday. 1993. $14.95; $11.95 (paper). 160 pages. Provides information about careers and job opportunities in such areas as fine and applied arts, antiques and collectibles, ceramics, woodworking, sewing and needlecraft, and more. Illustrated.

★8840★ Opportunities in Drafting Careers

VGM Career Horizons
4255 W. Touhy Ave.
Lincolnwood, IL 60646-1975
Ph: (847)679-5500   Fax: (847)679-2494
Fr: 800-323-4900

Mark Rowh. 1994. $14.95; $11.95 (paper). Provides information on opportunities in mechanical, landscape, marine, and topographical drafting in civil service, architecture, electronics, and other fields. Contains index and illustrations.

★8841★ Opportunities in Magazine Publishing Careers

VGM Career Horizons
4255 W. Touhy Ave.
Lincolnwood, IL 60646-1975
Ph: (847)679-5500   Fax: (847)679-2494
Fr: 800-323-4900

S. William Pattis. 1992. $14.95; $11.95 (paper). 160 pages. Covers the scope of magazine publishing and addresses how to identify and pursue available positions. Illustrated.

★8842★ Opportunities in Printing Careers

VGM Career Horizons
4255 W. Touhy Ave.
Lincolnwood, IL 60646-1975
Ph: (847)679-5500   Fax: (847)679-2494
Fr: 800-323-4900

Irvin J. Borowsky. 1992. $14.95; $11.95 (paper). 160 pages. Offers detailed information on the variety of pre-press, press, and post-press jobs available. Covers apprenticeships, unions, salaries, and how to get ahead. Illustrated.

★8843★ Opportunities in Publishing Careers

VGM Career Horizons
4255 W. Touhy Ave.
Lincolnwood, IL 60646-1975
Ph: (847)679-5500   Fax: (847)679-2494
Fr: 800-323-4900

Robert A. Carter and S. William Pattis. 1995. $11.95 paperback. $14.95 hardcover. 160 pages. Covers all positions in book and magazine publishing, including new opportunities in multimedia publishing.

★8844★ Opportunities in Visual Arts Careers

VGM Career Horizons
4255 W. Touhy Ave.
Lincolnwood, IL 60646-1975
Ph: (847)679-5500   Fax: (847)679-2494
Fr: 800-323-4900

Mark Salmon. 1993. $14.95; $11.95 (paper). Points the way to a career in the visual arts, examining opportunities for designers, painters, sculptors, illustrators, animators, photographers, art therapists, educators, and others. Offers a view of the pros and cons of working for an art or design company or on your own.

★8845★ Opportunities in Vocational and Technical Careers

VGM Career Horizons
4255 W. Touhy Ave.
Lincolnwood, IL 60646-1975
Ph: (847)679-5500   Fax: (847)679-2494
Fr: 800-323-4900

Adrian A. Paradis. 1992. $14.95; $11.95 (paper). 160 pages. Provides information on a variety of opportunities and advice on breaking into the field.

EMPLOYMENT AGENCIES AND SEARCH FIRMS

★8846★ Alden and Clark, Inc.

PO Box 180177
Boston, MA 02118
Ph: (617)247-1147

★8847★ Claremont-Branan, Inc.

2150 Parklake Dr., Ste. 212
Atlanta, GA 30345
Ph: (404)491-1292

Employment agency. Executive search firm.

★8848★ Creative Options, Inc.

50 Washington St.
Norwalk, CT 06854
Ph: (203)854-9393

Employment agency and search firm. Places staff on a regular and temporary basis.

★8849★ Graphic Arts Employment Service, Inc.

2530 Central Pkwy.
Cincinnati, OH 45214
Ph: (513)241-2201

Employment agency.

★8850★ Graphic Search Associates Inc.

PO Box 373
Newtown Square, PA 19073
Ph: (610)359-1234   Fax: (610)353-8120

Executive search firm.

★8851★ Randolph Associates, Inc.

950 Massachusetts Ave., Ste. 105
Cambridge, MA 02139-3174
Ph: (617)441-8777   Fax: (617)441-8778

Employment agency. Provides regular or temporary placement of staff.

OTHER SOURCES

★8852★ Aid to Artisans (ATA)

14 Brick Walk Ln.
Farmington, CT 06032
Ph: (203)677-1649   Fax: (203)676-2170

Purpose: Dedicated to creating employment opportunities for disadvantaged artisans worldwide. Functions as a consultative agency, helping other organizations establish craft programs and market Third World crafts. Provides technical assistance to needy craft producers in impoverished areas of the U.S. and other countries.

★8853★ American Center for Design (ACD)

233 E. Ontario, Ste. 500
Chicago, IL 60611
Ph: (312)787-2018   Fax: (312)649-9518
Fr: 800-257-8657

Members: Design professionals, educators, and students. **Purpose:** Objectives are to: promote high standards of design practice and education; elevate public, business, and governmental awareness of design. Acts as informational, technical, and educational resource to the design community. **E-Mail:** acdchicago@aol.com **Website:** http://www.design.chi.ll.us/ac4d/

★8854★ American Institute of Graphic Arts (AIGA)

164 5th Ave.
New York, NY 10010
Ph: (212)807-1990   Fax: (212)807-1799
Fr: 800-548-1634

Purpose: Graphic designers, art directors, illustrators, packaging designers, and craftsmen involved in printing and allied graphic fields. Sponsors exhibits and projects in the public interest. Sponsors traveling exhibitions. Operates gallery. Maintains library of design books and periodicals; offers slide archives.

★8855★ American Society of Artists (ASA)

PO Box 1326
Palatine, IL 60078
Ph: (312)751-2500

Members: Professional artists and craftspeople. **Purpose:** Maintains art referral service and information exchange service. Sponsors art and craft festivals and a Lecture and Demonstration Service. Offers ac-

cess to discounted supplies. The Special Arts Services Division aids handicapped individuals to either practice or enjoy the visual arts. Presents demonstrations in visual arts to better acquaint the public with various processes in different media.

★8856★ Career Connections Video Series

Cambridge Career Products
PO Box 2153
Dept. CC15
Charleston, WV 25328-2153
Ph: (304)744-9323   Fax: (304)744-9351
Fr: 800-468-4227

Series of six videos. 1993. $219.95/set. $39.95/each. 15-20 minutes. Each video contains interviews with workers and on-the-job footage. Titles include Graphic Design, Welding, Electrician, Plumber, Pipefitter, and HVAC.

★8857★ Careers in Art

Cambridge Career Products
PO Box 2153
Dept. CC15
Charleston, WV 25328-2153
Ph: (304)744-9323   Fax: (304)744-9351
Fr: 800-468-4227

Video. $49.95. 21 minutes. Covers many professional options available in the world of art.

★8858★ College Art Association (CAA)

275 7th Ave.
New York, NY 10001
Ph: (212)691-1051   Fax: (212)627-2381

Members: Professional organization of artists, art historians and fine art educators, museum directors, and curators. **Purpose:** Seeks to raise the standards of scholarship and of the teaching of art and art history throughout the country. **E-Mail:** cad@pipeline.com

★8859★ Getting Exposure: The Artists's Guide to Exhibiting the Work

Art Calendar
PO Box 199
Upper Fairmount, MD 21867
Ph: (410)651-9150

Carolyn Blakeslee, editor. 1995. $17.95 (paper).

★8860★ Getting the Word Out: The Artist's Guide to Self Promotion

Art Calendar
PO Box 199
Upper Fairmount, MD 21867
Ph: (410)651-9150

Carolyn Blakeslee, editor. 1995. $17.95 (paper).

★8861★ Graphic Arts Technical Foundation (GATF)

4615 Forbes Ave.
Pittsburgh, PA 15213
Ph: (412)621-6941   Fax: (412)621-3049

Members: Scientific, research, technical, and educational organization serving the international graphic communications industries. **Purpose:** Conducts research in all graphic processes and their commercial applications.

Conducts seminars, workshops, and forums on graphic arts and environmental subjects. Conducts educational programs, including the publishing of graphic arts textbooks and learning modules, audiovisuals, videotapes, aptitude testing, in-plant and school counseling, and national career and manpower recruitment program. Conducts the GATF training and certification program in sheet-fed offset press operating, Web Offset press operating, Image Assembly, and desktop publishing. Produces test images and quality control devices for the industry. Performs technical services for the graphic arts industry, including problem-solving, material evaluation, and plant audits. Compiles statistics.

★8862★ National Artists Equity Association (NAEA)

PO Box 28068, Central Sta.
Washington, DC 20038-8068
Ph: (202)628-9633

Members: Professional society of visual artists. **Purpose:** Seeks to: promote and protect the interests of visual arts professionals; advocate for appropriate legislation to benefit the profession; safeguard against abuses to the artist in dealings with persons or organizations connected directly or indirectly with the visual arts. The educational and charitable arm of the association is called the Artists Equity Fund. Offers fine art insurance, group health and life insurance, discounts, technical assistance, and legal referrals.

★8863★ National Association of Artists' Organizations (NAAO)

918 F St. NW
Washington, DC 20004
Ph: (202)347-6350   Fax: (202)393-1230

Members: Contemporary art centers and individuals committed to supporting artists and their work. **Purpose:** Serves as clearinghouse for information on legislation and activities of interest to artist organizations. Promotes public awareness of the role of artists organizations; provides technical assistance; conducts networking among artists organizations.

★8864★ National Directory of Arts Internships

National Network for Artist Placement
935 W. Ave. 37
Los Angeles, CA 90065
Ph: (213)222-4035   Fax: (213)222-4035

Biennial, odd years. $40.00, postpaid; payment with order. Covers Approximately 2,000 internship opportunities in dance, music, theater, art, design, film, and video. Entries include: Name of sponsoring organization, address, name of contact; description of positions available, eligibility requirements, stipend or salary (if any), application procedures. Arrangement: Classified by discipline, then geographical.

★8865★ Society of Illustrators (SI)

128 E. 63rd St.
New York, NY 10021
Ph: (212)838-2560   Fax: (212)838-2561

Members: Professional society of illustrators and art directors. **Purpose:** Maintains Museum of American Illustration which sponsors continuous exhibits; holds annual exhibit (February-April) of best illustrations of the year; conducts benefit and sale in gallery in December. Awards annual scholarships to students of accredited college-level art schools. **Activities:** Participates in annual U.S. Air Force exhibits. Maintains hall of fame.

★8866★ Society of Newspaper Design Foundation—Internship Project

Society of Newspaper Design Foundation
The Newspaper Center
Box 4075
Reston, VA 22090
Ph: (703)648-1308   Fax: (703)620-1083

Annual, fall. Free. Covers about 75 organizations offering 150 internships in the graphic arts and design fields, including paid and minority internships; limited international coverage. Entries include: Organization name, address, phone, name and title of contact. Arrangement: Geographical.

★8867★ Student Guide to Mass Media Internships

Intern Research Group
Box 52, Regent Hall
University of Colorado
Boulder, CO 80309
Ph: (303)442-8340

Annual, latest edition 1995. $35.00, payment with order; $40.00, billed. Covers about 10,000 internships offered by 2,700 newspapers, radio and television stations, cable television companies, magazines, advertising agencies, and other firms. Entries include: Organization name, address, type and number of internships offered, eligibility requirements, application deadline, salary or other stipend offered, name and title of contact; many listings also include description of intern's duties. Arrangement: Classified by type of medium, then geographical.

★8868★ Women's Caucus for Art (WCA)

Moore College of Art
20th The Parkway
Philadelphia, PA 19103
Ph: (215)854-0922   Fax: (215)854-0915

Members: Professional women in visual art fields: artists, critics, art historians, museum and gallery professionals, arts administrators, educators and students, and collectors of art. **Purpose:** Objectives are to: increase recognition for contemporary and historical achievements of women in art; ensure equal opportunity for employment, art commissions, and research grants; encourage professionalism and shared information among women in art; stimulate and publicize research and publications on women in the visual arts. **Activities:** Conducts workshops, periodic affirmative action research, and statistical surveys. Presents annual honor awards to senior women in the visual arts.

Wedding Consultants

PLACEMENT AND JOB REFERRAL SERVICES

★8869★ American Society of Wedding Professionals (ASWP)

268 Griggs Ave.
Teaneck, NJ 07666
Ph: (201)836-8895   Fax: (201)525-0692

Members: Professionals in the wedding industry. **Purpose:** Promotes the wedding professional and educates brides on the experience of working with a consultant. **Activities:** Provides trends, etiquette, marketing, consulting information, directory listing, referrals, networking, and co-op advertising. Offers local forums for information exchange among members. Compiles statistics and conducts educational programs and seminars.

★8870★ Association of Bridal Consultants (ABC)

200 Chestnutland Rd.
New Milford, CT 06776-2521
Ph: (203)355-0464   Fax: (203)354-1404

Members: Independent bridal and wedding consultants; persons employed by companies in wedding-related businesses. **Purpose:** Strives to improve professionalism and recognition of bridal and wedding consultants. **Activities:** Offers professional development program, start-up manual and seminars. Provides advertising, publicity, referrals, and information services. Operates speakers' bureau; compiles statistics. **E-Mail:** bridalassn@acl.com

EMPLOYER DIRECTORIES AND NETWORKING LISTS

★8871★ Wedding Consultants Directory

American Business Directories, Inc.
American Business Information, Inc.
5711 S. 86th Cir.
Omaha, NE 68127
Ph: (402)593-4600   Fax: (402)331-1505

Annual. $610.00, payment with order. Entries include: Name, address, phone (including area code), size of advertisement, year first in Yellow Pages, name of owner or manager, number of employees. Compiled from telephone company Yellow Pages, nationwide. Arrangement: Geographical.

HANDBOOKS AND MANUALS

★8872★ The Best Home-Based Businesses for the 90s

G.P. Putnam's Sons
Putnam Berkley Group
200 Madison Ave.
New York, NY 10016
Ph: (212)951-8400   Fr: 800-631-8571

Paul Edwards and Sarah Edwards. Second edition, 1994. $12.95. 400 pages. Profiles 95 businesses and careers that can be conducted from one's home. Lists sources of additional information.

★8873★ Complete Wedding Planner

Wings Books
Random House Value Publishing
400 Hahn Rd.
Westminster, MD 21157
Fr: 800-733-3000

Edith Gilbert. 1994. $8.99.

★8874★ Consulting: Is Consulting for You?

Chronicle Guidance Publications, Inc.
66 Aurora St.
PO Box 1190
Moravia, NY 13118-1190
Ph: (315)497-0330   Fax: (315)497-3359
Fr: 800-622-7284

Chronicle Guidance Staff. 1995. $2.00. Reprint of a journal article.

★8875★ Jobs Rated Almanac: Ranks the Best and Worst Jobs by More Than a Dozen Vital Criteria

John Wiley and Sons
605 Third Ave.
New York, NY 10158-0012
Ph: (212)850-6000   Fr: 800-225-5945

Les Krantz. Third edition, 1995. $16.95. 340 pages. Ranks 250 jobs by environment, salary, outlook, physical demands, stress, security, travel opportunities, and geographic location.

★8876★ Jumping the Job Track: Security, Satisfaction, and Success as an Independent Consultant

Crown Publishers
Covers issues related to establishing an independent consulting practice, with stories and advice from practicing consultants.

★8877★ Planning a Wedding to Remember

Wilshire Publications
275 Battery St., Ste 1860
San Francisco, CA 94111
Ph: (310)455-2706

Beverly Clark. Fourth edition, 1995. $16.95.

★8878★ Small Business Profiles

Gale Research
835 Penobscot Bldg.
Detroit, MI 48226-4094
Ph: (313)961-2242   Fax: (313)961-6083
Fr: 800-877-GALE

Volume 1, 1994. Volume 2, 1995. $90.00 per volume. About 275 pages per volume. Volume 1 includes a chapter on wedding planning services.

★8879★ Wedding Consultants

Chronicle Guidance Publications, Inc.
66 Aurora St.
PO Box 1190
Moravia, NY 13118-1190
Ph: (315)497-0330   Fax: (315)497-3359
Fr: 800-622-7284

Chronicle Guidance Staff. 1993. $2.00. Provides concise career information and sources of additional information.

OTHER SOURCES

★8880★ How to Become a Successful Consultant in Your Own Field

Prima Publishing
3875 Atherton Rd.
Rocklin, CA 95765
Ph: (916)632-4400

Hubert Bermont. Third edition, 1991. $21.95. 240 pages.

★8881★ How to Succeed as an Independent Consultant

John Wiley and Sons
605 3rd Ave.
New York, NY 10158
Ph: (212)850-6000   Fr: 800-225-5945

Herman Holtz. Third edition, 1993. $29.95. 416 pages. Presents information on launching a consulting venture, how to identify and secure clients, and how to build a practice.

★8882★ The Independent Consultant's Q&A Book

Bob Adams, Inc.
260 Center St.
Holbrook, MA 02343
Ph: (617)767-8100   Fax: (617)767-0994
Fr: 800-872-5627

Lawrence Tuller. 1992. $10.95. 300 pages. Directed at those considering entering consulting, consultants in the early stages of developing their practice, and experienced consultants in search of new ideas or direc-tions. Designed in a question-and-answer format to enable the reader to scan and focus on particular topics of interest.

★8883★ Marketing Your Consulting and Professional Services

John Wiley and Sons, Inc.
605 3rd Ave.
New York, NY 10158
Ph: (212)850-6000   Fr: 800-225-5945

Richard A. Connor. Second edition, 1990. $29.95. Step-by-step guide to entering the consulting field including developing a marketing plan.

★8884★ National Directory of Bridal Directors

National Tabletop Association
355 Lexington Ave., 17th Fl.
New York, NY 10017
Ph: (212)661-4261   Fax: (212)370-9047

Annual, January. $50.00. Covers Approximately 120 retail and specialty stores with bridal gift registry services in the U.S. Entries include: Store name, address, phone, names and titles of key personnel. Arrangement: Alphabetical. Indexes: Geographical.

★8885★ Wedding Announcements & Invitations Directory

American Business Directories, Inc.
American Business Information, Inc.
5711 S. 86th Cir.
Omaha, NE 68127
Ph: (402)593-4600   Fax: (402)331-1505

Updated continuously; printed on request. Entries include: Name, address, phone (in-cluding area code), size of advertisement, year first in Yellow Pages, name of owner or manager, number of employees. Compiled from telephone company Yellow Pages, nationwide. Arrangement: Geographical.

★8886★ The Wedding Sourcebook

Contemporary Books
2 Prudential Plaza, Ste. 1200
Chicago, IL 60601-6790
Fax: (312)540-4687

Madeline Barilo. 1996. $25.00.

★8887★ Wedding Supplies and Services Directory

American Business Directories, Inc.
American Business Information, Inc.
5711 S. 86th Cir.
Omaha, NE 68127
Ph: (402)593-4600   Fax: (402)331-1505

Latest edition, September 1989. $1,000.00, U.S. edition; $240.00, (Canad. ed.); payment with order. Entries include: Name, address, phone (including area code). Regional editions available: Eastern, $685.00; Western, $515.00. Compiled from telephone company Yellow Pages, nationwide. Arrangement: Geographical.

Wholesale and Retail Buyers

SOURCES OF HELP-WANTED ADS

★8888★ Aftermarket Business

Advanstar Communications, Inc.
7600 Old Oak Blvd.
Cleveland, OH 44130
Ph: (216)243-8100   Fax: (216)891-2733

Monthly. Magazine (tabloid) for purchasing professionals in the retail automotive aftermarket.

★8889★ AudioVideo International

Dempa Publications, Inc.
275 Madison Ave.
New York, NY 10016
Ph: (212)682-5953   Fax: (212)682-2730

Monthly. Magazine for domestic retailers of consumer electronics products. Feature stories include trends and developments in audio, hi-fi, TV, video, car stereo, and home and personal electronics products.

★8890★ Chain Store Age Executive

Lebhar-Friedman, Inc.
425 Park Ave.
New York, NY 10022
Ph: (212)756-5257   Fax: (212)756-5270

Monthly. $79.00/year for individuals. Magazine for management of retail chain headquarters. Reports on marketing, merchandising, strategic planning, physical supports, and shopping center developments.

★8891★ Children's Business

Fairchild Publications
7 W. 34th St.
New York, NY 10001
Ph: (212)630-4580   Fax: (212)630-4879

Monthly. Serves retailers and wholesalers in the children's apparel, furniture and footwear markets.

★8892★ Daily News Record

Fairchild Publications
7 W. 34th St.
New York, NY 10001
Ph: (212)630-4580   Fax: (212)630-4879
Fr: 800-360-1700

Daily (morn.). $62.00/year. Newspaper reporting on men's and boys' clothing and textiles.

★8893★ Discount Store News

Lebhar-Friedman, Inc.
425 Park Ave.
New York, NY 10022
Ph: (212)756-5257   Fax: (212)756-5270

Semimonthly. $99.00/year.

★8894★ Earnshaw's Review

Earnshaw Publications, Inc.
225 W. 34th St., Rm. 1212
New York, NY 10001
Ph: (212)563-2742   Fax: (212)629-3249

Monthly. Fashion and business magazine for retailers, manufacturers, licensees, and fiber companies in the children's apparel industry.

★8895★ Electronic Business Buyer

Cahners Publishing Co.
275 Washington St.
Newton, MA 02158-1630
Ph: (617)964-3030   Fax: (617)558-4470

Monthly. Magazine for purchasing managers and buyers of electronic components and materials used in end product manufacture.

★8896★ Electronic Buyers' News

CMP Publications
600 Community Dr.
Manhasset, NY 11030
Ph: (516)562-5000   Fax: (516)562-5016

Weekly.

★8897★ Fashion Market Directory

330 W. 38th St., 15th Fl.
New York, NY 10018
Ph: (212)760-5100   Fax: (212)760-5112

Seven times/year.

★8898★ Gifts and Decorative Accessories

Geyer-McAllister Publications, Inc.
51 Madison Ave.
New York, NY 10010
Ph: (212)689-7929

Monthly. $37.00/year.

★8899★ Juvenile Merchandising

Columbia Communications, Inc.
370 Lexington Ave.
New York, NY 10017-6558
Ph: (212)532-9290   Fax: (212)779-8345

Monthly. Magazine featuring juvenile furniture and wheel goods.

★8900★ Kids Fashions

Larkin Publications, Inc.
485 7th Ave., Ste. 1400
New York, NY 10018
Ph: (212)594-0880

Monthly. $26.00/year.

★8901★ LDB Interior Textiles Magazine

Columbia Communications, Inc.
342 Madison Ave., Ste. 1901
New York, NY 10017
Ph: (212)661-1516   Fax: (212)661-1713

Monthly. Magazine for buyers of home fashions, including linens, domestics and bath products, window treatments, home fragrances, decorative pillows and accessories.

★8902★ Modern Jeweler

Vance Publishing Corp.
10901 W. 84th Terr.
Lenexa, KS 66214
Ph: (913)438-8700   Fax: (913)438-0692
Fr: 800-255-5113

Monthly. $25.00/year for individuals; $4.00 for single issue; $100.00/year for other countries. Trade magazine for retail jewelers.

★8903★ Motor/Age

Chilton Publications
825 7th Ave.
New York, NY 10019
Ph: (212)887-8400   Fax: (212)887-8484

Monthly. Trade magazine for the automotive service industry.

★8904★ Music, Inc.

Maher Publications
102 N. Haven Rd.
Elmhurst, IL 60126
Ph: (708)941-2030   Fax: (708)941-3210

Eleven times/year. $16.50/year.

★8905★ Music Trades

Music Trades Corporation
80 West St.
PO Box 432
Englewood, NJ 07631
Ph: (201)871-1965   Fax: (201)871-0455

Monthly. Music trade magazine.

★8906★ National Jeweler

Miller Freeman, Inc.
1515 Broadway
New York, NY 10036
Ph: (212)626-2380   Fax: (212)944-7164
Fr: 800-950-1314

Semimonthly. Jewelry industry magazine.

★8907★ Purchasing

Cahners Publishing Co.
275 Washington St.
Newton, MA 02158-1630
Ph: (617)964-3030   Fax: (617)558-4470

Semimonthly. Magazine for buying professionals.

★8908★ Small World

Earnshaw Publications, Inc.
225 W. 34th St., Rm. 1212
New York, NY 10122
Ph: (212)563-2742   Fax: (212)629-3249

Monthly. Product and business magazine for retailers and manufacturers of juvenile products.

★8909★ Specialty and Custom Dealer

Babcox Publications
11 S. Forge St.
Akron, OH 44304
Ph: (216)535-7011   Fax: (216)535-0874

Monthly. Magazine serving owners and managers of automotive specialty/performance retail and wholesale operations.

★8910★ Sporting Goods Dealer

Times Mirror Magazines, Inc.
2 Park Ave.
New York, NY 10016
Ph: (212)779-5285   Fax: (212)779-5465

Monthly. Magazine providing merchandising information, market data, and new product information to retailers of sporting goods.

★8911★ Tire Business

Crain Communications Inc
1725 Merriman Rd., Ste. 300
Akron, OH 44313-5251
Ph: (216)836-9180   Fax: (216)836-2831

Semimonthly. $50.00/year for individuals; $92.00. for two years. Newspaper (tabloid) serving independent tire dealers.

★8912★ Tire Review

Babcox Publications
11 S. Forge St.
Akron, OH 44304
Ph: (216)535-7011   Fax: (216)535-0874

Monthly. Magazine containing news and business information about the tire, custom wheel, automotive service, and retreading industries.

★8913★ TWICE

Cahners Publishing Co.
249 W. 17th St.
New York, NY 10010
Ph: (212)645-0067   Fax: (212)337-7066

Semiweekly. Trade tabloid covering consumer electronics, appliance, and camera industries for retailers, manufacturers, and distributors.

★8914★ Video Business

Chilton Publications
825 7th Ave.
New York, NY 10019
Ph: (212)887-8400   Fax: (212)887-8484

Weekly. Magazine for retailers of pre-recorded video software and related goods and services.

★8915★ Video Software

825 7th Ave., 6th Fl.
New York, NY 10019
Ph: (212)887-8400   Fax: (212)887-8384

Monthly. $60.00/year. Magazine for retailers and wholesalers of prerecorded video programming.

PLACEMENT AND JOB REFERRAL SERVICES

★8916★ National Association of College Stores (NACS)

500 E. Lorain St.
Oberlin, OH 44074
Ph: (216)775-7777   Fax: (216)775-4769
Fr: 800-622-7498

Members: Institutional, private, leased, and cooperative college stores selling books, supplies, and other merchandise to college students, faculty, and staff; associate members include publishers and suppliers. **Purpose:** Seeks to effectively serve higher education by providing educational opportunities, services, and products to college stores and their suppliers. **Activities:** Maintains NAC-SCORP, Inc., a wholly owned subsidiary corporation, which distributes trade and mass market books and educational software. Operates placement service. Maintains College Stores Research and Educational Foundation which provides grants for NACS educational programs and conducts research.

EMPLOYER DIRECTORIES AND NETWORKING LISTS

★8917★ Directory of Department Stores

Chain Store Guide Information Services
3922 Coconut Palm Dr.
Tampa, FL 33619
Ph: (813)664-6700   Fax: 800-846-8047
Fr: 800-925-2288

Updated continuously; printed on request. $260.00. Covers over 600 department store companies operating over 6,800 stores; over 900 mail order firms; resident buying organizations; and major industry trade shows. Entries include: For department store companies, company name, address, phone, fax, number of stores, sales, total square feet, resident buyer, store locations; private labels, leased departments; names and titles of executives, merchandise managers, and buyers. For mail order firms, company name, address, phone, sales, product lines, year established, catalog name(s), whether company also operates retail stores, names and titles of executives. For resident buyers, company name, address, phone, department store companies represented. For shows, name, location, dates, contact phone. Arrangement: Separate geographical sections for department stores, mail order firms, and resident buyers; shows are chronological. Indexes: Company/resident buyer name; top 75 department stores and top 100 mail order companies ranked by sales (with number of stores).

★8918★ Directory of Drug Store & HBC Chains

Chain Store Guide Information Services
3922 Coconut Palm Dr.
Tampa, FL 33619
Ph: (813)664-6868   Fax: (813)664-6810
Fr: 800-925-2288

Annual, November. $290.00. Covers drug store chains operating two or more units; mass merchants with pharmacies; and wholesale drug companies. Arrangement: Separate geographical sections for chains and wholesalers.

★8919★ Directory of General Merchandise/Variety & Specialty Stores

Chain Store Guide Information Services
3922 Coconut Palm Dr.
Tampa, FL 33619
Ph: (813)664-6700   Fax: (813)664-6810
Fr: 800-925-2288

Updated continuously; printed on request. $245.00, plus $5.00 shipping. Covers about 700 general merchandise and variety store companies; approximately 1,400 housewares and giftwares chains; over 2,200 novelty card and gift shop companies; over 1,422 toy, hobby, and craft retail operations and 500 wholesalers; and nearly 2,600 stationery and office products store companies. Entries include: Company name, headquarters address, phone, fax, number of units, store names, names and titles of key personnel, sales volume, products, year founded, ownership. Arrangement: Classified by line of business, then geographical. Indexes: Product, alphabetical.

★8920★ **Discount Store News—Top Chains Issue**

Chain Store Guides, Inc.
Lebhar-Friedman, Inc.
425 Park Ave.
New York, NY 10022
Ph: (212)756-5000

Annual, July. $79.00. Entries include: Chain name, location, sales and earnings for the past two years, number of stores, net store square footage. Arrangement: Ranked by sales volume.

★8921★ **Stores—Top 100 Issue**

National Retail Federation
100 W. 31st St.
New York, NY 10001
Ph: (212)244-8780   Fax: (212)594-0487

Annual, July. $5.00, pre-paid. Publication includes: 100 U.S. retail companies having largest estimated sales during preceding year. Entries include: Name of store, city, number of stores included, and total sales. Arrangement: Ranked by sales.

★8922★ **Variety Stores Directory**

American Business Directories, Inc.
American Business Information, Inc.
5711 S. 86th Cir.
Omaha, NE 68127
Ph: (402)593-4600   Fax: (402)331-1505

Annual. $760.00, U.S. edition. Number of listings: 10,682 (U.S. edition); 3,545 (Canadian edition). Entries include: Name, address, phone (including area code), size of advertisement, year first in Yellow Pages, name of owner or manager, number of employees. Compiled from telephone company Yellow Pages, nationwide. Arrangement: Geographical.

★8923★ **Wholesaler—Wholesaling 100 Issue**

TMB Publishing Inc.
1838 Techny Ct.
Northbrook, IL 60062
Ph: (708)564-1127   Fax: (708)564-1264

Annual, July. $25.00. Publication includes: List of 100 leading wholesalers of plumbing, heating, air conditioning, refrigeration equipment, and supplies such as industrial pipe, valves and fittings. Entries include: Company name, address, phone, fax, names and titles of key personnel, number of employees, business breakdown (percentage). Arrangement: Ranked by sales.

HANDBOOKS AND MANUALS

★8924★ **Career Choices for the 90's for Students of Art**

Walker and Company
435 Hudson St.
New York, NY 10014
Ph: (212)727-8300   Fax: (212)727-0984
Fr: 800-289-2553

Prepared by the Career Associates staff.

1990. $9.95. 166 pages. Discusses alternatives for students of art. Offers advice on how to break into the field and how to move up. Covers where and who the employers are, internship possibilities, and professional networking associations. Comprehensive guide to career and job search planning.

★8925★ **Career Choices for the 90's for Students of Business**

Walker and Company
435 Hudson St.
New York, NY 10014
Ph: (212)727-8300   Fax: (212)727-0984
Fr: 800-289-2553

Prepared by the Career Associates staff. 1990. $9.95. 166 pages. Discusses alternatives for students of business. Offers advice on how to break into the field and how to move up. Covers where and who the employers are, internship possibilities, and professional networking associations. Comprehensive guide to career and job search planning.

★8926★ **Career Choices for the 90's for Students of English**

Walker and Company
435 Hudson St.
New York, NY 10014
Ph: (212)727-8300   Fax: (212)727-0984
Fr: 800-289-2553

Prepared by the Career Associates staff. 1990. $8.95. 166 pages. Discusses alternatives for students of English. Offers advice on how to break into the field and how to move up. Covers where and who the employers are, internship possibilities, and professional networking associations. Comprehensive guide to career and job search planning.

★8927★ **Career Choices for the 90's for Students of Mathematics**

Walker and Company
435 Hudson St.
New York, NY 10014
Ph: (212)727-8300   Fax: (212)727-0984
Fr: 800-289-2553

Prepared by the Career Associates staff. 1990. $8.95. 166 pages. Discusses alternatives for students of mathematics. Offers advice on how to break into the field and how to move up. Covers where and who the employers are, internship possibilities, and professional networking associations. Comprehensive guide to career and job search planning.

★8928★ **Career Choices for the 90's for Students of Political Science and Government**

Walker and Company
435 Hudson St.
New York, NY 10014
Ph: (212)727-8300   Fax: (212)727-0984
Fr: 800-289-2553

Prepared by the Career Associates staff. 1990. $8.95. 166 pages. Discusses alternatives for students of political science and government. Offers advice on how to break into the field and how to move up. Covers where and who the employers are, internship possibilities, and professional networking associations. Comprehensive guide to career and job search planning.

★8929★ **Career Choices for the 90's for Students of Psychology**

Walker and Company
435 Hudson St.
New York, NY 10014
Ph: (212)727-8300   Fax: (212)727-0984
Fr: 800-289-2553

Prepared by the Career Associates staff. 1990. $9.95. 166 pages. Discusses alternatives for students of psychology. Offers advice on how to break into the field and how to move up. Covers where and who the employers are, internship possibilities, and professional networking associations. Comprehensive guide to career and job search planning.

★8930★ **The Encyclopedia of Career Choices for the 1990s: Guide to Entry-Level Jobs**

Perigree Books
The Berkley Publishing Group
PO Box 506
East Rutherford, NJ 07073
Ph: (201)933-9292   Fr: 800-223-0510

Career Associates Staff. 1992. $19.95. 862 pages. Describes 500 entry-level careers in a variety of industries. Presents qualifications required, working conditions, salary, internships, and professional associations.

★8931★ **Encyclopedia of Careers and Vocational Guidance**

J. G. Ferguson Publishing Co.
200 W. Monroe, Ste. 250
Chicago, IL 60606
Ph: (312)580-5480

William E. Hopke. Ninth edition, 1993. $129.95; $199.95 (CD-ROM). Four-volume set that profiles 900 occupations and describes job trends in 71 industries. Includes career description, educational requirements, history of the job, methods of entry, advancement, employment outlook, earnings, conditions of work, social and psychological factors, and sources of further information. Contains career and employment information for this field.

★8932★ **Liberal Arts Jobs: What They Are and How to Get Them**

Peterson's
PO Box 2123
Princeton, NJ 08543-2123
Ph: (609)243-9111   Fax: (609)243-9150
Fr: 800-338-3282

Burton Jay Nadler. Second edition, 1989. $9.95. 153 pages. Presents a list of the top 20 fields for liberal arts majors, covering more than 300 job opportunities. Discusses strategies for going after those jobs, including guidance on the language of a successful job search, informational interviews, and making networking work.

★8933★ **Opportunities in Fashion Careers**

VGM Career Horizons
4255 W. Touhy Ave.
Lincolnwood, IL 60646-1975
Ph: (847)679-5500   Fax: (847)679-2494
Fr: 800-323-4900

Roslyn Dolber. 1993. $14.95; $11.95 (paper).

160 pages. Covers job opportunities in the textile industry, design and manufacturing, apparel production, and fashion merchandising, and how to pursue them. Illustrated.

★8934★ *Opportunities in Retailing Careers*

VGM Career Horizons
4255 W. Touhy Ave.
Lincolnwood, IL 60646-1975
Ph: (847)679-5500   Fax: (847)679-2494
Fr: 800-323-4900

Roslyn Dolber. 1994. $14.95; $11.95 (paper). Discusses a number of opportunities in retailing, from entry-level to retail management.

★8935★ *Opportunities in Vocational and Technical Careers*

VGM Career Horizons
4255 W. Touhy Ave.
Lincolnwood, IL 60646-1975
Ph: (847)679-5500   Fax: (847)679-2494
Fr: 800-323-4900

Adrian A. Paradis. 1992. $14.95; $11.95 (paper). 160 pages. Provides information on a variety of opportunities and advice on breaking into the field.

★8936★ *Retailing*

Prentice Hall
113 Sylvan Ave.
Rte. 9W
Englewood Cliffs, NJ 07632
Ph: (201)592-2000   Fr: 800-922-0579

Gerald Pintel and Jay Diamond. Fifth edition, 1991. $72.00. 544 pages. Includes an index.

EMPLOYMENT AGENCIES AND SEARCH FIRMS

★8937★ **B and M Associates, Inc.**
199 Cambridge Rd.
Woburn, MA 01801-4705
Ph: (617)938-9120

Employment agency.

★8938★ **Britt Associates Inc.**
2709 Black Rd.
Joliet, IL 60435
Ph: (815)744-7200

Employment agency.

★8939★ **Colli Associates of Tampa**
PO Box 2865
Tampa, FL 33601
Ph: (813)681-2145

Employment agency. Executive search firm.

★8940★ **Hayden and Associates, Inc.**
7825 Washington Ave. S., Ste. 120
Minneapolis, MN 55439-2431
Ph: (612)941-6300   Fax: (612)941-9602

Employment agency. Executive search firm. Fills openings in a variety of fields.

★8941★ **T.R. Employment Agency**
409 Wilshire Blvd.
Santa Monica, CA 90401
Ph: (310)393-4107

Employment agency.

OTHER SOURCES

★8942★ **National Retail Federation (NRF)**

325 7th St. NW, Ste. 1000
Washington, DC 20004-2802
Ph: (202)783-7971   Fax: (202)737-2849

Purpose: Represents 50 state retail association, several dozen national retail associations as well as large and small corporate members representing the breadth and diversity of the retail industry's establishment and employees. **Activities:** Conducts informational and educational conferences related to all phases of retailing including financial planning and cash management, taxation, economic forecasting, expense planning, shortage control, credit, electronic data processing, telecommunications, merchandise management, buying, traffic, security, supply, materials handling, store planning and construction, personnel administration, recruitment and training, and advertising and display.

★8943★ *Resumes for Sales and Marketing Careers*

VGM Career Horizons
4255 W. Touhy Ave.
Lincolnwood, IL 60646-1975
Ph: (847)679-5500   Fax: (847)679-2494
Fr: 800-323-4900

1991. $9.95. 128 pages. Sample resumes and cover letters from all levels of the sales and marketing field.

Writers and Editors

SOURCES OF HELP-WANTED ADS

★8944★ Adweek

Billboard Magazine
33 Commercial St.
Gloucester, MA 01930
Ph: (508)281-3110   Fax: (508)281-0136

Weekly (Mon.). $99.00/year for individuals. Advertising news magazine.

★8945★ Art Direction

Advertising Trade Publications, Inc.
10 E. 39th St., 6th Fl.
New York, NY 10016-0199
Ph: (212)889-6500   Fax: (212)889-6504

Monthly. Magazine on advertising art and photography.

★8946★ ARTJOB

Western States Arts Federation
236 Montezuma Ave.
Santa Fe, NM 87501
Ph: (505)988-1166

Biweekly. $45.00, for 24-issue subscription. Covers national full- and part-time positions and temporary paid positions in visual, performing, and literary arts, arts education, and general arts administration, competitions, internships, conferences. Entries include: Job title, salary, description of responsibilities, qualifications, application procedure and deadline, name and address of contact. Arrangement: Classified by field.

★8947★ Aviation Digest

Aviation Digest Associates
288 Christian St.
Oxford, CT 06478
Ph: (203)264-4333   Fax: (203)264-4511

Monthly. $19.95/year for individuals; $36.95 for two years. Magazine for aircraft owners and pilots.

★8948★ Columbia Journalism Review

Columbia Journalism Review
700 Journalism Bldg.
Columbia University
New York, NY 10027
Ph: (212)854-1881   Fax: (212)854-8580

Bimonthly. Magazine focusing on journalism.

★8949★ Daily Variety

Cahners Business Newspapers
5700 Wilshire Blvd., Ste. 120
Los Angeles, CA 90036
Ph: (213)857-6600   Fax: (213)857-0494

Daily (morn.). Global entertainment newspaper (tabloid).

★8950★ Editor & Publisher

Editor & Publisher Co.
11 W. 19th St.
New York, NY 10011
Ph: (212)675-4380   Fax: (212)929-1259

Weekly (Sat.). Magazine focusing on journalism, advertising, and printing equipment.

★8951★ History News

American Association for State and Local History
530 Church St., #600
Nashville, TN 37219-2325
Ph: (615)255-2971   Fax: (615)255-2979

Bimonthly. Magazine for employees of historic sites, museums, and public history agencies. Coverage includes museum education programs and techniques for working with volunteers.

★8952★ HOW

F&W Publications, Inc.
1507 Dana Ave.
Cincinnati, OH 45207
Ph: (513)531-2222   Fax: (513)531-1843

Bimonthly. $49.00/year for individuals. Instructional trade magazine.

★8953★ Metro Magazine

Bobit Publishing
2512 Artesia Blvd.
Redondo Beach, CA 90278
Ph: (310)376-8788   Fax: (310)374-7878

$25.00/year for individuals; $4.00 for single issue. Magazine on public transportation.

★8954★ The New Republic

New Republic, Inc.
1220 19th St. NW, 600
Washington, DC 20036
Ph: (202)331-7494   Fax: (202)331-0275

Weekly (Mon.). $69.67/year for individuals; $84.97/year for Canada; $99.97/year for other countries; $2.95 for single issue.

★8955★ PR Marcom Jobs East

Rachel PR Services
208 E. 51st St., No. 1600
New York, NY 10022
Ph: (212)962-9100

Biweekly. Provides news of job openings in public relations, marketing, journalism, communications, public relations agencies and corporations, and freelance and temporary writing positions. Focuses on the New York City, Washington, DC, and Boston, and surrounding areas.

★8956★ PR Marcom Jobs West: Northern California–Pacific Northwest

Rachel PR Services
298 4th Ave., No. 344
San Francisco, CA 94118
Ph: (415)334-7124

Biweekly. Provides information concerning job openings in public relations, journalism, marketing, communications, public relations agencies and corporations, and freelance and temporary writing positions. Focuses on opportunities in Northern California and Pacific Northwest areas.

★8957★ PR Marcom Jobs West: Southern California

Rachel PR Services
1650 S. Pacific Coast Hwy., Ste. 200-C
Redondo Beach, CA 90277
Ph: (310)792-1313

Biweekly. Provides information concerning job openings in public relations, journalism, marketing, communications, public relations agencies and corporations, and freelance and temporary writing positions. Focuses on opportunities in Southern California.

★8958★ Producer's Masterguide

Producer's Masterguide
60 E. 8th St., 31st Fl.
New York, NY 10003-6514
Ph: (212)777-4002   Fax: (212)777-4101
Fr: 800-622-6111

Annual. $125.00/year for individuals; $145.00/year for out of country. Magazine for the professional motion picture, TV commercial, cable, and videotape industries in the U.S. Canada, the U.K., the Caribbean Islands, Mexico, Europe, Israel, the Far East and South America.

★8959★ The Professional Communicator

Women in Communications, Inc.
10605 Judicial Dr., Ste. A4
Fairfax, VA 22030-5167
Ph: (703)920-5555   Fax: (703)920-5556

Magazine covering communications issues, trends and news.

★8960★ Publishers Weekly

Publisher's Weekly
249 W. 17th St.
New York, NY 10011
Ph: (212)463-6758   Fax: (212)463-6631

Weekly (Mon.).

★8961★ The Quill

Russell Sage College
Box 2134
Troy, NY 12180
Ph: (518)270-2259

Weekly (Thurs.). Collegiate newspaper.

★8962★ Signature

South Wind Publishing Co.
PO Box 6808
Leawood, KS 66206-0808
Ph: (913)642-6611   Fax: (913)642-6676

Periodic. Free to qualified subscribers; $48.00/year for institutions; $58.00/year for Canada and Mexico. Publishing industry magazine and catalog.

★8963★ Small Press

Moyer Bell Ltd.
Kymbolde Way
Wakefield, RI 02879-1915
Ph: (401)789-0074   Fax: (401)789-3793

Quarterly. $29.00/year for individuals; $7.50 for single issue. Book Reviews and articles about independent publishing.

★8964★ Sojourners

Sojurners
2401 15th St. NW
Washington, DC 20009
Ph: (202)328-8842   Fax: (202)328-8757

Bimonthly. Magazine endorsing the coming together of Christians in a movement of biblical faith and political conscience.

★8965★ The Writer

The Writer, Inc.
120 Boylston St.
Boston, MA 02116-4615
Ph: (617)423-3157   Fax: (617)423-2168

Monthly. $28.00/year for individuals; $3.50/year for single issue. Magazine for free-lance writers. Publishing practical information and advice on how to write publishable material and where to sell it.

★8966★ Writer's Digest

F&W Publications, Inc.
1507 Dana Ave.
Cincinnati, OH 45207
Ph: (513)531-2222   Fax: (513)531-1843

Monthly. $27.00/year for individuals. Professional magazine for writers.

PLACEMENT AND JOB REFERRAL SERVICES

★8967★ American Society of Journalists and Authors (ASJA)

1501 Broadway, Ste. 302
New York, NY 10036
Ph: (212)997-0947   Fax: (212)768-7414

Members: Freelance writers of nonfiction magazine articles and books. **Purpose:** Seeks to elevate the professional and economic position of nonfiction writers, provide a forum for discussion of common problems among writers and editors, and promote a code of ethics for writers and editors. **Activities:** Operates Dial-A-Writer Service for individuals, institutions, or companies seeking writers for special projects; sponsors Llewellyn Miller Fund to aid professional writers no longer able to work due to age, disability, or extraordinary professional crisis.

★8968★ Asian American Journalists Association (AAJA)

1765 Sutter St., Ste. 1000
San Francisco, CA 94115
Ph: (415)346-2051   Fax: (415)931-4671

Members: Journalists, educator, employees of news organizations, public relations specialists, and students. **Purpose:** Seeks to increase employment of Asian Pacific American journalists; provides journalism students with career advice and aid; encourages fair and accurate news coverage of Asian and Asian Pacific American issues; provides support and fellowship for Asian Pacific American journalists. **Activities:** Maintains resource file of resumes for potential employers. Compiles statistics; operates speakers' bureau.

★8969★ Associated Writing Programs (AWP)

George Mason University
Tallwood House, Mail Stop 1E3
Fairfax, VA 22030
Ph: (703)993-4301   Fax: (703)993-4302

Members: Writers; students and teachers in creative writing programs in university departments of English; editors, publishers, and freelance creative and professional writers. **Purpose:** Fosters literary talent and achievement; advocates the craft of writing as primary to a liberal and humane education; provides services to the makers and readers of contemporary literature. **Activities:** Operates job placement service; sponsors literary competitions.

★8970★ Association for Documentary Editing (ADE)

George C. Marshall Foundation
PO Box 1600
Lexington, VA 24450
Ph: (703)463-7103   Fax: (703)464-5229

Members: Editors of historical, literary, scientific, and philosophical documents; historical societies; representatives of university presses; persons with an interest in documentary editing. **Purpose:** Encourages excellence in documentary editing by offering a means of communication and cooperation and by promoting understanding of the principles and values inherent in documentary editing. **Activities:** Operates placement service.

★8971★ Aviation/Space Writers Association (AWA)

6540 50th St. N.
Oakdale, MN 55128
Ph: (612)779-9390

Members: Aviation/space writers and editors of newspapers, magazines, books, radio, television, and press services; public relations representatives and other writers associated with the aviation/space industry. **Activities:** Operates placement service.

★8972★ Black Women in Publishing (BWIP)

10 E. 87th St.
New York, NY 10128
Ph: (212)427-8100

Purpose: Works to create, develop, and maintain a network which provides information, encouragement, and support for professionals, students, and others interested in publishing, writing, and marketing books, magazines, newspapers, and new media products. **Activities:** Acts as a support group in relation to career planning and job security. Promotes, enhances, and recognizes the achievements of African Americans in the media; works for a free and responsible press.

★8973★ Catholic Press Association (CPA)

3555 Veterans Hwy., Unit 10
Ronkonkoma, NY 11779
Ph: (516)471-4730   Fax: (516)471-4804

Members: Publishers of Catholic newspapers, magazines, pamphlets, and books; Catholic writers, illustrators, and teachers. **Purpose:** Sponsors research and specialized education programs. **Activities:** Maintains placement service. Maintains 25 committees, including Freedom of Information, News Service Liaison, and Research.

★8974★ Computer Press Association (CPA)

3661 W. 4th Ave., No. 8
Vancouver, BC, Canada V6R 1P2
Ph: (604)733-5596   Fax: (604)732-4280

Members: Journalists and other individuals who write or report regularly about the computer industry. **Purpose:** Established to provide a forum for professional communication. **Activities:** Operates job listings service.

★8975★ Dow Jones Newspaper Fund (DJNF)

PO Box 300
Princeton, NJ 08543
Ph: (609)452-2820   Fax: (609)520-5804

Purpose: Established by Dow Jones and Company to encourage careers in journalism among young people. Operates Editing Internship Program for all junior, senior, and graduate level college students interested in journalism. Also offers On-Line Newspaper Program; Part-Time Information Intern Program; and Business Intern Program. Students work as copy editors during the summer for a daily newspaper or wire service and receive monetary scholarships to return to school in the fall. Offers information on careers in print journalism.

★8976★ Editorial Freelancers Association (EFA)

71 W. 23rd St., Ste. 1504
New York, NY 10010
Ph: (212)929-5400   Fax: (212)929-5439

Members: Persons who work full- or part-time as editorial freelancers. **Purpose:** Promotes professionalism and facilitates the exchange of information and support. **Activities:** Conducts professional training seminars; offers job phone. Compiles statistics.

★8977★ Education Writers Association (EWA)

1001 Connecticut Ave. NW, Ste. 310
Washington, DC 20036
Ph: (202)429-9680   Fax: (202)872-4016

Members: Education writers and reporters of daily and weekly newspapers, national magazines of general circulation, and radio and television stations; associate members are school and college public relations personnel and others with a serious interest in education writing. **Purpose:** Improves the quality of education reporting and interpretation; encourages the development of education coverage by the press; to help attract top-notch writers and reporters to the education field. **Activities:** Sponsors regional and special workshops. Provides job referral/bank services.

★8978★ Evangelical Press Association (EPA)

485 Panorama Rd.
Earlysville, VA 22936
Ph: (804)973-5941   Fax: (804)973-2710

Members: Editors and publishers of Christian periodicals. **Activities:** Maintains placement service.

★8979★ Health Sciences Communications Association (HESCA)

1 Wedgewood Dr.
Jewett City, CT 06351
Ph: (203)376-5915   Fax: (203)376-6621

Members: Media managers, graphic artists, biomedical librarians, producers, faculty members of health science and veterinary medicine schools, health professional organizations, and industry representatives. **Purpose:** Acts as a clearinghouse for information used by professionals engaged in health science communications. Coordinates Media Festivals Program which recognizes outstanding media productions in the health sciences. **Activities:** Offers placement service.

★8980★ International Black Writers (IBW)

PO Box 1030
Chicago, IL 60690
Ph: (708)331-6421

Purpose: Seeks to discover and support new black writers. **Activities:** Offers referral service. Conducts research and monthly seminars in poetry, fiction, nonfiction, music, and jazz. Operates a lending library of 500 volumes on black history for members only. Provides writing services and children's services. Maintains library and speakers' bureau.

★8981★ International Women's Writing Guild (IWWG)

Box 810, Gracie Sta.
New York, NY 10028-0082
Ph: (212)737-7536   Fax: (212)737-9469

Members: Women writers in 24 countries interested in expressing themselves through the written word professionally and for personal growth. **Purpose:** Seeks to empower women personally and professionally through writing. **Activities:** Facilitates manuscript submissions to literary agents. Participates in international network.

★8982★ Media Alliance (MA)

814 Mission St., Ste. 205
San Francisco, CA 94103

Members: Writers, photographers, editors, broadcast workers, public relations people, and others who support free press and independent journalism. **Purpose:** Seeks to change what the alliance calls the characteristic cutthroat competitive attitude among its practitioners by encouraging contact and discussion and developing structures enabling members to assist each other and to mobilize the group's resources on behalf of mutually agreed-upon projects. **Activities:** Maintains job file. Conducts continuing professional education classes. Maintains speakers' bureau.

★8983★ National Association of Hispanic Journalists (NAHJ)

Natl. Press Bldg., Ste. 1193
529 14th St. NW
Washington, DC 20045
Ph: (202)662-7145   Fax: (202)662-7144
Fr: 800-708-2774

Purpose: To organize and support Hispanics involved in news gathering and dissemination. Encourages journalism and communications study and practice by Hispanics. Seeks recognition for Hispanic members of the profession regarding their skills and achievements. Promotes fair and accurate media treatment of Hispanics; opposes job discrimination and demeaning stereotypes. Works to increase educational and career opportunities and development for Hispanics in the field. Seeks to foster greater awareness of members' cultural identity, interests, and concerns. Provides a united voice for Hispanic journalists with the aim of achieving national visibility. **Activities:** Offers placement services to Hispanic students.

★8984★ Society of American Business Editors and Writers (SABEW)

PO Box 838
Columbia, MO 65205
Ph: (314)882-7862   Fax: (314)882-9002

Members: Active business, economic, and financial news writers and editors for newspapers, magazines, and other publications; broadcasters of business news; teachers of business or journalism at colleges and universities. **Activities:** Plans periodic seminars on problems and techniques in business news coverage and occasional special meetings with business, financial, government and labor leaders, and other experts. Organized following a series of business news seminars sponsored by Society of Professional Journalists. Maintains the Resume Bank, a service which keeps resumes of SABEW members on file. Editors looking for job candidates can request the resumes of candidates that meet their requirements.

★8985★ Society of Professional Journalists (SPJ)

16 S. Jackson
Greencastle, IN 46135
Ph: (317)653-3333   Fax: (317)653-4631

Members: Professional society - journalism. **Purpose:** Promotes a free and unfettered press; high professional standards and ethical behavior; journalism as a career. Conducts lobbying activities; maintains legal defense fund. Sponsors Barney/Kilgore Freedom of Information Internships in Washington, DC. **Activities:** Holds forums on the free press. Maintains placement service. **E-Mail:** address spj@internetmci.com

★8986★ Women in Scholarly Publishing (WISP)

Duke University Press
Box 90660
Durham, NC 27708-0660
Ph: (919)687-3600   Fax: (919)688-4574

Members: Women involved in scholarly publishing and men who support the organization's goals. **Purpose:** Promotes professional development and advancement, management skills, and opportunities for women in scholarly publishing. Concerns include career development, job sharing information, surveys of salaries and job opportunities for women, and practical workshops or other training opportunities. Provides a forum and network for communication among women in presses throughout the U.S. **Activities:** Sponsors educational workshops, programs, and seminars, in conjunction with the Association of American University Presses. Compiles statistics.

★8987★ Writers Alliance (WA)

12 Skylark Ln.
Stony Brook, NY 11790
Ph: (516)751-7080

Members: Writers and artists. **Purpose:** Fosters communication, discussion, and literary support. Provides marketing information and writer referral service; suggests research techniques. **Activities:** Offers critique and editing service. Plans to conduct workshops. The alliance is expanding its membership, which was originally limited to the Long Island, NY area, to include women and men throughout the nation.

EMPLOYER DIRECTORIES AND NETWORKING LISTS

★8988★ American Society of Journalists and Authors—Directory

American Society of Writers, Journalists and Authors
1501 Broadway, Ste. 302
New York, NY 10036
Ph: (212)997-0947   Fax: (212)768-7414

Annual, November. $75.00. Covers 900 member freelance nonfiction writers. Entries include: Writer's name, home and office addresses and phone numbers, specialties, areas of expertise; name, address and phone of agent; memberships; books; periodicals to which contributed; awards. Arrangement: Alphabetical. Indexes: Subject specialty, type of material written, geographical.

★8989★ Association of American University Presses—Directory

Association of American University Presses
584 Broadway, Ste. 410
New York, NY 10012
Ph: (212)941-6610   Fax: (212)941-6618

Annual, November. $14.95; $18.00, postpaid. Covers 114 presses and affiliates worldwide. Entries include: Press name, address, phone, telex, cable address; titles and names of complete editorial and managerial staffs; editorial program; mailing, warehouse, printing, and/or customer service addresses; other details. Arrangement: Classified by press affiliation. Indexes: Personal name.

★8990★ Association of Professional Writing Consultants—Membership Directory

Association of Professional Writing Consultants
c/o Barbara Shwom
Northwestern University
1902 Sheridan Rd.
Evanston, IL 60208
Ph: (708)491-4969   Fax: (708)328-5536

Annual. $75.00. Covers 300 members. Entries include: Company or individual name, address, phone, areas of consulting expertise, services. Arrangement: Geographical.

★8991★ Author & Audience: A Readings and Workshops Guide

Poets & Writers, Inc.
72 Spring St.
New York, NY 10012
Ph: (212)226-3586   Fax: (212)226-3963
Fr: 800-666-2268

Triennial, 1993. $10.00. Covers Approximately 350 national venues which sponsor readings, workshops, and performances and accept queries, writing samples, and resumes from poets, fiction writers, and perfor-

mance poets. Entries include: Organization name, address, name of contact, description of activities, types of queries accepted, payment. Separate list of venues that sponsor performance poetry to cross-reference. Arrangement: Geographical.

★8992★ Burrelle's New York Media Directory

Burrelle's Information Services
75 E. Northfield Rd.
Livingston, NJ 07039
Ph: (201)992-6600   Fr: 800-876-3342

Annual. $95.00. Includes information on radio and television stations, newspapers, and other media companies. Regional editions available for some Northeastern states.

★8993★ Canadian Writer's Guide: Official Handbook of the Canadian Authors Association

Canadian Authors Association
275 Slater St.
Ottawa, ON, Canada K1P 5H9
Ph: (613)233-2846   Fax: (613)235-8237

Irregular, latest edition 1992. $21.95. Publication includes: List of over 500 market opportunities for Canadian freelance writers. Entries include: Company name, address, description of specific interests and services, payment schedules. Arrangement: Classified by type of publication. Indexes: Subject, product/service, award categories.

★8994★ Chicago Media Directory

Chicago Convention and Tourism Bureau
McCormick Place-on-the-Lake
Chicago, IL 60616
Ph: (312)567-8500   Fax: (312)567-8533

Quarterly. $5.00. Covers executive and editorial personnel at Chicago's major daily newspapers, downtown weeklies, and wire services, as well as radio and television station personnel. Entries include: For newspapers: publication name, address, phone, names and titles of key personnel. For radio and TV Station: name, address, phone, names and titles of key personnel. Arrangement: Classified by type of medium or outlet.

★8995★ Children's Writers & Illustrators Market

Writer's Digest Books
1507 Dana Ave.
Cincinnati, OH 45207
Ph: (513)531-2690   Fax: (513)531-4744
Fr: 800-289-0963

Annual, January. $19.99, plus $3.00 shipping. Covers about 600 book and magazine publishers that publish works by authors and illustrators for young audiences; sponsors of writing and illustrating contests and awards; writers' organizations; and workshops. Entries include: For Publishers Name, address, phone, name and title of contact, type of business, type and number of books published annually, average length of material bought, list of recently published material, reporting times, terms of payment to authors. Arrangement: Separate sections for book and magazine publishers. Indexes: Age level for books, general, magazine.

★8996★ Directory of Leading Magazines and Newspapers

Publisher Media
1136 Broadway
El Cajon, CA 92021
Ph: (619)469-2610

Annual, January. $12.95. Covers over 300 newspapers and 700 consumer and trade magazines; coverage also includes Canada. Entries include: Company name, address, description of services, circulation figures advertising information. Arrangement: Classified by subject.

★8997★ Directory of Poetry Publishers

Dustbooks
PO Box 100
Paradise, CA 95967
Ph: (916)877-6110   Fax: (916)877-0222
Fr: 800-477-6110

Annual, September. $18.95. Covers about 2,100 magazines, small presses, commercial presses, and university presses that accept poetry for publication. Entries include: Publisher name and address, number of submissions accepted, percentage of submissions published, deadlines, reporting time, list of recent contributors, rights purchased, and method of payment. Arrangement: Alphabetical. Indexes: Subject, geographical.

★8998★ Directory of Small Magazine— Press Editors and Publishers

Dustbooks
PO Box 100
Paradise, CA 95967
Ph: (916)877-6110   Fax: (916)877-0222
Fr: 800-477-6110

Annual, September. $23.95. Covers about 5,000 publishers and editors. Entries include: Individual name, title of press or magazine, address and phone number. Arrangement: Alphabetical.

★8999★ Do the Write Thing

Myriad Press
12535 Chandler Blvd., No. 3
North Hollywood, CA 91607
Ph: (818)508-6296   Fax: (818)508-6296

Published 1994. $18.95. Publication includes: Lists of publishers, trade associations, and government agencies of interest to aspiring professional writers. Entries include: company, organization, or personal name, address, and service provided. Indexes: Organization name, subject.

★9000★ Editor & Publisher—Directory of Syndicated Services Issue

Editor & Publisher Co., Inc.
11 W. 19th St., 10th Fl.
New York, NY 10011
Ph: (212)675-4380   Fax: (212)691-6939

Annual, July. $8.00. Publication includes: Directory of several hundred syndicates serving newspapers in the United States and abroad with news, columns, features, comic strips, editorial cartoons, etc. Entries include: Syndicate name, address, phone, names of executives. Arrangement: Alphabetical. Indexes: Personnel, feature title.

★9001★ Editor & Publisher International Year Book

Editor & Publisher Co., Inc.
11 W. 19th St., 10th Fl.
New York, NY 10011
Ph: (212)675-4380   Fax: (212)691-6939

Annual, April. $100.00. Covers daily and Sunday newspapers in the United States and Canada; weekly newspapers; foreign daily newspapers; special service newspapers; newspaper syndicates; news services; journalism schools; foreign language and Black newspapers in the United States; news, picture, and press services; feature and news syndicates; comic and magazine services; advertising clubs; trade associations; clipping bureaus; house organs; journalism awards; also lists manufacturers of equipment and supplies. Arrangement: Publications and schools are geographical; most other lists are alphabetical.

★9002★ Editorial Freelancers Association—Membership Directory

Editorial Freelancers Association
71 W. 23 St.
New York, NY 10011
Ph: (212)929-5400   Fax: (212)929-5439

Annual, spring. $25.00, plus $3.00 shipping. Covers 1,100 member editorial freelancers. Entries include: Personal name, address, phone, services provided, specialties. Arrangement: Alphabetical. Indexes: Product/service, special interest, geographical, computer skills.

★9003★ Freelance Editorial Association Yellow Pages & Code of Fair Practice

Freelance Editorial Association
PO Box 380835
Cambridge, MA 02238-0835
Ph: (617)729-8164

Annual. $47.50. Covers services offered by hundreds of freelance editors, indexers, proofreaders, translators, desktop publishers, researchers, illustrators, and writers; member are located throughout the United States. Entries include: Name, address, phone, and brief descriptions. Arrangement: Classified by editorial skill. Indexes: Name, geographical, specialty.

★9004★ Hudson's Washington News Media Contacts Directory

Howard Penn Hudson Associates, Inc.
44 W. Market St.
PO Box 311
Rhinebeck, NY 12572
Ph: (914)876-2081   Fax: (914)876-2561

Annual, November; updates in February, May, and August. $155.00. Covers nearly 5,000 editors, free-lance writers, and news correspondents, plus 4,624 United States, Canadian, and foreign newspapers, radio-TV networks and stations, magazines, and periodicals based or represented in Washington, D.C. Entries include: For publications and companies: name, address, phone, and name of editor or key personnel. For individuals: name, assignment. Arrangement: Classified by activity (e.g., correspondents), media type, etc; newspapers and radio-TV stations sections are arranged geographically; spe-

cialized periodicals section is arranged by subject. Indexes: Subject.

★9005★ Insider's Guide to Book Editors, Publishers, and Literary Agents

Prima Publishing
PO Box 1260
Rocklin, CA 95677-1260
Ph: (916)632-4400   Fax: (916)632-4405
Fr: 800-255-8989

Annual, latest edition October, 1995. $19.95. Covers more than 200 publishing houses and their editors. Entries include: Name of press, description, editors and their specialties. Appendixes list agents, model book proposal, and author-agency agreement.

★9006★ International Directory of Children's Literature

George Kurian Reference Books
Box 519
Baldwin Place, NY 10505
Ph: (914)962-3287

Irregular, latest edition 1993. $34.95. Covers about 5,000 children's book and magazine publishers, organizations, children's libraries and special collections, fairs, seminars, and conferences concerned with children's literature; worldwide coverage. Entries include: For book publishers, children's literature organizations, and major children's libraries and special collections: Name, address, purpose of activity. For periodicals, prizes, and events: Name, responsible organization, address, frequency or time period, subject. Arrangement: Geographical.

★9007★ International Directory of Little Magazines and Small Presses

Dustbooks
PO Box 100
Paradise, CA 95967
Ph: (916)877-6110   Fax: (916)877-0222
Fr: 800-477-6110

Annual, September. $44.95. Covers over 5,000 small, independent magazines, presses, and papers. Entries include: Name, address, size, circulation, frequency, price, type of material used, number of issues or books published annually, and other pertinent data. Arrangement: Alphabetical. Indexes: Subject, regional.

★9008★ International Literary Market Place

R. R. Bowker Co.
Reed Reference Publishing
121 Chanlon Rd.
New Providence, NJ 07974
Ph: (908)464-6800   Fax: (908)771-7704
Fr: 800-521-8110

Annual, Fall. $179.95. Covers more than 9,200 publishers in over 170 countries outside the United States and Canada, and about 1,150 trade and professional organizations related to publishing abroad; includes major printers, binders, typesetters, book manufacturers, book dealers, libraries, literary agencies, translators, book clubs, reference books and journals, periodicals, prizes, and international reference section. Entries include: For publishers Name, address, phone, fax, telex, names and titles of key

personnel, branches, type of publications, subjects, ISBN prefix. Arrangement: Classified by business activities, then geographical. Indexes: Company name, subject, type of publication.

★9009★ International Media Guide: Newspapers Worldwide

International Media Guides, Inc.
Macair Bldg.
85 Perimeter Rd.
Nashua, NH 03063
Ph: (603)882-9576   Fax: (603)595-0437
Fr: 800-964-6334

Annual. $150.00. Covers newspapers and color newspaper magazines/supplements from 200 countries, including the United States. Entries include: Publication name; publisher name, address, phone, fax, names of editor, advertising manager, and representatives in the United States and worldwide; advertising rates in U.S. dollars and/or local currency, circulation, mechanical data, ad closing, readership description, etc. Arrangement: Geographical.

★9010★ Literary Market Place

R. R. Bowker Co.
Reed Reference Publishing
121 Chanlon Rd.
New Providence, NJ 07974
Ph: (908)464-6800   Fax: (908)771-7704
Fr: 800-521-8110

Annual, September. $165.00. Covers over 15,000 firms or organizations offering services related to the publishing industry, including 3,800 book publishers in the United States and Canada who issued three or more books during the preceding year, plus a small press section of publishers who publish less than three titles per year or those who are self-published. Also included: book printers and binders; book clubs; book trade and literary associations; selected syndicates, newspapers, periodicals, and radio and TV programs that use book reviews or book publishing news; translators and literary agents. Arrangement: Classified by line of business. Indexes: Principal index is 35,000-item combined index of publishers, publications, and personnel; several sections have geographical and/or subject indexes; translators are indexed by source and target language.

★9011★ Midwest Travel Writers Association—Roster

Midwest Travel Writers Association
c/o Beverly Hurley Public Relations
12724 Sagamore
Leawood, KS 66209
Ph: (913)451-9023   Fax: (913)451-9023

Annual, September. $25.00. Covers over 100 travel writers, editors, and representatives of the travel and tourism industry, located in 13 midwestern states. Entries include: Name, spouse's name, address, phone; title, year membership began, publications, professional affiliations. Arrangement: Alphabetical. Indexes: Geographical.

★9012★ Mystery Writer's Market Place and Sourcebook

Writer's Digest Books
1507 Dana Ave.
Cincinnati, OH 45207
Ph: (513)531-2690   Fax: (513)531-4744
Fr: 800-289-0963

Published 1993. $17.95. Publication includes: Profiles of about 50 publishers of mystery and crime books; lists of magazines, organizations, conventions, workshops, awards, and bookstores of interest to mystery writers and other devotees. Entries include: For publishers Name, address, phone, editorial requirements, usual purchase terms, tips from the editor (do's and don'ts). Arrangement: Classified by type of entry. Indexes: General, category.

★9013★ National Directory of Community Newspapers

American Newspaper Representatives, Inc.
1000 Shelard Pkwy., Ste. 360
Minneapolis, MN 55426
Ph: (612)545-1116   Fax: (612)545-1481
Fr: 800-752-6237

Annual, March. $75.00, postpaid, payment with order. Number of listings: 7,000. Entries include: Name of newspaper, address, county, type of area, circulation, day published, name of publisher, and information on advertising and production. Arrangement: Geographical.

★9014★ National Directory of Magazines

Oxbridge Communications, Inc.
150 5th Ave., Ste. 301
New York, NY 10011
Ph: (212)741-0231

Annual. $445.00. Covers approximately 30,000 magazines.

★9015★ Northwest Publishing Marketplace

Writers Connection
PO Box 24770
San Jose, CA 95154
Ph: (408)554-2090   Fax: (408)554-2099

$14.95 plus $3.50 shipping. Covers book publishers, magazines, newspapers, literary agents, professional organizations, and writers conferences active in Alaska, Idaho, Montana, Oregon, Washington, and Wyoming. Arrangement: Classified by line of business. Indexes: Subject, geographical, alphabetical.

★9016★ Novel & Short Story Writer's Market

Writer's Digest Books
1507 Dana Ave.
Cincinnati, OH 45207
Ph: (513)531-2690   Fax: (513)531-4744
Fr: 800-289-0963

Annual, January. $19.99, plus 3.00 shipping. Publication includes: List of more than 1,900 literary magazines, general periodicals, small presses, book publishers, and authors' agents; contests awards; and writers' organizations. Entries include: For markets: publication name (if a periodical), publisher name and address, phone, name of editor or other

contact; description of periodical or type of work published; frequency and circulation for periodicals, number of titles published for others; needs, method of contact, terms, payment, advice, comments, or tips given by firm. For contests and awards: name, sponsoring organization name and address, name and title of contact, frequency; purpose, requirements, other information. Arrangement: Contests and awards are alphabetical; markets are classified by type of publisher or type of periodical. Indexes: Market category.

★9017★ Periodical Writers Association of Canada—Directory of Professional Members

Periodical Writers Association of Canada
24 Ryerson Ave.
Toronto, ON, Canada M5T 2P3
Ph: (416)868-6913   Fax: (416)860-0826

Annual, January. $15.00. Covers over 350 professional writer members. Membership is based on publication credits. Entries include: Name of writer, address, home and business phone numbers, periodicals in which published, subject expertise, experience, related interests and skills, languages, awards, books published, and writer's statement of skills. Arrangement: Geographical by region. Indexes: Alphabetical, subject specialty, skill.

★9018★ Poet's Handbook

Fine Arts Press
Box 3491
Knoxville, TN 37927
Ph: (615)637-9243

Annual, Autumn. $20.00. Covers magazines, book publishers, and greeting card companies that publish or use poetry submissions; limited international coverage. All entries include company name and address; entries for magazines and some book publishers also specify type of material accepted and arrangements for payment. Arrangement: Classified by line of business.

★9019★ Poet's Market

Writer's Digest Books
1507 Dana Ave.
Cincinnati, OH 45207
Ph: (513)531-2690   Fax: (513)531-4744
Fr: 800-289-0963

Annual, September. $21.99. Covers 1,700 publishers, periodicals, and other markets accepting poetry for publication. Entries include: Name, address, phone, name and title of contact, types of poetry accepted, submission requirements. Arrangement: Alphabetical. Indexes: Subject, geographical, chapbook publishers.

★9020★ PR Profitcenter

Ad-Lib Publications
51 1/2 W. Adams
PO Box 1102
Fairfield, IA 52556-1102
Ph: (515)472-6617   Fax: (515)472-3186
Fr: 800-669-0773

Monthly. $150.00. Diskette. Covers over 13,500 media, including 4,100 magazine editors, 5,500 newspaper editors, 2,300 radio shows, 975 TV shows, and 703 syndicated columnists. Database includes: Name of newspaper, magazine, station, or network;

name and title of editor, columnist, or contact person; address, phone, audience in subject and categories covered. Additional details may include show host, format, circulation, frequency.

★9021★ Professional Freelance Writers Directory

National Writers Club
1450 S. Havana, Ste. 620
Aurora, CO 80012
Ph: (303)751-7844   Fax: (303)751-8593

Annual, March. $12.50. Covers about 200 professional members selected from the club's membership on the basis of significant articles or books, or production of plays or movies. Entries include: Name, address, phone (home and business numbers), special fields of writing competence, titles of books published by royalty firms, mention of contributions to specific magazines, journals, newspapers or anthologies, recent awards received, relevant activities and skills (photography, etc.). Arrangement: Alphabetical. Indexes: Geographical and subject specialty.

★9022★ Publishers Directory

Gale Research
835 Penobscot Bldg.
Detroit, MI 48226-4094
Ph: (313)961-2242   Fax: (313)961-6083
Fr: 800-877-GALE

Annual, fall. $275.00. Covers approximately 20,000 new and established, commercial and nonprofit, private and alternative, corporate and association, government and institution publishing programs and their distributors; includes producers of books, classroom materials, prints, reports, and databases. Entries include: Firm name, address, phone, fax, year founded, ISBN prefix, Standard Address Number, whether firm participates in the Cataloging in Publication program of the Library of Congress, names of principal executives, number of titles in print, description of firm and its main subject interests, discount and returns policies, affiliated and parent companies, mergers and amalgamations, principal markets, imprints and divisions; distributors also list firms for which they distribute, special services, terms to publishers and regional offices. Arrangement: Alphabetical; distributors listed separately. Indexes: Subject, geographical, publisher name (including imprints).

★9023★ Publishers, Distributors, and Wholesalers of the United States

R. R. Bowker Co.
Reed Reference Publishing
121 Chanlon Rd.
New Providence, NJ 07974
Ph: (908)464-6800   Fax: (908)655-3502
Fr: 800-521-8110

Annual, October. $175.00. Covers Over 64,500 publishers, distributors, and wholesalers; includes associations, museums, software producers and manufacturers, and others not included in Books in Print. Entries include: Publisher name, editorial and ordering addresses, phone, Standard Address Numbers (SANs), International Standard Book Number prefix. Arrangement: Alphabetical; distributors and wholesalers are listed separately. Indexes: ISBN prefix, abbreviation, type of business, imprint name, geographical, inactive and out of business company name, toll-free phone and fax, wholesaler and distributor.

★9024★ Self-Publishing Manual: How to Write, Print & Sell Your Own Book

Para Publishing
PO Box 4232
Santa Barbara, CA 93140-4232
Ph: (805)968-7277　　Fax: (805)968-1379
Fr: 800-PARA-PUB

Biennial, odd years. $21.95, 1995 edition, postpaid. Publication includes: Lists of wholesalers, reviewers, exporters, suppliers, direct mailing list sources, publishing organizations, and others of assistance in publishing. Entries include: Organization or company name, address. Arrangement: Classified by ZIP code. Indexes: General subject.

★9025★ Society of American Travel Writers—Membership Directory

Society of American Travel Writers
4101 Lake Boone Trail, Ste. 201
Raleigh, NC 27607
Ph: (919)787-5181　　Fax: (919)787-4916

Annual, February. $95.00. Covers about 550 newspaper and magazine travel editors, writers, columnists, photo journalists, and broadcasters in the United States and Canada. Also covers separately 300 executives in public relations who handle tourist attractions and travel industry accounts. Entries include: For regular members: name, business address, phone, year joined; awards, publications, specialties, publications contributed to; spouse's name. For public relations executives: name, address, phone, year joined, clients. Arrangement: Classified by type of membership. Indexes: Geographical, travel editor affiliation, free lance travel writers, public relations executive affiliation.

★9026★ Southwest Publishing Marketplace

Writers Connection
PO Box 24770
San Jose, CA 95154
Ph: (408)554-2090　　Fax: (408)554-2099

$14.95, plus $3.50 shipping. Covers book publishers, magazines, newspapers, literary agents, professional organizations, and writers conferences in Arizona, Colorado, Nevada, New Mexico, Texas, and Utah. Arrangement: Classified by line of business. Indexes: Subject, geographical, alphabetical.

★9027★ Space Coast Writers Guild—Organization, Activities, Awards, and Membership

Space Coast Writers Guild
Box 804
Melbourne, FL 32902
Ph: (305)727-0051

Annual, January. Available to members only. Covers about 350 professional and aspiring writers in Florida. Entries include: Name, address, phone, area and form of specialty. Arrangement: Alphabetical.

★9028★ Technical Communication—Special Issue/Membership Directory

Society for Technical Communication
901 N. Stuart St., Ste. 904
Arlington, VA 22203-1854
Ph: (703)522-4114　　Fax: (703)522-2075

Annual, September. Available to members only. Covers Approximately 18,000 writers, editors, educators, scientists, engineers, artists, designers, publishers, and others involved in technical writing and communication. Entries include: Name, address, phone, chapter. Arrangement: Alphabetical; geographical, by state; classified by affiliation. Indexes: Geographical.

★9029★ Travel Editors U.S.A. & Canada

Rocky Point Press
PO Box 602
Santa Monica, CA 90406
Ph: (310)829-0590

Biennial, March of odd years. $7.95. Covers Approximately 400 travel editors of newspapers; coverage includes Canada. Entries include: Publication name, address, phone, travel editor name. Arrangement: Geographical.

★9030★ Ulrich's International Periodicals Directory

R. R. Bowker Co.
Reed Reference Publishing
121 Chanlon Rd.
New Providence, NJ 07974
Ph: (908)665-2847　　Fax: (908)771-7725
Fr: 800-521-8110

Annual, updates three times per year under. $415.00, includes updates. Covers nearly 126,000 current periodicals published worldwide; 7,000 newspapers published in the U.S. Entries include: In main list: publication title; Dewey Decimal Classification number, Library of Congress Classification Number (where applicable), CODEN designation (for sci-tech serials), British Library Document Supply Centre shelfmark number, country code, ISSN; subtitle, language(s) of text, year first published, frequency, subscription price in country of origin and U.S. rate, sponsoring organization, publisher name and address, editor; regular features (reviews, advertising, abstracts, bibliographies, trade literature, etc.), indexes, circulation, format, brief description of content; availability of microforms and reprints; whether refereed; CD-ROM availability with vendor name; online availability with host name; services that index or abstract the periodical, with years covered; advertising rates and contact; availability through document delivery services; Copyright Clearance Center participation; document type; former title. Arrangement: Main listing is classified by subject; newspapers are listed in a separate volume; lists of cessations, online hosts, and CD-ROM vendors are alphabetical. Indexes: International organization publication title, online periodical title, ISSN, periodicals available on CD-ROM refereed serial, controlled circulation serial, cumulative title changes.

★9031★ Washington Independent Writers—Directory

Washington Independent Writers
733 15th St. NW, Ste. 220
Washington, DC 20005
Ph: (202)347-4973　　Fax: (202)628-0298

Biennial, March of even years. $15.00. Covers about 2,500 member freelance writers in the Washington, D.C. area. Entries include: Name, address, home and office phone, area of specialization; personal and career data usually included. Arrangement: Alphabetical. Indexes: Specialty.

★9032★ Who's Who in Canadian Film and Television

Academy of Canadian Cinema and Television
158 Pearl St.
Toronto, ON, Canada M5H 1L3
Ph: (416)591-2040

Irregular, latest edition 1991. $39.95. Covers over 2,000 writers, producers, directors, art directors, editors, composers, and others involved in the television and film industry in Canada. Entries include: Name, address, phone; agent name, address, phone; union or guild affiliation, types and genres of work, biographical data, filmography. Arrangement: Classified by line of business. Indexes: Alphabetical.

★9033★ Who's Who in the Motion Picture Industry

Packard Publishing Co.
PO Box 2187
Beverly Hills, CA 90213
Ph: (310)854-0276　　Fax: (818)501-7392

Annual, February; supplement. $29.00. Covers about 1,200 cinematographers, directors, producers, writers, and studio executives in the theatrical and television motion picture industries. Entries include: For production companies and studios: name, address, phone, names and titles of key personnel. For others: name, company or agent name, address, phone, credits. Arrangement: Classified by professional status (director, studio executive, etc.) in separate sections for theatrical and television films. Indexes: Alphabetical.

★9034★ Working Press of the Nation

Reed Reference Publishing
121 Chanlon Rd.
New Providence, NJ 07974
Ph: (908)665-3561　　Fax: (908)665-2894
Fr: 800-521-8110

Annual, September. $385.00, four-volume set; Covers in four separate volumes, syndicates and over 8,400 daily and weekly newspapers; 1,400 newsletters; over 14,900 radio and television stations; 10,600 magazines; 3,200 feature writers, photographers, and professional speakers; and 2,700 internal house organs. Entries include: All listings include name of publication or station, address, phone, names of executives, editors, writers, etc., as appropriate. Broadcasting and magazine volumes include data on kinds of material needed. Technical and mechanical requirements for publications are given. Arrangement: Magazines are classified by audience; newspapers and broadcasting stations are geographical.

★9035★ **World Book of IABC Communicators**

International Association of Business Communicators
1 Hallidie Plaza, Ste. 600
San Francisco, CA 94102
Ph: (415)433-3400   Fax: (415)362-8762

Annual, January. $100.00. Covers about 13,000 association members involved with organizational, corporate, and public relations and other communications fields. Entries include: Name, address, title, code indicating type of business or organization, phone. Arrangement: Alphabetical. Indexes: Geographical, then classified by type of business.

★9036★ **The Writer— Special Market Lists Section**

The Writer, Inc.
120 Boylston St.
Boston, MA 02116-4615
Ph: (617)423-3157

Appears in regular monthly issues. $2.25 per copy; $27.00 per year, postpaid. Publication includes: Section on markets for freelance writers, with focus on a different type of market each month. Included is a short description of the particular market and its general editorial requirements, followed by a list of publications in that market. Entries include: Publication name, address, name and title of contact, specific interests, editorial requirements, and payment policies. Arrangement: Alphabetical.

★9037★ **Writers Directory**

American Business Directories, Inc.
American Business Information, Inc.
5711 S. 86th Cir.
Omaha, NE 68127
Ph: (402)593-4600   Fax: (402)331-1505

Updated continuously; printed on request. Please inquire. Entries include: Name, address, phone, size of advertisement, name of owner or manager, number of employees, year first in Yellow Pages. Compiled from telephone company Yellow Pages, nationwide. Arrangement: Geographical.

★9038★ **Writers Guild Directory**

Writers Guild of America, West
8955 Beverly Blvd.
West Hollywood, CA 90048
Ph: (310)550-1000   Fax: (310)550-8185

Annual, January. $17.00 plus 3.00 shipping. Covers about 12,000 writers for motion pictures, television, and radio; includes listings for members of Writers Guild of America, East; total listings are about 90% of the combined membership of the two organizations. Entries include: Name, biographical data, name of agent, recent work. Arrangement: Alphabetical.

★9039★ **The Writer's Handbook**

The Writer, Inc.
120 Boylston St.
Boston, MA 02116
Ph: (617)423-3157

Annual, January. $29.95. Publication includes: List of more than 3,000 markets for the sale of manuscripts, plus lists of American literary agents, syndicates, writers' organizations, literary prizes and awards. Entries include: For markets: name of firm or publication, address, editorial requirements, payment rate, name and title of contact editor. For agents: name, address. For organizations Name, address, key official, description of purpose and activities. Main content is 110 chapters on writing for publication, many by recognized authors and editors. Arrangement: Markets are classified by type (popular, specialized magazine, book, syndicate, etc.); agents and organizations are alphabetical. Indexes: Alphabetical.

★9040★ **Writer's Market: Where and How to Sell What You Write**

Writer's Digest Books
1507 Dana Ave.
Cincinnati, OH 45207
Ph: (513)531-2690   Fax: (513)531-4744
Fr: 800-289-0963

Annual, September. $26.99, plus 3.00 shipping. Covers more than 4,000 buyers of books, articles, short stories, plays, gags, verse, fillers, and other original written material. Includes book and periodical publishers, greeting card publishers, play producers and publishers, audiovisual material producers, syndicates, and contests and awards. Entries include: Name and address of buyer, phone, payment rates, editorial requirements, reporting time, how to break in. Arrangement: Classified by type of publication.

HANDBOOKS AND MANUALS

★9041★ **Be a Successful Writer: New Expanded Common Sense Program for Anyone Who Wants to Write**

Diamond Editions
2400 Kettner, Studio 233
San Diego, CA 92101
Ph: (619)237-8610

Carolan Gladden. 1995.

★9042★ **Book Publishing Career Directory**

Gale Research
835 Penobscot Bldg.
Detroit, MI 48226-4094
Ph: (313)961-2242   Fax: (313)961-6083
Fr: 800-877-GALE

Bradley Morgan. Fifth edition, 1992. $39.00. 292 pages. Features extensive listings of contacts and entry-level job opportunities at many book publishing firms. Includes articles by top professionals in the field and covers every area of book publishing, from editorial and sales to production and publicity.

★9043★ **Career Choices for the 90's for Students of Communications and Journalism**

Walker and Company
435 Hudson St.
New York, NY 10014
Ph: (212)727-8300   Fax: (212)727-0984
Fr: 800-289-2553

Prepared by the Career Associates staff. 1990. $8.95. 166 pages. Discusses alternatives for students of communications and journalism. Offers advice on how to break into the field and how to move up. Covers where and who the employers are, internship possibilities, and professional networking associations. Comprehensive guide to career and job search planning.

★9044★ **Career Choices for the 90's for Students of English**

Walker and Company
435 Hudson St.
New York, NY 10014
Ph: (212)727-8300   Fax: (212)727-0984
Fr: 800-289-2553

Prepared by the Career Associates staff. 1990. $8.95. 166 pages. Discusses alternatives for students of English. Offers advice on how to break into the field and how to move up. Covers where and who the employers are, internship possibilities, and professional networking associations. Comprehensive guide to career and job search planning.

★9045★ **Career Choices for the 90's for Students of History**

Walker and Company
435 Hudson St.
New York, NY 10014
Ph: (212)727-8300   Fax: (212)727-0984
Fr: 800-289-2553

Prepared by the Career Associates staff. 1990. $8.95. 166 pages. Discusses alternatives for students of history. Offers advice on how to break into the field and how to move up. Covers where and who the employers are, internship possibilities, and professional networking associations. Comprehensive guide to career and job search planning.

★9046★ **Career Choices for the 90's for Students of Political Science and Government**

Walker and Company
435 Hudson St.
New York, NY 10014
Ph: (212)727-8300   Fax: (212)727-0984
Fr: 800-289-2553

Prepared by the Career Associates staff. 1990. $8.95. 166 pages. Discusses alternatives for students of political science and government. Offers advice on how to break into the field and how to move up. Covers where and who the employers are, internship possibilities, and professional networking associations. Comprehensive guide to career and job search planning.

★9047★ Career Information Center

Macmillan Publishing Co.
200 Old Tappan Rd.
Old Tappan, NJ 07675
Ph: (609)461-6500   Fr: 800-223-2336

Visual Education Center Staff. Fifth edition, 1992. $229.00. This 13-volume set profiles over 600 occupations. Each occupational profile describes job duties, educational requirements, how to get the job, advancement possibilities, employment outlook, working conditions, earnings and benefits, and where to write for more information.

★9048★ Career Opportunities in Art

Facts on File, Inc.
11 Penn Plaza, 15th Fl.
New York, NY 10001-2006
Ph: (212)967-8800   Fax: 800-678-3633
Fr: 800-322-8755

Susan H. Haubenstock and David Joselit. Revised edition, 1994. $29.95; $15.95 (paper). 208 pages. This book profiles seventy-five jobs that can be found in the art field. Each profile includes a career description, career ladder, employment and advancement prospects, education, experience and skills required, salary range, and tips for entry into the field.

★9049★ Career Opportunities for Writers

Facts on File, Inc.
11 Penn Plaza, 15th Fl.
New York, NY 10001-2006
Ph: (212)967-8800   Fax: 800-678-3633
Fr: 800-322-8755

Rosemary Guiley. Third edition, 1995. $29.95; $15.95 (paper). Describes more than 100 jobs in eight major fields, offering such details as duties, salaries, perquisites, employment and advancement opportunities, organizations to join, and opportunities for women and minorities.

★9050★ Careers in Advertising

VGM Career Horizons
4255 W. Touhy Ave.
Lincolnwood, IL 60646-1975
Ph: (847)679-5500   Fax: (847)679-2494
Fr: 800-323-4900

S. William Pattis. Second edition, 1996. $17.95; $13.95 (paper). 192 pages. Explains the role of the media in advertising, personal characteristics needed to succeed in this field, educational requirements, and related jobs. Covers copy writing, art, design, account management, media, and research. Gives job hunting tips.

★9051★ Careers for Bookworms and Other Literary Types

VGM Career Horizons
4255 W. Touhy Ave.
Lincolnwood, IL 60646-1975
Ph: (847)679-5500   Fax: (847)679-2494
Fr: 800-323-4900

Marjorie Eberts and Margaret Gisler. Second edition, 1995. $14.95; $9.95 (paper). Details opportunities in education, publishing, libraries, journalism, think tanks, museums, film, broadcasting, the public sector, and other fields. Helps job seekers identify reading, writing, or research jobs.

★9052★ Careers in Communications

VGM Career Horizons
4255 W. Touhy Ave.
Lincolnwood, IL 60646-1975
Ph: (847)679-5500   Fax: (847)679-2494
Fr: 800-323-4900

Shonan Noronha. 1994. $17.95; $13.95 (paper). 176 pages. Examines the fields of journalism, photography, radio, television, film, public relations, and advertising. Gives concrete details on job locations and how to secure a job. Suggests many resources for job hunting.

★9053★ Careers for Culture Lovers and Other Artsy Types

VGM Career Horizons
4255 W. Touhy Ave.
Lincolnwood, IL 60646-1975
Ph: (847)679-5500   Fax: (847)679-2494
Fr: 800-323-4900

Marjorie Eberts and Margaret Gisler. 1994. $14.95; $9.95 (paper). Describes how to get work in a variety of fields related to art and culture. Opportunities include picture framer, curator, art restorer, symphony manager, disk jockey, music reviewer, dance teacher, choreographer, costume designer, theater manager, light designer, drama teacher, bookstore owner, interior decorator, antique store owner, and others.

★9054★ Careers in Health Care

VGM Career Horizons
4255 W. Touhy Ave.
Lincolnwood, IL 60646-1975
Ph: (847)679-5500   Fax: (847)679-2494
Fr: 800-323-4900

Barbara M. Swanson. 1995. $17.95; $13.95 (paper). Describes job duties, work settings, salaries, licensing and certification requirements, educational preparation, and future outlook. Gives ideas on how to secure a job.

★9055★ Careers for Sports Nuts and Other Athletic Types

VGM Career Horizons
4255 W. Touhy Ave.
Lincolnwood, IL 60646-1975
Ph: (847)679-5500   Fax: (847)679-2494
Fr: 800-323-4900

William Ray Heitzmann. 1994. Profiles sports enthusiasts who make their livings in a variety of ways in the world of sports. Explores opportunities in such sports-related fields as sports marketing, sports equipment sales, sports writing and photography, and sports management.

★9056★ Careers for Travel Buffs and Other Restless Types

VGM Career Horizons
4255 W. Touhy Ave.
Lincolnwood, IL 60646-1975
Ph: (847)679-5500   Fax: (847)679-2494
Fr: 800-323-4900

Paul Plawin. 1992. $14.95; $9.95 (paper). Includes a variety of travel and open-road careers, such as travel writers and photographers, tour bus drivers, entertainers, cruise line staff, travel agents, tour guides, sports writers, sales, the military, trucking, and meeting planning.

★9057★ Editorial Freelancing: A Practical Guide

Aletheia Publications
38-15 Corporal Kennedy St.
Bayside, NY 11361
Ph: (718)281-0403

Trumbull Rogers. 1995.

★9058★ The Encyclopedia of Career Choices for the 1990s: Guide to Entry-Level Jobs

Perigree Books
The Berkley Publishing Group
PO Box 506
East Rutherford, NJ 07073
Ph: (201)933-9292   Fr: 800-223-0510

Career Associates Staff. 1992. $19.95. 862 pages. Describes 500 entry-level careers in a variety of industries. Presents qualifications required, working conditions, salary, internships, and professional associations.

★9059★ Exploring High-Tech Careers

Rosen Publishing Group, Inc.
29 E. 21st St.
New York, NY 10010
Ph: (212)777-3017   Fax: (212)777-0277
Fr: 800-237-9932

Scott Southworth. Revised edition, 1993. $14.95; $9.95 (paper). 118 pages. Gives an orientation to the field of high technology and high-tech jobs. Describes educational preparation and job hunting. Includes a glossary and bibliography.

★9060★ Flying High in Travel

John Wiley and Sons
605 3rd Ave.
New York, NY 10158
Ph: (212)850-6000   Fr: 800-225-5945

Karen Rubin. Second edition, 1992. $19.95. 336 pages. A guide to careers and job hunting in the travel industry. Describes the many job opportunities available, from writing to hotel management to law. Includes information on educational preparation, training, and job hunting.

★9061★ A Guide to Careers in Science Writing

National Association of Science Writers, Inc.
PO Box 294
Greenlawn, NY 11740
Ph: (516)757-5664

Booklet. Free. 12 pages. Offers guidance on finding a job.

★9062★ Guide to Careers in World Affairs

Impact Publications
9104-N Manassas Dr.
Manassas Park, VA 22111-5211
Ph: (703)361-7300   Fax: (703)335-9486

Foreign Policy Association. 1993. $14.95. 331 pages. Describes jobs in business, government, and nonprofit organizations. Explains the methods and credentials required to secure a job in many fields, including international law and journalism. Contains sections on internships and graduate programs.

★9063★ **The Harvard Guide to Careers in the Mass Media**

Bob Adams, Inc.
260 Center St.
Holbrook, MA 02343
Ph: (617)767-8100   Fax: (617)767-0994
Fr: 800-872-5627

John Noble. 1989. $7.95. 202 pages. Each section of the book evaluates one media profession in depth and contains an industry profile, a career profile that describes positions available in that area, information about current salary ranges, industry-specific job-hunting tips and strategies, and a case study outlining the methods that were used in a successful job hunt.

★9064★ **How to Make a Living as a Travel Writer**

Marlowe & Company
632 Broadway, 7th Fl.
New York, NY 10012
Ph: (212)460-5742   Fax: (212)460-5796

Farewell. 1994. $9.95 (paper).

★9065★ **Jobs for English Majors and Other Smart People**

Peterson's
PO Box 2123
Princeton, NJ 08543-2123
Ph: (609)243-9111   Fax: (609)243-9150
Fr: 800-338-3282

John L. Munschauer. Third edition, 1991. $11.95. 174 pages. Shows job seekers how to position themselves in the marketplace and how to demonstrate the ability to meet the needs of prospective employers.

★9066★ **Liberal Arts Jobs: What They Are and How to Get Them**

Peterson's
PO Box 2123
Princeton, NJ 08543-2123
Ph: (609)243-9111   Fax: (609)243-9150
Fr: 800-338-3282

Burton Jay Nadler. Second edition, 1989. $9.95. 153 pages. Presents a list of the top 20 fields for liberal arts majors, covering more than 300 job opportunities. Discusses strategies for going after those jobs, including guidance on the language of a successful job search, informational interviews, and making networking work.

★9067★ **Magazines Career Directory**

Gale Research
835 Penobscot Bldg.
Detroit, MI 48226-4094
Ph: (313)961-2242   Fax: (313)961-6083
Fr: 800-877-GALE

Bradley Morgan. Fifth edition, 1993. $39.00. Features extensive listings of contacts and entry-level job opportunities at many magazine publishing organizations. Includes articles by top professionals in the field on some of the industry's varied career paths: art, editorial, sales, and business management.

★9068★ **Newspapers Career Directory**

Gale Research
835 Penobscot Bldg.
Detroit, MI 48226-4094
Ph: (313)961-2242   Fax: (313)961-6083
Fr: 800-877-GALE

Bradley Morgan. Fourth edition, 1993. $39.00. 344 pages. Features extensive listings of contacts and entry-level job opportunities at many newspaper organizations. Focuses on each area of the business, from reporting and editorial to sales and marketing to promotion and production.

★9069★ **Newspapers, Diversity, and You**

Dow Jones Newspaper Fund
PO Box 300
Princeton, NJ 08543-0300
Ph: (609)452-2820   Fr: 800-369-3863

Updated biennially. Free. 71 pages. Provides information to minorities on how to prepare for a career in journalism. Includes list of newspaper groups that actively recruit minorities.

★9070★ **100 Best Careers for the Year 2000**

Prentice Hall General Reference
15 Columbus Cir.
New York, NY 10023
Ph: (212)373-8500   Fr: 800-223-2348

Shelly Field. 1992. $15.00 (paper). Covers 100 of the fastest growing jobs. The publication is divided into 11 general employment sections. Specific careers are covered within each section. Provides job description, responsibilities, employment opportunities, earnings, education and training, advancement opportunities, and experience and qualifications for each occupation.

★9071★ **Opportunities in High Tech Careers**

VGM Career Horizons
4255 W. Touhy Ave.
Lincolnwood, IL 60646-1975
Ph: (847)679-5500   Fax: (847)679-2494
Fr: 800-323-4900

Gary D. Golter and Deborah Yanuck. 1995. $14.95; $11.95 (paper). 160 pages. Explores high technology careers. Describes job opportunities, how to make a career decision, how to prepare for high technology jobs, job hunting techniques, and future trends.

★9072★ **Opportunities in Journalism Careers**

VGM Career Horizons
4255 W. Touhy Ave.
Lincolnwood, IL 60646-1975
Ph: (847)679-5500   Fax: (847)679-2494
Fr: 800-323-4900

Jim Patten and Donald L. Ferguson. 1993. $14.95; $11.95 (paper). 160 pages. Outlines opportunities in every field of journalism, including newspaper reporting and editing, magazine and book publishing, corporate communications, advertising and public relations, freelance writing, and teaching. Covers how to prepare for and enter each field, outlining responsibilities, salaries, benefits, and job outlook for each specialty. Illustrated.

★9073★ **Opportunities in Magazine Publishing Careers**

VGM Career Horizons
4255 W. Touhy Ave.
Lincolnwood, IL 60646-1975
Ph: (847)679-5500   Fax: (847)679-2494
Fr: 800-323-4900

S. William Pattis. 1992. $14.95; $11.95 (paper). 160 pages. Covers the scope of magazine publishing and addresses how to identify and pursue available positions. Illustrated.

★9074★ **Opportunities in Newspaper Publishing Careers**

VGM Career Horizons
4255 W. Touhy Ave.
Lincolnwood, IL 60646-1975
Ph: (847)679-5500   Fax: (847)679-2494
Fr: 800-323-4900

John Tebbel. 1989. $14.95; $11.95 (paper). 160 pages. Tells how to land a newspaper job, describing editorial and noneditorial positions at big city and small city papers and syndicated wire services. Career preparation chapters address the need to anticipate changing newspaper technology while acquiring fundamental news skills. Illustrated.

★9075★ **Opportunities in Publishing Careers**

VGM Career Horizons
4255 W. Touhy Ave.
Lincolnwood, IL 60646-1975
Ph: (847)679-5500   Fax: (847)679-2494
Fr: 800-323-4900

Robert A. Carter and S. William Pattis. 1995. $11.95 paperback. $14.95 hardcover. 160 pages. Covers all positions in book and magazine publishing, including new opportunities in multimedia publishing.

★9076★ **Opportunities in Technical Writing and Communications Careers**

VGM Career Horizons
4255 W. Touhy Ave.
Lincolnwood, IL 60646-1975
Ph: (847)679-5500   Fax: (847)679-2494
Fr: 800-323-4900

Jay Gould and Wayne Losano. 1994. $14.95; $11.95 (paper). 160 pages. Provides advice on acquiring a position in medical, engineering, pharmaceutical, and other technical fields. Illustrated.

★9077★ **Opportunities in Writing Careers**

VGM Career Horizons
4255 W. Touhy Ave.
Lincolnwood, IL 60646-1975
Ph: (847)679-5500   Fax: (847)679-2494
Fr: 800-323-4900

Elizabeth Foote-Smith. 1989. $14.95; $11.95 (paper). 160 pages. Discusses opportunities in the print media, broadcasting, advertising or publishing. Business writing, public relations, and technical writing are among the careers covered. Contains bibliography and illustrations.

★9078★ Power Freelancing: Home-Based Careers for Writers, Designers, & Consultants

Mid-List Press
4324 12th Ave., S
Minneapolis, MN 55407-3218
Ph: (612)822-3733

George Sorenson. 1995. $14.95 (paper).

★9079★ Radio and Television Career Directory

Gale Research
835 Penobscot Bldg.
Detroit, MI 48226-4094
Ph: (313)961-2242   Fax: (313)961-6083
Fr: 800-877-GALE

Bradley Morgan. Second edition, 1993. $39.00. 334 pages. Features extensive listings of contacts and entry-level job opportunities. Provides information on internships and sources of help-wanted ads.

★9080★ Stein on Writing: A Master Editor of Some of the Most Successful Writers of Our Century Shares His Craft Techniques & Strategies

St. Martin's Press, Inc.
175 5th Ave., Rm. 1715
New York, NY 10010
Ph: (212)674-5151   Fax: (212)420-9314
Fr: 800-221-7945

Sol Stein. 1995.

★9081★ The Tech Writing Game

Facts on File, Inc.
11 Penn Plaza, 15th Fl.
New York, NY 10001-2006
Ph: (212)967-8800   Fax: 800-678-3633
Fr: 800-322-8755

Janet Van Wicklen. 1992. $22.95. 192 pages. Subtitled *A Comprehensive Career Guide for Aspiring Technical Writers*. Contains advice on how to break into the field and how to weigh the advantages and drawbacks of a staff position as opposed to freelancing.

★9082★ Technical Writing for Technicians: How to Build a Career As a Hardware Technical Writer

Contemax Publishers
17815 24th Ave., N.
Plymouth, MN 55447
Ph: (612)473-6436

Warren R. Freeman. 1995. $19.95 (paper).

★9083★ 30-Minute Writer: How to Write & Sell Short Pieces

Writer's Digest Books
1507 Dana Ave.
Cincinnati, OH 45207
Ph: (513)531-2690   Fax: (513)531-4082
Fr: 800-289-0963

Connie Emerson. 1993. $17.95.

★9084★ 30 Steps to Becoming a Writer & Getting Published

Writer's Digest Books
1507 Dana Ave.
Cincinnati, OH 45207
Ph: (513)531-2690   Fax: (513)531-4082
Fr: 800-289-0963

Scott Edelstein. 1993. $16.99.

★9085★ Where the Jobs Are: The Hottest Careers for the '90s

The Career Press, Inc.
3 Tice Rd.
PO Box 687
Franklin Lakes, NJ 07417
Ph: (201)848-0310   Fax: (201)848-1727
Fr: 800-237-3371

Joyce Hadley. Second edition, 1995. $9.99. 300 pages. Describes careers in fifteen general fields, from accounting to travel and hospitality.

★9086★ Writer's Northwest Handbook

Media Weavers
Blue Heron Publishing, Inc.
1738 NE 24th
Portland, OR 97212
Ph: (503)771-5166

Biennial, March of odd years. $18.95. Covers Approximately 2,800 markets for writers, including newspapers, magazines, and book publishers in Alaska, British Columbia, Idaho, Montana, Oregon, and Washington; approximately 500 workshops, conference, and related events. Entries include: Company name, address, phone, names and titles of key personnel, types of material solicited, form of reimbursement, rights purchased. Arrangement: Alphabetical. Indexes: Geographical, subject.

EMPLOYMENT AGENCIES AND SEARCH FIRMS

★9087★ Amtec Engineering Corp.

2749 Saturn St.
Brea, CA 92621
Ph: (714)993-1900   Fax: (714)993-2419

Employment agency.

★9088★ Bert Davis Publishing Placement Consultants

485 Madison Ave., Ste. 14A
New York, NY 10017
Ph: (212)838-4000

Executive search firm.

★9089★ Blair Personnel of Parsippany, Inc.

1130 U.S. Hwy 46
Parsippany, NJ 07054-2158
Ph: (201)335-6150   Fax: (201)335-4657

Employment agency. Focuses on regular and temporary placement.

★9090★ Calvert Associates, Inc.

202 E. Washington St., Ste. 304
Ann Arbor, MI 48104
Ph: (313)769-5413

Employment agency.

★9091★ Career Development Services

14 Franklin St., Ste. 1200
Rochester, NY 14604
Ph: (716)325-2275   Fax: (716)325-2133

Employment agency.

★9092★ Chaloner Associates

PO Box 1097, Back Bay Station
Boston, MA 02117
Ph: (617)451-5170   Fax: (617)451-8160

Executive search firm.

★9093★ Creative Options, Inc.

50 Washington St.
Norwalk, CT 06854
Ph: (203)854-9393

Employment agency and search firm. Places staff on a regular and temporary basis.

★9094★ Editorial Services of New England

126 Prospect St.
Cambridge, MA 02139
Ph: (617)254-2828

Provides placement on a temporary basis to a variety of industries.

★9095★ Esquire Personnel Services, Inc.

222 S. Riverside Plaza, Ste. 320
Chicago, IL 60606-5804
Ph: (312)648-4600   Fax: (312)648-4637

Employment agency.

★9096★ Howard-Sloan Associates, Inc.

353 Lexington Ave., 11th Fl.
New York, NY 10016
Ph: (212)661-5250   Fax: (212)687-5760
Fr: 800-221-1326

Executive search firm.

★9097★ Industrial Recruiters Associates, Inc.

630 Oakwood Ave., Ste. 318
West Hartford, CT 06110
Ph: (203)953-3643

Employment agency.

★9098★ The Pathfinder Group

295 Danbury Rd.
Wilton, CT 06897-3095
Ph: (203)834-2467

Employment agency. Executive search firm. Recruits staff in a variety of fields.

★9099★ Remer-Ribolow and Associates

230 Park Ave., Ste. 222
New York, NY 10169
Ph: (212)808-0580

Employment agency.

★9100★ **Technical Talent Locators Ltd.**
8850 Stanford Blvd., Ste. 3400
Columbia, MD 21045
Ph: (410)995-6051 Fax: (410)995-6281
Executive search firm.

OTHER SOURCES

★9101★ *American Almanac of Jobs and Salaries 1994-95*
Avon Books
1350 Avenue of the Americas, 2nd Fl.
New York, NY 10019
Ph: (212)261-6800 Fr: 800-238-0658
John Wright. Revised edition, 1993. $17.00. 704 pages. This is a comprehensive guide to the wages of hundreds of occupations in a wide variety of industries and organizations.

★9102★ **American Society of Business Press Editors (ASBPE)**
376 E. St. Charles Rd.
Lombard, IL 60148
Ph: (708)889-4141
Members: Executive, managing, and working editors of business, trade, and technical publications. **Purpose:** Serves as forum for exchange of ideas; carries out educational program with journalism societies and schools of journalism. **Activities:** Conducts research on editorial problems and practices. Provides educational events, annual contest, and program of discounts for members.

★9103★ **American Society of Magazine Editors (ASME)**
919 3rd Ave.
New York, NY 10022
Ph: (212)872-3700 Fax: (212)906-0128
Purpose: Professional organization of chief and senior magazine editors. **Activities:** Sponsors annual editorial internship program for college juniors.

★9104★ **Associated Business Writers of America (ABWA)**
1450 S. Havana, Ste. 424
Aurora, CO 80012
Ph: (303)751-7844 Fax: (303)751-8593
Members: Professional full- or part-time freelance writers who specialize in business writing. **Purpose:** Objective is to serve as a marketplace whereby business editors can easily locate competent writing talent. **Activities:** Establishes communication among editors and writers.

★9105★ **Association for Business Communication (ABC)**
University of North Texas
College of Bus.
Department of Management
Denton, TX 76203
Ph: (817)565-4423 Fax: (817)565-4930
Members: College teachers of business communication; management consultants in business communications; training directors and correspondence supervisors of business firms, direct mail copywriters, public relations writers, and others interested in communication for business. **Activities:** Sponsors research programs.

★9106★ **Copywriter's Council of America (CCA)**
Communications Bldg. 102
7 Putter Ln., Box 102
Middle Island, NY 11953-0102
Ph: (516)924-8555 Fax: (516)924-3890
Members: Advertising copywriters, marketing and public relations consultants, copyeditors, proofreaders, and other individuals involved in print, radio, broadcast, video, and telecommunications. **Purpose:** Provides freelance work; acts as agent for members; negotiates on members' behalf. Serves as a forum for professional and social contact between freelance communications professionals. **Activities:** Offers courses on copywriting, direct marketing, mail order, publishing screenplays, and how to get published. Conducts charitable programs. Maintains speakers' bureau, hall of fame, and word processing consultation service.

★9107★ **Council of Writers Organizations (CWO)**
972 Valley Rd.
Marquette, MI 49855
Ph: (906)249-3156
Purpose: Serves as an umbrella agency for organizations representing writers. Provides a means of sharing information among the organizations and their members as well as a voice for professional writers. Promotes and monitors pertinent legislation.

★9108★ *The Fictional Writer's Primer: And How to Become a Rich & Famous Author Without Ever Really Writing a Book*
Rabid Rhino Publishing
PO Box 5013
Huntington, IN 46750
Ph: (219)356-3091
Darvin P. Harfield. 1994. $6.95 (paper).

★9109★ *Freelance Writing Business Guide*
Entrepreneur, Inc.
2392 Morse Ave.
Box 19787
Irvine, CA 92713-9787
Fax: (714)851-9088 Fr: 800-421-2300
$79.50 (includes business guide and software). A step-by-step guide to starting a freelance writing business, as well as information on market potential, profits, advertising and promotion, and related topics.

★9110★ *How to Write Your Novel*
Writer, Inc.
120 Boylston St.
Boston, MA 02116
Ph: (617)423-3157 Fax: (617)423-2168
Margaret Chittenden. 1995. $12.00 (paper).

★9111★ *How You Can Make $25,000 a Year Writing (No Matter Where You Live)*
Writer's Digest Books
1507 Dana Ave.
Cincinnati, OH 45207
Ph: (513)531-2690 Fr: 800-289-0963
Nancy Edmonds Hanson. 1990. $12.95; $6.95 (paper). 224 pages. Discussion of the freelance market for writing.

★9112★ *Magazine & Bookseller—Who's Who of the Publishing & Distribution Industry Issue*
North American Publishing Co.
322 8th Ave.
New York, NY 10001
Ph: (212)886-9657 Fax: (212)620-7335
Annual, December. $49.00, included in subscription, per year. Publication includes: Lists of magazine publishers, paperback publishers, national distributors, industry services associations and magazine paperback wholesalers. Most listings include company name, address, phone, and key personnel; other details such as magazine frequency, name of distributor, cover price or distributor's number of titles carried may also be given. Arrangement: Classified by type of magazine or line of business.

★9113★ *National Directory of Arts Internships*
National Network for Artist Placement
935 W. Ave. 37
Los Angeles, CA 90065
Ph: (213)222-4035 Fax: (213)222-4035
Biennial, odd years. $40.00, postpaid; payment with order. Covers Approximately 2,000 internship opportunities in dance, music, theater, art, design, film, and video. Entries include: Name of sponsoring organization, address, name of contact; description of positions available, eligibility requirements, stipend or salary (if any), application procedures. Arrangement: Classified by discipline, then geographical.

★9114★ *Resumes for Communications Careers*
VGM Career Horizons
4255 W. Touhy Ave.
Lincolnwood, IL 60646-1975
Ph: (847)679-5500 Fax: (847)679-2494
Fr: 800-323-4900
1991. $9.95. 160 pages. Includes sample resumes representing journalists, writers, publicists, and other communications specialists.

★9115★ *Start and Run a Profitable Freelance Writing Business: Your Step-by-Step Business Plan*
Self-Counsel Press, Inc.
1704 N. State St.
Bellingham, WA 98225
Ph: (360)676-4530 Fax: (360)676-4549
Fr: 800-663-3007
Christine Adamec. 1994. $14.95 (paper).

★9116★ Student Guide to Mass Media Internships

Intern Research Group
Box 52, Regent Hall
University of Colorado
Boulder, CO 80309
Ph: (303)442-8340

Annual, latest edition 1995. $35.00, payment with order; $40.00, billed. Covers about 10,000 internships offered by 2,700 newspapers, radio and television stations, cable television companies, magazines, advertising agencies, and other firms. Entries include: Organization name, address, type and number of internships offered, eligibility requirements, application deadline, salary or other stipend offered, name and title of contact; many listings also include description of intern's duties. Arrangement: Classified by type of medium, then geographical.

★9117★ Women in Communications

10605 Judicial Dr., Ste. A4
Fairfax, VA 22030-5167
Ph: (703)359-9000   Fax: (703)359-0603

Members: Professional association of journalism and communications.

★9118★ Writer's Yellow Pages

Steve Davis Publishing
Box 190831
Dallas, TX 75204
Ph: (214)954-4469

$19.95. Covers over 23,000 companies and freelance professionals providing products or services of use to writers; includes publishers, producers, editors, ghost writers, researchers, illustrators, photographers, typesetters, bookstores and distributors, libraries, media contacts, relevant computer software and equipment suppliers, on-line databases, and writers' organizations. Entries include: Company, organization, or personal name, address, phone. Arrangement: CLS product or service. Indexes: Product/service, subject.

Part Two:
Sources of Essential Job-Hunting Information

Includes reference works; newspapers, magazines, and journals; audio/visual resources; online and database services; software; and other sources about the following topics:

Broad Sources of Job-Hunting Information

REFERENCE WORKS

★9119★ Adventure Careers

The Career Press, Inc.
3 Tice Rd.
PO Box 687
Franklin Lakes, NJ 07417
Ph: (201)848-0310   Fax: (201)848-1727
Fr: 800-237-3371

Susan Angle and Alex Hiam. Third edition, 1995. $11.99. 288 pages. Contains practical how-to information, lists of contacts and phone numbers, and first-hand experiences from a number of adventurers who tread "off the beaten career path".

★9120★ American Directory of Job and Labor Market Information

Career Communications
PO Box 169
Harleysville, PA 19438

$29.95. Covers resources providing information on jobs and labor markets, including state and federal government personnel departments, job information centers, employment service centers, databases, libraries, and publications. Arrangement: Classified by type of resource.

★9121★ The Best Home-Based Businesses for the 90s

G.P. Putnam's Sons
Putnam Berkley Group
200 Madison Ave.
New York, NY 10016
Ph: (212)951-8400   Fr: 800-631-8571

Paul Edwards and Sarah Edwards. Second edition, 1994. $12.95. 400 pages. Profiles 95 businesses and careers that can be conducted from one's home. Lists sources of additional information.

★9122★ The Career Fitness Program: Exercising Your Options

Gorsuch Scarisbrick, Publishers
8233 Via Paseo del Norte, Ste. F-400
Scottsdale, AZ 85258
Ph: (602)991-7881

Diane Sukiennik et al. Fourth edition, 1995. $16.00. 288 pages. Textbook, with second half devoted to the job search process.

★9123★ Career Information Center

Macmillan Publishing Co.
200 Old Tappan Rd.
Old Tappan, NJ 07675
Ph: (609)461-6500   Fr: 800-223-2336

Visual Education Center Staff. Fifth edition, 1992. $229.00. This 13-volume set profiles over 600 occupations. Each occupational profile describes job duties, educational requirements, how to get the job, advancement possibilities, employment outlook, working conditions, earnings and benefits, and where to write for more information.

★9124★ Change Your Job, Change Your Life: High Impact Strategies for Finding Great Jobs in the 90's

Impact Publications
9104-N Manassas Dr.
Manassas Park, VA 22111-5211
Ph: (703)361-7300   Fax: (703)335-9486

Ronald Krannich. Fourth edition, 1994. $14.95. 368 pages. Details trends in the marketplace, how to identify opportunities, how to retrain for them, and how to land jobs. Includes a chapter on starting a business. Contains index, bibliography, and illustrations.

★9125★ Chronicle Career Index

Chronicle Guidance Publications, Inc.
PO Box 1190
Moravia, NY 13118
Ph: (315)497-0330   Fax: (315)497-3359
Fr: 800-622-7284

Annual, September. $14.25, plus $1.43 shipping. Covers over 500 government agencies, nonprofit organizations, trade associations, and other groups that offer occupational and educational guidance materials. Entries include: Source name, address, materials offered, with brief description and price. Arrangement: Alphabetical. Indexes: Occupation/profession, subject, organization name.

★9126★ College Placement Council Directory: Who's Who in Career Planning, Placement, and Recruitment

College Placement Council (CPC)
62 Highland Ave.
Bethlehem, PA 18017
Ph: (610)868-1421   Fax: (610)868-0208
Fr: 800-544-5272

Annual, January. $47.95, plus $4.50 shipping. Covers about 2,400 college and university offices concerned with securing employment for graduates and about 2,300 companies with staff assigned to recruiting and hiring college graduates. Entries include: For colleges: college name and address; names, titles, phone, fax, and e-mail addresses of career planning and placement personnel; interview dates for undergraduates and graduates; months of graduation; whether alumni placement is also handled, student enrollment (including minority data), and dates of career/job fairs. For employers: company name; names, addresses, phone, and fax of recruitment staff; names of secondary contacts; nature of business; number of employees. Arrangement: Colleges are geographical; employers are alphabetical. Indexes: Institutional name, personal name (college personnel); geographical, personal name (in company recruitment).

★9127★ Coming Alive from Nine to Five

Mayfield Publishing
1280 Villa St.
Mountain View, CA 94041
Ph: (415)960-3222   Fr: 800-433-1279

Betty N. Michelozzi. Fourth edition, 1992. $19.95. 294 pages. In addition to general job-hunting advice, provides special information for women, young adults, minorities, older workers, and persons with handicaps.

★9128★ Complete Job and Career Handbook: 101 Ways to Get from Here to There

Garrett Park Press
PO Box 190F
Garrett Park, MD 20896
Ph: (301)946-2553

$15.00. Publication includes: Lists of organizations that may be of assistance to persons pursuing a career or looking for a job.

Principal content of publication is suggestions and techniques for finding a job or advancing a career. Entries include: Organization name, address, description. Arrangement: Alphabetical within topical sections. Indexes: Product/service, organization name, subject.

★9129★ **Dr. Job's Complete Career Guide: Advice for Getting Ahead in Your Career**

NTC Publishing Group
4255 W. Touhy Ave.
Lincolnwood, IL 60646-1975
Ph: (847)679-5500   Fax: (847)679-2494
Fr: 800-323-4900

Sandra Pesmen. 1995. $14.95 (paper).

★9130★ **Encyclopedia of Careers and Vocational Guidance**

J. G. Ferguson Publishing Co.
200 W. Monroe, Ste. 250
Chicago, IL 60606
Ph: (312)580-5480

William E. Hopke. Ninth edition, 1993. $129.95; $199.95 (CD-ROM). Four-volume set that profiles 900 occupations and describes job trends in 71 industries. Includes career description, educational requirements, history of the job, methods of entry, advancement, employment outlook, earnings, conditions of work, social and psychological factors, and sources of further information. Contains career and employment information for this field.

★9131★ **The Enhanced Guide for Occupational Exploration**

American Guidance Service (AGS)
4201 Woodland Rd.
PO Box 99
Circle Pines, MN 55014-1796
Fax: (612)786-9077   Fr: 800-328-2560

Marilyn Maze. $29.95 (paper). Provides descriptions for 2500 jobs. Each description includes skills, abilities, academic and physical requirements, work environment, salary, and outlook. Contains indices to career alternatives based on interests, skills, industry, and education.

★9132★ **From Campus to Corporation**

The Career Press, Inc.
3 Tice Rd.
PO Box 687
Franklin Lakes, NJ 07417
Ph: (201)848-0310   Fax: (201)848-1727
Fr: 800-237-3371

Stephen Strasser and John Sena. Second edition, 1993. $10.95. 192 pages. Helps jobseekers negotiate the obstacles from classroom to career and beyond.

★9133★ **Getting Hired in the '90s**

Dearborn Trade
155 N. Wacker Dr.
Chicago, IL 60606
Fax: (312)836-1146   Fr: 800-245-2665

Vickie Spina. $15.95 (paper).

★9134★ **Graduating Into the Nineties: Getting the Most Out of Your First Job After College**

Farrar, Straus & Giroux, Inc.
19 Union Sq., W.
New York, NY 10003
Ph: (212)741-6900   Fax: (212)633-9385
Fr: 800-788-6262

Carol Carter. 1993. $10.00.

★9135★ **The Hidden Job Market: A Job Seeker's Guide to America's 2,000 Little-Known, Fastest-Growing High-Tech Companies**

Peterson's Guides, Inc.
202 Carnegie Center
PO Box 2123
Princeton, NJ 08543-2123
Ph: (609)243-9111   Fax: (609)243-9150
Fr: 800-338-3282

Annual, October. $16.95. Covers Approximately 2,000 technology firms with under 1,000 employees, which have added the most employees in the survey year. Entries include: Company name, address, phone, fax, name and title of contact, number of employees, year founded, number of employees added in last year, percentage of growth, line of business. Arrangement: Geographical by state, then by area code. Indexes: Alphabetical by industry.

★9136★ **High-Impact Telephone Networking for Job Hunters**

Bob Adams, Inc.
260 Center St.
Holbrook, MA 02343
Ph: (617)767-8100   Fax: (617)767-0994
Fr: 800-872-5627

Howard Armstrong. 1992. $6.95. 132 pages. Examines the challenges associated with phone networking, shows the reader how to use "positive errors" to generate referrals, and offers hints on how to deal with "getting the runaround". Includes advice on how to ask for the meeting and addresses long-distance job searches by phone.

★9137★ **Hot Tips, Sneaky Tricks and Last-Ditch Tactics**

John Wiley and Sons, Inc.
605 3rd Ave.
New York, NY 10158
Ph: (212)850-6000   Fr: 800-225-5945

Jeff B. Speck. 1989. $12.95. Subtitled: "An Insider's Guide to Getting Your First Corporate Job". Gives an inside glimpse of the recruiting process and provides tips on using this knowledge to get the interview or the job.

★9138★ **How to Get a Better Job Quick**

NAL-Dutton (Signet)
375 Hudson St.
New York, NY 10014-3657
Ph: (212)366-2000   Fr: 800-331-4624

Richard A. Payne. 1991. $5.99.

★9139★ **How to Get a Better Job in This Crazy World**

NAL-Dutton (Signet)
375 Hudson St.
New York, NY 10014-3657
Ph: (212)366-2000   Fr: 800-331-4624

Robert Half. 1994. $5.50. 256 pages.

★9140★ **How to Get a Good Job and Keep It**

VGM Career Horizons
4255 W. Touhy Ave.
Lincolnwood, IL 60646-1975
Ph: (847)679-5500   Fax: (847)679-2494
Fr: 800-323-4900

Deborah Perlmutter Bloch. 1993. $7.95. Aimed at the recent high school or college graduate, this guide provides advice on finding out about jobs, completing applications and resumes, and managing successful interviews.

★9141★ **How to Get Hired Today!**

VGM Career Horizons
4255 W. Touhy Ave.
Lincolnwood, IL 60646-1975
Ph: (847)679-5500   Fax: (847)679-2494
Fr: 800-323-4900

George E. Kent. 1991. $7.95. 128 pages. Directed at individuals who know the type of job they are looking for. Focuses the reader on activities that are likely to lead to a job and eliminates those that won't. Shows how to establish productive contacts and discover, evaluate, and pursue strong job leads.

★9142★ **How to Get Interviews from Classified Job Ads**

Impact Publications
9104-N Manassas Dr.
Manassas Park, VA 22111-5211
Ph: (703)361-7300   Fax: (703)335-9486

Kenton W. Elderkin. Second edition, 1993. $14.95. 270 pages. Outlines how to select and follow up ads to get the job. Includes unique ways to get interview offers and how to incorporate the use of a computer and a fax machine in arranging interviews. Illustrated.

★9143★ **How to Land a Better Job**

VGM Career Horizons
4255 W. Touhy Ave.
Lincolnwood, IL 60646-1975
Ph: (847)679-5500   Fax: (847)679-2494
Fr: 800-323-4900

Catherine S. Lott and Oscar C. Lott. Third edition, 1994. $8.95. 144 pages. Tells the job seeker how to enhance his or her credentials, overcome past weaknesses, uncover job leads, get appointments, organize an appealing resume, and score points in interviews. A special section devoted to getting a better job without changing companies covers the process of transferring departments and gives pointers on moving up to the boss's job.

★9144★ How to Locate Jobs and Land Interviews

The Career Press, Inc.
3 Tice Rd.
PO Box 687
Franklin Lakes, NJ 07417
Ph: (201)848-0310   Fax: (201)848-1727
Fr: 800-237-3371

Albert L. French. Second edition, 1993. $10.95. 192 pages. Shows readers how to tap into the unadvertised, hidden job market and guides them through the resume, cover letter, and interview preparation process.

★9145★ How to Market Your College Degree

VGM Career Horizons
4255 W. Touhy Ave.
Lincolnwood, IL 60646-1975
Ph: (847)679-5500   Fax: (847)679-2494
Fr: 800-323-4900

Dorothy Rogers and Craig Bettinson. 1992. $12.95. Provides a guide to self-marketing as a key component of an effective job search. Helps job seekers to develop a strategic marketing plan that targets niches with needs that match their skills, differentiate themselves from the competition by positioning themselves against other candidates, evaluate their potential worth from the employer's perspective, and manage their careers as they move up the career ladder or into another field.

★9146★ How to Move from College into a Secure Job

NTC Publishing Group
4255 W. Touhy Ave.
Lincolnwood, IL 60646-1975
Ph: (708)679-5500   Fax: (708)679-6375
Fr: 800-323-4900

Mary Dehner. 1993. $12.95 (paper).

★9147★ How to Win Your Job Search: National Edition

ACES-American Computerized Employment Service
PO Box 27907
Santa Ana, CA 92799-7907
Ph: (714)250-0221

1994. $49.95 (paper).

★9148★ I Got the Job!

Crisp Publications, Inc.
1200 Hamilton Ct.
Menlo Park, CA 94025
Ph: (415)323-6100   Fr: 800-442-7477

Elwood N. Chapman. Revised edition, 1992. $9.95. 64 pages. Provides case studies and demonstrates how to plan a targeted job search.

★9149★ Job Hotlines USA: A National Telephone Directory of Employer Joblines

Career Communications
PO Box 169
Harleysville, PA 19438

Published 1994. $24.95. Covers over 1,000 government agencies, hospitals, colleges, companies, and federal job information centers that have employment hotlines. Entries include: company name, address, voice telephone number, job hotline number, and industry classification.

★9150★ The Job Hunter's Catalog

John Wiley & Sons, Inc.
605 3rd Ave.
New York, NY 10158-0012
Ph: (212)850-6000   Fr: 800-225-5945

Peggy Schmidt. $10.95 (paper).

★9151★ The Job Hunter's Final Exam

Surrey Books, Inc.
230 E. Ohio St., Ste. 120
Chicago, IL 60611
Ph: (312)661-0050

Thomas Camden. Second edition, 1990. $18.95. 130 pages. Helps job seeker quiz self about resumes, interviews, and general job-hunting strategies.

★9152★ Job Hunting Made Easy

NTC Publishing Group
4255 W. Touhy Ave.
Lincolnwood, IL 60646-1975
Ph: (847)679-5500   Fax: (847)679-2494
Fr: 800-323-4900

1995. $6.95 (paper). Part of series for job hunters.

★9153★ Job Search: Career Planning Guidebook, Book II

Brooks/Cole Publishing Company
Marketing Dept.
511 Forest Lodge Rd.
Pacific Grove, CA 93950
Ph: (408)373-0728

Robert D. Lock. Second edition, 1992. $17.95. Assists the reader in a productive job search.

★9154★ Joyce Lain Kennedy's Career Book

VGM Career Horizons
4255 W. Touhy Ave.
Lincolnwood, IL 60646-1975
Ph: (847)679-5500   Fax: (847)679-2494
Fr: 800-323-4900

Joyce Lain Kennedy. Co-authored by Dr. Darryl Laramore. 1993. $29.95; $17.95 (paper). 448 pages. Guides the reader through the entire career-planning and job-hunting process. Addresses how to find the kinds of jobs available and what to do once the job is secured. Provides a number of case histories to give examples.

★9155★ Liberal Arts Jobs: What They Are and How to Get Them

Peterson's
PO Box 2123
Princeton, NJ 08543-2123
Ph: (609)243-9111   Fax: (609)243-9150
Fr: 800-338-3282

Burton Jay Nadler. Second edition, 1989. $9.95. 153 pages. Presents a list of the top 20 fields for liberal arts majors, covering more than 300 job opportunities. Discusses strategies for going after those jobs, including guidance on the language of a successful job search, informational interviews, and making networking work.

★9156★ Merchandising Your Job Talents

U.S. Government Printing Office
Superintendent of Documents
Washington, DC 20402
Ph: (202)512-1800

Booklet. $2.75. 21 pages. General advice for job seekers. Illustrated.

★9157★ Network Your Way to Job and Career Success

Consultants Bookstore
Templeton Rd.
Fitzwilliam, NH 03447
Ph: (603)585-6544   Fax: (603)585-9555
Fr: 800-531-0007

Ron Krannich and Caryl Krannich. 1989. $11.95. 180 pages. Based on a comprehensive career planning framework, each chapter outlines the best strategies for identifying, finding, and transforming networks to gather information and obtain advice and referrals that lead to job interviews and offers. Includes exercises, sample interviewing dialogues, and a directory of organizations for initiating and sustaining networking activities.

★9158★ The New Quick Job-Hunting Map

Ten Speed Press
PO Box 7123
Berkeley, CA 94707
Ph: (510)559-1600   Fax: (510)559-1629
Fr: 800-841-BOOK

Richard N. Bolles. 1990. $3.95. 64 pages. Trade version of "The Quick Job-Hunting Map" in "What Color Is Your Parachute?" Provides a personal blueprint for the job search.

★9159★ The 1996 What Color Is Your Parachute?

Ten Speed Press
PO Box 7123
Berkeley, CA 94707
Ph: (510)559-1600   Fax: (510)559-1629
Fr: 800-841-BOOK

Richard N. Bolles. 1995. $21.95; $14.95 (paper). 480 pages. Subtitled: "A Practical Manual for Job-Hunters and Career-Changers". One of the best-known works on job hunting, this book provides detailed and strategic advice on all aspects of the job search.

★9160★ Occupational Outlook Handbook

U.S. Bureau of Labor Statistics
2 Massachusetts Ave. NE
Washington, DC 20212
Ph: (202)606-5703

Biennial, May of even years. $26.00, hardcover; $23.00, softcover. Publication includes: List of over 100 state employment agencies and State Occupational Information Coordinating Committees (SOICC) that provide state and local job market and career information; various occupational organizations that provide career information on about 250 occupations. Entries include: For agencies and committees: agency or committee name, address, phone, director name. For organizations: organization name, address. Principal content of publication is profiles of various occupations, which include description of occupation, educational requirements, job outlook, and expected earnings. Arrangement: Agencies and committees are geographical; organizations are classified by occupation.

★9161★ **The Only Job Hunting Guide You'll Ever Need**

Simon and Schuster Trade/Fireside
Simon and Schuster Bldg.
1230 Avenue of the Americas
New York, NY 10020
Ph: (212)698-7290

Kathryn and Ross Petras. 1995. $15.00. Covers the full range of the job search process for job hunters and career switchers.

★9162★ **The Overnight Job Change Strategy**

Ten Speed Press
PO Box 7123
Berkeley, CA 94707
Ph: (510)559-1600   Fax: (510)559-1629
Fr: 800-841-BOOK

Donald Asher. 1993. $7.95. 96 pages. Subtitled "How to Plan a Comprehensive, Systematic Job Search in One Evening". Incorporates sales and marketing techniques into a six-stage job search process.

★9163★ **The Perfect Job Reference**

John Wiley and Sons
605 Third Ave.
New York, NY 10158-0012
Ph: (212)850-6000   Fr: 800-225-5945

Jeffrey G. Allen. $9.95. Step-by-step methods for securing a written or verbal recommendation.

★9164★ **The Practical Job Search Guide**

Ten Speed Press
PO Box 7123
Berkeley, CA 94707
Fax: (510)559-1629   Fr: 800-841-BOOK

Donna Ferris. 1995. $14.95 (paper). Includes action plan and workbook for job hunters.

★9165★ **Professional's Job Finder**

Planning/Communications
7215 Oak Ave.
River Forest, IL 60305-1935
Ph: (708)366-5200   Fr: (888)366-5200

Daniel Lauber. 1996. $36.95; $18.95 (paper). 520 pages. Covers 2600 sources. Discusses how to use sources of private sector job vacancies in a number of specialties and state-by-state, including job-matching services, job hotlines, specialty periodicals with job ads, salary surveys, and directories. Covers a variety of fields from health care to sales. Includes chapters on resume and cover letter preparation and interviewing.

★9166★ **The Right Place at the Right Time: Finding a Job in the 1990s**

Ten Speed Press
PO Box 7123
Berkeley, CA 94707
Ph: (510)559-1600   Fax: (510)559-1629
Fr: 800-841-BOOK

Robert G. Wegmann. 1990. $11.95. 192 pages. A comprehensive approach to career planning and job seeking developed to find the right job in the new economy.

★9167★ **Rites of Passage at $100,000-Plus: The Insider's Guide to Absolutely Everything About Executive Job-Changing**

Henry Holt
John Lucht. Revised edition, 1993. $29.95. 640 pages. Aimed at top executives, this book covers a range of topics from networking and personal contacts to direct mail, resumes, references, interviewing, and negotiating. Includes large section on dealing with recruiters.

★9168★ **Self-Help Job Search: Ten Easy Steps to Your Future**

JEM Job Educational Materials
PO Box 4356
West Covina, CA 91791-0356
Ph: (818)308-7642   Fax: (818)282-9558

Donald L. Wilkes. 1992. $12.95 (paper).

★9169★ **Skills in Action: A Job-Finding Workbook**

University of Akron
Adult Resource Ctr.
Akron, OH 44325

J.H. Selden. $5.50. 75 pages. Workbook format; aimed at job seekers looking for initial or transitional employment.

★9170★ **The Student's Guide to Finding a Superior Job**

Slawson Communications
PO Box 28459
San Diego, CA 92198-0459

William A. Cohen. Second edition, 1993. $9.95. 108 pages. Aimed at the new college graduate.

★9171★ **The Successful Job Search: A Step-by-Step Guide for a Successful Job Search in the 1990s**

Rogers Resource, Inc.
3737 Woodland Ave., Ste. 410
West Des Moines, IA 50266
Ph: (515)225-1650   Fax: (515)225-6835

Roxanne S. Rogers. 1993. $29.95 (paper).

★9172★ **Super Job Search: The Complete Manual for Job-Seekers and Career-Changers**

Jamenair Ltd.
PO Box 241957
Los Angeles, CA 90024-9757
Ph: (310)470-6688   Fax: (310)470-8106

Peter Studner. Second edition, 1995. $22.95. 352 pages. A step-by-step guidebook for getting a job, with sections on getting started, how to present accomplishments, networking strategies, telemarketing tips, and negotiating tactics.

★9173★ **Taking Charge of Your Career Direction**

Brooks/Cole Publishing Company
Marketing Dept.
511 Forest Lodge Rd.
Pacific Grove, CA 93950
Ph: (408)373-0728

Robert D. Lock. Second edition, 1992. $21.95. 377 pages. Provides guidance for the job search process.

★9174★ **300 New Ways to Get a Better Job**

Bob Adams, Inc.
260 Center St.
Holbrook, MA 02343
Ph: (617)767-8100   Fax: (617)767-0994
Fr: 800-872-5627

Eleanor Baldwin. 1991. $7.95. 384 pages. Advocates a job search approach designed to meet the changing nature of the job market.

★9175★ **The Very Quick Job Search: Get a Good Job in Less Time**

JIST Works, Inc.
720 N. Park Ave.
Indianapolis, IN 46202
Fr: 800-648-5478

J. Michael Farr. Second edition, 1995. $14.95 (paper).

★9176★ **Where the Jobs Are: The Hottest Careers for the '90s**

The Career Press, Inc.
3 Tice Rd.
PO Box 687
Franklin Lakes, NJ 07417
Ph: (201)848-0310   Fax: (201)848-1727
Fr: 800-237-3371

Joyce Hadley. Second edition, 1995. $9.99. 300 pages. Describes careers in fifteen general fields, from accounting to travel and hospitality.

★9177★ **Who's Hiring Who**

Ten Speed Press
PO Box 7123
Berkeley, CA 94707
Ph: (510)559-1600   Fax: (510)559-1629
Fr: 800-841-BOOK

Richard Lathrop. 1989. $9.95. 268 pages. Provides advice on finding a better job faster and at a higher rate of pay.

★9178★ **Work in the New Economy: Careers and Job Seeking into the 21st Century**

JIST Works
720 N. Park Ave.
Indianapolis, IN 46202
Ph: (317)264-3720   Fr: 800-648-5478

Robert G. Wegmann et al. Second edition, 1989. $15.95. 303 pages.

NEWSPAPERS, MAGAZINES, AND JOURNALS

★9179★ Career Opportunities News
Garrett Park Press
PO Box 190
Garrett Park, MD 20896-0190
Ph: (301)946-2553

Bimonthly. $30.00/year. Each issue covers such things as resources to job seekers, special opportunities for minorities, women's career notes, and the current outlook in various occupations. Cites free and inexpensive job-hunting materials and new reports and books.

★9180★ Careers Unlimited
Target Marketing Inc.
5 Victory Ln.
Liberty, MO 64068
Ph: (816)781-7557   Fax: (816)792-3892
                    Publication focusing on careers.

★9181★ Kennedy's Career Strategist
Career Strategies
714 Sheridan Rd.
Wilmette, IL 60091

Twelve issues/year. $59.00/year. Offers job search guidance.

★9182★ Managing Your Career
Dow Jones and Co.
PO Box 300
Princeton, NJ 08543
Ph: (609)520-4305

Quarterly. Career guidance magazine for college students.

★9183★ Occupational Outlook Quarterly
U.S. Government Printing Office
Superintendent of Documents
Washington, DC 20402-9322
Ph: (202)512-1800   Fax: (202)512-2250

Quarterly. $9.50/year. Magazine providing occupational and employment information.

★9184★ Self-Help Reporter
National Self-Help Clearinghouse (NSHC)
25 W. 43rd St., Rm. 620
New York, NY 10036-7406
Ph: (212)354-8525   Fax: (212)642-1956

Quarterly. Newsletter.

AUDIO/VISUAL RESOURCES

★9185★ Career Assessment Video
Careers, Inc.
PO Box 135
Largo, FL 34649-0135
Ph: (813)584-7333   Fr: 800-726-0441

Video, software, test booklet, and worksheet. $395.00 (available in Apple, IBM, or Macintosh versions). Includes 40 minute live action video covering 100 occupational situations. Software management system allows on-site scoring of test results.

★9186★ Career Assessment Video
Cambridge Career Products
PO Box 2153
Dept. CC15
Charleston, WV 25328-2153
Ph: (304)744-9323   Fax: (304)744-9351
Fr: 800-468-4227

Video and software. $395.00. Available in Apple II or IBM versions. A group administered assessment which addresses 12 major worker trait clusters in a video presentation. Can be used in conjunction with state career information systems.

★9187★ The Career Coach
Kuselias Enterprises, Inc.
91 State St.
North Haven, CT 06473
Ph: (203)469-6700   Fr: 800-237-8562

Set of 6 audiocassettes. 1995. $39.95 plus $4.95 shipping and handling. Includes 100-page workbook. This step-by-step audio program helps job seekers decide on a career goal and then achieve it.

★9188★ Career Connections Video Series
Cambridge Career Products
PO Box 2153
Dept. CC15
Charleston, WV 25328-2153
Ph: (304)744-9323   Fax: (304)744-9351
Fr: 800-468-4227

Series of six videos. 1993. $219.95/set. $39.95/each. 15-20 minutes. Each video contains interviews with workers and on-the-job footage. Titles include Graphic Design, Welding, Electrician, Plumber, Pipefitter, and HVAC.

★9189★ Career Exploration: A Job Seeker's Guide to the OOH, DOT, and GOE
Cambridge Career Products
PO Box 2153
Dept. CC15
Charleston, WV 25328-2153
Ph: (304)744-9323   Fax: (304)744-9351
Fr: 800-468-4227

Video. $89.00. 21 minutes. Demonstrates four ways of finding information about careers.

★9190★ Career Exploration Video Series
Chronicle Guidance
66 Aurora St.
PO Box 1190
Moravia, NY 13118-1190
Ph: (315)497-0330   Fax: (315)497-3359
Fr: 800-622-7284

Series of 5 videos. Appalachia Educational Laboratory. 1993. $389.00/set. $95.00/each. 13-22 minutes each. Introduces career exploration concepts and vocabulary for middle school students through young adults. Five titles cover your future, your interests, your aptitudes, your temperaments, and educational planning.

★9191★ Career Self-Assessment: Where Do You Fit?
Cambridge Career Products
PO Box 2153
Dept. CC15
Charleston, WV 25328-2153
Ph: (304)744-9323   Fax: (304)744-9351
Fr: 800-468-4227

Video. 1993. $99.00. 25 minutes. Connect talents and interests to real career opportunities. Student guide included.

★9192★ Careers Without College: Jobnet
Cambridge Career Products
PO Box 2153
Dept. CC15
Charleston, WV 25328-2153
Ph: (304)744-9323   Fax: (304)744-9351
Fr: 800-468-4227

Video. 1995. $79.95. Covers career opportunities and other options for high school graduates.

★9193★ The CDM-R Career Video Set
American Guidance Service, Inc.
4201 Woodland Rd.
Circle Pines, MN 55014
Fr: 800-328-2560

Video. $149.00 (2 cassettes). 40 minutes.

★9194★ Choices Today Video Series
Cambridge Career Products
PO Box 2153
Dept. CC15
Charleston, WV 25328-2153
Ph: (304)744-9323   Fax: (304)744-9351
Fr: 800-468-4227

Series of three 30-minute videos. $275.00/set. Includes "Self-Awareness and Your Career Options," "Investigating the World of Work," and "Occupational Preparation." Includes student/teacher manual with each video.

★9195★ Dialing for Jobs
Career Communications, Inc.
PO Box 169
Harleysville, PA 19438
Ph: (215)256-3130   Fax: (215)256-3136
Fr: 800-346-1848

Video. $159.00. Shows how to cut job search time in half by using the telephone to obtain interviews.

★9196★ Directing Your Successful Job Search
Cambridge Career Products
PO Box 2153
Dept. CC15
Charleston, WV 25328-2153
Ph: (304)744-9323   Fax: (304)744-9351
Fr: 800-468-4227

Video. $98.00. 45 minutes. Describes the tools needed for a successful job search, networking, traditional sources of leads, and interviewing. Comes with an adapted version of the Cambridge Job Search Guide.

★9197★ Finding the Perfect Job

Cambridge Career Products
PO Box 2153
Dept. CC15
Charleston, WV 25328-2153
Ph: (304)744-9323   Fax: (304)744-9351
Fr: 800-468-4227

Video. $98.00. 30 minutes. Covers job search strategies.

★9198★ Get a Job

The Media Guild
11722 Sorrento Valley Rd., Ste. E
San Diego, CA 92121

Video. $160.00. 11 minutes. Animated color video covers career education and job placement for middle and high school students.

★9199★ Get the Job You Want

Cambridge Career Products
PO Box 2153
Dept. CC15
Charleston, WV 25328-2153
Ph: (304)744-9323   Fax: (304)744-9351
Fr: 800-468-4227

Video. $98.00. 120 minutes. Designed for job seekers who didn't attend or finish college.

★9200★ Getting a Job

Educational Design, Inc.
345 Hudson St.
New York, NY 10014

Four-video instructional program. 1993. $299.00.

★9201★ A Good Job After College: How to Get One!

Cambridge Career Products
PO Box 2153
Dept. CC15
Charleston, WV 25328-2153
Ph: (304)744-9323   Fax: (304)744-9351
Fr: 800-468-4227

Video. $69.95/each. 80 minutes. Senior recruiters and vice presidents from leading companies answer questions most often asked by college students.

★9202★ How to Get Interviews and Organize Your Time

Career Communications, Inc.
PO Box 169
Harleysville, PA 19438
Ph: (215)256-3130   Fax: (215)256-3136
Fr: 800-346-1848

Video. $225.00. Discusses using the telephone, contacting employers in person, organizing a job search, and other techniques.

★9203★ Investigating the World of Work

Cambridge Career Products
PO Box 2153
Dept. CC15
Charleston, WV 25328-2153
Ph: (304)744-9323   Fax: (304)744-9351
Fr: 800-468-4227

Video. $98.00. 30 minutes. Demonstrates techniques for relating knowledge of oneself to the world of work. Includes student/teacher manual.

★9204★ JIST Job Search Series

Cambridge Career Products
PO Box 2153
Dept. CC15
Charleston, WV 25328-2153
Ph: (304)744-9323   Fax: (304)744-9351
Fr: 800-468-4227

Series of 5 videos. $399.00/set. 20-30 minutes each. Available in adult and first-time job-seeker versions. Individual titles cover identifying your skills, job search methods, resumes and job applications, effective interviewing, and organizing a job search.

★9205★ JIST Video Guide to Occupational Exploration

JIST Works, Inc.
720 N. Park Ave.
Indianapolis, IN 46202
Ph: (317)264-3720   Fax: 800-547-8329
Fr: 800-648-5478

Series of 15 videos. 1995. $729.00/set. $69.00/each. 25-30 minutes each. Shows real people in their work settings.

★9206★ Job Hunting: Advice from Personnel Directors

CareerLab Books
9085 E. Mineral Circle, Ste. 330
Englewood, CO 80112
Ph: (303)790-0505   Fax: (303)790-0606
Fr: 800-723-9675

Audiotape. $14.95. 55 minutes. Comes with study guide. Two top personnel directors talk about job hunting.

★9207★ Job Hunting in Tough Times

Ready Reference Press
PO Box 5249
Santa Monica, CA 90409
Fax: (310)475-4895   Fr: 800-424-5627

Series of 3 videos. $239.00/set. $89.00/each. Separate titles cover job search skills, resume preparation, and interview techniques.

★9208★ Job Search in Action

Career Communications, Inc.
PO Box 169
Harleysville, PA 19438
Ph: (215)256-3130   Fax: (215)256-3136
Fr: 800-346-1848

Series of 4 videos. $595.00/set. For college and technical school students. Includes student workbooks and instructor manuals.

★9209★ Job Search Series

Cambridge Career Products
PO Box 2153
Dept. CC15
Charleston, WV 25328-2153
Ph: (304)744-9323   Fax: (304)744-9351
Fr: 800-468-4227

Series of 3 videos. $179.00/set. $69.95/each. 15-20 minutes each. Individual titles cover job search preparation, successful interviewing, and negotiating the job offer. Each video follows a recent college graduate through a job search.

★9210★ Job Search Series

Cambridge Career Products
PO Box 2153
Dept. CC15
Charleston, WV 25328-2153
Ph: (304)744-9323   Fax: (304)744-9351
Fr: 800-468-4227

Series of 12 videos. $695.00/set. $69.00/each. 30 minutes each. Individual titles cover knowing your skills, locating potential employers, job applications, interviewing, and more.

★9211★ Job Search Skills for Adults

Ready Reference Press
PO Box 5249
Santa Monica, CA 90409
Fax: (310)475-4895   Fr: 800-424-5627

Series of 3 videos. $239.00/set. $89.00/each. Separate titles cover job search skills, resume preparation, and interview techniques.

★9212★ Job Search Strategies

Learning Seed
330 Telser Rd.
Lake Zurich, IL 60047
Fr: 800-634-4941

Video. $89.00. 23 minutes.

★9213★ Job Search Success System

Career Communications, Inc.
PO Box 169
Harleysville, PA 19438
Ph: (215)256-3130   Fax: (215)256-3136
Fr: 800-346-1848

Series of 6 videos. $450.00/set. For high school and youth programs. Includes student workbooks and instructor manuals.

★9214★ Job Search: The Inside Track

Career Communications, Inc.
PO Box 169
Harleysville, PA 19438
Ph: (215)256-3130   Fax: (215)256-3136
Fr: 800-346-1848

Series of 6 videos. $1195.00/set. A video/workbook-based training program used primarily as the basis of a workshop.

★9215★ Job Search Training Program (JSTP)

Careers, Inc.
PO Box 135
Largo, FL 34649-0135
Ph: (813)584-7333   Fr: 800-726-0441

Video. $249.00. 35 minutes. Includes printed support materials. Designed for conducting a group or individual job search training program.

★9216★ Looking Ahead

Impact Publications
9104-N Manassas Dr.
Manassas Park, VA 22111-5211
Ph: (703)361-7300   Fax: (703)335-9486

Video. Video Initiatives. 1993. $129.95. 60 minutes. Covers all aspects of a positive job search. With noted authors Richard N. Bolles, William J. Morin, and Dr. Denis Waitley.

★9217★ Networking: Connections to Employment

Career Communications, Inc.
PO Box 169
Harleysville, PA 19438
Ph: (215)256-3130   Fax: (215)256-3136
Fr: 800-346-1848

Video. $79.00. 12 minutes. Explains the benefits of networking and how to present oneself to potential employers.

★9218★ Networking for Interviews

CareerLab Books
9085 E. Mineral Circle, Ste. 330
Englewood, CO 80112
Ph: (303)790-0505   Fax: (303)790-0606
Fr: 800-723-9675

Video. $59.95. 30 minutes.

★9219★ The Networking Process

DBM Publishing
Drake Beam Morin, Inc.
100 Park Ave., 4th Fl.
New York, NY 10164-0791
Fax: (212)972-2120   Fr: 800-345-5627

Video. $95.00. Presents networking techniques to find the job of your choice.

★9220★ Occupational Preparation

Cambridge Career Products
PO Box 2153
Dept. CC15
Charleston, WV 25328-2153
Ph: (304)744-9323   Fax: (304)744-9351
Fr: 800-468-4227

Video. $98.00. 30 minutes. Shows how to develop and implement an effective educational and training program. Includes student/teacher manual.

★9221★ Researching the Job Market

DBM Publishing
Drake Beam Morin, Inc.
100 Park Ave., 4th Fl.
New York, NY 10164-0791
Fax: (212)972-2120   Fr: 800-345-5627

Video. $95.00. Follows three successful job seekers who use careful, planned research.

★9222★ School to Work: Communication Connections for the Real World

Cambridge Career Products
PO Box 2153
Dept. CC15
Charleston, WV 25328-2153
Ph: (304)744-9323   Fax: (304)744-9351
Fr: 800-468-4227

Series of 10 videos. 1993. $1,399.00/set. $149.00/each. 1520 minutes each. Demonstrates how specific communication skills are important to each occupational area covered.

★9223★ Self-Awareness and Your Career Options

Cambridge Career Products
PO Box 2153
Dept. CC15
Charleston, WV 25328-2153
Ph: (304)744-9323   Fax: (304)744-9351
Fr: 800-468-4227

Video. $98.00. 30 minutes. Focuses on organizing information about yourself for career planning. Includes student/teacher manual.

★9224★ Setting Career Goals

Cambridge Career Products
PO Box 2153
Dept. CC15
Charleston, WV 25328-2153
Ph: (304)744-9323   Fax: (304)744-9351
Fr: 800-468-4227

Video, $98.00. Laserdisc, $199.00. Learn how to set four types of career goals.

★9225★ Shhh! I'm Finding a Job: The Library and Your Self-Directed Job Search

Cambridge Career Products
PO Box 2153
Dept. CC15
Charleston, WV 25328-2153
Ph: (304)744-9323   Fax: (304)744-9351
Fr: 800-468-4227

Video. 1993. $79.95. 40 minutes. A practical guide to using library resources to conduct a successful job search.

★9226★ Strategic Job Search

American Media Inc.
4900 University Ave., Ste. 100
West Des Moines, IA 50266-6769
Ph: (515)224-0919   Fax: (515)224-0256
Fr: 800-262-2557

Two video cassettes. John Gordon. 25 minutes each. Video 1 covers the development of job leads through a variety of sources such as networks, placement services, publications; video 2 covers the interviewing process.

★9227★ Strategy: Planning Your Job Search

Career Communications, Inc.
PO Box 169
Harleysville, PA 19438
Ph: (215)256-3130   Fax: (215)256-3136
Fr: 800-346-1848

Video. $79.00. 12 minutes. Designed for the mature job seeker suffering job loss.

★9228★ Success Without College

Ready Reference Press
PO Box 5249
Santa Monica, CA 90409
Fax: (310)475-4895   Fr: 800-424-5627

Video. $169.00 (2 cassettes). Designed for the non-college bound student.

★9229★ Ten Ways to a Better Job

Cambridge Career Products
PO Box 2153
Dept. CC15
Charleston, WV 25328-2153
Ph: (304)744-9323   Fax: (304)744-9351
Fr: 800-468-4227

Video. 1994. $79.95. 30 minutes. Reminds viewers of job search basics.

★9230★ The Tough New Labor Market Video

JIST Works, Inc.
720 N. Park Ave.
Indianapolis, IN 46202
Ph: (317)264-3720   Fax: 800-547-8329
Fr: 800-648-5478

Video. 1995. $195.00. 30 minutes. Explains how major changes in the economy affect the labor market.

★9231★ The Tough New Labor Market and What it Takes to Succeed

Careers, Inc.
PO Box 135
Largo, FL 34649-0135
Ph: (813)584-7333   Fr: 800-726-0441

Video. $195.00. 30 minutes. An introduction to labor market trends that discusses the fastest growing jobs for the 1990s.

★9232★ Tough Times Job Strategies

Cambridge Career Products
PO Box 2153
Dept. CC15
Charleston, WV 25328-2153
Ph: (304)744-9323   Fax: (304)744-9351
Fr: 800-468-4227

Series of two videos. 1993. $129.00/set. $69.95/each. 30 minutes each. Includes "Tough Times: Finding the Jobs" and "Tough Times: Making the Most of Your Job." Examines factors influencing today's job market.

★9233★ The Very Quick Job Search Video

Career Communications, Inc.
PO Box 169
Harleysville, PA 19438
Ph: (215)256-3130   Fax: (215)256-3136
Fr: 800-346-1848

Video. $169.00. 32 minutes. Teaches essential job seeking skills in a half hour.

★9234★ The Video Guide to JIST's Self-Directed Job Search

JIST Works, Inc.
720 N. Park Ave.
Indianapolis, IN 46202
Ph: (317)264-3720   Fax: 800-547-8329
Fr: 800-648-5478

Series of 10 videos. 1994. $795.00/set. $99.00/each. 25 minutes each.

★9235★ Video Guide to Occupational Exploration (Video GOE)

Cambridge Career Products
PO Box 2153
Dept. CC15
Charleston, WV 25328-2153
Ph: (304)744-9323   Fax: (304)744-9351
Fr: 800-468-4227

Series of 14 videos. $749.00/set. $69.95/each. Series covers 14 occupational clusters, such as artistic, scientific, mechanical, etc. Set includes Enhanced Guide for Occupational Exploration and the Worker Trait Group Guide.

★9236★ Vocational and Career Planning Video Series

Cambridge Career Products
PO Box 2153
Dept. CC15
Charleston, WV 25328-2153
Ph: (304)744-9323   Fax: (304)744-9351
Fr: 800-468-4227

Series of four 25-minute videos. $325.00/set. Includes "Career Planning Steps," "Plans for Success," "Keys to Job Success," and "The Quiz Master." Manual included with each video.

★9237★ Vocational Inventory Video

Cambridge Career Products
PO Box 2153
Dept. CC15
Charleston, WV 25328-2153
Ph: (304)744-9323   Fax: (304)744-9351
Fr: 800-468-4227

Video. $295.00. 30 minutes. Helps students understand vocational training and their own vocational preferences. Comes with 500-page book on exploring careers, instructor's guide, and student workbook.

★9238★ Where (and How) to Look for Job Leads

Career Communications, Inc.
PO Box 169
Harleysville, PA 19438
Ph: (215)256-3130   Fax: (215)256-3136
Fr: 800-346-1848

Video. $225.00. Covers traditional and non-traditional methods.

★9239★ Winning at Job Hunting in the '90s

Baker & Taylor Video
501 S. Gladiolus
Momence, IL 60954
Fax: 800-775-3500   Fr: 800-775-2300

1991. Video cassette. Mel Schnapper. $59.95. Combines with a workbook approach to help the reader make the connection between accomplishments and employer needs. Demonstrates how to sell accomplishments in the interview.

★9240★ Your Vocational Job Search Campaign: Successful Guerilla Tactics

Cambridge Career Products
PO Box 2153
Dept. CC15
Charleston, WV 25328-2153
Ph: (304)744-9323   Fax: (304)744-9351
Fr: 800-468-4227

Video. $79.95. 30 minutes.

ONLINE AND DATABASE SERVICES

★9241★ Career Information System (CIS)

Career Information System
1177 Pearl St.
Eugene, OR 97401
Ph: (503)346-3872

Online database. Provides career planning information, including occupational profiles; local, state, and national labor market trends; job search techniques; and self-employment options.

★9242★ College Recruitment Database (CRD)

TimePlace, Inc.
Human Resource Information Network (HRIN)
7-4 Metropolitan Ct.
Gaithersburg, MD 20878
Ph: (301)590-2300   Fr: 800-638-8094

Online database. Contains more than 10,000 resumes of undergraduate and graduate students in a wide range of disciplines. Includes college, degree, major, grade point average, activities and honors, employment history, and date available for employment. Also provides contact information, including placement director's name, address, and telephone number for participating schools. Currently covers 14 colleges and universities.

★9243★ Dr. Job

GE Information Services
GEnie
401 N. Washington Blvd.
Rockville, MD 20850
Ph: (301)340-4000   Fr: 800-638-9636

Online database. Bulletin board featuring a question-and-answer column covering work-related topics ranging from corporate politics to communications and career decisions. Coverage includes career listings, employment, and business communications.

★9244★ The Guidance Information System (GIS)

Houghton Mifflin Co.
Educational Software Div.
222 Berkeley St.
Boston, MA 02116-3764
Ph: (617)252-3000   Fax: (617)252-3145

Online database. Comprises a series of cross-referenced files on occupations, two- and four-year colleges, graduate schools, and sources of scholarships and financial aid. Contains the following five files: Occupational Information File—contains information on 1025 occupations with cross-references to 3000 related jobs. Armed Services Information File—contains information on 215 jobs for which training is available in the armed services, includes cross-references to related civilian occupations. Two- and Four-Year College Information Files—contain information on 1800 two-year colleges and 1750 four-year colleges. Graduate School Information File—contains information on more than 1550 graduate and professional schools. Financial

Aids Information File—contains information on state, federal, and private sources of financial aid. The Career Decision-Making System—a system designed to assist in making career decisions. Provides a list of possible career choices.

★9245★ Online Hotline News Service

Information Intelligence, Inc.
PO Box 31098
Phoenix, AZ 85046
Ph: (602)996-2283   Fr: 800-228-9982

Online database containing five files, one of which is Joblines, which features listings of employment and resume services available in voice, print, and online throughout North America. Joblines focuses on the online, library automation, and information-related fields.

★9246★ Workplace Roundtable

GE Information Services (GEIS)
GEnie
401 N. Washington Blvd.
Rockville, MD 20850
Ph: (301)340-4000   Fr: 800-638-9636

Bulletin board providing a forum for participants to discuss and find information and tips on all aspects of the workplace. Features information on careers, management styles, customer relations, on-the-job problems, and other workplace issues.

SOFTWARE

★9247★ Adams JobBank Software

Planning/Communications
7215 Oak Ave.
River Forest, IL 60305-1935
Ph: (708)366-5200   Fr: (888)366-5200

Adams New Media. 1996. $59.95. Requires Windows 3.1 or higher, 3.5 inch disks only. Users can search from 11,000 U.S. companies by industry, state, or type of job. Includes 7,500 company profiles, 1,900 job hotlines, 300 fastest-growing companies, 1,100 executive search firms, and 1,100 employment agencies.

★9248★ Career Assessment Video

Cambridge Career Products
PO Box 2153
Dept. CC15
Charleston, WV 25328-2153
Ph: (304)744-9323   Fax: (304)744-9351
Fr: 800-468-4227

Video and software. $395.00. Available in Apple II or IBM versions. A group administered assessment which addresses 12 major worker trait clusters in a video presentation. Can be used in conjunction with state career information systems.

★9249★ Career Compass

Meridian Education Corp.
236 E. Front St.
Bloomington, IL 61701

$95.00. Available in IBM, Apple II, and TRS 80 versions. Covers general career clusters, major work groups, and specific occupations based on student responses to 70 work activity questions.

★9250★ Career CompuSearch

Meridian Education Corp.
236 E. Front St.
Bloomington, IL 61701

1993. $249.00. Users can assess interests, temperaments, and aptitudes to identify and explore related occupations and work groups.

★9251★ CareerSearch

The Guidance Shoppe
2909 Brandemere Dr.
Tallahassee, FL 32312
Ph: (904)385-6717

Interactive software program. $149.95 (Apple II or IBM versions). Game format helps middle and high school students explore 400 career areas.

★9252★ *DISCovering Careers & Jobs*

Gale Research
835 Penobscot Bldg.
Detroit, MI 48226-4094
Ph: (313)961-2242   Fax: (313)961-6083
Fr: 800-877-GALE

Annual. $495.00, single user; $700.00, network. Database covers: Descriptions of over 1,400 job titles in some 250 career areas; over 1,000 abstracts, excerpts, and selected articles on various job issues; listings of informational and training programs, trade directories, certification agencies, profesional associations, periodicals, career and test guides, employment agencies, sources of want ads, scholarships and awards; and information on over 30,000 companies that might be considered as prospective employers.

★9253★ Job Hunter's Survival Kit

The Guidance Shoppe
2909 Brandemere Dr.
Tallahassee, FL 32312
Ph: (904)385-6717

Interactive software program. $149.95 (Apple II or IBM versions). Two modules help students match skills with occupations and learn to write resumes.

★9254★ Vocational Biographies Career Finder

Vocational Biographies, Inc.
PO Box 31
Sauk Centre, MN 56378-0031
Fr: 800-255-0752

Software suitable for IBM, Apple II, or Macintosh. Students can find 20 careers that most closely match their interests, based on an 18-question quiz.

OTHER SOURCES

★9255★ *The Job Search Organizer*

Miranda Associates
2000 L St. NW, Ste. 408
Washington, DC 20036
Ph: (202)822-6399

Jack O'Brien. 1990. $24.95; $14.95 (paper). 55 pages. A combination job search manual/workbook/organizer to help the reader plan and manage the job campaign.

★9256★ The National Resume Bank

The National Resume Bank
3637 4th St. N, Ste. 330
St. Petersburg, FL 33704
Ph: (813)896-3694

Online database containing qualifications summmaries submitted by those seeking employment in the following sectors: Aerospace, Airlines, Clerical, Communications, Creative, Data Processing, Education, Engineering, Financial, General, Government, Health Care, Hospitality, Human Resources, Insurance, Legal, Management, Manufacturing, Marketing, Real Estate, Research, Retail, Sales, Technical, and Trades. The summaries are accessed by employers seeking candidates for open positions within their organizations who then may request the resumes of listed individuals.

★9257★ National Self-Help Clearinghouse (NSHC)

25 W. 43rd St., Rm. 620
New York, NY 10036-7406
Ph: (212)354-8525   Fax: (212)642-1956

Purpose: Clearinghouse on selfhelp groups; provides referral services. Conducts research and training activities. Maintains speakers' bureau.

★9258★ Options Inc.

225 S. 15th St., Ste. 1635
Philadelphia, PA 19102-3916
Ph: (215)735-2202   Fax: (215)735-8097

Purpose: Career advisory and human resource consulting service. Provides consulting and training programs on the changing workforce and workplace. Offers counseling on career issues such as job searches, career changes, and career management. Provides consultation in the areas of managing change, career management, mentoring, effective communication, outplacement, managing diversity, and spouse employment assistance. Offers training to professionals. Conducts studies on employment-related issues; maintains speakers' bureau.

Career Transitions and Alternatives

REFERENCE WORKS

★9259★ Adventure Careers

The Career Press, Inc.
3 Tice Rd.
PO Box 687
Franklin Lakes, NJ 07417
Ph: (201)848-0310   Fax: (201)848-1727
Fr: 800-237-3371

Susan Angle and Alex Hiam. Third edition, 1995. $11.99. 288 pages. Contains practical how-to information, lists of contacts and phone numbers, and first-hand experiences from a number of adventurers who tread "off the beaten career path".

★9260★ Between Opportunities: A Survival Guide for Job Seekers & Career Changers

Aar Dee Aar Publishing, Inc.
4410 Bay Ln.
White Bear Lake, MN 55110-6760
Ph: (612)426-0164

Robert D. Riskin. 1992. $14.95 (paper).

★9261★ Career Directions

Richard D. Irwin
1333 Burr Ridge Pkwy.
Burr Ridge, IL 60521
Ph: (708)789-4000   Fax: (708)789-9841
Fr: 800-634-3961

Donna J. Yena. 1993. $19.50 (paper).

★9262★ Career Guide to Industries

U.S. Government Printing Office
Superintendent of Documents
Mail Stop: SM
Washington, DC 20401
Ph: (202)512-1800   Fax: (202)512-2250

1994. $14.00. Companion to the Occupational Outlook Handbook. Provides descriptions for occupations in more than 40 industries. Includes information on working conditions, training, earnings, and outlook.

★9263★ Career & Vocational Counseling Directory

American Business Directories, Inc.
American Business Information, Inc.
5711 S. 86th Cir.
Omaha, NE 68127
Ph: (402)593-4600   Fax: (402)331-1505

Annual. $290.00, payment with order. Entries include: Name, address, phone (including area code), size of advertisement, year first in Yellow Pages, name of owner or manager, number of employees. Compiled from telephone company Yellow Pages, nationwide. Arrangement: Geographical.

★9264★ Careers in Medicine: Traditional and Alternative Opportunities

Garrett Park Press
PO Box 190 C
Garrett Park, MD 20896-0190
Ph: (301)946-2553

Donald T. Rucker and Martin D. Keller. 1990. $15.95. 346 pages. Cites training requirements, illustrative work activities, and a summary of the advantages and disadvantages in a variety of specialized areas. Includes hundreds of career alternatives and discusses ways to break into these fields for persons trained in medicine. Features contributions from over 40 professionals in all phases of medicine and provides 200 sources of information on specialties and subspecialties.

★9265★ Change Your Job, Change Your Life: High Impact Strategies for Finding Great Jobs in the 90's

Impact Publications
9104-N Manassas Dr.
Manassas Park, VA 22111-5211
Ph: (703)361-7300   Fax: (703)335-9486

Ronald Krannich. Fourth edition, 1994. $14.95. 368 pages. Details trends in the marketplace, how to identify opportunities, how to retrain for them, and how to land jobs. Includes a chapter on starting a business. Contains index, bibliography, and illustrations.

★9266★ College Majors and Careers: A Resource Guide for Effective Life Planning

Garrett Park Press
PO Box 190D
Garrett Park, MD 20896
Ph: (301)946-2553

Irregular, latest edition 1993. $14.00, payment must accompany order. Publication includes: Lists of organizations and other sources of information on choosing a college field of concentration and a subsequent career path. Entries include: Organization name, address, phone. Principal content of publication is descriptions of 60 of the most popular major fields and discussions of their attributes.

★9267★ The Enhanced Guide for Occupational Exploration

American Guidance Service (AGS)
4201 Woodland Rd.
PO Box 99
Circle Pines, MN 55014-1796
Fax: (612)786-9077   Fr: 800-328-2560

Marilyn Maze. $29.95 (paper). Provides descriptions for 2500 jobs. Each description includes skills, abilities, academic and physical requirements, work environment, salary, and outlook. Contains indices to career alternatives based on interests, skills, industry, and education.

★9268★ The 40+ Job Hunting Guide

Facts on File, Inc.
11 Penn Plaza, 15th Fl.
New York, NY 10001-2006
Ph: (212)967-8800   Fax: 800-678-3633
Fr: 800-322-8755

E. Patricia Birsner. Third edition, 1995. $24.95. Approaches job search as a business problem-solving activity and provides advice on emotional and practical aspects of searching and interviewing.

★9269★ Get a Job You Love!

Dearborn Trade
155 N. Wacker Dr.
Chicago, IL 60606
Fax: (312)836-1146   Fr: 800-245-2665
Roxanne S. Rogers. $19.95 (paper).

★9270★ **How to Change Your Career**

VGM Career Horizons
4255 W. Touhy Ave.
Lincolnwood, IL 60646-1975
Ph: (847)679-5500   Fax: (847)679-2494
Fr: 800-323-4900

Kent Banning and Ardelle Friday. 1991. $9.95. 160 pages. Provides checklists, worksheets, and exercises to help career-changers identify and successfully enter new careers. Guides the the reader in the production of a career-change resume.

★9271★ **How to Find the Work You Love**

Penguin USA
375 Hudson St.
New York, NY 10014
Ph: (212)366-2000   Fax: (212)366-2666

Laurence G. Boldt. $9.95 (paper).

★9272★ **The Mentorship Guide: A Directory of Advisors and Resource People in Social Change**

Student Pugwash USA
1638 R St. NW, Ste. 32
Washington, DC 20009
Ph: (202)328-6555   Fax: (202)797-4664
Fr: 800-969-2784

Irregular, latest edition 1991. $6.00. Covers over 160 professionals in the fields of science, technology, public policy, education, global security, social sciences, and the environment in the U.S. and abroad who are willing to speak with and advise students and recent graduates on career alternatives that integrate academic interests with social and humanitarian concern. Entries include: Name, address, phone, telex, name and title of contact, previous involvement with Student Pugwash USA, education and employment background, personal and professional interests. Arrangement: Alphabetical. Indexes: Subject, geographical.

★9273★ **Mid-Career Changes: Strategies for Success**

Career Publishing, Inc.
910 Main St.
PO Box 5486
Orange, CA 92613
Ph: (714)771-5155   Fax: (714)532-0180
Fr: 800-854-4014

John D. Shingleton and James Anderson. 1994. $16.95 (paper). Provides information about today's changing workplace. Offers advice on identifying goals and adjusting to change.

★9274★ **Mid-Career Job Hunting**

Consultants Bookstore
Templeton Rd.
Fitzwilliam, NH 03447
Ph: (603)585-6544   Fax: (603)585-9555
Fr: 800-531-0007

E. Patricia Birsner. 1991. $14.00. 272 pages. Approaches the job search as a business problem-solving activity.

★9275★ **Occupational Outlook Handbook**

U.S. Bureau of Labor Statistics
2 Massachusetts Ave. NE
Washington, DC 20212
Ph: (202)606-5703

Biennial, May of even years. $26.00, hardcover; $23.00, softcover. Publication includes: List of over 100 state employment agencies and State Occupational Information Coordinating Committees (SOICC) that provide state and local job market and career information; various occupational organizations that provide career information on about 250 occupations. Entries include: For agencies and committees: agency or committee name, address, phone, director name. For organizations: organization name, address. Principal content of publication is profiles of various occupations, which include description of occupation, educational requirements, job outlook, and expected earnings. Arrangement: Agencies and committees are geographical; organizations are classified by occupation.

★9276★ **Offbeat Careers**

Kogan Page Ltd.
120 Pentonville Rd.
London N1 9JN, England
Ph: 071 278 0433

$6.99. Covers 60 alternative careers, such mushroom farmer and mime animateur. Entries include: Job description, contact names, necessary skills, salary.

★9277★ **Out the Organization: New Career Opportunities for the 1990's**

Consultants Bookstore
Templeton Rd.
Fitzwilliam, NH 03447
Ph: (603)585-6544   Fax: (603)585-9555
Fr: 800-531-0007

Madeleine Swain. 1992. $12.95. 250 pages. Offers advice to the mid-career executive whose job is no longer satisfying or safe. Discusses survival strategies, getting fired and its resulting emotions, and options, counseling, and strategy for the future.

★9278★ **Outside the Ivory Tower: A Guide for Academics Considering Alternative Careers**

Harvard University, Office of Career Services
54 Dunster St.
Cambridge, MA 02138
Ph: (617)495-2595   Fax: (617)495-3584

Margaret Newhouse. 1993. $13.00 (paper).

★9279★ **The Overnight Job Change Strategy**

Ten Speed Press
PO Box 7123
Berkeley, CA 94707
Ph: (510)559-1600   Fax: (510)559-1629
Fr: 800-841-BOOK

Donald Asher. 1993. $7.95. 96 pages. Subtitled "How to Plan a Comprehensive, Systematic Job Search in One Evening". Incorporates sales and marketing techniques into a six-stage job search process.

★9280★ **Professional Careers Sourcebook**

Gale Research
835 Penobscot Bldg.
Detroit, MI 48226-4094
Ph: (313)961-2242   Fax: (313)961-6083
Fr: 800-877-GALE

Fourth edition, 1995. $85.00. 1,000 pages. Directs users to career information sources related to specific professions, such as civil engineering, psychology, law, public relations, dance and choreography, and more. Provides a listing of state professional and occupational licensing agencies and occupational rankings and statistics. Includes over 110 professional career profiles containing information on general career guides, career information and services provided by professional associations, standards and certification agencies, directories of educational programs and institutions, basic reference guides and handbooks related to the profession, professional and trade periodicals, and more. Indexes: Alphabetical.

★9281★ **Rites of Passage at $100,000-Plus: The Insider's Guide to Absolutely Everything About Executive Job-Changing**

Henry Holt
John Lucht. Revised edition, 1993. $29.95. 640 pages. Aimed at top executives, this book covers a range of topics from networking and personal contacts to direct mail, resumes, references, interviewing, and negotiating. Includes large section on dealing with recruiters.

★9282★ **Shifting Gears: Planning a New Career for Midlife and After**

Crown Publishing Group
201 E. 50th St.
New York, NY 10003
Ph: (212)254-1600   Fr: 800-726-0600

Andrea Gross. 1992. $19.00. 224 pages. Offers guidance for those hoping to master career change and find fulfilling work.

★9283★ **Skills in Action: A Job-Finding Workbook**

University of Akron
Adult Resource Ctr.
Akron, OH 44325

J.H. Selden. $5.50. 75 pages. Workbook format; aimed at job seekers looking for initial or transitional employment.

★9284★ **Starting Over: You in the New Workplace**

Palomino Press
86-07 144 St.
Briarwood, NY 11435
Ph: (718)297-5053

Jo Danna. $12.95. 260 pages.

★9285★ **Take This Job and Love It: A Personal Guide to Career Empowerment**

McGraw-Hill
1221 Avenue of the Americas
New York, NY 10020
Ph: (212)512-2000   Fr: 800-262-4729

Diane Tracy. 1994. $19.95.

★9286★ Taking Charge of Your Career Direction

Brooks/Cole Publishing Company
Marketing Dept.
511 Forest Lodge Rd.
Pacific Grove, CA 93950
Ph: (408)373-0728

Robert D. Lock. Second edition, 1992. $21.95. 377 pages. Provides guidance for the job search process.

★9287★ VGM's Careers Encyclopedia

VGM Career Books
National Textbook Co.
4255 W. Touhy Ave.
Lincolnwood, IL 60646
Ph: (708)679-5500   Fax: (708)679-6375
Fr: 800-323-4900

Irregular, latest edition spring 1991. $39.95. Publication includes: List of over 200 professional associations that provide career guidance information. Entries include: Association name, address. Principal content is information on 200 careers, including qualifications needed, educational requirements, and salary. Arrangement: Alphabetical.

★9288★ Vocational Careers Sourcebook

Gale Research
835 Penobscot Bldg.
Detroit, MI 48226-4094
Ph: (313)961-2242   Fax: (313)961-6083
Fr: 800-877-GALE

Second edition, 1995. $79.00. 1,100 pages. Directs users to career information sources related to specific occupations, such as insurance and real estate sales, corrections and police work, mechanics, armed forces options, agriculture and forestry, production work, and the trades. Contains information on general career guides, career information and services provided by trade associations, standards and certification agencies, directories of educational programs and institutions, basic reference guides and handbooks related to the occupation, trade periodicals, and more. Indexes: Alphabetical.

AUDIO/VISUAL RESOURCES

★9289★ Fired and Re-focused

CareerLab Books
9085 E. Mineral Cir., Ste. 330
Englewood, CO 80112
Ph: (303)790-0505   Fax: (303)790-0606
Fr: 800-723-9675

Video. $59.95. 30 minutes. Discusses job search strategies following job loss.

★9290★ From Pink Slip to Paycheck

Career Communications, Inc.
PO Box 169
Harleysville, PA 19438
Ph: (215)256-3130   Fax: (215)256-3136
Fr: 800-346-1848

Series of 5 videos. $349.00/set. $79.00/each. 12 minutes each. Designed for mature job seekers suffering job loss. Individual titles cover job search strategies, feeling positive, interviewing, resume writing, and networking.

★9291★ Getting Fired, Getting Hired: Job Hunting from A to Z

CareerLab Books
9085 E. Mineral Circle, Ste. 330
Englewood, CO 80112
Ph: (303)790-0505   Fax: (303)790-0606
Fr: 800-723-9675

Series of 6 videos. $249.95/set. $59.95/each. 30 minutes each. Individual titles cover aspects of the job search following job loss.

★9292★ Strategy: Planning Your Job Search

Career Communications, Inc.
PO Box 169
Harleysville, PA 19438
Ph: (215)256-3130   Fax: (215)256-3136
Fr: 800-346-1848

Video. $79.00. 12 minutes. Designed for the mature job seeker suffering job loss.

OTHER SOURCES

★9293★ Career Planning and Adult Development Network (CPADN)

4965 Sierra Rd.
San Jose, CA 95132
Ph: (408)559-4946   Fax: (408)559-8211

Members: Counselors, trainers, consultants, therapists, educators, personnel specialists, and graduate students who work in business, educational, religious, and governmental organizations, and focus on career planning and adult development issues. **Purpose:** Seeks to: establish a link between professionals working with adults in a variety of settings; identify and exchange effective adult development methods and techniques; develop a clearer understanding of the directions and objectives of the career planning and the adult development movement. Keeps members informed of developments in career decision-making, career values clarification, preretirement counseling, dual-career families, job search techniques, and mid-life transitions. Cosponsors professional seminars; maintains biographical archives.

★9294★ New Ways to Work (NWW)

985 Market St., Ste 950
San Francisco, CA 94103
Ph: (415)995-9860   Fax: (415)995-9867

Purpose: Goal is to provide a work world that responds to the needs of both workers and institutions. Provides information, training, and support to individuals and organizations interested in new work options. Promotes the concepts of flextime, compressed work weeks, job sharing, work sharing, and voluntary reduced work time to satisfy the requirements of people who want and need flexible schedules. **Activities:** Offers technical assistance, including problem analysis and assistance in program facilitation for interested employees, employers, or unions.

★9295★ Options Inc.

225 S. 15th St., Ste. 1635
Philadelphia, PA 19102-3916
Ph: (215)735-2202   Fax: (215)735-8097

Purpose: Career advisory and human resource consulting service. Provides consulting and training programs on the changing workforce and workplace. Offers counseling on career issues such as job searches, career changes, and career management. Provides consultation in the areas of managing change, career management, mentoring, effective communication, outplacement, managing diversity, and spouse employment assistance. Offers training to professionals. Conducts studies on employment-related issues; maintains speakers' bureau.

Electronic Job Search Information

REFERENCE WORKS

★9296★ *Be Your Own Headhunter Online*

Planning/Communications
7215 Oak Ave.
River Forest, IL 60305-1935
Ph: (708)366-5200   Fr: (888)366-5200

Pam Dixon and Sylvia Tiersten. 1995. $16.00. 398 pages. Provides details on more than 250 online places to find job openings, including online services, usenet groups, the Internet and World Wide Web, and dial-up eomployment bulletin boards.

★9297★ *Electronic Job Search Revolution*

Consultants Bookstore
Templeton Rd.
Fitzwilliam, NH 03447
Ph: (603)585-6544   Fax: (603)585-9555
Fr: 800-531-0007

Joyce Lain Kennedy and Thomas J. Morrow. Second edition, 1995. $12.95 (paper). 183 pages. Discusses new technologies being used in job searching.

★9298★ *Electronic Resume Revolution*

Consultants Bookstore
Templeton Rd.
Fitzwilliam, NH 03447
Ph: (603)585-6544   Fax: (603)585-9555
Fr: 800-531-0007

Joyce Lain Kennedy and Thomas J. Morrow. Second edition, 1995. $12.95 (paper). 228 pages. Explains how to write a resume that a computer can read. Includes 30 model resumes.

★9299★ *Electronic Resumes*

Planning/Communications
7215 Oak Ave.
River Forest, IL 60305-1935
Ph: (708)366-5200   Fr: (888)366-5200

Wayne Gonyea and James Gonyea. 1996. $19.95 (book and MS-DOS disk). 224 pages. Explains the basics of online, multimedia, video, and audio resumes in nontechnical language. Disk includes software that enables users to create their own electronic resume to upload via modem onto online resume databases.

★9300★ *Electronic Resumes for the New Job Market*

Impact Publications
9104-N Manassas Dr.
Manassas Park, VA 22111-5211
Ph: (703)361-7300   Fax: (703)335-9486

Peter D. Weddle. 1995. $11.95. 154 pages. Explains how to use electronic job banks and design resumes that best meet electronic job bank specifications.

★9301★ *Finding a Job on the Internet*

TAB Electronics
PO Box 182607
Columbus, OH 43218
Fr: 800-822-8158

Alfred and Emily Glossbrenner. 1995. $15.25. 272 pages. Describes how to use the Internet to find job openings. Covers online database searches, posting your resume online, researching employers and unannounced job openings, and tapping newsgroups, mailing lists, and World Wide Web sites.

★9302★ *The Guide to Internet Job Searching*

VGM Career Books
NTC Publishing Group
4255 W. Touhy Ave.
Lincolnwood, IL 60646-1975
Ph: (847)679-5500   Fax: (847)679-2494
Fr: 800-323-4900

Margaret Riley et al. 1996. $12.95. 192 pages. Written by a team of information professionals, this book helps readers develop an effective Internet job application, quickly locate major job listing sites in each career area, and use the computer to search for job opportunities.

★9303★ *Hook Up, Get Hired! The Internet Job Search Revolution*

Consultants Bookstore
Templeton Rd.
Fitzwilliam, NH 03447
Ph: (603)585-6544   Fax: (603)585-9555
Fr: 800-531-0007

Joyce Lain Kennedy. 1995. $12.95 (paper). 250 pages. Provides an Internet roadmap for networking, researching companies, searching job ads, and creating an Internet-friendly resume. Includes e-mail addresses and access numbers to online career centers, newsgroups, bulletin boards, and resume marquees.

★9304★ *How to Get Your Dream Job Using the Internet*

Coriolis Group Books
7339 E. Acoma Dr., Ste. 7
Scottsdale, AZ 85260
Ph: (602)483-0192   Fax: (602)483-0193

Shannon Bounds and Arthur Karl. 1996. $29.99. 336 pages. Includes CD-ROM containing web page creation software, interview simulator, resume tools, and direct links to online recruiters, job and resume banks, etc.

★9305★ *Internet Guide to International Career Information and Job Opportunities*

Jeffries & Associates, Inc.
17200 Hughes Rd.
Poolesville, MD 20837
Ph: (301)972-8034

Francis M. Jeffries. 1995. $15.00.

★9306★ *Job-Seeker's Guide to On-Line Resources*

Consultants Bookstore
Templeton Rd.
Fitzwilliam, NH 03447
Ph: (603)585-6544   Fax: (603)585-9555
Fr: 800-531-0007

Alice Snell. 1995. $14.95. 64 pages. Describes available services and how to use them. Identifies 140 candidate databsaes, job-posting services, and related resources accessible with a computer and modem.

★9307★ *NetJobs: Use the Internet to Land Your Dream Job*

Michael Wolff and Co.
1633 Broadway, 27th Fl.
New York, NY 10019
Ph: (212)841-1572   Fax: (212)841-1556

Mary Goodwin et al. 1996. $12.95. 184 pages. Provides an overview of career resources on the Internet.

★9308★ Point and Click Jobfinder

Dearborn Trade
155 N. Wacker Dr.
Chicago, IL 60606
Ph: (312)836-4400   Fax: (312)836-1146
Fr: 800-245-2665

Seth Godin. 1996. $14.95. A guide to online services providing job listings, resume banks, and similar services. Comes with America Online diskette.

★9309★ Professional's Private Sector Job Finder

Planning/Communications
7215 Oak Ave.
River Forest, IL 60305
Ph: (708)366-5200   Fax: (708)366-5280
Fr: 800-829-5220

Biennial, February of even years. $18.95 plus $3.75 shipping; includes free update sheet. Covers over 2,500 sources of jobs in the private sector of the United States and abroad, including job matching services, job hotlines, periodicals and directories, salary surveys, databases, and electronic online job services. Entries include: For job services: name, sponsor or operator name, address, phone, length of registration period, cost, description (including number of job vacancies listed). For publications: title, publisher name, address, phone, frequency of publication, price, description (including number of job vacancies listed). Arrangement: Classified by occupational specialty; geographical by state. Indexes: Subject.

★9310★ Using the Internet in Your Job Search

Career Communications, Inc.
PO Box 169
Harleysville, PA 19438
Ph: (215)256-3130   Fax: (215)256-3136
Fr: 800-346-1848

Fred Jandt and Mary Nemnich. $19.95. 1995. 240 pages. Explains how to connect to the Internet, find job listings, research potential employers, use news groups to get leads, and adapt standard resumes to electronic formats.

NEWSPAPERS, MAGAZINES, AND JOURNALS

★9311★ Internet Job Classifieds

Career Communications, Inc.
PO Box 169
Harleysville, PA 19438
Ph: (215)256-3130   Fax: (215)256-3136
Fr: 800-346-1848

Weekly. $295.00/year. Delivered via fax to subscribers once a week. Includes e-mail and web site addresses of hiring companies in the United States.

AUDIO/VISUAL RESOURCES

★9312★ Connect on the Net: Online Employment

Planning/Communications
7215 Oak Ave.
River Forest, IL 60305-1935
Ph: (708)366-5200   Fr: (888)366-5200

Cambridge Educational. 1995. $79.95. This 30-minute video shows how to use a modem and the Internet to find job vacancies and information on bulletin board services, Internet and World Wide Web sites, online job databases, posting resumes, and networking.

ONLINE AND DATABASE SERVICES

★9313★ Academic Position Network

Gopher: wcni.cis.umn.edu • **URL:** gopher://wcni.cis.umn.edu:11111 • **Description:** Online position announcement service. Announcements include faculty, administration, and staff positions as well as announcements for graduate assistant and fellowship positions. **Fee:** Free searching and browsing features. **E-Mail:** apn@epx.cis.umn.edu

★9314★ Adams JobBank

URL: http://www.adamsonline.com/ • **Description:** Users can search current job openings by occupational field. They can also access the Career Center which includes areas for graduating students and women and minorities.

★9315★ America's Employers

URL: http://www.americasemployers.com/ • **Description:** Site offering job listings, employment agencies and recruiters, company databases, resume bank, and business and franchise offerings.

★9316★ America's Help Wanted!

URL: http://www.jobquest.com/ • **Description:** Provides job listings for searching. Offers jobQuest resume service for job seekers.

★9317★ America's Job Bank

URL: http://www.ajb.dni.us/index.html • **Description:** Provides detailed job listings in all areas. Use the site's self-directed search feature to find a job opening in a particular field. Or, browse by company name, or connect to one of the local job banks in each state. **Main files include:** About America's Job Bank; About This Service; Job Search; and Customer Comments. **Fee:** Free.

★9318★ Best Jobs in The USA Today

URL: http://www.bestjobsusa.com/ • **Description:** Database offering employment ads from *Employment Review Magazine* and *Employment Review's* recruitment section in the *USA Today* newspaper. Also features a resume service and a career store.

★9319★ BSA CareerMart

URL: http://www.careermart.com • **Description:** Site where users can scan job postings and learn about specific employers. Users can conduct job searches customized by state/region, job catagory, and company.

★9320★ Business Job Finder

URL: http://www.cob.ohio-state.edu/dept/fin/osujobs.htm • **Description:** Site contains information on jobs in the business sector, primarily in accounting, finance, and consulting. Links to many corporations who hire extensively in this are are included for those wishing to make contacts and/or mail out resumes. Provides detailed information on job search aids and employer profiles, with job areas broken down into subject. Data on salaries, skill requirements, trends and other important factors are expanded from each subject-specific occupation listing. There are also many links to other job-seeking related sites and dozens of company sites on the Internet. **Main files include:** What's the Job Market Like This Year for College Seniors?; 1995 Salaries for Undergraduate Business and Liberal Arts Students; MBA Page; Finance; Accounting; Management; Visit With Employers and Check Out Jobs; and Check Out Cool Career Sites.

★9321★ Career Shop

URL: http://www.tenkey.com/cshop/ • **Description:** Database of resume profiles and employment opportunites. Job hunters can post resumes and perform job searches. Employers can search resumes and post job openings.

★9322★ CareerMosaic

URL: http://www.careermosaic.com/cm/ • **Description:** Contains a help-wanted database and other information on careers, employers, and human resources. Also includes a library of employment related seminars and publications, special events listings, and employer information. **Fee:** Free. **E-Mail:** feedback@pa.hodes.com

★9323★ CareerPath.com

URL: http://www.careerpath.com • **Description:** Employment database featuring job listings from six newspapers: *The Boston Globe, Chicago Tribune, Los Angeles Times, The New York Times, San Jose Mercury News,* and *The Washington Post.* Listings are updated on a daily basis.

★9324★ Careers On-Line

URL: http://www.disserv.stu.umn.edu/TC/Grants/COL/ • **Description:** Site offering employment and career-related information to job seekers with disabilities. Databases include: Adaptive Technology Products and Resources; Job Internships and Postings; Resume Information Database; and the online version version of the Job Accomodation Handbook from Career Connections.

★9325★ CareerSite

URL: http://www.careersite.com/ • **Description:** Job seekers can scan job opportunities either by employer or by type of work, and reply electronically to job listings. They can submit a resume and confidential profile to be placed in the database. The job seeker's identity is released to employers only with the listee's permission.

★9326★ CareerSurf Recruiting Network

URL: http://www.careersurf.com/ • **Description:** Services offered to job seekers include: CompanySurf–listings of recruiting firms, employers, and career service provides; ResumeDock–resume database; LibrarySurf–online job search information.

★9327★ CareerWEB

URL: http://www.cweb.com/ • **Description:** Users can search job listings, store their resume online, and browse the "Bookstore" or the online newsletter for other career information. Also offers a Career Inventory to assess the user's skills.

★9328★ Contract Employment Weekly's Jobs Online

Gopher: gopher.ceweekly.wa.com • **URL:** gopher://ceweekly.wa.com • **Description:** Contains information on immediate and anticipated job openings throughout the United States, Canada, and overseas. All jobs listed are temporary technical jobs that are usually higher paying that similar direct jobs. **Main files include:** About Contract Employment Weekly's Job Online Gopher; AOL Subscribers Read This!!; How to Specify Keywords for the Jobs Database; Job Search and Information for Non-subscribers to C.E. Weekly; Job Search, and Other Services for C.E. Weekly Subscribers; and Publications and Services of C.E. **E-Mail:** ceweekly@eskimo.com

★9329★ Corporate Web Register

URL: http://www.hoovers.com/bizreg.html • **Description:** Directory of corporate Web presences for all major public, private, and international firms. Listed are more than 1700 sites that have company news as well as information on products, investor relations, and job opportunites. **Fee:** Free. **E-Mail:** info@hoovers.com

★9330★ DICE (Data Processing Consultants Exchange)

URL: http://www.dice.dlinc.com:8181/ • **Description:** Job search database for computer consultants and high-tech professionals. Users can search the company database by name, region, and logo, and then perform searches for job opportunities within each company.

★9331★ E-SPAN Interactive Employment Network

URL: http://www.espan.com • **Description:** Provides current, authoritative resources for the job seeker and for the employer, including resumes, job search tips, interview practice exercises, employment listings, salary guides, career fair calendars, and discussion forums. Includes more than 10,000 job openings and company profiles of more than 40 corporations advertising on the site, mainly for technical positions. **Fee:** Free to job seekers. **E-Mail:** info@espan3.espan.com

★9332★ Electric Ideas Clearinghouse Bulletin Board System

Telnet: eicbbs.wseo.wa.gov; Remarks: tel net login: new • **URL:** http://www.eicbbs.wseo.wa.gov/ • **Modem:** 800762-3319 (Pacific); 206956-2212 (Other areas) • **Description:** This site provides training, jobs and resumes, and up-to-date information for energy professionals and students in energy-related college and univeristy programs. Major features include a technical assistance hotline and an electronic bulletin board. Also includes job listings and online publications. **Main files include:** About the Clearinghouse; News, Bulletins, and Press Releases; Journals and Newsletters; Newsgroups; Conferences and Training Events; Accredited Courses Online; Publications; Reference Tools; Software; Job Listings; and Links to Other Web Sites. **Fee:** Free. **E-Mail:** grewar@wseo.wa.gov

★9333★ Employment Directory Guide to North American Markets

URL: http://www.careermosaic.com/ cm/directory/ed1.html • **Description:** This is the HTML edition of the Recruitment Directory of employment information on markets. (The print version is published annually.) The Directory is intended to assist to individuals in managing their careers. It also provides information for recruiters. It includes demographic information, an employment analysis, chambers of commerce, and convention and visitors bureaus. Also provides the top 25 U.S. markets college data (and will soon have links to each school's home page that hosts a www or gopher server.) The Cosumer Price Index (CPI) for select U.S. cities follows the top market data. A list of government sources of labor information also appears. **Main files include:** The Top 50 U.S. Markets; The Top 10 Canadian Markets; The Consumer Price Index (CPI). **E-Mail:** tgibbon@hodes.com

★9334★ The ESL Virtual Catalog

URL: http://www.pvp.com/esl.htm • **Description:** Designed for students and teachers of ESL (English as a Second Lanuguage), the ESL catalog provides links to related Web sites and electronic publications; a guide to instructional materials available from ESL publishers; related newsgroups, mailing lists, conferences, and study programs, a directory of ESL membership organizations; and job listings in the ESL field; as well as other information. **Main files include:** Directory of Internet Resources; Directory of Publishers and Distributors; Directory of Professional Organizations. **Fee:** Free. **E-Mail:** pvp@pvp.com

★9335★ Federal Job Announcements

Telnet: fedworld.gov • **URL:** http://www.fedworld.gov/pub/jobs/jobs.htm • **Modem:** 703321-8020 • **Anonymous ftp:** ftp.fedworld.gov; Path: jobs • **Description:** Database containing employment information in the public sector. Listings include address, job title and information, contact information, geographic location, and data of availability, among others. **Main files include:** NTIS Federal Job Opportunities; Atlanta Regional Federal Jobs; Chicago Regional Federal Jobs; Dallas Regional Federal Jobs; Philadel-

phia Regional Federal Jobs; San Francisco Regional Federal Jobs; Washington DC Regional Federal Jobs; National Federal Jobs; S&S Federal Positions Available; Public Health Service Positions; Federal Jobs Listed by State; Atlantic Overseas; Pacific Overseas; Puerto Rico; Virgin Islands; Information on Downloading Files; Federal Jobs EMail Forum; Exit to Main Menu; and Enter Jobs File Library. **Fee:** Free. **E-Mail:** webmaster@fedworld.gov

★9336★ Federal Job Opportunity Board

Telnet: fjob.mail.opm.gov; Login: first name; Password: last name; Remarks: System will automatically register names it doesn't recognize. • **Modem:** 912757-3100 N,8,1 F; 912757-3115 N,8,1 F (for high-speed modems) • **Description:** Provides information about jobs that are available in the Federal government. The online search program allows users to search job announcements on the bulletin board by either series number or job title. **Fee:** Free.

★9337★ First Steps in the Hunt: A Web Guide to The Employment Search

URL: http://www.interbiznet.com/hunt/index.html • **Description:** Database provides a wide variety of information on job hunting on the Internet, as well as links to other sources of information. Included are examples of online web page resumes and links to information about publishing them. Also includes an archive of articles, a listing of job hunting tools and products that may help in the job search. **Main files include:** Sponsors; Tools; Archives; Products; and Info. **E-Mail:** huntsuggest@interbiznet.com

★9338★ Global Job Net

URL: http://www.globaljobnet.com/index.shtml • **Description:** Provides a means for businesses and corporations to list job openings and business opportunities and individuals to post resumes and register as consultants. Fees are charged to post openings/requirements/resumes. Browsing the various files is free. **Main files include:** Business Opportunities; Consultant/Contractor Registry; Jobs Available Listing; and Resume Posting Service.

★9339★ HEART

URL: http://www.career.com/PUB/heart.html • **Description:** Users can perform job searches by company, location, discipline, and for new graduates. Other features include "Hot Jobs" and a resume save option.

★9340★ helpwanted.com

URL: http://www.helpwanted.com/ • **Description:** Site providing job postings, resume service, and listing of employment agencies and recruiters. Other features include "Job of the Week" and "Company of the Week."

★9341★ Industry.Net

URL: http://www.industry.net/c/mn/°co • **Description:** Users can search for career opportunities in technical catagories including: Engineering, Sales/Marketing, Programmers/Analysts, Computer Hardware, MIS Professionals, Manufacturing, and Administration.

★9342★ IntelliMatch

URL: http://www.intellimatch.com/ • **Description:** Offers a job matching service. Job seekers can create an online resume using a structured form focusing on skills rather than experience.

★9343★ Internet Career Connection

URL: http://www.iccweb.com/welcome.html • **Description:** Online career and employment guidance agency. Site's services include: Career Analysis Service–a personality assessment to identify the user's future career direction; Career Resource Mall–offers resources such as books, newsletters, etc.; Employment Recruiter Service–identifies recruiters, search firms, and placement services; Help Wanted-USA Ads–job seekers can access help wanted ads; U.S. Government Employment Opportunitities; Worldwide Resume/Talent Bank–job seekers can post resumes.

★9344★ itCareers

URL: http://careers.computerworld.com/ • **Description:** Subtitled: *Computerworld's* Center for Professional Development. Offers career opportunities for IT (information technology) professionals. Job seekers can search on their own for current listings or they can utilize the automated career search system, CareerMail.

★9345★ Job Listings Database

Gopher: University of Texas, Austin - Gopher Central; gopher.utexas.edu; Choose: World/Jobs • **URL:** gopher://gopher.utexas.edu/11/world/jobs • **Description:** Database containing job listings from various sources in the United States. Data providers include some 40 universities, state and U.S. government agencies and other miscellaneous data providers. **Main files include:** Jobs: Universities; Jobs: U.S. Government; Jobs: Miscellaneous; Job-related information. **Fee:** Free. **E-Mail:** gopher@gopher.utexas.edu

★9346★ Job Openings in Academe

Gopher: Academe This Week; chronicle.merit.edu; Choose: JOBS in and out of Academe: more than 1,040 openings • **URL:** gopher://chronicle.merit.edu:70/11/.ads • http://chronicle.merit.edu/.ads/.links.html • **Description:** Provided by the Chronicle of Higher Education, Job Openings in Academe is a fully searchable online listing of jobs currently available at univeristies and colleges in the U.S. and abroad. Position listings include faculty, research, administrative and executive openings. **Main files include:** Faculty and Research Positions; Administrative Positions; Executive Positions; Positions Outside Academe; and SEARCH using any word or words of the user's choosing. **Fee:** Free. **E-Mail:** info@merit.edu

★9347★ Job Openings in the Federal Government

Gopher: gopher.dartmouth.edu; Choose: Career Services • **URL:** gopher://caligari.dartmouth.edu/11/fedjobs • **Description:** Database containing copies of the electronic postings of federal job openings obtained by downloading the dialup Public OPM and other government agency bulletin boards.

Main files include: Gopher and the Federal Job Openings Files; About the Federal Job Openings Files; Federal Gov't Position Announcements; Private Industry Position Announcements; Salary Pay Tables for Federal Civilian Employees; Specific Locality Pay Tables for Federal Employees; Federal Job Classification; Federal Group Occupational Requirements; Miscellaneous info useful to job applicants.

★9348★ Job Search and Employment Opportunities: Best Bets from the Net

URL: gopher://una.hh.lib.umich.edu/00/inetdirsstacks/employment%3araytay • **Description:** Database providing a resource guide to information about job opportunities and employment found on the Internet. Leads users to job postings; places to submit a resume electronically; and career information resources. **Fee:** Free. **E-Mail:** job guide@umich.educ

★9349★ JobCenter Employment Service

URL: http://www.jobcenter.com/ • **Description:** Job seekers can post resumes and perform searches for job openings. Once a resume is posted, the site will send matching job ads to the user's e-mail address.

★9350★ JobWeb

URL: http://www.jobweb.org/ • **Description:** Site maintained by the National Association of Colleges and Employers (NACE). Provides career-related information and job listings to college students and graduates.

★9351★ Library and Information Science JobSearch

Telnet: alexia.lis.uiuc.edu; Login: jobs; Password: Urbaign • **URL:** http://carousel.lis.uiuc.edu/~jobs/ • **Description:** Database containing all professional job announcements received by the University of Illinois GSLIS (Graduate School of Library and Information Science) Placement Office. This site allows the user to perform searches of LIS-related jobs from the database. The user can search by given criteria, including library type, experience level, geographical area, salary, date, and job type. **Main files include:** Search Job Notices by Certain Criteria; Review All Job Notices in the Database; and Review New Job Notices in the Database. **Fee:** Free. **E-Mail:** lisjobs@uiuc.edu

★9352★ MedSearch America, Inc.

Gopher: gopher.medsearch.com • **URL:** gopher://gopher.medsearch.com/ • **Description:** MedSearch America delivers nationwide access to healthcare recruiting. Employers can post job listings or ads with private e-mail box responses; search resumes; and offer outplacement services, custom search and pre-screening services, company profiles and recruitment imformation, and direct dial-up accounts. Job seekers can post and code resumes, and search healthcare job listings, healthcare career advice columns, career resources information, member employer profiles and services, and a schedule of healthcare events. **Main files include:** What's New on MedSearch America; All About MedSearch America; How to Post Your Resume Online; MedSearch America

Membership; Featured Employers; Search Jobs; Search Resumes; Recruitment Services Network; Frequently Asked Questions; Limitation and Disclaimer of Liability. **E-Mail:** office@medsearch.com

★9353★ The Monster Board

URL: http://www.monster.com • **Description:** An interactive, continually expanding database of current job openings, including an online career fair, career search help, employer profiles, and a resume posting service. Searching is available by industry, location, company, discipline and keyword. Users can search tens of thousands of position openings, advertise openings, or submit resumes. Employers pay a fee for posting position openings and company profiles. An online form allows for contact with the producers of the database. **Main files include:** Career Search; Employer Profiles; Resume On-line; Career Events; Roar; HR HQ; and Virtual Help. **Fee:** Free to job seekers; fees for job advertisers. **E-Mail:** webmaster@monster.com

★9354★ NationJob Network

URL: http://www.nationjob.com/ • **Description:** Online job database containing job listings and company profiles. Job openings are from across the country, but focus primarily on the Midwest.

★9355★ NCS Career Magazine

URL: http://www.careermag.com/index.html • **Description:** Users can search the Jobline Database by location, job title, and skills required. In addition to a resume bank, the site also provides news articles, employer profiles, and other career-related information.

★9356★ NetJobs

URL: http://www.netjobs.com:8000/index.html • **Description:** Job seekers can post resumes online and search for job openings. Searches can be performed by job category, company name or location, and listings posted within the last ten days.

★9357★ nonPROFIT JOBS: The Employment Resource

URL: http://www.nonprofitjobs.com/ • **Description:** Database of resumes submitted by nonprofit professionals. Job seekers pay a fee to include their resumes in the database.

★9358★ Online Career Center Database

Gopher: MSEN Gopher; occ.com • **URL:** gopher://occ.com/11/occ • **Description:** Contains searchable job postings, employment events, and a list of resumes of job seekers. Most of the job postings are computer-related. **Main files include:** Search Jobs: Online Career Center; Search Resumes: Online Career Center; Search Chronicle of Higher Education; Search MedSearch America; About Online Career Center; Career Assistance; College & University; Resume Books/Diskettes; Company Sponsors and Profiles; Employment Events; FAQ–Frequently Asked Questions About OCC; Help Files: Keyword Search/Enter Resume/Print; How to Enter A Resume; Online Career Center–On Campus; Online Career Center Liability Policy; Recruitment Advertising Agencies. **Fee:** Free. **E-Mail:** occ@occ.com

★9359★ Resume'Net
URL: http://www.resumenet.com/ • **Description:** Online resume publishing service. Assists job seekers in creating online resumes.

★9360★ Saludos Web: Careers, Employment, and Culture
URL: http://www.hooked.net/saludos/index.html • **Description:** Supported by *Saludos Hispanos* magazine, this site is devoted to promoting Hispanic careers and education. Online job postings and resume services are offered. Educational resources include lists of grants and scholarships for Hispanic students, and interships. Links to other Hispanic sites on the Net are provided. **Main files include:** Career Center; Education Center; Article Archive; Resume Pool; and the

Hispanic Resource Index. **Fee:** Free. **E-Mail:** staff@hooked.net

★9361★ Summer Jobs
URL: http://www.summerjobs.com/ • **Description:** Database listing seasonal and part-time job opportunities. Job listings are organized by country, state, region, and city. Primary focus is on summer jobs for students and education professionals.

★9362★ The Virtual Job Fair
URL: http://www.careerexpo.com/ • **Description:** Site offers a database of over 15,000 high-tech job listings searchable by job title, technology, and location/company. Also provides a resume posting service, the *High Technology Careers Magazine,* Library and Resource Center, Human Resource Center, as well as schedules for career fairs and expos.

SOFTWARE

★9363★ The Job Finder's Tool Kit
Planning/Communications
7215 Oak Ave.
River Forest, IL 60305-1935
Ph: (708)366-5200   Fr: (888)366-5200

WinWay Corporation. 1996. $69.95 (CD-ROM version); $79.95 (Windows version on seven diskettes). Hypertext version of three books on one database: *Government Job Finder, Professional's Job Finder,* and *Non-Profit and Education Job Finder.* CD-ROM version includes 45-minute video on using electronic job search tools. CD-ROM version requires sound card; Windows version requires 14 MB of hard drive space.

Environmental Opportunities

REFERENCE WORKS

★9364★ Agricultural Research Institute—Membership Directory

Agricultural Research Institute
9650 Rockville Pke.
Bethesda, MD 20814
Ph: (301)530-7122   Fax: (301)530-7007

Annual. $10.00, postpaid. Covers 125 member institutions; also lists study panels and committees interested in environmental issues, pest control, agricultural meteorology, biotechnology, food irradiation, agricultural policy, research and development, food safety, technology transfer, and remote sensing. Entries include: Name, title of primary contact, address, phone. fax. Arrangement: Alphabetical.

★9365★ Association of Consulting Foresters—Membership Specialization Directory

Association of Consulting Foresters
5400 Grosvenor Ln., Ste. 300
Bethesda, MD 20814-2198
Ph: (301)530-6795   Fax: (301)530-5128

Annual, August. $18.00, postpaid. Covers nearly 450 member forestry consulting firms and professional foresters who earn the largest part of their income from consulting. Entries include: Name, address, phone, specialties, background, career data, staff (if a consulting firm), geographic area served, capabilities, including equipment available and foreign language proficiency. Arrangement: Alphabetical. Indexes: Name, office location, language, international capability.

★9366★ Canadian Environmental Directory

Gale Research
835 Penobscot Bldg.
Detroit, MI 48226-4094
Ph: (313)961-2242   Fax: (313)961-6083
Fr: 800-877-GALE

Fourth edition, 1994. $225.00. Directory of individuals, agencies, firms, and associations active in environment-related activities in Canada. Main alphabetical listings are organized by government, organization, and education/research establishments. Provides list-

ing of legal, ecological, and management consultants.

★9367★ Careers in the Environment

VGM Career Horizons
NTC Publishing Group
4255 W. Touhy Ave.
Lincolnwood, IL 60646-1975
Ph: (847)679-5500   Fax: (847)679-2494
Fr: 800-323-4900

Michael Fasulo and Paul Walker. 1995. $17.95; $13.95 (paper). 160 pages. Comprehensive information on the diverse career opportunities available in environmental services.

★9368★ Careers for Environmental Types and Others Who Respect the Earth

VGM Career Horizons
NTC Publishing Group
4255 W. Touhy Ave.
Lincolnwood, IL 60646-1975
Ph: (847)679-5500   Fax: (847)679-2494
Fr: 800-323-4900

Jane Kinney and Mike Fasulo. 1993. $14.95; $9.95 (paper). 160 pages. Describes environmentally friendly positions with corporations, government, and environmental organizations.

★9369★ Careers in National Park Service

National Park Service
U.S. Department of the Interior
Public Information Office
PO Box 37127
Washington, DC 20013-7127
Ph: (202)208-5228

Booklet. Free. 20 pages. Information about the hiring process for park service opportunities.

★9370★ Careers for Nature Lovers and Other Outdoor Types

VGM Career Horizons
4255 W. Touhy Ave.
Lincolnwood, IL 60646-1975
Ph: (847)679-5500   Fax: (847)679-2494
Fr: 800-323-4900

Louise Miller. 1992. $12.95; $9.95 (paper). Examines career opportunities in biology, agriculture, landscaping, forestry and conser-

vation, geology, and waste management, and pollution control. Offers insight into preparing for and finding outdoor jobs in federal and state government, as well as private industry.

★9371★ Conservation Directory

National Wildlife Federation
1400 16th St. NW
Washington, DC 20036
Ph: (202)790-4402   Fax: (202)442-7332
Fr: 800-432-6564

Annual, January. $20.00, plus shipping; payment with orders from individuals. Covers about 90 federal agencies, 600 national and international organizations, over 1,000 state government agencies and citizens groups, and 117 Canadian agencies and groups concerned with conservation of natural resources and preservation of the environment; colleges and universities with environmental education programs. Entries include: Agency name, address, branch or subsidiary office name and address, names and titles of key personnel, interests, activities, publications. Arrangement: Classified by type of organization. Indexes: Personal name, subject, publication title.

★9372★ Directory of Internships

Ready Reference Press
PO Box 5249
Santa Monica, CA 90409
Ph: (213)474-5175   Fr: 800-424-5627

$89.50. Out of print. Lists internship opportunities in many fields of interest, including, but not limited to arts, journalism, public relations, education, law, environmental affairs, business, engineering, and computer science. In addition, cites summer internship opportunities, work/study programs, and specialized opportunities for high school and undergraduate students. Indexed by subject, geography, and program.

★9373★ Directory of National Environmental Organizations

U.S. Environmental Directories
Box 65156
St. Paul, MN 55165
Ph: (612)331-6050

Irregular, latest edition October 1994. $59.00, postpaid; payment must accompany order. Covers over 775 organizations outside of government concerned with the environment and conservation. Entries include: Organization name, address, phone, contact name, year established, number of members, short description of activities and aims. Arrangement: Alphabetical. Indexes: Subject, geographical, federal agency (with address and phone numbers).

★9374★ **Education for the Earth: The College Guide for Careers in the Environment**

Peterson's Guides, Inc.
202 Carnegie Center
PO Box 2123
Princeton, NJ 08543-2123
Ph: (609)243-9111   Fax: (609)243-9150
Fr: 800-338-3282

Published 1994. $14.95. Covers over 300 colleges and universities offering programs in environmental studies. Entries include: College or university name, address, phone, description of program, major area of concentration, employment results, names of employers who recently recruited on campus. Arrangement: Classified by area of study. Indexes: Geographical; alphabetical.

★9375★ **EI Environmental Services Directory**

Environmental Information Ltd.
4801 W. 81st St., Ste. 119
Bloomington, MN 55437
Ph: (612)831-2473   Fax: (612)831-6550

Biennial, December of even years. $495.00, postpaid; payment with order. Covers over 620 waste-handling facilities, 600 transportation firms, 500 spill response firms, 2,100 consultants, 470 laboratories, 450 soil boring/well drilling firms; also includes incineration services, polychlorinated biphenyl (PCB) detoxification and mobile solvent-recovery services, asbestos services and underground tank services, summaries of states' regulatory programs. Entries include: Company name, address, phone, service, regulatory status, on and off site processes used, type of waste handled. Arrangement: Geographical. Indexes: Service.

★9376★ **Environmental Career Directory**

Gale Research
835 Penobscot Bldg.
Detroit, MI 48226-4094
Ph: (313)961-2242   Fax: (313)961-6083
Fr: 800-877-GALE

Latest edition 1993. $34.00; $17.95 (paper). Covers over 250 companies and organizations offering entry-level positions in environment-related careers, including forestry management, fish and wildlife management, and air and water quality control; sources of help-wanted ads, professional associations, producers of videos, databases, career guides, and professional guides and handbooks. Entries include: For companies: name, address, phone, business description, names and titles of key personnel, number of employees, average number of entry-level positions available, human resources contact, description of internship opportunities including contact, type and number available, application procedures, qualifications, and duties. For others: name or title, address, phone,

description. Paperback edition is available from Visible Ink Press. Arrangement: Companies are alphabetical; others are classified by type of resource. Indexes: Name, keyword.

★9377★ **Environmental Industry Directory**

Gale Research
835 Penobscot Bldg.
Detroit, MI 48226-4094
Ph: (313)961-2242   Fax: (313)961-6083
Fr: 800-877-GALE

1992. $195.00. Covers 6,000 organizations, state and federal government agencies, private institutions and services, research and educational facilities, and publications and information services involved with environmental issues and topics. Entries include organization name, address, and contact person.

★9378★ **Hazardous Waste Consultant— Directory of Commercial Hazardous Waste Management Facilities Issue**

Physical Sciences Group
Elsevier Science, Inc.
655 Ave. of the Americas
New York, NY 10010
Ph: (212)633-3827   Fax: (212)633-3795

Annual, March-April. $100.00. Publication includes: List of nearly 160 licensed commercial facilities that treat and/or dispose of hazardous waste material. Entries include: Facility name, address, phone, contact name, type of waste handled, methods of on-site treatment and/or disposal, Environmental Protection Agency permit status and identification number, restrictions, description of other services. Arrangement: Geographical. Indexes: Organization name.

★9379★ **The Hidden Job Market: A Job Seeker's Guide to America's 2,000 Little-Known, Fastest-Growing High-Tech Companies**

Peterson's Guides, Inc.
202 Carnegie Center
PO Box 2123
Princeton, NJ 08543-2123
Ph: (609)243-9111   Fax: (609)243-9150
Fr: 800-338-3282

Annual, October. $16.95. Covers Approximately 2,000 technology firms with under 1,000 employees, which have added the most employees in the survey year. Entries include: Company name, address, phone, fax, name and title of contact, number of employees, year founded, number of employees added in last year, percentage of growth, line of business. Arrangement: Geographical by state, then by area code. Indexes: Alphabetical by industry.

★9380★ **Job Opportunities in the Environment 1995**

Peterson's Guides, Inc.
PO Box 2123
Princeton, NJ 08543-2123
Ph: (609)243-9111   Fax: (609)243-9150
Fr: 800-225-0261

1994. $18.95 (paper).

★9381★ **Jobs from Recyclables Possibility Newsletter**

Prosperity & Profits Unlimited Distribution Services
PO Box 416
Denver, CO 80201
Ph: (303)575-5676

Annual. $4.50. Describes employment options for environmentalists, waste management, and businesses.

★9382★ **Life Sciences Organizations and Agencies Directory**

Gale Research
835 Penobscot Bldg.
Detroit, MI 48226-4094
Ph: (313)961-2242   Fax: (313)961-6083
Fr: 800-877-GALE

$175.00. Covers about 7,500 associations, government agencies, research centers, educational institutions, libraries and information centers, museums, consultants, electronic information services, and other organizations and agencies active in agriculture, biology, ecology, forestry, marine science, nutrition, wildlife and animal sciences, and other natural and life sciences. Entries include: Organization or agency name, address, phone, name and title of contact, description. Arrangement: Classified by type of organization. Indexes: Organization/agency name and keyword.

★9383★ **National Directory Conservation Land Trusts**

Land Trust Alliance
1319 F St. NW, Ste. 510
Washington, DC 20004-1106
Ph: (202)638-4725   Fax: (202)638-4730

Biennial, even years. Formerly *National Directory of Local and Regional Land Conservation Organizations*. Profiles 900 nonprofit land conservation organizations at the local and regional levels.

★9384★ **National Parks: Index**

U.S. National Park Service
1849 C St. NW
Washington, DC 20240
Ph: (202)512-2250

Biennial, odd years. $5.00, payment with order. Covers over 368 areas administered by the National Park Service, including parks, shores, historic sites, 80 national trails, and wild and scenic rivers. Entries include: Name, location, address, acreage (federal, non-federal, and gross), federal facilities, brief description. Arrangement: Most areas are geographical; wild and scenic rivers and national trails are alphabetical. Indexes: Alphabetical by area name.

★9385★ **Nature (Career Portraits)**

VGM Career Horizons
NTC Publishing Group
4255 W. Touhy Ave.
Lincolnwood, IL 60646-1975
Ph: (847)679-5500   Fax: (847)679-2494
Fr: 800-323-4900

Marjorie Eberts. 1996. $13.95. 96 pages. Highlights a range of careers that focus on the environment, with descriptions of a typical day on the job and interactive exercises for readers.

★9386★ New Careers Directory: Internships and Professional Opportunities in Technology and Social Change

Student Pugwash USA
815 15th St. NW, Ste. 814
Washington, DC 20005
Ph: (202)393-6555   Fax: (202)393-6550
Fr: 800-WOW-A-PUG

Irregular; latest edition spring 1993. $13.00 for students; $21.00 for institutions, plus $3.00 shipping. Covers about 300 research institutes, think tanks, laboratories, government agencies, professional, science, and other non-profit organizations offering public policy, science, and technology internships and jobs. Entries include: Sponsoring organization name, description of organization, programs offered, work environment and application procedures, compensation offered. Arrangement: Alphabetical and classified by subject. Indexes: Geographical, subject.

★9387★ Now Hiring! Outdoor Jobs: The Insider's Guide to Gaining Seasonal & Year-Round Employment in America's National Parks and Forests

Progressive Media, Inc.
4556 University Way NE., STE. 2222
Seattle, WA 98105
Ph: (206)545-7950   Fax: (206)545-7951

Kevin Lustgarten. 1993. $17.95 (paper).

★9388★ Opportunities in Energy Careers

VGM Career Horizons
4255 W. Touhy Ave.
Lincolnwood, IL 60646-1975
Ph: (847)679-5500   Fax: (847)679-2494
Fr: 800-323-4900

John Woodburn. 1992. $13.95; $10.95 (paper). 160 pages. Discusses opportunities in a variety of fields, including petroleum, nuclear, and thermal energy, and how to pursue employment. Illustrated.

★9389★ Opportunities in Environmental Careers

VGM Career Horizons
4255 W. Touhy Ave.
Lincolnwood, IL 60646-1975
Ph: (847)679-5500   Fax: (847)679-2494
Fr: 800-323-4900

Odom Fanning. 1995. $14.95; $11.95 (paper). 160 pages. Describes a broad range of opportunities in fields such as environmental health, recreation, physics, and hygiene, and provides job search advice.

★9390★ Opportunities in Forestry Careers

VGM Career Horizons
4255 W. Touhy Ave.
Lincolnwood, IL 60646-1975
Ph: (847)679-5500   Fax: (847)679-2494
Fr: 800-323-4900

Christopher M. Wille. 1992. $13.95; $10.95 (paper). 160 pages. Describes the forestry opportunities available in governmental agencies, commercial enterprises, education, and private conservation association, and how to pursue openings. Illustrated.

★9391★ Opportunities in Waste Management Careers

VGM Career Horizons
4255 W. Touhy Ave.
Lincolnwood, IL 60646-1975
Ph: (847)679-5500   Fax: (847)679-2494
Fr: 800-323-4900

Mark Rowh. 1992. $13.95; $10.95 (paper). Outlines the diverse opportunities in waste management and examines the duties, working conditions, salaries, and future of a variety of positions. Profiles jobs and opportunities in solid waste and waste water management, environmental engineering, soil and wildlife conservation, and related career areas.

★9392★ Peterson's Hidden Job Market 1996

Peterson's
PO Box 2123
Princeton, NJ 08543-2123
Ph: (609)243-9111   Fax: (609)243-9150
Fr: 800-338-3282

Fifth edition, 1995. $17.95. Guide to 2,000 fast-growing companies that are hiring now. Focuses on high technology companies in such fields as environmental consulting, genetic engineering, home health care, telecommunications, alternative energy systems, and others.

★9393★ Peterson's Job Opportunities in the Environment

Peterson's Guides, Inc.
202 Carnegie Ctr.
Box 2123
Princeton, NJ 08543-2123
Ph: (609)243-9111   Fax: (609)243-9150
Fr: 800-338-3282

Annual, August. $18.95. Covers Approximately 1,500 companies and government agencies hiring environmental professionals, including waste-management companies, state and federal agencies, advocacy groups, and environmental design firms. Entries include: Organization name, address, phone, name and title of contact, type of organization, number of employees, Standard Industrial Classification (SIC) code; description of opportunities available including desciplines, level of education required, starting locations and salaries, level of experience accepted, benefits. Arrangement: Alphabetical. Indexes: Employer by type of organization, industry classification, number of employees, starting location, special interest area; education level, company.

★9394★ Resumes for Environmental Careers

VGM Career Horizons
NTC Publishing Group
4255 W. Touhy Ave.
Lincolnwood, IL 60646-1975
Ph: (847)679-5500   Fax: (847)679-2494
Fr: 800-323-4900

1994. $9.95. 160 pages. Provides resume advice tailored to people pursuing careers focusing on the environment. Includes sample resumes and cover letters.

★9395★ Seasonal Employment

U.S. National Park Service
PO Box 37127
Washington, DC 20013-7127
Ph: (202)208-5074

Updated as needed. Free. Publication includes: List of 10 regional offices and branches of the National Park Service that accept applications for seasonal jobs. Entries include: Name, address, phone, geographical area served. Principal content of publication is information on seasonal jobs offered by the National Park Services, with description of duties, qualifications, and application procedures for each type of job offered. Arrangement: Geographical.

★9396★ So You Want to Be a Forester

American Forestry Assn.
PO Box 2000
Washington, DC 20013
Ph: (202)667-3300

Booklet. Free. 16 pages. Includes information on job prospects and opportunities.

★9397★ Summer Opportunities in Marine and Environmental Science

Summer Opportunities Guide
38 Litchfield Rd.
Londonderry, NH 03053

Herriott and Herrin. Second edition, 1994. $14.95. 60 pages. Subtitled: "A Student's Guide to Jobs, Internships and Study, Camp and Travel Programs". Prepared for both high school and college students.

★9398★ A Wildlife Conservation Career for You

The Wildlife Society, Inc.
5410 Grosvenor Lane
Bethesda, MD 20814-2197
Ph: (301)897-9770

Booklet. $.50. 12 pages. Describes career opportunities in wildlife conservation.

NEWSPAPERS, MAGAZINES, AND JOURNALS

★9399★ Appalachian Trailway News

Appalachian Trail Conference
PO Box 807
Harpers Ferry, WV 25425
Ph: (304)535-6331   Fax: (304)535-2667

$15.00/year for individuals. Magazine on hiking, Appalachian Trail protection, and general conservation issues.

★9400★ Applied Occupational & Environmental Hygiene

Applied Industrial Hygiene, Inc.
1330 Kemper Meadow Dr., Ste. 600
Cincinnati, OH 45240
Ph: (513)742-2020   Fax: (513)742-3355

Monthly. $85.00/year for individuals; $155.00/year for institutions. Magazine presenting solutions in occupational and environmental hygiene.

★9401★ **Community Jobs: The Employment Newspaper for the Non-Profit Sector**

ACCESS: Networking in the Public Interest
30 Irving Pl.
New York, NY 10003
Ph: (212)475-1001   Fax: (212)475-1199

Monthly. $69.00. Covers jobs and internships available with nonprofit organizations active in issues such as the environment, foreign policy, consumer advocacy, housing, education, etc. Entries include: Position title; name, address, and phone of contact; description, responsibilities; requirements; salary. Arrangement: Geographical.

★9402★ **Earth Work**

Student Conservation Association
PO Box 550, Rte. 12A, River Rd.
Charlestown, NH 03603-0550
Ph: (603)543-1700

Eleven issues/year. $29.95/year. Includes career information for those working in conservation.

★9403★ **Environment Today**

Enterprise Communications Inc.
1483 Chain Bridge Rd., Ste. 202
McLean, VA 22101-4599
Ph: (703)448-0322   Fax: (703)448-0270

Monthly. Magazine for environmental professionals, including corporate waste generators, municipal utilities managers, and governmental decisionmakers. Focuses on trend-spotting and problem-solving.

★9404★ **Environmental Lab**

Leo Douglas Publications
9609 Gayton Rd., Ste. 100
Richmond, VA 23233
Ph: (804)741-6704

Semimonthly. $62.00/year; $12.00/single issue.

★9405★ **Environmental Opportunities**

Environmental Opportunities
PO Box 788
Walpole, NH 03608
Ph: (603)756-4553

Monthly. $47.00/year. Lists full-time openings in environmental positions as well as short-term opportunities and internships.

★9406★ **Environmental Protection**

Stevens Publishing Corp.
PO Box 2573
Waco, TX 76702-2573
Ph: (817)776-9000   Fax: (817)662-7075
Fr: 800-727-7573

Monthly.

★9407★ **Environmental Science & Technology**

American Chemical Society
1155 16th St. NW
Washington, DC 20036
Ph: (202)872-4600   Fax: (202)872-4615

Monthly. $44.00/year for members; $90.00/year for nonmembers.

★9408★ **In Business**

The JG Press, Inc.
419 State Ave.
Emmaus, PA 18049
Ph: (215)967-4135

Bimonthly. Small business management magazine.

★9409★ **Job Opportunities Bulletin**

National Recreation and Park Association (NRPA)
2775 S. Quincy St., Ste. 300
Arlington, VA 22206
Ph: (703)820-4940   Fr: 800-626-6772

Bimonthly $30.00/year.

★9410★ **The Job Seeker**

The Job Seeker
Rt. 2, Box 16, Dept. J
Warrens, WI 54666
Ph: (608)378-4290

Semimonthly. $19.50/year. Specializes "in environmental and natural resource vacancies nationwide." Lists current vacancies from federal, state, local, private, and nonprofit employers.

★9411★ **Journal of Forestry**

Society of American Foresters
5400 Grosvenor Ln.
Bethesda, MD 20814-2198
Ph: (301)897-8720   Fax: (301)897-3690

Monthly. Journal covering measurement, protection, management, and use of forests for wildlife, recreation, water, wilderness, and graying, as well as the growing and harvesting for timber and energy.

★9412★ **Nature: International Weekly Journal of Science**

Nature Publishing Co.
65 Bleecker St.
New York, NY 10012-2467
Ph: (212)477-9600   Fax: (212)505-1364

Weekly. Magazine covering science and technology, including the fields of biology, biochemistry, genetics, medicine, earth sciences, physics, pharmacology, and behavioral sciences.

★9413★ **Park and Grounds Management**

Madisen Publishing Division
PO Box 1936
Appleton, WI 54913-1936
Ph: (414)733-2301

Bimonthly. $16.00/year for individuals. Magazine for managers of large outdoor grounds areas: college campuses, public parks and schools, resort hotels, and golf courses, covering technical material relating to turf, trees, facilities, equipment, and products.

★9414★ **Recycling Today, Municipal-Market Edition**

GIE Publishing Co.
4012 Bridge Ave.
Cleveland, OH 44113
Ph: (216)961-4130   Fax: (216)961-0364
Fr: 800-456-0707

Monthly. Magazine covering recycling of secondary raw materials and solid-waste management.

★9415★ **Resource Recycling**

Resource Recycling Inc.
PO Box 10540
Portland, OR 97210
Ph: (503)227-1319   Fax: (503)227-6135

Journal reporting on the recycling and composting of solid waste.

★9416★ **Water Environment Research**

Water Environment Federation
601 Wythe St.
Alexandria, VA 22314
Ph: (703)684-2400   Fax: (703)684-2492
Fr: 800-666-0206

Bimonthly. Technical journal covering municipal and industrial water pollution control, water quality, and hazardous wastes.

AUDIO/VISUAL RESOURCES

★9417★ **Career Profiles: Environmental Series**

Cambridge Career Products
PO Box 2153
Dept. CC15
Charleston, WV 25328-2153
Ph: (304)744-9323   Fax: (304)744-9351
Fr: 800-468-4227

Video cassette. 1989. 15 minutes. Examines environmental careers of all sorts.

OTHER SOURCES

★9418★ **Air and Waste Management Association (A&WMA)**

1 Gateway Ctr., 3rd Fl.
Pittsburgh, PA 15222
Ph: (412)232-3444   Fax: (412)232-3450
Fr: 800-270-3444

Purpose: Environmental, educational, and technical organization. Seeks to provide a neutral forum for the exchange of technical information on a wide variety of environmental topics.

★9419★ **American Academy of Environmental Engineers (AAEE)**

130 Holiday Ct., No. 100
Annapolis, MD 21401
Ph: (410)266-3311   Fax: (410)266-7653

Members: Environmentally oriented registered professional engineers certified by examination as diplomates of the academy.
Purpose: to improve the stan-

dards of environmental engineering; to certify those with special knowledge of environmental engineering; to furnish lists of those certified to the public. **Activities:** Maintains speakers' bureau. Recognizes areas of specialization: Air Pollution Control; General Environmental; Hazardous Waste Management; Industrial Hygiene; Radiation Protection; Solid Waste Management; Water Supply and Wastewater. Requires written and oral examinations for certification. Works with other professional organizations on environmentally oriented activities. Identifies potential employment candidates through Talent Search Service.

★9420★ American Public Health Association (APHA)

1015 15th St. NW
Washington, DC 20005
Ph: (202)789-5600   Fax: (202)789-5681

Members: Professional organization of physicians, nurses, educators, academicians, environmentalists, epidemiologists, new professionals, social workers, health administrators, optometrists, podiatrists, pharmacists, dentists, nutritionists, health planners, other community and mental health specialists, and interested consumers. **Purpose:** Seeks to protect and promote personal, mental, and environmental health. **Activities:** Services include: promulgation of standards; establishment of uniform practices and procedures; development of the etiology of communicable diseases; research in public health; exploration of medical care programs and their relationships to public health. Sponsors job placement service.

★9421★ Environmental Careers Organization (ECO)

286 Congress St., 3rd Fl.
Boston, MA 02210-1038
Ph: (617)426-4375   Fax: (617)423-0998

Members: Seeks to protect and enhance the environment through the development of professionals, the promotion of careers, and the inspiration of individual action. **Activities:** Offers placement series, career advisement, career publications, and research and consulting. Participants in programs are mostly upper-level undergraduate, graduate, and doctoral students, or recent graduates seeking professional experience relevant to careers in the environmental fields. Individual subject areas of placement service include biology, chemistry, community development, hazardous waste, natural resources, pollution, public/occupational health, transportation, and wildlife. Maintains high-school speaker's bureau, leadership training, mentoring, outreach to minority institutions, and the Technical Advisor Program for Toxics Use Reduction. **Website:** http://www.eco.org.

★9422★ Environmental Professional Associates

3857 Birch St., Ste. 186
Newport Beach, CA 92660
Ph: (310)273-5320

Executive search firm. Focuses on environmental positions.

★9423★ Hazardous Waste Treatment Council (HWTC)

915 15th St. NW, 5th Fl.
Washington, DC 20005
Ph: (202)783-0870   Fax: (202)737-2038

Purpose: Firms dedicated to the use of high technology treatment in the management of hazardous wastes and to the restricted use of land disposal facilities in the interests of protecting human health and the environment. Advocates minimization of hazardous wastes and the use of alternative technologies in their treatment, including chemical and biological treatments, fixation, neutralization, reclamation, recycling, and thermal treatments such as incineration. Encourages land disposal prohibitions. Promotes reductions in the volume of hazardous waste generated annually and expansion of EPA hazardous waste list. Advocates use of treatment technology as a more cost-effective approach to Superfund site cleanups. Works with state, national, and international officials and firms to assist in development of programs that utilize treatment and minimize land disposal. **Activities:** Provides technical and placement assistance to members; sponsors special studies, technical seminars, and workshops; participates in federal legislation, litigation, and regulatory development.

★9424★ National Association of Conservation Districts (NACD)

509 Capitol Ct. NE
Washington, DC 20002
Ph: (202)547-6223   Fax: (202)547-6450

Members: Soil and water conservation districts organized by the citizens of watersheds, counties, or communities under provisions of state laws. **Purpose:** Directs and coordinates, through local self-government efforts, the conservation and development of soil, water, and related natural resources. Districts include over 90% of the nation's privately owned land. **Activities:** Conducts educational programs and children's services.

★9425★ National Environmental Health Association (NEHA)

720 S. Colorado Blvd., Ste. 970, S. Tower
Denver, CO 80222
Ph: (303)756-9090   Fax: (303)691-9490

Purpose: Professional society of persons engaged in environmental health and protection for governmental agencies, public health and environmental protection agencies, industry, colleges, and universities. Conducts national professional registration program and continuing education programs. Provides self-paced learning modules for field professionals. **Activities:** Offers placement service; compiles statistics. Maintains speakers' bureau. Plans to offer an electronic bulletin board service.

★9426★ Student Conservation Association (SCA, Inc.)

PO Box 550, Rte. 12A, River Rd.
Charlestown, NH 03603-0550
Ph: (603)543-1700   Fax: (603)543-1828

Members: Individuals, foundations, corporations, and groups who support the associa-

tion's programs. **Purpose:** In cooperation with the National Park Service, the U.S. Forest Service, and other federal, state, local, and private agencies which manage public lands and natural resources, the association offers educational programs for high school and college students and other adults to assist with the stewardship of national parks, forests, and other resource areas. **Activities:** High school participants build and repair structures and trails, and carry out ecological restoration work. College students and other adults assist professionals with wildlife research, wilderness management, environmental education, archaeological surveys, and other tasks. Conducts educational and vocational programs providing job skill training, work experience, and exposure to career options in natural resource fields. Operates AmeriCorps programs for Corporation for National Service.

★9427★ United States Committee for the United Nations Environment Program (US UNEP)

2013 Que St. NW
Washington, DC 20009
Ph: (202)234-3600   Fax: (202)332-3221

Members: Individuals interested in raising public awareness of the importance of a global environmental effort. **Purpose:** Encourages activism in support of the United Nations Environment Program. Acts as a liason between the UNEP and the public. Sponsors educational programs and children's services. **Activities:** Offers placement services to job seekers in international environmental work. Maintains speakers' bureau.

★9428★ U.S. Public Interest Research Group (USPIRG)

218 D. St. SE
Washington, DC 20003
Ph: (202)546-9707   Fax: (202)546-2461

Members: Individuals who contribute time, effort, or funds toward public interest research and advocacy. **Activities:** Conducts research, monitors corporate and government actions, and lobbies for reforms on consumer, environmental, energy, and governmental issues. Current efforts include support for: laws to protect consumers from unsafe products and unfair banking practices; laws to reduce the use of toxic chemicals; renewal of the Clean Air Act; efforts to reduce global warming and ozone depletion; energy conservation and use of safe, renewable energy sources. Sponsors internships for college students; provides opportunities for students to receive academic credit for activities such as investigative journalism, legislative research, lobbying, and public education and organizing. Offers summer jobs.

★9429★ Water Environment Federation (WEF)

601 Wythe St.
Alexandria, VA 22314-1994
Ph: (703)684-2400   Fax: (703)684-2492
Fr: 800-666-0206

Members: Technical societies representing chemists, biologists, ecologists, geologists, operators, educational and research personnel, industrial wastewater engineers, consultant engineers, municipal officials, equipment manufacturers, and university professors and students dedicated to the ehancement and preservation of water quality and resources. **Purpose:** Seeks to advance fundamental and practical knowledge concerning the nature, collection, treatment, and disposal of domestic and industrial wastewaters, and the design, construction, operation, and management of facilities for these purposes. Disseminates technical information; promotes good public relations and regulations that improve water quality and the status of individuals working in this field. **Activities:** Conducts educational and research programs.

Government Employment Opportunities

REFERENCE WORKS

★9430★ The Access Guide to International Affairs Internships in The Washington, DC, Area

Access: A Security Information Service
1511 K St. NW, No. 643
Washington, DC 20005-1401
Ph: (202)785-6630   Fax: (202)785-3607

Bruce Seymore, editor. 1994. $17.95 (paper).

★9431★ Career Choices for the 90's for Students of Political Science and Government

Walker and Company
435 Hudson St.
New York, NY 10014
Ph: (212)727-8300   Fax: (212)727-0984
Fr: 800-289-2553

Prepared by the Career Associates staff. 1990. $8.95. 166 pages. Discusses alternatives for students of political science and government. Offers advice on how to break into the field and how to move up. Covers where and who the employers are, internship possibilities, and professional networking associations. Comprehensive guide to career and job search planning.

★9432★ Careers in Law

VGM Career Horizons
4255 W. Touhy Ave.
Lincolnwood, IL 60646-1975
Ph: (847)679-5500   Fax: (847)679-2494
Fr: 800-323-4900

Gary Munneke. 1992. $17.95; $13.95 (paper). Overview of opportunities available to lawyers in private practice, corporate law, in federal, state, and local governments, and in teaching. Provides information on the typical law school curriculum plus opportunities in internships and clerkships.

★9433★ Carroll's Federal Directory

Carroll Publishing
1058 Thomas Jefferson St. NW
Washington, DC 20007
Ph: (202)333-8620   Fax: (202)337-7020
Fr: 800-336-4240

Bimonthly. $197.00, includes CD-ROM or diskette in subscription. Covers about 35,000 executive managers in federal government offices in Washington, DC, including executive, congressional and judicial branches; members of Congress and Congressional committees and staff. Entries include: Agency names, titles, office address (including room numbers), e-mail addresses, and telephone and fax numbers. Available as part of a library edition titled, *Federal Executive Directory Annual*. Arrangement: By cabinet department or administrative agency. Indexes: Keyword, personal name (with phone).

★9434★ Carroll's State Directory

Carroll Publishing
1058 Thomas Jefferson St. NW
Washington, DC 20007
Ph: (202)333-8620   Fax: (202)337-7020
Fr: 800-336-4240

Three times per year. $180.00, includes CD-ROM or diskette. Covers about 37,000 state government officials in all branches of government and members of authorities. Entries include: Name, address, phone, fax,title. Arrangement: Geographical; separate sections for state offices and legislatures. Indexes: Personal name (with phone), organizational, keyword.

★9435★ Civil Service Handbook

Prentice Hall General Reference
15 Columbus Cir.
New York, NY 10023
Ph: (212)373-8500   Fr: 800-223-2348

Hy Hammer. Eleventh edition, 1994. $10.00. Subtitled: "How to Get a Civil Service Job." Comprehensive guide to working in state and federal government. Includes sample exams for postal clerks and police officers.

★9436★ Complete Guide to Public Employment

Impact Publications
9104-N Manassas Dr.
Manassas Park, VA 22111-5211
Ph: (703)361-7300   Fax: (703)335-9486

Ron and Caryl Krannich. Third edition, 1995. $19.95 (paper). List of federal, state, and local government agencies and departments, trade and professional associations, contracting and consulting firms, nonprofit organizations, foundations, research organizations, political support groups, and other organizations offering public service career opportunities. Entries include: Organization name, address, phone, name and title of contact. Arrangement: Classified by type of service. Indexes: Subject.

★9437★ Congressional Directory

Capitol Advantage
PO Box 1223
Order Department
McLean, VA 22101
Ph: (703)734-3266   Fax: (703)847-0573
Fr: 800-659-8708

Annual. $8.95, spiral or perfect bound. Covers 100 current senators and 395 House of Representative members. Entries include: Name, district office address, phone, fax; names and titles of key staff; committee and subcommittee assignments; photo. Arrangement: Available in separate alphabetical or geographical editions. Indexes: Name.

★9438★ Construction Employment Guide in the National and International Field

World Trade Academy Press
50 E. 42nd St., Ste. 509
New York, NY 10017
Ph: (212)697-4999

$16.50. Covers More than 200 U.S. and international construction, engineering and design companies. Also covers U.S. government construction employment opportunities, job centers and employment agencies. Entries include: Company name, address, specialties.

★9439★ Contractor's Directory

Government Data Publications, Inc.
1661 McDonald Ave.
Brooklyn, NY 11230
Ph: (718)627-0819   Fax: (718)998-5960

Annual, February. $15.00. Covers contractors who have received government contracts under Public Law 95-507, which requires preferential treatment of small business for subcontracts. Entries include: Contractor name and address. Supplementary to *Small Business Preferential Subcontracts Opportunities Monthly*, which lists companies with government contracts over $500,000 ($1,000,000 for construction). Arrangement: Same information given alphabetically and by ZIP code.

★9440★ Directory of Federal Women's Program Managers

Office of Affirmative Recruiting and Employment
U.S. Office of Personnel Management
1900 E St. NW, Rm. 6336
Washington, DC 20415
Ph: (202)606-0870

Annual, November. Covers about 95 federal government departments, agencies, bureaus, etc., with equal employment opportunity programs concerned specifically with women. Entries include: Department or agency name, address, phone, and name of program manager. Arrangement: Alphabetical.

★9441★ Employment Opportunities, USA

Washington Research Associates
1660 S. Albion, Ste. 390
Denver, CO 80222
Ph: (303)756-9038   Fax: (303)770-1945

Annual, quarterly updates. $184.00, includes quarterly updates. Publication includes: List of over 1,000 employment contacts in companies and agencies in the banking, arts, telecommunications, education, and 14 other industries and professions, including the federal government. Entries include: Company name, name of representative, address, description of products or services, hiring and recruiting practices, training programs, and year established. Principal content is industry overviews, carrer news, and employment opportunity information on 14 different job markets. Arrangement: Classified by industry. Indexes: Occupation.

★9442★ Employment Service—Government Company Fraternal Directory

American Business Directories, Inc.
American Business Information, Inc.
5711 S. 86th Cir.
Omaha, NE 68127
Ph: (402)593-4600   Fax: (402)331-1505

Updated continuously; printed on request. Entries include: Name, address, phone, size of advertisement, name of owner or manager, number of employees, year first in Yellow Pages. Compiled from telephone company Yellow Pages, nationwide. Arrangement: Geographical.

★9443★ Encyclopedia of Governmental Advisory Organizations

Gale Research
835 Penobscot Bldg.
Detroit, MI 48226-4094
Ph: (313)961-2242   Fax: (313)961-6083
Fr: 800-877-GALE

Biennial, odd years. $505.00, base edition; $375.00, supplement. Covers Approximately 7,000 boards, panels, commissions, committees, presidential conferences, and other groups that advise the President, Congress, and departments and agencies of federal government; includes interagency committees and federally sponsored conferences. Also includes historically significant organizations. Entries include: Unit name, address (if active), name of principal executive, legal basis for the unit, purpose, reports and publications, findings and recommendations, description of activities, members. Arrangement: Classified by general subject. Indexes: Alphabetical/keyword, personnel, publication, federal department/agency, presidential administration.

★9444★ Federal Career Directory

Superintendent of Documents
Government Printing Office
732 N. Capitol St. NW
Washington, DC 20401
Ph: (202)512-1991   Fax: (202)512-2034

Published 1990. $31.00. Covers over 160 agencies and bureaus within the federal government offering employment opportunities. Entries include: Agency or bureau name, contact name, address, phone.

★9445★ Federal Careers for Attorneys

Federal Reports Inc.
1010 Vermont Ave. NW, Ste. 408
Washington, DC 20005
Ph: (202)393-3311   Fax: (202)393-1553
Fr: 800-296-9611

Latest edition 1991. $23.95. Covers over 300 U.S. government general counsel and other legal offices throughout the Federal system. Entries include: Agency's name, address, mission, work of the office, divisions/structures, number of attorneys, hiring procedures, special recruitment programs, and locations of regional/field offices. Arrangement: Geographical. Indexes: Legal specialty and geographical.

★9446★ Federal Contracting Careers

Federal Acquisition Institute
General Services Administration
18th & F Sts. NW, Rm. 4019
Washington, DC 20405
Ph: (202)501-0964

This nine-page booklet describes working for the federal government as a contract specialist; explains intern programs, advancement, and career development and training, as well as how to apply for programs.

★9447★ Federal Job Winner's Tips Series

Federal Research Service
PO Box 1059CG
Vienna, VA 22183
Ph: (703)281-0200

Series of 5 booklets. $17.50/set. $4.00/each. 16 pages/each. Booklets are entitled: "How to Start Your Job Search; How to Select Your Federal Occupation; How to Prepare Your SF-171; How to Interview for Job Openings; How to Change Careers within Government".

★9448★ Federal Law-Related Careers Directory

Federal Reports Inc.
1010 Vermont Ave. NW, Ste. 408
Washington, DC 20005
Ph: (202)393-3311   Fax: (202)393-1553
Fr: 800-296-9611

Irregular. $16.95 postpaid. Publication includes: Listings of over 1,000 federal government recruiting offices. Entries include: Agency name, address, how to apply, and hiring procedure. Principal content of publication is the description of over 150 law-related careers in the U.S. government for which a law degree is an asset, but not a requirement, including contract specialist, criminal investigator, legal research analyst, and labor relations specialist. Arrangement: Classified by by subject.

★9449★ Federal Staff Directory

Staff Directories Ltd.
PO Box 62
Mount Vernon, VA 22121-0062
Ph: (703)739-0900   Fax: (703)739-0234

Semiannual, March and September. $79.00. Covers Approximately 33,000 persons in federal government offices and independent agencies, with biographies of 2,800 key executives; includes officials at policy level in agencies of the Office of the President, Cabinet-level departments, independent and regulatory agencies, military commands, federal information centers, and libraries, and United States attorneys, marshals, and ambassadors. Entries include: Name, title, location (indicating building, address, and/or room), phone, symbols indicating whether position is a presidential appointment and whether senate approval is required. Arrangement: Classified by department/agency. Indexes: Personal name, subject.

★9450★ Federal Yellow Book

Leadership Directories, Inc.
104 5th Ave., 2nd Fl.
New York, NY 10011
Ph: (212)627-4140   Fax: (212)645-0931

Quarterly. $235.00. Covers federal departments, including the Executive Office of the President, the Office of the Vice President, the Office of Management and Budget, the Cabinet, and the National Security Council, and over 35,000 key personnel; over 70 independent federal agencies. Entries include: For personnel: name, address, phone, fax, titles. For departments and agencies. office, or branch name and address; names and titles of principal personnel, with their room numbers and direct-dial phone numbers. Arrangement: Classified by by department or agency.

★9451★ **Find a Federal Job Fast! How to Cut the Red Tape and Get Hired**

The Career Press Inc.
3 Tice Rd.
PO Box 687
Franklin Lakes, NJ 07417
Ph: (201)848-0310   Fax: (201)848-1727
Fr: 800-237-3371

Ron Krannich and Caryl Krannich. Third edition, 1995. $12.95. 196 pages. Presents advice on cutting through the red tape, locating job vacancies, completing the SF-171 form, marketing oneself to the federal job market, and obtaining information quickly on a wide variety of jobs.

★9452★ **Government Job Finder**

Planning/Communications
7215 Oak Ave.
River Forest, IL 60305-1935
Ph: (708)366-5200   Fr: (888)366-5200

Daniel Lauber. Third edition, 1996. $32.95; $16.95 (paper). 352 pages. Covers 1800 sources. Discusses how to use sources of local, state, and federal government job vacancies in a number of specialties and state-by-state, including job-matching services, job hotlines, specialty periodicals with job ads, salary surveys, and directories. Explains how local, state, and federal hiring systems work. Includes chapters on resume and cover letter preparation and interviewing.

★9453★ **How to Get a Federal Job**

Fedhelp Publications
1354 Emerald St. NE
Washington, DC 20002
Ph: (202)397-7704

David E. Waelde. 1989. $15.00. 186 pages. Thorough guide to the civil service employment process.

★9454★ **Internships in Congress**

The Graduate Group
86 Norwood Rd.
West Hartford, CT 06117-2236
Ph: (203)232-3100

1994. $27.50.

★9455★ **Internships in Federal Government**

The Graduate Group
86 Norwood Rd.
West Hartford, CT 06117-2236
Ph: (203)232-3100

1994. $27.50.

★9456★ **Internships and Fellowships Information Pack**

U.S. Capitol
Washington, DC 20510
Ph: (202)224-3121

Congressional Research Service. Ask for Report No. IPO631. Request from your representative in Congress at the address given above.

★9457★ **Internships in State Government**

The Graduate Group
86 Norwood Rd.
West Hartford, CT 06117-2236
Ph: (203)232-3100

1995. $27.50.

★9458★ **Job Hotlines USA: A National Telephone Directory of Employer Joblines**

Career Communications
PO Box 169
Harleysville, PA 19438

Published 1994. $24.95. Covers over 1,000 government agencies, hospitals, colleges, companies, and federal job information centers that have employment hotlines. Entries include: company name, address, voice telephone number, job hotline number, and industry classification.

★9459★ **J.O.B.S. Job Opportunities and Business Series: The Employment Guide to the Washington, D.C., Metropolitan Area**

JSI Network
PO Box 231
Woodbridge, VA 22194-0231
Ph: (703)680-9611

Imelda R. Roberts. 1989. $17.95. 319 pages. Describes a number of opportunities in D.C. and the surrounding Maryland and Virginia area. Jobs include the public and private sector, the military, embassies, and international opportunities.

★9460★ **Municipal/County Directory Library Edition**

Carroll Publishing
1058 Thomas Jefferson St. NW
Washington, DC 20007
Ph: (202)333-8620   Fax: (202)337-7020
Fr: 800-336-4240

Annual, July. $137.00, plus $8.00 shipping; payment must accompany order. Covers officials of 1,400 county governments (with populations over 25,000) and 2,000 municipalities (with populations over 1,000); includes elected, appointed, and career office holders. Entries include: Name, title, agency, address, phone. Arrangement: County officials are geographical, then by agency; municipal officials are by city. Indexes: personal name (with phone), agency.

★9461★ **Municipal Year Book**

Newman Books Ltd.
32 Vauxhall Bridge Rd.
London SW1V 2SS, England
Ph: 71 9736400   Fax: 71 2335057

Annual, December. $140.00, postpaid. Covers local and central government agencies and officials of the United Kingdom; municipal art galleries, associations, development organizations, fairs, libraries, museums, airports, and other local authorities. Entries include: Name of authority or governing agency, address, phone, fax, names of elected councillors, officers, names and titles of key personnel, contacts, population, and pay. Arrangement: Geographical. Indexes: Subject, place names.

★9462★ **Now Hiring: Government Jobs for Lawyers**

American Bar Association (ABA)
750 N. Lake Shore Dr.
Chicago, IL 60611
Ph: (312)988-5555   Fax: (312)988-6281

Irregular, latest edition 1991. $14.95, plus $3.95 shipping. Covers over 100 offices of the federal government, quasi-government, and independent agencies. Entries include: Organization name, contact name and address, application deadline, number of attorneys employed and number of anticipated openings, location of positions, salaries and qualifications, nature of legal work performed by office, advancement opportunities. Arrangement: By government agency.

★9463★ **Opportunities in Federal Government Careers**

VGM Career Horizons
4255 W. Touhy Ave.
Lincolnwood, IL 60646-1975
Ph: (847)679-5500   Fax: (847)679-2494
Fr: 800-323-4900

Neale Baxter. 1992. $13.95; $10.95 (paper). 160 pages. Describes the spectrum of government employment, including professional, administrative, scientific, blue-collar, clerical, and technical opportunities, and how to land a job. Illustrated.

★9464★ **Opportunities in State and Local Government Careers**

VGM Career Horizons
4255 W. Touhy Ave.
Lincolnwood, IL 60646-1975
Ph: (847)679-5500   Fax: (847)679-2494
Fr: 800-323-4900

Neale Baxter. 1993. $13.95; $10.95 (paper). 160 pages. Points out the incentives and drawbacks of a government career. Describes hiring procedures and provides tips on filling out applications, taking physical and aptitude tests, handling interviews, and finding jobs. Describes the jobs in which 75% of all state and local government workers are employed. For each occupation, covers the nature of the work and the training required.

★9465★ **The Paralegal's Guide to U.S. Government Jobs: How to Land a Job in 70 Law-Related Career Fields**

Federal Reports, Inc.
1010 Vermont Ave. NW, Ste. 408
Washington, DC 20005
Ph: (202)393-3311

Richard L. Hermann and Linda P. Sutherland. Sixth edition, 1993. $16.00. 132 pages. Explains U.S. Government procedures and describes 70 law-related federal careers for which paralegals may qualify. Includes a directory of several hundred Federal Agency personnel offices that hire the most paralegal and law-related talents.

★9466★ Public Administration Career Directory

Gale Research
835 Penobscot Bldg.
Detroit, MI 48226-4094
Ph: (313)961-2242   Fax: (313)961-6083
Fr: 800-877-GALE

First edition March 1994. $34.00; $17.95 (paper). Covers over 210 U.S. federal government departments and agencies and other public organizations offering entry-level positions and internships; sources of help-wanted ads, professional associations, producers of videos, databases, career guides, and professional guides and handbooks. Entries include: For employers: Name, address, phone, fax, business description, names and titles of key personnel, number of employees, average number of entry-level positions available, human resources contact, description of internship opportunities including contact, type and number available, application procedures, qualifications, and duties. For others: Name or title, address, phone, description. Paperback edition is available from Visible Ink Press. Arrangement: Employers are alphabetical; others are classified by type of resource. Indexes: Name and keyword.

★9467★ State Directory Library Edition

Carroll Publishing
1058 Thomas Jefferson St. NW
Washington, DC 20007
Ph: (202)333-8620   Fax: (202)337-7020
Fr: 800-336-4240

Annual, July. $137.00, plus $8.00 shipping. Covers 37,000 state government officials in all branches of government and members of authorities. Entries include: Name, address, phone, fax, title. Arrangement: Geographical, then by agency within each state. Indexes: Personal name (with phone) organizational, keyword.

★9468★ State Yellow Book

Leadership Directories, Inc.
104 5th Ave., 2nd Fl.
New York, NY 10011
Ph: (212)627-4140   Fax: (212)645-0931

Quarterly. $235.00. Covers over 35,000 key officials in the executive and legislative branches of all 50 states, the District of Columbia, and the four insular U.S. territories. Entries include: Official name, address, phone, fax. Arrangement: Alphabetical. Indexes: Subject; geographical by state.

★9469★ Storming Washington: An Intern's Guide to National Government

American Political Science Association
1527 New Hampshire Ave., NW
Washington, DC 20036
Ph: (202)483-2512

Stephen E. Frantzich. Fourth edition, 1994. $3.00. 63 pages.

★9470★ Summer Jobs: Opportunities in the Federal Government

Office of Personnel Management
1900 E St. NW
Washington, DC 20415
Ph: (202)606-0950

Formerly annual; latest edition January 1993; suspended indefinitely. Free. Covers GS-1 through GS-4 clerical jobs and other jobs at GS-5 and above which are expected to be available in federal agencies and departments throughout the United States during the season. Most jobs are in Metropolitan Washington, D.C. Latest application date is generally April 15; many are earlier. Includes general information on applying for jobs in trades and labor occupations and summer employment for needy youth programs. Entries include: Agency name, filing deadline, titles of jobs available, brief information on qualifications needed, location, etc. Complete agency names and addresses are given in separate list. Publication is available from Federal Employment Information Center offices and agency personnel offices. Arrangement: By job level, then alphabetical by agency name.

★9471★ United States Government Manual

Office of the Federal Register
National Archives and Records Administration
Washington, DC 20408
Ph: (202)523-5230

Annual, September. $30.00. The manual is the official handbook of the United States government, and includes descriptions and lists of principal personnel of agencies and other bodies in the legislative, judicial, and executive branches; the executive branch is covered in greatest depth. The Congressional Directory and the Manual comprise the database for principal federal government organizations and personnel. Entries include: For each cabinet department and independent agency or other unit, titles of major administrative posts and the names of incumbents are given, along with a description of the unit's responsibilities. Additional listings of subordinate offices and bureaus give similar information. Addresses and phone numbers are provided for units at most levels. Arrangement: Classified by department and agency. Indexes: Personal name, agency/subject.

★9472★ Washington Information Directory

Congressional Quarterly Inc.
1414 22nd St. NW
Washington, DC 20037
Ph: (202)887-8500   Fr: 800-638-1710

Annual. $99.95. 1,100 pages. Guide to the people and activities of government agencies and committees.

★9473★ Washington Job Source: Everything You Need to Land the Internship, Entry-Level or Middle Management Job of Your Choice

Metcom, Inc.
1708 Surrey Ln., NW
Washington, DC 20007
Ph: (202)337-7800   Fax: (202)337-3121

Benjamin S. Psillas. 1995. $15.95 (paper).

★9474★ Who's Who in Local Government Management

International City/County Management Association (ICMA)
777 N. Capitol St. NE, Ste. 500
Washington, DC 20002-4201
Ph: (202)289-4262   Fax: (202)962-3500

Annual, September. Available to members only. Covers 8,000 appointed administrators of cities, counties, and councils of governments. Entries include: Name, position, office address, educational history, career data, offices held in ICMA. Arrangement: Alphabetical by individual name.

NEWSPAPERS, MAGAZINES, AND JOURNALS

★9475★ Bridging the Gap

Section for Women in Public Administration
c/o Debra Martin
3214 McClure Ave.
Flint, MI 48502

Three issues/year. Included in membership. Disseminates information relating to the organization's efforts to initiate action programs appropriate to the needs and concerns of women in public administration. Discusses the equality of educational and employment opportunities for women in public service and government. Acts as a forum for communication among professionals and students interested in women in public service administration. Recurring features include news of research, news of members, news of opportunities available for women, and recognition of achievement and awards received.

★9476★ Federal Career Opportunities

Federal Research Service, Inc.
243 Church St. NW
PO Box 1059
Vienna, VA 22183
Ph: (703)281-0200   Fax: (703)281-7639
Fr: 800-822-5627

Biweekly. $7.95, per copy; $39.00, 6 issues; $77.00, 12 issues; $175.00, 26 issues. Covers more than 4,000 current federal job vacancies in the United States and overseas; includes permanent, part-time, and temporary positions. Entries include: Position title, location, series and grade, job requirements, special forms, announcement number, closing date, application address. Arrangement: Classified by federal agency and occupation.

★9477★ Federal Jobs Digest

Federal Jobs Digest
325 Pennsylvania Ave. SE
Washington, DC 20003
Ph: (202)762-5111   Fax: (202)762-4818
Fr: 800-824-5000

Biweekly. $4.50, per issue; $29.00, for three months; $110.00, per year. Covers over 10,000 specific job openings in the federal government in each issue. Entries include: Position name, title, General Schedule (GS) grade, and Wage Grade (WG), closing date for applications, announcement number, application address, phone, and name of contact. Arrangement: By federal department or agency, then geographical.

★9478★ Federal Times

Times-Journal Co.
6883 Commercial Dr.
Springfield, VA 22159
Ph: (703)750-2000   Fax: (703)750-8622

Weekly (Mon.). Federal bureaucracy; technology in government.

★9479★ The Job Finder

Western Governmental Research
  Association
10900 Los Alamitos Blvd., Ste. 201
Los Alamitos, CA 90720
Ph: (310)795-6694   Fax: (310)795-6697
Fr: 800-700-WGRA

Monthly. Included in membership; $35.00. for other; $20.00, for students. Covers about 50 openings for administrative and governmental research employment in the western United States. Entries include: Position title, population of town or unit (if available), description of responsibilities, requirements, salary, application deadline; name, address, and phone of contact or agency. Arrangement: Classified by field (budget, data processing, engineering, etc.).

★9480★ The Municipality

League of Wisconsin Municipalities
122 W. Washington Ave., Ste. 301
Madison, WI 53703-2757
Ph: (608)267-2380   Fax: (608)267-0645

Monthly. Magazine for officials of Wisconsin's local municipal governments.

★9481★ Postal Record

National Association of Letter Carriers
100 Indiana Ave. NW
Washington, DC 20001-2144
Ph: (202)393-4695   Fax: (202)737-1540

Monthly. $16.00/year for individuals. Magazine for active and retired letter carriers.

SOFTWARE

★9482★ Quick and Easy Federal Jobs Kit

Planning/Communications
7215 Oak Ave.
River Forest, IL 60305-1935
Ph: (708)366-5200   Fr: (888)366-5200

Datatech. 1995. $49.95 (single user), $59.95 (two users), $129.95 (eight users), $399.95

(unlimited number of users). Requires Windows 3.1 or higher, 3.5 inch disks only. Designed to ensure that federal job applicants include all of the required information on the necessary forms.

★9483★ Quick and Easy for the SF 171

Planning/Communications
7215 Oak Ave.
River Forest, IL 60305-1935
Ph: (708)366-5200   Fr: (888)366-5200

Datatech. 1995. $49.95 (single user), $59.95 (two users), $129.95 (eight users), $399.95 (unlimited number of users). Available in DOS or Windows versions. Designed to ensure that federal job applicants include all of the required information on the old SF 171 form.

OTHER SOURCES

★9484★ African Studies Association (ASA)

Emory University
Credit Union Bldg.
Atlanta, GA 30322
Ph: (404)329-6410   Fax: (404)329-6433

Members: Persons specializing in teaching, writing, or research on Africa including political scientists, historians, geographers, anthropologists, economists, librarians, linguists, and government officials; persons who are studying African subjects; institutional members are universities, libraries, government agencies, and others interested in receiving information about Africa. **Purpose:** Seeks to foster communication and to stimulate research among scholars on Africa. **Activities:** Sponsors placement service; conducts panels and discussion groups; presents exhibits and films. **E-Mail:** africa@mony.edu

★9485★ Civil Service Employees Association (CSEA)

PO Box 7125, Capitol Sta.
Albany, NY 12210
Ph: (518)434-0191   Fax: (518)462-3639
Fr: 800-342-4146

Members: Members are state and local government employees from all public employee classifications. **Purpose:** Negotiates work contracts; represents members in grievances; provides legal assistance for on-the-job problems; provides advice and assistance on federal, state, and local laws affecting public employees. Conducts training and education programs.

★9486★ Federally Employed Women (FEW)

1400 Eye St. NW, Ste. 425
Washington, DC 20005
Ph: (202)898-0994   Fax: (202)898-0998

Members: Men and women employed by the federal government; associate members are persons who support the goals and objectives of FEW. **Purpose:** Seeks to end sex discrimination in government service; to increase job opportunities for women in government service and to further the potential

of all women in the government; to improve the merit system in government employment; to assist present and potential government employees who are discriminated against because of sex; to work with other organizations and individuals concerned with equal employment opportunity in the government. **Activities:** Informs members of opportunities for training to improve their job potential; issues fact sheets interpreting civil service rules and regulations and other legislative issues.

★9487★ National Alliance of Postal and Federal Employees (NAPFE)

1628 11th St. NW
Washington, DC 20001
Ph: (202)939-6325   Fax: (202)939-6389

Purpose: Works to eliminate employment discrimination.

★9488★ National Association of Civil Service Employees (NACSE)

7185 Navajo Rd., Ste. C
San Diego, CA 92119
Ph: (619)464-1014

Members: Federal, state, county, and city civil service employees; association employees and counselors. **Purpose:** Assists nonprofit charitable, educational, and scientific organizations in promoting social welfare. Conducts service and product consumer research and educational programs and symposia; sponsors competitions; maintains placement service.

★9489★ National Association of County Training and Employment Professionals (NACTEP)

c/o National Association of Counties
440 1st St. NW, 8th fl.
Washington, DC 20001
Ph: (202)393-6226   Fax: (202)737-0480

Members: County employment and training administrators. **Purpose:** To stimulate and contribute to the improvement of counties, county employment and training programs, and county employment practices. **E-Mail:** gorten@spaceworks.com

★9490★ National Association of Government Communicators (NAGC)

669 S. Washington St.
Alexandria, VA 22314
Ph: (703)519-3902   Fax: (703)519-7732

Members: Government employees, retired persons, non-government affiliates, and students. **Purpose:** Seeks to advance communications as an essential professional resource at every level of national, state, and local government by: disseminating information; encouraging professional development, public awareness, and exchange of ideas and experience; improving internal communications. **Activities:** Maintains placement service.

★9491★ National Association of Government Employees (NAGE)

2011 Crystal Dr., Ste. 206
Arlington, VA 22202
Ph: (703)979-0290   Fax: (703)979-0294

Members: Union of civilian federal government employees with locals and members in military agencies, Internal Revenue Service, Post Office, Veterans Administration, General Services Administration, Federal Aviation Administration, and other federal agencies, as well as state and local agencies. **Activities:** Activities include direct legal assistance, information service, legislative lobbying and representation, trained leadership in contract negotiations, employment protection, and insurance. Offers seminars; sponsors competitions.

★9492★ National Association of Hispanic Federal Executives (NAHFE)

PO Box 469
Herndon, VA 22070
Ph: (703)787-0291   Fax: (703)787-4675

Members: Hispanic and other federal employees ranked GM-13 and above; individuals in the private sector whose positions are equivalent to rank GM-13. **Purpose:** Promotes the federal government as a model employer by encouraging qualified individuals to apply for federal government positions. **Activities:** Offers increased productivity training to federal employees. Maintains speakers' bureau and placement service. Offers educational programs; compiles statistics; conducts research.

★9493★ U.S. Office of Personnel Management Job Information Center

1900 E St. NW
Washington, DC 20415-1000
Ph: (703)908-8566

In addition to the phone number provided above, check your telephone directory, under U.S. Government, Office of Personnel Management, to obtain a local Job Information Center telephone number. Each center provides information about government jobs and instructions for submitting an application.

Help-Wanted Ads

REFERENCE WORKS

★9494★ Help Yourself to the Help Wanted Ads

Chronicle Guidance Publications, Inc.
66 Aurora St.
PO Box 1190
Moravia, NY 13118-1190
Ph: (315)497-0330   Fax: (315)497-3359
Fr: 800-622-7284

Chronicle Guidance Staff. 1991. $2.00. Reprint of a journal article.

★9495★ Where the Jobs Are: A Comprehensive Directory of 1200 Journals Listing Career Opportunities

Garrett Park Press
PO Box 190
Garrett Park, MD 20896
Ph: (301)946-2553

1989. $15.00; $14.00, prepaid. 128 pages. Contains list of approximately 1,200 journals that publish advertisements announcing job opportunities. Arranged alphabetically. Indexes: Occupational field.

NEWSPAPERS, MAGAZINES, AND JOURNALS

★9496★ Affirmative Action Register

Affirmative Action, Inc.
8356 Olive Blvd.
St. Louis, MO 63132
Ph: (314)991-1335   Fax: (314)997-1788
Fr: 800-537-0655

Monthly. $1.50 for single issue. Free, to women, minority, handicapped candidate sources. Covers in each issue, about 300 positions at a professional level (most requiring advanced study) available to women, minorities, veterans, and the handicapped; listings are advertisements placed by employers with affirmative action programs. Entries include: Company or organization name, address, contact name; description of position including title, requirements, duties, application procedure, salary, etc. Arrangement: Classified by profession.

★9497★ The Black Collegian

Black Collegiate Services, Inc.
140 Carondelet St.
New Orleans, LA 70130-2526
Ph: (504)523-0154   Fax: (504)523-0271

Semiannual. $8.00/year for individuals; $4.00 for single issue. Career opportunity magazine featuring job searching role models, interviews, entertainment, art, and African-American history.

★9498★ Community Jobs: The Employment Newspaper for the Non-Profit Sector

ACCESS: Networking in the Public Interest
30 Irving Pl.
New York, NY 10003
Ph: (212)475-1001   Fax: (212)475-1199

Monthly. $69.00. Covers jobs and internships available with nonprofit organizations active in issues such as the environment, foreign policy, consumer advocacy, housing, education, etc. Entries include: Position title; name, address, and phone of contact; description, responsibilities; requirements; salary. Arrangement: Geographical.

★9499★ EEO Bi-monthly

Cass Recruitment Publications
1800 Sherman Pl., No.300
Evanston, IL 60201-3769
Ph: (708)475-8800   Fax: (708)475-8807

Bimonthly. $10.00, per issue; $42.00, per year. Covers about 100 employers nationwide who anticipate having technical, professional or management employment opportunities in the coming six months; five regional editions for Pacific, Western, Midwestern, Southern, and Eastern states. Entries include: Company name, address, phone, name of contact, date established, number of employees, description of the company and its products, and general description of openings expected. Arrangement: Alphabetical and geographical.

★9500★ Equal Opportunity

Equal Opportunity Publications
150 Motor Pky., Ste. 420
Hauppauge, NY 11788-5145
Ph: (516)273-8743

Quarterly. Career guidance magazine for college students and professionals.

★9501★ Federal Career Opportunities

Federal Research Service, Inc.
243 Church St. NW
PO Box 1059
Vienna, VA 22183
Ph: (703)281-0200   Fax: (703)281-7639
Fr: 800-822-5627

Biweekly. $7.95, per copy; $39.00, 6 issues; $77.00, 12 issues; $175.00, 26 issues. Covers more than 4,000 current federal job vacancies in the United States and overseas; includes permanent, part-time, and temporary positions. Entries include: Position title, location, series and grade, job requirements, special forms, announcement number, closing date, application address. Arrangement: Classified by federal agency and occupation.

★9502★ Federal Jobs Digest

Federal Jobs Digest
325 Pennsylvania Ave. SE
Washington, DC 20003
Ph: (202)762-5111   Fax: (202)762-4818
Fr: 800-824-5000

Biweekly. $4.50, per issue; $29.00, for three months; $110.00, per year. Covers over 10,000 specific job openings in the federal government in each issue. Entries include: Position name, title, General Schedule (GS) grade, and Wage Grade (WG), closing date for applications, announcement number, application address, phone, and name of contact. Arrangement: By federal department or agency, then geographical.

★9503★ International Employment Hotline

International Employment Hotline
PO Box 3030
Oakton, VA 22124
Ph: (703)620-1972   Fax: (703)620-1973

Monthly. $39.00, per year. Covers temporary and career job openings overseas and advice for international job hunters. Entries include: Company name, address, job title, description of job, requirements, geographic location of job. Arrangement: Geographical.

★9504★ The Job Finder

Western Governmental Research Association
10900 Los Alamitos Blvd., Ste. 201
Los Alamitos, CA 90720
Ph: (310)795-6694   Fax: (310)795-6697
Fr: 800-700-WGRA

Monthly. Included in membership; $35.00. for other; $20.00, for students. Covers about 50 openings for administrative and governmental research employment in the western United States. Entries include: Position title, population of town or unit (if available), description of responsibilities, requirements, salary, application deadline; name, address, and phone of contact or agency. Arrangement: Classified by field (budget, data processing, engineering, etc.).

★9505★ National Ad Search

National Ad Search, Inc.
PO Box 2083
Milwaukee, WI 53201
Ph: (414)351-1398   Fax: (414)351-0836
Fr: 800-992-2832

Weekly. Magazine (tabloid) on occupations, careers, and professional employment.

★9506★ National Business Employment Weekly

Dow Jones & Co., Inc.
PO Box 300
Princeton, NJ 08543
Ph: (609)520-4306   Fax: (609)520-4309
Fr: 800-323-NBEW

Weekly. $52.00/year. Magazine (tabloid) containing help-wanted advertising from the regional editions of the Wall Street Journal. Includes statistics and articles about employment opportunities and career advancement.

★9507★ The NonProfit Times

The Davis Information Group, Inc.
190 Tamarack Cir.
Skillman, NJ 08558-9662
Ph: (609)466-4600

Monthly. $39.00/year.

★9508★ Rocky Mountain Employment Newsletter

Intermountain Publishing & Referral
311-NP 14th St.
Glenwood Springs, CO 81601
Ph: (303)945-8991   Fax: (303)945-5140

Semimonthly. $13.00/year, per month for one edition; $16.00/year, for two editions; $19.00/year, for three editions; $21.00/year, for four editions. Lists information on current job openings in Colorado, Idaho, Montana, Arizona, New Mexico, Washington, Oregon, and Wyoming. Provides job titles, descriptions, requirements, and employer name and address or telephone number. Covers all occupational fields. Specializes in summer-winter seasonal openings, and in ranch, horse, livestock and farm opportunities. Available in four editions: Colorado-Wyoming, Arizona-New Mexico, Idaho-Montana, and Washington-Oregon.

ONLINE AND DATABASE SERVICES

★9509★ CSI National Career Network

Star Temporaries Inc.
8133 Leesburg Pke., Ste. 305
Vienna, VA 22182

Online database. An employee recruiting and job-listing service that contains resumes of job-seekers and lists of employment opportunities from potential employers. The resumes and job openings are classified into 40 technical and managerial job categories. Job descriptions include salary range offered, geographic location, job title and description, type of business, education level required, and experience desired. Resume information includes position and salary range desired, preferred geographic location, educational level attained, professional certification, employment background, and employment firm's comments.

★9510★ E-Span Job Search

E-Span
8440 Woodfield Crossing, Ste. 170
Indianapolis, IN 46240
Ph: (317)579-6922   Fax: (317)579-6933
Fr: 800-682-2901

Online database. Provides descriptions of job openings listed by subscribing organizations. Enables each job candidate to identify positions for which they qualify. Contains job openings in the fields of engineering, architecture, data processing, telecommunications, sales, advertising and marketing, human resources, administration, finance, accounting, banking, industry, manufacturing, health care, and management.

★9511★ Job Ads USA Database (JOBADS)

MILITRAN, Inc.
PO Box 490
Southeastern, PA 19399-0490
Ph: (610)687-3900   Fax: (610)296-7332
Fr: 800-426-9954

Online database providing listings of current job openings advertised in newspaper classified sections throughout the United States. Includes job postings from the U.S. Office of Personnel Management (OPM), the federal government's staffing department.

★9512★ Jobs Database

American Institute of Physics
Robert Ubell Associates
111 8th Ave., Ste. 1503
New York, NY 10011
Ph: (212)645-3303   Fax: (212)463-8645

Online database providing more than 200 job listings for positions in academia, industry, and government, especially in the fields of geophysics, astronomy, and materials research.

Identifying Prospective Employers

★9513★ **American Manufacturers Directory**

American Business Directories, Inc.
  American Business Information, Inc.
5711 S. 86th Cir.
Omaha, NE 68127
Ph: (402)593-4600   Fax: (402)331-5481

Annual, January. $495.00, lease basis. Covers more than 120,000 manufacturing companies with 25 or more employees. Entries include: Company name, address, phone, contact name, Standard Industrial Classification (SIC) codes, number of employees, sales volume code. Arrangement: Entries listed alphabetically, geographically, and by Standard Industrial Classification (SIC) code. Indexes: Geographical.

★9514★ **America's Corporate Families: The Billion Dollar Directory**

Dun & Bradstreet Information Services
899 Eaton Ave.
Bethlehem, PA 18025
Ph: (610)882-7000   Fr: 800-526-0651

Annual. Volume I lists all American divisions and subsidiaries; volume II lists all international divisions and subsidiaries.

★9515★ **America's Fastest Growing Employers**

Bob Adams, Inc.
260 Center St.
Holbrook, MA 02343
Ph: (617)298-9570   Fax: (617)767-0994
Fr: 800-872-5627

Irregular, latest edition 1994. $30.00; $16.00 (paper). Covers over 700 U.S. companies with at least 50 employees and a minimum growth rate of 20 percent over the last three to five years. Entries include: Name, address, phone, number of employees, year founded, economic outlook; some entries include name and title of contact, common positions, backgrounds sought, benefits offered. Indexes: Geographical, industry classification.

★9516★ **Career Employment Opportunities Directory**

Ready Reference Press
Box 5169
Santa Monica, CA 90405
Ph: (213)474-5175

Biennial, October of odd years. $47.50, per volume; $190.00, per four volume set; postpaid, payment with order. Covers about 1,250 companies that employ college graduates; separate editions available for Liberal Arts and Social Sciences, Business Administration, Engineering and Computer Sciences, and Sciences. Entries include: Company name, general description of company and career opportunities, job locations, special programs, and contact address. Arrangement: Alphabetical. Indexes: Discipline, geographical.

★9517★ **The Career Guide—Dun's Employment Opportunities Directory**

Dun & Bradstreet Information Services
Dun & Bradstreet Corp.
3 Sylvan Way
Parsippany, NJ 07054-3896
Ph: (201)605-6000   Fax: (201)605-6911
Fr: 800-526-0651

Annual, December. $385.00, to public libraries; $450.00, to others (lease basis). Covers more than 5,000 companies on leading employers throughout the U.S. that provide career opportunities in sales, marketing, management, engineering, life and physical sciences, computer science, mathematics, statistics planning, accounting and finance, liberal arts fields, and other technical and professional areas; based on data supplied on questionnaires and through personal interviews. Also covers personnel consultants; includes some public sector employers (governments, schools, etc.) usually not found in similar lists. Entries include: Company name, location of headquarters and other offices or plants; entries may also include name, title, address, and phone of employment contact; disciplines or occupational groups hired; brief overview of company, discussion of types of positions that may be available, training and career development programs, benefits offered. Arrangement: Companies are alphabetical; consultants are geographical. Indexes: Geographical, SIC code.

★9518★ **Careers and the MBA**

Bob Adams, Inc.
260 Center St.
Holbrook, MA 02343
Ph: (617)767-8100   Fax: (617)767-0994
Fr: 800-872-5627

Twice per year, January and September. $12.95. Publication includes: List of over 200 companies that employ people with Master of Business Administration degrees. Entries include: For companies: name, address, phone, name of contact person or office, description of company, possible positions open, and when to contact about them. For recruiters: name, address. Arrangement: Alphabetical.

★9519★ **College Placement Council Directory: Who's Who in Career Planning, Placement, and Recruitment**

College Placement Council (CPC)
62 Highland Ave.
Bethlehem, PA 18017
Ph: (610)868-1421   Fax: (610)868-0208
Fr: 800-544-5272

Annual, January. $47.95, plus $4.50 shipping. Covers about 2,400 college and university offices concerned with securing employment for graduates and about 2,300 companies with staff assigned to recruiting and hiring college graduates. Entries include: For colleges: college name and address; names, titles, phone, fax, and e-mail addresses of career planning and placement personnel; interview dates for undergraduates and graduates; months of graduation; whether alumni placement is also handled, student enrollment (including minority data), and dates of career/job fairs. For employers: company name; names, addresses, phone, and fax of recruitment staff; names of secondary contacts; nature of business; number of employees. Arrangement: Colleges are geographical; employers are alphabetical. Indexes: Institutional name, personal name (college personnel); geographical, personal name (in company recruitment).

★9520★ The Corporate Directory of U.S. Public Companies

Gale Research
835 Penobscot Bldg.
Detroit, MI 48226-4094
Ph: (313)961-2242   Fax: (313)961-6083
Fr: 800-877-GALE

Annual. $360.00. Provides information on more than 9,500 publicly-traded firms having at least $5,000,000 in assets. Entries include: General background, including name, address and phone, number of employees; stock data; description of areas of business; major subsidiaries; officers; directors; owners; and financial data. Indexes: Officers and directors, owners, subsidiary/parent, geographic, SIC, stock exchange, company rankings, and newly registered corporations.

★9521★ Directory of Career Training and Development Programs

Ready Reference Press
PO Box 5249
Santa Monica, CA 90409
Ph: (213)474-5175   Fr: 800-424-5627

$95.00. Out of print. Provides details on hundreds of professional career training programs offered by some of America's top corporations. Each company profile contains type of training, length of training, and qualifications.

★9522★ Directory of Corporate Affiliations

National Register Publishing Co.
Reed Reference Publishing
121 Chanlon Rd.
New Providence, NJ 07974
Ph: (908)464-6800   Fax: (908)771-7704
Fr: 800-521-8110

Annual, February; quarterly supplements. $950.00, per set (including Master Index); $795.00, U.S. Public Companies; $685.00, U.S. Private Companies; $685.00, International Public and Private Companies, a six-volume set listing public and private companies worldwide. Arrangement: Alphabetical within each volume. Indexes: Each volume includes company name, Standard Industrial Classification (SIC) code, geographical, and personnel indexes; separate Master Index volume lists all companies and brand names in the set in one alphabetic sequence.

★9523★ Dun & Bradstreet Reference Book of Corporate Managements

Dun & Bradstreet Information Services
Dun & Bradstreet Corp.
3 Sylvan Way
Parsippany, NJ 07054-3896
Ph: (201)605-6000   Fax: (201)605-6911
Fr: 800-526-0651

Annual, April. $785.00, lease basis; $635.00, for public libraries, lease basis. Covers nearly 200,000 presidents, directors, vice presidents, officers, and managers in 12,000 companies of greatest economic, marketing, and investment interests; those firms whose revenues are the highest in the United States. Arrangement: Alphabetical by company name. Indexes: Personal name (with abbreviated title and company affiliation), geographical, SIC code, advanced education institution, military affiliation.

★9524★ Employment Opportunities, USA

Washington Research Associates
1660 S. Albion, Ste. 390
Denver, CO 80222
Ph: (303)756-9038   Fax: (303)770-1945

Annual, quarterly updates. $184.00, includes quarterly updates. Publication includes: List of over 1,000 employment contacts in companies and agencies in the banking, arts, telecommunications, education, and 14 other industries and professions, including the federal government. Entries include: Company name, name of representative, address, description of products or services, hiring and recruiting practices, training programs, and year established. Principal content is industry overviews, carrer news, and employment opportunity information on 14 different job markets. Arrangement: Classified by industry. Indexes: Occupation.

★9525★ Financial World—FW 500 Fastest Growing Companies

Financial World Partners
1328 Broadway, 3rd Fl.
New York, NY 10001
Ph: (212)594-5030   Fax: (212)629-0026
Fr: 800-829-5916

Annual, every January. $3.95. Publication includes: Lists of 500 United States firms showing greatest growth in net earnings for the year. Entries include: Company name, rank, net earnings for two previous years, total assets, other financial and statistical data. Arrangement: Main list arranged by net earnings, other lists arranged by return on equity and other measures and by industry.

★9526★ Financial World—FW 200 Hottest Growth Companies

Financial World Partners
1328 Broadway, 3rd Fl.
New York, NY 10001
Ph: (212)594-5030   Fax: (212)629-0026

Annual, May. $3.95. Publication includes: List of companies selected on the basis of earnings per share growth rate over a 10-year period ending with current year; minimum growth rate used is 5 percent. Entries include: Company name, current and prior year's ranking, earnings growth rate (over prior 10 years), number of years of increase over prior 10 years, revenues, dividends per share, earnings per share for current year and 10 years ago. Arrangement: Classified by sales and earnings growth rate. Indexes: Company ranked within industry.

★9527★ Forbes—Up-and-Comers 200: Best Small Companies in America Issue

Forbes, Inc.
60 5th Ave.
New York, NY 10011
Ph: (212)620-2200   Fax: (212)620-1863

Annual, November. $4.50. Publication includes: List of 200 small companies judged to be exceptionally fast-growing on the basis of 5-year return on equity and other qualitative measurements. Entries include: Company name, address; biographical data and compensation data on chief executive officer; financial data. Arrangement: Alphabetical. Indexes: Ranking.

★9528★ Fortune Directory

Fortune Directories
Time, Inc.
Time Life Bldg.
Rockefeller Center
New York, NY 10020
Ph: (212)586-1212

Annual, August. $25.00, payment with order. Covers combined, in a fall reprint, 500 largest United States industrial corporations (published in an April issue each year) and the Service 500 (published in a June issue). The Service 500 comprises 100-company rankings of each of the largest diversified service, and commercial banking companies, and 50-company rankings each of the largest, diversified financial, savings institutions, life insurance, retailing, transportation, and utility companies. Entries include: Company name, address, headquarters city, sales, assets, net income, market value, comparative earnings per share for ten years, names and titles of key personnel, phone, and various other statistical and financial information. Arrangement: Classified by annual sales, where appropriate; otherwise by assets; chart format. Indexes: Separate alphabetical indexes for industrials and service companies.

★9529★ The Hidden Job Market: A Job Seeker's Guide to America's 2,000 Little-Known, Fastest-Growing High-Tech Companies

Peterson's Guides, Inc.
202 Carnegie Center
PO Box 2123
Princeton, NJ 08543-2123
Ph: (609)243-9111   Fax: (609)243-9150
Fr: 800-338-3282

Annual, October. $16.95. Covers Approximately 2,000 technology firms with under 1,000 employees, which have added the most employees in the survey year. Entries include: Company name, address, phone, fax, name and title of contact, number of employees, year founded, number of employees added in last year, percentage of growth, line of business. Arrangement: Geographical by state, then by area code. Indexes: Alphabetical by industry.

★9530★ Hoover's Directory of Human Resources Executives 1996

The Reference Press, Inc.
PO Box 140375
Austin, TX 78714-0375
Fax: (512)454-9401   Fr: 800-486-8666

1996. $39.95 (paper). Lists names of key hiring executives for over 5,000 companies. Includes company profiles.

★9531★ How to Locate Jobs and Land Interviews

The Career Press, Inc.
3 Tice Rd.
PO Box 687
Franklin Lakes, NJ 07417
Ph: (201)848-0310   Fax: (201)848-1727
Fr: 800-237-3371

Albert L. French. Second edition, 1993. $10.95. 192 pages. Shows readers how to tap into the unadvertised, hidden job market and guides them through the resume, cover letter, and interview preparation process.

★9532★ How and Where to Get the Best Computer Jobs

Information Resource Group
50495 Corporate Dr., Ste. 112
Shelby Township, MI 48315
Ph: (810)254-8500   Fax: (810)254-8500

Annual. $69.95 per directory. Publication includes: Listing of the top dataprocessing employers in United States and Canada. Information divided among 67 editions, according to state/province. Principal content of publication is hiring/interview tips, salary surveys. Entries include: Company name, address, phone, name and title of contact. Arrangement: Geographical.

★9533★ Inc.—The Inc. 500 Issue

Inc. Publishing Corp.
38 Commercial Wharf
Boston, MA 02110
Ph: (617)248-8000   Fax: (617)248-8090
Fr: 800-842-1343

Annual, October. $3.50 postpaid. Publication includes: List of 500 fastest-growing privately held companies based on percentage increase in sales over the five year period prior to compilation of current year's list. Entries include: Company name, headquarters city, description of business, year founded, number of employees, sales five years earlier and currently, profitability range, and growth statistics. Arrangement: Ranked by sales growth.

★9534★ Inc.—The Inc. 100 Issue

The Goldhirsh Group
38 Commercial Wharf
Boston, MA 02110
Ph: (617)248-8000   Fax: (617)248-8090
Fr: 800-842-1343

Annual, May. $3.50, postpaid. Publication includes: List of 100 fastest-growing publicly held companies in manufacturing and service industries that had revenues greater than $100,000 but less than $25 million five years prior to compilation of current year's list. Entries include: Company name, headquarters city, type of business, date incorporated, date public, number of employees, return on equity, sales, and net income five years earlier and currently, and five-year growth rate. Arrangement: Ranked by sales growth.

★9535★ International Directory of Company Histories

St. James Press
Gale Research
835 Penobscot Bldg.
Detroit, MI 48226-4094
Ph: (313)961-2242   Fax: (313)961-6083
Fr: 800-877-GALE

Most recent volume (11) published May 1995. $140.00. Covers in eleven volumes, about 2,200 leading companies of Australia, Canada, Europe, Great Britain, Japan, the Middle East, and the United States. Entries include: Company name, address, phone, names of subsidiaries, SICs, products or services, company history, sources for further reading. Arrangement: Alphabetical.

★9536★ The Job Bank Series

Bob Adams, Inc.
260 Center St.
Holbrook, MA 02343
Ph: (617)767-8100   Fax: (617)767-0994
Fr: 800-872-5627

$15.95/volume. There are 20 volumes in the Job Bank Series, each covering a different job market. Volumes exist for the following areas: Atlanta, Boston, the Carolinas, Chicago, Dallas/Fort Worth, Denver, Detroit, Florida, Houston, Los Angeles, Minneapolis, New York, Ohio, Philadelphia, Phoenix, San Francisco, Seattle, St. Louis, Tennessee, and Washington D.C. Each directory lists employers and provides name, address, telephone number, and contact information. Many entries include common positions, educational backgrounds sought, and fringe benefits provided. Cross-indexed by industry and alphabetically by company name. Profiles of professional associations, a section on the region's economic outlook, and listings of executive search and job placement agencies are included. Features sections on conducting a successful job search campaign and writing resumes and cover letters.

★9537★ Job Seeker's Guide to 1000 Top Employers

Visible Ink Press
Gale Research
835 Penobscot Bldg.
Detroit, MI 48226-4094
Ph: (313)961-2242   Fr: 800-735-4686

First edition 1993. $22.95. Covers 1,000 large or prominent private and public companies in the U.S. Entries include: Company name, address, phone, fax, year founded, type of company, stock exchanges on which traded, stock symbol, description, locations of operating units, subsidiaries and affiliated companies, corporate officers, financial data, number of employees, human resources contact, job application procedures. Arrangement: Alphabetical. Indexes: Geographical, industry.

★9538★ Job Seeker's Guide to Private and Public Companies

Gale Research
835 Penobscot Bldg.
Detroit, MI 48226-4094
Ph: (313)961-2242   Fax: (313)961-6083
Fr: 800-877-GALE

Annual. $99.00, per volume; $365.00, per set. Covers in four volumes, over 17,000 employers in all industries. Volume 1 covers the West; Volume 2, the Midwest; Volume 3, the Northeast; Volume 4, the South. Entries include: Company name, address, phone, fax; number of employees; company history and former or variant names; business description; ticker symbol and stock exchange information; main products, services, or accounts; parent company; subsidiary and branch names and locations; founding date; names and titles of key personnel; financial data; company perspective; employee information; job titles; benefits and features of employment; human resources contacts; application procedures; internship information. Arrangement: Geographical by state, then by city. Indexes: Industry, cumulative corporate name index.

★9539★ MacRae's Blue Book

MacRae's Blue Book, Inc.
Business Research Publications, Inc.
65 Bleecker St.
New York, NY 10012
Ph: (212)673-4700   Fax: (212)475-1790
Fr: 800-622-7237

Annual, March. $165.00, plus $5.00 shipping (1995 edition). Covers about 50,000 manufacturing firms. Entries include: Company name, address, products or services, phone, locations and phone numbers of branches and sales outlets. Arrangement: Alphabetical. Indexes: Corporate, Product/service (with address and financial key), trade name.

★9540★ Manufacturing USA: Industry Analyses, Statistics, and Leading Companies

Gale Research
835 Penobscot Bldg.
Detroit, MI 48226-4094
Ph: (313)961-2242   Fax: (313)961-6083
Fr: 800-877-GALE

Every 18 months; latest edition July 1994. $175.00, two-volume set. Publication includes: Lists of up to 75 leading companies for each manufacturing industry selected on the basis of annual sales. Entries include: Company name, address, phone, name of chief executive, type of company, annual sales, number of employees. Principal content of publication is statistical profiles of 459 manufacturing industries and over 26,000 public and private companies. Each industry division includes tables, graphs, and maps that provide general statistics on number of firms and employees, compensation, and production; change in these statistics since 1987 (through 1996 where available); materials consumed statistics; outputs; product share breakdowns by subsector; occupations of employees in the industry, and industry data by state. Arrangement: Classified by industry, then ranked by annual sales. Indexes: Company name, product, occupation, SIC.

★9541★ Million Dollar Directory Series

Dun & Bradstreet Information Services
Dun & Bradstreet Corp.
3 Sylvan Way
Parsippany, NJ 07054-3896
Ph: (201)605-6000   Fax: (201)605-6911
Fr: 800-526-0651

Annual, March. $1,350.00, lease basis; $1,225.00, for public libraries, lease basis. Covers 160,000 businesses with either a net worth of $500,000 or more, 250 or more employees at that location, or $25,000,000 or more in sales volume; includes industrial corporations, utilities, transportation companies, bank and trust companies, stock brokers, mutual and stock insurance companies, wholesalers, retailers, and domestic subsidiaries of foreign corporations. Arrangement: Alphabetical. Indexes: Geographical (with address and SIC), product by SIC (with address).

★9542★ National Directory of Addresses and Telephone Numbers

Omnigraphics Inc.
2500 Penobscot Bldg.
Detroit, MI 48226
Ph: (313)961-1340   Fax: (313)961-1383
Fr: 800-875-1340

Annual, November. $95.00. Covers about 140,000 U.S. businesses, federal, state, and local government offices, banks, colleges and universities, associations, labor unions, political organizations, newspapers, magazines, TV and radio stations, foundations, postal and shipping services, hospitals, office equipment suppliers, airlines, hotels and motels, profiles of top cities, accountants, law firms, computer firms, foreign corporations, overseas trade contacts, and other professional services. Also covers Internet access providers; Internet mailing lists, publications, and sources; freenets; e-mail addresses. Entries include: Company, organization, agency, or firm name, address, phone, fax, toll-free phone. Arrangement: Corporations are listed both alphabetically and classified by line of business; colleges and universities, travel services, media, and other professional services are geographical; associations and publications are classified by subject. Indexes: Product/service, Standard Industrial Classification (SIC) code, subject.

★9543★ National Directory of Minority-Owned Business Firms

Business Research Services, Inc.
4201 Connecticut Ave. NW, Ste. 610
Washington, DC 20008-1158
Ph: (202)364-6473   Fax: (202)686-3228
Fr: 800-325-8720

Annual. $245.00, plus $5.00 shipping. Covers over 48,000 minority-owned businesses. Entries include: Company name, address, phone, name and title of contact, minority group, certification status, date founded, number of employees, description of products or services, sales volume, government contracting experience, references. Arrangement: Standard Industrial Classification (SIC) code, geographical. Indexes: Alphabetical.

★9544★ National Directory of Nonprofit Organizations

Gale Research
835 Penobscot Bldg.
Detroit, MI 48226-4094
Ph: (313)961-2242   Fax: (313)961-6083
Fr: 800-877-GALE

Annual, spring. $425.00. Covers over 260,000 nonprofit organizations; volume 1 covers organizations with annual incomes of over $100,000; volume 2 covers organizations with incomes between $25,000 and $99,999. Entries include: Organization name, address, phone, annual income, IRS filing status, employer identification number, tax deductible status, activity description. Arrangement: Alphabetical. Indexes: Area of activity, geographical.

★9545★ National Directory of Woman-Owned Business Firms

Business Research Services, Inc.
4201 Connecticut Ave. NW, Ste. 610
Washington, DC 20008-1158
Ph: (202)364-6473   Fax: (202)686-3228
Fr: 800-325-8720

Annual. $245.00, plus $5.00 shipping. Covers over 30,000 woman-owned businesses. Entries include: Company name, address, phone, name and title of contact, minority group, certification status, date founded, number of employees, description of products or services, sales volume, government contracting experience, references. Arrangement: Standard Industrial Classification (SIC) code, geographical. Indexes: Alphabetical.

★9546★ Network of Small Businesses—Membership Directory

Network of Small Businesses (NSB)
5420 Mayfield Rd., Ste. 205
Lyndhurst, OH 44124
Ph: (216)442-5600   Fax: (216)449-3227

Approximately annual; previous edition April 1992; latest edition August 1993. Covers owners and others involved in small businesses (defined as 500 employees or less). Includes lists of inventors, innovators, engineers, and scientists. Entries include: Company name, address, phone, names and titles of key personnel. Arrangement: Alphabetical. Indexes: Company owner.

★9547★ The 100 Best Companies to Work for in America

Doubleday & Co., Inc.
1540 Broadway
New York, NY 10036-4094
Ph: (212)354-6500   Fr: 800-223-6834

Robert Levering and Milton Moskowitz. 1993. $27.50. Describes the best companies to work for in America, based on such factors as salary, benefits, job security, and ambience. The authors base their 'top 100' rating on surveys and personal visits to hundreds of firms.

★9548★ Peterson's Hidden Job Market 1996

Peterson's
PO Box 2123
Princeton, NJ 08543-2123
Ph: (609)243-9111   Fax: (609)243-9150
Fr: 800-338-3282

Fifth edition, 1995. $17.95. Guide to 2,000 fast-growing companies that are hiring now. Focuses on high technology companies in such fields as environmental consulting, genetic engineering, home health care, telecommunications, alternative energy systems, and others.

★9549★ Peterson's Job Opportunities in Business 1996

Peterson's
PO Box 2123
Princeton, NJ 08543-2123
Ph: (609)243-9111   Fax: (609)243-9150
Fr: 800-338-3282

Compiled by the Peterson's staff. Annual. $19.95 (paper). 416 pages. Profiles 2,000 companies that are hiring employees in a number of nontechnical fields, including financial services, management consulting, retailers, utilities, and consumer products companies. Contains job-search strategies and career options to help match education and expertise to the job market. Indexed geographically, by industry, and by hiring needs.

★9550★ Peterson's Job Opportunities in Engineering and Technology 1996

Peterson's
PO Box 2123
Princeton, NJ 08543-2123
Ph: (609)243-9111   Fax: (609)243-9150
Fr: 800-338-3282

Compiled by the Peterson's staff. Annual. $19.95 paperback. 432 pages. Profiles 2,000 high-tech companies looking primarily for technical personnel in such fields as biotechnology, telecommunications, software, computers and peripherals, defense, and aerospace. Contains job-search strategies and career options to help match education and expertise to the job market. Indexed geographically, by industry, and by hiring needs.

★9551★ Standard & Poor's Register of Corporations, Directors and Executives

Standard & Poor's
25 Broadway, 14th Fl.
New York, NY 10004
Ph: (212)208-8283   Fax: (212)412-0305

Annual, January; supplements in April, July, and October. $595.00, lease basis. Covers over 55,000 public and privately held corporations in the United States, including names and titles of over 400,000 officials (Volume 1); 70,000 biographies of directors and executives (Volume 2). Entries include: For companies, Name, address, phone, names of principal executives and accountants; primary bank, primary law firm, number of employees, estimated annual sales, outside directors, Standard Industrial Classification (SIC) code, product or service provided. For directors and executives, name, home and principal business addresses, date and place of birth, fraternal organization memberships, business affiliations. Arrangement: Alphabetical. Indexes: Volume 3 indexes companies geographically, by Standard Industrial Classification (SIC) code, and by corporate family groups.

★9552★ Thomas Register of American Manufacturers

Thomas Publishing Co.
5 Penn Plaza
New York, NY 10001
Ph: (212)695-0500   Fax: (212)290-7365
Fr: 800-222-7900

Annual, January. $240.00, plus $15.80 shipping. More than 149,000 manufacturing firms are listed in this 29 volume set. Volumes 1-19 list the firms under 50,000 product headings. Volumes 20 and 21 contain company profiles and a brand name section with more than 105,000 listings. Volumes 22-29 comprise prefiled catalogs from more than 1,700 firms. Arrangement: Volumes 1-19, classified by product or service; Volumes 20-29 alphabetical by company. Indexes: Product/service, brand/trade name (volume 19).

★9553★ Walker's Manual of Western Corporations

Walker's Western Research
1650 Borel Pl., #130
San Mateo, CA 94402-3506
Ph: (415)341-1110   Fr: 800-258-5737

1995. $390.00. (Supplement, $90.00.) 2400 pages. Publicly-held corporations in 13 western states. Indexed geographically and by industry.

★9554★ Ward's Business Directory of U.S. Private and Public Companies 1996

Gale Research
835 Penobscot Bldg.
Detroit, MI 48226-4094
Ph: (313)961-2242   Fax: (313)961-6083
Fr: 800-877-GALE

Annual. Six volumes. Volumes 1-3 lists companies alphabetically and Volume 4 lists companies geographically in ZIP code order by state; Volumes 1-4, $1,635.00/set (includes mid-year supplement). Volume 5 ranks companies by sales within 4-digit SIC; Volume 5, $850.00. Volumes 1-5, $1,845.00/set (includes mid-year supplement). Volume 6 provides state rankings by sales within 4-diogit SIC; $850.00. Volumes 1-6, $1,995.00/set (includes mid-year supplement). Contains information on over 142,000 U.S. businesses, over 90% of which are privately held. Entries include company name, address, and phone; sales; employees; description; names of officers; fiscal year end information; etc.

NEWSPAPERS, MAGAZINES, AND JOURNALS

★9555★ Georgia Technology Sourcebook

Jaye Communications, Inc.
550 Interstate North Pkwy., Ste. 150
Atlanta, GA 30339
Ph: (404)984-9444   Fax: (404)612-0780

Publication listing Georgia's high technology firms.

ONLINE AND DATABASE SERVICES

★9556★ Corporate Jobs Outlook!

Corporate Jobs Outlook, Inc. (CJOI)
PO Drawer 100
Boerne, TX 78006
Ph: (512)755-8810

Online database. Contains the complete text of *Corporate Jobs Outlook!*, a newsletter about career opportunities at 500 leading corporations. Includes salaries and benefits, advancement opportunities, research and development, growth plans, financial stability, and industry outlook. Contains details on national employers from 45 areas of business, including banking, aerospace, insurance, pharmaceuticals, retailing, and computers.

★9557★ Moody's Corporate Profiles

Moody's Investors Service, Inc.
99 Church St.
New York, NY 10007
Ph: (212)553-0300   Fax: (212)553-4700
Fr: 800-955-8080

Weekly. Database covers: more than 9,000 publicly held companies listed on the New York Stock Exchange or the American Stock Exchange or NMS companies traded on the National Association of Securities Dealers Automated Quotations. Database includes: Company name, address, phone, D-U-N-S number, Moody's number, stock exchange, ticker symbol, primary and secondary Standard Industrial Classification (SIC) codes and industries; line of business analysis, annual earnings and dividends per share and other financial and stock trading data for five-year period.

International Job Opportunities

REFERENCE WORKS

★9558★ A-Z of Careers and Jobs

Kogan Page Ltd.
120 Pentonville Rd.
London N1 9JN, England
Ph: 71 2780433   Fax: 71 8376348

Irregular, latest edition April 1994. $9.99. Publication includes: Lists of British sources for further information on careers and jobs; these lists are found at the ends of chapters dealing with various careers. Entries include: Name of source, address, phone, starting salary, qualifications, training. Principal content is information on over 350 jobs and careers. Arrangement: Alphabetical. Indexes: Subject.

★9559★ Almanac of International Jobs & Careers: A Guide to Over 1001 Employers

Impact Publications
9104 N Manassas Dr.
Manassas Park, VA 22111-5211
Ph: (703)361-7300   Fax: (703)335-9486

Ronald L. Krannich. 1994. $34.95; $19.95 (paper).

★9560★ American Jobs Abroad

Gale Research
835 Penobscot Bldg.
Detroit, MI 48226-4094
Ph: (313)961-2242   Fax: (313)961-6083
Fr: 800-877-GALE

First edition May 1994. $55.00. Covers over 800 U.S. corporations and 100 government agencies, associations, and other organizations that employ Americans overseas, generally on an ongoing or long-term basis at wages or salaries comparable to those in the U.S. Entries include: Company or organization name, address; recruiter's name, address, phone, fax, title; name of CEO; products and services; profile, annual sales, number of employees, number of U.S. employees abroad and countries where employed, application information, salaries, job categories, general requirements, length of assignment, language requirement, training, benefits. Arrangement: Alphabetical within sections cov-

ering companies and organizations. Indexes: Job category.

★9561★ Career Opportunities for Bilinguals and Multilinguals

Scarecrow Press
PO Box 4167
Metuchen, NJ 08840
Ph: (908)548-8600   Fax: (908)548-5767
Fr: 800-537-7107

Published 1994. $35.00. Covers 3,800 companies and organizations that hire people who are fluent in languages other than English; colleges and universities, libraries, books, and other educational resources for those wishing to learn other languages. Entries include: For employers: name, address, phone, description of work, languages sought. For educational resources: name, address, phone, languages. Arrangement: Separate sections for educational resources, U.S. opportunities, and overseas opportunities. Indexes: Language, educational background, geographical.

★9562★ Careers for Foreign Language Aficionados and Other Multilingual Types

VGM Career Horizons
4255 W. Touhy Ave.
Lincolnwood, IL 60646-1975
Ph: (847)679-5500   Fax: (847)679-2494
Fr: 800-323-4900

Ned H. Seelye and J. Laurence Day. 1992. $14.95; $9.95 (paper). Outlines mainstream and unusual jobs for teachers, translators, tour guides, and others who want to use a foreign language on the job.

★9563★ Careers in International Affairs

Georgetown University
Institute for the Study of Diplomacy
423 Intercultural Ctr.
Washington, DC 20057-1052
Ph: (202)687-8971

Mario Pinto Carland and Daniel H. Spatz, Jr. 1991. $15.00. 307 pages. Includes index and bibliography.

★9564★ The Complete Guide to International Jobs and Careers

Consultants Bookstore
Templeton Rd.
Fitzwilliam, NH 03447
Ph: (603)585-6544   Fax: (603)585-9555
Fr: 800-531-0007

Ron Krannich and Caryl Krannich. 1990. $13.95. 320 pages. Directed towards job seekers interested in learning the 'what', 'where', and 'how' of working in today's competitive international job market.

★9565★ Computer Jobs Worldwide: Support Staff Plus Electronics Plus Telecommunications

Zinks International Career Guidance
PO Box 790
Richland, MI 49083
Ph: (313)584-7529

Richard M. Zink. 1995. $14.95 (paper).

★9566★ Craighead's International Business, Travel, and Relocation Guide to 81 Countries 1996-97

Gale Research
835 Penobscot Bldg.
Detroit, MI 48226-4094
Ph: (313)961-2242   Fax: (313)961-6083
Fr: 800-877-GALE

Eighth edition. $460.00. 2,500 pages. Arranged geographically into regions of Asia, Africa, Europe, the Mideast, and the Americas. Profiles include information on maps, statistics, travel restrictions, currency, transportation, and health. A separate section covers details of international travel such as instructions for passports and visas and information on transportation and shopping. An international relocation chapter covers financial planning, legal matters, insurance, education, housing, and other family concerns.

★9567★ Directory of American Firms Operating in Foreign Countries

Uniworld Business Publications Inc.
50 E. 42nd St., Ste. 509
New York, NY 10017
Ph: (212)697-4999   Fax: (212)949-4001

Irregular, previous edition September 1991; latest edition 1994. $200.00, plus 7.50 shipping. Covers about 2,560 American corporations with 18,340 factories, branch offices, or other facilities outside the United States. Entries include: Company name, address, phone; names and titles of key personnel; locations and types of facilities in foreign countries, number of employees, product/service. Arrangement: Alphabetical (volume 1). Indexes: Foreign operation by country (volumes 2 and 3).

★9568★ **Directory of International Internships**

Dean's Office of International Studies and Programs
Michigan State University
International Center, Rm. 207
East Lansing, MI 48824
Ph: (517)353-5589   Fax: (517)353-7254

Irregular, latest edition 1994; new edition expected 1996. $25.00. Covers international internships sponsored by academic institutions, private corporations, and the federal government. Entries include: Institution name, address, phone, names and titles of key personnel, subject areas in which internships are available, number available, location, duration, financial data, academic credit available, evaluation procedures, application deadline, requirements of participation. Arrangement: Classified by type of sponsor, then alphabetical. Indexes: Sponsor, subject, geographical.

★9569★ **Directory of Jobs & Careers Abroad**

Vacation-Work Publications
9 Park End St.
Oxford OX1 1HJ, England
Ph: 865 241978   Fax: 865 790885

Quadrennial, latest edition 1993. $16.95. Publication includes: List of about 500 agencies; consultants; associations; government agencies; overseas branches; affiliates; and subsidiaries of British companies; and other organizations that offer or assist in locating permanent jobs abroad; worldwide coverage. Entries include: Company or organization name, address, phone, contact name, geographical and career areas covered. Principal content of publication is information on how to seek work abroad. Arrangement: Classified by type of career, then geographical. Indexes: Organization or company name.

★9570★ **The Directory of Schools, Colleges, and Universities Overseas**

Overseas Employment Services
PO Box 460
Mount Royal, PQ, Canada H3P 3C7
Ph: (514)739-1108   Fax: (514)739-0795

Annual. $15.00, postpaid. Covers Approximately 300 educational institutions worldwide that hire teachers to teach various subjects in English.

★9571★ **Directory of Summer Jobs Abroad**

Vacation-Work Publications
9 Park End St.
Oxford OX1 1HJ, England
Ph: 865 241978   Fax: 865 790885

Annual, November; supplement in May. $7.95, base edition; $6.00, supplement. Covers more than 30,000 jobs worldwide. En-

tries include: Name of employer, address, length of employment, number of positions available, pay rates, how and when to apply, name of contact. Arrangement: Geographical, then classified by type of job.

★9572★ **Directory of Work and Study in Developing Countries**

Vacation-Work Publications
9 Park End St.
Oxford OX1 1HJ, England
Ph: 865 241978   Fax: 865 790855

Quadrennial, latest edition 1994. $8.95. Covers about 420 organizations worldwide offering employment and study opportunities in over 100 developing countries; includes about 80 United States organizations. Entries include: Organization name, address, name and title of contact, geographical area covered, eligibility requirements, description of activities, qualifications needed, duration of assignments, travel costs, accommodations. Arrangement: Geographical. Indexes: Alphabetical.

★9573★ **Educational Placement Sources Abroad**

Education Information Services (EIS)
PO Box 660662
Newton, MA 02162-0662
Ph: (617)443-0125

Annual, August. Includes about 150 organizations in the United States and abroad which place English-speaking teachers and education administrators in positions abroad. Provides organization name and address. Classified by type of organization.

★9574★ **Educational Travel Resource Guide**

Transition Abroad Publishing, Inc
18 Hulst Rd
PO Box 1300
Amherst, MA 01004-1300
Ph: (413)256-3414   Fax: (413)256-0373

Annual, June. $7.50. Covers over 600 sources of information on international employment, education, and specialty travel opportunities. Entries include: Source name, address, phone. Arrangement: Classified by subject and country.

★9575★ **English in Asia: Teaching Tactics for New English Teachers**

Global Press
697 College Pkwy.
Rockville, MD 20850-1135
Ph: (202)466-1663

Irregular, latest edition 1992. $12.95. Publication includes: Directory covering over 1,000 private English-language schools in Asia to which applications can be made to teach. Entries include: School name, address, phone, contact.

★9576★ **Evaluating an Overseas Job Opportunity**

Pilot Books, Inc.
103 Cooper St.
Babylon, NY 11702
Ph: (516)422-2225

John Williams. 1990. $5.95. 39 pages.

★9577★ **Executive Grapevine: The Directory of Executive Recruitment Consultants**

Executive Grapevine International Ltd.
4 Theobald Ct.
Theobald St.
Borehamwood, Herts. WD6 4RN, England
Ph: 81 9539939   Fax: 81 9539808

Annual, July. $99.00. Covers about 750 executive search firms in the United Kingdom. Entries include: Firm name, address, phone, telex, names and titles of key personnel, year established, description of services, job function and industry handled, salary range, geographic area covered, fees, guarantees, associations with other firms, branch offices and phones. Arrangement: Alphabetical. Indexes: Product/service, name, subject, geographical.

★9578★ **Graduate Employment & Training**

Hobsons Publishing PLC
Bateman St.
Cambridge CB2 1LZ, England
Ph: 223 354551   Fax: 223 323154

Annual, September. $13.99. Covers about 5,000 firms offering more than 70,000 jobs in the United Kingdom to recent graduates. Entries include: Company name, address, phone, name and title of contact, area of interest, disciplines required, area of recruiting, number of vacancies per year. Arrangement: Alphabetical. Indexes: Degree subject, occupation, type of employer, geographical.

★9579★ **Great Jobs for Foreign Language Majors**

NTC Publishing Group
4255 W. Touhy Ave.
Lincolnwood, IL 60646-1975
Ph: (708)679-5500   Fax: (708)679-6375
Fr: 800-323-4900

Julie DeGalan. 1994. $11.95 (paper).

★9580★ **Guide to Careers in World Affairs**

Impact Publications
9104-N Manassas Dr.
Manassas Park, VA 22111-5211
Ph: (703)361-7300   Fax: (703)335-9486

Foreign Policy Association. 1993. $14.95. 331 pages. Describes jobs in business, government, and nonprofit organizations. Explains the methods and credentials required to secure a job in many fields, including international law and journalism. Contains sections on internships and graduate programs.

★9581★ **How to Get a Job in Europe**

Surrey Books, Inc.
230 E. Ohio St.
PO Box 11326
Chicago, IL 60611-9496
Ph: (312)751-7334   Fax: (312)751-7334
Fr: 800-326-4430

Robert Sanborn. Third edition, 1995. $17.95. 450 pages. Directory of employers, associations, job referral services, and other sources of employment information.

★9582★ How to Get a Job in the Pacific Rim

Surrey Books, Inc.
230 E. Ohio St.
PO Box 11326
Chicago, IL 60611-9496
Ph: (312)751-7334   Fax: (312)751-7334
Fr: 800-326-4430

Robert Sanborn. 1992. $17.95. Directory of employers, associations, job referral services, and other sources of employment information.

★9583★ How to Get the Job You Want Overseas

Pilot Books
103 Cooper St.
Babylon, NY 11702
Ph: (516)422-2225   Fax: (516)422-2227

$4.95. Covers Overseas jobs in private industry, as well as salary scales and benefits, and employment agencies specializing in overseas placement.

★9584★ International Directory of Employment Agencies

Overseas Employment Services
PO Box 460
Mount Royal, PQ, Canada H3P 3C7
Ph: (514)739-1108   Fax: (514)739-0795

Annual, January. $15.00. Covers Approximately 500 employment agencies and recruitment firms in fifty countries located in Western Europe, the Far and Middle East, South Africa, South America, Central America, Australia, and southeast Asia. Entries include: Company name, address, geographical area served, and product/service. Arrangement: Geographical.

★9585★ International Jobs: Where They Are & How to Get Them

Addison-Wesley Publishing Co., Inc.
1 Jacob Way
Reading, MA 01867
Ph: (617)944-3700

Eric Kocher. 1993. $14.95 (paper). 440 pages. Discusses over 500 different job opportunities in a variety of sectors.

★9586★ Jobs in Japan

Global Press
697 College Pkwy.
Rockville, MD 20850-1135

Irregular, latest edition 1993. $14.95. Publication includes: Lists of private schools in Japan and other organizations useful to native English-speaking job-seekers; directory of Japanese companies that hire non-Japanese workers. Entries include: Organization or company name, address, phone, name and title of contact. Principal content of publication is advice on jobs available for foreigners in Japan including teaching journalism, acting, office work, etc. It also explains how to negotiate with employers and obtain the right visas, and gives tips on living and working in Japan.

★9587★ J.O.B.S. Job Opportunities and Business Series: The Employment Guide to the Washington, D.C., Metropolitan Area

JSI Network
PO Box 231
Woodbridge, VA 22194-0231
Ph: (703)680-9611

Imelda R. Roberts. 1989. $17.95. 319 pages. Describes a number of opportunities in D.C. and the surrounding Maryland and Virginia area. Jobs include the public and private sector, the military, embassies, and international opportunities.

★9588★ Key European Executive Search Firms and Their U.S. Links

Consultants Bookstore
Templeton Rd.
Fitzwilliam, NH 03447
Ph: (603)585-6544   Fax: (603)585-9555
Fr: 800-531-0007

James H. Kennedy. 1991. $39.00. 210 pages. Identifies linkages between more than 500 search offices in the United States and many European countries.

★9589★ Looking for Employment in Foreign Countries

World Trade Academy Press, Inc.
50 E. 42nd St., Ste. 509
New York, NY 10017
Ph: (212)697-4999   Fax: (212)949-4001

Irregular, latest edition September 1992; new edition expected, date not set. $16.50, plus $3.50 shipping. Covers United States government agencies, religious and non-profit organizations, and private corporations offering overseas employment opportunities in 46 countries.

★9590★ Major Business Organizations of Eastern Europe and the Commonwealth of Independent States

Graham & Trotman Ltd.
Sterling House
66 Wilton Rd.
London SW1V 1DE, England
Ph: 71 8211123   Fax: 71 6305229

Annual, September. $685.00. Covers Approximately 3,000 ministries, chambers of commerce, financial institutions, manufacturing companies, and trading organizations in Albania, Bulgaria, Czech Republic, Slovakia, Hungary, Poland, Romania, Yugoslavia, Baltic Republics, and the Commonwealth of Independent States. Entries include: Organization name, address, phone, telex, names and titles of key personnel, number of employees, financial data, subsidiary and branch names and locations, product/service. Arrangement: Geographical. Indexes: Product/service, name, geographical.

★9591★ Major Companies of the Arab World

Graham & Trotman Ltd.
Sterling House
66 Wilton Rd.
London SW1V 1DE, England
Ph: 71 8211123   Fax: 71 6305229

Annual, October. $685.00. Covers about 6,500 companies in all lines of business, including finance, manufacturing, agriculture, retail, technology, service, and public utility; and professional firms and government agencies in Algeria, Bahrain, Egypt, Iraq, Jordan, Kuwait, Lebanon, Libya, Mauritania, Morocco, Oman, Qatar, Saudi Arabia, Somalia, Sudan, Syria, Tunisia, the United Arab Emirates, and the People's Democratic Republic of Yemen. Entries include: Company name, address, phone, telex, cable address, names and titles of key personnel, line of business and activities, firms represented, subsidiary and branch names and locations, associated company names, banking references, number of employees, financial data, principal shareholders, year established. Arrangement: Geographical. Indexes: Company name, company name within country, line of business within country.

★9592★ Major Companies of Europe

Gale Research
835 Penobscot Bldg.
Detroit, MI 48226-4094
Ph: (313)961-2242   Fax: (313)961-6083
Fr: 800-877-GALE

1994. Four volumes. Volume 1, "Austria, Belgium, Denmark, Ireland, Finland, France"; $450.00. Volume 2, "Germany, Greece, Italy, Liechtenstein, Luxembourg"; $450.00. Volume 3, "Netherlands, Norway, Portugal, Spain, Sweden, Switzerland"; $450.00. Volume 4, "United Kingdom"; $450.00. $1,440.00/set. Covers thousands of Europe's major companies, including information on corporate finances, personnel, structure, products, profitability, and key executives. Arrangement: By country. Indexes: Company name, business activities, and countries.

★9593★ Major Companies of the Far East and Australasia

Gale Research
835 Penobscot Bldg.
Detroit, MI 48226-4094
Ph: (313)961-2242   Fax: (313)961-6083
Fr: 800-877-GALE

1994. Three volumes. Volume 1, "South East Asia", $405.00. Volume 2, "East Asia", $405.00 Volume 3, "Australia and New Zealand", $290.00. $1,110.00/set. Provides information on some 5,000 major companies of the Far East. Entries include: Company finances and profitability, personnel, structure, key people, and products. Arrangement: By country. Indexes: Company names, business activities, and countries.

★9594★ Medium Companies of Europe

Graham & Trotman Ltd.
Sterling House
66 Wilton Rd.
London SW1V 1DE, England
Ph: 71 8211123   Fax: 71 6305229

Annual, July. $1,198.00, for set; $598.00, volume 1; $300.00, volume 2; $300.00, volume 3. Covers Approximately 8,000 medium-sized companies in western Europe. Entries include: Company name, address, phone, telex, names and titles of key personnel, number of employees, financial data, subsidiary and branch names and locations, product/service. Arrangement: Geographical.

Indexes: Product/service, company name, geographical.

★9595★ Middle East Employment Guide

Overseas Employment Services
PO Box 460
Mount Royal, PQ, Canada H3P 3C7
Ph: (514)739-1108   Fax: (514)739-0795

Annual, January. $15.00. Covers Approximately 500 North American, foreign, and local regional companies, institutions, and personnel recruitment firms that are hiring for positions in the Middle East. Entries include: Company name, address, geographical area served, and product/service. Arrangement: Alphabetical.

★9596★ The New Relocating Spouse's Guide to Employment: Options and Strategies in the U.S. and Abroad

Impact Publications
9104-N Manassas Dr.
Manassas Park, VA 22111
Ph: (703)361-7300   Fax: (703)335-9486

1993. $14.95. Publication includes: List of 133 professional associations and 54 federal job centers. Entries include: Organization name, address, phone. Principal content of publication is discussion of the job market, employment trends, and other useful information for those facing a move to a city where they have no job waiting. Arrangement: Alphabetical.

★9597★ Opening List of Professional Openings in American Overseas & International Schools

Education Information Services
Instant Alert
PO Box 662
Newton, MA 02162-0002
Ph: (617)237-0887

Every 6 weeks. $9.00. Covers about 150 current professional openings for teachers, administrators, counselors, librarians, and educational specialists in American overseas schools and international schools at which the teaching language is primarily English. Also covers English as a Second/Foreign Language (ESL-EFL) at all age levels. Entries include: Institute name, address, names and titles of key personnel, positions available.

★9598★ Opportunities Abroad for Educators

Fulbright Teacher Exchange Program
600 Maryland Ave., SW, Rm. 235
Washington, DC 20024-2520
Ph: (202)382-8586   Fax: (202)426-0657
Fr: 800-726-0479

Annual, May. Free. Covers opportunities available for elementary and secondary teachers, college and university instructors and professors, and school administrators to attend seminars or to teach abroad under the Mutual Educational and Cultural Exchange Act of 1961. Entries include: Countries of placement, dates, eligibility requirements, teaching assignments. Arrangement: Geographical.

★9599★ Opportunities in International Business Careers

VGM Career Horizons
4255 W. Touhy Ave.
Lincolnwood, IL 60646-1975
Ph: (847)679-5500   Fax: (847)679-2494
Fr: 800-323-4900

Jeffrey Arpan. 1995. $14.95; $11.95 (paper). 160 pages. Describes what types of jobs exist in international business, where they are located, what challenges and rewards they bring, and how to prepare for and obtain jobs in international business.

★9600★ Overseas Exotic Jobs–$100 to $1000 Daily: For Unskilled, Skilled, Professionals

Zinks International Career Guidance
PO Box 790
Richland, MI 49083
Ph: (313)584-7529

Richard M. Zink. 1995. $9.95 (paper).

★9601★ Overseas Jobs: The New Offshore & Oilfield Manual

Zinks International Career Guidance
PO Box 790
Richland, MI 49083
Ph: (313)584-7529

Richard M. Zink. 1995. $14.95 (paper).

★9602★ Overseas Summer Jobs, 1995

Peterson's Guides, Inc.
PO Box 2123
Princeton, NJ 08543-2123
Ph: (609)243-9111   Fax: (609)243-9150
Fr: 800-338-3282

1995. $14.95 (paper).

★9603★ Peterson's Job Opportunities in Business 1996

Peterson's
PO Box 2123
Princeton, NJ 08543-2123
Ph: (609)243-9111   Fax: (609)243-9150
Fr: 800-338-3282

Compiled by the Peterson's staff. Annual. $19.95 (paper). 416 pages. Profiles 2,000 companies that are hiring employees in a number of nontechnical fields, including financial services, management consulting, retailers, utilities, and consumer products companies. Contains job-search strategies and career options to help match education and expertise to the job market. Indexed geographically, by industry, and by hiring needs.

★9604★ Peterson's Job Opportunities in Engineering and Technology 1996

Peterson's
PO Box 2123
Princeton, NJ 08543-2123
Ph: (609)243-9111   Fax: (609)243-9150
Fr: 800-338-3282

Compiled by the Peterson's staff. Annual. $19.95 paperback. 432 pages. Profiles 2,000 high-tech companies looking primarily for technical personnel in such fields as biotechnology, telecommunications, software, computers and peripherals, defense, and aerospace. Contains job-search strategies and career options to help match education and expertise to the job market. Indexed geographically, by industry, and by hiring needs.

★9605★ Recruiting Fairs for Overseas Teaching

Education Information Services
Instant Alert
865 Central Ave., Ste. L-504
Needham, MA 02192-1344
Ph: (617)433-0125

Covers recruiting fairs and sponsors in the U.S. and elsewhere for American educators who wish to teach outside the U.S. Entries include: Fair sponsor, name, address, and phone; fair dates and locations are given in a separate list.

★9606★ Resumes for Overseas & Stateside Jobs

Zinks International Career Guidance
PO Box 790
Richland, MI 49083
Ph: (313)584-7529

Richard M. Zink. 1994. $14.94 (paper).

★9607★ Strategies for Getting an Overseas Job

Pilot Books
103 Cooper St.
Babylon, NY 11702
Ph: (516)422-2225   Fax: (516)422-2227

$3.95. Covers Over 150 U.S. firms that operate overseas along with their specific activities, as well as specialized personnel agencies, overseas job-finding associations and other foreign employment services.

★9608★ Summer Jobs in Britain

Vacation-Work Publications
9 Park End St.
Oxford OX1 1HJ, England
Ph: 865 241978   Fax: 865 790885

Annual, November. $15.95. Covers over 30,000 farm, hotel, au pair, voluntary, and other summer jobs in Scotland, Wales, England, the Channel Islands and Northern Ireland. Entries include: Employer name, address, positions offered, description of duties, length of service, wages, other amenities. Arrangement: Classified by line of work.

★9609★ Vacation Work's Overseas Summer Jobs

Peterson's Guides, Inc.
202 Carnegie Center
PO Box 2123
Princeton, NJ 08543-2123
Ph: (609)243-9111   Fax: (609)243-9150
Fr: 800-338-3282

$14.95. Covers Over 30,000 summer jobs worldwide. Entries include: Complete job data, length of employment, number of openings, pay, job description, qualifications needed, application/contact information.

★9610★ Work, Study, Travel Abroad: The Whole World Handbook

St. Martin's Press, Inc.
175 5th Ave.
New York, NY 10010
Ph: (212)674-5151   Fax: (212)420-9314
Fr: 800-221-7945

Biennial, January of even years. $13.95, plus

$3.00 shipping. Covers more than 1,000 work, travel, and study opportunities abroad, selected and described from the viewpoint of the United States student. Entries include: Name and description of program, address for information. Arrangement: Geographical. Indexes: Organization, publication.

★9611★ Work Your Way Around the World

Vacation-Work Publications
9 Park End St.
Oxford OX1 1HJ, England
Ph: 865 241978   Fax: 865 790885

Biennial, February of odd years. $17.95. Covers temporary employment opportunities worldwide. Entries include: Name and address of employer, description of position. Arrangement: Geographical.

★9612★ Working Holidays

Central Bureau for Educational Visits & Exchanges
Seymour Mews House
Seymour Mews
London W1H 9PE, England
Ph: 71 4865101   Fax: 71 9355741

Annual, November. $9.99, postpaid. Covers 1,000 organizations offering short-term paid and voluntary work opportunities in Britain and over 70 countries worldwide, for periods of three days to a year or longer; jobs include archeological digs, au pair/childcare, children's projects, couriers, guides, monitors, teachers, work camps, conservation, community works, hotel work, farm work, teaching, simple construction, etc. Entries include: Organization name, address, name of contact, objectives, projects available, conditions and terms of work. Arrangement: Geographical, then by type of work. Indexes: Organization name.

★9613★ A Year Off–A Year On: A Guide to Jobs, Voluntary Service, and Working Holidays in the U.K. and Overseas During Your Education

Hobsons Publishing PLC
Bateman St.
Cambridge CB2 1LZ, England
Ph: 223 354551

Irregular, latest edition May 1993; new edition expected April 1995. $7.99. Publication includes: Names and addresses of organizations providing information about short-term employment opportunities in the United Kingdom and overseas. Principal content of publication is discussion of opportunities for short-term employment, particularly as a supplement to formal education.

NEWSPAPERS, MAGAZINES, AND JOURNALS

★9614★ EIS Current Openings in Education Abroad

Education Information Services (EIS)
PO Box 660662
Newton, MA 02162-0662
Ph: (617)443-0125

$10.95. Monthly. List providing teaching and other professional education openings in American overseas schools and international schools.

★9615★ Federal Career Opportunities

Federal Research Service, Inc.
243 Church St. NW
PO Box 1059
Vienna, VA 22183
Ph: (703)281-0200   Fax: (703)281-7639
Fr: 800-822-5627

Biweekly. $7.95, per copy; $39.00, 6 issues; $77.00, 12 issues; $175.00, 26 issues. Covers more than 4,000 current federal job vacancies in the United States and overseas; includes permanent, part-time, and temporary positions. Entries include: Position title, location, series and grade, job requirements, special forms, announcement number, closing date, application address. Arrangement: Classified by federal agency and occupation.

★9616★ Foreign Faculty and Administrative Openings

Education Information Service
Box 662
Newton, MA 02162
Ph: (617)237-0887

Approximately every six weeks. $9.00. Covers approximately 150 specific openings in administration, counseling, library, teaching and other disciplines for American teachers in American schools overseas and in international schools, both of which must teach English as a primarily language. Entries include: Institution name, address.

★9617★ International Employment Hotline

International Employment Hotline
PO Box 3030
Oakton, VA 22124
Ph: (703)620-1972   Fax: (703)620-1973

Monthly. $39.00, per year. Covers temporary and career job openings overseas and advice for international job hunters. Entries include: Company name, address, job title, description of job, requirements, geographic location of job. Arrangement: Geographical.

★9618★ Overseas Employment Newsletter

Overseas Employment Services
PO Box 460
Mount Royal, PQ, Canada H3P 3C7
Ph: (514)739-1108   Fax: (514)739-0795

Biweekly. $39.00 for three months; $65.00 for 6 months; $105.00. Covers Approximately 300 available jobs in Europe, Asia, the Middle East, Africa, South America, Mexico, Australia/New Zealand, Bermuda, the Carri-

bean, etc. Entries include: Company name, address, phone, names and titles of key personnel, description of positions available and application requirements.

OTHER SOURCES

★9619★ Association for International Practical Training (AIPT)

10400 Little Patuxent Pky. Ste. 250
Columbia, MD 21044
Ph: (410)997-2200   Fax: (410)992-3924

Purpose: Helps coordinate training around the world in fields such as travel, the culinary arts, and hotel management. **Activities:** Conducts programs in career development and hospitality/tourism exchanges. Operates a student exchange program. Provides reciprocal practical training experience for recent graduates from the U.S., Austria, Germany, Finland, France, Hungary, Ireland, Japan, Malaysia, Netherlands, Switzerland, and the United Kingdom. Arranges training programs in the U.S. and abroad. Serves as U.S. affiliate to IAESTE (International Association for the Exchange of Students for Technical Experience) and operates a Professional Visitors Program to arrange short-term educational and training visits to the U.S. **E-Mail:** aipt@aipt.org

★9620★ Chinese Christian Mission (CCM)

PO Box 750759
Petaluma, CA 94975
Ph: (707)762-1314   Fax: (707)762-1713

Purpose: Serves as an evangelical faith mission dedicated to reaching Chinese people around the world with the gospel of Jesus Christ. Broadcasts radio programs to foster Christianity in China. **Activities:** Operates placement service providing ministers with churches. Sponsors short-term mission trips to Latin America and East Asia.

★9621★ Federation of Recruitment and Employment Services—Directory of Members

Federation of Recruitment and Employment Services
36-38 Mortimer St.
London W1N 7RB, England
Ph: 71 3234300   Fax: 71 2552878

Biennial. $8.00. Covers employment agencies and other member firms. Entries include: Agency or firm name, address, phone, type of job placement handled. Arrangement: Alphabetical. Indexes: Geographical.

★9622★ International Educator's Institute (TIE)

PO Box 513
Cummaquid, MA 02637
Ph: (508)362-1414

Purpose: Facilitates the placement of teachers and administrators in American, British, and international schools. Seeks to create a network that provides for professional development opportunities and improved financial security of members. Offers advice and information on international school news, recent educational developments, job placement, and investment, consumer, and professional development opportunities. Makes available insurance and travel benefits. Operates International Schools Internship Program. Sponsors competitions. Bestows awards.

★9623★ NAFSA/Association of International Educators (NAFSA)

1875 Connecticut Ave. NW, Ste. 1000
Washington, DC 20009
Ph: (202)462-4811   Fax: (202)667-3419

Members: Individuals, organizations, and institutions dealing with international educational exchange, including foreign student advisers, overseas educational advisers, credentials and admissions officers, administrators and teachers of English as a second language, community support personnel, study-abroad administrators, and embassy cultural or educational personnel. **Purpose:** Promotes self-regulation standards and responsibilities in international educational exchange; offers professional development opportunities primarily through publications, workshops, grants, and regional and national conferences. Advocates for increased awareness and support of international education and exchange on campuses, in government, and in communities. **Activities:** Offers services including: a job registry for employers and professionals involved with international education; a consultant referral service. Sponsors joint liaison activities with

a variety of other educational and government organizations to conduct a census of foreign student enrollment in the U.S.; conducts workshops about specific subjects and countries.

★9624★ Overseas Employment Opportunities for Educators: Department of Defense Dependents Schools

Diane Publishing Co.
600 Upland Ave.
Upland, PA 19015
Ph: (610)499-7415

1993. $29.95. 52 pages.

★9625★ U.S.-China Education Foundation (USCEF)

5345 Light Circle
Norcross, GA 30071
Ph: (770)729-1779   Fax: (770)448-1859

A project of the Society for the Advancement of Global Education. **Purpose:** To promote the learning of the Chinese languages (including Mandarin, Cantonese, and minority languages such as Mongolian) by Americans, and the learning of English by Chinese. **Activities:** Operates teacher placement service. Conducts short-term travel-study program to prepare Americans and Chinese for stays of four, six, or eight months or one to four years in China or the U.S., respectively. A project of S.A.G.E. the Society for the Development of Global Education.

★9626★ United States Committee for the United Nations Environment Program (US UNEP)

2013 Que St. NW
Washington, DC 20009
Ph: (202)234-3600   Fax: (202)332-3221

Members: Individuals interested in raising public awareness of the importance of a global environmental effort. **Purpose:** Encourages activism in support of the United Nations Environment Program. Acts as a liason between the UNEP and the public. Sponsors educational programs and children's services. **Activities:** Offers placement services to job seekers in international environmental work. Maintains speakers' bureau.

★9627★ YMCA International Camp Counselor Program (ICCP)

71 W. 23rd St., Ste. 1904
New York, NY 10010
Ph: (212)727-8800   Fax: (212)727-8814

Purpose: A work-travel program designed to introduce international university students and teachers and social workers aged 19-30 to life in America. The students spend 8 to 9 weeks counseling in children's camps across the country, followed by a period of independent or group travel. Also sponsors ICCP-Abroad placement service for American university students aged 18-25 wishing to serve as camp counselors in Africa, Asia, Australia, Hungary, New Zealand, and South America.

Interviewing Skills

REFERENCE WORKS

★9628★ Effective Interviewing for Paralegals

Anderson Publishing Co.
PO Box 1576
Cincinnati, OH 45201-1576
Ph: (513)421-4142   Fr: (513)562-8180

Fred E. Jandt. 1994.

★9629★ Essential Interviewing: A Programmed Approach to Effective Communication

Brooks Cole Publishing Co.
511 Forest Lodge Rd.
Pacific Grove, CA 93950
Ph: (408)373-0728   Fax: (408)375-6414

David Evans. 1993. $29.95 (paper).

★9630★ Fifty Winning Answers to Interview Questions: Everything You Need to Know to Prepare Yourself for the Job Interview

D B M Publishing
100 Park Ave., 4th Fl.
New York, NY 10017
Ph: (212)692-7715   Fax: (212)972-2120
Fr: 800-345-5627

Charles F. Albrecht, Jr. 1995. $10.95 (paper).

★9631★ Get That Interview: The Indispensable Guide for College Grads

Barron's Educational Series, Inc.
250 Wireless Blvd.
Hauppauge, NY 11788
Fr: 800-645-3476

R. Theodore Moock, Jr. $8.95 (paper) Offers strategies, tactics, and advice for the recent college graduate.

★9632★ Government Job Finder

Planning/Communications
7215 Oak Ave.
River Forest, IL 60305-1935
Ph: (708)366-5200   Fr: (888)366-5200

Daniel Lauber. Third edition, 1996. $32.95; $16.95 (paper). 352 pages. Covers 1800 sources. Discusses how to use sources of local, state, and federal government job vacancies in a number of specialties and state-by-state, including job-matching services, job hotlines, specialty periodicals with job ads, salary surveys, and directories. Explains how local, state, and federal hiring systems work. Includes chapters on resume and cover letter preparation and interviewing.

★9633★ Help Wanted: All the Help You'll Ever Need for Resume & Interview Preparation

Executive Type
PO Box 1315
Manhattan Beach, CA 90267-1315
Ph: (310)370-7332

Janet A. McKane. 1995. $12.00 (paper).

★9634★ How to Get Interviews from Classified Job Ads

Impact Publications
9104-N Manassas Dr.
Manassas Park, VA 22111-5211
Ph: (703)361-7300   Fax: (703)335-9486

Kenton W. Elderkin. Second edition, 1993. $14.95. 270 pages. Outlines how to select and follow up ads to get the job. Includes unique ways to get interview offers and how to incorporate the use of a computer and a fax machine in arranging interviews. Illustrated.

★9635★ How to Have a Winning Job Interview

VGM Career Horizons
4255 W. Touhy Ave.
Lincolnwood, IL 60646-1975
Ph: (847)679-5500   Fax: (847)679-2494
Fr: 800-323-4900

Deborah Perlmutter Bloch. Second edition, 1992. $8.95. 128 pages. Guides the reader through the steps of making the best impression on a future employer, including getting the appointment for the interview and planning an approach, what to emphasize, and what to minimize.

★9636★ How to Locate Jobs and Land Interviews

The Career Press, Inc.
3 Tice Rd.
PO Box 687
Franklin Lakes, NJ 07417
Ph: (201)848-0310   Fax: (201)848-1727
Fr: 800-237-3371

Albert L. French. Second edition, 1993. $10.95. 192 pages. Shows readers how to tap into the unadvertised, hidden job market and guides them through the resume, cover letter, and interview preparation process.

★9637★ Information Interviewing: What It Is and How to Use It in Your Career

Garrett Park Press
PO Box 190
Garrett Park, MD 20896-0190
Ph: (301)946-2553

Martha Stoodley. 1990. $10.95. 126 pages. Details the why, how, and where of information interviewing and provides suggestions for incorporating this technique into an effective job search.

★9638★ Interview Handbook

Kendall Hunt Publishing Co.
4050 Westmark Dr.
PO Box 1840
Dubuque, IA 52004-1840
Ph: (319)589-1000   Fax: 800-772-9165
Fr: 800-228-0810

1993. $8.95.

★9639★ Interview Strategies That Will Get You the Job You Want

Betterway Books
1507 Dana Ave.
Cincinnati, OH 45207
Ph: (513)717-0488   Fax: (513)531-4082
Fr: 800-289-0963

1995. $12.99 (paper).

★9640★ Interview for Success

Impact Publications
9104-N Manassas Dr.
Manassas Park, VA 22111-5211
Ph: (703)361-7300   Fax: (703)335-9486

Ronald Krannich and Caryl Krannich. 1990. $15.95. 212 pages. Subtitled: "A Practical

Guide to Increasing Job Interviews, Offers and Salaries". Offers hundreds of tips for more successful job interviews.

★9641★ **Interviewing & Helping Skills**

Jones & Bartlett Publishers, Inc.
40 Tall Pine Dr.
Sudbury, MA 01776
Ph: (508)443-5000   Fax: (508)443-8000
Fr: 800-832-0034

Cormier. 1995. $37.50 (paper).

★9642★ **Interviewing Principles and Practices**

Brown and Benchmark
25 Kessel Ct.
Madison, WI 53711
Ph: (608)273-0040   Fr: 800-338-5578

Charles J. Stewart. 1993.

★9643★ **Interviewing: Skills & Applications**

Gorsuch Scarisbrick Publishers
8233 Via Paseo del Norte, Ste. F400
Scottsdale, AZ 85258
Ph: (602)991-7881   Fax: (602)991-4770

James E. Sayer. 1993. $28.00 (paper).

★9644★ **Interviewing Skills for Nurses & Other Health Care Professionals: A Structured Approach**

Routledge
29 W. 35th St.
New York, NY 10001-2299
Ph: (212)244-3336   Fax: 800-248-4724

Robert Newell. 1994. $65.00; $18.95 (paper).

★9645★ **Interviewing Techniques for Newspapers**

State Mutual Book & Periodical Service, Ltd.
521 5th Ave., 17th Fl.
New York, NY 10175
Ph: (718)261-1704   Fax: (516)537-0412

Maurice Dunlevy. 1995. $20.00 (paper).

★9646★ **Job Interviewing for College Students**

NTC Publishing Group
4255 W. Touhy Ave.
Lincolnwood, IL 60646-1975
Ph: (847)679-5500   Fax: (847)679-2494
Fr: 800-323-4900

1995. $11.95 (paper).

★9647★ **Job Interviews: How to Win the Offer**

Consultants Bookstore
Templeton Rd.
Fitzwilliam, NH 03447
Ph: (603)585-6544   Fax: (603)585-9555
Fr: 800-531-0007

Joyce Lain Kennedy. 1990. $5.95. 28 pages.

★9648★ **Knock 'Em Dead: The Ultimate Job Seeker's Handbook**

Bob Adams, Inc.
260 Center St.
Holbrook, MA 02343
Ph: (617)767-8100   Fax: (617)767-0994
Fr: 800-872-5627

Martin John Yate. 1994. $20.00; $10.95 (paper). Prepares the job seeker for the interview with advice on dress, manner, how to answer the toughest questions, and how to spot illegal questions. Discusses how to respond to questions of salary to maximize income. Features sections on executive search firms and drug testing.

★9649★ **Make Your Job Interview a Success**

Prentice Hall General Reference
15 Columbus Cir.
New York, NY 10023
Ph: (212)373-8500   Fr: 800-223-2348

J.I. Biegeleisen. 1994. $12.00.

★9650★ **More Successful Less Stressful Interviewing for Women: A Guide to Improving Your Interviewing Skills While Reducing Stress**

StellWest Publishing Co., Inc.
PO Box 190
River Edge, NJ 07661
Ph: (201)692-8306   Fax: (201)692-0302

Jessica Woods. 1995. $9.95 (paper).

★9651★ **The New Job Interview**

P P I Publishing
PO Box 292239
Kettering, OH 45429
Ph: (513)294-5057

Dinah Tallent. 1995.

★9652★ **The 90 Minute Interview Prep Book**

Peterson's Guides, Inc.
PO Box 2123
Princeton, NJ 08543-2123
Ph: (609)243-9111   Fax: (609)243-9150
Fr: 800-338-3282

Peggy Schmidt. 1996. $15.95 (paper). Includes diskette. Provides step-by-step instructions for conducting practice interviews. Software allows users to evaluate the practice interviews.

★9653★ **101 Great Answers to the Toughest Interview Questions**

The Career Press, Inc.
3 Tice Rd.
PO Box 687
Franklin Lakes, NJ 07417
Ph: (201)848-0310   Fax: (201)848-1727
Fr: 800-237-3371

Ron Fry. Second edition, 1994. $8.95. 192 pages. Identifies some of the toughest interview questions and provides proven responses.

★9654★ **The Perfect Interview: How to Get the Job You Really Want**

Consultants Bookstore
Templeton Rd.
Fitzwilliam, NH 03447
Ph: (603)585-6544   Fax: (603)585-9555
Fr: 800-531-0007

John D. Drake. 1991. $17.95. 189 pages. Contains skill-building exercises and tips on preparing for the interview, framing good questions, and following through.

★9655★ **The Quick Interview & Salary Negotiation Book: Dramatically Improve Your Interviewing Skills & Pay in a Matter of Hours**

JIST Works, Inc.
720 N. Park Ave.
Indianapolis, IN 46202-3431
Ph: (317)264-3720   Fax: (317)264-3709
Fr: 800-648-5478

Michael J. Farr. 1995. $12.95 (paper).

★9656★ **Resume Writing, Interviewing and Role-playing Skills for Salespeople Looking for New Jobs**

J B & Me
PO Box 3879
Manhattan Beach, CA 90266
Ph: (310)546-1255

Jack Bernstein. 1993. $12.50.

★9657★ **A Road Map to Your Job Search: A Complete Guide to Finding & Keeping a Job**

Godfred T. Ansah
124 Monroe St.
East Hartford, CT 06118
Ph: (203)568-5801   Fax: (203)722-8042

Godfred T. Ansah. 1995.

★9658★ **The Smart Woman's Guide to Interviewing and Salary Negotiation**

Career Press, Inc.
3 Tice Rd.
PO Box 687
Franklin Lakes, NJ 07417-1322
Ph: (201)848-0310   Fax: (201)848-1727
Fr: 800-227-3371

Julie A. King. 1995. $12.99 (paper).

★9659★ **Successful Interviewing for College Seniors**

VGM Career Horizons
4255 W. Touhy Ave.
Lincolnwood, IL 60646-1975
Ph: (847)679-5500   Fax: (847)679-2494
Fr: 800-323-4900

John Shingleton. 1992. $11.95. Specifically tailored to the needs of college seniors and recent graduates. Includes what to expect in an interview, how to prepare for it, and how to excel in a sometimes tense situation.

★9660★ **Sweaty Palms: The Neglected Art of Being Interviewed**

Ten Speed Press
PO Box 7123
Berkeley, CA 94707
Ph: (510)559-1600   Fax: (510)559-1629
Fr: 800-841-BOOK

H. Anthony Medley. 1992. $8.95. 194 pages.

Offers a guide for several types of interviews, including stress and group sessions.

★9661★ **Your First Interview**

The Career Press, Inc.
3 Tice Rd.
PO Box 687
Franklin Lakes, NJ 07417
Ph: (201)848-0310   Fax: (201)848-1727
Fr: 800-237-3371

Ron Fry. Third edition, 1995. $9.99. 192 pages. Takes the reader from making the initial contact with a prospective employer to negotiating salary.

AUDIO/VISUAL RESOURCES

★9662★ **Advice from Hiring Experts**

CareerLab Books
9085 E. Mineral Circle, Ste. 330
Englewood, CO 80112
Ph: (303)790-0505   Fax: (303)790-0606
Fr: 800-723-9675

Video. $59.95. 30 minutes.

★9663★ **The Art of Interviewing**

Marketing Directions, Inc.
PO Box 715
Avon, CT 06001

Brian Jud. 1993. $39.95. 34 minutes. Demonstrates successful job interviewing techniques.

★9664★ **Common Mistakes People Make in Interviews**

Cambridge Career Products
PO Box 2153
Dept. CC15
Charleston, WV 25328-2153
Ph: (304)744-9323   Fax: (304)744-9351
Fr: 800-468-4227

Video. 1995. $79.95. 40 minutes. Helps job seekers anticipate what interviewers are looking for.

★9665★ **Extraordinary Answers to Common Interview Questions**

Cambridge Career Products
PO Box 2153
Dept. CC15
Charleston, WV 25328-2153
Ph: (304)744-9323   Fax: (304)744-9351
Fr: 800-468-4227

Video. 1995. $79.95. 30 minutes. Follows a quiz format, with advice from career experts.

★9666★ **Face to Face Video Series**

Cambridge Career Products
PO Box 2153
Dept. CC15
Charleston, WV 25328-2153
Ph: (304)744-9323   Fax: (304)744-9351
Fr: 800-468-4227

Series of five videos. $149.95/set. $39.95/each. 25 minutes each. Documents unrehearsed interviews and provides strategies for improving an interviewing style. Five titles: Commercial Banking, Retailing, Teach-

ing, Consumer Marketing, and Computer Science.

★9667★ **Getting Ready for the Interview**

Cambridge Career Products
PO Box 2153
Dept. CC15
Charleston, WV 25328-2153
Ph: (304)744-9323   Fax: (304)744-9351
Fr: 800-468-4227

Video. $98.00. 30 minutes. Show vocational students how to prepare for interviews.

★9668★ **How to Get Interviews and Organize Your Time**

Career Communications, Inc.
PO Box 169
Harleysville, PA 19438
Ph: (215)256-3130   Fax: (215)256-3136
Fr: 800-346-1848

Video. $225.00. Discusses using the telephone, contacting employers in person, organizing a job search, and other techniques.

★9669★ **The Insider's Guide to Competitive Interviewing**

Cambridge Career Products
PO Box 2153
Dept. CC15
Charleston, WV 25328-2153
Ph: (304)744-9323   Fax: (304)744-9351
Fr: 800-468-4227

Video. 1992. $49.95. 60 minutes. Peter Leffkowitz, a professional recruiter, presents strategies to prepare for even the toughest interviews.

★9670★ **The Interview**

Cambridge Career Products
PO Box 2153
Dept. CC15
Charleston, WV 25328-2153
Ph: (304)744-9323   Fax: (304)744-9351
Fr: 800-468-4227

Series of 2 videos. $69.00/each. 30 minutes each. Parts 1 and 2 observe three job seekers as they go through the interview process.

★9671★ **The Interview Edge: The Edge That Gets the Job**

Cranbrook Learning Systems, Inc.
12950 Capital
Oak Park, MI 48237
Ph: (313)542-8270   Fax: (313)564-6488
Fr: 800-368-5627

Larry Korn. 1994. $14.95 (audio cassette).

★9672★ **Interview to Win Your First Job**

Cambridge Career Products
PO Box 2153
Dept. CC15
Charleston, WV 25328-2153
Ph: (304)744-9323   Fax: (304)744-9351
Fr: 800-468-4227

Video. 1994. $98.95. 33 minutes. Instructional program for recent college, technical school, and community college graduates.

★9673★ **Interviewing for a Job**

Cambridge Career Products
PO Box 2153
Dept. CC15
Charleston, WV 25328-2153
Ph: (304)744-9323   Fax: (304)744-9351
Fr: 800-468-4227

Video. $59.95. 30 minutes. Shows how to communicate with an interviewer while assessing your interest in the position.

★9674★ **Interviewing for Success**

Golden West College
15744 Golden West St.
Huntington Beach, CA 92647
Ph: (714)892-7711   Fax: (714)895-8243

Video cassette. Series of 30-minute videos helps jobseekers in various fields prepare for the job interview.

★9675★ **Interviewing: The Key to Employment**

Career Communications, Inc.
PO Box 169
Harleysville, PA 19438
Ph: (215)256-3130   Fax: (215)256-3136
Fr: 800-346-1848

Video. $79.00. 12 minutes. Advice from Eileen Hahn, a human resources director, and Richard N. Bolles, author of *What Color Is Your Parachute?*

★9676★ **Interviews and the Job Offer**

CareerLab Books
9085 E. Mineral Circle, Ste. 330
Englewood, CO 80112
Ph: (303)790-0505   Fax: (303)790-0606
Fr: 800-723-9675

Video. $59.95. 30 minutes.

★9677★ **Job Hunting in Tough Times**

Ready Reference Press
PO Box 5249
Santa Monica, CA 90409
Fax: (310)475-4895   Fr: 800-424-5627

Series of 3 videos. $239.00/set. $89.00/each. Separate titles cover job search skills, resume preparation, and interview techniques.

★9678★ **The Job Interview and You**

Cambridge Career Products
PO Box 2153
Dept. CC15
Charleston, WV 25328-2153
Ph: (304)744-9323   Fax: (304)744-9351
Fr: 800-468-4227

Video. 1992. $79.95. 60 minutes. Jim Barton presents a sevenstep process for successful job interviews.

★9679★ **Job Search Skills for Adults**

Ready Reference Press
PO Box 5249
Santa Monica, CA 90409
Fax: (310)475-4895   Fr: 800-424-5627

Series of 3 videos. $239.00/set. $89.00/each. Separate titles cover job search skills, resume preparation, and interview techniques.

★9680★ Job Search Skills for Teens

Ready Reference Press
PO Box 5249
Santa Monica, CA 90409
Fax: (310)475-4895   Fr: 800-424-5627

Series of 3 videos. $239.00/set. $89.00/each. Separate titles cover job search skills, resume preparation, and interview techniques.

★9681★ Job Search Skills for Women

Ready Reference Press
PO Box 5249
Santa Monica, CA 90409
Fax: (310)475-4895   Fr: 800-424-5627

Series of 3 videos. $239.00/set. $89.00/each. Separate titles cover job search skills, resume preparation, and interview techniques.

★9682★ Job Search Skills for Women in Non-Traditional Occupations

Ready Reference Press
PO Box 5249
Santa Monica, CA 90409
Fax: (310)475-4895   Fr: 800-424-5627

Series of 3 videos. $239.00/set. $89.00/each. Separate titles cover job search skills, resume preparation, and interview techniques.

★9683★ Power Interviewing

Cambridge Career Products
PO Box 2153
Dept. CC15
Charleston, WV 25328-2153
Ph: (304)744-9323   Fax: (304)744-9351
Fr: 800-468-4227

Video. $49.95. 55 minutes. Instructional video on the art of getting hired.

★9684★ Preparing for the Interview

Cambridge Career Products
PO Box 2153
Dept. CC15
Charleston, WV 25328-2153
Ph: (304)744-9323   Fax: (304)744-9351
Fr: 800-468-4227

Series of 2 videos. $69.00/each. 30 minutes each. Part 1 covers recommended answers to 16 common interview questions and discusses body language. Part 2 covers more difficult questions and answers.

★9685★ Sell Yourself: Successful Job Interviewing

Learning Seed
330 Telser Rd.
Lake Zurich, IL 60047
Fr: 800-634-4941

Video. $89.00. 23 minutes.

★9686★ Seven Phases of a Job Interview

Cambridge Career Products
PO Box 2153
Dept. CC15
Charleston, WV 25328-2153
Ph: (304)744-9323   Fax: (304)744-9351
Fr: 800-468-4227

Video. $195.00. 38 minutes. Includes instructor's guide.

★9687★ Strategic Job Search

American Media Inc.
4900 University Ave., Ste. 100
West Des Moines, IA 50266-6769
Ph: (515)224-0919   Fax: (515)224-0256
Fr: 800-262-2557

Two video cassettes. John Gordon. 25 minutes each. Video 1 covers the development of job leads through a variety of sources such as networks, placement services, publications; video 2 covers the interviewing process.

★9688★ Succeeding in Your Interview

Cambridge Career Products
PO Box 2153
Dept. CC15
Charleston, WV 25328-2153
Ph: (304)744-9323   Fax: (304)744-9351
Fr: 800-468-4227

Video. $98.00. 30 minutes. Provides vocational students with necessary interviewing skills.

★9689★ Successful Interviewing

Cambridge Career Products
PO Box 2153
Dept. CC15
Charleston, WV 25328-2153
Ph: (304)744-9323   Fax: (304)744-9351
Fr: 800-468-4227

Video. $69.95. 15-20 minutes. Follows a recent college graduate.

★9690★ The Video Guide to Interviewing Series

Cambridge Career Products
PO Box 2153
Dept. CC15
Charleston, WV 25328-2153
Ph: (304)744-9323   Fax: (304)744-9351
Fr: 800-468-4227

Series of three videos. $275.00/set. $98.00/each. 30 minutes each. Three titles: "Four Stages of Interviewing," "Interview Preparation," and "Handling Difficult Questions." Workbook included with each video.

SOFTWARE

★9691★ Adams Job Interview Pro

Planning/Communications
7215 Oak Ave.
River Forest, IL 60305-1935
Ph: (708)366-5200   Fr: (888)366-5200

Adams New Media and Peter Veruki. 1996. $49.95 (CD-ROM). Available in Windows or Macintosh versions. Users can watch, listen, and respond to 11 short tutorials, 300 interview questions, 300 video clips, and 200 audio clips. Includes free access to Adams JobBank Online.

OTHER SOURCES

★9692★ A Funny Thing Happened at the Interview: Wit, Wisdom, and War Stories from the Job Hunt

Publishers Marketing Association (PMA)
2401 Pacific Coast Hwy., Ste. 102
Hermosa Beach, CA 90254
Ph: (310)372-2732   Fax: (310)374-3342

Gregory F. Farrell. $12.95 (paper). Humorous, true job interview stories.

Looking to Relocate

★9693★ Atlanta JobBank

Bob Adams, Inc.
260 Center St.
Holbrook, MA 02343
Ph: (617)767-8100   Fax: (617)767-0994
Fr: 800-872-5627

Annual, December. $15.95, payment with order. Covers about 5,300 employers in the Atlanta, Georgia area. Entries include: Firm or organization name, address, phone, description of organization, name and title of contact, typical titles for entry-level and middle-level positions, educational backgrounds desired, employment outlook, number of employees, benefits offered, training programs, internships, parent company, projected hiring, number of employees, revenues. Arrangement: Classified by industry. Indexes: Alphabetical.

★9694★ Boston JobBank

Bob Adams, Inc.
260 Center St.
Holbrook, MA 02343
Ph: (617)767-8100   Fax: (617)767-0994
Fr: 800-872-5627

Annual, December. $15.95, payment with order. Covers over 4,500 Boston area employers. Entries include: Firm or organization name, address, name and title of contact, entry-level positions, fringe benefits offered, stock exchange listing, phone desription of organization, location of headquarters, educational background desired, training programs, internships, parent company, projected hiring, number of employees, revenues. Arrangement: Classified by industry. Indexes: Alphabetical.

★9695★ Carolina JobBank

Bob Adams, Inc.
260 Center St.
Holbrook, MA 02343
Ph: (617)767-8100   Fax: (617)767-0994
Fr: 800-872-5627

Annual, March. $15.95. Covers 13,900 employers in North Carolina and South Carolina. Entries include: Firm or organization name, address, phone, description of organization, name and title of contact, location of headquarters, typical titles for entry-level and middle-level positions, educational backgrounds desired, company benefits, stock exchange listing, training programs and internships, parent company, projected hiring, number of employees, revenues. Arrangement: Classified by industry. Indexes: Alphabetical.

★9696★ Central Florida Career Guide

Edge Publishing
739 Little Wekiva Cir.
Altamonte Springs, FL 32714
Ph: (407)788-6357   Fax: (407)539-2966

Semiannual, January and November. $19.95. Covers employment needs of over 400 firms in the Orlando metropolitan area. Entries include: Company name, address, phone, name and title of contact, number of employees, products or services provided, staffing needs. Arrangement: Classified by line of business.

★9697★ Chicago JobBank

Bob Adams, Inc.
260 Center St.
Holbrook, MA 02343
Ph: (617)767-8100   Fax: (617)767-0994
Fr: 800-872-5627

Annual, August. $15.95, payment with order. Covers about 9,200 major employers in the Chicago area. Entries include: Firm or organization name, address, phone, description of organization, name and title of contact, headquarters locations, typical titles for entry-level and middle-level positions, educational backgrounds desired, company benefits, stock exchange listing, training programs, internships, parent company, projected hiring, number of employees, revenues. Arrangement: Classified by industry. Indexes: Alphabetical.

★9698★ Columbus Employment Resources Directory

Columbus Area Chamber of Commerce
37 N. High St.
Columbus, OH 43215
Ph: (614)221-2747   Fax: (614)469-8250

Biennial. $12.00. Covers about 200 employers and 70 employment services; also includes about 20 colleges, universities, and technical schools in central Ohio. Entries include: Company or firm name, address, phone, name of contact, company overview, positions hired, and training, education, and other benefits. Arrangement: Separate alphabetical sections for employers, employment services, and colleges.

★9699★ Craighead's International Business, Travel, and Relocation Guide to 81 Countries 1996-97

Gale Research
835 Penobscot Bldg.
Detroit, MI 48226-4094
Ph: (313)961-2242   Fax: (313)961-6083
Fr: 800-877-GALE

Eighth edition. $460.00. 2,500 pages. Arranged geographically into regions of Asia, Africa, Europe, the Mideast, and the Americas. Profiles include information on maps, statistics, travel restrictions, currency, transportation, and health. A separate section covers details of international travel such as instructions for passports and visas and information on transportation and shopping. An international relocation chapter covers financial planning, legal matters, insurance, education, housing, and other family concerns.

★9700★ Dallas/Ft. Worth JobBank

Bob Adams, Inc.
260 Center St.
Holbrook, MA 02343
Ph: (617)767-8100   Fax: (617)767-0994
Fr: 800-872-5627

Annual, September. $15.95. Covers 4,700 employers in the Dallas/Ft. Worth, Texas, area. Entries include: Firm or organization name, address, phone, description of organization, name and title of contact, location of headquarters, typical titles for entry-level and middle-level positions, educational backgrounds desired, company benefits, stock exchange listing, training programs, internships, parent company, projected hiring, number of employees, revenues. Arrangement: Classified by industry. Indexes: Alphabetical.

★9701★ Denver JobBank

Bob Adams, Inc.
260 Center St.
Holbrook, MA 02343
Ph: (617)767-8100   Fax: (617)767-0994
Fr: 800-872-5627

Annual, March. $15.95, payment with order. Covers 3,100 employers in Denver, Colorado. Entries include: Firm or organization name, address, phone, description of organization, name and title of contact, headquarters location; listings may also include typical titles for entry-level and middle-level positions, educational backgrounds desired, company benefits, stock exchange listing, training programs, internships, parent company, projected hiring, number of employees, revenues. Arrangement: Classified by industry. Indexes: Alphabetical.

★9702★ Detroit JobBank

Bob Adams, Inc.
260 Center St.
Holbrook, MA 02343
Ph: (617)767-8100   Fax: (617)767-0994
Fr: 800-872-5627

Annual, April. $15.95. Covers 6,300 employers in the Detroit, Michigan, area. Entries include: Firm or organization name, address, phone, description of organization, name and title of contact, location of headquarters, typical titles for entry-level and middle-level positions, educational backgrounds desired, company benefits, stock exchange listing, training programs, internships, parent company projected hiring, number of employees, revenues. Arrangement: Classified by industry. Indexes: Alphabetical.

★9703★ Finding a Job in Florida

Pineapple Press, Inc.
PO Drawer 16008, Southside Sta.
Sarasota, FL 34239
Ph: (813)359-0955   Fax: (813)359-0886

Latest edition 1994. $14.95. Covers major employers, career information sources, schools and training programs, chambers of commerce, personal consultants, newspapers, and state government agencies in Florida of interest to job seekers. Entries include: Organization name, address; some include phone. Arrangement: geographical and classified by type or work.

★9704★ Florida JobBank

Bob Adams, Inc.
260 Center St.
Holbrook, MA 02343
Ph: (617)767-8100   Fax: (617)767-0994
Fr: 800-872-5627

Annual, December. $15.95, payment with order. Covers 8,300 employers in Florida. Entries include: Firm or organization name, address, phone, description of organization, name and title of contact, headquarters location, typical titles for entry-level and middle-level positions, educational backgrounds desired, company benefits, stock exchange listing, training programs, internships, parent company, projected hiring, number of employees, revenues. Arrangement: Classified by industry. Indexes: Alphabetical.

★9705★ Getting Started: North Carolina Jobs and Careers

North Carolina Occupational Information Coordinating Committee (NCOICC)
PO Box 25903
Raleigh, NC 27611

Booklet. 1995-97. Free. 26 pages. A job search resource for readers seeking work in North Carolina.

★9706★ Greater Orlando Major Employers Guide

Greater Orlando Chamber of Commerce
75 E. Ivanhoe Blvd.
PO Box 1234
Orlando, FL 32802
Ph: (407)425-1234   Fax: (407)839-5020

Latest edition 1992. $10.60 plus $4.40 shipping. Covers over 500 firms in metropolitan Orlando that have 100 or more employees. Entries include: Company name, address, phone, Standard Industrial Classification (SIC) code, name and title of contacts, number of employees. Arrangement: Alphabetical. Indexes: Line of business.

★9707★ High-Impact Telephone Networking for Job Hunters

Bob Adams, Inc.
260 Center St.
Holbrook, MA 02343
Ph: (617)767-8100   Fax: (617)767-0994
Fr: 800-872-5627

Howard Armstrong. 1992. $6.95. 132 pages. Examines the challenges associated with phone networking, shows the reader how to use "positive errors" to generate referrals, and offers hints on how to deal with "getting the runaround". Includes advice on how to ask for the meeting and addresses long-distance job searches by phone.

★9708★ Houston JobBank

Bob Adams, Inc.
260 Center St.
Holbrook, MA 02343
Ph: (617)767-8100   Fax: (617)767-0994
Fr: 800-872-5627

Annual, September. $15.95, payment with order. Covers over 4,600 employers in Houston, Texas. Entries include: Firm or organization name, address, phone, name and title of contact; description of organization; headquarters location, typical titles for entry-level and middle-level positions, educational backgrounds desired, fringe benefits offered, stock exchange listing, training programs, internships, parent company, projected hiring, number of employees, revenues. Arrangement: Classified by industry. Indexes: Alphabetical.

★9709★ How to Get a Job in Atlanta

Surrey Books, Inc.
230 E. Ohio St.
PO Box 11326
Chicago, IL 60611-9496
Ph: (312)751-7334   Fax: (312)751-7334
Fr: 800-326-4430

Thomas M. Camden. Third edition, 1994. $15.95. 500 pages. Directory of employers, associations, job referral services, and other sources of employment information.

★9710★ How to Get a Job in Boston

Surrey Books, Inc.
230 E. Ohio St.
PO Box 11326
Chicago, IL 60611-9496
Ph: (312)751-7334   Fax: (312)751-7334
Fr: 800-326-4430

Thomas M. Camden. Second edition, 1994. $15.95. Directory of employers, associations, job referral services, and other sources of employment information.

★9711★ How to Get a Job in Chicago

Surrey Books, Inc.
230 E. Ohio St.
PO Box 11326
Chicago, IL 60611-9496
Ph: (312)751-7334   Fax: (312)751-7334
Fr: 800-326-4430

Thomas M. Camden. Sixth edition, 1995. $15.95. 500 pages. Directory of employers, associations, job referral services, and other sources of employment information.

★9712★ How to Get a Job in Dallas/Fort Worth

Surrey Books, Inc.
230 E. Ohio St.
PO Box 11326
Chicago, IL 60611-9496
Ph: (312)751-7334   Fax: (312)751-7334
Fr: 800-326-4430

Robert Sanborn. Sixth edition, 1996. $16.95. 500 pages. Directory of employers, associations, job referral services, and other sources of employment information.

★9713★ How to Get a Job in Europe

Surrey Books, Inc.
230 E. Ohio St.
PO Box 11326
Chicago, IL 60611-9496
Ph: (312)751-7334   Fax: (312)751-7334
Fr: 800-326-4430

Robert Sanborn. Third edition, 1995. $17.95. 450 pages. Directory of employers, associations, job referral services, and other sources of employment information.

★9714★ How to Get a Job in Houston

Surrey Books, Inc.
230 E. Ohio St.
PO Box 11326
Chicago, IL 60611-9496
Ph: (312)751-7334   Fax: (312)751-7334
Fr: 800-326-4430

Thomas M. Camden. Second edition, 1995. $15.95. 500 pages. Directory of employers, associations, job referral services, and other sources of employment information.

★9715★ How to Get a Job in New York

Surrey Books, Inc.
230 E. Ohio St.
PO Box 11326
Chicago, IL 60611-9496
Ph: (312)751-7334   Fax: (312)751-7334
Fr: 800-326-4430

Robert Sanborn. Fifth edition, 1996. $16.95. 500 pages. Directory of employers, associations, job referral services, and other sources of employment information.

★9716★ How to Get a Job in the Pacific Rim

Surrey Books, Inc.
230 E. Ohio St.
PO Box 11326
Chicago, IL 60611-9496
Ph: (312)751-7334   Fax: (312)751-7334
Fr: 800-326-4430

Robert Sanborn. 1992. $17.95. Directory of employers, associations, job referral services, and other sources of employment information.

★9717★ How to Get a Job in the San Francisco Bay Area

Surrey Books, Inc.
230 E. Ohio St.
PO Box 11326
Chicago, IL 60611-9496
Ph: (312)751-7334   Fax: (312)751-7334
Fr: 800-326-4430

Robert Sanborn. Fifth edition, 1996. $16.95. 500 pages. Directory of employers, associations, job referral services, and other sources of employment information.

★9718★ How to Get a Job in Seattle/ Portland

Surrey Books, Inc.
230 E. Ohio St.
PO Box 11326
Chicago, IL 60611-9496
Ph: (312)751-7334   Fax: (312)751-7334
Fr: 800-326-4430

Robert Sanborn. Third edition, 1996. $16.95. 500 pages. Directory of employers, associations, job referral services, and other sources of employment information.

★9719★ How to Get a Job in Southern California

Surrey Books, Inc.
230 E. Ohio St.
PO Box 11326
Chicago, IL 60611-9496
Ph: (312)751-7334   Fax: (312)751-7334
Fr: 800-326-4430

Thomas M. Camden. Fifth edition, 1993. $15.95. 500 pages. Directory of employers, associations, job referral services, and other sources of employment information.

★9720★ How to Get a Job in Washington, D.C.

Surrey Books, Inc.
230 E. Ohio St.
PO Box 11326
Chicago, IL 60611-9496
Ph: (312)751-7334   Fax: (312)751-7334
Fr: 800-326-4430

Thomas M. Camden. Second edition, 1993. $15.95. Directory of employers, associations, job referral services, and other sources of employment information.

★9721★ The Job Bank Series

Bob Adams, Inc.
260 Center St.
Holbrook, MA 02343
Ph: (617)767-8100   Fax: (617)767-0994
Fr: 800-872-5627

$15.95/volume. There are 20 volumes in the Job Bank Series, each covering a different job market. Volumes exist for the following areas: Atlanta, Boston, the Carolinas, Chicago, Dallas/Fort Worth, Denver, Detroit, Florida, Houston, Los Angeles, Minneapolis, New York, Ohio, Philadelphia, Phoenix, San Francisco, Seattle, St. Louis, Tennessee, and Washington D.C. Each directory lists employers and provides name, address, telephone number, and contact information. Many entries include common positions, educational backgrounds sought, and fringe benefits provided. Cross-indexed by industry and alphabetically by company name. Profiles of professional associations, a section on the region's economic outlook, and listings of executive search and job placement agencies are included. Features sections on conducting a successful job search campaign and writing resumes and cover letters.

★9722★ Job Catalog

Mail Order USA
1255 Wisconsin Ave. NW, Rm. 6
Washington, DC 20007
Ph: (202)686-9521

Annual, March. $9.50. Covers 840 magazine publishers, 250 book and newsletter publishers, 300 trade and professional associations, 250 industrial employers, and additional cultural, education, public interest groups, and other organizations which offer social and job opportunities in Washington, D.C., and Baltimore, Maryland; does not deal with federal government employment. Entries include: Name, address, phone; professional organization listings include dues, membership benefits, and other descriptive information. Arrangement: Classified by type of industry.

★9723★ Job Hunter's Guide to Florida

Brattle Communications, Inc.
24 Computer Dr. W
Albany, NY 12205
Ph: (518)482-1596   Fax: (518)482-1998
Fr: 800-724-5318

Published 1992. $18.95. Covers resources of interest to those seeking employment in Florida, including chambers of commerce, government agencies, business and trade associations and publications, employment and temporary agencies, and major area employers. Entries include: Resource name, address, phone, name and title of contact. Arrangement: Geographical by city.

★9724★ Job Hunter's Guide to One Hundred Great American Cities

Brattle Communications, Inc.
24 Computer Dr. W
Albany, NY 12205-1607
Ph: (518)482-1596   Fax: (518)482-1998
Fr: 800-724-5318

Latest edition 1991. $17.95. Covers government agencies, employment agencies, executive recruiters, temporary help agencies, business and trade organizations, top 300 employers, and other firms, including agencies providing aid to women, veterans, minorities, the disabled, and senior citizens, of possible interest to the job hunter in 100 markets in the U.S. Entries include: Agency, organization, or firm name, address, phone, and products or services. Arrangement: Geographical by city.

★9725★ Job Relocation: Managing People on the Move

John Wiley & Sons, Inc.
605 3rd Ave.
New York, NY 10158-0012
Fr: 800-225-5945

Anthony G. Munton. 1993. $36.95 (paper).

★9726★ Los Angeles JobBank

Bob Adams, Inc.
260 Center St.
Holbrook, MA 02343
Ph: (617)767-8100   Fax: (617)767-0994
Fr: 800-872-5627

Annual, December. $15.95, payment with order. Covers over 12,900 southern California employers. Entries include: Firm or organization name, address, phone, name and title of contact, description of organization headquarters location, typical titles for entry-level and middle-level positions, educational backgrounds desired, fringe benefits offered, stock exchange listing, training programs, internships, parent company, projected hiring, number of employees, revenues. Arrangement: Classified by industry. Indexes: Alphabetical.

★9727★ Metro Washington DC JobBank

Bob Adams, Inc.
260 Center St.
Holbrook, MA 02343
Ph: (617)767-8100   Fax: (617)767-0994
Fr: 800-872-5627

Annual, December. $15.95, payment with order. Covers about 5,000 employers in Washington, D.C., Baltimore, Maryland, and northern Virginia. Entries include: Firm or organization name, address, phone, name and title of contact, description of organization, titles for entry-level and middle-level positions, educational backgrounds desired, company benefits, stock exchange listing, location of headquarters, training programs, internships, parent company, projected hiring, number of employees, revenues. Arrangement: Classified by industry. Indexes: Alphabetical.

★9728★ Michigan Centennial Business Directory

Historical Society of Michigan
2117 Washtenaw Ave.
Ann Arbor, MI 48104
Ph: (313)769-1828   Fax: (313)769-4267

Irregular. Covers over 500 firms that have been operating continuously in Michigan for at least 100 years; also includes list of about 15 business archives. Entries include: For firms: firm name, address, phone, date founded, name and title of chief executive officer. For archives: facility name, address, date established, description of holdings. Arrangement: Firms are geographical; archives are alphabetical. Indexes: Alphabetical.

★9729★ Michigan Connections: A Resource Directory

Michigan Jobs Commission
201 N. Washington Sq.
Lansing, MI 48913
Ph: (517)373-4600   Fax: (517)335-0198

Irregular, latest edition 1993. Free. Covers over 50 job training programs and their sponsoring organizations; programs listed are partially funded by a government agency and deemed employer-specific to meet needs of displaced workers, young, aged, and handicapped groups, and others. Also lists contact agencies, Service Delivery Area Offices, and Michigan Employment Security Commission Offices. Entries include: For programs: program name, name and address of contact, services provided, category of need (keyed to appropriate agencies), eligibility requirements. For others: name, address, phone. Arrangement: Separate alphabetical lists for programs and agencies to contact; geographical for area offices and MESC branches.

★9730★ Minneapolis/St. Paul JobBank

Bob Adams, Inc.
260 Center St.
Holbrook, MA 02343
Ph: (617)767-8100   Fax: (617)767-0994
Fr: 800-872-5627

Annual, November. $15.95, payment with order. Covers Approximately 4,500 employers in Minneapolis-St. Paul, Minnesota. Entries include: Firm or organization name, address, phone, description of organization, name and title of contact, location of headquarters, typical titles for entry-level and middle-level positions, educational backgrounds desired, company benefits, stock exchange listing, training programs, internships, parent company, projected hiring, number of employees, revenues. Arrangement: Classified by industry. Indexes: Alphabetical.

★9731★ Multinational Firms & International Relocation

Ashgate Publishing Co.
Old Post Rd.
Brookfield, VT 05036
Ph: (802)276-3162   Fax: (802)276-3837

Peter J. Buckley. 1996.

★9732★ National JobBank

Bob Adams, Inc.
260 Center St.
Holbrook, MA 02343
Ph: (617)767-8100   Fax: (617)767-0994
Fr: 800-872-5627

Annual, September. $250.00, payment with order. Covers over 17,000 employers nationwide. Entries include: Firm or organization name, address, phone, contact name and title, description of organization, headquarters location, typical titles for entry-level and middle-level positions, educational backgrounds desired, stock exchange (if listed), fringe benefits offered. Several state and regional volumes are available and described separately. Arrangement: Geographical. Indexes: Geographical and classified by industry.

★9733★ The New Relocating Spouse's Guide to Employment: Options and Strategies in the U.S. and Abroad

Impact Publications
9104-N Manassas Dr.
Manassas Park, VA 22111
Ph: (703)361-7300   Fax: (703)335-9486

1993. $14.95. Publication includes: List of 133 professional associations and 54 federal job centers. Entries include: Organization name, address, phone. Principal content of publication is discussion of the job market, employment trends, and other useful information for those facing a move to a city where they have no job waiting. Arrangement: Alphabetical.

★9734★ New York JobBank

Bob Adams, Inc.
260 Center St.
Holbrook, MA 02343
Ph: (617)767-8100   Fax: (617)767-0994
Fr: 800-872-5627

Annual, November. $15.95, payment with order. Covers over 1,900 New York City area employers. Entries include: Firm or organization name, address, phone, name and title of contact; description of organization, headquarters location, typical titles for entry-level and middle-level positions, educational backgrounds desired, fringe benefits offered, stock exchange listing, training programs, internships, parent company, projected hiring, number of employees, revenues. Arrangement: Classified by industry. Indexes: Alphabetical.

★9735★ Ohio JobBank

Bob Adams, Inc.
260 Center St.
Holbrook, MA 02343
Ph: (617)767-8100   Fax: (617)767-0994
Fr: 800-872-5627

Annual, December. $15.95, payment with order. Covers 9,600 employers in Ohio. Entries include: Firm or organization name, address, phone, description of organization, name and title of contact, headquarters location, typical titles for entry-level and middle-level positions, educational backgrounds desired, company benefits, stock exchange listing, training programs, internships, parent company, projected hiring, number of employees, revenues. Arrangement: Classified by industry. Indexes: Alphabetical.

★9736★ Passport to Overseas Employment

ARCO
Simon & Schuster/Prentice Hall
15 Columbus Cir.
New York, NY 10023
Ph: (212)373-8931   Fax: (212)373-8642
Fr: 800-428-5331

First edition 1990; new edition possible, date not set. $15.00. Covers sources of information on obtaining employment outside the U.S. Entries include: Company or organization name, address, phone, name and title of contact, biographical data, geographical area served, requirements for eligibility, description of services. Arrangement: Alphabetical.

★9737★ Philadelphia JobBank

Bob Adams, Inc.
260 Center St.
Holbrook, MA 02343
Ph: (617)767-8100   Fax: (617)767-0994
Fr: 800-872-5627

Annual, August. $15.95. Covers 8,200 employers in the Philadelphia, Pennsylvania, area. Entries include: Firm or organization name, address, phone, description of organization, name and title of contact, location of headquarters, typical titles for entry-level and middle-level positions, educational backgrounds desired, company benefits, stock exchange listing, training programs, internships, parent company, projected hirings, number of employees, revenues. Arrangement: Classified by industry. Indexes: Alphabetical.

★9738★ Phoenix JobBank

Bob Adams, Inc.
260 Center St.
Holbrook, MA 02343
Ph: (617)767-8100   Fax: (617)767-0994
Fr: 800-872-5627

Annual, April. $15.95. Covers 2,900 employers in the Phoenix, Arizona, area. Entries include: Firm or organization name, address, phone, description of organization, name and title of contact, location of headquarters, typical titles for entry-level and middle-level positions, educational backgrounds desired, company benefits, stock exchange listing, training programs, internships, parent company projected hiring, number of employees, revenues. Arrangement: Classified by industry. Indexes: Alphabetical.

★9739★ St. Louis JobBank

Bob Adams, Inc.
260 Center St.
Holbrook, MA 02343
Ph: (617)767-8100   Fax: (617)767-0994
Fr: 800-872-5627

Annual, April. $15.95. Cover 2,900 employers in the St. Louis, Missouri, area. Entries include: Firm or organization name, address, phone, description of organization, name and title of contact, location of headquarters, typical titles for entry-level and middle-level positions, educational backgrounds desired, company benefits, stock exchange listing, training programs, internships, parent company, projected hiring, number of employees, revenues. Arrangement: Classified by industry. Indexes: Alphabetical.

★9740★ San Francisco Bay Area JobBank

Bob Adams, Inc.
260 Center St.
Holbrook, MA 02343
Ph: (617)767-8100   Fax: (617)767-0994
Fr: 800-872-5627

Annual, December. $15.95, payment with order. Covers about 6,900 employers in the San Francisco Bay area. Entries include: Firm or organization name, address, phone, description of organization; name and title of contact, headquarters location, typical titles for entry-level and middle-level positions, educational backgrounds desired, company benefits, stock exchange listing, training programs, internships, parent company, projected hiring, number of employees, revenues. Arrangement: Classified by industry. Indexes: Alphabetical.

★9741★ **Seattle JobBank**

Bob Adams, Inc.
260 Center St.
Holbrook, MA 02343
Ph: (617)767-8100   Fax: (617)767-0994
Fr: 800-872-5627

Annual, October. $15.95, payment with order. Covers about 2,000 employers in Seattle, Washington. Entries include: Firm or organization name, address, phone, description of organization, name and title of contact, headquarters location, typical titles for entry-level and middle-level positions, educational backgrounds desired, company benefits, stock exchange listing, training programs, internships, parent company, projected hiring number of employees, revenues. Arrangement: Classified by industry. Indexes: Alphabetical.

★9742★ **Tampa Bay Career Guide**

Edge Publishing
739 Little Wekiva Cir.
Altamonte Springs, FL 32714
Ph: (407)788-6357

Semiannual, January and June. $19.95. Covers Approximately 450 companies in over 12 industries in the Florida counties of Hillsborough, Pinellas, and Pasco. Entries include: Company name, address, phone, name and title of contact, number of employees, subsidiary and branch names and locations, description, projected recruitment needs. Arrangement: Classified by line of business.

★9743★ **Tennessee JobBank**

Bob Adams, Inc.
260 Center St.
Holbrook, MA 02343
Ph: (617)767-8100   Fax: (617)767-0994
Fr: 800-872-5627

Annual, March. $15.95. Covers 5,400 employers in Tennessee. Entries include: Firm or organization name, address, phone, description of organization, name and title of contact, location of headquarters, typical titles for entry-level and middle-level positions, educational backgrounds desired, company benefits, stock exchange listing, training programs, internships, parent company, projected hiring, number of employees, revenues. Arrangement: Classified by industry. Indexes: Alphabetical.

NEWSPAPERS, MAGAZINES, AND JOURNALS

★9744★ **Arizona Business Gazette**

Phoenix Newspapers, Inc.
400 E. Van Buren, Ste. 900
PO Box 1950
Phoenix, AZ 85004
Ph: (602)271-7300   Fax: (602)271-7363

Weekly (Fri.). $45.00/year for individuals. Business and legal newspaper.

★9745★ **Arkansas Business**

Arkansas Business
201 E. Markham
PO Box 3686
Little Rock, AR 72203
Ph: (501)372-1443   Fax: (501)375-3623

Weekly. $48.95/year for individuals. Business magazine on the Arkansas business community, covering people and recent news events.

★9746★ **Atlanta Business Chronicle**

American City Business Journals
First Citizen Plaza
128 S. Tryon, Ste. 2300
Charlotte, NC 28202
Ph: (704)375-7404   Fax: (704)371-3299

Weekly. $54.00/year for individuals. Local business newspaper.

★9747★ **Austin Business Journal**

Austin Business Journal, Inc.
1301 Capital of Texas Hwy., B-224
Austin, TX 78746
Ph: (512)328-0180   Fax: (512)328-7304

Weekly. Newspaper (tabloid) serving business and industry in Central Texas.

★9748★ **Baltimore Business Journal**

American City Business Journals
First Citizen Plaza
128 S. Tryon, Ste. 2300
Charlotte, NC 28202
Ph: (704)375-7404   Fax: (704)371-3299

Weekly. $53.00/year for individuals. Newspaper reporting Baltimore business news.

★9749★ **Boston Business Journal**

MCP, Inc.
200 High St.
Boston, MA 02110
Ph: (617)330-1000   Fax: (617)330-1016

Weekly. $64.00/year for individuals. Business newspaper specializing in local and regional business for upper management and CEO's of large and mid-sized businesses.

★9750★ **Business First**

American City Business Journals
First Citizen Plaza
128 S. Tryon, Ste. 2300
Charlotte, NC 28202
Ph: (704)375-7404   Fax: (704)371-3299

Weekly (Mon.). $50.00/year by mail. Business newspaper of Greater Columbus featuring breaking news and analysis of local commerce.

★9751★ **Business First of Buffalo**

American City Business Journals
First Citizen Plaza
128 S. Tryon, Ste. 2300
Charlotte, NC 28202
Ph: (704)375-7404   Fax: (704)371-3299

Weekly. $55.00/year for individuals. Western New Yorks Business Newspaper.

★9752★ **The Business Journal of Charlotte**

American City Business Journals
First Citizen Plaza
128 S. Tryon, Ste. 2300
Charlotte, NC 28202
Ph: (704)375-7404   Fax: (704)371-3299

Weekly. $44.00/year. News journal aimed at the Charlotte business community and surrounding area.

★9753★ **The Business Journal Serving Greater Milwaukee**

American City Business U.S.A.
2025 N. Summit Ave.
Milwaukee, WI 53202
Ph: (414)278-7788   Fax: (414)278-7028

Weekly (Mon.). Business newspaper. Subscribers are business decisionmakers in the metro area of Milwaukee.

★9754★ **Business Times**

Business Times, Inc.
315 Peck St., Bldg. 24
New Haven, CT 06513-0580
Ph: (203)782-1420

Monthly. $18.00/year for individuals. Business journal (tabloid).

★9755★ **California Job Journal**

Job Journal, Inc.
1800 Tribute Rd.
Sacramento, CA 95815-4314
Ph: (916)925-0800   Fax: (916)925-0101
Fr: 800-655-JOBS

Weekly. $99.00, per year. Covers job openings in California from entry-level to executive positions. Entries include: Company name, address, phone, type of business, name and title of contact; description of position and required skills/background, salary and/or benefits offered. Arrangement: Classified by field of employment.

★9756★ **Capital District Business Review**

American City Business Journals
First Citizen Plaza
128 S. Tryon, Ste. 2300
Charlotte, NC 28202
Ph: (704)375-7404   Fax: (704)371-3299

Weekly. $53.00/year for individuals. Business tabloid providing local business news for Capital Region area.

★9757★ **Corporate Report Minnesota**

City Media, Inc.
527 Marquette Ave. S
Ste. 300, Rand Tower
Minneapolis, MN 55402
Ph: (612)288-2100   Fax: (612)288-2121

Monthly. Business magazine.

★9758★ **Crain's Chicago Business**

Crain Communications, Inc.
740 N. Rush St.
Chicago, IL 60611
Ph: (312)649-5260   Fax: (312)649-5228

Weekly (Mon.). $73.00/year for individuals. Newspaper covering news stories about various aspects of business and labor activity in the Chicago market.

★9759★ Crain's Cleveland Business

Crain Communications, Inc.
700 W. St. Clair, Ste. 310
Cleveland, OH 44113
Ph: (216)522-1383   Fax: (216)694-4264

Weekly (Mon.). Metropolitan business newspaper serving seven counties.

★9760★ Crain's Detroit Business

Crain Communications, Inc.
1400 Woodbridge Ave.
Detroit, MI 48207
Ph: (313)446-1600   Fax: (313)446-0383

Weekly (Mon.). $40.00/year for individuals.
Local business tabloid covering Wayne, Ma-
comb, Oakland, Livingston, and Washtenaw
counties.

★9761★ Crain's New York Business

Crain Communications, Inc.
220 E. 42nd St.
New York, NY 10017
Ph: (212)210-0259   Fax: (212)210-0499

Weekly (Mon.). Regional business tabloid.

★9762★ Daily Journal of Commerce

Guide Publishing Co., Inc.
PO Box 52031
New Orleans, LA 70152
Ph: (504)368-8900   Fax: (504)368-8999

$270.00/year for individuals. Trade newspa-
per covering construction news in Louisiana
and Mississippi.

★9763★ Dallas Business Journal

American City Business Journals
First Citizen Plaza
128 S. Tryon, Ste. 2300
Charlotte, NC 28202
Ph: (704)375-7404   Fax: (704)371-3299

Weekly. Metro business journal.

★9764★ Des Moines Business Record

Business Publications Corp.
100 4th St.
Des Moines, IA 50309
Ph: (515)288-3336   Fax: (515)288-0309

Weekly (Mon.). $39.95/year; Free to qualified
subscribers; $47.50/year by mail. Newspaper
covering local business news.

**★9765★ Fairfield County Business
Journal**

Westfair Communications, Inc.
22 Saw Mill River Rd.
Hawthorne, NY 10532
Ph: (914)347-5200   Fax: (914)347-5576

Weekly (Mon.). $48.00/year for individuals.
Business and financial weekly newspaper of
Fairfield county.

★9766★ Florida Trend

Trend Magazines, Inc.
PO Box 611
St. Petersburg, FL 33731
Ph: (813)821-5800   Fax: (813)822-5083

Monthly. $27.00/year for individuals; $3.50
for single issue.

**★9767★ Georgia Technology
Sourcebook**

Jaye Communications, Inc.
550 Interstate North Pkwy., Ste. 150
Atlanta, GA 30339
Ph: (404)984-9444   Fax: (404)612-0780

Publication listing Georgia's high technology
firms.

★9768★ Houston Business Journal

American City Business Journals
First Citizen Plaza
128 S. Tryon, Ste. 2300
Charlotte, NC 28202
Ph: (704)375-7404   Fax: (704)371-3299

Weekly (Mon.). $49.00/year. Magazine (tab-
loid) for metropolitan Houston business community.

★9769★ Indianapolis Business Journal

IBJ Corp.
431 N. Pennsylvania
Indianapolis, IN 46204
Ph: (317)634-6200   Fax: (317)263-5060

Weekly. $59.00/year. Journal focusing on the
central Indiana business community.

★9770★ Long Island

Long Island Association
80 Hauppage Rd.
Commack, NY 11725-4495
Ph: (516)499-4400

Monthly. $30.00/year; $2.95/single issue.
Business journal for the Long Island area.

★9771★ Long Island Business News

2150 Smithtown Ave.
Ronkonkoma, NY 11779-7327
Ph: (516)737-1700   Fax: (516)737-1890
Fr: 800-LIB-NEWS

Weekly (Mon.). Business tabloid serving
Long Island.

**★9772★ The Los Angeles Business
Journal**

The Los Angeles Business Journal
5700 Wilshire, No. 170
Los Angeles, CA 90036
Ph: (213)549-5255   Fax: (213)549-5255

Weekly (Mon.). $48.00/year for individuals.
Newspaper (tabloid) covering local business
news, business trends, executive profiles,
and information for the Los Angeles area
executive.

★9773★ Memphis Business Journal

Mid-South Communications, Inc.
88 Union, Ste. 102
Memphis, TN 38103-5195
Ph: (901)523-1000   Fax: (901)526-5240

Weekly (Mon.). Magazine (tabloid) serving
the Mid-South business community.

★9774★ Miami Today

Today Enterprises, Inc.
PO Box 1368
Miami, FL 33101
Ph: (305)579-0211

Weekly (Thurs.). $90.00/year; $1.00 for single issue. Newspaper (tabloid) covering busi-

ness and community information targeted to
the upper management levels.

★9775★ Nashville Business Journal

1 Church St., Ste. 402
Nashville, TN 37202
Ph: (615)254-9154   Fax: (615)256-9080

Weekly. $39.00/year. Business news source
for Nashville business people.

**★9776★ Northeast Pennsylvania
Business Journal**

403 3rd Ave.
Kingston, PA 18704
Ph: (717)253-0271

Monthly. $18.00/year. Business journal fo-
cusing on regional business issues and
trends in the northeastern Pennsylvania area.

★9777★ Orlando Business Journal

American City Business Journals
First Citizen Plaza
128 S. Tryon, Ste. 2300
Charlotte, NC 28202
Ph: (704)375-7404   Fax: (704)371-3299

Weekly. $45.00/year for individuals. Newspa-
per (tabloid) covering local business news,
trends, and ideas of interest to industry,
trade, agribusiness, finance, and commerce.

★9778★ Orlando Magazine

Orlando Media Affiliates
422 W. Fairbanks Ave., Ste. 300
Winter Park, FL 32789-5079
Ph: (407)539-3939   Fax: (407)539-0533

Monthly. Free to qualified subscribers;
$14.90/year for individuals; $2.95 for single
issue. Regional magazine.

★9779★ Pacific Business News

American City Business Journals
First Citizen Plaza
128 S. Tryon, Ste. 2300
Charlotte, NC 28202
Ph: (704)375-7404   Fax: (704)371-3299

Weekly (Mon.). $48.00/year for individuals.
Business tabloid.

★9780★ Philadelphia Business Journal

Philadelphia Business Journal
400 Market St., Ste. 300
Philadelphia, PA 19106
Ph: (215)238-1450   Fax: (215)238-1466

Weekly. Regional and general business magazine.

★9781★ Pittsburgh Business Times, Inc.

Pittsburg Business Times, Inc.
2313 E. Carson St., Ste. 200
Pittsburgh, PA 15203
Ph: (412)481-6397   Fax: (412)481-9956

Weekly. $60.00/year. Metropolitan business
newspaper (tabloid).

★9782★ Providence Business News

Providence Business News
300 Richmond St, Ste. 202
Providence, RI 02903
Ph: (401)273-2201   Fax: (401)274-0270

Weekly (Mon.). Newspaper (tabloid) covering
business news in Southeastern New En-

gland. Regular editorial focus sections include banking/finance, computers, boating, industry, real estate and health care.

★9783★ **Puget Sound Business Journal**

American City Business Journals
First Citizen Plaza
128 S. Tryon, Ste. 2300
Charlotte, NC 28202
Ph: (704)375-7404   Fax: (704)371-3299

Weekly (Fri.). $49.00/year. Regional business newspaper (tabloid).

★9784★ **Rocky Mountain Employment Newsletter**

Intermountain Publishing & Referral
311-NP 14th St.
Glenwood Springs, CO 81601
Ph: (303)945-8991   Fax: (303)945-5140

Semimonthly. $13.00/year, per month for one edition; $16.00/year, for two editions; $19.00/year, for three editions; $21.00/year, for four editions. Lists information on current job openings in Colorado, Idaho, Montana, Arizona, New Mexico, Washington, Oregon, and Wyoming. Provides job titles, descriptions, requirements, and employer name and address or telephone number. Covers all occupational fields. Specializes in summer-winter seasonal openings, and in ranch, horse, livestock and farm opportunities. Available in four editions: Colorado-Wyoming, Arizona-New Mexico, Idaho-Montana, and Washington-Oregon.

★9785★ **St. Louis Business Journal**

American City Business Journals
First Citizen Plaza
128 S. Tryon, Ste. 2300
Charlotte, NC 28202
Ph: (704)375-7404   Fax: (704)371-3299

Weekly (Mon.). $54.00/year. Business newspaper.

★9786★ **St. Louis Countain**

Legal Communications Corporation
612 N. 2nd St., 4th Fl.
PO Box 88910
St. Louis, MO 63102
Ph: (314)421-1880   Fax: (314)421-0436

$175.00/year. Business and legal newspaper.

★9787★ **The San Antonio Business Journal**

American City Business Journals
First Citizen Plaza
128 S. Tryon, Ste. 2300
Charlotte, NC 28202
Ph: (704)375-7404   Fax: (704)371-3299

Weekly. $48.50/year for individuals. Newspaper featuring news and commentary about the San Antonio and south Texas business community.

★9788★ **San Diego Business Journal**

San Diego Business Journal
4909 Murphy Canyon Rd., No. 200
San Diego, CA 92123
Ph: (619)277-6359   Fax: (619)571-3628

Weekly (Mon.). $58.00/year for individuals. Metropolitan business newspaper specializing in investigative and enterprise reporting on San Diego County businesses and related issues.

★9789★ **San Diego Daily Transcript**

San Diego Daily Transcript
2131 3rd Ave.
PO Box 85469
San Diego, CA 92101
Ph: (619)232-4381   Fax: (619)239-5716
Fr: 800-697-6397

Daily. $131.00/year for individuals. Local business and financial newspaper.

★9790★ **San Francisco Business Times**

American City Business Journals
First Citizen Plaza
128 S. Tryon, Ste. 2300
Charlotte, NC 28202
Ph: (704)375-7404   Fax: (704)371-3299

Weekly (Fri.). $55.00/year for individuals; $93.00 for two years. Local business newspaper (tabloid) serving the San Francisco Bay Area.

★9791★ **South Florida Business Journal**

American City Business Journals
First Citizen Plaza
128 S. Tryon, Ste. 2300
Charlotte, NC 28202
Ph: (704)375-7404   Fax: (704)371-3299

Weekly (Fri.). $49.00/year for individuals. Newspaper covering business in Miami, Fort Lauderdale, and West Palm Beach.

★9792★ **Tampa Business Journal**

American City Business Journals
First Citizen Plaza
128 S. Tryon, Ste. 2300
Charlotte, NC 28202
Ph: (704)375-7404   Fax: (704)371-3299

Weekly. $42.00/year for individuals. Tampa Bay business news and information.

★9793★ **Vermont Business Magazine**

Lake Iroquois Publishing
2 Church St.
Burlington, VT 05401
Ph: (802)863-8038   Fax: (802)863-8069

Monthly. $25.00/year for individuals. Regional business magazine.

★9794★ **Washington Business Journal**

American City Business Journals
First Citizen Plaza
128 S. Tryon, Ste. 2300
Charlotte, NC 28202
Ph: (704)375-7404   Fax: (704)371-3299

Weekly. $54.60/year for individuals. Metropolitan business newspaper (tabloid).

ONLINE AND DATABASE SERVICES

★9795★ **L.A. Job Fair**

LA ONLINE
1332 Hermosa Ave., Ste. 7
Hermosa Beach, CA 90254
Ph: (310)372-9364   Fax: (310)374-6588

Online database containing information on career opportunities in technical and non-technical fields at Los Angeles-area companies. Listings include job descriptions and benefits. Enables the user to submit resumes directly to companies online.

SOFTWARE

★9796★ **Adams JobBank Software**

Planning/Communications
7215 Oak Ave.
River Forest, IL 60305-1935
Ph: (708)366-5200   Fr: (888)366-5200

Adams New Media. 1996. $59.95. Requires Windows 3.1 or higher, 3.5 inch disks only. Users can search from 11,000 U.S. companies by industry, state, or type of job. Includes 7,500 company profiles, 1,900 job hotlines, 300 fastest-growing companies, 1,100 executive search firms, and 1,100 employment agencies.

Negotiating Compensation Packages

REFERENCE WORKS

★9797★ American Almanac of Jobs and Salaries 1994-95

Avon Books
1350 Avenue of the Americas, 2nd Fl.
New York, NY 10019
Ph: (212)261-6800   Fr: 800-238-0658

John Wright. Revised edition, 1993. $17.00. 704 pages. This is a comprehensive guide to the wages of hundreds of occupations in a wide variety of industries and organizations.

★9798★ American Salaries and Wages Survey

Gale Research
835 Penobscot Bldg.
Detroit, MI 48226-4094
Ph: (313)961-2242   Fax: (313)961-6083
Fr: 800-877-GALE

Third edition, 1995. $105.00. About 1,000 pages. Provides salary information for thousands of occupations at different experience levels, as well as for specific areas of the country. Entries include occupation, specialization, and industry; location; frequency of salary cited; the low, mid, and/or high salary ranges; source, and survey or publication date.

★9799★ Dynamite Salary Negotiations: Know What You're Worth and Get It

Impact Publications
9104N Manassas Dr.
Manassas Park, VA 22111-5211
Ph: (703)361-7300   Fax: (703)335-9486

Ronald L. Krannich. 1994. $13.95 (paper).

★9800★ How to Make $1000 a Minute

Ten Speed Press
PO Box 7123
Berkeley, CA 94707
Ph: (510)559-1600   Fax: (510)559-1629
Fr: 800-841-BOOK

Jack Chapman. $8.95. 148 pages. A step-by-step guide to what to do and say in negotiating salaries and raises.

★9801★ How to Negotiate the Raise You Deserve

NTC Publishing Group
4255 W. Touhy Ave.
Lincolnwood, IL 60646-1975
Ph: (708)679-5500   Fax: (708)679-6375
Fr: 800-323-4900

Mark Satterfield. 1994. $9.95 (paper).

★9802★ Interview for Success

Impact Publications
9104-N Manassas Dr.
Manassas Park, VA 22111-5211
Ph: (703)361-7300   Fax: (703)335-9486

Ronald Krannich and Caryl Krannich. 1990. $15.95. 212 pages. Subtitled: "A Practical Guide to Increasing Job Interviews, Offers and Salaries". Offers hundreds of tips for more successful job interviews.

★9803★ Knock 'Em Dead: The Ultimate Job Seeker's Handbook

Bob Adams, Inc.
260 Center St.
Holbrook, MA 02343
Ph: (617)767-8100   Fax: (617)767-0994
Fr: 800-872-5627

Martin John Yate. 1994. $20.00; $10.95 (paper). Prepares the job seeker for the interview with advice on dress, manner, how to answer the toughest questions, and how to spot illegal questions. Discusses how to respond to questions of salary to maximize income. Features sections on executive search firms and drug testing.

★9804★ The Quick Interview & Salary Negotiation Book: Dramatically Improve Your Interviewing Skills & Pay in a Matter of Hours

JIST Works, Inc.
720 N. Park Ave.
Indianapolis, IN 46202-3431
Ph: (317)264-3720   Fax: (317)264-3709
Fr: 800-648-5478

Michael J. Farr. 1995. $12.95 (paper).

★9805★ The Smart Woman's Guide to Interviewing and Salary Negotiation

Career Press, Inc.
3 Tice Rd.
PO Box 687
Franklin Lakes, NJ 07417-1322
Ph: (201)848-0310   Fax: (201)848-1727
Fr: 800-227-3371

Julie A. King. 1995. $12.99 (paper).

AUDIO/VISUAL RESOURCES

★9806★ Advice from Hiring Experts

CareerLab Books
9085 E. Mineral Circle, Ste. 330
Englewood, CO 80112
Ph: (303)790-0505   Fax: (303)790-0606
Fr: 800-723-9675

Video. $59.95. 30 minutes.

★9807★ Interviews and the Job Offer

CareerLab Books
9085 E. Mineral Circle, Ste. 330
Englewood, CO 80112
Ph: (303)790-0505   Fax: (303)790-0606
Fr: 800-723-9675

Video. $59.95. 30 minutes.

★9808★ Negotiating the Job Offer

Cambridge Career Products
PO Box 2153
Dept. CC15
Charleston, WV 25328-2153
Ph: (304)744-9323   Fax: (304)744-9351
Fr: 800-468-4227

Video. $69.95. 15-20 minutes. Follows a recent college graduate.

★9809★ Negotiating Your Job Offer

DBM Publishing
Drake Beam Morin, Inc.
100 Park Ave., 4th Fl.
New York, NY 10164-0791
Fax: (212)972-2120   Fr: 800-345-5627

Video. $95.00. Shows an actual job offer negotiation session.

Non-Profit Opportunities

REFERENCE WORKS

★9810★ Alternatives to the Peace Corps: A Directory of Third World and U.S. Volunteer Opportunities

Institute for Food and Development Policy
398 60th St.
Oakland, CA 94618
Ph: (510)654-4400   Fax: (510)654-4551
Fr: 800-888-3314

Annual, latest edition winter 1994. $6.95, plus $2.50 shipping. Covers more than 60 foreign service organizations (excluding the Peace Corps) that offer long- or short-term volunteer service or travel opportunities in developing countries and U.S.-based volunteer opportunities. Entries include: Program name, address, phone, description of program, including geographical areas served and admission requirements. Arrangement: Classified by type of program. Indexes: Organization.

★9811★ Careers for Good Samaritans and Other Humanitarian Types

VGM Career Horizons
4255 W. Touhy Ave.
Lincolnwood, IL 60646-1975
Ph: (847)679-5500   Fax: (847)679-2494
Fr: 800-323-4900

Marjorie Eberts and Margaret Gisler. 1991. $12.95; $9.95 (paper). Contains hundreds of ideas for turning good work into paid work. Inventories opportunities in service organizations like the Red Cross, Goodwill, and the Salvation Army; religious groups, VISTA, the Peace Corps, and UNICEF; and agencies at all levels of the government.

★9812★ Charitable Organizations of the U.S.

Gale Research
835 Penobscot Bldg.
Detroit, MI 48226-4094
Ph: (313)961-2242   Fax: (313)961-6083
Fr: 800-877-GALE

Latest edition 1992. $150.00. Covers Approximately 800 organizations in the U.S. actively soliciting funds from the public to support their charitable programs and activities. Entries include: Organization name, ad-

dress, phone, telex, names and titles of key personnel, number of employees, financial data, description of services, projects, charitable programs, activities, product/service provided, history/purpose, fundraising methods, funding application information, supporters. Arrangement: Alphabetical. Indexes: Personal name, geographical, alphabetical/subject.

★9813★ Compensation in Nonprofit Organizations

Abbott, Langer & Associates
548 1st St.
Crete, IL 60417
Ph: (708)672-4200   Fax: (708)672-4674

Steven Langer. 1994. $225.00 (paper).

★9814★ Complete Guide to Public Employment

Impact Publications
9104-N Manassas Dr.
Manassas Park, VA 22111-5211
Ph: (703)361-7300   Fax: (703)335-9486

Ron and Caryl Krannich. Third edition, 1995. $19.95 (paper). List of federal, state, and local government agencies and departments, trade and professional associations, contracting and consulting firms, nonprofit organizations, foundations, research organizations, political support groups, and other organizations offering public service career opportunities. Entries include: Organization name, address, phone, name and title of contact. Arrangement: Classified by type of service. Indexes: Subject.

★9815★ Directory of Catholic Charities Diocesan Agencies and Organizations

Catholic Charities USA
1731 King St., Ste. 200
Alexandria, VA 22314
Ph: (703)549-1390   Fax: (703)549-1656

Biennial, odd years. $20.00 for members; $35.00 for nonmembers; $10.00, update supplement. Covers nearly 1,200 Catholic community and social service agencies and residential and non-residential institutions and facilities. Listings include diocesan agencies, institutions for the elderly, handicapped, and youth, Catholic schools of social work, and state Catholic conferences. Entries include: Organization name, address, name

and title of director, phone, fax, public relations contact. Arrangement: Geographical by diocese then classified by type of organization.

★9816★ Directory of Work and Study in Developing Countries

Vacation-Work Publications
9 Park End St.
Oxford OX1 1HJ, England
Ph: 865 241978   Fax: 865 790855

Quadrennial, latest edition 1994. $8.95. Covers about 420 organizations worldwide offering employment and study opportunities in over 100 developing countries; includes about 80 United States organizations. Entries include: Organization name, address, name and title of contact, geographical area covered, eligibility requirements, description of activities, qualifications needed, duration of assignments, travel costs, accommodations. Arrangement: Geographical. Indexes: Alphabetical.

★9817★ Federal Support for Nonprofits 1996

Gale Research
835 Penobscot Bldg.
Detroit, MI 48226-4094
Ph: (313)961-2242   Fax: (313)961-6083
Fr: 800-877-GALE

Cynthia R. Spomer. 1995. $150.00.

★9818★ Finding a Job in the Nonprofit Sector

The Taft Group
Gale Research
835 Penobscot Bldg.
Detroit, MI 48226-4094
Ph: (313)961-2242   Fax: (313)961-6083
Fr: 800-877-GALE

Published 1990. $95.00. Covers nearly 5,000 educational institutions, health and human services organizations, charities, social and recreational organizations, and cultural and historical societies in the U.S. Entries include: Organization name, address, phone, estimated annual income, description of activities, name and title of contact, representative job titles, typical employment requirements, application guidelines, number of employees, benefits, internship and training opportunities. Arrangement: Alphabetical. Indexes: Geographical, subject.

★9819★ **Guide to Careers in World Affairs**

Impact Publications
9104-N Manassas Dr.
Manassas Park, VA 22111-5211
Ph: (703)361-7300   Fax: (703)335-9486

Foreign Policy Association. 1993. $14.95. 331 pages. Describes jobs in business, government, and nonprofit organizations. Explains the methods and credentials required to secure a job in many fields, including international law and journalism. Contains sections on internships and graduate programs.

★9820★ **How to Successfully Start a Grassroots Non-Profit Organization**

Achievement U.S.A. Corp.
PO Box 9328
Washington, DC 20005
Fr: 800-891-3296

Darryl Webster. 1993. $20.00.

★9821★ **Jobs & Careers with Nonprofit Organizations**

Impact Publications
9104N Manassas Dr.
Manassas Park, VA 22111-5211
Ph: (703)361-7300   Fax: (703)335-9486

Ron Krannich. 1995. $15.95 (paper).

★9822★ **A Legal Guide to Starting and Managing a Nonprofit Organization**

John Wiley & Sons
605 3rd Ave.
New York, NY 10158-0012
Ph: (908)469-4400   Fr: 800-225-5945

Bruce R. Hopkins. 1993. $59.95; $19.95 (paper).

★9823★ **National Directory of Nonprofit Organizations**

Gale Research
835 Penobscot Bldg.
Detroit, MI 48226-4094
Ph: (313)961-2242   Fax: (313)961-6083
Fr: 800-877-GALE

Annual, spring. $425.00. Covers over 260,000 nonprofit organizations; volume 1 covers organizations with annual incomes of over $100,000; volume 2 covers organizations with incomes between $25,000 and $99,999. Entries include: Organization name, address, phone, annual income, IRS filing status, employer identification number, tax deductible status, activity description. Arrangement: Alphabetical. Indexes: Area of activity, geographical.

★9824★ **National Directory of Private Social Agencies**

Croner Publications, Inc.
34 Jericho Tpke.
Jericho, NY 11753
Ph: (516)333-9085   Fax: (516)338-4986
Fr: 800-441-4033

Base edition supplied upon order; monthly updates. $74.95, plus $4.95 shipping. Number of listings: Over 15,000. Entries include: Agency name, address, phone, name and title of contact, description of services. Arrangement: Geographical. Indexes: Service, agency type.

★9825★ **New Careers Directory: Internships and Professional Opportunities in Technology and Social Change**

Student Pugwash USA
815 15th St. NW, Ste. 814
Washington, DC 20005
Ph: (202)393-6555   Fax: (202)393-6550
Fr: 800-WOW-A-PUG

Irregular; latest edition spring 1993. $13.00 for students; $21.00 for institutions, plus $3.00 shipping. Covers about 300 research institutes, think tanks, laboratories, government agencies, professional, science, and other non-profit organizations offering public policy, science, and technology internships and jobs. Entries include: Sponsoring organization name, description of organization, programs offered, work environment and application procedures, compensation offered. Arrangement: Alphabetical and classified by subject. Indexes: Geographical, subject.

★9826★ **Non-Profits and Education Job Finder**

Planning/Communications
7215 Oak Ave.
River Forest, IL 60305-1935
Ph: (708)366-5200   Fr: (888)366-5200

Daniel Lauber. 1996. $32.95; $16.95 (paper). 350 pages. Covers 1600 sources. Discusses how to use sources of non-profit sector job vacancies in a number of specialties and state-by-state, including job-matching services, job hotlines, specialty periodicals with job ads, salary surveys, and directories. Covers a variety of fields from education to religion. Includes chapters on resume and cover letter preparation and interviewing.

★9827★ **Opportunities in Nonprofit Organizations**

VGM Career Horizons
NTC Publishing Group
4255 W. Touhy Ave.
Lincolnwood, IL 60646-1975
Ph: (847)679-5500   Fax: (847)679-2494
Fr: 800-323-4900

Adrian Paradis. 1994. $14.95; $11.95 (paper). 160 pages. Covers a range of career opportunities with nonprofit organizations.

★9828★ **Public Welfare Directory**

American Public Welfare Association
810 1st St. NE, Ste. 500
Washington, DC 20002-4267
Ph: (202)682-0100   Fax: (202)289-6555

Annual, August. $70.00, postpaid, payment with order; $75.00, billed. Covers federal, state, territorial, county, and major municipal human service agencies; coverage includes Canadian federal and provincial agencies. Entries include: Agency name, address, phone, names of key personnel, type of service or clientele. Arrangement: Geographical.

NEWSPAPERS, MAGAZINES, AND JOURNALS

★9829★ **The Chronicle of Philanthropy**

The Chronicle of Philanthrophy
1255 23rd St. NW, Ste. 775
Washington, DC 20037
Ph: (202)466-1200   Fax: (202)466-2078

Biweekly. Magazine covering fundraising, philanthropy, and non-profit organizations. Includes information on tax rulings, new grants, and statistics, reports on grant makers, and profiles of foundations.

★9830★ **Community Jobs: The Employment Newspaper for the Non-Profit Sector**

ACCESS: Networking in the Public Interest
30 Irving Pl.
New York, NY 10003
Ph: (212)475-1001   Fax: (212)475-1199

Monthly. $69.00. Covers jobs and internships available with nonprofit organizations active in issues such as the environment, foreign policy, consumer advocacy, housing, education, etc. Entries include: Position title; name, address, and phone of contact; description, responsibilities; requirements; salary. Arrangement: Geographical.

★9831★ **The NonProfit Times**

The Davis Information Group, Inc.
190 Tamarack Cir.
Skillman, NJ 08558-9662
Ph: (609)466-4600

Monthly. $39.00/year.

★9832★ **Public Interest Employment Service Job Alert**

Public Interest Clearing House
200 McAllister St.
San Francisco, CA 94102-4978
Ph: (415)255-1714

Semimonthly. $120.00/year for employed persons; $60.00/year for unemployed. Lists job openings in legal aid offices, public interest law firms, and nonprofit organizations.

OTHER SOURCES

★9833★ **ACCESS: Networking in the Public Interest**

30 Irving Pl.
New York, NY 10003
Ph: (212)475-1001   Fax: (212)475-1199

Purpose: Serves as a clearinghouse of information related to employment opportunities in the non-profit sector and public interest law. Seeks to increase and strengthen citizen involvement in public and community service.

★9834★ *Development Resource Group*
104 E. 40th St., Rm. 806
New York, NY 10016
Ph: (212)983-1600

Executive search firm specializing in the nonprofit sector.

★9835★ Intercristo
PO Box 33487
19303 Fremont Ave. N
Seattle, WA 98133
Ph: (206)546-7330   Fax: (206)546-7375
Fr: 800-251-7740

Members: Division of CRISTA Ministries.

Purpose: Provides job exploration and job information service with computerized referrals on current openings with Christian organizations. **Activities:** Distributes Career Kit, a home study career-building program.

★9836★ U.S. Public Interest Research Group (USPIRG)
218 D. St. SE
Washington, DC 20003
Ph: (202)546-9707   Fax: (202)546-2461

Members: Individuals who contribute time, effort, or funds toward public interest research and advocacy. **Activities:** Conducts research, monitors corporate and government actions, and lobbies for reforms on consumer, environmental, energy, and governmental issues. Current efforts include support for: laws to protect consumers from unsafe products and unfair banking practices; laws to reduce the use of toxic chemicals; renewal of the Clean Air Act; efforts to reduce global warming and ozone depletion; energy conservation and use of safe, renewable energy sources. Sponsors internships for college students; provides opportunities for students to receive academic credit for activities such as investigative journalism, legislative research, lobbying, and public education and organizing. Offers summer jobs.

Opportunities for Disabled Workers

REFERENCE WORKS

★9837★ Career Planning and Employment Strategies for Postsecondary Students with Disabilities

National Clearinghouse on Postsecondary Education for Individuals with Disabilities
1 Dupont Cir. NW, Ste. 800
Washington, DC 20036
Ph: (202)939-9320   Fax: (202)833-4760
Fr: 800-544-3284

Annual. Free. Covers about 30 educational institutions and organizations offering career placement programs for handicapped postsecondary students. Entries include: Institution name, address, phone, name and title of contact, program name, description of program. Arrangement: Classified by type of program.

★9838★ Coming Alive from Nine to Five

Mayfield Publishing
1280 Villa St.
Mountain View, CA 94041
Ph: (415)960-3222   Fr: 800-433-1279

Betty N. Michelozzi. Fourth edition, 1992. $19.95. 294 pages. In addition to general job-hunting advice, provides special information for women, young adults, minorities, older workers, and persons with handicaps.

★9839★ Job-Hunting Tips for the So-Called Handicapped

Ten Speed Press
PO Box 7123
Berkeley, CA 94707
Ph: (510)559-1600   Fax: (510)559-1629
Fr: 800-841-BOOK

Richard Nelson Bolles. 1992. $4.95. This book, originally published as an appendix to "What Color is Your Parachute", focuses on empowering disabled job seekers to reach their career goals and change the perceptions of employers.

★9840★ Job Strategies for People with Disabilities

Peterson's
PO Box 2123
Princeton, NJ 08543-2123
Ph: (609)243-9111   Fax: (609)243-9150
Fr: 800-338-3282

Melanie Astaire Witt. 1992. $14.95. 304 pages. Offers guidance to disabled jobseekers in uncovering the best career possibilities, determining job accommodations employers can be asked to provide for various positions, discovering their marketable skills, and locating organizations, publications, and other job hunting resources.

★9841★ Resources for the Handicapped

Ready Reference Press
PO Box 5249
Santa Monica, CA 90409
Ph: (213)474-5175   Fr: 800-424-5627

$139.50. Out of print. Three separate volumes provide a guide to information resources and services for the handicapped, covering the fields of employment, vocational rehabilitation, and education and training, among others. Discusses how to locate specialized career placement services.

★9842★ Shoot for the Moon

Saunderstown Press
1600 Boston Neck Rd.
PO Box 307
Saunderstown, RI 02874

Allen A. Johnson. 1993. $12.95. 37 pages. Designed for people starting or reentering employment, with special emphasis on handicapped and minorities.

★9843★ So You're "On Disability"...& You Think You Might Want to Get Back into Action

Daniel Thomas McAneny
2190 Anderson Ln.
Charlottesville, VA 22901

Daniel T. McAneny. 1995. $7.95 (paper).

NEWSPAPERS, MAGAZINES, AND JOURNALS

★9844★ Affirmative Action Register

Affirmative Action, Inc.
8356 Olive Blvd.
St. Louis, MO 63132
Ph: (314)991-1335   Fax: (314)997-1788
Fr: 800-537-0655

Monthly. $1.50 for single issue. Free, to women, minority, handicapped candidate sources. Covers in each issue, about 300 positions at a professional level (most requiring advanced study) available to women, minorities, veterans, and the handicapped; listings are advertisements placed by employers with affirmative action programs. Entries include: Company or organization name, address, contact name; description of position including title, requirements, duties, application procedure, salary, etc. Arrangement: Classified by profession.

★9845★ Careers and the Disabled

Equal Opportunity Publications
150 Motor Pky., Ste. 420
Hauppauge, NY 11788-5145
Ph: (516)273-8743

Quarterly. $10.00/year.

★9846★ MAINSTREAM

Exploding Myths, Inc.
2973 Beech St.
San Diego, CA 92102
Ph: (619)234-3138   Fax: (619)234-3155

Monthly. $16.98/year for individuals; $3.00 for single issue. Magazine reporting on successful disabled individuals and information on political realities, products, employment, sports, recreation, computer assistive devices, and personal relations concerning the disability rights and independent living movement.

★9847★ *Rehab Review*

California State Department of
Rehabilitation
830 K St. Rm. 320
Sacramento, CA 95814
Ph: (916)445-8638

Bimonthly. Free. Discusses issues affecting employment opportunities for persons with severe disabilities, including program descriptions, changing policies, employers, perspectives, upcoming events, and related information.

OTHER SOURCES

★9848★ **Christian League for the Handicapped (CLH)**

PO Box 948
Walworth, WI 53184-0943
Ph: (414)275-6131   Fax: (414)275-3355

Members: Christian people of all faiths with disabilities. **Purpose:** Provides opportunities for people with disabilities to pursue employment and housing independence. **Activities:** Maintains the Occupational Home and the Christian League apartments, residential facilities for persons with handicaps in southern Wisconsin. Offers job opportunities for persons with disabilities. Conducts summer camp; operates book and gift store.

★9849★ **Dole Foundation For Employment of People With Disabilities**

1819 H St. NW, Ste. 340
Washington, DC 20006-3603
Ph: (202)457-0318   Fax: (202)457-0473

Purpose: Promotes the employment of people with disabilities. **Activities:** Bestows grants to organizations that conduct innovative job training and placement programs.

★9850★ **Goodwill Industries International (GII)**

9200 Wisconsin Ave.
Bethesda, MD 20814
Ph: (301)530-6500   Fax: (301)530-1516

Purpose: Federation of Goodwill Industries organizations across North America and the world are concerned primarily with providing employment, training, evaluation, counseling, placement, job training, and other vocational rehabilitation services and opportunities for individual growth for people with disabilities and other special needs. Member Goodwill Industries organizations collect donated goods and sell them in Goodwill retail stores as a means of providing employment and generating income. Conducts seminars and training programs; compiles statistics.

★9851★ **Helen Keller National Center for Deaf-Blind Youths and Adults (HKNC)**

111 Middle Neck Rd.
Sands Point, NY 11050
Ph: (516)944-8900   Fax: (516)944-7302

Purpose: Established to provide and develop maximum support and training to deaf-blind individuals. Objectives are to: evaluate the degree of physical and psychosocial functioning of deaf-blind individuals; determine rehabilitation needs, interests, and potential; design and improve rehabilitation techniques. **Activities:** Job placement for people who are deaf-blind. Acts as a resource center. Is operated by Helen Keller Services for the Blind. Sponsors annual National Helen Keller Deaf-Blind Awareness Week.

★9852★ **Human Resources Development Institute (HRDI)**

815 16th St. NW
Washington, DC 20006
Ph: (202)638-3912   Fax: (202)783-6536

Purpose: Serves as the employment and training arm of the AFL-CIO. Works to assure full labor participation in employment and training programs funded under the Job Training Partnership Act. Assists in developing JTPA dislocated and economically disadvantaged workers; provides technical services in support of labor-operated programs. **Activities:** Offers job search and placement services for disabled persons and early intervention and return-to-work services for recently disabled union members.

★9853★ **Industry-Labor Council (ILC)**

National Center for Disability Services
201 I.U. Willets Rd.
Albertson, NY 11507-1599
Ph: (516)747-6323   Fax: (516)747-2046

Members: Corporations and labor unions committed to improving employment opportunities for persons with disabilities. **Purpose:** Acts as consultant and technical assistant on matters concerning employment of persons with disabilities; provides a clearinghouse for information on topics such as the Americans With Disabilities Act, accessibility, outreach and recruiting, reasonable accommodation, legislation, and disability management; encourages discussion of critical issues. Offers in-house training programs and audiovisual training packages; conducts research projects. **Activities:** Refers industry and labor to recruiting sources nationwide that in turn refer disabled applicants; operates placement service.

★9854★ **Job Accommodation Network (JAN)**

West Virginia University
PO Box 6080
Morgantown, WV 26506
Ph: (304)293-7186   Fax: (304)293-5407
Fr: 800-526-7234

Purpose: International information and referral service for employers, rehabilitation and social service counselors, and persons with disabilities. **Activities:** Offers information and counseling service to employers interested in learning how to hire, retain, or promote disabled persons. Compiles statistics.

★9855★ **Just One Break (JOB)**

373 Park Ave. S
New York, NY 10016
Ph: (212)725-2500   Fax: (212)213-6791

Purpose: Employment service for people with disabilities. Works to place job-ready people with disabilities into competitive employment. Concentrates efforts in New York, New Jersey, and Connecticut, but advises companies nationwide. Offers placement services, employment counseling, skills evaluation, college recruitment, a summer intern program, and an annual jobs fair. Conducts on-site Americans with Disabilities Act accessibility studies and advisory assistance for human resources managers to help them ease the transition of people with disabilities into their workforce.

★9856★ **Mainstream**

3 Bethesda Metro Ctr., Ste. 830
Bethesda, MD 20814
Ph: (301)654-2400   Fax: (301)654-2403

Purpose: Offers services and products to increase employment opportunities for people with disabilities. Assists companies and organizations in their efforts to "mainstream" people with disabilities into employment. Operates Mainstream Disablity Employment Network, which makes referrals to placement services around the country. Also operates Project LINK (linking individuals with disabilities with competitive employment), which helps place job-ready disabled applicants in the Dallas, TX and Washington, DC areas. Provides in-house training; conducts workshops, seminars and annual conference. Telecommunications Device for the Deaf (202)654-2400

★9857★ **National Association of the Deaf (NAD)**

814 Thayer Ave.
Silver Spring, MD 20910
Ph: (301)587-1788   Fax: (301)587-1791

Members: Adult deaf persons, parents of deaf children, professionals and students in the field of deafness, and interested individuals; organizations of and for deaf people. **Purpose:** Protects the civil rights of people who are deaf and hard of hearing in the areas of employment, elimination of communication barriers, and full citizenship benefits and obligations; promotes legislation and programs that benefit deaf and hard of hearing people. **Activities:** Maintains a legal defense fund. Promotes legislation to benefit deaf and hard of hearing persons. Supports improved programs in vocational training, rehabilitative services, educational opportunities, and mental health services.

★9858★ **National Center for Disability Services (NCDS)**

201 I.U. Willets Rd.
Albertson, NY 11507
Ph: (516)747-5400   Fax: (516)747-5378

Purpose: Serves as a center providing educational, vocational, rehabilitation, and research opportunities for persons with disabilities. Work is conducted through the following: Abilities Health and Rehabilitation Services, a New York state licensed diagnostic and treatment center which offers comprehensive outpatient programs in physical therapy, occupational therapy, speech therapy, and psychological services; Career and Employment Institute, which evaluates, trains, and counsels more than 600 adults with disabilities each year, with the goal of productive competitive employment; Henry Viscardi School, which conducts early childhood, elementary, and secondary programs, as well as adult and continuing education programs; Research and Training Institute, which conducts research on the education, employment, and career development of persons with disabilities, and holds seminars and workshops for rehabilitation services professionals. Maintains library and speakers' bureau; compiles statistics; offers placement service.

★9859★ NTID's Center on Employment (NCE)

Rochester Institute of Technology
52 Lomb Memorial Dr.
Rochester, NY 14623-5604
Ph: (716)475-6219   Fax: (716)475-6500

Members: Operated by the National Technical Institute for the Deaf. **Purpose:** Promotes successful employment of Rochester Institute of Technology's deaf students and graduates. Also offers resources and training for employers and deaf professionals.

★9860★ Special Interest Group for Computers and the Physically Handicapped (SISCAPH)

Association for Computing Machinery
1515 Broadway, 17th Fl.
New York, NY 10036
Ph: (212)626-0613   Fax: (212)302-5826

Members: A special interest group of the Association of Computing Machinery. Physically disabled computer professionals; persons involved in the application of computers to aid the disabled; persons involved in the training or employment of physically disabled computer professionals; others interested in aiding the disabled. **Purpose:** To promote application of computer technology to aid the physically disabled; to educate the public about disabled computer professionals. **Activities:** Sponsors lectures and sessions at computer conferences on hiring and training disabled computer professionals. Compiles statistics.

Opportunities for Gay and Lesbian Workers

REFERENCE WORKS

★9861★ Community Yellow Pages
Cordova Publications
2305 Canyon Dr.
Los Angeles, CA 90068
Ph: (213)469-4454   Fax: (213)469-2531
Fr: 800-745-5669

Annual, December. Free. Covers Approximately 2,500 gay and lesbian-owned businesses; professionals and organizations serving the gay and lesbian community in the Los Angeles, Ventura, Inland Empire, and Long Beach/Orange County, areas. Entries include: Company, organization, or individual name, address, phone. Arrangement: Classified by type of service or profession.

★9862★ Gayellow Pages: A Classified Directory of Gay Services and Businesses in USA and Canada
Gayellow Pages
Box 533, Village Sta.
New York, NY 10014-0533
Ph: (212)674-0120   Fax: (212)420-1126

Annual, May; regional editions vary. $12.00, national edition postpaid; $5.00 regional editions. Covers gay- or lesbian-oriented business enterprises, organizations, resources, churches, bars, restaurants, and publications; many AIDS/HIV resources. Includes a separate listing of national organizations. Entries include: Name, address, phone, business hours, and an annotation describing programs, products, or services. Arrangement: Geographical; national listings are classified by subject category.

★9863★ The 100 Best Companies for Gay Men and Lesbians
Pocket Books
1230 Avenue of the Americas
New York, NY 10020
Ph: (212)698-7000   Fr: 800-223-2348

Ed Mickens. 1994. $12.00 (paper). 275 pages. Provides profiles of 100 "gay-friendly" companies and their policies and benefits. Also includes a discussion of gay and lesbian workplace issues and opportunities.

★9864★ Out in the Workplace: Gay and Lesbian Professionals Tell Their Stories
Alyson Publications
40 Plympton St.
Boston, MA 02118
Ph: (617)542-5679   Fr: 800-825-9766

Richard A. Rasi and Lourdes Rodriguez-Nogues. 1995. $12.95. 220 pages.

NEWSPAPERS, MAGAZINES, AND JOURNALS

★9865★ Working It Out: The Newsletter for Gay and Lesbian Employment Issues
PO Box 2079
New York, NY 10108
Ph: (212)769-2384   Fax: (212)721-2680

Quarterly. Ed Mickens, editor and publisher. Newsletter covering employment-related issues such as law, policy, education, and benefits.

OTHER SOURCES

★9866★ Association for Gay, Lesbian, and Bisexual Issues in Counseling (AGLBIC)
Box 216
Jenkintown, PA 19046
Members: Counselors and personnel and guidance workers concerned with lesbian and gay issues. **Purpose:** Seeks to eliminate discrimination against and stereotyping of gay and lesbian individuals, particularly gay counselors. Works to educate heterosexual counselors on how to overcome homophobia and to best help homosexual clients. **Activities:** Provides a referral network and support for gay counselors and administrators; encourages objective research on gay issues.

★9867★ "Benefits for the Fringe" in The Advocate—Special Double Issue: The Year in Review (January 1994, p.56)
Liberation Publications, Inc.
6922 Hollywood Blvd., 10th Fl.
Los Angeles, CA 90028
Ph: (213)871-1225   Fax: (213)467-6805
Fr: 800-827-0561

John Gallagher. Article about employee benefits for same-sex partners.

★9868★ Career and Life Planning With Gay, Lesbian, and Bisexual Persons
American Counseling Association
ACA Distribution Center
PO Box 531
Annapolis Junction, MD 20701-0531
Fax: (301)604-0158   Fr: 800-422-2648

Susan Owre Gelberg and Joseph T. Chojnacki. 1996. $19.95. Addresses the issues of overt and covert discrimination in the workplace. Designed by combining career theory and application within a counseling framework specific to the needs of gay, lesbian, and bisexual persons.

★9869★ "Disney's Health Policy for Gay Employees Angers Religious Right in Florida" in The New York Times (November 29, 1995)
The New York Times Co.
229 W. 43rd St.
New York, NY 10036
Ph: (212)556-1234

Mireya Navarro. Article discussing the opposition Walt Disney Co. faces to its progressive health policy.

★9870★ "ENDA Promises to Ban Employment Discrimination for Gays" in Personnel Journal (August 1995, p.48)
ACC Communications, Inc.
245 Fischer Ave., B-2
Costa Mesa, CA 92626
Ph: (714)751-1883   Fax: (714)751-4106

Kenneth A. Kovach. Article covering the Employment Non-Discrimination Act (ENDA).

★9871★ Gay and Lesbian Medical Association

211 Church St., Ste. C
San Francisco, CA 94114
Ph: (415)255-4547   Fax: (415)255-4784
Members: Physicians and medical students. **Purpose:** Seeks elimination of discrimination on the basis of sexual orientation in the health professions; promotes unprejudiced medical care for gay and lesbian patients. Maintains a referral and support program for HIV infected physicians. Sponsors annual symposium on lesbian and gay health issues. Offers support to homosexual physicians; encourages research into the health needs of gays and lesbians. Maintains liaison with medical schools and other organizations concerning needs of gay patients and professionals; fosters communication and cooperation among members and other groups and individuals supportive of gay and lesbian physicians. **Activities:** Offers referral service. Sponsors lesbian health fund.

★9872★ "Gays at Home in High Tech" in *Computerworld* (September 1994, p.1)

International Data Group
375 Cochituate Rd.
PO Box 9171
Framingham, MA 01701
Ph: (508)879-0700   Fax: (508)875-8931
Ellis Booker. Article describing the visibility of gays in high technology fields.

★9873★ Lesbian, Bisexual, and Gay United Employees at AT&T (LEAGUE)

11900 Pecos St., No. 3OH-078
Denver, CO 80234-2703
Ph: (303)538-4430   Fax: (303)538-3564
Members: Individuals employed at or retired from AT&T or any of its subsidiaries. **Purpose:** Fosters the value of mutual respect and appreciation of cultural differences among employees. **Activities:** Offers educational programs and support groups to address issues that affect lesbian, gay, and bisexual employees, and their friends and families. Acts as an information clearinghouse on homosexuality, bisexuality, and lesbian and gay issues. Provides referral services to support groups and community and service organizations.

★9874★ Lesbian, Gay and Bisexual People in Medicine (LGBPM)

c/o American Medical Student Association
1902 Association Dr.
Reston, VA 22091
Ph: (703)620-6600   Fax: (703)620-5873
Members: Standing committee of the American Medical Student Association Physicians and physicians in training; others interested in gay/lesbian issues. **Purpose:** To improve the quality of health care for gay patients; to improve working conditions and professional status of gay health professionals and students. Administers educational workshops for health professionals; designs training materials; conducts research on the health problems of gay people and surveys on admissions, hiring, and promotion policies of medical schools and hospitals; provides referrals; sponsors support groups for gay professionals to meet, socialize, and orga-

nize; presses for legislative and political action to end discrimination against gay people. Maintains speakers' bureau.

★9875★ Lesbian Resource Center (LRC)

1808 Bellevue Ave., Ste. 204
Seattle, WA 98122
Ph: (206)322-3953
Purpose: Provides classes, support groups, workshops, social activities, and information on employment, housing, and lesbian community groups and events. Operates speakers' bureau. Represents the lesbian community in areas of political and social concern.

★9876★ "Making Sexual Orientation Part of Diversity" in *Training & Development* (April 1995, p.50)

American Society for Training and Development
1640 King St.
PO Box 1443
Alexandria, VA 22313
Ph: (703)683-8100   Fax: (703)683-8103
Liz Winfield and Susan Spielman. Article.

★9877★ NASW Lesbian and Gay Issues: A Resource Manual

National Association of Social Workers National Committee on Lesbian and Gay Issues (NASW)
750 1st St. NE, Ste. 700
Washington, DC 20002-4241
Ph: (202)336-8287

★9878★ National Association of Social Workers National Committee on Lesbian and Gay Issues (NASW)

750 1st St. NE, Ste. 700
Washington, DC 20002-4241
Ph: (202)336-8287
A committee of the National Association of Social Workers. **Purpose:** Seeks to ensure equal employment opportunities for lesbian and gay individuals. Informs the NASW about: domestic, racial, and antigay violence; civil rights; family and primary associations. Encourages the NASW to support legislation, regulations, policies, judicial review, political action, and other activities that seek to establish and protect equal rights for all persons without regard to their affectional and/or sexual orientation.

★9879★ National Organization of Gay and Lesbian Scientists and Technical Professionals (NOGLSTP)

c/o Rochelle Diamond
PO Box 91803
Pasadena, CA 91109
Ph: (818)791-7689   Fax: (818)791-7689
Members: Gay and lesbian individuals employed or interested in high-technology or scientific fields; interested organizations. **Purpose:** Works to educate the public, especially the gay and scientific communities; improve members' employment and professional environment; oppose anti-gay discrimination and stereotypes; interact with professional organizations; foster intercity contacts among members. **Activities:** Addresses issues of discrimination in the provision of security clearances, employment, and immigration. Disseminates information. Organizes

symposiums and workshops. **E-Mail:** Internet/Bitnet Distribution List noglstp@elroy.jpl.nasa.gov

★9880★ Network of Gay and Lesbian Alumni/ae Associations (NetGALA)

PO Box 53188
Washington, DC 20009
Ph: (202)691-4339
Purpose: Provides leadership and support to gay, lesbian, and bisexual alum groups. Works to create a greater understanding between academic institutions and gay and lesbian graduates, students, faculty, and staff. Acts as a clearinghouse for information and ideas in the gay and lesbian community. **Activities:** Offers referral and placement service. **E-Mail:** netgala@aol.com

★9881★ Out in All Directions: The Almanac of Gay and Lesbian America

Warner Books
1271 Avenue of the Americas
New York, NY 10020
Ph: (212)522-7200
Lynn Witt et al. 1995. $24.95.

★9882★ "Out at Work" in *Training Magazine* (June 1995, p.53)

Adams Recreation Pub.
50 S. 9th St.
Minneapolis, MN 55402
Ph: (612)342-2121   Fax: (612)342-2480
Fr: 800-923-2326
Marc Hequet. Article covering homosexuality in the workplace.

★9883★ Outing Yourself: How to Come Out to Your Family, Your Friends, and Your Coworkers

Random House
201 E. 50th St., 22nd Fl.
New York, NY 10022
Ph: (212)751-2600   Fr: 800-733-3000
Michelangelo Signorile. 1995. $20.00.

★9884★ Personal Financial Planning for Gays and Lesbians

Irwin Professional Publishing
1333 Burr Ridge Pkwy.
Burr Ridge, IL 60521
Fax: 800-926-9495   Fr: 800-634-3966
Peter M. Berkery, Jr. 1996. $24.95. Addresses challenges of financial planning and achieving financial goals.

★9885★ "Some Gay Workers Keep Dual Resumes" in *The Wall Street Journal* (January 2, 1996)

Dow Jones & Co., Inc.
420 Lexington Ave.
New York, NY 10170
Ph: (212)808-6600   Fax: (212)808-6898
Emily Nelson. Newspaper column discussing why some gay job seekers keep dual resumes (one "gay identifiable," one not).

★9886★ **"The Wage Effects of Sexual Orientation Discrimination"** in *Industrial and Labor Relations Review* (July 1995, pp. 726-739)
Cornell University
201 ILR Research Bldg.
Ithaca, NY 14853-3901
Ph: (607)255-3295   Fax: (607)255-8016
M.V. Lee Badgett. Article.

★9887★ **"Top 10"** in *The Advocate* (June 1992, p.56)
Liberation Publications, Inc.
6922 Hollywood Blvd., 10th Fl.
Los Angeles, CA 90028
Ph: (213)871-1225   Fax: (213)467-6805
Fr: 800-827-0561

Paul Katzeff. Article covering corporations that grant health benefits to gays, lesbians, and heterosexuals.

★9888★ **"Unlocking the Corporate Closet"** in *Training & Development* (January 1994, p.34)
American Society for Training and Development
1640 King St.
PO Box 1443
Alexandria, VA 22313
Ph: (703)683-8100   Fax: (703)683-8103
Jay H. Lucas and Mark G. Kaplan. Article about gays and lesbians in the workplace.

Opportunities for Liberal Arts Graduates

REFERENCE WORKS

★9889★ Career Choices for the 90's for Students of Art

Walker and Company
435 Hudson St.
New York, NY 10014
Ph: (212)727-8300   Fax: (212)727-0984
Fr: 800-289-2553

Prepared by the Career Associates staff. 1990. $9.95. 166 pages. Discusses alternatives for students of art. Offers advice on how to break into the field and how to move up. Covers where and who the employers are, internship possibilities, and professional networking associations. Comprehensive guide to career and job search planning.

★9890★ Career Choices for the 90's for Students of Communications and Journalism

Walker and Company
435 Hudson St.
New York, NY 10014
Ph: (212)727-8300   Fax: (212)727-0984
Fr: 800-289-2553

Prepared by the Career Associates staff. 1990. $8.95. 166 pages. Discusses alternatives for students of communications and journalism. Offers advice on how to break into the field and how to move up. Covers where and who the employers are, internship possibilities, and professional networking associations. Comprehensive guide to career and job search planning.

★9891★ Career Choices for the 90's for Students of English

Walker and Company
435 Hudson St.
New York, NY 10014
Ph: (212)727-8300   Fax: (212)727-0984
Fr: 800-289-2553

Prepared by the Career Associates staff. 1990. $8.95. 166 pages. Discusses alternatives for students of English. Offers advice on how to break into the field and how to move up. Covers where and who the employers are, internship possibilities, and professional networking associations. Comprehensive guide to career and job search planning.

★9892★ Career Employment Opportunities Directory

Ready Reference Press
Box 5169
Santa Monica, CA 90405
Ph: (213)474-5175

Biennial, October of odd years. $47.50, per volume; $190.00, per four volume set; postpaid, payment with order. Covers about 1,250 companies that employ college graduates; separate editions available for Liberal Arts and Social Sciences, Business Administration, Engineering and Computer Sciences, and Sciences. Entries include: Company name, general description of company and career opportunities, job locations, special programs, and contact address. Arrangement: Alphabetical. Indexes: Discipline, geographical.

★9893★ The Career Guide—Dun's Employment Opportunities Directory

Dun & Bradstreet Information Services
Dun & Bradstreet Corp.
3 Sylvan Way
Parsippany, NJ 07054-3896
Ph: (201)605-6000   Fax: (201)605-6911
Fr: 800-526-0651

Annual, December. $385.00, to public libraries; $450.00, to others (lease basis). Covers more than 5,000 companies on leading employers throughout the U.S. that provide career opportunities in sales, marketing, management, engineering, life and physical sciences, computer science, mathematics, statistics planning, accounting and finance, liberal arts fields, and other technical and professional areas; based on data supplied on questionnaires and through personal interviews. Also covers personnel consultants; includes some public sector employers (governments, schools, etc.) usually not found in similar lists. Entries include: Company name, location of headquarters and other offices or plants; entries may also include name, title, address, and phone of employment contact; disciplines or occupational groups hired; brief overview of company, discussion of types of positions that may be available, training and career development programs, benefits offered. Arrangement: Companies are alphabetical; consultants are geographical. Indexes: Geographical, SIC code.

★9894★ Career Planning & Development for College Students & Recent Graduates

NTC Publishing Group
4255 W. Touhy Ave.
Lincolnwood, IL 60646-1975
Ph: (708)679-5500   Fax: (708)679-6375
Fr: 800-323-4900

John E. Steele. 1994. $29.95; $12.94 (paper).

★9895★ Careers for Bookworms and Other Literary Types

VGM Career Horizons
4255 W. Touhy Ave.
Lincolnwood, IL 60646-1975
Ph: (847)679-5500   Fax: (847)679-2494
Fr: 800-323-4900

Marjorie Eberts and Margaret Gisler. Second edition, 1995. $14.95; $9.95 (paper). Details opportunities in education, publishing, libraries, journalism, think tanks, museums, film, broadcasting, the public sector, and other fields. Helps job seekers identify reading, writing, or research jobs.

★9896★ Careers for Culture Lovers and Other Artsy Types

VGM Career Horizons
4255 W. Touhy Ave.
Lincolnwood, IL 60646-1975
Ph: (847)679-5500   Fax: (847)679-2494
Fr: 800-323-4900

Marjorie Eberts and Margaret Gisler. 1994. $14.95; $9.95 (paper). Describes how to get work in a variety of fields related to art and culture. Opportunities include picture framer, curator, art restorer, symphony manager, disk jockey, music reviewer, dance teacher, choreographer, costume designer, theater manager, light designer, drama teacher, bookstore owner, interior decorator, antique store owner, and others.

★9897★ College Grad Job Hunter: Insider Techniques and Tactics for Finding a Top-Paying Entry Level Job

Quantum Leap Publishing
6910 W. Brown Deer Rd., No. 210
Milwaukee, WI 53223-2104
Ph: (414)377-8720

Brian D. Krueger, CPC. 1995. $14.95 (paper).

★9898★ **The Encyclopedia of Career Choices for the 1990s: Guide to Entry-Level Jobs**

Perigree Books
The Berkley Publishing Group
PO Box 506
East Rutherford, NJ 07073
Ph: (201)933-9292   Fr: 800-223-0510

Career Associates Staff. 1992. $19.95. 862 pages. Describes 500 entry-level careers in a variety of industries. Presents qualifications required, working conditions, salary, internships, and professional associations.

★9899★ **Great Jobs for Foreign Language Majors**

NTC Publishing Group
4255 W. Touhy Ave.
Lincolnwood, IL 60646-1975
Ph: (708)679-5500   Fax: (708)679-6375
Fr: 800-323-4900

Julie DeGalan. 1994. $11.95 (paper).

★9900★ **How You Can Make $25,000 a Year Writing (No Matter Where You Live)**

Writer's Digest Books
1507 Dana Ave.
Cincinnati, OH 45207
Ph: (513)531-2690   Fr: 800-289-0963

Nancy Edmonds Hanson. 1990. $12.95; $6.95 (paper). 224 pages. Discussion of the freelance market for writing.

★9901★ **Jobs for English Majors and Other Smart People**

Peterson's
PO Box 2123
Princeton, NJ 08543-2123
Ph: (609)243-9111   Fax: (609)243-9150
Fr: 800-338-3282

John L. Munschauer. Third edition, 1991. $11.95. 174 pages. Shows job seekers how to position themselves in the marketplace and how to demonstrate the ability to meet the needs of prospective employers.

★9902★ **Liberal Arts Jobs: What They Are and How to Get Them**

Peterson's
PO Box 2123
Princeton, NJ 08543-2123
Ph: (609)243-9111   Fax: (609)243-9150
Fr: 800-338-3282

Burton Jay Nadler. Second edition, 1989.

$9.95. 153 pages. Presents a list of the top 20 fields for liberal arts majors, covering more than 300 job opportunities. Discusses strategies for going after those jobs, including guidance on the language of a successful job search, informational interviews, and making networking work.

★9903★ **Liberal Arts Power!: What It Is and How to Sell It on Your Resume**

Peterson's
PO Box 2123
Princeton, NJ 08543-2123
Ph: (609)243-9111   Fax: (609)243-9150
Fr: 800-338-3282

Burton Jay Nadler. Second edition, 1989. $9.95. 174 pages. Stresses the value of a liberal arts education and shows how to demonstrate that value to potential employers through a well-crafted resume.

★9904★ **Liberal Education and Careers Today**

Garrett Park Press
PO Box 190 C
Garrett Park, MD 20896-0190
Ph: (301)946-2553

Howard Figler. 1989. $10.95 108 pages. Shows job seekers with liberal arts education how to link their majors to the specific needs of employers.

★9905★ **Path: A Career Workbook for Liberal Arts Students**

Sulzburger & Graham Publishing, Ltd.
165 W. 91st St.
New York, NY 10024
Ph: (212)769-9738   Fax: (212)769-9675
Fr: 800-366-7086

Howard E. Figler. 1993. $13.50.

★9906★ **Peterson's Job Opportunities in Business 1996**

Peterson's
PO Box 2123
Princeton, NJ 08543-2123
Ph: (609)243-9111   Fax: (609)243-9150
Fr: 800-338-3282

Compiled by the Peterson's staff. Annual. $19.95 (paper). 416 pages. Profiles 2,000 companies that are hiring employees in a number of nontechnical fields, including financial services, management consulting, retailers, utilities, and consumer products companies. Contains job-search strategies

and career options to help match education and expertise to the job market. Indexed geographically, by industry, and by hiring needs.

★9907★ **The Student's Guide to Finding a Superior Job**

Slawson Communications
PO Box 28459
San Diego, CA 92198-0459

William A. Cohen. Second edition, 1993. $9.95. 108 pages. Aimed at the new college graduate.

AUDIO/VISUAL RESOURCES

★9908★ **Interviewing for Success**

Golden West College
15744 Golden West St.
Huntington Beach, CA 92647
Ph: (714)892-7711   Fax: (714)895-8243

Video cassette. Series of 30-minute videos helps jobseekers in various fields prepare for the job interview.

OTHER SOURCES

★9909★ **Career Placement Registry/Student**

Career Placement Registry, Inc.
3202 Kirkwood Hwy.
Wilmington, DE 19808
Ph: (302)998-0478   Fax: (302)998-0733
Fr: 800-331-4955

Weekly. Database covers: more than 10,000 college and university seniors and recent graduates with degrees of associate or higher; persons listed pay a nominal registration fee. Database includes: Name, permanent and current addresses and phone numbers, citizenship status, colleges attended, degrees received, academic major and minor, grade point average, occupational preferences and experience, function and geographical preferences, date available, foreign language proficiency, special skills and achievements.

Opportunities for Military Personnel and Veterans

REFERENCE WORKS

★9910★ America's Top Military Careers: The Official Guide to Occupations in the Armed Forces
JIST Works, Inc.
720 N. Park Ave.
Indianapolis, IN 46202-3431
Ph: (317)264-3720   Fax: (317)264-3709
Fr: 800-648-5478

Compiled by JIST editorial staff. 1993. $19.95 (paper).

★9911★ Careers in Engineering
VGM Career Horizons
4255 W. Touhy Ave.
Lincolnwood, IL 60646-1975
Ph: (847)679-5500   Fax: (847)679-2494
Fr: 800-323-4900

Geraldine O. Gardner. 1994. $17.95; $13.95 (paper). Covers careers in the public or private sector, in industry, the university, or the military, from applications in computer architecture design to high temperature ceramics.

★9912★ Careers for Travel Buffs and Other Restless Types
VGM Career Horizons
4255 W. Touhy Ave.
Lincolnwood, IL 60646-1975
Ph: (847)679-5500   Fax: (847)679-2494
Fr: 800-323-4900

Paul Plawin. 1992. $14.95; $9.95 (paper). Includes a variety of travel and open-road careers, such as travel writers and photographers, tour bus drivers, entertainers, cruise line staff, travel agents, tour guides, sports writers, sales, the military, trucking, and meeting planning.

★9913★ Citizen Soldier: Opportunities in the Reserves
Rosen Publishing Group, Inc.
29 E. 21st St.
New York, NY 10010
Ph: (212)777-3017   Fax: (212)777-0277
Fr: 800-237-9932

Carl White. 1990. $14.95. Describes the function of the armed forces reserve units,
pay, retirement income, basic and specialty training, and ROTC programs.

★9914★ The Civilian Career Guide
Grant's Guide, Inc.
PO Box 613
Lake Placid, NY 12946
Ph: (518)523-3498   Fax: (518)523-2974
Fr: 800-922-1923

James Grant, editor. 1993. $9.95 (paper).

★9915★ Does Your Resume Wear Combat Boots? How to Turn Your Military Experience into a Good Civilian Job Offer
Prima Publishing
3875 Atherton Rd.
Rocklin, CA 95765
Ph: (916)632-4400   Fax: (916)624-2385

William G. Fitzpatrick. 1993. $9.95 (paper).

★9916★ Exploring Careers in the Military Services
Rosen Publishing Group, Inc.
29 E. 21st St.
New York, NY 10010
Ph: (212)777-3017   Fax: (212)777-0277
Fr: 800-237-9932

Robert W. MacDonald. 1991. $14.95. 190 pages. Describes the role of the military services, how to begin a military career, and taking the armed services vocational aptitude battery. Lists military occupations and equivalent civilian jobs. A separate chapter covers each branch of the military, what they do, organization, enlistment, training, advancement and career development, and becoming an officer.

★9917★ Exploring Careers Using Foreign Languages
Rosen Publishing Group, Inc.
29 E. 21st St.
New York, NY 10010
Ph: (212)777-3017   Fax: (212)777-0277
Fr: 800-237-9932

E.W. Edwards. Revised edition, 1990. $14.95. Explores careers in teaching, translating, interpreting, business and finance, government, the military, communications, and the media. Covers employment ideas, salaries, job duties, and educational prepara-
tion. Contains information on accreditation and job hunting.

★9918★ From Air Blue to Corporate Gray: A Career Transition Guide for Air Force Personnel
Impact Publications
9104 N Manassas Dr.
Manassas Park, VA 22111-5211
Ph: (703)361-7300   Fax: (703)335-9486

Carl S. Savino. 1995. $17.95 (paper).

★9919★ From Army Green to Corporate Gray: A Career Transition Guide for Army Personnel
Impact Publications
9104 N. Manassas Dr.
Manassas Park, VA 22111-5211
Ph: (703)361-7300   Fax: (703)335-9486

Carl S. Savino. 1994. $13.95 (paper).

★9920★ From Navy Blue to Corporate Gray: A Career Transition Guide for Navy & Marine Corps Personnel
Impact Publications
9104 N. Manassas Dr.
Manassas Park, VA 22111-5211
Ph: (703)361-7300   Fax: (703)335-9486

Carl S. Savino. 1995. $17.95 (paper).

★9921★ Future Career Management Systems for U.S. Military Officers
Rand Corp.
PO Box 2138
Santa Monica, CA 90407-2138
Ph: (310)393-0411   Fax: (310)451-6920

Harry Thie. 1994. $15.00 (cloth).

★9922★ In or Out of the Military: How to Make Your Own Best Decision
Pepper Press
1254 W. Pioneer Way, Ste. A266
Oak Harbor, WA 98277-3288
Ph: (360)675-7196   Fax: (360)679-3131
Fr: 800-678-5519

D.F. Reardon. 1993. $14.95 (paper).

★9923★ Job Search: Marketing Your Military Experience

Stackpole Books
5067 Ritter Rd.
Mechanicsburg, PA 17055
Ph: (717)796-0411   Fax: (717)796-0412
Fr: 800-732-3669

David G. Henderson. 1995. $14.95 (paper).

★9924★ J.O.B.S. Job Opportunities and Business Series: The Employment Guide to the Washington, D.C., Metropolitan Area

JSI Network
PO Box 231
Woodbridge, VA 22194-0231
Ph: (703)680-9611

Imelda R. Roberts. 1989. $17.95. 319 pages. Describes a number of opportunities in D.C. and the surrounding Maryland and Virginia area. Jobs include the public and private sector, the military, embassies, and international opportunities.

★9925★ Military Careers

U.S. Department of Defense
U.S. Military Entrance Processing Command
2500 Green Bay Rd.
North Chicago, IL 60064
Fr: 800-323-0513

Free. 223 pages. Focuses on variety of employment opportunities in the Armed Forces.

★9926★ Military Careers: A Guide to Military Occupations & Selected Military Career Paths

Gordon Press Publishers
PO Box 459, Bowling Green Station
New York, NY 10004
Ph: (718)624-8419

1995. $259.99.

★9927★ Opportunities in Aerospace Careers

VGM Career Horizons
4255 W. Touhy Ave.
Lincolnwood, IL 60646-1975
Ph: (847)679-5500   Fax: (847)679-2494
Fr: 800-323-4900

Wallace R. Maples. 1995. $14.95; $11.95 (paper). Surveys jobs with the airlines, airports, the government, the military, in manufacturing, and in research and development. Includes information on job opportunities with NASA in the U.S. space program.

★9928★ Opportunities in Law Enforcement and Criminal Justice

VGM Career Horizons
4255 W. Touhy Ave.
Lincolnwood, IL 60646-1975
Ph: (847)679-5500   Fax: (847)679-2494
Fr: 800-323-4900

James Stinchcomb. 1994. $14.95; $11.95 (paper). Offers information on opportunities at the city, county, state, military, and federal levels. Contains bibliography and illustrations.

★9929★ Opportunities in Military Careers

VGM Career Horizons
4255 W. Touhy Ave.
Lincolnwood, IL 60646-1975
Ph: (847)679-5500   Fax: (847)679-2494
Fr: 800-323-4900

Adrian Paradis. 1989. $14.95; $11.95 (paper). 160 pages. Illustrates what it's like to work in a variety of job situations unique to the armed forces. Opportunities for civilian employment are also included. Illustrated.

★9930★ Opportunities in Vocational and Technical Careers

VGM Career Horizons
4255 W. Touhy Ave.
Lincolnwood, IL 60646-1975
Ph: (847)679-5500   Fax: (847)679-2494
Fr: 800-323-4900

Adrian A. Paradis. 1992. $14.95; $11.95 (paper). 160 pages. Provides information on a variety of opportunities and advice on breaking into the field.

★9931★ Out of Uniform: A Career Transition Guide for Ex-Military Personnel

NTC Publishing Group
4255 W. Touhy Ave.
Lincolnwood, IL 60646-1975
Ph: (708)679-5500   Fax: (708)679-6375
Fr: 800-323-4900

1994. $12.95 (paper).

★9932★ Punching Out: Launching a Post-Military Career

St. Martin's Press, Inc.
175 Fifth Ave., Rm. 1715
New York, NY 10010
Ph: (212)674-5151   Fax: (212)420-9314
Fr: 800-221-7945

Fred Mastin. 1994. $22.00 (cloth).

★9933★ Resumes for Ex-Military Personnel

NTC Publishing Group
4255 W. Touhy Ave.
Lincolnwood, IL 60646-1975
Ph: (847)679-5500   Fax: (847)679-2494
Fr: 800-323-4900

1995. $9.95 (paper).

★9934★ Yes, There Is Life after Aerospace: Career Transition from Military Defense–Aerospace to Commercial Civilian Life

A B P Associates
758 N. Quince Ave.
Upland, CA 91786
Ph: (909)982-7595

Marie H. Reichelt. 1994. $14.95 (paper).

NEWSPAPERS, MAGAZINES, AND JOURNALS

★9935★ Affirmative Action Register

Affirmative Action, Inc.
8356 Olive Blvd.
St. Louis, MO 63132
Ph: (314)991-1335   Fax: (314)997-1788
Fr: 800-537-0655

Monthly. $1.50 for single issue. Free, to women, minority, handicapped candidate sources. Covers in each issue, about 300 positions at a professional level (most requiring advanced study) available to women, minorities, veterans, and the handicapped; listings are advertisements placed by employers with affirmative action programs. Entries include: Company or organization name, address, contact name; description of position including title, requirements, duties, application procedure, salary, etc. Arrangement: Classified by profession.

★9936★ Air Force Times

Army Times Publishing Co.
6883 Commercial Dr.
Springfield, VA 22159
Ph: (703)750-8646   Fax: (703)750-8622
Fr: 800-424-9335

Weekly (Mon.). Independent newspaper serving Air Force personnel worldwide.

★9937★ Armed Forces Journal International

Armed Forces Journal International
2000 L St. NW, Ste. 520
Washington, DC 20036
Ph: (202)296-0450   Fax: (202)296-4872

Monthly. $35.00/year for individuals. Magazine concerning the armed services, national security, and defense.

★9938★ Army Aviation Magazine

Army Aviation Publications, Inc.
49 Richmondville Ave.
Westport, CT 06880
Ph: (203)226-8184   Fax: (203)222-9863

$25.00/year for individuals; $42.00 for two years; $3.00 for single issue.

★9939★ Military Market Magazine

Army Times Publishing Co.
6883 Commercial Dr.
Springfield, VA 22159-0210
Ph: (703)750-8676   Fax: (703)750-8622

Monthly. Magazine covering military commissaries and post exchanges.

★9940★ Military Medicine

Association of Military Surgeons of the U.S.
9320 Old Georgetown Rd.
Bethesda, MD 20814
Ph: (301)897-8800   Fax: (301)530-5446

Monthly. $35.00/year for individuals; $40.00/year for other countries; $4.50 for single issue. Journal for professional personnel affiliated with the Federal medical services.

★9941★ Navy Times

Army Times Publishing Co.
6883 Commercial Dr.
Springfield, VA 22159
Ph: (703)750-8646   Fax: (703)750-8622
Fr: 800-424-9335

Weekly (Mon.). Independent newspaper serving Navy, Marine, and Coast Guard personnel.

★9942★ The Officer

Reserve Officers Association
1 Constitution Ave. NE
Washington, DC 20002
Ph: (202)479-2200   Fax: (202)479-0416

Monthly. $12.00/year for individuals; $1.15/year for single issue. Magazine for active and reserve officers of all military branches.

ONLINE AND DATABASE SERVICES

★9943★ JFAIR

MILITRAN, Inc.
PO Box 490
Southeastern, PA 19399-0490
Ph: (610)687-3900   Fax: (610)296-7332
Fr: 800-426-9954

Online database containing information on more than 1000 job fairs available to U.S. military personnel entering the civilian workforce and firms interested in hiring them. Includes location, occupations represented, and skill categories and expected numbers of military personnel attending.

★9944★ Military in Transition Database (MILITRAN)

MILITRAN, Inc.
PO Box 490
Southeastern, PA 19399
Ph: (610)687-3900   Fax: (610)296-7332
Fr: 800-426-9954

Online database containing approximately 30,000 resumes of military personnel, covering the occupational skills of all rank, grade, and service of retired, separating, and separated military personnel, including Guard and Reserve, seeking civilian employment.

SOFTWARE

★9945★ COIN Career Guidance System

COIN Educational Products
3361 Executive Pky., Ste. 302
Toledo, OH 43606
Ph: (419)536-5353   Fr: 800-274-8515

CD-ROM product; also available on diskette. Provides career information through seven cross-referenced files covering postsecondary schools, college majors, vocational programs, military service, apprenticeship programs, financial aid, and scholarships. Apprenticeship file describes national apprenticeship training programs, including informa-tion on how to apply, contact agencies, and program content. Military file describes more than 200 military occupations and training opportunities related to civilian employment.

OTHER SOURCES

★9946★ Air Force Association (AFA)

1501 Lee Hwy.
Arlington, VA 22209
Ph: (703)247-5800

Purpose: U.S. citizens, both civilian and military, united to address the responsibilities imposed by the impact of aerospace technology on modern society. Supports armed strength adequate to maintain the security and peace of the United States and the Free World; promotes public education about the development of adequate aerospace power. Works to develop friendly relations among free nations based on respect for the principle of freedom and equal rights for all mankind. **Activities:** Provides resume writing service and assistance with college planning.

★9947★ Air Force Sergeants Association

PO Box 50
Temple Hills, MD 20757
Ph: (301)899-3500   Fax: (301)899-8136

Members: Any enlisted man or woman, active or retired, in the Air Force, Air National Guard, Air Force Reserve, Army Air Corps, or Army Air Forces; ladies auxiliaries. **Purpose:** Works to: promote, preserve, and uphold fair and equitable legislation as it pertains to the welfare of the airmen who served and are serving in the U.S.A.F.; maintain the highest professional standards and integrity among members; promote the interests of members, the U.S., and the rest of the "free world"; promote religious, educational, and recreational activities among members, in order to develop a better understanding and mutual respect. **Activities:** JOBCAP–a job placement service, educational seminars, Air Force training, and programs for retired members.

★9948★ American Military Retirees Association (AMRA)

68 Clinton St.
Plattsburgh, NY 12901
Ph: (518)563-9479   Fax: (518)563-9479
Fr: 800-638-2610

Members: Persons honorably retired for length of service or disability from all branches and grades of the armed forces and their widows or widowers; persons still on active duty. **Purpose:** Goals: to maintain "COLA" Program; authorization for CHAMPUS for all military retirees regardless of age; to maintain adequate care at military/VA medical facilities. Works to support or oppose legislation in the best interests of members and to protect the earned privileges and benefits of military retirees. Testifies before Congress on legislation affecting members. **Activities:** Operates placement service and job resume bank; maintains speakers' bureau, biographical archives, and library.

★9949★ Armed Forces Broadcasters Association (AFBA)

PO Box 335
Sun Valley, CA 91353-0335
Ph: (213)256-3482   Fax: (213)256-3482

Members: Former and current military and commercial broadcasters. **Purpose:** Provides an opportunity for military broadcasters and supporters to meet and socialize. Assists broadcasters returning to the U.S. from overseas. **Activities:** Provides job information center.

★9950★ Army Aviation Association of America (AAAA)

49 Richmondville Ave.
Westport, CT 06880-2000
Ph: (203)226-8184   Fax: (203)222-9863

Members: Commissioned officers, warrant officers, and enlisted personnel serving in U.S. Army aviation assignments in the active U.S. Army, Army National Guard, and Army Reserve; Department of Army civilian personnel and industry representatives affiliated with army aviation. **Purpose:** Fosters fellowship among military and civilian persons connected with army aviation, past or present; seeks to advance status, overall esprit, and general knowledge of professionals engaged in army aviation. **Activities:** Include locator and placement services, technical assistance, and biographical archives.

★9951★ Army and Navy Union, U.S.A. (ANU)

1391 Main St.
PO Box 537
Lakemore, OH 44250
Ph: (216)733-3113

Members: Servicemen and veterans of the armed forces during peace or war. **Activities:** Participates in veterans service work of all types. Provides children's services. Maintains nine county councils and 11 departments.

★9952★ Association of Graduates of the United States Air Force Academy (AOG)

3116 Academy Dr.
USAF Academy, CO 80840-4475
Ph: (719)472-0300   Fax: (719)472-4194

Members: Graduates and friends of the U.S. Air Force Academy. **Purpose:** Promotes interest in and dedication to the mission, ideals, objectives, activities, and history of the Academy; encourages young people to attend the Academy; encourages and supports fundraising for the Academy; fosters camaraderie among Academy graduates and U.S. armed forces officer corps; professional development of the armed forces officer corps. Sponsors annual class reunions/homecomings. **Activities:** Offers scholarships to graduates of the academy and their dependents; provides placement service. Operates charitable program, including humanitarian support for next-of-kin of academy graduates. Compiles statistics.

★9953★ Association of the United States Army (AUSA)

2425 Wilson Blvd.
Arlington, VA 22201-3385
Ph: (703)841-4300   Fax: (703)525-9039
Fr: 800-336-4570

Members: Professional society of: active, retired, and reserve military personnel; West Point and Army ROTC cadets; civilians interested in national defense. **Purpose:** Seeks to advance the security of the United States and consolidate the efforts of all who support the United States Army as an indispensable instrument of national security. **Activities:** Conducts industrial symposia for manufacturers of Army weapons and equipment, and those in the Department of the Army who plan, develop, test, and use weapons and equipment.

★9954★ Blinded Veterans Association (BVA)

477 H St. NW
Washington, DC 20001
Ph: (202)371-8880   Fax: (202)371-8258
Fr: 800-669-7079

Members: Veterans who lost their sight as a result of military service in the armed forces of the U.S.; associate members are veterans whose loss of sight was not connected with military service. **Purpose:** Assists blinded veterans in attaining benefits and employment and with reestablishing themselves as adjusted, active, and productive citizens in their communities. **Activities:** Offers placement service; supports research programs; compiles statistics.

★9955★ Federal Employees Veterans Association (FEVA)

PO Box 183
Merion Station, PA 19066
Ph: (215)224-9235

Members: Federal government employees who have veterans' preference in federal employment under the G. I. Bill. **Purpose:** Works to maintain and increase veterans' preference in federal employment and prevent "the discrimination against the veteran that was rampant in federal agencies in the post-World War II era."

★9956★ Financial Aid for Veterans, Military Personnel, and Their Dependents

Reference Service Press
1100 Industrial Rd., Ste. 9
San Carlos, CA 94070
Ph: (415)594-0743   Fax: (415)594-0411

Biennial, January of even years. $38.50 plus $4.00 shipping. Covers organizations that offer approximately 950 scholarships, fellowships, loans, grants, awards, and internships to veterans, military personnel, and their families. Entries include: Organization name, address, phone, financial data, requirements for eligibility, duration, special features and limitations, deadline, number of awards. Arrangement: Classified by type of program and target audience. Indexes: Organization name, program, geographical, subject, and deadline date.

★9957★ IMCEA—Membership Directory

International Military Community Executives Association (IMCEA)
1800 Diagonal Rd., Ste. 285
Alexandria, VA 22314-2840
Ph: (703)548-0093   Fax: (703)548-0095

Annual, May. $200.00. Covers about 1,000 Navy, Army, Air Force, Marine Corps, and Coast Guard personnel who manage military clubs and golf and bowling centers; supplier members are also listed. Entries include: For military club and Morale, Welfare and Recreation (MWR) personnel, name, office address and phone. For suppliers, company name, address, product or service. Arrangement: Personnel are alphabetical; suppliers are classified by product, then alphabetical. Indexes: Geographical, product.

★9958★ Marine Corps Association (MCA)

Box 1775, Marine Corps Base
Quantico, VA 22134-0775
Ph: (703)640-6161   Fax: (703)640-0823
Fr: 800-336-0291

Members: Comprised of active duty, reserve, retired, Fleet Reserve, honorably discharged Marines, and members of other services who have served with Marine Corps units. **Purpose:** Disseminates information about the military arts and sciences to members; assists members' professional advancement; fosters the spirit and works to preserve the traditions of the United States Marine Corps. **Activities:** Maintains discount book service and group insurance plan for members. Association founded by members of the Second Provisional Marine Brigade at Guantanamo Bay, Cuba.

★9959★ Marine Corps Reserve Officers' Association (MCROA)

201 N. Washington St., Ste. 206
Alexandria, VA 22314
Ph: (703)548-7607   Fax: (703)319-8779

Members: Marine Corps Reserve officers who have served on active duty in peace or war. **Purpose:** Seeks to: advance the professional and technical skills of reserve officers; promote the interest of reserve officers in the U.S. Marine Corps and the interest of the Marine Corps in its reserve officers; represent and assist individual members; promote the interests of the U.S. Marine Corps in order to advance the welfare and preserve the security of the United States. **Activities:** Maintains placement service.

★9960★ National Association for Uniformed Services (NAUS)

5535 Hempstead Way
Springfield, VA 22151
Ph: (703)750-1342   Fax: (703)354-4380

Members: Members of the uniformed military services, active, retired or reserve, veteran, enlisted and officers, and their spouses or widows. **Purpose:** To develop and support legislation that upholds the security of the U.S., sustains the morale of the uniformed services, and provides fair and equitable consideration for all service people. Primary function is protection and improvement of compensation, entitlements, and benefits. **Activities:** Provides discount rates on travel, insurance, auto rentals, charge cards, prescription medicine, and legal services.

★9961★ National Naval Officers Association (NNOA)

40 Lake Edge Dr.
Euclid, OH 44123
Ph: (216)261-2941   Fax: (216)261-2828
Fr: 800-772-6662

Members: Active, reserve, and retired Navy, Marine, and Coast Guard officers and students in college and military sea service programs. **Purpose:** Promotes and assists recruitment, retention, and retirement of minorities in naval service. **Activities:** Conducts specialized education; maintains counseling, referral, and children's services. Makes available non-ROTC grants-in-aid. Sponsors competitions; operates charitable program.

★9962★ National Veteran's Outreach Program (NVOP)

206 San Pedro, Ste. 200
San Antonio, TX 78205-1100
Ph: (210)223-4096   Fax: (210)223-4970

A program sponsored by the American G.I. Forum of United States, funded by local, state, and national government contracts. **Purpose:** Provides services to the economically disadvantaged, recently separated veterans (within the last 48 months), and Vietnam era veterans. **Activities:** Counsels veterans in making a smooth transition to the civilian community and mobilizes and coordinates all available resources serving veterans. Provides family counseling to Vietnam veterans who served in or near Vietnam between 1961-1972. Works with the private sector and local, state, and national employment services in order to place the economically disadvantaged and veterans in meaningful jobs.

★9963★ Non Commissioned Officers Association of the United States of America (NCOA)

PO Box 33610
San Antonio, TX 78265
Ph: (210)653-6161   Fax: (210)656-6225
Fr: 800-662-2620

Members: Noncommissioned and petty officers of the United States military serving in grades E1 through E9 from all five branches of the U.S. Armed Forces; includes active duty and retired personnel, members of the Reserve and National Guard components, and associate members who were in pay grades E1 through E9 inclusive at the time of application for membership. **Purpose:** Formed for patriotic, fraternal, social, and benevolent purposes. **Activities:** Offers veterans job assistance, legislative representation, and grants. Conducts charitable program.

★9964★ Organization of African-American Veterans (AAV)

PO Box 873
Fort Huachuca, AZ 85613
Ph: (602)458-7245   Fax: (602)458-7245

Members: Veterans and active personnel of all branches of the U.S. military. **Purpose:** Promotes the physical, mental, social, and economic rehabilitation of veterans; works to obtain compensation, medical care, employment, and business assistance for veterans. Assists and represents veterans and their families in filing benefit claims. Sponsors and supports beneficial legislation.

★9965★ The Retired Officers Association (TROA)
201 N. Washington St.
Alexandria, VA 22314-2539
Ph: (703)549-2311   Fax: (703)838-8173
Fr: 800-245-8762

Members: Men and women who are or have been commissioned or warrant officers in any component of the Army, Navy, Air Force, Marine Corps, Coast Guard, National Oceanic and Atmospheric Administration, and Public Health Service. **Purpose:** Supports strong national defense and represents and assists members and their dependents and survivors with retirement issues and benefits. **Activities:** Sponsors educational assistance program, survivor assistance, and travel, insurance, and retiree employment services. **E-Mail:** troa@troa.org. **Website:** http://www.troa.org

★9966★ Vietnam Veterans Against the War (VVAW)
PO Box 408594
Chicago, IL 60640
Ph: (312)761-8248

Purpose: Works for: improved VA conditions and job opportunities; eliminating the possibility of future military conflicts such as Vietnam; no draft or registration; testing and treatment of Agent Orange poisoning. Offers traumatic stress disorder counseling and discharge upgrading; provides Agent Orange selfhelp information.

★9967★ Vietnam Veterans of America (VVA)
1224 M St. NW
Washington, DC 20005-5783
Ph: (202)628-2700   Fax: (202)628-5880
Fr: 800-VVA-1316

Members: Congressionally chartered, nationwide veterans service organization formed specifically for Vietnam veterans. **Purpose:** Objectives are to work for the employment, education benefits, improved psychological assistance, and health care of Vietnam veterans. **Activities:** Provides referral services and research and public information programs to help veterans in developing a positive identification with their Vietnam service and with fellow veterans. Offers annual training for veterans service representatives.

Opportunities for Minorities

REFERENCE WORKS

★9968★ The Big Book of Minority Opportunities: The Directory of Special Programs for Minority Group Members
Garrett Park Press
PO Box 190
Garrett Park, MD 20896
Ph: (301)946-2553
Willis L. Johnson. 1995. $39.00 (paper).

★9969★ Black Enterprise—Top Black Businesses Issue
Earl G. Graves Publishing Co.
130 5th Ave., 10th Fl.
New York, NY 10011
Ph: (212)242-8000   Fax: (212)886-9610
Fr: 800-727-7777

Annual, June. $3.95. Lists 100 Black-owned industrial/service companies with sales of $5 million or above, more than 35 banks with total assets of $1.6 billion or more, nearly 35 savings and loan associations with total assets of $1.15 billion or more, about 30 insurance companies with total assets of about $830 million or more, and 100 auto dealers with sales of $10 million or above. Entries include: Company name, city and state, name of chief executive, year founded, number of employees, financial data. Back issues available, $5.00 each. Arrangement: In categories, with rankings by financial size.

★9970★ Career Opportunities for Minority College Graduates
Paoli Publishing, Inc.
1708 E. Lancaster Ave., Ste. 287
Paoli, PA 19301
Ph: (215)640-9889   Fax: (610)296-9266

Annual, January. Free, plus $3.00 shipping. Covers over 900 companies, organizations and schools representing 24 occupational fields and five continuing educational alternatives. Entries include: Name, address, personnel contact name or department; phone and fax number listed in many entries. Arrangement: Classified by occupation then geographical.

★9971★ Coming Alive from Nine to Five
Mayfield Publishing
1280 Villa St.
Mountain View, CA 94041
Ph: (415)960-3222   Fr: 800-433-1279

Betty N. Michelozzi. Fourth edition, 1992. $19.95. 294 pages. In addition to general job-hunting advice, provides special information for women, young adults, minorities, older workers, and persons with handicaps.

★9972★ Council of Asian American Business Associations —Directory
Council of Asian American Business Associations
1670 Pine St.
San Francisco, CA 94109
Ph: (415)921-5910   Fax: (415)921-0182

Annual. $50.00, plus $3.25 shipping. Covers over 1,100 Asian-American professional, commercial, and industrial firms; trade associations. Entries include: Company name, address, phone, name of contact, product or service provided, number of employees, whether minority certified, market area, licenses; some listings include clients. Arrangement: Classified by Standard Industrial Classification (SIC) code. Indexes: Company name, association name, SIC number.

★9973★ Directory of Career Resources for Minorities
Ready Reference Press
PO Box 5249
Santa Monica, CA 90409
Ph: (213)474-5175   Fr: 800-424-5627

$98.00. Out of print. Offers details on hundreds of programs and services, including job referral services, talent banks, re-entry programs, special training programs, career counseling, resume preparation, workshops, and others. Entries include organization name, general information, resources offered, special features, hours, fees (if any), and address. Subject and geographic indexes.

★9974★ Directory of Special Programs for Minority Group Members: Career Information Services, Employment Skills Banks, Financial Aid Sources
Garrett Park Press
PO Box 190F
Garrett Park, MD 20896
Ph: (301)946-2553

Irregular, latest edition 1994. $27.00, payment with order. Covers About 2,000 private and governmental agencies offering 4,000 financial aid, employment assistance, and career guidance programs for minorities. Entries include: Organization or agency name, address, phone, contact name, type of organization, purpose, description of services and activities in the equal opportunity employment area. Arrangement: Alphabetical. Indexes: Alphabetical, type of program.

★9975★ Finding a Job in the United States
VGM Career Horizons
4255 W. Touhy Ave.
Lincolnwood, IL 60646-1975
Ph: (847)679-5500   Fax: (847)679-2494
Fr: 800-323-4900

John E. Friedenberg and Curtis H. Bradley. 1993. $7.95. 112 pages. Written for those whose native language is not English. Contains job information based on the successful experience of job seekers, plus advice from the U.S. Department of Labor. Includes information about American job customs and laws related to immigration, as well as a systematic plan for job hunting.

★9976★ The Minority Career Book
Bob Adams, Inc.
260 Center St.
Holbrook, MA 02343
Ph: (617)767-8100   Fax: (617)767-0994
Fr: 800-872-5627

Miquela Rivera. 1991. $9.95. Addresses the unique challenges facing minority workers and shows how to bridge cultural gaps to gain legitimacy and recognition.

★9977★ The Minority Career Guide: What African Americans, Hispanics, & Asian Americans Must Know to Succeed in Corporate America

Peterson's Guides, Inc.
PO Box 2123
Princeton, NJ 08543-2123
Ph: (609)243-9111   Fax: (609)243-9150
Fr: 800-338-3282

Michael Kastre. 1993. $12.95 (paper).

★9978★ The Minority Executives' Handbook: The Complete Guide to Career Success in Today's Culturally-Diverse Workforce

Amistad Press, Inc.
Time & Life Bldg.
Rockefeller Ctr., Rm. 3845
New York, NY 10020
Ph: (212)522-6936   Fax: (212)522-7853

Randolph W. Cameron. 1993. $9.95 (paper).

★9979★ National Directory of Minority-Owned Business Firms

Business Research Services, Inc.
4201 Connecticut Ave. NW, Ste. 610
Washington, DC 20008-1158
Ph: (202)364-6473   Fax: (202)686-3228
Fr: 800-325-8720

Annual. $245.00, plus $5.00 shipping. Covers over 48,000 minority-owned businesses. Entries include: Company name, address, phone, name and title of contact, minority group, certification status, date founded, number of employees, description of products or services, sales volume, government contracting experience, references. Arrangement: Standard Industrial Classification (SIC) code, geographical. Indexes: Alphabetical.

★9980★ SER Network Directory

SER-Jobs for Progress National, Inc.
100 Decker Dr., Ste. 200
Irving, TX 75062
Ph: (214)541-0616   Fax: (214)650-1860
Fr: 800-749-1355

Annual, April. Free. Covers Approximately 130 affiliated agencies in 90 U.S. cities of SER (Service, Employment, Redevelopment)-Jobs for Progress National, Inc., an organization of Hispanics that provides employment and training, services to disadvantaged youth and adults. Entries include: Organization name, address, phone, name of president, services provided, satellite offices, if any. Arrangement: Geographical.

★9981★ Shoot for the Moon

Saunderstown Press
1600 Boston Neck Rd.
PO Box 307
Saunderstown, RI 02874

Allen A. Johnson. 1993. $12.95. 37 pages. Designed for people starting or reentering employment, with special emphasis on handicapped and minorities.

★9982★ Try Us: National Minority Business Directory

Try Us Resources, Inc.
2105 Central Ave. NE
Minneapolis, MN 55418
Ph: (612)781-6819   Fax: (612)781-0109
Fr: 800-627-4347

Annual, January. $49.00. Covers over 6,000 minority-owned companies capable of supplying their goods and services on national or regional levels. Entries include: Company name, address, phone, fax, name of principal executive, number of employees, date established, trade and brand names, financial keys, products or services, names of three customers, certification status, minority identification, gross sales. Arrangement: Classified by product or service, then geographical and alphabetical. Indexes: Company, product/service.

NEWSPAPERS, MAGAZINES, AND JOURNALS

★9983★ Affirmative Action Register

Affirmative Action, Inc.
8356 Olive Blvd.
St. Louis, MO 63132
Ph: (314)991-1335   Fax: (314)997-1788
Fr: 800-537-0655

Monthly. $1.50 for single issue. Free, to women, minority, handicapped candidate sources. Covers in each issue, about 300 positions at a professional level (most requiring advanced study) available to women, minorities, veterans, and the handicapped; listings are advertisements placed by employers with affirmative action programs. Entries include: Company or organization name, address, contact name; description of position including title, requirements, duties, application procedure, salary, etc. Arrangement: Classified by profession.

★9984★ The Black Collegian

Black Collegiate Services, Inc.
140 Carondelet St.
New Orleans, LA 70130-2526
Ph: (504)523-0154   Fax: (504)523-0271

Semiannual. $8.00/year for individuals; $4.00 for single issue. Career opportunity magazine featuring job searching role models, interviews, entertainment, art, and African-American history.

★9985★ Equal Opportunity

Equal Opportunity Publications
150 Motor Pky., Ste. 420
Hauppauge, NY 11788-5145
Ph: (516)273-8743

Quarterly. Career guidance magazine for college students and professionals.

★9986★ Hispanic Times Magazine

PO Box 579
Winchester, CA 92596
Ph: (909)926-2119

$30.00/year for individuals; $3.50 for single issue. Magazine focusing on business and careers (in English and Spanish).

★9987★ JCC Association Personnel Reporter

Jewish Community Center Association
15 E. 26th St.
New York, NY 10010-1579

Quarterly. Free. Covers opportunities in Jewish community centers and camps.

★9988★ Saludos Hispanos

41-550 Eclectic A, No. 260
Palm Desert, CA 92260
Ph: (619)342-9994   Fax: (619)776-1214

Quarterly. Magazine showcasing successful Hispanic Americans and promoting higher education (English and Spanish).

ONLINE AND DATABASE SERVICES

★9989★ Minority Graduate Database (MGDB)

McClure-Lundberg Associates, Inc.
1515 U St. NW
Washington, DC 20009
Ph: (202)483-4107   Fax: (202)328-8572
Fr: 800-762-2023

Online database containing approximately 13,000 names of college graduates who are members of minority ethnic groups and are seeking employment.

OTHER SOURCES

★9990★ American Indian Science and Engineering Society (AISES)

1630 30th St., Ste. 301
Boulder, CO 80301
Ph: (303)492-8658   Fax: (303)492-3400

Members: American Indian and non-Indian students and professionals in science, technology, and engineering fields; corporations representing energy, mining, aerospace, electronic, and computer fields. **Purpose:** Seeks to motivate and encourage students to pursue undergraduate and graduate studies in science, engineering, and technology. **Activities:** Sponsors science fairs in grade schools, teacher training workshops, summer math/science sessions for 8th-12th graders, professional chapters, and student chapters in colleges. Offers scholarships. Adult members serve as role models, advisers, and mentors for students. Operates placement service. **E-Mail:** aise sha@spot.colorado.edu

★9991★ Asian American Architects and Engineers

1670 Pine St.
San Francisco, CA 94109
Ph: (415)928-5910   Fax: (415)921-0182

Members: Minorities. **Purpose:** Provides contracts and job opportunities for minorities in the architectural and engineering fields. **Activities:** Serves as a network for the promotion in professional fields.

★9992★ Black Citizens for a Fair Media (BCFM)

156-20 Riverside Dr., No. 13L
New York, NY 10032
Ph: (212)568-3168

Purpose: Community organizations concerned with employment practices in the television industry, images of black people projected by television, and how those images affect viewers. Works to improve programming, employment proctices, and training of blacks; evaluates compliance with the Federal Communication Commission's equal opportunity rules for the electronic media. Believes that the airways belong to the people and seeks to prevent any change in that ownership. Has established advisory boards with New York City television stations which meet quarterly to discuss programming and employment.

★9993★ Blackbook Business and Entertainment Reference Guide

National Publications Sales Agency, Inc.
1610 E. 79th St.
Chicago, IL 60649
Ph: (312)375-6800   Fax: (312)375-7149

Annual, March. $14.95. Covers about 6,000 African-American businesses and organizations, including local affiliates; African-Americans on boards of major corporations; in the food, beverage, and tobacco industries; elected officials and in the defense industry. Entries include: Firm name, address, phone, key personnel, history.

★9994★ Chinese for Affirmative Action (CAA)

17 Walter U. Lum Pl.
San Francisco, CA 94108
Ph: (415)274-6750   Fax: (415)397-8770

Members: Individuals and corporations seeking equal opportunity for and the protection of the civil rights of Asian-Americans. **Purpose:** Works with the larger community to help insure fair treatment under the law in employment matters; has cooperated with state and local governmental agencies to help develop bilingual materials to aid Asian-American job applicants; encourages the appointment and participation of Asian-Americans on public boards and commissions; works to secure a fair share of public resources for Asian-Americans. Seeks to influence broadcasting stations to produce Asian-American public affairs programming and to present accurate portrayals of Asian-Americans. **Activities:** Provides counseling information on workers' rights and makes referrals to sources of additional assistance; assists employers in meeting affirmative action goals. Trains Asian-Americans to be

public speakers and community spokespersons.

★9995★ Consortium of Doctors (COD)

PO Box 20402
Savannah, GA 31404
Ph: (912)354-4634

Members: Minority women who have earned a doctorate degree from an established, accredited institution. **Purpose:** Assists members in finding jobs suitable to their training. **Activities:** Conducts charitable, educational, and inspirational programs.

★9996★ Directorio Profesional Hispano

Blanca Balbi
PO Box 408
Flushing, NY 11352
Ph: (718)762-1432

Annual, January. ; Restricted circulation. Covers about 3,500 Hispanic doctors, optometrists, dentists, lawyers, architects, and accountants, with offices in the eastern United States. Entries include: Name, address, phone. Arrangement: Classified by profession. Indexes: Medical specialists.

★9997★ Directory of Indian Owned Businesses

All Indian Pueblo Council, Inc.
New Mexico Native American Business Development Center
3939 San Pedro NE, Ste. D
PO Box 3256
Albuquerque, NM 87190
Ph: (505)889-9092

Annual. $5.00. Covers about 200 firms offering professional, commercial, and industrial products and services in New Mexico. Entries include: Firm name, address, phone, name and title of owner or chief executive, product or service. Arrangement: Classified by Standard Industrial Classification (SIC) code. Indexes: Product/service.

★9998★ Ethnic Employees of the Library of Congress (EELC)

6100 Eastview St.
Bethesda, MD 20817
Ph: (301)229-6366

Members: Ethnic and racial minority employees and majority employees of the Library of Congress. **Purpose:** Objectives are to promote and strengthen brotherhood among ethnic employees and ethnic members of society, and to ensure equal employment opportunities in the Library of Congress and elsewhere. Monitors the Library of Congress with regard to its policies and practices affecting minority and majority employees through the American Black and Ethnic Helsinki Monitoring Group made up of leadership from EELC and Black Employees of the Library of Congress (BELC). Works with BELC to obtain equal employment of minority employees at the Library of Congress through a long-standing class action lawsuit against the Library of Congress. Testifies annually before Congress; compiles statistics; provides statistical background material for court litigation; assists attorneys defending employees in racial, ethnic, and sex discrimination cases. Conducts research program on Library of Congress budget.

★9999★ Interracial Council for Business Opportunity

51 Madison Ave., Ste. 2212
New York, NY 10010
Ph: (212)779-4360   Fax: (212)779-4365

Purpose: Assists minority businessmen and women in developing, owning, and managing business ventures with substantial employment and economic impact. **Activities:** Services include business feasibility studies, financing, market development, and other technical assistance to start or expand minority-owned compaines. Offers free management training courses.

★10000★ Minority Business Information System (MBISYS)

National Minority Supplier Development Council (NMSDC)
15 W. 39th St., 9th Fl.
New York, NY 10018
Ph: (212)944-2430

Current. Updated as needed. Database covers: Approximately 15,000 companies that are certified by the NMSDC as minority owned. Database includes: Company name, address, phone, parent company name, Standard Industrial Classification (SIC) code, description of products and services, year founded, ownership structure, number of employees; name, title, ethnicity, and sex of owners; major customers, annual sales, geographical area served, most recent certification date and accrediting council.

★10001★ National Association for the Advancement of Colored People (NAACP)

4805 Mt. Hope Dr.
Baltimore, MD 21215
Ph: (410)358-8900   Fax: (410)486-9257

Members: Persons "of all races and religions" who believe in the objectives and methods of the NAACP. **Purpose:** To achieve equal rights through the democratic process and eliminate racial prejudice by removing racial discrimination in housing, employment, voting, schools, the courts, transportation, recreation, prisons, and business enterprises. **Activities:** Offers referral services, tutorials, job referrals, and day care. Sponsors seminars; maintains law library. Sponsors the NAACP National Housing Corporation to assist in the development of low and moderate income housing for families. Compiles statistics.

★10002★ National Association of Cuban-American Women of the U.S.A. (NACAW-USA)

2513 S. Calhoun St.
Fort Wayne, IN 46807-1305
Ph: (219)745-5421   Fax: (219)744-1363

Purpose: Addresses current issues, concerns, and problems affecting Hispanic and minority women, and to achieve goals such as equal education and training, fair immigration policy, and meaningful work with adequate compensation. Coordinates activities with national Hispanic and other minority organizations; responds to female concerns from minority and majority populations; encourages participation in related task forces, legislative activities, and professional endeavors; acts as clearinghouse and referral center. Supports bilingual and bicultural education at the local, state, and national levels. Disseminates information on postsecondary educational opportunities and sources of financial aid in particular cities. Produces biweekly bilingual radio program. **Activities:** Conducts placement service; compiles statistics.

★10003★ National Association of Hispanic Journalists (NAHJ)

Natl. Press Bldg., Ste. 1193
529 14th St. NW
Washington, DC 20045
Ph: (202)662-7145   Fax: (202)662-7144
Fr: 800-708-2774

Purpose: To organize and support Hispanics involved in news gathering and dissemination. Encourages journalism and communications study and practice by Hispanics. Seeks recognition for Hispanic members of the profession regarding their skills and achievements. Promotes fair and accurate media treatment of Hispanics; opposes job discrimination and demeaning stereotypes. Works to increase educational and career opportunities and development for Hispanics in the field. Seeks to foster greater awareness of members' cultural identity, interests, and concerns. Provides a united voice for Hispanic journalists with the aim of achieving national visibility. **Activities:** Offers placement services to Hispanic students.

★10004★ National Black MBA Association (NBMBAA)

180 N. Michigan Ave., Ste. 1515
Chicago, IL 60601
Ph: (312)236-2622   Fax: (312)236-4131

Members: Business professionals, lawyers, accountants, and engineers concerned with the role of blacks who hold advanced management degrees. **Purpose:** Works to create economic and intellectual wealth for the black community. Encourages blacks to pursue continuing business education; assists students preparing to enter the business world. Provides programs for minority youths, students, and professionals, and entrepreneurs including workshops, panel discussions, and Destination MBA seminar. **Activities:** Sponsors job fairs. Works with graduate schools. Operates job placement service.

★10005★ National Coalition of 100 Black Women (NCBW)

38 W. 32nd St., 16th Fl.
New York, NY 10001-3816

Members: African-American women actively involved with issues such as economic development, health, employment, education, voting, housing, criminal justice, the status of black families, and the arts. **Purpose:** Seeks to provide networking and career opportunities for African-American women in the process of establishing links between the organization and the corporate and political arenas. Encourages leadership development; sponsors role-model and mentor programs to provide guidance to teenage mothers and young women in high school or who have graduated from college and are striving for career advancement.

★10006★ National Federation of Hispanics in Communications (NFHC)

PO Box 21032, Kalorama Sta.
Washington, DC 20009
Ph: (202)332-0019   Fax: (703)978-4633

Members: Professionals in Hispanic media and related fields including writers, editors, audiovisual specialists, cinematographers, photographers, and public information specialists; non-Hispanic support groups. **Purpose:** Works to form a network to: increase public awareness of Hispanic media; improve media coverage of the Hispanic community; provide programs and materials for and about the Hispanic community; project the needs and views of the Hispanic people; interpret and disseminate various sources of information at the community level. Promotes interchange of skills and experience among Hispanic communicators for mutual professional and career development. Encourages Hispanics to enter media-related education and training programs. Fosters collaboration among members to ensure the use of Hispanic media components in all programs affecting the Hispanic-American as a consumer. **Activities:** Disseminates information on training, jobs, professional development, national events, and other pertinent information. Conducts seminars and presentations.

★10007★ National Indian Business Directory

National Center for American Indian
Enterprise Development
953 E. Juanita Ave.
Mesa, AZ 85204
Ph: (602)831-7524   Fax: (602)491-1332
Fr: 800-462-2433

Annual, April. $25.00. Covers firms offering professional, commercial, and industrial products and services. Entries include: Firm name, address, phone, name and title of owner or chief executive, product or service, year established, work locations, license type/specialty, bonding capacity/sales. Arrangement: Classified by line of business.

★10008★ National Puerto Rican Forum (NPRF)

31 E. 32nd St., 4th Fl.
New York, NY 10016
Ph: (212)685-2311   Fax: (212)689-5034

Purpose: Concerned with the overall improvement of Puerto Rican and Hispanic communities throughout the U.S. Seeks to identify the obstacles preventing the advancement of the Puerto Rican and Hispanic communities and to develop strategies to remove them. **Activities:** Designs and implements programs in areas of job counseling, training and placement, and English language skills, to deal effectively with the problems of Puerto Ricans and other Hispanics. Sponsors Career Services and Job Placement Program at the national level. Also provides specialized programs in New York, such as: Employment Placement Initiative, Access and Family Services in the schools, and job counseling.

★10009★ National Society of Hispanic MBAs (NSHMBA)

PO Box 2903
Chicago, IL 60690-2903
Ph: (312)472-5545

Members: Hispanic individuals with Master of Business Administration degrees; MBA candidates; interested others. **Purpose:** Promotes business education among hispanics; works to increase hispanic representation in business. **Activities:** Sponsors speaker series and educational programs; maintains job bank.

★10010★ National Urban Affairs Council (NUAC)

2330 Shawnee Mission Pky.
Westwood, KS 66205
Ph: (908)561-6989

Purpose: Promotes the employment and corporate advancement of minority and economically disadvantaged individuals; works to identify these individuals. Develops and funds related educational programs for businesses.

★10011★ North American Indian Association (NAIA)

22720 Plymouth Rd.
Detroit, MI 48239
Ph: (313)535-2966   Fax: (313)535-8060

Members: Individuals of at least one-quarter North American Indian blood and their families. Membership centered in the Detroit, MI, area; open to natives and non-natives. **Purpose:** Objectives are to: establish a meeting center for North American Indians; preserve and promote Indian culture; assist Indians in obtaining higher education; help each other in time of need; work for the betterment of all Indians. **Activities:** Provides employment and training programs, adult counseling services, and children's services. Operates Native American Gallery. Offers speakers' bureau.

★10012★ Organization of Chinese American Women (OCAW)

1300 N St. NW, Ste. 100
Washington, DC 20005
Ph: (202)638-0330   Fax: (202)638-2196

Purpose: Advances the cause of Chinese American women in the U.S. and fosters public awareness of their special needs and concerns. Seeks to integrate Chinese American women into the mainstream of women's activities and programs. Addresses issues such as equal employment opportunities at both the professional and nonprofessional levels; overcoming stereotypes; racial and sexual discrimination and restrictive traditional beliefs; assistance to poverty-stricken recent immigrants; access to leadership and policymaking positions. Develops training models for Chinese and Asian American women. **Activities:** Conducts training and job placement for class participants, widening teenage women's career choices, and networking for Chinese American women.

★10013★ **SER–Jobs for Progress National**
100 Decker Dr., Ste. 200
Irving, TX 75062
Ph: (214)541-0616   Fax: (214)650-1860
Fr: 800-374-2SER

Purpose: Aims to provide employment training and opportunities for Spanish-speaking and disadvantaged Americans. Seeks to increase business and economic opportunities for minority communities and ensure optimum participation by the Hispanic community in public policy forums. Most SER performance contracts are funded by the federal government. (The acronym SER stands for service, employment, and redevelopment.) Each local office organizes its own training and management program and is responsible for recruitment and selection of job trainees, counseling, pre-job orientation and vocational preparation, basic education, employer relations, and follow-up services to trainees after training and job placement.

Opportunities for Older Workers

NEWSPAPERS, MAGAZINES, AND JOURNALS

★10028★ *Affirmative Action Register*

Affirmative Action, Inc.
8356 Olive Blvd.
St. Louis, MO 63132
Ph: (314)991-1335   Fax: (314)997-1788
Fr: 800-537-0655

Monthly. $1.50 for single issue. Free, to women, minority, handicapped candidate sources. Covers in each issue, about 300 positions at a professional level (most requiring advanced study) available to women, minorities, veterans, and the handicapped; listings are advertisements placed by employers with affirmative action programs. Entries include: Company or organization name, address, contact name; description of position including title, requirements, duties, application procedure, salary, etc. Arrangement: Classified by profession.

★10029★ *Working Age*

American Association of Retired Persons
601 E St. NW
Washington, DC 20049
Ph: (202)434-2040

Six issues/year. Free to institutions only. Focuses on pre-retirement and older worker issues. Discusses retirement planning programs, innovations and technology in the workplace affecting older workers, and retraining. Recurring features include legislative updates, research and survey results, and case studies.

OTHER SOURCES

★10030★ Asociacion Nacional pro Personas Mayores (ANPPM)

3325 Wilshire Blvd., Ste. 800
Los Angeles, CA 90010
Ph: (213)487-1922   Fax: (213)385-3014

Members: Older persons and organizations concerned with aging and social service groups. **Purpose:** Articulates needs of Hispanic and other low-income elderly; seeks to include the Hispanic elderly in social service programs aimed at older Americans. **Activities:** Administers the Senior Community Service Employment Program, funded by the Department of Labor, which provides employment to more than 1900 low-income people over 55 years of age in 11 states.

★10031★ Green Thumb (GT)

2000 N. 14th St., Ste. 800
Arlington, VA 22201
Ph: (703)522-7272   Fax: (703)522-0141

Purpose: Sponsored by the National Farmers Union; funded primarily by the U.S. Department of Labor. Provides job placement services, training, and part-time community service employment for unemployed persons 55 years of age or older, having income at or near poverty income level.

★10032★ National Institute on Age, Work and Retirement (NIAWR)

409 3rd St. SW, Ste. 200
Washington, DC 20024
Ph: (202)479-1200   Fax: (202)479-0735

Purpose: Promotes opportunities for middle-aged and older workers. Provides information on organizations serving older workers and technical assistance to older worker program directors. Conducts research on work/retirement behavior and attitudes. Advises corporations on employment practices and retirement planning programs.

Opportunities for Teenagers

REFERENCE WORKS

★10033★ Career Action Plan

Meridian Education Corporation
236 E. Front St.
Bloomington, IL 61701
Ph: (309)827-5455   Fr: 800-727-5507

William Bloomfield. 1989. $9.95. 160 pages. Aimed at giving students general career-planning and job-hunting skills. Also available: Implementation Guide, $12.95.

★10034★ Cents-Able Summer Self-Employment: An Entrepreneurial Guide for High School & College Students

Tamarax Press
PO Box 450
2A Taylor Way
Washington Crossing, PA 18977
Ph: (215)493-2136   Fax: (215)493-2057

E.K. Shepard. 1994. $12.95 (paper).

★10035★ Coming Alive from Nine to Five

Mayfield Publishing
1280 Villa St.
Mountain View, CA 94041
Ph: (415)960-3222   Fr: 800-433-1279

Betty N. Michelozzi. Fourth edition, 1992. $19.95. 294 pages. In addition to general job-hunting advice, provides special information for women, young adults, minorities, older workers, and persons with handicaps.

★10036★ Directory of Internships

Ready Reference Press
PO Box 5249
Santa Monica, CA 90409
Ph: (213)474-5175   Fr: 800-424-5627

$89.50. Out of print. Lists internship opportunities in many fields of interest, including, but not limited to arts, journalism, public relations, education, law, environmental affairs, business, engineering, and computer science. In addition, cites summer internship opportunities, work/study programs, and specialized opportunities for high school and undergraduate students. Indexed by subject, geography, and program.

★10037★ Focus on Careers

ABC-CLIO
PO Box 1911
Santa Barbara, CA 93116-1911
Ph: (805)968-1991   Fax: (805)658-9685
Fr: 800-422-2546

Published 1991. $39.50. Publication includes: Lists of hotlines, and print and non-print resources for teens investigating career options. Principal content of publication is an examination of career choices and plans, including definitions and statistics. Part of the Teenage Perspective Series.

★10038★ Free (& Almost Free) Adventures for Teenagers: Your Guide to the Top Low-Cost, Year-Round Programs & Internships

John Wiley & Sons, Inc.
605 3rd Ave.
New York, NY 10158-0012
Ph: (212)850-6000   Fr: 800-225-5945

Gail L. Grand. 1995. $14.95 (paper).

★10039★ How to Get a Good Job and Keep It

VGM Career Horizons
4255 W. Touhy Ave.
Lincolnwood, IL 60646-1975
Ph: (847)679-5500   Fax: (847)679-2494
Fr: 800-323-4900

Deborah Perlmutter Bloch. 1993. $7.95. Aimed at the recent high school or college graduate, this guide provides advice on finding out about jobs, completing applications and resumes, and managing successful interviews.

★10040★ The Job Hunter's Workbook

Johnson/Rudolph Educational Resources, Inc.
1004 State St.
Bowling Green, KY 42101
Fr: 800-248-5212

Workbook approach. 1989. $10.95. 90 pages. Aimed at the high school student.

★10041★ Peterson's Guide to College for Careers in Allied Health

Peterson's Guides, Inc.
202 Carnegie Center
PO Box 2123
Princeton, NJ 08543-2123
Ph: (609)243-9111   Fax: (609)243-9150
Fr: 800-338-3282

$14.95. Publication includes: College-level programs in allied health. Principal content of publication is career information on what it's like to work in the field, skills required, job outlook, career paths, education needed, and where to get more information.

★10042★ Peterson's Guide to College for Careers in Business

Peterson's Guides, Inc.
202 Carnegie Center
PO Box 2123
Princeton, NJ 08543-2123
Ph: (609)243-9111   Fax: (609)243-9150
Fr: 800-338-3282

$14.95. Publication includes: College-level programs in business. Principal content of publication is career information on what it's like to work in the field, skills required, job outlook, career paths, education needed, and where to get more information.

★10043★ Peterson's Guide to College for Careers in Computing

Peterson's Guides, Inc.
202 Carnegie Center
PO Box 2123
Princeton, NJ 08543-2123
Ph: (609)243-9111   Fax: (609)243-9150
Fr: 800-338-3282

$14.95. Publication includes: College-level programs in computing. Principal content of publication is career information on what it's like to work in the field, skills required, job outlook, career paths, education needed, and where to get more information.

★10044★ **Peterson's Guide to College for Careers in Teaching**

Peterson's Guides, Inc.
202 Carnegie Center
PO Box 2123
Princeton, NJ 08543-2123
Ph: (609)243-9111   Fax: (609)243-9150
Fr: 800-338-3282

$14.95. Publication includes: College-level programs in the field of teaching. Principal content of publication is career information on what it's like to work in the field, skills required, job outlook, career paths, education needed, and where to get more information.

★10045★ **Peterson's International Directory of Summer Opportunities for Kids & Teenagers**

Peterson's Guides, Inc.
PO Box 2123
Princeton, NJ 08543-2123
Ph: (609)243-9111   Fax: (609)243-9150
Fr: 800-338-3282

1995. $29.95 (paper).

★10046★ **Peterson's Summer Opportunities for Kids and Teenagers 1996**

Peterson's
PO Box 2123
Princeton, NJ 08543-2123
Ph: (609)243-9111   Fax: (609)243-9150
Fr: 800-338-3282

Annual. $23.95 (paper). 1,000 pages. In addition to information about 1,400 summer activities and programs, covers job opportunities for high school and college students.

★10047★ **Resumes for High School Graduates**

VGM Career Horizons
4255 W. Touhy Ave.
Lincolnwood, IL 60646-1975
Ph: (847)679-5500   Fax: (847)679-2494
Fr: 800-323-4900

1993. $9.95. Designed for the person with little or no full-time work experience. Shows how to emphasize part-work experience and highlight educational, extra-curricular and volunteer experience. Provides sample resumes and cover letters.

★10048★ **Your First Interview**

The Career Press, Inc.
3 Tice Rd.
PO Box 687
Franklin Lakes, NJ 07417
Ph: (201)848-0310   Fax: (201)848-1727
Fr: 800-237-3371

Ron Fry. Third edition, 1995. $9.99. 192 pages. Takes the reader from making the initial contact with a prospective employer to negotiating salary.

AUDIO/VISUAL RESOURCES

★10049★ **Job Search Skills for Teens**

Ready Reference Press
PO Box 5249
Santa Monica, CA 90409
Fax: (310)475-4895   Fr: 800-424-5627

Series of 3 videos. $239.00/set. $89.00/each. Separate titles cover job search skills, resume preparation, and interview techniques.

★10050★ **Teenage Entrepreneurs**

Educational Video Network
1401 Nineteenth St.
Huntsville, TX 77340
Ph: (409)295-5767   Fax: (409)294-0233

$79.95. Profiles teenage entrepreneurs who have found success in owning their own businesses.

OTHER SOURCES

★10051★ **National Employment and Training Association (NETA)**

2815 25th St.
Meridian, MS 39305
Ph: (601)484-5165   Fax: (601)484-4999

Members: Persons involved in: manpower and job training; public or private vocational education; employment services; apprenticeship and training programs; Job Training Partnership Act programs; business and industry; and private training schools. **Purpose:** Encourages development of quality training programs for youths and adults, regardless of race, color, creed, or national origin. Sponsors educational and leadership development programs. Maintains speakers' bureau.

★10052★ **National Youth Employment Coalition (NYEC)**

1001 Connecticut Ave. NW, Ste. 719
Washington, DC 20009
Ph: (202)659-1064   Fax: (202)775-9733

Members: Representatives of community-based organizations, research organizations, public interest groups, and policy analysis organizations. **Purpose:** Promotes improved policies and practices related to youth employment. **Activities:** Encourages local grass roots organizing and information exchange. Conducts forums.

★10053★ **Operation Enterprise (OE)**

PO Box 88
Hamilton, NY 13346
Ph: (315)824-2000   Fax: (315)824-6785
Fr: 800-634-4262

Purpose: Division of the American Management Association. Gives high school and college students an opportunity to learn about management by working with executives and managers. Learning techniques used include small group discussions, a computerized business simulation, and role playing. Sponsors two programs: Operation Enterprise, in which top managers and executives help students explore the concepts and skills of professional management, and Career Skills, to encourage development of job skills. Candidates are sponsored in a variety of ways by companies, civic organizations, or individuals.

★10054★ **Vocational Foundation, Inc. (VFI)**

902 Broadway, 15th Fl.
New York, NY 10010
Ph: (212)777-0700   Fax: (212)673-8975

Purpose: A free voluntary vocational training, guidance, and job placement service for economically and educationally disadvantaged young people (ages 16-21) who are referred by other accredited public and voluntary agencies in New York City. Seeks to aid high school dropouts and young people with correctional and drug abuse histories.

★10055★ **WAVE**

501 School St. SW, Ste. 600
Washington, DC 20024
Ph: (202)484-0103   Fax: (202)488-7595
Fr: 800-274-2005

Purpose: Organization, funded in part by the U.S. Department of Labor and grants from corporations and foundations, that helps disadvantaged 16-21 year old high school dropouts and students at risk of dropping out to find unsubsidized jobs and careers. Dropouts attend classes to prepare for their high school equivalency diplomas and to learn basic living skills, such as how to find an apartment, how to dress for a job interview, and how to balance a checkbook. High school students at risk of dropping out enroll in WAVE (Work, Achievement, and Values in Education). In schools WAVE's youth organization, holds seminars and competitions that foster motivation and leadership and conducts national employment and training seminars for enrollees, and annual staff training institutes.

★10056★ **World Impact Services (WIS)**

2001 S. Vermont Ave.
Los Angeles, CA 90007
Ph: (213)735-1137   Fax: (213)735-2576

Purpose: A project of World Impact. Vocational training ministry for teens and young adults, providing work experience and helping them prepare for their first entry-level job. Encourages teen responsibility.

Opportunities for Women

REFERENCE WORKS

★10057★ Coming Alive from Nine to Five

Mayfield Publishing
1280 Villa St.
Mountain View, CA 94041
Ph: (415)960-3222   Fr: 800-433-1279

Betty N. Michelozzi. Fourth edition, 1992. $19.95. 294 pages. In addition to general job-hunting advice, provides special information for women, young adults, minorities, older workers, and persons with handicaps.

★10058★ Directory of Career Resources for Women

Ready Reference Press
PO Box 5249
Santa Monica, CA 90409
Ph: (213)474-5175   Fr: 800-424-5627

$98.00. Out of print. Offers details on hundreds of programs and services, including job referral services, talent banks, re-entry programs, special training programs, career counseling, resume preparation, workshops, and others. Entries include organization name, general information, resources offered, special features, hours, fees (if any), and address. Subject and geographic indexes.

★10059★ Directory of Federal Women's Program Managers

Office of Affirmative Recruiting and Employment
U.S. Office of Personnel Management
1900 E St. NW, Rm. 6336
Washington, DC 20415
Ph: (202)606-0870

Annual, November. Covers about 95 federal government departments, agencies, bureaus, etc., with equal employment opportunity programs concerned specifically with women. Entries include: Department or agency name, address, phone, and name of program manager. Arrangement: Alphabetical.

★10060★ Directory of Non-Traditional Training and Employment Programs Serving Women

Diane Publishing Co.
600 Upland Ave.
Upland, PA 19015
Ph: (610)499-7415   Fax: (610)499-7429

1993. $45.00 (paper).

★10061★ Directory of Nontraditional Training and Employment Programs

Women's Bureau
Department of Labor
200 Constitution Ave. NW, Rm. S-3311
Washington, DC 20210
Ph: (202)523-6652   Fax: (202)219-6652

Published 1991. Free. Covers 125 programs in 32 states designed to assist women in obtaining training and employment in skilled nontraditional jobs. Entries include: Program name, address, phone, administrative agency, name and title of contact, program services, eligibility, program locations. Arrangement: Geographical.

★10062★ Directory of Wisconsin Women's Services and Organizations

Wisconsin Women's Council
16 N. Carroll St., Rm. 720
Madison, WI 53702
Ph: (608)266-2285

Biennial, latest edition Oct 1994. Free. Covers about 400 agencies, organizations, services, and other programs of interest to and concerned with women, including career planning, displaced homemaker services, legal aid, women's studies programs, child care services, etc. Entries include: Organization name, address, phone, purpose. Arrangement: Classified by area of concern.

★10063★ Directory of Women Entrepreneurs

Wind River Publications, Inc.
PO Box 450827, Northlake Branch
Atlanta, GA 30345
Fax: (404)496-5986

Annual, February. $79.95. Covers Approximately 3,200 women-owned businesses; companies with minority and women professional development programs, women's groups and organizations, and minority business assistance offices. Entries include: For women-owned businesses: company name, address, phone, names and titles of key personnel, year founded, financial data, Standard Industrial Classification (SIC) code, description of products or services. For others: name, address, phone. Arrangement: Alphabetical. Indexes: Geographical, Standard Industrial Classification (SIC) code.

★10064★ Displaced Homemaker/Single Parent Program Directory

WomenWork! The National Network for Women's Employment
1625 K St. NW
Washington, DC 20006
Ph: (202)467-6346   Fax: (202)467-5366

Annual. $49.95, plus $7.50 shipping; payment with order. Covers over 1,200 counseling and career assistance centers for women who are (primarily) widowed, divorced, separated, or abandoned after full-time careers as wives and mothers. Entries include: Center name, address, phone, name of contact. Arrangement: Geographical.

★10065★ Every Woman's Essential Job Hunting & Resume Book

Adams Publishing
260 Center St.
Holbrook, MA 02343-1074
Ph: (617)767-8100   Fax: (617)767-0994
Fr: 800-872-5627

Laura Morin. 1994. $10.95 (paper).

★10066★ Exploring Nontraditional Jobs for Women

Rosen Publishing Group, Inc.
29 E. 21st St.
New York, NY 10010
Ph: (212)777-3017   Fax: (212)777-0277
Fr: 800-237-9932

Rose Neufeld. 1989. $14.95. Describes occupations where few women are found. Covers job duties, training routes, where to apply for jobs, tools used, salary, and advantages and disadvantages of the job.

★10067★ **Finding the Work You Love: A Woman's Career Guide**

Resource Publications, Inc.
160 E. Virginia St., No. 290
San Jose, CA 95112-5876
Ph: (408)286-8505   Fax: (408)287-8748
Fr: 800-736-7600

Astrid Berg. 1994. $15.95 (paper).

★10068★ **National Council of Career Women—Membership Directory**

National Council of Career Women
4200 Wisconsin Ave. NW, Ste. 106-210
Washington, DC 20016
Ph: (202)310-4200

Annual, summer. Available to members only. Covers 450 members. Entries include: Name, address, title, and affiliation. Arrangement: Alphabetical.

★10069★ **National Directory of Woman-Owned Business Firms**

Business Research Services, Inc.
4201 Connecticut Ave. NW, Ste. 610
Washington, DC 20008-1158
Ph: (202)364-6473   Fax: (202)686-3228
Fr: 800-325-8720

Annual. $245.00, plus $5.00 shipping. Covers over 30,000 woman-owned businesses. Entries include: Company name, address, phone, name and title of contact, minority group, certification status, date founded, number of employees, description of products or services, sales volume, government contracting experience, references. Arrangement: Standard Industrial Classification (SIC) code, geographical. Indexes: Alphabetical.

★10070★ **The New Relocating Spouse's Guide to Employment: Options and Strategies in the U.S. and Abroad**

Impact Publications
9104-N Manassas Dr.
Manassas Park, VA 22111
Ph: (703)361-7300   Fax: (703)335-9486

1993. $14.95. Publication includes: List of 133 professional associations and 54 federal job centers. Entries include: Organization name, address, phone. Principal content of publication is discussion of the job market, employment trends, and other useful information for those facing a move to a city where they have no job waiting. Arrangement: Alphabetical.

★10071★ **Professional by Choice: Milady's Career Development Guide**

Milady Publishing Co.
3 Columbia Cir., Box 15015
Albany, NY 12212
Ph: (518)464-3500   Fax: (518)459-3552
Fr: 800-347-7707

Victoria Harper. 1994. $18.95.

★10072★ **Resumes for Women**

Macmillan Publishing Co., Inc.
200 Old Tappan Rd.
Old Tappan, NJ 07675
Fax: 800-445-6991   Fr: 800-223-2336

Eva Shaw. 1995.

★10073★ **The Smart Woman's Guide to Career Success**

Career Press, Inc.
3 Tice Rd.
PO Box 687
Franklin Lakes, NJ 07417-1322
Ph: (201)848-0310   Fax: (201)848-1727
Fr: 800-227-3371

Janet Hauter. 1993. $11.95 (paper).

★10074★ **The Smart Woman's Guide to Interviewing and Salary Negotiation**

Career Press, Inc.
3 Tice Rd.
PO Box 687
Franklin Lakes, NJ 07417-1322
Ph: (201)848-0310   Fax: (201)848-1727
Fr: 800-227-3371

Julie A. King. 1995. $12.99 (paper).

★10075★ **The Smart Woman's Guide to Resumes and Job Hunting**

The Career Press, Inc.
3 Tice Rd.
PO Box 687
Franklin Lakes, NJ 07417
Ph: (201)848-0310   Fax: (201)848-1727
Fr: 800-237-3371

Julie Adair King and Betsy Sheldon. Third edition, 1995. $9.99. 224 pages. Addresses job-search challenges unique to women in the '90s. Discusses breaking through the glass ceiling and other gender barriers, commanding a fair salary, networking to hidden job opportunities, using "power language", translating volunteer experiences into powerful accomplishments, and offers other guidance. Takes the reader through a resume-creating process.

★10076★ **Starting Over: You in the New Workplace**

Palomino Press
86-07 144 St.
Briarwood, NY 11435
Ph: (718)297-5053

Jo Danna. $12.95. 260 pages.

★10077★ **Women in Construction: A Resource Guide**

Her Own Words
PO Box 5264
Madison, WI 53705
Ph: (608)271-7083

Jocelyn Riley. 1995. $20.00.

★10078★ **Women's Business Resource Guide: A National Directory of Over 600 Programs, Resources & Organizations to Help Women Start or Expand a Business**

The Resource Group
PO Box 25505
Eugene, OR 97402
Ph: (503)683-5330   Fax: (503)683-5330

Biennial, June of even years. $19.95. Covers Over 600 training, technical assistance, and counseling programs, information sources, government agencies, membership organizations, and other associations of interest to women in business. Entries include: Resource name, address, phone, geographical area served, description. Arrangement: Clas-

sified by topic. Indexes: Product/service, organization name, subject.

★10079★ **Work of Her Own: A Woman's Guide to Success off the Career Track**

Putnam Publishing Group
200 Madison Ave.
New York, NY 10016
Ph: (212)951-8400   Fax: (212)213-6706
Fr: 800-631-8571

Susan W. Albert. 1994. $12.95 (paper).

NEWSPAPERS, MAGAZINES, AND JOURNALS

★10080★ **Affirmative Action Register**

Affirmative Action, Inc.
8356 Olive Blvd.
St. Louis, MO 63132
Ph: (314)991-1335   Fax: (314)997-1788
Fr: 800-537-0655

Monthly. $1.50 for single issue. Free, to women, minority, handicapped candidate sources. Covers in each issue, about 300 positions at a professional level (most requiring advanced study) available to women, minorities, veterans, and the handicapped; listings are advertisements placed by employers with affirmative action programs. Entries include: Company or organization name, address, contact name; description of position including title, requirements, duties, application procedure, salary, etc. Arrangement: Classified by profession.

★10081★ **Bridging the Gap**

Section for Women in Public Administration
c/o Debra Martin
3214 McClure Ave.
Flint, MI 48502

Three issues/year. Included in membership. Disseminates information relating to the organization's efforts to initiate action programs appropriate to the needs and concerns of women in public administration. Discusses the equality of educational and employment opportunities for women in public service and government. Acts as a forum for communication among professionals and students interested in women in public service administration. Recurring features include news of research, news of members, news of opportunities available for women, and recognition of achievement and awards received.

★10082★ **Homeworking Mothers**

Mother's Home Business Network
PO Box 423
East Meadow, NY 11554
Ph: (516)997-7394   Fax: (516)997-0839

Quarterly. Included in membership. Aims to inform and inspire mothers who choose to work at home. Explains how to get started in specific businesses and offers articles written by women who successfully combine motherhood with a money-making home business. Recurring features include book excerpts and columns titled: Take Note, It's My Business, Considering the Possibilities, Time Out for Kids, and Advice for Home-working Mothers.

★10083★ **National Business Woman**

National Federation of Business and Professional Women's Clubs
2012 Massachusetts Ave. NW
Washington, DC 20036
Ph: (202)293-1100   Fax: (202)861-0298

Quarterly. Magazine for working women that promotes workplace equity issues.

★10084★ **Successful Woman in Business**

American Society of Professional and Executive Women (ASPEW)
1429 Walnut St.
Philadelphia, PA 19102
Ph: (215)563-6005

Quarterly. $48.00/year. Contains advice on resources, management strategies, personal finance, and career development for professional and executive women.

★10085★ **Tradeswomen**

Tradeswomen, Inc.
PO Box 2622
Berkeley, CA 94702
Ph: (510)649-6260

Bimonthly. $35.00/year. Subtitled: "A Quarterly Magazine for Women in Blue Collar Work". Reports activities of the organization and other events in the California Bay Area and of national interest to women working or wishing to work in nontraditional and blue collar jobs. Recurring features include announcements of apprenticeship opportunities and job openings, information on unions and government agencies, and U.S. Department of Labor statistics.

★10086★ **WIT**

Northern New England Tradeswomen
26 Railroad St.
St. Johnsbury, VT 05819
Ph: (802)748-3308   Fax: (802)748-1768

Quarterly. Included in membership; $10.00/year for nonmembers. Provides a network of support, information, and skill sharing for women in trade professions.

★10087★ **Women in Business**

The ABWA Co., Inc.
9100 Ward Pkwy.
PO Box 8728
Kansas City, MO 64114-0728
Ph: (816)361-6621   Fax: (816)361-4991

Bimonthly. $16.00/year for individuals; $20.00/year for other countries. Women's business magazine for members of the American Business Women's Association.

★10088★ **Working at Home**

Mrs. H.C. McGarity
PO Box 200504
Cartersville, GA 30120
Ph: (404)386-1257

Quarterly. $12.00 for five issues. Provides short articles about work-at-home opportunities for women who are unable to work outside the home.

AUDIO/VISUAL RESOURCES

★10089★ **Aspire Higher: Sports Careers for Women**

Cambridge Career Products
PO Box 2153
Dept. CC15
Charleston, WV 25328-2153
Ph: (304)744-9323   Fax: (304)744-9351
Fr: 800-468-4227

Video. $29.95. 24 minutes. This motivational video includes profiles of women who have succeeded in sports careers such as marketing, corporate fitness, sports journalism, coaching, and officiating.

★10090★ **Career Close-ups: Women in Science**

AIMS Media
9710 DeSoto Ave.
Chatsworth, CA 91311
Fax: (818)341-6700   Fr: 800-367-2467

Video. 1993. $195.00. 19 minutes. Profiles a marine biologist, industrial forester, and astronomer.

★10091★ **Career Encounters: Women in Engineering**

Cambridge Career Products
PO Box 2153
Dept. CC15
Charleston, WV 25328-2153
Ph: (304)744-9323   Fax: (304)744-9351
Fr: 800-468-4227

Video. $99.95. 25 minutes. Professionals shown in a variety of settings discuss different aspects of their careers.

★10092★ **Job Search Skills for Women**

Ready Reference Press
PO Box 5249
Santa Monica, CA 90409
Fax: (310)475-4895   Fr: 800-424-5627

Series of 3 videos. $239.00/set. $89.00/each. Separate titles cover job search skills, resume preparation, and interview techniques.

★10093★ **Job Search Skills for Women in Non-Traditional Occupations**

Ready Reference Press
PO Box 5249
Santa Monica, CA 90409
Fax: (310)475-4895   Fr: 800-424-5627

Series of 3 videos. $239.00/set. $89.00/each. Separate titles cover job search skills, resume preparation, and interview techniques.

OTHER SOURCES

★10094★ **American Women Managers and Administrators: A Selective Biographical Dictionary**

Greenwood Publishing Group, Inc.
88 Post Rd. W
PO Box 5007
Westport, CT 06881
Ph: (203)226-3571   Fax: (203)222-1502
Fr: 800-225-5800

Published June 1985. $65.00. Covers 225 twentieth-century women who hold or have held administrative, managerial, or leadership positions in business, education, or government, including founders and presidents of colleges and companies, vice presidents of major corporations, and women who were first in their profession or position. Entries include: Name, vital statistics, education and career information, bibliography. Arrangement: Alphabetical.

★10095★ **Business and Professional Women's Foundation (BPWF)**

2012 Massachusetts Ave. NW
Washington, DC 20036
Ph: (202)293-1100   Fax: (202)861-0298

Purpose: Dedicated to improving the economic status of working women through their integration into all occupations. **Activities:** Conducts and supports research on women and work, with special emphasis on economic issues. Maintains Marguerite Rawalt Resource Center of 20,000 items on economic issues involving women and work and provides public reference and referral service. Sponsors BPW Foundation Loan Fund for Women in Engineering and BPW/Sears-Roebuck Loan Fund for Women in Graduate Business Studies. Established by BPW/USA, the National Federation of Business and Professional Women's Clubs.

★10096★ **Capitol Hill Women's Political Caucus (CHWPC)**

Longworth House Office Bldg.
PO Box 599
Washington, DC 20515
Ph: (202)986-0994

A chapter of the National Women's Political Caucus. **Members:** Individuals dedicated to equal rights and equal opportunities for all people. **Purpose:** Purpose is to promote and increase the election, appointment, and participation of women in local, state, and national political and governing processes. Works to increase the political power of women and to combat the inequities of employment and salaries for women on Capitol Hill. Believes equal political and governmental participation will enhance the quality of life for all Americans. **Activities:** Monitors and encourages the enactment of legislation beneficial to women; acts as clearinghouse of legislative information. Sponsors job seminars and programs in personal and professional development. Promotes national organization's goals and works closely with NWPC in its efforts.

★10097★ Catalyst

250 Park Ave. S.
New York, NY 10003
Ph: (212)777-8900   Fax: (212)477-4252

Purpose: Catalyst is the leading nonprofit organization focusing the attention of business leaders and public policy makers on women's workplace issues. Catalyst has a dual mission: (1) to enable women in business and the professions to achieve their maximum potential and (2) to help employers capitalize on the talents of their female employees. **Activities:** Conducts national research and works with individual corporations and professional firms to provide environmental assessments and tailored advice on women's advancement. Other Services include: Corporate Board Placement to assist employers in locating qualified women for board directorships; speakers' bureau; Women's Workplace Networks Resource, an information-sharing link between women's employee groups within corporations and firms across the country; and the Information Center, housing current statistics, print media, and research materials on issues related to women in business.

★10098★ Center for Economic Options

601 Delaware Ave.
Charleston, WV 25302
Ph: (304)345-1298

Purpose: Seeks to improve the economic position and quality of life for women, especially low-income and minority women. Works to provide access to job training and employment options to women. Supports self-employed women and small business owners by offering training and technical assistance and information. Advocates women's legal right to employment, training, education, and credit. Seeks to inform the public on economic issues related to women.

★10099★ Consortium of Doctors (COD)

PO Box 20402
Savannah, GA 31404
Ph: (912)354-4634

Members: Minority women who have earned a doctorate degree from an established, accredited institution. **Purpose:** Assists members in finding jobs suitable to their training. **Activities:** Conducts charitable, educational, and inspirational programs.

★10100★ Federally Employed Women (FEW)

1400 Eye St. NW, Ste. 425
Washington, DC 20005
Ph: (202)898-0994   Fax: (202)898-0998

Members: Men and women employed by the federal government; associate members are persons who support the goals and objectives of FEW. **Purpose:** Seeks to end sex discrimination in government service; to increase job opportunities for women in government service and to further the potential of all women in the government; to improve the merit system in government employment; to assist present and potential government employees who are discriminated against because of sex; to work with other organizations and individuals concerned with equal employment opportunity in the government.

Activities: Informs members of opportunities for training to improve their job potential; issues fact sheets interpreting civil service rules and regulations and other legislative issues.

★10101★ Federation of Organizations for Professional Women (FOPW)

1825 Eye St. NW, Ste. 400
Washington, DC 20006
Ph: (202)328-1415   Fax: (202)949-3459

Members: Affiliate groups and associates. **Purpose:** Women's groups concerned with economic, educational, and professional equality for women. Works to enhance the educational and employment status of women. **Activities:** Acts as a forum for the exchange of ideas and to provide mutual support. Provides information on selected public policy issues to affiliate groups. Offers research and policy analyses. Emphasizes integrity in the workplace. Accepts internships. Conducts training programs; compiles statistics. Maintains referral service. Sponsors networking events. Provides information and support for cases of gender discrimination and harassment. Affiliated with 30 women's groups and organizations.

★10102★ National Association of Cuban-American Women of the U.S.A. (NACAW-USA)

2513 S. Calhoun St.
Fort Wayne, IN 46807-1305
Ph: (219)745-5421   Fax: (219)744-1363

Purpose: Addresses current issues, concerns, and problems affecting Hispanic and minority women, and to achieve goals such as equal education and training, fair immigration policy, and meaningful work with adequate compensation. Coordinates activities with national Hispanic and other minority organizations; responds to female concerns from minority and majority populations; encourages participation in related task forces, legislative activities, and professional endeavors; acts as clearinghouse and referral center. Supports bilingual and bicultural education at the local, state, and national levels. Disseminates information on postsecondary educational opportunities and sources of financial aid in particular cities. Produces biweekly bilingual radio program. **Activities:** Conducts placement service; compiles statistics.

★10103★ National Association for Women in Careers (NAFWIC)

783 Forest Ridge Ct.
Oconomowoc, WI 53066
Ph: (414)778-1919   Fax: (414)778-1638

Purpose: Service organization for women representing various economic sectors including corporations, personally-owned businesses, nonprofit and sales organizations, retail outlets, financial institutions including government and health agencies, educational institutions, and associations. Provides support, networking, and skill-development services for all women to enhance their potential for greater success and enable them to meet future challenges for personal and career growth. Attempts to help women integrate who they are with what they do and to balance the demands of career growth and

private life. **Activities:** Conducts seminars and charitable programs; provides job referral, career planning, and professional speakers.

★10104★ National Coalition of 100 Black Women (NCBW)

38 W. 32nd St., 16th Fl.
New York, NY 10001-3816

Members: African-American women actively involved with issues such as economic development, health, employment, education, voting, housing, criminal justice, the status of black families, and the arts. **Purpose:** Seeks to provide networking and career opportunities for African-American women in the process of establishing links between the organization and the corporate and political arenas. Encourages leadership development; sponsors role-model and mentor programs to provide guidance to teenage mothers and young women in high school or who have graduated from college and are striving for career advancement.

★10105★ Nine to Five, National Association of Working Women

614 Superior Ave. NW, Rm. 852
Cleveland, OH 44113
Ph: (216)566-9308   Fax: (216)566-0192

Members: Women office workers. **Purpose:** Seeks to build a national network of local office worker chapters that strives to gain better pay, proper use of office automation, opportunities for advancement, elimination of sex and race discrimination, and improved working conditions for women office workers. Works to introduce legislation or regulations at state level to protect video display terminal operators. Produces studies and research in areas such as reproductive hazards of Video Display Terminals (VDTs), automation's effect on clerical employment, family and medical leaves, and stress.

★10106★ Nine to Five Working Women Education Fund (WWEF)

614 Superior Ave. NW
Cleveland, OH 44113
Ph: (216)274-0933   Fax: (216)272-2870

Purpose: Conducts research on the concerns of women office workers. Topics include: the future of office work; automation; health and safety issues; affirmative action; family and medical leave; pay equity; flextime; job-sharing. **Activities:** Conducts public presentations and seminars upon request; provides speakers. Compiles statistics; has conducted a national survey on women and stress.

★10107★ Organization of Chinese American Women (OCAW)

1300 N St. NW, Ste. 100
Washington, DC 20005
Ph: (202)638-0330   Fax: (202)638-2196

Purpose: Advances the cause of Chinese American women in the U.S. and fosters public awareness of their special needs and concerns. Seeks to integrate Chinese American women into the mainstream of women's activities and programs. Addresses issues such as equal employment opportunities at both the professional and nonprofessional levels; overcoming stereotypes; racial and sexual discrimination and restrictive traditional beliefs; assistance to poverty-stricken recent immigrants; access to leadership and policymaking positions. Develops training models for Chinese and Asian American women. **Activities:** Conducts training and job placement for class participants, widening teenage women's career choices, and networking for Chinese American women.

★10108★ Tradeswomen, Inc.

PO Box 40664 B
San Francisco, CA 94140
Ph: (415)821-7334   Fax: (415)861-8969

Members: Women who work in nontraditional, blue-collar occupations including construction, transportation, and industrial work; women who seek to enter these fields or who support the right of others to do so. **Purpose:** Serves as a network for women in the trades. Conducts social gatherings and local and regional forums on topics such as: health and safety on the job; racism and sexism in the trades; sexual harassment; working within unions. Makes available children's services; maintains speakers' bureau. Compiles statistics.

★10109★ Wider Opportunities for Women (WOW)

1325 G St. NW, Lower Level
Washington, DC 20005
Ph: (202)638-3143   Fax: (202)638-4885

Purpose: To expand employment opportunities for women through information, employment training, technical assistance, and advocacy. Works to overcome barriers to women's employment and economic equity, including occupational segregation, sex stereotypic education and training, discrimination in employment practices and wages. Sponsors Women's Work Force Network, a national network of 500 women's employment programs and advocates. The network monitors current policies to increase the priority given to employment needs of women; provides information to congressional staffs to clarify the impact of various legislative proposals on women; issues public policy alerts and informational materials when relevant federal policy is being proposed or undergoing revision; conducts investigative projects to assess how legislative programs are im-

plemented and their impact on women. Offers technical assistance to education institutions, government agencies, and private industry on programs to increase women's participation in non-traditional employment and training. Maintains National Commission on Working Women and Industry Advisory Council.

★10110★ Women Employed (WE)

22 W. Monroe, Ste. 1400
Chicago, IL 60603
Ph: (312)782-3902   Fax: (312)782-5249

Members: Working women and women seeking employment. **Purpose:** Helps women improve their jobs and employment opportunities. **Activities:** Conducts advocacy efforts on issues including pay equity, sexual harassment, and nontraditional jobs for women. Offers career development services that include seminars, counseling, networking opportunities and a job-bank. Monitors government enforcement of equal opportunity laws. Conducts public education programs on issues concerning working women. Sponsors Women Employed Institute.

★10111★ Women Employed Institute (WEI)

22 W. Monroe, Ste. 1400
Chicago, IL 60603
Ph: (312)782-3902   Fax: (312)782-5249

Purpose: Research and education division of Women Employed devoted to promoting economic equity for women. Analyzes government programs and employer policies; develops recommendations for public and corporate policy to promote equal opportunity. Sponsors advocacy programs to increase women's accessibility to vocational education and training for higher paying, nontraditional jobs. Develops model employment awareness/readiness programs for disadvantaged women. Conducts research projects; compiles statistics on women's economic status.

★10112★ Women Work! The National Network for Women's Employment

1625 K St. NW, Ste. 300
Washington, DC 20006
Ph: (202)467-6346   Fax: (202)467-5366
Fr: 800-235-2732

Members: Displaced homemakers and single

parents, women's training services, persons from related organizations, and supporters. **Purpose:** Fosters development of programs and services for women preparing for the workforce. Acts as clearinghouse to provide communications, technical assistance, public information, data collection, legislative monitoring, funding information, and other services. Compiles statistics. Provides referrals, information on research in progress, and publication distribution.

★10113★ Women's Information Bank (WIB)

3918 W St. NW
Washington, DC 20007
Ph: (202)338-8163   Fax: (202)337-9096

Purpose: Informal network of individuals who aid women seeking business partners and start-up capital, freelance work opportunities, short-term housing and home exchanges in Washington and other major cities, travel partners, and employment and educational opportunities. **Activities:** Operates Global Women's Network, which helps women travelers locate individuals with similar interests in several American cities. Maintains placement services.

★10114★ Women's Yellow Pages

Nancy Sardella
13601 Ventura Blvd., No. 374
Sherman Oaks, CA 91423
Ph: (818)995-6646

Annual, April. $10.95, plus $1.00 shipping. Covers over 1,400 women's businesses, services, and organizations in Los Angeles and Orange counties and nearby areas of southern California; includes lists of Equal Opportunity Employers and community resources, such as other women's directories. Entries include: Company or organization name, address, phone; product or service provided, field of interest. Alternate phone number is (714)520-4620 or (909)467-1439. Arrangement: Classified by type of business or organization.

Outplacement

REFERENCE WORKS

★10115★ Directory of Outplacement Firms

Kennedy Publications
Templeton Rd.
Fitzwilliam, NH 03447
Ph: (603)585-6544   Fax: (603)585-9555
Fr: 800-531-0007

Biennial, August of even years. $74.95, plus $7.00 shipping. Covers over 240 consulting firms with special interest in outplacement or de-hiring counseling executive employees being terminated because of poor performance, plant closings, etc., and assisting them in finding new jobs; firms that are compensated only by employers and those that also accept compensation from individuals are listed. Entries include: Firm name, address, phone, description of philosophy and services, names and titles of principals, branches, area served, year established, revenue (within wide ranges), professional affiliations, minimum salary of positions handled, number of staff, percentage of business devoted to outplacement. Arrangement: Separate sections on basis of compensation arrangements, then alphabetical. Indexes: Geographical, personal name.

★10116★ The 40+ Job Hunting Guide

Facts on File, Inc.
11 Penn Plaza, 15th Fl.
New York, NY 10001-2006
Ph: (212)967-8800   Fax: 800-678-3633
Fr: 800-322-8755

E. Patricia Birsner. Third edition, 1995. $24.95. Approaches job search as a business problem-solving activity and provides advice on emotional and practical aspects of searching and interviewing.

★10117★ Out the Organization: New Career Opportunities for the 1990's

Consultants Bookstore
Templeton Rd.
Fitzwilliam, NH 03447
Ph: (603)585-6544   Fax: (603)585-9555
Fr: 800-531-0007

Madeleine Swain. 1992. $12.95. 250 pages. Offers advice to the mid-career executive whose job is no longer satisfying or safe. Discusses survival strategies, getting fired and its resulting emotions, and options, counseling, and strategy for the future.

★10118★ Rites of Passage at $100,000-Plus: The Insider's Guide to Absolutely Everything About Executive Job-Changing

Henry Holt
John Lucht. Revised edition, 1993. $29.95. 640 pages. Aimed at top executives, this book covers a range of topics from networking and personal contacts to direct mail, resumes, references, interviewing, and negotiating. Includes large section on dealing with recruiters.

★10119★ Starting Over: You in the New Workplace

Palomino Press
86-07 144 St.
Briarwood, NY 11435
Ph: (718)297-5053

Jo Danna. $12.95. 260 pages.

NEWSPAPERS, MAGAZINES, AND JOURNALS

★10120★ Self-Help Reporter

National Self-Help Clearinghouse (NSHC)
25 W. 43rd St., Rm. 620
New York, NY 10036-7406
Ph: (212)354-8525   Fax: (212)642-1956

Quarterly. Newsletter.

AUDIO/VISUAL RESOURCES

★10121★ Fired and Re-focused

CareerLab Books
9085 E. Mineral Cir., Ste. 330
Englewood, CO 80112
Ph: (303)790-0505   Fax: (303)790-0606
Fr: 800-723-9675

Video. $59.95. 30 minutes. Discusses job search strategies following job loss.

★10122★ From Pink Slip to Paycheck

Career Communications, Inc.
PO Box 169
Harleysville, PA 19438
Ph: (215)256-3130   Fax: (215)256-3136
Fr: 800-346-1848

Series of 5 videos. $349.00/set. $79.00/each. 12 minutes each. Designed for mature job seekers suffering job loss. Individual titles cover job search strategies, feeling positive, interviewing, resume writing, and networking.

★10123★ Getting Fired, Getting Hired: Job Hunting from A to Z

CareerLab Books
9085 E. Mineral Circle, Ste. 330
Englewood, CO 80112
Ph: (303)790-0505   Fax: (303)790-0606
Fr: 800-723-9675

Series of 6 videos. $249.95/set. $59.95/each. 30 minutes each. Individual titles cover aspects of the job search following job loss.

OTHER SOURCES

★10124★ Association of Outplacement Consulting Firms International (AOCFI)

1200 19th St. NW, Ste. 300
Washington, DC 20036
Ph: (202)857-1185   Fax: (202)857-1115

Members: Firms providing displaced employees, who are sponsored by their organization, with counsel and assistance in job searching and the techniques and practices of choosing a career. **Purpose:** To develop, improve, and encourage the art and science of outplacement consulting and the professional standards of competence, objectivity, and integrity in the service of clients. Cooperates with other industrial, technical, educational, professional, and governmental bodies in areas of mutual interest and concern.

★10125★ International Association of Career Consulting Firms (IACCF)
11250 Roger Bacon Dr., Ste. 8
Reston, VA 22090-5202
Ph: (703)525-1191   Fax: (703)276-8146

Members: Firms offering career counseling and outplacement services to business executives. (Outplacement services constitute training designed to prepare individuals for new careers while easing them out of their present jobs.) **Purpose:** Works to establish and advocate adherence to industry ethics; provides professional training and certification. Helps prepare legislation pertinent to the industry. Seeks to increase public acceptance of outplacement programs.

★10126★ National Self-Help Clearinghouse (NSHC)
25 W. 43rd St., Rm. 620
New York, NY 10036-7406
Ph: (212)354-8525   Fax: (212)642-1956

Purpose: Clearinghouse on selfhelp groups; provides referral services. Conducts research and training activities. Maintains speakers' bureau.

Self Employment

★10127★ Becoming Self-Employed
Live Oak Publications
1515 23rd St.
PO Box 2193
Boulder, CO 80306
Ph: (303)447-1087

Susan Elliot. Second edition, 1994. $9.95. 160 pages. Illustrated.

★10128★ Change Your Job, Change Your Life: High Impact Strategies for Finding Great Jobs in the 90's
Impact Publications
9104-N Manassas Dr.
Manassas Park, VA 22111-5211
Ph: (703)361-7300   Fax: (703)335-9486

Ronald Krannich. Fourth edition, 1994. $14.95. 368 pages. Details trends in the marketplace, how to identify opportunities, how to retrain for them, and how to land jobs. Includes a chapter on starting a business. Contains index, bibliography, and illustrations.

★10129★ Entrepreneur's Buyer's Guide to Franchise and Business Opportunities
Entrepreneur, Inc.
2392 Morse Ave.
Irvine, CA 92714
Ph: (714)261-2325   Fax: (714)755-4211
Fr: 800-421-2300

Annual, September. $3.95, plus $3.00 shipping. Covers over 15,000 franchise and business opportunities; coverage includes Canada. Entries include: Company name, address, phone, name of contact, description of opportunity, geographical areas available, costs. Arrangement: Classified by line of business.

★10130★ Franchise Opportunities Handbook
U.S. International Trade Administration
14th St. & Constitution Ave. NW
USDOC/TOP, Rm. 1322
Washington, DC 20230
Ph: (202)377-4203

Annual, fall. $15.00, payment with order. Covers over 1,400 franchisors in some 40 lines of business (auto rentals, campgrounds, foods, security systems, etc.). Entries include: Company name, address, name of contact, description of the business operation franchised, number of franchisees, date company began, amount of capital needed, whether financial assistance is available, and what training and managerial assistance are provided. Also includes general information on securing franchises and operating franchised businesses. Users of the directory are cautioned that the Commerce Department has not verified statements in the listings for the various franchisors. Arrangement: Classified by type of business.

★10131★ Free Help from Uncle Sam to Start Your Own Business or Expand the One You Have
Puma Publishing
1670 Coral Dr.
Santa Maria, CA 93454
Ph: (805)925-3216   Fr: 800-255-5730

William M. Alarid and Gustav Berle. Third edition, 1992. $13.95. 300 pages.

★10132★ Government Giveaways for Entrepreneurs
Information USA, Inc.
PO Box E
Kensington, MD 20895
Ph: (301)942-0556   Fax: (301)924-1329
Fr: 800-955-POWER

Biennial, even years. $37.95. Covers about 300 government programs and 9,000 sources of free help for persons wanting to start or expand a business. Arrangement: Geographical.

★10133★ Guide to Self-Employment
John Wiley & Sons, Inc.
605 3rd Ave.
New York, NY 10158-0012
Ph: (212)850-6000   Fr: 800-225-5945

National Business Employment Weekly. $12.95 (paper).

★10134★ Home Business Made Easy
Todd Publications
PO Box 301
West Nyack, NY 10994
Fax: (914)358-6213   Fr: 800-747-1056

$15.00. Covers 153 different business that can be run from home full or part time based on interest, lifestyle, and finances.

★10135★ Home Businesses for Under $5,000.00
Sun Features Inc.
Box 368-P
Cardiff, CA 92007
Ph: (619)431-1660

Kennedy and Arden. 1995. $5.95.

★10136★ The Home Office and Small Business Success Book
Henry Holt Reference Books
Henry Holt & Co., Inc.
115 W. 18th St.
New York, NY 10012

Janet Attard. 1996. $19.95 (paper). Guide covering telecommunications and telecommuting trends.

★10137★ How to Become Self-Employed
Gordon Press Publishers
PO Box 459
Bowling Green Sta.
New York, NY 10004
Ph: (718)624-8419

1991. $66.95.

★10138★ How to Become Successfully Self-Employed

Bob Adams, Inc.
260 Center St.
Holbrook, MA 02343
Ph: (617)767-8100   Fax: (617)767-0994
Fr: 800-872-5627

Brian R. Smith. Second edition, 1993. $9.95. 360 pages. Offers practical advice and removes the myths surrounding self-employment.

★10139★ How to Have a Brilliant Career Without Ever Having a Proper Job: The Active Guide to Self-Employment

Trans-Atlantic Publications, Inc.
311 Bainbridge St.
Philadelphia, PA 19147
Ph: (215)925-5083   Fax: (215)925-1912

Stuart Crainer. 1995. $43.50 (paper).

★10140★ How to Leave Your Job and Buy a Business of Your Own

McGraw Hill
1221 Avenue of the Americas
New York, NY 10020
Ph: (212)512-2000   Fr: 800-262-4726

C.D. Peterson. 1992. $14.95. 224 pages. Provides advice on how to buy a business while still employed.

★10141★ How to Run Your Own Home Business

VGM Career Horizons
4255 W. Touhy Ave.
Lincolnwood, IL 60646-1975
Ph: (847)679-5500   Fax: (847)679-2494
Fr: 800-323-4900

Coralee Smith Kern and Tammara Hoffman Wolfgram. Third edition, 1994. $9.95. 192 pages. Helps the reader determine if he/she is suited to working at home, choose a product or service, set up a comfortable, efficient working environment, and keep abreast of zoning and tax laws.

★10142★ How to Start and Operate a Home-Based Word Processing or Desktop Publishing Business

Bob Adams, Inc.
260 Center St.
Holbrook, MA 02343
Ph: (617)767-8100   Fax: (617)767-0994
Fr: 800-872-5627

Michele Loftus. 1990. $9.95. 192 pages. Offers advice on making advertising decisions, obtaining clients, developing a business identity, setting prices, keeping the books, rating and selecting software and equipment, and keeping client relationships strong.

★10143★ How You Can Buy a Business Without Overpaying

The Consultant Press Ltd.
163 Amsterdam Ave., No. 201
PO Box 687
New York, NY 10023
Ph: (212)838-8640

Gary L. Schine. 1991. $24.95. 128 pages. Includes sources for finding businesses that are available to buy, categories of business,

an understanding of the psychology of the seller, methods for determining what the business is worth, advice on negotiating and financing the deal, and sample forms.

★10144★ The Ideal Entrepreneurial Business for You

John Wiley & Sons, Inc.
605 3rd Ave.
New York, NY 10158-0012
Ph: (212)850-6000   Fr: 800-225-5945

Glenn Desmond and Monica Faulkner. $16.95 (paper).

★10145★ Inc. Your Dreams

Penguin USA
375 Hudson St.
New York, NY 10014
Ph: (212)366-2000   Fax: (212)366-2666

Rebecca Maddox. $11.95 (paper).

★10146★ Marketing for the Home-based Business

Bob Adams, Inc.
260 Center St.
Holbrook, MA 02343
Ph: (617)767-8100   Fax: (617)767-0994
Fr: 800-872-5627

Jeffrey P. Davidson. 1990. $9.95. 204 pages. Addresses how to market the home-based business after you've started it.

★10147★ Minority Business Information Resource Directory

Try Us Resources, Inc.
2105 Central Ave. NE
Minneapolis, MN 55418
Ph: (612)781-6819   Fax: (612)781-0109
Fr: 800-627-4347

Annual, January. $27.00. Covers business opportunity fairs, seminars, and workshops; National Supplier Development Council regional offices; Small Business Administration and Minority Business Development Administration offices; minority business directories; and other resources for minority businesses.

★10148★ Money Sources for Small Business—How You Can Find Private, State, Federal, and Corporate Financing

Puma Publishing
1670 Coral Dr.
Santa Maria, CA 93454
Ph: (805)925-3216   Fax: (805)925-2656
Fr: 800-255-5730

Published January 1991. $19.95. Covers sources of financing for small businesses. Entries include: Company or organization name, address, phone, name and title of contact, geographical area served, financial data. Arrangement: Classified by line of funding. Indexes: Subject, company or organization, name, geographical.

★10149★ NBIA Directory of Business Incubators and Members

National Business Incubation Association (NBIA)
20 Circle Ln., Ste. 190
Athens, OH 45701-3211
Ph: (614)593-4331   Fax: (614)593-1996

Annual, October. Available to members only. Covers approximately 520 facilities that house small businesses in the beginning stage of development; coverage includes Canada. Entries include: Facility name, address, phone; name and title of contact; year opened; sponsorship; square footage; type and number of clients; incubator sponsor information. Arrangement: Geographical.

★10150★ Network of Small Businesses—Membership Directory

Network of Small Businesses (NSB)
5420 Mayfield Rd., Ste. 205
Lyndhurst, OH 44124
Ph: (216)442-5600   Fax: (216)449-3227

Approximately annual; previous edition April 1992; latest edition August 1993. Covers owners and others involved in small businesses (defined as 500 employees or less). Includes lists of inventors, innovators, engineers, and scientists. Entries include: Company name, address, phone, names and titles of key personnel. Arrangement: Alphabetical. Indexes: Company owner.

★10151★ On Your Own: A Guide to Working Happily, Productively & Successfully at Home

Prentice Hall
113 Sylvan Ave., Rte. 9W
Englewood Cliffs, NJ 07632
Ph: (201)592-2000   Fax: 800-445-6991
Fr: 800-922-0579

Lionel L. Fisher. 1994. $10.95 (paper),

★10152★ The Perfect Business: How to Make a Million from Home with No Payroll, No Employee Headaches, No Debt, and No Sleepless Nights

Simon & Schuster, Inc.
1230 Avenue of the Americas
New York, NY 10020
Ph: (212)698-7000   Fr: 800-223-2348

Michael LeBoeuf. $22.00

★10153★ Resource Guide for the Self-Employed

Ingraham Computer Services
13439 Elevation Ln.
Herndon, VA 22071
Ph: (703)318-0634

Latest edition November 1991; new edition expected. $10.00 postpaid. Covers 125 nationwide associations, government agencies, periodicals, books, catalogs and online services of interest to self-employed people. Arrangement: Classified by category.

★10154★ The Self-Employment Survival Manual: How to Start and Operate a One-Person Business Successfully

A. William Benitez Ltd.
PO Box 43233
Austin, TX 78745
Ph: (512)447-4744   Fax: (512)292-1778
Fr: 800-887-4017

A. William Benitez. 1993. $18.95 (paper).

★10155★ Selling Your Services: Proven Strategies for Getting Clients to Hire You (Or Your Firm)

Henry Holt & Company, Inc.
115 W. 18th St.
New York, NY 10011
Ph: (212)886-9200   Fax: (212)633-0748
Fr: 800-488-5233

Robert W. Bly. 1991. $24.95; $14.95 (paper).

★10156★ Small Business Network— National Directory

Small Business Network
Box 30149
Baltimore, MD 21270
Ph: (410)581-1373

Annual, summer. Available to members only. Covers businesses involved in assisting the development and support of small business.

★10157★ Small Business Sourcebook

Gale Research
835 Penobscot Bldg.
Detroit, MI 48226-4094
Ph: (313)961-2242   Fax: (313)961-6083
Fr: 800-877-GALE

Annual, October. $260.00. Contains profiles for 322 specific types of small business. Each profile contains sources of start-up information, associations, educational programs, reference works, sources of supplies, statistical sources, trade periodicals, videos, trade shows and conventions, consultants, franchises, databases, business systems and software, information services, libraries, and research centers. Publication also lists sources of general small business information and assistance, including federal and state government agencies; professional associations; small business development centers; educational programs; consultants; venture capital firms; SCORE (Service Corps of Retired Executives) offices; incubators; and related publications. Entries include: Generally, entries list organization, event, or publication name, address, phone; description of contents, activities, services, publication, or programs; and other details relevant to the type of source, such as show dates and location, investment preferences and limitations, etc. Arrangement: Volume 1 contains small business profiles A-O; volume 2 contains profiles P-Z, plus general small business topics, state listings, federal government assistance. Indexes: Alphabetical.

★10158★ Small Time Operator: How to Start Your Own Small Business, Keep Your Books, Pay Your Taxes, and Stay out of Trouble!

Bell Springs Publishing
Box 640
Bell Springs Rd.
Laytonville, CA 95454
Ph: (707)984-6746

Bernard Kamoroff. Nineteenth edition, 1995. $16.95. 224 pages.

★10159★ Start Up: An Entrepreneur's Guide to Launching and Managing a New Business

The Career Press, Inc.
3 Tice Rd.
PO Box 687
Franklin Lakes, NJ 07417
Ph: (201)848-0310   Fax: (201)848-1727
Fr: 800-237-3371

William Stolze. Third edition, 1994. $16.95. Written for the reader about to embark on a new venture or who has started a business within the past few years. Addresses key problems crucial to the small business owner, such as adequacy of funding and how to write a business plan.

★10160★ The States and Small Business: A Directory of Programs and Activities

Office of Advocacy
Small Business Administration
Mail Code 3114
Washington, DC 20416
Ph: (202)205-6958   Fax: (202)512-2250

Irregular, latest edition March 1993. $21.00. Covers over 750 state government small business offices, legislative committees, small business conferences. Entries include: Agency name, address, phone; name and title of contact; description of activities; summary of small business legislation, etc. Arrangement: Geographical.

★10161★ Successfully Self-Employed

Dearborn Trade
155 N. Wacker Dr.
Chicago, IL 60606
Fax: (312)836-1146   Fr: 800-245-2665

Gregory Brennan. 1996. $16.95 (paper).

★10162★ Venture Capital Directory

Forum Publishing Co.
383 E. Main St.
Centerport, NY 11721
Ph: (516)754-5000

Annual, February. $12.95. Covers over 500 members of the Small Business Administration and the Small Business Investment Company that provide funding for small and minority businesses. Entries include: Company name, address, phone, names and titles of key personnel, geographical area served, financial data, branch office or subsidiary names, description of services and projects. Arrangement: Alphabetical.

★10163★ Working Solo Sourcebook: Essential Resources for Independent Entrepreneurs

Portico Press
PO Box 190
New Paltz, NY 12561-0190
Ph: (914)255-7165   Fax: (914)255-2116
Fr: 800-222-7656

Terri Lonier. 1995. $24.95.

★10164★ Worldwide Franchise Directory

Gale Research
835 Penobscot Bldg.
Detroit, MI 48226-4094
Ph: (313)961-2242   Fax: (313)961-6083
Fr: 800-877-GALE

1991. $129.50. Lists over 2,000 franchises, including U.S. and Canadian companies and those based in other countries. Covers franchisors that operate internationally, plan to expand internationally, or have at least 10 outlets currently operating in their home country. Each profile provides 'highlights' and a general description, a background sketch on the franchisor, start-up and agreement information, foreign outlet contacts, and profile sources. Arrangement: Alphabetically under a primary franchise type category. Indexes: Master name and keyword, geographic, and personal name.

NEWSPAPERS, MAGAZINES, AND JOURNALS

★10165★ Entrepreneur Magazine

Entrepreneur, Inc.
2392 Morse Ave.
Irvine, CA 92714
Ph: (714)261-2325   Fax: (714)755-4211

Monthly. $19.97/year for individuals. Magazine covering small business management and operation.

★10166★ Franchising World

International Franchise Association
1350 New York Ave. NW, Ste. #900
Washington, DC 20005
Ph: (202)628-8000   Fax: (202)628-0812

Bimonthly. $12.00/year for individuals; $2.50/year for single issue. Trade magazine covering topics of interest to franchise company executives and the business world.

★10167★ Homeworking Mothers

Mother's Home Business Network
PO Box 423
East Meadow, NY 11554
Ph: (516)997-7394   Fax: (516)997-0839

Quarterly. Included in membership. Aims to inform and inspire mothers who choose to work at home. Explains how to get started in specific businesses and offers articles written by women who successfully combine motherhood with a money-making home business. Recurring features include book excerpts and columns titled: Take Note, It's My Business, Considering the Possibilities, Time Out for Kids, and Advice for Homeworking Mothers.

★10168★ *In Business*

The JG Press, Inc.
419 State Ave.
Emmaus, PA 18049
Ph: (215)967-4135

Bimonthly. Small business management magazine.

★10169★ *Income Opportunities*

IO Publications, Inc.
1500 Broadway
New York, NY 10036-4015
Ph: (212)642-0600   Fax: (212)302-8269

$19.95/year. Magazine focusing on money-making opportunities.

★10170★ *Spare Time*

Kipen Publishing Corp.
5810 W. Oklahoma Ave.
Milwaukee, WI 53219-4384
Ph: (414)543-8110   Fax: (414)543-9767

$16.95/year for individuals. Magazine featuring articles on business start-up and money-making opportunities.

AUDIO/VISUAL RESOURCES

★10171★ *Day in a Career: Entrepreneur*

Cambridge Career Products
PO Box 2153
Dept. CC15
Charleston, WV 25328-2153
Ph: (304)744-9323   Fax: (304)744-9351
Fr: 800-468-4227

Video. 1994. $89.00. 15-22 minutes. Includes candid interviews and work situations, plus outlines of relevant career information.

★10172★ *Teenage Entrepreneurs*

Educational Video Network
1401 Nineteenth St.
Huntsville, TX 77340
Ph: (409)295-5767   Fax: (409)294-0233

$79.95. Profiles teenage entrepreneurs who have found success in owning their own businesses.

ONLINE AND DATABASE SERVICES

★10173★ **Career Information System (CIS)**

Career Information System
1177 Pearl St.
Eugene, OR 97401
Ph: (503)346-3872

Online database. Provides career planning information, including occupational profiles; local, state, and national labor market trends; job search techniques; and self-employment options.

OTHER SOURCES

★10174★ *Contemporary Entrepreneurs*

Omnigraphics Inc.
2500 Penobscot Bldg.
Detroit, MI 48226
Ph: (313)961-1340   Fax: (313)961-1383
Fr: 800-875-1340

Published 1992. $95.00. Covers Approximately 74 companies often cited as successful and the entrepreneurs who founded them. Entries include: Entrepreneur's name, year of birth, marital status, number of children, type of venture; venture's address, phone, founding, incorporation, revenues, number of employees, original investment, net worth; text describing the history, growth, and vision of the company and entrepreneurial lessons.

Arrangement: Alphabetical by entrepreneur. Indexes: Combined company name, personal name, geographical, and product type index.

★10175★ *Directory of Business Incubators and University Research & Science Parks*

International Venture Capital Institute, Inc. (IVCI)
Baxter Associates, Inc.
PO Box 1333
Stamford, CT 06904
Ph: (203)323-3143   Fax: (203)838-5714

Annual. Covers Over 900 business incubators, university research parks, and science parks in the U.S. and Canada, that provide new businesses with such services as low-rent office space, accounting and legal services, business and financial advice, research and development, and marketing services. Entries include: Organization name, address, phone, services provided.

★10176★ **National Association for the Self-Employed (NASE)**

PO Box 612067
Dallas, TX 75261-2067
Fax: 800-551-4446   Fr: 800-232-NASE

Members: Self-employed and small independent businesspersons. **Purpose:** Acts as an advocate at the state and federal levels for self-employed people. Provides educational funding.

★10177★ *Small Business Reference Guide*

Bluechip Books
2606 3rd Ave.
Seattle, WA 98121
Ph: (206)448-0428

Irregular, latest edition 1991. $14.95. Covers over 350 firms, associations, and government agencies offering products and services of assistance to small businesses. Entries include: Organization name, address, phone; most listings also include description of services, products, or activities. Arrangement: Classified by product, service, or activity. Indexes: Book title, magazine title, publisher name, company name/subject.

Using Recruiters and Employment Agencies

847

REFERENCE WORKS

★10178★ American Directory of Job and Labor Market Information

Career Communications
PO Box 169
Harleysville, PA 19438

$29.95. Covers resources providing information on jobs and labor markets, including state and federal government personnel departments, job information centers, employment service centers, databases, libraries, and publications. Arrangement: Classified by type of resource.

★10179★ Atlanta Employment Services

Atlanta Chamber of Commerce
235 International Blvd.
Atlanta, GA 30301-1740
Ph: (404)880-9000   Fax: (404)586-8464

Annual. $2.00. Covers over 100 member executive search services, personnel consultants, personnel management, personnel services, and temporary personnel services in Atlanta, Georgia. Entries include: Company name, address, phone, description of employment specialty. Arrangement: Classified by type of service. Indexes: Organization name.

★10180★ The Best Directory of Recruiters, Agencies, Consultants

Gove Publishing Co.
1105 Lakeview Ave.
Dracut, MA 01826
Ph: (508)957-6600   Fax: (508)957-6605

Thomas P. Gove. 1993. $69.95 (paper).

★10181★ The Career Makers: America's Top 150 Executive Recruiters

Consultants Bookstore
Templeton Rd.
Fitzwilliam, NH 03447
Ph: (603)585-6544   Fax: (603)585-9555
Fr: 800-531-0007

John Sibbald. Second edition, 1995. $28.00. 408 pages. Profiles of top recruiters and guidance for working with search firms. Includes industry/functional cross-indexing.

★10182★ Directory of American Employment Agencies

Overseas Employment Services
PO Box 460
Mount Royal, PQ, Canada H3P 3C7
Ph: (514)739-1108   Fax: (514)739-0795

Annual, January. $15.00, postpaid. Covers Approximately 850 employment agencies and recruitment firms in the United States. Entries include: Company name, address, geographical area served, and description of services. Arrangement: Geographical.

★10183★ Directory of Canadian Employment Agencies

Overseas Employment Services
PO Box 460
Mount Royal, PQ, Canada H3P 3C7
Ph: (514)739-1108   Fax: (514)739-0795

Annual, January. $15.00. Covers about 600 employment agencies or recruitment firms located in the principal cities and towns of Canada. Entries include: Company name, address, geographical area served, and description of services. Arrangement: Geographical.

★10184★ The Directory of Employment Agencies

Overseas Employment Services
PO Box 460
Mount Royal, PQ, Canada H3P 3C7
Ph: (514)739-1108   Fax: (514)739-1108

Annual. $15.00. Covers 335 employment agencies in Canada, the U.S., and western Europe that specialize in overseas recruitment.

★10185★ The Directory of Executive Recruiters

Consultants Bookstore
Templeton Rd.
Fitzwilliam, NH 03447
Ph: (603)585-6544   Fax: (603)585-9555
Fr: 800-531-0007

James H. Kennedy. Twenty-fifth edition, 1995. $44.95 (paper). 900 pages. Lists and describes more than 3,200 firms in North America and indexes these by function, industry, and geographic area. Names key principals of recruiting firms. Includes narrative section on executive search and how it affects job candidates. Also available: Corpo-

rate Edition, expanded for use by corporate staffs, $99.00 (hardcover).

★10186★ Directory of U.S. Executive Search Firms

Market Advantage Group
51 Meadow Ridge
Avon, CT 06001
Ph: (203)673-2124   Fax: (203)593-5028

Biennial. $45.00. Covers over 2,700 executive search firms in the U.S., half of which work on a retained basis, the other half of which work mainly on a contingency basis. Entries include: Company name, address, phone, name and title of contact, description of firm, codes indicating firm's industry and functional specialization, minimum salary level handled. Arrangement: Alphabetical. Indexes: Geographical, industry specialization, functional specialization.

★10187★ Employment Agencies Directory

American Business Directories, Inc.
American Business Information, Inc.
5711 S. 86th Cir.
Omaha, NE 68127
Ph: (402)593-4600   Fax: (402)331-1505

Annual. $1,185.00, U.S. edition. Number of listings: 16,550 (U.S. edition); 1,780 (Canadian edition). Entries include: Name, address, phone (including area code), size of advertisement, year first in Yellow Pages, name of owner or manager, number of employees. Compiled from telephone company Yellow Pages, nationwide. Arrangement: Geographical.

★10188★ Employment Contractors-Temporary Help Directory

American Business Directories, Inc.
American Business Information, Inc.
5711 S. 86th Cir.
Omaha, NE 68127
Ph: (402)593-4600   Fax: (402)331-1505

Annual. $1,040.00, U.S. edition. Number of listings: 14,511 (U.S. edition); 730 (Canadian edition). Entries include: Name, address, phone (including area code), size of advertisement, year first in Yellow Pages, name of owner or manager, number of employees. Compiled from telephone company Yellow

Pages, nationwide. Arrangement: Geographical.

★10189★ **Executive Employment Guide**
AMACOM Books
American Management Association
135 W. 50th St.
New York, NY 10020
Ph: (212)903-7912   Fax: (212)903-8163

Monthly. $20.00. Covers over 150 executive search firms, personnel agencies, outplacement services, job registers, job counselors, resume writers, pre-employment investigators, and salary survey corporate guides. Entries include: Firm name, address, phone, subsidiary and branch names and locations, type of firm, kinds of positions handled, minimum salary of jobs handled, whether firm will review resumes and interview uninvited applicants, geographic placement capability. Arrangement: Alphabetical.

★10190★ **Executive Grapevine: The Directory of Executive Recruitment Consultants**
Executive Grapevine International Ltd.
4 Theobald Ct.
Theobald St.
Borehamwood, Herts. WD6 4RN, England
Ph: 81 9539939   Fax: 81 9539808

Annual, July. $99.00. Covers about 750 executive search firms in the United Kingdom. Entries include: Firm name, address, phone, telex, names and titles of key personnel, year established, description of services, job function and industry handled, salary range, geographic area covered, fees, guarantees, associations with other firms, branch offices and phones. Arrangement: Alphabetical. Indexes: Product/service, name, subject, geographical.

★10191★ **Executive Recruitment Firms**
JNN International, Inc.
6821 Sutherland Ct.
Mentor, OH 44060
Ph: (216)974-1959

Annual, September. $7.00, per volume. Covers firms providing services such as executive search, job counseling, and marketing (resume preparation, mailing, etc.); personnel agencies and job registers. Published in 18 industry-specific volumes under title, "Executive Recruitment Firms Specializing in (industry name)" and a general volume titled, "Executive Recruitment Firms Specializing in Most Industries". Entries include: Company name, contact name, address. Arrangement: Separate geographical sections for firms that do not charge fees and those that do charge.

★10192★ **Executive Search Consultants Directory**
American Business Directories, Inc.
American Business Information, Inc.
5711 S. 86th Cir.
Omaha, NE 68127
Ph: (402)593-4600   Fax: (402)331-1505

Annual. $460.00, payment with order. Entries include: Name, address, phone (including area code), size of advertisement, year first in Yellow Pages, name of owner or manager, number of employees. Compiled from telephone company Yellow Pages, nationwide. Arrangement: Geographical.

★10193★ **Executive Search Research Directory**
The Recruiting & Search Report
Box 9433
Panama City Beach, FL 32407
Ph: (904)235-3733   Fax: (904)233-9695
Fr: 800-634-4548

Biennial, with yearly updates. $88.00 postpaid. Covers over 300 freelance executive search researchers or independent executive search research firms that specialize in candidate locating, screening, and development for executive recruiters and corporate (inhouse) recruiters; publishers of directories, books, periodicals, and other resources related to recruitment research. Entries include: For researchers: name, address, phone, rates, year established, first year listed, whether a retainer relationship with the search firm is required, description of services and specialties, hourly rates. For resource publishers: name, address, phone, evaluation of publication. Arrangement: Researchers are geographical by zip code; publishers are classified by subject. Indexes: Geographical; means of industry or functional concentration; unusual expertise; specialty.

★10194★ **How to Get a Headhunter to Call**
Consultants Bookstore
Templeton Rd.
Fitzwilliam, NH 03447
Ph: (603)585-6544   Fax: (603)585-9555
Fr: 800-531-0007

Howard Freedman. 1989. $12.95. 165 pages.

★10195★ **International Directory of Employment Agencies**
Overseas Employment Services
PO Box 460
Mount Royal, PQ, Canada H3P 3C7
Ph: (514)739-1108   Fax: (514)739-0795

Annual, January. $15.00. Covers Approximately 500 employment agencies and recruitment firms in fifty countries located in Western Europe, the Far and Middle East, South Africa, South America, Central America, Australia, and southeast Asia. Entries include: Company name, address, geographical area served, and product/service. Arrangement: Geographical.

★10196★ **Job-Hunting: Should You Pay?**
Federal Trade Commission
Bureau of Consumer Protection
Public Reference, Rm. 130
Washington, DC 20580
Ph: (202)326-2222

Pamphlet. Free. 2 pages. Discusses criteria to use when selecting an employment service and when and whether the job seeker should pay the fee.

★10197★ **JobBank Guide to Employment Services**
Bob Adams, Inc.
260 Center St.
Holbrook, MA 02343
Ph: (617)767-8100   Fax: (617)767-0994
Fr: 800-872-5627

$150.00. Covers over 6,000 employment agencies, temporary help services, executive search firms, and career counseling services. Entries include: Company name, address, phone, fax, contact person, type of company, when founded, areas of specialization, positions filled, fee and appointment information, number of placements per year. Arrangement: Separate geographical and specialization sections.

★10198★ **Key European Executive Search Firms and Their U.S. Links**
Consultants Bookstore
Templeton Rd.
Fitzwilliam, NH 03447
Ph: (603)585-6544   Fax: (603)585-9555
Fr: 800-531-0007

James H. Kennedy. 1991. $39.00. 210 pages. Identifies linkages between more than 500 search offices in the United States and many European countries.

★10199★ **Knock 'Em Dead: The Ultimate Job Seeker's Handbook**
Bob Adams, Inc.
260 Center St.
Holbrook, MA 02343
Ph: (617)767-8100   Fax: (617)767-0994
Fr: 800-872-5627

Martin John Yate. 1994. $20.00; $10.95 (paper). Prepares the job seeker for the interview with advice on dress, manner, how to answer the toughest questions, and how to spot illegal questions. Discusses how to respond to questions of salary to maximize income. Features sections on executive search firms and drug testing.

★10200★ **National Directory of Personnel Service Firms**
National Association of Personnel Services
3133 Mt. Vernon Ave.
Alexandria, VA 22305
Ph: (703)684-0180   Fax: (703)684-0071

Annual, spring. $15.95, plus $5.00 shipping. Covers over 1,100 member private (for-profit) personnel service firms and temporary service firms. Entries include: Firm name, address, phone, fax, contact, area of specialization. Arrangement: Same information given geographically by employment specialty.

★10201★ **Rites of Passage at $100,000-Plus: The Insider's Guide to Absolutely Everything About Executive Job-Changing**
Henry Holt
John Lucht. Revised edition, 1993. $29.95. 640 pages. Aimed at top executives, this book covers a range of topics from networking and personal contacts to direct mail, resumes, references, interviewing, and negotiating. Includes large section on dealing with recruiters.

Working at Home

REFERENCE WORKS

★10202★ Complete Work-at-Home Companion: Everything You Need to Know to Prosper as a Home-Based Entrepreneur or Employee

Prima Publishing
3875 Atherton Rd.
Rocklin, CA 95765
Ph: (916)632-4400   Fax: (916)624-2385

Herman Holtz. 1993. $14.95.

★10203★ Complete Work-at-Home Directory and Idea Book

E. A. Morgan Publishing Co.
PO Box 1375
Huntington, NY 11743
Ph: (516)493-0285

Annual, March. $15.00. Covers about 275 organizations and companies that offer work at home business opportunities, information, and employment including mail order, dealer-ship/distributorship, and franchises. Entries include: Company or organization name, address, description of services, employment or business opportunity offered. Arrange-ment: Alphabetical.

★10204★ The Home-Based Entrepreneur: The Complete Guide to Working at Home

Upstart Publishing Co., Inc.
163 Central Ave., Ste. 4
Dover, NH 03820-4043
Ph: (603)749-5071   Fax: (603)742-9121
Fr: 800-235-8866

Linda Pinson. 1993. $19.95 (paper).

★10205★ Home Business Made Easy

Todd Publications
PO Box 301
West Nyack, NY 10994
Fax: (914)358-6213   Fr: 800-747-1056

$15.00. Covers 153 different business that can be run from home full or part time based on interest, lifestyle, and finances.

★10206★ Home Businesses for Under $5,000.00

Sun Features Inc.
Box 368-P
Cardiff, CA 92007
Ph: (619)431-1660

Kennedy and Arden. 1995. $5.95.

★10207★ The Home Office and Small Business Success Book

Henry Holt Reference Books
Henry Holt & Co., Inc.
115 W. 18th St.
New York, NY 10012

Janet Attard. 1996. $19.95 (paper). Guide covering telecommunications and telecom-muting trends.

★10208★ Home Work: Starting a Small Business-Starting at Home

Corey Stevens Publishing, Inc.
2111 E. Burnside St.
Portland, OR 97214
Ph: (503)230-4895   Fax: (503)230-9062

Jay Kimmel. 1994. $25.00 (paper).

★10209★ Homemade Money

Betterway Books
1507 Dana Ave.
Cincinnati, OH 45207
Ph: (513)717-0488   Fax: (513)531-4082
Fr: 800-289-0963

Irregular, latest edition February 1994. $19.95. Publication includes: List of more than 300 suppliers of information for owners of home-based businesses, including pub-lishers of books and periodicals, trade orga-nizations and associations, and government offices. Entries include: Supplier name, ad-dress, description of information, price, order information. Principal content of the book is editorial matter on beginning and developing a home-based business. Arrangement: Clas-sified by subject. Indexes: Alphabetical.

★10210★ How to Run Your Own Home Business

VGM Career Horizons
4255 W. Touhy Ave.
Lincolnwood, IL 60646-1975
Ph: (847)679-5500   Fax: (847)679-2494
Fr: 800-323-4900

Coralee Smith Kern and Tammara Hoffman

Wolfgram. Third edition, 1994. $9.95. 192 pages. Helps the reader determine if he/she is suited to working at home, choose a product or service, set up a comfortable, efficient working environment, and keep abreast of zoning and tax laws.

★10211★ How to Start and Operate a Home-Based Word Processing or Desktop Publishing Business

Bob Adams, Inc.
260 Center St.
Holbrook, MA 02343
Ph: (617)767-8100   Fax: (617)767-0994
Fr: 800-872-5627

Michele Loftus. 1990. $9.95. 192 pages. Offers advice on making advertising deci-sions, obtaining clients, developing a busi-ness identity, setting prices, keeping the books, rating and selecting software and equipment, and keeping client relationships strong.

★10212★ The Ideal Entrepreneurial Business for You

John Wiley & Sons, Inc.
605 3rd Ave.
New York, NY 10158-0012
Ph: (212)850-6000   Fr: 800-225-5945

Glenn Desmond and Monica Faulkner. $16.95 (paper).

★10213★ Jobs for People Who Love to Work from Home

Impact Publications
9104N Manassas Dr.
Manassas Park, VA 22111-5211
Ph: (703)361-7300   Fax: (703)335-9486

Krannich. 1996. $13.95 (paper).

★10214★ The Joy of Working from Home: Making a Life While Making a Living

Berrett-Koehler Publishers
155 Montgomery St.
San Francisco, CA 94104-4109
Ph: (415)288-0260   Fax: (415)362-2512
Fr: 800-929-2929

Jeff Berner. 1994. $12.95 (paper).

★**10215**★ *Marketing for the Home-based Business*

Bob Adams, Inc.
260 Center St.
Holbrook, MA 02343
Ph: (617)767-8100   Fax: (617)767-0994
Fr: 800-872-5627

Jeffrey P. Davidson. 1990. $9.95. 204 pages. Addresses how to market the home-based business after you've started it.

★**10216**★ *On Your Own: A Guide to Working Happily, Productively & Successfully at Home*

Prentice Hall
113 Sylvan Ave., Rte. 9W
Englewood Cliffs, NJ 07632
Ph: (201)592-2000   Fax: 800-445-6991
Fr: 800-922-0579

Lionel L. Fisher. 1994. $10.95 (paper),

★**10217**★ *100 Best Careers for the Year 2000*

Prentice Hall General Reference
15 Columbus Cir.
New York, NY 10023
Ph: (212)373-8500   Fr: 800-223-2348

Shelly Field. 1992. $15.00 (paper). Covers 100 of the fastest growing jobs. The publication is divided into 11 general employment sections. Specific careers are covered within each section. Provides job description, responsibilities, employment opportunities, earnings, education and training, advancement opportunities, and experience and qualifications for each occupation.

★**10218**★ *The Perfect Business: How to Make a Million from Home with No Payroll, No Employee Headaches, No Debt, and No Sleepless Nights*

Simon & Schuster, Inc.
1230 Avenue of the Americas
New York, NY 10020
Ph: (212)698-7000   Fr: 800-223-2348

Michael LeBoeuf. $22.00

★**10219**★ *The Selling-From-Home Sourcebook*

Betterway Books
1507 Dana Ave.
Cincinnati, OH 45207
Ph: (513)717-0488   Fax: (513)531-4082
Fr: 800-289-0963

Kathryn Caputo. 1995. $17.99 (paper).

★**10220**★ *Starting a Home Based Business (Full or Part-Time)*

Carol Publishing Group
600 Madison Ave., 11th Fl.
New York, NY 10022
Ph: (212)486-2200   Fax: (212)486-2231

Irene Korn. 1993. $8.95 (paper).

★**10221**★ *Thy Neighbor's Talent— Directory of Cottage Industry Show Dates*

Zoe McClintock
HCR 1, Box 75
Baldwin, ND 58521
Ph: (701)255-0352

Monthly. $18.95. Covers over 1,000 arts and crafts fairs, flea markets, and specialty show dates in Idaho, Minnesota, Montana, North Dakota, South Dakota, Washington, Wisconsin, and Wyoming. Entries include: Event name, date of occurrence, location, phone, and contact name and address. Arrangement: Chronological.

★**10222**★ *Work-at-Home Sourcebook*

Live Oak Publications
Box 2193
Boulder, CO 80306
Ph: (303)447-1087   Fax: (303)447-8684

Biennial, January of even years. $16.95, plus 3.00 shipping. Covers over 1,000 companies and home business franchises that employ home workers. Entries include: Company name, address, contact person, description of job position, pay scale, requirements, equipment, and training provided. Arrangement: Classified by occupational category. Indexes: Alphabetical, geographical.

★**10223**★ *Working From Home: Everything You Need to Know About Living and Working Under the Same Roof*

Jeremy P. Tarcher, Inc.
11150 W. Olympic Blvd., Ste. 600
Los Angeles, CA 90064-1823
Ph: (213)935-9980   Fax: (310)273-5732

Paul Edwards. 1990. $14.95 (paper).

★**10224**★ *Working from Home: Telecommuting*

Crisp Publications, Inc.
1200 Hamilton Ct.
Menlo Park, CA 94025
Ph: (415)323-6100   Fax: (415)323-5800
Fr: 800-442-7477

Philip Gerould, editor. 1994. $9.95 (paper).

Newspapers, Magazines, and Journals

★**10225**★ *Homeworking Mothers*

Mother's Home Business Network
PO Box 423
East Meadow, NY 11554
Ph: (516)997-7394   Fax: (516)997-0839

Quarterly. Included in membership. Aims to inform and inspire mothers who choose to work at home. Explains how to get started in specific businesses and offers articles written by women who successfully combine motherhood with a money-making home business. Recurring features include book excerpts and columns titled: Take Note, It's My Business, Considering the Possibilities, Time Out for Kids, and Advice for Homeworking Mothers.

★**10226**★ *The National Work at Home Catalog*

U.M.R.C., Inc.
PO Box 2712
Huntington Beach, CA 92647

Quarterly. $6.00/year; $3.00 for single issue. Pamphlet listing companies that offer work-at-home business opportunities.

★**10227**★ *Spare Time*

Kipen Publishing Corp.
5810 W. Oklahoma Ave.
Milwaukee, WI 53219-4384
Ph: (414)543-8110   Fax: (414)543-9767

$16.95/year for individuals. Magazine featuring articles on business start-up and money-making opportunities.

★**10228**★ *Working at Home*

Mrs. H.C. McGarity
PO Box 200504
Cartersville, GA 30120
Ph: (404)386-1257

Quarterly. $12.00 for five issues. Provides short articles about work-at-home opportunities for women who are unable to work outside the home.

Online and Database Services

★**10229**★ **Working From Home Forum**

CompuServe Information Service
5000 Arlington Centre Blvd.
PO Box 20212
Columbus, OH 43220
Ph: (614)457-8600   Fax: (614)457-0348
Fr: 800-848-8199

Bulletin board. Contains information of interest to people working from home. Covers home-based businesses and telecommuting, consulting, freelancing, information brokering, publishing and mail order, marketing, accounting, insurance issues, legal and tax issues, and industry trends and developments.

Working Part-Time, Summer Employment, and Internships

REFERENCE WORKS

★10230★ The Access Guide to International Affairs Internships in The Washington, DC, Area
Access: A Security Information Service
1511 K St. NW, No. 643
Washington, DC 20005-1401
Ph: (202)785-6630   Fax: (202)785-3607
Bruce Seymore, editor. 1994. $17.95 (paper).

★10231★ Cents-Able Summer Self-Employment: An Entrepreneurial Guide for High School & College Students
Tamarax Press
PO Box 450
2A Taylor Way
Washington Crossing, PA 18977
Ph: (215)493-2136   Fax: (215)493-2057
E.K. Shepard. 1994. $12.95 (paper).

★10232★ Creating a Flexible Workplace: How to Select & Manage Alternative Work Options
AMACOM
135 W. 50th St., 15th Fl.
New York, NY 10020
Ph: (212)903-8315   Fax: (212)903-8168
Fr: 800-225-3215
Barney Olmsted. 1994. $59.95.

★10233★ Directory of Child Life Programs
Child Life Council
7910 Woodmont Ave., Ste. 310
Bethesda, MD 20814
Ph: (301)654-1343   Fax: (301)654-4964
Irregular. $22.00, plus $3.00 shipping. Covers Nearly 150 internships, fellowships, and other practical teaching experiences in hospitals for students of child life activity. Entries include: Facility name, address, phone, name of individual in charge of the practicum; number of hours and number of weeks for practicum; beginning dates, if specified; number of students accepted each term; total number of students accepted for the year; colleges from which students are generally referred; areas of study from which students

generally come; fees; stipend and other benefits; prerequisites; whether application is to be made to college or hospital; level of student generally accepted; practicum experiences available; form of evaluation. Arrangement: Geographical.

★10234★ Directory of International Internships
Dean's Office of International Studies and Programs
Michigan State University
International Center, Rm. 207
East Lansing, MI 48824
Ph: (517)353-5589   Fax: (517)353-7254
Irregular, latest edition 1994; new edition expected 1996. $25.00. Covers international internships sponsored by academic institutions, private corporations, and the federal government. Entries include: Institution name, address, phone, names and titles of key personnel, subject areas in which internships are available, number available, location, duration, financial data, academic credit available, evaluation procedures, application deadline, requirements of participation. Arrangement: Classified by type of sponsor, then alphabetical. Indexes: Sponsor, subject, geographical.

★10235★ Directory of Internships
Ready Reference Press
PO Box 5249
Santa Monica, CA 90409
Ph: (213)474-5175   Fr: 800-424-5627
$89.50. Out of print. Lists internship opportunities in many fields of interest, including, but not limited to arts, journalism, public relations, education, law, environmental affairs, business, engineering, and computer science. In addition, cites summer internship opportunities, work/study programs, and specialized opportunities for high school and undergraduate students. Indexed by subject, geography, and program.

★10236★ Free (& Almost Free) Adventures for Teenagers: Your Guide to the Top Low-Cost, Year-Round Programs & Internships
John Wiley & Sons, Inc.
605 3rd Ave.
New York, NY 10158-0012
Ph: (212)850-6000   Fr: 800-225-5945
Gail L. Grand. 1995. $14.95 (paper).

★10237★ Guide to Volunteer and Internship Programs in Public Broadcasting
Corporation for Public Broadcasting
Publications Dept.
901 E St. NW
Washington, DC 20004-2037
Ph: (202)879-9600
1991. Free.

★10238★ The Higher Education MoneyBook for Women & Minorities: A Directory of Scholarships, Fellowships, Internships, Grants & Loans
Young Enterprises International, Inc.
5937 16th. St., NW
Washington, DC 20011
Ph: (202)829-0039   Fax: (202)829-7809
Fr: 800-516-9960
Doris M. Young. 1996. $25.00 (paper).

★10239★ The Imaginative Soul's Guide to Foreign Internships: A Roadmap to Envision, Create and Arrange Your Own Experience
Ivy House
15 Sartwell Ave.
Somerville, MA 02144
Ph: (617)666-0216
Laura Hitchcock. 1993. $16.95 (paper).

★10240★ International Directory for Youth Internships
Council on International & Public Affairs
777 United Nations Plaza
New York, NY 10017
Ph: (212)972-9877   Fr: 800-316-2739
Latest edition 1993. $7.50, plus $3.00 shipping. Covers United Nations agencies and nongovernmental organizations offering intern and volunteer opportunities. Entries include: Agency, organization, or office name,

address, description of internship. Arrangement: Classified by type of organization.

★10241★ Internship Directory: Internships and Summer Jobs at Public Gardens

American Association of Botanical Gardens and Arboreta (AABGA)
786 Church Rd.
Wayne, PA 19087
Ph: (610)688-1120   Fax: (610)293-0149

Annual, October. $5.00. Covers over 130 gardens, arboreta, and other horticultural organizations that offer student internships and summer jobs. Entries include: Name of institution, address, name of contact, deadline for application, number of students hired, whether internships are available, employment period, hours, rate of pay, whether housing is available, other comments. Arrangement: Alphabetical.

★10242★ Internship Opportunities at the Smithsonian Institution

Office of Museum Programs
Smithsonian Institution
900 Jefferson Dr. SW, Rm. 2235
MRC 427
Washington, DC 20560
Ph: (202)357-3101   Fax: (202)357-3346

Irregular, latest edition 1994. $5.00. Covers Internship programs and projects in Washington DC, New York City, and Panama through the Smithsonian Institution. Entries include: Program name, address, phone, eligibility requirements, description. Arrangement: Classified by subject. Indexes: Subject.

★10243★ Internships

Peterson's Guides, Inc.
202 Carnegie Center
PO Box 2123
Princeton, NJ 08543-2123
Ph: (609)243-9111   Fax: (609)243-9150
Fr: 800-338-3282

Annual, October. $29.95. Covers 35,000 career-oriented internship positions with over 1,700 organizations in the U.S. ranging from business to theater, communications to science. Entries include: Company name, address, phone, name and title of contact, types of internships available, number of internships offered, salary where applicable, qualifications, how to apply. Arrangement: Classified by career field. Indexes: Geographical.

★10244★ Internships

Macmillan Publishing Co., Inc.
200 Old Tappan Rd.
Old Tappan, NJ 07675
Fax: 800-445-6991   Fr: 800-223-2336

Sara D. Gilbert. 1995. $18.95 (paper).

★10245★ Internships: A Directory for Career-Finders & Career-Changers

Macmillan Publishing Company, Inc.
200 Old Tappan Rd.
Old Tappan, NJ 07675
Fax: 800-445-6991   Fr: 800-223-2336

Sara D. Gilbert. 1994. $19.00.

★10246★ Internships for College Students Interested in Law, Medicine, and Politics

The Graduate Group
86 Norwood Rd.
West Hartford, CT 06117-2236
Ph: (203)232-3100

1994. $27.50.

★10247★ Internships in Communications

Iowa State University Press
2121 S. State Ave.
Ames, IA 50014
Ph: (515)292-0140   Fax: (515)292-3348
Fr: 800-862-6657

James P. Alexander. 1995. $14.95 (paper).

★10248★ Internships in Congress

The Graduate Group
86 Norwood Rd.
West Hartford, CT 06117-2236
Ph: (203)232-3100

1994. $27.50.

★10249★ Internships in Federal Government

The Graduate Group
86 Norwood Rd.
West Hartford, CT 06117-2236
Ph: (203)232-3100

1994. $27.50.

★10250★ Internships and Fellowships Information Pack

U.S. Capitol
Washington, DC 20510
Ph: (202)224-3121

Congressional Research Service. Ask for Report No. IPO631. Request from your representative in Congress at the address given above.

★10251★ Internships in Hawaii and California

The Graduate Group
86 Norwood Rd.
West Hartford, CT 06117-2236
Ph: (203)232-3100

1995. $27.50.

★10252★ Internships and Job Opportunities in New York City and Washington, DC

The Graduate Group
86 Norwood Rd.
West Hartford, CT 06117-2236
Ph: (203)232-3100

1994. $27.50.

★10253★ Internships for Law Students

The Graduate Group
86 Norwood Rd.
West Hartford, CT 06117-2236
Ph: (203)232-3100

1995. $27.50.

★10254★ Internships Leading to Careers

The Graduate Group
86 Norwood Rd.
West Hartford, CT 06117-2236
Ph: (203)232-3100

1994. $27.50.

★10255★ Internships: Learning by Doing

Chronicle Guidance Publications, Inc.
66 Aurora St.
PO Box 1190
Moravia, NY 13118-1190
Ph: (315)497-0330   Fax: (315)497-3359
Fr: 800-622-7284

Chronicle Guidance Staff. 1993. $2.00. Reprint of a journal article.

★10256★ Internships in State Government

The Graduate Group
86 Norwood Rd.
West Hartford, CT 06117-2236
Ph: (203)232-3100

1995. $27.50.

★10257★ Internships for 2-Year College Students

The Graduate Group
86 Norwood Rd.
West Hartford, CT 06117-2236
Ph: (203)232-3100

1995. $27.50.

★10258★ Jobs in Arts and Media Management: What They Are and How to Get One!

American Council for the Arts
1 E. 53rd St.
New York, NY 10022-4201
Ph: (212)223-2787   Fr: 800-321-4510

Stephen Langley and James Abruzzo. Revised edition, 1990. $21.95. 281 pages. Includes lists of about 150 sources of information on job opportunities in the arts, including organizations offering internships, job listings, graduate programs, and short-term study; professional groups concerned with theater, music, dance, opera, museum and gallery management, film, and telecommunication management. (Does not include popular music performing or music recording.) Entries include: For internships Organization name, address, phone, description, requirements. For job referral associations and periodicals - Association or publisher name, address, fields covered, services offered, turn-around time, average number of jobs, cost of subscription or dues, comments. Arrangement: Classified by type of source.

★10259★ Jobs in Paradise

HarperCollins Publishers, Inc.
10 E. 53rd St.
New York, NY 10022-5299
Ph: (212)207-7000   Fax: (212)207-7145
Fr: 800-331-3761

Jeffrey Maltzman. 1993. $13.00 (paper).

★10260★ *Magazines Career Directory*

Gale Research
835 Penobscot Bldg.
Detroit, MI 48226-4094
Ph: (313)961-2242   Fax: (313)961-6083
Fr: 800-877-GALE

Bradley Morgan. Fifth edition, 1993. $39.00. Features extensive listings of contacts and entry-level job opportunities at many magazine publishing organizations. Includes articles by top professionals in the field on some of the industry's varied career paths: art, editorial, sales, and business management.

★10261★ *National Directory of Arts Internships*

National Network for Artist Placement
935 W. Ave. 37
Los Angeles, CA 90065
Ph: (213)222-4035   Fax: (213)222-4035

Biennial, odd years. $40.00, postpaid; payment with order. Covers Approximately 2,000 internship opportunities in dance, music, theater, art, design, film, and video. Entries include: Name of sponsoring organization, address, name of contact; description of positions available, eligibility requirements, stipend or salary (if any), application procedures. Arrangement: Classified by discipline, then geographical.

★10262★ *National Directory of Internships*

National Society for Experiential Education
3509 Haworth Dr., Ste. 207
Raleigh, NC 27609-7229
Ph: (919)787-3263   Fax: (919)787-3381

Biennial, fall of odd years. $26.50, postpaid. Covers over 40,000 educational internship opportunities in 85 fields with over 670 organizations in the U.S. for youth and adults. Entries include: Organization name, address, phone, contact name, description of internship opportunities, including application procedures and deadlines, remuneration, and eligibility requirements. Arrangement: Classified by type of organization. Indexes: Geographical, organization name, career field.

★10263★ *New Careers Directory: Internships and Professional Opportunities in Technology and Social Change*

Student Pugwash USA
815 15th St. NW, Ste. 814
Washington, DC 20005
Ph: (202)393-6555   Fax: (202)393-6550
Fr: 800-WOW-A-PUG

Irregular; latest edition spring 1993. $13.00 for students; $21.00 for institutions, plus $3.00 shipping. Covers about 300 research institutes, think tanks, laboratories, government agencies, professional, science, and other non-profit organizations offering public policy, science, and technology internships and jobs. Entries include: Sponsoring organization name, description of organization, programs offered, work environment and application procedures, compensation offered. Arrangement: Alphabetical and classified by subject. Indexes: Geographical, subject.

★10264★ *New Internships for 1994-1995*

The Graduate Group
86 Norwood Rd.
West Hartford, CT 06117-2236
Ph: (203)232-3100

Robert Whitman, editor. 1995. $27.50.

★10265★ *989 Great Part-Time Jobs in Seattle: How to Find Internships, Temporary, Seasonal, Student & Free-Lance Work*

Barrett Street Productions
PO Box 99642
Seattle, WA 98199
Ph: (206)284-8202   Fax: (206)284-9928

Linda Carlson. 1994. $19.95 (paper).

★10266★ *Overseas Summer Jobs, 1995*

Peterson's Guides, Inc.
PO Box 2123
Princeton, NJ 08543-2123
Ph: (609)243-9111   Fax: (609)243-9150
Fr: 800-338-3282

1995. $14.95 (paper).

★10267★ *Paralegal Internships Manual*

Pearson Publications Co.
5910 N. Central Expy., Ste. 1070
Dallas, TX 75206
Ph: (214)891-6332   Fax: (214)891-6335

Charles P. Nemeth. 1995.

★10268★ *Peterson's Internships, 1996*

Peterson's Guides, Inc.
PO Box 2123
Princeton, NJ 08543-2123
Ph: (609)243-9111   Fax: (609)243-9150
Fr: 800-338-3282

1995. $21.95 (paper). Lists 35,000 paid and unpaid internships.

★10269★ *Peterson's Job Opportunities in Business 1996*

Peterson's
PO Box 2123
Princeton, NJ 08543-2123
Ph: (609)243-9111   Fax: (609)243-9150
Fr: 800-338-3282

Compiled by the Peterson's staff. Annual. $19.95 (paper). 416 pages. Profiles 2,000 companies that are hiring employees in a number of nontechnical fields, including financial services, management consulting, retailers, utilities, and consumer products companies. Contains job-search strategies and career options to help match education and expertise to the job market. Indexed geographically, by industry, and by hiring needs.

★10270★ *Peterson's Job Opportunities in Engineering and Technology 1996*

Peterson's
PO Box 2123
Princeton, NJ 08543-2123
Ph: (609)243-9111   Fax: (609)243-9150
Fr: 800-338-3282

Compiled by the Peterson's staff. Annual. $19.95 paperback. 432 pages. Profiles 2,000 high-tech companies looking primarily for technical personnel in such fields as biotechnology, telecommunications, software, computers and peripherals, defense, and aerospace. Contains job-search strategies and career options to help match education and expertise to the job market. Indexed geographically, by industry, and by hiring needs.

★10271★ *Peterson's Summer Jobs USA*

Peterson's Guides, Inc.
202 Carnegie Center
PO Box 2123
Princeton, NJ 08543-2123
Ph: (609)243-9111   Fax: (609)243-9150
Fr: 800-338-3282

$16.95. Covers 20,000 summer jobs in the U.S. for first-time employees to professionals. Entries include: Full descriptions of employers and jobs, contact information.

★10272★ *Peterson's Summer Opportunities for Kids and Teenagers 1996*

Peterson's
PO Box 2123
Princeton, NJ 08543-2123
Ph: (609)243-9111   Fax: (609)243-9150
Fr: 800-338-3282

Annual. $23.95 (paper). 1,000 pages. In addition to information about 1,400 summer activities and programs, covers job opportunities for high school and college students.

★10273★ *Princeton Review Student Access Guide: America's Top 100 Internships, Counselors, and Employers*

Random House, Inc.
201 E. 50th St., 22nd Fl.
New York, NY 10022
Ph: (212)751-2600   Fr: 800-733-3000

Mark Oldman. 1994. $16.00 (paper).

★10274★ *Seasonal Employment*

U.S. National Park Service
PO Box 37127
Washington, DC 20013-7127
Ph: (202)208-5074

Updated as needed. Free. Publication includes: List of 10 regional offices and branches of the National Park Service that accept applications for seasonal jobs. Entries include: Name, address, phone, geographical area served. Principal content of publication is information on seasonal jobs offered by the National Park Services, with description of duties, qualifications, and application procedures for each type of job offered. Arrangement: Geographical.

★10275★ *Storming Washington: An Intern's Guide to National Government*

American Political Science Association
1527 New Hampshire Ave., NW
Washington, DC 20036
Ph: (202)483-2512

Stephen E. Frantzich. Fourth edition, 1994. $3.00. 63 pages.

★10276★ Student Guide to Mass Media Internships

Intern Research Group
Box 52, Regent Hall
University of Colorado
Boulder, CO 80309
Ph: (303)442-8340

Annual, latest edition 1995. $35.00, payment with order; $40.00, billed. Covers about 10,000 internships offered by 2,700 newspapers, radio and television stations, cable television companies, magazines, advertising agencies, and other firms. Entries include: Organization name, address, type and number of internships offered, eligibility requirements, application deadline, salary or other stipend offered, name and title of contact; many listings also include description of intern's duties. Arrangement: Classified by type of medium, then geographical.

★10277★ Student Science Opportunities: Your Guide to Over 300 Exciting National Programs, Competitions, Internships, and Scholarships

John Wiley & Sons, Inc.
605 3rd Ave.
New York, NY 10158-0012
Ph: (212)850-6000   Fr: 800-225-5945

Gail L. Grand. 1994. $14.95 (paper).

★10278★ Summer Jobs in Britain

Vacation-Work Publications
9 Park End St.
Oxford OX1 1HJ, England
Ph: 865 241978   Fax: 865 790885

Annual, November. $15.95. Covers over 30,000 farm, hotel, au pair, voluntary, and other summer jobs in Scotland, Wales, England, the Channel Islands and Northern Ireland. Entries include: Employer name, address, positions offered, description of duties, length of service, wages, other amenities. Arrangement: Classified by line of work.

★10279★ Summer Jobs: Opportunities in the Federal Government

Office of Personnel Management
1900 E St. NW
Washington, DC 20415
Ph: (202)606-0950

Formerly annual; latest edition January 1993; suspended indefinitely. Free. Covers GS-1 through GS-4 clerical jobs and other jobs at GS-5 and above which are expected to be available in federal agencies and departments throughout the United States during the season. Most jobs are in Metropolitan Washington, D.C. Latest application date is generally April 15; many are earlier. Includes general information on applying for jobs in trades and labor occupations and summer employment for needy youth programs. Entries include: Agency name, filing deadline, titles of jobs available, brief information on qualifications needed, location, etc. Complete agency names and addresses are given in separate list. Publication is available from Federal Employment Information Center offices and agency personnel offices. Arrangement: By job level, then alphabetical by agency name.

★10280★ Summer Jobs USA

Peterson's Guides, Inc.
202 Carnegie Center
PO Box 2123
Princeton, NJ 08543-2123
Ph: (609)243-9111   Fax: (609)243-9150
Fr: 800-338-3282

Annual, October. $16.95. Covers over 488 camps, resorts, amusement parks, hotels, businesses, national parks, conference and training centers, ranches, and restaurants offering about 20,000 temporary summer jobs; listings are paid. Entries include: Name and address, length of employment, pay rate, fringe benefits, duties, qualifications, application deadline and procedure. Arrangement: Geographical, then type of job. Indexes: Job title.

★10281★ Summer Legal Employment Guide

Federal Reports Inc.
1010 Vermont Ave. NW, Ste. 408
Washington, DC 20005
Ph: (202)393-3311   Fax: (202)393-1553
Fr: 800-296-9611

Annual, October. $18.00. Covers more than 100 U.S. government summer legal internship and clerkship programs for 1st-year, 2nd-year, and 3rd-year law students, including programs offered by international organizations with which the U.S. is affiliated. Entries include: Organization name, address, phone, salary or stipend, requirements for eligibility, number of positions, application deadline, program description, and required application forms. Arrangement: Alphabetical.

★10282★ Summer Opportunities in Marine and Environmental Science

Summer Opportunities Guide
38 Litchfield Rd.
Londonderry, NH 03053

Herriott and Herrin. Second edition, 1994. $14.95. 60 pages. Subtitled: "A Student's Guide to Jobs, Internships and Study, Camp and Travel Programs". Prepared for both high school and college students.

★10283★ Summer Theater Directory

American Theatre Works, Inc.
PO Box 519
Dorset, VT 05251
Ph: (802)867-2223   Fax: (802)867-0144

Annual, December. $15.95. Covers summer theater companies that offer employment opportunities in acting, design, production, and management; summer theater training programs. Entries include: Company name, address, phone, name and title of contact; type of company, activities and size of house; whether union affiliated, whether nonprofit or commercial; year established; hiring procedure and number of positions hired annually, season; description of stage; internships; description of company's artistic goals and audience. Arrangement: Geographical. Indexes: Company name.

★10284★ Summer Time, Summer Work: A Quick Guide to Finding a Summer Job

Chronicle Guidance Publications, Inc.
66 Aurora St.
PO Box 1190
Moravia, NY 13118-1190
Ph: (315)497-0330   Fax: (315)497-3359
Fr: 800-622-7284

Chronicle Guidance Staff. 1993. $2.00. Reprint of a journal article.

★10285★ Vacation Work's Overseas Summer Jobs

Peterson's Guides, Inc.
202 Carnegie Center
PO Box 2123
Princeton, NJ 08543-2123
Ph: (609)243-9111   Fax: (609)243-9150
Fr: 800-338-3282

$14.95. Covers Over 30,000 summer jobs worldwide. Entries include: Complete job data, length of employment, number of openings, pay, job description, qualifications needed, application/contact information.

★10286★ Washington Job Source: Everything You Need to Land the Internship, Entry-Level or Middle Management Job of Your Choice

Metcom, Inc.
1708 Surrey Ln., NW
Washington, DC 20007
Ph: (202)337-7800   Fax: (202)337-3121

Benjamin S. Psillas. 1995. $15.95 (paper).

★10287★ Win With Internships

Chronicle Guidance Publications, Inc.
66 Aurora St.
PO Box 1190
Moravia, NY 13118-1190
Ph: (315)497-0330   Fax: (315)497-3359
Fr: 800-622-7284

Chronicle Guidance Staff. 1993. $2.00. Reprint of a journal article.

★10288★ Work Your Way Around the World

Vacation-Work Publications
9 Park End St.
Oxford OX1 1HJ, England
Ph: 865 241978   Fax: 865 790885

Biennial, February of odd years. $17.95. Covers temporary employment opportunities worldwide. Entries include: Name and address of employer, description of position. Arrangement: Geographical.

★10289★ Working Holidays

Central Bureau for Educational Visits & Exchanges
Seymour Mews House
Seymour Mews
London W1H 9PE, England
Ph: 71 4865101   Fax: 71 9355741

Annual, November. $9.99, postpaid. Covers 1,000 organizations offering short-term paid and voluntary work opportunities in Britain and over 70 countries worldwide, for periods of three days to a year or longer; jobs include archeological digs, au pair/childcare, children's projects, couriers, guides, monitors, teachers, work camps, conservation, community works, hotel work, farm work, teaching, simple construction, etc. Entries include: Organization name, address, name of contact, objectives, projects available, conditions and terms of work. Arrangement: Geographical, then by type of work. Indexes: Organization name.

★10290★ A Year Off–A Year On: A Guide to Jobs, Voluntary Service, and Working Holidays in the U.K. and Overseas During Your Education

Hobsons Publishing PLC
Bateman St.
Cambridge CB2 1LZ, England
Ph: 223 354551

Irregular, latest edition May 1993; new edition expected April 1995. $7.99. Publication includes: Names and addresses of organizations providing information about short-term employment opportunities in the United Kingdom and overseas. Principal content of publication is discussion of opportunities for short-term employment, particularly as a supplement to formal education.

NEWSPAPERS, MAGAZINES, AND JOURNALS

★10291★ Community Jobs: The Employment Newspaper for the Non-Profit Sector

ACCESS: Networking in the Public Interest
30 Irving Pl.
New York, NY 10003
Ph: (212)475-1001   Fax: (212)475-1199

Monthly. $69.00. Covers jobs and internships available with nonprofit organizations active in issues such as the environment, foreign policy, consumer advocacy, housing, education, etc. Entries include: Position title; name, address, and phone of contact; description, responsibilities; requirements; salary. Arrangement: Geographical.

★10292★ Environmental Opportunities

Environmental Opportunities
PO Box 788
Walpole, NH 03608
Ph: (603)756-4553

Monthly. $47.00/year. Lists full-time openings in environmental positions as well as short-term opportunities and internships.

★10293★ Job Opportunities Bulletin

National Recreation and Park Association (NRPA)
2775 S. Quincy St., Ste. 300
Arlington, VA 22206
Ph: (703)820-4940   Fr: 800-626-6772

Bimonthly $30.00/year.

★10294★ Rocky Mountain Employment Newsletter

Intermountain Publishing & Referral
311-NP 14th St.
Glenwood Springs, CO 81601
Ph: (303)945-8991   Fax: (303)945-5140

Semimonthly. $13.00/year, per month for one edition; $16.00/year, for two editions; $19.00/year, for three editions; $21.00/year, for four editions. Lists information on current job openings in Colorado, Idaho, Montana, Arizona, New Mexico, Washington, Oregon, and Wyoming. Provides job titles, descriptions, requirements, and employer name and address or telephone number. Covers all occupational fields. Specializes in summer-winter seasonal openings, and in ranch, horse, livestock and farm opportunities. Available in four editions: Colorado-Wyoming, Arizona-New Mexico, Idaho-Montana, and Washington-Oregon.

★10295★ Spare Time

Kipen Publishing Corp.
5810 W. Oklahoma Ave.
Milwaukee, WI 53219-4384
Ph: (414)543-8110   Fax: (414)543-9767

$16.95/year for individuals. Magazine featuring articles on business start-up and money-making opportunities.

OTHER SOURCES

★10296★ Association of Part-Time Professionals (APTP)

Crescent Plz.
7700 Leesburg Pke., No. 216
Falls Church, VA 22043
Ph: (703)734-7975   Fax: (703)734-7975

Purpose: Promotes employment opportunities for qualified men and women interested in part-time professional positions. Primary goals are to upgrade the status of part-time employment by providing a professional association that represents all part-time professionals, permanent part-timers, job-sharers, free-lancers, and consultants; to educate employers, employees, and the community about the advantages of increased flexibility in working patterns; to advocate prorated benefits for part-timers and a work environment responsive to individual and family needs. Works to develop a constituency of professional men and women nationwide who want the part-time employment option available to them. Operates as an information resource center; conducts research; maintains speakers' bureau.

★10297★ Association of Psychology Postdoctoral and Internship Centers (APPIC)

733 15th St. NW, Ste. 717
Washington, DC 20005
Ph: (202)347-0022   Fax: (202)347-8480

Members: Veterans Administration hospitals, medical centers, state hospitals, university counseling centers, and other facilities that provide internship and postdoctoral programs in professional psychology. **Purpose:**

Promotes activities that assist in the development of professional psychology training programs. **Activities:** Serves as a clearinghouse to provide college students with internship placement assistance at member facilities. Conducts workshops and seminars on training procedures in professional psychology.

★10298★ Convention II (CII)

PO Box 1987
Washington, DC 20013
Ph: (202)544-1789

Members: High school participants in the annual model Constitutional Convention that convenes in the Halls of the U.S. Congress. **Purpose:** A national political/citizenship education program aimed at teaching American youth about the rule of law and politics. Delegates propose, debate, and vote on amendments to the Constitution as possible solutions to major challenges confronting the nation. Findings are presented at the White House and Congress, and sent to other American leaders. Sponsors internship program, placing former delegates in jobs on Capitol Hill, with the goal of increasing congressional support for the organization. Facilitates interaction between members and members of Congress. Communicates and collaborates with individuals, institutions, and organizations involved with business, education, government, humanities, politics, and youth.

★10299★ Inroads

10 S. Broadway
St. Louis, MO 63102
Ph: (314)241-7488   Fax: (314)241-9325

Members: Participants are U.S. corporations that sponsor internships for minority students and pledge to develop career opportunities for the interns. **Purpose:** Prepares black, Hispanic, and Native American high school and college students for leadership positions within major American business corporations in their own communities. Screens and places over 4000 individuals for internships with more than 1000 American business corporations per year. Offers professional training seminars on time management, business presentation skills, team building, and decision making. Provides personal and professional guidance to pre-college and college interns.

★10300★ National Association of Part-Time and Temporary Employees (NAPTE)

5800 Barton, Ste. 201
PO Box 3805
Shawnee, KS 66203
Ph: (913)762-7740

Purpose: Promotes the economic and social interests of persons working on a part-time, contingent, or temporary basis through research, advocacy, and member services. **Activities:** Operates resume referral service.

★10301★ New Ways to Work (NWW)
985 Market St., Ste 950
San Francisco, CA 94103
Ph: (415)995-9860   Fax: (415)995-9867
Purpose: Goal is to provide a work world that responds to the needs of both workers and institutions. Provides information, training, and support to individuals and organizations interested in new work options. Promotes the concepts of flextime, compressed work weeks, job sharing, work sharing, and voluntary reduced work time to satisfy the requirements of people who want and need flexible schedules. **Activities:** Offers techni-cal assistance, including problem analysis and assistance in program facilitation for interested employees, employers, or unions.

★10302★ U.S. Public Interest Research Group (USPIRG)
218 D. St. SE
Washington, DC 20003
Ph: (202)546-9707   Fax: (202)546-2461
Members: Individuals who contribute time, effort, or funds toward public interest research and advocacy. **Activities:** Conducts research, monitors corporate and government actions, and lobbies for reforms on consumer, environmental, energy, and governmental issues. Current efforts include support for: laws to protect consumers from unsafe products and unfair banking practices; laws to reduce the use of toxic chemicals; renewal of the Clean Air Act; efforts to reduce global warming and ozone depletion; energy conservation and use of safe, renewable energy sources. Sponsors internships for college students; provides opportunities for students to receive academic credit for activities such as investigative journalism, legislative research, lobbying, and public education and organizing. Offers summer jobs.

Writing Resumes and Other Job-Search Correspondence

REFERENCE WORKS

★10303★ Adams Cover Letter Almanac

Planning/Communications
7215 Oak Ave.
River Forest, IL 60305-1935
Ph: (708)366-5200   Fr: (888)366-5200

Adams New Media. 1996. $10.95 (book only); $19.95 (book and FastLetter Windows software). 762 pages. Contains more than 600 sample cover letters. Software includes word processing, tutorial, and suggested opening sentences, following paragraphs, and closings for cover letters.

★10304★ Adams Resume Almanac

Planning/Communications
7215 Oak Ave.
River Forest, IL 60305-1935
Ph: (708)366-5200   Fr: (888)366-5200

Adams New Media. 1996. $10.95 (book only); $19.95 (book and FastResume Windows software). 762 pages. Contains more than 600 sample resumes. Software includes word processing and tutorial.

★10305★ The Advanced 90 Minute Resume

Peterson's
PO Box 2123
Princeton, NJ 08543-2123
Ph: (609)243-9111   Fax: (609)243-9150
Fr: 800-338-3282

Peggy Schmidt. 1992. $7.95. 128 pages. Features guidance on upgrading and strengthening an existing resume.

★10306★ The Best Resumes for Scientists and Engineers

John Wiley and Sons
605 3rd Ave.
New York, NY 10158
Ph: (212)850-6000   Fr: 800-225-5945

Adele Lewis. Second edition, 1993. $37.50; $14.95 (paper). Presents an extensive collection of scientific and engineering resumes, highlighting the important differences between these and resumes written for other occupations.

★10307★ Better Resumes for Executives and Professionals

Barron's Educational Series, Inc.
250 Wireless Blvd.
PO Box 8040
Hauppauge, NY 11788
Ph: (516)434-3311   Fr: 800-645-3476

Robert F. Wilson. Second edition, 1991. $11.95 (paper). Explains how to write resumes and cover letters for executives and professionals in most fields.

★10308★ The Complete Resume Book and Job Getters Guide

Pocket Books
200 Old Tappan Rd.
Old Tappan, NJ 07675
Ph: (201)767-5937   Fr: 800-223-2336

Juvenal L. Angel. 1990. $5.99 (paper).

★10309★ The Complete Resume Guide

Macmillan General Reference
201 W. 103rd St.
Indianapolis, IN 46290
Fax: 800-882-8583   Fr: 800-428-5331

Marian Faux. Fifth edition, 1995. $8.95.

★10310★ Cover Letters Made Easy

NTC Publishing Group
4255 W. Touhy Ave.
Lincolnwood, IL 60646-1975
Ph: (847)679-5500   Fax: (847)679-2494
Fr: 800-323-4900

1995. $6.95 (paper). Part of series for job hunters.

★10311★ Cover Letters That Knock 'em Dead

Bob Adams, Inc.
260 Center St.
Holbrook, MA 02343
Ph: (617)767-8100   Fax: (617)767-0994
Fr: 800-872-5627

Martin Yate. Second edition, 1995. $9.95. Discusses the fundamentals of writing a superior cover letter; how to match the letter style with the resume it accompanies; which format is right for which applicant; what always goes in, what always stays out, and why. Includes a number of samples.

★10312★ Customizing Your Resume for Teaching Positions

University Press of America
4720 Boston Way
Lanham, MD 20706
Ph: (301)459-3366   Fax: (301)459-2118
Fr: 800-462-6420

Edward G. Pultorak. 1993. $17.50 (paper).

★10313★ The Damn Good Resume Guide

Ten Speed Press
PO Box 7123
Berkeley, CA 94707
Ph: (510)559-1600   Fax: (510)559-1629
Fr: 800-841-BOOK

Yana Parker. Third edition, 1996. $7.95. 80 pages. Concentrates on producing an effective resume, with examples of functional and chronological resumes.

★10314★ Designing Creative Resumes and Portfolios

Crisp Publications, Inc.
1200 Hamilton Ct.
Menlo Park, CA 94025
Ph: (415)323-6100   Fr: 800-442-7477

Gregg Berryman. 1991. $15.95 (paper). Presents different methods of designing resumes. Includes sample resumes and cover letters. Also discusses employment objectives and interview preparation.

★10315★ Designing the Perfect Resume

Barron's Educational Series, Inc.
250 Wireless Blvd.
Hauppauge, NY 11788
Fr: 800-645-3476

Pat Criscito, CPA. 1995. $12.95 (paper). Focuses on resume appearance. Includes hundreds of sample resumes created using WordPerfect software.

★10316★ Developing a Professional Vita or Resume

Garrett Park Press
PO Box 190 C
Garrett Park, MD 20896-0190
Ph: (301)946-2553

Carl McDaniels. 1990. $10.95. 108 pages. Prepared for the professional person who needs a detailed summary of educational, employment, and other qualifications. Vitas are used frequently to locate professional employment, to support nominations for advisory committees or consulting positions, to summarize background for review by professional societies, and to provide a summary for introductions.

★10317★ Dynamic Cover Letters

Ten Speed Press
PO Box 7123
Berkeley, CA 94707
Ph: (510)559-1600   Fax: (510)559-1629
Fr: 800-841-BOOK

Katherine Hansen. Revised edition, 1995. $7.95. Helps sell the employer with a cover letter that will get a resume read, get an interview, and get the job.

★10318★ Electronic Resume Revolution

Consultants Bookstore
Templeton Rd.
Fitzwilliam, NH 03447
Ph: (603)585-6544   Fax: (603)585-9555
Fr: 800-531-0007

Joyce Lain Kennedy and Thomas J. Morrow. Second edition, 1995. $12.95 (paper). 228 pages. Explains how to write a resume that a computer can read. Includes 30 model resumes.

★10319★ Electronic Resumes

Planning/Communications
7215 Oak Ave.
River Forest, IL 60305-1935
Ph: (708)366-5200   Fr: (888)366-5200

Wayne Gonyea and James Gonyea. 1996. $19.95 (book and MS-DOS disk). 224 pages. Explains the basics of online, multimedia, video, and audio resumes in nontechnical language. Disk includes software that enables users to create their own electronic resume to upload via modem onto online resume databases.

★10320★ Electronic Resumes for the New Job Market

Impact Publications
9104-N Manassas Dr.
Manassas Park, VA 22111-5211
Ph: (703)361-7300   Fax: (703)335-9486

Peter D. Weddle. 1995. $11.95. 154 pages. Explains how to use electronic job banks and design resumes that best meet electronic job bank specifications.

★10321★ Every Woman's Essential Job Hunting & Resume Book

Adams Publishing
260 Center St.
Holbrook, MA 02343-1074
Ph: (617)767-8100   Fax: (617)767-0994
Fr: 800-872-5627

Laura Morin. 1994. $10.95 (paper).

★10322★ The Executive Resume Book

Consultants Bookstore
Templeton Rd.
Fitzwilliam, NH 03447
Ph: (603)585-6544   Fax: (603)585-9555
Fr: 800-531-0007

Loretta Foxman. Second edition, 1989. $39.95; $14.95 (paper). 210 pages. Positions

the resume as a strategic tool and demonstrates how to use it effectively to land the job.

★10323★ From College to Career: Entry-Level Resumes for Any Major from Accounting to Zoology

Ten Speed Press
PO Box 7123
Berkeley, CA 94707
Ph: (510)559-1600   Fax: (510)559-1629
Fr: 800-841-BOOK

Donald Asher. 1992. $7.95. 128 pages. Addresses the needs of college students, particularly how to deal with little experience and how to present education in the strongest light. Covers technical resumes and academic/scientific curricula vitae.

★10324★ Government Job Finder

Planning/Communications
7215 Oak Ave.
River Forest, IL 60305-1935
Ph: (708)366-5200   Fr: (888)366-5200

Daniel Lauber. Third edition, 1996. $32.95; $16.95 (paper). 352 pages. Covers 1800 sources. Discusses how to use sources of local, state, and federal government job vacancies in a number of specialties and state-by-state, including job-matching services, job hotlines, specialty periodicals with job ads, salary surveys, and directories. Explains how local, state, and federal hiring systems work. Includes chapters on resume and cover letter preparation and interviewing.

★10325★ Guide to Basic Resume Writing

VGM Career Horizons
4255 W. Touhy Ave.
Lincolnwood, IL 60646-1975
Ph: (847)679-5500   Fax: (847)679-2494
Fr: 800-323-4900

Public Library Association Job and Career Information Services Committee. 1991. $7.95. 96 pages. Important resource for semiskilled and unskilled workers who need to compile a simple resume and write a cover letter.

★10326★ High Impact Resumes and Letters: How to Communicate Your Qualifications to Employers

Impact Publications
9104-N Manassas Dr.
Manassas Park, VA 22111-5211
Ph: (703)361-7300   Fax: (703)335-9486

Ronald L. Krannich and William J. Banis. Sixth edition, 1994. $14.95. 289 pages.

★10327★ How to Prepare Your Curriculum Vitae

VGM Career Horizons
4255 W. Touhy Ave.
Lincolnwood, IL 60646-1975
Ph: (847)679-5500   Fax: (847)679-2494
Fr: 800-323-4900

Acy L. Jackson. 1993. $14.95. Dozens of examples from academics in all disciplines and at all career levels illustrate the principles of writing an effective C.V. Worksheets guide the reader through a step-by-step process that begins with describing, in draft form, all

pertinent experiences, and then helps shape, organize, and edit experiences and credentials into a professional curriculum vitae. Includes sample cover letters tailored to academic institutions.

★10328★ How to Write an Effective Resume

Saunderstown Press
1600 Boston Neck Rd.
PO Box 307
Saunderstown, RI 02874

Allen A. Johnson, $7.95. 17 pages.

★10329★ How to Write a Winning Resume

VGM Career Horizons
4255 W. Touhy Ave.
Lincolnwood, IL 60646-1975
Ph: (847)679-5500   Fax: (847)679-2494
Fr: 800-323-4900

Deborah Perlmutter Bloch. Third edition, 1993. $6.95. 128 pages. Explains what a resume does, the various kinds that exist, and occasions where it should be used. Contains advice on what and what not to include in a resume, how to respond to the want ads, and an appendix of job descriptions.

★10330★ The Job Hunter's Word Finder

Peterson's Guides, Inc.
PO Box 2123
Princeton, NJ 08543-2123
Ph: (609)243-9111   Fax: (609)243-9150
Fr: 800-338-3282

James Bluemond. 1996. $9.95 (paper). Lists alternatives to frequently used resume words. Includes industry "buzzwords" for various fields. Provides examples of resumes.

★10331★ Liberal Arts Power! What It Is and How to Sell It on Your Resume

Peterson's
PO Box 2123
Princeton, NJ 08543-2123
Ph: (609)243-9111   Fax: (609)243-9150
Fr: 800-338-3282

Burton Jay Nadler. Second edition, 1989. $9.95. 174 pages. Stresses the value of a liberal arts education and shows how to demonstrate that value to potential employers through a well-crafted resume.

★10332★ The New 90 Minute Resume: For Job Hunters Who Want Top Notch Results−Fast!

Peterson's
PO Box 2123
Princeton, NJ 08543-2123
Ph: (609)243-9111   Fax: (609)243-9150
Fr: 800-338-3282

Peggy Schmidt. Revised edition, 1996. $15.95 (includes software). Provides step-by-step approach to resume writing. Software allows users to customize their resume.

★10333★ Non-Profits and Education Job Finder

Planning/Communications
7215 Oak Ave.
River Forest, IL 60305-1935
Ph: (708)366-5200   Fr: (888)366-5200

Daniel Lauber. 1996. $32.95; $16.95 (paper). 350 pages. Covers 1600 sources. Discusses how to use sources of non-profit sector job vacancies in a number of specialties and state-by-state, including job-matching services, job hotlines, specialty periodicals with job ads, salary surveys, and directories. Covers a variety of fields from education to religion. Includes chapters on resume and cover letter preparation and interviewing.

★10334★ 175 High-Impact Resumes

John Wiley & Sons, Inc.
605 3rd Ave.
New York, NY 10158-0012
Ph: (212)850-6000   Fr: 800-225-5945

Richard H. Beatty. $10.95 (paper).

★10335★ The Overnight Resume

Ten Speed Press
PO Box 7123
Berkeley, CA 94707
Ph: (510)559-1600   Fax: (510)559-1629
Fr: 800-841-BOOK

Donald Asher. 1990. $7.95. Discusses how to write aggressive business resumes, with additional information on special styles for technical, legal, and advertising personnel, actors, speakers, and students with no experience. Covers medical curricula vitae.

★10336★ The Perfect Cover Letter

John Wiley and Sons
605 Third Ave.
New York, NY 10158-0012
Ph: (212)850-6000   Fr: 800-225-5945

Richard H. Beatty. 1989. $34.95; $9.95 (paper). 192 pages. Provides examples and analysis of a range of letters, including executive search, advertising response, networking, personal introduction, and general broadcast targeted pieces. Also contains tips on what information to include or omit, as well as proper letter design.

★10337★ PLA Guide to Basic Resume Writing

NTC Publishing Group
4255 W. Touhy Ave.
Lincolnwood, IL 60646-1975
Ph: (708)679-5500   Fax: (708)679-6375
Fr: 800-323-4900

Compiled by the Public Library Association (PLA), Job and Career Infromation Committee Staff. 1995. $7.95 (paper).

★10338★ Professional's Job Finder

Planning/Communications
7215 Oak Ave.
River Forest, IL 60305-1935
Ph: (708)366-5200   Fr: (888)366-5200

Daniel Lauber. 1996. $36.95; $18.95 (paper). 520 pages. Covers 2600 sources. Discusses how to use sources of private sector job vacancies in a number of specialties and state-by-state, including job-matching services, job hotlines, specialty periodicals with

job ads, salary surveys, and directories. Covers a variety of fields from health care to sales. Includes chapters on resume and cover letter preparation and interviewing.

★10339★ The Resume Catalog: 200 Damn Good Examples

Ten Speed Press
PO Box 7123
Berkeley, CA 94707
Ph: (510)559-1600   Fax: (510)559-1629
Fr: 800-841-BOOK

Yana Parker. $15.95. 316 pages. Contains a range and variety of 200 sample resumes. Indexed and cross-referenced for ease of use.

★10340★ The Resume Handbook

Bob Adams, Inc.
260 Center St.
Holbrook, MA 02343
Ph: (617)767-8100   Fax: (617)767-0994
Fr: 800-872-5627

Arthur D. Rosenberg and David V. Hizer. Second edition, 1990. $5.95. 144 pages. Includes specific examples of excellent resumes and cover letters and examples of how weaker resumes and cover letters can be improved. Presents resumes for many types of job hunters, including recent college graduates, seasoned professionals, and women re-entering the job market. Chapters on cover letters and 'personal sales' letters and design and layout of resumes are also included.

★10341★ The Resume Kit

John Wiley and Sons, Inc.
605 3rd Ave.
New York, NY 10158
Ph: (212)850-6000   Fr: 800-225-5945

Richard H. Beatty. Third edition, 1995. $29.95; $10.95 (paper). Details effective resume preparation. Discusses both chronological and functional resumes. Includes sample resumes and cover letters.

★10342★ The Resume Makeover: The Resume Writing Guide That Includes Personalized Feedback

John Wiley & Sons, Inc.
605 3rd Ave.
New York, NY 10158-0012
Ph: (212)850-6000   Fr: 800-225-5945

Jeffrey G. Allen. 1995. $24.95; $9.95 (paper).

★10343★ Resume Power: Selling Yourself on Paper

Mount Vernon Press
1750 112th St. NE, C-224
Bellevue, WA 98004
Ph: (206)454-6982

Tom Washington. 1993. $8.95 (paper).

★10344★ The Resume Writer's Handbook

Consultants Bookstore
Templeton Rd.
Fitzwilliam, NH 03447
Ph: (603)585-6544   Fax: (603)585-9555
Fr: 800-531-0007

Michael Holley Smith. 1994. $4.99. A writing guide aimed at people at all job levels.

Provides examples and advice on common problems.

★10345★ Resume Writing: A Comprehensive, How-to-Do-It Guide

John Wiley & Sons
605 3rd Ave.
New York, NY 10158
Ph: (212)850-6000   Fax: (212)850-6088

Burdette E. Bostwick. Fourth edition, 1990. $34.95; $12.95 (paper). Covers resume style, format, and language. Includes sample resumes and cover letters.

★10346★ Resume Writing, Interviewing and Role-playing Skills for Salespeople Looking for New Jobs

J B & Me
PO Box 3879
Manhattan Beach, CA 90266
Ph: (310)546-1255

Jack Bernstein. 1993. $12.50.

★10347★ Resume Writing Made Easy

Gorsuch Scarisbrick, Publishers
8233 Via Paseo del Norte, Ste. F-400
Scottsdale, AZ 85258
Ph: (602)991-7881

Lola Coxford. Fifth edition, 1994. $11.95.

★10348★ Resume Writing for the Professional Nurse

CES Associates
112 S. Grant St.
Hinsdale, IL 60521
Ph: (708)654-2596

Nancy Kuzmich. Revised edition, 1995. $39.95. 110 pages. Self-study guide written for the professional nurse on how to set career goals, interview for a job, and select the best job offer. Includes sample resumes and cover letters.

★10349★ Resume Writing for Results: A Workbook

Wadsworth Publishing Co.
10 Davis Dr.
Belmont, CA 94002
Ph: (415)595-2350

Pat Brett. 1993. $16.95 (paper).

★10350★ Resumes for Advertising Careers

VGM Career Horizons
4255 W. Touhy Ave.
Lincolnwood, IL 60646-1975
Ph: (847)679-5500   Fax: (847)679-2494
Fr: 800-323-4900

1993. $9.95. Aimed at job seekers trying to enter or advance in advertising. Provides sample resumes for copywriters, art directors, account managers, ad managers, and media perople at all levels of experience. Furnishes sample cover letters.

★10351★ Resumes for Better Jobs

Prentice Hall General Reference
15 Columbus Cir.
New York, NY 10023
Ph: (212)373-8500   Fr: 800-223-2348

Lawrence D. Brennen et al. Second edition, 1994. $10.00. Sample resumes that correspond to over 200 jobs.

★10352★ Resumes for Business Management Careers

VGM Career Horizons
4255 W. Touhy Ave.
Lincolnwood, IL 60646-1975
Ph: (847)679-5500   Fax: (847)679-2494
Fr: 800-323-4900

1992. $9.95. 160 pages. Resume guide for supervisors and line and staff managers. Provides advice on compiling a business management resume; includes a number of sample resumes and cover letters.

★10353★ Resumes for College Students and Recent Graduates

VGM Career Horizons
4255 W. Touhy Ave.
Lincolnwood, IL 60646-1975
Ph: (847)679-5500   Fax: (847)679-2494
Fr: 800-323-4900

1992. $9.95. Shows how to write a resume that capitalizes on pertinent work experience, academic background, and volunteer and extracurricular activities. Includes sample resumes and cover letters.

★10354★ Resumes for Communications Careers

VGM Career Horizons
4255 W. Touhy Ave.
Lincolnwood, IL 60646-1975
Ph: (847)679-5500   Fax: (847)679-2494
Fr: 800-323-4900

1991. $9.95. 160 pages. Includes sample resumes representing journalists, writers, publicists, and other communications specialists.

★10355★ Resumes for Education Careers

VGM Career Horizons
4255 W. Touhy Ave.
Lincolnwood, IL 60646-1975
Ph: (847)679-5500   Fax: (847)679-2494
Fr: 800-323-4900

1992. $9.95. Sample resumes cover a variety of education careers and reflect education professionals at all levels of experience.

★10356★ Resumes for Engineering Careers

VGM Career Horizons
NTC Publishing Group
4255 W. Touhy Ave.
Lincolnwood, IL 60646-1975
Ph: (847)679-5500   Fax: (847)679-2494
Fr: 800-323-4900

1994. $9.95. 160 pages. Contains sample resumes and cover letters applicable to any engineering field.

★10357★ Resumes for Environmental Careers

VGM Career Horizons
NTC Publishing Group
4255 W. Touhy Ave.
Lincolnwood, IL 60646-1975
Ph: (847)679-5500   Fax: (847)679-2494
Fr: 800-323-4900

1994. $9.95. 160 pages. Provides resume advice tailored to people pursuing careers focusing on the environment. Includes sample resumes and cover letters.

★10358★ Resumes for Ex-Military Personnel

4255 W. Touhy Ave.
Lincolnwood, IL 60646-1975
Ph: (847)679-5500   Fax: (847)679-2494
Fr: 800-323-4900

1995. $9.95 (paper).

★10359★ Resumes for the 50 Plus Job Hunter

4255 W. Touhy Ave.
Lincolnwood, IL 60646-1975
Ph: (708)679-5500   Fax: (708)679-6375
Fr: 800-323-4900

1994. $9.95 (paper).

★10360★ Resumes for Health and Medical Careers

4255 W. Touhy Ave.
Lincolnwood, IL 60646-1975
Ph: (708)679-5500   Fax: (708)679-6375
Fr: 800-323-4900

Compiled by VGM Career Horizons Staff 1995. $9.95 (paper).

★10361★ Resumes for High School Graduates

VGM Career Horizons
4255 W. Touhy Ave.
Lincolnwood, IL 60646-1975
Ph: (847)679-5500   Fax: (847)679-2494
Fr: 800-323-4900

1993. $9.95. Designed for the person with little or no full-time work experience. Shows how to emphasize part-work experience and highlight educational, extra-curricular and volunteer experience. Provides sample resumes and cover letters.

★10362★ Resumes for High Tech Careers

VGM Career Horizons
4255 W. Touhy Ave.
Lincolnwood, IL 60646-1975
Ph: (847)679-5500   Fax: (847)679-2494
Fr: 800-323-4900

1992. $9.95. 160 pages. Demonstrates how to tailor a resume that catches a high tech employer's attention.

★10363★ Resumes for Overseas & Stateside Jobs

Zinks International Career Guidance
PO Box 790
Richland, MI 49083
Ph: (313)584-7529

Richard M. Zink. 1994. $14.94 (paper).

★10364★ Resumes & Personal Statements for Health Professionals

Galen Press, Ltd.
PO Box 64400
Tucson, AZ 85728-4400
Ph: (520)577-8363   Fax: (520)529-6459

James W. Tysinger. 1994. $15.95 (paper).

★10365★ Resumes for Re-Entering the Job Market

NTC Publishing Group
4255 W. Touhy Ave.
Lincolnwood, IL 60646-1975
Ph: (847)679-5500   Fax: (847)679-2494
Fr: 800-323-4900

1995. $9.95 (paper).

★10366★ Resumes! Resumes! Resumes!

The Career Press, Inc.
3 Tice Rd.
PO Box 687
Franklin Lakes, NJ 07417
Ph: (201)848-0310   Fax: (201)848-1727
Fr: 800-237-3371

Second edition, 1995. $9.99. 192 pages. A collection of job-winning resumes as selected by the country's leading employment, placement, and counseling professionals. Samples cover a variety of situations - from displaced homemakers reentering the work force to seasoned professionals looking to make a career change to hard-to-place, mid-level managers.

★10367★ Resumes for Sales and Marketing Careers

VGM Career Horizons
4255 W. Touhy Ave.
Lincolnwood, IL 60646-1975
Ph: (847)679-5500   Fax: (847)679-2494
Fr: 800-323-4900

1991. $9.95. 128 pages. Sample resumes and cover letters from all levels of the sales and marketing field.

★10368★ Resumes for Scientific and Technical Careers

VGM Career Horizons
NTC Publishing Group
4255 W. Touhy Ave.
Lincolnwood, IL 60646-1975
Ph: (847)679-5500   Fax: (847)679-2494
Fr: 800-323-4900

1994. $9.95. 160 pages. Provides resume advice for individuals interested in working in scientific and technical careers. Includes sample resumes and cover letters.

★10369★ Resumes for the Smart Job Search: The Ultimate Guide to Writing Resumes in the 90s

H D Publishing
PO Box 2171
Boston, MA 02106
Ph: (617)536-0169   Fax: (617)536-5090

Marc L. Makos. 1993. $14.95 (paper).

★10370★ Resumes That Get Jobs

Planning/Communications
7215 Oak Ave.
River Forest, IL 60305-1935
Ph: (708)366-5200   Fr: (888)366-5200

Jean Reed and Ray Potter. Eighth edition, 1996. $24.95 (book and disk); $9.95 (book only). 216 pages. Techniques for constructing resumes. Software includes electronic worksheets for assembling career information and searchable model resumes.

★10371★ Resumes That Knock 'Em Dead

Bob Adams, Inc.
260 Center St.
Holbrook, MA 02343
Ph: (617)767-8100   Fax: (617)767-0994
Fr: 800-872-5627

Martin John Yate. Second edition, 1994. $10.95. 216 pages. Presents resumes that were successfully used by individuals to obtain jobs. Resumes target the most commonly-sought positions on all levels.

★10372★ Resumes That Work: How to Sell Yourself on Paper

John Wiley & Sons
605 3rd Ave.
New York, NY 10158
Ph: (212)850-6000   Fax: (212)850-6088

Loretta Foxman. Second edition, 1993. $10.95 (paper). A guide for college graduates and those interested in changing careers. Discusses cover letters, resumes, broadcast letters, and resume logs. Assists in career planning. Includes employment sources.

★10373★ Resumes for Women

Macmillan Publishing Co., Inc.
200 Old Tappan Rd.
Old Tappan, NJ 07675
Fax: 800-445-6991   Fr: 800-223-2336

Eva Shaw. 1995.

★10374★ The Smart Woman's Guide to Resumes and Job Hunting

The Career Press, Inc.
3 Tice Rd.
PO Box 687
Franklin Lakes, NJ 07417
Ph: (201)848-0310   Fax: (201)848-1727
Fr: 800-237-3371

Julie Adair King and Betsy Sheldon. Third edition, 1995. $9.99. 224 pages. Addresses job-search challenges unique to women in the '90s. Discusses breaking through the glass ceiling and other gender barriers, commanding a fair salary, networking to hidden job opportunities, using "power language", translating volunteer experiences into powerful accomplishments, and offers other guidance. Takes the reader through a resume-creating process.

★10375★ Sure-Hire Resumes

AMACOM
135 W. 50th St., 15th Fl.
New York, NY 10020
Ph: (212)903-8315   Fr: 800-262-9699

Robbie M. Kaplan. 1994. $10.95. Includes 'ideal' cover letters written by personnel directors. Presents 25 actual resumes (indexed by occupation) and includes discussions of useful resume-writing software and word processing.

★10376★ Top Secret Resumes and Cover Letters

Planning/Communications
7215 Oak Ave.
River Forest, IL 60305-1935
Ph: (708)366-5200   Fr: (888)366-5200

Steven Provenzano. 1995. $12.95 (book only); $34.95 (CD-ROM and book); $19.95 (CD-ROM only). 208 pages. Provides detailed instructions on writing resumes. Multimedia CD-ROM (Windows 3.1 or higher) contains full text of the book plus software for creating resumes and cover letters and a video from the author.

★10377★ 200 Letters for Job Hunters

Ten Speed Press
PO Box 7123
Berkeley, CA 94707
Ph: (510)559-1600   Fax: (510)559-1629
Fr: 800-841-BOOK

William S. Frank. Revised edition, 1993. $17.95. Provides over 250 letters to cover a variety of situations.

★10378★ 201 Killer Cover Letters

Planning/Communications
7215 Oak Ave.
River Forest, IL 60305-1935
Ph: (708)366-5200   Fr: (888)366-5200

Sandra Podesta and Andrea Paxton. 1996. $16.95 (book and MSDOS disk). Includes worksheets to translate strengths into benefits to an employer. Disk contains all of the letters in the book.

★10379★ Your First Resume

The Career Press Inc.
3 Tice Rd.
PO Box 687
Franklin Lakes, NJ 07417
Ph: (201)848-0310   Fax: (201)848-1727
Fr: 800-237-3371

Ronald W. Fry. Fourth edition, 1995. $9.99. 192 pages. Subtitled: "The Comprehensive Guide for College Students or Anyone Preparing to Enter or Reenter the Job Market."

★10380★ Your Resume: Key to a Better Job

Prentice Hall General Reference and Travel
15 Columbus Cir.
New York, NY 10023
Ph: (212)373-8500

Leonard Corwen. Fifth edition, 1993. $11.00. Provides guidelines for resume writing; explains what employers look for in a resume, including contents and style. Includes model resumes for high-demand careers such as computer programmers, health administra-

tors, and high-tech professionals. Notes basic job-getting information and strategies.

AUDIO/VISUAL RESOURCES

★10381★ The Complete Job Application: Filling in the Blanks

Cambridge Career Products
PO Box 2153
Dept. CC15
Charleston, WV 25328-2153
Ph: (304)744-9323   Fax: (304)744-9351
Fr: 800-468-4227

Video. 1994. $99.00. 25 minutes. Learn how to avaoid common mistakes and make the best possible impression.

★10382★ Does Your Resume Wear Blue Jeans?

Cambridge Career Products
PO Box 2153
Dept. CC15
Charleston, WV 25328-2153
Ph: (304)744-9323   Fax: (304)744-9351
Fr: 800-468-4227

Video. $139.00 (book and video). Two 45-minute cassettes. A comprehensive resume preparation workshop.

★10383★ Effective Resumes and Job Applications

Cambridge Career Products
PO Box 2153
Dept. CC15
Charleston, WV 25328-2153
Ph: (304)744-9323   Fax: (304)744-9351
Fr: 800-468-4227

Video. 1992. $99.00. 32 minutes. Provides practical advice for writing resumes, cover letters, and job applications.

★10384★ Effective Resumes and Job Applications

Learning Seed
330 Telser Rd.
Lake Zurich, IL 60047
Fr: 800-634-4941

Video. $89.00. 32 minutes.

★10385★ Effective Resumes: Reading Between the Lines

Cambridge Career Products
PO Box 2153
Dept. CC15
Charleston, WV 25328-2153
Ph: (304)744-9323   Fax: (304)744-9351
Fr: 800-468-4227

Video. $79.95. 65 minutes. Employers discuss what they look for in a resume.

★10386★ High Impact Cover Letters

CareerLab Books
9085 E. Mineral Circle, Ste. 330
Englewood, CO 80112
Ph: (303)790-0505   Fax: (303)790-0606
Fr: 800-723-9675

Video. $59.95. 30 minutes.

★10387★ Job Hunting in Tough Times

Ready Reference Press
PO Box 5249
Santa Monica, CA 90409
Fax: (310)475-4895   Fr: 800-424-5627

Series of 3 videos. $239.00/set. $89.00/each. Separate titles cover job search skills, resume preparation, and interview techniques.

★10388★ Job Search Skills for Adults

Ready Reference Press
PO Box 5249
Santa Monica, CA 90409
Fax: (310)475-4895   Fr: 800-424-5627

Series of 3 videos. $239.00/set. $89.00/each. Separate titles cover job search skills, resume preparation, and interview techniques.

★10389★ Job Search Skills for Teens

Ready Reference Press
PO Box 5249
Santa Monica, CA 90409
Fax: (310)475-4895   Fr: 800-424-5627

Series of 3 videos. $239.00/set. $89.00/each. Separate titles cover job search skills, resume preparation, and interview techniques.

★10390★ Job Search Skills for Women

Ready Reference Press
PO Box 5249
Santa Monica, CA 90409
Fax: (310)475-4895   Fr: 800-424-5627

Series of 3 videos. $239.00/set. $89.00/each. Separate titles cover job search skills, resume preparation, and interview techniques.

★10391★ Job Search Skills for Women in Non-Traditional Occupations

Ready Reference Press
PO Box 5249
Santa Monica, CA 90409
Fax: (310)475-4895   Fr: 800-424-5627

Series of 3 videos. $239.00/set. $89.00/each. Separate titles cover job search skills, resume preparation, and interview techniques.

★10392★ The Power Resume

CareerLab Books
9085 E. Mineral Circle, Ste. 330
Englewood, CO 80112
Ph: (303)790-0505   Fax: (303)790-0606
Fr: 800-723-9675

Video. $59.95. 30 minutes.

★10393★ Resume Ready

Cambridge Career Products
PO Box 2153
Dept. CC15
Charleston, WV 25328-2153
Ph: (304)744-9323   Fax: (304)744-9351
Fr: 800-468-4227

Video. 1993. $99.00. 28 minutes. Step-by-step guide to writing a resume. Comes with book, *The Resume Solution*.

★10394★ Writing Resumes and Cover Letters

Career Communications, Inc.
PO Box 169
Harleysville, PA 19438
Ph: (215)256-3130   Fax: (215)256-3136
Fr: 800-346-1848

Video. $79.00. 12 minutes.

★10395★ Your Resume: A Self-Portrait

Cambridge Career Products
PO Box 2153
Dept. CC15
Charleston, WV 25328-2153
Ph: (304)744-9323   Fax: (304)744-9351
Fr: 800-468-4227

Video, $98.00. Interactive laserdisc, $199.00. 30 minutes. Takes viewers through the process of composing an effective resume.

SOFTWARE

★10396★ Adams Cover Letter Almanac

Planning/Communications
7215 Oak Ave.
River Forest, IL 60305-1935
Ph: (708)366-5200   Fr: (888)366-5200

Adams New Media. 1996. $10.95 (book only); $19.95 (book and FastLetter Windows software). 762 pages. Contains more than 600 sample cover letters. Software includes word processing, tutorial, and suggested opening sentences, following paragraphs, and closings for cover letters.

★10397★ Adams Resume Almanac

Planning/Communications
7215 Oak Ave.
River Forest, IL 60305-1935
Ph: (708)366-5200   Fr: (888)366-5200

Adams New Media. 1996. $10.95 (book only); $19.95 (book and FastResume Windows software). 762 pages. Contains more than 600 sample resumes. Software includes word processing and tutorial.

★10398★ Adams Resumes and Cover Letters

Planning/Communications
7215 Oak Ave.
River Forest, IL 60305-1935
Ph: (708)366-5200   Fr: (888)366-5200

Adams New Media and Peter Veruki. 1996. $39.95. Requires Windows 3.1 or higher, 3.5 inch disks only. Users can customize any of the 1,200 sample resumes and cover letters by choosing suggested phrases or paragraphs. Includes tutorials and contact management software.

★10399★ Electronic Resumes

Planning/Communications
7215 Oak Ave.
River Forest, IL 60305-1935
Ph: (708)366-5200   Fr: (888)366-5200

Wayne Gonyea and James Gonyea. 1996. $19.95 (book and MS-DOS disk). 224 pages.

Explains the basics of online, multimedia, video, and audio resumes in nontechnical language. Disk includes software that enables users to create their own electronic resume to upload via modem onto online resume databases.

★10400★ Resumes That Get Jobs

Planning/Communications
7215 Oak Ave.
River Forest, IL 60305-1935
Ph: (708)366-5200   Fr: (888)366-5200

Jean Reed and Ray Potter. Eighth edition, 1996. $24.95 (book and disk); $9.95 (book only). 216 pages. Techniques for constructing resumes. Software includes electronic worksheets for assembling career information and searchable model resumes.

★10401★ Top Secret Resumes and Cover Letters

Planning/Communications
7215 Oak Ave.
River Forest, IL 60305-1935
Ph: (708)366-5200   Fr: (888)366-5200

Steven Provenzano. 1995. $12.95 (book only); $34.95 (CD-ROM and book); $19.95 (CD-ROM only). 208 pages. Provides detailed instructions on writing resumes. Multimedia CD-ROM (Windows 3.1 or higher) contains full text of the book plus software for creating resumes and cover letters and a video from the author.

★10402★ 201 Killer Cover Letters

Planning/Communications
7215 Oak Ave.
River Forest, IL 60305-1935
Ph: (708)366-5200   Fr: (888)366-5200

Sandra Podesta and Andrea Paxton. 1996. $16.95 (book and MSDOS disk). Includes worksheets to translate strengths into benefits to an employer. Disk contains all of the letters in the book.

OTHER SOURCES

★10403★ Resume Service Directory

American Business Directories, Inc.
American Business Information, Inc.
5711 S. 86th Cir.
Omaha, NE 68127
Ph: (402)593-4600   Fax: (402)331-1505

Annual. $515.00, U.S. edition. Number of listings: 7,209 (U.S. edition); 685 (Canadian edition). Entries include: Name, address, phone (including area code), size of advertisement, year first in Yellow Pages, name of owner or manager, number of employees. Compiled from telephone company Yellow Pages, nationwide. Arrangement: Geographical.

Index to Information Sources

Index to Information Sources

This Index is an alphabetical listing of all entries contained in both Parts One and Two. Index references are to **entry numbers** rather than to page numbers. Publication and film titles are rendered in italics.

American Manufacturers Directory **4948, 9513**
American Marketing Association **5017, 5068**
American Marketing Association—Yellow Pages and International Membership Directory **5086**
American Mathematical Society **5167**
American Medical Association **6399, 6610**
American Medical Peer Review Association **6400**
American Medical Technologists **1459, 2233, 5270**
American Men and Women of Science **337, 405, 767, 825, 1122, 1225, 1357, 2865, 3129, 3404, 3561, 3949, 5168, 5214, 5370, 5416, 5454, 5641, 5963, 6536, 8052, 8246**
American Metal Market **4881, 5334**
American Meteorological Society **5413**
American Microchemical Society **1210**
American Military Retirees Association **9948**
American Montessori Society **4180, 6698, 8375**
American Nuclear Society **5675**
American Nurseryman **4304**
American Nurses Association **7439**
American Nurses in Business Association **4686, 7368**
American Nursing Assistant's Foundation **5773**
American Occupational Therapy Association **5816**
American Oil Chemists' Society **1115, 1211**
American Optometric Association **5859**
American Optometric Student Association **5877**
American Orff-Schulwerk Association **5502, 7775**
American Organization of Nurse Executives **7369**
American Osteopathic Association **6401**
American Osteopathic Association—Yearbook and Directory of Osteopathic Physicians **6440**
American Osteopathic College of Pathologists **6402**
American Paint and Coatings Journal **1177**
American Papermaker **4882**
American Pharmaceutical Association—Academy of Pharmacy Practice and Management **6056**
American Pharmacy **6009, 6064**
American Philological Association **563**
American Philosophical Association **1519**
American Photographers: An Illustrated Who's Who **6113**
American Physical Society **6556**
American Physical Therapy Association **6197**
American Planning Association **8700**
American Podiatric Medical Association **6644**
American Police Academy **4349**
American Political Science Association **1520, 6648, 6663**
American Political Science Association—Biographical Directory **6668**
American Political Science Association—Membership Directory **6669**
American Printer **6716, 8577**
American Psychological Association **6870**
American Psychological Association—APA Membership Register **6838**
American Psychologist **6808**
American Public Health Association **2234, 2268, 2337, 2454, 3665, 3786, 3878, 4013, 4687, 5724, 5784, 5860, 6022, 6067, 6198, 6403, 6611, 6826, 7370, 7538, 7974, 9420**
American Purchasing Society **6950**
American Real Estate Guide **7141**
American Registry of Diagnostic Medical Sonographers **7131**
American Registry of Radiologic Technologists **5703, 7132**

American Review of Respiratory Disease **6292, 7534**
American Sail Training Association **7240, 8186**
American Salaries and Wages Survey **9798**
American Salon **1938**
American Salon's Green Book **4949**
American School Board Journal **2619**
American School Health Association **2235, 2269, 2338, 2455, 4688, 5725, 6404, 7371**
American School and University **2620**
American Showcase Illustration **8793**
American Society for Adolescent Psychiatry—Membership Directory **2020**
American Society of Agronomy **394, 7724**
American Society of Anesthesiologists **6405**
American Society of Artists **8855**
American Society of Association Executives **3486, 5069**
American Society of Bank Directors **3234**
American Society for Biochemistry and Molecular Biology **750**
American Society of Business Press Editors **9102**
American Society of Cardiovascular Professionals **2768**
American Society for Cell Biology **751**
American Society of Certified Engineering Technicians **3061**
American Society of Civil Engineers **1408**
American Society of Civil Engineers—Official Register **1358**
American Society for Clinical Laboratory Science **1488**
American Society of CLU and ChFC **4078, 8681**
American Society of Colon and Rectal Surgeons **6406**
American Society of Consultant Pharmacists **6023**
American Society of Criminology **1922, 4350, 6827, 8017**
American Society of Cytopathology **1489**
American Society of Dentistry for Children **2365**
American Society for Eighteenth-Century Studies **3775**
American Society of Electroneurodiagnostic Technologists **2721**
American Society of Extra-Corporeal Technology **6407, 7372**
American Society of Farm Managers and Rural Appraisers **7189**
American Society of Furniture Designers **2389**
American Society of Hand Therapists **5817, 6238**
American Society of Handicapped Physicians **6408**
American Society for Healthcare Environmental Services of the American Hospital Association **3666**
American Society for Healthcare Human Resources Administration **5889**
American Society for Histocompatibility and Immunogenetics **752, 6409, 7725**
American Society of Home Inspectors **1910**
American Society of Home Inspectors—Membership Directory **1893**
American Society for Horticultural Science **395**
American Society of Hospital Pharmacists **6024**
American Society for Industrial Security **7879**
American Society for Information Science **650, 4578, 4631**
American Society of Interior Designers **4102**
American Society of Interpreters **8499**
American Society of Interpreters—Membership List **8501**
American Society of Journalists and Authors **8967**

American Society of Journalists and Authors—Directory **8988**
American Society of Landscape Architects **4281**
American Society of Landscape Architects—Members' Handbook **4282**
American Society of Magazine Editors **9103**
American Society of Mechanical Engineers **5259**
American Society of Media Photographers **6172**
American Society of Media Photographers—Membership Directory **6114**
American Society for Microbiology **753**
American Society of Nephrology **6410**
American Society for Neurochemistry **1212**
American Society of Ophthalmic Administrators **3667**
American Society of Pension Actuaries **220**
American Society for Photogrammetry and Remote Sensing **574, 2914, 3440, 3539, 3585, 5428, 6557, 8361, 8714**
American Society of Plant Physiologists **754, 1213**
American Society of Plumbing Engineers **6592**
American Society of Podiatric Medical Assistants **5307**
American Society of Primatologists **552**
American Society of Professional Estimators **1986**
American Society of Radiologic Technologists **5704, 7133**
American Society for Reproductive Medicine **6411**
American Society of Safety Engineers **4014**
American Society of Sanitary Engineering **6593**
American Society of Tax Professionals **71**
American Society of Test Engineers **2855**
American Society for Training and Development **5925**
American Society of Travel Agents **8572**
American Society of Travel Agents—Membership Directory **8534**
American Society of T.V. Cameramen and International Society of Videographers **6173**
American Society of Veterinary Ophthalmology—Directory **8733**
American Society of Wedding Professionals **8869**
American Society of Women Accountants—Membership Directory **25**
American Sociological Association **8032**
American Sociological Association—Biographical Directory of Members **8021**
American Speech-Language-Hearing Association **8174**
American Sportscasters Association **7014, 7468**
American Statistical Association **8261**
American Supplier Institute **3993, 5837**
The American Surgeon **6293**
American Swimming Coaches Association **8187**
American Symphony Orchestra League **5563**
American Telemarketing Association—Membership Services Referral Directory **8425**
American Therapeutic Recreation Association **7307**
American Trade Schools Directory **277**
American Translators Association—Membership Directory **8502**
American Universities and Colleges **1550**
American Urological Association **6412**
American Veterinary Medical Association **521, 8728**
American Veterinary Medical Association—Directory **8734**
American Vocational Association **303**
American Watchmakers Institute **4150**

Association of Human Resource Systems Professionals **5890**
Association for Humanistic Education and Development **2061, 2704, 6872, 8008**
Association of Image Consultants International **3918**
Association of Independent Video and Filmmakers **176**
Association of Industry Manufacturer's Representatives **5000**
Association for International Practical Training **378, 437, 639, 805, 1078, 1168, 1270, 1409, 2915, 3104, 3442, 3587, 3866, 3994, 5181, 5260, 5402, 5429, 5491, 5676, 6001, 6558, 7618, 7744, 9619**
Association for Investment Management and Research **8281**
Association for Investment Management and Research—Membership Directory **3247**
Association of Jewish Libraries **4581**
Association of Laban Movement Analysts **2134**
Association for Library and Information Science Education **1524, 4582**
Association of Management **5926**
Association of Management Consulting Firms **4818**
Association of Medical Illustrators **8783**
Association for Multicultural Counseling and Development **2010**
Association of North American Missions **5503**
Association of Outplacement Consulting Firms International **3028, 10124**
Association of Part-Time Professionals **10296**
Association of Philippine Physicians in America **6415**
Association of Physician Assistant Programs **6245**
Association of Physician Assistants in Cardiovascular Surgery **6274**
Association of Physician's Assistants in Cardiovascular Surgery—Membership Directory **6248**
Association of Professional Researchers for Advancement **3455**
Association of Professional Writing Consultants—Membership Directory **8990**
Association of Psychology Postdoctoral and Internship Centers **6873, 10297**
Association for Quality and Participation **5927**
Association of Records Managers and Administrators **5309**
Association for Research in Vision and Ophthalmology **6416**
Association for School, College and University Staffing **1584**
Association of Seventh-Day Adventist Librarians **4583**
Association of Southern Baptist Campus Ministers **5504**
Association of Southern Baptist Colleges and Schools **1525, 2644, 7777**
Association for Specialists in Group Work **2011**
Association for the Study of Higher Education **2705**
Association for the Study of Jewish Languages **6977**
Association of Surgical Technologists **8337**
Association for Systems Management **1863, 2220**
Association of Technical Personnel in Ophthalmology **5842**
Association for Theatre in Higher Education **101**
Association of Training and Employment Professionals **5928**
Association of the United States Army **9953**
Association of Unity Churches **5505**

Association for University Business and Economic Research—Membership Directory **2577**
Association of University Interior Designers— Membership List **606, 4107, 4283**
Association of University Professors of Ophthalmology **1526**
Association of Water Transportation Accounting Officers **17**
Association for Women in Computing **1730, 1864, 8120**
Association for Women Geoscientists **3555, 5958**
Association for Women Veterinarians **8756**
Association for Worksite Health Promotion **7271, 8233**
ASTM Standardization News **1084, 1180, 5335**
Astronomical League **6559**
Astronomy **6515**
ATA Translation Services Directory **8503**
Athletic Business—Professional Directory Section **607**
Athletic Equipment Managers Association **8188**
Atlanta Business Chronicle **9746**
Atlanta Employment Services **10179**
Atlanta JobBank **9693**
ATPO Placement **5849**
ATPO Viewpoints **5850**
Attorney Resource, Inc. **4475, 4541, 8271**
Attorneys Directory **4424**
Attorneys—Firms Directory **4425**
Attorneys' Service Bureaus Directory **4426**
Au Pair & Nanny's Guide to Working Abroad **1300**
Audio **83, 919**
AudioVideo International **8889**
Audit Data Search Ltd. **2214**
Austin Business Journal **9747**
Author & Audience: A Readings and Workshops Guide **8991**
Automatic Machining **8430**
Automotive Body Repair News **687**
Automotive Booster Clubs International **4940**
Automotive Cooling Journal **688**
Automotive Engineering **2811, 3035, 3927, 5187**
Automotive Fleet **689**
Automotive News **690**
Automotive Parts and Accessories Association **5001, 7683**
Automotive Parts & Accessories Association—Manufacturers' Representatives Roster, Aftermarket Resource Bibliography **4951**
Automotive Rebuilder **691**
Automotive Service Association **718**
Automotive Service Industry Association— Guide to Manufacturers' Representatives **4952**
Automotive Technicians Association International **709**
AV Video **84, 920, 6089**
Avery Crafts Associates, Ltd. **207, 1431, 4066, 8666**
Aviation Digest **8947**
Aviation Equipment Maintenance **316, 445**
Aviation Maintenance Foundation International **451**
Aviation/Space Writers Association **7470, 8971**
Aviation Week and Space Technology **317**

B

B and M Associates, Inc. **362, 1624, 1707, 1841, 2425, 2556, 2891, 3020, 3089, 3970, 5237, 5824, 5914, 6961, 8625, 8937**
B W and Associates, Inc. **630, 1392, 1905, 1982, 5989, 8357**

Bacon's Radio/TV/Cable Directory, Volume 1 **943, 7026**
Bader Research Corp. **4476**
Baker Scott and Co. **8307**
Bakers and Bakery Products Workers **724**
Bakery Technology and Engineering **732**
Baltimore Business Journal **9748**
Bank Administration Institute **3293, 4811**
Bank Marketing Association **5148, 6939**
Bank Systems and Technology **3214**
Bankers Monthly **2079, 3215, 4772**
Banner Personnel Service **7737**
Barbizon School of Modeling **3210**
Barron's National Business and Financial Weekly **3216**
Base Line **3540, 4564, 4624**
Be a Successful Writer: New Expanded Common Sense Program for Anyone Who Wants to Write **9041**
Be Your Own Headhunter Online **9296**
Beard Management, Inc. **1708, 1842, 8105**
Beauty Salons Directory **1945**
Become a Successful Consultant: Manage & Market Your Skills Effectively **4839**
Becoming a Chef **1061**
Becoming a Helper **3799, 3891**
Becoming a Lawyer: A Humanistic Perspective on Legal Education, Professionalism **4496**
Becoming a Minister **5542**
Becoming a Public Relations Writer: A Writing Process Workbook for the Profession **6940**
Becoming a Real Estate Professional **6777, 7155, 7203**
Becoming a Secondary School Science Teacher **7822**
Becoming Self-Employed **10127**
Becoming a Teacher **4227, 7823**
BedTimes **4883**
Beginner's Guide to Model Photography: Techniques for the Photographer and Tips for the Aspiring Model **3203**
Beginnings: Teaching & Learning in the Kindergarten **4228**
Being a Long-Term Care Nursing Assistant **5743**
Bell Oaks Co. **2892, 3171, 3971, 5238**
Bellon and Associates, Inc. **4477**
"Benefits for the Fringe" in The Advocate— Special Double Issue: The Year in Review (January 1994, p.56) **9867**
Bert Davis Publishing Placement Consultants **9088**
The Best Directory of Recruiters, Agencies, Consultants **10180**
Best Doctors in America **6441**
The Best Home-Based Businesses for the 90s **1023, 2495, 3330, 3908, 8073, 8872, 9121**
Best Impressions in Hospitality: Your Professional Image for Excellence **3836**
Best Jobs in The USA Today **9318**
Best Lawyers in America **4427**
Best Personnel Services **58, 1432, 2111, 8626, 8667**
The Best Resumes for Scientists and Engineers **347, 413, 773, 831, 1136, 1239, 1375, 2878, 3141, 3416, 3571, 3627, 3957, 5223, 5379, 5422, 5467, 5651, 5975, 6543, 7732, 10306**
Best's Agents Guide **191, 1421, 4034, 8649**
Best's Insurance Reports **192, 1422, 4035, 8650**
Best's Review (Life/Health Edition) **185, 1417, 4025, 8643**
Better Resumes for Executives and Professionals **3501, 10307**
Better Roads **1329**
Between Opportunities: A Survival Guide for Job Seekers & Career Changers **9260**
Between People and Nature: The Profession of Landscape Architecture **4290**